KEY TO WORLD MAP PAGES

- **Large scale maps**
  (> 1:3 500 000)
- **Medium scale maps**
  (1:4 000 000 – 1:9 000 000)
- **Small scale maps**
  (< 1:10 000 000)

64-65

55

88-89

84-85

79

80-81

78

82-83

86-87

66-67

68-69

60-61

62-63

76-77

70-71

72-73

74-75

ASIA
54-91

NORTH AMERICA
124-149 126-127

128-129

138-139

134-135

136-137

140-141

148-149

SOUTH AMERICA
150-160

152-153

154-155

156-157

158-159

160

PHILIP'S

ATLAS
OF THE
WORLD

PHILIP'S
ATLAS
OF THE
WORLD

LONDON NEW YORK SYDNEY TORONTO

This edition published 1993
by BCA by arrangement with
George Philip Limited,
an imprint of Reed Consumer Books Limited

Cartography by Philip's

Copyright © 1993 Reed International Books Limited

CN 4870

Printed in Italy

PHILIP'S WORLD MAPS

The reference maps which form the main body of this atlas have been prepared in accordance with the highest standards of international cartography to provide an accurate and detailed representation of the earth. The scales and projections used have been carefully chosen to give balanced coverage of the world, while emphasizing the most densely populated and economically significant regions. A hallmark of Philip's mapping is the use of hill shading and relief colouring to create a graphic impression of landforms: this makes the maps exceptionally easy to read. However, knowledge of the key features employed in the construction and presentation of the maps will enable the reader to derive the fullest benefit from the atlas.

Map sequence

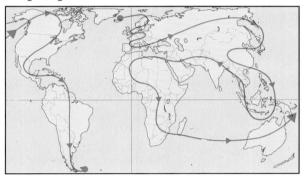

The atlas covers the earth continent by continent: first Europe; then its land neighbour Asia (mapped north before south, in a clockwise sequence), then Africa, Australia and Oceania, North America and South America. This is the classic arrangement adopted by most cartographers since the 16th century. For each continent, there are maps at a variety of scales. First, physical relief and political maps of the whole continent. Then a series of larger-scale maps of the regions within the continent, each followed, where required, by still larger-scale maps of the most important or densely populated areas. The governing principle is that by turning the pages of the atlas, the reader moves steadily from north to south through each continent, with each map overlapping its neighbours. A key map showing this sequence, and the area covered by each map, can be found on the endpapers of the atlas.

Map presentation

With very few exceptions (eg for the Arctic and Antarctic), the maps are drawn with north at the top, regardless of whether they are presented upright or sideways on the page. In the borders will be found the map title; a locator diagram showing the area covered and the page numbers for maps of adjacent areas; the scale; the projection used; the degrees of latitude and longitude; and the letters and figures used in the index for locating place names and geographical features. Physical relief maps also have a height reference panel identifying the colours used for each layer of contouring.

Map symbols

Each map contains a vast amount of detail which can only be conveyed clearly and accurately by the use of symbols. Points and circles of varying sizes locate and identify the relative importance of towns and cities; different styles of type are employed for administrative, geographical and regional place names. A variety of pictorial symbols denote landscape features such as glaciers, marshes and reefs, and man-made structures including roads, railways, airports, canals and dams. International borders are shown by red lines. Where neighbouring countries are in dispute, for example in the Middle East, the maps show the *de facto* boundary between nations, regardless of the legal or historical situation. The symbols are explained on the first page of the World Maps section of the atlas.

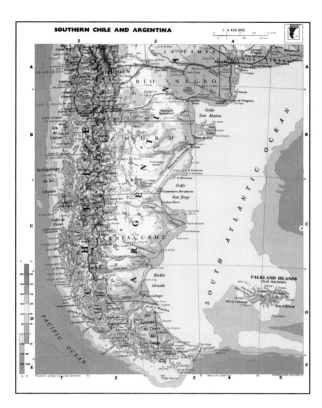

Map scales

1: 16 000 000
1 inch = 252 statute miles

The scale of each map is given in the numerical form known as the 'representative fraction'. The first figure is always one, signifying one unit of distance on the map; the second figure, usually in millions, is the number by which the map unit must be multiplied to give the equivalent distance on the earth's surface. Calculations can easily be made in centimetres and kilometres, by dividing the earth units figure by 100 000 (ie deleting the last five 0s). Thus 1:1 000 000 means 1 cm = 10 km. The calculation for inches and miles is more laborious, but 1 000 000 divided by 63 360 (the number of inches in a mile) shows that 1:1 000 000 means approximately 1 inch = 16 miles. The table below provides distance equivalents for scales down to 1:50 000 000.

LARGE SCALE		
1: 1 000 000	1 cm = 10 km	1 inch = 16 miles
1: 2 500 000	1 cm = 25 km	1 inch = 39.5 miles
1: 5 000 000	1 cm = 50 km	1 inch = 79 miles
1: 6 000 000	1 cm = 60 km	1 inch = 95 miles
1: 8 000 000	1 cm = 80 km	1 inch = 126 miles
1: 10 000 000	1 cm = 100 km	1 inch = 158 miles
1: 15 000 000	1 cm = 150 km	1 inch = 237 miles
1: 20 000 000	1 cm = 200 km	1 inch = 316 miles
1: 50 000 000	1 cm = 500 km	1 inch = 790 miles
SMALL SCALE		

Measuring distances

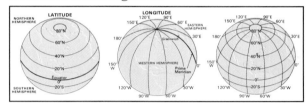

Although each map is accompanied by a scale bar, distances cannot always be measured with confidence because of the distortions involved in portraying the curved surface of the earth on a flat page. As a general rule, the larger the map scale (ie the lower the number of earth units in the representative fraction), the more accurate and reliable will be the distance measured. On small-scale maps such as those of the world and of entire continents, measurement may only be accurate along the 'standard parallels', or central axes, and should not be attempted without considering the map projection.

Map projections

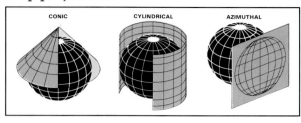

Unlike a globe, no flat map can give a true scale representation of the world in terms of area, shape and position of every region. Each of the numerous systems that have been devised for projecting the curved surface of the earth on to a flat page involves the sacrifice of accuracy in one or more of these elements. The variations in shape and position of landmasses such as Alaska, Greenland and Australia, for example, can be quite dramatic when different projections are compared.

For this atlas, the guiding principle has been to select projections that involve the least distortion of size and distance. The projection used for each map is noted in the border. Most fall into one of three categories - conic, cylindrical or azimuthal - whose basic concepts are shown above. Each involves plotting the forms of the earth's surface on a grid of latitude and longitude lines, which may be shown as parallels, curves or radiating spokes.

Latitude and longitude

Accurate positioning of individual points on the earth's surface is made possible by reference to the geometrical system of latitude and longitude. Latitude *parallels* are drawn west-east around the earth and numbered by degrees north and south of the Equator, which is designated 0° of latitude. Longitude *meridians* are drawn north-south and numbered by degrees east and west of the *prime meridian*, 0° of longitude, which passes through Greenwich in England. By referring to these co-ordinates and their sub-divisions of minutes (1/60th of a degree) and seconds (1/60th of a minute), any place on earth can be located to within a few hundred yards. Latitude and longitude are indicated by blue lines on the maps; they are straight or curved according to the projection employed. Reference to these lines is the easiest way of determining the relative positions of places on different maps, and for plotting compass directions.

Name forms

For ease of reference, both English and local name forms appear in the atlas. Oceans, seas and countries are shown in English throughout the atlas; country names may be abbreviated to their commonly accepted form (eg Germany, not Federal Republic of Germany). Conventional English forms are also used for place names on the smaller-scale maps of the continents. However, local name forms are used on all large-scale and regional maps, with the English form given in brackets only for important cities - the large-scale map of European Russia thus shows Moskva (Moscow). For countries which do not use a Roman script, place names have been transcribed according to the systems adopted by the British and US Geographic Names Authorities. For China, the Pin Yin system has been used, with some more widely known forms appearing in brackets, as with Beijing (Peking). Both English and local names appear in the index, the English form being cross-referenced to the local form.

V

CONTENTS

NOTE
The titles to the World Maps
list the main countries, states
and provinces covered by
each map. A name given in
italics indicates that only part
of the country is shown on
the map.

Netherlands, Belgium and Luxembourg
1:1 000 000

20-21

Northern France
1:2 000 000

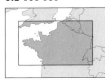

22-23

Southern France
1:2 000 000
Corsica, Monaco

24-25

Germany 1:2 000 000

26-27

Switzerland 1:800 000
Liechtenstein

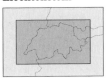

28-29

Austria, Czech Republic, Slovak Republic and Hungary 1:2 000 000
Poland

30-31

Malta, Crete, Corfu, Rhodes and Cyprus
1:800 000 / 1:1 040 000

32

Balearics, Canaries and Madeira 1:800 000 / 1:1 600 000
Mallorca, Menorca, Ibiza

33

Eastern Spain 1:2 000 000
Andorra

34-35

Western Spain and Portugal 1:2 000 000

36-37

Northern Italy, Slovenia and Croatia
1:2 000 000
San Marino, Slovenia, *Croatia*

38-39

Southern Italy 1:2 000 000
Sardinia, Sicily

40-41

The Lower Danube
1:2 000 000
Bosnia-Herzegovina, Yugoslavia, Macedonia

42-43

Greece and Albania
1:2 000 000

44-45

Romania 1:2 000 000

46

Poland 1:2 000 000

47

Eastern Europe and Turkey
1:8 000 000

48-49

Western Russia, Belorussia and the Baltic States 1:4 000 000
Russia, Estonia, Latvia, Lithuania, Belorussia, *Ukraine*

50-51

Ukraine, Moldavia and the Caucasus 1:4 000 000
Russia, Ukraine, Georgia, *Armenia, Azerbaijan,* Moldavia

52-53

ASIA

Southern Urals 1:4 000 000
Russia

54

Central Asia 1:4 000 000
Kazakhstan, Kirghizia, Tajikistan, *Uzbekistan*

55

Russia and Central Asia
1:16 000 000
Russia, Kazakhstan, Turkmenistan, Uzbekistan

56-57

Asia: Physical
1:40 000 000
58

Asia: Political
1:40 000 000
59

Japan 1:4 000 000
Ryukyu Islands

60-61

Southern Japan 1:2 000 000

62-63

China 1:12 000 000
Mongolia

64-65

Northern China and Korea 1:4 800 000
North Korea, South Korea

66-67

Southern China 1:4 800 000
Hong Kong, Taiwan, Macau

68-69

Philippines 1:3 200 000

70-71

Eastern Indonesia
1:5 600 000

72-73

Western Indonesia
1:5 600 000
Malaysia, Singapore, Brunei

74-75

Mainland South-East Asia 1:4 800 000
Thailand, Vietnam, Cambodia, Laos

76-77

Bangladesh, North-Eastern India and Burma
1:4 800 000
Bhutan

78

Afghanistan and Pakistan
1:5 600 000

79

The Indo-Gangetic Plain
1:4 800 000
India, Nepal, *Pakistan*, Kashmir

80-81

Southern India and Sri Lanka 1:4 800 000

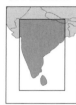

82-83

The Middle East 1:5 600 000
Iran, Iraq, *Saudi Arabia*, Kuwait

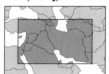

84-85

Southern Arabian Peninsula 1:5 600 000
Saudi Arabia, Yemen, United Arab Emirates, Oman, Qatar

86-87

Turkey 1:4 000 000
Syria

88-89

Arabia and the Horn of Africa 1:12 000 000
Saudi Arabia, Oman, Yemen, *Somalia*, Ethiopia, Eritrea, Djibouti

90

The Near East 1:2 000 000
Israel, Lebanon, *Jordan*

91

AFRICA

Africa: Physical
1:32 000 000

92

Africa: Political
1:32 000 000

93

The Nile Valley 1:6 400 000
Egypt, Sudan, Eritrea, *Ethiopia*
The Nile Delta 1:3 200 000

94-95

Central North Africa
1:6 400 000
Libya, Chad, *Niger*

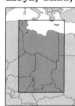

96-97

North-West Africa
1:6 400 000
Algeria, Morocco, Tunisia, *Mauritania, Niger, Mali*

98-99

West Africa 1:6 400 000
Nigeria, Ivory Coast, Ghana, Senegal, Guinea, Burkina Faso

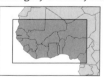

100-101

Central Africa 1:6 400 000
Zaïre, Angola, Cameroon, Congo, Gabon, Central African Republic

102-103

Southern Africa 1:6 400 000
South Africa, Zimbabwe, Madagascar, *Mozambique*, Botswana, Namibia

104-105

East Africa 1:6 400 000
Kenya, Tanzania, Zambia, Uganda, Malawi

106-107

Horn of Africa 1:6 400 000
Somalia, *Eritrea, Ethiopia*, Djibouti

108

Indian Ocean 1:40 000 000
Mauritius, Réunion, Seychelles, Maldives

109

AUSTRALIA AND OCEANIA

Australia and Oceania: Physical and Political
1:16 000 000

110-111

Western Australia
1:6 400 000
Northern Territory

112-113

Eastern Australia
1:6 400 000
Queensland, Tasmania, New South Wales

114-115

South-East Australia
1:3 200 000
New South Wales, Victoria, *South Australia*

116-117

New Zealand – North Island 1:2 800 000

118

New Zealand – South Island 1:2 800 000

119

Papua New Guinea
1:5 200 000

120

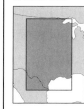

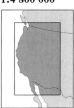

IX

World Statistics: Countries

This alphabetical list includes all the countries and territories of the world. If a territory is not completely independent, then the country it is associated with is named. The area figures give the total area of land, inland water and ice. Units for areas and populations are thousands. The annual income is the Gross National Product per capita in US dollars. The figures are the latest available, usually 1991.

Country/Territory	Area km² Thousands	Area miles² Thousands	Population Thousands	Capital	Annual Income US $
Adélie Land (Fr.)	432	167	0.03	-	-
Afghanistan	652	252	16,433	Kabul	450
Albania	28.8	11.1	3,250	Tirana	1,000
Algeria	2,382	920	24,960	Algiers	2,020
American Samoa (US)	0.20	0.08	39	Pago Pago	6,000
Amsterdam Is. (Fr.)	0.05	0.02	0.03	-	-
Andorra	0.45	0.17	52	Andorre-la-Vella	-
Angola	1,247	481	10,020	Luanda	620
Anguilla (UK)	0.09	0.04	8	The Valley	-
Antigua & Barbuda	0.44	0.17	77	St John's	4,770
Argentina	2,767	1,068	32,322	Buenos Aires	2,780
Armenia	29.8	11.5	3,416	Yerevan	2,150
Aruba (Neths.)	0.19	0.07	60	Oranjestad	6,000
Ascension Is. (UK)	0.09	0.03	1.5	Georgetown	-
Australia	7,687	2,968	17,086	Canberra	16,590
Australian Antarctic Territory	6,120	2,363	0	-	-
Austria	83.9	32.4	7,712	Vienna	20,380
Azerbaijan	86.6	33.4	7,451	Baku	1,670
Azores (Port.)	2.2	0.87	260	Ponta Delgada	-
Bahamas	13.9	5.4	253	Nassau	11,720
Bahrain	0.68	0.26	503	Manama	6,910
Bangladesh	144	56	115,594	Dacca	220
Barbados	0.43	0.17	255	Bridgetown	6,630
Belau (US)	0.46	0.18	15	Koror	-
Belgium	30.5	11.8	9,845	Brussels	19,300
Belize	23	8.9	188	Belmopan	2,050
Belorussia	207.6	80.1	10,374	Minsk	3,110
Benin	113	43	4,736	Porto-Novo	380
Bermuda (UK)	0.05	0.02	61	Hamilton	25,000
Bhutan	47	18.1	1,517	Thimphu	180
Bolivia	1,099	424	7,400	La Paz/Sucre	650
Bosnia-Herzegovina	51.2	19.8	4,364	Sarajevo	-
Botswana	582	225	1,291	Gaborone	2,590
Bouvet Is. (Nor.)	0.05	0.02	0.02	-	-
Brazil	8,512	3,286	153,322	Brasilia	2,920
British Antarctic Terr. (UK)	1,709	660	0.3	Stanley	-
British Indian Ocean Terr. (UK)	0.08	0.03	3	-	-
Brunei	5.8	2.2	266	Bandar Seri Begawan	6,000
Bulgaria	111	43	9,011	Sofia	1,840
Burkina Faso	274	106	9,001	Ouagadougou	350
Burma (Myanmar)	677	261	41,675	Rangoon	500
Burundi	27.8	10.7	5,438	Bujumbura	210
Cambodia	181	70	8,246	Phnom Penh	200
Cameroon	475	184	11,834	Yaoundé	940
Canada	9,976	3,852	26,522	Ottawa	21,260
Canary Is. (Spain)	7.3	2.8	1,700	Las Palmas/Santa Cruz	-
Cape Verde Is.	4	1.6	370	Praia	750
Cayman Is. (UK)	0.26	0.10	27	Georgetown	-
Central African Republic	623	241	3,039	Bangui	390
Chad	1,284	496	5,679	Ndjamena	220
Chatham Is. (NZ)	0.96	0.37	0.05	Waitangi	-
Chile	757	292	13,386	Santiago	2,160
China	9,597	3,705	1,139,060	Beijing (Peking)	370
Christmas Is. (Aus.)	0.14	0.05	2.3	The Settlement	-
Cocos (Keeling) Is. (Aus.)	0.01	0.005	0.70	-	-
Colombia	1,139	440	32,987	Bogotá	1,280
Comoros	2.2	0.86	551	Moroni	500
Congo	342	132	2,271	Brazzaville	1,120
Cook Is. (NZ)	0.24	0.09	18	Avarua	900
Costa Rica	51.1	19.7	2,994	San José	1,930
Croatia	56.5	21.8	4,784	Zagreb	-
Crozet Is. (Fr.)	0.51	0.19	35	-	-
Cuba	111	43	10,609	Havana	3,000
Cyprus	9.3	3.6	702	Nicosia	8,640
Czech Republic	78.9	30.4	10,299	Prague	2,370
Denmark	43.1	16.6	5,140	Copenhagen	23,660
Djibouti	23.2	9	409	Djibouti	1,000
Dominica	0.75	0.29	83	Roseau	2,440
Dominican Republic	48.7	18.8	7,170	Santo Domingo	950
Ecuador	284	109	10,782	Quito	1,020
Egypt	1,001	387	53,153	Cairo	620
El Salvador	21	8.1	5,252	San Salvador	1,070
Equatorial Guinea	28.1	10.8	348	Malabo	330
Estonia	44.7	17.3	1,600	Tallinn	3,830
* Ethiopia	1,222	472	50,974	Addis Ababa	120
Falkland Is. (UK)	12.2	4.7	2	Stanley	-
Faroe Is. (Den.)	1.4	0.54	47	Tórshavn	23,660
Fiji	18.3	7.1	765	Suva	1,830
Finland	338	131	4,986	Helsinki	24,400
France	552	213	56,440	Paris	20,600
French Guiana (Fr.)	90	34.7	99	Cayenne	2,500
French Polynesia (Fr.)	4	1.5	206	Papeete	6,000
Gabon	268	103	1,172	Libreville	3,780
Gambia, The	11.3	4.4	861	Banjul	360
Georgia	69.7	26.9	5,571	Tbilisi	1,640
Germany	357	138	79,479	Berlin	17,000
Ghana	239	92	15,028	Accra	400
Gibraltar (UK)	0.007	0.003	31	-	4,000
Greece	132	51	10,269	Athens	6,230
Greenland (Den.)	2,176	840	57	Godthåb	6,000
Grenada	0.34	0.13	85	St George's	2,180
Guadeloupe (Fr.)	1.7	0.66	344	Basse-Terre	7,000
Guam (US)	0.55	0.21	119	Agana	6,000
Guatemala	109	42	9,197	Guatemala City	930
Guinea	246	95	5,756	Conakry	450
Guinea-Bissau	36.1	13.9	965	Bissau	190
Guyana	215	83	796	Georgetown	290
Haiti	27.8	10.7	6,486	Port-au-Prince	370
Honduras	112	43	5,105	Tegucigalpa	570
Hong Kong (UK)	1.1	0.40	5,801	-	13,200
Hungary	93	35.9	10,344	Budapest	2,690
Iceland	103	40	255	Reykjavik	22,580
India	3,288	1,269	843,931	Delhi	330
Indonesia	1,905	735	179,300	Jakarta	610
Iran	1,648	636	58,031	Tehran	2,320
Iraq	438	169	18,920	Baghdad	2,000
Ireland	70.3	27.1	3,523	Dublin	10,780
Israel	27	10.3	4,659	Jerusalem	11,330
Italy	301	116	57,663	Rome	18,580
Ivory Coast	322	125	11,998	Abidjan	690
Jamaica	11	4.2	2,420	Kingston	1,380
Jan Mayen Is. (Nor.)	0.38	0.15	0.06	-	-
Japan	378	146	123,537	Tokyo	26,920
Johnston Is. (US)	0.002	0.0009	0.30	-	-
Jordan	89.2	34.4	4,009	Amman	1,120
Kazakhstan	2,717	1,049	17,104	Alma Ata	2,470
Kenya	580	224	24,032	Nairobi	340
Kerguelen Is. (Fr.)	7.2	2.8	0	-	-
Kermadec Is. (NZ)	0.03	0.01	0	-	-
Kirghizia	198.5	76.6	4,568	Bishkek	1,550
Kiribati	0.72	0.28	66	Tarawa	750
Korea, North	121	47	21,773	Pyongyang	900
Korea, South	99	38.2	43,302	Seoul	6,340
Kuwait	17.8	6.9	2,143	Kuwait City	16,380
Laos	237	91	4,139	Vientiane	230
Latvia	63.1	24.4	2,700	Riga	3,410
Lebanon	10.4	4	2,701	Beirut	2,000

Country/Territory	Area km² Thousands	Area miles² Thousands	Population Thousands	Capital	Annual Income US $
Lesotho	30.4	11.7	1,774	Maseru	580
Liberia	111	43	2,607	Monrovia	500
Libya	1,760	679	4,545	Tripoli	5,800
Liechtenstein	0.16	0.06	29	Vaduz	33,000
Lithuania	65.2	25.2	3,751	Vilnius	2,710
Luxembourg	2.6	1	384	Luxembourg	31,080
Macau (Port.)	0.02	0.006	479	-	2,000
Macedonia	25.3	9.8	2,174	Skopje	-
Madagascar	587	227	11,197	Antananarivo	210
Madeira (Port.)	0.81	0.31	280	Funchal	-
Malawi	118	46	8,556	Lilongwe	230
Malaysia	330	127	17,861	Kuala Lumpur	2,490
Maldives	0.30	0.12	215	Malé	460
Mali	1,240	479	8,156	Bamako	280
Malta	0.32	0.12	354	Valletta	6,850
Mariana Is. (US)	0.48	0.18	22	Saipan	-
Marshall Is.	0.18	0.07	42	Dalap-Uliga-Darrit	-
Martinique (Fr.)	1.1	0.42	341	Fort-de-France	4,000
Mauritania	1,025	396	2,050	Nouakchott	510
Mauritius	1.9	0.72	1,075	Port Louis	2,420
Mayotte (Fr.)	0.37	0.14	84	Mamoundzou	-
Mexico	1,958	756	86,154	Mexico City	2,870
Micronesia, Fed. States	0.70	0.27	103	Palikir	-
Midway Is. (US)	0.005	0.002	0.45	-	-
Moldavia	33.7	13	4,458	Kishinev	2,170
Monaco	0.002	0.0001	29	-	20,000
Mongolia	1,567	605	2,190	Ulan Bator	400
Montserrat (UK)	0.10	0.04	13	Plymouth	-
Morocco	447	172	25,061	Rabat	1,030
Mozambique	802	309	15,656	Maputo	70
Namibia	824	318	1,781	Windhoek	1,120
Nauru	0.02	0.008	10	Domaneab	-
Nepal	141	54	18,916	Katmandu	180
Netherlands	41.9	16.2	15,019	Amsterdam	18,560
Neths. Antilles (Neths.)	0.99	0.38	189	Willemstad	6,000
New Caledonia (Fr.)	19	7.3	168	Nouméa	4,000
New Zealand	269	104	3,429	Wellington	12,140
Nicaragua	130	50	3,871	Managua	340
Niger	1,267	489	7,732	Niamey	300
Nigeria	924	357	108,542	Lagos/Abuja	290
Niue (NZ)	0.26	0.10	3	Alofi	-
Norfolk Is. (Aus.)	0.03	0.01	2	Kingston	-
Norway	324	125	4,242	Oslo	24,160
Oman	212	82	1,502	Muscat	5,220
Pakistan	796	307	112,050	Islamabad	400
Panama	77.1	29.8	2,418	Panama City	2,180
Papua New Guinea	463	179	3,699	Port Moresby	820
Paraguay	407	157	4,277	Asunción	1,210
Peru	1,285	496	22,332	Lima	1,020
Peter 1st Is. (Nor.)	0.18	0.07	0	-	-
Philippines	300	116	61,480	Manila	740
Pitcairn Is. (UK)	0.03	0.01	0.06	Adamstown	-
Poland	313	121	38,180	Warsaw	1,830
Portugal	92.4	35.7	10,525	Lisbon	5,620
Puerto Rico (US)	8.9	3.4	3,599	San Juan	6,330
Qatar	11	4.2	368	Doha	15,860
Queen Maud Land (Nor.)	2,800	1,081	0	-	-
Réunion (Fr.)	2.5	0.97	599	St-Denis	4,000
Romania	238	92	23,200	Bucharest	1,340
Ross Dependency (NZ)	435	168	0	-	-
Russia	17,075	6,592	149,527	Moscow	3,220
Rwanda	26.3	10.2	7,181	Kigali	260
St Christopher/Nevis	0.36	0.14	44	Basseterre	3,960
St Helena (UK)	0.12	0.05	7	Jamestown	-
St Lucia	0.62	0.24	151	Castries	2,500
St Paul Is. (Fr.)	0.007	0.003	0	-	-
St Pierre & Miquelon (Fr.)	0.24	0.09	7	St-Pierre	-
St Vincent/Grenadines	0.39	0.15	116	Kingstown	1,730
San Marino	0.06	0.02	24	San Marino	-
São Tomé & Príncipe	0.96	0.37	121	São Tomé	350
Saudi Arabia	2,150	830	14,870	Riyadh	7,070
Senegal	197	76	7,327	Dakar	720
Seychelles	0.46	0.18	67	Victoria	5,110
Sierra Leone	71.7	27.7	4,151	Freetown	210
Singapore	0.62	0.24	3,003	Singapore	12,890
Slovak Republic	49	18.9	5,269	Bratislava	1,650
Slovenia	20.3	7.8	1,963	Ljubljana	-
Solomon Is.	28.9	11.2	321	Honiara	560
Somalia	638	246	7,497	Mogadishu	150
South Africa	1,221	471	35,282	Pretoria	2,530
South Georgia (UK)	3.8	1.4	0.05	-	-
South Sandwich Is. (UK)	0.38	0.15	0	-	-
Spain	505	195	38,959	Madrid	12,460
Sri Lanka	65.6	25.3	16,993	Colombo	500
Sudan	2,506	967	25,204	Khartoum	400
Surinam	163	63	422	Paramaribo	3,610
Svalbard (Nor.)	62.9	24.3	4	Longyearbyen	-
Swaziland	17.4	6.7	768	Mbabane	1,060
Sweden	450	174	8,618	Stockholm	25,490
Switzerland	41.3	15.9	6,712	Bern	33,510
Syria	185	71	12,116	Damascus	1,110
Taiwan	36	13.9	20,300	Taipei	6,600
Tajikistan	143.1	55.2	5,680	Dushanbe	1,050
Tanzania	945	365	25,635	Dar es Salaam	100
Thailand	513	198	57,196	Bangkok	1,580
Togo	56.8	21.9	3,531	Lomé	410
Tokelau (NZ)	0.01	0.005	2	Nukunonu	-
Tonga	0.75	0.29	95	Nuku'alofa	1,100
Trinidad & Tobago	5.1	2	1,227	Port of Spain	3,620
Tristan da Cunha (UK)	0.11	0.04	0.33	Edinburgh	-
Tunisia	164	63	8,180	Tunis	1,510
Turkey	779	301	57,326	Ankara	1,820
Turkmenistan	488.1	188.5	3,838	Ashkhabad	1,700
Turks & Caicos Is. (UK)	0.43	0.17	10	Grand Turk	-
Tuvalu	0.03	0.01	10	Funafuti	600
Uganda	236	91	18,795	Kampala	160
Ukraine	603.7	233.1	51,940	Kiev	2,340
United Arab Emirates	83.6	32.3	1,589	Abu Dhabi	19,860
United Kingdom	243.3	94	54,889	London	16,750
United States	9,373	3,619	249,975	Washington	22,560
Uruguay	177	68	3,094	Montevideo	2,860
Uzbekistan	447.4	172.7	21,627	Tashkent	1,350
Vanuatu	12.2	4.7	147	Port Vila	1,120
Vatican City	0.0004	0.0002	1	-	-
Venezuela	912	352	19,735	Caracas	2,610
Vietnam	332	127	66,200	Hanoi	300
Virgin Is. (UK)	0.15	0.06	13	Road Town	-
Virgin Is. (US)	0.34	0.13	117	Charlotte Amalie	12,000
Wake Is.	0.008	0.003	0.30	-	-
Wallis & Futuna Is. (Fr.)	0.20	0.08	18	Mata-Utu	-
Western Sahara	266	103	179	El Aaiún	-
Western Samoa	2.8	1.1	164	Apia	930
Yemen	528	204	11,282	Sana	540
Yugoslavia	102.3	39.5	10,642	Belgrade	2,940
Zaire	2,345	906	35,562	Kinshasa	230
Zambia	753	291	8,073	Lusaka	420
Zimbabwe	391	151	9,369	Harare	620

** Eritrea formally declared full independence from Ethiopia on 24th May 1993*

WORLD STATISTICS: CITIES

This list shows the principal cities with more than 500,000 inhabitants (for China only cities with more than 1 million are included). The figures are taken from the most recent census or estimate available, and as far as possible are the population of the metropolitan area, e.g. greater New York, Mexico or London. All the figures are in thousands. The top 20 world cities are indicated with their rank in brackets following the name.

Afghanistan
Kabul 1,127
Algeria
Algiers 1,722
Oran 664
Angola
Luanda 1,200
Argentina
Buenos Aires [8] 10,728
Cordoba 1,055
Rosario 1,016
Mendoza 668
La Plata 611
San Miguel de Tucumán 571
Armenia
Yerevan 1,199
Australia
Sydney 3,531
Melbourne 2,965
Brisbane 1,215
Perth 1,083
Adelaide 1,013
Austria
Vienna 1,483
Azerbaijan
Baku 1,757
Bangladesh
Dacca 4,770
Chittagong 1,840
Khulna 860
Rajshahi 430
Belgium
Brussels 970
Antwerp 500
Belorussia
Minsk 1,589
Gomel 500
Bolivia
La Paz 993
Brazil
São Paulo [3] 16,832
Rio de Janeiro [7] 11,141
Belo Horizonte 3,446
Recife 2,945
Pôrto Alegre 2,924
Salvador 2,362
Fortaleza 2,169
Çuritiba 1,926
Brasilia 1,557
Nova Iguaçu 1,325
Belem 1,296
Santos 1,200
Goiâna 928
Campinas 845
Manaus 834
São Gonçalo 731
Guarulhos 718
Duque de Caxias 666
Santo Andre 637
Osasco 594
São Bernado do Campo 566
São Luis 564
Natal 512
Bulgaria
Sofia 1,129
Burma (Myanmar)
Rangoon 2,459
Mandalay 533
Cambodia
Phnom Penh 500
Cameroon
Douala 1,030
Yaoundé 654
Central African Rep.
Bangui 597
Chad
Ndjamena 512
Canada
Toronto 3,427
Montréal 2,921
Vancouver 1,381
Ottawa-Hull 819
Edmonton 785
Calgary 671
Winnipeg 623
Québec 603
Hamilton 557

Chile
Santiago 4,858
China
Shanghai [5] 12,320
Beijing (Peking)[10] 9,750
Tianjin 5,459
Shenyang 4,285
Wuhan 3,493
Guangzhou 3,359
Chongqing 2,832
Harbin 2,668
Chengdu 2,642
Xi'an 2,387
Zibo 2,329
Nanjing 2,290
Nanchang 2,289
Lupanshui 2,247
Taiyuan 1,929
Changchun 1,908
Dalian 1,682
Zhaozhuang 1,612
Zhengzhou 1,610
Kunming 1,516
Jinan 1,464
Tangshan 1,410
Guiyang 1,403
Lanzhou 1,391
Linyi 1,385
Pingxiang 1,305
Qiqihar 1,301
Anshan 1,298
Qingdao 1,273
Xintao 1,272
Hangzhou 1,271
Fushun 1,270
Yangcheng 1,265
Yulin 1,255
Dongguang 1,230
Chao'an 1,227
Xiaogan 1,219
Fuzhou 1,205
Suining 1,195
Changsha 1,193
Shijiazhuang 1,187
Jilin 1,169
Xintai 1,167
Puyang 1,125
Baotou 1,119
Bozhou 1,112
Zhongshan 1,073
Luoyang 1,063
Laiwu 1,054
Leshan 1,039
Urumchi 1,038
Ningbo 1,033
Datong 1,020
Huainan 1,019
Heze 1,017
Handan 1,014
Linhai 1,012
Macheng 1,010
Changshu 1,004
Colombia
Bogotá 4,185
Medellin 1,506
Cali 1,397
Barranquilla 920
Cartagena 560
Congo
Brazzaville 596
Croatia
Zagreb 1,175
Cuba
Havana 2,059
Czech Republic
Prague 1,215
Denmark
Copenhagen 1,339
Dominican Rep.
Santo Domingo 1,313
Ecuador
Guayaquil 1,301
Quito 1,110
Egypt
Cairo [18] 6,325
Alexandria 2,893
El Giza 1,858
Shubra el Kheima 711
El Salvador
San Salvador 973

Ethiopia
Addis Ababa 1,686
Finland
Helsinki 987
France
Paris [13] 8,510
Lyons 1,170
Marseilles 1,080
Lille 935
Bordeaux 628
Toulouse 523
Georgia
Tbilisi 1,194
Germany
Berlin 3,301
Hamburg 1,594
Munich 1,189
Cologne 928
Essen 623
Frankfurt 619
Dortmund 584
Düsseldorf 563
Stuttgart 552
Leipzig 545
Bremen 533
Duisburg 525
Dresden 518
Hanover 500
Ghana
Accra 965
Greece
Athens 3,027
Thessalonika 872
Guatemala
Guatemala 2,000
Guinea
Conakry 705
Haiti
Port-au-Prince 1,144
Honduras
Tegucigalpa 605
Hong Kong
Kowloon 2,302
Hong Kong 1,176
Tsuen Wan 690
Hungary
Budapest 2,115
India
Calcutta [11] 9,194
Bombay [14] 8,243
Delhi 5,729
Madras 4,289
Bangalore 2,922
Ahmadabad 2,548
Hyderabad 2,546
Poona 1,686
Kanpur 1,639
Nagpur 1,302
Jaipur 1,015
Lucknow 1,008
Coimbatore 920
Patna 919
Surat 914
Madurai 908
Indore 829
Varanasi 797
Jabalpur 757
Agra 747
Vadodara 744
Cochin 686
Dhanbad 678
Bhopal 671
Jamshedpur 670
Allahabad 650
Ulhasnagar 649
Tiruchchirappalli 610
Ludhiana 606
Srinagar 606
Vishakhapatnam 604
Amritsar 595
Gwalior 556
Calicut 546
Vijayawada 543
Meerut 537
Dharwad 527
Trivandrum 520
Salem 519
Solapur 515
Jodhpur 506
Ranchi 503

Indonesia
Jakarta [16] 7,348
Surabaya 2,224
Medan 1,806
Bandung 1,567
Semarang 1,026
Palembang 787
Ujung Pandang 709
Malang 512
Iran
Tehran [20] 6,043
Mashhad 1,464
Esfahan 987
Tabriz 971
Shiraz 848
Ahvaz 580
Bakhtaran 561
Qom 543
Iraq
Baghdad 4,649
Basra 617
Mosul 571
Ireland
Dublin 921
Italy
Rome 2,817
Milan 1,464
Naples 1,203
Turin 1,012
Palermo 731
Genoa 715
Ivory Coast
Abidjan 1,850
Bouaké 640
Jamaica
Kingston 525
Japan
Tokyo [6] 11,829
Yokohama 2,993
Osaka 2,636
Nagoya 2,116
Sapporo 1,543
Kyoto 1,479
Kobe 1,411
Fukuoka 1,160
Kawasaki 1,089
Kitakyushu 1,056
Hiroshima 1,044
Sakai 818
Chiba 789
Sendai 700
Okayama 572
Kumamoto 556
Kagoshima 531
Higashiosaka 523
Hamamatsu 514
Amagasaki 509
Funabashi 507
Jordan
Amman 1,160
Irbid 680
Kazakhstan
Alma Ata 1,108
Karaganda 614
Astrakhan 509
Kenya
Nairobi 1,429
Mombasa 500
Kirghizia
Bishkek 616
Korea, North
Pyongyang 2,639
Hamhung 775
Chongjin 754
Chinnampo 691
Sinuiju 500
Korea, South
Seoul [9] 10,513
Pusan 3,754
Taegu 2,206
Inchon 1,604
Kwangju 1,165
Taejon 866
Ulsan 551
Latvia
Riga 915
Lebanon
Beirut 702
Libya
Tripoli 980

Benghazi 650
Lithuania
Vilnius 582
Macedonia
Skopje 505
Madagascar
Antananarivo 703
Malaysia
Kuala Lumpur 1,103
Mali
Bamako 646
Mauritania
Nouakchott 500
Mexico
Mexico City [1] 18,748
Guadalajara 2,587
Monterrey 2,335
Puebla 1,218
León 947
Torreón 730
San Luis Potosi 602
Ciudad Juárez 596
Mérida 580
Culiacán Rosales 560
Mexicali 511
Moldavia
Kishinev 565
Mongolia
Ulan Bator 500
Morocco
Casablanca 2,158
Rabat-Salé 893
Fès 548
Mozambique
Maputo 1,070
Netherlands
Rotterdam 1,040
Amsterdam 1,038
The Hague 684
Utrecht 526
New Zealand
Auckland 885
Nicaragua
Managua 682
Nigeria
Lagos 1,097
Ibadan 1,060
Ogbomosho 527
Norway
Oslo 643
Pakistan
Karachi 5,208
Lahore 2,953
Faisalabad 1,104
Rawalpindi 795
Hyderabad 752
Multan 722
Gujranwala 659
Peshawar 556
Panama
Panama City 625
Paraguay
Asunción 708
Peru
Lima-Callao 4,605
Arequipa 592
Philippines
Manila 1,728
Quezon City 1,326
Cebu 552
Caloocan 525
Poland
Warsaw 1,671
Lodz 852
Krakow 744
Wroclaw 640
Poznan 586
Portugal
Lisbon 1,612
Oporto 1,315
Puerto Rico
San Juan 1,816
Romania
Bucharest 2,014
Russia
Moscow [12] 8,967
St Petersburg 5,020
Nizhniy Novgorod 1,438
Novosibirsk 1,436
Yekaterinburg 1,367

Samara 1,257
Chelyabinsk 1,179
Omsk 1,148
Kazan 1,094
Perm 1,091
Ufa 1,083
Rostov 1,020
Volgograd 999
Krasnoyarsk 912
Saratov 905
Voronezh 887
Vladivostok 648
Izhevsk 635
Yaroslavl 633
Togliatti 630
Irkutsk 626
Simbirsk 625
Krasnodar 620
Barnaul 602
Khabarovsk 601
Novokuznetsk 600
Orenburg 547
Penza 543
Tula 540
Kemerovo 520
Ryazan 515
Tomsk 502
Naberezhniye-Chelni 501
Saudi Arabia
Riyadh 2,000
Jedda 1,400
Mecca 618
Medina 500
Senegal
Dakar 1,382
Singapore
Singapore 2,680
Somali Republic
Mogadishu 1,000
South Africa
Cape Town 1,912
Johannesburg 1,726
East Rand 1,038
Durban 982
Pretoria 823
Port Elizabeth 652
West Rand 647
Vereeniging 540
Spain
Madrid 3,123
Barcelona 1,694
Valencia 739
Seville 668
Zaragoza 596
Malaga 595
Sri Lanka
Colombo 1,412
Sudan
Omdurman 600
Khartoum 510
Sweden
Stockholm 1,471
Gothenburg 720
Malmö 500
Switzerland
Zurich 839
Syria
Damascus 1,361
Aleppo 1,308
Taiwan
Taipei 2,680
Kaohsiung 1,343
Taichung 715
Tainan 657
Panchiao 506
Tajikistan
Dushanbe 595
Tanzania
Dar es Salaam 1,100
Thailand
Bangkok 5,609
Tunisia
Tunis 774
Turkey
Istanbul 5,495
Ankara 2,252
Izmir 1,490
Adana 776
Bursa 614

Uganda
Kampala 500
Ukraine
Kiev 2,587
Kharkov 1,611
Dnepropetrovsk 1,179
Odessa 1,115
Donetsk 1,110
Zaporozhye 884
Lvov 790
Krivoy Rog 713
Mariupol 529
Lugansk 509
Nikolayev 503
United Kingdom
London [17] 6,378
Manchester 1,669
Birmingham 1,400
Liverpool 1,060
Glasgow 730
Newcastle 617
Uruguay
Montevideo 1,248
United States
New York [2] 18,087
Los Angeles [4] 14,532
Chicago [15] 8,066
San Francisco [19] 6,253
Philadelphia 5,899
Detroit 4,665
Boston 4,172
Washington 3,924
Dallas 3,885
Houston 3,711
Miami 3,193
Atlanta 2,834
Cleveland 2,760
Seattle 2,559
San Diego 2,498
Minneapolis-SP. 2,464
St Louis 2,444
Baltimore 2,382
Pittsburgh 2,243
Phoenix 2,122
Tampa 2,068
Denver 1,858
Cincinnati 1,729
Kansas City 1,575
Milwaukee 1,572
Portland 1,414
Sacramento 1,385
Norfolk 1,380
Columbus 1,344
San Antonio 1,323
New Orleans 1,307
Indianapolis 1,237
Buffalo 1,176
Providence 1,118
Charlotte 1,112
Hartford 1,108
Salt Lake City 1,065
San Jose 712
Memphis 653
Jacksonville 610
Uzbekistan
Tashkent 2,073
Venezuela
Caracas 3,247
Maracaibo 1,295
Valencia 1,135
Maracay 857
Barquisimeto 718
Vietnam
Ho Chi Minh 3,900
Hanoi 3,100
Haiphong 1,279
Da Nang 500
Yemen
San'a 500
Yugoslavia
Belgrade 1,470
Zaïre
Kinshasa 2,654
Lubumbashi 543
Zambia
Lusaka 900
Zimbabwe
Harare 681
Bulawayo 500

WORLD STATISTICS: DISTANCES

The table shows air distances in miles and kilometres between thirty major cities. Known as 'Great Circle' distances, these measure the shortest routes between the cities, which aircraft use where possible. The maps show the world centred on six individual cities, and illustrate, for example, why direct flights from Japan to northern America and Europe are across the Arctic regions, and Singapore is on the direct line route from Europe to Australia. The maps have been constructed on an Azimuthal Equidistant projection, on which all distances measured through the centre point are true to scale. The circular lines are drawn at 5,000, 10,000 and 15,000 km from the central city.

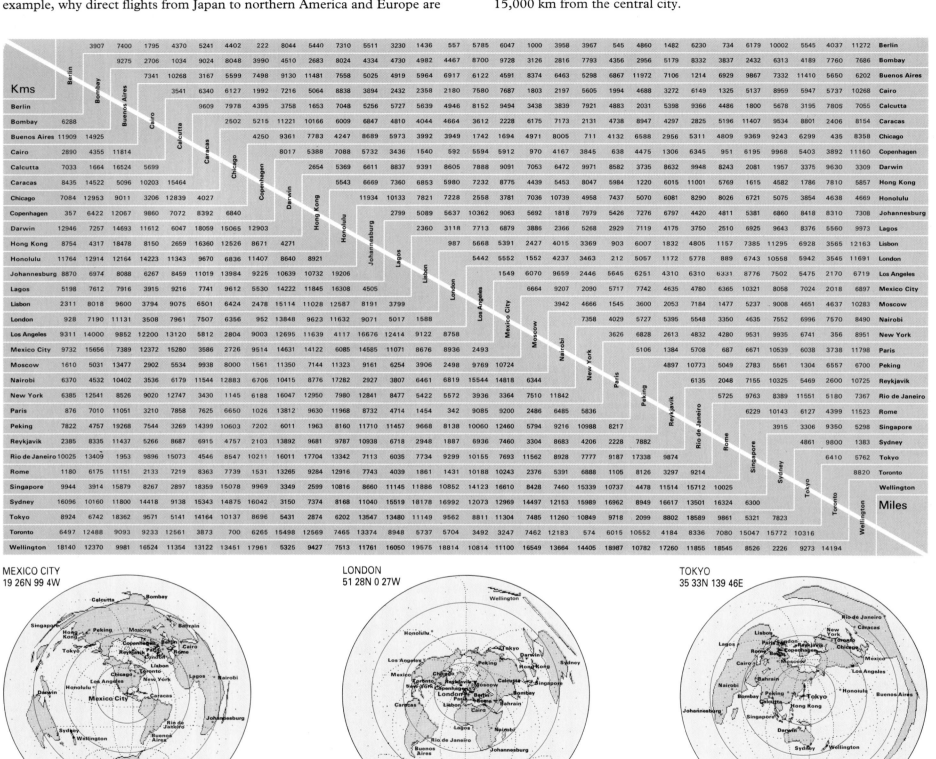

Distance table — upper-right triangle values are in **Miles**, lower-left triangle values are in **Kms**. Diagonal cells give the city name.

	Berlin	Bombay	Buenos Aires	Cairo	Calcutta	Caracas	Chicago	Copenhagen	Darwin	Hong Kong	Honolulu	Johannesburg	Lagos	Lisbon	London	Los Angeles	Mexico City	Moscow	Nairobi	New York	Paris	Peking	Reykjavik	Rio de Janeiro	Rome	Singapore	Sydney	Tokyo	Toronto	Wellington
Berlin	Berlin	3907	7400	1795	4370	5241	4402	222	8044	5440	7310	5511	3230	1436	557	5785	6047	1000	3958	3967	545	4860	1482	6230	734	6179	10002	5545	4037	11272
Bombay	6288	Bombay	9275	2706	1034	9024	8048	3990	4510	2683	8024	4334	4730	4982	4467	8700	9728	3126	2816	7793	4356	2956	5179	8332	3837	2432	6313	4189	7760	7686
Buenos Aires	11909	14925	Buenos Aires	7341	10268	3167	5599	7498	9130	11481	7558	5025	4919	5964	6917	6122	4591	8374	6463	5298	6867	11972	7106	1214	6929	9867	7332	11410	5650	6202
Cairo	2890	4355	11814	Cairo	3541	6340	6127	1992	7216	5064	8838	3894	2432	2358	2180	7580	7687	1803	2197	5605	1994	4688	3272	6149	1325	5137	8959	5947	5737	10268
Calcutta	7033	1664	16524	5699	Calcutta	9609	7978	4395	3758	1653	7048	5256	5727	5639	4946	8152	9494	3438	3839	7921	4883	2031	5398	9366	4486	1800	5678	3195	7805	7055
Caracas	8435	14522	5096	10203	15464	Caracas	2502	5215	11221	10166	6009	6847	4810	4044	4664	3612	6175	7173	2131	4738	4297	2825	5196	11407	9534	8801	2406	8154		
Chicago	7084	12953	9011	3206	12839	4027	Chicago	8017	5388	7088	5732	3436	1540	592	5594	5912	970	4167	3845	638	4475	1306	6345	951	6195	9968	5403	3892	11160	
Copenhagen	357	6422	12067	9860	7072	8392	6840	Copenhagen	2654	5369	6611	8837	9391	8605	7888	9091	7053	6472	9971	8582	3735	8632	9948	8243	2081	1957	3375	9630	3309	
Darwin	12946	7257	14693	11612	6047	18059	15065	12903	Darwin	5543	6669	7360	6853	5980	7232	8775	4439	5453	8047	5984	1220	6015	11001	5769	1615	4582	1786	7810	5857	
Hong Kong	8754	4317	18478	8150	2659	16360	12526	8671	4271	Hong Kong	11934	10133	7821	7228	2558	3781	7036	10739	4958	7437	5070	6081	8290	8026	6721	5075	3854	4638	4669	
Honolulu	11764	12914	12164	14223	11343	9670	6836	11407	8640	8921	Honolulu	2799	5089	5637	10362	9063	5692	1818	7979	5426	7276	6797	4420	4811	5381	6860	8418	8310	7308	
Johannesburg	8870	6974	8088	6267	8459	11019	13984	9225	10639	10732	19206	Johannesburg	2360	3118	7713	6879	3886	2366	5268	2929	7119	4175	3750	2510	6925	9643	8376	5560	9973	
Lagos	5198	7612	7916	3915	9216	7741	9612	5530	14222	11845	16308	4505	Lagos	987	5668	5391	2427	4015	3369	903	6007	1832	4805	1157	7385	11295	6928	3565	12163	
Lisbon	2311	8018	9600	3794	9075	6501	6424	2478	15114	11028	12587	8191	3799	Lisbon	5442	5552	1552	4237	3463	212	5057	1172	5778	889	6743	10558	5942	3545	11691	
London	928	7190	11131	3508	7961	7507	6356	952	13848	9623	11632	9071	5017	1588	London	1549	6070	9659	2446	5645	6251	6310	6331	8776	7502	5475	2170	6719		
Los Angeles	9311	14000	9852	12200	13120	5812	2804	9003	12695	11639	4117	16676	12414	9122	8758	Los Angeles	7358	4029	5727	5395	5548	3350	4635	7552	6996	7570	8490			
Mexico City	9732	15656	7389	12372	15280	3586	2726	9514	14631	14122	6085	14585	11071	8676	8936	2493	Mexico City	3942	4666	1545	3600	2053	7184	1477	5237	9008	4651	4637	10283	
Moscow	1610	5031	13477	2902	5534	9938	8000	1561	11350	7144	11323	9161	6254	3906	2498	9769	10724	Moscow	3626	6828	2613	4832	4280	9531	9935	6741	356	8951		
Nairobi	6370	4532	10402	3536	6179	11544	12883	6706	10415	8776	17282	2927	3807	6461	6819	15544	14818	6344	Nairobi	5106	1384	5708	687	6671	10539	6038	3738	11798		
New York	6385	12541	8526	9020	12747	3430	1145	6188	16047	12950	7980	12841	8477	5422	5572	3936	3364	7510	11842	New York	4897	10773	5049	2783	5561	1304	6557	6700		
Paris	876	7010	11051	3210	7858	7625	6650	1026	13812	9630	11968	8732	4714	1454	342	9085	9200	2486	6485	5836	Paris	6135	2048	7155	10325	5449	2600	10725		
Peking	7822	4757	19268	7544	3269	14399	10603	7202	6011	1963	8160	11710	11457	9668	8138	10060	12460	5794	9216	10988	8217	Peking	5725	9763	8389	11551	5180	7367	8490	
Reykjavik	2385	8335	11437	5266	8687	6915	4757	2103	13892	9681	9787	10938	6718	2948	1887	6936	7460	3304	8683	4206	2228	7882	Reykjavik	6229	10143	6127	4399	11523		
Rio de Janeiro	10025	13409	1953	9896	15073	4546	8547	10211	16011	17704	13342	7113	6035	7734	9299	10155	7693	11562	8928	7777	9187	17338	9874	Rio de Janeiro	3915	3306	9350	5298		
Rome	1180	6175	11151	2133	7219	8363	7739	1531	13265	9284	12916	7743	4039	1861	1431	10188	10243	2376	5391	6888	1105	8126	3297	9214	Rome	6229	10143	6127	4861	9800	1383
Singapore	9944	3914	15879	8267	2897	18359	15078	9969	3349	2599	10816	8660	11145	11886	10852	14123	16610	8428	7460	15339	10737	4478	11514	15712	10025	Singapore	3915	3306	9350	5298
Sydney	16096	10160	11800	14418	9138	15343	14875	16042	3150	7374	8168	11040	15519	18178	16992	12073	12969	14497	12153	15989	16962	8949	16617	13501	16324	6300	Sydney	4861	9800	1383
Tokyo	8924	6742	18362	9571	5141	14164	10137	8696	5431	2874	6202	13547	13480	11149	9562	8811	11304	7485	11260	10849	9718	2099	8802	18589	9861	5321	7823	Tokyo	6410	5762
Toronto	6497	12488	9093	9233	12561	700	6265	15498	12569	7465	13374	8948	5704	3492	3247	7462	12183	574	6015	10552	4184	8336	7080	15047	15772	10316			Toronto	8820
Wellington	18140	12370	9981	16524	11354	13122	13451	17961	5325	9427	7513	11761	16050	18814	10814	11100	16549	13664	14405	18987	10782	17260	11855	18545	8526	2226	9273	14194		Wellington

MEXICO CITY
19 26N 99 4W

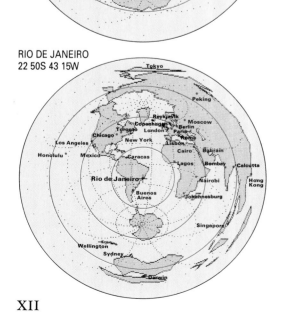

LONDON
51 28N 0 27W

TOKYO
35 33N 139 46E

RIO DE JANEIRO
22 50S 43 15W

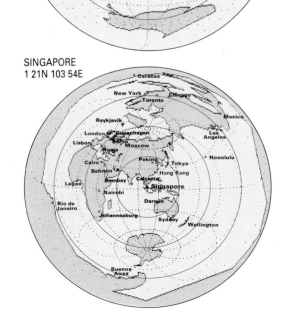

SINGAPORE
1 21N 103 54E

SYDNEY
33 56S 151 10E

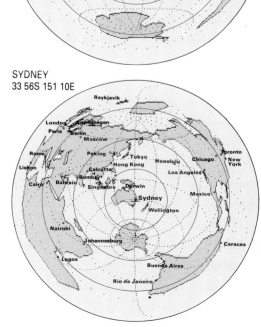

WORLD STATISTICS: CLIMATE

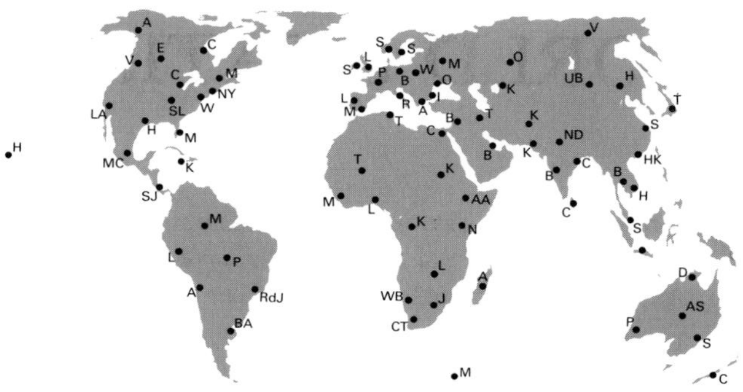

Rainfall and temperature figures are provided for more than 70 cities around the world. As climate is affected by altitude, the height of each city is shown in metres beneath its name. For each month, the figures in red show average temperature in degrees Celsius or centigrade, and in blue the total rainfall or snow in millimetres; the average annual temperature and total annual rainfall are at the end of the rows.

EUROPE	Jan.	Feb.	Mar.	Apr.	May	June	July	Aug.	Sept.	Oct.	Nov.	Dec.	Year
Athens, Greece	62	37	37	23	23	14	6	7	15	51	56	71	402
107 m	10	10	12	16	20	25	28	28	24	20	15	11	18
Berlin, Germany	46	40	33	42	49	65	73	69	48	49	46	43	603
55 m	-1	0	4	9	14	17	19	18	15	9	5	1	9
Istanbul, Turkey	109	92	72	46	38	34	34	30	58	81	103	119	816
114 m	5	6	7	11	16	20	23	23	20	16	12	8	14
Lisbon, Portugal	111	76	109	54	44	16	3	4	33	62	93	103	708
77 m	11	12	14	16	17	20	22	23	21	18	14	12	17
London, UK	54	40	37	37	46	45	57	59	49	57	64	48	593
5 m	4	5	7	9	12	16	18	17	15	11	8	5	11
Málaga, Spain	61	51	62	46	26	5	1	3	29	64	64	62	474
33 m	12	13	16	17	19	29	25	26	23	20	16	13	18
Moscow, Russia	39	38	36	37	53	58	88	71	58	45	47	54	624
156 m	-13	-10	-4	6	13	16	18	17	12	6	-1	-7	4
Odessa, Ukraine	57	62	30	21	34	34	42	37	37	13	35	71	473
64 m	-3	-1	2	9	15	20	22	22	18	12	9	1	10
Paris, France	56	46	35	42	57	54	59	64	55	50	51	50	619
75 m	3	4	8	11	15	18	20	19	17	12	7	4	12
Rome, Italy	71	62	57	51	46	37	15	21	63	99	129	93	744
17 m	8	9	11	14	18	22	25	25	22	17	13	10	16
Shannon, Irish Republic	94	67	56	53	61	57	77	79	86	86	96	117	929
2 m	5	5	7	9	12	14	16	16	14	11	8	6	10
Stockholm, Sweden	43	30	25	31	34	45	61	76	60	48	53	48	554
44 m	-3	-3	-1	5	10	15	18	17	12	7	3	0	7
ASIA													
Bahrain	8	18	13	8	<3	0	0	0	0	0	18	18	81
5 m	17	18	21	25	29	32	33	34	31	28	24	19	26
Bangkok, Thailand	8	20	36	58	198	160	160	175	305	206	66	5	1,397
2 m	26	28	29	30	29	29	28	28	28	28	26	25	28
Beirut, Lebanon	191	158	94	53	18	3	<3	<3	5	51	132	185	892
34 m	14	14	16	18	22	24	27	28	26	24	19	16	21
Bombay, India	3	3	3	<3	18	485	617	340	264	64	13	3	1,809
11 m	24	24	26	28	30	29	27	27	27	28	27	26	27
Calcutta, India	10	31	36	43	140	297	325	328	252	114	20	5	1,600
6 m	20	22	27	30	30	30	29	29	29	28	23	19	26
Colombo, Sri Lanka	89	69	147	231	371	224	135	109	160	348	315	147	2,365
7 m	26	26	27	28	28	27	27	27	27	27	26	26	27
Harbin, China	6	5	10	23	43	94	112	104	46	33	8	5	488
160 m	-18	-15	-5	6	13	19	22	21	14	4	-6	-16	3
Ho Chi Minh, Vietnam	15	3	13	43	221	330	315	269	335	269	114	56	1,984
9 m	26	27	29	30	29	28	28	28	27	27	27	26	28
Hong Kong	33	46	74	137	292	394	381	361	257	114	43	31	2,162
33 m	16	15	18	22	26	28	28	28	27	25	21	18	23
Jakarta, Indonesia	300	300	211	147	114	97	64	43	66	112	142	203	1,798
8 m	26	26	27	27	27	27	27	27	27	27	27	26	27
Kabul, Afghanistan	31	36	94	102	20	5	3	3	<3	15	20	10	338
1,815 m	-3	-1	6	13	18	22	25	24	20	14	7	3	12
Karachi, Pakistan	13	10	8	3	3	18	81	41	13	<3	3	5	196
4 m	19	20	24	28	30	31	30	29	28	28	24	20	26
Kazalinsk, Kazakhstan	10	10	13	13	15	5	5	8	8	10	13	15	125
63 m	-12	-11	-3	6	18	23	25	23	16	8	-1	-7	7
New Delhi, India	23	18	13	8	13	74	180	172	117	10	3	10	640
218 m	14	17	23	28	33	34	31	30	29	26	20	15	25
Omsk, Russia	15	8	8	13	31	51	51	51	28	25	18	20	318
85 m	-22	-19	-12	-1	10	16	18	16	10	1	-11	-18	-1
Shanghai, China	48	58	84	94	94	180	147	142	130	71	51	36	1,135
7 m	4	5	9	14	20	24	28	28	23	19	12	7	16
Singapore	252	173	193	188	173	173	170	196	178	208	254	257	2,413
10 m	26	27	28	28	28	28	28	27	27	27	27	27	27
Tehran, Iran	46	38	46	36	13	3	3	3	3	8	20	31	246
1,220 m	2	5	9	16	21	26	30	29	25	18	12	6	17
Tokyo, Japan	48	74	107	135	147	165	142	152	234	208	97	56	1,565
6 m	3	4	7	13	17	21	25	26	23	17	11	6	14
Ulan Bator, Mongolia	<3	<3	3	5	10	28	76	51	23	5	5	3	208
1,325 m	-26	-21	-13	-1	6	14	16	14	8	-1	-13	-22	-3
Verkhoyansk, Russia	5	5	3	5	8	23	28	25	13	8	8	5	134
100 m	-50	-45	-32	-15	0	12	14	9	2	-15	-38	-48	-17
AFRICA													
Addis Ababa, Ethiopia	<3	3	25	135	213	201	206	239	102	28	<3	0	1,151
2,450 m	19	20	20	20	19	18	18	19	21	22	21	20	20
Antananarivo, Madagas.	300	279	178	53	18	8	8	10	18	61	135	287	1,356
1,372 m	21	21	21	19	18	15	14	15	17	19	21	21	19
Cairo, Egypt	5	5	5	3	3	<3	0	0	<3	<3	3	5	28
116 m	13	15	18	21	25	28	28	28	26	24	20	15	22
Cape Town, South Africa	15	8	18	48	79	84	89	66	43	31	18	10	508
17 m	21	21	20	17	14	13	12	13	14	16	18	19	17
Johannesburg, S. Africa	114	109	89	38	25	8	8	8	23	56	107	125	709
1,665 m	20	20	18	16	13	10	11	13	16	18	19	20	16
Khartoum, Sudan	<3	<3	<3	<3	3	8	53	71	18	5	<3	0	158
390 m	24	25	28	31	33	34	32	31	32	32	28	25	29
Kinshasa, Zaïre	135	145	196	196	158	8	3	3	31	119	221	142	1,354
325 m	26	26	27	27	26	24	23	24	25	26	26	26	25
Lagos, Nigeria	28	46	102	150	269	460	279	64	140	206	69	25	1,836
3 m	27	28	29	28	28	26	26	25	26	26	28	28	27
Lusaka, Zambia	231	191	142	18	3	<3	<3	0	<3	10	91	150	836
1,277 m	21	22	21	21	19	16	16	18	22	24	23	22	21
Monrovia, Liberia	31	56	97	216	516	973	996	373	744	772	236	130	5,138
23 m	26	26	27	27	26	25	24	25	25	25	26	26	26
Nairobi, Kenya	38	64	125	211	158	46	15	23	31	53	109	86	958
1,820 m	19	19	19	19	18	16	16	16	18	19	18	18	18
Timbuktu, Mali	<3	<3	3	<3	5	23	79	81	38	3	<3	<3	231
301 m	22	24	28	32	34	35	32	30	32	31	28	23	29
Tunis, Tunisia	64	51	41	36	18	8	3	8	33	51	48	61	419
66 m	10	11	13	16	19	23	26	27	25	20	16	11	18
Walvis Bay, South Africa	<3	5	8	3	3	<3	<3	3	<3	<3	<3	<3	23
7 m	19	19	19	18	17	16	15	14	14	15	17	18	18
AUSTRALIA, NEW ZEALAND AND ANTARCTICA													
Alice Springs, Australia	43	33	28	10	15	13	8	8	8	18	31	38	252
579 m	29	28	25	20	15	12	12	14	18	23	26	28	21
Christchurch, N. Zealand	56	43	48	48	66	66	69	48	46	43	48	56	638
10 m	16	16	14	12	9	6	6	7	9	12	14	16	11
Darwin, Australia	386	312	254	97	15	3	<3	3	13	51	119	239	1,491
30 m	29	29	29	29	28	26	25	26	28	29	30	29	28
Mawson, Antarctica	11	30	20	10	44	180	4	40	3	20	0	0	362
14 m	0	-5	-10	-14	-15	-16	-18	-18	-19	-13	-5	-1	-11
Perth, Australia	8	10	20	43	130	180	170	149	86	56	20	13	881
60 m	23	23	22	19	16	14	13	13	15	16	19	22	18
Sydney, Australia	89	102	127	135	127	117	117	76	73	71	73	73	1,181
42 m	22	22	21	18	15	13	12	13	15	18	19	21	17
NORTH AMERICA													
Anchorage, Alaska, USA	20	18	15	10	13	18	41	66	66	56	25	23	371
40 m	-11	-8	-5	2	7	12	14	13	9	2	-5	-11	2
Chicago, Ill., USA	51	51	66	71	86	89	84	81	79	66	61	51	836
251 m	-4	-3	2	9	14	20	23	22	19	12	5	-1	10
Churchill, Man., Canada	15	13	18	23	32	44	46	58	51	43	39	21	402
13 m	-28	-26	-20	-10	-2	6	12	11	5	-2	-12	-22	-7
Edmonton, Alta., Canada	25	19	19	22	43	77	89	78	39	17	16	25	466
676 m	-15	-10	-5	4	11	15	17	16	11	6	-4	-10	3
Honolulu, Hawaii, USA	104	66	79	48	25	18	23	28	36	48	64	104	643
12 m	23	18	19	20	22	24	25	26	26	24	22	19	22
Houston, Tex., USA	89	76	84	91	119	117	99	99	104	94	89	109	1,171
12 m	12	13	17	21	24	27	28	29	26	22	16	12	21
Kingston, Jamaica	23	15	23	31	102	89	38	91	99	180	74	36	800
34 m	25	25	25	26	26	28	28	28	27	27	26	26	26
Los Angeles, Calif., USA	79	76	71	25	10	3	<3	<3	5	15	31	66	381
95 m	13	14	14	16	17	19	21	22	21	18	16	14	17
Mexico City, Mexico	13	5	10	20	53	119	170	152	130	51	18	8	747
2,309 m	12	13	16	18	19	19	17	18	18	16	14	13	16
Miami, Fla., USA	71	53	64	81	173	178	155	160	203	234	71	51	1,516
8 m	20	20	22	23	25	27	28	28	27	25	22	21	24
Montréal, Que., Canada	72	65	74	74	66	82	90	92	88	76	81	87	946
57 m	-10	-9	-3	-6	13	18	21	20	15	9	2	-7	6
New York, N.Y., USA	94	97	91	81	81	84	107	109	86	89	76	91	1,092
96 m	-1	-1	3	10	16	20	23	23	21	15	7	2	11
St Louis, Mo., USA	58	64	89	97	114	114	89	86	81	74	71	64	1,001
173 m	0	1	7	13	19	24	26	26	22	15	8	2	14
San José, Costa Rica	15	5	20	46	229	241	211	241	305	300	145	41	1,798
1,146 m	19	19	21	21	22	21	21	21	21	20	20	19	20
Vancouver, B.C., Canada	154	115	101	60	52	45	32	41	67	114	150	182	1,113
14 m	3	5	6	9	12	15	17	17	14	10	6	4	10
Washington, D.C., USA	86	76	91	84	94	99	112	109	94	74	66	79	1,064
22 m	1	2	7	12	18	23	25	24	20	14	8	3	13
SOUTH AMERICA													
Antofagasta, Chile	0	0	0	<3	<3	3	5	3	<3	3	<3	0	13
94 m	21	21	20	18	16	15	14	14	15	16	18	19	17
Buenos Aires, Argentina	79	71	109	89	76	61	56	61	79	86	84	99	950
27 m	23	23	21	17	13	9	10	11	13	15	19	22	16
Lima, Peru	3	<3	<3	<3	5	5	8	8	8	3	3	<3	41
120 m	23	24	24	22	19	17	17	16	17	18	19	21	20
Manaus, Brazil	249	231	262	221	170	84	58	38	46	107	142	203	1,811
44 m	28	28	28	27	28	28	28	28	29	29	29	28	28
Paraná, Brazil	287	236	239	102	13	<3	3	5	28	127	231	310	1,582
260 m	23	23	23	23	23	21	21	22	24	24	24	23	23
Rio de Janeiro, Brazil	125	122	130	107	79	53	41	43	66	79	104	137	1,082
61 m	26	26	25	24	22	21	21	21	21	22	23	25	23

WORLD STATISTICS: PHYSICAL DIMENSIONS

Each topic list is divided into continents and within a continent the items are listed in order of size. The order of the continents is as in the atlas, Europe through to South America. Certain lists down to this mark > are complete; below they are selective. The world top ten are shown in square brackets; in the case of mountains this has not been done because the world top 30 are all in Asia. The figures are rounded as appropriate.

WORLD, CONTINENTS, OCEANS

	km²	miles²	%
The World	509,450,000	196,672,000	-
Land	149,450,000	57,688,000	29.3
Water	360,000,000	138,984,000	70.7
Asia	44,500,000	17,177,000	29.8
Africa	30,302,000	11,697,000	20.3
North America	24,241,000	9,357,000	16.2
South America	17,793,000	6,868,000	11.9
Antarctica	14,100,000	5,443,000	9.4
Europe	9,957,000	3,843,000	6.7
Australia & Oceania	8,557,000	3,303,000	5.7
Pacific Ocean	179,679,000	69,356,000	49.9
Atlantic Ocean	92,373,000	35,657,000	25.7
Indian Ocean	73,917,000	28,532,000	20.5
Arctic Ocean	14,090,000	5,439,000	3.9

SEAS

Pacific	km²	miles²
South China Sea	2,318,000	895,000
Bering Sea	2,268,000	875,000
Sea of Okhotsk	1,528,000	590,000
East China & Yellow	1,249,000	482,000
Sea of Japan	1,008,000	389,000
Gulf of California	162,000	62,500
Bass Strait	75,000	29,000

Atlantic	km²	miles²
Caribbean Sea	2,766,000	1,068,000
Mediterranean Sea	2,516,000	971,000
Gulf of Mexico	1,543,000	596,000
Hudson Bay	1,232,000	476,000
North Sea	575,000	223,000
Black Sea	452,000	174,000
Baltic Sea	397,000	153,000
Gulf of St Lawrence	238,000	92,000

Indian	km²	miles²
Red Sea	438,000	169,000
The Gulf	239,000	92,000

MOUNTAINS

Europe		m	ft
Mont Blanc	France/Italy	4,807	15,771
Monte Rosa	Italy/Switzerland	4,634	15,203
Dom	Switzerland	4,545	14,911
Weisshorn	Switzerland	4,505	14,780
Matterhorn/Cervino	Italy/Switzerland	4,478	14,691
Mt Maudit	France/Italy	4,465	14,649
Finsteraarhorn	Switzerland	4,275	14,025
Aletschhorn	Switzerland	4,182	13,720
Jungfrau	Switzerland	4,158	13,642
Barre des Ecrins	France	4,103	13,461
Gran Paradiso	Italy	4,061	13,323
Piz Bernina	Italy/Switzerland	4,052	13,294
Ortles	Italy	3,899	12,792
Monte Viso	Italy	3,841	12,602
Grossglockner	Austria	3,797	12,457
Wildspitze	Austria	3,774	12,382
Weisskügel	Austria/Italy	3,736	12,257
Dammastock	Switzerland	3,640	11,942
Tödi	Switzerland	3,623	11,886
Presanella	Italy	3,556	11,667
Monte Adamello	Italy	3,554	11,660
Mulhacén	Spain	3,478	11,411
Pico de Aneto	Spain	3,404	11,168
Marmolada	Italy	3,342	10,964
Etna	Italy	3,340	10,958
> Musala	Bulgaria	2,925	9,596
Olympus	Greece	2,917	9,570
Gerlachovka	Slovak Republic	2,655	8,711
Galdhöpiggen	Norway	2,469	8,100
Pietrosul	Romania	2,305	7,562
Hvannadalshnúkur	Iceland	2,119	6,952
Narodnaya	Russia	1,894	6,214
Ben Nevis	UK	1,343	4,406

Asia		m	ft
Everest	China/Nepal	8,848	29,029
Godwin Austen (K2)	China/Kashmir	8,611	28,251
Kanchenjunga	India/Nepal	8,598	28,208
Lhotse	China/Nepal	8,516	27,939
Makalu	China/Nepal	8,481	27,824
Cho Oyu	China/Nepal	8,201	26,906
Dhaulagiri	Nepal	8,172	26,811
Manaslu	Nepal	8,156	26,758
Nanga Parbat	Kashmir	8,126	26,660
Annapurna	Nepal	8,078	26,502
Gasherbrum	China/Kashmir	8,068	26,469
Broad Peak	India	8,051	26,414
Gosainthan	China	8,012	26,286
Disteghil Sar	Kashmir	7,885	25,869
Nuptse	Nepal	7,879	25,849
Masherbrum	Kashmir	7,826	25,676
Nanda Devi	India	7,817	25,646
Rakaposhi	Kashmir	7,788	25,551
Kamet	India	7,756	25,446
Namcha Barwa	China	7,756	25,446
Gurla Mandhata	China	7,728	25,354
Muztag	China	7,723	25,338
Kongur Shan	China	7,719	25,324
Tirich Mir	Pakistan	7,690	25,229
> Saser	Kashmir	7,672	25,170
Pik Kommunizma	Tajikistan	7,495	24,590
Aling Gangri	China	7,315	23,999
Elbrus	Russia	5,633	18,481
Demavand	Iran	5,604	18,386
Ararat	Turkey	5,165	16,945
Gunong Kinabalu	Malaysia (Borneo)	4,101	13,455
Yu Shan	Taiwan	3,997	13,113
Fuji-san	Japan	3,776	12,388
Rinjani	Indonesia	3,726	12,224
Mt Rajang	Philippines	3,364	11,037
Pidurutalagala	Sri Lanka	2,524	8,281

Africa		m	ft
Kilimanjaro	Tanzania	5,895	19,340
Mt Kenya	Kenya	5,199	17,057
Ruwenzori	Uganda/Zaïre	5,109	16,762
Ras Dashan	Ethiopia	4,620	15,157
Meru	Tanzania	4,565	14,977
Karisimbi	Rwanda/Zaïre	4,507	14,787
Mt Elgon	Kenya/Uganda	4,321	14,176
Batu	Ethiopia	4,307	14,130
Gughe	Ethiopia	4,200	13,779
Toubkal	Morocco	4,165	13,665
Irhil Mgoun	Morocco	4,071	13,356
Mt Cameroon	Cameroon	4,070	13,353
Teide	Spain (Tenerife)	3,718	12,198
Thabana Ntlenyana	Lesotho	3,482	11,424
> Emi Kussi	Chad	3,415	11,204
Mt aux Sources	Lesotho/S. Africa	3,282	10,768
Mt Piton	Réunion	3,069	10,069

Oceania		m	ft
Puncak Jaya	Indonesia	5,029	16,499
Puncak Mandala	Indonesia	4,760	15,617
Puncak Trikora	Indonesia	4,750	15,584
Mt Wilhelm	Papua New Guinea	4,508	14,790
> Mauna Kea	USA (Hawaii)	4,208	13,806
Mauna Loa	USA (Hawaii)	4,169	13,678
Mt Cook	New Zealand	3,753	12,313
Mt Balbi	Solomon Is.	2,743	8,999
Orohena	Tahiti	2,241	7,352
Mt Kosciusko	Australia	2,230	7,316

North America		m	ft
Mt McKinley	USA (Alaska)	6,194	20,321
Mt Logan	Canada	6,050	19,849
Citlaltepetl	Mexico	5,700	18,701
Mt St Elias	USA/Canada	5,489	18,008
Popocatepetl	Mexico	5,452	17,887
Mt Foraker	USA (Alaska)	5,304	17,401
Ixtaccihuatl	Mexico	5,286	17,342
Lucania	USA (Alaska)	5,226	17,145
Mt Steele	Canada	5,011	16,440
Mt Bona	USA (Alaska)	5,005	16,420
Mt Blackburn	USA (Alaska)	4,996	16,391
Mt Sanford	USA (Alaska)	4,949	16,237
Mt Wood	Canada	4,848	15,905
Nevado de Toluca	Mexico	4,670	15,321
Mt Fairweather	USA (Alaska)	4,663	15,298
Mt Whitney	USA	4,418	14,495
Mt Elbert	USA	4,399	14,432
Mt Harvard	USA	4,395	14,419
Mt Rainier	USA	4,392	14,409
Blanca Peak	USA	4,364	14,317
Long's Peak	USA	4,345	14,255
Nevado de Colima	Mexico	4,339	14,235
Mt Shasta	USA	4,317	14,163
Tajumulco	Guatemala	4,217	13,835
> Gannett Peak	USA	4,202	13,786
Mt Waddington	Canada	3,994	13,104
Mt Robson	Canada	3,954	12,972
Chirripó Grande	Costa Rica	3,837	12,589
Loma Tinta	Haiti	3,175	10,417

South America		m	ft
Aconcagua	Argentina	6,960	22,834
Illimani	Bolivia	6,882	22,578
Bonete	Argentina	6,872	22,546
Ojos del Salado	Argentina/Chile	6,863	22,516
Tupungato	Argentina/Chile	6,800	22,309
Pissis	Argentina	6,779	22,241
Mercedario	Argentina/Chile	6,770	22,211
Huascaran	Peru	6,768	22,204
Llullaillaco	Argentina/Chile	6,723	22,057
Nudo de Cachi	Argentina	6,720	22,047
Yerupaja	Peru	6,632	21,758
N. de Tres Cruces	Argentina/Chile	6,620	21,719
Incahuasi	Argentina/Chile	6,601	21,657
Ancohuma	Bolivia	6,550	21,489
Sajama	Bolivia	6,520	21,391
Coropuna	Peru	6,425	21,079
Ausangate	Peru	6,384	20,945
Cerro del Toro	Argentina	6,380	20,932
Ampato	Peru	6,310	20,702
> Chimborasso	Ecuador	6,267	20,561
Cotopaxi	Ecuador	5,897	19,347
Cayambe	Ecuador	5,796	19,016
S. Nev. de S. Marta	Colombia	5,775	18,947
Pico Bolivar	Venezuela	5,007	16,427

Antarctica		m	ft
Vinson Massif		4,897	16,066
Mt Kirkpatrick		4,528	14,855
Mt Markham		4,349	14,268

OCEAN DEPTHS

Atlantic Ocean	m	ft	
Puerto Rico (Milwaukee) Deep	9,200	30,183	[7]
Cayman Trench	7,680	25,197	[10]
Gulf of Mexico	5,203	17,070	
Mediterranean Sea	5,121	16,801	
Black Sea	2,211	7,254	
North Sea	310	1,017	
Baltic Sea	294	965	
Hudson Bay	111	364	

Indian Ocean	m	ft
Java Trench	7,450	24,442
Red Sea	2,266	7,434
Persian Gulf	73	239

Pacific Ocean	m	ft	
Mariana Trench	11,022	36,161	[1]
Tonga Trench	10,822	35,505	[2]
Japan Trench	10,554	34,626	[3]
Kuril Trench	10,542	34,586	[4]
Mindanao Trench	10,497	34,439	[5]
Kermadec Trench	10,047	32,962	[6]
Peru-Chile Trench	8,050	26,410	[8]
Aleutian Trench	7,822	25,662	[9]
Middle American Trench	6,662	21,857	

Arctic Ocean	m	ft
Molloy Deep	5,608	18,399

LAND LOWS

		m	ft
Caspian Sea	Europe	-28	-92
Dead Sea	Asia	-400	-1,312
Lake Assal	Africa	-156	-512
Lake Eyre North	Oceania	-16	-52
Death Valley	N. America	-86	-282
Valdés Peninsula	S. America	-40	-131

Rivers

Europe

		km	miles	
Volga	Caspian Sea	3,700	2,300	
Danube	Black Sea	2,850	1,770	
Ural	Caspian Sea	2,535	1,574	
Dnieper	Volga	2,285	1,420	
Kama	Volga	2,030	1,260	
Don	Volga	1,990	1,240	
Petchora	Arctic Ocean	1,790	1,110	
Oka	Volga	1,480	920	
Belaya	Kama	1,420	880	
Dniester	Black Sea	1,400	870	
Vyatka	Kama	1,370	850	
Rhine	North Sea	1,320	820	
N. Dvina	Arctic Ocean	1,290	800	
Desna	Dnieper	1,190	740	
Elbe	North Sea	1,145	710	
Vistula	Baltic Sea	1,090	675	
Loire	Atlantic Ocean	1,020	635	
W. Dvina	Baltic Sea	1,019	633	

Asia

		km	miles	
Yangtze	Pacific Ocean	6,380	3,960	[3]
Yenisey-Angara	Arctic Ocean	5,550	3,445	[5]
Ob-Irtysh	Arctic Ocean	5,410	3,360	[6]
Hwang Ho	Pacific Ocean	4,840	3,005	[7]
Amur	Pacific Ocean	4,510	2,800	[9]
Mekong	Pacific Ocean	4,500	2,795	[10]
Lena	Arctic Ocean	4,400	2,730	
Irtysh	Ob	4,250	2,640	
Yenisey	Arctic Ocean	4,090	2,540	
Ob	Arctic Ocean	3,680	2,285	
Indus	Indian Ocean	3,100	1,925	
Brahmaputra	Indian Ocean	2,900	1,800	
Syr Darya	Aral Sea	2,860	1,775	
Salween	Indian Ocean	2,800	1,740	
Euphrates	Indian Ocean	2,700	1,675	
Vilyuy	Lena	2,650	1,645	
Kolyma	Arctic Ocean	2,600	1,615	
Amu Darya	Aral Sea	2,540	1,575	
Ural	Caspian Sea	2,535	1,575	
Ganges	Indian Ocean	2,510	1,560	
Si Kiang	Pacific Ocean	2,100	1,305	
Irrawaddy	Indian Ocean	2,010	1,250	
Tarim-Yarkand	Lop Nor	2,000	1,240	
Tigris	Indian Ocean	1,900	1,180	
Angara	Yenisey	1,830	1,135	
Godavari	Indian Ocean	1,470	915	
Sutlej	Indian Ocean	1,450	900	
Yamuna	Indian Ocean	1,400	870	

Africa

		km	miles	
Nile	Mediterranean	6,670	4,140	[1]
Zaïre/Congo	Atlantic Ocean	4,670	2,900	[8]
Niger	Atlantic Ocean	4,180	2,595	
Zambezi	Indian Ocean	2,740	1,700	
Oubangi/Uele	Zaïre	2,250	1,400	
Kasai	Zaïre	1,950	1,210	
Shaballe	Indian Ocean	1,930	1,200	
Orange	Atlantic Ocean	1,860	1,155	
Cubango	Okavango Swamps	1,800	1,120	
Limpopo	Indian Ocean	1,600	995	
Senegal	Atlantic Ocean	1,600	995	
Volta	Atlantic Ocean	1,500	930	
Benue	Niger	1,350	840	

Australia

		km	miles	
Murray-Darling	Indian Ocean	3,720	2,310	
Darling	Murray	3,070	1,905	
Murray	Indian Ocean	2,575	1,600	
Murrumbidgee	Murray	1,690	1,050	

North America

		km	miles	
Mississippi-Missouri	Gulf of Mexico	6,020	3,740	[4]
Mackenzie	Arctic Ocean	4,240	2,630	
Mississippi	Gulf of Mexico	3,780	2,350	
Missouri	Mississippi	3,725	2,310	
Yukon	Pacific Ocean	3,185	1,980	
Rio Grande	Gulf of Mexico	3,030	1,880	
Arkansas	Mississippi	2,340	1,450	
Colorado	Pacific Ocean	2,330	1,445	
Red	Mississippi	2,040	1,270	
Columbia	Pacific Ocean	1,950	1,210	
Saskatchewan	Lake Winnipeg	1,940	1,205	
Snake	Columbia	1,670	1,040	
Churchill	Hudson Bay	1,600	990	
Ohio	Mississippi	1,580	980	
Brazos	Gulf of Mexico	1,400	870	
St Lawrence	Atlantic Ocean	1,170	730	

South America

		km	miles	
Amazon	Atlantic Ocean	6,430	3,990	[2]
Paraná-Plate	Atlantic Ocean	4,000	2,480	
Purus	Amazon	3,350	2,080	
Madeira	Amazon	3,200	1,990	
São Francisco	Atlantic Ocean	2,900	1,800	
Paraná	Plate	2,800	1,740	
Tocantins	Atlantic Ocean	2,640	1,640	
Paraguay	Paraná	2,550	1,580	
Orinoco	Atlantic Ocean	2,500	1,550	
Pilcomayo	Paraná	2,500	1,550	
Araguaia	Tocantins	2,250	1,400	
Juruá	Amazon	2,000	1,240	
Xingu	Amazon	1,980	1,230	
Ucayali	Amazon	1,900	1,180	
Marañón	Amazon	1,600	990	
Uruguay	Plate	1,600	990	
Magdalena	Caribbean Sea	1,540	960	

Lakes

Europe

		km²	miles²	
Lake Ladoga	Russia	18,400	7,100	
Lake Onega	Russia	9,700	3,700	
Saimaa system	Finland	8,000	3,100	
Vänern	Sweden	5,500	2,100	
Rybinsk Res.	Russia	4,700	1,800	

Asia

		km²	miles²	
Caspian Sea	Asia	371,000	143,000	[1]
Aral Sea	Kazakh./Uzbek.	36,000	13,900	[6]
Lake Baykal	Russia	31,500	12,200	[9]
Tonlé Sap	Cambodia	20,000	7,700	
Lake Balkhash	Kazakhstan	18,500	7,100	
Dongting Hu	China	12,000	4,600	
Issyk Kul	Kirghizia	6,200	2,400	
Lake Urmia	Iran	5,900	2,300	
Koko Nur	China	5,700	2,200	
Poyang Hu	China	5,000	1,900	
Lake Khanka	China/Russia	4,400	1,700	
Lake Van	Turkey	3,500	1,400	
Ubsa Nur	China	3,400	1,300	

Africa

		km²	miles²	
Lake Victoria	E. Africa	68,000	26,000	[3]
Lake Tanganyika	C. Africa	33,000	13,000	[7]
Lake Malawi/Nyasa	E. Africa	29,000	11,000	[10]
Lake Chad	C. Africa	25,000	9,700	
Lake Turkana	Ethiopia/Kenya	8,500	3,300	
Lake Volta	Ghana	8,500	3,300	
Lake Bangweulu	Zambia	8,000	3,100	
Lake Rukwa	Tanzania	7,000	2,700	
Lake Mai-Ndombe	Zaïre	6,500	2,500	
Lake Kariba	Zambia/Zimbabwe	5,300	2,000	
Lake Mobutu	Uganda/Zaïre	5,300	2,000	
Lake Nasser	Egypt/Sudan	5,200	2,000	
Lake Mweru	Zambia/Zaïre	4,900	1,900	
Lake Cabora Bassa	South Africa	4,500	1,700	
Lake Kyoga	Uganda	4,400	1,700	
Lake Tana	Ethiopia	3,630	1,400	
Lake Kivu	Rwanda/Zaïre	2,650	1,000	
Lake Edward	Uganda/Zaïre	2,200	850	

Australia

		km²	miles²	
Lake Eyre	Australia	9,000	3,500	
Lake Torrens	Australia	5,800	2,200	
Lake Gairdner	Australia	4,800	1,900	

North America

		km²	miles²	
Lake Superior	Canada/USA	82,200	31,700	[2]
Lake Huron	Canada/USA	59,600	23,000	[4]
Lake Michigan	USA	58,000	22,400	[5]
Great Bear Lake	Canada	31,500	12,200	[8]
Great Slave Lake	Canada	28,700	11,100	
Lake Erie	Canada/USA	25,700	9,900	
Lake Winnipeg	Canada	24,400	9,400	
Lake Ontario	Canada/USA	19,500	7,500	
Lake Nicaragua	Nicaragua	8,200	3,200	
Lake Athabasca	Canada	8,000	3,100	
Smallwood Res.	Canada	6,530	2,520	
Reindeer Lake	Canada	6,400	2,500	
Lake Winnipegosis	Canada	5,400	2,100	
Nettilling Lake	Canada	5,500	2,100	
Lake Nipigon	Canada	4,850	1,900	
Lake Manitoba	Canada	4,700	1,800	

South America

		km²	miles²	
Lake Titicaca	Bolivia/Peru	8,200	3,200	
Lake Poopo	Peru	2,800	1,100	

Islands

Europe

		km²	miles²	
Great Britain	UK	229,880	88,700	[8]
Iceland	Atlantic Ocean	103,000	39,800	
Ireland	Ireland/UK	84,400	32,600	
Novaya Zemlya (N.)	Russia	48,200	18,600	
W. Spitzbergen	Norway	39,000	15,100	
Novaya Zemlya (S.)	Russia	33,200	12,800	
Sicily	Italy	25,500	9,800	
Sardinia	Italy	24,000	9,300	
N. E. Spitzbergen	Norway	15,000	5,600	
Corsica	France	8,700	3,400	
Crete	Greece	8,350	3,200	
Zealand	Denmark	6,850	2,600	

Asia

		km²	miles²	
Borneo	S. E. Asia	737,000	284,000	[3]
Sumatra	Indonesia	425,000	164,000	[6]
Honshu	Japan	230,000	88,800	[7]
Celebes	Indonesia	189,000	73,000	
Java	Indonesia	126,700	48,900	
Luzon	Philippines	104,700	40,400	
Mindanao	Philippines	95,000	36,700	
Hokkaido	Japan	78,400	30,300	
Sakhalin	Russia	76,400	29,500	
Sri Lanka	Indian Ocean	65,600	25,300	
Taiwan	Pacific Ocean	36,000	13,900	
Kyushu	Japan	35,700	13,800	
Hainan	China	34,000	13,100	
Timor	Indonesia	33,600	13,000	
Shikoku	Japan	18,800	7,300	
Halmahera	Indonesia	18,000	6,900	
Ceram	Indonesia	17,150	6,600	
Sumbawa	Indonesia	15,450	6,000	
Flores	Indonesia	15,200	5,900	
Samar	Philippines	13,100	5,100	
Negros	Philippines	12,700	4,900	
Bangka	Indonesia	12,000	4,600	
Palawan	Philippines	12,000	4,600	
Panay	Philippines	11,500	4,400	
Sumba	Indonesia	11,100	4,300	
Mindoro	Philippines	9,750	3,800	
Buru	Indonesia	9,500	3,700	
Bali	Indonesia	5,600	2,200	
Cyprus	Mediterranean	3,570	1,400	
Wrangel Is.	Russia	2,800	1,000	

Africa

		km²	miles²	
Madagascar	Indian Ocean	587,000	226,600	[4]
Socotra	Indian Ocean	3,600	1,400	
Réunion	Indian Ocean	2,500	965	
Tenerife	Atlantic Ocean	2,350	900	
Mauritius	Indian Ocean	1,865	720	

Oceania

		km²	miles²	
New Guinea	Indon./Pap. NG	780,000	301,080	[2]
New Zealand (S.)	New Zealand	150,500	58,100	
New Zealand (N.)	New Zealand	114,400	44,200	
Tasmania	Australia	67,800	26,200	
New Britain	Papua NG	37,800	14,600	
New Caledonia	Pacific Ocean	16,100	6,200	
Viti Levu	Fiji	10,500	4,100	
Hawaii	Pacific Ocean	10,450	4,000	
Bougainville	Papua NG	9,600	3,700	
Guadalcanal	Solomon Is.	6,500	2,500	
Vanua Levu	Fiji	5,550	2,100	
New Ireland	Papua NG	3,200	1,200	

North America

		km²	miles²	
Greenland	Greenland	2,175,600	839,800	[1]
Baffin Is.	Canada	508,000	196,100	[5]
Victoria Is.	Canada	212,200	81,900	[9]
Ellesmere Is.	Canada	212,000	81,800	[10]
Cuba	Cuba	114,500	44,200	
Newfoundland	Canada	96,000	37,100	
Hispaniola	Atlantic Ocean	76,200	29,400	
Banks Is.	Canada	67,000	25,900	
Devon Is.	Canada	54,500	21,000	
Melville Is.	Canada	42,400	16,400	
Vancouver Is.	Canada	32,150	12,400	
Somerset Is.	Canada	24,300	9,400	
Jamaica	Caribbean Sea	11,400	4,400	
Puerto Rico	Atlantic Ocean	8,900	3,400	
Cape Breton Is.	Canada	4,000	1,500	

South America

		km²	miles²	
Tierra del Fuego	Argentina/Chile	47,000	18,100	
Falkland Is. (E.)	Atlantic Ocean	6,800	2,600	
South Georgia	Atlantic Ocean	4,200	1,600	
Galapagos (Isabela)	Pacific Ocean	2,250	870	

INTRODUCTION TO WORLD GEOGRAPHY

THE UNIVERSE

About 15 billion years ago, time and space began with the most colossal explosion in cosmic history: the 'Big Bang' that initiated the universe. According to current theory, in the first millionth of a second of its existence it expanded from a dimensionless point of infinite mass and density into a fireball about 30 billion kilometres across; and it has been expanding ever since.

It took almost a million years for the primal fireball to cool enough for atoms to form. They were mostly hydrogen, still the most abundant material in the universe. But the new matter was not evenly distributed around the young universe, and a few billion years later atoms in relatively dense regions began to cling together under the influence of gravity, forming distinct masses of gas separated by vast expanses of empty space. These first proto-galaxies, to begin with, were dark places: the universe had cooled. But gravitational attraction continued its work, condensing matter into coherent lumps inside the galactic gas clouds. About three billion years later, some of these masses had contracted so much that internal pressure produced the high temperatures necessary to bring about nuclear fusion: the first stars were born.

There were several generations of stars, each feeding on the wreckage of its extinct predecessors as well as the original galactic gas swirls. With each new generation, progressively larger atoms were forged in stellar furnaces and the galaxy's range of elements, once restricted to hydrogen, grew larger. About ten billion years after the Big Bang, a star formed on the outskirts of our galaxy with enough matter left over to create a retinue of planets. Some 4.7 billion years after that, a few planetary atoms had evolved into structures of complex molecules that lived, breathed and eventually pointed telescopes at the sky.

They found that their Sun is just one of more than 100 billion stars in the home galaxy alone. Our galaxy, in turn, forms part of a local group of 25 or so similar structures, some much larger than our own; there are at least 100 million other galaxies in the universe as a whole. The most distant ever observed, a highly energetic galactic core known only as Quasar PKS 2000-330, lies about 15 billion light-years away.

LIFE OF A STAR

For most of its existence, a star produces energy by the nuclear fusion of hydrogen into helium at its core. The duration of this hydrogen-burning period – known as the main sequence – depends on the star's mass; the greater the mass, the higher the core temperatures and the sooner the star's supply of hydrogen is exhausted. Dim, dwarf stars consume their hydrogen slowly, eking it out over a thousand billion years or more. The Sun, like other stars of its mass, should spend about 10 billion years on the main sequence; since it was formed less than five billion years ago, it still has half its life left.

Once all a star's core hydrogen has been fused into helium, nuclear activity moves outward into layers of unconsumed hydrogen. For a time, energy production sharply increases: the star grows hotter and expands enormously, turning into a so-called red giant. Its energy output will increase a thousandfold, and it will swell to a hundred times its present diameter.

After a few hundred million years, helium in the core will become sufficiently compressed to initiate a new cycle of nuclear fusion: from helium to carbon. The star will contract somewhat, before beginning its last expansion, in the Sun's case engulfing the Earth and perhaps Mars. In this bloated condition, the Sun's outer layers will break off into space, leaving a tiny inner core, mainly of carbon, that shrinks progressively under the force of its own gravity: dwarf stars can attain a density more than 10,000 times that of normal matter, with crushing surface gravities to match. Gradually, the nuclear fires will die down, and the Sun will reach its terminal stage: a black dwarf, emitting insignificant amounts of energy.

However, stars more massive than the Sun may undergo another transformation. The additional mass allows gravitational collapse to continue indefinitely: eventually, all the star's remaining matter shrinks to a point, and its density approaches infinity – a state that will not permit even sub-atomic structures to survive.

The star has become a black hole: an anomalous 'singularity' in the fabric of space and time. Although vast coruscations of radiation will be emitted by any matter falling into its grasp, the singularity itself has an escape velocity that exceeds the speed of light, and nothing can ever be released from it. Within the boundaries of the black hole, the laws of physics are suspended, but no physicist can ever observe the extraordinary events that may occur.

THE END OF THE UNIVERSE

The likely fate of the universe is disputed. One theory (top) dictates that the expansion begun at the time of the Big Bang will continue 'indefinitely', with ageing galaxies moving farther and farther apart in an immense, dark graveyard. Alternately, (bottom) gravity may overcome the expansion. Galaxies will fall back together until everything is again concentrated at a single point, followed by a new Big Bang and a new expansion, in an endlessly repeated cycle. The first theory is supported by the amount of visible matter in the universe; the second assumes there is enough dark material to bring about the gravitational collapse.

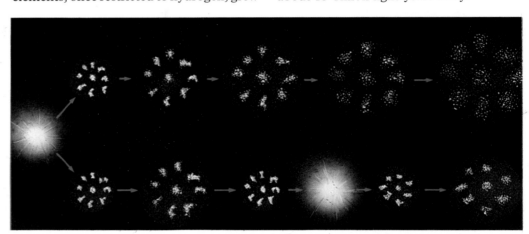

GALACTIC STRUCTURES

The universe's 100 million galaxies show clear structural patterns, originally classified by the American astronomer Edwin Hubble in 1925. Spiral galaxies like our own (top row) have a central, almost spherical bulge and a surrounding disc composed of spiral arms. Barred spirals (bottom row) have a central bar of stars across the nucleus, with spiral arms trailing from the ends of the bar. Elliptical galaxies (far left) have a uniform appearance, ranging from a flattened disc to a near sphere. So-called SO galaxies (left row, right) have a central bulge, but no spiral arms. A few have no discernible structure at all. Galaxies also vary enormously in size, from dwarfs only 2,000 light-years across to great assemblies of stars 80 or more times larger.

THE HOME GALAXY

The Sun and its planets are located in one of the spiral arms, a little less than 30,000 light-years from the galactic centre and orbiting around it in a period of more than 200 million years. The centre is invisible from the Earth, masked by vast, light-absorbing clouds of interstellar dust. The galaxy is probably around 12 billion years old and, like other spiral galaxies, has three distinct regions. The central bulge is about 30,000 light-years in diameter. The disc in which the Sun is located is not much more than 1,000 light-years thick but 100,000 light-years from end to end. Around the galaxy is the halo, a spherical zone 150,000 light-years across studded with globular star-clusters and sprinkled with individual suns.

Globular clusters

Bulge

Disc

Solar System

Star charts are drawn as projections of a vast, hollow sphere with the observer in the middle. Each circle below represents one hemisphere, centred on the north and south celestial poles respectively – projections of the Earth's poles in the heavens. At the present era, the north pole is marked by the star Polaris; the south pole has no such convenient reference point. The rectangular map shows the stars immediately above and below the celestial equator.

Astronomical coordinates are normally given in terms of 'Right Ascension' for longitude and 'Declination' for latitude or altitude. Since the stars appear to rotate around the Earth once every 24 hours, Right Ascension is measured eastward – anti-clockwise – in hours and minutes. One hour is equivalent to 15 angular degrees; zero on the scale is the point at which the Sun crosses the celestial equator at the spring equinox, known to astronomers as the First Point in Aries. Unlike the Sun, stars always rise and set at the same point on the horizon. Declination measures (in degrees) a star's angular distance above or below the celestial equator.

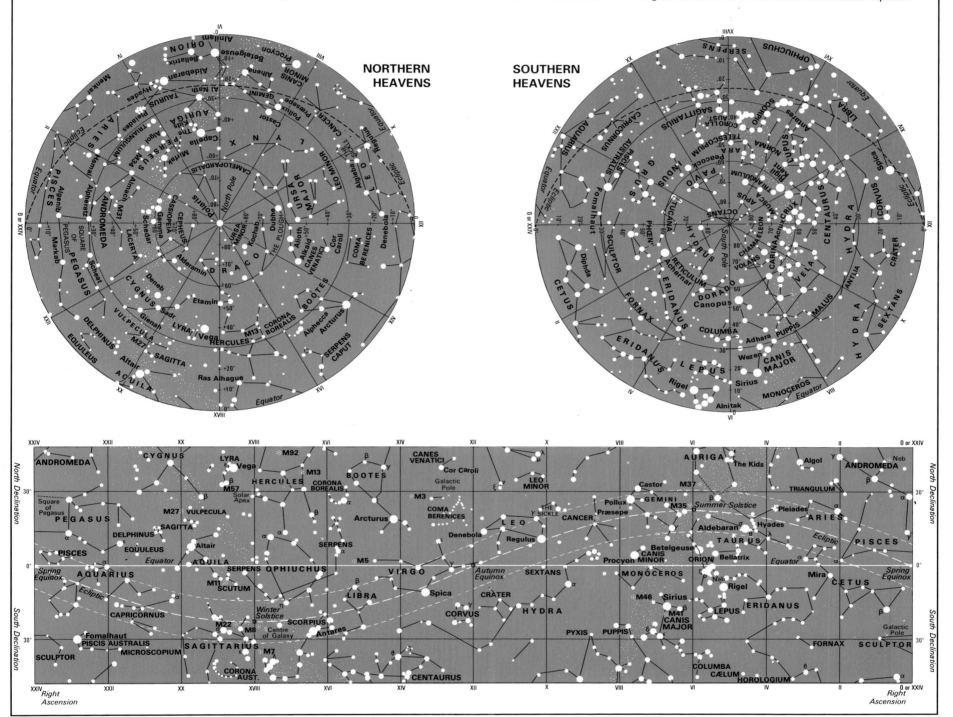

NORTHERN HEAVENS

SOUTHERN HEAVENS

THE CONSTELLATIONS

The constellations and their English names

Andromeda	Andromeda	Circinus	Compasses	Lacerta	Lizard	Piscis Austrinus	Southern Fish
Antila	Air Pump	Columba	Dove	Leo	Lion	Puppis	Ship's Stern
Apus	Bird of Paradise	Coma Berenices	Berenice's Hair	Leo Minor	Little Lion	Pyxis	Mariner's Compass
Aquarius	Water-carrier	Corona Australis	Southern Crown	Lepus	Hare	Reticulum	Net
Aquila	Eagle	Corona Borealis	Northern Crown	Libra	Scales	Sagitta	Arrow
Ara	Altar	Corvus	Crow	Lupus	Wolf	Sagittarius	Archer
Aries	Ram	Crater	Cup	Lynx	Lynx	Scorpius	Scorpion
Auriga	Charioteer	Crux	Southern Cross	Lyra	Harp	Sculptor	Sculptor
Boötes	Herdsman	Cygnus	Swan	Mensa	Table	Scutum	Shield
Caelum	Chisel	Delphinus	Dolphin	Microscopium	Microscope	Serpens	Serpent
Camelopardalis	Giraffe	Dorado	Swordfish	Monoceros	Unicorn	Sextans	Sextant
Cancer	Crab	Draco	Dragon	Musca	Fly	Taurus	Bull
Canes Venatici	Hunting Dogs	Equuleus	Little House	Norma	Level	Telescopium	Telescope
Canis Major	Great Dog	Eridanus	Eridanus	Octans	Octant	Triangulum	Triangle
Canis Minor	Little Dog	Fornax	Furnace	Ophiuchus	Serpent Bearer	Triangulum Australe	Southern Triangle
Capricornus	Goat	Gemini	Twins	Orion	Orion	Tucana	Toucan
Carina	Keel	Grus	Crane	Pavo	Peacock	Ursa Major	Great Bear
Cassiopeia	Cassiopeia	Hercules	Hercules	Pegasus	Winged Horse	Ursa Minor	Little Bear
Centaurus	Centaur	Horologium	Clock	Perseus	Perseus	Vela	Sails
Cepheus	Cepheus	Hydra	Water Snake	Phoenix	Phoenix	Virgo	Virgin
Cetus	Whale	Hydrus	Sea Serpent	Pictor	Easel	Volans	Flying Fish
Chamaeleon	Chameleon	Indus	Indian	Pisces	Fishes	Vulpecula	Fox

THE NEAREST STARS

The 20 nearest stars, excluding the Sun, with their distance from Earth in light-years*

Proxima Centauri	4.3
Alpha Centauri A	4.3
Alpha Centauri B	4.3
Barnard's Star	6.0
Wolf 359	8.1
Lal 21185	8.2
Sirius A	8.7
Sirius B	8.7
UV Ceti A	9.0
UV Citi B	9.0
Ross 154	9.3
Ross 248	10.3
Epsilon Eridani	10.8
L 789-6	11.1
Ross 128	11.1
61 Cygni A	11.2
61 Cygni B	11.2
Procyon A	11.3
Procyon B	11.3
Epsilon Indi	11.4

Many of the nearest stars, like Alpha Centauri A and B, are doubles, orbiting about the common centre of gravity and to all intents and purposes equidistant from Earth. Many of them are dim objects, with no name other than the designation given by the astronomers who investigated them. However, they include Sirius, the brightest star in the sky, and Procyon, the seventh brightest. Both are far larger than the Sun: of the nearest stars only Epsilon Eridani is similar in size and luminosity.

* A light-year equals approx. 9,500,000,000,000 kilometres

THE SOLAR SYSTEM

Lying 27,000 light years from the centre of one of billions of galaxies that comprise the observable universe, our solar system contains nine planets and their moons, innumerable asteroids and comets and a miscellany of dust and gas, all tethered by the immense gravitational field of the Sun, the middling-sized star whose thermonuclear furnaces provide them all with heat and light. The solar system was probably formed about 4.6 billion years ago, when a spinning cloud of gas, mostly hydrogen but seeded with other, heavier elements, condensed enough to ignite a nuclear reaction and create a star. The Sun still accounts for almost 99.9% of the system's total mass; one planet, Jupiter, contains most of the remainder.

By composition as well as distance, the planetary array divides quite neatly in two: an inner system of four small, solid planets, including the Earth, and an outer system, from Jupiter to Neptune, of four huge gas giants. Between the two groups lies a scattering of asteroids, perhaps as many as 40,000; possibly the remains of a planet destroyed by some unexplained catastrophe, they are more likely to be debris left over from the solar system's formation, prevented by the gravity of massive Jupiter from coalescing into a larger body. The ninth planet, Pluto, seems to be a world of the inner system type: small, rocky and something of an anomaly.

By the 1990s, the solar system also included some newer anomalies: several thousand spacecraft. Most were in orbit around the Earth, but some had probed far and wide around the system. The information beamed back by these robotic investigators has transformed our knowledge of our celestial environment.

Much of the early history of science is the story of people trying to make sense of the errant points of light that were all they knew of the planets. Now, people have themselves stood on the Earth's Moon; probes have landed on Mars and Venus and orbiting radars have mapped far distant landscapes with astonishing accuracy. In the 1980s, the US Voyagers skimmed all four major planets of the outer system, bringing new revelations with each close approach. Only Pluto, inscrutably distant in an orbit that takes it 50 times the Earth's distance from the Sun, remains unvisited by our messengers.

ORBITS OF THE PLANETS

The solar planets and their orbits, showing the relative position of each planet at the vernal equinox of 1992.

Orbits are drawn to exact scale, with Sun and planets greatly enlarged for clarity. The solar system is shown from the viewpoint of an observer a few light-hours distant in the direction of the constellation Hercules. Seen from such a position, above the plane of the ecliptic, all the planets revolve about the Sun in an anti-clockwise direction. The perspective view exaggerates the elliptical form of all the planetary orbits: only Pluto and Mercury follow paths that deviate noticeably from circularity. Near perihelion – its closest approach to the Sun – Pluto actually passes inside the orbit of Neptune, an event that last occurred in 1983. Pluto will not regain its station as the Sun's outermost planet until February, 1999.

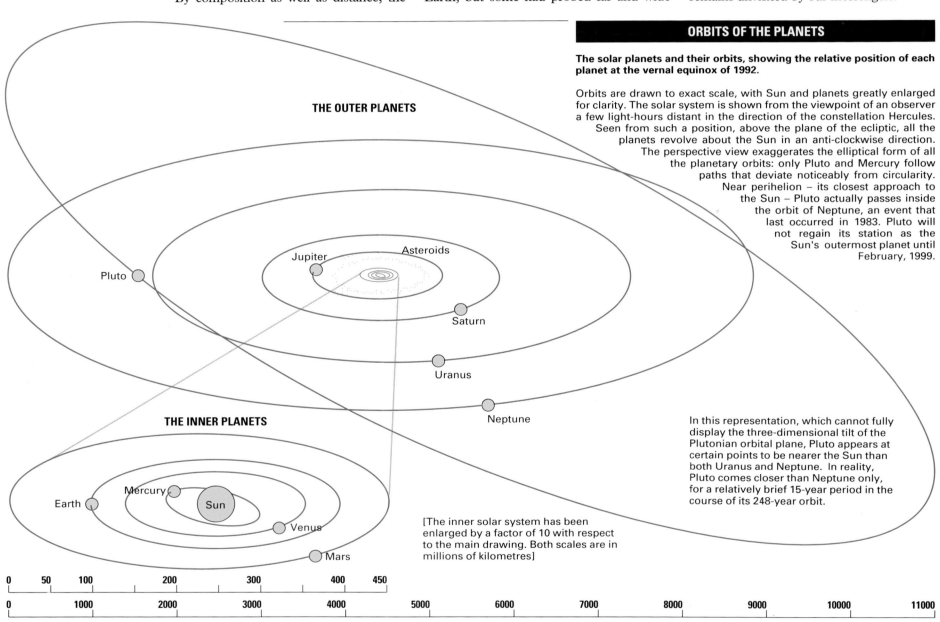

THE OUTER PLANETS

THE INNER PLANETS

Pluto · Jupiter · Asteroids · Saturn · Uranus · Neptune · Earth · Mercury · Sun · Venus · Mars

In this representation, which cannot fully display the three-dimensional tilt of the Plutonian orbital plane, Pluto appears at certain points to be nearer the Sun than both Uranus and Neptune. In reality, Pluto comes closer than Neptune only, for a relatively brief 15-year period in the course of its 248-year orbit.

[The inner solar system has been enlarged by a factor of 10 with respect to the main drawing. Both scales are in millions of kilometres]

| 0 | 50 | 100 | 200 | 300 | 400 | 450 |

| 0 | 1000 | 2000 | 3000 | 4000 | 5000 | 6000 | 7000 | 8000 | 9000 | 10000 | 11000 |

PLANETARY DATA

	Mean distance from Sun (million km)	Mass (Earth = 1)	Period of orbit (Earth years)	Period of rotation (Earth days)	Equatorial diameter (km)	Average density (water = 1)	Surface gravity (Earth = 1)	Escape velocity (km/sec)	Number of known satellites
Sun	-	332,946	-	25.38	1,392,000	1.41	27.9	617.5	-
Mercury	58.3	0.06	0.241	58.67	4,878	5.5	0.38	4.27	0
Venus	107.7	0.8	0.615	243	12,104	5.25	0.90	10.36	0
Earth	149.6	1.0	1.00	0.99	12,756	5.52	1.00	11.18	1
Mars	227.3	0.1	1.88	1.02	6,794	3.94	0.38	5.03	2
Jupiter	777.9	317.8	11.86	0.41	142,800	1.33	2.64	60.22	16
Saturn	1,427.1	95.2	29.63	0.42	120,000	0.706	1.16	36.25	17
Uranus	2,872.3	14.5	83.97	0.45	52,000	1.70	1.11	22.4	15
Neptune	4,502.7	17.2	164.8	0.67	48,400	1.77	1.21	23.9	8
Pluto	5,894.2	0.002	248.63	6.38	3,000	5.50	0.47	5.1	1

Planetary days are given in sidereal time -- that is, with respect to the stars rather than the Sun. Most of the information in the table was confirmed by spacecraft and often obtained from photographs and other data transmitted back to the Earth. In the case of Pluto, however, only earthbound observations have been made, and no spacecraft can hope to encounter it until well into the next century. Given the planet's small size and great distance, figures for its diameter and rotation period cannot be definitive.

Since Pluto does not appear to be massive enough to account for the perturbations in the orbits of Uranus and Neptune that led to its 1930 discovery, it is quite possible that a tenth and even more distant planet may exist. Once Pluto's own 248-year orbit has been observed for long enough, further discrepancies may give a clue as to any tenth planet's whereabouts. Even so, distance alone would make it very difficult to locate, especially since telescopes powerful enough to find it are normally engaged in galactic study.

Mercury is the closest planet to the Sun and hence the fastest-moving. It has no significant atmosphere and a cratered, wrinkled surface very similar to that of Earth's moon.

Venus has much the same physical dimensions as Earth. However, its carbon dioxide atmosphere is 90 times as dense, accounting for a runaway greenhouse effect that makes the Venusian surface, at 475°C, the hottest of all the planets. Radar mapping shows relatively level land with volcanic regions whose sulphurous discharges explain the sulphuric acid rains reported by soft-landing space probes before they succumbed to Venus's fierce climate.

Earth seen from space is easily the most beautiful of the inner planets; it is also, and more objectively, the largest, as well the only home of known life. Living things are the main reason why the Earth is able to retain a substantial proportion of corrosive and highly reactive oxygen in its atmosphere, a state of affairs that contradicts the laws of chemical equilibrium; the oxygen in turn supports the life that constantly regenerates it.

Mars was once considered the likeliest of the other planets to share Earth's cargo of life: seasonal expansion of dark patches strongly suggested vegetation and the planet's apparent icecaps indicated the vital presence of water. But close inspection by spacecraft brought disappointment: chemical reactions account for the seeming vegetation, the icecaps are mainly frozen carbon dioxide and whatever oxygen the planet once possessed is now locked up in the iron-bearing rock that covers its cratered surface and gives it its characteristic red hue.

Jupiter masses almost three times as much as all the other planets together; had it scooped up a little more matter during its formation, it might have evolved into a small companion star for the Sun. The planet is mostly gas, under intense pressure in the lower atmosphere above a core of fiercely compressed hydogen and helium. The upper layers form strikingly-coloured rotating belts, the outward sign of the intense storms created by Jupiter's rapid diurnal rotation. Close approaches by spacecraft have shown an orbiting ring system, and discovered several previously unknown moons: Jupiter has at least 16.

Saturn is structurally similar to Jupiter, rotating fast enough to produce an obvious bulge at its equator. Ever since the invention of the telescope, however, Saturn's rings have been the feature that has attracted most observers. Voyager probes in 1980 and 1981 sent back detailed pictures that showed them to be composed of thousands of separate ringlets, each in turn made up of tiny icy particles, interacting in a complex dance that may serve as a model for the study of galactic and even larger structures.

Uranus was unknown to the ancients: although it is faintly visible to the naked eye, it was not discovered until 1781. Its composition is broadly similar to Jupiter and Saturn, though its distance from the Sun ensures an even colder surface temperature. Observations in 1977 suggested the presence of a faint ring system, amply confirmed when Voyager 2 swung past the planet in 1986.

Neptune is always more than four billion kilometres from Earth, and despite its diameter of almost 50,000 km it can only be seen by telescope. Its 1846 discovery was the result of mathematical predictions by astronomers seeking to explain irregularities in the orbit of Uranus, but until Voyager 2 closed with the planet in 1989 little was known of it. Like Uranus, it has a ring system; Voyager's photographs revealed a total of eight moons.

Pluto is the most mysterious of the solar planets, if only because even the most powerful telescopes can scarcely resolve it from a point of light to a disc. It was discovered as recently as 1930, like Neptune as the result of perturbations in the orbits of the two then outermost planets. Its small size as well as its eccentric and highly tilted orbit have led to suggestions that it is a former satellite of Neptune, somehow liberated from its primary. In 1978 Pluto was found to have a moon of its own, Charon, apparently half the size of Pluto itself.

Mean distance from
Sun in million
kilometres

Mercury	58.3
Venus	107.7
Earth	149.6
Mars	227.9
Jupiter	777.9
Saturn	1,427.1
Uranus	2,872.3
Neptune	4,502.7
Pluto	5,894.2

THE EARTH: TIME & MOTION

The basic unit of time measurement is the day, one rotation of the Earth on its axis. The subdivision of the day into hours, minutes and seconds is arbitrary and simply for our convenience. Our present calendar is based on the solar year of 365.24 days, the time taken by the Earth to orbit the Sun. As the Earth rotates from west to east, the Sun appears to rise in the east and set in the west. When the Sun is setting in Shanghai, on the opposite side of the world New York is just emerging into sunlight. Noon, when the sun is directly overhead, is coincident at all places on the same meridian, with shadows pointing directly toward the poles.

Calendars based on the movements of the Sun and Moon have been used since ancient times. The Julian Calendar, with its leap year, introduced by Julius Caesar, fixed the average length of the year at 365.25 days, which was about 11 minutes too long (the Earth completes its orbit in 365 days, 5 hours, 48 minutes and 46 seconds of mean solar time). The cumulative error was rectified by the Gregorian Calendar, introduced by Pope Gregory XIII in 1582, when he decreed that the day following October 4 was October 15, and that century years do not count as leap years unless divisible by 400. England did not adopt the reformed calendar until 1752, when it found itself 11 days behind the continent.

Britain imposed the Gregorian Calendar on all its possessions, including the American colonies. All dates preceding September 2 were marked O.S., for Old Style.

EARTH DATA

Maximum distance from the Sun (Aphelion): 152,007,016 km.
Minimum distance from Sun (Perihelion): 147,000,830 km.
Obliquity of the ecliptic: 23° 27' 08".
Length of year - solar tropical (equinox to equinox): 365.24 days
Length of year - sidereal (fixed star to fixed star): 365.26 days
Length of day - mean solar day: 24h, 03m, 56s.
Length of day - mean sidereal day: 23h, 56m, 04s.

Superficial area: 510,000,000 sq. km.
Land surface: 149,000,000 sq. km. (29.2%)
Water surface: 361,000,000 sq. km. (70.8%)
Equatorial circumference: 40,077 km.
Polar circumference: 40,009 km.
Equatorial diameter: 12,756.8 km.
Polar diameter: 12,713.8 km.
Equatorial radius: 6,378.4 km.
Polar radius: 6,356.9 km.
Volume of the Earth: $1,083,230 \times 10^6$ cu. km.
Mass of the Earth: 5.9×10^{21} tonnes

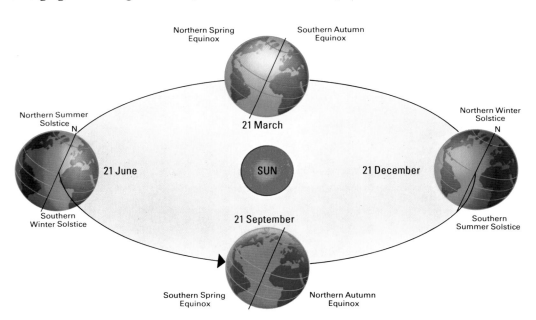

THE SEASONS

The Earth revolves around the Sun once a year in an 'anti-clockwise' direction, tilted at a constant angle 66½°. In June, the northern hemisphere is tilted towards the Sun: as a result it receives more hours of sunshine in a day and therefore has its warmest season, summer. By December, the Earth has rotated halfway round the Sun so that the southern hemisphere that is tilted towards the Sun has its summer; the hemisphere that is tilted away from the Sun has winter. On 21 June the Sun is directly overhead at the Tropic of Cancer (23½° N), and this is midsummer in the northern hemisphere. Midsummer in the southern hemisphere occurs on 21 December, when the Sun is overhead at the Tropic of Capricorn (23½° S).

DAY & NIGHT

The Sun appears to rise in the east, reach its highest point at noon, and then set in the west, to be followed by night. In reality it is not the Sun that is moving but the Earth revolving from west to east.

At the summer solstice in the northern hemisphere (21 June), the Arctic has total daylight and the Antarctic total darkness. The opposite occurs at the winter solstice (21 December). At the equator, the length of day and night are almost equal all year.

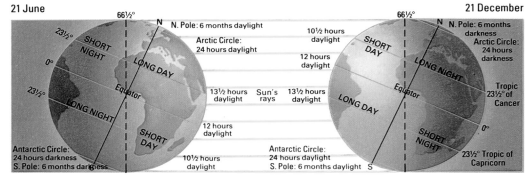

THE SUN'S PATH

The diagrams on the left illustrate the apparent path of the Sun at (A) the equator, (B) in mid-latitude (45°), (C) at the Arctic Circle (66½°) and (D) at the North Pole, where there are six months of continuous daylight and six months of continuous night.

MEASUREMENTS OF TIME

Astronomers distinguish between solar time and sidereal time. Solar time derives from the period taken by the Earth to rotate on its axis: one rotation defines a solar day. But the speed of the Earth along its orbit around the Sun is not constant. The length of day - or 'apparent solar day' - as defined by the apparent successive transits of the Sun - is irregular because the Earth must complete more than one rotation before the Sun returns to the same meridian. The constant sidereal day is defined as the interval between two successive apparent transits of a star, or the first point of Aries, across the same meridian. If the Sun is at the equinox and overhead at a meridian one day, then the next day it will be to the east by approximately 1°. Thus the Sun will not cross the meridian until four minutes after the sidereal noon.

From the diagrams on the right it is possible to discover the time of sunrise or sunset on a given date and for latitudes between 60°N and 60°S.

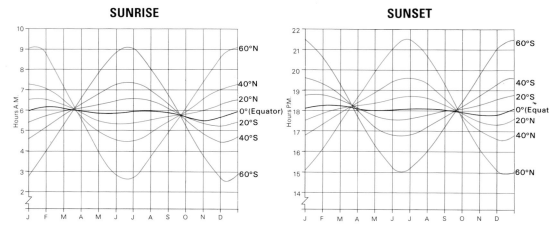

SUNRISE

SUNSET

THE MOON

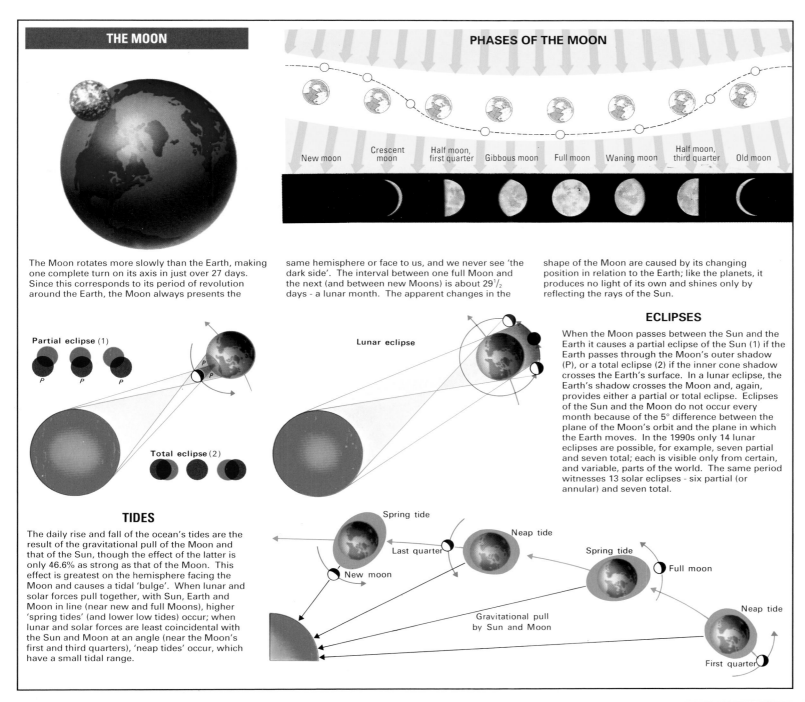

The Moon rotates more slowly than the Earth, making one complete turn on its axis in just over 27 days. Since this corresponds to its period of revolution around the Earth, the Moon always presents the same hemisphere or face to us, and we never see 'the dark side'. The interval between one full Moon and the next (and between new Moons) is about 29½ days - a lunar month. The apparent changes in the shape of the Moon are caused by its changing position in relation to the Earth; like the planets, it produces no light of its own and shines only by reflecting the rays of the Sun.

PHASES OF THE MOON

New moon — Crescent moon — Half moon, first quarter — Gibbous moon — Full moon — Waning moon — Half moon, third quarter — Old moon

ECLIPSES

When the Moon passes between the Sun and the Earth it causes a partial eclipse of the Sun (1) if the Earth passes through the Moon's outer shadow (P), or a total eclipse (2) if the inner cone shadow crosses the Earth's surface. In a lunar eclipse, the Earth's shadow crosses the Moon and, again, provides either a partial or total eclipse. Eclipses of the Sun and the Moon do not occur every month because of the 5° difference between the plane of the Moon's orbit and the plane in which the Earth moves. In the 1990s only 14 lunar eclipses are possible, for example, seven partial and seven total; each is visible only from certain, and variable, parts of the world. The same period witnesses 13 solar eclipses - six partial (or annular) and seven total.

Partial eclipse (1)

Total eclipse (2)

Lunar eclipse

TIDES

The daily rise and fall of the ocean's tides are the result of the gravitational pull of the Moon and that of the Sun, though the effect of the latter is only 46.6% as strong as that of the Moon. This effect is greatest on the hemisphere facing the Moon and causes a tidal 'bulge'. When lunar and solar forces pull together, with Sun, Earth and Moon in line (near new and full Moons), higher 'spring tides' (and lower low tides) occur; when lunar and solar forces are least coincidental with the Sun and Moon at an angle (near the Moon's first and third quarters), 'neap tides' occur, which have a small tidal range.

Spring tide — Neap tide — Last quarter — New moon — Spring tide — Full moon — Neap tide — Gravitational pull by Sun and Moon — First quarter

MOON DATA

Distance from Earth: The Moon orbits at a mean distance of 384,199.1 km, at an average speed of 3,683 km/h in relation to the Earth.

Size & mass: The average diameter of the Moon is 3,475.1 km. It is 400 times smaller than the Sun but is about 400 times closer to the Earth, so we see them as the same size. The Moon has a mass of 7.348×10^{19} tonnes, with a density 3.344 times that of water.

Visibility: Only 59% of the Moon's surface is directly visible from Earth. Reflected light takes 1.25 seconds to reach Earth - compared to 8 minutes 27.3 seconds for light from the Sun.

Temperature: With the Sun overhead the temperature on the lunar equator can reach 117.2°C [243°F]. At night it can sink to -162.7°C [-261°F].

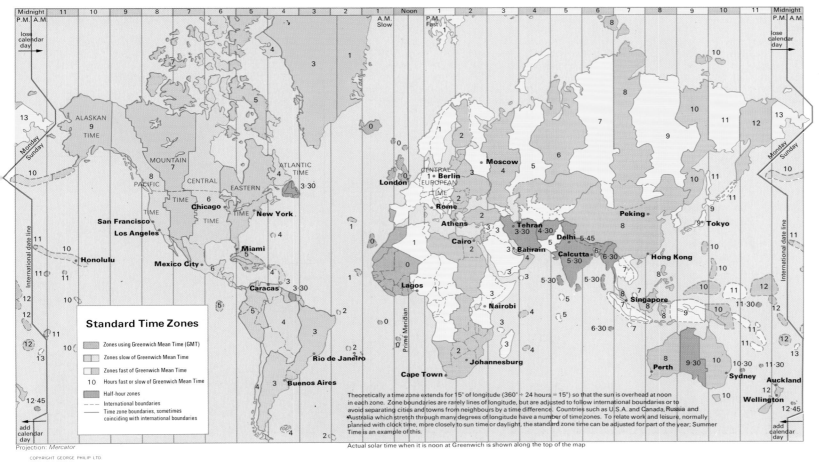

Standard Time Zones
- Zones using Greenwich Mean Time (GMT)
- Zones slow of Greenwich Mean Time
- Zones fast of Greenwich Mean Time
- 10 Hours fast or slow of Greenwich Mean Time
- Half-hour zones
- International boundaries
- Time zone boundaries, sometimes coinciding with international boundaries

Theoretically a time zone extends for 15° of longitude (360° ÷ 24 hours = 15°) so that the sun is overhead at noon in each zone. Zone boundaries are rarely lines of longitude, but are adjusted to follow international boundaries or to avoid separating cities and towns from neighbours by a time difference. Countries such as U.S.A. and Canada, Russia and Australia which stretch through many degrees of longitude have a number of time zones. To relate work and leisure, normally planned with clock time, more closely to sun time or daylight, the standard zone time can be adjusted for part of the year; Summer Time is an example of this.

Actual solar time when it is noon at Greenwich is shown along the top of the map

Projection: Mercator
COPYRIGHT GEORGE PHILIP LTD.

TIME ZONES

The Earth rotates through 360° in 24 hours, and therefore it moves 15° every hour. The world is divided into 24 standard time zones, each centred on lines of longitude at 15° intervals, so that every country falls within one or more agreed zones. The Greenwich meridian, based on the location of the Royal Observatory in London, lies at the centre of the first zone. All places to the west of Greenwich are one hour behind for every 15° of longitude; places to the east are ahead by one hour for every 15°.
When it is 12 noon at the Greenwich meridian, 180° east it is midnight of the same day – while 180° west the day is only just beginning. To overcome this the International Date Line was established, approximately following the 180° meridian. Thus if you travelled eastwards from Japan (140° East) to Samoa (170° West) you would pass from Sunday night into Sunday morning.

THE EARTH: GEOLOGY

The complementary, almost jigsaw-puzzle fit of the Atlantic coasts led to Alfred Wegener's proposition of continental drift in Germany (1915). His theory suggested that an ancient super-continent, which he called Pangaea, incorporating all the Earth's land masses, gradually split up to form the continents we know today. By 180 million years ago Pangaea had divided into two major groups and the southern part, Gondwanaland, had itself begun to break up with India and Antarctica-Australia becoming isolated. By 135 million years ago the widening of the splits in the North Atlantic and Indian Oceans persisted, a South Atlantic gap had appeared and India continued to move 'north' towards Asia. By 65 million years ago South America had completely split from Africa.
To form today's pattern India 'collided' with Asia (crumpling up sediments to form the Himalayas); South America rotated and moved west to connect with North America; Australia separated from Antarctica and moved north; and the familiar gap developed between Greenland and Europe.

The origin of the Earth is still open to conjecture, although the most widely accepted theory is that it was formed from a solar cloud consisting mainly of hydrogen 4,600 million years ago. The cloud condensed, forming the planets. The lighter elements floated to the surface of the Earth, where they cooled to form a crust; the inner material remained hot and molten. The first rocks were formed over 3,500 million years ago, but the Earth's surface has since been constantly altered.

The crust consists of a brittle, low-density material varying from 5 to 50 kilometres deep beneath the continents, consisting predominately of silica and aluminum: hence its name, 'sial'. Below the sial is a basaltic layer known as 'sima', comprising mainly silica and magnesium. The crust accounts for only 1.5 per cent of the Earth's volume.

Immediately below the crust the mantle begins, with a distinct change in density and chemical properties. The rock is rich in iron and magnesium silicates, and temperatures reach 1,600°C. The rigid upper mantle extends down to a depth of about 1,000 kilometres, below which is a more viscous lower mantle about 1,900 kilometres thick.

The outer core, measuring about 2,310 kilometres thick, consists of molten iron and nickel at 2,100°C to 5,000°C, possibly separated from the less dense mantle by an oxidized shell. About 5,000 kilometres below the surface is a liquid transition zone, below which is the solid inner core, a sphere of about 2,700 kilometres diameter where rock is three times as dense as in the crust. The temperature at the centre of the Earth is probably about 5,000°C.

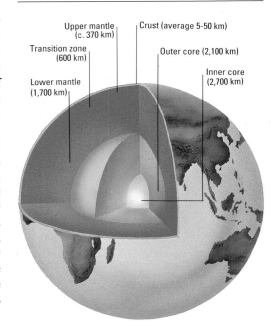

Upper mantle (c. 370 km)
Crust (average 5-50 km)
Transition zone (600 km)
Outer core (2,100 km)
Lower mantle (1,700 km)
Inner core (2,700 km)

CONTINENTAL DRIFT

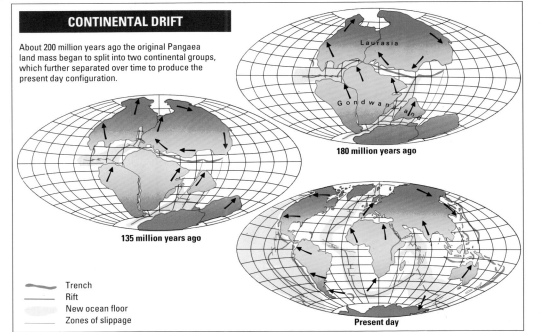

About 200 million years ago the original Pangaea land mass began to split into two continental groups, which further separated over time to produce the present day configuration.

Laurasia

Gondwanaland

180 million years ago

135 million years ago

Present day

⌇ Trench
∿ Rift
New ocean floor
Zones of slippage

PLATE TECTONICS

The original debate about the drift theory of Wegener and others formed a long prelude to a more radical idea: plate tectonics. The discovery that the continents are carried along on the top of slowly-moving crustal plates (which float on heavier liquid material – the lower mantle – much as icebergs do on water) provided the mechanism for the drift theories to work. The plates converge and diverge along margins marked by seismic and volcanic activity. Plates diverge from mid-ocean ridges where molten lava pushes up and forces the plates apart at a rate of up to 40 mm a year; converging plates form either a trench (where the oceanic plates sink below the lighter continental rock) or mountain ranges (where two continents collide).

The debate about plate tectonics is not over, however. In addition to abiding questions such as what force actually moves the plates (massive convection currents in the Earth's interior is the most popular explanation), and why many volcanoes and earthquakes occur in mid-plate (such as Hawaii and central China), evidence began to emerge in the early 1990s that, with more sophisticated equipment and models, the whole theory might be in doubt.

EARTHQUAKES

Earthquake magnitude is usually rated according to either the Richter or the Modified Mercalli scale, both devised by seismologists in the 1930s. The Richter scale measures absolute earthquake power with mathematical precision: each step upwards represents a ten-fold increase in shockwave amplitude. Theoretically, there is no upper limit, but the largest earthquakes measured have been rated at between 8.8 and 8.9. The 12–point Mercalli scale, based on observed effects, is often more meaningful, ranging from I (earthquakes noticed only by seismographs) to XII (total destruction); intermediate points include V (people awakened at night; unstable objects overturned), VII (collapse of ordinary buildings; chimneys and monuments fall); and IX (conspicuous cracks in ground; serious damage to reservoirs).

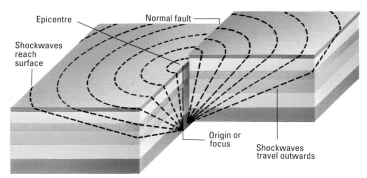

Epicentre
Normal fault
Shockwaves reach surface
Origin or focus
Shockwaves travel outwards

DISTRIBUTION

NOTABLE EARTHQUAKES SINCE 1900

Year	Location	Mag.	Deaths
1906	San Francisco, USA	8.3	503
1906	Valparaiso, Chile	8.6	22,000
1908	Messina, Italy	7.5	83,000
1915	Avezzano, Italy	7.5	30,000
1920	Gansu, China	8.6	180,000
1923	Yokohama, Japan	8.3	143,000
1927	Nan Shan, China	8.3	200,000
1932	Gansu, China	7.6	70,000
1934	Bihar, India/Nepal	8.4	10,700
1935	Quetta, India*	7.5	60,000
1939	Chillan, Chile	8.3	28,000
1939	Erzincan, Turkey	7.9	30,000
1960	Agadir, Morocco	5.8	12,000
1962	Khorasan, Iran	7.1	12,230
1963	Skopje, Yugoslavia	6.0	1,000
1964	Anchorage, Alaska	8.4	131
1968	N. E. Iran	7.4	12,000
1970	N. Peru	7.7	66,794
1972	Managua, Nicaragua	6.2	5,000
1974	N. Pakistan	6.3	5,200
1976	Guatemala	7.5	22,778
1976	Tangshan, China	8.2	650,000
1978	Tabas, Iran	7.7	25,000
1980	El Asnam, Algeria	7.3	20,000
1980	S. Italy	7.2	4,800
1985	Mexico City, Mexico	8.1	4,200
1988	N.W. Armenia	6.8	55,000
1990	N. Iran	7.7	36,000

The highest magnitude recorded on the Richter scale is 8.9, in Japan on 2 March 1933 (2,990 deaths). The most devastating quake ever was at Shaanxi (Shensi), central China, on 24 January 1566, when an estimated 830,000 people were killed.

* now Pakistan

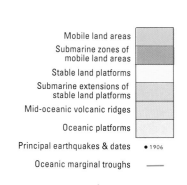

Mobile land areas
Submarine zones of mobile land areas
Stable land platforms
Submarine extensions of stable land platforms
Mid-oceanic volcanic ridges
Oceanic platforms
• 1906 Principal earthquakes & dates
— Oceanic marginal troughs

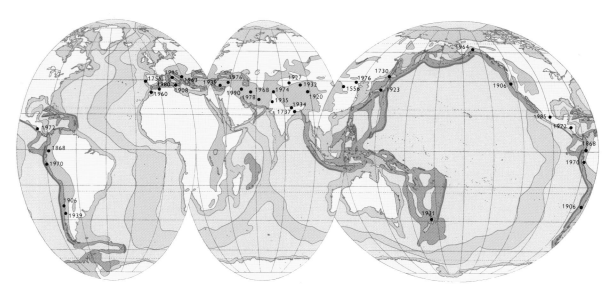

Earthquakes are a series of rapid vibrations originating from the the slipping or faulting of parts of the Earth's crust when stresses within build to breaking point, and usually occur at depths between 8 and 30 kilometres.

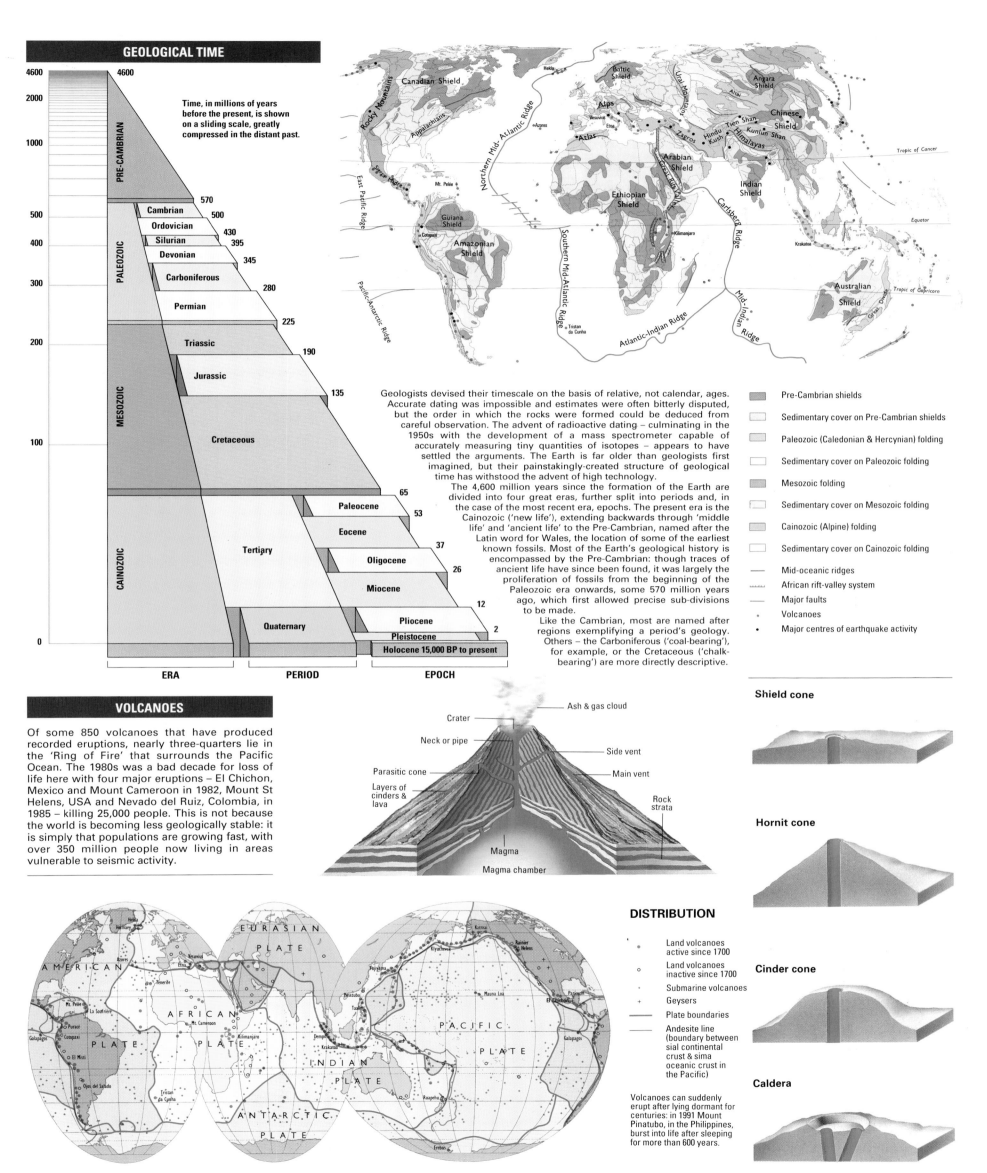

GEOLOGICAL TIME

Time, in millions of years before the present, is shown on a sliding scale, greatly compressed in the distant past.

4600
2000
1000
500
400
300
200
100
0

PRE-CAMBRIAN		4600
		570
PALEOZOIC	Cambrian	500
	Ordovician	430
	Silurian	395
	Devonian	345
	Carboniferous	280
	Permian	225
MESOZOIC	Triassic	190
	Jurassic	135
	Cretaceous	65
CAINOZOIC	Tertiary	Paleocene 53
		Eocene 37
		Oligocene 26
		Miocene 12
	Quaternary	Pliocene 2
		Pleistocene
		Holocene 15,000 BP to present

ERA   PERIOD   EPOCH

Geologists devised their timescale on the basis of relative, not calendar, ages. Accurate dating was impossible and estimates were often bitterly disputed, but the order in which the rocks were formed could be deduced from careful observation. The advent of radioactive dating – culminating in the 1950s with the development of a mass spectrometer capable of accurately measuring tiny quantities of isotopes – appears to have settled the arguments. The Earth is far older than geologists first imagined, but their painstakingly-created structure of geological time has withstood the advent of high technology.

The 4,600 million years since the formation of the Earth are divided into four great eras, further split into periods and, in the case of the most recent era, epochs. The present era is the Cainozoic ('new life'), extending backwards through 'middle life' and 'ancient life' to the Pre-Cambrian, named after the Latin word for Wales, the location of some of the earliest known fossils. Most of the Earth's geological history is encompassed by the Pre-Cambrian: though traces of ancient life have since been found, it was largely the proliferation of fossils from the beginning of the Paleozoic era onwards, some 570 million years ago, which first allowed precise sub-divisions to be made.

Like the Cambrian, most are named after regions exemplifying a period's geology. Others – the Carboniferous ('coal-bearing'), for example, or the Cretaceous ('chalk-bearing') are more directly descriptive.

Pre-Cambrian shields

Sedimentary cover on Pre-Cambrian shields

Paleozoic (Caledonian & Hercynian) folding

Sedimentary cover on Paleozoic folding

Mesozoic folding

Sedimentary cover on Mesozoic folding

Cainozoic (Alpine) folding

Sedimentary cover on Cainozoic folding

— Mid-oceanic ridges

···· African rift-valley system

— Major faults

• Volcanoes

● Major centres of earthquake activity

VOLCANOES

Of some 850 volcanoes that have produced recorded eruptions, nearly three-quarters lie in the 'Ring of Fire' that surrounds the Pacific Ocean. The 1980s was a bad decade for loss of life here with four major eruptions – El Chichon, Mexico and Mount Cameroon in 1982, Mount St Helens, USA and Nevado del Ruiz, Colombia, in 1985 – killing 25,000 people. This is not because the world is becoming less geologically stable: it is simply that populations are growing fast, with over 350 million people now living in areas vulnerable to seismic activity.

Ash & gas cloud
Crater
Neck or pipe
Parasitic cone
Layers of cinders & lava
Side vent
Main vent
Rock strata
Magma
Magma chamber

DISTRIBUTION

• Land volcanoes active since 1700

∘ Land volcanoes inactive since 1700

· Submarine volcanoes

+ Geysers

— Plate boundaries

— Andesite line (boundary between sial continental crust & sima oceanic crust in the Pacific)

Volcanoes can suddenly erupt after lying dormant for centuries: in 1991 Mount Pinatubo, in the Philippines, burst into life after sleeping for more than 600 years.

Shield cone

Hornit cone

Cinder cone

Caldera

THE EARTH: OCEANS

The Earth is a misnamed planet: almost 71% of its total surface area – 360,059,000 square kilometres – is covered by its oceans and seas. This great cloak of liquid water gives the planet its characteristic blue appearance from space, and is one of two obvious differences between the Earth and its near-neighbours in space, Mars and Venus. The other difference is the presence of life, and the two are closely linked.

In a strict geographical sense, the Earth has only three oceans: the Atlantic, the Pacific and the Indian. Sub-divided vertically instead of horizontally, however, there are many more. The most active is the sunlit upper layer, home of most sea-life and the vital interface between air and water. In this surface zone, huge energies are exchanged between the oceans and the atmosphere above; it is also a kind of membrane through which the ocean breathes, absorbing enormous quantities of carbon dioxide and partially exchanging them for oxygen, largely through the phytoplankton, tiny plants that photosynthesize solar energy and provide the food base for all other marine life.

As depth increases, light and colour fade away, the longer wavelengths dying first. At 50 metres, the ocean is a world of green and blue and violet; at 100 metres, only blue remains; by 200 metres, there is only a dim twilight. The temperature falls away with the light until some time before 1,000 metres – the precise depth varies – there occurs a temperature change almost as abrupt as the transition between air and water far above.

Below this thermocline, at a near-stable 3°C, the waters are forever unmoved by the winds of the upper world and are stirred only by the slow action of deep ocean currents. The pressure is crushing, touching 1,000 atmospheres in the deepest trenches: a force of one tonne bearing down on every square centimetre.

Yet even here the oceans support life, and not only the handful of strange, deep-sea creatures that find a living in the near-empty abyss. The deep ocean serves as a gigantic storehouse both for heat and for assorted atmospheric chemicals, regulating and balancing the proportions of various trace compounds and elements and ensuring a large measure of stability for both the climate and the ecology that depend on it.

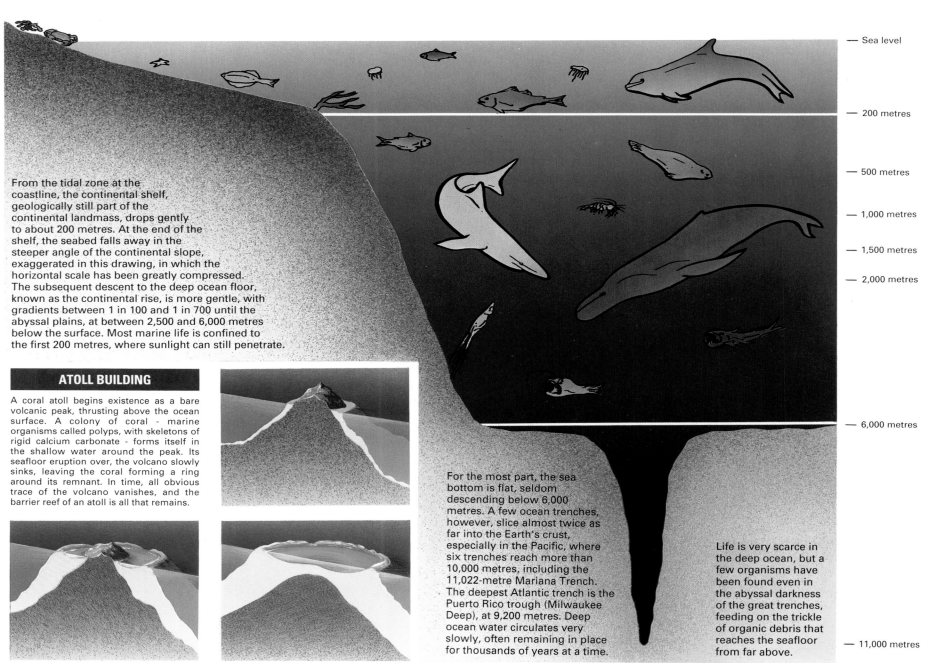

From the tidal zone at the coastline, the continental shelf, geologically still part of the continental landmass, drops gently to about 200 metres. At the end of the shelf, the seabed falls away in the steeper angle of the continental slope, exaggerated in this drawing, in which the horizontal scale has been greatly compressed. The subsequent descent to the deep ocean floor, known as the continental rise, is more gentle, with gradients between 1 in 100 and 1 in 700 until the abyssal plains, at between 2,500 and 6,000 metres below the surface. Most marine life is confined to the first 200 metres, where sunlight can still penetrate.

— Sea level
— 200 metres
— 500 metres
— 1,000 metres
— 1,500 metres
— 2,000 metres
— 6,000 metres
— 11,000 metres

For the most part, the sea bottom is flat, seldom descending below 6,000 metres. A few ocean trenches, however, slice almost twice as far into the Earth's crust, especially in the Pacific, where six trenches reach more than 10,000 metres, including the 11,022-metre Mariana Trench. The deepest Atlantic trench is the Puerto Rico trough (Milwaukee Deep), at 9,200 metres. Deep ocean water circulates very slowly, often remaining in place for thousands of years at a time.

Life is very scarce in the deep ocean, but a few organisms have been found even in the abyssal darkness of the great trenches, feeding on the trickle of organic debris that reaches the seafloor from far above.

ATOLL BUILDING

A coral atoll begins existence as a bare volcanic peak, thrusting above the ocean surface. A colony of coral - marine organisms called polyps, with skeletons of rigid calcium carbonate - forms itself in the shallow water around the peak. Its seafloor eruption over, the volcano slowly sinks, leaving the coral forming a ring around its remnant. In time, all obvious trace of the volcano vanishes, and the barrier reef of an atoll is all that remains.

PROFILE OF AN OCEAN

The deep ocean floor is no more uniform than the surface of the continents, although it was not until the development of effective sonar equipment that it was possible to examine submarine contours in detail. The Atlantic (right) and the Pacific show similar patterns. Off-shore comes the continental shelf, sliding downwards to the continental slope and the steeper continental rise, after which the seabed rolls onward into the abyssal plains. In the wide Pacific, these are interrupted by gently-rising abyssal hills; in both oceans, the plains extend all the way to the mid-oceanic ridges, where the upwelling of new crustal material is constantly forcing the oceans wider. Volcanic activity is responsible for the formation of seamounts and tablemounts or guyots, their flat-topped equivalents. In this cross-section, only the Azores are high enough to break the surface and become islands.

Massachusetts (Nantucket sound)

Kelvin seamounts

Corne seamou

2,000 metres

4,000 metres

Abyssal plain

OCEAN CURRENTS

NORTH		SOUTH
Arctic	Atlantic Ocean	Antarctic

Warm tropical water

Antarctic intermediate current

North Atlantic deep water

Antarctic bottom water

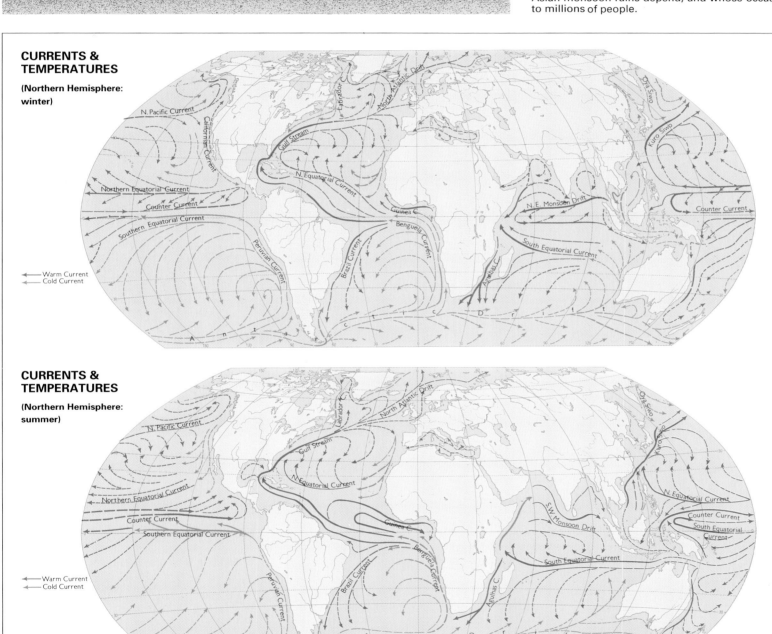

Moving immense quantities of energy as well as billions of tonnes of water every hour, the ocean currents are a vital part of the great heat engine that drives the Earth's climate. They themselves are produced by a twofold mechanism. At the surface, winds push huge masses of water before them; in the deep ocean, below an abrupt temperature gradient that separates the churning surface waters from the still depths, density variations cause slow vertical movements.

The pattern of circulation of the great surface currents is determined by the displacement known as the Coriolis effect. As the Earth turns beneath a moving object - whether it is a tennis ball or a vast mass of water - it appears to be deflected to one side. The deflection is most obvious near the equator, where the Earth's surface is spinning eastward at 1700 km/h; currents moving poleward are curved clockwise in the northern hemisphere and anti-clockwise in the southern.

The result is a system of spinning circles known as gyres. The Coriolis effect piles up water on the left of each gyre, creating a narrow, fast-moving stream that is matched by a slower, broader returning current on the right. North and south of the equator, the fastest currents are located in the west and in the east respectively. In each case, warm water moves from the equator and cold water returns to it. Cold currents often bring an upwelling of nutrients with them, supporting the world's most economically important fisheries.

Depending on the prevailing winds, some currents on or near the equator may reverse their direction in the course of the year - a seasonal variation on which Asian monsoon rains depend, and whose occasional failure can bring disaster to millions of people.

CURRENTS & TEMPERATURES

(Northern Hemisphere: winter)

Warm Current
Cold Current

CURRENTS & TEMPERATURES

(Northern Hemisphere: summer)

Warm Current
Cold Current

SEAWATER

The chemical composition of the sea, in grams per tonne of seawater, excluding the elements of water itself

Chlorine	19400
Sodium	10800
Magnesium	1290
Sulphur	904
Calcium	411
Potassium	392
Bromine	67
Strontium	8.1
Boron	4.5
Fluorine	1.3
Lithium	0.17
Rubidium	0.12
Phosphorus	0.09
Iodine	0.06
Barium	0.02
Arsenic	0.003
Cesium	0.0003

Seawater also contains virtually every other element, although the quantities involved are too small for reliable measurement. In natural conditions, its composition is broadly consistent across the world's seas and oceans; but especially in coastal areas, variations, sometimes substantial, may be caused by the presence of industrial waste and sewage sludge.

Mid-Atlantic ridge | Atlantic seamount | Azores | Josephine seamounts | Gettysburg seamounts | Gibraltar

THE EARTH: ATMOSPHERE

Extending from the surface far into space, the atmosphere is a meteor shield, a radiation deflector, a thermal blanket and a source of chemical energy for the Earth's diverse inhabitants. Five-sixths of its mass is found in the first 15 kilometres, the troposphere, no thicker in relative terms than the skin of an onion. Clouds, cyclonic winds, precipitation and virtually all the phenomena we call weather occur in this narrow layer. Above, a thin layer of ozone blocks ultra-violet radiation. Beyond 100 kilometres, atmospheric density is lower than most laboratory vacuums, yet these tenuous outer reaches, composed largely of hydrogen and helium, trap cosmic debris and incoming high-energy particles alike.

CIRCULATION OF THE AIR

STRUCTURE OF ATMOSPHERE

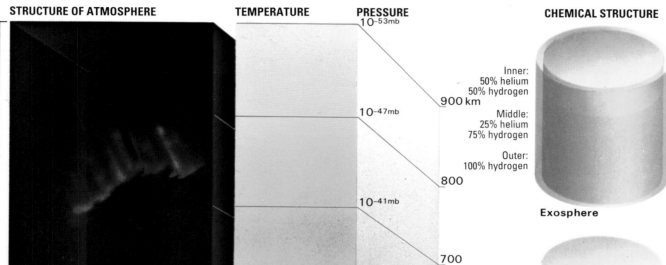

F2

F1

E

D

Mesosphere
Ozone layer
Tropopause

TEMPERATURE

ca. 2 200 °C

ca. 1 500 °C

ca. 750 °C

−58 °C
−91 °C
−93 °C
−33 °C
−8 °C
−12 °C
−38 °C
−53 °C
15 °C

PRESSURE

10^{-53}mb

10^{-47}mb

10^{-41}mb

10^{-35}mb

10^{-28}mb

10^{-22}mb

10^{-16}mb

10^{-10}mb

10^{-3}mb

10^{3}mb

900 km

800

700

600

500

400

300

200

100

0

CHEMICAL STRUCTURE

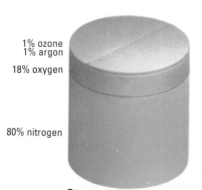

Inner:
50% helium
50% hydrogen

Middle:
25% helium
75% hydrogen

Outer:
100% hydrogen

Exosphere

15% helium

15% oxygen
& atomic
oxygen

70% nitrogen

Ionosphere

1% ozone
1% argon

18% oxygen

80% nitrogen

Stratosphere

1% argon

21% oxygen

78% nitrogen

Troposphere

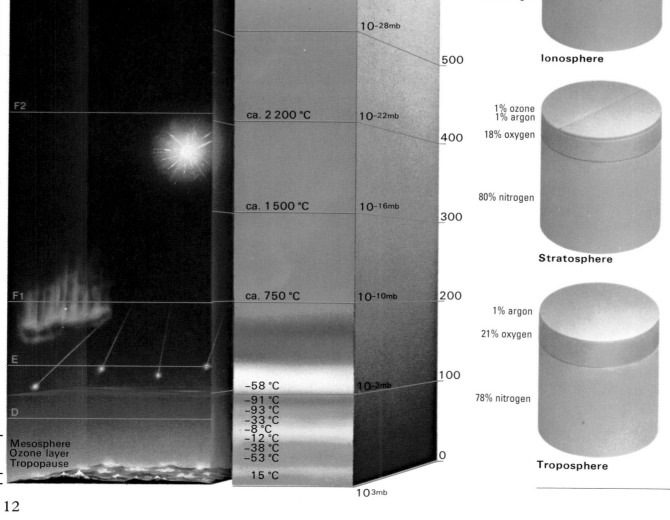

Exosphere

The atmosphere's upper layer has no clear outer boundary, merging imperceptibly with interplanetary space. Its lower boundary, at an altitude of approximately 600 kilometres, is almost equally vague. The exosphere is mainly composed of hydrogen and helium in changing proportions, with a small quantity of atomic oxygen up to 600 kilometres. Helium vanishes with increasing altitude, and above 2,400 kilometres the exosphere is almost entirely hydrogen.

Ionosphere

Gas molecules in the ionosphere, mainly helium, oxygen and nitrogen, are electrically charged - ionized - by the Sun's radiation. Within the ionosphere's range of 50 to 600 kilometres in altitude, they group themselves into four layers, known conventionally as D, E, F1 and F2, all of which can reflect radio waves of differing frequencies. The high energy of ionospheric gas gives it a notional temperature of more than 2,000°C, although its density is negligible. The auroras - *aurora borealis* and its southern counterpart, *aurora australis* - occur in the ionosphere when charged particles from the Sun interact with the Earth's magnetic fields, at their strongest near the poles.

Stratosphere

Separated at its upper and lower limits by the distinct thresholds of the stratopause and the tropopause, the stratosphere is a remarkably stable layer between 50 kilometres and about 15 kilometres. Its temperature rises from -55°C at its lower extent to approximately 0°C near the stratopause, where a thin layer of ozone absorbs ultra-violet radiation. "Mother-of-pearl" or nacreous cloud occurs at about 25 kilometres' altitude. Stratospheric air contains enough ozone to make it poisonous, although it is in any case far too rarified to breathe.

Troposphere

The narrowest of all the atmospheric layers, the troposphere extends up to 15 kilometres at the equator but only 8 kilometres at the poles. Since this thin region contains about 85% of the atmosphere's total mass and almost all of its water vapour, it is also the realm of the Earth's weather. Temperatures fall steadily with increasing height by about 1°C for every 100 metres above sea level.

Heated by the relatively high surface temperatures near the Earth's equator, air expands and rises to create a belt of low pressure. Moving northward towards the poles, it gradually cools, sinking once more and producing high pressure belts at about latitudes 30° North and South. Water vapour carried with the air falls as rain, releasing vast quantities of energy as well as liquid water when it condenses.

The high and low pressure belts are both areas of comparative calm, but between them, blowing from high to low pressure areas, are the prevailing winds. The atmospheric circulatory system is enormously complicated by the Coriolis effect brought about by the spinning Earth: winds are deflected to the right in the northern hemisphere and to the left in the southern, giving rise to the typically cyclonic pattern of swirling clouds carried by the moving masses of air.

Although clouds appear in an almost infinite variety of shapes and sizes, there are recognizable features that form the basis of a classification first put forward by Luke Howard, a London chemist, in 1803 and later modified by the World Meteorological Organization. The system derives from the altitude of clouds and whether they form hairlike filaments ('cirrus'), heaps or piles ('cumulus') or layers ('stratus'). Each characteristic carries some kind of message – not always a clear one – to forecasters about the weather to come.

CLASSIFICATION OF CLOUDS

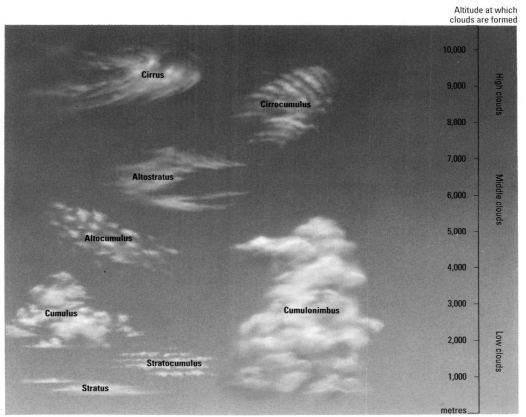

Altitude at which clouds are formed

Clouds form when damp, usually rising, air is cooled. Thus they form when a wind rises to cross hills or mountains; when a mass of air rises over, or is pushed up by, another mass of denser air; or when local heating of the ground causes convection currents. The types of clouds are classified according to altitude as high, middle, or low. The high ones, composed of ice crystals, are cirrus, cirrostratus and cirrocumulus. The middle clouds are altostratus, a grey or bluish striated, fibrous, or uniform sheet producing light drizzle, and altocumulus, a thicker and fluffier version of cirrocumulus. The low clouds include nimbostratus, a dark grey layer that brings almost continuous rain or snow; cumulus, a detached 'heap' – brilliant white in sunlight but dark and flat at the base; and stratus, which forms dull, overcast skies at low altitudes. Cumulonimbus, associated with storms and rains, heavy and dense with flat base and a high, fluffy outline, can be tall enough to occupy middle as well as low altitudes.

PRESSURE & WINDS

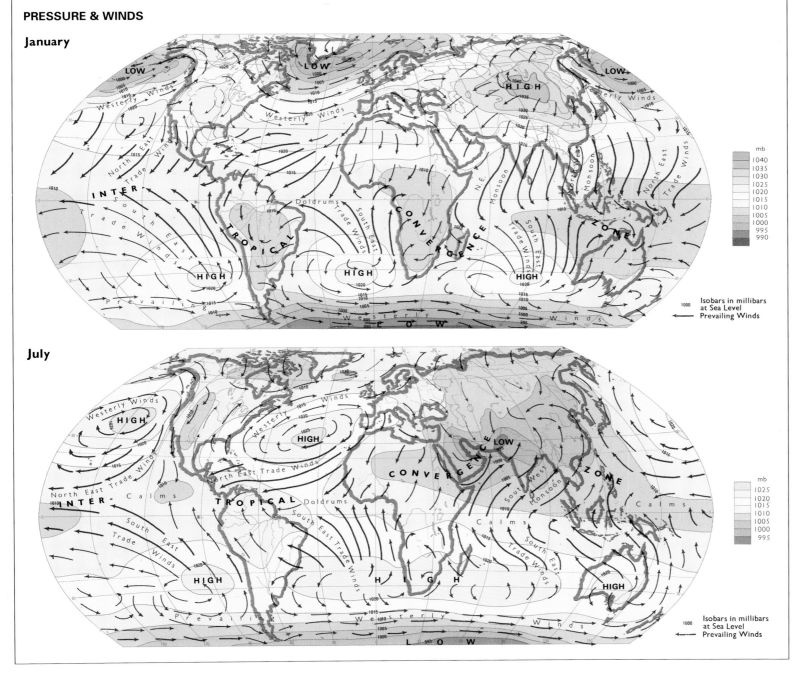

January

July

THE EARTH: CLIMATE

Climate is weather in the long term: the seasonal pattern of hot and cold, wet and dry, averaged over time. At the simplest level, it is caused by the uneven heating of the Earth. Surplus heat at the equator passes towards the poles, levelling out the energy differential. Its passage is marked by a ceaseless churning of the atmosphere and the oceans, further agitated by the the Earth's diurnal spin and the motion it imparts to moving air and water. The heat's means of transport – by winds and ocean currents, by the continual evaporation and recondensation of water molecules – is the weather itself.

There are four basic types of climate, each open to considerable sub-division: tropical, desert, temperate and polar. But although latitude is obviously a critical factor, it is not the only determinant. The differential heating of land and sea, the funnelling and interruption of winds and ocean currents by landmasses and mountain ranges, and the transpiration of vegetation: all combine to add complexity. New York, Naples and the Gobi Desert share almost the same latitude, for example, but their climates are very different. And although the sheer intricacy of the weather system often defies day-to-day prediction in these or any other places – despite the satellites and number-crunching supercomputers with which present-day meteorologists are equipped – their climatic patterns retain a year-on-year stability.

They are not indefinitely stable, however. The planet regularly passes through long, cool periods of around 100,000 years: these are the ice ages, probably caused by recurring long-term oscillations in the Earth's orbital path and fluctuations in the Sun's energy output. In the present era, the Earth is nearest to the Sun in the middle of the northern hemisphere's winter; 11,000 years ago, at the end of the last ice age, the northern winter fell with the Sun at its most distant.

Left to its own devices, the climate even now should be drifting towards another glacial period. But global warming caused by increasing carbon dioxide levels in the atmosphere, largely the result of 20th-century fuel-burning and deforestation, may well precipitate change far faster than the great, slow cycles of the solar system.

CLIMATE REGIONS

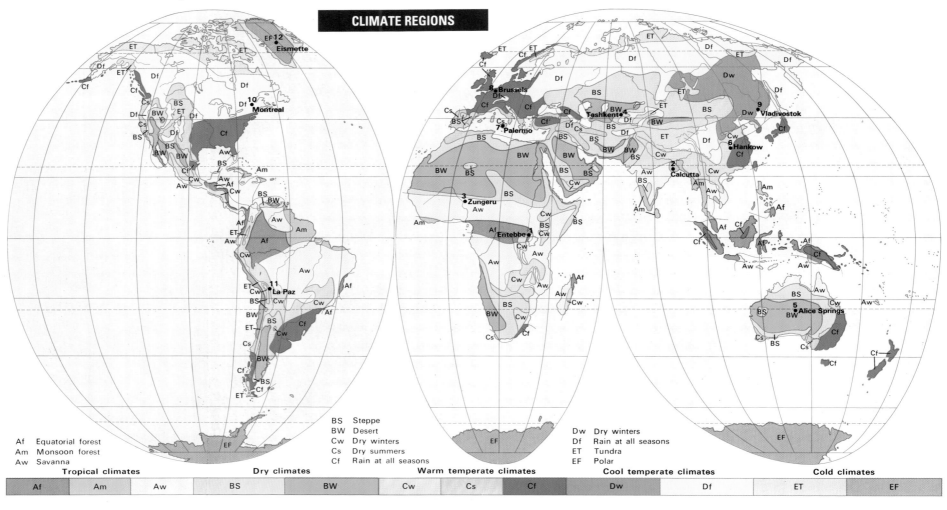

Af Equatorial forest
Am Monsoon forest
Aw Savanna

BS Steppe
BW Desert
Cw Dry winters
Cs Dry summers
Cf Rain at all seasons

Dw Dry winters
Df Rain at all seasons
ET Tundra
EF Polar

Tropical climates			Dry climates		Warm temperate climates			Cool temperate climates			Cold climates
Af	Am	Aw	BS	BW	Cw	Cs	Cf	Dw	Df	ET	EF

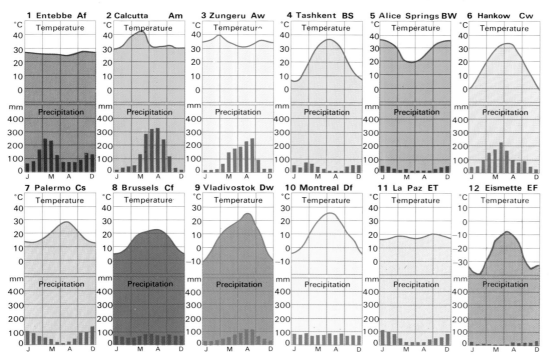

CLIMATE & WEATHER TERMS

Absolute humidity: amount of water vapour contained in a given volume of air.
Cloud cover: amount of cloud in the sky; measured in oktas (from 1 - 8), with 0 clear, & 8 total cover.
Condensation: the conversion of water vapour, moisture in the air into liquid.
Cyclone: violent storm resulting from counter clockwise rotation of winds in the northern hemisphere & clockwise in the southern: called hurricane in N. America, typhoon in the Far East.
Depression: approximately circular area of low pressure.
Dew: water droplets condensed out of the air after the ground has cooled at night.
Dew point: temperature at which air becomes saturated (reaches a relative humidity of 100%) at a constant pressure.
Drizzle: precipitation where drops are less than 0.5 mm (0.02 in) in diameter.
Evaporation: conversion of water from liquid into vapour, or moisture in the air.
Frost: dew that has frozen when the air temperature falls below freezing point.
Hail: frozen rain; small balls of ice, often falling during thunder storms.
Hoar frost: formed on objects when the dew point is below freezing point.
Humidity: amount of moisture in the air.
Isobar: cartographic line connecting places of equal atmospheric pressure.
Isotherm: cartographic line connecting places of equal temperature.
Lightning: massive electrical discharge released in thunderstorm from cloud to cloud or cloud to ground, the result of the tip becoming positively charged & the bottom negatively charged.
Precipitation: measurable rain, snow, sleet or hail.
Prevailing wind: most common direction of wind at a given location.
Rain: precipitation of liquid particles with diameter larger than 0.5 mm (0.02 in).
Relative humidity: amount of water vapour contained in a given volume of air at a given temperature.
Sleet: translucent or transparent ice-pellets (partially melted snow).
Snow: formed when water vapour condenses below freezing point.
Thunder: sound produced by the rapid expansion of air heated by lightning.
Tidal wave: giant ocean wave generated by earthquakes (tsunami) or cyclonic winds.
Tornado: severe funnel-shaped storm that twists as hot air spins vertically (waterspout at sea).
Whirlwind: rapidly rotating column of air, only a few metres across made visible by dust.

WINDCHILL FACTOR

In sub-zero weather, even moderate winds significantly reduce effective temperatures. The chart below shows the windchill effect across a range of speeds. Figures in the pink zone are not dangerous to well-clad people; in the blue zone, the risk of serious frostbite is acute.

	Wind speed (km/h)				
	16	**32**	**48**	**64**	**80**
0°C	-8	-14	-17	-19	-20
-5°C	-14	-21	-25	-27	-28
-10°C	-20	-28	-33	-35	-36
-15°C	-26	-36	-40	-43	-44
-20°C	-32	-42	-48	-51	-52
-25°C	-38	-49	-56	-59	-60
-30°C	-44	-57	-63	-66	-68
-35°C	-51	-64	-72	-74	-76
-40°C	-57	-71	-78	-82	-84
-45°C	-63	-78	-86	-90	-92
-50°C	-69	-85	-94	-98	-100

BEAUFORT WIND SCALE

Named for the 19th-century British naval officer who devised it, the Beaufort Scale assesses wind speed according to its effects. It was originally designed as an aid for sailors, but has since been adapted for use on land.

Scale	Wind speed kph	mph	Effect
0	0-1	0-1	**Calm** Smoke rises vertically
1	1-5	1-3	**Light air** Wind direction shown only by smoke drift
2	6-11	4-7	**Light breeze** Wind felt on face; leaves rustle; vanes moved by wind
3	12-19	8-12	**Gentle breeze** Leaves and small twigs in constant motion; wind extend small flag
4	20-28	13-18	**Moderate** Raises dust and loose paper; small branches move
5	29-38	19-24	**Fresh** Small trees in leaf sway; crested wavelets on inland waters
6	39-49	25-31	**Strong** Large branches move; difficult to use umbrellas; overhead wires whistle
7	50-61	32-38	**Near gale** Whole trees in motion; difficult to walk against wind
8	62-74	39-46	**Gale** Twigs break from trees; walking very difficult
9	75-88	47-54	**Strong gale** Slight structural damage
10	89-102	55-63	**Storm** Trees uprooted; serious structural damage
11	103-117	64-72	**Violent Storm** Widespread damage
12	118+	73+	**Hurricane**

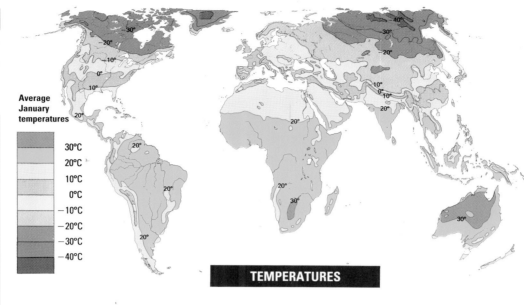

TEMPERATURES

Average January temperatures

- 30°C
- 20°C
- 10°C
- 0°C
- -10°C
- -20°C
- -30°C
- -40°C

Average July temperatures

- 30°C
- 20°C
- 10°C
- 0°C
- -10°C

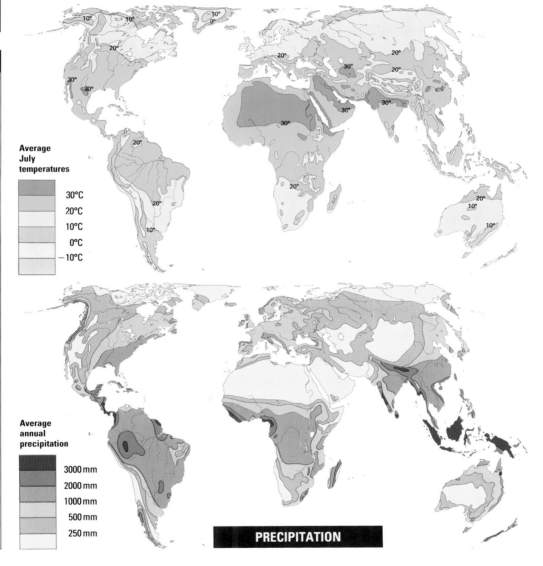

Average annual precipitation

- 3000 mm
- 2000 mm
- 1000 mm
- 500 mm
- 250 mm

PRECIPITATION

CLIMATE RECORDS

Temperature

Highest recorded temperature: Al Aziziyah, Libya, 58°C [136.4°F], 13 Sep. 1922.

Highest mean annual temperature: Dallol, Ethiopia, 34.4°C [94°F], 1960-66.

Longest heatwave: Marble Bar, W. Australia, 162 days over 38°C [100°F], 23 Oct. 1923 - 7 Apr. 1924.

Lowest recorded temperature (outside poles): Verkhoyansk, Siberia, USSR -68°C [-90°F], 6 Feb. 1933. Verkhoyansk also registered the greatest annual range of temperature: - 70°C to 37°C [-94°F to 98°F].

Lowest mean annual temperature: Polus Nedostupnosti, Pole of Cold, Antarctica, -57.8°C [-72°F].

Precipitation

Driest place: Arica, N. Chile, 0.8mm [0.03 in] per year (60-year average).

Longest drought: Calama, N. Chile: no recorded rainfall in 400 years to 1971.

Wettest place (average): Tututendo, Colombia: mean annual rainfall 11,770 mm [463.4 in].

Wettest place (12 months): Cherrapunji, Meghalaya, N.E. India, 26,470 mm [1,040 in], Aug. 1860 to Aug. 1861. Cherrapunji also holds the record for rainfall in one month: 930 mm [37 in] July 1861.

Wettest place (24 hours): Cilaos, Réunion, Indian Ocean, 1,870 mm [73.6 in], 15-16 Mar. 1952.

Heaviest hailstones: Gopalganj, Bangladesh, up to 1.02 kg [2.25 lb], 14 Apr. 1986 (killed 92 people).

Heaviest snowfall (continuous): Bessans, Savoie, France, 1730 mm [68 in] in 19 hours, 5-6 Apr. 1969.

Heaviest snowfall (season/year): Paradise Ranger Station, Mt Rainier, Washington, USA, 31,102 mm [1,224.5 in], 19 Feb. 1971 to 18 Feb. 1972.

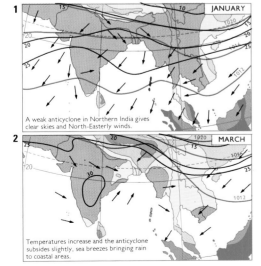

1 — JANUARY

A weak anticyclone in Northern India gives clear skies and North-Easterly winds.

2 — MARCH

Temperatures increase and the anticyclone subsides slightly, sea breezes bringing rain to coastal areas.

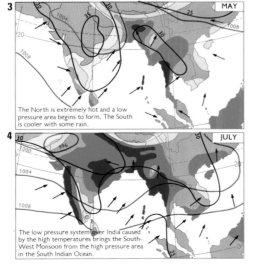

3 — MAY

The North is extremely hot and a low pressure area begins to form. The South is cooler with some rain.

4 — JULY

The low pressure system over India caused by the high temperatures brings the South-West Monsoon from the high pressure area in the South Indian Ocean.

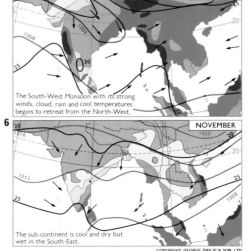

5 — SEPTEMBER

The South-West Monsoon with its strong winds, cloud, rain and cool temperatures begins to retreat from the North-West.

6 — NOVEMBER

The sub-continent is cool and dry but wet in the South-East.

THE MONSOON

While it is crucial to the agriculture of South Asia, the monsoon that follows the dry months is unpredictable - in duration as well as intensity. A season of very heavy rainfall, causing disastrous floods, can be succeeded by years of low precipitation, leading to serious drought.

Monthly rainfall

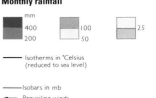

mm
- 400
- 200
- 100
- 50
- 25

— Isotherms in °Celsius (reduced to sea level)

— Isobars in mb

← Prevailing winds

15

THE EARTH: WATER

Fresh water is essential to all terrestrial life, from the humblest bacterium to the most advanced technological society. Yet freshwater resources form a minute fraction of the Earth's 1.41 billion cubic kilometres of water: most human needs must be met from the 2,000 cubic kilometres circulating in rivers at any one time. Agriculture accounts for huge quantities: without large-scale irrigation, most of the world's people would starve. And since fresh water is just as essential for most industrial processes – smelting a tonne of nickel, for example, requires about 4,000 tonnes of water – the combination of growing population and advancing industry has put water supplies under strain.

Fortunately water is seldom used up: the planet's hydrological cycle circulates it with benign efficiency, at least on a global scale. More locally, though, human activity can cause severe shortages: water for industry and agriculture is being withdrawn from many river basins and underground aquifers faster than natural recirculation can replace it.

THE HYDROLOGICAL CYCLE

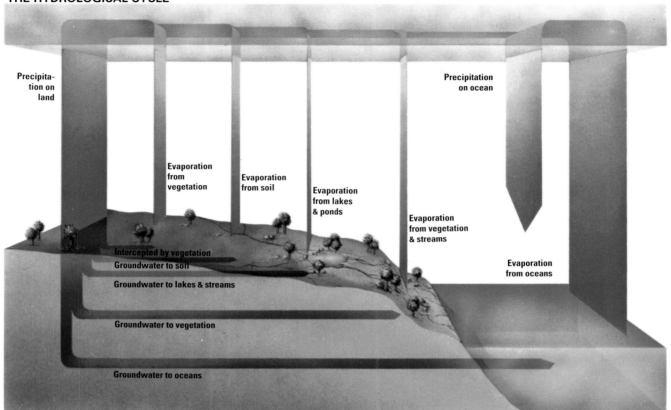

Water vapour is constantly drawn into the air from the Earth's rivers, lakes, seas and plant transpiration. In the atmosphere, it circulates around the planet, transporting energy as well as water itself. When the vapour cools it falls as rain or snow, and returns to the surface to evaporate once more. The whole cycle is driven by the Sun.

WATER DISTRIBUTION

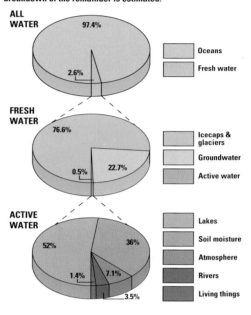

The distribution of planetary water, by percentage. Oceans and icecaps together account for more than 99% of the total; the breakdown of the remainder is estimated.

ALL WATER — 97.4% / 2.6% — Oceans, Fresh water

FRESH WATER — 76.6% / 0.5% / 22.7% — Icecaps & glaciers, Groundwater, Active water

ACTIVE WATER — 52% / 36% / 1.4% / 7.1% / 3.5% — Lakes, Soil moisture, Atmosphere, Rivers, Living things

Almost all the world's water is 3,000 million years old, and all of it cycles endlessly through the hydrosphere, though at different rates. Water vapour circulates over days, even hours, deep ocean water circulates over millenia and ice-cap water remains solid for millions of years.

WATER RUNOFF

Annual freshwater runoff by continent in cubic kilometres

- Asia
- North America
- South America
- Australasia
- Europe
- Africa

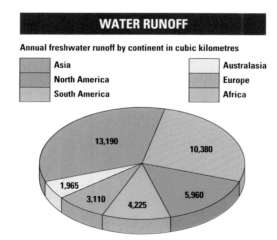

13,190 · 10,380 · 1,965 · 3,110 · 4,225 · 5,960

WATER UTILIZATION

The percentage breakdown of water usage by sector, selected countries (1980s)

Domestic · Industrial · Agriculture

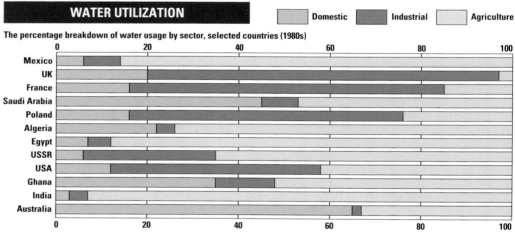

Mexico, UK, France, Saudi Arabia, Poland, Algeria, Egypt, USSR, USA, Ghana, India, Australia

WATER SUPPLY

Percentage of total population with access to safe drinking water (latest available year, 1980s)

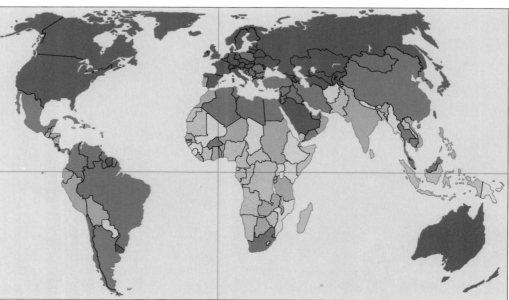

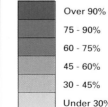

- Over 90%
- 75 – 90%
- 60 – 75%
- 45 – 60%
- 30 – 45%
- Under 30%

Least well provided countries (rural areas only):

Paraguay	8%	Guinea	15%
Mozambique	12%	Mauritania	17%
Uganda	12%	Malawi	17%
Angola	15%	Morocco	17%

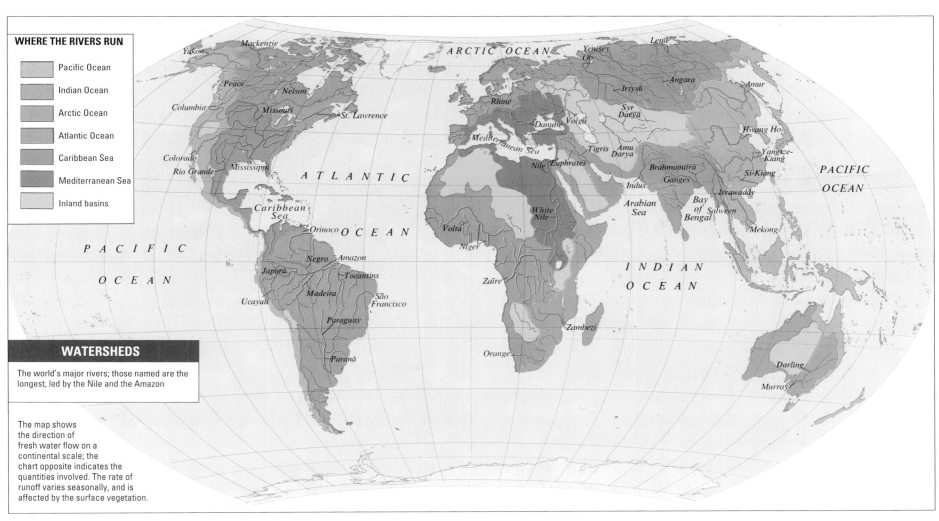

WHERE THE RIVERS RUN

- Pacific Ocean
- Indian Ocean
- Arctic Ocean
- Atlantic Ocean
- Caribbean Sea
- Mediterranean Sea
- Inland basins

WATERSHEDS

The world's major rivers; those named are the longest, led by the Nile and the Amazon

The map shows the direction of fresh water flow on a continental scale; the chart opposite indicates the quantities involved. The rate of runoff varies seasonally, and is affected by the surface vegetation.

LAND USE BY CONTINENT

- Forest
- Permanent pasture & rough grazing
- Permanent crops & plantations
- Arable
- Non-productive

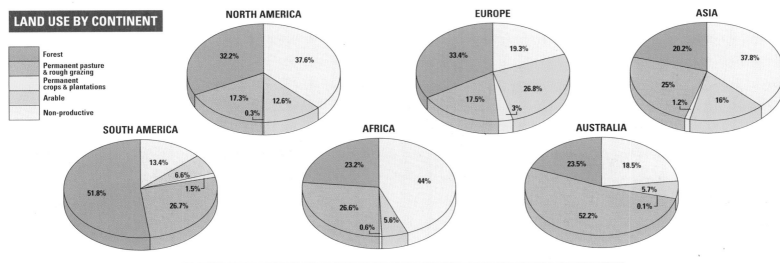

The proportion of productive land has reached its upper limit in Europe, and in Asia more than 80% of potential cropland is already under cultivation. Elsewhere, any increase is often matched by corresponding losses due to desertification and erosion; projections for 2025 show a decline in cropland per capita for all continents, most notably in Africa.

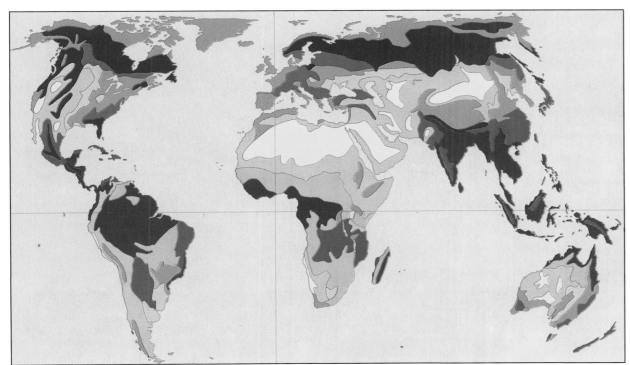
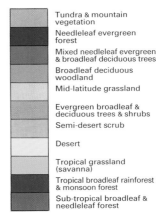

NATURAL VEGETATION

Regional variation in vegetation

- Tundra & mountain vegetation
- Needleleaf evergreen forest
- Mixed needleleaf evergreen & broadleaf deciduous trees
- Broadleaf deciduous woodland
- Mid-latitude grassland
- Evergreen broadleaf & deciduous trees & shrubs
- Semi-desert scrub
- Desert
- Tropical grassland (savanna)
- Tropical broadleaf rainforest & monsoon forest
- Sub-tropical broadleaf & needleleaf forest

The map illustrates the natural climax vegetation of a region, as dictated by its climate and topography. In most cases, human agricultural activity has drastically altered the vegetation pattern. Western Europe, for example, lost most of its broadleaf forest many centuries ago, and irrigation has turned some natural semi-desert into productive land.

THE EARTH: LANDSCAPE

Above and below the surface of the oceans, the features of the Earth's crust are constantly changing. The phenomenal forces generated by convection currents in the molten core of our planet carry the vast segments or 'plates' of the crust across the globe in an endless cycle of creation and destruction. New crust emerges along the central depths of the oceans, where molten magma flows from the margins of neighbouring plates to form the massive mid-ocean ridges. The sea floor spreads, and where ocean plates meet continental plates, they dip back into the earth's core to melt once again into magma.

Less dense, the continental plates 'float' among the oceans, drifting into and apart from each other at a rate which is almost imperceptibly slow. A continent may travel little more than 25 millimetres per year – in an average lifetime, Europe will move no more than a man's height – yet in the vast span of geological time, this process throws up giant mountain ranges and opens massive rifts in the land's surface.

The world's greatest mountain ranges have been formed in this way – the Himalayas by the collision of the Indo-Australian and Eurasian plates, the Andes by the meeting of the Nazca and South American plates. The Himalayas are a classic example of 'fold mountains', formed by the crumpling of the Earth's surface where two land masses have been driven together. The coastal range of the Andes, by contrast, was formed by the upsurge of molten volcanic rock created by the friction of the continent 'overriding' the ocean plate.

Destruction of the landscape, however, begins as soon as it is formed. Wind, water, ice and sea, the main agents of erosion, mount a constant assault that even the hardest rocks cannot withstand. Mountain peaks may dwindle by as little as a few millimetres each year, but if they are not uplifted by further movements of the crust they will eventually be reduced to rubble. Water is the most powerful destroyer – it has been estimated that 100 billion tonnes of rock is washed into the oceans every year.

When water freezes, its volume increases by about nine per cent, and no rock is strong enough to resist this pressure. Where water has penetrated tiny fissures or seeped into softer rock, a severe freeze followed by a thaw may result in rockfalls or earth-slides, creating major destruction in a few minutes. Over much longer periods, acidity in rainwater breaks down the chemical composition of porous rocks like limestone, eating away the rock to form deep caves and tunnels. Chemical decomposition also occurs in riverbeds and glacier valleys, hastening the process of mechanical erosion.

Rivers and glaciers, like the sea itself, generate much of their effect through abrasion – pounding the landscape with the debris they carry with them. But as well as destroying they also create new landscapes, many of them spectacular : vast deltas, as at the mouth of the Mississippi or the Nile; cliffs, rock arches and stacks, as on the south coast of Australia; and the fjords cut by long-melted glaciers in British Columbia, Norway and New Zealand.

The vast ridges that divide the Earth's crust beneath each of the world's major oceans mark the boundaries between tectonic plates which are moving very gradually in opposite directions. As the plates shift apart, molten magma rises from the Earth's core to seal the rift and the sea floor slowly spreads towards the continental landmasses. The rate of sea floor spreading has been calculated by magnetic analysis of the rock – at about 40 mm [1.5 in] a year in the North Atlantic. Near the ocean shore, underwater volcanoes mark the line where the continental rise begins. As the plates meet, much of the denser ocean crust dips beneath the continental plate and is melted back into the magma.

THE SPREADING EARTH

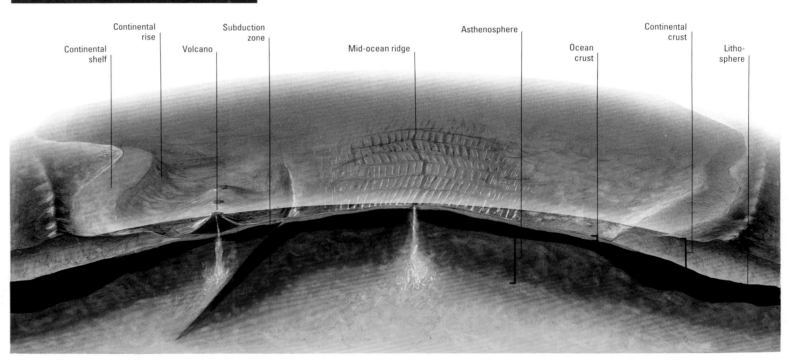

Continental shelf · Continental rise · Volcano · Subduction zone · Mid-ocean ridge · Asthenosphere · Ocean crust · Continental crust · Litho-sphere

TYPES OF ROCK

Rocks are divided into three types, according to the way in which they are formed:

Igneous rocks, including granite and basalt, are formed by the cooling of magma from within the Earth's crust.

Metamorphic rocks, such as slate, marble and quartzite, are formed below the Earth's surface by the compression or baking of existing rocks.

Sedimentary rocks, like sandstone and limestone, are formed on the surface of the Earth from the remains of living organisms and eroded fragments of older rocks.

MOUNTAIN BUILDING

Mountains are formed when pressures on the Earth's crust caused by continental drift become so intense that the surface buckles or cracks. This happens most dramatically where two tectonic plates collide : the Rockies, Andes, Alps, Urals and Himalayas resulted from such impacts. These are all known as fold mountains, because they were formed by the compression of the rocks, forcing the surface to bend and fold like a crumpled rug.

The other main building process is when the crust fractures to create faults, allowing rock to be forced upwards in large blocks; or when the pressure of magma within the crust forces the surface to bulge into a dome, or erupts to form a volcano. Large mountain ranges may reveal a combination of those features; the Alps, for example, have been compressed so violently that the folds are fragmented by numerous faults and intrusions of molten rock.

Over millions of years, even the greatest mountain ranges can be reduced by erosion to a rugged landscape known as a peneplain.

Types of fold: Geographers give different names to the degrees of fold that result from continuing pressure on the rock strata. A simple fold may be symmetric, with even slopes on either side, but as the pressure builds up, one slope becomes steeper and the fold becomes asymmetric. Later, the ridge or 'anticline' at the top of the fold may slide over the lower ground or 'syncline' to form a recumbent fold. Eventually, the rock strata may break under the pressure to form an overthrust and finally a nappe fold.

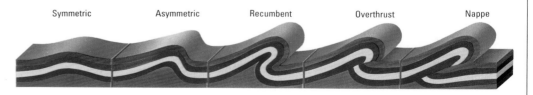

Symmetric · Asymmetric · Recumbent · Overthrust · Nappe

Types of fault: Faults are classified by the direction in which the blocks of rock have moved. A normal fault results when a vertical movement causes the surface to break apart; compression causes a reverse fault. Sideways movement causes shearing, known as a strike-slip fault. When the rock breaks in two places, the central block may be pushed up in a horst fault, or sink in a graben fault.

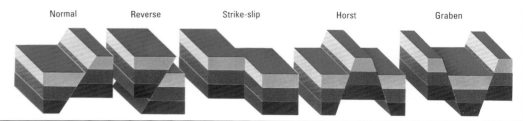

Normal · Reverse · Strike-slip · Horst · Graben

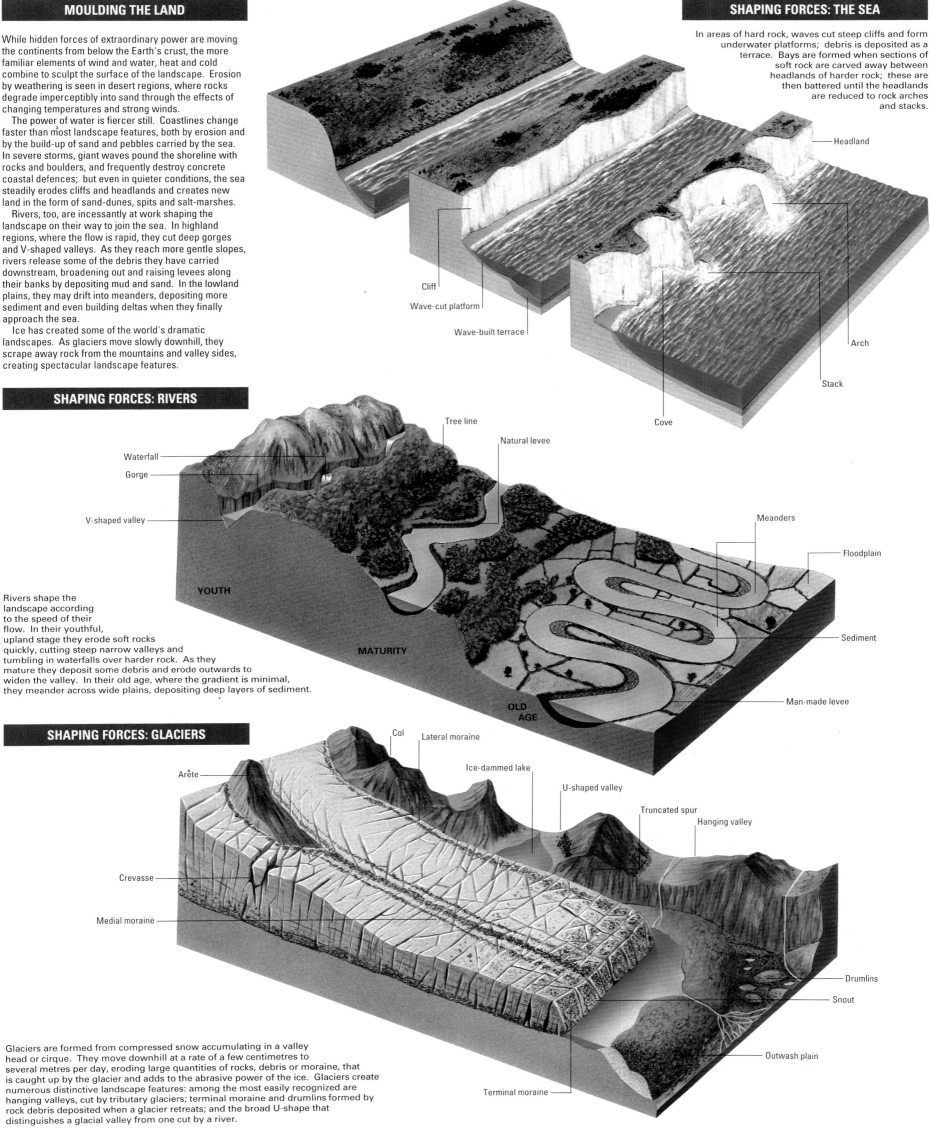

MOULDING THE LAND

While hidden forces of extraordinary power are moving the continents from below the Earth's crust, the more familiar elements of wind and water, heat and cold combine to sculpt the surface of the landscape. Erosion by weathering is seen in desert regions, where rocks degrade imperceptibly into sand through the effects of changing temperatures and strong winds.

The power of water is fiercer still. Coastlines change faster than most landscape features, both by erosion and by the build-up of sand and pebbles carried by the sea. In severe storms, giant waves pound the shoreline with rocks and boulders, and frequently destroy concrete coastal defences; but even in quieter conditions, the sea steadily erodes cliffs and headlands and creates new land in the form of sand-dunes, spits and salt-marshes.

Rivers, too, are incessantly at work shaping the landscape on their way to join the sea. In highland regions, where the flow is rapid, they cut deep gorges and V-shaped valleys. As they reach more gentle slopes, rivers release some of the debris they have carried downstream, broadening out and raising levees along their banks by depositing mud and sand. In the lowland plains, they may drift into meanders, depositing more sediment and even building deltas when they finally approach the sea.

Ice has created some of the world's dramatic landscapes. As glaciers move slowly downhill, they scrape away rock from the mountains and valley sides, creating spectacular landscape features.

SHAPING FORCES: THE SEA

In areas of hard rock, waves cut steep cliffs and form underwater platforms; debris is deposited as a terrace. Bays are formed when sections of soft rock are carved away between headlands of harder rock; these are then battered until the headlands are reduced to rock arches and stacks.

Headland

Cliff

Wave-cut platform

Wave-built terrace

Arch

Stack

Cove

SHAPING FORCES: RIVERS

Waterfall

Gorge

V-shaped valley

Tree line

Natural levee

Meanders

Floodplain

Sediment

YOUTH

MATURITY

OLD AGE

Man-made levee

Rivers shape the landscape according to the speed of their flow. In their youthful, upland stage they erode soft rocks quickly, cutting steep narrow valleys and tumbling in waterfalls over harder rock. As they mature they deposit some debris and erode outwards to widen the valley. In their old age, where the gradient is minimal, they meander across wide plains, depositing deep layers of sediment.

SHAPING FORCES: GLACIERS

Col

Lateral moraine

Arête

Ice-dammed lake

U-shaped valley

Truncated spur

Hanging valley

Crevasse

Medial moraine

Drumlins

Snout

Outwash plain

Terminal moraine

Glaciers are formed from compressed snow accumulating in a valley head or cirque. They move downhill at a rate of a few centimetres to several metres per day, eroding large quantities of rocks, debris or moraine, that is caught up by the glacier and adds to the abrasive power of the ice. Glaciers create numerous distinctive landscape features: among the most easily recognized are hanging valleys, cut by tributary glaciers; terminal moraine and drumlins formed by rock debris deposited when a glacier retreats; and the broad U-shape that distinguishes a glacial valley from one cut by a river.

THE EARTH: ENVIRONMENT

Unique among the planets, the Earth has been the home of living creatures for most of its existence. Precisely how these improbable assemblies of self-replicating chemicals ever began remains a matter of conjecture, but the planet and its passengers have matured together for a very long time. Over three billion years, life has not only adapted to its environment: it has also slowly changed that environment to suit itself.

The planet and its biosphere – the entirety of its living things – function like a single organism. The British scientist James Lovelock, who first stated this 'Gaia hypothesis' in the 1970s, went further: the planet, he declared, actually was a living organism, equipped on a colossal scale with the same sort of stability-seeking mechanisms used by lesser lifeforms like bacteria and humans to keep themselves running at optimum efficiency.

Lovelock's theory was inspired by a study of the Earth's atmosphere, whose constituents he noted are very far from the state of chemical equilibrium observed elsewhere in the solar system. The atmosphere has contained a substantial amount of free oxygen for the last two billion years; yet without constant renewal, the oxygen molecules would soon be locked permanently in oxides. The nitrogen, too, would find chemical stability, probably in nitrates (accounting for some of the oxygen). Without living plants and algae to remove it, carbon dioxide would steadily increase from its present-day 0.03%; in a few million years, it would form a thick blanket similar to the atmosphere of lifeless Venus, where surface temperatures reach 475°C.

It is not enough, however, for the biosphere simply to produce oxygen. While falling concentrations would be first uncomfortable and ultimately fatal for most contemporary life, at levels above the current 21% even moist vegetation is highly inflammable, and a massive conflagration becomes almost inevitable – a violent form of negative feedback to set the atmosphere on the path back to sterile equilibrium.

Fortunately, the biosphere has evolved over eons into a subtle and complex control system, sensing changes and reacting to them quickly but gently, tending always to maintain the balance it has achieved.

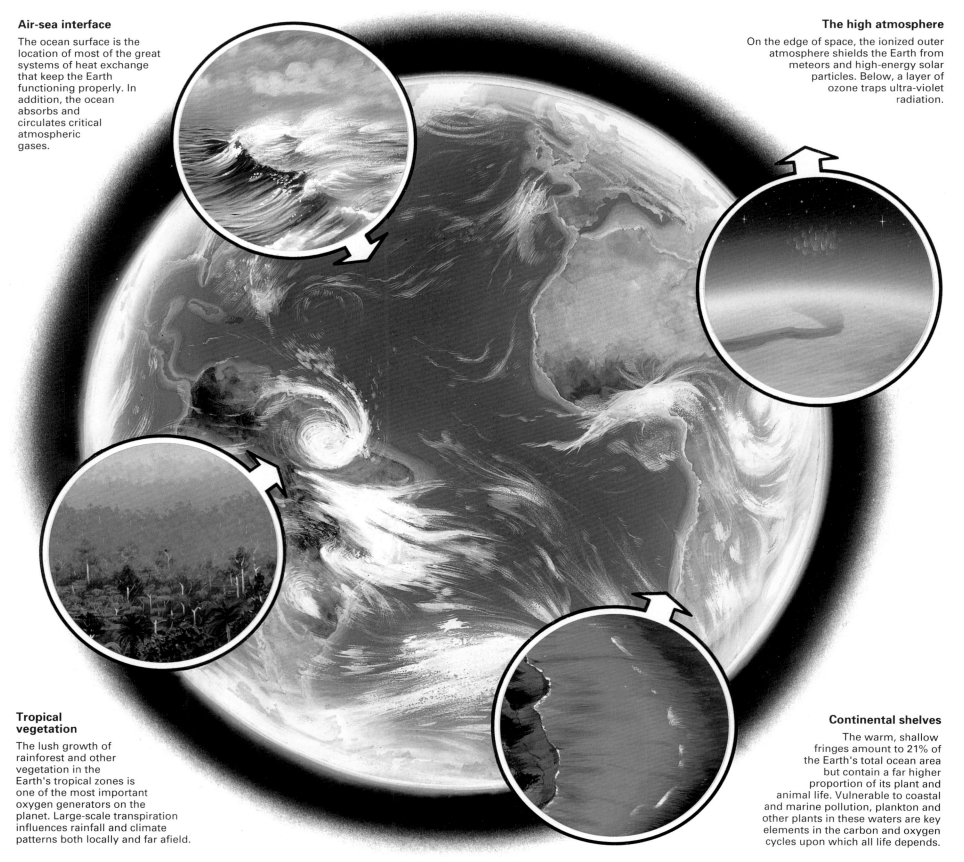

Air-sea interface

The ocean surface is the location of most of the great systems of heat exchange that keep the Earth functioning properly. In addition, the ocean absorbs and circulates critical atmospheric gases.

The high atmosphere

On the edge of space, the ionized outer atmosphere shields the Earth from meteors and high-energy solar particles. Below, a layer of ozone traps ultra-violet radiation.

Tropical vegetation

The lush growth of rainforest and other vegetation in the Earth's tropical zones is one of the most important oxygen generators on the planet. Large-scale transpiration influences rainfall and climate patterns both locally and far afield.

Continental shelves

The warm, shallow fringes amount to 21% of the Earth's total ocean area but contain a far higher proportion of its plant and animal life. Vulnerable to coastal and marine pollution, plankton and other plants in these waters are key elements in the carbon and oxygen cycles upon which all life depends.

20

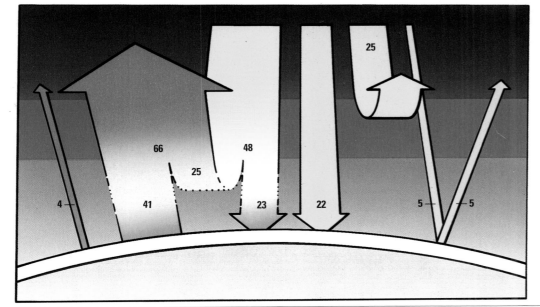

Apart from a modest quantity of internal heat from its molten core, the Earth receives all its energy from the Sun. If the planet is to remain at a constant temperature, it must re-radiate exactly as much as it receives. Even a minute surplus would lead to a warmer Earth, a deficit to a cooler one; because the planetary energy budget is constantly audited by the laws of physics, which do not permit juggling, it must balance with absolute precision. The temperature at which thermal equilibrium is reached depends on a multitude of interconnected factors. Two of the most important are the relative brightness of the Earth – its index of reflectivity, called the albedo – and the heat-trapping capacity of the atmosphere – the celebrated 'greenhouse effect'.

Because the Sun is very hot, most of its energy arrives in the form of relatively short-wave radiation: the shorter the waves, the more energy they carry. Some of the incoming energy is reflected straight back into space, exactly as it arrived; some is absorbed by the atmosphere on its way towards the surface; some is absorbed by the earth itself. Absorbed energy heats the Earth and its atmosphere alike. But since its temperature is very much lower than that of the Sun, outgoing energy is emitted at much longer infra-red wavelengths. Some of the outgoing radiation escapes directly into outer space; some of it is reabsorbed by the atmosphere. Atmospheric energy eventually finds its way back into space, too, after a complex series of interactions. These include the air movements we call the weather and, almost incidentally, the maintenance of life on Earth.

This diagram does not attempt to illustrate the actual mechanisms of heat exchange, but gives a reasonable account (in percentages) of what happens to 100 energy 'units'. Short-wave radiation is shown in yellow, long-wave in red.

THE CARBON CYCLE

Most of the constituents of the atmosphere are kept in constant balance by complex cycles in which life plays an essential and indeed a dominant part. The control of carbon dioxide, which left to its own devices would be the dominant atmospheric gas, is possibly the most important, although since all the Earth's biological and geophysical cycles interact and interlock, it is hard to separate them even in theory and quite impossible in practice.

The Earth has a huge supply of carbon, only a small quantity of which is in the form of carbon dioxide. Of that, around 98% is dissolved in the sea; the fraction circulating in the air amounts to only 340 parts per million of the atmosphere, where its capacity as a greenhouse gas is the key regulator of the planetary temperature. In turn, life regulates the regulator, keeping carbon dioxide concentrations below danger level.

If all life were to vanish tomorrow from the Earth, the atmosphere would begin the process of change immediately, although it might take several million years to achieve a new, inorganic stability. First, the oxygen content would begin to fall away; with no more assistance than a little solar radiation, a few electrical storms and its own high chemical potential, oxygen would steadily combine with atmospheric nitrogen and volcanic outgassing. In doing so, it would yield sufficient acid to react with carbonaceous rocks such as limestone, releasing carbon dioxide. Once carbon dioxide levels exceeded about 1%, its greenhouse power would increase disproportionately. Rising temperatures – well above the boiling point of water would speed chemical reactions; in time, the Earth's atmosphere would consist of little more than carbon dioxide and superheated water vapour.

Living things, however, circulate carbon. They do so first by simply existing: after all, the carbon atom is the basic building block of living matter. During life, plants absorb atmospheric carbon dioxide, incorporating the carbon itself into their structure – leaves and trunks in the case of land plants, shells

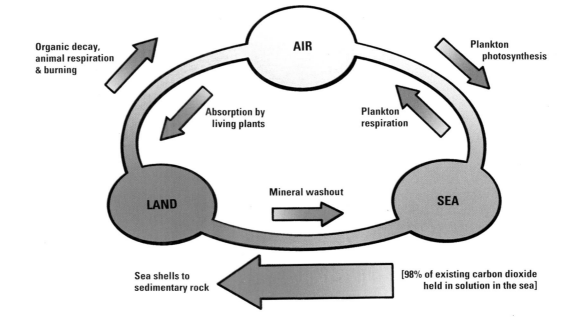

in the case of plankton and the tiny creatures that feed on it. The oxygen thereby freed is added to the atmosphere, at least for a time. Most plant carbon is returned to circulation when the plants die and decay, combining once more with the oxygen released during life. However, a small proportion – about one part in 1000 – is removed almost permanently, buried beneath mud on land, at sea sinking as dead matter to the ocean floor. In time, it is slowly compressed into sedimentary rocks such as limestone and chalk.

But in the evolution of the Earth, nothing is quite permanent. On an even longer timescale, the planet's crustal movements force new rock upward in mid-ocean ridges. Limestone deposits are

moved, and sea levels change; ancient limestone is exposed to weathering, and a little of its carbon is released to be fixed in turn by the current generation of plants.

The carbon cycle has continued quietly for an immensely long time, and without gross disturbance there is no reason why it would not continue almost indefinitely in the future. However, human beings have found a way to release fixed carbon at a rate far faster than existing global systems can recirculate it. Oil and coal deposits represent the work of millions of years of carbon accumulation; but it has taken only a few human generations of high-energy scavenging to endanger the entire complex regulatory cycle.

THE GREENHOUSE EFFECT

Constituting barely 0.03% of the atmosphere, carbon dioxide has a hugely disproportionate effect on the Earth's climate and even its habitability. Like the glass panes in a greenhouse, it is transparent to most incoming short-wave radiation, which passes freely to heat the planet beneath. But when the warmed earth re-transmits that energy, in the form of longer-wave infra-red radiation, the carbon dioxide functions as an opaque shield, so that the planetary surface (like the interior of a greenhouse) stays relatively hot.

Recent increases in CO_2 levels are causing alarm: global warming associated with a runaway greenhouse effect could bring disaster. But a serious reduction would be just as damaging, with surface temperatures falling dramatically; during the last ice age, for example, the carbon dioxide concentration was around 180 parts per million, and a total absence of the gas would likely leave the planet a ball of ice, or at best frozen tundra.

The diagram shows incoming sunlight as yellow; high-energy ultra-violet (blue) is trapped by the ozone layer while outgoing heat from the warmed Earth (red) is partially retained by carbon dioxide.

PEOPLE: DEMOGRAPHY

As the 20th century draws to its close, the Earth's population increases by nearly 10,000 every hour – enough to fill a new major city every week. The growth is almost entirely confined to the developing world, which accounted for 67% of total population in 1950 and is set to reach 84% by 2025. In developed countries, populations are almost static, and in some places, such as Germany, are actually falling. In fact, there is a clear correlation between wealth and low fertility: as incomes rise, reproduction rates drop.

The decline is already apparent. With the exception of Africa, the actual rates of increase are falling nearly everywhere. The structure of populations, however, ensures that human numbers will continue to rise even as fertility diminishes. Developed nations, like the UK, have an even spread across ages, and usually a growing proportion of elderly people: the over-75s often outnumber the under-5s, and women of child-bearing age form only a modest part of the total. Developing nations fall into a pattern somewhere between that of Kenya and Brazil: the great majority of their people are in the younger age groups, about to enter their most fertile years. In time, even Kenya's population profile should resemble the developed model, but the transition will come about only after a few more generations' growth.

It remains to be seen whether the planet will tolerate the population growth that seems inevitable before stability is reached. More people consume more resources, increasing the strain on an already troubled environment. However, more people should mean a greater supply of human ingenuity – the only commodity likely to resolve the crisis .

LARGEST NATIONS

The world's most populous nations, in millions (1989)

1.	China	1120
2.	India	812
3.	USA	250
4.	Indonesia	179
5.	Brazil	147
6.	Russia	147
7.	Japan	123
8.	Nigeria	109
9.	Pakistan	109
10.	Bangladesh	107
11.	Mexico	84
12.	Germany	79
13.	Vietnam	66
14.	Philippines	60
15.	Italy	58
16.	UK	57
17.	Turkey	57
18.	France	56
19.	Thailand	55
20.	Iran	55
21.	Egypt	53
22.	Ukraine	52
23.	Ethiopia	51
24.	S. Korea	43
25.	Burma	41

CROWDED NATIONS

Population per square kilometre (1989), exc. nations of less than one million

1.	Hong Kong	5826.2
2.	Singapore	4401.6
3.	Bangladesh	795.4
4.	Mauritius	577.3
5.	Taiwan	554.2
6.	Netherlands	439.0
7.	S. Korea	432.3
8.	Puerto Rico	412.9
9.	Belgium	328.5
10.	Japan	327.0
11.	Lebanon	283.2
12.	Rwanda	280.1
13.	India	273.1
14.	Sri Lanka	259.6
15.	El Salvador	251.3
16.	Trinidad & Tobago	246.2
17.	UK	236.8
18.	Germany	224.9
19.	Israel	224.6
20.	Jamaica	219.3

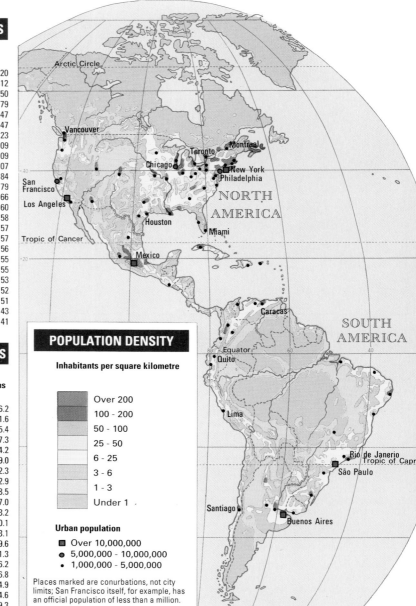

POPULATION DENSITY

Inhabitants per square kilometre

- Over 200
- 100 - 200
- 50 - 100
- 25 - 50
- 6 - 25
- 3 - 6
- 1 - 3
- Under 1

Urban population
- ◼ Over 10,000,000
- ⬤ 5,000,000 - 10,000,000
- • 1,000,000 - 5,000,000

Places marked are conurbations, not city limits; San Francisco itself, for example, has an official population of less than a million.

Projection : Mollweide's Interrupted Homolographic

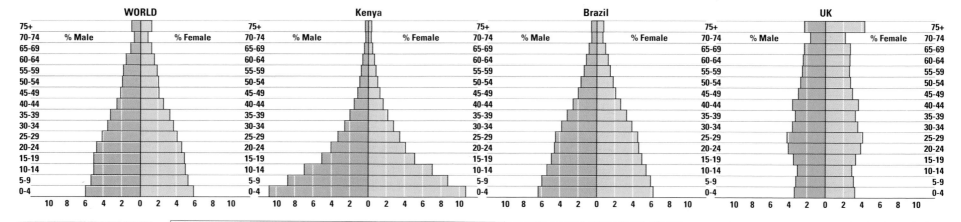

WORLD | Kenya | Brazil | UK

% Male | % Female (75+, 70-74, 65-69, 60-64, 55-59, 50-54, 45-49, 40-44, 35-39, 30-34, 25-29, 20-24, 15-19, 10-14, 5-9, 0-4)

RATES OF GROWTH

Apparently small rates of population growth lead to dramatic increases over two or three generations. The table below translates annual percentage growth into the number of years required to double a population.

% change	Doubling time
0.5	139.0
1.0	69.7
1.5	46.6
2.0	35.0
2.5	28.1
3.0	23.4
3.5	20.1
4.0	17.7

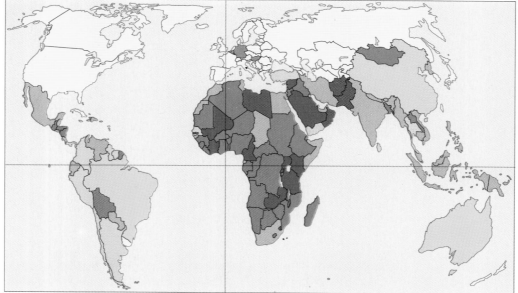

POPULATION CHANGE

Estimated percentage change in total population, between 1990 and 2000

- Over 40% gain
- 30 - 40% gain
- 20 - 30% gain
- 10 - 20% gain
- 0 - 10% gain
- No change or population loss

Top 5 countries		Bottom 5 countries	
Afghanistan	+60%	Hungary	-0.2%
Mali	+56%	Singapore	-0.2%
Tanzania	+55%	Grenada	-2.4%
Ivory Coast	+47%	Tonga	-3.2%
Saudi Arabia	+46%	Germany	-3.2%

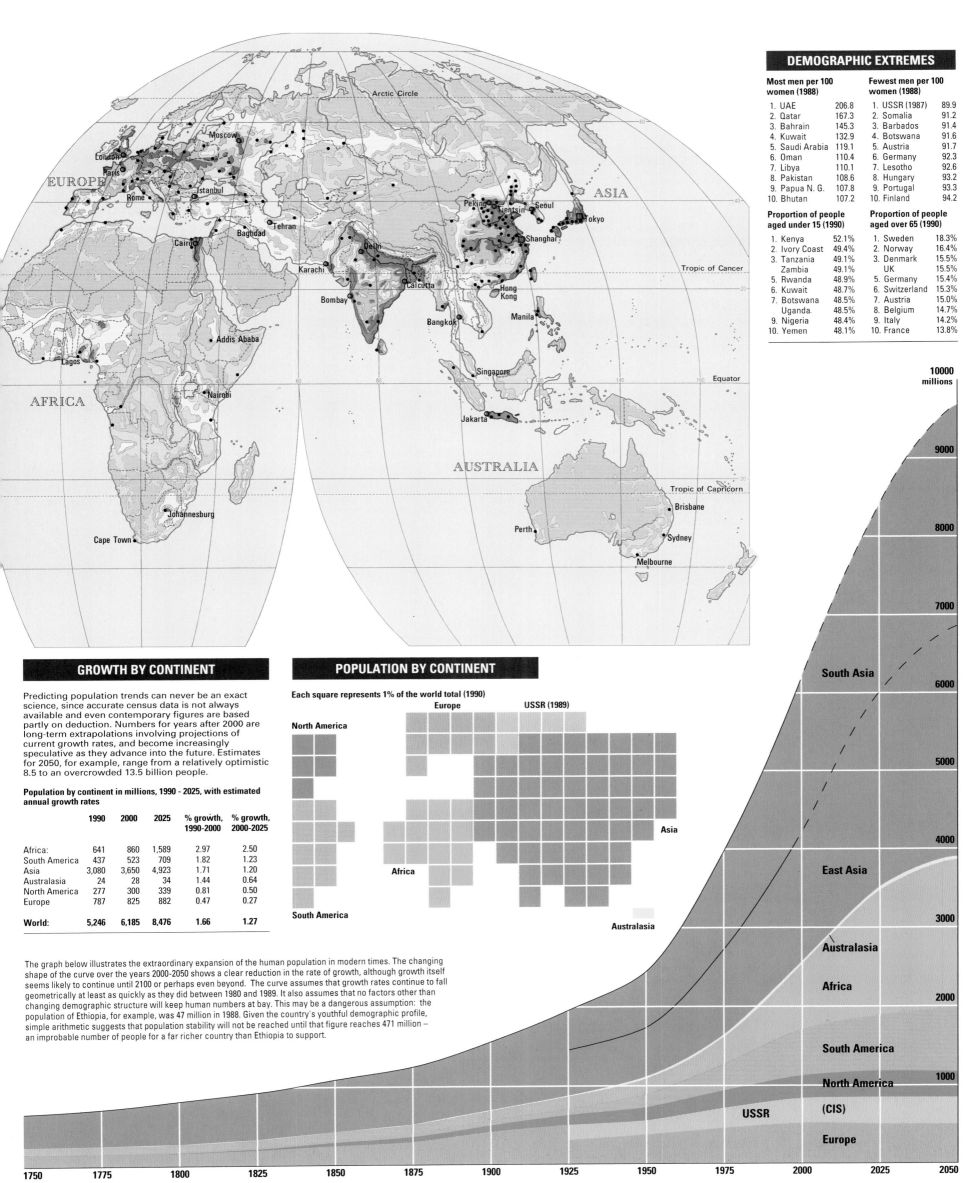

DEMOGRAPHIC EXTREMES

Most men per 100 women (1988)		Fewest men per 100 women (1988)	
1. UAE	206.8	1. USSR (1987)	89.9
2. Qatar	167.3	2. Somalia	91.2
3. Bahrain	145.3	3. Barbados	91.4
4. Kuwait	132.9	4. Botswana	91.6
5. Saudi Arabia	119.1	5. Austria	91.7
6. Oman	110.4	6. Germany	92.3
7. Libya	110.1	7. Lesotho	92.6
8. Pakistan	108.6	8. Hungary	93.2
9. Papua N. G.	107.8	9. Portugal	93.3
10. Bhutan	107.2	10. Finland	94.2

Proportion of people aged under 15 (1990)		Proportion of people aged over 65 (1990)	
1. Kenya	52.1%	1. Sweden	18.3%
2. Ivory Coast	49.4%	2. Norway	16.4%
3. Tanzania	49.1%	3. Denmark	15.5%
Zambia	49.1%	UK	15.5%
5. Rwanda	48.9%	5. Germany	15.4%
6. Kuwait	48.7%	6. Switzerland	15.3%
7. Botswana	48.5%	7. Austria	15.0%
Uganda	48.5%	8. Belgium	14.7%
9. Nigeria	48.4%	9. Italy	14.2%
10. Yemen	48.1%	10. France	13.8%

GROWTH BY CONTINENT

Predicting population trends can never be an exact science, since accurate census data is not always available and even contemporary figures are based partly on deduction. Numbers for years after 2000 are long-term extrapolations involving projections of current growth rates, and become increasingly speculative as they advance into the future. Estimates for 2050, for example, range from a relatively optimistic 8.5 to an overcrowded 13.5 billion people.

Population by continent in millions, 1990 - 2025, with estimated annual growth rates

	1990	2000	2025	% growth, 1990-2000	% growth, 2000-2025
Africa:	641	860	1,589	2.97	2.50
South America	437	523	709	1.82	1.23
Asia	3,080	3,650	4,923	1.71	1.20
Australasia	24	28	34	1.44	0.64
North America	277	300	339	0.81	0.50
Europe	787	825	882	0.47	0.27
World:	**5,246**	**6,185**	**8,476**	**1.66**	**1.27**

The graph below illustrates the extraordinary expansion of the human population in modern times. The changing shape of the curve over the years 2000-2050 shows a clear reduction in the rate of growth, although growth itself seems likely to continue until 2100 or perhaps even beyond. The curve assumes that growth rates continue to fall geometrically at least as quickly as they did between 1980 and 1989. It also assumes that no factors other than changing demographic structure will keep human numbers at bay. This may be a dangerous assumption: the population of Ethiopia, for example, was 47 million in 1988. Given the country's youthful demographic profile, simple arithmetic suggests that population stability will not be reached until that figure reaches 471 million – an improbable number of people for a far richer country than Ethiopia to support.

POPULATION BY CONTINENT

Each square represents 1% of the world total (1990)

PEOPLE: CITIES

In 1750, barely three humans in every hundred lived in a city; by 2000, more than half of a vastly greater world population will find a home in some kind of urban area. In 1850, only London and Paris had more than a million inhabitants; by 2000, at least 24 cities will each contain over ten million people. The increase is concentrated in the Third World, if only because levels of urbanization in most developed countries - more than 90% in the UK and Belgium, and almost 75% in the USA, despite that country's great open spaces - have already reached practical limits.

Such large-scale concentration is relatively new to the human race. Although city life has always attracted country-dwellers in search of trade, employment or simply human contact, until modern times they paid a high price. Crowding and poor sanitation ensured high death rates, and until about 1850, most cities needed a steady flow of incomers simply to maintain their populations: there were 600,000 more deaths than births in 18th-century London, for example, and some other large cities showed an even worse imbalance.

With improved public health, cities could grow from their own human resources, and large-scale urban living became a commonplace in the developed world. Since about 1950, the pattern has been global. Like their counterparts in 19th-century Europe and the USA, the great new cities are driven into rapid growth by a kind of push-pull mechanism. The push is generated by agricultural overcrowding: only so many people can live from a single plot of land, and population pressure drives many into towns; The pull comes from the possibilities of economic improvement, an irresistible lure to the world's rural hopefuls.

Such improvement is not always obvious: the typical Third World city, with millions of people living (often illegally) in shanty towns and many thousands existing homelessly on the ill-made streets, does not present a great image of prosperity. Yet modern shanty towns are healthier than industrializing Pittsburgh or Manchester in the last century, and these human ant-hills teem with industry as well as squalor: throughout the world, above-average rates of urbanization have gone hand-in-hand with above-average economic growth. Surveys consistently demonstrate that Third World city-dwellers are generally better off than their rural counterparts, whose poverty is less concentrated but often more desperate. This only serves to in crease the attraction of the city for the rural poor.

However, the sheer speed of the urbanization process threatens to overwhelm the limited abilities of city authorities to provide even rudimentary services and administration. The 24 million people expected to live in Mexico City by 2000, for example, would swamp a more efficient local government than Mexico can provide. Improvements are often swallowed up by the relentless rise in urban population: although safe drinking water should reach 75% of Third World city-dwellers by the end of the century - a considerable achievement - population growth will add 100 million to the list of those without it.

THE URBANIZATION OF THE EARTH

City-building, 1850-2000; each white spot represents a city of at least one million inhabitants.

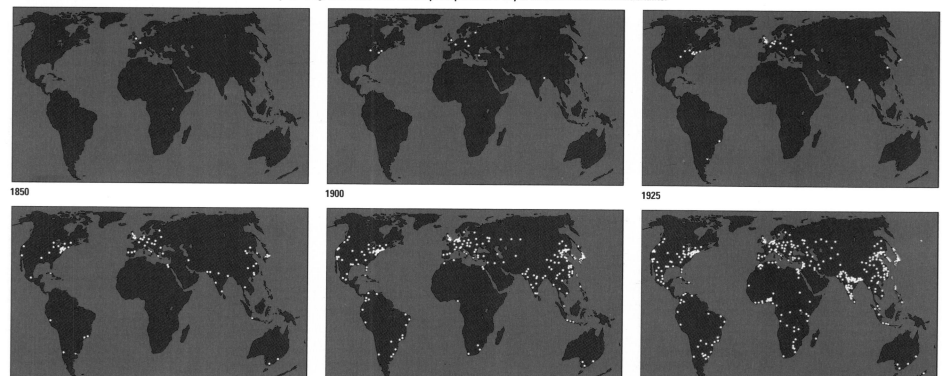

1850

1900

1925

1950

1975

2000

URBAN POPULATION

Percentage of total population living in towns & cities (1990)

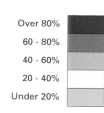

Over 80%
60 - 80%
40 - 60%
20 - 40%
Under 20%

Most urbanized		Least urbanized	
Singapore	100%	Nepal	10%
Belgium	97%	Burkina Faso	9%
Kuwait	96%	Rwanda	8%
Hong Kong	93%	Burundi	7%
UK	93%	Bhutan	5%

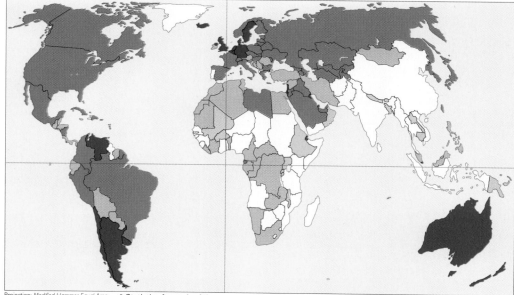

Projection: Modified Hammer Equal Area   * Statistics for each of the new republics of the former U.S.S.R. and Yugoslavia are not yet available.
The map shows the statistics for the entire U.S.S.R. and Yugoslavia.

EXPANDING CITIES

The growth of the world's largest cities, 1950-2000. Intermediate rings indicate relative size in 1970 & 1985.

New York
1950: 14.83 million
2000: 16.10 million
Average annual growth: 0.16%

Tokyo

London
1950: 8.35 million
2000: 10.79 million
Average annual growth: 0.51%

1950: 6.25 million
2000: 21.32 million
Average annual growth: 2.5%

Buenos Aires
1950: 5.25 million
2000: 13.05 million
Average annual growth: 1.8%

Calcutta
1950: 4.45 million
2000: 15.94 million
Average annual growth: 2.6%

Shanghai
1950: 4.3 million
2000: 14.69 million
Average annual growth: 2.5%

Mexico City
1950: 2.97 million
2000: 24.44 million
Average annual growth: 4.3%

Rio de Janeiro
1950: 2.94 million
2000: 13.0 million
Average annual growth: 3.0%

São Paulo
1950: 2.28 million
2000: 23.6 million
Average annual growth: 4.8%

Seoul
1950: 1.45 million
2000: 12.97 million
Average annual growth: 4.5%

Each set of circles illustrates a city's size in 1950, 1970, 1985 and 2000. In most cases, expansion has been steady and, often, explosive. New York and London, however, went through patches of negative growth during the period. In New York, the world's largest city in 1950, population reached a peak around 1970. London shrank slightly between 1970 and 1985 before resuming a very modest rate of increase. In both cases, the divergence from world trends can be explained in part by counting methods: each is at the centre of a great agglomeration, and definitions of where 'city limits' lie may vary over time. But their relative decline also matches a pattern often seen in mature cities in the developed world, where urbanization, already at a very high level, has reached a plateau.

CITIES IN DANGER

As the 1980s advanced, most industrial countries, alarmed by acid rain and urban smog, took significant steps to limit air pollution. These controls, however, are expensive to install and difficult to enforce, and clean air remains a luxury most developed as well as developing cities must live without.

Those taking part in the United Nations' Global Environment Monitoring System (right) frequently show dangerous levels of pollutants ranging from soot to sulphur dioxide and photochemical smog; air in the majority of cities without such sampling equipment is likely to be at least as bad.

URBAN AIR POLLUTION

The world's most polluted cities: number of days each year when sulphur dioxide levels exceeded the WHO threshold of 150 micrograms per cubic metre (averaged over 4 to 15 years, 1970s - 1980s)

Sulphur dioxide is the main pollutant associated with industrial cities. According to the World Health Organization, more than seven days in a year above 150 µg per cubic metre bring a serious risk of respiratory disease: at least 600 million people live in urban areas where SO_2 concentrations regularly reach damaging levels.

Manila, Philippines
Calcutta, India
Milan, Italy
Zagreb, Yugoslavia
Guangzhou, China
Madrid, Spain
Peking (Beijing), China
Xian, China
Seoul, South Korea
Tehran, Iran
Shenyang, China

120   90   60   30

LARGEST CITIES

The world's most populous cities, in millions of inhabitants, based on estimates for the year 2000*

1. Mexico City   24.4
2. São Paulo   23.6
3. Tokyo-Yokohama   21.3
4. New York   16.1
5. Calcutta   15.9
6. Bombay   15.4
7. Shanghai   14.7
8. Tehran   13.7
9. Jakarta   13.2
10. Buenos Aires   13.1
11. Rio de Janeiro   13.0
12. Seoul   13.0
13. Delhi   12.8
14. Lagos   12.4
15. Cairo-Giza   11.8
16. Karachi   11.6
17. Manila-Quezon   11.5
18. Peking (Beijing) 11.5
19. Dhaka   11.3
20. Osaka-Kobe   11.2
21. Los Angeles   10.9
22. London   10.8
23. Bangkok   10.3
24. Moscow   10.1
25. Tientsin (Tianjin) 10.0
26. Lima-Callao   8.8
27. Paris   8.8
28. Milan   8.7
29. Madras   7.8
30. Baghdad   7.7
31. Chicago   7.0
32. Bogotá   6.9
33. Hong Kong   6.1
34. St Petersburg   5.8
35. Pusan   5.8
36. Santiago   5.6
37. Shenyang   5.5
38. Madrid   5.4
39. Naples   4.5
40. Philadelphia   4.3

[City populations are based on urban agglomerations rather than legal city limits. In some cases, such as Tokyo-Yokohama and Cairo-Giza, where two adjacent cities have merged into one concentration, they have been regarded as a single unit]

* For list of largest cities in 1990, see page XI

INFORMAL CITIZENS

Proportion of population living in squatter settlements, selected cities in the developing world (1980s)

Urbanization in most Third World countries has been coming about far faster than local governments can provide services and accommodation for the new city-dwellers. Many – in some cities, most – find their homes in improvised squatter settlements, often unconnected to power, water and sanitation networks. Yet despite their ramshackle housing and marginal legality, these communities are often the most dynamic part of a city economy. They are also growing in size; and given the squatters' reluctance to be counted by tax-demanding authorities, the percentages shown here are likely to be underestimates.

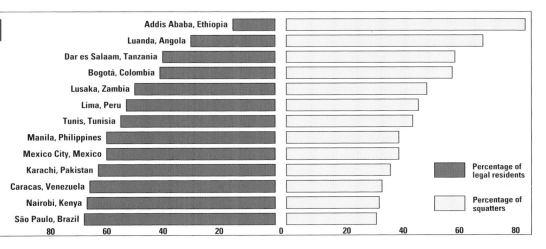

Addis Ababa, Ethiopia
Luanda, Angola
Dar es Salaam, Tanzania
Bogotá, Colombia
Lusaka, Zambia
Lima, Peru
Tunis, Tunisia
Manila, Philippines
Mexico City, Mexico
Karachi, Pakistan
Caracas, Venezuela
Nairobi, Kenya
São Paulo, Brazil

80   60   40   20   0   20   40   60   80

Percentage of legal residents

Percentage of squatters

URBAN ADVANTAGES

Despite overcrowding and poor housing, living standards in the developing world's cities are almost invariably better than in the surrounding countryside. Resources - financial, material and administrative - are concentrated in the towns, which are usually also the centres of political activity and pressure. Governments - frequently unstable, and rarely established on a solid democratic base - are usually more responsive to urban discontent than rural misery. In many countries, especially in Africa, food prices are often kept artificially low, appeasing underemployed urban masses at the expense of agricultural development. The imbalance encourages further cityward migration, helping to account for the astonishing rate of post-1950 urbanization and putting great strain on the ability of many nations to provide even modest improvements for their people.

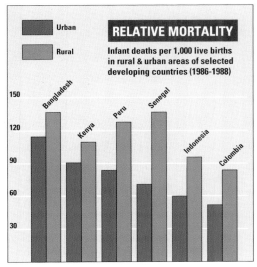

Urban
Rural

RELATIVE MORTALITY

Infant deaths per 1,000 live births in rural & urban areas of selected developing countries (1986-1988)

Bangladesh
Kenya
Peru
Senegal
Indonesia
Colombia

150
120
90
60
30

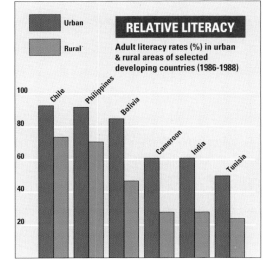

Urban
Rural

RELATIVE LITERACY

Adult literacy rates (%) in urban & rural areas of selected developing countries (1986-1988)

Chile
Philippines
Bolivia
Cameroon
India
Tunisia

100
80
60
40
20

PEOPLE: THE HUMAN FAMILY

Strictly speaking, all human beings belong to a single race: *Homo sapiens* has no sub-species. But although all humans are inter-fertile, anthropologists and geneticists distinguish three main racial types, whose differences reflect not so much evolutionary origin as long periods of separation.

Racial affinities are not always obvious. The Caucasoid group stems from Europe, North Africa and India, but still includes Australian aboriginals within its broad type; Mongoloid peoples comprise American Indians and Eskimos as well as most Chinese, central Asians and Malays; Negroids are mostly of African origin, but also include the Papuan peoples of New Guinea.

Migration in modern times has mingled racial groups to an unprecedented extent, and most nations now have some degree of racially mixed population.

Language is almost the definition of a particular human culture; the world has well over 5,000, most of them with only a few hundred thousand speakers. In one important sense, all languages are equal: although different vocabularies and linguistic structures greatly influence patterns of thought, all true human languages can carry virtually unlimited information. But even if there is no theoretical difference in the communicative power of English and one of the 500 or more tribal languages of Papua New Guinea, for example, an English speaker has access to very much more of the global culture than a Papuan who knows no other tongue.

Like language, religion encourages the internal cohesion of a single human group at the expense of creating gulfs of incomprehension between different groups. All religions satisfy a deep-seated human need, assigning men and women to a comprehensible place in what most of them still consider a divinely ordered world. But religion is also a means by which a culture can assert its individuality: the startling rise of Islam in the late 20th century is partly a response by large sections of the developing world to the secular, Western-inspired world order from which many non-Western peoples feel excluded. Like uncounted millions of human beings before them, they find in their religion not only a personal faith but a powerful group identity.

RACE

- European (Caucasoid)
- Mixed European and Asiatic
- Mixed European and African
- Indian
- Aboriginals
- African (Negroid)
- Asiatic (Mongoloid)
- Pacific races

MOVEMENTS OF POPULATION

1. Africa to America (slaves), c. 1500-1860
2. Western Russia to Siberia, c. 1850-1950
3. W., E. & N. Europe to N. America, c. 1850-1900
4. From East Coast N. America, c. 1860-1960
5. Southern Europe to America, c. 1880-1920
6. Europe to S., E. & Central Africa, c. 1880-1950
7. Europe to Australia & N. Zealand, c. 1840-1950
8. China to S-E Asia & N. America, c. 1900-1950
9. India to Africa & South-East Asia, c. 1860-1910

Major migrations of peoples since 600 AD

10. European & N. American Jews to Israel, 1948-
11. Japan to N. & S. America, c. 1870-1910
12. Arabs to North Africa, 7th-9th centuries
13. C. America to N. America & Europe, c. 1950-1970
14. Migration in the Middle East, c. 1950-
15. Refugees from Afghanistan, 1979-
16. Migration in India, 1946-
17. Migration in & from South-East Asia, c. 1960-
18. Spread of the Bantu peoples, c. 1700-1900

BUILDING THE USA

U.S. Immigration 1820-1990

'Give me your tired, your poor/Your huddled masses yearning to breathe free....'

So starts Emma Lazarus's poem *The New Colossus*, inscribed on the Statue of Liberty. For decades the USA was the magnet that attracted millions of immigrants, notably from Central and Eastern Europe, the flow peaking in the early years of this century.

- Germany 7,047,000
- Italy 5,333,000
- UK 5,064,000
- Austria/Hungary 4,322,000
- Canada 4,290,000
- Ireland 4,077,000
- Russia 3,433,000
- Mexico 2,802,000
- West Indies 2,520,000
- Sweden 1,281,000
- Others 14,259,000

MIGRATION

The movement of migrants in thousands (1985-1990)

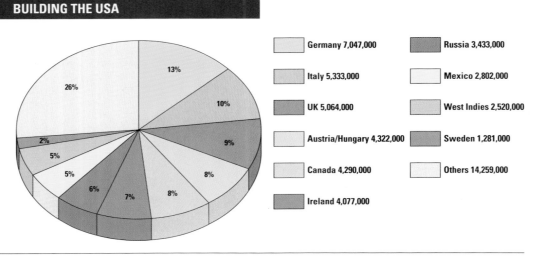

Emigrants: Mexico, Philippines, Lebanon, China, Pakistan, India, El Salvador, Colombia, Sri Lanka, Ethiopia, South Korea, UK, Mali, Dominican Republic, Guatemala, Haiti, Jamaica, Egypt, Vietnam

Immigrants: USA, Australia, Canada, Saudi Arabia, Ivory Coast, France, United Arab Emirates

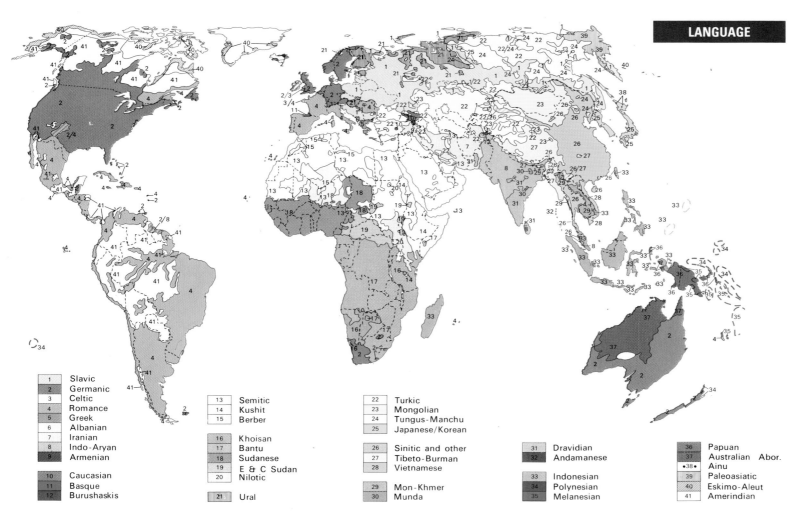

LANGUAGE

OFFICIAL LANGUAGES

Language	Total population	World %
English	1400m	27.0%
Chinese	1070m	19.1%
Hindi	700m	13.5%
Spanish	280m	5.4%
Russian	270m	5.2%
French	220m	4.2%
Arabic	170m	3.3%
Portuguese	160m	3.0%
Malay	160m	3.0%
Bengali	150m	2.9%
Japanese	120m	2.3%

1	Slavic
2	Germanic
3	Celtic
4	Romance
5	Greek
6	Albanian
7	Iranian
8	Indo-Aryan
9	Armenian
10	Caucasian
11	Basque
12	Burushaskis

13	Semitic
14	Kushit
15	Berber
16	Khoisan
17	Bantu
18	Sudanese
19	E & C Sudan
20	Nilotic
21	Ural

22	Turkic
23	Mongolian
24	Tungus-Manchu
25	Japanese/Korean
26	Sinitic and other
27	Tibeto-Burman
28	Vietnamese
29	Mon-Khmer
30	Munda

31	Dravidian
32	Andamanese
33	Indonesian
34	Polynesian
35	Melanesian

36	Papuan
37	Australian Abor.
38	Ainu
39	Paleoasiatic
40	Eskimo-Aleut
41	Amerindian

Languages form a kind of tree of development, splitting from a few ancient proto-tongues into branches that have grown apart and further divided with the passage of time. English and Hindi, for example, both belong to the great Indo-European family, although the relationship is only apparent after much analysis and comparison with non-Indo-European languages such as Chinese or Arabic; Hindi is part of the Indo-Aryan subgroup; English is a member of Indo-European's Germanic branch; French, another Indo-European tongue, traces its descent through the Latin, or Romance, branch. A few languages – Basque is one example – have no apparent links with any other, living or dead. Most modern languages, of course, have acquired enormous quantities of vocabulary from each other.

MOTHER TONGUES

Native speakers of the major languages, in millions (1989)

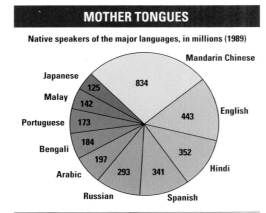

- Mandarin Chinese — 834
- English — 443
- Hindi — 352
- Spanish — 341
- Russian — 293
- Arabic — 197
- Bengali — 184
- Portuguese — 173
- Malay — 142
- Japanese — 125

Religions are not as easily mapped as the physical contours of landscape. Divisions are often blurred and frequently overlapping: most nations include people of many different faiths – or no faith at all. Some religions, like Islam and Christianity, have proselytes worldwide; others, like Hinduism and Confucianism, are restricted to a particular area, though modern migrations have taken some Indians and Chinese very far from their cultural origins. It is also difficult to show the degree to which religion exercises control over daily life: Christian Western Europe, for example, is nowadays far less dominated by its religion than are the Islamic nations of the Middle East. Similarly, figures for the major faiths' adherents make no distinction between nominal believers enrolled at birth and those for whom religion is a vital part of existence.

RELIGION

RELIGIOUS ADHERENTS

Christian	1667m
Roman Catholic	952m
Protestant	337m
Orthodox	162m
Anglican	70m
Other Christian	148m
Muslim	881m
Sunni	841m
Shia	40m
Hindu	663m
Buddhist	312m
Chinese folk	172m
Tribal	92m
Jewish	18m
Sikhs	17m

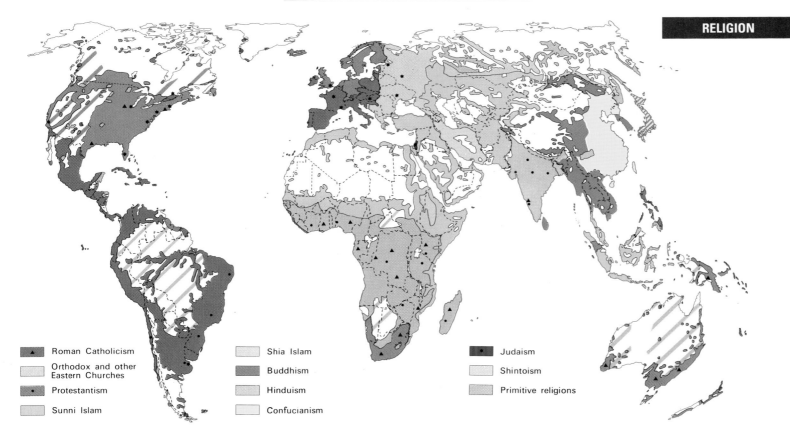

▲ Roman Catholicism	
Orthodox and other Eastern Churches	
Protestantism	
Sunni Islam	

Shia Islam	
Buddhism	
Hinduism	
Confucianism	

✶ Judaism	
Shintoism	
Primitive religions	

PEOPLE: CONFLICT & COOPERATION

Humans are social animals, rarely functioning well except in groups. Evolution has made them so: hunter-gatherers in cooperative bands were far more effective than animals that prowled alone. Agriculture, the building of cities and industrialization are all developments that depended on human cooperative ability – and in turn increased the need for it.

Unfortunately, human groups do not always cooperate so well with other human groups, and friction between them sometimes leads to cooperatively organized violence. War is itself a very human activity, with no real equivalent in any other species. Always murderous, it is sometimes purposeful and may even be very effective. The colonization of the Americas and Australia, for example, was in effect the waging of aggressive war by well-armed Europeans against indigenous peoples incapable of offering a serious defence.

More often, war achieves little but death and ruin. However, the great 20th-century wars appear to have cured the notoriously aggressive Europeans of their previous bad habits, although at the cost of between 50 and 100 million dead. The relative peace in the postwar developed world is at least partly due to the nuclear weapons with which rival powers have armed themselves – weapons so powerful that their use would leave a scarcely habitable planet with no meaningful distinction between victor and vanquished.

Yet warfare remains endemic: the second half of the 20th century was one of the bloodiest periods in history, and death by organized violence remains unhappily common. The map below attempts to show the serious conflicts that have scarred the Earth since 1945. Most are civil wars in poor countries, rather than international conflicts between rich ones; some of them are still unresolved, while others, like apparently extinct volcanoes, may erupt again at intervals, adding to the world's miserable population of refugees.

THE WORLD'S REFUGEES

Refugees and their national origin; the host nations and the relative size of their refugee populations (1991)

Refugees in millions

Refugees as a proportion of host country's population

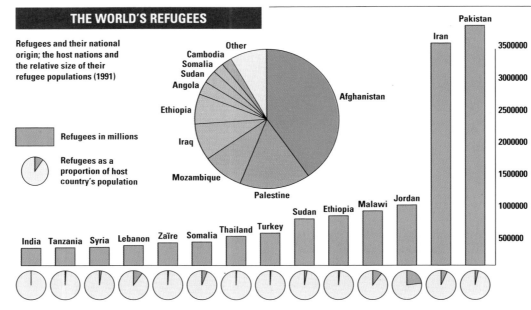

The pie-chart shows the origins of the world's refugees, the bar-chart their destinations. According to the United Nations High Commissioner for Refugees in 1990, there were almost 15 million of them, a number that continued to increase and was almost certain to be amplified during the decade. Some have fled from climatic change, some from economic disaster and others from political persecution; the great majority are the victims of war.
All but a few who make it overseas seek asylum in neighbouring countries, which are often the least equipped to deal with them and where they are rarely welcome. Lacking any rights or power, they frequently become an embarrassment and a burden to their reluctant hosts.
Usually, the best any refugee can hope for is rudimentary food and shelter in temporary camps that all to often become semi-permanent, with little prospect of assimilation by host populations: many Palestinians, for example, have been forced to live in camps since 1948.

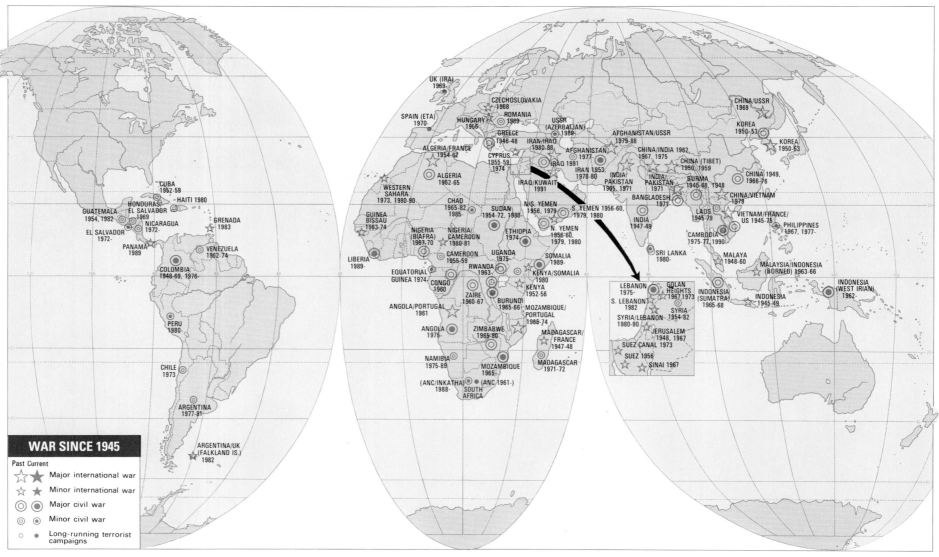

WAR SINCE 1945

Past / Current

☆ ★ Major international war

☆ ★ Minor international war

◎ ◉ Major civil war

◎ ◉ Minor civil war

○ ● Long-running terrorist campaigns

The United Nations Organization was born as World War II drew to its conclusion. Six years of strife had strengthened the world's desire for peace, but an effective international organization was needed to help achieve it. That body would replace the League of Nations which, since its inception in 1920, had signally failed to curb the aggression of at least some of its member nations. At the United Nations Conference on International Organization held in San Francisco, the United Nations Charter was drawn up. Ratified by the Security Council and signed by 51 nations, it came into effect on 24 October 1945.

The Charter set out the aims of the organization: to maintain peace and security, and develop friendly relations between nations; to achieve international cooperation in solving economic, social, cultural and humanitarian problems; to promote respect for human rights and fundamental freedoms; and to harmonize the activities of nations in order to achieve these common goals.

By 1992, the UN had expanded to more than 160 member countries; it is the largest international political organization, employing 23,000 people worldwide; its headquarters in New York accounts for 7,000 staff and it also has major offices in Rome, Geneva and Vienna.

The United Nations has six principal organs:

The General Assembly

The forum at which member nations discuss moral and political issues affecting world development, peace and security meets annually in September, under a newly-elected President whose tenure lasts one year. Any member can bring business to the agenda, and each member nation has one vote. Decisions are made by simple majority, save for matters of very great importance, when a two-thirds majority is required. While the General Assembly has no powers of enforcement, its recommendations to member nations are regarded as persuasive and it is empowered to instruct UN organs or agencies to implement its decisions.

The Security Council

A legislative and executive body, the Security Council is the primary instrument for establishing and maintaining international peace by attempting to settle disputes between nations. It has the power to dispatch UN forces to stop aggression, and member nations undertake to make armed forces, assistance and facilities available as required. The Security Council has ten temporary members elected by the General Assembly for two-year terms, and five permanent members - China, France, Russia, UK and USA. On questions of substance, the vote of each of the permanent members is required within the necessary nine-vote majority.

The Economic and Social Council

By far the largest United Nations executive, the Council operates as a conduit between the General Assembly and the many United Nations agencies it instructs to implement Assembly decisions, and whose work it coordinates. The Council also sets up commissions to examine economic conditions, collects data and issues studies and reports, and may make recommendations to the Assembly. The Council's overall aim is to help the peoples of the world with education, health and human rights. It has 54 member countries, elected by the General Assembly to three-year terms.

The Secretariat

This is the staff of the United Nations, and its task is to administer the policies and programmes of the UN and its organs, and assist and advise the Head of the Secretariat, the Secretary-General – a full-time, non-political, appointment made by the General Assembly.

The Trusteeship Council

The Council administers trust territories with the aim of promoting their advancement. Only one remains - the Trust Territory of the Pacific Is. (Palau), administered by the USA.

The International Court of Justice (the World Court)

The World Court is the judicial organ of the United Nations. It deals only with United Nations disputes and all members are subject to its jurisdiction, which includes both cases submitted to it by member nations and matters especially provided for in the Charter or in treaties. The Court's decisions are only binding in respect of a particular dispute; failure to heed a judgement may involve recourse to the Security Council. There are 15 judges, elected for nine-year terms by the General Assembly and the Security Council. The Court sits in The Hague.

United Nations agencies and programmes, and inter-governmental agencies coordinated by the UN, contribute to harmonious world development. Social and humanitarian operations include:

United Nations Development Programme (UNDP): plans and funds projects to help developing countries make better use of resources. Voluntary pledges of $1·3 billion were made for 1990, to fund almost 7,000 projects in 152 countries.

United Nations International Childrens' Fund (UNICEF): created at the General Assembly's first session in 1945 to help children in the aftermath of World War II, it now provides basic healthcare and aid worldwide. Voluntarily funded, three-quarters of its income is derived from government donations.

United Nations Fund for Population Activities (UNFPA): promotes awareness of population issues and family planning, providing appropriate assistance.

Food & Agriculture Organization (FAO): aims to raise living standards and nutrition levels in rural areas by improving food production and distribution.

United Nations Educational, Scientific & Cultural Organization (UNESCO): promotes international cooperation through broader and better education.

World Health Organization (WHO): promotes and provides for better health care, public and environmental health and medical research.

Membership: There are 13 independent states who are not members of the UN – Andorra, Kiribati, Liechtenstein, N. Korea, S. Korea, Monaco, Nauru, San Marino, Switzerland, Taiwan, Tonga, Tuvalu and Vatican City. By 1992, the successor states of the former USSR had either joined or were planning to join. There were 51 members in 1945. Official languages are Chinese, English, French, Russian, Spanish and (a recent addition) Arabic.

Funding: The UN budget for 1988-1989 was US $ 1,788,746,000. Contributions are assessed by members' ability to pay, with the maximum 25% of the total, the minimum 0.01%. Contributions for 1988-1989 were: USA 25%, Japan 11.38%, USSR 9.99%, W. Germany 8.08%, France 6.25%, UK 4.86%, Italy 3.99%, Canada 3.09%, Spain 1.95%, Netherlands 1.65% (others 23.75%).

Peacekeeping: The UN has been involved in 18 peacekeeping operations worldwide since 1945, five of which (Afghanistan/Pakistan, Iran/Iraq, Angola, Namibia and Honduras) were initiated in 1988-1989. In June 1991 UN personnel totalling over 11,000 were working in eight separate areas.

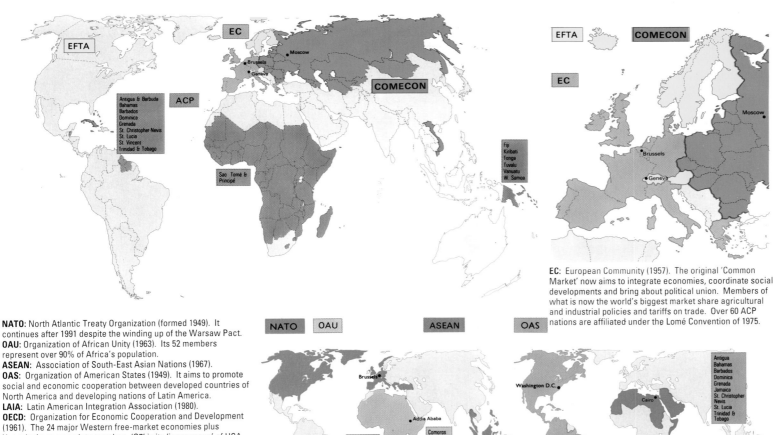

NATO: North Atlantic Treaty Organization (formed 1949). It continues after 1991 despite the winding up of the Warsaw Pact.

OAU: Organization of African Unity (1963). Its 52 members represent over 90% of Africa's population.

ASEAN: Association of South-East Asian Nations (1967).

OAS: Organization of American States (1949). It aims to promote social and economic cooperation between developed countries of North America and developing nations of Latin America.

LAIA: Latin American Integration Association (1980).

OECD: Organization for Economic Cooperation and Development (1961). The 24 major Western free-market economies plus Yugoslavia as associate member. 'G7' is its 'inner group' of USA, Canada, Japan, UK, Germany, Italy and France.

COMMONWEALTH: The Commonwealth of Nations evolved from the British Empire; it comprises 18 nations recognizing the British monarch as head of state and 32 with their own heads of state.

OPEC: Organization of Petroleum Exporting Countries (1960). It controls about three-quarters of the world's oil supply.

EC: European Community (1957). The original 'Common Market' now aims to integrate economies, coordinate social developments and bring about political union. Members of what is now the world's biggest market share agricultural and industrial policies and tariffs on trade. Over 60 ACP nations are affiliated under the Lomé Convention of 1975.

United Nations agencies are involved in many aspects of international trade, safety and security:

General Agreement on Tariffs and Trade (GATT): sponsors international trade negotiations and advocates a common code of conduct.

International Maritime Organization (IMO): promotes unity amongst merchant shipping, especially in regard to safety, marine pollution and standardization.

International Labour Organization (ILO): seeks to improve labour conditions and promote productive employment to raise living standards.

World Meteorological Organization (WMO): promotes cooperation in weather observation, reporting and forecasting.

World Intellectual Property Organization (WIPO): seeks to protect intellectual property such as artistic copyright, scientific patents and trademarks.

Disarmament Commission: considers and makes recommendations to the General Assembly on disarmament issues.

International Atomic Energy Agency (IAEA): fosters development of peaceful uses for nuclear energy, establishes safety standards and monitors the destruction of nuclear material designed for military use.

The World Bank comprises three United Nations agencies:

International Monetary Fund (IMF): cultivates international monetary cooperation and expansion of trade.

International Bank for Reconstruction & Development (IBRD): provides funds and technical assistance to developing countries.

International Finance Corporation (IFC): Encourages the growth of productive private enterprise in less developed countries.

OECD: Organization for Economic Cooperation and Development (1961). The 24 major Western free-market economies plus Yugoslavia as an associate member. 'G7' is its 'inner group' of USA, Canada, Japan, UK, Germany, Italy and France.

COMMONWEALTH: The Commonwealth of Nations evolved from the British Empire; it comprises 18 nations recognizing the British monarch as head of state and 32 nations with their own heads of state.

OPEC: Organization of Petroleum Exporting Countries (1960). It controls three-quarters of the world's oil supply.

PRODUCTION: AGRICULTURE

The invention of agriculture transformed human existence more than any other development, though it may not have seemed much of an improvement to its first practitioners. Primitive farming required brutally hard work, and it tied men and women to a patch of land, highly vulnerable to local weather patterns and to predators, especially human predators – drawbacks still apparent in much of the world today. It is difficult to imagine early humans being interested in such an existence while there were still animals around to hunt and wild seeds and berries to gather. Probably the spur was population pressure, with consequent overhunting and scarcity.

Despite its difficulties, the new life-style had a few overwhelming advantages. It supported far larger populations, eventually including substantial cities, with all the varied cultural and economic activities they allowed. Later still, it furnished the surpluses that allowed industrialization, another enormous step in human development.

Machines relieved many farmers of their burden of endless toil, and made it possible for relatively small numbers to provide food for more than five billion people.

Then as now, the whole business of farming involves the creation of a severely simplified ecology, under the tutelage and for the benefit of the farmer. Natural plant life is divided into crops, to be protected and nurtured, and weeds, the rest, to be destroyed. From the earliest days, crops were selectively bred to increase their food yield, usually at the expense of their ability to survive, which became the farmer's responsibility; 20th-century plant geneticists have carried the technique to highly productive extremes. Due mainly to new varieties of rice and wheat, world grain production has increased by 70% since 1965, more than doubling in the developing countries, although such high yields demand equally high consumption of fertilizers and pesticides to maintain them. Mechanized farmers in North America and Europe continue to turn out huge surpluses, although not without environmental costs.

Where production is inadequate, the reasons are as likely to be political as agricultural. Africa, the only continent where food production per capita is actually falling, suffers acutely from economic mis-management, as well as from the perennial problems of war and banditry. Dismal harvests in the USSR, despite its excellent farmland, helped bring about the collapse of the Soviet system.

There are other limits to progress. Increasing population puts relentless pressure on farmers not only to maintain high yields but also to increase them. Most of the world's potential cropland is already under the plough. The over-working of marginal land is one of the prime causes of desertification; new farmlands burned out of former rainforests are seldom fertile for long. Human numbers may yet outrun the land's ability to feed them, as they did almost 10,000 years ago.

SELF-SUFFICIENCY IN FOOD

Balance of trade in food products as a percentage of total trade in food products (1988)

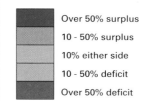

- Over 50% surplus
- 10 - 50% surplus
- 10% either side
- 10 - 50% deficit
- Over 50% deficit

Most self-sufficient		Least self-sufficient	
Uganda	93%	Algeria	-97%
Argentina	92%	Saudi Arabia	-95%
Burma	86%	Czechoslovakia	-92%
Chile	82%	Venezuela	-92%
Iceland	82%	Gabon	-88%
Uruguay	82%	Oman	-88%
Kenya	80%	Syria	-88%
New Zealand	80%	Egypt	-86%
Costa Rica	79%	Japan	-85%

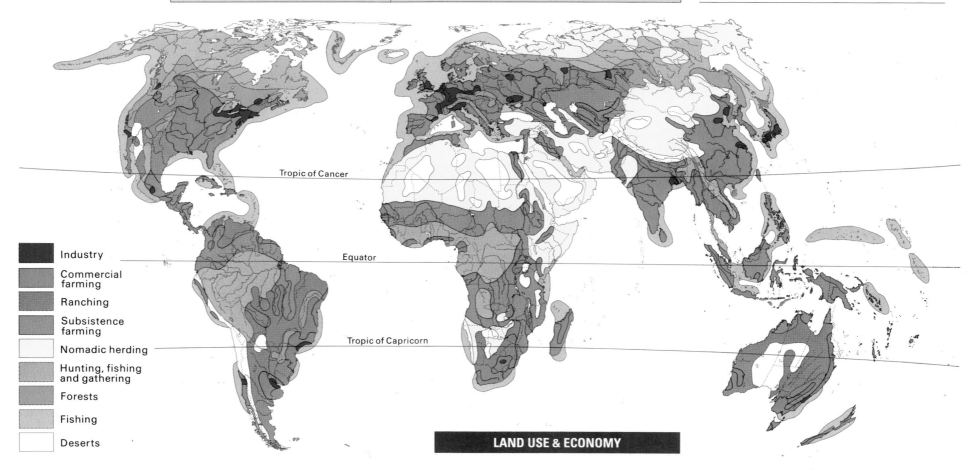

Tropic of Cancer

Equator

Tropic of Capricorn

- Industry
- Commercial farming
- Ranching
- Subsistence farming
- Nomadic herding
- Hunting, fishing and gathering
- Forests
- Fishing
- Deserts

LAND USE & ECONOMY

STAPLE CROPS

Separate figures for Russia, Ukraine and the other successors of the defunct USSR are not yet available

Cereals are grasses with starchy, edible seeds; every important civilization has depended on them as a source of food. The major cereal grains contain about 10% protein and 75% carbohydrate; grain is easy to store, handle and transport, and contributes more than any other group of foods to the energy and protein content of human diet. If all the cereals were consumed directly by man, there would be no shortage of food in the world, but a considerable proportion of the total output is used as animal feed.

Starchy tuber crops or root crops, represented here by potatoes and cassava, are second in importance only to cereals as staple foods; easily cultivated, they provide high yields for little effort and store well – potatoes for up to six months, cassava for up to a year in the ground. Protein content is low (2% or less), and starch content high; some minerals and vitamins are present, but populations that rely heavily on these crops may suffer from malnutrition.

Wheat: Grown in a range of climates, with most varieties - including the highest-quality bread wheats - requiring temperate conditions. Mainly used in baking, it is also used for pasta and breakfast cereals.

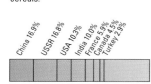

World total (1989): 538,056,000 tonnes

Maize: Originating in the New World and still an important human food in Africa and Latin America, in the developed world it is processed into breakfast cereals, oil, starches and adhesives. It is also used for animal feed.

World total (1989): 470,318,000 tonnes

Oats: Most widely used to feed livestock, but eaten by humans as oatmeal or porridge. Oats have a beneficial effect on the cardio-vascular system, and human consumption is likely to increase.

World total (1989): 42,197,000 tonnes

Millet: The name covers a number of small grained cereals, members of the grass family with a short growing season. Used to produce flour and meal, animal feed and fermented to make beer, especially in Africa.

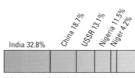

World total (1989): 30,512,000 tonnes

Cassava: A tropical shrub that needs high rainfall (over 1000 mm annually) and a 10 - 30 month growing season to produce its large, edible tubers. Used as flour by humans, as cattle feed and in industrial starches.

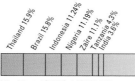

World total (1989): 147,500,000 tonnes

Rice: Thrives on the high humidity and temperatures of the Far East, where it is the traditional staple food of half the human race. Usually grown standing in water, rice responds well to continuous cultivation, with three or four crops annually.

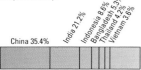

World total (1989): 506,291,000 tonnes

Barley: Primarily used as animal feed, but widely eaten by humans in Africa and Asia. Elsewhere, malted barley furnishes beer and spirits. Able to withstand the dry heat of sub-arid tropics, its growing season is only 80 days.

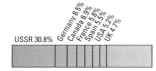

World total (1989): 168,964,000 tonnes

Rye: Hardy and tolerant of poor and sandy soils, it is an important foodstuff and animal feed in Central and Eastern Europe and the USSR. Rye produces a dark, heavy bread as well as alcoholic drinks.

World total (1989): 34,893,000 tonnes

Potatoes: The most important of the edible tubers, potatoes grow in well-watered, temperate areas. Weight for weight less nutritious than grain, they are a human staple as well as an important animal feed.

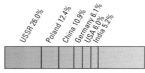

World total (1989): 276,740,000 tonnes

Soya: Beans from soya bushes are very high - 30-40% - in protein. Most are processed into oil and proprietary protein foods. Consumption since 1950 has tripled, mainly due to the health-conscious developed world.

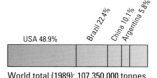

World total (1989): 107,350,000 tonnes

IMPORTANCE OF AGRICULTURE

Percentage of the total population dependent on agriculture (1990)

- Over 75% dependent
- 50 - 75% dependent
- 25 - 50% dependent
- 10 - 25% dependent
- Under 10% dependent

Top 5 countries		Bottom 5 countries	
Nepal	92%	UK	2.0%
Rwanda	91%	Belgium	1.8%
Burundi	91%	Bahrain	1.7%
Bhutan	91%	Hong Kong	1.2%
Niger	87%	Singapore	1.0%

FOOD & POPULATION

Comparison of food production and population by continent (1989). The left column indicates percentage shares of total world food production; the right shows population in proportion.

FOOD		POPULATION
1.2%	Australasia	0.4%
27.6%	Europe	15.5%
44.5%	Asia	58.3%
6.5%	S. America	6.7%
13.8%	N. America	7.1%
6.7%	Africa	12.0%

ANIMAL PRODUCTS

Separate figures for Russia, Ukraine and the other successors of the defunct USSR are not yet available

Traditionally, food animals subsisted on land unsuitable for cultivation, supporting agricultural production with their fertilizing dung. But free-ranging animals grow slowly and yield less meat than those more intensively reared; the demands of urban markets in the developed world have encouraged the growth of factory-like production methods. A large proportion of staple crops, especially cereals, are fed to animals, an inefficient way to produce protein but one likely to continue as long as people value meat and dairy products in their diet.

Milk: Many human groups, including most Asians, find raw milk indigestible after infancy, and it is often only the starting point for other dairy products such as butter, cheese and yoghurt. Most world production comes from cows, but sheep's milk and goats' milk are also important.

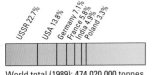

World total (1989): 474,020,000 tonnes

Cheese: Least perishable of all dairy products, cheese is milk fermented with selected bacterial strains to produce a foodstuff with a potentially immense range of flavours and textures. The vast majority of cheeses are made from cow's milk, although sheep and goat cheeses are highly prized.

World total (1989): 14,475,276 tonnes

Butter: A traditional source of vitamin A as well as calories, butter has lost much popularity in the developed world for health reasons, although it remains a valuable food. Most butter from India, the world's second-largest producer, is clarified into ghee, which has religious as well as nutritional importance.

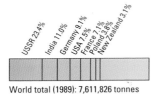

World total (1989): 7,611,826 tonnes

Lamb & Mutton: Sheep are the least demanding of domestic animals. Although unsuited to intensive rearing, they can thrive on marginal pastureland incapable of supporting beef cattle on a commercial scale. Sheep are raised as much for their valuable wool as for the meat that they provide, with Australia the world leader.

World total (1989): 6,473,000 tonnes

Pork: Although pork is forbidden to many millions, notably Muslims, on religious grounds, more is produced than any other meat in the world, mainly because it is the cheapest. It accounts for about 90% of China's meat output, although per capita meat consumption is relatively low.

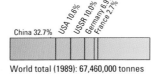

World total (1989): 67,460,000 tonnes

Beef & Veal: Most beef and veal is reared for home markets, and the top five producers are also the biggest consumers. The USA produces nearly a quarter of the world's beef and eats more. Australia, with its small domestic market, is by far the largest exporter.

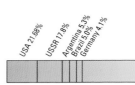

World total (1989): 49,436,000 tonnes

Fish: Commercial fishing requires large shoals of fish, often of only one species, within easy reach of markets. Although the great majority are caught wild in the sea, fish-farming of both marine and freshwater species is assuming increasing importance, especially as natural stocks become depleted.

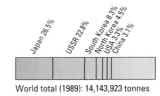

World total (1989): 14,143,923 tonnes

SUGARS

Sugar cane: Confined to tropical regions, cane sugar accounts for the bulk of international trade in the commodity. Most is produced as a foodstuff, but some countries, notably Brazil and South Africa, distil sugar cane and use the resulting ethyl alcohol to make motor fuels.

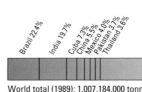

World total (1989): 1,007,184,000 tonnes

Sugar beet: A temperate crop closely related to the humble beetroot, sugar beet's yield after processing is indistinguishable from cane sugar. Sugar beet is steadily replacing sugar cane imports in Europe, to the detriment of the developing countries that rely on it as a major cash crop.

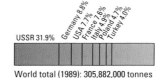

World total (1989): 305,882,000 tonnes

31

PRODUCTION: ENERGY

We live in a high-energy civilization. While vast discrepancies exist between rich and poor – a North American consumes 13 times as much energy as a Chinese, for example – even developing nations have more power at their disposal than was imaginable a century ago. Abundant energy supplies keep us warm or cool, fuel our industries and our transport systems, even feed us: high-intensity agriculture, with its fertilizers, pesticides and machinery, is heavily energy-dependent.

Unfortunately, most of the world's energy comes from fossil fuels: coal, oil and gas deposits laid down over many millions of years. These are the Earth's capital, not its income, and we are consuming that capital at an alarming rate. New discoveries have persistently extended the known reserves: in 1989, the reserves-to-production ratio for oil assured over 45 years' supply, an improvement of almost a decade on the 1970 situation. But despite the effort and ingenuity of prospectors, stocks are clearly limited. They are also very unequally distributed, with the Middle East accounting for most oil reserves, and the CIS, especially Russia, possessing an even higher proportion of the world's natural gas. Coal reserves are more evenly shared, and also more plentiful: coal will outlast oil and gas by a very wide margin.

It is possible to reduce energy demand by improving efficiency: most industrial nations have dramatically increased output since the 1970s without a matching rise in energy consumption. But as fossil stocks continue to diminish, renewable energy sources – solar, wave and wind power, as well as more conventional hydroelectricity – must take on steadily greater importance.

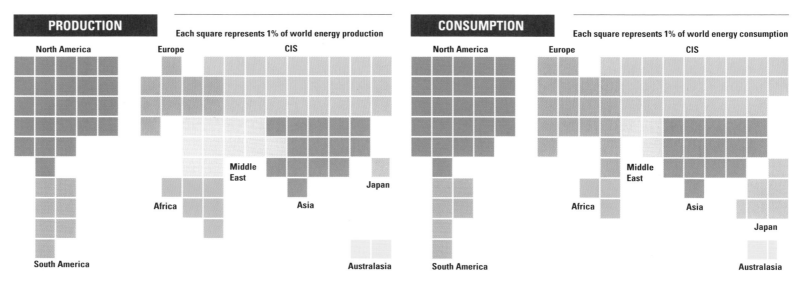

PRODUCTION
Each square represents 1% of world energy production

North America · Europe · CIS · Middle East · Japan · Africa · Asia · South America · Australasia

CONSUMPTION
Each square represents 1% of world energy consumption

North America · Europe · CIS · Middle East · Japan · Africa · Asia · South America · Australasia

CONVERSIONS

For historical reasons, oil is still traded in 'barrels'. The weight and volume equivalents shown below are all based on average density 'Arabian light' crude oil, and should be considered approximate.

The energy equivalents given for a tonne of oil are also somewhat imprecise: oil and coal of different qualities will have varying energy contents, a fact usually reflected in their price on world markets.

1 barrel:

    0.136 tonnes
    159 litres
    35 Imperial gallons
    42 US gallons

1 tonne:

    7.33 barrels
    1185 litres
    256 Imperial gallons
    261 US gallons

1 tonne oil:

    1.5 tonnes hard coal
    3.0 tonnes lignite
    12,000 kWh

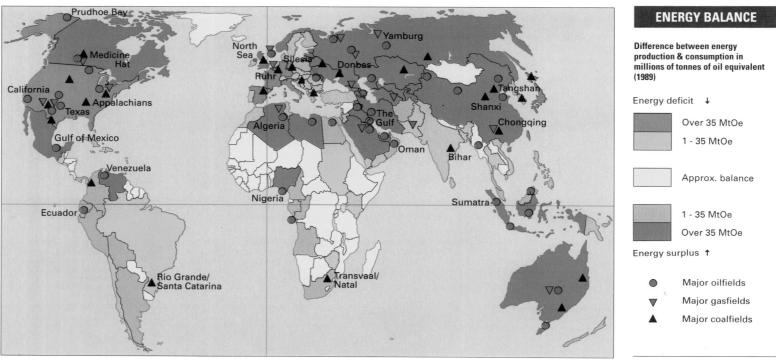

Map labels: Prudhoe Bay · Medicine Hat · California · Texas · Appalachians · Gulf of Mexico · Venezuela · Ecuador · Rio Grande/Santa Catarina · North Sea · Ruhr · Silesia · Donbas · Yamburg · Tangshan · Shanxi · Chongqing · The Gulf · Algeria · Oman · Bihar · Nigeria · Sumatra · Transvaal/Natal

ENERGY BALANCE

Difference between energy production & consumption in millions of tonnes of oil equivalent (1989)

Energy deficit ↓

  Over 35 MtOe
  1 - 35 MtOe

  Approx. balance

  1 - 35 MtOe
  Over 35 MtOe

Energy surplus ↑

● Major oilfields
▽ Major gasfields
▲ Major coalfields

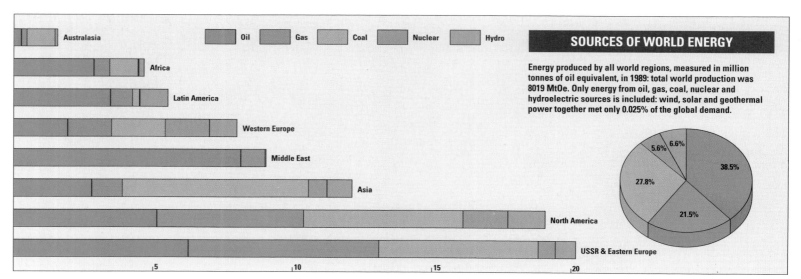

Bar chart regions: Australasia · Africa · Latin America · Western Europe · Middle East · Asia · North America · USSR & Eastern Europe

Legend: Oil · Gas · Coal · Nuclear · Hydro

SOURCES OF WORLD ENERGY

Energy produced by all world regions, measured in million tonnes of oil equivalent, in 1989: total world production was 8019 MtOe. Only energy from oil, gas, coal, nuclear and hydroelectric sources is included: wind, solar and geothermal power together met only 0.025% of the global demand.

Pie chart: 38.5% · 21.5% · 27.8% · 5.6% · 6.6%

Bar chart axis: 5 · 10 · 15 · 20

FOSSIL FUEL RESERVES

Known world reserves in years as a multiple of annual production, 1970, 1980 and 1989

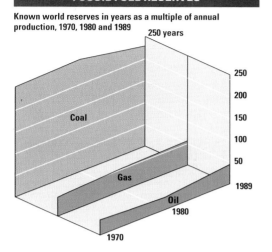

ENERGY AND OUTPUT

Tonnes of oil equivalent consumed to produce US $1000 of GDP, four industrial nations (1973-89)

Intensity of energy use is a rough indicator of efficiency: the 1973-4 oil crisis caused a dramatic improvement in each of the countries illustrated, though the USA remains relatively profligate. Exactly comparable figures for communist economies are not available, but estimates suggest that for equivalent production, the USSR and China use between two and four times as much energy as the USA.

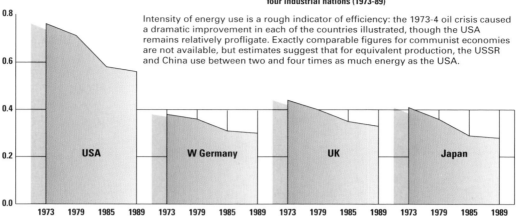

COAL RESERVES

World coal reserves by region & country, thousand million tonnes (1988)

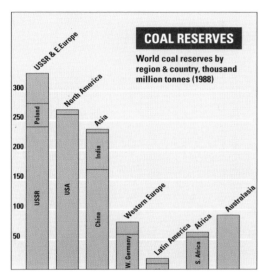

GAS RESERVES

World natural gas reserves by region & country, thousand million tonnes (1988)

Ca: Canada
In: Indonesia
Ma: Malaysia
AD: Abu Dhabi
SA: Saudi Arabia
Qa: Qatar
Iq: Iraq
No: Norway
Ne: Netherlands
Ve: Venezuela
Mx: Mexico
Al: Algeria
Ni: Nigeria

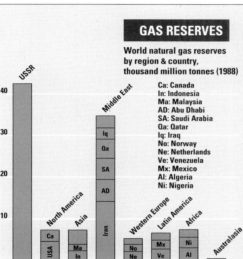

OIL RESERVES

World oil reserves by region & country, thousand million tonnes (1988)

AD: Abu Dhabi
Ve: Venezuela
Mx: Mexico

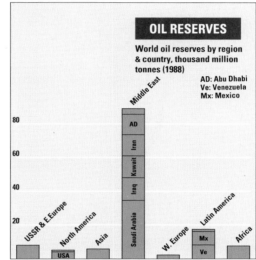

OIL MOVEMENTS

Major world movements of oil in millions of tonnes (1989)

Middle East to Western Europe 195.5
Middle East to Japan 150.0
Middle East to Asia (exc. Japan and China) 127.5
Latin America to USA 126.1
Middle East to USA 94.1
USSR to Western Europe 78.1
North Africa to Western Europe 93.5
West Africa to Western Europe 39.6
West Africa to USA 59.8
Canada to USA 45.0
South-East Asia to Japan 42.2
Latin America to Western Europe 28.7
Western Europe to USA 28.7
Middle East to Latin America 20.5

Total world movements: 1577 million tonnes

Only inter-regional movements in excess of 20 million tonnes are shown. Other Middle Eastern oil shipments throughout the world totalled 47.4 million tonnes; miscellaneous USSR oil exports amounted to 88.8 million tonnes.

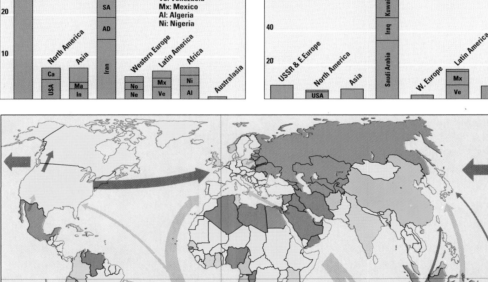

FUEL EXPORTS

Fuels as a percentage of total value of all exports (1986)

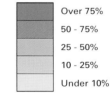

Over 75%
50 - 75%
25 - 50%
10 - 25%
Under 10%

Direction of trade

Coal
Oil

Arrows show the major trade direction of selected fuels, & are proportional to export value

NUCLEAR POWER

Percentage of electricity generated by nuclear power stations, leading nations (1988)

1.	France 70%	11.	W. Germany 34%
2.	Belgium 66%	12.	Japan 28%
3.	Hungary 49%	13.	Czechoslovakia .. 27%
4.	South Korea 47%	14.	UK 18%
5.	Sweden 46%	15.	USA 17%
6.	Taiwan 41%	16.	Canada 16%
7.	Switzerland 37%	17.	Argentina 12%
8.	Finland 36%	18.	USSR 11%
9.	Spain 36%	19.	Yugoslavia 6%
10.	Bulgaria 36%	20.	Netherlands 5%

The decade 1980-1990 was a bad time for the nuclear power industry. Major projects regularly ran vastly over-budget, and fears of long-term environmental damage were heavily reinforced by the 1986 Soviet disaster at Chernobyl. Although the number of reactors in service continued to increase throughout the period, orders for new plant shrank dramatically, and most countries cut back on their nuclear programmes.

HYDROELECTRICITY

Percentage of electricity generated by hydroelectrical power stations, leading nations (1988)

1.	Paraguay 99.9%	11.	Laos 95.5%
2.	Zambia 99.6%	12.	Nepal 95.2%
3.	Norway 99.5%	13.	Iceland 94.0%
4.	Congo 99.1%	14.	Uruguay 93.0%
5.	Costa Rica 98.3%	15.	Brazil 91.7%
6.	Uganda 98.3%	16.	Albania 87.2%
7.	Rwanda 97.7%	17.	Fiji 81.4%
8.	Malawi 97.6%	18.	Ecuador 80.7%
9.	Zaïre 97.4%	19.	C. African Rep. 80.4%
10.	Cameroon 97.2%	20.	Sri Lanka 80.4%

Countries heavily reliant on hydroelectricity are usually small and non-industrial: a high proportion of hydroelectric power more often reflects a modest energy budget than vast hydroelectric resources. The USA, for instance, produces only 8% of power requirements from hydroelectricity; yet that 8% amounts to more than three times the hydro-power generated by all of Africa.

ALTERNATIVE ENERGY SOURCES

Solar: Each year the sun bestows upon the Earth almost a million times as much energy as is locked up in all the planet's oil reserves, but only an insignificant fraction is trapped and used commercially. In some experimental installations, mirrors focus the sun's rays on to boilers, whose steam generates electricity by spinning turbines. Solar cells turn the sunlight into electricity directly, and although efficiencies are still low, advancing technology offers some prospect of using the sun as the main world electricity source by 2100.
Wind: Caused by uneven heating of the Earth, winds are themselves a form of solar energy. Windmills have been used for centuries to turn wind power into mechanical work; recent models, often arranged in banks on gust-swept high ground, usually generate electricity.
Tidal: The energy from tides is potentially enormous, although only a few installations have been built to exploit it. In theory at least, waves and currents could also provide almost unimaginable power, and the thermal differences in the ocean depths are another huge well of potential energy. But work on extracting it is still in the experimental stage.
Geothermal: The Earth's temperature rises by 1°C for every 30 metres' descent, with much steeper temperature gradients in geologically active areas. El Salvador, for example, produces 39% of its electricity from geothermal power stations. More than 130 are operating worldwide.
Biomass: The oldest of human fuels ranges from animal dung, still burned in cooking fires in much of North Africa and elsewhere, to sugar cane plantations feeding high-technology distilleries to produce ethanol for motor vehicle engines. In Brazil and South Africa, plant ethanol provides up to 25% of motor fuel. Throughout the developing world most biomass energy comes from firewood: although accurate figures are impossible to obtain, it may yield as much as 10% of the world's total energy consumption.

PRODUCTION: MINERALS

Even during the Stone Age, when humans often settled near the outcrops of flint on which their technology depended, mineral resources have attracted human exploiters. Their descendants have learned how to make use of almost every known element. These elements can be found, in one form or another, somewhere in the Earth's bountiful crust. Iron remains the most important, but modern industrial civilization has a voracious appetite for virtually all of them.

Mineral deposits once dictated the site of new industries; today, most industrial countries are heavily dependent on imports for many of their key materials. Most mining, and much refining of raw ores, is done in developing countries, where labour is cheap.

The main map below shows the richest sources of the most important minerals at present; some reserves – lead and mercury, for example – are running very low. The map takes no account of undersea deposits, most of which are considered inaccessible. Growing shortages, though, may encourage submarine mining: plans have already been made to recover the nodules of manganese found widely scattered on ocean floors.

MINERAL EXPORTS

Minerals & metals as a percentage of total exports (1986)

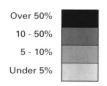

- Over 50%
- 10 - 50%
- 5 - 10%
- Under 5%

Direction of trade

- Copper
- Iron
- Bauxite (Aluminium)

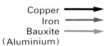

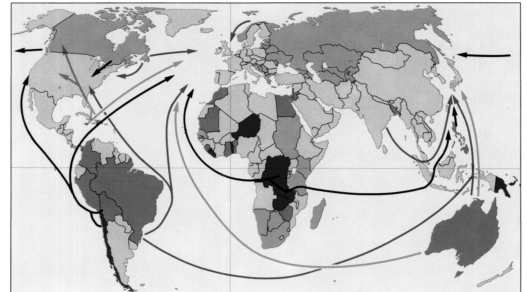

URANIUM

In its pure state, uranium is an immensely heavy, white metal; but although spent uranium is employed as projectiles in anti-missile cannon, where its mass ensures a lethal punch, its main use is as a fuel in nuclear reactors, and in nuclear weaponry. Uranium is very scarce: the main source is the rare ore pitchblende, which itself contains only 0.2% uranium oxide. Only a minute fraction of that is the radioactive U^{235} isotope, though so-called breeder reactors can transmute the more common U^{238} into highly radioactive plutonium.

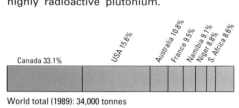

Canada 33.1% | USA 15.6% | Australia 10.8% | France 9.5% | Namibia 9.1% | Niger 8.8% | S. Africa 8.6%

World total (1989): 34,000 tonnes

METALS

Separate figures for Russia, Ukraine and the other successors of the defunct USSR are not as yet available

Aluminium: Produced mainly from its oxide, bauxite, which yields 25% of its weight in aluminium. The cost of refining and production is often too high for producer-countries to bear, so bauxite is largely exported. Lightweight and corrosion resistant, aluminium alloys are widely used in aircraft, vehicles, cans and packaging.

USA 22.4% | USSR 13.2% | Canada 8.6% | Australia 6.9% | Brazil 4.9% | Norway 4.8% | Germany 4.4%

World total (1989): 18,000,000 tonnes *

Copper: Derived from low-yielding sulphide ores, copper is an important export for several developing countries. An excellent conductor of heat and electricity, it forms part of most electrical items, and is used in the manufacture of brass and bronze. Major importers include Japan and Germany.

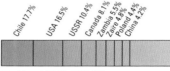

Chile 17.7% | USA 16.5% | USSR 10.4% | Canada 8.1% | Zambia 5.5% | Zaïre 4.8% | Poland 4.4% | China 4.2%

World total (1989): 9,100,000 tonnes *

Lead: A soft metal, obtained mainly from galena (lead sulphide), which occurs in veins associated with iron, zinc and silver sulphides. Its use in vehicle batteries accounts for the USA's prime consumer status; lead is also made into sheeting and piping. Its use as an additive to paints and petrol is decreasing.

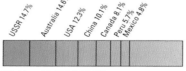

USSR 14.7% | Australia 14.6% | USA 12.3% | China 10.1% | Canada 8.1% | Peru 5.7% | Mexico 4.8%

World total (1989): 3,400,000 tonnes *

Mercury: The only metal that is liquid at normal temperatures, most is derived from its sulphide, cinnabar, found only in small quantities in volcanic areas. Apart from its value in thermometers and other instruments, most mercury production is used in anti-fungal and anti-fouling preparations, and to make detonators.

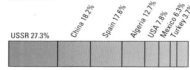

USSR 27.3% | China 18.2% | Spain 17.6% | Algeria 12.7% | USA 7.8% | Mexico 6.3% | Turkey 3.7%

World total (1989): 5,500,000 kilograms *

DIAMOND

Most diamond is found in kimberlite, or 'blue ground', a basic peridotite rock; erosion may wash the diamond from its kimberlite matrix and deposit it with sand or gravel on river beds. Only a small proportion of the world's diamond, the most flawless, is cut into gemstones - 'diamonds'; most is used in industry, where the material's remarkable hardness and abrasion resistance finds a use in cutting tools, drills and dies, as well as in styluses. Australia, not among the top 12 producers at the beginning of the 1980s, had by 1986 become world leader and by 1989 was the source of 37.5% of world production. The other main producers were Zaïre (18.9%), Botswana (16.3%), the then USSR (11.8%) and South Africa (9.7%). Between them, these five nations accounted for over 94% of the world total of 96,600,000 carats - at 0.2 grams per carat, almost one tonne.

Tin: Soft, pliable and non-toxic, used to coat 'tin' (tin-plated steel) cans, in the manufacture of foils and in alloys. The principal tin-bearing mineral is cassiterite (SnO_2), found in ore formed from molten rock. Producers and refiners were hit by a price collapse in 1991.

Brazil 22.5% | China 14.8% | Malaysia 14.4% | Indonesia 14.2% | Bolivia 7.1% | Thailand 6.6% | USSR 6.3%

World total (1989): 223,000 tonnes *

Zinc: Often found in association with lead ores, zinc is highly resistant to corrosion, and about 40% of the refined metal is used to plate sheet steel, particularly vehicle bodies – a process known as galvanizing. Zinc is also used in dry batteries, paints and dyes.

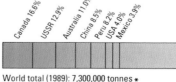

Canada 16.6% | USSR 12.9% | Australia 11.0% | China 8.5% | Peru 8.2% | USA 4.0% | Mexico 3.9%

World total (1989): 7,300,000 tonnes *

Gold: Regarded for centuries as the most valuable metal in the world and used to make coins, gold is still recognized as the monetary standard. A soft metal, it is alloyed to make jewellery; the electronics industry values its corrosion resistance and conductivity.

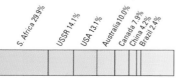

S. Africa 29.9% | USSR 14.1% | USA 13.1% | Australia 10.0% | Canada 7.9% | China 4.2% | Brazil 4.2%

World total (1989): 2,026,000 kilograms *

Silver: Most silver comes from ores mined and processed for other metals (including lead and copper). Pure or alloyed with harder metals, it is used for jewellery and ornaments. Industrial use includes dentistry, electronics, photography and as a chemical catalyst.

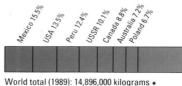

Mexico 15.5% | USA 13.5% | Peru 12.4% | USSR 10.1% | Canada 8.8% | Australia 7.2% | Poland 6.7%

World total (1989): 14,896,000 kilograms *

* Figures for aluminium are for refined metal, all other figures refer to ore production.

STRUCTURAL REGIONS

- Pre-Cambrian shields
- Sedimentary cover on Pre-Cambrian shields
- Palæozoic (Caledonian and Hercynian) folding
- Sedimentary cover on Palæozoic folding
- Mesozoic folding
- Sedimentary cover on Mesozoic folding
- Cainozoic (Alpine) folding
- Sedimentary cover on Cainozoic folding

Tropic of Cancer

Sullivan · Sudbury · Asbestos · Bingham · Great Lakes · Arizona · Florida · Jamaica · Carajas · Rondonia · Minas Gerais

IRON & FERRO-ALLOYS

Ever since the art of high-temperature smelting was discovered, some time in the second millennium BC, iron has been by far the most important metal known to man. The earliest iron ploughs transformed primitive agriculture and led to the first human population explosion, while iron weapons - or the lack of them - ensured the rise or fall of entire cultures.

Widely distributed around the world, iron ores usually contain 25-60% iron; blast furnaces process the raw product into pig-iron, which is then alloyed with carbon other minerals to produce steels of various qualities. From the time of the Industrial Revolution steel has been almost literally the backbone of modern civilization, the prime structural material on which all else is built.

Iron-smelting usually developed close to sources of ore and, later, to the coalfields that fueled the furnaces. Today, most ore comes from a few richly-endowed locations where large-scale mining is possible. Iron and steel plants are generally built at coastal sites so that giant ore carriers, which account for a sizeable proportion of the world's merchant fleet, can easily discharge their cargoes.

World production of pig iron and ferro-alloys (1988). All countries with an annual output of more than one million tonnes are shown

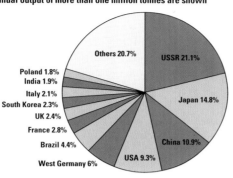

- USSR 21.1%
- Japan 14.8%
- China 10.9%
- USA 9.3%
- West Germany 6%
- Brazil 4.4%
- France 2.8%
- UK 2.4%
- South Korea 2.3%
- Italy 2.1%
- India 1.9%
- Poland 1.8%
- Others 20.7%

Total world production: 545 million tonnes

Development of world production of pig iron and ferro-alloys (1945-1988) in million tonnes

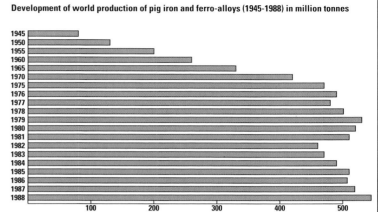

Chromium: Most of the world's chromium production is alloyed with iron and other metals to produce steels with various different properties. Combined with iron, nickel, cobalt and tungsten, chromium produces an exceptionally hard steel, resistant to heat; chrome steels are used for many household items where utility must be matched with appearance - cutlery, for example. Chromium is also used in production of refractory bricks, and its salts for tanning and dyeing leather and cloth.

Manganese: In its pure state, manganese is a hard, brittle metal. Alloyed with chrome, iron and nickel, it produces abrasion-resistant steels; manganese-aluminium alloys are light but tough. Found in batteries and inks, manganese is also used in glass production. Manganese ores are frequently found in the same location as sedimentary iron ores. Pyrolusite (MnO_2) and psilomelane are the main economically-exploitable sources.

Nickel: Combined with chrome and iron, nickel produces stainless and high-strength steels; similar alloys go to make magnets and electrical heating elements. Nickel combined with copper is widely used to make coins; cupro-nickel alloy is very resistant to corrosion. Its ores yield only modest quantities of nickel - 0.5 to 3.0% - but also contain copper, iron and small amounts of precious metals. Japan, the USA, the UK, Germany and France are the principal importers.

| USSR 24.4% | China 17.2% | Brazil 15.5% | Australia 10.7% | USA 5.8% | India 5.2% | Canada 4.1% | South Africa 3.0% | Sweden 2.2% |

World total production of iron ore (1989): 989,000,000 tonnes

| S. Africa 33.7% | USSR 29.9% | India 7.9% | Turkey 6.7% | Albania 5.5% | Zimbabwe 4.9% | Finland 3.9% |

World total (1989): 12,700,000 tonnes

| USSR 36.7% | S. Africa 15.1% | China 11.3% | Gabon 9.7% | Australia 8.9% | India 5.6% |

World total (1989): 24,000,000 tonnes

| USSR 23.1% | Canada 22.3% | New Caledonia 10.6% | Australia 7.1% | Indonesia 6.6% | Cuba 4.9% | S. Africa 3.7% |

World total (1989): 910,000 tonnes

DISTRIBUTION

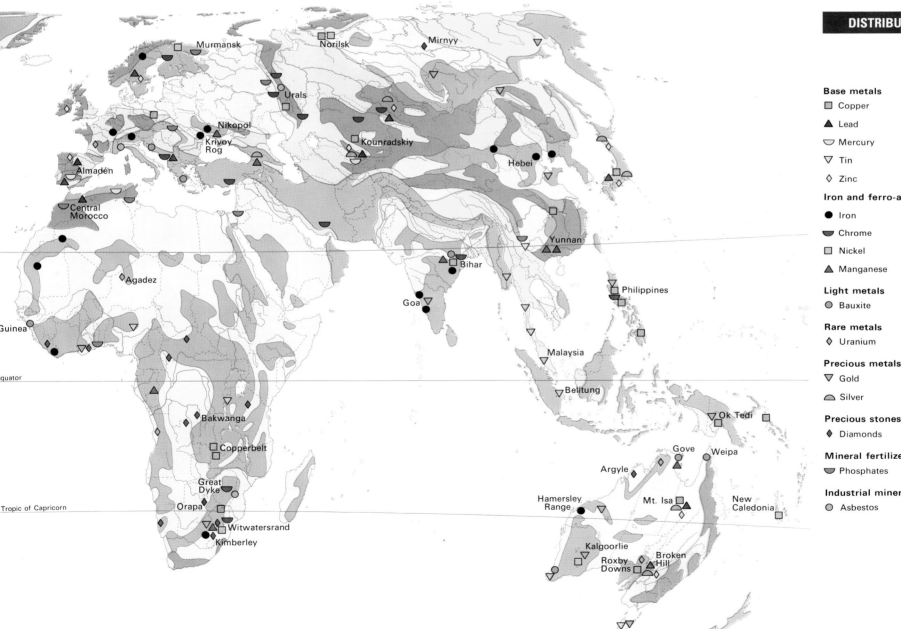

Base metals
- ▢ Copper
- ▲ Lead
- ◡ Mercury
- ▽ Tin
- ◇ Zinc

Iron and ferro-alloys
- ● Iron
- ◖ Chrome
- ▢ Nickel
- ▲ Manganese

Light metals
- ● Bauxite

Rare metals
- ◇ Uranium

Precious metals
- ▽ Gold
- ◠ Silver

Precious stones
- ◆ Diamonds

Mineral fertilizers
- ◡ Phosphates

Industrial minerals
- ● Asbestos

35

PRODUCTION: MANUFACTURING

In its broadest sense, manufacturing is the application of energy, labour and skill to raw materials in order to transform them into finished goods with a higher value than the various elements used in production.

Since the early days of the Industrial Revolution, manufacturing has implied the use of an organized workforce harnessed to some form of machine. The tendency has consistently been for increasingly expensive human labour to be replaced by increasingly complex machinery, which has evolved over time from water-powered looms to fully-integrated robotic plants.

Obviously, not all industries – or manufacturing countries - have reached the same level. Textiles, for example, the foundation of the early industrial revolution in the West, can be mass-produced with fairly modest technology; today, they are usually produced in developing countries, mostly in Asia, where low labour costs compensate for the large workforce the relatively simple machinery requires. Nevertheless, the trend towards high-technology production, however uneven, seems inexorable. Gains in efficiency make up for the staggering cost of the equipment itself, and the outcome is that fewer and fewer people are employed to produce more and more goods.

One paradoxical result of the increase in industrial efficiency is a relative decline in the importance of the industrial sector of a nation's economy. The economy has already passed through one transition, generations past, when workers were drawn from the land into factories. The second transition releases labour into what is called the service sector of the economy: a diffuse but vital concept that includes not only such obvious services as transport and administration, but also finance, insurance and activities as diverse as fashion design or the writing of computer software.

The process is far advanced in the mature economies of the West, with Japan not far behind. Almost two-thirds of US wealth, for example, is now generated in the service sector, and less than half of Japanese Gross National Product comes from industry. The shrinkage, though, is only relative: between them, these two industrial giants produce almost twice as much manufactured goods as the rest of the world put together. And it is on the solid base of production that the rest of their prosperity rests.

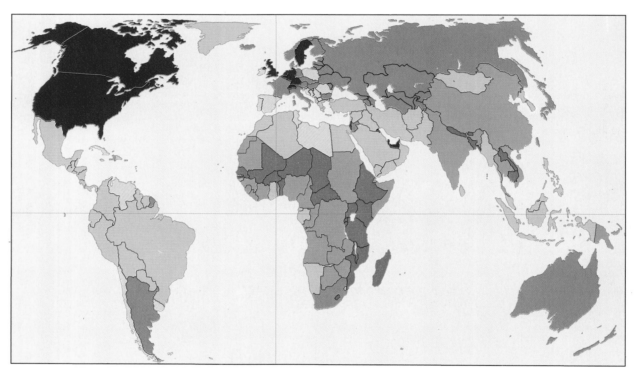

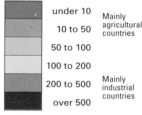

EMPLOYMENT

The number of workers employed in manufacturing for every 100 workers engaged in agriculture

under 10	Mainly agricultural countries
10 to 50	
50 to 100	
100 to 200	
200 to 500	Mainly industrial countries
over 500	

Selected countries (latest available figure, 1986-1989)

Singapore	6,166
Hong Kong	2,632
UK	912
Belgium	751
Germany (W)	749
USA	641
Sweden	615
France	331
Japan	320
Czechoslovakia	286

DIVISION OF EMPLOYMENT

Distribution of workers between agriculture, industry and services, selected countries (late 1980s)

The six countries selected illustrate the usual stages of economic development, from dependence on agriculture through industrial growth to the expansion of the services sector.

- Agriculture
- Industry
- Services

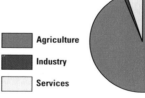

Nepal 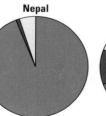 Nigeria  Pakistan 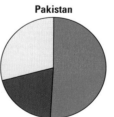 Brazil  Hong Kong 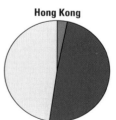 USA

THE WORKFORCE

Percentages of men and women between 15 and 64 in employment, selected countries (late 1980s)

The figures include employees and self-employed, who in developing countries are often subsistence farmers. People in full-time education are excluded. Because of the population age structure in developing countries, the employed population has to support a far larger number of non-workers than its industrial equivalent. For example, more than 52% of Kenya's people are under 15, an age group that makes up less than a tenth of the UK population.

- Men
- Women

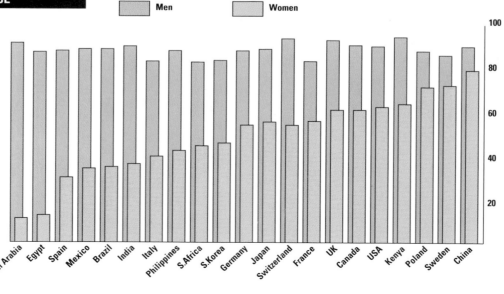

WEALTH CREATION

The Gross National Product (GNP) of the world's largest economies, US $ billion (1989)

1.	USA	5,237,707	21.	Denmark	105,263
2.	Japan	2,920,310	22.	Norway	92,097
3.	Germany	1,272,959	23.	Saudi Arabia	89,986
4.	France	1,000,866	24.	Indonesia	87,936
5.	Italy	871,955	25.	South Africa	86,029
6.	UK	834,166	26.	Turkey	74,731
7.	Canada	500,337	27.	Argentina	68,780
8.	China	393,006	28.	Poland	66,974
9.	Brazil	375,146	29.	Thailand	64,437
10.	Spain	358,352	30.	Hong Kong	59,202
11.	India	287,383	31.	Yugoslavia	59,080
12.	Australia	242,131	32.	Greece	53,626
13.	Netherlands	237,451	33.	Algeria	53,116
14.	Switzerland	197,984	34.	Venezuela	47,164
15.	South Korea	186,467	35.	Israel	44,131
16.	Sweden	184,230	36.	Portugal	44,058
17.	Mexico	170,053	37.	Philippines	42,754
18.	Belgium	162,026	38.	Pakistan	40,134
19.	Austria	131,899	39.	New Zealand	39,437
20.	Finland	109,705	40.	Colombia	38,607

There are no accurate figures available for either the USSR or its successor nations.

PATTERNS OF PRODUCTION

Breakdown of industrial output by value, selected countries (1987)

	Food & agriculture	Textiles & clothing	Machinery & transport	Chemicals	Other
Algeria	26%	20%	11%	1%	41%
Argentina	24%	10%	16%	12%	37%
Australia	18%	7%	21%	8%	45%
Austria	17%	8%	25%	6%	43%
Belgium	19%	8%	23%	13%	36%
Brazil	15%	12%	24%	9%	40%
Burkina Faso	62%	18%	2%	1%	17%
Canada	15%	7%	25%	9%	44%
Denmark	22%	6%	23%	10%	39%
Egypt	20%	27%	13%	10%	31%
Finland	13%	6%	24%	7%	50%
France	18%	7%	33%	9%	33%
Germany	12%	5%	38%	10%	36%
Greece	20%	22%	14%	7%	38%
Hong Kong	6%	40%	20%	2%	33%
Hungary	6%	11%	37%	11%	35%
India	11%	16%	26%	15%	32%
Indonesia	23%	11%	10%	10%	47%
Iran	13%	22%	22%	7%	36%
Israel	13%	10%	28%	8%	42%
Ireland	28%	7%	20%	15%	28%
Italy	7%	13%	32%	10%	38%
Japan	10%	6%	38%	10%	37%
Kenya	35%	12%	14%	9%	29%
Malaysia	21%	5%	23%	14%	37%
Mexico	24%	12%	14%	12%	39%
Netherlands	19%	4%	28%	11%	38%
New Zealand	26%	10%	16%	6%	43%
Norway	21%	3%	26%	7%	44%
Pakistan	34%	21%	8%	12%	25%
Philippines	40%	7%	7%	10%	35%
Poland	15%	16%	30%	6%	33%
Portugal	17%	22%	16%	8%	38%
Singapore	6%	5%	46%	8%	36%
South Africa	14%	8%	17%	11%	49%
South Korea	15%	17%	24%	9%	35%
Spain	17%	9%	22%	9%	43%
Sweden	10%	2%	35%	8%	44%
Thailand	30%	17%	14%	6%	33%
Turkey	20%	14%	15%	8%	43%
UK	14%	6%	32%	11%	36%
USA	12%	5%	35%	9%	38%
Venezuela	23%	8%	9%	11%	49%
Yugoslavia	13%	17%	25%	6%	39%

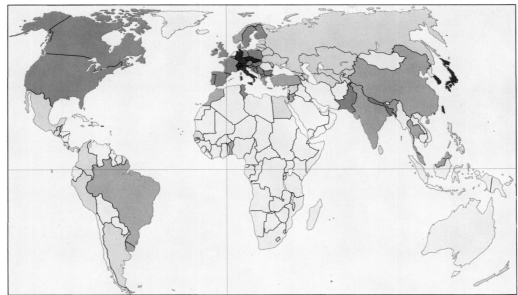

INDUSTRY & TRADE

Manufactured goods as a percentage of total exports (1989)

- Over 75%
- 50 - 75% [USA 69%]
- 25 - 50% [UK 67%]
- 10 - 25%
- Under 10%

The Far East & South-East Asia (Japan 99.5%, Macau 98.5%, Taiwan 96.8%, Hong Kong 96.1%, S. Korea 95.9%) is most dominant, but many countries in Europe (eg Austria 98.4%) are also heavily dependent on manufactured goods.

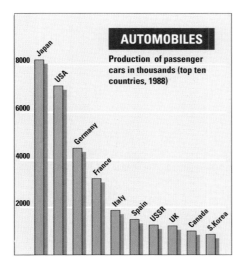

AUTOMOBILES
Production of passenger cars in thousands (top ten countries, 1988)

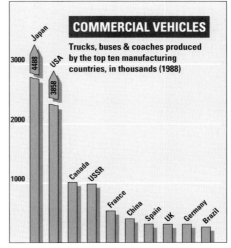

COMMERCIAL VEHICLES
Trucks, buses & coaches produced by the top ten manufacturing countries, in thousands (1988)

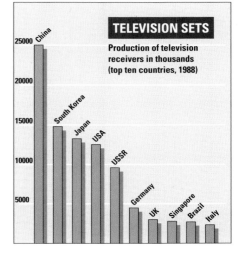

TELEVISION SETS
Production of television receivers in thousands (top ten countries, 1988)

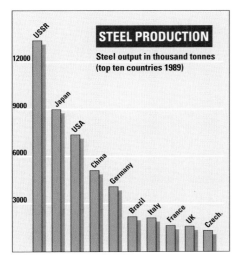

STEEL PRODUCTION
Steel output in thousand tonnes (top ten countries 1989)

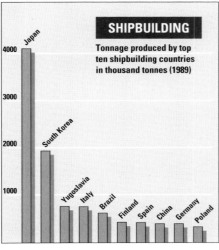

SHIPBUILDING
Tonnage produced by top ten shipbuilding countries in thousand tonnes (1989)

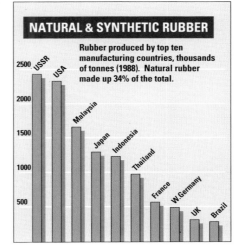

NATURAL & SYNTHETIC RUBBER
Rubber produced by top ten manufacturing countries, thousands of tonnes (1988). Natural rubber made up 34% of the total.

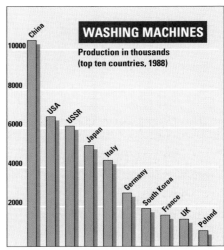

WASHING MACHINES
Production in thousands (top ten countries, 1988)

INDUSTRIAL POWER

Industrial output (mining, manufacturing, construction, energy & water production), top 40 nations, US $ billion (1988)

1.	USA	1,249.54	21.	Austria	50.63
2.	Japan	1,155.41	22.	Belgium	46.88
3.	Germany	479.69	23.	Poland	39.52
4.	USSR	326.54	24.	Finland	35.50
5.	France	304.95	25.	South Africa	35.46
6.	UK	295.00	26.	Saudi Arabia	33.36
7.	Italy	286.00	27.	Denmark	30.79
8.	China	174.05	28.	Iraq	30.27
9.	Canada	171.06	29.	Czechoslovakia	30.18
10.	Spain	126.60	30.	Yugoslavia	29.32
11.	Brazil	116.13	31.	Indonesia	29.03
12.	Netherlands	76.48	32.	Norway	28.74
13.	Sweden	75.17	33.	Argentina	26.27
14.	South Korea	74.00	34.	Turkey	26.07
15.	India	72.69	35.	Israel	24.15
16.	Australia	72.63	36.	Algeria	22.88
17.	E. Germany	64.66	37.	Venezuela	22.70
18.	Switzerland	63.37	38.	Romania	22.19
19.	Mexico	61.57	39.	Iran	19.90
20.	Taiwan	54.81	40.	Thailand	18.62

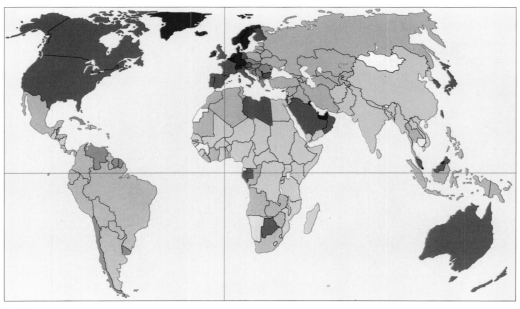

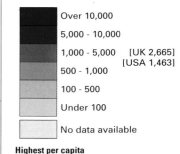

EXPORTS PER CAPITA

Value of exports in US $, divided by total population (1988)

- Over 10,000
- 5,000 - 10,000
- 1,000 - 5,000 [UK 2,665]
- 500 - 1,000 [USA 1,463]
- 100 - 500
- Under 100
- No data available

Highest per capita

Singapore	16,671
Hong Kong	12,676
UAE	10,217
Belgium	10,200
Bahamas	8,580
Qatar	8,431

PRODUCTION: TRADE

Thriving international trade is the outward sign of a healthy world economy – the obvious indicator that some countries have goods to sell and others the wherewithal to buy them. Despite local fluctuations, trade throughout the 1980s grew consistently faster than output, increasing in value by almost 50% in the decade 1979-89. It remains dominated by the wealthy, industrialized countries of the Organization for Economic Development: between them, the 24 OECD members account for almost 75% of world imports and exports in most years. OECD dominance is just as marked in the trade in 'invisibles' - a column in the balance sheet that includes, among other headings, the export of services, interest payments on overseas investments, tourism and even remittances from migrant workers abroad. In the UK, 'invisibles' account for more than half all trading income.

However, the size of these great trading economies means that imports and exports usually comprise a fraction of their total wealth: in the case of the export-conscious Japanese, trade in goods and services amounts to less than 18% of GDP. In poorer countries, trade - often in a single commodity - may amount to 50% GDP or more. And there are oddities: import-export figures for the entrepôt economy of Singapore, for example, the transit point for much Asian trade, are almost double that small nation's total earnings.

WORLD TRADE

Percentage of total world exports by value (1989)

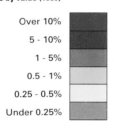

- Over 10%
- 5 - 10%
- 1 - 5%
- 0.5 - 1%
- 0.25 - 0.5%
- Under 0.25%

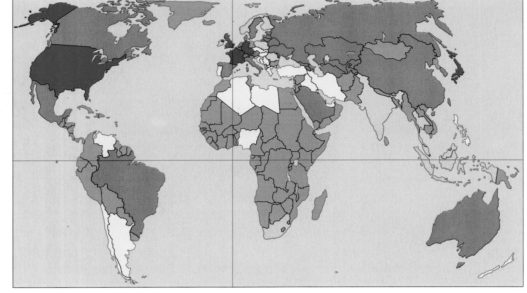

[USA 15.7%]   [UK 6.3%]

THE GREAT TRADING NATIONS

The imports and exports of the top ten trading nations as a percentage of world trade (1989). Each country's trade in manufactured goods is shown in orange.

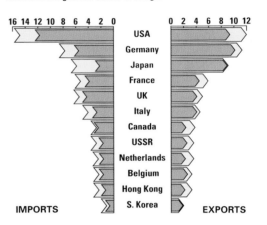

IMPORTS — 16 14 12 10 8 6 4 2 0 | 0 2 4 6 8 10 12 — EXPORTS

USA
Germany
Japan
France
UK
Italy
Canada
USSR
Netherlands
Belgium
Hong Kong
S. Korea

MAJOR EXPORTS

Leading manufactured items and their exporters, by percentage of world total in US dollars (late 1980s)

AIRCRAFT
- USA 51%
- UK 13%
- W. Germany 9%
- France 8%
- Canada 5%
- Italy 3%
- Other 11%

TELECOMMUNICATIONS GEAR
- Japan 33%
- USA 14%
- W.Germany 9%
- France 5%
- UK 5%
- Sweden 4%
- Hong Kong 4%
- Canada 4%
- Italy 3%
- Other 19%

DATA PROCESSING EQUIPMENT
- USA 24%
- Japan 22%
- W.Germany 11%
- France 6%
- UK 6%
- Ireland 5%
- Canada 4%
- Italy 4%
- Singapore 4%
- Other 14%

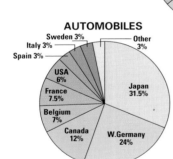

AUTOMOBILES
- Japan 31.5%
- W.Germany 24%
- Canada 12%
- Belgium 7%
- France 7.5%
- USA 6%
- Spain 3%
- Italy 3%
- Sweden 3%
- Other 3%

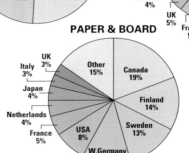

PAPER & BOARD
- Canada 19%
- Finland 14%
- Sweden 13%
- W.Germany 12%
- USA 8%
- France 5%
- Netherlands 4%
- Japan 4%
- Italy 3%
- UK 3%
- Other 15%

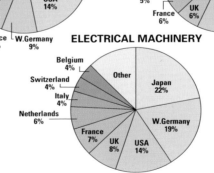

ELECTRICAL MACHINERY
- Japan 22%
- W.Germany 19%
- USA 14%
- UK 8%
- France 7%
- Netherlands 6%
- Italy 4%
- Switzerland 4%
- Belgium 4%
- Other

TRADED PRODUCTS

Top ten manufactures traded, by value in billions of US $ (late 1980s)

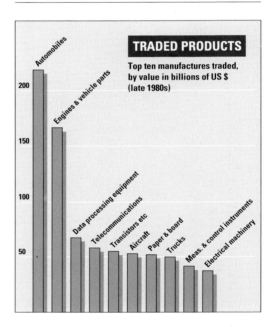

- Automobiles
- Engines & vehicle parts
- Data processing equipment
- Telecommunications
- Transistors etc
- Aircraft
- Paper & board
- Trucks
- Meas. & control instruments
- Electrical machinery

DEPENDENCE ON TRADE

Value of exports as a percentage of Gross Domestic Product (1988)

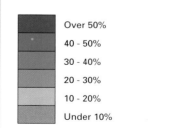

- Over 50%
- 40 - 50%
- 30 - 40%
- 20 - 30%   [UK 21%]
- 10 - 20%   [USA 6.5%]
- Under 10%

- Most dependent on industrial exports (over 75% of total exports)
- Most dependent on fuel exports (over 75% of total exports)
- Most dependent on mineral & metal exports (over 75% of total exports)

WORLD SHIPPING

While ocean passenger traffic is now relatively modest, sea transport still carries most of world trade. Oil and bulk carriers make up the majority of the world fleet, although the general cargo category was the fastest growing in 1989, a year in which total tonnage increased by 1.5%.

Almost 30% of world shipping sails under a 'flag of convenience', whereby owners take advantage of low taxes by registering their vessels in a foreign country the ships will never see, notably Panama and Liberia.

MERCHANT FLEETS

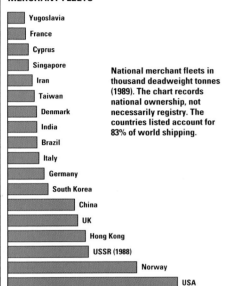

Yugoslavia
France
Cyprus
Singapore
Iran
Taiwan
Denmark
India
Brazil
Italy
Germany
South Korea
China
UK
Hong Kong
USSR (1988)
Norway
USA
Japan
Greece

20,000   40,000   60,000   80,000

National merchant fleets in thousand deadweight tonnes (1989). The chart records national ownership, not necessarily registry. The countries listed account for 83% of world shipping.

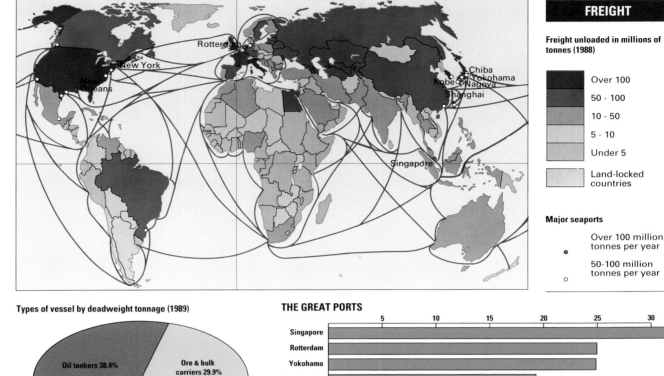

Rotterdam
New York
New Orleans
Chiba
Yokohama
Kobe Nagoya
Shanghai
Singapore

Freight unloaded in millions of tonnes (1988)

Over 100
50 - 100
10 - 50
5 - 10
Under 5
Land-locked countries

Major seaports

● Over 100 million tonnes per year
○ 50-100 million tonnes per year

Types of vessel by deadweight tonnage (1989)

Oil tankers 38.4%
Ore & bulk carriers 29.9%
Others 9.7%
General cargo 16.1%
Ferries & passenger ships 0.5%
Liquid gas carriers 1.6%
Container ships 3.8%

THE GREAT PORTS

5   10   15   20   25   30

Singapore
Rotterdam
Yokohama
Los Angeles
Antwerp
Hong Kong
Europoort
New Orleans
Hamburg
Kobe

The world's ten busiest ports by million tonnes of shipping arrivals (late 1980s)

TRADE IN PRIMARY PRODUCTS

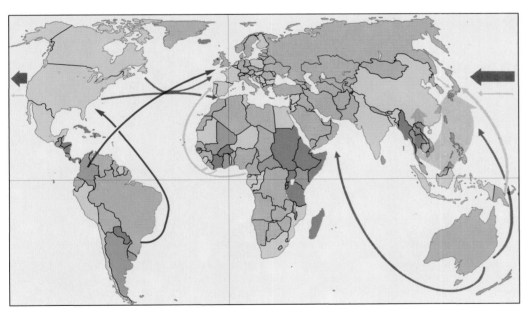

Exports in primary products (excluding fuels, minerals & metals) as a percentage of total exports (1988)

Over 75%
50 - 75%
25 - 50%
10 - 25%   [USA 17.6%]
Under 10%   [UK 9%]

Direction of trade

 Major movements of wheat
 Major movements of coffee
Major movements of hardwoods

Arrows show the major trade direction of selected primary products, & are proportional to export value

BALANCE OF TRADE

Value of exports in proportion to the value of imports (1988)

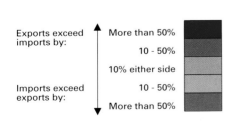

Exports exceed imports by:
More than 50%
10 - 50%
10% either side
Imports exceed exports by:
10 - 50%
More than 50%

The total world trade balance should amount to zero, since exports must equal imports on a global scale. In practice, at least $100 billions in exports go unrecorded, leaving the world with an apparent deficit and many countries in a better position than public accounting reveals. However, a favourable trade balance is not necessarily a sign of prosperity: many poorer countries must maintain a high surplus in order to service debts, and do so by restricting imports below their real requirements.

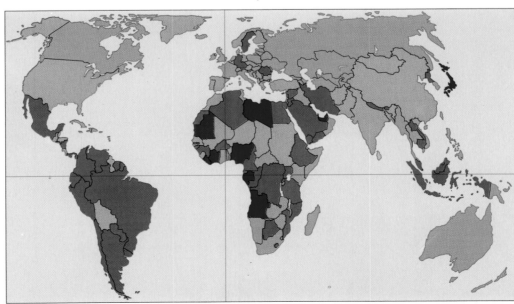

QUALITY OF LIFE: WEALTH

Throughout the 1980s, most of the world became at least slightly richer. There were exceptions: in Africa, the poorest of the continents, many incomes actually fell, and the upheavals in Eastern Europe in 1989 left whole populations awash with political freedom but worse off financially in economies still teetering towards capitalism.

Most of the improvements, however, came to those who were already, in world terms, extremely affluent: the gap between rich and poor grew steadily wider. And in those developing countries that showed significant statistical progress, advances were often confined to a few favoured areas while conditions in other, usually rural, districts went from bad to worse.

The pattern of world poverty varies from region to region. In most of Asia, the process of recognized development is generally under way, with production increases outpacing population growth. By 2000, less than 10% of the Chinese population should be officially rated 'poor': without the means to buy either adequate food or the basic necessities required to take a full part in everyday life. Even India's lower growth rate should be enough to reduce the burden of poverty for at least some of its people. In Latin America, average per capita production is high enough for most countries to be considered 'middle income' in world rankings. But although adequate resources exist, Latin American wealth is distributed with startling inequality. According to a 1990 World Bank report, a tax of only 2% on the richest fifth would raise enough money to pull every one of the continent's 437 million people above the poverty line.

In Africa, solutions will be harder to find. The bane of high population growth has often been aggravated by incompetent administration, a succession of natural disasters and war. Population is the crux of the problem: numbers are growing anything up to twice as fast as the economies that try to support them. Aid from the developed world is only a partial solution; although Africa receives more than any other continent, much has been wasted on over-ambitious projects or lost in webs of inexperienced or corrupt bureaucracy. Yet without aid, Africa seems doomed to permanent crisis.

The rich countries can afford to increase their spending. The 24 members of the Organization for Economic Cooperation and Development comprise only 16% of the world's population, yet between them the nations accounted for almost 80% of total world production in 1988, a share that is likely to increase as 2000 approaches.

CURRENCIES

Currency units of the world's most powerful economies

1. USA: US Dollar($,US$) = 100 cents
2. Japan: Yen (Y,¥) = 100 sen
3. Germany: Deutsche Mark (DM) = 100 Pfennige
4. France: French Franc (Fr) = 100 centimes
5. Italy: Italian Lira (L, £, Lit)
6. UK: Pound Sterling (£) = 100 pence
7. Canada: Canadian Dollar (C$, Can$) = 100 cents
8. China: Renminbi Yuan (RMBY, $, Y) = 10 jiao = 100 fen
9. Brazil: Cruzado (Cr$) = 100 centavos
10. Spain: Peseta (Pta, Pa) = 100 céntimos
11. India: Indian Rupee (Re, Rs) = 100 paisa
12. Australia: Australian Dollar ($A) = 100 cents
13. Netherlands: Guilder, Florin (Gld, f) = 100 centimes
14. Switzerland: Swiss Franc (SFr, SwF) = 100 centimes
15. South Korea: Won (W) = 100 Chon
16. Sweden: Swedish Krona (SKr) = 100 ore
17. Mexico: Mexican Pesos (Mex$) = 100 centavos
18. Belgium: Belgian Franc (BFr) = 100 centimes
19. Austria: Schilling (S, Sch) = 100 groschen
20. Finland: Markka (FMk) = 100 penni
21. Denmark: Danish Krone (DKr) = 100 ore
22. Norway: Norwegian Krone (NKr) = 100 ore
23. Saudi Arabia: Riyal (SAR, SRI$) = 100 halalah
24. Indonesia: Rupiah (Rp) = 100 sen
25. South Africa: Rand (R) = 100 cents

CONTINENTAL SHARES

Shares of population and of wealth (GNP) by continent

Generalized continental figures show the startling difference between rich and poor but mask the successes or failures of individual countries. Japan, for example, with less than 4% of Asia's population, produces almost 70% of the continent's output.

POPULATION

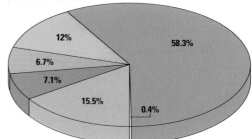

GNP

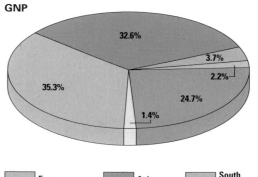

Europe   Asia   South America
Australia   Africa   North America

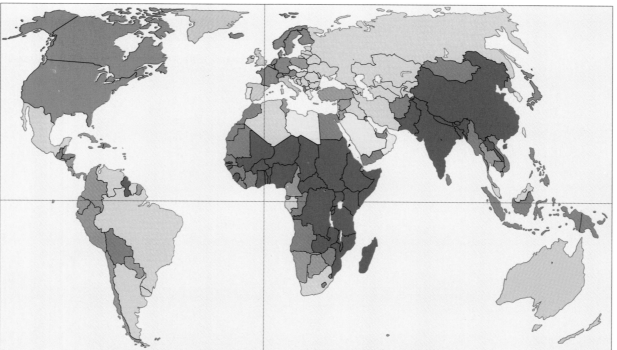

LEVELS OF INCOME

Gross National Product per capita: the value of total production divided by population (1989)

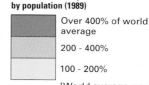

Over 400% of world average

200 - 400%

100 - 200%

[World average wealth per person US $3,980]

50 - 100%

25 - 50%

10 - 25%

Under 10%

Richest countries

Switzerland	$30,270
Luxembourg	$24,860
Japan	$23,730
Finland	$22,060

Poorest countries

Somalia	$170
Ethiopia	£120
Tanzania	$120
Mozambique	$80

INDICATORS

The gap between the world's rich and poor is now so great that it is difficult to illustrate it on a single graph. Car ownership in the USA, for example, is almost 2,000 times as common as it is in Bangladesh. Within each income group, however, comparisons have some meaning: the affluent Japanese on their overcrowded island have far fewer cars than the Americans; the Chinese, perhaps because of propaganda value, have more television sets than the Indians, whose per capita income is similar, while Nigerians prefer to spend their money on vehicles.

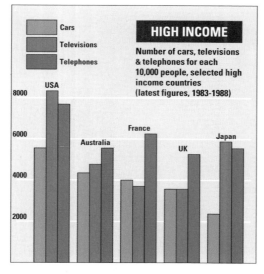

HIGH INCOME

Cars / Televisions / Telephones

Number of cars, televisions & telephones for each 10,000 people, selected high income countries (latest figures, 1983-1988)

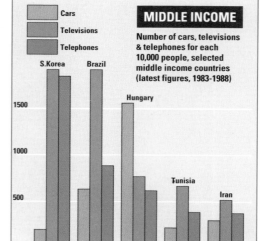

MIDDLE INCOME

Cars / Televisions / Telephones

Number of cars, televisions & telephones for each 10,000 people, selected middle income countries (latest figures, 1983-1988)

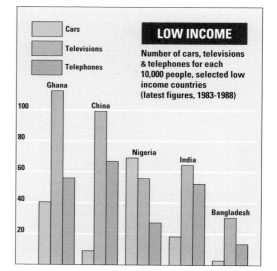

LOW INCOME

Cars / Televisions / Telephones

Number of cars, televisions & telephones for each 10,000 people, selected low income countries (latest figures, 1983-1988)

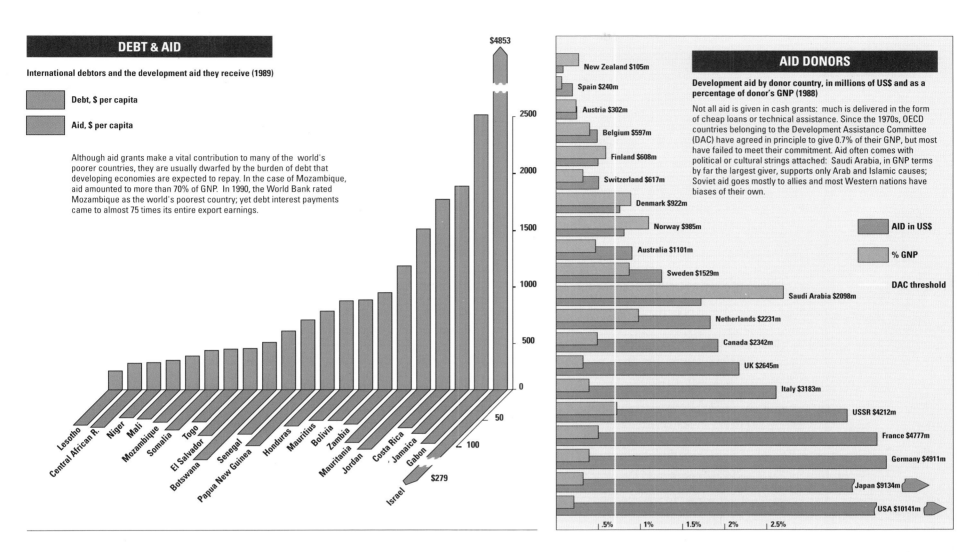

DEBT & AID

International debtors and the development aid they receive (1989)

- Debt, $ per capita
- Aid, $ per capita

Although aid grants make a vital contribution to many of the world's poorer countries, they are usually dwarfed by the burden of debt that developing economies are expected to repay. In the case of Mozambique, aid amounted to more than 70% of GNP. In 1990, the World Bank rated Mozambique as the world's poorest country; yet debt interest payments came to almost 75 times its entire export earnings.

$4853

$279

Lesotho, Central African R., Niger, Mali, Mozambique, Somalia, Togo, El Salvador, Botswana, Senegal, Papua New Guinea, Honduras, Mauritius, Bolivia, Zambia, Mauritania, Jordan, Costa Rica, Jamaica, Gabon, Israel

AID DONORS

Development aid by donor country, in millions of US$ and as a percentage of donor's GNP (1988)

Not all aid is given in cash grants: much is delivered in the form of cheap loans or technical assistance. Since the 1970s, OECD countries belonging to the Development Assistance Committee (DAC) have agreed in principle to give 0.7% of their GNP, but most have failed to meet their commitment. Aid often comes with political or cultural strings attached: Saudi Arabia, in GNP terms by far the largest giver, supports only Arab and Islamic causes; Soviet aid goes mostly to allies and most Western nations have biases of their own.

- AID in US$
- % GNP

DAC threshold

New Zealand $105m
Spain $240m
Austria $302m
Belgium $597m
Finland $608m
Switzerland $617m
Denmark $922m
Norway $985m
Australia $1101m
Sweden $1529m
Saudi Arabia $2098m
Netherlands $2231m
Canada $2342m
UK $2645m
Italy $3183m
USSR $4212m
France $4777m
Germany $4911m
Japan $9134m
USA $10141m

.5% 1% 1.5% 2% 2.5%

Inflation (right) is an excellent index of a country's financial stability, and usually its prosperity or at least its prospects. Inflation rates above 20% are generally matched by slow or even negative growth; above 50%, an economy is left reeling. Most advanced countries during the 1980s had to wrestle with inflation that occasionally touched or even exceeded 10%; in Japan, the growth leader, price increases averaged only 1.8% between 1980 and 1988.

Government spending (below right) is more difficult to interpret. Obviously, very low levels indicate a weak state, and high levels a strong one; but in poor countries, the 10-20% absorbed by the government may well amount to most of the liquid cash available, whereas in rich countries most of the 35-50% typically in government hands is returned in services. GNP per capita figures (below) should also be compared with caution. They do not reveal the vast differences in living costs between different countries: the equivalent of US $100 is worth considerably more in poorer nations than it is in the USA itself.

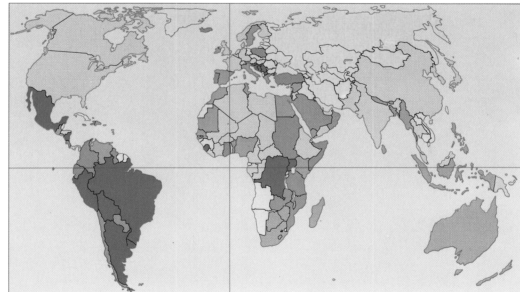

INFLATION

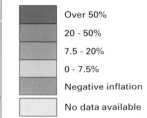

Average annual rate of inflation (1980-1988)

- Over 50%
- 20 - 50%
- 7.5 - 20%
- 0 - 7.5%
- Negative inflation
- No data available

Highest inflation
Bolivia 483%
Argentina 291%
Brazil 189%

Lowest inflation
Oman .... -6.5%
Saudi Arabia .... -4.2%
Kuwait .... -3.9%

[UK 5.7%] [USA 4.0%]

THE WEALTH GAP

The world's richest & poorest countries, by Gross National Product per capita in US $ (1989)

1.	Liechtenstein	33,000	1.	Mozambique	80
2.	Switzerland	30,270	2.	Ethiopia	120
3.	Bermuda	25,000	3.	Tanzania	120
4.	Luxembourg	24,860	4.	Laos	170
5.	Japan	23,730	5.	Nepal	170
6.	Finland	22,060	6.	Somalia	170
7.	Norway	21,850	7.	Bangladesh	180
8.	Sweden	21,710	8.	Malawi	180
9.	Iceland	21,240	9.	Bhutan	190
10.	USA	21,100	10.	Chad	190
11.	Denmark	20,510	11.	Sierra Leone	200
12.	Canada	19,020	12.	Burundi	220
13.	UAE	18,430	13.	Gambia	230
14.	France	17,830	14.	Madagascar	230
15.	Austria	17,360	15.	Nigeria	250
16.	Germany	16,500	16.	Uganda	250
17.	Belgium	16,390	17.	Mali	260
18.	Kuwait	16,380	18.	Zaire	260
19.	Netherlands	16,010	19.	Niger	290
20.	Italy	15,150	20.	Burkina Faso	310

GNP per capita is calculated by dividing a country's Gross National Product by its population. The UK ranks 21st, with US $14,570.

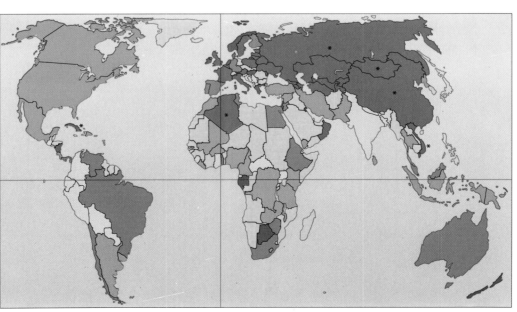

STATE REVENUE

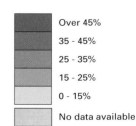

Central government revenue as a percentage of GNP (1988) [* estimate]

- Over 45%
- 35 - 45%
- 25 - 35%
- 15 - 25%
- 0 - 15%
- No data available

Highest proportion
Botswana 74%
Hungary 58%
Kuwait 52%
Netherlands 51%
Gabon 47%

[UK 36.4%] [USA 19.7%]

QUALITY OF LIFE: STANDARDS

At first sight, most international contrasts are swamped by differences in wealth. The rich not only have more money, they have more of everything, including years of life. Those with only a little money are obliged to spend most of it on food and clothing, the basic maintenance costs of existence; air travel and tourism are unlikely to feature on the lists of their expenditure. However, poverty and wealth are both relative: slum-dwellers living on social security payments in an affluent industrial country have far more resources at their disposal than an average African peasant, but feel their own poverty none the less acutely. A middle-class Indian lawyer cannot command a fraction of the earnings of a counterpart in New York, London or Rome; nevertheless, he rightly sees himself as prosperous.

In 1990 the United Nations Development Programme published its first Human Development Index, an attempt to construct a comparative scale by which at least a simplified form of well-being might be measured. The index, running from 1 to 100, combined figures for life expectancy and literacy with a wealth scale that matched incomes against the official poverty lines of a group of industrialized nations. National scores ranged from a startling 98.7 for

Sweden to a miserable 11.6 for Niger, reflecting the all too familiar gap between rich and poor.

Comparisons between nations with similar incomes are more interesting, showing the effect of government policies. For example, Sri Lanka was awarded 78.9 against 43.9 for its only slightly poorer neighbour, India; Zimbabwe, at 57.6, had more than double the score of Senegal, despite no apparent disparities in average income. Some development indicators may be interpreted in two ways. There is a very clear correlation, for example, between the wealth of a nation and the level of education that its people enjoy. Education helps create wealth, of course; but are rich countries wealthy because they are educated, or well-educated because they are rich? Women's fertility rates appear to fall almost in direct proportion to the amount of secondary education they receive; but high levels of female education are associated with rich countries, where fertility is already low.

Not everything, though, is married to wealth. The countries cited on these pages have been chosen, representatively, to give a range covering different cultures as well as different economic power, revealing disparities among rich and among poor as well as between the two obvious groups.

Income distribution, for example, shows that in Brazil (following the general pattern of Latin America) most national wealth is concentrated in a few hands; Bangladesh is much poorer, but what little wealth there is, is more evenly spread.

Among the developed countries the USA, with its poorest 20% sharing less than 5% of the national cake, has a noticeably less even distribution than Japan, where despite massive industrialization traditional values act as a brake against poverty. Hungary, still enmeshed in Communism when these statistics were compiled, shows the most even distribution of all, which certainly matches with Socialist theory. However, the inequalities in Communist societies, a contributing factor in the demise of most of them in the late 1980s, are not easily measured in money terms: Communist élites are less often rewarded with cash than with power and privilege, commodities not easily expressed statistically.

There are other limits to statistical analysis. Even without taking account of such imponderables as personal satisfaction, it will always be more difficult to measure a reasonable standard of living than a nation's income or its productivity. Lack of money certainly brings misery, but its presence does not guarantee contentment.

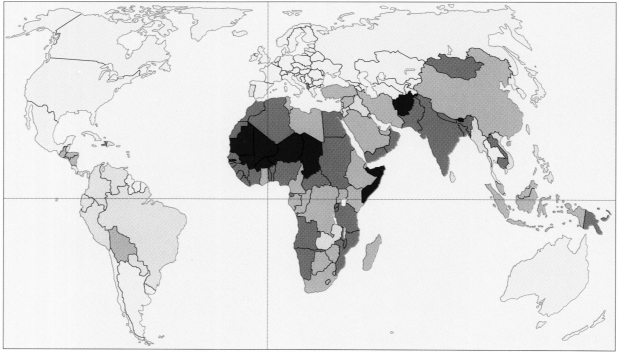

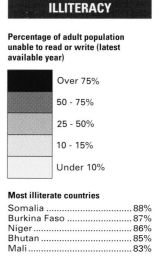

ILLITERACY

Percentage of adult population unable to read or write (latest available year)

- Over 75%
- 50 - 75%
- 25 - 50%
- 10 - 15%
- Under 10%

Most illiterate countries
Somalia 88%
Burkina Faso 87%
Niger 86%
Bhutan 85%
Mali 83%

Least illiterate countries
Canada 5%
Denmark 5%
Finland 5%
Guyana 4%
Trinidad & Tobago 4%

EDUCATION

The developing countries made great efforts in the 1970s and 1980s to bring at least a basic education to their people. Primary school enrolments rose above 60% in all but the poorest nations. Figures often include teenagers or young adults, however, and there are still an estimated 300 million children worldwide who receive no schooling at all. Secondary and higher education are expanding far more slowly, and the gap between rich and poor is probably even larger than it appears from the charts here, while the bare statistics provide no real reflection of educational quality.

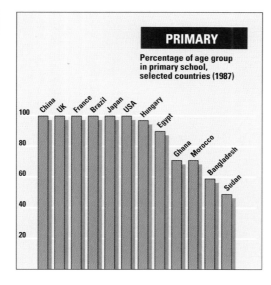

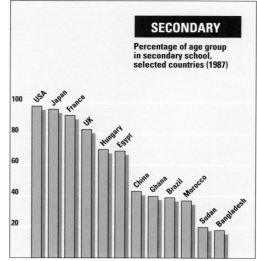

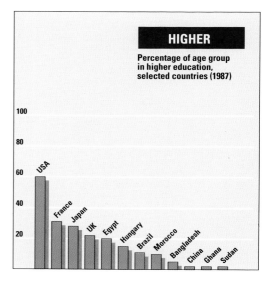

DISTRIBUTION OF SPENDING

Percentage share of household spending, (1989)

- Food
- Medicine & Education
- Clothing
- Transport
- Energy & Housing
- Other

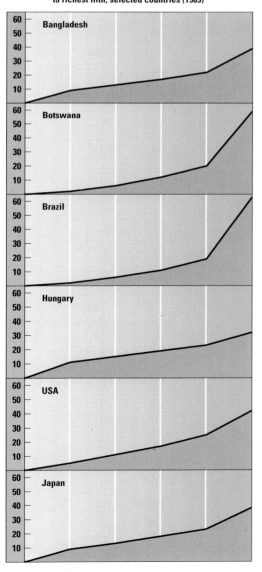

UK USA Japan Hungary Brazil Egypt Nigeria B'desh

DISTRIBUTION OF INCOME

Percentage share of household income from poorest fifth to richest fifth, selected countries (1989)

Bangladesh

Botswana

Brazil

Hungary

USA

Japan

FERTILITY & EDUCATION

Fertility rate: average number of children borne per woman

Percentage of female age group in secondary education

Fertility rates compared with female education, selected countries (1988)

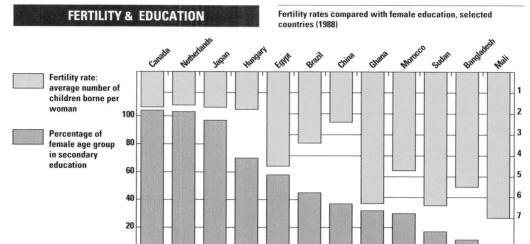

Canada Netherlands Japan Hungary Egypt Brazil China Ghana Morocco Sudan Bangladesh Mali

Since the age group for secondary schooling is usually defined as 12 to 17 years, percentages for countries with a significant number of 11- or 18-year-olds in secondary school may actually exceed 100. A high proportion of employed women may indicate either an advanced, industrial economy where female opportunities are high, or a poor country where many women's lives are dominated by agricultural toil. The lowest rates are found in Islamic nations, whose religious precepts often exclude women even from field-work.

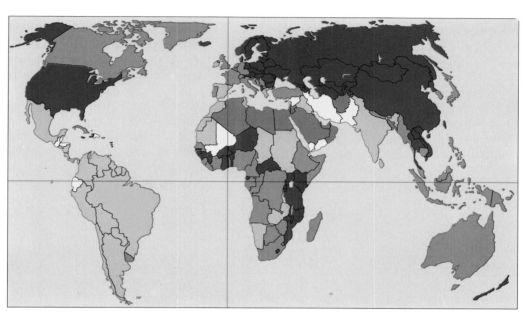

WOMEN AT WORK

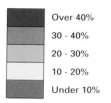

Women in paid employment as a percentage of the total workforce (1989)

- Over 40%
- 30 - 40%
- 20 - 30%
- 10 - 20%
- Under 10%

Highest proportion

Burundi	53%
Ghana	51%
Mozambique	48%

Lowest proportion

UAE	6%
Saudi Arabia	7%
Bangladesh	7%

[UK 42%] [USA 44%]

TOURIST SPENDING

Countries spending the most on overseas tourism US $ million (1987)

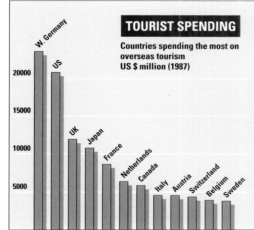

W. Germany US UK Japan France Netherlands Canada Italy Austria Switzerland Belgium Sweden

TOURIST EARNING

Countries receiving the most from overseas tourism US $ million (1987)

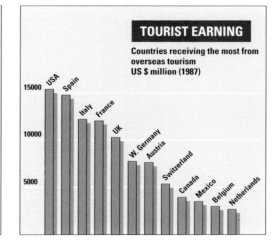

USA Spain Italy France UK W. Germany Austria Switzerland Canada Mexico Belgium Netherlands

Small economies in attractive areas are often completely dominated by tourism: in some West Indian islands, tourist spending provides over 90% of total income. In cash terms the USA is the world leader: its 1987 earnings exceeded 15 billion dollars, though that sum amounted to only 0.4% of its GDP.

AIR TRAVEL

Millions of passenger km [number carried, international & domestic, multiplied by distance flown by each from airport of origin] (1988)

- Over 100,000
- 50,000 - 100,000
- 10,000 - 50,000
- 1,000 - 10,000
- 500 - 1,000
- Under 500

○ Major airports (over 20 million passengers a year)

The world's busiest airport in terms of total passengers is Chicago's O'Hare; the busiest international airport is Heathrow, the largest of London's airports.

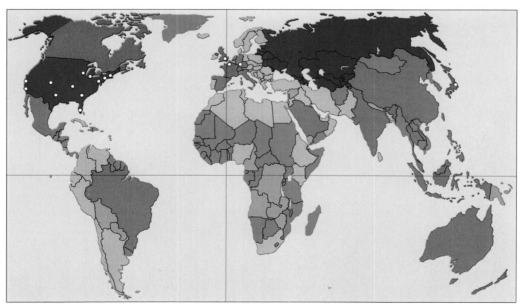

43

QUALITY OF LIFE: HEALTH

According to statistics gathered in the late 1980s and early 1990s, a third of the world's population has no access to safe drinking water: malaria is on the increase; cholera, thought vanquished, is reappearing in South America; an epidemic of the terrifying AIDS virus is gathering force in Africa; and few developing countries can stretch their health care budgets beyond US $2 per person per year.

Yet human beings, by every statistical index, have never been healthier. In the richest nations, where food is plentiful, the demands of daily work are rarely onerous and medical care is both readily available and highly advanced, the average life expectancy is often more than 75 years – approaching the perceived limits for human longevity. In middle-income nations such as Brazil and the Philippines, life expectancy usually extends at least to the mid-60s; in China, it has already reached 70. Even in poverty-stricken Ethiopia and Chad, lifespans are close to 50. Despite economic crisis, drought, famine and even war, every country in the world reported an increase between 1965 and 1990.

It was not always so, even in countries then considered rich. By comparison, in 1880 the life expectancy of an average Berliner was under 30 years and infant mortality in the United Kingdom, then the wealthiest nation, stood at 144 per thousand births – a grim toll exceeded today only by three of the poorest African countries (Mali, Sierra Leone and Guinea). Even by 1910, European death rates were almost twice as high as the world average less than 80 years later; infant mortality in Norway, Europe's healthiest country, was then higher than in present-day Indonesia. In far less than a century, human prospects have improved beyond recognition.

In global terms, the transformation is less the result of high technology medicine – still too expensive for all but a minority, even in rich countries – than of improvements in agriculture and hence nutrition, matched by the widespread diffusion of the basic concepts of disease and public health. One obvious consequence, as death rates everywhere continue to fall, is sustained population growth. Another is the rising expectation of continued improvement felt by both rich and poor nations alike.

In some ways, the task is easier for developing countries, striving with limited resources to attain health levels to which the industrialized world has only recently become accustomed. As the tables below illustrate, infectious disease is rare among the richer nations, while ailments such as cancer, which tend to kill in advanced years, do not seriously impinge on populations with shorter lifespans.

Yet infectious disease is relatively cheap to eliminate, or at least reduce, and it is likely to be easier to raise life expectancy from 60 to 70 than from 75 to 85. The ills of the developed world and its ageing population are more expensive to treat – though most poor countries would be happy to suffer from the problems of the affluent. Western nations regularly spend more money on campaigns to educate their citizens out of over-eating and other bad habits than many developing countries can devote to an entire health budget – an irony that marks the dimensions of the rich-poor divide.

Indeed, wealth itself may be the most reliable indicator of longevity. Harmful habits are usually the province of the rich; yet curiously, though the dangerous effects of tobacco have been proved beyond doubt, the affluent Japanese combine very high cigarette consumption with the longest life expectancy of all the major nations. Similarly, heavy alcohol consumption seems to have no effect on longevity: the French, world leaders in 1988 and in most previous surveys, outlive the more moderate British by a year, and the abstemious Indians by almost two decades.

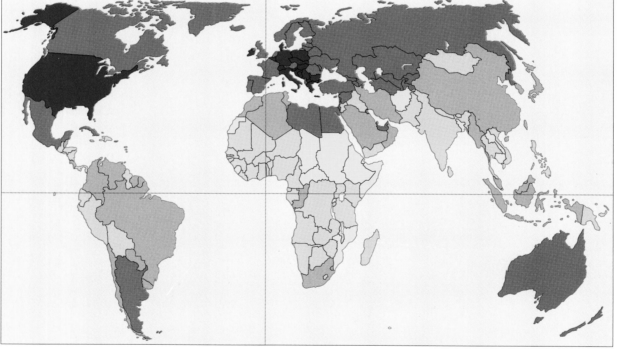

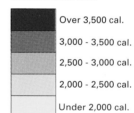

FOOD CONSUMPTION

Average daily food intake per person in calories (1986-1988)

- Over 3,500 cal.
- 3,000 - 3,500 cal.
- 2,500 - 3,000 cal.
- 2,000 - 2,500 cal.
- Under 2,000 cal.

Top 5 countries

Belgium	3,901 cal.
Greece	3,702 cal.
Ireland	3,688 cal.
Bulgaria	3,650 cal.
Germany	3,650 cal.

Bottom 5 countries

Bangladesh	1,925 cal.
Rwanda	1,817 cal.
Sierra Leone	1,813 cal.
Somalia	1,781 cal.
Mozambique	1,604 cal.

[USA 3,645] [UK 3,256]

CAUSES OF DEATH

The rich not only live longer, on average, than the poor; they also die from different causes. Infectious and parasitic diseases, all but eliminated in the developed world, remain a scourge in poorer countries. On the other hand, more than two-thirds of the populations of OECD nations eventually succumb to cancer or circulatory disease; the proportion in Latin America is only about 45%. In addition to the three major diseases shown here, respiratory infection and injury also claim more lives in developing nations, which lack the drugs and medical skills required to treat them.

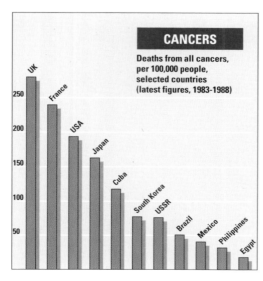

CANCERS

Deaths from all cancers, per 100,000 people, selected countries (latest figures, 1983-1988)

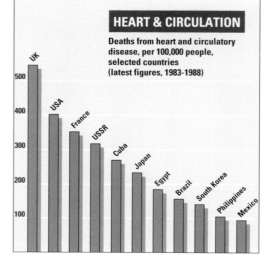

HEART & CIRCULATION

Deaths from heart and circulatory disease, per 100,000 people, selected countries (latest figures, 1983-1988)

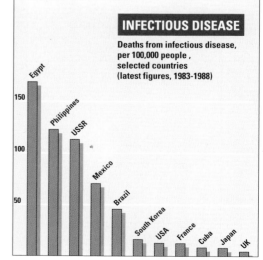

INFECTIOUS DISEASE

Deaths from infectious disease, per 100,000 people, selected countries (latest figures, 1983-1988)

LIFE EXPECTANCY

Years of life expectancy at birth, selected countries (1988-1989)

The chart shows combined data for both sexes. On average, women live longer than men worldwide, even in developing countries with high maternal mortality rates. Overall, life expectancy is steadily rising, though the difference between rich and poor nations remains dramatic.

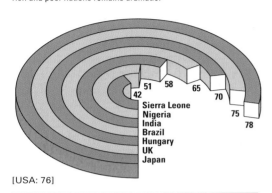

42 Sierra Leone
51 Nigeria
58 India
65 Brazil
70 Hungary
75 UK
78 Japan

[USA: 76]

HOSPITAL CAPACITY

Hospital beds available for each 1,000 people (1983-1988)

Highest capacity		Lowest capacity	
Finland	14.9	Bangladesh	0.2
Sweden	13.2	Nepal	0.2
France	12.9	Ethiopia	0.3
USSR	12.8	Mauritania	0.4
Netherlands	12.0	Mali	0.5
North Korea	11.7	Burkina Faso	0.6
Switzerland	11.3	Pakistan	0.6
Austria	10.4	Niger	0.7
Czechoslovakia	10.1	Haiti	0.8
Hungary	9.1	Chad	0.8

[UK 8] [USA 5.9]

The availability of a bed can mean anything from a private room in a well-equipped Californian teaching hospital to a place in the overcrowded annexe of a rural African clinic. In the Third World especially, quality of treatment can vary enormously from place to place within the same country.

CHILD MORTALITY

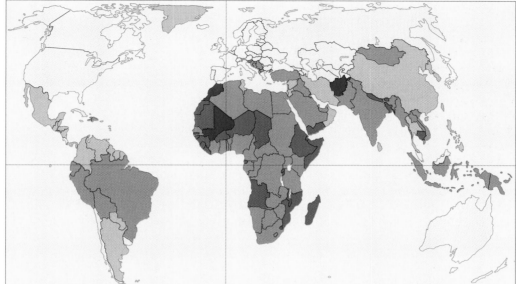

Number of babies who will die before the age of one year, per 1,000 live births (average 1990-95)

- Over 150
- 100 - 150
- 50 - 100
- 20 - 50
- 10 - 20
- Under 10

Highest child mortality

Afghanistan	162
Mali	159

Lowest child mortality

Iceland	5
Finland	5

[USA 9] [UK 8]

MEDICAL PROVISION

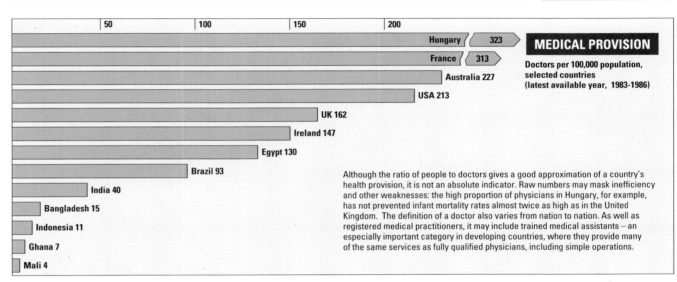

Hungary	323
France	313
Australia	227
USA	213
UK	162
Ireland	147
Egypt	130
Brazil	93
India	40
Bangladesh	15
Indonesia	11
Ghana	7
Mali	4

Doctors per 100,000 population, selected countries (latest available year, 1983-1986)

Although the ratio of people to doctors gives a good approximation of a country's health provision, it is not an absolute indicator. Raw numbers may mask inefficiency and other weaknesses: the high proportion of physicians in Hungary, for example, has not prevented infant mortality rates almost twice as high as in the United Kingdom. The definition of a doctor also varies from nation to nation. As well as registered medical practitioners, it may include trained medical assistants – an especially important category in developing countries, where they provide many of the same services as fully qualified physicians, including simple operations.

THE AIDS CRISIS

The Acquired Immune Deficiency Syndrome was first identified in 1981, when American doctors found otherwise healthy young men succumbing to rare infections. By 1984, the cause had been traced to the Human Immunodeficiency Virus (HIV), which can remain dormant for many years and perhaps indefinitely: only half of those known to carry the virus in 1981 had developed AIDS ten years later.

By 1991 the World Health Organization knew of more than 250,000 AIDS cases worldwide and suspected the true number to be at least four times as high. In Western countries in the early 1990s, most AIDS deaths were among male homosexuals or needle-sharing drug-users. However, the disease is spreading fastest among heterosexual men and women, which is its usual vector in the Third World, where most of its victims live. Africa is the most severely hit: a 1992 UN report estimated that 2 million African children will die of AIDS before the year 2000 – and some 10 million will be orphaned.

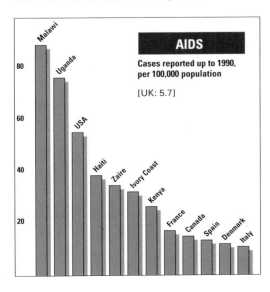

AIDS

Cases reported up to 1990, per 100,000 population

[UK: 5.7]

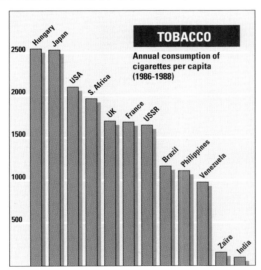

TOBACCO

Annual consumption of cigarettes per capita (1986-1988)

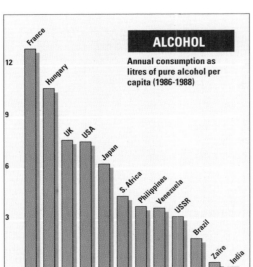

ALCOHOL

Annual consumption as litres of pure alcohol per capita (1986-1988)

CRIME & PUNISHMENT

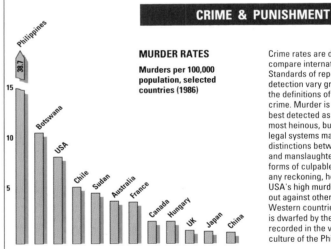

MURDER RATES

Murders per 100,000 population, selected countries (1986)

Crime rates are difficult to compare internationally. Standards of reporting and detection vary greatly, as do the definitions of many types of crime. Murder is probably the best detected as well as the most heinous, but different legal systems make different distinctions between murder and manslaughter or other forms of culpable homicide. By any reckoning, however, the USA's high murder rate stands out against otherwise similar Western countries, although it is dwarfed by the killings recorded in the very different culture of the Philippines.

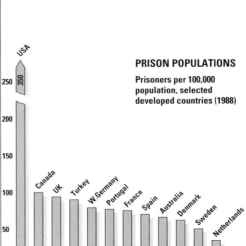

PRISON POPULATIONS

Prisoners per 100,000 population, selected developed countries (1988)

Differences in prison population reflect penal policies as much as the relative honesty or otherwise of different nations, and by no means all governments publish accurate figures. In more than 50 countries, people are still regularly imprisoned without trial, in 60 torture is a normal part of interrogation, and some 130 retain the death penalty, often administered for political crimes and in secret. Over 2,000 executions were recorded in 1990 by the civil rights organization Amnesty International; the real figure, as Amnesty itself maintains, was almost certainly much higher.

QUALITY OF LIFE: ENVIRONMENT

Humans have always had a dramatic effect on their environment, at least since the invention of agriculture almost 10,000 years ago. Generally, the Earth has accepted human interference without obvious ill effects: the complex systems that regulate the global environment have absorbed substantial damage while maintaining a stable and comfortable home for the planet's trillions of lifeforms. But advancing human technology and the rapidly expanding populations it supports are now threatening to overwhelm the Earth's ability to cope.

Industrial wastes, acid rainfall, expanding deserts and large-scale deforestation all combine to create environmental change at a rate far faster than the Earth can accommodate. Equipped with chain-saws and flame-throwers, humans can now destroy more forest in a day than their ancestors could in a century, upsetting the balance between plant and animal, carbon dioxide and oxygen, on which all life ultimately depends. The fossil fuels that power industrial civilization have pumped enough carbon dioxide and other greenhouse gases into the atmosphere to make climatic change a near-certainty. Chlorofluorocarbons (CFCs) and other man-made chemicals are rapidly eroding the ozone layer, the planet's screen against ultra-violet radiation.

As a result, the Earth's average temperature has risen by approximately 0.5°C since the beginning of this century. Further rises seem inevitable, with 1990 marked as the hottest year worldwide since records began. A warmer Earth probably means a wetter Earth, with melting icecaps raising sea levels and causing severe flooding in some of the world's most densely populated regions. Other climatic models suggest an alternative doom: rising temperatures could increase cloud cover, reflecting more solar energy back into space and causing a new ice age.

Either way, the consequences for humans could be disastrous – perhaps the Earth's own way of restoring ecological balance over the next few thousand years. Fortunately, there is a far faster mechanism available. Human ingenuity has provoked the present crisis; but human ingenuity, inspired if need be by fear, can respond to it. Production of CFCs is already almost at a standstill, and the first faltering steps towards stabilization and ultimately reduction of carbon dioxide have been taken, with Denmark pioneering the way by taxing emissions in 1991.

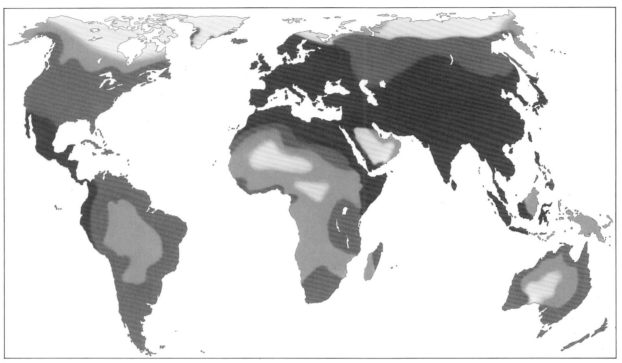

THE HISTORY OF HUMAN EXPANSION

The growth of ecological control: areas where human activity dominates the environment, from primitive times to the year 2000

By 1500 AD

By 1900 AD

By 2000 AD

Areas not dominated by human activity

THE RISE IN CARBON DIOXIDE

Emissions of carbon dioxide in millions of tonnes, 1950-1991

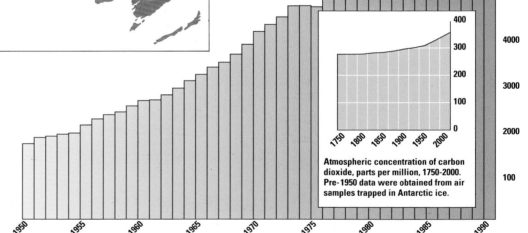

Atmospheric concentration of carbon dioxide, parts per million, 1750-2000. Pre-1950 data were obtained from air samples trapped in Antarctic ice.

Since the beginning of the Industrial Revolution, human activity has pumped steadily more carbon dioxide into the atmosphere. Most was quietly absorbed by the oceans, whose immense 'sink' capacity meant that 170 years were needed for levels to increase from the pre-industrial 280 parts per million to 300 (inset graph). But the vast increase in fuel-burning since 1950 (main graph) has overwhelmed even the oceanic sink. Atmospheric concentrations are now rising almost as steeply as carbon dioxide emissions themselves.

GREENHOUSE POWER

Relative contributions to the greenhouse effect by the major heat-absorbing gases in the atmosphere

The chart combines greenhouse potency and volume. Carbon dioxide has a greenhouse potential of only 1 but its concentration of 350 parts per million, makes it predominate. CFC 12 , with 25,000 times the absorption capacity of CO_2, is present only as 0.00044 ppm.

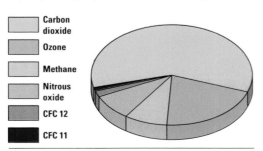

Carbon dioxide

Ozone

Methane

Nitrous oxide

CFC 12

CFC 11

CARBON DIOXIDE

Carbon dioxide released in millions of tonnes (1980s)

Although most of the net increase in atmospheric carbon dioxide comes from fossil fuel combustion, deforestation and changing land use also contribute

Fuel burning

Deforestation

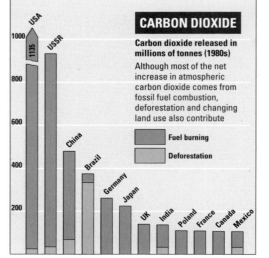

GLOBAL WARMING

The rise in average temperatures caused by carbon dioxide and other greenhouse gases (1960-2020)

assumes present trends continue

assumes drastic emissions cuts in the 1990s

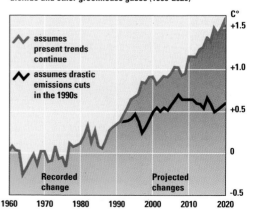

COPYRIGHT GEORGE PHILIP LTD.

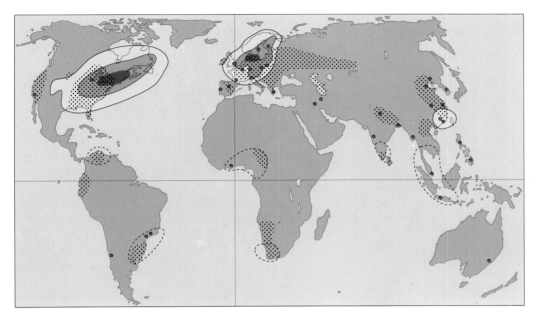

ACID RAIN

Acid rainfall & sources of acidic emissions (1980s)

Acid rain is caused when sulphur & nitrogen oxides in the air combine with water vapour to form sulphuric, nitric & other acids.

 Regions where sulphur and nitrogen oxides are released in high concentrations, mainly from fossil fuel combustion.

• Major cities with high levels of air pollution (including nitrogen & sulphur emissions)

Areas of heavy acid deposition

pH numbers indicate acidity, decreasing from a neutral 7. Normal rain, slightly acid from dissolved carbon dioxide, never exceeds a pH of 5.6.

pH less than 4.0 (most acidic)
pH 4.0 to 4.5
pH 4.5 to 5.0

- - - Areas where acid rain is a potential danger

THE ANTARCTIC

The vast Antarctic ice-sheet, containing some 70% of the Earth's fresh water, plays a crucial role in the circulation of atmosphere and oceans and hence in determining the planetary climate. The frozen southern continent is also the last remaining wilderness – the largest area to remain free from human colonization.

Ever since Amundsen and Scott raced for the South Pole in 1911, various countries have pressed territorial claims over sections of Antarctica, spurred in recent years by its known and suspected mineral wealth: enough iron ore to supply the world at present levels for 200 years, large oil reserves and, probably, the biggest coal deposits on Earth.

However, the 1961 Antarctic Treaty set aside the area for peaceful uses only, guaranteeing freedom of scientific investigation, banning waste disposal and nuclear testing, and suspending the issue of territorial rights. By 1990, the original 12 signatories had grown to 25, with a further 15 nations granted observer status in subsequent deliberations. However, the Treaty itself was threatened by wrangles between different countries, government agencies and international pressure groups.

Finally, in July, 1991, the belated agreement of the UK and the US assured unanimity on a new accord to ban all mineral exploration for a further 50 years. The ban can only be rescinded if all present signatories, plus a majority of any future adherents, agree. While the treaty has always lacked a formal mechanism for enforcement, it is firmly underwritten by public concern generated by the efforts of environmental pressure groups such as Greenpeace, foremost in the campaign to have Antarctica declared a 'World Park'.

It seems likely that the virtually uninhabited continent will remain untouched by tourism, nuclear-free and dedicated to peaceful scientific research.

DESERTIFICATION

Existing deserts
Areas with a high risk of desertification
Areas with a moderate risk of desertification
Former areas of rainforest
Existing rainforest

DEFORESTATION

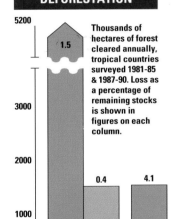

Thousands of hectares of forest cleared annually, tropical countries surveyed 1981-85 & 1987-90. Loss as a percentage of remaining stocks is shown in figures on each column.

	Brazil	India	Indonesia	Burma	Thailand	Vietnam	Philippines	Costa Rica	Cameroon
1987-90	1.5	4.1	0.8	2.1	2.5	2.0	1.5	7.6	0.6
1981-85	0.4	0.3	0.5	0.3	2.4	0.7	1.0	4.0	0.4

WATER POLLUTION

Severely polluted sea areas & lakes
Less polluted sea areas & lakes
Areas of frequent oil pollution by shipping
Major oil tanker spills ◣
Major oil rig blow outs ▲
Offshore dumpsites for industrial & municipal waste ▼
Severely polluted rivers & estuaries ───

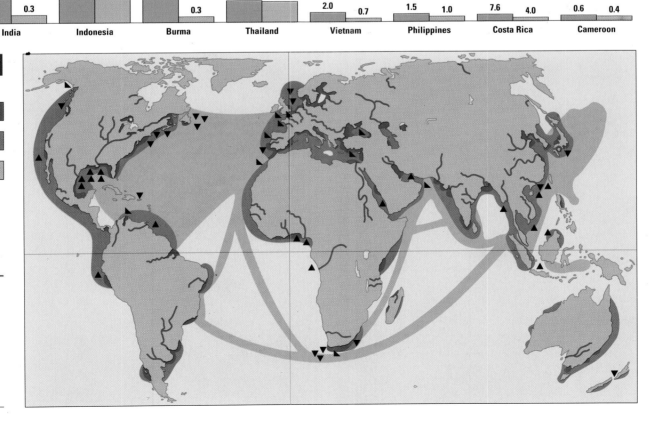

Poisoned rivers, domestic sewage and oil spillage have combined in recent years to reduce the world's oceans to a sorry state of contamination, notably near the crowded coasts of industrialized nations. Shipping routes, too, are constantly affected by tanker discharges. Oil spills of all kinds, however, declined significantly during the 1980s, from a peak of 750,000 tonnes in 1979 to under 50,000 tonnes in 1990. The most notorious tanker spill of that period – when the *Exxon Valdez* (94,999 gross registered tonnes) ran aground in Prince William Sound, Alaska, in March 1989 – released only 267,000 barrels, a relatively small amount compared to the results of blow-outs and war damage (see table). The worst tanker accident in history occurred in July 1979, when the *Atlantic Empress* and the *Aegean Captain* collided off Trinidad.

CITY MAPS

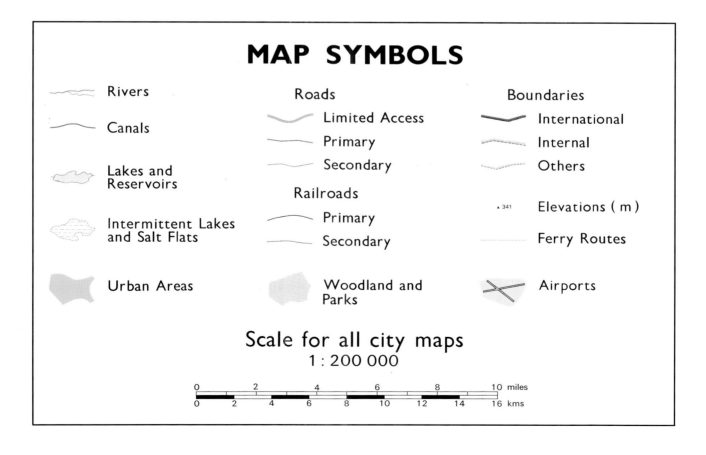

MAP SYMBOLS

Rivers	Roads	Boundaries
Canals	Limited Access	International
	Primary	Internal
Lakes and Reservoirs	Secondary	Others
Intermittent Lakes and Salt Flats	Railroads	• 341 Elevations (m)
	Primary	Ferry Routes
	Secondary	
Urban Areas	Woodland and Parks	Airports

Scale for all city maps
1 : 200 000

0	2	4	6	8	10 miles
0	2 4	6 8	10 12	14	16 kms

1: 200 000

5 miles
8 km

Grid columns (top): 1 2 3 4 5 6

Utvika
Bruløkka
Nordmarka
Glosli
Frog
Venner
Slakteren
Turter
Slattum
Nittedal
Huseby
Sørkedalen
Sandermosen
451
Skytta
60
Tryvass-høgda
531
Maridalen
407
Skedsmo
Homledal
418
Bogstadvatnet
Sognsvatn
Kjeller
Sollihøgda
Holmenkollen
Kjelsås
Alnsjøen
Vestli
Lillestrøm
Burudvatn
Røa
Ris
Ullevål
Grorud
Stovner
Strømmen
Bærums Verk
Ila
OSLO
Høybråten
Rud
Rustad
Lijordet
Skøyen
Ulleväl
Akerselva
Grefsen
Alnabru
Øyeren
Smestad
Haslum
Sagene
Bryn
Kolsås
Universitetet
Tøyen
Østre Aker
363
Lørenskog
B
379
Bærum
Lysaker
Bygdøy
Domkirke
Sentrist
Gamlebyen
Lutvatn
Skui
Stabekk
Akerhus Festning
Oppsal
Nordre Elvåga
Ärnes
Toverud
Hovik
Hovedøya
Lindøya
Ekeberg
Bøler
Rælingen
Sylling
Sandvika
Snarøya
Ormøya
Lambert Seter
Nøklevatn
Ramstadsjøen
Slependen
Nesøya
Ostøya
Fornebu
Nordstrand
Østmark-kapellet
Semsvän
Brønnøya
Nesoddtangen
Malmøya
Ljan
Søndre Elvåga
Nordbysjøen
Hvalstad
Flaskebekk
Oksval
Skullerud
Asker
Skoklefall
Hauketo
Sørsdal
Hvalstrand
59 50
Bonnefjorden
Klemetsrud
Tonekollen 368
Lierskogen
Blakstad
215
Sandbakken
Mosjøen
Tranby
Vollen
Oslofjorden
Sørby
Ingierstrand
Vardåsen 374
Skogen
Dikemark
Nesodden
Kolbotn
Krokhol
Lie
Gjellumvatn
Fjellstrand
Hasle
Gjersjøen
Siggerud
Bru
Børtervatna
Frogner
Reistad
Svestad
Oppegård
Myrvoll
Binningsvatna
Nærsnes
Slemmestad
Garder
134
Oppegård
Langen

Grid columns (bottom): 7 8 9 10 11

Gerlev
Øverød
Jægersborg
Skodsborg
Oslo
Stavnsholt
Søllerød
Hegn
Snostrup
Holte
Nærum
Farum
Ørholm
Møllea
Lille Rørbæk
Ganløse Orned
Lundtofte
Ølstykke
Farum Sø
Furesø
Brede
Hjortekær
Tårbæk
Skuldelev
Ganløse
Lille Værløse
Virum
Jægersborg Dyrehave
Svestrup
Frederiksdal
Klampenborg
Østby
Stenløse
Søndersø
Store Hareskov 42
Kongens Lyngby
Jyllinge
Jonstrup
Bagsværd Sø
Ordrup
Skovshoved
Roskilde Fjord
Værebro Å
Hareskovby
Vangede
Jægersborg
Sønderby
Måløv
Bagsværd
Gentofte
Charlottenlund
Smørumnedre
Gladsakse
Buddinge
Hellerup
Hove Å
Pederstrup
Hjortespring
Søborg
Bognæs
Ågerup
Ballerup
Herlev
Svanemøllen
Kattinge Vig
Skovlunde
Husum
Bispebjerg
Nybølle
Ledøje
Utterslev Mose
Trekroner
Risby
Ejby
Brønshøj
Refshaleøen
KØBENHAVN
Fælled-parken
Sengeløse
Vestskoven
Islev
Lillebavfrue
Herstedøster
Vanløse
Rosenborg Have
Vasby
Rødovre
Frederiksberg
Amalienborg Slot
Zoo
Hovedbanegård
Christianshavn
55 40
Store Kattingesø
Glostrup
Brøndbyøster
Valby
Sundbyerne
Albertslund
Svogerslev
Tåstrup
Hvidovre
Kastrup
Drogden
Saltholm
Roskilde
Hedehusene
Vallensbæk
Avedøre
Kalveboderne
Tårnby
Tranegilde
Brøndbyvester
Store Magleby
Kastrup Lufthavn
Sterkende
Ishøj Strand
Brøndby Strand
Amager
Vallensbæk Strand
Hundige
Ullerup
Dragør
Tune
Hundige Strand
Kongelunden
Sydstranden
Gadstrup
Mosede
Mosede Strand
Søvang
Snoldelev
Greve Strand
Viby
Havdrup
Karlslunde Strand
Køge Bugt
AFLANDSHAGE

East from Greenwich

COPYRIGHT GEORGE PHILIP & SON LTD

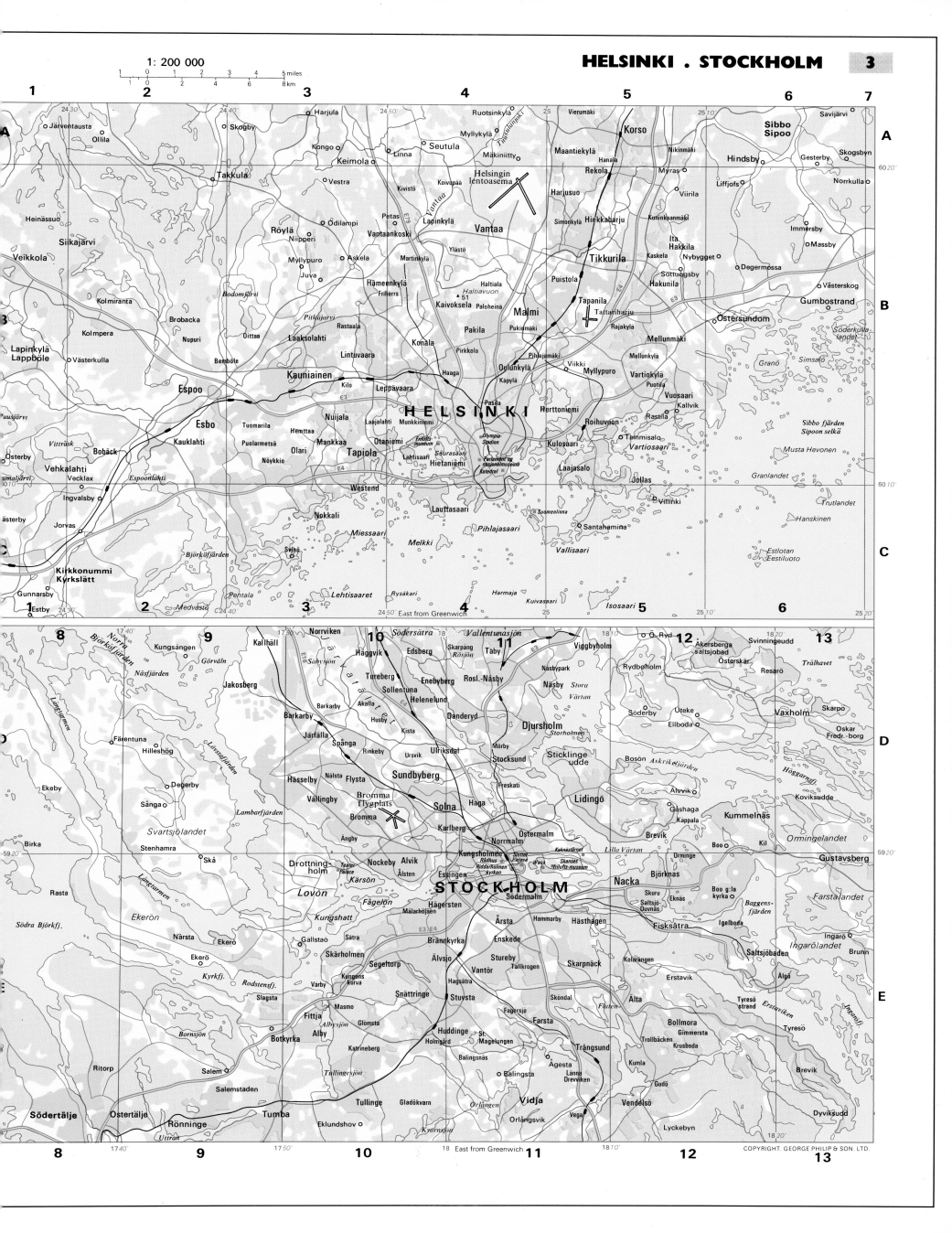

1: 200 000

5 miles
8 km

A B C D

7 7

Blackmore · Heybridge · Doddinghurst · Mountnessing · Ingrave · Herongate · Shenfield · **Brentwood** · Orsett · Chadwell St. Mary · Little Thurrock · Tilbury · Northfleet · Singlewell · Istead Rise · Meopham · Culverstone Green · Stanstead · Trottiscliffe · Borough Green

Chipping Ongar · Kelvedon Hatch · Pilgrims Hatch · Weald Park · Brook Street · Cranham · Corbets Tey · South Ockendon · North Stifford · West Thurrock · Grays · Greenhithe · Stone · Swanscombe · New Ash Green · West Kingsdown · Kemsing · Sevenoaks

6 6

Toot Hill · Stapleford Abbotts · Harold Hill · Harold Wood · Gallows Corner · Squirrel's Heath · Heath Park · Emerson Park · **Upminster** · **Hornchurch** · Rainham · Wennington · Purfleet · Aveley · **Dartford** · Sutton at Hone · Horton Kirby · South Darenth · Bank Hatch · Hartley · Farningham · Eynsford · Shoreham · Otford · Dunton Green · Riverhead

Epping · Theydon Bois · Abridge · Chigwell · **Rowhatch** · Hainault · Newbury Park · Seven Kings · Rush Green · **Dagenham** · Beacontree Heath · Chadwell Heath · Creekmouth · Thamesmead · Belvedere · Erith · Northumberland Heath · Slade Green · Barnehurst · **Bexleyheath** · Welling · East Wickham · Crayford · Hextable · Wilmington · **Bexley** · North Cray · St. Paul's Cray · Swanley · Crockenhill · Badgers Mount · Chelsfield Village · Pratts Bottom · Knockholt Pound · Westerham

5 5

Cheshunt · Waltham Abbey · High Beach · **Loughton** · **Woodford** · Woodford Green · **Chingford** · Buckhurst Hill · **Ilford** · **Redbridge** · Gants Hill · Barkingside · Clayhall · **Barking** · East Ham · **Woolwich** · Plumstead · Abbey Wood · West Heath · **Eltham** · Blackfen · Sidcup · Foots Cray · Longlands · Chislehurst · Mottingham · St. Mary Cray · **Orpington** · Petts Wood · Chislehurst West · Bickley · Southborough · Locksbottom · Farnborough · Keston Mark · Leaves Green · Downe · Cudham · Tatsfield

4 4

Potters Bar · **Enfield** · Ponders End · Upper Edmonton · Lower Edmonton · **Tottenham** · **Walthamstow** · **Stratford** · **Leyton** · **Hackney** · **Poplar** · **Greenwich** · **Lewisham** · **Catford** · Charlton · Blackheath · Lee · Hither Green · Grove Park · Bellingham · **Bromley** · Shortlands · Hayes · West Wickham · Addington · New Addington · Selsdon · Sanderstead · **Warlingham** · **Caterham** · Woldingham

Barnet · East Barnet · **Wood Green** · **Haringey** · Hornsey · Crouch End · **Islington** · Finsbury Park · Holborn · **City** · Shoreditch · **Stepney** · Bermondsey · Rotherhithe · Deptford · **Camberwell** · **Peckham** · Nunhead · Dulwich · Forest Hill · Sydenham · Penge · **Beckenham** · Elmers End · Shirley · Woodside · **Croydon** · Addiscombe · **Purley** · Kenley · Whyteleafe · Coulsdon · Old Coulsdon

3 3

Borehamwood · Edgware · **Hendon** · **Wembley** · **Willesden** · Acton · **Hammersmith** · **Kensington** · **Chelsea** · **Fulham** · **Wandsworth** · **Battersea** · Clapham · Brixton · **Streatham** · Balham · Tooting · **Mitcham** · Wallington · Carshalton · Beddington · **Sutton** · **Banstead** · Burgh Heath · Kingswood · Chipstead

Stanmore · **Harrow** · Pinner · Northolt · **Greenford** · **Ealing** · **Chiswick** · **Brentford** · **Richmond** · Barnes · Roehampton · Putney · **Wimbledon** · Merton · Morden · New Malden · **Kingston upon Thames** · Surbiton · Tolworth · Worcester Park · North Cheam · Cheam · **Epsom** · Ashtead · Tadworth · **Leatherhead** · Headley

2 2

Chipperfield · Abbots Langley · **Watford** · Croxley Green · **Rickmansworth** · Bushey · South Oxhey · Ruislip · Eastcote · Hayes · **Hillingdon** · **Uxbridge** · West Drayton · Yiewsley · **Staines** · East Bedfont · **Heathrow Airport** · Hatton · Cranford · **Hounslow** · Heston · Isleworth · **Twickenham** · Teddington · Hampton · Sunbury · Shepperton · **Walton on the Hill** · Hampton Court Palace · **Thames Ditton** · **Long Ditton** · East Molesey · **Esher** · Hersham · **Claygate** · Oxshott · Cobham · Stoke D'Abernon · **Weybridge** · Byfleet · **Great Bookham** · **Fetcham** · **East Horsley** · Ripley

1 1

1 : 200 000

0 1 2 3 4 5 miles
1 0 2 4 6 8 km

PARIS

East from Greenwich

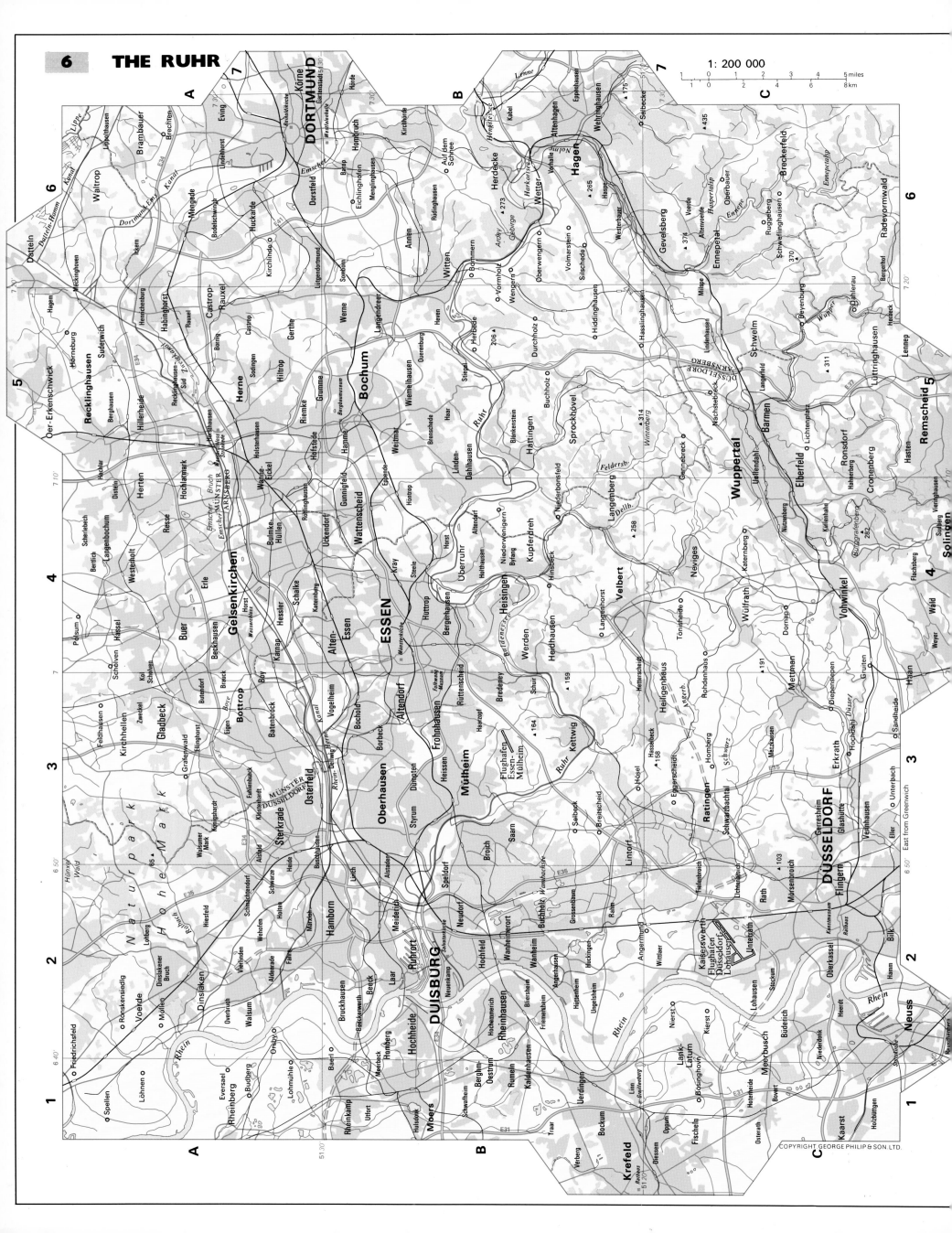

1 : 200 000

0 1 2 3 4 5 miles
0 2 4 6 8 km

BERLIN

Potsdam · Hennigsdorf · Falkensee · Spandau · Charlottenburg · Tiergarten · Wedding · Reinickendorf · Pankow · Weissensee · Mitte · Kreuzberg · Schöneberg · Neukölln · Treptow · Steglitz · Zehlendorf · Tempelhof · Köpenick · Wannsee · Nikolassee · Grunewald

Flughafen Tegel · Flughafen Tempelhof · Flughafen Schönefeld

Olympic Stadium · Teufelsberg · Müggelberge · Grosse Müggelsee

HAMBURG

Quickborn · Norderstedt · Pinneberg · Garstedt · Langenhorn · Poppenbüttel · Sasel · Fuhlsbüttel · Ohlsdorf · Brämfeld · Farmsen · Wandsbek · Eidelstedt · Stellingen · Eimsbüttel · Bahrenfeld · Altona · St. Pauli · Blankenese · Harvestehude · Barmbek · Winterhude · Billstedt · Billbrook · Wilhelmsburg · Harburg · Neu Wulmstorf · Neugraben-Fischbek

Flughafen Hamburg

MÜNCHEN

Dachau · Unterschleissheim · Oberschleissheim · Garching · Karlsfeld · Feldmoching · Ismaning · Allach · Moosach · Milbertshofen · Schwabing · Bogenhausen · Nymphenburg · Neuhausen · Pasing · Laim · Sendling · Giesing · Gräfelfing · Planegg · Krailling · Harlaching · Solln · Grünwald · Pullach · Oberhaching · Unterhaching · Ottobrunn · Neubiberg · Hohenbrunn · Taufkirchen

Flughafen München-Riem · Englischer Garten · Deutsches Museum · Forstenrieder Park

East from Greenwich

1: 200 000

5 miles
8 km

MADRID . BARCELONA . LISBON . ATHENS

MEDITERRANEAN SEA

BARCELONA
Badalona
San Adrián de Besós
Sta. Coloma de Gramanet
San Joan
La Puntuala
Cian
303 Poyo
151
Mongat
Besós
Santa Eulalia
Llano de Can Gineu
La Taxonera
Vallcalca
La Floresta
Sant Cugat
Valldoreix
Santa Cruz de Olorde
Tibidabo
512
S. Pedro de Bertí
Vallvidrera
435
La Sagrera
Guinardó
Gracia
San Martín
La Llacuna
Pueblo Nuevo
Barceloneta
Puxet
Sarriá
Las Corts
Sans
Pedralbes
387
389
San Martin
S. Just Martir
Desvern
Esplugas
Hospitalet
Cornellá
S. Feliu de Llobregat
Joan Despi
Molins de Rey
336
Madrona
Papiol
Torrellas de Llobregat
Colonia Güell
Beri
Sant Boi de Llobregat
Santa Coloma de Cervelló
S. Vicenc dels Horts
Palleja
Castelbisbal
Prat de Llobregat
Viladecans
Gavá
Gavamar
S. Clemente del Llobregat
La Pineda
Aeropuerto da Barcelona-Prat
Laguna de la Ricarda
Laguna del Rémola
Río Llobregat
East from Greenwich
2° 10′
41° 20′

MADRID
El Pardo
Las Rozas de Madrid
Majadahonda
Boadilla del Monte
Pozuelo de Alarcón
El Plantío
Aravaca
La Estación
Fuencarral
La Moraleja
680
Valdeveba
Barajas
Hortaleza
Canillas
Mamoteras
Almaira
Tetuán
Chamartín
Ciudad Lineal
Canillejas
Ciudad Fin de Semana
703
Guardias
Paracuellos del Jarama
Aeropuerto Transoceánico de Barajas
San Fernando de Henares
Barrio de La Estación
Rivas de Jarama
Rivas-Vaciamadrid
Cumbres de Vallecas
655
Vicálvaro
San Cristobal
Canteras de Vallecas
633
Salmedina
581
Pueblo Nuevo
Moratalaz
Vicálvaro
Vallecas
Mediodia
Mercamadrid
Perales del Rio
Cerro de los Angeles
Villaverde Bajo
Villaverde
Getafe
Leganés
Alcorcón
Móstoles
Campamento
Carabanchel Bajo
Carabanchel Alto
Cuatro Vientos
La Fortuna
705
Ventorro del Cano
Chamberi
Universidad
Latina
Usera
Retiro
Argüelles
Legazpi
Los Angeles
Entrevias
Palomeras
Buenavista
Progreso
Ventas
Manzanares
Casa de Campo
Avda. de Andalucía
West from Greenwich
3° 40′
40° 30′
40° 20′

LISBOA
Moscavide
Sacavém
S. João da Talha
Olivais
Beato
Apelação
163
Fetelas
Camarate
108
Olhos
Povoa de Santo Adrião
Charneca
Amexoeira
Campo Grande
Lumiar
Pontinha
Carnide
Benfica
228
Monsanto
Alcántara
Santo Amaro
Ajuda
Belém
Algés
Caxias
Paço de Arcos
Oeiras
Cruz de Pau
Amora
Seixal
Arrentela
Paio Pires
Amora
Sobreda
125
Raposo
Cova da Piedade
Almada
Cacilhas
Trafaria
Costa da Caparica
Caparica
Capuchos
Porto Brandão
Torre de Belém
Camarões
357
Queluz
Massamá
Agualva-Cacem
Río de Mouro
Telhal
Venda Seca
Tapada
283
Belas
Barcarena
Linda-a-Pastora
Queijas
210
Sabugo
Piedade
220
Talaíde
Leião
Barcarena
Terrugem
Bucelas
Amadora
Damaia
Buraca
Amoreira
Paia
Odivelas
Lisboa
Airoporto da Portela
Alto do Pina
B. Lopes
Sta. Apolonia Station
Barreiro
Montijo
Base Aérea
Alcochete
Lagoa da Pedra
Montio
Samoueo
Sarilhos Pequenos
Sarilhos Grandes
Moita
Rosairinho
Lavradio
Baixa da Banheira
Alhos Vedros
Santo António da Charneca
Santo André
Palhais
Coina
Tejo
Atlantic Ocean
West from Greenwich
9° 10′
38° 40′

ATHÍNAI
Drafi
Pallini
Hristoupoli
Spata
Gerakas
Pikermi
Markopoulo
Koropi
Peania
Karellas
Kitsi
Batako
230
Kalivia Thorikou
Vari
Khalándrion
Filothéi
Psikhikón
Kholargós
Zografos
Néa Ionía
Néa Lionía
Filadhelfia
Kipseli
Neapolis
Galátsion
Patisia
Kaisariani
Viron
Imittós
Ilioúpolis
N. Alexandhria
765
1026
Évzonos
Vouliagménis
Petroupolis
Verdi
Peristérion
Ayialeo
Tavros
Kallithéa
N. Smírni
P. Faliron
Kalamákion
Elliniko
Athinai Ellinikón Airport
Voula
Glifada
Voúla
Vouliagméni
Dháfni
Áy. Dhimitrios
Áyios Rendis
N. Faliron
Nikaia
Koridhallós
Khaidhárion
468
Dhrapetsóna
Piraévs
Skaramangás
Ag Ghergios
Dhifistina
Aigáleos Oros
Ormos Falírou
Imittós Oros
Sarónikós Kólpos
Kíthnos
Sífnos
Kithnos
East from Greenwich
23° 40′
23° 50′
37° 50′

COPYRIGHT GEORGE PHILIP AND SON LTD.

1 : 200 000

5 miles
8 km

Major places:

Monza, Lissone, Desio, **Cinisello Balsamo**, **Sesto S. Giovanni**, Brugherio, Cologno Monz., Cernusco s. Nav., Pioltello, Segrate, **Aeroporto di Linate**, **MILANO**, **Baggio**, **Córsico**, **Rho**, Bollate, Baréggio, Cornaredo

TORINO, **Settimo Tor.**, **Caselle Tor.**, **Aeroporto di Caselle**, **Chieri**, **Moncalieri**, **Nichelino**, **Mirafiori**, **Grugliasco**, Collegno, **Venaria**, **Alpignano**, **Rivoli**, Rivalta di Torino, Orbassano, Pianezza

NÁPOLI, **Torre del Greco**, **Torre Annunziata**, **Bosco-trecase**, **Boscoreale**, Ercolano, Pórtici, Barra, **S. Giorgio a Crem.**, Pompei, **Acerra**, **Afragola**, **Casória**, **Arzano**, **Frattamaggiore**, **Giugliano in Camp.**, **Caivano**, **Marano di Náp.**, Ottaviano, S. Giuseppe Vesuviano, **Vesuvio**, Mte Somma 1132, Vómero, Posíllipo, **Campi Flegrei**

ROMA, **CITTÀ DEL VATICANO**, **E.U.R.**, Ostiense, Cinecittà, Centocelle, Quadraro, Acília, Torrevécchia, Primavalle, Montespaccato, Monteverde Nuovo, Magliana, **Aeroporto Intercontinentale Leonardo da Vinci**, **Aeroporto di Ciampino**, Ponte Galéria

Golfo di Nápoli

COPYRIGHT GEORGE PHILIP & SON LTD.

1 : 200 000

1 0 1 2 3 4 5 miles
1 0 1 2 3 4 5 6 7 8 km

WARSZAWA

Wołomin, Kobyłka, Maciołki, Grabicz, Turów, Ossów, Zielonka, Wesoła, Stara Miłosna, Sulejówek, Groszówka, Zbójna Góra, Michalin, Otwock, Józefów, Falenica, Radość, Międzylesie, Anin, Marysin Wawerski, Rembertów, Marki, Ząbki, Drewnica, Kawęczyn, Wygoda, Grochów, Wawer, Zerzeń, Błota, Bartyki, Powsin, Okrzeszyn, Ulrata, Targówek, Praga, Saska, Kępa, Sielce, Czerniaków, Sadyba, Wilanów, Powsinek, Wolica, Natolin, Kabaty, Pyry, Wyczółki, Imielin, Moczydło, Grabów, Grodzisk, Brzeziny, Białołęka Dworska, Bródno, Henryków, Marcelin, Pelcowizna, Stare Miasto, Muranów, Powiśle, Śródmieście, Mokotów, Wierzbno, Służew, Raków, Okęcie, Okęcie Airport, Jaworowa, Dawidy, Łady, Falenty, Marymont, Żoliborz, Wola, Ochota, Szczęśliwice, Czyste, Włochy, Ursus, Opacz, Michałowice, Sokołów, Janki, Wolica, Tarchomin, Bielany, Młociny, Koło, Bemowo, Górce, Jelonki, Odolany, Raszyn, Salomea, Zatusy, Opo, Golabki, Nowe-Babice, Blizne, Chrzanów, Wieruchów, Komorów, Wólka Węglowa, Wawrzyszew, Laski, Klaudyn, Macierzysz, Ożarów-Franciszków, Piastów, Pruszków, Dąbrowa, Sieraków, Izabelin, Homówek, Lipków, Janów, Stare Babice, Tworki

PRAHA

Stará Boleslav, Brandýs nad Labem, Zápy, Jirný, N. Šibřina, Šibřina, Roztoky, Libeznice, Měšice, Sluhy, Zeleneč, Újezd nad Lesy, Říčany, Koloděje, Kolovraty, Libčice nad Vltavou, Hovorčovice, Radonice, Horní Počernice, Klánovice, Šestajovice, Přezletice, Vinoř, Chvaly, Dolní Počernice, Běchovice, Uhříněves, Petrovice, Průhonice, Zdiby, Klecany, Čakovice, Kbely, Letňany, Dolní, Horní, Kyje, Měcholupy, Michovice, Satalice, Klíčov, Štěrboholy, Hostivař, Dubeč, Čimice, Kobylisy, Troja, Dolní Chabry, Prosek, Vysočany, Žižkov, Hloubětín, Hostavice, Hrdlořezy, Malešice, Strašnice, Zábehlice, Hostivař, Spořilov, Kunratice, Šeberov, Suchdol, Děvice, Dejvice, Střešovice, Holešovice, Karlín, Libeň, Vinohrady, Nusle, Michle, Krč, Libuš, Písnice, Roztoky, Bubeneč, Veleslavín, Střešovice, Hradčany, Staré Město, Nové Město, Vyšehrad, Podolí, Braník, Modřany, Horoměřice, Lysolaje, Radlice, Smíchov, Velká Chuchle, Statenice, Nebušice, Praha-Ruzyně Airport, Ruzyně, Řepy, Zličín, Jinonice, Stodůlky, Hlubočepy, Košíře, Jinočany, Zbuzany, Ořech, Slivenec, Lochkov, Radotín, Réporyje, Třebonice, Zbraslav

WIEN

Deutsch-Wagram, Helmahof, Parbasdorf, Aderklaa, Raasdorf, Grossenzersdorf, Oberhausen, Mühlleiten, Essling, Aspern, Breitenlee, Süssenbrunn, Neusiessenbrunn, Kapellerfeld, Gerasdorf bei Wien, Hirschstetten, Stadlau, Biberhaufen, Mannsworth, Schwechat, Föhrenhain, Deutsch-Wagram, Oberlisse, Stammersdorf, Leopoldau, Kagran, Donaufeld, Floridsdorf, Kaisermühlen, Simmering, Zentralfriedhof, Nordbahn, Jedlesee, Messe, Freudenau, Kaiserebersdorf, Kledering, Rannersdorf, Bisamberg, Langenzersdorf, Strebersdorf, Grossjedlersdorf, Nussdorf, Heiligenstadt, Brigittenau, Leopoldstadt, Landstrasse, Favoriten, Rothneusiedl, Unterlaa, Oberlaa, Klosterneuburg, Kritzendorf, Kierling, Weidling, Grinzing, Sievering, Döbling, Währing, Hernals, Ottakring, Alsergrund, Margareten, Meidling, Penzing, Atzgersdorf, Inzersdorf, Vösendorf, Erlaa, Liesing, Perchtoldsdorf, St. Andrä, Wolfpassing, Kierlingbach, Weidlingbach, Salmannsdorf, Neustift am Walde, Neuwaldegg, Dornbach, Rudolfsheim, Hütteldorf, Hietzing, St. Veit, Speising, Mauer, Kalksburg, Rodaun, Siebenhirten, Unterkirchbach, Oberkirchbach, Scheiblingstein, Hadersdorf, Mauerbach, Steinbach, Am Steinhof, Baumgarten, Lainz, Herzogberg, Altmannsdorf, Hinterhainbach, Vordereinbach, Untermauerbach, Steinriegel, Kaltenleutgeben, Wiener Wald, Lainzer Tiergarten, Laab im Walde, Eigentum Sdlg., Purkersdorf

BUDAPEST

Pécel, Maglód, Ecser, Üllő, Kerepes, Kistarcsa, Nagytarcsa, Rákoscsaba, Vecsés, Gyál, Pestimre, Pestlőrinc, Pestszentimre, Szilasliget, Csömör, Mátyásföld, Cinkota, Rákoskeresztúr, Rákoskert, Rákosliget, Rákoshegy, Sashalom, Rákoskeresztúr, Ferihegy Airport, Sóskút, Mogyoród, Sikátorpuszta, Árpádföld, Pestújhely, Rákospalota, Palota-Újfalu, Rákosszentmihály, Zugló, Kőbánya, Kispest, Pesterzsébet, Újpest, Angyalföld, Pest, Ferencváros, Soroksár, Soroksár Újtelep, Csillagtelep, Óbuda, Buda, Kelenföld, Budafok, Budatétény, Csepel, Csepel sziget, Üröm, Békásmegyer, Római-Fürdő, Aquincum, Vörösvölgy, Nagytétény, Solymár, Pesthidegkút, Hűvösvölgy, Sasad, Budaörs, Budakeszi, Budafok, Diósd, Érd, Kamaraerdő

COPYRIGHT. GEORGE PHILIP AND SON. LTD.

1: 200 000

1 0 1 2 3 4 5 miles
1 0 2 4 6 8 km

1 **2** **3** **4** **5** **6**

A

60

Lisiy Nos
O. Verperluda
Primorskoye Prospekt
Olgino
Oz. Lakhtinskiy Razliv
Kolomyagi
Novaya Derevnya
Udelnaya
Ruchyi
Gorelïy
Berngardovka
Lubya
Vsevolozhsk

Bobylyskaya
Lakhtinskiy
Lesnoy
Grazhdanka
Rybatskaya
Rzhevka
Noyoye Kovalyova
Kalytino

Staraya Derevnya
Bolshaya Nevka
O. Trudyashchikhsya
Kirov Stadium
Ostrova Kirovskiye
Apterkarskiy Ostrov
Petrogradskaya Storona
Vyborgskaya Storona
Polyustrovo
Krasnaya Gorka

O. Volynnyy
Malaya Neva
Dekabristov
Finland Station
Bolshaya-Okhta
Selytsy

B

Gulf of Finland

Ostrov Vasilyevskiy
Fortress of St. Peter & St. Paul
Neva
Hermitage & Winter Palace
Old Admiralty
Admiralteyskaya Storona
Khirvosti
Koltushi
Pavlovo

St. Isaac's Cathedral
SANKT-PETERBURG
Moskva Station
Alexander Nevskiy Abbey
Malaya-Okhta
Okkervil
Zanevka
Yanino
Staraya

Fontanka
Vitebsk Station
Kudrovo
Novosergiyevka
Razmitelevo
Oz. Korkinskoye
Tavry

Obvodnyy Kanal
Ostrov Kanonerskiy
Ostrov Gutuyevskiy
Baltic Station
Volynkina-Derevnya
Warszawa Station
Volodarskoye
Vesolyy Posolok
LENINGRAD OBLAST
GOROD ST-PETERBURG
Myaglovo
Khaboye

Obukhovo
Cornaya
Ozerki

Avtovo
Volkovka
Farforovskaya
Lesnozavodskaya
Neva

Aleksandrovskoye
Kupchino
Novoaleksandrovskoye
Novosaratovka

59 50
Strelyna
Kikenka
Posolok Lenina
Sosnovaya
Uritsk
Ulyanka
Ligovo
Dakhnoye
Airport
Srednaya Rogatka
Rybatskoye
Ust-Slavyanka

C
1 30 **2** 30 10 **3** Airport 30 20 **4** 30 30 **5** 30 40' East from Greenwich **6** 59 50

7 Sheremetyevo Airport 37 20' **8** Khimki 37 30' Moskovskaya **9** Kolytsevaya Avtomobïlynaya Doroga 37 40' **10** Mytishchi 37 50' **11** 38 Zhegalovo **12**

Saburovo
Kurkino
Lianozovo
Chelobityevo
Yauza
Tayninka
Tsentralynyy
Oboldino

D

Maryino
Putilkovo
Novokhovrino
Beskudnikovo
Medvedkovo
Vatutino
Druzhba
MOSKVA OBLAST
GOROD MOSKVA
Medvezhiy Ozyora
Medvezhiy Ozyora

Novonikolyskoye
Chernyovo
Mitino
Bratsevo
Degunino
Vladykino
Babushkin
157
Pekhra-Pokrovskoye
Almazovo

Penyagino
Khimki-Khovrino
Nikolskiy
Dzerzhinskiy Park
Likhoborka
Abramtsevo
Vostochnyy

55 50
Krasnogorsk
Tushino
Petrovsko-Razumovskoye
Timiryazev Park
Ostankino
Sosenka
Galyanovo
140
Balashikha
Novaya

Pavshino
Myakinino
Strogino
Pokrovsko-Sresnevo
Petrovskiy Park
Bogorodskoye
Gorenki

Golyevo
Troitse-Lykovo
Sokolniki Park
Izmaylovo
Vishnyaki
Pekhra-Yakovievskaya

Arkhangelyskoye
Rublovo
Frunze
Riga Station
Sokolniki
Serebryanka
Nikolskoye
Pekhorka

Zakharkovo
Tatarovo
Khorosovo
Dzerzhinskiy
MOSKVA
Izmayloskiy Park
Izmaylovo Shosse
Saltykovka

Mnevniki
Krasno-Presnenskaya
Bolshoi Theatre
Leningrad Station
Kazan Station
Leportovo
150
Entuziastov Shosse
Novogireyevo
Reutov

E
Razdory
Cherepkovo
Sverdlov
Kremlin
Bauman
Perovo
Kuskovo
Serebryanka
Kutsino

Barvikha
Setuny
Krylatskoye
Red Square
St. Basil's Cathedral
Lenin Mausoleum
Zhdanov
Plyushchevo
Veshnyaki
Zheleznodorozhnyy

Romashkovo
Kuntsevo
Fili-Mazilovo
Kirov Sta.
Tretyakov Art Gallery
Vykhino
Kosino
94
Kozhukhovo
Fenino
Temnikovo

Poduskino
Nemchinovka
Davydkovo
Lenin
Pavelets Station
Moskvoretskiy
Plyushchevo
Kuzyminki
Zhulebino
Mikhelysona
Rudnevka
Marusino

Novoivanovskoye
Aminyevo
Lomonosov University
Leninskiye Gory
Gorkiy Park
Tekstilyshchik
Nekrasova
Chornaya

Lochino
Odintsovo
Meshcherskiy
Nikulino
Ochakovo
Ramenki
Yugo-Zarad
150
Nogatino
Kolomenskoye
Lyublino
Lyubertsy

Mamonovo
Bakovka
Zarechye
Cheryomushki
Dyakovo
Volkhonka-Zil
Maryino
Koreneyo

55 40'
Choboty
Solntsevo
Rumyantsevo
Troparevo
Zyuzino
Kuryanovo
Kapotnya
Tomilino
Kotelyniki
Malakhovka

Peredelkino
Rasskazovka
Orlovo
Belyayevo Bogorodskoye
Certanovka
Lenino
Brateyevo
Chkalova
Dzerzhinskiy
Kraskovo

Vnukovo
Vnukovo Airport
Salaryevo
250
Certanovo
Borisovo
Besedy
Tokareva
Udelnaya

F
Seredneyo
Valuyevo
Peredelytsy
Nikolo-Khovanskoye
Teplyy Star
Yasenevo
Kr. Stroitel
Pokrovskoye
Lenino
GOROD MOSKVA
MOSKVA OBLAST
Mamonovo
Ashcherino
Oktyabrskiy
Petrovskoye
Ostrov
Lytkarino
Vereya
Pechorka

Likova
Letovo
Baturino
Kommunarka
Mikhaylovskoye
Bitsa
Biryulyovo
Molokovo
Ostrovtsy
Zaozerye
38

7 37 20' **8** 37 30' **9** 37 40' East from Greenwich **10** 37 50' **11** COPYRIGHT GEORGE PHILIP & SON. LTD. **12**

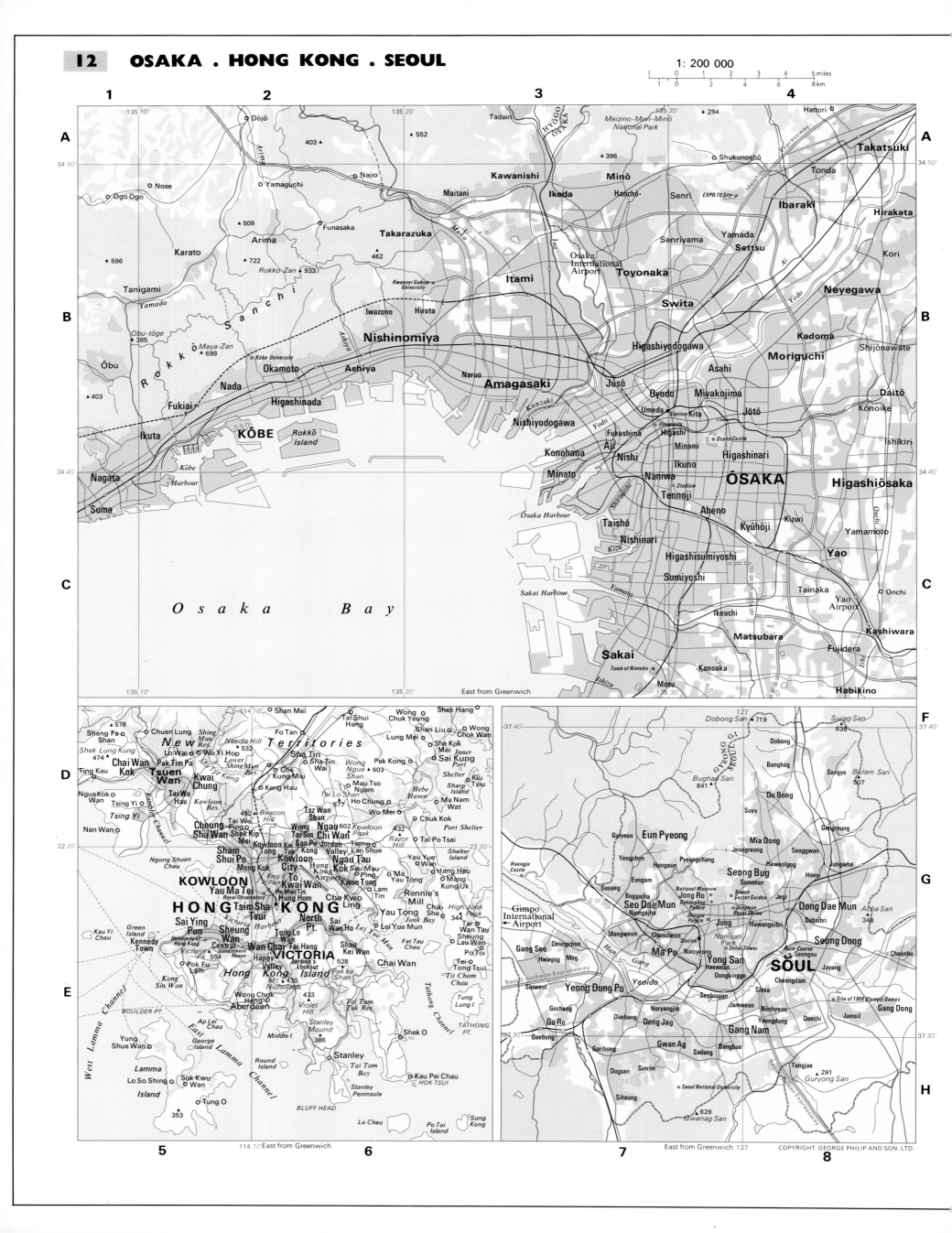

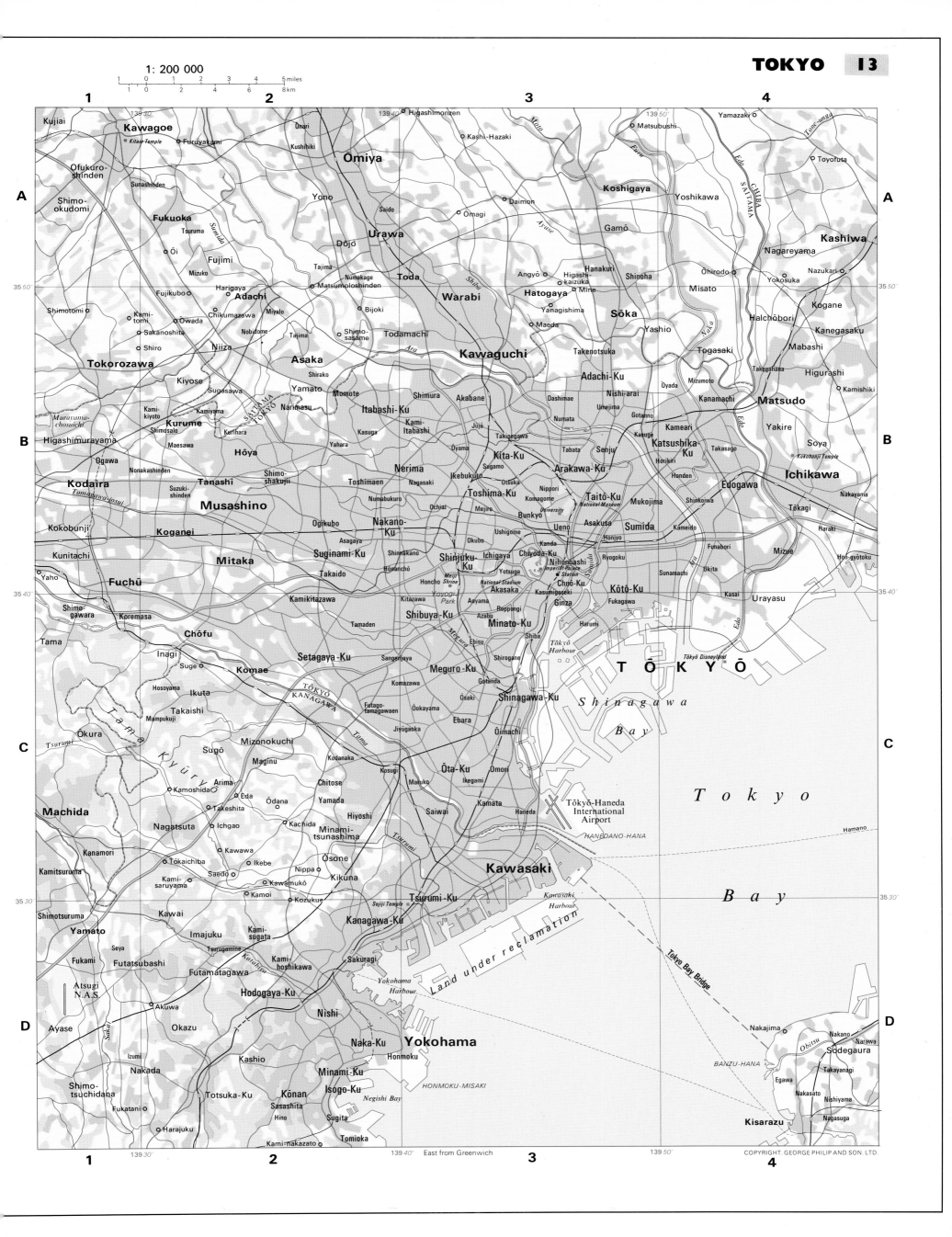

1 : 200 000

5 miles
8 km

1   **2**   **3**   **4**

Kujiai
Kawagoe
Kitaun Temple
Furuyakami
Higashimonzen
Yamazaki
Matsubushi
Toyofuta

Ofukuro-
shinden
Ūnari
Kushihiki
Kashi-Hazaki
Sunashinden
Omiya
Koshigaya
Yoshikawa

A   Shimo-
okudomi
Yono
Saido
Daimon
Gamō
Nagareyama
Kashiwa   **A**

Fukuoka
Tsuruma
Urawa
Ōmagi
Angyō
Higashi-
kaizuka
Shinoha
Ōhirodo
Yokosuka
Nazukari

Ōi
Dōjō
Tajima
Numakage
Toda
Warabi
Hatogaya
Mine
Misato
Kogane

Mizuko
Fujimi
Matsumoloshinden
Shiba
Yanagishima
Sōka
Halchōbori
Kanegasaku

35 50'   Shimotomi
Fujikubo
Harigaya
Adachi
Bijoki
Maeda
Yashio
Togasaki
Takegahana
Higurashi
35 50'

Kami-
tomi
Miyalo
Shimo-
sasome
Todamachi
Takenotsuka
Mabashi

Ōwada
Chikumazawa
Nobidome
Kawaguchi
Adachi-Ku
Nishi-arai
Ōyada
Kanamachi
Kamishiki

Sakanoshita
Tajima
Shirako
Shimura
Akabane
Dashimae
Numata
Ōyama
Umejima
Gotanno

Shiro
Niiza
Yamato
Momote
Akabane
Jūjā
Takinegawa
Senju
Kameari
Yakire

Tokorozawa
Asaka
Sugasawa
Nanmasu
Itabashi-Ku
Kami-
Itabashi
Tabata
Kasuge
Katsushika-
Ku
Takasago
Sōya

Kiyose
Kami-
kiyoto
Kamiyama
Kurihara
Yahara
Kita-Ku
Sugamo
Nippori
Horikiri
Honden

B   Higashimurayama
Kurume
Shimosalo
Maesawa
Hōya
Ūyama
Kasuga
Nerima
Ikebukuro
Ōtsuka
Arakawa-Ku
Mukojima
Shinkoiwa
Ichikawa   **B**

Ogawa
Nonakashinden
Suzuki-
shinden
Shimo-
shakujii
Toshimaen
Nagasaki
Toshima-Ku
Nippori
Komagome
Taitō-Ku
Edogawa

Kodaira
Tanashi
Numabukuro
University
National
Museum
Sumida
Tōkagi

Kokobunji
Musashino
Ogikubo
Nakano-
Ku
Ochiai
Mejiro
Bunkyo
Ueno
Asakusa
Kāmeito
Haraki

Koganei
Asagaya
Shinnakano
Okubo
Ushigome
Kanda
Honjyo
Funabori

Kunitachi
Mitaka
Suginami-Ku
Shinjuku-
Ku
Ichigaya
Chiyoda-Ku
Ryogoku
Ukita

Yaho
Takaido
Hōranchō
Yotsuga
Imperial Palace
Station
Kōtō-Ku
Mizue
Hon-gyōtoku

35 40'   Shimo-
gawara
Kamikitazawa
Honcho
Meiji
Shrine
National Stadium
Akasaka
Kasumigaseki
Fukagawa
Kasai
35 40'

Koremasa
Kitazawa
Yayogi
Park
Auyama
Ginza
Urayasu

Tama
Chōfu
Tamaden
Shibuya-Ku
Roppongi
Minato-Ku
Harumi

Inagi
Suge
Sangenjaya
Azabu
Mēguro
Shiba
Tōkyō
Harbour
Tōkyā Disneyland

Komae
Komazawa
Meguro-Ku
Ebisu
Shirogane

Hosoyama
Ikuta
Setagaya-Ku
Futago-
tamagawaen
Shinagawa
Bay

Takaishi
Mampukuji
Kodanaka
Ōokayama
Ōsaki
Gotanda

C   Ōkura
Sugō
Mizonokuchi
Maginu
Shinagawa-Ku
TŌKYŌ   **C**

Tsurumi
Arima
Eda
Chitose
Yamada
Kosugi
Matuko
Ōta-Ku
Omori

Kamoshida
Takeshita
Ōdana
Ikegami
Tokyo

Machida
Nagatsuta
Ichgao
Kachida
Hiyoshi
Saiwai
Kamata
Tōkyō-Haneda
International
Airport
Bay

Kanamori
Tōkaichiba
Kawawa
Ikebe
Minami-
tsunashima
Haneda
HANEDANO-HANA
Hamano

Kamitsuruma
Saedo
Nippa
Ōsone
Kikuna

Kami-
saruyama
Kawamukō
Kamoi
Kozukue
Kawasaki
Kawasaki
Harbour

35 30'   Shimotsuruma
Kawai
Kami-
sugata
Tsurumi-Ku
35 30'

Yamato
Imajuku
Tsurugemine
Kami-
hoshikawa
Kanagawa-Ku
Land under reclamation
Bay

Seya
Fukami
Futatsubashi
Futamatagawa
Sakuragi
Tokyo Bay Bridge

Atsugi
N.A.S.
Hodogaya-Ku
Yokohama
Harbour
Nakajima

Akuwa
Nishi
Nakano
Narawa
Sodegaura

D   Ayase
Okazu
Naka-Ku
Yokohama
Honmoku
BANZU-HANA
Obitsu
Egawa
Takayanagi   **D**

Izumi
Kashio
Minami-Ku
Isogo-Ku
HONMOKU-MISAKI
Nakasato
Nishiyama

Nakada
Kōnan
Sasashita
Negishi Bay

Shimo-
tsuchidana
Totsuka-Ku
Hino
Sugita
Kisarazu
Nagasuga

Fukatani
Harajuku
Kami-nakazato
Tomioka

1   **2**   East from Greenwich   **3**   **4**

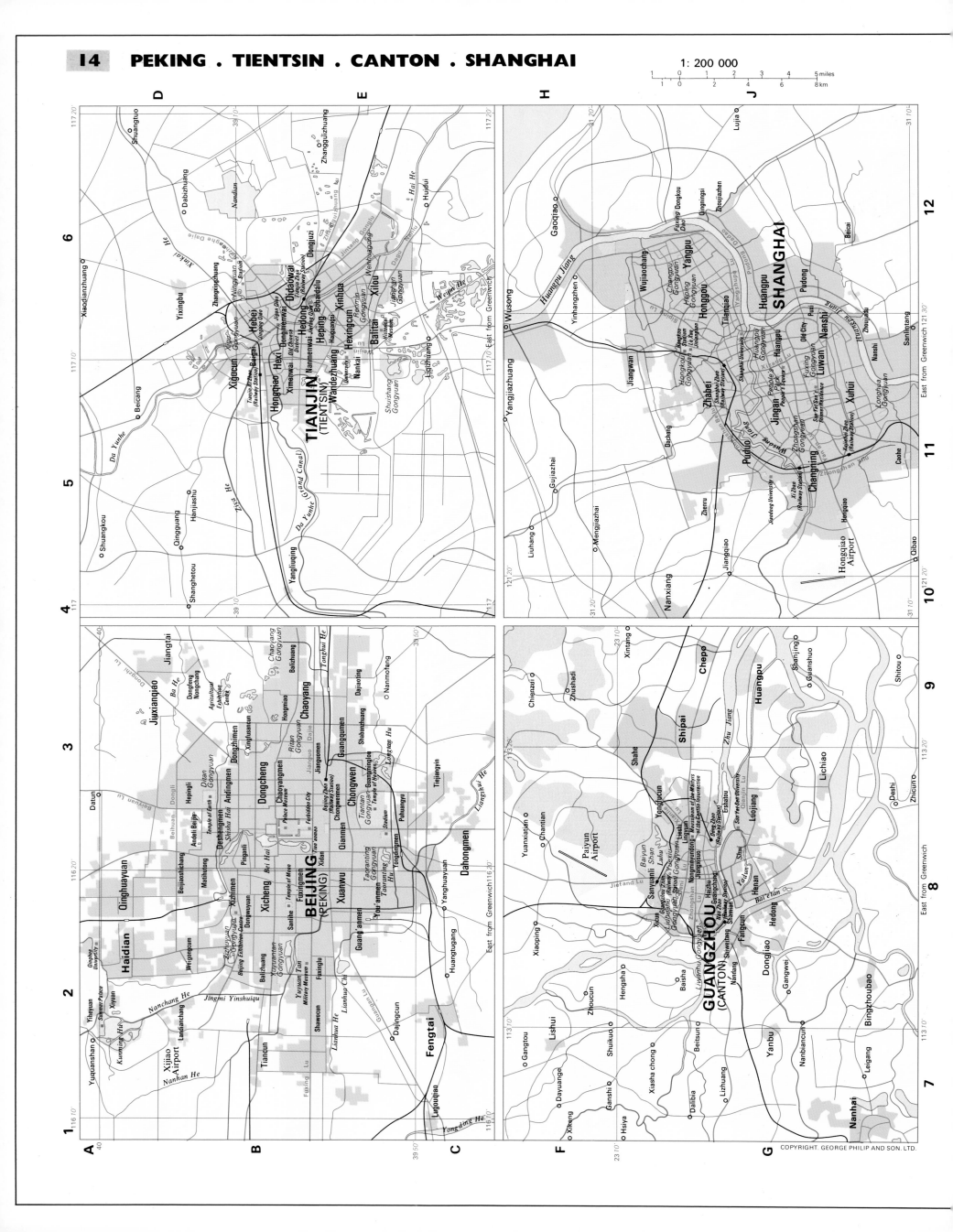

1 : 200 000

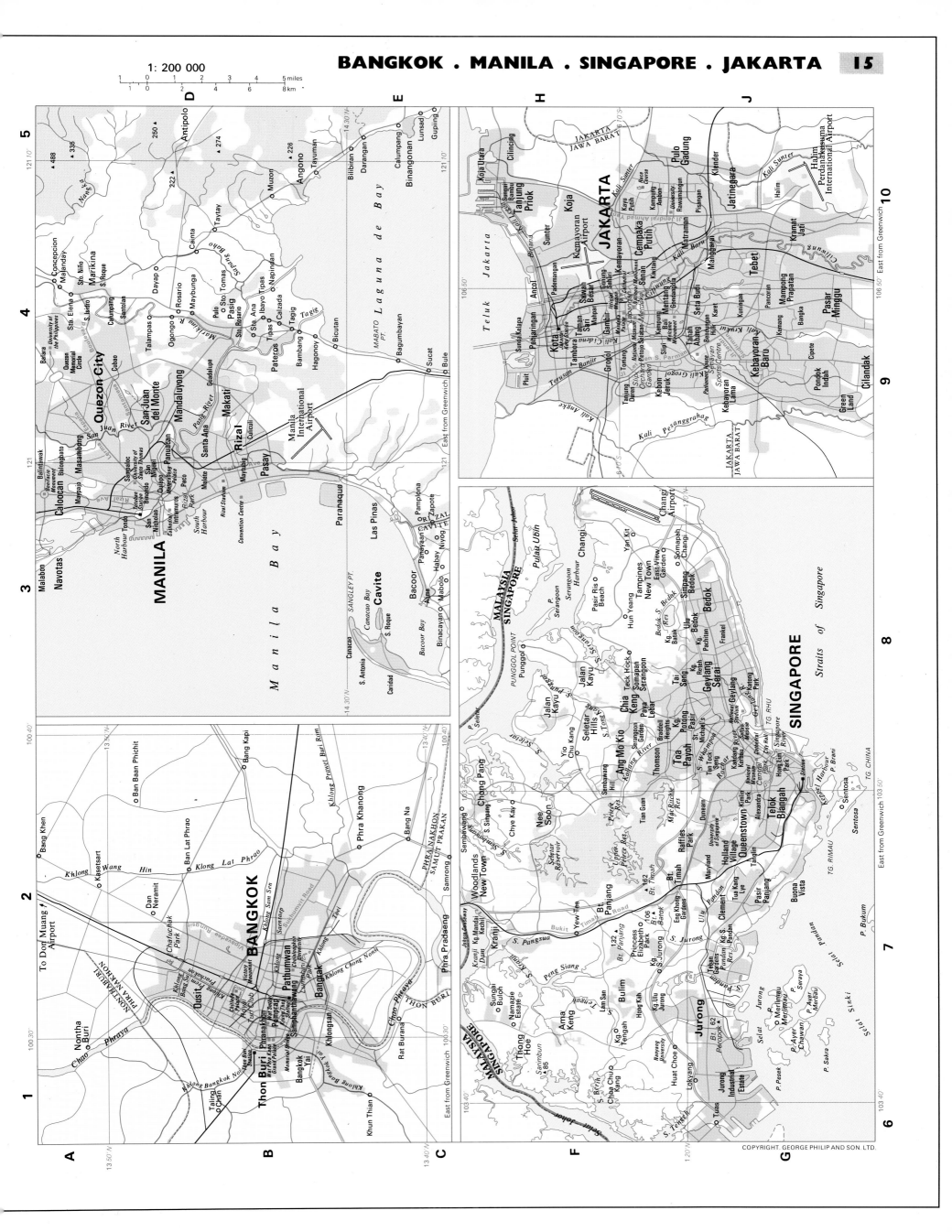

1: 200 000

5 miles
8 km

DELHI

DELHI
New Delhi
UTTAR PRADESH
DELHI
Shahdara
Palam Int. Airport
Safdar Jang Airport
Delhi Cantonment
Yamuna
Agra Canal
Grand Trunk Road
Ring Road
The Ridge

Daulatpur, Nangloi Jat, Nithari, Sahibabad, Rithala, Puth Kalan, Nangloi, Khayala, Asalatpur, Badahela, Nangal Dewat, Palam, Bagraula, Tehar, Basai Darapur, Madipur, Pira, Tatarpur, Garhi Naraina, Naraina, Mehpalpur, Mehram Nagar, Der Sarai, Munirka, Akarpur, Kalkaji, Shalpur Jat, Mujakipur, Kilokri, Okhla, Chilla Saroda, Shamspur, Khichripur, Mandaoli, Khuraii Khas, Ghazipur, Kondli, Nithari, Atta, Aganpur, Karkar Duman, Chhalera Bangal, Maharajpur, Saboli, Babarpur, Ghonda, Ghondao, Mustafabad, Silampur, Shakarpur Khas, Kath Wara, Shastrinagar, Wazirpur, Rajpur, Shadipur, Sadar Bazar, Sabzi Mandi, Dahirpur, Malagur, Jahangirpur, Mukandpur, Coronation Memorial, Bhalswa, Shalimar Bagh, Subhepur, Loni, Rampur, Jauli, Bhopura, Atzalpur, Tela, Azadpur, Wazirabad, Jagatpur, Shakurpur, Haidarpur, Pitampura Kalan, Magholpur, Jwalahari, Bedli Tail, Delhi Tail, Nangal

BOMBAY

BOMBAY
Salsette Island
Bombay Harbour
Thana Creek
Panvel Creek
ARABIAN SEA
Elephanta Island (Gharapuri) 169
Elephanta Caves
Gharapuri
Shet Bandar
Butcher Island (Dia Deva)
Cross Island
Oyster Rock
COLABA POINT
BANDRA POINT
Bandra, Colaba, Worli, Mahim Bay, Back Bay, Malabar Hill, Towers of Silence, Tardeo, Byculla, Mazagaon, Parel, Sewri, Dadar, Kurla, Ghatkopar, Chembur, Trombay, Mahul, Mankhurd, Man Budrukh, Vadaul, Nanole, Borle, Dharavi, Sion, Matunga, Shahar, Brahmapur, Mohili, Kurnuri, Maradli, Anik, Santa Cruz Int. Airport, Juhu, Khairna, Koparkhairna 73, Vashi, Turambhe, Sanpada, Sarsol, Shiraone, Bonsari, Pavne, Nerul, Belopurpada, Karave, Barave, Gavanpada, Shahabad, Vahal, Bamondongri, Selghar, Chirle, Dhutunikhar, Jasai, Jashkar, Pagote, Sonari, More, Panje, Dongri, Punde, Nhava, Sheva Nhava, Sheva, Kharavli 211, Kharavli 305
Santa Cruz, Kalyan, Kole, Dada, Naupada, Tara

CALCUTTA

CALCUTTA
Hooghly
Grand Trunk Rd.
North Rd.
Dum Dum
Dum Dum Int. Airport
Barrackpore Airport
Howrah Bridge
Salt Water Lake
New Canal
Saraswati
East from Greenwich

Chunchura, Bhatpara, Naihati, Madatpur, Panpur, Chandernagore, Mankundu, Garulia, Ichapur, Barakpur, Bhadreswar, Baidyabati, Champdani, Shrirampur, Titagarh, Khardah, Sukchar, Panihati, Kamarhati, Baranagar, Cossipure, Chatpur, Belur, Bally, Uttarpara, Konnagar, Kotrang, Rishra, Ballabhpur, Satghara, Liluah, Golabari, Salkhia, Sibpur, Haora, Bantra, Kidderpore, Alipore, Bhawanipore, Ballygunge, Tollygunge, Behala, Garden Reach, Panchur, Batanagar, Maheshtala, Nangi, Baj Baj, Baurla, Syampur, Chakdapa
Madhyamgram, Dum Dum, Nimta, Sodpur, Bhatpur, Telinipara, Niaganj, Bidyadharpur, Basudebpur, Berabari, Balagarh, Bandipur, Phinga, Nimta, Baguiati, Kankurgachi, Beliaghata, Sura, Banstale, Madhudaha, Naoabad, Dhakuria, Raypur, Russa, Chinguipota, Asati, Kendua, Deulpur, Rajapur, Santoshpur, Bhadua, Ramanathpur, Chanditala, Parbatipur, Dumjor, Depharpur, Nibria, Bartala, Sankrail, Sarenga, Sapa, Bahgio

COPYRIGHT. GEORGE PHILIP AND SON. LTD.

1: 200 000

5 miles
8 km

TEHRAN

Tehrān Pars
Qasr-e-Firūzeh
Qasemābād
Niávarān
Shemīrānāt
Ekhtiyarieh
Dolhak
Dāvudiyeh
Magidiyeh
Najmak
Eshratābād
Dulāb
Dowlatābād
Mesgarābād
Farahābād
Doshan Tappeh Airfield
Niru-ye Hava'i
Sepah Salar Mosque
Majlis
Gulistan Palace
Bāzār
Ewir
Park-e-Shāhanshāhī
Vanak
Yusofā'd
Amīrābād
University
Shah Mosque
Kuy-e-Mekānir
Kuy-e-Gīshā
Reza Course
Shahr-e-Rey
Imperial Palace
Bāgh-e-Feiz
Jamshīdābād
Jawādiyeh
Qual'eh Murgeh Airfield
Hasanābād
Akbabābād
Wastanād
Nematabād
Tepe Saif
Kan
▲1214
Mehrābād Airport
Yaffābād
Guldasteh
Fīrūz Bahram

ISTANBUL

Beykoz
Paşabahçe
Çubuklu
Kanlica
Anadoluhisari
Kandilli
▲438
Yeniköy
İstinye
Boyacıköy
Rumelihisari
Kandilli
Yaniköy
Cengelköy
Umraniye
Kuleli Dere
İçerenköy
Erenköy
Bostanci
Bebek
Boğazı
Beylerbeyi
Kisikli
Kandilli
Kızıltoprak
Avazağa
Mecidiyeköy
Ortaköy
Üsküdar
Fenerbahçe
Salacak
Kağithane
Şişli
Beyoğlu
Kadıköy
Alibey
▲128
Hurriyet Abidesi
Taksim
Haskőy
Galata
Küçüksu
Alibeyköy
Beşiktaş
Dolmabahçe Sarayı
Kız Kulesi
Cebeciköy
Küçükköy
Eyüp
Fener
Balat
Eminönü
Selimiye Kışlası
Mahmutbey
Atışalan
Esenler
Topkapı
Fatih
Kapalı Çarşı
Atikali
Yeni Cami
Yenikapı
Lâleli
Ahmet Camii
Karagümrük
Haydarpaşa Gar.
Kocasinan
Hazreti Eyüp Camii
Karagümrük
Safratya
Yedikule
Zeytinburnu
Bakırköy
Havaalimani
İstanbul Hava Alani
Yeşilköy
Şafraköy
Şenlikköy
Çaruşabaşı
Güngören

MARMARA DENIZI

BAGHDAD

Saddām City
Khansā
Amin
New Baghdad
Humaydi
Riyad
Muthana
Khalij
Nazal Hikmat Beg
Isbhilīya
Idris
Shebāb
Wahda
Quds
Nil
Mustansirīya
Jizīra
Dōra
Al 'Azamīyah
Ubaidīya
Saadūn
Aalām
Tishtiyaa
Jizā'er
Maghreb
Shaikh Amar
Rusāfa
Liberation Monument
Karrādah
Jia'ir
Maarifa
Tunis
Iraqi Mus.
Sūq
Gaylani
Um Al Khanazir Island
Karkh
Karama
Kindi
Fālih
Baghdad Univ.
Salam
Madinat Al Mansur
Ramadān
Yarmūk
Amal Qādisīya
Site of Ancient Round
Mutanabi
City of Baghdad
'Andalus
Jizīra
Zahra
Adel
Khudrā
Huriya
Arbatash
Hamra
Jihad
Firdows
Shaala
Saddam Intl. Airport
AMANAT AL ASIMA

KARACHI

Malir Cantonment
Karachi Intl. Airport
Drigh Road
Phihāi
Bhambo Khān Qarmati
Korangi
Shāre'i Faisal
Ghizri Creek
Mahmoodabad
Tower of Silence
Malir R.
Nazimabad
Lūlūkhet
Pīpāpur
Goth Goti Mār
Thaie Faurza
Sadr
Fqir Hall
Ghizri
Goth Shet Shāh
Clifton
University
Lavāri
Zoological
Gulbai
City
Sind
Gandhi Zoo
Bahri
Quaid-i-Azam
Chhota Andai
Oyster Rocks
Barra Andai
Chauki
Masroor
Napier Mole
Kiamari
Bunker
Manora
West Wharf
Babel.
Mauripur

ARABIAN SEA

East from Greenwich

1 : 200 000

5 miles
8 km

LAGOS

Lagos Lagoon

IKORODU

LAGOS MUNICIPALITY

Bight of Benin

Lagos Island
Victoria Island
Ebute-Metta
Yaba
Apapa
Mushin
Shomolu
Ikeja
Oshodi
Lagos-Ikeja Airport
University of Lagos
Lagos State University
National Stadium
Eko Bridge
Lagos Harbour
Tarqua Bay
Porto Novo Creek

Ebute-Ikorodu
Gbogbo
Májèkete
Ason
Igbopa
Oreta
Ofin
Osorun
Ibese
Ogoyo
Moba
Alaguntan
Iboju
Oworonsoki
Ikoyi
Falomo
Obalende
Ogogoro
Okoogbe
Erunkan
Onisigun
Ojota
Ogudu
Okota
Iponri
Iddo
Idi-Oro
Igbobi
Ijora
Ajegunle
Coker
Isolo
Isagatedo
Idimu
Shogunle
Ewu
Eregun
Ikeja
BADAGRI
Ikotun
Cardoso
Arida
Iseri-Osun
Okunola
Olsheri-Olofin
Eijgbo
Agboju
Olute
Amuwo
Isunba
Kirikiri
Ijesa-Tedo
Iksata
Igbologun
Imore
Badagri

EL QÂHIRA

Masr el Gedida (Heliopolis)
Cairo International Airport
Almaza Airport
EL QÂHIRA
Mâdinet el Qadîma
Masr el Qadîma (Old Cairo)
EL GÎZA
EL BAHR EL AHMAR
EL QÂHIRA
El Ma'âdi
Gebel el Ahmar
Gebel el Muqattam
Gebel et Tura
Wâdi Digla
Nahr en-Nil en-Nîl

El Abbâsîya
El Gamâlîya
El Mosk
Ghurîya
Bûlâq
Shubra el Kheima
El Zamâlik
Imbâba
Gezîra
Warrâq Muhammad el Hadar
Warrâq el Arab
Warrâq el Hadf
El Dubba
El Wâqi el Kubra
El Zeitûn
El Matarîya
El Duqqi
El Awkâl
El Abbin
Abdîn
Garden City
Gezîret el Rauda
Zoological Gardens
University
Egyptian Museum
Presidential Palace
El Talibîya
Minshât el Bekkâri
Pyramids
Sphinx
Cheops Khefren Mykerinos
Saft el Laban
El Kôm el Ahmar
El Barâgil
Birak el Kiyam
Nahia
Kirdâsa
Hakim
Ausim
Burtus
El Muhit Idku el Gharbi
Bahr el Lubeini
Kafr es Sammân
Zâwiyet Abû Musallam
Abû en Nymrus
Tirsa
Shabrâmant
El Basâtin
Tammûh
Tura
Maadî Nasr
Hilmîya
Himîya
Bahtim
Musturud
Basus
Sireil
Stireil
Zâwiyet Abû Musallam

JOHANNESBURG

Springs
Brakpan
Kwa-Thema
Benoni
Boksburg
Germiston
Alberton
Kempton Park
Jan Smuts Airport
Rand Airport
Sandton
Randburg
Roodepoort
Soweto
Krugersdorp
Modderfontein
Witfield
Bedford View
Edenvale
Daveyton
Brenthurst
Gedult Dam
New Modder
New Kleinfontein
Benoni South
Boksburg North
Boksburg South
Parkdene
Cinderella
Elspark
Elsburg
Wadeville
Roodekop
Rynfield
Rusville
Lakefield
Brentwood Park
Moehill
Van Ryn Dam
Modderfontein Deep Levels
Bonaero Park
Rhodesfield
Allengrove
Cresslawn
Edleen
Isando
Sunnyridge
Fisher's Hill
Primrose
North Germiston
South Germiston
Delville
Klippoortjie
Lambton
Parkhill Gardens
Dinwiddie
Randhart
Alrode
Alberante
New Redruth
Florentia
Victoria Lake
Roodekop
Linbropark
Lakeside
Thornhill
Ahnwerp
Dunvegan
Eastleigh
Edendale
Lombardy East
St. Andrews
Sandringham
Malvern East
Kensington
Malvern
Troyeville
Observatory
Orange Grove
Highlands North
Oaklands
Orchards
Norwood
Houghton
Berea
Parktown
Saxonwold
Westcliff
Parkview
Parktown North
Greenside
Emmarentia
Linden
Greymont
Mayfair
Fordsburg
Doornfontein
Jeppestown
Wemmer
Turffontein
Rosettenville
La Rochelle
Regents Park
Robertsham
Mondeor
Ophirton
Crown Mines
Booysens
Nasrec
Baragwanath Airfield
Diepkloof
Meredale
Nancefield
Moroka
Molapo
Meadowlands
Orlando West
Orlando East
Mofolo
Jabavu
Chiawelo
Klipspruit
Pimville
Morningside
Bramley
Kew
Wynberg
Kelvin
Alexandra
Sandown
Waverley
Sydenham
Cyrildene
Sunningdale
Parkmore
Hurlingham
Hyde Park
Sandhurst
Illovo
Craighall
Craighall Park
Dunkeld
Rosebank
Illovo
Florence Bloom Bird Sanctuary
The Wilds
Bordeaux
Blairgowrie
Ferndale
Randpark
Fontainebleau
Northcliff
Blackheath
Robin Hills
Windsor Cresta
Weltevreden Park Ext.
Fairland
Quellerina
Discovery
Florida
Hamberg
Klopperpark
Kloofendal
Honeydew
Poortview
Amorosa
Helderkruin
Roodepoort West
Manufacta
Witpoortjie
Kenmare
Luipaardsvlei
Silverfields
Lewisham
Culemborck
Emdeni
Jabulani
Moletsane
Mapetla
Petit
New Canada
Crown Gardens
Glenvista
Mulbarton
Klipriviersberg
Bassonia

Newlands
Maraisburg
Triomf
Westdene
Newclare
Crosby
Vrededorp
Bezuidenhout Valley
Berario
Kleif
Auckland Park
Melville
University
Franklin Roosevelt Park
Montgomery Park
Klip River
Natalspruit
Klipspruit
Elandsfontein

COPYRIGHT. GEORGE PHILIP AND SON. LTD.

1: 200 000

1   0   1   2   3   4   5 miles
1   0   2   4   6   8 km

Sydney map (top)

1 | 2 | 3 | 4

150 50' Doonside
Rooty Hill
Wallgrove
Western Freeway
Great Western Highway
Prospect
Prospect Reservoir
Horsley Park
Greystanes
Wentworthville
Parramatta
Parramatta North Park
Parramatta River
Granville
Merrylands
Smithfield
Fairfield
Yennora
Villawood
Carramar
Regents Park
Guildford
Auburn
Bonnyrigg
Cabramatta
Bossley Park
Cecil Park
Green Valley
Hoxton Park Aerodrome
West Hoxton
Hoxton Park
Liverpool
Warwick Farm Race Track
Georges Hall
Bankstown Aerodrome
Lurnea
Moorebank
Georges River
Glenfield
Macquarie Fields
Ingleburn
Minto
Military Reserve
South Western Freeway

Blacktown
Winston Hills
Severn Hills
Northmead
Carlingford
Eastwood
Dundas
Rydalmere
Ermington
Epping
Marsfield
North Ryde
Ryde
Gladesville
Mortlake
Drummoyne
Concord
Five Dock
Strathfield
Burwood
Flemington
Enfield
Ashfield
Bass Hill
Chullora
Belfield
Campsie
Bankstown
Yagoona
Belmore
Canterbury
Lakemba
Punchbowl
Milperra
Revesby
Padstow
Riverwood
East Hills
Peakhurst
Hurstville
Beverly Hills
Beverley Hills
Bexley
Rockdale
Arncliffe
Brighton le Sands
Kogarah
Ramsgate
Lugarno
Oatley
Blakehurst
San Souci
Como
Oyster Bay
Jannali
Georges River Bridge
Sylvania
Captain Cook Bridge
Woolooware Bay
Menai
Woronora
Sutherland
Gynea
Miranda
East from Greenwich

Macquarie University
Pennant Hills Park
Gordon
Killara
Lindfield
Lane Cove National Park
Chatswood
Lane Cove
Willoughby
Middle Cove
Northbridge
Baronia Park
Gore Hill
North Sydney
Crows Nest
St Leonards
Greenwich
Hunters Hill
Balmain
Sydney Harbour Bridge
Opera House
Government House
Observatory
Kings Cross
Royal Botanic Gardens
Parliament House
SYDNEY
Leichhardt
Camperdown
Univ. of Sydney
Hyde Park
Surrey Hills
Waterloo
Newtown
S. Peters
Enmore
Marrickville
Erskineville
Kensington
Randwick
Earlwood
Roseberry
Mascot
Univ. of N.S.W.
Kingsford
Barton Park
Sydney Airport
Botany
Banksmeadow
Beverly Park
Malabar
Phillip Bay
Little Bay
Long Bay
La Perouse
Botany Bay
Captain Cook Landing Place Park
Kurnell
Potter Point

Forestville
Manly Warringah War Memorial Park
Dee Why
North Manly
Allambie Heights
Queenscliffe
Seaforth
Manly
Clontarf
Balgowlah Heights
Balgowlah
North Point
North Head
Middle Head
South Head
Watsons Bay
Mosman
Taronga Zoological Park
Port Jackson
Rose Bay
Double Bay
Dover Heights
Paddington
Woollahra
Bondi
Centennial Park
Waverley
Clovelly
Coogee
Pagewood
Maroubra
Cape Banks

SOUTH PACIFIC OCEAN

Melbourne map (bottom)

5 | 6 | 7 | 8 | 9

144 50' Westmeadows
Broadmeadows
Campbellfield
Melbourne Airport
Tullamarine
Keilor
Glenroy
Fawkner
Airport West
Essendon Airport
Pascoe Vale
Keilor East
Niddrie
Essendon
Coburg
Preston
Avondale Heights
Moonee Ponds
Brunswick
Braybrook
Maidstone
Ascot Vale
Flemington Racecourse
Moonee Valley Racecourse
Royal Park Zoo
Carlton
Northcote
Fairfield
Thornbury
Sunshine
Brooklyn
Tottenham
Footscray
Yarraville
Melb. Uni.
MELBOURNE
Richmond
Kew
Newport
Spotswood
Fishermans Bend
Albert Park
Port Melbourne
Middle Park
St. Kilda
Toorak
Malvern
Armadale
Elwood
Caulfield
Elsternwick
Glenhuntly
Ormond
Carnegie
Murrumbeena
Caulfield Racecourse
Bentleigh
McKinnon
Brighton
Bentleigh East
Clayton

Lalor
Epping
Mill Park
Plenty
Thomastown
Greensborough
Bundoora
Bundoora Park
Reservoir
Watsonia
Heidelberg West
Macleod
View Bank
Rosanna
Heidelberg
Ivanhoe
Bulleen
Balwyn North
Box Hill
Blackburn
Mitcham
Nunawading
Canterbury
Surrey Hills
Camberwell
Burwood
Ashburton
Ashwood
Mt. Waverley
Chadstone
Oakleigh
Monash Uni.
Notting Hill
Mulgrave

Wattle Glen
Diamond Creek
Watsons Creek
Kangaroo Ground
Research
Eltham
Templestowe
Warrandyte
Lower Plenty
Yarra River
Templestowe Lower
Doncaster East
Doncaster
Donvale
Ringwood
Blackburn South
Forest Hill
Vermont
Glen Waverley
Wheelers Hill
Scoresby
Rowville

Little Sugarloaf
Mt. Lofty
Wonga Park
Warrandyte South
Lilydale
Chirnside Park
Croydon North
Mooroolbark
Warranwood
Park Orchards
East Ringwood
Croydon
Kilsyth
Mt. Dandenong
Montrose
Bayswater
Boronia
Wantirna
The Basin
Olinda
One Tree Hill
Sassafras
Ferntree Gully
Knoxfield
Tremont
Upper Ferntree Gully
Belgrave
Tecoma
Upwey
Dongala Forest Res.

East from Greenwich

1: 200 000

1 : 200 000

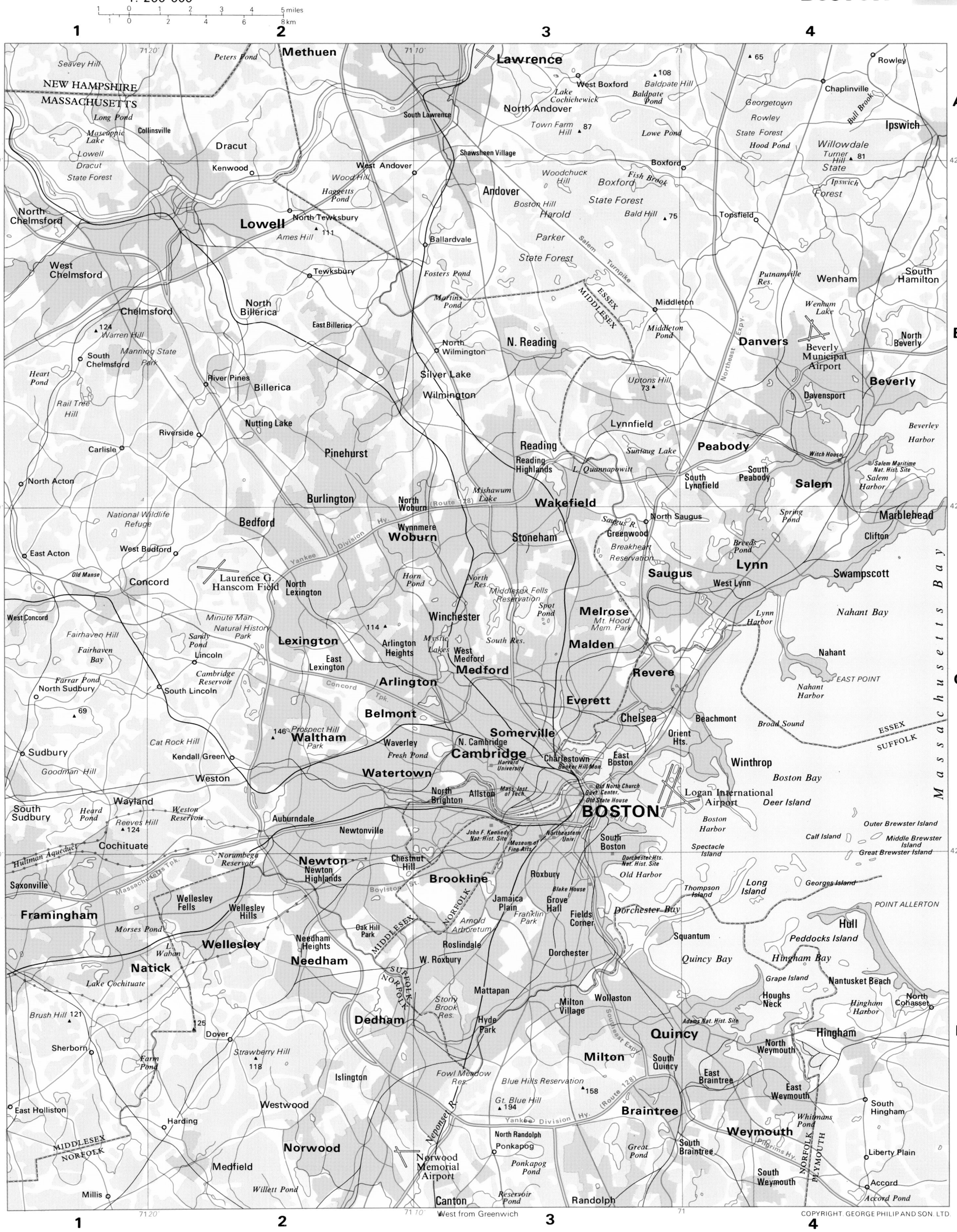

0 1 2 3 4 5 miles
0 2 4 6 8 km

1   2   3   4

A

Seavey Hill
Peters Pond
Methuen
Lawrence
West Boxford
▲108 Baldpate Hill
▲65
Rowley
NEW HAMPSHIRE
MASSACHUSETTS
Lake Cochichewick
Baldpate Pond
Georgetown
Rowley
Chaplinville
Long Pond
North Andover
State Forest
Bull Brook
Museippic Lake
Collinsville
Town Farm Hill ▲87
Lowe Pond
Hood Pond
Ipswich
Dracut
Lowell Dracut State Forest
Kenwood
West Andover
Shawsheen Village
Boxford
▲81 State
Willowdale Turner Hill
Ipswich Forest

42 40'

B

North Chelmsford
Wood Hill
Haggetts Pond
Andover
Woodchuck Hill
Boxford State Forest
Fish Brook
Putnamville Res.
Wenham
South Hamilton
Lowell
North Tewksbury
▲111
Ballardvale
Boston Hill
Harold
Bald Hill ▲75
Topsfield
West Chelmsford
Ames Hill
Tewksbury
Fosters Pond
Parker State Forest
Salem Turnpike
Middleton
Wenham Lake
▲124 Warren Hill
North Billerica
Martins Pond
Middleton Pond
Danvers
Beverly Municipal Airport
North Beverly
South Chelmsford
Manning State Park
East Billerica
North Wilmington
N. Reading
Uptons Hill ▲73
Beverly
Heart Pond
Billerica
Silver Lake
Lynnfield
Davensport
Rail Tree Hill
River Pines
Wilmington
Beverley Harbor
Nutting Lake
Reading
Suntaug Lake
Peabody
Witch House
Salem Maritime Nat. Hist. Site

42 30'

C

North Acton
Carlisle
Riverside
Pinehurst
Reading Highlands
L. Quannapowitt
South Lynnfield
South Peabody
Salem
Salem Harbor
Marblehead
East Acton
Burlington
North Woburn
(Route 28)
Mishawum Lake
Wakefield
Saugus R.
North Saugus
Greenwood
Spring Pond
Old Manse
Bedford
Wynmere
Woburn
Stoneham
Breakheart Reservation
Breeds Pond
Lynn
Clifton
Concord
Laurence G. Hanscom Field
North Lexington
Horn Pond
North Res.
Middlesex Fells Reservation
Spot Pond
Saugus
West Lynn
Swampscott
West Concord
Minute Man Natural History Park
▲114
Winchester
Melrose Mt. Hood Mem. Park
Lynn Harbor
Nahant Bay
Fairhaven Hill
Sandy Pond
Lexington
Arlington Heights
Mystic Lakes
South Res.
Malden
Nahant
Fairhaven Bay
Lincoln
East Lexington
West Medford
Medford
Revere
EAST POINT
Farrar Pond
Cambridge Reservoir
Arlington
Nahant Harbor
North Sudbury
South Lincoln
Concord Tpk.
Belmont
Everett
Chelsea
Beachmont
Broad Sound
ESSEX
SUFFOLK

42 20'

D

▲69
Cat Rock Hill
Prospect Hill
▲146 **Waltham** Park
Waverley
Fresh Pond
Somerville
Orient Hts.
Winthrop
Boston Bay
Sudbury
Kendall Green
Cambridge
Charlestown Bunker Hill Mon.
East Boston
Goodman Hill
Weston
Watertown
Harvard University
Old North Church
Govt. Center
Old State House
Winthrop
South Sudbury
Heard Pond
Wayland
North Brighton
Allston
Mass. Inst. of Tech.
BOSTON
Logan International Airport
Deer Island
Reeves Hill ▲124
Weston Reservoir
Auburndale
Newton
Newtonville
John F. Kennedy Nat. Hist. Site
Museum of Fine Arts
Northeastern Univ.
South Boston
Boston Harbor
Outer Brewster Island
Cochituate
Norumbega Reservoir
Newton Highlands
Chestnut Hill
Boylston St.
Brookline
Roxbury
Spectacle Island
Middle Brewster Island
Great Brewster Island
Saxonville
Framingham
Morses Pond
Wellesley Fells
Wellesley Hills
Oak Hill Park
Jamaica Plain
Blake House
Grove Hall
Fields Corner
Old Harbor
Dorchester Bay
Thompson Island
Long Island
Georges Island
POINT ALLERTON
Arnold Arboretum
Franklin Park
Hull
Peddocks Island
Needham Heights
Wellesley
Needham
W. Roxbury
Roslindale
Dorchester
Squantum
Quincy Bay
Hingham Bay
Grape Island
Nantusket Beach
Brush Hill ▲121
L. Wabon
Natick
Lake Cochituate
Story Brook Res.
Mattapan
Wollaston
Milton Village
Houghs Neck
Hingham Harbor
North Cohasset
Sherborn
▲25
Dover
Strawberry Hill ▲118
Hyde Park
Milton
Quincy
Adams Nat. Hist. Site
South Quincy
North Weymouth
Hingham
Farm Pond
Islington
Dedham
Fowl Meadow Res.
Blue Hills Reservation
East Braintree
East Weymouth
East Holliston
Harding
Westwood
Gt. Blue Hill ▲194
▲158 (Route 128)
Braintree
Weymouth
South Hingham
MIDDLESEX
NORFOLK
Medfield
Norwood
Norwood Memorial Airport
North Randolph
Ponkapog
Yankee Division Hy.
Great Pond
South Braintree
Whitmans Pond
Liberty Plain
Millis
Willett Pond
Canton
West from Greenwich
Randolph
Ponkapog Pond
Reservoir Pond
South Weymouth
South Braintree
Accord
Accord Pond

42 20'

1   2   3   4

71 20'   71 10'   71

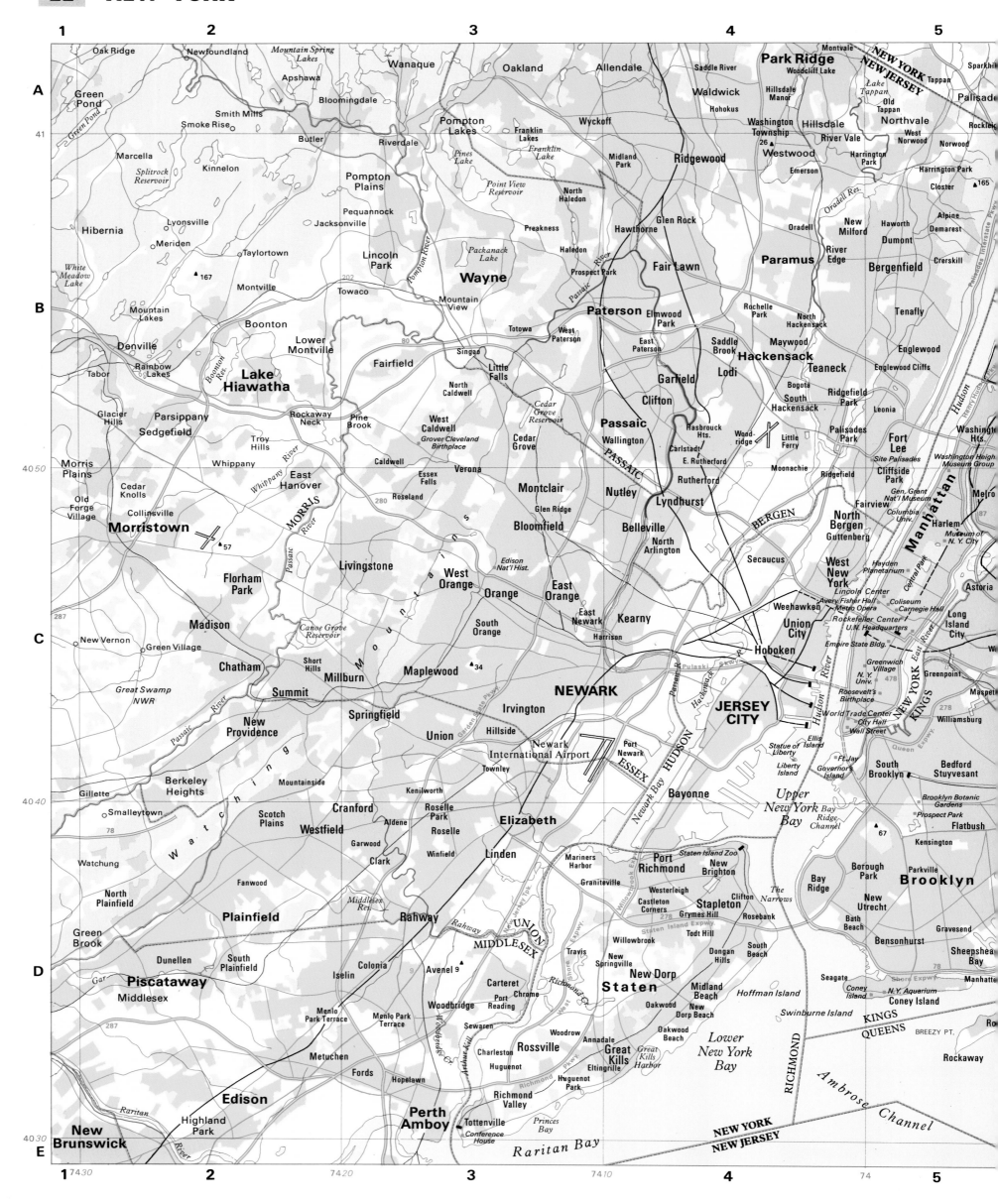

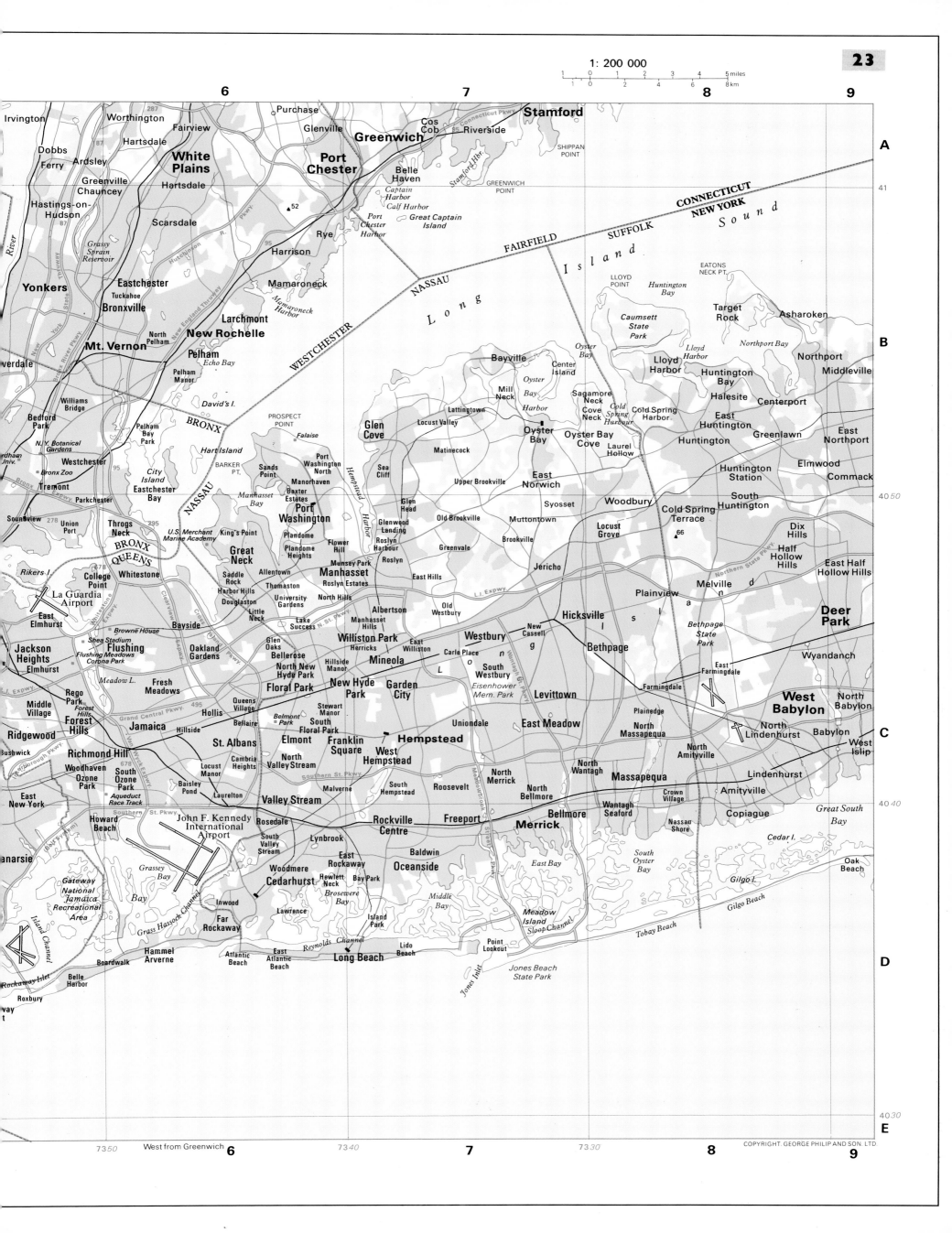

1 : 200 000

5 miles
8 km

PHILADELPHIA

Camden
Norristown
King of Prussia
Conshohocken
Bryn Mawr
Upper Darby
Havertown
Drexel Hill
Lansdowne
Darby
Yeadon
Collingdale
Swarthmore
Media
Chester
Newtown Square
Broomall
Wayne
Malvern
West Chester
Dulworthtown
Phoenixville

Woodbury
Gloucester City
Haddonfield
Cherry Hill
Palmyra
Pennsauken
Willingboro
Burlington
Bristol
Willow Grove

Wilmington
Fairfax
Talleyville
Penns Grove
Paulsboro
Pitman
Sewell
Mullica Hill
Clementon
Lindenwold
West Berlin
Berlin
Atco

Philadelphia Airport
Philadelphia International Airport

NEW JERSEY
PENNSYLVANIA
DELAWARE
MONTGOMERY
CHESTER
BUCKS
BURLINGTON
CAMDEN
GLOUCESTER

Delaware River
Schuylkill River
Pennypack Creek
Wissahickon Cr.
Cooper River
Ridley Creek
Darby Creek
Brandywine Cr.
Raccoon Creek
Oldmans Creek

West from Greenwich

1: 200 000

0 1 2 3 4 5 miles
0 2 4 6 8 km

1 **2** **3** **4**

Owings Mills
213
Liberty Reservoir
Falls Run
Garrison
Scotts Level Br.
170
Harrisonville
Hernwood Hts.
Woodmore
Randallstown
Rockdale
Granite
Milford
Hebbville
Woodstock
Daniels
Patapsco State Park
Patapsco River
Baltimore National Pike
Normandy Heights
Valley Mede
Pine Orchard
Columbia Hills
128
Little Patuxent River
Oakland Mills
Jonestown
Worthington
Ilchester
112
Columbia

Brooklandville
Riderwood
Stevenson
Ruxton
Towson
Pikesville
BALTIMORE
CITY OF BALTIMORE
Western Run
Pimlico Racetrack
Locheam
Woodlawn
Gwynns Falls
Catonsville Manor
West Edmondale
Catonsville
Bloomsbury
Arbutus
Ellicott City
BALTIMORE
HOWARD
Halethorpe
Rockburn Branch
Elkridge
Linthicum Heights
Baltimore Washington Int'l Airport
Ferndale
Shipley
Pumphrey
Arundel Gardens
Rippling Ridge

Lutherville-Timonium
Providence
Hampton Nat'l History Site
Minebank Run
Robert E. Lee Mem. Park
Lake Roland
Roland Park
John Hopkins Univ. & Art Museum
Memorial Stadium
Druid Hill Park
Druid Lake
Lake Ashburton
Leakin Park
North Ave.
Greenmount Ave.
Peabody Inst.
Franklin St.
Civic Center
BALTIMORE
Carroll Park
Fort McHenry Nat. Mon. & Hist. Shrine
Middle Branch
Baltimore Highlands
Brooklyn
Arundel Village
Foremans Corner
Curtis Bay
Francis Scott Key Bridge
Patapsco River

102
Graham Mem. Park
Germantown
Perry Hall
67
White Marsh
Carney
Parkville
Loch Raven Village
Rodgers Forge
Mount Pleasant Park
Clifton Park
Clifton
Herring Run
Overlea
Linbigh
Elmwood
Rossville
Kenwood
Chesaco Park
Essex
Middleborough
Rosedale
Eastpoint
Patterson Park
Northwest Branch
Dundalk
Inverness
Turner
Patapsco River
Sparrows Point
Bethlehem Steel Plant
Old Road Bay
Fort Howard
BALTIMORE
ANNE ARUNDEL

Whitemarsh
Putty Hill
Fullerton
John F. Kennedy Mem. Hwy.
Pulaski Hwy.
Middle River
Martin State Nat'l Airport
North Point
Back River
Back Cr.
Edgemere
Bear Cr.
Sparrows Point

Gunpowder Falls
Loreley
Joppatowne
Bird River
Harewood Park
HARFORD
BALTIMORE
Bowleys Quarters
Carroll Island
Miller Island
Hart Island
Bay Shore Park
Chesapeake Bay

5 **6** **7** **8** **9**

Travilah Regional Park
Travilah
Rockville
Foxhall
Meadowood
Fairland
Montpelier
Muirkirk
Randolph Hills
Glenmont
LOUDOUN
FAIRFAX
The Glen
Watkins Island
Montrose
Wheaton Regional Park
Calverton
Wheaton
MONTGOMERY
PRINCE GEORGES
Beltsville
Cabin John Nat'l Pke.
Kemp Mill
White Oak
Oak View
Beltsville Airport
Shady Oak
Cabin John Regional Park
Kensington
Chevy Chase View
Northwest Branch
Little Paint Br.
Dranesville
Great Falls
Potomac
Silver Spring
Adelphi
College Park
Greenbelt
39
99
Great Falls Park
Bethesda
Woodmont
Chevy Chase
Avenel
Langley Park
Berwyn Hts.
Greenbelt Park
Nichols Run
Rock Run
MARYLAND
VIRGINIA
Cabin John
Glen Echo
Somerset
Takoma Park
Lewisdale
Univ. of Maryland
East Pines
Lanham
Reston
Potomac River
Langley
Brookmont
Chillum
University Park
Riverdale
New Carrollton
Seabrook
Dulles Airport Access Rd.
Belleview
Brightwood
Rock Creek Park
Hyattsville
Edmondston
John Hanson Hwy.
Wolf Trap Farm Park
Capital Beltway
McLean
American University
Mt. Rainier
Bladensburg
Landover Hills
Glenarden
126
Pimmit Hills
Franklin Park
Georgetown
WASHINGTON
Trinidad Nat'l Arboretum
MARYLAND
DISTRICT OF COLUMBIA
Cheverly
Kentland
Palmer Park
Hunters Valley
Vienna
Dunn Loring
Theodore Roosevelt Memorial
The White House
Anacostia River Park
Fairmount Heights
Seat Pleasant
Vale
Difficult Run
Arlington
Rosslyn
Lincoln Memorial
The Mall
U.S. Capitol
Library of Congress
Trinidad
Ft. du Pont Park
Capitol Hts.
Millwood
Kettering
Falls Church
Seven Corners
Hillwood
Arlington Nat'l Cemetery
Pentagon
G. Mason Mem. Br.
East Potomac Park
Oakland
District Hts.
Ritchie
Fairfax
Broyhill Park
ARLINGTON
FAIRFAX
East Arlington
Anacostia River
Coral Hills
Accotink Creek
Annalee Hts.
L. Burcroft
Baileys Crossroads
Washington Nat'l Airport
Anacostia
PRINCE GEORGES
Suitland
Forestville
Holmes Acres
Parklawn
Potomac River
Little River Hwy.
Annandale
Fourmile Run
38 50
Long Br.
Alexandria
Hillcrest Hts.
Morningside
Glassmanor
Silver Hill
Fairfax Station
416
Kings Park
North Springfield
Forest Heights
Temple Hills Park
Camp Springs
Andrews Air Force Base
Butts Corner
Pollick Cr.
West Springfield
Franconia
Rose Hill
Huntington
South Lawn
Oxon Hill
Henson Cr.
Oaklawn
85
Springfield
Groveton
Belle Haven
W. Wilson Mem. Hwy.
Fort Foote Village
Henry G. Shirley Mem. Hwy.
Holmes Run

5 **6** **7** **8** **9**

West from Greenwich

1: 200 000

5 miles
8 km

1   2   3

Potawatomi Woods
208 ▲
Chicago Botanic Garden
Wheeling
Northbrook
Chipilly Woods
Techny
Glencoe
Skokie Lagoons

Prospect Heights
Winnetka
Glenview N.A.S.
Northfield
Kenilworth

A — Arlington Heights
Lake Avenue Woods
Beck Lake
Glenview Woods
Wilmette
Wilmette Harbor
Baha'i Temple — A

Mount Prospect
Glenview
Glenview Countryside
Morton Grove
Northwestern University

Des Plaines
Weller Cr.
Skokie R.
Niles
Skokie
Evanston

Edison Park
Lincolnwood
Rogers Park

42
Park Ridge
Edens Expwy
Smith Forest Preserve
Norwood Park
North Shore Channel
Loyola University
42

Rosemont
Chicago-O'Hare International Airport
Jefferson Park
North Branch Chicago River
Uptown

Bensenville
Norridge
Lake O'Hare
Harwood Heights
Irving Park
Lincoln Park

Schiller Woods
Dunning
Portage Park
Avondale
Belmont Harbor

Schiller Park
Des Plaines R.
Belmont Cragin
Lakeview

B — Westdale
Franklin Park
River Grove
Elmwood Park
Logan Square — B

Northlake
198 ▲
Stone Park
Humboldt Park
Old Town
John Hancock Center
Water Tower

Elmhurst
Melrose Park
Austin
West Town
Art Institute
Northwestern Station
Sears Tower
Chicago Harbor

Berkeley
River Forest
Frank Lloyd Wright Home
Garfield Park
The Loop
La Salle St. Station
Chicago Fire Market

Bellwood
Dwight D. Eisenhower Expwy
Oak Park
Grant Park
Adler Planetarium

Hillside
Maywood
Douglas Park
Burnham Park Harbor

Broadview
Miller Meadow
Forest Park
Lawndale
Bridgeport
CHICAGO

Westchester
North Riverside
Cicero
S. Branch Chicago R.

41 50
Bemis Woods
La Grange Park
Berwyn
Stickney
Dan Ryan Expressway
41 50

Salt Creek
Riverside
Forest View
Brighton Park
Michigan Ave

Brookfield
Lyons
Chicago Sanitary and Ship Canal
A. E. Stevenson Expwy

La Grange
Chicago Portage National Historical Site
Gage Park
Hyde Park

Hinsdale
Western Springs
McCook
Clearing
Washington Park
Museum of Science and Industry

Countryside
Summit
Chicago-Midway Airport
Chicago Lawn
Englewood
University of Chicago

Burr Ridge
La Grange Highlands
Bedford Park
Jackson Park

Hodgkins
Bridgeview
Ashburn
Hayford

C — *Cook County / DuPage County*
Des Plaines
Justice
Burbank
Hometown
Chatham — C

Willow Springs
Dan Ryan Woods
South Shore

Maple Lake
Hickory Hills
185 ▲
Oak Lawn
Evergreen Park
South Chicago

Longjohn Slough
Palos Hills
Beverley
Roseland
Calumet Park
Calumet Harbor

Argonne Forest
Sag Bridge
Mount Greenwood
South Deering
ILLINOIS / INDIANA

Saganashkee Slough
Chicago Ridge
Merrionette Park
Morgan Park
Whiting

Palos Hills Forest
Worth
Calumet Sag Channel
Stony Creek
Lake Calumet
Robertsdale

Palos Park
Alsip
Blue Island
Calumet Park
Wolf Lake
Indiana Harbor

41 40
Tampier Slough
Palos Heights
Robbins
Riverdale
Hegewisch
Powderhorn Lake
41 40

221 ▲
Tinley Creek
Rubio Woods
Crestwood
Little Calumet River
Burnham

Orland Lake
Midlothian
Posen
Dolton
Calumet City

D — Orland Park
Tinley Creek Woods
Goeselville
Oak Forest
Dixmoor
Harvey
Phoenix
Shabbona Woods
East Chicago — D

Tinley Park
Markham
South Holland
Hammond
Gary

87 50   87 40 West from Greenwich   87 30

LAKE

MICHIGAN

COOK COUNTY / LAKE COUNTY

1   2   3   4

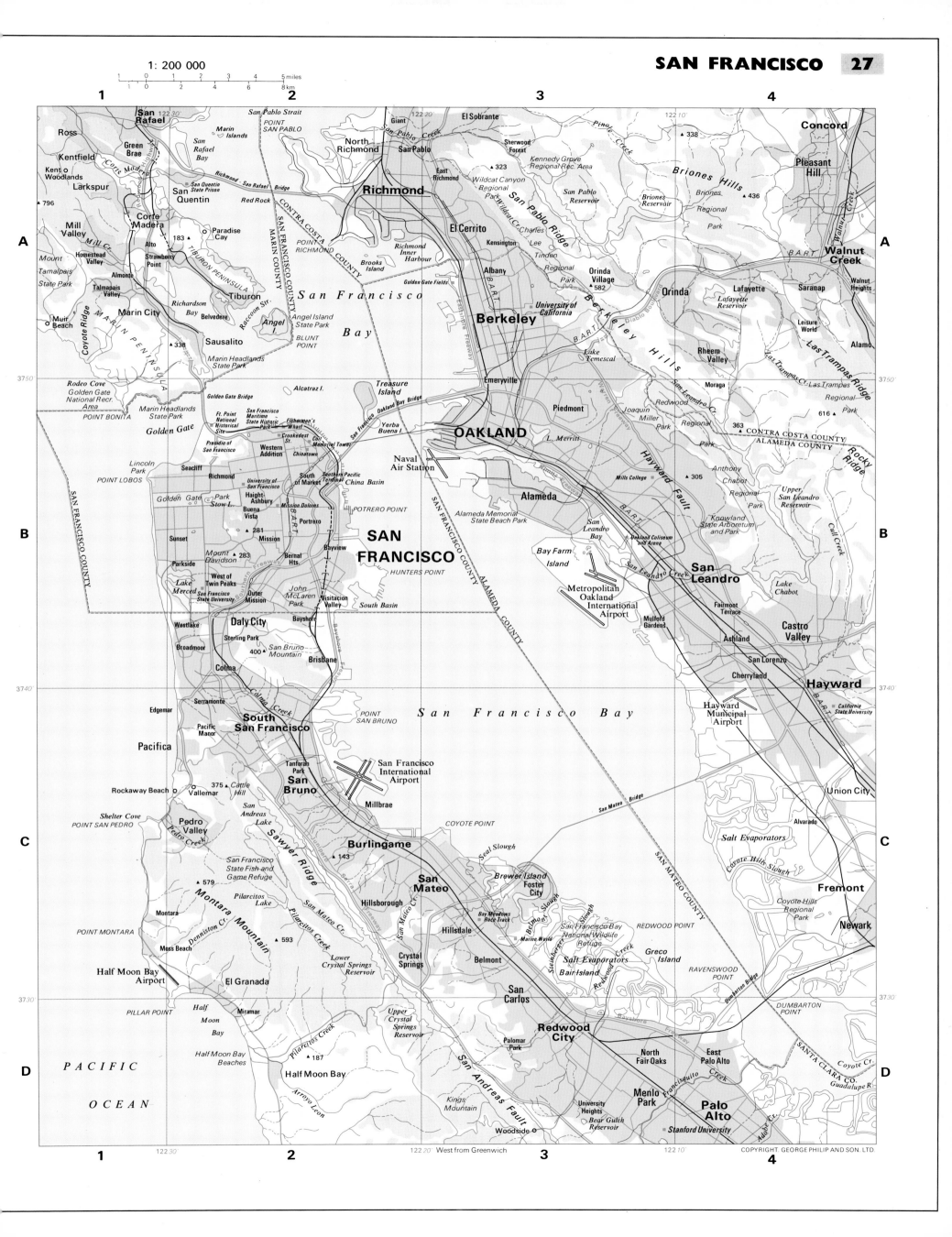

1: 200 000

0   1   2   3   4   5 miles
0   2   4   6   8 km

PACIFIC

OCEAN

COPYRIGHT. GEORGE PHILIP AND SON. LTD.

122 20' West from Greenwich

1: 200 000

5 miles
8 km

COPYRIGHT. GEORGE PHILIP AND SON. LTD.

Angeles National Forest

Waterman Mountain
Silver Mountain
Josephine Pk.
Strawberry Peak 1879
San Gabriel Peak 1877
Mount Markham
Mount Lowe
Mt. Wilson
Mt. Wilson Observatory
Mount Harvard
Mount Disappointment
Echo Mountain
Mount Lukens
Big Tujunga Canyon
San Gabriel River

Azusa
Irwindale
Duarte
Las Lomas
Monrovia
Sierra Madre
Arcadia
Temple City
Baldwin Park
West Covina
La Puente
Rowland
Fallon
Santa Fe Flood Control Basin
Bassett
Hillgrove District
Puente Hills
Hacienda Hts.
La Habre Heights
Sunshine Acres
La Habra
LOS ANGELES
ORANGE
Fuller Park
Buena Park

Altadena
Pasadena
California Inst. of Tech.
San Marino
San Gabriel
Rosemead
El Monte
South San Gabriel
Monterey Park
Whittier
Santa Fe Springs
Los Nietos
Pico Rivera
Rio Hondo
Rosemead Blvd
Norwalk
Artesia
San Gabriel River

La Canada
Montrose
La Crescenta
Tujunga
Highway Highlands
San Rafael Hills
Eagle Rock
Highland Park
Garvanza
El Sereno
Alhambra
California State University
Boyle Heights
Lincoln Heights
East Los Angeles
Commerce
Montebello
Bell Gardens
Maywood
Huntington Park
Florence
South Gate
Lynwood
Downey
Bellflower
Clearwater
Hynes
North Long Beach
Hollydale
Paramount
Compton
Willowbrook

Glendale
Los Angeles River
Golden State Fwy.
Dodger Stadium
Civic Center
LOS ANGELES
Harbour Fwy.
Los Angeles River Long Beach Fwy.
Gardena
Flint Peak 575
Rose Bowl

Burbank
Verdugo Mountains
Sunland
Stonehurst
Hansen Flood Control Basin
San Fernando Airport
San Fernando
Pacoima
Panorama City
North Hollywood
Sun Valley
Hollywood-Burbank Airport
Lockheed Aircraft Corporation
NBC
Universal City
Cahuenga Peak 555
Griffith Park
Hollywood Fwy.
Hollywood Bowl
West Hollywood
Beverly Hills
The Coliseum
The Forum
Inglewood
Lennox
Hawthorne
Lawndale
Hermosa Beach

Granada Hills
Northridge
Winnetka
Reseda
Sepulveda
Van Nuys Airport
Van Nuys
Sherman Oaks
Encino
Tarzana
Aliso Canyon Wash
San Fernando Valley
Lower Van Norman Luke
Tujunga Wash
Ventura Fwy.
Studio City
Glen Aire Golf Club
Sepulveda Flood Control Basin
Encino Reservoir
Stone Canyon Reservoir
Santa Monica Mts.
Beverly Glen
Bel Air
Franklin Reservoir
Twentieth Century Fox
Westwood Village
Brentwood Park
Santa Monica
Culver City
Baldwin Hills
Baldwin Hills Reservoir
Santa Monica Fwy.
San Diego Fwy.
Santa Monica Municipal Airport
Venice
Los Angeles Intl. Airport
El Segundo
Manhattan Beach
Pacific Palisades
Will Rogers State Historical Park
J. Paul Getty Museum
Santa Ynez Canyon

Santa Monica Bay

West from Greenwich

1 : 200 000

1 0 1 2 3 4 5 miles
1 0 2 4 6 8 km

1 **2** **3** **4**

Hila
La Colmena
San Mateo Tecoloapan
Barrientos
Cerro el Picacho 2968
Ecatepec de Morelos
Santa Isabel Ixtapan
Santa María Tulpetlac
Planta de Evaporación
Río Nestinoyac
Ciudad López Mateos
Cuautepec El Alto
Santa Clara
San Andrés Atenco
Santa Cecilia
Cuautepec de Madero
Ciudad Azteca

A

San Nicolás Viejo
Tlalnepantla
La Loma
Pirámide de Tenayuca
Ticomán
Lago de Texcoco
San Juan Ixtacala
Progreso Nacional
San Pedro Zacatenco
Juan González Romero
Presa de Rancho Colorado
Ciudad Satélite
Reynosa Tamaulipas
Indios Verdes
Nueva Aztacoalco
Santiago Tepatlaxco
Río Tlalnepantla
Azcapotzalco
Villa Gustavo A. Madero
Villa de Guadalupe
Basílica de Guadalupe
San Juan de Aragón
Naucalpan de Juárez
CIUDAD DE MÉXICO
Zoológica
Parque San Juan de Aragón
San Juan Toltotepec
Presa Tenantongo
Parque Nacional de los Remedios
El Toreo
Nueva Tenochtitlán
Río Sn. Lorenzo
San Rafael Chamapa
Tacuba
Central Station
Venustiano Carranza
San Francisco Chimalpa
San José Río Hondo
Hipódromo de las Américas
Tlatelolco
Catedral
Tenochtitlán
Palacio Nacional
Lomas Chapultepec
Bellas Artes
Tecamachaleo
Paseo de la Reforma
Ciudadela
B
La Magdalena Chichicaspa
Presa Los Jazmines
Bosque de Chapultepec
Castillo de Chapultepec
Tlacoaque
Chimalhuacán
San Pablo San Pedro
Xochitenco
Xochiaca
Lomas Reforma
Av. Constituyentes
Tacubaya
Viaducto Presidente Miguel Alemán
Ciudad de los Deportes
Palacio de los Deportes
Pantitlán
Netzahualcóyotl
San Lorenzo Chimalco
San Bartolomé Coatepec
Unidad Santa Fe
Ciudad Deportiva
Los Pirules
Santa Cruz Ayotusco
Iztacalco
Agrícola Oriental
San Agustín Atlapulco
Dos Ríos
Olivar del Conde
Juan Escutia
Tepalcates
La Magdalena Atlipac
Molino de Rosas
Mixcoac
Héroes de Churubusco
Santa Martha Acatitla
Huixquilucan Chimalpa
Presa de Mixcoac
Presa Tarango
Iztapalapa
Santa María Aztahuacán
Los Reyes
Cuajimalpa
Olivar de los Padres
Villa Obregón
Coyoacán
Av. Río Churubusco
Universidad Ibero-Americana
Santiago Acahualtepec
General Ignacio Allende
Contadero
Lomas San Angel Inn
San Angel
Rosedal
Prado Churubusco
Los Reyes
Santa Cruz Meyehualco
Tlaltenango
Santa Rosa Xochiac
San Bartolo Ameyalco
Tizapán
La Candelaria
Ciudad Universitaria
Parque Nacional 2460 Cerro de la Estrella
Tlalpitzáhuac
San Lorenzo Acopilco
Estadio Olímpico
Jardines del Pedregal de San Angel
San Francisco Culhuacán
San Lorenzo Tezonco
Iztapalapa Tlahuac
Parque Nacional Desierto de los Leones
San Jerónimo Lidice
El Reloj
El Vergel
La Marquesa
La Magdalena Contreras
Pirámide de Cuicuilco
Tlalpan
Estadio Azteca
La Nopalera
Zapotitlán
Tlaltenco
Parque Nacional del Insurgente Miguel Hidalgo
Las Fuentes Brotantes
Santa Úrsula Xitla
Tepepan
Lago de Xochimilco
Jardines Flotantes
Tlahuac
San Nicolás Totolapan
San Pedro Martir
Gran Canal
Cerro Xico 2346
Xitle
San Luis Tlaxialtemalco
Cerro Xitle 3128
San Andrés Totoltepec
Xochitepec
San Gregorio Atlapulco
Santiago Tepalcatlalpan
Nativitas
Tulyehualco
San Juan Ixtayopan
Xochimilco
Santa Cruz Alcapixca
La Magdalena Petlalco
San Miguel Xicalco
San Mateo Xalpa
San Antonio Tecómitl
Mixquic
San Andrés Ahuayucan
Santa Cecilia Tepetlapa
Tetelco
San Miguel Ajusco
San Francisco Tecoxpa
San Jerónimo Miacatlán
San Juan y San Pedro Tezompa
Parque Nacional de Ajusco
Cerro Ajusco 3937
Topilejo
San Pedro Actopan
San Augustín Ohtenco
Milpa Alta
San Francisco Tlalnepantla
San Salvador Cuauhtenco
San Pablo Ostotepec
Santa Ana Tlacotenco
San Lorenzo Tlacoyucan
Aserradero
Cerro Pelado 3620
Cerro Cuautzin 3497
Cerro Tláloc 3690
D
El Guarda Parres
DISTRITO FEDERAL ESTADO DE MORELOS
Cerro Chichinautzin 3476
DISTRITO FEDERAL ESTADO DE MORELOS
Parque Nacional de las Lagunas de Zempoala
Tres Marias
Parque Nacional del Tepozteco

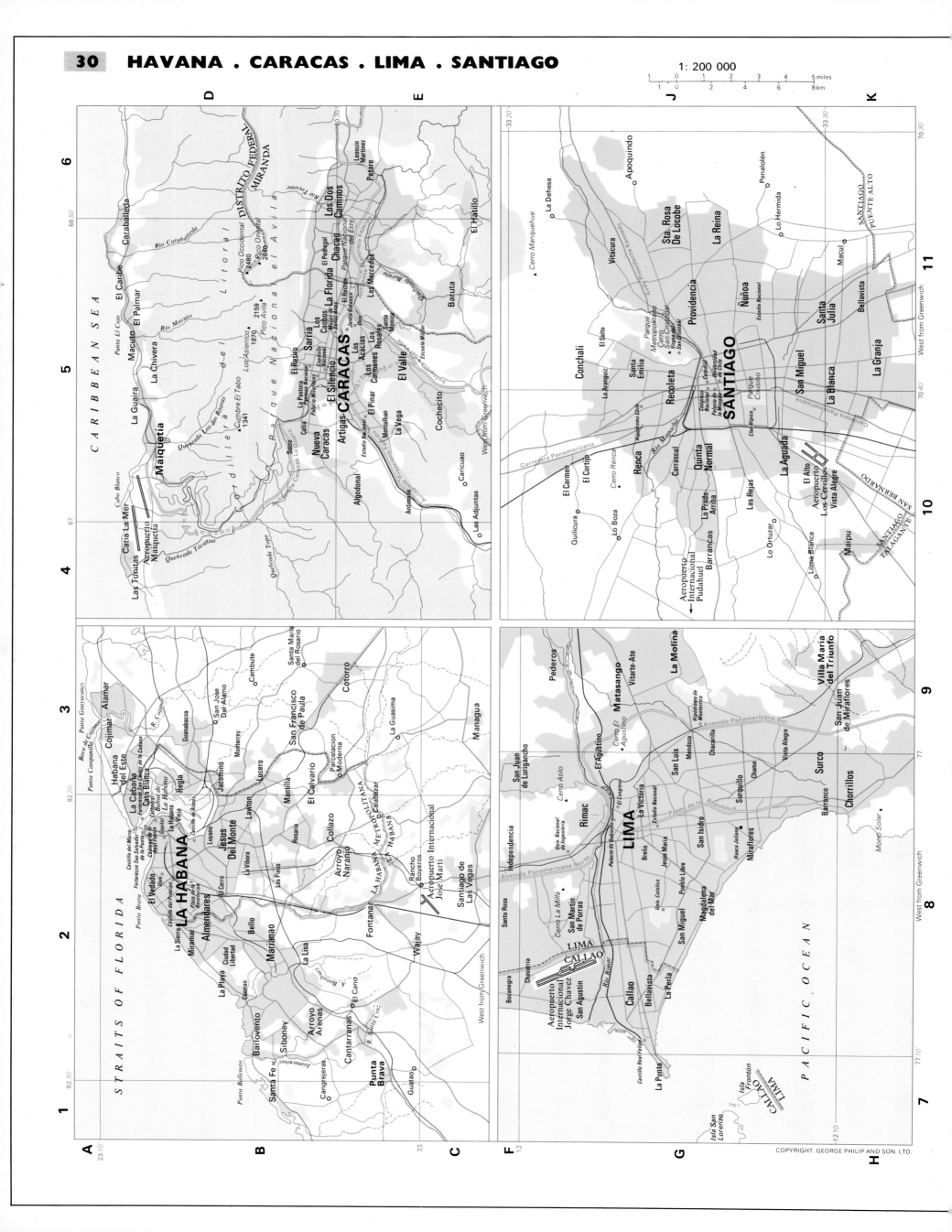

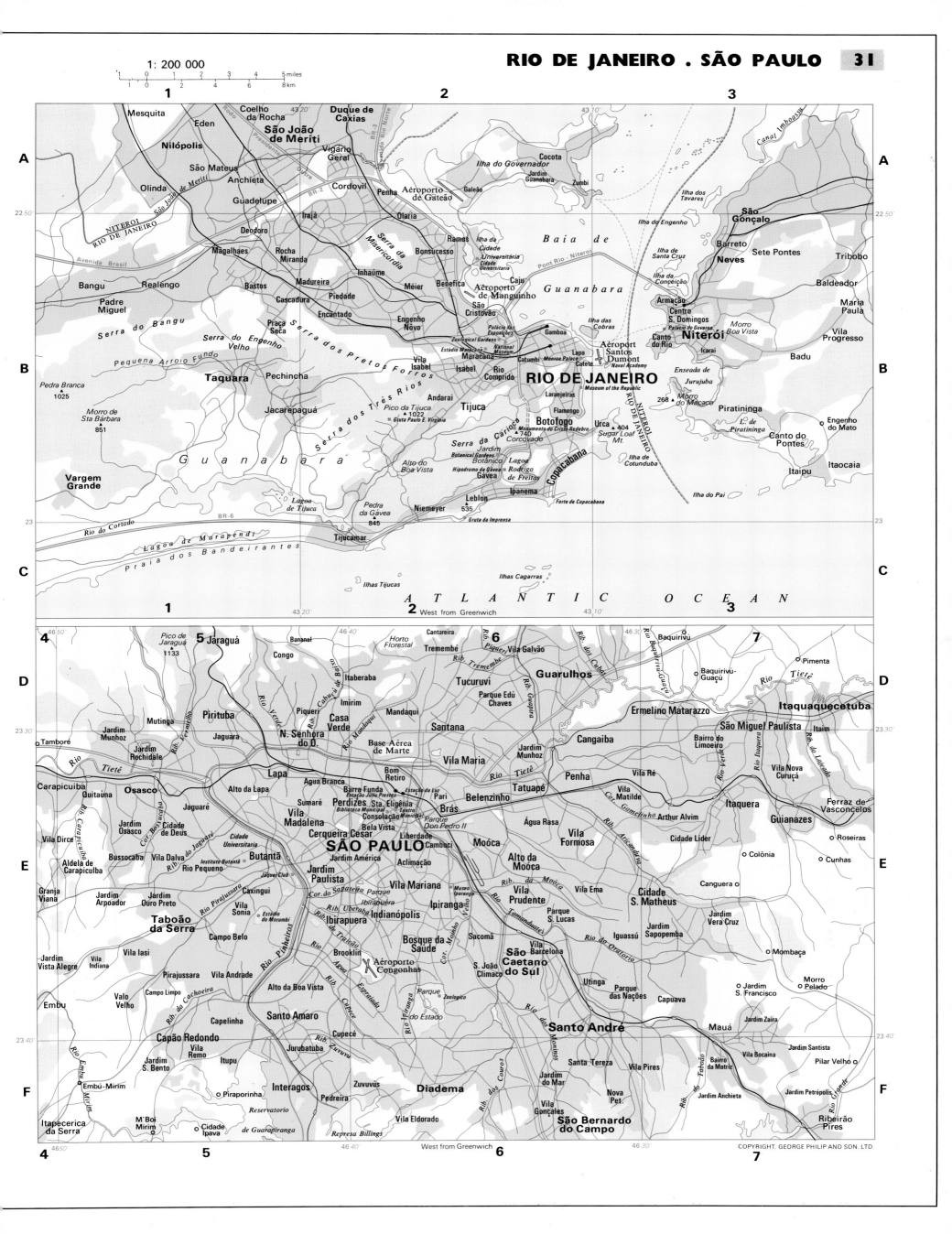

1: 200 000

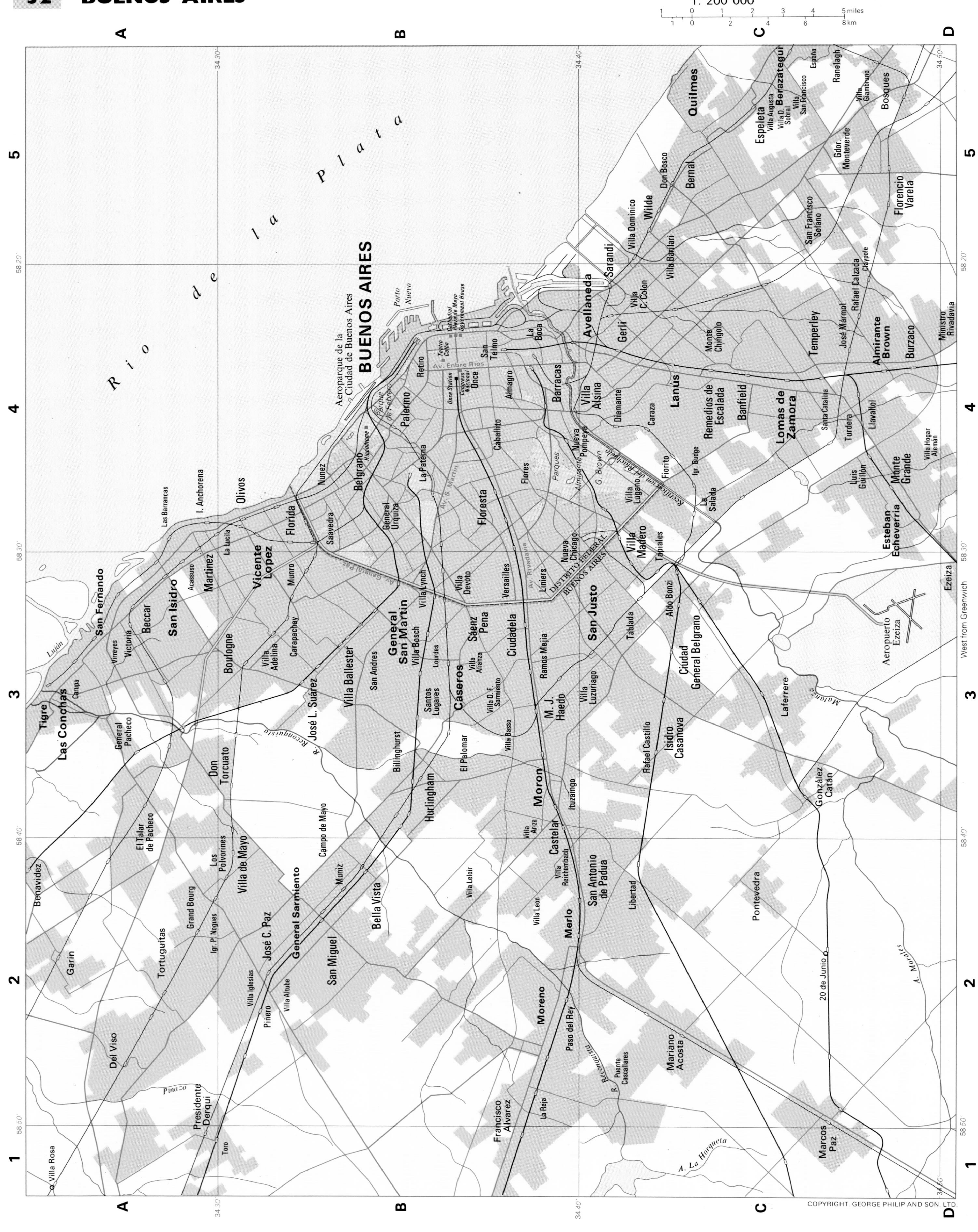

5 miles
8 km

Rio de la Plata

BUENOS AIRES

Aeroparque de la Ciudad de Buenos Aires

Catedral
Plaza de Mayo
Government House
Teatro Colón
San Telmo
La Boca
Retiro
Once Station
Congreso Nacional
Onse Station
Av. Entre Ríos
Porto Nuevo

Quilmes

Espeleta
Villa D. Berazategui
Sobral
San Francisco
España
Ranelagh
San Augusta

Villa
Giambuena
Bosques
Gdor. Monteverde
Florencio Varela

Bernal
Wilde
Don Bosco
Villa Dominico
San Francisco Solano
Villa Bazlari
Rafael Calzada
Claypole

Sarandí
Avellaneda
Gerli
Villa C. Colon
Lanús
Monte Chingolo
Remedios de Escalada
Banfield
Temperley
José Marmot
Almirante Brown
Burzaco
Ministro Rivadavia

Barracas
Villa Alsina
Diamante
Caraza
Ing. Budge
Santa Catalina
Lomas de Zamora
Turdera
Llavallol
Villa Hogar Aleman

Almagro
Cabalito
Flores
Parques
Nueva Pompeya
Almacene
G. Brown
Fiorito
La Salada
Villa Lugano
Luis Guillón
Esteban Echeverría
Monte Grande

Floresta
Villa Madero
Tapiales
Aeropuerto Ezeiza
Ezeiza

Belgrano
Núñez
Palermo
La Paternal
General Urquiza
Villa Devoto
Versailles
Liniers
Nueva Chicago
San Justo
Tablada
Aldo Bonzi
Ciudad General Belgrano
Laferrere
González Catán
West from Greenwich

Olivos
Las Barrancas
I. Anchorena
Florida
Saavedra
Villa Lynch
Villa Bosch
Saenz Peña
Ciudadela
Ramos Mejia
San Justo
DISTRITO FEDERAL BUENOS AIRES

San Fernando
San Isidro
Beccar
Martínez
La Lucila
Vicente López
Munro
General San Martín
Villa Ballester
San Andres
Lourdes
Villa D.F. Sarmiento
Caseros
Santos Lugares
M. J. Haedo
Villa Luzuriago
Isidro Casanova
Rafael Castillo

Tigre
Las Conchas
Victoria
Vireyes
Carupa
General Pacheco
Boulogne
Villa Adelina
Carapachay
José L. Suárez
Billinghurst
Hurlingham
El Palomar
Villa Basso
Villa Ariza
Moron
Ituzaingó
Pontevedra

Benavidez
Garín
El Talar de Pacheco
Don Torcuato
Los Polvorines
Campo de Mayo
Villa Leloir
Castelar
Villa Reichenbaah
San Antonio de Padua
Libertad

Tortuguitas
Grand Bourg
Igr. P. Nogues
Villa de Mayo
José C. Paz
General Sarmiento
Bella Vista
Muniz
San Miguel
Merlo
Mariano Acosta

Del Viso
Pinero
Villa Altube
Villa Iglesias
Paso del Rey
Moreno
20 de Junio

Presidente Derqui
Pinazo
Toro
Francisco Alvarez
La Reja
Marcos Paz

Villa Rosa
A. La Horqueta

INDEX TO CITY MAPS

Place names in this index are given a letter-figure reference to a map square made from the lines of latitude and longitude that appear on the city maps. The full geographic reference is provided in the border of each map. The letter-figure reference will take the reader directly to the square, and by using the geographical coordinates the place sought can be pinpointed within that square.

The location given is the city or suburban center, and not necessarily the name. Lakes, airports and other features having a large area are given coordinates for their centers. Rivers that enter the sea, lake or main stream within the map area have the coordinates of that entrance.

If the river flows through the map, then the coordinates are given to the name. The same rule applies to canals. A river carries the symbol → after its name.

As an aid to identification, every place name is followed by the city map name or its abbreviation; for example, Oakland in California will be followed by S.F. Some of the place names so described will be completely independent of the main city.

An explanation of the alphabetical order rules is to be found at the beginning of the World Map Index.

ABBREVIATIONS USED IN THE INDEX

Ath. – Athinai (Athens)
B. – Baie, Bahía, Bay, Bucht
B.A. – Buenos Aires
Bagd. – Baghdad
Balt. – Baltimore
Bangk. – Bangkok
Barc. – Barcelona
Beij. – Beijing (Peking)
Berl. – Berlin
Bomb. – Bombay
Bost. – Boston
Bud. – Budapest
C. – Cabo, Cap, Cape
Calc. – Calcutta
Car. – Caracas
Chan. – Channel
Chic. – Chicago
Cr. – Creek
E. – East
El Qâ. – El Qâhira (Cairo)
G. – Golfe, Golfo, Gulf, Guba
Gzh. – Guangzhou (Canton)
H.K. – Hong Kong
Hbg. – Hamburg
Hd. – Head
Hels. – Helsinki
Hts. – Heights
I.(s) – Île, Ilha, Insel, Isla, Island, Isle
Ist. – Istanbul
J. – Jabal, Jebel
Jak. – Jakarta
Jobg. – Johannesburg
K. – Kap, Kapp
Kar. – Karachi
Kep. – Kepulauan
Købn. – København (Copenhagen)
L. – Lac, Lacul, Lago, Lagoa, Lake
L.A. – Los Angeles
La Hab. – La Habana (Havana)
Lisb. – Lisboa (Lisbon)
Lon. – London
Mdrd. – Madrid
Melb. – Melbourne
Méx. – México
Mil. – Milano
Mos. – Moskva (Moscow)
Mt. (e) – Mont, Monte, Monti, Montaña, Mountain
Mtrl. – Montréal
Mün. – München (Munich)
N. – Nord, Norte, North, Northern, Nouveau
Nápl. – Nápoli (Naples)
N.Y. – New York City
Os. – Ostrov
Oz. – Ozero
Pen. – Peninsula, Peninsule
Phil. – Philadelphia
Pk. – Park, Peak
Pra. – Praha (Prague)
Pt. – Point
Pta. – Ponta, Punta
Pte. – Pointe
R. – Rio, River
Ra. (s) – Range(s)
Res. – Reserve, Reservoir
Rio J. – Rio de Janeiro
S. – San, South
S.F. – San Francisco
S. Pau. – São Paulo
Sa. – Serra, Sierra
Sd. – Sound
Shang. – Shanghai
Sing. – Singapore
St. – Saint, Sankt, Sint
St-Pet. – St-Peterburg
Sta. – Santa, Station
Ste. – Sainte
Stgo. – Santiago
Sto. – Santo
Stock. – Stockholm
Str. – Strait, Stretto
Syd. – Sydney
Tehr. – Tehran
Tianj. – Tianjin (Tientsin)
Tori. – Torino (Turin)
Trto. – Toronto
W. – West
Wash. – Washington
Wsaw. – Warszawa (Warsaw)

A

Aalām, *Bagd.* 17 F8 33 19N 44 23 E
Abada, *Calc.* 16 E5 22 32N 88 13 E
Abbadia di Stura, *Tori.* 9 B3 45 7N 7 44 E
Abbey Wood, *Lon.* 4 C5 51 29N 0 7 E
Abbots Langley, *Lon.* 4 A2 51 42N 0 25W
Abeno, *Ōsaka* 12 C4 34 38N 135 31 E
Aberdeen, *H.K.* 12 E6 22 14N 114 8 E
Abfanggraben, *Mün.* 7 F11 48 10N 11 41 E
Abington, *Phil.* 24 A4 40 7N 75 7W
Ablon-sur-Seine, *Paris* 5 C4 48 43N 2 25 E
Abord à Plouffe, *Mtrl.* 20 A3 43 32N 73 43W
Abramtsevo, *Mos.* 11 E10 55 49N 37 49 E
Abridge, *Lon.* 4 B5 51 38N 0 7 E
Abû en Numrus, *El Qâ.* 18 D5 29 57N 31 12 E
Acassuso, *B.A.* 32 A3 34 29 S 58 30W
Accord, *Bost.* 21 D4 42 10N 70 52W
Accord Pond, *Bost.* 21 D4 42 10N 70 53W
Accotink Cr. →, *Wash.* 25 D6 38 51N 77 15W
Acerra, *Nápl.* 9 H13 40 56N 14 22 E
Acha San, *Sŏul* 12 G8 37 33N 127 5 E
Acheres, *Paris* 5 B2 48 57N 2 3 E
Acília, *Rome* 9 G9 41 47N 12 21 E
Aclimação, *S. Pau.* 31 E6 23 34 S 46 37W
Acostia →, *Wash.* 25 D8 38 51N 77 1W
Acton, *Lon.* 4 B3 51 30N 0 16W
Açúcar, Pão de, *Rio J.* 31 B3 22 56 S 43 9W
Ada Beja, *Lisb.* 8 F7 38 47N 9 13W
Adabe Cr. →, *S.F.* 27 D4 37 26N 122 6W
Adachi, *Tōkyō* 13 B2 35 49N 139 34 E
Adachi-Ku, *Tōkyō* 13 B3 35 47N 139 47 E
Adams Nat. Hist. Site, *Bost.* 21 D4 42 15N 71 0W
Addington, *Lon.* 4 C4 51 21N 0 1W
Addiscombe, *Lon.* 4 C4 51 22N 0 4W
Adel, *Bagd.* 17 E7 33 20N 44 17 E
Adelphi, *Wash.* 25 C8 39 0N 76 58W
Aderklaa, *Wien* 10 G11 48 17N 16 32 E
Admiralteyskaya Storona, *St-Pet.* 11 B4 59 56N 30 20 E
Áffori, *Mil.* 9 D6 45 31N 9 10 E
Aflandshage, *Købn.* 2 E10 55 33N 12 35 E
Afragola, *Nápl.* 9 H12 40 55N 14 18 E
Aganpur, *Delhi* 16 B3 28 33N 77 20 E
Agboju, *Lagos* 18 B1 6 27N 7 16 E
Agboyi Cr. →, *Lagos* 18 A2 6 33N 7 24 E
Ågerup, *Købn.* 2 D8 55 43N 12 19 E
Ågesta, *Stock.* 3 E11 59 12N 18 6 E
Agincourt, *Trto.* 20 D9 43 47N 79 16W
Agnano Terme, *Nápl.* 9 J12 40 49N 14 10 E
Agora, *Ath.* 8 J11 37 57N 23 43 E
Agra Canal, *Delhi* 16 B2 28 33N 77 17 E
Agricola Oriental, *Méx.* 29 B3 19 23N 99 4W
Agro Romano, *Rome* 9 F8 41 56N 12 17 E
Agua Branca, *S. Pau.* 31 E5 23 31 S 46 40W
Agua Espraiada →, *S. Pau.* 31 E6 23 36 S 46 41W
Água Rasa, *S. Pau.* 31 E6 23 32 S 46 33W
Agualva-Cacem, *Lisb.* 8 F7 38 46N 9 15W
Agustino, Cerro El, *Lima* 30 G8 12 3 S 76 59W
Ahrensfelde, *Berl.* 7 A4 52 34N 13 34 E
Ahuntsic, *Mtrl.* 20 A3 43 32N 73 41W
Ai →, *Ōsaka* 12 B4 34 46N 135 35 E
Aigremont, *Paris* 5 B2 48 54N 2 1 E
Airport West, *Melb.* 19 E6 37 42 S 144 52 E
Aiyaleo, *Ath.* 8 J11 37 59N 23 40 E
Ajegunle, *Lagos* 18 B2 6 26N 7 20 E
Aji, *Ōsaka* 12 B3 34 40N 135 27 E
Ajuda, *Lisb.* 8 F7 38 42N 9 12W
Ajusco, Parque Nacional de, *Méx.* 29 C2 19 12N 99 15W
Akabane, *Tōkyō* 13 B3 35 46N 139 42 E
Akalla, *Stock.* 3 D10 59 24N 17 55 E
Akasaka, *Tōkyō* 13 B3 35 40N 139 43 E
Akbarābād, *Tehr.* 17 C5 35 40N 51 20 E
Åkersberga Saltsjobad, *Stock.* 3 D12 59 26N 18 15 E
Akerselva →, *Oslo* 2 B4 59 54N 10 45 E
Akrópolis, *Ath.* 8 J11 37 57N 23 43 E
Akuwa, *Tōkyō* 13 D2 35 26N 139 30 E
Al 'Azamiyah, *Bagd.* 17 E8 33 22N 44 22 E
Alaguntan, *Lagos* 18 B2 6 25N 7 29 E
Alamar, *La Hab.* 30 B3 23 9N 82 16W
Alameda, *S.F.* 27 B3 37 46N 122 15W
Alameda Memorial State Beach Park, *S.F.* 27 B3 37 45N 122 16W
Alamo, *S.F.* 27 A4 37 51N 122 2W
Albany, *S.F.* 27 A3 37 53N 122 17W
Alberante, *Jobg.* 18 F9 26 16 S 28 7 E
Albern, *Wien* 10 H10 48 9N 16 29 E
Albert Hall, *Lon.* 4 C3 51 29N 0 10W
Albert Park, *Melb.* 19 F6 37 51 S 144 58 E
Albertfalva, *Bud.* 10 K13 47 26N 19 3 E
Alberton, *Jobg.* 18 F9 26 15 S 28 7 E
Albertslund, *Købn.* 2 E9 55 39N 12 21 E
Albertson, *N.Y.* 23 C7 40 46N 73 38W
Albertville, *Jobg.* 18 E8 26 9 S 27 58 E
Albion, *Phil.* 24 C5 39 46N 74 57W
Alby, *Stock.* 3 E10 59 14N 17 51 E
Albysjön, *Stock.* 3 E10 59 14N 17 52 E
Alcantara, *Lisb.* 8 F7 38 43N 9 10W
Alcatraz I., *S.F.* 27 B2 37 49N 122 25W
Alcochete, *Lisb.* 8 F9 38 45N 8 58W
Alcorcón, *Mdrd.* 8 B2 40 20N 3 48W
Aldan, *Phil.* 24 B3 39 55N 75 17W
Aldela de Carapiculba, *S. Pau.* 31 E5 23 34 S 46 49W
Aldene, *N.Y.* 22 D3 40 39N 74 17W
Aldenrade, *Ruhr* 6 A2 51 31N 6 44 E
Alder Planetarium, *Chic.* 26 B3 41 5N 87 36W
Aldershof, *Berl.* 7 B4 52 26N 13 33 E
Aldo Bonzi, *B.A.* 32 C3 34 42 S 58 31W
Aleksandrovskoye, *St-Pet.* 11 B4 59 51N 30 20 E
Aleksandrów, *Wsaw.* 10 E8 52 10N 21 14 E
Alexander Nevsky Abbey, *St-Pet.* 11 B4 59 54N 30 23 E
Alexandra, *Jobg.* 18 E9 26 6 S 28 5 E
Alexandra, *Sing.* 15 G7 1 17N 103 49 E
Alexandria, *Wash.* 25 E7 38 49N 77 5W
Alfortville, *Paris* 5 C4 48 48N 2 24 E
Algés, *Lisb.* 8 F7 38 42N 9 13W
Älgo, *Stock.* 3 E13 59 16N 18 20 E
Algodonal, *Car.* 30 E5 10 29N 66 58W
Alhambra, *L.A.* 28 B4 34 5N 118 7W
Alhos Vedros, *Lisb.* 8 G8 38 39N 9 1W
Alibey →, *Ist.* 17 A2 41 3N 28 56 E
Alibeyköy, *Ist.* 17 A2 41 4N 28 56 E
Alima, *Manila* 15 E3 14 27N 120 55 E
Alimos, *Ath.* 8 J11 37 52N 23 43 E
Aliperti, *Nápl.* 9 H13 40 53N 14 28 E
Alipore, *Calc.* 16 E6 22 31N 88 20 E
Alipur, *Calc.* 16 D5 22 43N 88 12 E
Aliso Canyon Wash →, *L.A.* 28 A1 34 15N 118 31W
Allach, *Mün.* 7 F9 48 11N 11 27 E
Allambie Heights, *Syd.* 19 A4 33 46 S 151 15 E
Allendale, *N.Y.* 22 A4 41 1N 74 9W
Allengrove, *Jobg.* 18 E10 26 5 S 28 14 E
Allentown, *N.Y.* 23 C6 40 47N 73 43W
Allermohe, *Hbg.* 7 E8 53 29N 10 7 E
Allerton, Pt., *Bost.* 21 D4 42 18N 70 52W
Allston, *Bost.* 21 C3 42 21N 71 7W
Alluets, Forêt des, *Paris* 5 B1 48 56N 1 55 E
Almada, *Lisb.* 8 F8 38 41N 9 8W
Almagro, *B.A.* 32 B4 34 38 S 58 24W
Almanara, *Mdrd.* 8 B2 40 28N 3 41W
Almaza Airport, *El Qâ.* 18 C6 30 5N 31 21 E
Almazovo, *Mos.* 11 D12 55 50N 38 3 E
Almendares, *La Hab.* 30 B2 23 6N 82 23W
Almendares →, *La Hab.* 30 B2 23 7N 82 24W
Almirante Brown, *B.A.* 32 C4 34 48 S 58 23W
Almirante G. Brown, Parques, *B.A.* 32 C4 34 40 S 58 28W
Almonesson, *Phil.* 24 C4 39 48N 75 5W
Almonte, *S.F.* 27 A1 37 53N 122 31W
Alnabru, *Oslo* 2 B5 59 55N 10 50 E
Alnsjøen, *Oslo* 2 B5 59 57N 10 51 E
Alperton, *Lon.* 4 B3 51 32N 0 17W
Alpignano, *Tori.* 9 B1 45 6N 7 31 E
Alpine, *N.Y.* 22 B5 40 57N 73 57W
Alpur, *Calc.* 16 C6 22 50N 88 23 E
Alrode, *Jobg.* 18 F9 26 17 S 28 7 E
Alsergrund, *Wien* 10 G10 48 13N 16 21 E
Alsfeld, *Ruhr* 6 A3 51 31N 6 50 E
Alsip, *Chic.* 26 C2 41 40N 87 44W
Alstaden, *Ruhr* 6 B2 51 28N 6 49 E
Ålsten, *Stock.* 3 E10 59 19N 17 57 E
Alster →, *Hbg.* 7 D8 53 38N 10 4 E
Alsterdorf, *Hbg.* 7 D8 53 36N 10 0 E
Älta, *Stock.* 3 E12 59 15N 18 11 E
Altadena, *L.A.* 28 A4 34 11N 118 8W
Alte-Donau →, *Wien* 10 G10 48 14N 16 25 E
Alte Süderelbe, *Hbg.* 7 D7 53 31N 9 52 E
Alten-Essen, *Ruhr* 6 B4 51 29N 7 1 E
Altendorf, *Ruhr* 6 B3 51 27N 6 58 E
Altenhagen, *Ruhr* 6 B6 51 22N 7 27 E
Altenvoerde, *Ruhr* 6 C6 51 18N 7 22 E
Altenwerder, *Hbg.* 7 D7 53 30N 9 55 E
Alter Finkenkrug, *Berl.* 7 A1 52 35N 13 3 E
Altglenicke, *Berl.* 7 B4 52 25N 13 32 E
Altlandsberg Nord, *Berl.* 7 A5 52 34N 13 43 E
Altmannsdorf, *Wien* 10 H9 48 9N 16 18 E
Alto, *S.F.* 27 A1 37 54N 122 30W
Alto da Boa Vista, *S. Pau.* 31 E5 23 38 S 46 42W
Alto da Lapa, *S. Pau.* 31 E5 23 31 S 46 43W
Alto da Moóca, *S. Pau.* 31 E6 23 34 S 46 33W
Alto do Pina, *Lisb.* 8 F8 38 44N 9 7W
Altona, *Hbg.* 7 D7 53 32N 9 56 E
Altona, *Melb.* 19 F5 37 51 S 144 49 E
Altona B., *Melb.* 19 F6 37 52 S 144 51 E
Altona North, *Melb.* 19 F5 37 50 S 144 49 E
Altona Sports Park, *Melb.* 19 F6 37 51 S 144 51 E
Altstadt, *Hbg.* 7 D8 53 32N 10 0 E
Alvarado, *S.F.* 27 C4 37 35N 122 4W
Alvik, *Stock.* 3 E10 59 19N 17 58 E
Älvsjo, *Stock.* 3 E11 59 16N 18 0 E
Älvvik, *Stock.* 3 D12 59 21N 18 15 E
Am Hasenbergl, *Mün.* 7 F10 48 12N 11 33 E
Am Steinhof, *Wien* 10 G9 48 12N 16 17 E
Am Wald, *Mün.* 7 G10 48 3N 11 36 E
Ama Keng, *Sing.* 15 F7 1 23N 103 41 E
Amadora, *Lisb.* 8 F7 38 45N 9 13W
Amagasaki, *Ōsaka* 12 B3 34 42N 135 23 E
Amager, *Købn.* 2 E10 55 36N 12 35 E
Amāl Qādisiya, *Bagd.* 17 F8 33 16N 44 20 E
Amalienborg Slott, *Købn.* 2 D10 55 41N 12 35 E
Amata, *Mil.* 9 D5 45 34N 9 8 E
Ambler, *Phil.* 24 A3 40 9N 75 13W
Ambrose Channel, *N.Y.* 22 D5 40 31N 73 50W
Ameixoeira, *Lisb.* 8 F8 38 46N 9 8W
Ames Hill, *Bost.* 21 B2 42 38N 71 13W
Amin, *Bagd.* 17 F8 33 19N 44 29 E
Aminyevo, *Mos.* 11 E8 55 41N 37 25 E
Amirābād, *Tehr.* 17 C5 35 43N 51 24 E
Amityville, *N.Y.* 23 C8 40 40N 73 23W
Ammersbek →, *Hbg.* 7 C8 53 42N 10 7 E
Amora, *Lisb.* 8 G8 38 37N 9 6W
Amoreira, *Lisb.* 8 F7 38 48N 9 11W
Amorosa, *Jobg.* 18 E8 26 5 S 27 52 E
Ampelokipi, *Ath.* 8 J11 37 58N 23 47 E
Amper →, *Mün.* 7 F9 48 14N 11 25 E
Amselhain, *Berl.* 7 A5 52 38N 13 43 E
Amuwo, *Lagos* 18 B1 6 28N 7 18 E
Anacostia, *Wash.* 25 D8 38 51N 76 59W
Anacostia River Park, *Wash.* 25 D8 38 54N 76 57W
Anadoluhisari, *Ist.* 17 A3 41 4N 29 3 E
Anandanagar, *Calc.* 16 C5 22 51N 88 16 E
Anchieta, *Rio J.* 31 A1 22 48 S 43 21W
Ancol, *Jak.* 15 H9 6 7 S 106 49 E
Andalus, *Bagd.* 17 F7 33 19N 44 18 E
Andalusia, *Phil.* 24 A5 40 4N 74 58W
Andarai, *Rio J.* 31 B2 22 56 S 43 14W
Andeli Beijie, *Beij.* 14 B3 39 57N 116 21 E
Anderson Cr. →, *Melb.* 19 E8 37 44 S 145 12 E
Andilly, *Paris* 5 A3 49 0N 2 17 E
Andingmen, *Beij.* 14 B3 39 55N 116 23 E
Andover, *Bost.* 21 B3 42 39N 71 7W
Andrésy, *Paris* 5 B2 48 58N 2 3 E
Andrews Air Force Base, *Wash.* 25 E8 38 48N 76 52W
Ang Mo Kio, *Sing.* 15 F8 1 22N 103 50 E
Ängby, *Stock.* 3 D10 59 20N 17 53 E
Angel I., *S.F.* 27 A2 37 52N 122 25W
Angel Island State Park, *S.F.* 27 A2 37 52N 122 25W
Angerbruch →, *Ruhr* 6 C3 51 18N 6 59 E
Angerhausen, *Ruhr* 6 B2 51 22N 6 43 E
Angermund, *Ruhr* 6 C2 51 19N 6 46 E
Angke, Kali →, *Jak.* 15 H9 6 6 S 106 46 E
Angono, *Manila* 15 D4 14 31N 121 8 E
Angyalföld, *Bud.* 10 J13 47 32N 19 5 E
Angyō, *Tōkyō* 13 A3 35 50N 139 45 E
Aniene →, *Rome* 9 F10 41 56N 12 35 E
Anik, *Bomb.* 16 G8 19 1N 72 53 E
Anin, *Wsaw.* 10 E7 52 13N 21 9 E
Anjou, *Mtrl.* 20 A4 43 36N 73 33W
Annadale, *N.Y.* 22 D3 40 32N 74 10W
Annalee Heights, *Wash.* 25 D6 38 51N 77 10W
Annandale, *Wash.* 25 D6 38 50N 77 11W
Annen, *Ruhr* 6 B6 51 27N 7 22 E
Annet-sur-Marne, *Paris* 5 B6 48 55N 2 43 E
Anthony Chabot Regional Park, *S.F.* 27 B4 37 46N 122 7W
Antignano, *Nápl.* 9 H12 40 51N 14 13 E
Antimano, *Car.* 30 E5 10 27N 66 59W
Antipolo, *Manila* 15 D5 14 35N 121 10 E
Antony, *Paris* 5 C3 48 44N 2 17 E
Antwerp, *Jobg.* 18 E9 26 5 S 28 9 E
Aoyama, *Tōkyō* 13 C3 35 39N 139 42 E
Ap Lei Chau, *H.K.* 12 E5 22 14N 114 9 E
Apapa, *Lagos* 18 B2 6 26N 7 21 E
Apelacão, *Lisb.* 8 F8 38 48N 9 7W
Apoquindo, *Stgo* 30 J11 33 23 S 70 30W
Apshawa, *N.Y.* 22 A2 41 1N 74 22W
Apterkarskiy Os., *St-Pet.* 11 B4 59 57N 30 20 E
Aquincum, *Bud.* 10 J13 47 33N 19 3 E
Ara →, *Tōkyō* 13 B4 35 41N 139 50 E
Arakawa-Ku, *Tōkyō* 13 B3 35 44N 139 48 E
Arakpur, *Delhi* 16 B2 28 35N 77 11 E
Arany-hegyi-patak →, *Bud.* 10 J13 47 34N 19 4 E
Aravaca, *Mdrd.* 8 B2 40 27N 3 47W
Arbataash, *Bagd.* 17 E7 33 20N 44 19 E
Arbutus, *Balt.* 25 B2 39 15N 76 41W
Arc de Triomphe, *Paris* 5 B3 48 52N 2 17 E
Arcadia, *L.A.* 28 B4 34 7N 118 1W
Arceuil, *Paris* 5 C3 48 48N 2 19 E
Arden, *Phil.* 24 C2 39 48N 75 29W
Ardey Gebirge, *Ruhr* 6 B6 51 24N 7 23 E
Ardmore, *Phil.* 24 A3 40 0N 75 17W
Ardsley, *N.Y.* 23 A5 41 0N 73 50W
Arese, *Mil.* 9 D5 45 32N 9 4 E
Arganzuela, *Mdrd.* 8 B2 40 23N 3 42W
Argenteuil, *Paris* 5 B3 48 56N 2 15 E
Argonne Forest, *Chic.* 26 C1 41 42N 87 53W
Ariadana, *Calc.* 16 E6 22 39N 88 22 E
Aricanduva →, *S. Pau.* 31 E6 23 31 S 46 33W
Arida, *Lagos* 18 A1 6 33N 7 16 E
Arima, *Ōsaka* 12 B2 34 47N 135 15 E
Arima, *Tōkyō* 13 C2 35 33N 139 33 E
Arima →, *Ōsaka* 12 A2 34 50N 135 14 E
Arkhangelyskoye, *Mos.* 11 E7 55 47N 37 17 E
Arkley, *Lon.* 4 B3 51 38N 0 13W
Arlington, *Bost.* 21 C2 42 24N 71 10W
Arlington, *Wash.* 25 D7 38 53N 77 7W
Arlington Heights, *Bost.* 21 C2 42 25N 71 10W
Arlington Heights, *Chic.* 26 A1 42 5N 87 55W
Arlington Nat. Cemetery, *Wash.* 25 D7 38 52N 77 4W
Armação, *Rio J.* 31 B3 22 52 S 43 6W
Armadale, *Melb.* 19 F7 37 51 S 145 0 E
Armadale, *Trto.* 20 C9 43 50N 79 14W
Armainvilliers, Forêt d', *Paris* 5 C6 48 46N 2 42 E
Armour Heights, *Trto.* 20 D8 43 45N 79 25W
Arncliffe, *Syd.* 19 B3 33 56 S 151 8 E
Arnold Arboretum, *Bost.* 21 D3 42 18N 71 8W
Arnouville-les-Gonesse, *Paris* 5 B4 48 59N 2 24 E
Arrentela, *Lisb.* 8 G8 38 37N 9 6W
Arrone →, *Rome* 9 F8 41 55N 12 16 E
Arroyo Arenas, *La Hab.* 30 B2 23 3N 82 27W
Arroyo Cr. →, *S.F.* 26 D2 37 27N 122 25W
Arroyo Naranjo, *La Hab.* 30 B2 23 2N 82 21W
Årsta, *Stock.* 3 E11 59 17N 18 3 E
Artesia, *L.A.* 28 C4 33 51N 118 4W
Arthur Alvim, *S. Pau.* 31 E7 23 32 S 46 28W
Arthur Kill →, *N.Y.* 22 D3 40 32N 74 15W
Artigas, *Car.* 30 E5 10 29N 66 56W
Arundel Gardens, *Balt.* 25 B3 39 12N 76 37W
Arundel Village, *Balt.* 25 B3 39 13N 76 35W
Aryiróupolis, *Ath.* 8 J11 37 52N 23 44 E
Arzano, *Nápl.* 9 H12 40 54N 14 16 E
Asagaya, *Tōkyō* 13 B2 35 41N 139 38 E
Asahi, *Ōsaka* 12 B4 34 43N 135 31 E
Asaka, *Tōkyō* 13 B2 35 47N 139 35 E
Asakusa, *Tōkyō* 13 B3 35 42N 139 47 E
Asalatpur, *Delhi* 16 B1 28 37N 77 4 E
Asati, *Calc.* 16 F5 22 28N 88 15 E
Aschheim, *Mün.* 7 F11 48 10N 11 42 E
Ascot Vale, *Melb.* 19 E6 37 46 S 144 53 E
Aserradero, *Méx.* 29 D2 19 10N 99 16W
Asharoken, *N.Y.* 23 B8 40 55N 73 21W
Ashburn, *Chic.* 26 C2 41 45N 87 43W
Ashburton, *Melb.* 19 F7 37 51 S 145 4 E

34 Ashburton, L.

Ashburton, L., Balt. 25 B2 39 19N 76 40W
Ashchherino, Mos. 11 F10 55 36N 37 46 E
Ashfield, Syd. 19 B3 33 53 S 151 7 E
Ashford, Lon. 4 C2 51 25N 0 26W
Ashiya, Ōsaka 12 B2 34 43N 135 18 E
Ashiya →, Ōsaka 12 B2 34 42N 135 18 E
Ashland, S.F. 27 B4 37 41N 122 7W
Ashstead, Lon. 4 D3 51 18N 0 17W
Ashwood, Melb. 19 F7 37 52 S 145 5 E
Asker, Oslo 2 B2 59 50N 10 25 E
Askisto, Hels. 3 B3 60 16N 24 47 E
Askrikefjärden, Stock. 3 D12 59 22N 18 13 E
Asnieres, Paris 5 B3 48 54N 2 16 E
Ason, Lagos 18 A3 6 34N 7 31 E
Aspern, Wien 10 G10 48 13N 16 29 E
Aspern, Flugplatz, Wien 10 G11 48 13N 16 30 E
Assiano, Mil. 9 E5 45 27N 9 3 E
Aston Mills, Phil. 24 B2 39 52N 75 26W
Astoria, N.Y. 22 C5 40 46N 73 55W
Atares, Castillo de, La Hab. 30 B2 23 7N 82 21W
Atco, Phil. 24 C5 39 46N 74 53W
Atghara, Calc. 16 E6 22 37N 88 26 E
Athens = Athínai, Ath. 8 J11 37 58N 23 43 E
Athínai, Ath. 8 J11 37 58N 23 43 E
Athinai-Ellinikón Airport, Ath. 8 J2 37 51N 23 44 E
Athis-Mons, Paris 5 C4 48 42N 2 23 E
Atīfiya, Bagd. 17 E8 33 21N 44 21 E
Atikali, Ist. 17 A2 41 1N 28 56 E
Atilo, Cerro, Lima 30 G8 12 2 S 77 2W
Atişalen, Ist. 17 A2 41 3N 28 52 E
Atlandsberg, Berl. 7 A5 52 33N 13 43 E
Atlantic Beach, N.Y. 23 D6 40 35N 73 44W
Atta, Delhi 16 B2 28 34N 77 19 E
Attiki, Ath. 8 H11 38 0N 23 43 E
Atzalpur, Delhi 16 A3 28 43N 77 20 E
Atzgersdorf, Wien 10 H9 48 8N 16 18 E
Aubervilliers, Paris 5 B4 48 54N 2 22 E
Aubing, Mün. 7 G9 48 9N 11 25 E
Auburn, Syd. 19 B3 33 51 S 151 1 E
Auburndale, Bost. 21 C2 42 20N 71 14W
Auckland Park, Jobg. 18 F9 26 11 S 28 0 E
Audubon, Phil. 24 A2 40 7N 75 25W
Auf-dem-Schnee, Ruhr 6 B6 51 26N 7 25 E
Auffargis, Paris 5 C1 48 42N 1 53 E
Augustówka, Wsaw. 10 E7 52 11N 21 5 E
Aulnay-sous-Bois, Paris 5 B4 48 56N 2 29 E
Aurelio, Rome 9 F9 51 54N 12 26 E
Ausîm, El Qâ. 18 C4 30 7N 31 8 E
Aussen Alster, Hbg. 7 D8 53 33N 10 0 E
Austerlitz, Gare d', Paris 5 B4 48 50N 2 22 E
Austin, Chic. 26 B2 41 53N 87 45W
Auteuil, Mtrl. 20 A3 43 37N 73 44W
Avedøre, Købn. 2 E9 55 37N 12 27 E
Aveley, Lon. 4 C6 51 29N 0 15 E
Avellaneda, B.A. 32 C4 34 40 S 58 22W
Avenel, N.Y. 22 D3 40 34N 74 16W
Avenel, Wash. 25 D8 38 59N 76 59W
Avila, Parque National el, Car. 30 D5 10 31N 66 52W
Avila, Pico, Car. 30 D5 10 32N 66 52W
Avini, Nápl. 9 J13 40 48N 14 28 E
Avondale, Chic. 26 B2 41 56N 87 41W
Avondale Heights, Melb. 19 E6 37 45 S 144 52 E
Avtovo, St-Pet. 11 B3 59 51N 30 16 E
Ayase, Tōkyō 13 D1 35 25N 139 26 E
Ayase →, Tōkyō 13 A3 35 52N 139 45 E
Ayazaga, Ist. 17 A2 41 6N 28 59 E
Ayer Chawan, P., Sing. 15 G7 1 16N 103 41 E
Ayer Merbau, P., Sing. 15 G7 1 16N 103 42 E
Ayía Paraskeví, Ath. 8 H11 38 1N 23 49 E
Áyios Dhimítrios, Ath. 8 J11 37 53N 23 44 E
Áyios Ioánnis Rendis, Ath. 8 J10 37 57N 23 39 E
Azabu, Tōkyō 13 C3 35 39N 139 43 E
Azadpur, Delhi 16 A2 28 42N 77 10 E
Azcapotzalco, Méx. 29 B2 19 28N 99 10W
Azteca, Estadia, Méx. 29 C3 19 8N 99 9W
Azusa, L.A. 28 B5 34 7N 117 54W

B

Ba He →, Beij. 14 B3 39 57N 116 27 E
Baba I., Kar. 17 H10 24 49N 66 57 E
Babarpur, Delhi 16 A2 28 41N 77 16 E
Babelsberg, Berl. 7 B1 52 22N 13 7 E
Babushkin, Mos. 11 D10 55 51N 37 42 E
Babylon, N.Y. 23 C9 40 42N 73 19W
Back →, Balt. 25 B4 39 17N 76 27W
Back B., Bomb. 16 H7 18 56N 72 48 E
Bacoor, Manila 15 E3 14 27N 120 56 E
Bacoor B., Manila 15 E3 14 27N 120 54 E
Badagri Cr. →, Lagos 18 B1 6 24N 7 17 E
Badahela, Delhi 16 B1 28 38N 77 4 E
Badalona, Barc. 8 D6 41 26N 2 14 E
Badersfeld, Mün. 7 F10 48 15N 11 31 E
Badgers Mt., Lon. 4 C5 51 20N 0 8 E
Badi, Delhi 16 A1 28 44N 77 8 E
Badinan, Calc. 16 C5 22 53N 88 14 E
Badu, Rio J. 31 B3 22 54 S 43 3W
Baerl, Ruhr 6 B2 51 29N 6 40 E
Bærum, Oslo 2 B3 59 54N 10 36 E
Bærums Verk, Oslo 2 B2 59 56N 10 28 E
Baggensfjärden, Stock. 3 E12 59 18N 18 19 E
Bàggio, Mil. 9 E5 45 27N 9 6 E
Bāgh-e-Feiz, Tehr. 17 C4 35 44N 51 19 E
Baghdād, Bagd. 17 E8 33 20N 44 23 E
Bagmari, Calc. 16 E6 22 34N 88 23 E
Bagneux, Paris 5 C3 48 47N 2 18 E
Bagnolet, Paris 5 B4 48 52N 2 25 E
Bagnoli, Nápl. 9 J11 40 48N 14 9 E
Bagraula, Delhi 16 B1 28 34N 77 4 E
Bagsværd, Købn. 2 D9 55 45N 12 27 E
Bagsværd Sø, Købn. 2 D9 55 46N 12 28 E
Baguiati, Calc. 16 E6 22 36N 88 25 E
Bagumbayan, Manila 15 E4 14 28N 121 3 E
Baha'i Temple, Chic. 26 A2 42 4N 87 41W
Bahrenfeld, Hbg. 7 D7 53 34N 9 55 E
Bahtīm, El Qâ. 18 C5 30 8N 31 16 E
Bahu Bheri, Calc. 16 C5 22 50N 88 14 E
Baidyabati, Calc. 16 C5 22 48N 88 20 E
Baie-d'Urfé, Mtrl. 20 B2 43 25N 73 53W
Baierbrunn, Mün. 7 G10 48 1N 11 29 E
Baijala, Calc. 16 C5 22 51N 88 16 E
Baileys Crossroads, Wash. 25 D7 38 50N 77 6W
Bailly, Paris 5 B2 48 50N 2 4 E
Bainchipota, Calc. 16 C5 22 51N 88 16 E
Bair I., S.F. 27 C3 37 30N 122 13W
Bairro da Matriz, S. Pau. 31 F7 23 40 S 46 27W
Bairro do Limoeiro, S. Pau. 31 E7 23 30 S 46 27W
Baisha, Gzh. 14 G8 23 8N 113 11 E
Baisley Pond, N.Y. 23 C6 40 40N 73 47W
Baixa da Banheira, Lisb. 8 G8 38 39N 9 2W
Baiyun Shan, Gzh. 14 G8 23 8N 113 15 E
Baj Baj, Calc. 16 F5 22 28N 88 11 E
Bakirkoy, Ist. 17 B2 40 58N 28 52 E
Bakovka, Mos. 11 E8 55 40N 37 19 E
Bala-Cynwyd, Phil. 24 A3 40 0N 75 15W
Balagarh, Calc. 16 D6 22 44N 88 27 E
Balara, Manila 15 D4 14 39N 121 3 E
Balarambati, Calc. 16 D5 22 48N 88 12 E
Balashikha, Mos. 11 E11 55 48N 37 58 E
Bald Hill, Bost. 21 B3 42 38N 71 0W
Baldeador, Rio J. 31 B3 22 51 S 43 1W
Baldeneysee, Ruhr 6 B4 51 24N 7 1 E
Baldissero Torinese, Tori. 9 B3 45 4N 7 48 E
Baldpate Hill, Bost. 21 A3 42 42N 71 0W
Baldpate Pond, Bost. 21 A3 42 41N 71 0W
Baldwin, N.Y. 23 D7 40 38N 73 37W
Baldwin Hills, L.A. 28 B2 34 0N 118 21W
Baldwin Hills Res., L.A. 28 B2 34 0N 118 21W
Baldwin Park, L.A. 28 B5 34 5N 117 57W
Bal'etan →, Gzh. 14 G8 23 5N 113 14 E
Balgowlah, Syd. 19 A4 33 47 S 151 16 E
Balgowlah Heights, Syd. 19 A4 33 48 S 151 16 E
Balham, Lon. 4 C4 51 26N 0 8W
Balihati, Calc. 16 D5 22 44N 88 18 E
Balingsnäs, Stock. 3 E11 59 13N 18 0 E
Balingsta, Stock. 3 E11 59 12N 18 3 E
Balintawak, Manila 15 D3 14 39N 120 59 E
Balitai, Tianj. 14 E6 39 5N 117 11 E
Balizhuang, Beij. 14 B3 39 53N 116 28 E
Ballabhpur, Calc. 16 D6 22 44N 88 20 E
Ballainvilliers, Paris 5 C3 48 40N 2 17 E
Ballardvale, Bost. 21 B3 42 37N 71 9W
Ballenato, Pta., La Hab. 30 B2 23 55N 82 28W
Ballerup, Købn. 2 D9 55 43N 12 21 E
Bally, Calc. 16 E6 22 38N 88 20 E
Ballygunge, Calc. 16 E6 22 31N 88 21 E
Balmain, Syd. 19 B4 33 51 S 151 11 E
Balmumcu, Ist. 17 A3 41 3N 29 2 E
Balongbato, Manila 15 D3 14 39N 120 59 E
Baltikri, Calc. 16 E5 22 36N 88 18 E
Baltimore, Balt. 25 B3 39 17N 76 37W
Baltimore Highlands, Balt. 25 B3 39 14N 76 38W
Baltimore-Washington Int. Airport, Balt. 25 B3 39 11N 76 39W
Baluhati, Calc. 16 E5 22 39N 88 15 E
Balwyn, Melb. 19 E7 37 48 S 145 4 E
Balwyn North, Melb. 19 E7 37 47 S 145 4 E
Bambang, Manila 15 D4 14 31N 121 4 E
Bamondongri, Bomb. 16 H9 18 58N 73 1 E
Ban Baan Phichit, Bangk. 15 B2 13 49N 100 37 E
Ban Hugli, Calc. 16 E6 22 38N 88 22 E
Ban Lat Phrao, Bangk. 15 B2 13 47N 100 35 E
Banabuey →, La Hab. 30 B2 23 5N 82 27W
Bananal, S. Pau. 31 D5 23 27 S 46 41W
Banática, Lisb. 8 F7 38 40N 9 11W
Bandeirantes, Praia dos, Rio J. 31 C1 23 0 S 43 23W
Bandipur, Calc. 16 D6 22 43N 88 26 E
Bandipur, Calc. 16 C4 22 50N 88 9 E
Bandra, Bomb. 16 G7 19 3N 72 49 E
Bandra Pt., Bomb. 16 G7 19 2N 72 49 E
Banfield, B.A. 32 C4 34 44 S 58 24W
Bang Kapi, Bangk. 15 B2 13 45N 100 38 E
Bang Khen, Bangk. 15 A2 13 52N 100 35 E
Bang Na, Bangk. 15 B2 13 40N 100 36 E
Bang Su, Khlong →, Bangk. 15 B2 13 47N 100 31 E
Bangbae, Sŏul 12 H7 37 29N 126 59 E
Banghag, Sŏul 12 G8 37 38N 127 1 E
Bangka, Jak. 15 J9 6 15 S 106 48 E
Bangkok, Bangk. 15 B2 13 44N 100 30 E
Bangkok Noi, Khlong →, Bangk. 15 B1 13 45N 100 29 E
Bangkok Yai, Bangk. 15 B1 13 43N 100 29 E
Bangkok Yai, Khlong →, Bangk. 15 B1 13 44N 100 29 E
Banglo, Calc. 16 E5 22 31N 88 14 E
Bangrak, Bangk. 15 B2 13 43N 100 31 E
Bangu, Rio J. 31 B2 22 52 S 43 26W
Bangu, Sa. do, Rio J. 31 B1 22 53 S 43 24W
Bankipur, Calc. 16 D5 22 47N 88 13 E
Bankra, Calc. 16 E5 22 36N 88 17 E
Banks, C., Syd. 19 C4 34 0 S 151 16 E
Bankstown, Syd. 19 B3 33 55 S 151 2 E
Bankstown Aerodrome, Syd. 19 B2 33 55 S 150 59 E
Banna →, Tori. 9 A3 45 12N 7 42 E
Banstala, Calc. 16 E6 22 31N 88 24 E
Banstead, Lon. 4 D3 51 18N 0 12W
Bantra, Calc. 16 E5 22 35N 88 18 E
Banyule Flats Res., Melb. 19 E7 37 44 S 145 5 E
Baquirivú, S. Pau. 31 D7 23 26 S 46 28W
Baquirivú-Guaçu, S. Pau. 31 D7 23 28 S 46 28W
Bara, Calc. 16 D5 22 45N 88 16 E
Baragwanath Airfield, Jobg. 18 F8 26 14 S 27 58 E
Barai, Calc. 16 C6 22 52N 88 22 E
Barajas, Mdrd. 8 B3 40 28N 3 34W
Barajas, Aeropuerto Transoceanico de, Mdrd. 8 B3 40 28N 3 33W
Barakpur, Calc. 16 D6 22 47N 88 21 E
Baranagar, Calc. 16 E6 22 38N 88 22 E
Barbaiana, Mil. 9 D5 45 32N 9 1 E
Barca, Tori. 9 B3 45 6N 7 43 E
Barcarena, Lisb. 8 F7 38 43N 9 16W
Barcarena →, Lisb. 8 F7 38 41N 9 16W
Barcelona, Barc. 8 D6 41 22N 2 10 E
Barcelona-Prat, Aeropuerta de, Barc. 8 E5 41 17N 2 5 E
Barceloneta, Barc. 8 D6 41 22N 2 11 E
Barcroft, L., Wash. 25 D6 38 50N 77 9W
Baréggio, Mil. 9 E5 45 28N 9 0 E
Bariti Bil, Calc. 16 D6 22 48N 88 26 E
Barkarby, Stock. 3 D10 59 24N 17 52 E
Barker Pt., N.Y. 23 B6 40 51N 73 44W
Barking, Lon. 4 B5 51 32N 0 5 E
Barkingside, Lon. 4 B5 51 35N 0 4 E
Barlovento, La Hab. 30 B2 23 5N 82 28W
Barmbek, Hbg. 7 D8 53 34N 10 2 E
Barmen, Ruhr 6 C5 51 16N 7 12 E
Barneau, Paris 5 D6 48 38N 2 43 E
Barnes, Lon. 4 C3 51 28N 0 14W
Barnet, Lon. 4 B3 51 39N 0 11W
Barnsboro, Phil. 24 C4 39 45N 75 9W
Baronia Park, Syd. 19 A3 33 49 S 151 8 E
Barop, Ruhr 6 B6 51 29N 7 25 E
Barra, Nápl. 9 H12 40 50N 14 19 E
Barra Andai, Kar. 17 H11 24 47N 66 59 E
Barra Funda, S. Pau. 31 E6 23 31 S 46 39W
Barracas, B.A. 32 B4 34 39 S 58 24W
Barrackpore Airport, Calc. 16 D6 22 46N 88 21 E
Barrancas, Stgo 30 J10 33 26 S 70 44W
Barranco, Lima 30 G8 12 9 S 77 2W
Barreiro, Lisb. 8 G8 38 39N 9 5W
Barreto, Rio J. 31 B3 22 50 S 43 5W
Barrientos, Méx. 29 A2 19 34N 99 11W
Barrington, Phil. 24 B4 39 52N 75 3W
Barrio de La Estación, Mdrd. 8 B3 40 26N 3 32W
Bartala, Calc. 16 E5 22 32N 88 15 E
Barton Park, Syd. 19 B3 33 56 S 151 9 E
Bartyki, Wsaw. 10 F7 52 10N 21 6 E
Baru, Kali →, Jak. 15 J10 6 12 S 106 51 E
Baruipara, Calc. 16 E5 22 45N 88 13 E
Baruta, Car. 30 E5 10 26N 66 52W
Barvikha, Mos. 11 E7 55 44N 37 16 E
Basai Darapur, Delhi 16 B1 28 38N 77 6 E
Bass Hill, Syd. 19 B3 33 54 S 151 0 E
Bassett, L.A. 28 B5 34 3N 117 59W
Bastille, Place de la, Paris 5 B4 48 51N 2 22 E
Bastos, Rio J. 31 B1 22 52 S 43 21W
Basudebpur, Calc. 16 D6 22 49N 88 24 E
Basus, El Qâ. 18 C5 30 7N 31 12 E
Batanagar, Calc. 16 E5 22 31N 88 15 E
Batenbrock, Ruhr 6 A3 51 31N 6 57 E
Bath Beach, N.Y. 22 D4 40 36N 74 0W
Bath I., Kar. 17 H11 24 49N 67 1 E
Batok, Bukit, Sing. 15 F7 1 21N 103 46 E
Battersea, Lon. 4 C4 51 28N 0 9W
Baturino, Mos. 11 F9 55 35N 37 30 E
Bauman, Mos. 11 E10 55 45N 37 40 E
Baumgarten, Wien 10 G9 48 12N 16 17 E
Bauria, Calc. 16 E5 22 30N 88 10 E
Baxter Estates, N.Y. 23 B6 40 50N 73 41W
Bay Farm I., S.F. 27 B3 37 44N 122 14W
Bay Meadows Race Track, S.F. 27 C3 37 32N 122 17W
Bay Park, N.Y. 23 D7 40 37N 73 39W
Bay Ridge, N.Y. 22 D4 40 37N 74 1W
Bay Ridge Channel, N.Y. 22 D4 40 39N 74 1W
Bay Shore Park, Balt. 25 B4 39 13N 76 25W
Baykoz, Ist. 17 A3 41 7N 29 7 E
Bayonne, N.Y. 22 C4 40 40N 74 6W
Bayshore, S.F. 27 B2 37 42N 122 24W
Bayside, N.Y. 23 C6 40 45N 73 46W
Bayswater, Lon. 4 B3 51 30N 0 10W
Bayswater, Melb. 19 F8 37 50 S 145 17 E
Bayview, S.F. 27 B2 37 44N 122 23W
Bayville, N.Y. 23 B7 40 54N 73 33W
Bāzār, Tehr. 17 C5 35 40N 51 25 E
Beachmont, Bost. 21 C4 42 23N 70 59W
Beacon Hill, H.K. 12 D6 22 21N 114 10 E
Beaconsfield, Mtrl. 20 B2 43 25N 73 53W
Beacontree Heath, Lon. 4 B6 51 33N 0 9 E
Beam →, Lon. 4 B6 51 30N 0 10 E
Bear Cr. →, Balt. 25 B3 39 13N 76 30W
Bear Gulch Res., S.F. 27 D3 37 26N 122 13W
Beato, Lisb. 8 F8 38 44N 9 5W
Beauchamp, Paris 5 A3 49 0N 2 11 E
Beaumonte Heights, Trto. 20 D7 43 45N 79 34W
Beaverdam Cr. →, Wash. 25 C8 39 0N 76 5W
Bebek, Ist. 17 A3 41 4N 29 2 E
Beccar, B.A. 32 A3 34 27 S 58 32W
Běchovice, Pra. 10 B3 50 4N 14 36 E
Beck L., Chic. 26 A1 42 4N 87 52W
Beckenham, Lon. 4 C4 51 24N 0 1W
Beckhausen, Ruhr 6 A4 51 33N 7 1 E
Beckton, Lon. 4 B5 51 30N 0 4 E
Beddington, Lon. 4 C4 51 21N 0 8W
Beddington Corner, Lon. 4 C4 51 23N 0 9W
Bedford, Bost. 21 C2 42 27N 71 15W
Bedford Park, Chic. 26 C2 41 46N 87 46W
Bedford Park, N.Y. 23 B5 40 52N 73 52W
Bedford Stuyvesant, N.Y. 22 C5 40 41N 73 56W
Bedford View, Jobg. 18 F9 26 10 S 28 7 E
Bedok, Sing. 15 G8 1 19N 103 56 E
Beeck, Ruhr 6 B2 51 28N 6 44 E
Beeckerwerth, Ruhr 6 B2 51 28N 6 42 E
Behala, Calc. 16 E5 22 30N 88 18 E
Bei Hai, Beij. 14 B3 39 54N 116 21 E
Beicai, Shang. 14 J12 31 11N 121 32 E
Beicun, Beij. 14 D5 39 13N 117 7 E
Beigai, Tianj. 14 E6 39 9N 117 10 E
Beijiaoshichang, Beij. 14 B2 39 57N 116 19 E
Beijing, Beij. 14 B2 39 53N 116 21 E
Beinasco, Tori. 9 B2 45 1N 7 34 E
Beirolas, Lisb. 8 F8 38 46N 9 5W
Beitsun, Gzh. 14 G8 23 7N 113 10 E
Békásmegyer, Bud. 10 J13 47 35N 19 3 E
Bekkelaget, Oslo 2 B4 59 53N 10 47 E
Bel Air, L.A. 28 B2 34 4N 118 27W
Bela Vista, S. Pau. 31 E6 23 33 S 46 38W
Bélanger, Mtrl. 20 A3 43 35N 73 42W
Belas, Lisb. 8 F7 38 46N 9 15W
Belém, Lisb. 8 F7 38 41N 9 12W
Belém, Torre de, Lisb. 8 F7 38 41N 9 12W
Belenzinho, S. Pau. 31 E6 23 32 S 46 34W
Belfield, Syd. 19 B3 33 53 S 151 6 E
Belgachi, Calc. 16 E5 22 36N 88 18 E
Belgharia, Calc. 16 E6 22 39N 88 22 E
Belgrano, B.A. 32 B4 34 33 S 58 27W
Belgrave, Melb. 19 F9 37 54 S 145 21 E
Bell Gardens, L.A. 28 C4 33 58N 118 9W
Bella Vista, B.A. 32 B2 34 34 S 58 41W
Bellaire, N.Y. 23 C6 40 42N 73 44W
Bellavista, Lima 30 G8 12 4 S 77 8W
Bellavista, Stgo 30 K11 33 31 S 70 35W
Belle Harbour, N.Y. 23 D5 40 34N 73 51W
Belle Haven, N.Y. 23 A7 41 0N 73 37W
Belle Haven, Wash. 25 E7 38 46N 77 3W
Bellefonte, Phil. 24 C1 39 45N 75 30W
Bellerose, N.Y. 23 C6 40 44N 73 42W
Belleview, Wash. 25 D6 38 57N 77 14W
Belleville, N.Y. 22 C4 40 48N 74 8W
Bellflower, L.A. 28 C4 33 53N 118 7W
Bellingham, Lon. 4 C4 51 25N 0 1W
Bellmawr, Phil. 24 B4 39 52N 75 5W
Bellmore, N.Y. 23 D7 40 39N 73 31W
Bello, La Hab. 30 B2 23 5N 82 24W
Bells Lake, Phil. 24 C4 39 45N 75 3W
Bellwood, Chic. 26 B1 41 52N 87 53W
Belmont, Bost. 21 C2 42 23N 71 10W
Belmont, Lon. 4 B3 51 36N 0 18W
Belmont, S.F. 27 C3 37 31N 122 17W
Belmont Cragin, Chic. 26 B2 41 56N 87 45W
Belmont Harbor, Chic. 26 B3 41 56N 87 38W
Belmont Hills, Phil. 24 A3 40 1N 75 15W
Belmont Slough, S.F. 27 C3 37 32N 122 15W
Belmore, Syd. 19 B3 33 55 S 151 5 E
Belopurpada, Bomb. 16 G9 19 0N 73 1 E
Beltsville, Wash. 25 C8 39 2N 76 54W
Beltsville Airport, Wash. 25 C9 39 1N 76 49W
Belur, Calc. 16 E6 22 37N 88 21 E
Belvedere, Lon. 4 C5 51 29N 0 9 E
Belvedere, S.F. 27 A2 37 52N 122 27W
Belyayevo Bogorodskoye, Mos. 11 F9 55 39N 37 31 E
Bemböle, Hels. 3 B2 60 13N 24 39 E
Bemis Woods, Chic. 26 C1 41 49N 87 54W
Bemowo, Wsaw. 10 E6 52 15N 20 53 E
Benavidez, B.A. 32 A2 34 24 S 58 41W
Bendale, Trto. 20 D9 43 45N 79 15W
Bendungan Hilir, Jak. 15 J9 6 12 S 106 48 E
Benefica, Rio J. 31 B2 22 52 S 43 14W
Benfica, Lisb. 8 F7 38 45N 9 11W
Benin B., Lagos 18 B2 6 24N 7 28 E
Benjamin Franklin Br., Phil. 24 B4 39 57N 75 8W
Benoni, Jobg. 18 F10 26 11 S 28 18 E
Benoni South, Jobg. 18 F10 26 12 S 28 17 E
Bensenville, Chic. 26 B1 41 57N 87 56W
Bensonhurst, N.Y. 22 D5 40 35N 73 59W
Bentleigh, Melb. 19 F7 37 54 S 145 2 E
Bentleigh East, Melb. 19 F7 37 54 S 145 4 E
Beraberi, Calc. 16 D6 22 46N 88 27 E
Berario, Jobg. 18 E8 26 7 S 27 57 E
Berazategui, B.A. 32 C5 34 45 S 58 15W
Berea, Jobg. 18 F9 26 10 S 28 3 E
Berg am Laim, Mün. 7 G10 48 7N 11 38 E
Bergbaumuseum, Ruhr 6 B5 51 29N 7 13 E
Bergenfield, N.Y. 22 B5 40 55N 73 59W
Berger, Oslo 2 B6 59 56N 11 7 E
Bergerhausen, Ruhr 6 B4 51 26N 7 2 E
Bergerhof, Ruhr 6 C6 51 12N 7 21 E
Bergham, Mün. 7 G10 48 2N 11 37 E
Berghausen, Ruhr 6 A5 51 36N 7 12 E
Berghm-Oestrum, Ruhr 6 B1 51 25N 6 39 E
Bergstedt, Hbg. 7 C8 53 40N 10 7 E
Beri, Barc. 8 D5 41 20N 2 1 E
Berih, Sungei →, Sing. 15 F7 1 22N 103 40 E
Berkeley, Chic. 26 B1 41 53N 87 54W
Berkeley, S.F. 27 A3 37 51N 122 16W
Berkeley Heights, N.Y. 22 C2 40 40N 74 26W
Berkeley Hills, S.F. 27 A3 37 51N 122 11W
Berlin, Berl. 7 A3 52 31N 13 23 E
Berlin, Phil. 24 C5 39 47N 74 55W
Bermondsey, Lon. 4 C4 51 29N 0 3W
Bernabeu, Estadio, Mdrd. 8 B2 40 27N 3 41W
Bernal, B.A. 32 C5 34 43 S 58 17W
Bernal Heights, S.F. 27 B2 37 44N 122 24W
Berne, Hbg. 7 D8 53 38N 10 8 E
Berngardovka, St-Pet. 11 A5 60 0N 30 34 E
Berthpage, N.Y. 23 C8 40 45N 73 29W
Bertlich, Ruhr 6 A4 51 36N 7 4 E
Bertolla Barca, Tori. 9 B3 45 6N 7 44 E
Berwyn, Chic. 26 B2 41 50N 87 47W
Berwyn, Phil. 24 A2 40 2N 75 26W
Berwyn Heights, Wash. 25 D8 38 59N 76 55W
Besedy, Mos. 11 F10 55 38N 37 47 E
Besiktas, Ist. 17 A3 41 2N 29 0 E
Beskudnikovo, Mos. 11 D9 55 52N 37 34 E
Besós →, Barc. 8 D6 41 24N 2 13 E
Bessancourt, Paris 5 A3 49 2N 2 12 E
Bestazzo, Mil. 9 E5 45 25N 9 0 E
Bethayres, Phil. 24 A4 40 7N 75 3W
Bethesda, Wash. 25 D7 38 59N 77 6W
Bethlehem Steel Plant, Balt. 25 B4 39 13N 76 29W
Bethnal Green, Lon. 4 B4 51 31N 0 2W
Bethpage State Park, N.Y. 23 C8 40 45N 73 25W
Betor, Calc. 16 E5 22 34N 88 17 E
Beuvronne →, Paris 5 B6 48 59N 2 40 E
Beverley, Chic. 26 C3 41 42N 87 39W
Beverley Hills, Syd. 19 B3 33 56 S 151 5 E
Beverley Park, Syd. 19 B3 33 58 S 151 8 E
Beverly, Bost. 21 B4 42 34N 70 53W
Beverly, Phil. 24 A5 40 3N 74 55W
Beverly Glen, L.A. 28 B2 34 6N 118 26W
Beverly Harbor, Bost. 21 B4 42 32N 70 51W
Beverly Hills, L.A. 28 B2 34 5N 118 24W
Beverly Municipal Airport, Bost. 21 B4 42 36N 70 55W
Bexley, Lon. 4 C5 51 26N 0 8 E
Bexley, Syd. 19 B3 33 56 S 151 7 E
Bexleyheath, Lon. 4 C5 51 27N 0 8 E
Beyenburg, Ruhr 6 C5 51 15N 7 19 E
Beylerbeyi, Ist. 17 A3 41 2N 29 2 E
Beyoğlu, Ist. 17 A2 41 1N 28 58 E
Bezons, Paris 5 B3 48 56N 2 13 E
Bhadrakali, Calc. 16 D6 22 40N 88 20 E
Bhadreswar, Calc. 16 D5 22 49N 88 22 E
Bhadua, Calc. 16 D5 22 40N 88 12 E
Bhalswa, Delhi 16 A2 28 44N 77 10 E
Bhambo Khān Qarmati, Kar. 17 H11 24 49N 67 7 E
Bhandardaha, Calc. 16 E5 22 37N 88 12 E
Bhatpara, Calc. 16 C6 22 52N 88 25 E
Bhatpur, Calc. 16 D6 22 43N 88 25 E
Bhatsala, Calc. 16 E5 22 30N 88 16 E
Bhawanipore, Calc. 16 E6 22 32N 88 21 E
Bhopura, Delhi 16 A2 28 41N 77 19 E
Białołeka Dworska, Wsaw. 10 E7 52 19N 21 1 E
Bickley, Lon. 4 C5 51 23N 0 3 E
Bicutan, Manila 15 D4 14 30N 121 3 E
Bidyadharpur, Calc. 16 C6 22 50N 88 24 E
Bielany, Wsaw. 10 E6 52 17N 20 57 E
Biesdorf, Berl. 7 A4 52 30N 13 33 E
Bièvre →, Paris 5 C2 48 44N 2 9 E
Bièvres, Paris 5 C3 48 45N 2 13 E
Big Timber Cr. →, Phil. 24 B4 39 52N 75 7W
Big Tujunga Canyon →, L.A. 28 A3 34 16N 118 12W
Biggin Hill, Lon. 4 D5 51 18N 0 1 E
Bijoki, Tōkyō 13 B2 35 49N 139 38 E
Bilibiran, Manila 15 E5 14 29N 121 10 E
Bilk, Ruhr 6 C2 51 12N 6 46 E
Billbrook, Hbg. 7 D8 53 31N 10 4 E
Bille →, Hbg. 7 D8 53 32N 10 4 E
Billerica, Bost. 21 B2 42 33N 71 16W
Billinghurst, B.A. 32 B3 34 34 S 58 37W
Billings, Represa, S. Pau. 31 F6 23 42 S 46 39W
Billstedt, Hbg. 7 D8 53 32N 10 6 E
Billwerder, Hbg. 7 D8 53 30N 10 7 E
Billwerder B., Hbg. 7 D8 53 31N 10 3 E
Binacayan, Manila 15 E3 14 27N 120 55 E
Binangonan, Manila 15 E5 14 28N 121 10 E
Binaria, Jak. 15 H10 6 7 S 106 51 E
Bingzhoubao, Gzh. 14 G8 23 2N 113 11 E
Binningsvatna, Oslo 2 C6 50 46N 11 3 E
Binondo, Manila 15 D3 14 36N 120 58 E
Binzago, Mil. 9 D5 45 37N 9 8 E
Birak el Kiyam, El Qâ. 18 C4 30 2N 31 9 E
Birch Cliff, Trto. 20 D9 43 41N 79 16W
Bird →, Balt. 25 A4 39 22N 76 22W
Birka, Stock. 3 D8 59 20N 17 33 E
Birkenhöhe, Berl. 7 A4 52 38N 13 36 E
Birkenstein, Berl. 7 A5 52 31N 13 40 E
Birkholz, Berl. 7 A4 52 37N 13 34 E
Birkholzaue, Berl. 7 A4 52 38N 13 36 E
Biryulyovo, Mos. 11 F10 55 35N 37 40 E
Bisamberg, Wien 10 G10 48 19N 16 21 E
Bispebjerg, Købn. 2 D10 55 42N 12 32 E
Bitsa, Mos. 11 F9 55 35N 37 36 E
Biwon Secret Garden, Sŏul 12 G7 37 34N 126 59 E
Bizard, Î., Mtrl. 20 B2 43 29N 73 53W
Björknas, Stock. 3 E12 59 19N 18 13 E
Björköfjärden, Hels. 3 C2 60 7N 24 38 E
Black Cr. →, Trto. 20 D8 43 40N 79 30W
Blackburn, Melb. 19 E7 37 48 S 145 9 E
Blackburn L., Melb. 19 E7 37 49 S 145 9 E
Blackburn South, Melb. 19 F7 37 50 S 145 9 E
Blackfen, Lon. 4 C5 51 26N 0 6 E
Blackheath, Jobg. 18 E8 26 8 S 27 57 E
Blackheath, Lon. 4 C5 51 28N 0 0 E
Blackmore, Lon. 4 A6 51 41N 0 19 E
Blacktown, Syd. 19 A2 33 46 S 150 56 E
Blackwall, Lon. 4 B4 51 30N 0 0 E
Blackwood, Phil. 24 C4 39 47N 75 4W
Bladensburg, Wash. 25 D8 38 55N 76 55W
Blairgowrie, Jobg. 18 E9 26 6 S 28 0 E
Blakehurst, Syd. 19 B3 33 59 S 151 6 E
Blakstad, Oslo 2 C2 50 49N 10 28 E
Blanco, C., Car. 30 D5 10 36N 66 59W
Blankenburg, Berl. 7 A3 52 35N 13 27 E
Blankenese, Hbg. 7 D6 53 33N 9 48 E
Blankenfelde, Berl. 7 A3 52 37N 13 23 E
Blankenstein, Ruhr 6 B5 51 24N 7 11 E
Blenheim, Phil. 24 C4 39 48N 75 4W
Bliersheim, Ruhr 6 B2 51 23N 6 42 E
Blind Cr. →, Melb. 19 F8 37 53 S 145 12 E
Blizne, Wsaw. 10 E6 52 14N 20 52 E
Bloomfield, N.Y. 22 C3 40 48N 74 12W
Bloomingdale, N.Y. 22 A3 41 0N 74 19W
Bloomsbury, Balt. 25 B2 39 15N 76 44W
Blota, Wsaw. 10 F8 52 9N 21 11 E
Bloubosspruit →, Jobg. 18 F9 26 16 S 28 0 E
Blue Hills Reservation, Bost. 21 D3 42 13N 71 5W
Blue Island, Chic. 26 C2 41 40N 87 40W
Bluff Hd., H.K. 12 E6 22 11N 114 12 E
Blumberg, Berl. 7 A4 52 36N 13 39 E
Blunt Pt., S.F. 27 A2 37 51N 122 25W
Blutenberg, Mün. 7 G9 48 9N 11 27 E
Blylaget, Oslo 2 C4 59 46N 10 41 E
Boa Vista, Alto do, Rio J. 31 B2 22 58 S 43 16W
Boa Vista, Morro, Rio J. 31 B3 22 53 S 43 5W
Boadilla del Monte, Mdrd. 8 B1 40 24N 3 52W
Boardwalk, N.Y. 23 D6 40 34N 73 49W
Boavista, Lisb. 8 F8 38 48N 9 8W
Bobäck, Hels. 3 B2 60 10N 24 31 E
Boberg, Hbg. 7 D8 53 30N 10 9 E
Bobigny, Paris 5 B4 48 54N 2 26 E
Bobylskaya, St-Pet. 11 B3 59 59N 30 10 E
Bocanegra, Lima 30 F8 11 59 S 77 7W
Boccea, Rome 9 F8 41 57N 12 19 E
Bochold, Ruhr 6 B3 51 28N 6 57 E
Bochum, Ruhr 6 B5 51 28N 7 13 E
Bockum, Ruhr 6 B1 51 21N 6 37 E
Bodelschwingh, Ruhr 6 A6 51 33N 7 22 E
Bodomjärvi, Hels. 3 B3 60 15N 24 40 E
Bogenhausen, Mün. 7 G10 48 8N 11 36 E
Bognæs, Købn. 2 D7 55 41N 12 1 E
Bogorodskoye, Mos. 11 E10 55 48N 37 42 E
Bogota, N.Y. 22 B4 40 52N 74 2W
Bogstadvatnet, Oslo 2 B3 59 58N 10 37 E
Bohaidalu, Tianj. 14 E6 39 7N 117 12 E
Bohnsdorf, Berl. 7 B4 52 23N 13 34 E
Bois-Colombes, Paris 5 B3 48 55N 2 16 E
Bois-d'Arcy, Paris 5 C2 48 48N 2 1 E
Boisement, Paris 5 A2 49 1N 2 0 E
Boissy-St.-Léger, Paris 5 C5 48 44N 2 31 E
Boksburg, Jobg. 18 F10 26 12 S 28 15 E
Boksburg North, Jobg. 18 F10 26 12 S 28 15 E
Boksburg South, Jobg. 18 F10 26 13 S 28 16 E
Boldinasco, Mil. 9 E5 45 29N 9 8 E
Bøler, Oslo 2 B5 59 53N 10 50 E
Bollate, Mil. 9 D5 45 32N 9 7 E
Bollensdorf, Berl. 7 A5 52 30N 13 42 E
Bollmora, Stock. 3 E12 59 14N 18 14 E
Bolshaya Nevka, St-Pet. 11 B3 59 58N 30 18 E
Bolshaya-Okhta, St-Pet. 11 B4 59 56N 30 26 E
Bolshoi Theatre, Mos. 11 E9 55 45N 37 37 E
Bom Retiro, S. Pau. 31 E6 23 31 S 46 38W
Bombay, Bomb. 16 H8 18 56N 72 50 E
Bombay Harbour, Bomb. 16 H8 18 58N 72 55 E
Bombay Univ., Bomb. 16 H7 18 55N 72 49 E
Bommern, Ruhr 6 B6 51 25N 7 20 E
Bonaero Park, Jobg. 18 E10 26 7 S 28 15 E
Bondi, Syd. 19 B4 33 53 S 151 16 E
Bondoufle, Paris 5 D4 48 36N 2 22 E
Bondy, Paris 5 B4 48 54N 2 28 E
Bondy, Forêt de, Paris 5 B5 48 54N 2 33 E
Bonifacio Monument, Manila 15 D3 14 38N 120 58 E
Bonifica di Maccarese, Rome 9 F8 41 50N 12 15 E
Bonifica di Porto, Rome 9 G8 41 48N 12 16 E
Bonita, Pt., S.F. 27 B1 37 48N 122 31W
Bonnelles, Paris 5 D2 48 37N 2 1 E
Bonneuil-sur-Marne, Paris 5 C5 48 46N 2 30 E
Bönningstedt, Hbg. 7 C7 53 40N 9 54 E
Bonnyrigg, Syd. 19 B2 33 53 S 150 54 E
Bonsari, Bomb. 16 G9 19 4N 73 1 E
Bonsucesso, Rio J. 31 B2 22 51 S 43 15W
Boo, Stock. 3 D12 59 20N 18 16 E
Boonton, N.Y. 22 B2 40 54N 74 24W
Boonton Res., N.Y. 22 B2 40 53N 74 24W
Booth Corner, Phil. 24 B2 39 50N 75 29W
Boothwyn, Phil. 24 C2 39 49N 75 26W
Borbeck, Ruhr 6 B3 51 28N 6 56 E
Bordeaux, Jobg. 18 E9 26 5 S 28 1 E
Bordeaux, Mtrl. 20 A3 43 31N 73 43W
Borehamwood, Lon. 4 B3 51 39N 0 15W
Borgaretto, Tori. 9 B2 45 0N 7 35 E
Bórgaro Torinese, Tori. 9 B2 45 9N 7 39 E
Borghese, Villa, Rome 9 F9 41 54N 12 29 E
Borisovo, Mos. 11 F10 55 37N 37 44 E
Borle, Bomb. 16 G8 19 2N 72 54 E
Bornig, Ruhr 6 A5 51 33N 7 16 E
Bornsjön, Stock. 3 E9 59 14N 17 44 E
Boronia, Melb. 19 F8 37 51 S 145 17 E
Borough Green, Lon. 4 D6 51 17N 0 18 E
Borough Park, N.Y. 22 D5 40 38N 73 59W
Børtervatna, Oslo 2 C6 59 47N 11 4 E
Boscoreale, Nápl. 9 J13 40 46N 14 28 E
Boscotrecase, Nápl. 9 J13 40 46N 14 27 E
Bösinghovn, Ruhr 6 C1 51 18N 6 38 E
Bosmont, Jobg. 18 F8 26 10 S 27 57 E
Bosön, Stock. 3 D12 59 22N 18 11 E
Bosporus = Istanbul Boğazi, Ist. 17 A3 41 5N 29 3 E
Bosque da Saúde, S. Pau. 31 E6 23 36 S 46 37W
Bosques, B.A. 32 C5 34 48 S 58 15W
Bossley Park, Syd. 19 B2 33 51 S 150 53 E
Bossucaba →, S. Pau. 31 E5 23 31 S 46 46W
Bostanci, Ist. 17 B3 40 57N 29 5 E
Bostelbek, Hbg. 7 E7 53 28N 9 55 E
Boston, Bost. 21 C3 42 21N 71 3W
Boston B., Bost. 21 C4 42 22N 70 55W
Boston Harbor, Bost. 21 C4 42 20N 70 58W
Boston Hill, Bost. 21 A3 42 38N 71 5W
Botany, Syd. 19 B4 33 56 S 151 12 E
Botany B., Lon. 4 A4 51 40N 0 7W
Botany B., Syd. 19 B4 33 58 S 151 11 E
Botič →, Pra. 10 B3 50 4N 14 26 E
Botkyrka, Stock. 3 E9 59 15N 17 49 E
Botofogo, Rio J. 31 B2 22 56 S 43 10W
Bottrop, Ruhr 6 A3 51 32N 6 57 E
Bötzow, Berl. 7 A1 52 39N 13 8 E
Bouafle, Paris 5 B1 48 57N 1 54 E
Boucherville, Mtrl. 20 A5 43 36N 73 28W
Boucherville, Îs. de, Mtrl. 20 A5 43 36N 73 28W
Bougival, Paris 5 B2 48 51N 2 8 E
Boulder Pt., H.K. 12 E5 22 14N 114 6 E

Choisy-le-Roi 35

Boullay-les-Troux, *Paris* 5 C2 48 40N 2 2 E
Boulogne, *B.A.* 32 B3 34 30 S 58 33W
Boulogne, Bois de, *Paris* 5 B3 48 51N 2 14 E
Boulogne-Billancourt, *Paris* 5 B3 48 50N 2 14 E
Bouqueval, *Paris* 5 A4 49 1N 2 25 E
Bourg-la-Reine, *Paris* 5 C3 48 46N 2 19 E
Boussy-St.-Antoine, *Paris* 5 C5 48 41N 2 33 E
Bouviers, *Paris* 5 C2 48 46N 2 4 E
Bovert, *Ruhr* 6 C1 51 16N 6 37 E
Bovisa, *Mil.* 9 D6 45 30N 9 10 E
Bovísio-Masciago, *Mil.* 9 D5 45 36N 9 8 E
Bow, *Lon.* 4 B4 51 31N 0 1W
Bowleys Quarters, *Balt.* 25 A4 39 20N 76 24W
Box Hill, *Melb.* 19 E7 37 48 S 145 6 E
Boxford State Forest, *Bost.* 21 B3 42 39N 71 2W
Boy, *Ruhr* 6 A3 51 31N 7 0 E
Boyaciköy, *Ist.* 17 A3 41 5N 29 2 E
Boye →, *Ruhr* 6 A3 51 30N 6 59 E
Boyle Heights, *L.A.* 28 B3 34 1N 118 12 E
Braddell Heights, *Sing.* 15 F8 1 20N 103 51 E
Brahmanpur, *Bomb.* 16 G8 19 5N 72 52 E
Braintree, *Bost.* 21 D3 42 12N 71 0W
Brakpan, *Jobg.* 18 F11 26 14 S 28 20 E
Brambauer, *Ruhr* 6 A6 51 35N 7 26 E
Bramfeld, *Hbg.* 7 D8 53 36N 10 5 E
Bramley, *Jobg.* 18 E9 26 7 S 28 4 E
Brande, *Hbg.* 7 D6 53 37N 9 49 E
Brandenburg Gate, *Berl.* 7 A3 52 30N 13 21 E
Brandizzo, *Tori.* 9 A3 45 10N 7 49 E
Brands Hatch, *Lon.* 4 C6 51 21N 0 15 E
Brandýs nad Labem, *Pra.* 10 A3 50 10N 14 39 E
Brandywine, *Phil.* 24 C1 39 49N 75 32W
Brandywine Cr. →, *Phil.* 24 C1 39 43N 75 31W
Brani, P., *Sing.* 15 G8 1 15N 103 50 E
Branik, *Pra.* 10 B2 50 1N 14 25 E
Brännkyrka, *Stock.* 3 E11 59 17N 18 0 E
Brás, *S. Pau.* 31 E6 23 32 S 46 36W
Brateyevo, *Mos.* 11 F10 55 39N 37 45 E
Bratsevo, *Mos.* 11 D8 55 51N 37 24 E
Brauck, *Ruhr* 6 A3 51 32N 7 0 E
Brava, Pta., *La Hab.* 30 B2 23 8N 82 23W
Braybrook, *Melb.* 19 E6 37 46 S 144 51 E
Brázdim, *Pra.* 10 A3 50 10N 14 35 E
Breakheart Reservation, *Bost.* 21 C3 42 28N 71 1W
Brechten, *Ruhr* 6 A6 51 34N 7 27 E
Breckerfeld, *Ruhr* 6 C6 51 15N 7 28 E
Brede, *Købn.* 2 D10 55 47N 12 30 E
Bredeney, *Ruhr* 6 B3 51 24N 6 59 E
Breeds Pond, *Bost.* 21 C4 42 28N 70 58W
Breezy Pt., *N.Y.* 22 D5 40 33N 73 56W
Breitenlee, *Wien* 10 G11 48 15N 16 30 E
Breitscheid, *Ruhr* 6 B3 51 21N 6 51 E
Breña, *Lima* 30 G8 12 3 S 77 3W
Brenschede, *Ruhr* 6 B5 51 26N 7 12 E
Brent, *Lon.* 4 B3 51 33N 0 15W
Brent →, *Lon.* 4 B2 51 30N 0 20W
Brent Res., *Lon.* 4 B3 51 34N 0 14W
Brentford, *Lon.* 4 C3 51 28N 0 18W
Brenthurst, *Jobg.* 18 F11 26 15 S 28 21 E
Brentwood, *Lon.* 4 B6 51 36N 0 18 E
Brentwood Park, *Jobg.* 18 E10 26 7 S 28 17 E
Brentwood Park, *L.A.* 28 B2 34 3N 118 29W
Brera, *Mil.* 9 E6 45 28N 9 11 E
Bresso, *Mil.* 9 D6 45 32N 9 11 E
Brétigny-sur-Orge, *Paris* 5 D3 48 36N 2 18 E
Brevik, *Stock.* 3 D12 59 20N 18 12 E
Břevnov, *Pra.* 10 B2 50 4N 14 22 E
Brewer I., *S.F.* 27 C3 37 33N 122 16W
Bricket Wood, *Lon.* 4 A2 51 42N 0 21W
Bridesburg, *Phil.* 24 B4 39 59N 75 4W
Bridgeport, *Chic.* 26 B3 41 50N 87 38W
Bridgeport, *Phil.* 24 A2 40 6N 75 21W
Bridgeview, *Chic.* 26 C2 41 45N 87 48W
Brie-Comte-Robert, *Paris* 5 C5 48 41N 2 36 E
Brighton, *Melb.* 19 F6 37 55 S 144 59 E
Brighton le Sands, *Syd.* 19 B3 33 57 S 151 9 E
Brighton Park, *Chic.* 26 C2 41 48N 87 41W
Brightwood, *Wash.* 25 D7 38 57N 77 1W
Brigittenau, *Wien* 10 G10 48 14N 16 22 E
Briis-sous-Forges, *Paris* 5 D2 48 37N 2 7 E
Brimbank Park, *Melb.* 19 E6 37 43 S 144 50 E
Brimsdown, *Lon.* 4 B4 51 39N 0 1W
Brione, *Tori.* 9 B1 45 8N 7 28 E
Briones Hills, *S.F.* 27 A4 37 56N 122 8W
Briones Regional Park, *S.F.* 27 A4 37 55N 122 8W
Briones Res., *S.F.* 27 A3 37 55N 122 11W
Brisbane, *S.F.* 27 B2 37 40N 122 24W
Bristol, *Phil.* 24 A5 40 6N 74 53W
Britz, *Berl.* 7 B3 52 26N 13 27 E
Brixton, *Lon.* 4 C4 51 27N 0 8W
Broad Axe, *Phil.* 24 A3 40 8N 75 14W
Broad Sd., *Bost.* 21 C4 42 23N 70 56W
Broadmeadows, *Melb.* 19 E6 37 40 S 144 55 E
Broadmoor, *S.F.* 27 B2 37 41N 122 29W
Broadview, *Chic.* 26 B1 41 51N 87 52W
Brobacka, *Hels.* 3 B2 60 15N 24 36 E
Brockley, *Lon.* 4 C4 51 27N 0 2W
Bródno, *Wsaw.* 10 E7 52 17N 21 1 E
Bródnowski, Kanal, *Wsaw.* 10 E7 52 17N 21 3 E
Broich, *Ruhr* 6 B3 51 25N 6 50 E
Bromley, *Lon.* 4 C5 51 24N 0 0 E
Bromley-by-Bow, *Lon.* 4 B4 51 31N 0 0 E
Bromley Common, *Lon.* 4 C5 51 22N 0 2 E
Bromma, *Stock.* 3 D10 59 21N 17 55 E
Bromma flygplats, *Stock.* 3 D10 59 21N 17 56 E
Brompton, *Lon.* 4 C3 51 29N 0 10W
Brøndby Strand, *Købn.* 2 E9 55 36N 12 25 E
Brøndbyøster, *Købn.* 2 E9 55 39N 12 26 E
Brøndbyvester, *Købn.* 2 E9 55 37N 12 23 E
Brondesbury, *Lon.* 4 B3 51 32N 0 12W
Brønnøya, *Oslo* 2 C3 59 51N 10 32 E
Brønshøj, *Købn.* 2 D9 55 41N 12 29 E
Bronx Zoo, *N.Y.* 23 B5 40 50N 73 51W
Bronxville, *N.Y.* 23 B6 40 56N 73 49W
Brook Street, *Lon.* 4 B6 51 36N 0 17 E
Brookfield, *Chic.* 26 C1 41 48N 87 50W
Brookhaven, *Phil.* 24 B2 39 52N 75 23W
Brooklandville, *Balt.* 25 A2 39 25N 76 40W
Brooklin, *S. Pau.* 31 E6 23 37 S 46 39W
Brookline, *Bost.* 21 D3 42 19N 71 8W
Brooklyn, *Balt.* 25 B3 39 13N 76 36W
Brooklyn, *Melb.* 19 E5 37 49 S 144 49 E
Brooklyn, *N.Y.* 22 D5 40 37N 73 57W
Brookmont, *Wash.* 25 D7 38 57N 77 7W
Brooks I., *S.F.* 27 A2 37 53N 122 21W
Brookville, *N.Y.* 23 C7 40 48N 73 33W
Broomall, *Phil.* 24 B2 39 58N 75 22W
Brosewere B., *N.Y.* 23 D6 40 37N 73 40W
Brossard, *Mtrl.* 20 B5 43 27N 73 28W
Brou-sur-Chantereine, *Paris* 5 B5 48 53N 2 37 E
Brown, *Trto.* 20 D9 43 48N 79 14W
Browns Line, *Trto.* 20 E7 43 36N 79 32W
Broyhill Park, *Wash.* 25 D6 38 52N 77 12W
Bru, *Oslo* 2 C5 59 47N 10 54 E
Bruckhausen, *Ruhr* 6 B2 51 29N 6 43 E
Brughério, *Mil.* 9 D6 45 33N 9 17 E
Bruino, *Tori.* 9 B1 45 1N 7 27 E
Bruløkka, *Oslo* 2 A2 60 1N 10 22 E
Brunn, *Stock.* 3 E13 59 17N 18 25 E
Brunnthal, *Mün.* 7 G11 48 0N 11 41 E
Brunoy, *Paris* 5 C4 48 41N 2 29 E
Brunswick, *Melb.* 19 E6 37 45 S 144 57 E
Brusciano, *Nápl.* 9 H13 40 55N 14 25 E
Brush Hill, *Bost.* 21 D1 42 15N 71 22W
Bruzzano, *Mil.* 9 D6 45 31N 9 10 E
Bry-sur-Marne, *Paris* 5 B5 48 50N 2 32 E
Bryn, *Oslo* 2 B2 59 55N 10 27 E
Bryn Athyn, *Phil.* 24 A4 40 8N 75 3W
Bryn Mawr, *Phil.* 24 A3 40 1N 75 19W
Brzeziny, *Wsaw.* 10 E7 52 19N 21 2 E
Bubeneč, *Pra.* 10 B2 50 6N 14 24 E
Buc, *Paris* 5 C2 48 46N 2 7 E
Buch, *Berl.* 7 A3 52 38N 13 29 E
Buchburg, *Wien* 10 G9 48 13N 16 11 E
Buchenhain, *Mün.* 7 G9 48 1N 11 29 E
Buchholz, *Berl.* 7 A3 52 36N 13 25 E
Buchholz, *Ruhr* 6 B2 51 23N 6 46 E
Buckhurst Hill, *Lon.* 4 B5 51 37N 0 2 E
Buckingham Palace, *Lon.* 4 B4 51 30N 0 8W
Buckow, *Berl.* 7 B3 52 25N 13 26 E
Buda, *Bud.* 10 J13 47 30N 19 2 E
Budafok, *Bud.* 10 K13 47 25N 19 2 E
Budakeszi, *Bud.* 10 J12 47 30N 18 56 E
Budaörs, *Bud.* 10 K12 47 27N 18 57 E
Budapest, *Bud.* 10 K13 47 29N 19 3 E
Budatétény, *Bud.* 10 K13 47 25N 19 1 E
Budberg, *Ruhr* 6 A1 51 32N 6 38 E
Buddinge, *Købn.* 2 D10 55 44N 12 30 E
Büderich, *Ruhr* 6 C2 51 15N 6 41 E
Buena Park, *L.A.* 28 C4 33 51N 118 1W
Buena Vista, *S.F.* 27 B2 37 45N 122 26W
Buenavista, *Mdrd.* 8 B2 40 25N 3 40W
Buenos Aires, *B.A.* 32 B4 34 36 S 58 22W
Buenos Aires, Aeroparque de la Ciudad de, *B.A.* 32 B4 34 34 S 58 25W
Buer, *Ruhr* 6 A4 51 34N 7 2 E
Bufalotta, *Rome* 9 F10 41 59N 12 33 E
Buggajha, *Sŏul* 12 G7 37 34N 126 55 E
Bughan San, *Sŏul* 12 G7 37 38N 126 58 E
Bugio, *Lisb.* 8 G7 38 39N 9 18W
Bukit Panjang, *Sing.* 15 F7 1 22N 103 45 E
Bukit Timah, *Sing.* 15 F7 1 20N 103 47 E
Bulam San, *Sŏul* 12 G8 37 38N 127 4 E
Bûlâq, *El Qâ.* 18 C5 30 3N 31 14 E
Bule, *Manila* 15 E4 14 26N 121 2 E
Bulim, *Sing.* 15 F7 1 22N 103 43 E
Bull Brook →, *Bost.* 21 A4 42 41N 70 52W
Bulleen, *Melb.* 19 E7 37 46 S 145 4 E
Bullen Park, *Melb.* 19 E7 37 46 S 145 4 E
Bullion, *Paris* 5 D1 48 37N 1 59 E
Bulmke-Hüllen, *Ruhr* 6 A4 51 31N 7 7 E
Bulphan, *Lon.* 4 B7 51 32N 0 21 E
Bundoora, *Melb.* 19 E7 37 41 S 145 2 E
Bundoora Park, *Melb.* 19 E7 37 42 S 145 2 E
Bunker I., *Kar.* 17 H10 24 48N 66 57 E
Bunkyo, *Tōkyō* 13 B3 35 42N 139 45 E
Bunnefjorden, *Oslo* 2 B4 59 50N 10 44 E
Buona Vista, *Sing.* 15 G7 1 16N 103 47 E
Buquirivú-Guaçu →, *S. Pau.* 31 D7 23 28 S 46 28W
Burbank, *Chic.* 26 C2 41 44N 87 46W
Burbank, *L.A.* 28 A3 34 12N 118 18W
Bures, *Paris* 5 B1 48 56N 1 57 E
Bures-sur-Yvette, *Paris* 5 C2 48 41N 2 9 E
Burggrafenberg, *Ruhr* 6 C4 51 13N 7 3 E
Burgh Heath, *Lon.* 4 D3 51 18N 0 13W
Burlingame, *S.F.* 27 C2 37 34N 122 20W
Burlington, *Bost.* 21 B2 42 30N 71 13W
Burlington, *Phil.* 24 A5 40 4N 74 53W
Burnham, *Chic.* 26 D3 41 38N 87 33W
Burnham Park Harbor, *Chic.* 26 B3 41 51N 87 36W
Burnhamthorpe, *Trto.* 20 E7 43 37N 79 35W
Burnt Oak, *Lon.* 4 B3 51 36N 0 15W
Burr Ridge, *Chic.* 26 C1 41 46N 87 54W
Burtus, *El Qâ.* 18 C4 30 8N 31 8 E
Burudvatn, *Oslo* 2 B3 59 58N 10 35 E
Burwood, *Melb.* 19 F7 37 50 S 145 6 E
Burwood, *Syd.* 19 B3 33 52 S 151 5 E
Burwood East, *Melb.* 19 F7 37 51 S 145 8 E
Burzaco, *B.A.* 32 C4 34 49 S 58 23W
Buschhausen, *Ruhr* 6 A3 51 30N 6 50 E
Bush Hill Park, *Lon.* 4 B4 51 38N 0 4W
Bushey, *Lon.* 4 B2 51 38N 0 22W
Bushwick, *N.Y.* 23 C5 40 41N 73 54W
Bushy Cr. →, *Melb.* 19 E8 37 42 S 145 17 E
Bushy Park, *Lon.* 4 C2 51 24N 0 20W
Bussocaba, *S. Pau.* 31 E5 23 34 S 46 47W
Bussy-St.-Georges, *Paris* 5 B6 48 50N 2 41 E
Bussy-St.-Martin, *Paris* 5 B6 48 50N 2 41 E
Bustleton, *Phil.* 24 A4 40 4N 75 2W
Butantã, *S. Pau.* 31 E5 23 34 S 46 42W
Butcher I., *Bomb.* 16 H8 18 57N 72 53 E
Butendorf, *Ruhr* 6 A3 51 33N 6 59 E
Butler, *N.Y.* 22 B2 40 59N 74 20W
Buttonville, *Trto.* 20 C8 43 51N 79 21W
Butts Corner, *Wash.* 25 E6 38 46N 77 19W
Byailla, *Bomb.* 16 H8 18 58N 72 50 E
Byberry, *Phil.* 24 A5 40 6N 74 59W
Byfang, *Ruhr* 6 B4 51 24N 7 5 E
Byfleet, *Lon.* 4 D1 51 19N 0 28W
Bygdøy, *Oslo* 2 B4 59 54N 10 40 E

C

C.N. Tower, *Trto.* 20 E8 43 38N 79 23W
Caballito, *B.A.* 32 B4 34 37 S 58 25W
Cabin John, *Wash.* 25 D6 38 58N 77 10W
Cabin John Cr. →, *Wash.* 25 C7 39 2N 77 8W
Cabin John Regional Park, *Wash.* 25 C6 39 0N 77 10W
Cabramatta, *Syd.* 19 B2 33 53 S 150 56 E
Cabuçú de Baixo →, *S. Pau.* 31 D5 23 30 S 46 40W
Cachan, *Paris* 5 C3 48 47N 2 19 E
Cachenka →, *Mos.* 11 E7 55 46N 37 17 E
Cachoeira →, *S. Pau.* 31 E5 23 38 S 46 43W
Cacilhas, *Lisb.* 8 F8 38 41N 9 8W
Cadieux, Î., *Mtrl.* 20 B1 43 25N 74 1W
Cagarras, Is., *Rio J.* 31 C2 23 1 S 43 12W
Cahuenga Pk., *L.A.* 28 B3 34 8N 118 19 E
Cainta, *Manila* 15 D4 14 34N 121 6 E
Cairo = El Qâhira, *El Qâ.* 18 C5 30 2N 31 13 E
Cairo Int. Airport, *El Qâ.* 18 C6 30 7N 31 23 E
Caivano, *Nápl.* 9 H12 40 57N 14 18 E
Caju, *Rio J.* 31 B2 22 52 S 43 12W
Čakovice, *Pra.* 10 B3 50 9N 14 31 E
Calabazar, *La Hab.* 30 B2 23 1N 82 20W
Calcutta, *Calc.* 16 E6 22 34N 88 21 E
Caldwell, *N.Y.* 22 B3 40 50N 74 19W
Calf Harbour, *N.Y.* 23 B7 40 59N 73 37W
Calf I., *Bost.* 21 C4 42 20N 70 53W
Calhua, *Lisb.* 8 F8 38 44N 9 9W
California, Univ. of, *S.F.* 27 A3 37 52N 122 16W
California Inst. of Tech., *L.A.* 28 B4 34 8N 118 8W
California State Univ., *L.A.* 28 B3 34 4N 118 10W
California State Univ., *S.F.* 27 C4 37 39N 122 6W
Callao, *Lima* 30 G8 12 3 S 77 8W
Caloocan, *Manila* 15 D3 14 39N 120 58 E
Calumet →, *Chic.* 26 C3 41 43N 87 31W
Calumet, L., *Chic.* 26 C3 41 40N 87 35W
Calumet City, *Chic.* 26 D3 41 36N 87 32W
Calumet Harbor, *Chic.* 26 C3 41 43N 87 30W
Calumet Park, *Chic.* 26 C3 41 40N 87 39W
Calumet Sag Channel →, *Chic.* 26 C2 41 40N 87 47W
Calumpang, *Manila* 15 D4 14 37N 121 5 E
Calvairate, *Mil.* 9 E6 45 27N 9 13 E
Calverton, *Wash.* 25 C8 39 3N 76 56W
Calvizzano, *Nápl.* 9 H12 40 54N 14 11 E
Calzada, *Manila* 15 D4 14 32N 121 4 E
Camarate, *Lisb.* 8 F8 38 48N 9 7W
Camaroes, *Lisb.* 8 F7 38 49N 9 14W
Camberwell, *Lon.* 4 C4 51 28N 0 5W
Camberwell, *Melb.* 19 F7 37 50 S 145 5 E
Cambria Heights, *N.Y.* 23 C6 40 41N 73 44W
Cambridge, *Bost.* 21 C3 42 23N 71 7W
Cambridge Res., *Bost.* 21 C2 42 24N 71 16W
Cambuci, *S. Pau.* 31 E6 23 33 S 46 47W
Cambute, *La Hab.* 30 B3 23 5N 82 16W
Camden, *Lon.* 4 B4 51 32N 0 8W
Camden, *Phil.* 24 B4 39 56N 75 7W
Camp Springs, *Wash.* 25 E8 38 48N 76 55W
Campamento, *Mdrd.* 8 B2 40 23N 3 46W
Campanilla, Pta., *La Hab.* 30 A3 23 10N 82 18W
Campbellfield, *Melb.* 19 E6 37 40 S 144 57 E
Camperdown, *Syd.* 19 B4 33 53 S 151 11 E
Campi Flegrei, *Nápl.* 9 H11 40 50N 14 9 E
Campo, Casa de, *Mdrd.* 8 B2 40 25N 3 45W
Campo Belo, *S. Pau.* 31 E5 23 36 S 46 44W
Campo de Mayo, *B.A.* 32 B2 34 32 S 58 40W
Campo Grando, *Lisb.* 8 F8 38 45N 9 9W
Campo Limpo, *S. Pau.* 31 E5 23 38 S 46 46W
Campo Pequeño, *Lisb.* 8 F8 38 44N 9 8W
Campolide, *Lisb.* 8 F8 38 43N 9 9W
Campsie, *Syd.* 19 B3 33 54 S 151 6 E
C'an San Joan, *Barc.* 8 D6 41 28N 2 11 E
Canacao, *Manila* 15 E3 14 29N 120 54 E
Canacao B., *Manila* 15 E3 14 29N 120 54 E
Cañada de los Helechos →, *Méx.* 29 B2 19 21N 99 15W
Canarsie, *N.Y.* 23 D5 40 38N 73 53W
Candiac, *Mtrl.* 20 B5 43 23N 73 29W
Caneças, *Lisb.* 8 F7 38 48N 9 13W
Cangaiba, *S. Pau.* 31 E6 23 30 S 46 31W
Cangrejeras, *La Hab.* 30 B1 23 3N 82 30W
Canguera, *S. Pau.* 31 E2 23 34 S 46 26W
Canillas, *Mdrd.* 8 B3 40 27N 3 38W
Canillejas, *Mdrd.* 8 B3 40 26N 3 36W
Cann Hall, *Lon.* 4 B5 51 33N 0 0 E
Canning Town, *Lon.* 4 B5 51 30N 0 1 E
Canoe Grove Res., *N.Y.* 22 C2 40 45N 74 21W
Cantalupo, *Mil.* 9 D4 45 34N 8 58 E
Cantareira, *S. Pau.* 31 D6 23 26 S 46 36W
Cantarranas, *La Hab.* 30 B2 23 2N 82 28W
Canteras de Vallecas, *Mdrd.* 8 B3 40 20N 3 37W
Canterbury, *Melb.* 19 E7 37 49 S 145 4 E
Canterbury, *Syd.* 19 B3 33 55 S 151 7 E
Canto do Rio, *Rio J.* 31 B3 22 54 S 43 7W
Canton, *Bost.* 21 D3 42 10N 71 8W
Caohe, *Shang.* 14 J11 31 10N 121 24 E
Caonao, *La Hab.* 30 B2 23 5N 82 24W
Capão Redondo, *S. Pau.* 31 E5 23 39 S 46 45W
Caparica, *Lisb.* 8 F8 38 40N 9 9W
Caparica, Costa da, *Lisb.* 8 G7 38 38N 9 15W
Capelinha, *S. Pau.* 31 E5 23 39 S 46 44W
Capitol Heights, *Wash.* 25 D8 38 52N 76 55W
Capodichino, Aeroporto di, *Nápl.* 9 H12 40 52N 14 17 E
Capodimonte, *Nápl.* 9 H12 40 52N 14 14 E
Capodimonte, Bosco di, *Nápl.* 9 H12 40 52N 14 15 E
Captain Cook Bridge, *Syd.* 19 C3 34 0 S 151 7 E
Captain Cook Landing Place Park, *Syd.* 19 C4 34 1 S 151 14 E
Captain Harbour, *N.Y.* 23 B7 40 59N 73 37W
Capuava, *S. Pau.* 31 E7 23 38 S 46 28W
Capuchos, *Lisb.* 8 G7 38 38N 9 16W
Caraballeda, *Car.* 30 D5 10 36N 66 50W
Carabanchel Alto, *Mdrd.* 8 B2 40 22N 3 44W
Carabanchel Bajo, *Mdrd.* 8 B2 40 23N 3 44W
Carabatteda →, *Car.* 30 D5 10 37N 66 51W
Caracas, *Car.* 30 E5 10 30N 66 54W
Carapachay, *B.A.* 32 B3 34 31 S 58 32W
Carapicuiba, *S. Pau.* 31 E5 23 31 S 46 49W
Carapicuiba →, *S. Pau.* 31 E5 23 31 S 46 49W
Caravita, *Nápl.* 9 H13 40 52N 14 21 E
Caraza, *B.A.* 32 C4 34 41 S 58 25W
Cardito, *Nápl.* 9 H12 40 56N 14 17 E
Cardoso, *Lagos* 18 A1 6 34N 7 16 E
Caribbean Gardens, *Melb.* 19 F8 37 54 S 145 12 E
Caricuao, *Car.* 30 E5 10 25N 66 58W
Caridad, *Manila* 15 E3 14 28N 120 53 E
Carioca, Sa. da, *Rio J.* 31 B2 22 57 S 43 13W
Carle Place, *N.Y.* 23 C7 40 44N 73 35W
Carlingford, *Syd.* 19 A3 33 46 S 151 3 E
Carlisle, *Bost.* 21 B1 42 31N 71 20W
Carlshof, *Mün.* 7 F11 48 15N 11 41 E
Carlstadt, *N.Y.* 22 B4 40 50N 74 6W
Carlton, *Melb.* 19 E6 37 47 S 144 57 E
Carnaxide, *Lisb.* 8 F7 38 43N 9 14W
Carnegie, *Melb.* 19 F7 37 53 S 145 3 E
Carnegie Hall, *N.Y.* 22 C5 40 45N 73 59W
Carnetin, *Paris* 5 B6 48 54N 2 42 E
Carney, *Balt.* 25 A3 39 23N 76 31W
Carnide, *Lisb.* 8 F7 38 45N 9 10W
Caronno Pert, *Mil.* 9 D5 45 35N 9 2 E
Carramar, *Syd.* 19 B2 33 51 S 150 58 E
Carrascal, *Stgo.* 30 J10 33 25 S 70 42W
Carrières-sous-Bois, *Paris* 5 B2 48 55N 2 6 E
Carrières-sous-Poissy, *Paris* 5 B2 48 56N 2 2 E
Carrières-sur-Seine, *Paris* 5 B3 48 55N 2 11 E
Carroll I., *Balt.* 25 B4 39 19N 76 20W
Carroll Park, *Balt.* 25 B3 39 16N 76 38W
Carshalton, *Lon.* 4 C3 51 22N 0 10W
Carshalton on the Hill, *Lon.* 4 C4 51 20N 0 9W
Carteret, *N.Y.* 22 D3 40 34N 74 13W
Cartierville, Aéroport de, *Mtrl.* 20 A3 43 31N 73 42 E
Carugate, *Mil.* 9 D6 45 32N 9 20 E
Carupa, *B.A.* 32 A3 34 25 S 58 33W
Casa Blanca, *La Hab.* 30 B3 23 8N 82 19W
Casa Verde, *S. Pau.* 31 D5 23 29 S 46 40W
Casalnuovo di Nápoli, *Nápl.* 9 H12 40 54N 14 20 E
Casalotti, *Rome* 9 F9 41 54N 12 22 E
Casandrino, *Nápl.* 9 H12 40 56N 14 15 E
Casavatore, *Nápl.* 9 H12 40 53N 14 15 E
Cascadura, *Rio J.* 31 B2 22 52 S 43 19W
Caselette, *Tori.* 9 B1 45 6N 7 28 E
Caselette, Laghi di, *Tori.* 9 B1 45 7N 7 29 E
Caselle Torinese, *Tori.* 9 A3 45 10N 7 38 E
Caseros, *B.A.* 32 B3 34 36 S 58 34W
Casória, *Nápl.* 9 H12 40 54N 14 17 E
Cassignanica, *Mil.* 9 E7 45 27N 9 20 E
Cassiobury Park, *Lon.* 4 B2 51 39N 0 25W
Castel di Camerletto, *Tori.* 9 B1 45 6N 7 27 E
Castel di Guido, *Rome* 9 F8 41 53N 12 17 E
Castel Malnome, *Rome* 9 F8 41 50N 12 19 E
Castel San Cristina, *Tori.* 9 B3 45 8N 7 40 E
Castel Sant'Angelo, *Rome* 9 F9 41 54N 12 27 E
Castelar, *B.A.* 32 B3 34 39 S 58 39W
Castellbisbal, *Barc.* 8 D4 41 28N 1 58 E
Castello di Cisterna, *Nápl.* 9 H13 40 54N 14 24 E
Castelvécchio, *Tori.* 9 B3 45 1N 7 46 E
Castiglione Torinese, *Tori.* 9 B3 45 6N 7 48 E
Castleton Corners, *N.Y.* 22 D4 40 36N 74 8W
Castro Valley, *S.F.* 27 B4 37 41N 122 5W
Castrop, *Ruhr* 6 A5 51 32N 7 18 E
Castrop-Rauxel, *Ruhr* 6 A5 51 33N 7 18 E
Cat Rock Hill, *Bost.* 21 C2 42 23N 71 18W
Caterham, *Lon.* 4 D4 51 16N 0 5W
Catete, *Rio J.* 31 B2 22 54 S 43 10W
Catford, *Lon.* 4 C4 51 26N 0 1W
Catia, *Car.* 30 D5 10 31N 66 56W
Catia La Mer, *Car.* 30 D4 10 36N 67 0W
Catonsville, *Balt.* 25 B2 39 16N 76 43W
Catonsville Manor, *Balt.* 25 B2 39 17N 76 44W
Cattle Hill, *S.F.* 27 C2 37 36N 122 27W
Catumbi, *Rio J.* 31 B2 22 54 S 43 12W
Caughnawaga, *Mtrl.* 20 B3 43 24N 73 40W
Caulfield, *Melb.* 19 F7 37 52 S 145 1 E
Caulfield Racecourse, *Melb.* 19 F7 37 53 S 145 4 E
Caumsett State Park, *N.Y.* 23 B8 40 55N 73 27W
Cavite, *Manila* 15 E3 14 29N 120 54 E
Cavoretto, *Tori.* 9 B3 45 1N 7 41 E
Caxias, *Lisb.* 8 F7 38 42N 9 16W
Caxingui, *S. Pau.* 31 E5 23 35 S 46 43W
Cebeciköy, *Ist.* 17 A2 41 7N 28 53 E
Cecchignola, *Rome* 9 G10 41 48N 12 29 E
Cecil Park, *Syd.* 19 B2 33 52 S 150 51 E
Cecilienhof, *Berl.* 7 B1 52 35N 13 5 E
Cedar Grove, *N.Y.* 22 B3 40 50N 74 13W
Cedar Grove Res., *N.Y.* 22 B3 40 51N 74 12W
Cedar I., *N.Y.* 23 D8 40 38N 73 22W
Cedar Knolls, *N.Y.* 22 C2 40 49N 74 27W
Cedarhurst, *N.Y.* 23 D6 40 37N 73 43W
Cedarvale, *Trto.* 20 D8 43 41N 79 26W
Celle →, *Paris* 5 D1 48 36N 1 59 E
Cempaka Putih, *Jak.* 15 J10 6 10 S 106 51 E
Çengelköy, *Ist.* 17 A3 41 2N 29 3 E
Centennial Park, *Syd.* 19 B4 33 53 S 151 14 E
Center Square, *Phil.* 24 C2 39 48N 75 22W
Centerport, *N.Y.* 23 B8 40 53N 73 22W
Centerton, *Phil.* 24 B5 39 59N 74 53W
Centocelle, *Rome* 9 F10 41 52N 12 34 E
Central Park, *N.Y.* 22 C5 40 47N 73 58W
Central Park, *Sing.* 15 G8 1 17N 103 50 E
Centre City, *Phil.* 24 C3 39 46N 75 11W
Centre I., *N.Y.* 23 B7 40 54N 73 31W
Cércola, *Nápl.* 9 H13 40 51N 14 21 E
Cergy-Pontoise, *Paris* 5 A2 49 1N 2 4 E
Cernay-la-Ville, *Paris* 5 C1 48 40N 1 58 E
Cernusco sul Navíglio, *Mil.* 9 D6 45 31N 9 19 E
Cerqueira Cesar, *S. Pau.* 31 E5 23 33 S 46 40W
Cerro Ajusco, *Méx.* 29 C2 19 12N 99 15W
Cerro de la Estrella, *Méx.* 29 B3 19 20N 99 5W
Cerro de los Angeles, *Mdrd.* 8 C2 40 18N 3 41W
Cerro el Picacho, *Méx.* 29 A3 19 35N 99 6W
Cerro Maggiore, *Mil.* 9 D4 45 35N 8 57 E
Certanovka →, *Mos.* 11 F9 55 38N 37 48 E
Certanovo, *Mos.* 11 F9 55 38N 37 36 E
Cesano Boscone, *Mil.* 9 E5 45 26N 9 5 E
Cesate, *Mil.* 9 D5 45 35N 9 4 E
Cha Kwo Ling, *H.K.* 12 E6 22 18N 114 13 E
Chabot, L., *S.F.* 27 B4 37 43N 122 6W
Chacao, *Car.* 30 E5 10 30N 66 50W
Chacarilla, *Lima* 30 G9 12 6 S 76 59W
Chadds Ford, *Phil.* 24 B1 39 52N 75 35W
Chadstone, *Melb.* 19 F7 37 52 S 145 5 E
Chadwell Heath, *Lon.* 4 B5 51 34N 0 8 E
Chadwell St. Mary, *Lon.* 4 C7 51 29N 0 20 E
Chai Wan, *H.K.* 12 E6 22 16N 114 14 E
Chai Wan Kok, *H.K.* 12 D5 22 22N 114 6 E
Chakdaha, *Calc.* 16 F5 22 28N 88 19 E
Chama, *Lima* 30 G8 12 7 S 77 0W
Chamartin, *Mdrd.* 8 B2 40 27N 3 40W
Chamberi, *Mdrd.* 8 B2 40 26N 3 42W
Chambourcy, *Paris* 5 B2 48 54N 2 2 E
Champdani, *Calc.* 16 D5 22 48N 88 19 E
Champigny-sur-Marne, *Paris* 5 C5 48 49N 2 30 E
Champlain, Pont, *Mtrl.* 20 B4 43 28N 73 31W
Champlan, *Paris* 5 C3 48 42N 2 16 E
Champrosay, *Paris* 5 D4 48 39N 2 25 E
Champs-sur-Marne, *Paris* 5 B5 48 50N 2 34 E
Chamrail, *Calc.* 16 E5 22 38N 88 17 E
Chancheon, *Sŏul* 12 G7 37 33N 126 56 E
Chandernagore, *Calc.* 16 C6 22 51N 88 21 E
Chanditala, *Calc.* 16 D5 22 41N 88 15 E
Changi, *Sing.* 15 F8 1 23N 103 59 E
Changi Airport, *Sing.* 15 F8 1 21N 103 59 E
Changning, *Shang.* 14 J11 31 13N 121 24 E
Changpu Gongyuan, *Shang.* 14 J12 31 17N 121 31 E
Chanteloup-les-Vignes, *Paris* 5 B2 48 58N 2 1 E
Chantereine, *Paris* 5 B5 48 53N 2 37 E
Chantian, *Gzh.* 14 F8 23 12N 113 16 E
Chao Phraya →, *Bangk.* 15 B2 13 40N 100 31 E
Chaoyang, *Beij.* 14 B3 39 53N 116 26 E
Chaoyang Gongyuan, *Beij.* 14 B3 39 54N 116 28 E
Chaoyangmen, *Beij.* 14 B3 39 54N 116 25 E
Chapel End, *Lon.* 4 B4 51 35N 0 1W
Chapet, *Paris* 5 B1 48 58N 1 55 E
Chaplinville, *Bost.* 21 A4 42 42N 70 54W
Chapultepec, Bosque de, *Méx.* 29 B2 19 25N 99 11W
Chapultepec, Castillo de, *Méx.* 29 B2 19 25N 99 10W
Charenton-le-Pont, *Paris* 5 C4 48 49N 2 25 E
Charles-de-Gaulle, Aéroport, *Paris* 5 A5 49 0N 2 33 E
Charles Lee Tinden Regional Park, *S.F.* 27 A3 37 53N 122 14W
Charleston, *N.Y.* 22 D3 40 32N 74 14W
Charlestown, *Bost.* 21 C3 42 22N 71 4W
Charlottenburg, *Berl.* 7 A2 52 31N 13 14 E
Charlottenburg, Schloss, *Berl.* 7 A2 52 31N 13 18 E
Charlottenlund, *Købn.* 2 D10 55 44N 12 35 E
Charlton, *Lon.* 4 C5 51 29N 0 1 E
Charneca, *Lisb.* 8 F8 38 47N 9 8W
Charneca, *Lisb.* 8 G7 38 37N 9 12W
Chase Side, *Lon.* 4 B4 51 39N 0 4W
Châteaufort, *Paris* 5 C2 48 44N 2 5 E
Châtenay-Malabry, *Paris* 5 C3 48 46N 2 16 E
Chatham, *Chic.* 26 C3 41 45N 87 36W
Chatham, *N.Y.* 22 C2 40 44N 74 23W
Châtillon, *Paris* 5 C3 48 48N 2 17 E
Chatou, *Paris* 5 B2 48 53N 2 9 E
Chatpur, *Calc.* 16 E6 22 36N 88 22 E
Chatra, *Calc.* 16 D5 22 45N 88 19 E
Chatswood, *Syd.* 19 A4 33 47 S 151 11 E
Chauki, *Kar.* 17 G10 24 55N 66 56 E
Chavarria, *Lima* 30 G8 12 0 S 77 1W
Chavenay, *Paris* 5 B1 48 51N 1 59 E
Chavenay-Villepreux, Aérodrôme de, *Paris* 5 B1 48 50N 1 58 E
Chaville, *Paris* 5 C3 48 48N 2 11 E
Che Kung Miu, *H.K.* 12 D6 22 22N 114 10 E
Cheam, *Lon.* 4 C3 51 21N 0 12W
Chelles, *Paris* 5 B5 48 53N 2 35 E
Chelles, Canal de, *Paris* 5 B5 48 51N 2 35 E
Chells-le-Pin, Aérodrome, *Paris* 5 B5 48 53N 2 36 E
Chelmsford, *Bost.* 21 B1 42 35N 71 20W
Chelobityevo, *Mos.* 11 D10 55 54N 37 40 E
Chelsea, *Bost.* 21 C3 42 23N 71 1W
Chelsea, *Lon.* 4 C3 51 29N 0 10W
Chelsea, *Phil.* 24 B2 39 51N 75 27W
Chelsfield Village, *Lon.* 4 C5 51 21N 0 8 E
Cheltenham, *Phil.* 24 A4 40 3N 75 6W
Chembur, *Bomb.* 16 G8 19 3N 72 53 E
Chennevières, *Paris* 5 A2 49 0N 2 6 E
Chennevières-sur-Marne, *Paris* 5 C5 48 47N 2 31 E
Cheongdam, *Sŏul* 12 G8 37 31N 127 2 E
Cheonho, *Sŏul* 12 G8 37 32N 127 6 E
Cheops, *El Qâ.* 18 D4 29 58N 31 8 E
Chepo, *Gzh.* 14 G9 23 7N 113 23 E
Cherepkovo, *Mos.* 11 E8 55 45N 37 21 E
Chernyovo, *Mos.* 11 D7 55 50N 37 17 E
Cherry Hill, *Phil.* 24 B4 39 54N 75 1W
Cherry L., *Melb.* 19 F5 37 51 S 144 49 E
Cherryland, *S.F.* 27 B4 37 40N 122 7W
Cherrywood, *Trto.* 20 C10 43 51N 79 8W
Chertsey, *Lon.* 4 C2 51 23N 0 29W
Cheryomushki, *Mos.* 11 E9 55 40N 37 35 E
Chesaco Park, *Balt.* 25 B3 39 18N 76 30W
Chesapeake B., *Balt.* 25 B4 39 12N 76 22W
Cheshunt, *Lon.* 4 A4 51 42N 0 0 E
Chess →, *Lon.* 4 B2 51 38N 0 27W
Chessington, *Lon.* 4 C3 51 21N 0 18W
Chessington Zoo, *Lon.* 4 C3 51 20N 0 19W
Chester, *Phil.* 24 B2 39 50N 75 23W
Chester Cr. →, *Phil.* 24 B2 39 50N 75 21W
Chester Heights, *Phil.* 24 B2 39 53N 75 27W
Chestnut, *Phil.* 24 A3 40 4N 75 13W
Chestnut Hill, *Bost.* 21 D2 42 19N 71 10W
Cheung Sha Wan, *H.K.* 12 D5 22 20N 114 8 E
Cheverly, *Wash.* 25 D8 38 55N 76 54W
Chevilly-Larue, *Paris* 5 C4 48 46N 2 21 E
Chevreuse, *Paris* 5 C2 48 42N 2 2 E
Chevry-Cossigny, *Paris* 5 C5 48 43N 2 39 E
Chevy Chase, *Wash.* 25 D7 38 59N 77 4W
Chevy Chase View, *Wash.* 25 C7 39 0N 77 4W
Cheyney, *Phil.* 24 B1 39 55N 75 31W
Chhalera Bangar, *Delhi* 16 B2 28 33N 77 17 E
Chhinamor, *Calc.* 16 D5 22 48N 88 17 E
Chhota Andai, *Kar.* 17 H11 24 48N 66 59 E
Chia Keng, *Sing.* 15 F8 1 21N 103 52 E
Chiaiano, *Nápl.* 9 H12 40 53N 14 13 E
Chiaravalle Milanese, *Mil.* 9 E6 45 24N 9 16 E
Chiawelo, *Jobg.* 18 F8 26 17 S 27 51 E
Chicago, *Chic.* 26 B3 41 52N 87 38W
Chicago, Univ. of, *Chic.* 26 C3 41 47N 87 35W
Chicago Harbor, *Chic.* 26 B3 41 52N 87 36W
Chicago Lawn, *Chic.* 26 C2 41 47N 87 42W
Chicago-Midway Airport, *Chic.* 26 C2 41 47N 87 45W
Chicago-O'Hare Int. Airport, *Chic.* 26 B1 41 58N 87 53W
Chicago Ridge, *Chic.* 26 C2 41 41N 87 46W
Chicago Sanitary and Ship Canal, *Chic.* 26 C2 41 49N 87 45W
Chichinautzin, Cerro, *Méx.* 29 D3 19 6N 99 8W
Chicot, *Mtrl.* 20 A2 43 35N 73 56W
Chicot →, *Mtrl.* 20 A2 43 34N 73 51W
Chienzui, *Gzh.* 14 F9 23 12N 113 22 E
Chieri, *Tori.* 9 B3 45 0N 7 49 E
Chigwell, *Lon.* 4 B5 51 36N 0 5 E
Chigwell Row, *Lon.* 4 B5 51 37N 0 7 E
Chik Sha, *H.K.* 12 E6 22 17N 114 16 E
Chikumazawa, *Tōkyō* 13 B2 35 49N 139 32 E
Childs Hill, *Lon.* 4 B3 51 33N 0 12W
Chilla Saroda, *Delhi* 16 B2 28 35N 77 18 E
Chillum, *Wash.* 25 D8 38 57N 76 58W
Chilly-Mazarin, *Paris* 5 C3 48 42N 2 17 E
Chimalhuacán, *Méx.* 29 B4 19 25N 89 57 E
Chimalpa, *Méx.* 29 B2 19 21N 99 19W
China, Tg., *Sing.* 15 G8 1 14N 103 50 E
China Basin, *S.F.* 27 B2 37 46N 122 22W
Chingford, *Lon.* 4 B5 51 37N 0 0 E
Chingupota, *Calc.* 16 F5 22 29N 88 14 E
Chipilly Woods, *Chic.* 26 A2 42 8N 87 48W
Chipperfield, *Lon.* 4 A2 51 42N 0 29W
Chipping Ongar, *Lon.* 4 A6 51 41N 0 15 E
Chipstead, *Lon.* 4 D4 51 17N 0 8W
Chirle, *Bomb.* 16 H9 18 55N 73 2 E
Chirnside Park, *Melb.* 19 E8 37 45 S 145 18 E
Chislehurst, *Lon.* 4 C5 51 24N 0 6 E
Chislehurst West, *Lon.* 4 C5 51 25N 0 3 E
Chiswick, *Lon.* 4 C3 51 29N 0 16W
Chiswick House, *Lon.* 4 C3 51 28N 0 15W
Chitlade Palace, *Bangk.* 15 B2 13 45N 100 31 E
Chitose, *Tōkyō* 13 C2 35 33N 139 37 E
Chiyoda-Ku, *Tōkyō* 13 B3 35 41N 139 44 E
Chkalova, *Mos.* 11 F11 55 39N 37 56 E
Choa Chu Kang, *Sing.* 15 F7 1 22N 103 40 E
Choboty, *Mos.* 11 F8 55 38N 37 22 E
Chodov u Prahy, *Pra.* 10 B3 50 1N 14 30 E
Chōfu, *Tōkyō* 13 C2 35 38N 139 32 E
Choisel, *Paris* 5 C2 48 41N 2 1 E
Choisy-le-Roi, *Paris* 5 C4 48 46N 2 24 E

36 Chomedey

Chomedey, Mtrl. 20 A3 43 32N 73 45W
Chong Nonsi, Khlong →, Bangk. 15 B2 13 42N 100 32 E
Chong Pang, Sing. 15 F7 1 26N 103 49 E
Chongwen, Beij. 14 B3 39 52N 116 23 E
Chongwenmen, Beij. 14 B3 39 52N 116 22 E
Chorleywood, Lon. 4 B2 51 39N 0 29W
Chornaya →, Mos. 11 E12 55 41N 38 0 E
Chorrillos, Lima 30 H8 12 10 S 77 1W
Christianshavn, Købn. 2 D10 55 40N 12 35 E
Chrome, N.Y. 22 D3 40 34N 74 13W
Chrzanów, Wsaw. 10 E6 52 13N 20 53 E
Chuen Lung, H.K. 12 D5 22 23N 114 6 E
Chuk Kok, H.K. 12 D6 22 20N 114 15 E
Chulalongkon Univ., Bangk. 15 B2 13 44N 100 31 E
Chullora, Syd. 19 B3 33 54 S 151 5 E
Chunchura, Calc. 16 C6 22 53N 88 23 E
Chuō-Ku, Tōkyō 13 B3 35 40N 139 46 E
Church End, Lon. 4 B3 51 35N 0 11W
Chvaly, Pra. 10 B3 50 6N 14 35 E
Chye Kay, Sing. 15 F7 1 25N 103 49 E
Ciampino, Rome 9 G10 41 47N 12 36 E
Ciampino, Aeroporto di, Rome 9 G10 41 47N 12 35 E
Cicero, Chic. 26 B2 41 51N 87 44W
Cidade, I. da, Rio J. 31 B2 22 51 S 43 13W
Cidade de Deus, S. Pau. 31 E5 23 33 S 46 45W
Cidade Ipava, S. Pau. 31 F5 23 42 S 46 45W
Cidade Lider, S. Pau. 31 E7 23 33 S 46 27W
Cidade São Matheus, S. Pau. 31 E7 23 35 S 46 29W
Cidena, Kali →, Jak. 15 H9 6 9 S 106 48 E
Cilandak, Jak. 15 J9 6 17 S 106 47 E
Cilincing, Jak. 15 H10 6 6 S 106 54 E
Ciliwung →, Jak. 15 J10 6 6 S 106 47 E
Čimice, Pra. 10 B2 50 8N 14 25 E
Cinderella, Jobg. 18 F10 26 14 S 28 15 E
Cinderella Dam, Jobg. 18 F10 26 14 S 28 14 E
Cinecittà, Rome 9 F10 41 51N 12 34 E
Cinisello Bálsamo, Mil. 9 D6 45 33N 9 13 E
Cinkota, Bud. 10 J14 47 31N 19 14 E
Cinnaminson, Phil. 24 B5 39 59N 74 59W
Cipete, Jak. 15 J9 6 15 S 106 47 E
Cipresso, Tori. 9 B3 45 2N 7 48 E
Cisliano, Mil. 9 E4 45 26N 8 59 E
Citta degli Studi, Mil. 9 E6 45 28N 9 12 E
Città del Vaticano, Rome 9 F9 41 54N 12 26 E
City I., N.Y. 23 B6 40 50N 73 47W
Ciudad Azteca, Méx. 29 A3 19 32N 99 1W
Ciudad Fin de Semana, Mdrd. 8 B3 40 26N 3 34W
Ciudad General Belgrano, B.A. 32 C3 34 43 S 58 33W
Ciudad Libertad, La Hab. 30 B2 23 5N 82 25W
Ciudad Lineál, Mdrd. 8 B3 40 26N 3 38W
Ciudad López Mateos, Méx. 29 A2 19 33N 99 16W
Ciudad Satélite, Méx. 29 A2 19 30N 99 13W
Ciudad Universitaria, Méx. 29 C2 19 9N 99 10W
Ciudadela, B.A. 32 B3 34 38 S 58 32W
Ciudadela, Parque de la, Barc. 8 D6 41 23N 2 11 E
Clairefontaine, Paris 5 D1 48 36N 1 54 E
Clamart, Paris 5 C3 48 48N 2 15 E
Clapham, Lon. 4 C4 51 27N 0 8W
Clapton, Lon. 4 B4 51 33N 0 3W
Clark, N.Y. 22 D3 40 38N 74 18W
Clarksboro, Phil. 24 C3 39 48N 75 13W
Claye-Souilly, Paris 5 B6 48 56N 2 41 E
Claygate, Lon. 4 C3 51 21N 0 19W
Clayhall, Lon. 4 B5 51 35N 0 3 E
Clayhill, Lon. 4 A4 51 40N 0 5W
Claymont, Phil. 24 C2 39 48N 75 27W
Claypole, B.A. 32 C4 34 48 S 58 20W
Clayton, Melb. 19 F7 37 55 S 145 7 E
Clearing, Chic. 26 C2 41 47N 87 45W
Clearwater, L.A. 28 C3 33 52N 118 10W
Clement, Sing. 15 G7 1 18N 103 46 E
Clementon, Phil. 24 C5 39 48N 74 59W
Clichy, Paris 5 B3 48 54N 2 18 E
Clichy-sous-Bois, Paris 5 B5 48 54N 2 32 E
Cliffside, Trto. 20 D9 43 44N 79 14W
Cliffside Park, N.Y. 22 C5 40 49N 73 59W
Clifton, Bost. 21 C4 42 29N 70 52W
Clifton, Kar. 17 H11 24 48N 67 1 E
Clifton, N.Y. 22 D4 40 37N 74 4W
Clifton, N.Y. 22 B4 40 51N 74 7W
Clifton, L., Balt. 25 B3 39 19N 76 35W
Clifton Heights, Phil. 24 B3 39 55N 75 17W
Clifton Park, Balt. 25 A3 39 20N 76 35W
Clontarf, Syd. 19 A4 33 48 S 151 16 E
Closter, N.Y. 22 B5 40 58N 73 57W
Clovelly, Syd. 19 B4 33 54 S 151 15 E
Cobbin's Brook →, Lon. 4 A5 51 40N 0 0 E
Cobbs Cr. →, Phil. 24 B3 39 58N 75 18W
Cobham, Lon. 4 D2 51 19N 0 23W
Cobras, I. das, Rio J. 31 B3 22 53 S 43 9W
Coburg, Melb. 19 E6 37 44 S 144 56 E
Cochecito, Car. 30 E5 10 26N 66 55W
Cochichewick, L., Bost. 21 A3 42 42N 71 5W
Cochituate, Bost. 21 C1 42 20N 71 21W
Cochituate, L., Bost. 21 D1 42 16N 71 21W
Cockfosters, Lon. 4 B4 51 39N 0 8W
Cocota, Rio J. 31 A2 22 48 S 43 11W
Coelho da Rocha, Rio J. 31 A1 22 46 S 43 21W
Cœuilly, Paris 5 C5 48 48N 2 32 E
Coignières, Paris 5 C1 48 44N 1 55 E
Coina, Lisb. 8 G8 38 39N 9 5W
Cojimar, La Hab. 30 B3 23 9N 82 17W
Cojimar →, La Hab. 30 B3 23 9N 82 17W
Cojimar, Boca de, La Hab. 30 A3 23 10N 82 17W
Coker, Lagos 18 B2 6 28N 7 20 E
Colaba, Bomb. 16 H7 18 53N 72 48 E
Colaba Pt., Bomb. 16 H7 18 53N 72 48 E
Cold Spring Harbor, N.Y. 23 B8 40 52N 73 27W
Cold Spring Terrace, N.Y. 23 C8 40 49N 73 25W
Coleraine, Trto. 20 D6 43 49N 79 40W
Colindale, Lon. 4 B3 51 35N 0 15W
Collazo, La Hab. 30 B2 23 2N 82 21W
College Park, Wash. 25 D8 38 59N 76 55W
College Point, N.Y. 23 C5 40 47N 73 50W
Collégien, Paris 5 B6 48 50N 2 41 E
Collegno, Tori. 9 B2 45 5N 7 34 E
Collier Row, Lon. 4 B5 51 35N 0 9 E
Colliers Wood, Lon. 4 C3 51 24N 0 10W
Collingdale, Phil. 24 B3 39 54N 75 17W
Collingswood, Phil. 24 B4 39 55N 75 5W
Collinsville, Bost. 21 A1 42 40N 71 20W
Collinsville, N.Y. 22 C2 40 48N 74 26W
Colma, S.F. 27 B2 37 40N 122 27W
Colma Cr. →, S.F. 27 C2 37 38N 122 23W
Colney Hatch, Lon. 4 B4 51 36N 0 9W
Cologno Monzese, Mil. 9 D6 45 31N 9 16 E
Colombes, Paris 5 B3 48 55N 2 15 E
Colonia, N.Y. 22 D3 40 35N 74 18W
Colônia, S. Pau. 31 E7 23 33 S 46 27W
Colonia Güell, Barc. 8 D5 41 21N 2 2 E
Colonia Puerta de Hierro, Mdrd. 8 B2 40 27N 3 43W
Colonial Manor, Phil. 24 B4 39 51N 75 9W
Colorado →, Méx. 29 B4 19 23N 89 58 E
Colosseo, Rome 9 F9 41 53N 12 29 E
Columbia, Balt. 25 B1 39 12N 76 50W
Columbia Hills, Balt. 25 B1 39 14N 76 51W
Columbia Univ., N.Y. 22 C5 40 48N 73 58W
Colwyn, Phil. 24 B3 39 54N 75 14W
Combault, Paris 5 C5 48 48N 2 37 E
Combs-la-Ville, Paris 5 D5 48 39N 2 33 E
Comércio, Praça do, Lisb. 8 F8 38 41N 9 9W
Commack, N.Y. 23 B9 40 50N 73 19W
Commerce, L.A. 28 B4 34 0N 118 9W
Como, Syd. 19 C3 34 0 S 151 4 E
Compans, Paris 5 B5 48 59N 2 39 E
Compton, L.A. 28 C3 33 53N 118 14W
Conceição, I. da, Rio J. 31 B3 22 52 S 43 6W
Concepcion, Manila 15 D4 14 39N 121 6 E
Conchali, Stgo 30 J11 33 22 S 70 39W
Concord, Bost. 21 C1 42 27N 71 20W
Concord, S.F. 27 A4 37 58N 122 3W
Concord, Syd. 19 B3 33 52 S 151 6 E
Concord, Trto. 20 D8 43 48N 79 29W
Concordville, Phil. 24 B1 39 53N 75 31W
Concorezzo, Mil. 9 D6 45 35N 9 19 E
Condécourt, Paris 5 A1 49 2N 1 56 E
Coney Island, N.Y. 22 D4 40 34N 74 0W
Conflans-Ste.-Honorine, Paris 5 B2 48 59N 2 5 E
Congo, S. Pau. 31 D5 23 27 S 46 42W
Congonhas, Aéroporto, S. Pau. 31 E6 23 38 S 46 39W
Conshohocken, Phil. 24 A3 40 4N 75 18W
Contadero, Méx. 29 B2 19 20N 99 17W
Convento de Valverde, Mdrd. 8 A2 40 30N 3 40W
Coogee, Syd. 19 B4 33 55 S 151 16 E
Cooksville, Trto. 20 E7 43 35N 79 38W
Cooper →, Phil. 24 B4 39 57N 75 6W
Copacabana, Rio J. 31 B2 22 58 S 43 11W
Copenhagen = København, Købn. 2 D9 55 40N 12 26 E
Copiague, N.Y. 23 D8 40 39N 73 23W
Coral Hills, Wash. 25 D8 38 51N 76 55W
Corbeil-Essonnes, Paris 5 D4 48 36N 2 29 E
Corbets Tey, Lon. 4 B6 51 32N 0 15 E
Corbiglia, Tori. 9 B1 45 3N 7 29 E
Corcovado, Rio J. 31 B2 22 57 S 43 12W
Cordon, Paris 5 D6 48 39N 2 41 E
Córdova, Tori. 9 B3 45 5N 7 48 E
Cordovil, Rio J. 31 A2 22 49 S 43 18W
Cormano, Mil. 9 D6 45 32N 9 10 E
Cormeilles-en-Parisis, Paris 5 B3 48 58N 2 11 E
Cornaredo, Mil. 9 D5 45 30N 9 1 E
Cornaya →, St-Pet. 11 B5 59 53N 30 35 E
Cornellá, Barc. 8 D5 41 21N 2 4 E
Cornwells Heights, Phil. 24 A5 40 4N 74 57W
Coróglio, Nápl. 9 J12 40 48N 14 10 E
Coronation Memorial, Delhi 16 A2 28 42N 77 12 E
Córsico, Mil. 9 E5 45 25N 9 6 E
Corte Madera, S.F. 27 A1 37 55N 122 30W
Corte Madera →, S.F. 27 A1 37 55N 122 30W
Corviale, Rome 9 F9 41 51N 12 25 E
Cos Cob, N.Y. 23 A7 41 1N 73 36W
Cossigny, Paris 5 C6 48 43N 2 40 E
Cossipure, Calc. 16 E6 22 37N 88 22 E
Cotao, Lisb. 8 F7 38 45N 9 17W
Côte St.-Luc, Mtrl. 20 B4 43 28N 73 39W
Cotorro, La Hab. 30 B3 23 2N 82 15W
Cotunduba, I. de, Rio J. 31 B3 22 57 S 43 8W
Coubert, Paris 5 C6 48 40N 2 41 E
Coubron, Paris 5 B5 48 54N 2 34 E
Coulsdon, Lon. 4 D4 51 18N 0 7W
Countryside, Chic. 26 C1 41 47N 87 52W
Courbevoie, Paris 5 B3 48 53N 2 14 E
Courcouronnes, Paris 5 D4 48 37N 2 24 E
Courdimanche, Paris 5 A1 49 2N 2 0 E
Courellle, Paris 5 C2 48 43N 2 7 E
Couros →, S. Pau. 31 F6 23 37 S 46 34W
Courtry, Paris 5 B5 48 55N 2 35 E
Cousino, Parque, Stgo 30 J11 33 27 S 70 40W
Cove Neck, N.Y. 23 B8 40 52N 73 29W
Cowley, Lon. 4 B2 51 31N 0 28W
Coyoacan, Méx. 29 B3 19 21N 99 9W
Coyote Cr. →, S.F. 27 D4 37 28N 122 4W
Coyote Hills Regional Park, S.F. 27 C4 37 32N 122 7W
Coyote Hills Slough, S.F. 27 C4 37 33N 122 7W
Coyote Pt., S.F. 27 C3 37 35N 122 18W
Coyote Ridge, S.F. 27 A1 37 51N 122 33W
Craighall Park, Jobg. 18 E9 26 7 S 28 1 E
Crane →, Lon. 4 C2 51 29N 0 29W
Cranford, Lon. 4 C2 51 29N 0 25W
Cranford, N.Y. 22 D3 40 39N 74 19W
Cranham, Lon. 4 B6 51 33N 0 16 E
Cray →, Lon. 4 C5 51 28N 0 8 E
Crayford, Lon. 4 C6 51 27N 0 11 E
Creekmouth, Lon. 4 B5 51 30N 0 6 E
Crerskill, N.Y. 22 B5 40 56N 73 57W
Crescenzago, Mil. 9 D6 45 30N 9 14 E
Crespières, Paris 5 B1 48 52N 1 55 E
Cressely, Paris 5 C2 48 44N 2 6 E
Cresslawn, Jobg. 18 E10 26 6 S 28 13 E
Crestwood, Chic. 26 D2 41 38N 87 43W
Creteil, Paris 5 C4 48 47N 2 27 E
Cricklewood, Lon. 4 B3 51 33N 0 13W
Crispano, Nápl. 9 H12 40 57N 14 17 E
Cristo Redebro, Monumento do, Rio J. 31 B2 22 56 S 43 12W
Crockenhill, Lon. 4 C5 51 22N 0 9 E
Croissy-Beaubourg, Paris 5 C5 48 49N 2 39 E
Croissy-sur-Seine, Paris 5 B2 48 52N 2 8 E
Cronenberg, Ruhr 6 C4 51 12N 7 9 E
Crosby, Jobg. 18 F8 26 11 S 27 59 E
Crosne, Paris 5 C4 48 43N 2 27 E
Cross I., Bomb. 16 H8 18 56N 72 51 E
Crouch End, Lon. 4 B4 51 34N 0 7W
Croud →, Paris 5 B4 48 57N 2 24 E
Crown Gardens, Jobg. 18 F9 26 15 S 28 0 E
Crown Mines, Jobg. 18 F8 26 12 S 27 57 E
Crown Village, N.Y. 23 C8 40 40N 73 26W
Crows Nest, Syd. 19 A4 33 49 S 151 12 E
Croxley Green, Lon. 4 B2 51 38N 0 26W
Croydon, Lon. 4 C4 51 22N 0 5W
Croydon, Melb. 19 E8 37 48 S 145 17 E
Croydon, Phil. 24 A5 40 5N 74 54W
Croydon North, Melb. 19 E8 37 46 S 145 16 E
Cruz de Pau, Lisb. 8 G8 38 37N 9 7W
Crystal Palace, Lon. 4 C4 51 25N 0 4W
Crystal Springs, S.F. 27 C2 37 31N 122 20W
Csepel, Bud. 10 K13 47 25N 19 4 E
Csepelsziget, Bud. 10 K13 47 25N 19 4 E
Csillaghegy, Bud. 10 J13 47 35N 19 2 E
Csillagtelep, Bud. 10 K13 47 24N 19 5 E
Cski-hegyek, Bud. 10 K12 47 30N 18 57 E
Csömör, Bud. 10 J14 47 33N 19 14 E
Cuajimalpa, Méx. 29 B2 19 21N 99 17W
Cuatro Vientos, Mdrd. 8 B2 40 22N 3 47W
Cuautepec de Madero, Méx. 29 A3 19 32N 99 8W
Cuautepec El Alto, Méx. 29 A3 19 33N 99 7W
Cuautzin, Cerro, Méx. 29 D3 19 10N 99 8W
Cubao, Manila 15 D4 14 37N 121 3 E
Cubas →, S. Pau. 31 D6 23 28 S 46 31W
Cubuklu, Ist. 17 A3 41 5N 29 4 E
Cudham, Lon. 4 D5 51 19N 0 4 E
Cuffley, Lon. 4 A4 51 42N 0 6W
Cuicuilco, Pirámido de, Méx. 29 C2 19 17N 99 10W
Culembeeck, Jobg. 18 E7 26 9 S 27 49 E
Culiculi, Manila 15 D4 14 33N 121 0 E
Cull Creek, S.F. 27 B4 37 45N 122 2W
Culver City, L.A. 28 B2 34 1N 118 24W
Culverstone Green, Lon. 4 C7 51 20N 0 20 E
Cumbre El Tabo, Car. 30 D5 10 33N 66 56W
Cumbres de Vallecas, Mdrd. 8 B3 40 20N 3 33W
Cunhas, S. Pau. 31 E7 23 34 S 46 23W
Cupecé, S. Pau. 31 E5 23 39 S 46 40W
Cupece →, S. Pau. 31 E6 23 37 S 46 42W
Curtis B., Balt. 25 B3 39 13N 76 34W
Curtis Cr. →, Balt. 25 B3 39 12N 76 34W
Cusago, Mil. 9 E5 45 26N 9 1 E
Cusano Milanese, Mil. 9 D6 45 33N 9 11 E
Çuvuşabaşi →, Ist. 17 A2 40 58N 28 51 E
Cyrildene, Jobg. 18 F9 26 10 S 28 6 E
Czernrakow, Wsaw. 10 E7 52 11N 21 3 E
Czyste, Wsaw. 10 E6 52 13N 20 57 E

D

Da Yunhe →, Tianj. 14 D5 39 19N 117 10 E
Dabizhuang, Tianj. 14 D6 39 11N 117 16 E
Ďablice, Pra. 10 B2 50 8N 14 29 E
Dabsibri, Sŏul 12 G8 37 33N 127 2 E
Dachang, Shang. 14 J11 31 17N 121 24 E
Dachau, Mün. 7 F9 48 15N 11 27 E
Dachau-Ost, Mün. 7 F9 48 15N 11 27 E
Dachauer Moos, Mün. 7 F9 48 13N 11 27 E
Daebang, Sŏul 12 G7 37 30N 126 55 E
Daechi, Sŏul 12 G8 37 30N 127 2 E
Dagenham, Lon. 4 B5 51 32N 0 8 E
Daglfing, Mün. 7 G10 48 8N 11 39 E
Dahirpur, Delhi 16 A2 28 43N 77 11 E
Dahlem, Berl. 7 B2 52 27N 13 16 E
Dahlerau, Ruhr 6 C5 51 13N 7 18 E
Dahlwitz-Hoppegarten, Berl. 7 A5 52 30N 13 41 E
Dahongmen, Beij. 14 C3 39 48N 116 21 E
Daiman, Tōkyō 13 A3 35 53N 139 44 E
Daitō, Ōsaka 12 B4 34 42N 135 38 E
Dajiaoting, Beij. 14 B3 39 51N 116 27 E
Dajingcun, Beij. 14 B2 39 50N 116 13 E
Dakhnoye, St-Pet. 11 C3 59 49N 30 15 E
Dalar, Bomb. 16 G7 19 0N 72 49 E
Dalejsky →, Pra. 10 B2 50 2N 14 24 E
Dalibia, Gzh. 14 G7 23 2N 113 6 E
Dallgow, Berl. 7 A1 52 32N 13 5 E
Dalston, Lon. 4 B4 51 32N 0 4W
Dalview, Jobg. 18 F11 26 14 S 28 20 E
Daly City, S.F. 27 B2 37 42N 122 27W
Damaia, Lisb. 8 F7 38 44N 9 12W
Dämeritzsee, Berl. 7 B5 52 34N 13 43 E
Damiette, Paris 5 C2 48 41N 2 7 E
Dampierre, Paris 5 C1 48 42N 1 59 E
Dan Neramit, Bangk. 15 B2 13 48N 100 34 E
Dan Ryan Woods, Chic. 26 C2 41 44N 87 40W
Dandenong, Mt., Melb. 19 E9 37 49 S 145 21 E
Danderyd, Stock. 3 D11 59 24N 18 1 E
Danforth, Trto. 20 D9 43 43N 79 16W
Daniels, Balt. 25 B2 39 19N 76 48W
Danvers, Bost. 21 B4 42 34N 70 56W
Dapharpur, Calc. 16 E5 22 38N 88 14 E
Darangan, Manila 15 E5 14 29N 121 10 E
Darave, Bomb. 16 G9 19 1N 73 1 E
Darby, Phil. 24 B3 39 55N 75 15W
Darby Cr. →, Phil. 24 B3 39 54N 75 15W
Darent →, Lon. 4 C6 51 21N 0 12 E
Darling, Phil. 24 B2 39 54N 75 28W
Darlington Corners, Phil. 24 B1 39 55N 75 34W
Dartford, Lon. 4 C6 51 26N 0 13 E
Dashi, Gzh. 14 G8 23 1N 113 17 E
Dashimae, Tōkyō 13 B3 35 46N 139 46 E
Datteln, Ruhr 6 A6 51 39N 7 20 E
Datteln-Hamm Kanal, Ruhr 6 A6 51 38N 7 28 E
Datun, Beij. 14 A3 40 0N 116 23 E
Dauko, Calc. 16 E5 22 31N 88 12 E
Daulatpur, Delhi 16 A1 28 44N 77 6 E
Davensport, Bost. 21 B4 42 33N 70 54W
Daveyton, Jobg. 18 E11 26 9 S 28 24 E
Davidkovo, Mos. 11 E8 55 43N 37 29 E
David's I., N.Y. 23 B6 40 53N 73 46W
Davidson, Mt., S.F. 27 B2 37 44N 122 27W
Davron, Paris 5 B1 48 52N 1 56 E
Dāvudiyeh, Tehr. 17 C5 35 45N 51 25 E
Dawidy, Wsaw. 10 F6 52 8N 20 58 E
Dayap, Manila 15 D4 14 35N 121 4 E
Dayuange, Gzh. 14 F7 23 11N 113 7 E
Dead Run →, Balt. 25 B2 39 18N 76 41W
Dedham, Bost. 21 D2 42 15N 71 10W
Dee Why, Syd. 19 A4 33 46 S 151 17 E
Deer I., Bost. 21 C4 42 21N 70 57W
Deer Park, N.Y. 23 C9 40 46N 73 19W
Degerby, Stock. 3 D9 59 22N 17 42 E
Degermossa, Hels. 3 B6 60 17N 25 12 E
Degunino, Mos. 11 D9 55 52N 37 33 E
Deisenhofen, Mün. 7 G10 48 0N 11 35 E
Dejvice, Pra. 10 B2 50 6N 14 23 E
Dekabristov, Os., St-Pet. 11 B3 59 56N 30 15 E
Del Viso, B.A. 32 A2 34 27 S 58 47W
Delanco, Phil. 24 A5 40 2N 74 57W
Delaware →, Phil. 24 A4 40 1N 75 0W
Delbruch, Ruhr 6 B4 51 22N 7 8 E
Delhi, Delhi 16 B2 28 39N 77 13 E
Delhi Cantonment, Delhi 16 B1 28 35N 77 7 E
Delhi Univ., Delhi 16 A2 28 41N 77 12 E
Dellwig, Ruhr 6 B3 51 29N 6 55 E
Delran, Phil. 24 A5 40 0N 74 57W
Delville, Jobg. 18 F10 26 11 S 28 13 E
Demarest, N.Y. 22 B5 40 57N 73 57W
Denham, Lon. 4 B1 51 35N 0 30W
Denham Green, Lon. 4 B2 51 34N 0 29W
Denniston Cr. →, S.F. 27 C2 37 30N 122 29W
Dentonia Park, Trto. 20 D9 43 42N 79 17W
Denville, N.Y. 22 B2 40 53N 74 28W
Deodoro, Rio J. 31 B1 22 50 S 43 21W
Depgsu Palace, Sŏul 12 G7 37 34N 126 58 E
Deptford, Lon. 4 C4 51 28N 0 1W
Der Sarai, Delhi 16 B2 28 33N 77 10 E
Des Plaines, Chic. 26 A1 42 2N 87 54W
Des Plaines →, Chic. 26 B1 41 48N 87 49W
Deshengmen, Beij. 14 B3 39 56N 116 21 E
Desierto de los Leones, Parque Nacional, Méx. 29 C2 19 18N 99 18W
Desio, Mil. 9 D6 45 36N 9 12 E
Deuil-la-Barre, Paris 5 B3 48 58N 2 19 E
Deulpur, Calc. 16 E5 22 36N 88 10 E
Deungchon, Sŏul 12 G7 37 33N 126 52 E
Deutsch-Wagram, Wien 10 G11 48 17N 16 33 E
Deutsche Oper, Berl. 7 A2 52 30N 13 19 E
Deutscher Museum, Mün. 7 G10 48 7N 11 35 E
Deux-Montagnes, Mtrl. 20 A2 43 32N 73 53W
Deux Montagnes, L. des, Mtrl. 20 B2 43 27N 73 59W
Devault, Phil. 24 A1 40 4N 75 32W
Dháfni, Ath. 8 J11 37 55N 23 44 E
Dhakuria, Calc. 16 E6 22 30N 88 22 E
Dhakuria L., Calc. 16 E6 22 30N 88 21 E
Dhamarakia, Ath. 8 J10 37 58N 23 39 E
Dharava, Bomb. 16 G8 19 1N 72 51 E
Dhrapersón, Ath. 8 J10 37 56N 23 37 E
Dhutumkhar, Bomb. 16 H9 18 54N 73 1 E
Dia Deva, Bomb. 16 H8 18 57N 72 53 E
Diadema, S. Pau. 31 F6 23 41 S 46 37W
Diamante, B.A. 32 C4 34 41 S 58 25W
Diamond Cr. →, Melb. 19 E7 37 44 S 145 9 E
Diamond Creek, Melb. 19 E8 37 40 S 145 10 E
Didaowai, Tianj. 14 E6 39 8N 117 12 E
Diepensiepen, Ruhr 6 C3 51 14N 6 58 E
Diepkloof, Jobg. 18 F8 26 14 S 27 57 E
Diessem, Ruhr 6 C1 51 19N 6 34 E
Difficult Run →, Wash. 25 D6 38 55N 77 18W
Digla, W. →, El Qâ. 18 D6 29 58N 31 22 E
Digra, Calc. 16 D5 22 49N 88 19 E
Dikemark, Oslo 2 C2 59 48N 10 22 E
Dilerpur, Calc. 16 C5 22 51N 88 10 E
Dinslaken, Ruhr 6 A2 51 33N 6 43 E
Dinslakener Bruch, Ruhr 6 A2 51 34N 6 44 E
Dinwiddie, Jobg. 18 F9 26 16 S 28 9 E
Diósd, Bud. 10 K12 47 24N 18 57 E
Dirnismaning, Mün. 7 F10 48 13N 11 38 E
Disappointment, Mt., L.A. 28 A4 34 15N 118 7W
Discovery, Jobg. 18 E8 26 8 S 27 54 E
Disteln, Ruhr 6 A4 51 36N 7 9 E
District Heights, Wash. 25 D8 38 51N 76 53W
Ditan Gongyuan, Beij. 14 B3 39 56N 116 23 E
Dix Hills, N.Y. 23 C8 40 48N 73 21W
Dixmoor, Chic. 26 D2 41 37N 87 40W
Diyala →, Bagd. 17 F9 33 13N 44 30 E
Djakarta = Jakarta, Jak. 15 H10 6 9 S 106 52 E
Djursholm, Stock. 3 D11 59 24N 18 5 E
Do Bong, Sŏul 12 G8 37 37N 127 1 E
Dobbs, N.Y. 23 A5 41 1N 73 52W
Döberitz, Berl. 7 A1 52 32N 13 3 E
Döbling, Wien 10 G10 48 14N 16 20 E
Dobong, Sŏul 12 G8 37 39N 127 2 E
Dobong San, Sŏul 12 F8 37 40N 127 0 E
Dōbrowa, Wsaw. 10 E6 52 19N 20 52 E
Doddinghurst, Lon. 4 A6 51 40N 0 18 E
Dodger Stadium, L.A. 28 B3 34 4N 118 14W
Dogsan, Sŏul 12 H7 37 28N 126 54 E
Doirone, Tori. 9 B2 45 3N 7 32 E
Dōjō, Ōsaka 12 A2 34 51N 135 14 E
Dōjō, Tōkyō 13 A2 35 51N 139 37 E
Dollard-des-Ormeaux, Mtrl. 20 B3 43 29N 73 49W
Dollis Hill, Lon. 4 B3 51 33N 0 13W
Dolni, Pra. 10 B3 50 3N 14 33 E
Dolni Chabry, Pra. 10 B2 50 8N 14 26 E
Dolni Počernice, Pra. 10 B3 50 5N 14 34 E
Dolton, Chic. 26 D3 41 37N 87 35W
Domont, Paris 5 A3 49 2N 2 19 E
Don Bosco, B.A. 32 C5 34 42 S 58 17W
Don Mills, Trto. 20 D8 43 44N 79 21W
Don Pedro II, Parque, S. Pau. 31 E6 23 33 S 46 36W
Don Torcuato, B.A. 32 A3 34 29 S 58 38W
Donau →, Bud. 10 J13 47 33N 19 4 E
Donau-Oder Kanal, Wien 10 G11 48 12N 16 32 E
Donaufeld, Wien 10 G10 48 15N 16 24 E
Donaukanal, Wien 10 G10 48 10N 16 27 E
Donaupark, Wien 10 G10 48 14N 16 24 E
Donaustadt, Wien 10 G10 48 13N 16 29 E
Doncaster, Melb. 19 E7 37 47 S 145 8 E
Doncaster East, Melb. 19 E7 37 46 S 145 8 E
Dong Dae Mun, Sŏul 12 G8 37 34N 127 2 E
Dong Jag, Sŏul 12 G7 37 30N 126 56 E
Dongala Forest Reserve, Melb. 19 F9 37 50 S 145 20 E
Dongan Hills, N.Y. 22 D4 40 35N 74 5W
Dongbinggo, Sŏul 12 G7 37 31N 126 58 E
Dongcheng, Beij. 14 B3 39 54N 116 23 E
Dongfeng Nongchang, Beij. 14 B3 39 57N 116 28 E
Dongjiao, Gzh. 14 G8 23 5N 113 12 E
Dongjuzi, Tianj. 14 E6 39 7N 117 14 E
Dongkou, Shang. 14 J12 31 17N 121 33 E
Dongmenwai, Tianj. 14 E6 39 8N 117 11 E
Dongri, Bomb. 16 H8 18 53N 72 57 E
Dongwuyuan, Beij. 14 B2 39 55N 116 18 E
Dongzhimen, Beij. 14 B3 39 55N 116 24 E
Donvale, Melb. 19 E8 37 47 S 145 11 E
Doonside, Syd. 19 A2 33 46 S 150 51 E
Doornfontein, Jobg. 18 F9 26 11 S 28 3 E
Dōra, Bagd. 17 F8 33 15N 44 25 E
Dora Riparia →, Tori. 9 B2 45 4N 7 38 E
Dorchester, Bost. 21 D3 42 17N 71 4W
Dorchester B., Bost. 21 D3 42 18N 71 1W
Dorchester Heights Nat. Hist. Site, Bost. 21 D3 42 19N 71 2W
Dorion, Mtrl. 20 B1 43 23N 74 1W
Dornach, Mün. 7 G11 48 9N 11 41 E
Dornap, Ruhr 6 C4 51 15N 7 3 E
Dornbach, Wien 10 G9 48 13N 16 18 E
Dorsey Run →, Balt. 25 B2 39 11N 76 47W
Dorstfeld, Ruhr 6 A6 51 30N 7 24 E
Dortmund, Ruhr 6 A6 51 30N 7 28 E
Dorval, Mtrl. 20 B3 43 26N 73 45W
Dorval, Aéroport de, Mtrl. 20 B3 43 28N 73 44 E
Dos Rios, Méx. 29 B1 19 22N 99 20W
Doshan Tappeh Airport, Tehr. 17 C5 35 41N 51 28 E
Dotmund-Ems Kanal, Ruhr 6 A6 51 35N 7 24 E
Double B., Syd. 19 B4 33 52 S 151 15 E
Douglas Park, Chic. 26 B2 41 51N 87 42W
Douglaston, N.Y. 23 C6 40 46N 73 44W
Dove Elbe →, Hbg. 7 E8 53 28N 10 7 E
Dover, Bost. 21 D2 42 14N 71 16W
Dover Heights, Syd. 19 B4 33 52 S 151 16 E
Dowlatābād, Tehr. 17 D5 35 38N 51 27 E
Downe, Lon. 4 C5 51 20N 0 3 E
Downey, L.A. 28 C4 33 56N 118 9W
Downsview, Trto. 20 D7 43 43N 79 30W
Downsview Dells Park, Trto. 20 D7 43 44N 79 30W
Dracut, Bost. 21 A2 42 40N 71 17W
Dragør, Købn. 2 E10 55 35N 12 38 E
Drancy, Paris 5 B4 48 55N 2 26 E
Dranesville, Wash. 25 C5 39 0N 77 20W
Draveil, Paris 5 C4 48 41N 2 23 E
Drayton Green, Lon. 4 B3 51 30N 0 19W
Dreilinden, Berl. 7 B2 52 24N 13 10 E
Dresher, Phil. 24 A4 40 9N 75 9W
Drewnica, Wsaw. 10 E7 52 18N 21 6 E
Drexel Hill, Phil. 24 B3 39 56N 75 18W
Drexel Inst. of Technology, Phil. 24 B3 39 57N 75 11W
Drigh Road, Kar. 17 G11 24 52N 67 7 E
Drogden, Købn. 2 E11 55 37N 12 42 E
Drottningholm, Stock. 3 E10 59 19N 17 53 E
Druento, Tori. 9 B2 45 8N 7 34 E
Druid Hill Park, Balt. 25 B3 39 19N 76 38W
Druid Lake, Balt. 25 B3 39 19N 76 38W
Drummoyne, Syd. 19 B3 33 51 S 151 8 E
Druzhba, Mos. 11 D10 55 52N 37 44 E
Duarte, L.A. 28 B5 34 8N 117 57W
Dubeč, Pra. 10 B3 50 3N 14 35 E
Dubi Bheri, Calc. 16 C5 22 52N 88 16 E
Duffryn Mawr, Phil. 24 A2 40 2N 75 27W
Dugnano, Mil. 9 D6 45 33N 9 11 E
Dugny, Paris 5 B4 48 57N 2 24 E
Duiha, Calc. 16 E5 22 34N 88 15 E
Duisburg, Ruhr 6 B2 51 26N 6 45 E
Dulāb, Tehr. 17 D5 35 39N 51 27 E
Dulworthtown, Phil. 24 B1 39 54N 75 33W
Dum Dum, Calc. 16 E6 22 38N 88 25 E
Dum Dum Int. Airport, Calc. 16 E6 22 38N 88 26 E
Dumbarton Pt., S.F. 27 D4 37 29N 122 6W
Dumjor, Calc. 16 E5 22 37N 88 13 E
Dumont, N.Y. 22 B5 40 56N 73 59W
Dümpten, Ruhr 6 B3 51 27N 6 54 E
Duna →, Bud. 10 J13 47 33N 19 4 E
Dunbarton, Trto. 20 C10 43 50N 79 6W
Dundalk, Balt. 25 B3 39 17N 76 31W
Dundas, Syd. 19 A3 33 47 S 151 3 E
Dunearn, Sing. 15 G7 1 19N 103 49 E
Dunellen, N.Y. 22 D2 40 35N 74 26W
Dunn Loring, Wash. 25 D6 38 54N 77 13W
Dunning, Chic. 26 B2 41 56N 87 48W
Dunton Green, Lon. 4 D6 51 17N 0 11 E
Dunvegan, Jobg. 18 E9 26 9 S 28 8 E
Duomo, Mil. 9 E6 45 28N 9 11 E
Duomo, Nápl. 9 H12 40 51N 14 15 E
Duomo, Tori. 9 B3 45 4N 7 45 E
Duque de Caxias, Rio J. 31 A2 22 46 S 43 18W
Durban Roodepoort Deep Gold Mines, Jobg. 18 F8 26 11 S 27 52 E
Durchholz, Ruhr 6 B5 51 23N 7 18 E
Düssel →, Ruhr 6 C3 51 13N 6 58 E
Düsseldorf, Ruhr 6 C2 51 13N 6 46 E
Düsseldorf-Lohausen, Flughafen, Ruhr 6 C2 51 17N 6 45 E
Duvenstedt, Hbg. 7 C8 53 42N 10 6 E
Duvenstedter Brook, Hbg. 7 C8 53 43N 10 8 E
Duvernay, Mtrl. 20 A3 43 35N 73 40W
Dyakovo, Mos. 11 E9 55 40N 37 39 E
Dyviksudd, Stock. 3 E13 59 11N 18 23 E
Dzerzhinskiy, Mos. 11 F11 55 38N 37 51 E
Dzerzhinskiy, Mos. 11 E9 55 47N 37 37 E
Dzerzhinskiy Park, Mos. 11 E9 55 50N 37 37 E

E

Eagle Rock, L.A. 28 B3 34 8N 118 12 E
Ealing, Lon. 4 B3 51 30N 0 18W
Earls Court, Lon. 4 C3 51 29N 0 11W
Earlsfield, Lon. 4 C3 51 26N 0 10W
Earlwood, Syd. 19 B3 33 55 S 151 8 E
East Acton, Bost. 21 C1 42 28N 71 24W
East Acton, Lon. 4 B3 51 30N 0 14W
East Arlington, Wash. 25 D7 38 51N 77 4W
East Atlantic Beach, N.Y. 23 D6 40 35N 73 43W
East B., N.Y. 23 D7 40 38N 73 32W
East Barnet, Lon. 4 B4 51 38N 0 9W
East Bedfont, Lon. 4 C2 51 26N 0 28W
East Billerica, Bost. 21 B2 42 35N 71 13W
East Boston, Bost. 21 C3 42 22N 71 1W
East Braintree, Bost. 21 D4 42 13N 70 58W
East Chicago, Chic. 26 D4 41 38N 87 26W
East Don →, Trto. 20 D8 43 48N 79 25W
East Dulwich, Lon. 4 C4 51 26N 0 4W
East Elmhurst, N.Y. 23 C5 40 45N 73 52W
East Farmingdale, N.Y. 23 C8 40 44N 73 25W
East Finchley, Lon. 4 B3 51 35N 0 10W
East Half Hollow Hills, N.Y. 23 C9 40 47N 73 19W
East Ham, Lon. 4 B5 51 32N 0 3 E
East Hanover, N.Y. 22 C2 40 49N 74 21W
East Hills, N.Y. 23 C7 40 47N 73 37W
East Hills, Syd. 19 B2 33 57 S 150 59 E
East Holliston, Bost. 21 D1 42 12N 71 25W
East Horsley, Lon. 4 D2 51 16N 0 25W
East Humber →, Trto. 20 D7 43 47N 79 35W
East Huntington, N.Y. 23 B8 40 52N 73 24W
East Lamma Channel, H.K. 12 E5 22 13N 114 9 E
East Lexington, Bost. 21 C2 42 25N 71 12W
East Los Angeles, L.A. 28 B3 34 1N 118 10 E
East Meadow, N.Y. 23 C7 40 42N 73 31W
East Molesey, Lon. 4 C2 51 24N 0 21W
East New York, N.Y. 23 C5 40 40N 73 53W
East Newark, N.Y. 22 C3 40 45N 74 10W
East Northport, N.Y. 23 B9 40 52N 73 18W
East Norwich, N.Y. 23 B7 40 50N 73 31W
East Orange, N.Y. 22 C3 40 46N 74 11W
East Palo Alto, S.F. 27 D4 37 28N 122 8W
East Paterson, N.Y. 22 B4 40 53N 74 8W
East Pines, Wash. 25 D8 38 57N 76 54W
East Point, Bost. 21 C4 42 25N 70 54W
East Potomac Park, Wash. 25 D7 38 52N 77 1W
East Richmond, S.F. 27 A3 37 56N 122 19W
East Ringwood, Melb. 19 E8 37 48 S 145 15 E
East River →, N.Y. 22 C5 40 44N 73 58W
East Rockaway, N.Y. 23 D6 40 38N 73 40W
East Rutherford, N.Y. 22 B4 40 50N 74 5W
East Sheen, Lon. 4 C3 51 27N 0 16W
East View Garden, Sing. 15 F8 1 20N 103 57 E
East Weymouth, Bost. 21 D4 42 13N 70 55W
East Wickham, Lon. 4 C5 51 28N 0 5 E
East Williston, N.Y. 23 C7 40 45N 73 37W
East York, Trto. 20 D8 43 40N 79 22W
Eastchester, N.Y. 23 B6 40 56N 73 49W
Eastchester B., N.Y. 23 B6 40 50N 73 47W
Eastcote, Lon. 4 B2 51 34N 0 23W
Eastleigh, Jobg. 18 E9 26 7 S 28 9 E
Eastpoint, Balt. 25 B3 39 17N 76 34W
Eastwood, Syd. 19 A3 33 47 S 151 4 E
Eatons Neck Pt., N.Y. 23 B8 40 57N 73 24W
Eaubonne, Paris 5 B3 48 59N 2 16 E
Ebara, Tōkyō 13 C3 35 35N 139 42 E
Ebisu, Tōkyō 13 C3 35 38N 139 42 E
Ebute-Ikorodu, Lagos 18 A2 6 35N 7 29 E

Gerthe 37

Ebute-Metta, Lagos 18 B2 6 28N 7 23 E
Ecatepec de Morelos, Méx. 29 A3 19 35N 99 2W
Echo B., N.Y. 23 B6 40 54N 73 45W
Echo Mt., L.A. 28 A4 34 12N 118 8W
Écouen, Paris 5 A4 49 1N 2 22 E
Ecquevilly, Paris 5 B1 48 57N 1 55 E
Ecser, Bud. 10 K14 47 26N 19 19 E
Eda, Tōkyō 13 C2 35 33N 139 33 E
Eddington, Phil. 24 A5 40 5N 74 55W
Eddystone, Phil. 24 B2 39 51N 75 20W
Eden, Rio J. 31 A1 22 47 S 43 23W
Edendale, Jobg. 18 E9 26 8 S 28 9 E
Edenvale, Jobg. 18 E9 26 8 S 28 9 E
Edgars Cr. →, Melb. 19 E6 37 43 S 144 58 E
Edge Hill, Phil. 24 A4 40 7N 75 9W
Edgeley, Trto. 20 D7 43 47N 79 31W
Edgemar, S.F. 27 C2 37 39N 122 29W
Edgemere, Balt. 25 B4 39 14N 76 26W
Edgemont, Phil. 24 B2 39 58N 75 26W
Edgewater Park, Phil. 24 A5 40 3N 74 54W
Edgware, Lon. 4 B3 51 36N 0 15W
Edison, N.Y. 22 D2 40 31N 74 23W
Edison Park, Chic. 26 A2 42 1N 87 48W
Edleen, Jobg. 18 E10 26 5 S 28 12 E
Edmondston, Wash. 25 D8 38 56N 76 54W
Edo →, Tōkyō 13 C4 35 38N 139 52 E
Edogawa, Tōkyō 13 B4 35 43N 139 52 E
Edsberg, Stock. 3 D10 59 26N 17 57 E
Edwards L., Melb. 19 E6 37 42 S 144 59 E
Eestiluoto, Hels. 3 C6 60 7N 25 13 E
Egawa, Tōkyō 13 D4 35 22N 139 54 E
Egenbüttel, Hbg. 7 D7 53 39N 9 51 E
Eggerscheidt, Ruhr 6 C3 51 19N 6 53 E
Egham, Lon. 4 C1 51 25N 0 30W
Eiche, Berl. 7 A4 52 33N 13 35 E
Eiche Sud, Berl. 7 A4 52 33N 13 35 E
Eichlinghofen, Ruhr 6 B6 51 29N 7 24 E
Eichwalde, Berl. 7 B4 52 22N 13 37 E
Eidelstedt, Hbg. 7 D7 53 36N 9 54 E
Eiffel, Tour, Paris 5 B3 48 51N 2 17 E
Eigen, Ruhr 6 A3 51 32N 6 56 E
Eilbek, Hbg. 7 D8 53 34N 10 2 E
Eimsbüttel, Hbg. 7 D7 53 34N 9 57 E
Eissendorf, Hbg. 7 E7 53 27N 9 57 E
Ejby, Købn. 2 D9 55 41N 12 24 E
Ejigbo, Lagos 18 A1 6 33N 7 18 E
Ekeberg, Oslo 2 B4 59 53N 10 46 E
Ekeby, Stock. 3 D8 59 21N 17 35 E
Ekerö, Stock. 3 E9 59 17N 17 46 E
Ekerön, Stock. 3 E9 59 18N 17 41 E
Ekhtiyarieh, Tehr. 17 C5 35 46N 51 28 E
Eklundshov, Stock. 3 E10 59 11N 17 54 E
Eknäs, Stock. 3 E12 59 18N 18 13 E
El 'Abbasiya, El Qâ. 18 C5 30 3N 31 16 E
El Agustino, Lima 30 G8 12 2 S 77 0W
El Alto, Stgo 30 J10 33 29 S 70 42W
El Awkal, El Qâ. 18 C5 30 2N 31 12 E
El Baragil, El Qâ. 18 C4 30 4N 31 9 E
El Basâtîn, El Qâ. 18 C5 29 58N 31 16 E
El Calvario, La Hab. 30 B3 23 3N 82 19W
El Cano, La Hab. 30 B2 23 2N 82 27W
El Caribe, Car. 30 D5 10 36N 66 52W
El Carmen, Stgo 30 J10 33 22 S 70 43W
El Cerrito, S.F. 27 A3 37 54N 122 18W
El Cerro, La Hab. 30 B2 23 6N 82 23W
El Cojo, Pta., Car. 30 D5 10 36N 66 53W
El Cortijo, Stgo 30 J10 33 22 S 70 42W
El Duqqi, El Qâ. 18 C5 30 1N 31 12 E
El Gamâlîya, El Qâ. 18 C5 30 2N 31 15 E
El Ghurîya, El Qâ. 18 C5 30 2N 31 15 E
El Gîza, El Qâ. 18 C5 30 0N 31 12 E
El Granada, S.F. 27 C2 37 30N 122 27W
El Guarda Parres, Méx. 29 D2 19 9N 99 11W
El Hatillo, Car. 30 E6 10 25N 66 49W
El Khalîfa, El Qâ. 18 C5 30 0N 31 15 E
El Kôm el Ahmar, El Qâ. 18 C5 30 6N 31 10 E
El Ma'âdi, El Qâ. 18 C5 29 57N 31 15 E
El Matarîya, El Qâ. 18 C5 30 7N 31 18 E
El Monte, L.A. 28 B4 34 3N 118 1W
El Muhît Idkû el Gharbi →, El Qâ. 18 C4 30 6N 31 6 E
El Mûskî, El Qâ. 18 C5 30 3N 31 15 E
El Palmar, Car. 30 D5 10 36N 66 53W
El Palomar, B.A. 32 B3 34 36 S 58 37W
El Pardo, Mdrd. 8 A2 40 30N 3 46W
El Pedregal, Car. 30 D5 10 30N 66 51W
El Pinar, Car. 30 E5 10 28N 66 56W
El Plantio, Mdrd. 8 B1 40 28N 3 51W
El Qâhira, El Qâ. 18 C5 30 2N 31 13 E
El Qubba, El Qâ. 18 C5 30 4N 31 16 E
El Recreo, Car. 30 E5 10 29N 66 52W
El Reloj, Méx. 29 C3 19 19N 99 9W
El Retiro, Car. 30 D5 10 31N 66 54W
El Salto, Stgo 30 J11 33 22 S 70 38W
El Segundo, L.A. 28 C2 33 55N 118 24W
El Sereno, L.A. 28 B3 34 6N 118 10 E
El Silencio, Car. 30 D5 10 30N 66 55W
El Sobrante, S.F. 27 A3 37 58N 122 17W
El Talar de Pacheco, B.A. 32 A3 34 27 S 58 38W
El Talibîya, El Qâ. 18 C5 29 59N 31 10 E
El Valle, Car. 30 E5 10 29N 66 54W
El Vedado, La Hab. 30 B2 23 8N 82 23W
El Vergel, Méx. 29 C3 19 18N 99 5W
El Wâyli el Kubra, El Qâ. 18 C5 30 5N 31 17 E
El Zamalik, El Qâ. 18 C5 30 3N 31 12 E
Elam, Phil. 24 B1 39 51N 75 32W
Élancourt, Paris 5 C1 48 47N 1 57 E
Elandsfortein, Jobg. 18 E10 26 9 S 28 13 E
Elbe →, Hbg. 7 D6 53 32N 9 49 E
Elberfeld, Ruhr 6 C4 51 15N 7 9 E
Elephanta Caves, Bomb. 16 H8 18 57N 72 57 E
Elephanta I., Bomb. 16 H8 18 57N 72 56 E
Elisenau, Berl. 7 A4 52 38N 13 37 E
Elizabeth, N.Y. 22 D3 40 39N 74 13W
Elkins Park, Phil. 24 A4 40 4N 75 8W
Elkridge, Balt. 25 B2 39 13N 76 42W
Ellboda, Stock. 3 D12 59 24N 18 15 E
Eller, Ruhr 6 C3 51 12N 6 51 E
Ellerbek, Hbg. 7 D7 53 39N 9 52 E
Ellicott City, Balt. 25 B2 39 15N 76 49W
Ellinghorst, Ruhr 6 A3 51 33N 6 57 E
Ellinikón, Ath. 8 J11 37 50N 23 45 E
Ellis I., N.Y. 22 C4 40 41N 74 2W
Elm Park, Lon. 4 B6 51 32N 0 12 E
Elmers End, Lon. 4 C4 51 23N 0 2W
Elmhurst, Chic. 26 B1 41 53N 87 55W
Elmhurst, N.Y. 23 C5 40 44N 73 53W
Elmont, N.Y. 23 C6 40 42N 73 42W
Elmstead, Lon. 4 C5 51 24N 0 2 E
Elmwood, Balt. 25 A3 39 20N 76 31W
Elmwood, N.Y. 23 B8 40 51N 73 20W
Elmwood Park, Chic. 26 B2 41 55N 87 48W
Elmwood Park, N.Y. 22 B4 40 54N 74 7W
Elsburg, Jobg. 18 F10 26 15 S 28 13 E
Elsburgspruit →, Jobg. 18 F10 26 15 S 28 12 E
Elsnere, Phil. 24 C1 39 44N 75 35W
Elspark, Jobg. 18 F10 26 15 S 28 13 E
Elsternwick, Melb. 19 F7 37 52 S 145 0 E
Eltham, Lon. 4 C5 51 27N 0 3 E
Eltham, Melb. 19 E7 37 42 S 145 9 E
Elthorn Heights, Lon. 4 B2 51 31N 0 20W
Eltingrille, N.Y. 22 D4 40 32N 74 9W
Elwood, Melb. 19 F6 37 53 S 144 59 E
Élysée, Paris 5 B3 48 52N 2 19 E
Embu, S. Pau. 31 E4 23 38 S 46 50W
Embu-Mirim, S. Pau. 31 F5 23 41 S 46 49W
Embu Mirim →, S. Pau. 31 F5 23 43 S 46 47W
Emdeni, Jobg. 18 F7 26 14 S 27 49 E
Émerainville, Paris 5 C5 48 48N 2 37 E
Emerson, N.Y. 22 B4 40 57N 74 2W
Emerson Park, Lon. 4 B6 51 34N 0 13 E
Emeryville, S.F. 27 B3 37 49N 122 17W
Eminonu, Ist. 17 A2 41 0N 28 57 E
Emmarentia, Jobg. 18 E9 26 9 S 28 0 E
Emperor's Palace, Tōkyō 13 B3 35 40N 139 45 E
Empire State Building, N.Y. 22 C5 40 44N 73 59W
Emscher →, Ruhr 6 A6 51 30N 7 26 E
Emscher Bruch, Ruhr 6 A4 51 33N 7 8 E
Emscher Zweigkanal, Ruhr 6 A4 51 33N 7 9 E
Encantado, Rio J. 31 B2 22 53 S 43 19W
Encino, L.A. 28 B2 34 9N 118 28W
Encino Res., L.A. 28 B1 34 8N 118 30W
Enebyberg, Stock. 3 D10 59 25N 17 59 E
Enfield, Lon. 4 B4 51 39N 0 4W
Enfield, Phil. 24 A3 40 6N 75 11W
Enfield, Syd. 19 B3 33 53 S 151 6 E
Enfield Chase, Lon. 4 A4 51 40N 0 8W
Enfield Highway, Lon. 4 B4 51 39N 0 2W
Enfield Lock, Lon. 4 A4 51 40N 0 1W
Enfield Wash, Lon. 4 B4 51 39N 0 2W
Eng Khong Gardens, Sing. 15 F7 1 20N 103 46 E
Engenho, I. do, Rio J. 31 B3 22 50 S 43 6W
Engenho Nôvo, Rio J. 31 B2 22 53 S 43 17W
Engenho Velho, Sa. do, Rio J. 31 B1 22 54 S 43 21W
Engenno do Mato, Rio J. 31 B3 22 56 S 43 2W
Enghein-les-Bains, Paris 5 B3 48 58N 2 18 E
Englewood, Chic. 26 C3 41 46N 87 38W
Englewood, N.Y. 22 B5 40 53N 73 58W
Englewood Cliffs, N.Y. 22 B5 40 53N 73 59W
Englischer Garten, Mün. 7 G10 48 9N 11 35 E
Enmore, Syd. 19 B4 33 54 S 151 10 E
Ennepe →, Ruhr 6 C6 51 17N 7 23 E
Ennepetal, Ruhr 6 C6 51 17N 7 21 E
Ennepetalsp →, Ruhr 6 C6 51 14N 7 24 E
Enskede, Stock. 3 E11 59 17N 18 4 E
Entrevias, Mdrd. 8 B2 40 22N 3 40W
Épiais-les-Louvres, Paris 5 A5 49 1N 2 33 E
Epinay, Paris 5 B3 48 57N 2 19 E
Epinay-sous-Sénart, Paris 5 C5 48 41N 2 30 E
Epinay-sur-Orge, Paris 5 C3 48 40N 2 19 E
Eppende, Ruhr 6 B4 51 28N 7 9 E
Eppenhausen, Ruhr 6 B6 51 22N 7 29 E
Epping, Lon. 4 A5 51 41N 0 6 E
Epping, Melb. 19 D7 37 39 S 145 1 E
Epping, Syd. 19 A3 33 46 S 151 5 E
Epping Forest, Lon. 4 B5 51 39N 0 2 E
Epsom, Lon. 4 D3 51 19N 0 15W
Epsom Racecourse, Lon. 4 D3 51 18N 0 15W
Éragny, Paris 5 A2 49 1N 2 5 E
Ercolano, Nápl. 9 J13 40 48N 14 21 E
Érd, Bud. 10 K12 47 23N 18 56 E
Erdenheim, Phil. 24 A3 40 5N 75 12W
Eregun, Lagos 18 A2 6 35N 7 22 E
Erenköy, Ist. 17 B3 40 58N 29 3 E
Ergal, Paris 5 C1 48 47N 1 55 E
Erial, Phil. 24 C4 39 46N 75 0W
Erith, Lon. 4 C6 51 28N 0 11 E
Erkner, Berl. 7 B5 52 25N 13 44 E
Erkrath, Ruhr 6 C3 51 13N 6 54 E
Erlaa, Wien 10 H9 48 9N 16 19 E
Erle, Ruhr 6 A4 51 33N 7 4 E
Ermelino Matarazzo, S. Pau. 31 D7 23 29 S 46 28W
Ermington, Syd. 19 A3 33 48 S 151 4 E
Ermont, Paris 5 B3 48 59N 2 15 E
Ersébet-Telep, Bud. 10 K14 47 27N 19 10 E
Ershatou, Gzh. 14 G8 23 6N 113 18 E
Erskineville, Syd. 19 B4 33 54 S 151 12 E
Erstavik, Stock. 3 E12 59 16N 18 14 E
Erstaviken, Stock. 3 E12 59 16N 18 20 E
Erunkan, Lagos 18 A2 6 36N 7 23 E
Eschenried, Mün. 7 F9 48 13N 11 25 E
Esenler, Ist. 17 A2 41 1N 28 52 E
Esher, Lon. 4 C2 51 22N 0 20W
Eshratābād, Tehr. 17 C5 35 42N 51 27 E
España, B.A. 32 C5 34 46 S 58 14W
Espeleta, B.A. 32 C5 34 45 S 58 15W
Esplugas, Barc. 8 D5 41 22N 2 5 E
Espoo, Hels. 3 B2 60 13N 24 38 E
Espoonlahti, Hels. 3 B2 60 9N 24 31 E
Esposizione Univ. di Roma (E.U.R.), Rome 9 G9 41 49N 12 28 E
Essen, Ruhr 6 B4 51 27N 7 0 E
Essen-Mülheim, Flughafen, Ruhr 6 B3 51 24N 6 56 E
Essendon, Melb. 19 E6 37 44 S 144 55 E
Essendon Airport, Melb. 19 E6 37 43 S 144 54 E
Essex, Balt. 25 B4 39 18N 76 28W
Essex Falls, N.Y. 22 C3 40 49N 74 16W
Essingen, Stock. 3 E10 59 19N 17 59 E
Essling, Wien 10 G11 48 12N 16 31 E
Est, Gare de l', Paris 5 B4 48 52N 2 21 E
Estado, Parque do, S. Pau. 31 E6 23 38 S 46 38W
Estby, Hels. 3 C1 60 5N 24 27W
Este, Parque Nacional del, Car. 30 E5 10 29N 66 50W
Esteban Echeverria, B.A. 32 C4 34 48 S 58 29W
Estlotan, Hels. 3 C6 60 7N 25 13 E
Estrela, Basilica da, Lisb. 8 F8 38 42N 9 9W
Étiolles, Paris 5 D4 48 38N 2 28 E
Etobicoke, Trto. 20 E7 43 39N 79 34W
Etobicoke Cr. →, Trto. 20 E7 43 35N 79 32W
Etzenhausen, Mün. 7 F9 48 16N 11 27 E
Eun Pyeong, Sŏul 12 G7 37 36N 126 56 E
Eungam, Sŏul 12 G7 37 34N 126 55 E
Evanston, Chic. 26 A2 42 3N 87 40W
Évecquemont, Paris 5 A1 49 0N 1 56 E
Everett, Bost. 21 C3 42 24N 71 3W
Evergreen Park, Chic. 26 C2 41 43N 87 42W
Eversael, Ruhr 6 A1 51 32N 6 39 E
Evesboro, Phil. 24 B5 39 54N 74 55W
Eving, Ruhr 6 A6 51 33N 7 28 E
Evry, Paris 5 D4 48 38N 2 26 E
Évry-les-Châteaux, Paris 5 D5 48 39N 2 38 E
Évzonos, Ath. 8 J11 37 55N 23 49 E
Ewin, Tehr. 17 C5 35 47N 51 23 E
Ewu, Lagos 18 A1 6 33N 7 19 E
Exelberg, Wien 10 G9 48 14N 16 15 E
Eynsford, Lon. 4 C6 51 21N 0 12 E
Eyup, Ist. 17 A2 41 2N 28 55 E
Ez Zeitûn, El Qâ. 18 C5 30 6N 31 18 E
Ézanville, Paris 5 A4 49 1N 2 21 E
Ezeiza, B.A. 32 D3 34 50 S 58 31W
Ezeiza, Aeropuerto, B.A. 32 C3 34 48 S 58 32W

F

Fabreville, Mtrl. 20 A2 43 33N 73 51W
Fælledparken, Købn. 2 D10 55 42N 12 34 E
Fågelön, Stock. 3 E10 59 18N 17 55 E
Fagersjo, Stock. 3 E11 59 14N 18 4 E
Fagnano, Mil. 9 E4 45 24N 8 59 E
Fahrn, Ruhr 6 A2 51 30N 6 45 E
Faibano, Nápl. 9 H13 40 55N 14 27 E
Fair Lawn, N.Y. 22 B4 40 55N 74 7W
Fairfax, Phil. 24 C1 39 47N 75 33W
Fairfax, Wash. 25 D6 38 50N 77 19W
Fairfax Station, Wash. 25 E6 38 48N 77 19W
Fairfield, Melb. 19 E7 37 46 S 145 2 E
Fairfield, N.Y. 22 B3 40 53N 74 17W
Fairfield, Syd. 19 B2 33 52 S 150 56 E
Fairhaven B., Bost. 21 C1 42 25N 71 21W
Fairhaven Hill, Bost. 21 C1 42 26N 71 21W
Fairland, Jobg. 18 E8 26 8 S 27 57 E
Fairland, Wash. 25 C8 39 4N 76 57W
Fairmont Terrace, S.F. 27 B4 37 42N 122 7W
Fairmount Heights, Wash. 25 D8 38 54N 76 54W
Fairmount Park, Phil. 24 A3 40 3N 75 13W
Fairport, Trto. 20 D10 43 49N 79 4W
Fairview, N.Y. 22 C5 40 48N 73 59W
Fairview, N.Y. 23 A6 41 1N 73 46W
Falenica, Wsaw. 10 F8 52 9N 21 12 E
Falenty, Wsaw. 10 F6 52 8N 20 55 E
Falkenburg, Berl. 7 A4 52 34N 13 32 E
Falkenhagen, Berl. 7 A1 52 34N 13 5 E
Falkensee, Berl. 7 A1 52 34N 13 4 E
Fallon, L.A. 28 C5 33 59N 117 54W
Falls Church, Wash. 25 D6 38 53N 77 12W
Falls Run →, Balt. 25 A1 39 21N 76 52W
Falomo, Lagos 18 B2 6 26N 7 26 E
Fangcun, Gzh. 14 G8 23 6N 113 13 E
Fanwood, N.Y. 22 D2 40 37N 74 23W
Far Rockaway, N.Y. 23 D6 40 36N 73 45W
Farahābād, Tehr. 17 C5 35 41N 51 29 E
Färentuna, Stock. 3 D8 59 23N 17 39 E
Farforovskaya, St-Pet. 11 B4 59 52N 30 27 E
Farm Pond, Bost. 21 D2 42 13N 71 20W
Farmingdale, N.Y. 23 C8 40 43N 73 27W
Farmsen, Hbg. 7 D8 53 36N 10 8 E
Farnborough, Lon. 4 C5 51 21N 0 3 E
Farningham, Lon. 4 C6 51 23N 0 12 E
Farrar Pond, Bost. 21 C1 42 24N 71 21W
Farrarmere, Jobg. 18 E10 26 9 S 28 18 E
Farsta, Stock. 3 E11 59 14N 18 5 E
Farstalandet, Stock. 3 E13 59 18N 18 23 E
Farum, Købn. 2 D8 55 48N 12 21 E
Farum Sø, Købn. 2 D9 55 48N 12 21 E
Fasanerie-Nord, Mün. 7 F10 48 11N 11 32 E
Fasangarten, Mün. 7 G10 48 5N 11 36 E
Fat Tau Chau, H.K. 12 E6 22 16N 114 16 E
Fatih, Ist. 17 A2 41 0N 28 56 E
Favoriten, Wien 10 H10 48 9N 16 23 E
Fawkner, Melb. 19 E6 37 42 S 144 56 E
Fawkner Park, Melb. 19 F6 37 50 S 144 58 E
Feasterville, Phil. 24 A4 40 9N 75 0W
Febrero, Parque de, B.A. 32 B4 34 36 S 58 25W
Feijó, Lisb. 8 G8 38 39N 9 9W
Feldersbruch →, Ruhr 6 B5 51 23N 7 4 E
Feldhausen, Ruhr 6 A3 51 36N 6 58 E
Feldkirchen, Mün. 7 G11 48 8N 11 43 E
Feldmoching, Mün. 7 F10 48 14N 11 32 E
Fellowship, Phil. 24 B5 39 56N 74 57W
Feltham, Lon. 4 C2 51 26N 0 24W
Feltonville, Phil. 24 A4 40 1N 75 8W
Fenerbahce, Ist. 17 B3 40 58N 29 2 E
Fengtai, Beij. 14 C2 39 49N 116 14 E
Fenino, Mos. 11 E11 55 43N 37 56 E
Ferencváros, Bud. 10 K13 47 29N 19 5 E
Ferihegyi Airport, Bud. 10 K14 47 26N 19 14 E
Ferndale, Balt. 25 B3 39 11N 76 38W
Ferndale, Jobg. 18 E9 26 5 S 28 0 E
Ferntree Gully, Melb. 19 F8 37 52 S 145 17 E
Ferntree Gully Nat. Park, Melb. 19 F8 37 52 S 145 19 E
Ferny Cr. →, Melb. 19 F8 37 54 S 145 16 E
Férolles-Attilly, Paris 5 C5 48 44N 2 37 E
Ferraz de Vasconcelos, S. Pau. 31 E7 23 32 S 46 22W
Ferrières-en-Brie, Paris 5 C6 48 49N 2 42 E
Ferry, N.Y. 23 A5 41 0N 73 52W
Fetcham, Lon. 4 D2 51 17N 0 21W
Feucherolles, Paris 5 B1 48 52N 1 58 E
Fichtenau, Berl. 7 B5 52 27N 13 42 E
Fields Corner, Bost. 21 D3 42 18N 71 3W
Fiera Camp, Mil. 9 E5 45 28N 9 9 E
Figino, Mil. 9 E5 45 29N 9 4 E
Fijir, Bagd. 17 E8 33 21N 44 21 E
Filadhélfia, Ath. 8 H11 38 2N 23 43 E
Fili-Mazilovo, Mos. 11 E8 55 44N 37 29 E
Filothei, Ath. 8 H11 38 1N 23 46 E
Finalspan, Jobg. 18 F10 26 16 S 28 16 E
Finchley, Lon. 4 B3 51 36N 0 11W
Finkenkrug, Berl. 7 A1 52 33N 13 3 E
Finkenwerder, Hbg. 7 D7 53 32N 9 51 E
Finsbury, Lon. 4 B4 51 31N 0 6W
Finsbury Park, Lon. 4 B4 51 34N 0 6W
Fiorito, B.A. 32 C4 34 42 S 58 26W
Firdows, Bagd. 17 F7 33 17N 44 17 E
Firōz Bahram, Tehr. 17 D4 35 37N 51 14 E
Fischeln, Ruhr 6 C1 51 18N 6 35 E
Fish Brook →, Bost. 21 B1 42 39N 71 1W
Fishermans Bend, Melb. 19 E6 37 49 S 144 55 E
Fisher's Hill, Jobg. 18 E10 26 10 S 28 10 E
Fisherville, Trto. 20 D8 43 46N 79 28W
Fisksätra, Stock. 3 E12 59 17N 18 13 E
Fittja, Stock. 3 E10 59 14N 17 51 E
Fitzroy Gardens, Melb. 19 E7 37 48 S 144 58 E
Five Cowrie Cr. →, Lagos 18 B2 6 26N 7 25 E
Five Dock, Syd. 19 B3 33 52 S 151 8 E
Fjellstrand, Oslo 2 C3 59 47N 10 36 E
Flachsberg, Ruhr 6 C4 51 11N 7 4 E
Flag →, Chic. 26 C1 41 43N 87 55W
Flamengo, Rio J. 31 B2 22 56 S 43 11W
Flaminio, Rome 9 F9 41 55N 12 28 E
Flaskebekk, Oslo 2 B3 59 51N 10 39 E
Flatbush, N.Y. 22 D5 40 39N 73 56W
Flaten, Stock. 3 E11 59 15N 18 9 E
Flemington, Syd. 19 B3 33 53 S 151 4 E
Flemington Racecourse, Melb. 19 E6 37 47 S 144 54 E
Fleury-Mérogis, Paris 5 D4 48 37N 2 21 E
Flingern, Ruhr 6 C2 51 14N 6 48 E
Flint Pk., L.A. 28 B3 34 9N 118 11 E
Floral Park, N.Y. 23 C6 40 43N 73 42W
Florence, L.A. 28 C3 33 57N 118 13W
Florence, Phil. 24 C5 39 44N 74 55W
Florence Bloom Bird Sanctuary, Jobg. 18 E9 26 7 S 28 0 E
Florencio Varela, B.A. 32 C5 34 49 S 58 18W
Florentia, Jobg. 18 F9 26 16 S 28 8 E
Flores, B.A. 32 B4 34 38 S 58 27W
Floresta, B.A. 32 B4 34 37 S 58 27W
Florham Park, N.Y. 22 C2 40 46N 74 23W
Florida, B.A. 32 B4 34 31 S 58 28W
Florida, Jobg. 18 F8 26 10 S 27 55 E
Florida L., Jobg. 18 F8 26 10 S 27 54 E
Floridsdorf, Wien 10 G10 48 15N 16 26 E
Flourtown, Phil. 24 A3 40 6N 75 13W
Flower Hill, N.Y. 23 C6 40 48N 73 40W
Flushing, N.Y. 23 C6 40 45N 73 49W
Flushing Meadows Corona Park, N.Y. 23 C5 40 44N 73 50W
Flysta, Stock. 3 D10 59 22N 17 54 E
Fo Tan, H.K. 12 D6 22 23N 114 11 E
Föhrenhain, Wien 10 G10 48 19N 16 26 E
Folcroft, Phil. 24 B3 39 53N 75 16W
Folsom, Phil. 24 B3 39 53N 75 19W
Fontainbleau, Jobg. 18 E8 26 6 S 27 57 E
Fontana, La Hab. 30 B2 23 1N 82 24W
Fontanka, St-Pet. 11 B3 59 54N 30 16 E
Fontenay-aux-Roses, Paris 5 C3 48 47N 2 17 E
Fontenay-le-Fleury, Paris 5 C2 48 48N 2 2 E
Fontenay-lès-Briis, Paris 5 D2 48 37N 2 9 E
Fontenay-sous-Bois, Paris 5 B4 48 51N 2 28 E
Foots Cray, Lon. 4 C5 51 24N 0 7 E
Footscray, Melb. 19 E6 37 48 S 144 56 E
Forbidden City, Beij. 14 B3 39 53N 116 21 E
Fordham Univ., N.Y. 23 B5 40 51N 73 51W
Fords, N.Y. 22 D3 40 31N 74 19W
Fordsburg, Jobg. 18 F9 26 12 S 28 2 E
Foremans Corner, Balt. 25 B3 39 11N 76 33W
Forest Gate, Lon. 4 B5 51 32N 0 1 E
Forest Heights, Wash. 25 E7 38 48N 77 0W
Forest Hill, Lon. 4 C4 51 26N 0 2W
Forest Hill, Melb. 19 F8 37 50 S 145 10 E
Forest Hill, Trto. 20 D8 43 41N 79 25W
Forest Hills, N.Y. 23 C5 40 42N 73 51W
Forest Park, Chic. 26 B2 41 51N 87 47W
Forest View, Chic. 26 C2 41 48N 87 47W
Forestville, Syd. 19 A4 33 46 S 151 12 E
Forestville, Wash. 25 D8 38 50N 76 52W
Forges-les-Bains, Paris 5 D2 48 37N 2 5 E
Fornacino, Tori. 9 B3 45 9N 7 44 E
Fornebu, Oslo 2 B3 59 53N 10 36 E
Fornebu Airport, Oslo 2 B3 59 56N 10 37 E
Foro Italico, Rome 9 F9 41 56N 12 26 E
Foro Romano, Rome 9 F9 41 53N 12 29 E
Forst Rantzau, Hbg. 7 C6 53 43N 9 49 E
Forstenried, Mün. 7 G9 48 5N 11 29 E
Forstenrieder Park, Mün. 7 G9 48 3N 11 27 E
Fort du Pont Park, Wash. 25 D8 38 52N 76 56W
Fort Foote Village, Wash. 25 E7 38 46N 77 1W
Fort Howard, Balt. 25 B4 39 12N 76 26W
Fort Lee, N.Y. 22 B5 40 50N 73 58W
Fort McHenry Nat. Mon., Balt. 25 B3 35 15N 76 35W
Fort Washington, Phil. 24 A3 40 8N 75 13W
Fort William, Calc. 16 E6 22 33N 88 20 E
Foster City, S.F. 27 C3 37 33N 122 15W
Fosters Pond, Bost. 21 B3 42 36N 71 8W
Fourcherolle, Paris 5 C1 48 42N 1 58 E
Fourmile Run →, Wash. 25 D7 38 50N 77 2W
Fourqueux, Paris 5 B2 48 53N 2 3 E
Fowl Meadow Res., Bost. 21 D3 42 13N 71 8W
Fox Chase, Phil. 24 A4 40 4N 75 5W
Foxhall, Wash. 25 C7 39 4N 77 3W
Framingham, Bost. 21 D1 42 18N 71 24W
Francisco Álvarez, B.A. 32 B1 34 38 S 58 50W
Francisquito Cr. →, S.F. 27 D4 37 27N 122 9W
Franconia, Wash. 25 E7 38 47N 77 7W
Franconville, Paris 5 B3 48 59N 2 13 E
Francop, Hbg. 7 D7 53 30N 9 51 E
Frankel, Sing. 15 G8 1 18N 103 55 E
Frankford, Phil. 24 A4 40 1N 75 5W
Franklin L., N.Y. 22 B3 40 59N 74 13W
Franklin Lakes, N.Y. 22 B3 40 59N 74 13W
Franklin Park, Bost. 21 D3 42 18N 71 5W
Franklin Park, Chic. 26 B1 41 55N 87 52W
Franklin Park, Wash. 25 D7 38 55N 77 9W
Franklin Res., L.A. 28 B2 34 5N 118 24W
Franklin Roosevelt Park, Jobg. 18 E8 26 8 S 27 59 E
Franklin Roosevelt Park, Phil. 24 B3 39 54N 75 10W
Franklin Square, N.Y. 23 C6 40 42N 73 40W
Frattamaggiore, Nápl. 9 H12 40 56N 14 16 E
Frauenkirche, Mün. 7 G10 48 8N 11 34 E
Frederiksberg, Købn. 2 D10 55 40N 12 33 E
Frederiksdal, Købn. 2 D9 55 46N 12 25 E
Fredersdorf, Berl. 7 A5 52 31N 13 45 E
Fredersdorf Nord, Berl. 7 A5 52 32N 13 43 E
Freeport, N.Y. 23 D7 40 39N 73 35W
Freidrichshain, Volkspark, Berl. 7 A3 52 31N 13 25 E
Freiham, Mün. 7 G9 48 8N 11 25 E
Freimann, Mün. 7 F10 48 11N 11 37 E
Fremont, S.F. 27 C4 37 33N 122 2W
Fresh Meadows, N.Y. 23 C6 40 43N 73 47W
Fresh Pond, Bost. 21 C3 42 22N 71 8W
Freskati, Stock. 3 D11 59 22N 18 3 E
Fresnes, Paris 5 C3 48 45N 2 18 E
Fretay, Paris 5 C3 48 40N 2 12 E
Freudenau, Wien 10 G10 48 11N 16 25 E
Friedenau, Berl. 7 B3 52 28N 13 20 E
Friederikenhof, Berl. 7 B3 52 23N 13 21 E
Friedrichsfeld, Ruhr 6 A1 51 37N 6 39 E
Friedrichsfelde, Berl. 7 B4 52 30N 13 33 E
Friedrichshagen, Berl. 7 B4 52 27N 13 37 E
Friedrichshain, Berl. 7 A3 52 31N 13 27 E
Friedrichshulde, Hbg. 7 D7 53 36N 9 51 E
Friedrichstadt, Berl. 7 A5 52 31N 13 43 E
Frielas, Lisb. 8 F8 38 49N 9 6W
Friemersheim, Ruhr 6 B2 51 23N 6 42 E
Friern Barnet, Lon. 4 B4 51 37N 0 9W
Friherrs, Hels. 3 B3 60 16N 24 49 E
Frogner, Oslo 2 A6 60 1N 11 6 E
Frohnau, Berl. 7 A2 52 38N 13 18 E
Frohnhausen, Ruhr 6 B3 51 26N 6 56 E
Frontón, I., Lima 30 G7 12 7 S 77 11W
Frunze, Mos. 11 E9 55 47N 37 33 E
Fuchū, Tōkyō 13 B1 35 40N 139 29 E
Fuencarral, Mdrd. 8 B2 40 29N 3 42W
Fuhlenbrock, Ruhr 6 A3 51 32N 6 54 E
Fuhlsbüttel, Hbg. 7 D8 53 37N 10 1 E
Fujidera, Ōsaka 12 C4 34 34N 135 36 E
Fujikubo, Tōkyō 13 B2 35 49N 139 31 E
Fujimi, Tōkyō 13 B2 35 51N 139 32 E
Fukagawa, Tōkyō 13 C3 35 40N 139 48 E
Fukami, Tōkyō 13 D1 35 28N 139 27 E
Fukiai, Ōsaka 12 B2 34 42N 135 12 E
Fukuoka, Tōkyō 13 A2 35 52N 139 31 E
Fukushima, Ōsaka 12 B3 34 41N 135 28 E
Fulatani, Tōkyō 13 D1 35 22N 139 30 E
Fulham, Lon. 4 C3 51 28N 0 12W
Fuller Park, L.A. 28 C5 33 51N 117 56W
Fullerton, Balt. 25 A3 39 22N 76 30W
Funabori, Tōkyō 13 B4 35 41N 139 52 E
Funasaka, Ōsaka 12 B2 34 48N 135 16 E
Fünfhaus, Wien 10 G10 48 11N 16 20 E
Fünfhausen, Hbg. 7 E8 53 27N 10 2 E
Furesø, Købn. 2 D9 55 47N 12 25 E
Fürstenried, Mün. 7 G9 48 5N 11 28 E
Furth, Mün. 7 G10 48 2N 11 35 E
Furu →, Tōkyō 13 A3 35 54N 139 49 E
Furuyakami, Tōkyō 13 A2 35 54N 139 31 E
Futago-tamagawaen, Tōkyō 13 C2 35 36N 139 39 E
Futamatagawa, Tōkyō 13 D2 35 27N 139 31 E
Futatsubashi, Tōkyō 13 D1 35 28N 139 29 E
Fuxing Dao, Shang. 14 J12 31 16N 121 33 E
Fuxing Gongyuan, Shang. 14 J11 31 13N 121 27 E
Fuxinglu, Beij. 14 B2 39 52N 116 16 E
Fuxingmen, Beij. 14 B2 39 53N 116 19 E

G

Gadstrup, Købn. 2 E7 55 34N 12 5 E
Gaebong, Sŏul 12 H7 37 29N 126 52 E
Gage Park, Chic. 26 C2 41 47N 87 42W
Gagny, Paris 5 B5 48 53N 2 32 E
Gaillon, Paris 5 A1 49 1N 1 53 E
Galata, Ist. 17 A2 41 1N 28 58 E
Galátsion, Ath. 8 H11 38 1N 23 45 E
Galeão, Rio J. 31 A2 22 49 S 43 14W
Galéria →, Rome 9 F9 41 57N 12 20 E
Gallows Corner, Lon. 4 B6 51 35N 0 13 E
Gällstaö, Stock. 3 E10 59 17N 17 51 E
Galyanovo, Mos. 11 E10 55 48N 37 47 E
Galyeon, Sŏul 12 G7 37 36N 126 55 E
Gambir, Jak. 15 H9 6 9 S 106 48 E
Gamboa, Rio J. 31 B2 22 53 S 43 11W
Gamboloita, Mil. 9 E6 45 26N 9 13 E
Gamelinha →, S. Pau. 31 E6 23 31 S 46 31W
Gamlebyen, Oslo 2 B4 59 54N 10 46 E
Gamlebyen, Shang. 14 J11 31 13N 121 29 E
Gamō, Tōkyō 13 A3 35 52N 139 48 E
Gang Dong, Sŏul 12 G8 37 30N 127 5 E
Gang Nam, Sŏul 12 G7 37 30N 126 59 E
Gang Sea, Sŏul 12 G7 37 32N 126 51 E
Gangadharpur, Calc. 16 E5 22 35N 88 11 E
Gangtou, Gzh. 14 F7 23 13N 113 8 E
Gangwei, Gzh. 14 G8 23 4N 113 11 E
Ganløse, Købn. 2 D8 55 47N 12 15 E
Ganløse Orned, Købn. 2 D8 55 48N 12 18 E
Ganshi, Gzh. 14 F7 23 10N 113 8 E
Gants Hill, Lon. 4 B5 51 34N 0 4 E
Gaoqiao, Shang. 14 H12 31 21N 121 34 E
Garbagnate Milanese, Mil. 9 D5 45 34N 9 4 E
Garbatella, Rome 9 F10 41 51N 12 30 E
Garches, Paris 5 B3 48 50N 2 11 E
Garching, Mün. 7 F11 48 14N 11 39 E
Garden City, El Qâ. 18 C5 30 2N 31 14 E
Garden City, N.Y. 23 C7 40 43N 73 37W
Garden Reach, Calc. 16 E5 22 33N 88 15 E
Gardena, L.A. 28 C3 33 53N 118 18W
Garder, Oslo 2 C3 59 45N 10 38 E
Garfield, N.Y. 22 B4 40 52N 74 7W
Garfield Park, Chic. 26 B2 41 52N 87 42W
Gargareta, Ath. 8 J11 37 57N 23 43 E
Garges-lès-Gonesse, Paris 5 B4 48 58N 2 25 E
Garhi Naraina, Delhi 16 B1 28 37N 77 8 E
Garibong, Sŏul 12 H7 37 29N 126 54 E
Garin, B.A. 32 A2 34 25 S 58 44W
Gariya, Calc. 16 F6 22 28N 88 23 E
Garji, Calc. 16 C5 22 50N 88 19 E
Garne, Paris 5 C1 48 41N 1 58 E
Garrison, Balt. 25 A2 39 24N 76 45W
Garstedt, Hbg. 7 C7 53 40N 9 59 E
Gartenstadt, Ruhr 6 B6 51 30N 7 30 E
Garulia, Calc. 16 D6 22 48N 88 22 E
Garvanza, L.A. 28 B3 34 6N 118 11 E
Garwood, N.Y. 22 D3 40 38N 74 18W
Gary, Chic. 26 D4 41 35N 87 23W
Gåshaga, Stock. 3 D12 59 21N 18 13 E
Gassino Torinese, Tori. 9 B3 45 7N 7 49 E
Gästerby, Hels. 3 C1 60 8N 24 27 E
Gateão, Aéroporto de, Rio J. 31 A2 22 49 S 43 15W
Gateway of India, Bomb. 16 H8 18 55N 72 50 E
Gatow, Berl. 7 B1 52 29N 13 11 E
Gaurhati, Calc. 16 D6 22 48N 88 21 E
Gauripur, Calc. 16 C6 22 53N 88 25 E
Gavá, Barc. 8 E5 41 18N 2 0 E
Gavamar, Barc. 8 E4 41 16N 1 58 E
Gavanpada, Bomb. 16 H9 18 57N 73 0 E
Gávea, Rio J. 31 B2 22 58 S 43 13W
Gávea, Pedra da, Rio J. 31 B2 22 59 S 43 18W
Gbogbo, Lagos 18 A3 6 35N 7 31 E
Gebel el Ahmar, El Qâ. 18 C5 30 2N 31 16 E
Gebel el Muqattam, El Qâ. 18 C5 30 1N 31 17 E
Gebel et Tura, El Qâ. 18 D5 29 56N 31 15 E
Geduld Dam, Jobg. 18 F11 26 12 S 28 24 E
Geiselgasteig, Mün. 7 G10 48 3N 11 33 E
Geist Res., Phil. 24 B2 39 57N 75 24W
Gellért hegy, Bud. 10 K13 47 29N 19 2 E
Gelsenkirchen, Ruhr 6 A4 51 32N 7 2 E
General Ignacio Allende, Méx. 29 B1 19 20N 99 21W
General Pacheco, B.A. 32 A3 34 27 S 58 36W
General San Martín, B.A. 32 B3 34 35 S 58 32W
General Sarmiento, B.A. 32 B2 34 32 S 58 43W
General Urquiza, B.A. 32 B4 34 34 S 58 28W
Gennebreck, Ruhr 6 C5 51 18N 7 12 E
Gennevilliers, Paris 5 B3 48 56N 2 17 E
Gentilly, Paris 5 C4 48 48N 2 21 E
Gentofte, Købn. 2 D10 55 44N 12 32 E
Georges →, Syd. 19 B2 33 56 S 150 55 E
Georges Hall, Syd. 19 B2 33 54 S 150 59 E
Georges I., Bost. 21 D4 42 19N 70 55W
Georges River Bridge, Syd. 19 C3 34 0 S 151 6 E
Georgetown, Wash. 25 D7 38 54N 77 3W
Georgetown Rowley State Forest, Bost. 21 A4 42 41N 70 56W
Georgsweide, Hbg. 7 D8 53 30N 10 1 E
Gerasdorf bei Wein, Wien 10 G10 48 17N 16 28 E
Gerberau, Mün. 7 G10 48 12N 11 27 E
Gérbido, Tori. 9 B2 45 2N 7 36 E
Gerlev, Købn. 2 D7 55 49N 12 0 E
Gerli, B.A. 32 C4 34 41 S 58 22W
Germantown, Balt. 25 A4 39 24N 76 25W
Germantown, Phil. 24 A3 40 2N 75 11W
Germiston, Jobg. 18 F9 26 13 S 28 10 E
Gerresheim, Ruhr 6 C3 51 14N 6 52 E
Gersthof, Wien 10 G9 48 14N 16 18 E
Gerthe, Ruhr 6 A5 51 31N 7 16 E

38 Gesîrat el Rauda

Gesîrat el Rauda, *El Qâ.* 18 C5 30 1N 31 13 E
Gesîrat Muhammad, *El Qâ.* 18 C5 30 6N 31 11 E
Gesterby, *Hels.* 3 A6 60 20N 25 17 E
Getafe, *Mdrd.* 8 C2 40 18N 3 43W
Gevelsberg, *Ruhr* 6 C6 51 19N 7 21 E
Geylang, *Sing.* 15 G8 1 18N 103 53 E
Geylang →, *Sing.* 15 G8 1 18N 103 52 E
Geylang Serai, *Sing.* 15 G8 1 19N 103 53 E
Gezîrat edn Dhahab, *El Qâ.* 18 D5 29 59N 31 13 E
Gezîrat Warrâq el Hadar, *El Qâ.* 18 C5 30 6N 31 13 E
Gharapuri, *Bomb.* 16 H8 18 57N 72 57 E
Ghatkopar, *Bomb.* 16 G8 19 4N 72 54 E
Ghazipur, *Delhi* 16 B2 28 37N 77 19 E
Ghizri, *Kar.* 17 H11 24 49N 67 2 E
Ghizri Cr. →, *Kar.* 17 H11 24 47N 67 5 E
Ghonda, *Delhi* 16 A2 28 41N 77 16 E
Ghushuri, *Calc.* 16 E6 22 37N 88 21 E
Gianicolense, *Rome* 9 F9 51 53N 12 28 E
Giant, *S.F.* 27 A2 37 58N 122 20W
Gibbsboro, *Phil.* 24 B5 39 50N 74 57W
Gibbstown, *Phil.* 24 C3 39 49N 75 17W
Gibraltar Pt., *Trto.* 20 E8 43 36N 79 23W
Gidea Park, *Lon.* 4 B6 51 35N 0 11 E
Giesing, *Mün.* 7 G10 48 6N 11 35 E
Gif-sur-Yvette, *Paris* 5 C2 48 42N 2 8 E
Gilgo Beach, *N.Y.* 23 D8 40 36N 73 24W
Gilgo I., *N.Y.* 23 D8 40 37N 73 23W
Gillette, *N.Y.* 22 C2 40 40N 74 29W
Gimmersta, *Stock.* 3 E12 59 14N 18 14 E
Ginza, *Tōkyō* 13 C3 35 39N 139 46 E
Girgaum, *Bomb.* 16 H8 18 57N 72 50 E
Giugliano in Campània, *Nápl.* 9 H12 40 55N 14 12 E
Givoletto, *Tori.* 9 B1 45 9N 7 29 E
Gjellumvatn, *Oslo* 2 C2 59 47N 10 26 E
Gjersjøen, *Oslo* 2 C4 59 47N 10 47 E
Glacier Hills, *N.Y.* 22 B2 40 51N 74 28W
Gladbeck, *Ruhr* 6 A3 51 34N 6 58 E
Gladesville, *Syd.* 19 B3 33 50 S 151 8 E
Gladökvarn, *Stock.* 3 E10 59 11N 17 59 E
Gladsakse, *Købn.* 2 D9 55 45N 12 25 E
Glashutte, *Hbg.* 7 C8 53 41N 10 2 E
Glashütte, *Ruhr* 6 C3 51 13N 6 51 E
Glasmoor, *Hbg.* 7 C8 53 42N 10 1 E
Glassmanor, *Wash.* 25 E7 38 49N 77 0W
Glen Cove, *N.Y.* 23 B7 40 52N 73 38W
Glen Echo, *Wash.* 25 D7 38 58N 77 8W
Glen Hd., *N.Y.* 23 C7 40 49N 73 37W
Glen Iris, *Melb.* 19 F7 37 51 S 145 3 E
Glen Mills, *Phil.* 24 B2 39 55N 75 29W
Glen Oaks, *N.Y.* 23 C6 40 45N 73 43W
Glen Riddle, *Phil.* 24 B2 39 53N 75 26W
Glen Ridge, *N.Y.* 22 C3 40 48N 74 12W
Glen Rock, *N.Y.* 22 B4 40 57N 74 7W
Glen Waverley, *Melb.* 19 F8 37 52 S 145 10 E
Glenardon, *Wash.* 25 D8 38 56N 76 51W
Glencoe, *Chic.* 26 A2 42 7N 87 44W
Glendale, *L.A.* 28 B3 34 9N 118 15 E
Glendora, *Phil.* 24 B4 39 50N 75 4W
Glenfield, *Syd.* 19 B2 33 58 S 150 53 E
Glenhazel, *Jobg.* 18 E9 26 8 S 28 6 E
Glenhuntly, *Melb.* 19 F7 37 52 S 145 1 E
Glenmont, *Wash.* 25 C7 39 3N 77 4W
Glenolden, *Phil.* 24 B3 39 54N 75 17W
Glenroy, *Melb.* 19 E6 37 42 S 144 55 E
Glenside, *Phil.* 24 A4 40 6N 75 9W
Glenview, *Chic.* 26 A2 42 3N 87 48W
Glenview Countryside, *Chic.* 26 A2 42 3N 87 49W
Glenview Woods, *Chic.* 26 A2 42 4N 87 46W
Glenville, *N.Y.* 23 A6 41 1N 73 41W
Glenvista, *Jobg.* 18 F9 26 17 S 28 3 E
Glenwood Landing, *N.Y.* 23 C7 40 48N 73 38W
Glienicke, *Berl.* 7 A2 52 38N 13 18 E
Glömsta, *Stock.* 3 E10 59 14N 17 55 E
Glosli, *Oslo* 2 A5 60 1N 10 55 E
Glostrup, *Købn.* 2 E9 55 39N 12 23 E
Gloucester City, *Phil.* 24 B4 39 53N 75 7W
Gocheog, *Sŏul* 12 G7 37 30N 126 52 E
Gocławek, *Wsaw.* 10 E7 52 14N 21 7 E
Goeselville, *Chic.* 26 D2 41 37N 87 46W
Goetjensort, *Hbg.* 7 E8 53 29N 10 2 E
Golabari, *Calc.* 16 E6 22 35N 88 20 E
Golabki, *Wsaw.* 10 E6 52 12N 20 52 E
Golden Gate, *S.F.* 27 B2 37 48N 122 29W
Golden Gate Bridge, *S.F.* 27 B2 37 49N 122 28W
Golden Gate National Recreation Area, *S.F.* 27 B1 37 49N 122 31W
Golden Gate Park, *S.F.* 27 B2 37 46N 122 28W
Golden Horn, *Ist.* 17 A2 41 1N 28 57 E
Golders Green, *Lon.* 4 B3 51 34N 0 11W
Golyevo, *Mos.* 11 E7 55 48N 37 18 E
Gometz-la-Ville, *Paris* 5 C2 48 40N 2 7 E
Gometz-le-Châtel, *Paris* 5 C2 48 40N 2 8 E
Gondangdia, *Jak.* 15 J9 6 11 S 106 49 E
Gonesse, *Paris* 5 A4 48 59N 2 26 E
Gongreung, *Sŏul* 12 G8 37 36N 127 3 E
González Catán, *B.A.* 32 C3 34 46 S 58 38W
Goodman Hill, *Bost.* 21 C1 42 22N 71 23W
Goodmayes, *Lon.* 4 B5 51 33N 0 6 E
Gopalnagar, *Calc.* 16 C5 22 50N 88 13 E
Gopalpur, *Calc.* 16 C6 22 38N 88 26 E
Górce, *Wsaw.* 10 E6 52 15N 20 55 E
Gordon, *Syd.* 19 A3 33 45 S 151 8 E
Gore Hill, *Syd.* 19 A4 33 49 S 151 10 E
Gorelyy →, *St-Pet.* 11 A5 60 1N 30 30 E
Gorenki, *Mos.* 11 E11 55 47N 37 53 E
Gorkiy Park, *Mos.* 11 E9 55 43N 37 36 E
Görväln, *Stock.* 3 D9 59 26N 17 45 E
Gose Elbe →, *Hbg.* 7 E8 53 28N 10 6 E
Gosen, *Berl.* 7 B5 52 23N 13 43 E
Gosener kanal, *Berl.* 7 B5 52 24N 13 42 E
Goshenville, *Phil.* 24 B1 39 59N 75 32W
Gospel Oak, *Lon.* 4 B4 51 32N 0 9W
Gotanda, *Tōkyō* 13 C3 35 37N 139 43 E
Gotanno, *Tōkyō* 13 B3 35 45N 139 49 E
Goth Goli Mār, *Kar.* 17 G11 24 53N 67 1 E
Goth Sher Shāh, *Kar.* 17 G10 24 53N 66 59 E
Gournay-sur-Marne, *Paris* 5 B5 48 51N 2 34 E
Goussainville, *Paris* 5 A4 49 1N 2 27 E
Gouvernes, *Paris* 5 B6 48 51N 2 41 E
Governador, I. do, *Rio J.* 31 A2 22 48 S 43 13W
Governor's I., *N.Y.* 22 C4 40 41N 74 1W
Grabicz, *Wsaw.* 10 E8 52 19N 21 12 E
Grabów, *Wsaw.* 10 F6 52 8N 20 59 E
Gracia, *Barc.* 8 D6 41 24N 2 10 E
Gradyville, *Phil.* 24 B2 39 56N 75 27W
Gräfelfing, *Mün.* 7 G9 48 7N 11 25 E
Grafenwald, *Ruhr* 6 A3 51 34N 6 54 E
Graham Memorial Park, *Balt.* 25 A4 39 25N 76 29W
Gran Canal, *Méx.* 29 A3 19 34N 99 1W
Granada Hills, *L.A.* 28 A1 34 16N 118 30W
Grand Bourg, *B.A.* 32 A2 34 29 S 58 42W
Grand Calumet →, *Chic.* 26 D4 41 37N 87 28W
Grand Union Canal, *Lon.* 4 A2 51 42N 0 26W
Grande →, *S. Pau.* 31 F7 23 43 S 46 24W
Grange, *Tori.* 9 B1 45 7N 7 29 E
Grange Hill, *Lon.* 4 B5 51 36N 0 5 E
Granite, *Balt.* 25 A1 39 20N 76 51W
Graniteville, *N.Y.* 22 D3 40 37N 74 10W
Granja Viana, *S. Pau.* 31 E4 23 35 S 46 50W
Granlandet, *Hels.* 3 B6 60 10N 25 15 E
Granö, *Hels.* 3 B6 60 13N 25 14 E
Grant Park, *Chic.* 26 B3 41 52N 87 37W
Granville, *Syd.* 19 A3 33 49 S 151 1 E
Grape I., *Bost.* 21 D4 42 16N 70 55W
Grass Hassock Channel, *N.Y.* 23 D6 40 36N 73 47W
Grassey B., *N.Y.* 23 D6 40 37N 73 47W
Grassy Sprain Res., *N.Y.* 23 B5 40 58N 73 50W
Gratosóglio, *Mil.* 9 E6 45 24N 9 1 E
Gratzwalde, *Berl.* 7 B5 52 28N 13 42 E
Gravesend, *N.Y.* 22 D5 40 36N 73 56W
Grays, *Lon.* 4 C6 51 28N 0 19 E
Grazhdanka, *St-Pet.* 11 B4 59 59N 30 24 E
Great Blue Hill, *Bost.* 21 D3 42 12N 71 4W
Great Bookham, *Lon.* 4 D2 51 16N 0 21W
Great Brewster I., *Bost.* 21 C4 42 19N 70 53W
Great Captain I., *N.Y.* 23 B7 40 59N 73 37W
Great Falls, *Wash.* 25 D6 38 59N 77 17W
Great Falls Park, *Wash.* 25 D6 38 59N 77 14W
Great Kills, *N.Y.* 22 D4 40 32N 74 9W
Great Kills Harbour, *N.Y.* 22 D4 40 32N 74 8W
Great Neck, *N.Y.* 23 C6 40 48N 73 44W
Great Pond, *Bost.* 21 D3 42 11N 71 2W
Great South B., *N.Y.* 23 D9 40 39N 73 19W
Greco, *Mil.* 9 D6 45 30N 9 12 E
Greco I., *S.F.* 27 C3 37 30N 122 10W
Green Brae, *S.F.* 27 A1 37 57N 122 31W
Green Brook, *N.Y.* 22 D2 40 35N 74 26W
Green I., *H.K.* 12 E5 22 17N 114 6 E
Green Land, *Jak.* 15 J9 6 17 S 106 46 E
Green Pond, *N.Y.* 22 A2 41 1N 74 29W
Green Street, *Lon.* 4 A3 51 40N 0 16W
Green Street Green, *Lon.* 4 C5 51 21N 0 5 E
Green Valley, *Syd.* 19 B2 33 54 S 150 53 E
Green Village, *N.Y.* 22 C2 40 44N 74 27W
Greenbelt, *Wash.* 25 C8 39 0N 76 52W
Greenbelt Park, *Wash.* 25 D8 38 58N 76 53W
Greenfield Park, *Mtrl.* 20 B5 43 29N 73 28W
Greenfields Village, *Phil.* 24 C4 39 49N 75 9W
Greenford, *Lon.* 4 B2 51 31N 0 21W
Greenhithe, *Lon.* 4 C6 51 27N 0 17 E
Greenlawn, *N.Y.* 23 B8 40 52N 73 22W
Greenpoint, *N.Y.* 22 C5 40 43N 73 57W
Greensborough, *Melb.* 19 E7 37 41 S 145 5 E
Greenside, *Jobg.* 18 E9 26 8 S 28 1 E
Greenvale, *N.Y.* 23 C7 40 48N 73 38W
Greenville Chauncey, *N.Y.* 23 B5 40 59N 73 50W
Greenwich, *Lon.* 4 C4 51 28N 0 0 E
Greenwich, *N.Y.* 23 A7 41 1N 73 37W
Greenwich, *Syd.* 19 B4 33 50 S 151 11 E
Greenwich Observatory, *Lon.* 4 C4 51 28N 0 0 E
Greenwich Pt., *N.Y.* 23 A7 41 0N 73 34W
Greenwich Village, *N.Y.* 22 C5 40 44N 73 59W
Greenwood, *Bost.* 21 C3 42 29N 71 2W
Grefsen, *Oslo* 2 B4 59 56N 10 47 E
Grégy-sur-Yerres, *Paris* 5 C5 48 40N 2 37 E
Greiffenburg, *Ruhr* 6 B1 51 20N 6 37 E
Gressy, *Paris* 5 A5 48 58N 2 40 E
Greve Strand, *Købn.* 2 E8 55 34N 12 18 E
Greystanes, *Syd.* 19 A2 33 49 S 150 58 E
Griebnitzsee, *Berl.* 7 B1 52 23N 13 8 E
Griffith Park, *L.A.* 28 B3 34 7N 118 18 E
Grignon, *Paris* 5 B1 48 50N 1 56 E
Grigny, *Paris* 5 D4 48 39N 2 23 E
Grinzing, *Wien* 10 G10 48 15N 16 20 E
Grisy-Suisnes, *Paris* 5 C6 48 41N 2 40 E
Gröbenried, *Mün.* 7 F9 48 13N 11 25 E
Grochów, *Wsaw.* 10 E7 52 15N 21 4 E
Grodzisk, *Wsaw.* 10 E7 52 19N 21 4 E
Grogol, *Jak.* 15 H9 6 9 S 106 47 E
Grogol, Kali →, *Jak.* 15 J9 6 11 S 106 47 E
Gronsdorf, *Mün.* 7 G11 48 7N 11 42 E
Grorud, *Oslo* 2 B5 59 57N 10 52 E
Gross Borstel, *Hbg.* 7 D7 53 36N 9 58 E
Gross Flottbek, *Hbg.* 7 D7 53 33N 9 53 E
Gross Glienicke, *Berl.* 7 B1 52 28N 13 6 E
Gross-Hadern, *Mün.* 7 G9 48 6N 11 29 E
Gross-Lappen, *Mün.* 7 F10 48 11N 11 35 E
Grosse Krampe, *Berl.* 7 B5 52 23N 13 40 E
Grosse Müggelsee, *Berl.* 7 B4 52 26N 13 38 E
Grossenbaum, *Ruhr* 6 B2 51 22N 6 46 E
Grossenzersdorf, *Wien* 10 G11 48 12N 16 33 E
Grossenzersdorfer Arm →, *Wien* 10 G11 48 12N 16 31 E
Grosser Biberhaufen, *Wien* 10 G10 48 12N 16 28 E
Grosser Wannsee, *Berl.* 7 B2 52 25N 13 10 E
Grossfeld-Siedlung, *Wien* 10 G10 48 16N 16 26 E
Grosshesselohe, *Mün.* 7 G10 48 3N 11 32 E
Grossjedlersdorf, *Wien* 10 G10 48 16N 16 23 E
Grossziethen, *Berl.* 7 B3 52 23N 13 26 E
Groszówka, *Wsaw.* 10 E8 52 13N 21 13 E
Grove Hall, *Bost.* 21 D3 42 18N 71 4W
Grove Park, *Lon.* 4 C5 51 25N 0 1 E
Grove Park, *Lon.* 4 C3 51 28N 0 15W
Groveton, *Wash.* 25 E7 38 46N 77 6W
Grugliasco, *Tori.* 9 B1 45 5N 7 34 E
Gruiten, *Ruhr* 6 C4 51 12N 7 0 E
Grumme, *Ruhr* 6 B5 51 30N 7 13 E
Grumo Nevano, *Nápl.* 9 H12 40 56N 14 15 E
Grünau, *Berl.* 7 B4 52 25N 13 34 E
Grunewald, *Berl.* 7 B2 52 28N 13 15 E
Grünwald, *Mün.* 7 G10 48 2N 11 31 E
Grünwalder Forst, *Mün.* 7 G10 48 2N 11 33 E
Grymes Hill, *N.Y.* 22 D4 40 36N 74 6W
Gu Ro, *Sŏul* 12 G7 37 30N 126 51 E
Guadalupe, *Manila* 15 D4 14 34N 121 2 E
Guadalupe →, *S.F.* 27 D4 37 28N 122 4W
Guadalupe, Basilica de, *Méx.* 29 B3 19 29N 99 7W
Guadelupe, *Rio J.* 31 A1 22 49 S 43 20W
Guanabacoa, *La Hab.* 30 B3 23 7N 82 17W
Guanabara, *Rio J.* 31 B1 22 57 S 43 20W
Guanabara, B. de, *Rio J.* 31 B2 22 52 S 43 10W
Guanabara, Jardim, *Rio J.* 31 A2 22 48 S 43 11W
Guang'anmen, *Beij.* 14 B2 39 51N 116 18 E
Guangminglou, *Beij.* 14 B3 39 51N 116 23 E
Guangqumen, *Beij.* 14 B3 39 52N 116 25 E
Guangzhou, *Gzh.* 14 G8 23 4N 113 22 E
Guanshuo, *Gzh.* 14 G9 23 4N 113 25 E
Guantai, *Nápl.* 9 H12 40 52N 14 11 E
Guapira →, *S. Pau.* 31 D6 23 30 S 46 33W
Guarapiranga, Res. de, *S. Pau.* 31 E5 23 42 S 46 43W
Guardias, *Mdrd.* 8 B3 40 29N 3 31W
Guarulhos, *S. Pau.* 31 D6 23 28 S 46 32W
Guatao, *La Hab.* 30 B2 23 0N 82 29W
Guayacanes, Pta., *La Hab.* 30 A3 23 10N 82 16W
Gubernador Monteverde, *B.A.* 32 C5 34 47 S 58 16W
Gudö, *Stock.* 3 E12 59 12N 18 12 E
Güell, Parque de, *Barc.* 8 D6 41 24N 2 10 E
Guermantes, *Paris* 5 B6 48 51N 2 42 E
Gugging, *Wien* 10 G9 48 18N 16 15 E
Guianazes, *S. Pau.* 31 E7 23 32 S 46 24W
Guildford, *Syd.* 19 B2 33 51 S 150 59 E
Guinardó, *Barc.* 8 D6 41 24N 2 10 E
Gujiazhai, *Shang.* 14 H11 31 21N 121 23 E
Gulbāi, *Kar.* 17 G10 24 52N 66 58 E
Guldasteh, *Tehr.* 17 D4 35 36N 51 15 E
Gulistan Palace, *Tehr.* 17 C5 35 40N 51 24 E
Gulph Mills, *Phil.* 24 A2 40 4N 75 20W
Gumbostrand, *Hels.* 3 B6 60 15N 25 17 E
Güngören, *Ist.* 17 A2 41 1N 28 52 E
Gunnarsby, *Hels.* 3 C1 60 6N 24 28W
Gunnersbury, *Lon.* 4 C3 51 29N 0 17W
Gunnigfeld, *Ruhr* 6 B4 51 29N 7 8 E
Gunpowder Falls →, *Balt.* 25 A4 39 23N 76 36W
Gunung Sahari, *Jak.* 15 H9 6 9 S 106 49 E
Gupiing, *Manila* 15 E5 14 27N 121 12 E
Guryong San, *Sŏul* 12 H8 37 28N 127 3 E
Gustavsberg, *Stock.* 3 E13 59 19N 18 23 E
Guttenberg, *N.Y.* 22 C4 40 48N 74 0W
Gutuyevskiy, Os., *St-Pet.* 11 B3 59 53N 30 15 E
Guyancourt, *Paris* 5 C2 48 46N 2 4 E
Guyancourt, Aérodrome de, *Paris* 5 C2 48 45N 2 3 E
Gvali-patak →, *Bud.* 10 K13 47 23N 19 7 E
Gwan Ag, *Sŏul* 12 H7 37 28N 126 57 E
Gwanag San, *Sŏul* 12 H7 37 27N 126 58 E
Gwynns Falls →, *Balt.* 25 B2 39 19N 76 42W
Gyál, *Bud.* 10 K14 47 23N 19 13 E
Gyeongbong Palace, *Sŏul* 12 G7 37 34N 126 58 E
Gynea, *Syd.* 19 C3 34 1 S 151 5 E

H

Haaga, *Hels.* 3 B4 60 13N 24 53 E
Haan, *Ruhr* 6 C3 51 11N 6 59 E
Haar, *Mün.* 7 G11 48 6N 11 43 E
Haar, *Ruhr* 6 B5 51 26N 7 13 E
Haarzopf, *Ruhr* 6 B3 51 25N 6 57 E
Habana del Este, *La Hab.* 30 B3 23 9N 82 19W
Habay, *Manila* 15 E3 14 27N 120 56 E
Habikino, *Ōsaka* 12 C4 34 33N 135 36 E
Habinghorst, *Ruhr* 6 A5 51 34N 7 18 E
Hacienda Heights, *L.A.* 28 C5 33 59N 117 59W
Hackbridge, *Lon.* 4 C4 51 23N 0 9W
Hackensack, *N.Y.* 22 B4 40 52N 74 4W
Hackney, *Lon.* 4 B4 51 32N 0 3W
Hackney Wick, *Lon.* 4 B4 51 32N 0 1W
Haddon Heights, *Phil.* 24 B4 39 53N 75 3W
Haddonfield, *Phil.* 24 B4 39 53N 75 3W
Hadersdorf, *Wien* 10 G9 48 12N 16 14 E
Hadley Wood, *Lon.* 4 B3 51 39N 0 10W
Haga, *Stock.* 3 D11 59 21N 18 1 E
Hagem, *Ruhr* 6 A5 51 38N 7 19 E
Hagen, *Ruhr* 6 B6 51 21N 7 27 E
Hägersten, *Stock.* 3 E10 59 18N 17 59 E
Haggetts Pond, *Bost.* 21 B2 42 39N 71 11W
Häggvik, *Stock.* 3 D10 59 26N 17 56 E
Hagonoy, *Manila* 15 D4 14 30N 121 4 E
Hagsätra, *Stock.* 3 E11 59 15N 18 0 E
Hahipur, *Calc.* 16 D5 22 47N 88 10 E
Hahnerberg, *Ruhr* 6 C4 51 12N 7 9 E
Hai He →, *Tianj.* 14 E6 39 4N 117 17 E
Haidarpur, *Delhi* 16 A1 28 43N 77 8 E
Haidhausen, *Mün.* 7 G10 48 7N 11 36 E
Haidian, *Beij.* 14 B2 39 59N 116 16 E
Haight-Ashbury, *S.F.* 27 B2 37 46N 122 26W
Haiguangsi, *Tianj.* 14 E6 39 7N 117 11 E
Hainault, *Lon.* 4 B5 51 36N 0 6 E
Haizhu Guangchang, *Gzh.* 14 G8 23 6N 113 14 E
Hakim, *El Qâ.* 18 C4 30 4N 31 7 E
Hakunila, *Hels.* 3 B5 60 16N 25 6 E
Halchōbori, *Tōkyō* 13 B4 35 48N 139 55 E
Haledon, *N.Y.* 22 B3 40 57N 74 11W
Halesite, *N.Y.* 23 B8 40 53N 73 24W
Halethorpe, *Balt.* 25 B2 39 15N 76 40W
Half Hollow Hills, *N.Y.* 23 C8 40 48N 73 23W
Half Moon B., *S.F.* 26 D2 37 27N 122 25W
Half Moon Bay Airport, *S.F.* 27 C1 37 31N 122 30W
Half Moon Beaches, *S.F.* 26 D2 37 28N 122 28W
Halim, *Jak.* 15 J10 6 15 S 106 53 E
Halim Perdanakusuma Airport, *Jak.* 15 J10 6 16 S 106 53 E
Halstead, *Lon.* 4 D5 51 19N 0 8 E
Halstenbeck, *Hbg.* 7 D7 53 38N 9 50 E
Haltiala, *Hels.* 3 B4 60 16N 24 57 E
Haltiavuori, *Hels.* 3 B4 60 16N 24 56 E
Ham, *Lon.* 4 C3 51 25N 0 18W
Ham, *Paris* 5 A2 49 1N 2 3 E
Hamberg, *Jobg.* 18 E8 26 9 S 27 54 E
Hamborn, *Ruhr* 6 B2 51 29N 6 46 E
Hamburg, *Hbg.* 7 D8 53 33N 10 0 E
Hamburg Flughafen, *Hbg.* 7 D7 53 38N 9 59 E
Hämeenkylä, *Hels.* 3 B3 60 16N 24 48 E
Hamm, *Hbg.* 7 D8 53 33N 10 2 E
Hamm, *Ruhr* 6 C2 51 12N 6 44 E
Hammarby, *Stock.* 3 E11 59 17N 18 5 E
Hamme, *Ruhr* 6 B5 51 29N 7 12 E
Hammel Arverne, *N.Y.* 23 D6 40 35N 73 48W
Hammerbrook, *Hbg.* 7 D8 53 32N 10 1 E
Hammersmith, *Lon.* 4 C3 51 29N 0 14W
Hammond, *Chic.* 26 D4 41 36N 87 29W
Hampstead, *Lon.* 4 B3 51 33N 0 10W
Hampstead, *Mtrl.* 20 B4 43 28N 73 37W
Hampstead Garden Suburb, *Lon.* 4 B3 51 34N 0 11W
Hampstead Heath, *Lon.* 4 B3 51 33N 0 10W
Hampton Court Palace, *Lon.* 4 C2 51 24N 0 20W
Hampton Hill, *Lon.* 4 C2 51 25N 0 21W
Hampton Wick, *Lon.* 4 C3 51 24N 0 18W
Hamrā, *Bagd.* 17 F7 33 18N 44 18 E
Han Gang →, *Sŏul* 12 G7 37 32N 126 55 E
Hanakuri, *Tōkyō* 13 A3 35 50N 139 47 E
Hanala, *Hels.* 3 A5 60 20N 25 4 E
Hancho, *Ōsaka* 12 B3 34 48N 135 28 E
Haneda, *Tōkyō* 13 C3 35 32N 139 44 E
Hang Hau, *H.K.* 12 E6 22 19N 114 16 E
Hanjiashu, *Tianj.* 14 E5 39 11N 117 4 E
Hanlon, *Trto.* 20 E7 43 38N 79 39W
Hansen Flood Control Basin, *L.A.* 28 A2 34 15N 118 23W
Hansia, *Calc.* 16 D6 22 48N 88 24 E
Hanskinen, *Hels.* 3 C6 60 8N 25 15 E
Hanwell, *Lon.* 4 B2 51 30N 0 20W
Hanworth, *Lon.* 4 C2 51 25N 0 23W
Haora, *Calc.* 16 E5 22 34N 88 18 E
Happy Valley, *H.K.* 12 E6 22 16N 114 10 E
Harajuku, *Tōkyō* 13 D2 35 22N 139 30 E
Haraki, *Tōkyō* 13 B4 35 42N 139 56 E
Harat, *Calc.* 16 C5 22 52N 88 11 E
Harbor Hills, *N.Y.* 23 C6 40 46N 73 44W
Harburg, *Hbg.* 7 E7 53 27N 9 59 E
Harding, *Bost.* 21 D2 42 12N 71 19W
Hardricourt, *Paris* 5 A1 49 0N 1 53 E
Harefield, *Lon.* 4 B2 51 36N 0 28W
Hareskovby, *Købn.* 2 D9 55 45N 12 23 E
Harewood Park, *Balt.* 25 A4 39 22N 76 21W
Harigaya, *Tōkyō* 13 B2 35 49N 139 33 E
Haringey, *Lon.* 4 B4 51 34N 0 4W
Haripur, *Calc.* 16 D5 22 42N 88 10 E
Harjula, *Hels.* 3 A3 60 21N 24 45 E
Harjusuo, *Hels.* 3 B5 60 19N 25 0 E
Harkortsee, *Ruhr* 6 B6 51 23N 7 24 E
Harksheide, *Hbg.* 7 C8 53 43N 10 0 E
Harlaching, *Mün.* 7 G10 48 5N 11 33 E
Harlem, *N.Y.* 22 C5 40 48N 73 56W
Harlesden, *Lon.* 4 B3 51 32N 0 14W
Harlington, *Lon.* 4 C2 51 29N 0 25W
Harmaja, *Hels.* 3 C4 60 6N 24 58 E
Harmashatar hegy, *Bud.* 10 J13 47 33N 19 0 E
Harmondsworth, *Lon.* 4 C2 51 29N 0 29W
Harmonville, *Phil.* 24 A3 40 5N 75 18W
Harold Hill, *Lon.* 4 B6 51 36N 0 14 E
Harold Parker State Forest, *Bost.* 21 B3 42 37N 71 4W
Harold Wood, *Lon.* 4 B6 51 35N 0 14 E
Harrington Park, *N.Y.* 22 B5 40 59N 73 58W
Harrison, *N.Y.* 22 C4 40 44N 74 9W
Harrison, *N.Y.* 23 B6 40 57N 73 42W
Harrisonville, *Balt.* 25 A2 39 22N 76 49W
Harrow, *Lon.* 4 B2 51 34N 0 20W
Harrow on the Hill, *Lon.* 4 B2 51 34N 0 21W
Harrow School, *Lon.* 4 B2 51 34N 0 20W
Harrow Weald, *Lon.* 4 B2 51 36N 0 20W
Hart I., *Balt.* 25 B4 39 14N 76 23W
Hart I., *N.Y.* 23 B6 40 51N 73 46W
Hartford, *Phil.* 24 B5 39 58N 74 53W
Hartley, *Lon.* 4 C6 51 22N 0 18 E
Hartsdale, *N.Y.* 23 A6 41 1N 73 48W
Harumi, *Tōkyō* 13 C3 35 38N 139 47 E
Harvard, Mt., *L.A.* 28 A4 34 12N 118 4W
Harvard Univ., *Bost.* 21 C3 42 23N 71 7W
Harvestehude, *Hbg.* 7 D7 53 34N 9 58 E
Harvey, *Chic.* 26 D3 41 36N 87 39W
Harwood Heights, *Chic.* 26 B2 41 57N 87 46W
Hasanābād, *Tehr.* 17 C4 35 44N 51 16 E
Hasbrouck Heights, *N.Y.* 22 B4 40 51N 74 6W
Haselbach, *Wien* 10 G9 48 18N 16 14 E
Haselhorst, *Berl.* 7 A2 52 33N 13 14 E
Hasköy, *Ist.* 17 A2 41 2N 28 57 E
Hasle, *Oslo* 2 C3 59 46N 10 38 E
Hasloh, *Hbg.* 7 C7 53 41N 9 54 E
Haslohfeld, *Hbg.* 7 C7 53 41N 9 56 E
Haslum, *Oslo* 2 B3 59 55N 10 34 E
Haspe, *Ruhr* 6 B6 51 21N 7 25 E
Haspertalsp., *Ruhr* 6 C6 51 17N 7 24 E
Hasselbeck, *Ruhr* 6 C3 51 19N 6 56 E
Hässelby, *Stock.* 3 D10 59 22N 17 50 E
Hasslinghausen, *Ruhr* 6 C5 51 20N 7 16 E
Hasten, *Ruhr* 6 C5 51 11N 7 11 E
Hästhagen, *Stock.* 3 E11 59 18N 18 9 E
Hastings-on-Hudson, *N.Y.* 23 B5 40 59N 73 51W
Hatch End, *Lon.* 4 B2 51 36N 0 22W
Hatiara, *Calc.* 16 E6 22 36N 88 26 E
Hatogaya, *Tōkyō* 13 B3 35 49N 139 44 E
Hattingen, *Ruhr* 6 B5 51 23N 7 11 E
Hatton, *Lon.* 4 C2 51 28N 0 25W
Hattori, *Ōsaka* 12 A4 34 51N 135 36 E
Hauketo, *Oslo* 2 B4 59 50N 10 48 E
Hauldres →, *Paris* 5 D5 48 37N 2 37 E
Hausbruch, *Hbg.* 7 E7 53 28N 9 53 E
Havalimani, *Ist.* 17 B2 40 59N 28 50 E
Havana = La Habana, *La Hab.* 30 B2 23 7N 82 21W
Havdrup, *Købn.* 2 E7 55 33N 12 7 E
Havel →, *Berl.* 7 A2 52 37N 13 11 E
Havelkanal, *Berl.* 7 A2 52 36N 13 10 E
Haverford, *Phil.* 24 A3 40 0N 75 18W
Havering, *Lon.* 4 B6 51 33N 0 12 E
Havering-atte-Bower, *Lon.* 4 B6 51 37N 0 11 E
Havertown, *Phil.* 24 B3 39 58N 75 18W
Hawangsibri, *Sŏul* 12 G8 37 33N 127 1 E
Haweolgog, *Sŏul* 12 G8 37 36N 127 1 E
Haworth, *N.Y.* 22 B5 40 57N 73 59W
Hawthorne, *L.A.* 28 C2 33 54N 118 21W
Hawthorne, *N.Y.* 22 B4 40 57N 74 8W
Hayes, *Lon.* 4 C5 51 22N 0 0 E
Hayes, *Lon.* 4 B2 51 30N 0 23W
Hayes End, *Lon.* 4 B2 51 31N 0 25W
Hayford, *Chic.* 26 C2 41 45N 87 42W
Hayward, *S.F.* 27 B4 37 40N 122 4W
Hayward Fault, *S.F.* 27 B3 37 46N 122 10W
Haywood Municipal Airport, *S.F.* 27 C4 32 39N 122 9W
Headley, *Lon.* 4 D3 51 16N 0 16W
Headstone, *Lon.* 4 B2 51 35N 0 21W
Heard Pond, *Bost.* 21 C1 42 20N 71 23W
Heart Pond, *Bost.* 21 B1 42 33N 71 23W
Heath Park, *Lon.* 4 B6 51 34N 0 12 E
Heathmont, *Melb.* 19 E8 37 49 S 145 14 E
Heathrow Airport, *Lon.* 4 C2 51 28N 0 27W
Hebbville, *Balt.* 25 A2 39 20N 76 45W
Hebe Haven, *H.K.* 12 D6 22 21N 114 15 E
Hebei, *Tianj.* 14 E6 39 9N 117 11 E
Hedehusene, *Købn.* 2 E8 55 39N 12 11 E
Hedong, *Gzh.* 14 G8 23 5N 113 14 E
Hedong, *Tianj.* 14 E6 39 7N 117 11 E
Heerdt, *Ruhr* 6 C2 51 13N 6 42 E
Hegewisch, *Chic.* 26 D3 41 39N 87 32W
Heggelielva →, *Oslo* 2 A3 60 1N 10 36 E
Heide, *Ruhr* 6 A3 51 31N 6 50 E
Heidelberg, *Melb.* 19 E7 37 45 S 145 4 E
Heidelberg West, *Melb.* 19 E7 37 43 S 145 2 E
Heidemühle, *Berl.* 7 B5 52 29N 13 40 E
Heidhausen, *Ruhr* 6 B4 51 22N 7 1 E
Heiligenhaus, *Ruhr* 6 C3 51 19N 6 57 E
Heiligensee, *Berl.* 7 A2 52 36N 13 13 E
Heiligenstadt, *Wien* 10 G10 48 14N 16 21 E
Heimfeld, *Hbg.* 7 E7 53 28N 9 57 E
Heinässuo, *Hels.* 3 B1 60 18N 24 27 E
Heinersdorf, *Berl.* 7 A3 52 34N 13 26 E
Heisingen, *Ruhr* 6 B4 51 24N 7 3 E
Heissen, *Ruhr* 6 B3 51 26N 6 54 E
Helderkruin, *Jobg.* 18 E8 26 7 S 27 51 E
Helenelund, *Stock.* 3 D10 59 24N 17 58 E
Heliopolis, *El Qâ.* 18 C5 30 5N 31 19 E
Hellersdorf, *Berl.* 7 A4 52 32N 13 35 E
Hellerup, *Købn.* 2 D10 55 44N 12 33 E
Helmahof, *Wien* 10 G11 48 18N 16 34 E
Helsingfors = Helsinki, *Hels.* 3 B4 60 10N 24 55 E
Helsinki, *Hels.* 3 B4 60 10N 24 55 E
Helsinki Airport, *Hels.* 3 B4 60 18N 24 58 E
Hempstead, *N.Y.* 23 C7 40 42N 73 37W
Hempstead Harbor, *N.Y.* 23 B7 40 50N 73 39W
Henan, *Gzh.* 14 G8 23 5N 113 14 E
Hendon, *Lon.* 4 B3 51 35N 0 14W
Hengsha, *Gzh.* 14 G8 23 9N 113 12 E
Hengsteysee, *Ruhr* 6 B6 51 24N 7 27 E
Hennigsdorf, *Berl.* 7 A2 52 38N 13 12 E
Henrichenburg, *Ruhr* 6 A5 51 35N 7 19 E
Henriville, *Paris* 5 C1 48 44N 1 56 E
Henrykow, *Wsaw.* 10 E6 52 19N 20 58 E
Henson Cr. →, *Wash.* 25 E8 38 47N 76 58W
Henttaa, *Hels.* 3 B3 60 11N 24 45 E
Heping, *Tianj.* 14 E6 39 7N 117 11 E
Heping Gongyuan, *Shang.* 14 J12 31 16N 121 30 E
Hepingli, *Beij.* 14 B3 39 57N 116 23 E
Herbeck, *Ruhr* 6 C5 51 12N 7 18 E
Herbede, *Ruhr* 6 B5 51 25N 7 16 E
Herblay, *Paris* 5 B2 48 59N 2 9 E
Herdecke, *Ruhr* 6 B6 51 24N 7 25 E
Herlev, *Købn.* 2 D9 55 43N 12 27 E
Hermannskogel, *Wien* 10 G9 48 16N 16 17 E
Hermitage and Winter Palace, *St-Pet.* 11 B3 59 55N 30 19 E
Hermosa Beach, *L.A.* 28 C2 33 51N 118 23W
Hermsdorf, *Berl.* 7 A2 52 37N 13 18 E
Hernals, *Wien* 10 G10 48 13N 16 20 E
Herne, *Ruhr* 6 A5 51 32N 7 13 E
Herne Hill, *Lon.* 4 C4 51 27N 0 6W
Hernwood Heights, *Balt.* 25 A2 39 22N 76 49W
Héroes de Churubusco, *Méx.* 29 B3 19 21N 99 6W
Herongate, *Lon.* 4 B7 51 35N 0 21 E
Herons, Î. aux, *Mtrl.* 20 B4 43 25N 73 34W
Herricks, *N.Y.* 23 C7 40 45N 73 39W
Herring Run →, *Balt.* 25 B3 39 18N 76 30W
Hersham, *Lon.* 4 C2 51 21N 0 22W
Herstedøster, *Købn.* 2 D9 55 40N 12 22 E
Herten, *Ruhr* 6 A4 51 35N 7 8 E
Herttoniemi, *Hels.* 3 B5 60 12N 25 2 E
Hessler, *Ruhr* 6 A4 51 31N 7 3 E
Heston, *Lon.* 4 C2 51 28N 0 22W
Hetterscheidt, *Ruhr* 6 B3 51 20N 6 59 E
Hetzendorf, *Wien* 10 H9 48 9N 16 17 E
Heuberg, *Wien* 10 G9 48 13N 16 16 E
Heven, *Ruhr* 6 B5 51 26N 7 18 E
Hewlett Neck, *N.Y.* 23 D6 40 37N 73 41W
Hexi, *Tianj.* 14 E5 39 8N 117 9 E
Hexingcun, *Tianj.* 14 E6 39 8N 117 10 E
Hextable, *Lon.* 4 C6 51 24N 0 10 E
Heybridge, *Lon.* 4 B7 51 39N 0 22 E
Hibernia, *N.Y.* 22 B2 40 57N 74 29W
Hickory Hills, *Chic.* 26 C2 41 43N 87 49W
Hicksville, *N.Y.* 23 C7 40 46N 73 30W
Hiddinghausen, *Ruhr* 6 B5 51 21N 7 17 E
Hiekkaharju, *Hels.* 3 B5 60 18N 25 2 E
Hiesfeld, *Ruhr* 6 A2 51 33N 6 46 E
Hietaniemi, *Hels.* 3 B4 60 10N 24 54 E
Hietzing, *Wien* 10 G9 48 10N 16 17 E
Higashi, *Ōsaka* 12 B4 34 41N 135 30 E
Higashi-kaizuka, *Tōkyō* 13 A3 35 50N 139 46 E
Higashimonzen, *Tōkyō* 13 A3 35 55N 139 40 E
Higashimurayama, *Tōkyō* 13 B1 35 45N 139 26 E
Higashinada, *Ōsaka* 12 B2 34 42N 135 15 E
Higashinari, *Ōsaka* 12 B4 34 40N 135 32 E
Higashiōsaka, *Ōsaka* 12 C4 34 39N 135 37 E
Higashisumiyoshi, *Ōsaka* 12 C4 34 37N 135 31 E
Higashiyodogawa, *Ōsaka* 12 B3 34 44N 135 28 E
High Beach, *Lon.* 4 B5 51 39N 0 1 E
High Junk Pk., *H.K.* 12 E6 22 17N 114 17 E
High Park, *Trto.* 20 E8 43 38N 79 27W
Higham Hill, *Lon.* 4 B4 51 35N 0 2W
Highbury, *Lon.* 4 B4 51 33N 0 6W
Highgate, *Lon.* 4 B4 51 34N 0 8W
Highland Cr. →, *Trto.* 20 D9 43 45N 79 13W
Highland Creek, *Trto.* 20 D9 43 46N 79 8W
Highland Park, *L.A.* 28 B3 34 7N 118 13 W
Highland Park, *N.Y.* 22 D2 40 30N 74 25W
Highlands North, *Jobg.* 18 E9 26 8 S 28 5 E
Highway Highlands, *L.A.* 28 A3 34 14N 118 16W
Higurashi, *Tōkyō* 13 B4 35 47N 139 55 E
Hila, *Méx.* 29 A2 19 35N 99 17W
Hillcrest Heights, *Wash.* 25 E8 38 49N 76 57W
Hillerheide, *Ruhr* 6 A5 51 35N 7 12 E
Hilleshög, *Stock.* 3 D9 59 23N 17 42 E
Hillgrove District, *L.A.* 28 B5 34 1N 117 58W
Hillingdon, *Lon.* 4 B2 51 32N 0 27W
Hillingdon Heath, *Lon.* 4 B2 51 31N 0 26W
Hillsborough, *S.F.* 27 C2 37 32N 122 21W
Hillsdale, *N.Y.* 22 A4 41 0N 74 1W
Hillsdale, *S.F.* 27 C3 37 32N 122 18W
Hillsdale Manor, *N.Y.* 22 A4 41 1N 74 3W
Hillside, *Chic.* 26 B1 41 52N 87 55W
Hillside, *N.Y.* 23 C6 40 42N 73 46W
Hillside Manor, *N.Y.* 23 C6 40 44N 73 40W
Hilltop, *Phil.* 24 C4 39 49N 75 4W
Hillwood, *Wash.* 25 D7 38 52N 77 9W
Hilmîya, *El Qâ.* 18 C5 30 6N 31 14 E
Hiltrop, *Ruhr* 6 A5 51 31N 7 15 E
Hindsby, *Hels.* 3 A6 60 20N 25 13 E
Hingham, *Bost.* 21 D4 42 14N 70 54W
Hingham B., *Bost.* 21 D4 42 17N 70 56W
Hingham Harbor, *Bost.* 21 D4 42 15N 70 53W
Hino, *Tōkyō* 13 D2 35 39N 139 23 E
Hinsbeck, *Ruhr* 6 B4 51 22N 7 4 E
Hinschenfelde, *Hbg.* 7 D8 53 35N 10 0 E
Hinsdale, *Chic.* 26 C1 41 47N 87 55W
Hinterhainbach, *Wien* 10 G9 48 14N 16 10 E
Hintersdorf, *Wien* 10 G9 48 18N 16 13 E
Hirakata, *Ōsaka* 12 B4 34 48N 135 38 E
Hirota, *Ōsaka* 12 B4 34 45N 135 20 E
Hirschstetten, *Wien* 10 G10 48 14N 16 27 E
Hither Green, *Lon.* 4 C4 51 26N 0 0 E
Hiyoshi, *Tōkyō* 13 C2 35 32N 139 38 E
Hjortekær, *Købn.* 2 D10 55 47N 12 32 E
Hjortespring, *Købn.* 2 D9 55 44N 12 25 E
Hlubočepy, *Pra.* 10 B2 50 2N 14 23 E
Ho Chung, *H.K.* 12 D6 22 21N 114 14 E
Ho Man Tin, *H.K.* 12 E6 22 18N 114 10 E
Hoboken, *N.Y.* 22 C4 40 44N 74 3W
Hobsons B., *Melb.* 19 F6 37 51 S 144 55 E
Hochbrück, *Mün.* 7 F10 48 14N 11 37 E
Hochdahl, *Ruhr* 6 C3 51 13N 6 55 E
Hochemmerich, *Ruhr* 6 B2 51 24N 6 41 E
Hochfeld, *Ruhr* 6 B2 51 25N 6 45 E
Hochheide, *Ruhr* 6 B2 51 27N 6 40 E
Hochlar, *Ruhr* 6 A5 51 36N 7 11 E
Hochlarmark, *Ruhr* 6 A5 51 34N 7 11 E
Hodgkins, *Chic.* 26 C1 41 46N 87 53W
Hodogaya-Ku, *Tōkyō* 13 D2 35 26N 139 35 E
Hoegi, *Sŏul* 12 G8 37 35N 127 3 E
Hofberg, *Wien* 10 G10 48 12N 16 21 E
Hoffman I., *N.Y.* 22 D4 40 34N 74 3W
Hofstede, *Ruhr* 6 A5 51 30N 7 11 E
Höggarnsfjärden, *Stock.* 3 D13 59 22N 18 22 E
Hohe Mark, Naturpark, *Ruhr* 6 A2 51 35N 6 49 E
Hohe Schaar, *Hbg.* 7 E7 53 29N 9 58 E
Hohenbrunn, *Mün.* 7 G11 48 2N 11 42 E
Hohenfelde, *Hbg.* 7 D8 53 33N 10 1 E
Höhenkirchen, *Mün.* 7 G11 48 1N 11 42 E
Hohenraden, *Hbg.* 7 C6 53 41N 9 49 E
Hohenschönhausen, *Berl.* 7 A4 52 33N 13 30 E
Hohenwisch, *Hbg.* 7 E7 53 29N 9 53 E

Kennedy Grove Regional Rec. Area 39

Hohokus, N.Y. 22 A4 41 0N 74 5W
Hok Tsui, H.K. 12 E6 22 12N 114 15 E
Holborn, Lon. 4 B4 51 31N 0 7W
Holešovice, Pra. 10 B2 50 6N 14 28 E
Holland Village, Sing. 15 G7 1 18N 103 47 E
Hollis, N.Y. 23 C6 40 42N 73 45W
Höllriegelskreuth, Mün. 7 G9 48 2N 11 30 E
Holly Oak, Phil. 24 C2 39 47N 75 27W
Hollydale, L.A. 28 C4 33 55N 118 10W
Hollywood Bowl, L.A. 28 B2 34 6N 118 21W
Hollywood-Burbank Airport, L.A. 28 A2 34 11N 118 21W
Holmenkollen, Oslo 2 B4 59 57N 10 41 E
Holmes, Phil. 24 B3 39 53N 75 18W
Holmes Acres, Wash. 25 D6 38 51N 77 13W
Holmes Run →, Wash. 25 E7 38 48N 77 6W
Holmesburg, Phil. 24 A4 40 2N 75 2W
Holmgård, Stock. 3 E10 59 14N 18 0 E
Holsfjorden, Oslo 2 B1 59 58N 10 17 E
Holsterhausen, Ruhr 6 A5 51 32N 7 11 E
Holte, Købn. 2 D9 55 48N 12 27 E
Holten, Ruhr 6 A2 51 31N 6 47 E
Holthausen, Ruhr 6 B4 51 25N 7 5 E
Holzbüttgen, Ruhr 6 C1 51 13N 6 37 E
Homberg, Ruhr 6 B2 51 27N 6 41 E
Hombruch, Ruhr 6 B6 51 28N 7 27 E
Homerton, Lon. 4 B4 51 32N 0 2W
Homestead Lake, Jobg. 18 F10 26 10 S 28 17 E
Homestead Valley, S.F. 27 A1 37 53N 122 32W
Hometown, Chic. 26 C2 41 44N 87 42W
Homledal, Oslo 2 B1 59 59N 10 18 E
Homówek, Wsaw. 10 E5 52 17N 20 48 E
Hon-gyōtoku, Tōkyō 13 B4 35 41N 139 57 E
Hōnanchō, Tōkyō 13 B2 35 40N 139 39 E
Honcho, Tōkyō 13 B3 35 40N 139 41 E
Honden, Tōkyō 13 B4 35 43N 139 50 E
Honeydew, Jobg. 18 E8 26 4 S 27 55 E
Hong Kah, Sing. 15 F7 1 21N 103 43 E
Hong Kong, H.K. 12 E5 22 17N 114 11 E
Hong Kong, Univ. of, H.K. 12 E5 22 16N 114 8 E
Hong Kong Airport, H.K. 12 E6 22 19N 114 11 E
Hong Kong I., H.K. 12 E6 22 16N 114 11 E
Hong Lim Park, Sing. 15 G8 1 17N 103 50 E
Hongeun, Sŏul 12 G7 37 35N 126 56 E
Honggiao, Shang. 14 J11 31 12N 121 22 E
Honggou, Shang. 14 J11 31 16N 121 29 E
Hongkou Gongyuan, Shang. 14 J11 31 17N 121 28 E
Hongmiao, Beij. 14 B3 39 54N 116 26 E
Hongqiao, Tianj. 14 E5 39 8N 117 9 E
Hongqiao Airport, Shang. 14 J10 31 12N 121 19 E
Honjyo, Tōkyō 13 B3 35 41N 139 48 E
Honmoku, Tōkyō 13 D2 35 24N 139 39 E
Hönow, Berl. 7 A4 52 32N 13 38 E
Höntrop, Ruhr 6 B4 51 27N 7 9 E
Hood Pond, Bost. 21 A4 42 40N 70 57W
Hooghly →, Calc. 16 D6 22 41N 88 21 E
Hook, Lon. 4 C3 51 22N 0 17W
Hopelawn, N.Y. 22 D3 40 31N 74 17W
Hörde, Ruhr 6 B7 51 29N 7 30 E
Horikiri, Tōkyō 13 B4 35 44N 139 50 E
Horn, Hbg. 7 D8 53 33N 10 5 E
Horn Pond, Bost. 21 C2 42 28N 71 9W
Hornchurch, Lon. 4 B6 51 33N 0 14 E
Horneburg, Ruhr 6 A5 51 37N 7 17 E
Horni, Pra. 10 B3 50 2N 14 33 E
Horni Počernice, Pra. 10 B3 50 6N 14 36 E
Hornsey, Lon. 4 B4 51 35N 0 7W
Horoměřice, Pra. 10 B1 50 8N 14 20 E
Horsley Park, Syd. 19 B2 33 50 S 150 51 E
Horst, Ruhr 6 B4 51 26N 7 6 E
Horsthausen, Ruhr 6 A5 51 33N 7 12 E
Hortaleza, Mdrd. 8 B3 40 28N 3 38W
Horto Florestal, S. Pau. 31 D6 23 27 S 46 38W
Horton Kirby, Lon. 4 C6 51 23N 0 14 E
Hösel, Ruhr 6 B3 51 20N 6 53 E
Hosoyama, Tōkyō 13 C2 35 36N 139 31 E
Hospitalet, Barc. 8 D5 41 21N 2 6 E
Hostafranchs, Barc. 8 D5 41 21N 2 8 E
Hoterheide, Ruhr 6 C1 51 16N 6 37 E
Houbetin, Pra. 10 B3 50 6N 14 33 E
Houghs Neck, Bost. 21 D4 42 15N 70 57W
Houghton, Jobg. 18 F9 26 10 S 28 3 E
Houilles, Paris 5 B3 48 56N 2 11 E
Hounslow, Lon. 4 C2 51 28N 0 21W
Houses of Parliament, Lon. 4 C4 51 29N 0 7W
Hove Å →, Købn. 2 D8 55 43N 12 7 E
Hovedøya, Oslo 2 B4 59 53N 10 43 E
Høvik, Oslo 2 B3 59 54N 10 34 E
Hovorčovice, Pra. 10 A3 50 10N 14 31 E
Howard Beach, N.Y. 23 D5 40 39N 73 50W
Hoxton Park, Syd. 19 B2 33 55 S 150 51 E
Hoxton Park Aerodrome, Syd. 19 B2 33 54 S 150 50 E
Hōya, Tōkyō 13 B2 35 44N 139 34 E
Høybråten, Oslo 2 B5 59 56N 10 55 E
Hradčany, Pra. 10 B2 50 5N 14 24 E
Hsiya, Gzh. 14 G7 23 9N 113 6 E
Huangpu, Gzh. 14 G9 23 5N 113 23 E
Huangpu, Shang. 14 J12 31 14N 121 30 E
Huangpu Gongyuan, Shang. 14 J11 31 14N 121 29 E
Huangpu Jiang →, Shang. 14 J11 31 11N 121 29 E
Huangtugang, Beij. 14 C2 39 49N 116 15 E
Huat Choe, Sing. 15 F7 1 20N 103 41 E
Huckarde, Ruhr 6 A6 51 32N 7 24 E
Huckingen, Ruhr 6 B2 51 21N 6 44 E
Huddinge, Stock. 3 E11 59 14N 18 0 E
Hudson →, N.Y. 22 B5 40 43N 73 6W
Huertas de San Beltran, Barc. 8 D5 41 22N 2 9 E
Huguenot, N.Y. 22 D3 40 32N 74 13W
Huguenot Park, N.Y. 22 D3 40 31N 74 12W
Huidui, Tianj. 14 E6 39 4N 117 16 E
Huisquilucan →, Méx. 29 B2 19 24N 99 17W
Huixquilucan, Méx. 29 B1 19 21N 99 21W
Hull, Bost. 21 D4 42 18N 70 54W
Hulman Aqueduct, Bost. 21 C1 42 20N 71 23W
Hulmeville, Phil. 24 A5 40 8N 74 55W
Hulsdonk, Ruhr 6 B1 51 27N 6 36 E
Humaljärvi, Hels. 3 B1 60 10N 24 26 E
Humber →, Trto. 20 D7 43 47N 79 38W
Humber B., Trto. 20 E8 43 37N 79 27W
Humber Bay, Trto. 20 E8 43 38N 79 29W
Humber Summit, Trto. 20 D7 43 45N 79 32W
Humber Valley Park, Trto. 20 E8 43 39N 79 29W
Humber Valley Village, Trto. 20 D7 43 40N 79 31W
Humberlea, Trto. 20 D7 43 43N 79 31W
Humboldt Park, Chic. 26 B2 41 54N 87 42W
Humera, Mdrd. 8 B2 40 25N 3 46W
Hummelsbüttel, Hbg. 7 D8 53 39N 10 4 E
Hun Yeang, Sing. 15 F8 1 21N 103 55 E
Hunaydī, Bagd. 17 F8 33 18N 44 29 E
Hundige, Købn. 2 E8 55 35N 12 18 E
Hundige Strand, Købn. 2 E9 55 35N 12 20 E
Hung Hom, H.K. 12 E6 22 18N 114 11 E
Hunters Hill, Syd. 19 B3 33 50 S 151 9 E
Hunters Pt., S.F. 27 B2 37 43N 122 21W
Hunters Valley, Wash. 25 D6 38 54N 77 17W
Huntington, N.Y. 23 B8 40 51N 73 25W
Huntington, Wash. 25 E7 38 47N 77 4W
Huntington B., N.Y. 23 B8 40 54N 73 24W
Huntington Bay, N.Y. 23 B8 40 56N 73 26W
Huntington Park, L.A. 28 C3 33 58N 118 13W
Huntington Station, N.Y. 23 B8 40 50N 73 23W
Hünxer Wald, Ruhr 6 A2 51 37N 6 49 E
Hurffville, Phil. 24 C4 39 45N 75 6W
Hurīya, Bagd. 17 E7 33 21N 44 19 E
Hurlingham, B.A. 32 B3 34 35 S 58 37W
Hurlingham, Jobg. 18 E9 26 6 S 28 2 E
Hurstville, Syd. 19 B3 33 57 S 151 6 E
Husby, Stock. 3 D10 59 24N 17 56 E
Huseby, Oslo 2 A6 60 0N 11 1 E
Hustivař, Pra. 10 B3 50 3N 14 31 E
Husum, Købn. 2 D9 55 42N 12 27 E
Hütteldorf, Wien 10 G9 48 12N 16 15 E
Hüttenheim, Ruhr 6 B2 51 21N 6 43 E
Huttrop, Ruhr 6 B4 51 26N 7 3 E
Hüvösvölgy, Bud. 10 J13 47 32N 19 0 E
Hvalstad, Oslo 2 B2 59 51N 10 27 E
Hvalstrand, Oslo 2 B3 59 50N 10 30 E
Hvidovre, Købn. 2 E9 55 38N 12 27 E
Hwagog, Sŏul 12 G7 37 32N 126 51 E
Hyattsville, Wash. 25 D8 38 57N 76 57W
Hyde Park, Bost. 21 D3 42 15N 71 7W
Hyde Park, Chic. 26 C3 41 47N 87 35W
Hyde Park, Jobg. 18 E9 26 6 S 28 2 E
Hyde Park, Lon. 4 B3 51 30N 0 10W
Hyde Park, Syd. 19 B4 33 52 S 151 12 E
Hynes, L.A. 28 C3 33 52N 118 10W

I

Ibaraki, Ōsaka 12 B4 34 48N 135 34 E
Ibayo Tipas, Manila 15 D4 14 32N 121 4 E
Ibese, Lagos 18 A2 6 33N 7 28 E
Ibirapuera, S. Pau. 31 E5 23 36 S 46 40W
Ibirapuera, Parque, S. Pau. 31 E6 23 35 S 46 38W
Iboju, Lagos 18 B3 6 25N 7 31 E
Icarai, Rio J. 31 B3 22 54 S 43 6W
Icerenköy, Ist. 17 B3 40 58N 29 6 E
Ichapur, Calc. 16 D6 22 48N 88 22 E
Ichgao, Tōkyō 13 C2 35 32N 139 32 E
Ichigaya, Tōkyō 13 B3 35 41N 139 43 E
Ichikawa, Tōkyō 13 B4 35 43N 139 54 E
Ickenham, Lon. 4 B2 51 33N 0 26W
Ickern, Ruhr 6 A6 51 35N 7 21 E
Iddo, Lagos 18 B2 6 28N 7 22 E
Idi-Oro, Lagos 18 A2 6 31N 7 21 E
Idimu, Lagos 18 A1 6 34N 7 17 E
Idrīs, Bagd. 17 E8 33 22N 44 27 E
Iganmu, Lagos 18 B2 6 28N 7 22 E
Igbobi, Lagos 18 A2 6 31N 7 22 E
Igbologun, Lagos 18 B1 6 24N 7 19 E
Igbopa, Lagos 18 A3 6 32N 7 31 E
Igelboda, Stock. 3 E12 59 17N 18 17 E
Igny, Paris 5 C3 48 44N 2 13 E
Iguassú, S. Pau. 31 E6 23 36 S 46 30W
Ijesa-Tedo, Lagos 18 B1 6 29N 7 19 E
Ijora, Lagos 18 B2 6 27N 7 22 E
Ikebe, Tōkyō 13 C2 35 31N 139 34 E
Ikebukuro, Tōkyō 13 B3 35 43N 139 42 E
Ikeda, Ōsaka 12 B3 34 48N 135 25 E
Ikegami, Tōkyō 13 C3 35 33N 139 42 E
Ikeja, Lagos 18 A2 6 35N 7 20 E
Ikeuchi, Ōsaka 12 C4 34 35N 135 32 E
Ikotun, Lagos 18 A1 6 32N 7 16 E
Ikoyi, Lagos 18 B2 6 27N 7 26 E
Ikuata, Lagos 18 B2 6 24N 7 21 E
Ikuno, Ōsaka 12 B4 34 40N 135 30 E
Ikuta, Ōsaka 12 B4 34 41N 135 30 E
Ikuta, Tōkyō 13 C2 35 36N 139 32 E
Ila, Oslo 2 B3 59 57N 10 35 E
Ilchester, Balt. 25 B2 39 14N 76 46W
Ilford, Lon. 4 B5 51 33N 0 4 E
Ilioúpolis, Ath. 8 J11 37 54N 23 47 E
Illovo, Jobg. 18 E9 26 7 S 28 3 E
Ilsós →, Ath. 8 J11 37 55N 23 41 E
Imajuku, Tōkyō 13 D2 35 28N 139 32 E
Imbâba, El Qâ. 18 C5 30 3N 31 12 E
Imielin, Wsaw. 10 F7 52 9N 21 0 E
Imirim, S. Pau. 31 D6 23 29 S 46 39W
Imittós, Ath. 8 J11 37 55N 23 45 E
Immersby, Hels. 3 B6 60 18N 25 16 E
Imore, Lagos 18 B3 6 25N 7 31 E
Imperial Palace, Tōkyō 13 B3 35 41N 139 45 E
Ina →, Ōsaka 12 B3 34 48N 135 27 E
Inagi, Tōkyō 13 C2 35 38N 139 31 E
Incirano, Mil. 9 D5 45 34N 9 9 E
Independencia, Lima 30 F8 11 59 S 77 3W
Indian Gabe, Delhi 16 B2 28 36N 77 13 E
Indian Museum, Calc. 16 E6 22 33N 88 21 E
Indiana Harbor, Chic. 26 C4 41 40N 87 26W
Indiana Harbor Canal, Chic. 26 D4 41 39N 87 26W
Indianópolis, S. Pau. 31 E6 23 35 S 46 38W
Indios Verdes, Méx. 29 B3 19 29N 99 6W
Ingarö, Stock. 3 E13 59 17N 18 24 E
Ingaröfjärden, Stock. 3 E13 59 14N 18 25 E
Ingarölandet, Stock. 3 E13 59 17N 18 22 E
Ingenieur Budge, B.A. 32 C4 34 43 S 58 27W
Ingierstrand, Oslo 2 C4 59 49N 10 46 E
Ingleburn, Syd. 19 C2 34 0 S 150 52 E
Inglewood, L.A. 28 C3 33 57N 118 19W
Ingrave, Lon. 4 B7 51 35N 0 20 E
Ingvalsby, Hels. 3 C2 60 9N 24 32 E
Inhaúme, Rio J. 31 B2 22 51 S 43 17W
Inner Port Shelter, H.K. 12 D6 22 22N 114 17 E
Interagos, S. Pau. 31 E5 23 41 S 46 42W
Intramuros, Manila 15 D3 14 35N 120 57 E
Invalides, Paris 5 B3 48 51N 2 18 E
Inverness, Balt. 25 B4 39 15N 76 29W
Inwood, N.Y. 23 D6 40 36N 73 45W
Inzersdorf, Wien 10 H10 48 8N 16 21 E
Ipanema, Rio J. 31 B2 22 59 S 43 12W
Ipiranga, S. Pau. 31 E6 23 35 S 46 36W
Ipiranga →, S. Pau. 31 E6 23 34 S 46 36W
Iponri, Lagos 18 B2 6 28N 7 22 E
Ipswich, Bost. 21 A4 42 41N 70 50W
Ipswich →, Bost. 21 A4 42 41N 70 50W
Irajá, Rio J. 31 B2 22 50 S 43 19W
Irving Park, Chic. 26 B2 41 57N 87 42W
Irvington, N.Y. 23 A5 41 2N 73 52W
Irwindale, L.A. 28 B5 34 6N 117 54W
Isabel, Rio J. 31 B2 22 55 S 43 14W
Isagatedo, Lagos 18 A1 6 31N 7 19 E
Isando, Jobg. 18 E10 26 8 S 28 12 E
Isar →, Mün. 7 F11 48 15N 11 47 E
Iselin, N.Y. 22 D3 40 34N 74 19W
Iserbrook, Hbg. 7 D6 53 34N 9 49 E
Iseri-Osun, Lagos 18 A1 6 30N 7 16 E
Ishbīliya, Bagd. 17 E8 33 21N 44 26 E
Isheri-Olofin, Lagos 18 A1 6 34N 7 13 E
Ishi →, Ōsaka 12 B4 34 34N 135 37 E
Ishikiri, Ōsaka 12 B4 34 40N 135 39 E
Ishizu →, Ōsaka 12 C3 34 33N 135 26 E
Ishøj Strand, Købn. 2 E9 55 36N 12 20 E
Isidro Casanova, B.A. 32 C3 34 42 S 58 36W
Island Channel, N.Y. 23 D5 40 35N 73 52W
Island Park, N.Y. 23 D7 40 36N 73 38W
Island Park, Trto. 20 E8 43 37N 79 22W
Islev, Købn. 2 D9 55 41N 12 27 E
Isleworth, Lon. 4 C3 51 28N 0 19W
Islington, Bost. 21 D2 42 13N 71 13W
Islington, Lon. 4 B4 51 32N 0 6W
Islington, Trto. 20 E7 43 38N 79 30W
Ismaning, Mün. 7 F11 48 13N 11 40 E
Ismayloskiypark, Mos. 11 E10 55 46N 37 46 E
Isogo-Ku, Tōkyō 13 D2 35 23N 139 37 E
Isolo, Lagos 18 A1 6 31N 7 19 E
Isosaari, Hels. 3 C5 60 6N 25 3 E
Issy-les-Moulineaux, Paris 5 C3 48 49N 2 15 E
Istanbul, Ist. 17 B2 41 0N 28 58 E
Istanbul Boğazi, Ist. 17 A3 41 5N 29 3 E
Istanbul Hava Alani, Ist. 17 B2 40 58N 28 50 E
Istead Rise, Lon. 4 C7 51 24N 0 21 E
Istinye, Ist. 17 A3 41 6N 29 3 E
Isunba, Lagos 18 B1 6 25N 7 17 E
Itä Hakkila, Hels. 3 B5 60 17N 25 7 E
Itabashi-Ku, Tōkyō 13 B2 35 46N 139 38 E
Itaberaba, S. Pau. 31 D6 23 28 S 46 39W
Itaewon, Sŏul 12 G7 37 32N 126 58 E
Itaim, S. Pau. 31 D7 23 29 S 46 23W
Itaipu, Rio J. 31 B3 22 58 S 43 2W
Italie, Place d', Paris 5 C4 48 49N 2 22 E
Itami, Ōsaka 12 B3 34 46N 135 24 E
Itaocaia, Rio J. 31 B3 22 58 S 43 2W
Itapecerica da Serra, S. Pau. 31 F5 23 42 S 46 50W
Itaquaquecetuba, S. Pau. 31 D7 23 29 S 46 23W
Itaquera, S. Pau. 31 E7 23 32 S 46 27W
Itaquera →, S. Pau. 31 E7 23 28 S 46 26W
Ithan, Phil. 24 A2 40 1N 75 21W
Itupu, S. Pau. 31 F5 23 40 S 46 43W
Ituzaingo, B.A. 32 B3 34 39 S 58 38W
Ivanhoe, Melb. 19 E7 37 45 S 145 3 E
Iver, Lon. 4 B1 51 32N 0 30W
Ivry-sur-Seine, Paris 5 C4 48 49N 2 22 E
Iwazono, Ōsaka 12 B2 34 45N 135 18 E
Izabelin, Wsaw. 10 E5 52 17N 20 48 E
Izmaylovo, Mos. 11 E10 55 47N 37 47 E
Iztacalco, Méx. 29 B3 19 23N 99 6W
Iztapalapa, Méx. 29 B3 19 21N 99 6W
Izumi, Tōkyō 13 D1 35 25N 139 29 E

J

J. G. Strijdom Post Office Tower, Jobg. 18 F9 26 11 S 28 2 E
J. Paul Getty Museum, L.A. 28 B1 34 2N 118 33W
Jabavu, Jobg. 18 F8 26 14 S 27 52 E
Jabulani, Jobg. 18 F8 26 14 S 27 51 E
Jacarepaguá, Rio J. 31 B1 22 56 S 43 20W
Jackson Heights, N.Y. 23 C5 40 44N 73 53W
Jackson Park, Chic. 26 C3 41 46N 87 34W
Jacksonville, N.Y. 22 B3 40 57N 74 18W
Jacomino, La Hab. 30 B3 23 6N 82 19W
Jacques Cartier, Mtrl. 20 A5 43 31N 73 27W
Jægersborg, Købn. 2 D10 55 45N 12 31 E
Jægersborg Dyrehave, Købn. 2 D10 55 46N 12 33 E
Jægersborg Hegn, Købn. 2 D10 55 49N 12 33 E
Jafarpur, Calc. 16 D6 22 45N 88 22 E
Jagacha, Calc. 16 E5 22 35N 88 17 E
Jagannathpur, Calc. 16 D5 22 43N 88 18 E
Jagatdal, Calc. 16 C6 22 51N 88 23 E
Jagatmagar, Calc. 16 D5 22 46N 88 13 E
Jagatpur, Delhi 16 A2 28 44N 77 13 E
Jagdispur, Calc. 16 E2 22 39N 88 17 E
Jaguara, S. Pau. 31 E5 23 30 S 46 45W
Jaguaré, S. Pau. 31 E5 23 33 S 46 45W
Jaguaré →, S. Pau. 31 E5 23 32 S 46 45W
Jahangirpur, Delhi 16 A2 28 43N 77 12 E
Jaimanitas →, La Hab. 30 B2 23 5N 82 29W
Jakarta, Jak. 15 H10 6 9 S 106 52 E
Jakarta, Teluk, Jak. 15 H9 6 5 S 106 50 E
Jakobsberg, Stock. 3 D9 59 25N 17 47 E
Jalan Kayu, Sing. 15 F8 1 24N 103 52 E
Jamaica, N.Y. 23 C6 40 42N 73 48W
Jamaica B., N.Y. 23 D6 40 36N 73 49W
Jamaica Plain, Bost. 21 D3 42 18N 71 6W
Jamshīdābād, Tehr. 17 C5 35 42N 51 22 E
Jamsil, Sŏul 12 G8 37 30N 127 4 E
Jamweon, Sŏul 12 G8 37 30N 127 0 E
Jan Smuts Airport, Jobg. 18 E10 26 7 S 28 14 E
Janai, Calc. 16 E5 22 43N 88 15 E
Janā'in, Bagd. 17 F8 33 18N 44 22 E
Janki, Wsaw. 10 F6 52 8N 20 52 E
Jannali, Syd. 19 C3 34 0 S 151 4 E
Jánoshegy, Bud. 10 J12 47 31N 18 57 E
Janów, Wsaw. 10 E6 52 16N 20 50 E
Janvry, Paris 5 D2 48 38N 2 9 E
Jaraguá, S. Pau. 31 D5 23 27 S 46 44W
Jaraguá, Pico de, S. Pau. 31 D5 23 27 S 46 46W
Jarama →, Mdrd. 8 B3 40 29N 3 32W
Jardim América, S. Pau. 31 E6 23 34 S 46 39W
Jardim Anchieta, S. Pau. 31 F7 23 41 S 46 27W
Jardim Arpoador, S. Pau. 31 E5 23 35 S 46 48W
Jardim do Mar, S. Pau. 31 F6 23 41 S 46 33W
Jardim Munhoz, S. Pau. 31 E6 23 30 S 46 32W
Jardim Osasco, S. Pau. 31 E5 23 33 S 46 47W
Jardim Ouro Preto, S. Pau. 31 E5 23 35 S 46 46W
Jardim Paulista, S. Pau. 31 E5 23 34 S 46 41W
Jardim Petrópolis, S. Pau. 31 F7 23 41 S 46 23W
Jardim Rochidale, S. Pau. 31 E5 23 30 S 46 46W
Jardim Santista, S. Pau. 31 F7 23 40 S 46 25W
Jardim São Bento, S. Pau. 31 E5 23 30 S 46 46W
Jardim São Francisco, S. Pau. 31 E7 23 38 S 46 26W
Jardim Sapopemba, S. Pau. 31 E7 23 36 S 46 29W
Jardim Vera Cruz, S. Pau. 31 E7 23 36 S 46 27W
Jardim Vista Alegre, S. Pau. 31 E5 23 37 S 46 49W
Jardim Zaira, S. Pau. 31 E7 23 39 S 46 25W
Jardines Flotantes, Méx. 29 C3 19 16N 99 6W
Jardine's Lookout, H.K. 12 E6 22 16N 114 11 E
Järfälla, Stock. 3 D10 59 23N 17 51 E
Järvafältet, Stock. 3 D10 59 26N 17 54 E
Järventausta, Hels. 3 A1 60 21N 24 28 E
Jasai, Bomb. 16 H9 18 56N 73 1 E
Jaskhar, Bomb. 16 H8 18 54N 72 58 E
Jatinegara, Jak. 15 J10 6 13 S 106 52 E
Jauli, Delhi 16 A3 28 44N 77 20 E
Jawādiyeh, Tehr. 17 D5 35 39N 51 22 E
Jaworowa, Wsaw. 10 F6 52 9N 20 56 E
Jayang, Sŏul 12 G8 37 32N 127 3 E
Jedlesee, Wien 10 G10 48 15N 16 23 E
Jefferson, Phil. 24 C3 39 45N 75 12W
Jefferson Park, Chic. 26 B2 41 58N 87 46W
Jeffersonville, Phil. 24 A2 40 8N 75 23W
Jegi, Sŏul 12 G8 37 34N 127 1 E
Jells Park, Melb. 19 F8 37 53 S 145 11 E
Jelonki, Wsaw. 10 E6 52 14N 20 54 E
Jenfeld, Hbg. 7 D8 53 34N 10 8 E
Jenkintown, Phil. 24 A4 40 6N 75 8W
Jeongreung, Sŏul 12 G8 37 35N 127 0 E
Jericho, N.Y. 23 C7 40 47N 73 32W
Jerónimes, Mosteiro dos, Lisb. 8 F7 38 41N 9 11W
Jersey City, N.Y. 22 C4 40 42N 74 4W
Jésus, Î., Mtrl. 20 A3 43 36N 73 44W
Jesus Del Monte, La Hab. 30 B2 23 6N 82 21W
Jesús Maria, Lima 30 G8 12 4 S 77 3W
Jhenkari, Calc. 16 D5 22 45N 88 18 E
Jhil Kuranga, Delhi 16 B2 28 39N 77 14 E
Jiangqiao, Shang. 14 J11 31 15N 121 20 E
Jiangtai, Beij. 14 B3 39 57N 116 28 E
Jianguomen, Beij. 14 B3 39 53N 116 24 E
Jiangwan, Shang. 14 J11 31 18N 121 28 E
Jianshan Gongyuan, Tianj. 14 E6 39 5N 117 12 E
Jihād, Bagd. 17 F7 33 17N 44 19 E
Jingan, Shang. 14 J11 31 14N 121 25 E
Jinočany, Pra. 10 B1 50 2N 14 16 E
Jinonice, Pra. 10 B2 50 3N 14 22 E
Jirny, Pra. 10 B4 50 7N 14 41 E
Jiuxianqiao, Beij. 14 B3 39 58N 116 28 E
Jiyūgaoka, Tōkyō 13 C3 35 35N 139 40 E
Jizā'er, Bagd. 17 F8 33 15N 44 23 E
Jizīra, Bagd. 17 F8 33 15N 44 25 E
Joan Despi, Barc. 8 D5 41 22N 2 2 E
Joaquin Miller Park, S.F. 27 B3 37 48N 122 11W
Johannesburg, Jobg. 18 F9 26 11 S 28 2 E
Johanneskirchen, Mün. 7 F10 48 10N 11 38 E
Johannesstift, Berl. 7 A2 52 34N 13 12 E
Johannisthal, Berl. 7 B4 52 26N 13 30 E
John F. Kennedy Int. Airport, N.Y. 23 D6 40 39N 73 45W
John F. Kennedy Nat. Hist. Site, Bost. 21 C3 42 20N 71 7W
John Hancock Center, Chic. 26 B3 41 53N 87 37W
John Hopkins Univ., Balt. 25 B3 39 19N 76 37W
John McLaren Park, S.F. 27 B2 37 43N 122 24W
Joinville-le-Pont, Paris 5 C4 48 49N 2 27 E
Jollas, Hels. 3 B5 60 10N 25 5 E
Jones Beach State Park, N.Y. 23 D7 40 35N 73 32W
Jones Falls →, Balt. 25 B3 39 20N 76 36W
Jones Inlet, N.Y. 23 D7 40 34N 73 34W
Jonestown, Balt. 25 B2 39 13N 76 48W
Jong Ro, Sŏul 12 G7 37 34N 126 58 E
Jongmyo Royal Shrine, Sŏul 12 G7 37 34N 126 59 E
Jonstrup, Købn. 2 D9 55 45N 12 20 E
Joppatowne, Balt. 25 A4 39 24N 76 20W
Jordan Valley, H.K. 12 D6 22 20N 114 12 E
Jorge Chavez, Aeropuerto Int., Lima 30 G8 12 2 S 77 8W
Jorvas, Hels. 3 C2 60 8N 24 30 E
José C. Paz, B.A. 32 B2 34 31 S 58 44W
José L. Suárez, B.A. 32 B3 34 32 S 58 34W
José Mármol, B.A. 32 C4 34 47 S 58 22W
Jose Martí, Aeropuerto Int., La Hab. 30 C2 22 59N 82 22W
Josephine Pk., L.A. 28 A4 34 17N 118 7W
Jōsō, Ōsaka 12 B3 34 42N 135 27 E
Jōtō, Ōsaka 12 B4 34 42N 135 33 E
Jouars-Pontchartrain, Paris 5 C1 48 47N 1 53 E
Jouy-en-Josas, Paris 5 C3 48 46N 2 10 E
Jouy-le-Moutier, Paris 5 A2 49 0N 2 2 E
Józefów, Wsaw. 10 F8 52 8N 21 13 E
Juan Escutia, Méx. 29 B3 19 23N 99 3W
Juan González Romero, Méx. 29 A3 19 30N 99 3W
Juhu, Bomb. 16 G9 19 5N 73 0 E
Juilly, Paris 5 A6 49 0N 2 42 E
Jūjā, Tōkyō 13 B3 35 45N 139 43 E
Jukskeirivier →, Jobg. 18 E9 26 5 S 28 6 E
Julianów, Wsaw. 10 E7 52 10N 21 9 E
Jung, Sŏul 12 G7 37 33N 126 59 E
Jungfernheide, Volkspark, Berl. 7 A2 52 32N 13 18 E
Jungfernsee, Berl. 7 B1 52 25N 13 6 E
Jungwha, Sŏul 12 G8 37 35N 127 3 E
Junk B., H.K. 12 E6 22 17N 114 15 E
Jurong, Sing. 15 G7 1 19N 103 40 E
Jurong, Selat, Sing. 15 G7 1 17N 103 42 E
Jurong, Sungei →, Sing. 15 G7 1 17N 103 45 E
Jurubatuba, S. Pau. 31 F5 23 40 S 46 41W
Jurujuba, Enseada de, Rio J. 31 B3 22 54 S 43 6W
Justice, Chic. 26 C2 41 44N 87 49W
Juusjärvi, Hels. 3 B1 60 12N 24 26 E
Juva, Hels. 3 B3 60 16N 24 45 E
Juvisy-sur-Orge, Paris 5 C4 48 41N 2 21 E
Jwalahari, Delhi 16 B1 28 40N 77 6 E
Jyllinge, Købn. 2 D7 55 45N 12 6 E

K

Kaarst, Ruhr 6 C1 51 13N 6 36 E
Kabaty, Wsaw. 10 F7 52 8N 21 4 E
Kabel, Ruhr 6 B6 51 24N 7 28 E
Kadiköy, Ist. 17 B3 40 59N 29 1 E
Kadoma, Ōsaka 12 B4 34 44N 135 35 E
Kafr es Sammân, El Qâ. 18 D4 29 58N 31 8 E
Kâğithane, Ist. 17 A2 41 4N 28 58 E
Kâğithane →, Ist. 17 A2 41 9N 28 56 E
Kagran, Wien 10 G10 48 14N 16 26 E
Kahlenberg, Wien 10 G9 48 16N 16 19 E
Kai Tak, H.K. 12 D6 22 20N 114 11 E
Kaisariani, Ath. 8 J11 37 57N 23 46 E
Kaiser-Mühlen, Wien 10 G10 48 13N 16 25 E
Kaiserebersdorf, Wien 10 H10 48 9N 16 26 E
Kaiserswerth, Ruhr 6 C2 51 18N 6 44 E
Kaivoksela, Hels. 3 B4 60 15N 24 53 E
Kakukk-hegy, Bud. 10 K12 47 29N 18 57 E
Kalachhara, Calc. 16 D5 22 42N 88 15 E
Kalamákion, Ath. 8 J11 37 52N 23 43 E
Kaldenhausen, Ruhr 6 B1 51 23N 6 39 E
Kalipur, Calc. 16 D5 22 40N 88 17 E
Kalkaji, Delhi 16 B2 28 32N 77 12 E
Kalksburg, Wien 10 H9 48 8N 16 15 E
Kallang →, Sing. 15 F8 1 21N 103 51 E
Kallhäll, Stock. 3 D9 59 26N 17 48 E
Kallithéa, Ath. 8 J11 37 56N 23 43 E
Kallvik, Hels. 3 B5 60 12N 25 8 E
Kaltbründsberg, Wien 10 G9 48 10N 16 13 E
Kaltenleutgeben, Wien 10 H9 48 7N 16 11 E
Kalveboderne, Købn. 2 E10 55 37N 12 31 E
Kalytino, St-Pet. 11 B5 59 59N 30 39 E
Kamaraerdö, Bud. 10 K12 47 26N 18 59 E
Kamarhati, Calc. 16 D6 22 40N 88 23 E
Kamarkunda, Calc. 16 D5 22 49N 88 12 E
Kamata, Tōkyō 13 C3 35 33N 139 43 E
Kamdebpur, Calc. 16 C5 22 53N 88 19 E
Kameari, Tōkyō 13 B4 35 45N 139 50 E
Kameido, Tōkyō 13 B4 35 42N 139 50 E
Kami-hoshikawa, Tōkyō 13 D2 35 27N 139 35 E
Kami-Itabashi, Tōkyō 13 B3 35 45N 139 40 E
Kami-nakazato, Tōkyō 13 D2 35 22N 139 36 E
Kami-saruyama, Tōkyō 13 C2 35 30N 139 31 E
Kami-sugata, Tōkyō 13 D2 35 28N 139 34 E
Kami-tomi, Tōkyō 13 B1 35 48N 139 29 E
Kamikitazawa, Tōkyō 13 C2 35 39N 139 36 E
Kamikiyoto, Tōkyō 13 B2 35 45N 139 30 E
Kamishiki, Tōkyō 13 B4 35 46N 139 57 E
Kamitsuruma, Tōkyō 13 C1 35 30N 139 26 E
Kamiyama, Tōkyō 13 B2 35 46N 139 32 E
Kamoi, Tōkyō 13 C2 35 30N 139 34 E
Kamoshida, Tōkyō 13 C2 35 33N 139 31 E
Kampong Batak, Sing. 15 F8 1 20N 103 54 E
Kampong Mandai Kechil, Sing. 15 F7 1 26N 103 46 E
Kampong Pachitan, Sing. 15 G8 1 19N 103 54 E
Kampong Potong Pasir, Sing. 15 F8 1 20N 103 52 E
Kampong Reteh, Sing. 15 G8 1 19N 103 53 E
Kampong Tengah, Sing. 15 F7 1 22N 103 42 E
Kampong Ulu Jurong, Sing. 15 F7 1 20N 103 42 E
Kampung Ambon, Jak. 15 J10 6 11 S 106 53 E
Kampung Bali, Jak. 15 J9 6 11 S 106 48 E
Kan, Tehr. 17 C4 35 45N 51 16 E
Kanagawa-Ku, Tōkyō 13 D2 35 29N 139 38 E
Kanamachi, Tōkyō 13 B4 35 46N 139 52 E
Kanamori, Tōkyō 13 C1 35 31N 139 27 E
Kanda, Tōkyō 13 B3 35 41N 139 45 E
Kandang Kerbau, Sing. 15 G8 1 18N 103 51 E
Kandilli, Ist. 17 A3 41 4N 29 3 E
Kanegasaku, Tōkyō 13 B4 35 48N 139 56 E
Kangaroo Ground, Melb. 19 E8 37 41 S 145 13 E
Kankinara, Calc. 16 C6 22 51N 88 24 E
Kankurgachi, Calc. 16 E6 22 34N 88 23 E
Kanlica, Ist. 17 A3 41 5N 29 3 E
Kanoaka, Ōsaka 12 C4 34 33N 135 31 E
Kanonerskiy, Os., St-Pet. 11 B3 59 53N 30 13 E
Kanzaki →, Ōsaka 12 B3 34 41N 135 24 E
Kapellerfeld, Wien 10 G10 48 18N 16 29 E
Kapotnya, Mos. 11 F10 55 39N 37 48 E
Käppala, Stock. 3 D12 59 21N 18 13 E
Käpylä, Hels. 3 B4 60 13N 24 57 E
Karachi, Kar. 17 G11 24 50N 67 0 E
Karachi Int. Airport, Kar. 17 G11 24 51N 67 9 E
Karachi Univ., Kar. 17 G11 24 56N 67 0 E
Karagümrük, Ist. 17 A2 41 1N 28 56 E
Karāma, Bagd. 17 E8 33 20N 44 22 E
Karato, Ōsaka 12 B2 34 46N 135 12 E
Karave, Bomb. 16 G9 19 0N 73 0 E
Karet, Jak. 15 J9 6 12 S 106 49 E
Karkar Duman, Delhi 16 B2 28 39N 77 18 E
Karkh, Bagd. 17 E8 33 20N 44 22 E
Karlberg, Stock. 3 D11 59 20N 18 1 E
Karlin, Pra. 10 B2 50 5N 14 26 E
Karlsfeld, Mün. 7 F9 48 13N 11 28 E
Karlshorst, Berl. 7 B4 52 29N 13 31 E
Karlslunde Strand, Købn. 2 E8 55 33N 12 15 E
Karnap, Ruhr 6 A4 51 31N 7 0 E
Karolinenhof, Berl. 7 B4 52 23N 13 38 E
Karow, Berl. 7 A3 52 36N 13 29 E
Karrādah, Bagd. 17 F8 33 17N 44 23 E
Kärsön, Stock. 3 E10 59 19N 17 54 E
Kasai, Tōkyō 13 C4 35 39N 139 52 E
Kasetsart, Bangk. 15 A2 13 50N 100 34 E
Kashi-Hazaki, Tōkyō 13 A3 35 54N 139 42 E
Kashio, Tōkyō 13 D2 35 24N 139 34 E
Kashiwa, Tōkyō 13 A4 35 51N 139 57 E
Kashiwara, Ōsaka 12 C4 34 34N 135 37 E
Kaskela, Hels. 3 B5 60 17N 25 6 E
Kastrup, Købn. 2 E10 55 38N 12 39 E
Kastrup Lufthavn, Købn. 2 E11 55 37N 12 14 E
Kasuga, Tōkyō 13 B2 35 45N 139 38 E
Kasuge, Tōkyō 13 B3 35 45N 139 49 E
Kasumigasek, Tōkyō 13 C3 35 40N 139 46 E
Katabira →, Tōkyō 13 D2 35 27N 139 38 E
Katernberg, Ruhr 6 A4 51 30N 7 4 E
Katong Park, Sing. 15 G8 1 18N 103 53 E
Katrineberg, Stock. 3 E10 59 13N 17 54 E
Katsushika-Ku, Tōkyō 13 B4 35 44N 139 50 E
Kattinge Vig, Købn. 2 D7 55 40N 12 1 E
Kau Pei Chau, H.K. 12 E6 22 12N 114 15 E
Kau Yi Chau, H.K. 12 E5 22 17N 114 4 E
Kauklahti, Hels. 3 B2 60 11N 24 36 E
Kaulsdorf, Berl. 7 B4 52 29N 13 34 E
Kauniainen, Hels. 3 B3 60 13N 24 44 E
Kawagoe, Tōkyō 13 A1 35 54N 139 29 E
Kawaguchi, Tōkyō 13 B3 35 47N 139 43 E
Kawai, Tōkyō 13 D2 35 29N 139 31 E
Kawamukō, Tōkyō 13 C2 35 30N 139 34 E
Kawanishi, Ōsaka 12 B3 34 49N 135 24 E
Kawasaki, Tōkyō 13 C3 35 31N 139 43 E
Kawasaki Harbour, Tōkyō 13 D3 35 30N 139 47 E
Kawawa, Tōkyō 13 C2 35 31N 139 33 E
Kawęczyn, Wsaw. 10 E7 52 16N 21 5 E
Kayu Putih, Jak. 15 J10 6 10 S 106 53 E
Kbely, Pra. 10 B3 50 8N 14 32 E
Kearny, N.Y. 22 C4 40 45N 74 8W
Kebayoran Baru, Jak. 15 J9 6 14 S 106 47 E
Kebayoran Lama, Jak. 15 J9 6 13 S 106 46 E
Kebon Jeruk, Jak. 15 J9 6 11 S 106 46 E
Keferloh, Mün. 7 G11 48 5N 11 43 E
Keilor, Melb. 19 E6 37 42 S 144 50 E
Keilor East, Melb. 19 E6 37 44 S 144 51 E
Keimola, Hels. 3 A3 60 20N 24 49 E
Kelenföld, Bud. 10 K13 47 27N 19 2 E
Kelvedon Hatch, Lon. 4 A6 51 40N 0 15 E
Kelvin, Jobg. 18 E9 26 4 S 28 5 E
Kemang, Jak. 15 J9 6 15 S 106 48 E
Kemayoran, Jak. 15 J10 6 10 S 106 51 E
Kemayoran Airport, Jak. 15 H10 6 8 S 106 50 E
Kemp Mill, Wash. 25 C7 39 0N 77 1W
Kempton Park, Jobg. 18 E10 26 5 S 28 14 E
Kempton Racecourse, Lon. 4 C2 51 24N 0 23W
Kemsing, Lon. 4 D6 51 18N 0 12 E
Kendall Green, Bost. 21 C2 42 22N 71 16W
Kendua, Calc. 16 E5 22 34N 88 10 E
Keng Hau, H.K. 12 D6 22 22N 114 10 E
Kenilworth, Chic. 26 A2 42 5N 87 42W
Kenilworth, N.Y. 22 C3 40 40N 74 17W
Kenley, Lon. 4 D4 51 19N 0 5W
Kenmare, Jobg. 18 E7 26 6 S 27 48 E
Kennedy Grove Regional Rec. Area, S.F. 27 A3 37 56N 122 14W

40 Kennedy Town

Kennedy Town, *H.K.* 12 E5 22 16N 114 6 E
Kensal Green, *Lon.* 4 B3 51 32N 0 13W
Kensington, *Jobg.* 18 F9 26 11 S 28 6 E
Kensington, *Lon.* 4 C3 51 29N 0 10W
Kensington, *N.Y.* 22 D5 40 38N 73 57W
Kensington, *Phil.* 24 B4 39 59N 75 6W
Kensington, *S.F.* 27 A3 37 54N 122 17W
Kensington, *Syd.* 19 B4 33 54 S 151 13 E
Kensington, *Wash.* 25 C7 39 1N 77 4W
Kensington Palace, *Lon.* 4 B3 51 30N 0 11W
Kent Woodlands, *S.F.* 27 A1 37 56N 122 34W
Kentfield, *S.F.* 27 A1 37 57N 122 33W
Kentish Town, *Lon.* 4 B4 51 32N 0 8W
Kentland, *Wash.* 25 D8 38 55N 76 53W
Kenton, *Lon.* 4 B3 51 34N 0 17W
Kenwood, *Balt.* 25 A4 39 20N 76 30W
Kenwood, *Bost.* 21 B2 42 40N 71 14W
Kenwood House, *Lon.* 4 B4 51 34N 0 9W
Kepa, *Wsaw.* 10 E7 52 13N 21 3 E
Keppel Harbour, *Sing.* 15 G7 1 15N 103 49 E
Kerameikos, *Ath.* 8 J11 37 58N 23 42 E
Kerepes, *Bud.* 10 J14 47 33N 19 17 E
Keston, *Lon.* 4 C5 51 21N 0 1 E
Keston Mark, *Lon.* 4 C5 51 21N 0 2 E
Keth Wara, *Delhi* 16 A2 28 40N 77 13 E
Kettering, *Wash.* 25 D9 38 53N 76 49W
Kettwig, *Ruhr* 6 B3 51 22N 6 56 E
Kew, *Jobg.* 18 E9 26 7 S 28 5 E
Kew, *Lon.* 4 C3 51 28N 0 17W
Kew, *Melb.* 19 E7 37 48 S 145 2 E
Kew Gardens, *Lon.* 4 C3 51 28N 0 17W
Key Gardens, *Trto.* 20 E9 43 39N 79 18W
Khaboye, *St-Pet.* 11 B6 59 53N 30 44 E
Khaidhárion, *Ath.* 8 H10 38 2N 23 38 E
Khairna, *Bomb.* 16 G9 19 5N 73 0 E
Khalándrion, *Ath.* 8 H11 38 3N 23 48 E
Khalīj, *Bagd.* 17 E8 33 18N 44 28 E
Khansā, *Bagd.* 17 E8 33 21N 44 28 E
Kharavli, *Bomb.* 16 H8 18 54N 72 55 E
Khardah, *Calc.* 16 D6 22 43N 88 22 E
Khayala, *Delhi* 16 B1 28 39N 77 6 E
Khefren, *El Qâ.* 18 D4 29 58N 31 8 E
Khichripur, *Delhi* 16 B2 28 37N 77 18 E
Khimki, *Mos.* 11 D8 55 53N 37 24 E
Khimki-Khovrino, *Mos.* 11 D9 55 51N 37 31 E
Khimkinskoye Vdkr., *Mos.* 11 D8 55 51N 37 27 E
Khirvosti, *St-Pet.* 11 B5 59 56N 30 37 E
Khlongsan, *Bangk.* 15 B1 13 43N 100 29 E
Kholargós, *Ath.* 8 J11 37 59N 23 48 E
Khorel, *Calc.* 16 D5 22 41N 88 18 E
Khorosovo, *Mos.* 11 E8 55 46N 37 27 E
Khudrā, *Bagd.* 17 F7 33 19N 44 17 E
Khun Thian, *Bangk.* 15 B1 13 41N 100 27 E
Khuraiji Khas, *Delhi* 16 B2 28 38N 77 16 E
Khurigachi, *Calc.* 16 D5 22 48N 88 21 E
Kiamari, *Kar.* 17 H10 24 49N 66 58 E
Kidderpore, *Calc.* 16 E5 22 32N 88 19 E
Kienwerder, *Berl.* 7 B2 52 22N 13 11 E
Kierling, *Wien* 10 G9 48 18N 16 16 E
Kierlingbach →, *Wien* 10 G9 48 18N 16 19 E
Kierlinger Forst, *Wien* 10 G9 48 17N 16 14 E
Kierst, *Ruhr* 6 C2 51 18N 6 42 E
Kifisós →, *Ath.* 8 J11 37 58N 23 42 E
Kikenka →, *St-Pet.* 11 B2 59 50N 30 3 E
Kikuna, *Tōkyō* 13 C2 35 30N 139 37 E
Kil, *Stock.* 3 D12 59 20N 18 19 E
Kilburn, *Lon.* 4 B3 51 32N 0 11W
Killara, *Syd.* 19 A4 33 46 S 151 10 E
Kilo, *Hels.* 3 B3 60 13N 24 47 E
Kilokri, *Delhi* 16 B2 28 34N 77 15 E
Kilsyth, *Melb.* 19 E8 37 48 S 145 18 E
Kimberton, *Phil.* 24 A1 40 7N 75 34W
Kimlin Park, *Sing.* 15 G7 1 18N 103 50 E
Kindi, *Bagd.* 17 F8 33 18N 44 22 E
King of Prussia, *Phil.* 24 A2 40 5N 75 22W
Kings Cross, *Syd.* 19 B4 33 52 S 151 12 E
Kings Domain, *Melb.* 19 E6 37 49 S 144 58 E
Kings Mt., *S.F.* 27 D3 37 27N 122 19W
King's Park, *H.K.* 12 E6 22 18N 114 10 E
Kings Park, *Wash.* 25 E6 38 48N 77 17W
King's Point, *N.Y.* 23 C6 40 48N 73 45W
Kingsbury, *Lon.* 4 B3 51 34N 0 15W
Kingsford, *Syd.* 19 B4 33 55 S 151 14 E
Kingston upon Thames, *Lon.* 4 C3 51 24N 0 17W
Kingston Vale, *Lon.* 4 C3 51 25N 0 25W
Kingsway, *Trto.* 20 E7 43 38N 79 32W
Kingswood, *Lon.* 4 D3 51 17N 0 13W
Kinnelon, *N.Y.* 22 B2 40 59N 74 23W
Kipling Heights, *Trto.* 20 D7 43 43N 79 34W
Kipséli, *Ath.* 8 J11 37 59N 23 45 E
Kirchhellen, *Ruhr* 6 A3 51 36N 6 56 E
Kirchhörde, *Ruhr* 6 B6 51 27N 7 27 E
Kirchlinde, *Ruhr* 6 A6 51 31N 7 22 E
Kirchof, *Hbg.* 7 E8 53 29N 10 1 E
Kirchsteinbek, *Hbg.* 7 D8 53 31N 10 7 E
Kirchstockbach, *Mün.* 7 G11 48 1N 11 40 E
Kirchtrudering, *Mün.* 7 G11 48 7N 11 40 E
Kirdasa, *El Qâ.* 18 C4 30 2N 31 6 E
Kirikiri, *Lagos* 18 B1 6 26N 7 18 E
Kirkkonummi, *Hels.* 3 C1 60 6N 24 28W
Kirkland, *Mtrl.* 20 B2 43 26N 73 51W
Kirovskiye, Os., *St-Pet.* 11 B3 59 57N 30 14 E
Kisarazu, *Tōkyō* 13 D4 35 21N 139 54 E
Kisikli, *Ist.* 17 A3 41 1N 29 2 E
Kispest, *Bud.* 10 K13 47 27N 19 8 E
Kista, *Stock.* 3 D10 59 24N 17 57 E
Kistarcsa, *Bud.* 10 J14 47 32N 19 16 E
Kita, *Ōsaka* 12 B4 34 41N 135 30 E
Kita-Ku, *Tōkyō* 13 B3 35 44N 139 44 E
Kitain-Temple, *Tōkyō* 13 A1 35 54N 139 29 E
Kitazawa, *Tōkyō* 13 C3 35 39N 139 40 E
Kiu Tsiu, *H.K.* 12 D6 22 22N 114 17 E
Kivistö, *Hels.* 3 B4 60 18N 24 50 E
Kiyose, *Tōkyō* 13 B2 35 46N 139 31 E
Kiziltoprak, *Ist.* 17 B3 40 58N 29 3 E
Kizu →, *Ōsaka* 12 C3 34 37N 135 27 E
Kizuri, *Ōsaka* 12 C4 34 38N 135 34 E
Kjeller, *Oslo* 2 B6 59 58N 11 1 E
Kjelsås, *Oslo* 2 B4 59 57N 10 47 E
Kladow, *Berl.* 7 B1 52 27N 13 9 E
Klampenborg, *Købn.* 2 D10 55 46N 12 35 E
Klánovice, *Pra.* 10 B3 50 5N 14 40 E
Klaudyń, *Wsaw.* 10 E6 52 17N 20 50 E
Klecany, *Pra.* 10 A2 50 10N 14 24 E
Kledering, *Wien* 10 H10 48 8N 16 26 E
Klein Gleinicke, *Berl.* 7 B1 52 23N 13 5 E
Klein-Hadern, *Mün.* 7 G9 48 7N 11 28 E
Klein Jukskei →, *Jobg.* 18 E8 26 6 S 27 57 E
Kleinburg, *Trto.* 20 C7 43 51N 79 37W
Kleine Grasbrook, *Hbg.* 7 D7 53 31N 9 59 E
Kleinmachnow, *Berl.* 7 B2 52 24N 13 14 E
Kleinschönebeck, *Berl.* 7 B5 52 29N 13 42 E
Kleinziethen, *Berl.* 7 B3 52 22N 13 27 E
Klemetsrud, *Oslo* 2 B5 59 50N 10 51 E
Klender, *Jak.* 15 J10 6 12 S 106 53 E
Klippoortje, *Jobg.* 18 F10 26 14 S 28 10 E
Klipriviersberg, *Jobg.* 18 F9 26 16 S 28 2 E
Klipspruit →, *Jobg.* 18 F8 26 14 S 27 53 E
Kloofendal, *Jobg.* 18 E8 26 8 S 27 52 E
Klosterhardt, *Ruhr* 6 A3 51 32N 6 52 E
Klosterneuburg, *Wien* 10 G9 48 18N 16 19 E
Knockholt Pound, *Lon.* 4 D5 51 18N 0 7 E
Knowland State Arboretum and Park, *S.F.* 27 B4 37 45N 122 7W
Knox Park, *Melb.* 19 F8 37 54 S 145 15 E
Knoxville, *Melb.* 19 F8 37 53 S 145 14 E
Kōbanya, *Bud.* 10 K13 47 28N 19 9 E
Kobe, *Ōsaka* 12 B2 34 41N 135 13 E
Kōbe Harbour, *Ōsaka* 12 C2 34 39N 135 11 E
København, *Købn.* 2 D9 55 40N 12 26 E
Kobylisy, *Pra.* 10 B2 50 7N 14 26 E
Kobyłka, *Wsaw.* 10 D8 52 20N 21 10 E
Kocasinan, *Ist.* 17 A2 41 1N 28 50 E
Kočife, *Pra.* 10 B2 50 3N 14 21 E
Kodaira, *Tōkyō* 13 B1 35 43N 139 28 E
Kodanaka, *Tōkyō* 13 C2 35 34N 139 37 E
Kogane, *Tōkyō* 13 B4 35 49N 139 55 E
Koganei, *Tōkyō* 13 B2 35 42N 139 31 E
Kogarah, *Syd.* 19 B3 33 57 S 151 8 E
Køge Bugt, *Købn.* 2 E9 55 34N 12 24 E
Köhlbrand Rethe, *Hbg.* 7 D7 53 31N 9 56 E
Köhlfleet, *Hbg.* 7 D7 53 32N 9 53 E
Koivupää, *Hels.* 3 B4 60 18N 24 53 E
Koja, *Jak.* 15 H10 6 8 S 106 52 E
Koja Utara, *Jak.* 15 H10 6 5 S 106 53 E
Kokobunji, *Tōkyō* 13 B1 35 42N 139 27 E
Kokobunji-Temple, *Tōkyō* 13 B4 35 44N 139 55 E
Kol Scholven, *Ruhr* 6 A3 51 35N 6 59 E
Kolarängen, *Stock.* 3 E12 59 16N 18 10 E
Kolbotn, *Oslo* 2 C4 59 48N 10 48 E
Kole Kalyan, *Bomb.* 16 G8 19 5N 72 50 E
Kolmiranta, *Hels.* 3 B2 60 15N 24 31 E
Kolmperä, *Hels.* 3 B2 60 15N 24 32 E
Koło, *Wsaw.* 10 E6 52 14N 20 56 E
Kolodeje, *Pra.* 10 B3 50 3N 14 38 E
Kolokinthou, *Ath.* 8 J11 38 0N 23 42 E
Kolomenskoye, *Mos.* 11 E10 55 40N 37 40 E
Kolomyagi, *St-Pet.* 11 A3 60 0N 30 19 E
Kolónos, *Ath.* 8 J11 37 59N 23 43 E
Kolovraty, *Pra.* 10 B3 50 0N 14 37 E
Kolsås, *Oslo* 2 B3 59 55N 10 30 E
Koltushi, *St-Pet.* 11 B5 59 55N 30 38 E
Komae, *Tōkyō* 13 C2 35 37N 139 34 E
Komagome, *Tōkyō* 13 B3 35 43N 139 45 E
Komazawa, *Tōkyō* 13 C3 35 37N 139 40 E
Komdhara, *Calc.* 16 C5 22 52N 88 14 E
Kommunarka, *Mos.* 11 F8 55 35N 37 29 E
Komorów, *Wsaw.* 10 F5 52 9N 20 48 E
Kona, *Calc.* 16 E5 22 37N 88 18 E
Konala, *Hels.* 3 B4 60 14N 24 52 E
Kōnan, *Tōkyō* 13 D2 35 23N 139 35 E
Kondli, *Delhi* 16 B2 28 36N 77 19 E
Kong Sin Wan, *H.K.* 12 E5 22 15N 114 7 E
Kongelunden, *Købn.* 2 E10 55 34N 12 34 E
Kongens Lyngby, *Købn.* 2 D10 55 46N 12 30 E
Kongo, *Hels.* 3 A3 60 20N 24 47 E
Königshardt, *Ruhr* 6 A3 51 33N 6 51 E
Konnagar, *Calc.* 16 D6 22 42N 88 21 E
Konohana, *Ōsaka* 12 B3 34 40N 135 26 E
Kōnoike, *Ōsaka* 12 B4 34 42N 135 37 E
Konradshöhe, *Berl.* 7 A2 52 35N 13 13 E
Koonung Cr. →, *Melb.* 19 E7 37 46 S 145 4 E
Kopanina, *Pra.* 10 B1 50 3N 14 17 E
Koparkhairna, *Bomb.* 16 G8 19 6N 72 59 E
Köpenick, *Berl.* 7 B4 52 26N 13 35 E
Korangi, *Kar.* 17 H11 24 47N 67 8 E
Koremasa, *Tōkyō* 13 C1 35 39N 139 29 E
Korenevo, *Mos.* 11 E12 55 40N 38 0 E
Kori, *Ōsaka* 12 B4 34 47N 135 38 E
Koridhallós, *Ath.* 8 J10 37 59N 23 39 E
Korkinskoye, Oz., *St-Pet.* 11 B6 59 55N 30 42 E
Korne, *Ruhr* 6 A7 51 30N 7 30 E
Korso, *Hels.* 3 A5 60 21N 25 5 E
Koshigaya, *Tōkyō* 13 A3 35 53N 139 47 E
Kosino, *Mos.* 11 E11 55 43N 37 50 E
Kosugi, *Tōkyō* 13 C2 35 34N 139 39 E
Kota, *Jak.* 15 H9 6 7 S 106 48 E
Kotelyniki, *Mos.* 11 F11 55 39N 37 52 E
Kōtō-Ku, *Tōkyō* 13 B3 35 40N 139 48 E
Kotrang, *Calc.* 16 D6 22 41N 88 20 E
Kouponia, *Ath.* 8 J11 37 57N 23 47 E
Koviksudde, *Stock.* 3 D13 59 21N 18 21 E
Kowloon, *H.K.* 12 E5 22 18N 114 10 E
Kowloon City, *H.K.* 12 E6 22 19N 114 11 E
Kowloon Pk., *H.K.* 12 D6 22 20N 114 13 E
Kowloon Res., *H.K.* 12 D5 22 21N 114 9 E
Kowloon Tong, *H.K.* 12 D6 22 20N 114 10 E
Kozhukhovo, *Mos.* 11 E11 55 43N 37 53 E
Kozukue, *Tōkyō* 13 C2 35 30N 139 36 E
Krailling, *Mün.* 7 G9 48 5N 11 25 E
Kramat Jati, *Jak.* 15 J10 6 15 S 106 51 E
Krampnitz, *Berl.* 7 B1 52 27N 13 3 E
Krampnitzsee, *Berl.* 7 B1 52 27N 13 1 E
Kranji, *Sing.* 15 F7 1 26N 103 45 E
Kranji, Sungei →, *Sing.* 15 F7 1 26N 103 44 E
Kranji Dam, *Sing.* 15 F7 1 26N 103 44 E
Kraskovo, *Mos.* 11 F11 55 39N 37 58 E
Krasnaya Gorka, *St-Pet.* 11 B5 59 58N 30 38 E
Krasno-Presnenskaya, *Mos.* 11 E9 55 45N 37 32 E
Krasnogorsk, *Mos.* 11 E7 55 49N 37 18 E
Krasnyj Stroitel, *Mos.* 11 F9 55 36N 37 35 E
Kray, *Ruhr* 6 B4 51 27N 7 4 E
Krč, *Pra.* 10 B2 50 2N 14 26 E
Krefeld, *Ruhr* 6 B1 51 20N 6 34 E
Kremlin, *Mos.* 11 E9 55 45N 37 38 E
Kresson, *Phil.* 24 B5 39 51N 74 54W
Kreuzberg, *Berl.* 7 A3 52 30N 13 24 E
Krishnarampur, *Calc.* 16 D5 22 43N 88 13 E
Kritzendorf, *Wien* 10 G9 48 19N 16 18 E
Krokhol, *Oslo* 2 C5 59 48N 10 55 E
Krugersdorp, *Jobg.* 18 E7 26 6 S 27 48 E
Krukut, Kali →, *Jak.* 15 J9 6 13 S 106 48 E
Krumme Lanke, *Berl.* 7 B2 52 27N 13 14 E
Krummensee, *Berl.* 7 A5 52 35N 13 42 E
Krupunder, *Hbg.* 7 D7 53 37N 9 53 E
Krusboda, *Stock.* 3 E12 59 13N 18 14 E
Krylatskoye, *Mos.* 11 E8 55 45N 37 23 E
Küçükkoy, *Ist.* 17 A2 41 3N 28 52 E
Kudrovo, *St-Pet.* 11 B5 59 54N 30 30 E
Kuivasaari, *Hels.* 3 C5 60 8N 25 0 E
Kujiai, *Tōkyō* 13 A1 35 57N 139 26 E
Küllenhahn, *Ruhr* 6 C4 51 14N 7 8 E
Kulosaari, *Hels.* 3 B5 60 11N 25 0 E
Kulturpalasset, *Wsaw.* 10 E7 52 14N 21 0 E
Kumla, *Stock.* 3 E12 59 13N 18 11 E
Kummelnäs, *Stock.* 3 D12 59 21N 18 16 E
Kungens kurva, *Stock.* 3 E10 59 15N 17 53 E
Kungsängen, *Stock.* 3 D9 59 26N 17 43 E
Kungshatt, *Stock.* 3 E10 59 17N 17 51 E
Kungsholmen, *Stock.* 3 D11 59 20N 18 1 E
Kuningan, *Jak.* 15 J9 6 13 S 106 49 E
Kuninkaanmäki, *Hels.* 3 B5 60 18N 25 7 E
Kunitachi, *Tōkyō* 13 B1 35 41N 139 27 E
Kunming Hu, *Beij.* 14 B2 39 59N 116 13 E
Kunratice, *Pra.* 10 B3 50 0N 14 29 E
Kunratický →, *Pra.* 10 B2 50 1N 14 24 E
Kunsthalle, *Hbg.* 7 D8 53 33N 10 0 E
Kuntsevo, *Mos.* 11 E8 55 43N 37 23 E
Kupchino, *St-Pet.* 11 B4 59 50N 30 23 E
Kupferdreh, *Ruhr* 6 B4 51 23N 7 5 E
Kurbali Dere →, *Ist.* 17 B3 40 58N 29 1 E
Kurihara, *Tōkyō* 13 B2 35 45N 139 34 E
Kurkino, *Mos.* 11 D8 55 53N 37 22 E
Kurla, *Bomb.* 16 G8 19 4N 72 52 E
Kurmuri, *Bomb.* 16 G8 19 4N 72 53 E
Kurnell, *Syd.* 19 C4 34 0 S 151 10 E
Kurume, *Tōkyō* 13 B2 35 45N 139 31 E
Kuryanovo, *Mos.* 11 F10 55 39N 37 42 E
Kushihiki, *Tōkyō* 13 A2 35 54N 139 36 E
Kushtia, *Calc.* 16 E6 22 31N 88 23 E
Kuskovo, *Mos.* 11 E10 55 44N 37 48 E
Kutsino, *Mos.* 11 E11 55 44N 37 55 E
Kuy-e-Gīshā, *Tehr.* 17 C5 35 44N 51 23 E
Kuy-e-Mekānir, *Tehr.* 17 C5 35 46N 51 22 E
Kuzyminki, *Mos.* 11 E10 55 42N 37 46 E
Kvarnsjön, *Stock.* 3 E10 59 11N 17 58 E
Kwa-Thema, *Jobg.* 18 F11 26 17 S 28 23 E
Kwai Chung, *H.K.* 12 D5 22 22N 114 7 E
Kwitang, *Jak.* 15 J10 6 11 S 106 50 E
Kwun Tong, *H.K.* 12 E6 22 18N 114 13 E
Kyje, *Pra.* 10 B3 50 6N 14 33 E
Kyōhōji, *Tōkyō* 12 C4 34 38N 135 33 E
Kyrkfjärden, *Stock.* 3 E9 59 16N 17 45 E
Kyrkslätt, *Hels.* 3 C1 60 6N 24 28W

L

La Aguada, *Stgo* 30 J10 33 28 S 70 40W
La Blanca, *Stgo* 30 K11 33 30 S 70 40W
La Boca, *B.A.* 32 B4 34 38 S 58 22W
La Bottáccia, *Rome* 9 F8 41 54N 12 18 E
La Bretèche, *Paris* 5 B2 48 51N 2 1 E
La Brosse, *Paris* 5 C1 48 43N 1 20 E
La Cabana, *La Hab.* 30 B3 23 8N 82 20W
La Canada, *L.A.* 28 A3 34 12N 118 12W
La Cassa, *Tori.* 9 A2 45 11N 7 30 E
La Celle-les-Bordes, *Paris* 5 D1 48 38N 1 57 E
La Celle-St.-Cloud, *Paris* 5 B2 48 50N 2 9 E
La Chivera, *Car.* 30 D5 10 35N 66 54W
La Colmena, *Méx.* 29 A2 19 35N 99 16W
La Courneuve, *Paris* 5 B4 48 55N 2 22 E
La Crescenta, *L.A.* 28 A3 34 13N 118 14W
La Défense, *Paris* 5 B3 48 53N 2 12 E
La Dehesa, *Stgo* 30 J11 33 21 S 70 33W
La Estación, *Mdrd.* 8 B2 40 27N 3 48W
La Floresta, *Barc.* 8 D5 41 26N 2 3 E
La Florida, *Car.* 30 D5 10 30N 66 52W
La Fortuna, *Mdrd.* 8 B2 40 21N 3 46W
La Fransa, *Barc.* 8 D5 41 22N 2 9 E
La Fresnière, *Mtrl.* 20 A2 43 33N 73 58W
La Frette-sur-Seine, *Paris* 5 B3 48 58N 2 11 E
La Garenne-Colombes, *Paris* 5 B3 48 54N 2 15 E
La Giustiniana, *Rome* 9 F8 41 59N 12 24 E
La Grange, *Chic.* 26 C1 41 48N 87 53W
La Grange des Noues, *Paris* 5 A4 49 1N 2 28 E
La Grange Highlands, *Chic.* 26 C1 41 46N 87 53W
La Grange Park, *Chic.* 26 C1 41 49N 87 51W
La Granja, *Stgo* 30 K11 33 31 S 70 38W
La Guaira, *Car.* 30 D5 10 36N 66 55W
La Guardia Airport, *N.Y.* 23 C5 40 46N 73 52W
La Guasima, *La Hab.* 30 B3 23 0N 82 17W
La Habana, *La Hab.* 30 B2 23 7N 82 21W
La habana, B. de, *La Hab.* 30 B3 23 7N 82 20W
La Habana Vieia, *La Hab.* 30 B2 23 7N 82 20W
La Habra, *L.A.* 28 C5 33 56N 117 57W
La Habre Heights, *L.A.* 28 C5 33 59N 117 56W
La Horqueta →, *B.A.* 32 C1 34 43 S 58 51W
La Lisa, *La Hab.* 30 B2 23 3N 82 25W
La Llacuna, *Barc.* 8 D6 41 24N 2 12 E
La Loma, *Méx.* 29 A2 19 31N 99 11W
La Lucila, *B.A.* 32 B4 34 30 S 58 29W
La Magdalena Atlipac, *Méx.* 29 B4 19 22N 89 56 E
La Magdalena Chichicaspa, *Méx.* 29 B2 19 24N 99 18W
La Magdalena Contreras, *Méx.* 29 C2 19 17N 99 13W
La Magdalena Petlalco, *Méx.* 29 C2 19 13N 99 10W
La Maison Blanche, *Paris* 5 C1 48 44N 1 54 E
La Maladrerie, *Paris* 5 B2 48 54N 2 1 E
La Marquesa, *Méx.* 29 C1 19 18N 99 22W
La Milla, Cerro, *Lima* 30 G8 12 3 S 77 5W
La Molina, *Lima* 30 G9 12 4 S 76 56W
La Monachina, *Rome* 9 F9 41 53N 12 21 E
La Moraleja, *Mdrd.* 8 A3 40 30N 30 38W
La Nopalera, *Méx.* 29 C3 19 18N 99 5W
La Pastora, *Car.* 30 D5 10 31N 66 55W
La Paterna, *B.A.* 32 B4 34 35 S 58 26W
La Patte-d'Oie, *Paris* 5 A3 49 0N 2 10 E
La Perla, *Lima* 30 G8 12 4 S 77 7W
La Perouse, *Syd.* 19 B4 33 59 S 151 14 E
La Pineda, *Barc.* 8 E5 41 15N 2 1 E
La Pisana, *Rome* 9 F9 41 51N 12 23 E
La Playa, *La Hab.* 30 B2 23 6N 82 26W
La Prairie, *Mtrl.* 20 B5 43 25N 73 29W
La Puente, *L.A.* 28 B5 34 1N 117 54W
La Punta, *Lima* 30 G7 12 4 S 77 10W
La Puntigala, *Barc.* 8 D6 41 27N 2 13 E
La Queue-en-Brie, *Paris* 5 C5 48 47N 2 34 E
La Reina, *Stgo* 30 J11 33 26 S 70 33W
La Reja, *B.A.* 32 B2 34 38 S 58 48W
La Ribera, *Barc.* 8 D5 41 21N 2 4 E
La Romanie, *Paris* 5 C1 48 43N 1 53 E
La Rústica, *Rome* 9 F10 41 54N 12 36 E
La Sagrera, *Barc.* 8 D6 41 25N 2 11 E
La Salada, *B.A.* 32 C4 34 43 S 58 27W
La Scala, *Mil.* 9 E6 45 28N 9 11 E
La Selce, *Rome* 9 F9 41 53N 12 20 E
La Sierra, *La Hab.* 30 B2 23 7N 82 24W
La Taxonera, *Barc.* 8 D6 41 25N 2 8 E
La Vega, *Car.* 30 E5 10 28N 66 56W
La Verrière, *Paris* 5 C1 48 45N 1 57 E
La Vibora, *La Hab.* 30 B3 23 5N 82 21W
La Victoria, *Lima* 30 G8 12 3 S 77 2W
La Ville-du-Bois, *Paris* 5 D3 48 39N 2 16 E
Laab im Walde, *Wien* 10 H9 48 9N 16 10 E
Laaer Berg, *Wien* 10 H10 48 9N 16 23 E
Laajalahti, *Hels.* 3 B3 60 11N 24 48 E
Laajasalo, *Hels.* 3 B5 60 10N 25 1 E
Laaksolahti, *Hels.* 3 B3 60 14N 24 45 E
Laar, *Ruhr* 6 B2 51 27N 6 44 E
Lablâba, W. el →, *El Qâ.* 18 C5 30 1N 31 19 E
Lachine, *Mtrl.* 20 B3 43 26N 73 42W
Ládví, *Pra.* 10 B2 50 8N 14 27 E
Łady, *Wsaw.* 10 F6 52 8N 20 57 E
Lafayette, *S.F.* 27 A4 37 52N 122 6W
Lafayette Hill, *Phil.* 24 A3 40 5N 75 15W
Lafayette Res., *S.F.* 27 A4 37 52N 122 8W
Laferrere, *B.A.* 32 C3 34 45 S 58 35W
Lagny, *Paris* 5 B6 48 52N 2 42 E
Lagoa da Pedra, *Lisb.* 8 F9 38 43N 8 58W
Lagos, *Lagos* 18 B2 6 27N 7 23 E
Lagos Harbour, *Lagos* 18 B2 6 26N 7 23 E
Lagos-Ikeja Airport, *Lagos* 18 A1 6 34N 7 19 E
Lagos Island, *Lagos* 18 B2 6 26N 7 23 E
Lagos Lagoon, *Lagos* 18 B2 6 30N 7 28 E
Laguna de B., *Manila* 15 E4 14 29N 121 6 E
Laim, *Mün.* 7 G10 48 7N 11 30 E
Lainate, *Mil.* 9 D5 45 34N 9 1 E
Lainz, *Wien* 10 H9 48 10N 16 16 E
Lainzer Tiergarten, *Wien* 10 G9 48 10N 16 13 E
Lajeado →, *S. Pau.* 31 E7 23 28 S 46 24W
Lake Avenue Woods, *Chic.* 26 A1 42 4N 87 53W
Lake Hiawatha, *N.Y.* 22 B2 40 52N 74 23W
Lakefield, *Jobg.* 18 F10 26 11 S 28 17 E
Lakemba, *Syd.* 19 B3 33 55 S 151 5 E
Lakeside, *Jobg.* 18 E9 26 5 S 28 8 E
Lakeview, *Chic.* 26 B3 41 56N 87 38W
Lakeview, *Trto.* 20 E7 43 35N 79 32W
Lakhtinskiy, *St-Pet.* 11 B2 59 59N 30 9 E
Lakhtinskiy Razliv, Oz., *St-Pet.* 11 B3 59 59N 30 12 E
Lakshmanpur, *Calc.* 16 E5 22 38N 88 16 E
Laleham, *Lon.* 4 C2 51 24N 0 29W
Lâleli, *Ist.* 17 A2 41 0N 28 57 E
Lalor, *Melb.* 19 E6 37 40 S 144 59 E
Lam San, *Sing.* 15 F7 1 22N 103 43 E
Lam Tin, *H.K.* 12 E6 22 18N 114 14 E
Lambarfjärden, *Stock.* 3 D9 59 21N 17 48 E
Lambert, *Oslo* 2 B4 59 52N 10 48 E
Lambeth, *Lon.* 4 C4 51 28N 0 6W
Lambrate, *Mil.* 9 E6 45 28N 9 16 E
Lambro →, *Mil.* 9 E6 45 24N 9 17 E
Lambro, Parco, *Mil.* 9 E6 45 29N 9 14 E
Lambton, *Jobg.* 18 F10 26 14 S 28 10 E
Lambton Hills, *Trto.* 20 E7 43 39N 79 30W
Lamma I., *H.K.* 12 E5 22 12N 114 7 E
Lampton, *Lon.* 4 C2 51 28N 0 21W
Landianchang, *Beij.* 14 B2 39 57N 116 13 E
Landover Hills, *Wash.* 25 D8 38 56N 76 54W
Landstrasse, *Wien* 10 G10 48 12N 16 23 E
Landwehr kanal, *Berl.* 7 B3 52 29N 13 24 E
Lane Cove, *Syd.* 19 A3 33 48 S 151 9 E
Lane Cove National Park, *Syd.* 19 A3 33 47 S 151 8 E
Langen, *Oslo* 2 C5 59 44N 10 57 E
Langenberg, *Ruhr* 6 B4 51 20N 7 7 E
Langenbochum, *Ruhr* 6 A4 51 36N 7 7 E
Langendreer, *Ruhr* 6 B5 51 28N 7 18 E
Langenhorn, *Hbg.* 7 D7 53 39N 9 59 E
Langenhorst, *Ruhr* 6 B4 51 21N 7 1 E
Langenzersdorf, *Wien* 10 G10 48 18N 16 21 E
Langer See, *Berl.* 7 B4 52 24N 13 37 E
Langerfeld, *Ruhr* 6 C5 51 16N 7 14 E
Langley, *Wash.* 25 D6 38 57N 77 11W
Langley Park, *Wash.* 25 D8 38 59N 76 58W
Langstaff, *Trto.* 20 C8 43 50N 79 26W
Längtarmen, *Stock.* 3 D8 59 24N 17 36 E
Langwald, *Mün.* 7 F9 48 10N 11 25 E
Lanham, *Wash.* 25 D8 38 59N 76 51W
Lank-Latum, *Ruhr* 6 C2 51 18N 6 40 E
Lankwitz, *Berl.* 7 B3 52 25N 13 21 E
Länna Drevviken, *Stock.* 3 E11 59 12N 18 8 E
L'Annunziatella, *Rome* 9 G10 41 49N 12 33 E
Lansdowne, *Balt.* 25 B3 39 14N 76 38W
Lansdowne, *Phil.* 24 B3 39 56N 75 16W
Lansing, *Trto.* 20 D8 43 45N 79 24W
Lanús, *B.A.* 32 C4 34 42 S 58 23W
Lapa, *Rio J.* 31 B2 22 54 S 43 10W
Lapa, *S. Pau.* 31 E5 23 31 S 46 42W
Lapangan Merdeka, *Jak.* 15 J9 6 10 S 106 49 E
Lapinkylä, *Hels.* 3 B4 60 18N 24 51 E
Lapinkylä, *Hels.* 3 B1 60 13N 24 27 E
Lappböle, *Hels.* 3 B1 60 13N 24 27 E
Laranjeiras, *Rio J.* 31 B2 22 55 S 43 10W
Larchmont, *N.Y.* 23 B6 40 55N 73 44W
Larkspur, *S.F.* 27 A1 37 55N 122 31W
Las, *Wsaw.* 10 E7 52 13N 21 6 E
Las Acacias, *Car.* 30 E5 10 29N 66 54W
Las Adjuntas, *Car.* 30 E4 10 25N 67 0W
Las Barrancas, *B.A.* 32 A4 34 28 S 58 29W
Las Conchas, *B.A.* 32 A3 34 25 S 58 34W
Las Corts, *Barc.* 8 D5 41 23N 2 9 E
Las Fuentes Brotantes, *Méx.* 29 C2 19 16N 99 11W
Las Kabacki, *Wsaw.* 10 F7 52 7N 21 2 E
Las Lomas, *L.A.* 28 B5 34 8N 117 59W
Las Mercedes, *Car.* 30 E5 10 29N 66 51W
Las Pinas, *Manila* 15 E3 14 29N 120 58 E
Las Rejas, *Stgo* 30 J10 33 27 S 70 42W
Las Rozas de Madrid, *Mdrd.* 8 B1 40 29N 3 52W
Las Trampas Cr. →, *S.F.* 27 A4 37 53N 122 6W
Las Trampas Regional Park, *S.F.* 27 B4 37 49N 122 3W
Las Trampas Ridge, *S.F.* 27 A4 37 50N 122 3W
Las Tunitas, *Car.* 30 D4 10 36N 67 1W
Lasalle, *Mtrl.* 20 B4 43 26N 73 37W
Lasek Bielański, *Wsaw.* 10 E6 52 17N 20 57 E
Lasek Na Kole, *Wsaw.* 10 E6 52 15N 20 56 E
Laski, *Wsaw.* 10 E6 52 18N 20 50 E
Latina, *Mdrd.* 8 B2 40 24N 3 44W
Latrobe Univ., *Melb.* 19 E7 37 43 S 145 3 E
Lattingtown, *N.Y.* 23 B7 40 52N 73 34W
Laufzorn, *Mün.* 7 G10 48 0N 11 33 E
Laurel Hollow, *N.Y.* 23 B8 40 51N 73 28W
Laurel Springs, *Phil.* 24 C4 39 49N 75 0W
Laurelton, *N.Y.* 23 C6 40 40N 73 45W
Laurence Hanscom Field, *Bost.* 21 C2 42 28N 71 16W
Lausdomini, *Nápl.* 9 H13 40 55N 14 26 E
Lauttasaari, *Hels.* 3 C4 60 9N 24 53 E
Lava Nuova, *Nápl.* 9 J13 40 47N 14 23 E
Laval-des-Rapides, *Mtrl.* 20 A3 43 33N 73 41W
Laval-Ouest, *Mtrl.* 20 A3 43 33N 73 52W
Laval-sur-le-Lac, *Mtrl.* 20 A2 43 32N 73 52W
Lavradio, *Lisb.* 8 F8 38 40N 9 2W
Lawndale, *Chic.* 26 B2 41 50N 87 42W
Lawndale, *L.A.* 28 C2 33 52N 118 22W
Lawndale, *Phil.* 24 A4 40 3N 75 5W
Lawnside, *Phil.* 24 B4 39 51N 75 1W
Lawrence, *Bost.* 21 A3 42 42N 71 10W
Lawrence, *N.Y.* 23 D6 40 36N 73 43W
Lawrence Heights, *Trto.* 20 D8 43 43N 79 25W
Lawrence Park, *Phil.* 24 B2 39 57N 75 20W
Lawton, *La Hab.* 30 B2 23 5N 82 20W
Layāri, *Kar.* 17 G11 24 52N 67 0 E
Layāri →, *Kar.* 17 G10 24 52N 66 58 E
Lazienkowski Park, *Wsaw.* 10 E7 52 13N 21 1 E
Le Blanc-Mesnil, *Paris* 5 B4 48 56N 2 27 E
Le Bourget, *Paris* 5 B4 48 56N 2 25 E
Le Chesnay, *Paris* 5 C2 48 49N 2 8 E
Le Christ de Saclay, *Paris* 5 C3 48 43N 1 59 E
Le Kremlin-Bicêtre, *Paris* 5 C4 48 48N 2 21 E
Le Mesnil-Amelot, *Paris* 5 A5 49 1N 2 35 E
Le Mesnil-le-Roi, *Paris* 5 B2 48 56N 2 7 E
Le Mesnil-St.-Denis, *Paris* 5 C1 48 44N 1 57 E
Le Pecq, *Paris* 5 B2 48 53N 2 6 E
Le Perreux, *Paris* 5 B4 48 50N 2 29 E
Le Pin, *Paris* 5 B5 48 54N 2 37 E
Le Plessis-Bouchard, *Paris* 5 A3 49 0N 2 14 E
Le Plessis-Gassot, *Paris* 5 A4 49 2N 2 24 E
Le Plessis-Pâté, *Paris* 5 D3 48 36N 2 19 E
Le Plessis-Robinson, *Paris* 5 C3 48 47N 2 15 E
Le Plessis-Trévise, *Paris* 5 C5 48 48N 2 34 E
Le Port-Marly, *Paris* 5 B2 48 52N 2 6 E
Le Pré-St.-Gervais, *Paris* 5 B4 48 53N 2 23 E
Le Raincy, *Paris* 5 B5 48 53N 2 31 E
Le Thillay, *Paris* 5 A4 49 0N 2 28 E
Le Trappe, *Mtrl.* 20 B1 43 30N 74 1W
Le Val d'Enfer, *Paris* 5 C3 48 45N 2 11 E
Le Vésinet, *Paris* 5 B2 48 54N 2 8 E
Lea →, *Lon.* 4 B4 51 30N 0 2W
Lea Bridge, *Lon.* 4 B4 51 33N 0 2W
Leakin Park, *Balt.* 25 B2 39 18N 76 41W
Leaside, *Trto.* 20 D8 43 42N 79 22W
Leatherhead, *Lon.* 4 D3 51 17N 0 19W
Leaves Green, *Lon.* 4 D5 51 19N 0 1 E
Leblon, *Rio J.* 31 B2 22 59 S 43 14W
Léchelle, Forêt de la, *Paris* 5 C6 48 43N 2 41 E
Ledøje, *Købn.* 2 D8 55 42N 12 18 E
Lee, *Lon.* 4 C5 51 27N 0 0 E
Leeupan, *Jobg.* 18 F10 26 13 S 28 18 E
Leganes, *Mdrd.* 8 C2 40 19N 3 45W
Legazpi, *Mdrd.* 8 B2 40 23N 3 41W
Legoa, Kali →, *Jak.* 15 H10 6 6 S 106 52 E
Lehtisaaret, *Hels.* 3 C3 60 6N 24 46 E
Lehtisaari, *Hels.* 3 B4 60 10N 24 51 E
Lei Yue Mun, *H.K.* 12 E6 22 17N 114 14 E
Leião, *Lisb.* 8 F7 38 43N 9 17W
Leichhardt, *Syd.* 19 B3 33 53 S 151 9 E
Leigang, *Gzh.* 14 G7 23 2N 113 6 E
Léini, *Tori.* 9 A3 45 11N 7 42 E
Leisure World, *S.F.* 27 A4 37 51N 122 4W
Lemoyne, *Mtrl.* 20 B5 43 29N 73 29W
Lemsahl, *Hbg.* 7 C8 53 41N 10 5 E
Lenin, *Mos.* 11 E9 55 43N 37 34 E
Leningrad = St. Petersburg, *St-Pet.* 11 B3 59 55N 30 15 E
Lenino, *Mos.* 11 F9 55 38N 37 39 E
Leninskiye Gory, *Mos.* 11 E9 55 41N 37 32 E
Lenne →, *Ruhr* 6 B7 51 25N 7 30 E
Lennep, *Ruhr* 6 C5 51 11N 7 15 E
Lenni, *Phil.* 24 B2 39 53N 75 27W
Lennox, *L.A.* 28 C2 33 56N 118 20W
Leonardo da Vinci, Aeroporto Int., *Rome* 9 G8 41 47N 12 15 E
Leoncio Martinez, *Car.* 30 E6 10 29N 66 48W
Leonia, *N.Y.* 22 B5 40 51N 73 59W
Leopard, *Phil.* 24 A2 40 1N 75 26W
Leopardi, *Nápl.* 9 J13 40 45N 14 24 E
Leopoldau, *Wien* 10 G10 48 15N 16 26 E
Leopoldstadt, *Wien* 10 G10 48 13N 16 22 E
Leportovo, *Mos.* 11 E10 55 46N 37 43 E
Leppävaara, *Hels.* 3 B3 60 13N 24 49 E
Lera, Mte., *Tori.* 9 A1 45 10N 7 27 E
L'Éremo, *Tori.* 9 B3 45 2N 7 44 E
Les Alluets-le-Roi, *Paris* 5 B1 48 54N 1 55 E
Les Clayes-sous-Bois, *Paris* 5 C1 48 49N 1 59 E
Les Essarts-le-Roi, *Paris* 5 C1 48 42N 1 53 E
Les Gâtines, *Paris* 5 C1 48 48N 1 58 E
Les Grésillons, *Paris* 5 B2 48 56N 2 1 E
Les Layes, *Paris* 5 C1 48 43N 1 55 E
Les Lilas, *Paris* 5 B4 48 52N 2 25 E
Les Loges-en-Josas, *Paris* 5 C2 48 45N 2 8 E
Les Molières, *Paris* 5 C2 48 40N 2 4 E
Les Mureaux, *Paris* 5 B1 48 59N 1 54 E
Les Pavillons-sous-Bois, *Paris* 5 B5 48 54N 2 30 E
Les Vaux de Cernay →, *Paris* 5 C1 48 41N 1 59 E
Lésigny, *Paris* 5 C5 48 44N 2 37 E
Lesnosavodskaya, *St-Pet.* 11 B4 59 51N 30 29 E
Lesnoy, *St-Pet.* 11 B4 59 59N 30 22 E
Lester B. Pearson Int. Airport, *Trto.* 20 D7 43 40N 79 38 E
L'Étang-la-Ville, *Paris* 5 B2 48 52N 2 4 E
Letná, *Pra.* 10 B2 50 0 S 14 26 E
Letňany, *Pra.* 10 B3 50 8N 14 30 E
Letovo, *Mos.* 11 F8 55 34N 37 24 E
Leuville-sur-Orge, *Paris* 5 D3 48 36N 2 15 E
Levallois-Perret, *Paris* 5 B3 48 53N 2 16 E
Lévis St.-Nom, *Paris* 5 C1 48 43N 1 57 E
Levittown, *N.Y.* 23 C7 40 43N 73 31W
Lewisdale, *Wash.* 25 D8 38 58N 76 59W
Lewisham, *Jobg.* 18 E7 26 7 S 27 49 E
Lewisham, *Lon.* 4 C4 51 27N 0 1W
Lexington, *Bost.* 21 C2 42 25N 71 12W
Leyton, *Lon.* 4 B4 51 33N 0 1W
Leytonstone, *Lon.* 4 B5 51 34N 0 0 E
L'Hautil, *Paris* 5 A2 49 0N 2 0 E
L'Hay-les-Roses, *Paris* 5 C4 48 46N 2 20 E
Lhotka, *Pra.* 10 B2 50 1N 14 26 E
Liangshui He →, *Beij.* 14 C3 39 48N 116 23 E
Lianhua Chi, *Beij.* 14 B2 39 52N 116 16 E
Lianhua He →, *Beij.* 14 B2 39 52N 116 22 E
Lianozovo, *Mos.* 11 D9 55 53N 37 34 E
Libčice nad Vitavou, *Pra.* 10 A2 50 11N 14 22 E
Liben, *Pra.* 10 B2 50 6N 14 27 E
Liberdade, *S. Pau.* 31 E6 23 33 S 46 37W
Libertad, *B.A.* 32 C2 34 41 S 58 41W
Liberty I., *N.Y.* 22 C4 40 41N 74 2W
Liberty Plain, *Bost.* 21 D4 42 11N 70 52W
Liberty Res., *Balt.* 25 A1 39 23N 76 52W
Libeznice, *Pra.* 10 A2 50 11N 14 29 E
Library of Congress, *Wash.* 25 D7 38 53N 77 0W
Libuč, *Pra.* 10 B2 50 0N 14 27 E
Lichiao, *Gzh.* 14 G8 23 3N 113 18 E
Lichtenbroich, *Ruhr* 6 C2 51 17N 6 49 E
Lichtenburg, *Berl.* 7 A4 52 31N 13 30 E
Lichtenplatz, *Ruhr* 6 C5 51 14N 7 11 E
Lichtenrade, *Berl.* 7 B3 52 23N 13 24 E
Lichterfelde, *Berl.* 7 B2 52 25N 13 19 E
Licignano di Nápoli, *Nápl.* 9 H13 40 54N 14 21 E
Lidcombe, *Syd.* 19 B3 33 52 S 151 3 E
Lidingö, *Stock.* 3 D11 59 21N 18 8 E
Lido Beach, *N.Y.* 23 D7 40 35N 73 37W
Lier, *Oslo* 2 C1 59 47N 10 13 E
Lierskogen, *Oslo* 2 C1 59 49N 10 18 E
Lieshi Lingyuan, *Gzh.* 14 G8 23 7N 113 16 E
Liesing, *Wien* 10 H9 48 8N 16 17 E
Liesing →, *Wien* 10 H10 48 8N 16 28 E
Lieusant, *Paris* 5 D5 48 38N 2 33 E
Liffjofs, *Hels.* 3 B6 60 19N 25 12 E
Ligovo, *St-Pet.* 11 B3 59 50N 30 13 E
Lijordet, *Oslo* 2 B3 59 56N 10 31 E
Likhoborka →, *Mos.* 11 D9 55 50N 37 37 E
Likova →, *Mos.* 11 F8 55 36N 37 20 E
Lilla Värtan, *Stock.* 3 D12 59 20N 18 11 E
Lille Rørbæk, *Købn.* 2 D7 55 47N 12 6 E

42 Midlothian

Midlothian, Chic. 26 D2 41 37N 87 43W
Miedzeszyn, Wsaw. 10 E8 52 10N 21 11 E
Międzylesie, Wsaw. 10 E8 52 12N 21 10 E
Miessaari, Hels. 3 C3 60 8N 24 47 E
Mikhaylovskoye, Mos. 11 F9 55 35N 37 35 E
Mikhelysona, Mos. 11 E11 55 42N 37 52 E
Milano, Mil. 9 E5 45 28N 9 10 E
Milano Due, Mil. 9 E6 45 29N 9 16 E
Milano San Felice, Mil. 9 E6 45 28N 9 18 E
Milanolago, Mil. 9 E6 45 27N 9 17 E
Milbertshofen, Mün. 7 F10 48 10N 11 34 E
Milburn, N.Y. 22 C3 40 43N 74 19W
Milford, Balt. 25 A2 39 21N 76 43W
Mill Cr. →, S.F. 27 A1 37 53N 122 31W
Mill Hill, Lon. 4 B3 51 37N 0 14W
Mill Neck, N.Y. 23 B7 40 53N 73 33W
Mill Park, Melb. 19 E7 37 40 S 145 3 E
Mill Valley, S.F. 27 A1 37 54N 122 33W
Millbrae, S.F. 27 C2 37 35N 122 22W
Mille-Iles, R. des →, Mtrl. 20 A3 43 39N 73 46W
Miller I., Balt. 25 B4 39 15N 76 21W
Miller Meadow, Chic. 26 B2 41 51N 87 49W
Milliken, Trto. 20 D9 43 49N 79 17W
Millis, Bost. 21 D1 42 10N 71 21W
Mills College, S.F. 27 B3 37 46N 122 10W
Milltown, Phil. 24 B1 39 57N 75 32W
Millwall, Lon. 4 C4 51 29N 0 0 E
Millwood, Wash. 25 D8 38 52N 76 52W
Milon-la-Chapelle, Paris 5 C2 48 43N 2 3 E
Milpa Alta, Méx. 29 C3 19 11N 99 0W
Milperra, Syd. 19 B2 33 56 S 150 59 E
Milspe, Ruhr 6 C5 51 18N 7 19 E
Milton, Bost. 21 D3 42 14N 71 2W
Milton Village, Bost. 21 D3 42 15N 71 4W
Mimico, Trto. 20 E8 43 36N 79 29W
Mimico Cr. →, Trto. 20 E7 43 37N 79 33W
Minami, Ōsaka 12 B4 34 40N 135 30 E
Minami-Ku, Tōkyō 13 D2 35 24N 139 37 E
Minami-tsunashima, Tōkyō 13 C2 35 32N 139 37 E
Minato, Ōsaka 12 C3 34 39N 135 25 E
Minato-Ku, Tōkyō 13 C3 35 39N 139 44 E
Mine, Tōkyō 13 B3 35 49N 139 46 E
Minebank Run →, Balt. 25 A3 39 24N 76 33W
Mineola, N.Y. 23 C7 40 44N 73 38W
Ministro Rivadavia, B.A. 32 D4 34 50 S 58 22W
Minō, Ōsaka 12 B3 34 49N 135 28 E
Minshât el Bekkarî, El Qâ. 18 C4 30 0N 31 8 E
Minto, Syd. 19 C2 34 1 S 150 51 E
Minute Man Nat. Hist. Park, Bost. 21 C2 42 25N 71 16W
Mirafiori, Tori. 9 B2 45 1N 7 36 E
Miraflores, Lima 30 G8 12 7 S 77 2W
Miramar, La Hab. 30 B2 23 7N 82 25W
Miramar, S.F. 27 D2 37 29N 122 27W
Miranda, Syd. 19 C3 34 2 S 151 6 E
Mirzapur, Calc. 16 D6 22 49N 88 24 E
Misato, Tōkyō 13 B4 35 49N 139 51 E
Misericordia, Sa. da, Rio J. 31 B2 22 51 S 43 17W
Mishawum L., Bost. 21 B3 42 30N 71 8W
Mission, S.F. 27 B2 37 44N 122 25W
Mississauga, Trto. 20 E7 43 35N 79 34W
Mitaka, Tōkyō 13 B2 35 41N 139 34 E
Mitcham, Lon. 4 C3 51 23N 0 10W
Mitcham, Melb. 19 E8 37 48 S 145 12 E
Mitcham Common, Lon. 4 C4 51 23N 0 8W
Mitino, Mos. 11 D8 55 51N 37 20 E
Mitry, Paris 5 B5 48 59N 2 36 E
Mitry-Mory, Paris 5 B5 48 59N 2 38 E
Mitry-Mory, Aérodrome de, Paris 5 B5 48 59N 2 37 E
Mitte, Berl. 7 A3 52 32N 13 24 E
Mittel Isarkanal, Mün. 7 F11 48 12N 11 40 E
Mittenheim, Mün. 7 F10 48 15N 11 33 E
Mixcoac, Presa de, Méx. 29 B2 19 21N 99 14W
Mixquic, Méx. 29 C4 19 13N 98 58W
Miyakojima, Ōsaka 12 B4 34 42N 135 31 E
Miyalo, Tōkyō 13 B2 35 49N 139 35 E
Mizonokuchi, Tōkyō 13 C2 35 35N 139 34 E
Mizue, Tōkyō 13 B4 35 41N 139 54 E
Mizuko, Tōkyō 13 A2 35 50N 139 32 E
Mizumoto, Tōkyō 13 B4 35 46N 139 52 E
Młocinski Park, Wsaw. 10 E6 52 19N 20 57 E
Młociny, Wsaw. 10 E6 52 18N 20 55 E
Mnevniki, Mos. 11 E8 55 45N 37 28 E
Moba, Lagos 18 B2 6 26N 7 28 E
Moczydło, Wsaw. 10 F7 52 8N 21 2 E
Modderfontein, Jobg. 18 E10 26 5 S 28 10 E
Modderfontein →, Jobg. 18 E9 26 5 S 28 10 E
Modřany, Pra. 10 B2 50 0N 14 24 E
Moers, Ruhr 6 B1 51 26N 6 37 E
Moffat Park, Jobg. 18 F9 26 15 S 28 4 E
Mofolo, Jobg. 18 F8 26 13 S 27 53 E
Mog, Sŏul 12 G7 37 32N 126 52 E
Mogyorod, Bud. 10 J14 47 35N 19 14 E
Mohili, Bomb. 16 G8 19 5N 72 52 E
Moinho Velho →, S. Pau. 31 E6 23 35 S 46 35W
Moissy-Cramayel, Paris 5 D5 48 37N 2 35 E
Moita, Lisb. 8 G9 38 39N 8 59W
Mokotów, Wsaw. 10 E7 52 12N 21 0 E
Molapo, Jobg. 18 F8 26 15 S 27 51 E
Mole →, Lon. 4 D2 51 14N 0 20W
Moletsane, Jobg. 18 F8 26 14 S 27 50 E
Molino de Rosas, Méx. 29 B2 19 21N 99 14W
Mølleå →, Købn. 2 D10 55 48N 12 35 E
Möllen, Ruhr 6 A2 51 35N 6 41 E
Mollins de Rey, Barc. 8 D5 41 24N 2 1 E
Molokovo, Mos. 11 F11 55 35N 37 53 E
Mombaça, S. Pau. 31 E7 23 37 S 46 25W
Mombello, Mil. 9 D5 45 36N 9 7 E
Momote, Tōkyō 13 B2 35 46N 139 37 E
Monash Univ., Melb. 19 F7 37 54 S 145 8 E
Monbulk Cr. →, Melb. 19 F8 37 55 S 145 12 E
Moncalieri, Tori. 9 B3 45 0N 7 41 E
Moncolombone, Tori. 9 A1 45 12N 7 28 E
Mondeor, Jobg. 18 F9 26 16 S 28 0 E
Moneda, Palacio de la, Stgo 30 J11 33 26 S 70 39W
Mong Kok, H.K. 12 E6 22 19N 114 10 E
Mongat, Barc. 8 D6 41 27N 2 16 E
Mongreno, Tori. 9 B3 45 3N 7 45 E
Moninos →, S. Pau. 31 F6 23 40 S 46 33W
Monrovia, L.A. 28 B4 34 9N 118 1W
Monsanto, Lisb. 8 F7 38 44N 9 12W
Monsanto, Parque Florestal de, Lisb. 8 F7 38 43N 9 11W
Mont Royal, Mtrl. 20 A4 43 30N 73 38W
Mont-Royal, Parc, Mtrl. 20 A4 43 30N 73 36W
Montalban, Car. 30 E5 10 28N 66 56W
Montana de Montjuich, Barc. 8 D5 41 21N 2 9 E
Montara, S.F. 27 C2 37 32N 122 30W
Montara, Pt., S.F. 27 C1 37 32N 122 31W
Montara Mt., S.F. 27 C2 37 32N 122 27W
Montchanin, Phil. 24 C1 39 47N 75 35W
Montclair, N.Y. 22 C3 40 49N 74 12W
Monte Chingolo, B.A. 32 C4 34 43 S 58 22W
Monte Grande, B.A. 32 C4 34 48 S 58 27W
Monte Sacro, Rome 9 F10 41 56N 12 32 E
Montebello, L.A. 28 B4 34 1N 118 8W
Montelera, Tori. 9 B1 45 9N 7 26 E
Montemor, Lisb. 8 F7 38 49N 9 12W
Monterey Park, L.A. 28 B4 34 3N 118 7W
Monterrey, La Hab. 30 B3 23 5N 82 18W
Montespaccato, Rome 9 F9 41 54N 12 23 E
Montesson, Paris 5 B2 48 54N 2 8 E
Monteverde Nuovo, Rome 9 F9 41 52N 12 26 E
Montfermeil, Paris 5 B5 48 54N 2 33 E
Montgeron, Paris 5 C4 48 42N 2 27 E
Montigny-le-Bretonneux, Paris 5 C2 48 46N 2 1 E
Montigny-les-Cormeilles, Paris 5 B3 48 59N 2 11 E
Montijo, Lisb. 8 F9 38 42N 8 58W
Montjay-la-Tour, Paris 5 B6 48 54N 2 40 E
Montlhéry, Paris 5 D3 48 38N 2 16 E
Montlignon, Paris 5 A3 49 0N 2 16 E
Montmagny, Paris 5 B4 48 58N 2 21 E
Montmorency, Paris 5 B3 48 59N 2 19 E
Montmorency, Forêt de, Paris 5 A3 49 2N 2 16 E
Montparnasse, Gare, Paris 5 B3 48 50N 2 19 E
Montpelier, Wash. 25 C8 39 3N 76 50W
Montréal, Mtrl. 20 A4 43 30N 73 33W
Montréal, Î. de, Mtrl. 20 A4 43 30N 73 40W
Montréal, Univ. de, Mtrl. 20 B4 43 29N 73 37W
Montréal-Est, Mtrl. 20 A4 43 37N 73 31W
Montréal Nord, Mtrl. 20 A4 43 36N 73 36W
Montreuil, Paris 5 B4 48 51N 2 27 E
Montrose, L.A. 28 A3 34 12N 118 12W
Montrose, Melb. 19 E8 37 49 S 145 19 E
Montrose, Wash. 25 C7 39 2N 77 7W
Montrouge, Paris 5 C3 48 48N 2 18 E
Montvale, N.Y. 22 A4 41 2N 74 1W
Montville, N.Y. 22 B2 40 55N 74 23W
Monza, Mil. 9 D6 45 35N 9 16 E
Monzoro, Mil. 9 E5 45 27N 9 2 E
Moóca, S. Pau. 31 E6 23 33 S 46 35W
Moóca →, S. Pau. 31 E6 23 35 S 46 35W
Moonachie, N.Y. 22 C4 40 50N 74 2W
Moonee Ponds, Melb. 19 E6 37 45 S 144 53 E
Moonee Valley Racecourse, Melb. 19 E6 37 45 S 144 55 E
Moorbek, Hbg. 7 C7 53 41N 9 58 E
Moorburg, Hbg. 7 E7 53 29N 9 55 E
Moorebank, Syd. 19 B2 33 56 S 150 56 E
Moorestown, Phil. 24 B5 39 58N 74 56W
Moorfleet, Hbg. 7 D8 53 30N 10 4 E
Mooroolbark, Melb. 19 E8 37 46 S 145 19 E
Moorwerder, Hbg. 7 E8 53 28N 10 3 E
Moosach, Mün. 7 F10 48 10N 11 30 E
Mora, Bomb. 16 H8 18 54N 72 55 E
Moraga, S.F. 27 B4 37 49N 122 7W
Morainvilliers, Paris 5 B1 48 55N 1 56 E
Morales →, B.A. 32 C2 34 47 S 58 35W
Morangis, Paris 5 C4 48 42N 2 20 E
Moratalaz, Mdrd. 8 B3 40 24N 3 39W
Morbras →, Paris 5 C5 48 46N 2 30 E
Mörby, Stock. 3 D11 59 23N 18 3 E
Morce →, Paris 5 B4 48 57N 2 25 E
Morden, Lon. 4 C3 51 24N 0 13W
Morehill, Jobg. 18 F11 26 10 S 28 20 E
Moreno, B.A. 32 B2 34 38 S 58 45W
Moreno, Rome 9 G10 41 48N 12 37 E
Morgan Park, Chic. 26 C3 41 41N 87 38W
Moriguchi, Ōsaka 12 B4 34 43N 135 34 E
Morivione, Mil. 9 E6 45 26N 9 12 E
Morningside, Jobg. 18 E9 26 4 S 28 3 E
Morningside, Wash. 25 E8 38 49N 76 53W
Morningside Park, Trto. 20 D9 43 46N 79 12W
Moroka, Jobg. 18 F8 26 15 S 27 52 E
Moron, B.A. 32 B3 34 39 S 58 37W
Morris Plains, N.Y. 22 C2 40 49N 74 29W
Morristown, N.Y. 22 C2 40 47N 74 28W
Morro, Castillo del, La Hab. 30 B2 23 8N 82 21W
Morro Pelado, S. Pau. 31 E7 23 38 S 46 24W
Morro Solar, Lima 30 H8 12 11 S 77 1W
Morsang-sur-Orge, Paris 5 D4 48 39N 2 21 E
Mörsenbroich, Ruhr 6 C2 51 15N 6 48 E
Morses Pond, Bost. 21 D2 42 17N 71 19W
Morte →, Paris 5 C3 48 40N 2 16 E
Mortlake, Lon. 4 C3 51 27N 0 15W
Mortlake, Syd. 19 B3 33 50 S 151 6 E
Morton, Phil. 24 B2 39 54N 75 20W
Morton Grove, Chic. 26 A2 42 2N 87 46W
Mory, Paris 5 B5 48 58N 2 37 E
Moscavide, Lisb. 8 F8 38 47N 9 6W
Moscow = Moskva, Mos. 11 E9 55 45N 37 37 E
Mosede, Købn. 2 E8 55 34N 12 17 E
Mosede Strand, Købn. 2 E8 55 34N 12 17 E
Mosjøen, Oslo 2 C6 50 49N 11 0 E
Moskhaton, Ath. 8 J11 37 55N 23 40 E
Moskva, Mos. 11 E9 55 45N 37 37 E
Moskvoretskiy, Mos. 11 E9 55 42N 37 37 E
Mosman, Syd. 19 A4 33 49 S 151 15 E
Moss Beach, S.F. 27 C2 37 31N 122 30W
Móstoles, Mdrd. 8 C1 40 18N 3 51W
Moto →, Tōkyō 13 A3 35 53N 139 45 E
Motol, Pra. 10 B1 50 3N 14 19 E
Motspur Park, Lon. 4 C3 51 23N 0 14W
Mottingham, Lon. 4 C5 51 26N 0 1 E
Mount Airy, Phil. 24 A3 40 3N 75 10W
Mount Dennis, Trto. 20 D8 43 40N 79 28W
Mount Ephraim, Phil. 24 B4 39 52N 75 5W
Mount Greenwood, Chic. 26 C2 41 42N 87 42W
Mount Hood Memorial Park, Bost. 21 C3 42 26N 71 1W
Mount Pleasant, Lon. 4 B2 51 30N 0 22W
Mount Pleasant Park, Balt. 25 A3 39 22N 76 34W
Mount Prospect, Chic. 26 A1 42 3N 87 54W
Mount Royal, Phil. 24 C3 39 48N 75 12W
Mount Tamalpais State Park, S.F. 27 A1 37 53N 122 34W
Mount Vernon, N.Y. 23 B6 40 54N 73 49W
Mount Waverley, Melb. 19 F7 37 52 S 145 7 E
Mount Wilson Observatory, L.A. 28 A4 34 13N 118 4W
Mountain Lakes, N.Y. 22 B2 40 54N 74 27W
Mountain Spring Ls., N.Y. 22 A2 41 2N 74 21W
Mountain View, N.Y. 22 B3 40 55N 74 15W
Mountainside, N.Y. 22 C2 40 40N 74 21W
Mountnessing, Lon. 4 B7 51 39N 0 21 E
Moûtiers, Paris 5 D1 48 36N 1 58 E
Mozu, Ōsaka 12 C3 34 33N 135 29 E
Müggelberge, Berl. 7 B4 52 25N 13 37 E
Müggelheim, Berl. 7 B5 52 24N 13 40 E
Muggiò, Mil. 9 D6 45 35N 9 13 E
Mugnano di Nápoli, Nápl. 9 H12 40 54N 14 12 E
Mühleiten, Wien 10 G11 48 10N 16 33 E
Mühlenau →, Hbg. 7 C7 53 41N 9 56 E
Mühlenfliess →, Berl. 7 A5 52 32N 13 42 E
Muir Beach, S.F. 27 A1 37 51N 122 34W
Muirkirk, Wash. 25 C8 39 3N 76 53W
Mujahidpur, Delhi 16 B2 28 33N 77 14 E
Mukandpur, Delhi 16 A2 28 44N 77 10 E
Muko →, Ōsaka 12 B3 34 48N 135 22 E
Mukojima, Tōkyō 13 B3 35 43N 139 49 E
Mulbarton, Jobg. 18 F9 26 17 S 28 3 E
Mulford Gardens, S.F. 27 B3 37 42N 122 10W
Mulgrave, Melb. 19 F8 37 55 S 145 12 E
Mülheim, Ruhr 6 B3 51 25N 6 53 E
Mullica Hill, Phil. 24 C3 39 44N 75 13W
Mullum Mullum Cr. →, Melb. 19 E8 37 44 S 145 10 E
Münchehofe, Berl. 7 B5 52 29N 13 40 E
München, Mün. 7 G10 48 8N 11 34 E
Munchen-Riem, Flughafen, Mün. 7 G11 48 7N 11 42 E
Munich = München, Mün. 7 G10 48 8N 11 34 E
Munirka, Delhi 16 B2 28 33N 77 10 E
Muniz, B.A. 32 B2 34 33 S 58 41W
Munkkiniemi, Hels. 3 B4 60 11N 24 52 E
Munro, B.A. 32 B3 34 31 S 58 31W
Munsey Park, N.Y. 23 C6 40 47N 73 40W
Münsterkirche, Ruhr 6 B4 51 27N 7 0 E
Muranów, Wsaw. 10 E6 52 14N 20 58 E
Murayama-chosuichi, Tōkyō 13 B1 35 45N 139 26 E
Murrumbeena, Melb. 19 F7 37 53 S 145 4 E
Musashino, Tōkyō 13 B2 35 42N 139 33 E
Mushin, Lagos 18 A2 6 31N 7 21 E
Musinè, Mte., Tori. 9 B1 45 7N 7 27 E
Musocco, Mil. 9 E5 45 29N 9 8 E
Musta Hevonen, Hels. 3 B6 60 11N 25 14 E
Mustafabad, Delhi 16 A2 28 43N 77 13 E
Mustansiriya, Bagd. 17 E8 33 22N 44 24 E
Musturud, El Qâ. 18 C5 30 8N 31 17 E
Muswell Hill, Lon. 4 B4 51 35N 0 8W
Mutanabi, Bagd. 17 F8 33 19N 44 21 E
Muthana, Bagd. 17 F8 33 19N 44 27 E
Mutinga, S. Pau. 31 D5 23 29 S 46 46W
Muttontown, N.Y. 23 C7 40 49N 73 32W
Muzon, Manila 15 D4 14 32N 121 8 E
Myaglovo, St-Pet. 11 B5 59 53N 30 39 E
Myakinino, Mos. 11 E8 55 48N 37 22 E
Mykerinos, El Qâ. 18 D4 29 28N 31 8 E
Myllykylä, Hels. 3 A4 60 21N 24 57 E
Myllypuro, Hels. 3 B5 60 13N 25 3 E
Myras, Hels. 3 B5 60 19N 25 6 E
Myrvoll, Oslo 2 C4 59 47N 10 48 E
Mystic Lakes, Bost. 21 C3 42 26N 71 8W
Mytishchi, Mos. 11 D10 55 53N 37 44 E

N

Nababpur, Calc. 16 D5 22 42N 88 12 E
Nações, Parque das, S. Pau. 31 E6 23 38 S 46 30W
Nachstebreck, Ruhr 6 C5 51 17N 7 14 E
Nacka, Stock. 3 E12 59 19N 18 10 E
Nada, Ōsaka 12 B2 34 42N 135 13 E
Nærsnes, Oslo 2 C2 59 45N 10 27 E
Nærum, Købn. 2 D10 55 48N 12 33 E
Nagareyama, Tōkyō 13 A4 35 51N 139 54 E
Nagasaki, Tōkyō 13 B3 35 43N 139 40 E
Nagasuga, Tōkyō 13 D4 35 21N 139 57 E
Nagata, Ōsaka 12 C1 34 39N 135 8 E
Nagatsuta, Tōkyō 13 C2 35 32N 139 31 E
Nagytarcsa, Bud. 10 J14 47 31N 19 17 E
Nagytétény, Bud. 10 K12 47 23N 18 59 E
Nahant, Bost. 21 C4 42 25N 70 54W
Nahant B., Bost. 21 C4 42 26N 70 54W
Nahant Harbor, Bost. 21 C4 42 25N 70 55W
Nahdein, W. el →, El Qâ. 18 C5 30 3N 31 19 E
Nahia, El Qâ. 18 C4 30 2N 31 7 E
Naihati, Calc. 16 C6 22 53N 88 25 E
Najafgarh Drain →, Delhi 16 B1 28 39N 77 4 E
Najio, Ōsaka 12 B2 34 49N 135 18 E
Naka →, Tōkyō 13 B4 35 49N 139 52 E
Naka-Ku, Tōkyō 13 D2 35 25N 139 38 E
Nakada, Tōkyō 13 D2 35 24N 139 30 E
Nakajima, Tōkyō 13 D4 35 25N 139 54 E
Nakano, Tōkyō 13 D4 35 25N 139 56 E
Nakano-Ku, Tōkyō 13 B2 35 42N 139 39 E
Nakasato, Tōkyō 13 D4 35 22N 139 55 E
Nakayama, Tōkyō 13 B4 35 43N 139 57 E
Nalikul, Calc. 16 D5 22 49N 88 10 E
Nalpur, Calc. 16 E5 22 31N 88 10 E
Namazie Estate, Sing. 15 F7 1 25N 103 42 E
Namgajha, Sŏul 12 G7 37 33N 126 55 E
Namsan Park, Sŏul 12 G7 37 32N 126 59 E
Namyeong, Sŏul 12 G7 37 32N 126 57 E
Nan Wan, H.K. 12 D5 22 20N 114 5 E
Nanbiancun, Gzh. 14 G7 23 4N 113 10 E
Nancefield, Jobg. 18 F8 26 17 S 27 54 E
Nanchang He →, Beij. 14 B2 39 58N 116 14 E
Nandaha, Calc. 16 D5 22 49N 88 18 E
Nandang, Gzh. 14 G8 23 6N 113 12 E
Nandian, Tianj. 14 D6 39 10N 117 16 E
Nangal Dewat, Delhi 16 B1 28 33N 77 5 E
Nangi, Calc. 16 E5 22 30N 88 13 E
Nangka →, Manila 15 D4 14 38N 121 8 E
Nangloi, Delhi 16 A1 28 41N 77 4 E
Nangloi Jat, Delhi 16 A1 28 41N 77 3 E
Nanhai, Gzh. 14 G7 23 2N 113 6 E
Nanhan He →, Beij. 14 B2 39 57N 116 11 E
Naniwa, Ōsaka 12 C3 34 39N 135 29 E
Nankai, Tianj. 14 E5 39 7N 117 10 E
Nanmenwai, Tianj. 14 E6 39 8N 117 10 E
Nanole, Bomb. 16 G8 19 0N 72 55 E
Nanshi, Shang. 14 J11 31 12N 121 29 E
Nanterre, Paris 5 B3 48 53N 2 12 E
Nantouillet, Paris 5 A6 49 0N 2 42 E
Nantusket Beach, Bost. 21 D4 42 16N 70 52W
Nanxiang, Shang. 14 J10 31 17N 121 18 E
Naoabad, Calc. 16 F6 22 28N 88 26 E
Napara, Calc. 16 E6 22 38N 88 23 E
Napier Mole, Kar. 17 H10 24 49N 66 58 E
Napindan, Manila 15 D4 14 32N 121 5 E
Naples = Nápoli, Nápl. 9 J12 40 50N 14 14 E
Nápoli, Nápl. 9 J12 40 50N 14 14 E
Nápoli, G. di, Nápl. 9 J12 40 46N 14 15 E
Naraina, Delhi 16 B1 28 36N 77 8 E
Narawa, Tōkyō 13 D4 35 25N 139 58 E
Narayanpara, Calc. 16 C5 22 53N 88 18 E
Narberth, Phil. 24 A3 40 0N 75 16W
Narimasu, Tōkyō 13 B2 35 46N 139 35 E
Nārmak, Tehr. 17 C5 35 42N 51 28 E
Närsta, Stock. 3 E9 59 17N 17 43 E
Naruo, Ōsaka 12 B3 34 43N 135 22 E
Näsby, Stock. 3 D11 59 25N 18 5 E
Näsbypark, Stock. 3 D11 59 25N 18 5 E
Näsfjärden, Stock. 3 D9 59 25N 17 41 E
Nassau Shore, N.Y. 23 D8 40 39N 73 26W
Natick, Bost. 21 D2 42 16N 71 19W
Nation, Place de la, Paris 5 B4 48 51N 2 23 E
National Arboretum, Wash. 25 D8 39 54N 76 59W
Nativitas, Méx. 29 C3 19 15N 99 5W
Natolin, Wsaw. 10 F7 52 8N 21 4 E
Naucalpan de Juárez, Méx. 29 B2 19 28N 99 14W
Naupada, Bomb. 16 G8 19 3N 72 50 E
Navíglio di Pavia, Mil. 9 E5 45 24N 9 9 E
Navíglio Grande, Mil. 9 E5 45 25N 9 5 E
Navotas, Manila 15 D3 14 39N 120 56 E
Nazal Hikmat Beg, Bagd. 17 E8 33 23N 44 25 E
Nazimabad, Kar. 17 G11 24 54N 67 1 E
Nazukari, Tōkyō 13 A4 35 50N 139 57 E
Néa Alexandhria, Ath. 8 J11 37 52N 23 46 E
Néa Faliron, Ath. 8 J10 37 55N 23 39 E
Néa Ionía, Ath. 8 H11 38 3N 23 45 E
Néa Liósia, Ath. 8 H11 38 3N 23 43 E
Néa Smirni, Ath. 8 J11 37 54N 23 43 E
Neapolis, Ath. 8 J11 37 58N 23 45 E
Neasden, Lon. 4 B3 51 35N 0 16W
Neauphle-le-Château, Paris 5 C1 48 48N 1 53 E
Nebučice, Pra. 10 B1 50 6N 14 19 E
Nedlitz, Berl. 7 B1 52 25N 13 3 E
Nee Soon, Sing. 15 F7 1 24N 103 49 E
Needham, Bost. 21 D2 42 16N 71 13W
Needham Heights, Bost. 21 D2 42 17N 71 14W
Needle Hill, H.K. 12 D5 22 23N 114 9 E
Negishi B., Tōkyō 13 D2 35 23N 139 38 E
Nehiti, Calc. 16 D5 22 42N 88 16 E
Nekrasovka, Mos. 11 E11 55 41N 37 55 E
Nematābād, Tehr. 17 D5 35 38N 51 21 E
Nemchinovka, Mos. 11 E7 55 42N 37 19 E
Népliget, Bud. 10 K13 47 29N 19 7 E
Neponset →, Bost. 21 D3 42 12N 71 9W
Nerima, Tōkyō 13 B3 35 44N 139 40 E
Nerul, Bomb. 16 G9 19 2N 73 0 E
Nerviano, Mil. 9 D4 45 32N 8 58 E
Nesodden, Oslo 2 C4 59 48N 10 41 E
Nesoddtangen, Oslo 2 B4 59 52N 10 41 E
Nesøya, Oslo 2 B3 59 52N 10 31 E
Nestipayac →, Méx. 29 A4 19 33N 89 57W
Netzahualcóyotl, Méx. 29 B3 19 24N 99 2W
Neu Aubing, Mün. 7 G9 48 8N 11 25 E
Neu Buch, Berl. 7 A4 52 37N 13 31 E
Neu Buchhorst, Berl. 7 B5 52 24N 13 44 E
Neu Fahrland, Berl. 7 B1 52 26N 13 3 E
Neu Lindenberg, Berl. 7 A4 52 36N 13 33 E
Neu Wulmstorf, Hbg. 7 E6 53 27N 9 48 E
Neu Zittau, Berl. 7 B5 52 23N 13 44 E
Neubiberg, Mün. 7 G11 48 4N 11 40 E
Neudorf, Hbg. 7 E8 53 27N 10 4 E
Neudorf, Ruhr 6 B2 51 25N 6 47 E
Neuegenbüttel, Hbg. 7 D7 53 38N 9 54 E
Neuenfelde, Hbg. 7 D6 53 31N 9 48 E
Neuenhagen, Berl. 7 A4 52 32N 13 38 E
Neuenkamp, Ruhr 6 B2 51 26N 6 43 E
Neuessling, Wien 10 G11 48 15N 16 32 E
Neugraben-Fischbek, Hbg. 7 E6 53 28N 9 49 E
Neuhausen, Mün. 7 G10 48 9N 11 32 E
Neuherberg, Mün. 7 F10 48 13N 11 35 E
Neuhönow, Berl. 7 A5 52 34N 13 44 E
Neuilly-Plaisance, Paris 5 B5 48 51N 2 30 E
Neuilly-sur-Marne, Paris 5 B5 48 51N 2 31 E
Neuilly-sur-Seine, Paris 5 B3 48 53N 2 15 E
Neukagran, Wien 10 G10 48 14N 16 27 E
Neukettenhof, Wien 10 H10 48 7N 16 28 E
Neukölln, Berl. 7 B3 52 28N 13 25 E
Neuland, Hbg. 7 E8 53 27N 10 0 E
Neuperlach, Mün. 7 G10 48 6N 11 37 E
Neuried, Mün. 7 G9 48 5N 11 27 E
Neuss, Ruhr 6 C2 51 12N 6 42 E
Neustift am Walde, Wien 10 G9 48 14N 16 17 E
Neusüssenbrunn, Wien 10 G10 48 16N 16 29 E
Neuville-sur-Oise, Paris 5 A2 49 0N 2 3 E
Neuwaldegg, Wien 10 G9 48 14N 16 17 E
Neuwiedenthal, Hbg. 7 E7 53 28N 9 52 E
Neva →, St-Pet. 11 B4 59 56N 30 20 E
Neves, Rio J. 31 B3 22 51 S 43 5W
Neviges, Ruhr 6 C4 51 18N 7 6 E
New Addington, Lon. 4 C4 51 20N 0 0 E
New Ash Green, Lon. 4 C6 51 22N 0 18 E
New Baghdād, Bagd. 17 F8 33 18N 44 28 E
New Barnet, Lon. 4 B3 51 38N 0 10W
New Brighton, N.Y. 22 D4 40 38N 74 5W
New Brunswick, N.Y. 22 D2 40 30N 74 29W
New Canada, Jobg. 18 F8 26 12 S 27 56 E
New Canada Dam, Jobg. 18 F8 26 12 S 27 56 E
New Canal →, Calc. 16 E6 22 33N 88 25 E
New Carrollton, Wash. 25 D8 38 58N 76 52W
New Cassell, N.Y. 23 C7 40 45N 73 32W
New Cross, Lon. 4 C4 51 28N 0 1W
New Delhi, Delhi 16 B2 28 36N 77 11 E
New Dorp, N.Y. 22 D4 40 34N 74 7W
New Dorp Beach, N.Y. 22 D4 40 33N 74 6W
New Hyde Park, N.Y. 23 C7 40 43N 73 39W
New Kleinfontein, Jobg. 18 F11 26 11 S 20 20 E
New Malden, Lon. 4 C3 51 24N 0 15W
New Milford, N.Y. 22 B4 40 56N 74 0W
New Modder, Jobg. 18 F11 26 10 S 28 21 E
New Providence, N.Y. 22 C2 40 42N 74 23W
New Redruth, Jobg. 18 F9 26 15 S 28 7 E
New Rochelle, N.Y. 23 B6 40 55N 73 45W
New South Wales, Univ. of, Syd. 19 B4 33 55 S 151 14 E
New Southgate, Lon. 4 B4 51 37N 0 7W
New Springville, N.Y. 22 D4 40 35N 74 9W
New Territories, H.K. 12 D5 22 23N 114 10 E
New Toronto, Trto. 20 E7 43 35N 79 30W
New Utrecht, N.Y. 22 D5 40 36N 73 59W
New Vernon, N.Y. 22 C2 40 44N 74 30W
New York Aquarium, N.Y. 22 D5 40 33N 73 59W
New York Botanical Gdns., N.Y. 23 B5 40 51N 73 51W
New York Univ., N.Y. 22 C5 40 43N 74 59W
Newabgarj, Calc. 16 D6 22 47N 88 23 E
Newark, N.Y. 22 C3 40 43N 74 10W
Newark, S.F. 27 C4 37 32N 122 2W
Newark B., N.Y. 22 C4 40 40N 74 8W
Newark Int. Airport, N.Y. 22 C3 40 41N 74 10W
Newbury Park, Lon. 4 B5 51 34N 0 5 E
Newclare, Jobg. 18 F8 26 11 S 27 58 E
Newfoundland, N.Y. 22 A2 41 2N 74 25W
Newham, Lon. 4 B5 51 31N 0 1 E
Newlands, Jobg. 18 F8 26 10 S 27 57 E
Newport, Melb. 19 F6 37 50 S 144 51 E
Newportville, Phil. 24 A5 40 7N 74 53W
Newton, Bost. 21 D2 42 19N 71 13W
Newton Brook, Trto. 20 D8 43 47N 79 24W
Newton Highlands, Bost. 21 D2 42 19N 71 13W
Newtonville, Bost. 21 C2 42 20N 71 11W
Newtown, Syd. 19 B4 33 54 S 151 11 E
Newtown Square, Phil. 24 B2 39 59N 75 24W
Neyegawa, Ōsaka 12 B4 34 45N 135 36 E
Ngau Chi Wan, H.K. 12 D6 22 20N 114 12 E
Ngau Tau Kok, H.K. 12 E6 22 19N 114 12 E
Ngong Shuen Chau, H.K. 12 E5 22 19N 114 8 E
Ngua Kok Wan, H.K. 12 D5 22 21N 114 5 E
Niāvarān, Tehr. 17 C5 35 47N 51 29 E
Nibria, Calc. 16 E5 22 36N 88 15 E
Nichelino, Tori. 9 C2 44 59N 7 38 E
Nichols Run →, Wash. 25 C6 39 2N 77 17W
Nicholson, Mt., H.K. 12 E6 22 15N 114 11 E
Nidāl, Bagd. 17 F8 33 19N 44 25 E
Niddrie, Melb. 19 E6 37 44 S 144 51 E
Nieder Neuendorf, Berl. 7 A2 52 36N 13 12 E
Niederbonsfeld, Ruhr 6 B4 51 22N 7 8 E
Niederdonk, Ruhr 6 C2 51 14N 6 41 E
Niederschöneweide, Berl. 7 B3 52 27N 13 30 E
Niederschönhausen, Berl. 7 A3 52 35N 13 25 E
Niederwenigern, Ruhr 6 B4 51 24N 7 8 E
Niemeyer, Rio J. 31 B2 22 59 S 43 16W
Niendorf, Hbg. 7 D7 53 37N 9 57 E
Nienstedten, Hbg. 7 D7 53 33N 9 51 E
Nierst, Ruhr 6 C2 51 19N 6 43 E
Nihonbashi, Tōkyō 13 B3 35 41N 139 46 E
Niipperi, Hels. 3 B3 60 18N 24 45 E
Niiza, Tōkyō 13 B2 35 48N 139 33 E
Nikaia, Ath. 8 J10 37 57N 23 38 E
Nikinmäki, Hels. 3 A5 60 20N 25 8 E
Nikolassee, Berl. 7 B2 52 25N 13 12 E
Nikolo-Khovanskoye, Mos. 11 F8 55 36N 37 27 E
Nikolskiy, Mos. 11 E8 55 49N 37 29 E
Nikolyskoye, Mos. 11 E11 55 46N 37 53 E
Nikulino, Mos. 11 E8 55 40N 37 25 E
Nil, Bagd. 17 E8 33 21N 44 25 E
Nil, Nahr en →, El Qâ. 18 D5 29 57N 31 14 E
Nile = Nil, Nahr en →, El Qâ. 18 D5 29 57N 31 14 E
Niles, Chic. 26 A2 42 1N 87 48W
Nilganj, Calc. 16 D6 22 45N 88 25 E
Nilópolis, Rio J. 31 A1 22 47 S 43 23W
Nimta, Calc. 16 D6 22 40N 88 24 E
Nincop, Hbg. 7 D6 53 30N 9 48 E
Ningyuan, Tianj. 14 E6 39 9N 117 12 E
Nippa, Tōkyō 13 C2 35 31N 139 36 E
Nippori, Tōkyō 13 B3 35 43N 139 45 E
Niru-ye-Hava'i, Tehr. 17 C5 35 41N 51 26 E
Nishi, Ōsaka 12 B3 34 40N 135 28 E
Nishi, Tōkyō 13 D2 35 26N 139 37 E
Nishi-arai, Tōkyō 13 B3 35 46N 139 48 E
Nishinari, Ōsaka 12 C3 34 37N 135 28 E
Nishinomiya, Ōsaka 12 B2 34 44N 135 18 E
Nishiyama, Tōkyō 13 D4 35 22N 139 57 E
Nishiyodogawa, Ōsaka 12 B3 34 41N 135 24 E
Nisida, I. di, Nápl. 9 J11 40 47N 14 10 E
Niterói, Rio J. 31 B3 22 53 S 43 7W
Nithari, Delhi 16 B3 28 34N 77 20 E
Nittedal, Oslo 2 A5 60 0N 10 57 E
Niyog, Manila 15 E3 14 27N 120 57 E
Noapara, Calc. 16 D6 22 49N 88 22 E
Nobidome, Tōkyō 13 B2 35 48N 139 34 E
Nockeby, Stock. 3 E10 59 19N 17 56 E
Noel Park, Lon. 4 B4 51 35N 0 5W
Nogatino, Mos. 11 E10 55 41N 37 41 E
Nogent-sur-Marne, Paris 5 B4 48 50N 2 28 E
Noiseau, Paris 5 C5 48 46N 2 32 E
Noisiel, Paris 5 B5 48 51N 2 37 E
Noisy-le-Grand, Paris 5 B5 48 50N 2 33 E
Noisy-le-Roi, Paris 5 B2 48 50N 2 3 E
Noisy-le-Sec, Paris 5 B4 48 53N 2 27 E
Nokkala, Hels. 3 C3 60 8N 24 45 E
Nøklevatn, Oslo 2 B5 59 52N 10 52 E
Nolme →, Ruhr 6 B6 51 23N 7 26 E
Nomentano, Rome 9 F10 41 55N 12 30 E
Nonakashinden, Tōkyō 13 B2 35 44N 139 30 E
Nongminyundong Jiangxisuo, Gzh. 14 G8 23 7N 113 15 E
Nonhyeon, Sŏul 12 G8 37 30N 127 1 E
Nontha Buri, Bangk. 15 A1 13 50N 100 29 E
Noordgesig, Jobg. 18 F8 26 13 S 27 56 E
Nord, Gare du, Paris 5 B4 48 52N 2 21 E
Nordbysjøen, Oslo 2 B6 59 51N 11 1 E
Nordereble, Hbg. 7 D7 53 32N 9 59 E
Norderelbe →, Hbg. 7 E8 53 29N 10 3 E
Norderstedt, Hbg. 7 C7 53 42N 9 59 E
Nordmarka, Oslo 2 A4 60 1N 10 38 E
Nordrand-Seidlung, Wien 10 G10 48 16N 16 26 E
Nordre Elvåga, Oslo 2 B5 59 53N 10 54 E
Nordstrand, Oslo 2 B4 59 52N 10 48 E
Normandy Heights, Balt. 25 B2 39 17N 76 48W
Norra Björköfjärden, Stock. 3 D8 59 26N 17 39 E
Norridge, Chic. 26 B2 41 57N 87 49W
Norristown, Phil. 24 A2 40 7N 75 20W
Norrkula, Hels. 3 B6 60 19N 25 20 E
Norrmalm, Stock. 3 D11 59 20N 18 3 E
Norrviken, Stock. 3 D10 59 27N 17 52 E
North Acton, Bost. 21 B1 42 30N 71 23W
North Amityville, N.Y. 23 C8 40 41N 73 25W
North Andover, Bost. 21 A3 42 41N 71 7W
North Arlington, N.Y. 22 C4 40 47N 74 7W
North Auburn, Syd. 19 B3 33 50 S 151 3 E
North Babylon, N.Y. 23 C9 40 43N 73 19W
North Bellmore, N.Y. 23 C7 40 40N 73 32W
North Bergen, N.Y. 22 C4 40 48N 74 0W
North Beverly, Bost. 21 B4 42 34N 70 51W
North Billerica, Bost. 21 B2 42 35N 71 16W
North Branch →, Phil. 24 C4 39 50N 75 5W
North Branch Chicago River →, Chic. 26 B2 41 53N 87 42W
North Brighton, Bost. 21 C3 42 21N 71 8W
North Caldwell, N.Y. 22 B3 40 52N 74 15W
North Cambridge, Bost. 21 C3 42 23N 71 7W
North Cheam, Lon. 4 C3 51 22N 0 11W
North Chelmsford, Bost. 21 B1 42 38N 71 23W
North Cohasset, Bost. 21 D4 42 15N 70 50W
North Cray, Lon. 4 C5 51 25N 0 8 E
North Fair Oaks, S.F. 27 D3 37 28N 122 11W
North Finchley, Lon. 4 B3 51 36N 0 10W
North Germiston, Jobg. 18 F9 26 12 S 28 9 E
North Hackensack, N.Y. 22 B4 40 54N 74 2W
North Haledon, N.Y. 22 B3 40 58N 74 11W
North Harbour, Manila 15 D3 14 37N 120 57 E
North Hd., Syd. 19 A4 33 49 S 151 18 E
North Hills, N.Y. 23 C6 40 46N 73 40W
North Hollywood, L.A. 28 B2 34 9N 118 22W
North Lexington, Bost. 21 C2 42 27N 71 14W
North Lindenhurst, N.Y. 23 C8 40 42N 73 22W
North Long Beach, L.A. 28 C3 33 53N 118 10W
North Manly, Syd. 19 A4 33 46 S 151 17 E
North Massapequa, N.Y. 23 C8 40 42N 73 27W
North Merrick, N.Y. 23 C7 40 41N 73 33W
North New Hyde Park, N.Y. 23 C6 40 44N 73 42W
North Pelham, N.Y. 23 B6 40 54N 73 46W
North Plainfield, N.Y. 22 D2 40 37N 74 27W
North Point, Balt. 25 B4 39 16N 76 29W
North Pt., H.K. 12 E6 22 17N 114 12 E
North Pt., Syd. 19 A4 33 48 S 151 18 E
North Randolph, Bost. 21 D3 42 11N 71 5W
North Reading, Bost. 21 B3 42 34N 71 5W
North Res., Bost. 21 C3 42 27N 71 6W
North Richmond, S.F. 27 A2 37 57N 122 22W
North Riverside, Chic. 26 B2 41 50N 87 48W
North Ryde, Syd. 19 A3 33 47 S 151 7 E
North Saugus, Bost. 21 C3 42 29N 71 0W
North Shore Channel →, Chic. 26 B2 41 58N 87 42W

Pitampura Kalan 43

North Springfield, Wash. 25 E6 38 48N 77 11W
North Stifford, Lon. 4 B6 51 30N 0 18 E
North Sudbury, Bost. 21 C1 42 24N 71 24W
North Sydney, Syd. 19 B4 33 50 S 151 13 E
North Tewksbury, Bost. 21 B2 42 38N 71 14W
North Valley Stream, N.Y. 23 C6 40 41N 73 42W
North Wantagh, N.Y. 23 C7 40 41N 73 30W
North Weymouth, Bost. 21 D4 42 14N 70 56W
North Wilmington, Bost. 21 B3 42 34N 71 9W
North Woburn, Bost. 21 B2 42 30N 71 10W
North Woolwich, Lon. 4 B5 51 30N 0 3 E
North York, Trto. 20 D8 43 45N 79 27W
Northaw, Lon. 4 A4 51 42N 0 8W
Northbridge, Syd. 19 A4 33 49 S 151 15 E
Northbrook, Chic. 26 A1 42 7N 87 50W
Northcliff, Jobg. 18 E8 26 8 S 27 58 E
Northcote, Melb. 19 E7 37 46 S 145 0 E
Northeastern Univ., Bost. 21 C3 42 20N 71 4W
Northfield, Chic. 26 A2 42 5N 87 45W
Northfleet, Lon. 4 C7 51 26N 0 21 E
Northlake, Chic. 26 B1 41 54N 87 53W
Northmead, Jobg. 18 E10 26 9 S 28 19 E
Northmead, Syd. 19 A3 33 47 S 151 0 E
Northmount, Trto. 20 D8 43 46N 79 23W
Northolt, Lon. 4 B2 51 32N 0 22W
Northport, N.Y. 23 B8 40 54N 73 20W
Northport B., N.Y. 23 B8 40 54N 73 22W
Northridge, L.A. 28 A1 34 14N 118 30W
Northumberland Heath, Lon. 4 C6 51 28N 0 10 E
Northvale, N.Y. 22 A5 41 0N 73 59W
Northwest Branch →, Balt. 25 B3 39 16N 76 35W
Northwest Branch →, Wash. 25 C8 39 2N 76 56W
Northwestern Univ., Chic. 26 A2 42 3N 87 40W
Northwood, Lon. 4 B2 51 36N 0 25W
Norumbega Res., Bost. 21 D2 42 19N 71 17W
Norwalk, L.A. 28 C4 33 53N 118 4W
Norwood, Bost. 21 D2 42 11N 71 13W
Norwood, Jobg. 18 E9 26 9 S 28 4 E
Norwood, N.Y. 22 B5 40 59N 73 57W
Norwood, Phil. 24 B3 39 53N 75 17W
Norwood Memorial Airport, Bost. 21 D3 42 11N 71 9W
Norwood Park, Chic. 26 B2 41 59N 87 48W
Noryangjin, Sŏul 12 G7 37 30N 126 56 E
Nose, Ōsaka 12 B2 34 49N 135 10 E
Nossa Senhora do Ó, S. Pau. 31 E5 23 30 S 46 41W
Notre-Dame, Mtrl. 20 B5 43 28N 73 28W
Notre-Dame, Paris 5 B4 48 51N 2 21 E
Notre-Dame, Bois, Paris 5 C5 48 45N 2 34 E
Notre Dame de L'Île Perrot, Mtrl. 20 B2 43 23N 73 53W
Notting Hill, Lon. 4 B3 51 30N 0 12W
Notting Hill, Melb. 19 F7 37 54 S 145 9 E
Nottingham, Phil. 24 A5 40 7N 74 58W
Nova Milanese, Mil. 9 D6 45 35N 9 12 E
Novate Milanese, Mil. 9 D5 45 30N 9 8 E
Novaya Derevnya, St-Pet. 11 A3 60 0N 30 19 E
Nové Mesto, Pra. 10 B2 50 4N 14 25 E
Novoaleksandrovskoye, St-Pet. 11 B4 59 50N 30 31 E
Novogireyevo, Mos. 11 E10 55 45N 37 46 E
Novoivanovskoye, Mos. 11 E7 55 42N 37 21 E
Novokhovrino, Mos. 11 D8 55 53N 37 27 E
Novonikolskoye, Mos. 11 D7 55 50N 37 14 E
Novosaratovka, St-Pet. 11 B5 59 50N 30 32 E
Novosergiyevka, St-Pet. 11 B5 59 54N 30 34 E
Nowe-Babice, Wsaw. 10 E6 52 15N 20 51 E
Nöykkiö, Hels. 3 B3 60 10N 24 42 E
Noyoye Kovalyova, St-Pet. 11 B5 59 58N 30 34 E
Nozay, Paris 5 D3 48 39N 2 14 E
Nueva Atzacoalco, Méx. 29 B3 19 29N 99 4W
Nueva Caracas, Car. 30 D5 10 30N 66 57W
Nueva Chicago, B.A. 32 B4 34 39 S 58 29W
Nueva Pompeya, B.A. 32 C4 34 40 S 58 25W
Nueva Tenochtitlán, Méx. 29 B3 19 27N 99 5W
Nuijala, Hels. 3 B3 60 12N 24 46 E
Numabukuro, Tōkyō 13 B2 35 43N 139 39 E
Numakage, Tōkyō 13 A2 35 50N 139 37 E
Numata, Tōkyō 13 B3 35 45N 139 46 E
Nunawading, Melb. 19 E8 37 49 S 145 10 E
Nunez, B.A. 32 B4 34 32 S 58 27W
Nunhead, Lon. 4 C4 51 27N 0 3W
Ñuñoa, Stgo 30 J11 33 27 S 70 35W
Nupuri, Hels. 3 B2 60 14N 24 36 E
Nusle, Pra. 10 B2 50 3N 14 26 E
Nussdorf, Wien 10 G10 48 15N 16 21 E
Nuthe →, Berl. 7 B1 52 22N 13 5 E
Nutley, N.Y. 22 C4 40 49N 74 9W
Nutting L., Bost. 21 B2 42 32N 71 16W
Nützenberg, Ruhr 6 C4 51 15N 7 8 E
Nybølle, Købn. 2 D8 55 42N 12 15 E
Nybygget, Hels. 3 B6 60 17N 25 11 E
Nymphenburg, Mün. 7 G10 48 9N 11 30 E
Nymphenburg, Schloss, Mün. 7 G10 48 9N 11 30 E

O

Oak Beach, N.Y. 23 D9 40 38N 73 19W
Oak Forest, Chic. 26 D2 41 36N 87 44W
Oak Hill Park, Bost. 21 D2 42 17N 71 11W
Oak Lane, Phil. 24 A4 40 3N 75 8W
Oak Lawn, Chic. 26 C2 41 42N 87 45W
Oak Park, Chic. 26 B2 41 52N 87 47W
Oak Ridge, N.Y. 22 A2 41 2N 74 28W
Oak Valley, Phil. 24 C4 39 48N 75 9W
Oak View, Wash. 25 D8 39 1N 76 58W
Oakland, N.Y. 22 A3 41 1N 74 13W
Oakland, S.F. 27 B3 37 48N 122 18W
Oakland, Wash. 25 D8 38 52N 76 54W
Oakland Coliseum, S.F. 27 B3 37 44N 122 11W
Oakland Gardens, N.Y. 23 C6 40 45N 73 46W
Oakland Int. Airport, S.F. 27 B3 37 43N 122 12W
Oakland Mills, Balt. 25 B2 39 13N 76 49W
Oakland Naval Air Station, S.F. 27 B3 37 47N 122 19W
Oaklands, Jobg. 18 E9 26 8 S 28 4 E
Oaklawn, Wash. 25 E8 38 46N 76 56W
Oakleigh, Melb. 19 F7 37 54 S 145 5 E
Oaks, Phil. 24 A2 40 8N 75 26W
Oakwood, N.Y. 22 D4 40 33N 74 7W
Oakwood Beach, N.Y. 22 D4 40 33N 74 7W
Oatley, Syd. 19 B3 33 59 S 151 4 E
Obalende, Lagos 18 B2 6 26N 7 25 E
Oba's Palace, Lagos 18 B2 6 27N 7 24 E
Oberbauer, Ruhr 6 C6 51 17N 7 25 E
Oberföhring, Mün. 7 G10 48 10N 11 37 E
Oberhaching, Mün. 7 G10 48 1N 11 35 E
Oberhausen, Ruhr 6 B3 51 28N 6 54 E
Oberhausen, Wien 10 G11 48 10N 16 34 E
Oberkassel, Ruhr 6 C2 51 14N 6 45 E
Oberkirchbach, Wien 10 G9 48 17N 16 12 E
Oberlaa, Wien 10 H10 48 8N 16 24 E
Oberlisse, Wien 10 G10 48 17N 16 26 E
Obermenzing, Mün. 7 F9 48 10N 11 28 E
Obermoos Schwaige, Mün. 7 F9 48 14N 11 27 E
Oberschleissheim, Mün. 7 F10 48 15N 11 33 E
Oberschöneweide, Berl. 7 B4 52 27N 13 31 E
Oberwengern, Ruhr 6 B6 51 23N 7 22 E
Obitsu →, Tōkyō 13 D4 35 25N 139 56 E
Oboldino, Mos. 11 D11 55 53N 37 56 E
Observatory, Jobg. 18 F9 26 10 S 28 4 E
Ōbu, Ōsaka 12 B1 34 43N 135 8 E
Obu-tōge, Ōsaka 12 B1 34 44N 135 9 E
Óbuda, Bud. 10 J13 47 33N 19 2 E
Obudaisziget, Bud. 10 J13 47 33N 19 3 E
Obukhovo, St-Pet. 11 B4 59 53N 30 22 E
Occidental, Pico, Car. 30 D5 10 32N 66 51W
Oceanside, N.Y. 23 D7 40 38N 73 37W
Ochakovo, Mos. 11 E8 55 41N 37 26 E
Ochiai, Tōkyō 13 B3 35 43N 139 42 E
Ochota, Wsaw. 10 E6 52 13N 20 58 E
Ochsenwerder, Hbg. 7 E8 53 28N 10 4 E
Ochsenzoll, Hbg. 7 C8 53 41N 10 0 E
Odana, Tōkyō 13 C2 35 33N 139 35 E
Oden-Stockach, Mün. 7 G11 48 5N 11 41 E
Odilampi, Hels. 3 B3 60 18N 24 45 E
Odintsovo, Mos. 11 E7 55 40N 37 16 E
Odivelas, Lisb. 8 F7 38 47N 9 10W
Odolany, Wsaw. 10 E6 52 13N 20 55 E
Oeiras, Lisb. 8 F7 38 41N 9 18W
Oella, Balt. 25 B2 39 16N 76 46W
Oer-Erkenschwick, Ruhr 6 A5 51 38N 7 15 E
Oern, Mün. 7 G10 48 10N 11 32 E
Ofin, Lagos 18 A3 6 32N 7 30 E
Ofukuro-shinden, Tōkyō 13 A1 35 53N 139 28 E
Ogawa, Tōkyō 13 B1 35 44N 139 28 E
Ogden, Phil. 24 C2 39 49N 75 27W
Ogikubo, Tōkyō 13 B2 35 42N 139 37 E
Ogo Ogo, Ōsaka 12 B1 34 49N 135 8 E
Ogogoro, Lagos 18 B2 6 25N 7 24 E
Ogongo, Manila 15 D4 14 35N 121 4 E
Ogoyo, Lagos 18 B2 6 25N 7 29 E
Ogudu, Lagos 18 A2 6 34N 7 24 E
O'Hare, L., Chic. 26 B1 41 57N 87 53W
Ōhirodo, Tōkyō 13 A4 35 50N 139 53 E
Ohlsdorf, Hbg. 7 D8 53 37N 10 3 E
Ōi, Tōkyō 13 A2 35 51N 139 31 E
Ōimachi, Tōkyō 13 C3 35 35N 139 43 E
Oise →, Paris 5 A2 49 2N 2 5 E
Oittaa, Hels. 3 B3 60 15N 24 42 E
Ojota, Lagos 18 A2 6 35N 7 23 E
Okamoto, Ōsaka 12 B2 34 43N 135 15 E
Okazu, Tōkyō 13 D2 35 25N 139 31 E
Okęcie, Wsaw. 10 E6 52 11N 20 56 E
Okęcie Airport, Wsaw. 10 E6 52 10N 20 57 E
Okelra, Lagos 18 B2 6 29N 7 22 E
Okeogbe, Lagos 18 B2 6 24N 7 23 E
Okhla, Delhi 16 B2 28 33N 77 16 E
Okhta →, St-Pet. 11 B4 59 56N 30 25 E
Okkervil →, St-Pet. 11 B4 59 56N 30 30 E
Okrzeszyn, Wsaw. 10 F7 52 8N 21 8 E
Oksval, Oslo 2 B4 59 51N 10 40 E
Oktyabrskiy, Mos. 11 F11 55 37N 37 58 E
Oktyabrskiy, Mos. 11 E9 55 41N 37 35 E
Okubo, Tōkyō 13 A2 35 41N 139 42 E
Okunola, Lagos 18 A1 6 35N 7 17 E
Ōkura, Tōkyō 13 C1 35 35N 139 27 E
Olari, Hels. 3 B3 60 10N 24 44 E
Olaria, Rio J. 31 B2 22 50 S 43 16W
Old Brookville, N.Y. 23 C7 40 49N 73 35W
Old Cairo, El Qâ. 18 C5 30 0N 31 14 E
Old Coulsdon, Lon. 4 D4 51 17N 0 6W
Old Forge Village, N.Y. 22 C2 40 48N 74 29W
Old Harbor, Bost. 21 D3 42 19N 71 1W
Old Road B., Balt. 25 B4 39 12N 76 27W
Old Tappan, N.Y. 22 A5 41 0N 73 59W
Old Town, Chic. 26 B3 41 54N 87 37W
Old Westbury, N.Y. 23 C7 40 47N 73 35W
Oldmans Cr. →, Phil. 24 C2 39 47N 75 26W
Olgino, St-Pet. 11 A3 60 0N 30 10 E
Olimpico, Estadio, Méx. 29 C2 19 19N 99 11W
Olinda, Melb. 19 F9 37 51 S 145 21 E
Olinda, Rio J. 31 A1 22 49 S 43 25W
Olivais, Lisb. 8 F8 38 45N 9 7W
Olivar de los Padres, Méx. 29 B2 19 21N 99 14W
Olivar del Conde, Méx. 29 B2 19 22N 99 12W
Olivos, B.A. 32 B4 34 30 S 58 28W
Ollila, Hels. 3 A2 60 20N 24 32 E
Olney, Phil. 24 A4 40 2N 75 7W
Olona →, Mil. 9 E5 45 29N 9 6 E
Ølstykke, Købn. 2 D7 55 47N 12 8 E
Olute, Lagos 18 B1 6 27N 7 17 E
Olympia-Stadion, Hels. 3 B4 60 11N 24 55 E
Olympique Parc, Mtrl. 20 A4 43 33N 73 33W
Ōmagi, Tōkyō 13 A3 35 52N 139 43 E
Ōmiya, Tōkyō 13 A2 35 54N 139 37 E
Ōmori, Tōkyō 13 C3 35 34N 139 43 E
Ōnari, Tōkyō 13 B3 35 55N 139 36 E
Once, B.A. 32 B4 34 37 S 58 24W
Onchi, Ōsaka 12 C4 34 36N 135 38 E
Onchi →, Ōsaka 12 C4 34 38N 135 37 E
One Tree Hill, Melb. 19 F8 37 52 S 145 19 E
Onisigun, Lagos 18 A2 6 32N 7 22 E
Ōokayama, Tōkyō 13 C3 35 36N 139 40 E
Opacz, Wsaw. 10 E6 52 8N 20 55 E
Ophirton, Jobg. 18 F9 26 13 S 28 1 E
Oppegård, Oslo 2 C4 59 45N 10 49 E
Oppsal, Oslo 2 B5 59 53N 10 51 E
Oppum, Ruhr 6 C1 51 19N 6 36 E
Oradell, N.Y. 22 B4 40 57N 74 2W
Oradell Res., N.Y. 22 B4 40 58N 74 0W
Orange, N.Y. 22 C3 40 45N 74 15W
Orange Grove, Jobg. 18 E9 26 9 S 28 5 E
Oratorio →, S. Pau. 31 E6 23 36 S 46 32W
Orbassano, Tori. 9 B2 45 0N 7 31 E
Orchards, Jobg. 18 E9 26 9 S 28 4 E
Ordrup, Købn. 2 D10 55 46N 12 34 E
Orech, Pra. 10 B2 50 1N 14 18 E
Orekhovo, Mos. 11 E9 55 38N 37 39 E
Oreta, Lagos 18 A3 6 31N 7 31 E
Orge →, Paris 5 D3 48 36N 2 17 E
Orgeval, Paris 5 B2 48 55N 1 58 E
Orholm, Købn. 2 D10 55 46N 12 30 E
Orient Heights, Bost. 21 C4 42 23N 70 59W
Oriental, Pico, Car. 30 D5 10 32N 66 51W
Origgio, Mil. 9 D5 45 35N 9 1 E
Orinda, S.F. 27 A3 37 52N 122 10W
Orinda Village, S.F. 27 A3 37 53N 122 10W
Orland L., Chic. 26 D1 41 38N 87 52W
Orland Park, Chic. 26 D1 41 37N 87 52W
Orlando Dam, Jobg. 18 F8 26 15 S 27 55 E
Orlando East, Jobg. 18 F8 26 14 S 27 55 E
Orlando West, Jobg. 18 F8 26 13 S 27 54 E
Orlången, Stock. 3 E11 59 11N 18 0 E
Orlångsvik, Stock. 3 E11 59 11N 18 3 E
Orlovo, Mos. 11 F8 55 38N 37 22 E
Orly, Paris 5 C4 48 45N 2 23 E
Ormesson-sur-Marne, Paris 5 C5 48 47N 2 32 E
Orminge, Stock. 3 E12 59 19N 18 14 E
Ormingelandet, Stock. 3 D13 59 20N 18 22 E
Ormond, Melb. 19 F7 37 54 S 145 1 E
Ormos Fáliriou, Ath. 8 J11 37 54N 23 40 E
Ormøya, Oslo 2 B4 59 52N 10 45 E
Oros Aiyáleos, Ath. 8 J10 38 0N 23 36 E
Oros Imittós, Ath. 8 J11 37 53N 23 48 E
Örpadfold, Bud. 10 J14 47 32N 19 12 E
Orpington, Lon. 4 C5 51 22N 0 6 E
Orsay, Paris 5 C3 48 41N 2 11 E
Orsby, Ruhr 6 A2 51 31N 6 41 E
Orsett, Lon. 4 B7 51 30N 0 22 E
Ortaköy, Ist. 17 A3 41 3N 29 1 E
Ortica, Mil. 9 E6 45 28N 9 16 E
Oruba, Lagos 18 A2 6 34N 7 24 E
Ōsaka, Ōsaka 12 C4 34 42N 135 30 E
Ōsaka B., Ōsaka 12 C2 34 35N 135 18 E
Ōsaka Castle, Ōsaka 12 B4 34 41N 135 30 E
Ōsaka Harbour, Ōsaka 12 C3 34 38N 135 25 E
Ōsaka Univ., Ōsaka 12 B3 34 41N 135 29 E
Ōsaki, Tōkyō 13 C3 35 36N 139 42 E
Osasco, S. Pau. 31 E5 23 31 S 46 46W
Osdorf, Berl. 7 B3 52 24N 13 20 E
Osdorf, Hbg. 7 D7 53 34N 9 50 E
Oshodi, Lagos 18 A2 6 33N 7 21 E
Oskar Frederikborg, Stock. 3 D13 59 24N 18 24 E
Oslo, Oslo 2 B4 59 54N 10 43 E
Oslofjorden, Oslo 2 C3 59 40N 10 35 E
Ōsone, Tōkyō 13 C2 35 31N 139 37 E
Osorun, Lagos 18 A2 6 33N 7 29 E
Ospiate, Mil. 9 D5 45 32N 9 6 E
Ossów, Wsaw. 10 E8 52 18N 21 12 E
Ostankino, Mos. 11 E9 55 49N 37 37 E
Østby, Købn. 2 D7 55 45N 12 2 E
Osterath, Ruhr 6 C1 51 16N 6 36 E
Österby, Hels. 3 B1 60 10N 24 25 E
Osterfeld, Ruhr 6 A3 51 30N 6 53 E
Osterley, Lon. 4 C2 51 28N 0 21W
Osterley Park, Lon. 4 C2 51 29N 0 21W
Östermalm, Stock. 3 D11 59 20N 18 4 E
Österåker, Stock. 3 D12 59 26N 18 16 E
Östersundom, Hels. 3 B6 60 15N 25 10 E
Östertälje, Stock. 3 E8 59 11N 17 39 E
Ostiense, Rome 9 F9 41 51N 12 29 E
Østmarkkapellet, Oslo 2 B5 59 52N 10 51 E
Østøya, Oslo 2 B3 59 52N 10 34 E
Östra Ryd, Stock. 3 D12 59 27N 18 11 E
Østre Aker, Oslo 2 B4 59 54N 10 49 E
Ostrov, Mos. 11 F11 55 36N 37 50 E
Ostrovtsy, Mos. 11 F12 55 36N 38 0 E
Ōta-Ku, Tōkyō 13 C3 35 34N 139 41 E
Otaniemi, Hels. 3 B3 60 11N 24 49 E
Otford, Lon. 4 D6 51 18N 0 11 E
Othmarschen, Hbg. 7 D7 53 33N 9 53 E
Otsuka, Tōkyō 13 B3 35 43N 139 44 E
Ottakring, Wien 10 G9 48 12N 16 18 E
Ottávia, Rome 9 F9 41 57N 12 24 E
Ottaviano, Nápl. 9 H13 40 50N 14 28 E
Ottensen, Hbg. 7 D7 53 33N 9 55 E
Ottobrunn, Mün. 7 G11 48 3N 11 40 E
Ottocalli, Nápl. 9 H12 40 52N 14 17 E
Otwock, Wsaw. 10 F8 52 8N 21 13 E
Ouerenburg, Ruhr 6 B5 51 27N 7 16 E
Ouiapo, Manila 15 D3 14 35N 120 59 E
Oulunkylä, Hels. 3 B4 60 13N 24 58 E
Ourcq, Canal de l', Paris 5 B4 48 54N 2 28 E
Ousit, Bangk. 15 B2 13 47N 100 31 E
Outer Brewster I., Bost. 21 C4 42 20N 70 52W
Outer Mission, S.F. 27 B2 37 43N 122 26W
Outremont, Mtrl. 20 A4 43 31N 73 36W
Overbruch, Ruhr 6 A2 51 32N 6 43 E
Overlea, Balt. 25 A3 39 21N 76 32W
Øverød, Købn. 2 D9 55 48N 12 28 E
Ōwada, Tōkyō 13 B2 35 48N 139 31 E
Owings Mills, Balt. 25 A2 39 25N 76 47W
Oworonsoki, Lagos 18 A2 6 32N 7 24 E
Oxon Hill, Wash. 25 E8 38 48N 76 59W
Oxshott, Lon. 4 D2 51 19N 0 21W
Oyada, Tōkyō 13 B4 35 46N 139 50 E
Ōyama, Tōkyō 13 B3 35 44N 139 42 E
Øyeren, Oslo 2 B6 59 55N 11 6 E
Oyodo, Ōsaka 12 B3 34 42N 135 29 E
Oyster B., N.Y. 23 B7 40 52N 73 31W
Oyster B., Syd. 19 C3 34 0 S 151 5 E
Oyster Bay Cove, N.Y. 23 B8 40 51N 73 29W
Oyster Bay Harbour, N.Y. 23 B7 40 53N 73 32W
Oyster Rock, Bomb. 16 H7 18 54N 72 49 E
Oyster Rocks, Kar. 17 H11 24 48N 66 59 E
Ozarów-Franciszków, Wsaw. 10 E5 52 13N 20 48 E
Ozerki, St-Pet. 11 B6 59 53N 30 42 E
Ozoir-la-Ferrière, Paris 5 C6 48 46N 2 40 E
Ozone Park, N.Y. 23 C5 40 40N 73 50W

P

Pacific Manor, S.F. 27 C2 37 38N 122 27W
Pacific Palisades, L.A. 28 B1 34 2N 118 32W
Pacifica, S.F. 27 C2 37 37N 122 27W
Packanack L., N.Y. 22 B3 40 56N 74 15W
Paco, Manila 15 D3 14 35N 120 59 E
Paco de Arcos, Lisb. 8 G7 38 41N 9 17W
Paddington, Lon. 4 B3 51 30N 0 10W
Paddington, Syd. 19 B4 33 53 S 151 14 E
Pademangan, Jak. 15 H9 6 7 S 106 49 E
Paderno, Mil. 9 D5 45 33N 9 9 E
Padre Miguel, Rio J. 31 B1 22 52 S 43 25W
Padstow, Syd. 19 B3 33 57 S 151 2 E
Pagewood, Syd. 19 B4 33 56 S 151 14 E
Pagote, Bomb. 16 H8 18 53N 73 59 E
Pai, I. do, Rio J. 31 B3 22 59 S 43 5W
Paia, Lisb. 8 F7 38 46N 9 11W
Paikpara, Calc. 16 E6 22 36N 88 23 E
Paint Br. →, Wash. 25 C8 38 57N 76 55W
Paiyun Airport, Gzh. 14 F8 23 10N 113 15 E
Pak Ka Shan, H.K. 12 E6 22 16N 114 13 E
Pak Kong, H.K. 12 D6 22 22N 114 15 E
Pak Tim Pa, H.K. 12 D5 22 22N 114 7 E
Pakila, Hels. 3 B4 60 15N 24 55 E
Palace Museum, Beij. 14 B3 39 54N 116 21 E
Palaión Fáliron, Ath. 8 J11 37 53N 23 42 E
Palaiseau, Paris 5 C3 48 42N 2 14 E
Palam, Delhi 16 B1 28 35N 77 4 E
Palam Int. Airport, Delhi 16 B1 28 32N 77 8 E
Palazzo Reale, Nápl. 9 H12 40 50N 14 15 E
Palazzo Reale, Tori. 9 B3 45 4N 7 40 E
Palazzolo, Mil. 9 D5 45 34N 9 9 E
Palazzuolo, Nápl. 9 H13 40 54N 14 28 E
Palermo, B.A. 32 B4 34 35 S 58 24W
Palhais, Lisb. 8 G8 38 37N 9 2W
Palisades, N.Y. 22 A5 41 1N 73 55W
Palisades Park, N.Y. 22 B4 40 50N 74 1W
Palleja, Barc. 8 D5 41 25N 2 0 E
Palmer Park, Wash. 25 D8 38 55N 76 52W
Palmers Green, Lon. 4 B4 51 36N 0 6W
Palmyra, Phil. 24 A4 40 0N 75 1W
Palo Alto, S.F. 27 D4 37 26N 122 8W
Paloheinä, Hels. 3 B4 60 15N 24 56 E
Palomar Park, S.F. 27 D3 37 29N 122 16W
Palomeras, Mdrd. 8 B3 40 22N 3 39W
Palos Heights, Chic. 26 D2 41 39N 87 47W
Palos Hills, Chic. 26 C2 41 42N 87 49W
Palos Hills Forest, Chic. 26 C1 41 40N 87 52W
Palos Park, Chic. 26 C1 41 40N 87 50W
Palota-Újfalu, Bud. 10 J13 47 33N 19 7 E
Palpara, Calc. 16 E6 22 38N 88 22 E
Palta, Calc. 16 D6 22 46N 88 23 E
Pamplona, Manila 15 E3 14 27N 120 58 E
Panayaan, Manila 15 E3 14 27N 120 57 E
Panchghara, Calc. 16 D5 22 44N 88 16 E
Panchur, Calc. 16 E5 22 32N 88 16 E
Pancoran, Jak. 15 J9 6 14 S 106 49 E
Pandan, Selat, Sing. 15 G7 1 16N 103 45 E
Pandan, Sungei →, Sing. 15 G7 1 18N 103 43 E
Pandan Res., Sing. 15 G7 1 18N 103 44 E
Panehpara, Calc. 16 E5 22 34N 88 15 E
Pangrati, Ath. 8 J11 37 56N 23 45 E
Pangsua, Sungei →, Sing. 15 F7 1 25N 103 45 E
Panihati, Calc. 16 D6 22 41N 88 22 E
Panjang, Bukit, Sing. 15 F7 1 22N 103 45 E
Panje, Bomb. 16 H8 18 54N 72 57 E
Panke →, Berl. 7 A3 52 31N 13 22 E
Pankow, Berl. 7 A3 52 34N 13 23 E
Panorama City, L.A. 28 A2 34 13N 118 26W
Panpur, Calc. 16 C6 22 51N 88 26 E
Pantheon, Rome 9 F9 41 53N 12 28 E
Pantin, Paris 5 B4 48 53N 2 24 E
Pantitlán, Méx. 29 B3 19 24N 99 4W
Panuacan, Manila 15 D4 14 35N 121 0 E
Panvel Cr. →, Bomb. 16 H9 18 59N 73 0 E
Paoli, Phil. 24 A2 40 2N 75 28W
Papiol, Barc. 8 D5 41 25N 2 0 E
Paracuellos del Jarama, Mdrd. 8 A3 40 30N 3 31W
Paradise Cay, S.F. 27 A2 37 54N 122 28W
Paramount, L.A. 28 C3 33 53N 118 11W
Paramus, N.Y. 22 B4 40 56N 74 2W
Paranaque, Manila 15 D3 14 30N 120 59 E
Paray-Vieille-Poste, Paris 5 C4 48 42N 2 20 E
Parbasdorf, Wien 10 G11 48 16N 16 35 E
Parbatipur, Calc. 16 E5 22 39N 88 13 E
Parcelacion Moderna, La Hab. 30 B3 23 2N 82 19W
Parco Regionale, Mil. 9 D5 45 35N 9 5 E
Parel, Bomb. 16 H7 18 59N 72 49 E
Pari, S. Pau. 31 E6 23 32 S 46 36W
Parioli, Rome 9 F9 41 55N 12 29 E
Paris, Paris 5 B4 48 53N 2 20 E
Paris-Le Bourget, Aéroport de, Paris 5 B4 48 58N 2 26 E
Paris-Orly, Aéroport de, Paris 5 C4 48 43N 2 22 E
Pārk-e-Shahānshāh, Tehr. 17 C5 35 46N 51 24 E
Park Orchards, Melb. 19 E8 37 46 S 145 13 E
Park Ridge, Chic. 26 A1 42 0N 87 50W
Park Ridge, N.Y. 22 A4 41 2N 74 2W
Park Royal, Lon. 4 B3 51 31N 0 16W
Parkchester, N.Y. 23 C5 40 49N 73 50W
Parkdale, Trto. 20 E8 43 38N 79 25W
Parkdene, Jobg. 18 F10 26 11 S 28 15 E
Parkhafen, Hbg. 7 D7 53 32N 9 54 E
Parkhill Gardens, Jobg. 18 F10 26 14 S 28 11 E
Parkhurst, Jobg. 18 E9 26 8 S 28 1 E
Parklawn, Wash. 25 D7 38 50N 77 7W
Parkmore, Jobg. 18 E9 26 5 S 28 2 E
Parkside, S.F. 27 B2 37 44N 122 29W
Parktown, Jobg. 18 E9 26 10 S 28 2 E
Parktown North, Jobg. 18 E9 26 8 S 28 2 E
Parkview, Jobg. 18 E9 26 9 S 28 1 E
Parkville, Balt. 25 A3 39 23N 76 34W
Parkville, N.Y. 22 D5 40 38N 73 57W
Parkwood, Jobg. 18 E9 26 9 S 28 2 E
Parque Edú Chaves, S. Pau. 31 D6 23 29 S 46 34W
Parramatta, Syd. 19 A2 33 49 S 150 59 E
Parramatta →, Syd. 19 A3 33 49 S 151 3 E
Parramatta North, Syd. 19 A3 33 48 S 151 0 E
Parramatta Park, Syd. 19 A3 33 48 S 151 0 E
Parsippany, N.Y. 22 B2 40 51N 74 26W
Paşabahçe, Ist. 17 A3 41 6N 29 5 E
Pasadena, L.A. 28 B4 34 9N 118 8W
Pasar Minggu, Jak. 15 J9 6 16 S 106 49 E
Pasay, Manila 15 D3 14 32N 120 59 E
Pascoe Vale, Melb. 19 E6 37 43 S 144 55 E
Pasig, Manila 15 D4 14 33N 121 4 E
Pasig →, Manila 15 D4 14 31N 121 6 E
Pasila, Hels. 3 B4 60 12N 24 56 E
Pasing, Mün. 7 G9 48 8N 11 28 E
Pasir Panjang, Sing. 15 G7 1 17N 103 46 E
Pasir Ris Beach, Sing. 15 F8 1 22N 103 56 E
Paso del Rey, B.A. 32 B2 34 38 S 58 45W
Passaic, N.Y. 22 B4 40 51N 74 9W
Passaic →, N.Y. 22 B3 40 42N 74 10W
Passirana, Mil. 9 D5 45 32N 9 2 E
Patapsco →, Balt. 25 B2 39 19N 76 49W
Patapsco State Park, Balt. 25 B2 39 18N 76 47W
Pateres, Manila 15 D4 14 32N 121 3 E
Paterson, N.Y. 22 B4 40 54N 74 9W
Pathumwan, Bangk. 15 B2 13 44N 100 31 E
Patipukur, Calc. 16 E6 22 36N 88 24 E
Patisia, Ath. 8 H11 38 2N 23 45 E
Patterson Park, Balt. 25 B3 39 17N 76 34W
Patul, Calc. 16 D4 22 45N 88 9 E
Paulo E. Virginia, Gruta, Rio J. 31 B2 22 56 S 43 16W
Paulsboro, Phil. 24 C3 39 49N 75 14W
Paulshof, Berl. 7 A5 52 38N 13 42 E
Pausin, Berl. 7 A1 52 38N 13 3 E
Pavarolo, Tori. 9 B3 45 4N 7 49 E
Pavlovo, St-Pet. 11 B5 59 55N 30 38 E
Pavne, Bomb. 16 G9 19 5N 73 1 E
Pavshino, Mos. 11 E7 55 49N 37 20 E
Paya Lebar, Sing. 15 F8 1 21N 103 52 E
Paylampur, Calc. 16 D5 22 46N 88 15 E
Peabody, Bost. 21 B4 42 32N 70 57W
Peabody Inst., Balt. 25 B3 39 17N 76 37W
Peakhurst, Syd. 19 B3 33 57 S 151 3 E
Pécel, Bud. 10 K14 47 29N 19 20 E
Pecetto Torinese, Tori. 9 B3 45 1N 7 44 E
Pechincha, Rio J. 31 B1 22 55 S 43 20W
Pechorka →, Mos. 11 F12 55 37N 38 2 E
Peckham, Lon. 4 C4 51 28N 0 3W
Pecqueuse, Paris 5 D2 48 38N 2 3 E
Peddocks I., Bost. 21 D4 42 17N 70 56W
Pederstrup, Købn. 2 D9 55 44N 12 20 E
Pedra Branca, Rio J. 31 B1 22 55 S 43 26W
Pedralbes, Barc. 8 D5 41 23N 2 7 E
Pedregal de San Angel, Jardines del, Méx. 29 C2 19 19N 99 12W
Pedreira, S. Pau. 31 F5 23 41 S 46 40W
Pedreros, Lima 30 G8 12 2 S 76 57W
Pedricktown, Phil. 24 C2 39 45N 75 24W
Pedro Cr. →, S.F. 27 C2 37 35N 122 30W
Pedro Valley, S.F. 27 C2 37 35N 122 29W
Peirce Res., Sing. 15 F7 1 22N 103 49 E
Pekhra-Pokrovskoye, Mos. 11 D11 55 50N 37 56 E
Pekhra-Yakovlevskaya, Mos. 11 E11 55 47N 37 57 E
Peking = Beijing, Beij. 14 B2 39 53N 116 21 E
Pelado, Cerro, Méx. 29 D2 19 10N 99 14W
Pelcowizna, Wsaw. 10 E7 52 17N 21 0 E
Pelham, N.Y. 23 B6 40 54N 73 46W
Pelham B. Park, N.Y. 23 B6 40 52N 73 48W
Pelham Manor, N.Y. 23 B6 40 53N 73 46W
Penalolén, Stgo 30 J11 33 28 S 70 30W
Peng Siang →, Sing. 15 F7 1 24N 103 43 E
Penge, Lon. 4 C4 51 24N 0 3W
Penha, Rio J. 31 A2 22 49 S 43 17W
Penha, S. Pau. 31 E6 23 31 S 46 32W
Penjaringan, Jak. 15 H9 6 7 S 106 48 E
Penn Square, Phil. 24 A3 40 8N 75 19W
Penn Wynne, Phil. 24 B3 39 59N 75 16W
Pennant Hills Park, Syd. 19 A3 33 46 S 151 6 E
Penndel, Phil. 24 A5 40 9N 74 54W
Penns Grove, Phil. 24 C2 39 44N 75 27W
Pennsauken, Phil. 24 B4 39 57N 75 5W
Pennsauken Cr. →, Phil. 24 B4 39 59N 75 3W
Pennsylvania, Univ. of, Phil. 24 B3 39 51N 75 11W
Pennypack Cr. →, Phil. 24 A4 40 0N 75 3W
Pentala, Hels. 3 C3 60 6N 24 40 E
Penyagino, Mos. 11 D8 55 50N 37 20 E
Penzing, Wien 10 G9 48 11N 16 18 E
Pequannock, N.Y. 22 B3 40 57N 74 17W
Pequena Arroio Fundo →, Rio J. 31 B1 22 58 S 43 21W
Perales del Rio, Mdrd. 8 C3 40 18N 3 38W
Perchtoldsdorf, Wien 10 H9 48 7N 16 17 E
Perdizes, S. Pau. 31 E6 23 32 S 46 39W
Peredelkino, Mos. 11 F8 55 38N 37 20 E
Peredelytsy, Mos. 11 F8 55 36N 37 21 E
Peristérion, Ath. 8 H11 38 1N 23 42 E
Perivale, Lon. 4 B3 51 31N 0 18W
Perlach, Mün. 7 G10 48 5N 11 37 E
Perlacher Forst, Mün. 7 G10 48 4N 11 34 E
Pero, Mil. 9 D5 45 30N 9 5 E
Peropok, Bukit, Sing. 15 G7 1 19N 103 42 E
Perovo, Mos. 11 E10 55 44N 37 45 E
Perrot, Î., Mtrl. 20 B2 43 23N 73 56W
Perry Hall, Balt. 25 A4 39 24N 76 28W
Perth Amboy, N.Y. 22 D3 40 30N 74 16W
Pertusella, Mil. 9 D5 45 35N 9 3 E
Pesanggrahag, Kali →, Jak. 15 J9 6 10 S 106 44 E
Peschiera Borromeo, Mil. 9 E6 45 26N 9 19 E
Pesek, P., Sing. 15 G7 1 17N 103 41 E
Pest, Bud. 10 K13 47 29N 19 4 E
Pesterzsébet, Bud. 10 K13 47 26N 19 6 E
Pesthidegkút, Bud. 10 J12 47 33N 18 57 E
Pestimre, Bud. 10 K14 47 24N 19 11 E
Pestlörinc, Bud. 10 K14 47 26N 19 11 E
Pestujhely, Bud. 10 J13 47 32N 19 7 E
Petare, Car. 30 E6 10 29N 66 48W
Petas, Hels. 3 B4 60 15N 24 59 E
Peters Pond, Bost. 21 A2 42 43N 71 15W
Petit, Jobg. 18 E11 26 6 S 28 22 E
Petit-Brûlé, Mtrl. 20 A1 43 35N 74 2W
Petojo Selatan, Jak. 15 J9 6 10 S 106 48 E
Petrograd = St. Petersburg, St-Pet. 11 B3 59 55N 30 15 E
Petrogradskaya Storona, St-Pet. 11 B4 59 56N 30 20 E
Petroúpolis, Ath. 8 H11 38 3N 23 40 E
Petrovice, Pra. 10 B3 50 2N 14 33 E
Petrovsko-Rasumovskoye, Mos. 11 E9 55 49N 37 34 E
Petrovskoye, Mos. 11 F11 55 36N 37 53 E
Petrovsky Park, Mos. 11 E9 55 47N 37 54 E
Pfaueninsel, Berl. 7 B1 52 26N 13 7 E
Phihāi, Kar. 17 G11 24 50N 67 8 E
Philadelphia, Phil. 24 B3 39 57N 75 11W
Philadelphia Airport, Phil. 24 A5 40 4N 75 0W
Philadelphia Int. Airport, Phil. 24 B3 39 52N 75 16W
Phillip B., Syd. 19 B4 33 58 S 151 14 E
Phinga, Calc. 16 D6 22 41N 88 25 E
Phoenix, Chic. 26 D3 41 36N 87 37W
Phoenixville, Phil. 24 A1 40 7N 75 31W
Phra Khanong, Bangk. 15 B2 13 40N 100 36 E
Phra Pradaeng, Bangk. 15 C2 13 39N 100 33 E
Phranakhon, Bangk. 15 B1 13 44N 100 29 E
Pianezza, Tori. 9 B2 45 6N 7 32 E
Pianura, Nápl. 9 H11 40 51N 14 10 E
Piaslów, Wsaw. 10 E5 52 11N 20 49 E
Pico Rivera, L.A. 28 C4 33 59N 118 5W
Piedade, Lisb. 8 F7 38 49N 9 16W
Piedade, Rio J. 31 B2 22 52 S 43 18W
Piedade, Cova da, Lisb. 8 F8 38 40N 9 8W
Piedmont, S.F. 27 B3 37 49N 122 14W
Pierrefitte, Paris 5 B4 48 58N 2 21 E
Pierrefonds, Mtrl. 20 A3 43 29N 73 52W
Pierrelaye, Paris 5 A2 49 1N 2 8 E
Pietralata, Rome 9 F10 41 55N 12 33 E
Pihlajamäki, Hels. 3 B4 60 14N 24 58 E
Pihlajasaari, Hels. 3 C4 60 8N 24 55 E
Pikesville, Balt. 25 A2 39 22N 76 42W
Pilar Velho, S. Pau. 31 F7 23 40 S 46 22W
Pilarcitos Cr. →, S.F. 27 C2 37 33N 122 24W
Pilarcitos L., S.F. 27 C2 37 33N 122 25W
Pilgrim Corner, Phil. 24 B3 39 57N 75 19W
Pilgrims Hatch, Lon. 4 B6 51 37N 0 17 E
Pillar Pt., S.F. 26 D2 37 29N 122 30W
Pimenta, S. Pau. 31 D7 23 27 S 46 24W
Pimlico, Lon. 4 C4 51 29N 0 8W
Pimmit Hills, Wash. 25 D6 38 54N 77 12W
Pimville, Jobg. 18 F8 26 16 S 27 54 E
Pinazo →, B.A. 32 A2 34 29 S 58 49W
Pine Brook, N.Y. 22 B3 40 51N 74 18W
Pine Grove, Trto. 20 D7 43 47N 79 34W
Pine Hill, Phil. 24 C5 39 47N 74 59W
Pine Orchard, Balt. 25 B1 39 16N 76 52W
Pinehurst, Bost. 21 B2 42 31N 71 12W
Piñero, B.A. 32 B2 34 31 S 58 46W
Pines Lake, N.Y. 22 B3 40 59N 74 15W
Piney Run →, Wash. 25 D6 38 58N 77 14W
Pinganli, Beij. 14 B3 39 56N 116 20 E
Pinheiros →, S. Pau. 31 E5 23 37 S 46 44W
Pinjrāpur, Kar. 17 G11 24 53N 67 4 E
Pinn →, Lon. 4 B2 51 30N 0 28W
Pinnau →, Hbg. 7 C6 53 40N 9 48 E
Pinneberg, Hbg. 7 C6 53 40N 9 48 E
Pinner, Lon. 4 B2 51 35N 0 23W
Pinner Green, Lon. 4 B2 51 35N 0 23W
Pino Torinese, Tori. 9 B3 45 2N 7 46 E
Pinole Cr. →, S.F. 27 A3 37 58N 122 12W
Pioltello, Mil. 9 D6 45 30N 9 19 E
Piossasco, Tori. 9 C1 44 59N 7 27 E
Piqueri, S. Pau. 31 D5 23 29 S 46 40W
Piqueri →, S. Pau. 31 D6 23 27 S 46 34W
Pira, Delhi 16 A1 28 40N 77 7 E
Piraévs, Ath. 8 J10 37 54N 23 39 E
Pirajussara, S. Pau. 31 E5 23 37 S 46 46W
Pirajussara →, S. Pau. 31 E5 23 33 S 46 42W
Piraporinha, S. Pau. 31 F5 23 40 S 46 42W
Piratininga, Rio J. 31 B3 22 56 S 43 4W
Piratininga, L. de, Rio J. 31 B3 22 56 S 43 4W
Pirituba, S. Pau. 31 D5 23 29 S 46 44W
Pirkkola, Hels. 3 B4 60 14N 24 55 E
Pisangan, Jak. 15 J10 6 12 S 106 52 E
Piscataway, N.Y. 22 D2 40 34N 74 27W
Pisnice, Pra. 10 C2 49 59N 14 28 E
Pitampura Kalan, Delhi 16 A1 28 41N 77 8 E

44 Pitkäjärvi

Pitkäjärvi, *Hels.* 3 B3 60 15N 24 45 E
Pitman, *Phil.* 24 C4 39 44N 75 7W
Plainedge, *N.Y.* 23 C8 40 43N 73 27W
Plainfield, *N.Y.* 22 D2 40 36N 74 23W
Plainview, *N.Y.* 23 C8 40 46N 73 27W
Plaisir, *Paris* 5 C1 48 49N 1 56 E
Plandome, *N.Y.* 23 C6 40 48N 73 42W
Plandome Heights, *N.Y.* 23 C6 40 48N 73 42W
Planegg, *Mün.* 7 G9 48 6N 11 25 E
Plazo Mayor, *Mdrd.* 8 B2 40 25N 3 43W
Pleasant Hill, *S.F.* 27 A4 37 56N 122 4W
Plenty, *Melb.* 19 E7 37 40 S 145 5 E
Pluit, *Jak.* 15 H9 6 7 S 106 47 E
Plumsock, *Phil.* 24 B2 39 58N 75 28W
Plumstead, *Lon.* 4 C5 51 29N 0 5 E
Plymouth Meeting, *Phil.* 24 A3 40 6N 75 16W
Plyushchevo, *Mos.* 11 E10 55 44N 37 45 E
Po →, *Tori.* 9 B3 45 7N 7 46 E
Po Toi, *H.K.* 12 E6 22 16N 114 17 E
Po Toi I., *H.K.* 12 E6 22 10N 114 15 E
Podbaba, *Pra.* 10 B2 50 7N 14 22 E
Podoli, *Pra.* 10 B2 50 2N 14 25 E
Podra, *Calc.* 16 E5 22 33N 88 16 E
Poduskino, *Mos.* 11 E7 55 43N 37 15 E
Poggioreale, *Nápl.* 9 H12 40 51N 14 17 E
Pogliano Milanese, *Mil.* 9 D4 45 32N 8 59 E
Pohick Cr. →, *Wash.* 25 E6 38 47N 77 16W
Point Breeze, *Phil.* 24 B3 39 54N 75 13W
Point Lookout, *N.Y.* 23 D7 40 35N 73 34W
Point View Res., *N.Y.* 22 B3 40 58N 74 14W
Pointe-Aux-Trembles, *Mtrl.* 20 A4 43 38N 73 30W
Pointe-Calumet, *Mtrl.* 20 B2 43 29N 73 58W
Pointe-Claire, *Mtrl.* 20 B3 43 27N 73 48W
Poissy, *Paris* 5 B2 48 55N 2 2 E
Pok Fu Lam, *H.K.* 12 E5 22 16N 114 7 E
Pokrovsko-Sresnevo, *Mos.* 11 E8 55 48N 37 27 E
Pokrovskoye, *Mos.* 11 F9 55 37N 37 36 E
Póllena, *Nápl.* 9 H13 40 51N 14 22 E
Polsum, *Ruhr* 6 A4 51 37N 7 2 E
Polyustrovo, *St-Pet.* 11 B4 59 57N 30 25 E
Pomigliano d'Arco, *Nápl.* 9 H13 40 54N 14 23 E
Pompei, *Nápl.* 9 J13 40 45N 14 29 E
Pomponne, *Paris* 5 B6 48 52N 2 40 E
Pomprap, *Bangk.* 15 B2 13 44N 100 30 E
Pompton →, *N.Y.* 22 B3 40 53N 74 16W
Pompton Lakes, *N.Y.* 22 A3 41 0N 74 15W
Pompton Plains, *N.Y.* 22 B3 40 58N 74 18W
Ponders End, *Lon.* 4 B4 51 38N 0 2W
Pondok Indah, *Jak.* 15 J9 6 16 S 106 46 E
Ponkapog, *Bost.* 21 D3 42 11N 71 4W
Ponkapog Pond, *Bost.* 21 D3 42 11N 71 5W
Pont-Viau, *Mtrl.* 20 A3 43 34N 73 41W
Pontault-Combault, *Paris* 5 C5 48 47N 2 36 E
Pontcarré, *Paris* 5 C6 48 47N 2 42 E
Pontchartrain, *Paris* 5 C1 48 48N 1 54 E
Ponte Galéria, *Rome* 9 G8 41 48N 12 19 E
Pontes, Canto do, *Rio J.* 31 B3 22 56 S 43 3W
Pontevedra, *B.A.* 32 C2 34 44 S 58 41W
Ponticelli, *Nápl.* 9 H12 40 51N 14 19 E
Pontinha, *Lisb.* 8 F7 38 45N 9 11W
Pontoise, *Paris* 5 A2 49 2N 2 4 E
Poortview, *Jobg.* 18 E8 26 5 S 27 51 E
Poplar, *Lon.* 4 B4 51 30N 0 0 E
Poppenbüttel, *Hbg.* 7 D8 53 39N 10 4 E
Port Chester, *N.Y.* 23 A6 41 0N 73 40W
Port Chester Harbour, *N.Y.* 23 B7 40 58N 73 38W
Port Jackson, *Syd.* 19 B4 33 51 S 151 14 E
Port Kennedy, *Phil.* 24 A2 40 6N 75 25W
Port Melbourne, *Melb.* 19 F6 37 50 S 144 54 E
Port Newark, *N.Y.* 22 C4 40 41N 74 9W
Port Reading, *N.Y.* 22 D3 40 34N 74 13W
Port Richmond, *N.Y.* 22 D4 40 38N 74 7W
Port Shelter, *H.K.* 12 D6 22 20N 114 17 E
Port Union, *Trto.* 20 D10 43 47N 79 7W
Port Washington, *N.Y.* 23 B7 40 49N 73 42W
Port Washington North, *N.Y.* 23 B6 40 50N 73 41W
Portage Park, *Chic.* 26 B2 41 56N 87 45W
Portela, Aeroporto da, *Lisb.* 8 F8 38 46N 9 7W
Pórtici, *Nápl.* 9 J12 40 48N 14 19 E
Porto Brandão, *Lisb.* 8 F7 38 40N 9 12W
Porto Novo Cr. →, *Lagos* 18 B2 6 25N 7 22 E
Porto Nuevo, *B.A.* 32 B4 34 35 S 58 22W
Portrero, *S.F.* 27 B3 37 46N 122 25W
Posen, *Chic.* 26 D2 41 38N 87 41W
Posíllipo, *Nápl.* 9 J12 40 49N 14 13 E
Posíllipo, C. di, *Nápl.* 9 J12 40 48N 14 12 E
Posolok Lenina, *St-Pet.* 11 C2 59 50N 30 5 E
Potawatomi Woods, *Chic.* 26 A1 42 8N 87 53W
Potomac, *Wash.* 25 D6 38 59N 77 13W
Potomac →, *Wash.* 25 D7 38 58N 77 9W
Potrero Pt., *S.F.* 27 B2 37 45N 122 22W
Potsdam, *Berl.* 7 B1 52 23N 13 3 E
Potter Pt., *Syd.* 19 C4 34 2 S 151 13 E
Potters Bar, *Lon.* 4 A4 51 41N 0 10W
Potzham, *Mün.* 7 G10 48 1N 11 36 E
Pötzleinsdorf, *Wien* 10 G9 48 14N 16 17 E
Povoa de Santo Adriao, *Lisb.* 8 F8 38 47N 9 9W
Powderhorn L., *Chic.* 26 D3 41 38N 87 31W
Powiĉle, *Wsaw.* 10 E7 52 14N 21 1 E
Powôzki, *Wsaw.* 10 E6 52 15N 20 58 E
Powsin, *Wsaw.* 10 F7 52 8N 21 6 E
Powsinek, *Wsaw.* 10 F7 52 9N 21 6 E
Poyo, *Barc.* 8 D6 41 28N 2 12 E
Pozuelo de Alarcón, *Mdrd.* 8 B2 40 25N 3 48W
Praça Seca, *Rio J.* 31 B1 22 53 S 43 20W
Prado, Museo del, *Mdrd.* 8 B2 40 25N 3 42W
Prado Churubusco, *Méx.* 29 B3 19 20N 99 8W
Praga, *Wsaw.* 10 E7 52 15N 21 2 E
Prague = Praha, *Pra.* 10 B2 50 4N 14 25 E
Praha, *Pra.* 10 B2 50 4N 14 25 E
Praha-Ruzyně Airport, *Pra.* 10 B1 50 6N 14 16 E
Praires, R. des →, *Mtrl.* 20 A4 43 38N 73 36W
Prat de Llobregat, *Barc.* 8 E5 41 19N 2 5 E
Prater, *Wien* 10 G10 48 12N 16 25 E
Pratts Bottom, *Lon.* 4 C5 51 20N 0 7 E
Prawet Buri Rom, Khlong →, *Bangk.* 15 B2 13 43N 100 38 E
Preakness, *N.Y.* 22 B3 40 56N 74 12W
Precotto, *Mil.* 9 D6 45 30N 9 13 E
Prédecelles →, *Paris* 5 D2 48 36N 2 7 E
Pregnana Milanese, *Mil.* 9 D4 45 30N 9 0 E
Prem Prachakan, Khlong →, *Bangk.* 15 B2 13 46N 100 35 E
Prenestino Labicano, *Rome* 9 F10 41 53N 12 33 E
Prenzlauerberg, *Berl.* 7 A3 52 32N 13 24 E
Presidente Derqui, *B.A.* 32 A1 34 29 S 58 50W
Presidente Outra, Rodo, *Rio J.* 31 A1 22 47 S 43 21W
Preston, *Melb.* 19 E6 37 44 S 144 59 E
Pretos Forros, Sa. dos, *Rio J.* 31 B2 22 54 S 43 17W
Préville, *Mtrl.* 20 B5 43 28N 73 29W
Přezletice, *Pra.* 10 B3 50 9N 14 34 E
Primavalle, *Rome* 9 F9 41 55N 12 25 E
Primrose, *Jobg.* 18 F9 26 11 S 28 9 E
Princes B., *N.Y.* 22 D3 40 30N 74 12W
Princess Elizabeth Park, *Sing.* 15 F7 1 21N 103 45 E
Progreso, *Mdrd.* 8 B3 40 27N 3 39W
Progreso Nacional, *Méx.* 29 A3 19 30N 99 9W
Prosek, *Pra.* 10 B3 50 7N 14 30 E
Prospect, *Syd.* 19 A2 33 48 S 150 55 E
Prospect Heights, *Chic.* 26 A1 42 5N 87 55W
Prospect Hill Park, *Bost.* 21 C2 42 23N 71 13W
Prospect Park, *N.Y.* 22 B3 40 55N 74 10W
Prospect Park, *Phil.* 24 B3 39 53N 75 18W
Prospect Pt., *N.Y.* 23 B6 40 52N 73 42W
Prospect Res., *Syd.* 19 A2 33 49 S 150 53 E
Providence, *Balt.* 25 A3 39 25N 76 34W
Providencia, *Stgo* 30 J11 33 25 S 70 36W
Průhonice, *Pra.* 10 C3 50 0N 14 33 E
Pruszków, *Wsaw.* 10 E5 52 10N 20 48 E
Psikhikón, *Ath.* 8 H11 38 1N 23 46 E
Pudong, *Shang.* 14 J12 31 13N 121 30 E
Puduo, *Shang.* 14 J11 31 15N 121 24 E
Pueblo Libre, *Lima* 30 G8 12 5 S 77 4W
Pueblo Nuevo, *Barc.* 8 D6 41 23N 2 11 E
Pueblo Nuevo, *Mdrd.* 8 B3 40 25N 3 37W
Puente Cascallares, *B.A.* 32 C2 34 41 S 58 48W
Puente Hills, *L.A.* 28 C5 33 59N 117 59W
Puffing Billy Station, *Melb.* 19 F9 37 54 S 145 20 E
Puhuangyu, *Beij.* 14 B3 39 50N 116 22 E
Puistola, *Hels.* 3 B5 60 16N 25 2 E
Pukinmäki, *Hels.* 3 B4 60 15N 24 57 E
Pullach, *Mün.* 7 G9 48 3N 11 31 E
Pulo, *Manila* 15 D4 14 34N 121 4 E
Pulo Gadung, *Jak.* 15 J10 6 11 S 106 54 E
Pumphrey, *Balt.* 25 B3 39 13N 76 39W
Punchbowl, *Syd.* 19 B3 33 55 S 151 3 E
Punde, *Bomb.* 16 H8 18 53N 72 57 E
Punggol, *Sing.* 15 F8 1 23N 103 54 E
Punggol, Sungei →, *Sing.* 15 F8 1 24N 103 53 E
Punggol Pt., *Sing.* 15 F8 1 24N 103 54 E
Punta Brava, *La Hab.* 30 B2 23 1N 82 29W
Puolarmetsä, *Hels.* 3 B3 60 11N 24 41 E
Puotila, *Hels.* 3 B5 60 13N 25 6 E
Purchase, *N.Y.* 23 A6 41 2N 73 43W
Purfleet, *Lon.* 4 C5 51 29N 0 14 E
Purkersdorf, *Wien* 10 G9 48 12N 16 11 E
Purley, *Lon.* 4 C4 51 20N 0 6W
Puteaux, *Paris* 5 B3 48 53N 2 14 E
Puth Kalan, *Delhi* 16 A1 28 42N 77 4 E
Putilkovo, *Mos.* 11 D8 55 51N 37 22 E
Putnamville Res., *Bost.* 21 B4 42 36N 70 56W
Putney, *Lon.* 4 C3 51 27N 0 13W
Putty Hill, *Balt.* 25 A3 39 22N 76 30W
Putxet, *Barc.* 8 D5 41 24N 2 8 E
Putzbrunn, *Mün.* 7 G11 48 4N 11 42 E
Pyeongchang, *Sŏul* 12 G7 37 35N 126 57 E
Pyramids, *El Qâ.* 18 D4 29 58N 31 7 E
Pyry, *Wsaw.* 10 F6 52 8N 21 0 E

Q

Qanât el Ismâ'îliya, *El Qâ.* 18 C5 30 7N 31 17 E
Qasemābād, *Tehr.* 17 C6 35 4N 51 3 E
Qasr-e-Firōzeh, *Tehr.* 17 D6 35 29N 51 31 E
Qianmen, *Beij.* 14 B3 39 51N 116 21 E
Qibao, *Shang.* 14 K11 31 9N 121 20 E
Qingguang, *Tianj.* 14 D5 39 11N 117 2 E
Qinghua Univ., *Beij.* 14 A2 40 0N 116 17 E
Qinghuayuan, *Beij.* 14 B2 39 59N 116 19 E
Qingningsi, *Shang.* 14 J12 31 16N 121 33 E
Qolhak, *Tehr.* 17 C5 35 45N 51 26 E
Quadraro, *Rome* 9 F10 41 51N 12 33 E
Quaid-i-Azam, *Kar.* 17 G10 24 50N 66 59 E
Qual'eh Murgeh Airport, *Tehr.* 17 D5 35 38N 51 22 E
Qualiano, *Nápl.* 9 H11 40 55N 14 9 E
Quannapowitt, L., *Bost.* 21 B3 42 30N 71 4W
Quartiere Zingone, *Mil.* 9 E5 45 25N 9 3 E
Quarto, *Nápl.* 9 H11 40 52N 14 8 E
Quds, *Bagd.* 17 E8 33 23N 44 24 E
Quebrada Baruta →, *Car.* 30 E5 10 29N 66 53W
Quebrada Tácagua →, *Car.* 30 D4 10 36N 67 1W
Quebrada Topo →, *Car.* 30 D4 10 32N 67 0W
Queen Mary Res., *Lon.* 4 C2 51 24N 0 27W
Queens Village, *N.Y.* 23 C6 40 43N 73 44W
Queensbury, *Lon.* 4 B3 51 35N 0 16W
Queenscliffe, *Syd.* 19 A4 33 47 S 151 17 E
Queenstown, *Sing.* 15 G7 1 18N 103 48 E
Quellerina, *Jobg.* 18 E8 26 9 S 27 55 E
Queluz, *Lisb.* 8 F7 38 45N 9 14W
Quezon City, *Manila* 15 D4 14 37N 121 2 E
Quickborn, *Hbg.* 7 C7 53 43N 9 54 E
Quilicura, *Stgo* 30 J10 33 22 S 70 43W
Quilmes, *B.A.* 32 C5 34 43 S 58 15W
Quincy, *Bost.* 21 D3 42 14N 71 0W
Quincy B., *Bost.* 21 D4 42 16N 70 59W
Quincy-sous-Sénart, *Paris* 5 C5 48 40N 2 32 E
Quinta Normal, *Stgo* 30 J10 33 26 S 70 40W
Quinto Romano, *Mil.* 9 E5 45 28N 9 5 E
Quirinale, *Rome* 9 F9 41 53N 12 29 E
Quitaúna, *S. Pau.* 31 E5 23 31 S 46 48W

R

Raasdorf, *Wien* 10 G11 48 14N 16 33 E
Raccoon Cr. →, *Phil.* 24 C3 39 48N 75 21W
Raccoon Str., *S.F.* 27 A2 37 52N 122 26W
Radevormwald, *Ruhr* 6 C6 51 12N 7 22 E
Radlett, *Lon.* 4 A3 51 41N 0 19W
Radlice, *Pra.* 10 B2 50 3N 14 23 E
Radnor, *Phil.* 24 A2 40 2N 75 21W
Radonice, *Pra.* 10 B3 50 8N 14 36 E
Radotin, *Pra.* 10 C2 49 59N 14 21 E
Rælingen, *Oslo* 2 B6 59 53N 11 5 E
Rafael Calzada, *B.A.* 32 C4 34 47 S 58 21W
Rafael Castillo, *B.A.* 32 C3 34 42 S 58 36W
Raffles Park, *Sing.* 15 G7 1 19N 103 48 E
Raghunathpur, *Calc.* 16 D5 22 41N 88 14 E
Rahlstedt, *Hbg.* 7 D8 53 35N 10 7 E
Rahm, *Ruhr* 6 B2 51 21N 6 47 E
Rahnsdorf, *Berl.* 7 B5 52 25N 13 41 E
Rahway, *N.Y.* 22 D3 40 36N 74 17W
Rail Tree Hill, *Bost.* 21 B2 42 33N 71 13W
Rainbow Lakes, *N.Y.* 22 B2 40 53N 74 27W
Rainham, *Lon.* 4 B6 51 31N 0 11 E
Rainier, Mt., *Wash.* 25 D8 38 56N 76 57W
Raj Bhawan, *Calc.* 16 E6 22 33N 88 20 E
Rajakylä, *Hels.* 3 B5 60 15N 25 5 E
Rajapur, *Calc.* 16 E5 22 39N 88 11 E
Rajganj, *Calc.* 16 E5 22 34N 88 14 E
Rajpur, *Delhi* 16 A2 28 41N 77 12 E
Rákos-patak →, *Bud.* 10 K14 47 29N 19 12 E
Rákoscsaba, *Bud.* 10 K14 47 28N 19 17 E
Rákoshegy, *Bud.* 10 K14 47 27N 19 14 E
Rákoskér, *Bud.* 10 K14 47 28N 19 14 E
Rákoskert, *Bud.* 10 K14 47 27N 19 18 E
Rákosliget, *Bud.* 10 K14 47 29N 19 16 E
Rákospalota, *Bud.* 10 J13 47 34N 19 7 E
Rákosszentmihály, *Bud.* 10 J13 47 31N 19 8 E
Raków, *Wsaw.* 10 E6 52 11N 20 56 E
Rakowiec, *Wsaw.* 10 E6 52 12N 20 58 E
Ramadān, *Bagd.* 17 F8 33 19N 44 20 E
Ramanathpur, *Calc.* 16 D5 22 41N 88 14 E
Rambler Channel, *H.K.* 12 D5 22 21N 114 6 E
Ramblewood, *Phil.* 24 B5 39 55N 74 56W
Ramenki, *Mos.* 11 E8 55 41N 37 28 E
Ramersdorf, *Mün.* 7 G10 48 6N 11 35 E
Ramnathpur, *Calc.* 16 E5 22 35N 88 18 E
Ramos, *Rio J.* 31 B2 22 50 S 43 14W
Ramos Mejía, *B.A.* 32 B3 34 39 S 58 33W
Rampur, *Delhi* 16 A2 28 44N 77 18 E
Ramsgate, *Syd.* 19 B3 33 58 S 151 8 E
Ramstadjøen, *Oslo* 2 B6 59 53N 11 3 E
Rancho Boyeros, *La Hab.* 30 C2 22 59N 82 22W
Rancho Colorado, Presa de, *Méx.* 29 B2 19 29N 99 16W
Rancocas Cr. →, *Phil.* 24 A5 40 2N 74 58W
Rand Afrikaans Univ., *Jobg.* 18 F9 26 11 S 28 0 E
Rand Airport, *Jobg.* 18 F9 26 14 S 28 8 E
Randallstown, *Balt.* 25 A2 39 21N 76 46W
Randburg, *Jobg.* 18 E8 26 5 S 27 57 E
Randhart, *Jobg.* 18 F9 26 16 S 28 7 E
Randolph, *Bost.* 21 D3 42 10N 71 3W
Randolph Hills, *Wash.* 25 C7 39 3N 77 6W
Randpark, *Jobg.* 18 E8 26 6 S 27 58 E
Randwick, *Syd.* 19 B4 33 54 S 151 14 E
Ranelagh, *B.A.* 32 C5 34 47 S 58 14W
Rannersdorf, *Wien* 10 H10 48 7N 16 27 E
Raparkrif, *Jobg.* 18 E8 26 5 S 27 58 E
Raposo, *Lisb.* 8 F7 38 40N 9 11W
Raritan →, *N.Y.* 22 D2 40 30N 74 27W
Raritan B., *N.Y.* 22 E3 40 29N 74 12W
Rasskazovka, *Mos.* 11 F8 55 38N 37 20 E
Rasta, *Stock.* 3 E8 59 18N 17 37 E
Rastaala, *Hels.* 3 B3 60 15N 24 48 E
Rastila, *Hels.* 3 B5 60 12N 25 7 E
Raszyn, *Wsaw.* 10 F6 52 9N 20 54 E
Rat Burana, *Bangk.* 15 B2 13 40N 100 30 E
Ratanpur, *Calc.* 16 D5 22 49N 88 14 E
Rath, *Ruhr* 6 C2 51 16N 6 49 E
Ratingen, *Ruhr* 6 C3 51 18N 6 52 E
Rato, *Lisb.* 8 F8 38 43N 9 8W
Rauxel, *Ruhr* 6 A5 51 34N 7 18 E
Ravenswood Pt., *S.F.* 27 C4 37 30N 122 8W
Rawamangun, *Jak.* 15 J10 6 11 S 106 52 E
Rayners Lane, *Lon.* 4 B2 51 34N 0 23W
Raynes Park, *Lon.* 4 C3 51 24N 0 12W
Raypur, *Calc.* 16 F6 22 28N 88 22 E
Razdory, *Mos.* 11 E7 55 44N 37 17 E
Razmitelevo, *St-Pet.* 11 B5 59 54N 30 39 E
Razor Hill, *H.K.* 12 D6 22 20N 114 15 E
Reading, *Bost.* 21 B3 42 31N 71 5W
Reading Highlands, *Bost.* 21 B3 42 31N 71 5W
Reáglie, *Tori.* 9 B3 45 3N 7 44 E
Real, Palacio, *Mdrd.* 8 B2 40 25N 3 43W
Real Felipe, Castillo, *Lima* 30 G8 12 4 S 77 9W
Real Fuerta, Château de la, *La Hab.* 30 B2 23 8N 82 20W
Realengo, *Rio J.* 31 B1 22 52 S 43 24W
Réau, *Paris* 5 D5 48 36N 2 37 E
Recklinghausen, *Ruhr* 6 A5 51 37N 7 12 E
Recklinghausen-Süd, *Ruhr* 6 A5 51 34N 7 14 E
Recoleta, *Stgo* 30 J11 33 25 S 70 40W
Reconquista →, *B.A.* 32 B3 34 35 S 58 35W
Red Bank Battle Mon., *Phil.* 24 B3 39 52N 75 11W
Red Fort, *Delhi* 16 B2 28 39N 77 14 E
Red Rock, *S.F.* 27 A2 37 55N 122 25W
Red Square, *Mos.* 11 E9 55 45N 37 37 E
Redbridge, *Lon.* 4 B5 51 34N 0 3 E
Redwood City, *S.F.* 27 D3 37 29N 122 14W
Redwood Cr. →, *S.F.* 27 C3 37 31N 122 11W
Redwood Pt., *S.F.* 27 C3 37 32N 122 11W
Redwood Regional Park, *S.F.* 27 B4 37 48N 122 8W
Reeves Hill, *Bost.* 21 C1 42 20N 71 20W
Refshaleøen, *Købn.* 2 D10 55 41N 12 36 E
Regents Park, *Jobg.* 18 F9 26 14 S 28 3 E
Regents Park, *Lon.* 4 B4 51 31N 0 9W
Regents Park, *Syd.* 19 B3 33 52 S 151 1 E
Regi Lagni →, *Nápl.* 9 H13 40 56N 14 23 E
Regina Margherita, *Tori.* 9 B2 45 4N 7 34 E
Regla, *La Hab.* 30 B3 23 7N 82 19W
Rego Park, *N.Y.* 23 C5 40 43N 73 51W
Reiherstieg, *Hbg.* 7 D7 53 30N 9 58 E
Reinickendorf, *Berl.* 7 A3 52 34N 13 22 E
Reinoldikirche, *Ruhr* 6 A6 51 30N 7 28 E
Reistad, *Oslo* 2 C1 59 46N 10 16 E
Reitbrook, *Hbg.* 7 E8 53 28N 10 8 E
Rekola, *Hels.* 3 B5 60 19N 25 4 E
Rellingen, *Hbg.* 7 D7 53 39N 9 50 E
Rembertów, *Wsaw.* 10 E7 52 15N 21 9 E
Remedios de Escalada, *B.A.* 32 C4 34 43 S 58 24W
Rémola, Laguna del, *Barc.* 8 E5 41 16N 2 4 E
Remscheid, *Ruhr* 6 C5 51 11N 7 11 E
Renca, *Stgo* 30 J10 33 24 S 70 42W
Renca, Cerro, *Stgo* 30 J10 33 23 S 70 44W
Rener, *Ist.* 17 A2 41 1N 28 56 E
Renmin Gongyuan, *Tianj.* 14 E6 39 6N 117 12 E
Rennemoulin, *Paris* 5 B2 48 50N 2 2 E
Rennie's Mill, *H.K.* 12 E6 22 18N 114 15 E
Renzel, *Hbg.* 7 D8 53 36N 10 5 E
Repaupo, *Phil.* 24 C3 39 48N 75 19W
Repaupo Cr. →, *Phil.* 24 C3 39 49N 75 20W
Řeporyje, *Pra.* 10 B1 50 1N 14 18 E
République, Place de la, *Paris* 5 B4 48 52N 2 22 E
Repy, *Pra.* 10 B1 50 4N 14 17 E
Resarö, *Stock.* 3 D13 59 25N 18 20 E
Rescaldina, *Mil.* 9 D4 45 36N 8 57 E
Research, *Melb.* 19 E8 37 42 S 145 10 E
Reseda, *L.A.* 28 A1 34 12N 118 31W
Reservoir, *Melb.* 19 E7 37 42 S 145 1 E
Reservoir Pond, *Bost.* 21 D3 42 10N 71 7W
Residenz, *Mün.* 7 G10 48 8N 11 34 E
Resse, *Ruhr* 6 A4 51 34N 7 6 E
Reston, *Wash.* 25 D6 38 57N 77 20W
Retiro, *B.A.* 32 B4 34 35 S 58 22W
Retiro, *Mdrd.* 8 B2 40 24N 3 40W
Reutov, *Mos.* 11 E11 55 45N 37 50 E
Réveillon →, *Paris* 5 C5 48 42N 2 30 E
Revere, *Bost.* 21 C3 42 25N 71 0W
Revesby, *Syd.* 19 B3 33 57 S 151 0 E
Revolucion, Plaza de la, *La Hab.* 30 B2 23 7N 82 23W
Rexdale, *Trto.* 20 D7 43 43N 79 35W
Reynolds Channel, *N.Y.* 23 D6 40 35N 73 41W
Reynosa Tamaulipas, *Méx.* 29 A2 19 30N 99 10W
Rheem Valley, *S.F.* 27 A4 37 50N 122 8W
Rhein-Herne Kanal, *Ruhr* 6 B3 51 29N 6 59 E
Rheinberg, *Ruhr* 6 A1 51 32N 6 37 E
Rheinhausen, *Ruhr* 6 B2 51 24N 6 43 E
Rheinkamp, *Ruhr* 6 B1 51 29N 6 36 E
Rho, *Mil.* 9 D5 45 31N 9 2 E
Rhodes, *Syd.* 19 A3 33 49 S 151 6 E
Rhodesfield, *Jobg.* 18 E10 26 6 S 28 14 E
Rhodon, *Paris* 5 C2 48 42N 2 3 E
Rhodon →, *Paris* 5 C2 48 42N 2 4 E
Rhu, Tg., *Sing.* 15 G8 1 17N 103 51 E
Ribeirão Pires, *S. Pau.* 31 F7 23 42 S 46 23W
Ričanský →, *Pra.* 10 B3 50 5N 14 36 E
Říčany, *Pra.* 10 C3 49 59N 14 39 E
Ricarda, Laguna de la, *Barc.* 8 E5 41 17N 2 6 E
Richardson B., *S.F.* 27 A2 37 52N 122 29W
Richmond, *Lon.* 4 C3 51 27N 0 17W
Richmond, *Melb.* 19 E7 37 48 S 145 0 E
Richmond, *S.F.* 27 B2 37 46N 122 27W
Richmond, *S.F.* 27 A2 37 56N 122 21W
Richmond →, *N.Y.* 22 D3 40 34N 74 11W
Richmond, Pt., *S.F.* 27 A2 37 54N 122 23W
Richmond Hill, *N.Y.* 23 C5 40 41N 73 51W
Richmond Hill, *Trto.* 20 C8 43 51N 79 24W
Richmond Inner Harbour, *S.F.* 27 A2 37 54N 122 20W
Richmond Park, *Lon.* 4 C3 51 26N 0 16W
Richmond Valley, *N.Y.* 22 D3 40 31N 74 13W
Richvale, *Trto.* 20 C8 43 51N 79 26W
Rickers I., *N.Y.* 23 C5 40 47N 73 53W
Rickmansworth, *Lon.* 4 B2 51 38N 0 28W
Riddel Cr. →, *Melb.* 19 F8 37 52 S 145 13 E
Riderwood, *Balt.* 25 A3 39 24N 76 37W
Ridgefield, *N.Y.* 22 C4 40 49N 74 0W
Ridgefield Park, *N.Y.* 22 B4 40 52N 74 1W
Ridgewood, *N.Y.* 23 C5 40 42N 73 53W
Ridley Cr. →, *Phil.* 24 B2 39 51N 75 20W
Ridley Creek State Park, *Phil.* 24 B2 39 57N 75 26W
Ridley Park, *Phil.* 24 B3 39 52N 75 19W
Riedmoos, *Mün.* 7 F10 48 16N 11 32 E
Riem, *Mün.* 7 G11 48 8N 11 41 E
Riemke, *Ruhr* 6 A5 51 30N 7 12 E
Rimac, *Lima* 30 G8 12 2 S 77 2W
Rimau, Tg., *Sing.* 15 G7 1 15N 103 48 E
Ringwood, *Melb.* 19 E8 37 48 S 145 4 E
Rinkeby, *Stock.* 3 D10 59 23N 17 55 E
Rio Comprido, *Rio J.* 31 B2 22 55 S 43 12W
Rio de Janeiro, *Rio J.* 31 B2 22 54 S 43 12W
Rio de Mouro, *Lisb.* 8 F7 38 46N 9 15W
Rio Hondo →, *L.A.* 28 B4 34 2N 118 5W
Rio Pequeno, *S. Pau.* 31 E5 23 34 S 46 44W
Rione Trieste, *Nápl.* 9 H13 40 52N 14 27 E
Ripley, *Lon.* 4 D2 51 17N 0 29W
Rippling Ridge, *Balt.* 25 B3 39 11N 76 37W
Ris, *Oslo* 2 B4 59 56N 10 41 E
Ris-Orangis, *Paris* 5 D4 48 38N 2 24 E
Risby, *Købn.* 2 D8 55 41N 12 19 E
Rishra, *Calc.* 16 D6 22 42N 88 20 E
Ritan Gongyuan, *Beij.* 14 B3 39 53N 116 24 E
Ritchie, *Wash.* 25 D8 38 52N 76 51W
Rithala, *Delhi* 16 A1 28 43N 77 6 E
Ritorp, *Stock.* 3 E8 59 12N 17 38 E
Rivalta di Torino, *Tori.* 9 B1 45 2N 7 31 E
Rivas de Jarama, *Mdrd.* 8 B3 40 22N 3 31W
Rivas-Vaciamadrio, *Mdrd.* 8 C3 40 19N 3 30W
Rivasacco, *Tori.* 9 A1 45 10N 7 29 E
Rive Sud, Canal de la, *Mtrl.* 20 B4 43 24N 73 31W
River Edge, *N.Y.* 22 B4 40 56N 74 1W
River Forest, *Chic.* 26 B2 41 53N 87 49W
River Grove, *Chic.* 26 B1 41 55N 87 50W
River Pines, *Bost.* 21 B2 42 33N 71 17W
River Vale, *N.Y.* 22 B4 40 59N 74 1W
Riverdale, *Chic.* 26 D3 41 38N 87 37W
Riverdale, *N.Y.* 22 B3 40 59N 74 17W
Riverdale, *Trto.* 20 E8 43 39N 79 21W
Riverdale, *Wash.* 25 D8 38 57N 76 54W
Riverdale Park, *Trto.* 20 D8 43 40N 79 21W
Riverhead, *Lon.* 4 D5 51 16N 0 10 E
Riverlea, *Jobg.* 18 F8 26 12 S 27 58 E
Riverside, *Bost.* 21 B2 42 32N 71 18W
Riverside, *Chic.* 26 C2 41 49N 87 48W
Riverside, *N.Y.* 23 B5 40 47N 73 54W
Riverside, *N.Y.* 23 A7 41 1N 73 34W
Riverside, *Phil.* 24 A5 40 2N 74 57W
Riverton, *Phil.* 24 A4 40 0N 75 1W
Riverwood, *Syd.* 19 B3 33 57 S 151 3 E
Rivière-des-Praires, *Mtrl.* 20 A4 43 38N 73 34W
Rivodora, *Tori.* 9 B3 45 5N 7 47 E
Rivoli, *Tori.* 9 B1 45 4N 7 30 E
Riyad, *Bagd.* 17 F8 33 18N 44 27 E
Rizal, *Manila* 15 D4 14 33N 121 0 E
Rizal Park, *Manila* 15 D3 14 35N 120 58 E
Rizel Stadium, *Manila* 15 D3 14 34N 120 59 E
Røa, *Oslo* 2 B3 59 57N 10 39 E
Robassomero, *Tori.* 9 A1 45 11N 7 34 E
Robbins, *Chic.* 26 D2 41 38N 87 42W
Robert E. Lee Memorial Park, *Balt.* 25 A3 39 23N 76 40 E
Robertsdale, *Chic.* 26 C3 41 40N 87 30W
Robertsham, *Jobg.* 18 F9 26 15 S 28 1 E
Robin Hills, *Jobg.* 18 E8 26 6 S 27 58 E
Rocha Miranda, *Rio J.* 31 B2 22 51 S 43 20W
Rochar →, *Sing.* 15 G8 1 18N 103 52 E
Rochelle Park, *N.Y.* 22 B4 40 54N 74 4W
Rock Cr. →, *Wash.* 25 D7 38 54N 77 3W
Rock Creek Park, *Wash.* 25 D7 38 56N 77 2W
Rockaway, *N.Y.* 22 D5 40 32N 73 56W
Rockaway Beach, *S.F.* 27 C2 37 36N 122 29W
Rockaway Islet, *N.Y.* 23 D5 40 34N 73 53W
Rockaway Neck, *N.Y.* 22 B2 40 51N 74 21W
Rockaway Point, *N.Y.* 22 D5 40 33N 73 55W
Rockburn Branch →, *Balt.* 25 B2 39 13N 76 43W
Rockdale, *Balt.* 25 A2 39 21N 76 46W
Rockdale, *Syd.* 19 B3 33 57 S 151 8 E
Rockland, *Phil.* 24 C1 39 47N 75 34W
Rocklege, *Phil.* 24 A4 40 4N 75 5W
Rockleigh, *N.Y.* 22 A5 41 0N 73 55W
Rockville, *Wash.* 25 C6 39 4N 77 10W
Rockville Centre, *N.Y.* 23 D6 40 39N 73 38W
Rocky Hill, *Phil.* 24 B1 39 55N 75 30W
Rocky Ridge, *S.F.* 27 B4 37 47N 122 2W
Rocky Run →, *Wash.* 25 D6 38 58N 77 14W
Rodaon, *Wien* 10 H9 48 8N 16 13 E
Rodeo Cove, *S.F.* 27 B1 37 49N 122 32W
Rodgers Forge, *Balt.* 25 A3 39 22N 76 36W
Roding →, *Lon.* 4 B5 51 30N 0 1 E
Rodošć, *Wsaw.* 10 E6 52 11N 20 59 E
Rødovre, *Købn.* 2 D9 55 40N 12 26 E
Rodrigo de Freitas, L., *Rio J.* 31 B2 22 58 S 43 12W
Rodstensfjärden, *Stock.* 3 E9 59 16N 17 48 E
Roehampton, *Lon.* 4 C3 51 27N 0 15W
Rogers Park, *Chic.* 26 A2 42 0N 87 40W
Rohdenhaus, *Ruhr* 6 C4 51 18N 7 0 E
Röhlinghausen, *Ruhr* 6 A4 51 30N 7 9 E
Roihuvuori, *Hels.* 3 B5 60 11N 25 2 E
Roissy, *Paris* 5 C5 48 47N 2 39 E
Roissy-en-France, *Paris* 5 A5 49 0N 2 30 E
Rokkō Sanchi, *Ōsaka* 12 B2 34 44N 135 13 E
Rokko-Zan, *Ōsaka* 12 B2 34 46N 135 16 E
Rokytka →, *Pra.* 10 B3 50 6N 14 27 E
Roland Lake, *Balt.* 25 A3 39 23N 76 38W
Roland Park, *Balt.* 25 A3 39 20N 76 39W
Roma, *Rome* 9 F9 41 54N 12 28 E
Római-Fürdö, *Bud.* 10 J13 47 34N 19 4 E
Romainville, *Paris* 5 B4 48 52N 2 26 E
Romani, *Nápl.* 9 H13 40 52N 14 22 E
Romano Banco, *Mil.* 9 E5 45 25N 9 6 E
Romashkovo, *Mos.* 11 E7 55 43N 37 19 E
Rome = Roma, *Rome* 9 F9 41 54N 12 28 E
Romford, *Lon.* 4 B6 51 34N 0 11 E
Roncáglia, *Tori.* 9 B1 45 2N 7 29 E
Rönninge, *Stock.* 3 E9 59 12N 17 45 E
Ronsdorf, *Ruhr* 6 C5 51 13N 7 11 E
Ronskensiedlg, *Ruhr* 6 A2 51 36N 6 41 E
Rontgental, *Berl.* 7 A4 52 38N 13 31 E
Roodekop, *Jobg.* 18 F10 26 17 S 28 11 E
Roodepoort, *Jobg.* 18 E8 26 9 S 27 53 E
Roodepoort-Wes, *Jobg.* 18 E8 26 8 S 27 51 E
Roosevelt, *N.Y.* 23 C7 40 40N 73 35W
Rooty Hill, *Syd.* 19 A2 33 46 S 150 50 E
Roppongi, *Tōkyō* 13 C3 35 39N 139 44 E
Rosairinho, *Lisb.* 8 F8 38 40N 9 0W
Rosanna, *Melb.* 19 E7 37 44 S 145 4 E
Rosario, *La Hab.* 30 B2 23 3N 82 21W
Rosario, *Manila* 15 D4 14 35N 121 4 E
Rose B., *Syd.* 19 B4 33 51 S 151 16 E
Rose Hill, *Wash.* 25 E7 38 47N 77 6W
Rose Tree, *Phil.* 24 B2 39 56N 75 23W
Rosebank, *N.Y.* 22 D4 40 36N 74 4W
Rosebery, *Syd.* 19 B4 33 55 S 151 12 E
Rosedal La Candelaria, *Méx.* 29 B3 19 20N 99 10W
Rosedale, *Balt.* 25 B3 39 19N 76 31W
Rosedale, *N.Y.* 23 D6 40 39N 73 43W
Roseiras, *S. Pau.* 31 E7 23 33 S 46 23W
Roseland, *Chic.* 26 C3 41 42N 87 37W
Roseland, *N.Y.* 22 C3 40 49N 74 17W
Roselle, *N.Y.* 22 D3 40 39N 74 15W
Roselle Park, *N.Y.* 22 C3 40 39N 74 15W
Rosemead, *L.A.* 28 B4 34 4N 118 4W
Rosemere, *Mtrl.* 20 A2 43 34N 73 50W
Rosemont, *Chic.* 26 B1 41 59N 87 52W
Rosemont, *Phil.* 24 A3 40 1N 75 19W
Rosenborg Have, *Købn.* 2 D10 55 41N 12 33 E
Rosengarten, *Hbg.* 7 D6 53 31N 9 49 E
Rosenthal, *Berl.* 7 A3 52 35N 13 22 E
Rosettenville, *Jobg.* 18 F9 26 15 S 28 3 E
Rosherville Dam, *Jobg.* 18 F9 26 13 S 28 6 E
Rósio, *Mil.* 9 E4 45 25N 8 57 E
Rösjön, *Stock.* 3 D11 59 26N 18 0 E
Roskilde, *Købn.* 2 E7 55 38N 12 5 E
Roskilde Fjord, *Købn.* 2 D7 55 45N 12 4 E
Roslags-Näsby, *Stock.* 3 D11 59 26N 18 3 E
Roslindale, *Bost.* 21 D3 42 17N 71 7W
Roslyn, *N.Y.* 23 C7 40 47N 73 38W
Roslyn, *Phil.* 24 A4 40 7N 75 8W
Roslyn Estates, *N.Y.* 23 C6 40 47N 73 40W
Roslyn Harbour, *N.Y.* 23 C7 40 48N 73 38W
Rosne →, *Paris* 5 B4 48 58N 2 25 E
Rosny-sous-Bois, *Paris* 5 B5 48 52N 2 30 E
Ross, *S.F.* 27 A1 37 57N 122 33W
Rosslyn, *Wash.* 25 D7 38 53N 77 4W
Rossville, *Balt.* 25 A4 39 20N 76 28W
Rossville, *N.Y.* 22 D3 40 32N 74 12W
Rosta, *Tori.* 9 B1 45 4N 7 27 E
Rotbach →, *Ruhr* 6 A2 51 34N 6 41 E
Rothenburgsort, *Hbg.* 7 D8 53 32N 10 2 E
Rotherbaum, *Hbg.* 7 D7 53 33N 9 58 E
Rotherhithe, *Lon.* 4 C4 51 29N 0 2W
Rothneusiedl, *Wien* 10 H10 48 8N 16 23 E
Rothschmaige, *Mün.* 7 F9 48 14N 11 27 E
Rouge →, *Trto.* 20 D9 43 47N 79 6W
Rouge Hill, *Trto.* 20 D10 43 48N 79 7W
Round I., *H.K.* 12 E6 22 13N 114 11 E
Roundshaw, *Lon.* 4 C4 51 20N 0 7W
Roussigny, *Paris* 5 D2 48 38N 2 6 E
Rowland, *L.A.* 28 B5 34 0N 117 55W
Rowley, *Bost.* 21 A4 42 43N 70 52W
Rowville, *Melb.* 19 F8 37 55 S 145 14 E
Roxboro, *Mtrl.* 20 A3 43 30N 73 48W
Roxborough, *Phil.* 24 A3 40 1N 75 13W
Roxbury, *Bost.* 21 D3 42 19N 71 5W
Roxbury, *N.Y.* 23 D5 40 33N 73 53W
Roxeth, *Lon.* 4 B2 51 33N 0 20W
Royal Observatory, *H.K.* 12 E6 22 18N 114 10 E
Royal Park, *Melb.* 19 E6 37 46 S 144 57 E
Röylä, *Hels.* 3 B3 60 18N 24 42 E
Royston Park, *Lon.* 4 B2 51 36N 0 22W
Rozas, Portilleros de las, *Mdrd.* 8 B2 40 29N 3 49W
Roztoky, *Pra.* 10 B2 50 9N 14 23 E
Rubbianetta, *Tori.* 9 B2 45 9N 7 34 E
Rubi →, *Barc.* 8 D5 41 26N 2 3 E
Rubio Woods, *Chic.* 26 D2 41 38N 87 45W
Rublovo, *Mos.* 11 E8 55 47N 37 21 E
Ruchyi, *St-Pet.* 11 A4 60 0N 30 25 E
Rud, *Oslo* 2 B3 59 56N 11 0 E
Rüdinghausen, *Ruhr* 6 B6 51 26N 7 24 E
Rudnevka →, *Mos.* 11 E11 55 43N 37 56 E
Rudolfsheim, *Wien* 10 G10 48 12N 16 20 E
Rudolfshöhe, *Berl.* 7 A5 52 37N 13 44 E
Rudow, *Berl.* 7 B3 52 24N 13 29 E
Rueil-Malmaison, *Paris* 5 B3 48 52N 2 11 E
Ruffys Cr. →, *Melb.* 19 E7 37 45 S 145 7 E
Ruggeberg, *Ruhr* 6 C6 51 16N 7 23 E
Ruhlsdorf, *Berl.* 7 B2 52 22N 13 15 E
Ruhr →, *Ruhr* 6 B3 51 27N 6 56 E
Ruhrort, *Ruhr* 6 B2 51 27N 6 44 E
Ruislip, *Lon.* 4 B2 51 34N 0 24W
Rumelihisari, *Ist.* 17 A3 41 4N 29 2 E
Rumeln, *Ruhr* 6 B1 51 24N 6 39 E
Rumyantsevo, *Mos.* 11 F8 55 38N 37 25 E
Rungis, *Paris* 5 C4 48 44N 2 20 E
Runnemede, *Phil.* 24 B4 39 50N 75 4W
Ruotsinkylä, *Hels.* 3 A4 60 21N 24 57 E
Rusāfa, *Bagd.* 17 E8 33 21N 44 23 E
Rush Green, *Lon.* 4 B6 51 33N 0 10 E
Russa, *Calc.* 16 F6 22 29N 88 21 E
Russell Lea, *Syd.* 19 B4 33 52 S 151 10 E
Rustad, *Oslo* 2 B2 59 56N 10 30 E
Rustenfeld, *Wien* 10 H10 48 7N 16 23 E
Rusville, *Jobg.* 18 E10 26 9 S 28 18 E
Rutherford, *N.Y.* 22 C4 40 49N 74 6W
Rüttenscheid, *Ruhr* 6 B3 51 25N 6 59 E
Ruxton, *Balt.* 25 A3 39 23N 76 38W
Ruzyně, *Pra.* 10 B1 50 5N 14 17 E
Rybatskaya, *St-Pet.* 11 B4 59 59N 30 51 E
Rybatskoye, *St-Pet.* 11 B4 59 50N 30 29 E
Rydalmere, *Syd.* 19 A3 33 48 S 151 2 E
Rydboholm, *Stock.* 3 D12 59 26N 18 12 E
Ryde, *Syd.* 19 A3 33 49 S 151 6 E
Rye, *N.Y.* 23 B6 40 58N 73 40W
Rynfield, *Jobg.* 18 E10 26 9 S 28 19 E
Ryogoku, *Tōkyō* 13 B3 35 40N 139 48 E
Rysäkari, *Hels.* 3 C4 60 8N 25 0 E
Rzhevka, *St-Pet.* 11 B5 59 59N 30 31 E

S

Saadōn, Bagd. — 17 F8 33 19N 44 25 E
Saarn, Ruhr — 6 B3 51 24N 6 51 E
Saavedra, B.A. — 32 B4 34 33 S 58 29W
Saboli, Delhi — 16 A2 28 42N 77 18 E
Sabugo, Lisb. — 8 F7 38 49N 9 17W
Saburovo, Mos. — 11 D7 55 53N 37 15 E
Säbysjön, Stock. — 3 D10 59 26N 17 52 E
Sacavém, Lisb. — 8 F8 38 47N 9 5W
Saclay, Paris — 5 C3 48 43N 2 10 E
Saclay, Étang de, Paris — 5 C2 48 44N 2 9 E
Sacoma, S. Pau. — 31 E6 23 36 S 46 35W
Sacré-Coeur, Paris — 5 B4 48 53N 2 20 E
Sacrow, Berl. — 7 B1 52 25N 13 6 E
Sacrower See, Berl. — 7 B1 52 26N 13 6 E
Sadang, Sŏul — 12 H7 37 29N 126 58 E
Sadar Bazar, Delhi — 16 B2 28 39N 77 11 E
Saddām City, Bagd. — 17 E8 33 23N 44 27 E
Saddle Brook, N.Y. — 22 B4 40 53N 74 5W
Saddle River, N.Y. — 22 A4 41 1N 74 6W
Saddle Rock, N.Y. — 23 C6 40 47N 73 45W
Sadr, Kar. — 17 G11 24 51N 67 2 E
Sadyba, Wsaw. — 10 E7 52 11N 21 3 E
Saedo, Tōkyō — 13 C2 35 30N 139 33 E
Saensaep, Khlong →, Bangk. — 15 B2 13 44N 100 32 E
Sáenz Pena, B.A. — 32 B3 34 37 S 58 32W
Safdar Jang Airport, Delhi — 16 B2 28 35N 77 12 E
Safdar Jangs Tomb, Delhi — 16 B2 28 35N 77 12 E
Safráköy, Ist. — 17 A1 41 0N 28 48 E
Saft el Laban, El Qâ. — 18 C5 30 1N 31 10 E
Sag Bridge, Chic. — 26 C1 41 41N 87 55W
Sagamore Neck, N.Y. — 23 B8 40 53N 73 29W
Saganashkee Slough, Chic. — 26 C1 41 41N 87 53W
Sagene, Oslo — 2 B4 59 55N 10 46 E
Sagrada Família, Temple de, Barc. — 8 D6 41 24N 2 10 E
Sahapur, Calc. — 16 E5 22 31N 88 11 E
Sahibabad, Delhi — 16 A1 28 45N 77 4 E
Sai Kung, H.K. — 12 D6 22 22N 114 16 E
Sai Wan Ho, H.K. — 12 E6 22 17N 114 12 E
Sai Ying Pun, H.K. — 12 E6 22 17N 114 8 E
Saido, Tōkyō — 13 A2 35 52N 139 39 E
Sailmouille →, Paris — 5 D3 48 42N 73 44W
St. Albans, Wien — 10 G9 48 19N 16 12 E
St. Andrä, Wien — 10 G9 48 19N 16 12 E
St. Andrews, Jobg. — 18 E9 26 9 S 28 7 E
St. Aubin, Paris — 5 C2 48 44N 2 8 E
St. Augustin, Mtrl. — 20 A2 43 37N 73 58W
St. Basil's Cathedral, Mos. — 11 E9 55 45N 37 38 E
St.-Benoit, Paris — 5 C1 48 40N 1 54 E
St.-Brice-sous-Forêt, Paris — 5 A4 49 0N 2 21 E
St.-Cloud, Paris — 5 B3 48 50N 2 12 E
St.-Cyr-l'École, Paris — 5 C2 48 47N 2 4 E
St.-Cyr-l'École, Aérodrome de, Paris — 5 C2 48 48N 2 4 E
St. Davids, Phil. — 24 A2 40 2N 75 23W
St.-Denis, Mtrl. — 5 B4 48 56N 2 20 E
St. Eustache, Mtrl. — 20 A2 43 53N 73 54W
St.-Forget, Paris — 5 C2 48 42N 2 0 E
St. Georg, Hbg. — 7 D8 53 33N 10 1 E
St.-Germain, Forêt de, Paris — 5 B2 48 57N 2 5 E
St. Germain-en-Laye, Paris — 5 B2 48 53N 2 4 E
St.-Germain-lès-Corbeil, Paris — 5 D4 48 37N 2 29 E
St.-Gratien, Paris — 5 B4 48 58N 2 17 E
St. Helier, Lon. — 4 C3 51 23N 0 11W
St.-Hubert, Mtrl. — 20 B5 43 29N 73 25W
St. Isaac's Cathedral, St-Pet. — 11 B3 59 55N 30 19 E
St. Jacques →, Mtrl. — 20 B5 43 26N 73 29W
St. Jean-de-Beauregard, Paris — 5 D3 48 39N 2 10 E
St.-Jean-de-Dieu, Mtrl. — 20 A4 43 34N 73 31W
St. Joseph-du-Lac, Mtrl. — 20 A1 43 32N 74 0W
St. Katherine's Dock, Lon. — 4 B4 51 30N 0 4W
St. Kilda, Melb. — 19 F6 37 51 S 144 58 E
St. Lambert, Mtrl. — 20 A5 43 30N 73 29W
St.-Lambert, Paris — 5 C2 48 45N 2 1 E
St.-Laurent, Mtrl. — 20 A3 43 30N 73 43W
St. Lawrence, Mtrl. — 20 A5 43 30N 73 44W
St.-Lazare, Gare, Paris — 5 B4 48 52N 2 19 E
St.-Léonard, Mtrl. — 20 A4 43 35N 73 34W
St. Leonards, Syd. — 19 B4 33 50 S 151 12 E
St. Leu-la-Forêt, Paris — 5 A3 49 1N 2 14 E
St.-Louis, L., Mtrl. — 20 B3 43 24N 73 44W
St. Magnloren, Stock. — 3 E11 59 13N 18 4 E
St.-Mandé, Paris — 5 B4 48 50N 2 24 E
St.-Mard, Paris — 5 A6 49 22N 2 41 E
St.-Martin, Mtrl. — 20 A3 43 33N 73 45W
St.-Martin, Bois, Paris — 5 C5 48 48N 2 35 E
St. Mary Cray, Lon. — 4 C5 51 23N 0 7 E
St.-Maur-des-Fossés, Paris — 5 C4 48 48N 2 29 E
St.-Maurice, Paris — 5 C4 48 49N 2 24 E
St.-Mesmes, Paris — 5 B6 48 59N 2 41 E
St. Michaëliskirche, Hbg. — 7 D7 53 32N 9 59 E
St. Michael's, Sing. — 15 G8 1 19N 103 51 E
St.-Michel, Mtrl. — 20 A4 43 34N 73 37W
St.-Michel-sur-Orge, Paris — 5 D3 48 38N 2 18 E
St. Nikolaus-Kirken, Pra. — 10 B2 50 5N 14 23 E
St. Nom-la-Bretèche, Paris — 5 B2 48 51N 2 1 E
St.-Ouen, Paris — 5 B4 48 56N 2 20 E
St. Ouen-l'Aumône, Paris — 5 A2 49 2N 2 6 E
St. Pauli, Hbg. — 7 D7 53 33N 9 57 E
St. Pauls Cathedral, Lon. — 4 B4 51 30N 0 5W
St. Paul's Cray, Lon. — 4 C5 51 23N 0 6 E
St. Petersburg, St-Pet. — 11 B3 59 55N 30 15 E
St.-Pierre, Mtrl. — 20 A3 43 27N 73 38W
St. Prix, Paris — 5 A3 49 0N 2 15 E
St.-Quentin, Étang de, Paris — 5 C2 48 47N 2 0 E
St. Quentin-en-Yvelines, Paris — 5 C1 48 46N 1 57 E
St.-Rémy-lès-Chevreuse, Paris — 5 C2 48 42N 2 4 E
St.-Thibault-des-Vignes, Paris — 5 B6 48 52N 2 41 E
St. Veit, Wien — 10 G9 48 11N 16 16 E
St.-Vincent-de-Paul, Mtrl. — 20 A4 43 36N 73 39W
Ste.-Anne-de-Bellevue, Mtrl. — 20 B2 43 24N 73 39W
Ste.-Catherine, Mtrl. — 20 A4 43 24N 73 34W
Ste.-Dorothée, Mtrl. — 20 A3 43 31N 73 48W
Ste.-Gemme, Paris — 5 B1 48 52N 1 59 E
Ste.-Geneviève, Mtrl. — 20 B2 43 39N 73 51W

Ste.-Geneviève-des-Bois, Paris — 5 D3 48 38N 2 19 E
Ste.-Hélène, Î., Mtrl. — 20 A4 43 31N 73 32W
Ste. Marthe-sur-le-Lac, Mtrl. — 20 A2 43 31N 73 56W
Ste.-Rose, Mtrl. — 20 A3 43 37N 73 46W
Ste. Thérèse, Mtrl. — 20 A3 43 38N 73 49W
Ste.-Thérèse-Ouest, Mtrl. — 20 A2 43 36N 73 50W
Saiwai, Tōkyō — 13 C3 35 32N 139 41 E
Sakai, Ōsaka — 12 C3 34 34N 135 27 E
Sakai →, Tōkyō — 13 C1 35 27N 139 29 E
Sakai Harbour, Ōsaka — 12 C3 34 36N 135 26 E
Sakanoshita, Tōkyō — 13 B2 35 48N 139 30 E
Sakra, P., Sing. — 15 G7 1 15N 103 41 E
Sakuragi, Tōkyō — 13 D2 35 28N 139 38 E
Salam, Bagd. — 17 E8 33 20N 44 20 E
Salaryevo, Mos. — 11 F8 55 37N 37 25 E
Salem, Bost. — 21 B4 42 30N 70 54W
Salem, Stock. — 3 E9 59 13N 17 46 E
Salem Harbor, Bost. — 21 B4 42 30N 70 52W
Salem Maritime Nat. Hist. Site, Bost. — 21 B4 42 31N 70 52W
Salemstaden, Stock. — 3 E9 59 13N 17 46 E
Salkhia, Calc. — 16 E6 22 36N 88 21 E
Salmannsdorf, Wien — 10 G9 48 14N 16 14 E
Salmdorf, Mün. — 7 G11 48 7N 11 43 E
Salmedina, Mdrd. — 8 B3 40 18N 3 35W
Salomea, Wsaw. — 10 E6 52 11N 20 55 E
Salsette I., Bomb. — 16 G8 19 12N 72 53 E
Salt Cr. →, Chic. — 26 C1 41 51N 87 54W
Salt Cr. →, Melb. — 19 E7 37 45 S 145 4 E
Salt Water L., Calc. — 16 E6 22 33N 88 26 E
Saltholm, Køb. — 2 E11 55 38N 12 46 E
Saltsjö-Duvnäs, Stock. — 3 E12 59 18N 18 12 E
Saltsjöbaden, Stock. — 3 E12 59 15N 18 18 E
Saltykovka, Mos. — 11 E11 55 45N 37 54 E
Salvatorkirche, Mün. — 6 B2 51 26N 6 45 E
Sam Sen, Khlong →, Bangk. — 15 B2 13 45N 100 33 E
Samatya, Ist. — 17 B2 40 59N 28 55 E
Samouco, Lisb. — 8 F9 38 41N 8 59W
Sampaloc, Manila — 15 D3 14 36N 120 59 E
Samphanthawong, Bangk. — 15 C2 13 44N 100 31 E
Samrong, Bangk. — 15 C2 13 39N 100 35 E
Samseon, Sŏul — 12 G8 37 34N 127 2 E
San Agustin, Lima — 30 G8 12 1 S 77 9W
San Agustin Atlapulco, Méx. — 29 B4 19 23N 99 7W
San Andreas Fault, S.F. — 27 D3 37 27N 122 28W
San Andreas L., S.F. — 27 D3 37 35N 122 25W
San Andres, B.A. — 32 B3 34 34 S 58 33W
San Andrés, Barc. — 8 D6 41 26N 2 11 E
San Andrés Ahuayucan, Méx. — 29 C3 19 13N 99 7W
San Andrés Atenco, Méx. — 29 A2 19 32N 99 13W
San Andrés Totoltepec, Méx. — 29 C2 19 15N 99 10W
San Andrián de Besós, Barc. — 8 D6 41 25N 2 13 E
San Angel, Méx. — 29 B2 19 20N 99 11W
San Antonia, Manila — 15 E3 14 29N 120 53 E
San Antonio de Padua, B.A. — 32 C2 34 40 S 58 42W
San Agustin Ohtenco, Méx. — 29 C2 19 12N 99 0W
San Bartolo Ameyalco, Méx. — 29 C2 19 19N 99 16W
San Bartolomé Coatepec, Méx. — 29 B2 19 23N 99 18W
San Basilio, Rome — 9 F10 41 56N 12 35 E
San Bóvio, Mil. — 9 E6 45 27N 9 18 E
San Bruno, S.F. — 27 C2 37 38N 122 24W
San Bruno, Pt., S.F. — 27 C2 37 39N 122 22W
San Bruno Mt., S.F. — 27 B2 37 41N 122 26W
San Carlos, S.F. — 27 C2 37 30N 122 16W
San Carlos de la Cabana, Forteresse, La Hab. — 30 B2 23 8N 82 20W
San Clemente del Llobregat, Barc. — 8 E4 41 19N 1 59 E
San Cristobal, Mdrd. — 8 B3 40 25N 3 35W
San Cristobal, Cerro, Stgo — 30 J11 33 25 S 70 38W
San Cristoforo, Mil. — 9 E5 45 26N 9 9 E
San Donato Milanese, Mil. — 9 E6 45 24N 9 16 E
San Felice, Tori. — 9 B3 45 1N 7 46 E
San Feliu de Llobregat, Barc. — 8 D5 41 22N 2 2 E
San Fernando, B.A. — 32 A3 34 26 S 58 32W
San Fernando, L.A. — 28 A2 34 17N 118 26W
San Fernando Airport, L.A. — 28 A2 34 17N 118 26W
San Fernando de Henares, Mdrd. — 8 B3 40 25N 3 31W
San Fernando Valley, L.A. — 28 A1 34 12N 118 31W
San Francisco, S.F. — 27 B2 37 46N 122 23W
San Francisco, Univ. of, S.F. — 27 B2 37 47N 122 27W
San Francisco B., S.F. — 27 C3 37 39N 122 14W
San Francisco Chimalpa, Méx. — 29 B1 19 26N 99 8W
San Francisco Culhuacán, Méx. — 29 C3 19 19N 99 8W
San Francisco de Paula, La Hab. — 30 B3 23 3N 82 17W
San Francisco Int. Airport, S.F. — 27 C2 37 37N 122 22W
San Francisco Solano, B.A. — 32 C5 34 46 S 58 19W
San Francisco State Univ., S.F. — 27 B2 37 43N 122 28W
San Francisco Tecoxpa, Méx. — 29 C3 19 12N 99 0W
San Francisco Tlalnepantla, Méx. — 29 C3 19 12N 99 4W
San Fruttuoso, Mil. — 9 D6 45 34N 9 14 E
San Gabriel, L.A. — 28 B4 34 5N 118 5W
San Gabriel →, L.A. — 28 C4 33 55N 118 6W
San Gabriel Pk., L.A. — 28 A4 34 14N 118 6W
San Giacomo, Tori. — 9 A2 45 11N 7 36 E
San Gillio, Tori. — 9 B2 45 8N 7 32 E
San Giórgio a Crem, Nápl. — 9 J13 40 50N 14 20 E
San Giovanni a Teduccio, Nápl. — 9 H13 40 49N 14 14 E
San Giuseppe Vesuviano, Nápl. — 9 H13 40 50N 14 29 E
San Gregorio Atlapulco, Méx. — 29 C3 19 15N 99 4W
San Isidro, B.A. — 32 A3 34 28 S 58 30W
San Isidro, Lima — 30 G8 12 5 S 77 2W
San Isidro, Manila — 15 D4 14 38N 121 5 E
San Jerónimo Lidice, Méx. — 29 C2 19 19N 99 14W
San Jerónimo Miacatlán, Méx. — 29 B2 19 48N 98 59W
San Jorge, Castelo de, Lisb. — 8 F8 38 42N 9 8W
San Jose Del Alamo, La Hab. — 30 B3 23 6N 82 17W

San José Rio Hondo, Méx. — 29 B2 19 26N 99 14W
San Juan →, Manila — 15 D4 14 35N 121 0 E
San Juan de Aragón, Méx. — 29 B3 19 28N 99 4W
San Juan de Aragón, Parque, Méx. — 29 B3 19 27N 99 4W
San Juan de Lurigancho, Lima — 30 F8 11 59 S 77 0W
San Juan de Miraflores, Lima — 30 H9 12 10 S 76 58W
San Juan del Monte, Manila — 15 D4 14 36N 121 1 E
San Juan Ixtacala, Méx. — 29 A2 19 31N 99 10W
San Juan Ixtayopan, Méx. — 29 C4 19 14N 98 59W
San Juan Toltotepec, Méx. — 29 B2 19 28N 99 15W
San Juan y San Pedro Tezompa, Méx. — 29 C4 19 12N 98 57W
San Justo, B.A. — 32 C3 34 40 S 58 33W
San Leandro, S.F. — 27 B4 37 43N 122 9W
San Leandro B., S.F. — 27 B3 37 45N 122 13W
San Leandro Cr. →, S.F. — 27 B3 37 44N 122 12W
San Lorenzo, Mil. — 9 D4 45 34N 8 57 E
San Lorenzo, S.F. — 27 B4 37 41N 122 6W
San Lorenzo →, Méx. — 29 B2 19 28N 99 17W
San Lorenzo, I., Lima — 30 G7 12 6 S 77 12W
San Lorenzo Acopilco, Méx. — 29 C1 19 19N 99 20W
San Lorenzo Chimalco, Méx. — 29 B2 19 24N 99 58W
San Lorenzo Tezonco, Méx. — 29 C3 19 19N 99 3W
San Lorenzo Tlacoyucan, Méx. — 29 C3 19 10N 99 2W
San Lucas Xochimanca, Méx. — 29 C3 19 15N 99 6W
San Luis, Lima — 30 G8 12 4 S 77 0W
San Luis Tlaxialtemalco, Méx. — 29 C3 19 16N 99 2W
San Marino, L.A. — 28 B4 34 7N 118 5W
San Martin, Barc. — 8 D6 41 24N 2 11 E
San Martin de Porras, Lima — 30 G8 12 1 S 77 5W
San Martino, Tori. — 9 B3 45 6N 7 47 E
San Mateo, S.F. — 27 C3 37 33N 122 19W
San Mateo Cr. →, S.F. — 27 C2 37 31N 122 22W
San Mateo Tecoloapan, Méx. — 29 A2 19 35N 99 14W
San Mateo Xalpa, Méx. — 29 C3 19 13N 99 8W
San Máuro Torinese, Tori. — 9 B3 45 6N 7 45 E
San Miguel, B.A. — 32 B2 34 32 S 58 43W
San Miguel, Lima — 30 G8 12 5 S 77 6W
San Miguel, Manila — 15 D3 14 36N 120 59 E
San Miguel, Stgo — 30 J11 33 29 S 70 39W
San Miguel Ajusco, Méx. — 29 C2 19 13N 99 11W
San Miguel Xicalco, Méx. — 29 C3 19 13N 99 11W
San Nicholas, Manila — 15 D3 14 36N 120 57 E
San Nicola, Rome — 9 F9 41 58N 12 21 E
San Nicolás Totolapan, Méx. — 29 C2 19 17N 99 9W
San Nicolás Viejo, Méx. — 29 A1 19 31N 99 21W
San Onófrio, Rome — 9 F9 41 57N 12 25 E
San Pablo, S.F. — 27 B4 37 57N 122 20W
San Pablo, Pt., S.F. — 27 A2 37 58N 122 22W
San Pablo Cr. →, S.F. — 27 A2 37 58N 122 22W
San Pablo Ostotepec, Méx. — 29 C3 19 11N 99 3W
San Pablo Res., S.F. — 27 A3 37 55N 122 14W
San Pablo Ridge, S.F. — 27 A3 37 55N 122 15W
San Pablo Str., S.F. — 27 A2 37 58N 122 22W
San Pancrázio, Tori. — 9 B2 45 6N 7 32 E
San Pedro, L.A. — 28 C4 33 44N 118 17W
San Pedro, Pt., S.F. — 27 C1 37 35N 122 31W
San Pedro Actopan, Méx. — 29 C3 19 12N 99 2W
San Pedro Martir, Barc. — 8 D5 41 23N 2 6 E
San Pedro Martir, Méx. — 29 C2 19 16N 99 10W
San Pedro Zacatenco, Méx. — 29 B3 19 30N 99 6W
San Pietro, Rome — 9 F9 41 53N 12 27 E
San Pietro a Patierno, Nápl. — 9 H12 40 53N 14 17 E
San Pietro all'Olmo, Mil. — 9 E5 45 29N 9 1 E
San Po Kong, H.K. — 12 D6 22 20N 114 11 E
San Quentin, S.F. — 27 B2 37 56N 122 27W
San Rafael, S.F. — 27 A1 37 58N 122 30W
San Rafael B., S.F. — 27 A2 37 57N 122 28W
San Rafael Chamapa, Méx. — 29 B2 19 27N 99 15W
San Rafael Hills, L.A. — 28 A3 34 10N 118 12W
San Roque, Manila — 15 D4 14 37N 121 5 E
San Salvador Cuauhtenco, Méx. — 29 C3 19 11N 99 8W
San Salvador de la Punta, Forteresse, La Hab. — 30 B2 23 8N 82 21W
San Sebastiano al Vesúvio, Nápl. — 9 H13 40 50N 14 22 E
San Siro, Mil. — 9 E5 45 28N 9 7 E
San Souci, Syd. — 19 B3 33 59 S 151 8 E
San Telmo, B.A. — 32 B4 34 37 S 58 23W
San Vicenc dels Horts, Barc. — 8 D5 41 23N 2 0 E
San Vitaliano, Nápl. — 9 H13 40 55N 14 28 E
San Vito, Mil. — 9 E5 45 24N 9 0 E
San Vito, Nápl. — 9 J13 40 49N 14 14 E
San Vito, Tori. — 9 B3 45 2N 7 43 E
Sandbakken, Oslo — 2 C5 59 49N 10 54 E
Sandermoen, Oslo — 2 A4 60 0N 10 8 E
Sanderstead, Lon. — 4 C4 51 19N 0 4W
Sandheide, Ruhr — 6 C3 51 12N 6 56 E
Sandhurst, Jobg. — 18 E9 26 6 S 28 3 E
Sandown, Jobg. — 18 E9 26 5 S 28 4 E
Sandown Racecourse, Lon. — 4 C2 51 22N 0 21W
Sandringham, Jobg. — 18 E9 26 8 S 28 5 E
Sands Point, N.Y. — 23 B6 40 50N 73 43W
Sandton, Jobg. — 18 E9 26 5 S 28 4 E
Sandungen, Oslo — 2 B2 59 52N 10 21 E
Sandvika, Oslo — 2 B3 59 54N 10 31 E
Sandy Pond, Bost. — 21 C2 42 26N 71 18W
Sânga, Stock. — 3 D9 59 21N 17 42 E
Sangano, Tori. — 9 B1 45 1N 7 26 E
Sangenjaya, Tōkyō — 13 C2 35 37N 139 39 E
Sangley Pt., Manila — 15 E3 14 29N 120 53 E
Sangye, Sŏul — 12 G8 37 33N 127 4 E
Sankrail, Calc. — 16 E5 22 33N 88 13 E
Sanlihe, Beij. — 14 B3 39 55N 116 18 E
Sanlintang, Shang. — 14 K11 31 9N 121 26 E
Sannō, Tōkyō — 13 B2 35 35N 139 42 E
Sannois, Paris — 5 B3 48 58N 2 3 E
Sanpada, Bomb. — 16 G9 19 3N 73 0 E
Sans, Barc. — 8 D5 41 22N 2 7 E
Sant Ambrogio, Basilica di, Mil. — 9 E6 45 27N 9 10 E

Sant Boi de Llobregat, Barc. — 8 D5 41 20N 2 2 E
Sant Cugat, Barc. — 8 D5 41 28N 2 5 E
Santa Ana, Manila — 15 D4 14 34N 121 0 E
Santa Ana Tlacotenco, Méx. — 29 C4 19 11N 98 58W
Santa Bárbara, Morro de, Rio J. — 31 B1 22 56 S 43 26W
Santa Catalina, B.A. — 32 C4 34 47 S 58 24W
Santa Cecilia Tepetlapa, Méx. — 29 C3 19 13N 99 5W
Santa Clara, Méx. — 29 A3 19 33N 99 3W
Santa Coloma de Cerelló, Barc. — 8 D5 41 21N 2 1 E
Santa Coloma de Gramanet, Barc. — 8 D6 41 27N 2 12 E
Santa Cruz, Bomb. — 16 G7 19 4N 72 51 E
Santa Cruz, La Hab. — 30 B2 23 4N 82 29W
Santa Cruz, Ilhe de, Rio J. — 31 B3 22 51 S 43 7W
Santa Cruz Alcapixca, Méx. — 29 C3 19 14N 99 4W
Santa Cruz Ayotusco, Méx. — 29 B1 19 22N 99 21W
Santa Cruz de Olorde, Barc. — 8 D5 41 25N 2 3 E
Santa Cruz Int. Airport, Bomb. — 16 G8 19 5N 72 51 E
Santa Cruz Meyehualco, Méx. — 29 B3 19 20N 99 3W
Santa Elena, Manila — 15 D4 14 38N 121 5 E
Santa Eligênia Consolação, S. Pau. — 31 E6 23 32 S 46 38W
Santa Emilia, Stgo — 30 J11 33 23 S 70 39W
Santa Eulalia, Barc. — 8 D6 41 25N 2 12 E
Santa Fe, La Hab. — 30 B2 23 4N 82 30W
Santa Fe Flood Control Basin, L.A. — 28 B5 34 7N 117 57W
Santa Fe Springs, L.A. — 28 C4 33 56N 118 3W
Santa Isabel Ixtapan, Méx. — 29 A4 19 35N 98 57W
Santa Julia, Stgo — 30 K11 33 30 S 70 35W
Santa Lucia, Nápl. — 9 J12 40 49N 14 15 E
Santa Margherita, Tori. — 9 B3 45 3N 7 43 E
Santa Maria Aztahuacán, Méx. — 29 B3 19 21N 99 2W
Santa Maria del Rosario, La Hab. — 30 B3 23 3N 82 15W
Santa Maria Tulpetlac, Méx. — 29 A3 19 34N 99 3W
Santa Martha Acatitla, Méx. — 29 B3 19 21N 99 2W
Santa Monica, Car. — 30 E5 10 28N 66 53W
Santa Monica, L.A. — 28 B2 34 1N 118 29W
Santa Monica B., L.A. — 28 C1 33 58N 118 30W
Santa Monica Mt., L.A. — 28 B2 34 4N 118 39W
Santa Rosa, Lima — 30 F8 11 59 S 77 5W
Santa Rosa De Locobe, Stgo — 30 J11 33 25 S 70 33W
Santa Rosa Xochiac, Méx. — 29 C2 19 19N 99 17W
Santa Tereza, S. Pau. — 31 F6 23 40 S 46 33W
Santa Ursula Xitla, Méx. — 29 C2 19 16N 99 11W
Santa Ynez Canyon →, L.A. — 28 B1 34 2N 118 33W
Santahamina, Hels. — 3 C5 60 8N 25 2 E
Santana, S. Pau. — 31 D6 23 29 S 46 38W
Sant'Anastasia, Nápl. — 9 H13 40 51N 14 24 E
Sant'Ántimo, Nápl. — 9 H12 40 56N 14 4 E
Santeny, Paris — 5 C5 48 43N 2 34 E
Santiago, Stgo — 30 J11 33 26 S 70 40W
Santiago Acahualtepec, Méx. — 29 B3 19 20N 99 0W
Santiago de Las Vegas, La Hab. — 30 C2 22 58N 82 22W
Santiago Tepalcatlalpan, Méx. — 29 C3 19 14N 99 9W
Santiago Tepetlaxco, Méx. — 29 B1 19 28N 99 20W
Sant'Ilário, Mil. — 9 D4 45 34N 8 59 E
Santo Amaro, Lisb. — 8 F7 38 42N 9 11W
Santo Amaro, S. Pau. — 31 E5 23 39 S 46 42W
Santo Andre, Lisb. — 8 G8 38 38N 9 3W
Santo André, S. Pau. — 31 E6 23 39 S 46 41W
Santo António, Qta. de, Lisb. — 8 G7 38 39N 9 15W
Santo António da Charneca, Lisb. — 8 G8 38 37N 9 1W
Santo Niño, Manila — 15 D4 14 38N 121 1 E
Santo Rosario, Manila — 15 D4 14 33N 121 4 E
Santo Thomas, Univ. of, Manila — 15 D3 14 36N 120 59 E
Santo Tomas, Manila — 15 D4 14 33N 121 4 E
Santolan, Manila — 15 D4 14 36N 121 4 E
Santos Dumont, Aéroport, Rio J. — 31 B2 22 54 S 43 9W
Santos Lugares, B.A. — 32 B3 34 35 S 58 35W
Santoshpur, Calc. — 16 E5 22 31N 88 16 E
Santragachi, Calc. — 16 E5 22 35N 88 17 E
Sanyuanli, Gzh. — 14 G8 23 8N 113 14 E
São Bernardo do Campo, S. Pau. — 31 F6 23 42 S 46 32W
São Caetano do Sul, S. Pau. — 31 E6 23 37 S 46 34W
São Cristovão, Rio J. — 31 B2 22 53 S 43 13W
São Domingos, Centro, Rio J. — 31 B3 22 53 S 43 6W
São Gonçalo, Rio J. — 31 A3 22 49 S 43 4W
São João Climaco, S. Pau. — 31 E6 23 37 S 46 36W
São João da Talha, Lisb. — 8 F8 38 49N 9 5W
São João de Meriti, Rio J. — 31 A1 22 47 S 43 18W
São Lucas, Parque, S. Pau. — 31 E6 23 35 S 46 36W
São Mateus, Rio J. — 31 A1 22 48 S 43 22W
São Miguel Paulista, S. Pau. — 31 D7 23 29 S 46 26W
São Paulo, S. Pau. — 31 E6 23 32 S 46 38W
Sapa, Calc. — 16 E5 22 30N 88 15 E
Sapang Baho →, Manila — 15 D4 14 33N 121 4 E
Sapateiro →, S. Pau. — 31 E6 23 35 S 46 41W
Sarandi, Jobg. — 18 E9 26 8 S 28 4 E
Sarandí, B.A. — 32 C4 34 40 S 58 20W
Saraswati →, Calc. — 16 D5 22 48N 88 18 E
Sarcelles, Paris — 5 B4 48 59N 2 22 E
Sarenga, Calc. — 16 E5 22 31N 88 12 E
Sarilhos Grandes, Lisb. — 8 F9 38 40N 8 58W
Sarilhos Pequenos, Lisb. — 8 F9 38 40N 8 58W
Sarımbun, Sing. — 15 F7 1 24N 103 40 E
Saronikòs Kólpos, Ath. — 8 J10 37 52N 23 30 E
Saronno, Mil. — 9 D5 45 37N 9 2 E
Sárria, Car. — 30 E5 10 25N 66 55W
Sarsol, Bomb. — 16 G9 19 3N 73 1 E
Sartrouville, Paris — 5 B3 48 56N 2 10 E
Sasad, Bud. — 10 K13 47 28N 19 0 E
Sasashita, Tōkyō — 13 D3 35 29N 139 43 E
Sashalom, Bud. — 10 K14 47 31N 19 11 E
Saska, Wsaw. — 10 E7 52 14N 21 3 E
Sassafras, Melb. — 19 F9 37 52 S 145 20 E

Satalice, Pra. — 10 B3 50 7N 14 34 E
Satgachi, Calc. — 16 E6 22 37N 88 25 E
Satghara, Calc. — 16 D6 22 43N 88 21 E
Satpukur, Calc. — 16 E6 22 37N 88 24 E
Sätra, Stock. — 3 E10 59 17N 17 54 E
Satsuna, Calc. — 16 F5 22 28N 88 17 E
Sau Mau Ping, H.K. — 12 E6 22 19N 114 13 E
Saugus, Bost. — 21 C3 42 28N 71 0W
Saugus →, Bost. — 21 C3 42 27N 70 58W
Saulx-les-Chartreux, Paris — 5 C3 48 41N 2 16 E
Sausalito, S.F. — 27 A2 37 51N 122 28W
Sausset →, Paris — 5 B5 48 56N 2 2 E
Savigny-sur-Orge, Paris — 5 C4 48 40N 2 21 E
Savijärvi, Hels. — 3 A6 60 21N 25 19 E
Savonera, Tori. — 9 B2 45 7N 7 36 E
Sawah Besar, Jak. — 15 H9 6 8 S 106 49 E
Sawyer Ridge, S.F. — 27 C2 37 34N 122 24W
Saxonville, Bost. — 21 D1 42 19N 71 24W
Saxonwold, Jobg. — 18 E9 26 9 S 28 2 E
Scarborough, Trto. — 20 D9 43 44N 79 14W
Scarsdale, N.Y. — 23 B6 40 58N 73 47W
Sceaux, Paris — 5 C4 48 46N 2 1 E
Schalke, Ruhr — 6 A4 51 35N 7 4 E
Schapenrust, Jobg. — 18 F11 26 15 S 28 21 E
Scharfenberg, Berl. — 7 A2 52 35N 13 15 E
Scheiblingstein, Wien — 10 G9 48 16N 16 13 E
Schenefeld, Hbg. — 7 D7 53 36N 9 52 E
Scherlebech, Ruhr — 6 A4 51 37N 7 8 E
Schildow, Berl. — 7 A3 52 38N 13 22 E
Schiller Park, Chic. — 26 B1 41 56N 87 52W
Schiller Woods, Chic. — 26 B1 41 57N 87 51W
Schlachtensee, Berl. — 7 B2 52 26N 13 13 E
Schlossgarten, Berl. — 7 A2 52 31N 13 18 E
Schmachtendorf, Ruhr — 6 A2 51 32N 6 48 E
Schmargendorf, Berl. — 7 B2 52 28N 13 17 E
Schmöckwitz, Berl. — 7 B5 52 22N 13 38 E
Schnelsen, Hbg. — 7 D7 53 38N 9 54 E
Scholven, Ruhr — 6 A4 51 36N 7 0 E
Schönblick, Berl. — 7 A4 51 36N 7 0 E
Schönbrunn, Schloss, Wien — 10 G9 48 10N 16 19 E
Schöneberg, Berl. — 7 B3 52 28N 13 20 E
Schönefeld, Berl. — 7 B4 52 23N 13 30 E
Schöneiche, Berl. — 7 B5 52 28N 13 41 E
Schönwalde, Berl. — 7 A1 52 37N 13 7 E
Schottenwald, Wien — 10 G9 48 13N 16 16 E
Schuir, Ruhr — 6 B3 51 23N 6 59 E
Schulzendorf, Berl. — 7 A2 52 36N 13 16 E
Schuylkill →, Phil. — 24 B3 39 53N 75 11W
Schwabing, Mün. — 7 G10 48 10N 11 35 E
Schwafheim, Ruhr — 6 B1 51 25N 6 36 E
Schwanebeck, Berl. — 7 A4 52 37N 13 32 E
Schwanenwerder, Berl. — 7 B2 52 26N 13 10 E
Schwarz →, Ruhr — 6 C3 51 17N 6 51 E
Schwarzbachtal, Ruhr — 6 C3 51 17N 6 51 E
Schwarze Berge, Hbg. — 7 E7 53 27N 9 54 E
Schwarzlackenau, Wien — 10 G9 48 16N 16 23 E
Schwechat, Wien — 10 H10 48 8N 16 28 E
Schwellingshausen, Ruhr — 6 C6 51 15N 7 24 E
Schwelm, Ruhr — 6 C5 51 17N 7 18 E
Sciisciano, Nápl. — 9 H13 40 54N 14 28 E
Scoresby, Melb. — 19 F8 37 54 S 145 14 E
Scotch Plains, N.Y. — 22 D2 40 39N 74 22W
Scotts Level Br. →, Balt. — 25 A2 39 23N 76 45W
Sea Cliff, N.Y. — 23 B7 40 50N 73 38W
Seabrook, Wash. — 25 D3 38 58N 76 49W
Seacliff, S.F. — 27 B2 37 47N 122 28W
Seaforth, Syd. — 19 B3 33 48 S 151 15 E
Seagate, N.Y. — 22 D4 40 34N 73 59W
Seal Slough, S.F. — 27 C3 37 34N 122 17W
Sears Tower, Chic. — 26 B3 41 52N 87 38W
Searsport, Wash. — 25 D8 38 53N 76 53W
Seavey Hill, Bost. — 21 A1 42 42N 71 23W
Šeberov, Pra. — 10 B3 50 0N 14 30 E
Secaucus, N.Y. — 22 C4 40 47N 74 3W
Secondigliano, Nápl. — 9 H12 40 53N 14 15 E
Seddinsee, Berl. — 7 B5 52 23N 13 41 E
Sedgefield, N.Y. — 22 B2 40 51N 74 26W
Sedriano, Mil. — 9 E4 45 29N 8 58 E
Seeburg, Berl. — 7 A5 52 33N 13 7 E
Seefeld, Berl. — 7 A5 52 33N 13 40 E
Seegefeld, Berl. — 7 A1 52 33N 13 8 E
Seehof, Berl. — 3 E10 59 16N 17 56 E
Segeltorp, Stock. — 3 E10 59 16N 17 56 E
Seguro, Mil. — 9 E5 45 28N 9 17 E
Seine →, Paris — 5 C4 48 48N 2 25 E
Seixal, Lisb. — 8 G8 38 38N 9 6W
Selbeck, Ruhr — 6 B2 51 22N 6 51 E
Selbecke, Ruhr — 6 C5 51 20N 7 28 E
Selby, Jobg. — 18 F9 26 12 S 28 2 E
Seletar →, Sing. — 15 F8 1 26N 103 51 E
Seletar, P., Sing. — 15 F8 1 24N 103 52 E
Seletar, Sungei →, Sing. — 15 F7 1 26N 103 49 E
Seletar Hills, Sing. — 15 F8 1 23N 103 52 E
Seletar Res., Sing. — 15 F7 1 24N 103 48 E
Selghar, Bomb. — 16 H9 18 57N 73 1 E
Selhurst, Lon. — 4 C4 51 23N 0 5W
Selsdon, Lon. — 4 C4 51 20N 0 3W
Selston, Car. — 30 E5 10 30N 66 52W
Selsytsy, St-Pet. — 11 B6 59 56N 30 42 E
Sembawang, Sing. — 15 F7 1 26N 103 49 E
Sembawang, Sungei →, Sing. — 15 F7 1 26N 103 48 E
Sembawang Hill, Sing. — 15 F7 1 22N 103 49 E
Semsvatn, Oslo — 2 B2 59 51N 10 25 E
Senago, Mil. — 9 D5 45 34N 9 7 E
Senan, Jak. — 15 J10 6 10 S 106 50 E
Sénart, Forêt de, Paris — 5 D4 48 40N 2 28 E
Senayan Sports Centre, Jak. — 15 J9 6 12 S 106 47 E
Sendling, Mün. — 7 G10 48 7N 11 31 E
Sengeløse, Køben. — 2 D8 55 40N 12 14 E
Senju, Tōkyō — 13 B3 35 44N 139 48 E
Senlikköy, Ist. — 17 B1 40 58N 28 48 E
Senlisse, Paris — 5 C1 48 41N 1 59 E
Senneville, Mtrl. — 20 B2 43 24N 73 57W
Senri, Ōsaka — 12 B4 34 49N 135 30 E
Senriyama, Ōsaka — 12 B4 34 47N 135 30 E
Sentosa, Sing. — 15 G7 1 15N 103 49 E
Seo Dae Mun, Sŏul — 12 G7 37 34N 126 55 E
Seobinngo, Sŏul — 12 G7 37 31N 126 58 E
Seoggwan, Sŏul — 12 G8 37 35N 127 8 E
Seong Bug, Sŏul — 12 G8 37 35N 127 0 E
Seong Dong, Sŏul — 12 G8 37 33N 127 1 E
Seoul = Sŏul, Sŏul — 12 G8 37 34N 127 1 E
Seoul National Univ., Sŏul — 12 H7 37 28N 126 57 E
Sepah Salar Mosque, Tehr. — 17 C5 35 40N 51 25 E
Sepolia, Ath. — 8 H11 38 1N 23 43 E
Sepulveda, L.A. — 28 A2 34 13N 118 27W
Sepulveda Flood Control Basin, L.A. — 28 A2 34 10N 118 28W
Serangoon, P., Sing. — 15 F8 1 23N 103 55 E
Serangoon, Sungei →, Sing. — 15 F8 1 23N 103 53 E
Serangoon Garden, Sing. — 15 F8 1 21N 103 51 E

46 Serangoon Harbour

Serangoon Harbour, Sing. 15 F8 1 23N 103 57 E
Seraya, P., Sing. 15 G7 1 16N 103 43 E
Serebryanka, Mos. 11 E11 55 44N 37 53 E
Serebryanka →, Mos. 11 E10 55 47N 37 44 E
Serednevo, Mos. 11 F7 55 35N 37 18 E
Serramonte, S.F. 27 C2 37 39N 122 28W
Servon, Paris 5 C5 48 43N 2 35 E
Šestajovice, Pra. 10 B3 50 6N 14 40 E
Sesto San Giovanni, Mil. 9 D6 45 31N 9 13 E
Seta Budi, Jak. 15 J9 6 12 S 106 49 E
Setagaya-Ku, Tōkyō 13 C2 35 37N 139 36 E
Sete Pontes, Rio J. 31 B3 22 50 S 43 4W
Seter, Oslo 2 B4 59 52N 10 47 E
Séttimo Milanese, Mil. 9 E5 45 28N 9 3 E
Séttimo Torinese, Tori. 9 B3 45 8N 7 46 E
Settsu, Ōsaka 12 B4 34 47N 135 33 E
Setuny →, Mos. 11 E8 55 43N 37 21 E
Seurasaari, Hels. 3 B4 60 11N 24 53 E
Seutula; Hels. 3 A4 60 20N 24 52 E
Seven Corners, Wash. 25 D7 38 53N 77 9W
Seven Kings, Lon. 4 B5 51 33N 0 5 E
Sevenoaks, Lon. 4 D6 51 16N 0 11 E
Severn Hills, Syd. 19 A2 33 46 S 150 57 E
Sévesco →, Mil. 9 D5 45 35N 9 9 E
Sevran, Paris 5 B5 48 56N 2 31 E
Sèvres, Paris 5 C3 48 49N 2 13 E
Sewaren, N.Y. 22 D3 40 33N 74 15W
Sewell, Phil. 24 C4 39 46N 75 8W
Sewri, Bomb. 16 H8 18 59N 72 50 E
Seya, Tōkyō 13 D1 35 28N 139 28 E
Sforzesso, Castello, Mil. 9 E6 45 28N 9 10 E
Sha Kok Mei, H.K. 12 D6 22 23N 114 16 E
Sha Tin, H.K. 12 D6 22 23N 114 11 E
Sha Tin Wai, H.K. 12 D6 22 22N 114 11 E
Shaala, Bagd. 17 E7 33 22N 44 16 E
Shabanzhuang, Beij. 14 B3 39 51N 116 25 E
Shabbona Woods, Chic. 26 D3 41 36N 87 33W
Shabrâmant, El Qâ. 18 D5 29 56N 31 11 E
Shadipur, Delhi 16 B2 28 38N 77 11 E
Shady Oak, Wash. 25 C6 39 1N 77 17W
Shahabad, Bomb. 16 G9 19 0N 73 2 E
Shahar, Bomb. 16 G8 19 5N 72 52 E
Shahdara, Delhi 16 A2 28 40N 77 18 E
Shahe, Gzh. 14 G8 23 9N 113 19 E
Shahpur Jel, Delhi 16 B2 28 33N 77 12 E
Shahr-e-Rey, Tehr. 17 D5 35 36N 51 25 E
Shaikh Aomar, Bagd. 17 E8 33 20N 44 23 E
Shakarpor Khas, Delhi 16 B2 28 37N 77 14 E
Shakurpur, Delhi 16 A1 28 40N 77 8 E
Sham Shui Po, H.K. 12 E5 22 19N 114 9 E
Shamepur, Delhi 16 A1 28 44N 77 8 E
Shamian, Gzh. 14 G8 23 6N 113 13 E
Shamspur, Delhi 16 B2 28 36N 77 17 E
Shan Liu, H.K. 12 D6 22 23N 114 16 E
Shan Mei, H.K. 12 D6 22 24N 114 10 E
Shanghai, Shang. 14 J12 31 14N 121 28 E
Shanghetou, Tianj. 14 D5 39 11N 117 0 E
Shanjing, Gzh. 14 G9 23 4N 113 23 E
Sharea Faisal, Kar. 17 G11 24 52N 67 8 E
Sharon Hill, Phil. 24 B3 39 54N 75 16W
Sharp I., H.K. 12 D6 22 21N 114 17 E
Sharp Park, S.F. 27 C2 37 38N 122 29W
Shau Kei Wan, H.K. 12 E6 22 16N 114 13 E
Shawocun, Beij. 14 B2 39 53N 116 13 E
Shawsheen Village, Bost. 21 A3 42 40N 71 7W
Shea Stadium, N.Y. 23 C5 40 45N 73 50W
Sheakhala, Calc. 16 D5 22 45N 88 10 E
Shebāb, Bagd. 17 E8 33 20N 44 26 E
Sheepshead B., N.Y. 22 D5 40 35N 73 55W
Shek Hang, H.K. 12 D6 22 24N 114 17 E
Shek Kip Mei, H.K. 12 D5 22 20N 114 9 E
Shek Lung Kung, H.K. 12 D5 22 23N 114 5 E
Shek O, H.K. 12 E6 22 13N 114 15 E
Shellpot Cr. →, Phil. 24 C1 39 44N 75 30W
Shelter Cove, S.F. 27 C1 37 35N 122 30W
Shelter I., H.K. 12 E6 22 19N 114 17 E
Shemirānāt, Tehr. 17 C5 35 47N 51 25 E
Shenfield, Lon. 4 B6 51 37N 0 19 E
Sheng Fa Shan, H.K. 12 D5 22 23N 114 5 E
Shenley, Lon. 4 A3 51 41N 0 16W
Shepherds Bush, Lon. 4 B3 51 30N 0 13W
Shepperton, Lon. 4 C2 51 23N 0 26W
Sherborn, Bost. 21 D1 42 14N 71 22W
Sherman Oaks, L.A. 28 B2 34 8N 118 29W
Sherwood Forest, S.F. 27 A3 37 57N 122 16W
Shet Bandar, Bomb. 16 H8 18 57N 72 55 E
Sheung Lau Wan, H.K. 12 E6 22 16N 114 16 E
Sheung Wan, H.K. 12 E5 22 16N 114 9 E
Sheva, Bomb. 16 H8 18 56N 72 57 E
Sheva Nhava, Bomb. 16 H8 18 57N 72 57 E
Shiba, Tōkyō 13 C3 35 38N 139 45 E
Shiba →, Tōkyō 13 A3 35 50N 139 44 E
Shibuya-Ku, Tōkyō 13 C3 35 39N 139 41 E
Shijōnawate, Ōsaka 12 B4 34 44N 135 37 E
Shimo-okudomi, Tōkyō 13 A1 35 52N 139 27 E
Shimo-tsuchidana, Tōkyō 13 D1 35 24N 139 27 E
Shimogawara, Tōkyō 13 C1 35 39N 139 27 E
Shimosalo, Tōkyō 13 B2 35 45N 139 31 E
Shimosasame, Tōkyō 13 B2 35 48N 139 37 E
Shimoshakujii, Tōkyō 13 B2 35 43N 139 35 E
Shimotomi, Tōkyō 13 B1 35 49N 139 27 E
Shimotsuruma, Tōkyō 13 D1 35 29N 139 26 E
Shimura, Tōkyō 13 B3 35 46N 139 41 E
Shinagawa B., Tōkyō 13 C3 35 35N 139 48 E
Shinagawa-Ku, Tōkyō 13 C3 35 36N 139 44 E
Shing Mun Res., H.K. 12 D5 22 23N 114 8 E
Shinjuku-Ku, Tōkyō 13 B3 35 41N 139 42 E
Shinkoiwa, Tōkyō 13 B4 35 43N 139 51 E
Shinnakano, Tōkyō 13 B3 35 41N 139 40 E
Shinoha, Tōkyō 13 A3 35 50N 139 49 E
Shipai, Gzh. 14 G9 23 8N 113 20 E
Shipley, Balt. 25 B3 39 12N 76 39W
Shippan Pt., N.Y. 23 A7 41 1N 73 31W
Shirako, Tōkyō 13 B2 35 47N 139 36 E
Shiraone, Bomb. 16 G9 19 2N 73 1 E
Shirinashi →, Ōsaka 12 C3 34 38N 135 27 E
Shirley, Lon. 4 C4 51 22N 0 2W
Shiro, Tōkyō 13 B2 35 48N 139 30 E
Shirogane, Tōkyō 13 C3 35 37N 139 44 E
Shisha Hai, Beij. 14 B3 39 55N 116 21 E
Shitou, Gzh. 14 G9 23 1N 113 23 E
Shiweitang, Gzh. 14 G8 23 6N 113 12 E
Shogunle, Lagos 18 A2 6 34N 7 20 E
Shomolu, Lagos 18 A2 6 32N 7 22 E
Shooters Hill, Lon. 4 C5 51 28N 0 4 E
Shoreditch, Lon. 4 B4 51 31N 0 4W
Shoreham, Lon. 4 D6 51 19N 0 10 E
Short Hills, N.Y. 22 C2 40 44N 74 21W
Shortlands, Lon. 4 C5 51 23N 0 0 E
Shrirampur, Calc. 16 D5 22 45N 88 21 E
Shuangkou, Tianj. 14 D5 39 14N 117 2 E
Shuangtuo, Tianj. 14 D6 39 13N 117 19 E
Shubrâ el Kheima, El Qâ. 18 C5 30 6N 31 14 E
Shuikuo, Gzh. 14 F8 23 10N 113 10 E
Shuishang Gongyuan, Tianj. 14 E5 39 5N 117 9 E
Shukunoshō, Ōsaka 12 A4 34 50N 135 31 E
Sibbo, Hels. 3 A6 60 21N 25 14 E
Sibbo fjärden, Hels. 3 B6 60 11N 25 17 E
Siboney, La Hab. 30 B2 23 4N 82 28W
Sibpur, Calc. 16 E5 22 34N 88 19 E
Sibřina, Pra. 10 B4 50 3N 14 40 E
Sidcup, Lon. 4 C5 51 25N 0 6 E
Siebenhirten, Wien 10 H9 48 8N 16 17 E
Siedlung, Berl. 7 A1 52 35N 13 7 E
Siekierki, Wsaw. 10 E7 52 12N 21 4 E
Sielce, Wsaw. 10 E7 52 12N 21 2 E
Siemensstadt, Berl. 7 A2 52 32N 13 16 E
Sieraków, Wsaw. 10 E5 52 19N 20 48 E
Sierra Madre, L.A. 28 B4 34 9N 118 3W
Sievering, Wien 10 G10 48 15N 16 20 E
Siggerud, Oslo 2 C5 59 47N 10 52 E
Siheung, Sŏul 12 H7 37 28N 126 54 E
Siikajärvi, Hels. 3 B2 60 17N 24 31 E
Sikátorpuszta, Bud. 10 J14 47 34N 19 10 E
Silampur, Delhi 16 B2 28 39N 77 16 E
Silschede, Ruhr 6 B6 51 21N 7 22 E
Silver Hill, Wash. 25 E8 38 49N 76 55W
Silver L., Bost. 21 B3 42 33N 71 9W
Silver Mt., L.A. 28 A5 34 12N 117 55W
Silver Spring, Wash. 25 D7 38 59N 77 2W
Silverfields, Jobg. 18 E7 26 7 S 27 49 E
Silvertown, Lon. 4 C5 51 29N 0 1 E
Simla, Calc. 16 E6 22 35N 88 22 E
Simmer and Jack Mines, Jobg. 18 F9 26 12 S 28 8 E
Simmering, Wien 10 G10 48 10N 16 24 E
Simmering Heide, Wien 10 G10 48 10N 16 26 E
Simonkylä, Hels. 3 B5 60 18N 25 1 E
Simpang Bedok, Sing. 15 G8 1 19N 103 56 E
Simsalö, Hels. 3 B6 60 14N 25 17 E
Singao, N.Y. 22 B3 40 53N 74 14W
Singapore, Sing. 15 G8 1 17N 103 51 E
Singapore →, Sing. 15 G8 1 17N 103 51 E
Singapore, Univ. of, Sing. 15 G7 1 19N 103 49 E
Singapore Airport, Sing. 15 F8 1 21N 103 54 E
Singlewell, Lon. 4 C7 51 25N 0 21 E
Singur, Calc. 16 D5 22 48N 88 13 E
Sinicka →, Mos. 11 D7 55 52N 37 18 E
Sinki, Selat, Sing. 15 G7 1 15N 103 42 E
Sinrim, Sŏul 12 H7 37 28N 126 56 E
Sinsa, Sŏul 12 G8 37 31N 127 0 E
Sinthi, Calc. 16 E6 22 37N 88 23 E
Sinweol, Sŏul 12 G7 37 31N 126 51 E
Sipoo, Hels. 3 A6 60 21N 25 14 E
Sipoon selkä, Hels. 3 B6 60 11N 25 17 E
Sipson, Lon. 4 C2 51 29N 0 26W
Siqeil, El Qâ. 18 C4 30 7N 31 10 E
Şişli, Ist. 17 A2 41 3N 28 58 E
Skå, Stock. 3 E9 59 19N 17 44 E
Skärholmen, Stock. 3 E10 59 16N 17 53 E
Skarpäng, Stock. 3 D11 59 26N 18 0 E
Skarpnäck, Stock. 3 E11 59 16N 18 7 E
Skarpö, Stock. 3 D13 59 24N 18 22 E
Skedsmo, Oslo 2 B6 59 59N 11 2 E
Skhodnya →, Mos. 11 D8 55 53N 37 23 E
Skodsborg, Købn. 2 D10 55 49N 12 34 E
Skogby, Hels. 3 A2 60 21N 24 40 E
Skogen, Oslo 2 C1 59 48N 10 18 E
Skogsbyn, Hels. 3 A6 60 20N 25 18 E
Skokie, Chic. 26 A2 42 2N 87 43W
Skokie →, Chic. 26 A2 42 3N 87 46W
Skokie Lagoons, Chic. 26 A2 42 7N 87 46W
Skoklefall, Oslo 2 B4 59 50N 10 40 E
Sköndal, Stock. 3 E11 59 15N 18 6 E
Skovlunde, Købn. 2 D9 55 42N 12 25 E
Skovshoved, Købn. 2 D10 55 45N 12 35 E
Skøyen, Oslo 2 B4 59 55N 10 40 E
Skui, Oslo 2 B2 59 55N 10 25 E
Skuldelev, Købn. 2 D7 55 46N 12 1 E
Skullerud, Oslo 2 B5 59 51N 10 50 E
Skuru, Stock. 3 E12 59 18N 18 12 E
Skytta, Oslo 2 B5 59 59N 10 54 E
Slade Green, Lon. 4 C6 51 27N 0 11 E
Slagsta, Stock. 3 E9 59 15N 17 48 E
Slakteren, Oslo 2 A4 60 1N 10 40 E
Slattum, Oslo 2 A5 60 0N 10 55 E
Slemmestad, Oslo 2 C2 59 46N 10 29 E
Slependen, Oslo 2 B3 59 52N 10 30 E
Sligo Cr. →, Wash. 25 C7 39 0N 77 1W
Slipi, Jak. 15 J9 6 11 S 106 47 E
Slipi Orchard Garden, Jak. 15 J9 6 10 S 106 46 E
Slivenec, Pra. 10 B2 50 1N 14 21 E
Slone Canyon Res., L.A. 28 B2 34 6N 118 27W
Sloop Channel, N.Y. 23 D7 40 36N 73 31W
Sluhy, Pra. 10 A3 50 11N 14 33 E
Służew, Wsaw. 10 E7 52 10N 21 1 E
Służewiec, Wsaw. 10 E7 52 10N 21 0 E
Smalleytown, N.Y. 22 D2 40 39N 74 28W
Smestad, Oslo 2 B2 59 55N 10 25 E
Smíchov, Pra. 10 B2 50 4N 14 23 E
Smith Forest Preserve, Chic. 26 B2 41 59N 87 45W
Smith Mills, N.Y. 22 A2 41 0N 74 23W
Smithfield, Syd. 19 B2 33 51 S 150 56 E
Smoke Rise, N.Y. 22 A2 41 0N 74 24W
Smørumnedre, Købn. 2 D8 55 44N 12 7 E
Snakeden Br. →, Wash. 25 D6 38 58N 77 17W
Snarøya, Oslo 2 B3 59 52N 10 33 E
Snättringe, Stock. 3 E10 59 15N 17 58 E
Snoldelev, Købn. 2 E8 55 33N 12 10 E
Snostrup, Købn. 2 D7 55 48N 12 7 E
Søborg, Købn. 2 D9 55 43N 12 29 E
Sobreda, Lisb. 8 G7 38 39N 9 11W
Soccavo, Nápl. 9 H12 40 50N 14 11 E
Sodegaura, Tōkyō 13 D4 35 24N 139 57 E
Söderby, Stock. 3 D12 59 24N 18 12 E
Söderkullalandet, Hels. 3 B6 60 14N 25 19 E
Södermalm, Stock. 3 E11 59 18N 18 4 E
Södersätra, Stock. 3 D10 59 27N 17 56 E
Södertälje, Stock. 3 E8 59 11N 17 36 E
Sodingen, Ruhr 6 A5 51 32N 7 15 E
Sodpur, Calc. 16 D6 22 42N 88 24 E
Södra Björkfjärden, Stock. 3 E8 59 17N 17 34 E
Soeurs, Î. des, Mtrl. 20 B4 43 27N 73 32W
Sognsvatn, Oslo 2 B4 59 58N 10 43 E
Soignolles-en-Brie, Paris 5 D6 48 39N 2 43 E
Soisy-sous-Montmorency, Paris 5 B3 48 59N 2 17 E
Soisy-sur-Seine, Paris 5 D4 48 39N 2 27 E
Sojiji Temple, Tōkyō 13 D3 35 29N 139 40 E
Sok Kwu Wan, H.K. 12 E5 22 12N 114 7 E
Sōka, Tōkyō 13 B3 35 49N 139 48 E
Sokolniki, Mos. 11 E10 55 47N 37 40 E
Sokolniki Park, Mos. 11 E10 55 48N 37 40 E
Sokołów, Wsaw. 10 F6 52 9N 20 51 E
Solalinden, Mün. 7 G11 48 5N 11 42 E
Solaro, Mil. 9 D5 45 36N 9 6 E
Solers, Paris 5 D6 48 39N 2 43 E
Solingen, Ruhr 6 C4 51 10N 7 5 E
Sollentuna, Stock. 3 D10 59 25N 17 56 E
Søllerød, Købn. 2 D9 55 48N 12 29 E
Sollihøgda, Oslo 2 B2 59 58N 10 21 E
Solln, Mün. 7 G10 48 4N 11 31 E
Solna, Stock. 3 D10 59 21N 17 59 E
Solntsevo, Mos. 11 F8 55 39N 37 24 E
Solymár, Bud. 10 J12 47 35N 18 56 E
Somapah Changi, Sing. 15 F8 1 20N 103 57 E
Somapan Serangoon, Sing. 15 F8 1 21N 103 53 E
Somborn, Ruhr 6 B6 51 29N 7 20 E
Somerdale, Phil. 24 B4 39 50N 75 1W
Somerset, Wash. 25 D7 38 57N 77 5W
Somerton, Phil. 24 A4 40 7N 75 1W
Somerville, Bost. 21 C3 42 22N 71 5W
Somma, Mte., Nápl. 9 H13 40 50N 14 25 E
Somma Vesuviana, Nápl. 9 H13 40 52N 14 26 E
Sonari, Bomb. 16 H8 18 54N 72 59 E
Sønderby, Købn. 2 D7 55 44N 12 2 E
Søndersø, Købn. 2 D9 55 46N 12 21 E
Sondre Elvåga, Oslo 2 B5 59 51N 10 54 E
Sonnberg, Wien 10 G9 48 19N 16 15 E
Sørby, Oslo 2 C4 59 49N 10 41 E
Sørkedalen, Oslo 2 A3 60 1N 10 37 E
Soroksár, Bud. 10 K13 47 24N 19 7 E
Soroksár-Újtelep, Bud. 10 K13 47 25N 19 7 E
Soroksari Duna →, Bud. 10 K13 47 25N 19 5 E
Sørsdal, Oslo 2 B1 59 50N 10 16 E
Sosenka →, Mos. 11 E10 55 46N 37 42 E
Sosnovaya, St-Pet. 11 C2 59 49N 30 8 E
Sottungsby, Hels. 3 B5 60 16N 25 8 E
Sŏul, Sŏul 12 G8 37 34N 127 51 E
Soundview, N.Y. 23 C5 40 49N 73 53W
South Basin, S.F. 27 B2 37 42N 122 22W
South Beach, N.Y. 22 D4 40 35N 74 4W
South Boston, Bost. 21 C3 42 20N 71 2W
South Braintree, Bost. 21 D4 42 11N 70 59W
South Branch →, Phil. 24 C4 39 50N 75 5W
South Brooklyn, N.Y. 22 C5 40 41N 73 59W
South Chelmsford, Bost. 21 B1 42 34N 71 22W
South Chicago, Chic. 26 C3 41 44N 87 32W
South Darenth, Lon. 4 C6 51 23N 0 15 E
South Deering, Chic. 26 C3 41 42N 87 33W
South Floral Park, N.Y. 23 C6 40 42N 73 41W
South Gate, L.A. 28 C3 33 56N 118 12W
South Germiston, Jobg. 18 F10 26 11 S 28 13 E
South Hackensack, N.Y. 22 B4 40 51N 74 2W
South Hamilton, Bost. 21 B4 42 36N 70 52W
South Harbour, Manila 15 D3 14 34N 120 58 E
South Harrow, Lon. 4 B2 51 33N 0 21W
South Hd., Syd. 19 B4 33 50 S 151 16 E
South Hempstead, N.Y. 23 C7 40 40N 73 37W
South Hills, Jobg. 18 F9 26 14 S 28 5 E
South Hingham, Bost. 21 D4 42 12N 70 53W
South Holland, Chic. 26 D3 41 36N 87 35W
South Hornchurch, Lon. 4 B6 51 32N 0 11 E
South Huntington, N.Y. 23 C8 40 49N 73 23W
South Lawn, Wash. 25 E7 38 47N 77 0W
South Lawrence, Bost. 21 A3 42 41N 71 9W
South Lincoln, Bost. 21 C2 42 24N 71 19W
South Lynnfield, Bost. 21 B4 42 30N 70 59W
South Norwood, Lon. 4 C4 51 23N 0 3W
South Ockendon, Lon. 4 B6 51 30N 0 16 E
South of Market, S.F. 27 B2 37 46N 122 24W
South Orange, N.Y. 22 C3 40 45N 74 14W
South Oxley, Lon. 4 B2 51 37N 0 23W
South Oyster B., N.Y. 23 D8 40 38N 73 27W
South Ozone Park, N.Y. 23 C6 40 41N 73 49W
South Pasadena, L.A. 28 B4 34 7N 118 8W
South Peabody, Bost. 21 B4 42 30N 70 57W
South Peters, Syd. 19 B4 33 54 S 151 11 E
South Plainfield, N.Y. 22 D2 40 35N 74 24W
South Quincy, Bost. 21 D3 42 13N 71 0W
South Res., Bost. 21 C3 42 26N 71 6W
South San Francisco, S.F. 27 C2 37 38N 122 26W
South San Gabriel, L.A. 28 B4 34 3N 118 6W
South Shore, Chic. 26 C3 41 45N 87 34W
South Sudbury, Bost. 21 C1 42 21N 71 24W
South Valley Stream, N.Y. 23 D6 40 38N 73 43W
South Westbury, N.Y. 23 C7 40 44N 73 34W
South Weymouth, Bost. 21 D4 42 10N 70 56W
South Wimbledon, Lon. 4 C3 51 24N 0 11W
South Yarra, Melb. 19 F6 37 50 S 144 59 E
Southall, Lon. 4 B2 51 30N 0 22W
Southborough, Lon. 4 C5 51 23N 0 3 E
Southcrest, Jobg. 18 F9 26 15 S 28 5 E
Southend, Lon. 4 C4 51 25N 0 0 E
Southfields, Lon. 4 C3 51 26N 0 11W
Southgate, Lon. 4 B4 51 38N 0 7W
Southwark, Lon. 4 C4 51 29N 0 5W
Søvang, Købn. 2 E10 55 34N 12 37 E
Soweto, Jobg. 18 F8 26 14 S 27 52 E
Soya, Tōkyō 13 B4 35 44N 139 55 E
Spadenland, Hbg. 7 E8 53 28N 10 3 E
Spandau, Berl. 7 A1 52 33N 13 9 E
Spånga, Stock. 3 D10 59 23N 17 53 E
Sparkhill, N.Y. 22 A5 41 1N 73 55W
Sparrows Point, Balt. 25 B4 39 13N 76 29W
Spectacle I., Bost. 21 C4 42 19N 70 59W
Speicher-See, Mün. 7 F11 48 12N 11 42 E
Speising, Wien 10 H9 48 10N 16 17 E
Speldorf, Ruhr 6 B2 51 26N 6 49 E
Spellen, Ruhr 6 A1 51 36N 6 36 E
Sphinx, El Qâ. 18 D4 29 58N 31 8 E
Spinaceto, Rome 9 G9 41 47N 12 27 E
Splitrock Res., N.Y. 22 B2 40 58N 74 26W
Spořilov, Pra. 10 B3 50 2N 14 29 E
Spot Pond, Bost. 21 C3 42 26N 71 4W
Spotswood, Melb. 19 F6 37 50 S 144 52 E
Spree →, Berl. 7 A2 52 32N 13 12 E
Spreehafen, Hbg. 7 D7 53 31N 9 59 E
Spring Pond, Bost. 21 C4 42 29N 70 56W
Springeberg, Berl. 7 B5 52 26N 13 43 E
Springfield, N.Y. 22 C3 40 42N 74 18W
Springfield, Phil. 24 B3 39 56N 75 19W
Springfield, Wash. 25 E6 38 46N 77 10W
Springs, Jobg. 18 F11 26 15 S 28 23 E
Sprockhövel, Ruhr 6 B5 51 22N 7 14 E
Squantum, Bost. 21 D3 42 17N 71 0W
Squirrel's Heath, Lon. 4 B6 51 34N 0 12 E
Srednaya Rogatka, St-Pet. 11 C4 59 49N 30 22 E
Sródmiečcie, Wsaw. 10 E7 52 13N 21 0 E
Staaken, Berl. 7 A1 52 31N 13 8 E
Staatsoper, Wien 10 G10 48 12N 16 21 E
Stabekk, Oslo 2 B3 59 54N 10 36 E
Stadlau, Wien 10 G10 48 13N 16 27 E
Stahnsdorf, Berl. 7 B2 52 23N 13 12 E
Staines, Lon. 4 C2 51 26N 0 29W
Stains, Paris 5 B4 48 57N 2 22 E
Stamford, N.Y. 23 A7 41 2N 73 32W
Stamford Harbor, N.Y. 23 A7 41 0N 73 34W
Stamford Hill, Lon. 4 B4 51 34N 0 4W
Stammersdorf, Wien 10 G10 48 18N 16 24 E
Stanford Univ., S.F. 27 D4 37 26N 122 10W
Stanley, H.K. 12 E6 22 13N 114 12 E
Stanley Mound, H.K. 12 E6 22 13N 114 12 E
Stanley Pen., H.K. 12 E6 22 12N 114 12 E
Stanmore, Lon. 4 B3 51 37N 0 18W
Stansted, Lon. 4 C6 51 20N 0 18 E
Stapleford Abbotts, Lon. 4 B6 51 37N 0 10 E
Stapleton, N.Y. 22 D4 40 36N 74 5W
Stará Boleslav, Pra. 10 A3 50 11N 14 39 E
Stara Milosna, Wsaw. 10 E8 52 15N 21 12 E
Staraya, St-Pet. 11 B5 59 55N 30 37 E
Staraya Derevnya, St-Pet. 11 B3 59 58N 30 15 E
Stare, Wsaw. 10 E7 52 15N 21 0 E
Stare Babice, Wsaw. 10 E5 52 15N 20 49 E
Staré Mesto, Pra. 10 B2 50 5N 14 25 E
State House, Lagos 18 B2 6 26N 7 24 E
Staten, N.Y. 22 D4 40 34N 74 7W
Staten Island Zoo, N.Y. 22 D4 40 38N 74 6W
Statenice, Pra. 10 B1 50 9N 14 19 E
Stavnsholt, Købn. 2 D9 55 48N 12 24 E
Steele, Ruhr 6 B4 51 27N 7 4 E
Steele Creek, Melb. 19 E6 37 44 S 144 52 E
Steglitz, Berl. 7 B2 52 27N 13 19 E
Stehstücken, Berl. 7 B1 52 23N 13 7 E
Steilshoop, Hbg. 7 D8 53 36N 10 2 E
Steinberger Slough, S.F. 27 C3 37 32N 122 13W
Steinriegel, Wien 10 G9 48 16N 16 12 E
Steinstücken, Berl. 7 B1 52 21N 13 7 E
Steinwerder, Hbg. 7 D7 53 32N 9 57 E
Stellingen, Hbg. 7 D7 53 35N 9 56 E
Stenhamra, Stock. 3 D9 59 20N 17 40 E
Stenløse, Købn. 2 D8 55 46N 12 11 E
Stephansdom, Wien 10 G10 48 12N 16 21 E
Stepney, Lon. 4 B4 51 30N 0 3W
Sterkende, Købn. 2 E8 55 36N 12 10 E
Sterkrade, Ruhr 6 A3 51 31N 6 52 E
Sterling Park, S.F. 27 B2 37 41N 122 27W
Stevenson, Balt. 25 A2 39 24N 76 42W
Stewart Manor, N.Y. 23 C6 40 43N 73 40W
Sticklinge udde, Stock. 3 D11 59 23N 18 6 E
Stickney, Chic. 26 C2 41 49N 87 46W
Stienitzaue, Berl. 7 A5 52 38N 13 44 E
Stiepel, Ruhr 6 B5 51 25N 7 14 E
Stiftskirche, Ruhr 6 C2 51 12N 6 41 E
Still Run →, Phil. 24 C3 39 47N 75 16W
Stockholm, Stock. 3 E11 59 19N 18 4 E
Stocksund, Stock. 3 D11 59 23N 18 3 E
Stockum, Ruhr 6 C2 51 16N 6 44 E
Stodůlky, Pra. 10 B1 50 3N 14 19 E
Stoke D'Abernon, Lon. 4 D2 51 19N 0 23W
Stoke Newington, Lon. 4 B4 51 33N 0 4W
Stolpe-Süd, Berl. 7 A2 52 37N 13 14 E
Stone, Lon. 4 C6 51 26N 0 16 E
Stone Grove, Lon. 4 B3 51 37N 0 16W
Stone Park, Chic. 26 B1 41 53N 87 52W
Stonebridge, Lon. 4 B3 51 32N 0 16W
Stoneham, Bost. 21 C3 42 29N 71 5W
Stonehurst, L.A. 28 A2 34 15N 118 21W
Stony Brook Res., Bost. 21 D3 42 15N 71 8W
Stony Cr. →, Chic. 26 C2 41 40N 87 45W
Stony Cr. →, Melb. 19 E6 37 49 S 144 53 E
Stora Värtan, Stock. 3 D11 59 25N 18 7 E
Store Hareskov, Købn. 2 D9 55 46N 12 23 E
Store Kattingesø, Købn. 2 E7 55 39N 12 0 E
Store Magleby, Købn. 2 E10 55 35N 12 35 E
Storholmen, Stock. 3 D11 59 23N 18 8 E
Stovivatn, Oslo 2 B2 59 54N 10 26 E
Stovner, Oslo 2 B5 59 57N 10 55 E
Stow L., S.F. 27 B2 37 46N 122 28W
Stračnice, Pra. 10 B2 50 4N 14 28 E
Strandbad Gansehäufe, Wien 10 G10 48 13N 16 26 E
Strasslach, Mün. 7 G10 48 0N 11 30 E
Strasstrudering, Mün. 7 G11 48 6N 11 41 E
Stratford, Lon. 4 B5 51 33N 0 0 E
Stratford, Phil. 24 C4 39 49N 75 0W
Strathfield, Syd. 19 B3 33 52 S 151 5 E
Strawberry Hill, Bost. 21 D2 42 14N 71 15W
Strawberry Pk., L.A. 28 A4 34 16N 118 7W
Strawberry Pt., S.F. 27 A1 37 53N 122 30W
Streatham, Lon. 4 C4 51 25N 0 7W
Streatham Vale, Lon. 4 C4 51 24N 0 8W
Strebersdorf, Wien 10 G10 48 17N 16 23 E
Střečovice, Pra. 10 B2 50 5N 14 23 E
Strelyna, St-Pet. 11 C1 59 49N 30 0 E
Střížkov, Pra. 10 B2 50 7N 14 28 E
Strogino, Mos. 11 E8 55 48N 37 24 E
Strømmen, Oslo 2 B5 59 56N 10 59 E
Stromovka, Pra. 10 B2 50 6N 14 25 E
Strunkede Wasserschloss, Ruhr 6 A5 51 33N 7 12 E
Studio City, L.A. 28 B2 34 8N 118 24W
Stupinigi, Tori. 9 C2 44 59N 7 36 E
Stura di Lanzo →, Tori. 9 A2 45 11N 7 47 E
Stureby, Stock. 3 E11 59 15N 18 4 E
Stuvsta, Stock. 3 E11 59 15N 18 0 E
Styrum, Ruhr 6 B3 51 27N 6 52 E
Subhepur, Delhi 16 A2 28 44N 77 15 E
Sucat, Manila 15 E4 14 27N 121 2 E
Success, L., N.Y. 23 C6 40 45N 73 42W
Suchdol, Pra. 10 B2 50 8N 14 22 E
Sucre, Car. 30 D5 10 31N 66 57W
Sucy-en-Brie, Paris 5 C5 48 46N 2 31 E
Sudberg, Ruhr 6 C4 51 10N 7 6 E
Sudbury, Bost. 21 C1 42 22N 71 24W
Suderelbe →, Hbg. 7 E7 53 28N 9 58 E
Suderwich, Ruhr 6 A5 51 36N 7 16 E
Sugamo, Tōkyō 13 B3 35 44N 139 43 E
Sugar Loaf Mt. = Açúcar, Pão de, Rio J. 31 B3 22 56 S 43 9W
Sugartown, Phil. 24 B1 39 59N 75 30W
Sugasawa, Tōkyō 13 B2 35 46N 139 32 E
Suge, Tōkyō 13 C2 35 37N 139 32 E
Suginami-Ku, Tōkyō 13 B2 35 41N 139 37 E
Sugita, Tōkyō 13 D2 35 22N 139 37 E
Sugō, Tōkyō 13 C2 35 34N 139 33 E
Suitland, Wash. 25 D8 38 50N 76 55W
Sukchar, Calc. 16 D6 22 42N 88 22 E
Sulejówek, Wsaw. 10 E8 52 14N 21 14 E
Sulldorf, Hbg. 7 D6 53 34N 9 49 E
Sultan Mosque, Sing. 15 G8 1 18N 103 51 E
Suma, Ōsaka 12 C1 34 38N 135 8 E
Sumaré, S. Pau. 31 E5 23 32 S 46 41W
Sumida, Tōkyō 13 B3 35 42N 139 49 E
Sumida →, Tōkyō 13 B3 35 39N 139 45 E
Sumiyoshi, Ōsaka 12 C4 34 36N 135 30 E
Summer Palace, Beij. 14 B2 39 59N 116 13 E
Summerville, Trto. 20 E7 43 37N 79 33W
Summit, Chic. 26 C2 41 47N 87 47W
Summit, N.Y. 22 C2 40 43N 74 22W
Sun Valley, L.A. 28 A2 34 13N 118 21W
Sunamachi, Tōkyō 13 B4 35 40N 139 50 E
Sunashinden, Tōkyō 13 A2 35 53N 139 30 E
Sunbury, Lon. 4 C2 51 25N 0 26W
Sunda Kelapa, Jak. 15 H9 6 6 S 106 48 E
Sundbyberg, Stock. 3 D10 59 22N 17 57 E
Sundbyerne, Købn. 2 E10 55 39N 12 36 E
Sung Kong, H.K. 12 E6 22 11N 114 17 E
Sungai Bambu, Jak. 15 H10 6 6 S 106 53 E
Sungai Buloh, Sing. 15 F7 1 25N 103 42 E
Sungei Simpang, Sing. 15 F7 1 26N 103 49 E
Sunland, L.A. 28 A3 34 15N 118 18W
Sunnyridge, Jobg. 18 F10 26 10 S 28 10 E
Sunset, S.F. 27 B2 37 44N 122 29W
Sunshine, Melb. 19 E5 37 48 S 144 49 E
Sunshine Acres, L.A. 28 C5 33 56N 117 59W
Suntaug L., Bost. 21 B3 42 31N 71 0W
Sunter, Jak. 15 H10 6 7 S 106 51 E
Sunter, Kali, Jak. 15 J10 6 10 S 106 53 E
Suomenlinna, Hels. 3 C4 60 9N 24 59 E
Superga, Tori. 9 B3 45 4N 7 46 E
Superga, Basilica di, Tori. 9 B3 45 5N 7 45 E
Sura, Calc. 16 E6 22 33N 88 24 E
Surag San, Sŏul 12 F8 37 40N 127 4 E
Surbiton, Lon. 4 C3 51 23N 0 17W
Surco, Lima 30 G8 12 9 S 77 0W
Suresnes, Paris 5 B3 48 52N 2 13 E
Surquillo, Lima 30 G8 12 6 S 77 1W
Surrey Hills, Melb. 19 F7 37 50 S 145 5 E
Surrey Hills, Syd. 19 B4 33 53 S 151 13 E
Surrey Park, Melb. 19 E7 37 49 S 145 6 E
Susaeg, Sŏul 12 G7 37 34N 126 54 E
Süssenbrunn, Wien 10 G10 48 16N 16 29 E
Sutherland, Syd. 19 C3 34 2 S 151 3 E
Sutton, Lon. 4 C3 51 21N 0 11W
Sutton at Hone, Lon. 4 C6 51 24N 0 14 E
Suyu, Sŏul 12 G8 37 37N 127 0 E
Suzukishinden, Tōkyō 13 B2 35 43N 139 31 E
Svanemøllen, Købn. 2 D10 55 43N 12 34 E
Svartsjölandet, Stock. 3 D9 59 20N 17 43 E
Sverdlov, Mos. 11 E9 55 46N 37 36 E
Svestad, Oslo 2 C3 59 46N 10 36 E
Svestrup, Købn. 2 D7 55 46N 12 8 E
Svinningeudd, Stock. 3 D12 59 26N 18 17 E
Švinö, Hels. 3 C3 60 7N 24 44 E
Svogerslev, Købn. 2 E7 55 38N 12 0 E
Swampscott, Bost. 21 C4 42 28N 70 53W
Swanley, Lon. 4 C5 51 23N 0 9 E
Swanscombe, Lon. 4 C6 51 26N 0 18 E
Swansea, Trto. 20 E8 43 39N 79 27W
Swarthmore, Phil. 24 B2 39 54N 75 22W
Swedesboro, Phil. 24 C3 39 45N 75 17W
Swedesburg, Phil. 24 A3 40 5N 75 19W
Swinburne I., N.Y. 22 D4 40 33N 74 3W
Swita, Ōsaka 12 B4 34 45N 135 30 E
Syampur, Calc. 16 F5 22 28N 88 12 E
Sycamore Mills, Phil. 24 B2 39 57N 75 25W
Sydenham, Jobg. 18 E9 26 9 S 28 5 E
Sydney, Syd. 19 B4 33 52 S 151 12 E
Sydney, Univ. of, Syd. 19 B4 33 54 S 151 11 E
Sydney Airport, Syd. 19 B4 33 56 S 151 10 E
Sydney Harbour Bridge, Syd. 19 B4 33 51 S 151 12 E
Sydstranden, Købn. 2 E10 55 34N 12 38 E
Sylling, Oslo 2 B1 59 54N 10 16 E
Sylvania, Syd. 19 C3 34 0 S 151 7 E
Syndal, Melb. 19 F7 37 52 S 145 9 E
Syon House, Lon. 4 C3 51 28N 0 18W
Syosset, N.Y. 23 C7 40 49N 73 30W
Szabadság-hegy, Bud. 10 J12 47 30N 18 59 E
Szczęsliwice, Wsaw. 10 E6 52 12N 20 57 E
Szemere-Telep, Bud. 10 K14 47 26N 19 13 E
Sźephalom, Bud. 10 J12 47 34N 18 57 E
Szilasliget, Bud. 10 J14 47 34N 19 16 E

T

Tabata, Tōkyō 13 B3 35 44N 139 46 E
Tablada, B.A. 32 C3 34 41 S 58 32W
Taboão →, S. Pau. 31 F7 23 40 S 46 27W
Taboão da Serra, S. Pau. 31 E5 23 36 S 46 45W
Tabor, N.Y. 22 B2 40 52N 74 28W
Täby, Stock. 3 D11 59 26N 18 2 E
Tacony, Phil. 24 A4 40 1N 75 2W
Tacuba, Méx. 29 B2 19 26N 99 11W
Tacubaya, Méx. 29 B2 19 24N 99 10W
Tadain, Ōsaka 12 A3 34 51N 135 24 E
Tadworth, Lon. 4 D3 51 17N 0 14W
Tagig, Manila 15 D4 14 31N 121 4 E
Tagig →, Manila 15 D4 14 31N 121 5 E
Tai Hang, H.K. 12 E6 22 16N 114 11 E
Tai Lo Shan, H.K. 12 D6 22 21N 114 13 E
Tai Po Tsai, H.K. 12 D6 22 20N 114 15 E
Tai Seng, Sing. 15 F8 1 20N 103 53 E
Tai Shui Hang, H.K. 12 D6 22 24N 114 13 E
Tai Tam B., H.K. 12 E6 22 12N 114 13 E
Tai Tam Tuk Res., H.K. 12 E6 22 14N 114 13 E
Tai Wan Tau, H.K. 12 E6 22 17N 114 17 E
Tai Wo Hau, H.K. 12 D5 22 21N 114 7 E
Tai Wo Ping, H.K. 12 D5 22 20N 114 9 E
Ta'imim, Bagd. 17 F8 33 15N 44 21 E
Tainaka, Ōsaka 12 C4 34 36N 135 35 E
Taishō, Ōsaka 12 C3 34 38N 135 27 E
Taitō-Ku, Tōkyō 13 B3 35 43N 139 47 E
Tajima, Tōkyō 13 B2 35 48N 139 36 E
Tajpur, Calc. 16 D5 22 44N 88 15 E
Takaido, Tōkyō 13 B2 35 40N 139 37 E
Takaishi, Tōkyō 13 C2 35 36N 139 31 E
Takarazuka, Ōsaka 12 B2 34 47N 135 20 E
Takasago, Tōkyō 13 B4 35 44N 139 52 E
Takatsuki, Ōsaka 12 A4 34 50N 135 37 E
Takayanagi, Tōkyō 13 D4 35 23N 139 57 E
Takegahana, Tōkyō 13 B4 35 47N 139 54 E
Takenotsuka, Tōkyō 13 B3 35 47N 139 47 E
Takeshita, Tōkyō 13 C2 35 33N 139 32 E
Takinegawa, Tōkyō 13 B3 35 45N 139 44 E
Takkula, Hels. 3 B2 60 19N 24 38 E
Takoma Park, Wash. 25 D7 38 58N 77 0W
Taksim, Ist. 17 A2 41 2N 28 58 E
Talaide, Lisb. 8 F7 38 44N 9 18W
Talampas, Manila 15 D4 14 36N 121 4 E
Taling Chan, Bangk. 15 B1 13 46N 100 27 E
Talleyville, Phil. 24 C1 39 48N 75 32W
Tallkrogen, Stock. 3 E11 59 16N 18 4 E
Talmapais Valley, S.F. 27 A1 37 52N 122 32W
Tama, Tōkyō 13 C1 35 38N 139 26 E
Tama →, Tōkyō 13 C2 35 32N 139 39 E
Tama Kyźryō, Tōkyō 13 C2 35 34N 139 30 E
Tamaden, Tōkyō 13 C2 35 39N 139 38 E
Tamagawa-josui →, Tōkyō 13 B1 35 41N 139 47 E
Taman Sari, Jak. 15 H9 6 8 S 106 48 E
Tamanduatei →, S. Pau. 31 E6 23 37 S 46 38W
Tambora, Jak. 15 H9 6 8 S 106 47 E
Tamboré, S. Pau. 31 E4 23 30 S 46 50W
Tammisalo, Hels. 3 B5 60 11N 25 5 E
Tammûh, El Qâ. 18 D5 29 55N 31 15 E
Tampier Slough, Chic. 26 D1 41 39N 87 54W
Tan Tock Seng, Sing. 15 G8 1 19N 103 50 E
Tanah Abang, Jak. 15 J9 6 12 S 106 48 E
Tanashi, Tōkyō 13 B2 35 43N 139 32 E
Tanforan Park, S.F. 27 C2 37 37N 122 24W
Tangjae, Sŏul 12 H8 37 29N 127 2 E
Tanglin, Sing. 15 G7 1 18N 103 47 E
Tangstedt, Hbg. 7 C7 53 40N 9 51 E
Tangstedter Forst, Hbg. 7 C8 53 43N 10 3 E
Tanigami, Ōsaka 12 B2 34 45N 135 10 E
Tanjung Duren, Jak. 15 J9 6 10 S 106 46 E
Tanjung Priok, Jak. 15 H10 6 6 S 106 52 E
Tanum, Oslo 2 B2 59 53N 10 28 E
Taoranting Gongyuan, Beij. 14 B3 39 51N 116 20 E
Taoranting Hu, Beij. 14 B3 39 50N 116 20 E
Tapada, Lisb. 8 F7 38 49N 9 16W
Tapanila, Hels. 3 B5 60 15N 25 2 E
Tapiales, B.A. 32 C3 34 42 S 58 30W
Tapiola, Hels. 3 B3 60 10N 24 48 E
Tappan, N.Y. 22 A5 41 1N 73 57W
Tappan, L., N.Y. 22 A5 41 1N 73 59W
Tappeh, Tehr. 17 C5 35 41N 51 29 E
Tapsia, Calc. 16 E6 22 32N 88 23 E
Taquara, Rio J. 31 B1 22 55 S 43 21W
Tara, Bomb. 16 G7 19 5N 72 49 E
Tarāblus, Bagd. 17 F8 33 19N 44 21 E
Tarango, Presa, Méx. 29 B2 19 21N 99 12W
Tårbæk, Købn. 2 D10 55 46N 12 35 E
Tarchomin, Wsaw. 10 E6 52 19N 20 58 E
Tardeo, Bomb. 16 H7 18 57N 72 48 E
Target Rock, N.Y. 23 B8 40 55N 73 24W
Targówek, Wsaw. 10 E7 52 16N 21 3 E
Tårnby, Købn. 2 E10 55 37N 12 35 E

Villecresnes 47

Taronga Zoo. Park, Syd. 19 B4 33 50 S 151 14 E
Tarqua B., Lagos 18 B2 6 24N 7 23 E
Tarzana, L.A. 28 A1 34 10N 118 32W
Tåstrup, Købn. 2 E8 55 39N 12 18 E
Tatarovo, Mos. 11 E8 55 45N 37 24 E
Tatarpur, Delhi 16 B1 28 38N 77 9 E
Tatenberg, Hbg. 7 E8 53 29N 10 3 E
Tathong Channel, H.K. 12 E6 22 15N 114 16 E
Tathong Pt., H.K. 12 E6 22 14N 114 17 E
Tatsfield, Lon. 4 D5 51 17N 0 1 E
Tattariharju, Hels. 3 B5 60 15N 25 2 E
Tatuapé, S. Pau. 31 E6 23 31 S 46 33W
Taufkirchen, Mün. 7 G10 48 2N 11 36 E
Tavares, I. dos, Rio J. 31 A3 22 49 S 43 6W
Tavernanova, Nápl. 9 H13 40 54N 14 21 E
Taverny, Paris 5 A3 49 1N 2 13 E
Távros, Ath. 8 J11 37 57N 23 43 E
Tavry, St-Pet. 11 B6 59 54N 30 40 E
Taylortown, N.Y. 22 B2 40 56N 74 23W
Tayninka, Mos. 11 D10 55 53N 37 45 E
Taytay, Manila 15 D4 14 34N 121 7 E
Tayuman, Manila 15 D4 14 31N 121 9 E
Teaneck, N.Y. 22 B4 40 52N 74 1W
Teatro Colón, B.A. 32 B4 34 36 S 58 23 E
Teban Gardens, Sing. 15 G7 1 19N 103 44 E
Tebet, Jak. 15 J10 6 14 S 106 50 E
Tecamachaleo, Méx. 29 B2 19 25N 99 14W
Techny, Chic. 26 A2 42 6N 87 48W
Teck Hock, Sing. 15 F8 1 21N 103 54 E
Tecoma, Melb. 19 F9 37 54 S 145 20 E
Teddington, Lon. 4 C2 51 25N 0 20W
Tegel, Berl. 7 A2 52 34N 13 16 E
Tegel, Flughafen, Berl. 7 A2 52 35N 13 15 E
Tegeler Fliess →, Berl. 7 A3 52 37N 13 21 E
Tegeler See, Berl. 7 A2 52 34N 13 15 E
Tegelort, Berl. 7 A2 52 34N 13 13 E
Tehar, Delhi 16 B1 28 37N 77 7 E
Tehrān, Tehr. 17 C5 35 41N 51 25 E
Tehrān Pars, Tehr. 17 C6 35 44N 51 32 E
Tei Tong Tsui, H.K. 12 E6 22 16N 114 17 E
Tejo →, Lisb. 8 F8 38 45N 9 3W
Tekstilyshchik, Mos. 11 E10 55 42N 37 41 E
Tela, Delhi 16 A2 28 43N 77 19 E
Telhal, Lisb. 8 F7 38 48N 9 18W
Telinipara, Calc. 16 D6 22 46N 88 23 E
Telok Blangah, Sing. 15 G7 1 17N 103 49 E
Teltow, Berl. 7 B2 52 23N 13 17 E
Teltow kanal, Berl. 7 B3 52 26N 13 29 E
Temescal, L., S.F. 27 A3 37 50N 122 13W
Temnikovo, Mos. 11 E12 55 43N 38 1 E
Tempelhof, Berl. 7 B3 52 27N 13 23 E
Tempelhof, Flughafen, Berl. 7 B3 52 28N 13 27 E
Temperley, B.A. 32 C4 34 46 S 58 22W
Temple City, L.A. 28 B4 34 6N 118 3W
Temple Hills Park, Wash. 25 E8 38 48N 76 56W
Templestowe, Melb. 19 E7 37 45 S 145 8 E
Templestowe Lower, Melb. 19 E7 37 45 S 145 6 E
Tenafly, N.Y. 22 B5 40 54N 73 58W
Tenantongo, Presa, Méx. 29 B2 19 28N 99 15W
Tengah →, Sing. 15 F7 1 23N 103 43 E
Tengeh, Sungei →, Sing. 15 F6 1 20N 103 39 E
Tennoji, Ōsaka 12 C4 34 39N 135 30 E
Tenochtitlán, Méx. 29 B3 19 26N 99 7W
Tepalcates, Méx. 29 B3 19 23N 99 3W
Tepe Saif, Tehr. 17 D4 35 36N 51 17 E
Tepepan, Méx. 29 C3 19 16N 99 9W
Teplyy Star, Mos. 11 F9 55 37N 37 30 E
Tepozteco, Parque Nac. del, Méx. 29 D3 19 3N 99 5W
Terrasse Vaudreuil, Mtrl. 20 B2 43 23N 73 59W
Terrazzano, Mil. 9 D5 45 32N 9 4 E
Terrugem, Lisb. 8 F7 38 41N 9 17W
Terusan Banjir, Jak. 15 H9 6 7 S 106 46 E
Terzigno, Nápl. 9 J13 40 48N 14 29 E
Tessancourt-sur-Aubette, Paris 5 A1 49 1N 1 55 E
Testona, Tori. 9 C3 44 59N 7 42 E
Tetelco, Méx. 29 C4 19 12N 98 57W
Tetreauville, Mtrl. 20 A4 43 35N 73 32W
Tetti Neirotti, Tori. 9 B2 45 3N 7 32 E
Tetuán, Mdrd. 8 B2 40 27N 3 42W
Teufelsberg, Berl. 7 B2 52 29N 13 14 E
Tévere →, Rome 9 F9 41 56N 12 27 E
Tewksbury, Bost. 21 B2 42 37N 71 13W
Texcoco, L. de, Méx. 29 B4 19 30N 89 58 E
Thalkirchen, Mün. 7 G10 48 6N 11 32 E
Thames Ditton, Lon. 4 C2 51 23N 0 20W
Thamesmead, Lon. 4 B5 51 30N 0 7 E
Thana Cr. →, Bomb. 16 G8 19 4N 72 54 E
The Basin, Melb. 19 F8 37 51 S 145 19 E
The Glen, Wash. 25 C6 39 2N 77 12W
The Loop, Chic. 26 B3 41 52N 87 37W
The Narrows, N.Y. 22 D4 40 37N 74 3W
The Ridge, Delhi 16 B2 28 37N 77 10 E
The White House, Wash. 25 D7 38 53N 77 1W
The Wilds, Jobg. 18 F9 26 10 S 28 2 E
Theseión, Ath. 8 J11 37 57N 23 43 E
Theydon Bois, Lon. 4 A5 51 40N 0 6 E
Thiais, Paris 5 C4 48 46N 2 23 E
Thieux, Paris 5 A6 49 0N 2 40 E
Thistletown, Trto. 20 D7 43 44N 79 34W
Thiverval-Grignon, Paris 5 B1 48 51N 1 55 E
Thomaston, N.Y. 23 C6 40 47N 73 43W
Thomastown, Melb. 19 E7 37 40 S 145 2 E
Thompson I., Bost. 21 D4 42 19N 70 59W
Thomson, Sing. 15 F8 1 20N 103 50 E
Thon Buri, Bangk. 15 B1 13 45N 100 29 E
Thong Hoe, Sing. 15 F7 1 25N 103 42 E
Thorigny-sur-Marne, Paris 5 B6 48 53N 2 41 E
Thornbury, Melb. 19 E7 37 44 S 145 1 E
Thorncliffe, Trto. 20 D8 43 42N 79 20W
Thornhill, Jobg. 18 E9 26 6 S 28 9 E
Thornhill, Trto. 20 D8 43 48N 79 25W
Thornton, Phil. 24 B1 39 54N 75 31W
Thornton Heath, Lon. 4 C4 51 23N 0 6W
Thorofare, Phil. 24 B3 39 50N 75 11W
Throgs Neck, N.Y. 23 C6 40 48N 73 49W
Tian Guan, Sing. 15 F7 1 21N 103 49 E
Tian'anmen, Beij. 14 B3 39 53N 116 21 E
Tiancun, Beij. 14 B2 39 54N 116 12 E
Tianjin, Tianj. 14 E5 39 7N 117 12 E
Tiantan Gongyuan, Beij. 14 B3 39 51N 116 22 E
Tiateloco, Méx. 29 B3 19 27N 99 8W
Tibidabo, Barc. 8 D5 41 25N 2 6 E
Tiburon, S.F. 27 A2 37 52N 122 27W
Tiburon Pen., S.F. 27 A2 37 53N 122 28W
Tiburtino, Rome 9 F10 41 53N 12 30 E
Ticomán, Méx. 29 A3 19 31N 99 8W
Tiefenbroich, Ruhr 6 C2 51 18N 6 49 E
Tiefersee, Berl. 7 B1 52 24N 13 5 E
Tiejiangyin, Beij. 14 C3 39 49N 116 23 E
Tientsin = Tianjin, Tianj. 14 E5 39 7N 117 12 E
Tiergarten, Berl. 7 A3 52 31N 13 20 E
Tietê →, S. Pau. 31 D7 23 28 S 46 24W
Tigery, Paris 5 D5 48 38N 2 30 E
Tigre, B.A. 32 A3 34 25 S 58 34W
Tigris →, Bagd. 17 F8 33 17N 44 23 E
Tijuca, Rio J. 31 B2 22 56 S 43 13W
Tijuca, L. de, Rio J. 31 B2 22 59 S 43 20W
Tijuca, Pico da, Rio J. 31 B2 22 56 S 43 15W
Tijucamar, Rio J. 31 C2 23 0 S 43 18W
Tijucas, Is., Rio J. 31 C2 23 1 S 43 17W
Tikkurila, Hels. 3 B5 60 17N 25 2 E
Tilanqiao, Shang. 14 J11 31 15N 121 29 E
Tilbury, Lon. 4 C7 51 27N 0 21 E
Timah, Bukit, Sing. 15 F7 1 21N 103 46 E
Timiryazev Park, Mos. 11 E9 55 49N 37 33 E
Ting Kau, H.K. 12 D5 22 22N 114 4 E
Tinley Cr. →, Chic. 26 D2 41 39N 87 45W
Tinley Creek Woods, Chic. 26 D2 41 38N 87 48W
Tinley Park, Chic. 26 D2 41 35N 87 46W
Tipas, Manila 15 D4 14 32N 121 4 E
Tirsa, El Qâ. 18 D5 29 57N 31 12 E
Tishrīyaa, Bagd. 17 F8 33 18N 44 24 E
Tit Cham Chau, H.K. 12 E6 22 15N 114 17 E
Titagarh, Calc. 16 D6 22 44N 88 22 E
Tivoli, Købn. 2 D10 55 40N 12 35 E
Tizapán, Méx. 29 C2 19 19N 99 13W
Tlalnepantla, Méx. 29 A2 19 32N 99 11W
Tlalnepantla →, Méx. 29 A2 19 30N 99 18W
Tláloc, Cerro, Méx. 29 D3 19 7N 99 3W
Tlalpan, Méx. 29 C2 19 17N 99 10W
Tlalpitzáhuac, Méx. 29 C4 19 19N 98 56W
Tlaltenango, Méx. 29 B2 19 20N 99 17W
Tlaltenco, Méx. 29 C3 19 19N 99 0W
Tlaxcoaque, Méx. 29 B3 19 25N 99 8W
To Kwai Wan, H.K. 12 E6 22 18N 114 11 E
Toa Payoh, Sing. 15 F8 1 20N 103 50 E
Tobay Beach, N.Y. 23 D8 40 36N 73 26W
Točná, Pra. 10 C2 49 58N 14 25 E
Tocome →, Car. 30 D6 10 28N 66 49W
Toda, Tōkyō 13 A3 35 50N 139 40 E
Todamachī, Tōkyō 13 B2 35 48N 139 39 E
Todt Hill, N.Y. 22 D4 40 36N 74 6W
Toei, Khlong →, Bangk. 15 B2 13 43N 100 32 E
Togasaki, Tōkyō 13 B4 35 47N 139 51 E
Tōkagi, Tōkyō 13 B4 35 42N 139 55 E
Tōkaichiba, Tōkyō 13 C2 35 31N 139 30 E
Tokarevo, Mos. 11 F11 55 38N 37 54 E
Tokorozawa, Tōkyō 13 B1 35 47N 139 28 E
Tōkyō, Tōkyō 13 C3 35 43N 139 45 E
Tōkyō B., Tōkyō 13 C4 35 33N 139 53 E
Tōkyō-Haneda Int. Airport, Tōkyō 13 C3 35 33N 139 45 E
Tōkyō Harbour, Tōkyō 13 C3 35 38N 139 46 E
Tokyo Univ., Tōkyō 13 B3 35 42N 139 46 E
Tollygunge, Calc. 16 F6 22 29N 88 21 E
Tolly's Nala, Calc. 16 E6 22 33N 88 19 E
Tolworth, Lon. 4 C3 51 22N 0 17W
Tomang, Jak. 15 J9 6 10 S 106 47 E
Tomba di Nerone, Rome 9 F9 41 58N 12 26 E
Tomilino, Mos. 11 F11 55 39N 37 55 E
Tomioka, Tōkyō 13 D2 35 22N 139 37 E
Tonda, Ōsaka 12 B4 34 49N 135 35 E
Tondo, Manila 15 D3 14 36N 120 57 E
Tone-unga →, Tōkyō 13 A4 35 55N 139 56 E
Tonekollen, Oslo 2 C6 50 49N 11 0 E
Tong Kang, Sungei →, Sing. 15 F8 1 23N 103 53 E
Tonghui He →, Beij. 14 B3 39 53N 116 28 E
Tönisheide, Ruhr 6 C4 51 18N 7 3 E
Tonndorf, Hbg. 7 D8 53 35N 10 8 E
Toorak, Melb. 19 F7 37 50 S 145 1 E
Toot Hill, Lon. 4 A6 51 41N 0 11 E
Topilejo, Méx. 29 C3 19 12N 99 9W
Topkapi, Ist. 17 A2 41 1N 28 55 E
Topsfield, Bost. 21 B4 42 38N 70 57W
Tor di Quinto, Rome 9 F9 41 56N 12 27 E
Tor Pignattara, Rome 9 F10 41 52N 12 31 E
Tor Sapienza, Rome 9 F10 41 53N 12 35 E
Torcy, Paris 5 B5 48 51N 2 39 E
Torino, Tori. 9 B2 45 5N 7 39 E
Toro, B.A. 32 B1 34 30 S 58 50W
Toronto, Trto. 20 E9 43 39N 79 23W
Toronto, Univ. of, Trto. 20 E8 43 39N 79 23W
Toronto Harbour, Trto. 20 E8 43 38N 79 21W
Toronto I., Trto. 20 E8 43 37N 79 23W
Toronto Int. Airport, Trto. 20 D7 43 40N 79 38 E
Torre Annunziata, Nápl. 9 J13 40 45N 14 26 E
Torre Cervara, Rome 9 F10 41 55N 12 35 E
Torre del Greco, Nápl. 9 J13 40 47N 14 21 E
Torre Novo, Rome 9 F10 41 51N 12 36 E
Torrellas →, Barc. 8 D5 41 23N 2 1 E
Torrellas del Llobregat, Barc. 8 D4 41 20N 1 59 E
Torresdale, Phil. 24 A5 40 3N 74 59W
Torrevécchia, Rome 9 F9 41 55N 12 25 E
Tortuguitas, B.A. 32 A2 34 28 S 58 44W
Toshima-Ku, Tōkyō 13 B3 35 43N 139 43 E
Toshimaen, Tōkyō 13 B2 35 43N 139 38 E
Totowa, N.Y. 22 B3 40 54N 74 13W
Totsuka-Ku, Tōkyō 13 D2 35 23N 139 32 E
Tottenham, Lon. 4 B4 51 35N 0 4W
Tottenham, Melb. 19 E6 37 48 S 144 51 E
Tottenville, N.Y. 22 D3 40 30N 74 14W
Totteridge, Lon. 4 B3 51 37N 0 11W
Toussus-le-Noble, Paris 5 C2 48 44N 2 6 E
Toussus-le-Noble, Aérodrome de, Paris 5 C2 48 44N 2 6 E
Toverud, Oslo 2 B5 59 55N 10 20 E
Towaco, N.Y. 22 B3 40 55N 74 18W
Tower Hamlets, Lon. 4 B4 51 31N 0 2W
Town Farm Hill, Bost. 21 A3 42 40N 71 3W
Townley, N.Y. 22 C3 40 41N 74 14W
Towra Pt., Syd. 19 C4 34 0 S 151 10 E
Towson, Balt. 25 A3 39 24N 76 36W
Tøyen, Oslo 2 B4 59 55N 10 46 E
Toyofuta, Tōkyō 13 A4 35 54N 139 55 E
Toyonaka, Ōsaka 12 B3 34 46N 135 28 E
Traar, Ruhr 6 B1 51 22N 6 36 E
Trafaria, Lisb. 8 F7 38 40N 9 13W
Tragliata, Rome 9 F8 41 58N 12 14 E
Traicão →, S. Pau. 31 E6 23 35 S 46 41W
Trälhavet, Stock. 3 D13 59 26N 18 20 E
Tranby, Oslo 2 C1 59 49N 10 14 E
Tranegilde, Købn. 2 E9 55 36N 12 19 E
Trångsund, Stock. 3 E11 59 13N 18 8 E
Trappenfelde, Berl. 7 A4 52 34N 13 35 E
Trappes, Paris 5 C1 48 46N 1 59 E
Trastévere, Rome 9 F9 51 53N 12 28 E
Travilah, Wash. 25 C6 39 4N 77 15W
Travilah Regional Park, Wash. 25 C6 39 4N 77 17W
Travis, N.Y. 22 D3 40 35N 74 11W
Treasure I., S.F. 27 B2 37 49N 122 22W
Třeboradice, Pra. 10 B3 50 9N 14 31 E
Třebotov, Pra. 10 C1 49 58N 14 17 E
Trecase, Nápl. 9 J13 40 46N 14 26 E
Trekroner, Købn. 2 D10 55 42N 12 20 E
Tremblay-lès-Gonesse, Paris 5 B5 48 58N 2 30 E
Tremembé, S. Pau. 31 D6 23 27 S 46 36W
Tremembe →, S. Pau. 31 D6 23 27 S 46 34W
Tremont, Melb. 19 F9 37 53 S 145 20 E
Tremont, N.Y. 23 B5 40 50N 73 52W
Trenno, Mil. 9 E5 45 29N 9 6 E
Treptow, Berl. 7 B3 52 29N 13 27 E
Tres Marias, Méx. 29 D2 19 3N 99 15W
Trés Rios, Sa. dos, Rio J. 31 B2 22 56 S 43 17W
Tretiakov Art Gallery, Mos. 11 E9 55 44N 37 38 E
Trevose, Phil. 24 A5 40 8N 74 59W
Trezzano sul Naviglio, Mil. 9 E5 45 24N 9 4 E
Tribobo, Rio J. 31 B3 22 50 S 43 0W
Triel-sur-Seine, Paris 5 B2 48 58N 2 0 E
Trieste, Rome 9 F10 41 55N 12 30 E
Trinidad, Wash. 25 D8 38 54N 76 59W
Triome, Jobg. 18 F8 26 10 S 27 58 E
Trionfale, Rome 9 F9 41 54N 12 26 E
Triulzo, Mil. 9 E6 45 25N 9 16 E
Trócchia, Nápl. 9 H13 40 51N 14 23 E
Troitse-Lykovo, Mos. 11 E8 55 47N 37 23 E
Troja, Pra. 10 B2 50 7N 14 25 E
Trollbäcken, Stock. 3 E12 59 14N 18 12 E
Trombay, Bomb. 16 G8 19 2N 72 56 E
Troparevo, Mos. 11 F8 55 39N 37 29 E
Trottiscliffe, Lon. 4 D7 51 18N 0 21 E
Troy Hills, N.Y. 22 B3 40 50N 74 23W
Troyeville, Jobg. 18 F9 26 11 S 28 4 E
Truc di Miola, Tori. 9 A2 45 11N 7 30 E
Trudyashchikhsya, Os., St-Pet. 11 B3 59 58N 30 18 E
Trutlandet, Hels. 3 C6 60 9N 25 17 E
Tryvasshøgda, Oslo 2 B4 59 59N 10 40 E
Tseng Lan Shue, H.K. 12 D6 22 20N 114 14 E
Tsentralynyy, Mos. 11 D11 55 53N 37 51 E
Tsim Sha Tsui, H.K. 12 E6 22 17N 114 10 E
Tsing Yi, H.K. 12 D5 22 21N 114 6 E
Tsuen Wan, H.K. 12 D5 22 22N 114 7 E
Tsurugamine, Tōkyō 13 D2 35 28N 139 33 E
Tsuruma, Tōkyō 13 A2 35 52N 139 31 E
Tsurumi →, Tōkyō 13 C3 35 32N 139 40 E
Tsurumi-Ku, Tōkyō 13 D3 35 30N 139 41 E
Tsz Wan Shan, H.K. 12 D6 22 20N 114 11 E
Tua Kang Lye, Sing. 15 G7 1 18N 103 46 E
Tuas, Sing. 15 G6 1 19N 103 39 E
Tuchoměřice, Pra. 10 B1 50 7N 14 16 E
Tuckahoe, N.Y. 23 B6 40 56N 73 49W
Tucuruvi, S. Pau. 31 D6 23 28 S 46 35W
Tufello, Rome 9 F10 41 56N 12 32 E
Tufnell Park, Lon. 4 B4 51 33N 0 8W
Tujunga, L.A. 28 A3 34 15N 118 16W
Tujunga Wash →, L.A. 28 A2 34 12N 118 23W
Tullamarine, Melb. 19 E6 37 41 S 144 50 E
Tullinge, Stock. 3 E10 59 12N 17 54 E
Tullingesjön, Stock. 3 E10 59 12N 17 52 E
Tulse Hill, Lon. 4 C4 51 26N 0 6W
Tulyehualco, Méx. 29 C3 19 15N 99 0W
Tumba, Stock. 3 E9 59 12N 17 49 E
Tune, Købn. 2 E8 55 35N 12 10 E
Tung Lo Wan, H.K. 12 E6 22 17N 114 11 E
Tung Lung I., H.K. 12 E6 22 15N 114 17 E
Tung O, H.K. 12 E5 22 11N 114 8 E
Tunis, Bagd. 17 E8 33 23N 44 21 E
Tuomarila, Hels. 3 B3 60 11N 24 41 E
Tura, El Qâ. 18 D5 29 55N 31 16 E
Turambhe, Bomb. 16 G9 19 4N 73 0 E
Turdera, B.A. 32 C4 34 48 S 58 26W
Tureberg, Stock. 3 D10 59 25N 17 55 E
Turffontein, Jobg. 18 F9 26 14 S 28 2 E
Turin = Torino, Tori. 9 B2 45 5N 7 39 E
Turner, Balt. 25 B3 39 14N 76 31W
Turner Hill, Bost. 21 A4 42 40N 70 53W
Turnersville, Phil. 24 C4 39 46N 75 3W
Turnham Green, Lon. 4 C3 51 29N 0 16W
Turów, Wsaw. 10 E8 52 19N 21 12 E
Turter, Oslo 2 A4 60 0N 10 46 E
Tuscolano, Rome 9 F10 41 52N 12 31 E
Tushino, Mos. 11 D8 55 50N 37 24 E
Tuusulanjoki →, Hels. 3 A4 60 20N 24 54 E
Twickenham, Lon. 4 C2 51 26N 0 20W
Twickenham Rugby Ground, Lon. 4 C2 51 27N 0 20W
Twin Oaks, Phil. 24 B2 39 50N 75 25W
Twórki, Wsaw. 10 E5 52 10N 20 49 E
Tyresö, Stock. 3 E13 59 14N 18 20 E
Tyresö strand, Stock. 3 E12 59 15N 18 17 E

U

Uberaba →, S. Pau. 31 E6 23 35 S 46 41W
Uberruhr, Ruhr 6 B4 51 25N 7 4 E
Ubin, P., Sing. 15 F8 1 24N 103 57 E
Uboldo, Mil. 9 D5 45 36N 9 0 E
Uckendorf, Ruhr 6 B4 51 29N 7 7 E
Udelnaya, St-Pet. 11 A4 60 0N 30 21 E
Udelynaya, Mos. 11 F11 55 38N 37 59 E
Udlding, Mün. 7 F9 48 15N 11 25 E
Uellendahl, Ruhr 6 C5 51 16N 7 10 E
Ueno, Tōkyō 13 B3 35 42N 139 46 E
Uerdingen, Ruhr 6 B1 51 21N 6 38 E
Uhlenhorst, Hbg. 7 D8 53 34N 10 1 E
Úholičky, Pra. 10 B1 50 9N 14 19 E
Uhříněves, Pra. 10 B3 50 2N 14 35 E
Újezd nad Lesy, Pra. 10 B3 50 4N 14 39 E
Újpalota, Bud. 10 J13 47 32N 19 8 E
Újpest, Bud. 10 J13 47 35N 19 6 E
Ukita, Tōkyō 13 B4 35 40N 139 51 E
Ullerup, Købn. 2 E10 55 34N 12 36 E
Ullevål, Oslo 2 B4 59 56N 10 43 E
Üllo, Bud. 10 K14 47 23N 19 20 E
Ulriksdal, Stock. 3 D10 59 23N 17 59 E
Ulu Bedok, Sing. 15 G8 1 19N 103 55 E
Ulu Pandan →, Sing. 15 G7 1 19N 103 45 E
Ulyanka, St-Pet. 11 B3 59 50N 30 14 E
Um Al-Khanazir, Bagd. 17 F8 33 17N 44 22 E
Umeda, Ōsaka 12 B3 34 41N 135 29 E
Umejima, Tōkyō 13 B3 35 46N 139 48 E
Umraniye, Ist. 17 A3 41 1N 29 4 E
Unětický →, Pra. 10 B2 50 9N 14 24 E
Ungelsheim, Ruhr 6 B2 51 21N 6 43 E
Unhos, Lisb. 8 F8 38 49N 9 7W
Unidad Santa Fe, Méx. 29 B2 19 23N 99 13W
Union, N.Y. 22 C3 40 42N 74 16W
Union City, N.Y. 22 C4 40 45N 74 2W
Union City, S.F. 27 C4 37 36N 122 2W
Union Port, N.Y. 23 C5 40 49N 73 51W
Uniondale, N.Y. 23 C7 40 42N 73 35W
United Nations H.Q., N.Y. 22 C5 40 45N 73 59W
Universal City, L.A. 28 B2 34 8N 118 21W
Universidad de Chila, Stgo 30 J11 33 26 S 70 39W
University Gardens, N.Y. 23 C6 40 46N 73 42W
University Heights, S.F. 27 D3 37 26N 122 13W
University Park, Wash. 25 D8 38 58N 76 56W
Unsani, Calc. 16 E5 22 35N 88 15 E
Unterbach, Ruhr 6 C3 51 12N 6 53 E
Unterbiberg, Mün. 7 G10 48 6N 11 38 E
Unterföhring, Mün. 7 F11 48 11N 11 38 E
Unterhaching, Mün. 7 G10 48 3N 11 37 E
Unterkirchbach, Wien 10 G9 48 17N 16 12 E
Unterlaa, Wien 10 H10 48 8N 16 24 E
Untermauerbach, Wien 10 G9 48 14N 16 11 E
Untermenzing, Mün. 7 F9 48 10N 11 28 E
Unterrath, Ruhr 6 C2 51 16N 6 45 E
Unterschleissheim, Mün. 7 F10 48 16N 11 35 E
Upminster, Lon. 4 B6 51 33N 0 14 E
Upper Brookville, N.Y. 23 B7 40 50N 73 35W
Upper Crystal Springs Res., S.F. 26 D2 37 28N 122 20W
Upper Darby, Phil. 24 B3 39 57N 75 16W
Upper Edmonton, Lon. 4 B4 51 36N 0 3W
Upper Elmers End, Lon. 4 C4 51 23N 0 1W
Upper Fern Tree Gully, Melb. 19 F8 37 53 S 145 18 E
Upper New York B., N.Y. 22 D4 40 39N 74 3W
Upper Norwood, Lon. 4 C4 51 24N 0 6W
Upper Peirce Res., Sing. 15 F7 1 22N 103 47 E
Upper San Leandro Res., S.F. 27 B4 37 46N 122 6W
Upper Sydenham, Lon. 4 C4 51 26N 0 4W
Upper Tooting, Lon. 4 C4 51 25N 0 9W
Upton, Lon. 4 B5 51 32N 0 1 E
Uptons Hill, Bost. 21 B3 42 33N 71 0W
Uptown, Chic. 26 B2 41 58N 87 40W
Upwey, Melb. 19 F9 37 53 S 145 20 E
Urawa, Tōkyō 13 A2 35 51N 139 39 E
Urayasu, Tōkyō 13 C4 35 39N 139 53 E
Urbe, Aeroporto d', Rome 9 F10 41 57N 12 30 E
Urca, Rio J. 31 B3 22 56 S 43 9W
Uritsk, St-Pet. 11 C3 59 49N 30 10 E
Üröm, Bud. 10 J13 47 35N 19 1 E
Ursus, Wsaw. 10 E6 52 11N 20 52 E
Ursvik, Stock. 3 D10 59 23N 17 57 E
Usera, Mdrd. 8 B2 40 22N 3 42W
Ushigome, Tōkyō 13 B3 35 42N 139 44 E
Usküdar, Ist. 17 A3 41 1N 29 0 E
Ust-Slavyanka, St-Pet. 11 C5 59 51N 30 32 E
Uteke, Stock. 3 D12 59 24N 18 15 E
Utfort, Ruhr 6 B1 51 28N 6 37 E
Utinga, S. Pau. 31 E6 23 38 S 46 31W
Utrata, Wsaw. 10 E7 52 15N 21 4 E
Uttarpara, Calc. 16 E5 22 39N 88 21 E
Utterslev Mose, Købn. 2 D9 55 42N 12 29 E
Uttran, Stock. 3 E9 59 12N 17 43 E
Utvika, Oslo 2 A1 60 2N 10 15 E
Uxbridge, Lon. 4 B2 51 32N 0 28W
Uzkoye, Mos. 11 F9 55 37N 37 32 E
Uzunca →, Ist. 17 A1 41 54N 28 50 E

V

Vadaul, Bomb. 16 G8 19 2N 72 55 E
Værebro Å →, Købn. 2 D8 55 47N 12 7 E
Vahal, Bomb. 16 H9 18 58N 73 2 E
Vaires-sur-Marne, Paris 5 B5 48 52N 2 38 E
Val della Torre, Tori. 9 B1 45 8N 7 27 E
Valby, Købn. 2 E9 55 39N 12 29 E
Valcannuta, Rome 9 F9 41 52N 12 25 E
Valdeveba, Mdrd. 8 B3 40 29N 3 39W
Vale, Wash. 25 D5 38 55N 77 20W
Valentino, Parco del, Tori. 9 B3 45 3N 7 41 E
Valenton, Paris 5 C4 48 44N 2 27 E
Valera, Mil. 9 D5 45 33N 9 3 E
Vallcarca, Barc. 8 D5 41 25N 2 9 E
Valldoreix, Barc. 8 D5 41 27N 2 3 E
Vallecas, Mdrd. 8 B3 40 22N 3 37W
Vallemar, S.F. 27 C2 37 36N 122 28W
Vallensbæk, Købn. 2 E9 55 38N 12 21 E
Vallensbæk Strand, Købn. 2 E9 55 36N 12 23 E
Vallentunasjön, Stock. 3 D11 59 27N 18 1 E
Valleranello, Rome 9 G9 41 46N 12 29 E
Valley Forge, Phil. 24 A2 40 5N 75 27W
Valley Forge Hist. State Park, Phil. 24 A2 40 5N 75 27W
Valley Mede, Balt. 25 B1 39 16N 76 50W
Valley Stream, N.Y. 23 C6 40 40N 73 43W
Vällingby, Stock. 3 D10 59 21N 17 52 E
Vallisaari, Hels. 3 C5 60 7N 25 0 E
Vallvidrera, Barc. 8 D5 41 24N 2 6 E
Valo Velho, S. Pau. 31 E5 23 38 S 46 47W
Valuyevo, Mos. 11 F8 55 30N 37 21 E
Valvidrera →, Barc. 8 D5 41 25N 2 0 E
Van Dyks Park, Jobg. 18 F10 26 15 S 28 18 E
Van Nuys, L.A. 28 A2 34 11N 118 27W
Van Nuys Airport, L.A. 28 A2 34 12N 118 29W
Van Ryn Dam, Jobg. 18 E11 26 8 S 28 21 E
Vanak, Tehr. 17 C5 35 45N 51 23 E
Vangede, Købn. 2 D10 55 45N 12 30 E
Vaniköy, Ist. 17 A3 41 3N 29 3 E
Vanløse, Købn. 2 D9 55 41N 12 28 E
Vantaa, Hels. 3 B4 60 18N 24 56 E
Vantaa →, Hels. 3 B4 60 13N 24 53 E
Vantaankoski, Hels. 3 B4 60 18N 24 51 E
Vantör, Stock. 3 E11 59 16N 18 2 E
Vanves, Paris 5 C3 48 49N 2 17 E
Vanzago, Mil. 9 D4 45 31N 8 59 E
Värby, Stock. 3 E10 59 15N 17 52 E
Vardåsen, Oslo 2 C6 50 48N 11 6 E
Varedo, Mil. 9 D5 45 35N 9 8 E
Varennes-Jarcy, Paris 5 C5 48 40N 2 33 E
Vargem Grande, Rio J. 31 B1 22 58 S 43 27W
Városliget, Bud. 10 J13 47 30N 19 5 E
Vartiokylä, Hels. 3 B5 60 13N 25 6 E
Vartiosaari, Hels. 3 B5 60 11N 25 5 E
Vasby, Købn. 2 D8 55 40N 12 12 E
Vashi, Bomb. 16 G8 19 4N 72 59 E
Vasilyevskiy, Os., St-Pet. 11 B3 59 55N 30 16 E
Västerkulla, Hels. 3 B2 60 16N 24 31 E
Västerskog, Hels. 3 B6 60 16N 25 17 E
Vasto, Nápl. 9 H12 40 51N 14 16 E
Vatutino, Mos. 11 D10 55 52N 37 40 E
Vaucresson, Paris 5 B2 48 50N 2 9 E
Vaudreuil, Mtrl. 20 B1 43 24N 74 1W
Vaudreuil-sur-le Lac, Mtrl. 20 B1 43 25N 74 1W
Vauhallan, Paris 5 C3 48 44N 2 12 E
Vaujours, Paris 5 B5 48 56N 2 34 E
Vauréal, Paris 5 A2 49 2N 2 1 E
Vaux-sur-Seine, Paris 5 A1 49 0N 1 57 E
Vauxhall, Lon. 4 C4 51 29N 0 7W
Vaxholm, Stock. 3 D13 59 24N 18 20 E
Vecklax, Hels. 3 B2 60 10N 24 31 E
Vecsés, Bud. 10 K14 47 24N 19 16 E
Vedano al Lissone, Mil. 9 D6 45 36N 9 16 E
Veddel, Hbg. 7 D8 53 31N 10 1 E
Vega, Stock. 3 E11 59 11N 18 8 E
Vehkalahti, Hels. 3 B2 60 11N 24 30 E
Veikkola, Hels. 3 B1 60 17N 24 26 E
Velbert, Ruhr 6 B4 51 21N 7 1 E
Veleň, Pra. 10 A3 50 10N 14 33 E
Veleslavin, Pra. 10 B2 50 5N 14 21 E
Vélizy-Villacoublay, Paris 5 C3 48 47N 2 11 E
Velka-Chuchle, Pra. 10 B2 50 0N 14 23 E
Venaria, Tori. 9 B2 45 8N 7 37 E
Venda Seca, Lisb. 8 F7 38 46N 9 15W
Vendelsö, Stock. 3 E12 59 12N 18 11 E
Venice, L.A. 28 C2 33 59N 118 27W
Venner, Oslo 2 A3 60 1N 10 36 E
Vennhausen, Ruhr 6 C3 51 13N 6 51 E
Ventas, Mdrd. 8 B2 40 26N 3 40W
Ventorro del Cano, Mdrd. 8 B2 40 23N 3 49W
Verberg, Ruhr 6 B1 51 21N 6 34 E
Verde →, S. Pau. 31 E7 23 29 S 46 27W
Verdi, Ath. 8 H11 38 2N 23 40 E
Verdugo Mt., L.A. 28 A3 34 12N 118 17W
Verdun, Mtrl. 20 B4 43 27N 73 35W
Vereya, Mos. 11 F12 55 37N 38 2 E
Vérhalom, Bud. 10 J13 47 31N 19 1 E
Vermelho →, S. Pau. 31 E5 23 30 S 46 46W
Vermont, Melb. 19 F8 37 50 S 145 12 E
Vermont South, Melb. 19 F8 37 51 S 145 11 E
Verneuil-sur-Seine, Paris 5 B1 48 58N 1 59 E
Vernouillet, Paris 5 B1 48 58N 1 56 E
Verona, N.Y. 22 C3 40 49N 74 15W
Verperluda, Os., St-Pet. 11 B2 59 59N 30 0 E
Verrières-le-Buisson, Paris 5 C3 48 44N 2 16 E
Versailles, B.A. 32 B3 34 38 S 58 31W
Versailles, Paris 5 C2 48 48N 2 7 E
Veshnyaki, Mos. 11 E10 55 43N 37 48 E
Vesolyy Posolok, St-Pet. 11 B4 59 53N 30 28 E
Vestli, Oslo 2 B5 59 58N 10 55 E
Vestra, Hels. 3 B3 60 19N 24 46 E
Vestskoven, Købn. 2 D9 55 41N 12 23 E
Vesuvio, Nápl. 9 J13 40 49N 14 25 E
Vets Stadium, Phil. 24 B3 39 54N 75 10W
Viby, Købn. 2 E7 55 33N 12 1 E
Vicálvaro, Mdrd. 8 B3 40 24N 3 36W
Vicente Lopez, B.A. 32 B4 34 31 S 58 30W
Victoria, B.A. 32 A3 34 27 S 58 32W
Victoria, H.K. 12 E6 22 17N 114 11 E
Victoria, Pont, Mtrl. 20 B4 43 29N 73 32W
Victoria Gardens, Bomb. 16 H8 18 58N 72 50 E
Victoria Harbour, H.K. 12 E5 22 17N 114 10 E
Victoria Island, Lagos 18 B2 6 25N 7 25 E
Victoria L., Jobg. 18 F9 26 13 S 28 9 E
Victoria Lawn Tennis Courts, Melb. 19 F7 37 50 S 145 1 E
Victoria Park, H.K. 12 E5 22 16N 114 8 E
Vidja, Stock. 3 E11 59 12N 18 4 E
Vidrholec, Pra. 10 B3 50 5N 14 39 E
Vienna = Wien, Wien 10 G10 48 12N 16 22 E
Vienna, Wash. 25 D6 38 54N 77 16W
Vieringhausen, Ruhr 6 C4 51 10N 7 9 E
Vierlinden, Ruhr 6 A2 51 32N 6 45 E
Vierumäki, Hels. 3 A5 60 21N 25 2 E
Vierzigstücken, Hbg. 7 D6 53 30N 9 49 E
View Bank, Melb. 19 E7 37 43 S 145 6 E
Vigário Geral, Rio J. 31 A2 22 48 S 43 18W
Vigentino, Mil. 9 E6 45 26N 9 13 E
Viggbyholm, Stock. 3 D11 59 26N 18 7 E
Vighignolo, Mil. 9 E5 45 29N 9 2 E
Vigneux-sur-Seine, Paris 5 C4 48 42N 2 24 E
Viikki, Hels. 3 B5 60 13N 25 1 E
Viirilä, Hels. 3 B5 60 19N 25 8 E
Vila Andrade, S. Pau. 31 E5 23 37 S 46 44W
Vila Barcelona, S. Pau. 31 E6 23 37 S 46 33W
Vila Bocaina, S. Pau. 31 F7 23 40 S 46 26W
Vila Dalva, S. Pau. 31 E4 23 34 S 46 46W
Vila Dirce, S. Pau. 31 E4 23 33 S 46 50W
Vila Eldorado, S. Pau. 31 F6 23 42 S 46 38W
Vila Ema, S. Pau. 31 E6 23 36 S 46 31W
Vila Formosa, S. Pau. 31 E6 23 36 S 46 44W
Vila Galvão, S. Pau. 31 D6 23 27 S 46 34W
Vila Gonçales, S. Pau. 31 F6 23 42 S 46 33W
Vila Iasi, S. Pau. 31 E5 23 37 S 46 47W
Vila Indiana, S. Pau. 31 E5 23 37 S 46 48W
Vila Isabel, Rio J. 31 B2 22 54 S 43 15W
Vila Madalena, S. Pau. 31 E5 23 32 S 46 41W
Vila Maria, S. Pau. 31 E6 23 31 S 46 36W
Vila Mariana, S. Pau. 31 E6 23 34 S 46 36W
Vila Matilde, S. Pau. 31 E6 23 31 S 46 30W
Vila Nova Curuçá, S. Pau. 31 E7 23 31 S 46 25W
Vila Pires, S. Pau. 31 F6 23 41 S 46 30W
Vila Progresso, Rio J. 31 B3 22 53 S 43 1W
Vila Prudente, S. Pau. 31 E6 23 35 S 46 33W
Vila Ré, S. Pau. 31 E7 23 31 S 46 29W
Vila Remo, S. Pau. 31 F5 23 40 S 46 45W
Vila Sonia, S. Pau. 31 E5 23 35 S 46 44W
Viladecans, Barc. 8 E5 41 18N 2 1 E
Villa Ada, Rome 9 F10 41 55N 12 30 E
Villa Adelina, B.A. 32 B3 34 31 S 58 33W
Villa Alianza, B.A. 32 B3 34 37 S 58 35W
Villa Alsina, B.A. 32 C4 34 40 S 58 24W
Villa Altube, B.A. 32 B2 34 31 S 58 45W
Villa Ariza, B.A. 32 B3 34 38 S 58 39W
Villa Augusta, B.A. 32 C5 34 45 S 58 15W
Villa Ballester, B.A. 32 B3 34 33 S 58 33W
Villa Barilari, B.A. 32 C4 34 42 S 58 20W
Villa Basso, B.A. 32 B3 34 35 S 58 33W
Villa Bosch, B.A. 32 B3 34 35 S 58 33W
Villa C. Colon, B.A. 32 C4 34 41 S 58 21W
Villa D. F. Sarmiento, B.A. 32 B3 34 38 S 58 35W
Villa D. Sobral, B.A. 32 C5 34 45 S 58 15W
Villa de Guadalupe, Méx. 29 B3 19 29N 99 6W
Villa de Mayo, B.A. 32 B2 34 30 S 58 40W
Villa Devoto, B.A. 32 B3 34 36 S 58 31W
Villa Dominico, B.A. 32 C5 34 41 S 58 19W
Villa Giambruno, B.A. 32 C5 34 48 S 58 15W
Villa Gustavo A. Madero, Méx. 29 B3 19 29N 99 8W
Villa Hogar Alemán, B.A. 32 C4 34 49 S 58 26W
Villa Iglesias, B.A. 32 B2 34 30 S 58 45W
Villa Leloir, B.A. 32 B3 34 36 S 58 41W
Villa Leon, B.A. 32 B2 34 31 S 58 41W
Villa Lugano, B.A. 32 C4 34 41 S 58 28W
Villa Luzuriago, B.A. 32 C4 34 40 S 58 35W
Villa Lynch, B.A. 32 B3 34 35 S 58 31W
Villa Madero, B.A. 32 C3 34 41 S 58 30W
Villa Maria del Triunfo, Lima 30 G9 12 9 S 76 57W
Villa Obregon, Méx. 29 B2 19 20N 99 12W
Villa Reichembach, B.A. 32 B2 34 39 S 58 41W
Villa Rosa, B.A. 32 A1 34 25 S 58 5W
Villa San Francisco, B.A. 32 C5 34 46 S 58 15W
Villacoublay, Aérodrome de, Paris 5 C3 48 46N 2 12 E
Village Green, Phil. 24 B2 39 52N 75 26W
Villanova, Phil. 24 A2 40 1N 75 20W
Villarbasse, Tori. 9 B1 45 2N 7 27 E
Villaretto, Tori. 9 B3 45 8N 7 41 E
Villaricca, Nápl. 9 H12 40 55N 14 11 E
Villaroche, Paris 5 D5 48 37N 2 39 E
Villaroy, Paris 5 C2 48 46N 2 5 E
Villasanta, Mil. 9 D6 45 36N 9 18 E
Villastanza, Mil. 9 D4 45 32N 8 57 E
Villaverde, Mdrd. 8 B2 40 21N 3 42W
Villaverde Bajo, Mdrd. 8 B2 40 20N 3 40W
Villawood, Syd. 19 B2 33 52 S 150 58 E
Ville-d'Avray, Paris 5 C2 48 49N 2 11 E
Ville de Laval, Mtrl. 20 A3 43 34N 73 43W
Villebon-sur-Yvette, Paris 5 C3 48 41N 2 14 E
Villecresnes, Paris 5 C5 48 43N 2 31 E

48 Villejuif

Villejuif, Paris 5 C4 48 47N 2 21 E
Villejust, Paris 5 C3 48 41N 2 15 E
Villemoisson-sur-Orge, Paris 5 C3 48 40N 2 19 E
Villemomble, Paris 5 B5 48 52N 2 30 E
Villeneuve-la-Garenne, Paris 5 B3 48 56N 2 19 E
Villeneuve-le-Roi, Paris 5 C4 48 43N 2 24 E
Villeneuve-St.-Georges, Paris 5 C4 48 43N 2 27 E
Villeneuve-sous-Dammartin, Paris 5 A5 49 2N 2 38 E
Villennes-sur-Seine, Paris 5 B1 48 56N 2 0 E
Villeparisis, Paris 5 B5 48 56N 2 36 E
Villepinte, Paris 5 B5 48 57N 2 30 E
Villepreux, Paris 5 C1 48 49N 1 59 E
Villevaudé, Paris 5 B5 48 55N 2 39 E
Villeziers, Paris 5 C3 48 40N 2 10 E
Villiers-le-Bâcle, Paris 5 C2 48 44N 2 8 E
Villiers-le-Bel, Paris 5 A4 49 0N 2 23 E
Villiers-St. Frédéric, Paris 5 C1 48 49N 1 53 E
Villiers-sur-Marne, Paris 5 C5 48 49N 2 32 E
Villiers-sur-Orge, Paris 5 D3 48 39N 2 18 E
Villinki, Hels. 3 C5 60 9N 25 6 E
Villoresi, Canale, Mil. 9 D4 45 33N 8 59 E
Vimodrone, Mil. 9 D6 45 30N 9 16 E
Vimont, Mtrl. 20 A3 43 36N 73 43W
Vincennes, Paris 5 B4 48 51N 2 26 E
Vincennes, Bois de, Paris 5 C4 48 49N 2 26 E
Vinohrady, Pra. 10 B2 50 4N 14 26 E
Vinoř, Pra. 10 B3 50 8N 14 34 E
Vinořský →, Pra. 10 A3 50 11N 14 39 E
Violet Hill, H.K. 12 E6 22 15N 114 11 E
Virányos, Bud. 10 J12 47 31N 18 59 E
Virgeo del San Cristóbal, Stgo 30 J11 33 25 S 70 38W
Viroflay, Paris 5 C3 48 48N 2 10 E
Viron, Ath. 8 J11 37 55N 23 46 E
Virreyes, B.A. 32 A3 34 27 S 58 33W
Virum, Købn. 2 D9 55 47N 12 27 E
Viry-Châtillon, Paris 5 C4 48 40N 2 21 E
Vishnyaki, Mos. 11 E11 55 46N 37 53 E
Visitacion Valley, S.F. 27 B2 37 42N 122 23W
Vista Alegre, Lima 30 G9 12 8 S 76 59W
Vista Alegre, Stgo 30 K10 33 30 S 70 43W
Vitacura, Stgo 30 J11 33 23 S 70 35W
Vitarte-Ate, Lima 30 G9 12 3 S 76 57W
Vitinia, Rome 9 G9 41 47N 12 24 E
Vitry-sur-Seine, Paris 5 C4 48 47N 2 23 E
Vittråsk, Hels. 3 B1 60 11N 24 29 E
Vittuone, Mil. 9 E4 45 28N 8 57 E
Vladykino, Mos. 11 D9 55 51N 37 35 E
Vltava →, Pra. 10 A2 50 10N 14 2 E
Vnukovo, Mos. 11 F7 55 37N 37 17 E
Voerde, Ruhr 6 C6 51 18N 7 23 E
Voerde, Ruhr 6 A2 51 35N 6 42 E
Vogelheim, Ruhr 6 B3 51 29N 6 59 E
Vohwinkel, Ruhr 6 C4 51 13N 7 4 E
Voisins-le-Bretonneux, Paris 5 C2 48 45N 2 3 E
Vokovice, Pra. 10 B2 50 5N 14 21 E
Volgelsdorf, Berl. 7 B5 52 30N 13 44 E
Volkhonka-Zil, Mos. 11 F9 55 39N 37 37 E
Volkovka →, St-Pet. 11 B4 59 54N 30 25 E
Volksdorf, Hbg. 7 D8 53 39N 10 8 E
Volla, Nápl. 9 H13 40 52N 14 20 E
Vollen, Oslo 2 C2 59 48N 10 27 E
Volmarstein, Ruhr 6 B6 51 22N 7 22 E
Volodarskoye, St-Pet. 11 B4 59 54N 30 23 E
Volpiano, Tori. 9 A3 45 12N 7 46 E
Volynkina-Derevnya, St-Pet. 11 B3 59 53N 30 18 E
Volynyy, Os., St-Pet. 11 B3 59 57N 30 14 E
Vômero, Nápl. 9 H12 40 50N 14 13 E
Vorderhainbach, Wien 10 G9 48 13N 16 12 E
Vorhalle, Ruhr 6 B6 51 23N 7 26 E
Vormholz, Ruhr 6 B5 51 24N 7 19 E
Vösendorf, Wien 10 H10 48 7N 16 20 E
Vostochnyy, Mos. 11 E11 55 49N 37 51 E
Vouliagmeni, Ath. 8 K11 37 50N 23 46 E
Vrčovice, Pra. 10 B2 50 4N 14 28 E
Vsevolozhsk, St-Pet. 11 A5 60 0N 30 39 E
Vuosaari, Hels. 3 B5 60 13N 25 8 E
Vyborgskaya Storona, St-Pet. 11 B4 59 57N 30 22 E
Vyčehrad, Pra. 10 B2 50 3N 14 25 E
Vykhino, Mos. 11 E10 55 42N 37 48 E
Vysočany, Pra. 10 B2 50 6N 14 29 E

W

Waban, L., Bost. 21 D2 42 17N 71 18W
Wachterhof, Mün. 7 G11 48 2N 11 42 E
Waddington, Lon. 4 D4 51 18N 0 7W
Wadeville, Jobg. 18 F10 26 15 S 28 11 E
Wahda, Bagd. 17 F8 33 18N 44 26 E
Währing, Wien 10 G10 48 14N 16 20 E
Waidmannslust, Berl. 7 A3 52 36N 13 20 E
Wajay, La Hab. 30 B2 23 0N 82 25W
Wakefield, Bost. 21 B3 42 30N 71 5W
Wald, Ruhr 6 C4 51 11N 7 3 E
Waldesruh, Berl. 7 B4 52 28N 13 37 E
Waldheim, Berl. 7 A1 52 34N 13 3 E
Waldperlach, Mün. 7 G11 48 4N 11 40 E
Waldtrudering, Mün. 7 G11 48 6N 11 42 E
Waldwick, N.Y. 22 A4 41 1N 74 5W
Wall Street, N.Y. 22 C4 40 42N 74 0W
Wallgrove, Syd. 19 A2 33 47 S 150 51 E
Wallington, Lon. 4 C4 51 21N 0 8W
Wallington, N.Y. 22 B4 40 50N 74 8W
Walnut Cr. →, S.F. 27 A4 37 55N 122 3W
Walnut Creek, S.F. 27 A4 37 53N 122 3W
Walnut Heights, S.F. 27 A4 37 52N 122 2W
Walsum, Ruhr 6 A2 51 32N 6 42 E
Walsumer Mark, Ruhr 6 A3 51 33N 6 50 E
Walt Whitman Br., Phil. 24 B4 39 4N 75 9W
Waltershof, Hbg. 7 D7 53 31N 9 54 E
Waltham, Bost. 21 C2 42 23N 71 14W
Waltham Abbey, Lon. 4 A5 51 41N 0 1 E
Waltham Forest, Lon. 4 B4 51 36N 0 0 E
Walthamstow, Lon. 4 B4 51 34N 0 1W
Walton on Thames, Lon. 4 C2 51 22N 0 23W
Walton on the Hill, Lon. 4 D3 51 16N 0 14W
Waltrop, Ruhr 6 A6 51 36N 7 25 E
Walworth, Lon. 4 C4 51 29N 0 5W
Wambachsee, Ruhr 6 B2 51 23N 6 47 E
Wan Chai, H.K. 12 E6 22 16N 114 10 E
Wanaque, N.Y. 22 A3 41 1N 74 17W
Wandezhuang, Tianj. 14 E5 39 6N 117 10 E
Wandle →, Lon. 4 C3 51 27N 0 11W
Wandsbek, Hbg. 7 D8 53 34N 10 4 E
Wandsworth, Lon. 4 C3 51 27N 0 11W
Wang Hin, Khlong →, Bangk. 15 A2 13 50N 100 35 E
Wanheim, Ruhr 6 B2 51 23N 6 45 E
Wanheimerort, Ruhr 6 B2 51 24N 6 45 E
Wanne-Eickel, Ruhr 6 A4 51 31N 7 9 E
Wannsee, Berl. 7 B1 52 25N 13 9 E
Wansdorf, Berl. 7 A1 52 38N 13 5 E
Wanstead, Lon. 4 B5 51 34N 0 1 E
Wantagh Seaford, N.Y. 23 D8 40 39N 73 28W
Wantirna, Melb. 19 F8 37 50 S 145 14 E
Wapping, Lon. 4 B4 51 30N 0 3W
Warabi, Tōkyō 13 B3 35 49N 139 42 E
Ward, Phil. 24 B1 39 52N 75 30W
Warlingham, Lon. 4 D4 51 18N 0 2W
Warnberg, Mün. 7 G10 48 4N 11 31 E
Warngal Park, Melb. 19 E7 37 45 S 145 4 E
Warrandyte, Melb. 19 E8 37 43 S 145 13 E
Warrandyte Park, Melb. 19 E8 37 44 S 145 14 E
Warrandyte South, Melb. 19 E8 37 44 S 145 14 E
Warranwood, Melb. 19 E8 37 46 S 145 14 E
Warrâq el 'Arab, El Qâ. 18 C5 30 4N 31 11 E
Warrâq el Hadf, El Qâ. 18 C5 30 5N 31 12 E
Warren Hill, Bost. 21 B1 42 35N 71 21W
Warsaw = Warszawa, Wsaw. 10 E7 52 14N 21 0 E
Warszawa, Wsaw. 10 E7 52 14N 21 0 E
Wartenberg, Berl. 7 A4 52 34N 13 31 E
Warwick Farm Racetrack, Syd. 19 B2 33 54 S 150 56 E
Wasa, Stock. 3 E11 59 19N 18 5 E
Wasfanârd, Tehr. 17 D5 35 38N 51 20 E
Washington, Wash. 25 D7 38 53N 77 2W
Washington Heights, N.Y. 22 B5 40 51N 73 56W
Washington Memorial Museum, Phil. 24 A2 40 5N 75 26W
Washington Nat. Airport, Wash. 25 D7 38 51N 77 2W
Washington Park, Chic. 26 C3 41 47N 87 36W
Washington Square, Phil. 24 A3 40 9N 75 19W
Washington Township, N.Y. 22 A4 41 0N 74 3W
Wasserschloss, Ruhr 6 A4 51 32N 7 1 E
Watching Mts., N.Y. 22 C2 40 43N 74 20W
Watchung, N.Y. 22 D2 40 38N 74 29W
Waterloo, Syd. 19 B4 33 53 S 151 12 E
Waterman Mt., L.A. 28 A5 34 14N 117 56W
Watertown, Bost. 21 C2 42 22N 71 10W
Watford, Lon. 4 A2 51 40N 0 27W
Watkins Island, Wash. 25 C6 39 2N 77 15W
Watsonia, Melb. 19 E7 37 43 S 145 6 E
Watsons B., Syd. 19 B4 33 50 S 151 18 E
Watsons Creek, Melb. 19 E8 37 40 S 145 13 E
Wattenscheid, Ruhr 6 B4 51 28N 7 8 E
Wattle Glen, Melb. 19 E8 37 39 S 145 11 E
Wattle Park, Melb. 19 F7 37 50 S 145 6 E
Watts →, Wash. 25 C6 39 2N 77 15W
Waverley, Bost. 21 C2 42 23N 71 10W
Waverley, Jobg. 18 E9 26 7 S 28 4 E
Waverley, Syd. 19 B4 33 53 S 151 16 E
Wawer, Wsaw. 10 E7 52 13N 21 8 E
Wawrzyszew, Wsaw. 10 E6 52 17N 20 53 E
Wayland, Bost. 21 C1 42 21N 71 20W
Wayne, N.Y. 22 B3 40 55N 74 15W
Wayne, Phil. 24 A2 40 2N 75 24W
Wazirabad, Delhi 16 A2 28 43N 77 13 E
Wazîrîya, Bagd. 17 E8 33 22N 44 23 E
Wazirpur, Delhi 16 A2 28 41N 77 10 E
Weald Park, Lon. 4 B6 51 37N 0 16 E
Wedding, Berl. 7 A3 52 32N 13 21 E
Weehawken, N.Y. 22 C4 40 45N 74 2W
Wegendorf, Berl. 7 A5 52 36N 13 45 E
Wehofen, Ruhr 6 A2 51 31N 6 46 E
Wehringhausen, Ruhr 6 B6 51 21N 7 28 E
Weidling, Wien 10 G9 48 17N 16 18 E
Weidling →, Wien 10 G9 48 17N 16 19 E
Weidlingbach, Wien 10 G9 48 16N 16 15 E
Weigongcun, Beij. 14 B2 39 57N 116 16 E
Weijin He →, Tianj. 14 E6 39 3N 117 12 E
Weissensee, Berl. 7 A3 52 33N 13 27 E
Weitmar, Ruhr 6 B5 51 27N 7 11 E
Welcome Monument, Jak. 15 J9 6 12N 106 49 E
Weller Creek, Chic. 26 A1 42 2N 87 52W
Wellesley, Bost. 21 D2 42 17N 71 17W
Wellesley Fells, Bost. 21 D2 42 18N 71 18W
Wellesley Hills, Bost. 21 D2 42 18N 71 16W
Welling, Lon. 4 C5 51 27N 0 6 E
Wellingsbüttel, Hbg. 7 D8 53 38N 10 6 E
Weltevreden Park Extension, Jobg. 18 E8 26 7 S 27 56 E
Wembley, Lon. 4 B3 51 33N 0 17W
Wembley Stadium, Jobg. 18 F9 26 13 S 28 1 E
Wembley Stadium, Lon. 4 B3 51 33N 0 16W
Wemmer Pan, Jobg. 18 F9 26 13 S 28 3 E
Wendenschloss, Berl. 7 B4 52 24N 13 35 E
Wengern, Ruhr 6 B6 51 24N 7 20 E
Wenham, Bost. 21 A4 42 36N 70 53W
Wenham L., Bost. 21 B4 42 35N 70 53W
Wenhuagong, Tianj. 14 E6 39 5N 117 14 E
Wennington, Lon. 4 B6 51 30N 0 12 E
Wenonah, Phil. 24 C4 39 47N 75 9W
Wentworthville, Syd. 19 A3 33 48 S 150 58 E
Werden, Ruhr 6 B4 51 23N 7 1 E
Werne, Ruhr 6 B5 51 29N 7 18 E
Werneuchen, Berl. 7 A5 52 38N 13 44 E
Wesola, Wsaw. 10 E8 52 15N 21 13 E
West Andover, Bost. 21 B2 42 39N 71 10W
West Babylon, N.Y. 23 C8 40 43N 73 21W
West Bedford, Bost. 21 C2 42 29N 71 18W
West Berlin, Phil. 24 C5 39 48N 74 56W
West Boxford, Bost. 21 A3 42 41N 71 3W
West Caldwell, N.Y. 22 B3 40 51N 74 16W
West Chelmsford, Bost. 21 B1 42 36N 71 23W
West Chester, Phil. 24 B1 39 57N 75 35W
West Concord, Bost. 21 C1 42 27N 71 24W
West Covina, L.A. 28 B5 34 4N 117 55W
West Don →, Trto. 20 D8 43 44N 79 24W
West Drayton, Lon. 4 C2 51 30N 0 28W
West Dulwich, Lon. 4 C4 51 26N 0 5W
West Edmondale, Balt. 25 B2 39 17N 76 42W
West Ham, Lon. 4 B5 51 31N 0 1 E
West Harrow, Lon. 4 B2 51 34N 0 21W
West Heath, Lon. 4 C5 51 29N 0 7 E
West Hempstead, N.Y. 23 C7 40 41N 73 38W
West Hill, Trto. 20 D9 43 46N 79 10W
West Hollywood, L.A. 28 B2 34 5N 118 22W
West Hoxton, Syd. 19 B2 33 55 S 150 49 E
West Islip, N.Y. 23 C9 40 41N 73 18W
West Kingsdown, Lon. 4 C6 51 20N 0 15 E
West Lamma Channel, H.K. 12 E5 22 14N 114 4 E
West Lynn, Bost. 21 C4 42 27N 70 58W
West Medford, Bost. 21 C3 42 25N 71 7W
West New York, N.Y. 22 C4 40 46N 74 1W
West Norwood, N.Y. 22 B5 40 59N 73 58W
West of Twin Peaks, S.F. 27 B2 37 43N 122 27W
West Orange, N.Y. 22 C3 40 46N 74 15W
West Park, Jobg. 18 E8 26 9 S 27 59 E
West Paterson, N.Y. 22 B3 40 54N 74 11W
West Rouge, Trto. 20 D10 43 48N 79 7W
West Roxbury, Bost. 21 D3 42 16N 71 9W
West Springfield, Wash. 25 E6 38 47N 77 13W
West Thurrock, Lon. 4 C6 51 28N 0 16 E
West Town, Chic. 26 B2 41 53N 87 42W
West Wharf, Kar. 17 H10 24 49N 66 58 E
West Wickham, Lon. 4 C4 51 22N 0 0 E
Westbury, N.Y. 23 C7 40 45N 73 34W
Westchester, Chic. 26 B1 41 51N 87 53W
Westchester, N.Y. 23 B5 40 51N 73 51W
Westcliff, Jobg. 18 F9 26 10 S 28 1 E
Westdale, Chic. 26 B1 41 55N 87 54W
Westdene, Jobg. 18 F8 26 10 S 27 59 E
Westend, Hels. 3 C3 60 9N 24 48 E
Westerbauer, Ruhr 6 B6 51 20N 7 23 E
Westerham, Lon. 4 D5 51 16N 0 4 E
Westerham, Mün. 7 G10 48 3N 11 36 E
Westerholt, Ruhr 6 A4 51 36N 7 5 E
Westerleigh, N.Y. 22 D4 40 37N 74 7W
Western Addition, S.F. 27 B2 37 47N 122 25W
Western Run →, Balt. 25 A2 39 22N 76 39W
Western Springs, Chic. 26 C1 41 47N 87 52W
Westfalenhalle, Ruhr 6 B6 51 29N 7 27 E
Westfield, N.Y. 22 D2 40 39N 74 21W
Westlake, S.F. 27 B2 37 42N 122 29W
Westmeadows, Melb. 19 D6 37 39 S 144 55 E
Westminster, Lon. 4 B4 51 30N 0 7W
Westminster Abbey, Lon. 4 C4 51 29N 0 7W
Westmont, Phil. 24 B4 39 54N 75 3W
Westmount, Mtrl. 20 B4 43 29N 73 35W
Weston, Bost. 21 C2 42 22N 71 16W
Weston, Trto. 20 D7 43 42N 79 30W
Weston Res., Bost. 21 C2 42 21N 71 11W
Westover Hills, Phil. 24 C1 39 45N 75 35W
Westtown, Phil. 24 B1 39 56N 75 32W
Westville, Phil. 24 B4 39 52N 75 7W
Westville Grove, Phil. 24 B4 39 51N 75 7W
Westwood, Bost. 21 D2 42 12N 71 14W
Westwood, N.Y. 22 B4 40 59N 74 3W
Westwood Village, L.A. 28 B2 34 3N 118 26W
Wetter, Ruhr 6 B6 51 23N 7 23 E
Wexford, Trto. 20 D9 43 45N 79 18W
Wey →, Lon. 4 D2 51 18N 0 27W
Weybridge, Lon. 4 C2 51 22N 0 27W
Weyer, Ruhr 6 C4 51 10N 7 1 E
Weymouth, Bost. 21 D4 42 12N 70 57W
Whampoa, Sungei →, Sing. 15 G8 1 18N 103 52 E
Wheaton, Wash. 25 C7 39 2N 77 2W
Wheaton Regional Park, Wash. 25 C7 39 3N 77 1W
Wheelers Hill, Melb. 19 F8 37 53 S 145 10 E
Wheeling, Chic. 26 A1 42 8N 87 54W
Whetstone, Lon. 4 B3 51 37N 0 10W
Whippany, N.Y. 22 B2 40 49N 74 24W
Whippany →, N.Y. 22 B2 40 50N 74 20W
White Marsh, Balt. 25 A4 39 23N 76 28W
White Meadow L., N.Y. 22 B1 40 55N 74 30W
White Oak, Wash. 25 C8 39 2N 76 59W
White Plains, N.Y. 23 A6 41 2N 73 46W
Whitechapel, Lon. 4 B4 51 31N 0 3W
Whitehorse, Phil. 24 B2 39 59N 75 28W
Whiteley Village, Lon. 4 C2 51 21N 0 25W
Whitemarsh →, Balt. 25 A4 39 22N 76 29W
Whitestone, N.Y. 23 C6 40 47N 73 48W
Whiting, Chic. 26 C4 41 41N 87 29W
Whitmans Pond, Bost. 21 D4 42 12N 70 55W
Whittier, L.A. 28 C4 33 58N 118 2W
Whitton, Lon. 4 C2 51 27N 0 21W
Whyteleafe, Lon. 4 D4 51 18N 0 5W
Wieden, Wien 10 G10 48 11N 16 22 E
Wiemelhausen, Ruhr 6 B5 51 27N 7 13 E
Wien, Wien 10 G10 48 12N 16 22 E
Wien-Schwechat, Flughafen, Wien 10 H11 48 6N 16 34 E
Wiener Berg, Wien 10 H10 48 9N 16 21 E
Wiener Wald, Wien 10 G9 48 10N 16 14 E
Wieruchów, Wsaw. 10 E5 52 14N 20 49 E
Wierzbno, Wsaw. 10 E7 52 11N 21 1 E
Wilanów, Wsaw. 10 E7 52 10N 21 4 E
Wilanówka →, Wsaw. 10 F7 52 8N 21 5 E
Wildcat Canyon Regional Park, S.F. 27 A3 37 56N 122 17W
Wildcat Cr. →, S.F. 27 A3 37 57N 122 15W
Wilde, B.A. 32 C5 34 24 S 58 18W
Wilhelmsburg, Hbg. 7 E7 53 29N 9 59 E
Wilhelmshagen, Berl. 7 B5 52 26N 13 42 E
Wilket Creek Park, Trto. 20 D8 43 43N 79 21W
Willesden, Lon. 4 B3 51 32N 0 15W
Willesden Green, Lon. 4 B3 51 32N 0 13W
Willett Pond, Bost. 21 D2 42 10N 71 14W
William Girling Res., Lon. 4 B4 51 38N 0 1W
Williams Bridge, N.Y. 23 B5 40 52N 73 51W
Williamsburg, N.Y. 22 C5 40 42N 73 56W
Williamstown, Melb. 19 F6 37 51 S 144 52 E
Williamstown Junction, Phil. 24 C5 39 45N 74 56W
Willingboro, Phil. 24 A5 40 2N 74 53W
Williston Park, N.Y. 23 C7 40 45N 73 38W
Willoughby, Syd. 19 A4 33 48 S 151 12 E
Willow Grove, Phil. 24 A4 40 8N 75 7W
Willow Springs, Chic. 26 C1 41 44N 87 51W
Willowbrook, L.A. 28 C3 33 54N 118 13W
Willowbrook, N.Y. 22 D4 40 35N 74 8W
Willowdale, Phil. 24 B5 39 52N 74 58W
Willowdale, Trto. 20 D8 43 46N 79 25W
Willowdale State Forest, Bost. 21 B4 42 39N 70 54W
Wilmette, Chic. 26 A2 42 4N 87 42W
Wilmette Harbor, Chic. 26 A2 42 4N 87 41W
Wilmington, Bost. 21 B3 42 33N 71 9W
Wilmington, Lon. 4 C6 51 25N 0 12 E
Wilmington, Phil. 24 C1 39 44N 75 33W
Wilson, Mt., L.A. 28 A4 34 13N 118 4W
Wimbledon, Lon. 4 C3 51 25N 0 13W
Wimbledon Common, Lon. 4 C3 51 26N 0 14W
Wimbledon Park, Lon. 4 C3 51 25N 0 11W
Wimbledon Tennis Ground, Lon. 4 C3 51 25N 0 12W
Winchester, Bost. 21 C3 42 26N 71 8W
Winchmore Hill, Lon. 4 B4 51 38N 0 5W
Windsor Cresta, Jobg. 18 E8 26 7 S 27 59 E
Winfield, N.Y. 22 D3 40 38N 74 17W
Winnetka, Chic. 26 A2 42 6N 87 43W
Winnetka, L.A. 28 A1 34 10N 118 32W
Winning, Mün. 7 G10 48 2N 11 37 E
Winston Hills, Syd. 19 A2 33 46 S 150 57 E
Winterberg, Ruhr 6 C5 51 19N 7 12 E
Winterhude, Hbg. 7 D8 53 35N 10 0 E
Winterthur, Phil. 24 C1 39 48N 75 35W
Winthrop, Bost. 21 C4 42 22N 70 58W
Winzeldorf, Hbg. 7 C7 53 40N 9 54 E
Wisley Gardens, Lon. 4 D2 51 18N 0 28W
Wiśniowa Góra, Wsaw. 10 E8 52 13N 21 12 E
Wissahickon Cr. →, Phil. 24 A3 40 0N 75 12W
Wissinoming, Phil. 24 A4 40 1N 75 4W
Wissous, Paris 5 C3 48 44N 2 19 E
Witch House, Bost. 21 B4 42 31N 70 54W
Witfield, Jobg. 18 F10 26 11 S 28 12 E
Witpoortjie, Jobg. 18 E8 26 8 S 27 50 E
Witten, Ruhr 6 B6 51 26N 7 20 E
Wittenau, Berl. 7 A3 52 35N 13 19 E
Wittlaer, Ruhr 6 C2 51 19N 6 44 E
Witwatersrand, Univ. of, Jobg. 18 F9 26 11 S 28 1 E
Włochy, Wsaw. 10 E6 52 12N 20 56 E
Wo Mei, H.K. 12 D6 22 21N 114 15 E
Wo Yi Hop, H.K. 12 D5 22 23N 114 8 E
Woburn, Bost. 21 C3 42 29N 71 9W
Woburn, Trto. 20 D9 43 46N 79 12W
Wohldorf-Ohlstedt, Hbg. 7 C8 53 41N 10 7 E
Wola, Wsaw. 10 E6 52 14N 20 57 E
Woldingham, Lon. 4 D4 51 16N 0 1W
Wolf Lake, Chic. 26 D3 41 39N 87 31W
Wolf Trap Farm Park, Wash. 25 D6 38 56N 77 17W
Wolfpassing, Wien 10 G9 48 18N 16 10 E
Wolica, Wsaw. 10 F7 52 9N 21 3 E
Wolica, Wsaw. 10 F6 52 7N 20 51 E
Wólka Węglowa, Wsaw. 10 E6 52 18N 20 52 E
Wollaston, Bost. 21 D3 42 15N 71 2W
Wolomin, Wsaw. 10 D8 52 20N 21 12 E
Woltersdorf, Berl. 7 B5 52 27N 13 44 E
Wong Chuk Hang, H.K. 12 E6 22 15N 114 10 E
Wong Chuk Wan, H.K. 12 D6 22 23N 114 17 E
Wong Chuk Yeung, H.K. 12 D6 22 24N 114 15 E
Wong Nai Shan, H.K. 12 D6 22 22N 114 14 E
Wong Tai Sin, H.K. 12 D6 22 20N 114 11 E
Wonga Park, Melb. 19 E8 37 44 S 145 17 E
Wood End, Lon. 4 B2 51 33N 0 21W
Wood Green, Lon. 4 B4 51 36N 0 6W
Wood Hill, Bost. 21 B2 42 39N 71 11W
Woodbridge, N.Y. 22 D3 40 33N 74 16W
Woodbridge, Trto. 20 D7 43 47N 79 35W
Woodbridge Cr. →, N.Y. 22 D3 40 32N 74 15W
Woodbury, N.Y. 23 C8 40 49N 73 28W
Woodbury, Phil. 24 B4 39 50N 75 9W
Woodbury Cr. →, Phil. 24 B4 39 51N 75 11W
Woodbury Heights, Phil. 24 C4 39 49N 75 7W
Woodchuck Hill, Bost. 21 B3 42 39N 71 4W
Woodcliff Lake, N.Y. 22 A4 41 1N 74 2W
Woodford, Lon. 4 B5 51 36N 0 1 E
Woodford Bridge, Lon. 4 B5 51 36N 0 3 E
Woodford Green, Lon. 4 B5 51 36N 0 1 E
Woodford Wells, Lon. 4 B5 51 37N 0 1 E
Woodhaven, N.Y. 23 C5 40 41N 73 51W
Woodlands, Sing. 15 F7 1 26N 103 46 E
Woodlawn, Balt. 25 B2 39 19N 76 44W
Woodlyn, Phil. 24 B2 39 52N 75 21W
Woodlynne, Phil. 24 B4 39 54N 75 6W
Woodmere, N.Y. 23 D6 40 38N 73 43W
Woodmont, Wash. 25 D7 38 59N 77 5W
Woodmore, Balt. 25 A2 39 22N 76 47W
Woodridge, N.Y. 22 B4 40 50N 74 4W
Woodrow, N.Y. 22 D3 40 32N 74 11W
Woodside, Lon. 4 C4 51 23N 0 4W
Woodside, N.Y. 23 C5 40 44N 73 54W
Woodside, S.F. 27 D3 37 26N 122 16W
Woodstock, Balt. 25 B1 39 19N 76 52W
Woodstream, Phil. 24 B5 39 54N 74 57W
Woollahra, Syd. 19 B4 33 53 S 151 15 E
Woolooware B., Syd. 19 C3 34 1 S 151 8 E
Woolwich, Lon. 4 C5 51 29N 0 4 E
Wördern, Wien 10 G9 48 19N 16 12 E
World Trade Center, N.Y. 22 C4 40 42N 74 0W
Worli, Bomb. 16 G7 19 1N 72 49 E
Woronora, Syd. 19 C3 34 1 S 151 2 E
Worth, Chic. 26 C2 41 41N 87 47W
Worthington, Balt. 25 B2 39 14N 76 47W
Worthington, N.Y. 23 A6 41 2N 73 49W
Wrotham, Lon. 4 D6 51 18N 0 18 E
Wrotham Park, Lon. 4 A3 51 40N 0 10W
Wuhlgarten, Berl. 7 A4 52 31N 13 34 E
Wujiaochang, Shang. 14 J12 31 18N 121 31 E
Wülfrath, Ruhr 6 C4 51 16N 7 2 E
Wulfsmühle, Hbg. 7 C7 53 41N 9 51 E
Wulksfelde, Hbg. 7 C8 53 42N 10 6 E
Wupper →, Ruhr 6 C5 51 14N 7 18 E
Wuppertal, Ruhr 6 C5 51 17N 7 10 E
Würm →, Mün. 7 G9 48 8N 11 27 E
Würm-kanal, Mün. 7 F9 48 13N 11 29 E
Wusong, Shang. 14 H11 31 22N 121 29 E
Wusong Jiang →, Shang. 14 J11 31 15N 121 29 E
Wyandanch, N.Y. 23 C8 40 44N 73 20W
Wyckoff, N.Y. 22 A3 41 0N 74 10W
Wyczółki, Wsaw. 10 F6 52 9N 20 59 E
Wygoda, Wsaw. 10 E7 52 15N 21 7 E
Wyncote, Phil. 24 A4 40 5N 75 8W
Wynnewood, Phil. 24 A3 40 0N 75 17W
Wynnmere, Bost. 21 C3 42 29N 71 7W
Wyola, Phil. 24 A2 40 0N 75 24W

X

Xabregas, Lisb. 8 F8 38 43N 9 6W
Xiaodianzhuang, Tianj. 14 D6 39 14N 117 14 E
Xiaoping, Gzh. 14 F8 23 12N 113 13 E
Xiasha chong, Gzh. 14 G7 23 8N 113 9 E
Xicheng, Beij. 14 B2 39 54N 116 19 E
Xico, Cerro, Méx. 29 C4 19 15N 98 56W
Xicun, Gzh. 14 G8 23 8N 113 13 E
Xidan, Beij. 14 B2 39 52N 116 20 E
Xigu Gongyuan, Tianj. 14 D6 39 10N 117 10 E
Xigucun, Tianj. 14 D5 39 10N 117 9 E
Xijiao Airport, Beij. 14 B2 39 57N 116 12 E
Xikeng, Gzh. 14 F7 23 11N 113 6 E
Xilou, Tianj. 14 E5 39 8N 117 9 E
Ximenwai, Tianj. 14 E5 39 8N 117 9 E
Xingfusancun, Beij. 14 B3 39 55N 116 25 E
Xinhua, Tianj. 14 E6 39 6N 117 12 E
Xinkai He →, Tianj. 14 D6 39 12N 117 15 E
Xintang, Gzh. 14 G9 23 9N 113 24 E
Xitle, Méx. 29 C2 19 15N 99 12W
Xitle, Cerro, Méx. 29 C2 19 14N 99 12W
Xiyuan, Beij. 14 B2 39 59N 116 14 E
Xizhimen, Beij. 14 B2 39 55N 116 19 E
Xochiaca, Méx. 29 B4 19 24N 89 58 E
Xochimilco, Méx. 29 C3 19 15N 99 5W
Xochimilco, L. de, Méx. 29 C3 19 16N 99 7W
Xochitenco, Méx. 29 B4 19 24N 89 58 E
Xochitepec, Méx. 29 C3 19 15N 99 9W
Xuanwu, Beij. 14 B2 39 52N 116 19 E
Xuhui, Shang. 14 J11 31 11N 121 26 E

Y

Yaba, Lagos 18 A2 6 30N 7 22 E
Yadun Shui, Gzh. 14 G8 23 5N 113 15 E
Yaftābād, Tehr. 17 D4 35 37N 51 17 E
Yagoona, Syd. 19 B3 33 54 S 151 2 E
Yahara, Tōkyō 13 B3 35 44N 139 37 E
Yaho, Tōkyō 13 B1 35 40N 139 26 E
Yakire, Tōkyō 13 B4 35 45N 139 54 E
Yamada, Ōsaka 12 B4 34 47N 135 32 E
Yamada, Tōkyō 13 C2 35 33N 139 37 E
Yamada →, Ōsaka 12 B2 34 45N 135 10 E
Yamaguchi, Ōsaka 12 B2 34 49N 135 14 E
Yamamoto, Ōsaka 12 C4 34 38N 135 37 E
Yamato, Tōkyō 13 B2 35 46N 139 36 E
Yamato, Tōkyō 13 D1 35 29N 139 27 E
Yamato →, Ōsaka 12 C3 34 36N 135 26 E
Yamazaki, Tōkyō 13 A4 35 55N 139 53 E
Yamuna →, Delhi 16 B2 28 37N 77 15 E
Yan Kit, Sing. 15 F8 1 21N 103 58 E
Yanagishima, Tōkyō 13 B3 35 49N 139 45 E
Yanbu, Gzh. 14 G7 23 5N 113 9 E
Yanghuayuan, Beij. 14 C2 39 49N 116 18 E
Yangjiazhuang, Shang. 14 H11 31 22N 121 25 E
Yangliuqing, Tianj. 14 E5 39 8N 117 0 E
Yangpu, Shang. 14 J12 31 16N 121 32 E
Yanino, St-Pet. 11 B5 59 55N 30 36 E
Yao, Ōsaka 12 C4 34 37N 135 36 E
Yao Airport, Ōsaka 12 C4 34 35N 135 36 E
Yarmūk, Bagd. 17 F7 33 18N 44 19 E
Yarra →, Melb. 19 E6 37 51 S 144 53 E
Yarra Bend Nat. Park, Melb. 19 E7 37 47 S 145 0 E
Yarraville, Melb. 19 E6 37 48 S 144 53 E
Yasenevo, Mos. 11 F9 55 36N 37 21 E
Yashio, Tōkyō 13 B3 35 48N 139 49 E
Yau Ma Tei, H.K. 12 E5 22 18N 114 10 E
Yau Tong, H.K. 12 E6 22 17N 114 14 E
Yau Yue Wan, H.K. 12 E6 22 19N 114 15 E
Yauza →, Mos. 11 D10 55 54N 37 43 E
Yeading, Lon. 4 B2 51 31N 0 23W
Yeadon, Phil. 24 B3 39 55N 75 15W
Yedikule, Ist. 17 B2 40 59N 28 55 E
Yenikapi, Ist. 17 A2 41 0N 28 56 E
Yeniköy, Ist. 17 A3 41 6N 29 3 E
Yennora, Syd. 19 B2 33 51 S 150 58 E
Yeongchon, Sŏul 12 G7 37 35N 126 55 E
Yeoido, Sŏul 12 G7 37 31N 126 55 E
Yeong Dung Po, Sŏul 12 G7 37 31N 126 54 E
Yeongdong, Sŏul 12 G8 37 30N 127 1 E
Yerba Buena I., S.F. 27 B2 37 48N 122 21W
Yerres, Paris 5 C5 48 43N 2 30 E
Yerres →, Paris 5 C5 48 43N 2 26 E
Yesilköy, Ist. 17 B2 40 57N 28 50 E
Yew Tee, Sing. 15 F7 1 23N 103 45 E
Yiewsley, Lon. 4 B2 51 31N 0 27W
Yiheyuan, Beij. 14 A2 40 0N 116 14 E
Yinhangzhen, Shang. 14 H12 31 20N 121 31 E
Yio Chu Kang, Sing. 15 F8 1 23N 103 51 E
Yixingbu, Tianj. 14 D6 39 11N 117 12 E
Ylästö, Hels. 3 B4 60 17N 24 35 E
Yodo →, Ōsaka 12 B4 34 45N 135 35 E
Yokohama, Tōkyō 13 D3 35 26N 139 41 E
Yokohama Harbour, Tōkyō 13 D2 35 27N 139 39 E
Yokosuka, Tōkyō 13 A4 35 50N 139 54 E
Yong San, Sŏul 12 G7 37 32N 126 58 E
Yongding He →, Beij. 14 C1 39 49N 116 10 E
Yongdingmen, Beij. 14 B3 39 51N 116 20 E
Yongfucun, Gzh. 14 G8 23 8N 113 17 E
Yonkers, N.Y. 23 B5 40 56N 73 52W
Yono, Tōkyō 13 A2 35 52N 139 37 E
York, Trto. 20 D8 43 40N 79 26W
York Mills, Trto. 20 D8 43 45N 79 22W
Yoshikawa, Tōkyō 13 A4 35 53N 139 50 E
Yotsuga, Tōkyō 13 B3 35 40N 139 44 E
You'anmen, Beij. 14 B2 39 51N 116 20 E
Yoyogi Park, Tōkyō 13 C3 35 40N 139 41 E
Yuanxiatian, Gzh. 14 F8 23 12N 113 17 E
Yuexiu Gongyuan, Gzh. 14 G8 23 8N 113 16 E
Yugo-Zarad, Mos. 11 E9 55 40N 37 30 E
Yung Shue Wan, H.K. 12 E5 22 13N 114 6 E
Yuquanshan, Beij. 14 A2 40 0N 116 14 E
Yusofābād, Tehr. 17 C5 35 44N 51 24 E
Yuyuan Tan, Beij. 14 B2 39 53N 116 16 E
Yuyuantan Gongyuan, Beij. 14 B2 39 54N 116 16 E
Yvelines, Forêt des, Paris 5 D1 48 38N 1 53 E
Yvette →, Paris 5 C1 48 43N 1 57 E

Z

Záběhlice, Pra. 10 B2 50 3N 14 29 E
Żacisze, Wsaw. 10 E7 52 17N 21 4 E
Zahrā, Bagd. 17 E7 33 22N 44 19 E
Zakharkovo, Mos. 11 E7 55 46N 37 18 E
Zalov, Pra. 10 A2 50 10N 14 22 E
Załuski, Wsaw. 10 F6 52 9N 20 55 E
Zamdorf, Mün. 7 G10 48 8N 11 35 E
Zanevka, St-Pet. 11 B5 59 55N 30 31 E
Zaozerye, Mos. 11 F12 55 35N 38 1 E
Zapote, Manila 15 E3 14 27N 120 56 E
Zapotitlán, Méx. 29 C3 19 18N 99 2W
Zápy, Pra. 10 B4 50 9N 14 40 E
Zarechye, Mos. 11 E8 55 41N 37 22 E
Zawady, Wsaw. 10 E7 52 13N 21 6 E
Zâwiyet Abû Musallam, El Qâ. 18 D4 29 56N 31 9 E
Zawrā Park, Bagd. 17 F8 33 18N 44 23 E
Zbójna Góra, Wsaw. 10 E8 52 11N 21 13 E
Zbraslav, Pra. 10 C2 49 58N 14 23 E
Zbuzany, Pra. 10 B1 50 1N 14 17 E
Zdiby, Pra. 10 B2 50 9N 14 27 E
Zehlendorf, Berl. 7 B2 52 26N 13 16 E
Zeleneč, Pra. 10 B3 50 8N 14 39 E
Zempoala, Parque Nac. de las Lagunas de, Méx. 29 D2 19 5N 99 18W
Zepernick, Berl. 7 A4 52 38N 13 33 E
Żerań, Wsaw. 10 E6 52 18N 20 58 E
Zerzeń, Wsaw. 10 E7 52 12N 21 7 E
Zeytinburnu, Ist. 17 B2 40 58N 28 53 E
Zhabei, Shang. 14 J11 31 16N 121 26 E
Zhangguizhuang, Tianj. 14 E6 39 7N 117 19 E
Zhangxingzhuang, Tianj. 14 D6 39 10N 117 12 E
Zhdanov, Mos. 11 E10 55 44N 37 41 E
Zhegalovo, Mos. 11 D11 55 54N 37 59 E
Zheleznodorozhnyy, Mos. 11 E12 55 45N 38 0 E
Zhenru, Shang. 14 J11 31 16N 121 22 E
Zhicun, Gzh. 14 G8 23 0N 113 18 E
Zhongshan Gongyuan, Shang. 14 J11 31 13N 121 24 E
Zhoucun, Gzh. 14 F8 23 11N 113 11 E
Zhoujiadu, Shang. 14 J11 31 11N 121 28 E
Zhoujiazhen, Shang. 14 J12 31 16N 121 33 E
Zhu Jiang →, Gzh. 14 G8 23 6N 113 20 E
Zhulebino, Mos. 11 E11 55 42N 37 50 E
Zhushadi, Gzh. 14 G8 23 11N 113 22 E
Zielona, Wsaw. 10 E8 52 14N 21 11 E
Zielonka, Wsaw. 10 E7 52 18N 21 9 E
Zitadella, Berl. 7 A2 52 31N 13 11 E
Zizhuyuan Gongyuan, Beij. 14 B2 39 55N 116 17 E
Žižkov, Pra. 10 B2 50 5N 14 28 E
Zličín, Pra. 10 B1 50 3N 14 17 E
Ząbki, Wsaw. 10 E7 52 17N 21 12 E
Zografos, Ath. 8 J11 37 58N 23 47 E
Żoliborz, Wsaw. 10 E6 52 16N 20 57 E
Zugliget, Bud. 10 J12 47 30N 18 59 E
Zugló, Bud. 10 J13 47 31N 19 8 E
Zumbi, Rio J. 31 A2 22 49 S 43 10W
Zuvuvu →, S. Pau. 31 F5 23 40 S 46 42W
Zuvuvus, S. Pau. 31 F6 23 41 S 46 39W
Zweckel, Ruhr 6 A3 51 35N 6 57 E
Zyuzino, Mos. 11 F9 55 39N 37 34 E

WORLD MAPS

MAP SYMBOLS

SETTLEMENTS

⬢ **PARIS**   ◼ **Berne**   ◉ **Livorno**   ◎ Brugge   ⊚ Algeciras   ○ *Fréjus*   ○ *Oberammergau*   ○ *Thira*

Settlement symbols and type styles vary according to the scale of each map and indicate the importance of towns on the map rather than specific population figures

∴   Ruins or Archæological Sites   ᵛ   Wells in Desert

ADMINISTRATION

Boundaries	National Parks	Country Names
——— International		**NICARAGUA**
– – – International (Undefined or Disputed)	International boundaries show the *de facto* situation where there are rival claims to territory.	Administrative Areas
·········· Internal		KENT
		CALABRIA

COMMUNICATIONS

Roads	Railroads	✿ Airfields
——— Primary	⌒ Primary	⤫ Passes
⌒ Secondary	⌒ Secondary	϶--϶ Railroad Tunnels
·-·-· Trails and Seasonal	-·-·- Under Construction	·········· Principal Canals

PHYSICAL FEATURES

⌒ Perennial Streams	⬭ Intermittent Lakes	▲ 2259 Elevations (m)
········ Intermittent Streams	⬭ Swamps and Marshes	▼ 2604 Sea Depths (m)
⬭ Perennial Lakes	▭ Permanent Ice and Glaciers	*408* Elevation of Lake Surface Above Sea Level (m)

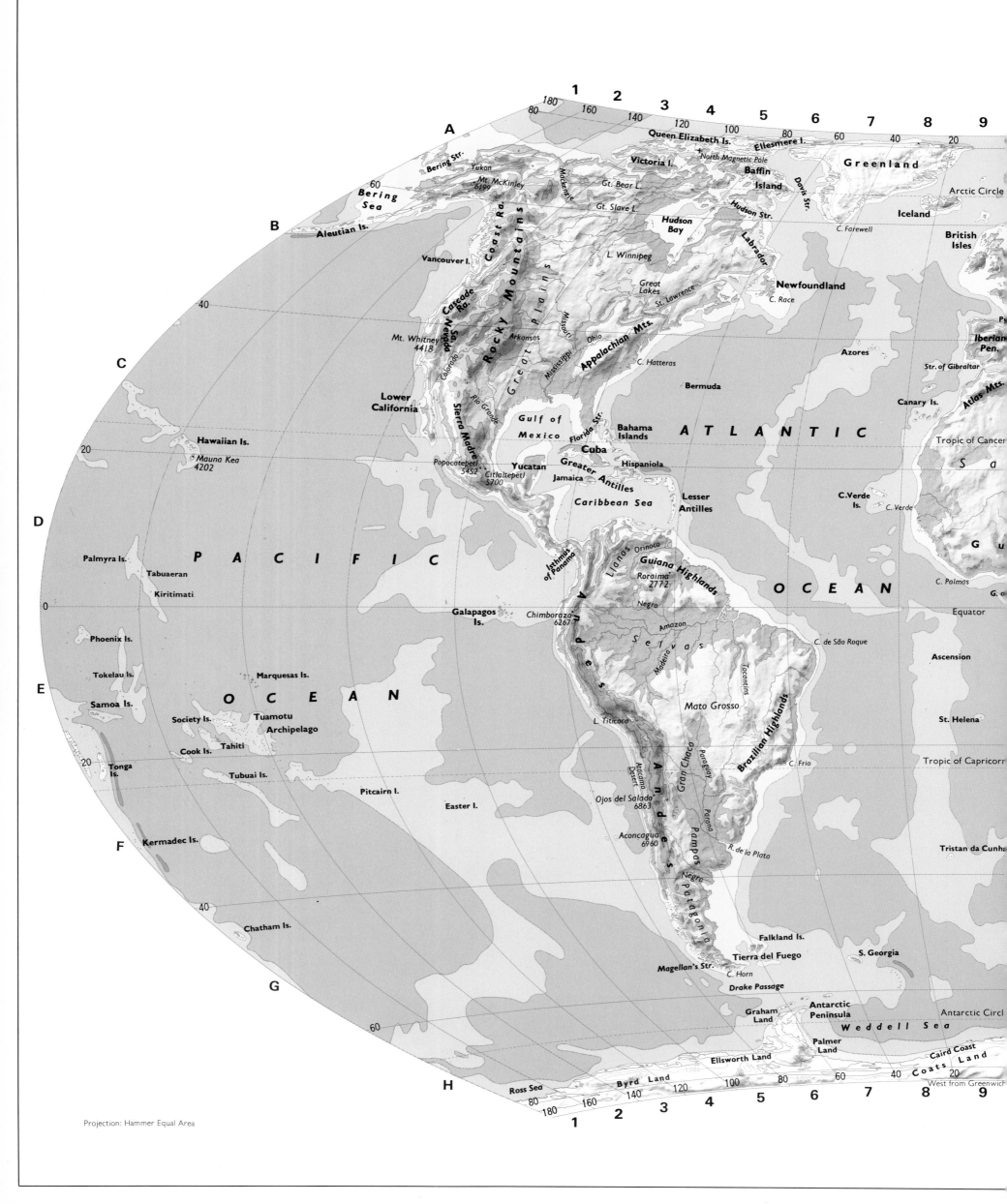

Projection: Hammer Equal Area

1 2 3 4 5 6 7 8 9

A

80 180 160 140 120 100 80 60 40 20

Bering Str.
Yukon
Mt. McKinley 6199
Mackenzie
Queen Elizabeth Is.
North Magnetic Pole
Victoria I.
Gt. Bear L.
Ellesmere I.
Greenland
Baffin Island
Davis Str.

Bering Sea
60
Gt. Slave L.
Hudson Str.
Arctic Circle

B
Aleutian Is.
Hudson Bay
Labrador
C. Farewell
Iceland
British Isles

Vancouver I.
L. Winnipeg
Newfoundland

Coast Ra.
Rocky Mountains
Great Lakes
St. Lawrence
C. Race

40
Cascade Ra.
Sierra Nevada
Missouri
Ohio
Appalachian Mts.
Pyr
Iberian Pen.

C
Mt. Whitney 4418
Arkansas
Mississippi
C. Hatteras
Azores
Str. of Gibraltar

Colorado
Great Plains
Bermuda
Atlas Mts.

Lower California
Sierra Madre
Rio Grande
Canary Is.
Tropic of Cancer

20
Hawaiian Is.
Gulf of Mexico
Florida Str.
Bahama Islands
A T L A N T I C
Sa

Mauna Kea 4202
Popocatepetl 5452
Citlaltepetl 5700
Cuba
Hispaniola
C. Verde Is.

Yucatan
Greater Antilles
Jamaica
Lesser Antilles
C. Verde

D
P A C I F I C
Caribbean Sea
Gu

Palmyra Is.
Isthmus of Panama
Llanos
Orinoco
Guiana Highlands
O C E A N

Tabuaeran
Roraima 2772
C. Palmas

Kiritimati
0
Negro
Equator
G. o

Galapagos Is.
Chimborazo 6267
Amazon
C. de São Roque

Phoenix Is.
Andes
Selvas
Madeira
Ascension

Tokelau Is.
Marquesas Is.
Tocantins

E
Samoa Is.
O C E A N
Mato Grosso
St. Helena

Society Is.
Tuamotu Archipelago
Brazilian Highlands

Cook Is.
Tahiti
L. Titicaca
Gran Chaco
Paraguay

20
Tonga Is.
Tubuai Is.
Atacama Desert
C. Frio
Tropic of Capricorn

Pitcairn I.
Ojos del Salado 6863
Paraná

Easter I.
Pampas
R. de la Plata

F
Kermadec Is.
Aconcagua 6960
Tristan da Cunha

Negro

40
Chatham Is.
Patagonia

G
Falkland Is.
S. Georgia

60
Magellan's Str.
Tierra del Fuego
C. Horn
Drake Passage
Antarctic Circle

H
Ross Sea
Byrd Land
Graham Land
Antarctic Peninsula
Weddell Sea

Ellsworth Land
Palmer Land
Caird Coast
Coats Land

80 180 160 140 120 100 80 60 40 20 West from Greenwich

1 2 3 4 5 6 7 8 9

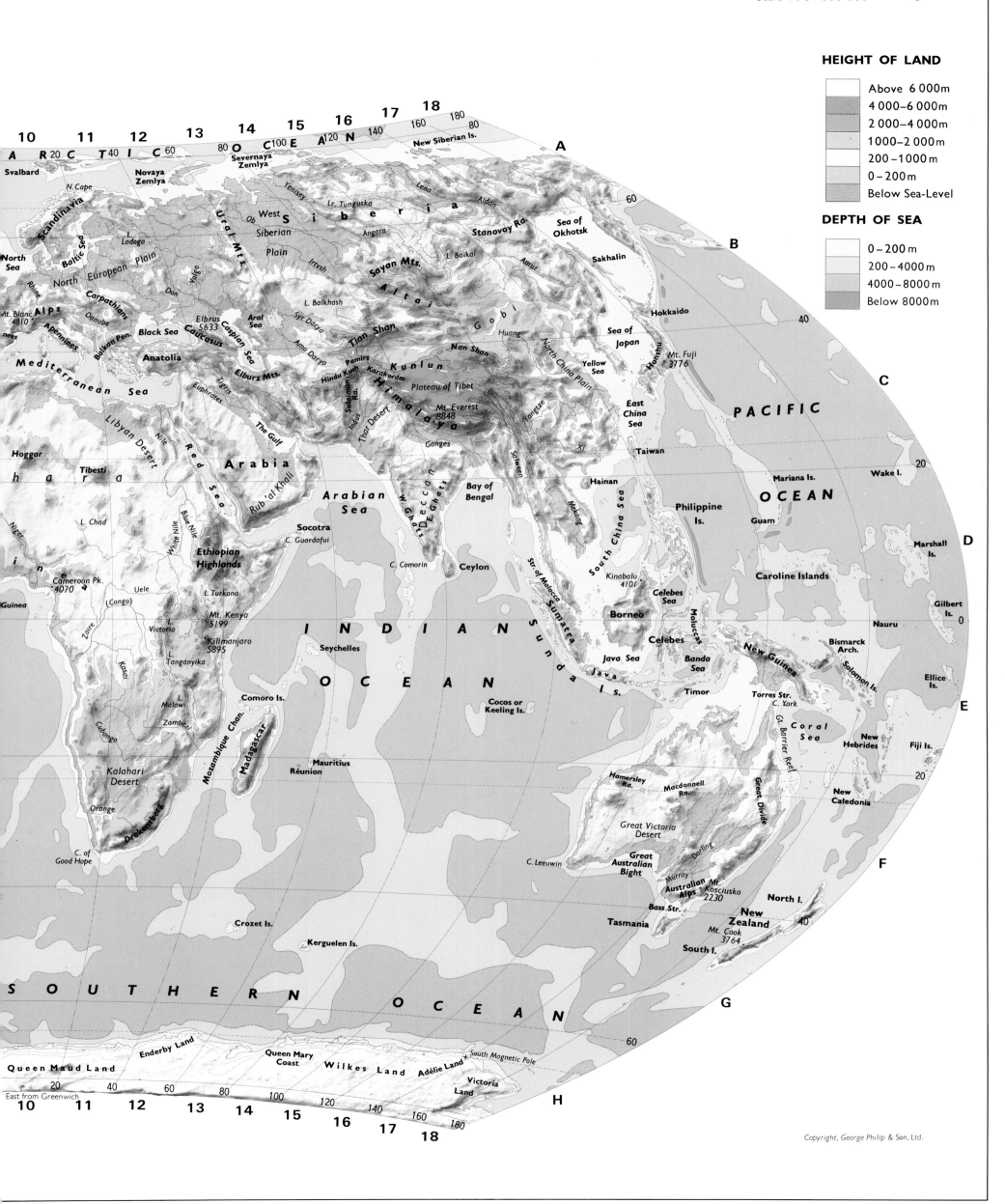

HEIGHT OF LAND

Above 6 000m
4 000 – 6 000m
2 000 – 4 000m
1000 – 2 000m
200 – 1000m
0 – 200m
Below Sea-Level

DEPTH OF SEA

0 – 200 m
200 – 4000 m
4000 – 8000 m
Below 8000m

ARCTIC OCEAN

Svalbard
N. Cape
Novaya Zemlya
Severnaya Zemlya
New Siberian Is.

Scandinavia
Ural Mts.
S i b e r i a
Yenisey
Lr. Tunguska
Lena
Aldan
Stanovoy Ra.
Sea of Okhotsk

North Sea
Baltic Sea
L. Ladoga
Ob
West Siberian Plain
Irtysh
Angara
Sayan Mts.
L. Baikal
Amur
Sakhalin
Hokkaido

North European Plain
Volga
Syr Darya
L. Balkhash
A l t a i
Gobi
Sea of Japan
Honshu

Carpathians
Don
Aral Sea
Tian Shan
Huang
North China Plain
Mt. Fuji 3776

Mt. Blanc 4810
Alps
Apennines
Danube
Elbrus 5633
Caspian Sea
Amu Darya
Pamirs
Kunlun
Nan Shan
Yellow Sea
East China Sea

Pyrenees
Black Sea
Caucasus
Elburz Mts.
Hindu Kush
Karakoram
Plateau of Tibet
Yangtze

Anatolia
Tigris
Euphrates
Sulaiman Ra.
Himalaya
Mt. Everest 8848
Salween
Xi

Mediterranean Sea
The Gulf
Thar Desert
Indus
Ganges
Taiwan

Libyan Desert
Red Sea
Arabia
Rub 'al Khali
Bay of Bengal
Hainan

Hoggar
Tibesti
Arabian Sea
W. Ghats
Deccan
E. Ghats
Mekong
South China Sea

S a h a r a
L. Chad
Socotra
C. Guardafui
Str. of Malacca
Kinabalu 4101

Niger
Ethiopian Highlands
C. Comorin
Ceylon
Sumatra
Borneo
Celebes Sea

Guinea
Cameroon Pk. 4070
L. Turkana
Mt. Kenya 5199
Celebes
Moluccas
Bismarck Arch.

(Congo)
Uele
Kilimanjaro 5895
I N D I A N
Java Sea
Banda Sea
New Guinea
Solomon Is.

Zaire
L. Victoria
L. Tanganyika
Seychelles
O C E A N
Java
Timor
Torres Str.

Kasai
L. Malawi
Comoro Is.
Cocos or Keeling Is.
S u n d a I s.
C. York
Coral Sea

Cubango
Zambezi
Madagascar
Mozambique Chan.
Mauritius
Réunion
Hamersley Ra.
Macdonnell Ra.
Great Divide
Gr. Barrier Reef

Kalahari Desert
Orange
Drakensberg
C. of Good Hope
Great Victoria Desert
Great Australian Bight
Darling
New Hebrides
New Caledonia

Crozet Is.
C. Leeuwin
Murray
Australian Alps
Mt. Kosciusko 2230
North I.
Fiji Is.

Kerguelen Is.
Bass Str.
Tasmania
New Zealand
Mt. Cook 3764
South I.

S O U T H E R N   O C E A N

Queen Maud Land
Enderby Land
Queen Mary Coast
Wilkes Land
Adélie Land
South Magnetic Pole
Victoria Land

East from Greenwich

P A C I F I C   O C E A N

Mariana Is.
Wake I.
Guam
Caroline Islands
Nauru
Gilbert Is.
Marshall Is.
Ellice Is.

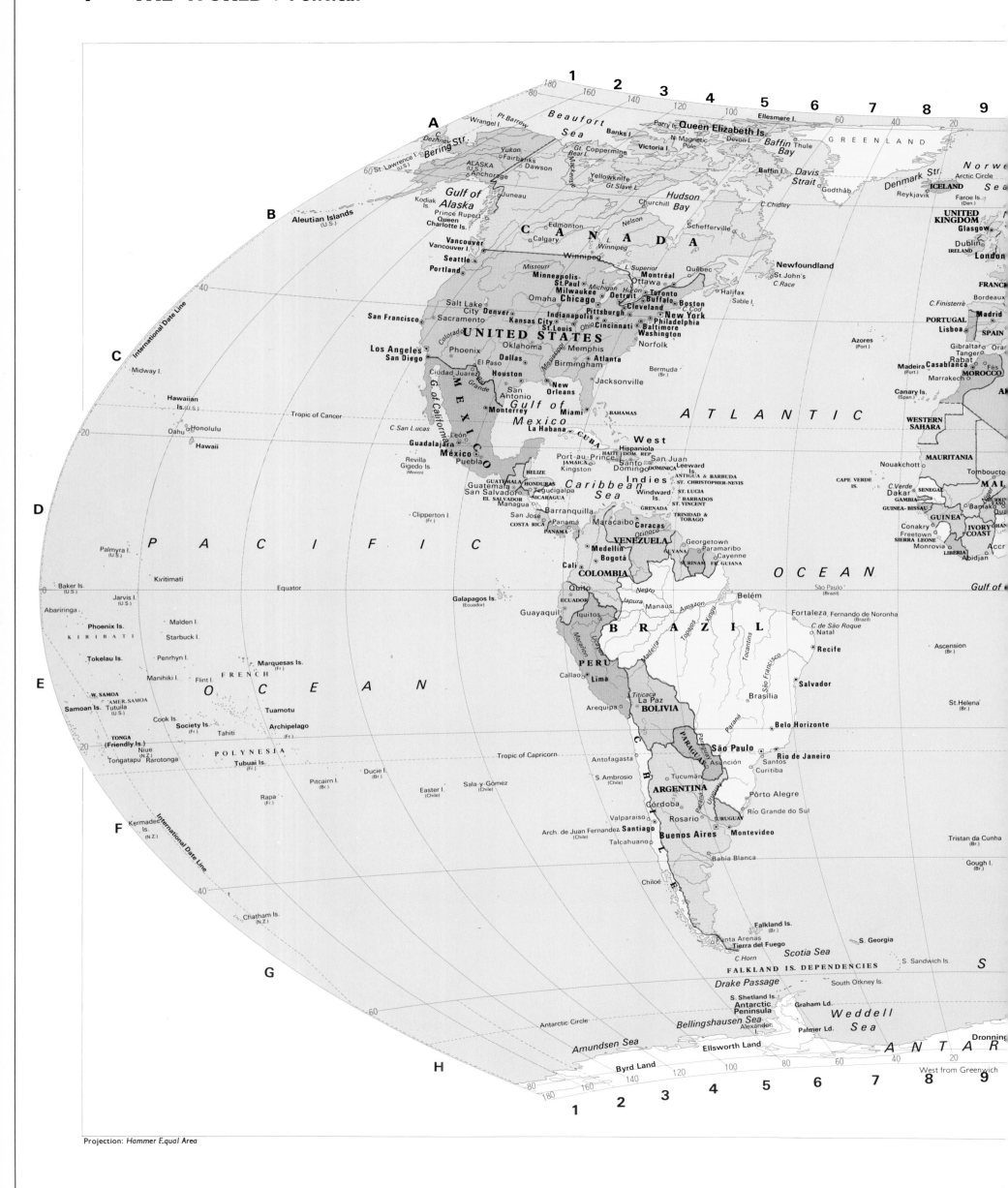

Projection: *Hammer Equal Area*

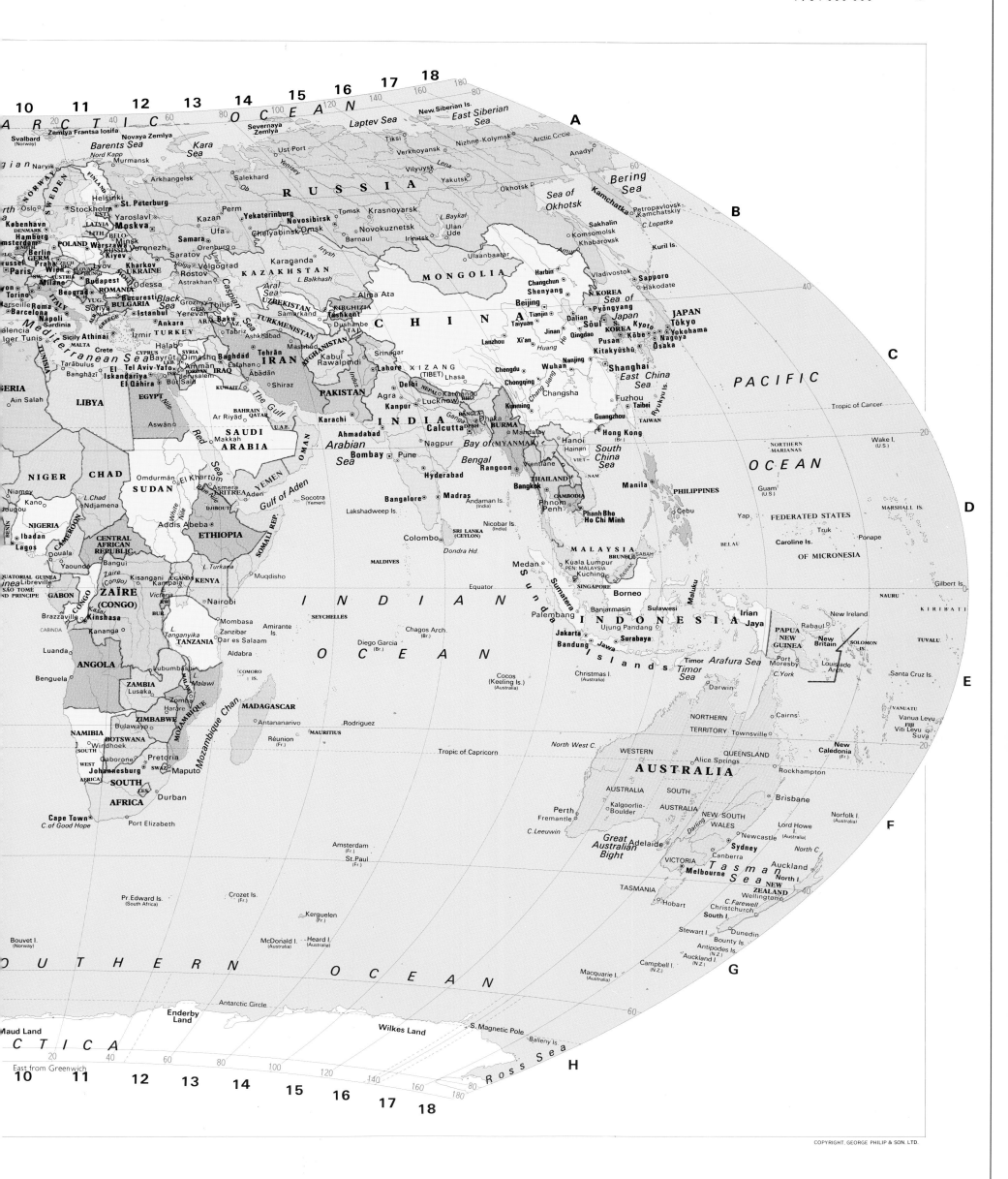

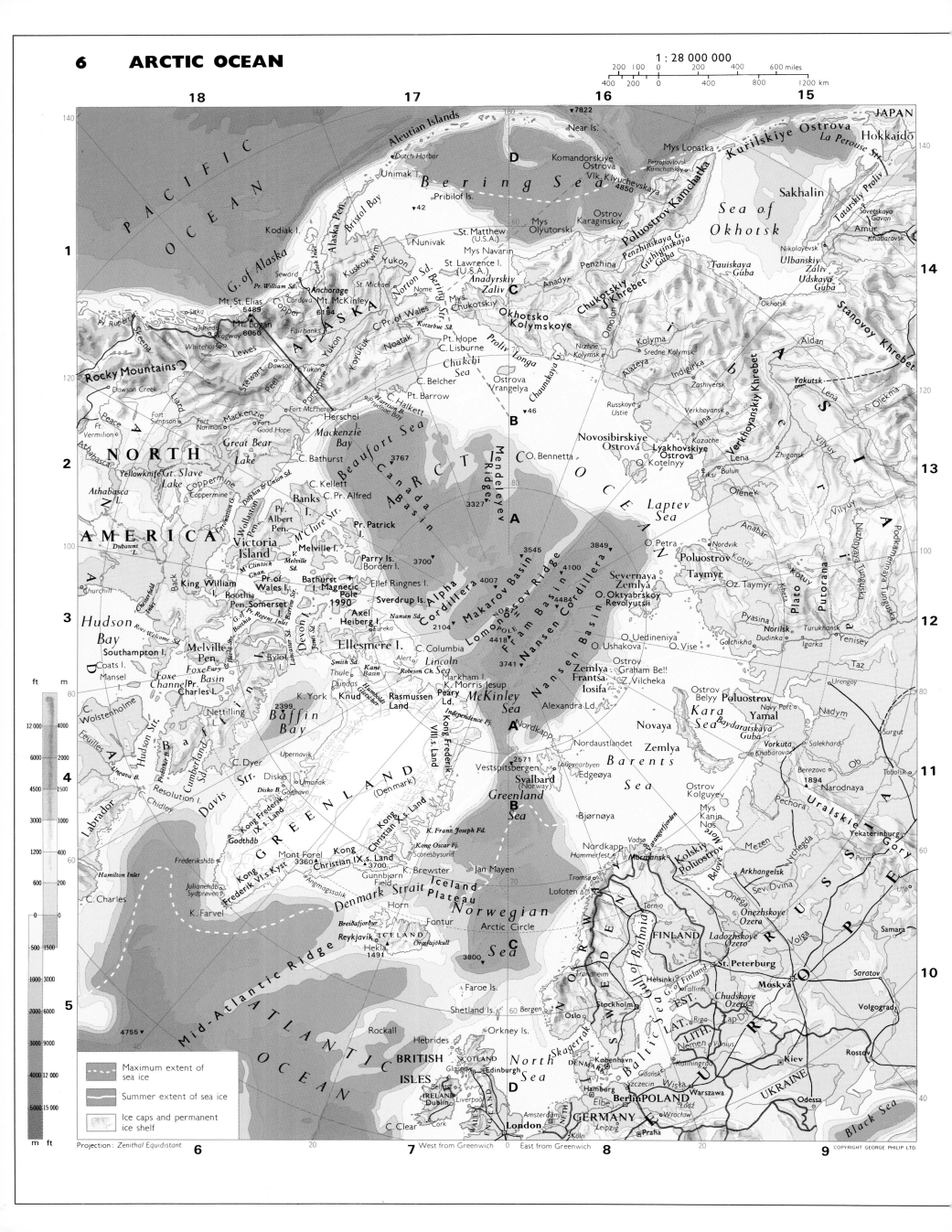

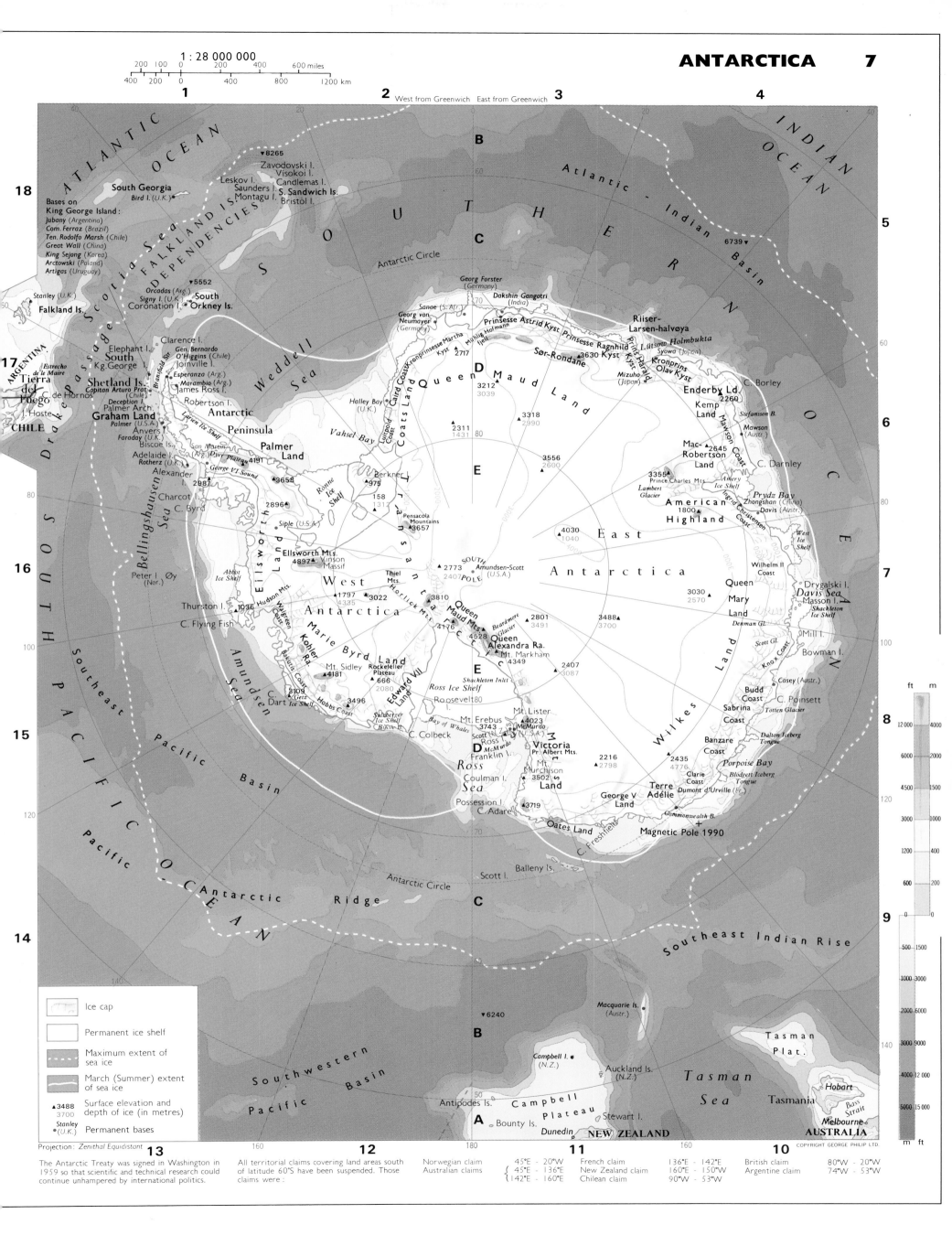

1 : 28 000 000

Projection: Zenithal Equidistant

The Antarctic Treaty was signed in Washington in
1959 so that scientific and technical research could
continue unhampered by international politics.

All territorial claims covering land areas south
of latitude 60°S have been suspended. Those
claims were :

Norwegian claim	45°E – 20°W	French claim	136°E – 142°E	British claim	80°W – 20°W
Australian claims	{ 45°E – 136°E	New Zealand claim	160°E – 150°W	Argentine claim	74°W – 53°W
	{ 142°E – 160°E	Chilean claim	90°W – 53°W	

COPYRIGHT GEORGE PHILIP LTD.

Legend

Ice cap

Permanent ice shelf

Maximum extent of
sea ice

March (Summer) extent
of sea ice

▲3488
3700 Surface elevation and
depth of ice (in metres)

Stanley
• (U.K.) Permanent bases

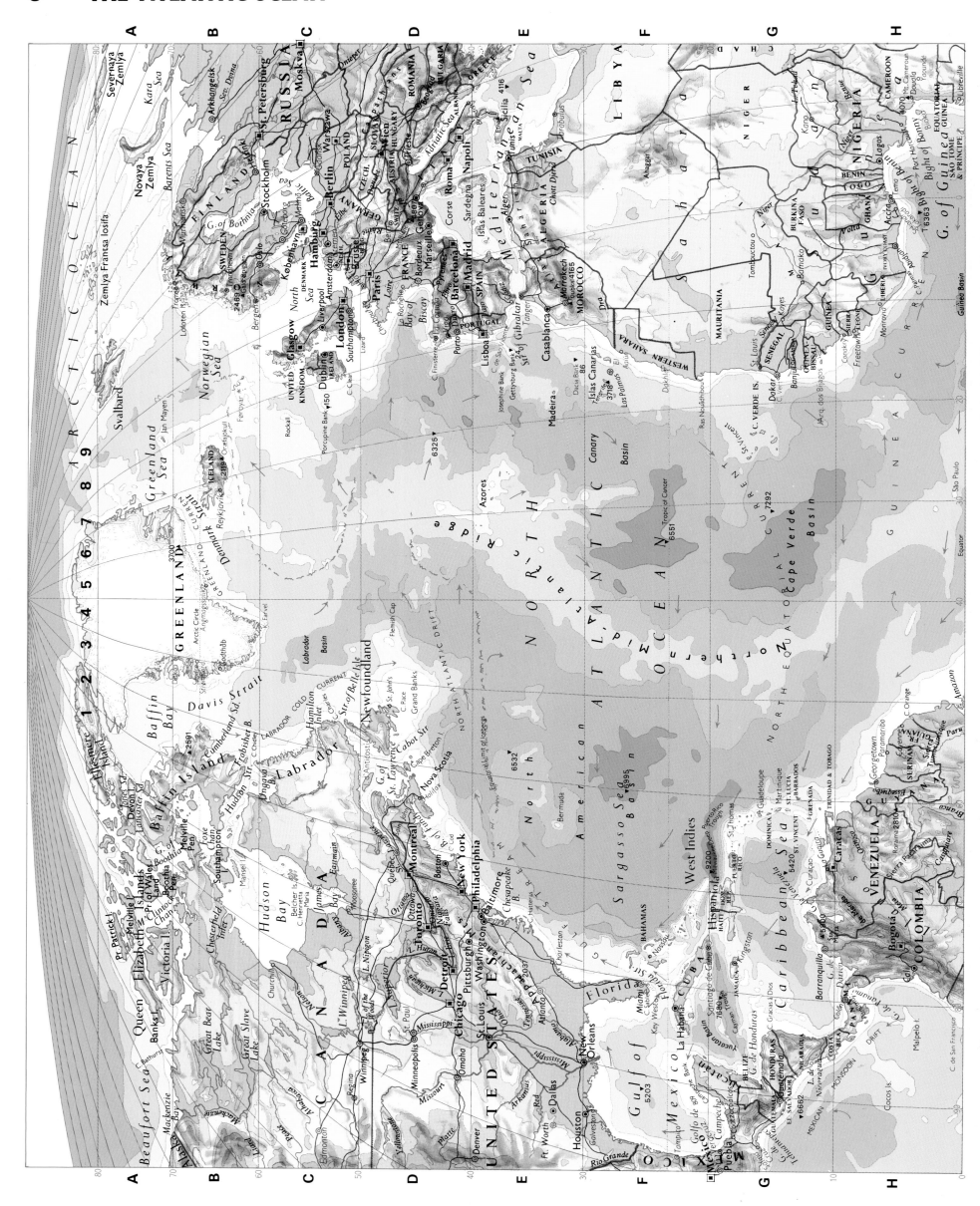

1 : 36 000 000

PACIFIC OCEAN

SOUTH ATLANTIC OCEAN

SOUTHERN OCEAN

CONGO
Brazzaville
Kinshasa
ANGOLA
Luanda
Benguela
Namibe
C. Frio
NAMIBIA (SOUTH WEST AFRICA)
Swakopmund
Walvisbaai
Windhoek
Lüderitz
Oranje
Port Nolloth
SOUTH AFRICA
Cape Town
Agulhas
Kaap die Goeie Hoop
Agulhas Bank

C. López
Annobón
Pointe Noire

BENGUELA COLD CURRENT

Angola Basin
6013

Walvis Ridge
5892

Cape Basin
5457

Agulhas Basin
6739

Atlantic Indian Ridge
Bouvetøya

WEST WIND DRIFT

Enderby Land

Dronning Maud Land

Coats Land

SOUTH EQUATORIAL CURRENT

Ascension
St. Helena
Tristan da Cunha
Gough I.

Tropic of Capricorn

Equatorial Limit of Icebergs

Mid-Atlantic Ridge
Southern

Fernando de Noronha
C. de São Roque
Martin Vaz
Trindade
6027
5755
302
411
638

Brazil Basin
6537

7758

Galápagos

Quito
ECUADOR
Guayaquil
Golfo de Guayaquil
Chimborazo
Cotopaxi 5897
Pta. Parinas

PERU
Lima
Callao
6369
Arequipa

Iquitos
Leticia
Negro
Japurá
Içá
Amazon
Madeira
Manaus
Aripuaná
Tapajós
Xingú
Araguaia
Tocantins
Purus
Juruá
Ucayali
Marañón
Napo

BRAZIL
Belém
São Luís
Fortaleza
Recife
Salvador
Brasília
Belo Horizonte
Rio de Janeiro
São Paulo
Santos
Pôrto Alegre

Mato Grosso
Goiânia
Serra do Espinhaço
São Francisco
Paraná
Paraná
Paranaíba

6550
L. Titicaca
La Paz
BOLIVIA
Sucre
Potosí
Pilcomayo
PARAGUAY
Asunción
Paraguay

Antofagasta
6723
Aconcagua 6960
CHILE
Valparaíso
Santiago
Concepción
Puerto Montt
Isla de Chiloé
Arch. de los Chonos
Pen. de Taitao
Arch. de Juan Fernández
S. Ambrosio
S. Félix

ARGENTINA
Córdoba
Rosario
Buenos Aires
Montevideo
URUGUAY
L. Mirim
L. dos Patos
Río de la Plata
Paraná
Salado
Colorado
Negro
Bahía Blanca
Pampas
Desaguadero
Bahía Grande
Golfo San Matías
Pen. Valdés
Chubut
Golfo San Jorge

PERUVIAN COLD CURRENT

South East Pacific Basin

Chile Rise
(Southern Pacific) Basin

Antarctic 5385

FALKLAND IS. DEPENDENCIES
Falkland Is. (Islas Malvinas)
6212

Tierra del Fuego
Estrecho de Magallanes
Drake Passage
CAPE HORN COLD CURRENT
Cabo de Hornos

FALKLAND IS. (Islas Malvinas)
South Georgia
Shag Rocks
South Orkney Is.
South Sandwich Is.
South Shetland Is.
8428

Scotia Sea
Argentine Basin

Weddell Sea

BRITISH ANTARCTIC TERRITORY

Antarctic Peninsula
Graham Land
Palmer Land
Alexander I.
Ellsworth Land

Byrd Land
Ross Sea

Antarctic Circle

Antarctic Drift Basin

PACIFIC OCEAN

→ Direction of Currents

Projection : Mollweide

COPYRIGHT GEORGE PHILIP & SON LTD

ft m
18,000 6000
12,000 4000
9000 3000
6000 2000
4500 1500
1200 400
600 200
0 0
200 600
1200 2000
4500 6000
5000 15,000
6000 18,000
8000 24,000
m ft

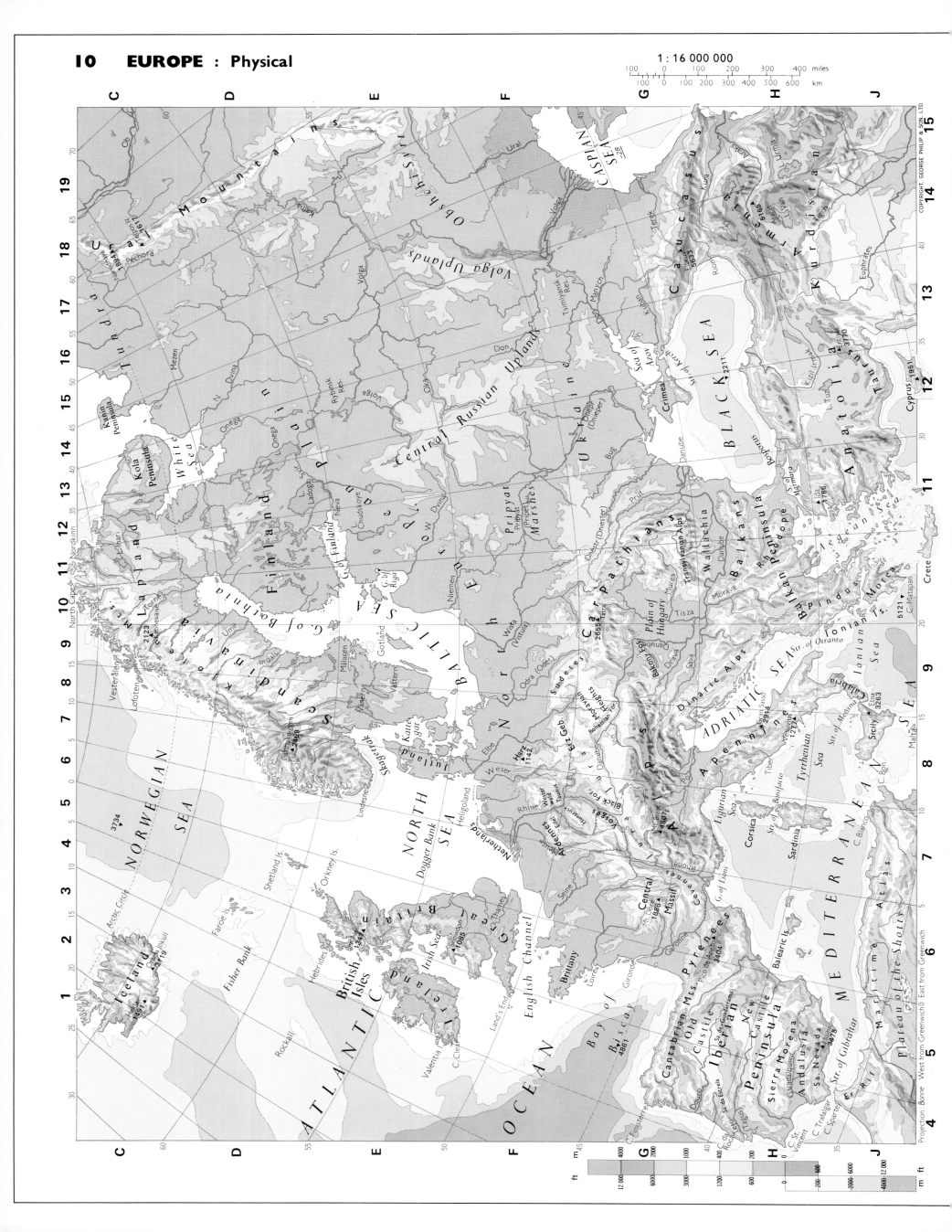

1 : 16 000 000

Projection: Bonne   West from Greenwich 0 East from Greenwich

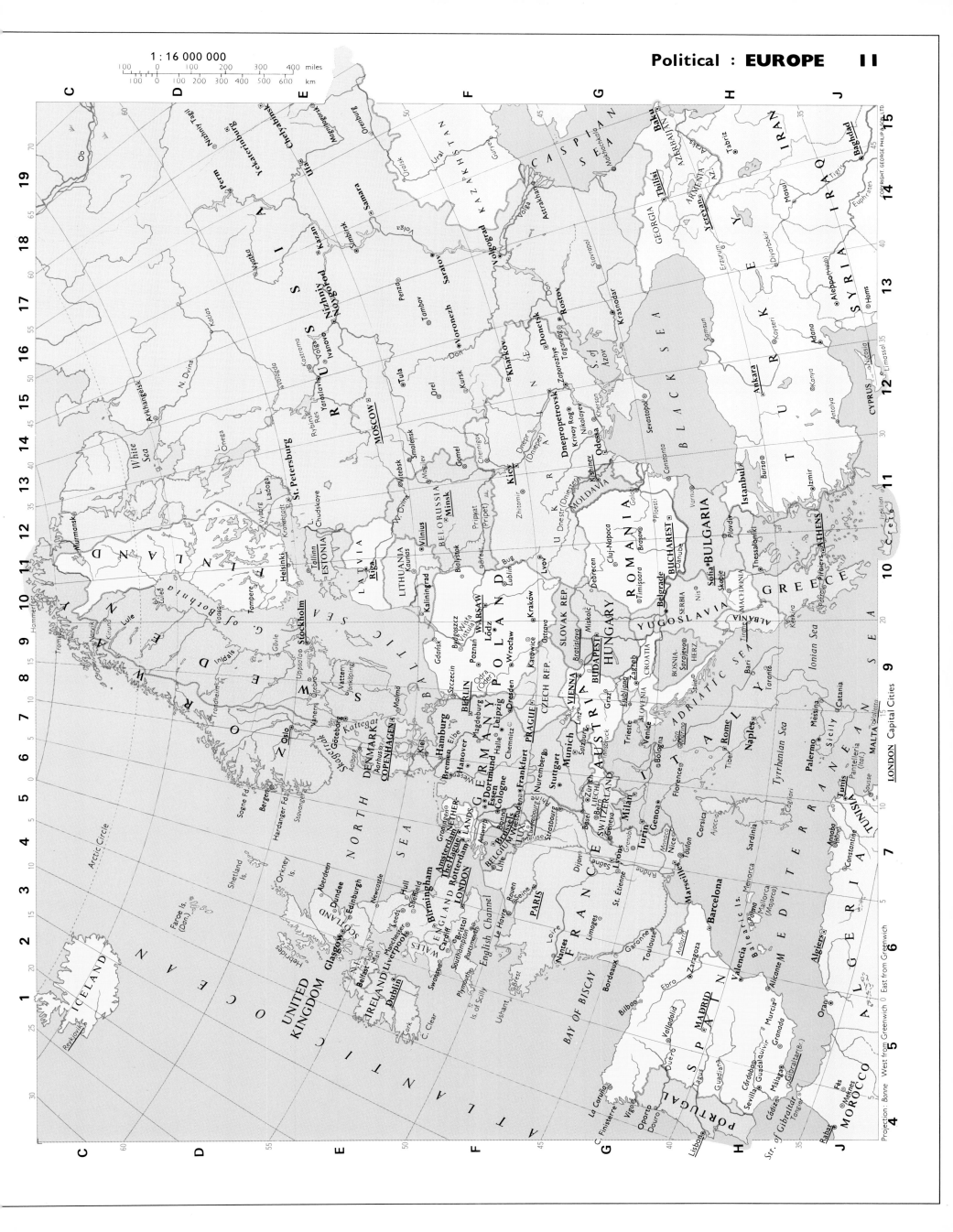

1 : 16 000 000

COPYRIGHT GEORGE PHILIP & SON, LTD

LONDON Capital Cities

Projection: Bonne   West from Greenwich 0 East from Greenwich

ICELAND
on the same scale
as general map

Norway / Sweden / Finland labels (selected):

L A P L A N D

N O R R B O T T E N

V Ä S T E R B O T T E N

Å N G E R M A N L A N D

J Ä M T L A N D

N. TRÖNDELAG

SÖR-TRÖNDELAG

GULF OF BOTHNIA

NORWEGIAN SEA

Towns / places (selected):

Vadsö, Vardö, Kirkenes, Hammerfest, Nordkapp, Tromsö, Narvik, Kiruna, Gällivare, Bodö, Luleå, Piteå, Skellefteå, Umeå, Örnsköldsvik, Härnösand, Sundsvall, Östersund, Steinkjer, Levanger, Trondheim, Kristiansund, Molde, Ålesund, Mo, Mosjöen, Namsos, Oulu, Kemi, Rovaniemi, Tornio, Haparanda, Kokkola, Jakobstad, Vaasa, Kristinestad, Kuopio, Kajaani, Mikkeli

Arctic Circle

Iceland (selected):

Reykjavik, Keflavik, Akranes, Akureyri, Saudárkrókur, Siglufjördur, Húsavik, Vatnajökull, Hekla, Myrdalsjökull, Langjökull, Hofsjökull, Snaefell, Vestmannaeyjar, Breidafjördur, Faxaflói, Húnaflói

West from 18 Greenwich

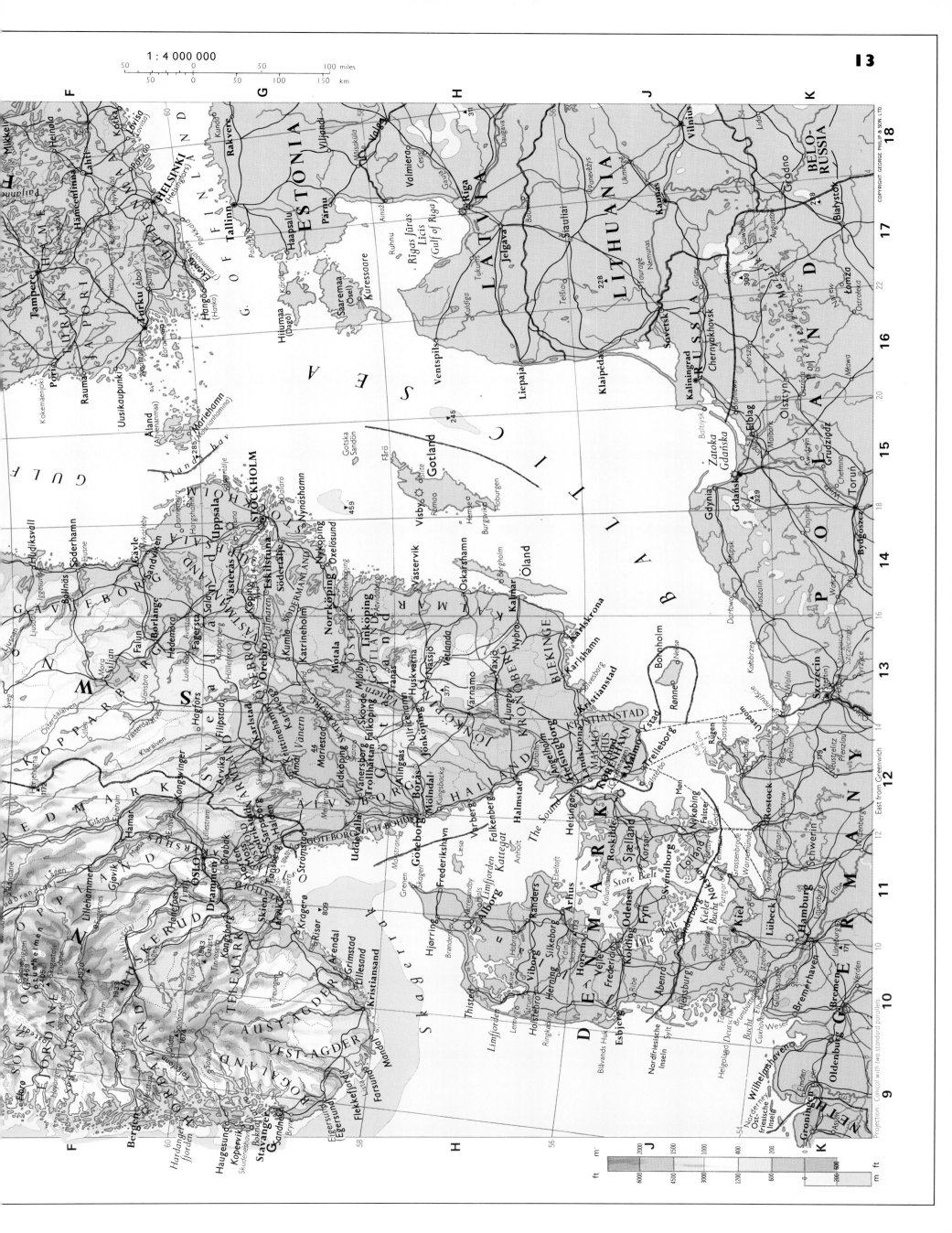

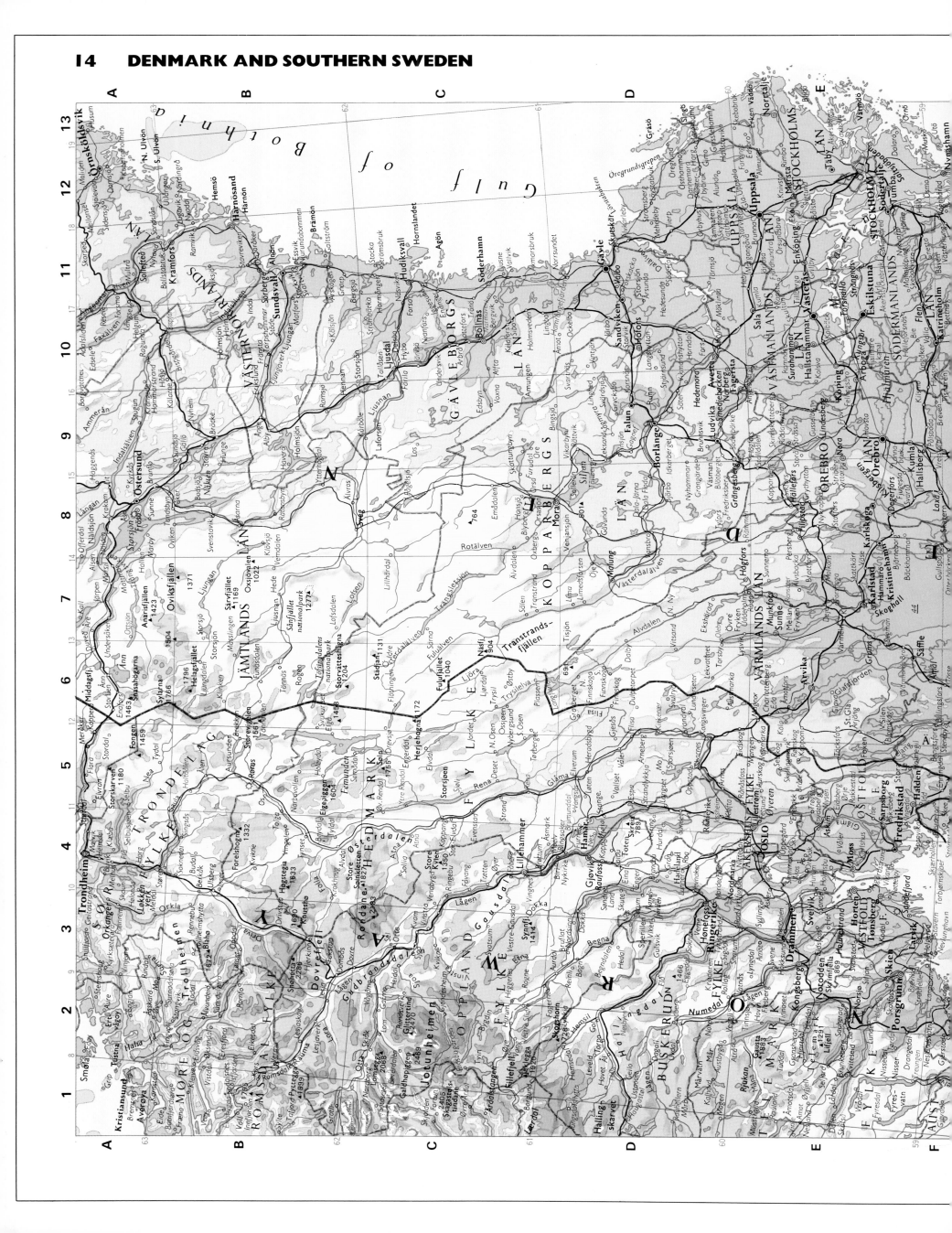

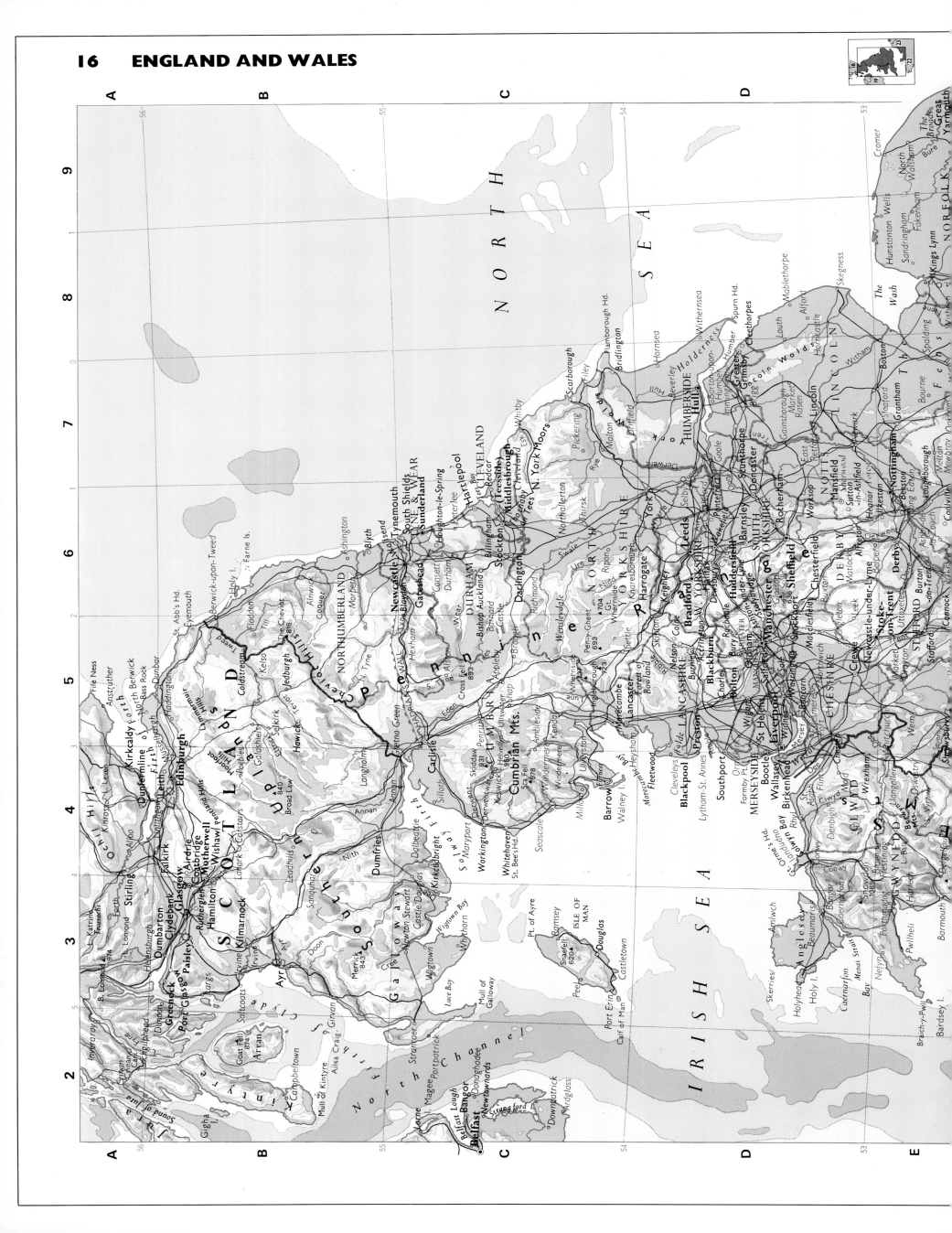

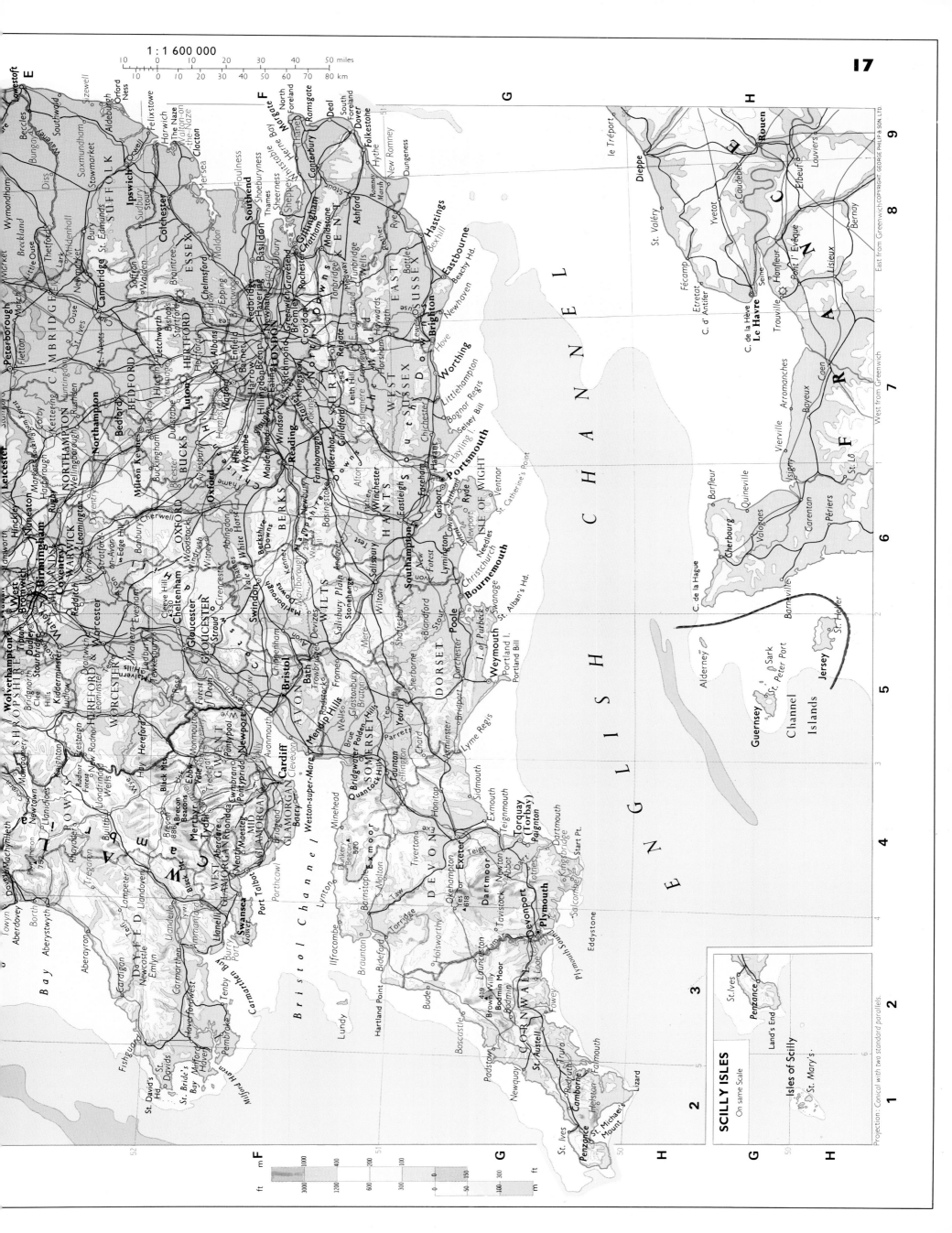

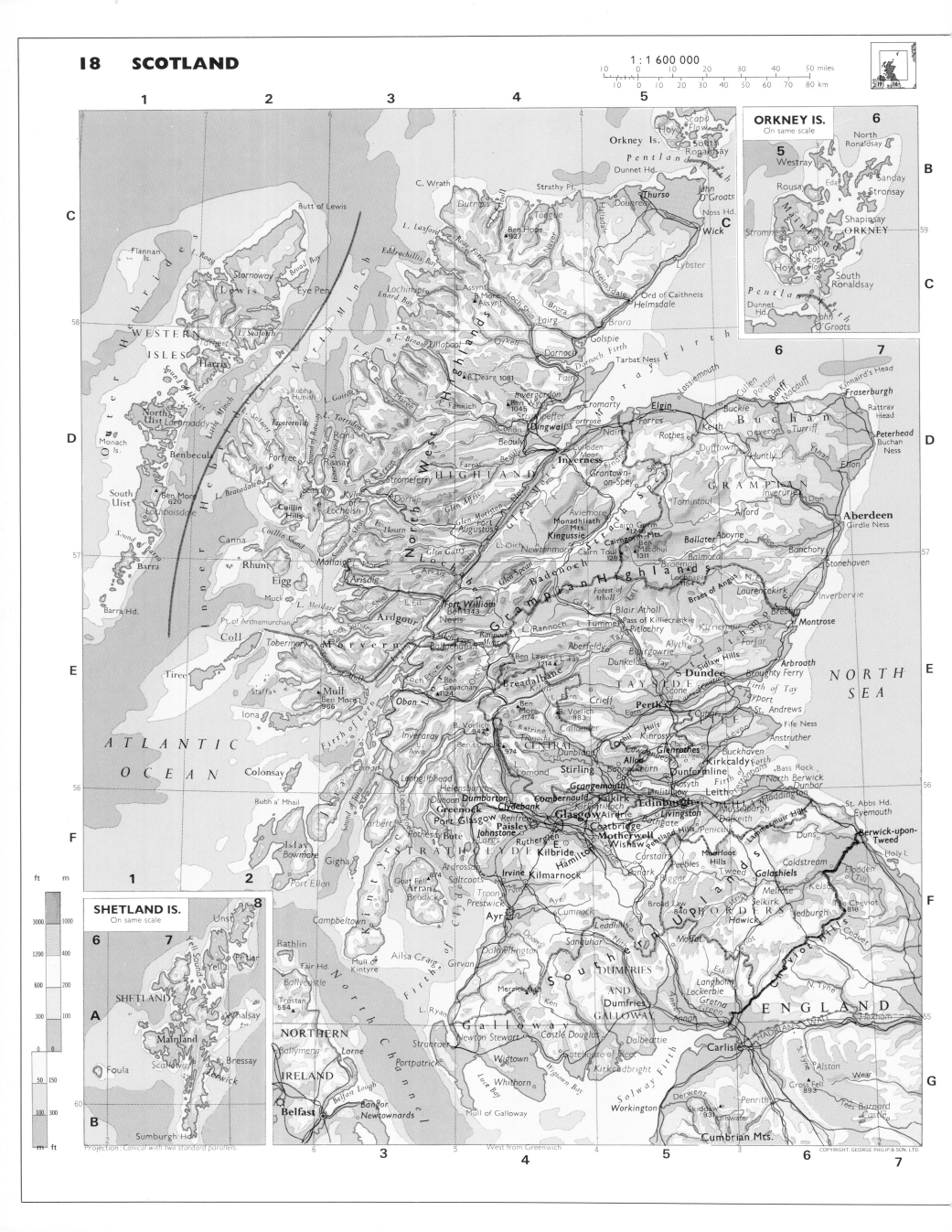

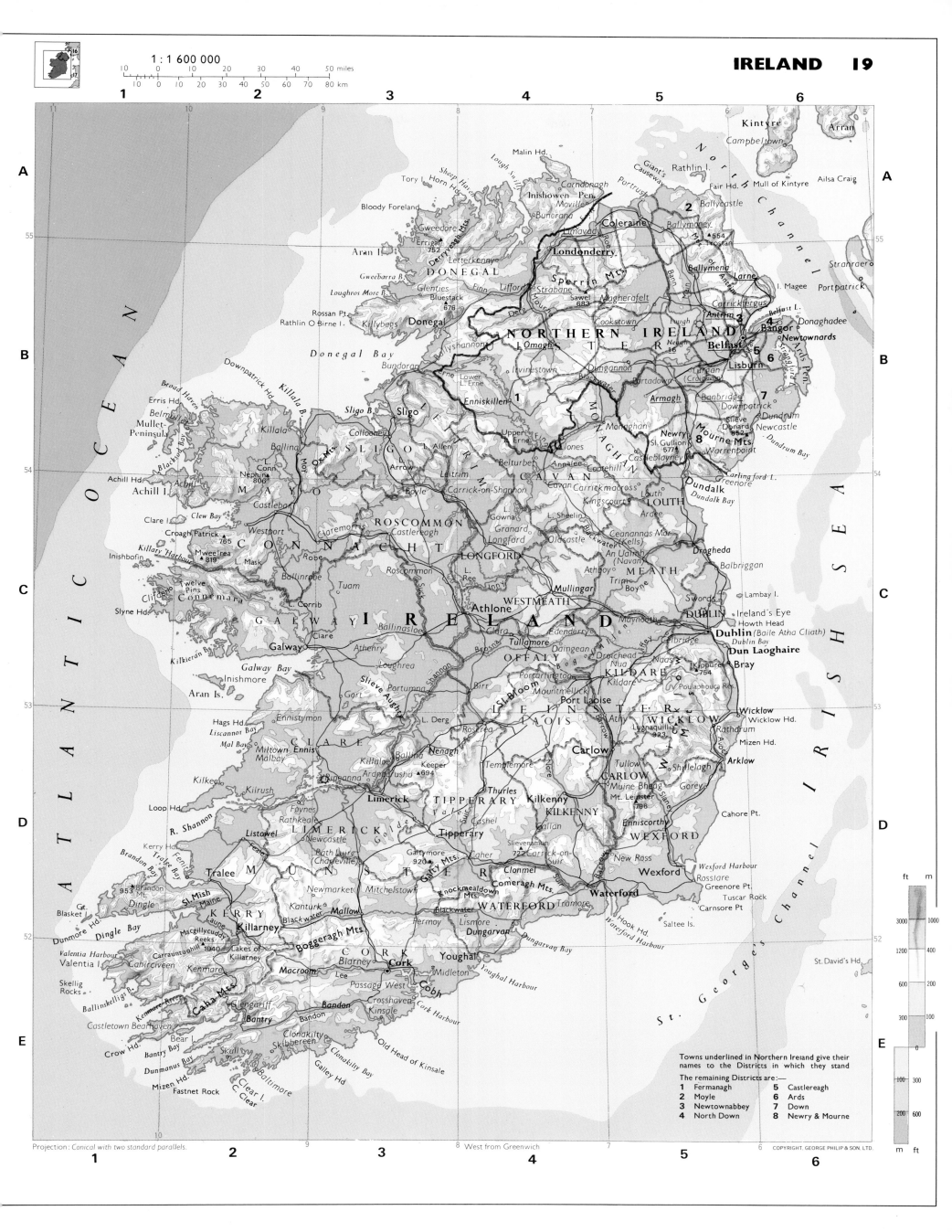

1 : 1 600 000

Towns underlined in Northern Ireland give their
names to the Districts in which they stand
The remaining Districts are:—

1 Fermanagh	5 Castlereagh
2 Moyle	6 Ards
3 Newtownabbey	7 Down
4 North Down	8 Newry & Mourne

Projection: Conical with two standard parallels.

West from Greenwich

COPYRIGHT. GEORGE PHILIP & SON. LTD.

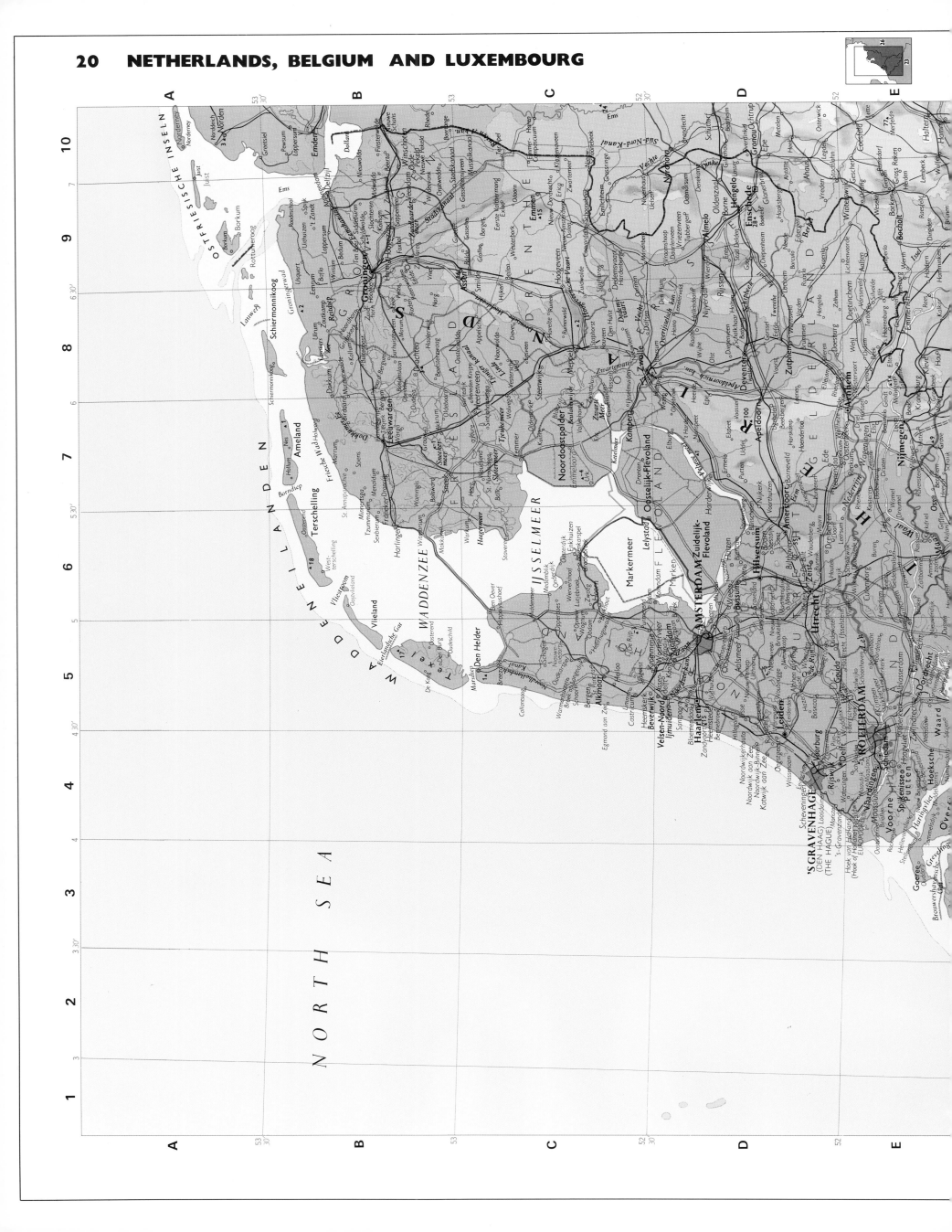

NORTH SEA

WADDENZEE

OSTFRIESISCHE INSELN

OSTFRIESISCHE INSELN

IJSSELMEER

Markermeer

WADDEN EILANDEN

Groningen

Leeuwarden

FRIESLAND

DRENTHE

Emmen

GRONINGEN

Zwolle

GELDERLAND

Deventer

Zutphen

Apeldoorn

Enschede

Hengelo

Almelo

OVERIJSSEL

Noordoostpolder

FLEVOLAND

Oostelijk-Flevoland

Zuidelijk-Flevoland

Lelystad

AMSTERDAM

Zuidelijk-Flevoland

Hilversum

Bussum

Utrecht

Zeist

Amersfoort

Nijmegen

Den Helder

Texel

Terschelling

Vlieland

Ameland

Schiermonnikoog

Alkmaar

Beverwijk

Velsen-Noord

IJmuiden

Haarlem

Leiden

ROTTERDAM

Schiedam

Dordrecht

Delft

'S GRAVENHAGE
(DEN HAAG)
(THE HAGUE)
('s-Gravenhage)

Scheveningen

Hoeksche
Waard

Voorne

Goeree

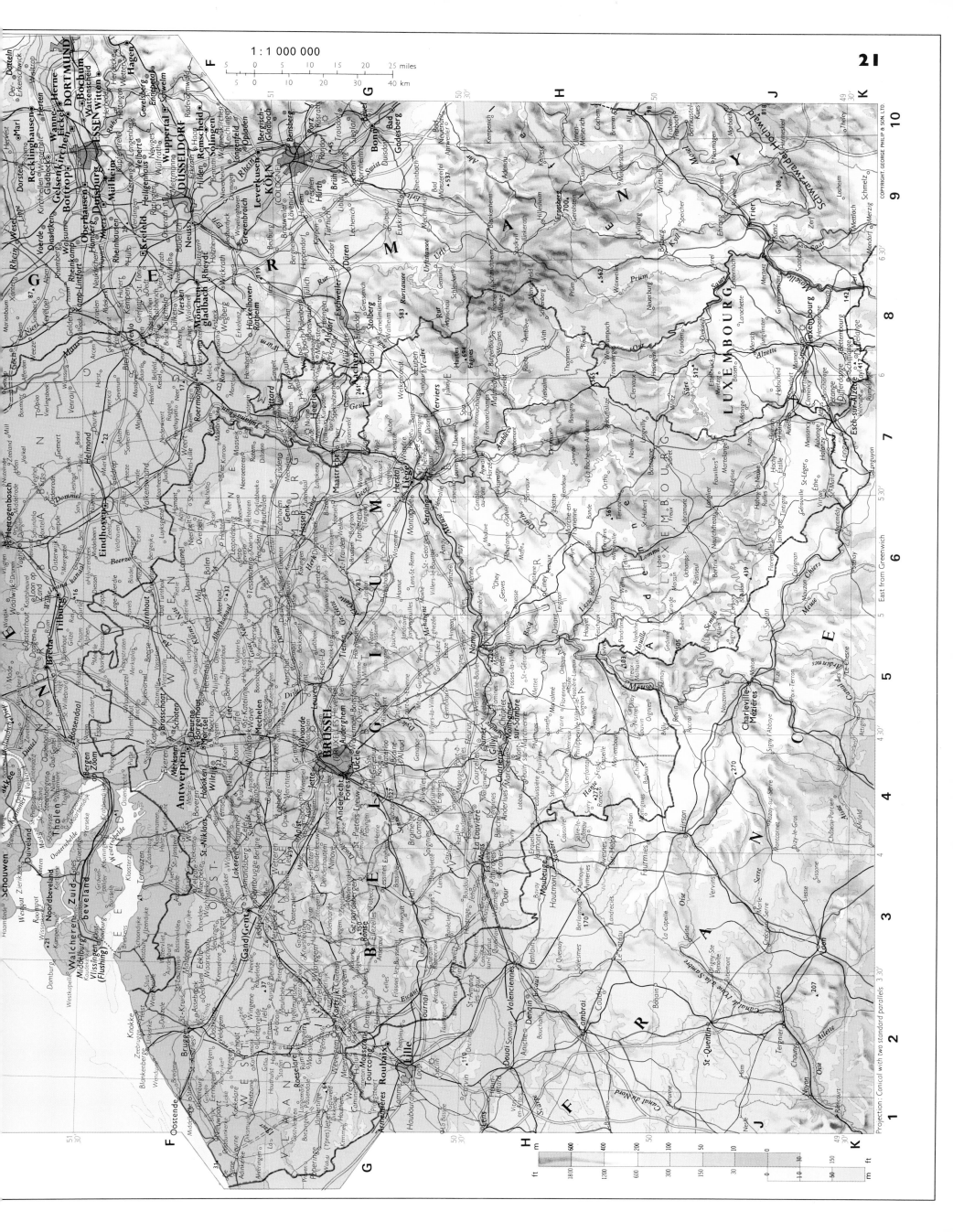

ENGLAND

English Channel

CHANNEL ISLANDS
Guernsey
St. Peter Port
Jersey
St. Helier
Alderney

Baie de la Seine

Le Havre
Rouen
Cherbourg
Caen
NORMANDIE
CALVADOS
Bayeux

Golfe de St-Malo
St-Malo
Dinard
Granville
Mont-St-Michel
Avranches

BRETAGNE
Brest
Quimper
Lorient
Vannes
Rennes
St-Brieuc
Morlaix
Lannion
Guingamp
CÔTES-D'ARMOR
MORBIHAN
Montagne Noire
Monts d'Arrée

Mer d'Iroise
Ile d'Ouessant
Pte. du Raz
Douarnenez
Audierne

Belle-Ile
Presqu'île de Quiberon
Ile de Groix

Le Mans
Laval
Mayenne
Alençon
Fougères
Vitré
ANJOU
Angers
MAINE

Nantes
St. Nazaire
LOIRE-ATLANTIQUE
Baie de Bourgneuf
Ile de Noirmoutier
Cholet
Saumur
Tours
TOURAINE
Blois
Chartres

VENDÉE
La Roche-sur-Yon
Ile d'Yeu
Les-Sables-d'Olonne
Châtellerault
Poitiers
DEUX-SÈVRES
Niort
VIENNE

Ile de Ré
La Rochelle
AUNIS
Rochefort
Ile d'Oléron
CHARENTE-MARITIME
Saintes
Cognac
ANGOUMOIS
Angoulême
CHARENTE
HAUTE-VIENNE
Limoges
LIMOUSIN

Plymouth
Exeter
Dartmoor
Torquay
Land's End
Penzance
Falmouth
Newquay
Bodmin
Bideford
Lyme Bay
Weymouth
Bournemouth
Southampton
Portsmouth
Isle of Wight
Brighton
Eastbourne
Hastings
South Downs

Dieppe
Le Tréport
Baie de la Somme

Projection: Conical with two standard parallels

West from Greenwich   East from Greenwich

DÉPARTEMENTS IN THE PARIS AREA
1 Ville de Paris   3 Val-de-Marne
2 Seine-St-Denis   4 Hauts-de-Seine

ft   m
12 000   4000
9000   3000
6000   2000
4500   1500
3000   1000
1200   400
600   200
0   0
200   600
2000   6000
m   ft

1 : 2 000 000

10 0 10 20 30 40 50 miles
10 0 10 20 30 40 50 60 70 80 km

BELGIUM

FRANCE

GERMANY

LUXEMBOURG

SAARLAND

SWITZERLAND

ITALY

Calais · Dunkerque · Gent · BRUSSEL (Bruxelles) · Mechelen · Leuven · Maastricht · Liège · Aachen · Bonn · FRANKFURT · Wiesbaden · Mainz · Worms

Lille · Tournai · Mons · Namur · Charleroi · Verviers · Koblenz · Ludwigshafen · Mannheim

Amiens · St Quentin · Charleville-Mézières · Luxembourg · Trier · Saarbrücken · Karlsruhe

Reims · Épernay · Châlons-sur-Marne · Verdun · Metz · Nancy · Strasbourg · Baden-Baden

PARIS · Versailles · St-Germain · Melun · Troyes · Chaumont · Épinal · Colmar · Freiburg

Orléans · Auxerre · Dijon · Besançon · Mulhouse · Belfort · Basel

Bourges · Nevers · Beaune · Chalon-sur-Saône · Neuchâtel · Bern

Montluçon · Moulins · Mâcon · Bourg-en-Bresse · Lausanne · Genève · Fribourg

Clermont-Ferrand · Vichy · Roanne · LYON (Lyons) · Annecy · Aosta

COPYRIGHT GEORGE PHILIP & SON LTD.

SOUTHERN FRANCE

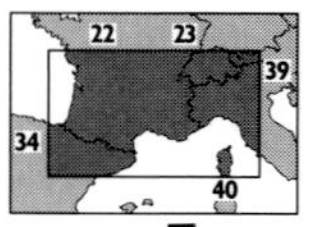

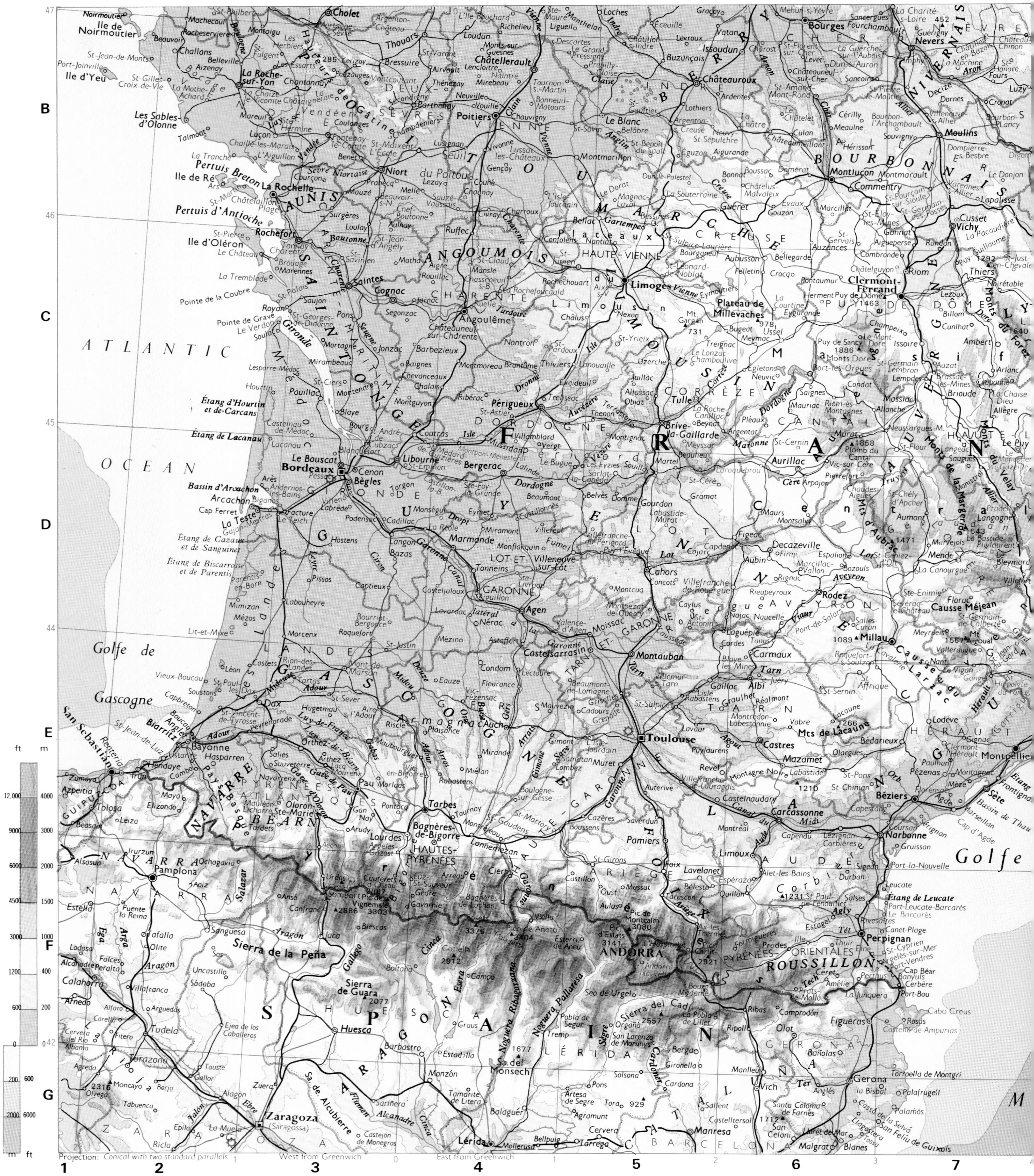

1 : 2 000 000

10   0   10   20   30   40   50 miles
10   0   10   20 30 40 50 60 70 80 km

8   9   10   11   12   13   14

SWITZERLAND

Bern   FRIBOURG   Fribourg   Thun   Interlaken   Luzern   Schwyz   GRAUBÜNDEN (GRISONS)   Davos   St. Moritz

FRANCHE-COMTÉ   Neuchâtel   La Chaux-de-Fonds

Chalon-sur-Saône   Lons-le-Saunier   Lausanne   Lac Léman   Montreux   VALAIS   Valaisannes   Zermatt

Mâcon   Bourg-en-Bresse   Genève   Annemasse   HAUTE-SAVOIE   Mont Blanc 4807   VAL D'AOSTA   Bellinzona   Lugano   Bergamo

LYON   Vienne   Chambéry   Annecy   SAVOIE   Aix-les-Bains   Albertville   TORINO   Milano (Milan)   Brescia

St-Étienne   Grenoble   Voiron   Novara   Vercelli   Pavia   Cremona

DAUPHINÉ   La Mure   Briançon   Massif du Pelvoux 4103   Pinerolo   Asti   Alessandria   Voghera   Parma

DRÔME   Valence   Crest   Die   Gap   PIEMONTE   Cúneo   Mondovì   ITALY

Montélimar   Sisteron   ALPES-DE-HAUTE-PROVENCE   Digne   ALPES-MARITIMES   Savona   GENOVA (Génova)   La Spezia   Carrara   Massa

Avignon   VAUCLUSE   Manosque   Castellane   Grasse   Nice   Monaco   Monte-Carlo   San Remo   Imperia (Maurizio-Oneglia)   Golfo di Génova   Livorno

Nîmes   Arles   Aix-en-Provence   PROVENCE   Draguignan   Cannes   Antibes   Agnes-sur-Mer

MARSEILLE   Aubagne   Toulon   Hyères   ILES D'HYÈRES   Fréjus   St-Raphaël   Ste-Maxime   St-Tropez

Golfe du Lion   LIGURIAN SEA

C. Corse   Capraia

G. de St-Florent   Bastia   Elba   Étang de Biguglia   Pianosa

L'Ile-Rousse   Calvi   Monte Cinto 2710   HAUTE CORSE   Corte 1766   CORSICA

MEDITERRANEAN SEA   G. de Porto   G. de Sagone   Ajaccio   G. d'Ajaccio   CORSE DU SUD   Propriano   Sartène   G. de Valinco   Bonifacio   I. de Cavallo

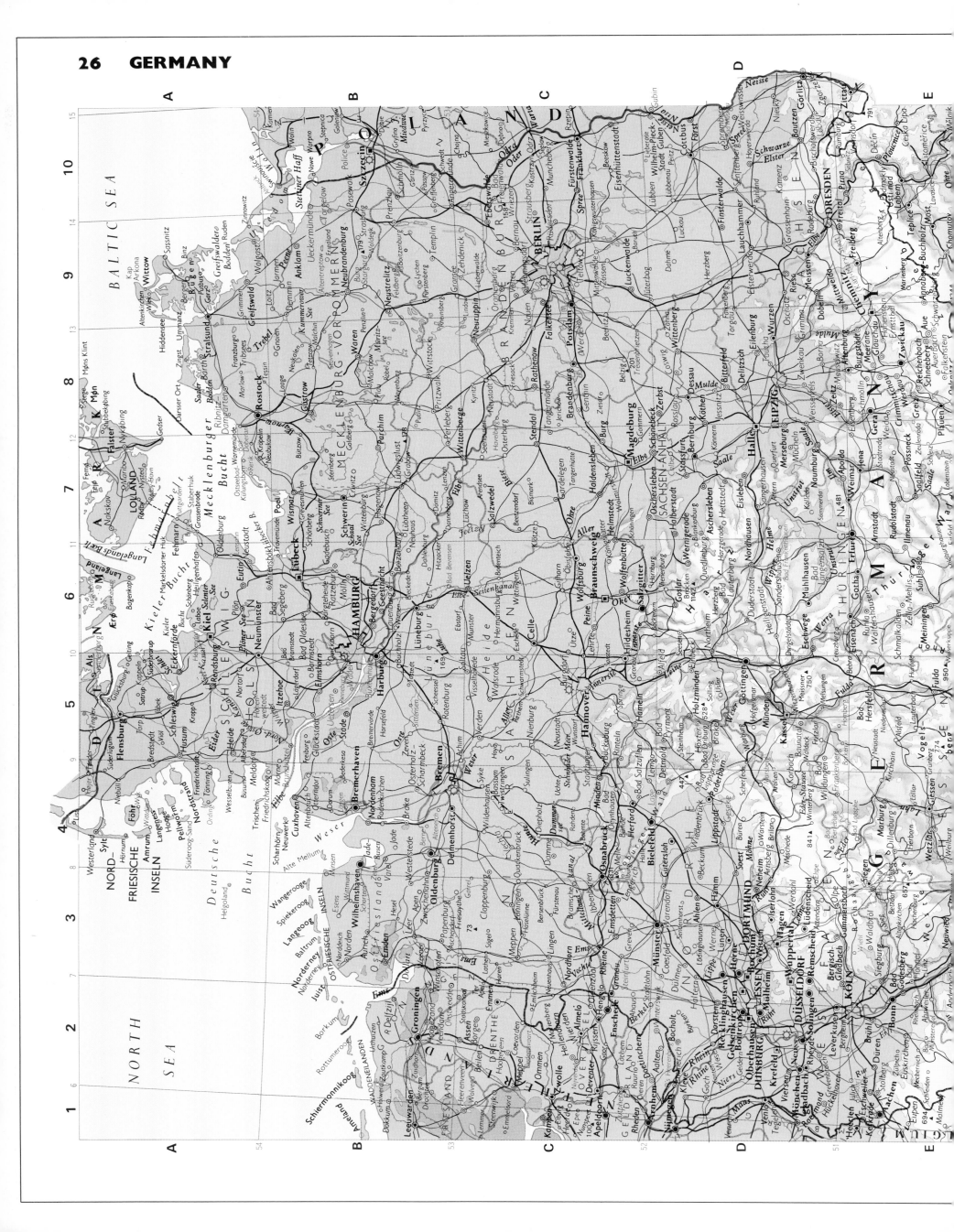

1 : 2 000 000

10   0   10   20   30   40   50 miles
10   0   10   20   30   40   50   60   70   80 km

East from Greenwich

Projection: Conical with two standard parallels.

ft   m
12000 4000
9000   3000
6000   2000
4500   1500
3000   1000
1200   400
600   200
0   0

1 2 3 4 5 6

FRANCE

HAUTE-SAÔNE

Vesoul

Belfort

BESANÇON

DOUBS

JURA

Pontarlier

MULHOUSE

HAUT-RHIN

BELFORT

BASEL (BASLE)

BASEL LANDSCHAFT

AARGAU

Olten

Solothurn

SOLOTHURN

Biel (Bienne)

La Chaux-de-Fonds

Le Locle

NEUCHÂTEL

Neuchâtel

BERN (BERNE)

Burgdorf

LUZERN

OBWALDEN

Lac de Neuchâtel

Fribourg (Freibourg)

FRIBOURG

Lausanne

VAUD

Yverdon

Morges

Vevey

Montreux

Léman (L. Geneva)

Thonon-les-Bains

Nyon

GENÈVE (GENEVA)

Annemasse

HAUTE-SAVOIE

Annecy

Lac d'Annecy

Albertville

SAVOIE

Thun

Thunersee

Brienzersee

Interlaken

Gstaad

Adelboden

BERNER OBERLAND

Frutigen

Grindelwald

Sierre

Sion

VALAIS

Martigny

Chamonix-Mont-Blanc

Mt. Blanc 4807

Monte Rosa

Matterhorn (Mte Cervino) 4478

Zermatt

VALLE D'AOSTA

Aosta

Simplon tunnel

Brig

PIEMONTE

ft m
9000 3000
6000 2000
4500 1500
3000 1000
1200 500
600 200

Projection: Conical with two standard parallels

1 2 3 4 5

Projection: Conical with two standard parallels

1 : 2 000 000

10 0 10 20 30 40 50 miles
10 0 10 20 30 40 50 60 70 80 km

POLAND

SLOVAK REP

HUNGARY

CROATIA

YUGOSLAVIA

Wrocław (Breslau)
Opole
Częstochowa
Katowice
Gliwice
Zabrze
Ruda Śląska
Chorzów
Kraków
Ostrava
Olomouc
Brno
Bielsko-Biała
Nowy Sącz
Przemyśl
Rzeszów
Krosno
WIEN (VIENNA)
Bratislava
Nitra
Trenčín
Žilina
Košice
Uzhgorod
Mukachevo
BUDAPEST
Győr
Miskolc
Debrecen
Nyíregyháza
Szolnok
Kecskemét
Szeged
Pécs
Nagykanizsa
Timişoara
Arad
Oradea

East from Greenwich

COPYRIGHT GEORGE PHILIP & SON. LTD

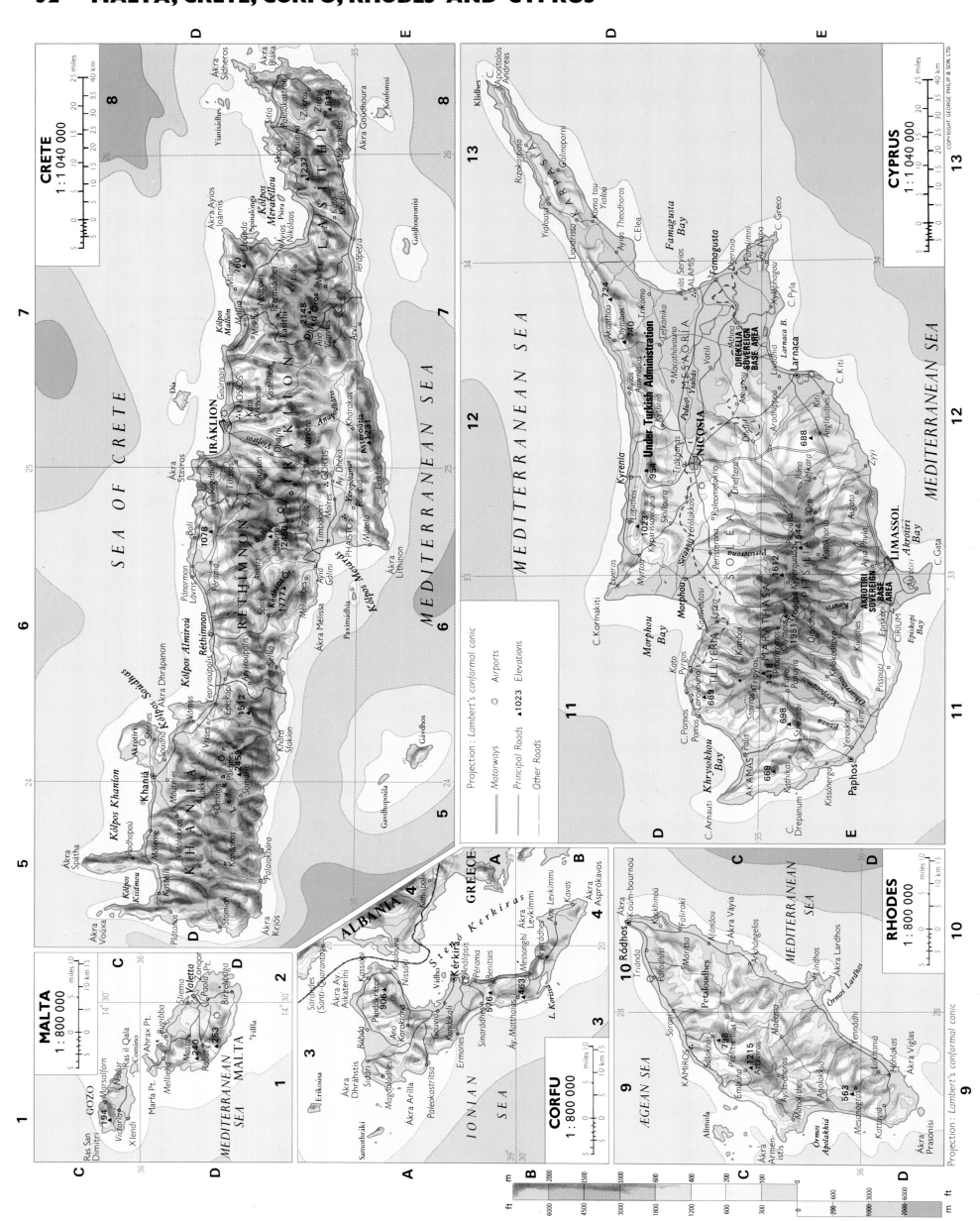

CRETE
1:1 040 000

MALTA
1:800 000

CORFU
1:800 000

RHODES
1:800 000

CYPRUS
1:1 040 000

Projection: Lambert's conformal conic

Motorways
Principal Roads
Other Roads
Airports
▲1023 Elevations

COPYRIGHT GEORGE PHILIP & SON LTD.

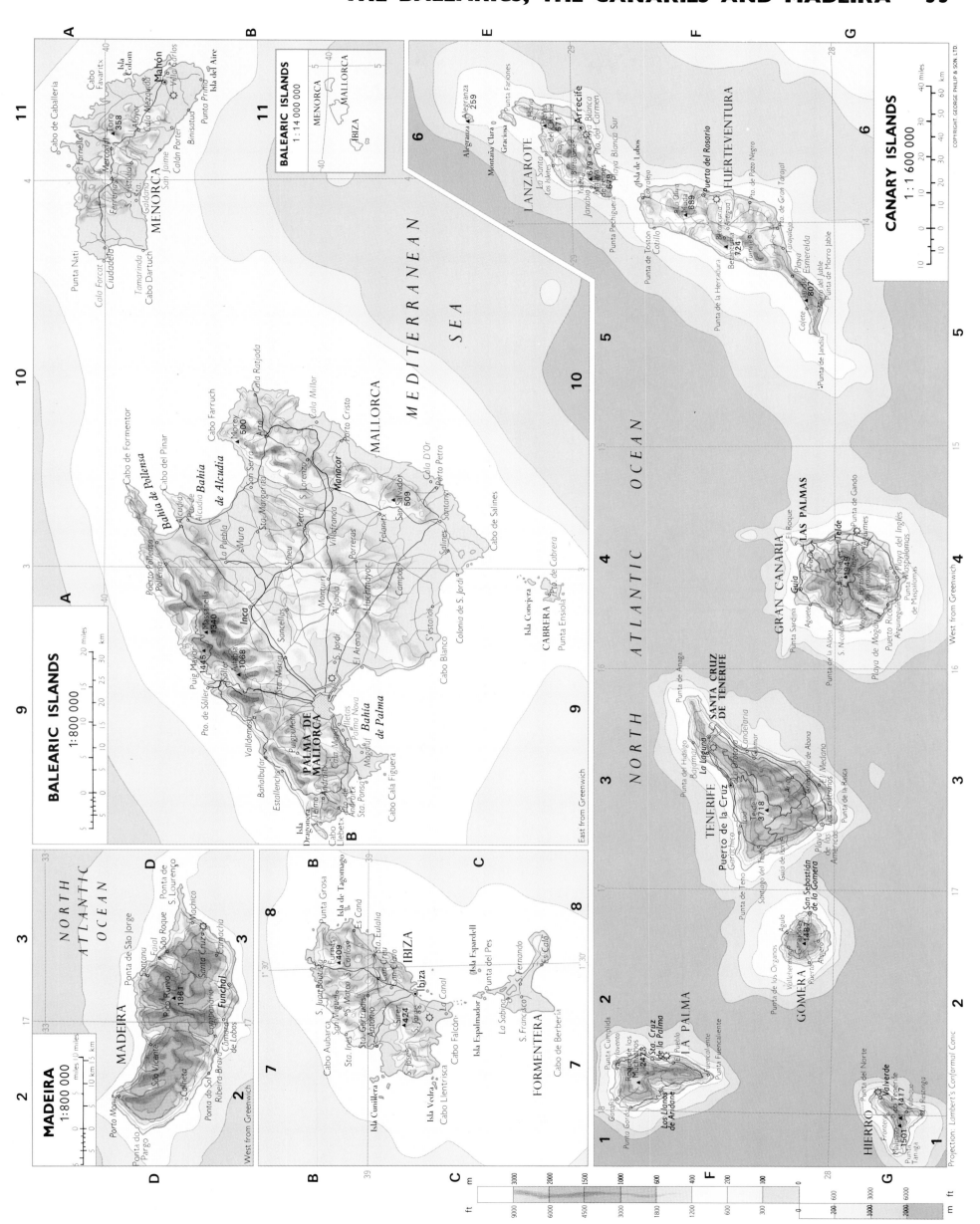

BALEARIC ISLANDS
1:800 000

BALEARIC ISLANDS
1:14 000 000

MENORCA

MALLORCA

IBIZA

MADEIRA
1:800 000

CANARY ISLANDS
1:1 600 000

COPYRIGHT GEORGE PHILIP & SON LTD

Projection Lambert's Conformal Conic

B A Y   O F   B I S C A Y

Golfe de Gascogne

F R A N C E

PYRÉNÉES

ANDORRA

ROUSSILLON

PAÍS VASCO

NAVARRA

A R A G Ó N

C A T A L U Ñ A

BARCELONA

Badalona
Sta. Colona de Gramanet
Hospitalet de Llobregat
Villafranca del Panadés
Villanueva y Geltrú

Tarragona
Reus
Tortosa

San Sebastián
Bilbao
Baracaldo
Santander
CANTABRIA

Pamplona
Logroño
Vitoria
Burgos

Zaragoza (Saragossa)
Huesca
Lérida

VALENCIA
Castellón de la Plana

MADRID
Segovia
Guadalajara
Aranjuez
Getafe

LA MANCHA

Montes Universales
Sierra de Albarracín

Golfo de San Jorge
Golfo de Valencia

ISLAS BALEARES

Menorca (Minorca)
Ciudadela
Mercadal
Mahón
C. Dartuch
Isla del Aire

Mallorca (Majorca)
Palma
Sóller
Manacor

Toulouse
Montauban
Carcassonne
Narbonne
Béziers
Castres
Perpignan
Gerona
Figueras

Tarbes
Lourdes
Bayonne
Biarritz
Pau

Costa Brava
Costa Dorada

1 : 2 000 000

10   0   10   20   30   40   50 miles
10   0   10   20   30   40   50   60   70   80 km

Projection: Conical with two standard parallels

M E D I T E R R A N E A N   S E A

B A L E A R I C   I S.

Cabo de Salines
Campos 509
Cabrera
Bahía de Palma
Lluchmayor
Isla Conejera
San Miguel
San Juan Bautista
Punta Grosa
Ibiza (Iviza)
Sta. Eulalia
Ibiza
Isla Espardell
Formentera 192
I. Espalmador
San Francisco
San Antonio
Isla del Vedra 475
Cabo Berbería
Punta de Cala Codolar

2850

A L G E R I A

ALGER (Algiers)
Boufarik
Blida
Koléa
Medéa
Berrouaghia
Cherchel
El Arba
Bou Ismael
Miliana
Khemis Miliana
Ech Cheliff
Ténès
Gouraya
1985
Tiaret
Hamadia
Ksar el Boukhari
Gueit es Stel
Ksar Chellala
Chabounia
Tissemsilt
Zemmora
Aïn Tédelès
Mostaganem
Mohammadia
Sig
ORAN
Arzew
Mascara
Ighil Izane
Sidi Ali
Sidi-Bel-Abbès
Aïn Témouchent
Misserghin
C. Caxine
C. Falcon
Misseghin
Beni Saf
Ghazzaouet
Nedroma
Berkane
Melilla (Sp.)
Nador
C. Tres Forcas
C. del Agua
Alborán (Sp.)
Punta del Sabinal

M O R O C C O

East from Greenwich
West from Greenwich

VALENCIA
Valencia
Albufera de Valencia
Sueca
Cullera
Alcira
Játiva
Tabernes de Valldigna
Cabo de San Antonio
Denia
Jávea
Cabo de la Nao
Gandía
Oliva
Pego
Benidorm
Villajoyosa
Alcoy
Alicante
Elche
Santa Pola
Isla de Tabarca
Villena
Elda
Petrel
Novelda
Aspe
Crevillente
Catral
Orihuela
Murcia
Cartagena
Cabo de Palos
Mar Menor
San Pedro del Pinatar
Torrevieja
Guardamar del Segura
Cartagena
Golfo de Mazarrón
Cabo Tiñoso
Mazarrón
Puerto Mazarrón
Cope
Aguilas
Lorca
Totana
Alhama de Murcia
Sierra Espuña 1584
Almería
Golfo de Almería
Sierra de Gádor
Sierra Nevada 3478
Granada
Guadix
Baza
Sierra de los Filabres 2043
Vélez Rubio
Vélez Blanco
Huércal Overa
Cabo de Gata
Adra
Motril
Las Alpujarras
Mulhacén 3478
Sierra de Segura
Sierra de Alcaraz
Albacete
Hellín
Almansa
Yecla
Jumilla
Cieza
Mula
Caravaca
Moratalla

Sierra Morena
Guadalquivir
Úbeda
Baeza
Linares
Albacete
Daimiel
Manzanares
Valdepeñas
Alcázar de San Juan
Tomelloso
Sierra Martés
Cabriel
Júcar

BAY OF BISCAY

ATLANTIC OCEAN

San Sebastián
Bilbao
Baracaldo
Santander
Gijón
Oviedo
Mieres
La Coruña (Corunna)
El Ferrol
Santiago de Compostela
Pontevedra
Vigo
Lugo
Orense
Vitoria
BURGOS
Logroño
Palencia
Valladolid
León
Zamora
Salamanca
Segovia
Avila
MADRID
Alcalá de Henares
Aranjuez
Toledo
Guadalajara
Porto (Oporto)
Vila Nova de Gaia
Matosinhos
Aveiro
Coimbra
Braga
Guimarães
Vila Real
Bragança

PAIS VASCO
LA RIOJA
CANTABRIA
ASTURIAS
LEÓN
CASTILLA
PALENCIA
BURGOS
VALLADOLID
SALAMANCA
GREDOS
GUADARRAMA
GALICIA
LUGO
ORENSE
PORTO
VISEU
GUARDA
BRAGANÇA
VILA REAL
CASTELO BRANCO

Picos de Europa
Sierra de la Demanda
Sierra de Gredos
Sierra de Guadarrama
Sierra de la Estrela
Sierra de la Culebra
Sierra de Gata

Duero
Ebro
Douro
Tajo
Pisuerga
Tormes
Mondego
Miño

2926
5000

1 : 2 000 000

10 0 10 20 30 40 50 miles

10 0 10 20 30 40 50 60 70 80 km

MEDITERRANEAN SEA

MOROCCO

Golfo de Cádiz

Golfo de Almería

Strait of Gibraltar

West from Greenwich

LISBOA (LISBON)

Sevilla (Seville)

Córdoba

Granada

Málaga

Cádiz

Huelva

Badajoz

Mérida

Jaén

Linares

Ciudad Real

Valdepeñas

Manzanares

Alcázar de San Juan

Daimiel

Antequera

Marbella

Gibraltar (Br.)

Algeciras

Ceuta (Sp.)

Tánger (Tangier)

Tétouan

Melilla (Sp.)

Alborán (Sp.)

Sierra Nevada

Sierra de Segura

Sierra de Alcaraz

Montes de Toledo

Évora

Setúbal

Faro

Sierra Morena

Projection: Conical with two standard parallels

COPYRIGHT GEORGE PHILIP & SON LTD

ft   m
9000 3000
6000 2000
4500 1500
3000 1000
        400
        200
          0

m   ft
2000 6000
600
200
0

SWITZERLAND

VORARLBERG

ST. GALLEN

LIECHTENSTEIN

GRAUBÜNDEN

FRANCHE-COMTÉ

BOURGOGNE

SAÔNE-ET-LOIRE

VAUD

FRIBOURG

VALAIS

TICINO

Bern

Lausanne

Genève

Lac Léman

Neuchâtel

Luzern

Zürich

Zug

Schwyz

Glarus

Vaduz

Interlaken

Lyon (Lyons)

Grenoble

Vienne

Chambéry

Annecy

Lac d'Annecy

Lac du Bourget

Aix-les-Bains

Valence

Gap

VAL D'AOSTA

PIEMONTE

LOMBARDIA

Lago Maggiore

Lago di Como

Lago d'Orta

Lago d'Iseo

Garda

TORINO (Turin)

Milano (Milan)

Novara

Vercelli

Biella

Varese

Como

Lecco

Bergamo

Bréscia

Monza

Pavia

Cremona

Piacenza

Mántova

Alessándria

Asti

Cúneo

Pinerolo

Tortona

Voghera

Parma

Réggio

Módena

EMILIA

Savona

GÉNOVA (Genoa)

Golfo di Génova

La Spézia

Carrara

Massa

LIGURIA

Imperia (Maurizio-Oneglia)

San Remo

Ventimiglia

Monte-Carlo

MONACO

Nice

Antibes

Cannes

Fréjus

St-Raphaël

Grasse

Draguignan

Ste-Maxime

St-Tropez

MARSEILLE (Marseilles)

Toulon

Hyères

ILES D'HYÈRES

Aix-en-Provence

Avignon

Arles

Salon

PROVENCE

BOUCHES-DU-RHÔNE

ALPES MARITIMES

ALPES-DE-HAUTE-PROVENCE

HAUTES-ALPES

DAUPHINÉ

Côte d'Azur

Var

LIGURIAN SEA

Livorno (Leghorn)

Pisa

Lucca

Péscia

Pistóia

Viaréggio

TOSCANA

Cécina

Piombino

Elba

Bastia

L'Ile Rousse

Calvi

Ajaccio

CORSE (CORSICA)

HAUTE-CORSE

CORSE-DU-SUD

Arcipelago Toscano

Montecristo

Giglio

Pianosa

Capraia

Gorgona

ft / m elevation scale: 12 000 / 4000, 9000 / 3000, 6000 / 2000, 4500 / 1500, 3000 / 1000, 1200 / 400, 600 / 200, 0 / 0, 600 / 200, 2000 / 6000

Projection: Conical with two standard parallels

East from Greenwich

1 : 2 000 000

10 0 10 20 30 40 50 miles
10 0 10 20 30 40 50 60 70 80 km

8   9   10   11   12   13   14

AUSTRIA

Innsbruck

Graz

HUNGARY

SOMOGY

Klagenfurt

Villach

Maribor

Bolzano

Merano

SLOVENIA

Ljubljana

Trieste

Zagreb

CROATIA

Udine

Gorízia

Pordenone

Monfalcone

Vittório Véneto

Belluno

Treviso

Vicenza

Pádova

Venézia (Venice)

Golfo di Venézia

Chióggia

Rovigo

Ferrara

Bologna

Ravenna

Banja Luka

BOSNIA-HERZEGOVINA

Bihać

Zadar

A D R I A T I C   S E A

Dugi Otok

Rímini

SAN MARINO

Pésaro

Fano

Firenze

Arezzo

Ancona

Perúgia

UMBRIA

MARCHE

Split

Brač

Hvar

Korčula

Mljet

Lastovo

Vis

Šibenik

Trogir

Drniš

Knin

Ascoli Piceno

Téramo

Pescara

Chieti

ABRUZZI

L'Aquila

Terni

Viterbo

Orvieto

Spoleto

Vasto

Térmoli

Vieste

Monte Sant'Angelo

MOLISE

ROMA (ROME)

Vatican City

Tívoli

Civitavécchia

COPYRIGHT GEORGE PHILIP & SON LTD.

8   9   10   11   12   13

CORSE / CORSICA

Iles Sanguinaires
G. d'Ajaccio
C. di Muro
Tarayo
Petreto
Incudine
Zonza
2136
Favone
Solenzara
CORSE-DU-SUD
G. de Valinco
Sartène
Levie
Propriano
Porto-Vecchio
Iles Cerbicales
Bonifacio
I. de Cavallo
Bouches de Bonifacio
Maddalena
Santa Teresa Gallura
La Maddalena
Caprera
Costa Smeralda

SARDEGNA / SARDINIA

Asinara
Punta dello Scorno
Golfo dell' Asinara
Porto Tórres
C. dell'Argentiera
Sássari
Ittiri
Fertília
Alghero
Villanova Monteleone
Temo
Bosa
Macomer
Coghinas
Aggius
Témpio Pausania
Sorso
Sennori
Ósilo
Oschiri
Ózieri
Pattada
Bonórva
1259
Tirso
Buddusò
Bitti
Orune
Núoro
Dorgali
G. di Ólbia
Golfo Aranci
Pto. Cervo
Arzachena
Ólbia
Tavolara
Posada
Siniscola
C. Comino
Golfo di Orosei
Oliena
Macomer
L. del Tirso
Fordni
Sorgono
Monti del Gennargentu
1834
Bauneí
C. di Monte Santo
C. Mannu
Ghilarza
Oristano
Sórgono
M. Arci
812
Láconi
Arbatax
Lanusei
Golfo di Oristano
Arborea
Terralba
Nurri
Ierzu
Gúspini
Arbus
Gonnosfanadiga
Sanluri
Villacidro
S. Vito
 Filaputzu
Muravera
S. Gavino
Monreale
Senorbi
C. Pécora
Fluminimaggiore
1236
M. Línas
Iglésias
Cíxerri
Gonnesa
Serramanna
Assémini
Sestu
Dolianova
Símaxis
1069
Quartu Sant'Elena
C. Ferrato
Portoscuso
Carloforte
Carbónia
1116
Síliqua
Seláreus
Cágliari
Serpentara
San Pietro
Sant'Antíoco
Santadi
Porto Botte
Pula
Golfo di Cágliari
C. Carbonara
Sant' Antíoco
Teulada
C. Spartivento

TYRRHENIAN SEA

3719
3589
Ustica

ROMA (Rome) area

Vatican City
Fregene
Lido di Óstia (Lido di Roma)
Prática di Mare
Ánzio
Nettuno
Tívoli
Subiaco
Frascati
Velletri
Albano
Aprília
Cisterna
Latina
Monte Círceo
541
Zannone
Palmarola
Ísole Ponziane
Ponza
283
Ventotene
Palestrina
Frosinone
Alatri
Véroli
Ceccano
Priverno
Sonnino
Pontínia
Sabáudia
Terracina
Gaeta
Fondi
Minturno
Fórmia
1633
Conca del Fúcino
2283
Sora
Isola del Liri
Arpino
Monte S. Giovanni
Cassino
Gargliano
Golfo di Gaeta
Mondragone
Volturno
Casal di Principe
Giugliano
Ísch ia (Naples)
788
Póz...
Procida

SICILIA / SICILY

C. San Vito
Castellammare del Golfo
Favorotta
Levanzo
Trápani
Érice
1110
PALERMO
Bagheria
Ísole Égadi
Maréttimo
Favignana
Paceco
Alcamo
Partinico
Montelepre
Monreale
Términi Imerese
Marsala
Castelvetrano
Salemi
Calatafimi
Gibellina
Partanna
Campobello di Mazara
Sambuca di Sicília
Mazara del Vallo
Menfi
Sciacca
Ribera
Cattólica Eraclea
Siculiana
Porto Empédocle
Agrigento
Favara
Camporeale
Corleone
Prizzi
1613
Bisacquino
Lercara
Marineo
Belsito
Belice
Caltabellotta
Búrgio
Platani
Racalmuto
Rafadali
Canicatti
Naro
Mussomeli
Caltanissetta
San Cataldo
Castelterminí
Licata
Campobello di Licata

TUNISIA

Iles de la Galite
El Kala
Tabarka
C. Serrat
Bizerte (Binzert)
C. Blanc
Cani
Menzel-Bourguiba
Plane
Mateur
ALGÉRIE
Bou Salem
Béja
Téboursouk
Medjerda
TUNIS
Halq el Oued
Zembra
Golfe de Tunis
C. Bon
Kelibia
Menzel-Temime
Soliman
Nabeul
Hammamet
Zaghouan

Sicilian Channel / MEDITERRANEAN

Pantelleria
836
Pantelleria (It.)
1319
Malta
MEDITE...

Scale:
ft / m
9000 / 3000
6000 / 2000
4500 / 1500
3000 / 1000
1200 / 400
600 / 200
0 / 0
37
m / ft
200 / 600
2000 / 6000
4000 / 12.000

1 : 2 000 000

10   0   10   20   30   40   50 miles
10 0 10 20 30 40 50 60 70 80 km

7 **8** **9** **10** **11** **12**

A D R I A T I C

S E A

I O N I A N

S E A

M E D I T E R R A N E A N   S E A

Channel

Golfo di Táranto

Golfo di Squillace

Golfo di Sant'Eufémia

G. di Salerno

G. di Policastro

G. di Gióia

Strait of Otranto

Str. di Messina

A L B A N I A

ABRUZZI

MOLISE

CAMPANIA

BASILICATA

CALABRIA

SICILIA

PUGLIA

Isole Eólie o Lípari (Æolian Is.)

Major towns and features:
NÁPOLI, Salerno, Benevento, Avellino, Caserta, Foggia, Lucera, Cerignola, Barletta, Trani, Andria, Corato, Bari, Molfetta, Bitonto, Bisceglie, Terlizzi, Ruvo, Canosa, Cengola, Minervino, Murge 686, Gravina, Altamura, Matera, Potenza, Marsico Nuovo, Táranto, Manduria, Brindisi, Mesagne, Francavilla Fontana, Lecce, Galatina, Nardò, Gallipoli, Galatone, Casarano, Otranto, C. Santa Maria di Leuca, Gagliano del Capo, Tricase, Ugento, Presicce

Cosenza, Catanzaro, Crotone, Crati, Neto, Sila, Monte Pollino 2271, Castrovillari, Rossano, Corigliano, Acri, Paola, Amantea, Nicastro, Pizzo, Vibo Valéntia, Palmi, Gióia Táuro, Bagnara, Villa S. Gio, Réggio, Messina, Milazzo, Barcellona, Taormina, Randazzo, Bronte, Etna 3340, Giarre, Riposto, Acireale, Paternò, Catánia, Golfo di Catánia, Lentini, Augusta, Siracusa, Avola, Noto, Pachino, C. Passero, Ragusa, Módica, Scicli, Vittória, Cómiso, Niscemi, Gela, Golfo di Gela, Caltagirone

Monte Sant'Ángelo, G. di Manfredónia, Manfredónia, Vieste, Testa del Gargano, L. di Lésina, S. Severo, Monti Nébrodi, Monti Iblei

TIRANA (Tiranë), Durrësi (Durazzo), Vlora (Valona), Berati, Shkumbini

Kérkira (Corfu), Othonoí

COPYRIGHT. GEORGE PHILIP & SON. LTD

East from Greenwich

1 : 2 000 000

ROMANIA

BULGARIA

TURKEY

GREECE

MOLDAVIA

UKRAINE

BLACK SEA

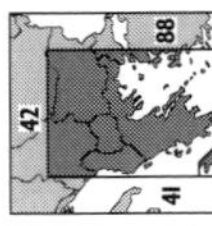

YUGOSLAVIA
MACEDONIA
ALBANIA
MONTENEGRO
Skopje
Tirana
Sofiya
Thessaloníki
Plovdiv
Thásos
Límnos
Samothráki
Thermaïkós Kólpos
Ioánnina
Kérkira
Lárisa
Vólos
Kateríni
Véroia
Kozáni
Kavála
Sérrai
Komotiní
Xánthi
Dráma
Edirne
Çanakkale
Vlora (Valona)
Durrësi (Durazzo)
Shkodra
Elbasani
Berati
Korça
Bitola
Prilep
Ohrid
Priština
Prizren
Niš
Leskovac
Pernik
Kyustendil
Blagoevgrad
Stara Zagora
Sliven
Yambol
Pleven
Lovech
Vratsa
Mikhaylovgrad
Kardzhali
Khaskovo
Smolyan

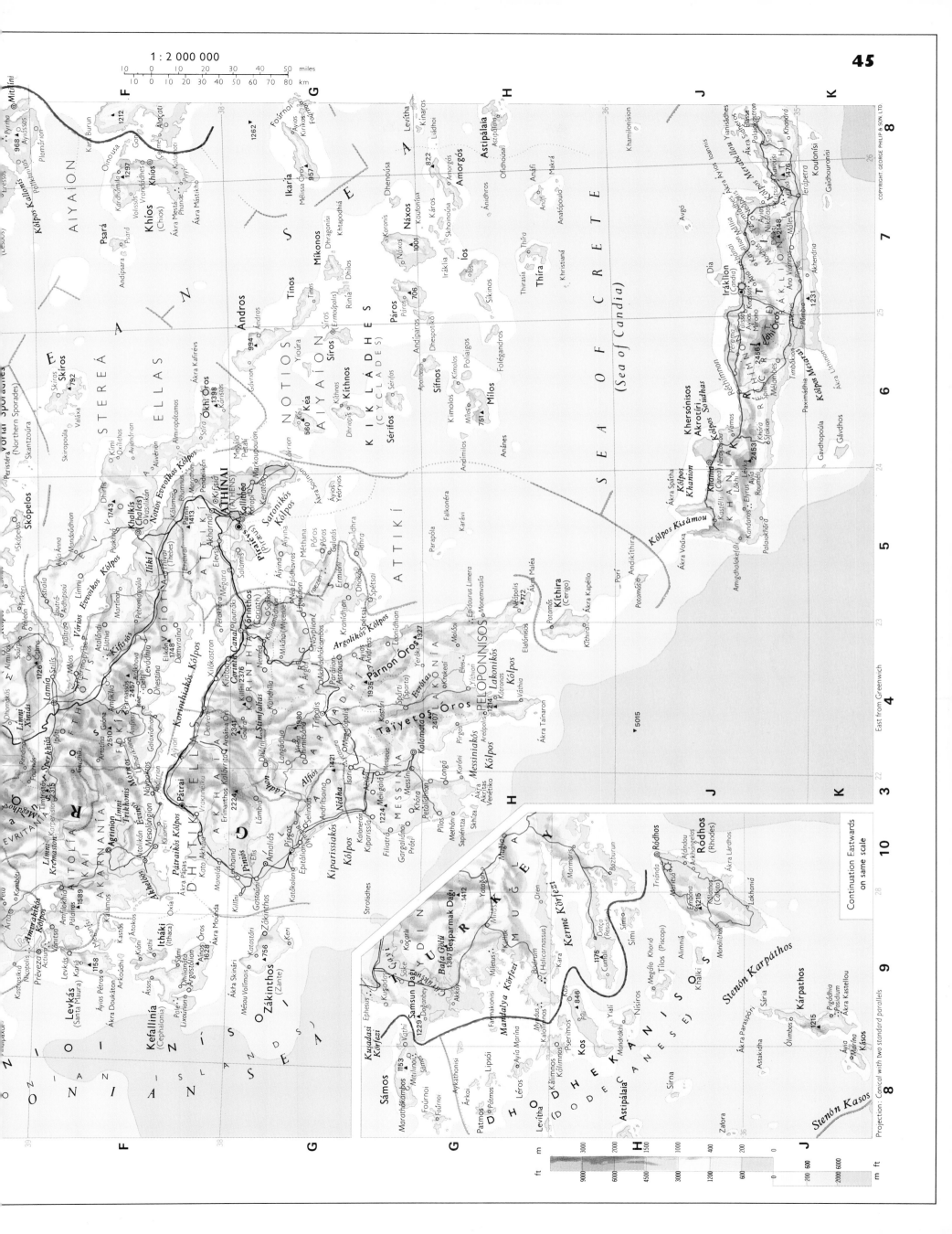

1 : 2 000 000

EXTENSION WESTWARDS
At the same scale as main map

ROMANIA

HUNGARY

YUGOSLAVIA

BULGARIA

UKRAINE

MOLDAVIA

BLACK SEA

TRANSILVANIA

MOLDOVA

MUNTENIA

OLTENIA

DOBROGEA

BUCUREȘTI
Constanța
Galați
Brăila
Timișoara
Arad
Oradea
Craiova
Sibiu
Brașov
Ploiești
Pitești
Iași
Suceava
Botoșani
Bacău
Focșani
Bârlad
Giurgiu
Ruse

Projection: Conical with two standard parallels

COPYRIGHT GEORGE PHILIP & SON, LTD.

East from Greenwich

ft m
6000
4500
3000
2000
1500
1000
600
400
200
0

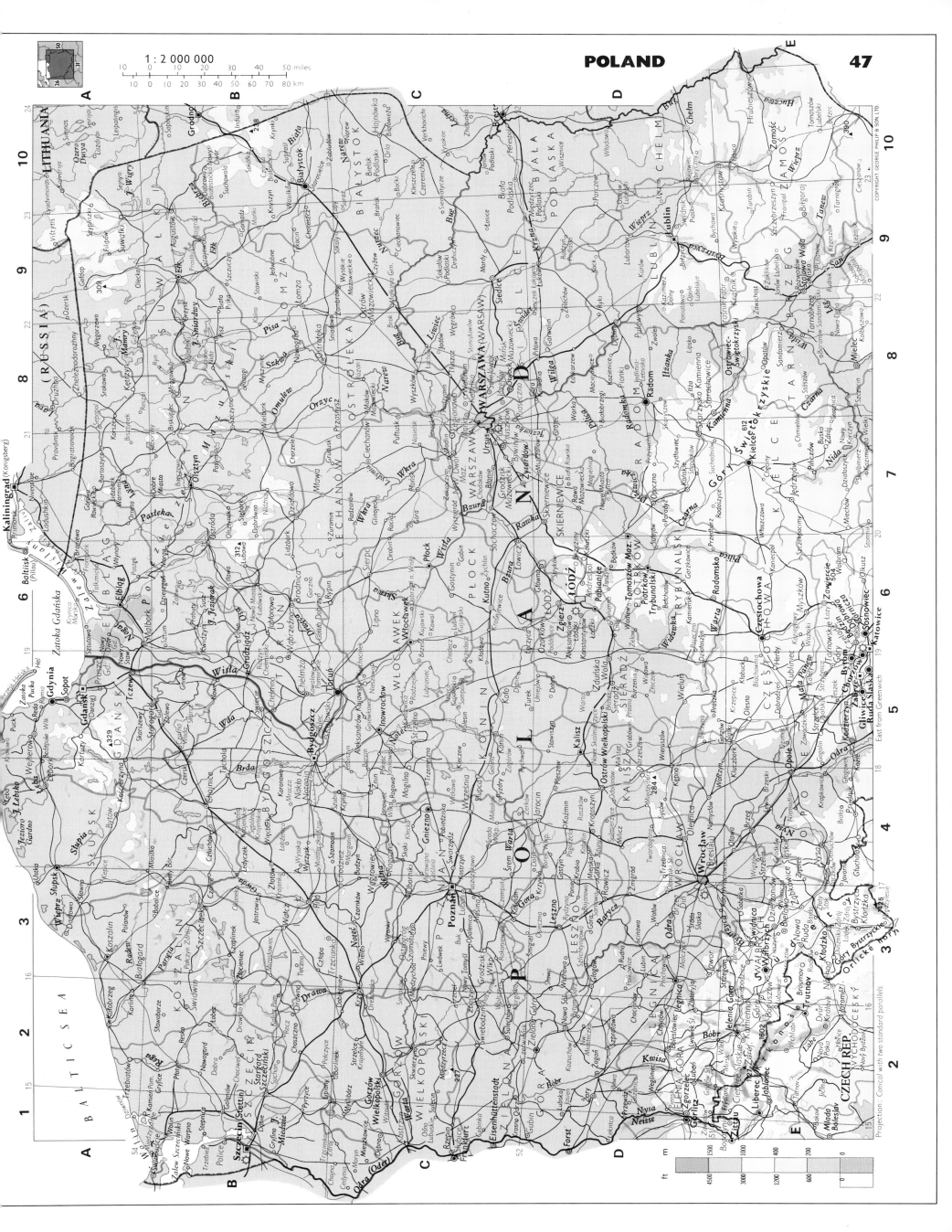

1 : 2 000 000

Projection: Conical with two standard parallels

East from Greenwich

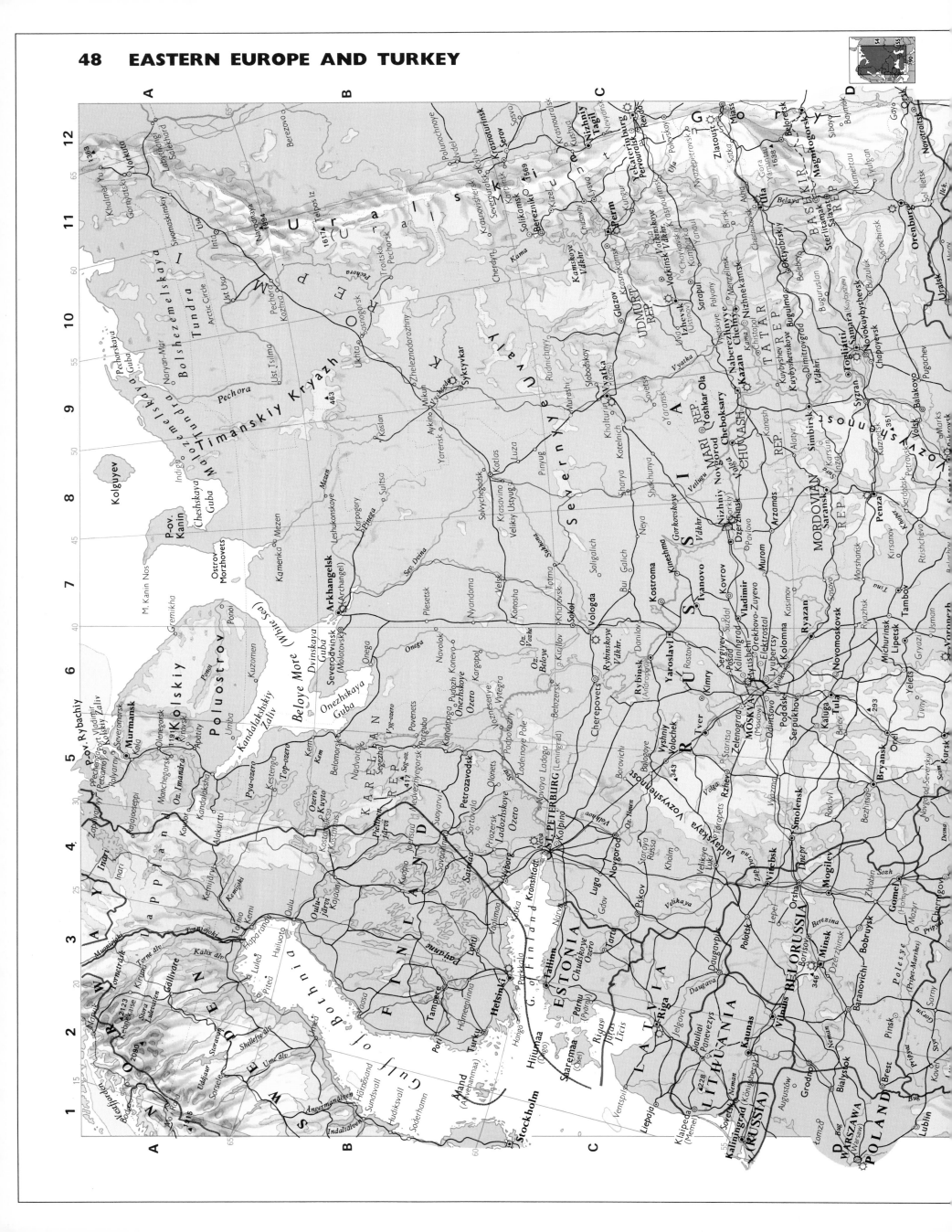

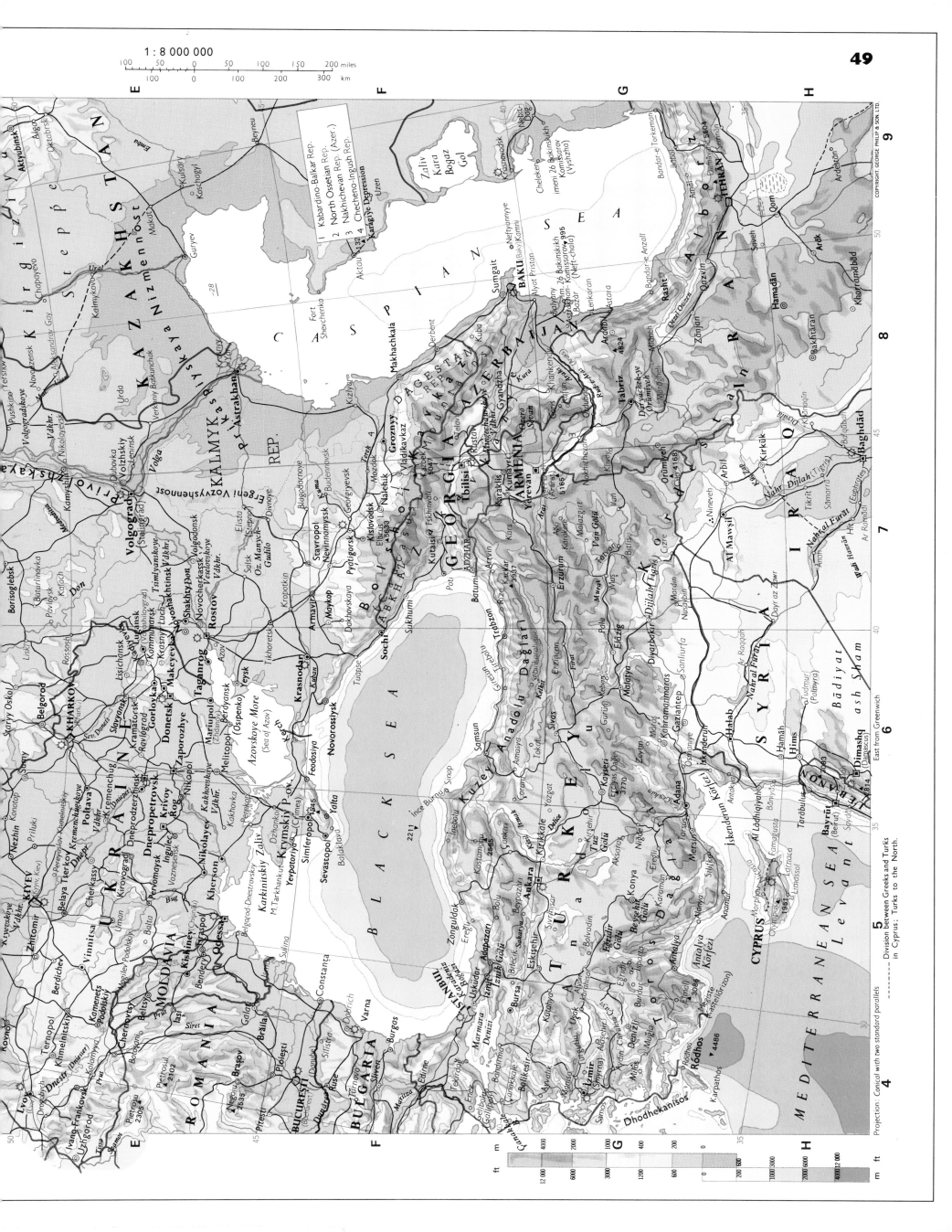

1 : 8 000 000

100   0   50   100   150   200 miles
100   0   100   200   300   km

1 Kabardino-Balkar Rep.
2 North Ossetian Rep. (Azer.)
3 Nakhichevan Rep.
4 Checheno-Ingush Rep.
Karagiye Depression

Projection: Conical with two standard parallels
------- Division between Greeks and Turks
in Cyprus; Turks to the North.

East from Greenwich

ft
12 000
6000
3000
1200
600
400
200
0
m

m
4000
2000
1000
600
400
200
0
ft

400 12 000
2000 6000
1000 3000
600
400
200
0

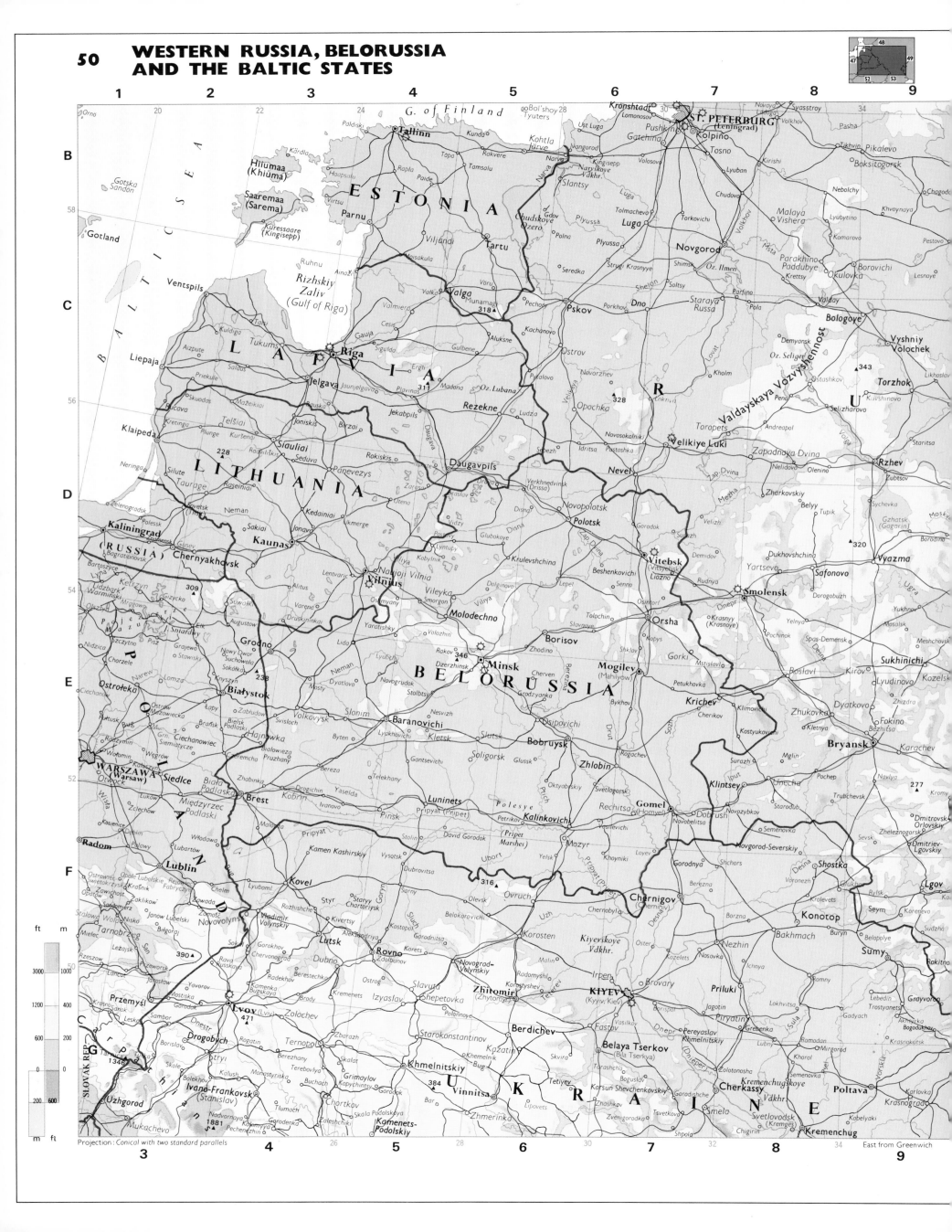

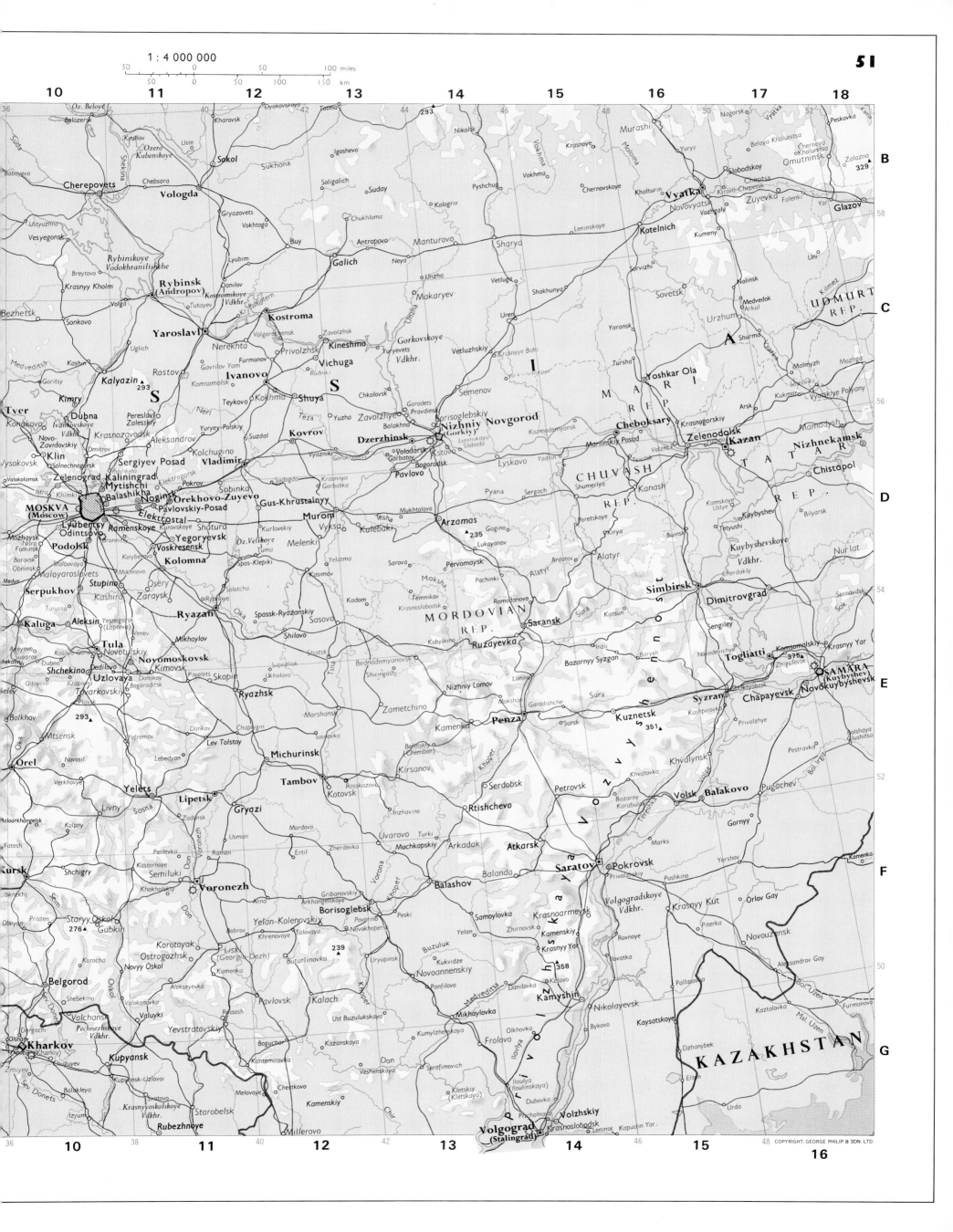

A B C D E F G

1 2 3 4 5 6 7

UKRAINE

MOLDAVIA

ROMANIA

BULGARIA

BLACK SEA

AZOVSKOYE MORE
(Sea of Azov)

Rovno · Aleksandriya · Korosten · Nezhin · Bakhmach · Sumy · Belgorod · Starry Oskol
Lvov · Dubno · Zolbunov · Zhitomir (Zhytomyr) · KIYEV (Kyyiv, Kiev) · Brovary · Priluki · Romny · Kharkov (Kharkiv) · Kupyansk
Ternopol · Berdichev · Fastov · Belaya Tserkov (Bila Tserkva) · Poltava · Krasnograd
Ivano-Frankovsk (Stanislav) · Vinnitsa · Cherkassy · Kremenchug · Rubezhnoye
Chernovtsy · Khmelnitskiy · Kirovograd · Kremenchugskoye Vdkhr. · Slavyansk · Kramatorsk
Iasi · Kishinev (Chişinău) · Uman · Novomirgorod · Dneprodzerzhinsk · Dnepropetrovsk · Artemovsk · Gorlovka · Yenakiyevo
Bacău · Bendery · Tiraspol · Nikolayev (Mykolayiv) · Krivoy Rog (Kryvyy Rih) · Zaporozhye · Krasnoarmeisk · Makeyevka · Donetsk (Stalino)
Galaţi · Odessa · Kherson · Nikopol · Melitopol · Mariupol (Zhdanov) · Berdyansk · Yeysk
Buzău · Braila · Ismail · Dzhankoi · Krymskiy P.-ov. (Crimea) · Kerch · Slavyansk-na-Kubani
Ploieşti · BUCUREŞTI (Bucharest) · Yevpatoriya · Simferopol · Feodosiya · Novorossiysk
Ruse (Ruşcuk) · Constanţa · Sevastopol · Yalta · Gelendzhik

Varna · Burgas · Karkinitskiy Zaliv

İstanbul · Üsküdar · İzmit · Adapazari · Bolu · Zonguldak · Ereğli · Karabük · Kastamonu · Samsun · Terme · Ordu · Giresun
Bursa · Balikesir · Ankara · Çorum · Amasya · Turhal · Tokat

MARMARA DENİZİ (Sea of Marmara)

Projection: Conical with two standard parallels

ft m
12,000 4000
9000 3000
6000 2000
4500 1500
3000 1000
1200 400
600 200
0 0
600 200
6000 2000
m ft

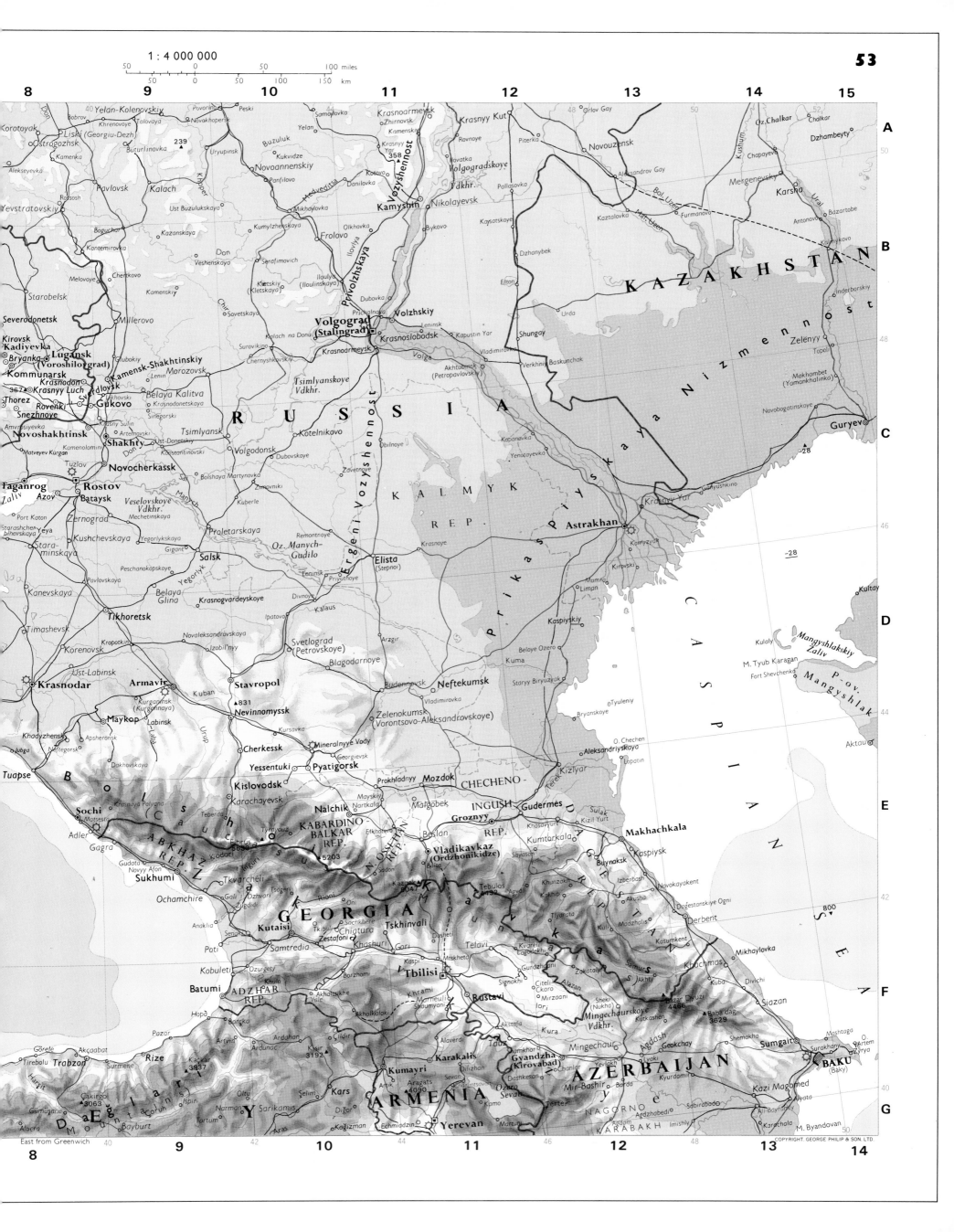

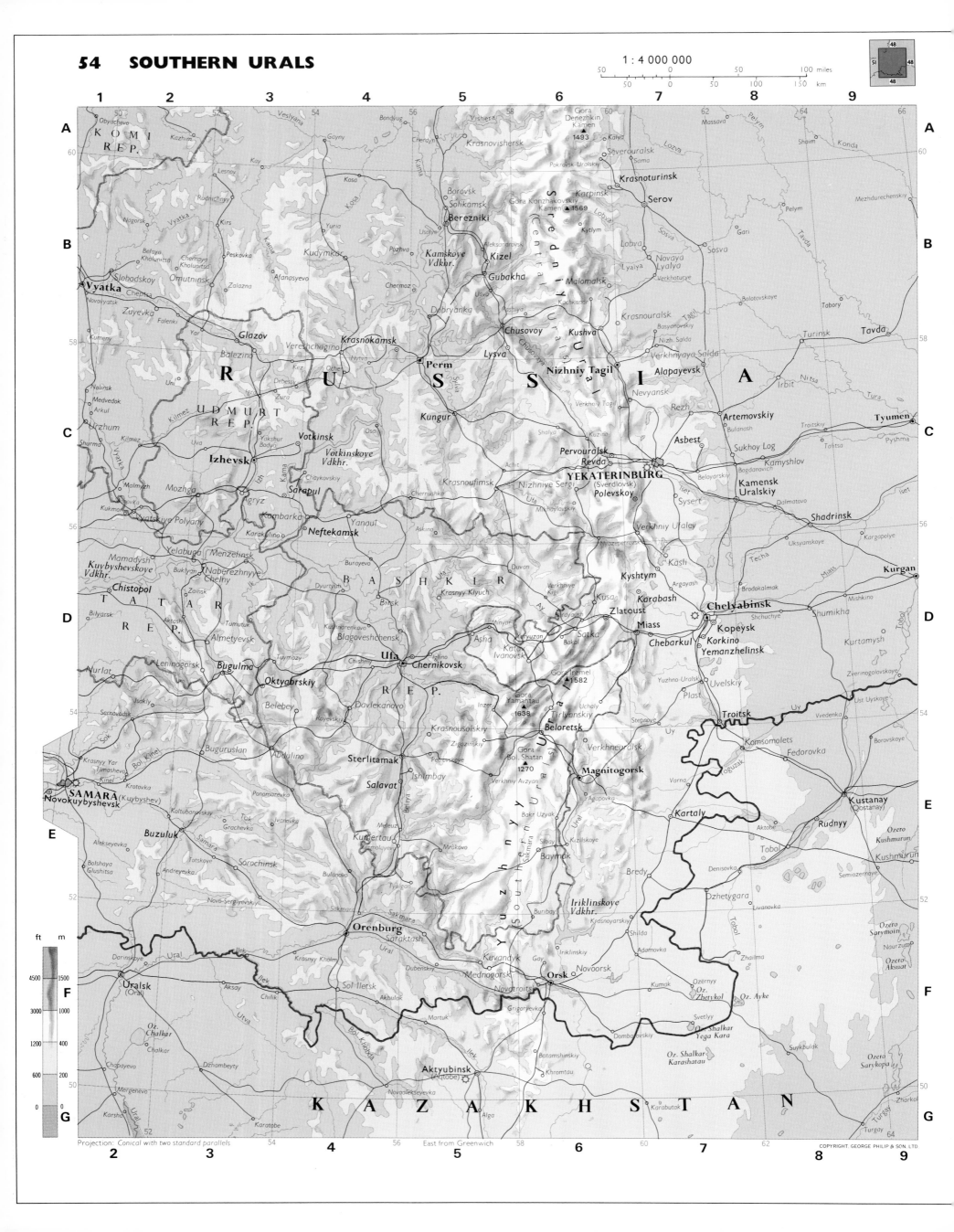

1 : 4 000 000

50   0   50   100 miles
50   0   50   100   150 km

A K O M I
   R E P.

Vyatka

R   U   S   S   I   A

UDMURT
REP.

Izhevsk

T A T A R
   R E P.

Chistopol

SAMARA
(Kuybyshev)
Novokuybyshevsk

Buzuluk

B A S H K I R

Ufa
Chernikovsk

REP.

Sterlitamak

Salavat

Orenburg

Uralsk
(Oral)

Perm

Nizhniy Tagil

YEKATERINBURG
(Sverdlovsk)

Chelyabinsk

Magnitogorsk

Orsk

Aktyubinsk
(Aqtöbe)

K   A   Z   A   K   H   S   T   A   N

Kurgan

Tyumen

Kustanay
(Qostanay)

ft   m

4500   1500

3000   1000

1200   400

600   200

0

Projection: Conical with two standard parallels

East from Greenwich

COPYRIGHT. GEORGE PHILIP & SON. LTD

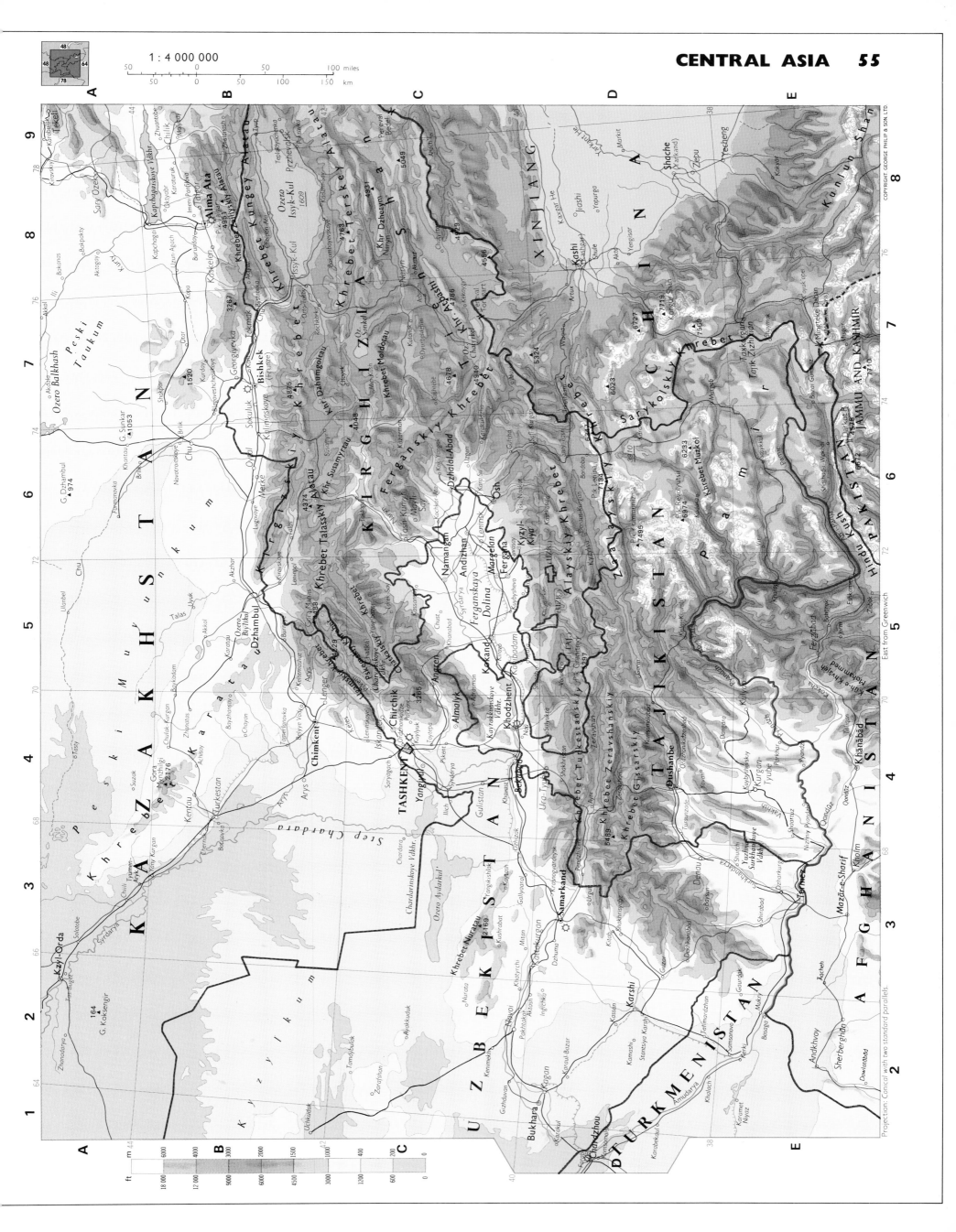

1 : 4 000 000

Projection: Conical with two standard parallels.

East from Greenwich

K A Z A K H S T A N

U Z B E K I S T A N

T U R K M E N I S T A N

K I R G H I Z I A

T A J I K I S T A N

X I N J I A N G

C H I N A

A F G H A N I S T A N

PAKISTAN

JAMMU AND KASHMIR

Ozero Balkhash

Peski Taukum

Ozero Issyk-Kul

TASHKENT

Bishkek (Frunze)

Alma Ata

Samarkand

Dushanbe

Bukhara

Kunlun Shan

Ferganskaya Dolina

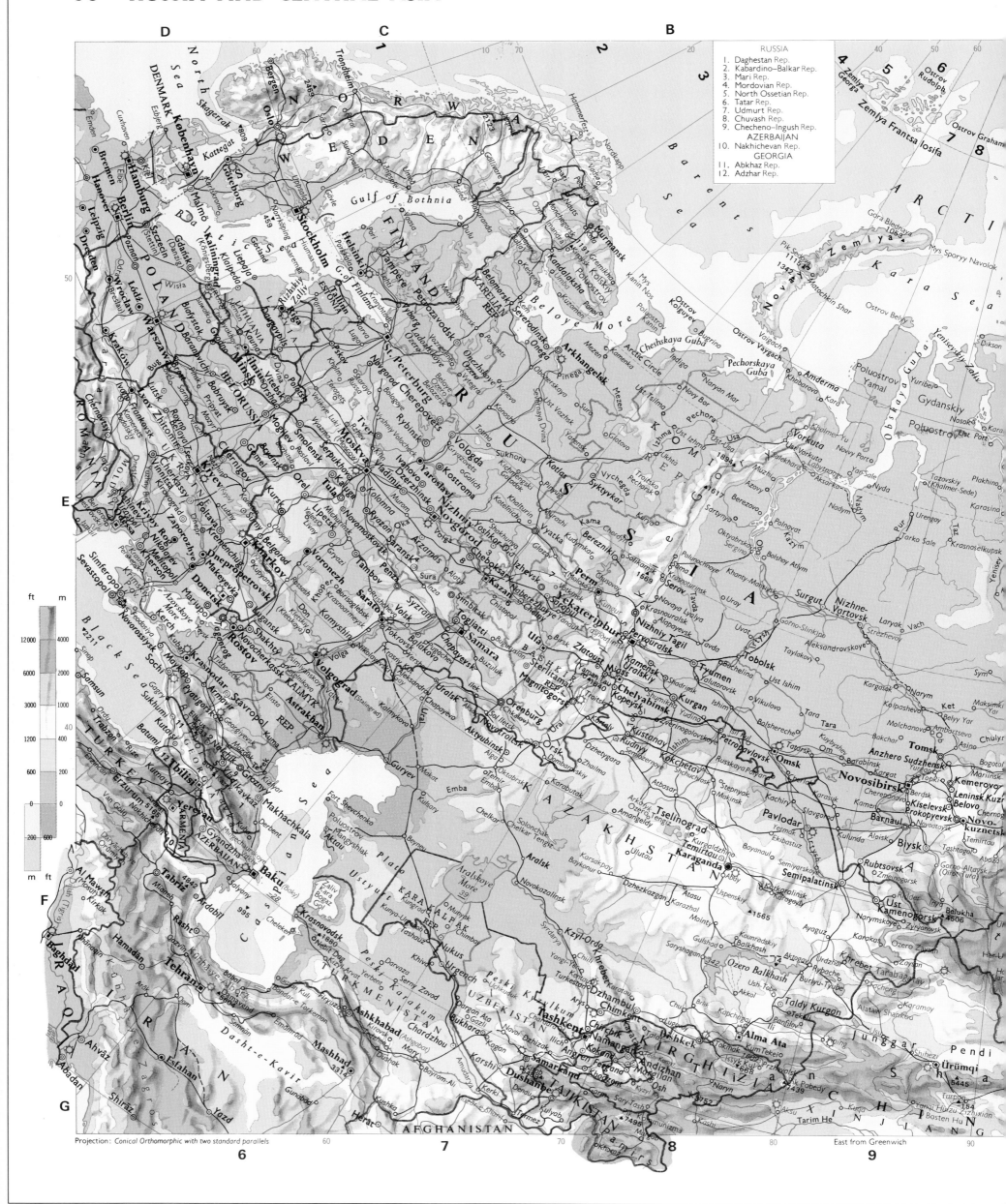

Projection: Conical Orthomorphic with two standard parallels

East from Greenwich

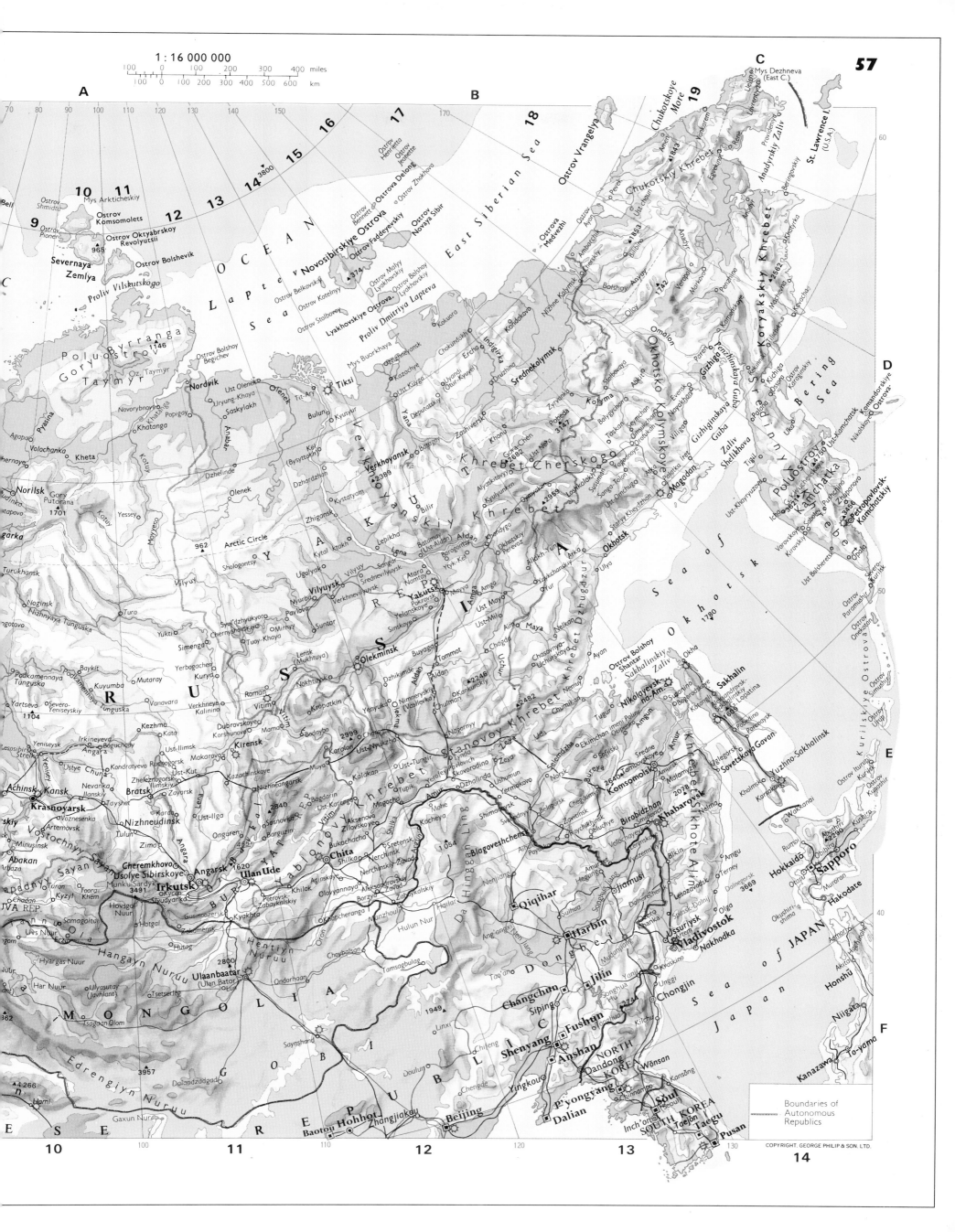

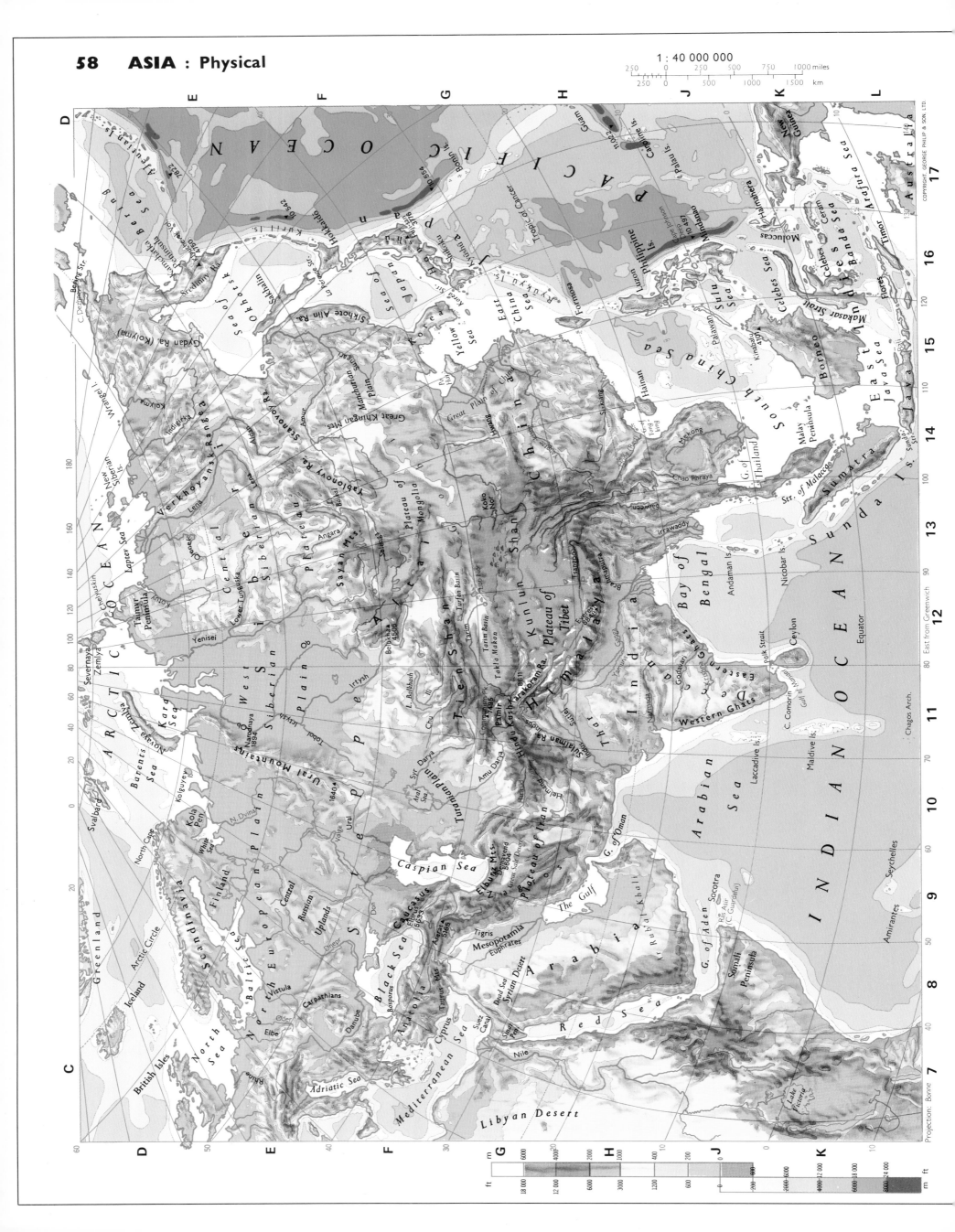

1 : 40 000 000

Projection: Bonne

1 : 40 000 000

250   0   250   500   750   1000 miles

250   0   500   1000   1500   km

D   E   F   G   H   J   K   L

17   16   15   14   13   12   11   10   9   8   7

PACIFIC OCEAN

ARCTIC OCEAN

INDIAN OCEAN

East from Greenwich

Projection: Bonne

R U S S I A

C H I N A

MONGOLIA

INDIA

KAZAKHSTAN

SAUDI ARABIA

IRAN

PAKISTAN

AFGHANISTAN

TURKEY

AUSTRALIA

E U R O P E

A F R I C A

Bering Sea
Sea of Okhotsk
Aleutian Is.
Kuril Is.
Sakhalin
Hokkaido
Honshu
Kyushu
Shikoku
East C. (C. Dezhnev)
Wrangel I.
New Siberian Is.
Severnaya Zemlya
Novaya Zemlya
Svalbard
Kara Sea
Barents Sea
White Sea
North Sea
Baltic Sea
Black Sea
Caspian Sea
Mediterranean Sea
Red Sea
Arabian Sea
Bay of Bengal
Yellow Sea
East China Sea
South China Sea
Sea of Japan
Philippine Sea
Java Sea
Celebes Sea
Banda Sea
Ceram Sea
Sulu Sea
Flores Sea
Andaman Is. (India)
Nicobar Is. (India)
Lakshadweep Is. (India)
MALDIVES
SRI LANKA
Tropic of Cancer
Equator
Arctic Circle

Cities:
London, Paris, Rome, Berlin, Vienna, Warsaw, Belgrade, Athens, Istanbul, Izmir, Ankara, Odessa, Moscow, St. Petersburg, Murmansk, Arkhangelsk, Yekaterinburg, Chelyabinsk, Omsk, Novosibirsk, Tomsk, Krasnoyarsk, Irkutsk, Yakutsk, Khabarovsk, Vladivostok, Petropavlovsk, Magadan, Magnitogorsk, Orenburg, Rostov, Astrakhan, Volgograd, Tbilisi, Baku, Yerevan, Tehran, Esfahan, Shiraz, Baghdad, Basra, Kuwait, Riyadh, Medina, Mecca, Jedda, Sana, Aden, Damascus, Beirut, Amman, Jerusalem, Nicosia, Cairo, Alexandria, Khartoum, Port Sudan, Addis Ababa, Djibouti, Mogadishu, Nairobi, Mombasa, Dar es Salaam, Kampala

TOKYO, Yokohama, Osaka, Kyoto, Pyongyang, Seoul, Dalian, Tientsin, Peking, Shenyang, Harbin, Tsingtao, Nanking, Shanghai, Wuhan, Sian, Lanchow, Chungking, Kunming, Canton, Hong Kong, Macau, Foochow, Taipei, Ulan Bator, Urumchi, Lhasa, Kathmandu, Thimphu, Dacca, Calcutta, Varanasi, Kanpur, Delhi, Lahore, Islamabad, Kabul, Qandahar, Herat, Mashhad, Zahidan, Karachi, Ahmadabad, Bombay, Hyderabad, Nagpur, Bangalore, Madras, Colombo, Kuala Lumpur, Singapore, Jakarta, Surabaya, Bangkok, Phnom Penh, Ho Chi Minh City, Hanoi, Vientiane, Rangoon, Manila, Mandalay, Medan, Palembang, Banjarmasin

Rivers: Lena, Ob, Yenisei, Amur, Aldan, Irtysh, Syr Darya, Amu Darya, Ural, Volga, Don, Dnieper, Danube, Rhine, Vistula, Tigris, Euphrates, Nile, Indus, Ganges, Brahmaputra, Irrawaddy, Mekong, Hwang Ho, Yangtze, Godavari, Narmada, Tarim

8 Peking   Capital Cities

MALAYSIA, INDONESIA, VIETNAM, THAILAND, CAMBODIA, LAOS, BURMA (MYANMAR), BANGLA., NEPAL, BHUTAN, KASHMIR, BRUNEI, PHILIPPINES, BORNEO, SUMATRA, JAVA, TIMOR, MOLUCCAS, Luzon, Mindanao, Hainan, New Guinea, Irian Jaya, Guam, Caroline Is., Belau, Bonin Is.

UZBEKISTAN, TURKMENISTAN, TAJIKISTAN, KIRGHIZIA, GEORGIA, AZER., ARMENIA, SYRIA, IRAQ, JORDAN, ISRAEL, LEBANON, CYPRUS, KUWAIT, BAHRAIN, QATAR, U.A.E., OMAN, YEMEN, EGYPT, LIBYA, SUDAN, ETHIOPIA, ERITREA, SOMALI REP., KENYA, TANZANIA, UGANDA, RWANDA, BURUNDI, ZAIRE, ZAMBIA, MALAWI, ICELAND, BRITISH ISLES

The Gulf, G. of Oman, G. of Aden, G. of Thailand, Socotra (Yemen), Kuria Muria Is., SEYCHELLES, Amirantes

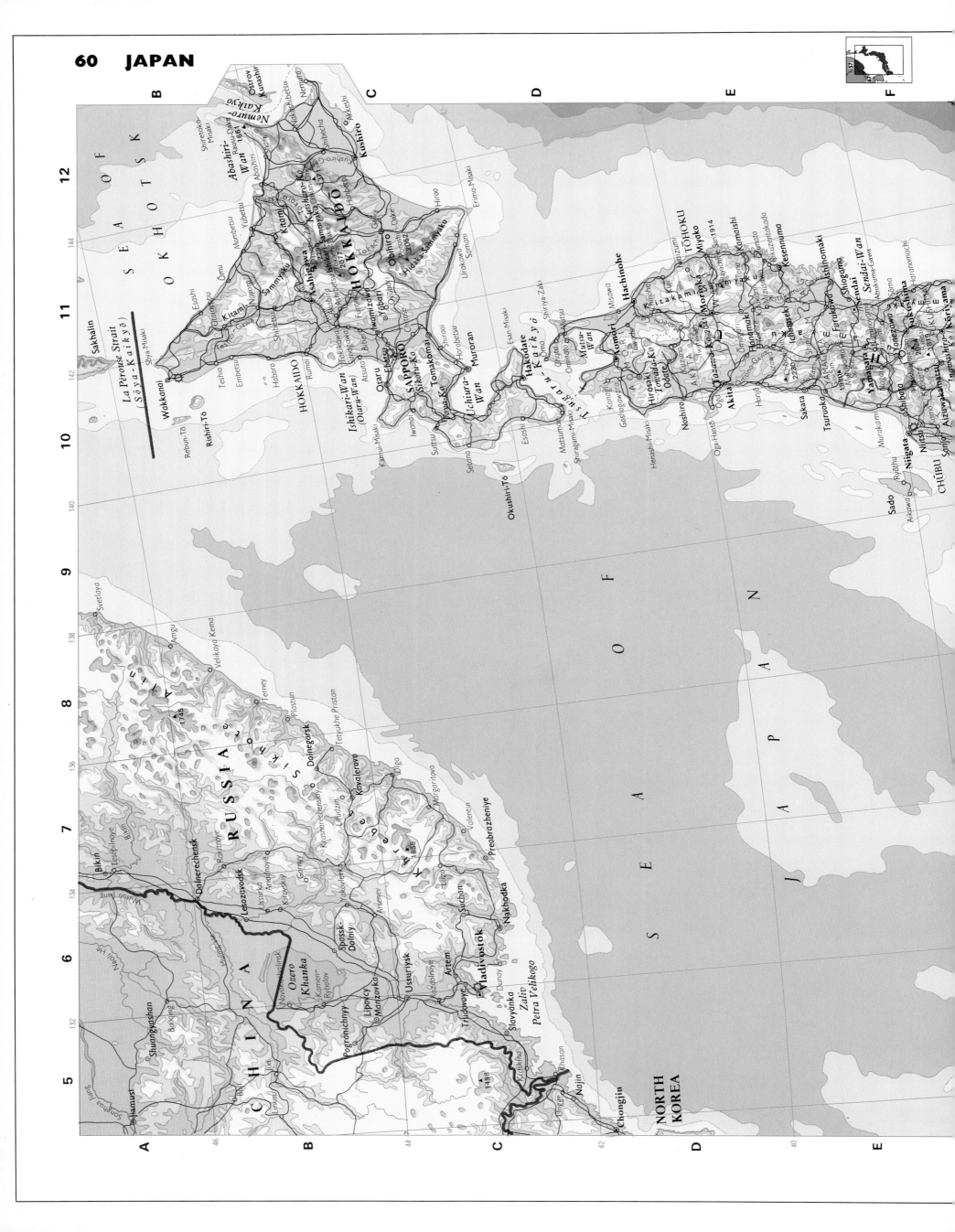

SEA OF OKHOTSK

HOKKAIDO

Sakhalin

La Pérouse Strait
(Sōya-Kaikyō)

Sōya-Misaki

Wakkanai

Rebun-Tō
Rishiri-Tō

Teshio

Embetsu

Hoboro

Ōmu

Esashi

Mombetsu

Yūbetsu

Abashiri
Abashiri-Wan 1661
Rausu-Dake

Shiretoko-Misaki

Ostrov Kunashir

Nemuro-Kaikyō

Nemuro

Nokke-Shibetsu

Akkeshi

Kushiro

Kushiro-Gawa

Shibecha

Hohetsi

Hiroo

Tokachi-Dake 2077
Obihiro

Hidaka-Sammyaku 2052

Erimo-Misaki

Samani

Urakawa

SAPPORO

Asahigawa

Ishikari-Dake 2290
Sammyaku

Kitami-Sammyaku

Kitami

Nayoro

Otoineppu

Rumoi

Teshio-Gawa

Ishikari-Gawa

Iwamizawa

Yūbari

Bibai

Shintotsu

Tomakomai

Shiraoi

Muroran

Horobetsu

Noboribetsu

Uchiura-Wan

Oshamambe

Otaru
Ishikari-Wan
(Otaru-Wan)

Yoichi-Ko

Iwanai

Kamui-Misaki

Suttsu

Setana

Okushiri-Tō

Esashi

Matsumae-Misaki

Shiragami-Misaki

Kikonai
Hakodate

Tsugaru-Kaikyō

Tappi-Saki

Tsugaru-Misaki

Esan-Misaki

Oma

Ohata

Ōminato

Mutsu-Wan

Shiriya-Zaki

Misawa

Towada-Ko

Hachinohe

TŌHOKU

Akita

Oga-Hantō

Oga

Noshiro

Odate

Hirosaki

Aomori

Towada 1614

Kuzumaki

Iwate-San 2041
Morioka

Kitakami-Gawa

Kitakami-Sammyaku

Miyako

Yamada

Kamaishi

Ōfunato

Rikuzentakada

Kesennuma

Ishinomaki

Sendai-Wan

Sendai

Shiogama

Furukawa

Naruko

Yamagata

Zaō-San 1841

Yonezawa

Shinjō

Mogami-Gawa

Sakata

Tsuruoka

Murakami

Niitsu

Niigata

Sado

Ryōtsu

Aikawa

CHŪBU

Shibata

Aizuwakamatsu

Fukushima

Kōriyama

Haranomachi

Abukuma-Gawa

Nikkō

San 1914

Bandai-San 1819

SEA OF JAPAN

RUSSIA

SIKHOTE ALIN'

1745

Svetlaya

Amgu

Velikaya Kema

Terney

Plastun

Tetyukhe Pristan

Dolnegorsk

Kavalerovo

Margaritovo

Olga

Valentin

Preobrazheniye

1855

Lazo

Arsenev

Yakovlevka

Lifudzin

Kirovskiy

Ussuriysk

Artem

Suchan

Nakhodka

Vladivostok

Zaliv Petra Velikogo

Zaliv Velikogo

Dunoy

Slavyanka

Trudovoye

Razdolnoye

Pogranichnyy

Spassk-Dalniy

Lipovcy

Marzovka

Ozero Khanka

Kamen'-Rybolov

Novonikolsk

Lesozavodsk

Dalnerechensk

Spalninoye

Bikin

Malinovka

Rakitnoye

Gornyy

Ariadnoye

CHINA

Khasan

Najin

Chongjin

NORTH KOREA

1498

Tumen-ula

Ungsang

Khasan

Nansin

Songhua Jiang

Jiamusi

Shuangyashan

Boqing

Naoli He

Usuri Jiang

Wusuli Jiang

Sōya-Misaki

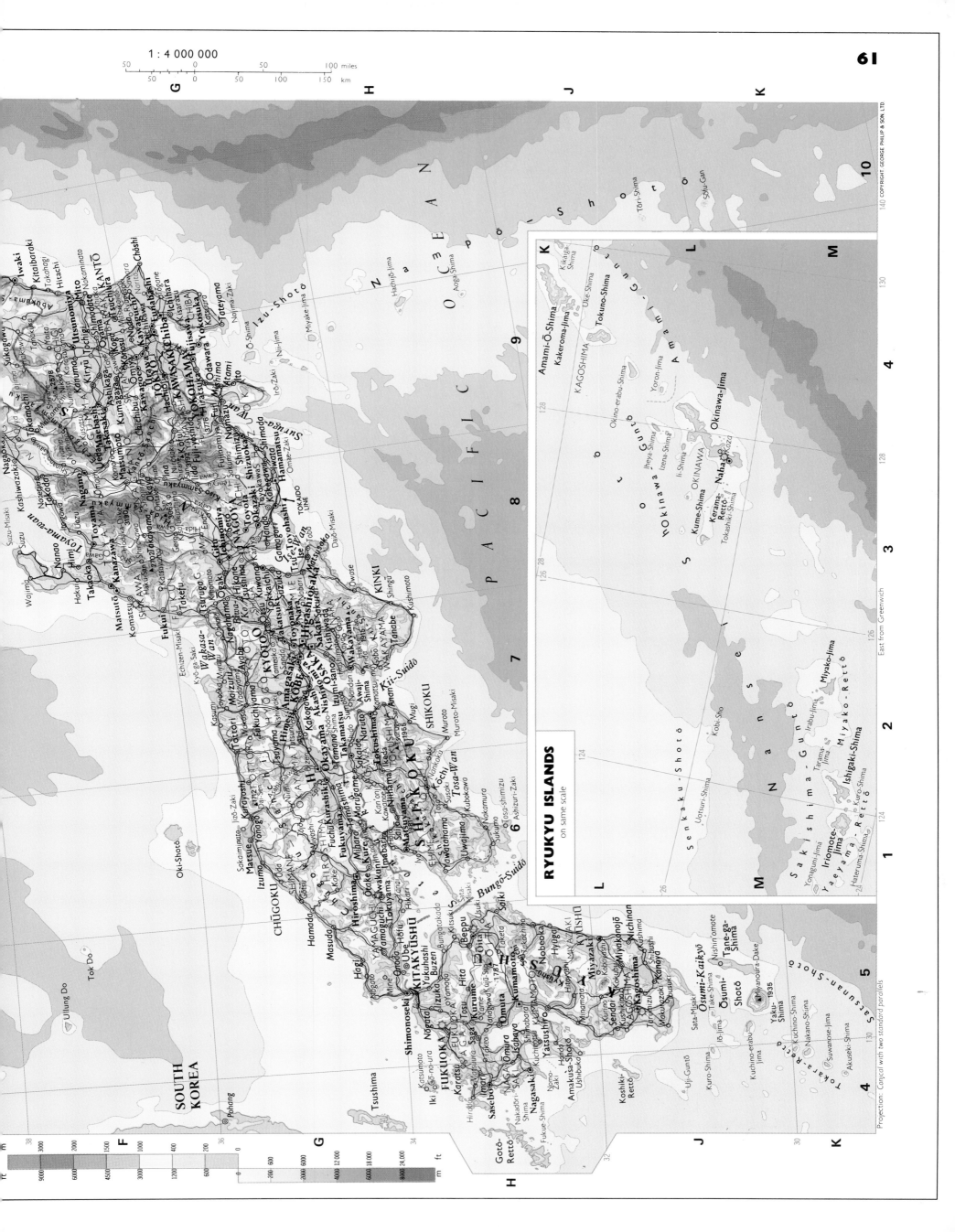

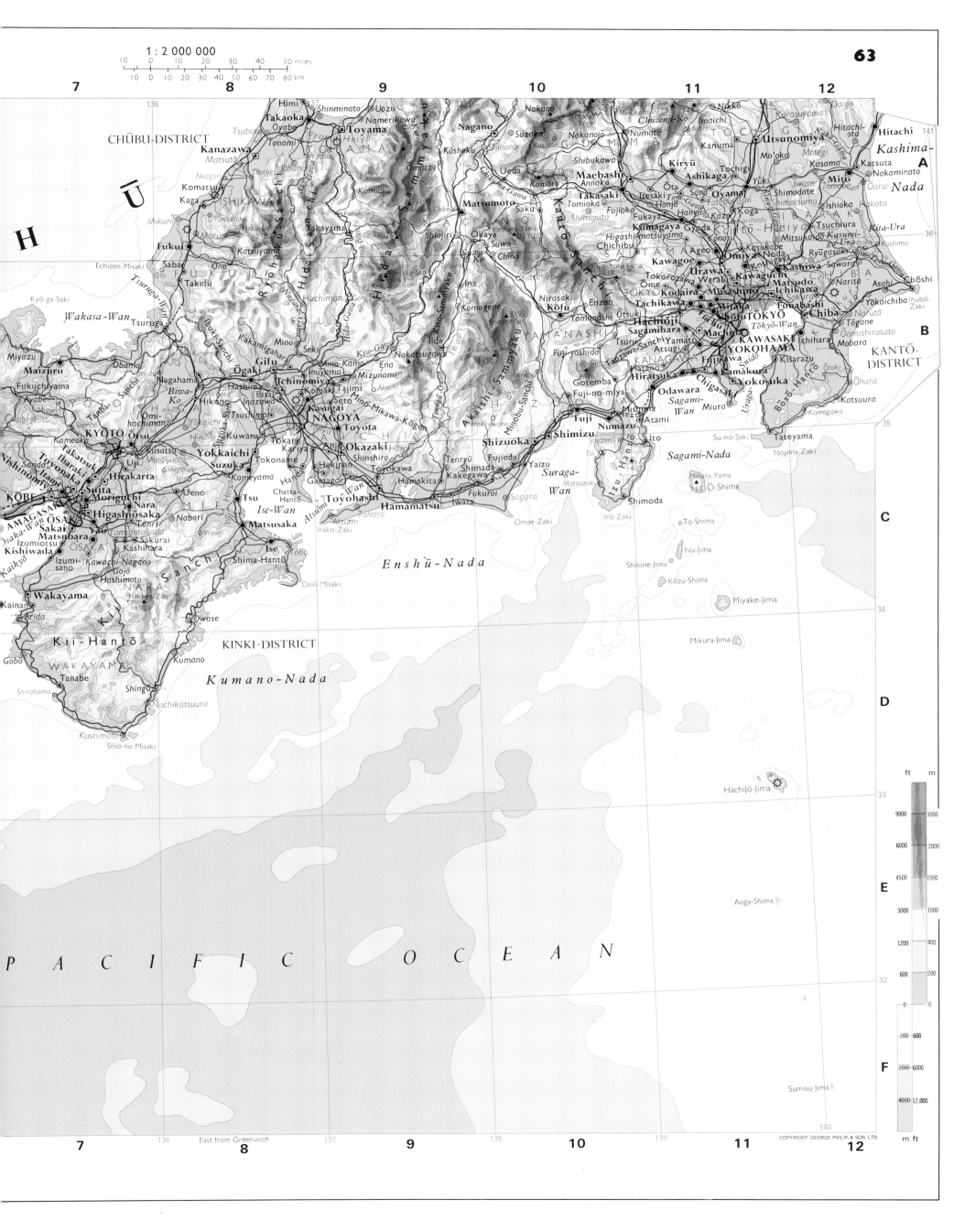

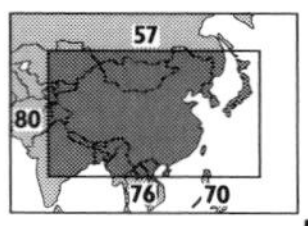

57
80 76 70

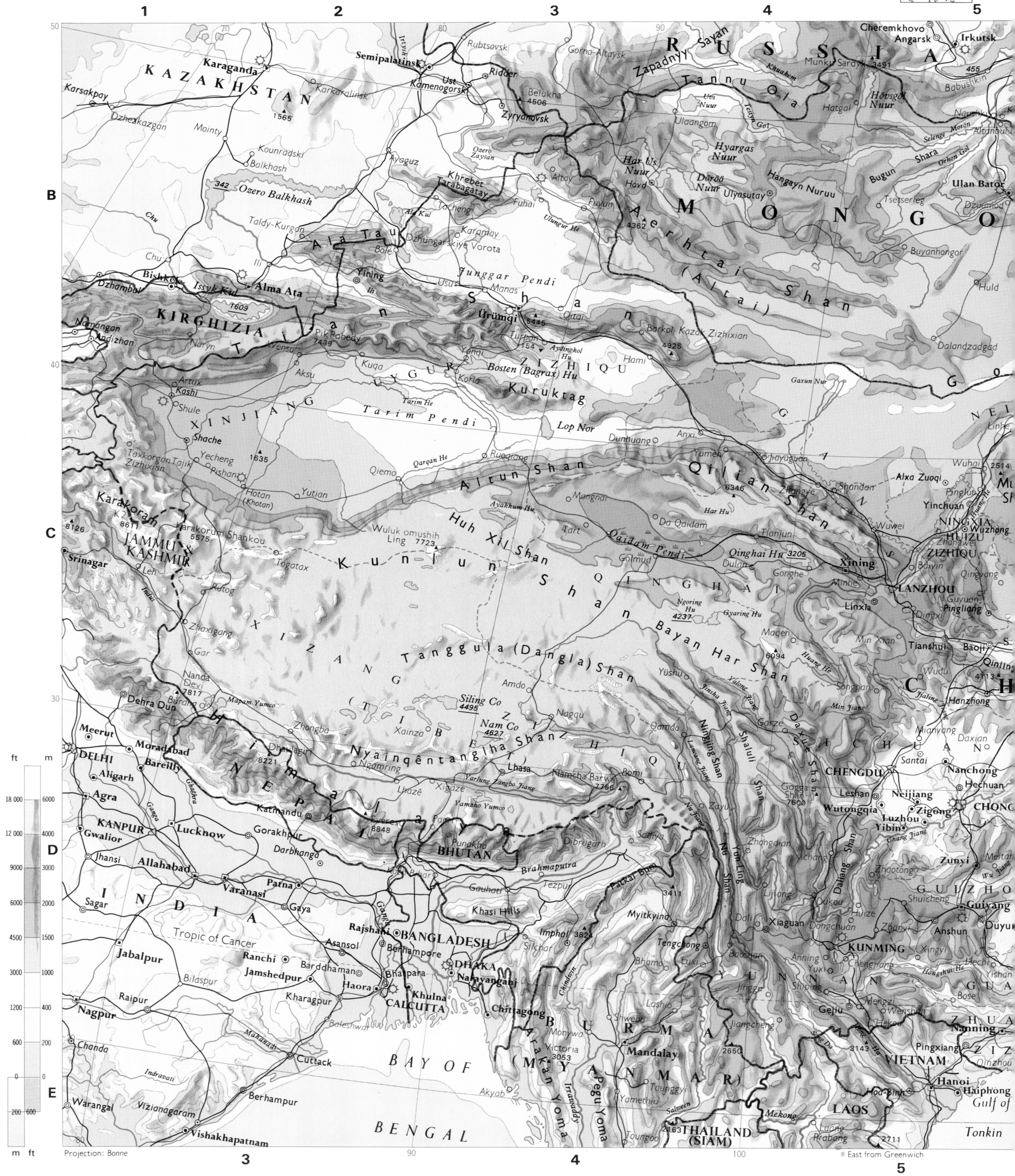

1 **2** **3** **4** **5**

50

B

C

D

E

KAZAKHSTAN

Karaganda
Karsakpay
Dzheskazgan
1565
Mointy
Kounradski
Balkhash
342 Ozero Balkhash
Taldy-Kurgan
Chu
Chu

Semipalatinsk
Ust Kamenogorsk
Ridder
Rubtsovsk
Zyryanovsk
Karkaralinsk
Ayaguz
Ozero Zaysan
Khrebet Tarabagatay
Tacheng
Ala Kul
Ali Kul
Belukha 4506
Altay
Fuhai
Ulungur He
Fuyun
4362

RUSSIA
Sayan
Zapadnyy
Tannu Ola
Gorno-Altaysk
Khuakm
Munku Sardyk 3491
Cheremkhovo
Angarsk
Irkutsk
455
Babushkin
Uus Nuur
Ulaangom
Har Us Nuur
Hovd
Hyargas Nuur
Döröö Nuur
Ulyasutay
Hangayn Nuruu
Bugun
Shara
Orhon Gol
Selenge Mörön
Altanbul
Hatgal
Hövsgöl Nuur
Tsetserleg
Ulan Bator
Dzuunhar

MONGOLIA
Buyanhongor
Hald
Dalandzadgad

Bishkek
Dzhambul
Issyk Kul
Alma Ata
Namangan
Andizhan
KIRGHIZIA
Naryn
Pik Pobedy 7439
Aksu
Artux
Kashi
Shule

Ili
Yining
Bole
Ala Tau
Usu
Manas
Dzhungarskiye Vorota
Karamay
Junggar Pendi
Shan
Ürümqi 5445
Qitai
Turpan 154
Aydingkol Hu
Barkol Kazak Zizhixian
Hami
4925

Gaxun Nur

Dalandzadgad
NEI

40

Tien Shan
Kensu
Kuqa
Yengi
Korla
Bosten (Bagrax) Hu
Kuruktag
ZIZHIQU
UYGUR
Tarim He
Tarim Pendi
XINJIANG
Shache
Yecheng
1635
Hotan (Khotan)
Yutian
Qiemo
Qarqan He
Ruoqiang
Altun Shan
Lop Nor
Dunhuang
Anxi
Yumen
Jiayuguan
Mangnai
6346
Shandan
Zhangye
QILIAN SHAN
Wuhai 2514
Alxa Zuoqi
Pingluo
Yinchuan
Wuwei
Wuzhong
NINGXIA
HUIZU
ZIZHIQU

Taxkorgan Tajik Zizhixian
K2 8611
8126
Karakorum
5575
Karakorum Shankou
JAMMU & KASHMIR
Srinagar
Leh
Togatax
Rutog
Zhaxigang
Gar

Wuluk omushih Ling 7723
Huh Xil Shan
Ayakkum Hu
Tart
Da Qaidam
Qaidam Pendi
Golmud
Dulan
Gonghe
Xining
QINGHAI
Qinghai Hu 3205
Tianjun
Minhe
Linxia
LANZHOU
Baiyin
Qingyang
Guyuan
Pingliang
ZIZHIQU

C

Kunlun Shan
Xizang
Tibet
Nanda Devi 7817
Dehra Dun
Burang
Mapam Yumco
Zhongba

Tanggula (Dangla) Shan
Siling Co 4495
Xainza
Nam Co 4627
Amdo
Naqu
Yushu
Bayan Har Shan
Ngoring Hu 4237
Gyaring Hu
Maqen
6094
Songpan
Hiuang He
Min Xian
Tianshui
Baoji
Wudu
Qinling
4113

30

Meerut
DELHI
Aligarh
Agra
KANPUR
Gwalior
Lucknow
Jhansi
Allahabad
Sagar
Jabalpur
Nagpur
Raipur
Chanda
Warangal
Vizianagaram
Vishakhapatnam

Moradabad
Bareilly
NEPAL
Dhaulagiri 8221
Ngamring
Katmandu
Gorakhpur
Darbhanga
Patna
Varanasi
Gaya
Ranchi
Barddhaman
Jamshedpur
Bilaspur
Mahanadi
Indravati
Cuttack
Berhampur

Zhongba
Lhaze
Xigaze
Yamzho Yumco
Himalaya
Everest 8848
Paro
Punakha
BHUTAN
Thimphu
Nyainqentanglha Shan
Lhasa
Yarlung Zangbo Jiang
Namcha Barwa 7756
Bomi
Zayu
Dibrugarh
Sadiya
Tezpur
Gauhati
Brahmaputra
Pakar Bum
3411
Myitkyina
Bhamo
Loshio
Shwebo
Monywa
Mandalay
Toungoo

Qamdo
Ningjing Shan
Shaluli Shan
Garze
Daxue Shan
Goggen Shan 7600
Kangding
Ya'an
Leshan
Neijiang
Wutongqiao
Zigong
Luzhou
Yibin
Chang Jiang
SICHUAN
CHENGDU
Santai
Mianyang
Daxian
Nanchong
Hechuan
CHONGQING

Dikou
3411
Daliang Shan
Xichang
Lijiang
Xiaguan
Dongchuan
Dali
Tengchong
Baoshan
Euxi
YUNNAN
Anning
KUNMING
Chenghang
Yuxi
Shiping
Gejiu
Mengzi
Wenshan

Zhaotong
Zunyi
Meitan
Wu
Huize
Shuicheng
GUIZHOU
Guiyang
Anshun
Duyun
Xingyi
Hechi
Yishan
Nanning
Pingxiang
ZHUANG
GUA

Tropic of Cancer
INDIA
Rajshahi
Asansol
Berhampore
Khulna
Haora
CALCUTTA
Kharagpur
Baleshwar
BAY OF
BENGAL

BANGLADESH
DHAKA
Narayanganj
Bhatpara
Chittagong
Khasi Hills
Silchar
Imphal 3821
Chindwin
Akyab
Arakan Yoma
Victoria 3053
MYANMAR (BURMA)
Pegu Yoma
Yamethin
Irrawaddy
Salween
Taunggyi
Mekong
Luang Prabang
2711
THAILAND (SIAM)
3163
LAOS
Jingpo
Jiangcheng
Shiping
Jinghong
Simao
Hongshui He
Bose
VIETNAM
Hanoi
Haiphong
Gulf of Tonkin
Hoa Binh
2650
2143
Pingxiang
Qinzhou
Nu Shan
Yun Ling
Nujiang

ft m
18 000 6000
12 000 4000
9000 3000
6000 2000
4500 1500
3000 1000
1200 400
600 200
0 0
200 600
600 1800

m ft

Projection: Bonne
East from Greenwich

3 **90** **4** **100** **5**

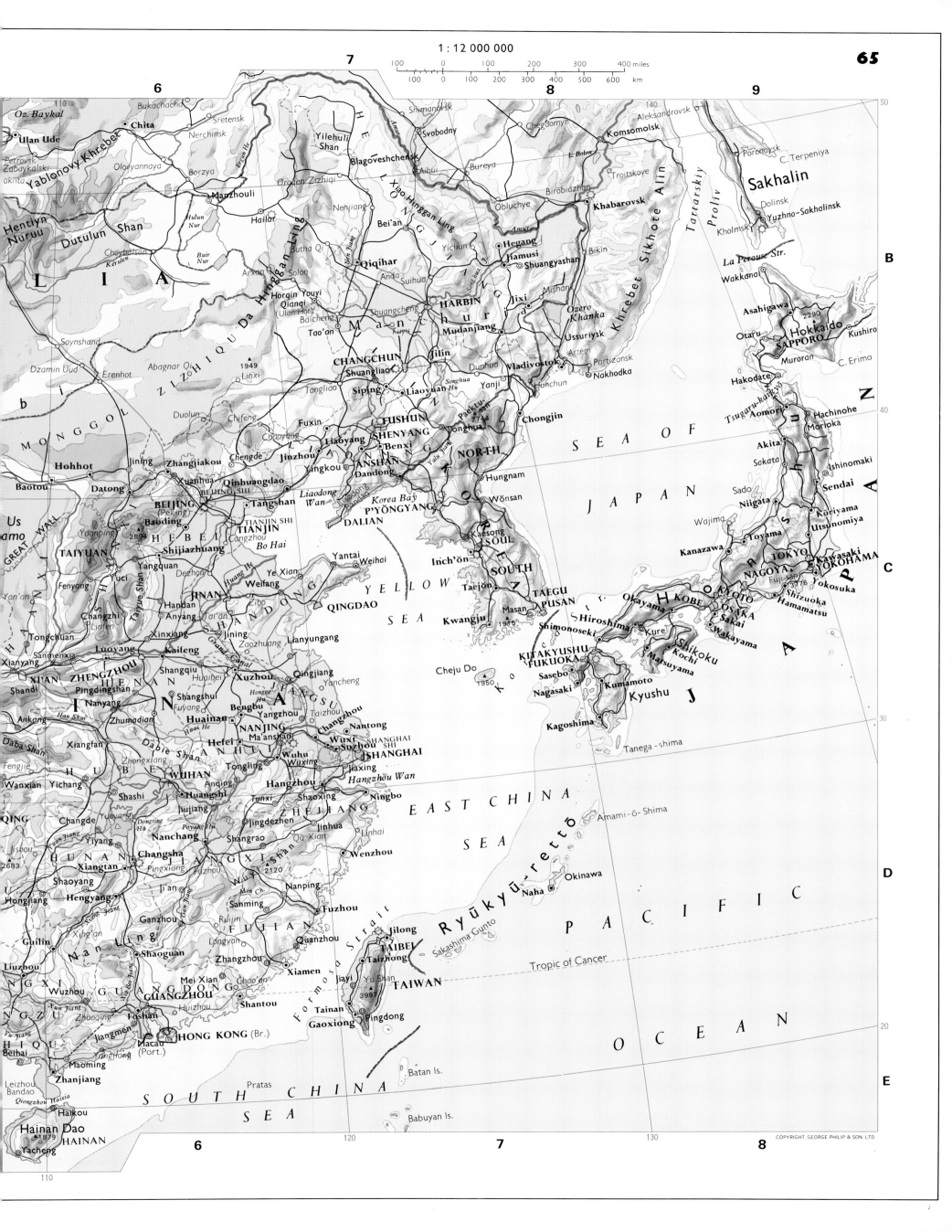

MONGOLIA

ÖVÖR HANGAY

DUNDGOVĬ

SÜHBAATAR

Arts Bogd Uul
▲3582

Sayhan-Ovoo

Mandalgovi

Har-Ayrag

Delgerhet

Hongor

Ongon

Dong Ujimqin Qi

Bayandalay
▲2825

Hanhongor

Huld

Öndörshil

Saynshand

Dariganga

ÖMNÖGOVĬ

DORNOGOVĬ

Nayon

Dalandzadgad

Tsogttsetsiy

Ulaan Nuur

Manlay

Sayhandulaan

Erdene

Abagnar Qi

Hanbogd

Hövsgöl

Dzamin Üüd
Erenhot

Qagan Nur

Dalai Nur

Nomgon

Bayan-Ovoo

Hatanbulag

ZI ZI

MONGGOL

NEI

Lang Shan

Bayan Obo

Darhan Muminggan Lianheqi

Duolun

Xianghuang Qi

Tabus Qi

Yabrai Shan

Wuyuan

Hanggin Hou Qi

Linhe

Guyang

Wulanbulang

▲2174

Qahar Youyi Zhongqi

Jining

Wanquan

Xinghe

Huade

Shangdu

Guyuan

Zhangbei

Fengning

Chongli

Chicheng

MONGGOL

Urad Qianqi

▲2187

Shiguaigou

Dashetai

Daqing Shan

Zhuozi

Hohhot

Xighe

Huai'an

Zhangjiakou (Changchak ou, Kalgan)

Longguan

Huang He (Hwang Ho)

Dengkou

Baotou (Pao'tou)

Tumd Youqi

Bikeqi

Horinger

Liangcheng

Fengzhen

Shahukou

Yanggao

Tianzhen

Zhuolu

Yanqing Miyun

Huairen

Datong

Yangyuan

▲2870

BEIJING (Peiping, Peking)

Changping

Jartai

Judengkou
▲2149

Hanggin Qi

Dongsheng

Qingshuihe

Togtoh

Youyu

Shanyin

Ping lu

Hunyuan

Yu Xian

Ying Xian

Guangling

Zhuo Xian

Laishui

Tong

Nanyuan

Fengtai

Langxiangzheng

Alxa Zuoqi (Bayan Hot)
▲3626
3556

Helan Shan

Huinong

Pingluo

Mu Us Shamo (Ordos)

Uxin Qi

GREAT

Hequ

Fugu

Baode

Wuzhai

Ningwu

Dai Xian

▲3058

Wutai

Fanshi

Qingxu

Fuping

Wan Xian

Quyang

Lingshou

Baoding

Xiong Xian

Daicheng

Yinchuan

Hengcheng

Taole

Yulin

Jia Xian

Kuye He

Kelan

Xing Xian

Lan Xian

Jingle

Dingxiang

Yu Xian

Ding Xian

Qing Xian

Cangzhou

Daman

Mingin

Yongning

Lingwu

Wuzhong

Qingtongxia Shuku

Yuchi

Jinji

Hengshan

Huang He Yellow River

Mizhi

Lin Xian

▲2831

TAIYUAN (Yangch'u)

Yangquan

SHIJIAZHUANG

Zhengding

Jin Xian

Anping

Hejian

Dezhou

Ling Xian

NINGXIA HUIZU ZIZHIQU (aut. reg.)

Zhongning

Bai Yu Shan

Dingbian

Jingbian

Suide

Wubu

Lishi

Xiaoyi

Jiexiu

Lingshi

Xiangyuan

Licheng

Zhao Xian

Pingding

Shouyang

Yuci

Taigu

Heshun

Yushe

Zuoquan

Wuan

Shahe

Julu

Wucheng

Nangong

Pingxiang

Xingtai

Jize

Linqing

Guantao

Gaotang

Jinan (Tsinan, Chinan)

Zhongwei

Haiyuan

Heichengzhen

Zhidan

Ansai

Yanchuan

Yonghe

Xi Xian

Fenxi

Huozhou

Hongtong

Anze

Tunliu

Changzhi

Lucheng

Lingchuan

Hui Xian

Fengfeng

Handan

Ci Xian

Daming

Shen Xian

Liaocheng

Jining

Lanzhou (Lanchow)

Dingxi

Huining

Guyuan

Huan Xian

Quzi

Qingyang

Yan'an

Yanchang

Yichuan

Daning

Linfen

Yicheng

Fushan

Jishan

Qwo
▲2322

Wanrong

Yuncheng

Hua Xian

Yuncheng

Xinxiang

Heze

Dingtao

Juxiang

Yutai

Lintao

Weiyuan

Longxi

Jingning

Pingliang
▲2942

Jingchuan

Jing He

Lingtai

Xifengzhen

Zhenyuan

Ning Xian

Huanglong

Huchuan

Fu Xian

Luochuan

Xianning

Hejin

Xinjiang

Qishui

Wenxi

Xia Xian

Yuanqu

Yangcheng

Qinyang

Wen Xian

Mengzhou

Huaxian

Boai

Xiuwu

Jiaozuo

Qinyang

Wei He

Xinxiang

Changyuan

Jinxiang

Tianshui

Qin'an

Qingshui

Changwu

Xunyi

Tongchuan

Yaoxian

Binxian

Chengcheng

Dali

Yongji

Zhongtiao Shan

Sanmenxia

Mianchi

Luoyang (Chengchow)

Sishui

Xingyang

Zhengzhou

Kaifeng

Chenliu

Cao Xian

Shangqiu

Dongshan

Li Xian
▲3100

Gangu

Wushan

Min Xian

Longdang

Cheng Xian

Hui Xian

Baoji

Fengxiang

Qianyang

Qishan

Qianxian

Liquan

Xingping

Xianyang

Sanyuan

Jingyang

Lintong

Weinan

Tongguan

Lingbao

Luoning

Yiyang

Dengfeng

Yu Xian

Xuchang

Yanling

Taikang

Huaiyang

Dingtao

Baishui

Chang'an

Qinling Shandi

▲3767

Wei He

XI'AN (Hsian, Sian)

Hu Xian

Lantian

Danfeng

Luoyang

Song Xian

Jia Xian

Lushan

Xiangcheng

Ye Xian

Pingdingshan

Xiangcheng

Fugou

Luohe

Shangshui

Su Xian

ANHUI

Wudu

Wen Xian
▲3002

Lüeyang

Mian Xian

Baocheng

Yong Xian

Niushan

Shanyang

Shangnan

Xixia

Zhenping

Neixiang

Fangcheng

Shangshui

Xiping

Yancheng

Shanghai

Zhoujiazhuang

Suiping

Runan

Zhengqiao

Jieshou

Mengcheng

Hanzhong

Chenggu

Shiquan

Zhen'an

Shanyang

Taipingzhen

Lushan

Zhenping

Tanghe

Shiqi

Xichuan

Nanyang

Zhumadian

Biyang

Pingli

Fuping

Pingwu

Ningqiang

Han Shui

Hanyin

Ziyang

Xunyang

Baihe

Yun Xi

Tanghe

Wodian

Biyang

Queshan

Xhei He

Fuyang

Ankang

Han Shui

Baihe

Hong He

Projection: Conical with two standard parallels

ft m
12,000 4000
9000 3000
6000 2000
4500 1500
3000 1000
1200 400
600 200
0 0
200 600
2000 6000
m ft

1 : 4 800 000

50   0   50   100   150 miles

50   0   50   100   150   200 250
km

9   10   11   12   13   14   15   16

HEILONGJIANG

JILIN

LIAONING

NORTH
KOREA

SOUTH
KOREA

Don bei (Manchuria)

Zhangguangcai Ling

Changbai Shan

RUSSIA

HARBIN
(Haerhpin)

Changchun

Jilin
(Kirin)

Shenyang
(Mukden)

Fushun

Liaoyang

Benxi

Anshan

Jinzhou

Jinxi

Yingkou

Dandong

Sinŭiju

P'YŎNGYANG

Chinnampo

Haeju

Kaesŏng

SEOUL
(Sŏul)

INCH'ŎN

Suwŏn

Hamhung

Hŭngnam

Wŏnsan

Tongjosŏn
Man

Chŏngjin

Kimchaek
(Songjin)

Nanam

Kyŏngsŏng

Vladivostok

Ussuriysk
(Voroshilov)

Artem

Ozero
Khanka

Tangshan

TIANJIN
(Tientsin
Tienching)

Qinhuangdao

Lüshun

DALIAN
(Lüda)

Bo Hai
(Gulf of Chihli)

Korea
Bay

Liaodong
Wan

Huang He

Yantai

Weihai

Laizhou
Wan

Shandong Bandao

Zibo

Weifang

Tai Shan
1524

QINGDAO
(Ch'ingtao)

Haizhou Wan

Lianyungang
(Hsinhailien)

Xuzhou

JIANGSU

Bengbu

HUANG HAI
(Yellow Sea)

Korea   Strait

Tsushima

Tsushima-kaikyō

Cheju   Cheju-do

Mokpo

KWANGJU

Sunchŏn

Yŏsu

PUSAN

Chungmu

Masan

Chinju

CHŎNJU

TAEGU

Kyongju

Ulsan

Pohang

Yŏngdŏk

TAEJŎN

Chŏngju

Chungju

Chŏchon

Wŏnju

Chunchŏn

Kangnŭng

Samchŏk

Ulchin

Ullung-do

Kunsan

SEA   OF
JAPAN

JAPAN

Nagasaki

Sasebo

Case Fire Line

East from Greenwich

COPYRIGHT. GEORGE PHILIP & SON. LTD.

9   10   11   12   13   14   15

B   C   D   E   F   G   H

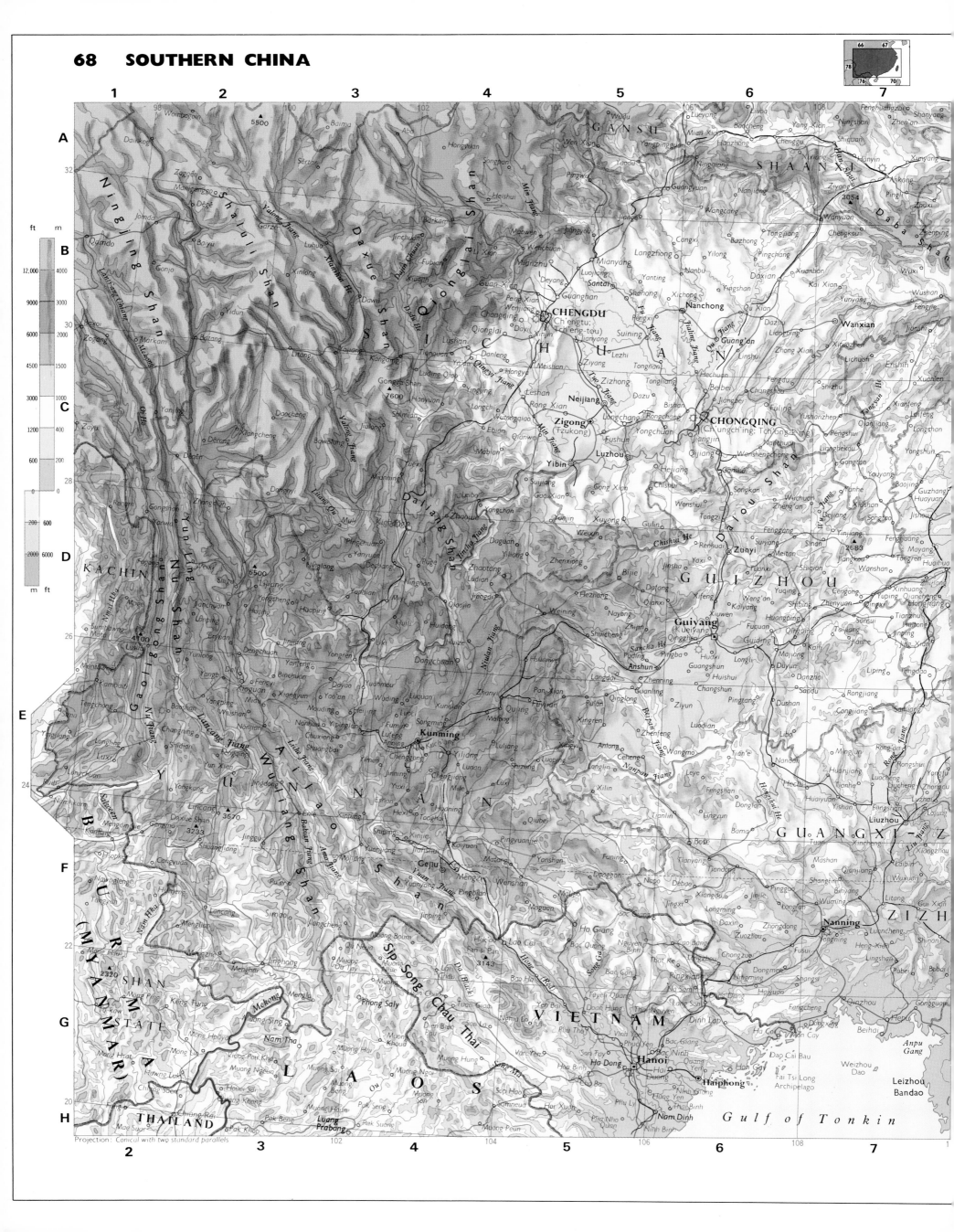

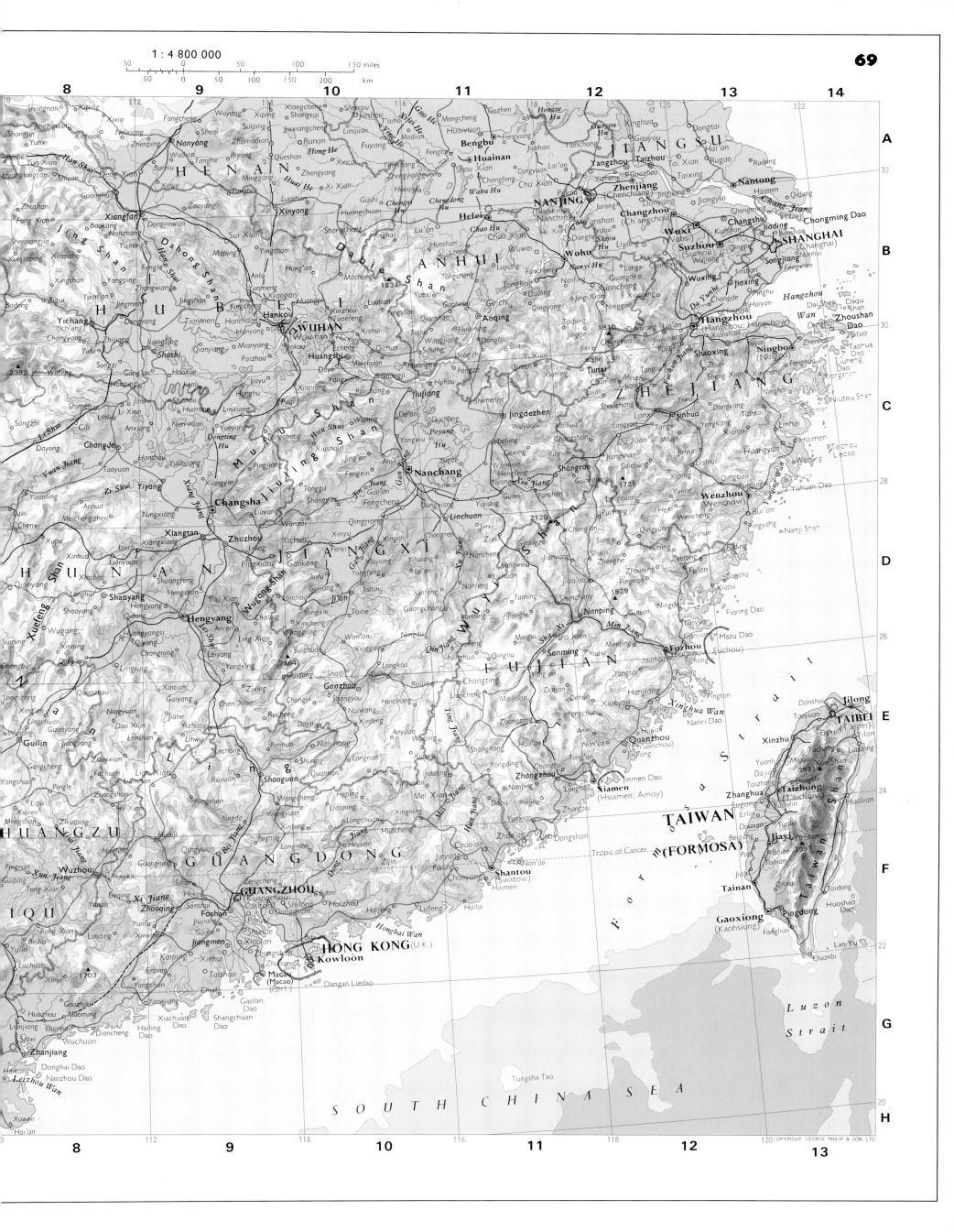

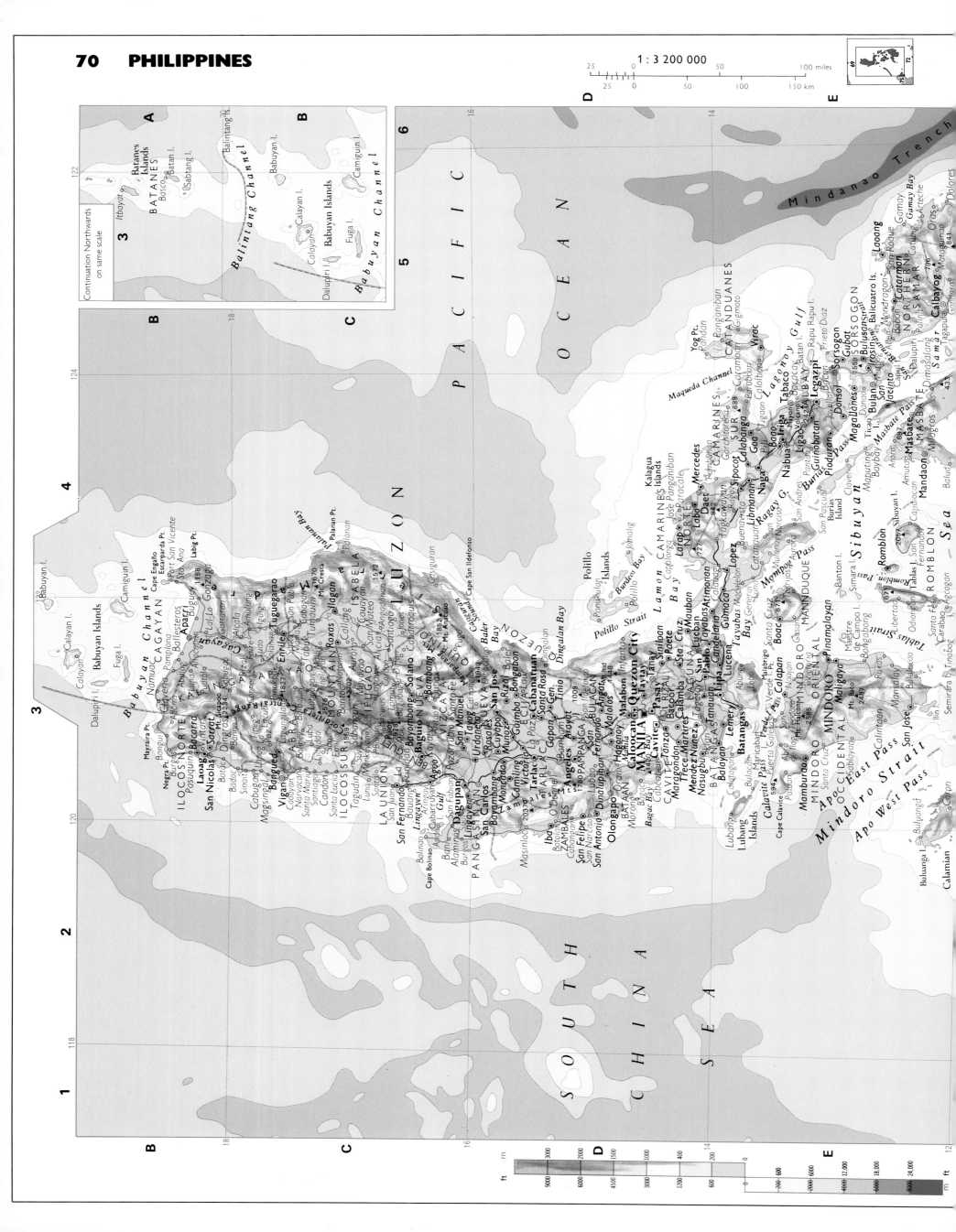

1 : 3 200 000

PACIFIC OCEAN

SOUTH CHINA SEA

LUZON

Mindanao Trench

Sibuyan Sea

ROMBLON

Continuation Northwards on same scale

BATANES

Batanes Islands

Babuyan Islands

Babuyan Channel

Balintang Channel

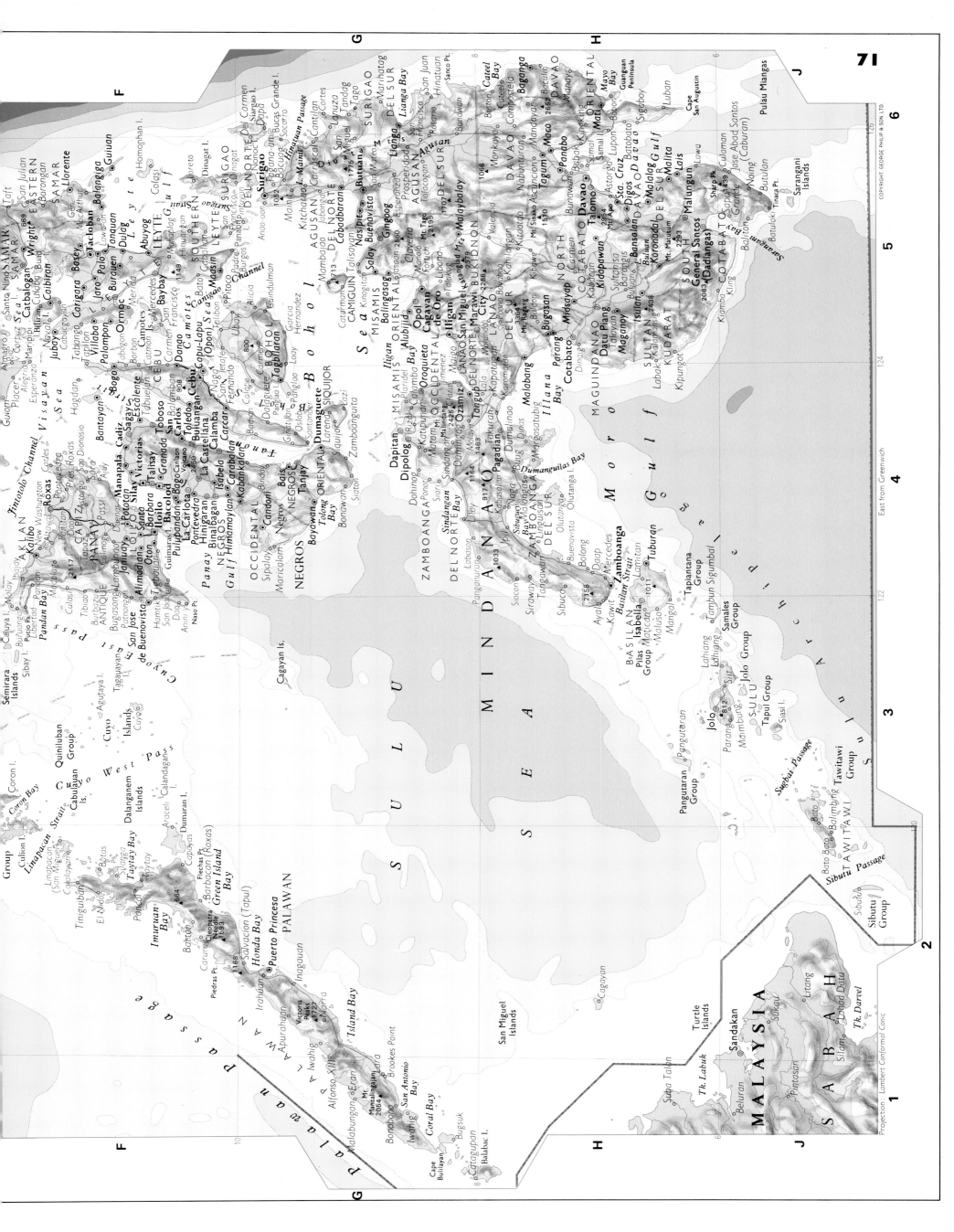

71

1 2 3

BORNEO

1346
Tawau
Teluk Sebuku Lama
Semporna
120

Malinau
Nomeh
Sesayap
Bunju
Tarakan
Tanjungselor
Tanjungbatu
Maratua

A

Kongkemul
2053
Berau
TIMUR
Tanjungredeb
Dumaring

S U L A W E S I

S E A

▾5315

Kepulauan Sangihe

Bulu
Karakelong
Beo
Kepulauan Talaud

Kaburuang

Tahuna
Sangihe

Siau
Tohulandang

Biaro

Bangka

Mayu

Morotai
Sopi
Rau
Berebere
Doi
Wayabula

M A L U K U S E A

Equator
Muarakaman
Telen
Samarinda
Tenggarong
Sangasanga
Sungaitiram
Balikpapan
Tanahgrogot
Jangeru
Bontang

Donggala
Toboli
Palu
3[1]7
Poso
Fojo

Teluk Tomini

Kepulauan Toglan

Poh
Maliku
Luwuk

Peleng
Toili
Banggai
Kepulauan Banggai

Taliabu
Mangole
Auponhia
Sanana
Kepulauan Sula
Sanana

Ibu
Jailolo
Akelamo
Tobelo
Ternate
Ternate
Spasui

Halmahera
Tidore
Makian
Kayoa

Weda
Teluk Weda
Patani
Teluk Buli

Kepulauan Bacan
Mandioli
Wosi
Gani
Labuha

Bacan
Bisa

Kepulauan Obilatu
Obi
Sesepe
Loji
Fluk

Fluk

0

Selat Makasar

B

Tolitoli
Teluk Dondo
Maling
2707
Ogomas
2913
Tomini

2300
Tentolomatinan

U T A R A
Sumalata
Kwandang
Gambuta
1954
Gorontalo
Tilamuta
Tg. Flesko

Buol
Paleleh

Kuandang
Kotamobagu

Amurang
Manado 2922
Kema
Tondano

Kepulauan
Balabalangan
(Paternoster)

Kotabaru
Sebuku
Karambu
Pulau Laut

Lariang
Mamuju
3074
Masamba
Makale
Onang
Polewali
SELATAN
Raatekombola
Majene
Teluk Mandar
Enrekang
Pinrang
Rappang

Masamba
Palopo
3016
Balease
Malili

Tangkeleboke
1782
Mekongga
2790
Kolaka

TENGAH
SULAWESI
(CELEBES)
Teluk Tolo

Mondeodo
Manui

Tenggara
Kendari

Kepulauan Molucca

Buru
Kaupalatmada
2429
Wamsasi
Namlea
Tifu
Leksula
Namrole
Kayeli
Lima

Piru

S E R A M

Ambon
Ambon

C

ft m

12,000 4000

9000 3000

6000 2000

4500 1500

3000 1000

1200 400

600 200

0 0

200 600

2000 6000

4000 12,000

6000 18,000

8000 24,000

m ft

Watangsoppeng
Sumpangbinangae
Pangkajene
Ujung Pandang
Maros
Sungguminasa
Pattallassang
Kepulauan
Masalima
Bantaeng
Bontosunggu
Lompobatang
2871
Bolukumba

Salayar
Benteng

Kabaena

Baubau
Cawele

Buapinang
Raha
Muna
Butung
Rising

Teluk Bone
Singkang
Pampanua
Watampone
Marek
Sinjai

Wowoni

I N D O N

Monse

Wangiwangi
Kepulauan Tukangbesi
Binongko

B A N D A

Gunungapi
5888

Damar

Kepulauan Romang

Wetar
Wesiri
Ilwaki

D

m ft

Projection: Mercator

FLORES SEA
Kepulauan
Bone Rate
Tanahjampea
Kalao
Bone Rate
Kalaotoa

Batuata
(Watuata I.)

L e s s e r S u n d a I s l a n d s

Lombok
Rinjani
3726
Selong
Mataram
Mojo
Sumbawa Besar
Tambora
2821
Dompu
Sape
Parado
Taliwang

Sumbawa
Raba
Komodo
Rinca
Labuhanbajo
Ruteng
Aimere
Ende
Flores
Maumere
Larantuka
Adonara
Pantar
Solor
Lomblen

Kalabahi
Atauro
Alor
Selat Ombai

Kisar
Leti
Moa
Lakar
Kepulauan Leti
Bacan
Tutuala

Dili
Pante Macassar
Atapupu
Atambua
TIMOR
Viqueque
Uato-Udo

Memboro
Waikabubak
Waingapu
Sumba
Melolo

NUSA TENGGARA TIMUR

Naikliu
Kefamenanu
Timor
Soe
Nikiniki

Sangeang

Baing

SAWU SEA

NUSA TENGGARA BARAT

Raijua
Sawu
Baa
Dana
Roti

Semau
Kupang
Pariti

T I M O R S E A

East from Greenwich

1 2 3

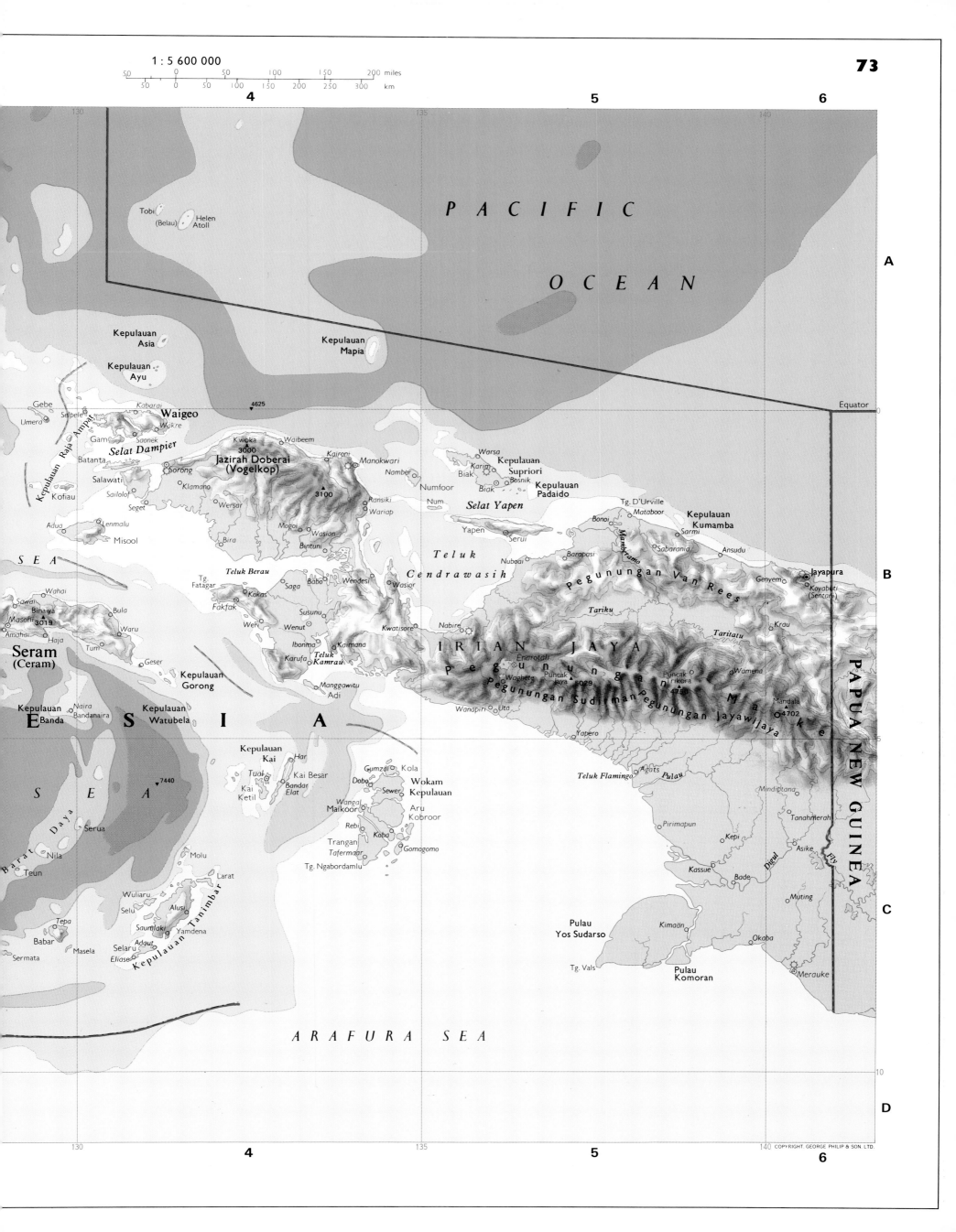

1 : 5 600 000

50   0   50   100   150   200 miles
50   0   50   100   150   200   250   300 km

4   **5**   **6**

130   135   140

P A C I F I C

O C E A N

Tobi
(Belau)   Helen
Atoll

Kepulauan
Asia

Kepulauan
Mapia

Kepulauan
Ayu

Equator

A

Gebe   Selpele   Kabarai   *4625*
Umera   Waigeo
Gam   Saonek   Wikre
Batanta   Selat Dampier
Kwoka   Waibeem
Sorong   3000   Kairoru
Salawati   Klamano   Jazirah Doberai   Manokwari
Sailolof   (Vogelkop)   Warsa
Kofiau   Seget   Wersar   *3100*   Ransiki   Namber   Kepulauan
Adua   Mogoi   Wariap   Numfoor   Biak   Supriori
Lenmalu   Bira   Wasian   Num   Karim   Bosnik
Misool   Bintuni   Selat Yapen   Kepulauan
Padaido

Kepulauan
Raja Ampat

S E A

Teluk Berau   Saga   Babo   Wendesi   Teluk   Yapen   Serui   Tg. D'Urville
Tg.   Kokas   Cendrawasih   Mataboor   Kepulauan
Wahai   Fatagar   Susunu   Wasior   Bonoi   Kumamba
Sawai   Bula   Fakfak   Weri   Nuboai   Sarmi
Binaiya   Waru   Wenut   Barapasi   Sabarania   Ansudu
Masohi   3019   Haja   Ibonma   Kaimana   Nabire   Pegunungan Van Rees   Genyem
Amahai   Tum   Karufa   Teluk   Kwatisore   Krau   Jayapura
Seram   Geser   Kamrau   Uta   Tariku   Koyabuti
(Ceram)   Kepulauan   Manggawitu   I R I A N   J A Y A   Taritatu   (Sentani)
Gorong   Adi   Endrotali   Puncak   Puncak
Naira   Enarotali   Trikora   Wamena
Kepulauan   Bandanaira   Waghete   Jaya   5029   Mandala
E   Banda   Watubela   Pegunungan   Sudirman   Pegunungan Jayawijaya   4702
Wanapiri   Yapero

B

Kepulauan   Kepulauan
Banda

S   E   S   I   A

7440   Kepulauan   Har
Kai   Kola   Teluk Flamingo   Agats
Tual   Gumzai   Wokam   Mindiptana
S   Kai Besar   Doba   Pulau
E   Kai   Bandar   Sewer   Kepulauan
A   Ketil   Elat   Aru   Kobroor   Pirimapun
Serua   Wangal   Rebi   Kassue   Tanahmerah
Maikoor   Koba   Kepi   Asike
Molu   Trangan   Koba   Pulau   Bade
Nila   Tafermaar   Gomagomo   Yos Sudarso   Muting
Teun   Tg. Ngabordamlu   Kimaän   Okaba
Wuliaru
Selu   Alusi   Pulau
Tepa   Saumlaki   Yamdena   Komoran
Babar   Masela   Adgut   Tg. Vals   Merauke
Sermata   Selaru
Eliase   Kepulauan Tanimbar

C

P A P U A   N E W   G U I N E A

B
a
r
a
t
      D
a
y
a

A R A F U R A   S E A

D

130   135   140   COPYRIGHT GEORGE PHILIP & SON LTD.

4   **5**   **6**

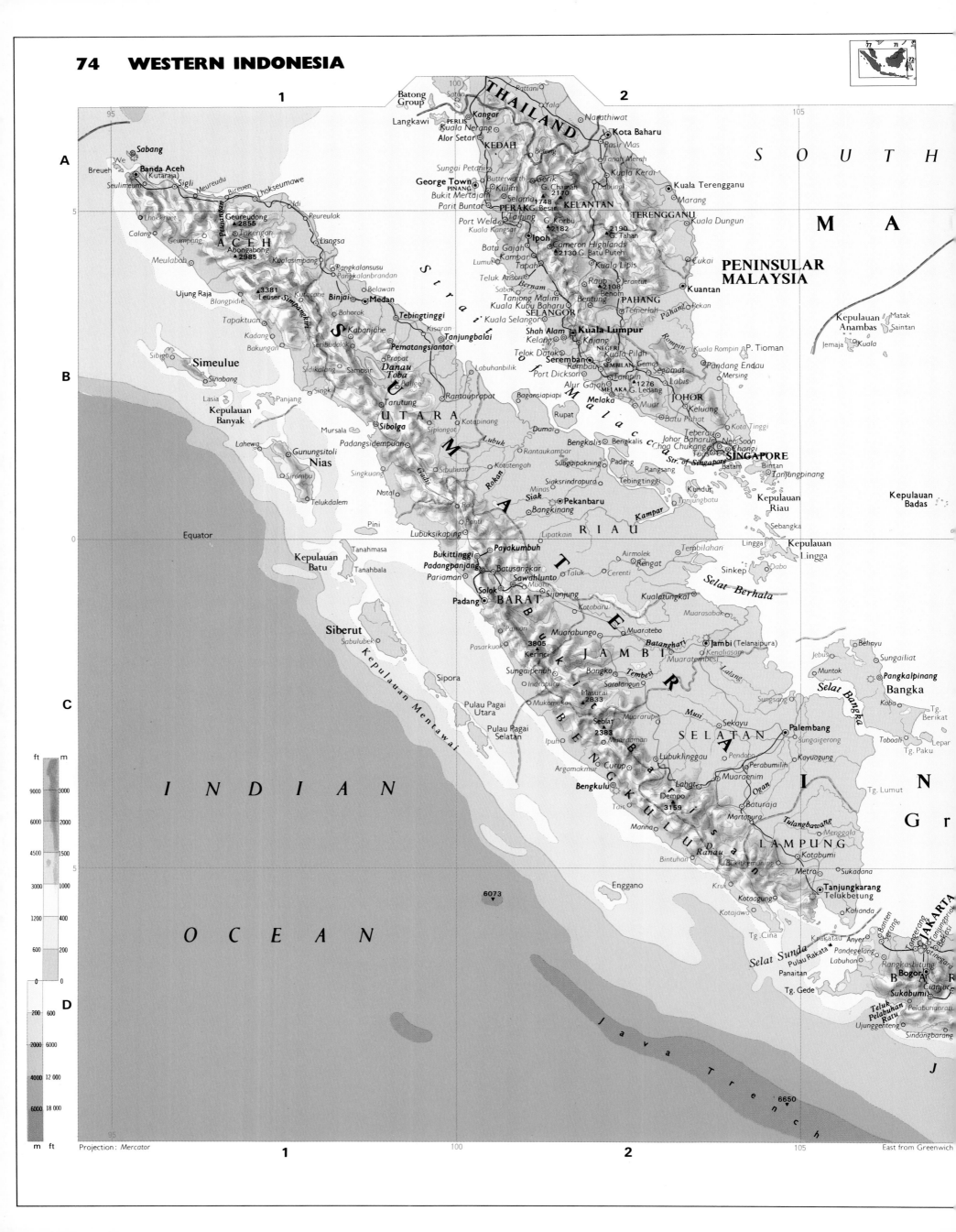

THAILAND

SOUTH

MALAYSIA

PENINSULAR
MALAYSIA

Batong
Group
Langkawi
PERLIS
Kuala Nerang
Alor Setar
KEDAH
George Town
PINANG
Bukit Mertajam
Parit Buntar
Port Weld
Kuala Kangsar
Batu Gajah
Lumut
Kampar
Teluk Anson
Bernam
Tanjong Malim
Kuala Kubu Baharu
Kuala Selangor
SELANGOR
Shah Alam
Kelang
Telok Datok
Port Dickson

Kangar
Kuala Nerang
Kota Baharu
Pasir Mas
Tanah Merah
Kuala Kerai
Gerik
G. Chamah 2170
748
Besar
KELANTAN
G. Korbu 2182
Cameron Highlands
2130 G. Batu Puteh
Kuala Lipis
Raub
Benom 2108
Bentung
PAHANG
Temerloh
Pahang
Kuala Lumpur
Kajang
NEGERI
Seremban
Kuala Pilah
SEMBILAN
Rembau
Gemas
Alur Gajah
Lampin 1276
MELAKA G. Ledang
Melaka
Muar

Narathiwat
Kota Baharu
Marang
Kuala Terengganu
TERENGGANU
Kuala Dungun
Cukai
G. Tahan 2190
Kuantan
Pekan
Kuala Rompin
P. Tioman
Kepulauan
Anambas
Matak
Saintan
Jemaja
Kuala
Pandang Endau
Mersing
JOHOR
Keluang
Batu Pahat
Kota Tinggi
Teberau
Johor Baharu
Nee Soon
Choa Chukang
Changi
Tuas
SINGAPORE
Batam
Bintan
Tanjungpinang
Kundur
Kepulauan
Riau
Kepulauan
Badas

Sabang
Breueh
We
Banda Aceh
(Kutaraja)
Seulimeum
Sigli
Meureudu
Bireuen
Lhokseumawe
Lhokkruet
Calang
Geureudong 2855
Takengon
ACEH
Abongabong
2985
Meulaboh
Ujung Raja
3381
Leuser
Blangpidie
Tapaktuan
Kadang
Bakungan
Sibigo
Simeulue
Sinabang
Lasia
Kepulauan
Banyak
Lahewa
Gunungsitoli
Nias
Sirombu
Telukdalem

Kualasimpang
Pangkalansusu
Pangkalanbrandan
Belawan
Binjai
Medan
Bohorok
Tebingtinggi
Kisaran
Tanjungbalai
Kabanjahe
Seribudolok
Pematangsiantar
Sidikalang
Samosir
Prapat
Danau
Toba
Balige
Singkil
Panjang
Tarutung
UTARA
Sibolga
Mursala
Padangsidempuan
Siborong

Langsa
Peureulak
Idi
Kuala

Str.
of
Malacca

S U M A T E R A
U T A R A

Singkuang
Natal
Gaib
Sibuhuan
Kotanopan
Lubuk
Rokan
Rantauprapat
Kotapinang
Siporok
Labuhanbilik
Dumai
Bengkalis
Bengkalis
Rupat
Bagansiapiapi
Siak
Rangsang
Tebingtinggi
Tanjungbatu
Sebangka
Sebangka
Pini
Lubuksikaping
Ponti
Rau
Pekanbaru
Bangkinang
RIAU
Kampar
Sungaipakning
Padang
Minas
Siaksrindrapura
Kotatengah
Rantaukampar
Lingga
Lingga
Selat Berhala
Sinkep
Dabo
Kepulauan
Lingga

Equator

Kepulauan
Batu
Tanahmasa
Tanahbala
Siberut
Sabulubek
Sipora
Pulau Pagai
Utara
Pulau Pagai
Selatan

Bukittinggi
Payakumbuh
Padangpanjang
Batusangkar
Pariaman
Sawahlunto
Solok
Muaro
Sijunjung
Padang
BARAT
Kotabaru
Pasarkuok
Panti
Muarabungo
3381
Bukit
Kerinci
Sungaipenuh
Indrapura
Masurai 2833
Mukomuko
Ipuh
Seblat 2383
Argamakmur
Bengkulu
Curup
Lahat
Dempo
3159
Kru
Bintuhan

Taluk
Cerenti
Airmolek
Rengat
Tembilahan
Kualatungkal
Muarasabak
Batanghari
Jambi (Telanaipura)
Kenaliasam
JAMBI
Muaratembesi
Sarolangun
Bangko
Tembesi
Latang
Sungsang
Muararupit
Muaraaman
Sekayu
Musi
Lubuklinggau
Perabumilih
Pendopo
Muaraenim
Ogan
Baturaja
Martapura
Manna
Ranau
Bintuhan
LAMPUNG
Kotabumi
Metro
Sukadana
Bukit Tumuing

Pangkalpinang
Bangka
Koba
Tg.
Berikat
Selat Bangka
Tobaali
Lepar
Tg. Paku
SELATAN
Palembang
Sungaigerong
Kayuagung
PALEMBANG
Tg. Lumut
Tg.
N

Muntok
Jebus
Belinyu
Sungailiat

G r

INDIAN

OCEAN

6073

6650

Enggano
Kotaagung
Kotajawa
Tanjungkarang
Telukbetung
Kalianda
Tg. Cina
Selat Sunda
Krakatau
Pulau Rakata
Pandeglang
Panaitan
Labuhan
Tg. Gede
Teluk
Pelabuhan
Ratu
Ujunggenteng
Sindangbarang
Anyer
Banten
Serang
Rangkasbitung
JAKARTA
Tangerang
Bekasi
Bogor
Cianjur
Sukabumi
B
R

Java Trench

Selat
Sindang

Projection: Mercator

East from Greenwich

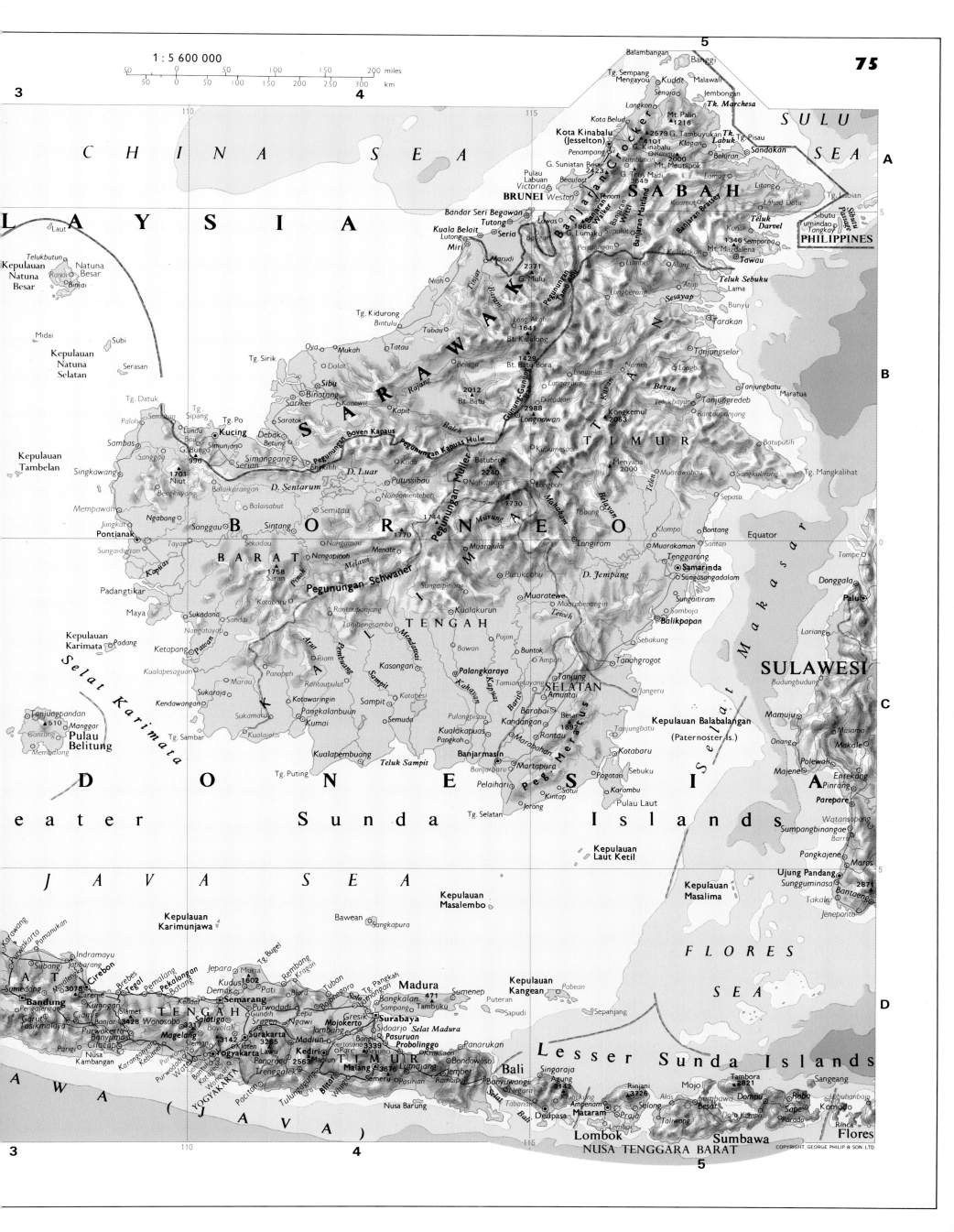

Gulf of Tonkin
HANOI
Haiphong
Hainan
Da Nang
Hue
Vientiane
BANGKOK
Rangoon
Mandalay
Gulf of Martaban
Mekong
CAMBODIA
THAILAND
BURMA
(MYANMAR)
YUNNAN
GUANGXI ZHUANGZU ZIZHIQU
AUTONOMOUS REGION
Phnom Dangrek
Tonle Sap
Moulmein
Chiang Mai
Luang Prabang

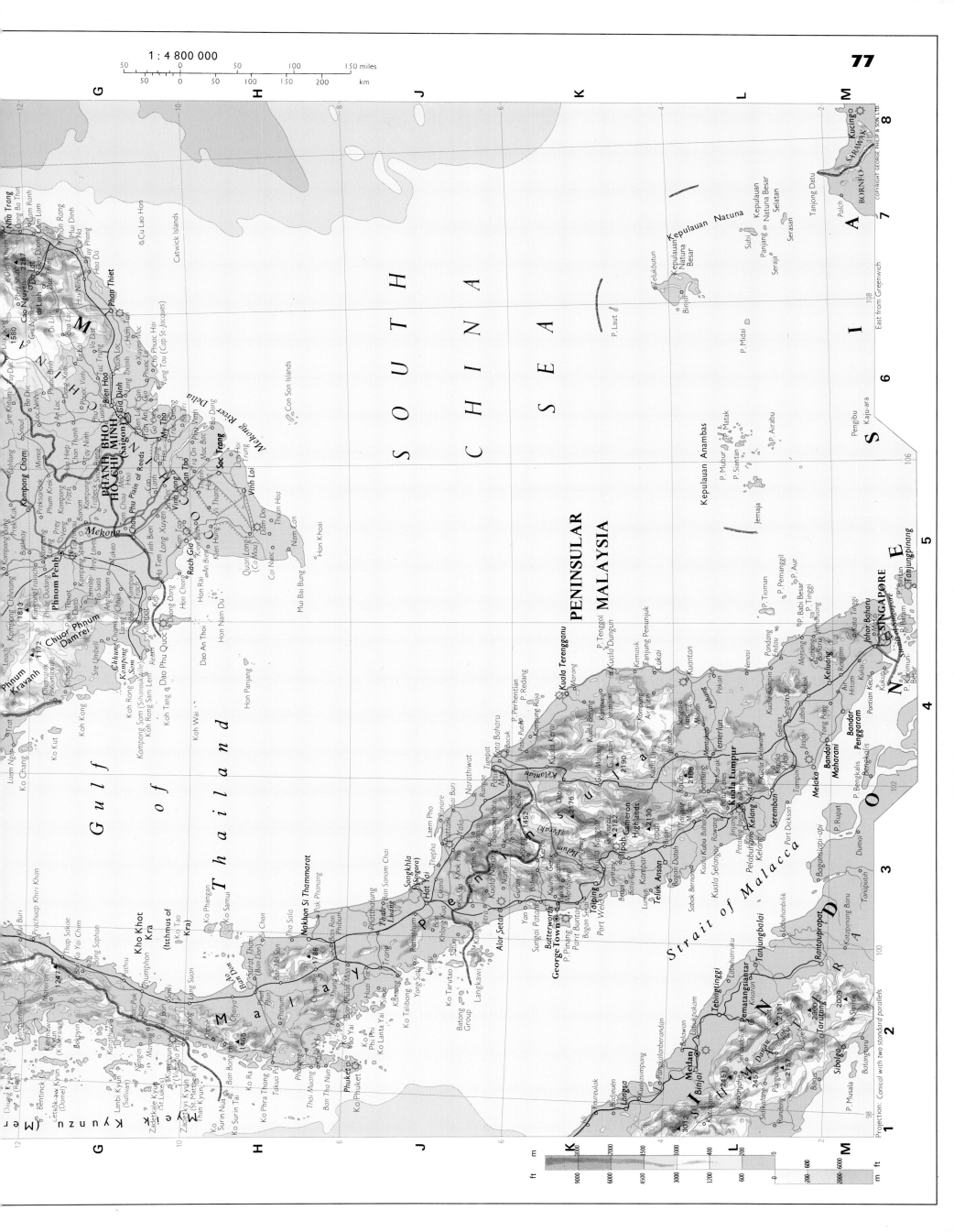

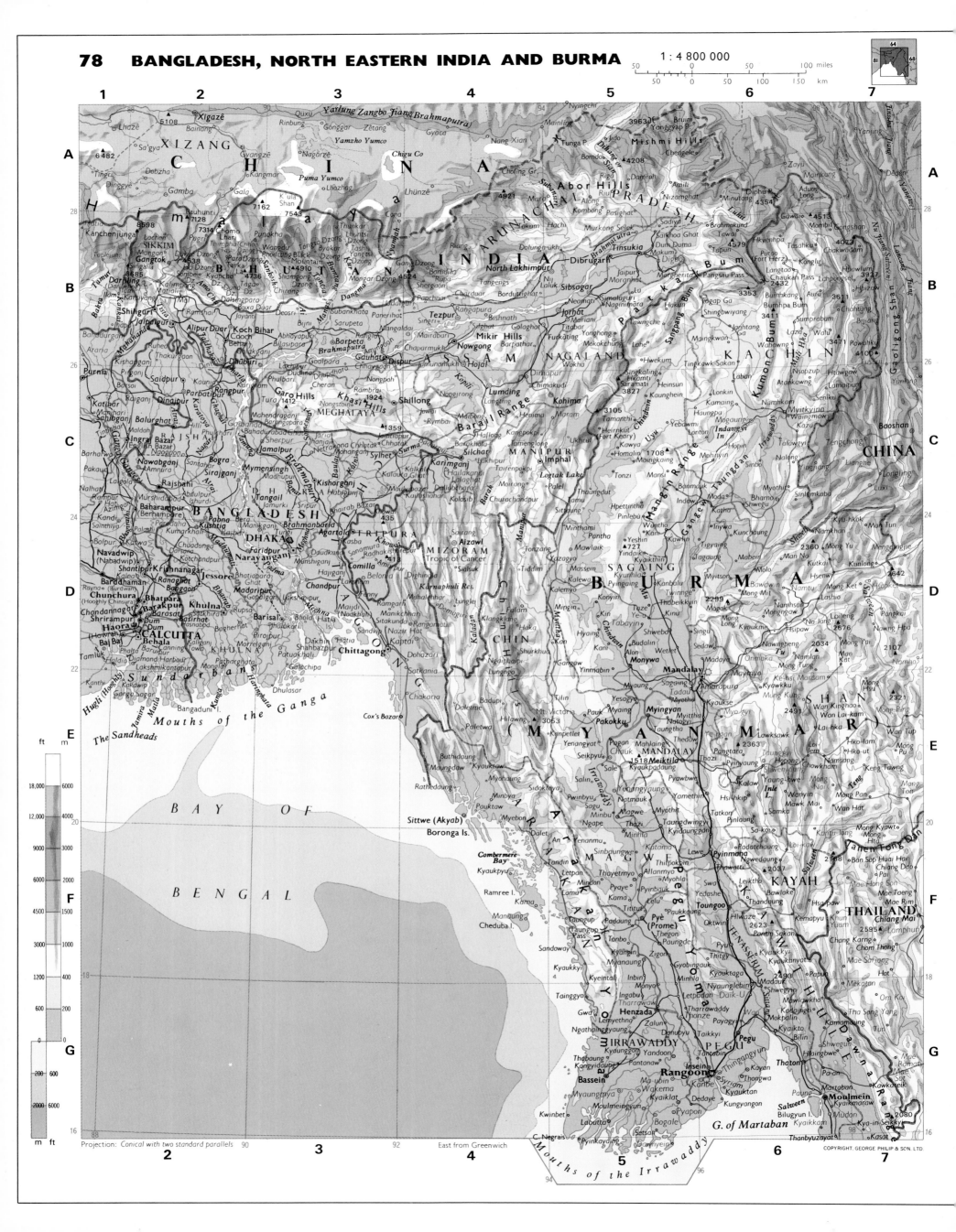

1 : 4 800 000

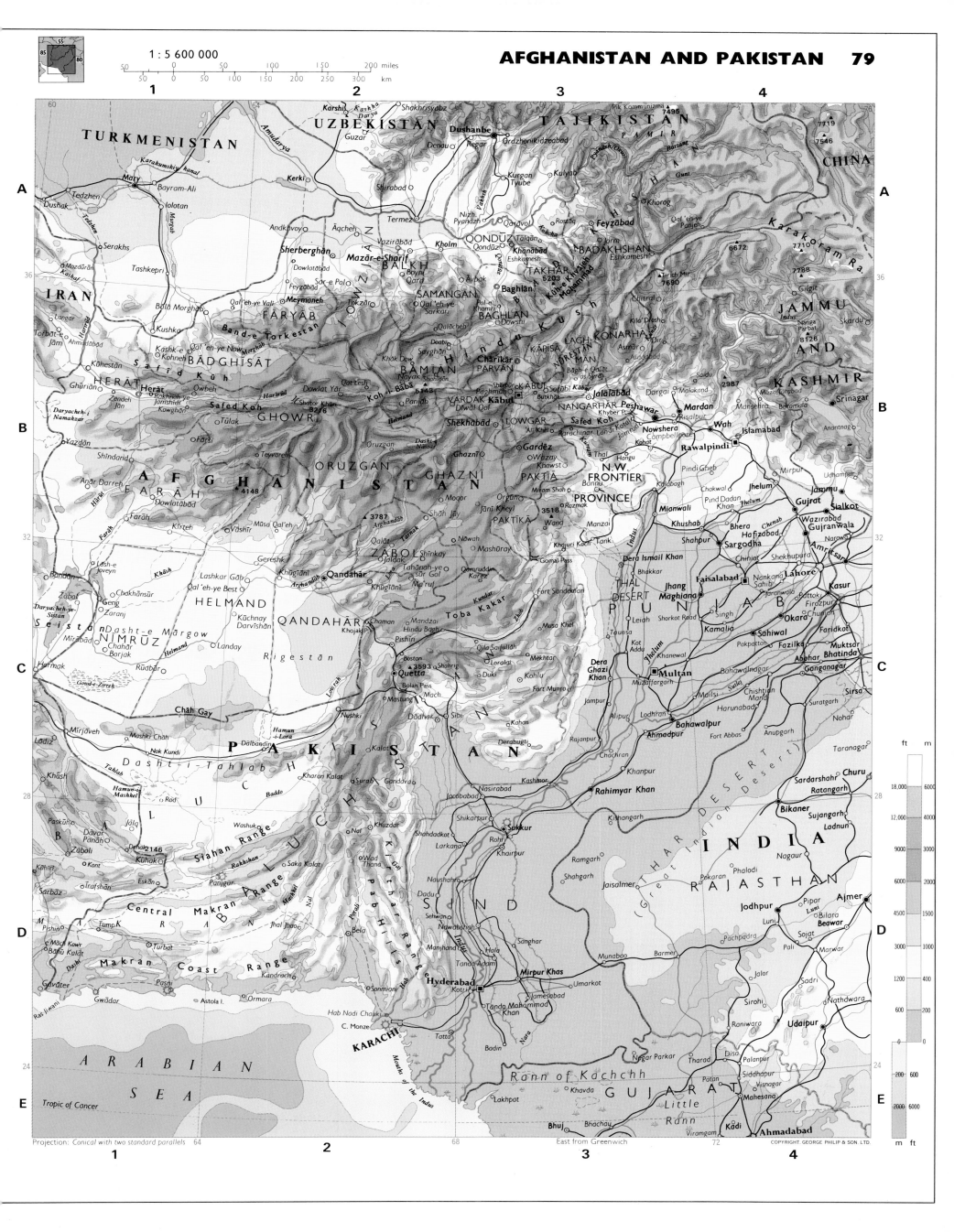

1 : 5 600 000

Projection: Conical with two standard parallels

East from Greenwich

COPYRIGHT. GEORGE. PHILIP & SON. LTD.

AFGHANISTAN

N.W. FRONTIER PROVINCE

Kabul

Peshawar
Rawalpindi
Islamabad
Srinagar

Mardan
Kohat

JAMMU AND KASHMIR

HIMACHAL PRADESH

Lahore
Amritsar
Jullundur
Ludhiana
Chandigarh
Dehra Dun

PUNJAB

Faisalabad
Gujranwala
Sialkot
Jammu

THAL DESERT

SALT RANGE

Multan
Dera Ghazi Khan
Bahawalpur

HARYANA

Patiala
Ambala
Meerut
DELHI
Faridabad

PAKISTAN

BALUCHISTAN

Quetta
Qandahar

SIND

RAJASTHAN

Great Indian (Thar) Desert

Bikaner
Jodhpur
Jaipur
Ajmer
Agra
Mathura
Alwar
Gwalior

Sukkur
Shikarpur
Larkana
Jacobabad
Khairpur
Jaisalmer
Barmer
Udaipur

Hyderabad
Mirpur Khas
Nawabshah

KARACHI

Mouths of the Indus

Rann of Kachchh

Little Rann

Gulf of Kachchh

Bhuj
Jamnagar
Rajkot
Porbandar
Junagadh
Bhavnagar
AHMADABAD
Vadodara
Bharuch

GUJARAT

MADHYA PRADESH

Ujjain
Indore
Bhopal
Dewas
Ratlam
Mandsaur

Tropic of Cancer

ARABIAN SEA

Gir Hills

Indus
Chenab
Sutlej
Luni
Banas
Chambal
Narmada
Tapi
Mahi

Kirthar Range

Pab Hills

Projection: Conical with two standard parallels

ft	m
18,000	6000
12,000	4000
9000	3000
6000	2000
4500	1500
3000	1000
1200	400
600	200
0	0

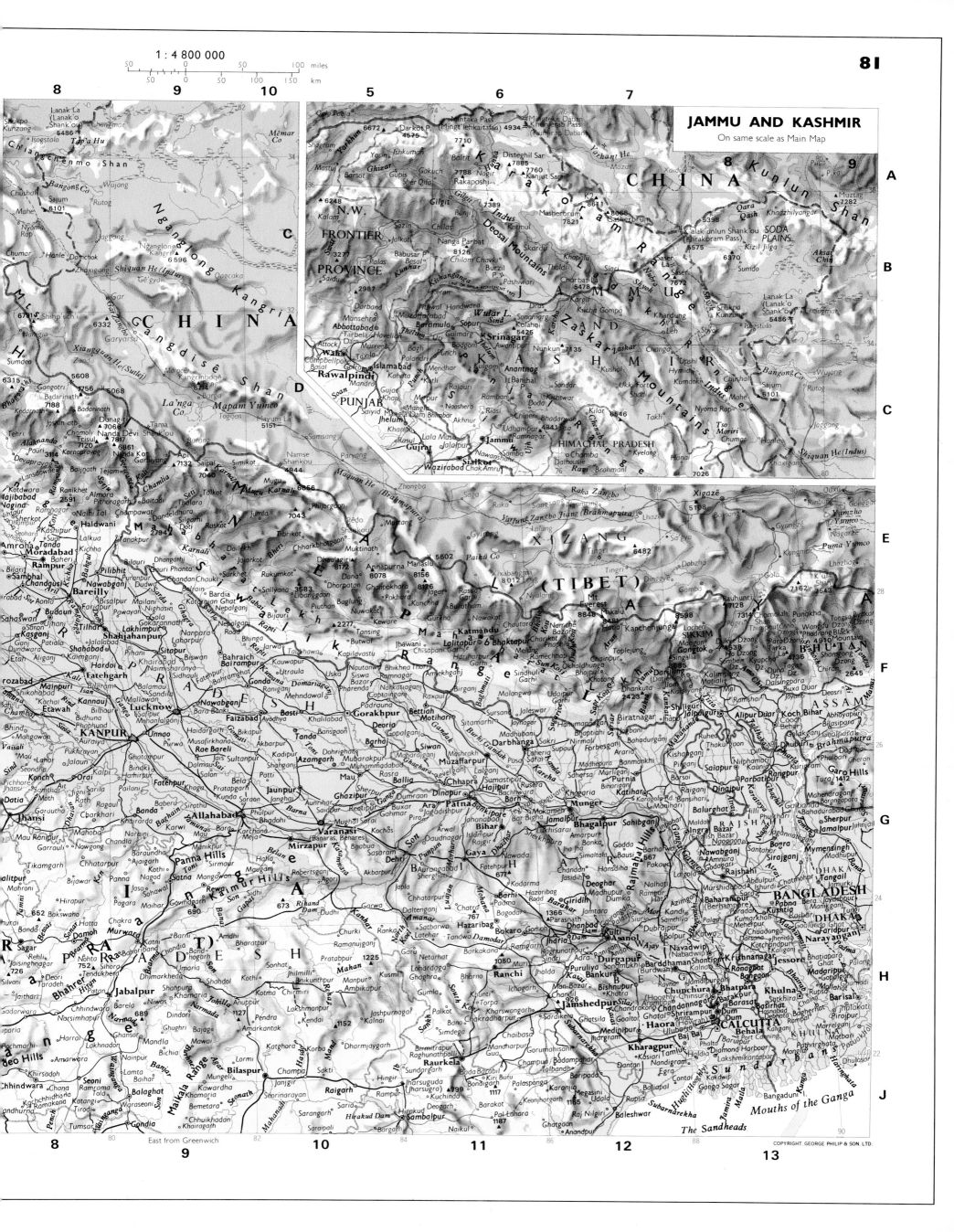

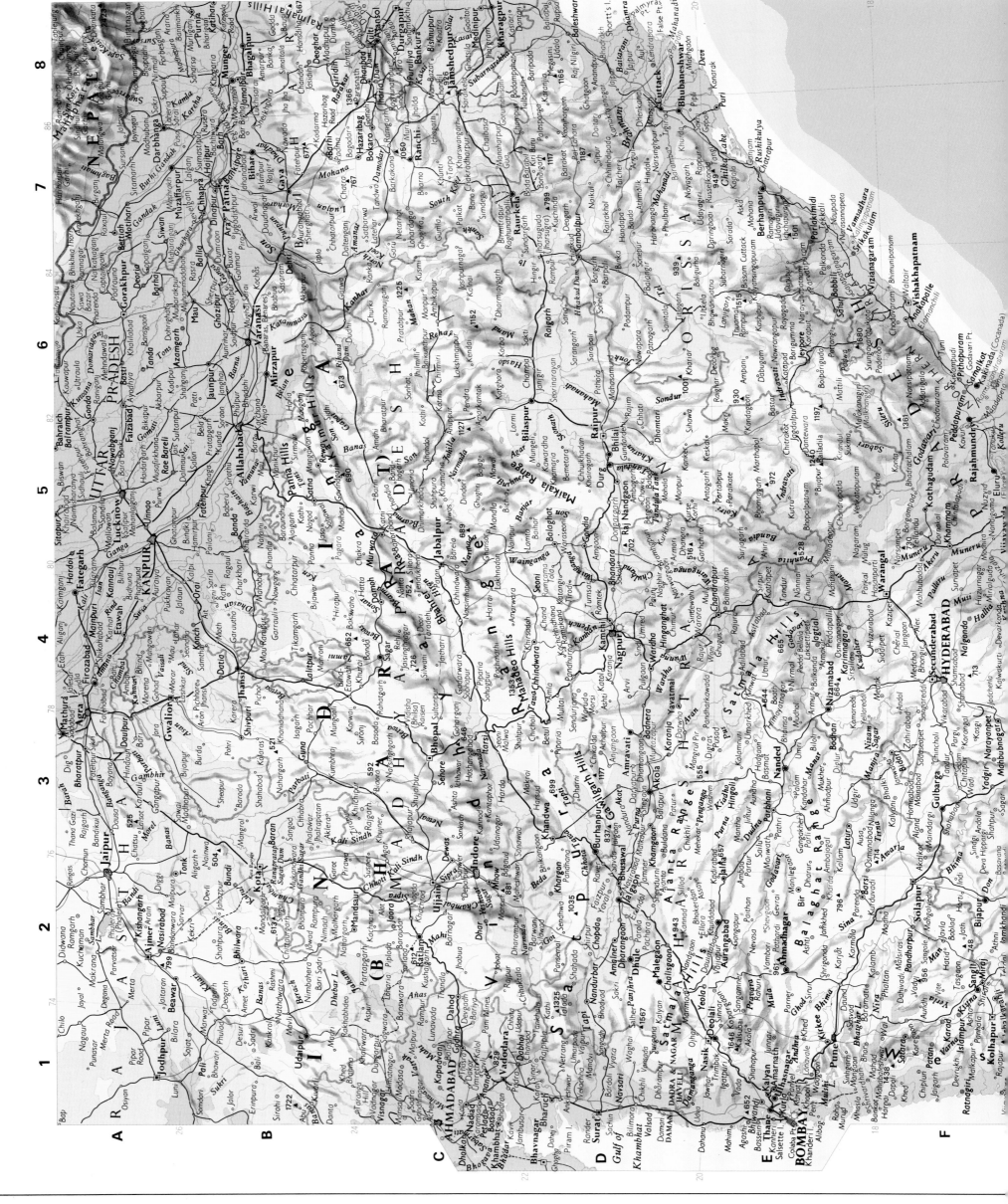

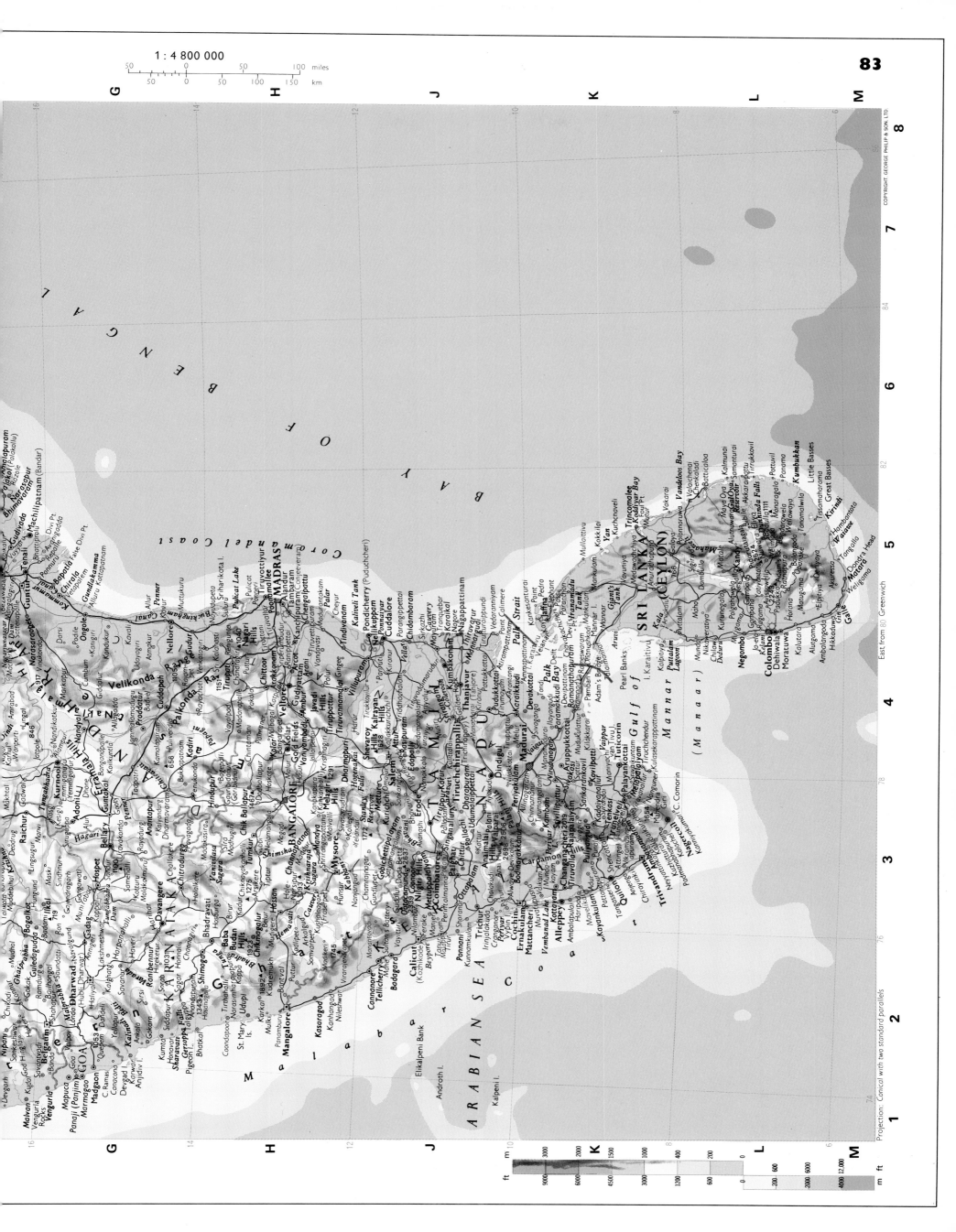

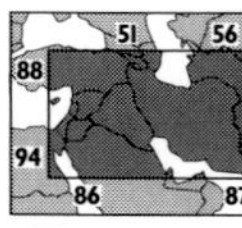

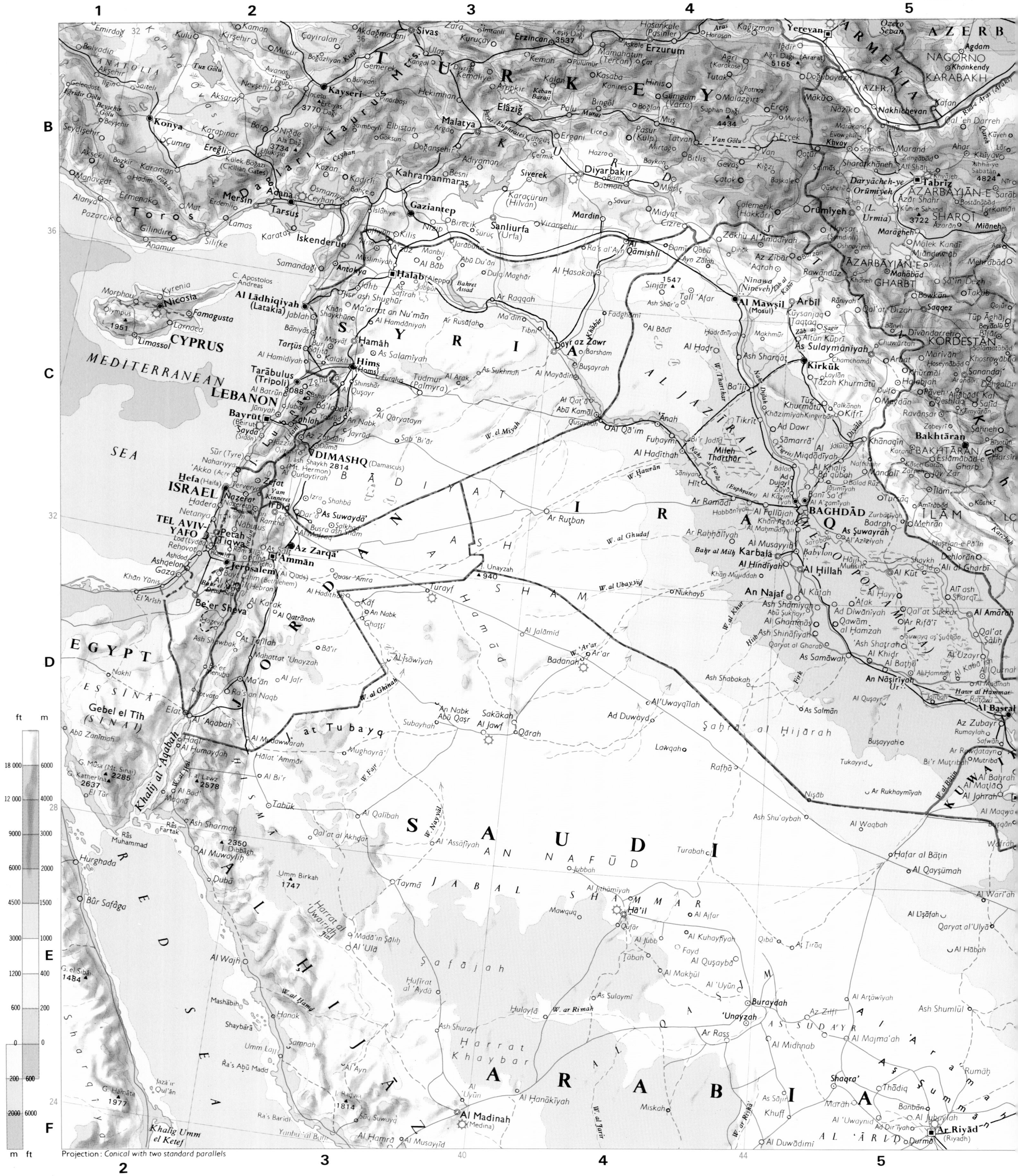

1 2 3 4 5

TURKEY

ANATOLIA

Konya Kayseri Sivas Erzurum Erzincan Yerevan **ARMENIA** **AZERB**

NAGORNO KARABAKH (AZER.) Khankendy

Mersin Tarsus Adana Gaziantep Kahramanmaras Malatya Elâziğ Diyarbakır Mardin Tabrīz **ĀZARBĀYJĀN-E SHARQĪ**

CYPRUS Nicosia Famagusta Limassol

MEDITERRANEAN SEA

SYRIA Halab (Aleppo) Al Lādhiqiyah (Latakia) Hamāh Hims Ar Raqqah Dayr az Zawr Al Ḩasakah Al Qāmishli Al Mawsil (Mosul) Arbīl **KORDESTĀN** As Sulaymānīyah Kirkūk

Tarābulus (Tripoli) **LEBANON** Bayrūt (Beirut) Sayda Sūr (Tyre)

DIMASHQ (Damascus)

ISRAEL Hefa (Haifa) Nazerat TEL AVIV-YAFO Jerusalem (Al Quds) Be'er Sheva

JORDAN **AMMAN** Az Zarqā'

IRAQ **BAGHDĀD** Karbalā' An Najaf Al Hillah Al Kūt Al 'Amārah An Nāşirīyah Al Basrah

ILĀM Bakhtārān Mehrān

EGYPT **E S S I N Â (SINAI)** Gebel el Tih Elat Al 'Aqabah

Tabūk

SAUDI ARABIA

AN NAFŪD

JABAL SHAMMAR Hā'il

HIJĀZ Al Wajh Al 'Ula

Buraydah 'Unayzah

KUWAIT Al Aḩmadī

Hafar al Bāţin

Al Madīnah (Medina)

AL 'ĀRIĐ **Ar Riyāḑ (Riyadh)** Shaqrā'

RED SEA **SHARM**

Hurghada Bûr Safâga

ft m
18 000 6000
12 000 4000
9000 3000
6000 2000
4500 1500
3000 1000
1200 400
600 200
0 0
200 600
2000 6000
m ft

Projection: Conical with two standard parallels

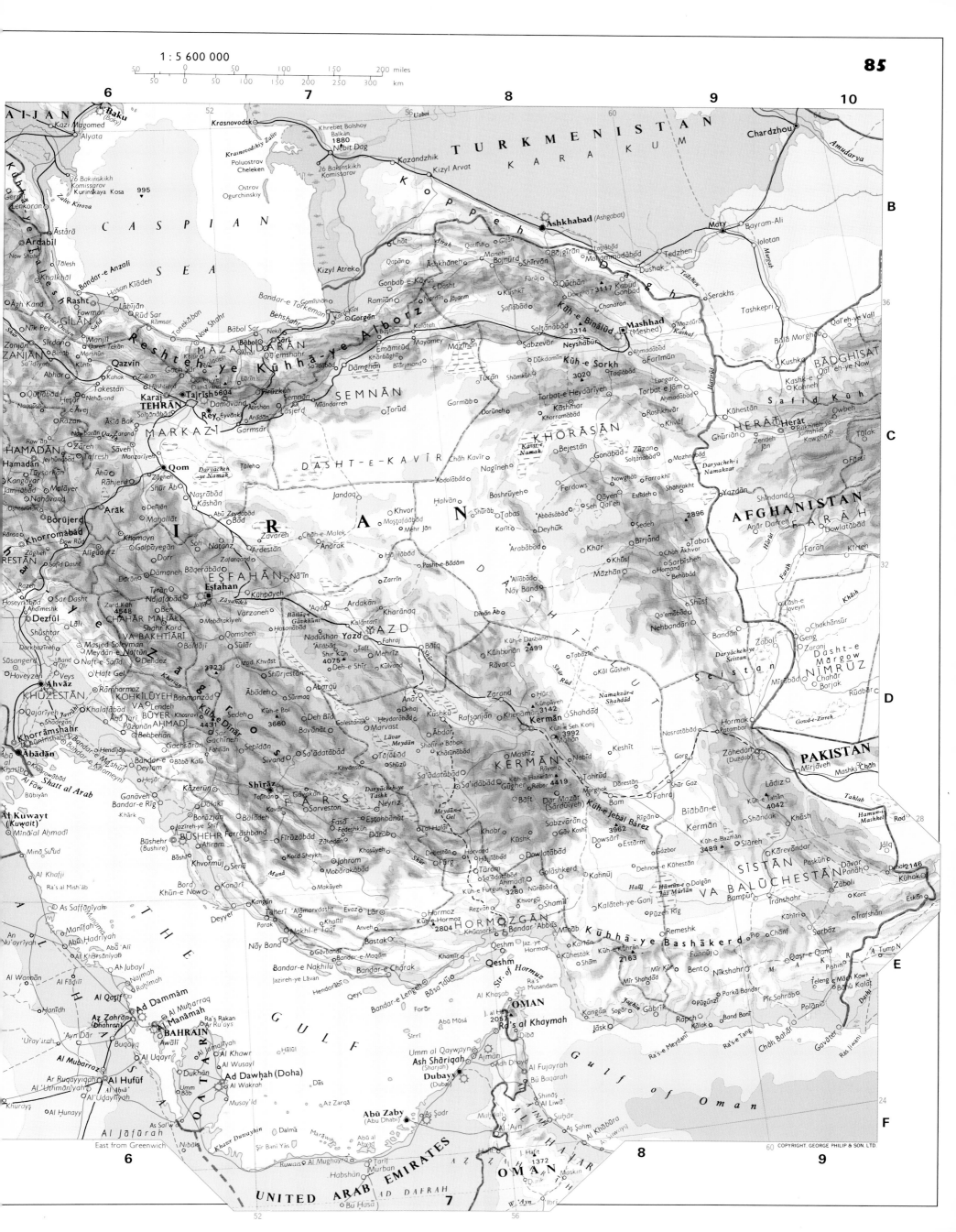

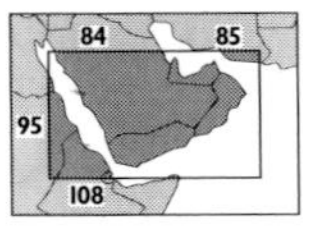

EGYPT

H I J A Z

R E D   S E A

SUDAN

Al Wajh
Madā'in Ṣāliḥ
Al 'Ulā
Ṣafājah
Al Jubb
Al Kuhayfīyah
Qiba
Aṭ Ṭirāq
Al Hōbah
G. el Sibāī 1484
Ḥulayfā'
Ṭābah
Fayd
Al Quṣayba
Mashābiha
Hanak
W. al Ḥamḍ
Al 'Uyūn
Buraydah
Az Zilfī
Ash Shumlūl
Shaybārā
Samnah
Ash Shurayf
As Sulaymī
'Unayzah
Al Arṭāwīyah
Umm Lajj
Harrat Khaybar
Al Midhnab
Al Majma'ah
Rumāḥ
Rā's Abū Madd
Al 'Ayn
Al Ḥanākīyah
Ar Rass
Shaqrā'
Thādiq
Banbān
Ra's Barīdī
Al Madīnah (Medina)
Miskah
As Sājir
Khuff
Māriḥ
Al Jubaylah
Jazā'ir Qul'ān
Khalig Umm el Ketef
Yanbu' al Baḥr
Al Qā'iyah
Al 'Uwaynid
Ad Dilam
Ar-Riyāḍ (Riyadh)
Al Ḥamrā
Abū Rubayq
Mahd adh Dhahab
Al Duwādimī
Al Quway'īyah
Durmā
As Salamīy
Al Yamā
Ra'īs
Ar Rayyānah
'Afif
Ar Ramāḍyāt
Ash Sha'rā'
As Sulaymī
Masṭūrah
Ar Rabad
Ḍafīnah
Sanām
Al Ḥarīq
AL ḤAWṬAH
Al Ḥillāh
Rābigh
Ḥarrat al Kishb
Ṭōlim
Halabān
Al Ḥulwah
Al Bi'ār
Muḥayriqah
Al Muwayh
 Khulays
Usfān
Dhahabān
Ra's Ḥāṭibah
Al Jumūm
Zaymān
Ushayrah
Sahl Rakbah
As Sūq
Harrat Nawāṣīf
As Sawādah
Al Hūwah
Ghayl
Al Ḥamar
Jiddah
Makkah
Medīnah
Sayl al Kabīr
W. al 'Aqīq
Khumrah
Ra's al Aswad
Shidād
At Ṭā'if
Turabah
'Umm Thalwīwah
W. Rānyah
Ar Rawdah
Al Kharfah
Layla
Al Badī
Masṭūrah
Al Līth
Ḥajrah
Banī Sār
Al 'Aqīq
W. Biṭḥah
Al Junaynah
Al Khamāsīn
Kumdah
Tamrah
Al Qunfudhah
Baljurshī
Qal'at Bīshah
Ar Rawshān
As Sulayyil
Ḥamdānah
Al 'Ulayyah
W. Tathlīth
Tathlīth
Sirrayn
Dawqah
Kudayṣ
An Nimāṣ
Ḥamdah
Khay
J. Ṣabāyā
Al Birk
Dirs
Ghurayrah
Bi'r Īdimah
Al Qaḥmah
Khamīs Mushayṭ
Abhā
Zahrān
W. Ḥabawnah
Abā as Su'ūd
Ash Shuqayq
Ad Darb
Sabyā
Āl 'Arīḍah
Su'dah
Wuday'ah
Jāzir Farasān (Farasan Is.)
Ra's Tārfa
Jīzān
Abū 'Arīsh 3200
Hayjān
Ṣabyā
Maydī
Hayrān
Fakam
Al Kharāb
Hūth
Harmil
Nora
Ḥarad
Khamir
W. al Jawf
Ḥiṣn al Abr
Harat
Dahlak Kebir
Sūd 'Abs
Antufash
Ḥayjah
Ḥajjah
Amrān
Ma'rib
Al Luḥayyah
Az Zaydīyah
Kawkabān 3600
Ṣan'ā 3770
Nuqūb
Shabwah
ERITREA
Nakfa
Keren
Mitsiwa (Massowa)
Kamarān (S. Yemen)
Ṣalif
Zubayr
Ḥamrā
Bājil
Manākhah
Ḥarīb
Bayḥān al Qiṣāb
Al Maghārim
Akordat
Asmera (Asmara)
Mersa Fatma
Al Ḥudaydah
Ma'bar
Dhamār 3350
Riḍā'
Niṣāb
Ar Rawdah
Al Ḥawṭah
Adi Ugri
Adi Keyih
Ras Shiakhs
Bayt al Faqīḥ
YEMEN
Bayhān
Al Baydā
Yashbum
Tessenei
Barentu
Om Hajer
Zabīd
W. Zabid
Hays
Ibb 3200
Al Manṣūrī
Qa'tabah
Al Qārah
Ḥubbān
Al Ḥuwaymī
Adwa
Aksum
Colulli
L. Asale
Mawshi
Rumaydah
Ta'izz
Al Dāli'
Lawdar
Aṣ Ṣurrah
Al 'Irqah
Mekele
Danakil Depression
Az Zuqur
Ḥanish
Mawṣil
Musaymīr
Aḥwar
Gallābāt
Adi Arkai
Ras Dashan 4620
Edd
Al Mukhā
Ubaydīyah
Madīnat ash Sha'b
Labī
Shaqrā'
Dabat
Dhubāb
At Turbah
Shaykh 'Uthmān
Al'Adan (Aden)
Gonder
1830 L. Tana
Sekota
Aṣeb (Assab)
Bab el Mandeb
Little Aden
ETHIOPIA
DJIBOUTI

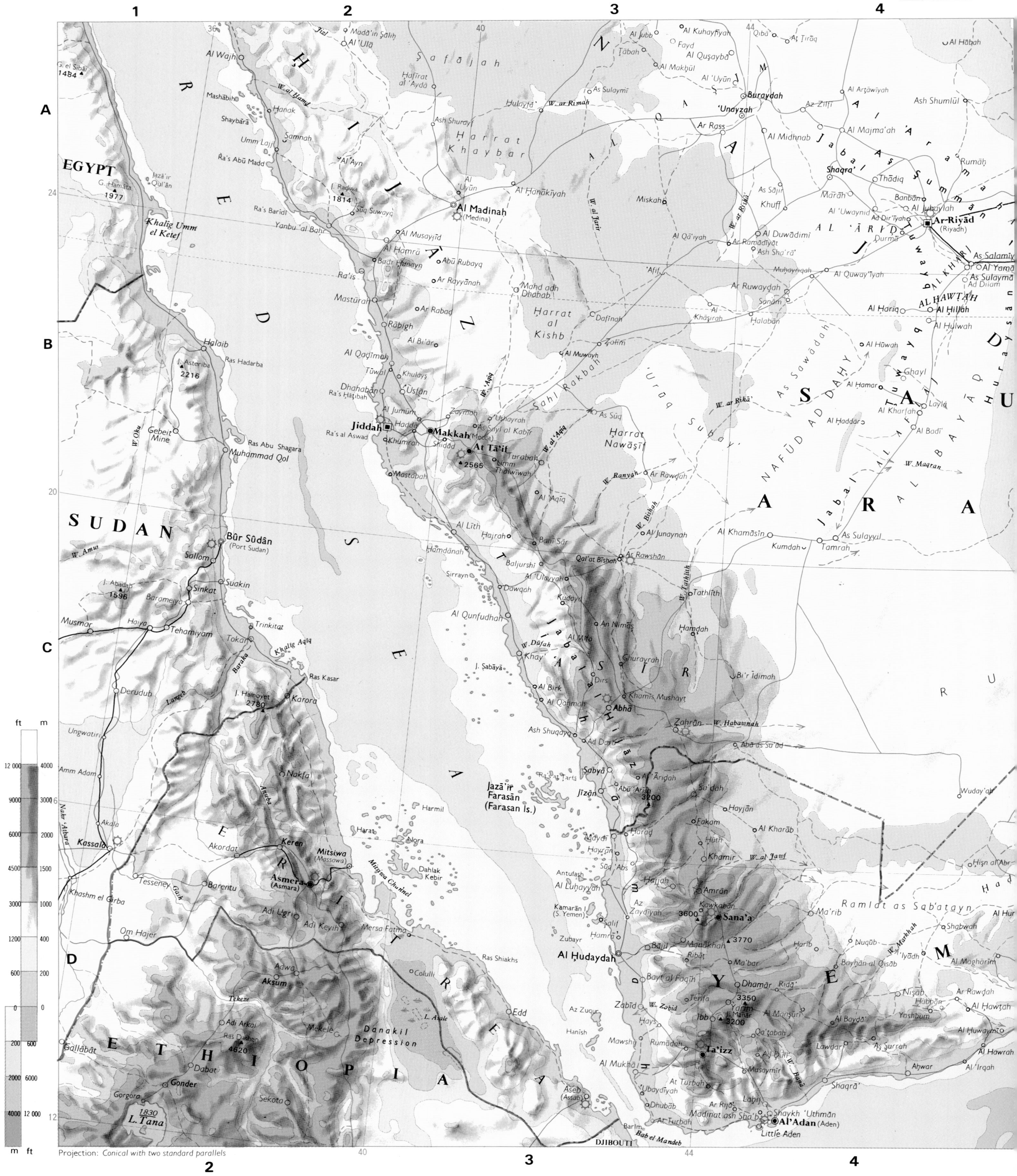

Projection: Conical with two standard parallels

ft / m scale:
12 000 / 4000
9000 / 3000
6000 / 2000
4500 / 1500
3000 / 1000
1200 / 400
600 / 200
0
200 / 600
2000 / 6000
4000 / 12000

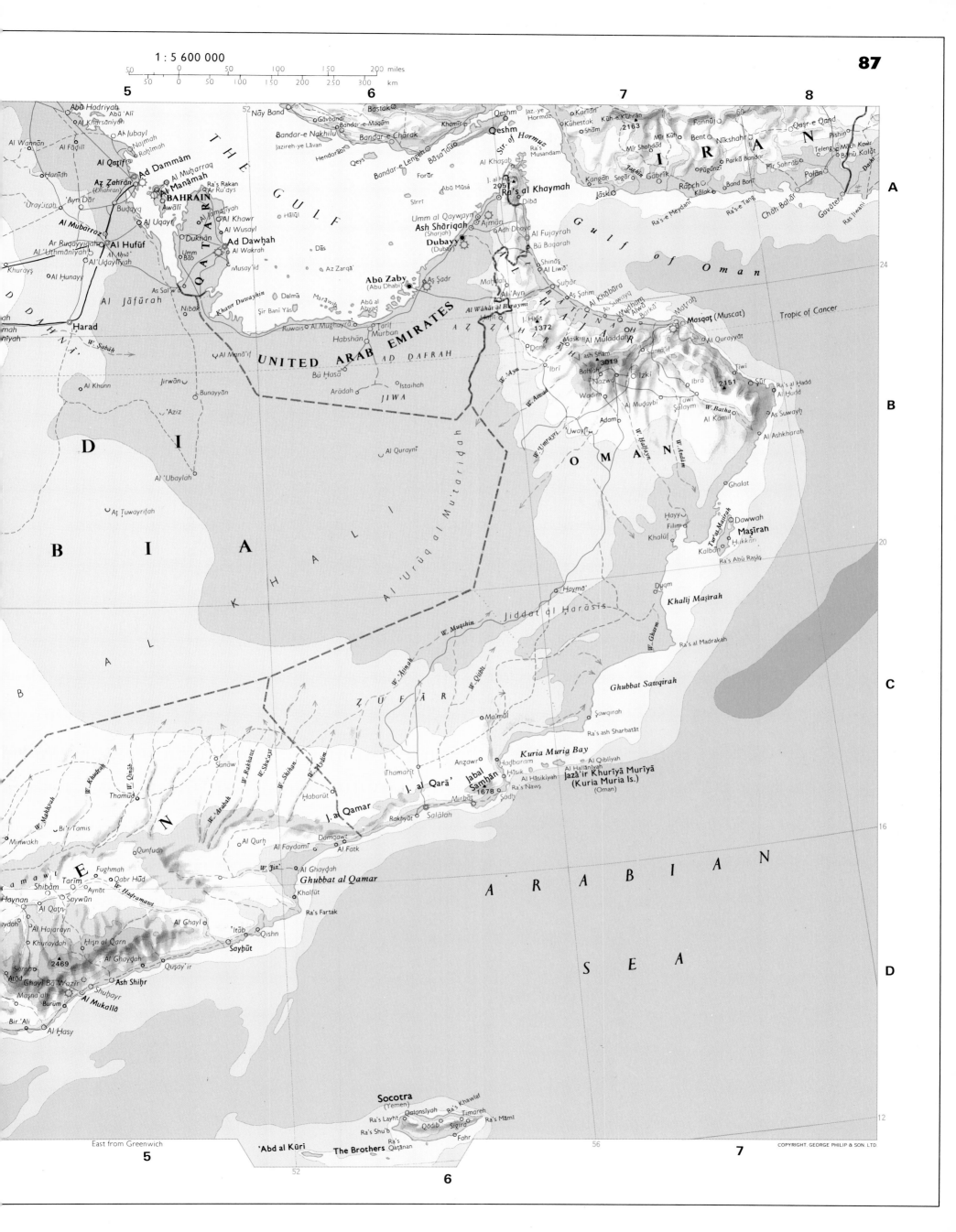

1 : 5 600 000

50   0   50   100   150   200 miles

50   0   50   100   150   200   250   300 km

5   **6**   **7**   **8**

Abū Hadrīyah
Abū 'Alī
Al Kharsānīyah
Al Jubayl
Najmah
Al Wannān
Al Faḍilī
Raḥīmah
Ḥanīdh
Al Qaṭīf
Ad Dammām
Al Muḥarraq
Az Zahrān
(Dhahran)
Al Manāmah
'Uray'irah
'Ayn Dār
BAHRAIN
Buqayq
Ar Ruqayyiqah
Al Muḇarraz
Al Uqayr
Al 'Uthmānīyah
Al Hufūf
Al Aḥsā'
'Udaylīyah
Khurays
Al Hunayy

THE GULF
Nāy Band
Gāvbandī
Bandar-e Māgām
Bastak
Bandar-e Nakhīlū
Bandar-e Chārak
Khamīr
Qeshm
Jazireh-ye Lāvan
Hendorābī
Bandar-e Lengeh
Bāsa'īdū
Qeshm
Str. of Hormuz
Qeys
Forūr
Abū Mūsā
Al Khaṣab
Ra's
Musandam
Sirrī
Dibā
Ra's al Khaymah
205 J. al Ḥarīm
Ḥālūl
Umm al Qaywayn
Ash Shāriqah
(Sharjah)
Adh Dhayd
Ajmān
Al Fujayrah
Dubayy
(Dubai)
Bū Baqarah
Shināṣ
Aṣ Ṣadr
Al Liwā'
Suḥār
Aṣ Ṣahm

IRAN
Kūhestak
Kārīān
Kūh-e Kührān
2163
Mīr Küh
Bent
Nīkshahr
Shām
Fannūj
Qasr-e Qand
Pishīn
Mīr Shahdād
Jāshm
IRAN
Kangān
Sogar
Gābrīk
Rāpch
Band Bonī
Jāsk
Ra's-e Meydānī
Kalāk
Chāh Bahār
Polān
Ra's-e Tang
Gavāter
Ras Jiwanī
Telengt
Mach Kowr
Bāhū Kalāt
Dashti
Pīr Sohrāb
pūgūnzī
Parkā Bandar

Al Qaṭrī
24

QATAR
Ra's Rakan
Ar Ru'ays
Al Khawr
Al Wusayl
Dukhān
Umm
Bāb
Ad Dawḥah
Al Wakrah
Das
Musay'īd
Az Zarqā'
Abū Zaby
(Abū Dhabī)
Dalmā
Marāwīh
Shīr Banī Yās
Abū
Abyaḍ
Al 'Ayn
Al Wāḥāt al Buraymī
Maṣīrah
As Suwayq
Wudhām
Alwā
Maṭraḥ
Masqaṭ (Muscat)
Al Quṟayyāt

Tropic of Cancer

Harad
Al Jāfūrah
Nibāk
Khawr Duwayhin
Ruwais
Al Mughayrā
Ṭarīf
Murbān
Habshān
Bū Ḥasā
UNITED ARAB EMIRATES
Ḥafīt
1372
Daṇk
Maskin
Al Muladdaḥr
ash Shām
Bahlah
3019
Ibrī
Nazwá
OMAN
Izki
Ṣūr
Ra's al Ḥadd
Al Ḥudd

RUB' AL KHĀLĪ
Al Khunn
Jirwān
Bunayyān
Arādah
Istaiḥah
JIWA
Al Quraynī
'Ayn
'Azīz
Al 'Ubaylah
Al 'Urūq al Mutarīḍah
W. Ḥalfayn
Wadīm
Adam
Al Muḍaybī
Tūwī
Ṣulaym
W. Baṭḥa
Al Kāmil
As Suwayḥ
Al Ashkharah

D I B I A
At Ṭuwayrīfah
KH
Ghalat

B

20

Hayy
Filim
Khalūf
Dawwah
Maṣīrah
Kalbān
Ḥukkān
Ra's Abū Raṣāṣ

Haymā'
Khalīj Maṣīrah
Duqm

A L   K H A L I
Jiddat al Ḥarāsis
W. Muqshin
Ra's al Madrakah

C

B
Z U F Ā R
W. 'Atīnah
W. Qitbīt
Ghubbat Sawqirah
Ma'mūl
Shawqirah
Ra's ash Sharbatāt

Sānaw
W. Rakhyūt
W. Shīḥan
W. Tthānī
Anzawr
Thamarīt
Kuria Muria Bay
Ḥaqbaram
Al Qibliyah
Thamūd
Ḥabarūt
J. al Qarā'
Jabal Samḥān
1678
Ḥāsik
Al Ḥallānīyah
Ḥāsikīyah
Jazā'ir Khurīyā Murīyā
(Kuria Muria Is.)
(Oman)
Bi'r Tamīs
J. al Qamar
Mirbāṭ
Rakhyūt
Ra's Nawṣ
Sādḥ
Minwakh
Fughmah
Qabr Hūd
Al Qurḥ
Al Faydamī
Al Fatk
Damqawt
Salālah

16

Ḥaḏramawt
Tarīm
Shibām
Aynāt
W. Jiz'
Al Ghaydah
W. Ḥaḏramawt
Haynan
Al Qaṭn
Qishn
Sayḥūt
Ghubbat al Qamar
Khalfūt
Ra's Fartak

A R A B I A N

Al Hajarayn
'Itāb
Saywūn
Al Ghayl
Khuraydah
Ḥiṣn al Qarn
2469
Al Ghaydah
Qusay'ir
Saraḇ
Ghayl Bā Wazīr
Ash Shihr
Maṣna'ah
Shuḇayr
Al Mukallā
Burum
Bīr 'Alī
Al Ḥasy

D

S E A

Socotra
(Yemen)
Ra's Layht
Qalansīyah
Ra's Khawlat
Timareh
Ra's Mami
Ra's Shu'b
Qādib
Sīgira
Fahr

12

'Abd al Kūri   **The Brothers**   Qatanan

B L A C K   S E A

MEDITERRANEAN SEA

BULGARIA
GREECE
THRACE
TURKEY

Projection : Conical with two standard parallels

Provinces in Turkey are named after the chief towns which are underlined.

Division between Greeks and Turks in Cyprus; Turks to the North.

Gorna Oryakhovitsa, Razgrad, Dobrich, Mangalia
Türnovo, Türgovishte, Kolarovgrad, Balchik
Gabrovo, Stara Planina (Balkan Mts), Nos Kaliakra
Yamrukchal, Sliven, Varna
Kazanlŭk, Stara Zagora, Yambol, Polianovgrad, Burgas
Dimitrovgrad, Elkhovo, Aytos
Khaskovo, Kŭrdzhali, Kirklareli, İğneada Burnu
Edirne, Babaeski, Vize, Demirköy
Komotini, Séta, Uzunköprü, Lüleburgaz
Alexandroúpolis, Keşan, Çorlu, Çatalca
Samothráki, Enez, Silivri, **İSTANBUL**
Gökçeada (İmroz), Tekirdağ, Büyükçekmece, Gebze, İzmit (Kocaeli), Adapazarı (Sakarya)
Gelibolu, Malkara, Marmara, İzmir Denizi (Sea of Marmara), Yalova, Gölcük, Sapanca
Limnos, Çanakkale, Bandırma, Mudanya, Orhangazi, Akyazı
Bozcaada, Troy, Biga, **Bursa**, İnegöl, Bilecik, Söğüt
Baba Burnu, Ezine, Edremit, Balya, Susurluk, Domaniç, Bozüyük, **Eskişehir**
Ayvacık, Edremit Körfezi, Balıkesir, Alaçam Dağları, Dursunbey, Tavşanlı
Lésvos (Lesbos), Bergama, Soma, **Kütahya**, Emet, Simav, Gediz, Altıntaş
Mitilíni, Akhisar, Demirci, Anadolu (Anatolia)
Khíos (Chios), Manisa, Turgutlu, Uşak, Afyonkarahisar
İzmir (Smyrna), Salihli, Eşme, Sandıklı
Çeşme, Sefarihisar, Torbalı, Ödemiş, Bozdoğan, Denizli
Sámos, Aydın, Nazilli, Pamukkale, Dinar, Burdur, Isparta, **Konya**
İkaría, Söke, Milas, Muğla, Tefenni, Beyşehir, Ereğli
Pátmos, Miletus, Ephesus, Çine, Bodrum, Göksu
Léros, Kos, Gökova Körfezi, Dalaman, Fethiye, Antalya, Aspendos
Dhodekánisos (Dodecanese), Marmaris, Köyceğiz, Kalkan, Finike, Kumluca
Ródhos (Rhodes), Datça, Xanthos, Kaş, Gelidonya Burnu, Kemer, Antalya Körfezi
Kárpathos, Megiste (Kastellórizon)

Zonguldak, Ereğli, Karabük, Bolu, İğaz Dağları, Kuzey Ana
PAPHLAGONIA, Kastamonu, Tosya, Samsun, Bafra
Küre Dağları, Devrekani, Sinop, Civa Burnu
Kerempe Burnu, İnce Burnu, Çatalzeytin, Gerze
BITHYNIA, Köroğlu Dağları, Çankırı, Çorum, Amasya, Turhal, Tokat
Köroğlu Dağları, Beypazarı, Kızılırmak, Çubuk
Sincan, Elmadağ, **Ankara**, Kırıkkale, Yozgat, Sorgun
GALATIA, Polatlı, Keskin, Kırşehir, CAPPADOCIA, **Sivas**
Hirfanlı Barajı, Kulu, Tuz Gölü, Mucur, Hacıbektaş
Şereflikoçhisar, Ortaköy, **Kayseri**, Nevşehir, Göreme
LYCAONIA, Aksaray, Niğde, Develi, Gürün, T U R
Obruk, Karapınar, Ereğli, **CATAONIA**, Kahramanmaraş
PISIDIA, Konya Ovası, Karaman, Kozan, Kadirli, Osmaniye, Gaziantep
PAMPHYLIA (Taurus), Toros Dağları, Adana, Ceyhan, Kilis
CILICIA, Tarsus, Mersin (İçel), İskenderun, Antakya (Hatay), Halab (Aleppo)
Anamur Burnu, Silifke, Kaş, Gülnar, İdlib

CYPRUS, K. Apóstolos Andreas, K. Kormakíti, Kyrenia, Nicosia, Famagusta, Morphou, Troodos, Larnaca, Paphos, Limassol, K. Gata, K. Greco

LEBANON, Tarābulus (Tripoli), Hamāh, Hims (Homs), Bāniyās, Maşyāf, Zghartā
Jubayl, Bayrut (Beirut), Zahlah, Dimashq (Damascus), Sayda (Sidon), Sūr (Tyre), Naharíyya, 'Akko (Acre), Zefat

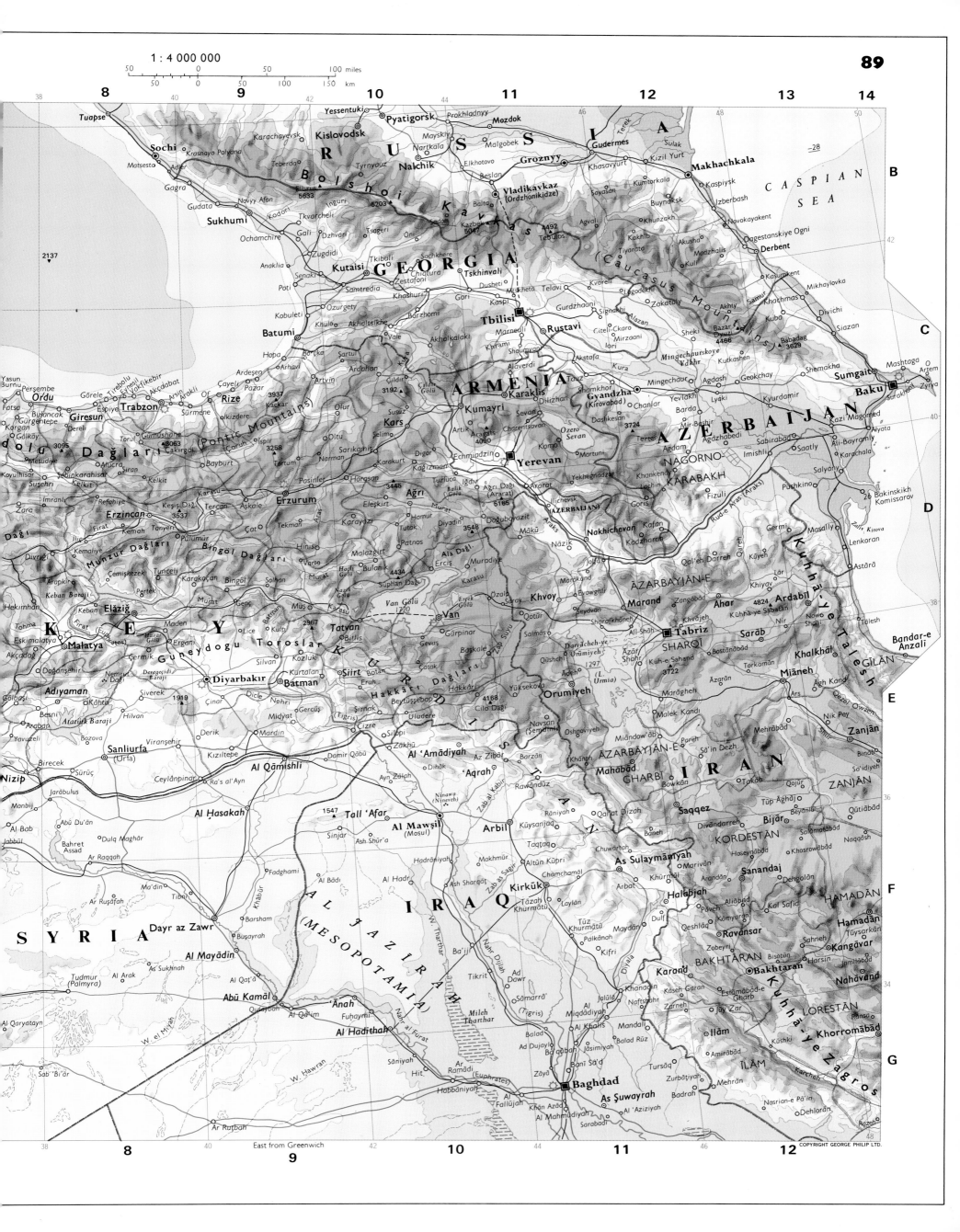

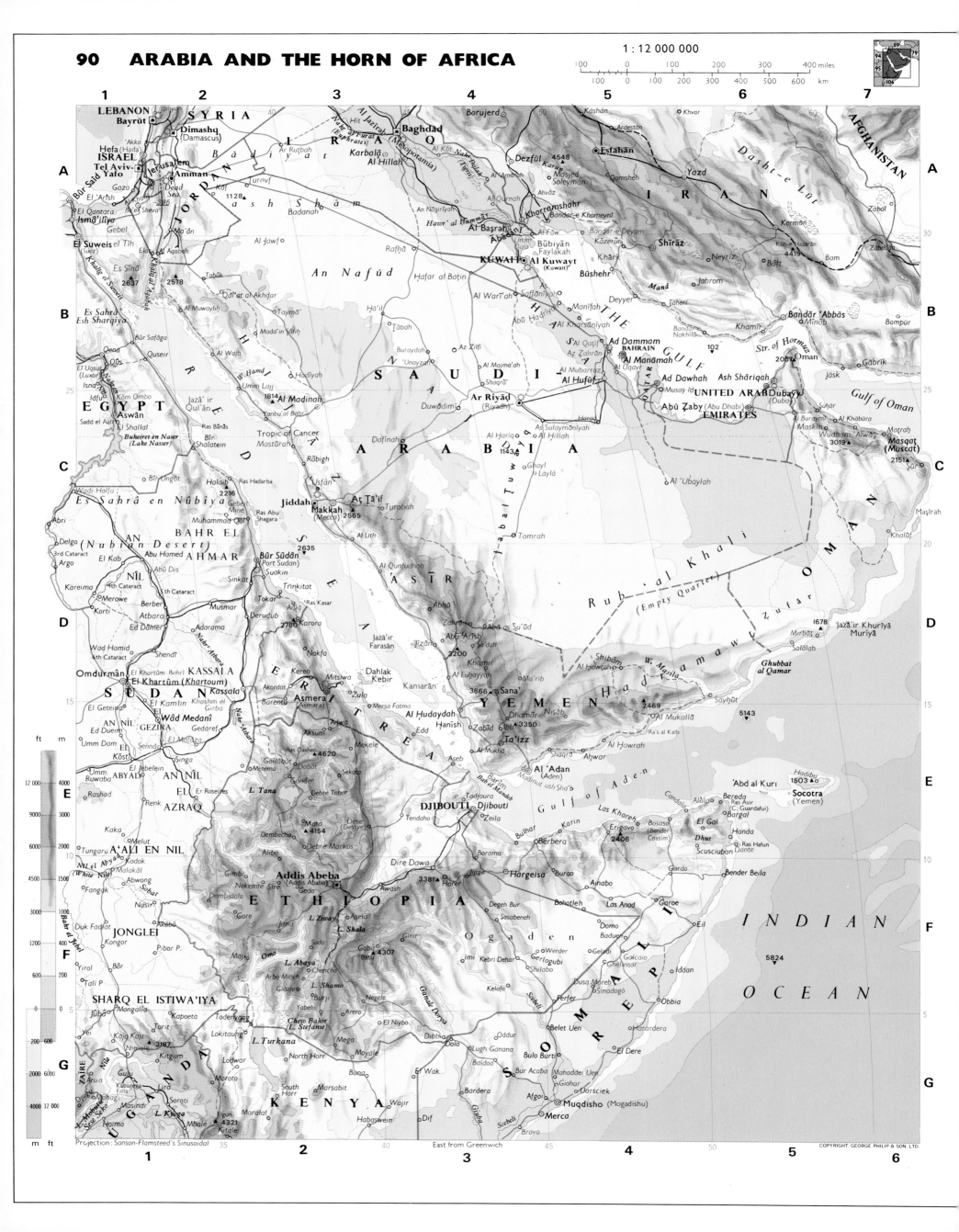

1 : 12 000 000

100   0   100   200   300   400 miles
100   0   100   200   300   400   500   600 km

1   2   3   4   5   6   7

LEBANON
Bayrūt
Hefa (Haifa)
Dimashq (Damascus)
ISRAEL
Tel Aviv-Yafo
Jerusalem
Amman
JORDAN
SYRIA
Hit
Al Jazīrah
Nahr al Furāt (Euphrates)
Baghdad (Mesopotamia)
Karbalā
Al Hillah
IRAQ
Borujerd
Eṣfahān
Dezfūl 4548
Kāshān
Khvor
Ardestān
IRAN
Dasht-e Lūt
AFGHANISTAN

Gaza
El 'Arīsh
Bûr Sa'îd
El Qantara
Ismaʿīliya
El Suweis (Suez)
Gebel el Tîh
Ma'ān
Badānah
An Nafūd
An Nāṣirīyah
Al Qurnah
Al Basrah
Khorramshahr
Ahvāz
Masjed Soleymān
Qomsheh
Yazd
Zābol

Es Sahrâ Esh Sharqiya
Tabūk 2578
2637
Qal'at al Akhdar
Madā'in Sālih
Taymā'
Tābah
Hafar al Batin
Rafhā
Hā'il
Al Warī'ah
Al Kharsānīyah
Manīfah
Deyyer
Būshehr
Khark
Mand
Tāheri
Bandar 'Abbās
Mināb
Khamīr
Bampūr

Es Sahrâ Esh Sharqiya
Bûr Safâga
Quseir
Al Wajh
Umm Lajj
Hodīyah
Buraydah
Az Zilfi
Al Majma'ah
Shaqrā'
'Unayzah
SAUDI
Ar Riyād (Riyadh)
S'Al Qatif
Az Zahrān
Al Mubarraz
Ad Dammam
BAHRAIN
Al Manāmah
Al Uqayr
Musay'īd
Ad Dawhah
QATAR
Ash Shāriqah
UNITED ARAB
Dubayy (Dubai)
Gulf of Oman
Str. of Hormuz
Jāsk
Gābrik
Oman
2057

EGYPT
Qena
Qūs
Aswan
Sadd el 'Ali
El Shallal
Buheiret en Naser (Lake Nasser)
Jazā'ir Qul'ān
Al Madinah 1814
Yanbu'al Bahr
Ras Bānās
Bîr Shalatein
Mastūrah
Tropic of Cancer
Rābigh
Usfān
ARABIA
Duwādimī
Dafīnah
1143
Al Hariq
Al Hillah
As Sulaymānīyah
Harad
Abū Zaby (Abu Dhabi)
EMIRATES
Al Buray" mī
Al Khābūra
Suhār
Maskin
Wudhām 'Alwá
3019
Maṣqat (Muscat)
2151
Sūr

Es Sahrâ en Nûbiya
Wadi Halfa
Bîr Ungāt
Halaib
Ras Hadarba
2216
Gebeit el Mine
Ras Abu Shagara
Jiddah
Makkah (Mecca) 2565
Aṭ Ṭā'if
Turabah
Al Lith
Tamrah
Ghayl o Laylá
Al 'Ubaylah
Maṣīrah
Khalūf

Abri
Delgo
3rd Cataract
Argo
El Kab
Abū Dis
Abū Hamed
BAHR EL AHMAR
(Nubian Desert)
AN
Kareima
Merowe
4th Cataract
Berber
5th Cataract
Musmar
Sinkat
Suakin
Trinkitat
2635
Bûr Sûdân (Port Sudan)
Al Qunfudhah
'ASĪR
OMAN
Rub'al Khali
(Empty Quarter)
Hadramawt
Zufār
1678
Mirbāt
Salālah
Jazā'ir Khurīyā Murīyā

Korti
Atbara
Ed Dāmer
Derudub
Karora
2780
Jazā'ir Farasān
Abū 'Arīsh
Sa'dah
3200
Zahrān
Abā as Su'ūd
Khamir
Shibām
Al Hawṭah
W. Masīla
Ghubbat al Qamar

Omdurmān
El Khartūm Bahrī
SUDAN
El Khartūm (Khartoum)
KASSALA
Kassala
Khashm el Girba
Nakfa
Keren
Mitsiwa
Dahlak Kebir
Al Luhayyah
Ma'rib
3666 Sana'
2469
Al Hawtah
Sāyhūt
5143

El Geteina
El Kamlin
Wâd Medanî
GEZIRA
Gedaref
ERITREA
Asmera (Asmara)
Barentu
Adwa
Zula
Mersa Fatma
YEMEN
Al Hudaydah
Hanish
Zabīd
Ilbb 3350
Dhamār
Niṣāb
Al Mukallā
Ra's al Kalb

AN NIL
El Dueim
Ed Duweim
Umm Dam
EL GEZIRA
El Mafaza
Sennâr
Singa
Aksum
Ras Dashen 4620
Mekele
Edd
Ta'izz
Al Mukhā
Shaqrā
Ahwar
Al Hawrah

Umm Ruwaba
Rashad
ABYAD
El Obeid
El Jebelein
Metema
Gondar
Dabat
Gallabāt
Aseb
Barīm
Bāb el Mandeb
Al 'Adan (Aden)
Madīnat ush Sha'b
'Abd al Kuri
Socotra (Yemen)
Hadiby 1503

AN NIL
Kaka
Renk
EL AZRAQ
Er Roseires
L. Tana
Debre Tabor
Mota 4154
Dese (Dessye)
Tadjoura
DJIBOUTI
Djibouti
Zeila
Gulf of Aden
Karin
Las Khoreh
Bosaso (Bender Cassim)
2406
El Gal
Candala
Alūla
Bereda
Ras Asir (C. Guardafui)
Bargal
Handa
Dhut

A'ALI EN NIL
Tungaru
Kodok
Nil el Abyad (White Nile)
Malakal
Abwong
Fangak
Nasir
Dembidolo
Nekemte
Sirè
Gimbi
Addis Abeba (Addis Ababa)
ETHIOPIA
Awash
3381 Harer
Jijiga
Dire Dawa
Hargeisa
Burao
Ainabo
Erigavo
Scusciuban
Dante
Ras Hafun
Bender Beila
Gardo

JONGLEI
Duk Fadiat
Kongor
Pibor P.
Bahr el Jebel
Gore
L. Ziway
L. Shala
Asela
Ginir
Degeh Bur
Sasabeneh
Bohotleh
Las Anod
Domo
Baduen
Eil
INDIAN
5824

Tirol
Bôr
Tali P
Majī
Omo
L. Abaya
Sodo
Chencha
Gaba 4307
Batu
Imi
Kebri Dehar
Gerlogubi
Shilabo
Geladi
Ghelinsor
Galcaio
Dusa Mareb
Sinadogo
Iddan
Obbia
OCEAN

SHARQ EL ISTIWA'IYA
Jūba
Mongalla
Kapoeta
Torit
Arbo Minch
Gidole
L. Shamo
Negele
Arero
Dibbisa
Kelafa
Ferfer
Belet Uen
Harardera

Yei
Kajo Kaji
3187
Taderkanp
Chezo Bahir (L. Stefanie)
Yabelo
Burti
El Niybo
Dolo
Lugh Ganana
Bulo Burti
El Dere

ZAIRE
Gulu
Kabalega Falls
Lira
Soroti
UGANDA
Moroto
Kitale
4321
Eldon
L. Kyoga
Mbale
Kitgum
Lokitaung
L. Turkana
North Horr
Marsabit
South Horr
Moyale
Boaa
El Wak
SOMALI
Bardera
Afgoi
Muqdisho (Mogadishu)
Merca
Brava
Mahaddei Uen
Giohar
Uarsciek
Scebeli
Bur Acaba
Baidoa

KENYA
Mbale
Kitale
Marsabit
Habaswein
Wajir
Dif
Gimba

Projection: Sanson-Flamsteed's Sinusoidal
East from Greenwich

ft   m
12 000   4000
9000   3000
6000   2000
4500   1500
3000   1000
1200   400
600   200
0   0
200   600
2000   6000
4000   12 000
m   ft

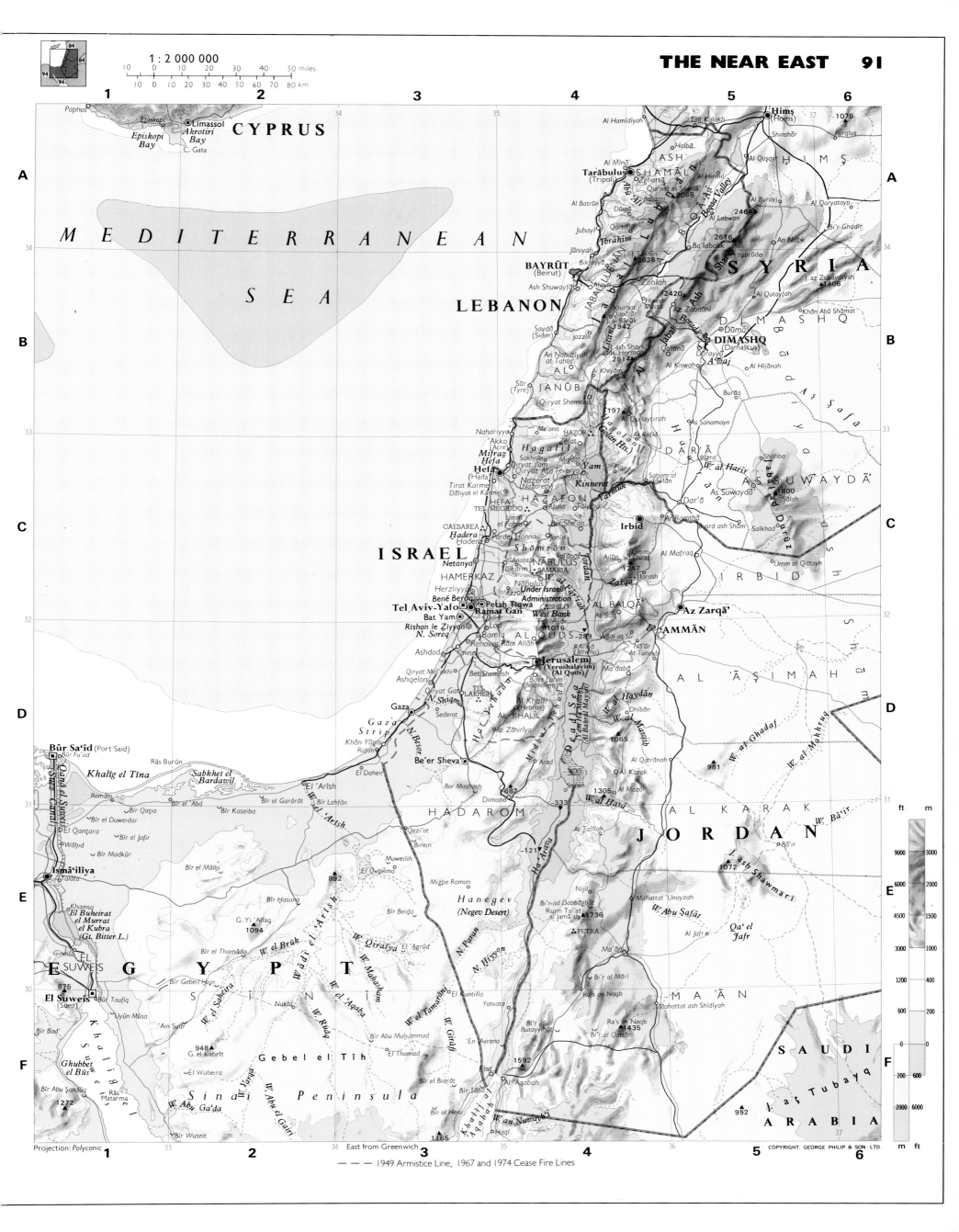

1 : 2 000 000

10   0   10   20   30   40   50 miles
10   0   10   20   30   40   50   60   70   80 km

CYPRUS

Paphos
Episkopi
Akrotiri Bay
Limassol
Episkopi Bay
C. Gata

M E D I T E R R A N E A N

S E A

Al Hamidiyah   Tall Kalakh   Ḥimṣ (Homs)   1075
                                                                 Furqlus
Al Minā'   Halba   Al Qusayr   ḤIMṢ   Al Qaryatayn
Ṭarābulus (Tripoli)   ASH SHAMĀL   Al Hirmil   Bi'r Ghadīr
Al Batrūn   Zghartā   Qurnat as Sawda'   3088   Al Buraij
Dūmā   Bsharri   Bᴇqaa Valley   An Nabk
Jubayl   Qarṭaba   Al Labwah   2646
Ibrāhīm   2616   Ba'labakk   2628   2420
Jūniyah   Bikfayyā   Ygbrūdo   **SYRIA**
BAYRŪT (Beirut)   Ash Shuwayfāt   Zaḥlah   Ash   J. az Zubaydīyah   1406
                                                                        Al Qutayfah
LEBANON   Sayda (Sidon)   Jazzīn   2814   Jabal Baradā   **DIMASHQ (Damascus)**
                                                                                              Dūmā   DIMASHQ
An Nabaṭīyah at Taḥtā   Ash Shaykh   Qaṭanā   Dārayyā   A'ṭaj   Al Hijānah
AL JANŪB   Sur (Tyre)   Al Khiyām   Al Kiswah   Al Ḥijānah
Qiryat Shemona   197   Qunayṭirah   As Sanamayn   Burāq   **AS SAFĀ**
Naharīyya   Ḥ   Golan Hts.   Al Rafīd   **DARʿĀ**
'Akko (Acre)   **Hagalil**   Zefat   W. al Ḥarīr   Shahba
Mifraz Hefa   Sakhnīn   Migdal   Fīq   As Suwaydā   **AS SUWAYDĀ**
Hefa (Haifa)   Qiryat Yam   Ṭeverya   Saham al Jawlān   Dar'ā   1800
Tirat Karmel   Qiryat Ata   **Yam**   **Kinneret**   Busrā ash Shām   Salah
Dāliyat el Karmel   Nazerat (Nazareth)   Yarmūk   Salkhad   **Jabal ad Durūz**
HEFA   HAZAFON   'Afula   Umm al Qittayn
TEL MEGIDDO   Umm al Fahm   Bet She'an   **Irbid**   Al Ramthā
CAESAREA   Janīn   **Shōmrōn**   Ajlūn   Al Mafraq   **IRBID**
Hadera   Pardes Hanna   'Arrabūn   Umm ad Daraj   Umm al Qittayn
ISRAEL   Ṭūlkarm   **NĀBULUS**   1247   Jarash
Netanya   **HAMERKAZ**   **SAMARIA**   Zarqā   **Az Zarqāʾ**
Herzliyya   Azzūn   Nāblus   W. al Far'ah   AL BALQĀ   **AMMĀN**
Benē Beraq   **Under Israeli Administration**   As Salṭ
Petah Tiqwa   **SHILO**   Wādī as Sīr   **AL ʿĀṢIMAH**
Tel Aviv-Yafo   Ramat Gan   **West Bank**   Tel Aṣūr   Na'ūr
Bat Yam   Rishon le Ziyyon   1016   'Arīḥā (Jericho)   At Tunayb   Ma'daba
N. Soreq   Lod   **AL QUDS**   289
Ashdod   Ramla   Ram Allāh   Ma'dabā
Rehovot   **Jerusalem (Yerushalayim) (Al Quds)**
Qiryat Mal'akhi   Qavnel   Bayt Laḥm (Bethlehem)
Ashqelon   Bet Shemesh   **Dead Sea**   W. al Ḥaydān
Qiryat Gat   **TEL LAKHISH**   Yam Ha Melaḥ (Al Baḥr al Mayyit)   1065
Gaza   N. Shiqma   Al Khalīl (Hebron)   **AL KARAK**   981
Gaza Strip   Sederot   **AL KHALIL**   Al Karak
Khān Yūnis   N. Besor   Az Ẓāhīrīya   Mu'tah
Rafaḥ   **Be'er Sheva**   Arad   1305   Al Mazar
Bûr Saʿîd (Port Said)   El Daheir   **Midbar Yehuda**   Al Qaṭrānah
Bûr Fu'ad   Bor Mashash   882   333
Khalîg el Tîna   El 'Arîsh   Dimona   **JORDAN**   W. al Ghadaf
Sabkhet el Bardawil   Romāni   Bir Lahfān   At Tafīlah   Bā'ir   W. al Makhrūq
Râs Burûn   Bir el 'Abd   W. el 'Arîsh   121   Bā'ir
Bir Qaṭia   **HADAROM**   Ha 'Arava   Jash Shawmari   W. Bā'ir
Ismâ'ilîya   El Qantara   Bir el Jafir   Bir Kaseiba   Qezi'ot   1072
El Qanṭara   Bir el Mālḥi   Birein   Mizbe Ramon   **MAʿĀN**
Wâḥid   Bir Madkûr   Muweilih   El Quseima   **Hanegev (Negev Desert)**   Bi'r ad Dabbāghāt   Qa' el Jafr
Khamsa   892   Bi'r al Mārī   Maḥaṭṭat 'Unayẓah
El Buheirat el Murrat el Kubra (Gt. Bitter L.)   G. Yi 'Allaq   Bir Beiḍa   Ru'im Tal'at al Jamā'a   1736   W. Abu Safār   **ʿAMMĀN**
                                                            1094   **PETRA**   Al Jafr
Ginefa   Bir el Thamāda   W. Qiraiya   El 'Agrūd   N. Paran   Ma'ān
EL SUWEIS   **E G Y P T**   W. el Brûk   W. Mahasham   N. Ḥiyyon   Nijil
El Suweis (Suez)   875   **S I N Â I**   Nakhl   W. el 'Aqaba   Bi'r al Māri   **MAʿĀN**   1435
Bûr Taufiq   'Uyûn Mûsa   W. el Sahêra   W. el Tamarīni   Bir al Qaṭṭar   Ra's an Naqb   Mahaṭṭat ash Shidīyah
'Ain Sudr   W. el Giraṭi   El Kuntilla   Ra's an Naqb   **SAUDI**
Bir Bad'   948   Bir Abu Muḥammad   Yotvata   Bir al Butayyihāt
Ghubbet el Bûs   G. el Kabrît   **Gebel el Tîh**   El Thamad   1592   **ARABIA**
Bir Abu Ṣandaq   El Wabeira   Bir el Biarât   **Elat**   **Jᴀl aṭ Tubayq**
1272   Bir Wuseit   W. Abu Ga'da   W. Abu el Giri   Bir el Heisi   Bor Ṭaba   Al 'Aqabah   952
                                                                                      Khalîg Aqaba   W. an Nuwaybi'
                                                            1165   Ḥaql

Projection: Polyconic   East from Greenwich   COPYRIGHT. GEORGE PHILIP & SON. LTD.

– – – – 1949 Armistice Line, 1967 and 1974 Cease Fire Lines

ft   m
9000   3000
6000   2000
4500   1500
3000   1000
1200   400
600   200
200   60
0
200   60
2000   6000
m   ft

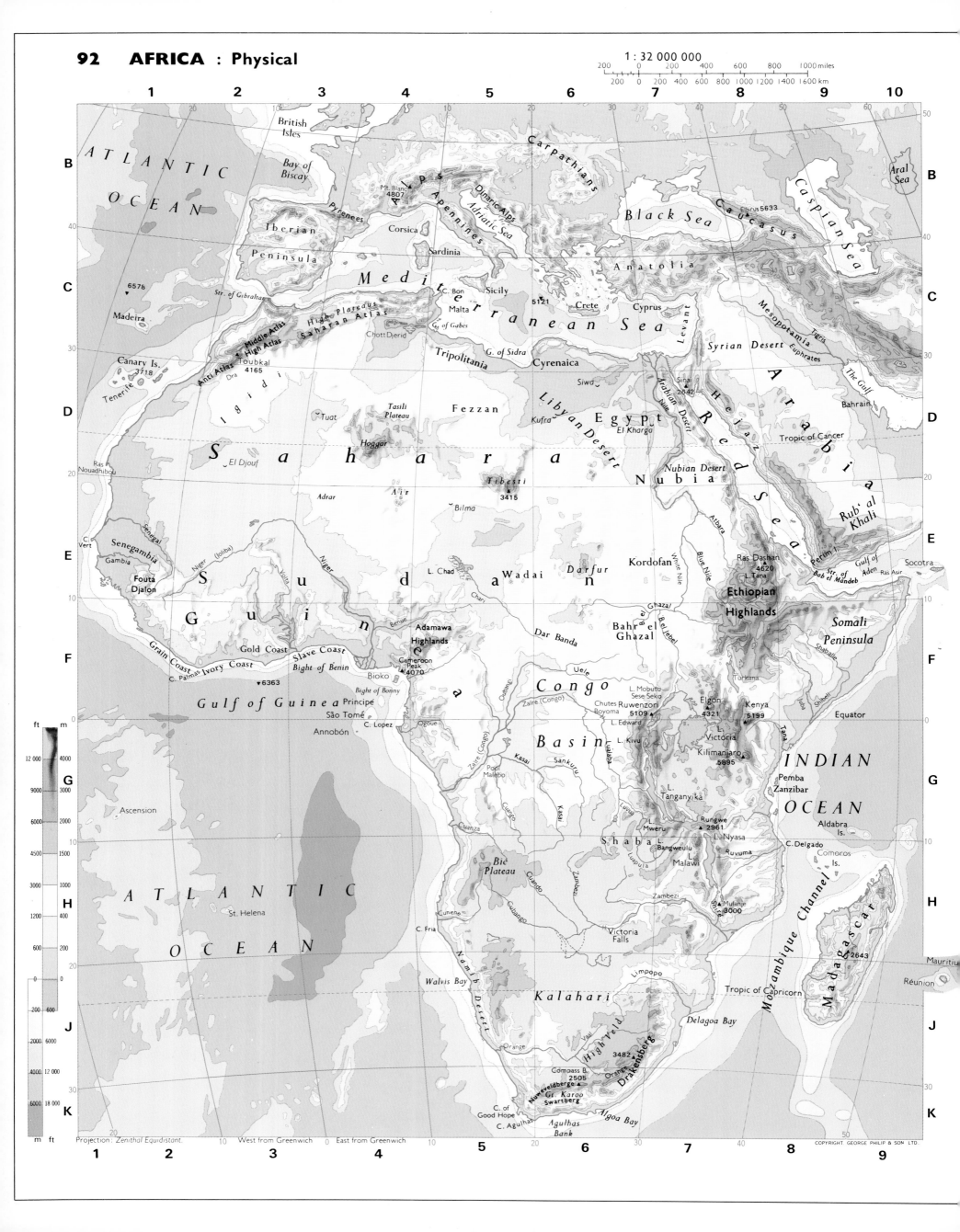

1 : 32 000 000

COPYRIGHT GEORGE PHILIP & SON LTD.

Projection: Zenithal Equidistant.

1 : 32 000 000

200   0   200   400   600   800   1000 miles
200 0 200 400 600 800 1000 1200 1400 1600 km

ATLANTIC

OCEAN

UNITED KINGDOM
□London
NETH.
BELG.
GERMANY
□Prague
CZECH
□Paris
FRANCE
SWITZ.
AUSTRIA
□Vienna
HUNGARY
POLAND
□Warsaw
SLOVAK
□Kiev
UKRAINE
RUSSIA
•Volgograd
KAZAKHSTAN
Aral Sea

Bay of Biscay
CROATIA
BOS. HERZ.
YUG.
ROMANIA
□Odessa
BULGARIA
□Istanbul
Black Sea
GEORGIA
ARM.
AZERB.
□Baku
Caspian Sea
TURKMEN.

Madrid
SPAIN
PORTUGAL
Lisbon
Corsica
ITALY
Rome
Adriatic Sea
ALB.
MAC.
GREECE
Athens
Crete
CYPRUS
TURKEY
Ankara
•Aleppo
Mosul
•Tehran
SYRIA
LEB.
Damascus
Baghdad
•Esfahan
IRAN

Madeira (Port.)
Tetouan
•Gibraltar (Br.)
Algiers
Annaba
Constantine
•Oran
Sicily
MALTA
Tunis
TUNISIA
Sfax
Mediterranean Sea
Tel Aviv -Jaffa
Port Said
ISRAEL
Jerusalem
JORDAN
Syrian Desert
Euphrates
Tigris
Basra
KUWAIT
Bahrain I.
QATAR

Casablanca
Rabat Fès
MOROCCO
•Marrakesh
Chott Djerid
Tripoli
Misratah
Benghazi
Alexandria
CAIRO
El Faiyum
Suez
SAUDI
•Riyadh
The Gulf

Canary Is. (Sp.)
El Aaiun
WESTERN SAHARA
Dra
ALGERIA
•In Salah
LIBYA
Marzuq
Ghadames
EGYPT
Asyut
Nile
Aswan
Tropic of Cancer
•Medina
ARABIA
•Mecca
Jedda

Ras Nouadhibou (Cap Blanc)
Dakhla
F'Dérik
Sahara
Al Jawf
Wadi Halfa
Pt. Sudan
Red Sea

Nouakchott
MAURITANIA
Tombouctou (Timbuktu)
Agades
NIGER
CHAD
El Fasher
SUDAN
Khartoum
Omdurman
Atbara
Kassala
Atbara
•Mesewa
Asmera
ERITREA
YEMEN
G. of Aden
Socotra (Yemen)
Ras Asir (C. Guardafui)

St. Louis
C. Vert
Dakar
SENEGAL
Senegal
MALI
Niger
Niamey
Bamako
BURKINA FASO
Ouagadougou
Kano
Maiduguri
L. Chad
Abéché
Ndjamena (Ft. Lamy)
El Obeid
Wad Medani
L. Tana
DJIBOUTI
Djibouti
Berbera

GAMBIA
Banjul
GUINEA-BISSAU
Bissau
GUINEA
Bobo-Dioulasso
Kaduna
BENIN
NIGERIA
Abuja
Benue
Wau
Bahr el Jebel
Addis Ababa
Malakal
ETHIOPIA
Harer
Shabelle
SOMALI REP.

Conakry
Freetown
SIERRA LEONE
IVORY COAST
Kumasi
Bouake
GHANA
TOGO
Lomé
Ibadan
Lagos
Enugu
Port Harcourt
CAMEROON
CENTRAL AFRICAN REPUBLIC
Bangui
Ubangi
Zaire (Congo)
L. Turkana
L. Tana

Monrovia
LIBERIA
Abidjan
Accra
Yamoussoukro
Porto-Novo
Sekondi Takoradi
Bight of Benin
Douala
Yaoundé
Bioko
EQUATORIAL GUINEA
SAO TOMÉ & PRINCIPE
Rio Muni
Kisangani
Mbandaka
L. Mobutu Sese Seko
L. Edward
L. Kivu
RWANDA
Kigali
BURUNDI
Bujumbura
UGANDA
Kampala
KENYA
Kisumu
L. Victoria
Nairobi
Mombasa
Jubba
Tana
Kismayu
Mogadishu (Mogadiscio)

Gulf of Guinea
Annobon
C. Lopez
Libreville
GABON
CONGO
Equator
Brazzaville
Pointe Noire
CABINDA
Kinshasa
Matadi
ZAÏRE
Kananga
Kasai
Lualaba
Mwanza
TANZANIA
Dodoma
Zanzibar
Dar-es-Salaam
INDIAN OCEAN

Luanda
ANGOLA
Lobito
Huambo
Namibe
L. Tanganyika
L. Mweru
L. Nyasa
L. Malawi
Ruvuma
C. Delgado
COMOROS
Aldabra Is.
Antsiranana

ATLANTIC
St. Helena (Br.)
Ascension (Br.)
Likasi
Lubumbashi
Ndola
ZAMBIA
Lilongwe
MALAWI
Blantyre
Mozambique
Mahajanga

NAMIBIA
Cunene
Cubango
Cuango
Lusaka
Zambezi
Harare
Livingstone
ZIMBABWE
Bulawayo
MOZAMBIQUE
Beira
Mozambique Channel
Antananarivo
MADAGASCAR
MAURITIUS
Réunion (Fr)
Toamasina
Fianarantsoa

OCEAN
Walvis Bay (South Africa)
Windhoek
BOTSWANA
C. Fria
Limpopo
Tropic of Capricorn

Gaborone
TRANSVAAL
Pretoria
Mbabane
SWAZILAND
Maputo
Johannesburg
ORANGE FREE STATE
Vaal
Orange
Kimberley
Bloemfontein
Maseru
LESOTHO
NATAL
Durban
SOUTH AFRICA
CAPE PROVINCE
East London
Cape Town
C. of Good Hope
Port Elizabeth
C. Agulhas

Nairobi Capital Cities
West from Greenwich   East from Greenwich
COPYRIGHT GEORGE PHILIP & SON. LTD

1 : 6 400 000

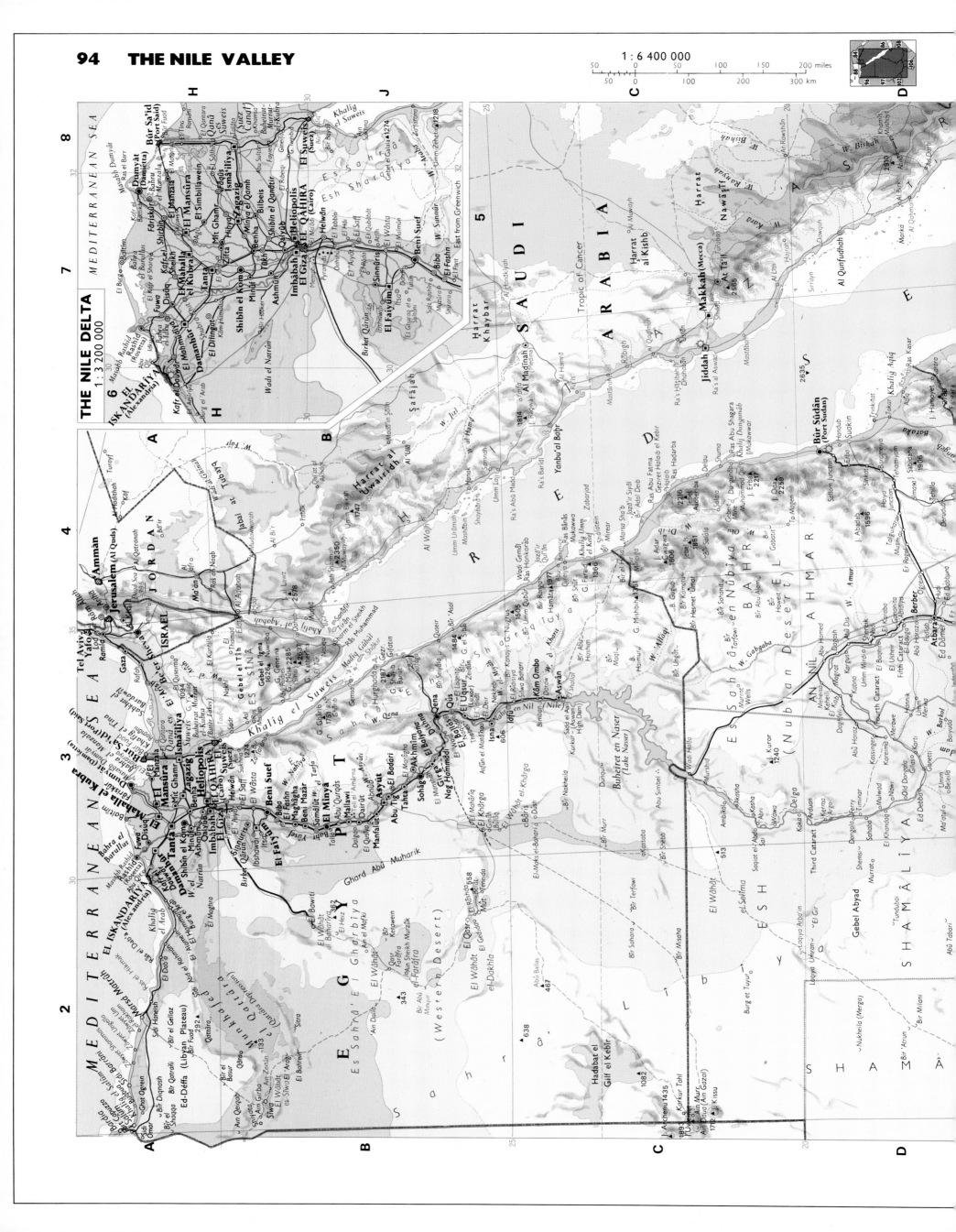

THE NILE DELTA
1 : 3 200 000

YEMEN

Jazā'ir Faraṣān al Kabir

ERITREA

DJIBOUTI

Mitsiwa
ASMERA (Asmara)
Keren

Mekele
Aksum
Adwa

GONDER
L. Tana
Gonder

ETHIOPIA

Dese

ADDIS ABEBA (Addis Ababa)
Nazret
Debre Zeyt

Dire Dawa
HARGE

SHEWA

WELEGA
Nekemte
 Gore
ILUBABOR

KEFA
Jima

GAMO-GOFA

SIDAMO

L. Turkana (L. Rudolf)

KENYA

SOMALI REP.

SUDAN

KASSALA
Kassala
Gedaref

Khashm el Girba

Shendi
Omdurmān
El Khartûm Bahrî
El Khartûm (Khartoum)
Wad Medanî
Singa

EL KHARTÛM
GEZIRA
EN NIL EL AZRAQ

Ed Dueim
El Kôsti
EN NIL EL ABYAD

El Obeid
KORDOFÂN
ESH SHAMÂL

Jibalan Nubah (Nuba Mts.)

En Nahud

DÂRFÛR
El Fâsher

BAHR EL GHAZAL
Wâw

AALI EN NIL
Malakâl

Jûba
EQUATORIA

UGANDA

ZAIRE

CENTRAL AFRICAN REPUBLIC

Buta

Projection: Lambert's Equivalent Azimuthal

East from Greenwich

COPYRIGHT GEORGE PHILIP & SON LTD

EGYPT

MEDITERRANEAN SEA

LIBYA

TUNISIA

ALGERIA

SICILIA (It.)

MALTA

Sahra

Sahara

Tarābulus (Tripoli)

Banghāzī (Benghazi)

Darnah

Miṣrātah

Surt

Khalīj Surt (Gulf of Sidra)

Zāwiyat al Bayḍā

Al Marj

Ajdābiyah

Al Jaghbūb

Siwa

Al Kufrah

Rebiana

Sabhah (Sebha)

Marzūq

Ghadāmis

Ghāt

Sfax

Gabès

Sousse

Kairouan

TUNIS

Bizerte

CONSTANTINE

Annaba

Iráklion

Kríti

Kikládhes

Pelopónnisos

Tripolis

Catánia

Siracusa

Ragusa

Caltanissetta

Agrigento

Pantelleria

Valletta

Djerba

Zuwārah

Al Khums

Zlīṭan

Tājūrā

Gharyān

Miżdah

Nālūt

Al Hammādah al Ḥamrā'

Sarīr Tibastī

Ténéré

Tropic of Cancer

Idehan Marzūq

Al Haruj al Aswad

Waddān

Hūn

Zillah

Sarīr Calanscio

Al Jabal al Akhḍar

Ad Diffah

Marsā al Burayqah

Bi'r Zaltan

Tmassah

Al Qaṭrūn

Erg d'Admer

Tassili n'Ajjer

Plateau du Tinrhert

Grand Erg Oriental

Chott Djerid

El Oued

Gafsa

Médenine

Zarzis

Tozeur

Nefta

Adrar 2254

Waw an Nāmūs

El Wāḥāt (Libyan Plateau)

Tūbruq

Wādān

Al Jufrah

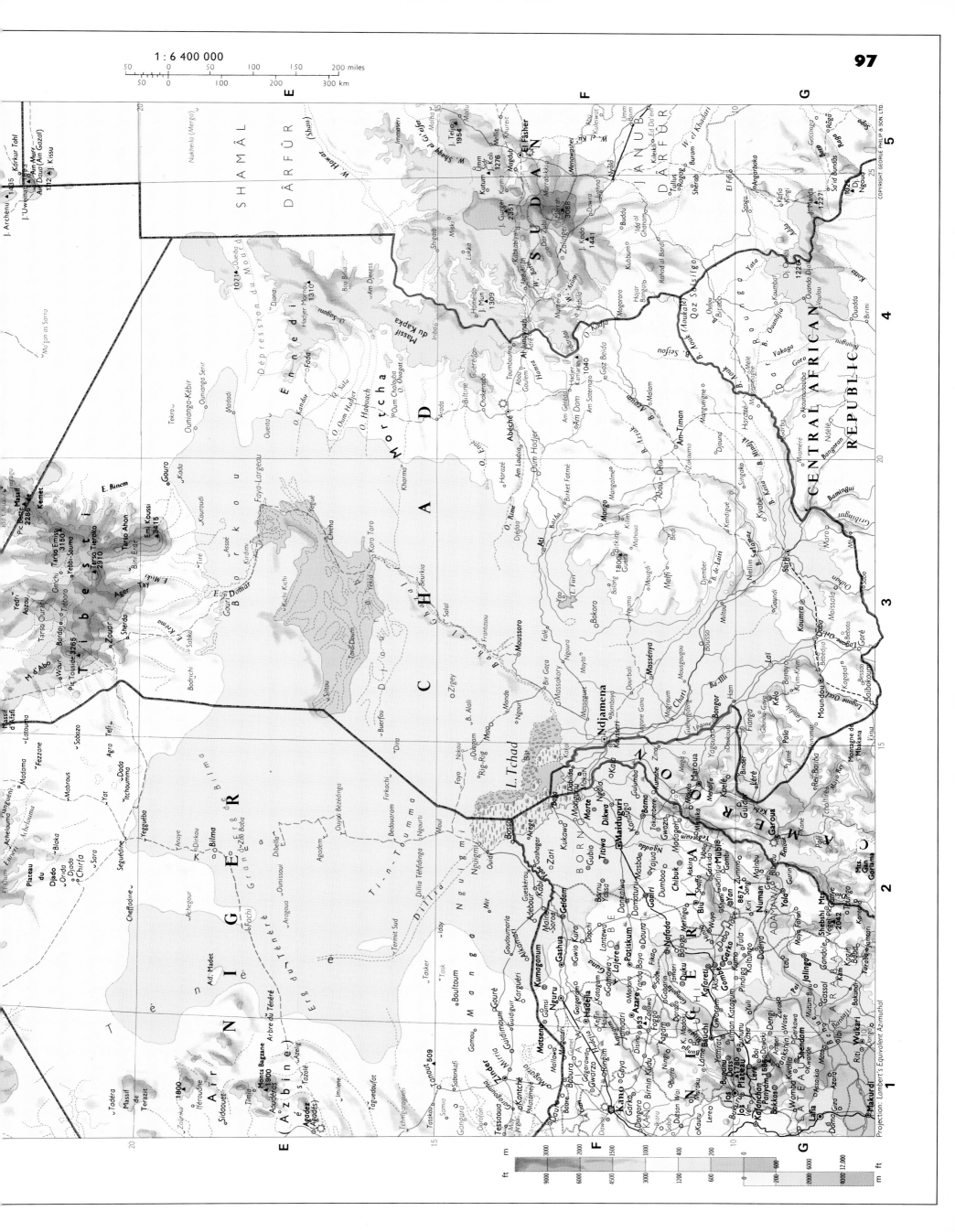

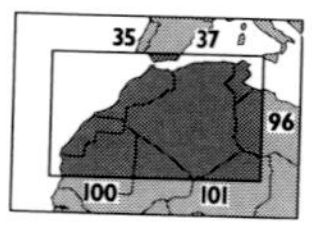

A
B
C
D
E

1   2   3

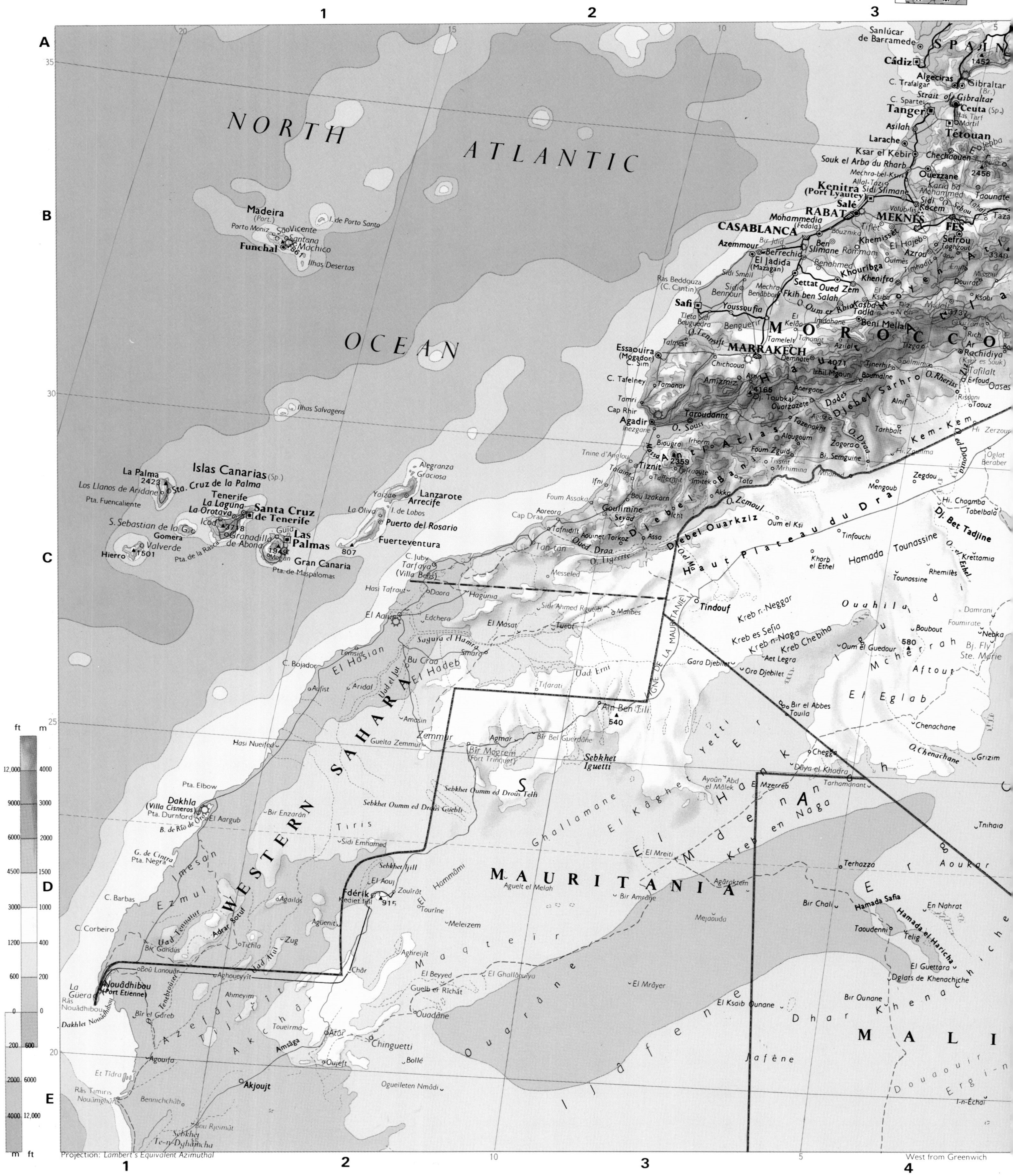

NORTH

ATLANTIC

OCEAN

SPAIN
Sanlúcar de Barramede
Cádiz
Algeciras
Gibraltar (Br.)
C. Trafalgar
Ceuta (Sp.)
Strait of Gibraltar
Tanger
Ras Tarf
Martil
Asilah
Tétouan
Larache
Chechaouen
Ksar el Kebir
Jebha
Souk el Arba du Rharb
Ouezzane
Taounate
Mechra-bel-Ksiri
Allal-Tazi
Kenitra (Port Lyautey)
Sidi Slimane
Taza
Salé
Sebou
RABAT
MEKNES
Mohammedia (Fedala)
FES
CASABLANCA
Sefrou
Azemmour
Berrechid
Ben Slimane
El Hajeb
Azrou
Khemisset
Khouribga
Khenifra
El Jadida (Mazagan)
Benahmed
Settat Oued Zem
Fkih ben Salah
Kasba
Beni Mellal
Safi
Youssoufia
Oum er Rbia
Essaouira (Mogador)
MARRAKECH
Demnate
Boumalne
C. Tafelney
Chichaoua
Rachidia
Erfoud
Oasis
Cap Rhir
Taroudannt
Ouarzazate
Alnif
Rissani
Taouz
Agadir
Inezgane
O. Souss
Dj. Toubkal
Zagora
O. Draa
Tiznit
Djebel Sarhro
Ifni
Goulimine
Tata
Cap Draa
Djebel Bani
Tan-tan
Oued Draa

Islas Canarias (Sp.)
La Palma
Sta. Cruz de la Palma
Los Llanos de Aridane
Pta. Fuencaliente
Tenerife
La Laguna
La Orotava
Santa Cruz de Tenerife
S. Sebastian de la G.
Gomera
Granadilla de Abona
Hierro
Valverde
Pta. de la Rasca
Lanzarote
Arrecife
Graciosa
Alegranza
I. de Lobos
La Oliva
Puerto del Rosario
Las Palmas
Gran Canaria
Fuerteventura
Pta. de Maspalomas
C. Juby
Tarfaya (Villa Bens)
Messeled

WESTERN SAHARA
El Aaiún
Edchera
Hagunia
Daora
Saguia el Hamra
Smara
Bu Craa
El Hasian
El Hadeb
C. Bojador
Aridal
Tindouf
Tifarati
Ain Ben Tili

Haut Plateau du Dra
Djebel Ouarzziz
Dj. Bet Tadjine
Hamada Tounassine
El Eglab
Chenachane

Dakhla (Villa Cisneros)
Pta. Durnford
El Argub
Bir Enzaran
Tiris
Sebkhet Iguetti
Bir Mogrein (Port Trinquet)
Zemmur
Guelta Zemmur
Sebkhet Oumm ed Drous Telli
Sebkhet Oumm ed Drous Guebli
Yetti
Chegga

MAURITANIA
G. de Cintra
Pta. Negra
Ezmul
Sidi Emhamed
Sebkhet Ijill
Zouîrat
Fdérik
Kediet Ijill
Tourine
Hammami
Aguelt el Melah
Bir Amrane
Mejaouda
Terhazza
Bir Chalir
Hamada Safia
En Nahrat
Taoudenni
Hamada el Haricha
C. Barbas
C. Corbeiro
Adrar Soutuf
Aguenit
Zug
Atar
Chinguetti
Ouadane
El Ksaib Ounane
Bir Ounane
Dglats de Khenachiche
Dhar

MALI

Nouâdhibou (Port Etienne)
La Güera
Ras Nouâdhibou
Dakhlet Nouâdhibou
Bir el Gareb
Akjoujt
Ras Tmimiss
Agouifa
Et Tidra
Chinguetti
Bollé
Oujeft
Oueilen Nmâdi

Madeira (Port.)
Porto Moniz
São Vicente
Santana
Machico
Funchal
Ilhas Desertas
I. de Porto Santo
Ilhas Salvagens

West from Greenwich

ft   m
12,000   4000
9000   3000
6000   2000
4500   1500
3000   1000
1200   400
600   200
0   0
200   600
2000   6000
4000   12,000
m   ft

1 : 6 400 000

50   0   50   100   150   200 miles

50   0   100   200   300 km

MEDITERRANEAN SEA

MÁLAGA

Granada
Almería
Antequera
Motril
Huércal Overa

SICILIA
Marsala

Al Hoceima
Nador
Melilla (Sp.)
C. de Gata
Ténès
ALGER (Algiers)
Bou Ismail
Cherchell
Dellys
Tizi-Ouzou
Bejaia
Jijel
Collo
Skikda
Annaba
Bizerte (Binzert)
TUNIS

Oujda
Tlemcen
Sidi-Bel-Abbès
Mostaganem
Arzew (Arzeu)
ORAN (Ouahran)
Mascara
Tiaret
Mohammadia
Saïda
BLIDA
Médéa
Miliana
CONSTANTINE
Guelma
Souk Ahras
El Kef
Sousse
Monastir
Mahdia
Sfax

Béchar
Aïn Sefra
El Bayadh
Laghouat
Ghardaïa
Biskra
El Oued
Touggourt
Ouargla
Gafsa
Gabès
Djerba
Zarzis
Tarābulus (Tripoli)

A L G E R I A

L I B Y A

Grand Erg Occidental

Grand Erg Oriental

Plateau du Tademaït

El Goléa

Timimoun

In Salah

Ghudāmis

Plateau du Tinrhert

Hammādah al Hamrā'

GHARYĀN

AWBĀRI

Idehan Marzūq

Zaouiet Reggane

Tassili-n-Ajjer

Ahaggar

Mt. Tahat 2918

Tamanrasset

Djanet

Ghat

Adrar des Iforhas

Tassili-n-Ahaggar

N I G E R

Plateau du Djado

In-Guezzam

Massif de Terazit

East from Greenwich

1 2 3

B

MAURITANIA

Et Tidra
Râs Timirist
Nouâmghâr
Akjoujt
Oujeft
Ogueïlet en Nmâdi
Bennichâb
Bouraga
Araouane
Azo
Guir
Akortäl
Sidi Moktar
Bou

Sebkhet Te-n-Dghâmcha
Trarza
Rachid
Tidjikja
Gâneb
Tichît
Aratâne
Akreïjit
Touerat
In-Alei
Dayet en Naharat

Nouakchott
Idîni
Boutilimit
Moudjéria
Letfatar
522
Aoukâr
Iâfène El Mreyye
Tagourâret
Tombouctou (Timbuktu)
Goundam

Mederdra
Aleg
Mâl
Bôumdeïd
I-n-Ahmer
Tâmchekket
Oualâta
Néma
Râs el Mâ
L. Faguibine
Diré
Harchongo

Massène Dagana Bôdé
Bogué
El Ghabra
Kiffa
Tintâne
Ayoûn el 'Atroûs
Nampala
L. Tanda
Niafounké
L. Débo
Ngorkou

Rosso
Richard Toll
L. de Guiers
N'Dioum
Mbagne
Kaédi
Maghama
Seil
Boumdeïd
Bassikounou
Djiguéni
Kobenni
Akka
Korienzé
N. Kururu
Nokara

Sénégal
St. Louis
Mérinaguène
Ngoui
Ranérou
Kanel
Harr
El Gueïete
Kirané
Ballé
Sampaka
Karounga
Nara
Boulal
Akor
Ouro-Ndia
Baro
Barka
791
Mopti

Louga
Yang-Yang
Poute
Ouro Sogui
Loumboï
Sémé
Gandé
Sélibabi
Koussané
Dioka
Tangauga Ba
Dilly
Digna
Goumbou
Tenenkou
Bandiagara

DAKAR
Rufisque
Thiès
Tivaouane
Khombole
Bambey
Touba
Taltal
Sinc
Tiel
Namari
Fété Bowé
Bakel
Ambidédi
Maréna
Diéma
Koniakori
Lakamané
Diongoi
Fallou
Mourdiah
Sokolo
Ségou
Mpésoba
Gani

Diourbel
Tiadiaye
Gossas
Kolobane
Nhar
Gabou
Kidira
Naye
Kayes
Dinguira
Séféto
Dindanko
Maréna
Mercoya
Sagala
Say
Niono
Djenné
Diallassagou
Bankas

SENEGAL
Fatick
Kaolack
Nioro du Rip
Kounghel
Koumpentoum
Tambacounda
Maka
Goudiry
Bala
Koussané
Sadiola
584
Diala
Didiéni
Banamba
Niono
San
Tominian

GAMBIA
Banjul
Kerewan
Georgetown
Santa Su
Vélingara
Dialakoto
Kouniakari
Kita
Bafoulabé
Badoumbé
Kouroukoto
Sirakoro
Négala
Koulikoro
Fana
Baraoueli
Bla
Bani

Ziguinchor
Sédhiou
Kolda
Farim
Médina Gonasse
Kéniéba
Sollo
Sébékoro
Kati
Bamako
Dioïla
Koutiala
Réo
Ouaga
Koudougou

GUINEA-BISSAU
Arquipélago dos Bijagós
Bissau
Bolama
Gabú
Mali
1537
Faléa
Kangaba
Kourémalé
Kouroba
Sikasso
820
Bobo-Dioulasso

Boké
Télimélé
Pita
Labé
Fouta Djalon
Dinguiraye
Siguiri
Yanfolila
Bougouni
Kolondiéba
Banfora

Conakry
Kindia
Dabola
Dinguiraye
Kouroussa
Kankan
Mandiana
Tingréla
Niéllé
Korhogo
Ferkéssedougou
Kampti

NORTHERN
Kabala
Faranah
Tiro
Odienné
914
Boundiali
Niofoun
Kong
Bouna

SIERRA LEONE
Freetown
Waterloo
Makeni
Magburaka
Sefadu
Guékédou
Macenta
Beyla
Borotou
Touba
Séguéla
Mankono
Katiola
Bouaké
741
Bondoukou
Kumasi

Sherbro I.
Bonthe
Pujehun
Kenema
Zimmi
Gehlun
Ganta
Man
Fakobli
Zuénoula
Daloa
Dimbokro
Agboville
Abengourou

LIBERIA
Robertsport
Monrovia
Paynesville
Buchanan
Greenville
Sino Bay
Cape Palmas
Harper
San-Pédro
Tabou
6363

IVORY COAST
Gagnoa
Divo
Abidjan
Grand Bassam
Aboisso
Prestea

Grain Coast
Ivory Coast
GULF

West from Greenwich

1 2 10 3 5 4

1 : 6 400 000

50 0 50 100 150 200 miles
50 0 100 200 300 km

N. E. NIGERIA
on same scale
as general map

ALGERIA

NIGER

NIGERIA

BENIN

GHANA

CAMEROON

EQUATORIAL GUINEA

CHAD

Slave Coast

Bight of Benin

Niger Delta

Bight of Bonny

BIOKO
(FERNANDO POO)

East from Greenwich

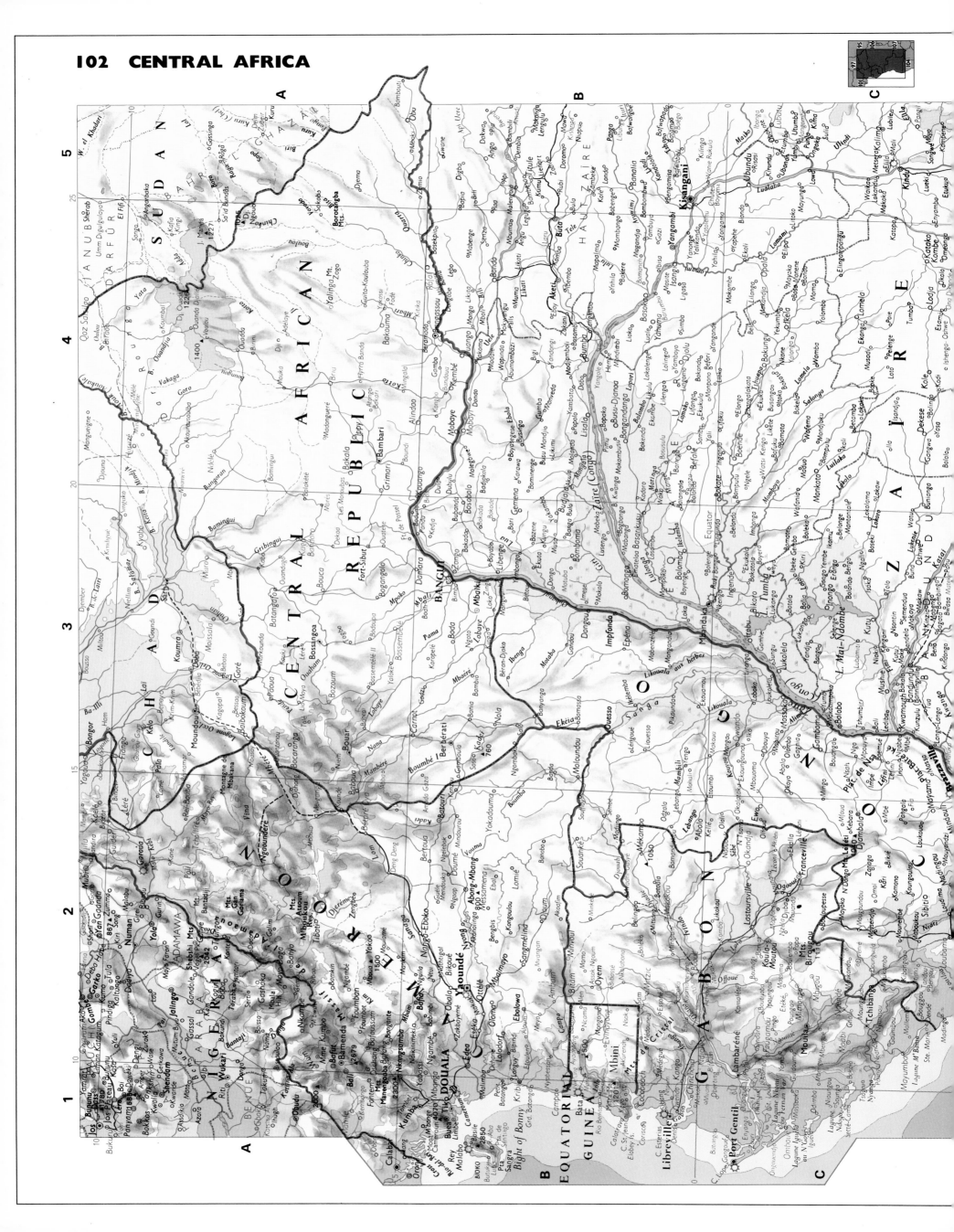

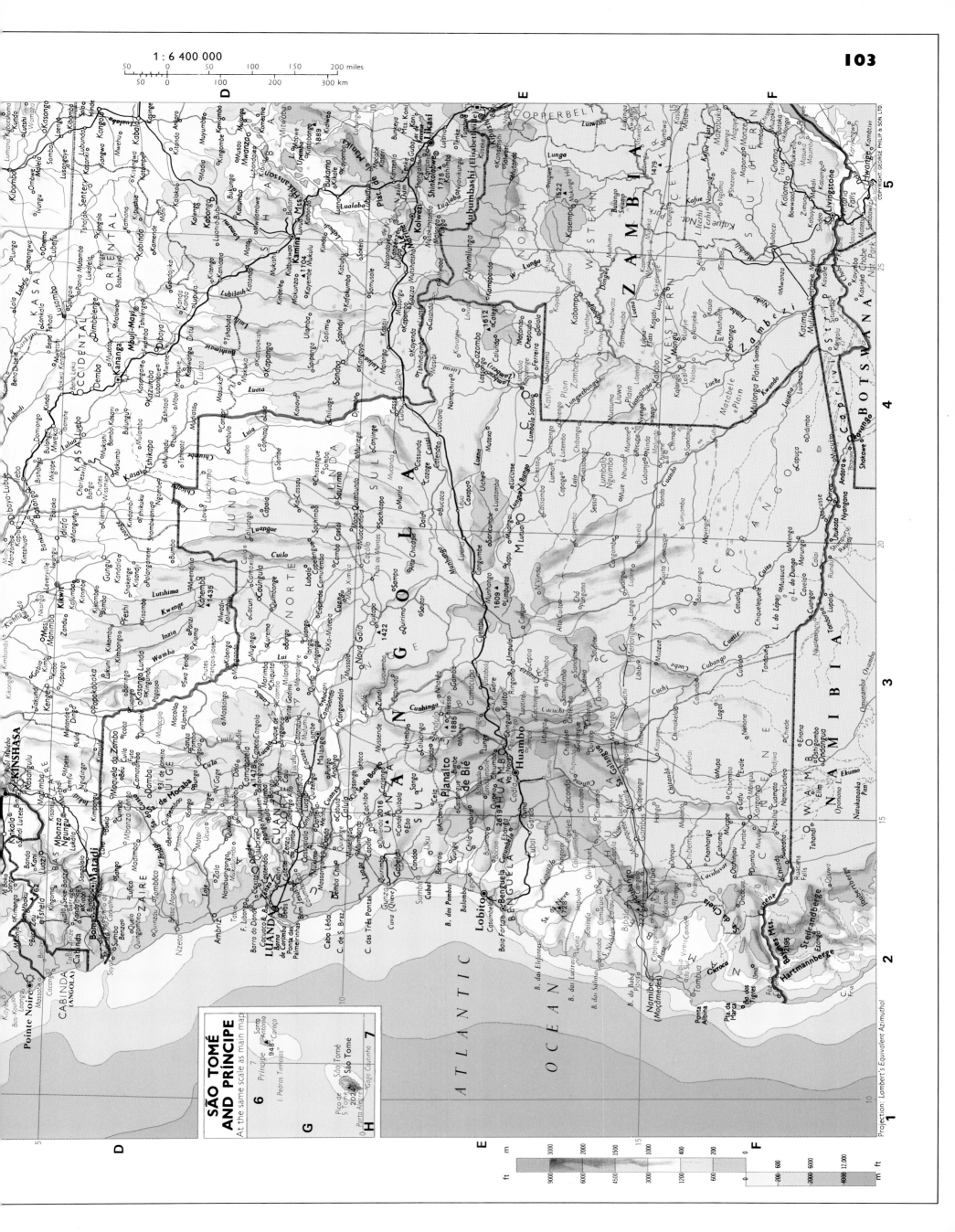

ZAMBIA

ANGOLA

CUANDO CUBANGO

Caprivi Strip

NAMIBIA

Etosha Pan

Tsumeb
Grootfontein
Otavi

Windhoek
Khomas Hochland

Swakopmund
Walvisbaai
(Cape Province)
Walvisbaai (Walvis Bay)
Sandwich B.

Tropic of Capricorn

BOTSWANA

Okavango Swamps

Maun

Kalahari

Gaborone

Rehoboth

Mariental

Keetmanshoop

Lüderitz
Lüderitzbaai

ATLANTIC

OCEAN

SOUTH AFRICA

Upington

ORANGE FREE STATE

Kimberley
Bloemfontein

BOPHUTHATSWANA

Krugersdorp
Potchefstroom
Klerksdorp
Welkom
Virginia
Kroonstad

Port Nolloth
Springbok
Namaqualand

CAPE PROVINCE

Great Karoo

De Aar

Queenstown

CISKEI

Beaufort West

Calvinia

George
Mosselbaai
Knysna

Vredenburg
Saldanha
Moorreesburg

Worcester
Paarl
CAPE TOWN (Kaapstad)
Table Mt. 1086
Stellenbosch
Somerset West
Strand
Simonstown
Kaap die Goeie Hoop
(Cape of Good Hope)

Oudtshoorn
Swartberge
Little Karoo

Uitenhage
PORT ELIZABETH
Algoa Bay

C. Agulhas

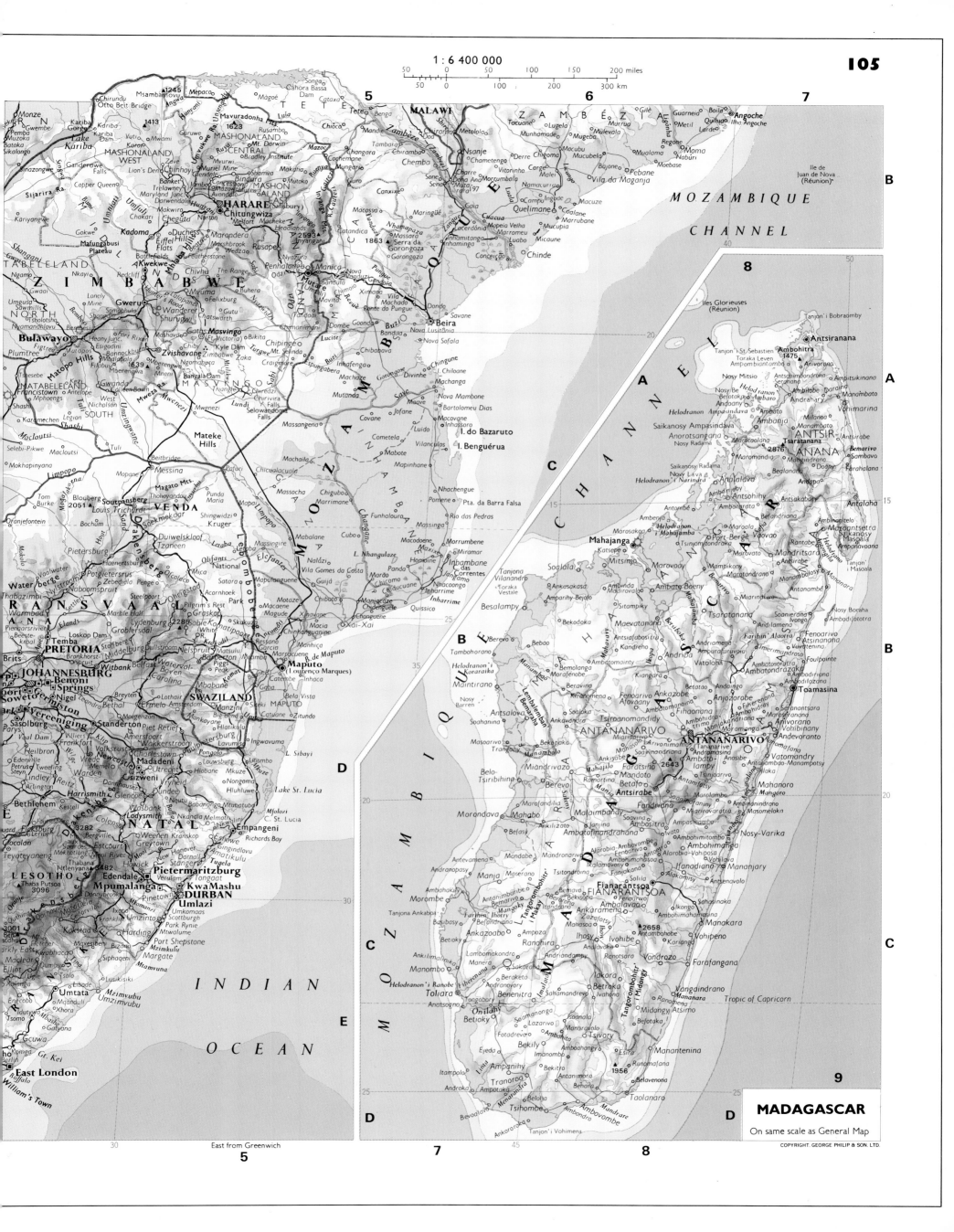

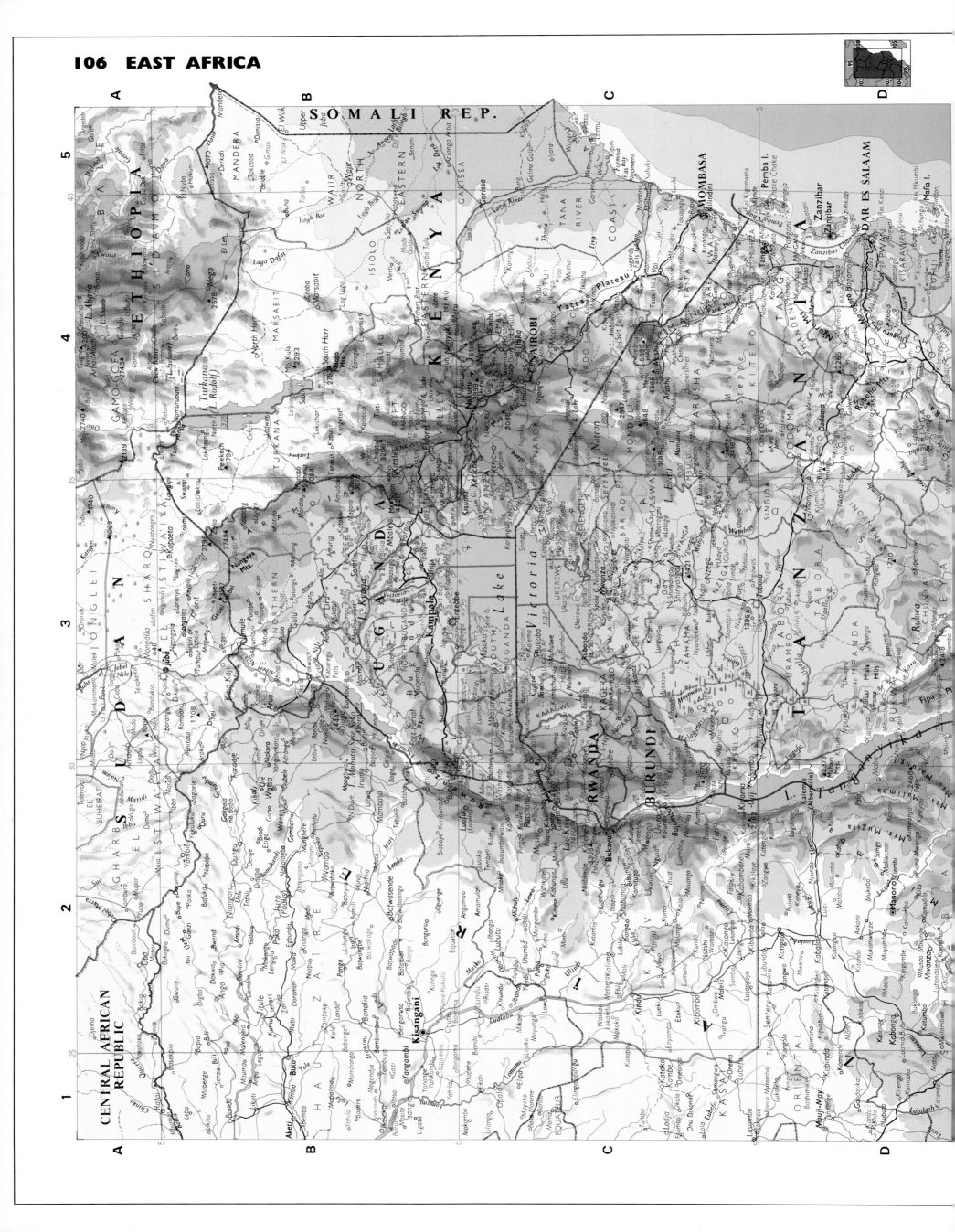

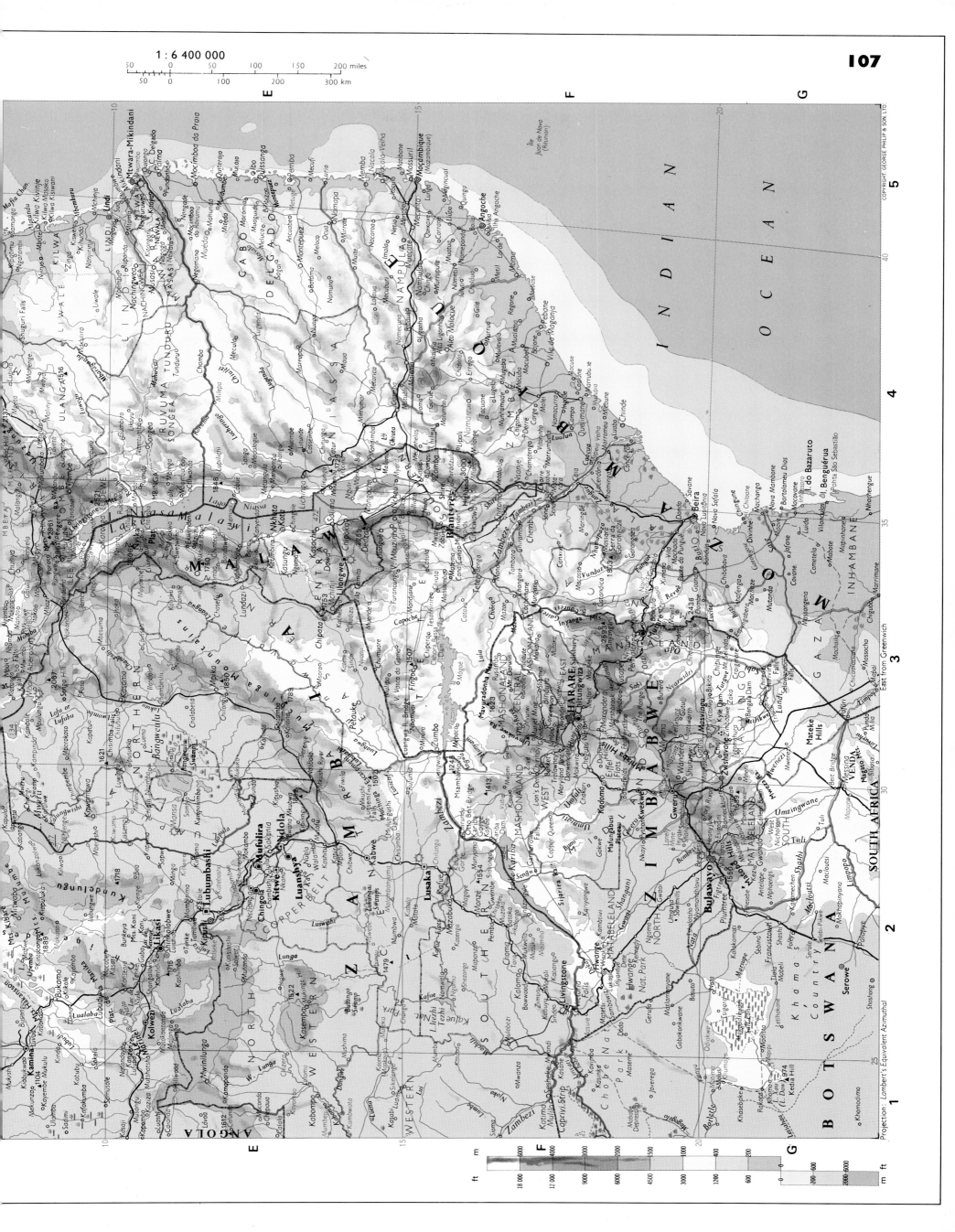

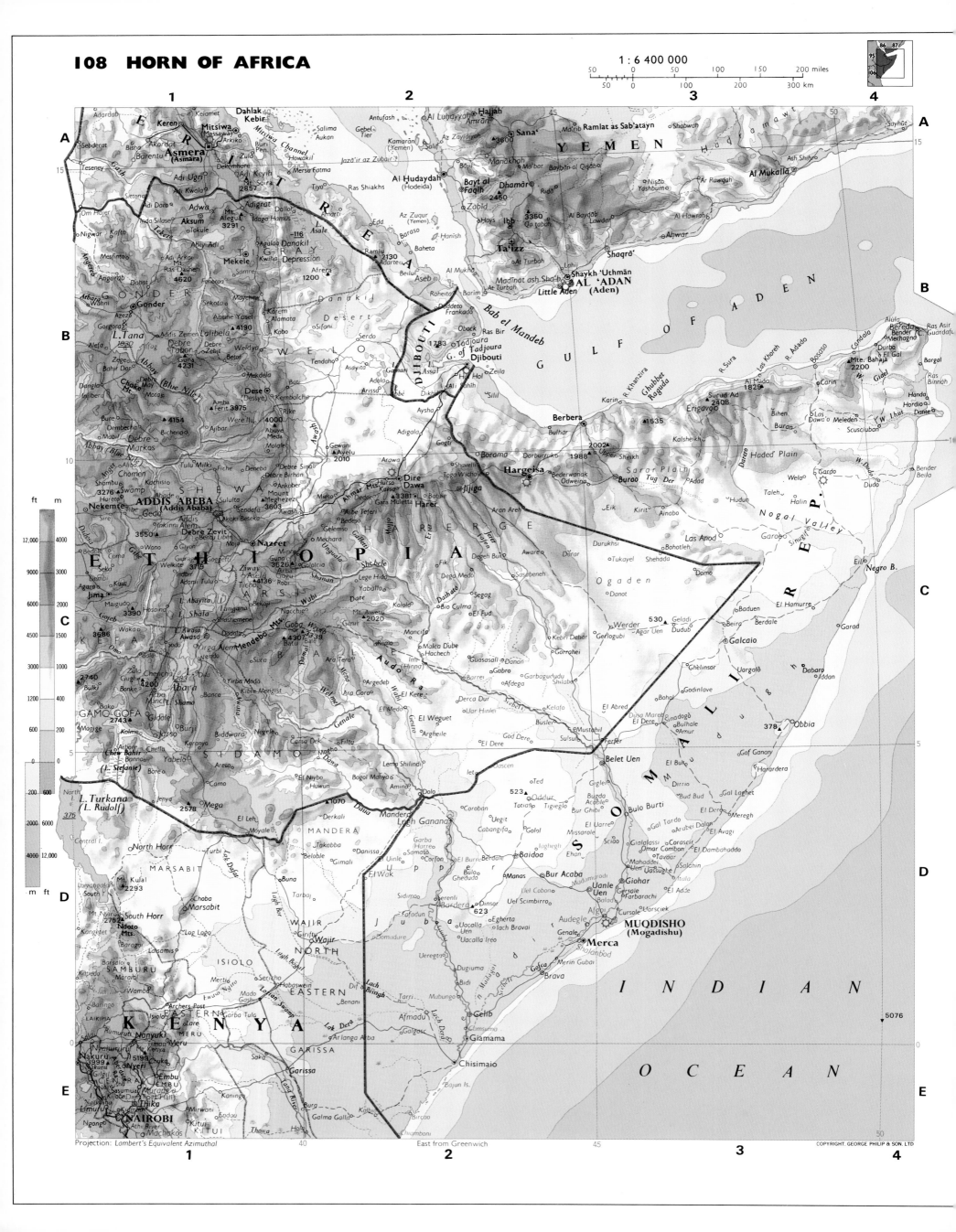

1 : 6 400 000

50 0 50 100 150 200 miles
50 0 100 200 300 km

86 87
95
106

1 **2** **3** **4**

YEMEN

Sana'

Al Hudaydah
(Hodeida)

Ta'izz

AL 'ADAN
(Aden)
Little Aden

GULF OF ADEN

ERITREA

Asmera
(Asmara)

Keren

TIGRAY

Mekele

GONDER

L.Tana

WELO

DJIBOUTI

Djibouti

Berbera

Hargeisa

Burao

SOMALI REP.

Nogal Valley

Las Anod

ETHIOPIA

ADDIS ABEBA
(Addis Ababa)

Nazret

SHEWA

ARSI

HARERGE

Harer
Dire Dawa
Jijiga

Ogaden

Werder

Galcaio

Obbia

SIDAMO

L. Turkana
(L. Rudolf)

BALE

GEMU GOFA

SOMALI

Belet Uen

Bulo Burti

Giohar

Baidoa

Bur Acaba

MUQDISHO
(Mogadishu)

Merca

KENYA

MARSABIT

WAJIR

NORTH
EASTERN

GARISSA

ISIOLO

SAMBURU

NAIROBI

Brava

Giamama

Chisimaio

INDIAN

OCEAN

Projection: Lambert's Equivalent Azimuthal

East from Greenwich

COPYRIGHT. GEORGE PHILIP & SON. LTD

ft m

12,000 4000

9000 3000

6000 2000

4500 1500

3000 1000

1200 400

600 200

0 0

200 600

2000 6000

4000 12,000

m ft

Equatorial Scale 1 : 40 000 000

1 2 3 4 5 6 7 8 9 10

A Mediterranean Sea · Bayrût · SYRIA · Baghdâd · IRAN · Kabul · Rawalpindi · XIZANG · CHINA · Xi'an · Nanjing · Shanghai
El Iskandariya · Tel Aviv-Yafo · ISRAEL · Dimashq · Karbala · Esfahan · AFGHANISTAN · Qandahâr · Lahore · Mt. Yarlung Zangbo · Chengdu · Wuhan · Hangzhou
El Qâhira · El Suweis · JORDAN · IRAQ · Al Basrah · Âbâdân · Quetta · Multan · Everest 8848 · Chongqing · Changsha · Nanchang

B LIBYA · EGYPT · Asyût · KUWAIT · SAUDI · BAHRAIN · Delhi · NEPAL · BHUTAN · Guiyang · Wenzhou
Aswân · Al Madinah · QATAR · UNITED ARAB EMIRATES · Agra · Katmandu · Ganga · Brahmaputra · Kunming · Fuzhou
L. Nasser · Tropic of Cancer · Ar Riyâd · Kanpur · Varanasi · Dhaka · Guangzhou
Wadi Halfa · ARABIA · OMAN · Karachi · INDIA · Chittagong · Mandalay · Hanoi · Hong Kong · TAIWAN
Jiddah · Makkah · G. of Kutch · Ahmadabad · Calcutta · BURMA · Chiang Mai · G. of Tonkin · Hainan

C Omdurmân · El Khartûm · ERITREA · Mitsiwa · YEMEN · Socotra (Yemen) · Arabian · Bombay · Godavari · Pune · Hyderabad · Bay of Bengal · Rangoon · THAILAND · Paracel Is. · South
SUDAN · Asmera · DJIBOUTI · Gulf of Aden · Ras Asir C. Guardafui · Sea · Narmada · Krishna · Andaman Is. (India) · Mergui Arch. · Bangkok · CAMBODIA · China
CHAD · Al 'Adan · Arabian · Bangalore · Madras · Isthmus of Kra · Phnom Penh · Phanh Bho · Sea
Addis Abeba · Berbera · Basin · Madurai · SRI LANKA (CEYLON) · Nicobar Is. (India) · Gulf of Thailand · Ho Chi Minh
CENTRAL AFRICA · ETHIOPIA 4307 · 5875 · Colombo · Pidurutalagala 2524

D Wâw · Mongalla · L. Tana · 5824 · Carlesberg · MALDIVES · George Town · SABAH · BORNEO
SOMALI REP. · L. Turkana · Somali · Ridge · Lakshadweep Is. (India) · Kuala Lumpur · MALAYSIA · SARAWAK · BRUNEI
UGANDA · L. Mobutu Sese Seko · Muqdisho · Basin · Nias · Kuching
ZAÏRE · Kisangani · Kampala · Entebbe · KENYA · Equator · SEYCHELLES · Singapore · Borneo
L. Edward · L. Kivu · RWANDA · Nairobi · Mt. Kenya 5199 · Amirante Is. · Mahe · Chagos Archipelago (Br.) · Mentawei Is. · Palembang · INDONESIA

E BURUNDI · Mwanza · Kilimanjaro 5895 · Victoria · Des Roches · Diego Garcia · Jakarta · Java Sea
TANZANIA · L. Victoria · Mombasa · Coetivy Is. · Bandung · Semarang · Surabaya · Flores Sea
Bukoba · L. Tanganyika · Dar es Salaam · Zanzibar · Pemba · Alphonse · Sunda Strait · Java · Bali · Lombok · Sumbawa
Aldabra Is. · St. Pierre · Providence · Cocos or Keeling Is. (Austral.) · Christmas I. (Austral.) 7450

F Lubumbashi · L. Mweru · L. Bangweulu · Runuma · Farquhar Is. · Agalega · 4819 · 6327
ANGOLA · ZAMBIA · Lusaka · MALAWI · COMOROS · Moçambique · Tromelin I. · Cargados Garajos
Lilongwe · Manjanga · Rodriquez · N.W. Cape · Onslow
ZIMBABWE · Blantyre · MADAGASCAR · 5322 · Port St. Louis · MAURITIUS · Mascarene Islands

G Harare · Beira · Antananarivo 2643 · Réunion (Fr.) · Tropic of Capricorn · Shark Bay · WESTERN AUSTRALIA
BOTSWANA · Bulawayo · Toliara · Mascarene Basin · Geraldton · Kalgoorlie
Gaborone · Maputo · 6400 · 1491 · 1104 · Perth · Fremantle
NAMIBIA · Pretoria · Johannesburg · SWAZI · Durban · Madagascar · Geographe Bay · Albany

H Cape Town · Port Elizabeth · East London · Basin · Equatorial Limit of Icebergs · 18 000 · 6000
SOUTH AFRICA · 5778 · Crozet · Amsterdam I. (Fr.) · St. Paul I. (Fr.) · 12 000 · 4000

J Agulhas · Basin · Pr. Edward Is. (S.A.) · Crozet Is. (Fr.) · Basin · 2899 · 3000 · 1000
Marion I. · Hög I. · Possession I. · 1200 · 400

K Kerguelen (Fr.) · Southeast Indian Rise · 600 · 200
McDonald Is. · Heard I. (Austral.) · 5141 · 5202 · 0 · 0
5848 · Extreme Limit of Pack Ice · 200 · 600

L 4850 · 4691 · 2000 · 6000
Antarctic Circle · Enderby Land · Wilkes Land · 4000 · 12 000

M Queen Maud Land · Adélie Land · 6000 · 18 000

Projection: Mollweide · 20 · 0 · 20 · 40 · 60 · 80 · 100 · 120 · 140 · 160

Oceans and Seas
Banda Sea
Timor Sea
Arafura Sea
Flores Sea
Coral Sea
Coral Sea Islands Territory
Gulf of Carpentaria
Gulf of Papua
Torres Strait
Great Australian Bight
Bass Strait
Spencer Gulf
Encounter B.
Solomon Sea
INDIAN OCEAN

Regions and Countries
INDONESIA
PAPUA NEW GUINEA
NEW GUINEA
Irian Barat
AUSTRALIA
WESTERN AUSTRALIA
NORTHERN TERRITORY
SOUTH AUSTRALIA
QUEENSLAND
NEW SOUTH WALES
VICTORIA
Australian Capital Territory
TASMANIA
Bismarck Archipelago
New Ireland
New Britain
Louisiade Archipelago
D'Entrecasteaux
Furneaux Group

Places and Features
Sulawesi (Celebes)
Maluku
Buru
Ceram
Butung
Kendari
Ujung Pandang (Makasar)
Sumbawa
Flores
Sumba
Raba
Ende
Kupang
Alor
Wetar
Leti
Babar
Timor
Dili
Kep. Kai
Kep. Aru
Kep. Tanimbar
Misool
Fakfak
Sorong
Vogelkop Peninsula
Vogelkop
Biak
Jayapura
Pegunungan Maoke
Puncak Jaya 5020
Pulau Yos Sudarso
Wewak
Madang
Mount Hagen
Mt. Wilhelm 4508
Lae
Owen Stanley Range
Port Moresby
Rabaul
Kavieng
Ambon
5300
7260
3350
3310
6204
9140

Melville
C. Croker
C. Arnhem
Darwin
Arnhem Land
C. Londonderry
Wyndham
Kimberley Plateau
Derby
Broome
Cambridge G.
Daly Waters
Larrimah
C. York
Weipa
Cape York Peninsula
Cooktown
Cairns
Bartle Frere 1611
Townsville
Charters Towers
Mackay
Mitchell
Normanton
Forsayth
Hughenden
Winton
Longreach
Yaraka
Rockhampton
Gladstone
Bundaberg
Maryborough
Gympie
QUEENSLAND
Great Dividing Range
Mount Isa
Kajaabi
Flinders
Barkly Tableland
Tennant Creek
Tanami Desert
Great Sandy Desert
L. Mackay
Lake Disappointment
Gibson Desert
Newman
Mt. Bruce 1226
Hamersley Range
Port Hedland
Dampier
N.W. Cape
Carnarvon
Meekatharra
Murchison
Leonora
L. Carnegie
Great Victoria Desert
Macdonnell Ranges
Mt. Ziel 1510
Alice Springs
Ayers Rock
Mt. Woodroffe 1440
Musgrave Ranges
Simpson Desert
Diamantina
Cooper Creek
Lake Eyre
Marree
Grey Range
Thargomindah
Quilpie
Charleville
Cunnamulla
Roma
Toowoomba
BRISBANE
Ipswich
Gold Coast
Lismore
Round Mt. 1615
Warrego
Bourke
Cobar
Dirranbandi
Walgett
Tamworth
Taree
NEW SOUTH WALES
Broken Hill
Darling
Flinders Range
Tarcoola
Deakin
Penong
Port Augusta
Port Pirie
Whyalla
Spencer Gulf
Port Lincoln
Port Lincoln
5632
Nullarbor Plain
Kalgoorlie-Boulder
Lake Barlee
Norseman
Esperance
Geraldton
Northam
Perth
Bunbury
Augusta
C. Leeuwin
Albany
Darling Range
AUSTRALIA
WESTERN
SOUTH AUSTRALIA
Dubbo
Orange
Bathurst
Cobar
Wagga Wagga
Mt. Kosciusko 2237
Albury
Mildura
Murray
Shepparton
Horsham
Bendigo
Ballarat
MELBOURNE
Geelong
VICTORIA
Australian Alps
Bombala
C. Howe
Mount Gambier
Warrnambool
Adelaide
Canberra
CAPITAL TERRITORY
Goulburn
SYDNEY
Wollongong
Shellharbour
Newcastle
King I.
Burnie
Launceston
Mt. Ossa 1617
Hobart
S.E. Cape
TASMANIA

Scale (elevation)
ft / m
6000 / 2000
4500 / 1500
3000 / 1000
1200 / 400
600 / 200
0 / 0
200 / 600
2000 / 6000
4000 / 12,000
6000 / 18,000
m / ft
35

Projection : Lambert's Equivalent Azimuthal
East from Greenwich

1 : 16 000 000

III

10   11   12   13   14   15   16

NAURU

Me **KIRIBATI**

Tamana

Baker

Equator

2743
Mt. Balbi Bougainville

6195

0

170

Choiseul

SOLOMON

Santa Isabel

Namumea

Abariringa

New Georgia

Malaita

l

Phoenix Is.

ISLANDS

Honiara 2331

Carondelet

A

Arch.

Guadalcanal

San Cristóbal

e

TUVALU

5

Rennell

7223

Santa Cruz Is.

n

(Ellice Is.) Funafuti Funafuti

Sea

Fataka

e

Nukulaelae

Tokelau Is.

B

(N.Z.)

Banks Is.

Rotuma

10

Espíritu Santo 1880

s

Mata-Utu Uvea

WESTERN

VANUATU

Wallis & Futuna

SAMOA

Malakula

(New Hebrides)

i

Horn (Fr.)

Savai'i Apia C

Port-Vila Efate

Vanua Levu

Niuafo'ou

Upolu **AMERICAN**

Îs. D'Entrecasteaux

a

Viti Levu

Tutuila **SAMOA**

Îs. Chesterfield

1324 **FIJI**

15

1628

Îs. Loyauté

Suva

Lau Is.

Vavau Is.

New Caledonia 7569

Ha'apai Is. **TONGA**

Niue

(Fr.)

(N.Z.)

Nouméa

Matthew

Ceve-i-Ra

D

Nuku'Alofa

P A C I F I C

Tongatapu Is.

Cook Is.

(N.Z.)

20

5303

10 882 Tonga Trench

O C E A N

Tropic of Capricorn

E

25

Norfolk

Raoul

(Austr.)

Kermadec Is.

Kermadec Trench

Lord Howe

(N.Z.)

(Austr.)

734

F

10 047

30

Tasman Sea

North C.

Kaitaia

Whangarei

Auckland

NORTH ISLAND

G

Hamilton

Bay of Plenty

New Plymouth

Rotorua

Gisborne

5267

Ruapehu

NEW

2797 Napier

Wanganui

35

ZEALAND

Palmerston North

Nelson

Cook Strait

Wellington

Greymouth

Blenheim

SOUTH ISLAND

International Date Line

H

Mt. Cook Southern Alps Christchurch

3783

Wakatipu Timaru

Chatham

(N.Z.)

40

Invercargill Dunedin

Stewart

J

155   10   160   11   165   12   13   175 West from Greenwich 170   17   165   18

COPYRIGHT, GEORGE PHILIP LTD.

Timor

INDONESIA

Lombok
Sumbawa
Sumba
Roti
Sawu
Semal
Raidjuah
Danu

TIMOR SEA

INDIAN OCEAN

Serinagapatam Reef
Scott Reef
Hibernia Reef
Ashmore Reef
Cartier I.
Browse I.
Lynher Reef
Mermaid Reef
Clerke Reef
Imperieuse Reef
Rowley Shoals

Monte Bello Is.
Barrow I.
Pasco

C. Croker
Grant I.
C. Don
P. Essington
Cobourg Pen.
Melville I.
Bathurst I.
C. Van Diemen
Dundas Str.
Van Diemen Gulf
C. Gambier St.
C. Hotham
Clarence Str.
Darwin
Port Darwin
Pt. Fawcett
Gordan B.
Peron Is.
Anson B.
Pt. Blaze
C. Scott
Noonamah
Rum Jungle
Batchelor
Adelaide River
Mt. Greenwood
152
Win Gate Mts.
Daly River
Joly River
Daly

Murgenella
Endyalgout I.
Oenpelli
Jabiru
480
Field Is.
Pine Creek
Katherine
Maranboy
Mataranka
Larrimah
Birdum
Birdum Creek

Joseph Bonaparte Gulf
Dussejour Hd.
Cambridge Gulf
Lesueur I. Rutherfords
Eclipse Is.
Vansittart B.
Sir Graham Moore Is.
Napier Broome B.
Talbot
Londonderry
C. Bougainville
C. Voltaire
Long Reef
Admiralty Gulf
Montague Sd.
Bigge I.
York Sd.
Prince Regent R.
Brunswick B.
Camden Sd.
Collier B.
Wood
Eagle I.
C. Leveque
Pender B.
Beagle Bay
Adele I.
Lacepede Is.
C. Boileau
Broome
Roebuck B.
C. Latouche Treville

Buccaneer Archipelago
Bonaparte Archipelago

Buckle Hd.
Kulumburu
Carson
Drysdale
King Edward
Mount Elizabeth
Mt. Hann
776
Durack
Gibb River
Glenelg
Napier Downs
Meda
Kimberley Downs
Liveringa
Myroodah
Noonkanbah
Jubilee Downs
Derby
Yeeda
Thangoo
Roebuck Plains
Anna Plains
Wallal Downs
Frazier Downs
Lagrange B.
Lagrange

Eighty Mile Beach

Oombulgurri
Wyndham
Carr Boyd Ra.
Ord
Ivanhoe
Queen Chan.
Ogin
C. Hay
Turkey Creek
Argyle
Rosewood
Bedford Downs
Bohemia Downs
Margaret River
Fitzroy Crossing
Christmas Creek
Fitzroy
St. George Ra.
Margaret
Mt. Ord
1000
Leopold Downs
Hann
Halls Creek
Mount Amherst
Alice Downs
Tableland
Mueller Ra.
Albert Edward Ra.
Alice
Springvale
McClintock Ra.
Billiluna

King Leopold Ranges

Cockburn Ra.
Chamberlain
Black Elvire Ra.

Sturt Creek
Gordon Downs
Nicholson
Carranya
Gregory Lake
Lake Gregory

Wave Hill
Inverway
Nicholson R.
Humbert River
Limbunya

Timber Creek
Auvergne
Victoria River Downs
Soaker's Ra.
Fitzmaurice R.
Newcastle Ra.
Victoria

Yilleroo
Top Springs
Montejinnie
Wilton
Hooker Creek
Winnecke Cr.

NORTHERN TERRITORY

Tanami Desert
Tanami
Willowra
Landers

Horden Hills
Mt. Leisler
901

Lake Mackay

L. White
L. Hazlett
Gregory Lake
Christmas Creek

Great Sandy Desert

Percival Lakes
L. Tobin
L. Auld
L. Dora
L. George
L. Blanche

Stansmore Ra.

Mt. Singleton
808
L. Bennett
Yuendumu
Mt. Liebig
1524
Haast Bluff
Papunya
L. Neale
Mt. Zeil
1540
Hermannsburg
George Gill Ra.
Macdonnell Ranges
James Ranges
Square Bluff Ra.
Reynolds Ra.
Anningie
Mt. Doreen

Bonython Ra.
Lewis Ra.
Baron Ra.
Angas Hills
L. Macdonald
Mt. Rason
L. Hopkins

Tropic of Capricorn

Gibson Desert

Gardiner Ra.
Ringer Soak
Paterson Ra.
Throssell Ra.
Poisonbush Ra.
Broadhurst Ra.
McKay Ra.
Rudall
Disappointment
Calvert Ra.
Lake Dora
Blanche Ra.

Gregory Ra.
Isabella Ra.
Oakover
L. Waukarlycarly
Nullagine
Boonedarrie Downs
Roy Hill
Ethel Creek
Newman
1053
Ophthalmia Ra.

Hamersley Range
Mt. Bruce
1235
Mt. Meharry
1251
Marillana
Wittenoom
Ashburton Downs
Kalgan Ck.
Capricorn Ra.

Port Hedland
Poissonier Pt.
C. Keraudren
De Grey
Goldsworthy
Pippingarra
Shaw
Mulline
Marble Bar
Woodstock
Hillside
Strelley
Nullagine
Shay Gap
Warrawagine
Callawa

Dampier Archipelago
Karratha
Roebourne
Cossack
Whim Creek
Mt. Price
Pyramid
Hooley
Tom Price
Paraburdoo
Rocklea
Yandeearra
Wyloo
Mt. Palgrave
704

Exmouth Gulf
Onslow
North West C.
Exmouth
Learmonth
Pt. Cloates
Ningaloo
Yanrey

INDIAN OCEAN

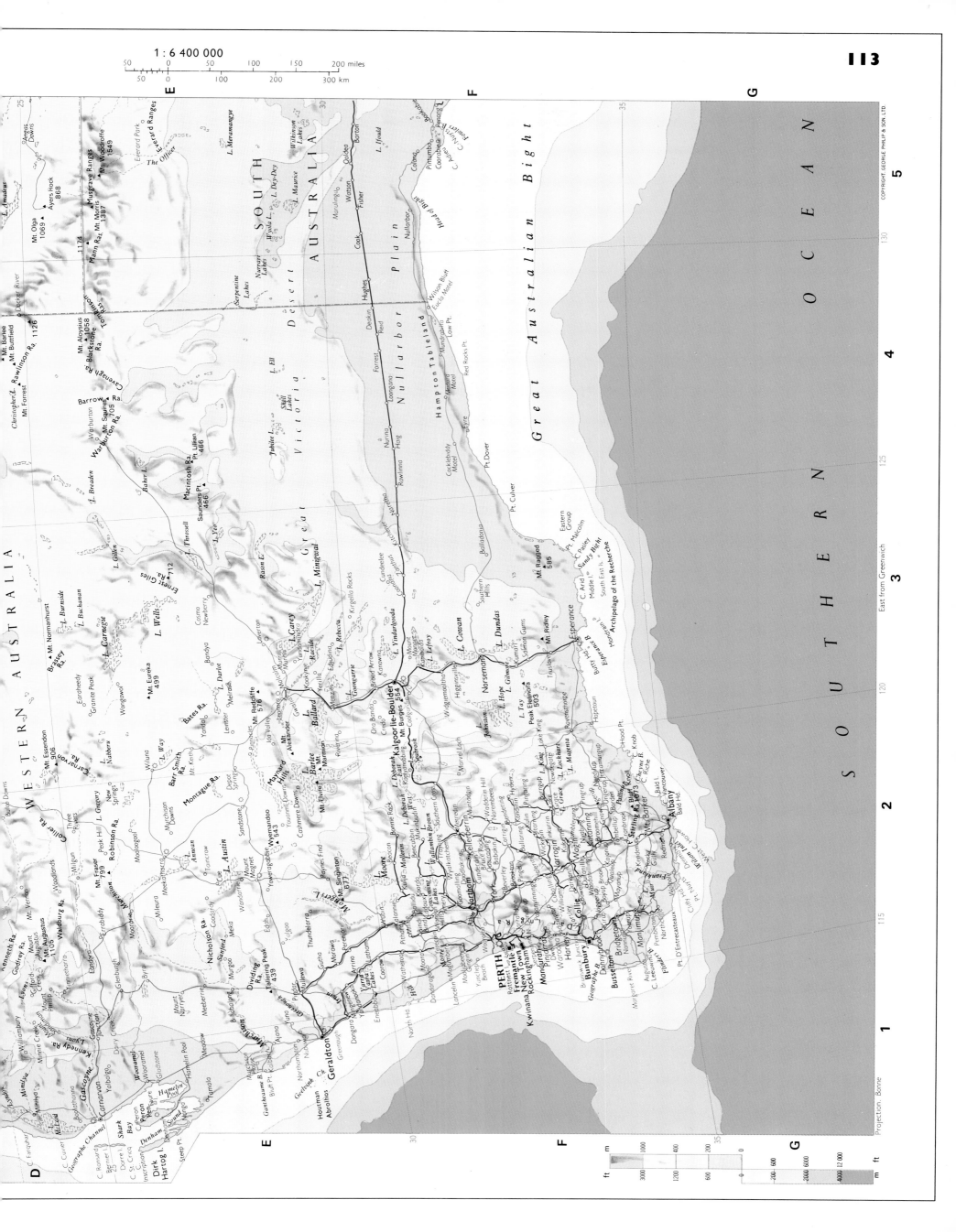

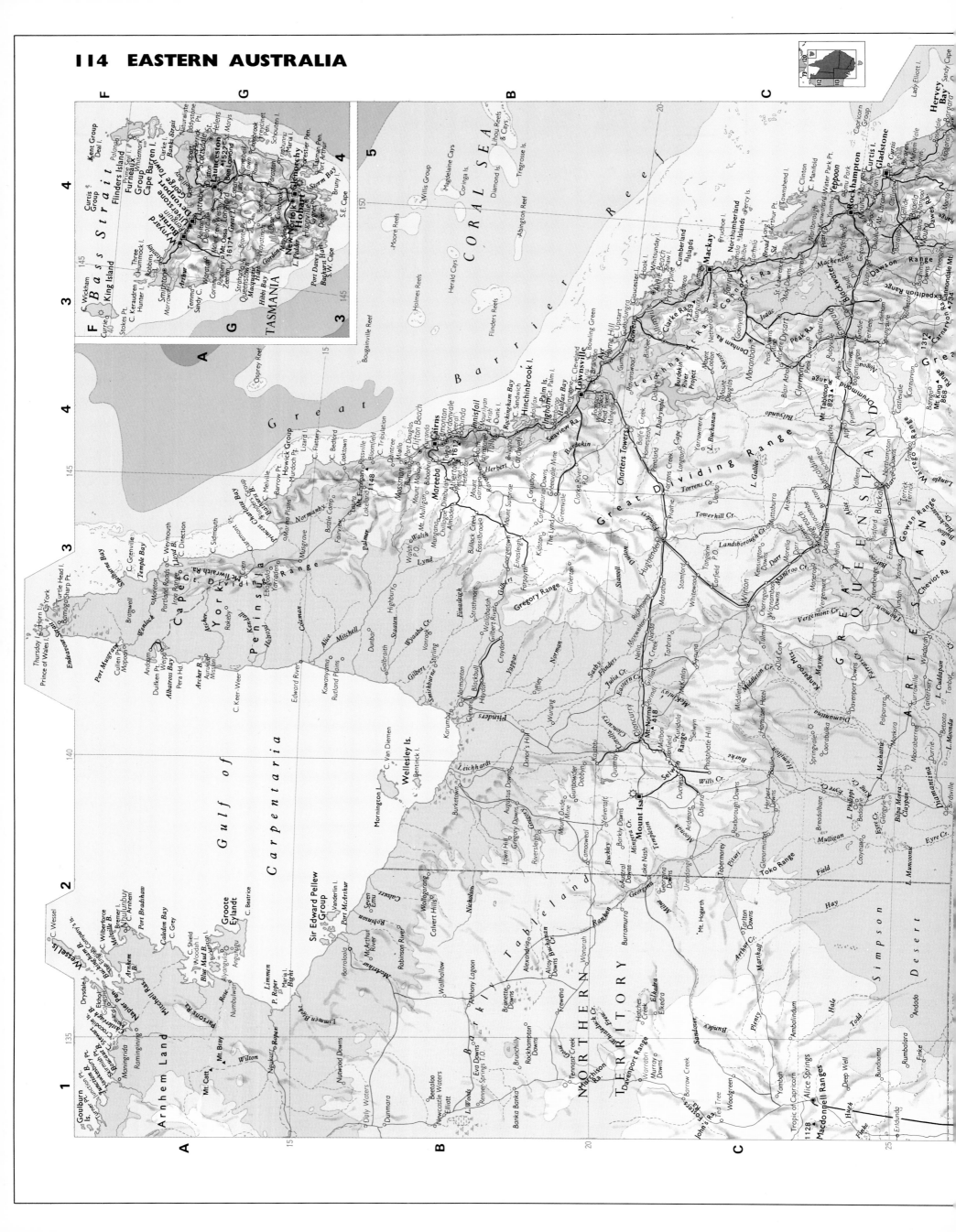

SOUTH AUSTRALIA

VICTORIA

N.S.W.

Parakylia · Leigh Creek South · Telford · Benbonyathe 1058 · Lake Frome · Packsaddle · Caraduc · Peri Lake

L. Younghusband · Mt. Deception 685 · Mt. Hack 1083 · Beltana · White Cliffs · Momba · Tilpa

L. Hanson · Arcoona · Nilpena · Parachilna · Broughams Gate · Koonawarra · Glen Gowrie · Kalkaroo

Wirraminna · Pimba · Woomera · Frome Downs · McDougalls Well · Mulga Valley · Grassmere · Menamurtee · Wongalarroo L. · Poopelloe L.

Island Lagoon · Pernatty Lagoon · St. Mary Pk. 1165 · Wilpena · Wilpena Cr. · Pasmore · Benagerie · Wilangee · Langidoon · Sturts Meadows · Cawkers Well · Volo · Goonalga

Lake Gairdner · Cotabena · Hawker · Siccus · Glenorchy · Boolcoomata · Silverton · Stephens Creek · Wahratta · Wilcannia

Mt. Ive · Hesso · Gordon · Mount Victor · Mingary · Cockburn · **Broken Hill** · Darnick · Beilpajah · Ivanhoe

L. Macfarlane · Mt. Brown 969 · Quorn · Carrieton · Olary · Mannahill · Mutooroo · Menindee L. · Menindee · Teryaweyna · Mount Manara

Port Augusta West · Wilmington · Eurelia · Yunta · Netley Gap · Leonora Downs · Cawndilla L. · Tandou L. · Boolaboolka L. · Gypsum Palace

Port Augusta · Orroroo · Black Rock · Nackara · Paratoo · Kimberley · Tartna Point · Gum Lake

Buckleboo · Nectar Brook · 969 Mt. Remarkable · Booleroo Centre · Peterborough · Oakbank · L. Popilta · Popio L. · Traveller's Lake · Manfred · Mossgiel

Lake Gilles · Iron Knob · Napperby · Jamestown · Terowie · Quondong · Morgan Vale · L. Popilta · Pooncarie · Clare

Siam · **Whyalla** · **Port Pirie** · Laura · Gladstone · Hallett · Braemar · Belmore · Lethero · Culpataro

Kimba · Iron Baron · Crystal Brook · Gulnare · Spalding · Mt. Bryan 934 · Canopus · Bulpunga · Burtundy · Arumpo · Magenta

Darke Peak · Pondooma · Port Broughton · Brinkworth · Burra · Gluepot · L. Victoria · Hatfield P.O.

Rudall · Cowell · Blyth · Clare · Farrell Flat · Wentworth · Bidura · Oxley

Arno Bay · Wallaroo · Bute · Snowtown · Robertstown · Morgan · Murray · Merbein · **Mildura** · Dymple · Pitarpunga L. · Murrumbidgee · Maude

Ungarra · Moonta · Balaklava · Point Pass · Waikerie · Renmark · Berri · Yamba · Red Cliffs · Nangiloc · Balranald

Koppio · Tumby Bay · Kadina · Bowmans · Hamley Bridge · Kapunda · Eudunda · Holder · Barmera · Loxton · Meringur · Werrimull · Nowing · Bannerton · Robinvale · Kooloonong

Poonindie · C. Donington · Maitland · Ardrossan · Mallala · Owen · Nuriootpa · Truro · Maggea · Taplan · Hattah · Annuello · Perekerten · Moulamein

Port Lincoln · Port Victoria · Minlaton · Tanunda · Angaston · Sedan · Swan Reach · Wanbi · Veitch · Meribah · Kulwin · Natya · Piangil · Edward

West Pt. · THISTLE I. · GAMBIER IS. · **Gulf** · Salisbury · **Port Adelaide** · **ADELAIDE** · Woodside · Mannum · Kalyan · Sandalwood · Peebinga · Walpeup · Ouyen · Speed · Waitchie · **Swan Hill** · Wakool

C. Spencer · Marion Bay · Edithburgh · **Glenelg** · **Elizabeth** · **Murray Bridge** · Karoonda · Marama · Pinnaroo · Cowangie · Tutye · Underbool · Piet Millan · Yarto · Nyah West · Ultima · Meatian · Koondrook · Cohuna

Yorke · St. Vincent · **Brighton** · Mt. Barker · McLaren Vale · Monteith · Tailem Bend · Peake · Geranium · Lameroo · Patchewollock · Berriwillock · Tyrrell · Kerang · Mincha

Investigator Strait · Vincent · Willunga · Strathalbyn · Cooke Plains · L. Tyrrell · Culgoa · Quambatook · Tragowel

Western River · Kingscote · Nepean Bay · Penneshaw · Normanville · Finniss · L. Alexandrina · Meningie · Coonalpyn · L. Albacutya · Hopetoun · Yaapeet · Curyo · Birchip · Wycheproof · Charlton · Mitiamo · Lockington

C. Borda · Vivonne · Victor Harbor · Goolwa · L. Albert · Culburra · Tintinara · Rainbow · Brim · Warracknabeal · Litchfield · Korong Vale · Rochester · Elmore

KANGAROO I. · D'Estrees Bay · Cape Jervis · Encounter Bay · Yumali · Jeparit · Antwerp · Wedderburn · Cope Cope · Bridgewater

Vivonne Bay · Backstairs Passage · The Coorong · Salt Creek · Keith · Bordertown · Diapur · Nhill · Kaniva · Dimboola · Murtoa · St. Arnaud · Eaglehawk · **Bendigo**

C. du Couedic · C. Gantheaume · Youngh · Lacepede Bay · Wolseley · Frances · Goroke · Natimuk · **Horsham** · Bolangum · Dunolly · Maldon · **VICTORIA**

Kingston S.E. · C. Jaffa · Reedy Creek · Kybybolite · Morea · Noradjuha (Carpolac) · Glenorchy · Wimmera · **Maryborough** · Avoca · **Castlemaine** · Kyneton · Woodend

WIMMERA · Toolondo · Naracoorte · Deep Lead · **Stawell** · Talbot · Clunes · Daylesford · Creswick

Beachport · L. George · Kalangadoo · Glenroy · Balmoral · Mt. William 1167 · **Ararat** · Maroona · Beaufort · **BALLARAT**

Rivoli B. · Millicent · Penola · Englefield · Casterton · Coleraine · Cavendish · Willaura · Mininera · Scarsdale · Elaine · Bacchus Marsh

L. Bonney · **Mount Gambier** · Nangwarry · **Hamilton** · Dunkeld · Penshurst · Skipton · Derrinallum · **Werribee** · Lara

Port MacDonnell · Dartmoor · Branxholme · Condah · Macarthur · Mortlake · Cressy · Inverleigh · **Williams**

C. Northumberland · Heywood · Koroit · Terang · Camperdown · Alvie · Winchelsea · **GEELONG** · Queenscliff

Discovery Bay · **Portland** · Portland Bay · Port Fairy · Cobden · Allansford · **Colac** · Torquay · Mo

C. Bridgewater · C. Nelson · **Warrnambool** · Timboon · Aireys Inlet · Lorne

Lavers Hill · Forrest · Apollo Bay · Port Campbell · C. Otway

Projection: Alber's Equal area with two standard parallels

1 : 3 200 000

20 0 20 40 60 miles
20 0 20 40 60 80 km

6   7   8   9   10

A

Louth, Curraweena, Byrock, Glenariff, Carinda, Gwabegar, Turrawan, Barraba, Black Mountain, Kingstown, 1684, Coffs Harbour, Dorrigo
Wilgaroon, Colossal, Quambone, Nelgowrie, Baradine, Upper Manilla, Namoi, Manilla, Attunga, Bendemeer, Walcha Road, Walcha, Chandlers Pk., Bellingen
Curranyalpa, Coolabah, Pine Ridge, Girilambone, Coonamble, Gombara, Yearinan, Boggabri, Gunnedah, Armidale, Uralla, Kentucky, Nambucca Heads, Macksville
Burnamwood, Booroomugga, Ulamambri, Coonabarabran, **Liverpool Plains**, Tamworth, Limbri, Tia, Mt. Banda Banda 1263, Macleay, Smithtown
Cobar, Canbelego, Hermidale, Nyngan, Haddon Rig, Armatree, Castlereagh, Binnaway, Ulinda, Currabubula, Werris Creek, Yarras, Wauchope, Kempsey
Barnato, Elsinore, Rest Downs, Mullengudgery, Warren, Collie, Gilgandra, Neilrex, Tamarang, Quirindi, Oakley Creek, Murrurundi, Wingen, Nowendoc, Comboyne, Port Macquarie, Kendall
Everdale, Buddabadah, Nevertire, Merrygoen, Dunedoo, Coolah, Hannahs Bridge, **Liverpool Range**, Ellerston, Elandos, Moorland

32

Nymagee, Taringa Downs, Bogan, Trangie, Brocklehurst, Dubbo, Minore, Narromine, Talbragar, Craboon, Merriwa, Aberdeen, Gungal, Scone, 1555, Denman, Ravensworth, Stratford, Wards River, Stroud Road, Gloucester, Taree, Tuncurry, Forster
Gilgunnia, Tottenham, Bobadah, Geurie, Toongi, Tallawang, Gulgong, Baerami Creek, Muswellbrook, Dungog, Bulahdelah, Booral
Wee Elwah, Mt. Hope, Melrose, Peak Hill, Yeoval, Wellington, Mudgee, Lake Burrendong, Rylstone, Lue, Kandos, 1257, Putty, Singleton, Paterson, Karuah

B

W, Tiarra, Conoble, Trida, Roto, Matakana, Gunebang, Trundle, Tomingley, **Hunter Range**, Store Creek, Olinda, Coricudgy, Branxton, Maitland, Cessnock, Kurri Kurri, Raymond Terrace, Thornton-Beresfield, Stockton
Billabong Cr., Gunnigulhra, Condobolin, Ootha, Bogan Gate, Goonumbla, Eucharena, Ben Bullen, Portland, Waller, Wallerawang, Lithgow, Kurri Kurri, Toronto, Wallsend, **NEWCASTLE**
SOUTH, 552 Ural, Lake Cargelligo, Tullibigeal, Burcher, Parkes, Molong, Cumnock, Orange, Spring Hill, Blue Mts., Richmond, Kurrajong, Windsor, Morisset, Belmont, Swansea, Budgewoi
Hillston, Naradhan, Ungarie, L. Cowal, Eugowra, Forbes, Bathurst, Blayney, Oberon, Penrith, Parramatta, Fairfield, Gosford, The Entrance, Woy Woy

34

Hay, Beabula, Merriwagga, Rankins Springs, Kikoira, West Wyalong, Marsden, Caragabal, Quandialla, Grenfell, Bribbaree, Billimari, Carcoar, Woodstock, Wyangala Res., Lake Burragorang, Camden, Picton, The Oaks, Liverpool, **SYDNEY**, Manly, Hornsby, Sutherland, Cronulla
Booligal, Goolgowi, Bellarwi, Barmedman, Mirrool, Reefton, Young, Koorawatha, Peelwood, Crookwell, Campbelltown, Helensburgh, Bulli, Woonona
Griffith, Hanwood, Yenda, Ardlethan, Barellan, Temora, Cootamundra, Boorowa, Frogmore, Roslyn, Mittagong, Bargo, **WOLLONGONG**, Port Kembla, Shellharbour
Willbriggie, **Leeton**, Yanco, Ganmain, Harden, Galong, Binalong, Moss Vale, Robertson, **Bowral**, Kiama
Narrandera, Coolamon, Junee, Pettitts, Yass, Murrumbateman, Marulan, Berry, Gerringong
Morundah, Kywong, Borea Creek, **Wagga Wagga**, Alfred Town, Gundagai, Murrumbidgee, **Goulburn**, Nowra, Bomaderry

C

Deniliquin, Finley, Berrigan, Jerilderie, Urana, The Rock, Adelong, Tumut, Burrinjuck Res., L. George, **CANBERRA**, **A.C.T.**, Bungendore, Wandanian, Jervis Bay (Commonwealth Territory)
Tocumwal, Mathoura, Oaklands, Pleasant Hills, Henty, Culcairn, Humula, Kunama, Batlow, Royalla, Queanbeyan, Braidwood, Marlow, St. Georges Hd., Ulladulla

36

Barnes, Numurkah, Nathalia, Cobram, Yarrawonga, Corowa, Rutherglen, **Albury**, Chiltern, Walla Walla, Rosewood, Holbrook, Tumbarumba, Bimberi Pk. 1910, Colinton, Captains Flat, Majors Creek, East Lynne, Batemans Bay, Bateman's Bay
Echuca, **Kyabram**, Yabba North, **Wodonga**, Yackandandah, Cudgewa, L. Hume (Res.), Tallangatta, Corryong, Mt. Jagungal 2060, L. Eucumbene, Adaminaby, **Cooma**, Yowrie, C. Dromedary, Narooma
Tatura, Mooroopna, **Shepparton**, **Wangaratta**, Beechworth, Everton, Glenrowan, Mt. Benambra 1476, Tooma, Murray, 2230 Mt. Kosciusko, Jindabyne, Rock Flat, Nimmitabel, Bega, Goalen Hd.
Stanhope, Rushworth, Colbinabbin, Violet Town, Ovens, Bright, Myrtleford, Mt. Bogong 1986, Mount Beauty, Jimenbuen, Bombala, Tathra

D

Nagambie, Euroa, **Benalla**, Whitfield, Glen Valley, 1836 Mt. Cobberas, Corrowidgie, Candelo, Cathcart, Candelo
Heathcote, **Seymour**, Carisbrook, Bonnie Doon, Mansfield, Mt. Buller 1806, Omeo, Bonang, Rowes, Delegate, Eden, Twofold Bay
VICTORIA, Bradford, Alexandra, Yea, L. Eildon, Eildon, Mt. Tamboritha 1646, Swifts Creek, Buchan, Mt. Ellery 1297, Bonang, Wonboyn, Green C., Disaster B., C. Howe
Kilmore Junc., Heathcote Junc., Glenburn, Cobbannah, Bruthen, Nowa Nowa, Orbost, Club Terrace, Towamba, Genoa, C. Conran
Whittlesea, **Sunbury**, Healesville, Warburton, Aberfeldy, Munro, Stratford, Lakes Entrance, Cann River, Mallacoota, Mallacoota Inlet, Ram Head
Sunshine, Eltham, **MELBOURNE**, **Dandenong**, Walhalla, Heyfield, Maffra, **Sale**, L. Wellington, Ninety Mile Beach

38

Chelsea, Seaford, **Frankston**, Hastings, Drouin, Yallourn, **Moe**, **Traralgon**, Seaspray
FRENCH I., **PHILLIP**, Korumburra, Mirboo North, **Morwell**, **Churchill**, Boolarra, Woodside, The Ninety Mile Beach
Rosebud, San Remo, Leongatha, Meeniyan, Yarram
C. Woolamai, **Wonthaggi**, Anderson, Koonwarra, Inverloch, Toora, Port Albert, **SNAKE I.**, Welshpool
C. Liptrap, Venus B., Waratah B., Wilsons Promontory

T A S M A N

S E A

COPYRIGHT. GEORGE PHILIP & SON. LTD

E

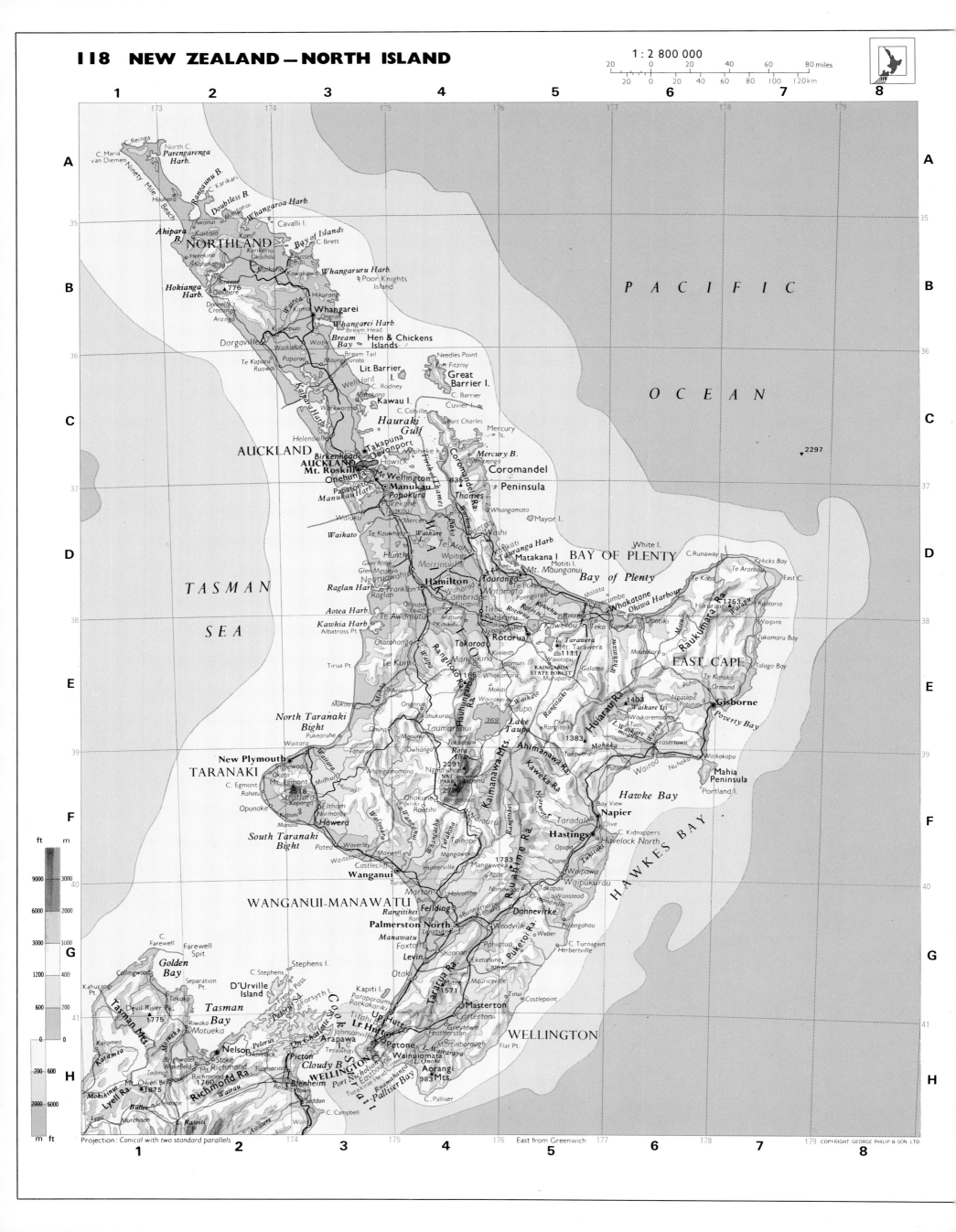

1 : 2 800 000

PACIFIC

OCEAN

NORTHLAND

TASMAN

SEA

AUCKLAND

Hauraki
Gulf

BAY OF PLENTY

Bay of Plenty

EAST CAPE

Hamilton

Tauranga

Rotorua

Lake
Taupo

TARANAKI

New Plymouth

Hawke Bay

Napier

Hastings

HAWKES BAY

Wanganui

WANGANUI-MANAWATU

Palmerston North

Gisborne

Poverty Bay

Mahia
Peninsula

Golden
Bay

Tasman
Bay

Nelson

WELLINGTON

WELLINGTON

Masterton

Projection: Conical with two standard parallels   East from Greenwich   COPYRIGHT. GEORGE PHILIP & SON. LTD.

1 : 2 800 000

20   0   20   40   60   80 miles
20   0   20 40 60 80 100 120km

NELSON-MARLBOROUGH

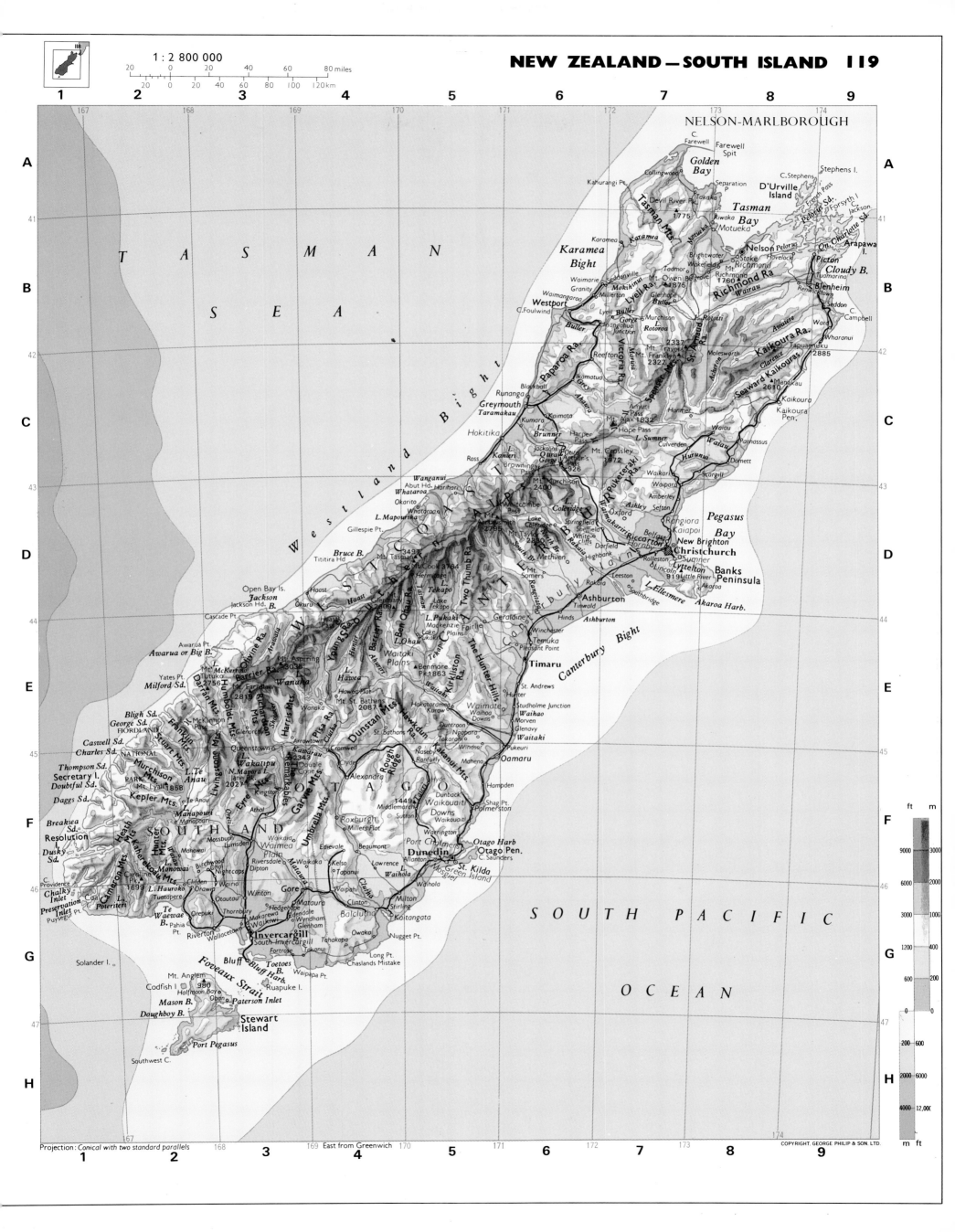

T A S M A N   S E A

Karamea Bight

Westland Bight

W E S T   C O A S T

Golden Bay

Tasman Bay

Cloudy B.

D'Urville Island

Richmond Ra.

Kaikoura Ra.

Seaward Kaikouras

Blenheim

Westport

Greymouth
Taramakau

Hokitika

Ross

Kanieri
L. Brunner

Pegasus Bay

New Brighton
Christchurch
Lyttelton
Banks Peninsula
Akaroa Harb.

Ashburton

C A N T E R B U R Y   P L A I N S

Timaru

Canterbury Bight

Geraldine
Temuka

Mt. Cook 3764

L. Tekapo
L. Pukaki
L. Ohau

Waitaki Plains

Waimate

Oamaru

Waitaki

S O U T H   P A C I F I C

O C E A N

O T A G O

Dunedin
Otago Pen.
St. Kilda
Green Island

Milford Sd.

Fiordland

Lake Wakatipu
Queenstown

L. Te Anau
Manapouri

S O U T H L A N D

Gore
Mataura

Invercargill
South Invercargill
Bluff
Foveaux Strait

Stewart Island
Port Pegasus
Southwest C.

Solander I.

Codfish I.
Oban
Paterson Inlet

ft   m

9000   3000

6000   2000

3000   1000

1200   400

600   200

0   0

200   600

2000   6000

4000   12,000

m   ft

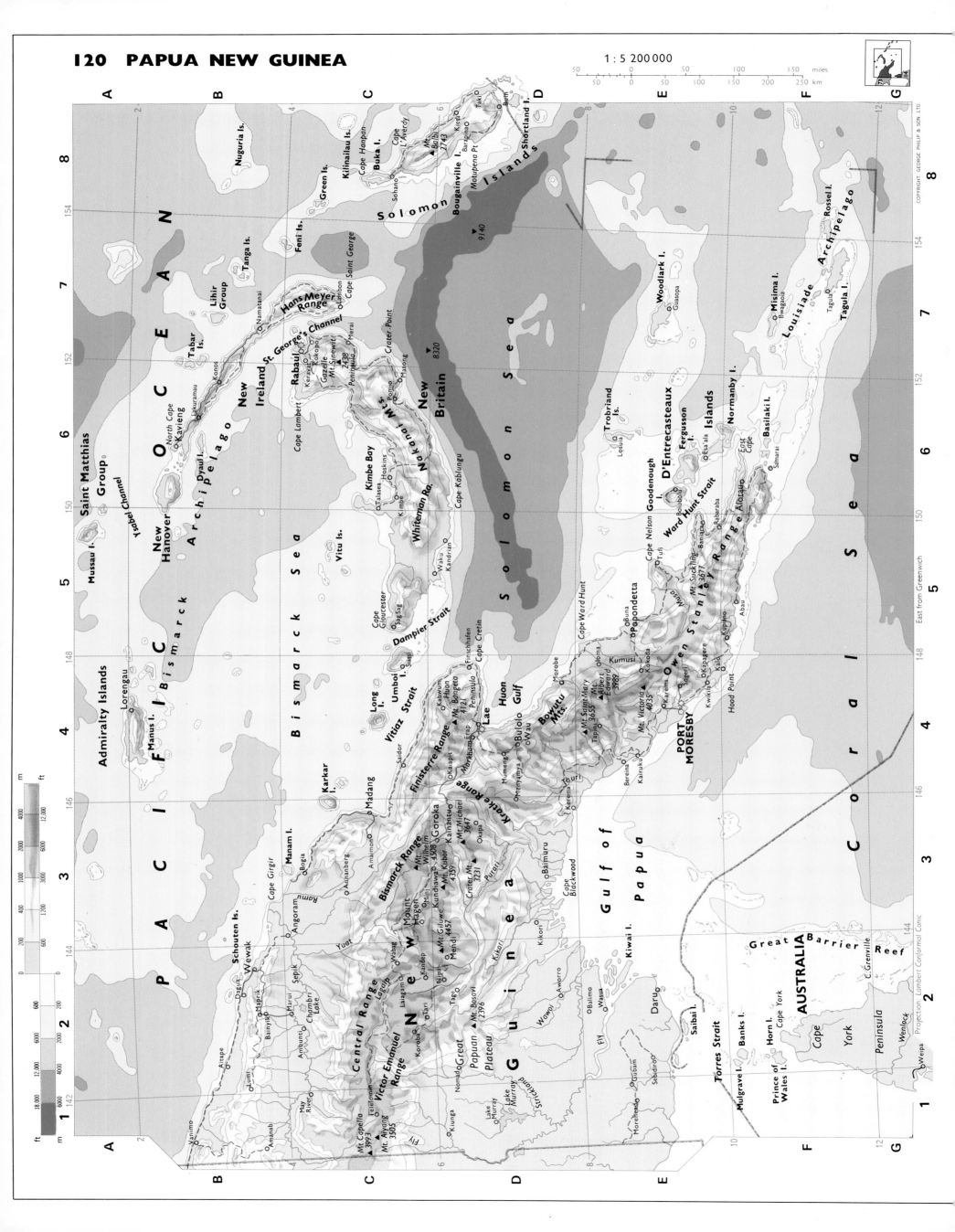

1 : 5 200 000

East from Greenwich

Projection: Lambert Conformal Conic

COPYRIGHT GEORGE PHILIP & SON LTD

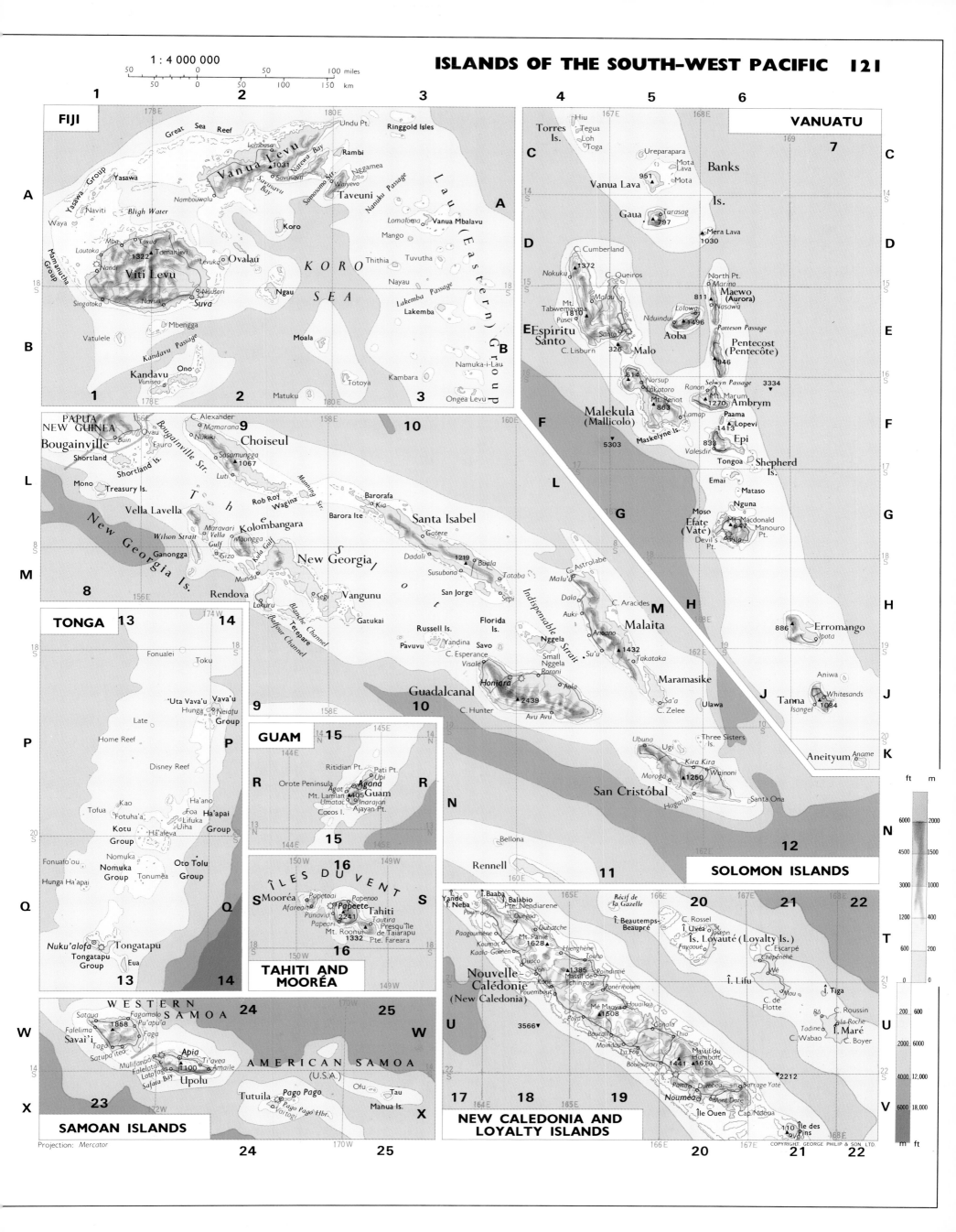

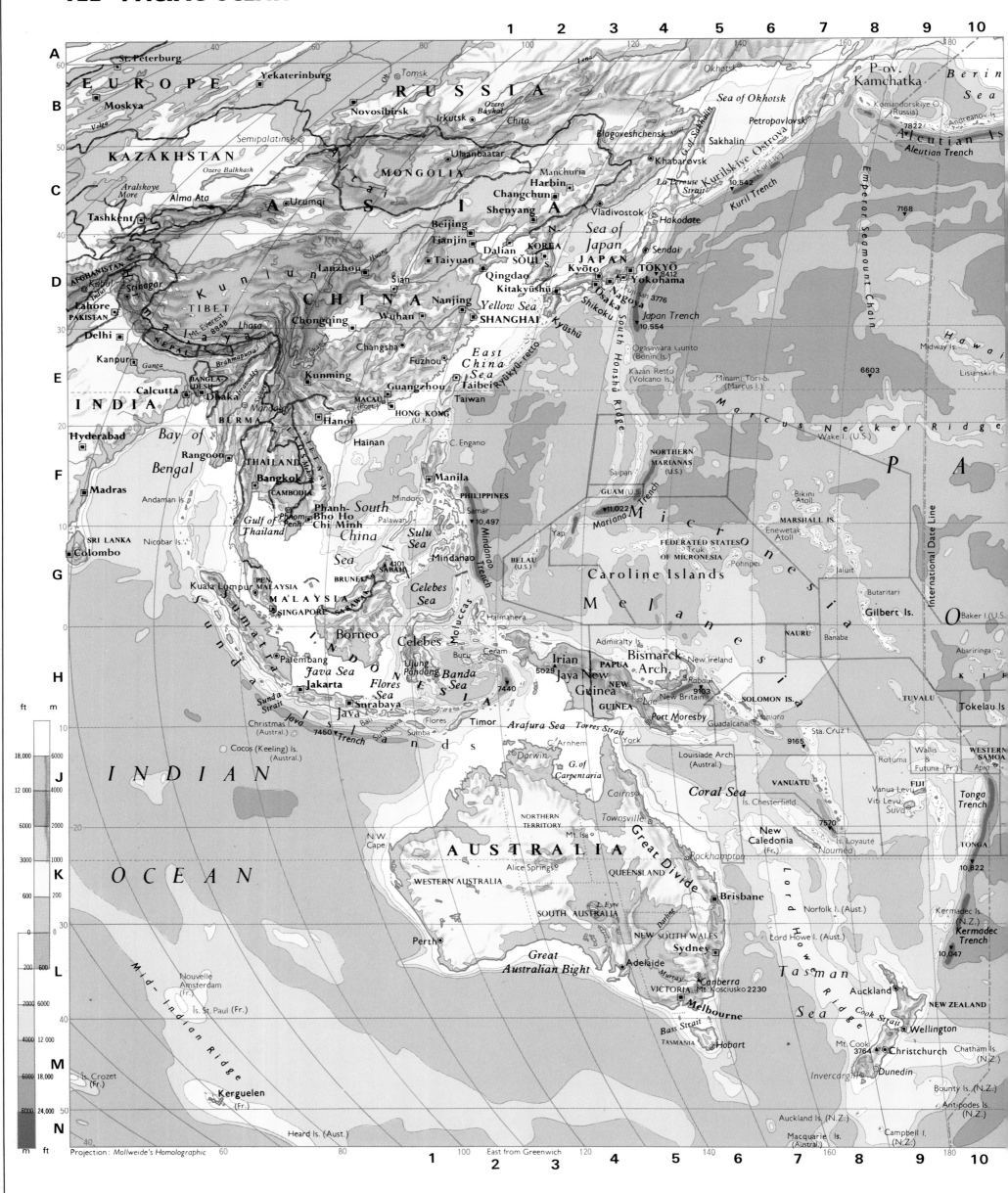

1 : 43 200 000

11 12 13 14 15 16 17 18 19 20

GREENLAND

C. Farewell — A — 60 — U.K.

Bristol Bay — ALASKA (U.S.) — 6050 — Juneau — Gulf of Alaska — Prince of Wales I. — Queen Charlotte Is. — Prince Rupert — Kitimat

Hudson Bay — NORTH

B

ROCKY — C A N A D A — Labrador — Newfoundland — NORTH

Edmonton — L. Winnipeg

Vancouver — NORTH — AMERICA — 50

Vancouver I. — Victoria — Calgary — Regina — Winnipeg — L. Superior — Montréal — Québec — St. Lawrence — Pr. Edward I. — Saint John

Seattle — Portland — Boise — Minneapolis — L. Huron — Ottawa — Toronto — L. Ontario — Boston — C. Sable — C

CHICAGO — L. Michigan — L. Erie — Buffalo

Salt Lake City — Denver — Kansas City — St. Louis — Cincinnati — Detroit — Pittsburgh — NEW YORK — Philadelphia — 40

San Francisco — 4418 — UNITED STATES — Baltimore — Washington — ATLANTIC — D

Los Angeles — Oklahoma — Memphis — Appalachian Mts. — Atlanta — C. Hatteras

San Diego — Dallas — Mississippi — Jacksonville — Bermuda (U.K.)

6741 — Ciudad Juárez — MEXICO — 6225 — Houston — New Orleans — OCEAN — 30 — E

Hawaiian Is. (U.S.) — Tropic of Cancer — San Antonio — Monterrey — Gulf of Mexico — Miami — Florida Strait — BAHAMAS

Honolulu — Oahu — Hawaii — Sierra Madre — Gulf of California — La Habana — CUBA — West Indies — Hispaniola — 9200 — 20

Is. Revilla Gigedo (Mexico) — México — 5700 — Yucatan Channel — Mérida — 7680 — DOM. REP. — Leeward Is.

Johnston I. (U.S.) — Guadalajara — Puebla — HAITI — JAMAICA — Kingston — PUERTO RICO (U.S.) — F

Acapulco — BELIZE — Caribbean Sea — BARBADOS

I. Clipperton (Fr.) — GUATEMALA — HONDURAS — Windward Is. — TRINIDAD & TOBAGO

Guatemala — San Salvador — NICARAGUA — Barranquilla — 10

EL SALVADOR — CENTRAL AMERICA — Managua — San José — Maracaibo — Caracas

COSTA RICA — PANAMA — Colón — Panama — VENEZUELA

Palmyra Is. (U.S.) — I. del Coco (Costa Rica) — Panama Canal — Orinoco — G

Teraina — Tabuaeran — Medellín — Bogotá

Kiritimati — Cali — COLOMBIA

Jarvis I. (U.S.) — Quito — ECUADOR — 0

Phoenix Is. — Equator — Galápagos (Ecuador) — Guayaquil — Amazonas — Manaus

Malden I. — C. Pariñas — Iquitos — BRAZIL — H

Starbuck I. — Î. Marquises — Trujillo — SOUTH

Tongareva — Penrhyn Is. — Caroline I. — Vostok I. — 6369 — PERU — 10

Manihiki — Lima — AMERICA

Pukapuka — Suwarrow Is. — Flint I. — Î. de la Société — Cuzco — J

Cook Islands (N.Z.) — Î. Tuamotu — Arequipa — Titicaca — Illampu & Ancohuma — 6550

AMER. SAMOA (U.S.) — Tahiti — Manuae — FRENCH POLYNESIA — Peru — 6866 — La Paz — BOLIVIA

Niue (N.Z.) — Austral — Î. Tuamotu — Iquique — Chile — 20

Rarotonga — Tropic of Capricorn — PARAGUAY

Î. Tubuai (Is. Australes) — Pitcairn I. (U.K.) — 8050 — Antofagasta Trench — Asunción — K

Rapa — Ducie I. (U.K.) — I. de Pascua (Easter I.) (Chile) — San Félix (Chile) — Tucumán

Sala-y-Gomez (Chile) — San Ambrosio (Chile) — 30

Arch. de Juan Fernández (Chile) — 6960 — Córdoba — Rosario — URUGUAY

Valparaíso — ARGENTINA — Montevideo — L

Santiago — Buenos Aires — Río de la Plata

Concepción — SOUTH

40 — ATLANTIC

Patagonia — M

OCEAN

6212

Falkland Is. (U.K.) — 50

Punta Arenas — Str. of Magellan — South Georgia — N

Tierra del Fuego — C. Horn

PACIFIC — OCEAN — East Pacific Ridge — Chile Rise — Pacific-Antarctic Ridge — Tuamotu Ridge — Seamount Chain

11 12 13 14 15 16 17 18 19 20

160 — 140 — 120 — West from Greenwich — 80 — 60 — 40 — 20

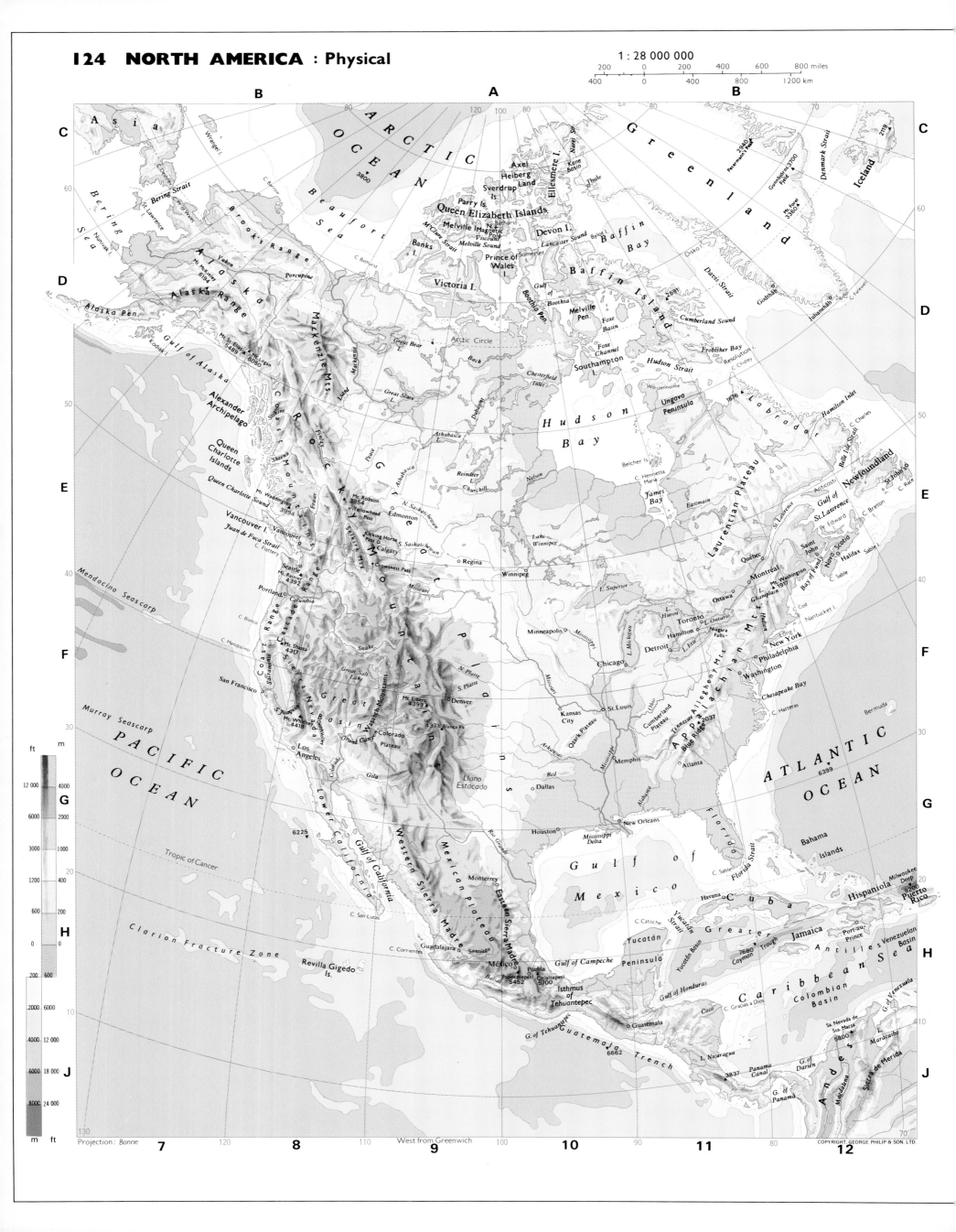

1 : 28 000 000

200   0   200   400   600   800 miles
400   0   200   400   800   1200 km

B   A   B

C   *Asia*   ARCTIC OCEAN   *Greenland*   C
Wrangel I.   C. Barrow   Beaufort Sea   3800   Axel Heiberg Land   Sverdrup Is.   Parry Is.   Queen Elizabeth Islands   Melville I.   N. Magnetic Pole   Thule   2940 Petermann Pk   3700   Denmark Strait   Iceland   2119
Bering Strait   St. Lawrence   Brooks Range   C. Bathurst   Banks I.   M'Clure Strait   Melville Sound   Devon I.   Lancaster Sound   Baffin Bay   Bylot I.   Disko I.   Mt. Forel 3360   Godthåb

D   Alaska Pen.   Kodiak I.   Gulf of Alaska   Mt. St. Elias 5489   Mt. Logan 6050   Alaska Range   C. Prince of Wales   Victoria I.   Gulf of Boothia   Melville Pen.   Foxe Basin   Baffin Island   2591   Cumberland Sound   Dubawnt Strait   C. Farewell   D
Alexander Archipelago   Mackenzie Mts.   Arctic Circle   Great Bear L.   Back   Foxe Channel   Frobisher Bay   Resolution   C. Chidley

E   Queen Charlotte Islands   Queen Charlotte Sound   Stikine   Skeena   Finlay   Liard   Mackenzie   Great Slave L.   Athabasca   Dubawnt   Chesterfield Inlet   Southampton   Hudson Strait   Wolstenholme   Hudson Bay   Ungava Peninsula   1676   Labrador   Hamilton Inlet   Newfoundland   E
Mt. Waddington 3994   Mt. Robson 3954   Yellowhead Pass   Peace   Athabasca   Reindeer L.   Nelson   Belcher Is.   C. Henrietta Maria   James Bay   Eastmain   Laurentian Plateau   Anticosti I.   Gulf of St. Lawrence   St. John's   C. Race

F   Vancouver I.   Juan de Fuca Strait   C. Flattery   Kicking Horse Pass   Calgary   N. Saskatchewan   S. Saskatchewan   Lake Winnipeg   L. Superior   Québec   Montreal   Mt. Washington 1917   Bay of Fundy   Nova Scotia   Halifax   F
Seattle   Mt. Rainier 4392   Portland   Crowsnest Pass   Regina   Winnipeg   Minneapolis   L. Michigan   L. Huron   Ottawa   Toronto   Hamilton   L. Ontario   Niagara Falls   L. Erie   Detroit   Champlain   Hudson   New York   Saint John   Pr. Edward I.   C. Breton   C. Sable   Cod   Nantucket I.
Mendocino Seascarp   C. Blanco   Missouri   Chicago   Philadelphia   Washington
C. Mendocino   Mt. Shasta 4317   Snake   Great Salt Lake   N. Platte   St. Louis   Cumberland Plateau   Allegheny Mts.   Appalachian Mts.   Chesapeake Bay

G   San Francisco   Coast Range   Sierra Nevada   Mt. Whitney 4418   Boundary Pk   Wasatch Mountains   Mt. Elbert 4399   Denver   S. Platte   Colorado   4378 Blanca Pk.   Kansas City   Arkansas   Ohio   Tennessee   Blue Ridge 2037   C. Hatteras   Bermuda   6399   G
PACIFIC OCEAN   Los Angeles   Great Basin   Grand Canyon   Colorado Plateau   Llano Estacado   Red   Memphis   Mississippi   Atlanta   ATLANTIC OCEAN
Murray Seascarp   San Joaquin   Gila   Dallas   Alabama   New Orleans

H   Tropic of Cancer   6225   Lower California   Gulf of California   Western Sierra Madre   Mexican Plateau   Eastern Sierra Madre   Rio Grande   Houston   Mississippi Delta   Gulf of Mexico   C. Sable   Florida   Bahama Islands   Milwaukee Deep 9700   Puerto Rico   H
Clarion Fracture Zone   C. San Lucas   C. San Lazaro   Havana   Cuba   Hispaniola   Venezuelan Basin
Revilla Gigedo Is.   C. Corrientes   Guadalajara   Santiago   Yucatán   C. Catoche   Yucatán Strait   Greater   Jamaica   Antilles   Port-au-Prince

J   México   Puebla   Popocatepetl 5452   Orizaba 5700   Isthmus of Tehuantepec   Yucatán Peninsula   Gulf of Campeche   Yucatán Basin   Cayman Trough 7680   Colombian Basin   Caribbean Sea   Sa. Nevada de Sta. Marta 5800   L. Maracaibo   G. of Venezuela   J
Balsas   Gulf of Honduras   Coco   C. Gracias á Dios   Sierra de Merida
G. of Tehuantepec   Guatemala   Guatemala Trench 6662   L. Nicaragua   Panama Canal   3837   Panama Basin   G. of Panama   G. of Darién   Andes   Magdalena

Projection: Bonne   West from Greenwich   COPYRIGHT. GEORGE PHILIP & SON. LTD.

7   8   9   10   11   12

ft   m
12 000   4000
6000   2000
3000   1000
1200   400
600   200
0   0
200   600
2000   6000
4000   12 000
6000   18 000
8000   24 000
m   ft

1 : 28 000 000

200   0   200   400   600   800 miles
400   0   400   800   1200 km

B   A   B

C   ARCTIC OCEAN   GREENLAND (Denmark)   ICELAND   Reykjavik   C

Bering Sea   Bering Strait   Beaufort Sea   Queen Elizabeth Is.   Ellesmere I.   Baffin Bay   Denmark Strait

ALASKA   Yukon   Fairbanks   Arctic Circle

D   Anchorage   INUVIK   Victoria I.   KITIKMEOT   BAFFIN   Baffin I.   Godthaab   C. Farewell   D

Gulf of Alaska   YUKON TERRITORY   Whitehorse   NORTHWEST TERRITORIES

Juneau   FORT SMITH   Yellowknife   Great Bear L.   Back   KEEWATIN   Hudson Strait   NEWFOUNDLAND

Great Slave L.   Dubawnt   Hudson Bay

50   BRITISH COLUMBIA   Peace   L. Athabasca   Churchill   Nelson   Labrador   50

ALBERTA   Edmonton   SASKATCHEWAN   MANITOBA   Eastmain   QUÉBEC   St. John's   SPM

Calgary   Regina   L. Winnipeg   ONTARIO   Québec   NEW BRUNSWICK   PR. EDWARD   Charlottetown   NOVA SCOTIA   Halifax

Vancouver   S. Saskatchewan   Winnipeg   Fredericton   MAINE

40   Victoria   WASHINGTON   Seattle   Montréal   Montpelier   Augusta   40

Olympia   Ottawa   VER. N.H.   Concord

Portland   Columbia   MONTANA   NORTH DAKOTA   MINNESOTA   L. Superior   Toronto   Buffalo   NEW YORK   Albany   MASS. Boston

Salem   Bismarck   L. Ontario   Hartford   R.I. Providence

OREGON   Helena   SOUTH DAKOTA   Minneapolis   St. Paul   WISCONSIN   MICHIGAN   Detroit   Cleveland   PENNSYLVANIA   NEW YORK

IDAHO   Boise   WYOMING   Pierre   Madison   Lansing   Milwaukee   Toledo   Pittsburgh   Harrisburg   N.J.   Philadelphia

F   Sacramento   Carson City   Salt Lake City   Cheyenne   NEBRASKA   Des Moines   IOWA   Chicago   INDIANA   Columbus   OHIO   Baltimore   Dover   F

San Francisco   CALIFORNIA   NEVADA   UTAH   Denver   Lincoln   Springfield   ILLINOIS   Indianapolis   Cincinnati   WEST VIRGINIA   D.C. Washington   Annapolis   M.

San Jose   COLORADO   Topeka   Kansas City   Jefferson City   Frankfort   Charleston   Richmond   Virginia

30   Las Vegas   Santa Fe   KANSAS   MISSOURI   St. Louis   KENTUCKY   NORTH CAROLINA   Raleigh   30

LOS ANGELES   ARIZONA   Albuquerque   OKLAHOMA   Oklahoma City   Nashville   TENNESSEE   Columbia   SOUTH CAROLINA   Bermuda (Br.)

San Diego   Phoenix   NEW MEXICO   Little Rock   ARKANSAS   Memphis   Birmingham   Atlanta   GEORGIA

G   Tucson   El Paso   TEXAS   Dallas   MISSISSIPPI   ALABAMA   Montgomery   FLORIDA   Jacksonville   ATLANTIC OCEAN   G

PACIFIC OCEAN   Gila   Red River   LOUISIANA   Jackson   Baton Rouge   Tallahassee

Austin   Houston   New Orleans   Tampa   Miami   Nassau   BAHAMAS

Rio Grande   Gulf of Mexico   C. Sable   Str. of Florida   Turks & Caicos (Br.)

20   Tropic of Cancer   Monterrey   Havana   CUBA   HAITI   DOMINICAN REP.   San Juan   PUERTO RICO   20

MEXICO   Cayman Is. (Br.)   Port-au-Prince   Santo Domingo

H   Revilla Gigedo Is. (Mexico)   Guadalajara   JAMAICA   Kingston   H

MEXICO   Caribbean Sea

Belmopan   BELIZE

10   GUATEMALA   HONDURAS   Maracaibo   10

Guatemala   Tegucigalpa   Barranquilla   VENEZUELA

San Salvador   NICARAGUA   Panamá

EL SALVADOR   Managua   L. Nicaragua   SOUTH

J   San José   COSTA RICA   PANAMA   Medellin   COLOMBIA   Bogotá   AMERICA   J

70

7   **Washington** Capital Cities
⊙ U.S. State Capitals and Canadian Provincial Capitals

C.   CONNECTICUT   N.H.   NEW HAMPSHIRE
D.   DELAWARE   N.J.   NEW JERSEY
D.C.   DISTRICT OF COLUMBIA   R.I.   RHODE ISLAND
M.   MARYLAND   VER.   VERMONT
MASS.   MASSACHUSETTS   SPM   ST. PIERRE ET MIQUELON

Projection : Bonne

120   110   West from Greenwich   90   70

8   **9**   **10**   **11**   **12**

COPYRIGHT. GEORGE PHILIP & SON. LTD.

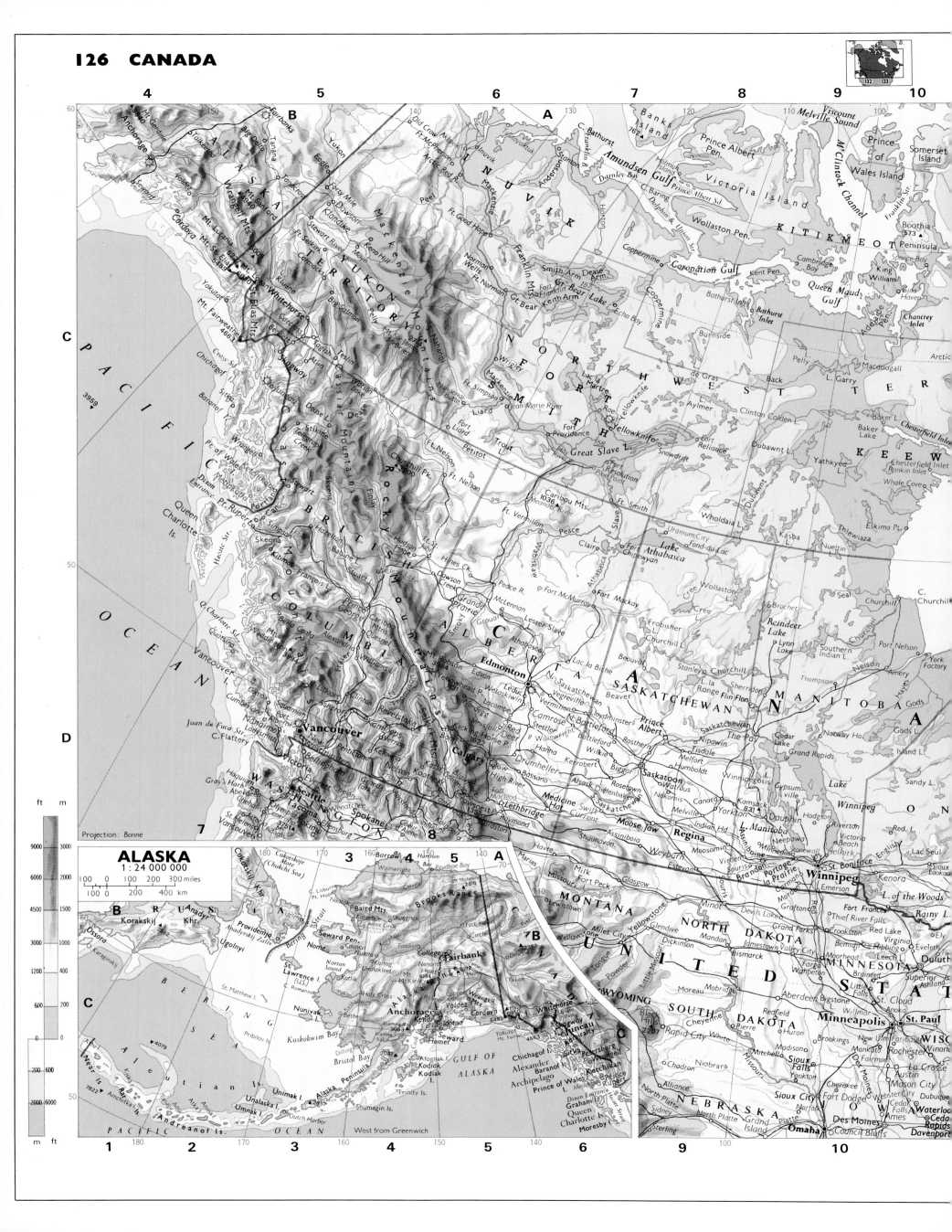

MANITOBA

ONTARIO

QUEBEC

N.W. TERRITORIES

HUDSON BAY

JAMES BAY

LAKE SUPERIOR

LAKE HURON

LAKE MICHIGAN

LAKE ERIE

LAKE ONTARIO

WISCONSIN

INDIANA

OHIO

PENNSYLVANIA

NEW YORK

Major cities: Duluth, Ashland, Milwaukee, Madison, Chicago, Detroit, Cleveland, Toronto, Hamilton, Buffalo, Ottawa, Montréal, Thunder Bay, Sault Ste. Marie, Sudbury, North Bay, Timmins, Kirkland Lake

Belcher Islands

Akimiski I.

Lambert's Equivalent Azimuthal

ft m
4500 1500
3000 1000
1200 400
600 200
0
200 600
2000 6000
4000 12 000
m ft

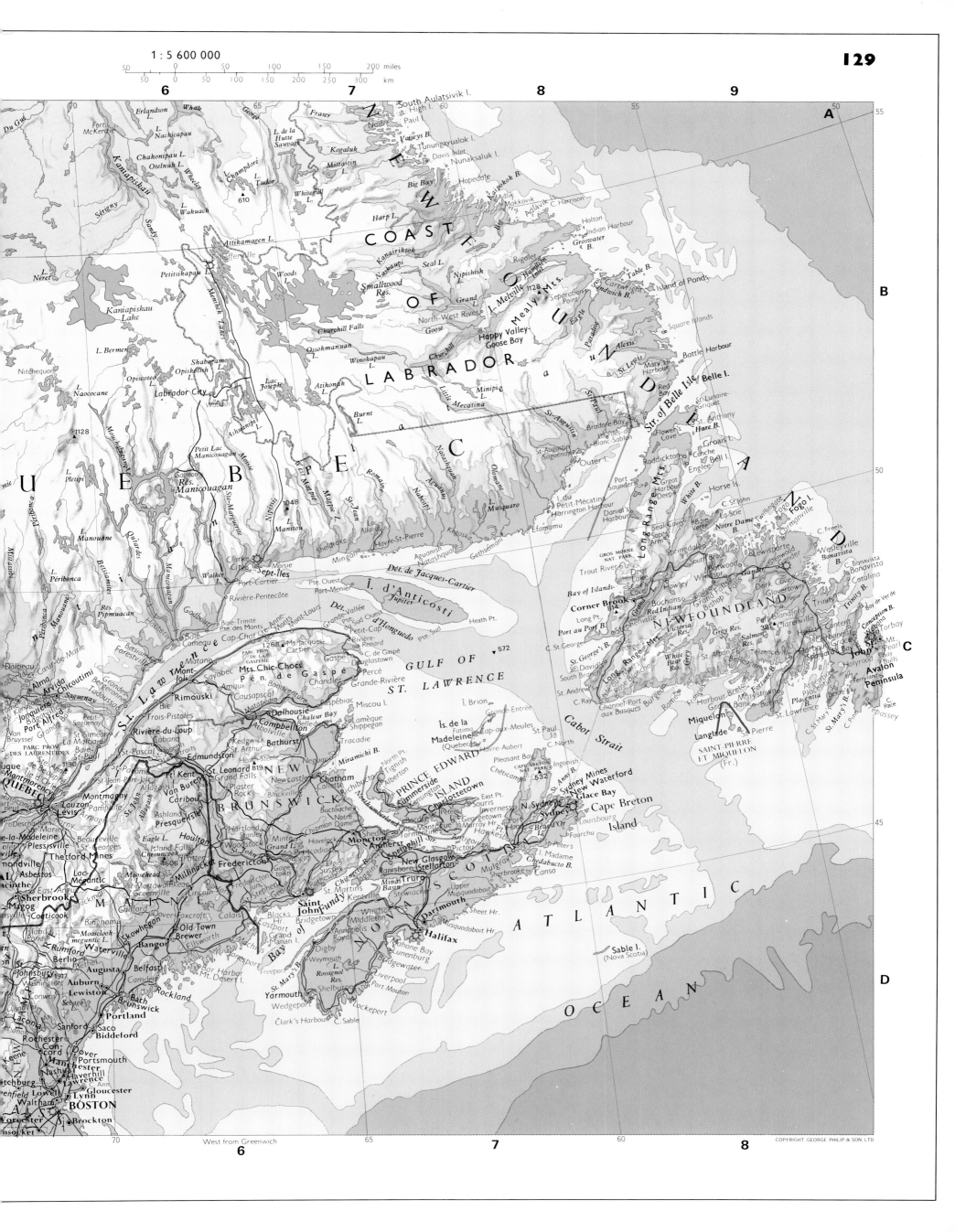

1　2　3　4　5　6

A

B

C

D

YUKON TERRITORY

ALASKA

NORTH WEST TERRITORIES

Great Slave Lake

WOOD BUFFALO NATIONAL PARK

BRITISH COLUMBIA

ALBERTA

Rocky Mountains

Cariboo Mountains

Coast Mountains

Skeena Mountains

Selkirk Mountains

Purcell Mts.

QUEEN CHARLOTTE ISLANDS

Graham I.

Moresby I.

HECATE STRAIT

ALEXANDER ARCH.

Chichagof I.

Baranof I.

Prince of Wales I.

Dall I.

VANCOUVER ISLAND

Nootka I.

Whitehorse

Juneau

Ketchikan

Prince Rupert

Kitimat

Terrace

Prince George

Quesnel

Williams Lake

Kamloops

VANCOUVER

New Westminster

Victoria

Nanaimo

Port Alberni

EDMONTON

St. Albert

Camrose

Red Deer

Calgary

Lethbridge

Medicine Hat

Grande Prairie

Dawson Creek

Fort St. John

Peace River

Fort McMurray

Fort Nelson

Jasper

Banff

Kelowna

Penticton

Cranbrook

Nelson

WASHINGTON

IDAHO

MONTANA

SEATTLE

Everett

Bellingham

Mount Vernon

OLYMPIC NATIONAL PARK

PACIFIC OCEAN

Dixon Entrance

PACIFIC

scale

ft / m

12 000 / 4000

9000 / 3000

6000 / 2000

4500 / 1500

3000 / 1000

1200 / 400

600 / 200

0 / 0

200 / 600

2000 / 6000

m / ft

Projection: Lambert's Equivalent Azimuthal

West from Greenwich

125　120　115

135　130

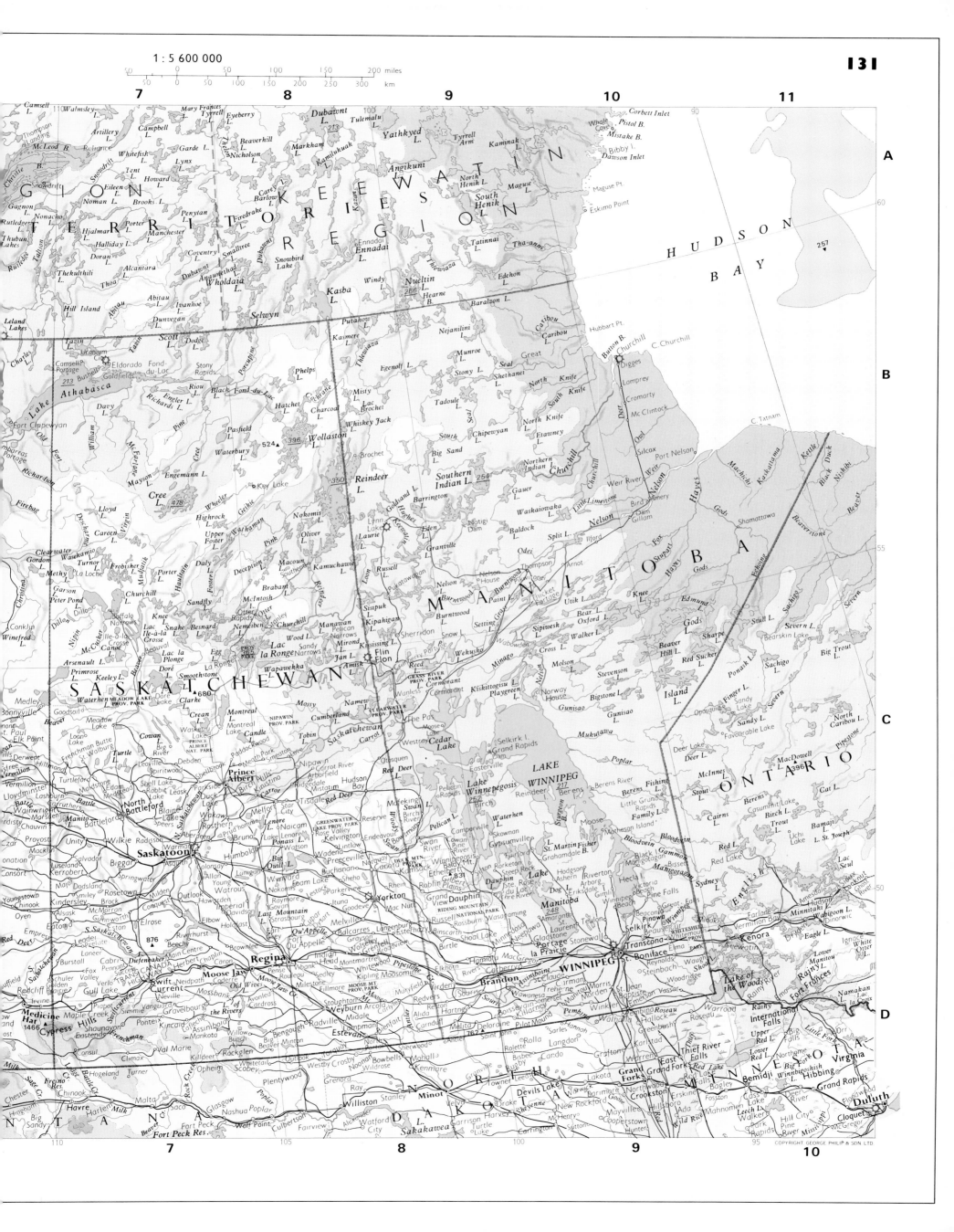

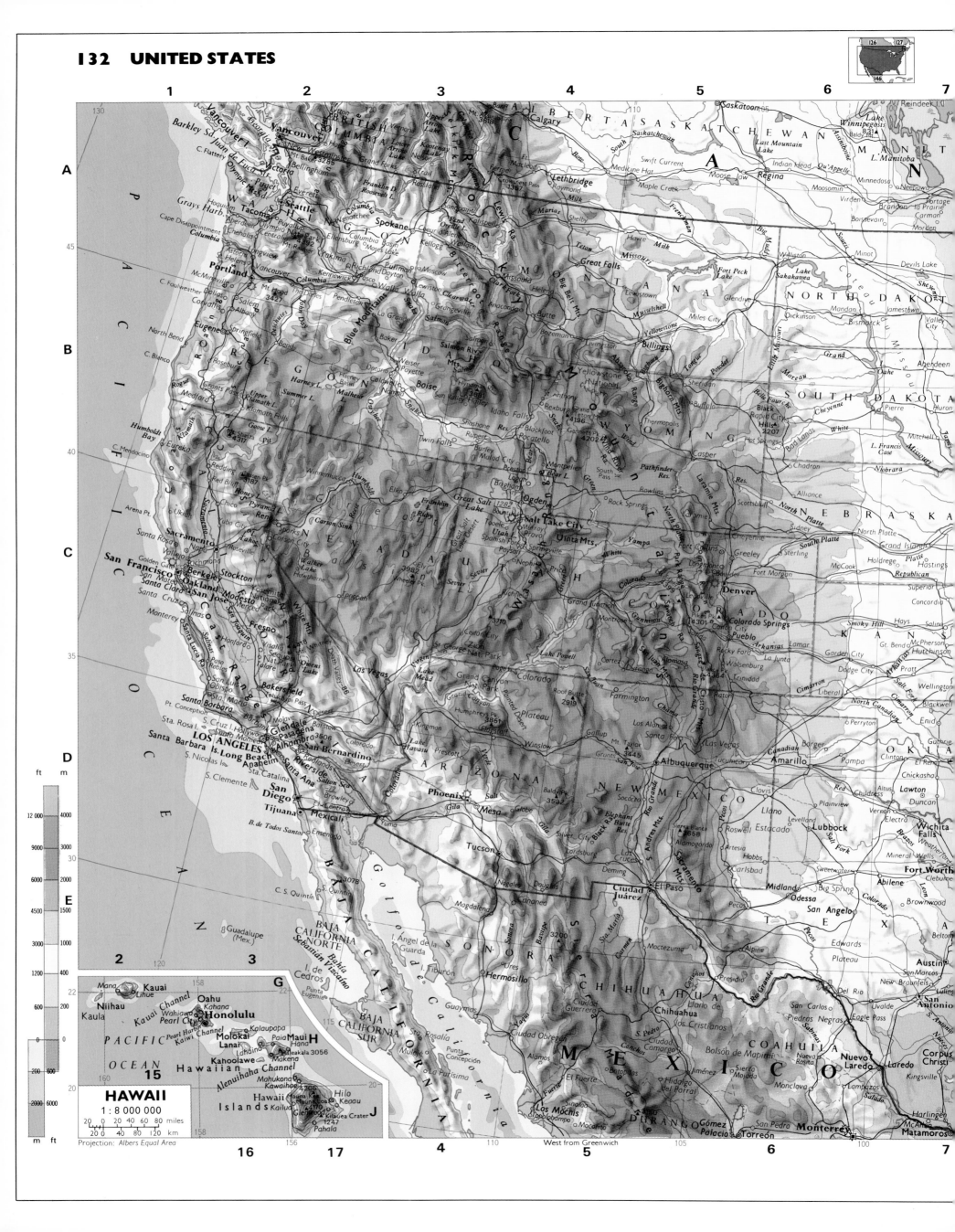

HAWAII

1 : 8 000 000

20 0 20 40 60 80 miles
20 0 40 80 120 km

Projection: Albers Equal Area

West from Greenwich

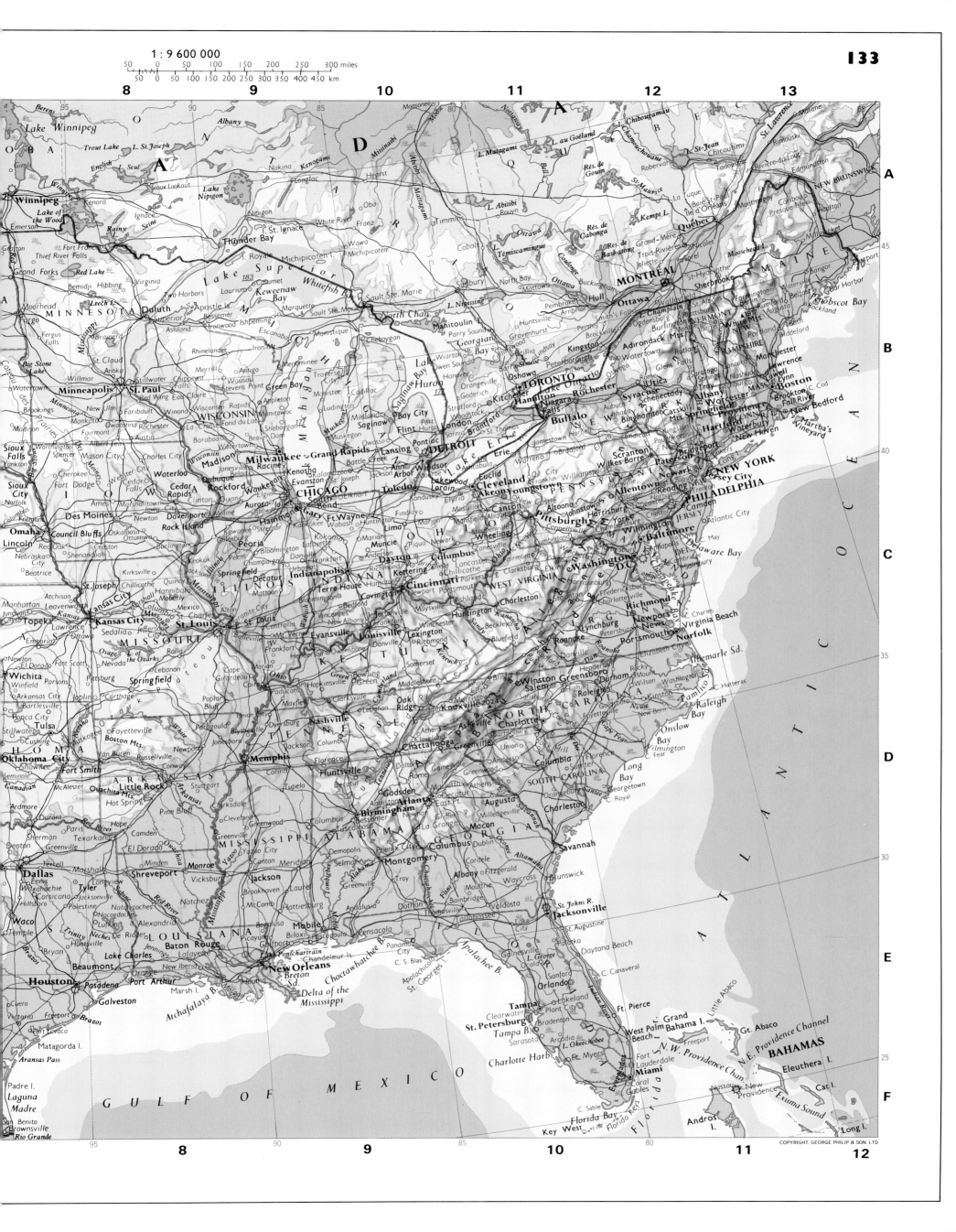

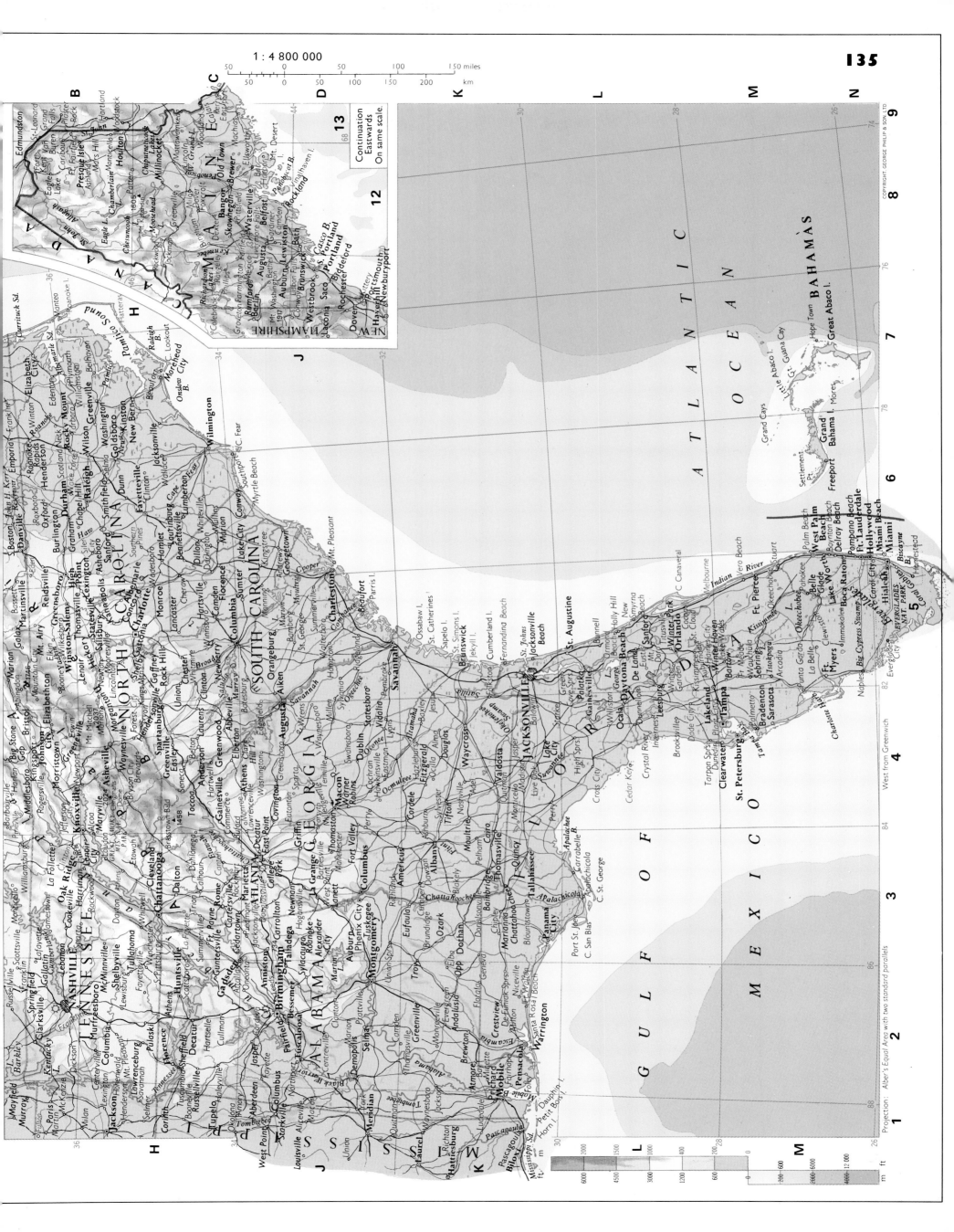

1 2 3 4 5 6 7

C A N A D A

O N T A R I O

Georgian Bay

LAKE HURON

Nottawasaga Bay

Bruce Peninsula

Owen Sound
Collingwood
Barrie
L. Simcoe
Orillia
Peterborough
Belleville
Trenton

TORONTO
Mississauga
Oshawa
Whitby
Bowmanville
Port Hope
Cobourg

Kitchener
Guelph
Cambridge
Hamilton
Burlington
Brantford
Woodstock

LAKE ONTARIO

St. Catharines
Niagara Falls
Welland
Port Colborne

BUFFALO
Lockport
Tonawanda
N. Tonawanda
Amherst
Lancaster
West Seneca
Lackawanna

Rochester
Greece
Irondequoit
Gates
Brighton
Canandaigua
Batavia

MICHIGAN

Port Huron
Sarnia
London
St. Thomas

Port Hope
Bad Axe
Harbor Beach

DETROIT
Windsor
Chatham
Lake St. Clair
Mt. Clemens

LAKE ERIE

Long Point Bay

Erie
Dunkirk
Fredonia
Jamestown
Olean

N E W   Y O R K

Elmira
Corning
Hornell
Salamanca

OHIO

CLEVELAND
Lakewood
Euclid
Cleveland Hts.
Shaker Hts.
Parma
Elyria
Lorain
Sandusky

Akron
Cuyahoga Falls
Kent
Barberton
Canton
Massillon
Mansfield

Warren
Youngstown
Boardman
Niles
Sharon
New Castle

PENNSYLVANIA

Meadville
Oil City
Franklin
Titusville
Bradford
Warren
Kane
Emporium

PITTSBURGH
McKeesport
Wilkinsburg
Penn Hills
Monroeville
Plum
New Kensington
Aliquippa
Beaver Falls
Ambridge
Butler
Indiana
Johnstown
Altoona
State College

Washington
Wheeling
W. VA.
Steubenville
Weirton
Zanesville
Cambridge

Projection: Bonne

ft m
6000 2000
4500 1500
1200 400
600 200
0 0
200 600
m ft

1 : 2 000 000

10 0 10 20 30 40 50 miles
10 0 10 20 30 40 50 60 70 80 km

8   9   10   11   12   13   14

ONTARIO CANADA QUEBEC

MONTREAL Longueuil Lachine Greenfield Park Chambly Granby Sherbrooke Lennoxville Cookshire

Ottawa Hull Cornwall

Kingston Watertown

NEW YORK

Syracuse Utica Rome

Adirondack Mountains

Mt. Marcy 1629 Lake Placid Saranac Lakes Plattsburgh

Lake Champlain

VERMONT

Burlington Montpelier Rutland

NEW HAMPSHIRE

White Mountains Mt. Washington 1917 Concord Manchester Nashua

MAINE

Albany Schenectady Troy Amsterdam Saratoga Springs Glens Falls

Gloversville Oneonta Binghamton Ithaca Cortland Auburn

MASSACHUSETTS

Pittsfield Springfield Worcester Framingham BOSTON Cambridge Quincy Lowell Lawrence Lynn Salem Gloucester

CONNECTICUT

Hartford New Britain Waterbury Danbury Bridgeport New Haven Norwalk Stamford New London

RHODE ISLAND

Providence Pawtucket Cranston Warwick Fall River Newport

Kingston Poughkeepsie Newburgh Middletown Kingston

White Plains Yonkers New Rochelle Mt. Vernon

Long Island Sound

Long Island

Block Island Sound Block I. Montauk Pt.

Martha's Vineyard Nantucket Sound

Buzzards Bay

NEW JERSEY

NEW YORK Jersey City Newark Elizabeth Bayonne Perth Amboy New Brunswick Paterson Passaic Hackensack Hoboken Union City

PENNSYLVANIA

Scranton Wilkes-Barre Allentown Bethlehem Easton Reading Trenton Levittown

PHILADELPHIA Camden

ATLANTIC OCEAN

Long Branch Asbury Park Lakewood Toms River Point Pleasant

Lancaster

West from Greenwich

8   9   10   11   12   13   14

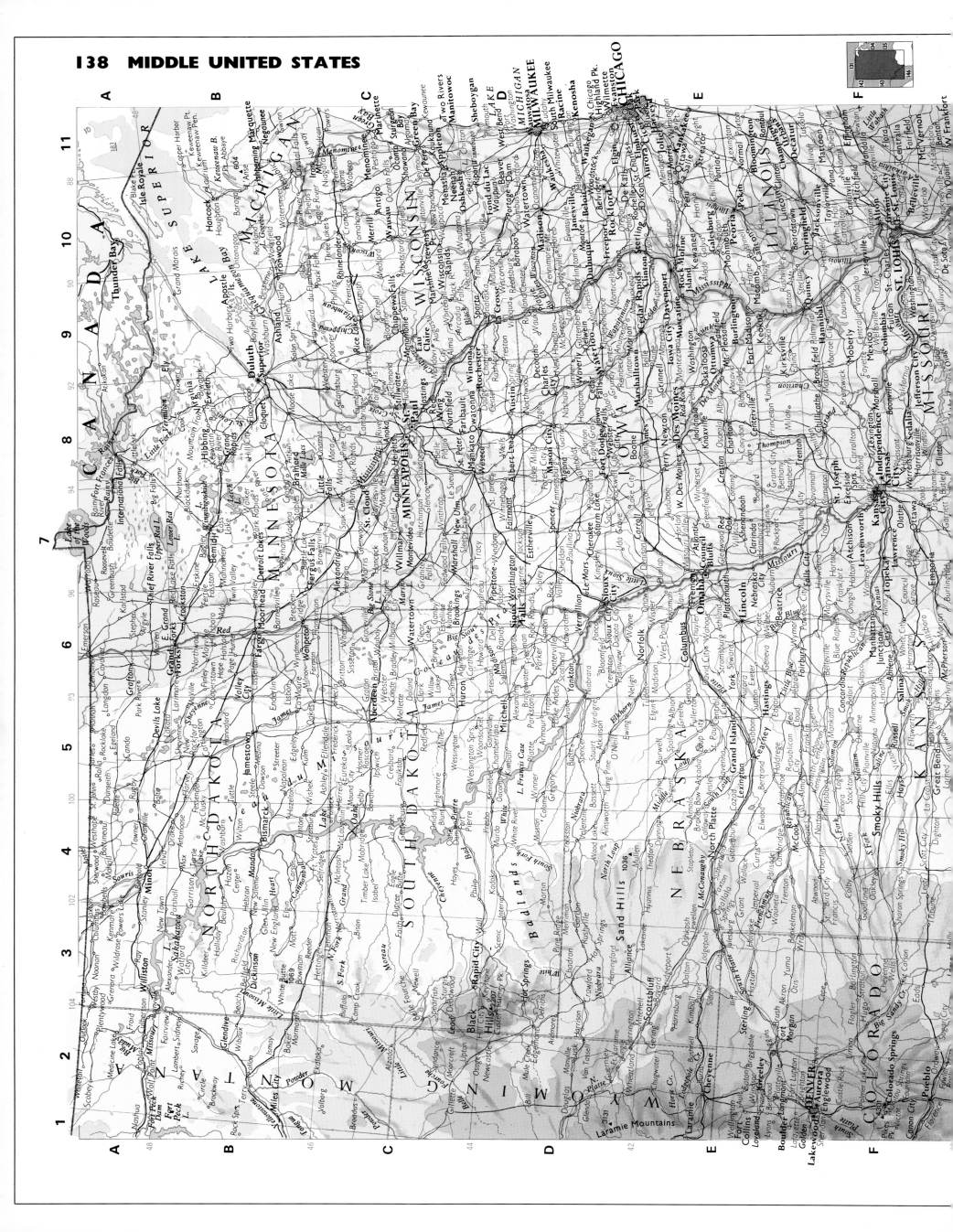

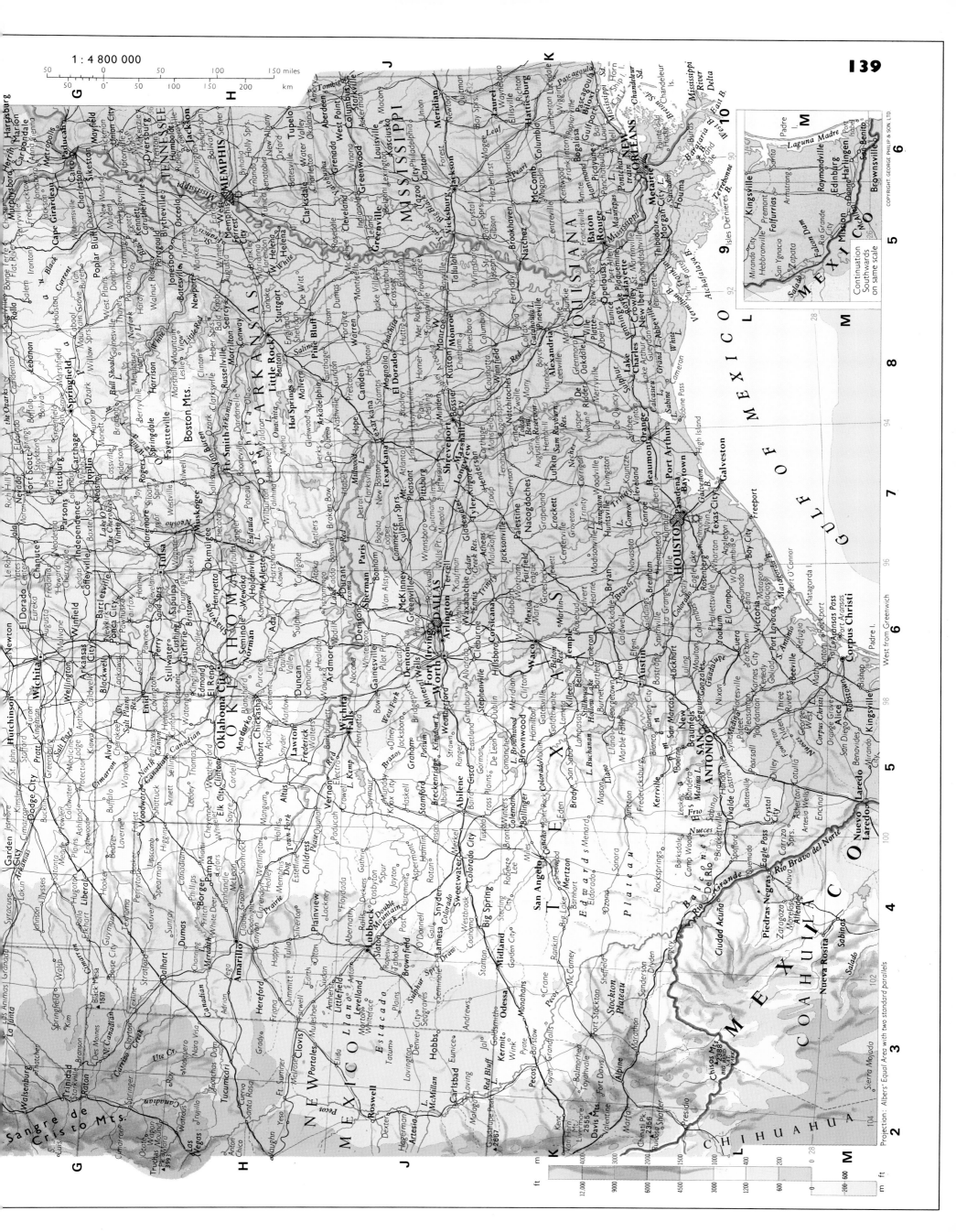

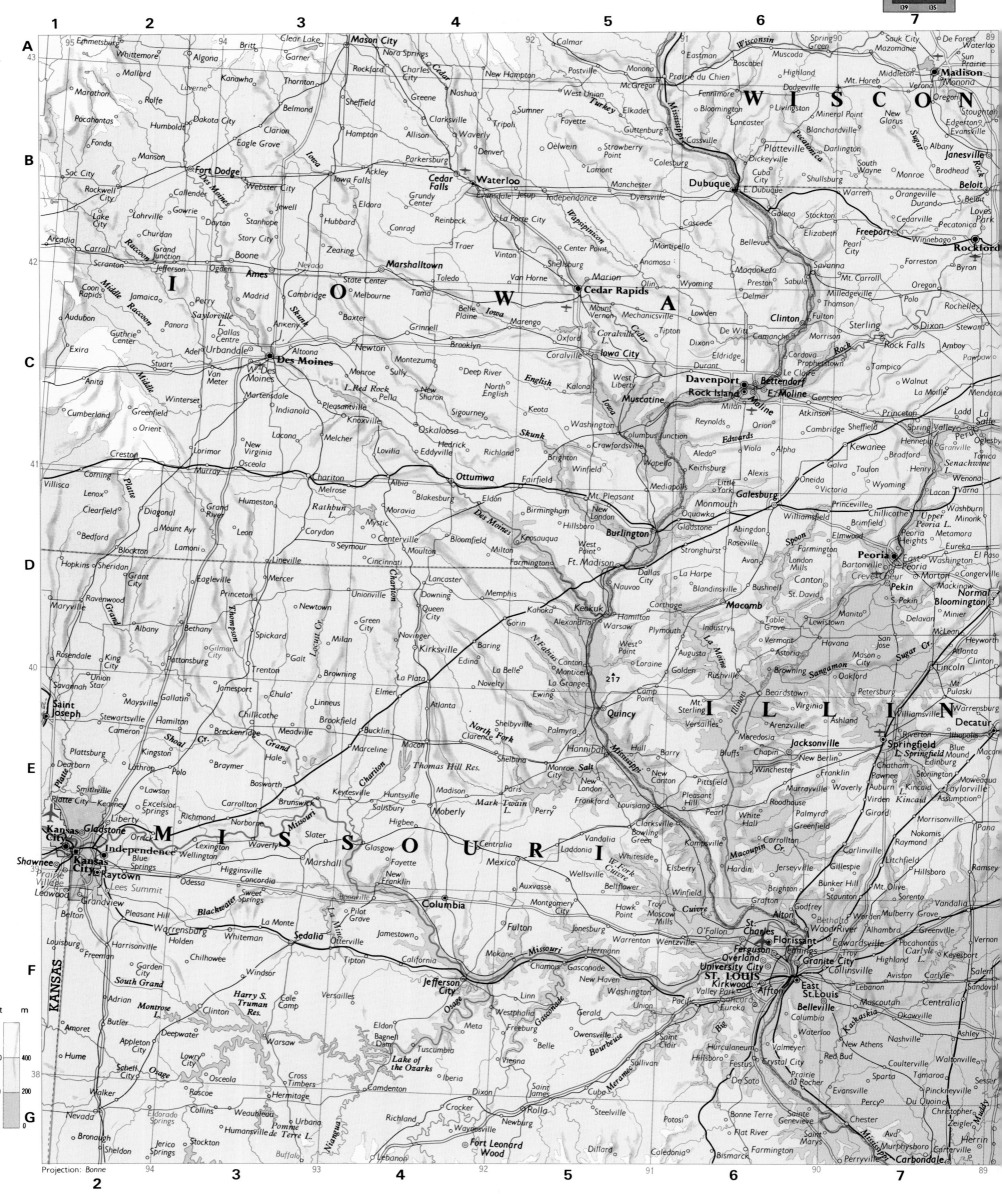

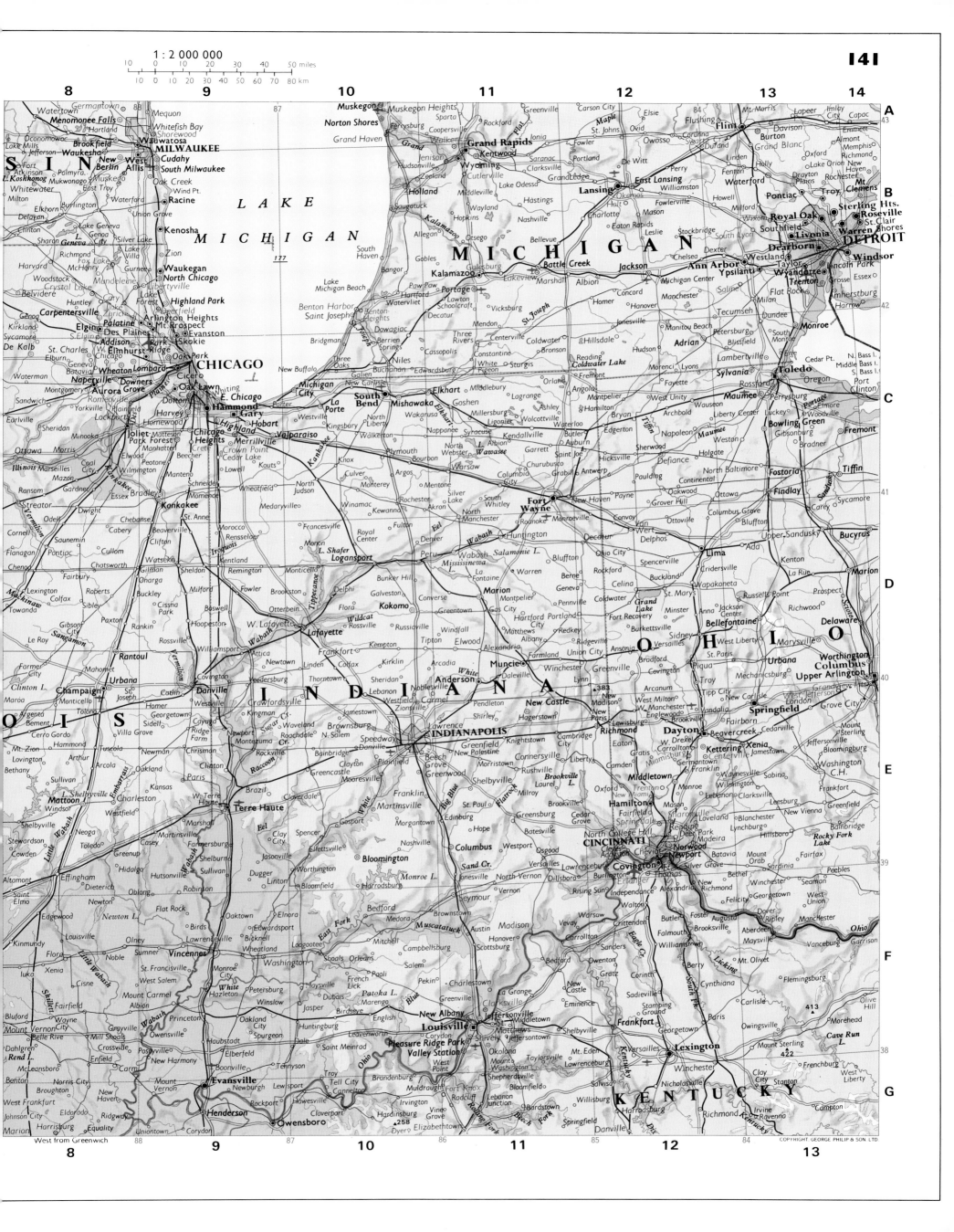

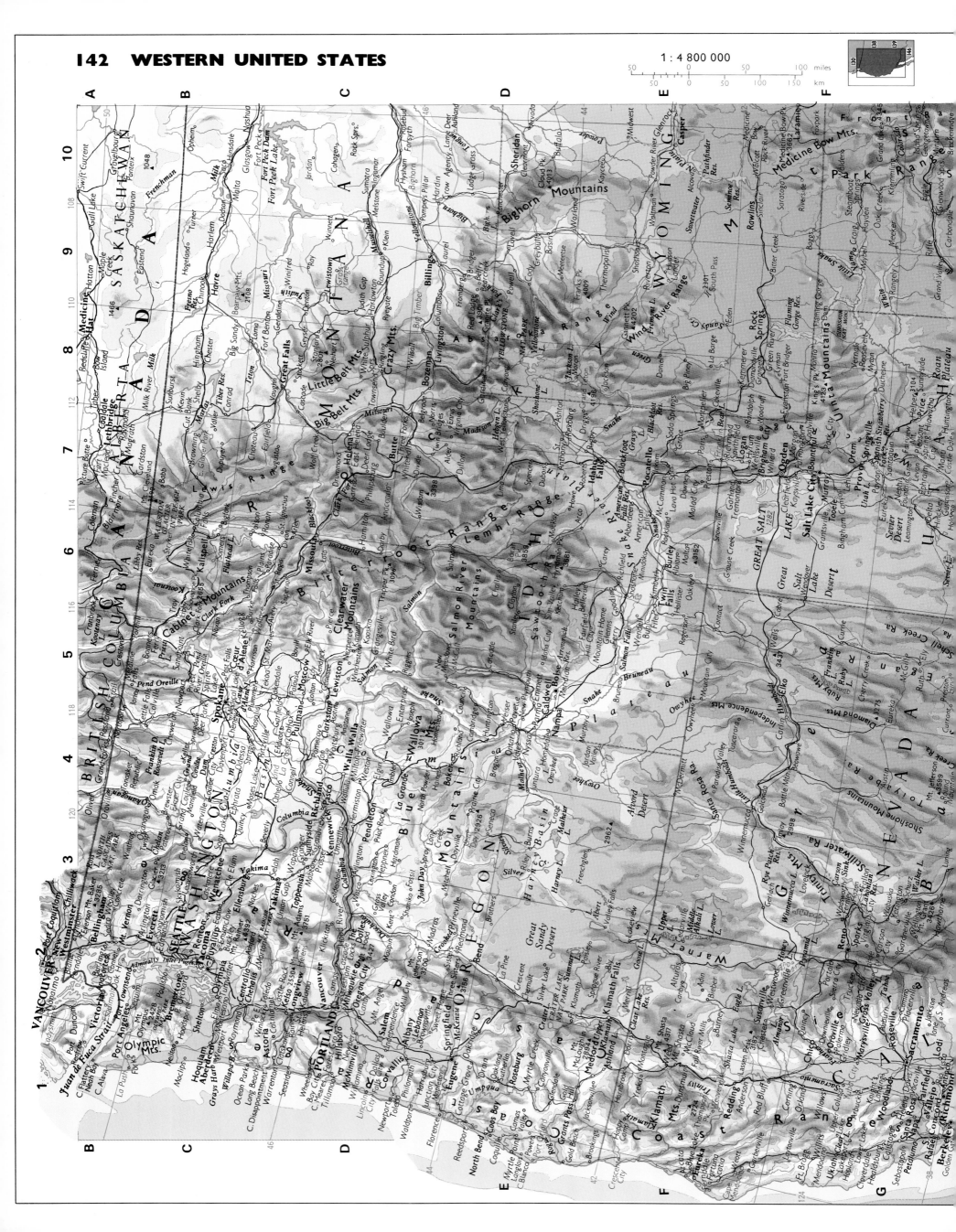

1 : 4 800 000

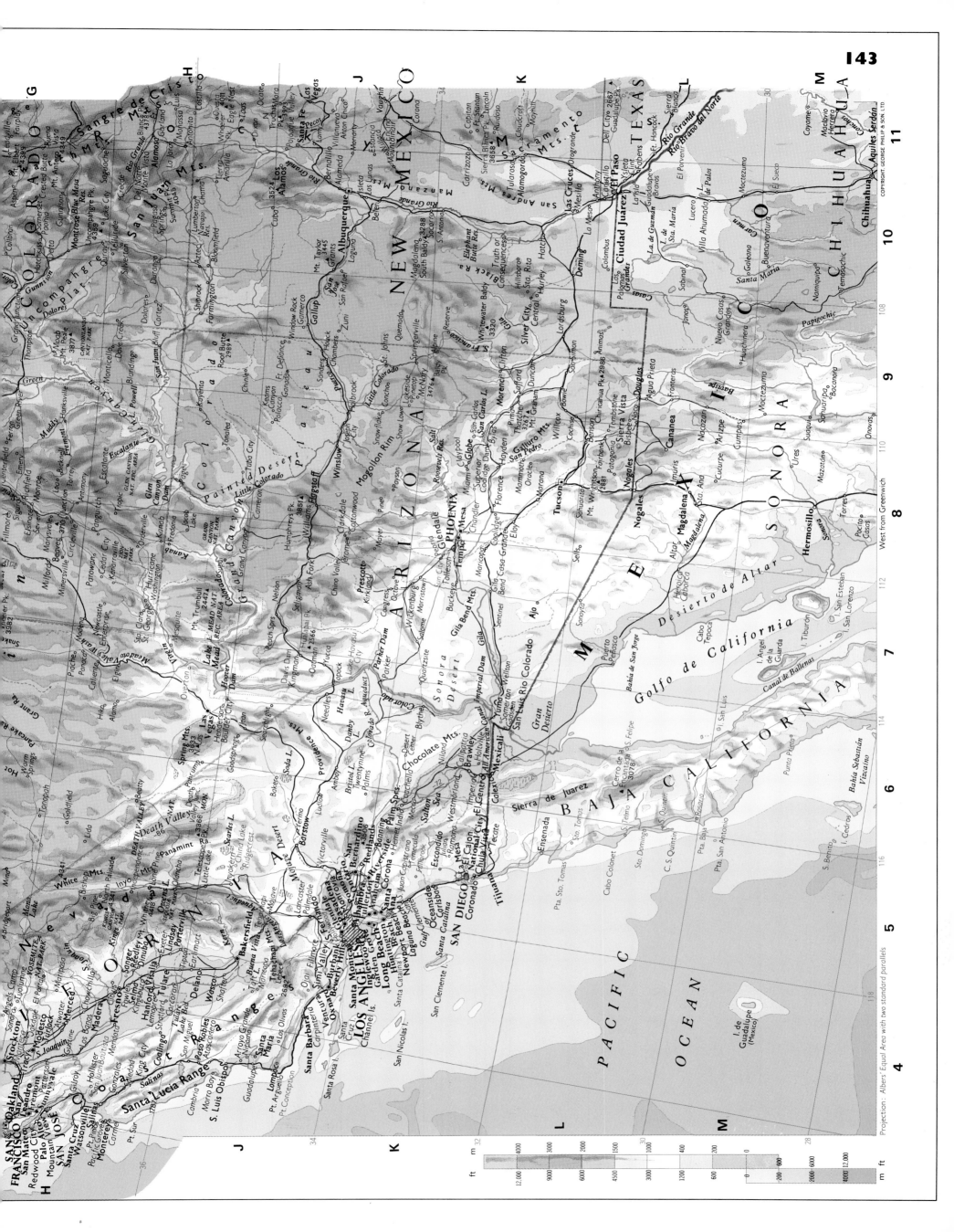

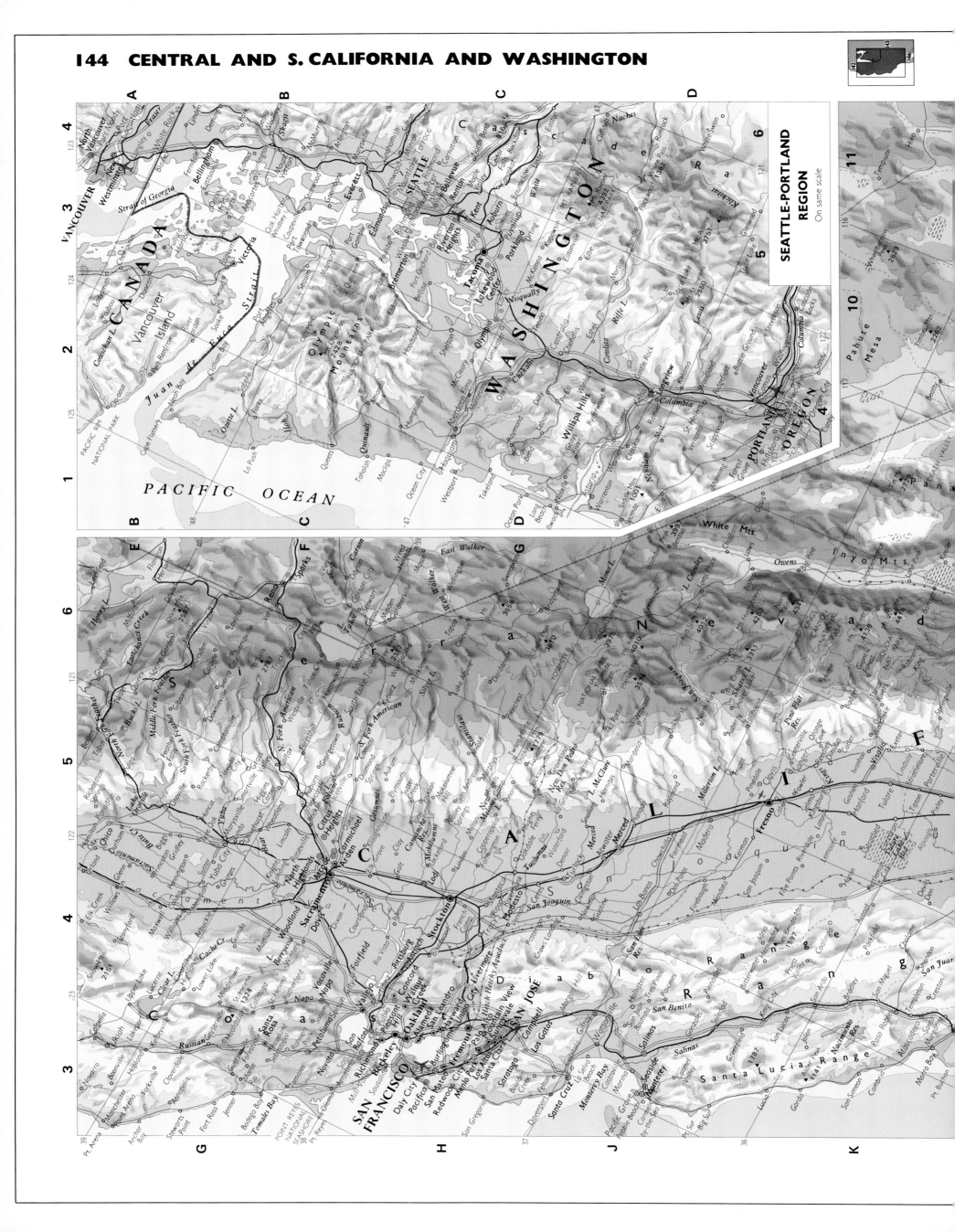

SEATTLE-PORTLAND REGION
On same scale

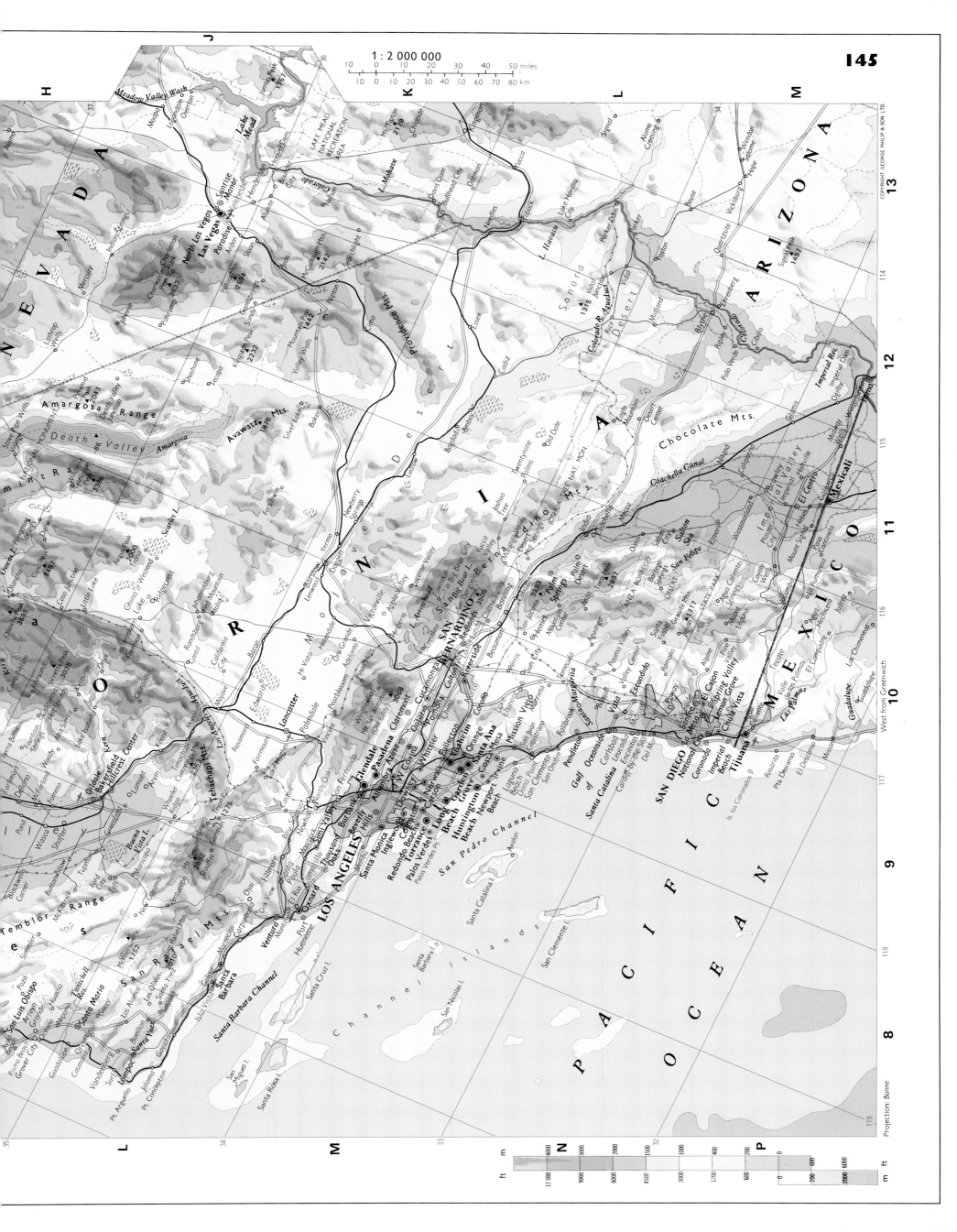

Major labels

PACIFIC OCEAN

GOLFO DE CALIFORNIA — Gulf of California

BAJA CALIFORNIA NORTE

BAJA CALIFORNIA SUR

SONORA

CHIHUAHUA

COAHUILA

DURANGO

SINALOA

NAYARIT

ZACATECAS

JALISCO

MICHOACAN

ARIZONA

NEW MEXICO

UNITED STATES

Cities and places

TIJUANA, MEXICALI, Ensenada, San Luis Río Colorado, Yuma, TUCSON, Nogales, Bisbee, Douglas, Agua Prieta, CIUDAD JUAREZ, EL PASO, Las Cruces, Deming, Lordsburg, Carlsbad, Hobbs, Big Spring, Sweetwater, Roswell, Lubbock, San Angelo

Santo Tomás, San Telmo, Santo Domingo, San Quintín, Rosario, San Fernando, Pta. Baja, Pta. Prieta, El Rosario, Punta Prieta, El Desemboque, Puerto Peñasco, Benjamín Hill, Santa Ana, Magdalena, Imuris, Cananea, Caborca, Altar, Cucurpe, Nacozari, Fronteras, Ascensión, Nuevo Casas Grandes, Villa Ahumada, Buenaventura, El Sueco, Janos, Sabinal, Lucero, Guadalupe Bravos, El Porvenir, Van Horn, Alpine, Sanderson, Del Río, Acuña, Eagle Pass, Piedras Negras, Allende, Sabinas

Hermosillo, Guaymas, Empalme, Ciudad Obregón, Navojoa, Alamos, Huatabampo, Yávaros, Ures, Mazatán, Sahuaripa, Tecoripa, Pocito Casas, San Luis, I. Tiburón, I. Angel de la Guarda, Bahía Sebastián Vizcaíno, Desierto de Vizcaíno, Sierra Vizcaíno, I. Cedros, Natividad, Pta. Falsa, Pta. Abreojos, Laguna San Ignacio, San Ignacio, La Purísima, Loreto, I. Carmen, I. Santa Catalina, Santa Rosalía, Mulegé, Comondú

Chihuahua, Cuauhtémoc, Aquiles Serdán, Meoqui, Delicias, Ciudad Camargo, Jiménez, Hidalgo del Parral, Santa Bárbara, San Francisco del Oro, Villa Ocampo, Conejos, Ciudad Guerrero, Madera, Ciudad Juárez

Nueva Rosita, Melchor Múzquiz, Monclova, Sabinas Hidalgo, MONTERREY, Saltillo, Parras, TORREÓN, Gómez Palacio, Lerdo, Matamoros, Francisco I. Madero, San Pedro de las Colonias, Matehuala

Los Mochis, Guasave, Guamúchil, Navolato, Culiacán, El Dorado, San Lorenzo, La Cruz, Topolobampo, El Fuerte, San Blas, Ahome, Guadalupe y Calvo, Badiraguato

Mazatlán, Villa Unión, Rosario, Escuinapa, Acaponeta, Tecuala, Santiago Ixcuintla, Tepic, Compostela, San Blas, Islas Tres Marías, Is. de Revillagigedo (Mexico), San Benedicto, Socorro, Roca Partida

Victoria de Durango, Río Grande, Sombrerete, Fresnillo, Zacatecas, Valparaíso, Jerez de García Salinas, Aguascalientes, Rincón de Romos, Ojocaliente, Salinas, San Luis Potosí, Cerritos, SAN LUIS POTOSI

GUADALAJARA, Tlaquepaque, Ameca, Ixtlán del Río, Etzatlán, Mascota, Ocotlán, Chapala, L. de Chapala, Zacoalco, Sayula, Autlán, Ciudad Guzmán, Colima, COLIMA, Manzanillo, Tecomán, Coalcomán, Apatzingán, Uruapan, Paracho, Zamora, La Piedad, Sahuayo, Jiquilpan, Los Reyes, Zacapu, Morelia, Zitácuaro, Huetamo, Arteaga, Tacámbaro, Ario de Rosales

Lagos de Moreno, LEÓN, Guanajuato, Irapuato, Celaya, Salamanca, Acámbaro, San Diego de la Unión, San Luis de la Paz

Puerto Vallarta, B. de Banderas, C. Corrientes, Barra de Navidad, Chamela, Zihuatanejo, Petatlán, Coahuayana, La Unión, Las Truchas

C. San Lázaro, I. Santa Magdalena, B. Magdalena, I. Santa Margarita, La Paz, San Pedro, I. Espíritu Santo, I. Cerralvo, I. San José, Todos Santos, San José del Cabo, San Lucas, C. San Lucas, Cabo San Lucas

Río Grande / Río Bravo del Norte, Río Conchos, Río Yaqui, Río Grande de Santiago, Balsas, Tropic of Cancer

Sierra Madre Occidental, Sierra de la Giganta, Llano de la Magdalena, Bolsón de Mapimí

Elevation scale (ft / m)

ft	m
12 000	4000
9000	3000
6000	2000
4500	1500
3000	1000
1200	400
600	200
0	0
600	200
6000	2000
12 000	4000

Reference to numbers

1 Federal District	5 México
2 Aguascalientes	6 Morelos
3 Guanajuato	7 Querétaro
4 Hidalgo	8 Tlaxcala

Projection: Bi-polar oblique Conical Orthomorphic

West from Greenwich

Grid references: 1 2 3 4 / A B C D

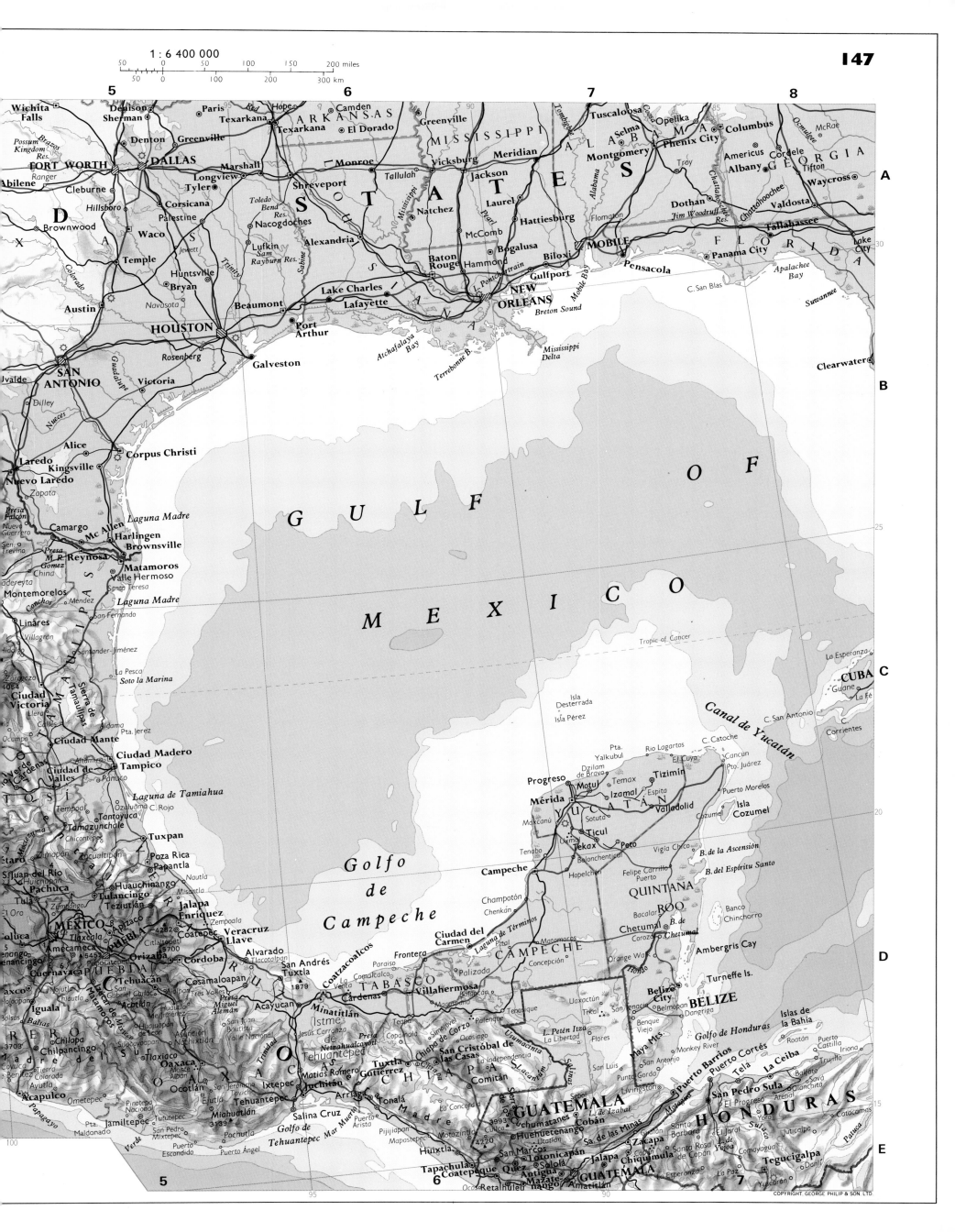

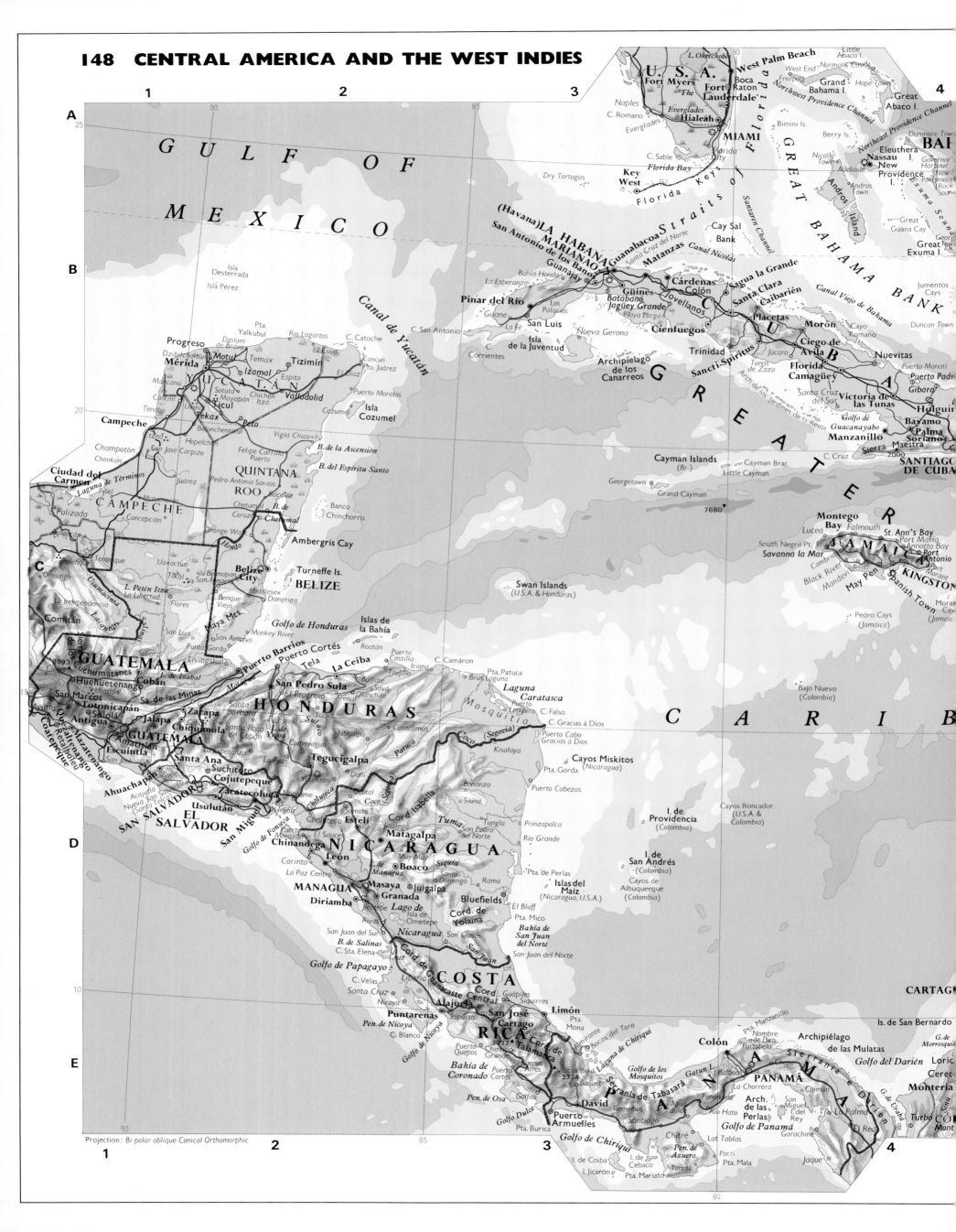

GULF OF MEXICO

Isla Desterrada

Isla Pérez

Canal de Yucatán

Progreso
Yalkubul
Dzilam de Bravo
Pta.
Río Lagartos
C. Catoche
Motul
Temax
Tizimín
Mérida
Izamal
Espita
Cancun
YUCATÁN
Sotuta
Chichén
Pto. Juárez
Maxcanú
Ticul
Mayapán
Itzá
El Díaz
Puerto Morelos
Campeche
Yekax
Peto
Valladolid
Tzucacab
Bolonchenticul
Hopelchén
Vigía Chico
Isla Cozumel
Champotón
Calkiní
San José Carpizo
QUINTANA
Chenkan
Felipe Carrillo
Puerto
B. de la Ascensión
Ciudad del Carmen
Juárez
Pedro Antonio Santos
ROO
B. del Espíritu Santo
Palizada
Matamoros
Bacalar
Chetumal
Banco Chinchorro
Aguada
CAMPECHE
Concepción
B. de Chetumal
Orange Walk
Ambergris Cay
Palenque
Tenosique
Hondo
Uaxactún
Belize
Turneffe Is.
Ocosingo
Tikal
City
Comitán
L. Petén Itzá
La Libertad
San Ignacio
Middlesex
BELIZE
La Independencia
Flores
Benque Viejo
Dangriga
Maya Mts.
San Luis
GUATEMALA
Golfo de Honduras
Islas de la Bahía
Cuchumatanes
Cobán
Punta Gorda
San Antonio
Monkey River
Roatán
Huehuetenango
L. de Izabal
Livingston
Puerto Barrios
Puerto Cortés
Puerto Castilla
San Marcos
Totonicapán
Zacapa
Tela
La Ceiba
Irlona
Trujillo
C. Camarón
Pta. Patuca
Sololá
Jalapa
Chiquimula
San Pedro Sula
Balfate
Savá
Olanchito
Brus Laguna
Antigua
El Progreso
HONDURAS
Mosquitia
GUATEMALA
Santa Barbara
Yoro
Laguna Caratasca
Mazatenango
Retalhuleu
Escuintla
Santa Rosa de Copán
Comayagua
Juticalpa
Puerto Lempira
C. Falso
Ahuachapán
Cojutepeque
Tegucigalpa
Catacamas
C. Gracias á Dios
Santa Ana
Suchitoto
Danlí
Coco
Puerto Cabo
Gracias á Dios
Zacatecoluca
Usulután
SAN SALVADOR
Cayos Miskitos
EL SALVADOR
San Miguel
Estelí
Cord. Isabella
Kisalaya
Pta. Gorda
Chinandega
Matagalpa
Tuma
Puerto Cabezas
NICARAGUA
Bonanza
León
Boaco
Siquia
Siuna
MANAGUA
Masaya
Juigalpa
Santo Domingo
Rama
Río Grande
Diriamba
Granada
Lago de
Bluefields
I. de Providencia (U.S.A. & Colombia)
Jinotepe
Nicaragua
Cord. de Yolaina
El Bluff
San Juan del Sur
Rivas
San Carlos
Bahía de San Juan del Norte
I. de San Andrés (Colombia)
B. de Salinas
San Juan
San Juan del Norte
Cayos de Albuquerque (Colombia)
Golfo de Papagayo
Cord. de Guanacaste
Liberia
Santa Cruz
COSTA
Cord. Central
Limón
Nicoya
Alajuela
San José
Cartago
Puntarenas
RICA
Pen. de Nicoya
C. Blanco
Cord. de Talamanca
Colón
Archipiélago de las Mulatas
Bahía de Coronado
David
PANAMÁ
Pen. de Osa
Puerto Armuelles
Golfo Dulce
Golfo de Chiriquí

GREATER

(Havana) LA HABANA
MARIANAO
Guanabacoa
Straits of Florida
San Antonio de los Baños
Guanajay
Matanzas
Canal Nicolás
Pinar del Río
Güines
Cárdenas
Colón
Sagua la Grande
Santa Clara
Caibarién
San Luis
Batabanó
Jagüey Grande
Jovellanos
Placetas
Morón
CUBA
Cienfuegos
Trinidad
Sancti-Spíritus
Ciego de Ávila
Nuevitas
Archipiélago de los Canarreos
Camagüey
Isla de la Juventud
Nueva Gerona
Victoria de las Tunas
Holguín
Bayamo
Manzanillo
Palma Soriano
SANTIAGO DE CUBA
Sierra Maestra

Cayman Islands (Br.)
Georgetown
Grand Cayman
Little Cayman
Cayman Brac

Swan Islands (U.S.A. & Honduras)

CARIB

Montego Bay
Falmouth
St. Ann's Bay
Lucea
Savanna la Mar
JAMAICA
Port Antonio
Black River
Mandeville
May Pen
KINGSTON
Spanish Town
Pedro Cays (Jamaica)

Bajo Nuevo (Colombia)

Cayos Roncador (U.S.A. & Colombia)

Islas del Maíz (Nicaragua, U.S.A.)

MIAMI
West Palm Beach
Boca Raton
Fort Lauderdale
U.S.A.
Fort Myers
Naples
Everglades
Hialeah
C. Romano
C. Sable
Key West
Florida Bay
Dry Tortugas
Florida Keys

Little Abaco I.
Grand Bahama I.
Great Abaco I.
Bimini Is.
Berry Is.
Eleuthera I.
Nassau
New Providence
Andros Island
Great Exuma I.
Exuma Sound
GREAT BAHAMA BANK

CARTAGE

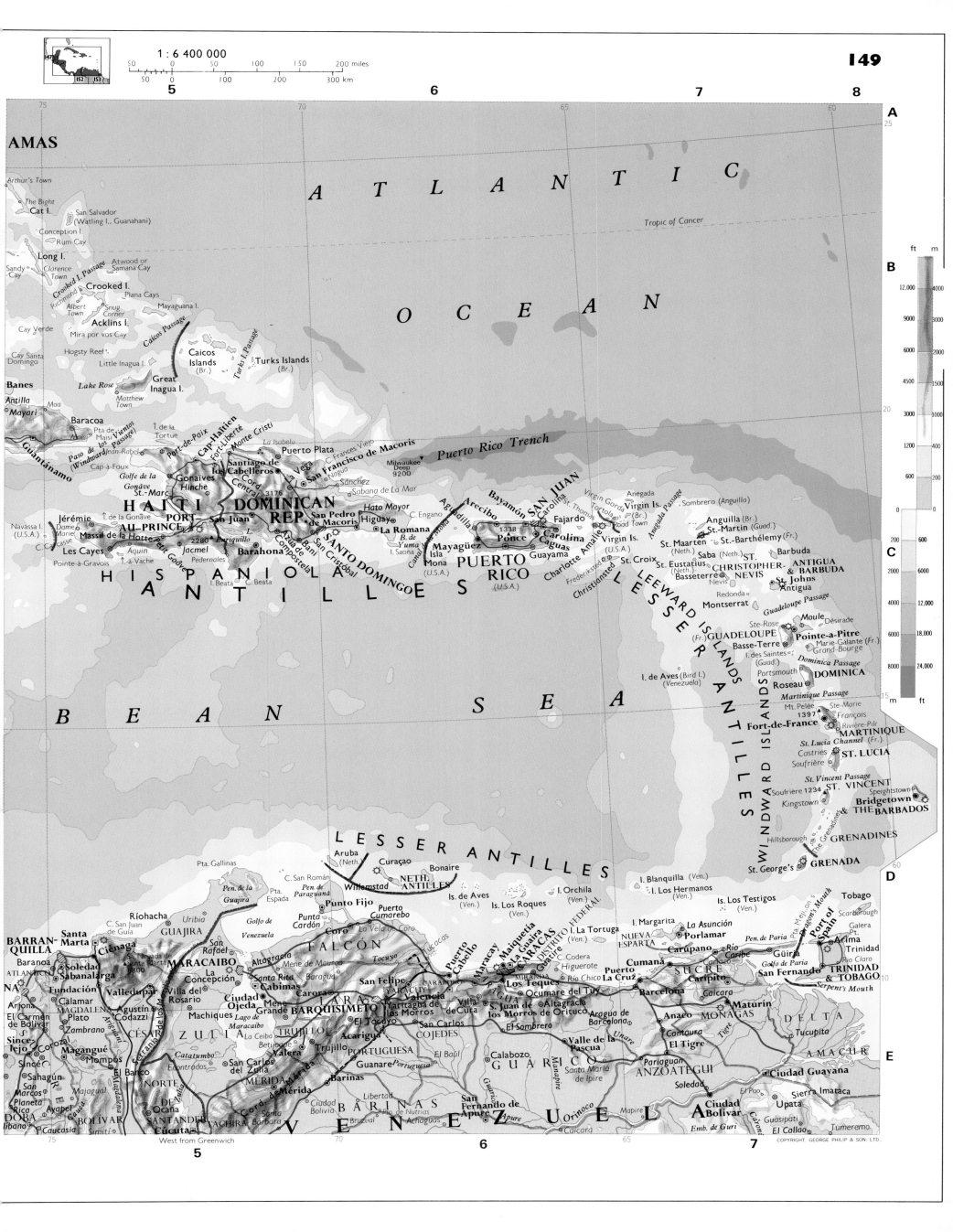

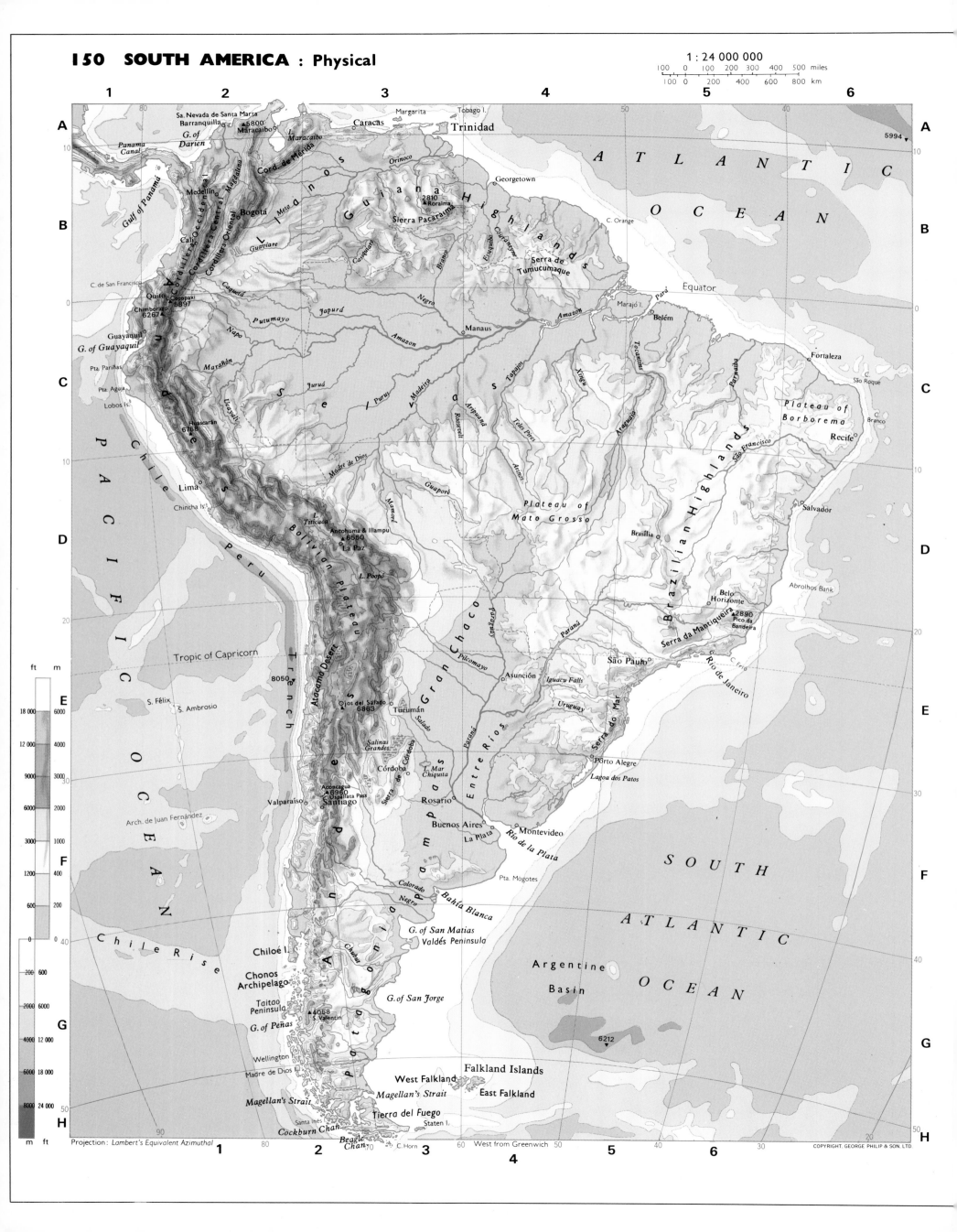

1 : 24 000 000

100   0   100   200   300   400   500 miles
100   0   200   400   600   800 km

ATLANTIC

OCEAN

Panama Canal

G. of Darien

Gulf of Panamá

Sa. Nevada de Santa Marta
Barranquilla
Maracaibo   5800
G. of
Maracaibo   Margarita
Cord. de Mérida   Tobago I.
Caracas   Trinidad

Medellín   Orinoco
Bogotá   Georgetown
Cali   Guaviare   Guiana
Meta   Highlands
2810
Roraima
Sierra Pacaraima   Serra de Tumucumaque
C. Orange

C. de San Francisco

Quito   Cotopaxi
Chimborazo   5897
6267   Napo   Amazon   Equator
Guayaquil   Marañón   Manaus   Marajó I.   Pará   Belém
G. of Guayaquil   Putumayo   Japurá
Pta. Pariñas   Juruá   Fortaleza
Pta. Aguja   Ucayali   Purus   Madeira   C. São Roque
Lobos Is.   C. Branco

Huascarán   Plateau of Borborema
6768   Recife

Chincha Is¹   Madre de Dios   Plateau of Mato Grosso   São Francisco   Salvador
Lima   L. Titicaca   Guaporé   Brasília   Abrolhos Bank
Ancohuma & Illampu   Mamoré   Brazilian Highlands
6550   Belo
La Paz   Horizonte
L. Poopó   Pilcomayo   2890
Pico da Bandeira
8050   Asunción   Iguaçu Falls   São Paulo   Serra da Mantiqueira
Salinas Grandes   Uruguay   Rio de Janeiro   C. Frio
Ojos del Salado   Salado   Entre Ríos   Serra do Mar
6863   Tucumán   Paraná   Pôrto Alegre
Córdoba   L. Mar Chiquita   Lagoa dos Patos
Aconcagua   Rosario
6960   Sierra de Córdoba
Uspallata Pass   Buenos Aires
Valparaíso   Santiago   Montevideo
La Plata   Río de la Plata   SOUTH
Arch. de Juan Fernández   Pta. Mogotes   ATLANTIC

Tropic of Capricorn
S. Félix
S. Ambrosio

Colorado   OCEAN
Negro   Bahía Blanca

G. of San Matías   Argentine
Valdés Peninsula   Basin
Chiloé I.   Chubut
Chonos Archipelago   G. of San Jorge
Taitao Peninsula   4058
G. of Peñas   S. Valentín   6212
Wellington
Madre de Dios   Falkland Islands
West Falkland
Magellan's Strait   East Falkland
Santa Inés   Tierra del Fuego
Cockburn Chan.   Staten I.
Beagle Chan.   C. Horn

Projection: Lambert's Equivalent Azimuthal   West from Greenwich   COPYRIGHT. GEORGE PHILIP & SON. LTD

PACIFIC   OCEAN

Chile Rise

Chile   Peru   Trench

Atacama Desert

Bolivian Plateau

Gran Chaco

Pampas

Patagonia

Andes

Llanos

Selvas

5994
A

ft   m
18 000   6000
12 000   4000
9000   3000
6000   2000
3000   1000
600   200
0   0
200   600
2000   6000
4000   12000
6000   18000
8000   24000
m   ft

1 : 24 000 000

100 0   100 200 300 400 500 miles
100 0   200   400   600   800 km

1   2   3   4   5   6

A
COSTA RICA
San José
PANAMA
Golfo de Darién
Golfo de Panamá
Colón
Panamá
Barranquilla
Cartagena
Maracaibo
Barquisimeto
Valencia
Caracas
Port of Spain
TRINIDAD AND TOBAGO
Medellín
Cúcuta
San Cristóbal
Bucaramanga
Bogotá
Orinoco
Ciudad Guayana
VENEZUELA
Georgetown
Paramaribo
Cayenne
GUYANA
SURINAM
FRENCH GUIANA
Maroni
C. Orange

NORTH
ATLANTIC
OCEAN

B
Cali
COLOMBIA
Orinoco
Esequibo
Courantyne
Branco
Magdalena
Meta
C. de San Francisco

Equator

Quito
ECUADOR
Guayaquil
G. de Guayaquil
Napo
Putumayo
Caquetá
Japurá
Negro
Iquitos
Marañón
Juruá
Madeira
Amazonas (Amazon)
Manaus
Santarem
Ilha de Marajó
Belém
São Luís
Teresina

C
Pta. Aguja
Chiclayo
Trujillo
Chimbote
PERU
Ucayali
Purus
Juruá
Madre de Dios
Aripuanã
Pôrto Velho
Guaporé
Tapajós
Xingu
Tocantins
Araguaia
Parnaíba
São Francisco
Fortaleza (Ceará)
C. de São Roque
Natal
Recife (Pernambuco)
João Pessoa
Maceió

D
Callao
Lima
Cuzco
L. Titicaca
Arequipa
La Paz
Cochabamba
BOLIVIA
Sucre
Santa Cruz
Mamoré
BRAZIL
Cuiabá
Brasília
Goiânia
Belo Horizonte
Aracaju
Salvador

E
Iquique
Antofagasta
Tropic of Capricorn
Campo Grande
PARAGUAY
Paraná
Paraguay
Pilcomayo
Asunción
Salta
San Miguel de Tucumán
Resistencia
Corrientes
Uruguay
Londrina
Ribeirão Prêto
Juiz de Fora
Campinas
Santos
SÃO PAULO
Curitiba
Vitória
Campos
Niterói
RIO DE JANEIRO

Isla San Felix (Chile)
Isla San Ambrosio (Chile)

PACIFIC OCEAN

SOUTH
ATLANTIC
OCEAN

F
CHILE
ARGENTINA
Córdoba
San Juan
Salado
Santa Fe
Paraná
Rosario
URUGUAY
Pôrto Alegre
Lagoa dos Patos
Pelotas
Mendoza
Viña del Mar
Valparaíso
Arch de Juan Fernández (Chile)
Santiago
Talca
BUENOS AIRES
La Plata
Río de la Plata
Montevideo
Concepción
Bahía Blanca
Colorado
Mar del Plata

G
Valdivia
Negro
Viedma
Puerto Montt
Chubut
Golfo Comodoro Rivadavia
San Jorge
G. de Penas

H
Punta Arenas
Strait of Magellan
Cape Horn
Tierra del Fuego
FALKLAND ISLANDS
West Falkland
Stanley
East Falkland
(U.K.)

West from Greenwich

Projection: Lambert's Equivalent Azimuthal

COPYRIGHT. GEORGE PHILIP & SON. LTD.

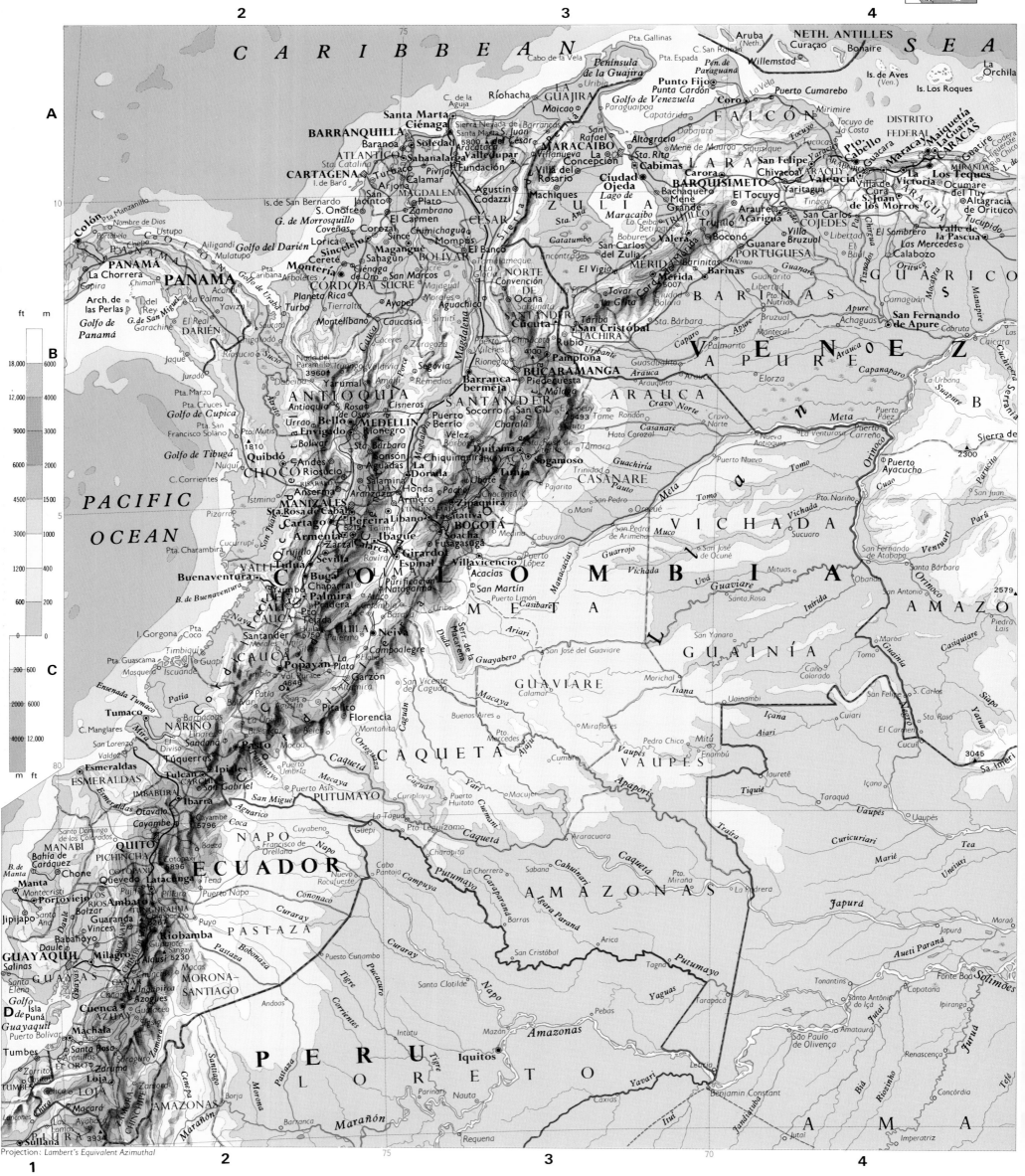

1 : 6 400 000

50   0   50   100   150   200 miles
50   0   100   200   300 km

5   **6**   **7**

65   60   55

GRENADA
St. George's

La Blanquilla (Ven.)
Los Hermanos (Ven.)
Is. Los Testigos (Ven.)
Tobago
Scarborough

A — 10

NUEVA ESPARTA
Margarita
La Asunción
Porlamar
I. La Tortuga (Ven.)
I. Coche
Pta. Arenas
Carúpano
Río Caribe
Pen. de Paria
Pta. Peñas
Boca del Dragón
Boca de la Sierpe
Dragon's Mouth
Arima
Port of Spain
TRINIDAD AND TOBAGO

ATLANTIC

Puerto La Cruz
Guanta
Barcelona
Cumaná
SUCRE
Pen. de Araya
S. Juan
Güiria
Golfo de San Fernando
Río Claro
Galeota Point
Trinidad

Aragua de Barcelona
Anaco
Cantaura
Caripito
Maturín
MONAGAS
Santa María de Ipire
Zaraza
ANZOÁTEGUI
El Tigre
Guanipa
Tigre
DELTA
AMACURO
Serpent's Mouth

OCEAN

Mapire
Soledad
Ciudad Bolívar
Caicara
Pao
Tembladar
Barrancas
Tucupita
Morichal Largo
Caño Manamo
Caño Macareo
Boca Grande
Curiapo
I. Corocoro
Boca Grande
Morawhanna

B

Pariaguán
Orinoco
Pta. Ordaz
Ciudad Guayana
Upata
El Palmar
Maburuma
Barima
Waini
Charity

Santa Cruz
Bonitas
El Pao
Guri Dam
Ciudad Piar
El Manteco
La Horqueta
Tumeremo
Matthew's Ridge
Kokerite
Anna Regina
Suddie

BOLÍVAR
de Mato
Serranía Turagua
La Paragua
Caparo
El Miamo
El Dorado
Cuyuni
Parika
Georgetown
Buxton
Mahaicony

Aro
Caura
Curatabaca
Caroní
Angel Falls 2580
Paca
Luepa
Imbaimadai
Issano
Mazaruni
Peter's Mine
Bartica
Wismar
Rosignol
New Amsterdam
Port Mourant
Hyde Park
Mara

GUYANA

Guampi
Sierra Maigualida
Erebato
Equeipa
La Gran Sabana
Mt. Roraima 2772
Arabopo
Tumatumari
Ituni
Skeldon
Nieuw Nickerie
Totness
Paramaribo
Alliance
Mana
Iracoubo

Guaina
Arabelo
Pakaraima
Kaieteur Falls
Sta. Teresa
Sierra del Zamuro
Sa. Tepequem
Orinduik
Ireng
Wandaik
Kurupukari
Tapoeripa
Epira
Wageningen
CORONIE
Groningen
Republiek
Kwakoegron
Brokopondo
Nieuw Amsterdam
Moengo
Albina
St. Laurent
Langatabbetje
Gare Tigre
Tonate
Cayenne
Remire
Roura

5

Motocurunya
Catisimina
Majari
Toka
Apoteri
Yupukari
Rewa
Nieuw River
Prof. Dr. Ir. W. J. Van Blommestein Meer
SARAMACCA
Posoegroenoe
Asidonhoppo
Gran Rio
Cacao
Kaw
Cabo Orange

NAS
Matacuni
Ocamo
Parima
Sa. Tepequem
Uraricaá
Boa Esperança
Boa Vista
Lethem
Shea
Isherton
Alalaparu
Coeroeni
Americankondre
Tapanahoni
Wilhelmina Geb.
Julianatop 1280
SURINAM
BROKOPONDO
Grand Santi
Paul Isnard
St. Élie
Benzdorp
Eau Claire
Saül
MAROWIJNE
Mariposoula
Bienvenue
FRENCH GUIANA
690
Camopi
Clevelândia do Norte
Vila Velho
Lourenço

C

Orinoco
Parima
Serra Curupira
Caracaraí
San José do Anauá
Demini
Catrimani
Serra do Apiaú
Serra do Mucajaí
RORAIMA
Anauá
Kamoa Mts.
Biloku
Essequibo
734
Serra Acaraí
Citaré
Jari
Paru
Merirumã
Serra Tumucumaque
AMAPÁ
I. de Maracá
Aporema

Sa. Tapirapecó
Araçá
Preto
Padauari
Serra Tabatinga
Anauá
Janaperi
Alalaú
Uatumã
Paru de Oeste
Maloca
Serra do Navio
Teresinha
Amapari
Pôrto Grande
Caviana

Tapurucuará
Ilha Grande
Urubaxi
Cuiuni
Moreira
Barcelos
Caurés
Negro
Jufari
Branco
Catrimani
Boiaçu
Uatumã
Mapuera
São Tiago
Cuminá
Jari
Amapá
Amapari
Macapá
Pôrto Santos
Furo do Janaucu

B R A Z I L

Agua Preta
Carvoeiro
Moura
Unini
Caapiranga
Santa Maria
Paru
Trombetas
Cuminapanema
Caruapanema
Almeirim
Gurupá
I. Grande de Gurupá
Ilha de Marajó
Anajás
Breves

L. Amana
L. Mucura
Manacapuru
Airão
Apuaú
Urubu
Urucara
Nhamundá
Faro
Óbidos
Alenquer
Monte Alegre
Prainha
Pôrto de Moz
Anapu
Portel

Piorini
L. Badajós
MANAUS
Manacapuru
Itacoatiara
Eva
Silves
Itapiranga
Urucurituba
Parintins
Juruti
Santarém
Belterra
Anajás

(Amazonas)
L. Piorini
Caapiranga
Anamã
Careiro
Ilha Tupinambaranas
Maués
Barreirinha
Amazonas
Jaraucu
Altamira
João

Tefé
L. de Coari
Coari
Codajás
Beruri
Nova Olinda
Autazes
Maués
Canumã
Xingu
Iriri
Carvalho
Sousel

D — 50

Itanhauá
L. de Coari
Purus
Arumã
Itaboca
Prêto do Igapó-Açu
Madeiras
Borba
Novo Aripuana
Abacaxis
Mundurucus
Itaituba
Tapajós
Pôrto Alegre
Bacajá
Teeré

Abufari
P A R Á

A M A Z O N A S

West from Greenwich

65   60   **6**   55   **7**

COPYRIGHT. GEORGE PHILIP & SON. LTD.

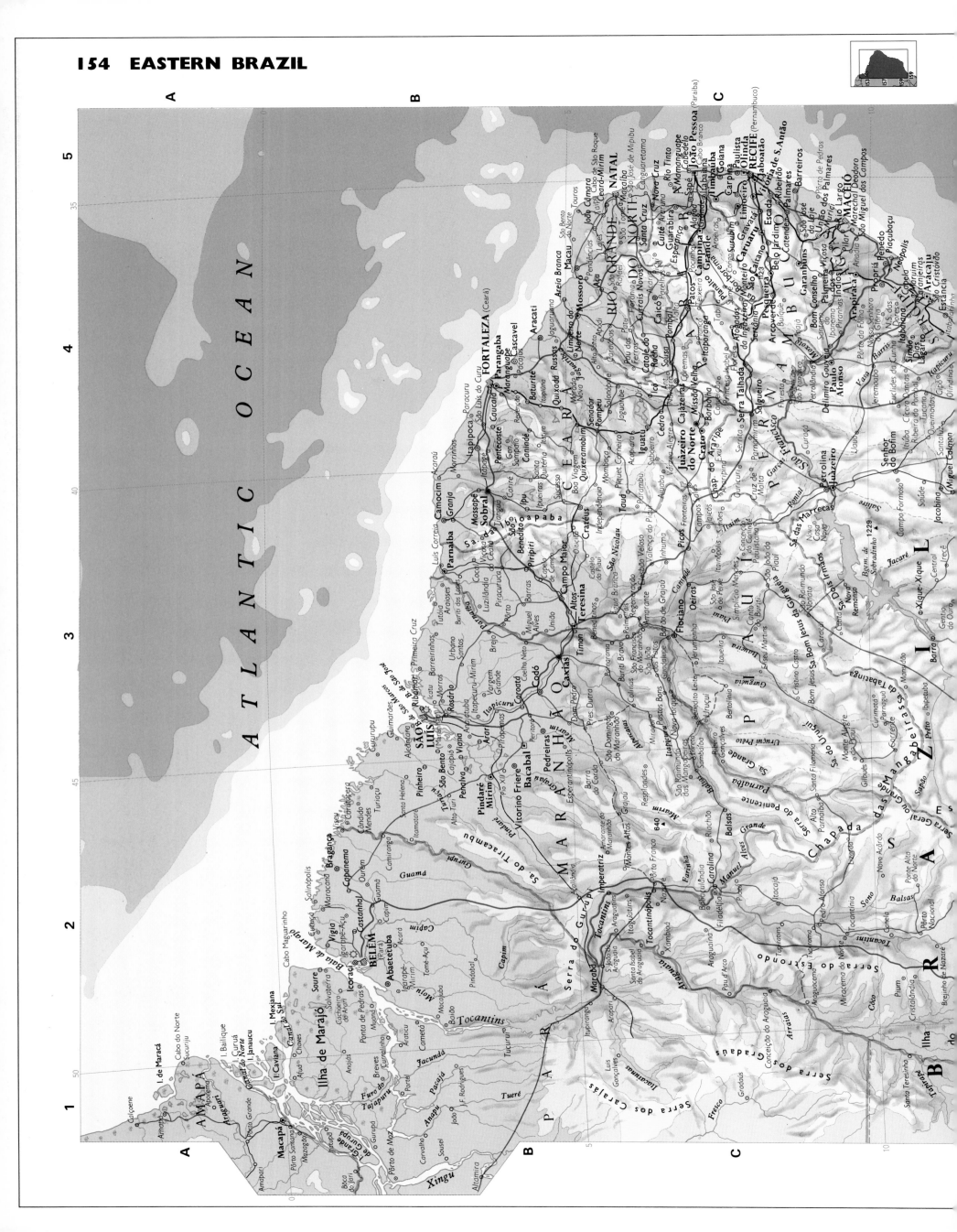

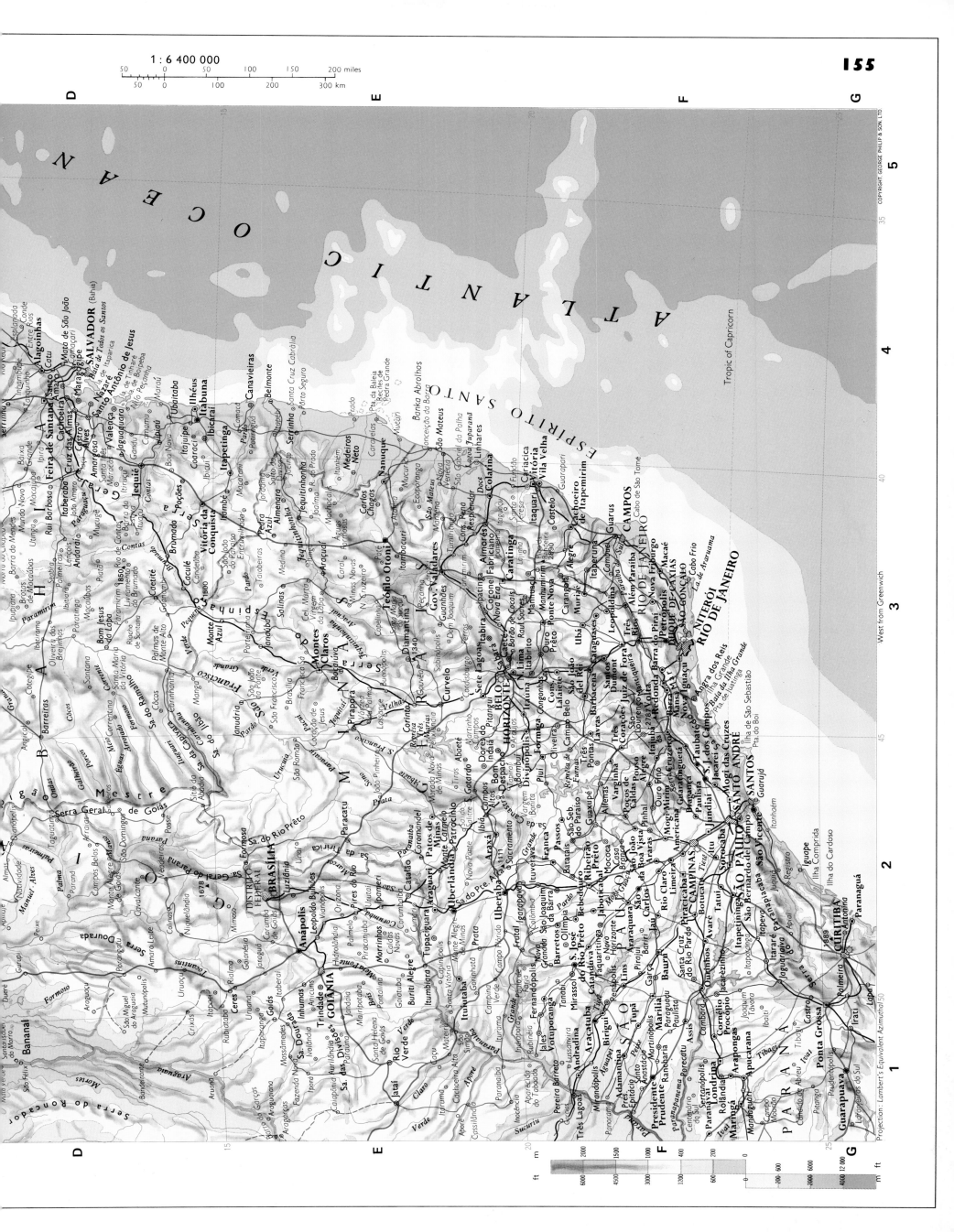

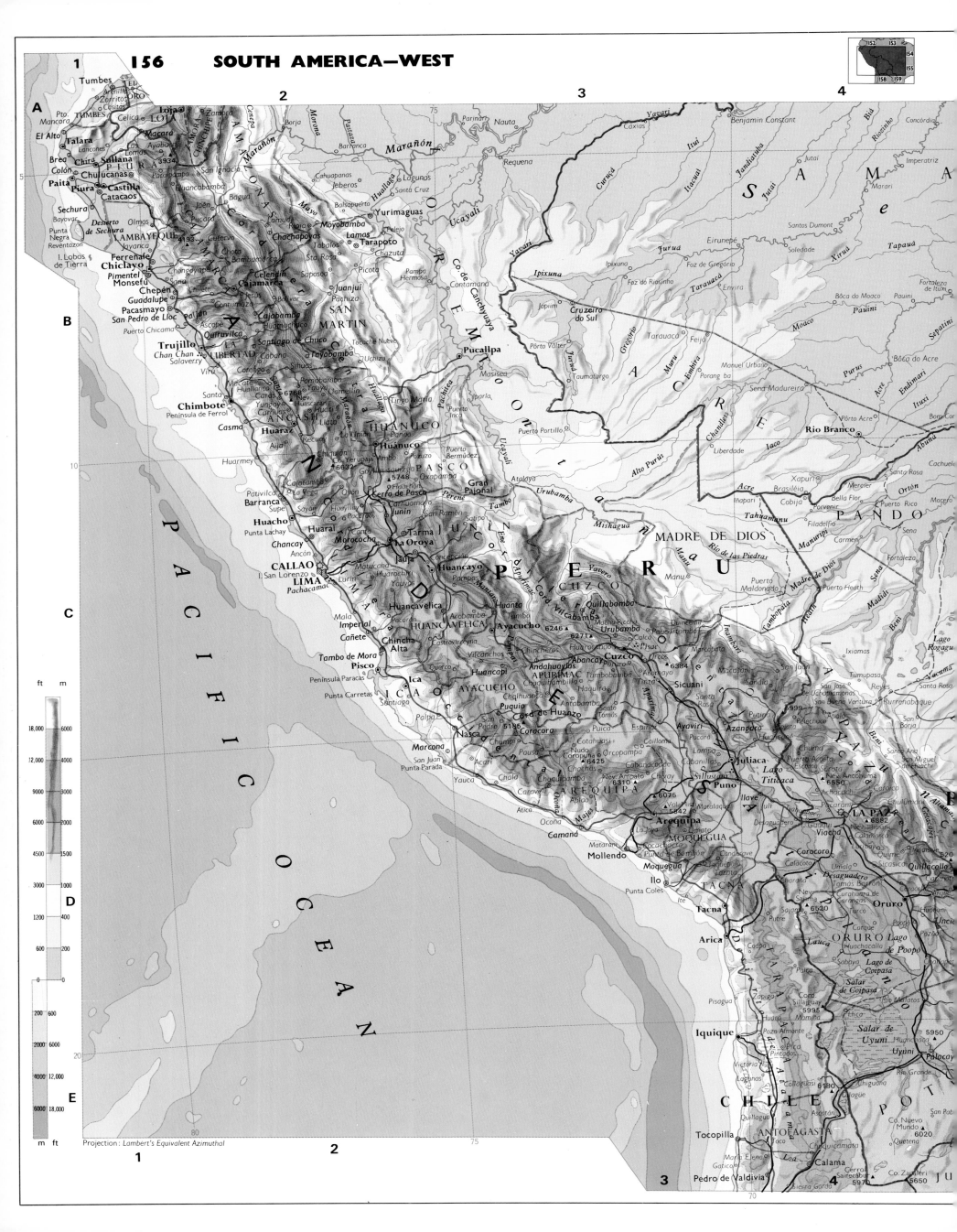

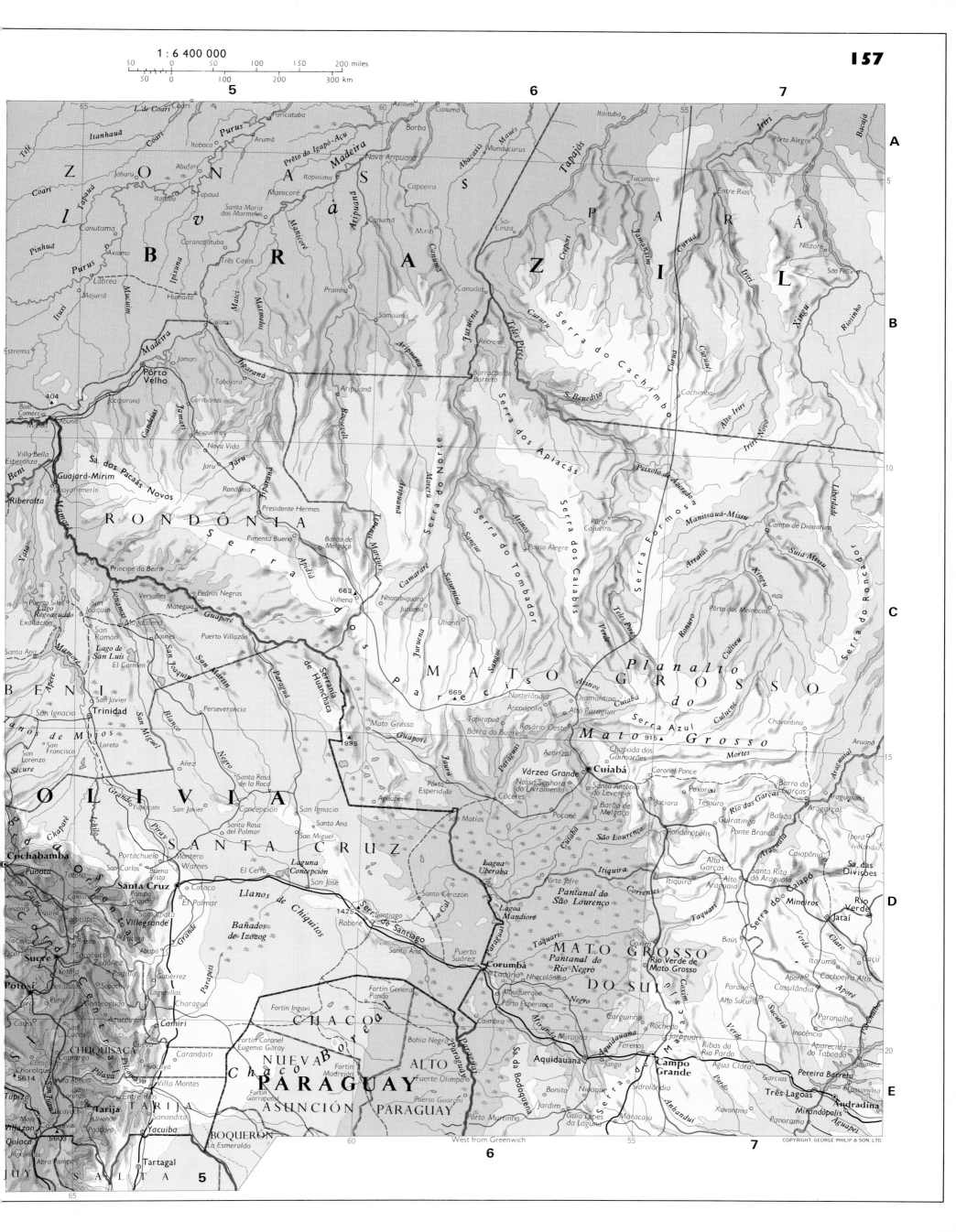

PACIFIC OCEAN

BOLIVIA

PARAGUAY

ASUNCIÓN

ALTO PARAGUAY

BOQUERÓN

PRESIDENTE HAYES

FORMOSA

CHACO

GRAN CHACO

CONCEPCIÓN

PARAGUARI

MISIONES

CORRIENTES

SANTA FE

ENTRE RÍOS

URU (Uruguay)

TARIJA

JUJUY

SALTA

TUCUMÁN

SAN MIGUEL DE TUCUMÁN

CATAMARCA

SANTIAGO DEL ESTERO

LA RIOJA

CÓRDOBA

SAN JUAN

SAN LUIS

MENDOZA

LA PAMPA

NEUQUÉN

BUENOS AIRES

ANTOFAGASTA

ATACAMA

COQUIMBO

CHILE

Iquique, Tocopilla, Antofagasta, Taltal, Chañaral, Copiapó, Caldera, Vallenar, La Serena, Coquimbo, Ovalle, Illapel, Valparaíso, Viña del Mar, Santiago, San Antonio, Rancagua, San Fernando, Curicó, Talca, Linares, Chillán, Concepción, Talcahuano, Los Ángeles

Salta, San Salvador de Jujuy, San Pedro de Jujuy, San Miguel de Tucumán, Catamarca, Santiago del Estero, La Rioja, San Juan, Mendoza, San Luis, Córdoba, Río Cuarto, Villa María, Rosario, San Lorenzo, Santa Fe, Paraná, Concordia, Salto, Paysandú, Gualeguaychú, Corrientes, Resistencia, Formosa, Goya, Reconquista, Asunción, Concepción, Mar del Plata, Bahía Blanca, Tres Arroyos, Santa Rosa, General Pico, Trenque Lauquen, Olavarría, Tandil

ft   m
18 000   6000
12 000   4000
9000   3000
6000   2000
4500   1500
3000   1000
1200   400
600   200
0   0
600   200
2000   6000
4000   12 000
6000   18 000
m   ft

Projection: Lambert's Equivalent Azimuthal

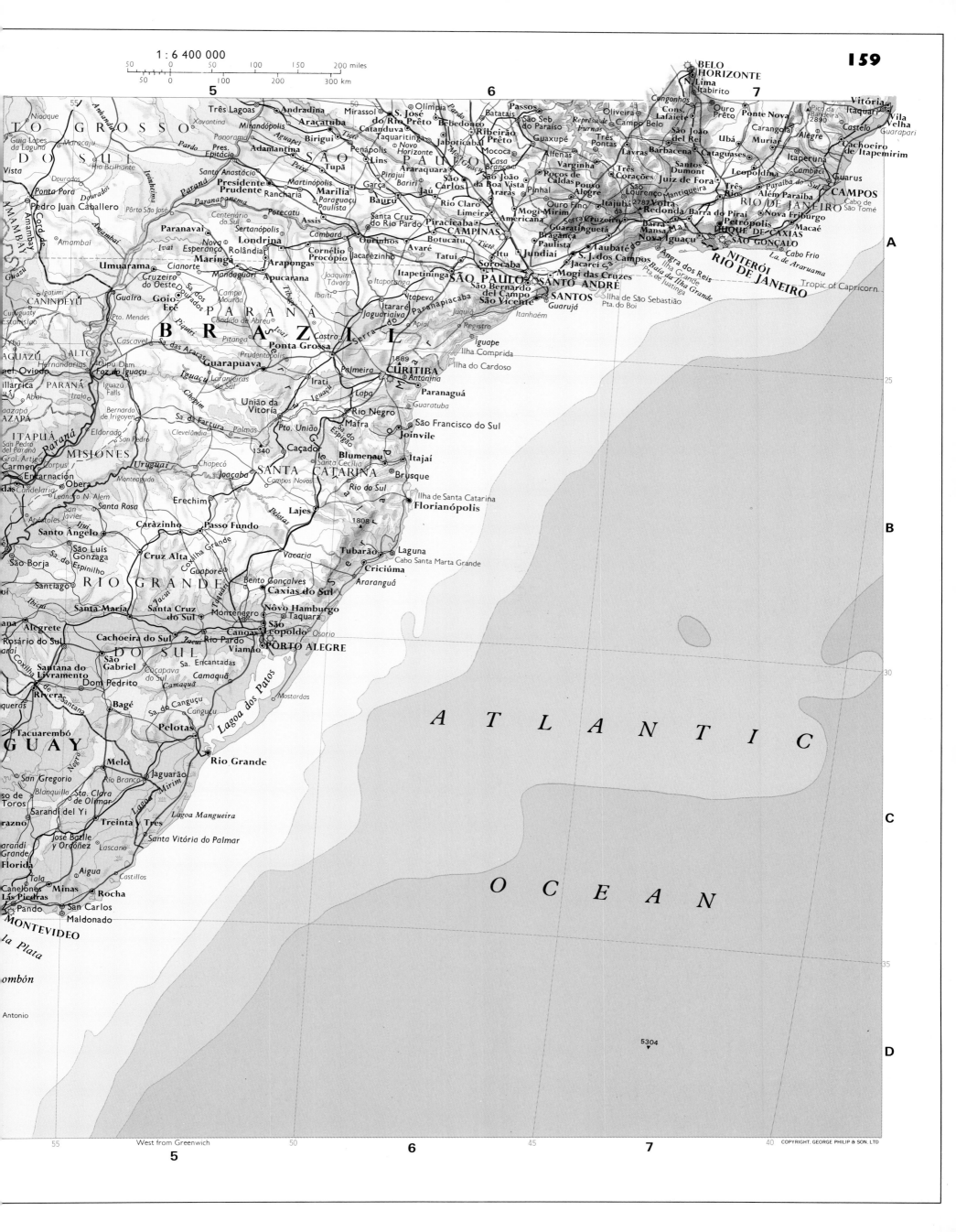

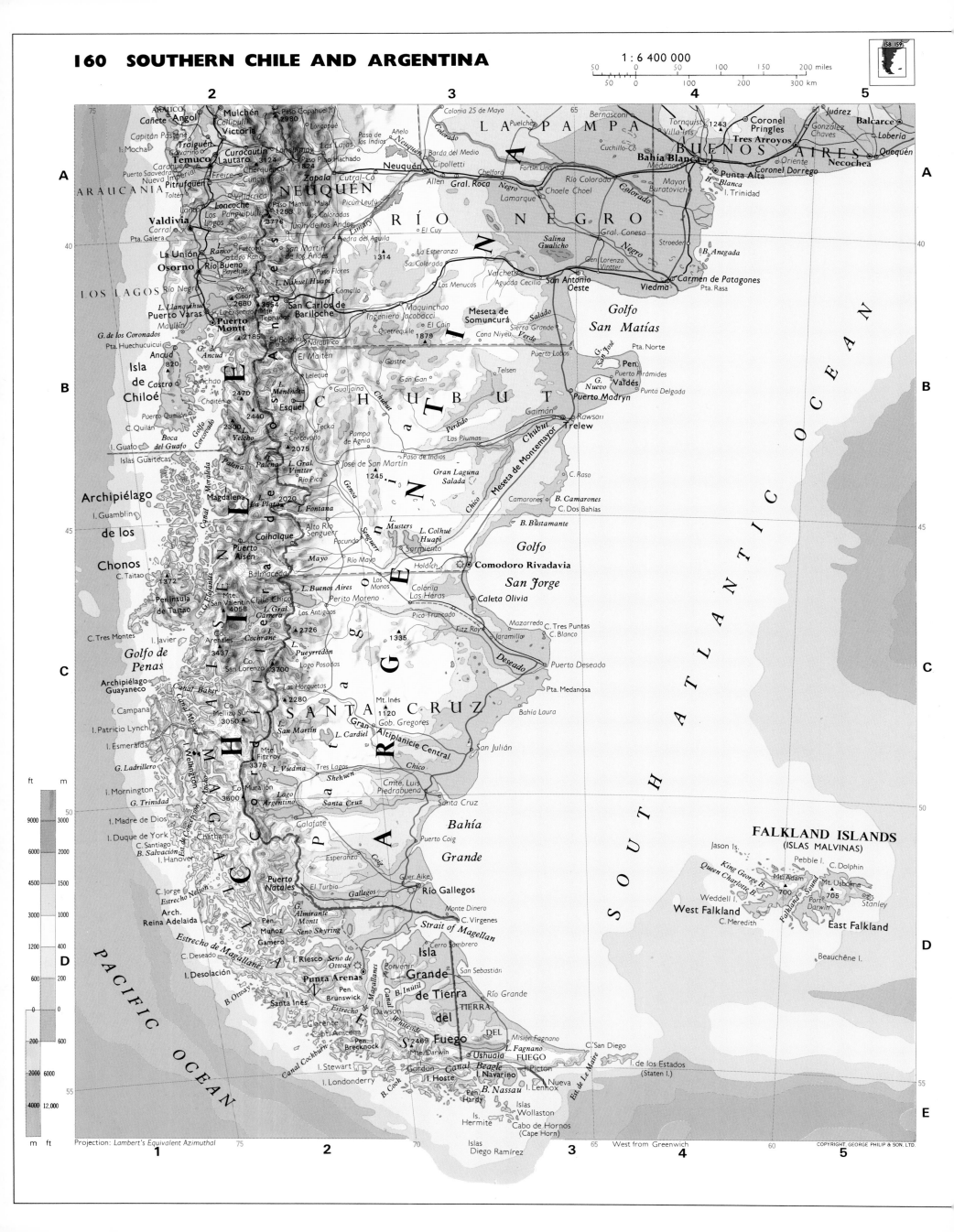

INDEX

The index contains the names of all the principal places and features shown on the World Maps. Each name is followed by an additional entry in italics giving the country or region within which it is located. The alphabetical order of names composed of two or more words is governed primarily by the first word and then by the second. This is an example of the rule:

Mīr Kūh, *Iran*	**85 E8**	26	22 N	58	55 E
Mīr Shahdād, *Iran*	**85 E8**	26	15 N	58	29 E
Miraj, *India*	**82 F2**	16	50 N	74	45 E
Miram Shah, *Pakistan*	**79 B3**	33	0 N	70	2 E
Miramar, *Mozam.*	**105 C6**	23	50 S	35	35 E

Physical features composed of a proper name (Erie) and a description (Lake) are positioned alphabetically by the proper name. The description is positioned after the proper name and is usually abbreviated:

Erie, L., *N. Amer.* . . . . **136 D3** 42 15 N 81 0 W

Where a description forms part of a settlement or administrative name however, it is always written in full and put in its true alphabetic position:

Mount Morris, *U.S.A.* . . . . . . **136 D7** 42 44 N 77 52 W

Names beginning with M' and Mc are indexed as if they were spelt Mac. Names beginning St. are alphabetised under Saint, but Sankt, Sint, Sant', Santa and San are all spelt in full and are alphabetised accordingly. If the same place name occurs two or more times in the index and all are in the same country, each is followed by the name of the administrative subdivision in which it is located. The names are placed in the alphabetical order of the subdivisions. For example:

Jackson, *Ky., U.S.A.*	**134 G4**	37	33 N	83	23 W
Jackson, *Mich., U.S.A.*	**141 B12**	42	15 N	84	24 W
Jackson, *Minn., U.S.A.*	**138 D7**	43	37 N	95	1 W

The number in bold type which follows each name in the index refers to the number of the map page where that feature or place will be found. This is usually the largest scale at which the place or feature appears.

The letter and figure which are in bold type immediately after the page number give the grid square on the map page, within which the feature is situated. The letter represents the latitude and the figure the longitude.

In some cases the feature itself may fall within the specified square, while the name is outside. This is usually the case only with features which are larger than a grid square.

For a more precise location the geographical coordinates which follow the letter/figure references give the latitude and the longitude of each place. The first set of figures represent the latitude which is the distance north or south of the Equator measured as an angle at the centre of the earth. The Equator is latitude 0°, the North Pole is 90°N, and the South Pole 90°S.

The second set of figures represent the longitude, which is the distance East or West of the prime meridian, which runs through Greenwich, England. Longitude is also measured as an angle at the centre of the earth and is given East or West of the prime meridian, from 0° to 180° in either direction.

The unit of measurement for latitude and longitude is the degree, which is subdivided into 60 minutes. Each index entry states the position of a place in degrees and minutes, a space being left between the degrees and the minutes.

The latitude is followed by N(orth) or S(outh) and the longitude by E(ast) or W(est).

Rivers are indexed to their mouths or confluences, and carry the symbol → after their names. A solid square ■ follows the name of a country while, an open square □ refers to a first order administrative area.

ABBREVIATIONS USED IN THE INDEX

A.C.T. — Australian Capital Territory
Afghan. — Afghanistan
Ala. — Alabama
Alta. — Alberta
Amer. — America(n)
Arch. — Archipelago
Ariz. — Arizona
Ark. — Arkansas
Atl. Oc. — Atlantic Ocean
B. — Baie, Bahía, Bay, Bucht, Bugt
B.C. — British Columbia
Bangla. — Bangladesh
Barr. — Barrage
Bos.-H. — Bosnia-Herzegovina
C. — Cabo, Cap, Cape, Coast
C.A.R. — Central African Republic
C. Prov. — Cape Province
Calif. — California
Cent. — Central
Chan. — Channel
Colo. — Colorado
Conn. — Connecticut
Cord. — Cordillera
Cr. — Creek
Czech. — Czech Republic
D.C. — District of Columbia
Del. — Delaware
Dep. — Dependency
Des. — Desert
Dist. — District
Dj. — Djebel
Domin. — Dominica
Dom. Rep. — Dominican Republic
E. — East
El Salv. — El Salvador

Eq. Guin. — Equatorial Guinea
Fla. — Florida
Falk. Is. — Falkland Is.
G. — Golfe, Golfo, Gulf, Guba, Gebel
Ga. — Georgia
Gt. — Great, Greater
Guinea-Biss. — Guinea-Bissau
H.K. — Hong Kong
H.P. — Himachal Pradesh
Hants. — Hampshire
Harb. — Harbor, Harbour
Hd. — Head
Hts. — Heights
I.(s). — Île, Ilha, Insel, Isla, Island, Isle
Ill. — Illinois
Ind. — Indiana
Ind. Oc. — Indian Ocean
Ivory C. — Ivory Coast
J. — Jabal, Jebel, Jazira
Junc. — Junction
K. — Kap, Kapp
Kans. — Kansas
Kep. — Kepulauan
Ky. — Kentucky
L. — Lac, Lacul, Lago, Lagoa, Lake, Limni, Loch, Lough
La. — Louisiana
Liech. — Liechtenstein
Lux. — Luxembourg
Mad. P. — Madhya Pradesh
Madag. — Madagascar
Man. — Manitoba
Mass. — Massachusetts
Md. — Maryland

Me. — Maine
Medit. S. — Mediterranean Sea
Mich. — Michigan
Minn. — Minnesota
Miss. — Mississippi
Mo. — Missouri
Mont. — Montana
Mozam. — Mozambique
Mt.(e). — Mont, Monte, Monti, Montaña, Mountain
N. — Nord, Norte, North, Northern, Nouveau
N.B. — New Brunswick
N.C. — North Carolina
N. Cal. — New Caledonia
N. Dak. — North Dakota
N.H. — New Hampshire
N.I. — North Island
N.J. — New Jersey
N. Mex. — New Mexico
N.S. — Nova Scotia
N.S.W. — New South Wales
N.W.T. — North West Territory
N.Y. — New York
N.Z. — New Zealand
Nebr. — Nebraska
Neths. — Netherlands
Nev. — Nevada
Nfld. — Newfoundland
Nic. — Nicaragua
O. — Oued, Ouadi
Occ. — Occidentale
O.F.S. — Orange Free State
Okla. — Oklahoma
Ont. — Ontario
Or. — Orientale

Oreg. — Oregon
Os. — Ostrov
Oz. — Ozero
P. — Pass, Passo, Pasul, Pulau
P.E.I. — Prince Edward Island
Pa. — Pennsylvania
Pac. Oc. — Pacific Ocean
Papua N.G. — Papua New Guinea
Pass. — Passage
Pen. — Peninsula, Péninsule
Phil. — Philippines
Pk. — Park, Peak
Plat. — Plateau
P-ov. — Poluostrov
Prov. — Province, Provincial
Pt. — Point
Pta. — Ponta, Punta
Pte. — Pointe
Qué. — Québec
Queens. — Queensland
R. — Rio, River
R.I. — Rhode Island
Ra.(s). — Range(s)
Raj. — Rajasthan
Reg. — Region
Rep. — Republic
Res. — Reserve, Reservoir
S. — San, South, Sea
Si. Arabia — Saudi Arabia
S.C. — South Carolina
S. Dak. — South Dakota
S.I. — South Island
S. Leone — Sierra Leone
Sa. — Serra, Sierra
Sask. — Saskatchewan
Scot. — Scotland

Sd. — Sound
Sev. — Severnaya
Sib. — Siberia
Sprs. — Springs
St. — Saint, Sankt, Sint
Sta. — Santa, Station
Ste. — Sainte
Sto. — Santo
Str. — Strait, Stretto
Switz. — Switzerland
Tas. — Tasmania
Tenn. — Tennessee
Tex. — Texas
Tg. — Tanjung
Trin. & Tob. — Trinidad & Tobago
U.A.E. — United Arab Emirates
U.K. — United Kingdom
U.S.A. — United States of America
Ut. P. — Uttar Pradesh
Va. — Virginia
Vdkhr. — Vodokhranilishche
Vf. — Vîrful
Vic. — Victoria
Vol. — Volcano
Vt. — Vermont
W. — Wadi, West
W. Va. — West Virginia
Wash. — Washington
Wis. — Wisconsin
Wlkp. — Wielkopolski
Wyo. — Wyoming
Yorks. — Yorkshire
Yug. — Yugoslavia

162 A Coruña

A

A Coruña = La Coruña, Spain 36 B2 43 20N 8 25W
Aachen, Germany 26 E2 50 47N 6 4 E
Aadorf, Switz. 29 B7 47 30N 8 55 E
Aalborg = Ålborg, Denmark 15 G3 57 2N 9 54 E
Aalen, Germany 27 G6 48 49N 10 6 E
A'âli en Nîl □, Sudan 95 F3 9 30N 31 30 E
Aalsmeer, Neths. 20 D5 52 17N 4 43 E
Aalst, Belgium 21 G4 50 56N 4 2 E
Aalst, Neths. 21 F6 51 23N 5 29 E
Aalten, Neths. 20 E9 51 56N 6 35 E
Aalter, Belgium 21 F2 51 5N 3 28 E
Aarau, Switz. 28 B6 47 23N 8 4 E
Aarberg, Switz. 28 B4 47 2N 7 16 E
Aardenburg, Belgium 21 F2 51 16N 3 28 E
Aare →, Switz. 28 A6 47 33N 8 14 E
Aargau □, Switz. 28 B6 47 26N 8 10 E
Aarhus = Århus, Denmark 15 H4 56 8N 10 11 E
Aarle, Neths. 21 E7 51 30N 5 38 E
Aarschot, Belgium 21 G5 50 59N 4 49 E
Aarsele, Belgium 21 G2 51 0N 3 26 E
Aartrijke, Belgium 21 F2 51 7N 3 6 E
Aarwangen, Switz. 28 B5 47 15N 7 46 E
Aba, China 68 A3 32 59N 101 42 E
Aba, Nigeria 101 D6 5 10N 7 19 E
Aba, Zaïre 106 B3 3 58N 30 17 E
Âbâ, Jazîrat, Sudan 95 E3 13 30N 32 31 E
Abacaxis →, Brazil 153 D6 3 54 S 58 47W
Ābādān, Iran 85 D6 30 22N 48 20 E
Abade, Ethiopia 95 F4 9 22N 38 3 E
Ābādeh, Iran 85 D7 31 8N 52 40 E
Abadin, Spain 36 B3 43 21N 7 29W
Abadla, Algeria 99 B4 31 2N 2 45W
Abaeté, Brazil 155 E2 19 9 S 45 27W
Abaeté →, Brazil 155 E2 18 2 S 45 12W
Abaetetuba, Brazil 154 B2 1 40 S 48 50W
Abagnar Qi, China 66 C9 43 52N 116 2 E
Abai, Paraguay 159 B4 25 58 S 55 54W
Abak, Nigeria 101 E6 4 58N 7 50 E
Abakaliki, Nigeria 101 D6 6 22N 8 2 E
Abakan, Russia 57 D10 53 40N 91 10 E
Abalemma, Niger 101 B6 16 12N 7 50 E
Abana, Turkey 88 C6 41 59N 34 1 E
Abancay, Peru 156 C3 13 35 S 72 55W
Abanilla, Spain 35 G3 38 12N 1 3W
Abano Terme, Italy 39 C8 45 22N 11 46 E
Abapó, Bolivia 157 D5 18 48 S 63 25W
Abarán, Spain 35 G3 38 12N 1 23W
Abariringa, Kiribati 122 H10 2 50 S 171 40W
Abarqū, Iran 85 D7 31 10N 53 20 E
Abashiri, Japan 60 B12 44 0N 144 15 E
Abashiri-Wan, Japan 60 B12 44 0N 144 30 E
Abau, Papua N. G. 120 F5 10 11 S 148 46 E
Abaújszántó, Hungary 31 C14 48 16N 21 12 E
Abay, Kazakhstan 56 E8 49 38N 72 53 E
Abaya, L., Ethiopia 95 F4 6 30N 37 50 E
Abaza, Russia 56 D10 52 39N 90 6 E
Abbadia San Salvatore, Italy 39 F8 42 53N 11 40 E
'Abbāsābād, Iran 85 C8 33 34N 58 23 E
Abbay = Nîl el Azraq →, Sudan 95 D3 15 38N 32 31 E
Abbaye, Pt., U.S.A. 134 B1 46 58N 88 8W
Abbé, L., Ethiopia 95 E5 11 8N 41 47 E
Abbeville, France 23 B8 50 6N 1 49 E
Abbeville, La., U.S.A. 139 K8 29 58N 92 8W
Abbeville, S.C., U.S.A. 135 H4 34 11N 82 23W
Abbiategrasso, Italy 38 C5 45 23N 8 55 E
Abbieglassie, Australia 115 D4 27 15 S 147 28 E
Abbot Ice Shelf, Antarctica 7 D16 73 0 S 92 0W
Abbotsford, Canada 130 D4 49 5N 122 20W
Abbotsford, U.S.A. 138 C9 44 57N 90 19W
Abbottabad, Pakistan 80 B5 34 10N 73 15 E
Abcoude, Neths. 20 D5 52 17N 4 59 E
Abd al Kūrī, Ind. Oc. 87 D6 12 5N 52 20 E
Ābdar, Iran 85 D7 30 16N 55 19 E
'Abdolābād, Iran 85 C8 34 12N 56 30 E
Abdulino, Russia 54 E3 53 42N 53 40 E
Abéché, Chad 97 F4 13 50N 20 35 E
Abejar, Spain 34 D2 41 48N 2 47W
Abekr, Sudan 95 E2 12 45N 28 50 E
Abêlessa, Algeria 99 D5 22 58N 4 47 E
Abengourou, Ivory C. 100 D4 6 42N 3 27W
Åbenrå, Denmark 15 J3 55 3N 9 25 E
Abensberg, Germany 27 G7 48 49N 11 51 E
Abeokuta, Nigeria 101 D5 7 3N 3 19 E
Aber, Uganda 106 B3 2 12N 32 25 E
Aberaeron, U.K. 17 E3 52 15N 4 16W
Aberayron = Aberaeron, U.K. 17 E3 52 15N 4 16W
Abercorn = Mbala, Zambia 107 D3 8 46 S 31 24 E
Abercorn, Australia 115 D5 25 12 S 151 5 E
Aberdare, U.K. 17 F4 51 43N 3 27W
Aberdare Ra., Kenya 106 C4 0 15 S 36 50 E
Aberdeen, Australia 117 B9 32 9 S 150 56 E
Aberdeen, Canada 131 C7 52 20N 106 8W
Aberdeen, S. Africa 104 E3 32 28 S 24 2 E
Aberdeen, U.K. 18 D6 57 9N 2 6W
Aberdeen, Ala., U.S.A. 135 J1 33 49N 88 33W
Aberdeen, Idaho, U.S.A. 142 E7 42 57N 112 50W
Aberdeen, Ohio, U.S.A. 141 F13 38 39N 83 46W
Aberdeen, S. Dak., U.S.A. 138 C5 45 28N 98 29W
Aberdeen, Wash., U.S.A. 144 D3 46 59N 123 50W
Aberdovey = Aberdyfi, U.K. 17 E3 52 33N 4 3W
Aberdyfi, U.K. 17 E3 52 33N 4 3W
Aberfeldy, Australia 117 D7 37 42 S 146 22 E
Aberfeldy, U.K. 18 E5 56 37N 3 50W
Abergaria-a-Velha, Portugal 36 E2 40 41N 8 32W
Abergavenny, U.K. 17 F4 51 49N 3 1W
Abernathy, U.S.A. 139 J4 33 50N 101 51W
Abert, L., U.S.A. 142 E3 42 38N 120 14W
Aberystwyth, U.K. 17 E3 52 25N 4 6W
Abha, Si. Arabia 94 D5 18 0N 42 34 E
Abhar, Iran 85 B6 36 9N 49 13 E
Abhayapuri, India 78 B3 26 24N 90 38 E
Abia □, Nigeria 101 D6 5 30N 7 35 E
Abidiya, Sudan 94 D3 18 18N 34 3 E
Abidjan, Ivory C. 100 D4 5 26N 3 58W
Abilene, Kans., U.S.A. 138 F6 38 55N 97 13W
Abilene, Tex., U.S.A. 139 J5 32 28N 99 43W
Abingdon, U.K. 17 F6 51 40N 1 17W
Abingdon, Ill., U.S.A. 140 D6 40 48N 90 24W
Abingdon, Va., U.S.A. 135 G5 36 43N 81 59W
Abington Reef, Australia 114 B4 18 0 S 149 35 E
Abitau →, Canada 131 B7 59 53N 109 3W
Abitau L., Canada 131 A7 60 27N 107 15W
Abitibi L., Canada 128 C4 48 40N 79 40W
Abiy Adi, Ethiopia 95 E4 13 39N 39 3 E
Abkhaz Republic □, Georgia 53 E9 43 0N 41 0 E
Abkit, Russia 57 C16 64 10N 157 10 E
Abminga, Australia 115 D1 26 8 S 134 51 E
Abnûb, Egypt 94 B3 27 18N 31 4 E
Abo, Massif d', Chad 97 D3 21 41N 16 8 E
Abocho, Nigeria 101 D6 7 35N 6 56 E
Abohar, India 80 D6 30 10N 74 10 E
Aboisso, Ivory C. 100 D4 5 30N 3 5W
Abolo, Congo 102 B2 0 8N 14 16 E
Aboméy, Benin 101 D5 7 10N 2 5 E
Abondance, France 25 B10 46 18N 6 43 E
Abong-Mbang, Cameroon 102 B2 4 0N 13 8 E
Abongabong, Indonesia 74 B1 4 15N 96 48 E
Abonnema, Nigeria 101 E6 4 41N 6 49 E
Abony, Hungary 31 D13 47 12N 20 3 E
Aboso, Ghana 100 D4 5 23N 1 57W
Abou-Deïa, Chad 97 F3 11 20N 19 20 E
Abou Goulem, Chad 97 F4 13 37N 21 38 E
Aboyne, U.K. 18 D6 57 4N 2 48W
Abra □, Phil. 70 C3 17 35N 120 45 E
Abra de Ilog, Phil. 70 E3 13 27N 120 44 E
Abra Pampa, Argentina 158 A2 22 43 S 65 42W
Abrantes, Portugal 37 F2 39 24N 8 7W
Abraveses, Portugal 36 E3 40 41N 7 55W
Abreojos, Pta., Mexico 146 B2 26 50N 113 40W
Abreschviller, France 23 D14 48 39N 7 6 E
Abri, Esh Shamâliya, Sudan 94 C3 20 50N 30 27 E
Abri, Janub Kordofân, Sudan 95 E3 11 40N 30 21 E
Abrolhos, Banka, Brazil 155 E4 18 0 S 38 0W
Abrud, Romania 46 C4 46 19N 23 5 E
Abruzzi □, Italy 39 F10 42 15N 14 0 E
Absaroka Range, U.S.A. 142 D9 44 45N 109 50W
Abū al Khaşīb, Iraq 85 D6 30 25N 48 0 E
Abū 'Alī, Si. Arabia 85 E6 27 20N 49 27 E
Abū 'Alī →, Lebanon 91 A4 34 25N 35 50 E
Abu 'Arīsh, Si. Arabia 86 C3 16 53N 42 48 E
Abû Ballas, Egypt 94 C2 24 26N 27 36 E
Abu Deleiq, Sudan 95 D3 15 57N 33 48 E
Abu Dhabi = Abū Ẓāby, U.A.E. 85 E7 24 28N 54 22 E
Abû Dis, Sudan 94 D3 19 12N 33 38 E
Abû Dom, Sudan 95 D3 16 18N 32 25 E
Abū Du'ān, Syria 84 B3 36 25N 38 15 E
Abu el Gairi, W. →, Egypt 91 F2 29 35N 33 30 E
Abû Gabra, Sudan 95 E2 11 2N 26 50 E
Abu Ga'da, W. →, Egypt 91 F1 29 15N 32 53 E
Abû Gubeiha, Sudan 95 E3 11 30N 31 15 E
Abu Habl, Khawr →, Sudan 95 E3 12 37N 31 0 E
Abū Ḩadrīyah, Si. Arabia 85 E6 27 20N 48 58 E
Abu Hamed, Sudan 94 D3 19 32N 33 13 E
Abu Haraz, An Nîl el Azraq, Sudan 95 E3 14 35N 33 30 E
Abû Haraz, Esh Shamâliya, Sudan 94 D3 19 8N 32 18 E
Abû Higar, Sudan 95 E3 12 50N 33 59 E
Abū Kamāl, Syria 84 C4 34 30N 41 0 E
Abū Madd, Ra's, Si. Arabia 84 E3 24 50N 37 7 E
Abu Matariq, Sudan 95 E2 10 59N 26 9 E
Abu Qir, Egypt 94 H7 31 18N 30 0 E
Abu Qireiya, Egypt 94 C4 24 5N 35 28 E
Abu Qurqâs, Egypt 94 J7 28 1N 30 44 E
Abū Raşāş, Ra's, Oman 87 B7 20 10N 58 38 E
Abū Rubayq, Si. Arabia 86 B2 23 44N 39 42 E
Abu Şafāt, W. →, Jordan 91 E5 30 24N 36 7 E
Abû Simbel, Egypt 94 C3 22 18N 31 40 E
Abū Şukhayr, Iraq 84 D5 31 54N 44 30 E
Abu Tig, Egypt 94 B3 27 4N 31 15 E
Abu Tiga, Sudan 95 E3 12 47N 34 12 E
Abû Zabad, Sudan 95 E2 12 25N 29 10 E
Abū Ẓāby, U.A.E. 85 E7 24 28N 54 22 E
Abū Zeydābād, Iran 85 C6 33 54N 51 45 E
Abufari, Brazil 157 B5 5 25 S 62 59W
Abuja, Nigeria 101 D6 9 16N 7 2 E
Abukuma-Gawa →, Japan 60 E10 38 6N 140 52 E
Abukuma-Sammyaku, Japan 60 F10 37 30N 140 45 E
Abulug, Phil. 70 B3 18 27N 121 27 E
Abumombazi, Zaïre 102 B4 3 42N 22 10 E
Abunã, Brazil 157 B4 9 40 S 65 20W
Abunã →, Brazil 157 B4 9 41 S 65 20W
Abung, Phil. 70 E3 13 46N 121 26 E
Aburatsu, Japan 62 F3 31 34N 131 24 E
Aburo, Zaïre 106 B3 2 4N 30 53 E
Abut Hd., N.Z. 119 D5 43 7 S 170 15 E
Abwong, Sudan 95 F3 9 2N 32 14 E
Åby, Sweden 15 F10 58 40N 16 10 E
Aby, Lagune, Ivory C. 100 D4 5 15N 3 14W
Acacías, Colombia 152 C3 3 59N 73 46W
Acajutla, El Salv. 148 D2 13 36N 89 50W
Açailândia, Brazil 154 C2 5 0 S 47 30W
Acámbaro, Mexico 146 C4 20 0N 100 40W
Acanthus, Greece 44 D5 40 27N 23 47 E
Acaponeta, Mexico 146 C3 22 30N 105 20W
Acapulco, Mexico 147 D5 16 51N 99 56W
Acarai, Serra, Brazil 153 C6 1 50N 57 50W
Acaraú, Brazil 154 B3 2 53 S 40 7W
Acari, Brazil 154 C4 6 31 S 36 38W
Acarí, Peru 156 D3 15 25 S 74 36W
Acarigua, Venezuela 152 B4 9 33N 69 12W
Acatlán, Mexico 147 D5 18 10N 98 3W
Acayucan, Mexico 147 D6 17 59N 94 58W
Accéglio, Italy 38 D3 44 28N 6 59 E
Accomac, U.S.A. 134 G8 37 43N 75 40W
Accous, France 24 E3 43 0N 0 36W
Accra, Ghana 101 D4 5 35N 0 6W
Accrington, U.K. 16 D5 53 46N 2 22W
Acebal, Argentina 158 C3 33 20 S 60 50W
Acerenza, Italy 41 B8 40 50N 15 58 E
Acerra, Italy 41 B7 40 57N 14 22 E
Aceuchal, Spain 37 G4 38 39N 6 30W
Achacachi, Bolivia 156 D4 16 3 S 68 43W
Achaguas, Venezuela 152 B4 7 46N 68 14W
Achalpur, India 82 D3 21 22N 77 32 E
Achao, Chile 160 B2 42 28 S 73 30W
Achel, Belgium 21 F6 51 15N 5 29 E
Acheng, China 67 B14 45 30N 126 58 E
Achenkirch, Austria 30 D4 47 32N 11 45 E
Achensee, Austria 30 D4 47 26N 11 45 E
Acher, India 80 H5 23 10N 72 32 E
Achern, Germany 27 G4 48 37N 8 5 E
Acheron →, N.Z. 119 C8 42 16 S 173 4 E
Achill, Ireland 19 C2 53 56N 9 55W
Achill Hd., Ireland 19 C1 53 59N 10 15W
Achill I., Ireland 19 C1 53 58N 10 5W
Achill Sd., Ireland 19 C2 53 53N 9 55W
Achim, Germany 26 B5 53 1N 9 2 E
Achinsk, Russia 57 D10 56 20N 90 20 E
Achisay, Kazakhstan 55 B4 43 35N 68 53 E
Achit, Russia 54 C5 56 48N 57 54 E
Achol, Sudan 95 F3 6 35N 31 32 E
Acıgöl, Turkey 88 E3 37 50N 29 50 E
Acireale, Italy 41 E8 37 37N 15 9 E
Ackerman, U.S.A. 139 J10 33 19N 89 11W
Ackley, U.S.A. 140 B3 42 33N 93 3W
Acklins I., Bahamas 149 B5 22 30N 74 0W
Acme, Canada 130 C6 51 33N 113 30W
Acobamba, Peru 156 C3 12 52 S 74 35W
Acomayo, Peru 156 C3 13 55 S 71 38W
Aconcagua □, Chile 158 C1 32 15 S 70 30W
Aconcagua, Cerro, Argentina 158 C2 32 39 S 70 0W
Aconquija, Mt., Argentina 158 B2 27 0 S 66 0W
Acopiara, Brazil 154 C4 6 6 S 39 27W
Açores, Is. dos = Azores, Atl. Oc. 8 E6 38 44N 29 0W
Acorizal, Brazil 157 D6 15 12 S 56 22W
Acquapendente, Italy 39 F8 42 45N 11 50 E
Acquasanta, Italy 39 F10 42 46N 13 24 E
Acquaviva delle Fonti, Italy 41 B9 40 53N 16 50 E
Acqui, Italy 38 D5 44 40N 8 28 E
Acraman, L., Australia 115 E2 32 2 S 135 23 E
Acre = 'Akko, Israel 91 C4 32 55N 35 4 E
Acre □, Brazil 156 B3 9 1 S 71 0W
Acre →, Brazil 156 B4 8 45 S 67 22W
Acri, Italy 41 C9 39 29N 16 23 E
Acs, Hungary 31 D11 47 42N 18 2 E
Actium, Greece 45 F2 38 57N 20 45 E
Acton, Canada 136 C4 43 38N 80 3W
Açu, Brazil 154 C4 5 34 S 36 54W
Ad Dahnā, Si. Arabia 87 A5 24 30N 48 10 E
Aḑ Ḑālī', Yemen 86 D4 13 42N 44 44 E
Ad Dammām, Si. Arabia 85 E6 26 20N 50 5 E
Ad Darb, Si. Arabia 86 C3 18 2N 43 7 E
Ad Dawhah, Qatar 85 E6 25 15N 51 35 E
Ad Dawr, Iraq 84 C4 34 27N 43 47 E
Aḑ Ḑiffah, Libya 96 B4 30 30N 24 30 E
Ad Dilam, Si. Arabia 86 B4 23 55N 47 10 E
Ad Dir'īyah, Si. Arabia 84 E5 24 44N 46 35 E
Ad Dīwānīyah, Iraq 84 D5 32 0N 45 0 E
Ad Dujayl, Iraq 84 C5 33 51N 44 14 E
Ad Durūz, J., Jordan 91 C5 32 35N 36 40 E
Ada, Ghana 101 D5 5 44N 0 40 E
Ada, Serbia 42 B5 45 49N 20 9 E
Ada, Minn., U.S.A. 138 B6 47 18N 96 31W
Ada, Ohio, U.S.A. 141 D13 40 46N 83 49W
Ada, Okla., U.S.A. 139 H6 34 46N 96 41W
Adad, Somali Rep. 108 C3 9 27N 46 49 E
Adaja →, Spain 36 D6 41 32N 4 52W
Ådalslinden, Sweden 14 A10 63 27N 16 55 E
Adam, Oman 87 B7 22 15N 57 28 E
Adam, Mt., Falk. Is. 160 D4 51 34 S 60 4W
Adamantina, Brazil 155 F1 21 42 S 51 4W
Adamaoua, Massif de l', Cameroon 101 D7 7 20N 12 20 E
Adamaoua □, Nigeria 101 D7 9 20N 12 30 E
Adamawa Highlands = Adamaoua, Massif de l', Cameroon 101 D7 7 20N 12 20 E
Adamello, Mt., Italy 38 B7 46 10N 10 34 E
Adami Tulu, Ethiopia 95 F4 7 53N 38 41 E
Adaminaby, Australia 117 D8 36 0 S 148 45 E
Adamovka, Russia 54 F6 51 32N 59 56 E
Adams, Phil. 70 B3 18 28N 120 54 E
Adams, Mass., U.S.A. 137 D11 42 38N 73 7W
Adams, N.Y., U.S.A. 137 C8 43 49N 76 1W
Adams, Wis., U.S.A. 138 D10 43 57N 89 49W
Adam's Bridge, Sri Lanka 83 K4 9 15N 79 40 E
Adams L., Canada 130 C5 51 10N 119 40W
Adams Mt., U.S.A. 144 D5 46 12N 121 30W
Adam's Peak, Sri Lanka 83 L5 6 48N 80 30 E
Adamuz, Spain 37 G6 38 2N 4 32W
Adana, Turkey 88 E6 37 0N 35 16 E
Adana □, Turkey 88 E6 37 0N 35 30 E
Adanero, Spain 36 E6 40 56N 4 36W
Adapazarı, Turkey 88 C4 40 48N 30 25 E
Adarama, Sudan 95 D3 17 10N 34 52 E
Adare, C., Antarctica 7 D11 71 0 S 171 0 E
Adaut, Indonesia 73 C4 8 8 S 131 7 E
Adavale, Australia 115 D3 25 52 S 144 32 E
Adda →, Italy 38 C6 45 8N 9 53 E
Addis Ababa = Addis Abeba, Ethiopia 95 F4 9 2N 38 42 E
Addis Abeba, Ethiopia 95 F4 9 2N 38 42 E
Addis Alem, Ethiopia 95 F4 9 0N 38 17 E
Addison, Ill., U.S.A. 141 C8 41 55N 88 0W
Addison, N.Y., U.S.A. 136 D7 42 1N 77 14W
Addo, S. Africa 104 E4 33 32 S 25 45 E
Addyston, U.S.A. 141 E12 39 8N 84 43W
Adebour, Niger 97 F2 13 17N 11 50 E
Ādeh, Iran 84 B5 37 42N 45 11 E
Adel, Ga., U.S.A. 135 K4 31 8N 83 25W
Adel, Iowa, U.S.A. 140 C2 41 37N 94 1W
Adelaide, Australia 116 C3 34 52 S 138 30 E
Adelaide, Bahamas 148 A4 25 4N 77 31W
Adelaide, S. Africa 104 E4 32 42 S 26 20 E
Adelaide I., Antarctica 7 C17 67 15 S 68 30W
Adelaide Pen., Canada 126 B10 68 15N 97 30W
Adelaide River, Australia 112 B5 13 15 S 131 7 E
Adelanto, U.S.A. 145 L9 34 35N 117 22W
Adelboden, Switz. 28 D5 46 29N 7 33 E
Adele I., Australia 112 C3 15 32 S 123 9 E
Adélie, Terre, Antarctica 7 C10 68 0 S 140 0 E
Adélie Land = Adélie, Terre, Antarctica 7 C10 68 0 S 140 0 E
Ademuz, Spain 34 E3 40 5N 1 13W
Aden = Al 'Adan, Yemen 86 D4 12 45N 45 0 E
Aden, G. of, Asia 90 E4 12 30N 47 30 E
Adendorp, S. Africa 104 E3 32 15 S 24 30 E
Adh Dhayd, U.A.E. 85 E7 25 17N 55 53 E
Adhoi, India 80 H4 23 26N 70 32 E
Adi, Indonesia 73 B4 4 15 S 133 30 E
Adi Daro, Ethiopia 95 E4 14 20N 38 14 E
Adi Keyih, Eritrea 95 E4 14 51N 39 22 E
Adi Kwala, Eritrea 95 E4 14 38N 38 48 E
Adi Ugri, Eritrea 95 E4 14 58N 38 48 E
Adieu, C., Australia 113 F5 32 0 S 132 10 E
Adieu Pt., Australia 112 C3 15 14 S 124 35 E
Adigala, Ethiopia 95 E5 10 24N 42 15 E
Adige →, Italy 39 C9 45 9N 12 20 E
Adigrat, Ethiopia 95 E4 14 20N 39 26 E
Adilabad, India 82 E4 19 33N 78 20 E
Adin, U.S.A. 142 F3 41 12N 120 57W
Adinkerke, Belgium 21 F1 51 5N 2 36 E
Adirondack Mts., U.S.A. 137 C10 44 0N 74 0W
Adıyaman, Turkey 89 E8 37 45N 38 16 E
Adiyaman □, Turkey 89 E8 37 30N 38 10 E
Adjim, Tunisia 96 B2 33 47N 10 50 E
Adjohon, Benin 101 D5 6 41N 2 32 E
Adjud, Romania 46 C8 46 7N 27 10 E
Adjumani, Uganda 106 B3 3 20N 31 50 E
Adlavik Is., Canada 129 B8 55 2N 57 45W
Adler, Russia 53 E8 43 28N 39 52 E
Adliswil, Switz. 29 B7 47 19N 8 32 E
Admer, Algeria 99 D6 20 21N 5 27 E
Admer, Erg d', Algeria 99 D6 24 0N 9 5 E
Admiralty G., Australia 112 B4 14 20 S 125 55 E
Admiralty I., U.S.A. 126 C6 57 30N 134 30W
Admiralty Inlet, U.S.A. 142 C2 48 8N 122 58W
Admiralty Is., Papua N. G. 120 B4 2 0 S 147 0 E
Ado, Nigeria 101 D5 6 36N 2 56 E
Ado Ekiti, Nigeria 101 D6 7 38N 5 12 E
Adok, Sudan 95 F3 8 10N 30 20 E
Adola, Ethiopia 95 E5 11 14N 41 44 E
Adonara, Indonesia 72 C2 8 15 S 123 5 E
Adoni, India 83 G3 15 33N 77 18 E
Adony, Hungary 31 D11 47 6N 18 52 E
Adour →, France 24 E2 43 32N 1 32W
Adra, India 81 H12 23 30N 86 42 E
Adra, Spain 35 J1 36 43N 3 3W
Adrano, Italy 41 E7 37 40N 14 49 E
Adrar, Algeria 99 C4 27 51N 0 11W
Adrasman, Tajikistan 55 C4 40 38N 69 58 E
Adré, Chad 97 F4 13 40N 22 20 E
Adrī, Libya 96 C2 27 32N 13 2 E
Ádria, Italy 39 C9 45 4N 12 3 E
Adrian, Mich., U.S.A. 141 C12 41 54N 84 2W
Adrian, Mo., U.S.A. 140 F2 38 24N 94 21W
Adrian, Tex., U.S.A. 139 H3 35 16N 102 40W
Adriatic Sea, Europe 10 G9 43 0N 16 0 E
Adua, Indonesia 73 B3 1 45 S 129 50 E
Adula, Switz. 29 D8 46 30N 9 3 E
Adung Long, Burma 78 A6 28 7N 97 42 E
Adur, India 83 K3 9 8N 76 40 E
Adwa, Ethiopia 95 E4 14 15N 38 52 E
Adzhar Republic □, Georgia 53 F10 41 30N 42 0 E
Adzopé, Ivory C. 100 D4 6 7N 3 49W
Ægean Sea, Europe 45 F7 38 30N 25 0 E
Æolian Is. = Eólie, Is., Italy 41 D7 38 30N 14 50 E
Aerhtai Shan, Mongolia 64 B4 46 40N 92 45 E
Ærø, Denmark 15 K4 54 52N 10 25 E
Ærøskøbing, Denmark 15 K4 54 53N 10 24 E
Aesch, Switz. 28 B5 47 28N 7 36 E
Aëtós, Greece 45 G3 37 15N 21 50 E
Afafi, Massif d', Niger 97 D3 22 11N 15 10 E
'Afak, Iraq 84 C5 32 4N 45 15 E
Afanasyevo, Russia 54 B3 58 52N 53 15 E
Afándou, Greece 32 C10 36 18N 28 12 E
Afarag, Erg, Algeria 99 D5 23 50N 2 47 E
Afars & Issas, Terr. of = Djibouti ■, Africa 90 E3 12 0N 43 0 E
Afdega, Ethiopia 108 C2 6 4N 43 30 E
Affreville = Khemis Miliana, Algeria 99 A5 36 11N 2 14 E
Affton, U.S.A. 140 F6 38 33N 90 20W
Afghanistan ■, Asia 79 B2 33 0N 65 0 E
Afgoi, Somali Rep. 90 G3 2 7N 44 59 E
'Afif, Si. Arabia 86 B3 23 53N 42 56 E
Afikpo, Nigeria 101 D6 5 53N 7 54 E
Aflou, Algeria 99 B5 34 7N 2 3 E
Afmadu, Somali Rep. 108 D2 0 31N 42 4 E
Afogados da Ingâzeira, Brazil 154 C4 7 45 S 37 39W
Afognak I., U.S.A. 126 C4 58 15N 152 30W
Afragola, Italy 41 B7 40 54N 14 15 E
Afrera, Ethiopia 95 E5 13 16N 41 5 E
Africa 92 E6 10 0N 20 0 E
'Afrīn, Syria 84 B3 36 32N 36 50 E
Afşin, Turkey 88 D7 38 14N 36 55 E
Afton, U.S.A. 137 D9 42 14N 75 32W
Aftout, Algeria 98 C4 26 50N 3 45W
Afuá, Brazil 153 D7 0 15 S 50 20W
Afula, Israel 91 C4 32 37N 35 17 E
Afyonkarahisar, Turkey 88 D4 38 45N 30 33 E
Afyonkarahisar □, Turkey 88 D4 38 45N 30 30 E
Aga, Egypt 94 H7 30 55N 31 10 E
Agadès = Agadez, Niger 97 E1 16 58N 7 59 E
Agadez, Niger 97 E1 16 58N 7 59 E
Agadir, Morocco 98 B3 30 28N 9 55W
Agaete, Canary Is. 33 F4 28 6N 15 43W
Agailás, Mauritania 98 D2 22 37N 14 22W
Agana, Guam 121 R15 13 28N 144 45 E
Agapa, Russia 57 B9 71 27N 89 15 E
Agapovka, Russia 54 E6 53 18N 59 8 E
Agar, India 80 H7 23 40N 76 2 E
Agaro, Ethiopia 95 F4 7 50N 36 38 E
Agartala, India 78 D3 23 50N 91 23 E
Agăş, Romania 46 C7 46 28N 26 15 E
Agassiz, Canada 130 D4 49 14N 121 46W
Agats, Indonesia 73 C5 5 33 S 138 0 E
Agbélouvé, Togo 101 D5 6 35N 1 14 E
Agboville, Ivory C. 100 D4 5 55N 4 15W

Al Khābūra 163

Agcogan, Phil. 70 E3 12 4N 121 57 E
Agdam, Azerbaijan 53 G12 40 0N 46 58 E
Agdash, Azerbaijan 53 F12 40 44N 47 22 E
Agde, France 24 E7 43 19N 3 28 E
Agde, C. d', France 24 E7 43 16N 3 28 E
Agdz, Morocco 98 B3 30 47N 6 30W
Agdzhabedi, Azerbaijan 53 F12 40 5N 47 27 E
Agen, France 24 D4 44 12N 0 38 E
Ageo, Japan 63 B11 35 58N 139 36 E
Ager Tay, Chad 97 E3 20 0N 17 41 E
Agersø, Denmark 15 J5 55 13N 11 12 E
Ageyevo, Russia 51 D10 54 10N 36 27 E
Agger, Denmark 15 H2 56 47N 8 13 E
Äggius, Italy 40 B2 40 56N 9 4 E
Āgh Kand, Iran 85 B6 37 15N 48 4 E
Aghoueyyît, Mauritania 98 D1 21 10N 15 6W
Aginskoye, Russia 57 D12 51 6N 114 32 E
Agira, Italy 41 E7 37 40N 14 30 E
Ağlasun, Turkey 88 E4 37 39N 30 31 E
Agly →, France 24 F7 42 46N 3 3 E
Agnibilékrou, Ivory C. 100 D4 7 10N 3 11W
Agnita, Romania 46 D5 45 59N 24 40 E
Agnone, Italy 41 A7 41 49N 14 20 E
Ago, Japan 63 C8 34 20N 136 51 E
Agofie, Ghana 101 D5 8 27N 0 15 E
Agogna →, Italy 38 C5 45 4N 8 52 E
Agogo, Sudan 95 F2 7 50N 28 45 E
Agon, France 22 C5 49 2N 1 34W
Agön, Sweden 14 C11 61 34N 17 23 E
Agoo, Phil. 70 C3 16 20N 120 22 E
Agordo, Italy 39 B9 46 18N 12 2 E
Agout →, France 24 E5 43 47N 1 41 E
Agra, India 80 F7 27 17N 77 58 E
Agramunt, Spain 34 D6 41 48N 1 6 E
Agreda, Spain 34 D3 41 51N 1 55W
Ağri, Turkey 89 D10 39 44N 43 4 E
Ağri □, Turkey 89 D10 39 45N 43 5 E
Agri →, Italy 41 B9 40 13N 16 44 E
Ağrı Dağı, Turkey 89 D11 39 50N 44 15 E
Ağrı Karakose, Turkey 89 D10 39 44N 43 3 E
Agrigento, Italy 40 E6 37 19N 13 33 E
Agrinion, Greece 45 F3 38 37N 21 27 E
Agrópoli, Italy 41 B7 40 23N 14 59 E
Agryz, Russia 54 C3 56 33N 53 2 E
Água Branca, Brazil 154 C3 5 50 S 42 40W
Agua Caliente, Baja Calif. N., Mexico 145 N10 32 29N 116 59W
Agua Caliente, Sinaloa, Mexico 146 B3 26 30N 108 20W
Agua Caliente Springs, U.S.A. 145 N10 32 56N 116 19W
Água Clara, Brazil 157 E7 20 25 S 52 45W
Agua Hechicero, Mexico 145 N10 32 26N 116 14W
Agua Preta →, Brazil 153 D5 1 41 S 63 48W
Agua Prieta, Mexico 146 A3 31 20N 109 32W
Aguachica, Colombia 152 B3 8 19N 73 38W
Aguada Cecilio, Argentina 160 B3 40 51 S 65 51W
Aguadas, Colombia 152 B2 5 40N 75 38W
Aguadilla, Puerto Rico 149 C6 18 26N 67 10W
Aguadulce, Panama 148 E3 8 15N 80 32W
Aguanga, U.S.A. 145 M10 33 27N 116 51W
Aguanish, Canada 129 B7 50 14N 62 2W
Aguanus →, Canada 129 B7 50 13N 62 5W
Aguapeí, Brazil 157 D6 16 12 S 59 43W
Aguapeí →, Brazil 155 F1 21 0 S 51 0W
Aguapey →, Argentina 158 B4 29 7 S 56 36W
Aguaray Guazú →, Paraguay 158 A4 24 47 S 57 19W
Aguarico →, Ecuador 152 D2 0 59 S 75 11W
Aguas →, Spain 34 D4 41 20N 0 30W
Aguas Blancas, Chile 158 A2 24 15 S 69 55W
Aguas Calientes, Sierra de, Argentina 158 B2 25 26 S 66 40W
Águas Formosas, Brazil 155 E3 17 5 S 40 57W
Aguascalientes, Mexico 146 C4 21 53N 102 12W
Aguascalientes □, Mexico 146 C4 22 0N 102 20W
Agudo, Spain 37 G6 38 59N 4 52W
Águeda, Portugal 36 E2 40 34N 8 27W
Agueda →, Spain 36 D4 41 2N 6 56W
Aguié, Niger 101 C6 13 31N 7 46 E
Aguilafuente, Spain 36 D6 41 13N 4 7W
Aguilar, Spain 37 H6 37 31N 4 40W
Aguilar de Campóo, Spain 36 C6 42 47N 4 15W
Aguilares, Argentina 158 B2 27 26 S 65 35W
Aguilas, Spain 35 H3 37 23N 1 35W
Agüimes, Canary Is. 33 G4 27 58N 15 27W
Aguja, C. de la, Colombia 152 A3 11 18N 74 12W
Agulaa, Ethiopia 95 E4 13 40N 39 40 E
Agulhas, C., S. Africa 104 E3 34 52 S 20 0 E
Agulo, Canary Is. 33 F2 28 11N 17 12W
Agung, Indonesia 75 D5 8 20 S 115 28 E
Agur, Uganda 106 B3 2 28N 32 55 E
Agusan →, Phil. 71 G5 9 0N 125 30 E
Agusan del Norte □, Phil. 71 G5 9 20N 125 10 E
Agusan del Sur □, Phil. 71 G5 8 30N 125 30 E
Agustín Codazzi, Colombia 152 A3 10 2N 73 14W
Agutaya I., Phil. 71 F3 11 9N 120 58 E
Agvali, Russia 53 E12 42 36N 46 8 E
Aha Mts., Botswana 104 B3 19 45 S 21 0 E
Ahaggar, Algeria 99 D6 23 0N 6 30 E
Ahamansu, Ghana 101 D5 7 38N 0 35 E
Ahar, Iran 84 B5 38 35N 47 0 E
Ahaura →, N.Z. 119 C6 42 21 S 171 34 E
Ahaus, Germany 26 C3 52 4N 7 1 E
Ahelledjem, Algeria 99 C6 26 37N 6 58 E
Ahimanawa Ra., N.Z. 118 F5 39 3 S 176 30 E
Ahipara B., N.Z. 118 B2 35 5 S 173 5 E
Ahiri, India 82 E5 19 30N 80 0 E
Ahlen, Germany 26 D3 51 45N 7 52 E
Ahmad Wal, Pakistan 80 E1 29 18N 65 58 E
Ahmadabad, India 80 H5 23 0N 72 40 E
Aḥmadābād, Khorāsān, Iran 85 C9 35 3N 60 50 E
Aḥmadābād, Khorāsān, Iran 85 C8 35 49N 59 42 E
Aḥmadī, Iran 85 E8 27 56N 56 42 E
Ahmadnagar, India 82 E2 19 7N 74 46 E
Ahmadpur, Pakistan 80 E4 29 12N 71 10 E
Ahmar, Ethiopia 95 F5 9 20N 41 15 E
Ahmedabad = Ahmadabad, India 80 H5 23 0N 72 40 E
Ahmednagar = Ahmadnagar, India 82 E2 19 7N 74 46 E
Ahoada, Nigeria 101 D6 5 8N 6 36 E
Ahome, Mexico 146 B3 25 55N 109 11W
Ahr →, Germany 26 E3 50 33N 7 17 E
Ahram, Iran 85 D6 28 52N 51 16 E
Ahrax Pt., Malta 32 D1 35 59N 14 22 E
Ahrensbök, Germany 26 A6 54 2N 10 34 E
Ahrweiler, Germany 26 E3 50 31N 7 3 E
Āhū, Iran 85 C6 34 33N 50 2 E
Ahuachapán, El Salv. 148 D2 13 54N 89 52W
Ahuriri →, N.Z. 119 E5 44 31 S 170 12 E
Ahvāz, Iran 85 D6 31 20N 48 40 E
Ahvenanmaa = Åland, Finland 13 F16 60 15N 20 0 E
Aḥwar, Yemen 86 D4 13 30N 46 40 E
Ahzar, Mali 101 B5 15 30N 3 20 E
Aiari →, Brazil 152 C4 1 22N 68 36W
Aichach, Germany 27 G7 48 28N 11 9 E
Aichi □, Japan 63 B9 35 0N 137 15 E
Aidone, Italy 41 E7 37 26N 14 26 E
Aiello Cálabro, Italy 41 C9 39 6N 16 12 E
Aigle, Switz. 28 D3 46 18N 6 58 E
Aignay-le-Duc, France 23 E11 47 40N 4 43 E
Aigoual, Mt., France 24 D7 44 8N 3 35 E
Aigre, France 24 C4 45 54N 0 1 E
Aigua, Uruguay 159 C5 34 13 S 54 46W
Aigueperse, France 24 B7 46 3N 3 13 E
Aigues →, France 25 D8 44 7N 4 43 E
Aigues-Mortes, France 25 E8 43 35N 4 12 E
Aigues-Mortes, G. d', France 25 E8 43 31N 4 3 E
Aiguilles, France 25 D10 44 47N 6 51 E
Aiguillon, France 24 D4 44 18N 0 21 E
Aigurande, France 24 B5 46 27N 1 49 E
Aihui, China 65 A7 50 10N 127 30 E
Aija, Peru 156 B2 9 50 S 77 45W
Aikawa, Japan 60 E9 38 2N 138 15 E
Aiken, U.S.A. 135 J5 33 34N 81 43W
Ailao Shan, China 68 F3 24 0N 101 20 E
Aillant-sur-Tholon, France 23 E10 47 52N 3 20 E
Aillik, Canada 129 A8 55 11N 59 18W
Ailly-sur-Noye, France 23 C9 49 45N 2 20 E
Ailsa Craig, U.K. 18 F3 55 15N 5 7W
'Ailūn, Jordan 91 C4 32 18N 35 47 E
Aim, Russia 57 D14 59 0N 133 55 E
Aimere, Indonesia 72 C2 8 45 S 121 3 E
Aimogasta, Argentina 158 B2 28 33 S 66 50W
Aimorés, Brazil 155 E3 19 30 S 41 4W
Ain □, France 25 B9 46 5N 5 20 E
Ain →, France 25 C9 45 45N 5 11 E
Aïn Beïda, Algeria 99 A6 35 50N 7 29 E
Aïn Ben Khellil, Algeria 99 B4 33 15N 0 49W
Aïn Ben Tili, Mauritania 98 C3 25 59N 9 27W
Aïn Beni Mathar, Morocco 99 B4 34 1N 2 0W
Aïn Benian, Algeria 99 A5 36 48N 2 55 E
Ain Dalla, Egypt 94 B2 27 20N 27 23 E
Ain el Mafki, Egypt 94 B2 27 30N 28 15 E
Ain Girba, Egypt 94 B2 29 20N 25 14 E
Aïn M'lila, Algeria 99 A6 36 2N 6 35 E
Ain Qeiqab, Egypt 94 B1 29 42N 24 55 E
Aïn-Sefra, Algeria 99 B4 32 47N 0 37W
Ain Sheikh Murzûk, Egypt 94 B2 26 47N 27 45 E
'Ain Sudr, Egypt 91 F2 29 50N 33 6 E
Ain Sukhna, Egypt 94 J8 29 32N 32 20 E
Aïn Tédelès, Algeria 99 A5 36 0N 0 21 E
Aïn-Témouchent, Algeria 99 A4 35 16N 1 8W
Aïn Touta, Algeria 99 A6 35 26N 5 54 E
Ain Zeitûn, Egypt 94 B2 29 10N 25 48 E
Aïn Zorah, Morocco 99 B4 34 37N 3 32W
Ainabo, Somali Rep. 90 F4 9 0N 46 25 E
Ainaži, Latvia 50 C4 57 50N 24 24 E
Aínos Óros, Greece 45 F2 38 10N 20 35 E
Ainsworth, U.S.A. 138 D5 42 33N 99 52W
Aioi, Japan 62 C6 34 48N 134 28 E
Aipe, Colombia 152 C2 3 13N 75 15W
Aiquile, Bolivia 157 D4 18 10 S 65 10W
Aïr, Niger 97 E1 18 30N 8 0 E
Air Hitam, Malaysia 77 M4 1 55N 103 11 E
Airaines, France 23 C8 49 58N 1 55 E
Airão, Brazil 153 D5 1 56 S 61 22W
Airdrie, U.K. 18 F5 55 53N 3 57W
Aire →, France 23 C11 49 18N 4 49 E
Aire →, U.K. 16 D7 53 42N 0 55W
Aire, I. del, Spain 33 B11 39 48N 4 16 E
Aire-sur-la-Lys, France 23 B9 50 37N 2 22 E
Aire-sur-l'Adour, France 24 E3 43 42N 0 15W
Aireys Inlet, Australia 116 E6 38 29 S 144 5 E
Airlie Beach, Australia 114 C4 20 16 S 148 43 E
Airolo, Switz. 29 C7 46 32N 8 37 E
Airvault, France 22 F6 46 50N 0 8W
Aisch →, Germany 27 F7 49 46N 11 1 E
Aisen □, Chile 160 C2 46 30 S 73 0W
Aisne □, France 23 C10 49 42N 3 40 E
Aisne →, France 23 C9 49 26N 2 50 E
Aitana, Sierra de, Spain 35 G4 38 35N 0 24W
Aitape, Papua N. G. 120 B2 3 11 S 142 22 E
Aitkin, U.S.A. 138 B8 46 32N 93 42W
Aitolía Kai Akarnanía □, Greece 45 F3 38 45N 21 18 E
Aitolikón, Greece 45 F3 38 26N 21 21 E
Aiuaba, Brazil 154 C3 6 38 S 40 7W
Aiud, Romania 46 C4 46 19N 23 44 E
Aix-en-Provence, France 25 E9 43 32N 5 27 E
Aix-la-Chapelle = Aachen, Germany 26 E2 50 47N 6 4 E
Aix-les-Bains, France 25 C9 45 41N 5 53 E
Aixe-sur-Vienne, France 24 C5 45 47N 1 9 E
Aiyang, Mt., Papua N. G. 120 C1 5 10 S 141 20 E
Aiyansh, Canada 130 B3 55 17N 129 2W
Áíyina, Greece 45 G5 37 45N 23 26 E
Aiyínion, Greece 44 D4 40 28N 22 28 E
Aiyion, Greece 45 F4 38 15N 22 5 E
Aizawl, India 78 D4 23 40N 92 44 E
Aizenay, France 22 F5 46 44N 1 38W
Aizpute, Latvia 50 C2 56 43N 21 40 E
Aizuwakamatsu, Japan 60 F9 37 30N 139 56 E
Ajaccio, France 25 G12 41 55N 8 40 E
Ajaccio, G. d', France 25 G12 41 52N 8 40 E
Ajaju →, Colombia 152 C3 0 59N 72 20W
Ajalpan, Mexico 147 D5 18 22N 97 15W
Ajanta Ra., India 82 D2 20 28N 75 50 E
Ajari Rep. = Adzhar Republic □, Georgia 53 F10 41 30N 42 0 E
Ajax, Canada 136 C5 43 50N 79 1W
Ajax, Mt., N.Z. 119 C7 42 35 S 172 5 E
Ajayan Pt., Guam 121 R15 13 15N 144 43 E
Ajdâbiyah, Libya 96 B4 30 54N 20 4 E
Ajdovščina, Slovenia 39 C10 45 54N 13 54 E
Ajibar, Ethiopia 95 E4 10 35N 38 36 E
Ajka, Hungary 31 D10 47 4N 17 31 E
'Ajmān, U.A.E. 85 E7 25 25N 55 30 E
Ajmer, India 80 F6 26 28N 74 37 E
Ajo, U.S.A. 143 K7 32 22N 112 52W
Ajoie, Switz. 28 B4 47 22N 7 0 E
Ajok, Sudan 95 F2 9 15N 28 28 E
Ajuy, Phil. 71 F4 11 10N 123 1 E
Ak Dağ, Antalya, Turkey 88 E3 36 30N 29 45 E
Ak Dağ, Sivas, Turkey 88 D7 39 40N 36 25 E
Akaba, Togo 101 D5 8 10N 1 2 E
Akabira, Japan 60 C11 43 33N 142 5 E
Akabli, Algeria 99 C5 26 49N 1 31 E
Akaishi-Dake, Japan 63 B10 35 27N 138 9 E
Akaishi-Sammyaku, Japan 63 B10 35 25N 138 10 E
Akaki Beseka, Ethiopia 95 F4 8 55N 38 45 E
Akala, Sudan 95 D4 15 39N 36 13 E
Akamas □, Cyprus 32 D11 35 3N 32 18 E
Akanthou, Cyprus 32 D12 35 22N 33 45 E
Akaroa, N.Z. 119 D7 43 49 S 172 59 E
Akaroa Harbour, N.Z. 119 D7 43 50 S 172 55 E
Akasha, Sudan 94 C3 21 10N 30 32 E
Akashi, Japan 62 C6 34 45N 134 58 E
Akbou, Algeria 99 A5 36 31N 4 31 E
Akbulak, Russia 54 F4 51 1N 55 37 E
Akçaabat, Turkey 89 C8 41 1N 39 34 E
Akçakoca, Turkey 88 C4 41 5N 31 8 E
Akchâr, Mauritania 98 D2 20 20N 14 28W
Akdağmadeni, Turkey 88 D6 39 39N 35 53 E
Akdala, Kazakhstan 55 A7 45 2N 74 35 E
Akechi, Japan 63 B9 35 18N 137 23 E
Akelamo, Indonesia 72 A3 1 35N 129 40 E
Akershus fylke □, Norway 14 E5 60 0N 11 10 E
Akeru →, India 82 F5 17 25N 80 5 E
Aketi, Zaïre 102 B4 2 38N 23 47 E
Akhaïa □, Greece 45 F3 38 5N 21 45 E
Akhalkalaki, Georgia 53 F10 41 27N 43 25 E
Akhaltsikhe, Georgia 53 F10 41 40N 43 0 E
Akharnaí, Greece 45 F5 38 5N 23 44 E
Akhelóös →, Greece 45 F3 38 36N 21 14 E
Akhendria, Greece 45 K7 34 58N 25 16 E
Akhéron →, Greece 44 E2 39 20N 20 29 E
Akhladhókambos, Greece 45 G4 37 31N 22 35 E
Akhmîm, Egypt 94 B3 26 31N 31 47 E
Akhnur, India 81 C6 32 52N 74 45 E
Akhtopol, Bulgaria 43 E12 42 6N 27 56 E
Akhtubinsk, Russia 53 B12 48 13N 46 7 E
Akhty, Russia 53 F12 41 30N 47 45 E
Akhtyrka, Ukraine 50 F9 50 25N 35 0 E
Aki, Japan 62 D5 33 30N 133 54 E
Aki-Nada, Japan 62 C4 34 5N 132 40 E
Akiéni, Gabon 102 C2 1 11 S 13 53 E
Akimiski I., Canada 128 B3 52 50N 81 30W
Akimovka, Ukraine 52 C6 46 44N 35 0 E
Akita, Japan 60 E10 39 45N 140 7 E
Akita □, Japan 60 E10 39 40N 140 30 E
Akjoujt, Mauritania 100 B2 19 45N 14 15W
Akka, Morocco 98 C3 29 22N 8 9W
Akkeshi, Japan 60 C12 43 2N 144 51 E
'Akko, Israel 91 C4 32 55N 35 4 E
Akkol, Kazakhstan 55 B5 43 36N 70 45 E
Akkol, Kazakhstan 56 E8 45 0N 75 39 E
Akköy, Turkey 45 G9 37 30N 27 18 E
Akkrum, Neths. 20 B7 53 3N 5 50 E
Aklampa, Benin 101 D5 8 15N 2 10 E
Aklan □, Phil. 71 F4 11 50N 122 30 E
Aklavik, Canada 126 B6 68 12N 135 0W
Akmolinsk = Tselinograd, Kazakhstan 56 D8 51 10N 71 30 E
Akmonte, Spain 37 H4 37 13N 6 38W
Akmuz, Kirghizia 55 C8 41 15N 76 10 E
Aknoul, Morocco 99 B4 34 40N 3 55W
Akō, Japan 62 C6 34 45N 134 24 E
Ako, Nigeria 101 C7 10 19N 10 48 E
Akobo →, Ethiopia 95 F3 7 48N 33 3 E
Akola, India 82 D3 20 42N 77 2 E
Akonolinga, Cameroon 101 E7 3 50N 12 18 E
Akordat, Eritrea 95 D4 15 30N 37 40 E
Akosombo Dam, Ghana 101 D5 6 20N 0 5 E
Akot, India 82 D3 21 10N 77 10 E
Akot, Sudan 95 F3 6 31N 30 9 E
Akpatok I., Canada 127 B13 60 25N 68 8W
Akranes, Iceland 12 D3 64 19N 22 5W
Akreïjit, Mauritania 100 B3 18 19N 9 11W
Akrítas Venétiko, Ákra, Greece 45 H3 36 43N 21 54 E
Akron, Colo., U.S.A. 138 E3 40 10N 103 13W
Akron, Ind., U.S.A. 141 C10 41 2N 86 1W
Akron, Ohio, U.S.A. 136 E3 41 5N 81 31W
Akrotiri, Cyprus 32 E11 34 36N 32 57 E
Akrotíri, Ákra, Greece 44 D7 40 26N 25 27 E
Akrotiri Bay, Cyprus 32 E12 34 35N 33 10 E
Aksai Chih, India 81 B8 35 15N 79 55 E
Aksaray, Turkey 88 D6 38 25N 34 2 E
Aksarka, Russia 56 C7 66 31N 67 50 E
Aksay, Kazakhstan 54 F3 51 11N 53 0 E
Akşehir, Turkey 88 D4 38 18N 31 30 E
Akşehir Gölü, Turkey 88 D4 38 30N 31 25 E
Aksenovo Zilovskoye, Russia 57 D12 53 20N 117 40 E
Akstafa, Azerbaijan 53 F11 41 7N 45 27 E
Aksu, China 64 B3 41 5N 80 10 E
Aksu →, Turkey 88 E4 36 41N 30 54 E
Aksuat, Ozero, Kazakhstan 54 F9 51 32N 64 34 E
Aksum, Ethiopia 95 E4 14 5N 38 40 E
Aktash, Russia 54 D3 55 2N 52 0 E
Aktash, Uzbekistan 55 D2 39 55N 65 55 E
Aktogay, Kazakhstan 55 A8 44 25N 76 44 E
Aktogay, Kazakhstan 56 E8 46 57N 79 40 E
Aktyubinsk, Kazakhstan 49 D10 50 17N 57 10 E
Aktyuz, Kirghizia 55 B8 42 54N 76 7 E
Aku, Nigeria 101 D6 6 40N 7 18 E
Akula, Zaïre 102 B4 2 22N 20 12 E
Akune, Japan 62 E2 32 1N 130 12 E
Akure, Nigeria 101 D6 7 15N 5 5 E
Akureyri, Iceland 12 D4 65 40N 18 6W
Akuseki-Shima, Japan 61 K4 29 27N 129 37 E
Akusha, Russia 53 E12 42 18N 47 30 E
Akwa-Ibom □, Nigeria 101 E6 4 30N 7 30 E
Akyab = Sittwe, Burma 78 E4 20 18N 92 45 E
Akyazı, Turkey 88 C4 40 40N 30 38 E
Akzhar, Kazakhstan 55 B5 43 8N 71 37 E
Al Abyār, Libya 96 B4 32 9N 20 29 E
Al 'Adan, Yemen 86 D4 12 45N 45 0 E
Al Aḥsā, Si. Arabia 85 E6 25 50N 49 0 E
Al Ajfar, Si. Arabia 84 E4 27 26N 43 0 E
Al Amādīyah, Iraq 84 B4 37 5N 43 30 E
Al Amārah, Iraq 84 D5 31 55N 47 15 E
Al 'Aqabah, Jordan 91 F4 29 31N 35 0 E
Al' Aqīq, Si. Arabia 86 B3 20 39N 41 25 E
Al Arak, Syria 84 C3 34 38N 38 35 E
Al 'Aramah, Si. Arabia 84 E5 25 30N 46 0 E
Al 'Ariḍah, Si. Arabia 86 C3 17 3N 43 5 E
Al Arṭāwīyah, Si. Arabia 84 E5 26 31N 45 20 E
Al Ashkhara, Oman 87 B7 21 50N 59 30 E
Al 'Āṣimah □, Jordan 91 D5 31 40N 36 30 E
Al' Assāfīyah, Si. Arabia 84 D3 28 17N 38 59 E
Al 'Ayn, Oman 85 E7 24 15N 55 45 E
Al 'Ayn, Si. Arabia 84 E3 25 4N 38 6 E
Al A'ẓamīyah, Iraq 84 C5 33 22N 44 22 E
Al 'Azīzīyah, Iraq 84 C5 32 54N 45 4 E
Al 'Azīzīyah, Libya 96 B2 32 30N 13 1 E
Al Bāb, Syria 84 B3 36 23N 37 29 E
Al Bad', Si. Arabia 84 D2 28 28N 35 1 E
Al Bādī, Iraq 84 C4 35 56N 41 32 E
Al Badī', Si. Arabia 86 B4 22 0N 46 35 E
Al Baḥrah, Kuwait 84 D5 29 40N 47 52 E
Al Balqā' □, Jordan 91 C4 32 5N 35 45 E
Al Barkāt, Libya 96 D2 24 56N 10 14 E
Al Bārūk, J., Lebanon 91 B4 33 39N 35 40 E
Al Başrah, Iraq 84 D5 30 30N 47 50 E
Al Baṭḥā, Iraq 84 D5 31 6N 45 53 E
Al Batrūn, Lebanon 91 A4 34 15N 35 40 E
Al Bayāḍ, Si. Arabia 86 B4 22 0N 47 0 E
Al Bayḍā', Yemen 86 D4 14 5N 45 42 E
Al Bayḍā □, Libya 96 B4 32 0N 21 30 E
Al Bi'ār, Si. Arabia 86 B2 22 39N 39 40 E
Al Bi'r, Si. Arabia 84 D3 28 51N 36 16 E
Al Birk, Si. Arabia 86 C3 18 13N 41 33 E
Al Bu'ayrāt, Libya 96 B3 31 24N 15 44 E
Al Burayj, Syria 91 A5 34 15N 36 46 E
Al Fallūjah, Iraq 84 C4 33 20N 43 55 E
Al Fatk, Yemen 87 C6 16 31N 52 41 E
Al Fāw, Iraq 85 D6 30 0N 48 30 E
Al Faydamī, Yemen 87 C6 16 25N 52 26 E
Al Fujayrah, U.A.E. 85 E8 25 7N 56 18 E
Al Ghadaf, W. →, Jordan 91 D5 31 26N 36 43 E
Al Ghammās, Iraq 84 D5 31 45N 44 37 E
Al Gharīb, Libya 96 B4 32 35N 21 11 E
Al Ghayḍah, Yemen 87 C6 16 13N 52 11 E
Al Ghayḍah, Yemen 87 D5 14 55N 50 0 E
Al Ghayl, Yemen 87 D5 15 30N 50 54 E
Al Hābah, Si. Arabia 84 E5 27 10N 47 0 E
Al Ḥadd, Oman 87 B7 22 32N 59 48 E
Al Ḥaddār, Si. Arabia 86 B4 21 58N 45 57 E
Al Ḥadīthah, Iraq 84 C4 34 0N 41 13 E
Al Ḥadīthah, Si. Arabia 84 D3 31 28N 37 8 E
Al Hājānah, Syria 91 B5 33 20N 36 33 E
Al Hajarayn, Yemen 87 D5 15 29N 48 20 E
Al Hallānīyah, Oman 87 C7 17 30N 56 1 E
Al Hāmad, Si. Arabia 84 D3 31 30N 39 30 E
Al Ḥamar, Si. Arabia 86 B4 22 26N 46 12 E
Al Hamdānīyah, Syria 84 C3 35 25N 36 50 E
Al Hamidīyah, Syria 91 A4 34 42N 35 57 E
Al Hammādah al Ḥamrā', Libya 96 C2 29 30N 12 0 E
Al Ḥammār, Iraq 84 D5 30 57N 46 51 E
Al Ḥamrā', Si. Arabia 86 A2 24 2N 38 55 E
Al Ḥarīq, Si. Arabia 86 B4 23 29N 46 27 E
Al Ḥarīr, W. →, Syria 91 C4 32 44N 35 59 E
Al Harūj al Aswad, Libya 96 C3 27 0N 17 10 E
Al Ḥasā, W. →, Jordan 91 D4 31 4N 35 29 E
Al Ḥasakah, Syria 84 B4 36 35N 40 45 E
Al Hāsikīyah, Oman 87 C6 17 28N 55 36 E
Al Ḥasy, Yemen 87 D5 14 3N 48 40 E
Al Ḥawrah, Yemen 86 D4 13 50N 47 35 E
Al Ḥawṭah, Yemen 86 D4 14 23N 47 24 E
Al Ḥawṭah □, Si. Arabia 86 B4 23 30N 47 0 E
Al Haydān, W. →, Jordan 91 D4 31 29N 35 34 E
Al Ḥayy, Iraq 84 C5 32 5N 46 5 E
Al Ḥijāz, Si. Arabia 86 A2 26 0N 37 30 E
Al Ḥillah, Iraq 84 C5 32 30N 44 25 E
Al Ḥillah, Si. Arabia 86 B4 23 35N 46 50 E
Al Hirmil, Lebanon 91 A5 34 26N 36 24 E
Al Hoceïma, Morocco 98 A4 35 8N 3 58W
Al Ḥudaydah, Yemen 86 D3 14 50N 43 0 E
Al Ḥufrah, Awbārī, Libya 96 C2 25 32N 14 1 E
Al Ḥufrah, Misrātah, Libya 96 C3 29 5N 18 3 E
Al Hufūf, Si. Arabia 85 E6 25 25N 49 45 E
Al Ḥulwah, Si. Arabia 86 B4 23 24N 46 48 E
Al Ḥumaydah, Si. Arabia 84 D2 29 14N 34 56 E
Al Ḥunayy, Si. Arabia 85 E6 25 58N 48 45 E
Al Ḥurayḍah, Yemen 87 D5 15 36N 48 12 E
Al Husayyāt, Libya 96 B4 30 24N 20 37 E
Al Hūwah, Si. Arabia 86 B4 23 2N 45 48 E
Al Ḥuwaymī, Yemen 86 D4 13 23N 44 28 E
Al Irq, Libya 96 C4 29 5N 21 35 E
Al 'Irqah, Yemen 86 D4 13 39N 47 22 E
Al Īsāwīyah, Si. Arabia 84 D3 30 43N 37 59 E
Al Ittihad = Madīnat ash Sha'b, Yemen 86 D4 12 50N 45 0 E
Al Jabal al Akhḍar, Libya 96 B4 32 0N 21 30 E
Al Jafr, Jordan 91 E5 30 18N 36 14 E
Al Jaghbūb, Libya 96 C4 29 42N 24 38 E
Al Jahrah, Kuwait 84 D5 29 25N 47 40 E
Al Jalāmīd, Si. Arabia 84 D3 31 20N 39 45 E
Al Jamalīyah, Qatar 85 E6 25 37N 51 5 E
Al Janūb □, Lebanon 91 B4 33 20N 35 20 E
Al Jawf, Libya 96 D4 24 10N 23 24 E
Al Jawf, Si. Arabia 84 D3 29 55N 39 40 E
Al Jazirah, Iraq 84 C5 33 30N 44 0 E
Al Jazirah, Libya 96 C4 26 10N 21 20 E
Al Jithāmīyah, Si. Arabia 84 E4 27 41N 41 43 E
Al Jubayl, Si. Arabia 85 E6 27 0N 49 50 E
Al Jubaylah, Si. Arabia 84 E5 24 55N 46 25 E
Al Jubb, Si. Arabia 84 E4 27 11N 42 17 E
Al Jumūm, Si. Arabia 86 B2 21 37N 39 42 E
Al Junaynah, Sudan 97 F4 13 27N 22 45 E
Al Kaba'ish, Iraq 84 D5 30 58N 47 0 E
Al Kāmil, Oman 87 B7 22 13N 59 12 E
Al Karak, Jordan 91 D4 31 11N 35 42 E
Al Karak □, Jordan 91 E5 31 0N 36 0 E
Al Kāzim Tyah, Iraq 84 C5 33 22N 44 12 E
Al Khābūra, Oman 87 B7 23 57N 57 5 E

Ampasindava, Helodranon' 165

Aliquippa, *U.S.A.* **136 F4** 40 37N 80 15W
Aliste →, *Spain* **36 D5** 41 34N 5 58W
Alitus, *Lithuania* **50 D4** 54 24N 24 3 E
Alivérion, *Greece* **45 F6** 38 24N 24 2 E
Aliwal North, *S. Africa* **104 E4** 30 45 S 26 45 E
Alix, *Canada* **130 C6** 52 24N 113 11W
Aljezur, *Portugal* **37 H2** 37 18N 8 49W
Aljustrel, *Portugal* **37 H2** 37 55N 8 10W
Alkamari, *Niger* **97 F2** 13 27N 11 10 E
Alken, *Belgium* **21 G6** 50 53N 5 18 E
Alkmaar, *Neths.* **20 C5** 52 37N 4 45 E
All American Canal, *U.S.A.* **143 K6** 32 45N 115 15W
Allacapan, *Phil.* **70 B3** 18 15N 121 35 E
Allada, *Benin* **101 D5** 6 41N 2 9 E
Allah Dad, *Pakistan* **80 G2** 25 38N 67 34 E
Allahabad, *India* **81 G9** 25 25N 81 58 E
Allakh-Yun, *Russia* **57 C14** 60 50N 137 5 E
Allal Tazi, *Morocco* **98 B3** 34 30N 6 20W
Allan, *Canada* **131 C7** 51 53N 106 4W
Allanche, *France* **24 C6** 45 14N 2 57 E
Allanmyo, *Burma* **78 F5** 19 30N 95 17 E
Allanridge, *S. Africa* **104 D4** 27 45 S 26 40 E
Allansford, *Australia* **116 E5** 38 26 S 142 39 E
Allanton, *N.Z.* **119 F5** 45 55 S 170 15 E
Allanwater, *Canada* **128 B1** 50 14N 90 10W
Allaqi, Wadi →, *Egypt* **94 C3** 23 7N 32 47 E
Allariz, *Spain* **36 C3** 42 11N 7 50W
Allassac, *France* **24 C5** 45 15N 1 29 E
Alle, *Belgium* **21 J5** 49 51N 4 58 E
Allegan, *U.S.A.* **141 B11** 42 32N 85 51W
Allegany, *U.S.A.* **136 D6** 42 6N 78 30W
Allegheny →, *U.S.A.* **136 F5** 40 27N 80 1W
Allegheny Plateau, *U.S.A.* **134 G6** 38 0N 80 0W
Allegheny Reservoir, *U.S.A.* **136 E6** 41 50N 79 0W
Allègre, *France* **24 C7** 45 12N 3 41 E
Allen, *Argentina* **160 A3** 38 58 S 67 50W
Allen, *Phil.* **70 E5** 12 30N 124 17 E
Allen, Bog of, *Ireland* **19 C4** 53 15N 7 0W
Allen, L., *Ireland* **19 B3** 54 12N 8 5W
Allende, *Mexico* **146 B4** 28 20N 100 50W
Allentown, *U.S.A.* **137 F9** 40 37N 75 29W
Allentsteig, *Austria* **30 C8** 48 41N 15 20 E
Alleppey, *India* **83 K3** 9 30N 76 28 E
Aller →, *Germany* **26 C5** 52 57N 9 10 E
Alleur, *Belgium* **21 G7** 50 39N 5 31 E
Allevard, *France* **25 C10** 45 24N 6 5 E
Alliance, *Surinam* **153 B7** 5 50N 54 50W
Alliance, *Nebr., U.S.A.* **138 D3** 42 6N 102 52W
Alliance, *Ohio, U.S.A.* **136 F3** 40 55N 81 6W
Allier □, *France* **24 B6** 46 25N 2 40 E
Allier →, *France* **23 F10** 46 57N 3 4 E
Allingåbro, *Denmark* **15 H4** 56 28N 10 20 E
Allison, *U.S.A.* **140 B4** 42 45N 92 48W
Alliston, *Canada* **128 D4** 44 9N 79 52W
Alloa, *U.K.* **18 E5** 56 7N 3 49W
Allora, *Australia* **115 D5** 28 2 S 152 0 E
Allos, *France* **25 D10** 44 15N 6 38 E
Alluitsup Paa = Sydprøven, *Greenland* **6 C5** 60 30N 45 35W
Alma, *Canada* **129 C5** 48 35N 71 40W
Alma, *Ga., U.S.A.* **135 K4** 31 33N 82 28W
Alma, *Kans., U.S.A.* **138 F6** 39 1N 96 17W
Alma, *Mich., U.S.A.* **134 D3** 43 23N 84 39W
Alma, *Nebr., U.S.A.* **138 E5** 40 6N 99 22W
Alma, *Wis., U.S.A.* **138 C9** 44 20N 91 55W
Alma Ata, *Kazakhstan* **55 B8** 43 15N 76 57 E
Almada, *Portugal* **37 G1** 38 40N 9 9W
Almaden, *Australia* **114 B3** 17 22 S 144 40 E
Almadén, *Spain* **37 G6** 38 49N 4 52W
Almagro, *Spain* **37 G7** 38 50N 3 45W
Almagro I., *Phil.* **71 F5** 11 56N 124 18 E
Almalyk, *Uzbekistan* **55 C4** 40 50N 69 35 E
Almanor, L., *U.S.A.* **142 F3** 40 14N 121 9W
Almansa, *Spain* **35 G3** 38 51N 1 5W
Almanza, *Spain* **36 C5** 42 39N 5 3W
Almanzor, Pico de, *Spain* **36 E5** 40 15N 5 18W
Almanzora →, *Spain* **35 H3** 37 14N 1 46W
Almas, *Brazil* **155 D2** 11 33 S 47 9W
Almaş, Mţii., *Romania* **46 E3** 44 49N 22 12 E
Almaty = Alma Ata, *Kazakhstan* **55 B8** 43 15N 76 57 E
Almazán, *Spain* **34 D2** 41 30N 2 30W
Almazora, *Spain* **34 F4** 39 57N 0 3W
Almeirim, *Brazil* **153 D7** 1 30 S 52 34W
Almeirim, *Portugal* **37 F2** 39 12N 8 37W
Almelo, *Neths.* **20 D9** 52 22N 6 42 E
Almenar, *Spain* **34 D2** 41 43N 2 12W
Almenara, *Brazil* **155 E3** 16 11 S 40 42W
Almenara, *Spain* **34 F4** 39 46N 0 14W
Almenara, Sierra de, *Spain* **35 H3** 37 34N 1 32W
Almendralejo, *Spain* **37 G4** 38 41N 6 26W
Almería, *Spain* **35 J2** 36 52N 2 27W
Almería □, *Spain* **35 H2** 37 20N 2 20W
Almería, G. de, *Spain* **35 J2** 36 41N 2 28W
Almetyevsk, *Russia* **54 D3** 54 53N 52 20 E
Almirante, *Panama* **148 E3** 9 10N 82 30W
Almirante Montt, G., *Chile* **160 D2** 51 52 S 72 50W
Almirópótamos, *Greece* **45 F6** 38 16N 24 11 E
Almirós, *Greece* **45 E4** 39 11N 22 45 E
Almiroú, Kólpos, *Greece* **32 D6** 35 23N 24 20 E
Almodôvar, *Portugal* **37 H2** 37 31N 8 2W
Almodóvar del Campo, *Spain* **37 G6** 38 43N 4 10W
Almogia, *Spain* **37 J6** 36 50N 4 32W
Almonaster la Real, *Spain* **37 H4** 37 52N 6 48W
Almont, *U.S.A.* **136 D1** 42 55N 83 3W
Almonte, *Canada* **137 A8** 45 14N 76 12W
Almonte →, *Spain* **37 F4** 39 41N 6 28W
Almora, *India* **81 E8** 29 38N 79 40 E
Almoradi, *Spain* **35 G4** 38 7N 0 46W
Almorox, *Spain* **36 E6** 40 14N 4 24W
Almoustarat, *Mali* **101 B5** 17 35N 0 8 E
Almuñécar, *Spain* **37 J7** 36 43N 3 41W
Alnif, *Morocco* **98 B3** 31 10N 5 8W
Alnwick, *U.K.* **16 B6** 55 25N 1 42W
Aloi, *Uganda* **106 B3** 2 16N 33 10 E
Alon, *Burma* **78 D5** 22 12N 95 5 E
Alor, *Indonesia* **72 C2** 8 15 S 124 30 E
Alor Setar, *Malaysia* **77 J3** 6 7N 100 22 E
Alora, *Spain* **37 J6** 36 49N 4 46W
Alosno, *Spain* **37 H3** 37 33N 7 7W
Alotau, *Papua N. G.* **120 F6** 10 16 S 150 30 E
Alougoum, *Morocco* **98 B3** 30 17N 6 56W
Aloysius, Mt., *Australia* **113 E4** 26 0 S 128 38 E
Alpaugh, *U.S.A.* **144 K7** 35 53N 119 29W
Alpedrinha, *Portugal* **36 E3** 40 6N 7 27W
Alpena, *U.S.A.* **134 C4** 45 4N 83 27W
Alpercatas →, *Brazil* **154 C3** 6 2 S 44 19W
Alpes-de-Haute-Provence □, *France* **25 D10** 44 8N 6 10 E
Alpes-Maritimes □, *France* **25 E11** 43 55N 7 10 E
Alpha, *Australia* **114 C4** 23 39 S 146 37 E
Alpha, *U.S.A.* **140 C6** 41 12N 90 23W
Alphen, *Neths.* **21 F5** 51 29N 4 58 E
Alphen aan den Rijn, *Neths.* **20 D5** 52 7N 4 40 E
Alphonse, *Seychelles* **109 E4** 7 0 S 52 45 E
Alpiarça, *Portugal* **37 F2** 39 15N 8 35W
Alpine, *Ariz., U.S.A.* **143 K9** 33 51N 109 9W
Alpine, *Calif., U.S.A.* **145 N10** 32 50N 116 46W
Alpine, *Tex., U.S.A.* **139 K3** 30 22N 103 40W
Alpnach, *Switz.* **29 C6** 46 57N 8 17 E
Alps, *Europe* **10 F7** 46 30N 9 30 E
Alpu, *Turkey* **88 D4** 39 46N 30 58 E
Alrø, *Denmark* **15 J4** 55 52N 10 5 E
Alroy Downs, *Australia* **114 B2** 19 20 S 136 5 E
Alsace, *France* **23 D14** 48 15N 7 25 E
Alsask, *Canada* **131 C7** 51 21N 109 59W
Alsásua, *Spain* **34 C2** 42 54N 2 10W
Alsen, *Sweden* **14 A7** 63 23N 13 56 E
Alsfeld, *Germany* **26 E5** 50 44N 9 19 E
Alsónémedi, *Hungary* **31 D12** 47 20N 19 15 E
Alsten, *Norway* **12 D12** 65 58N 12 40 E
Alta, *Norway* **12 B17** 69 57N 23 10 E
Alta, Sierra, *Spain* **34 E3** 40 31N 1 30W
Alta Gracia, *Argentina* **158 C3** 31 40 S 64 30W
Alta Lake, *Canada* **130 C4** 50 10N 123 0W
Alta Sierra, *U.S.A.* **145 K8** 35 42N 118 33W
Altaelva →, *Norway* **12 B17** 69 46N 23 45 E
Altafjorden, *Norway* **12 A17** 70 5N 23 5 E
Altagracia, *Venezuela* **152 A3** 10 45N 71 30W
Altagracia de Orituco, *Venezuela* **152 B4** 9 52N 66 23W
Altai = Aerhtai Shan, *Mongolia* **64 B4** 46 40N 92 45 E
Altamachi →, *Bolivia* **156 D4** 16 8 S 66 50W
Altamaha →, *U.S.A.* **135 K5** 31 20N 81 20W
Altamira, *Brazil* **153 D7** 3 12 S 52 10W
Altamira, *Chile* **158 B2** 25 47 S 69 51W
Altamira, *Colombia* **152 C2** 2 3N 75 47W
Altamira, *Mexico* **147 C5** 22 24N 97 55W
Altamira, Cuevas de, *Spain* **36 B6** 43 20N 4 5W
Altamont, *Ill., U.S.A.* **141 E8** 39 4N 88 45W
Altamont, *N.Y., U.S.A.* **137 D10** 42 43N 74 3W
Altamura, *Italy* **41 B9** 40 50N 16 33 E
Altanbulag, *Mongolia* **64 A5** 50 16N 106 30 E
Altar, *Mexico* **146 A2** 30 40N 111 50W
Altata, *Mexico* **146 C3** 24 30N 108 0W
Altavas, *Phil.* **71 F4** 11 32N 122 29 E
Altavista, *U.S.A.* **134 G6** 37 6N 79 17W
Altay, *China* **64 B3** 47 48N 88 10 E
Altdorf, *Switz.* **29 C7** 46 52N 8 36 E
Alte Mellum, *Germany* **26 B4** 53 45N 8 6 E
Altea, *Spain* **35 G4** 38 38N 0 2W
Altenberg, *Germany* **26 E9** 50 46N 13 47 E
Altenbruch, *Germany* **26 B4** 53 48N 8 44 E
Altenburg, *Germany* **26 E8** 50 59N 12 28 E
Altenkirchen, *Mecklenburg-Vorpommern, Germany* **26 A9** 54 38N 13 20 E
Altenkirchen, *Rhld-Pfz., Germany* **26 E3** 50 41N 7 38 E
Altenmarkt, *Austria* **30 D7** 47 43N 14 39 E
Altenteptow, *Germany* **26 B9** 53 42N 13 15 E
Alter do Chão, *Portugal* **37 F3** 39 12N 7 40W
Altıntaş, *Turkey* **88 D4** 39 4N 30 10 E
Altiplano, *Bolivia* **156 D4** 17 0 S 68 0W
Altkirch, *France* **23 E14** 47 37N 7 15 E
Altmühl →, *Germany* **27 G7** 48 54N 11 54 E
Alto Adige = Trentino-Alto Adige □, *Italy* **38 B8** 46 30N 11 0 E
Alto Araguaia, *Brazil* **157 D7** 17 15 S 53 20W
Alto Cuchumatanes = Cuchumatanes, Sierra de los, *Guatemala* **148 C1** 15 35N 91 25W
Alto Cuito, *Angola* **103 E3** 13 27 S 18 49 E
Alto del Inca, *Chile* **158 A2** 24 10 S 68 10W
Alto Garças, *Brazil* **157 D7** 16 56 S 53 32W
Alto Iriri →, *Brazil* **157 B7** 8 50 S 53 25W
Alto Ligonha, *Mozam.* **107 F4** 15 30 S 38 11 E
Alto Molocue, *Mozam.* **107 F4** 15 50 S 37 35 E
Alto Paraguai, *Brazil* **157 C6** 14 30 S 56 31W
Alto Paraguay □, *Paraguay* **158 A4** 21 0 S 58 30W
Alto Paraná □, *Paraguay* **159 B5** 25 30 S 54 50W
Alto Parnaíba, *Brazil* **154 C2** 9 6 S 45 57W
Alto Purús →, *Peru* **156 B3** 9 12 S 70 28W
Alto Río Senguerr, *Argentina* **160 C2** 45 2 S 70 50W
Alto Santo, *Brazil* **154 C4** 5 31 S 38 15W
Alto Sucuriú, *Brazil* **157 D7** 19 19 S 52 47W
Alto Turi, *Brazil* **154 B2** 2 54 S 45 38W
Alton, *Canada* **136 C4** 43 54N 80 5W
Alton, *U.S.A.* **140 F6** 38 53N 90 11W
Alton Downs, *Australia* **115 D2** 26 7 S 138 57 E
Altoona, *Iowa, U.S.A.* **140 C3** 41 39N 93 28W
Altoona, *Pa., U.S.A.* **136 F6** 40 31N 78 24W
Altopáscio, *Italy* **38 E7** 43 50N 10 40 E
Altos, *Brazil* **154 C3** 5 3 S 42 28W
Altötting, *Germany* **27 G8** 48 14N 12 41 E
Altstätten, *Switz.* **29 B9** 47 22N 9 33 E
Altūn Kūprī, *Iraq* **84 C5** 35 45N 44 9 E
Altun Shan, *China* **64 C3** 38 30N 88 0 E
Alturas, *U.S.A.* **142 F3** 41 29N 120 32W
Altus, *U.S.A.* **139 H5** 34 38N 99 20W
Alubijid, *Phil.* **71 G5** 8 35N 124 29 E
Alucra, *Turkey* **53 F8** 40 22N 38 47 E
Alūksne, *Latvia* **50 C5** 57 24N 27 3 E
Alùla, *Somali Rep.* **90 E5** 11 50N 50 45 E
Alunite, *U.S.A.* **145 K12** 35 59N 114 55W
Alupka, *Ukraine* **52 D6** 44 23N 34 2 E
Alur Gajah, *Malaysia* **74 B2** 2 23N 102 13 E
Alushta, *Ukraine* **52 D6** 44 40N 34 25 E
Alusi, *Indonesia* **73 C4** 7 35 S 131 40 E
Alustante, *Spain* **34 E3** 40 36N 1 40W
Al'Uzayr, *Iraq* **84 D5** 31 19N 47 25 E
Alva, *U.S.A.* **139 G5** 36 48N 98 40W
Alvaiázere, *Portugal* **36 F2** 39 49N 8 23W
Älvängen, *Sweden* **15 G6** 57 58N 12 8 E
Alvarado, *Mexico* **147 D5** 18 40N 95 50W
Alvarado, *U.S.A.* **139 J6** 32 24N 97 13W
Alvarães, *Brazil* **153 D5** 3 12 S 64 50W
Alvaro Obregón, Presa, *Mexico* **146 B3** 27 55N 109 52W
Alvdal, *Norway* **14 B4** 62 6N 10 37 E
Alvear, *Argentina* **158 B4** 29 5 S 56 30W
Alverca, *Portugal* **37 G1** 38 56N 9 1W
Alveringen, *Belgium* **21 F1** 51 1N 2 43 E
Alvesta, *Sweden* **13 H13** 56 54N 14 35 E
Alvie, *Australia* **116 E5** 38 14 S 143 30 E
Alvin, *U.S.A.* **139 L7** 29 26N 95 15W
Alvinston, *Canada* **136 D3** 42 49N 81 52W
Alvito, *Portugal* **37 G3** 38 15N 8 0W
Älvkarleby, *Sweden* **13 F14** 60 34N 17 26 E
Älvros, *Sweden* **14 B8** 62 3N 14 38 E
Älvsborgs län □, *Sweden* **15 F6** 58 30N 12 30 E
Älvsbyn, *Sweden* **12 D16** 65 40N 21 0 E
Älvsered, *Sweden* **15 G6** 57 14N 12 51 E
Alwar, *India* **80 F7** 27 38N 76 34 E
Alwaye, *India* **83 J3** 10 8N 76 24 E
Alxa Zuoqi, *China* **66 E3** 38 50N 105 40 E
Alyaskitovyy, *Russia* **57 C15** 64 45N 141 30 E
Alyata, *Azerbaijan* **53 G13** 39 58N 49 25 E
Alyth, *U.K.* **18 E5** 56 38N 3 15W
Alzada, *U.S.A.* **138 C2** 45 2N 104 25W
Alzano Lombardo, *Italy* **38 C6** 45 44N 9 43 E
Alzette →, *Lux.* **21 J8** 49 45N 6 6 E
Alzey, *Germany* **27 F4** 49 48N 8 4 E
Am Dam, *Chad* **97 F4** 12 40N 20 35 E
Am Géréda, *Chad* **97 F4** 12 53N 21 14 E
Am-Timan, *Chad* **97 F4** 11 0N 20 10 E
Amacuro □, *Venezuela* **153 B5** 8 50N 61 5W
Amadeus, L., *Australia* **113 D5** 24 54 S 131 0 E
Amâdi, *Sudan* **95 F3** 5 29N 30 25 E
Amadi, *Zaïre* **106 B2** 3 40N 26 40 E
Amadjuak, *Canada* **127 B12** 64 0N 72 39W
Amadjuak L., *Canada* **127 B12** 65 0N 71 8W
Amadora, *Portugal* **37 G1** 38 45N 9 13W
Amagasaki, *Japan* **63 C7** 34 42N 135 20 E
Amager, *Denmark* **15 J6** 55 37N 12 35 E
Amagi, *Japan* **62 D2** 33 25N 130 39 E
Amahai, *Indonesia* **73 B3** 3 20 S 128 55 E
Amaimon, *Papua N. G.* **120 C3** 5 12 S 145 30 E
Amakusa-Nada, *Japan* **62 E2** 32 35N 130 5 E
Amakusa-Shotō, *Japan* **62 E2** 32 15N 130 10 E
Amalapuram, *India* **83 F5** 16 35N 81 55 E
Amalfi, *Colombia* **152 B2** 6 55N 75 4W
Amalfi, *Italy* **41 B7** 40 39N 14 34 E
Amaliás, *Greece* **45 G3** 37 47N 21 22 E
Amalner, *India* **82 D2** 21 5N 75 5 E
Amambaí, *Brazil* **159 A4** 23 5 S 55 13W
Amambaí →, *Brazil* **159 A5** 23 22 S 53 56W
Amambay □, *Paraguay* **159 A4** 23 0 S 56 0W
Amambay, Cordillera de, *S. Amer.* **159 A4** 23 0 S 55 45W
Amami-Guntō, *Japan* **61 L4** 27 16N 129 21 E
Amami-Ō-Shima, *Japan* **61 L4** 28 0N 129 0 E
Amana →, *Venezuela* **153 B5** 9 45N 62 39W
Amanã, L., *Brazil* **153 D5** 2 35 S 64 40W
Amanab, *Papua N. G.* **120 B1** 3 40 S 141 14 E
Amanda Park, *U.S.A.* **144 C3** 47 28N 123 55W
Amándola, *Italy* **39 F10** 42 59N 13 21 E
Amangeldy, *Kazakhstan* **56 D7** 50 10N 65 10 E
Amantea, *Italy* **41 C9** 39 8N 16 3 E
Amapá, *Brazil* **153 C7** 2 5N 50 50W
Amapá □, *Brazil* **153 C7** 1 40N 52 0W
Amapari, *Brazil* **153 C7** 0 37N 51 39W
Amara, *Sudan* **95 E3** 10 25N 34 10 E
Amarante, *Brazil* **154 C3** 6 14 S 42 50W
Amarante, *Portugal* **36 D2** 41 16N 8 5W
Amarante do Maranhão, *Brazil* **154 C2** 5 36 S 46 45W
Amaranth, *Canada* **131 C9** 50 36N 98 43W
Amarapura, *Burma* **78 E6** 21 54N 96 3 E
Amaravati →, *India* **83 J4** 11 0N 78 15 E
Amareleja, *Portugal* **37 G3** 38 12N 7 13W
Amargosa, *Brazil* **155 D4** 13 2 S 39 36W
Amargosa →, *U.S.A.* **145 J10** 36 14N 116 51W
Amargosa Range, *U.S.A.* **145 J10** 36 20N 116 45W
Amári, *Greece* **32 D6** 35 13N 24 40 E
Amarillo, *U.S.A.* **139 H4** 35 13N 101 50W
Amarnath, *India* **82 E1** 19 12N 73 22 E
Amaro, Mt., *Italy* **39 F11** 42 5N 14 6 E
Amaro Leite, *Brazil* **155 D2** 13 58 S 49 9W
Amarpur, *India* **81 G12** 25 5N 87 0 E
Amasra, *Turkey* **88 C5** 41 45N 32 23 E
Amassama, *Nigeria* **101 D6** 5 1N 6 2 E
Amasya, *Turkey* **88 C6** 40 40N 35 50 E
Amasya □, *Turkey* **88 C6** 40 40N 35 50 E
Amataurá, *Brazil* **152 D4** 3 29 S 68 6W
Amatikulu, *S. Africa* **105 D5** 29 3 S 31 33 E
Amatitlán, *Guatemala* **148 D1** 14 29N 90 38W
Amatrice, *Italy* **39 F10** 42 38N 13 16 E
Amay, *Belgium* **21 G6** 50 33N 5 19 E
Amazon = Amazonas →, *S. Amer.* **153 D7** 0 5 S 50 0W
Amazonas □, *Brazil* **157 B5** 5 0 S 65 0W
Amazonas □, *Peru* **156 B2** 5 0 S 78 0W
Amazonas □, *Venezuela* **152 C4** 3 30N 66 0W
Amazonas →, *S. Amer.* **153 D7** 0 5 S 50 0W
Ambad, *India* **82 E2** 19 38N 75 50 E
Ambahakily, *Madag.* **105 C7** 21 36 S 43 41 E
Ambala, *India* **80 D7** 30 23N 76 56 E
Ambalangoda, *Sri Lanka* **83 L5** 6 15N 80 5 E
Ambalapulai, *India* **83 K3** 9 25N 76 25 E
Ambalavao, *Madag.* **105 C8** 21 50 S 46 56 E
Ambalindum, *Australia* **114 C2** 23 23 S 135 0 E
Ambam, *Cameroon* **102 B2** 2 20N 11 15 E
Ambanja, *Madag.* **105 A8** 13 40 S 48 27 E
Ambarchik, *Russia* **57 C17** 69 40N 162 20 E
Ambarijeby, *Madag.* **105 A8** 14 56 S 47 41 E
Ambaro, Helodranon', *Madag.* **105 A8** 13 23 S 48 38 E
Ambartsevo, *Russia* **56 D9** 57 30N 83 52 E
Ambasamudram, *India* **83 K3** 8 43N 77 25 E
Ambato, *Ecuador* **152 D2** 1 5 S 78 42W
Ambato, Sierra de, *Argentina* **158 B2** 28 25 S 66 10W
Ambato Boeny, *Madag.* **105 B8** 16 28 S 46 43 E
Ambatofinandrahana, *Madag.* **105 C8** 20 33 S 46 48 E
Ambatolampy, *Madag.* **105 B8** 19 20 S 47 35 E
Ambatondrazaka, *Madag.* **105 B8** 17 55 S 48 28 E
Ambatosoratra, *Madag.* **105 B8** 17 37 S 48 31 E
Ambenja, *Madag.* **105 B8** 15 17 S 46 58 E
Amberg, *Germany* **27 F7** 49 25N 11 52 E
Ambergris Cay, *Belize* **147 D7** 18 0N 88 0W
Ambérieu-en-Bugey, *France* **25 C9** 45 57N 5 20 E
Amberley, *N.Z.* **119 D7** 43 9 S 172 44 E
Ambert, *France* **24 C7** 45 33N 3 44 E
Ambidédi, *Mali* **100 C2** 14 35N 11 47W
Ambikapur, *India* **81 H10** 23 15N 83 15 E
Ambikol, *Sudan* **94 C3** 21 20N 30 50 E
Ambilobé, *Madag.* **105 A8** 13 10 S 49 3 E
Ambinanindrano, *Madag.* **105 C8** 20 5 S 48 23 E
Ambjörnarp, *Sweden* **15 G7** 57 25N 13 17 E
Ambleside, *U.K.* **16 C5** 54 26N 2 58W
Amblève, *Belgium* **21 H8** 50 21N 6 10 E
Amblève →, *Belgium* **21 H7** 50 25N 5 45 E
Ambo, *Ethiopia* **95 E4** 12 20N 37 30 E
Ambo, *Peru* **156 C2** 10 5 S 76 10W
Ambodifototra, *Madag.* **105 B8** 16 59 S 49 52 E
Ambodilazana, *Madag.* **105 B8** 18 6 S 49 10 E
Ambohimahasoa, *Madag.* **105 C8** 21 7 S 47 13 E
Ambohimanga, *Madag.* **105 C8** 20 52 S 47 36 E
Ambohitra, *Madag.* **105 A8** 12 30 S 49 10 E
Ambon, *Indonesia* **72 B3** 3 43 S 128 12 E
Ambon, *Indonesia* **72 B3** 3 35 S 128 20 E
Amboseli L., *Kenya* **106 C4** 2 40 S 37 10 E
Ambositra, *Madag.* **105 C8** 20 31 S 47 25 E
Ambovombé, *Madag.* **105 D8** 25 11 S 46 5 E
Amboy, *Calif., U.S.A.* **145 L11** 34 33N 115 45W
Amboy, *Ill., U.S.A.* **140 C7** 41 44N 89 20W
Ambridge, *U.S.A.* **136 F4** 40 36N 80 14W
Ambriz, *Angola* **103 D2** 7 48 S 13 8 E
Ambrym, *Vanuatu* **121 F6** 16 15 S 168 10 E
Ambunti, *Papua N. G.* **120 C2** 4 13 S 142 52 E
Ambur, *India* **83 H4** 12 48N 78 43 E
Amby, *Australia* **115 D4** 26 30 S 148 11 E
Amchitka I., *U.S.A.* **126 C1** 51 32N 179 0 E
Amderma, *Russia* **56 C7** 69 45N 61 30 E
Ameca, *Mexico* **146 C4** 20 30N 104 0W
Ameca →, *Mexico* **146 C3** 20 40N 105 15W
Amecameca, *Mexico* **147 D5** 19 7N 98 46W
Ameland, *Neths.* **20 B7** 53 27N 5 45 E
Amélia, *Italy* **39 F9** 42 33N 12 25 E
Amélie-les-Bains-Palalda, *France* **24 F6** 42 29N 2 41 E
Amen, *Russia* **57 C18** 68 45N 180 0 E
Amendolaro, *Italy* **41 C9** 39 58N 16 34 E
America, *Neths.* **21 F7** 51 27N 5 59 E
American Falls, *U.S.A.* **142 E7** 42 47N 112 51W
American Falls Reservoir, *U.S.A.* **142 E7** 42 47N 112 52W
American Highland, *Antarctica* **7 D6** 73 0 S 75 0 E
American Samoa ■, *Pac. Oc.* **121 X24** 14 20 S 170 40W
Americana, *Brazil* **159 A6** 22 45 S 47 20W
Americus, *U.S.A.* **135 J3** 32 4N 84 14W
Amersfoort, *Neths.* **20 D6** 52 9N 5 23 E
Amersfoort, *S. Africa* **105 D4** 26 59 S 29 53 E
Amery, *Australia* **113 F2** 31 9 S 117 5 E
Amery, *Canada* **131 B10** 56 34N 94 3W
Amery Ice Shelf, *Antarctica* **7 C6** 69 30 S 72 0 E
Ames, *U.S.A.* **140 B3** 42 2N 93 37W
Amesbury, *U.S.A.* **137 D14** 42 51N 70 56W
Amfíklia, *Greece* **45 F4** 38 38N 22 35 E
Amfilokhía, *Greece* **45 F3** 38 52N 21 9 E
Amfípolis, *Greece* **44 D5** 40 48N 23 52 E
Ámfissa, *Greece* **45 F4** 38 32N 22 22 E
Amga, *Russia* **57 C14** 60 50N 132 0 E
Amga →, *Russia* **57 C14** 62 38N 134 32 E
Amgu, *Russia* **57 E14** 45 45N 137 15 E
Amgun →, *Russia* **57 D14** 52 56N 139 38 E
Amherst, *Canada* **129 C7** 45 48N 64 8W
Amherst, *Mass., U.S.A.* **137 D12** 42 23N 72 31W
Amherst, *N.Y., U.S.A.* **136 D6** 42 59N 78 48W
Amherst, *Ohio, U.S.A.* **136 E2** 41 24N 82 14W
Amherst, *Tex., U.S.A.* **139 H3** 34 1N 102 25W
Amherst I., *Canada* **137 B8** 44 8N 76 43W
Amherstburg, *Canada* **128 D3** 42 6N 83 6W
Amiata, Mte., *Italy* **39 F8** 42 54N 11 40 E
Amiens, *France* **23 C9** 49 54N 2 16 E
Amigdhalokefáli, *Greece* **45 J5** 35 23N 23 30 E
Amili, *India* **78 A5** 28 25N 95 52 E
Amindaion, *Greece* **44 D3** 40 42N 21 42 E
Amīrābād, *Iran* **84 C5** 33 20N 46 16 E
Amirante Is., *Seychelles* **109 E4** 6 0 S 53 0 E
Amisk L., *Canada* **131 C8** 54 35N 102 15W
Amistad, Presa de la, *Mexico* **146 B4** 29 24N 101 0W
Amite, *U.S.A.* **139 K9** 30 44N 90 30W
Amizmiz, *Morocco* **98 B3** 31 12N 8 15W
Åmli, *Norway* **15 F2** 58 45N 8 32 E
Amlwch, *U.K.* **16 D3** 53 24N 4 21W
Amm Adam, *Sudan* **95 D4** 16 20N 36 1 E
'Ammān, *Jordan* **91 D4** 31 57N 35 52 E
Ammanford, *U.K.* **17 F3** 51 48N 4 4W
Ammassalik = Angmagssalik, *Greenland* **6 C6** 65 40N 37 20W
Ammerån, *Sweden* **14 A10** 63 9N 16 13 E
Ammerån →, *Sweden* **14 A10** 63 9N 16 13 E
Ammersee, *Germany* **27 G7** 48 0N 11 7 E
Ammerzoden, *Neths.* **20 E6** 51 45N 5 13 E
Amnat Charoen, *Thailand* **76 E5** 15 51N 104 38 E
Amo Jiang →, *China* **68 F3** 23 0N 101 50 E
Āmol, *Iran* **85 B7** 36 23N 52 20 E
Amorebieta, *Spain* **34 B2** 43 13N 2 44W
Amoret, *U.S.A.* **140 F2** 38 15N 94 35W
Amorgós, *Greece* **45 H7** 36 50N 25 57 E
Amory, *U.S.A.* **135 J1** 33 59N 88 29W
Amos, *Canada* **128 C4** 48 35N 78 5W
Åmot, *Buskerud, Norway* **14 E3** 59 54N 9 54 E
Åmot, *Telemark, Norway* **14 E2** 59 34N 8 0 E
Åmotsdal, *Norway* **14 E2** 59 37N 8 26 E
Amour, Djebel, *Algeria* **99 B5** 33 42N 1 37 E
Amoy = Xiamen, *China* **69 E12** 24 25N 118 4 E
Ampang, *Malaysia* **77 L3** 3 8N 101 45 E
Ampanihy, *Madag.* **105 C7** 24 40 S 44 45 E
Ampasindava, Helodranon', *Madag.* **105 A8** 13 40 S 48 15 E

166 Ampasindava, Saikanosy

Ampasindava, Saikanosy, *Madag.* 105 A8 13 42 S 47 55 E
Ampato, Nevado, *Peru* 156 D3 15 40 S 71 56W
Ampenan, *Indonesia* 75 D5 8 35 S 116 13 E
Amper, *Nigeria* 101 D6 9 25N 9 40 E
Amper →, *Germany* 27 G7 48 30N 11 57 E
Ampère, *Algeria* 99 A6 35 44N 5 27 E
Ampezzo, *Italy* 39 B9 46 25N 12 48 E
Amposta, *Spain* 34 E5 40 43N 0 34 E
Ampotaka, *Madag.* 105 D7 25 3 S 44 41 E
Ampoza, *Madag.* 105 C7 22 20 S 44 44 E
Amqui, *Canada* 129 C6 48 28N 67 27W
'Amrān, *Yemen* 86 D3 15 41N 43 55 E
Amravati, *India* 82 D3 20 55N 77 45 E
Amreli, *India* 80 J4 21 35N 71 17 E
Amrenene el Kasba, *Algeria* 99 D5 22 10N 0 30 E
Amriswil, *Switz.* 29 A8 47 33N 9 18 E
Amritsar, *India* 80 D6 31 35N 74 57 E
Amroha, *India* 81 E8 28 53N 78 30 E
Amrum, *Germany* 26 A4 54 37N 8 21 E
Amsel, *Algeria* 99 D6 22 47N 5 29 E
Amsterdam, *Neths.* 20 D5 52 23N 4 54 E
Amsterdam, *U.S.A.* 137 D10 42 56N 74 11W
Amsterdam, I., *Ind. Oc.* 109 H6 38 30 S 77 30 E
Amstetten, *Austria* 30 C7 48 7N 14 51 E
Amudarya →, *Uzbekistan* 56 E6 43 40N 59 0 E
Amulung, *Phil.* 70 C3 17 50N 121 43 E
Amundsen Gulf, *Canada* 126 A7 71 0N 124 0W
Amundsen Sea, *Antarctica* 7 D15 72 0 S 115 0W
Amuntai, *Indonesia* 75 C5 2 28 S 115 25 E
Amur, *Somali Rep.* 108 C3 5 16N 46 30 E
Amur →, *Russia* 57 D15 52 56N 141 10 E
Amurang, *Indonesia* 72 A2 1 5N 124 40 E
Amuri Pass, *N.Z.* 119 C7 42 31 S 172 11 E
Amurrio, *Spain* 34 B1 43 3N 3 0W
Amursk, *Russia* 57 D14 50 14N 136 54 E
Amurzet, *Russia* 57 E14 47 50N 131 5 E
Amusco, *Spain* 36 C6 42 10N 4 28W
Amutag, *Phil.* 70 E4 12 23N 123 16 E
Amvrakikós Kólpos, *Greece* 45 F2 39 0N 20 55 E
Amvrosiyevka, *Ukraine* 53 C8 47 43N 38 30 E
Amyderya = Amudarya →, *Uzbekistan* 56 E6 43 40N 59 0 E
Amzeglouf, *Algeria* 99 C5 26 50N 0 1 E
An, *Burma* 78 F5 19 48N 94 0 E
An Bien, *Vietnam* 77 H5 9 45N 105 0 E
An Hoa, *Vietnam* 76 E7 15 40N 108 5 E
An Khe, *Vietnam* 76 F7 13 57N 108 39 E
An Nabatīyah at Tahta, *Lebanon* 91 B4 33 23N 35 27 E
An Nabk, *Si. Arabia* 84 D3 31 20N 37 20 E
An Nabk, *Syria* 91 A5 34 2N 36 44 E
An Nabk Abū Qaşr, *Si. Arabia* 84 D3 30 21N 38 34 E
An Nafūd, *Si. Arabia* 84 D4 28 15N 41 0 E
An Najaf, *Iraq* 84 C5 32 3N 44 15 E
An Nāşirīyah, *Iraq* 84 D5 31 0N 46 15 E
An Nawfalīyah, *Libya* 96 B3 30 54N 17 58 E
An Nhon, *Vietnam* 76 F7 13 55N 109 7 E
An Nīl □, *Sudan* 94 D3 19 30N 33 0 E
An Nīl el Abyad □, *Sudan* 95 E3 14 0N 32 15 E
An Nīl el Azraq □, *Sudan* 95 E3 12 30N 34 30 E
An Nimāş, *Si. Arabia* 86 C3 19 7N 42 8 E
An Nu'ayrīyah, *Si. Arabia* 85 E6 27 30N 48 30 E
An Nuwaybʻī, W. →, *Si. Arabia* 91 F3 29 18N 34 57 E
An Thoi, Dao, *Vietnam* 77 H4 9 58N 104 0 E
An Uaimh, *Ireland* 19 C5 53 39N 6 40W
Anabar →, *Russia* 57 B12 73 8N 113 36 E
'Anabtā, *Jordan* 91 C4 32 19N 35 7 E
Anabuki, *Japan* 62 C6 34 2N 134 11 E
Anaco, *Venezuela* 153 B5 9 27N 64 28W
Anaconda, *U.S.A.* 142 C7 46 8N 112 57W
Anacortes, *U.S.A.* 144 B4 48 30N 122 37W
Anacuao, Mt., *Phil.* 70 C3 16 16N 121 53 E
Anadarko, *U.S.A.* 139 H5 35 4N 98 15W
Anadia, *Brazil* 154 C4 9 42 S 36 18W
Anadia, *Portugal* 36 E2 40 26N 8 27W
Anadolu, *Turkey* 88 D4 39 0N 30 0 E
Anadyr, *Russia* 57 C18 64 35N 177 20 E
Anadyr →, *Russia* 57 C18 64 55N 176 5 E
Anadyrskiy Zaliv, *Russia* 57 C19 64 0N 180 0 E
Anáfi, *Greece* 45 H7 36 22N 25 48 E
Anafópoulo, *Greece* 45 H7 36 17N 25 50 E
Anaga, Pta. de, *Canary Is.* 33 F3 28 34N 16 9W
Anagni, *Italy* 40 A6 41 44N 13 8 E
'Ānah, *Iraq* 84 C4 34 25N 42 0 E
Anaheim, *U.S.A.* 145 M9 33 50N 117 55W
Anahim Lake, *Canada* 130 C3 52 28N 125 18W
Anáhuac, *Mexico* 146 B4 27 14N 100 9W
Anai Mudi, Mt., *India* 83 J3 10 12N 77 4 E
Anaimalai Hills, *India* 83 J3 10 20N 76 40 E
Anajás, *Brazil* 154 B2 0 59 S 49 57W
Anajatuba, *Brazil* 154 B3 3 16 S 44 37W
Anakapalle, *India* 82 F6 17 42N 83 6 E
Anakie, *Australia* 114 C4 23 32 S 147 45 E
Anaklia, *Georgia* 53 E9 42 22N 41 35 E
Analalava, *Madag.* 105 A8 14 35 S 48 0 E
Análipsis, *Greece* 32 A3 39 36N 19 55 E
Anamã, *Brazil* 153 D5 3 35 S 61 22W
Anambar →, *Pakistan* 80 D3 30 15N 68 50 E
Anambas, Kepulauan, *Indonesia* 74 B3 3 20N 106 30 E
Anambas Is. = Anambas, Kepulauan, *Indonesia* 74 B3 3 20N 106 30 E
Anambra □, *Nigeria* 101 D6 6 20N 7 0 E
Aname, *Vanuatu* 121 K7 20 8 S 169 47 E
Anamoose, *U.S.A.* 138 B4 47 53N 100 15W
Anamosa, *U.S.A.* 140 B5 42 7N 91 17W
Anamur, *Turkey* 88 E5 36 8N 32 58 E
Anamur Burnu, *Turkey* 88 E5 36 2N 32 47 E
Anan, *Japan* 62 D6 33 54N 134 40 E
Anand, *India* 80 H5 22 32N 72 59 E
Anandpur, *India* 82 D8 21 16N 86 13 E
Anánes, *Greece* 45 H6 36 33N 24 9 E
Anantapur, *India* 83 G3 14 39N 77 42 E
Anantnag, *India* 81 C6 33 45N 75 10 E
Ananyev, *Ukraine* 52 C3 47 44N 29 47 E
Anao-aon, *Phil.* 71 G5 9 47N 125 25 E
Anapa, *Russia* 52 D7 44 55N 37 25 E
Anapodháris →, *Greece* 32 E7 34 59N 25 20 E
Anápolis, *Brazil* 155 E2 16 15 S 48 50W
Anapu →, *Brazil* 153 D7 1 53 S 50 53W
Anār, *Iran* 85 D7 30 55N 55 13 E
Anār Darreh, *Afghan.* 79 B1 32 46N 61 39 E
Anārak, *Iran* 85 C7 33 25N 53 40 E
Anatolia = Anadolu, *Turkey* 88 D4 39 0N 30 0 E
Anatone, *U.S.A.* 142 C5 46 8N 117 8W
Anatsogno, *Madag.* 105 C7 23 33 S 43 46 E
Añatuya, *Argentina* 158 B3 28 20 S 62 50W
Anauá →, *Brazil* 153 C5 0 58N 61 21W
Anaunethad L., *Canada* 131 A8 60 55N 104 25W
Anavilhanas, Arquipélago das, *Brazil* 153 D5 2 42 S 60 45W
Anaye, *Niger* 97 E2 19 15N 12 50 E
Anbyŏn, *N. Korea* 67 E14 39 1N 127 35 E
Ancash □, *Peru* 156 B2 9 30 S 77 45W
Ancenis, *France* 22 E5 47 21N 1 10W
Ancho, Canal, *Chile* 160 D2 50 0 S 74 20W
Anchor Bay, *U.S.A.* 144 G3 38 48N 123 34W
Anchorage, *U.S.A.* 126 B5 61 13N 149 54W
Anci, *China* 66 E9 39 20N 116 40 E
Ancohuma, Nevada, *Bolivia* 156 D4 16 0 S 68 50W
Ancón, *Peru* 156 C2 11 50 S 77 10W
Ancona, *Italy* 39 E10 43 37N 13 30 E
Ancud, *Chile* 160 B2 42 0 S 73 50W
Ancud, G. de, *Chile* 160 B2 42 0 S 73 0W
Anda, *China* 65 B7 46 24N 125 19 E
Anda, *Phil.* 70 C2 16 17N 119 57 E
Andacollo, *Argentina* 158 D1 37 10 S 70 42W
Andacollo, *Chile* 158 C1 30 5 S 71 10W
Andado, *Australia* 114 D2 25 25 S 135 15 E
Andahuaylas, *Peru* 156 C3 13 40 S 73 25W
Andalgalá, *Argentina* 158 B2 27 40 S 66 30W
Åndalsnes, *Norway* 14 B1 62 35N 7 43 E
Andalucía □, *Spain* 37 H6 37 35N 5 0W
Andalusia, *U.S.A.* 135 K2 31 18N 86 29W
Andalusia □ = Andalucía □, *Spain* 37 H6 37 35N 5 0W
Andaman Is., *Ind. Oc.* 58 H13 12 30N 92 30 E
Andara, *Namibia* 104 B3 18 2 S 21 9 E
Andaraí, *Brazil* 155 D3 12 48 S 41 20W
Andeer, *Switz.* 29 C8 46 36N 9 26 E
Andelfingen, *Switz.* 29 A7 47 36N 8 41 E
Andelot, *France* 23 D12 48 15N 5 18 E
Andenne, *Belgium* 21 H6 50 28N 5 5 E
Andéranboukane, *Mali* 101 B5 15 26N 3 2 E
Anderlecht, *Belgium* 21 G4 50 50N 4 19 E
Anderlues, *Belgium* 21 H4 50 25N 4 16 E
Andermatt, *Switz.* 29 C7 46 38N 8 35 E
Andernach, *Germany* 26 E3 50 24N 7 25 E
Andernos-les-Bains, *France* 24 D2 44 44N 1 6W
Anderslöv, *Sweden* 15 J7 55 26N 13 19 E
Anderson, *Calif., U.S.A.* 142 F2 40 27N 122 18W
Anderson, *Ind., U.S.A.* 141 D11 40 10N 85 41W
Anderson, *Mo., U.S.A.* 139 G7 36 39N 94 27W
Anderson, *S.C., U.S.A.* 135 H4 34 31N 82 39W
Anderson →, *Canada* 126 B7 69 42N 129 0W
Anderson, Mt., *S. Africa* 105 D5 25 5 S 30 42 E
Andes = Andes, Cord. de los, *S. Amer.* 156 C3 20 0 S 68 0W
Andes, *S. Amer.* 156 C2 10 0 S 75 53W
Andes, Cord. de los, *S. Amer.* 156 C3 20 0 S 68 0W
Andfjorden, *Norway* 12 B14 69 10N 16 20 E
Andhra, L., *India* 82 E1 18 54N 73 32 E
Andhra Pradesh □, *India* 83 F4 18 0N 79 0 E
Andijon = Andizhan, *Uzbekistan* 55 C6 41 10N 72 15 E
Andikíthira, *Greece* 45 J5 35 52N 23 15 E
Andīmeshk, *Iran* 85 C6 32 27N 48 21 E
Andímilos, *Greece* 45 H6 36 47N 24 12 E
Andíparos, *Greece* 45 H7 37 0N 25 3 E
Andípaxoi, *Greece* 45 E2 39 9N 20 13 E
Andípsara, *Greece* 45 F7 38 30N 25 29 E
Andírrion, *Greece* 45 F3 38 24N 21 46 E
Andizhan, *Uzbekistan* 55 C6 41 10N 72 15 E
Andkhvoy, *Afghan.* 79 A2 36 52N 65 8 E
Andoany, *Madag.* 105 A8 13 25 S 48 16 E
Andoas, *Peru* 152 D2 2 55 S 76 25W
Andol, *India* 82 F4 17 51N 78 4 E
Andong, *S. Korea* 67 F15 36 40N 128 43 E
Andongwei, *China* 67 G10 35 6N 119 20 E
Andorra ■, *Europe* 34 C6 42 30N 1 30 E
Andorra La Vella, *Andorra* 34 C6 42 31N 1 32 E
Andover, *U.K.* 17 F6 51 13N 1 29W
Andover, *Mass., U.S.A.* 137 D13 42 40N 71 8W
Andover, *N.Y., U.S.A.* 136 D7 42 10N 77 48W
Andover, *Ohio, U.S.A.* 136 E4 41 36N 80 34W
Andradina, *Brazil* 155 F1 20 54 S 51 23W
Andrahary, Mt., *Madag.* 105 A8 13 37 S 49 17 E
Andraitx, *Spain* 33 B9 39 39N 2 25 E
Andramasina, *Madag.* 105 B8 19 11 S 47 35 E
Andranopasy, *Madag.* 105 C7 21 17 S 43 44 E
Andreanof Is., *U.S.A.* 126 C2 52 0N 178 0W
Andreapol, *Russia* 50 C8 56 40N 32 17 E
Andrespol, *Poland* 47 D6 51 45N 19 34 E
Andrewilla, *Australia* 115 D2 26 31 S 139 17 E
Andrews, *S.C., U.S.A.* 135 J6 33 27N 79 34W
Andrews, *Tex., U.S.A.* 139 J3 32 19N 102 33W
Andreyevka, *Russia* 54 E2 52 19N 51 55 E
Ándria, *Italy* 41 A9 41 13N 16 17 E
Andriba, *Madag.* 105 B8 17 30 S 46 58 E
Andrijevica, *Montenegro* 42 E4 42 45N 19 48 E
Andrítsaina, *Greece* 45 G3 37 29N 21 52 E
Androka, *Madag.* 105 C7 24 58 S 44 2 E
Andropov = Rybinsk, *Russia* 51 B11 58 5N 38 50 E
Ándros, *Greece* 45 G6 37 50N 24 57 E
Andros I., *Bahamas* 148 B4 24 30N 78 0W
Andros Town, *Bahamas* 148 B4 24 43N 77 47W
Andrychów, *Poland* 31 B12 49 51N 19 18 E
Andújar, *Spain* 37 G6 38 3N 4 5W
Andulo, *Angola* 103 E3 11 25 S 16 45 E
Anegada, B., *Argentina* 160 B4 40 20 S 62 20W
Anegada I., *Virgin Is.* 149 C7 18 45N 64 20W
Anegada Passage, *W. Indies* 149 C7 18 15N 63 45W
Anécho, *Togo* 101 D5 6 12N 1 34 E
Aneityum, *Vanuatu* 121 K7 20 12 S 169 45 E
Añelo, *Argentina* 160 A3 38 20 S 68 45W
Anergane, *Morocco* 98 B3 31 4N 7 14W
Aneto, Pico de, *Spain* 34 C5 42 37N 0 40 E
Añez, *Bolivia* 157 D5 15 40 S 63 10W
Anfu, *China* 69 D10 27 21N 114 40 E
Ang Thong, *Thailand* 76 E3 14 35N 100 31 E
Angadanan, *Phil.* 70 C3 16 45N 121 45 E
Angamos, Punta, *Chile* 158 A1 23 1 S 70 32W
Angara →, *Russia* 57 D10 58 5N 94 20 E
Angarab, *Ethiopia* 95 E4 13 11N 37 7 E
Angarsk, *Russia* 57 D11 52 30N 104 0 E
Angas Downs, *Australia* 113 E5 25 2 S 132 14 E
Angas Hills, *Australia* 112 D4 23 0 S 127 50 E
Angaston, *Australia* 116 C3 34 30 S 139 8 E
Angat, *Phil.* 70 D3 14 56N 121 2 E
Ånge, *Sweden* 14 B9 62 31N 15 35 E
Ángel de la Guarda, I., *Mexico* 146 B2 29 30N 113 30W
Angel Falls, *Venezuela* 153 B5 5 57N 62 30W
Angeles, *Phil.* 70 D3 15 9N 120 33 E
Ängelholm, *Sweden* 15 H6 56 15N 12 58 E
Angellala, *Australia* 115 D4 26 24 S 146 54 E
Angels Camp, *U.S.A.* 144 G6 38 4N 120 32W
Anger →, *Ethiopia* 95 F4 9 37N 36 6 E
Angereb →, *Ethiopia* 95 E4 13 45N 36 40 E
Ångermanälven →, *Sweden* 14 B12 62 40N 18 0 E
Angermünde, *Germany* 26 B10 53 1N 14 0 E
Angers, *Canada* 137 A9 45 31N 75 29W
Angers, *France* 22 E6 47 30N 0 35W
Angerville, *France* 23 D8 48 19N 2 0 E
Ängesån →, *Sweden* 12 C17 66 50N 22 15 E
Anghiari, *Italy* 39 E9 43 32N 12 3 E
Angical, *Brazil* 155 D3 12 0 S 44 42W
Angikuni L., *Canada* 131 A9 62 0N 100 0W
Angkor, *Cambodia* 76 F4 13 22N 103 50 E
Anglem Mt., *N.Z.* 119 G2 46 45 S 167 53 E
Anglés, *Spain* 34 D7 41 57N 2 38 E
Anglesey, *U.K.* 16 D3 53 17N 4 20W
Anglet, *France* 24 E2 43 29N 1 31W
Angleton, *U.S.A.* 139 L7 29 10N 95 26W
Angleur, *Belgium* 21 G7 50 36N 5 35 E
Anglin →, *France* 24 B4 46 42N 0 52 E
Anglisidhes, *Cyprus* 32 E12 34 51N 33 27 E
Anglure, *France* 23 D10 48 35N 3 50 E
Angmagssalik, *Greenland* 6 C6 65 40N 37 20W
Ango, *Zaïre* 106 B2 4 10N 26 5 E
Angoche, *Mozam.* 107 F4 16 8 S 39 55 E
Angoche, I., *Mozam.* 107 F4 16 20 S 39 50 E
Angol, *Chile* 158 D1 37 56 S 72 45W
Angola, *Ind., U.S.A.* 141 C12 41 38N 85 0W
Angola, *N.Y., U.S.A.* 136 D5 42 38N 79 2W
Angola ■, *Africa* 103 E3 12 0 S 18 0 E
Angoon, *U.S.A.* 130 B2 57 30N 134 35W
Angoram, *Papua N. G.* 120 C3 4 4 S 144 4 E
Angoulême, *France* 24 C4 45 39N 0 10 E
Angoumois, *France* 24 C4 45 50N 0 25 E
Angra dos Reis, *Brazil* 159 A7 23 0 S 44 10W
Angren, *Uzbekistan* 55 C5 41 1N 70 12 E
Angtassom, *Cambodia* 77 G5 11 1N 104 41 E
Angu, *Zaïre* 106 B1 3 25N 24 28 E
Anguang, *China* 67 B12 45 15N 123 45 E
Anguilla ■, *W. Indies* 149 C7 18 14N 63 5W
Anguo, *China* 66 E8 38 28N 115 15 E
Angurugu, *Australia* 114 A2 14 0 S 136 25 E
Angus, Braes of, *U.K.* 18 E5 56 51N 3 10W
Anhanduí →, *Brazil* 159 A5 21 46 S 52 9W
Anhée, *Belgium* 21 H5 50 18N 4 53 E
Anholt, *Denmark* 15 H5 56 42N 11 33 E
Anhua, *China* 69 C8 28 23N 111 12 E
Anhui □, *China* 69 B11 32 0N 117 0 E
Anhwei □ = Anhui □, *China* 69 B11 32 0N 117 0 E
Anichab, *Namibia* 104 C1 21 0 S 14 46 E
Anicuns, *Brazil* 155 E2 16 28 S 49 58W
Ánidhros, *Greece* 45 H7 36 38N 25 43 E
Anie, *Togo* 101 D5 7 42N 1 8 E
Animas, *U.S.A.* 143 L9 31 57N 108 48W
Ånimskog, *Sweden* 15 F6 58 53N 12 35 E
Anina, *Romania* 42 B6 45 6N 21 51 E
Anini-y, *Phil.* 71 F3 10 25N 121 55 E
Anita, *U.S.A.* 140 C2 41 27N 94 46W
Anivorano, *Madag.* 105 B8 18 44 S 48 58 E
Aniwa, *Vanuatu* 121 J7 19 17 S 169 35 E
Anjangaon, *India* 82 D3 21 10N 77 20 E
Anjar, *India* 80 H4 23 6N 70 10 E
Anjidiv I., *India* 83 G2 14 40N 74 10 E
Anjō, *Japan* 63 C9 34 57N 137 5 E
Anjou, *France* 22 E6 47 20N 0 15W
Anjozorobe, *Madag.* 105 B8 18 22 S 47 52 E
Anju, *N. Korea* 67 E13 39 36N 125 40 E
Anka, *Nigeria* 101 C6 12 13N 5 58 E
Ankaboa, Tanjona, *Madag.* 105 C7 21 58 S 43 20 E
Ankang, *China* 66 H5 32 40N 109 1 E
Ankara, *Turkey* 88 D5 39 57N 32 54 E
Ankara □, *Turkey* 88 D5 39 55N 32 50 E
Ankaramena, *Madag.* 105 C8 21 57 S 46 39 E
Ankazoabo, *Madag.* 105 C7 22 18 S 44 31 E
Ankazobe, *Madag.* 105 B8 18 20 S 47 10 E
Ankeny, *U.S.A.* 140 C3 41 44N 93 36W
Ankisabe, *Madag.* 105 B8 19 17 S 46 29 E
Anklam, *Germany* 26 B9 53 48N 13 40 E
Ankleshwar, *India* 82 D1 21 38N 73 3 E
Ankober, *Ethiopia* 95 F4 9 35N 39 40 E
Ankoro, *Zaïre* 106 D2 6 45 S 26 55 E
Anlong, *China* 68 E5 25 2N 105 27 E
Anlu, *China* 69 B9 31 15N 113 45 E
Anmyŏn-do, *S. Korea* 67 F14 36 25N 126 25 E
Ånn, *Sweden* 14 A6 63 19N 12 34 E
Ann, C., *U.S.A.* 137 D14 42 38N 70 35W
Ann Arbor, *U.S.A.* 141 B13 42 17N 83 45W
Anna, *Russia* 51 F12 51 28N 40 23 E
Anna, *Ill., U.S.A.* 139 G10 37 28N 89 15W
Anna, *Ohio, U.S.A.* 141 D12 40 24N 84 11W
Anna Plains, *Australia* 112 C3 19 17 S 121 37 E
Anna Regina, *Guyana* 153 B6 7 10N 58 30W
Annaba, *Algeria* 99 A6 36 50N 7 46 E
Annaberg-Buchholz, *Germany* 26 E8 50 34N 12 58 E
Annaka, *Japan* 63 A10 36 19N 138 54 E
Annalee →, *Ireland* 19 B4 54 3N 7 15W
Annam = Trung-Phan, *Vietnam* 76 E7 16 0N 108 0 E
Annamitique, Chaîne, *Asia* 76 D6 17 0N 106 0 E
Annan, *U.K.* 18 G5 54 57N 3 17W
Annan →, *U.K.* 18 G5 54 58N 3 18W
Annanberg, *Papua N. G.* 120 C3 4 52 S 144 42 E
Annapolis, *U.S.A.* 134 F7 38 59N 76 30W
Annapolis Royal, *Canada* 129 D6 44 44N 65 32W
Annapurna, *Nepal* 81 E10 28 34N 83 50 E
Annean, L., *Australia* 113 E2 26 54 S 118 14 E
Anneberg, *Sweden* 15 G6 57 32N 12 6 E
Annecy, *France* 25 C10 45 55N 6 8 E
Annecy, L. d', *France* 25 C10 45 52N 6 10 E
Annemasse, *France* 25 B10 46 12N 6 16 E
Anning, *China* 68 E4 24 55N 102 26 E
Anningie, *Australia* 112 D5 21 50 S 133 7 E
Anniston, *U.S.A.* 135 J3 33 39N 85 50W
Annobón, *Atl. Oc.* 93 G4 1 25 S 5 36 E
Annonay, *France* 25 C8 45 15N 4 40 E
Annot, *France* 25 E10 43 58N 6 38 E
Annotto Bay, *Jamaica* 148 C4 18 17N 76 45W
Annuello, *Australia* 116 C5 34 53 S 142 55 E
Annville, *U.S.A.* 137 F8 40 20N 76 31W
Annweiler, *Germany* 27 F3 49 12N 7 58 E
Áno Arkhánai, *Greece* 45 J7 35 16N 25 11 E
Áno Porróia, *Greece* 44 C5 41 17N 23 2 E
Áno Viánnos, *Greece* 32 D7 35 2N 25 21 E
Anoano, *Solomon Is.* 121 M11 8 59 S 160 46 E
Anoka, *U.S.A.* 138 C8 45 12N 93 23W
Anorotsangana, *Madag.* 105 A8 13 56 S 47 55 E
Anóyia, *Greece* 32 D6 35 16N 24 52 E
Anping, *Hebei, China* 66 E8 38 15N 115 30 E
Anping, *Liaoning, China* 67 D12 41 5N 123 30 E
Anpu Gang, *China* 68 G7 21 25N 109 50 E
Anqing, *China* 69 B11 30 30N 117 3 E
Anqiu, *China* 67 F10 36 25N 119 10 E
Anren, *China* 69 D9 26 43N 113 18 E
Ans, *Belgium* 21 G7 50 39N 5 32 E
Ansai, *China* 66 F5 36 50N 109 20 E
Ansbach, *Germany* 27 F6 49 17N 10 34 E
Anseba →, *Eritrea* 95 D4 16 0N 38 30 E
Anserma, *Colombia* 152 B2 5 13N 75 48W
Anseroeul, *Belgium* 21 G3 50 43N 3 32 E
Anshan, *China* 65 B7 41 3N 122 58 E
Anshan, *Liaoning, China* 67 D12 41 5N 122 58 E
Anshun, *China* 68 D5 26 18N 105 57 E
Ansião, *Portugal* 36 F2 39 56N 8 27W
Ansirabe, *Madag.* 105 B8 19 55 S 47 2 E
Ansley, *U.S.A.* 138 E5 41 18N 99 23W
Ansó, *Spain* 34 C4 42 51N 0 48W
Anson, *U.S.A.* 139 J5 32 45N 99 54W
Anson B., *Australia* 112 B5 13 20 S 130 6 E
Ansongo, *Mali* 101 B5 15 25N 0 35 E
Ansonia, *Conn., U.S.A.* 137 E11 41 21N 73 5W
Ansonia, *Ohio, U.S.A.* 141 D12 40 13N 84 38W
Anstruther, *U.K.* 18 E6 56 14N 2 40W
Ansudu, *Indonesia* 73 B5 2 11 S 139 22 E
Antabamba, *Peru* 156 C3 14 40 S 73 0W
Antakya, *Turkey* 88 E7 36 14N 36 10 E
Antalaha, *Madag.* 105 A9 14 57 S 50 20 E
Antalya, *Turkey* 88 E4 36 52N 30 45 E
Antalya □, *Turkey* 88 E4 36 55N 30 45 E
Antalya Körfezi, *Turkey* 88 E4 36 15N 31 30 E
Antananarivo, *Madag.* 105 B8 18 55 S 47 31 E
Antananarivo □, *Madag.* 105 B8 19 0 S 47 0 E
Antanimbaribe, *Madag.* 105 C7 21 30 S 44 48 E
Antarctic Pen., *Antarctica* 7 C18 67 0 S 60 0W
Antarctica 7 E3 90 0 S 0 0 E
Antelope, *Zimbabwe* 107 G2 21 2 S 28 31 E
Antenor Navarro, *Brazil* 154 C4 6 44 S 38 27W
Antequera, *Paraguay* 158 A4 24 8 S 57 7W
Antequera, *Spain* 37 H6 37 5N 4 33W
Antero, Mt., *U.S.A.* 143 G10 38 41N 106 15W
Anthemoús, *Greece* 44 D5 40 31N 23 15 E
Anthony, *Kans., U.S.A.* 139 G5 37 9N 98 2W
Anthony, *N. Mex., U.S.A.* 143 K10 32 0N 106 36W
Anthony Lagoon, *Australia* 114 B2 18 0 S 135 30 E
Anti Atlas, *Morocco* 98 C2 30 0N 8 30W
Anti-Lebanon = Ash Sharqi, Al Jabal, *Lebanon* 91 B5 33 40N 36 10 E
Antibes, *France* 25 E11 43 34N 7 6 E
Antibes, C. d', *France* 25 E11 43 31N 7 7 E
Anticosti, I. d', *Canada* 129 C7 49 30N 63 0W
Antifer, C. d', *France* 22 C7 49 41N 0 10 E
Antigo, *U.S.A.* 138 C10 45 9N 89 9W
Antigonish, *Canada* 129 C7 45 38N 61 58W
Antigua, *Canary Is.* 33 F5 28 24N 14 1W
Antigua, *Guatemala* 148 D1 14 34N 90 41W
Antigua, *W. Indies* 149 C7 17 0N 61 50W
Antigua & Barbuda ■, *W. Indies* 149 C7 17 20N 61 48W
Antilla, *Cuba* 148 B4 20 40N 75 50W
Antimony, *U.S.A.* 143 G8 38 7N 112 0W
Antioch, *U.S.A.* 144 G5 38 1N 121 48W
Antioche, Pertuis d', *France* 24 B2 46 6N 1 20W
Antioquia, *Colombia* 152 B2 6 40N 75 55W
Antioquia □, *Colombia* 152 B2 7 0N 75 30W
Antipodes Is., *Pac. Oc.* 122 M9 49 45 S 178 40 E
Antique □, *Phil.* 71 F4 11 10N 122 5 E
Antler, *U.S.A.* 138 A4 48 59N 101 17W
Antler →, *Canada* 131 D8 49 8N 101 0W
Antlers, *U.S.A.* 139 H7 34 14N 95 37W
Antofagasta, *Chile* 158 A1 23 50 S 70 30W
Antofagasta □, *Chile* 158 A2 24 0 S 69 0W
Antofagasta de la Sierra, *Argentina* 158 B2 26 5 S 67 20W
Antofalla, *Argentina* 158 B2 25 30 S 68 5W
Antofalla, Salar de, *Argentina* 158 B2 25 40 S 67 45W
Antoing, *Belgium* 21 G2 50 34N 3 27 E
Anton, *U.S.A.* 139 J3 33 49N 102 10W
Anton Chico, *U.S.A.* 143 J11 35 12N 105 9W
Antongila, Helodrano, *Madag.* 105 B8 15 30 S 49 50 E
Antonibé, *Madag.* 105 B8 15 7 S 47 24 E
Antonibé, Presqu'île d', *Madag.* 105 A8 14 55 S 47 20 E
Antonina, *Brazil* 159 B6 25 26 S 48 42W
Antonito, *U.S.A.* 143 H10 37 5N 106 0W
Antonovo, *Kazakhstan* 53 B14 49 25N 51 42 E
Antrain, *France* 22 D5 48 28N 1 30W
Antrim, *U.K.* 19 B5 54 43N 6 13W
Antrim □, *U.K.* 19 B5 54 55N 6 20W
Antrim, Mts. of, *U.K.* 19 B5 55 3N 6 8W
Antrim Plateau, *Australia* 112 C4 18 8 S 128 20 E
Antrodoco, *Italy* 39 F10 42 25N 13 4 E
Antropovo, *Russia* 51 B13 58 26N 42 51 E

Arica 167

Antsalova, Madag. 105 B7 18 40 S 44 37 E
Antsiranana, Madag. 105 A8 12 25 S 49 20 E
Antsohihy, Madag. 105 A8 14 50 S 47 59 E
Antsohimbondrona Seranana, Madag. 105 A8 13 7 S 48 48 E
Antu, China 67 C15 42 30N 128 20 E
Antufash, Yemen 86 D3 15 42N 42 25 E
Antwerp = Antwerpen, Belgium 21 F4 51 13N 4 25 E
Antwerp, Australia 116 D5 36 17 S 142 4 E
Antwerp, N.Y., U.S.A. 137 B9 44 12N 75 37W
Antwerp, Ohio, U.S.A. 141 C12 41 11N 84 45W
Antwerpen, Belgium 21 F4 51 13N 4 25 E
Antwerpen □, Belgium 21 F5 51 15N 4 40 E
Anupgarh, India 80 E5 29 10N 73 10 E
Anuradhapura, Sri Lanka 83 K5 8 22N 80 28 E
Anveh, Iran 85 E7 27 23N 54 11 E
Anvers = Antwerpen, Belgium 21 F4 51 13N 4 25 E
Anvers I., Antarctica 7 C17 64 30 S 63 40W
Anxi, Fujian, China 69 E12 25 2N 118 12 E
Anxi, Gansu, China 64 B4 40 30N 95 43 E
Anxiang, China 69 C9 29 27N 112 11 E
Anxious B., Australia 115 E1 33 24 S 134 45 E
Anyama, Ivory C. 100 D4 5 30N 4 3W
Anyang, China 66 F8 36 5N 114 21 E
Anyer, Indonesia 74 D3 6 4 S 105 53 E
Anyi, Jiangxi, China 69 C10 28 49N 115 25 E
Anyi, Shanxi, China 66 G6 35 2N 111 2 E
Anyuan, China 69 E10 25 9N 115 21 E
Anza, U.S.A. 145 M10 33 35N 116 39W
Anẕawr, Oman 87 C6 17 28N 52 50 E
Anze, China 66 F7 36 10N 112 12 E
Anzhero-Sudzhensk, Russia 56 D9 56 10N 86 0 E
Ánzio, Italy 40 A5 41 28N 12 37 E
Anzoátegui □, Venezuela 153 B5 9 0N 64 30W
Aoba, Vanuatu 121 E5 15 25 S 167 50 E
Aoga-Shima, Japan 63 E11 32 28N 139 46 E
Aoiz, Spain 34 C3 42 46N 1 22W
Aomori, Japan 60 D10 40 45N 140 45 E
Aomori □, Japan 60 D10 40 45N 140 40 E
Aonla, India 81 E8 28 16N 79 11 E
Aono-Yama, Japan 62 C3 34 28N 131 48 E
Aorangi Mts., N.Z. 118 H4 41 28 S 175 22 E
Aosta, Italy 38 C4 45 43N 7 20 E
Aotea Harbour, N.Z. 118 D3 38 0 S 174 50 E
Aoudéras, Niger 97 E1 17 45N 8 20 E
Aouinet Torkoz, Morocco 98 C3 28 31N 9 46W
Aoukar, Mali 98 D4 23 50N 2 45W
Aouker, Mauritania 100 B3 17 40N 10 0W
Aoulef el Arab, Algeria 99 C5 26 55N 1 2 E
Apa →, S. Amer. 158 A4 22 6 S 58 2W
Apache, U.S.A. 139 H5 34 54N 98 22W
Apalachee B., U.S.A. 135 L3 30 0N 84 0W
Apalachicola, U.S.A. 135 L3 29 43N 84 59W
Apalachicola →, U.S.A. 135 L3 29 43N 84 58W
Apapa, Nigeria 101 D5 6 25N 3 25 E
Apaporis →, Colombia 152 D4 1 23 S 69 25W
Aparecida do Taboado, Brazil 155 F1 20 5 S 51 5W
Aparri, Phil. 70 B3 18 22N 121 38 E
Aparurén, Venezuela 153 B5 5 6N 62 8W
Apateu, Romania 46 C2 46 36N 21 47 E
Apatin, Serbia 42 B4 45 40N 19 0 E
Apàtity, Russia 48 A5 67 34N 33 22 E
Apatzingán, Mexico 146 D4 19 0N 102 20W
Apayao □, Phil. 70 B3 18 10N 121 10 E
Apeldoorn, Neths. 20 D7 52 13N 5 57 E
Apeldoornsch Kanal →, Neths. 20 D8 52 29N 6 5 E
Apen, Germany 26 B3 53 12N 7 47 E
Apennines = Appennini, Italy 38 D7 44 0N 10 0 E
Apere →, Bolivia 157 C4 13 44 S 65 18W
Apia, W. Samoa 121 W24 13 50 S 171 50W
Apiacás, Serra dos, Brazil 157 B6 9 50 S 57 0W
Apiaú →, Brazil 153 C5 2 39N 61 12W
Apiaú, Serra do, Brazil 153 C5 2 30N 62 0W
Apidiá →, Brazil 157 C5 11 39 S 61 11W
Apinajé, Brazil 155 D2 11 31 S 48 18W
Apiti, N.Z. 118 F4 39 58 S 175 54 E
Apizaco, Mexico 147 D5 19 26N 98 9W
Aplao, Peru 156 D3 16 0 S 72 40W
Apo, Mt., Phil. 71 H5 6 53N 125 14 E
Apo East Pass, Phil. 70 E3 12 40N 120 40 E
Apo West Pass, Phil. 70 E3 12 31N 120 22 E
Apodi, Brazil 154 C4 5 39 S 37 48W
Apolakkiá, Greece 32 C9 36 5N 27 48 E
Apolakkiá, Órmos, Greece 32 C9 36 5N 27 45 E
Apolda, Germany 26 D7 51 1N 11 30 E
Apollo Bay, Australia 116 E5 38 45 S 143 40 E
Apollonia = Marsá Susah, Libya 96 B4 32 52N 21 59 E
Apollonia, Greece 45 H6 36 58N 24 43 E
Apolo, Bolivia 156 C4 14 30 S 68 30W
Apónguao →, Venezuela 153 C5 4 48N 61 36W
Aporé, Brazil 157 D7 18 58 S 52 1W
Aporé →, Brazil 155 E1 19 27 S 50 57W
Aporema, Brazil 154 A1 1 14N 50 49W
Apostle Is., U.S.A. 138 B9 47 0N 90 40W
Apóstoles, Argentina 159 B4 28 0 S 56 0W
Apostolos Andreas, C., Cyprus 32 D13 35 42N 34 35 E
Apostolovo, Ukraine 52 C5 47 39N 33 39 E
Apoteri, Guyana 153 C6 4 2N 58 32W
Appalachian Mts., U.S.A. 124 F12 38 0N 80 0W
Appelscha, Neths. 20 C8 52 57N 6 21 E
Appennini, Italy 38 D7 44 0N 10 0 E
Appennino Ligure, Italy 38 D5 44 30N 9 0 E
Appenzell, Switz. 29 B8 47 20N 9 25 E
Appenzell-Ausser Rhoden □, Switz. 29 B8 47 23N 9 23 E
Appenzell-Inner Rhoden □, Switz. 29 B8 47 20N 9 25 E
Appiano, Italy 39 B8 46 27N 11 17 E
Appingedam, Neths. 20 B9 53 19N 6 51 E
Apple Hill, Canada 137 A10 45 13N 74 46W
Apple Valley, U.S.A. 145 L9 34 32N 117 14W
Appleby, U.K. 16 C5 54 35N 2 29W
Appleton, U.S.A. 134 C1 44 16N 88 25W
Appleton City, U.S.A. 140 F2 38 11N 94 2W
Approuague, Fr. Guiana 153 C7 4 20N 52 0W
Approuague →, Fr. Guiana 153 C7 4 30N 51 57W
Apricena, Italy 41 A8 41 47N 15 25 E
Aprigliano, Italy 41 C9 39 17N 16 19 E
Aprília, Italy 40 A5 41 38N 12 38 E
Apsheronsk, Russia 53 D8 44 28N 39 42 E
Apt, France 25 E9 43 53N 5 24 E
Apuane, Alpi, Italy 38 D7 44 7N 10 14 E
Apuaú, Brazil 153 D5 2 25 S 60 53W
Apucarana, Brazil 159 A5 23 55 S 51 33W
Apulia = Púglia □, Italy 41 B9 41 0N 16 30 E
Apurahuan, Phil. 71 G2 9 35N 118 20 E
Apure □, Venezuela 152 B4 7 10N 68 50W
Apure →, Venezuela 152 B4 7 37N 66 25W
Apurímac □, Peru 156 C3 14 0 S 73 0W
Apurimac →, Peru 156 C3 12 17 S 73 56W
Apuseni, Munţii, Romania 46 C3 46 30N 22 45 E
Aqabah = Al 'Aqabah, Jordan 91 F4 29 31N 35 0 E
'Aqabah, Khalīj al, Red Sea 84 D2 28 15N 33 20 E
Āqcheh, Afghan. 79 A2 36 56N 66 11 E
'Aqdā, Iran 85 C7 32 26N 53 37 E
Aqīq, Sudan 94 D4 18 14N 38 12 E
Aqīq, Khalīg, Sudan 94 D4 18 20N 38 10 E
'Aqīq, W. al →, Si. Arabia 86 B3 20 16N 41 40 E
Aqmola = Tselinograd, Kazakhstan 56 D8 51 10N 71 30 E
Aqrah, Iraq 84 B4 36 46N 43 45 E
Aqtöbe = Aktyubinsk, Kazakhstan 49 D10 50 17N 57 10 E
Aquidauana, Brazil 157 E6 20 30 S 55 50W
Aquidauana →, Brazil 157 D6 19 44 S 56 50W
Aquiles Serdán, Mexico 146 B3 28 37N 105 54W
Aquin, Haiti 149 C5 18 16N 73 24W
Ar Rabaḑ, Si. Arabia 86 B2 23 11N 39 52 E
Ar Rachidiya, Morocco 98 B4 31 58N 4 20W
Ar Rafīd, Syria 91 C4 32 57N 35 52 E
Ar Raḩḩālīyah, Iraq 84 C4 32 44N 43 23 E
Ar Ramādī, Iraq 84 C4 33 25N 43 20 E
Ar Ramādīyāt, Si. Arabia 86 A3 24 18N 43 52 E
Ar Raml, Libya 96 C3 26 45N 19 40 E
Ar Ramthā, Jordan 91 C5 32 34N 36 0 E
Ar Raqqah, Syria 84 C3 36 0N 38 55 E
Ar Rass, Si. Arabia 84 E4 25 50N 43 40 E
Ar Rawḑah, Si. Arabia 86 B3 21 16N 42 50 E
Ar Rawḑah, Yemen 86 D4 14 28N 47 17 E
Ar Rawshān, Si. Arabia 86 B3 20 2N 42 36 E
Ar Rayyānah, Si. Arabia 86 B2 23 32N 39 45 E
Ar Rifa'i, Si. Arabia 84 D5 31 50N 46 10 E
Ar Rijā', Yemen 86 D4 13 1N 44 35 E
Ar Riyāḑ, Si. Arabia 84 E5 24 41N 46 42 E
Ar Ru'ays, Qatar 85 E6 26 8N 51 12 E
Ar Rukhaymīyah, Iraq 84 D5 29 22N 45 38 E
Ar Ruqayyidah, Si. Arabia 85 E6 25 21N 49 34 E
Ar Ruşāfah, Syria 84 C3 35 52N 36 53 E
Ar Ruţbah, Iraq 84 C4 33 0N 40 15 E
Ar Ruwayḑah, Si. Arabia 86 B4 23 40N 44 40 E
Ara, India 81 G11 25 35N 84 32 E
'Arab, Bahr el →, Sudan 95 F2 9 0N 29 30 E
Arab, Khalîg el, Egypt 94 H6 30 55N 29 0 E
'Arabābād, Iran 85 C8 33 2N 57 41 E
'Arabah, W. →, Yemen 87 C5 18 5N 51 26 E
Araban, Turkey 89 E7 37 28N 37 3 E
Arabatskaya Strelka, Ukraine 52 D6 45 40N 35 0 E
Arabba, Italy 39 B8 46 30N 11 51 E
Arabelo, Venezuela 153 C5 4 55N 64 13W
Arabia, Asia 90 C4 25 0N 45 0 E
Arabian Desert = Es Sahrâ' Esh Sharqîya, Egypt 94 B3 27 30N 32 30 E
Arabian Gulf = Gulf, The, Asia 85 E6 27 0N 50 0 E
Arabian Sea, Ind. Oc. 58 H10 16 0N 65 0 E
Araç, Turkey 88 C5 41 15N 33 21 E
Aracaju, Brazil 154 D4 10 55 S 37 4W
Aracataca, Colombia 152 A3 10 38N 74 9W
Aracati, Brazil 154 B4 4 30 S 37 44W
Araçatuba, Brazil 159 A5 21 10 S 50 30W
Araceli, Phil. 71 F2 10 33N 119 59 E
Aracena, Spain 37 H4 37 53N 6 38W
Aracena, Sierra de, Spain 37 H4 37 50N 6 50W
Aracides, C., Solomon Is. 121 M11 8 21 S 161 0 E
Araçuaí, Brazil 155 E3 16 52 S 42 4W
Araçuaí →, Brazil 155 E3 16 46 S 42 2W
'Arad, Israel 91 D4 31 15N 35 12 E
Arad, Romania 46 C2 46 10N 21 20 E
Arad □, Romania 46 C2 46 20N 22 0 E
Arada, Chad 97 F4 15 0N 20 20 E
Aradhippou, Cyprus 32 E12 34 57N 33 36 E
Aradu Nou, Romania 46 C2 46 8N 21 20 E
Arafura Sea, E. Indies 73 C5 9 0 S 135 0 E
Aragarças, Brazil 157 D7 15 55 S 52 15W
Aragats, Armenia 53 F11 40 30N 44 15 E
Aragón □, Spain 34 D4 41 25N 0 40W
Aragón →, Spain 34 C3 42 13N 1 44W
Aragona, Italy 40 E6 37 24N 13 36 E
Aragua □, Venezuela 152 B4 10 0N 67 10W
Aragua de Barcelona, Venezuela 153 B5 9 28N 64 49W
Araguacema, Brazil 154 C2 8 50 S 49 20W
Araguaçu, Brazil 155 D2 12 49 S 49 51W
Araguaia →, Brazil 154 C2 5 21 S 48 41W
Araguaiana, Brazil 157 D7 15 43 S 51 51W
Araguaína, Brazil 154 C2 7 12 S 48 12W
Araguari, Brazil 155 E2 18 38 S 48 11W
Araguari →, Brazil 153 C8 1 15N 49 55W
Araguatins, Brazil 154 C2 5 38 S 48 7W
Araioses, Brazil 154 B3 2 53 S 41 55W
Arak, Algeria 99 C5 25 20N 3 45 E
Arāk, Iran 85 C6 34 0N 49 40 E
Arakan □, Burma 78 F5 19 0N 94 15 E
Arakan Yoma, Burma 78 F5 20 0N 94 40 E
Arákhova, Greece 45 F4 38 28N 22 35 E
Arakkonam, India 83 H4 13 7N 79 43 E
Arakli, Turkey 89 C9 41 6N 40 2 E
Araks = Aras, Rūd-e →, Iran 84 B5 39 10N 47 10 E
Aral Sea = Aralskoye More, Asia 56 E7 44 30N 60 0 E
Aralsk, Kazakhstan 56 E7 46 50N 61 20 E
Aralskoye More, Asia 56 E7 44 30N 60 0 E
Aramac, Australia 114 C4 22 58 S 145 14 E
Arambag, India 81 H12 22 53N 87 48 E
Aran Areh, Ethiopia 108 C2 9 2N 43 54 E
Aran I., Ireland 19 B3 55 0N 8 30W
Aran Is., Ireland 19 C2 53 5N 9 42W
Aranda de Duero, Spain 34 D1 41 39N 3 42W
Arandān, Iran 84 C5 35 23N 46 55 E
Aranđelovac, Serbia 42 C5 44 18N 20 27 E
Aranga, N.Z. 118 B2 35 44 S 173 40 E
Arani, India 83 H4 12 43N 79 19 E
Aranjuez, Spain 36 E7 40 1N 3 40W
Aranos, Namibia 104 C2 24 9 S 19 7 E
Aransas Pass, U.S.A. 139 M6 27 55N 97 9W
Aranzazu, Colombia 152 B2 5 16N 75 30W
Arao, Japan 62 E2 32 59N 130 25 E
Araouane, Mali 100 B4 18 55N 3 30W
Arapahoe, U.S.A. 138 E5 40 18N 99 54W
Arapari, Brazil 154 C2 5 34 S 49 15W
Arapawa I., N.Z. 119 B9 41 11 S 174 17 E
Arapey Grande →, Uruguay 158 C4 30 55 S 57 49W
Arapiraca, Brazil 154 C4 9 45 S 36 39W
Arapkir, Turkey 89 D8 39 5N 38 30 E
Arapongas, Brazil 159 A5 23 29 S 51 28W
Arapuni, N.Z. 118 E4 38 4 S 175 39 E
Ar'ar, Si. Arabia 84 D4 30 59N 41 2 E
Araracuara, Colombia 152 D3 0 24 S 72 17W
Araranguá, Brazil 159 B6 29 0 S 49 30W
Araraquara, Brazil 155 F2 21 50 S 48 0W
Ararás, Serra das, Brazil 159 B5 25 0 S 53 10W
Ararat, Australia 116 D5 37 16 S 143 0 E
Ararat, Mt. = Ağrı Dağı, Turkey 89 D11 39 50N 44 15 E
Arari, Brazil 154 B3 3 28 S 44 47W
Araria, India 81 F12 26 9N 87 33 E
Araripe, Chapada do, Brazil 154 C3 7 20 S 40 0W
Araripina, Brazil 154 C3 7 33 S 40 34W
Araruama, L. de, Brazil 155 F3 22 53 S 42 12W
Araruna, Brazil 154 C4 6 52 S 35 44W
Aras, Rūd-e →, Iran 84 B5 39 10N 47 10 E
Araticu, Brazil 154 B2 1 58 S 49 51W
Arauca, Colombia 152 B3 7 0N 70 40W
Arauca □, Colombia 152 B3 6 40N 71 0W
Arauca →, Venezuela 152 B4 7 24N 66 35W
Arauco, Chile 158 D1 37 16 S 73 25W
Arauco □, Chile 158 D1 37 40 S 73 25W
Araújos, Brazil 155 E2 19 56 S 45 14W
Arauquita, Colombia 152 B3 7 2N 71 25W
Araure, Venezuela 152 B4 9 34N 69 13W
Arawa, Ethiopia 95 F5 9 57N 41 58 E
Arawata →, N.Z. 119 E3 44 0 S 168 40 E
Araxá, Brazil 155 E2 19 35 S 46 55W
Araya, Pen. de, Venezuela 153 A5 10 40N 64 0W
Arayat, Phil. 70 D3 15 10N 120 46 E
Arba Minch, Ethiopia 95 F4 6 0N 37 30 E
Arbat, Iraq 84 C5 35 25N 45 35 E
Arbatax, Italy 40 C2 39 57N 9 42 E
Arbaza, Russia 57 D10 52 40N 92 30 E
Arbedo, Switz. 29 D8 46 12N 9 3 E
Arbīl, Iraq 84 B5 36 15N 44 5 E
Arbois, France 23 F12 46 55N 5 46 E
Arboletes, Colombia 152 B2 8 51N 76 26W
Arbon, Switz. 29 A8 47 31N 9 26 E
Arbore, Ethiopia 95 F4 5 3N 36 50 E
Arborea, Italy 40 C1 39 46N 8 34 E
Arborfield, Canada 131 C8 53 6N 103 39W
Arborg, Canada 131 C9 50 54N 97 13W
Arbrå, Sweden 14 C10 61 28N 16 22 E
Arbroath, U.K. 18 E6 56 34N 2 35W
Arbuckle, U.S.A. 144 F4 39 1N 122 3W
Arbus, Italy 40 C1 39 30N 8 33 E
Arbuzinka, Ukraine 52 C4 47 50N 31 59 E
Arc, France 23 E12 47 28N 5 34 E
Arc →, France 25 C10 45 34N 6 12 E
Arcachon, France 24 D2 44 40N 1 10W
Arcachon, Bassin d', France 24 D2 44 42N 1 10W
Arcade, U.S.A. 136 D6 42 32N 78 25W
Arcadia, Fla., U.S.A. 135 M5 27 13N 81 52W
Arcadia, Ind., U.S.A. 141 D10 40 11N 86 1W
Arcadia, Iowa, U.S.A. 140 B1 42 5N 95 3W
Arcadia, La., U.S.A. 139 J8 32 33N 92 55W
Arcadia, Nebr., U.S.A. 138 E5 41 25N 99 8W
Arcadia, Pa., U.S.A. 136 F6 40 47N 78 51W
Arcadia, Wis., U.S.A. 138 C9 44 15N 91 30W
Arcanum, U.S.A. 141 E12 39 59N 84 33W
Arcata, U.S.A. 142 F1 40 52N 124 5W
Arcévia, Italy 39 E9 43 29N 12 58 E
Archangel = Arkhangelsk, Russia 48 B7 64 40N 41 0 E
Archar, Bulgaria 42 D7 43 50N 22 54 E
Archbald, U.S.A. 137 E9 41 30N 75 32W
Archbold, U.S.A. 141 C12 41 32N 84 18W
Archena, Spain 35 G3 38 9N 1 16W
Archer →, Australia 114 A3 13 28 S 141 41 E
Archer B., Australia 114 A3 13 20 S 141 30 E
Archers Post, Kenya 106 B4 0 35N 37 35 E
Archidona, Spain 37 H6 37 6N 4 22W
Arci, Monte, Italy 40 C1 39 47N 8 44 E
Arcidosso, Italy 39 F8 42 51N 11 30 E
Arcila = Asilah, Morocco 98 A3 35 29N 6 0W
Arcis-sur-Aube, France 23 D11 48 32N 4 10 E
Arckaringa, Australia 115 D1 27 56 S 134 45 E
Arckaringa Cr. →, Australia 115 D2 28 10 S 135 22 E
Arco, Italy 38 C7 45 55N 10 54 E
Arco, U.S.A. 142 E7 43 38N 113 18W
Arcola, Canada 131 D8 49 40N 102 30W
Arcola, U.S.A. 141 E8 39 41N 88 19W
Arcoona, Australia 116 A2 31 2 S 137 1 E
Arcos, Spain 34 D2 41 12N 2 16W
Arcos de los Frontera, Spain 37 J5 36 45N 5 49W
Arcos de Valdevez, Portugal 36 D2 41 55N 8 22W
Arcot, India 83 H4 12 53N 79 20 E
Arcoverde, Brazil 154 C4 8 25 S 37 4W
Arctic Bay, Canada 127 A11 73 1N 85 7W
Arctic Ocean, Arctic 6 B18 78 0N 160 0W
Arctic Red River, Canada 126 B6 67 15N 134 0W
Arda →, Bulgaria 43 F11 41 40N 26 29 E
Arda →, Italy 38 D6 44 53N 9 52 E
Ardabīl, Iran 85 B6 38 15N 48 18 E
Ardahan, Turkey 89 C10 41 7N 42 41 E
Ardakān = Sepīdān, Iran 85 D7 30 20N 52 5 E
Ardales, Spain 37 J6 36 53N 4 51W
Ardalstangen, Norway 14 C1 61 14N 7 43 E
Ardatov, Russia 51 D15 54 51N 46 15 E
Ardea, Greece 44 D4 40 58N 22 3 E
Ardèche □, France 25 D8 44 42N 4 16 E
Ardèche →, France 25 D8 44 16N 4 39 E
Ardee, Ireland 19 C5 53 51N 6 32W
Arden, Canada 136 B8 44 43N 76 56W
Arden, Denmark 15 H3 56 46N 9 52 E
Arden, Calif., U.S.A. 144 G5 38 36N 121 33W
Arden, Nev., U.S.A. 145 J11 36 1N 115 14W
Ardenne, Belgium 23 C12 49 50N 5 5 E
Ardennes = Ardenne, Belgium 23 C12 49 50N 5 5 E
Ardennes □, France 23 C11 49 35N 4 40 E
Ardentes, France 23 F8 46 45N 1 50 E
Ardeşen, Turkey 89 C9 41 12N 41 2 E
Ardestān, Iran 85 C7 33 20N 52 25 E
Ardgour, U.K. 18 E3 56 45N 5 25W
Árdhas →, Greece 44 C8 41 36N 26 25 E
Ardila →, Portugal 37 G3 38 12N 7 28W
Ardino, Bulgaria 43 F10 41 34N 25 9 E
Ardlethan, Australia 117 C7 34 22 S 146 53 E
Ardmore, Australia 114 C2 21 39 S 139 11 E
Ardmore, Okla., U.S.A. 139 H6 34 10N 97 8W
Ardmore, Pa., U.S.A. 137 G9 39 58N 75 18W
Ardmore, S. Dak., U.S.A. 138 D3 43 1N 103 40W
Ardnacrusha, Ireland 19 D3 52 43N 8 38W
Ardnamurchan, Pt. of, U.K. 18 E2 56 44N 6 14W
Ardooie, Belgium 21 G2 50 59N 3 13 E
Ardore Marina, Italy 41 D9 38 11N 16 10 E
Ardres, France 23 B8 50 50N 1 59 E
Ardrossan, Australia 116 C2 34 26 S 137 53 E
Ardrossan, U.K. 18 F4 55 39N 4 50W
Ards □, U.K. 19 B6 54 35N 5 30W
Ards Pen., U.K. 19 B6 54 30N 5 25W
Ardud, Romania 46 B3 47 37N 22 52 E
Ardunac, Turkey 53 F10 41 8N 42 5 E
Åre, Sweden 14 A7 63 22N 13 15 E
Arecibo, Puerto Rico 149 C6 18 29N 66 43W
Areia Branca, Brazil 154 B4 5 0 S 37 0W
Arena, Pt., U.S.A. 144 G3 38 57N 123 44W
Arenales, Cerro, Chile 160 C2 47 5 S 73 40W
Arenápolis, Brazil 157 C6 14 26 S 56 49W
Arenas, Spain 36 B6 43 17N 4 50W
Arenas de San Pedro, Spain 36 E5 40 12N 5 5W
Arendal, Norway 15 F2 58 28N 8 46 E
Arendonk, Belgium 21 F6 51 19N 5 5 E
Arendsee, Germany 26 C7 52 52N 11 27 E
Arenillas, Ecuador 152 D1 3 33 S 80 10W
Arenys de Mar, Spain 34 D7 41 35N 2 33 E
Arenzano, Italy 38 D5 44 24N 8 40 E
Arenzville, U.S.A. 140 E6 39 53N 90 22W
Areópolis, Greece 45 H4 36 40N 22 22 E
Arequipa, Peru 156 D3 16 20 S 71 30W
Arequipa □, Peru 156 D3 16 0 S 72 50W
Arere, Brazil 153 D7 0 16 S 53 52W
Arero, Ethiopia 95 G4 4 41N 38 50 E
Arès, France 24 D2 44 47N 1 8W
Arévalo, Spain 36 D6 41 3N 4 43W
Arezzo, Italy 39 E8 43 28N 11 50 E
Arga →, Spain 34 C3 42 18N 1 47W
Argalastí, Greece 44 E5 39 13N 23 13 E
Argamakmur, Indonesia 74 C2 3 35 S 102 0 E
Argamasilla de Alba, Spain 35 F1 39 8N 3 5W
Arganda, Spain 34 E1 40 19N 3 26W
Arganil, Portugal 36 E2 40 13N 8 3W
Argayash, Russia 54 D7 55 29N 60 52 E
Argelès-Gazost, France 24 F3 43 0N 0 6W
Argelès-sur-Mer, France 24 F7 42 34N 3 1 E
Argens →, France 25 E10 43 24N 6 44 E
Argent-sur-Sauldre, France 23 E9 47 33N 2 25 E
Argenta, Italy 39 D8 44 37N 11 50 E
Argenta, U.S.A. 141 E8 39 59N 88 49W
Argentan, France 22 D6 48 45N 0 1W
Argentário, Mte., Italy 39 F8 42 23N 11 11 E
Argentat, France 24 C5 45 6N 1 56 E
Argentera, Italy 38 D3 44 23N 6 58 E
Argentera, Monte del, Italy 38 D4 44 12N 7 5 E
Argenteuil, France 23 D9 48 57N 2 14 E
Argentia, Canada 129 C9 47 18N 53 58W
Argentiera, C. dell', Italy 40 B1 40 44N 8 8 E
Argentière, Aiguilles d', Switz. 28 E4 45 58N 7 2 E
Argentina ■, S. Amer. 160 B3 35 0 S 66 0W
Argentina Is., Antarctica 7 C17 66 0 S 64 0W
Argentino, L., Argentina 160 D2 50 10 S 73 0W
Argenton-Château, France 22 F6 46 59N 0 27W
Argenton-sur-Creuse, France 24 B5 46 36N 1 30 E
Argeş □, Romania 46 D5 45 0N 24 45 E
Argeş →, Romania 46 E7 44 12N 26 14 E
Arghandab →, Afghan. 79 C2 31 30N 64 15 E
Argo, Sudan 94 D3 19 28N 30 30 E
Argolikós Kólpos, Greece 45 G4 37 20N 22 52 E
Argolís □, Greece 45 G4 37 38N 22 50 E
Argonne, France 23 C12 49 10N 5 0 E
Árgos, Greece 45 G4 37 40N 22 43 E
Argos, U.S.A. 141 C10 41 14N 86 15W
Árgos Orestikón, Greece 44 D3 40 27N 21 26 E
Argostólion, Greece 45 F2 38 12N 20 33 E
Arguedas, Spain 34 C3 42 11N 1 36W
Arguello, Pt., U.S.A. 145 L6 34 35N 120 39W
Arguineguín, Canary Is. 33 G4 27 46N 15 41W
Argun →, Russia 57 D13 53 20N 121 28 E
Argungu, Nigeria 101 C5 12 40N 4 31 E
Argus Pk., U.S.A. 145 K9 35 52N 117 26W
Argyle, U.S.A. 138 A6 48 20N 96 49W
Argyle, L., Australia 112 C4 16 20 S 128 40 E
Arhavi, Turkey 89 C9 41 21N 41 18 E
Århus, Denmark 15 H4 56 8N 10 11 E
Århus Amtskommune □, Denmark 15 H4 56 15N 10 15 E
Aria, N.Z. 118 E4 38 33 S 175 0 E
Ariadnoye, Russia 60 B7 45 8N 134 25 E
Ariamsvlei, Namibia 104 D2 28 9 S 19 51 E
Ariana, Tunisia 96 A2 36 52N 10 12 E
Ariano Irpino, Italy 41 A8 41 10N 15 4 E
Ariano nel Polèsine, Italy 39 D9 44 56N 12 5 E
Ariari →, Colombia 152 C3 2 35N 72 47W
Aribinda, Burkina Faso 101 C4 14 17N 0 52W
Arica, Chile 156 D3 18 32 S 70 20W
Arica, Colombia 152 D3 2 0 S 71 50W

168 Arico

Arico, Canary Is. 33 F3 28 9N 16 29W
Arid, C., Australia 113 F3 34 1S 123 10 E
Arida, Japan 63 C7 34 5N 135 8 E
Ariège □, France 24 F5 42 56N 1 30 E
Ariège →, France 24 E5 43 30N 1 25 E
Arieş →, Romania 46 C4 46 24N 23 20 E
Arīḩā, Syria 84 C3 35 49N 36 35 E
Arilje, Serbia 42 D5 43 44N 20 7 E
Arílla, Ákra, Greece 32 A3 39 43N 19 39 E
Arima, Trin. & Tob. 149 D7 10 38N 61 17W
Aringay, Phil. 70 C3 16 26N 120 21 E
Arinos →, Brazil 157 C6 10 25 S 58 20W
Ario de Rosales, Mexico 146 D4 19 12N 102 0W
Aripuanã, Brazil 157 B5 9 25 S 60 30W
Aripuanã →, Brazil 157 B5 5 7 S 60 25W
Ariquemes, Brazil 157 B5 9 55 S 63 6W
Arisaig, U.K. 18 E3 56 55N 5 50W
Arîsh, W. el →, Egypt 94 H8 31 9N 33 49 E
Arismendi, Venezuela 152 B4 8 29N 68 22W
Arissa, Ethiopia 95 E5 11 10N 41 35 E
Aristazabal I., Canada 130 C3 52 40N 129 10W
Arita, Japan 62 D1 33 11N 129 54 E
Aritao, Phil. 70 C3 16 18N 121 2 E
Arivaca, U.S.A. 143 L8 31 37N 111 25W
Arivonimamo, Madag. 105 B8 19 1 S 47 11 E
Ariyalur, India 83 J4 11 8N 79 8 E
Ariza, Spain 34 D2 41 19N 2 3W
Arizaro, Salar de, Argentina 158 A2 24 40 S 67 50W
Arizona, Argentina 158 D2 35 45 S 65 25W
Arizona □, U.S.A. 143 J8 34 0N 112 0W
Arizpe, Mexico 146 A2 30 20N 110 11W
Arjeplog, Sweden 12 C15 66 3N 18 2 E
Arjona, Colombia 152 A2 10 14N 75 22W
Arjona, Spain 37 H6 37 56N 4 4W
Arjuno, Indonesia 75 D4 7 49 S 112 34 E
Arka, Russia 57 C15 60 15N 142 0 E
Arkadak, Russia 51 F13 51 58N 43 19 E
Arkadelphia, U.S.A. 139 H8 34 7N 93 4W
Arkadhía □, Greece 45 G4 37 30N 22 20 E
Arkaig, L., U.K. 18 E3 56 58N 5 10W
Arkalyk, Kazakhstan 56 D7 50 13N 66 50 E
Arkansas □, U.S.A. 139 H8 35 0N 92 30W
Arkansas →, U.S.A. 139 J9 33 47N 91 4W
Arkansas City, U.S.A. 139 G6 37 4N 97 2W
Árkathos →, Greece 44 E3 39 20N 21 4 E
Arkhángelos, Greece 32 C10 36 13N 28 7 E
Arkhangelsk, Russia 48 B7 64 40N 41 0 E
Arkhangelskoye, Russia 51 F12 51 32N 40 58 E
Arkiko, Eritrea 95 D4 15 33N 39 30 E
Arklow, Ireland 19 D5 52 48N 6 10W
Árkoi, Greece 45 G8 37 24N 26 44 E
Arkona, Kap, Germany 26 A9 54 41N 13 26 E
Arkösund, Sweden 15 F10 58 29N 16 56 E
Arkoúdhi, Greece 45 F2 38 33N 20 43 E
Arkticheskiy, Mys, Russia 57 A10 81 10N 95 0 E
Arkul, Russia 54 C2 57 17N 50 3 E
Arlanc, France 24 C7 45 25N 3 42 E
Arlanza →, Spain 36 C6 42 6N 4 9W
Arlanzón →, Spain 36 C6 42 3N 4 17W
Arlberg Pass, Austria 27 H6 47 9N 10 12 E
Arlee, U.S.A. 142 C6 47 10N 114 5W
Arles, France 25 E8 43 41N 4 40 E
Arlesheim, Switz. 28 B5 47 30N 7 37 E
Arlington, S. Africa 105 D4 28 1 S 27 53 E
Arlington, Oreg., U.S.A. 142 D3 45 43N 120 12W
Arlington, S. Dak., U.S.A. 138 C6 44 22N 97 8W
Arlington, Va., U.S.A. 134 F7 38 53N 77 7W
Arlington, Wash., U.S.A. 144 B4 48 12N 122 8W
Arlington Heights, U.S.A. 141 B9 42 5N 87 59W
Arlon, Belgium 21 J7 49 42N 5 49 E
Arlöv, Sweden 15 J7 55 38N 13 5 E
Arly, Burkina Faso 101 C5 11 35N 1 28 E
Armagh, U.K. 19 B5 54 22N 6 40W
Armagh □, U.K. 19 B5 54 18N 6 37W
Armagnac, France 24 E4 43 50N 0 10 E
Armançon →, France 23 E10 47 59N 3 30 E
Armavir, Russia 53 D9 45 2N 41 7 E
Armenia, Colombia 152 C2 4 35N 75 45W
Armenia ■, Asia 53 F11 40 20N 45 0 E
Armeniş, Romania 46 D3 45 13N 22 17 E
Armenistís, Ákra, Greece 32 C9 36 8N 27 42 E
Armentières, France 23 B9 50 40N 2 50 E
Armidale, Australia 117 A9 30 30 S 151 40 E
Armour, U.S.A. 138 D5 43 19N 98 21W
Armstrong, B.C., Canada 130 C5 50 25N 119 10W
Armstrong, Ont., Canada 128 B2 50 18N 89 4W
Armstrong, U.S.A. 139 M6 26 56N 97 47W
Armstrong →, Australia 112 C5 16 35 S 131 40 E
Armur, India 82 E4 18 48N 78 16 E
Arnaía, Greece 44 D5 40 30N 23 40 E
Arnarfjörður, Iceland 12 D2 65 48N 23 40W
Arnaud →, Canada 127 B12 60 0N 70 0W
Arnauti, C., Cyprus 32 D11 35 6N 32 17 E
Arnay-le-Duc, France 23 E11 47 10N 4 27 E
Arnedillo, Spain 34 C2 42 13N 2 14W
Arnedo, Spain 34 C2 42 12N 2 5W
Arnemuiden, Neths. 21 F3 51 30N 3 40 E
Árnes, Iceland 12 C3 66 1N 21 31W
Årnes, Norway 14 D5 60 7N 11 28 E
Arnett, U.S.A. 139 G5 36 8N 99 46W
Arnhem, Neths. 20 E7 51 58N 5 55 E
Arnhem, C., Australia 114 A2 12 20 S 137 30 E
Arnhem B., Australia 114 A2 12 20 S 136 10 E
Arnhem Land, Australia 114 A1 13 10 S 134 30 E
Árnissa, Greece 44 D3 40 47N 21 49 E
Arno →, Italy 38 E7 43 41N 10 17 E
Arno Bay, Australia 116 B2 33 54 S 136 34 E
Arnold, Calif., U.S.A. 144 G6 38 15N 120 20W
Arnold, Nebr., U.S.A. 138 E4 41 26N 100 12W
Arnoldstein, Austria 30 E6 46 33N 13 43 E
Arnon →, France 23 E9 47 13N 2 1 E
Arnot, Canada 131 B9 55 56N 96 41W
Arnøy, Norway 12 A16 70 9N 20 40 E
Arnprior, Canada 128 C4 45 26N 76 21W
Arnsberg, Germany 26 D4 51 25N 8 2 E
Arnstadt, Germany 26 E6 50 50N 10 56 E
Aro →, Venezuela 153 B5 8 1N 64 11W
Aroab, Namibia 104 D2 26 41 S 19 39 E
Aroánia Óri, Greece 45 G4 37 56N 22 12 E
Aroche, Spain 37 H4 37 56N 6 57W
Aroeiras, Brazil 154 C4 7 31 S 35 41W
Arolla, Switz. 28 D4 46 2N 7 29 E
Arolsen, Germany 26 D5 51 23N 9 1 E
Aron →, France 24 B7 46 50N 3 28 E
Arona, Italy 38 C5 45 45N 8 32 E
Aroroy, Phil. 70 E4 12 31N 123 24 E
Arosa, Switz. 29 C9 46 47N 9 41 E
Arosa, Ria de, Spain 36 C2 42 28N 8 57W
Arpajon, France 23 D9 48 36N 2 15 E
Arpajon-sur-Cère, France 24 D6 44 53N 2 28 E
Arpino, Italy 40 A6 41 40N 13 35 E
Arque, Bolivia 156 D4 17 48 S 66 23W
Arrabury, Australia 115 D3 26 45 S 141 0 E
Arrah = Ara, India 81 G11 25 35N 84 32 E
Arraias, Brazil 155 D2 12 56 S 46 57W
Arraias →, Mato Grosso, Brazil 157 C7 11 10 S 53 35W
Arraias →, Pará, Brazil 154 C2 7 30 S 49 20W
Arraiolos, Portugal 37 G3 38 44N 7 59W
Arran, U.K. 18 F3 55 34N 5 12W
Arrandale, Canada 130 C3 54 57N 130 0W
Arras, France 23 B9 50 17N 2 46 E
Arrats →, France 24 D4 44 6N 0 52 E
Arreau, France 24 F4 42 54N 0 22 E
Arrecife, Canary Is. 33 F6 28 57N 13 37W
Arrecifes, Argentina 158 C3 34 6 S 60 9W
Arrée, Mts. d', France 22 D3 48 26N 3 55W
Arriaga, Chiapas, Mexico 147 D6 16 15N 93 52W
Arriaga, San Luis Potosí, Mexico 146 C4 21 55N 101 23W
Arrilalah P.O., Australia 114 C3 23 43 S 143 54 E
Arrino, Australia 113 E2 29 30 S 115 40 E
Arrojado →, Brazil 155 D3 13 24 S 44 20W
Arromanches-les-Bains, France 22 C6 49 20N 0 38W
Arronches, Portugal 37 F3 39 8N 7 16W
Arros →, France 24 E3 43 40N 0 2W
Arrou, France 22 D8 48 6N 1 8 E
Arrow, L., Ireland 19 B3 54 3N 8 20W
Arrow Rock Res., U.S.A. 142 E6 43 45N 115 50W
Arrowhead, Canada 130 C5 50 40N 117 55W
Arrowhead, L., U.S.A. 145 L9 34 16N 117 10W
Arrowsmith, Mt., N.Z. 119 D5 43 20 S 170 55 E
Arrowtown, N.Z. 119 E3 44 57 S 168 50 E
Arroyo de la Luz, Spain 37 F4 39 30N 6 38W
Arroyo Grande, U.S.A. 145 K6 35 7N 120 35W
Års, Denmark 15 H3 56 48N 9 30 E
Ars, Iran 84 B5 37 9N 47 46 E
Ars-en-Ré, France 24 B2 46 12N 1 31W
Ars-sur-Moselle, France 23 C13 49 5N 6 4 E
Arsenault L., Canada 131 B7 55 6N 108 32W
Arsenev, Russia 60 B6 44 10N 133 15 E
Arsi □, Ethiopia 95 F4 7 45N 39 0 E
Arsiero, Italy 39 C8 45 49N 11 22 E
Arsikere, India 83 H3 13 15N 76 15 E
Arsin, Turkey 89 C8 41 8N 39 55 E
Arsk, Russia 51 C16 56 10N 49 50 E
Árta, Greece 45 E3 39 8N 21 2 E
Artá, Spain 33 B10 39 41N 3 21 E
Árta □, Greece 44 E3 39 15N 21 5 E
Arteaga, Mexico 146 D4 18 50N 102 20W
Arteche, Phil. 70 E5 12 17N 125 22 E
Arteijo, Spain 36 B2 43 19N 8 29W
Artem, Russia 60 C6 43 22N 132 13 E
Artem, Ostrov, Azerbaijan 53 F14 40 28N 50 20 E
Artemovsk, Russia 57 D10 54 45N 93 35 E
Artemovsk, Ukraine 52 B8 48 35N 38 0 E
Artemovski, Russia 53 C9 47 45N 40 16 E
Artemovskiy, Russia 54 C7 57 21N 61 54 E
Artenay, France 23 D8 48 5N 1 50 E
Artern, Germany 26 D7 51 22N 11 18 E
Artesa de Segre, Spain 34 D6 41 54N 1 3 E
Artesia = Mosomane, Botswana 104 C4 24 2 S 26 19 E
Artesia, U.S.A. 139 J2 32 51N 104 24W
Artesia Wells, U.S.A. 139 L5 28 17N 99 17W
Artesian, U.S.A. 138 C6 44 1N 97 55W
Arth, Switz. 29 B7 47 4N 8 31 E
Arthez-de-Béarn, France 24 E3 43 29N 0 38W
Arthington, Liberia 100 D2 6 35N 10 45W
Arthur, U.S.A. 141 E8 39 43N 88 28W
Arthur →, Australia 114 G3 41 2 S 144 40 E
Arthur Cr. →, Australia 114 C2 22 30 S 136 25 E
Arthur Pt., Australia 114 C5 22 7 S 150 3 E
Arthur's Pass, N.Z. 119 C6 42 54 S 171 35 E
Arthur's Town, Bahamas 149 B4 24 38N 75 42W
Artigas, Uruguay 158 C4 30 20 S 56 30W
Artik, Armenia 53 F10 40 38N 43 58 E
Artillery L., Canada 131 A7 63 9N 107 52W
Artois, France 23 B9 50 20N 2 30 E
Artotína, Greece 45 F4 38 42N 22 2 E
Artsiz, Ukraine 52 C3 46 4N 29 26 E
Artvin, Turkey 53 F9 41 14N 41 44 E
Artvin □, Turkey 89 C9 41 10N 41 50 E
Aru, Kepulauan, Indonesia 73 C4 6 0 S 134 30 E
Aru Is. = Aru, Kepulauan, Indonesia 73 C4 6 0 S 134 30 E
Aru Meru □, Tanzania 106 C4 3 20 S 36 50 E
Arua, Uganda 106 B3 3 1N 30 58 E
Aruanã, Brazil 155 D1 14 54 S 51 10W
Aruba ■, W. Indies 149 D6 12 30N 70 0W
Arucas, Canary Is. 33 F4 28 7N 15 32W
Arudy, France 24 E3 43 7N 0 28W
Arumã, Brazil 153 D5 4 44 S 62 8W
Arumpo, Australia 116 B5 33 48 S 142 55 E
Arun →, Nepal 81 F12 26 55N 87 10 E
Arunachal Pradesh □, India 78 A5 28 0N 95 0 E
Aruppukkottai, India 83 K4 9 31N 78 8 E
Arusha, Tanzania 106 C4 3 20 S 36 40 E
Arusha □, Tanzania 106 C4 4 0 S 36 30 E
Arusha Chini, Tanzania 106 C4 3 32 S 37 20 E
Arut →, Indonesia 75 C4 2 42 S 111 34 E
Aruvi →, Sri Lanka 83 K4 8 48N 79 53 E
Aruwimi →, Zaïre 106 B1 1 13N 23 36 E
Arvada, U.S.A. 142 D10 44 39N 106 8W
Arvakalu, Sri Lanka 83 K4 8 20N 79 58 E
Arve →, France 25 B10 46 11N 6 8 E
Árvi, Greece 32 E7 34 59N 25 28 E
Arvi, India 82 D4 20 59N 78 16 E
Arvida, Canada 129 C5 48 25N 71 14W
Arvidsjaur, Sweden 12 D15 65 35N 19 10 E
Arvika, Sweden 13 G12 59 40N 12 36 E
Arvin, U.S.A. 145 K8 35 12N 118 50W
Arxan, China 65 B6 47 11N 119 57 E
Aryirádhes, Greece 32 B3 39 27N 19 58 E
Aryiroúpolis, Greece 32 D6 35 17N 24 20 E
Arys, Kazakhstan 55 B4 42 26N 68 48 E
Arys →, Kazakhstan 55 B4 42 45N 68 15 E
Arzachena, Italy 40 A2 41 5N 9 27 E
Arzamas, Russia 51 D13 55 27N 43 55 E
Arzew, Algeria 99 A4 35 50N 0 23W
Arzgir, Russia 53 D11 45 18N 44 23 E
Arzignano, Italy 39 C8 45 30N 11 20 E
As, Belgium 21 F7 51 1N 5 35 E
Aš, Czech. 30 A5 50 13N 12 12 E
Aş Şadr, U.A.E. 85 E7 24 40N 54 41 E
Aş Şafā, Syria 91 B6 33 10N 37 0 E
'As Saffānīyah, Si. Arabia 85 D6 28 5N 48 50 E
As Safīrah, Syria 84 B3 36 5N 37 21 E
Aş Şahm, Oman 85 E8 24 10N 56 53 E
As Sājir, Si. Arabia 84 E5 25 11N 44 36 E
As Salamīyah, Si. Arabia 86 A4 24 12N 47 18 E
As Salamīyah, Syria 84 C3 35 1N 37 2 E
As Salt, Jordan 91 C4 32 2N 35 43 E
As Sal'w'a, Qatar 85 E6 24 23N 50 50 E
As Samāwah, Iraq 84 D5 31 15N 45 15 E
As Sanamayn, Syria 91 B5 33 3N 36 10 E
As Sawādah, Si. Arabia 86 B4 22 30N 44 28 E
As Sayl al Kabīr, Si. Arabia 86 B3 21 38N 40 25 E
As Sukhnah, Syria 84 C3 34 52N 38 52 E
As Sulaymānīyah, Iraq 84 C5 35 35N 45 29 E
As Sulaymānīyah, Si. Arabia 86 A4 24 9N 47 18 E
As Sulaymī, Si. Arabia 84 E4 26 17N 41 21 E
As Sulayyil, Si. Arabia 86 B4 20 27N 45 34 E
As Sulṭan, Libya 96 B3 31 4N 17 8 E
As Summān, Si. Arabia 84 E5 25 0N 47 0 E
As Sūq, Si. Arabia 86 B3 21 54N 42 3 E
Aş Şurrah, Yemen 86 D4 13 57N 46 14 E
As Suwaydā', Syria 91 C5 32 40N 36 30 E
As Suwaydā' □, Syria 91 C5 32 45N 36 45 E
As Suwayh, Oman 87 B7 22 10N 59 33 E
As Suwayq, Oman 87 B7 23 51N 57 26 E
Aş Şuwayrah, Iraq 84 C5 32 55N 45 0 E
Asab, Namibia 104 D2 25 30 S 18 0 E
Asaba, Nigeria 101 D6 6 12N 6 38 E
Asafo, Ghana 100 D4 6 20N 2 40W
Asahi, Japan 63 B12 35 43N 140 39 E
Asahi-Gawa →, Japan 62 C5 34 36N 133 58 E
Asahigawa, Japan 60 C11 43 46N 142 22 E
Asale, L., Ethiopia 95 E5 14 0N 40 20 E
Asama-Yama, Japan 63 A10 36 24N 138 31 E
Asamankese, Ghana 101 D4 5 50N 0 40W
Asansol, India 81 H12 23 40N 87 1 E
Åsarna, Sweden 14 B8 62 39N 14 22 E
Asbe Teferi, Ethiopia 95 F5 9 4N 40 49 E
Asbesberge, S. Africa 104 D3 29 0 S 23 0 E
Asbest, Russia 54 C7 57 0N 61 30 E
Asbestos, Canada 129 C5 45 47N 71 58W
Asbury Park, U.S.A. 137 F10 40 13N 74 1W
Ascensión, Mexico 146 A3 31 6N 107 59W
Ascensión, B. de la, Mexico 147 D7 19 50N 87 20W
Ascension I., Atl. Oc. 9 J7 8 0 S 14 15W
Aschach, Austria 30 C7 48 22N 14 2 E
Aschaffenburg, Germany 27 F5 49 58N 9 8 E
Aschendorf, Germany 26 B3 53 2N 7 22 E
Aschersleben, Germany 26 D7 51 45N 11 28 E
Asciano, Italy 39 E8 43 14N 11 32 E
Áscoli Piceno, Italy 39 F10 42 51N 13 34 E
Áscoli Satriano, Italy 41 A8 41 11N 15 32 E
Ascona, Switz. 29 D7 46 9N 8 46 E
Ascope, Peru 156 B2 7 46 S 79 8W
Ascotán, Chile 158 A2 21 45 S 68 17W
Ascuncion, Phil. 71 H5 7 35N 125 45 E
Aseb, Eritrea 90 E3 13 0N 42 40 E
Asedjrad, Algeria 99 D5 24 51N 1 29 E
Asela, Ethiopia 95 F4 8 0N 39 0 E
Asenovgrad, Bulgaria 43 E9 42 1N 24 51 E
Asfeld, France 23 C11 49 27N 4 5 E
Asfûn el Matâ'na, Egypt 94 B3 25 26N 32 30 E
Åsgårdstrand, Norway 14 E4 59 22N 10 27 E
Asgata, Cyprus 32 E12 34 46N 33 15 E
Ash Fork, U.S.A. 143 J7 35 13N 112 29W
Ash Grove, U.S.A. 139 G8 37 19N 93 35W
Ash Shamāl □, Lebanon 91 A5 34 25N 36 0 E
Ash Shāmīyah, Iraq 84 D5 31 55N 44 35 E
Ash Sha'rā', Si. Arabia 86 A4 24 16N 44 11 E
Ash Shāriqah, U.A.E. 85 E7 25 23N 55 26 E
Ash Sharmah, Si. Arabia 84 D2 28 1N 35 16 E
Ash Sharqāt, Iraq 84 C4 35 27N 43 16 E
Ash Sharqi, Al Jabal, Lebanon 91 B5 33 40N 36 10 E
Ash Shaṭrah, Iraq 84 D5 31 30N 46 10 E
Ash Shawbak, Jordan 84 D2 30 32N 35 34 E
Ash Shawmari, J., Jordan 91 E5 30 35N 36 35 E
Ash Shaykh, J., Lebanon 91 B4 33 25N 35 50 E
Ash Shiḩr, Yemen 87 D5 14 45N 49 36 E
Ash Shināfīyah, Iraq 84 D5 31 35N 44 39 E
Ash Shu'aybah, Si. Arabia 84 E5 27 53N 44 43 E
Ash Shumlūl, Si. Arabia 84 E5 26 31N 47 20 E
Ash Shuqayq, Si. Arabia 86 C3 17 44N 42 1 E
Ash Shūr'a, Iraq 84 C4 35 58N 43 13 E
Ash Shurayf, Si. Arabia 84 E3 25 43N 39 14 E
Ash Shuwayfāt, Lebanon 91 B4 33 45N 35 30 E
Asha, Russia 54 D5 55 0N 57 16 E
Ashanti □, Ghana 101 D4 7 30N 1 30W
Ashau, Vietnam 76 D6 16 6N 107 22 E
Ashburn, U.S.A. 135 K4 31 43N 83 39W
Ashburton, N.Z. 119 D6 43 53 S 171 48 E
Ashburton →, Australia 112 D1 21 40 S 114 56 E
Ashburton, North Branch →, N.Z. 119 D6 43 54 S 171 44 E
Ashburton, South Branch →, N.Z. 119 D6 43 54 S 171 44 E
Ashburton Downs, Australia 112 D2 23 25 S 117 4 E
Ashby de la Zouch, U.K. 16 E6 52 45N 1 29W
Ashcroft, Canada 130 C4 50 40N 121 20W
Ashdod, Israel 91 D3 31 49N 34 35 E
Asheboro, U.S.A. 135 H6 35 43N 79 49W
Asherton, U.S.A. 139 L5 28 27N 99 46W
Asheville, U.S.A. 135 H4 35 36N 82 33W
Asheweig →, Canada 128 B2 54 17N 87 12W
Ashford, Australia 115 D5 29 15 S 151 3 E
Ashford, U.K. 17 F8 51 8N 0 53 E
Ashford, U.S.A. 142 C2 46 46N 122 2W
Ashgabat = Ashkhabad, Turkmenistan 56 F6 38 0N 57 50 E
Ashibetsu, Japan 60 C11 43 31N 142 11 E
Ashikaga, Japan 63 A11 36 28N 139 29 E
Ashio, Japan 63 A11 36 38N 139 27 E
Ashizuri-Zaki, Japan 62 E5 32 44N 133 0 E
Ashkarkot, Afghan. 80 C2 33 3N 67 58 E
Ashkhabad, Turkmenistan 56 F6 38 0N 57 50 E
Ashland, Ill., U.S.A. 140 E6 39 53N 90 1W
Ashland, Kans., U.S.A. 139 G5 37 11N 99 46W
Ashland, Ky., U.S.A. 134 F4 38 28N 82 38W
Ashland, Maine, U.S.A. 129 C6 46 38N 68 24W
Ashland, Mont., U.S.A. 142 D10 45 36N 106 16W
Ashland, Nebr., U.S.A. 138 E6 41 3N 96 23W
Ashland, Ohio, U.S.A. 136 F2 40 52N 82 19W
Ashland, Oreg., U.S.A. 142 E2 42 12N 122 43W
Ashland, Pa., U.S.A. 137 F8 40 45N 76 22W
Ashland, Va., U.S.A. 134 G7 37 46N 77 29W
Ashland, Wis., U.S.A. 138 B9 46 35N 90 53W
Ashley, Ill., U.S.A. 140 F7 38 20N 89 11W
Ashley, Ind., U.S.A. 141 C11 41 32N 85 4W
Ashley, N. Dak., U.S.A. 138 B5 46 2N 99 22W
Ashley, Pa., U.S.A. 137 E9 41 12N 75 55W
Ashley →, N.Z. 119 D7 43 17 S 172 44 E
Ashmont, Canada 130 C6 54 7N 111 35W
Ashmore Reef, Australia 112 B3 12 14 S 123 5 E
Ashmûn, Egypt 94 H7 30 18N 30 55 E
Ashq'elon, Israel 91 D3 31 42N 34 35 E
Ashtabula, U.S.A. 136 E4 41 52N 80 47W
Ashti, India 82 E2 18 50N 75 15 E
Ashton, S. Africa 104 E3 33 50 S 20 5 E
Ashton, U.S.A. 142 D8 44 4N 111 27W
Ashton under Lyne, U.K. 16 D5 53 30N 2 8W
Ashuanipi, L., Canada 129 B6 52 45N 66 15W
Ashurst, N.Z. 118 G4 40 16 S 175 45 E
Asia 58 E11 45 0N 75 0 E
Asia, Kepulauan, Indonesia 73 A4 1 0N 131 13 E
Āsīā Bak, Iran 85 C6 35 19N 50 30 E
Asiago, Italy 39 C8 45 52N 11 30 E
Asidonhoppo, Surinam 153 C6 3 50N 55 30W
Asifabad, India 82 E4 19 20N 79 24 E
Asike, Indonesia 73 C6 6 39 S 140 24 E
Asilah, Morocco 98 A3 35 29N 6 0W
Asinara, Italy 40 A1 41 5N 8 15 E
Asinara, G. dell', Italy 40 B1 41 0N 8 30 E
Asino, Russia 56 D9 57 0N 86 0 E
'Asīr □, Si. Arabia 86 C3 18 40N 42 30 E
Asir, Ras, Somali Rep. 90 E5 11 55N 51 10 E
Aska, India 82 E7 19 2N 84 42 E
Aşkale, Turkey 89 D9 39 55N 40 41 E
Asker, Norway 14 E4 59 50N 10 26 E
Askersund, Sweden 15 F8 58 53N 14 55 E
Askham, S. Africa 104 D3 26 59 S 20 47 E
Askim, Norway 14 E5 59 35N 11 10 E
Askino, Russia 54 C5 56 5N 56 34 E
Askja, Iceland 12 D5 65 3N 16 48W
Asl, Egypt 94 J8 29 33N 32 44 E
Asmār, Afghan. 79 B3 35 10N 71 27 E
Asmara = Asmera, Eritrea 95 D4 15 19N 38 55 E
Asmera, Eritrea 95 D4 15 19N 38 55 E
Asnæs, Denmark 15 J5 55 40N 11 0 E
Asni, Morocco 98 B3 31 17N 7 58W
Aso, Japan 62 E3 32 55N 131 5 E
Aso-Zan, Japan 62 E3 32 53N 131 6 E
Ásola, Italy 38 C7 45 12N 10 25 E
Asoteriba, Jebel, Sudan 94 C4 21 51N 36 30 E
Asotin, U.S.A. 142 C5 46 20N 117 3W
Aspe, Spain 35 G4 38 20N 0 40W
Aspen, U.S.A. 143 G10 39 11N 106 49W
Aspendos, Turkey 88 E4 36 54N 31 7 E
Aspermont, U.S.A. 139 J4 33 8N 100 14W
Aspiring, Mt., N.Z. 119 E3 44 23 S 168 46 E
Aspres-sur-Buëch, France 25 D9 44 32N 5 44 E
Asprókavos, Ákra, Greece 32 B4 39 21N 20 6 E
Aspromonte, Italy 41 D8 38 10N 15 55 E
Aspur, India 80 H6 23 58N 74 7 E
Asquith, Canada 131 C7 52 8N 107 13W
Assa, Morocco 98 C3 28 35N 9 6W
Assâba, Mauritania 100 B2 16 10N 11 45W
Assam □, India 78 B4 26 0N 93 0 E
Assamakka, Niger 101 B6 19 21N 5 38 E
Asse, Belgium 21 H4 50 24N 4 10 E
Assebroek, Belgium 21 F2 51 11N 3 17 E
Assekrem, Algeria 99 D6 23 16N 5 49 E
Assémini, Italy 40 C2 39 18N 9 0 E
Assen, Neths. 20 C9 53 0N 6 35 E
Assendelft, Neths. 20 D5 52 29N 4 45 E
Assenede, Belgium 21 F3 51 14N 3 46 E
Assens, Århus, Denmark 15 H4 56 41N 10 3 E
Assens, Fyn, Denmark 15 J3 55 16N 9 55 E
Assesse, Belgium 21 H6 50 22N 5 2 E
Assini, Ivory C. 100 D4 5 9N 3 17W
Assiniboia, Canada 131 D7 49 40N 105 59W
Assiniboine →, Canada 131 D9 49 53N 97 8W
Assis, Brazil 159 A5 22 40 S 50 20W
Assisi, Italy 39 E9 43 4N 12 36 E
Ássos, Greece 45 F2 38 22N 20 33 E
Assumption, U.S.A. 140 E7 39 31N 89 3W
Assus, Turkey 44 E8 39 32N 26 22 E
Assynt, L., U.K. 18 C3 58 25N 5 15W
Astaffort, France 24 D4 44 4N 0 40 E
Astakídha, Greece 45 J8 35 53N 26 50 E
Astara, Azerbaijan 89 D13 38 30N 48 50 E
Asten, Neths. 21 F7 51 24N 5 45 E
Asteroúsia, Greece 32 E7 34 59N 25 3 E
Asti, Italy 38 D5 44 54N 8 11 E
Astipálaia, Greece 45 H8 36 32N 26 22 E
Astorga, Mindanao, Phil. 71 H5 6 54N 125 27 E
Astorga, Panay, Phil. 71 F4 11 15N 122 48 E
Astorga, Spain 36 C4 42 29N 6 8W
Astoria, Ill., U.S.A. 140 D6 40 14N 90 21W
Astoria, Oreg., U.S.A. 144 D3 46 11N 123 50W
Åstorp, Sweden 15 H6 56 6N 12 55 E
Astrakhan, Russia 53 C13 46 25N 48 5 E
Astrakhan-Bazàr, Azerbaijan 49 G8 39 14N 48 30 E
Astudillo, Spain 36 C6 42 12N 4 22W
Asturias □, Spain 36 B5 43 15N 6 0W
Asunción, Paraguay 158 B4 25 10 S 57 30W
Asunción Nochixtlán, Mexico 147 D5 17 28N 97 14W
Asutri, Sudan 95 D4 15 25N 35 45 E
Aswa →, Uganda 106 B3 3 43N 31 55 E
Aswad, Ras al, Si. Arabia 86 B2 21 20N 39 0 E
Aswân, Egypt 94 C3 24 4N 32 57 E
Aswân High Dam = Sadd el Aali, Egypt 94 C3 23 54N 32 54 E

Azärbayjan 169

Asyût, *Egypt* 94 B3 27 11N 31 4 E
Asyûti, Wadi →, *Egypt* . 94 B3 27 11N 31 16 E
Aszód, *Hungary* 31 D12 47 39N 19 28 E
At Ţafīlah, *Jordan* 91 E4 30 45N 35 30 E
At Tā'if, *Si. Arabia* 86 B3 21 5N 40 27 E
At Tāj, *Libya* 96 D4 24 13N 23 18 E
At Tamīmī, *Libya* 96 B4 32 20N 23 4 E
Aţ Ţirāq, *Si. Arabia* 84 E5 27 19N 44 33 E
At Turbah, *Yemen* 86 D4 13 13N 44 7 E
At Turbah, *Yemen* 86 D3 12 40N 43 30 E
Aţ Ţuwayrifah, *Si. Arabia* 87 B5 21 30N 49 35 E
Atacama □, *Chile* 158 B2 27 30 S 70 0W
Atacama, Desierto de, *Chile* 158 A2 24 0 S 69 20W
Atacama, Salar de, *Chile* 158 A2 23 30 S 68 20W
Ataco, *Colombia* 152 C2 3 35N 75 23W
Atakor, *Algeria* 99 D6 23 27N 5 31 E
Atakpamé, *Togo* 101 D5 7 31N 1 13 E
Atalándi, *Greece* 45 F4 38 39N 22 58 E
Atalaya, *Peru* 156 C3 10 45 S 73 50W
Atalaya de Femes, *Canary Is.* 33 F6 28 56N 13 47W
Ataléia, *Brazil* 155 E3 18 3 S 41 6W
Atambua, *Indonesia* 72 C2 9 7 S 124 54 E
Atami, *Japan* 63 B11 35 5N 139 4 E
Atankawng, *Burma* 78 C6 25 50N 97 47 E
Atapupu, *Indonesia* 72 C2 9 0 S 124 51 E
Atâr, *Mauritania* 98 D2 20 30N 13 5W
Atara, *Russia* 57 C13 63 10N 129 10 E
Ataram, Erg n-, *Algeria* . 99 D5 23 57N 2 0 E
Atarfe, *Spain* 37 H7 37 13N 3 40W
Atascadero, *Calif., U.S.A.* 143 J3 35 32N 120 44W
Atascadero, *Calif., U.S.A.* 144 K6 35 29N 120 40W
Atasu, *Kazakhstan* 56 E8 48 30N 71 0 E
Atauro, *Indonesia* 72 C3 8 10 S 125 30 E
Atbara, *Sudan* 94 D3 17 42N 33 59 E
'Atbara →, *Sudan* 94 D3 17 40N 33 56 E
Atbasar, *Kazakhstan* 56 D7 51 48N 68 20 E
Atbashi, *Kirghizia* 55 C7 41 10N 75 48 E
Atbashi, Khrebet, *Kirghizia* 55 C7 40 50N 75 30 E
Atchafalaya B., *U.S.A.* 139 L9 29 25N 91 25W
Atchison, *U.S.A.* 138 F7 39 34N 95 7W
Atebubu, *Ghana* 101 D4 7 47N 1 0W
Ateca, *Spain* 34 D3 41 20N 1 49W
Aterno →, *Italy* 39 F10 42 11N 13 51 E
Atesine, Alpi, *Italy* 38 B8 46 55N 11 30 E
Atessa, *Italy* 39 F11 42 5N 14 27 E
Ath, *Belgium* 21 G3 50 38N 3 47 E
Athabasca, *Canada* 130 C6 54 45N 113 20W
Athabasca →, *Canada* 131 B6 58 40N 110 50W
Athabasca, L., *Canada* 131 B7 59 15N 109 15W
Athboy, *Ireland* 19 C5 53 37N 6 55W
Athenry, *Ireland* 19 C3 53 18N 8 45W
Athens = Athínai, *Greece* 45 G5 37 58N 23 46 E
Athens, *Ala., U.S.A.* 135 H2 34 48N 86 58W
Athens, *Ga., U.S.A.* 135 J4 33 57N 83 23W
Athens, *N.Y., U.S.A.* 137 D11 42 16N 73 49W
Athens, *Ohio, U.S.A.* 134 F4 39 20N 82 6W
Athens, *Pa., U.S.A.* 137 E8 41 57N 76 31W
Athens, *Tenn., U.S.A.* 135 H3 35 27N 84 36W
Athens, *Tex., U.S.A.* 139 J7 32 12N 95 51W
Atherley, *Canada* 136 B5 44 37N 79 20W
Atherton, *Australia* 114 B4 17 17 S 145 30 E
Athiéme, *Benin* 101 D5 6 37N 1 40 E
Athienou, *Cyprus* 32 D12 35 3N 33 32 E
Athínai, *Greece* 45 G5 37 58N 23 46 E
Athlone, *Ireland* 19 C4 53 26N 7 57W
Athna, *Cyprus* 32 D12 35 3N 33 47 E
Athni, *India* 82 F2 16 44N 75 6 E
Athol, *N.Z.* 119 F3 45 30 S 168 35 E
Atholl, Forest of, *U.K.* 18 E5 56 51N 3 50W
Atholville, *Canada* 129 C6 47 59N 66 43W
Áthos, *Greece* 44 D6 40 9N 24 22 E
Athus, *Belgium* 21 J7 49 34N 5 50 E
Athy, *Ireland* 19 D5 53 0N 7 0W
Ati, *Chad* 97 F3 13 13N 18 20 E
Ati, *Sudan* 95 E2 13 5N 29 2 E
Atiak, *Uganda* 106 B3 3 12N 32 2 E
Atiamuri, *N.Z.* 118 E5 38 24 S 176 5 E
Atico, *Peru* 156 D3 16 14 S 73 40W
Atienza, *Spain* 34 D2 41 12N 2 52W
Atikokan, *Canada* 128 C1 48 45N 91 37W
Atikonak L., *Canada* 129 B7 52 40N 64 32W
Atimonan, *Phil.* 70 D3 14 0N 121 55 E
'Ātinah, W. →, *Oman* 87 C6 18 23N 53 28 E
Atirampattinam, *India* 83 J4 10 28N 79 20 E
Atka, *Russia* 57 C16 60 50N 151 48 E
Atkarsk, *Russia* 51 F14 51 55N 45 2 E
Atkinson, *Ill., U.S.A.* 140 C6 41 25N 90 1W
Atkinson, *Nebr., U.S.A.* 138 D5 42 32N 98 59W
Atlanta, *Ga., U.S.A.* 135 J3 33 45N 84 23W
Atlanta, *Ill., U.S.A.* 140 D7 40 16N 89 14W
Atlanta, *Mo., U.S.A.* 140 E4 39 54N 92 29W
Atlanta, *Tex., U.S.A.* 139 J7 33 7N 94 10W
Atlantic, *U.S.A.* 138 E7 41 24N 95 1W
Atlantic City, *U.S.A.* 134 F8 39 21N 74 27W
Atlantic Ocean 8 H7 0 0 20 0W
Atlántico □, *Colombia* 152 A2 10 45N 75 0W
Atlas Mts. = Haut Atlas, *Morocco* 98 B3 32 30N 5 0W
Atlin, *Canada* 130 B2 59 31N 133 41W
Atlin, L., *Canada* 130 B2 59 26N 133 45W
Atmakur, *India* 83 G4 14 37N 79 40 E
Atmore, *U.S.A.* 135 K2 31 2N 87 29W
Atō, *Japan* 62 C3 34 25N 131 40 E
Atok, *Phil.* 70 C3 16 35N 120 41 E
Atoka, *U.S.A.* 139 H6 34 23N 96 8W
Átokos, *Greece* 45 F2 38 28N 20 49 E
Atolia, *U.S.A.* 145 K9 35 19N 117 37W
Atouguia, *Portugal* 37 F1 39 20N 9 20W
Atoyac →, *Mexico* 147 D5 16 30N 97 31W
Atrak →, *Iran* 85 B8 37 50N 57 0 E
Ätran, *Sweden* 15 G6 57 7N 12 57 E
Atrato →, *Colombia* 152 B2 8 17N 76 58W
Atrauli, *India* 80 E8 28 2N 78 20 E
Atri, *Italy* 39 F10 42 35N 14 0 E
Atsbi, *Ethiopia* 95 E4 13 52N 39 50 E
Atsoum, Mts., *Cameroon* 101 D7 6 41N 12 57 E
Atsugi, *Japan* 63 B11 35 25N 139 21 E
Atsumi, *Japan* 63 C9 34 35N 137 4 E
Atsumi-Wan, *Japan* 63 C9 34 44N 137 13 E
Atsuta, *Japan* 60 C10 43 24N 141 26 E
Attalla, *U.S.A.* 135 H2 34 1N 86 6W
Attáviros, *Greece* 32 C9 36 12N 27 50 E
Attawapiskat, *Canada* 128 B3 52 56N 82 24W
Attawapiskat →, *Canada* 128 B3 52 57N 82 18W
Attawapiskat, L., *Canada* 128 B2 52 18N 87 54W
Attendorn, *Germany* 26 D3 51 8N 7 54 E
Attersee, *Austria* 30 D6 47 55N 13 32 E
Attert, *Belgium* 21 J7 49 45N 5 47 E
Attica, *U.S.A.* 141 D9 40 18N 87 15W
Attichy, *France* 23 C10 49 25N 3 3 E
Attigny, *France* 23 C11 49 28N 4 35 E
Attikamagen L., *Canada* . 129 A6 55 0N 66 30W
Attikí □, *Greece* 45 F5 38 10N 23 40 E
Attleboro, *U.S.A.* 137 E13 41 57N 71 17W
Attock, *Pakistan* 80 C5 33 52N 72 20 E
Attopeu, *Laos* 76 E6 14 48N 106 50 E
Attunga, *Australia* 117 A9 30 55 S 150 50 E
Attur, *India* 83 J4 11 35N 78 30 E
'Atūd, *Yemen* 87 D5 14 53N 48 10 E
Atuel →, *Argentina* 158 D2 36 17 S 66 50W
Atvacik, *Turkey* 88 D2 39 36N 26 24 E
Åtvidaberg, *Sweden* 15 F10 58 12N 16 0 E
Atwater, *U.S.A.* 144 H6 37 21N 120 37W
Atwood, *Canada* 136 C3 43 40N 81 1W
Atwood, *U.S.A.* 138 F4 39 48N 101 3W
Atyrau, *Kazakhstan* 53 C14 47 5N 52 0 E
Au Sable →, *U.S.A.* 134 C4 44 25N 83 20W
Au Sable Pt., *U.S.A.* 128 C2 46 40N 86 10W
Aubagne, *France* 25 E9 43 17N 5 37 E
Aubange, *Belgium* 21 J7 49 34N 5 48 E
Aubarca, C., *Spain* 33 B7 39 4N 1 22 E
Aube □, *France* 23 D11 48 15N 4 10 E
Aube →, *France* 23 D10 48 34N 3 43 E
Aubel, *Belgium* 21 G7 50 42N 5 51 E
Aubenas, *France* 25 D8 44 37N 4 24 E
Aubenton, *France* 23 C11 49 50N 4 12 E
Auberry, *U.S.A.* 144 H7 37 7N 119 29W
Aubigny-sur-Nère, *France* 23 E9 47 30N 2 24 E
Aubin, *France* 24 D6 44 33N 2 15 E
Aubrac, Mts. d', *France* 24 D7 44 40N 3 2 E
Auburn, *Ala., U.S.A.* 135 J3 32 36N 85 29W
Auburn, *Calif., U.S.A.* 144 G5 38 54N 121 4W
Auburn, *Ill., U.S.A.* 140 E7 39 36N 89 45W
Auburn, *Ind., U.S.A.* 141 C11 41 22N 85 4W
Auburn, *N.Y., U.S.A.* 137 D8 42 56N 76 34W
Auburn, *Nebr., U.S.A.* 138 E7 40 23N 95 51W
Auburn, *Wash., U.S.A.* 144 C4 47 18N 122 14W
Auburn Ra., *Australia* 115 D5 25 15 S 150 30 E
Auburndale, *U.S.A.* 135 L5 28 4N 81 48W
Aubusson, *France* 24 C6 45 57N 2 11 E
Auch, *France* 24 E4 43 39N 0 36 E
Auchel, *France* 23 B9 50 30N 2 29 E
Auchi, *Nigeria* 101 D6 7 6N 6 13 E
Auckland, *N.Z.* 118 C3 36 52 S 174 46 E
Auckland □, *N.Z.* 118 E6 36 50 S 175 0 E
Auckland Is., *Pac. Oc.* 122 N8 50 40 S 166 5 E
Aude □, *France* 24 E6 43 8N 2 28 E
Aude →, *France* 24 E7 43 13N 3 14 E
Audegle, *Somali Rep.* 108 D2 1 59N 44 50 E
Auden, *Canada* 128 B2 50 14N 87 53W
Auderghem, *Belgium* 21 G4 50 49N 4 26 E
Auderville, *France* 22 C5 49 43N 1 57W
Audierne, *France* 22 D2 48 1N 4 34W
Audincourt, *France* 23 E13 47 30N 6 50 E
Audo, *Ethiopia* 95 F5 6 20N 41 50 E
Audubon, *U.S.A.* 140 C2 41 43N 94 56W
Aue, *Germany* 26 E8 50 34N 12 43 E
Auerbach, *Germany* 26 E8 50 30N 12 25 E
Aueti Paraná →, *Brazil* . 152 D4 1 51 S 65 37W
Aufist, *W. Sahara* 98 C2 25 44N 14 39W
Augathella, *Australia* 115 D4 25 48 S 146 35 E
Augrabies Falls, *S. Africa* 104 D3 28 35 S 20 20 E
Augsburg, *Germany* 27 G6 48 22N 10 54 E
Augusta, *Italy* 41 E8 37 14N 15 12 E
Augusta, *Ark., U.S.A.* 139 H9 35 17N 91 22W
Augusta, *Ga., U.S.A.* 135 J5 33 28N 81 58W
Augusta, *Ill., U.S.A.* 140 D6 40 14N 90 57W
Augusta, *Kans., U.S.A.* 139 G6 37 41N 96 59W
Augusta, *Ky., U.S.A.* 141 F12 38 47N 84 0W
Augusta, *Maine, U.S.A.* 129 D6 44 19N 69 47W
Augusta, *Mont., U.S.A.* 142 C7 47 30N 112 24W
Augusta, *Wis., U.S.A.* 138 C9 44 41N 91 7W
Augustenborg, *Denmark* 15 K3 54 57N 9 53 E
Augustów, *Poland* 47 B9 53 51N 23 0 E
Augustus, Mt., *Australia* 112 D2 24 20 S 116 50 E
Augustus Downs, *Australia* 114 B2 18 35 S 139 55 E
Augustus I., *Australia* 112 C3 15 20 S 124 30 E
Aukan, *Eritrea* 95 D5 15 29N 40 50 E
Auki, *Solomon Is.* 121 M11 8 45 S 160 42 E
Aukum, *U.S.A.* 144 G6 38 34N 120 43W
Auld, L., *Australia* 112 D3 22 25 S 123 50 E
Aulla, *Italy* 38 D6 44 12N 10 0 E
Aulnay, *France* 24 B3 46 2N 0 22W
Aulne →, *France* 22 D2 48 17N 4 16W
Aulnoye-Aymeries, *France* 23 B10 50 12N 3 50 E
Ault, *France* 22 B8 50 8N 1 26 E
Ault, *U.S.A.* 138 E2 40 35N 104 44W
Aulus-les-Bains, *France* 24 F5 42 49N 1 19 E
Aumale, *France* 23 C8 49 46N 1 46 E
Aumont-Aubrac, *France* 24 D7 44 43N 3 17 E
Auna, *Nigeria* 101 C5 10 9N 4 42 E
Aundh, *India* 82 F2 17 33N 74 23 E
Aunis, *France* 24 B3 46 5N 0 50W
Auponhia, *Indonesia* 72 B3 1 58 S 125 27 E
Aups, *France* 25 E10 43 37N 6 15 E
Aur, P., *Malaysia* 77 L5 2 35N 104 10 E
Aura, *Burma* 78 B6 26 59N 97 57 E
Auraiya, *India* 81 F8 26 28N 79 33 E
Aurangabad, *Bihar, India* 81 G11 24 45N 84 18 E
Aurangabad, *Maharashtra, India* 82 E2 19 50N 75 23 E
Auray, *France* 22 E4 47 40N 2 59W
Aurès, *Algeria* 99 A6 35 8N 6 30 E
Aurich, *Germany* 26 B3 53 28N 7 30 E
Aurilândia, *Brazil* 155 E1 16 44 S 50 28W
Aurillac, *France* 24 D6 44 55N 2 26 E
Auronza, *Italy* 39 B9 46 33N 12 27 E
Aurora = Maewo, *Vanuatu* 121 E6 15 10 S 168 10 E
Aurora, *Canada* 136 C5 44 0N 79 28W
Aurora, *Isabela, Phil.* 70 C3 16 59N 121 38 E
Aurora, *Quezon, Phil.* 70 E4 13 21N 122 31 E
Aurora, *S. Africa* 104 E2 32 40 S 18 29 E
Aurora, *Colo., U.S.A.* 138 F2 39 44N 104 52W
Aurora, *Ill., U.S.A.* 141 C8 41 45N 88 19W
Aurora, *Mo., U.S.A.* 139 G8 36 58N 93 43W
Aurora, *Nebr., U.S.A.* 138 E6 40 52N 98 0W
Aurora, *Ohio, U.S.A.* 136 E3 41 21N 81 20W
Aursmoen, *Norway* 14 E5 59 55N 11 26 E
Aurukun Mission, *Australia* 114 A3 13 20 S 141 45 E
Aus, *Namibia* 104 D2 26 35 S 16 12 E
Auschwitz = Oświecim, *Poland* 31 A12 50 2N 19 11 E
Aust-Agder fylke □, *Norway* 13 G9 58 55N 7 40 E
Austerlitz = Slavkov, *Czech.* 31 B9 49 10N 16 52 E
Austin, *Ind., U.S.A.* 141 F11 38 45N 85 49W
Austin, *Minn., U.S.A.* 138 D8 43 40N 92 58W
Austin, *Nev., U.S.A.* 142 G5 39 30N 117 4W
Austin, *Pa., U.S.A.* 136 E6 41 38N 78 6W
Austin, *Tex., U.S.A.* 139 K6 30 17N 97 45W
Austin, L., *Australia* 113 E2 27 40 S 118 0 E
Austral Downs, *Australia* 114 C2 20 30 S 137 45 E
Austral Is. = Tubuai Is., *Pac. Oc.* 123 K12 25 0 S 150 0W
Austral Seamount Chain, *Pac. Oc.* 123 K13 24 0 S 150 0W
Australia ■, *Oceania* 122 K5 23 0 S 135 0 E
Australian Alps, *Australia* 117 D8 36 30 S 148 30 E
Australian Capital Territory □, *Australia* . 115 F4 35 30 S 149 0 E
Austria ■, *Europe* 30 E7 47 0N 14 0 E
Austvågøy, *Norway* 12 B13 68 20N 14 40 E
Autazes, *Brazil* 153 D6 3 35 S 59 8W
Autelbas, *Belgium* 21 J7 49 39N 5 52 E
Auterive, *France* 24 E5 43 21N 1 29 E
Authie →, *France* 23 B8 50 22N 1 38 E
Authon-du-Perche, *France* 22 D7 48 12N 0 54 E
Autlán, *Mexico* 146 D4 19 40N 104 30W
Autun, *France* 23 F11 46 58N 4 17 E
Auvelais, *Belgium* 21 H5 50 27N 4 38 E
Auvergne, *Australia* 112 C5 15 39 S 130 1 E
Auvergne, *France* 24 C7 45 20N 3 15 E
Auvergne, Mts. d', *France* 24 C6 45 20N 2 55 E
Auvézére →, *France* 24 C4 45 12N 0 50 E
Auxerre, *France* 23 E10 47 48N 3 32 E
Auxi-le-Château, *France* . 23 B9 50 15N 2 8 E
Auxonne, *France* 23 E12 47 10N 5 20 E
Auxvasse, *U.S.A.* 140 E5 39 1N 91 54W
Auzances, *France* 24 B6 46 2N 2 30 E
Auzat-sur-Allier, *France* . 24 C7 45 27N 3 19 E
Ava, *U.S.A.* 140 G7 37 53N 89 30W
Avallon, *France* 23 E10 47 30N 3 53 E
Avalon, *U.S.A.* 145 M8 33 21N 118 20W
Avalon Pen., *Canada* 129 C9 47 30N 53 20W
Avanigadda, *India* 83 G5 16 0N 80 56 E
Avaré, *Brazil* 159 A6 23 4 S 48 58W
Ávas, *Greece* 44 D7 40 57N 25 56 E
Avawatz Mts., *U.S.A.* 145 K10 35 40N 116 30W
Aveiro, *Brazil* 153 D6 3 10 S 55 5W
Aveiro, *Portugal* 36 E2 40 37N 8 38W
Aveiro □, *Portugal* 36 E2 40 40N 8 35W
Āvej, *Iran* 85 C6 35 40N 49 15 E
Avelgem, *Belgium* 21 G2 50 47N 3 27 E
Avellaneda, *Argentina* 158 C4 34 50 S 58 10W
Avellino, *Italy* 41 B7 40 54N 14 46 E
Avenal, *U.S.A.* 144 K6 36 0N 120 8W
Avenches, *Switz.* 28 C4 46 53N 7 2 E
Averøya, *Norway* 14 A1 63 5N 7 35 E
Aversa, *Italy* 41 B7 40 58N 14 11 E
Avery, *U.S.A.* 142 C6 47 15N 115 49W
Aves, I. de, *W. Indies* 149 C7 15 45N 63 55W
Aves, Is. de, *Venezuela* 149 D6 12 0N 67 30W
Avesnes-sur-Helpe, *France* 23 B10 50 8N 3 55 E
Avesta, *Sweden* 13 F14 60 9N 16 10 E
Aveyron □, *France* 24 D6 44 22N 2 45 E
Aveyron →, *France* 24 D5 44 5N 1 16 E
Avezzano, *Italy* 39 F10 42 2N 13 24 E
Avgó, *Greece* 45 J7 35 33N 25 37 E
Aviá Terai, *Argentina* 158 B3 26 45 S 60 50W
Aviano, *Italy* 39 B9 46 3N 12 35 E
Avigliana, *Italy* 38 C4 45 7N 7 13 E
Avigliano, *Italy* 41 B8 40 44N 15 41 E
Avignon, *France* 25 E8 43 57N 4 50 E
Ávila, *Spain* 36 E6 40 39N 4 43W
Ávila □, *Spain* 36 E6 40 30N 5 0W
Ávila, Sierra de, *Spain* 36 E5 40 40N 5 15W
Avila Beach, *U.S.A.* 145 K6 35 11N 120 44W
Avilés, *Spain* 36 B5 43 35N 5 57W
Avionárion, *Greece* 45 F6 38 31N 24 8 E
Avisio →, *Italy* 39 B8 46 7N 11 5 E
Aviston, *U.S.A.* 140 F7 38 36N 89 36W
Aviz, *Portugal* 37 F3 39 4N 7 53W
Avize, *France* 23 D11 48 59N 4 1 E
Avoca, *Ireland* 19 D5 52 52N 6 13W
Avoca, *U.S.A.* 136 D7 42 25N 77 25W
Avoca →, *Australia* 116 C5 35 40 S 143 43 E
Avola, *Canada* 130 C5 51 45N 119 19W
Avola, *Italy* 41 F8 36 56N 15 7 E
Avon, *Ill., U.S.A.* 140 D6 40 40N 90 26W
Avon, *N.Y., U.S.A.* 136 D7 42 55N 77 45W
Avon, *S. Dak., U.S.A.* 138 D5 43 0N 98 4W
Avon □, *U.K.* 17 F5 51 30N 2 40W
Avon →, *Australia* 113 F2 31 40 S 116 7 E
Avon →, *Avon, U.K.* 17 F5 51 30N 2 43W
Avon →, *Hants., U.K.* 17 G6 50 44N 1 45W
Avon →, *Warks., U.K.* 17 F5 51 57N 2 9W
Avondale, *Zimbabwe* 107 F3 17 43 S 30 58 E
Avonlea, *Canada* 131 D7 50 0N 105 0W
Avonmore, *Canada* 137 A10 45 10N 74 58W
Avonmouth, *U.K.* 17 F5 51 30N 2 42W
Avramov, *Bulgaria* 43 E11 42 45N 26 38 E
Avranches, *France* 22 D5 48 40N 1 20W
Avre →, *France* 22 D8 48 47N 1 22 E
Avrig, *Romania* 46 D5 45 43N 24 21 E
Avtovac, *Bos.-H.* 42 D3 43 9N 18 35 E
Avu Avu, *Solomon Is.* 121 M11 9 50 S 160 22 E
Awag el Baqar, *Sudan* 95 E3 10 10N 33 10 E
A'waj →, *Syria* 91 B5 33 23N 36 20 E
Awaji, *Japan* 63 C7 34 32N 135 1 E
Awaji-Shima, *Japan* 62 C6 34 30N 134 50 E
'Awālī, *Bahrain* 85 E6 26 0N 50 30 E
Awantipur, *India* 81 C6 33 55N 75 3 E
Awanui, *N.Z.* 118 B2 35 4 S 173 17 E
Awarja →, *India* 82 F3 17 5N 76 15 E
Awarua B., *N.Z.* 119 E3 44 28 S 168 4 E
Awarua Pt., *N.Z.* 119 E3 44 15 S 168 5 E
Awasa, L., *Ethiopia* 95 F4 7 0N 38 30 E
Awash, *Ethiopia* 90 F3 9 1N 40 10 E
Awash →, *Ethiopia* 95 E5 11 45N 41 5 E
Awaso, *Ghana* 100 D4 6 15N 2 22W
Awatere →, *N.Z.* 119 B9 41 37 S 174 10 E
Awbārī, *Libya* 96 C2 26 46N 12 57 E
Awbārī □, *Libya* 96 C2 26 35N 12 46 E
Awe, L., *U.K.* 18 E3 56 15N 5 15W
Aweil, *Sudan* 95 F2 8 42N 27 20 E
Awgu, *Nigeria* 101 D6 6 4N 7 24 E
Awjilah, *Libya* 96 C4 29 8N 21 7 E
Aworro, *Papua N. G.* 120 D2 7 43 S 143 11 E
Ax-les-Thermes, *France* 24 F5 42 44N 1 50 E
Axarfjörður, *Iceland* 12 C5 66 15N 16 45W
Axel, *Neths.* 21 F3 51 16N 3 55 E
Axel Heiberg I., *Canada* . 6 B3 80 0N 90 0W
Axim, *Ghana* 100 E4 4 51N 2 15W
Axinim, *Brazil* 153 D6 4 2 S 59 22W
Axintele, *Romania* 46 E7 44 37N 26 47 E
Axioma, *Brazil* 157 B5 6 45 S 64 31W
Axiós →, *Greece* 44 D4 40 57N 22 35 E
Axminster, *U.K.* 17 G4 50 47N 3 1W
Axvall, *Sweden* 15 F7 58 23N 13 34 E
Aÿ, *France* 23 C11 49 3N 4 1 E
Ay →, *Russia* 54 C5 56 8N 57 40 E
Ayaantang, *Eq. Guin.* 102 B2 1 58N 10 24 E
Ayabaca, *Peru* 156 A2 4 40 S 79 53W
Ayabe, *Japan* 63 B7 35 20N 135 20 E
Ayacucho, *Argentina* 158 D4 37 5 S 58 20W
Ayacucho, *Peru* 156 C3 13 0 S 74 0W
Ayaguz, *Kazakhstan* 56 E9 48 10N 80 10 E
Ayakkuduk, *Uzbekistan* 55 C2 41 12N 65 12 E
Ayakudi, *India* 83 J3 10 28N 77 56 E
Ayala, *Phil.* 71 H3 6 57N 121 57 E
Ayamonte, *Spain* 37 H3 37 12N 7 24W
Ayan, *Russia* 57 D14 56 30N 138 16 E
Ayancık, *Turkey* 52 F6 41 57N 34 35 E
Ayapel, *Colombia* 152 B2 8 19N 75 9W
Ayas, *Turkey* 52 F5 40 2N 32 21 E
Ayaviri, *Peru* 156 C3 14 50 S 70 35W
Āybak, *Afghan.* 79 A3 36 15N 68 5 E
Aybastı, *Turkey* 88 C7 40 41N 37 23 E
Aydim, W. →, *Oman* 87 C6 18 8N 53 8 E
Aydın, *Turkey* 88 E2 37 51N 27 51 E
Aydin □, *Turkey* 88 E2 37 50N 28 0 E
Aye, *Belgium* 21 H6 50 14N 5 18 E
Ayenngré, *Togo* 101 D5 8 40N 1 1 E
Ayer's Cliff, *Canada* 137 A12 45 10N 72 3W
Ayers Rock, *Australia* 113 E5 25 23 S 131 5 E
Ayiá, *Greece* 44 E4 39 43N 22 45 E
Ayía Aikateríni, Ákra, *Greece* 32 A3 39 50N 19 50 E
Ayía Ánna, *Greece* 45 F5 38 52N 23 24 E
Ayia Dhéka, *Greece* 32 D6 35 3N 24 58 E
Ayia Gálini, *Greece* 32 D6 35 6N 24 41 E
Ayía Marína, *Kásos, Greece* 45 J8 35 27N 26 53 E
Ayía Marína, *Leros, Greece* 45 G8 37 11N 26 48 E
Ayia Napa, *Cyprus* 32 E13 34 59N 34 0 E
Ayía Paraskeví, *Greece* 44 E8 39 14N 26 16 E
Áyia Phyla, *Cyprus* 32 E12 34 43N 33 1 E
Ayía Rouméli, *Greece* 45 J5 35 14N 23 58 E
Ayia Varvára, *Greece* 32 D7 35 8N 25 1 E
Ayiássos, *Greece* 45 E8 39 5N 26 23 E
Áyion Óros, *Greece* 44 D6 40 25N 24 6 E
Áyios Amvrósios, *Cyprus* 32 D12 35 20N 33 35 E
Áyios Andréas, *Greece* 45 G4 37 21N 22 45 E
Áyios Evstrátios, *Greece* . 44 E6 39 34N 24 58 E
Áyios Ioánnis, Ákra, *Greece* 32 D7 35 20N 25 40 E
Áyios Isidhoros, *Greece* 32 C9 36 9N 27 51 E
Áyios Kiríkos, *Greece* 45 G8 37 34N 26 17 E
Áyios Matthaíos, *Greece* 32 B3 39 30N 19 47 E
Áyios Míronos, *Greece* 32 D7 35 15N 25 1 E
Áyios Nikólaos, *Greece* 32 D7 35 11N 25 41 E
Áyios Pétros, *Greece* 45 F2 38 38N 20 33 E
Áyios Seryios, *Cyprus* 32 D12 35 12N 33 53 E
Ayios Theodhoros, *Cyprus* 32 D13 35 22N 34 1 E
Áyios Yeóryios, *Greece* 45 G5 37 28N 23 57 E
Aykathonisi, *Greece* 45 G8 37 28N 27 0 E
Ayke, Ozero, *Kazakhstan* 54 F7 50 57N 61 36 E
Aykin, *Russia* 48 B8 62 15N 49 56 E
Aylesbury, *U.K.* 17 F7 51 48N 0 49W
Aylmer, *Canada* 136 D4 42 46N 80 59W
Aylmer, L., *Canada* 126 B8 64 0N 110 8W
'Ayn al Ghazālah, *Libya* 96 B4 32 10N 23 20 E
'Ayn Zaqqūt, *Libya* 96 C3 29 0N 19 30 E
Ayna, *Spain* 35 G2 38 34N 2 3W
Aynāt, *Yemen* 87 C5 16 4N 49 9 E
Ayni, *Tajikistan* 55 D4 39 23N 68 32 E
Ayolas, *Paraguay* 158 B4 27 10 S 56 59W
Ayom, *Sudan* 95 F2 7 49N 28 23 E
Ayon, Ostrov, *Russia* 57 C17 69 50N 169 0 E
Ayora, *Spain* 35 F3 39 3N 1 3W
Ayr, *Australia* 114 B4 19 35 S 147 25 E
Ayr, *U.K.* 18 F4 55 28N 4 37W
Ayr →, *U.K.* 18 F4 55 29N 4 40W
Ayrancı, *Turkey* 88 E5 37 21N 33 41 E
Ayre, Pt. of, *U.K.* 16 C3 54 27N 4 21W
Aysha, *Ethiopia* 95 E5 10 50N 42 23 E
Aytos, *Bulgaria* 43 E12 42 42N 27 16 E
Aytoska Planina, *Bulgaria* 43 E12 42 45N 27 30 E
Ayu, Kepulauan, *Indonesia* 73 A4 0 35N 131 5 E
Ayutla, *Guatemala* 148 D1 14 40N 92 10W
Ayutla, *Mexico* 147 D5 16 58N 99 17W
Ayvacık, *Turkey* 88 C7 40 59N 36 38 E
Ayvalık, *Turkey* 88 D2 39 20N 26 46 E
Aywaille, *Belgium* 21 H7 50 28N 5 40 E
Az Zabdānī, *Syria* 91 B5 33 43N 36 5 E
Az Ẓāhirīyah, *Jordan* 91 D3 31 25N 34 58 E
Az Ẓahrān, *Si. Arabia* 85 E6 26 10N 50 7 E
Az Zarqā, *Jordan* 91 C5 32 5N 36 4 E
Az Zāwiyah, *Libya* 96 B2 32 52N 12 56 E
Az Zaydīyah, *Yemen* 86 D3 15 20N 43 1 E
Az Zībār, *Iraq* 84 B5 36 52N 44 4 E
Az-Zilfī, *Si. Arabia* 84 E5 26 12N 44 52 E
Az Zubayr, *Iraq* 84 D5 30 20N 47 50 E
Az Zuqur, *Yemen* 86 D3 14 0N 42 45 E
Azambuja, *Portugal* 37 F2 39 4N 8 51W
Azamgarh, *India* 81 F10 26 5N 83 13 E
Azangaro, *Peru* 156 C3 14 55 S 70 13W
Azaouak, Vallée de l', *Mali* 101 B5 15 50N 3 20 E
Āzār Shahr, *Iran* 84 B5 37 45N 45 59 E
Azärbayjan = Azerbaijan ■, *Asia* 53 F12 40 20N 48 0 E

Baran 171

Balaguer, *Spain* 34 D5 41 50N 0 50 E
Balakété, *C.A.R.* 102 A3 6 56N 19 54 E
Balakhna, *Russia* 51 C13 56 25N 43 32 E
Balaklava, *Australia* 116 C3 34 7 S 138 22 E
Balaklava, *Ukraine* 52 D5 44 30N 33 30 E
Balakleya, *Ukraine* 52 B7 49 28N 36 55 E
Balakovo, *Russia* 51 E15 52 4N 47 55 E
Balamban, *Phil.* 71 F4 10 30N 123 43 E
Balambangan, *Malaysia* 75 A5 7 17N 116 55 E
Balancán, *Mexico* 147 D6 17 48N 91 32W
Balanda, *Russia* 51 F14 51 30N 44 40 E
Balangiga, *Phil.* 71 F5 11 7N 125 23 E
Balangir, *India* 82 D6 20 43N 83 35 E
Balapur, *India* 82 D3 20 40N 76 45 E
Balashikha, *Russia* 51 D10 55 49N 37 59 E
Balashov, *Russia* 51 F13 51 30N 43 10 E
Balasinor, *India* 80 H5 22 57N 73 23 E
Balasore = Baleshwar, *India* 82 D8 21 35N 87 3 E
Balassagyarmat, *Hungary* 31 C12 48 4N 19 15 E
Balât, *Egypt* 94 B2 25 36N 29 19 E
Balaton, *Hungary* 31 E10 46 50N 17 40 E
Balatonfüred, *Hungary* 31 E10 46 58N 17 54 E
Balatonszentgyörgy, *Hungary* 31 E10 46 41N 17 19 E
Balayan, *Phil.* 70 E3 13 57N 120 44 E
Balazote, *Spain* 35 G2 38 54N 2 9W
Balbalan, *Phil.* 70 C3 17 27N 121 12 E
Balbi, Mt., *Papua N. G.* 120 C8 5 55 S 154 58 E
Balboa, *Panama* 148 E4 8 57N 79 34W
Balbriggan, *Ireland* 19 C5 53 35N 6 10W
Balcarce, *Argentina* 158 D4 38 0 S 58 10W
Balcarres, *Canada* 131 C8 50 50N 103 35W
Balchik, *Bulgaria* 43 D13 43 28N 28 11 E
Balclutha, *N.Z.* 119 G4 46 15 S 169 45 E
Bald Hd., *Australia* 113 G2 35 6 S 118 1 E
Bald I., *Australia* 113 F2 34 57 S 118 27 E
Bald Knob, *U.S.A.* 139 H9 35 19N 91 34W
Baldock L., *Canada* 131 B9 56 33N 97 57W
Baldwin, *Fla., U.S.A.* 135 K4 30 18N 81 59W
Baldwin, *Mich., U.S.A.* 134 D3 43 54N 85 51W
Baldwinsville, *U.S.A.* 137 C8 43 10N 76 20W
Baldy Peak, *U.S.A.* 143 K9 33 54N 109 34W
Bale, *Croatia* 39 C10 45 4N 13 46 E
Bale □, *Ethiopia* 95 F5 6 20N 41 30 E
Baleares □, *Spain* 34 F7 39 30N 3 0 E
Baleares, Is., *Spain* 33 B10 39 30N 3 0 E
Balearic Is. = Baleares, Is., *Spain* 33 B10 39 30N 3 0 E
Baleia, Pta. da, *Brazil* 155 E4 17 40 S 39 7W
Balen, *Belgium* 21 F6 51 10N 5 10 E
Băleni, *Romania* 46 D8 45 48N 27 51 E
Baler, *Phil.* 70 D3 15 46N 121 34 E
Baler Bay, *Phil.* 70 D3 15 50N 121 35 E
Balerna, *Switz.* 29 E8 45 52N 9 0 E
Baleshwar, *India* 82 D8 21 35N 87 3 E
Balezino, *Russia* 54 B3 58 2N 53 6 E
Balfate, *Honduras* 148 C2 15 48N 86 25W
Balfe's Creek, *Australia* 114 C4 20 12 S 145 55 E
Balfour, *S. Africa* 105 D4 26 38 S 28 35 E
Balfour Channel, *Solomon Is.* 121 M9 8 43 S 157 27 E
Balharshah, *India* 82 E4 19 50N 79 23 E
Bali, *Cameroon* 101 D6 5 54N 10 0 E
Balí, *Greece* 32 D6 35 25N 24 47 E
Bali, *Indonesia* 75 D4 8 20 S 115 0 E
Bali □, *Indonesia* 75 D4 8 20 S 115 0 E
Bali, Selat, *Indonesia* 75 D4 8 18 S 114 25 E
Balicuatro Is., *Phil.* 70 E5 12 39N 124 24 E
Baligród, *Poland* 31 B15 49 20N 22 17 E
Balık Gölü, *Turkey* 89 D10 39 46N 43 34 E
Balikeşir, *Turkey* 88 D2 39 35N 27 58 E
Balikeşir □, *Turkey* 88 D2 39 45N 28 0 E
Balikpapan, *Indonesia* 75 C5 1 10 S 116 55 E
Balimbing, *Phil.* 71 J2 5 5N 119 58 E
Balimo, *Papua N. G.* 120 E2 8 6 S 142 57 E
Baling, *Malaysia* 77 K3 5 41N 100 55 E
Balintang Channel, *Phil.* 70 B3 19 49N 121 40 E
Balintang Is., *Phil.* 70 B4 19 58N 122 9 E
Baliton, *Phil.* 71 J5 5 44N 125 14 E
Baliza, *Brazil* 157 D7 16 0 S 52 20W
Baljurshi, *Si. Arabia* 86 C3 19 51N 41 33 E
Balk, *Neths.* 20 C7 52 54N 5 35 E
Balkan Mts. = Stara Planina, *Bulgaria* 43 D8 43 15N 23 0 E
Balkan Peninsula, *Europe* 10 G10 42 0N 23 0 E
Balkh □, *Afghan.* 79 A2 36 30N 67 0 E
Balkhash, *Kazakhstan* 56 E8 46 50N 74 50 E
Balkhash, Ozero, *Kazakhstan* 56 E8 46 0N 74 50 E
Ballachulish, *U.K.* 18 E3 56 40N 5 10W
Balladonia, *Australia* 113 F3 32 27 S 123 51 E
Ballara, *Australia* 116 B4 32 19 S 140 45 E
Ballarat, *Australia* 115 F3 37 33 S 143 50 E
Ballard, L., *Australia* 113 E3 29 20 S 120 40 E
Ballater, *U.K.* 18 D5 57 2N 3 2W
Balldale, *Australia* 117 C7 35 50 S 146 33 E
Ballenas, Canal de, *Mexico* 146 B2 29 10N 113 45W
Balleny Is., *Antarctica* 7 C11 66 30 S 163 0 E
Ballesteros, *Phil.* 70 B3 18 25N 121 31 E
Ballia, *India* 81 G11 25 46N 84 12 E
Ballidu, *Australia* 113 F2 30 35 S 116 45 E
Ballina, *Australia* 115 D5 28 50 S 153 31 E
Ballina, *Mayo, Ireland* 19 B2 54 7N 9 10W
Ballina, *Tipp., Ireland* 19 D3 52 49N 8 27W
Ballinasloe, *Ireland* 19 C3 53 20N 8 12W
Ballinger, *U.S.A.* 139 K5 31 45N 99 57W
Ballinrobe, *Ireland* 19 C2 53 36N 9 13W
Ballinskelligs B., *Ireland* 19 E1 51 46N 10 11W
Ballon, *France* 22 D7 48 10N 0 14 E
Ballycastle, *U.K.* 19 A5 55 12N 6 15W
Ballymena, *U.K.* 19 B5 54 53N 6 18W
Ballymena □, *U.K.* 19 B5 54 53N 6 18W
Ballymoney, *U.K.* 19 A5 55 5N 6 30W
Ballymoney □, *U.K.* 19 A5 55 5N 6 23W
Ballyshannon, *Ireland* 19 B3 54 30N 8 10W
Balmaceda, *Chile* 160 C2 46 0 S 71 50W
Balmazújváros, *Hungary* 31 D14 47 37N 21 21 E
Balmhorn, *Switz.* 28 D5 46 26N 7 42 E
Balmoral, *Australia* 116 D4 37 15 S 141 48 E
Balmoral, *U.K.* 18 D5 57 3N 3 13W
Balmorhea, *U.S.A.* 139 K3 30 59N 103 45W
Balombo, *Angola* 103 E2 12 21 S 14 46 E
Balonne →, *Australia* 115 D4 28 47 S 147 56 E
Balqash Kol = Balkhash, Ozero, *Kazakhstan* 56 E8 46 0N 74 50 E
Balrampur, *India* 81 F10 27 30N 82 20 E
Balranald, *Australia* 116 C5 34 38 S 143 33 E
Balş, *Romania* 46 E5 44 22N 24 5 E
Balsapuerto, *Peru* 156 B2 5 48 S 76 33W
Balsas, *Mexico* 147 D5 18 0N 99 40W
Balsas →, *Goiás, Brazil* 154 C2 9 58 S 47 52W
Balsas →, *Maranhão, Brazil* 154 C3 7 15 S 44 35W
Balsas →, *Mexico* 146 D4 17 55N 102 10W
Bålsta, *Sweden* 14 E11 59 35N 17 30 E
Balsthal, *Switz.* 28 B5 47 19N 7 41 E
Balston Spa, *U.S.A.* 137 D11 43 0N 73 52W
Balta, *Romania* 46 E3 44 54N 22 38 E
Balta, *Russia* 53 E11 42 58N 44 32 E
Balta, *Ukraine* 52 B3 48 2N 29 45 E
Balta, *U.S.A.* 138 A4 48 10N 100 2W
Baltanás, *Spain* 36 D6 41 56N 4 15W
Bălţi = Beltsy, *Moldavia* 52 C3 47 48N 28 0 E
Baltic Sea, *Europe* 13 H15 57 0N 19 0 E
Baltîm, *Egypt* 94 H7 31 35N 31 10 E
Baltimore, *Ireland* 19 E2 51 29N 9 22W
Baltimore, *U.S.A.* 134 F7 39 17N 76 37W
Baltit, *Pakistan* 81 A6 36 15N 74 40 E
Baltrum, *Germany* 26 B3 53 43N 7 25 E
Baluchistan □, *Pakistan* 79 D2 27 30N 65 0 E
Balud, *Phil.* 70 E4 12 2N 123 12 E
Balurghat, *India* 81 G13 25 15N 88 44 E
Balya, *Turkey* 88 D2 39 44N 27 35 E
Balygychan, *Russia* 57 C16 63 56N 154 12 E
Balzar, *Ecuador* 152 D2 2 2 S 79 54W
Bam, *Iran* 85 D8 29 7N 58 14 E
Bama, *China* 68 E6 24 8N 107 12 E
Bama, *Nigeria* 101 C7 11 33N 13 41 E
Bamako, *Mali* 100 C3 12 34N 7 55W
Bamba, *Mali* 101 B4 17 5N 1 24W
Bamba, *Zaïre* 103 D3 5 45 S 18 23 E
Bambam, *Phil.* 70 D3 15 40N 120 20 E
Bambamarca, *Peru* 156 B2 6 36 S 78 32W
Bambang, *Phil.* 70 C3 16 23N 121 6 E
Bambari, *C.A.R.* 102 A4 5 40N 20 35 E
Bambaroo, *Australia* 114 B4 18 50 S 146 10 E
Bamberg, *Germany* 27 F6 49 54N 10 53 E
Bamberg, *U.S.A.* 135 J5 33 18N 81 2W
Bambesi, *Ethiopia* 95 F3 9 45N 34 40 E
Bambey, *Senegal* 100 C1 14 42N 16 28W
Bambili, *Zaïre* 106 B2 3 40N 26 0 E
Bambuí, *Brazil* 155 F2 20 1 S 45 58W
Bamenda, *Cameroon* 101 D7 5 57N 10 11 E
Bamfield, *Canada* 130 D3 48 45N 125 10W
Bāmīān □, *Afghan.* 79 B2 35 0N 67 0 E
Bamiancheng, *China* 67 C13 43 15N 124 2 E
Bamingui, *C.A.R.* 102 A3 7 34N 20 11 E
Bamkin, *Cameroon* 101 D7 6 3N 11 27 E
Bampūr, *Iran* 85 E9 27 15N 60 21 E
Ban Aranyaprathet, *Thailand* 76 F4 13 41N 102 30 E
Ban Ban, *Laos* 76 C4 19 31N 103 30 E
Ban Bang Hin, *Thailand* 77 H2 9 32N 98 35 E
Ban Chiang Klang, *Thailand* 76 C3 19 25N 100 55 E
Ban Chik, *Laos* 76 D4 17 15N 102 22 E
Ban Choho, *Thailand* 76 E4 15 2N 102 9 E
Ban Dan Lan Hoi, *Thailand* 76 D2 17 0N 99 35 E
Ban Don = Surat Thani, *Thailand* 77 H2 9 6N 99 20 E
Ban Don, *Vietnam* 76 F6 12 53N 107 48 E
Ban Don, Ao, *Thailand* 77 H2 9 20N 99 25 E
Ban Dong, *Thailand* 76 C3 19 30N 100 59 E
Ban Hong, *Thailand* 76 C2 18 18N 98 50 E
Ban Kaeng, *Thailand* 76 D3 17 29N 100 7 E
Ban Keun, *Laos* 76 C4 18 22N 102 35 E
Ban Khai, *Thailand* 76 F3 12 46N 101 18 E
Ban Kheun, *Laos* 76 B3 20 13N 101 7 E
Ban Khlong Kua, *Thailand* 77 J3 6 57N 100 8 E
Ban Khuan Mao, *Thailand* 77 J2 7 50N 99 37 E
Ban Khun Yuam, *Thailand* 76 C1 18 49N 97 57 E
Ban Ko Yai Chim, *Thailand* 77 G2 11 17N 99 26 E
Ban Kok, *Thailand* 76 D4 16 40N 103 40 E
Ban Laem, *Thailand* 76 F2 13 13N 99 59 E
Ban Lao Ngam, *Laos* 76 E6 15 28N 106 10 E
Ban Le Kathe, *Thailand* 76 E2 15 49N 98 53 E
Ban Mae Chedi, *Thailand* 76 C2 19 11N 99 31 E
Ban Mae Laeng, *Thailand* 76 B2 20 1N 99 17 E
Ban Mae Sariang, *Thailand* 76 C1 18 10N 97 56 E
Ban Mê Thuôt = Buon Me Thuot, *Vietnam* 76 F7 12 40N 108 3 E
Ban Mi, *Thailand* 76 E3 15 3N 100 32 E
Ban Muong Mo, *Laos* 76 C4 19 4N 103 58 E
Ban Na Mo, *Laos* 76 D5 17 7N 105 40 E
Ban Na San, *Thailand* 77 H2 8 53N 99 52 E
Ban Na Tong, *Laos* 76 B3 20 56N 101 47 E
Ban Nam Bac, *Laos* 76 B4 20 38N 102 20 E
Ban Nam Ma, *Laos* 76 A3 22 2N 101 37 E
Ban Ngang, *Laos* 76 E6 15 59N 106 11 E
Ban Nong Bok, *Laos* 76 D5 17 5N 104 48 E
Ban Nong Boua, *Laos* 76 E6 15 40N 106 33 E
Ban Nong Pling, *Thailand* 76 E3 15 40N 100 10 E
Ban Pak Chan, *Thailand* 77 G2 10 32N 98 51 E
Ban Phai, *Thailand* 76 D4 16 4N 102 44 E
Ban Pong, *Thailand* 76 F2 13 50N 99 55 E
Ban Ron Phibun, *Thailand* 77 H2 8 9N 99 51 E
Ban Sanam Chai, *Thailand* 77 J3 7 33N 100 25 E
Ban Sangkha, *Thailand* 76 E4 14 37N 103 52 E
Ban Tak, *Thailand* 76 D2 17 2N 99 4 E
Ban Tako, *Thailand* 76 E4 14 5N 102 40 E
Ban Tha Dua, *Thailand* 76 D2 17 59N 98 39 E
Ban Tha Li, *Thailand* 76 D3 17 37N 101 25 E
Ban Tha Nun, *Thailand* 77 H2 8 12N 98 18 E
Ban Thahine, *Laos* 76 E5 14 12N 105 33 E
Ban Xien Kok, *Laos* 76 B3 20 54N 100 39 E
Ban Yen Nhan, *Vietnam* 76 B6 20 57N 106 2 E
Baña, Punta de la, *Spain* 34 E5 40 33N 0 40 E
Banā, W. →, *Yemen* 86 D4 13 3N 45 24 E
Banaba, *Kiribati* 122 H8 0 45 S 169 50 E
Bañalbufar, *Spain* 33 B9 39 42N 2 31 E
Banalia, *Zaïre* 106 B2 1 32N 25 5 E
Banam, *Cambodia* 77 G5 11 20N 105 17 E
Banamba, *Mali* 100 C3 13 29N 7 22W
Banana, *Australia* 114 C5 24 28 S 150 8 E
Bananal, I. do, *Brazil* 155 D1 11 30 S 50 30W
Banaras = Varanasi, *India* 81 G10 25 22N 83 0 E
Banas →, *Gujarat, India* 80 H4 23 45N 71 25 E
Banas →, *Mad. P., India* 81 G9 24 15N 81 30 E
Bânâs, Ras, *Egypt* 94 C4 23 57N 35 50 E
Banaz, *Turkey* 88 D3 38 44N 29 46 E
Banbān, *Si. Arabia* 84 E5 25 1N 46 35 E
Banbridge, *U.K.* 19 B5 54 21N 6 17W
Banbridge □, *U.K.* 19 B5 54 21N 6 16W
Banbury, *U.K.* 17 E6 52 4N 1 21W
Banchory, *U.K.* 18 D6 57 3N 2 30W
Bancroft, *Canada* 128 C4 45 3N 77 51W
Band, *Romania* 46 C5 46 30N 24 25 E
Band Bonī, *Iran* 85 E8 25 30N 59 33 E
Band-e Torkestān, *Afghan.* 79 B2 35 30N 64 0 E
Band Qīr, *Iran* 85 D6 31 39N 48 53 E
Banda, *Cameroon* 102 B2 3 58N 14 32 E
Banda, *India* 81 G9 25 30N 80 26 E
Banda, Kepulauan, *Indonesia* 73 B3 4 37 S 129 50 E
Banda Aceh, *Indonesia* 74 A1 5 35N 95 20 E
Banda Banda, Mt., *Australia* 117 A10 31 10 S 152 28 E
Banda Elat, *Indonesia* 73 C4 5 40 S 133 5 E
Banda Is. = Banda, Kepulauan, *Indonesia* 73 B3 4 37 S 129 50 E
Banda Sea, *Indonesia* 72 C3 6 0 S 130 0 E
Bandai-San, *Japan* 60 F10 37 36N 140 4 E
Bandama →, *Ivory C.* 100 D3 6 32N 5 30W
Bandān, *Iran* 85 D9 31 23N 60 44 E
Bandanaira, *Indonesia* 73 B3 4 32 S 129 54 E
Bandanwara, *India* 80 F6 26 9N 74 38 E
Bandar = Machilipatnam, *India* 83 F5 16 12N 81 8 E
Bandār 'Abbās, *Iran* 85 E8 27 15N 56 15 E
Bandar-e Anzalī, *Iran* 85 B6 37 30N 49 30 E
Bandar-e Chārak, *Iran* 85 E7 26 45N 54 20 E
Bandar-e Deylam, *Iran* 85 D6 30 5N 50 10 E
Bandar-e Khomeyni, *Iran* 85 D6 30 30N 49 5 E
Bandar-e Lengeh, *Iran* 85 E7 26 35N 54 58 E
Bandar-e Maqām, *Iran* 85 E7 26 56N 53 29 E
Bandar-e Ma'shur, *Iran* 85 D6 30 35N 49 10 E
Bandar-e Nakhīlū, *Iran* 85 E7 26 58N 53 30 E
Bandar-e Rīg, *Iran* 85 D6 29 29N 50 38 E
Bandar-e Torkeman, *Iran* 85 B7 37 0N 54 10 E
Bandar Maharani = Muar, *Malaysia* 77 L4 2 3N 102 34 E
Bandar Penggaram = Batu Pahat, *Malaysia* 77 M4 1 50N 102 56 E
Bandar Seri Begawan, *Brunei* 75 B4 4 52N 115 0 E
Bandawe, *Malawi* 107 E3 11 58 S 34 5 E
Bande, *Belgium* 21 H6 50 10N 5 25 E
Bande, *Spain* 36 C3 42 3N 7 58W
Bandeira, Pico da, *Brazil* 155 F3 20 26 S 41 47W
Bandeirante, *Brazil* 155 D1 13 41 S 50 48W
Bandera, *Argentina* 158 B3 28 55 S 62 20W
Bandera, *U.S.A.* 139 L5 29 44N 99 5W
Banderas, B. de, *Mexico* 146 C3 20 40N 105 30W
Bandia →, *India* 82 E5 19 2N 80 28 E
Bandiagara, *Mali* 100 C4 14 12N 3 29W
Bandırma, *Turkey* 88 C3 40 20N 28 0 E
Bandon, *Ireland* 19 E3 51 44N 8 45W
Bandon →, *Ireland* 19 E3 51 40N 8 41W
Bandoua, *C.A.R.* 102 B4 4 39N 21 42 E
Bandula, *Mozam.* 107 F3 19 0 S 33 7 E
Bandundu, *Zaïre* 102 C3 3 15 S 17 22 E
Bandung, *Indonesia* 75 D3 6 54 S 107 36 E
Bandya, *Australia* 113 E3 27 40 S 122 5 E
Băneasa, *Romania* 46 D8 45 56N 27 55 E
Bāneh, *Iran* 84 C5 35 59N 45 53 E
Bañeres, *Spain* 35 G4 38 44N 0 38W
Banes, *Cuba* 149 B4 21 0N 75 42W
Banff, *Canada* 130 C5 51 10N 115 34W
Banff, *U.K.* 18 D6 57 40N 2 32W
Banff Nat. Park, *Canada* 130 C5 51 30N 116 15W
Banfora, *Burkina Faso* 100 C4 10 40N 4 40W
Bang Fai →, *Laos* 76 D5 16 57N 104 45 E
Bang Hieng →, *Laos* 76 D5 16 10N 105 10 E
Bang Krathum, *Thailand* 76 D3 16 34N 100 18 E
Bang Lamung, *Thailand* 76 F3 13 3N 100 56 E
Bang Mun Nak, *Thailand* 76 D3 16 2N 100 23 E
Bang Pa In, *Thailand* 76 E3 14 14N 100 35 E
Bang Rakam, *Thailand* 76 D3 16 45N 100 7 E
Bang Saphan, *Thailand* 77 G2 11 14N 99 28 E
Bangala Dam, *Zimbabwe* 107 G3 21 7 S 31 25 E
Bangalore, *India* 83 H3 12 59N 77 40 E
Bangante, *Cameroon* 101 D7 5 8N 10 32 E
Bangaon, *India* 81 H13 23 0N 88 47 E
Bangassou, *C.A.R.* 102 B4 4 55N 23 7 E
Bangeta, Mt., *Papua N. G.* 120 D4 6 21 S 147 3 E
Banggai, Kepulauan, *Indonesia* 72 B2 1 40 S 123 30 E
Banggai Arch., *Indonesia* 72 B2 2 0 S 123 15 E
Banggi, P., *Malaysia* 75 A5 7 17N 117 12 E
Banghāzī, *Libya* 96 B4 32 11N 20 3 E
Banghāzī □, *Libya* 96 B4 32 7N 20 4 E
Bangil, *Indonesia* 75 D4 7 36 S 112 50 E
Bangjang, *Sudan* 95 E3 11 23N 32 41 E
Bangka, P., *Sulawesi, Indonesia* 72 A3 1 50N 125 5 E
Bangka, P., *Sumatera, Indonesia* 74 C3 2 0 S 105 50 E
Bangka, Selat, *Indonesia* 74 C3 2 30 S 105 30 E
Bangkalan, *Indonesia* 75 D4 7 2 S 112 46 E
Bangkinang, *Indonesia* 74 B2 0 18N 101 5 E
Bangko, *Indonesia* 74 C2 2 5 S 102 9 E
Bangkok, *Thailand* 76 F3 13 45N 100 35 E
Bangladesh ■, *Asia* 78 C3 24 0N 90 0 E
Bangolo, *Ivory C.* 100 D3 7 1N 7 29W
Bangong Co, *India* 81 B8 35 50N 79 20 E
Bangor, *Down, U.K.* 19 B6 54 40N 5 40W
Bangor, *Gwynedd, U.K.* 16 D3 53 13N 4 9W
Bangor, *Maine, U.S.A.* 129 D6 44 48N 68 46W
Bangor, *Mich., U.S.A.* 141 B10 42 18N 86 7W
Bangor, *Pa., U.S.A.* 137 F9 40 52N 75 13W
Bangu, *Zaïre* 102 C3 0 3N 19 12 E
Bangued, *Phil.* 70 C3 17 40N 120 37 E
Bangui, *C.A.R.* 102 B3 4 23N 18 35 E
Bangui, *Phil.* 70 B3 18 32N 120 46 E
Banguru, *Zaïre* 106 B2 0 30N 27 10 E
Bangweulu, L., *Zambia* 107 E3 11 0 S 30 0 E
Bangweulu Swamp, *Zambia* 107 E3 11 20 S 30 15 E
Bani, *Dom. Rep.* 149 C5 18 16N 70 22W
Bani, *Phil.* 70 C2 16 11N 119 52 E
Bani →, *Mali* 100 C4 14 30N 4 12W
Bani, Djebel, *Morocco* 98 C3 29 16N 8 0W
Bani Bangou, *Niger* 101 B5 15 3N 2 42 E
Banī Sa'd, *Iraq* 84 C5 33 34N 44 32 E
Banī Sār, *Si. Arabia* 86 B3 20 6N 41 27 E
Banī Walīd, *Libya* 96 B2 31 36N 13 53 E
Bania, *Ivory C.* 100 D4 9 4N 3 6W
Baniara, *Papua N. G.* 120 E5 9 44 S 149 54 E
Banihal Pass, *India* 81 C6 33 30N 75 12 E
Banīnah, *Libya* 96 B4 32 0N 20 12 E
Bāniyās, *Syria* 84 C3 35 10N 36 0 E
Banja Luka, *Bos.-H.* 42 C2 44 49N 17 11 E
Banjar, *Indonesia* 75 D3 7 24 S 108 30 E
Banjarmasin, *Indonesia* 75 C4 3 20 S 114 35 E
Banjarnegara, *Indonesia* 75 D3 7 24 S 109 42 E
Banjul, *Gambia* 100 C1 13 28N 16 40W
Banka Banka, *Australia* 114 B1 18 50 S 134 0 E
Banket, *Zimbabwe* 107 F3 17 27 S 30 19 E
Bankilaré, *Niger* 101 C5 14 35N 0 44 E
Bankipore, *India* 81 G11 25 35N 85 10 E
Banks, Is., *Vanuatu* 121 C5 13 50 S 167 30 E
Banks I., *B.C., Canada* 130 C3 53 20N 130 0W
Banks I., *N.W.T., Canada* 126 A7 73 15N 121 30W
Banks I., *Papua N. G.* 120 F2 10 10 S 142 15 E
Banks Pen., *N.Z.* 119 D8 43 45 S 173 15 E
Banks Str., *Australia* 114 G4 40 40 S 148 10 E
Bankura, *India* 81 H12 23 11N 87 18 E
Bankya, *Bulgaria* 42 E8 42 43N 23 8 E
Bann →, *Down, U.K.* 19 B5 54 30N 6 31W
Bann →, *L'derry., U.K.* 19 A5 55 10N 6 34W
Banna, *Phil.* 70 C3 17 59N 120 39 E
Bannalec, *France* 22 E3 47 57N 3 42W
Bannang Sata, *Thailand* 77 J3 6 16N 101 16 E
Bannerton, *Australia* 116 C5 34 42 S 142 47 E
Banning, *U.S.A.* 145 M10 33 56N 116 53W
Banningville = Bandundu, *Zaïre* 102 C3 3 15 S 17 22 E
Bannockburn, *Canada* 136 B7 44 39N 77 33W
Bannockburn, *U.K.* 18 E5 56 5N 3 55W
Bannockburn, *Zimbabwe* 107 G2 20 17 S 29 48 E
Bannu, *Pakistan* 79 B3 33 0N 70 18 E
Bañolas, *Spain* 34 C7 42 16N 2 44 E
Banon, *France* 25 D9 44 2N 5 38 E
Baños de la Encina, *Spain* 37 G7 38 10N 3 46W
Baños de Molgas, *Spain* 36 C3 42 15N 7 40W
Bánovce, *Slovak Rep.* 31 C11 48 44N 18 16 E
Bansilan □, *Phil.* 71 H3 6 40N 121 40 E
Banská Bystrica, *Slovak Rep.* 31 C12 48 46N 19 14 E
Banská Štiavnica, *Slovak Rep.* 31 C11 48 25N 18 55 E
Bansko, *Bulgaria* 43 F8 41 52N 23 28 E
Banswara, *India* 80 H6 23 32N 74 24 E
Bantayan, *Phil.* 71 F4 11 10N 123 43 E
Bantayan I., *Phil.* 71 F4 11 13N 123 44 E
Banten, *Indonesia* 74 D3 6 5 S 106 8 E
Banton I., *Phil.* 70 E4 12 56N 122 4 E
Bantry, *Ireland* 19 E2 51 40N 9 28W
Bantry B., *Ireland* 19 E2 51 35N 9 50W
Bantul, *Indonesia* 75 D4 7 55 S 110 19 E
Bantva, *India* 80 J4 21 29N 70 12 E
Bantval, *India* 83 H2 12 55N 75 0 E
Banya, *Bulgaria* 43 E9 42 33N 24 50 E
Banyak, Kepulauan, *Indonesia* 74 B1 2 10N 97 10 E
Banyo, *Cameroon* 101 D7 6 52N 11 45 E
Banyuls-sur-Mer, *France* 24 F7 42 28N 3 8 E
Banyumas, *Indonesia* 75 D3 7 32 S 109 18 E
Banyuwangi, *Indonesia* 75 D4 8 13 S 114 21 E
Banzare Coast, *Antarctica* 7 C9 68 0 S 125 0 E
Banzyville = Mobayi, *Zaïre* 102 B4 4 15N 21 8 E
Bao Ha, *Vietnam* 76 A5 22 11N 104 21 E
Bao Lac, *Vietnam* 76 A5 22 57N 105 40 E
Bao Loc, *Vietnam* 77 G6 11 32N 107 48 E
Bao'an, *China* 69 F10 22 27N 114 10 E
Baocheng, *China* 66 H4 33 12N 106 56 E
Baode, *China* 66 E6 39 1N 111 5 E
Baodi, *China* 67 E9 39 38N 117 20 E
Baoding, *China* 66 E8 38 50N 115 28 E
Baoji, *China* 66 G4 34 20N 107 5 E
Baojing, *China* 68 C7 28 45N 109 41 E
Baokang, *China* 69 B8 31 54N 111 12 E
Baoro, *C.A.R.* 102 A3 5 40N 15 58 E
Baoshan, *Shanghai, China* 69 B13 31 27N 121 26 E
Baoshan, *Yunnan, China* 68 E2 25 10N 99 5 E
Baotou, *China* 66 D6 40 32N 110 2 E
Baoying, *China* 67 H10 33 17N 119 20 E
Bap, *India* 80 F5 27 23N 72 18 E
Bapatla, *India* 83 G5 15 55N 80 30 E
Bapaume, *France* 23 B9 50 7N 2 50 E
Bāqerābād, *Iran* 85 C6 33 2N 51 58 E
Ba'qūbah, *Iraq* 84 C5 33 45N 44 50 E
Baquedano, *Chile* 158 A2 23 20 S 69 52W
Bar, *Montenegro* 42 E4 42 8N 19 8 E
Bar, *Ukraine* 52 B2 49 4N 27 40 E
Bar Bigha, *India* 81 G11 25 21N 85 47 E
Bar Harbor, *U.S.A.* 129 D6 44 23N 68 13W
Bar-le-Duc, *France* 23 D12 48 47N 5 10 E
Bar-sur-Aube, *France* 23 D11 48 14N 4 40 E
Bar-sur-Seine, *France* 23 D11 48 7N 4 20 E
Barabai, *Indonesia* 75 C5 2 32 S 115 34 E
Barabinsk, *Russia* 56 D8 55 20N 78 20 E
Baraboo, *U.S.A.* 138 D10 43 28N 89 45W
Baracaldo, *Spain* 34 B2 43 18N 2 59W
Baracoa, *Cuba* 149 B5 20 20N 74 30W
Baradero, *Argentina* 158 C4 33 52 S 59 29W
Baradine, *Australia* 117 A8 30 56 S 149 4 E
Baraga, *U.S.A.* 138 B10 46 47N 88 30W
Barahona, *Dom. Rep.* 149 C5 18 13N 71 7W
Barahona, *Spain* 34 D2 41 17N 2 39W
Baraka →, *Sudan* 94 D4 18 13N 37 35 E
Barakot, *India* 81 J11 21 33N 84 59 E
Barakpur, *India* 81 H13 22 44N 88 30 E
Barakula, *Australia* 115 D5 26 30 S 150 33 E
Baralaba, *Australia* 114 C4 24 13 S 149 50 E
Baralzon L., *Canada* 131 B9 60 0N 98 3W
Baram →, *Malaysia* 75 B4 4 35N 113 58 E
Baramati, *India* 82 E2 18 11N 74 33 E
Baramba, *India* 82 D7 20 25N 85 23 E
Barameiya, *Sudan* 94 D4 18 32N 36 38 E
Baramula, *India* 81 B6 34 15N 74 20 E
Baran, *India* 80 G7 25 9N 76 40 E

174 Belzoni

Belzoni, *U.S.A.* **139 J9** 33 11N 90 29W
Bełżyce, *Poland* **47 D9** 51 11N 22 17 E
Bemaraha, Lembalemban' i, *Madag.* **105 B7** 18 40 S 44 45 E
Bemarivo, *Madag.* **105 C7** 21 45 S 44 45 E
Bemarivo →, *Madag.* **105 B8** 15 27 S 47 40 E
Bemavo, *Madag.* **105 C8** 21 33 S 45 25 E
Bembéréke, *Benin* **101 C5** 10 11N 2 43 E
Bembesi, *Zimbabwe* **107 F2** 20 0 S 28 58 E
Bembesi →, *Zimbabwe* **107 F2** 18 57 S 27 47 E
Bembézar →, *Spain* **37 H5** 37 45N 5 13W
Bement, *U.S.A.* **141 E8** 39 55N 88 34W
Bemidji, *U.S.A.* **138 B7** 47 28N 94 53W
Bemmel, *Neths.* **20 E7** 51 54N 5 54 E
Ben, *Iran* **85 C6** 32 32N 50 45 E
Ben Bullen, *Australia* **117 B9** 33 12 S 150 2 E
Ben Cruachan, *U.K.* **18 E3** 56 26N 5 8W
Ben Dearg, *U.K.* **18 D4** 57 47N 4 58W
Ben Gardane, *Tunisia* **96 B2** 33 11N 11 11 E
Ben Hope, *U.K.* **18 C4** 58 24N 4 36W
Ben Lawers, *U.K.* **18 E4** 56 33N 4 13W
Ben Lomond, *N.S.W., Australia* **115 E5** 30 1 S 151 43 E
Ben Lomond, *Tas., Australia* **114 G4** 41 38 S 147 42 E
Ben Lomond, *U.K.* **18 E4** 56 12N 4 39W
Ben Luc, *Vietnam* **77 G6** 10 39N 106 29 E
Ben Macdhui, *U.K.* **18 D5** 57 4N 3 40W
Ben Mhor, *U.K.* **18 D1** 57 16N 7 21W
Ben More, *Central, U.K.* **18 E4** 56 23N 4 31W
Ben More, *Strath., U.K.* **18 E2** 56 26N 6 2W
Ben More Assynt, *U.K.* **18 C4** 58 7N 4 51W
Ben Nevis, *U.K.* **18 E4** 56 48N 4 58W
Ben Ohau Ra., *N.Z.* **119 E5** 44 1 S 170 4 E
Ben Quang, *Vietnam* **76 D6** 17 3N 106 55 E
Ben Slimane, *Morocco* **98 B3** 33 38N 7 7W
Ben Tre, *Vietnam* **77 G6** 10 3N 106 36 E
Ben Vorlich, *U.K.* **18 E4** 56 22N 4 15W
Ben Wyvis, *U.K.* **18 D4** 57 40N 4 35W
Bena, *Nigeria* **101 C6** 11 20N 5 50 E
Bena Dibele, *Zaïre* **103 C4** 4 4 S 22 50 E
Bena-Leka, *Zaïre* **103 D4** 5 8 S 22 10 E
Bena-Tshadi, *Zaïre* **103 C4** 4 40 S 22 49 E
Benadir, *Somali Rep.* **108 D2** 1 30N 44 30 E
Benagalbón, *Spain* **37 J6** 36 45N 4 15W
Benagerie, *Australia* **116 A4** 31 25 S 140 22 E
Benahmed, *Morocco* **98 B3** 33 4N 7 9W
Benalla, *Australia* **117 D7** 36 30 S 146 0 E
Benambra, Mt., *Australia* **117 D7** 36 31 S 147 34 E
Benamejí, *Spain* **37 H6** 37 16N 4 33W
Benares = Varanasi, *India* **81 G10** 25 22N 83 0 E
Bénat, C., *France* **25 E10** 43 5N 6 22 E
Benavente, *Portugal* **37 G2** 38 59N 8 49W
Benavente, *Spain* **36 C5** 42 2N 5 43W
Benavides, *Spain* **36 C5** 42 30N 5 54W
Benavides, *U.S.A.* **139 M5** 27 36N 98 25W
Benbecula, *U.K.* **18 D1** 57 26N 7 21W
Benbonyathe, *Australia* **116 A3** 30 25 S 139 11 E
Bencubbin, *Australia* **113 F2** 30 48 S 117 52 E
Bend, *U.S.A.* **142 D3** 44 4N 121 19W
Bendela, *Zaïre* **102 C3** 3 18 S 17 36 E
Bender Beila, *Somali Rep.* **90 F5** 9 30N 50 48 E
Bender Merchagno, *Somali Rep.* **108 B4** 11 41N 50 34 E
Bendering, *Australia* **113 F2** 32 23 S 118 18 E
Bendery, *Moldavia* **52 C3** 46 50N 29 30 E
Bendigo, *Australia* **116 D6** 36 40 S 144 15 E
Bendorf, *Germany* **26 E3** 50 26N 7 34 E
Benē Beraq, *Israel* **91 C3** 32 6N 34 51 E
Beneden Knijpe, *Neths.* **20 C7** 52 58N 5 59 E
Beneditinos, *Brazil* **154 C3** 5 27 S 42 22W
Benedito Leite, *Brazil* **154 C3** 7 13 S 44 34W
Bénéna, *Mali* **100 C4** 13 9N 4 17W
Benenitra, *Madag.* **105 C8** 23 27 S 45 5 E
Benešŏv, *Czech.* **30 B7** 49 46N 14 41 E
Bénestroff, *France* **23 D13** 48 54N 6 45 E
Benet, *France* **24 B3** 46 22N 0 35W
Benevento, *Italy* **41 A7** 41 7N 14 45 E
Benfeld, *France* **23 D14** 48 22N 7 34 E
Benga, *Mozam.* **107 F3** 16 11 S 33 40 E
Bengal, Bay of, *Ind. Oc.* **58 H13** 15 0N 90 0 E
Bengbu, *China* **67 H9** 32 58N 117 20 E
Benghazi = Banghāzī, *Libya* **96 B4** 32 11N 20 3 E
Bengkalis, *Indonesia* **74 B2** 1 30N 102 10 E
Bengkulu, *Indonesia* **74 C2** 3 50 S 102 12 E
Bengough, *Canada* **131 D7** 49 25N 105 10W
Benguela, *Angola* **103 E2** 12 37 S 13 25 E
Benguela □, *Angola* **103 E2** 13 0 S 13 30 E
Benguerir, *Morocco* **98 B3** 32 16N 7 56W
Benguérua, I., *Mozam.* **105 C6** 21 58 S 35 28 E
Benguet □, *Phil.* **70 C3** 16 30N 120 40 E
Benha, *Egypt* **94 H7** 30 26N 31 8 E
Beni, *Zaïre* **106 B2** 0 30N 29 27 E
Beni □, *Bolivia* **157 C4** 14 0 S 65 0W
Beni →, *Bolivia* **157 C4** 10 23 S 65 24W
Beni Abbès, *Algeria* **99 B4** 30 5N 2 5W
Beni-Haoua, *Algeria* **99 A5** 36 30N 1 30 E
Beni Mazâr, *Egypt* **94 J7** 28 32N 30 44 E
Beni Mellal, *Morocco* **98 B3** 32 21N 6 21W
Beni Ounif, *Algeria* **99 B4** 32 0N 1 10W
Beni Saf, *Algeria* **99 A4** 35 17N 1 15W
Beni Suef, *Egypt* **94 J7** 29 5N 31 6 E
Beniah L., *Canada* **130 A6** 63 23N 112 17W
Benicarló, *Spain* **34 E5** 40 23N 0 23 E
Benicia, *U.S.A.* **144 G4** 38 3N 122 9W
Benidorm, *Spain* **35 G4** 38 33N 0 9W
Benidorm, Islote de, *Spain* **35 G4** 38 31N 0 9W
Benin ■, *Africa* **101 D5** 10 0N 2 0 E
Benin, Bight of, *W. Afr.* **101 D5** 5 0N 3 0 E
Benin City, *Nigeria* **101 D6** 6 20N 5 31 E
Benisa, *Spain* **35 G5** 38 43N 0 3 E
Benitses, *Greece* **32 A3** 39 32N 19 55 E
Benjamin Aceval, *Paraguay* **158 A4** 24 58 S 57 34W
Benjamin Constant, *Brazil* **152 D3** 4 40 S 70 15W
Benjamin Hill, *Mexico* **146 A2** 30 10N 111 10W
Benkelman, *U.S.A.* **138 E4** 40 3N 101 32W
Benkovac, *Croatia* **39 D12** 44 2N 15 37 E
Benlidi, *Australia* **114 C3** 24 35 S 144 50 E
Benmore Pk., *N.Z.* **119 E5** 44 25 S 170 8 E
Bennebroek, *Neths.* **20 D5** 52 19N 4 36 E
Bennekom, *Neths.* **20 D7** 52 0N 5 41 E
Bennett, *Canada* **130 B2** 59 56N 134 53W
Bennett, L., *Australia* **112 D5** 22 50 S 131 2 E
Bennett, Ostrov, *Russia* **57 B15** 76 21N 148 56 E
Bennettsville, *U.S.A.* **135 H6** 34 37N 79 41W
Bennington, *U.S.A.* **137 D11** 43 0N 71 55W
Bénodet, *France* **22 E2** 47 53N 4 7W
Benoni, *S. Africa* **105 D4** 26 11 S 28 18 E
Benoud, *Algeria* **99 B5** 32 20N 0 16 E
Benoy, *Chad* **97 G3** 8 59N 16 19 E
Benque Viejo, *Belize* **147 D7** 17 5N 89 8W
Bensheim, *Germany* **27 F4** 49 40N 8 38 E
Benson, *U.S.A.* **143 L8** 31 58N 110 18W
Bent, *Iran* **85 E8** 26 20N 59 31 E
Benteng, *Indonesia* **72 C2** 6 10 S 120 30 E
Bentinck I., *Australia* **114 B2** 17 3 S 139 35 E
Bentiu, *Sudan* **95 F2** 9 10N 29 55 E
Bento Gonçalves, *Brazil* **159 B5** 29 10 S 51 31W
Benton, *Ark., U.S.A.* **139 H8** 34 34N 92 35W
Benton, *Calif., U.S.A.* **144 H8** 37 48N 118 32W
Benton, *Ill., U.S.A.* **140 G8** 38 0N 88 55W
Benton Harbor, *U.S.A.* **141 B10** 42 6N 86 27W
Bentu Liben, *Ethiopia* **95 F4** 8 32N 38 21 E
Bentung, *Malaysia* **77 L3** 3 31N 101 55 E
Benue □, *Nigeria* **101 D6** 7 20N 8 45 E
Benue →, *Nigeria* **101 D6** 7 48N 6 46 E
Benxi, *China* **67 D12** 41 20N 123 48 E
Benzdorp, *Surinam* **153 C7** 3 44N 54 5W
Beo, *Indonesia* **72 A3** 4 25N 126 50 E
Beograd, *Serbia* **42 C5** 44 50N 20 37 E
Beowawe, *U.S.A.* **142 F5** 40 35N 116 29W
Bepan Jiang →, *China* **68 E6** 24 55N 106 5 E
Beppu, *Japan* **62 D3** 33 15N 131 30 E
Beppu-Wan, *Japan* **62 D3** 33 18N 131 34 E
Bera, *Bangla.* **78 C2** 24 5N 89 37 E
Berati, *Albania* **44 D1** 40 43N 19 59 E
Berau →, *Indonesia* **75 B5** 2 10N 117 42 E
Berau, Teluk, *Indonesia* **73 B4** 2 30 S 132 30 E
Berber, *Sudan* **94 D3** 18 0N 34 0 E
Berbera, *Somali Rep.* **90 E4** 10 30N 45 2 E
Berbérati, *C.A.R.* **102 B3** 4 15N 15 40 E
Berberia, C. del, *Spain* **33 C7** 38 39N 1 24 E
Berbice →, *Guyana* **153 B6** 6 20N 57 32W
Berceto, *Italy* **38 D7** 44 30N 10 0 E
Berchtesgaden, *Germany* **27 H8** 47 37N 12 58 E
Berdale, *Somali Rep.* **108 C3** 7 4N 47 51 E
Berdichev, *Ukraine* **52 B3** 49 57N 28 30 E
Berdsk, *Russia* **56 D9** 54 47N 83 2 E
Berdyansk, *Ukraine* **52 C7** 46 45N 36 50 E
Berdyaush, *Russia* **54 D6** 55 9N 59 9 E
Berdychiv = Berdichev, *Ukraine* **52 B3** 49 57N 28 30 E
Berea, *U.S.A.* **134 G3** 37 34N 84 17W
Berebere, *Indonesia* **72 A3** 2 25N 128 45 E
Bereda, *Somali Rep.* **90 E5** 11 45N 51 0 E
Bereina, *Papua N. G.* **120 E4** 8 39 S 146 30 E
Berekum, *Ghana* **100 D4** 7 29N 2 34W
Berenice, *Egypt* **94 C4** 24 2N 35 25 E
Berens →, *Canada* **131 C9** 52 25N 97 2W
Berens I., *Canada* **131 C9** 52 18N 97 18W
Berens River, *Canada* **131 C9** 52 25N 97 0W
Berestechko, *Ukraine* **50 F4** 50 22N 25 5 E
Bereşti, *Romania* **46 C8** 46 6N 27 50 E
Beretău →, *Romania* **46 B2** 47 10N 21 50 E
Berettyo →, *Hungary* **31 E14** 46 59N 21 7 E
Berettyóújfalu, *Hungary* **31 D14** 47 13N 21 33 E
Berevo, *Mahajanga, Madag.* **105 B7** 17 14 S 44 17 E
Berevo, *Toliara, Madag.* **105 B7** 19 44 S 44 58 E
Bereza, *Belorussia* **50 E4** 52 31N 24 51 E
Berezhany, *Ukraine* **50 G4** 49 26N 24 58 E
Berezina →, *Belorussia* **50 E7** 52 33N 30 14 E
Berezna, *Ukraine* **50 F7** 51 35N 31 46 E
Berezniki, *Russia* **54 B5** 59 24N 56 46 E
Berezovka, *Ukraine* **52 C4** 47 14N 30 55 E
Berezovo, *Russia* **48 B11** 64 0N 65 0 E
Berga, *Spain* **34 C6** 42 6N 1 48 E
Bergama, *Turkey* **88 D2** 39 8N 27 15 E
Bergambacht, *Neths.* **20 E5** 51 56N 4 48 E
Bérgamo, *Italy* **38 C6** 45 42N 9 40 E
Bergantiños, *Spain* **36 B2** 43 20N 8 40W
Bergara, *Spain* **34 B2** 43 9N 2 28W
Bergedorf, *Germany* **26 B6** 53 28N 10 12 E
Bergeijk, *Neths.* **21 F6** 51 19N 5 21 E
Bergen, *Germany* **26 A9** 54 24N 13 26 E
Bergen, *Neths.* **20 C5** 52 40N 4 43 E
Bergen, *Norway* **13 F8** 60 23N 5 20 E
Bergen, *U.S.A.* **136 C7** 43 5N 77 57W
Bergen-op-Zoom, *Neths.* **21 F4** 51 28N 4 18 E
Bergerac, *France* **24 D4** 44 51N 0 30 E
Bergheim, *Germany* **26 E2** 50 57N 6 38 E
Berghem, *Neths.* **20 E7** 51 46N 5 33 E
Bergisch-Gladbach, *Germany* **26 E3** 50 59N 7 9 E
Bergschenhoek, *Neths.* **20 E5** 51 59N 4 30 E
Bergsjö, *Sweden* **14 C11** 61 59N 17 3 E
Bergues, *France* **23 B9** 50 58N 2 24 E
Bergum, *Neths.* **20 B7** 53 13N 5 59 E
Bergville, *S. Africa* **105 D4** 28 52 S 29 18 E
Berhala, Selat, *Indonesia* **74 C2** 1 0 S 104 15 E
Berhampore = Baharampur, *India* **81 G13** 24 2N 88 27 E
Berhampur, *India* **82 E7** 19 15N 84 54 E
Berheci →, *Romania* **46 C8** 46 7N 27 19 E
Bering Sea, *Pac. Oc.* **126 C1** 58 0N 171 0 E
Bering Strait, *U.S.A.* **126 B3** 65 30N 169 0W
Beringen, *Belgium* **21 F6** 51 3N 5 14 E
Beringen, *Switz.* **29 A7** 47 38N 8 34 E
Beringovskiy, *Russia* **57 C18** 63 3N 179 19 E
Berislav, *Ukraine* **52 C5** 46 50N 33 30 E
Berisso, *Argentina* **158 C4** 34 56 S 57 50W
Berja, *Spain* **35 J2** 36 50N 2 56W
Berkane, *Morocco* **99 B4** 34 52N 2 20W
Berkel →, *Neths.* **20 D8** 52 8N 6 12 E
Berkeley, *U.K.* **17 F5** 51 41N 2 28W
Berkeley, *U.S.A.* **144 H4** 37 52N 122 16W
Berkeley Springs, *U.S.A.* **134 F6** 39 38N 78 14W
Berkhout, *Neths.* **20 C5** 52 38N 4 59 E
Berkner I., *Antarctica* **7 D18** 79 30 S 50 0W
Berkovitsa, *Bulgaria* **43 D8** 43 16N 23 8 E
Berkshire □, *U.K.* **17 F6** 51 30N 1 20W
Berlaar, *Belgium* **21 F5** 51 7N 4 39 E
Berland →, *Canada* **130 C5** 54 0N 116 50W
Berlanga, *Spain* **37 G5** 38 17N 5 50W
Berlare, *Belgium* **21 F4** 51 2N 4 2 E
Berlenga, I., *Portugal* **37 F1** 39 25N 9 30W
Berlin, *Germany* **26 C9** 52 32N 13 24 E
Berlin, *Md., U.S.A.* **134 F8** 38 20N 75 13W
Berlin, *N.H., U.S.A.* **137 B13** 44 28N 71 11W
Berlin, *Wis., U.S.A.* **134 D1** 43 58N 88 57W
Bermeja, Sierra, *Spain* **37 J5** 36 30N 5 11W
Bermejo →, *Formosa, Argentina* **158 B4** 26 51 S 58 23W
Bermejo →, *San Juan, Argentina* **158 C2** 32 30 S 67 30W
Bermeo, *Spain* **34 B2** 43 25N 2 47W
Bermillo de Sayago, *Spain* **36 D4** 41 22N 6 8W
Bermuda ■, *Atl. Oc.* **8 E2** 32 45N 65 0W
Bern, *Switz.* **28 C4** 46 57N 7 28 E
Bern □, *Switz.* **28 C5** 46 45N 7 40 E
Bernado, *U.S.A.* **143 J10** 34 30N 106 53W
Bernalda, *Italy* **41 B9** 40 24N 16 44 E
Bernalillo, *U.S.A.* **143 J10** 35 18N 106 33W
Bernam →, *Malaysia* **74 B2** 3 45N 101 5 E
Bernardo de Irigoyen, *Argentina* **159 B5** 26 15 S 53 40W
Bernardo O'Higgins □, *Chile* **158 C1** 34 15 S 70 45W
Bernasconi, *Argentina* **158 D3** 37 55 S 63 44W
Bernau, *Bayern, Germany* **27 H8** 47 45N 12 20 E
Bernau, *Brandenburg, Germany* **26 C9** 52 40N 13 35 E
Bernay, *France* **22 C7** 49 5N 0 35 E
Bernburg, *Germany* **26 D7** 51 40N 11 42 E
Berndorf, *Austria* **30 D9** 47 59N 16 1 E
Berne = Bern, *Switz.* **28 C4** 46 57N 7 28 E
Berne = Bern □, *Switz.* **28 C5** 46 45N 7 40 E
Berne, *U.S.A.* **141 D12** 40 39N 84 57W
Berner Alpen, *Switz.* **28 D5** 46 27N 7 35 E
Bernese Oberland = Oberland, *Switz.* **28 C5** 46 35N 7 38 E
Bernier I., *Australia* **113 D1** 24 50 S 113 12 E
Bernina, Piz, *Switz.* **29 D9** 46 20N 9 54 E
Bernina, Pizzo, *Switz.* **29 D9** 46 22N 9 54 E
Bernissart, *Belgium* **21 H3** 50 28N 3 39 E
Bernkastel-Kues, *Germany* **27 F3** 49 55N 7 4 E
Beroroha, *Madag.* **105 C8** 21 40 S 45 10 E
Béroubouay, *Benin* **101 C5** 10 34N 2 46 E
Beroun, *Czech.* **30 B7** 49 57N 14 5 E
Berounka →, *Czech.* **30 B7** 50 0N 14 22 E
Berovo, *Macedonia* **42 F7** 41 38N 22 51 E
Berrahal, *Algeria* **99 A6** 36 54N 7 33 E
Berre, Étang de, *France* **25 E9** 43 27N 5 5 E
Berrechid, *Morocco* **98 B3** 33 18N 7 36W
Berri, *Australia* **116 C4** 34 14 S 140 35 E
Berriane, *Algeria* **99 B5** 32 50N 3 46 E
Berrien Springs, *U.S.A.* **141 C10** 41 57N 86 20W
Berrigan, *Australia* **117 C6** 35 38 S 145 49 E
Berriwillock, *Australia* **116 C5** 35 36 S 142 59 E
Berrouaghia, *Algeria* **99 A5** 36 10N 2 53 E
Berry, *Australia* **117 C9** 34 46 S 150 43 E
Berry, *France* **23 F8** 46 50N 2 0 E
Berry, *U.S.A.* **141 F12** 38 31N 84 23W
Berry Is., *Bahamas* **148 A4** 25 40N 77 50W
Berryessa L., *U.S.A.* **144 G4** 38 31N 122 6W
Berryville, *U.S.A.* **139 G8** 36 22N 93 34W
Bersenbrück, *Germany* **26 C3** 52 33N 7 56 E
Berthold, *U.S.A.* **138 A4** 48 19N 101 44W
Berthoud, *U.S.A.* **138 E2** 40 19N 105 5W
Bertincourt, *France* **23 B9** 50 5N 2 58 E
Bertoua, *Cameroon* **102 B2** 4 30N 13 45 E
Bertrand, *U.S.A.* **138 E5** 40 32N 99 38W
Bertrange, *Lux.* **21 J8** 49 37N 6 3 E
Bertrix, *Belgium* **21 J6** 49 51N 5 15 E
Berufjörður, *Iceland* **12 D6** 64 48N 14 29W
Beruri, *Brazil* **153 D5** 3 54 S 61 22W
Berwick, *U.S.A.* **137 E8** 41 3N 76 14W
Berwick-upon-Tweed, *U.K.* **16 B5** 55 47N 2 0W
Berwyn Mts., *U.K.* **16 E4** 52 54N 3 26W
Berzasca, *Romania* **42 C6** 44 39N 21 58 E
Berzence, *Hungary* **31 E10** 46 12N 17 11 E
Besal, *Pakistan* **81 B5** 35 4N 73 56 E
Besalampy, *Madag.* **105 B7** 16 43 S 44 29 E
Besançon, *France* **23 E13** 47 15N 6 2 E
Besar, *Indonesia* **75 C5** 2 40 S 116 0 E
Besar, Gunong, *Malaysia* **74 A2** 5 10N 101 18 E
Beshenkovichi, *Belorussia* **50 D6** 55 2N 29 29 E
Beška, *Serbia* **42 B5** 45 8N 20 6 E
Beskids = Beskydy, *Europe* **31 B11** 49 35N 18 40 E
Beskydy, *Europe* **31 B11** 49 35N 18 40 E
Beslan, *Russia* **53 E11** 43 15N 44 28 E
Besna Kobila, *Serbia* **42 E7** 42 31N 22 10 E
Besnard L., *Canada* **131 B7** 55 25N 106 0W
Besni, *Turkey* **89 E7** 37 41N 37 52 E
Besor, N. →, *Egypt* **91 D3** 31 28N 34 22 E
Beşparmak Dağı, *Turkey* **45 G9** 37 32N 27 30 E
Bessa Monteiro, *Angola* **103 D2** 7 7 S 13 44 E
Bessarabiya, *Moldavia* **46 C9** 47 0N 28 10 E
Bessarabka, *Moldavia* **52 C3** 46 21N 28 58 E
Bessèges, *France* **25 D8** 44 18N 4 8 E
Bessemer, *Ala., U.S.A.* **135 J2** 33 24N 86 58W
Bessemer, *Mich., U.S.A.* **138 B9** 46 29N 90 3W
Bessin, *France* **22 C5** 49 18N 1 0W
Bessines-sur-Gartempe, *France* **24 B5** 46 6N 1 22 E
Best, *Neths.* **21 E6** 51 31N 5 23 E
Bet She'an, *Israel* **91 C4** 32 30N 35 30 E
Bet Shemesh, *Israel* **91 D3** 31 44N 35 0 E
Bet Tadjine, Djebel, *Algeria* **98 C4** 29 0N 3 30W
Betafo, *Madag.* **105 B8** 19 50 S 46 51 E
Betancuria, *Canary Is.* **33 F5** 28 25N 14 3W
Betanzos, *Bolivia* **157 D4** 19 34 S 65 27W
Betanzos, *Spain* **36 B2** 43 15N 8 12W
Bétaré Oya, *Cameroon* **102 A2** 5 40N 14 5 E
Bétera, *Spain* **34 F4** 39 35N 0 28W
Bethal, *S. Africa* **105 D4** 26 27 S 29 28 E
Bethanien, *Namibia* **104 D2** 26 31 S 17 8 E
Bethany, *S. Africa* **104 D4** 29 34 S 25 59 E
Bethany, *Ill., U.S.A.* **141 E8** 39 39N 88 45W
Bethany, *Mo., U.S.A.* **140 D2** 40 16N 94 2W
Bethel, *Alaska, U.S.A.* **126 B3** 60 48N 161 45W
Bethel, *Ohio, U.S.A.* **141 F12** 38 58N 84 5W
Bethel, *Vt., U.S.A.* **137 C12** 43 50N 72 38W
Bethel Park, *U.S.A.* **136 F4** 40 20N 80 1W
Bethlehem = Bayt Lahm, *Jordan* **91 D4** 31 43N 35 12 E
Bethlehem, *S. Africa* **105 D4** 28 14 S 28 18 E
Bethlehem, *U.S.A.* **137 F9** 40 37N 75 23W
Bethulie, *S. Africa* **104 E4** 30 30 S 25 59 E
Béthune, *France* **23 B9** 50 30N 2 38 E
Béthune →, *France* **22 C8** 49 53N 1 9 E
Bethungra, *Australia* **117 C7** 34 45 S 147 51 E
Betijoque, *Venezuela* **152 B3** 9 23N 70 44W
Betim, *Brazil* **155 E3** 19 58 S 44 7W
Betioky, *Madag.* **105 C7** 23 48 S 44 20 E
Beton-Bazoches, *France* **23 D10** 48 42N 3 15 E
Betong, *Thailand* **77 K3** 5 45N 101 5 E
Betoota, *Australia* **114 D3** 25 45 S 140 42 E
Betroka, *Madag.* **105 C8** 23 16 S 46 0 E
Betsiamites, *Canada* **129 C6** 48 56N 68 40W
Betsiamites →, *Canada* **129 C6** 48 56N 68 38W
Betsiboka →, *Madag.* **105 B8** 16 3 S 46 36 E
Betsjoeanaland, *S. Africa* **104 D3** 26 30 S 22 30 E
Bettembourg, *Lux.* **21 J8** 49 31N 6 6 E
Bettendorf, *U.S.A.* **140 C6** 41 32N 90 30W
Bettiah, *India* **81 F11** 26 48N 84 33 E
Béttola, *Italy* **38 D6** 44 42N 9 32 E
Betul, *India* **82 D3** 21 58N 77 59 E
Betung, *Malaysia* **75 B4** 1 24N 111 31 E
Betzdorf, *Germany* **26 E3** 50 47N 7 53 E
Beuca, *Romania* **46 E5** 44 14N 24 56 E
Beuil, *France* **25 D10** 44 6N 6 59 E
Beulah, *U.S.A.* **138 B4** 47 16N 101 47W
Beuvron →, *France* **22 E8** 47 29N 1 15 E
Beveren, *Belgium* **21 F4** 51 12N 4 16 E
Beverley, *Australia* **113 F2** 32 9 S 116 56 E
Beverley, *U.K.* **16 D7** 53 52N 0 26W
Beverlo, *Belgium* **21 F6** 51 7N 5 13 E
Beverly, *Mass., U.S.A.* **137 D14** 42 33N 70 53W
Beverly, *Wash., U.S.A.* **142 C4** 46 50N 119 56W
Beverly Hills, *U.S.A.* **145 L8** 34 4N 118 25W
Beverwijk, *Neths.* **20 D5** 52 28N 4 38 E
Bex, *Switz.* **28 D4** 46 15N 7 0 E
Bey Dağları, *Turkey* **88 E4** 36 45N 30 15 E
Beyānlū, *Iran* **84 C5** 36 0N 47 51 E
Beyin, *Ghana* **100 D4** 5 1N 2 41W
Beykoz, *Turkey* **43 F14** 41 8N 29 7 E
Beyla, *Guinea* **100 D3** 8 30N 8 38W
Beynat, *France* **24 C5** 45 8N 1 44 E
Beyneu, *Kazakhstan* **49 E10** 45 10N 55 3 E
Beypazarı, *Turkey* **88 C4** 40 10N 31 56 E
Beypore →, *India* **83 J2** 11 10N 75 47 E
Beyşehir Gölü, *Turkey* **88 E4** 37 40N 31 45 E
Beytüşşebap, *Turkey* **89 E10** 37 35N 43 10 E
Bezdan, *Serbia* **42 B3** 45 50N 18 57 E
Bezhetsk, *Russia* **51 C10** 57 47N 36 39 E
Bezhitsa, *Russia* **50 E9** 53 19N 34 17 E
Béziers, *France* **24 E7** 43 20N 3 12 E
Bezwada = Vijayawada, *India* **83 F5** 16 31N 80 39 E
Bhadarwah, *India* **81 C6** 32 58N 75 46 E
Bhadra →, *India* **83 H2** 14 0N 75 20 E
Bhadrakh, *India* **82 D8** 21 10N 86 30 E
Bhadravati, *India* **83 H2** 13 49N 75 40 E
Bhagalpur, *India* **81 G12** 25 10N 87 0 E
Bhainsa, *India* **82 E3** 19 10N 77 58 E
Bhairab →, *Bangla.* **78 D2** 22 51N 89 34 E
Bhairab Bazar, *Bangla.* **78 C3** 24 4N 90 58 E
Bhakkar, *Pakistan* **79 C3** 31 40N 71 5 E
Bhakra Dam, *India* **80 D7** 31 30N 76 45 E
Bhamo, *Burma* **78 C6** 24 15N 97 15 E
Bhamragarh, *India* **82 E5** 19 30N 80 40 E
Bhandara, *India* **82 D4** 21 5N 79 42 E
Bhanrer Ra., *India* **80 H8** 23 40N 79 45 E
Bharat = India ■, *Asia* **59 H11** 20 0N 78 0 E
Bharatpur, *India* **80 F7** 27 15N 77 30 E
Bharuch, *India* **82 D1** 21 47N 73 0 E
Bhatghar L., *India* **82 E1** 18 10N 73 48 E
Bhatiapara Ghat, *Bangla.* **78 D2** 23 13N 89 42 E
Bhatinda, *India* **80 D6** 30 15N 74 57 E
Bhatkal, *India* **83 H2** 13 58N 74 35 E
Bhatpara, *India* **81 H13** 22 50N 88 25 E
Bhattiprolu, *India* **83 F5** 16 7N 80 45 E
Bhaun, *Pakistan* **80 C5** 32 55N 72 40 E
Bhaunagar = Bhavnagar, *India* **80 J5** 21 45N 72 10 E
Bhavani, *India* **83 J3** 11 27N 77 43 E
Bhavani →, *India* **83 J4** 11 0N 78 15 E
Bhavnagar, *India* **80 J5** 21 45N 72 10 E
Bhawanipatna, *India* **82 E6** 19 55N 80 10 E
Bhera, *Pakistan* **80 C5** 32 29N 72 57 E
Bhilsa = Vidisha, *India* **80 H7** 23 28N 77 53 E
Bhilwara, *India* **80 G6** 25 25N 74 38 E
Bhima →, *India* **82 F3** 16 25N 77 17 E
Bhimavaram, *India* **83 F5** 16 30N 81 30 E
Bhimbar, *Pakistan* **81 C6** 32 59N 74 3 E
Bhind, *India* **81 F8** 26 30N 78 46 E
Bhiwandi, *India* **82 E1** 19 20N 73 0 E
Bhiwani, *India* **80 E7** 28 50N 76 9 E
Bhola, *Bangla.* **78 D3** 22 45N 90 35 E
Bhongir, *India* **82 F4** 17 30N 78 56 E
Bhopal, *India* **80 H7** 23 20N 77 30 E
Bhor, *India* **82 E1** 18 12N 73 53 E
Bhubaneshwar, *India* **82 D7** 20 15N 85 50 E
Bhuj, *India* **80 H3** 23 15N 69 49 E
Bhumiphol Dam = Phumiphon, Khuan, *Thailand* **76 D2** 17 15N 98 58 E
Bhusaval, *India* **82 D2** 21 3N 75 46 E
Bhutan ■, *Asia* **78 B3** 27 25N 90 30 E
Biá →, *Brazil* **152 D4** 3 28 S 67 23W
Biafra, B. of = Bonny, Bight of, *Africa* **101 E6** 3 30N 9 20 E
Biak, *Indonesia* **73 B5** 1 10 S 136 6 E
Biała, *Poland* **47 E4** 50 24N 17 40 E
Biała →, *Białystok, Poland* **47 B10** 53 11N 23 4 E
Biała →, *Tarnów, Poland* **31 A13** 50 3N 20 55 E
Biała Piska, *Poland* **47 B9** 53 37N 22 5 E
Biała Podlaska, *Poland* **47 C10** 52 4N 23 6 E
Biała Podlaska □, *Poland* **47 D10** 52 0N 23 0 E
Biała Rawska, *Poland* **47 D7** 51 48N 20 29 E
Białobrzegi, *Poland* **47 C8** 52 27N 21 3 E
Białogard, *Poland* **47 A2** 54 2N 15 58 E
Białowieża, *Poland* **47 C10** 52 41N 23 49 E
Biały Bór, *Poland* **47 B3** 53 53N 16 51 E
Białystok, *Poland* **47 B10** 53 10N 23 10 E
Białystok □, *Poland* **47 B10** 53 9N 23 10 E
Biancavilla, *Italy* **41 E7** 37 39N 14 50 E
Bīārjmand, *Iran* **85 B7** 36 6N 55 53 E
Biaro, *Indonesia* **72 A3** 2 5N 125 26 E
Biarritz, *France* **24 E2** 43 29N 1 33W
Biasca, *Switz.* **29 D7** 46 22N 8 58 E
Biba, *Egypt* **94 J7** 28 55N 31 0 E
Bibai, *Japan* **60 C10** 43 19N 141 52 E

176 Black Mt.

Black Mt. = Mynydd Du, *U.K.* **17 F4** 51 45N 3 45W
Black Mountain, *Australia* **117 A9** 30 18 S 151 39 E
Black Mts., *U.K.* **17 F4** 51 52N 3 5W
Black Range, *U.S.A.* **143 K10** 33 15N 107 50W
Black River, *Jamaica* **148 C4** 18 0N 77 50W
Black River Falls, *U.S.A.* **138 C9** 44 18N 90 51W
Black Rock, *Australia* **116 B3** 32 50 S 138 44 E
Black Sea, *Europe* **52 E6** 43 30N 35 0 E
Black Volta →, *Africa* **100 D4** 8 41N 1 33W
Black Warrior →, *U.S.A.* **135 J2** 32 32N 87 51W
Blackall, *Australia* **114 C4** 24 25 S 145 45 E
Blackball, *N.Z.* **119 C6** 42 22 S 171 26 E
Blackbull, *Australia* **114 B3** 17 55 S 141 45 E
Blackburn, *U.K.* **16 D5** 53 44N 2 30W
Blackduck, *U.S.A.* **138 B7** 47 44N 94 33W
Blackfoot, *U.S.A.* **142 E7** 43 11N 112 21W
Blackfoot →, *U.S.A.* **142 C7** 46 52N 113 53W
Blackfoot River Reservoir, *U.S.A.* **142 E8** 43 0N 111 43W
Blackie, *Canada* **130 C6** 50 36N 113 37W
Blackpool, *U.K.* **16 D4** 53 48N 3 3W
Blackriver, *U.S.A.* **136 B1** 44 46N 83 17W
Blacks Harbour, *Canada* **129 C6** 45 3N 66 49W
Blacksburg, *U.S.A.* **134 G5** 37 14N 80 25W
Blacksod B., *Ireland* **19 B2** 54 6N 10 0W
Blackstone, *U.S.A.* **134 G6** 37 4N 78 0W
Blackstone →, *Canada* **130 A4** 61 5N 122 55W
Blackstone Ra., *Australia* **113 E4** 26 0 S 128 30 E
Blackville, *Canada* **129 C6** 46 44N 65 50W
Blackwater, *Australia* **114 C4** 23 35 S 148 53 E
Blackwater →, *Ireland* **19 E4** 51 55N 7 50W
Blackwater →, *U.K.* **19 B5** 54 31N 6 35W
Blackwater →, *U.S.A.* **140 F4** 38 59N 92 59W
Blackwater Cr. →, *Australia* **115 D3** 25 56 S 144 30 E
Blackwell, *U.S.A.* **139 G6** 36 48N 97 17W
Blackwells Corner, *U.S.A.* **145 K7** 35 37N 119 47W
Blackwood, C., *Papua N. G.* **120 D3** 7 49 S 144 31 E
Bladel, *Neths.* **21 F6** 51 22N 5 13 E
Blaenau Ffestiniog, *U.K.* **16 E4** 52 59N 3 57W
Blagaj, *Bos.-H.* **42 D2** 43 16N 17 55 E
Blagodarnoye, *Russia* **53 D10** 45 7N 43 37 E
Blagoevgrad, *Bulgaria* **42 E8** 42 2N 23 5 E
Blagoveshchensk, *Russia* **54 D4** 55 1N 55 59 E
Blagoveshchensk, *Amur, Russia* **57 D13** 50 20N 127 30 E
Blagoveshchenskoye, *Kazakhstan* **55 B7** 43 18N 74 12 E
Blain, *France* **22 E5** 47 29N 1 45W
Blaine, *U.S.A.* **144 B4** 48 59N 122 45W
Blaine Lake, *Canada* **131 C7** 52 51N 106 52W
Blainville-sur-l'Eau, *France* **23 D13** 48 33N 6 23 E
Blair, *U.S.A.* **138 E6** 41 33N 96 8W
Blair Athol, *Australia* **114 C4** 22 42 S 147 31 E
Blair Atholl, *U.K.* **18 E5** 56 46N 3 50W
Blairgowrie, *U.K.* **18 E5** 56 36N 3 20W
Blairmore, *Canada* **130 D6** 49 40N 114 25W
Blairsden, *U.S.A.* **144 F6** 39 47N 120 37W
Blairsville, *U.S.A.* **136 F5** 40 26N 79 16W
Blaj, *Romania* **46 C4** 46 10N 23 57 E
Blake Pt., *U.S.A.* **138 A10** 48 11N 88 25W
Blakely, *U.S.A.* **135 K3** 31 23N 84 56W
Blakesburg, *U.S.A.* **140 D4** 40 58N 92 38W
Blâmont, *France* **23 D13** 48 35N 6 50 E
Blanc, C., *Tunisia* **96 A1** 37 15N 9 56 E
Blanc, Mont, *Alps* **25 C10** 45 48N 6 50 E
Blanca, B., *Argentina* **160 A4** 39 10 S 61 30W
Blanca Peak, *U.S.A.* **143 H11** 37 35N 105 29W
Blanchard, *U.S.A.* **139 H6** 35 8N 97 39W
Blanchardville, *U.S.A.* **140 B7** 42 49N 89 52W
Blanche, C., *Australia* **115 E1** 33 1 S 134 9 E
Blanche, L., *S. Austral., Australia* **115 D2** 29 15 S 139 40 E
Blanche, L., *W. Austral., Australia* **112 D3** 22 25 S 123 17 E
Blanche Channel, *Solomon Is.* **121 M9** 8 30 S 157 30 E
Blanchester, *U.S.A.* **141 E13** 39 17N 83 59W
Blanco, *S. Africa* **104 E3** 33 55 S 22 23 E
Blanco, *U.S.A.* **139 K5** 30 6N 98 25W
Blanco →, *Argentina* **158 C2** 30 20 S 68 42W
Blanco, C., *U.S.A.* **142 E1** 42 51N 124 34W
Blanco, C., *Costa Rica* **148 E2** 9 34N 85 8W
Blanco, C., *Spain* **33 B9** 39 21N 2 51 E
Blanda →, *Iceland* **12 D4** 65 20N 19 40W
Blandford Forum, *U.K.* **17 G5** 50 52N 2 10W
Blanding, *U.S.A.* **143 H9** 37 37N 109 29W
Blandinsville, *U.S.A.* **140 D6** 40 33N 90 52W
Blanes, *Spain* **34 D7** 41 40N 2 48 E
Blangy-sur-Bresle, *France* **23 C8** 49 55N 1 37 E
Blanice →, *Czech.* **30 B7** 49 10N 14 5 E
Blankenberge, *Belgium* **21 F2** 51 20N 3 9 E
Blankenburg, *Germany* **26 D6** 51 46N 10 56 E
Blanquefort, *France* **24 D3** 44 55N 0 38W
Blanquillo, *Uruguay* **159 C4** 32 53 S 55 37W
Blansko, *Czech.* **31 B9** 49 22N 16 40 E
Blantyre, *Malawi* **107 F4** 15 45 S 35 0 E
Blaricum, *Neths.* **20 D6** 52 16N 5 14 E
Blarney, *Ireland* **19 E3** 51 57N 8 35W
Błaski, *Poland* **47 D5** 51 38N 18 30 E
Blatná, *Czech.* **30 B6** 49 25N 13 52 E
Blatnitsa, *Bulgaria* **43 D13** 43 41N 28 32 E
Blato, *Croatia* **39 F13** 42 56N 16 48 E
Blatten, *Switz.* **28 D5** 46 20N 7 50 E
Blaubeuren, *Germany* **27 G5** 48 24N 9 47 E
Blåvands Huk, *Denmark* **13 J10** 55 33N 8 4 E
Blaydon, *U.K.* **16 C6** 54 56N 1 47W
Blaye, *France* **24 C3** 45 8N 0 40W
Blaye-les-Mines, *France* **24 D6** 44 1N 2 8 E
Blayney, *Australia* **117 B8** 33 32 S 149 14 E
Blaze, Pt., *Australia* **112 B5** 12 56 S 130 11 E
Błazowa, *Poland* **31 B15** 49 53N 22 7 E
Bleckede, *Germany* **26 B6** 53 18N 10 43 E
Bled, *Slovenia* **39 B11** 46 27N 14 7 E
Blednaya, Gora, *Russia* **56 B7** 76 20N 65 0 E
Bléharis, *Belgium* **21 G2** 50 31N 3 25 E
Bleiburg, *Austria* **30 E7** 46 35N 14 49 E
Blejeşti, *Romania* **46 E6** 44 19N 25 27 E
Blekinge län □, *Sweden* **13 H13** 56 20N 15 20 E
Blenheim, *Canada* **136 D2** 42 20N 82 0W
Blenheim, *N.Z.* **119 B8** 41 38 S 173 57 E
Bléone →, *France* **25 D10** 44 5N 6 0 E
Blerick, *Neths.* **21 F8** 51 22N 6 9 E
Bletchley, *U.K.* **17 F7** 51 59N 0 44W
Blida, *Algeria* **99 A5** 36 30N 2 49 E
Blidet Amor, *Algeria* **99 B6** 32 59N 5 58 E
Blidö, *Sweden* **14 E12** 59 37N 18 53 E
Bligh Sound, *N.Z.* **119 E2** 44 47 S 167 32 E
Bligh Water, *Fiji* **121 A2** 17 0 S 178 0 E
Blind River, *Canada* **128 C3** 46 10N 82 58W
Blinishti, *Albania* **44 C1** 41 52N 19 58 E
Blinnenhorn, *Switz.* **29 D6** 46 26N 8 19 E
Blissfield, *U.S.A.* **141 C13** 41 50N 83 52W
Blitar, *Indonesia* **75 D4** 8 5 S 112 11 E
Blitta, *Togo* **101 D5** 8 23N 1 6 E
Block I., *U.S.A.* **137 E13** 41 11N 71 35W
Block Island Sd., *U.S.A.* **137 E13** 41 15N 71 40W
Blockton, *U.S.A.* **140 D2** 40 37N 94 29W
Blodgett Iceberg Tongue, *Antarctica* **7 C9** 66 8 S 130 35 E
Bloemendaal, *Neths.* **20 D5** 52 24N 4 39 E
Bloemfontein, *S. Africa* **104 D4** 29 6 S 26 7 E
Bloemhof, *S. Africa* **104 D4** 27 38 S 25 32 E
Blois, *France* **22 E8** 47 35N 1 20 E
Blokziji, *Neths.* **20 C7** 52 43N 5 58 E
Blönduós, *Iceland* **12 D3** 65 40N 20 12W
Błonie, *Poland* **47 C7** 52 12N 20 37 E
Bloodvein →, *Canada* **131 C9** 51 47N 96 43W
Bloody Foreland, *Ireland* **19 A3** 55 10N 8 18W
Bloomer, *U.S.A.* **138 C9** 45 6N 91 29W
Bloomfield, *Australia* **114 B4** 15 56 S 145 22 E
Bloomfield, *Canada* **136 C7** 43 59N 77 14W
Bloomfield, *Ind., U.S.A.* **141 E10** 39 1N 86 57W
Bloomfield, *Iowa, U.S.A.* **140 D4** 40 45N 92 25W
Bloomfield, *Ky., U.S.A.* **141 G11** 37 55N 85 19W
Bloomfield, *N. Mex., U.S.A.* **143 H10** 36 43N 107 59W
Bloomfield, *Nebr., U.S.A.* **138 D6** 42 36N 97 39W
Bloomingburg, *U.S.A.* **141 E13** 39 36N 83 24W
Bloomington, *Ill., U.S.A.* **140 D7** 40 28N 89 0W
Bloomington, *Ind., U.S.A.* **141 E10** 39 10N 86 32W
Bloomington, *Wis., U.S.A.* **140 B6** 42 53N 90 55W
Bloomsburg, *U.S.A.* **137 F8** 41 0N 76 27W
Blora, *Indonesia* **75 D4** 6 57 S 111 25 E
Blossburg, *U.S.A.* **136 E7** 41 41N 77 4W
Blouberg, *S. Africa* **105 C4** 23 8 S 28 59 E
Blountstown, *U.S.A.* **135 K3** 30 27N 85 3W
Bludenz, *Austria* **30 D2** 47 10N 9 50 E
Blue →, *U.S.A.* **141 F10** 38 11N 86 19W
Blue Island, *U.S.A.* **134 E2** 41 40N 87 40W
Blue Lake, *U.S.A.* **142 F2** 40 53N 123 59W
Blue Mesa Reservoir, *U.S.A.* **143 G10** 38 28N 107 20W
Blue Mound, *U.S.A.* **140 E7** 39 42N 89 7W
Blue Mts., *Australia* **117 B9** 33 40 S 150 0 E
Blue Mts., *Oreg., U.S.A.* **142 D4** 45 15N 119 0W
Blue Mts., *Pa., U.S.A.* **137 F8** 40 30N 76 30W
Blue Mud B., *Australia* **114 A2** 13 30 S 136 0 E
Blue Nile = An Nîl el Azraq □, *Sudan* **95 E3** 12 30N 34 30 E
Blue Nile = Nîl el Azraq →, *Sudan* **95 D3** 15 38N 32 31 E
Blue Rapids, *U.S.A.* **138 F6** 39 41N 96 39W
Blue Ridge Mts., *U.S.A.* **135 G5** 36 30N 80 15W
Blue Springs, *U.S.A.* **140 E2** 39 1N 94 17W
Blue Stack Mts., *Ireland* **19 B3** 54 46N 8 5W
Blueberry →, *Canada* **130 B4** 56 45N 120 49W
Bluefield, *U.S.A.* **134 G5** 37 15N 81 17W
Bluefields, *Nic.* **148 D3** 12 20N 83 50W
Blueskin B., *N.Z.* **119 F5** 45 44 S 170 38 E
Bluff, *Australia* **114 C4** 23 35 S 149 4 E
Bluff, *N.Z.* **119 G3** 46 37 S 168 20 E
Bluff, *U.S.A.* **143 H9** 37 17N 109 33W
Bluff Harbour, *N.Z.* **119 G3** 46 36 S 168 21 E
Bluff Knoll, *Australia* **113 F2** 34 24 S 118 15 E
Bluff Pt., *Australia* **113 E1** 27 50 S 114 5 E
Bluffs, *U.S.A.* **140 E6** 39 45N 90 32W
Bluffton, *Ind., U.S.A.* **141 D11** 40 44N 85 11W
Bluffton, *Ohio, U.S.A.* **141 D13** 40 54N 83 54W
Bluford, *U.S.A.* **141 F8** 38 20N 88 45W
Blumenau, *Brazil* **159 B6** 27 0 S 49 0W
Blümisalphorn, *Switz.* **28 D5** 46 28N 7 47 E
Blunt, *U.S.A.* **138 C4** 44 31N 99 59W
Bly, *U.S.A.* **142 E3** 42 24N 121 3W
Blyth, *Canada* **136 C3** 43 44N 81 26W
Blyth, *U.K.* **16 B6** 55 8N 1 32W
Blyth Bridge, *U.K.* **16 E5** 52 58N 2 4W
Blythe, *U.S.A.* **145 M12** 33 37N 114 36W
Bø, *Norway* **14 E3** 59 25N 9 3 E
Bo, *S. Leone* **100 D2** 7 55N 11 50W
Bo Duc, *Vietnam* **77 G6** 11 58N 106 50 E
Bo Hai, *China* **67 E10** 39 0N 119 0 E
Bō-no-Misaki, *Japan* **62 F2** 31 15N 130 13 E
Bo Xian, *China* **66 H8** 33 55N 115 41 E
Boa Esperança, *Brazil* **153 C5** 3 21N 61 23W
Boa Nova, *Brazil* **155 D3** 14 22 S 40 10W
Boa Viagem, *Brazil* **154 C4** 5 7 S 39 44W
Boa Vista, *Brazil* **153 C5** 2 48N 60 30W
Boac, *Phil.* **70 E3** 13 27N 121 50 E
Boaco, *Nic.* **148 D2** 12 29N 85 35W
Bo'ai, *China* **66 G7** 35 10N 113 3 E
Boal, *Spain* **36 B4** 43 25N 6 49W
Boali, *C.A.R.* **102 B3** 4 48N 18 7 E
Boardman, *U.S.A.* **136 E4** 41 2N 80 40W
Boatman, *Australia* **115 D4** 27 16 S 146 55 E
Bobadah, *Australia* **117 B7** 32 19 S 146 41 E
Bobai, *China* **68 F7** 22 17N 109 59 E
Bobbili, *India* **82 E6** 18 35N 83 30 E
Bóbbio, *Italy* **38 D6** 44 47N 9 22 E
Bobcaygeon, *Canada* **128 D4** 44 33N 78 33W
Böblingen, *Germany* **27 G5** 48 41N 9 1 E
Bobo-Dioulasso, *Burkina Faso* **100 C4** 11 8N 4 13W
Boboc, *Romania* **46 D7** 45 13N 26 59 E
Bobolice, *Poland* **47 B3** 53 58N 16 37 E
Bobon, *Davao, Phil.* **71 H6** 6 53N 126 19 E
Bobon, *Samar, Phil.* **70 E5** 12 32N 124 34 E
Bobonaza →, *Ecuador* **152 D2** 2 36 S 76 38W
Boboshevo, *Bulgaria* **42 E7** 42 9N 23 0 E
Bobov Dol, *Bulgaria* **42 E7** 42 20N 23 0 E
Bóbr →, *Poland* **47 C2** 52 4N 15 4 E
Bobraomby, Tanjon' i, *Madag.* **105 A8** 12 40 S 49 10 E
Bobrinets, *Ukraine* **52 B5** 48 4N 32 5 E
Bobrov, *Russia* **51 F12** 51 5N 40 2 E
Bobruysk, *Belorussia* **50 E6** 53 10N 29 15 E
Bobures, *Venezuela* **152 B3** 9 15N 71 11W
Boca de Drago, *Venezuela* **153 A5** 11 0N 61 50W
Bôca do Acre, *Brazil* **156 B4** 8 50 S 67 27W
Bôca do Jari, *Brazil* **153 D7** 1 7 S 51 58W
Bôca do Moaco, *Brazil* **156 B4** 7 41 S 68 17W
Boca Grande, *Venezuela* **153 B5** 8 40N 60 40W
Boca Raton, *U.S.A.* **135 M5** 26 21N 80 5W
Bocaiúva, *Brazil* **155 E3** 17 7 S 43 49W
Bocanda, *Ivory C.* **100 D4** 7 5N 4 31W
Bocaranga, *C.A.R.* **102 A3** 7 0N 15 35 E
Bocas del Toro, *Panama* **148 E3** 9 15N 82 20W
Boceguillas, *Spain* **34 D1** 41 20N 3 39W
Bochnia, *Poland* **31 B13** 49 58N 20 27 E
Bocholt, *Belgium* **21 F7** 51 10N 5 35 E
Bocholt, *Germany* **26 D2** 51 50N 6 35 E
Bochov, *Czech.* **30 A6** 50 9N 13 3 E
Bochum, *Germany* **26 D3** 51 28N 7 12 E
Bockenem, *Germany* **26 C6** 52 1N 10 8 E
Boćki, *Poland* **47 C10** 52 39N 23 3 E
Bocognano, *France* **25 F13** 42 5N 9 4 E
Boconó, *Venezuela* **152 B3** 9 15N 70 16W
Boconó →, *Venezuela* **152 B4** 8 43N 69 34W
Bocoyna, *Mexico* **146 B3** 27 52N 107 35W
Bocq →, *Belgium* **21 H5** 50 20N 4 55 E
Boçşa, *Romania* **42 B6** 45 21N 21 47 E
Boda, *C.A.R.* **102 B3** 4 19N 17 26 E
Bodaybo, *Russia* **57 D12** 57 50N 114 0 E
Boddington, *Australia* **113 F2** 32 50 S 116 30 E
Bodega Bay, *U.S.A.* **144 G3** 38 20N 123 3W
Bodegraven, *Neths.* **20 D5** 52 5N 4 46 E
Boden, *Sweden* **12 D16** 65 50N 21 42 E
Bodensee, *Europe* **29 A8** 47 35N 9 25 E
Bodenteich, *Germany* **26 C6** 52 49N 10 41 E
Bodhan, *India* **82 E3** 18 40N 77 44 E
Bodinayakkanur, *India* **83 J3** 10 2N 77 10 E
Bodinga, *Nigeria* **101 C6** 12 58N 5 10 E
Bodio, *Switz.* **29 D7** 46 23N 8 55 E
Bodmin, *U.K.* **17 G3** 50 28N 4 44W
Bodmin Moor, *U.K.* **17 G3** 50 33N 4 36W
Bodoquena, Serra da, *Brazil* **157 E6** 21 0 S 56 50W
Bodoupa, *C.A.R.* **102 A3** 5 43N 17 36 E
Bodrog →, *Hungary* **31 C14** 48 15N 21 35 E
Bodrum, *Turkey* **88 E2** 37 5N 27 30 E
Bódva →, *Hungary* **31 C13** 48 19N 20 45 E
Boechout, *Belgium* **21 F5** 51 10N 4 30 E
Boegoebergdam, *S. Africa* **104 D3** 29 7 S 22 9 E
Boekelo, *Neths.* **20 D9** 52 12N 6 49 E
Boelenslaan, *Neths.* **20 B8** 53 10N 6 10 E
Boembé, *Congo* **102 C3** 2 54 S 15 39 E
Boën, *France* **25 C8** 45 44N 4 0 E
Boende, *Zaïre* **102 C4** 0 24 S 21 12 E
Boerne, *U.S.A.* **139 L5** 29 47N 98 44W
Boertange, *Neths.* **20 B10** 53 1N 7 12 E
Boezinge, *Belgium* **21 G1** 50 54N 2 52 E
Boffa, *Guinea* **100 C2** 10 16N 14 3W
Bogale, *Burma* **78 G5** 16 17N 95 24 E
Bogalusa, *U.S.A.* **139 K10** 30 47N 89 52W
Bogan →, *Australia* **117 A7** 29 59 S 146 17 E
Bogan Gate, *Australia* **117 B7** 33 7 S 147 49 E
Bogangolo, *C.A.R.* **102 A3** 5 34N 18 15 E
Bogantungan, *Australia* **114 C4** 23 41 S 147 17 E
Bogata, *U.S.A.* **139 J7** 33 28N 95 13W
Bogatić, *Serbia* **42 C4** 44 51N 19 30 E
Boğazlıyan, *Turkey* **88 D6** 39 11N 35 14 E
Bogdanovitch, *Russia* **54 C8** 56 47N 62 1 E
Bogense, *Denmark* **15 J4** 55 34N 10 5 E
Boggabilla, *Australia* **115 D5** 28 36 S 150 24 E
Boggabri, *Australia* **117 A9** 30 45 S 150 5 E
Boggeragh Mts., *Ireland* **19 D3** 52 2N 8 55W
Bogia, *Papua N. G.* **120 C3** 4 9 S 145 0 E
Bognor Regis, *U.K.* **17 G7** 50 47N 0 40W
Bogø, *Denmark* **15 K6** 54 55N 12 2 E
Bogo, *Phil.* **71 F4** 11 3N 124 0 E
Bogodukhov, *Ukraine* **52 A6** 50 9N 35 33 E
Bogong, Mt., *Australia* **117 D7** 36 47 S 147 17 E
Bogor, *Indonesia* **74 D3** 6 36 S 106 48 E
Bogoroditsk, *Russia* **51 E11** 53 47N 38 8 E
Bogorodsk, *Russia* **51 C13** 56 4N 43 30 E
Bogorodskoye, *Russia* **57 D15** 52 22N 140 30 E
Bogoso, *Ghana* **100 D4** 5 38N 2 3W
Bogotá, *Colombia* **152 C3** 4 34N 74 0W
Bogotol, *Russia* **56 D9** 56 15N 89 50 E
Bogra, *Bangla.* **78 C2** 24 51N 89 22 E
Boguchany, *Russia* **57 D10** 58 40N 97 30 E
Boguchar, *Russia* **53 B9** 49 55N 40 32 E
Bogué, *Mauritania* **100 B2** 16 45N 14 10W
Boguslav, *Ukraine* **52 B4** 49 47N 30 53 E
Boguszów, *Poland* **47 E3** 50 45N 16 12 E
Bohain-en-Vermandois, *France* **23 C10** 49 59N 3 28 E
Bohemia, *Czech.* **30 B7** 50 0N 14 0 E
Bohemia Downs, *Australia* **112 C4** 18 53 S 126 14 E
Bohemian Forest = Böhmerwald, *Germany* **27 F8** 49 30N 12 40 E
Bohena Cr. →, *Australia* **115 E4** 30 17 S 149 42 E
Bohinjska Bistrica, *Slovenia* **39 B11** 46 17N 14 1 E
Böhmerwald, *Germany* **27 F8** 49 30N 12 40 E
Bohmte, *Germany* **26 C4** 52 24N 8 20 E
Bohol, *Phil.* **71 G5** 9 50N 124 10 E
Bohol, *Somali Rep.* **108 C3** 5 45N 46 9 E
Bohol Sea, *Phil.* **71 G5** 9 0N 124 0 E
Bohol Str., *Phil.* **71 G4** 9 45N 123 40 E
Bohotleh, *Somali Rep.* **90 F4** 8 20N 46 25 E
Boi, *Nigeria* **101 D6** 9 35N 9 27 E
Boi, Pta. de, *Brazil* **159 A6** 23 55 S 45 15W
Boiaçu, *Brazil* **153 D5** 0 27 S 61 46W
Boiano, *Italy* **41 A7** 41 28N 14 29 E
Boileau, C., *Australia* **112 C3** 17 40 S 122 7 E
Boinitsa, *Bulgaria* **42 D7** 43 58N 22 32 E
Boipeba, I. de, *Brazil* **155 D4** 13 39 S 38 55W
Bois →, *Brazil* **155 E1** 18 35 S 50 2W
Boischot, *Belgium* **21 F5** 51 3N 4 47 E
Boise, *U.S.A.* **142 E5** 43 37N 116 13W
Boise City, *U.S.A.* **139 G3** 36 44N 102 31W
Boissevain, *Canada* **131 D8** 49 15N 100 5W
Boite →, *Italy* **39 B9** 46 5N 12 5 E
Boitzenburg, *Germany* **26 B9** 53 16N 13 36 E
Boizenburg, *Germany* **26 B6** 53 22N 10 42 E
Bojador C., *W. Sahara* **98 C2** 26 0N 14 30W
Bojana →, *Albania* **42 F4** 41 52N 19 22 E
Bojanowo, *Poland* **47 D3** 51 43N 16 42 E
Bojnūrd, *Iran* **85 B8** 37 30N 57 20 E
Bojonegoro, *Indonesia* **75 D4** 7 11 S 111 54 E
Boju, *Nigeria* **101 D6** 7 22N 7 55 E
Boka, *Serbia* **42 B5** 45 22N 20 52 E
Boka Kotorska, *Montenegro* **42 E3** 42 23N 18 32 E
Bokada, *Zaïre* **102 B3** 4 8N 19 23 E
Bokala, *Ivory C.* **100 D4** 8 31N 4 33W
Bokatola, *Zaïre* **102 C3** 0 38 S 18 46 E
Boké, *Guinea* **100 C2** 10 56N 14 17W
Bokhara →, *Australia* **115 D4** 29 55 S 146 42 E
Bokkos, *Nigeria* **101 D6** 9 17N 9 1 E
Boknafjorden, *Norway* **13 G8** 59 14N 5 40 E
Bokombayevskoye, *Kirghizia* **55 B8** 42 10N 76 55 E
Bokoro, *Chad* **97 F3** 12 25N 17 14 E
Bokote, *Zaïre* **102 C4** 0 12 S 21 8 E
Boksitogorsk, *Russia* **50 B8** 59 32N 33 56 E
Bokungu, *Zaïre* **102 C4** 0 35 S 22 50 E
Bol, *Chad* **97 F2** 13 30N 14 40 E
Bol, *Croatia* **39 E13** 43 18N 16 38 E
Bolama, *Guinea-Biss.* **100 C1** 11 30N 15 30W
Bolan Pass, *Pakistan* **79 C2** 29 50N 67 20 E
Bolangum, *Australia* **116 D5** 36 42 S 142 54 E
Bolaños →, *Mexico* **146 C4** 21 14N 104 8W
Bolbec, *France* **22 C7** 49 30N 0 30 E
Boldājī, *Iran* **85 D6** 31 56N 51 3 E
Boldeşti, *Romania* **46 D7** 45 3N 26 2 E
Bole, *China* **64 B3** 45 11N 81 37 E
Bole, *Ethiopia* **95 F4** 6 36N 37 20 E
Bolekhov, *Ukraine* **50 G3** 49 0N 23 57 E
Bolesławiec, *Poland* **47 D2** 51 17N 15 37 E
Bolgatanga, *Ghana* **101 C4** 10 44N 0 53W
Bolgrad, *Ukraine* **52 D3** 45 40N 28 32 E
Boli, *Sudan* **95 F2** 6 2N 28 48 E
Bolinao, *Phil.* **70 C2** 16 23N 119 54 E
Bolinao C., *Phil.* **70 C2** 16 23N 119 55 E
Boliney, *Phil.* **70 C3** 17 24N 120 48 E
Bolívar, *Argentina* **158 D3** 36 15 S 60 53W
Bolívar, *Antioquía, Colombia* **152 B2** 5 50N 76 1W
Bolívar, *Cauca, Colombia* **152 C2** 2 0N 77 0W
Bolívar, *Peru* **156 B2** 7 18 S 77 48W
Bolivar, *Mo., U.S.A.* **139 G8** 37 37N 93 25W
Bolivar, *Tenn., U.S.A.* **139 H10** 35 12N 89 0W
Bolívar □, *Colombia* **152 B3** 9 0N 74 40W
Bolívar □, *Ecuador* **152 D2** 1 15 S 79 5W
Bolívar □, *Venezuela* **153 B5** 6 20N 63 30W
Bolivia ■, *S. Amer.* **157 D5** 17 6 S 64 0W
Bolivian Plateau, *S. Amer.* **150 D3** 20 0 S 67 30W
Boljevac, *Serbia* **42 D6** 43 51N 21 58 E
Bolkhov, *Russia* **51 E10** 53 25N 36 0 E
Bollène, *France* **25 D8** 44 18N 4 45 E
Bollnäs, *Sweden* **14 C10** 61 21N 16 24 E
Bollon, *Australia* **115 D4** 28 2 S 147 29 E
Bollstabruk, *Sweden* **14 A11** 63 1N 17 40 E
Bollullos, *Spain* **37 H4** 37 19N 6 32W
Bolobo, *Zaïre* **102 C3** 2 6 S 16 20 E
Bologna, *Italy* **39 D8** 44 30N 11 20 E
Bologne, *France* **23 D12** 48 10N 5 8 E
Bologoye, *Russia* **50 C9** 57 55N 34 5 E
Bolomba, *Zaïre* **102 B3** 0 35N 19 0 E
Bolonchenticul, *Mexico* **147 D7** 20 0N 89 49W
Bolong, *Phil.* **71 H4** 7 6N 122 14 E
Bolotovskoye, *Russia* **54 B8** 58 31N 62 28 E
Boloven, Cao Nguyen, *Laos* **76 E6** 15 10N 106 30 E
Bolpur, *India* **81 H12** 23 40N 87 45 E
Bolsena, *Italy* **39 F8** 42 40N 11 58 E
Bolsena, L. di, *Italy* **39 F8** 42 35N 11 55 E
Bolshaya Glushitsa, *Russia* **54 E2** 52 28N 50 30 E
Bolshaya Khobda →, *Kazakhstan* **54 F4** 50 56N 54 34 E
Bolshaya Kinel →, *Russia* **54 E2** 53 14N 50 30 E
Bolshaya Martynovka, *Russia* **53 C9** 47 12N 41 46 E
Bolshaya Shatan, Gora, *Russia* **54 E6** 53 37N 58 3 E
Bolshaya Vradiyevka, *Ukraine* **52 C4** 47 50N 30 40 E
Bolshereche, *Russia* **56 D8** 56 4N 74 45 E
Bolshevik, Ostrov, *Russia* **57 B11** 78 30N 102 0 E
Bolshezemelskaya Tundra, *Russia* **48 A10** 67 0N 56 0 E
Bolshoi Kavkas, *Asia* **53 E11** 42 50N 44 0 E
Bolshoy Anyuy →, *Russia* **57 C17** 68 30N 160 49 E
Bolshoy Atlym, *Russia* **56 C7** 62 25N 66 50 E
Bolshoy Begichev, Ostrov, *Russia* **57 B12** 74 20N 112 30 E
Bolshoy Lyakhovskiy, Ostrov, *Russia* **57 B15** 73 35N 142 0 E
Bolshoy Tokmak, *Ukraine* **52 C6** 47 16N 35 42 E
Bol'shoy Tyuters, *Estonia* **50 B5** 59 51N 27 13 E
Bolsward, *Neths.* **20 B7** 53 3N 5 32 E
Boltaña, *Spain* **34 C5** 42 28N 0 4 E
Boltigen, *Switz.* **28 C4** 46 38N 7 24 E
Bolton, *Canada* **136 C5** 43 54N 79 45W
Bolton, *U.K.* **16 D5** 53 35N 2 26W
Bolu, *Turkey* **88 C4** 40 45N 31 35 E
Bolu □, *Turkey* **88 C4** 40 40N 31 30 E
Bolubolu, *Papua N. G.* **120 E6** 9 21 S 150 20 E
Boluo, *China* **69 F10** 23 3N 114 21 E
Bolvadin, *Turkey* **88 D4** 38 45N 31 4 E
Bolzano, *Italy* **39 B8** 46 30N 11 20 E
Bom Comércio, *Brazil* **157 B4** 9 45 S 65 54W
Bom Conselho, *Brazil* **154 C4** 9 10 S 36 41W
Bom Despacho, *Brazil* **155 E2** 19 43 S 45 15W
Bom Jesus, *Brazil* **154 C3** 9 4 S 44 22W
Bom Jesus da Gurguéia, Serra, *Brazil* **154 C3** 9 0 S 43 0W
Bom Jesus da Lapa, *Brazil* **155 D3** 13 15 S 43 25W
Boma, *Zaïre* **103 D2** 5 50 S 13 4 E
Bomaderry, *Australia* **117 C9** 34 52 S 150 37 E
Bomandjokou, *Congo* **102 B2** 0 34N 14 23 E
Bomassa, *Congo* **102 B3** 2 12N 16 12 E
Bombala, *Australia* **117 D8** 36 56 S 149 15 E
Bombarral, *Portugal* **37 F1** 39 15N 9 9W
Bombay, *India* **82 E1** 18 55N 72 50 E
Bomboma, *Zaïre* **102 B3** 2 25N 18 55 E
Bombombwa, *Zaïre* **106 B2** 1 40N 25 40 E
Bomi Hills, *Liberia* **100 D2** 7 1N 10 38W
Bomili, *Zaïre* **106 B2** 1 45N 27 5 E
Bommel, *Neths.* **20 E4** 51 43N 4 26 E
Bomokandi →, *Zaïre* **106 B2** 3 39N 26 8 E
Bomongo, *Zaïre* **102 B3** 1 27N 18 21 E
Bomu →, *C.A.R.* **102 B4** 4 40N 22 30 E
Bon, C., *Tunisia* **96 A2** 37 1N 11 2 E

Bradford 177

Bon Sar Pa, *Vietnam* **76 F6** 12 24N 107 35 E
Bonaduz, *Switz.* **29 C8** 46 49N 9 25 E
Bonaire, *Neth. Ant.* **149 D6** 12 10N 68 15W
Bonang, *Australia* **117 D8** 37 11 S 148 41 E
Bonanza, *Nic.* **148 D3** 13 54N 84 35W
Bonaparte Arch., *Australia* **112 B3** 14 0 S 124 30 E
Boñar, *Spain* **36 C5** 42 52N 5 19W
Bonaventure, *Canada* **129 C6** 48 5N 65 32W
Bonavista, *Canada* **129 C9** 48 40N 53 5W
Bonavista, C., *Canada* **129 C9** 48 42N 53 5W
Bonawan, *Phil.* **71 G4** 9 8N 122 55 E
Bondeno, *Italy* **39 D8** 44 53N 11 22 E
Bondo, *Zaïre* **102 B4** 3 55N 23 53 E
Bondoukou, *Ivory C.* **100 D4** 8 2N 2 47W
Bondowoso, *Indonesia* **75 D4** 7 55 S 113 49 E
Bondyug, *Russia* **54 A4** 60 29N 55 56 E
Bone, Teluk, *Indonesia* **72 B2** 4 10 S 120 50 E
Bone Rate, *Indonesia* **72 C2** 7 25 S 121 5 E
Bone Rate, Kepulauan, *Indonesia* **72 C2** 6 30 S 121 10 E
Bonefro, *Italy* **41 A7** 41 42N 14 55 E
Bo'ness, *U.K.* **18 E5** 56 0N 3 38W
Bong Son = Hoai Nhon, *Vietnam* **76 E7** 14 28N 109 1 E
Bongabon, *Phil.* **70 D3** 15 38N 121 8 E
Bongabong, *Phil.* **70 E3** 12 45N 121 29 E
Bongandanga, *Zaïre* **102 B4** 1 24N 21 3 E
Bongo, *Zaïre* **102 C3** 1 47 S 17 41 E
Bongor, *Chad* **97 F3** 10 35N 15 20 E
Bongouanou, *Ivory C.* **100 D4** 6 42N 4 15W
Bonham, *U.S.A.* **139 J6** 33 35N 96 11W
Bonheiden, *Belgium* **21 F5** 51 1N 4 32 E
Bonifacio, *France* **25 G13** 41 24N 9 10 E
Bonifacio, Bouches de, *Medit. S.* **40 A2** 41 12N 9 15 E
Bonin Is. = Ogasawara Gunto, *Pac. Oc.* **122 E6** 27 0N 142 0 E
Bonke, *Ethiopia* **95 F4** 6 5N 37 16 E
Bonn, *Germany* **26 E3** 50 43N 7 6 E
Bonnat, *France* **24 B5** 46 20N 1 54 E
Bonne Terre, *U.S.A.* **139 G9** 37 55N 90 33W
Bonners Ferry, *U.S.A.* **142 B5** 48 42N 116 19W
Bonnétable, *France* **22 D7** 48 11N 0 25 E
Bonneuil-Matours, *France* **22 F7** 46 41N 0 34 E
Bonneval, *France* **22 D8** 48 11N 1 24 E
Bonneville, *France* **25 B10** 46 4N 6 24 E
Bonney, L., *Australia* **116 D4** 37 50 S 140 20 E
Bonnie Doon, *Australia* **117 D6** 37 2 S 145 53 E
Bonnie Downs, *Australia* **114 C3** 22 7 S 143 50 E
Bonnie Rock, *Australia* **113 F2** 30 29 S 118 22 E
Bonny, *Nigeria* **101 E6** 4 25N 7 13 E
Bonny →, *Nigeria* **101 E6** 4 20N 7 10 E
Bonny, Bight of, *Africa* **101 E6** 3 30N 9 20 E
Bonny-sur-Loire, *France* **23 E9** 47 33N 2 50 E
Bonnyville, *Canada* **131 C6** 54 20N 110 45W
Bonobono, *Phil.* **71 G1** 8 40N 117 36 E
Bonoi, *Indonesia* **73 B5** 1 45 S 137 41 E
Bonorva, *Italy* **40 B1** 40 25N 8 47 E
Bonsall, *U.S.A.* **145 M9** 33 16N 117 14W
Bontang, *Indonesia* **75 B5** 0 10N 117 30 E
Bonthain, *Indonesia* **72 C1** 5 34 S 119 56 E
Bonthe, *S. Leone* **100 D2** 7 30N 12 33W
Bontoc, *Phil.* **70 C3** 17 7N 120 58 E
Bonyeri, *Ghana* **100 D4** 5 1N 2 46W
Bonyhád, *Hungary* **31 E11** 46 18N 18 32 E
Bonython Ra., *Australia* **112 D4** 23 40 S 128 45 E
Bookabie, *Australia* **113 F5** 31 50 S 132 41 E
Booker, *U.S.A.* **139 G4** 36 27N 100 32W
Boolaboolka L., *Australia* **116 B5** 32 38 S 143 10 E
Boolarra, *Australia* **117 E7** 38 20 S 146 20 E
Boolcoomata, *Australia* **116 A4** 31 57 S 140 33 E
Booleroo Centre, *Australia* **116 B3** 32 53 S 138 21 E
Booligal, *Australia* **117 B6** 33 58 S 144 53 E
Boom, *Belgium* **21 F4** 51 6N 4 20 E
Boonah, *Australia* **115 D5** 27 58 S 152 41 E
Boone, *Iowa, U.S.A.* **140 B3** 42 4N 93 53W
Boone, *N.C., U.S.A.* **135 G5** 36 13N 81 41W
Booneville, *Ark., U.S.A.* **139 H8** 35 8N 93 55W
Booneville, *Miss., U.S.A.* **135 H1** 34 39N 88 34W
Boonville, *Calif., U.S.A.* **144 F3** 39 1N 123 22W
Boonville, *Ind., U.S.A.* **141 F9** 38 3N 87 16W
Boonville, *Mo., U.S.A.* **140 F4** 38 58N 92 44W
Boonville, *N.Y., U.S.A.* **137 C9** 43 29N 75 20W
Booral, *Australia* **117 B9** 32 30 S 151 56 E
Boorindal, *Australia* **115 E4** 30 22 S 146 11 E
Booroomugga, *Australia* **117 A7** 31 17 S 146 27 E
Boorowa, *Australia* **117 C8** 34 28 S 148 44 E
Boothia, Gulf of, *Canada* **127 A11** 71 0N 90 0W
Boothia Pen., *Canada* **126 A10** 71 0N 94 0W
Bootle, *Cumb., U.K.* **16 C4** 54 17N 3 24W
Bootle, *Mersey., U.K.* **16 D4** 53 28N 3 1W
Booué, *Gabon* **102 C2** 0 5S 11 55 E
Bophuthatswana □, *S. Africa* **104 D4** 25 49 S 25 30 E
Boppard, *Germany* **27 E3** 50 13N 7 36 E
Boquerón □, *Paraguay* **157 E5** 23 0 S 60 0W
Boquete, *Panama* **148 E3** 8 46N 82 27W
Boquilla, Presa de la, *Mexico* **146 B3** 27 40N 105 30W
Boquillas del Carmen, *Mexico* **146 B4** 29 17N 102 53W
Bor, *Czech.* **30 B5** 49 41N 12 45 E
Bor, *Serbia* **42 C7** 44 5N 22 7 E
Bôr, *Sudan* **95 F3** 6 10N 31 40 E
Bor, *Turkey* **88 E6** 37 54N 34 32 E
Bor Mashash, *Israel* **91 D3** 31 7N 34 50 E
Boradā →, *Syria* **91 B5** 33 33N 36 34 E
Borah Peak, *U.S.A.* **142 D7** 44 8N 113 47W
Borama, *Somali Rep.* **90 F3** 9 55N 43 7 E
Borang, *Sudan* **95 G3** 4 50N 30 59 E
Borangapara, *India* **78 C3** 25 14N 90 14 E
Borås, *Sweden* **15 G6** 57 43N 12 56 E
Borāzjān, *Iran* **85 D6** 29 22N 51 10 E
Borba, *Brazil* **153 D6** 4 12 S 59 34W
Borba, *Portugal* **37 G3** 38 50N 7 26W
Borbon, *Phil.* **71 F5** 10 50N 124 2 E
Borborema, Planalto da, *Brazil* **154 C4** 7 0 S 37 0W
Borçka, *Turkey* **53 F9** 41 25N 41 41 E
Borculo, *Neths.* **20 D9** 52 7N 6 31 E
Bord Khūn-e Now, *Iran* **85 D6** 28 3N 51 28 E
Borda, C., *Australia* **116 C2** 35 45 S 136 34 E
Bordeaux, *France* **24 D3** 44 50N 0 36W
Borden, *Australia* **113 F2** 34 3 S 118 12 E
Borden, *Canada* **129 C7** 46 18N 63 47W
Borden I., *Canada* **6 B2** 78 30N 111 30W
Borders □, *U.K.* **18 F6** 55 35N 2 50W
Bordertown, *Australia* **116 D4** 36 19 S 140 45 E
Borðeyri, *Iceland* **12 D3** 65 12N 21 6W
Bordighera, *Italy* **38 E4** 43 47N 7 40 E
Bordj bou Arreridj, *Algeria* **99 A5** 36 4N 4 45 E
Bordj Bourguiba, *Tunisia* **96 B2** 32 12N 10 2 E
Bordj el Hobra, *Algeria* **99 B5** 32 9N 4 51 E
Bordj Fly Ste. Marie, *Algeria* **98 C4** 27 19N 2 32W
Bordj-in-Eker, *Algeria* **99 D6** 24 9N 5 3 E
Bordj Menaiel, *Algeria* **99 A5** 36 46N 3 43 E
Bordj Messouda, *Algeria* **99 B6** 30 12N 9 25 E
Bordj Nili, *Algeria* **99 B5** 33 28N 3 2 E
Bordj Omar Driss, *Algeria* **99 C6** 28 10N 6 40 E
Bordj-Tarat, *Algeria* **99 C6** 25 55N 9 3 E
Bordj Zelfana, *Algeria* **99 B5** 32 27N 4 15 E
Bordoba, *Kirghizia* **55 D6** 39 31N 73 16 E
Borea Creek, *Australia* **117 C7** 35 5 S 146 35 E
Borek Wielkopolski, *Poland* **47 D4** 51 54N 17 11 E
Boremore, *Australia* **117 B8** 33 15 S 149 0 E
Boren Kapuas, Pegunungan, *Malaysia* **75 B4** 1 25N 113 15 E
Borensberg, *Sweden* **15 F9** 58 34N 15 17 E
Borgå, *Finland* **13 F18** 60 24N 25 40 E
Borgarnes, *Iceland* **12 D3** 64 32N 21 55W
Børgefjellet, *Norway* **12 D12** 65 20N 13 45 E
Borger, *Neths.* **20 C9** 52 54N 6 44 E
Borger, *U.S.A.* **139 H4** 35 39N 101 24W
Borgerhout, *Belgium* **21 F4** 51 12N 4 28 E
Borghamn, *Sweden* **15 F8** 58 23N 14 41 E
Borgholm, *Sweden* **13 H14** 56 52N 16 39 E
Bórgia, *Italy* **41 D9** 38 50N 16 30 E
Borgloon, *Belgium* **21 G6** 50 48N 5 21 E
Borgo San Dalmazzo, *Italy* **38 D4** 44 19N 7 29 E
Borgo San Lorenzo, *Italy* **39 E8** 43 57N 11 21 E
Borgo Valsugano, *Italy* **39 B8** 46 3N 11 27 E
Borgomanero, *Italy* **38 C5** 45 41N 8 28 E
Borgonovo Val Tidone, *Italy* **38 C6** 45 1N 9 28 E
Borgorose, *Italy* **39 F10** 42 12N 13 14 E
Borgosésia, *Italy* **38 C5** 45 43N 8 17 E
Borgvattnet, *Sweden* **14 A9** 63 26N 15 48 E
Borikhane, *Laos* **76 C4** 18 33N 103 43 E
Borislav, *Ukraine* **50 G3** 49 18N 23 28 E
Borisoglebsk, *Russia* **51 F13** 51 27N 42 5 E
Borisoglebskiy, *Russia* **51 C13** 56 28N 43 59 E
Borisov, *Belorussia* **50 D6** 54 17N 28 28 E
Borisovka, *Kazakhstan* **55 B4** 43 15N 68 10 E
Borispol, *Ukraine* **50 F7** 50 21N 30 59 E
Borja, *Peru* **152 D2** 4 20 S 77 40W
Borja, *Spain* **34 D3** 41 48N 1 34W
Borjas Blancas, *Spain* **34 D5** 41 31N 0 52 E
Borken, *Germany* **26 D2** 51 51N 6 52 E
Borkou, *Chad* **97 E3** 18 15N 18 50 E
Borkum, *Germany* **26 B2** 53 36N 6 42 E
Borlänge, *Sweden* **13 F13** 60 29N 15 26 E
Borley, C., *Antarctica* **7 C5** 66 15 S 52 30 E
Bormida →, *Italy* **38 D5** 44 23N 8 13 E
Bórmio, *Italy* **38 B7** 46 28N 10 22 E
Born, *Neths.* **21 F7** 51 2N 5 49 E
Borna, *Germany* **26 D8** 51 8N 12 31 E
Borndiep, *Neths.* **20 B7** 53 27N 5 35 E
Borne, *Neths.* **20 D9** 52 18N 6 45 E
Bornem, *Belgium* **21 F4** 51 6N 4 14 E
Borneo, *E. Indies* **75 B4** 1 0N 115 0 E
Bornholm, *Denmark* **13 J13** 55 10N 15 0 E
Borno □, *Nigeria* **101 C7** 11 30N 13 0 E
Bornos, *Spain* **37 J5** 36 48N 5 42W
Bornu Yassa, *Nigeria* **101 C7** 12 14N 12 25 E
Borobudur, *Indonesia* **75 D4** 7 36 S 110 13 E
Borodino, *Russia* **50 D9** 55 31N 35 40 E
Borogontsy, *Russia* **57 C14** 62 42N 131 8 E
Boromo, *Burkina Faso* **100 C4** 11 45N 2 58W
Boron, *U.S.A.* **145 L9** 35 0N 117 39W
Boronga Is., *Burma* **78 F4** 19 58N 93 6 E
Borongan, *Phil.* **71 F5** 11 37N 125 26 E
Bororen, *Australia* **114 C5** 24 13 S 151 33 E
Borotangba Mts., *C.A.R.* **95 F1** 6 30N 25 0 E
Borovan, *Bulgaria* **43 D8** 43 27N 23 45 E
Borovichi, *Russia* **50 B8** 58 25N 33 55 E
Borovsk, *Russia* **51 D10** 55 12N 36 24 E
Borovsk, *Russia* **54 B5** 59 43N 56 40 E
Borovskoye, *Kazakhstan* **54 E9** 53 48N 64 12 E
Borrego Springs, *U.S.A.* **145 M10** 33 15N 116 23W
Borriol, *Spain* **34 E4** 40 4N 0 4W
Borroloola, *Australia* **114 B2** 16 4 S 136 17 E
Borşa, *Romania* **46 B5** 47 41N 24 50 E
Borsod-Abaúj-Zemplén □, *Hungary* **31 C13** 48 20N 21 0 E
Borssele, *Neths.* **21 F3** 51 26N 3 45 E
Bort-les-Orgues, *France* **24 C6** 45 24N 2 29 E
Borth, *U.K.* **17 E3** 52 29N 4 3W
Borujerd, *Iran* **85 C6** 33 55N 48 50 E
Borzhomi, *Georgia* **53 F10** 41 48N 43 28 E
Borzna, *Ukraine* **50 F8** 51 18N 32 26 E
Borzya, *Russia* **57 D12** 50 24N 116 31 E
Bosa, *Italy* **40 B1** 40 17N 8 32 E
Bosaga, *Turkmenistan* **55 E2** 37 33N 65 41 E
Bosanska Brod, *Bos.-H.* **42 B3** 45 10N 18 0 E
Bosanska Dubica, *Bos.-H.* **39 C13** 45 10N 16 50 E
Bosanska Gradiška, *Bos.-H.* **42 B2** 45 10N 17 15 E
Bosanska Kostajnica, *Bos.-H.* **39 C13** 45 11N 16 33 E
Bosanska Krupa, *Bos.-H.* **39 D13** 44 53N 16 10 E
Bosanski Novi, *Bos.-H.* **39 C13** 45 2N 16 22 E
Bosanski Šamac, *Bos.-H.* **42 B3** 45 3N 18 29 E
Bosansko Grahovo, *Bos.-H.* **39 D13** 44 12N 16 26 E
Bosansko Petrovac, *Bos.-H.* **39 D13** 44 35N 16 21 E
Bosaso, *Somali Rep.* **90 E4** 11 12N 49 18 E
Bosavi, Mt., *Papua N. G.* **120 D2** 6 30 S 142 49 E
Boscastle, *U.K.* **17 G3** 50 42N 4 42W
Boscobel, *U.S.A.* **140 A6** 43 8N 90 42W
Boscotrecase, *Italy* **41 B7** 40 46N 14 28 E
Bose, *China* **68 F6** 23 53N 106 35 E
Boshan, *China* **67 F9** 36 28N 117 49 E
Boshoek, *S. Africa* **104 D4** 25 30 S 27 9 E
Boshof, *S. Africa* **104 D4** 28 31 S 25 13 E
Boshrūyeh, *Iran* **85 C8** 33 50N 57 30 E
Bosilegrad, *Serbia* **42 E7** 42 30N 22 27 E
Boskoop, *Neths.* **20 D5** 52 4N 4 40 E
Boskovice, *Czech.* **31 B9** 49 29N 16 40 E
Bosna →, *Bos.-H.* **42 B3** 45 4N 18 29 E
Bosna i Hercegovina = Bosnia-Herzegovina ■, *Europe* **42 D2** 44 0N 17 0 E
Bosnia-Herzegovina ■, *Europe* **42 D2** 44 0N 17 0 E
Bosnik, *Indonesia* **73 B5** 1 5 S 136 10 E
Bōsō-Hantō, *Japan* **63 B12** 35 20N 140 20 E
Bosobolo, *Zaïre* **102 B3** 4 15N 19 50 E
Bosporus = Karadeniz Boğazı, *Turkey* **88 C3** 41 10N 29 10 E
Bossangoa, *C.A.R.* **102 A3** 6 35N 17 30 E
Bossekop, *Norway* **12 B17** 69 57N 23 15 E
Bossembélé, *C.A.R.* **102 A3** 5 25N 17 40 E
Bossembélé II, *C.A.R.* **102 A3** 5 41N 16 38 E
Bossier City, *U.S.A.* **139 J8** 32 31N 93 44W
Bosso, *Niger* **97 F2** 13 43N 13 19 E
Bostānābād, *Iran* **84 B5** 37 50N 46 50 E
Bosten Hu, *China* **64 B3** 41 55N 87 40 E
Boston, *Phil.* **71 H6** 7 52N 126 22 E
Boston, *U.K.* **16 E7** 52 59N 0 2W
Boston, *U.S.A.* **137 D13** 42 22N 71 4W
Boston Bar, *Canada* **130 D4** 49 52N 121 30W
Bosusulu, *Zaïre* **102 B4** 0 50N 20 45 E
Bosut →, *Croatia* **42 B3** 45 20N 18 45 E
Boswell, *Canada* **130 D5** 49 28N 116 45W
Boswell, *Ind., U.S.A.* **141 D9** 40 31N 87 23W
Boswell, *Okla., U.S.A.* **139 H7** 34 2N 95 52W
Boswell, *Pa., U.S.A.* **136 F5** 40 10N 79 2W
Bosworth, *U.S.A.* **140 E3** 39 28N 93 20W
Botad, *India* **80 H4** 22 15N 71 40 E
Botan →, *Turkey* **89 E9** 37 44N 41 47 E
Botany B., *Australia* **115 E5** 34 0 S 151 14 E
Botene, *Laos* **76 D3** 17 35N 101 12 E
Botevgrad, *Bulgaria* **43 E8** 42 55N 23 47 E
Bothaville, *S. Africa* **104 D4** 27 23 S 26 34 E
Bothnia, G. of, *Europe* **12 E16** 63 0N 20 15 E
Bothwell, *Australia* **114 G4** 42 20 S 147 1 E
Bothwell, *Canada* **136 D3** 42 38N 81 52W
Boticas, *Portugal* **36 D3** 41 41N 7 40W
Botletle →, *Botswana* **104 C3** 20 10 S 23 15 E
Botolan, *Phil.* **70 D3** 15 17N 120 1 E
Botoroaga, *Romania* **46 E6** 44 8N 25 32 E
Botoşani, *Romania* **46 B7** 47 42N 26 41 E
Botoşani □, *Romania* **46 B7** 47 50N 26 50 E
Botro, *Ivory C.* **100 D3** 7 51N 5 19W
Botswana ■, *Africa* **104 C3** 22 0 S 24 0 E
Bottineau, *U.S.A.* **138 A4** 48 50N 100 27W
Bottrop, *Germany* **21 E9** 51 34N 6 59 E
Botucatu, *Brazil* **159 A6** 22 55 S 48 30W
Botwood, *Canada* **129 C8** 49 6N 55 23W
Bou Alam, *Algeria* **99 B5** 33 50N 1 26 E
Bou Ali, *Algeria* **99 C4** 27 11N 0 4W
Bou Djébéha, *Mali* **100 B4** 18 25N 2 45W
Bou Guema, *Algeria* **99 C5** 28 49N 0 19 E
Bou Ismael, *Algeria* **99 A5** 36 38N 2 42 E
Bou Izakarn, *Morocco* **98 C3** 29 12N 9 46W
Boû Lanouâr, *Mauritania* **98 D1** 21 12N 16 34W
Bou Saâda, *Algeria* **99 A5** 35 11N 4 9 E
Bou Salem, *Tunisia* **96 A1** 36 45N 9 2 E
Bouaké, *Ivory C.* **100 D3** 7 40N 5 2W
Bouanga, *Congo* **102 C3** 2 7 S 16 8 E
Bouar, *C.A.R.* **102 A3** 6 0N 15 40 E
Bouârfa, *Morocco* **99 B4** 32 32N 1 58W
Bouca, *C.A.R.* **102 A3** 6 45N 18 25 E
Boucau, *France* **24 E2** 43 32N 1 29W
Boucaut B., *Australia* **114 A1** 12 0 S 134 25 E
Bouches-du-Rhône □, *France* **25 E9** 43 37N 5 2 E
Bouda, *Algeria* **99 C4** 27 50N 0 27W
Boudenib, *Morocco* **98 B4** 31 59N 3 31W
Boudry, *Switz.* **28 C3** 46 57N 6 50 E
Boufarik, *Algeria* **99 A5** 36 34N 2 58 E
Bougainville, C., *Australia* **112 B4** 13 57 S 126 4 E
Bougainville I., *Solomon Is.* **121 L8** 6 0 S 155 0 E
Bougainville Reef, *Australia* **114 B4** 15 30 S 147 5 E
Bougainville Str., *Solomon Is.* **121 L9** 6 40 S 156 10 E
Bougaroun, C., *Algeria* **99 A6** 37 6N 6 30 E
Bougie = Bejaia, *Algeria* **99 A6** 36 42N 5 2 E
Bougouni, *Mali* **100 C3** 11 30N 7 20W
Bouillon, *Belgium* **21 J6** 49 44N 5 3 E
Bouïra, *Algeria* **99 A5** 36 20N 3 59 E
Boulder, *Colo., U.S.A.* **138 E2** 40 1N 105 17W
Boulder, *Mont., U.S.A.* **142 C7** 46 14N 112 7W
Boulder City, *U.S.A.* **145 K12** 35 59N 114 50W
Boulder Creek, *U.S.A.* **144 H4** 37 7N 122 7W
Boulder Dam = Hoover Dam, *U.S.A.* **145 K12** 36 1N 114 44W
Boulembo, *Gabon* **102 C2** 1 26 S 12 0 E
Bouli, *Mauritania* **100 B2** 15 17N 12 18W
Boulia, *Australia* **114 C2** 22 52 S 139 51 E
Bouligny, *France* **23 C12** 49 17N 5 45 E
Boulogne →, *France* **22 E5** 47 12N 1 47W
Boulogne-sur-Gesse, *France* **24 E4** 43 18N 0 38 E
Boulogne-sur-Mer, *France* **23 B8** 50 42N 1 36 E
Bouloire, *France* **22 E7** 47 59N 0 45 E
Bouloupari, *N. Cal.* **121 U20** 21 52 S 166 4 E
Boulsa, *Burkina Faso* **101 C4** 12 39N 0 34W
Boultoum, *Niger* **97 F2** 14 45N 10 25 E
Boumalne, *Morocco* **98 B3** 31 25N 6 0W
Boun Neua, *Laos* **76 B3** 21 38N 101 54 E
Boun Tai, *Laos* **76 B3** 21 23N 101 58 E
Bouna, *Ivory C.* **100 D4** 9 10N 3 0W
Boundary Peak, *U.S.A.* **144 H8** 37 51N 118 21W
Boundiali, *Ivory C.* **100 D3** 9 30N 6 20W
Bountiful, *U.S.A.* **142 F8** 40 53N 111 53W
Bounty Is., *Pac. Oc.* **122 M9** 48 0 S 178 30 E
Bourail, *N. Cal.* **121 U19** 21 34 S 165 30 E
Bourbeuse →, *U.S.A.* **140 F6** 38 24N 90 53W
Bourbon, *U.S.A.* **141 C10** 41 18N 86 7W
Bourbon-Lancy, *France* **24 B7** 46 37N 3 45 E
Bourbon-l'Archambault, *France* **24 B7** 46 36N 3 4 E
Bourbonnais, *France* **24 B7** 46 28N 3 0 E
Bourbonne-les-Bains, *France* **23 E12** 47 54N 5 45 E
Bourem, *Mali* **101 B4** 17 0N 0 24W
Bourg, *France* **24 C3** 45 3N 0 34W
Bourg-Argental, *France* **25 C8** 45 18N 4 32 E
Bourg-de-Péage, *France* **25 C9** 45 2N 5 3 E
Bourg-en-Bresse, *France* **25 B9** 46 13N 5 12 E
Bourg-St.-Andéol, *France* **25 D8** 44 23N 4 39 E
Bourg-St.-Maurice, *France* **25 C10** 45 35N 6 46 E
Bourg-St.-Pierre, *Switz.* **28 E4** 45 57N 7 12 E
Bourganeuf, *France* **24 C5** 45 57N 1 45 E
Bourges, *France* **23 E9** 47 9N 2 25 E
Bourget, *Canada* **137 A9** 45 26N 75 9W
Bourget, L. du, *France* **25 C9** 45 44N 5 52 E
Bourgneuf, B. de, *France* **22 E4** 47 3N 2 10W
Bourgneuf-en-Retz, *France* **22 E5** 47 2N 1 58W
Bourgogne, *France* **23 F11** 47 0N 4 50 E
Bourgoin-Jallieu, *France* **25 C9** 45 36N 5 17 E
Bourgueil, *France* **22 E7** 47 17N 0 10 E
Bourke, *Australia* **115 E4** 30 8 S 145 55 E
Bournemouth, *U.K.* **17 G6** 50 43N 1 53W
Bourriot-Bergonce, *France* **24 D3** 44 7N 0 14W
Bouse, *U.S.A.* **145 M13** 33 56N 114 0W
Boussac, *France* **24 B6** 46 22N 2 13 E
Boussens, *France* **24 E4** 43 12N 0 58 E
Bousso, *Chad* **97 F3** 10 34N 16 52 E
Boussu, *Belgium* **21 H3** 50 26N 3 48 E
Boutilimit, *Mauritania* **100 B2** 17 45N 14 40W
Bouvet I. = Bouvetøya, *Antarctica* **9 P9** 54 26 S 3 24 E
Bouvetøya, *Antarctica* **9 P9** 54 26 S 3 24 E
Bouznika, *Morocco* **98 B3** 33 46N 7 6W
Bouzonville, *France* **23 C13** 49 17N 6 32 E
Bova Marina, *Italy* **41 E8** 37 59N 15 56 E
Bovalino Marina, *Italy* **41 D9** 38 9N 16 10 E
Bovec, *Slovenia* **39 B10** 46 20N 13 33 E
Bovenkarspel, *Neths.* **20 C6** 52 41N 5 14 E
Bovigny, *Belgium* **21 H7** 50 12N 5 55 E
Bovill, *U.S.A.* **142 C5** 46 51N 116 24W
Bovino, *Italy* **41 A8** 41 15N 15 20 E
Bow Island, *Canada* **130 D6** 49 50N 111 23W
Bowbells, *U.S.A.* **138 A3** 48 48N 102 15W
Bowdle, *U.S.A.* **138 C5** 45 27N 99 39W
Bowelling, *Australia* **113 F2** 33 25 S 116 30 E
Bowen, *Australia* **114 C4** 20 0 S 148 16 E
Bowen Mts., *Australia* **117 D7** 37 0 S 147 50 E
Bowie, *Ariz., U.S.A.* **143 K9** 32 19N 109 29W
Bowie, *Tex., U.S.A.* **139 J6** 33 34N 97 51W
Bowkān, *Iran* **84 B5** 36 31N 46 12 E
Bowland, Forest of, *U.K.* **16 D5** 54 0N 2 30W
Bowling Green, *Ky., U.S.A.* **134 G2** 36 59N 86 27W
Bowling Green, *Mo., U.S.A.* **140 E5** 39 21N 91 12W
Bowling Green, *Ohio, U.S.A.* **141 C13** 41 23N 83 39W
Bowling Green, C., *Australia* **114 B4** 19 19 S 147 25 E
Bowman, *U.S.A.* **138 B3** 46 11N 103 24W
Bowman I., *Antarctica* **7 C8** 65 0 S 104 0 E
Bowmans, *Australia* **116 C3** 34 10 S 138 17 E
Bowmanville, *Canada* **128 D4** 43 55N 78 41W
Bowmore, *U.K.* **18 F2** 55 45N 6 18W
Bowral, *Australia* **117 C9** 34 26 S 150 27 E
Bowraville, *Australia* **115 E5** 30 37 S 152 52 E
Bowron →, *Canada* **130 C4** 54 3N 121 50W
Bowser L., *Canada* **130 B3** 56 30N 129 30W
Bowsman, *Canada* **131 C8** 52 14N 101 12W
Bowutu Mts., *Papua N. G.* **120 D4** 7 45 S 147 10 E
Bowwood, *Zambia* **107 F2** 17 5 S 26 20 E
Boxholm, *Sweden* **15 F9** 58 12N 15 3 E
Boxmeer, *Neths.* **21 E7** 51 38N 5 56 E
Boxtel, *Neths.* **21 E6** 51 36N 5 20 E
Boyabat, *Turkey* **52 F6** 41 28N 34 42 E
Boyabo, *Zaïre* **102 B3** 3 43N 18 46 E
Boyaca = Casanare □, *Colombia* **152 B3** 6 0N 73 0W
Boyce, *U.S.A.* **139 K8** 31 23N 92 40W
Boyer →, *Canada* **130 B5** 58 27N 115 57W
Boyer, C., *N. Cal.* **121 U22** 21 37 S 168 6 E
Boyle, *Ireland* **19 C3** 53 58N 8 19W
Boyne →, *Ireland* **19 C5** 53 43N 6 15W
Boyne City, *U.S.A.* **134 C3** 45 13N 85 1W
Boyni Qara, *Afghan.* **79 A2** 36 20N 67 0 E
Boynton Beach, *U.S.A.* **135 M5** 26 32N 80 4W
Boyolali, *Indonesia* **75 D4** 7 32 S 110 35 E
Boyoma, Chutes, *Zaïre* **102 B5** 0 35N 25 23 E
Boyup Brook, *Australia* **113 F2** 33 50 S 116 23 E
Boz Dağ, *Turkey* **88 E3** 37 18N 29 11 E
Boz Dağları, *Turkey* **88 D3** 38 20N 28 0 E
Bozburun, *Turkey* **45 H10** 36 43N 28 8 E
Bozcaada, *Turkey* **44 E8** 39 49N 26 3 E
Bozdoğan, *Turkey* **88 E3** 37 40N 28 17 E
Bozeman, *U.S.A.* **142 D8** 45 41N 111 2W
Bozen = Bolzano, *Italy* **39 B8** 46 30N 11 20 E
Bozene, *Zaïre* **102 B3** 2 56N 19 12 E
Bożepole Wielkopolski, *Poland* **47 A4** 54 33N 17 56 E
Boževac, *Serbia* **42 C6** 44 32N 21 24 E
Bozkır, *Turkey* **88 E5** 37 11N 32 14 E
Bozouls, *France* **24 D6** 44 28N 2 43 E
Bozoum, *C.A.R.* **102 A3** 6 25N 16 35 E
Bozova, *Turkey* **89 E8** 37 21N 38 32 E
Bozovici, *Romania* **46 E3** 44 56N 22 1 E
Bozüyük, *Turkey* **88 D4** 39 54N 30 3 E
Bra, *Italy* **38 D4** 44 41N 7 50 E
Brabant □, *Belgium* **21 G5** 50 46N 4 30 E
Brabant L., *Canada* **131 B8** 55 58N 103 43W
Brabrand, *Denmark* **15 H4** 56 9N 10 7 E
Brač, *Croatia* **39 E13** 43 20N 16 40 E
Bracadale, L., *U.K.* **18 D2** 57 20N 6 30W
Bracciano, *Italy* **39 F9** 42 6N 12 10 E
Bracciano, L. di, *Italy* **39 F9** 42 8N 12 11 E
Bracebridge, *Canada* **128 C4** 45 2N 79 19W
Brach, *Libya* **96 C2** 27 31N 14 20 E
Bracieux, *France* **23 E8** 47 30N 1 30 E
Bräcke, *Sweden* **14 B9** 62 45N 15 26 E
Brackettville, *U.S.A.* **139 L4** 29 19N 100 25W
Bracki Kanal, *Croatia* **39 E13** 43 24N 16 40 E
Brad, *Romania* **46 C3** 46 10N 22 50 E
Brådano →, *Italy* **41 B9** 40 23N 16 51 E
Bradenton, *U.S.A.* **135 M4** 27 30N 82 34W
Bradford, *Canada* **136 B5** 44 7N 79 34W
Bradford, *U.K.* **16 D6** 53 47N 1 45W
Bradford, *Ill., U.S.A.* **140 C7** 41 11N 89 39W
Bradford, *Ohio, U.S.A.* **141 D12** 40 8N 84 27W
Bradford, *Pa., U.S.A.* **136 E6** 41 58N 78 38W
Bradford, *Vt., U.S.A.* **137 C12** 43 59N 72 9W

178 Brădiceni

Brădiceni, *Romania* **46 D4** 45 3N 23 4 E
Bradley, *Ark., U.S.A.* **139 J8** 33 6N 93 39W
Bradley, *Calif., U.S.A.* **144 K6** 35 52N 120 48W
Bradley, *Ill., U.S.A.* **141 C9** 41 9N 87 52W
Bradley, *S. Dak., U.S.A.* **138 C6** 45 5N 97 39W
Bradley Institute, *Zimbabwe* **107 F3** 17 7 S 31 25 E
Bradore Bay, *Canada* **129 B8** 51 27N 57 18W
Bradshaw, *Australia* **112 C5** 15 21 S 130 16 E
Brady, *U.S.A.* **139 K5** 31 9N 99 20W
Brædstrup, *Denmark* **15 J3** 55 58N 9 37 E
Braemar, *Australia* **116 B3** 33 12 S 139 35 E
Braeside, *Canada* **137 A8** 45 28N 76 24W
Braga, *Portugal* **36 D2** 41 35N 8 25W
Braga □, *Portugal* **36 D2** 41 30N 8 30W
Bragado, *Argentina* **158 D3** 35 2 S 60 27W
Bragança, *Brazil* **154 B2** 1 0 S 47 2W
Bragança, *Portugal* **36 D4** 41 48N 6 50W
Bragança □, *Portugal* **36 D4** 41 30N 6 45W
Bragança Paulista, *Brazil* **159 A6** 22 55 S 46 32W
Brahmanbaria, *Bangla.* **78 D3** 23 58N 91 15 E
Brahmani →, *India* **82 D8** 20 39N 86 46 E
Brahmaputra →, *India* **78 D2** 23 58N 89 50 E
Braich-y-pwll, *U.K.* **16 E3** 52 47N 4 46W
Braidwood, *Australia* **117 C8** 35 27 S 149 49 E
Brăila, *Romania* **46 D8** 45 19N 27 59 E
Brăila □, *Romania* **46 D8** 45 5N 27 30 E
Braine-l'Alleud, *Belgium* **21 G4** 50 42N 4 23 E
Braine-le-Comte, *Belgium* **21 G4** 50 37N 4 8 E
Brainerd, *U.S.A.* **138 B7** 46 22N 94 12W
Braintree, *U.K.* **17 F8** 51 53N 0 34 E
Braintree, *U.S.A.* **137 D14** 42 13N 71 0W
Brak →, *S. Africa* **104 D3** 29 35 S 22 55 E
Brake, *Niedersachsen, Germany* **26 B4** 53 19N 8 30 E
Brake, *Nordrhein-Westfalen, Germany* **26 D5** 51 43N 9 12 E
Brakel, *Neths.* **20 E6** 51 49N 5 5 E
Brakwater, *Namibia* **104 C2** 22 28 S 17 3 E
Brålanda, *Sweden* **15 F6** 58 34N 12 21 E
Bralorne, *Canada* **130 C4** 50 50N 122 50W
Bramberg, *Germany* **27 E6** 50 6N 10 40 E
Bramminge, *Denmark* **15 J2** 55 28N 8 42 E
Brämön, *Sweden* **14 B11** 62 14N 17 40 E
Brampton, *Canada* **128 D4** 43 45N 79 45W
Bramsche, *Germany* **26 C3** 52 25N 7 58 E
Bramwell, *Australia* **114 A3** 12 8 S 142 37 E
Branco →, *Brazil* **153 D5** 1 20 S 61 50W
Branco, C., *Brazil* **154 C5** 7 9 S 34 47W
Brande, *Denmark* **15 J3** 55 57N 9 8 E
Brandenburg = Neubrandenburg, *Germany* **26 B9** 53 33N 13 17 E
Brandenburg, *Germany* **26 C8** 52 24N 12 33 E
Brandenburg, *U.S.A.* **141 G10** 38 0N 86 10W
Brandenburg □, *Germany* **26 C9** 52 15N 13 0 E
Brandfort, *S. Africa* **104 D4** 28 40 S 26 30 E
Brandon, *Canada* **131 D9** 49 50N 99 57W
Brandon, *U.S.A.* **137 C11** 43 48N 73 4W
Brandon B., *Ireland* **19 D1** 52 17N 10 8W
Brandon Mt., *Ireland* **19 D1** 52 15N 10 15W
Brandsen, *Argentina* **158 D4** 35 10 S 58 15W
Brandval, *Norway* **14 D6** 60 19N 12 1 E
Brandvlei, *S. Africa* **104 E3** 30 25 S 20 30 E
Brandýs, *Czech.* **30 A7** 50 10N 14 40 E
Branford, *U.S.A.* **137 E12** 41 17N 72 49W
Braniewo, *Poland* **47 A6** 54 25N 19 50 E
Bransfield Str., *Antarctica* **7 C18** 63 0 S 59 0W
Brańsk, *Poland* **47 C9** 52 45N 22 50 E
Branson, *Colo., U.S.A.* **139 G3** 37 1N 103 53W
Branson, *Mo., U.S.A.* **139 G8** 36 39N 93 13W
Brantford, *Canada* **128 D3** 43 10N 80 15W
Brantôme, *France* **24 C4** 45 22N 0 39 E
Branxholme, *Australia* **116 D4** 37 52 S 141 49 E
Branxton, *Australia* **117 B9** 32 38 S 151 21 E
Branzi, *Italy* **38 B6** 46 0N 9 46 E
Bras d'Or, L., *Canada* **129 C7** 45 50N 60 50W
Brasiléia, *Brazil* **156 C4** 11 0 S 68 45W
Brasília, *Brazil* **155 E2** 15 47 S 47 55W
Brasília Legal, *Brazil* **153 D6** 3 49 S 55 36W
Braslav, *Belorussia* **50 D5** 55 38N 27 0 E
Braslovce, *Slovenia* **39 B12** 46 21N 15 3 E
Braşov, *Romania* **46 D6** 45 38N 25 35 E
Braşov □, *Romania* **46 D6** 45 45N 25 15 E
Brass, *Nigeria* **101 E6** 4 35N 6 14 E
Brass →, *Nigeria* **101 E6** 4 15N 6 13 E
Brassac-les-Mines, *France* **24 C7** 45 24N 3 20 E
Brasschaat, *Belgium* **21 F4** 51 19N 4 27 E
Brassey, Banjaran, *Malaysia* **75 B5** 5 0N 117 15 E
Brassey Ra., *Australia* **113 E3** 25 8 S 122 15 E
Brasstown Bald, *U.S.A.* **135 H4** 34 53N 83 49W
Bratan = Morozov, *Bulgaria* **43 E10** 42 30N 25 10 E
Bratislava, *Slovak Rep.* **31 C10** 48 10N 17 7 E
Bratsigovo, *Bulgaria* **43 E9** 42 1N 24 22 E
Bratsk, *Russia* **57 D11** 56 10N 101 30 E
Brattleboro, *U.S.A.* **137 D12** 42 51N 72 34W
Bratunac, *Bos.-H.* **42 C4** 44 13N 19 21 E
Braunau, *Austria* **30 C6** 48 15N 13 3 E
Braunschweig, *Germany* **26 C6** 52 17N 10 28 E
Braunton, *U.K.* **17 F3** 51 6N 4 9W
Brava, *Somali Rep.* **90 G3** 1 20N 44 8 E
Bråviken, *Sweden* **14 F10** 58 38N 16 32 E
Bravo del Norte →, *Mexico* **146 B5** 25 57N 97 9W
Brawley, *U.S.A.* **145 N11** 32 59N 115 31W
Bray, *Ireland* **19 C5** 53 12N 6 6W
Bray, Mt., *Australia* **114 A1** 14 0 S 134 30 E
Bray, Pays de, *France* **23 C8** 49 46N 1 26 E
Bray-sur-Seine, *France* **23 D10** 48 25N 3 14 E
Braymer, *U.S.A.* **140 E3** 39 35N 93 48W
Brazeau →, *Canada* **130 C5** 52 55N 115 14W
Brazil, *U.S.A.* **141 E9** 39 32N 87 8W
Brazil ■, *S. Amer.* **155 D2** 12 0 S 50 0W
Brazo Sur →, *S. Amer.* **158 B4** 25 21 S 57 42W
Brazos →, *U.S.A.* **139 L7** 28 53N 95 23W
Brazzaville, *Congo* **103 C3** 4 9 S 15 12 E
Brčko, *Bos.-H.* **42 C3** 44 54N 18 46 E
Brda →, *Poland* **47 B5** 53 8N 18 8 E
Brea, *Peru* **156 A1** 4 40 S 81 7W
Breadalbane, *Australia* **114 C2** 23 50 S 139 35 E
Breadalbane, *U.K.* **18 E4** 56 30N 4 15W
Breaden, L., *Australia* **113 E4** 25 51 S 125 28 E
Breaksea Sd., *N.Z.* **119 F1** 45 35 S 166 35 E
Bream B., *N.Z.* **118 B3** 35 56 S 174 28 E
Bream Hd., *N.Z.* **118 B3** 35 51 S 174 36 E
Bream Tail, *N.Z.* **118 C3** 36 3 S 174 36 E
Breas, *Chile* **158 B1** 25 29 S 70 24W
Brebes, *Indonesia* **75 D3** 6 52 S 109 3 E
Brechin, *Canada* **136 B5** 44 32N 79 10W
Brechin, *U.K.* **18 E6** 56 44N 2 40W
Brecht, *Belgium* **21 F5** 51 21N 4 38 E
Breckenridge, *Colo., U.S.A.* **142 G10** 39 29N 106 3W
Breckenridge, *Minn., U.S.A.* **138 B6** 46 16N 96 35W
Breckenridge, *Mo., U.S.A.* **140 E3** 39 46N 93 48W
Breckenridge, *Tex., U.S.A.* **139 J5** 32 45N 98 54W
Breckland, *U.K.* **17 E8** 52 30N 0 40 E
Brecknock, Pen., *Chile* **160 D2** 54 35 S 71 30W
Břeclav, *Czech.* **31 C9** 48 46N 16 53 E
Brecon, *U.K.* **17 F4** 51 57N 3 23W
Brecon Beacons, *U.K.* **17 F4** 51 53N 3 27W
Breda, *Neths.* **21 E5** 51 35N 4 45 E
Bredasdorp, *S. Africa* **104 E3** 34 33 S 20 2 E
Bredbo, *Australia* **117 C8** 35 58 S 149 10 E
Bredene, *Belgium* **21 F1** 51 14N 2 59 E
Bredstedt, *Germany* **26 A4** 54 37N 8 59 E
Bredy, *Russia* **54 E7** 52 26N 60 21 E
Bree, *Belgium* **21 F7** 51 8N 5 35 E
Breezand, *Neths.* **20 C5** 52 53N 4 49 E
Bregalnica →, *Macedonia* **42 F7** 41 43N 22 9 E
Bregenz, *Austria* **30 D2** 47 30N 9 45 E
Bregovo, *Bulgaria* **42 C7** 44 9N 22 39 E
Bréhal, *France* **22 D5** 48 53N 1 30W
Bréhat, I. de, *France* **22 D4** 48 51N 3 0W
Breiðafjörður, *Iceland* **12 D2** 65 15N 23 15W
Breil-sur-Roya, *France* **25 E11** 43 56N 7 31 E
Breisach, *Germany* **27 G3** 48 2N 7 37 E
Brejinho de Nazaré, *Brazil* **154 D2** 11 1 S 48 34W
Brejo, *Brazil* **154 B3** 3 41 S 42 47W
Bremen, *Germany* **26 B4** 53 4N 8 47 E
Bremen □, *Germany* **26 B4** 53 6N 8 46 E
Bremer I., *Australia* **114 A2** 12 5 S 136 45 E
Bremerhaven, *Germany* **26 B4** 53 34N 8 35 E
Bremerton, *U.S.A.* **144 C4** 47 34N 122 38W
Bremervörde, *Germany* **26 B5** 53 28N 9 10 E
Bremsnes, *Norway* **14 A1** 63 6N 7 40 E
Brenes, *Spain* **37 H5** 37 32N 5 54W
Brenham, *U.S.A.* **139 K6** 30 10N 96 24W
Brenner Pass, *Austria* **30 D4** 47 2N 11 30 E
Breno, *Italy* **38 C7** 45 57N 10 20 E
Brent, *Canada* **128 C4** 46 2N 78 29W
Brent, *U.K.* **17 F7** 51 33N 0 18W
Brenta →, *Italy* **39 C9** 45 11N 12 18 E
Brentwood, *U.K.* **17 F8** 51 37N 0 19 E
Brentwood, *U.S.A.* **137 F11** 40 47N 73 15W
Bréscia, *Italy* **38 C7** 45 33N 10 13 E
Breskens, *Neths.* **21 F3** 51 23N 3 33 E
Breslau = Wrocław, *Poland* **47 D4** 51 5N 17 5 E
Bresle →, *France* **22 B8** 50 4N 1 22 E
Bresles, *France* **23 C9** 49 25N 2 13 E
Bressanone, *Italy* **39 B8** 46 43N 11 40 E
Bressay, *U.K.* **18 A7** 60 10N 1 5W
Bresse, *France* **23 F12** 46 50N 5 10 E
Bressuire, *France* **22 F6** 46 51N 0 30W
Brest, *Belorussia* **50 E3** 52 10N 23 40 E
Brest, *France* **22 D2** 48 24N 4 31W
Brest-Litovsk = Brest, *Belorussia* **50 E3** 52 10N 23 40 E
Bretagne, *France* **22 D4** 48 10N 3 0W
Bretçu, *Romania* **46 C7** 46 7N 26 18 E
Breteuil, *Eure, France* **22 D7** 48 50N 0 53 E
Breteuil, *Oise, France* **23 C9** 49 38N 2 18 E
Breton, *Canada* **130 C6** 53 7N 114 28W
Breton, Pertuis, *France* **24 B2** 46 17N 1 25W
Breton Sd., *U.S.A.* **139 L10** 29 35N 89 15W
Brett, C., *N.Z.* **118 B3** 35 10 S 174 20 E
Bretten, *Germany* **27 F4** 49 2N 8 43 E
Breukelen, *Neths.* **20 D6** 52 10N 5 0 E
Brevard, *U.S.A.* **135 H4** 35 14N 82 44W
Breves, *Brazil* **154 B1** 1 40 S 50 29W
Brevik, *Norway* **14 E3** 59 4N 9 42 E
Brewarrina, *Australia* **115 D4** 30 0 S 146 51 E
Brewer, *U.S.A.* **129 D6** 44 48N 68 46W
Brewer, Mt., *U.S.A.* **144 J8** 36 44N 118 28W
Brewster, *N.Y., U.S.A.* **137 E11** 41 23N 73 37W
Brewster, *Wash., U.S.A.* **142 B4** 48 6N 119 47W
Brewster, Kap, *Greenland* **6 B6** 70 7N 22 0W
Brewton, *U.S.A.* **135 K2** 31 7N 87 4W
Breyten, *S. Africa* **105 D4** 26 16 S 30 0 E
Breytovo, *Russia* **51 B10** 58 18N 37 50 E
Brezhnev = Naberezhnyye Chelny, *Russia* **54 D3** 55 42N 52 19 E
Brežice, *Slovenia* **39 C12** 45 54N 15 35 E
Brézina, *Algeria* **99 B5** 33 4N 1 14 E
Březnice, *Czech.* **30 B6** 49 32N 13 57 E
Breznik, *Bulgaria* **42 E7** 42 44N 22 50 E
Brezno, *Slovak Rep.* **31 C12** 48 50N 19 40 E
Brezovo, *Bulgaria* **43 E10** 42 21N 25 5 E
Bria, *C.A.R.* **102 A4** 6 30N 21 58 E
Briançon, *France* **25 D10** 44 54N 6 39 E
Briare, *France* **23 E9** 47 38N 2 45 E
Bribbaree, *Australia* **117 C7** 34 10 S 147 51 E
Bribie I., *Australia* **115 D5** 27 0 S 153 10 E
Bricquebec, *France* **22 C5** 49 28N 1 38W
Bridgehampton, *U.S.A.* **137 F12** 40 56N 72 19W
Bridgend, *U.K.* **17 F4** 51 30N 3 35W
Bridgeport, *Calif., U.S.A.* **144 G7** 38 15N 119 14W
Bridgeport, *Conn., U.S.A.* **137 E11** 41 11N 73 12W
Bridgeport, *Nebr., U.S.A.* **138 E3** 41 40N 103 6W
Bridgeport, *Tex., U.S.A.* **139 J6** 33 13N 97 45W
Bridger, *U.S.A.* **142 D9** 45 18N 108 55W
Bridgeton, *U.S.A.* **134 F8** 39 26N 75 14W
Bridgetown, *Australia* **113 F2** 33 58 S 116 7 E
Bridgetown, *Barbados* **149 D8** 13 5N 59 30W
Bridgetown, *Canada* **129 D6** 44 55N 65 18W
Bridgewater, *Australia* **116 D5** 36 36 S 143 59 E
Bridgewater, *Canada* **129 D7** 44 25N 64 31W
Bridgewater, *Mass., U.S.A.* **137 E14** 41 59N 70 58W
Bridgewater, *S. Dak., U.S.A.* **138 D6** 43 33N 97 30W
Bridgewater, C., *Australia* **116 E4** 38 23 S 141 23 E
Bridgman, *U.S.A.* **141 C10** 41 57N 86 33W
Bridgnorth, *U.K.* **17 E5** 52 33N 2 25W
Bridgton, *U.S.A.* **137 B14** 44 3N 70 42W
Bridgwater, *U.K.* **17 F4** 51 7N 3 0W
Bridlington, *U.K.* **16 C7** 54 6N 0 11W
Bridport, *Australia* **114 G4** 40 59 S 147 23 E
Bridport, *U.K.* **17 G5** 50 43N 2 45W
Brie, Plaine de la, *France* **23 D10** 48 35N 3 10 E
Brie-Comte-Robert, *France* **23 D9** 48 40N 2 35 E
Briec, *France* **22 D2** 48 6N 4 0W
Brielle, *Neths.* **20 E4** 51 54N 4 10 E
Brienne-le-Château, *France* **23 D11** 48 24N 4 30 E
Brienon-sur-Armançon, *France* **23 E10** 47 59N 3 38 E
Brienz, *Switz.* **28 C6** 46 46N 8 2 E
Brienzersee, *Switz.* **28 C5** 46 44N 7 53 E
Brig, *Switz.* **28 D5** 46 18N 7 59 E
Brigg, *U.K.* **16 D7** 53 33N 0 30W
Briggsdale, *U.S.A.* **138 E2** 40 38N 104 20W
Brigham City, *U.S.A.* **142 F7** 41 31N 112 1W
Bright, *Australia* **117 D7** 36 42 S 146 56 E
Brighton, *Australia* **116 C3** 35 5 S 138 30 E
Brighton, *Canada* **128 D4** 44 2N 77 44W
Brighton, *U.K.* **17 G7** 50 50N 0 9W
Brighton, *Colo., U.S.A.* **138 F2** 39 59N 104 49W
Brighton, *Ill., U.S.A.* **140 E6** 39 2N 90 8W
Brighton, *Iowa, U.S.A.* **140 C5** 41 10N 91 49W
Brightwater, *N.Z.* **119 B8** 41 22 S 173 9 E
Brignogan-Plage, *France* **22 D2** 48 40N 4 20W
Brignoles, *France* **25 E10** 43 25N 6 5 E
Brihuega, *Spain* **34 E2** 40 45N 2 52W
Brikama, *Gambia* **100 C1** 13 15N 16 45W
Brilliant, *Canada* **130 D5** 49 19N 117 38W
Brilliant, *U.S.A.* **136 F4** 40 15N 80 39W
Brilon, *Germany* **26 D4** 51 23N 8 32 E
Brim, *Australia* **116 D5** 36 3 S 142 27 E
Brimfield, *U.S.A.* **140 D7** 40 50N 89 53W
Bríndisi, *Italy* **41 B10** 40 39N 17 55 E
Brinje, *Croatia* **39 D12** 45 0N 15 9 E
Brinkley, *U.S.A.* **139 H9** 34 53N 91 12W
Brinkworth, *Australia* **116 B3** 33 42 S 138 26 E
Brinnon, *U.S.A.* **144 C4** 47 41N 122 54W
Brion, I., *Canada* **129 C7** 47 46N 61 26W
Brionne, *France* **22 C7** 49 11N 0 43 E
Brionski, *Croatia* **39 D10** 44 55N 13 45 E
Brioude, *France* **24 C7** 45 18N 3 24 E
Briouze, *France* **22 D6** 48 42N 0 23W
Brisbane, *Australia* **115 D5** 27 25 S 153 2 E
Brisbane →, *Australia* **115 D5** 27 24 S 153 9 E
Brisighella, *Italy* **39 D8** 44 14N 11 46 E
Bristol, *U.K.* **17 F5** 51 26N 2 35W
Bristol, *Conn., U.S.A.* **137 E12** 41 44N 72 57W
Bristol, *Pa., U.S.A.* **137 F10** 40 6N 74 51W
Bristol, *R.I., U.S.A.* **137 E13** 41 40N 71 16W
Bristol, *S. Dak., U.S.A.* **138 C6** 45 21N 97 45W
Bristol, *Tenn., U.S.A.* **135 G4** 36 36N 82 11W
Bristol B., *U.S.A.* **126 C4** 58 0N 160 0W
Bristol Channel, *U.K.* **17 F3** 51 18N 4 30W
Bristol I., *Antarctica* **7 B1** 58 45 S 28 0W
Bristol L., *U.S.A.* **143 J5** 34 23N 116 50W
Bristow, *U.S.A.* **139 H6** 35 50N 96 23W
British Columbia □, *Canada* **130 C3** 55 0N 125 15W
British Guiana = Guyana ■, *S. Amer.* **153 B6** 5 0N 59 0W
British Honduras = Belize ■, *Cent. Amer.* **147 D7** 17 0N 88 30W
British Isles, *Europe* **10 E5** 54 0N 4 0W
Brits, *S. Africa* **105 D4** 25 37 S 27 48 E
Britstown, *S. Africa* **104 E3** 30 37 S 23 30 E
Britt, *Canada* **128 C3** 45 46N 80 34W
Britt, *U.S.A.* **140 A3** 43 6N 93 48W
Brittany = Bretagne, *France* **22 D4** 48 10N 3 0W
Britton, *U.S.A.* **138 C6** 45 48N 97 45W
Brive-la-Gaillarde, *France* **24 C5** 45 10N 1 32 E
Briviesca, *Spain* **34 C1** 42 32N 3 19W
Brixton, *Australia* **114 C3** 23 32 S 144 57 E
Brlik, *Kazakhstan* **55 B6** 43 40N 73 49 E
Brlik, *Kazakhstan* **55 A6** 44 5N 73 31 E
Brno, *Czech.* **31 B9** 49 10N 16 35 E
Bro, *Sweden* **14 E11** 59 31N 17 38 E
Broach = Bharuch, *India* **82 D1** 21 47N 73 0 E
Broad →, *U.S.A.* **135 J5** 34 1N 81 4W
Broad Arrow, *Australia* **113 F3** 30 23 S 121 15 E
Broad B., *U.K.* **18 C2** 58 14N 6 16W
Broad Haven, *Ireland* **19 B2** 54 20N 9 55W
Broad Law, *U.K.* **18 F5** 55 30N 3 22W
Broad Sd., *Australia* **114 C4** 22 0 S 149 45 E
Broadford, *Australia* **117 D6** 37 14 S 145 4 E
Broadhurst Ra., *Australia* **112 D3** 22 30 S 122 30 E
Broads, The, *U.K.* **16 E9** 52 45N 1 30 E
Broadus, *U.S.A.* **138 C2** 45 27N 105 25W
Broadview, *Canada* **131 C8** 50 22N 102 35W
Broager, *Denmark* **15 K3** 54 53N 9 40 E
Broaryd, *Sweden* **15 G7** 57 7N 13 15 E
Brochet, *Canada* **131 B8** 57 53N 101 40W
Brochet, L., *Canada* **131 B8** 58 36N 101 35W
Brock, *Canada* **131 C7** 51 26N 108 43W
Brocken, *Germany* **26 D6** 51 48N 10 40 E
Brocklehurst, *Australia* **117 B8** 32 9 S 148 38 E
Brockport, *U.S.A.* **136 C7** 43 13N 77 56W
Brockton, *U.S.A.* **137 D13** 42 5N 71 1W
Brockville, *Canada* **128 D4** 44 35N 75 41W
Brockway, *Mont., U.S.A.* **138 B2** 47 18N 105 45W
Brockway, *Pa., U.S.A.* **136 E6** 41 15N 78 47W
Brocton, *U.S.A.* **136 D5** 42 23N 79 26W
Brod, *Macedonia* **42 F6** 41 35N 21 17 E
Brodarevo, *Serbia* **42 D4** 43 14N 19 44 E
Brodeur Pen., *Canada* **127 A11** 72 30N 88 10W
Brodhead, *U.S.A.* **140 B7** 42 37N 89 22W
Brodick, *U.K.* **18 F3** 55 34N 5 9W
Brodnica, *Poland* **47 B6** 53 15N 19 25 E
Brodokalmak, *Russia* **54 D8** 55 35N 62 6 E
Brody, *Ukraine* **50 F4** 50 5N 25 10 E
Broechem, *Belgium* **21 F5** 51 11N 4 38 E
Broek, *Neths.* **20 D6** 52 26N 5 0 E
Broek op Langedijk, *Neths.* **20 C5** 52 41N 4 49 E
Brogan, *U.S.A.* **142 D5** 44 15N 117 31W
Broglie, *France* **22 C7** 49 2N 0 30 E
Brok, *Poland* **47 C8** 52 43N 21 52 E
Broken Bow, *Nebr., U.S.A.* **138 E5** 41 24N 99 38W
Broken Bow, *Okla., U.S.A.* **139 H7** 34 2N 94 44W
Broken Hill = Kabwe, *Zambia* **107 E2** 14 30 S 28 29 E
Broken Hill, *Australia* **116 A4** 31 58 S 141 29 E
Brokind, *Sweden* **15 F9** 58 13N 15 42 E
Brokopondo, *Surinam* **153 B7** 5 3N 54 59W
Brokopondo □, *Surinam* **153 C6** 4 30N 55 30W
Bromfield, *U.K.* **17 E5** 52 25N 2 45W
Bromley, *U.K.* **17 F8** 51 20N 0 5 E
Bronaugh, *U.S.A.* **140 G2** 37 41N 94 28W
Brønderslev, *Denmark* **15 G3** 57 16N 9 57 E
Brong-Ahafo □, *Ghana* **100 D4** 7 50N 2 0W
Bronkhorstspruit, *S. Africa* **105 D4** 25 46 S 28 45 E
Bronnitsy, *Russia* **51 D11** 55 27N 38 10 E
Bronson, *U.S.A.* **141 C11** 41 52N 85 12W
Bronte, *Italy* **41 E7** 37 48N 14 49 E
Bronte, *U.S.A.* **139 K4** 31 53N 100 18W
Bronte Park, *Australia* **114 G4** 42 8 S 146 30 E
Brook Park, *U.S.A.* **136 E4** 41 24N 80 51W
Brookes Point, *Phil.* **71 G1** 8 47N 117 50 E
Brookfield, *U.S.A.* **140 E3** 39 47N 93 4W
Brookhaven, *U.S.A.* **139 K9** 31 35N 90 26W
Brookings, *Oreg., U.S.A.* **142 E1** 42 3N 124 17W
Brookings, *S. Dak., U.S.A.* **138 C6** 44 19N 96 48W
Brooklin, *Canada* **136 C6** 43 55N 78 55W
Brooklyn, *U.S.A.* **140 C4** 41 44N 92 27W
Brookmere, *Canada* **130 D4** 49 52N 120 53W
Brooks, *Canada* **130 C6** 50 35N 111 55W
Brooks B., *Canada* **130 C3** 50 15N 127 55W
Brooks L., *Canada* **131 A7** 61 55N 106 35W
Brooks Ra., *U.S.A.* **126 B5** 68 40N 147 0W
Brookston, *U.S.A.* **141 D10** 40 36N 86 52W
Brooksville, *Fla., U.S.A.* **135 L4** 28 33N 82 23W
Brooksville, *Ky., U.S.A.* **141 F12** 38 41N 84 4W
Brookville, *U.S.A.* **141 E11** 39 25N 85 1W
Brooloo, *Australia* **115 D5** 26 30 S 152 43 E
Broom, L., *U.K.* **18 D3** 57 55N 5 15W
Broome, *Australia* **112 C3** 18 0 S 122 15 E
Broomehill, *Australia* **113 F2** 33 51 S 117 39 E
Broons, *France* **22 D4** 48 20N 2 16W
Brora, *U.K.* **18 C5** 58 3N 3 50W
Brora →, *U.K.* **18 C5** 58 4N 3 52W
Brosna →, *Ireland* **19 C4** 53 8N 8 0W
Broşteni, *Romania* **46 B6** 47 14N 25 43 E
Brotas de Macaúbas, *Brazil* **155 D3** 12 0 S 42 38W
Brothers, *U.S.A.* **142 E3** 43 49N 120 36W
Brøttum, *Norway* **14 C4** 61 2N 10 34 E
Brou, *France* **22 D8** 48 13N 1 11 E
Brough, *U.K.* **16 C5** 54 32N 2 19W
Broughams Gate, *Australia* **116 A4** 30 51 S 140 59 E
Broughton, *U.S.A.* **141 G8** 37 56N 88 27W
Broughton Island, *Canada* **127 B13** 67 33N 63 0W
Broughty Ferry, *U.K.* **18 E6** 56 29N 2 50W
Broumov, *Czech.* **31 A9** 50 35N 16 20 E
Brouwershaven, *Neths.* **20 E3** 51 45N 3 55 E
Brouwershavensche Gat, *Neths.* **20 E3** 51 46N 3 50 E
Brovary, *Ukraine* **50 F7** 50 34N 30 48 E
Brovst, *Denmark* **15 G3** 57 6N 9 31 E
Browerville, *U.S.A.* **138 B7** 46 5N 94 52W
Brown, Mt., *Australia* **116 B2** 32 30 S 138 0 E
Brown, Pt., *Australia* **115 E1** 32 32 S 133 50 E
Brown Willy, *U.K.* **17 G3** 50 35N 4 34W
Brownfield, *U.S.A.* **139 J3** 33 11N 102 17W
Browning, *Ill., U.S.A.* **140 D6** 40 8N 90 22W
Browning, *Mo., U.S.A.* **140 D3** 40 3N 93 12W
Browning, *Mont., U.S.A.* **142 B7** 48 34N 113 1W
Browning Pass, *N.Z.* **119 C6** 42 55 S 171 22 E
Brownlee, *Canada* **131 C7** 50 43N 106 1W
Brownsburg, *U.S.A.* **141 E10** 39 51N 86 24W
Brownstown, *U.S.A.* **141 F10** 38 53N 86 3W
Brownsville, *Oreg., U.S.A.* **142 D2** 44 24N 122 59W
Brownsville, *Tenn., U.S.A.* **139 H10** 35 36N 89 16W
Brownsville, *Tex., U.S.A.* **139 N6** 25 54N 97 30W
Brownsweg, *Surinam* **153 B6** 5 5N 55 15W
Brownwood, *U.S.A.* **139 K5** 31 43N 98 59W
Brownwood, L., *U.S.A.* **139 K5** 31 51N 98 35W
Browse I., *Australia* **112 B3** 14 7 S 123 33 E
Broye →, *Switz.* **28 C3** 46 52N 6 58 E
Brozas, *Spain* **37 F4** 39 37N 6 47W
Bruas, *Malaysia* **77 K3** 4 30N 100 47 E
Bruay-en-Artois, *France* **23 B9** 50 29N 2 33 E
Bruce, Mt., *Australia* **112 D2** 22 37 S 118 8 E
Bruce B., *N.Z.* **119 D4** 43 35 S 169 42 E
Bruce Pen., *Canada* **136 A3** 45 0N 81 30W
Bruce Rock, *Australia* **113 F2** 31 52 S 118 8 E
Bruche →, *France* **23 D14** 48 34N 7 43 E
Bruchsal, *Germany* **27 F4** 49 9N 8 39 E
Bruck an der Leitha, *Austria* **31 C9** 48 1N 16 47 E
Bruck an der Mur, *Austria* **30 D8** 47 24N 15 16 E
Brue →, *U.K.* **17 F5** 51 10N 2 59W
Brugelette, *Belgium* **21 G3** 50 35N 3 52 E
Bruges = Brugge, *Belgium* **21 F2** 51 13N 3 13 E
Brugg, *Switz.* **28 B6** 47 29N 8 11 E
Brugge, *Belgium* **21 F2** 51 13N 3 13 E
Brühl, *Germany* **26 E2** 50 49N 6 51 E
Bruinisse, *Neths.* **21 E4** 51 40N 4 5 E
Brûlé, *Canada* **130 C5** 53 15N 117 58W
Brûlon, *France* **22 E6** 47 58N 0 15W
Brûly, *Belgium* **21 J5** 49 58N 4 32 E
Brumado, *Brazil* **155 D3** 14 14 S 41 40W
Brumado →, *Brazil* **155 D3** 14 13 S 41 40W
Brumath, *France* **23 D14** 48 43N 7 40 E
Brummen, *Neths.* **20 D8** 52 5N 6 10 E
Brumunddal, *Norway* **14 D4** 60 53N 10 56 E
Brunchilly, *Australia* **114 B1** 18 50 S 134 30 E
Brundidge, *U.S.A.* **135 K3** 31 43N 85 49W
Bruneau, *U.S.A.* **142 E6** 42 53N 115 48W
Bruneau →, *U.S.A.* **142 E6** 42 56N 115 57W
Brunei = Bandar Seri Begawan, *Brunei* **75 B4** 4 52N 115 0 E
Brunei ■, *Asia* **75 B4** 4 50N 115 0 E
Brunette Downs, *Australia* **114 B2** 18 40 S 135 55 E
Brunflo, *Sweden* **14 A8** 63 5N 14 50 E
Brunico, *Italy* **39 B8** 46 50N 11 55 E
Brünig, P., *Switz.* **28 C6** 46 46N 8 8 E
Brunkeberg, *Norway* **14 E2** 59 26N 8 28 E

Burullus, Bahra el 179

Brunna, *Sweden* **14 E11** 59 52N 17 25 E
Brunnen, *Switz.* **29 C7** 46 59N 8 37 E
Brunner, L., *N.Z.* **119 C6** 42 37 S 171 27 E
Bruno, *Canada* **131 C7** 52 20N 105 30W
Brunsbüttel, *Germany* **26 B5** 53 52N 9 13 E
Brunssum, *Neths.* **21 G7** 50 57N 5 59 E
Brunswick = Braunschweig, *Germany* **26 C6** 52 17N 10 28 E
Brunswick, *Ga., U.S.A.* **135 K5** 31 10N 81 30W
Brunswick, *Maine, U.S.A.* **129 D6** 43 55N 69 58W
Brunswick, *Md., U.S.A.* **134 F7** 39 19N 77 38W
Brunswick, *Mo., U.S.A.* **140 E3** 39 26N 93 8W
Brunswick, *Ohio, U.S.A.* **136 E3** 41 14N 81 51W
Brunswick, Pen. de, *Chile* **160 D2** 53 30 S 71 30W
Brunswick B., *Australia* **112 C3** 15 15 S 124 50 E
Brunswick Junction, *Australia* **113 F2** 33 15 S 115 50 E
Bruntál, *Czech.* **31 B10** 50 0N 17 27 E
Bruny I., *Australia* **114 G4** 43 20 S 147 15 E
Brus Laguna, *Honduras* **148 C3** 15 47N 84 35W
Brusartsi, *Bulgaria* **42 D8** 43 40N 23 5 E
Brush, *U.S.A.* **138 E3** 40 15N 103 37W
Brushton, *U.S.A.* **137 B10** 44 50N 74 31W
Brusio, *Switz.* **29 D10** 46 14N 10 8 E
Brusque, *Brazil* **159 B6** 27 5 S 49 0W
Brussel, *Belgium* **21 G4** 50 51N 4 21 E
Brussels = Brussel, *Belgium* **21 G4** 50 51N 4 21 E
Brussels, *Canada* **136 C3** 43 44N 81 15W
Brustem, *Belgium* **21 G6** 50 48N 5 14 E
Bruthen, *Australia* **117 D7** 37 42 S 147 50 E
Bruxelles = Brussel, *Belgium* **21 G4** 50 51N 4 21 E
Bruyères, *France* **23 D13** 48 10N 6 40 E
Brwinów, *Poland* **47 C7** 52 9N 20 40 E
Bryagovo, *Bulgaria* **43 F10** 41 58N 25 8 E
Bryan, *Ohio, U.S.A.* **141 C12** 41 28N 84 33W
Bryan, *Tex., U.S.A.* **139 K6** 30 40N 96 22W
Bryan, Mt., *Australia* **116 B3** 33 30 S 139 0 E
Bryanka, *Ukraine* **53 B8** 48 32N 38 45 E
Bryansk, *Russia* **50 E9** 53 13N 34 25 E
Bryanskoye, *Russia* **53 D12** 44 20N 47 10 E
Bryant, *U.S.A.* **138 C6** 44 35N 97 28W
Bryne, *Norway* **13 G8** 58 44N 5 38 E
Bryson City, *U.S.A.* **135 H4** 35 26N 83 27W
Brza Palanka, *Serbia* **42 C7** 44 28N 22 27 E
Brzava →, *Serbia* **42 B5** 45 21N 20 45 E
Brzeg, *Poland* **47 E4** 50 52N 17 30 E
Brzeg Din, *Poland* **47 D3** 51 16N 16 41 E
Brześć Kujawski, *Poland* **47 C5** 52 36N 18 55 E
Brzesko, *Poland* **31 B13** 49 59N 20 34 E
Brzeszcze, *Poland* **31 B12** 49 59N 19 10 E
Brzeziny, *Poland* **47 D6** 51 49N 19 42 E
Brzozów, *Poland* **31 B15** 49 41N 22 3 E
Bsharri, *Lebanon* **91 A5** 34 15N 36 0 E
Bū Athlah, *Libya* **96 B3** 30 9N 15 39 E
Bū Baqarah, *U.A.E.* **85 E8** 25 35N 56 25 E
Bu Craa, *W. Sahara* **98 C2** 26 45N 12 50W
Bū Ḩasā, *U.A.E.* **85 F7** 23 30N 53 20 E
Bua Yai, *Thailand* **76 E4** 15 33N 102 26 E
Buad I., *Phil.* **71 F5** 11 40N 124 51 E
Buala, *Solomon Is.* **121 M10** 8 10 S 159 35 E
Buapinang, *Indonesia* **72 B2** 4 40 S 121 30 E
Buba, *Guinea-Biss.* **100 C2** 11 40N 14 59W
Bubanda, *Zaïre* **102 B3** 4 14N 19 38 E
Bubanza, *Burundi* **106 C2** 3 6 S 29 23 E
Būbiyān, *Kuwait* **85 D6** 29 45N 48 15 E
Bucak, *Turkey* **88 E4** 37 28N 30 36 E
Bucaramanga, *Colombia* **152 B3** 7 0N 73 0W
Bucas Grande I., *Phil.* **71 G5** 9 40N 125 57 E
Buccaneer Arch., *Australia* **112 C3** 16 7 S 123 20 E
Bucchiánico, *Italy* **39 F11** 42 20N 14 10 E
Bucecea, *Romania* **46 B7** 47 47N 26 28 E
Buchach, *Ukraine* **50 G4** 49 5N 25 25 E
Buchan, *Australia* **117 D8** 37 30 S 148 12 E
Buchan, *U.K.* **18 D6** 57 32N 2 8W
Buchan Ness, *U.K.* **18 D7** 57 29N 1 48W
Buchanan, *Canada* **131 C8** 51 40N 102 45W
Buchanan, *Liberia* **100 D2** 5 57N 10 2W
Buchanan, *U.S.A.* **141 C10** 41 50N 86 22W
Buchanan, L., *Queens., Australia* **114 C4** 21 35 S 145 52 E
Buchanan, L., *W. Austral., Australia* **113 E3** 25 33 S 123 2 E
Buchanan, L., *U.S.A.* **139 K5** 30 45N 98 25W
Buchanan Cr. →, *Australia* **114 B2** 19 13 S 136 33 E
Buchans, *Canada* **129 C8** 48 50N 56 52W
Bucharest = Bucureşti, *Romania* **46 E7** 44 27N 26 10 E
Buchholz, *Germany* **26 B5** 53 19N 9 51 E
Buchloe, *Germany* **27 G6** 48 3N 10 45 E
Buchon, Pt., *U.S.A.* **144 K6** 35 15N 120 54W
Buchs, *Switz.* **29 B8** 47 10N 9 28 E
Bückeburg, *Germany* **26 C5** 52 16N 9 2 E
Buckeye, *U.S.A.* **143 K7** 33 22N 112 35W
Buckhannon, *U.S.A.* **134 F5** 39 0N 80 8W
Buckhaven, *U.K.* **18 E5** 56 10N 3 2W
Buckie, *U.K.* **18 D6** 57 40N 2 58W
Buckingham, *Canada* **128 C4** 45 37N 75 24W
Buckingham, *U.K.* **17 F7** 52 0N 0 59W
Buckingham B., *Australia* **114 A2** 12 10 S 135 40 E
Buckingham Canal, *India* **83 G5** 14 0N 80 5 E
Buckinghamshire □, *U.K.* **17 F7** 51 50N 0 55W
Buckland, *U.S.A.* **141 D12** 40 37N 84 16W
Buckle Hd., *Australia* **112 B4** 14 26 S 127 52 E
Buckleboo, *Australia* **116 B2** 32 54 S 136 12 E
Buckley, *Ill., U.S.A.* **141 D8** 40 36N 88 2W
Buckley, *Wash., U.S.A.* **142 C2** 47 10N 122 2W
Buckley →, *Australia* **114 C2** 20 10 S 138 49 E
Bucklin, *Kans., U.S.A.* **139 G5** 37 33N 99 38W
Bucklin, *Mo., U.S.A.* **140 E4** 39 47N 92 53W
Bucks L., *U.S.A.* **144 F5** 39 54N 121 12W
Buco Zau, *Angola* **103 C2** 4 46 S 12 33 E
Bucquoy, *France* **23 B9** 50 9N 2 43 E
Buctouche, *Canada* **129 C7** 46 30N 64 45W
Bucureşti, *Romania* **46 E7** 44 27N 26 10 E
Bucyrus, *U.S.A.* **141 D14** 40 48N 82 59W
Budafok, *Hungary* **31 D12** 47 26N 19 2 E
Budalin, *Burma* **78 D5** 22 20N 95 10 E
Budapest, *Hungary* **31 D12** 47 29N 19 5 E
Budaun, *India* **81 E8** 28 5N 79 10 E
Budd Coast, *Antarctica* **7 C8** 68 0 S 112 0 E
Buddabadah, *Australia* **117 A7** 31 56 S 147 14 E
Buddusò, *Italy* **40 B2** 40 35N 9 18 E
Bude, *U.K.* **17 G3** 50 49N 4 33W
Budel, *Neths.* **21 F7** 51 17N 5 34 E
Budennovsk, *Russia* **53 D11** 44 50N 44 10 E
Budeşti, *Romania* **46 E7** 44 13N 26 30 E
Budge Budge = Baj Baj, *India* **81 H13** 22 30N 88 5 E
Budgewoi, *Australia* **117 B9** 33 13 S 151 34 E
Búðareyri, *Iceland* **12 D6** 65 2N 14 13W
Búðir, *Iceland* **12 D2** 64 49N 23 23W
Budia, *Spain* **34 E2** 40 38N 2 46W
Budjala, *Zaïre* **102 B3** 2 50N 19 40 E
Búdrio, *Italy* **39 D8** 44 31N 11 31 E
Budva, *Montenegro* **42 E3** 42 17N 18 50 E
Budzyń, *Poland* **47 C3** 52 54N 16 59 E
Buea, *Cameroon* **101 E6** 4 10N 9 9 E
Buellton, *U.S.A.* **145 L6** 34 37N 120 12W
Buena Vista, *Bolivia* **157 D5** 17 27 S 63 40W
Buena Vista, *Colo., U.S.A.* **143 G10** 38 51N 106 8W
Buena Vista, *Va., U.S.A.* **134 G6** 37 44N 79 21W
Buena Vista L., *U.S.A.* **145 K7** 35 12N 119 18W
Buenaventura, *Colombia* **152 C2** 3 53N 77 4W
Buenaventura, *Mexico* **146 B3** 29 50N 107 30W
Buenaventura, B. de, *Colombia* **152 C2** 3 48N 77 17W
Buenavista, *Luzon, Phil.* **70 E4** 13 35N 122 34 E
Buenavista, *Mindanao, Phil.* **71 G5** 8 59N 125 24 E
Buenavista, *Zamboanga del S., Phil.* **71 H4** 7 15N 122 16 E
Buendía, Pantano de, *Spain* **34 E2** 40 25N 2 43W
Buenópolis, *Brazil* **155 E3** 17 54 S 44 11W
Buenos Aires, *Argentina* **158 C4** 34 30 S 58 20W
Buenos Aires, *Colombia* **152 C3** 1 36N 73 18W
Buenos Aires, *Costa Rica* **148 E3** 9 10N 83 20W
Buenos Aires □, *Argentina* **158 D4** 36 30 S 60 0W
Buenos Aires, L., *Chile* **160 C2** 46 35 S 72 30W
Buesaco, *Colombia* **152 C2** 1 23N 77 9W
Buffalo, *Mo., U.S.A.* **139 G8** 37 39N 93 6W
Buffalo, *N.Y., U.S.A.* **136 D6** 42 53N 78 53W
Buffalo, *Okla., U.S.A.* **139 G5** 36 50N 99 38W
Buffalo, *S. Dak., U.S.A.* **138 C3** 45 35N 103 33W
Buffalo, *Wyo., U.S.A.* **142 D10** 44 21N 106 42W
Buffalo →, *Canada* **130 A5** 60 5N 115 5W
Buffalo Head Hills, *Canada* **130 B5** 57 25N 115 55W
Buffalo L., *Canada* **130 C6** 52 27N 112 54W
Buffalo Narrows, *Canada* **131 B7** 55 51N 108 29W
Buffels →, *S. Africa* **104 D2** 29 36 S 17 3 E
Buford, *U.S.A.* **135 H4** 34 10N 84 0W
Bug →, *Poland* **47 C8** 52 31N 21 5 E
Bug →, *Ukraine* **52 C4** 46 59N 31 58 E
Buga, *Colombia* **152 C2** 4 0N 76 15W
Buganda, *Uganda* **106 C3** 0 0 31 30 E
Buganga, *Uganda* **106 C3** 0 3 S 32 0 E
Bugasan, *Phil.* **71 H5** 7 27N 124 14 E
Bugasong, *Phil.* **71 F4** 11 3N 122 4 E
Bugeat, *France* **24 C5** 45 36N 1 55 E
Bugel, Tanjung, *Indonesia* **75 D4** 6 26 S 111 3 E
Buggenhout, *Belgium* **21 F4** 51 1N 4 12 E
Bugibba, *Malta* **32 D1** 35 57N 14 25 E
Bugojno, *Bos.-H.* **42 C2** 44 2N 17 25 E
Bugsuk, *Phil.* **71 G1** 8 15N 117 15 E
Buguey, *Phil.* **70 B3** 18 17N 121 50 E
Bugulma, *Russia* **54 D3** 54 33N 52 48 E
Buguma, *Nigeria* **101 E6** 4 42N 6 55 E
Bugun Shara, *Mongolia* **64 B5** 49 0N 104 0 E
Bugun Shara, *Mongolia* **64 B5** 49 0N 104 0 E
Buguruslan, *Russia* **54 E3** 53 39N 52 26 E
Buhăeşti, *Romania* **46 C8** 46 47N 27 32 E
Buheirat-Murrat-el-Kubra, *Egypt* **94 H8** 30 15N 32 40 E
Buhl, *Idaho, U.S.A.* **142 E6** 42 36N 114 46W
Buhl, *Minn., U.S.A.* **138 B8** 47 30N 92 46W
Buhuşi, *Romania* **46 C7** 46 41N 26 45 E
Buick, *U.S.A.* **139 G9** 37 38N 91 2W
Builth Wells, *U.K.* **17 E4** 52 10N 3 26W
Buin, *Papua N. G.* **121 L8** 6 48 S 155 42 E
Buinsk, *Russia* **51 D16** 55 0N 48 18 E
Buíque, *Brazil* **154 C4** 8 37 S 37 9W
Buir Nur, *Mongolia* **65 B6** 47 50N 117 42 E
Buis-les-Baronnies, *France* **25 D9** 44 17N 5 16 E
Buitenpost, *Neths.* **20 B8** 53 15N 6 9 E
Buitrago, *Spain* **36 E7** 40 58N 3 38W
Bujalance, *Spain* **37 H6** 37 54N 4 23W
Buján, *Spain* **36 C2** 42 59N 8 36W
Bujanovac, *Serbia* **42 E6** 42 28N 21 44 E
Bujaraloz, *Spain* **34 D4** 41 29N 0 10W
Buje, *Croatia* **39 C10** 45 24N 13 39 E
Bujumbura, *Burundi* **106 C2** 3 16 S 29 18 E
Bük, *Hungary* **31 D9** 47 22N 16 45 E
Buk, *Poland* **47 C3** 52 21N 16 30 E
Buka I., *Papua N. G.* **120 C8** 5 10 S 154 35 E
Bukachacha, *Russia* **57 D12** 52 55N 116 50 E
Bukama, *Zaïre* **107 D2** 9 10 S 25 50 E
Bukavu, *Zaïre* **106 C2** 2 20 S 28 52 E
Bukene, *Tanzania* **106 C3** 4 15 S 32 48 E
Bukhara, *Uzbekistan* **55 D2** 39 48N 64 25 E
Bukhoro = Bukhara, *Uzbekistan* **55 D2** 39 48N 64 25 E
Bukidnon □, *Phil.* **71 G5** 8 0N 125 0 E
Bukima, *Tanzania* **106 C3** 1 50 S 33 25 E
Bukit Mertajam, *Malaysia* **77 K3** 5 22N 100 28 E
Bukittinggi, *Indonesia* **74 C2** 0 20 S 100 20 E
Bukkapatnam, *India* **83 G3** 14 14N 77 46 E
Buklyan, *Russia* **54 D3** 55 42N 52 10 E
Bukoba, *Tanzania* **106 C3** 1 20 S 31 49 E
Bukoba □, *Tanzania* **106 C3** 1 30 S 32 0 E
Bukowno, *Poland* **31 A12** 50 17N 19 35 E
Bukuru, *Nigeria* **101 D6** 9 42N 8 48 E
Bukuya, *Uganda* **106 B3** 0 40N 31 52 E
Bula, *Guinea-Biss.* **100 C1** 12 7N 15 43W
Bula, *Indonesia* **73 B4** 3 6 S 130 30 E
Bulacan, *Phil.* **70 E3** 13 40N 120 21 E
Bulacan □, *Phil.* **70 D3** 15 0N 121 5 E
Bülach, *Switz.* **29 A7** 47 31N 8 32 E
Bulahdelah, *Australia* **117 B10** 32 23 S 152 13 E
Bulalacao, *Phil.* **70 E3** 12 31N 121 26 E
Bulan, *Phil.* **70 E4** 12 40N 123 52 E
Bulanash, *Russia* **54 C8** 57 16N 62 0 E
Bulancak, *Turkey* **89 C8** 40 56N 38 14 E
Bulandshahr, *India* **80 E7** 28 28N 77 51 E
Bulanık, *Turkey* **89 D10** 39 4N 42 14 E
Bulanovo, *Russia* **54 E4** 52 27N 55 10 E
Bûlâq, *Egypt* **94 B3** 25 10N 30 38 E
Bulawayo, *Zimbabwe* **107 G2** 20 7 S 28 32 E
Buldan, *Turkey* **88 D3** 38 2N 28 50 E
Buldana, *India* **82 D3** 20 30N 76 18 E
Buldon, *Phil.* **71 H5** 7 33N 124 25 E
Bulgaria ■, *Europe* **43 E10** 42 35N 25 30 E
Bulgroo, *Australia* **115 D3** 25 47 S 143 58 E
Bulgunnia, *Australia* **115 E1** 30 10 S 134 53 E
Bulhale, *Somali Rep.* **108 C3** 5 20N 46 29 E
Bulhar, *Somali Rep.* **90 E3** 10 25N 44 30 E
Buli, Teluk, *Indonesia* **72 A3** 1 5N 128 25 E
Buliluyan, C., *Phil.* **71 G1** 8 20N 117 15 E
Bulki, *Ethiopia* **95 F4** 6 11N 36 31 E
Bulkley →, *Canada* **130 B3** 55 15N 127 40W
Bull Shoals L., *U.S.A.* **139 G8** 36 22N 92 35W
Bullange, *Belgium* **21 H8** 50 24N 6 15 E
Bullaque →, *Spain* **37 G6** 38 59N 4 17W
Bullara, *Australia* **112 D1** 22 40 S 114 3 E
Bullaring, *Australia* **113 F2** 32 30 S 117 45 E
Bullas, *Spain* **35 G3** 38 2N 1 40W
Bulle, *Switz.* **28 C4** 46 37N 7 3 E
Buller →, *N.Z.* **119 B6** 41 44 S 171 36 E
Buller, Mt., *Australia* **117 D7** 37 10 S 146 28 E
Buller Gorge, *N.Z.* **119 B7** 41 40 S 172 10 E
Bulli, *Australia* **117 C9** 34 15 S 150 57 E
Bullock Creek, *Australia* **114 B3** 17 43 S 144 31 E
Bulloo →, *Australia* **115 D3** 28 43 S 142 30 E
Bulloo Downs, *Queens., Australia* **115 D3** 28 31 S 142 57 E
Bulloo Downs, *W. Austral., Australia* **112 D2** 24 0 S 119 32 E
Bulloo L., *Australia* **115 D3** 28 43 S 142 25 E
Bulls, *N.Z.* **118 G4** 40 10 S 175 24 E
Bully-les-Mines, *France* **23 B9** 50 27N 2 44 E
Bulnes, *Chile* **158 D1** 36 42 S 72 19W
Bulo Burti, *Somali Rep.* **90 G4** 3 50N 45 33 E
Bulo Ghedudo, *Somali Rep.* **108 D2** 2 52N 43 1 E
Bulolo, *Papua N. G.* **120 D4** 7 10 S 146 40 E
Bulongo, *Zaïre* **103 C4** 4 45 S 21 30 E
Bulpunga, *Australia* **116 B4** 33 47 S 141 45 E
Bulqiza, *Albania* **44 C2** 41 30N 20 21 E
Bulsar = Valsad, *India* **82 D1** 20 40N 72 58 E
Bultfontein, *S. Africa* **104 D4** 28 18 S 26 10 E
Buluan, L., *Phil.* **71 H5** 6 40N 124 49 E
Buluangan, *Phil.* **71 F4** 10 24N 123 20 E
Bulukumba, *Indonesia* **72 C2** 5 33 S 120 11 E
Bulun, *Russia* **57 B13** 70 37N 127 30 E
Bulungu, *Zaïre* **103 D4** 6 4 S 21 54 E
Bulusan, *Phil.* **70 E5** 12 45N 124 8 E
Bumba, *Zaïre* **102 B4** 2 13N 22 30 E
Bumbiri I., *Tanzania* **106 C3** 1 40 S 31 55 E
Bumhkang, *Burma* **78 B6** 26 51N 97 40 E
Bumhpa Bum, *Burma* **78 B6** 26 51N 97 14 E
Bumi →, *Zimbabwe* **107 F2** 17 0 S 28 20 E
Bumtang →, *Bhutan* **78 B3** 26 56N 90 53 E
Buna, *Kenya* **106 B4** 2 58N 39 30 E
Buna, *Papua N. G.* **120 E5** 8 42 S 148 27 E
Bunawan, *Agusan del S., Phil.* **71 G5** 8 12N 125 57 E
Bunawan, *Davao del S., Phil.* **71 H5** 7 14N 125 38 E
Bunazi, *Tanzania* **106 C3** 1 3 S 31 23 E
Bunbah, Khalīj, *Libya* **96 B4** 32 20N 23 15 E
Bunbury, *Australia* **113 F2** 33 20 S 115 35 E
Buncrana, *Ireland* **19 A4** 55 8N 7 28W
Bundaberg, *Australia* **115 C5** 24 54 S 152 22 E
Bünde, *Germany* **26 C4** 52 11N 8 33 E
Bundey →, *Australia* **114 C2** 21 46 S 135 37 E
Bundi, *India* **80 G6** 25 30N 75 35 E
Bundooma, *Australia* **114 C1** 24 54 S 134 16 E
Bundoran, *Ireland* **19 B3** 54 24N 8 17W
Bundukia, *Sudan* **95 F3** 5 14N 30 55 E
Bundure, *Australia* **117 C7** 35 10 S 146 1 E
Bung Kan, *Thailand* **76 C4** 18 23N 103 37 E
Bungatakada, *Japan* **62 D3** 33 35N 131 25 E
Bungendore, *Australia* **117 C8** 35 14 S 149 30 E
Bungil Cr. →, *Australia* **114 D4** 27 5 S 149 5 E
Bungo, Gunong, *Malaysia* **75 B4** 1 16N 110 9 E
Bungo-Suidō, *Japan* **62 E4** 33 0N 132 15 E
Bungoma, *Kenya* **106 B3** 0 34N 34 34 E
Bungu, *Tanzania* **106 D4** 7 35 S 39 0 E
Bunia, *Zaïre* **106 B3** 1 35N 30 20 E
Bunji, *Pakistan* **81 B6** 35 45N 74 40 E
Bunker Hill, *Ill., U.S.A.* **140 E7** 39 3N 89 57W
Bunker Hill, *Ind., U.S.A.* **141 D10** 40 40N 86 6W
Bunkie, *U.S.A.* **139 K8** 30 57N 92 11W
Bunnell, *U.S.A.* **135 L5** 29 28N 81 16W
Bunnik, *Neths.* **20 D6** 52 4N 5 12 E
Bunnythorpe, *N.Z.* **118 G4** 40 16 S 175 39 E
Buñol, *Spain* **35 F4** 39 25N 0 47W
Bunsbeek, *Belgium* **21 G5** 50 50N 4 56 E
Bunschoten, *Neths.* **20 D6** 52 14N 5 22 E
Buntok, *Indonesia* **75 C4** 1 40 S 114 58 E
Bununu, *Nigeria* **101 D6** 9 51N 9 32 E
Bununu Dass, *Nigeria* **101 C6** 10 5N 9 31 E
Bünyan, *Turkey* **88 D6** 38 51N 35 51 E
Bunyu, *Indonesia* **75 B5** 3 35N 117 50 E
Bunza, *Nigeria* **101 C5** 12 8N 4 0 E
Buol, *Indonesia* **72 A2** 1 15N 121 32 E
Buon Brieng, *Vietnam* **76 F7** 13 9N 108 12 E
Buon Me Thuot, *Vietnam* **76 F7** 12 40N 108 3 E
Buong Long, *Cambodia* **76 F6** 13 44N 106 59 E
Buorkhaya, Mys, *Russia* **57 B14** 71 50N 132 40 E
Buqayq, *Si. Arabia* **85 E6** 26 0N 49 45 E
Buqbua, *Egypt* **94 A2** 31 29N 25 29 E
Bur Acaba, *Somali Rep.* **90 G3** 3 12N 44 20 E
Bûr Fuad, *Egypt* **94 H8** 31 15N 32 20 E
Bur Ghibi, *Somali Rep.* **108 D3** 3 56N 45 7 E
Bûr Safâga, *Egypt* **94 B3** 26 43N 33 57 E
Bûr Sa'îd, *Egypt* **94 H8** 31 16N 32 18 E
Bûr Sûdân, *Sudan* **94 D4** 19 32N 37 9 E
Bûr Taufiq, *Egypt* **94 J8** 29 54N 32 32 E
Bura, *Kenya* **106 C4** 1 4 S 39 58 E
Buran, *Somali Rep.* **108 B3** 10 14N 48 44 E
Burao, *Somali Rep.* **90 F4** 9 32N 45 32 E
Burāq, *Syria* **91 B5** 33 11N 36 29 E
Buras, *U.S.A.* **139 L10** 29 22N 89 32W
Burauen, *Phil.* **71 F5** 10 58N 124 53 E
Buraydah, *Si. Arabia* **84 E5** 26 20N 44 8 E
Burayevo, *Russia* **54 D4** 55 50N 55 24 E
Burbank, *U.S.A.* **145 L8** 34 11N 118 19W
Burcher, *Australia* **117 B7** 33 30 S 147 16 E
Burdekin →, *Australia* **114 B4** 19 38 S 147 25 E
Burdeos Bay, *Phil.* **70 D4** 14 44N 122 6 E
Burdett, *Canada* **130 D6** 49 50N 111 32W
Burdur, *Turkey* **88 E4** 37 45N 30 17 E
Burdur □, *Turkey* **88 E4** 37 45N 30 15 E
Burdur Gölü, *Turkey* **88 E4** 37 44N 30 10 E
Burdwan = Barddhaman, *India* **81 H12** 23 14N 87 39 E
Bure, *Ethiopia* **95 E4** 10 40N 37 4 E
Bure →, *U.K.* **16 E9** 52 38N 1 45 E
Büren, *Germany* **26 D4** 51 33N 8 34 E
Buren, *Neths.* **20 E6** 51 55N 5 20 E
Bureya →, *Russia* **57 E13** 49 27N 129 30 E
Burford, *Canada* **136 C4** 43 7N 80 27W
Burg, *Sachsen-Anhalt, Germany* **26 C7** 52 16N 11 50 E
Burg, *Schleswig-Holstein, Germany* **26 A7** 54 25N 11 10 E
Burg el Arab, *Egypt* **94 H6** 30 54N 29 32 E
Burg et Tuyur, *Sudan* **94 C2** 20 55N 27 56 E
Burg Stargard, *Germany* **26 B9** 53 29N 13 19 E
Burgas, *Bulgaria* **43 E12** 42 33N 27 29 E
Burgaski Zaliv, *Bulgaria* **43 E12** 42 30N 27 39 E
Burgdorf, *Germany* **26 C5** 52 27N 10 0 E
Burgdorf, *Switz.* **28 B5** 47 3N 7 37 E
Burgenland □, *Austria* **31 D9** 47 20N 16 20 E
Burgeo, *Canada* **129 C8** 47 37N 57 38W
Burgersdorp, *S. Africa* **104 E4** 31 0 S 26 20 E
Burges, Mt., *Australia* **113 F3** 30 50 S 121 5 E
Burghausen, *Germany* **27 G8** 48 10N 12 50 E
Búrgio, *Italy* **40 E6** 37 35N 13 18 E
Bürglen, *Switz.* **29 C7** 46 53N 8 40 E
Burglengenfeld, *Germany* **27 F8** 49 11N 12 2 E
Burgo de Osma, *Spain* **34 D1** 41 35N 3 4W
Burgohondo, *Spain* **36 E6** 40 26N 4 47W
Burgos, *Ilocos N., Phil.* **70 B3** 18 31N 120 39 E
Burgos, *Pangasinan, Phil.* **70 C2** 16 4N 119 52 E
Burgos, *Spain* **34 C1** 42 21N 3 41W
Burgos □, *Spain* **34 C1** 42 21N 3 42W
Burgstädt, *Germany* **26 E8** 50 55N 12 49 E
Burgsvik, *Sweden* **13 H15** 57 3N 18 19 E
Burguillos del Cerro, *Spain* **37 G4** 38 23N 6 35W
Burgundy = Bourgogne, *France* **23 F11** 47 0N 4 50 E
Burhanpur, *India* **82 D3** 21 18N 76 14 E
Burhou, *U.K.* **22 C4** 49 45N 2 15W
Buri Pen., *Eritrea* **95 D4** 15 25N 39 55 E
Burias, *Phil.* **70 E4** 12 55N 123 5 E
Burias Pass, *Phil.* **70 E4** 13 0N 123 15 E
Buribay, *Russia* **54 F6** 51 57N 58 10 E
Burica, Pta., *Costa Rica* **148 E3** 8 3N 82 51W
Burigi, L., *Tanzania* **106 C3** 2 2 S 31 22 E
Burin, *Canada* **129 C8** 47 1N 55 14W
Buriram, *Thailand* **76 E4** 15 0N 103 0 E
Buriti Alegre, *Brazil* **155 E2** 18 9 S 49 3W
Buriti Bravo, *Brazil* **154 C3** 5 50 S 43 50W
Buriti dos Lopes, *Brazil* **154 B3** 3 10 S 41 52W
Burj Sāfitā, *Syria* **84 C3** 34 48N 36 7 E
Burji, *Ethiopia* **95 F4** 5 29N 37 51 E
Burkburnett, *U.S.A.* **139 H5** 34 6N 98 34W
Burke, *U.S.A.* **142 C6** 47 31N 115 49W
Burke →, *Australia* **114 C2** 23 12 S 139 33 E
Burketown, *Australia* **114 B2** 17 45 S 139 33 E
Burkettsville, *U.S.A.* **141 D12** 40 21N 84 39W
Burkina Faso ■, *Africa* **100 C4** 12 0N 1 0W
Burk's Falls, *Canada* **128 C4** 45 37N 79 24W
Burley, *U.S.A.* **142 E7** 42 32N 113 48W
Burlingame, *U.S.A.* **144 H4** 37 35N 122 21W
Burlington, *Canada* **136 C5** 43 18N 79 45W
Burlington, *Colo., U.S.A.* **138 F3** 39 18N 102 16W
Burlington, *Ill., U.S.A.* **141 B8** 42 3N 88 33W
Burlington, *Iowa, U.S.A.* **140 D5** 40 49N 91 14W
Burlington, *Kans., U.S.A.* **138 F7** 38 12N 95 45W
Burlington, *Ky., U.S.A.* **141 E12** 39 2N 84 43W
Burlington, *N.C., U.S.A.* **135 G6** 36 6N 79 26W
Burlington, *N.J., U.S.A.* **137 F10** 40 4N 74 51W
Burlington, *Vt., U.S.A.* **137 B11** 44 29N 73 12W
Burlington, *Wash., U.S.A.* **144 B4** 48 28N 122 20W
Burlington, *Wis., U.S.A.* **134 D1** 42 41N 88 17W
Burlyu-Tyube, *Kazakhstan* **56 E8** 46 30N 79 10 E
Burma ■, *Asia* **78 E6** 21 0N 96 30 E
Burnaby I., *Canada* **130 C2** 52 25N 131 19W
Burnamwood, *Australia* **117 A6** 31 7 S 144 53 E
Burnet, *U.S.A.* **139 K5** 30 45N 98 14W
Burney, *U.S.A.* **142 F3** 40 53N 121 40W
Burngup, *Australia* **113 F2** 33 2 S 118 42 E
Burnham, *U.S.A.* **136 F7** 40 38N 77 34W
Burnie, *Australia* **114 G4** 41 4 S 145 56 E
Burnley, *U.K.* **16 D5** 53 47N 2 15W
Burnoye, *Kazakhstan* **55 B5** 42 36N 70 47 E
Burns, *Oreg., U.S.A.* **142 E4** 43 35N 119 3W
Burns, *Wyo., U.S.A.* **138 E2** 41 12N 104 21W
Burns Lake, *Canada* **130 C3** 54 20N 125 45W
Burnside →, *Canada* **126 B9** 66 51N 108 4W
Burnside, L., *Australia* **113 E3** 25 22 S 123 0 E
Burnt River, *Canada* **136 B6** 44 41N 78 42W
Burntwood →, *Canada* **131 B9** 56 8N 96 34W
Burntwood L., *Canada* **131 B8** 55 22N 100 26W
Burqān, *Kuwait* **84 D5** 29 0N 47 57 E
Burra, *Australia* **116 B3** 33 40 S 138 55 E
Burragorang, L., *Australia* **117 B9** 33 52 S 150 37 E
Burramurra, *Australia* **114 C2** 20 25 S 137 15 E
Burreli, *Albania* **44 C2** 41 36N 20 1 E
Burren Junction, *Australia* **115 E4** 30 7 S 148 59 E
Burrendong, L., *Australia* **117 B8** 32 45 S 149 10 E
Burrendong Dam, *Australia* **115 E4** 32 39 S 149 6 E
Burriana, *Spain* **34 F4** 39 50N 0 4W
Burrinjuck Res., *Australia* **117 C8** 35 0 S 148 36 E
Burro, Serranías del, *Mexico* **146 B4** 29 0N 102 0W
Burruyacú, *Argentina* **158 B3** 26 30 S 64 40W
Burry Port, *U.K.* **17 F3** 51 41N 4 17W
Bursa, *Turkey* **88 C3** 40 15N 29 5 E
Bursa □, *Turkey* **88 C3** 40 10N 30 0 E
Burseryd, *Sweden* **15 G7** 57 12N 13 17 E
Burstall, *Canada* **131 C7** 50 39N 109 54W
Burton, *U.S.A.* **141 B13** 43 0N 83 40W
Burton L., *Canada* **128 B4** 54 45N 78 20W
Burton upon Trent, *U.K.* **16 E6** 52 48N 1 39W
Burtundy, *Australia* **116 B5** 33 45 S 142 15 E
Buru, *Indonesia* **72 B3** 3 30 S 126 30 E
Buruanga, *Phil.* **71 F3** 11 51N 121 53 E
Burullus, Bahra el, *Egypt* **94 H7** 31 25N 31 0 E

180 Burūm

Burūm, *Yemen* **87 D5** 14 22N 48 59 E
Burûn, Râs, *Egypt* **91 D2** 31 14N 33 7 E
Burunday, *Kazakhstan* **55 B8** 43 20N 76 51 E
Burundi ■, *Africa* **106 C3** 3 15 S 30 0 E
Bururi, *Burundi* **106 C2** 3 57 S 29 37 E
Burutu, *Nigeria* **101 D6** 5 20N 5 29 E
Burwell, *U.S.A.* **138 E5** 41 47N 99 8W
Bury, *U.K.* **16 D5** 53 36N 2 19W
Bury St. Edmunds, *U.K.* **17 E8** 52 15N 0 42 E
Buryat Republic □, *Russia* **57 D11** 53 0N 110 0 E
Buryn, *Ukraine* **50 F8** 51 13N 33 50 E
Burzenin, *Poland* **47 D5** 51 28N 18 47 E
Busalla, *Italy* **38 D5** 44 34N 8 58 E
Busango Swamp, *Zambia* **107 E2** 14 15 S 25 45 E
Buşayrah, *Syria* **84 C4** 35 9N 40 26 E
Buşayyah, *Iraq* **84 D5** 30 0N 46 10 E
Busca, *Italy* **38 D4** 44 31N 7 29 E
Bushati, *Albania* **44 C1** 41 58N 19 34 E
Būshehr, *Iran* **85 D6** 28 55N 50 55 E
Būshehr □, *Iran* **85 D6** 28 20N 51 45 E
Bushell, *Canada* **131 B7** 59 31N 108 45W
Bushenyi, *Uganda* **106 C3** 0 35 S 30 10 E
Bushire = Būshehr, *Iran* **85 D6** 28 55N 50 55 E
Bushnell, *Ill., U.S.A.* **138 E9** 40 33N 90 31W
Bushnell, *Nebr., U.S.A.* **138 E3** 41 14N 103 54W
Busia □, *Kenya* **106 B3** 0 25N 34 6 E
Busie, *Ghana* **100 C4** 10 29N 2 22W
Businga, *Zaïre* **102 B4** 3 16N 20 59 E
Buskerud fylke □, *Norway* **14 D3** 60 13N 9 0 E
Busko Zdrój, *Poland* **47 E7** 50 28N 20 42 E
Buslei, *Ethiopia* **108 C2** 5 28N 44 25 E
Busoga □, *Uganda* **106 B3** 0 5N 33 30 E
Busovača, *Bos.-H.* **42 C2** 44 6N 17 53 E
Busra ash Shām, *Syria* **91 C5** 32 30N 36 25 E
Bussang, *France* **23 E13** 47 50N 6 50 E
Busselton, *Australia* **113 F2** 33 42 S 115 15 E
Busseto, *Italy* **38 D7** 44 59N 10 2 E
Bussigny, *Switz.* **28 C3** 46 33N 6 33 E
Bussum, *Neths.* **20 D6** 52 16N 5 10 E
Bustamante, B., *Argentina* **160 C3** 45 5 S 66 18W
Busto, C., *Spain* **36 B4** 43 34N 6 28W
Busto Arsizio, *Italy* **38 C5** 45 40N 8 50 E
Busu-Djanoa, *Zaïre* **102 B4** 1 43N 21 23 E
Busuanga, *Phil.* **70 E2** 12 10N 120 0 E
Busuanga, *Phil.* **70 E2** 12 14N 119 52 E
Büsum, *Germany* **26 A4** 54 7N 8 50 E
Buta, *Zaïre* **106 B1** 2 50N 24 53 E
Butare, *Rwanda* **106 C2** 2 31 S 29 52 E
Butaritari, *Kiribati* **122 G9** 3 30N 174 0 E
Bute, *Australia* **116 B3** 33 51 S 138 2 E
Bute, *U.K.* **18 F3** 55 48N 5 2W
Bute Inlet, *Canada* **130 C4** 50 40N 124 53W
Butemba, *Uganda* **106 B3** 1 9N 31 37 E
Butembo, *Zaïre* **106 B2** 0 9N 29 18 E
Butera, *Italy* **41 E7** 37 10N 14 10 E
Bütgenbach, *Belgium* **21 H8** 50 26N 6 12 E
Butha Qi, *China* **65 B7** 48 0N 122 32 E
Buthidaung, *Burma* **78 E4** 20 52N 92 32 E
Butiaba, *Uganda* **106 B3** 1 50N 31 20 E
Butkhāk, *Afghan.* **79 B3** 34 30N 69 22 E
Butler, *Ind., U.S.A.* **141 C12** 41 26N 84 52W
Butler, *Ky., U.S.A.* **141 F12** 38 47N 84 22W
Butler, *Mo., U.S.A.* **140 F2** 38 16N 94 20W
Butler, *Pa., U.S.A.* **136 F5** 40 52N 79 54W
Butom Odrzánski, *Poland* **47 D2** 51 44N 15 48 E
Bütschwil, *Switz.* **29 B8** 47 23N 9 5 E
Butte, *Mont., U.S.A.* **142 C7** 46 0N 112 32W
Butte, *Nebr., U.S.A.* **138 D5** 42 58N 98 51W
Butte Creek →, *U.S.A.* **144 F5** 39 12N 121 56W
Butterworth = Gcuwa, *S. Africa* **105 E4** 32 20 S 28 11 E
Butterworth, *Malaysia* **77 K3** 5 24N 100 23 E
Buttfield, Mt., *Australia* **113 D4** 24 45 S 128 9 E
Button B., *Canada* **131 B10** 58 45N 94 23W
Buttonwillow, *U.S.A.* **145 K7** 35 24N 119 28W
Butty Hd., *Australia* **113 F3** 33 54 S 121 39 E
Butuan, *Phil.* **71 G5** 8 57N 125 33 E
Butuku-Luba, *Eq. Guin.* **101 E6** 3 29N 8 33 E
Butulan, *Phil.* **71 J5** 5 38N 125 26 E
Butung, *Indonesia* **72 C2** 5 0S 122 45 E
Buturlinovka, *Russia* **51 F12** 50 50N 40 35 E
Butzbach, *Germany* **26 E4** 50 24N 8 40 E
Bützow, *Germany* **26 B7** 53 51N 11 59 E
Buug, *Phil.* **71 H4** 7 40N 123 2 E
Buxar, *India* **81 G10** 25 34N 83 58 E
Buxton, *Guyana* **153 B6** 6 48N 58 2W
Buxton, *S. Africa* **104 D3** 27 38 S 24 42 E
Buxton, *U.K.* **16 D6** 53 16N 1 54W
Buxy, *France* **23 F11** 46 44N 4 40 E
Buy, *Russia* **51 B12** 58 28N 41 28 E
Buyaga, *Russia* **57 D13** 59 50N 127 0 E
Buynaksk, *Russia* **53 E12** 42 48N 47 7 E
Büyük Kemikli Burun, *Turkey* **44 D8** 40 20N 26 15 E
Büyük Menderes →, *Turkey* **88 E2** 37 28N 27 11 E
Büyükçekmece, *Turkey* **43 F13** 41 2N 28 35 E
Buzançais, *France* **22 F8** 46 54N 1 25 E
Buzău, *Romania* **46 D7** 45 10N 26 50 E
Buzău □, *Romania* **46 D7** 45 20N 26 30 E
Buzău →, *Romania* **46 D8** 45 26N 27 44 E
Buzău, Pasul, *Romania* **46 D7** 45 35N 26 12 E
Buzen, *Japan* **62 D3** 33 35N 131 5 E
Buzet, *Croatia* **39 C10** 45 24N 13 58 E
Buzi →, *Mozam.* **107 F3** 19 50 S 34 43 E
Buziaş, *Romania* **46 D2** 45 38N 21 36 E
Buzuluk, *Russia* **54 E3** 52 48N 52 12 E
Buzuluk →, *Russia* **51 F13** 50 15N 42 7 E
Buzzards Bay, *U.S.A.* **137 E14** 41 45N 70 37W
Bwagaoia, *Papua N. G.* **120 F7** 10 40 S 152 52 E
Bwana Mkubwe, *Zaïre* **107 E2** 13 8 S 28 38 E
Byala, *Ruse, Bulgaria* **43 D10** 43 28N 25 44 E
Byala, *Varna, Bulgaria* **43 E12** 42 53N 27 55 E
Byala Slatina, *Bulgaria* **43 D8** 43 26N 23 55 E
Byandovan, Mys, *Azerbaijan* **53 G13** 39 45N 49 28 E
Bychawa, *Poland* **47 D9** 51 1N 22 36 E
Byczyna, *Poland* **47 D5** 51 7N 18 12 E
Bydgoszcz, *Poland* **47 B5** 53 10N 18 0 E
Bydgoszcz □, *Poland* **47 B4** 53 16N 17 33 E
Byelarus = Belorussia ■, *Europe* **50 E5** 53 30N 27 0 E
Byelorussia = Belorussia ■, *Europe* **50 E5** 53 30N 27 0 E
Byers, *U.S.A.* **138 F2** 39 43N 104 14W
Byesville, *U.S.A.* **136 G3** 39 58N 81 32W
Byhalia, *U.S.A.* **139 H10** 34 52N 89 41W
Bykhov, *Belorussia* **50 E7** 53 31N 30 14 E
Bykovo, *Russia* **53 B11** 49 50N 45 25 E
Bylas, *U.S.A.* **143 K8** 33 8N 110 7W
Bylderup, *Denmark* **15 K3** 54 57N 9 6 E
Bylot I., *Canada* **127 A12** 73 13N 78 34W
Byrd, C., *Antarctica* **7 C17** 69 38 S 76 7W
Byro, *Australia* **113 E2** 26 5 S 116 11 E
Byrock, *Australia* **117 A7** 30 40 S 146 27 E
Byron, *U.S.A.* **140 B7** 42 8N 89 15W
Byron Bay, *Australia* **115 D5** 28 43 S 153 37 E
Byrranga, Gory, *Russia* **57 B11** 75 0N 100 0 E
Byrranga Mts. = Byrranga, Gory, *Russia* **57 B11** 75 0N 100 0 E
Byrum, *Denmark* **15 G5** 57 16N 11 0 E
Byske, *Sweden* **12 D16** 64 57N 21 11 E
Byske älv →, *Sweden* **12 D16** 64 57N 21 13 E
Bystrovka, *Kirghizia* **55 B7** 42 47N 75 42 E
Bystrzyca →, *Lublin, Poland* **47 D9** 51 21N 22 46 E
Bystrzyca →, *Wrocław, Poland* **47 D3** 51 12N 16 55 E
Bystrzyca Kłodzka, *Poland* **47 E3** 50 19N 16 39 E
Byten, *Belorussia* **50 E4** 52 50N 25 27 E
Bytom, *Poland* **47 E5** 50 25N 18 54 E
Bytów, *Poland* **47 A4** 54 10N 17 30 E
Byumba, *Rwanda* **106 C3** 1 35 S 30 4 E
Bzenec, *Czech.* **31 C10** 48 58N 17 18 E
Bzura →, *Poland* **47 C7** 52 25N 20 15 E

C

C.I.S. = Commonwealth of Independent States ■, *Eurasia* **57 D11** 60 0N 100 0 E
Ca →, *Vietnam* **76 C5** 18 45N 105 45 E
Ca Mau = Quan Long, *Vietnam* **77 H5** 9 7N 105 8 E
Ca Mau, Mui = Bai Bung, Mui, *Vietnam* **77 H5** 8 38N 104 44 E
Ca Na, *Vietnam* **77 G7** 11 20N 108 54 E
Caacupé, *Paraguay* **158 B4** 25 23 S 57 5W
Caála, *Angola* **103 E3** 12 46 S 15 30 E
Caamano Sd., *Canada* **130 C3** 52 55N 129 25W
Caapiranga, *Brazil* **153 D5** 3 18 S 61 13W
Caazapá, *Paraguay* **158 B4** 26 8 S 56 19W
Caazapá □, *Paraguay* **159 B4** 26 10 S 56 0W
Cabadbaran, *Phil.* **71 G5** 9 10N 125 38 E
Cabagan, *Phil.* **70 C3** 17 26N 121 46 E
Cabalian, *Phil.* **71 F5** 10 16N 125 10 E
Caballeria, C. de, *Spain* **33 A11** 40 5N 4 5 E
Cabana, *Peru* **156 B2** 8 25 S 78 5W
Cabanaconde, *Peru* **156 D3** 15 38 S 71 58W
Cabañaquinta, *Spain* **36 B5** 43 10N 5 38W
Cabanatuan, *Phil.* **70 D3** 15 30N 120 58 E
Cabanes, *Spain* **34 E5** 40 9N 0 2 E
Cabangon, *Phil.* **70 D3** 15 10N 120 3 E
Cabanillas, *Peru* **156 D3** 15 36 S 70 28W
Cabano, *Canada* **129 C6** 47 40N 68 56W
Čabar, *Croatia* **39 C11** 45 36N 14 39 E
Cabarroquis, *Phil.* **70 C3** 16 50N 121 30 E
Cabarruyan I., *Phil.* **70 C2** 16 18N 119 59 E
Cabazon, *U.S.A.* **145 M10** 33 55N 116 47W
Cabcaben, *Phil.* **70 D3** 14 27N 120 35 E
Cabedelo, *Brazil* **154 C5** 7 0S 34 50W
Cabery, *U.S.A.* **141 D8** 41 0N 88 12W
Cabeza del Buey, *Spain* **37 G5** 38 44N 5 13W
Cabildo, *Chile* **158 C1** 32 30 S 71 5W
Cabimas, *Venezuela* **152 A3** 10 23N 71 25W
Cabinda, *Angola* **103 D2** 5 33 S 12 11 E
Cabinda □, *Angola* **103 D2** 5 0S 12 30 E
Cabinet Mts., *U.S.A.* **142 C6** 48 0N 115 30W
Cabiri, *Angola* **103 D2** 8 52 S 13 39 E
Cabo Blanco, *Argentina* **160 C3** 47 15 S 65 47W
Cabo Frio, *Brazil* **155 F3** 22 51 S 42 3W
Cabo Pantoja, *Peru* **152 D2** 1 0S 75 10W
Cabo Raso, *Argentina* **160 B3** 44 20 S 65 15W
Cabonga, Réservoir, *Canada* **128 C4** 47 20N 76 40W
Cabool, *U.S.A.* **139 G8** 37 7N 92 6W
Caboolture, *Australia* **115 D5** 27 5 S 152 58 E
Cabora Bassa Dam = Cahora Bassa Dam, *Mozam.* **107 F3** 15 20 S 32 50 E
Caborca, *Mexico* **146 A2** 30 40N 112 10W
Cabot, Mt., *U.S.A.* **137 B13** 44 30N 71 25W
Cabot Str., *Canada* **129 C8** 47 15N 59 40W
Cabra, *Spain* **37 H6** 37 30N 4 28W
Cabra del Santo Cristo, *Spain* **35 H1** 37 42N 3 16W
Cábras, *Italy* **40 C1** 39 57N 8 30 E
Cabrera, I., *Spain* **33 B9** 39 8N 2 57 E
Cabrera, Sierra, *Spain* **36 C4** 42 12N 6 40W
Cabri, *Canada* **131 C7** 50 35N 108 25W
Cabriel →, *Spain* **35 F3** 39 14N 1 3W
Cabruta, *Venezuela* **152 B4** 7 50N 66 10W
Cabucgayan, *Phil.* **71 F5** 11 29N 124 34 E
Cabugao, *Phil.* **70 C3** 17 48N 120 27 E
Cabulauan Is., *Phil.* **71 F3** 11 25N 120 8 E
Caburan = Jose Abad Santos, *Phil.* **71 J5** 5 55N 125 39 E
Cabuyaro, *Colombia* **152 C3** 4 18N 72 49W
Çacabelos, *Spain* **36 C4** 42 36N 6 44W
Čačak, *Serbia* **42 D5** 43 54N 20 20 E
Cacao, *Fr. Guiana* **153 C7** 4 33N 52 26W
Cáceres, *Brazil* **157 D6** 16 5 S 57 40W
Cáceres, *Colombia* **152 B2** 7 35N 75 20W
Cáceres, *Spain* **37 F4** 39 26N 6 23W
Cáceres □, *Spain* **37 F4** 39 45N 6 0W
Cache Bay, *Canada* **128 C4** 46 22N 80 0W
Cache Cr. →, *U.S.A.* **144 G5** 38 42N 121 42W
Cachepo, *Portugal* **37 H3** 37 20N 7 49W
Cachéu, *Guinea-Biss.* **100 C1** 12 14N 16 8W
Cachi, *Argentina* **158 B2** 25 5 S 66 10W
Cachimbo, *Brazil* **157 B7** 8 57 S 54 54W
Cachimbo, Serra do, *Brazil* **157 B6** 9 30 S 55 30W
Cachingues, *Angola* **103 E3** 13 5 S 16 43 E
Cachoeira, *Brazil* **155 D4** 12 30 S 39 0W
Cachoeira Alta, *Brazil* **155 E1** 18 48 S 50 58W
Cachoeira de Itapemirim, *Brazil* **155 F3** 20 51 S 41 7W
Cachoeira do Sul, *Brazil* **159 C5** 30 3 S 52 53W
Cachoeiro do Arari, *Brazil* **154 B2** 1 1 S 48 58W
Cachopo, *Portugal* **37 H3** 37 20N 7 49W
Cachuela Esperanza, *Bolivia* **157 C4** 10 32 S 65 38W
Cacólo, *Angola* **103 E3** 10 9 S 19 21 E
Caconda, *Angola* **103 E3** 13 48 S 15 8 E
Cacongo, *Angola* **103 D2** 5 11 S 12 5 E
Caçu, *Brazil* **155 E1** 18 37 S 51 4W
Cacula, *Angola* **103 E2** 14 29 S 14 10 E
Caculé, *Brazil* **155 D3** 14 30 S 42 13W
Cacuso, *Angola* **103 D3** 9 25 S 15 45 E
Çadarache, *France* **25 E9** 43 41N 5 43 E
Čadca, *Slovak Rep.* **31 B11** 49 26N 18 45 E
Caddo, *U.S.A.* **139 H6** 34 7N 96 16W
Cadell Cr. →, *Australia* **114 C3** 22 35 S 141 51 E
Cadenazzo, *Switz.* **29 D7** 46 9N 8 57 E
Cader Idris, *U.K.* **16 E4** 52 43N 3 56W
Cadí, Sierra del, *Spain* **34 C6** 42 17N 1 42 E
Cadibarrawirracanna, L., *Australia* **115 D2** 28 52 S 135 27 E
Cadillac, *Canada* **128 C4** 48 14N 78 23W
Cadillac, *France* **24 D3** 44 38N 0 20W
Cadillac, *U.S.A.* **134 C3** 44 15N 85 24W
Cadiz, *Phil.* **71 F4** 10 57N 123 15 E
Cádiz, *Spain* **37 J4** 36 30N 6 20W
Cadiz, *U.S.A.* **136 F4** 40 22N 81 0W
Cádiz □, *Spain* **37 J5** 36 36N 5 45W
Cádiz, G. de, *Spain* **37 J4** 36 40N 7 0W
Cadney Park, *Australia* **115 D1** 27 55 S 134 3 E
Cadomin, *Canada* **130 C5** 53 2N 117 20W
Cadotte →, *Canada* **130 B5** 56 43N 117 10W
Cadours, *France* **24 E5** 43 44N 1 2 E
Cadoux, *Australia* **113 F2** 30 46 S 117 7 E
Caen, *France* **22 C6** 49 10N 0 22W
Caernarfon, *U.K.* **16 D3** 53 8N 4 17W
Caernarfon B., *U.K.* **16 D3** 53 4N 4 40W
Caernarvon = Caernarfon, *U.K.* **16 D3** 53 8N 4 17W
Caerphilly, *U.K.* **17 F4** 51 34N 3 13W
Caesarea, *Israel* **91 C3** 32 30N 34 53 E
Caeté, *Brazil* **155 E3** 19 55 S 43 40W
Caetité, *Brazil* **155 D3** 13 50 S 42 32W
Cafayate, *Argentina* **158 B2** 26 2 S 66 0W
Cafifi, *Colombia* **152 B3** 5 13N 71 4W
Cafu, *Angola* **103 F3** 16 30 S 15 8 E
Cagayan □, *Phil.* **70 B3** 18 0N 121 50 E
Cagayan →, *Phil.* **70 B3** 18 25N 121 42 E
Cagayan de Oro, *Phil.* **71 G5** 8 30N 124 40 E
Cagayan Is., *Phil.* **71 G3** 9 40N 121 16 E
Cagayan Sulu I., *Phil.* **71 H2** 7 1N 118 30 E
Cagli, *Italy* **39 E9** 43 32N 12 38 E
Cágliari, *Italy* **40 C2** 39 15N 9 6 E
Cágliari, G. di, *Italy* **40 C2** 39 8N 9 10 E
Cagnano Varano, *Italy* **41 A8** 41 49N 15 47 E
Cagnes-sur-Mer, *France* **25 E11** 43 40N 7 9 E
Caguán →, *Colombia* **152 D3** 0 8 S 74 18W
Caguas, *Puerto Rico* **149 C6** 18 14N 66 2W
Caha Mts., *Ireland* **19 E2** 51 45N 9 40W
Cahama, *Angola* **103 F2** 16 17 S 14 19 E
Caher, *Ireland* **19 D4** 52 23N 7 56W
Cahersiveen, *Ireland* **19 E1** 51 57N 10 13W
Cahora Bassa Dam, *Mozam.* **107 F3** 15 20 S 32 50 E
Cahore Pt., *Ireland* **19 D5** 52 34N 6 11W
Cahors, *France* **24 D5** 44 27N 1 27 E
Cahuapanas, *Peru* **156 B2** 5 15 S 77 0W
Cahuinari →, *Colombia* **152 D3** 1 21 S 70 44W
Cai Bau, Dao, *Vietnam* **76 B6** 21 10N 107 27 E
Cai Nuoc, *Vietnam* **77 H5** 8 56N 105 1 E
Caia, *Mozam.* **107 F4** 17 51 S 35 24 E
Caiabis, Serra dos, *Brazil* **157 C6** 11 30 S 56 30W
Caianda, *Angola* **103 E4** 11 2 S 23 31 E
Caiapó, Serra do, *Brazil* **157 D7** 17 0 S 52 0W
Caiapônia, *Brazil* **157 D7** 16 57 S 51 49W
Caibarién, *Cuba* **148 B4** 22 30N 79 30W
Caibiran, *Phil.* **71 F5** 11 34N 124 35 E
Caicara, *Bolívar, Venezuela* **152 B4** 7 38N 66 10W
Caicara, *Monagas, Venezuela* **153 B5** 9 52N 63 38W
Caicó, *Brazil* **154 C4** 6 20 S 37 0W
Caicos Is., *W. Indies* **149 B5** 21 40N 71 40W
Caicos Passage, *W. Indies* **149 B5** 22 45N 72 45W
Cailloma, *Peru* **156 D3** 15 9 S 71 45W
Caine →, *Bolivia* **157 D4** 18 23 S 65 21W
Caird Coast, *Antarctica* **7 D1** 75 0 S 25 0W
Cairn Gorm, *U.K.* **18 D5** 57 7N 3 40W
Cairn Toul, *U.K.* **18 D5** 57 3N 3 44W
Cairngorm Mts., *U.K.* **18 D5** 57 6N 3 42W
Cairns, *Australia* **114 B4** 16 57 S 145 45 E
Cairo = El Qâhira, *Egypt* **94 H7** 30 1N 31 14 E
Cairo, *Ga., U.S.A.* **135 K3** 30 52N 84 13W
Cairo, *Ill., U.S.A.* **139 G10** 37 0N 89 11W
Cairo Montenotte, *Italy* **38 D5** 44 23N 8 16 E
Caithness, Ord of, *U.K.* **18 C5** 58 9N 3 37W
Caiundo, *Angola* **103 F3** 15 50 S 17 28 E
Caiza, *Bolivia* **157 E4** 20 2 S 65 40W
Cajabamba, *Peru* **156 B2** 7 38 S 78 4W
Cajamarca, *Peru* **156 B2** 7 5 S 78 28W
Cajamarca □, *Peru* **156 B2** 6 15 S 78 50W
Cajapió, *Brazil* **154 B3** 2 58 S 44 48W
Cajarc, *France* **24 D5** 44 29N 1 50 E
Cajatambo, *Peru* **156 C2** 10 30 S 77 2W
Cajàzeiras, *Brazil* **154 C4** 6 52 S 38 30W
Čajetina, *Serbia* **42 D4** 43 47N 19 42 E
Cajidiocan, *Phil.* **70 E4** 12 22N 122 41 E
Čajniče, *Bos.-H.* **42 D4** 43 34N 19 5 E
Çakirgol, *Turkey* **53 F8** 40 33N 39 40 E
Čakovec, *Croatia* **39 B13** 46 23N 16 26 E
Çal, *Turkey* **88 D3** 38 4N 29 23 E
Cala, *Spain* **37 H4** 37 59N 6 21W
Cala →, *Spain* **37 H4** 37 38N 6 5W
Cala Cadolar, Punta de, *Spain* **35 G6** 38 38N 1 35 E
Cala d'Or, *Spain* **33 B10** 39 23N 3 14 E
Cala Figuera, C., *Spain* **33 B9** 39 27N 2 31 E
Cala Forcat, *Spain* **33 A10** 40 0N 3 47 E
Cala Mayor, *Spain* **33 B9** 39 33N 2 37 E
Cala Mezquida, *Spain* **33 B11** 39 55N 4 16 E
Cala Millor, *Spain* **33 B10** 39 35N 3 22 E
Cala Ratjada, *Spain* **33 B10** 39 43N 3 27 E
Calabanga, *Phil.* **70 E4** 13 42N 123 17 E
Calabar, *Nigeria* **101 E6** 4 57N 8 20 E
Calabozo, *Venezuela* **152 B4** 9 0N 67 28W
Calábria □, *Italy* **41 C9** 39 24N 16 30 E
Calaburras, Pta. de, *Spain* **37 J6** 36 30N 4 38W
Calaceite, *Spain* **34 D5** 41 1N 0 11 E
Calacota, *Bolivia* **156 D4** 17 16 S 68 38W
Calafat, *Romania* **46 F3** 43 58N 22 59 E
Calafate, *Argentina* **160 D2** 50 19 S 72 15W
Calahorra, *Spain* **34 C3** 42 18N 1 59W
Calais, *France* **23 B8** 50 57N 1 56 E
Calais, *U.S.A.* **129 C6** 45 11N 67 17W
Calais, Pas de, *France* **23 B8** 50 30N 1 20 E
Calalaste, Cord. de, *Argentina* **158 B2** 25 0 S 67 0W
Calalayan, *Phil.* **71 F2** 11 30N 119 38 E
Calama, *Brazil* **157 B5** 8 0 S 62 50W
Calama, *Chile* **158 A2** 22 30 S 68 55W
Calamar, *Bolívar, Colombia* **152 A3** 10 15N 74 55W
Calamar, *Vaupés, Colombia* **152 C3** 1 58N 72 32W
Calamarca, *Bolivia* **156 D4** 16 55 S 68 9W
Calamba, *Cavite, Phil.* **71 G4** 8 35N 123 39 E
Calamba, *Misamis, Phil.* **71 F4** 10 11N 123 17 E
Calamba, *Negros, Phil.* **70 D3** 14 13N 121 10 E
Calamian Group, *Phil.* **71 F2** 11 50N 119 55 E
Calamocha, *Spain* **34 E3** 40 50N 1 17W
Calán Porter, *Spain* **33 B11** 39 52N 4 8 E
Calañas, *Spain* **37 H4** 37 40N 6 53W
Calanda, *Spain* **34 E4** 40 56N 0 15W
Calandagan I., *Phil.* **71 F3** 10 39N 120 15 E
Calandula, *Angola* **103 D3** 9 6 S 15 57 E
Calang, *Indonesia* **74 B1** 4 37N 95 37 E
Calangiánus, *Italy* **40 B2** 40 56N 9 12 E
Calanscio, Sarīr, *Libya* **96 C4** 27 0N 21 30 E
Calapan, *Phil.* **70 E3** 13 25N 121 7 E
Calape, *Phil.* **71 G4** 9 54N 123 52 E
Călăraşi, *Romania* **46 E8** 44 12N 27 20 E
Călăraşi □, *Romania* **46 E8** 44 10N 27 0 E
Calasparra, *Spain* **35 G3** 38 14N 1 41W
Calatafimi, *Italy* **40 E5** 37 56N 12 50 E
Calatagan, *Phil.* **70 E3** 13 50N 120 38 E
Calatayud, *Spain* **34 D3** 41 20N 1 40W
Calato = Kálathos, *Greece* **45 H10** 36 9N 28 8 E
Calauag, *Phil.* **70 E4** 13 55N 122 15 E
Calavà, C., *Italy* **41 D7** 38 11N 14 55 E
Calavite, C., *Phil.* **70 E3** 13 26N 120 20 E
Calavite Pass, *Phil.* **70 E3** 13 36N 120 25 E
Calayan, *Phil.* **70 B3** 19 16N 121 28 E
Calayan I., *Phil.* **70 B3** 19 20N 121 27 E
Calbayog, *Phil.* **70 E5** 12 4N 124 38 E
Calbe, *Germany* **26 D7** 51 57N 11 47 E
Calca, *Peru* **156 C3** 13 22 S 72 0W
Calcasieu L., *U.S.A.* **139 L8** 29 55N 93 18W
Calci, *Italy* **38 E7** 43 44N 10 31 E
Calcutta, *India* **81 H13** 22 36N 88 24 E
Caldaro, *Italy* **39 B8** 46 23N 11 15 E
Caldas □, *Colombia* **152 B2** 5 15N 75 30W
Caldas da Rainha, *Portugal* **37 F1** 39 24N 9 8W
Caldas de Reyes, *Spain* **36 C2** 42 36N 8 39W
Caldas Novas, *Brazil* **155 E2** 17 45 S 48 38W
Calder →, *U.K.* **16 D6** 53 44N 1 21W
Caldera, *Chile* **158 B1** 27 5 S 70 55W
Caldwell, *Idaho, U.S.A.* **142 E5** 43 40N 116 41W
Caldwell, *Kans., U.S.A.* **139 G6** 37 2N 97 37W
Caldwell, *Tex., U.S.A.* **139 K6** 30 32N 96 42W
Caledon, *S. Africa* **104 E2** 34 14 S 19 26 E
Caledon →, *S. Africa* **104 E4** 30 31 S 26 5 E
Caledon B., *Australia* **114 A2** 12 45 S 137 0 E
Caledonia, *Canada* **136 C5** 43 7N 79 58W
Caledonia, *Mo., U.S.A.* **140 G6** 37 45N 90 46W
Caledonia, *N.Y., U.S.A.* **136 D7** 42 58N 77 51W
Calella, *Spain* **34 D7** 41 37N 2 40 E
Calemba, *Angola* **104 B2** 16 0S 15 44 E
Calenzana, *France* **25 F12** 42 31N 8 51 E
Caleta Olivia, *Argentina* **160 C3** 46 25 S 67 25W
Calexico, *U.S.A.* **145 N11** 32 40N 115 30W
Calf of Man, *U.K.* **16 C3** 54 3N 4 49W
Calgary, *Canada* **130 C6** 51 0N 114 10W
Calheta, *Madeira* **33 D2** 32 44N 17 11W
Calhoun, *U.S.A.* **135 H3** 34 30N 84 57W
Cali, *Colombia* **152 C2** 3 25N 76 35W
Calicut, *India* **83 J2** 11 15N 75 43 E
Caliente, *U.S.A.* **143 H6** 37 37N 114 31W
California, *Mo., U.S.A.* **140 F4** 38 38N 92 34W
California, *Pa., U.S.A.* **136 F5** 40 4N 79 54W
California □, *U.S.A.* **143 H4** 37 30N 119 30W
California, Baja, *Mexico* **146 A1** 32 10N 115 12W
California, Baja, T.N. □, *Mexico* **146 B2** 30 0N 115 0W
California, Baja, T.S. □, *Mexico* **146 B2** 25 50N 111 50W
California, G. de, *Mexico* **146 B2** 27 0N 111 0W
California City, *U.S.A.* **145 K9** 35 10N 117 55W
California Hot Springs, *U.S.A.* **145 K8** 35 51N 118 41W
Călimăneşti, *Romania* **46 D5** 45 14N 24 20 E
Călimani, Munţii, *Romania* **46 B5** 47 12N 25 0 E
Călineşti, *Romania* **46 D5** 45 21N 24 18 E
Calingasta, *Argentina* **158 C2** 31 15 S 69 30W
Calinog, *Phil.* **71 F4** 11 7N 122 32 E
Calintaan, *Phil.* **70 E3** 12 35N 120 57 E
Calipatria, *U.S.A.* **145 M11** 33 8N 115 31W
Calistoga, *U.S.A.* **144 G4** 38 35N 122 35W
Calitri, *Italy* **41 B8** 40 54N 15 25 E
Calitzdorp, *S. Africa* **104 E3** 33 33 S 21 42 E
Callabonna, L., *Australia* **115 D3** 29 40 S 140 5 E
Callac, *France* **22 D3** 48 25N 3 27W
Callan, *Ireland* **19 D4** 52 33N 7 25W
Callander, *U.K.* **18 E4** 56 15N 4 14W
Callang, *Phil.* **70 C3** 17 2N 121 38 E
Callantsoog, *Neths.* **20 C5** 52 50N 4 42 E
Callao, *Peru* **156 C2** 12 0 S 77 0W
Callaway, *U.S.A.* **138 E5** 41 18N 99 56W
Callender, *U.S.A.* **140 B2** 42 22N 94 17W
Calles, *Mexico* **147 C5** 23 2N 98 42W
Callide, *Australia* **114 C5** 24 18 S 150 28 E
Calling Lake, *Canada* **130 B6** 55 15N 113 12W
Calliope, *Australia* **114 C5** 24 0 S 151 16 E
Callosa de Ensarriá, *Spain* **35 G4** 38 40N 0 8W
Callosa de Segura, *Spain* **35 G4** 38 1N 0 53W
Calmar, *U.S.A.* **140 A5** 43 11N 91 52W
Calola, *Angola* **103 F3** 16 25 S 17 48 E
Calolbon, *Phil.* **70 E5** 13 36N 124 6 E
Caloocan, *Phil.* **70 D3** 14 39N 120 58 E

Champagne, Plaine de 183

Castres, *France* 24 E6 43 37N 2 13 E
Castricum, *Neths.* 20 C5 52 33N 4 40 E
Castries, *St. Lucia* 149 D7 14 2N 60 58W
Castril, *Spain* 35 H2 37 48N 2 46W
Castro, *Brazil* 159 A5 24 45 S 50 0W
Castro, *Chile* 160 B2 42 30 S 73 50W
Castro Alves, *Brazil* 155 D4 12 46 S 39 33W
Castro del Río, *Spain* 37 H6 37 41N 4 29W
Castro Marim, *Portugal* 37 H3 37 13N 7 26W
Castro Urdiales, *Spain* 34 B1 43 23N 3 11W
Castro Verde, *Portugal* 37 H2 37 41N 8 4W
Castrojeriz, *Spain* 36 C6 42 17N 4 9W
Castropol, *Spain* 36 B3 43 32N 7 0W
Castroreale, *Italy* 41 D8 38 5N 15 15 E
Castrovillari, *Italy* 41 C9 39 49N 16 11 E
Castroville, *Calif., U.S.A.* 144 J5 36 46N 121 45W
Castroville, *Tex., U.S.A.* 139 L5 29 21N 98 53W
Castrovirreyna, *Peru* 156 C2 13 20 S 75 18W
Castuera, *Spain* 37 G5 38 43N 5 37W
Casummit Lake, *Canada* 128 B1 51 29N 92 22W
Caswell Sound, *N.Z.* 119 E2 44 59 S 167 8 E
Çat, *Turkey* 89 D9 39 40N 41 3 E
Cat Ba, Dao, *Vietnam* 76 B6 20 50N 107 0 E
Cat I., *Bahamas* 149 B4 24 30N 75 30W
Cat I., *U.S.A.* 139 K10 30 14N 89 6W
Cat L., *Canada* 128 B1 51 40N 91 50W
Čata, *Slovak Rep.* 31 D11 47 58N 18 38 E
Catabola, *Angola* 103 E3 12 9 S 17 16 E
Catacamas, *Honduras* 148 D2 14 54N 85 56W
Catacáos, *Peru* 156 B1 5 20 S 80 45W
Cataguases, *Brazil* 155 F3 21 23 S 42 39W
Catagupan, *Phil.* 71 G1 8 1N 116 58 E
Catahoula L., *U.S.A.* 139 K8 31 31N 92 7W
Çatak, *Turkey* 89 D10 38 1N 43 8 E
Catalão, *Brazil* 155 E2 18 10 S 47 57W
Çatalca, *Turkey* 88 C3 41 8N 28 27 E
Catalina, *Canada* 129 C9 48 31N 53 4W
Catalonia = Cataluña □, *Spain* 34 D6 41 40N 1 15 E
Cataluña □, *Spain* 34 D6 41 40N 1 15 E
Çatalzeytin, *Turkey* 88 C6 41 57N 34 12 E
Catamarca, *Argentina* 158 B2 28 30 S 65 50W
Catamarca □, *Argentina* 158 B2 27 0 S 65 50W
Catanauan, *Phil.* 70 E4 13 36N 122 19 E
Catanduanes, *Phil.* 70 E5 13 50N 124 20 E
Catanduva, *Brazil* 159 A6 21 5 S 48 58W
Catánia, *Italy* 41 E8 37 31N 15 4 E
Catánia, G. di, *Italy* 41 E8 37 25N 15 8 E
Catanzaro, *Italy* 41 D9 38 54N 16 38 E
Cataonia, *Turkey* 88 E6 37 30N 36 0 E
Catarman, *Camiguin, Phil.* 71 G5 9 8N 124 40 E
Catarman, *N. Samar, Phil.* 70 E5 12 28N 124 35 E
Catbalogan, *Phil.* 71 F5 11 46N 124 53 E
Cateel, *Phil.* 71 H6 7 47N 126 24 E
Cateel Bay, *Phil.* 71 H6 7 54N 126 25 E
Catende, *Angola* 103 E4 11 14 S 21 30 E
Catende, *Brazil* 154 C4 8 40 S 35 43W
Catete, *Angola* 103 D2 9 6 S 13 43 E
Cathcart, *Australia* 117 D8 36 52 S 149 24 E
Cathcart, *S. Africa* 104 E4 32 18 S 27 10 E
Cathlamet, *U.S.A.* 144 D3 46 12N 123 23W
Catio, *Guinea-Biss.* 100 C1 11 17N 15 15W
Catismiña, *Venezuela* 153 C5 4 5N 63 40W
Catita, *Brazil* 154 C3 9 31 S 43 1W
Catlettsburg, *U.S.A.* 134 F4 38 25N 82 36W
Catlin, *U.S.A.* 141 D9 40 4N 87 42W
Catmon, *Phil.* 71 F5 10 43N 124 1 E
Catoche, C., *Mexico* 147 C7 21 40N 87 8W
Catolé do Rocha, *Brazil* 154 C4 6 21 S 37 45W
Catral, *Spain* 35 G4 38 10N 0 47W
Catria, Mt., *Italy* 39 E9 43 28N 12 42 E
Catrimani, *Brazil* 153 C5 0 27N 61 41W
Catrimani →, *Brazil* 153 C5 0 28N 61 44W
Catskill, *U.S.A.* 137 D11 42 14N 73 52W
Catskill Mts., *U.S.A.* 137 D10 42 10N 74 25W
Catt, Mt., *Australia* 114 A1 13 49 S 134 23 E
Cattaraugus, *U.S.A.* 136 D6 42 22N 78 52W
Cattólica, *Italy* 39 E9 43 58N 12 43 E
Cattólica Eraclea, *Italy* 40 E6 37 27N 13 24 E
Catu, *Brazil* 155 D4 12 21 S 38 23W
Catuala, *Angola* 103 F3 16 25 S 19 2 E
Catumbela, *Angola* 103 E2 12 25 S 13 34 E
Catur, *Mozam.* 107 E4 13 45 S 35 30 E
Catwick Is., *Vietnam* 77 G7 10 0N 109 0 E
Cauayan, *Phil.* 70 C3 16 56N 121 46 E
Cauca □, *Colombia* 152 C2 2 30N 76 50W
Cauca →, *Colombia* 152 B3 8 54N 74 28W
Caucaia, *Brazil* 154 B4 3 40 S 38 35W
Caucasia, *Colombia* 152 B2 8 0N 75 12W
Caucasus = Bolshoi Kavkas, *Asia* 53 E11 42 50N 44 0 E
Caudebec-en-Caux, *France* 22 C7 49 30N 0 42 E
Caudete, *Spain* 35 G3 38 42N 1 2W
Caudry, *France* 23 B10 50 7N 3 22 E
Caulnes, *France* 22 D4 48 18N 2 10W
Caulónia, *Italy* 41 D9 38 23N 16 25 E
Caúngula, *Angola* 103 D3 8 26 S 18 38 E
Cauquenes, *Chile* 158 D1 36 0 S 72 22W
Caura →, *Venezuela* 153 B5 7 38N 64 53W
Caurés →, *Brazil* 153 D5 1 21 S 62 20W
Cauresi →, *Mozam.* 107 F3 17 8 S 33 0 E
Causapscal, *Canada* 129 C6 48 19N 67 12W
Caussade, *France* 24 D5 44 10N 1 33 E
Causse-Méjean, *France* 24 D7 44 18N 3 42 E
Cauterets, *France* 24 F3 42 52N 0 8W
Cautín □, *Chile* 160 A2 39 0 S 72 30W
Caux, Pays de, *France* 22 C7 49 38N 0 35 E
Cava dei Tirreni, *Italy* 41 B7 40 42N 14 42 E
Cávado →, *Portugal* 36 D2 41 32N 8 48W
Cavaillon, *France* 25 E9 43 50N 5 2 E
Cavalaire-sur-Mer, *France* 25 E10 43 10N 6 33 E
Cavalcante, *Brazil* 155 D2 13 48 S 47 30W
Cavalese, *Italy* 39 B8 46 17N 11 29 E
Cavalier, *U.S.A.* 138 A6 48 48N 97 37W
Cavalla = Cavally →, *Africa* 100 E3 4 22N 7 32W
Cavalli Is., *N.Z.* 118 B2 35 0 S 173 58 E
Cavallo, I. de, *France* 25 G13 41 22N 9 16 E
Cavally →, *Africa* 100 E3 4 22N 7 32W
Cavan, *Ireland* 19 C4 54 0N 7 22W
Cavan □, *Ireland* 19 C4 53 58N 7 10W
Cavárzere, *Italy* 39 C9 45 8N 12 6 E
Cave City, *U.S.A.* 134 G3 37 8N 85 58W
Cavenagh Ra., *Australia* 113 E4 26 12 S 127 55 E
Cavendish, *Australia* 116 D5 37 31 S 142 2 E
Caviana, I., *Brazil* 153 C7 0 10N 50 10W
Cavite, *Phil.* 70 D3 14 29N 120 55 E
Cavite □, *Phil.* 70 D3 14 15N 120 50 E
Cavour, *Italy* 38 D4 44 47N 7 22 E
Cavtat, *Croatia* 42 E3 42 35N 18 13 E
Cavuşcu Gölü, *Turkey* 88 D4 38 22N 31 53 E
Cawkers Well, *Australia* 116 A5 31 41 S 142 57 E
Cawndilla L., *Australia* 116 B5 32 30 S 142 15 E
Cawnpore = Kanpur, *India* 81 F9 26 28N 80 20 E
Caxias, *Brazil* 154 B3 4 55 S 43 20W
Caxias do Sul, *Brazil* 159 B5 29 10 S 51 10W
Caxine, C., *Algeria* 99 A4 35 56N 0 27W
Caxito, *Angola* 103 D2 8 30 S 13 30 E
Caxopa, *Angola* 103 E4 11 52 S 20 52 E
Çay, *Turkey* 88 D4 38 35N 31 1 E
Cay Sal Bank, *Bahamas* 148 B3 23 45N 80 0W
Cayambe, *Ecuador* 152 C2 0 2N 77 59W
Cayambe, *Ecuador* 152 C2 0 3N 78 8W
Çaycuma, *Turkey* 88 C5 41 25N 32 4 E
Çayeli, *Turkey* 89 C9 41 5N 40 45 E
Cayenne, *Fr. Guiana* 153 B7 5 5N 52 18W
Cayenne □, *Fr. Guiana* 153 C7 5 0N 53 0W
Cayeux-sur-Mer, *France* 23 B8 50 10N 1 30 E
Cayiralan, *Turkey* 88 D6 39 17N 35 38 E
Caylus, *France* 24 D5 44 15N 1 47 E
Cayman Brac, *Cayman Is.* 148 C4 19 43N 79 49W
Cayman Is. ■, *W. Indies* 148 C3 19 40N 80 30W
Cayo Romano, *Cuba* 149 B4 22 0N 78 0W
Cayuga, *Canada* 136 D5 42 59N 79 50W
Cayuga, *Ind., U.S.A.* 141 E9 39 57N 87 28W
Cayuga, *N.Y., U.S.A.* 137 D8 42 54N 76 44W
Cayuga L., *U.S.A.* 137 D8 42 41N 76 41W
Cazaje, *Angola* 103 E4 11 2 S 20 45 E
Cazalla de la Sierra, *Spain* 37 H5 37 56N 5 45W
Căzăneşti, *Romania* 46 E8 44 36N 27 3 E
Cazaux et de Sanguinet, Étang de, *France* 24 D2 44 29N 1 10W
Cazères, *France* 24 E5 43 13N 1 5 E
Cazin, *Bos.-H.* 39 D12 44 57N 15 57 E
Čazma, *Croatia* 39 C13 45 45N 16 39 E
Čazma →, *Croatia* 39 C13 45 35N 16 29 E
Cazombo, *Angola* 103 E4 11 54 S 22 56 E
Cazorla, *Spain* 35 H1 37 55N 3 2W
Cazorla, *Venezuela* 152 B4 8 1N 67 0W
Cazorla, Sierra de, *Spain* 35 G2 38 5N 2 55W
Cea →, *Spain* 36 C5 42 0N 5 36W
Ceamurlia de Jos, *Romania* 46 E9 44 43N 28 47 E
Ceanannus Mor, *Ireland* 19 C5 53 42N 6 53W
Ceará = Fortaleza, *Brazil* 154 B4 3 45 S 38 35W
Ceará □, *Brazil* 154 C4 5 0 S 40 0W
Ceará Mirim, *Brazil* 154 C4 5 38 S 35 25W
Ceauru, L., *Romania* 46 E4 44 58N 23 11 E
Cebaco, I. de, *Panama* 148 E3 7 33N 81 9W
Cebollar, *Argentina* 158 B2 29 10 S 66 35W
Cebollera, Sierra de, *Spain* 34 D2 42 0N 2 30W
Cebreros, *Spain* 36 E6 40 27N 4 28W
Cebu, *Phil.* 71 F4 10 18N 123 54 E
Ceccano, *Italy* 40 A6 41 34N 13 18 E
Cece, *Hungary* 31 E11 46 46N 18 39 E
Cechi, *Ivory C.* 100 D4 6 15N 4 25W
Čechy, *Czech.* 30 B6 49 58N 13 30 E
Cecil Plains, *Australia* 115 D5 27 30 S 151 11 E
Cécina, *Italy* 38 E7 43 19N 10 33 E
Cécina →, *Italy* 38 E7 43 19N 10 29 E
Ceclavin, *Spain* 36 F4 39 50N 6 45W
Cedar →, *U.S.A.* 140 C5 41 17N 91 21W
Cedar City, *U.S.A.* 143 H7 37 41N 113 4W
Cedar Creek Reservoir, *U.S.A.* 139 J6 32 11N 96 4W
Cedar Falls, *Iowa, U.S.A.* 140 B4 42 32N 92 27W
Cedar Falls, *Wash., U.S.A.* 144 C5 47 25N 121 45W
Cedar Grove, *U.S.A.* 141 E12 39 22N 84 56W
Cedar Key, *U.S.A.* 135 L4 29 8N 83 2W
Cedar L., *Canada* 131 C8 53 10N 100 0W
Cedar Lake, *U.S.A.* 141 C9 41 22N 87 26W
Cedar Point, *U.S.A.* 141 C13 41 44N 83 21W
Cedar Rapids, *U.S.A.* 140 C5 41 59N 91 40W
Cedartown, *U.S.A.* 135 H3 34 1N 85 15W
Cedarvale, *Canada* 130 B3 55 1N 128 22W
Cedarville, *S. Africa* 105 E4 30 23 S 29 3 E
Cedarville, *Calif., U.S.A.* 142 F3 41 32N 120 10W
Cedarville, *Ill., U.S.A.* 140 B7 42 23N 89 38W
Cedarville, *Ohio, U.S.A.* 141 E13 39 44N 83 49W
Cedeira, *Spain* 36 B2 43 39N 8 2W
Cedral, *Mexico* 146 C4 23 50N 100 42W
Cedrino →, *Italy* 40 B2 40 23N 9 44 E
Cedro, *Brazil* 154 C4 6 34 S 39 3W
Cedros, I. de, *Mexico* 146 B1 28 10N 115 20W
Ceduna, *Australia* 115 E1 32 7 S 133 46 E
Cedynia, *Poland* 47 C1 52 53N 14 12 E
Cefalù, *Italy* 41 D7 38 3N 14 1 E
Cega →, *Spain* 36 D6 41 33N 4 46W
Cegléd, *Hungary* 31 D12 47 11N 19 47 E
Céglie Messápico, *Italy* 41 B10 40 39N 17 31 E
Cehegín, *Spain* 35 G3 38 6N 1 48W
Ceheng, *China* 68 E5 24 58N 105 48 E
Cehu-Silvaniei, *Romania* 46 B4 47 24N 23 9 E
Ceica, *Romania* 46 C3 46 53N 22 10 E
Ceira →, *Portugal* 36 E2 40 13N 8 16W
Cekhira, *Tunisia* 96 B2 34 20N 10 5 E
Cela, *Angola* 103 E3 11 25 S 15 7 E
Celano, *Italy* 39 F10 42 6N 13 30 E
Celanova, *Spain* 36 C3 42 9N 7 58W
Celaya, *Mexico* 146 C4 20 31N 100 37W
Celbridge, *Ireland* 19 C5 53 20N 6 33W
Celebes = Sulawesi □, *Indonesia* 72 B2 2 0 S 120 0 E
Celebes Sea = Sulawesi Sea, *Indonesia* 72 A2 3 0N 123 0 E
Čelendín, *Peru* 156 B2 6 52 S 78 10W
Čelić, *Bos.-H.* 42 C3 44 43N 18 47 E
Celica, *Ecuador* 152 D2 4 7 S 79 59W
Celina, *U.S.A.* 141 D12 40 33N 84 35W
Celje, *Slovenia* 39 B12 46 16N 15 18 E
Celldömölk, *Hungary* 31 D10 47 16N 17 10 E
Celle, *Germany* 26 C6 52 37N 10 4 E
Celles, *Belgium* 21 G2 50 42N 3 28 E
Celorico da Beira, *Portugal* 36 E3 40 38N 7 24W
Cement, *U.S.A.* 139 H5 34 56N 98 8W
Çemişgezek, *Turkey* 89 D8 39 3N 38 56 E
Cenepa →, *Peru* 152 D2 4 40 S 78 10W
Cengong, *China* 68 D7 27 13N 108 44 E
Ceno →, *Italy* 38 D7 44 4N 10 5 E
Centallo, *Italy* 38 D4 44 30N 7 35 E
Centenário do Sul, *Brazil* 155 F1 22 48 S 51 36W
Center, *N. Dak., U.S.A.* 138 B4 47 7N 101 18W
Center, *Tex., U.S.A.* 139 K7 31 48N 94 11W
Center Point, *U.S.A.* 140 B5 42 12N 91 46W
Centerfield, *U.S.A.* 143 G8 39 8N 111 49W
Centerville, *Calif., U.S.A.* 144 J7 36 44N 119 30W
Centerville, *Iowa, U.S.A.* 140 D4 40 44N 92 52W
Centerville, *Mich., U.S.A.* 141 C11 41 55N 85 32W
Centerville, *Pa., U.S.A.* 136 F5 40 3N 79 59W
Centerville, *S. Dak., U.S.A.* 138 D6 43 7N 96 58W
Centerville, *Tenn., U.S.A.* 135 H2 35 47N 87 28W
Centerville, *Tex., U.S.A.* 139 K7 31 16N 95 59W
Cento, *Italy* 39 D8 44 43N 11 16 E
Central, *Brazil* 154 D3 11 8 S 42 8W
Central, *U.S.A.* 143 K9 32 47N 108 9W
Central □, *Kenya* 106 C4 0 30 S 37 30 E
Central □, *Malawi* 107 E3 13 30 S 33 30 E
Central □, *U.K.* 18 E4 56 10N 4 30W
Central □, *Zambia* 107 E2 14 25 S 28 50 E
Central, Cordillera, *Bolivia* 157 D5 18 30 S 64 55W
Central, Cordillera, *Colombia* 152 C2 5 0N 75 0W
Central, Cordillera, *Costa Rica* 148 D3 10 10N 84 5W
Central, Cordillera, *Dom. Rep.* 149 C5 19 15N 71 0W
Central, Cordillera, *Peru* 156 B2 7 0 S 77 30W
Central, Cordillera, *Phil.* 70 C3 17 20N 120 57 E
Central, Sistema, *Spain* 36 E5 40 40N 5 55W
Central African Rep. ■, *Africa* 102 A4 7 0N 20 0 E
Central City, *Ky., U.S.A.* 134 G2 37 18N 87 7W
Central City, *Nebr., U.S.A.* 138 E5 41 7N 98 0W
Central I., *Kenya* 106 B4 3 30N 36 0 E
Central Makran Range, *Pakistan* 79 D2 26 30N 64 15 E
Central Patricia, *Canada* 128 B1 51 30N 90 9W
Central Ra., *Papua N. G.* 120 C2 5 0 S 143 0 E
Central Russian Uplands, *Europe* 10 E13 54 0N 36 0 E
Central Siberian Plateau, *Russia* 58 C14 65 0N 105 0 E
Centralia, *Ill., U.S.A.* 140 F7 38 32N 89 8W
Centralia, *Mo., U.S.A.* 140 E4 39 13N 92 8W
Centralia, *Wash., U.S.A.* 144 D4 46 43N 122 58W
Centreville, *Ala., U.S.A.* 135 J2 32 57N 87 8W
Centreville, *Miss., U.S.A.* 139 K9 31 5N 91 4W
Centúripe, *Italy* 41 E7 37 37N 14 41 E
Cephalonia = Kefallinía, *Greece* 45 F2 38 20N 20 30 E
Čepin, *Croatia* 42 B3 45 32N 18 34 E
Ceprano, *Italy* 40 A6 41 33N 13 30 E
Ceptura, *Romania* 46 D7 45 1N 26 21 E
Cepu, *Indonesia* 75 D4 7 9 S 111 35 E
Ceram = Seram, *Indonesia* 73 B3 3 10 S 129 0 E
Ceram Sea = Seram Sea, *Indonesia* 72 B3 2 30 S 128 30 E
Cerbère, *France* 24 F7 42 26N 3 10 E
Cerbicales, Is., *France* 25 G13 41 33N 9 22 E
Cerbu, *Romania* 46 E5 44 46N 24 46 E
Cercal, *Portugal* 37 H2 37 48N 8 40W
Cercemaggiore, *Italy* 41 A7 41 27N 14 43 E
Cerdaña, *Spain* 34 C6 42 22N 1 35 E
Cerdedo, *Spain* 36 C2 42 33N 8 23W
Cère →, *France* 24 D5 44 55N 1 49 E
Cerea, *Italy* 39 C8 45 12N 11 13 E
Ceres, *Argentina* 158 B3 29 55 S 61 55W
Ceres, *Brazil* 155 E2 15 17 S 49 35W
Ceres, *Italy* 38 C4 45 19N 7 22 E
Ceres, *S. Africa* 104 E2 33 21 S 19 18 E
Ceres, *U.S.A.* 144 H6 37 35N 120 57W
Céret, *France* 24 F6 42 30N 2 42 E
Cereté, *Colombia* 152 B2 8 53N 75 48W
Cerfontaine, *Belgium* 21 H4 50 11N 4 26 E
Cerignola, *Italy* 41 A8 41 17N 15 53 E
Cerigo = Kíthira, *Greece* 45 H6 36 9N 23 12 E
Cérilly, *France* 24 B6 46 37N 2 50 E
Cerisiers, *France* 23 D10 48 8N 3 30 E
Cerizay, *France* 22 F6 46 50N 0 40W
Çerkeş, *Turkey* 88 C5 40 49N 32 52 E
Çerkezköy, *Turkey* 88 C2 41 17N 27 59 E
Cerknica, *Slovenia* 39 C11 45 48N 14 21 E
Cermerno, *Serbia* 42 D5 43 35N 20 25 E
Çermik, *Turkey* 89 D8 38 8N 39 26 E
Cerna, *Romania* 46 D9 45 4N 28 17 E
Cerna →, *Romania* 46 E5 44 15N 24 25 E
Cernavodă, *Romania* 46 E9 44 22N 28 3 E
Cernay, *France* 23 E14 47 44N 7 10 E
Cernik, *Croatia* 42 B2 45 17N 17 22 E
Cerralvo, I., *Mexico* 146 C3 24 20N 109 45W
Cerreto Sannita, *Italy* 41 A7 41 17N 14 34 E
Cerritos, *Mexico* 146 C4 22 27N 100 20W
Cerro Gordo, *U.S.A.* 141 E8 39 53N 88 44W
Cerro Sombrero, *Chile* 160 D3 52 45 S 69 15W
Certaldo, *Italy* 38 E8 43 32N 11 2 E
Cervaro →, *Italy* 41 A8 41 30N 15 52 E
Cervera, *Spain* 34 D6 41 40N 1 16 E
Cervera de Pisuerga, *Spain* 36 C6 42 51N 4 30W
Cervera del Río Alhama, *Spain* 34 C3 42 2N 1 58W
Cérvia, *Italy* 39 D9 44 15N 12 20 E
Cervignano del Friuli, *Italy* 39 C10 45 49N 13 20 E
Cervinara, *Italy* 41 A7 41 2N 14 36 E
Cervione, *France* 25 F13 42 20N 9 29 E
Cervo, *Spain* 36 B3 43 40N 7 24W
César □, *Colombia* 152 B3 9 0N 73 30W
Cesaro, *Italy* 41 E7 37 50N 14 38 E
Cesena, *Italy* 39 D9 44 9N 12 14 E
Cesenático, *Italy* 39 D9 44 12N 12 22 E
Cēsis, *Latvia* 50 C4 57 17N 25 28 E
Česká Lípa, *Czech.* 30 A7 50 45N 14 30 E
Česka Republika □, *Czech.* 30 B7 49 30N 14 40 E
Česká Třebová, *Czech.* 31 B9 49 54N 16 27 E
České Budějovice, *Czech.* 30 C7 48 55N 14 25 E
České Velenice, *Czech.* 30 C8 48 45N 15 1 E
Ceskomoravská Vrchovina, *Czech.* 30 B8 49 30N 15 40 E
Český Brod, *Czech.* 30 A7 50 4N 14 52 E
Český Krumlov, *Czech.* 30 C7 48 43N 14 21 E
Český Těšín, *Czech.* 31 B11 49 45N 18 39 E
Çeşme, *Turkey* 45 F8 38 20N 26 23 E
Cessnock, *Australia* 117 B9 32 50 S 151 21 E
Cestos →, *Liberia* 100 D3 5 40N 9 10W
Cetate, *Romania* 46 E4 44 7N 23 2 E
Cétin Grad, *Croatia* 39 C12 45 9N 15 45 E
Cetina →, *Croatia* 39 E13 43 26N 16 42 E
Cetinje, *Montenegro* 42 E3 42 23N 18 59 E
Cetraro, *Italy* 41 C8 39 30N 15 56 E
Ceuta, *Morocco* 98 A3 35 52N 5 18W
Ceva, *Italy* 38 D5 44 23N 8 3 E
Cévennes, *France* 24 D7 44 10N 3 50 E
Ceyhan, *Turkey* 88 E6 37 4N 35 47 E
Ceyhan →, *Turkey* 88 E6 36 38N 35 40 E
Ceylânpınar, *Turkey* 89 E9 36 50N 40 2 E
Ceylon = Sri Lanka ■, *Asia* 83 L5 7 30N 80 50 E
Cèze →, *France* 25 D8 44 6N 4 43 E
Cha-am, *Thailand* 76 F2 12 48N 99 58 E
Chá Pungana, *Angola* 103 E3 13 44 S 18 39 E
Chaam, *Neths.* 21 E5 51 30N 4 52 E
Chabeuil, *France* 25 D9 44 54N 5 3 E
Chablais, *France* 25 B10 46 20N 6 36 E
Chablis, *France* 23 E10 47 47N 3 48 E
Chabounia, *Algeria* 99 A5 35 30N 2 38 E
Chacabuco, *Argentina* 158 C3 34 40 S 60 27W
Chachapoyas, *Peru* 156 B2 6 15 S 77 50W
Chachasp, *Peru* 156 D3 15 30 S 72 15W
Chachoengsao, *Thailand* 76 F3 13 42N 101 5 E
Chachro, *Pakistan* 80 G4 25 5N 70 15 E
Chaco □, *Argentina* 158 B3 26 30 S 61 0W
Chaco □, *Paraguay* 158 B3 26 0 S 60 0W
Chad ■, *Africa* 97 F3 15 0N 17 15 E
Chad, L. = Tchad, L., *Chad* 97 F2 13 30N 14 30 E
Chadan, *Russia* 57 D10 51 17N 91 35 E
Chadileuvú →, *Argentina* 158 D2 37 46 S 66 0W
Chadiza, *Zambia* 107 E3 14 45 S 32 27 E
Chadron, *U.S.A.* 138 D3 42 50N 103 0W
Chadyr-Lunga, *Moldavia* 52 C3 46 3N 28 51 E
Chae Hom, *Thailand* 76 C2 18 43N 99 35 E
Chaem →, *Thailand* 76 C2 18 11N 98 38 E
Chaeryŏng, *N. Korea* 67 E13 38 24N 125 36 E
Chagda, *Russia* 57 D14 58 45N 130 38 E
Chagny, *France* 23 F11 46 57N 4 45 E
Chagoda, *Russia* 50 B9 59 10N 35 15 E
Chagos Arch., *Ind. Oc.* 58 K11 6 0 S 72 0 E
Chāh Ākhvor, *Iran* 85 C8 32 41N 59 40 E
Chāh Bahār, *Iran* 85 E9 25 20N 60 40 E
Chāh-e-Malek, *Iran* 85 D8 28 35N 59 7 E
Chāh Gay Hills, *Afghan.* 79 C1 29 30N 64 0 E
Chāh Kavīr, *Iran* 85 D7 31 45N 54 52 E
Chahār Borjak, *Afghan.* 79 C1 30 17N 62 3 E
Chahtung, *Burma* 78 B7 26 41N 98 10 E
Chaillé-les-Marais, *France* 24 B2 46 25N 1 2W
Chainat, *Thailand* 76 E3 15 11N 100 8 E
Chaitén, *Chile* 160 B2 42 55 S 72 43W
Chaiya, *Thailand* 77 H2 9 23N 99 14 E
Chaj Doab, *Pakistan* 80 C5 32 15N 73 0 E
Chajari, *Argentina* 158 C4 30 42 S 58 0W
Chakaria, *Bangla.* 78 E4 21 45N 92 5 E
Chake Chake, *Tanzania* 106 D4 5 15 S 39 45 E
Chakhānsūr, *Afghan.* 79 C1 31 10N 62 0 E
Chakonipau, L., *Canada* 129 A6 56 18N 68 30W
Chakradharpur, *India* 81 H11 22 45N 85 40 E
Chakwadam, *Burma* 78 B7 27 29N 98 31 E
Chakwal, *Pakistan* 79 B4 32 56N 72 53 E
Chala, *Peru* 156 D3 15 48 S 74 20W
Chalais, *France* 24 C4 45 16N 0 3 E
Chalakudi, *India* 83 J3 10 18N 76 20 E
Chalchihuites, *Mexico* 146 C4 23 29N 103 53W
Chalcis = Khalkís, *Greece* 45 F5 38 27N 23 42 E
Chaleur B., *Canada* 129 C6 47 55N 65 30W
Chalfant, *U.S.A.* 144 H8 37 32N 118 21W
Chalhuanca, *Peru* 156 C3 14 15 S 73 15W
Chalindrey, *France* 23 E12 47 43N 5 26 E
Chaling, *China* 69 D9 26 58N 113 30 E
Chalisgaon, *India* 82 D2 20 30N 75 10 E
Chalkar, *Kazakhstan* 53 A14 50 40N 51 53 E
Chalkar, Ozero, *Kazakhstan* 53 A14 50 50N 51 50 E
Chalky Inlet, *N.Z.* 119 G1 46 3 S 166 31 E
Challans, *France* 22 F5 46 50N 1 52W
Challapata, *Bolivia* 156 D4 18 53 S 66 50W
Challis, *U.S.A.* 142 D6 44 30N 114 14W
Chalna, *India* 81 H13 22 36N 89 35 E
Chalon-sur-Saône, *France* 23 F11 46 48N 4 50 E
Chalonnes-sur-Loire, *France* 22 E6 47 20N 0 45W
Châlons-sur-Marne, *France* 23 D11 48 58N 4 20 E
Châlus, *France* 24 C4 45 39N 0 58 E
Chalyaphum, *Thailand* 76 E4 15 48N 102 2 E
Cham, *Germany* 27 F8 49 12N 12 40 E
Cham, *Switz.* 29 B6 47 11N 8 28 E
Cham, Cu Lao, *Vietnam* 76 E7 15 57N 108 30 E
Chama, *U.S.A.* 143 H10 36 54N 106 35W
Chamah, Gunong, *Malaysia* 74 A2 5 13N 101 35 E
Chaman, *Pakistan* 79 C2 30 58N 66 25 E
Chamba, *India* 80 C7 32 35N 76 10 E
Chamba, *Tanzania* 107 E4 11 37 S 37 0 E
Chambal →, *India* 81 F8 26 29N 79 15 E
Chamberlain, *U.S.A.* 138 D5 43 49N 99 20W
Chamberlain →, *Australia* 112 C4 15 30 S 127 54 E
Chambers, *U.S.A.* 143 J9 35 11N 109 26W
Chambersburg, *U.S.A.* 134 F7 39 56N 77 40W
Chambéry, *France* 25 C9 45 34N 5 55 E
Chambly, *Canada* 137 A11 45 27N 73 17W
Chambord, *Canada* 129 C5 48 25N 72 6W
Chambri L., *Papua N. G.* 120 C2 4 15 S 143 10 E
Chamchamal, *Iraq* 84 C5 35 32N 44 50 E
Chamela, *Mexico* 146 D3 19 32N 105 5W
Chamical, *Argentina* 158 C2 30 22 S 66 27W
Chamkar Luong, *Cambodia* 77 G4 11 0N 103 45 E
Chamois, *U.S.A.* 140 F5 38 41N 91 46W
Chamonix-Mont-Blanc, *France* 25 C10 45 55N 6 51 E
Champa, *India* 81 H10 22 2N 82 43 E
Champagne, *Canada* 130 A1 60 49N 136 30W
Champagne, *France* 23 D11 48 40N 4 20 E
Champagne, Plaine de, *France* 23 D11 49 0N 4 30 E

184 Champagnole

Champagnole, *France* **23 F12** 46 45N 5 55 E
Champaign, *U.S.A.* **141 D8** 40 7N 88 15W
Champassak, *Laos* **76 E5** 14 53N 105 52 E
Champaubert, *France* **23 D10** 48 50N 3 45 E
Champdeniers, *France* **24 B3** 46 29N 0 25W
Champeix, *France* **24 C7** 45 37N 3 8 E
Champlain, *Canada* **134 B9** 46 27N 72 24W
Champlain, *U.S.A.* **137 B11** 44 59N 73 27W
Champlain, L., *U.S.A.* **137 B11** 44 40N 73 20W
Champotón, *Mexico* **147 D6** 19 20N 90 50W
Chamrajnagar, *India* **83 J3** 11 52N 76 52 E
Chamusca, *Portugal* **37 F2** 39 21N 8 29W
Chan Chan, *Peru* **156 B2** 8 7 S 79 0W
Chana, *Thailand* **77 J3** 6 55N 100 44 E
Chañaral, *Chile* **158 B1** 26 23 S 70 40W
Chanārān, *Iran* **85 B8** 36 39N 59 6 E
Chanasma, *India* **80 H5** 23 44N 72 5 E
Chancay, *Peru* **156 C2** 11 32 S 77 25W
Chancy, *Switz.* **28 D1** 46 8N 5 58 E
Chandannagar, *India* **81 H13** 22 52N 88 24 E
Chandausi, *India* **81 E8** 28 27N 78 49 E
Chandeleur Is., *U.S.A.* **139 L10** 29 55N 88 57W
Chandeleur Sd., *U.S.A.* **139 L10** 29 55N 89 0W
Chandigarh, *India* **80 D7** 30 43N 76 47 E
Chandler, *Australia* **115 D1** 27 0 S 133 19 E
Chandler, *Canada* **129 C7** 48 18N 64 46W
Chandler, *Ariz., U.S.A.* **143 K8** 33 18N 111 50W
Chandler, *Okla., U.S.A.* **139 H6** 35 42N 96 53W
Chandlers Pk., *Australia* **117 A9** 30 15 S 151 48 E
Chandless →, *Brazil* **156 B4** 9 8 S 69 51W
Chandpur, *Bangla.* **78 D3** 23 8N 90 45 E
Chandpur, *India* **80 E8** 29 8N 78 19 E
Chandrapur, *India* **82 E4** 19 57N 79 25 E
Chānf, *Iran* **85 E9** 26 38N 60 29 E
Chang, *Pakistan* **80 F3** 26 59N 68 30 E
Chang, Ko, *Thailand* **77 F4** 12 0N 102 23 E
Ch'ang Chiang = Chang Jiang →, *China* **69 B13** 31 48N 121 10 E
Chang Jiang →, *China* **69 B13** 31 48N 121 10 E
Changa, *India* **81 C7** 33 53N 77 35 E
Changanacheri, *India* **83 K3** 9 25N 76 31 E
Changane →, *Mozam.* **105 C5** 24 30 S 33 30 E
Changbai, *China* **67 D15** 41 25N 128 5 E
Changbai Shan, *China* **67 C15** 42 20N 129 0 E
Changchiak'ou = Zhangjiakou, *China* **66 D8** 40 48N 114 55 E
Ch'angchou = Changzhou, *China* **69 B12** 31 47N 119 58 E
Changchun, *China* **67 C13** 43 57N 125 17 E
Changchunling, *China* **67 B13** 45 18N 125 27 E
Changde, *China* **69 C8** 29 4N 111 35 E
Changdo-ri, *N. Korea* **67 E14** 38 30N 127 40 E
Changfeng, *China* **69 A11** 32 28N 117 10 E
Changhai = Shanghai, *China* **69 B13** 31 15N 121 26 E
Changhua, *China* **69 B12** 30 12N 119 12 E
Changhŭng, *S. Korea* **67 G14** 34 41N 126 52 E
Changhŭngni, *N. Korea* **67 D15** 40 24N 128 19 E
Changi, *Malaysia* **74 B2** 1 23N 103 59 E
Changjiang, *China* **76 C7** 19 20N 108 55 E
Changjin, *N. Korea* **67 D14** 40 23N 127 15 E
Changjin-chŏsuji, *N. Korea* **67 D14** 40 30N 127 15 E
Changle, *China* **69 E12** 25 59N 119 27 E
Changli, *China* **67 E10** 39 40N 119 13 E
Changling, *China* **67 B12** 44 20N 123 58 E
Changlun, *Malaysia* **77 J3** 6 25N 100 26 E
Changning, *Hunan, China* **69 D9** 26 28N 112 22 E
Changning, *Yunnan, China* **68 E2** 24 45N 99 30 E
Changping, *China* **66 D9** 40 14N 116 12 E
Changsha, *China* **69 C9** 28 12N 113 0 E
Changshan, *China* **69 C12** 28 55N 118 27 E
Changshou, *China* **68 C6** 29 51N 107 8 E
Changshu, *China* **69 B13** 31 38N 120 43 E
Changshun, *China* **68 D6** 26 3N 106 25 E
Changtai, *China* **69 E11** 24 35N 117 42 E
Changting, *China* **69 E11** 25 50N 116 22 E
Changwu, *China* **66 G4** 35 10N 107 45 E
Changxing, *China* **69 B12** 31 0N 119 55 E
Changyang, *China* **69 B8** 30 30N 111 10 E
Changyi, *China* **67 F10** 36 40N 119 30 E
Changyŏn, *N. Korea* **67 E13** 38 15N 125 6 E
Changyuan, *China* **66 G8** 35 15N 114 42 E
Changzhi, *China* **66 F7** 36 10N 113 6 E
Changzhou, *China* **69 B12** 31 47N 119 58 E
Chanhanga, *Angola* **103 F2** 16 0 S 14 8 E
Chanlar, *Azerbaijan* **53 F12** 40 25N 46 10 E
Channapatna, *India* **83 H3** 12 40N 77 15 E
Channel Is., *U.K.* **17 H5** 49 30N 2 40W
Channel Is., *U.S.A.* **145 M7** 33 40N 119 15W
Channel-Port aux Basques, *Canada* **129 C8** 47 30N 59 9W
Channing, *Mich., U.S.A.* **134 B1** 46 9N 88 5W
Channing, *Tex., U.S.A.* **139 H3** 35 41N 102 20W
Chantada, *Spain* **36 C3** 42 36N 7 46W
Chanthaburi, *Thailand* **76 F4** 12 38N 102 12 E
Chantilly, *France* **23 C9** 49 12N 2 29 E
Chantonnay, *France* **22 F5** 46 40N 1 3W
Chantrey Inlet, *Canada* **126 B10** 67 48N 96 20W
Chanute, *U.S.A.* **139 G7** 37 41N 95 27W
Chanza →, *Spain* **37 H3** 37 32N 7 30W
Chao Hu, *China* **69 B11** 31 30N 117 30 E
Chao Phraya →, *Thailand* **76 F3** 13 32N 100 36 E
Chao Phraya Lowlands, *Thailand* **76 E3** 15 30N 100 0 E
Chao Xian, *China* **69 B11** 31 38N 117 50 E
Chao'an, *China* **69 F11** 23 42N 116 32 E
Chaocheng, *China* **66 F8** 36 4N 115 37 E
Chaoyang, *Guangdong, China* **69 F11** 23 17N 116 30 E
Chaoyang, *Liaoning, China* **67 D11** 41 35N 120 22 E
Chapada dos Guimarães, *Brazil* **157 D6** 15 26 S 55 45W
Chapala, *Mozam.* **107 F4** 15 50 S 37 35 E
Chapala, L. de, *Mexico* **146 C4** 20 10N 103 20W
Chaparé →, *Bolivia* **157 D5** 15 58 S 64 42W
Chaparmukh, *India* **78 B4** 26 12N 92 31 E
Chaparral, *Colombia* **152 C2** 3 43N 75 28W
Chapayevo, *Kazakhstan* **53 A14** 50 25N 51 10 E
Chapayevsk, *Russia* **51 E16** 53 0N 49 40 E
Chapecó, *Brazil* **159 B5** 27 14 S 52 41W
Chapel Hill, *U.S.A.* **135 H6** 35 55N 79 4W
Chapeyevo, *Kazakhstan* **54 F2** 50 12N 51 10 E
Chapin, *U.S.A.* **140 E6** 39 46N 90 24W
Chapleau, *Canada* **128 C3** 47 50N 83 24W
Chaplin, *Canada* **131 C7** 50 28N 106 40W
Chaplino, *Ukraine* **52 B7** 48 8N 36 15 E
Chaplygin, *Russia* **51 E12** 53 15N 40 0 E
Chapra = Chhapra, *India* **81 G11** 25 48N 84 44 E
Châr, *Mauritania* **98 D2** 21 32N 12 45W
Chara, *Russia* **57 D12** 56 54N 118 20 E
Charadai, *Argentina* **158 B4** 27 35 S 59 55W
Charagua, *Bolivia* **157 D5** 19 45 S 63 10W
Charalá, *Colombia* **152 B3** 6 17N 73 10W
Charambirá, Punta, *Colombia* **152 C2** 4 16N 77 32W
Charaña, *Bolivia* **156 D4** 17 30 S 69 25W
Charapita, *Colombia* **152 D3** 0 37 S 74 21W
Charata, *Argentina* **158 B3** 27 13 S 61 14W
Charcas, *Mexico* **146 C4** 23 10N 101 20W
Charcoal L., *Canada* **131 B8** 58 49N 102 22W
Chard, *U.K.* **17 G5** 50 52N 2 59W
Chardara, *Kazakhstan* **55 C3** 41 16N 67 59 E
Chardara, Step, *Kazakhstan* **55 B4** 42 20N 68 0 E
Chardarinskoye Vdkhr., *Kazakhstan* **55 C4** 41 10N 68 15 E
Chardon, *U.S.A.* **136 E3** 41 35N 81 12W
Charduar, *India* **78 B4** 26 51N 92 46 E
Chardzhou, *Turkmenistan* **55 D1** 39 6N 63 34 E
Charente □, *France* **24 C4** 45 50N 0 16 E
Charente →, *France* **24 C2** 45 57N 1 5W
Charente-Maritime □, *France* **24 C3** 45 45N 0 45W
Charentsavan, *Armenia* **53 F11** 40 35N 44 41 E
Chari →, *Chad* **97 F2** 12 58N 14 31 E
Chārīkār, *Afghan.* **79 B3** 35 0N 69 10 E
Chariton, *U.S.A.* **140 C3** 41 1N 93 19W
Chariton →, *U.S.A.* **140 E4** 39 19N 92 58W
Charity, *Guyana* **153 B6** 7 24N 58 36W
Chärjew = Chardzhou, *Turkmenistan* **55 D1** 39 6N 63 34 E
Charkhari, *India* **81 G8** 25 24N 79 45 E
Charkhi Dadri, *India* **80 E7** 28 37N 76 17 E
Charleroi, *Belgium* **21 H4** 50 24N 4 27 E
Charleroi, *U.S.A.* **136 F5** 40 9N 79 57W
Charles, C., *U.S.A.* **134 G8** 37 7N 75 58W
Charles City, *U.S.A.* **140 A4** 43 4N 92 41W
Charles L., *Canada* **131 B6** 59 50N 110 33W
Charles Sound, *N.Z.* **119 F2** 45 2 S 167 4 E
Charles Town, *U.S.A.* **134 F7** 39 17N 77 52W
Charleston, *Ill., U.S.A.* **134 F1** 39 30N 88 10W
Charleston, *Ill., U.S.A.* **141 E8** 39 30N 88 10W
Charleston, *Miss., U.S.A.* **139 H9** 34 1N 90 4W
Charleston, *Mo., U.S.A.* **139 G10** 36 55N 89 21W
Charleston, *S.C., U.S.A.* **135 J6** 32 46N 79 56W
Charleston, *W. Va., U.S.A.* **134 F5** 38 21N 81 38W
Charleston Peak, *U.S.A.* **145 J11** 36 16N 115 42W
Charlestown, *S. Africa* **105 D4** 27 26 S 29 53 E
Charlestown, *U.S.A.* **141 F11** 38 27N 85 40W
Charlesville, *Zaïre* **103 D4** 5 27 S 20 59 E
Charleville = Rath Luirc, *Ireland* **19 D3** 52 21N 8 40W
Charleville, *Australia* **115 D4** 26 24 S 146 15 E
Charleville-Mézières, *France* **23 C11** 49 44N 4 40 E
Charlevoix, *U.S.A.* **134 C3** 45 19N 85 16W
Charlieu, *France* **25 B8** 46 10N 4 10 E
Charlotte, *Mich., U.S.A.* **141 B12** 42 34N 84 50W
Charlotte, *N.C., U.S.A.* **135 H5** 35 13N 80 51W
Charlotte Amalie, *Virgin Is.* **149 C7** 18 21N 64 56W
Charlotte Harbor, *U.S.A.* **135 M4** 26 50N 82 10W
Charlottesville, *U.S.A.* **134 F6** 38 2N 78 30W
Charlottetown, *Canada* **129 C7** 46 14N 63 8W
Charlton, *Australia* **116 D5** 36 16 S 143 24 E
Charlton, *U.S.A.* **138 E8** 40 59N 93 20W
Charlton I., *Canada* **128 B4** 52 0N 79 20W
Charmes, *France* **23 D13** 48 22N 6 17 E
Charny, *Canada* **129 C5** 46 43N 71 15W
Charolles, *France* **25 B8** 46 27N 4 16 E
Chârost, *France* **23 F9** 46 58N 2 7 E
Charouine, *Algeria* **99 C4** 29 0N 0 15W
Charre, *Mozam.* **107 F4** 17 13 S 35 10 E
Charroux, *France* **24 B4** 46 9N 0 25 E
Charsadda, *Pakistan* **80 B4** 34 7N 71 45 E
Charters Towers, *Australia* **114 C4** 20 5 S 146 13 E
Chartres, *France* **22 D8** 48 29N 1 30 E
Charvakskoye Vdkhr., *Uzbekistan* **55 C5** 41 35N 70 0 E
Chascomús, *Argentina* **158 D4** 35 30 S 58 0W
Chasefu, *Zambia* **107 E3** 11 55 S 33 8 E
Chaslands Mistake, *N.Z.* **119 G4** 46 38 S 169 22 E
Chasovnya-Uchurskaya, *Russia* **57 D14** 57 15N 132 50 E
Chasseneuil-sur-Bonnieure, *France* **24 C4** 45 52N 0 29 E
Chāt, *Iran* **85 B7** 37 59N 55 16 E
Chatal Balkan = Udvoy Balkan, *Bulgaria* **43 E11** 42 50N 26 50 E
Château-Arnoux, *France* **25 D10** 44 6N 6 0 E
Château-Chinon, *France* **23 E10** 47 4N 3 56 E
Château d'Oex, *Switz.* **28 D4** 46 28N 7 8 E
Château-du-Loir, *France* **22 E7** 47 40N 0 25 E
Château-Gontier, *France* **22 E6** 47 50N 0 48W
Château-la-Vallière, *France* **22 E7** 47 30N 0 20 E
Château-Landon, *France* **23 D9** 48 8N 2 40 E
Château-Porcien, *France* **23 C11** 49 31N 4 13 E
Château-Renault, *France* **22 E7** 47 36N 0 56 E
Château-Salins, *France* **23 D13** 48 50N 6 30 E
Château-Thierry, *France* **23 C10** 49 3N 3 20 E
Châteaubourg, *France* **22 D5** 48 7N 1 25W
Châteaubriant, *France* **22 E5** 47 43N 1 23W
Châteaudun, *France* **22 D8** 48 3N 1 20 E
Châteaugiron, *France* **22 D5** 48 3N 1 30W
Châteaulin, *France* **22 D2** 48 11N 4 8W
Châteaumeillant, *France* **24 B6** 46 35N 2 12 E
Châteauneuf-du-Faou, *France* **22 D3** 48 11N 3 50W
Châteauneuf-en-Thymerais, *France* **22 D8** 48 35N 1 13 E
Châteauneuf-sur-Charente, *France* **24 C3** 45 36N 0 3W
Châteauneuf-sur-Cher, *France* **23 F9** 46 52N 2 18 E
Châteauneuf-sur-Loire, *France* **23 E9** 47 52N 2 13 E
Châteaurenard, *Bouches-du-Rhône, France* **25 E8** 43 53N 4 51 E
Châteaurenard, *Loiret, France* **23 E9** 47 56N 2 55 E
Châteauroux, *France* **23 F8** 46 50N 1 40 E
Châtel-St.-Denis, *Switz.* **28 C3** 46 32N 6 54 E
Châtelaillon-Plage, *France* **24 B2** 46 5N 1 5W
Châtelaudren, *France* **22 D4** 48 33N 2 59W
Châtelet, *Belgium* **21 H5** 50 24N 4 32 E
Châtelguyon, *France* **24 C7** 45 55N 3 4 E
Châtellerault, *France* **22 F7** 46 50N 0 30 E
Châtelus-Malvaleix, *France* **24 B6** 46 18N 2 1 E
Chatfield, *U.S.A.* **138 D9** 43 51N 92 11W
Chatham, *N.B., Canada* **129 C6** 47 2N 65 28W
Chatham, *Ont., Canada* **128 D3** 42 24N 82 11W
Chatham, *U.K.* **17 F8** 51 22N 0 32 E
Chatham, *Ill., U.S.A.* **140 E7** 39 40N 89 42W
Chatham, *La., U.S.A.* **139 J8** 32 18N 92 27W
Chatham, *N.Y., U.S.A.* **137 D11** 42 21N 73 36W
Chatham, I., *Chile* **160 D2** 50 40 S 74 25W
Chatham Is., *Pac. Oc.* **122 M10** 44 0 S 176 40W
Chatham Str., *U.S.A.* **130 B2** 57 0N 134 40W
Chatillon, *Italy* **38 C4** 45 45N 7 40 E
Châtillon-Coligny, *France* **23 E9** 47 50N 2 51 E
Châtillon-en-Bazois, *France* **23 E10** 47 3N 3 39 E
Châtillon-en-Diois, *France* **25 D9** 44 41N 5 29 E
Châtillon-sur-Indre, *France* **22 F8** 46 59N 1 10 E
Châtillon-sur-Loire, *France* **23 E9** 47 35N 2 44 E
Châtillon-sur-Marne, *France* **23 C10** 49 6N 3 44 E
Châtillon-sur-Seine, *France* **23 E11** 47 50N 4 33 E
Chatkal →, *Uzbekistan* **55 C5** 41 38N 70 1 E
Chatkalskiy Khrebet, *Kirghizia* **55 C5** 41 30N 70 45 E
Chatmohar, *Bangla.* **81 G13** 24 15N 89 15 E
Chatra, *India* **81 G11** 24 12N 84 56 E
Chatrapur, *India* **82 E7** 19 22N 85 2 E
Chats, L. des, *Canada* **137 A8** 45 30N 76 20W
Chatsworth, *Canada* **136 B4** 44 27N 80 54W
Chatsworth, *U.S.A.* **141 D8** 40 45N 88 18W
Chatsworth, *Zimbabwe* **107 F3** 19 38 S 31 13 E
Chatta-Hantō, *Japan* **63 C8** 34 45N 136 55 E
Chattahoochee →, *U.S.A.* **135 K3** 30 54N 84 57W
Chattanooga, *U.S.A.* **135 H3** 35 3N 85 19W
Chaturat, *Thailand* **76 E3** 15 40N 101 51 E
Chatyrkel, Ozero, *Kirghizia* **55 C7** 40 40N 75 18 E
Chatyrtash, *Kirghizia* **55 C8** 40 55N 76 25 E
Chau Doc, *Vietnam* **77 G5** 10 42N 105 7 E
Chaudanne, Barr. de, *France* **25 E10** 43 51N 6 32 E
Chaudes-Aigues, *France* **24 D7** 44 51N 3 1 E
Chauffailles, *France* **25 B8** 46 13N 4 20 E
Chauk, *Burma* **78 E5** 20 53N 94 49 E
Chaukan Pass, *Burma* **78 B6** 27 8N 97 10 E
Chaulnes, *France* **23 C9** 49 48N 2 47 E
Chaumont, *France* **23 D12** 48 7N 5 8 E
Chaumont, *U.S.A.* **137 B8** 44 4N 76 8W
Chaumont-en-Vexin, *France* **23 C8** 49 16N 1 53 E
Chaumont-sur-Loire, *France* **22 E8** 47 29N 1 11 E
Chaunay, *France* **24 B4** 46 13N 0 9 E
Chauny, *France* **23 C10** 49 37N 3 12 E
Chausey, Is., *France* **22 D5** 48 52N 1 49W
Chaussin, *France* **23 F12** 46 59N 5 22 E
Chautauqua L., *U.S.A.* **136 D5** 42 10N 79 24W
Chauvigny, *France* **22 F7** 46 34N 0 39 E
Chauvin, *Canada* **131 C6** 52 45N 110 10W
Chavantina, *Brazil* **157 C7** 14 40 S 52 21W
Chaves, *Brazil* **154 B2** 0 15 S 49 55W
Chaves, *Portugal* **36 D3** 41 45N 7 32W
Chavuma, *Zambia* **103 E4** 13 4 S 22 40 E
Chawang, *Thailand* **77 H2** 8 25N 99 30 E
Chayan, *Kazakhstan* **55 B4** 43 5N 69 25 E
Chayek, *Kirghizia* **55 C7** 41 55N 74 30 E
Chaykovskiy, *Russia* **54 C4** 56 47N 54 9 E
Chazelles-sur-Lyon, *France* **25 C8** 45 39N 4 22 E
Chazuta, *Peru* **156 B2** 6 30 S 76 0W
Chazy, *U.S.A.* **137 B11** 44 53N 73 26W
Cheb, *Czech.* **30 A5** 50 9N 12 28 E
Chebanse, *U.S.A.* **141 C9** 41 0N 87 54W
Chebarkul, *Russia* **54 D7** 55 0N 60 25 E
Cheboksary, *Russia* **51 C15** 56 8N 47 12 E
Cheboygan, *U.S.A.* **134 C3** 45 39N 84 29W
Chebsara, *Russia* **51 B11** 59 10N 38 59 E
Chech, Erg, *Africa* **98 D4** 25 0N 2 15W
Chechaouen, *Morocco* **98 A3** 35 9N 5 15W
Chechen, Os., *Russia* **53 E12** 43 59N 47 40 E
Checheno-Ingush Republic □, *Russia* **53 E11** 43 30N 45 29 E
Chechon, *S. Korea* **67 F15** 37 8N 128 12 E
Chęciny, *Poland* **47 E7** 50 46N 20 28 E
Checleset B., *Canada* **130 C3** 50 5N 127 35W
Checotah, *U.S.A.* **139 H7** 35 28N 95 31W
Chedabucto B., *Canada* **129 C7** 45 25N 61 8W
Cheduba I., *Burma* **78 F4** 18 45N 93 40 E
Cheepie, *Australia* **115 D4** 26 33 S 145 1 E
Chef-Boutonne, *France* **24 B3** 46 7N 0 4W
Chegdomyn, *Russia* **57 D14** 51 7N 133 1 E
Chegga, *Mauritania* **98 C3** 25 27N 5 40W
Chegutu, *Zimbabwe* **107 F3** 18 10 S 30 14 E
Chehalis, *U.S.A.* **144 D4** 46 40N 122 58W
Cheiron, Mt., *France* **25 E10** 43 49N 6 58 E
Cheju Do, *S. Korea* **67 H14** 33 29N 126 34 E
Chekalin, *Russia* **51 D10** 54 10N 36 10 E
Chekiang = Zhejiang □, *China* **69 C13** 29 0N 120 0 E
Chel = Kuru, Bahr el →, *Sudan* **95 F2** 8 10N 26 50 E
Chela, Sa. da, *Angola* **103 F2** 16 20 S 13 20 E
Chelan, *U.S.A.* **142 C4** 47 51N 120 1W
Chelan, L., *U.S.A.* **142 C3** 48 11N 120 30W
Cheleken, *Turkmenistan* **49 G9** 39 26N 53 7 E
Chelforó, *Argentina* **160 A3** 39 0 S 66 33W
Chéliff, O. →, *Algeria* **99 A5** 36 0N 0 8 E
Chelkar, *Kazakhstan* **56 E6** 47 48N 59 39 E
Chelkar Tengiz, Solonchak, *Kazakhstan* **56 E7** 48 0N 62 30 E
Chellala Dahrania, *Algeria* **99 B5** 33 2N 0 1 E
Chelles, *France* **23 D9** 48 52N 2 33 E
Chełm, *Poland* **47 D10** 51 8N 23 30 E
Chełm □, *Poland* **47 D10** 51 15N 23 30 E
Chełmek, *Poland* **31 A12** 50 6N 19 16 E
Chełmno, *Poland* **47 B5** 53 20N 18 30 E
Chelmsford, *U.K.* **17 F8** 51 44N 0 29 E
Chelmsford Dam, *S. Africa* **105 D4** 27 55 S 29 59 E
Chełmża, *Poland* **47 B5** 53 10N 18 39 E
Chelsea, *Australia* **117 E6** 38 5 S 145 8 E
Chelsea, *Mich., U.S.A.* **141 B12** 42 19N 84 1W
Chelsea, *Okla., U.S.A.* **139 G7** 36 32N 95 26W
Chelsea, *Vt., U.S.A.* **137 C12** 43 59N 72 27W
Cheltenham, *U.K.* **17 F5** 51 55N 2 5W
Chelva, *Spain* **34 F4** 39 45N 1 0W
Chelyabinsk, *Russia* **54 D7** 55 10N 61 24 E
Chelyuskin, C., *Russia* **58 B14** 77 30N 103 0 E
Chemainus, *Canada* **130 D4** 48 55N 123 42W
Chembar = Belinskiy, *Russia* **51 E13** 53 0N 43 25 E
Chemillé, *France* **22 E6** 47 14N 0 45W
Chemnitz, *Germany* **26 E8** 50 50N 12 55 E
Chemult, *U.S.A.* **142 E3** 43 14N 121 47W
Chen, Gora, *Russia* **57 C15** 65 16N 141 50 E
Chen Xian, *China* **69 E9** 25 47N 113 1 E
Chenab →, *Pakistan* **79 C3** 30 23N 71 2 E
Chenachane, O. →, *Algeria* **98 C4** 25 20N 3 20W
Chenango Forks, *U.S.A.* **137 D9** 42 15N 75 51W
Chencha, *Ethiopia* **95 F4** 6 15N 37 32 E
Chenchiang = Zhenjiang, *China* **69 A12** 32 11N 119 26 E
Chênée, *Belgium* **21 G7** 50 37N 5 37 E
Cheney, *U.S.A.* **142 C5** 47 30N 117 35W
Cheng Xian, *China* **66 H3** 33 43N 105 42 E
Chengalpattu, *India* **83 H4** 12 42N 79 58 E
Chengbu, *China* **69 D8** 26 18N 110 16 E
Chengcheng, *China* **66 G5** 35 8N 109 56 E
Chengchou = Zhengzhou, *China* **66 G7** 34 45N 113 34 E
Chengde, *China* **67 D9** 40 59N 117 58 E
Chengdong Hu, *China* **69 A11** 32 15N 116 20 E
Chengdu, *China* **68 B5** 30 38N 104 2 E
Chengele, *India* **78 A6** 28 47N 96 16 E
Chenggong, *China* **68 E4** 24 52N 102 56 E
Chenggu, *China* **66 H4** 33 10N 107 21 E
Chengjiang, *China* **68 E4** 24 39N 103 0 E
Chengkou, *China* **68 B7** 31 54N 108 31 E
Ch'engtu = Chengdu, *China* **68 B5** 30 38N 104 2 E
Chengwu, *China* **66 G8** 34 58N 115 50 E
Chengxi Hu, *China* **69 A11** 32 15N 116 10 E
Chengyang, *China* **67 F11** 36 18N 120 21 E
Chenjiagang, *China* **67 G10** 34 23N 119 47 E
Chenkán, *Mexico* **147 D6** 19 8N 90 58W
Chenoa, *U.S.A.* **141 D8** 40 45N 88 43W
Chenxi, *China* **69 C8** 28 2N 110 12 E
Cheo Reo, *Vietnam* **76 F7** 13 25N 108 28 E
Cheom Ksan, *Cambodia* **76 E5** 14 13N 104 56 E
Chepelare, *Bulgaria* **43 F9** 41 44N 24 40 E
Chepén, *Peru* **156 B2** 7 15 S 79 23W
Chépénéhé, *Vanuatu* **121 K5** 20 47 S 167 9 E
Chepes, *Argentina* **158 C2** 31 20 S 66 35W
Chepo, *Panama* **148 E4** 9 10N 79 6W
Cheptsa →, *Russia* **51 B17** 58 36N 50 4 E
Cheptulil, Mt., *Kenya* **106 B4** 1 25N 35 35 E
Chequamegon B., *U.S.A.* **138 B9** 46 40N 90 30W
Cher □, *France* **23 E9** 47 10N 2 30 E
Cher →, *France* **22 E7** 47 21N 0 29 E
Cheran, *India* **78 C3** 25 45N 90 44 E
Cherasco, *Italy* **38 D4** 44 39N 7 50 E
Cheratte, *Belgium* **21 G7** 50 40N 5 41 E
Cheraw, *U.S.A.* **135 H6** 34 42N 79 53W
Cherbourg, *France* **22 C5** 49 39N 1 40W
Cherchell, *Algeria* **99 A5** 36 35N 2 12 E
Cherdakly, *Russia* **51 D16** 54 25N 48 50 E
Cherdyn, *Russia* **54 A5** 60 24N 56 29 E
Cheremkhovo, *Russia* **57 D11** 53 8N 103 1 E
Cherepanovo, *Russia* **56 D9** 54 15N 83 30 E
Cherepovets, *Russia* **51 B10** 59 5N 37 55 E
Chergui, Chott ech, *Algeria* **99 B5** 34 21N 0 25 E
Cherikov, *Belorussia* **50 E7** 53 32N 31 20 E
Cherkassy, *Ukraine* **52 B5** 49 27N 32 4 E
Cherkasy = Cherkassy, *Ukraine* **52 B5** 49 27N 32 4 E
Cherkessk, *Russia* **53 D10** 44 15N 42 5 E
Cherlak, *Russia* **56 D8** 54 15N 74 55 E
Chermoz, *Russia* **54 B5** 58 46N 56 10 E
Chernak, *Kazakhstan* **55 B4** 43 24N 68 2 E
Chernaya Kholunitsa, *Russia* **54 B2** 58 51N 51 52 E
Cherni, *Bulgaria* **43 E8** 42 35N 23 18 E
Chernigov, *Ukraine* **50 F7** 51 28N 31 20 E
Chernihiv = Chernigov, *Ukraine* **50 F7** 51 28N 31 20 E
Chernikovsk, *Russia* **54 D5** 54 48N 56 8 E
Chernivtsi = Chernovtsy, *Ukraine* **52 B1** 48 15N 25 52 E
Chernobyl, *Ukraine* **50 F7** 51 20N 30 15 E
Chernogorsk, *Russia* **57 D10** 53 49N 91 18 E
Chernomorskoye, *Ukraine* **52 D5** 45 31N 32 40 E
Chernovskoye, *Russia* **51 B15** 58 48N 47 20 E
Chernovtsy, *Ukraine* **52 B1** 48 15N 25 52 E
Chernoye, *Russia* **57 B9** 70 30N 89 10 E
Chernushka, *Russia* **54 C5** 56 29N 56 3 E
Chernyakhovsk, *Russia* **50 D2** 54 36N 21 48 E
Chernyshkovskiy, *Russia* **53 B10** 48 30N 42 13 E
Chernyshovskiy, *Russia* **57 C12** 63 0N 112 30 E
Cherokee, *Iowa, U.S.A.* **138 D7** 42 45N 95 33W
Cherokee, *Okla., U.S.A.* **139 G5** 36 45N 98 21W
Cherokees, Lake O' The, *U.S.A.* **139 G7** 36 28N 95 2W
Cherquenco, *Chile* **160 A2** 38 35 S 72 0W
Cherry Creek, *U.S.A.* **142 G6** 39 54N 114 53W
Cherry Valley, *U.S.A.* **145 M10** 33 59N 116 57W
Cherryvale, *U.S.A.* **139 G7** 37 16N 95 33W
Cherskiy, *Russia* **57 C17** 68 45N 161 18 E
Cherskogo Khrebet, *Russia* **57 C15** 65 0N 143 0 E
Chertkovo, *Russia* **53 B9** 49 25N 40 19 E
Cherven, *Belorussia* **50 E6** 53 45N 28 28 E
Cherven-Bryag, *Bulgaria* **43 D9** 43 17N 24 7 E
Chervonograd, *Ukraine* **50 F4** 50 25N 24 10 E
Cherwell →, *U.K.* **17 F6** 51 46N 1 18W
Chesapeake, *U.S.A.* **134 G7** 36 50N 76 17W
Chesapeake B., *U.S.A.* **134 F7** 38 0N 76 10W

Chunya 185

Cheshire □, *U.K.* **16 D5** 53 14N 2 30W
Cheshskaya Guba, *Russia* **48 A8** 67 20N 47 0 E
Cheslatta L., *Canada* **130 C3** 53 49N 125 20W
Chesley, *Canada* **136 B3** 44 17N 81 5W
Cheste, *Spain* **35 F4** 39 30N 0 41W
Chester, *U.K.* **16 D5** 53 12N 2 53W
Chester, *Calif., U.S.A.* **142 F3** 40 19N 121 14W
Chester, *Ill., U.S.A.* **139 G10** 37 55N 89 49W
Chester, *Mont., U.S.A.* **142 B8** 48 31N 110 58W
Chester, *Pa., U.S.A.* **134 F8** 39 51N 75 22W
Chester, *S.C., U.S.A.* **135 H5** 34 43N 81 12W
Chesterfield, *U.K.* **16 D6** 53 14N 1 26W
Chesterfield, Is., *N. Cal.* **122 J7** 19 52 S 158 15 E
Chesterfield Inlet, *Canada* **126 B10** 63 30N 90 45W
Chesterton Ra., *Australia* **115 D4** 25 30 S 147 27 E
Chesterville, *Canada* **137 A9** 45 6N 75 14W
Chesuncook L., *U.S.A.* **129 C6** 46 0N 69 21W
Chetaibi, *Algeria* **99 A6** 37 1N 7 20 E
Chéticamp, *Canada* **129 C7** 46 37N 60 59W
Chetumal, B. de, *Mexico* **147 D7** 18 40N 88 10W
Chetwynd, *Canada* **130 B4** 55 45N 121 36W
Chevanceaux, *France* **24 C3** 45 18N 0 14W
Cheviot, *U.S.A.* **141 E12** 39 10N 84 37W
Cheviot, The, *U.K.* **16 B5** 55 29N 2 8W
Cheviot Hills, *U.K.* **16 B5** 55 20N 2 30W
Cheviot Ra., *Australia* **114 D3** 25 20 S 143 45 E
Chew Bahir, *Ethiopia* **95 G4** 4 40N 36 50 E
Chewelah, *U.S.A.* **142 B5** 48 17N 117 43W
Cheyenne, *Okla., U.S.A.* **139 H5** 35 37N 99 40W
Cheyenne, *Wyo., U.S.A.* **138 E2** 41 8N 104 49W
Cheyenne →, *U.S.A.* **138 C4** 44 41N 101 18W
Cheyenne Wells, *U.S.A.* **138 F3** 38 49N 102 21W
Cheyne B., *Australia* **113 F2** 34 35 S 118 50 E
Chhabra, *India* **80 G7** 24 40N 76 54 E
Chhapra, *India* **81 G11** 25 48N 84 44 E
Chhata, *India* **80 F7** 27 42N 77 30 E
Chhatak, *Bangla.* **78 C3** 25 5N 91 37 E
Chhatarpur, *India* **81 G8** 24 55N 79 35 E
Chhep, *Cambodia* **76 F5** 13 45N 105 24 E
Chhindwara, *India* **81 H8** 22 2N 78 59 E
Chhlong, *Cambodia* **77 F5** 12 15N 105 58 E
Chhuk, *Cambodia* **77 G5** 10 46N 104 28 E
Chi →, *Thailand* **76 E5** 15 11N 104 43 E
Chiai, *Taiwan* **65 D7** 23 29N 120 25 E
Chiamussu = Jiamusi, *China* **65 B8** 46 40N 130 26 E
Chiang Dao, *Thailand* **76 C2** 19 22N 98 58 E
Chiang Kham, *Thailand* **76 C3** 19 32N 100 18 E
Chiang Khan, *Thailand* **76 D3** 17 52N 101 36 E
Chiang Khong, *Thailand* **76 B3** 20 17N 100 24 E
Chiang Mai, *Thailand* **76 C2** 18 47N 98 59 E
Chiang Saen, *Thailand* **76 B3** 20 16N 100 5 E
Chiange, *Angola* **103 F2** 15 35 S 13 40 E
Chiapa →, *Mexico* **147 D6** 16 42N 93 0W
Chiapa de Corzo, *Mexico* **147 D6** 16 42N 93 0W
Chiapas □, *Mexico* **147 D6** 17 0N 92 45W
Chiaramonte Gulfi, *Italy* **41 E7** 37 1N 14 41 E
Chiaravalle, *Italy* **39 E10** 43 38N 13 17 E
Chiaravalle Centrale, *Italy* **41 D9** 38 41N 16 25 E
Chiari, *Italy* **38 C6** 45 31N 9 55 E
Chiasso, *Switz.* **29 E8** 45 50N 9 2 E
Chiatura, *Georgia* **53 E10** 42 15N 43 17 E
Chiautla, *Mexico* **147 D5** 18 18N 98 34W
Chiávari, *Italy* **38 D6** 44 20N 9 20 E
Chiavenna, *Italy* **38 B6** 46 18N 9 23 E
Chiba, *Japan* **63 B12** 35 30N 140 7 E
Chiba □, *Japan* **63 B12** 35 30N 140 20 E
Chibabava, *Mozam.* **105 C5** 20 17 S 33 35 E
Chibemba, *Cunene, Angola* **103 F2** 15 48 S 14 8 E
Chibemba, *Huila, Angola* **103 F3** 16 20 S 15 20 E
Chibia, *Angola* **103 F2** 15 10 S 13 42 E
Chibougamau, *Canada* **128 C5** 49 56N 74 24W
Chibougamau L., *Canada* **128 C5** 49 50N 74 20W
Chibuk, *Nigeria* **101 C7** 10 52N 12 50 E
Chic-Chocs, Mts., *Canada* **129 C6** 48 55N 66 0W
Chicacole = Srikakulam, *India* **82 E6** 18 14N 83 58 E
Chicago, *U.S.A.* **141 C9** 41 53N 87 38W
Chicago Heights, *U.S.A.* **141 C9** 41 30N 87 38W
Chichagof I., *U.S.A.* **130 B1** 57 30N 135 30W
Chichaoua, *Morocco* **98 B3** 31 32N 8 44W
Chicheng, *China* **66 D8** 40 55N 115 55 E
Chichester, *U.K.* **17 G7** 50 50N 0 47W
Chichibu, *Japan* **63 A11** 36 5N 139 10 E
Ch'ich'ihaerh = Qiqihar, *China* **57 E13** 47 26N 124 0 E
Chickasha, *U.S.A.* **139 H5** 35 3N 97 58W
Chiclana de la Frontera, *Spain* **37 J4** 36 26N 6 9W
Chiclayo, *Peru* **156 B2** 6 42 S 79 50W
Chico, *U.S.A.* **144 F5** 39 44N 121 50W
Chico →, *Chubut, Argentina* **160 B3** 44 0 S 67 0W
Chico →, *Santa Cruz, Argentina* **160 C3** 50 0 S 68 30W
Chicomo, *Mozam.* **105 C5** 24 31 S 34 6 E
Chicontepec, *Mexico* **147 C5** 20 58N 98 10W
Chicopee, *U.S.A.* **137 D12** 42 9N 72 37W
Chicoutimi, *Canada* **129 C5** 48 28N 71 5W
Chicualacuala, *Mozam.* **105 C5** 22 6 S 31 42 E
Chidambaram, *India* **83 J4** 11 20N 79 45 E
Chidenguele, *Mozam.* **105 C5** 24 55 S 34 11 E
Chidley, C., *Canada* **127 B13** 60 23N 64 26W
Chiede, *Angola* **103 F3** 17 15 S 16 22 E
Chiefs Pt., *Canada* **136 B3** 44 41N 81 18W
Chiem Hoa, *Vietnam* **76 A5** 22 12N 105 17 E
Chiemsee, *Germany* **27 H8** 47 53N 12 27 E
Chiengi, *Zambia* **107 D2** 8 45 S 29 10 E
Chiengmai = Chiang Mai, *Thailand* **76 C2** 18 47N 98 59 E
Chiengo, *Angola* **103 E4** 13 20 S 21 55 E
Chienti →, *Italy* **39 E10** 43 18N 13 45 E
Chieri, *Italy* **38 D4** 45 0N 7 50 E
Chiers →, *France* **23 C11** 49 39N 4 59 E
Chiese →, *Italy* **38 C7** 45 8N 10 25 E
Chieti, *Italy* **39 F11** 42 22N 14 10 E
Chièvres, *Belgium* **21 G3** 50 35N 3 48 E
Chifeng, *China* **67 C10** 42 18N 118 58 E
Chigasaki, *Japan* **63 B11** 35 19N 139 24 E
Chigirin, *Ukraine* **52 B5** 49 4N 32 38 E
Chignecto B., *Canada* **129 C7** 45 30N 64 40W
Chigorodó, *Colombia* **152 B2** 7 41N 76 42W
Chiguana, *Bolivia* **158 A2** 21 0 S 67 58W
Chiha-ri, *N. Korea* **67 E14** 38 40N 126 30 E
Chihli, G. of = Bo Hai, *China* **67 E10** 39 0N 119 0 E
Chihuahua, *Mexico* **146 B3** 28 40N 106 3W
Chihuahua □, *Mexico* **146 B3** 28 40N 106 3W
Chiili, *Kazakhstan* **55 A3** 44 20N 66 15 E
Chik Bollapur, *India* **83 H3** 13 25N 77 45 E
Chikhli, *India* **82 D3** 20 20N 76 18 E
Chikmagalur, *India* **83 H2** 13 15N 75 45 E
Chikodi, *India* **83 F2** 16 26N 74 38 E
Chikugo, *Japan* **62 D2** 33 14N 130 28 E
Chikuma-Gawa →, *Japan* **63 A10** 36 59N 138 35 E
Chikwawa, *Malawi* **107 F3** 16 2 S 34 50 E
Chilac, *Mexico* **147 D5** 18 20N 97 24W
Chilako →, *Canada* **130 C4** 53 53N 122 57W
Chilam Chavki, *Pakistan* **81 B6** 35 5N 75 5 E
Chilanga, *Zambia* **107 F2** 15 33 S 28 16 E
Chilapa, *Mexico* **147 D5** 17 40N 99 11W
Chilas, *Pakistan* **81 B6** 35 25N 74 5 E
Chilcotin →, *Canada* **130 C4** 51 44N 122 23W
Childers, *Australia* **115 D5** 25 15 S 152 17 E
Childress, *U.S.A.* **139 H4** 34 25N 100 13W
Chile ■, *S. Amer.* **160 B2** 35 0 S 72 0W
Chile Chico, *Chile* **160 C2** 46 33 S 71 44W
Chile Rise, *Pac. Oc.* **123 L18** 38 0 S 92 0W
Chilecito, *Argentina* **158 B2** 29 10 S 67 30W
Chilete, *Peru* **156 B2** 7 10 S 78 50W
Chilhowee, *U.S.A.* **140 F3** 38 36N 93 51W
Chilia, Braţul →, *Romania* **46 D10** 45 25N 29 20 E
Chilik, *Kazakhstan* **54 F3** 51 7N 53 55 E
Chilik, *Kazakhstan* **55 B9** 43 33N 78 17 E
Chililabombwe, *Zambia* **107 E2** 12 18 S 27 43 E
Chilin = Jilin, *China* **67 C14** 43 44N 126 30 E
Chilka L., *India* **82 E7** 19 40N 85 25 E
Chilko →, *Canada* **130 C4** 52 0N 123 40W
Chilko, L., *Canada* **130 C4** 51 20N 124 10W
Chillagoe, *Australia* **114 B3** 17 7 S 144 33 E
Chillán, *Chile* **158 D1** 36 40 S 72 10W
Chillicothe, *Ill., U.S.A.* **140 D7** 40 55N 89 29W
Chillicothe, *Mo., U.S.A.* **140 E3** 39 48N 93 33W
Chillicothe, *Ohio, U.S.A.* **134 F4** 39 20N 82 59W
Chilliwack, *Canada* **130 D4** 49 10N 121 54W
Chilo, *India* **80 F5** 27 25N 73 32 E
Chiloane, I., *Mozam.* **105 C5** 20 40 S 34 55 E
Chiloé □, *Chile* **160 B2** 43 0 S 73 0W
Chiloé, I. de, *Chile* **160 B2** 42 30 S 73 50W
Chilonda, *Angola* **103 E3** 11 19 S 16 12 E
Chilpancingo, *Mexico* **147 D5** 17 30N 99 30W
Chiltern, *Australia* **117 D7** 36 10 S 146 36 E
Chiltern Hills, *U.K.* **17 F7** 51 44N 0 42W
Chilton, *U.S.A.* **134 C1** 44 2N 88 10W
Chiluage, *Angola* **103 D4** 9 30 S 21 50 E
Chilubi, *Zambia* **107 E2** 11 5 S 29 58 E
Chilubula, *Zambia* **107 E3** 10 14 S 30 51 E
Chilumba, *Malawi* **107 E3** 10 28 S 34 12 E
Chilung, *Taiwan* **65 D7** 25 3N 121 45 E
Chilwa, L., *Malawi* **107 F4** 15 15 S 35 40 E
Chimaltitán, *Mexico* **146 C4** 21 46N 103 50W
Chimán, *Panama* **148 E4** 8 45N 78 40W
Chimay, *Belgium* **21 H4** 50 3N 4 20 E
Chimbay, *Uzbekistan* **56 E6** 42 57N 59 47 E
Chimborazo, *Ecuador* **152 D2** 1 29 S 78 55W
Chimborazo □, *Ecuador* **152 D2** 1 0 S 78 40W
Chimbote, *Peru* **156 B2** 9 0 S 78 35W
Chimion, *Uzbekistan* **55 C5** 40 15N 71 32 E
Chimishliya, *Moldavia* **46 C9** 46 34N 28 44 E
Chimkent, *Kazakhstan* **55 B4** 42 18N 69 36 E
Chimoio, *Mozam.* **107 F3** 19 4 S 33 30 E
Chimpembe, *Zambia* **107 D2** 9 31 S 29 33 E
Chin □, *Burma* **78 D4** 22 0N 93 0 E
Chin Hills, *Burma* **78 D4** 22 30N 93 30 E
Chin Ling Shan = Qinling Shandi, *China* **66 H5** 33 50N 108 10 E
China, *Mexico* **147 B5** 25 40N 99 20W
China ■, *Asia* **66 E3** 30 0N 110 0 E
China Lake, *U.S.A.* **145 K9** 35 44N 117 37W
Chinacota, *Colombia* **152 B3** 7 37N 72 36W
Chinan = Jinan, *China* **66 F9** 36 38N 117 1 E
Chinandega, *Nic.* **148 D2** 12 35N 87 12W
Chinati Peak, *U.S.A.* **139 K2** 29 57N 104 29W
Chincha Alta, *Peru* **156 C2** 13 25 S 76 7W
Chinchilla, *Australia* **115 D5** 26 45 S 150 38 E
Chinchilla de Monte Aragón, *Spain* **35 G3** 38 53N 1 40W
Chinchón, *Spain* **34 E1** 40 9N 3 26W
Chinchorro, Banco, *Mexico* **147 D7** 18 35N 87 20W
Chinchou = Jinzhou, *China* **67 D11** 41 5N 121 3 E
Chinchoua, *Gabon* **102 B1** 0 1N 9 48 E
Chincoteague, *U.S.A.* **134 G8** 37 56N 75 23W
Chinde, *Mozam.* **107 F4** 18 35 S 36 30 E
Chindo, *S. Korea* **67 G14** 34 28N 126 15 E
Chindwin →, *Burma* **78 E5** 21 26N 95 15 E
Chineni, *India* **81 C6** 33 2N 75 15 E
Chinga, *Mozam.* **107 F4** 15 13 S 38 35 E
Chingola, *Zambia* **107 E2** 12 31 S 27 53 E
Chingole, *Malawi* **107 E3** 13 4 S 34 17 E
Chingoroi, *Angola* **103 E2** 13 37 S 14 1 E
Ch'ingtao = Qingdao, *China* **67 F11** 36 5N 120 20 E
Chinguar, *Angola* **103 E3** 12 25 S 16 45 E
Chinguetti, *Mauritania* **98 D2** 20 25N 12 24W
Chingune, *Mozam.* **105 C5** 20 33 S 34 58 E
Chinhae, *S. Korea* **67 G15** 35 9N 128 47 E
Chinhanguanine, *Mozam.* **105 D5** 25 21 S 32 30 E
Chinhoyi, *Zimbabwe* **107 F3** 17 20 S 30 8 E
Chiniot, *Pakistan* **79 C4** 31 45N 73 0 E
Chínipas, *Mexico* **146 B3** 27 22N 108 32W
Chinju, *S. Korea* **67 G15** 35 12N 128 2 E
Chinle, *U.S.A.* **143 H9** 36 9N 109 33W
Chinnamanur, *India* **83 K3** 9 50N 77 24 E
Chinnampo, *N. Korea* **67 E13** 38 52N 125 10 E
Chinnur, *India* **82 E4** 18 57N 79 49 E
Chino, *Japan* **63 B10** 35 59N 138 9 E
Chino, *U.S.A.* **145 L9** 34 1N 117 41W
Chino Valley, *U.S.A.* **143 J7** 34 45N 112 27W
Chinon, *France* **22 E7** 47 10N 0 15 E
Chinook, *Canada* **131 C6** 51 28N 110 59W
Chinook, *U.S.A.* **142 B9** 48 35N 109 14W
Chinsali, *Zambia* **107 E3** 10 30 S 32 2 E
Chintamani, *India* **83 H4** 13 26N 78 3 E
Chióggia, *Italy* **39 C9** 45 13N 12 15 E
Chíos = Khíos, *Greece* **45 F8** 38 27N 26 9 E
Chipata, *Zambia* **107 E3** 13 38 S 32 28 E
Chipewyan L., *Canada* **131 B9** 58 0N 98 27W
Chipinge, *Zimbabwe* **107 G3** 20 13 S 32 28 E
Chipiona, *Spain* **37 J4** 36 44N 6 26W
Chipley, *U.S.A.* **135 K3** 30 47N 85 32W
Chiplun, *India* **82 F1** 17 31N 73 34 E
Chipman, *Canada* **129 C6** 46 6N 65 53W
Chipoka, *Malawi* **107 E3** 13 57 S 34 28 E
Chippenham, *U.K.* **17 F5** 51 27N 2 7W
Chippewa →, *U.S.A.* **138 C8** 44 25N 92 5W
Chippewa Falls, *U.S.A.* **138 C9** 44 56N 91 24W
Chiprovtsi, *Bulgaria* **42 D7** 43 24N 22 52 E
Chiquián, *Peru* **156 C2** 10 10 S 77 0W
Chiquimula, *Guatemala* **148 D2** 14 51N 89 37W
Chiquinquira, *Colombia* **152 B3** 5 37N 73 50W
Chiquitos, Llanos de, *Bolivia* **157 D5** 18 0 S 61 30W
Chir →, *Russia* **53 B10** 48 30N 43 0 E
Chirala, *India* **83 G5** 15 50N 80 26 E
Chiramba, *Mozam.* **107 F3** 16 55 S 34 39 E
Chiran, *Japan* **62 F2** 31 22N 130 27 E
Chirawa, *India* **80 E6** 28 14N 75 42 E
Chirayinkil, *India* **83 K3** 8 41N 76 49 E
Chirchik, *Uzbekistan* **55 C4** 41 29N 69 35 E
Chirfa, *Niger* **97 D2** 20 55N 12 22 E
Chirgua →, *Venezuela* **152 B4** 8 54N 67 58W
Chiricahua Peak, *U.S.A.* **143 L9** 31 51N 109 18W
Chiriquí, G. de, *Panama* **148 E3** 8 0N 82 10W
Chiriquí, L. de, *Panama* **148 E3** 9 10N 82 0W
Chirivira Falls, *Zimbabwe* **107 G3** 21 10 S 32 12 E
Chirnogi, *Romania* **46 E7** 44 7N 26 32 E
Chirpan, *Bulgaria* **43 E10** 42 10N 25 19 E
Chirripó Grande, Cerro, *Costa Rica* **148 E3** 9 29N 83 29W
Chisamba, *Zambia* **107 E2** 14 55 S 28 20 E
Chishmy, *Russia* **54 D4** 54 35N 55 23 E
Chisholm, *Canada* **130 C6** 54 55N 114 10W
Chishtian Mandi, *Pakistan* **80 E5** 29 50N 72 55 E
Chishui, *China* **68 C5** 28 30N 105 42 E
Chishui He →, *China* **68 C5** 28 49N 105 50 E
Chisimaio, *Somali Rep.* **108 E2** 0 22 S 42 32 E
Chisimba Falls, *Zambia* **107 E3** 10 12 S 30 56 E
Chişinău = Kishinev, *Moldavia* **52 C3** 47 0N 28 50 E
Chisineu Criş, *Romania* **46 C2** 46 32N 21 37 E
Chisone →, *Italy* **38 D4** 44 49N 7 25 E
Chisos Mts., *U.S.A.* **139 L3** 29 5N 103 15W
Chistopol, *Russia* **51 D17** 55 25N 50 38 E
Chita, *Colombia* **152 B3** 6 11N 72 28W
Chita, *Russia* **57 D12** 52 0N 113 35 E
Chitado, *Angola* **103 F2** 17 10 S 14 8 E
Chitapur, *India* **82 F3** 17 10N 77 5 E
Chitembo, *Angola* **103 E3** 13 30 S 16 50 E
Chitipa, *Malawi* **107 D3** 9 41 S 33 19 E
Chitose, *Japan* **60 C10** 42 49N 141 39 E
Chitrakot, *India* **82 E5** 19 10N 81 40 E
Chitral, *Pakistan* **79 B3** 35 50N 71 56 E
Chitravati →, *India* **83 G4** 14 45N 78 15 E
Chitré, *Panama* **148 E3** 7 59N 80 27W
Chittagong, *Bangla.* **78 D3** 22 19N 91 48 E
Chittagong □, *Bangla.* **78 C3** 24 5N 91 0 E
Chittaurgarh, *India* **80 G6** 24 52N 74 38 E
Chittoor, *India* **83 H4** 13 15N 79 5 E
Chittur, *India* **83 J3** 10 40N 76 45 E
Chitungwiza, *Zimbabwe* **107 F3** 18 0 S 31 6 E
Chiumba, *Angola* **103 E3** 12 29 S 16 8 E
Chiume, *Angola* **103 F4** 15 3 S 21 14 E
Chiusa, *Italy* **39 B8** 46 38N 11 34 E
Chiusi, *Italy* **39 E8** 43 1N 11 58 E
Chiva, *Spain* **35 F4** 39 27N 0 41W
Chivacoa, *Venezuela* **152 A4** 10 10N 68 54W
Chivasso, *Italy* **38 C4** 45 10N 7 52 E
Chivay, *Peru* **156 D3** 15 40 S 71 35W
Chivhu, *Zimbabwe* **107 F3** 19 2 S 30 52 E
Chivilcoy, *Argentina* **158 C4** 34 55 S 60 0W
Chiwanda, *Tanzania* **107 E3** 11 23 S 34 55 E
Chixi, *China* **69 G9** 22 0N 112 58 E
Chizera, *Zambia* **107 E1** 13 10 S 25 0 E
Chkalov = Orenburg, *Russia* **54 F4** 51 45N 55 6 E
Chkolovsk, *Russia* **51 C13** 56 50N 43 10 E
Chloride, *U.S.A.* **145 K12** 35 25N 114 12W
Chlumec, *Czech.* **30 A8** 50 9N 15 29 E
Chmielnik, *Poland* **47 E7** 50 37N 20 43 E
Cho Bo, *Vietnam* **76 B5** 20 46N 105 10 E
Cho-do, *N. Korea* **67 E13** 38 30N 124 40 E
Cho Phuoc Hai, *Vietnam* **77 G6** 10 26N 107 18 E
Choa Chukang, *Malaysia* **74 B2** 1 22N 103 41 E
Choba, *Kenya* **106 B4** 2 30N 38 5 E
Chobe National Park, *Botswana* **104 B3** 18 0 S 25 0 E
Chochiwŏn, *S. Korea* **67 F14** 36 37N 127 18 E
Chocianów, *Poland* **47 D2** 51 27N 15 55 E
Chociwel, *Poland* **47 B2** 53 29N 15 21 E
Chocó □, *Colombia* **152 B2** 6 0N 77 0W
Chocontá, *Colombia* **152 B3** 5 9N 73 41W
Choctawhatchee B., *U.S.A.* **133 D9** 30 20N 86 20W
Chodaków, *Poland* **47 C7** 52 16N 20 18 E
Chodavaram, *India* **82 F6** 17 50N 82 57 E
Chodecz, *Poland* **47 C6** 52 24N 19 2 E
Chodziez, *Poland* **47 C3** 52 58N 16 58 E
Choele Choel, *Argentina* **160 A3** 39 11 S 65 40W
Chōfu, *Japan* **63 B11** 35 39N 139 33 E
Choiseul, *Solomon Is.* **121 L9** 7 0 S 156 40 E
Choisy-le-Roi, *France* **23 D9** 48 45N 2 24 E
Choix, *Mexico* **146 B3** 26 40N 108 23W
Chojna, *Poland* **47 C1** 52 58N 14 25 E
Chojnice, *Poland* **47 B4** 53 42N 17 32 E
Chojnów, *Poland* **47 D2** 51 18N 15 58 E
Chōkai-San, *Japan* **60 E10** 39 6N 140 3 E
Choke, *Ethiopia* **95 E4** 11 18N 37 15 E
Chokurdakh, *Russia* **57 B15** 70 38N 147 55 E
Cholame, *U.S.A.* **144 K6** 35 44N 120 18W
Cholet, *France* **22 E6** 47 4N 0 52W
Cholpon-Ata, *Kirghizia* **55 B8** 42 40N 77 6 E
Choluteca, *Honduras* **148 D2** 13 20N 87 14W
Choluteca →, *Honduras* **148 D2** 13 0N 87 20W
Chom Bung, *Thailand* **76 F2** 13 37N 99 36 E
Chom Thong, *Thailand* **76 C2** 18 25N 98 41 E
Choma, *Zambia* **107 F2** 16 48 S 26 59 E
Chomen Swamp, *Ethiopia* **95 F4** 9 20N 37 10 E
Chomun, *India* **80 F6** 27 15N 75 40 E
Chomutov, *Czech.* **30 A6** 50 28N 13 23 E
Chon Buri, *Thailand* **76 F3** 13 21N 101 1 E
Chon Thanh, *Vietnam* **77 G6** 11 24N 106 36 E
Chonan, *S. Korea* **67 F14** 36 48N 127 9 E
Chone, *Ecuador* **152 D2** 0 40 S 80 0W
Chong Kai, *Cambodia* **76 F4** 13 57N 103 35 E
Chong Mek, *Thailand* **76 E5** 15 10N 105 27 E
Chong'an, *China* **69 D12** 27 45N 118 0 E
Chongde, *China* **69 B13** 30 32N 120 26 E
Chŏngdo, *S. Korea* **67 G15** 35 38N 128 42 E
Chŏngha, *S. Korea* **67 F15** 36 12N 129 21 E
Chŏngjin, *N. Korea* **67 D15** 41 47N 129 50 E
Chŏngju, *N. Korea* **67 E13** 39 40N 125 5 E
Chŏngju, *S. Korea* **67 F14** 36 39N 127 27 E
Chongli, *China* **66 D8** 40 58N 115 15 E
Chongming, *China* **69 B13** 31 38N 121 23 E
Chongming Dao, *China* **69 B13** 31 40N 121 30 E
Chongoyape, *Peru* **156 B2** 6 35 S 79 25W
Chongqing, *Sichuan, China* **68 C6** 29 35N 106 25 E
Chongqing, *Sichuan, China* **68 B4** 30 38N 103 40 E
Chongren, *China* **69 D11** 27 46N 116 3 E
Chŏngŭp, *S. Korea* **67 G14** 35 35N 126 50 E
Chongzuo, *China* **68 F6** 22 23N 107 20 E
Chŏnju, *S. Korea* **67 G14** 35 50N 127 4 E
Chonos, Arch. de los, *Chile* **160 C2** 45 0 S 75 0W
Chopda, *India* **82 D2** 21 20N 75 15 E
Chopim →, *Brazil* **159 B5** 25 35 S 53 5W
Chorbat La, *India* **81 B7** 34 42N 76 37 E
Chorley, *U.K.* **16 D5** 53 39N 2 39W
Chornobyl = Chernobyl, *Ukraine* **50 F7** 51 20N 30 15 E
Chorolque, Cerro, *Bolivia* **158 A2** 20 59 S 66 5W
Choroszcz, *Poland* **47 B9** 53 10N 22 59 E
Chorregon, *Australia* **114 C3** 22 40 S 143 32 E
Chortkov, *Ukraine* **50 G4** 49 2N 25 46 E
Chŏrwŏn, *S. Korea* **67 E14** 38 15N 127 10 E
Chorzele, *Poland* **47 B7** 53 15N 20 55 E
Chorzów, *Poland* **47 E5** 50 18N 18 57 E
Chos-Malal, *Argentina* **158 D1** 37 20 S 70 15W
Chosan, *N. Korea* **67 D13** 40 50N 125 47 E
Chōshi, *Japan* **63 B12** 35 45N 140 51 E
Choszczno, *Poland* **47 B2** 53 7N 15 25 E
Chota, *Peru* **156 B2** 6 33 S 78 39W
Choteau, *U.S.A.* **142 C7** 47 49N 112 11W
Chotila, *India* **80 H4** 22 23N 71 15 E
Chowchilla, *U.S.A.* **144 H6** 37 7N 120 16W
Chowkham, *Burma* **78 E6** 20 52N 97 28 E
Choybalsan, *Mongolia* **65 B6** 48 4N 114 30 E
Chrisman, *U.S.A.* **141 E9** 39 48N 87 41W
Christchurch, *N.Z.* **119 D7** 43 33 S 172 47 E
Christchurch, *U.K.* **17 G6** 50 44N 1 45W
Christian I., *Canada* **136 B4** 44 50N 80 12W
Christiana, *S. Africa* **104 D4** 27 52 S 25 8 E
Christiansfeld, *Denmark* **15 J3** 55 21N 9 29 E
Christiansted, *Virgin Is.* **149 C7** 17 45N 64 42W
Christie B., *Canada* **131 A6** 62 32N 111 10W
Christina →, *Canada* **131 B6** 56 40N 111 3W
Christmas Cr. →, *Australia* **112 C4** 18 29 S 125 23 E
Christmas Creek, *Australia* **112 C4** 18 29 S 125 23 E
Christmas I. = Kiritimati, *Kiribati* **123 G12** 1 58N 157 27W
Christmas I., *Ind. Oc.* **109 F9** 10 30 S 105 40 E
Christopher L., *Australia* **113 D4** 24 49 S 127 42 E
Chrudim, *Czech.* **30 B8** 49 58N 15 43 E
Chrzanów, *Poland* **31 A12** 50 10N 19 21 E
Chtimba, *Malawi* **107 E3** 10 35 S 34 13 E
Chu, *Kazakhstan* **55 B6** 43 36N 73 42 E
Chu →, *Kazakhstan* **55 A3** 45 0N 67 44 E
Chu →, *Vietnam* **76 C5** 19 53N 105 45 E
Chu Chua, *Canada* **130 C4** 51 22N 120 10W
Chu Lai, *Vietnam* **76 E7** 15 28N 108 45 E
Chu Xian, *China* **69 A12** 32 19N 118 20 E
Chuadanga, *Bangla.* **78 D2** 23 38N 88 51 E
Ch'uanchou = Quanzhou, *China* **69 E12** 24 55N 118 34 E
Chuankou, *China* **66 G6** 34 20N 110 59 E
Chūbu □, *Japan* **63 A9** 36 45N 137 30 E
Chubut □, *Argentina* **160 B3** 43 30 S 69 0W
Chubut →, *Argentina* **160 B3** 43 20 S 65 5W
Chuchi L., *Canada* **130 B4** 55 12N 124 30W
Chudovo, *Russia* **50 B7** 59 10N 31 41 E
Chudskoye, Oz., *Estonia* **50 B5** 58 13N 27 30 E
Chūgoku □, *Japan* **62 C4** 35 0N 133 0 E
Chūgoku-Sanchi, *Japan* **62 C4** 35 0N 133 0 E
Chuguyev, *Ukraine* **52 B7** 49 55N 36 45 E
Chugwater, *U.S.A.* **138 E2** 41 46N 104 50W
Chukhloma, *Russia* **51 B13** 58 45N 42 40 E
Chukotskiy Khrebet, *Russia* **57 C18** 68 0N 175 0 E
Chukotskoye More, *Russia* **57 C19** 68 0N 175 0W
Chula, *U.S.A.* **140 E3** 39 55N 93 29W
Chula Vista, *U.S.A.* **145 N9** 32 39N 117 5W
Chulak-Kurgan, *Kazakhstan* **55 B4** 43 46N 69 9 E
Chulman, *Russia* **57 D13** 56 52N 124 52 E
Chulucanas, *Peru* **156 B1** 5 8 S 80 10W
Chulumani, *Bolivia* **156 D4** 16 24 S 67 31W
Chulym →, *Russia* **56 D9** 57 43N 83 51 E
Chum Phae, *Thailand* **76 D4** 16 40N 102 6 E
Chum Saeng, *Thailand* **76 E3** 15 55N 100 15 E
Chuma, *Bolivia* **156 D4** 15 24 S 68 56W
Chumar, *India* **81 C8** 32 40N 78 35 E
Chumbicha, *Argentina* **158 B2** 29 0 S 66 10W
Chumerna, *Bulgaria* **43 E10** 42 45N 25 55 E
Chumikan, *Russia* **57 D14** 54 40N 135 10 E
Chumphon, *Thailand* **77 G2** 10 35N 99 14 E
Chumpi, *Peru* **156 D3** 15 4 S 73 46W
Chumuare, *Mozam.* **107 E3** 14 31 S 31 50 E
Chumunjin, *S. Korea* **67 F15** 37 55N 128 54 E
Chuna →, *Russia* **57 D10** 57 47N 94 37 E
Chun'an, *China* **69 C12** 29 35N 119 3 E
Chunchŏn, *S. Korea* **67 F14** 37 58N 127 44 E
Chunchura, *India* **81 H13** 22 53N 88 27 E
Chunga, *Zambia* **107 F2** 15 0 S 26 2 E
Chunggang-ŭp, *N. Korea* **67 D14** 41 48N 126 48 E
Chunghwa, *N. Korea* **67 E13** 38 52N 125 47 E
Chungju, *S. Korea* **67 F14** 36 58N 127 58 E
Chungking = Chongqing, *China* **68 C6** 29 35N 106 25 E
Chungmu, *S. Korea* **67 G15** 34 50N 128 20 E
Chungt'iaoshan = Zhongtiao Shan, *China* **66 G6** 35 0N 111 10 E
Chunian, *Pakistan* **80 D6** 30 57N 74 0 E
Chunya, *Tanzania* **107 D3** 8 30 S 33 27 E

186 Chunya

Chunya □, *Tanzania* .... **106 D3** 7 48 S 33 0 E
Chunyang, *China* .... **67 C15** 43 38N 129 23 E
Chuquibamba, *Peru* ..... **156 D3** 15 47 S 72 44W
Chuquibambilla, *Peru* ..... **156 C3** 14 7 S 72 41W
Chuquicamata, *Chile* .... **158 A2** 22 15 S 69 0W
Chuquisaca □, *Bolivia* ... **157 E5** 20 30 S 63 30W
Chur, *Switz.* .... **29 C9** 46 52N 9 32 E
Churachandpur, *India* ... **78 C4** 24 20N 93 40 E
Churchill, *Canada* **131 B10** 58 47N 94 11W
Churchill →, *Man., Canada* **131 B10** 58 47N 94 12W
Churchill →, *Nfld., Canada* **129 B7** 53 19N 60 10W
Churchill, C., *Canada* ... **131 B10** 58 46N 93 12W
Churchill Falls, *Canada* .. **129 B7** 53 36N 64 19W
Churchill L., *Canada* **131 B7** 55 55N 108 20W
Churchill Pk., *Canada* ... **130 B3** 58 10N 125 10W
Churdan, *U.S.A.* **140 B2** 42 9N 94 29W
Churfisten, *Switz.* .... **29 B8** 47 8N 9 17 E
Churu, *India* .... **80 E6** 28 20N 74 50 E
Churubusco, *U.S.A.* **141 C11** 41 14N 85 19W
Churwalden, *Switz.* ..... **29 C9** 46 47N 9 33 E
Chushal, *India* .... **81 C8** 33 40N 78 40 E
Chusovaya →, *Russia* ... **54 B5** 58 18N 56 22 E
Chusovoy, *Russia* ...... **54 B5** 58 15N 57 40 E
Chust, *Uzbekistan* ...... **55 C5** 41 0N 71 13 E
Chuuronjang, *N. Korea* .. **67 D15** 41 35N 129 40 E
Chuvash Republic □, *Russia* .... **51 D15** 55 30N 47 0 E
Chuwārtah, *Iraq* .... **84 C5** 35 43N 45 34 E
Chuxiong, *China* .... **68 E3** 25 2N 101 28 E
Ci Xian, *China* .... **66 F8** 36 20N 114 25 E
Ciacova, *Romania* ...... **46 D2** 45 35N 21 10 E
Ciamis, *Indonesia* ...... **75 D3** 7 20 S 108 21 E
Cianjur, *Indonesia* ...... **74 D3** 6 49 S 107 8 E
Cibola, *U.S.A.* **145 M12** 33 17N 114 42W
Cicero, *U.S.A.* **134 E2** 41 48N 87 48W
Cicero, *Ill., U.S.A.* **141 C9** 41 51N 87 45W
Cícero Dantas, *Brazil* ... **154 D4** 10 36 S 38 23W
Cidacos →, *Spain* **34 C3** 42 21N 1 38W
Cide, *Turkey* .... **52 F5** 41 53N 33 1 E
Ciechanów, *Poland* ..... **47 C7** 52 52N 20 38 E
Ciechanów □, *Poland* ... **47 B7** 53 0N 20 30 E
Ciechanowiec, *Poland* ... **47 C9** 52 40N 22 31 E
Ciechocinek, *Poland* .... **47 C5** 52 53N 18 45 E
Ciego de Avila, *Cuba* ... **148 B4** 21 50N 78 50W
Ciénaga, *Colombia* **152 A3** 11 1N 74 15W
Ciénaga de Oro, *Colombia* **152 B2** 8 53N 75 37W
Cienfuegos, *Cuba* **148 B3** 22 10N 80 30W
Cieplice Sląskie Zdrój, *Poland* .... **47 E2** 50 50N 15 40 E
Cierp, *France* .... **24 F4** 42 55N 0 40 E
Cíes, Is., *Spain* **36 C2** 42 12N 8 55W
Cieszanów, *Poland* ..... **47 E10** 50 14N 23 8 E
Cieszyn, *Poland* .... **31 B11** 49 45N 18 35 E
Cieza, *Spain* **35 G3** 38 17N 1 23W
Çifteler, *Turkey* .... **88 D4** 39 22N 31 2 E
Cifuentes, *Spain* **34 E2** 40 47N 2 37W
Cihanbeyli, *Turkey* ...... **88 D5** 38 40N 32 55 E
Cihuatlán, *Mexico* **146 D4** 19 14N 104 35W
Cijara, Pantano de, *Spain* **37 F6** 39 18N 4 52W
Cilacap, *Indonesia* ...... **75 D3** 7 43 S 109 0 E
Çıldır, *Turkey* .... **53 F10** 41 7N 43 8 E
Çıldır Gölü, *Turkey* ..... **89 C10** 41 5N 43 15 E
Cili, *China* .... **69 C8** 29 30N 111 8 E
Cilicia, *Turkey* .... **88 E5** 36 30N 33 40 E
Cîlnicu, *Romania* .... **46 E4** 44 54N 23 4 E
Cilo Dağı, *Turkey* ...... **89 E10** 37 28N 43 55 E
Cima, *U.S.A.* **145 K11** 35 14N 115 30W
Cimarron, *Kans., U.S.A.* **139 G4** 37 48N 100 21W
Cimarron, *N. Mex., U.S.A.* **139 G2** 36 31N 104 55W
Cimarron →, *U.S.A.* **139 G6** 36 10N 96 17W
Cimone, Mte., *Italy* ..... **38 D7** 44 10N 10 40 E
Cîmpic Turzii, *Romania* . **46 C4** 46 34N 23 53 E
Cîmpina, *Romania* ...... **46 D6** 45 10N 25 45 E
Cîmpulung, *Argeş, Romania* .... **46 D6** 45 17N 25 3 E
Cîmpulung, *Suceava, Romania* .... **46 B6** 47 32N 25 30 E
Cîmpuri, *Romania* ...... **46 C7** 46 0N 26 50 E
Çinar, *Turkey* .... **89 E9** 37 46N 40 19 E
Cinca →, *Spain* .... **34 D5** 41 26N 0 21 E
Cincer, *Bos.-H.* .... **42 D2** 43 55N 17 5 E
Cincinnati, *Iowa, U.S.A.* **140 D4** 40 38N 92 56W
Cincinnati, *Ohio, U.S.A.* **141 E12** 39 6N 84 31W
Cîndeşti, *Romania* ...... **46 D7** 45 15N 26 42 E
Çine, *Turkey* .... **88 E3** 37 37N 28 2 E
Ciney, *Belgium* .... **21 H6** 50 18N 5 5 E
Cíngoli, *Italy* .... **39 E10** 43 23N 13 10 E
Cinigiano, *Italy* .... **39 F8** 42 53N 11 23 E
Cinto, Mte., *France* ..... **25 F12** 42 24N 8 54 E
Ciorani, *Romania* .... **46 E7** 44 45N 26 25 E
Čiovo, *Croatia* .... **39 E13** 43 30N 16 17 E
Cipó, *Brazil* .... **154 D4** 11 6 S 38 31W
Circeo, Monte, *Italy* .... **40 A6** 41 14N 13 3 E
Çirçir, *Turkey* .... **88 C7** 40 5N 36 47 E
Circle, *Alaska, U.S.A.* ... **126 B5** 65 50N 144 4W
Circle, *Mont., U.S.A.* **138 B2** 47 25N 105 35W
Circleville, *Ohio, U.S.A.* **134 F4** 39 36N 82 57W
Circleville, *Utah, U.S.A.* . **143 G7** 38 10N 112 16W
Cirebon, *Indonesia* ...... **75 D3** 6 45 S 108 32 E
Cirencester, *U.K.* **17 F6** 51 43N 1 59W
Cireşu, *Romania* .... **46 E3** 44 47N 22 31 E
Cirey-sur-Vezouze, *France* **23 D13** 48 35N 6 57 E
Ciriè, *Italy* .... **38 C4** 45 14N 7 35 E
Cirium, *Cyprus* .... **32 E11** 34 40N 32 53 E
Cirò, *Italy* .... **41 C10** 39 23N 17 3 E
Ciron →, *France* **24 D3** 44 36N 0 18W
Cisco, *U.S.A.* **139 J5** 32 23N 98 59W
Ciskei □, *S. Africa* ..... **105 E4** 33 0 S 27 0 E
Cislău, *Romania* .... **46 D7** 45 14N 26 20 E
Cisna, *Poland* .... **31 B15** 49 12N 22 20 E
Cisnădie, *Romania* ...... **46 D5** 45 42N 24 9 E
Cisne, *U.S.A.* **141 F8** 38 31N 88 26W
Cisneros, *Colombia* **152 B2** 6 33N 75 4W
Cissna Park, *U.S.A.* **141 D9** 40 34N 87 54W
Cisterna di Latina, *Italy* . **40 A5** 41 35N 12 50 E
Cisternino, *Italy* .... **41 B10** 40 45N 17 26 E
Citaré →, *Brazil* **153 C7** 1 11N 54 41W
Citeli-Ckaro, *Georgia* .... **53 F12** 41 33N 46 0 E
Citlaltépetl, *Mexico* **147 D5** 19 0N 97 20W
Citrus Heights, *U.S.A.* ... **144 G5** 38 42N 121 17W
Citrusdal, *S. Africa* ..... **104 E2** 32 35 S 19 0 E
Città della Pieve, *Italy* ... **39 F9** 42 57N 12 0 E
Città di Castello, *Italy* ... **39 E9** 43 27N 12 14 E
Città Sant' Angelo, *Italy* . **39 F11** 42 32N 14 5 E
Cittadella, *Italy* .... **39 C8** 45 39N 11 48 E
Cittaducale, *Italy* .... **39 F9** 42 24N 12 58 E
Cittanova, *Italy* .... **41 D9** 38 22N 16 5 E
Ciuc, Munţii, *Romania* .. **46 C7** 46 25N 26 5 E
Ciucaş, *Romania* .... **46 D6** 45 31N 25 56 E
Ciudad Altamirano, *Mexico* **146 D4** 18 20N 100 40W
Ciudad Bolívar, *Venezuela* **153 B5** 8 5N 63 36W
Ciudad Camargo, *Mexico* **146 B3** 27 41N 105 10W
Ciudad Chetumal, *Mexico* **147 D7** 18 30N 88 20W
Ciudad de Valles, *Mexico* **147 C5** 22 0N 99 0W
Ciudad del Carmen, *Mexico* **147 D6** 18 38N 91 50W
Ciudad Delicias = Delicias, *Mexico* **146 B3** 28 10N 105 30W
Ciudad Guayana, *Venezuela* **153 B5** 8 0N 62 30W
Ciudad Guerrero, *Mexico* **146 B3** 28 33N 107 28W
Ciudad Guzmán, *Mexico* . **146 D4** 19 40N 103 30W
Ciudad Juárez, *Mexico* .. **146 A3** 31 40N 106 28W
Ciudad Madero, *Mexico* . **147 C5** 22 19N 97 50W
Ciudad Mante, *Mexico* .. **147 C5** 22 50N 99 0W
Ciudad Obregón, *Mexico* **146 B3** 27 28N 109 59W
Ciudad Ojeda, *Venezuela* **152 A3** 10 12N 71 19W
Ciudad Real, *Spain* **37 G7** 38 59N 3 55W
Ciudad Real □, *Spain* ... **37 G7** 38 50N 4 0W
Ciudad Rodrigo, *Spain* .. **36 E4** 40 35N 6 32W
Ciudad Trujillo = Santo Domingo, *Dom. Rep.* . **149 C6** 18 30N 69 59W
Ciudad Victoria, *Mexico* . **147 C5** 23 41N 99 9W
Ciudadela, *Spain* .... **33 B10** 40 0N 3 50 E
Ciulnița, *Romania* ...... **46 E8** 44 26N 27 22 E
Civa Burnu, *Turkey* ..... **88 C7** 41 21N 36 38 E
Cividale del Friuli, *Italy* . **39 B10** 46 6N 13 25 E
Cívita Castellana, *Italy* .. **39 F9** 42 18N 12 24 E
Civitanova Marche, *Italy* . **39 E10** 43 18N 13 41 E
Civitavécchia, *Italy* ..... **39 F8** 42 6N 11 46 E
Civitella del Tronto, *Italy* **39 F10** 42 48N 13 40 E
Civray, *France* .... **24 B4** 46 10N 0 17 E
Çivril, *Turkey* .... **88 D3** 38 20N 29 43 E
Cixerri →, *Italy* .... **40 C1** 39 20N 8 40 E
Cizre, *Turkey* .... **89 E10** 37 19N 42 10 E
Clacton-on-Sea, *U.K.* ... **17 F9** 51 47N 1 10 E
Clain →, *France* .... **22 F7** 46 47N 0 33 E
Claire, L., *Canada* **130 B6** 58 35N 112 5W
Clairemont, *U.S.A.* **139 J4** 33 9N 100 44W
Clairton, *U.S.A.* **136 F5** 40 18N 79 53W
Clairvaux-les-Lacs, *France* **25 B9** 46 35N 5 45 E
Clallam Bay, *U.S.A.* **144 B2** 48 15N 124 16W
Clamecy, *France* .... **23 E10** 47 28N 3 30 E
Clanton, *U.S.A.* **135 J2** 32 51N 86 38W
Clanwilliam, *S. Africa* .. **104 E2** 32 11 S 18 52 E
Clara, *Ireland* **19 C4** 53 20N 7 38W
Clara →, *Australia* ..... **114 B3** 19 8 S 142 30 E
Claraville, *U.S.A.* **145 K8** 35 24N 118 20W
Clare, *Australia* .... **116 B3** 33 50 S 138 37 E
Clare, *U.S.A.* **134 D3** 43 49N 84 46W
Clare □, *Ireland* **19 D3** 52 45N 9 0W
Clare →, *Ireland* **19 C2** 53 22N 9 5W
Clare I., *Ireland* **19 C2** 53 48N 10 0W
Claremont, *Calif., U.S.A.* **145 L9** 34 6N 117 43W
Claremont, *N.H., U.S.A.* **137 C12** 43 23N 72 20W
Claremont Pt., *Australia* . **114 A3** 14 1 S 143 41 E
Claremore, *U.S.A.* **139 G7** 36 19N 95 36W
Claremorris, *Ireland* **19 C3** 53 45N 9 0W
Clarence, *U.S.A.* **140 E4** 39 45N 92 16W
Clarence →, *Australia* .. **115 D5** 29 25 S 153 22 E
Clarence →, *N.Z.* ...... **119 C8** 42 10 S 173 56 E
Clarence, I., *Chile* ...... **160 D2** 54 0 S 72 0W
Clarence I., *Antarctica* ... **7 C18** 61 10 S 54 0W
Clarence Str., *Australia* .. **112 B5** 12 0 S 131 0 E
Clarence Str., *U.S.A.* ... **130 B2** 55 40N 132 10W
Clarence Town, *Bahamas* **149 B5** 23 6N 74 59W
Clarendon, *Ark., U.S.A.* . **139 H9** 34 42N 91 19W
Clarendon, *Tex., U.S.A.* . **139 H4** 34 56N 100 53W
Clarenville, *Canada* **129 C9** 48 10N 54 1W
Claresholm, *Canada* **130 C6** 50 0N 113 33W
Clarie Coast, *Antarctica* . **7 C9** 68 0 S 135 0 E
Clarin, *Phil.* .... **71 G4** 8 12N 123 52 E
Clarinda, *U.S.A.* **138 E7** 40 44N 95 2W
Clarion, *Iowa, U.S.A.* ... **140 B3** 42 44N 93 44W
Clarion, *Pa., U.S.A.* **136 E5** 41 13N 79 23W
Clarion →, *U.S.A.* **136 E5** 41 7N 79 41W
Clark, *U.S.A.* **138 C6** 44 53N 97 44W
Clark, Pt., *Canada* **136 B3** 44 4N 81 45W
Clark Fork, *U.S.A.* **142 B5** 48 9N 116 11W
Clark Fork →, *U.S.A.* .. **142 B5** 48 9N 116 15W
Clark Hill Res., *U.S.A.* .. **135 J4** 33 45N 82 20W
Clarkdale, *U.S.A.* **143 J7** 34 46N 112 3W
Clarke City, *Canada* **129 B6** 50 12N 66 38W
Clarke I., *Australia* ..... **114 G4** 40 32 S 148 10 E
Clarke L., *Canada* **131 C7** 54 24N 106 54W
Clarke Ra., *Australia* ... **114 C4** 20 40 S 148 30 E
Clark's Fork →, *U.S.A.* . **142 D9** 45 39N 108 43W
Clark's Harbour, *Canada* **129 D6** 43 25N 65 38W
Clarks Summit, *U.S.A.* .. **137 E9** 41 30N 75 42W
Clarksburg, *U.S.A.* **134 F5** 39 17N 80 30W
Clarksdale, *U.S.A.* **139 H9** 34 12N 90 35W
Clarkston, *U.S.A.* **142 C5** 46 25N 117 3W
Clarksville, *Ark., U.S.A.* **139 H8** 35 28N 93 28W
Clarksville, *Iowa, U.S.A.* **140 B4** 42 47N 92 40W
Clarksville, *Mich., U.S.A.* **141 B11** 42 50N 85 15W
Clarksville, *Ohio, U.S.A.* **141 E13** 39 24N 83 59W
Clarksville, *Tenn., U.S.A.* **135 G2** 36 32N 87 21W
Clarksville, *Tex., U.S.A.* . **139 J7** 33 37N 95 3W
Claro →, *Brazil* .... **155 E1** 19 8 S 50 40W
Clatskanie, *U.S.A.* **144 D3** 46 6N 123 12W
Claude, *U.S.A.* **139 H4** 35 7N 101 22W
Claveria, *Cagayan, Phil.* . **70 E4** 12 54N 123 15 E
Claveria, *Masbate, Phil.* . **71 G5** 8 38N 124 55 E
Claveria, *Mindanao, Phil.* **70 B3** 18 37N 121 4 E
Clay, *U.S.A.* **144 G5** 38 17N 121 10W
Clay Center, *U.S.A.* **138 F6** 39 23N 97 8W
Clay City, *Ind., U.S.A.* .. **141 E9** 39 17N 87 7W
Clay City, *Ky., U.S.A.* ... **141 G13** 37 52N 83 55W
Claypool, *U.S.A.* **143 K8** 33 25N 110 51W
Claysville, *U.S.A.* **136 F4** 40 7N 80 25W
Clayton, *Idaho, U.S.A.* .. **142 D6** 44 16N 114 24W
Clayton, *Ind., U.S.A.* ... **141 E10** 39 41N 86 31W
Clayton, *N. Mex., U.S.A.* **139 G3** 36 27N 103 11W
Cle Elum, *U.S.A.* **142 C3** 47 12N 120 56W
Clear, C., *Ireland* **19 E2** 51 26N 9 30W
Clear I., *Ireland* **19 E2** 51 26N 9 30W
Clear L., *U.S.A.* **144 F4** 39 2N 122 47W
Clear Lake, *Iowa, U.S.A.* **140 A3** 43 8N 93 23W
Clear Lake, *S. Dak., U.S.A.* **138 C6** 44 45N 96 41W
Clear Lake, *Wash., U.S.A.* **142 B2** 48 27N 122 15W
Clear Lake Reservoir, *U.S.A.* **142 F3** 41 56N 121 5W
Clearfield, *Iowa, U.S.A.* . **140 D2** 40 48N 94 29W
Clearfield, *Pa., U.S.A.* .. **134 E6** 41 2N 78 27W
Clearfield, *Utah, U.S.A.* . **142 F7** 41 7N 112 2W
Clearlake Highlands, *U.S.A.* **144 G4** 38 57N 122 38W
Clearmont, *U.S.A.* **142 D10** 44 38N 106 23W
Clearwater, *Canada* **130 C4** 51 38N 120 2W
Clearwater, *U.S.A.* **135 M4** 27 58N 82 48W
Clearwater →, *Alta., Canada* **130 C6** 52 22N 114 57W
Clearwater →, *Alta., Canada* **131 B6** 56 44N 111 23W
Clearwater Cr. →, *Canada* **130 A3** 61 36N 125 30W
Clearwater Mts., *U.S.A.* . **142 C6** 46 5N 115 20W
Clearwater Prov. Park, *Canada* **131 C8** 54 0N 101 0W
Cleburne, *U.S.A.* **139 J6** 32 21N 97 23W
Cleethorpes, *U.K.* **16 D7** 53 33N 0 2W
Cleeve Hill, *U.K.* **17 F6** 51 54N 2 0W
Clelles, *France* .... **25 D9** 44 50N 5 38 E
Clemency, *Lux.* .... **21 J7** 49 35N 5 53 E
Cleopatra Needle, *Phil.* .. **71 F2** 10 7N 118 58 E
Clerke Reef, *Australia* ... **112 C2** 17 22 S 119 20 E
Clermont, *Australia* ..... **114 C4** 22 49 S 147 39 E
Clermont, *France* .... **23 C9** 49 23N 2 24 E
Clermont-en-Argonne, *France* .... **23 C12** 49 5N 5 4 E
Clermont-Ferrand, *France* **24 C7** 45 46N 3 4 E
Clermont-l'Hérault, *France* **24 E7** 43 38N 3 26 E
Clerval, *France* .... **23 E13** 47 25N 6 30 E
Clervaux, *Lux.* .... **21 H8** 50 4N 6 2 E
Cléry-St.-André, *France* . **23 E8** 47 50N 1 46 E
Cles, *Italy* .... **38 B8** 46 21N 11 4 E
Cleveland, *Australia* ..... **115 D5** 27 30 S 153 15 E
Cleveland, *Miss., U.S.A.* . **139 J9** 33 45N 90 43W
Cleveland, *Ohio, U.S.A.* . **136 E3** 41 30N 81 42W
Cleveland, *Okla., U.S.A.* . **139 G6** 36 19N 96 28W
Cleveland, *Tenn., U.S.A.* . **135 H3** 35 10N 84 53W
Cleveland, *Tex., U.S.A.* .. **139 K7** 30 21N 95 5W
Cleveland □, *U.K.* ...... **16 C9** 54 35N 1 8 E
Cleveland, C., *Australia* . **114 B4** 19 11 S 147 1 E
Cleveland Heights, *U.S.A.* **136 E3** 41 30N 81 34W
Clevelândia, *Brazil* ..... **159 B5** 26 24 S 52 23W
Clevelândia do Norte, *Brazil* **153 C7** 3 49N 51 52W
Cleves, *U.S.A.* **141 E12** 39 10N 84 45W
Clew B., *Ireland* **19 C2** 53 54N 9 50W
Clewiston, *U.S.A.* **135 M5** 26 45N 80 56W
Clifden, *Ireland* **19 C1** 53 30N 10 2W
Clifden, *N.Z.* .... **119 G2** 46 1 S 167 42 E
Cliffdell, *U.S.A.* **144 D5** 46 56N 121 5W
Clifton, *Australia* ...... **115 D5** 27 59 S 151 53 E
Clifton, *Ariz., U.S.A.* ... **143 K9** 33 3N 109 18W
Clifton, *Ill., U.S.A.* **141 D9** 40 56N 87 56W
Clifton, *Tex., U.S.A.* **139 K6** 31 47N 97 35W
Clifton Beach, *Australia* . **114 B4** 16 46 S 145 39 E
Clifton Forge, *U.S.A.* ... **134 G6** 37 49N 79 50W
Clifton Hills, *Australia* .. **115 D2** 27 1 S 138 54 E
Climax, *Canada* **131 D7** 49 10N 108 20W
Clinch →, *U.S.A.* **135 H3** 35 53N 84 29W
Clingmans Dome, *U.S.A.* **135 H4** 35 34N 83 30W
Clint, *U.S.A.* **143 L10** 31 35N 106 14W
Clinton, *B.C., Canada* ... **130 C4** 51 6N 121 35W
Clinton, *Ont., Canada* ... **128 D3** 43 37N 81 32W
Clinton, *N.Z.* .... **119 G4** 46 12 S 169 23 E
Clinton, *Ark., U.S.A.* ... **139 H8** 35 36N 92 28W
Clinton, *Ill., U.S.A.* **138 E10** 40 9N 88 57W
Clinton, *Ind., U.S.A.* **141 E9** 39 40N 87 24W
Clinton, *Iowa, U.S.A.* ... **140 C6** 41 51N 90 12W
Clinton, *Mass., U.S.A.* .. **137 D13** 42 25N 71 41W
Clinton, *Mo., U.S.A.* **140 F3** 38 22N 93 46W
Clinton, *N.C., U.S.A.* ... **135 H6** 35 0N 78 22W
Clinton, *Okla., U.S.A.* .. **139 H5** 35 31N 98 58W
Clinton, *S.C., U.S.A.* ... **135 H5** 34 29N 81 53W
Clinton, *Tenn., U.S.A.* .. **135 G3** 36 6N 84 8W
Clinton, *Wash., U.S.A.* .. **144 C4** 47 59N 122 21W
Clinton, *Wis., U.S.A.* ... **141 B8** 42 34N 88 52W
Clinton C., *Australia* .... **114 C5** 22 30 S 150 45 E
Clinton Colden L., *Canada* **126 B9** 63 58N 107 27W
Clintonville, *U.S.A.* **138 C10** 44 37N 88 46W
Clipperton, I., *Pac. Oc.* . **123 F17** 10 18N 109 13W
Clisson, *France* **22 E5** 47 5N 1 16W
Clive, *N.Z.* .... **118 F5** 39 36 S 176 58 E
Clive L., *Canada* **130 A5** 63 13N 118 54W
Cliza, *Bolivia* .... **157 D4** 17 36 S 65 56W
Cloates, Pt., *Australia* ... **112 D1** 22 43 S 113 40 E
Clocolan, *S. Africa* ..... **105 D4** 28 55 S 27 34 E
Clodomira, *Argentina* ... **158 B3** 27 35 S 64 14W
Clonakilty, *Ireland* **19 E3** 51 37N 8 53W
Clonakilty B., *Ireland* ... **19 E3** 51 33N 8 50W
Cloncurry, *Australia* .... **114 C3** 20 40 S 140 28 E
Cloncurry →, *Australia* . **114 B3** 18 37 S 140 40 E
Clones, *Ireland* **19 B4** 54 10N 7 13W
Clonmel, *Ireland* **19 D4** 52 22N 7 42W
Cloppenburg, *Germany* .. **26 C4** 52 50N 8 3 E
Cloquet, *U.S.A.* **138 B8** 46 43N 92 28W
Clorinda, *Argentina* ..... **158 B4** 25 16 S 57 45W
Cloud Peak, *U.S.A.* **142 D10** 44 23N 107 11W
Cloudcroft, *U.S.A.* **143 K11** 32 58N 105 45W
Cloudy B., *N.Z.* .... **119 B9** 41 25 S 174 10 E
Cloverdale, *Calif., U.S.A.* **144 G4** 38 48N 123 1W
Cloverdale, *Ind., U.S.A.* . **141 E10** 39 31N 86 48W
Cloverport, *U.S.A.* **141 G10** 37 50N 86 38W
Clovis, *Calif., U.S.A.* ... **144 J7** 36 49N 119 42W
Clovis, *N. Mex., U.S.A.* . **139 H3** 34 24N 103 12W
Cloyes-sur-le-Loir, *France* **22 E8** 48 0N 1 14 E
Club Terrace, *Australia* .. **117 D8** 37 35 S 148 58 E
Cluj □, *Romania* .... **46 C4** 46 45N 23 30 E
Cluj-Napoca, *Romania* .. **46 C4** 46 47N 23 38 E
Clunes, *Australia* ...... **116 D5** 37 20 S 143 45 E
Cluny, *France* .... **25 B8** 46 26N 4 38 E
Cluses, *France* .... **25 B10** 46 5N 6 35 E
Clusone, *Italy* .... **38 C6** 45 54N 9 58 E
Clutha →, *N.Z.* .... **119 G4** 46 20 S 169 49 E
Clwyd □, *U.K.* **16 D4** 53 5N 3 20W
Clwyd →, *U.K.* **16 D4** 53 20N 3 30W
Clyde, *N.Z.* .... **119 F4** 45 12 S 169 20 E
Clyde, *U.S.A.* **136 C8** 43 5N 76 52W
Clyde →, *U.K.* **18 F4** 55 56N 4 29W
Clyde, Firth of, *U.K.* **18 F4** 55 20N 5 0W
Clyde River, *Canada* **127 A13** 70 30N 68 30W
Clydebank, *U.K.* **18 F4** 55 54N 4 25W
Clymer, *U.S.A.* **136 D5** 40 40N 79 1W
Côa →, *Portugal* **36 D3** 41 5N 7 6W
Coachella, *U.S.A.* **145 M10** 33 41N 116 10W
Coachella Canal, *U.S.A.* . **145 N12** 32 43N 114 57W
Coahoma, *U.S.A.* **139 J4** 32 18N 101 18W
Coahuayana →, *Mexico* . **146 D4** 18 41N 103 45W
Coahuayutla, *Mexico* **146 D4** 18 19N 101 42W
Coahuila □, *Mexico* **146 B4** 27 0N 103 0W
Coal →, *Canada* **130 B3** 59 39N 126 57W
Coal City, *U.S.A.* **141 C8** 41 17N 88 17W
Coal I., *N.Z.* .... **119 G1** 46 8 S 166 40 E
Coalane, *Mozam.* .... **107 F4** 17 48 S 37 2 E
Coalcomán, *Mexico* **146 D4** 18 40N 103 10W
Coaldale, *Canada* **130 D6** 49 45N 112 35W
Coalgate, *U.S.A.* **139 H6** 34 32N 96 13W
Coalinga, *U.S.A.* **144 J6** 36 9N 120 21W
Coalville, *U.K.* **16 E6** 52 43N 1 21W
Coalville, *U.S.A.* **142 F8** 40 55N 111 24W
Coaraci, *Brazil* .... **155 D4** 14 38 S 39 32W
Coari, *Brazil* .... **153 D5** 4 8 S 63 7W
Coari →, *Brazil* .... **153 D5** 4 30 S 63 33W
Coari, L. de, *Brazil* ..... **153 D5** 4 15 S 63 22W
Coast □, *Kenya* .... **106 C4** 2 40 S 39 45 E
Coast Mts., *Canada* **130 C3** 55 0N 129 20W
Coast Ranges, *U.S.A.* ... **124 E7** 39 0N 123 0W
Coatbridge, *U.K.* **18 F4** 55 52N 4 2W
Coatepec, *Mexico* **147 D5** 19 27N 96 58W
Coatepeque, *Guatemala* . **148 D1** 14 46N 91 55W
Coatesville, *U.S.A.* **134 F8** 39 59N 75 50W
Coaticook, *Canada* **129 C5** 45 10N 71 46W
Coats I., *Canada* **127 B11** 62 30N 83 0W
Coats Land, *Antarctica* ... **7 D1** 77 0 S 25 0W
Coatzacoalcos, *Mexico* ... **147 D6** 18 7N 94 25W
Cobadin, *Romania* ...... **46 E9** 44 5N 28 13 E
Cobalt, *Canada* **128 C4** 47 25N 79 42W
Cobán, *Guatemala* **148 C1** 15 30N 90 21W
Cobar, *Australia* .... **117 A6** 31 27 S 145 48 E
Cobberas, Mt., *Australia* . **117 D8** 36 53 S 148 12 E
Cobden, *Australia* ...... **116 E5** 38 20 S 143 3 E
Cóbh, *Ireland* **19 E3** 51 50N 8 18W
Cobham, *Australia* ...... **115 E3** 30 18 S 142 7 E
Cobija, *Bolivia* .... **156 C4** 11 0 S 68 50W
Cobleskill, *U.S.A.* **137 D10** 42 41N 74 29W
Coboconk, *Canada* **136 B6** 44 39N 78 48W
Cobourg, *Canada* **128 D4** 43 58N 78 10W
Cobourg Pen., *Australia* . **112 B5** 11 20 S 132 15 E
Cobram, *Australia* ...... **117 C6** 35 54 S 145 40 E
Cobre, *U.S.A.* **142 F6** 41 7N 114 24W
Cóbué, *Mozam.* .... **107 E3** 12 0 S 34 58 E
Coburg, *Germany* .... **27 E6** 50 15N 10 58 E
Coca, *Spain* **36 D6** 41 13N 4 32W
Coca →, *Ecuador* ...... **152 D2** 0 29 S 76 58W
Cocachacra, *Peru* .... **156 D3** 17 5 S 71 45W
Cocal, *Brazil* .... **154 B3** 3 28 S 41 34W
Cocanada = Kakinada, *India* .... **82 F6** 16 57N 82 11 E
Cocentaina, *Spain* **35 G4** 38 45N 0 27W
Cochabamba, *Bolivia* .... **157 D4** 17 26 S 66 10W
Coche, I., *Venezuela* **153 A5** 10 47N 63 56W
Cochem, *Germany* ...... **27 E3** 50 8N 7 7 E
Cochemane, *Mozam.* .... **107 F3** 17 0 S 32 54 E
Cochin, *India* .... **83 K3** 9 59N 76 22 E
Cochin China = Nam-Phan, *Vietnam* .... **77 G6** 10 30N 106 0 E
Cochise, *U.S.A.* **143 K9** 32 7N 109 55W
Cochran, *U.S.A.* **135 J4** 32 23N 83 21W
Cochrane, *Alta., Canada* . **130 C6** 51 11N 114 30W
Cochrane, *Ont., Canada* . **128 C3** 49 0N 81 0W
Cochrane →, *Canada* **131 B8** 59 0N 103 40W
Cochrane, L., *Chile* ..... **160 C2** 47 10 S 72 0W
Cockburn, *Australia* ..... **116 B4** 32 5 S 141 0 E
Cockburn, Canal, *Chile* .. **160 D2** 54 30 S 72 0W
Cockburn I., *Canada* **128 C3** 45 55N 83 22W
Cockburn Ra., *Australia* . **112 C4** 15 46 S 128 0 E
Cocklebiddy Motel, *Australia* .... **113 F4** 32 0 S 126 3 E
Coco →, *Cent. Amer.* ... **148 D3** 15 0N 83 8W
Coco, Pta., *Colombia* ... **152 C2** 2 58N 77 43W
Cocoa, *U.S.A.* **135 L5** 28 21N 80 44W
Cocobeach, *Gabon* ...... **102 B1** 0 59N 9 34 E
Cocora, *Romania* .... **46 E8** 44 45N 27 3 E
Côcos, *Brazil* .... **155 D3** 14 10 S 44 33W
Côcos →, *Brazil* .... **155 D3** 12 44 S 44 48W
Cocos, I. del, *Pac. Oc.* .. **123 G19** 5 25N 87 55W
Cocos I., *Guam* .... **121 R15** 13 14N 144 39 E
Cocos Is., *Ind. Oc.* ...... **109 F8** 12 10 S 96 55 E
Cod, C., *U.S.A.* **133 B13** 42 5N 70 10W
Codajás, *Brazil* .... **153 D5** 3 55 S 62 0W
Codera, C., *Venezuela* ... **152 A4** 10 35N 66 4W
Coderre, *Canada* **131 C7** 50 11N 106 31W
Codfish I., *N.Z.* .... **119 G2** 46 47 S 167 38 E
Codigoro, *Italy* .... **39 D9** 44 50N 12 5 E
Codó, *Brazil* .... **154 B3** 4 30 S 43 55W
Codogno, *Italy* .... **38 C6** 45 10N 9 42 E
Codpa, *Chile* .... **156 D4** 18 50 S 69 44W
Codróipo, *Italy* .... **39 C10** 45 57N 13 0 E
Codru, Munţii, *Romania* . **46 C3** 46 30N 22 15 E
Cody, *U.S.A.* **142 D9** 44 32N 109 3W
Coe Hill, *Canada* **128 D4** 44 52N 77 50W
Coelemu, *Chile* .... **158 D1** 36 30 S 72 48W
Coelho Neto, *Brazil* .... **154 B3** 4 15 S 43 0W
Coen, *Australia* .... **114 A3** 13 52 S 143 12 E
Coeroeni →, *Surinam* ... **153 C6** 3 21N 57 31W
Coesfeld, *Germany* ...... **26 D3** 51 56N 7 10 E
Coetivy Is., *Seychelles* ... **109 E4** 7 8 S 56 16 E
Cœur d'Alene, *U.S.A.* ... **142 C5** 47 45N 116 51W
Cœur d'Alene L., *U.S.A.* **142 C5** 47 32N 116 48W
Coevorden, *Neths.* ...... **20 C9** 52 40N 6 44 E
Cofete, *Canary Is.* **33 F5** 28 6N 14 23W
Coffeyville, *U.S.A.* **139 G7** 37 2N 95 37W
Coffin B., *Australia* ..... **115 E2** 34 38 S 135 28 E
Coffin Bay Peninsula, *Australia* .... **115 E2** 34 32 S 135 15 E
Coffs Harbour, *Australia* . **117 A10** 30 16 S 153 5 E
Cofrentes, *Spain* **35 F3** 39 13N 1 5W
Cogealac, *Romania* ..... **46 E9** 44 36N 28 36 E
Coghinas →, *Italy* ...... **40 B1** 40 55N 8 48 E
Coghinas, L. di, *Italy* .... **40 B2** 40 46N 9 3 E

Copperopolis 187

Cognac, *France* **24 C3** 45 41N 0 20W
Cogne, *Italy* **38 C4** 45 37N 7 21 E
Cogolludo, *Spain* **34 E1** 40 59N 3 10W
Cohagen, *U.S.A.* **142 C10** 47 3N 106 37W
Cohoes, *U.S.A.* **137 D11** 42 46N 73 42W
Cohuna, *Australia* **116 C6** 35 45 S 144 15 E
Coiba, I., *Panama* **148 E3** 7 30N 81 40W
Coig →, *Argentina* **160 D3** 51 0 S 69 10W
Coihaique, *Chile* **160 C2** 45 30 S 71 45W
Coimbatore, *India* **83 J3** 11 2N 76 59 E
Coimbra, *Brazil* **157 D6** 19 55 S 57 48W
Coimbra, *Portugal* **36 E2** 40 15N 8 27W
Coimbra □, *Portugal* **36 E2** 40 12N 8 25W
Coín, *Spain* **37 J6** 36 40N 4 48W
Coipasa, L. de, *Bolivia* **156 D4** 19 12 S 68 7W
Coipasa, Salar de, *Bolivia* **156 D4** 19 26 S 68 9W
Cojata, *Peru* **156 D4** 15 2 S 69 25W
Cojedes □, *Venezuela* **152 B4** 9 20N 68 20W
Cojedes →, *Venezuela* **152 B4** 8 34N 68 5W
Cojimies, *Ecuador* **152 C1** 0 20N 80 0W
Cojocna, *Romania* **46 C4** 46 45N 23 50 E
Cojutepequé, *El Salv.* **148 D2** 13 41N 88 54W
Čoka, *Serbia* **42 B5** 45 57N 20 12 E
Cokeville, *U.S.A.* **142 E8** 42 5N 110 57W
Colaba Pt., *India* **82 E1** 18 54N 72 47 E
Colac, *Australia* **116 E5** 38 21 S 143 35 E
Colachel = Kolachel, *India* **83 K3** 8 10N 77 15 E
Colares, *Portugal* **37 G1** 38 48N 9 30W
Colasi, *Phil.* **71 F5** 10 43N 125 44 E
Colatina, *Brazil* **155 E3** 19 32 S 40 37W
Colbeck, C., *Antarctica* **7 D13** 77 6 S 157 48W
Colbinabbin, *Australia* **117 D6** 36 38 S 144 48 E
Colborne, *Canada* **136 B7** 44 0N 77 53W
Colby, *U.S.A.* **138 F4** 39 24N 101 3W
Colchagua □, *Chile* **158 C1** 34 30 S 71 0W
Colchester, *U.K.* **17 F8** 51 54N 0 55 E
Coldstream, *U.K.* **18 F6** 55 39N 2 14W
Coldwater, *Canada* **136 B5** 44 42N 79 40W
Coldwater, *Kans., U.S.A.* **139 G5** 37 16N 99 20W
Coldwater, *Mich., U.S.A.* **141 C11** 41 57N 85 0W
Coldwater, *Ohio, U.S.A.* **141 D12** 40 29N 84 38W
Coldwater, L., *U.S.A.* **141 C12** 41 48N 84 59W
Cole Camp, *U.S.A.* **140 F3** 38 28N 93 12W
Colebrook, *Australia* **114 G4** 42 31 S 147 21 E
Colebrook, *U.S.A.* **137 B13** 44 54N 71 30W
Coleman, *Canada* **130 D6** 49 40N 114 30W
Coleman, *U.S.A.* **139 K5** 31 50N 99 26W
Coleman →, *Australia* **114 B3** 15 6 S 141 38 E
Colenso, *S. Africa* **105 D4** 28 44 S 29 50 E
Coleraine, *Australia* **116 D4** 37 36 S 141 40 E
Coleraine, *U.K.* **19 A5** 55 8N 6 40W
Coleraine □, *U.K.* **19 A5** 55 8N 6 40W
Coleridge, L., *N.Z.* **119 D6** 43 17 S 171 30 E
Coleroon →, *India* **83 J4** 11 25N 79 50 E
Colesberg, *S. Africa* **104 E4** 30 45 S 25 5 E
Colesburg, *U.S.A.* **140 B5** 42 38N 91 12W
Coleville, *U.S.A.* **144 G7** 38 34N 119 30W
Colfax, *Calif., U.S.A.* **144 F6** 39 6N 120 57W
Colfax, *Ill., U.S.A.* **141 D8** 40 34N 88 37W
Colfax, *Ind., U.S.A.* **141 D10** 40 12N 86 40W
Colfax, *La., U.S.A.* **139 K8** 31 31N 92 42W
Colfax, *Wash., U.S.A.* **142 C5** 46 53N 117 22W
Colhué Huapi, L., *Argentina* **160 C3** 45 30 S 69 0W
Cólico, *Italy* **38 B6** 46 8N 9 22 E
Coligny, *France* **25 B9** 46 23N 5 21 E
Coligny, *S. Africa* **105 D4** 26 17 S 26 15 E
Colima, *Mexico* **146 D4** 19 10N 103 40W
Colima □, *Mexico* **146 D4** 19 10N 103 40W
Colima, Nevado de, *Mexico* **146 D4** 19 35N 103 45W
Colina, *Chile* **158 C1** 33 13 S 70 45W
Colina do Norte, *Guinea-Biss.* **100 C2** 12 28N 15 0W
Colinas, *Goiás, Brazil* **155 D2** 14 15 S 48 2W
Colinas, *Maranhão, Brazil* **154 C3** 6 0 S 44 10W
Colinton, *Australia* **117 C8** 35 50 S 149 10 E
Coll, *U.K.* **18 E2** 56 40N 6 35W
Collaguasi, *Chile* **158 A2** 21 5 S 68 45W
Collarada, Peña, *Spain* **34 C4** 42 43N 0 29W
Collarenebri, *Australia* **115 D4** 29 33 S 148 34 E
Collbran, *U.S.A.* **143 G10** 39 14N 107 58W
Colle di Val d'Elsa, *Italy* **39 E8** 43 25N 11 7 E
Colle Salvetti, *Italy* **38 E7** 43 34N 10 27 E
Colle Sannita, *Italy* **41 A7** 41 22N 14 48 E
Collécchio, *Italy* **38 D7** 44 45N 10 10 E
Colleen Bawn, *Zimbabwe* **107 G2** 21 0 S 29 12 E
College Park, *U.S.A.* **135 J3** 33 40N 84 27W
Collette, *Canada* **129 C6** 46 40N 65 30W
Collie, *N.S.W., Australia* **117 A8** 31 41 S 148 18 E
Collie, *W. Austral., Australia* **113 F2** 33 22 S 116 8 E
Collier B., *Australia* **112 C3** 16 10 S 124 15 E
Collier Ra., *Australia* **112 D2** 24 45 S 119 10 E
Colline Metallifere, *Italy* **38 E7** 43 10N 11 0 E
Collingwood, *Canada* **128 D3** 44 29N 80 13W
Collingwood, *N.Z.* **119 A7** 40 41 S 172 40 E
Collins, *Canada* **128 B2** 50 17N 89 27W
Collins, *U.S.A.* **140 G3** 37 54N 93 37W
Collinsville, *Australia* **114 C4** 20 30 S 147 56 E
Collinsville, *U.S.A.* **140 F7** 38 40N 89 59W
Collipulli, *Chile* **158 D1** 37 55 S 72 30W
Collo, *Algeria* **99 A6** 36 58N 6 37 E
Collonges, *France* **25 B9** 46 9N 5 52 E
Collooney, *Ireland* **19 B3** 54 11N 8 28W
Colmar, *France* **23 D14** 48 5N 7 20 E
Colmars, *France* **25 D10** 44 11N 6 39 E
Colmenar, *Spain* **37 J6** 36 54N 4 20W
Colmenar de Oreja, *Spain* **34 E1** 40 6N 3 25W
Colmenar Viejo, *Spain* **36 E7** 40 39N 3 47W
Colne, *U.K.* **16 D5** 53 51N 2 11W
Colo →, *Australia* **117 B9** 33 25 S 150 52 E
Cologna Véneta, *Italy* **39 C8** 45 19N 11 21 E
Cologne = Köln, *Germany* **26 E2** 50 56N 6 58 E
Colom, I., *Spain* **33 B11** 39 58N 4 16 E
Coloma, *U.S.A.* **144 G6** 38 48N 120 53W
Colomb-Béchar = Béchar, *Algeria* **99 B4** 31 38N 2 18W
Colombey-les-Belles, *France* **23 D12** 48 32N 5 54 E
Colombey-les-Deux-Églises, *France* **23 D11** 48 13N 4 50 E
Colômbia, *Brazil* **155 F2** 20 10 S 48 40W
Colombia ■, *S. Amer.* **152 C3** 3 45N 73 0W
Colombier, *Switz.* **28 C3** 46 58N 6 53 E
Colombo, *Sri Lanka* **83 L4** 6 56N 79 58 E
Colome, *U.S.A.* **138 D5** 43 16N 99 43W
Colón, *Argentina* **158 C4** 32 12 S 58 10W
Colón, *Cuba* **148 B3** 22 42N 80 54W
Colón, *Panama* **148 E4** 9 20N 79 54W
Colón, *Peru* **156 A1** 5 0 S 81 0W
Colona, *Australia* **113 F5** 31 38 S 132 4 E
Colonella, *Italy* **39 F10** 42 52N 13 50 E
Colonia, *Uruguay* **158 C4** 34 25 S 57 50W
Colonia de San Jordi, *Spain* **33 B9** 39 19N 2 59 E
Colonia Dora, *Argentina* **158 B3** 28 34 S 62 59W
Colonial Heights, *U.S.A.* **134 G7** 37 15N 77 25W
Colonne, C. delle, *Italy* **41 C10** 39 2N 17 11 E
Colonsay, *Canada* **131 C7** 51 59N 105 52W
Colonsay, *U.K.* **18 E2** 56 4N 6 12W
Colorado □, *U.S.A.* **143 G10** 39 30N 105 30W
Colorado →, *Argentina* **160 A4** 39 50 S 62 8W
Colorado →, *N. Amer.* **143 L6** 31 45N 114 40W
Colorado →, *U.S.A.* **139 L7** 28 36N 95 59W
Colorado City, *U.S.A.* **139 J4** 32 24N 100 52W
Colorado Desert, *U.S.A.* **132 D3** 34 20N 116 0W
Colorado Plateau, *U.S.A.* **143 H8** 37 0N 111 0W
Colorado River Aqueduct, *U.S.A.* **145 L12** 34 17N 114 10W
Colorado Springs, *U.S.A.* **138 F2** 38 50N 104 49W
Colorno, *Italy* **38 D7** 44 55N 10 21 E
Colotlán, *Mexico* **146 C4** 22 6N 103 16W
Colquechaca, *Bolivia* **157 D4** 18 40 S 66 1W
Colton, *Calif., U.S.A.* **145 L9** 34 4N 117 20W
Colton, *N.Y., U.S.A.* **137 B10** 44 33N 74 56W
Colton, *Wash., U.S.A.* **142 C5** 46 34N 117 8W
Columbia, *Ill., U.S.A.* **140 F6** 38 27N 90 12W
Columbia, *La., U.S.A.* **139 J8** 32 6N 92 5W
Columbia, *Miss., U.S.A.* **139 K10** 31 15N 89 50W
Columbia, *Mo., U.S.A.* **140 F4** 38 57N 92 20W
Columbia, *Pa., U.S.A.* **137 F8** 40 2N 76 30W
Columbia, *S.C., U.S.A.* **135 H5** 34 0N 81 2W
Columbia, *Tenn., U.S.A.* **135 H2** 35 37N 87 2W
Columbia →, *U.S.A.* **142 C1** 46 15N 124 5W
Columbia, C., *Canada* **6 A4** 83 0N 70 0W
Columbia, District of □, *U.S.A.* **134 F7** 38 55N 77 0W
Columbia, Mt., *Canada* **130 C5** 52 8N 117 20W
Columbia Basin, *U.S.A.* **142 C4** 46 45N 119 5W
Columbia Falls, *U.S.A.* **142 B6** 48 23N 114 11W
Columbia Heights, *U.S.A.* **138 C8** 45 3N 93 15W
Columbiana, *U.S.A.* **136 F4** 40 53N 80 42W
Columbretes, Is., *Spain* **34 F5** 39 50N 0 50 E
Columbus, *Ga., U.S.A.* **135 J3** 32 28N 84 59W
Columbus, *Ind., U.S.A.* **141 E11** 39 13N 85 55W
Columbus, *Kans., U.S.A.* **139 G7** 37 10N 94 50W
Columbus, *Miss., U.S.A.* **135 J1** 33 30N 88 25W
Columbus, *Mont., U.S.A.* **142 D9** 45 38N 109 15W
Columbus, *N. Dak., U.S.A.* **138 A3** 48 54N 102 47W
Columbus, *N. Mex., U.S.A.* **143 L10** 31 50N 107 38W
Columbus, *Nebr., U.S.A.* **138 E6** 41 26N 97 22W
Columbus, *Ohio, U.S.A.* **141 E13** 39 58N 83 0W
Columbus, *Tex., U.S.A.* **139 L6** 29 42N 96 33W
Columbus, *Wis., U.S.A.* **138 D10** 43 21N 89 1W
Columbus Grove, *U.S.A.* **141 D12** 40 55N 84 4W
Columbus Junction, *U.S.A.* **140 C5** 41 17N 91 22W
Colunga, *Spain* **36 B5** 43 29N 5 16W
Colusa, *U.S.A.* **144 F4** 39 13N 122 1W
Colville, *U.S.A.* **142 B5** 48 33N 117 54W
Colville →, *U.S.A.* **126 A4** 70 25N 150 30W
Colville, C., *N.Z.* **118 C4** 36 29 S 175 21 E
Colwyn Bay, *U.K.* **16 D4** 53 17N 3 44W
Coma, *Ethiopia* **95 F4** 8 29N 36 53 E
Comácchio, *Italy* **39 D9** 44 41N 12 10 E
Comalcalco, *Mexico* **147 D6** 18 16N 93 13W
Comallo, *Argentina* **160 B2** 41 0 S 70 5W
Comana, *Romania* **46 E7** 44 10N 26 10 E
Comanche, *Okla., U.S.A.* **139 H6** 34 22N 97 58W
Comanche, *Tex., U.S.A.* **139 K5** 31 54N 98 36W
Comandante Luis Piedrabuena, *Argentina* **160 C3** 49 59 S 68 54W
Comănești, *Romania* **46 C7** 46 25N 26 26 E
Comarapa, *Bolivia* **157 D5** 17 54 S 64 29W
Comayagua, *Honduras* **148 D2** 14 25N 87 37W
Combahee →, *U.S.A.* **135 J5** 32 30N 80 31W
Combara, *Australia* **117 A8** 31 10 S 148 22 E
Combeaufontaine, *France* **23 E12** 47 38N 5 54 E
Comber, *Canada* **136 D2** 42 14N 82 33W
Combermere Bay, *Burma* **78 F4** 19 37N 93 34 E
Comblain-au-Pont, *Belgium* **21 H7** 50 29N 5 35 E
Combles, *France* **23 B9** 50 2N 2 50 E
Combourg, *France* **22 D5** 48 25N 1 46W
Comboyne, *Australia* **117 A10** 31 34 S 152 27 E
Combronde, *France* **24 C7** 45 58N 3 5 E
Comeragh Mts., *Ireland* **19 D4** 52 17N 7 35W
Comet, *Australia* **114 C4** 23 36 S 148 38 E
Comilla, *Bangla.* **78 D3** 23 28N 91 10 E
Comines, *Belgium* **21 G1** 50 46N 3 0 E
Comino, *Malta* **32 C1** 36 2N 14 20 E
Comino, C., *Italy* **40 B2** 40 28N 9 47 E
Cómiso, *Italy* **41 F7** 36 57N 14 35 E
Comitán, *Mexico* **147 D6** 16 18N 92 9W
Commentry, *France* **24 B6** 46 20N 2 46 E
Commerce, *Ga., U.S.A.* **135 H4** 34 12N 83 28W
Commerce, *Tex., U.S.A.* **139 J7** 33 15N 95 54W
Commercy, *France* **23 D12** 48 43N 5 34 E
Commewijne □, *Surinam* **153 B7** 5 25N 54 45W
Committee B., *Canada* **127 B11** 68 30N 86 30W
Commonwealth B., *Antarctica* **7 C10** 67 0 S 144 0 E
Commonwealth of Independent States ■, *Eurasia* **57 D11** 60 0N 100 0 E
Commoron Cr. →, *Australia* **115 D5** 28 22 S 150 8 E
Communism Pk. = Kommunizma, Pik, *Tajikistan* **55 D6** 39 0N 72 2 E
Como, *Italy* **38 C6** 45 48N 9 5 E
Como, L. di, *Italy* **38 B6** 46 5N 9 17 E
Comodoro Rivadavia, *Argentina* **160 C3** 45 50 S 67 40W
Comorin, C., *India* **83 K3** 8 3N 77 40 E
Comoriște, *Romania* **46 D2** 45 10N 21 35 E
Comoro Is. = Comoros ■, *Ind. Oc.* **93 H8** 12 10 S 44 15 E
Comoros ■, *Ind. Oc.* **93 H8** 12 10 S 44 15 E
Comox, *Canada* **130 D4** 49 42N 124 55W
Compiègne, *France* **23 C9** 49 24N 2 50 E
Comporta, *Portugal* **37 G2** 38 22N 8 46W
Compostela, *Mexico* **146 C4** 21 15N 104 53W
Compostela, *Phil.* **71 H6** 7 40N 126 2 E
Comprida, I., *Brazil* **159 A6** 24 50 S 47 42W
Compton, *U.S.A.* **145 M8** 33 54N 118 13W
Compton Downs, *Australia* **115 E4** 30 28 S 146 30 E
Con Cuong, *Vietnam* **76 C5** 19 2N 104 54 E
Con Son, Is., *Vietnam* **77 H6** 8 41N 106 37 E
Cona Niyeu, *Argentina* **160 B3** 41 58 S 67 0W
Conakry, *Guinea* **100 D2** 9 29N 13 49W
Conara Junction, *Australia* **114 G4** 41 50 S 147 26 E
Conargo, *Australia* **117 C6** 35 16 S 145 10 E
Concarneau, *France* **22 E3** 47 52N 3 56W
Conceição, *Brazil* **154 C4** 7 33 S 38 31W
Conceição, *Mozam.* **107 F4** 18 47 S 36 7 E
Conceição da Barra, *Brazil* **155 E4** 18 35 S 39 45W
Conceição do Araguaia, *Brazil* **154 C2** 8 0 S 49 2W
Conceição do Canindé, *Brazil* **154 C3** 7 54 S 41 34W
Concepción, *Argentina* **158 B2** 27 20 S 65 35W
Concepción, *Bolivia* **157 D5** 16 15 S 62 8W
Concepción, *Chile* **158 D1** 36 50 S 73 0W
Concepción, *Mexico* **147 D6** 18 15N 90 5W
Concepción, *Paraguay* **158 A4** 23 22 S 57 26W
Concepción, *Peru* **156 C2** 11 54 S 75 19W
Concepción □, *Chile* **158 D1** 37 0 S 72 30W
Concepción →, *Mexico* **146 A2** 30 32N 113 2W
Concepción, Est. de, *Chile* **160 D2** 50 30 S 74 55W
Concepción, L., *Bolivia* **157 D5** 17 20 S 61 20W
Concepción, Punta, *Mexico* **146 B2** 26 55N 111 59W
Concepción del Oro, *Mexico* **146 C4** 24 40N 101 30W
Concepción del Uruguay, *Argentina* **158 C4** 32 35 S 58 20W
Conception, Pt., *U.S.A.* **145 L6** 34 27N 120 28W
Conception B., *Namibia* **104 C1** 23 55 S 14 22 E
Conception I., *Bahamas* **149 B4** 23 52N 75 9W
Concession, *Zimbabwe* **107 F3** 17 27 S 30 56 E
Conchas Dam, *U.S.A.* **139 H2** 35 22N 104 11W
Conche, *Canada* **129 B8** 50 55N 55 58W
Concho, *U.S.A.* **143 J9** 34 28N 109 36W
Concho →, *U.S.A.* **139 K5** 31 34N 99 43W
Conchos →, *Chihuahua, Mexico* **146 B4** 29 32N 105 0W
Conchos →, *Tamaulipas, Mexico* **147 B5** 25 9N 98 35W
Concord, *Calif., U.S.A.* **144 H4** 37 59N 122 2W
Concord, *Mich., U.S.A.* **141 B12** 42 11N 84 38W
Concord, *N.C., U.S.A.* **135 H5** 35 25N 80 35W
Concord, *N.H., U.S.A.* **137 C13** 43 12N 71 32W
Concordia, *Argentina* **158 C4** 31 20 S 58 2W
Concórdia, *Brazil* **152 D4** 4 36 S 66 36W
Concordia, *Mexico* **146 C3** 23 18N 106 2W
Concordia, *Kans., U.S.A.* **138 F6** 39 34N 97 40W
Concordia, *Mo., U.S.A.* **140 F3** 38 59N 93 34W
Concots, *France* **24 D5** 44 26N 1 40 E
Concrete, *U.S.A.* **142 B3** 48 32N 121 45W
Condah, *Australia* **116 D4** 37 57 S 141 44 E
Condamine, *Australia* **115 D5** 26 56 S 150 9 E
Condat, *France* **24 C6** 45 21N 2 46 E
Condé, *Angola* **103 E2** 10 50 S 14 37 E
Conde, *Brazil* **155 D4** 11 49 S 37 37W
Conde, *U.S.A.* **138 C5** 45 9N 98 6W
Condé-sur-l'Escaut, *France* **23 B10** 50 26N 3 34 E
Condé-sur-Noireau, *France* **22 D6** 48 51N 0 33W
Condeúba, *Brazil* **155 D3** 14 52 S 42 0W
Condobolin, *Australia* **115 E4** 33 4 S 147 6 E
Condom, *France* **24 E4** 43 57N 0 22 E
Condon, *U.S.A.* **142 D3** 45 15N 120 11W
Condove, *Italy* **38 C4** 45 8N 7 19 E
Conegliano, *Italy* **39 C9** 45 53N 12 18 E
Conejera, I., *Spain* **33 B9** 39 11N 2 58 E
Conejos, *Mexico* **146 B4** 26 14N 103 53W
Conflans-en-Jarnisy, *France* **23 C12** 49 10N 5 52 E
Confolens, *France* **24 B4** 46 2N 0 40 E
Confuso →, *Paraguay* **158 B4** 25 9 S 57 34W
Congjiang, *China* **68 E7** 25 43N 108 52 E
Congleton, *U.K.* **16 D5** 53 10N 2 12W
Congo = Zaïre →, *Africa* **103 D2** 6 4 S 12 24 E
Congo, *Brazil* **154 C4** 7 48 S 36 40W
Congo (Kinshasa) = Zaïre ■, *Africa* **103 C4** 3 0 S 23 0 E
Congo ■, *Africa* **102 C3** 1 0 S 16 0 E
Congo Basin, *Africa* **92 G6** 0 10 S 24 30 E
Congonhas, *Brazil* **155 F3** 20 30 S 43 52W
Congress, *U.S.A.* **143 J7** 34 9N 112 51W
Conil, *Spain* **37 J4** 36 17N 6 10W
Coniston, *Canada* **128 C3** 46 29N 80 51W
Conjeeveram = Kanchipuram, *India* **83 H4** 12 52N 79 45 E
Conjuboy, *Australia* **114 B3** 18 35 S 144 35 E
Conklin, *Canada* **131 B6** 55 38N 111 5W
Conlea, *Australia* **115 E3** 30 7 S 144 35 E
Conn, L., *Ireland* **19 B2** 54 3N 9 15W
Connacht, *Ireland* **19 C3** 53 23N 8 40W
Conneaut, *U.S.A.* **136 E4** 41 57N 80 34W
Connecticut □, *U.S.A.* **137 E12** 41 30N 72 45W
Connecticut →, *U.S.A.* **137 E12** 41 16N 72 20W
Connell, *U.S.A.* **142 C4** 46 40N 118 52W
Connellsville, *U.S.A.* **136 F5** 40 1N 79 35W
Connemara, *Ireland* **19 C2** 53 29N 9 45W
Connemaugh →, *U.S.A.* **136 F5** 40 28N 79 19W
Conner, *Phil.* **70 C3** 17 48N 121 19 E
Connerré, *France* **22 D7** 48 3N 0 30 E
Connersville, *U.S.A.* **141 E11** 39 39N 85 8W
Connors Ra., *Australia* **114 C4** 21 40 S 149 10 E
Conoble, *Australia* **117 B6** 32 55 S 144 33 E
Cononaco →, *Ecuador* **152 D2** 1 32 S 75 35W
Cononbridge, *U.K.* **18 D4** 57 32N 4 30W
Conquest, *Canada* **131 C7** 51 32N 107 14W
Conrad, *Iowa, U.S.A.* **140 B4** 42 14N 92 52W
Conrad, *Mont., U.S.A.* **142 B8** 48 10N 111 57W
Conran, C., *Australia* **117 D8** 37 49 S 148 44 E
Conroe, *U.S.A.* **139 K7** 30 19N 95 27W
Conselheiro Lafaiete, *Brazil* **155 F3** 20 40 S 43 48W
Conselheiro Pena, *Brazil* **155 E3** 19 10 S 41 30W
Consort, *Canada* **131 C6** 52 1N 110 46W
Constance = Konstanz, *Germany* **27 H5** 47 39N 9 10 E
Constance, L. = Bodensee, *Europe* **29 A8** 47 35N 9 25 E
Constanța, *Romania* **46 E9** 44 14N 28 38 E
Constanța □, *Romania* **46 E9** 44 15N 28 15 E
Constantina, *Spain* **37 H5** 37 51N 5 40W
Constantine, *Algeria* **99 A6** 36 25N 6 42 E
Constantine, *U.S.A.* **141 C11** 41 50N 85 40W
Constitución, *Chile* **158 D1** 35 20 S 72 30W
Constitución, *Uruguay* **158 C4** 31 0 S 57 50W
Consuegra, *Spain* **37 F7** 39 28N 3 36W
Consul, *Canada* **131 D7** 49 20N 109 30W
Contact, *U.S.A.* **142 F6** 41 46N 114 45W
Contai, *India* **81 J12** 21 54N 87 46 E
Contamana, *Peru* **156 B3** 7 19 S 74 55W
Contarina, *Italy* **39 C9** 45 2N 12 13 E
Contas →, *Brazil* **155 D4** 14 17 S 39 1W
Contes, *France* **25 E11** 43 49N 7 19 E
Conthey, *Switz.* **28 D4** 46 14N 7 18 E
Continental, *U.S.A.* **141 C12** 41 6N 84 16W
Contoocook, *U.S.A.* **137 C13** 43 13N 71 45W
Contra Costa, *Mozam.* **105 D5** 25 9 S 33 30 E
Contres, *France* **22 E8** 47 24N 1 26 E
Contrexéville, *France* **23 D12** 48 10N 5 53 E
Contumaza, *Peru* **156 B2** 7 23 S 78 57W
Convención, *Colombia* **152 B3** 8 28N 73 21W
Conversano, *Italy* **41 B10** 40 57N 17 8 E
Converse, *U.S.A.* **141 D11** 40 35N 85 52W
Convoy, *U.S.A.* **141 D12** 40 55N 84 43W
Conway = Conwy, *U.K.* **16 D4** 53 17N 3 50W
Conway = Conwy →, *U.K.* **16 D4** 53 18N 3 50W
Conway, *Ark., U.S.A.* **139 H8** 35 5N 92 26W
Conway, *N.H., U.S.A.* **137 C13** 43 59N 71 7W
Conway, *S.C., U.S.A.* **135 J6** 33 51N 79 3W
Conway, L., *Australia* **115 D2** 28 17 S 135 35 E
Conwy, *U.K.* **16 D4** 53 17N 3 50W
Conwy →, *U.K.* **16 D4** 53 18N 3 50W
Coober Pedy, *Australia* **115 D1** 29 1 S 134 43 E
Cooch Behar = Koch Bihar, *India* **78 B2** 26 22N 89 29 E
Coodardy, *Australia* **113 E2** 27 15 S 117 39 E
Cook, *Australia* **113 F5** 30 37 S 130 25 E
Cook, *U.S.A.* **138 B8** 47 49N 92 39W
Cook, B., *Chile* **160 E2** 55 10 S 70 0W
Cook, Mt., *N.Z.* **119 D5** 43 36 S 170 9 E
Cook Inlet, *U.S.A.* **126 C4** 60 0N 152 0W
Cook Is., *Pac. Oc.* **123 J11** 17 0 S 160 0W
Cook Strait, *N.Z.* **118 H3** 41 15 S 174 29 E
Cooke Plains, *Australia* **116 C3** 35 23 S 139 34 E
Cookeville, *U.S.A.* **135 G3** 36 10N 85 30W
Cookhouse, *S. Africa* **104 E4** 32 44 S 25 47 E
Cookshire, *Canada* **137 A13** 45 25N 71 38W
Cookstown, *U.K.* **19 B5** 54 40N 6 43W
Cookstown □, *U.K.* **19 B5** 54 40N 6 43W
Cooksville, *Canada* **136 C5** 43 36N 79 35W
Cooktown, *Australia* **114 B4** 15 30 S 145 16 E
Coolabah, *Australia* **117 A7** 31 1 S 146 43 E
Cooladdi, *Australia* **115 D4** 26 37 S 145 23 E
Coolah, *Australia* **117 A8** 31 48 S 149 41 E
Coolamon, *Australia* **115 E4** 34 46 S 147 8 E
Coolangatta, *Australia* **115 D5** 28 11 S 153 29 E
Coolgardie, *Australia* **113 F3** 30 55 S 121 8 E
Coolibah, *Australia* **112 C5** 15 33 S 130 56 E
Coolidge, *U.S.A.* **143 K8** 32 59N 111 31W
Coolidge Dam, *U.S.A.* **143 K8** 33 0N 110 20W
Cooma, *Australia* **117 D8** 36 12 S 149 8 E
Coon Rapids, *U.S.A.* **140 C2** 41 53N 94 41W
Coonabarabran, *Australia* **117 A8** 31 14 S 149 18 E
Coonalpyn, *Australia* **116 C3** 35 43 S 139 52 E
Coonamble, *Australia* **117 A8** 30 56 S 148 27 E
Coonana, *Australia* **113 F3** 31 0 S 123 0 E
Coondapoor, *India* **83 H2** 13 42N 74 40 E
Coongie, *Australia* **115 D3** 27 9 S 140 8 E
Coongoola, *Australia* **115 D4** 27 43 S 145 51 E
Cooninie, L., *Australia* **115 D2** 26 4 S 139 59 E
Coonoor, *India* **83 J3** 11 21N 76 45 E
Cooper, *U.S.A.* **139 J7** 33 23N 95 42W
Cooper →, *U.S.A.* **135 J6** 32 50N 79 56W
Cooper Cr. →, *N. Terr., Australia* **110 C5** 12 7 S 132 41 E
Cooper Cr. →, *S. Austral., Australia* **115 D2** 28 29 S 137 46 E
Cooperstown, *N. Dak., U.S.A.* **138 B5** 47 27N 98 8W
Cooperstown, *N.Y., U.S.A.* **137 D10** 42 42N 74 56W
Coopersville, *U.S.A.* **141 A11** 43 4N 85 57W
Coorabie, *Australia* **113 F5** 31 54 S 132 18 E
Coorabulka, *Australia* **114 C3** 23 41 S 140 20 E
Coorow, *Australia* **113 E2** 29 53 S 116 2 E
Cooroy, *Australia* **115 D5** 26 22 S 152 54 E
Coos Bay, *U.S.A.* **142 E1** 43 22N 124 13W
Cootamundra, *Australia* **117 C8** 34 36 S 148 1 E
Cootehill, *Ireland* **19 B4** 54 5N 7 5W
Cooyar, *Australia* **115 D5** 26 59 S 151 51 E
Cooyeana, *Australia* **114 C2** 24 29 S 138 45 E
Copahue Paso, *Argentina* **158 D1** 37 49 S 71 8W
Copainalá, *Mexico* **147 D6** 17 8N 93 11W
Copán, *Honduras* **148 D2** 14 50N 89 9W
Copatana, *Brazil* **152 D4** 2 48 S 67 4W
Cope, *U.S.A.* **138 F3** 39 40N 102 51W
Cope, C., *Spain* **35 H3** 37 26N 1 28W
Cope Cope, *Australia* **116 D5** 36 27 S 143 5 E
Copenhagen = København, *Denmark* **15 J6** 55 41N 12 34 E
Copertino, *Italy* **41 B11** 40 17N 18 2 E
Copeville, *Australia* **116 C3** 34 47 S 139 51 E
Copiapó, *Chile* **158 B1** 27 30 S 70 20W
Copiapó →, *Chile* **158 B1** 27 19 S 70 56W
Copley, *Australia* **116 A3** 30 36 S 138 26 E
Copp L., *Canada* **130 A6** 60 14N 114 40W
Copparo, *Italy* **39 D8** 44 52N 11 49 E
Coppename →, *Surinam* **153 B6** 5 48N 55 55W
Copper Center, *U.S.A.* **126 B5** 61 58N 145 18W
Copper Cliff, *Canada* **128 C3** 46 28N 81 4W
Copper Harbor, *U.S.A.* **134 B2** 47 28N 87 53W
Copper Queen, *Zimbabwe* **107 F2** 17 29 S 29 18 E
Copperbelt □, *Zambia* **107 E2** 13 15 S 27 30 E
Coppermine, *Canada* **126 B8** 67 50N 115 5W
Coppermine →, *Canada* **126 B8** 67 49N 116 4W
Copperopolis, *U.S.A.* **144 H6** 37 58N 120 38W

Dalgān 189

Cromarty, U.K. 18 D4 57 40N 4 2W
Cromer, U.K. 16 E9 52 56N 1 18 E
Cromwell, N.Z. 119 F4 45 3 S 169 14 E
Cronat, France 23 F10 46 43N 3 40 E
Cronulla, Australia 117 C9 34 3 S 151 8 E
Crooked →, Canada 130 C4 54 50N 122 54W
Crooked →, U.S.A. 142 D3 44 32N 121 16W
Crooked I., Bahamas 149 B5 22 50N 74 10W
Crooked Island Passage, Bahamas 149 B5 23 0N 74 30W
Crookston, Minn., U.S.A. 138 B6 47 47N 96 37W
Crookston, Nebr., U.S.A. 138 D4 42 56N 100 45W
Crooksville, U.S.A. 134 F4 39 46N 82 6W
Crookwell, Australia 117 C8 34 28 S 149 24 E
Crosby, Minn., U.S.A. 138 B8 46 29N 93 58W
Crosby, N. Dak., U.S.A. 131 D8 48 55N 103 18W
Crosby, Pa., U.S.A. 136 E6 41 45N 78 23W
Crosbyton, U.S.A. 139 J4 33 40N 101 14W
Cross →, Nigeria 101 E6 4 42N 8 21 E
Cross City, U.S.A. 135 L4 29 38N 83 7W
Cross Fell, U.K. 16 C5 54 44N 2 29W
Cross L., Canada 131 C9 54 45N 97 30W
Cross Plains, U.S.A. 139 J5 32 8N 99 11W
Cross River □, Nigeria 101 D6 6 0N 8 0 E
Cross Sound, U.S.A. 126 C6 58 0N 135 0W
Cross Timbers, U.S.A. 140 F3 38 1N 93 14W
Crossett, U.S.A. 139 J9 33 8N 91 58W
Crossfield, Canada 130 C6 51 25N 114 0W
Crosshaven, Ireland 19 E3 51 48N 8 19W
Crossley, Mt., N.Z. 119 C7 42 50 S 172 5 E
Crossville, U.S.A. 141 F8 38 10N 88 4W
Croton-on-Hudson, U.S.A. 137 E11 41 12N 73 55W
Crotone, Italy 41 C10 39 5N 17 6 E
Crow →, Canada 130 B4 59 41N 124 20W
Crow Agency, U.S.A. 142 D10 45 36N 107 28W
Crow Hd., Ireland 19 E1 51 34N 10 9W
Crowell, U.S.A. 139 J5 33 59N 99 43W
Crowl Creek, Australia 117 B6 32 0 S 145 30 E
Crowley, U.S.A. 139 K8 30 13N 92 22W
Crowley, L., U.S.A. 144 H8 37 35N 118 42W
Crown Point, U.S.A. 141 C9 41 25N 87 22W
Crows Landing, U.S.A. 144 H5 37 23N 121 6W
Crows Nest, Australia 115 D5 27 16 S 152 4 E
Crowsnest Pass, Canada 130 D6 49 40N 114 40W
Croydon, Australia 114 B3 18 13 S 142 14 E
Croydon, U.K. 17 F7 51 18N 0 5W
Crozet Is., Ind. Oc. 109 J4 46 27 S 52 0 E
Crozon, France 22 D2 48 15N 4 30W
Cruz, C., Cuba 148 C4 19 50N 77 50W
Cruz Alta, Brazil 159 B5 28 45 S 53 40W
Cruz das Almas, Brazil 155 D4 12 0 S 39 6W
Cruz de Malta, Brazil 154 C3 8 15 S 40 20W
Cruz del Eje, Argentina 158 C3 30 45 S 64 50W
Cruzeiro, Brazil 155 F2 22 33 S 45 0W
Cruzeiro do Oeste, Brazil 159 A5 23 46 S 53 4W
Cruzeiro do Sul, Brazil 156 B3 7 35 S 72 35W
Cry L., Canada 130 B3 58 45N 129 0W
Crystal Bay, U.S.A. 144 F7 39 15N 120 0W
Crystal Brook, Australia 116 B3 33 21 S 138 12 E
Crystal City, Mo., U.S.A. 140 F6 38 13N 90 23W
Crystal City, Tex., U.S.A. 139 L5 28 41N 99 50W
Crystal Falls, U.S.A. 134 B1 46 5N 88 20W
Crystal Lake, U.S.A. 141 B8 42 14N 88 19W
Crystal River, U.S.A. 135 L4 28 54N 82 35W
Crystal Springs, U.S.A. 139 K9 31 59N 90 21W
Csongrád, Hungary 31 E13 46 43N 20 12 E
Csongrád □, Hungary 31 E13 46 32N 20 15 E
Csorna, Hungary 31 D10 47 38N 17 18 E
Csurgo, Hungary 31 E10 46 16N 17 9 E
Cu Lao Hon, Vietnam 77 G7 10 54N 108 18 E
Cua Rao, Vietnam 76 C5 19 16N 104 27 E
Cuácua →, Mozam. 107 F4 17 54 S 37 0 E
Cuamato, Angola 103 F3 17 2 S 15 7 E
Cuamba, Mozam. 107 E4 14 45 S 36 22 E
Cuando →, Angola 103 F4 17 30 S 23 15 E
Cuando Cubango □, Angola 103 F3 16 25 S 20 0 E
Cuangar, Angola 103 F3 17 36 S 18 39 E
Cuango, Angola 103 D3 6 15 S 16 42 E
Cuanza →, Angola 92 G5 9 2 S 13 30 E
Cuanza Norte □, Angola 103 D2 8 50 S 14 30 E
Cuanza Sul □, Angola 103 E2 10 50 S 14 50 E
Cuarto →, Argentina 158 C3 33 25 S 63 2W
Cuatrociénegas, Mexico 146 B4 26 59N 102 5W
Cuauhtémoc, Mexico 146 B3 28 25N 106 52W
Cuba, Portugal 37 G3 38 10N 7 54W
Cuba, Mo., U.S.A. 140 F5 38 4N 91 24W
Cuba, N. Mex., U.S.A. 143 J10 36 1N 107 4W
Cuba, N.Y., U.S.A. 136 D6 42 13N 78 17W
Cuba ■, W. Indies 148 B4 22 0N 79 0W
Cuba City, U.S.A. 140 B6 42 36N 90 26W
Cubal, Angola 103 E2 12 26 S 14 3 E
Cuballing, Australia 113 F2 32 50 S 117 10 E
Cubango →, Africa 103 F4 18 50 S 22 25 E
Cubanja, Angola 103 E4 14 49 S 21 20 E
Cubia, Angola 103 F4 15 58 S 21 42 E
Çubuk, Turkey 88 C5 40 14N 33 3 E
Cucamonga, U.S.A. 145 L9 34 10N 117 30W
Cuchi, Angola 103 E3 14 37 S 16 58 E
Cuchillo-Có, Argentina 160 A4 38 20 S 64 37W
Cuchivero →, Venezuela 152 B4 7 40N 65 57W
Cuchumatanes, Sierra de los, Guatemala 148 C1 15 35N 91 25W
Cucuí, Brazil 152 C4 1 12N 66 50W
Cucurpe, Mexico 146 A2 30 20N 110 43W
Cucurrupí, Colombia 152 C2 4 23N 76 56W
Cúcuta, Colombia 152 B3 7 54N 72 31W
Cudahy, U.S.A. 141 B9 42 58N 87 52W
Cudalbi, Romania 46 D8 45 46N 27 41 E
Cuddalore, India 83 J4 11 46N 79 45 E
Cuddapah, India 83 G4 14 30N 78 47 E
Cuddapan, L., Australia 114 D3 25 45 S 141 26 E
Cudgewa, Australia 117 D7 36 10 S 147 42 E
Cudillero, Spain 36 B4 43 33N 6 9W
Cue, Australia 113 E2 27 25 S 117 54 E
Cuéllar, Spain 36 D6 41 23N 4 21W
Cuemba, Angola 103 E3 11 50 S 17 42 E
Cuenca, Ecuador 152 D2 2 50 S 79 9W
Cuenca, Spain 34 E2 40 5N 2 10W
Cuenca □, Spain 34 F2 40 0N 2 0W
Cuenca, Serranía de, Spain 34 F3 39 55N 1 50W
Cuerdo del Pozo, Pantano de la, Spain 34 D2 41 51N 2 44W
Cuernavaca, Mexico 147 D5 18 50N 99 20W
Cuero, U.S.A. 139 L6 29 6N 97 17W
Cuers, France 25 E10 43 14N 6 5 E
Cuervo, U.S.A. 139 H2 35 2N 104 25W
Cuesmes, Belgium 21 H3 50 26N 3 56 E
Cuevas, Cerro, Bolivia 157 E4 22 0 S 65 12W
Cuevas del Almanzora, Spain 35 H3 37 18N 1 58W
Cuevo, Bolivia 157 E5 20 15 S 63 30W
Cugir, Romania 46 D4 45 48N 23 25 E
Cuiabá, Brazil 157 D6 15 30 S 56 0W
Cuiabá →, Brazil 157 D6 17 5 S 56 36W
Cuilco, Guatemala 148 C1 15 24N 91 58W
Cuillin Hills, U.K. 18 D2 57 14N 6 15W
Cuillin Sd., U.K. 18 D2 57 4N 6 20W
Cuima, Angola 103 E3 13 25 S 15 45 E
Cuiseaux, France 25 B9 46 30N 5 22 E
Cuité, Brazil 154 C4 6 29 S 36 9W
Cuito →, Angola 103 F4 18 1 S 20 48 E
Cuito Cuanavale, Angola 103 F3 15 10 S 19 10 E
Cuitzeo, L. de, Mexico 146 D4 19 55N 101 5W
Cuiuni →, Brazil 153 D5 0 45 S 63 7W
Cuivre →, U.S.A. 140 F6 38 55N 90 44W
Cuivre, West Fork →, U.S.A. 140 E6 39 2N 90 58W
Cujmir, Romania 46 E3 44 13N 22 57 E
Cukai, Malaysia 77 K4 4 13N 103 25 E
Culaba, Phil. 71 F5 11 40N 124 32 E
Culan, France 24 B6 46 34N 2 20 E
Culasi, Phil. 71 F4 11 26N 122 3 E
Culauan, Phil. 71 J5 5 58N 125 40 E
Culbertson, U.S.A. 138 A2 48 9N 104 31W
Culburra, Australia 116 C3 35 50 S 139 58 E
Culcairn, Australia 115 F4 35 41 S 147 3 E
Culebra, Sierra de la, Spain 36 D4 41 55N 6 20W
Culemborg, Neths. 20 E6 51 58N 5 14 E
Culgoa, Australia 116 C5 35 44 S 143 6 E
Culgoa →, Australia 115 D4 29 56 S 146 20 E
Culiacán, Mexico 146 C3 24 50N 107 23W
Culiacán →, Mexico 146 C3 24 30N 107 42W
Culion, Phil. 71 F3 11 54N 120 1 E
Culiseu →, Brazil 157 C7 12 14 S 53 17W
Cúllar de Baza, Spain 35 H2 37 35N 2 34W
Cullarin Ra., Australia 117 C8 34 30 S 149 30 E
Cullen, U.K. 18 D6 57 45N 2 50W
Cullen Pt., Australia 114 A3 11 57 S 141 54 E
Cullera, Spain 35 F4 39 9N 0 17W
Cullman, U.S.A. 135 H2 34 11N 86 51W
Culloden Moor, U.K. 18 D4 57 29N 4 7W
Cullom, U.S.A. 141 D8 40 53N 88 16W
Culoz, France 25 C9 45 47N 5 46 E
Culpataro, Australia 116 B6 33 40 S 144 22 E
Culpeper, U.S.A. 134 F7 38 30N 78 0W
Culuene →, Brazil 157 C7 12 56 S 52 51W
Culver, U.S.A. 141 C10 41 13N 86 25W
Culver, Pt., Australia 113 F3 32 54 S 124 43 E
Culverden, N.Z. 119 C7 42 47 S 172 49 E
Cuma, Angola 103 E3 12 52 S 15 5 E
Cumali, Turkey 45 H9 36 42N 27 28 E
Cumaná, Venezuela 153 A5 10 30N 64 5W
Cumare, Colombia 152 C3 0 49N 72 32W
Cumari, Brazil 155 E2 18 16 S 48 11W
Cumberland, Canada 130 D3 49 40N 125 0W
Cumberland, Iowa, U.S.A. 140 C2 41 16N 94 52W
Cumberland, Md., U.S.A. 134 F6 39 39N 78 46W
Cumberland, Wis., U.S.A. 138 C8 45 32N 92 1W
Cumberland →, U.S.A. 135 G2 36 15N 87 0W
Cumberland, C., Vanuatu 121 D4 14 39 S 166 37 E
Cumberland I., U.S.A. 135 K5 30 50N 81 25W
Cumberland Is., Australia 114 C4 20 35 S 149 10 E
Cumberland L., Canada 131 C8 54 3N 102 18W
Cumberland Pen., Canada 127 B13 67 0N 64 0W
Cumberland Plateau, U.S.A. 135 H3 36 0N 85 0W
Cumberland Sd., Canada 127 B13 65 30N 66 0W
Cumborah, Australia 115 D4 29 40 S 147 45 E
Cumbres Mayores, Spain 37 G4 38 4N 6 39W
Cumbria □, U.K. 16 C5 54 35N 2 55W
Cumbrian Mts., U.K. 16 C4 54 30N 3 0W
Cumbum, India 83 G4 15 40N 79 10 E
Cuminá →, Brazil 153 D6 1 30 S 56 0W
Cuminapanema →, Brazil 153 D7 1 9 S 54 54W
Cummings Mt., U.S.A. 145 K8 35 2N 118 34W
Cummins, Australia 115 E2 34 16 S 135 43 E
Cumnock, Australia 117 B8 32 59 S 148 46 E
Cumnock, U.K. 18 F4 55 27N 4 18W
Cumpas, Mexico 146 A3 30 0N 109 48W
Cumplida, Pta., Canary Is. 33 F2 28 50N 17 48W
Çumra, Turkey 88 E5 37 34N 32 45 E
Cuncumén, Chile 158 C1 31 53 S 70 38W
Cundeelee, Australia 113 F3 30 43 S 123 26 E
Cunderdin, Australia 113 F2 31 37 S 117 12 E
Cundinamarca □, Colombia 152 C3 5 0N 74 0W
Cunene □, Angola 103 F3 16 30 S 15 0 E
Cunene →, Angola 103 F2 17 20 S 11 50 E
Cúneo, Italy 38 D4 44 23N 7 31 E
Cunhinga, Angola 103 E3 12 11 S 16 47 E
Cunillera, I., Spain 33 C7 38 59N 1 13 E
Cunjamba, Angola 103 F4 15 27 S 20 10 E
Cunlhat, France 24 C7 45 38N 3 32 E
Cunnamulla, Australia 115 D4 28 2 S 145 38 E
Cuorgnè, Italy 38 C4 45 23N 7 39 E
Cupar, Canada 131 C8 50 57N 104 10W
Cupar, U.K. 18 E5 56 20N 3 3W
Cupica, G. de, Colombia 152 B2 6 25N 77 30W
Ćuprija, Serbia 42 D6 43 57N 21 26 E
Curaçá, Brazil 154 C4 8 59 S 39 54W
Curaçao, Neth. Ant. 149 D6 12 10N 69 0W
Curacautín, Chile 160 A2 38 26 S 71 53W
Curahuara de Carangas, Bolivia 156 D4 17 52 S 68 26W
Curanilahue, Chile 158 D1 37 29 S 73 28W
Curaray →, Peru 152 D3 2 20 S 74 5W
Curatabaca, Venezuela 153 B5 6 19N 62 51W
Cure →, France 23 E10 47 40N 3 41 E
Curepto, Chile 158 D1 35 8 S 72 1W
Curiapo, Venezuela 153 B5 8 33N 61 5W
Curicó, Chile 158 C1 34 55 S 71 20W
Curicó □, Chile 158 C1 34 50 S 71 15W
Curicuriari →, Brazil 152 D4 0 14 S 66 48W
Curimatá, Brazil 154 D3 10 2 S 44 17W
Curiplaya, Colombia 152 C3 0 16N 74 52W
Curitiba, Brazil 159 B6 25 20 S 49 10W
Currabubula, Australia 117 A9 31 16 S 150 44 E
Currais Novos, Brazil 154 C4 6 13 S 36 30W
Curralinho, Brazil 154 B2 1 45 S 49 46W
Currant, U.S.A. 142 G6 38 51N 115 32W
Curranyalpa, Australia 117 A6 30 53 S 144 39 E
Curraweena, Australia 117 A6 30 47 S 145 54 E
Currawilla, Australia 114 D3 25 10 S 141 20 E
Current →, U.S.A. 139 G9 36 15N 90 55W
Currie, Australia 114 F3 39 56 S 143 53 E
Currie, U.S.A. 142 F6 40 16N 114 45W
Currie, Mt., S. Africa 105 E4 30 29 S 29 21 E
Currituck Sd., U.S.A. 135 G8 36 20N 75 52W
Cursole, Somali Rep. 108 D3 2 14N 45 25 E
Curtea de Argeş, Romania 46 D5 45 12N 24 42 E
Curtis, Spain 36 B2 43 7N 8 4W
Curtis, U.S.A. 138 E4 40 38N 100 31W
Curtis Group, Australia 114 F4 39 30 S 146 37 E
Curtis I., Australia 114 C5 23 35 S 151 10 E
Curuá →, Pará, Brazil 153 D7 2 24 S 54 5W
Curuá →, Pará, Brazil 157 B7 5 23 S 54 22W
Curuá, I., Brazil 154 A1 0 48N 50 10W
Curuaés →, Brazil 157 B7 7 30 S 54 45W
Curuápanema →, Brazil 153 D6 2 25 S 55 2W
Curuçá, Brazil 154 B2 0 43 S 47 50W
Curuguaty, Paraguay 159 A4 24 31 S 55 42W
Çürüksu Çayi →, Turkey 49 G4 37 27N 27 11 E
Curup, Indonesia 74 C2 4 26 S 102 13 E
Curupira, Serra, S. Amer. 153 C5 1 25N 64 30W
Cururu →, Brazil 157 B6 7 12 S 58 3W
Cururupu, Brazil 154 B3 1 50 S 44 50W
Curuzú Cuatiá, Argentina 158 B4 29 50 S 58 5W
Curvelo, Brazil 155 E3 18 45 S 44 27W
Curyo, Australia 116 C5 35 50 S 142 47 E
Cushing, U.S.A. 139 H6 35 59N 96 46W
Cushing, Mt., Canada 130 B3 57 35N 126 57W
Cusihuiriáchic, Mexico 146 B3 28 10N 106 50W
Cusna, Monte, Italy 38 D7 44 13N 10 25 E
Cusset, France 24 B7 46 8N 3 28 E
Custer, U.S.A. 138 D3 43 46N 103 36W
Cut Bank, U.S.A. 142 B7 48 38N 112 20W
Cutervo, Peru 156 B2 6 25 S 78 55W
Cuthbert, U.S.A. 135 K3 31 46N 84 48W
Cutler, U.S.A. 144 J7 36 31N 119 17W
Cutral-Có, Argentina 160 A3 38 58 S 69 15W
Cutro, Italy 41 C9 39 1N 16 58 E
Cuttaburra →, Australia 115 D3 29 43 S 144 22 E
Cuttack, India 82 D7 20 25N 85 57 E
Cuvelai, Angola 103 F3 15 44 S 15 50 E
Cuvier, C., Australia 113 D1 23 14 S 113 22 E
Cuvier I., N.Z. 118 C4 36 27 S 175 50 E
Cuxhaven, Germany 26 B4 53 51N 8 41 E
Cuyabeno, Ecuador 152 D2 0 16 S 75 53W
Cuyahoga Falls, U.S.A. 136 E3 41 8N 81 30W
Cuyapo, Phil. 70 D3 15 46N 120 40 E
Cuyo, Phil. 71 F3 10 50N 121 5 E
Cuyo East Pass, Phil. 71 F3 11 0N 121 28 E
Cuyo I., Phil. 71 F3 10 51N 121 2 E
Cuyo West Pass, Phil. 71 F3 11 0N 120 30 E
Cuyuni →, Guyana 153 B6 6 23N 58 41W
Cuzco, Bolivia 156 E4 20 0 S 66 50W
Cuzco, Peru 156 C3 13 32 S 72 0W
Cuzco □, Peru 156 C3 13 31 S 71 59W
Čvrsnica, Bos.-H. 42 D2 43 36N 17 35 E
Cwmbran, U.K. 17 F4 51 39N 3 3W
Cyangugu, Rwanda 106 C2 2 29 S 28 54 E
Cybinka, Poland 47 C1 52 12N 14 46 E
Cyclades = Kikládhes, Greece 45 G6 37 20N 24 30 E
Cygnet, Australia 114 G4 43 8 S 147 1 E
Cynthiana, U.S.A. 141 F12 38 23N 84 18W
Cypress Hills, Canada 131 D7 49 40N 109 30W
Cyprus ■, Asia 32 E12 35 0N 33 0 E
Cyrenaica, Libya 92 C6 27 0N 23 0 E
Cyrene = Shaḩḩāt, Libya 96 B4 32 48N 21 54 E
Czaplinek, Poland 47 B3 53 34N 16 14 E
Czar, Canada 131 C6 52 27N 110 50W
Czarna →, Piotrkow Trybunalski, Poland 47 D6 51 18N 19 55 E
Czarna →, Tarnobrzeg, Poland 47 E8 50 3N 21 21 E
Czarna Woda, Poland 47 B5 53 51N 18 6 E
Czarne, Poland 47 B3 53 42N 16 58 E
Czarnków, Poland 47 C3 52 55N 16 38 E
Czech Rep. ■, Europe 30 B7 50 0N 15 0 E
Czechowice-Dziedzice, Poland 31 B11 49 54N 18 59 E
Czeladz, Poland 47 E6 50 16N 19 2 E
Czempiń, Poland 47 C3 52 9N 16 33 E
Czeremcha, Poland 47 C10 52 31N 23 21 E
Czersk, Poland 47 B4 53 46N 17 58 E
Czerwieńsk, Poland 47 C2 52 1N 15 13 E
Czerwionka, Poland 31 A11 50 7N 18 37 E
Częstochowa, Poland 47 E6 50 49N 19 7 E
Częstochowa □, Poland 47 E6 50 45N 19 0 E
Człopa, Poland 47 B3 53 6N 16 6 E
Człuchów, Poland 47 B4 53 41N 17 22 E
Czyzew, Poland 47 C9 52 48N 22 19 E

D

Da →, Vietnam 76 B5 21 15N 105 20 E
Da Hinggan Ling, China 65 B7 48 0N 121 0 E
Da Lat, Vietnam 77 G7 11 56N 108 25 E
Da Nang, Vietnam 76 D7 16 4N 108 13 E
Da Qaidam, China 64 C4 37 50N 95 15 E
Da Yunhe →, China 67 G11 34 25N 120 5 E
Da'an, China 67 B13 45 30N 124 7 E
Daap, Phil. 71 H4 7 4N 122 12 E
Daarlerveen, Neths. 20 D9 52 26N 6 34 E
Dab'a, Râs el, Egypt 94 H6 31 3N 28 31 E
Daba Shan, China 68 B7 32 0N 109 0 E
Dabai, Nigeria 101 C6 11 25N 5 15 E
Dabajuro, Venezuela 152 A3 11 2N 70 40W
Dabakala, Ivory C. 100 D4 8 15N 4 20W
Dabaro, Somali Rep. 108 C3 6 21N 48 43 E
Dabeiba, Colombia 152 B2 7 1N 76 16W
Dabhoi, India 80 H5 22 10N 73 20 E
Dąbie, Konin, Poland 47 C5 52 5N 18 50 E
Dąbie, Szczecin, Poland 47 B1 53 27N 14 45 E
Dabie Shan, China 69 B10 31 20N 115 20 E
Dabo, Indonesia 74 C2 0 30 S 104 33 E
Dabola, Guinea 100 C2 10 50N 11 5W
Dabou, Ivory C. 100 D4 5 20N 4 23W
Daboya, Ghana 101 D4 9 30N 1 20W
Dabrowa Górnicza, Poland 47 E6 50 15N 19 10 E
Dabrowa Tarnówska, Poland 31 A13 50 10N 20 59 E
Dąbrówno, Poland 47 B7 53 27N 20 2 E
Dabu, China 69 E11 24 22N 116 41 E
Dabung, Malaysia 77 K4 5 23N 102 1 E
Dabus →, Ethiopia 95 E4 10 48N 35 10 E
Dacato →, Ethiopia 95 F5 7 25N 42 40 E
Dacca = Dhaka, Bangla. 78 D3 23 43N 90 26 E
Dacca = Dhaka □, Bangla. 78 C3 24 25N 90 25 E
Dachau, Germany 27 G7 48 16N 11 27 E
Dadale, Solomon Is. 121 M10 8 7 S 159 6 E
Dadanawa, Guyana 153 C6 2 50N 59 30W
Daday, Turkey 52 F5 41 28N 33 27 E
Dade City, U.S.A. 135 L4 28 22N 82 11W
Dades, Oued →, Morocco 98 B3 30 58N 6 44W
Dadiya, Nigeria 101 D7 9 35N 11 24 E
Dadra and Nagar Haveli □, India 82 D1 20 5N 73 0 E
Dadri = Charkhi Dadri, India 80 E7 28 37N 76 17 E
Dadu, Pakistan 79 D2 26 45N 67 45 E
Dadu He →, China 68 C4 29 31N 103 46 E
Dăeni, Romania 46 E9 44 51N 28 10 E
Daet, Phil. 70 D4 14 2N 122 55 E
Dafang, China 68 D5 27 9N 105 39 E
Dagana, Senegal 100 B1 16 30N 15 35W
Dagash, Sudan 94 D3 19 19N 33 25 E
Dagestanskiye Ogni, Russia 53 E13 42 6N 48 12 E
Dagg Sd., N.Z. 119 F1 45 23 S 166 45 E
Daggett, U.S.A. 145 L10 34 52N 116 52W
Daghestan Republic □, Russia 53 E12 42 30N 47 0 E
Daghfeli, Sudan 94 D3 19 18N 32 40 E
Dagö = Hiiumaa, Estonia 50 B3 58 50N 22 45 E
Dagu, China 67 E9 38 59N 117 40 E
Dagua, Papua N. G. 120 B2 3 27 S 143 20 E
Daguan, China 68 D4 27 43N 103 56 E
Dagupan, Phil. 70 C3 16 3N 120 20 E
Dahab, Egypt 94 B3 28 31N 34 31 E
Dahlak Kebir, Eritrea 90 D3 15 50N 40 10 E
Dahlenburg, Germany 26 B6 53 11N 10 43 E
Dahlgren, U.S.A. 141 F8 38 12N 88 41W
Dahlonega, U.S.A. 135 H4 34 32N 83 59W
Dahme, Germany 26 D9 51 51N 13 25 E
Dahod, India 80 H6 22 50N 74 15 E
Dahomey = Benin ■, Africa 101 D5 10 0N 2 0 E
Dahong Shan, China 69 B9 31 25N 113 0 E
Dahra, Senegal 100 B1 15 22N 15 30W
Dahra, Massif de, Algeria 99 A5 36 7N 1 21 E
Daḩy, Nafūd ad, Si. Arabia 86 B4 22 0N 45 25 E
Dai Hao, Vietnam 76 C6 18 1N 106 25 E
Dai-Sen, Japan 62 B5 35 22N 133 32 E
Dai Shan, China 69 B14 30 25N 122 10 E
Dai Xian, China 66 E7 39 4N 112 58 E
Daicheng, China 66 E9 38 42N 116 38 E
Daigo, Japan 63 A12 36 46N 140 21 E
Daimanji-San, Japan 62 A5 36 14N 133 20 E
Daimiel, Spain 35 F1 39 5N 3 35W
Daingean, Ireland 19 C4 53 18N 7 15W
Dainkog, China 68 A1 32 30N 97 58 E
Daintree, Australia 114 B4 16 20 S 145 20 E
Daiō-Misaki, Japan 63 C8 34 15N 136 45 E
Dairût, Egypt 94 B3 27 34N 30 43 E
Daisetsu-Zan, Japan 60 C11 43 30N 142 57 E
Daitari, India 82 D7 21 10N 85 46 E
Daito, Japan 62 B4 35 19N 132 58 E
Dajarra, Australia 114 C2 21 42 S 139 30 E
Dajia, Taiwan 69 E13 24 22N 120 37 E
Dajin Chuan →, China 68 B3 31 16N 101 59 E
Dak Dam, Cambodia 76 F6 12 20N 107 21 E
Dak Nhe, Vietnam 76 E6 15 28N 107 48 E
Dak Pek, Vietnam 76 E6 15 4N 107 44 E
Dak Song, Vietnam 77 F6 12 19N 107 35 E
Dak Sui, Vietnam 76 E6 14 55N 107 43 E
Dakar, Senegal 100 C1 14 34N 17 29W
Dakhla, W. Sahara 98 D1 23 50N 15 53W
Dakhla, El Wâhât el-, Egypt 94 B2 25 30N 28 50 E
Dakhovskaya, Russia 53 D9 44 13N 40 13 E
Dakingari, Nigeria 101 C5 11 37N 4 1 E
Dakor, India 80 H5 22 45N 73 11 E
Dakoro, Niger 101 C6 14 31N 6 46 E
Dakota City, Iowa, U.S.A. 140 B2 42 43N 94 12W
Dakota City, Nebr., U.S.A. 138 D6 42 25N 96 25W
Đakovica, Serbia 42 E5 42 22N 20 26 E
Đakovo, Croatia 42 B3 45 19N 18 24 E
Dala, Angola 103 E4 11 3 S 20 17 E
Dala, Solomon Is. 121 M11 8 30 S 160 41 E
Dalaba, Guinea 100 C2 10 42N 12 15W
Dalachi, China 66 F3 36 48N 105 0 E
Dalaguete, Phil. 71 G4 9 46N 123 32 E
Dalai Nur, China 66 C9 43 20N 116 45 E
Dālakī, Iran 85 D6 29 26N 51 17 E
Dalälven, Sweden 13 F14 60 12N 16 43 E
Dalaman, Turkey 88 E3 36 48N 28 47 E
Dalaman →, Turkey 88 E3 36 41N 28 43 E
Dalandzadgad, Mongolia 66 C3 43 27N 104 30 E
Dalanganem Is., Phil. 71 F3 10 40N 120 17 E
Dalarö, Sweden 13 G15 59 8N 18 24 E
Dalat, Malaysia 75 B4 2 44N 111 56 E
Dālbandīn, Pakistan 79 C2 29 0N 64 23 E
Dalbeattie, U.K. 18 G5 54 55N 3 50W
Dalbosjön, Sweden 15 F6 58 40N 12 45 E
Dalby, Australia 115 D5 27 10 S 151 17 E
Dalby, Sweden 15 J7 55 40N 13 22 E
Dale, U.S.A. 141 F10 38 10N 86 59W
Dalen, Neths. 20 C9 52 42N 6 46 E
Dalen, Norway 14 E2 59 26N 8 0 E
Dalet, Burma 78 F4 19 59N 93 51 E
Daletme, Burma 78 F4 21 36N 92 46 E
Daleville, U.S.A. 141 D11 40 7N 85 33W
Dalfsen, Neths. 20 C8 52 31N 6 16 E
Dalga, Egypt 94 B3 27 39N 30 41 E
Dalgān, Iran 85 E8 27 31N 59 19 E

Dîmboviţa 191

Dehgolān, *Iran* **84 C5** 35 17N 47 25 E
Dehibat, *Tunisia* **96 B2** 32 0N 10 47 E
Dehiwala, *Sri Lanka* **83 L4** 6 50N 79 51 E
Dehlorān, *Iran* **84 C5** 32 41N 47 16 E
Dehnow-e Kūhestān, *Iran* **85 E8** 27 58N 58 32 E
Dehra Dun, *India* **80 D8** 30 20N 78 4 E
Dehri, *India* **81 G11** 24 50N 84 15 E
Dehua, *China* **69 E12** 25 26N 118 14 E
Dehui, *China* **67 B13** 44 30N 125 40 E
Deinze, *Belgium* **21 G3** 50 59N 3 32 E
Dej, *Romania* **46 B4** 47 10N 23 52 E
Dejiang, *China* **68 C7** 28 18N 108 7 E
Dekemhare, *Eritrea* **95 D4** 15 6N 39 0 E
Dekese, *Zaïre* **102 C4** 3 24 S 21 24 E
Dekhkanabad, *Uzbekistan* **55 D3** 38 21N 66 30 E
Dekoa, *C.A.R.* **102 A3** 6 19N 19 4 E
Del Carmen, *Phil.* **71 G6** 9 50N 126 0 E
Del Mar, *U.S.A.* **145 N9** 32 58N 117 16W
Del Norte, *U.S.A.* **143 H10** 37 41N 106 21W
Del Rio, *U.S.A.* **139 L4** 29 22N 100 54W
Delai, *Sudan* **94 D4** 17 21N 36 6 E
Delano, *U.S.A.* **145 K7** 35 46N 119 15W
Delareyville, *S. Africa* **104 D4** 26 41 S 25 26 E
Delavan, *Ill., U.S.A.* **140 D7** 40 22N 89 33W
Delavan, *Wis., U.S.A.* **138 D10** 42 38N 88 39W
Delaware, *U.S.A.* **141 D13** 40 18N 83 4W
Delaware □, *U.S.A.* **134 F8** 39 0N 75 20W
Delaware ⟶, *U.S.A.* **134 F8** 39 15N 75 20W
Delaware B., *U.S.A.* **133 C12** 39 0N 75 10W
Delčevo, *Macedonia* **42 F7** 41 58N 22 46 E
Delegate, *Australia* **117 D8** 37 4 S 148 56 E
Delémont, *Switz.* **28 B4** 47 22N 7 20 E
Delft, *Neths.* **20 D4** 52 1N 4 22 E
Delft I., *Sri Lanka* **83 K4** 9 30N 79 40 E
Delfzijl, *Neths.* **20 B9** 53 20N 6 55 E
Delgado, C., *Mozam.* **107 E5** 10 45 S 40 40 E
Delgerhet, *Mongolia* **66 B6** 45 50N 110 30 E
Delgo, *Sudan* **94 C3** 20 6N 30 40 E
Delhi, *Canada* **136 D4** 42 51N 80 30W
Delhi, *India* **80 E7** 28 38N 77 17 E
Delhi, *U.S.A.* **137 D10** 42 17N 74 55W
Deli Jovan, *Serbia* **42 C7** 44 13N 22 9 E
Delia, *Canada* **130 C6** 51 38N 112 23W
Delice, *Turkey* **88 D6** 39 54N 34 2 E
Delice ⟶, *Turkey* **88 D6** 39 45N 34 15 E
Delicias, *Mexico* **146 B3** 28 10N 105 30W
Delījān, *Iran* **85 C6** 33 59N 50 40 E
Delitzsch, *Germany* **26 D8** 51 32N 12 22 E
Dell City, *U.S.A.* **143 L11** 31 56N 105 12W
Dell Rapids, *U.S.A.* **138 D6** 43 50N 96 43W
Delle, *France* **23 E14** 47 30N 7 2 E
Dellys, *Algeria* **99 A5** 36 57N 3 57 E
Delmar, *Iowa, U.S.A.* **140 C6** 42 0N 90 37W
Delmar, *N.Y., U.S.A.* **137 D11** 42 37N 73 47W
Delmenhorst, *Germany* **26 B4** 53 3N 8 37 E
Delmiro Gouveia, *Brazil* **154 C4** 9 24 S 38 6W
Delnice, *Croatia* **39 C11** 45 23N 14 50 E
Delong, Ostrova, *Russia* **57 B15** 76 40N 149 20 E
Deloraine, *Australia* **114 G4** 41 30 S 146 40 E
Deloraine, *Canada* **131 D8** 49 15N 100 29W
Delphi, *Greece* **45 F4** 38 28N 22 30 E
Delphi, *U.S.A.* **141 D10** 40 36N 86 41W
Delphos, *U.S.A.* **141 D12** 40 51N 84 21W
Delportshoop, *S. Africa* **104 D3** 28 22 S 24 20 E
Delray Beach, *U.S.A.* **135 M5** 26 28N 80 4W
Delsbo, *Sweden* **14 C10** 61 48N 16 32 E
Delta, *Colo., U.S.A.* **143 G9** 38 44N 108 4W
Delta, *Utah, U.S.A.* **142 G7** 39 21N 112 35W
Delta □, *Nigeria* **101 D6** 5 30N 6 0 E
Delta Amacuro □, *Venezuela* **153 B5** 8 30N 61 30W
Delungra, *Australia* **115 D5** 29 39 S 150 51 E
Delvina, *Albania* **44 E2** 39 59N 20 4 E
Delvinákion, *Greece* **44 E2** 39 57N 20 32 E
Demak, *Indonesia* **75 D4** 6 53 S 110 38 E
Demanda, Sierra de la, *Spain* **34 C1** 42 15N 3 0W
Demavand = Damāvand, *Iran* **85 C7** 35 47N 52 0 E
Demba, *Zaïre* **103 D4** 5 28 S 22 15 E
Demba Chio, *Angola* **103 D2** 9 41 S 13 41 E
Dembecha, *Ethiopia* **95 E4** 10 32N 37 30 E
Dembi, *Ethiopia* **95 F4** 8 5N 36 25 E
Dembia, *Zaïre* **106 B2** 3 33N 25 48 E
Dembidolo, *Ethiopia* **95 F3** 8 34N 34 50 E
Demer ⟶, *Belgium* **21 G5** 50 57N 4 42 E
Demetrias, *Greece* **44 E5** 39 22N 23 1 E
Demidov, *Russia* **50 D7** 55 16N 31 30 E
Deming, *N. Mex., U.S.A.* **143 K10** 32 16N 107 46W
Deming, *Wash., U.S.A.* **144 B4** 48 50N 122 13W
Demini ⟶, *Brazil* **153 D5** 0 46 S 62 56W
Demirci, *Turkey* **88 D3** 39 2N 28 38 E
Demirköy, *Turkey* **88 C2** 41 49N 27 45 E
Demmin, *Germany* **26 B9** 53 54N 13 2 E
Demnate, *Morocco* **98 B3** 31 44N 6 59W
Demonte, *Italy* **38 D4** 44 18N 7 18 E
Demopolis, *U.S.A.* **135 J2** 32 31N 87 50W
Dempo, *Indonesia* **74 C2** 4 2 S 103 15 E
Demyansk, *Russia* **50 C8** 57 40N 32 27 E
Den Burg, *Neths.* **20 B5** 53 3N 4 47 E
Den Chai, *Thailand* **76 D3** 17 59N 100 4 E
Den Dungen, *Neths.* **21 E6** 51 41N 5 22 E
Den Haag = 's-Gravenhage, *Neths.* **20 D4** 52 7N 4 17 E
Den Ham, *Neths.* **20 D8** 52 28N 6 30 E
Den Helder, *Neths.* **20 C5** 52 57N 4 45 E
Den Hulst, *Neths.* **20 C8** 52 36N 6 16 E
Den Oever, *Neths.* **20 C6** 52 56N 5 2 E
Denain, *France* **23 B10** 50 20N 3 22 E
Denair, *U.S.A.* **144 H6** 37 32N 120 48W
Denau, *Uzbekistan* **55 D3** 38 16N 67 54 E
Denbigh, *U.K.* **16 D4** 53 12N 3 26W
Dendang, *Indonesia* **75 C3** 3 7 S 107 56 E
Dender ⟶, *Belgium* **21 F4** 51 2N 4 6 E
Denderhoutem, *Belgium* **21 G4** 50 53N 4 2 E
Denderleeuw, *Belgium* **21 G4** 50 54N 4 5 E
Dendermonde, *Belgium* **21 F4** 51 2N 4 5 E
Deneba, *Ethiopia* **95 F4** 9 47N 39 10 E
Denekamp, *Neths.* **20 D10** 52 22N 7 1 E
Denezhkin Kamen, Gora, *Russia* **54 A6** 60 25N 59 32 E
Deng Deng, *Cameroon* **102 A2** 5 12N 13 31 E
Deng Xian, *China* **69 A9** 32 34N 112 4 E
Dengchuan, *China* **68 E3** 25 59N 100 3 E
Denge, *Nigeria* **101 C6** 12 52N 5 21 E
Dengfeng, *China* **66 G7** 34 25N 113 2 E
Dengi, *Nigeria* **101 D6** 9 25N 9 55 E
Dengkou, *China* **66 D4** 40 18N 106 55 E
Denham, *Australia* **113 E1** 25 56 S 113 31 E
Denham Ra., *Australia* **114 C4** 21 55 S 147 46 E
Denham Sd., *Australia* **113 E1** 25 45 S 113 15 E
Denia, *Spain* **35 G5** 38 49N 0 8 E
Denial B., *Australia* **115 E1** 32 14 S 133 32 E
Deniliquin, *Australia* **117 C6** 35 30 S 144 58 E
Denison, *Iowa, U.S.A.* **138 D7** 42 1N 95 21W
Denison, *Tex., U.S.A.* **139 J6** 33 45N 96 33W
Denison Plains, *Australia* **112 C4** 18 35 S 128 0 E
Denisovka, *Kazakhstan* **54 E7** 52 28N 61 46 E
Denizli, *Turkey* **88 E3** 37 42N 29 2 E
Denizli □, *Turkey* **88 E3** 37 45N 29 5 E
Denman, *Australia* **117 B9** 32 24 S 150 42 E
Denman Glacier, *Antarctica* **7 C7** 66 45 S 99 25 E
Denmark, *Australia* **113 F2** 34 59 S 117 25 E
Denmark ■, *Europe* **15 J3** 55 30N 9 0 E
Denmark Str., *Atl. Oc.* **124 C17** 66 0N 30 0W
Dennison, *U.S.A.* **136 F3** 40 24N 81 19W
Denton, *Mont., U.S.A.* **142 C9** 47 19N 109 57W
Denton, *Tex., U.S.A.* **139 J6** 33 13N 97 8W
D'Entrecasteaux, Pt., *Australia* **113 F2** 34 50 S 115 57 E
D'Entrecasteaux Is., *Papua N. G.* **120 E6** 9 0 S 151 0 E
Dents du Midi, *Switz.* **28 D3** 46 10N 6 56 E
Denu, *Ghana* **101 D5** 6 4N 1 8 E
Denver, *Colo., U.S.A.* **138 F2** 39 44N 104 59W
Denver, *Ind., U.S.A.* **141 D10** 40 52N 86 5W
Denver, *Iowa, U.S.A.* **140 B4** 42 40N 92 20W
Denver City, *U.S.A.* **139 J3** 32 58N 102 50W
Deoband, *India* **80 E7** 29 42N 77 43 E
Deobhog, *India* **82 E6** 19 53N 82 44 E
Deogarh, *India* **82 D7** 21 32N 84 45 E
Deoghar, *India* **81 G12** 24 30N 86 42 E
Deolali, *India* **82 E1** 19 58N 73 50 E
Deoli = Devli, *India* **80 G6** 25 50N 75 20 E
Deoria, *India* **81 F10** 26 31N 83 48 E
Deosai Mts., *Pakistan* **81 B6** 35 40N 75 0 E
Deping, *China* **67 F9** 37 25N 116 58 E
Deposit, *U.S.A.* **137 D9** 42 4N 75 25W
Depot Springs, *Australia* **113 E3** 27 55 S 120 3 E
Deputatskiy, *Russia* **57 C14** 69 18N 139 54 E
Dêqên, *China* **68 C2** 28 34N 98 51 E
Deqing, *China* **69 F8** 23 8N 111 42 E
Dera Ghazi Khan, *Pakistan* **79 C3** 30 5N 70 43 E
Dera Ismail Khan, *Pakistan* **79 C3** 31 50N 70 50 E
Derbent, *Russia* **53 E13** 42 5N 48 15 E
Derby, *Australia* **112 C3** 17 18 S 123 38 E
Derby, *U.K.* **16 E6** 52 55N 1 28W
Derby, *Conn., U.S.A.* **137 E11** 41 19N 73 5W
Derby, *N.Y., U.S.A.* **136 D6** 42 41N 78 58W
Derbyshire □, *U.K.* **16 E6** 52 55N 1 28W
Derecske, *Hungary* **31 D14** 47 20N 21 33 E
Dereli, *Turkey* **89 C8** 40 44N 38 26 E
Derg ⟶, *U.K.* **19 B4** 54 42N 7 26W
Derg, L., *Ireland* **19 D3** 53 0N 8 20W
Dergachi, *Ukraine* **52 A7** 50 9N 36 11 E
Derik, *Turkey* **89 E9** 37 21N 40 18 E
Derinkuyu, *Turkey* **88 D6** 38 22N 34 45 E
Dermantsi, *Bulgaria* **43 D9** 43 8N 24 17 E
Dernieres, Isles, *U.S.A.* **139 L9** 29 2N 90 50W
Dêrong, *China* **68 C2** 28 44N 99 9 E
Derrinallum, *Australia* **116 D5** 37 57 S 143 15 E
Derry = Londonderry, *U.K.* **19 B4** 55 0N 7 23W
Derryveagh Mts., *Ireland* **19 B3** 55 0N 8 4W
Derudub, *Sudan* **94 D4** 17 31N 36 7 E
Derval, *France* **22 E5** 47 40N 1 41W
Dervéni, *Greece* **45 F4** 38 8N 22 25 E
Derventa, *Bos.-H.* **42 C2** 44 59N 17 55 E
Derwent, *Canada* **131 C6** 53 41N 110 58W
Derwent ⟶, *Derby, U.K.* **16 E6** 52 53N 1 17W
Derwent ⟶, *N. Yorks., U.K.* **16 D7** 53 45N 0 57W
Derwent Water, *U.K.* **16 C4** 54 35N 3 9W
Des Moines, *Iowa, U.S.A.* **140 C3** 41 35N 93 37W
Des Moines, *N. Mex., U.S.A.* **139 G3** 36 46N 103 50W
Des Moines ⟶, *U.S.A.* **138 E9** 40 23N 91 25W
Des Plaines, *U.S.A.* **141 B9** 42 3N 87 52W
Des Plaines ⟶, *U.S.A.* **141 C8** 41 23N 88 15W
Desaguadero ⟶, *Argentina* **158 C2** 34 30 S 66 46W
Desaguadero ⟶, *Bolivia* **156 D4** 16 35 S 69 5W
Descanso, Pta., *Mexico* **145 N9** 32 21N 117 3W
Descartes, *France* **24 B4** 46 59N 0 42 E
Deschaillons, *Canada* **129 C5** 46 32N 72 7W
Descharme ⟶, *Canada* **131 B7** 56 51N 109 13W
Deschutes ⟶, *U.S.A.* **142 D3** 45 38N 120 55W
Dese, *Ethiopia* **90 E2** 11 5N 39 40 E
Deseado, C., *Chile* **160 D2** 52 45 S 74 42W
Desenzano del Gardo, *Italy* **38 C7** 45 28N 10 32 E
Desert Center, *U.S.A.* **145 M11** 33 43N 115 24W
Desert Hot Springs, *U.S.A.* **145 M10** 33 58N 116 30W
Désirade, I., *Guadeloupe* **149 C7** 16 18N 61 3W
Deskenatlata L., *Canada* **130 A6** 60 55N 112 3W
Desna ⟶, *Ukraine* **50 F7** 50 33N 30 32 E
Desnătui ⟶, *Romania* **46 E4** 44 15N 23 27 E
Desolación, I., *Chile* **160 D2** 53 0 S 74 0W
Despeñaperros, Paso, *Spain* **35 G1** 38 24N 3 30W
Despotovac, *Serbia* **42 C6** 44 6N 21 30 E
Dessau, *Germany* **26 D8** 51 49N 12 15 E
Dessel, *Belgium* **21 F6** 51 15N 5 7 E
Dessye = Dese, *Ethiopia* **90 E2** 11 5N 39 40 E
D'Estrees B., *Australia* **116 C2** 35 55 S 137 45 E
Desuri, *India* **80 G5** 25 18N 73 35 E
Desvres, *France* **23 B8** 50 40N 1 48 E
Det Udom, *Thailand* **76 E5** 14 54N 105 5 E
Deta, *Romania* **42 B6** 45 24N 21 13 E
Dete, *Zimbabwe* **107 F2** 18 38 S 26 50 E
Detinja ⟶, *Serbia* **42 D4** 43 51N 20 5 E
Detmold, *Germany* **26 D4** 51 58N 8 50 E
Detour, Pt., *U.S.A.* **134 C2** 45 40N 86 40W
Detroit, *Mich., U.S.A.* **128 D3** 42 20N 83 3W
Detroit, *Tex., U.S.A.* **139 J7** 33 40N 95 16W
Detroit Lakes, *U.S.A.* **138 B7** 46 49N 95 51W
Deurne, *Belgium* **21 F4** 51 12N 4 24 E
Deurne, *Neths.* **21 F7** 51 27N 5 49 E
Deutsche Bucht, *Germany* **26 A4** 54 15N 8 0 E
Deutschlandsberg, *Austria* **30 E8** 46 49N 15 14 E
Deux-Sèvres □, *France* **22 F6** 46 35N 0 20W
Deva, *Romania* **46 D3** 45 53N 22 55 E
Devakottai, *India* **83 K4** 9 55N 78 45 E
Devaprayag, *India* **81 D8** 30 13N 78 35 E
Dévaványa, *Hungary* **31 D13** 47 2N 20 59 E
Deveci Dağı, *Turkey* **52 F7** 40 10N 36 0 E
Deveci Dağları, *Turkey* **88 C6** 40 10N 35 50 E
Devecser, *Hungary* **31 D10** 47 6N 17 26 E
Develi, *Turkey* **88 D6** 38 23N 35 29 E
Deventer, *Neths.* **20 D8** 52 15N 6 10 E
Deveron ⟶, *U.K.* **18 D6** 57 40N 2 31W
Devesel, *Romania* **46 E3** 44 28N 22 41 E
Devgad I., *India* **83 G2** 14 48N 74 5 E
Devgadh Bariya, *India* **80 H5** 22 40N 73 55 E
Devil River Pk., *N.Z.* **119 A7** 40 56 S 172 37 E
Devils Den, *U.S.A.* **144 K7** 35 46N 119 58W
Devils Lake, *U.S.A.* **138 A5** 48 7N 98 52W
Devils Paw, *Canada* **130 B2** 58 47N 134 0W
Devil's Pt., *Sri Lanka* **83 K5** 9 26N 80 6 E
Devil's Pt., *Vanuatu* **121 G6** 17 44 S 168 11 E
Devin, *Bulgaria* **43 F9** 41 44N 24 24 E
Devizes, *U.K.* **17 F6** 51 21N 2 0W
Devli, *India* **80 G6** 25 50N 75 20 E
Devnya, *Bulgaria* **43 D12** 43 13N 27 33 E
Devolii ⟶, *Albania* **44 D2** 40 57N 20 15 E
Devon, *Canada* **130 C6** 53 24N 113 44W
Devon □, *U.K.* **17 G4** 50 50N 3 40W
Devon I., *Canada* **6 B3** 75 10N 85 0W
Devonport, *Australia* **114 G4** 41 10 S 146 22 E
Devonport, *N.Z.* **118 C3** 36 49 S 174 49 E
Devonport, *U.K.* **17 G3** 50 23N 4 11W
Devrek, *Turkey* **88 C4** 41 13N 31 57 E
Devrekâni, *Turkey* **88 C5** 41 36N 33 50 E
Devrez ⟶, *Turkey* **88 C6** 41 6N 34 25 E
Dewas, *India* **80 H7** 22 59N 76 3 E
Dewetsdorp, *S. Africa* **104 D4** 29 33 S 26 39 E
Dewsbury, *U.K.* **16 D6** 53 42N 1 38W
Dexing, *China* **69 C11** 28 46N 117 30 E
Dexter, *Mich., U.S.A.* **141 B13** 42 20N 83 53W
Dexter, *Mo., U.S.A.* **139 G9** 36 48N 89 57W
Dexter, *N. Mex., U.S.A.* **139 J2** 33 12N 104 22W
Dey-Dey, L., *Australia* **113 E5** 29 12 S 131 4 E
Deyang, *China* **68 B5** 31 3N 104 27 E
Deyhūk, *Iran* **85 C8** 33 15N 57 30 E
Deyyer, *Iran* **85 E6** 27 55N 51 55 E
Dezadeash L., *Canada* **130 A1** 60 28N 136 58W
Dezfūl, *Iran* **85 C6** 32 20N 48 30 E
Dezhneva, Mys, *Russia* **57 C19** 66 5N 169 40W
Dezhou, *China* **66 F9** 37 26N 116 18 E
Dháfni, *Greece* **45 G4** 37 48N 22 1 E
Dháfni, *Kríti, Greece* **32 D7** 35 13N 25 3 E
Dhahaban, *Si. Arabia* **86 B2** 21 58N 39 3 E
Dhahiriya = Aẓ Ẓāhirīyah, *Jordan* **91 D3** 31 25N 34 58 E
Dhahran = Aẓ Ẓahrān, *Si. Arabia* **85 E6** 26 10N 50 7 E
Dhaka, *Bangla.* **78 D3** 23 43N 90 26 E
Dhaka □, *Bangla.* **78 C3** 24 25N 90 25 E
Dhali, *Cyprus* **32 D12** 35 1N 33 25 E
Dhamangaon, *India* **82 D4** 20 45N 78 15 E
Dhamar, *Yemen* **86 D4** 14 30N 44 20 E
Dhamási, *Greece* **44 E4** 39 43N 22 11 E
Dhampur, *India* **81 E8** 29 19N 78 33 E
Dhamtari, *India* **82 D5** 20 42N 81 35 E
Dhanbad, *India* **81 H12** 23 50N 86 30 E
Dhankuta, *Nepal* **81 F12** 26 55N 87 40 E
Dhanora, *India* **82 D5** 20 20N 80 22 E
Dhar, *India* **80 H6** 22 35N 75 26 E
Dharampur, *Gujarat, India* **82 D1** 20 32N 73 17 E
Dharampur, *Mad. P., India* **80 H6** 22 13N 75 18 E
Dharamsala = Dharmsala, *India* **80 C7** 32 16N 76 23 E
Dharapuram, *India* **83 J3** 10 45N 77 34 E
Dharmapuri, *India* **83 H4** 12 10N 78 10 E
Dharmavaram, *India* **83 G3** 14 29N 77 44 E
Dharmsala, *India* **80 C7** 32 16N 76 23 E
Dharwad, *India* **83 G2** 15 22N 75 15 E
Dhaulagiri, *Nepal* **81 E10** 28 39N 83 28 E
Dhebar, L., *India* **80 G6** 24 10N 74 0 E
Dheftera, *Cyprus* **32 D12** 35 5N 33 16 E
Dhenkanal, *India* **82 D7** 20 45N 85 35 E
Dhenoúsa, *Greece* **45 G7** 37 8N 25 48 E
Dherinia, *Cyprus* **32 D12** 35 3N 33 57 E
Dheskáti, *Greece* **44 E3** 39 55N 21 49 E
Dhespotikó, *Greece* **45 H6** 36 57N 24 58 E
Dhestina, *Greece* **45 F4** 38 25N 22 31 E
Dhiarrizos ⟶, *Cyprus* **32 E11** 34 41N 32 34 E
Dhībān, *Jordan* **91 D4** 31 30N 35 46 E
Dhidhimótikhon, *Greece* **44 C8** 41 22N 26 29 E
Dhíkti Óros, *Greece* **32 D7** 35 8N 25 22 E
Dhilianáta, *Greece* **45 F2** 38 15N 20 34 E
Dhílos, *Greece* **45 G7** 37 23N 25 15 E
Dhimitsána, *Greece* **45 G4** 37 36N 22 3 E
Dhírfis, *Greece* **45 F5** 38 40N 23 54 E
Dhodhekánisos, *Greece* **45 H8** 36 35N 27 0 E
Dhokós, *Greece* **45 G5** 37 20N 23 20 E
Dholiana, *Greece* **44 E2** 39 54N 20 32 E
Dholka, *India* **80 H5** 22 44N 72 29 E
Dhomokós, *Greece* **45 E4** 39 10N 22 18 E
Dhoraji, *India* **80 J4** 21 45N 70 37 E
Dhoxáton, *Greece* **44 C6** 41 9N 24 16 E
Dhragonísi, *Greece* **45 G7** 37 27N 25 29 E
Dhráhstis, Ákra, *Greece* **32 A3** 39 48N 19 40 E
Dhrangadhra, *India* **80 H4** 22 59N 71 31 E
Dhrápanon, Ákra, *Greece* **32 D6** 35 28N 24 14 E
Dhriopís, *Greece* **45 G6** 37 25N 24 35 E
Dhrol, *India* **80 H4** 22 33N 70 25 E
Dhubāb, *Yemen* **86 D3** 12 56N 43 25 E
Dhuburi, *India* **78 B2** 26 2N 89 59 E
Dhulasar, *Bangla.* **78 E3** 21 52N 90 14 E
Dhule, *India* **82 D2** 20 58N 74 50 E
Dhupdhara, *India* **78 B3** 26 10N 91 4 E
Dhut ⟶, *Somali Rep.* **90 E5** 10 30N 50 0 E
Di Linh, *Vietnam* **77 G7** 11 35N 108 4 E
Di Linh, Cao Nguyen, *Vietnam* **77 G7** 11 30N 108 0 E
Día, *Greece* **32 D7** 35 28N 25 14 E
Diablo, Mt., *U.S.A.* **144 H5** 37 53N 121 56W
Diablo Range, *U.S.A.* **144 J5** 37 20N 121 25W
Diafarabé, *Mali* **100 C4** 14 9N 4 57W
Diagonal, *U.S.A.* **140 D2** 40 49N 94 20W
Diala, *Mali* **100 C3** 14 10N 9 58W
Dialakoro, *Mali* **100 C3** 12 18N 7 54W
Diallassagou, *Mali* **100 C4** 13 47N 3 41W
Diamante, *Argentina* **158 C3** 32 5 S 60 40W
Diamante ⟶, *Argentina* **158 C2** 34 30 S 66 46W
Diamantina, *Brazil* **155 E3** 18 17 S 43 40W
Diamantina ⟶, *Australia* **115 D2** 26 45 S 139 10 E
Diamantino, *Brazil* **157 C6** 14 30 S 56 30W
Diamond Harbour, *India* **81 H13** 22 11N 88 14 E
Diamond Is., *Australia* **114 B5** 17 25 S 151 5 E
Diamond Mts., *U.S.A.* **142 G6** 39 50N 115 30W
Diamond Springs, *U.S.A.* **144 G6** 38 42N 120 49W
Diamondville, *U.S.A.* **142 F8** 41 47N 110 32W
Dianbai, *China* **69 G8** 21 33N 111 0 E
Diancheng, *China* **69 G8** 21 30N 111 4 E
Diano Marina, *Italy* **38 E5** 43 55N 8 3 E
Dianópolis, *Brazil* **155 D2** 11 38 S 46 50W
Dianra, *Ivory C.* **100 D3** 8 45N 6 14W
Diapaga, *Burkina Faso* **101 C5** 12 5N 1 46 E
Diapangou, *Burkina Faso* **101 C5** 12 5N 0 10 E
Diapur, *Australia* **116 D4** 36 19 S 141 29 E
Diariguila, *Guinea* **100 C2** 10 35N 10 2W
Dībā, *Oman* **85 E8** 25 45N 56 16 E
Dibaya, *Zaïre* **103 D4** 6 30 S 22 57 E
Dibaya-Lubue, *Zaïre* **103 C3** 4 12 S 19 54 E
Dibbi, *Ethiopia* **90 G3** 4 10N 41 52 E
Dibete, *Botswana* **104 C4** 23 45 S 26 32 E
Dibrugarh, *India* **78 B5** 27 29N 94 55 E
Dickeyville, *U.S.A.* **140 B6** 42 38N 90 36W
Dickinson, *U.S.A.* **138 B3** 46 53N 102 47W
Dickson, *U.S.A.* **135 G2** 36 5N 87 23W
Dickson City, *U.S.A.* **137 E9** 41 29N 75 40W
Dicomano, *Italy* **39 E8** 43 53N 11 30 E
Didam, *Neths.* **20 E8** 51 57N 6 8 E
Didesa, W. ⟶, *Ethiopia* **95 E4** 10 2N 35 32 E
Didiéni, *Mali* **100 C3** 13 53N 8 6W
Didsbury, *Canada* **130 C6** 51 35N 114 10W
Didwana, *India* **80 F6** 27 23N 74 36 E
Die, *France* **25 D9** 44 47N 5 22 E
Diébougou, *Burkina Faso* **100 C4** 11 0N 3 15W
Diefenbaker L., *Canada* **131 C7** 51 0N 106 55W
Diego Garcia, *Ind. Oc.* **109 E6** 7 50 S 72 50 E
Diekirch, *Lux.* **21 J8** 49 52N 6 10 E
Diélette, *France* **22 C5** 49 33N 1 52W
Diéma, *Mali* **100 C3** 14 32N 9 12W
Diémbéring, *Senegal* **100 C1** 12 29N 16 47W
Diemen, *Neths.* **20 D5** 52 21N 4 58 E
Dien Ban, *Vietnam* **76 E7** 15 53N 108 16 E
Dien Bien, *Vietnam* **76 B4** 21 20N 103 0 E
Dien Khanh, *Vietnam* **77 F7** 12 15N 109 6 E
Diepenbeek, *Belgium* **21 G6** 50 54N 5 25 E
Diepenheim, *Neths.* **20 D9** 52 12N 6 33 E
Diepenveen, *Neths.* **20 D8** 52 18N 6 9 E
Diepholz, *Germany* **26 C4** 52 37N 8 22 E
Diepoldsau, *Switz.* **29 B9** 47 23N 9 40 E
Dieppe, *France* **22 C8** 49 54N 1 4 E
Dieren, *Neths.* **20 D8** 52 3N 6 6 E
Dierks, *U.S.A.* **139 H7** 34 7N 94 1W
Diessen, *Neths.* **21 F6** 51 29N 5 10 E
Diessenhofen, *Switz.* **29 A7** 47 42N 8 46 E
Diest, *Belgium* **21 G6** 50 58N 5 4 E
Dieterich, *U.S.A.* **141 E8** 39 4N 88 23W
Dietikon, *Switz.* **29 B6** 47 24N 8 24 E
Dieulefit, *France* **25 D9** 44 32N 5 4 E
Dieuze, *France* **23 D13** 48 49N 6 43 E
Diever, *Neths.* **20 C8** 52 51N 6 19 E
Differdange, *Lux.* **21 J7** 49 31N 5 54 E
Diffun, *Phil.* **70 C3** 16 36N 121 33 E
Dig, *India* **80 F7** 27 28N 77 20 E
Digba, *Zaïre* **106 B2** 4 25N 25 48 E
Digboi, *India* **78 B5** 27 23N 95 38 E
Digby, *Canada* **129 D6** 44 38N 65 50W
Digges, *Canada* **131 B10** 58 40N 94 0W
Digges Is., *Canada* **127 B12** 62 40N 77 50W
Dighinala, *Bangla.* **78 D4** 23 15N 92 5 E
Dighton, *U.S.A.* **138 F4** 38 29N 100 28W
Diglur, *India* **82 E3** 18 34N 77 33 E
Digne, *France* **25 D10** 44 5N 6 12 E
Digoin, *France* **24 B7** 46 29N 3 58 E
Digor, *Turkey* **89 C10** 40 22N 43 25 E
Digos, *Phil.* **71 H5** 6 45N 125 20 E
Digranes, *Iceland* **12 C6** 66 4N 14 44W
Digras, *India* **82 D3** 20 6N 77 45 E
Digul ⟶, *Indonesia* **73 C5** 7 7 S 138 42 E
Dīhōk, *Iraq* **84 B3** 36 55N 38 57 E
Dijlah, Nahr ⟶, *Asia* **84 D5** 31 0N 47 25 E
Dijle ⟶, *Belgium* **21 G5** 50 58N 4 41 E
Dijon, *France* **23 E12** 47 20N 5 3 E
Dikala, *Sudan* **95 G3** 4 45N 31 28 E
Dikkil, *Djibouti* **95 E5** 11 8N 42 20 E
Dikomu di Kai, *Botswana* **104 C3** 24 58 S 24 36 E
Diksmuide, *Belgium* **21 F1** 51 2N 2 52 E
Dikson, *Russia* **56 B9** 73 40N 80 5 E
Dikwa, *Nigeria* **101 C7** 12 4N 13 30 E
Dila, *Ethiopia* **95 F4** 6 21N 38 22 E
Dilbeek, *Belgium* **21 G4** 50 51N 4 17 E
Dili, *Indonesia* **72 C3** 8 39 S 125 34 E
Dilizhan, *Armenia* **53 F11** 40 46N 44 57 E
Dilj, *Croatia* **42 B3** 45 29N 18 1 E
Dillard, *U.S.A.* **140 G5** 37 44N 91 13W
Dillenburg, *Germany* **26 E4** 50 44N 8 17 E
Dilley, *U.S.A.* **139 L5** 28 40N 99 10W
Dilling, *Sudan* **95 E2** 12 3N 29 35 E
Dillingen, *Germany* **27 G6** 48 32N 10 29 E
Dillingham, *U.S.A.* **126 C4** 59 3N 158 28W
Dillon, *Canada* **131 B7** 55 56N 108 35W
Dillon, *Mont., U.S.A.* **142 D7** 45 13N 112 38W
Dillon, *S.C., U.S.A.* **135 H6** 34 25N 79 22W
Dillon ⟶, *Canada* **131 B7** 55 56N 108 56W
Dillsboro, *U.S.A.* **141 E11** 39 1N 85 4W
Dilolo, *Zaïre* **103 E4** 10 28 S 22 18 E
Dilsen, *Belgium* **21 F7** 51 2N 5 44 E
Dilston, *Australia* **114 G4** 41 22 S 147 10 E
Dimapur, *India* **78 C4** 25 54N 93 45 E
Dimas, *Mexico* **146 C3** 23 43N 106 47W
Dimasalang, *Phil.* **70 E4** 12 12N 123 51 E
Dimashq, *Syria* **91 B5** 33 30N 36 18 E
Dimashq □, *Syria* **91 B5** 33 30N 36 30 E
Dimbaza, *S. Africa* **105 E4** 32 50 S 27 14 E
Dimbelenge, *Zaïre* **103 D4** 5 33 S 23 7 E
Dimbokro, *Ivory C.* **100 D4** 6 45N 4 46W
Dimboola, *Australia* **116 D5** 36 28 S 142 7 E
Dîmboviţa □, *Romania* **46 E6** 45 0N 25 30 E
Dîmboviţa ⟶, *Romania* **46 E7** 44 5N 26 35 E

194 Dvinskaya Guba

Dvinskaya Guba, *Russia* . **48 B6** 65 0N 39 0 E
Dvor, *Croatia* **39 C13** 45 4N 16 22 E
Dvorce, *Czech.* **31 B10** 49 50N 17 34 E
Dvur Králové, *Czech.* **30 A8** 50 27N 15 50 E
Dwarka, *India* **80 H3** 22 18N 69 8 E
Dwellingup, *Australia* **113 F2** 32 43 S 116 4 E
Dwight, *Canada* **136 A5** 45 20N 79 1W
Dwight, *U.S.A.* **141 C8** 41 5N 88 26W
Dyakovskoya, *Russia* **51 A12** 60 5N 41 12 E
Dyatkovo, *Russia* **50 E9** 53 40N 34 27 E
Dyatlovo, *Belorussia* **50 E4** 53 28N 25 28 E
Dyer, *U.S.A.* **141 G10** 37 24N 86 13W
Dyer, C., *Canada* **127 B13** 66 40N 61 0W
Dyer Plateau, *Antarctica* . **7 D17** 70 45 S 65 30W
Dyerbeldzhin, *Kirghizia* . **55 C7** 41 13N 74 54 E
Dyersburg, *U.S.A.* **139 G10** 36 3N 89 23W
Dyersville, *U.S.A.* **140 B5** 42 29N 91 8W
Dyfed □, *U.K.* **17 E3** 52 0N 4 30W
Dyfi →, *U.K.* **17 E4** 52 32N 4 0W
Dyje →, *Czech.* **31 C9** 48 37N 16 56 E
Dyle →, *Belgium* **21 G5** 50 58N 4 41 E
Dynevor Downs, *Australia* **115 D3** 28 10 S 144 20 E
Dynów, *Poland* **31 B15** 49 50N 22 11 E
Dysart, *Canada* **131 C8** 50 57N 104 2W
Dyurtyuli, *Russia* **54 D4** 55 9N 54 40 E
Dzamin Üüd, *Mongolia* . **66 C6** 43 50N 111 58 E
Dzerzhinsk, *Belorussia* . **50 E5** 53 40N 27 1 E
Dzerzhinsk, *Russia* **51 C13** 56 14N 43 30 E
Dzhalal-Abad, *Kirghizia* . **55 C6** 40 56N 73 0 E
Dzhalinda, *Russia* **57 D13** 53 26N 124 0 E
Dzhambeyty, *Kazakhstan* **53 A15** 50 16N 52 35 E
Dzhambul, *Kazakhstan* . **55 B5** 42 54N 71 22 E
Dzhambul, Gora,
Kazakhstan **55 A6** 44 54N 73 0 E
Dzhankoi, *Ukraine* **52 D6** 45 40N 34 20 E
Dzhanybek, *Kazakhstan* . **53 B12** 49 25N 46 50 E
Dzhardzhan, *Russia* **57 C13** 68 10N 124 10 E
Dzharkurgan, *Uzbekistan* **55 E3** 37 31N 67 25 E
Dzhelinde, *Russia* **57 C12** 70 0N 114 20 E
Dzhetygara, *Kazakhstan* . **54 E7** 52 11N 61 12 E
Dzhetym, Khrebet,
Kirghizia **55 C8** 41 30N 77 0 E
Dzhezkazgan, *Kazakhstan* **56 E7** 47 44N 67 40 E
Dzhikimde, *Russia* **57 D13** 59 1N 121 47 E
Dzhizak, *Uzbekistan* **55 C3** 40 6N 67 50 E
Dzhugdzur, Khrebet,
Russia **57 D14** 57 30N 138 0 E
Dzhuma, *Uzbekistan* **55 D3** 39 42N 66 40 E
Dzhumgoltau, Khrebet,
Kirghizia **55 B7** 42 15N 74 30 E
Dzhungarskiye Vorota,
Kazakhstan **64 B3** 45 0N 82 0 E
Dzhvari, *Georgia* **53 E10** 42 42N 42 4 E
Działdowo, *Poland* **47 B7** 53 15N 20 15 E
Działoszyce, *Poland* **47 E7** 50 22N 20 20 E
Działoszyn, *Poland* **47 D5** 51 6N 18 50 E
Dzierzgoń, *Poland* **47 B6** 53 58N 19 20 E
Dzierzoniów, *Poland* **47 E3** 50 45N 16 39 E
Dzilam de Bravo, *Mexico* **147 C7** 21 24N 88 53W
Dzioua, *Algeria* **99 B6** 33 14N 5 14 E
Dziwnów, *Poland* **47 A1** 54 2N 14 45 E
Dzungaria = Junggar
Pendi, *China* **64 B3** 44 30N 86 0 E
Dzungarian Gates =
Dzhungarskiye Vorota,
Kazakhstan **64 B3** 45 0N 82 0 E
Dzuumod, *Mongolia* **64 B5** 47 45N 106 58 E

E

Eabamet, L., *Canada* **128 B2** 51 30N 87 46W
Eads, *U.S.A.* **138 F3** 38 29N 102 47W
Eagle, *U.S.A.* **142 G10** 39 39N 106 50W
Eagle →, *Canada* **129 B8** 53 36N 57 26W
Eagle Butte, *U.S.A.* **138 C4** 45 0N 101 10W
Eagle Cr. →, *U.S.A.* **141 F11** 38 36N 85 4W
Eagle Grove, *U.S.A.* **140 B3** 42 40N 93 54W
Eagle L., *Calif., U.S.A.* . **142 F3** 40 39N 120 45W
Eagle L., *Maine, U.S.A.* . **129 C6** 46 20N 69 22W
Eagle Lake, *U.S.A.* **139 L6** 29 35N 96 20W
Eagle Mountain, *U.S.A.* . **145 M11** 33 49N 115 27W
Eagle Nest, *U.S.A.* **143 H11** 36 33N 105 16W
Eagle Pass, *U.S.A.* **139 L4** 28 43N 100 30W
Eagle Pk., *U.S.A.* **144 G7** 38 10N 119 25W
Eagle Pt., *Australia* **112 C3** 16 11 S 124 23 E
Eagle River, *U.S.A.* **138 C10** 45 55N 89 15W
Eagleville, *U.S.A.* **140 D3** 40 28N 93 59W
Ealing, *U.K.* **17 F7** 51 30N 0 19W
Earaheedy, *Australia* **113 E3** 25 34 S 121 29 E
Earl Grey, *Canada* **131 C8** 50 57N 104 43W
Earle, *U.S.A.* **139 H9** 35 16N 90 28W
Earlimart, *U.S.A.* **145 K7** 35 53N 119 16W
Earlville, *U.S.A.* **141 C8** 41 35N 88 55W
Earn →, *U.K.* **18 E5** 56 20N 3 19W
Earn, L., *U.K.* **18 E4** 56 23N 4 14W
Earnslaw, Mt., *N.Z.* **119 E3** 44 32 S 168 27 E
Earth, *U.S.A.* **139 H3** 34 14N 102 24W
Easley, *U.S.A.* **135 H4** 34 50N 82 36W
East Angus, *Canada* **129 C5** 45 30N 71 40W
East Aurora, *U.S.A.* **136 D6** 42 46N 78 37W
East B., *U.S.A.* **139 L10** 29 0N 89 15W
East Beskids = Vychodné
Beskydy, *Europe* **31 B15** 49 20N 22 0 E
East Brady, *U.S.A.* **136 F5** 40 59N 79 36W
East C., *N.Z.* **118 D7** 37 42 S 178 35 E
East C., *Papua N. G.* **120 F6** 10 13 S 150 53 E
East Chicago, *U.S.A.* **141 C9** 41 38N 87 27W
East China Sea, *Asia* **65 C7** 30 5N 126 0 E
East Coast Bays, *N.Z.* **118 C3** 36 46 S 174 46 E
East Coulee, *Canada* **130 C6** 51 23N 112 27W
East Dubuque, *U.S.A.* **140 B6** 42 30N 90 39W
East Falkland, *Falk. Is.* . **160 D5** 51 30 S 58 30W
East Grand Forks, *U.S.A.* **138 B6** 47 56N 97 1W
East Greenwich, *U.S.A.* . **137 E13** 41 40N 71 27W
East Hartford, *U.S.A.* **137 E12** 41 46N 72 39W
East Helena, *U.S.A.* **142 C8** 46 35N 111 56W
East Indies, *Asia* **58 K15** 0 0 120 0 E
East Jordan, *U.S.A.* **134 C3** 45 10N 85 7W
East Lansing, *U.S.A.* **141 B12** 42 44N 84 29W
East Liverpool, *U.S.A.* . **136 F4** 40 37N 80 35W
East London, *S. Africa* . **105 E4** 33 0 S 27 55 E
East Lynne, *Australia* **117 C9** 35 35 S 150 16 E
East Main = Eastmain,
Canada **128 B4** 52 10N 78 30W
East Moline, *U.S.A.* **140 C6** 41 32N 90 26W
East Orange, *U.S.A.* **137 F10** 40 46N 74 13W
East Pacific Ridge,
Pac. Oc. **123 J17** 15 0 S 110 0W
East Pakistan =
Bangladesh ■, *Asia* **78 C3** 24 0N 90 0 E
East Palestine, *U.S.A.* **136 F4** 40 50N 80 33W
East Peoria, *U.S.A.* **140 D7** 40 40N 89 34W
East Pine, *Canada* **130 B4** 55 48N 120 12W
East Pt., *Canada* **129 C7** 46 27N 61 58W
East Point, *U.S.A.* **135 J3** 33 41N 84 27W
East Providence, *U.S.A.* . **137 E13** 41 49N 71 23W
East Retford, *U.K.* **16 D7** 53 19N 0 55W
East St. Louis, *U.S.A.* **140 F6** 38 37N 90 9W
East Schelde → =
Oosterschelde, *Neths.* . **21 E4** 51 33N 4 0 E
East Siberian Sea, *Russia* **57 B17** 73 0N 160 0 E
East Stroudsburg, *U.S.A.* **137 E9** 41 1N 75 11W
East Sussex □, *U.K.* **17 G8** 51 0N 0 20 E
East Tawas, *U.S.A.* **134 C4** 44 17N 83 29W
East Toorale, *Australia* . **115 E4** 30 27 S 145 28 E
East Troy, *U.S.A.* **141 B8** 42 47N 88 24W
East Walker →, *U.S.A.* . **144 G7** 38 52N 119 10W
Eastbourne, *N.Z.* **118 H3** 41 19 S 174 55 E
Eastbourne, *U.K.* **17 G8** 50 46N 0 18 E
Eastend, *Canada* **131 D7** 49 32N 108 50W
Easter Dal =
Österdalälven →,
Sweden **13 F12** 61 30N 13 45 E
Easter Islands = Pascua,
I. de, *Pac. Oc.* **123 K17** 27 0 S 109 0W
Eastern □, *Kenya* **106 B4** 0 0 38 30 E
Eastern □, *Uganda* **106 B3** 1 50N 33 45 E
Eastern Cr. →, *Australia* **114 C3** 20 40 S 141 35 E
Eastern Ghats, *India* **83 J4** 14 0N 78 50 E
Eastern Group = Lau
Group, *Fiji* **121 A3** 17 0 S 178 30W
Eastern Group, *Australia* **113 F3** 33 30 S 124 30 E
Eastern Province □,
S. Leone **100 D2** 8 15N 11 0W
Eastern Samar □, *Phil.* . **71 F5** 11 40N 125 40 E
Easterville, *Canada* **131 C9** 53 8N 99 49W
Easthampton, *U.S.A.* **137 D12** 42 16N 72 40W
Eastland, *U.S.A.* **139 J5** 32 24N 98 49W
Eastleigh, *U.K.* **17 G6** 50 58N 1 21W
Eastmain, *Canada* **128 B4** 52 10N 78 30W
Eastmain →, *Canada* **128 B4** 52 27N 78 26W
Eastman, *Canada* **137 A12** 45 18N 72 19W
Eastman, *Ga., U.S.A.* **135 J4** 32 12N 83 11W
Eastman, *Wis., U.S.A.* **140 A5** 43 10N 91 1W
Easton, *Md., U.S.A.* **134 F7** 38 47N 76 5W
Easton, *Pa., U.S.A.* **137 F9** 40 41N 75 13W
Easton, *Wash., U.S.A.* **144 C5** 47 14N 121 11W
Eastport, *U.S.A.* **129 D6** 44 56N 67 0W
Eastsound, *U.S.A.* **144 B4** 48 42N 122 55W
Eaton, *Colo., U.S.A.* **138 E2** 40 32N 104 42W
Eaton, *Ohio, U.S.A.* **141 E12** 39 45N 84 38W
Eaton Rapids, *U.S.A.* **141 B12** 42 31N 84 39W
Eatonia, *Canada* **131 C7** 51 13N 109 25W
Eatonton, *U.S.A.* **135 J4** 33 20N 83 23W
Eatontown, *U.S.A.* **137 F10** 40 19N 74 4W
Eatonville, *U.S.A.* **144 D4** 46 52N 122 16W
Eau Claire, *Fr. Guiana* **153 C7** 3 30N 53 40W
Eau Claire, *U.S.A.* **138 C9** 44 49N 91 30W
Eauze, *France* **24 E4** 43 53N 0 7 E
Ebagoola, *Australia* **114 A3** 14 15 S 143 12 E
Eban, *Nigeria* **101 D5** 9 40N 4 50 E
Ebangalakata, *Zaïre* **102 C4** 0 29 S 21 29 E
Ebbw Vale, *U.K.* **17 F4** 51 47N 3 12W
Ebebiyín, *Eq. Guin.* **102 B2** 2 9N 11 20 E
Ebeggui, *Algeria* **99 C6** 26 2N 6 0 E
Ebel, *Gabon* **102 B2** 0 7N 11 5 E
Ebeltoft, *Denmark* **13 H11** 56 12N 10 41 E
Ebensburg, *U.S.A.* **136 F6** 40 29N 78 44W
Ebensee, *Austria* **30 D6** 47 48N 13 46 E
Eber Gölü, *Turkey* **88 D4** 38 38N 31 11 E
Eberbach, *Germany* **27 F4** 49 27N 8 59 E
Eberswalde, *Germany* **26 C9** 52 49N 13 50 E
Ebetsu, *Japan* **60 C10** 43 7N 141 34 E
Ebian, *China* **68 C4** 29 11N 103 13 E
Ebikon, *Switz.* **29 B6** 47 5N 8 21 E
Ebingen, *Germany* **27 G5** 48 13N 9 1 E
Ebino, *Japan* **62 E2** 32 2N 130 48 E
Ebnat-Kappel, *Switz.* **29 B8** 47 16N 9 7 E
Eboli, *Italy* **41 B8** 40 39N 15 2 E
Ebolowa, *Cameroon* **101 E7** 2 55N 11 10 E
Ebrach, *Germany* **27 F6** 49 50N 10 30 E
Ébrié, Lagune, *Ivory C.* . **100 D4** 5 12N 4 26W
Ebro →, *Spain* **34 E5** 40 43N 0 54 E
Ebro, Pantano del, *Spain* **36 B7** 43 0N 3 58W
Ebstorf, *Germany* **26 B6** 53 2N 10 23 E
Ecaussines-d' Enghien,
Belgium **21 G4** 50 35N 4 11 E
Eceabat, *Turkey* **44 D8** 40 11N 26 21 E
Ech Cheliff, *Algeria* **99 A5** 36 10N 1 20 E
Echallens, *Switz.* **28 C3** 46 38N 6 38 E
Echeng, *China* **69 B10** 30 23N 114 50 E
Echigo-Sammyaku, *Japan* **61 F9** 36 50N 139 50 E
Echizen-Misaki, *Japan* **63 B7** 35 59N 135 57 E
Echmiadzin, *Armenia* **53 F11** 40 12N 44 19 E
Echo Bay, *N.W.T.,*
Canada **126 B8** 66 5N 117 55W
Echo Bay, *Ont., Canada* . **128 C3** 46 29N 84 4W
Echoing →, *Canada* **131 B10** 55 51N 92 5W
Echt, *Neths.* **21 F7** 51 7N 5 52 E
Echternach, *Lux.* **21 J8** 49 49N 6 25 E
Echuca, *Australia* **117 D6** 36 10 S 144 20 E
Ecija, *Spain* **37 H5** 37 30N 5 10W
Eckernförde, *Germany* **26 A5** 54 26N 9 50 E
Eclipse Is., *Australia* **112 B4** 13 54 S 126 19 E
Écommoy, *France* **22 E7** 47 50N 0 17 E
Ecoporanga, *Brazil* **155 E3** 18 23 S 40 50W
Écos, *France* **23 C8** 49 9N 1 35 E
Écouché, *France* **22 D6** 48 42N 0 10W
Ecuador ■, *S. Amer.* **152 D2** 2 0 S 78 0W
Écueillé, *France* **22 E8** 47 5N 1 21 E
Ed, *Sweden* **15 F5** 58 55N 11 55 E
Ed Dabbura, *Sudan* **94 D3** 17 40N 34 15 E
Ed Dâmer, *Sudan* **94 D3** 17 27N 34 0 E
Ed Debba, *Sudan* **94 D3** 18 0N 30 51 E
Ed-Déffa, *Egypt* **94 A2** 30 40N 26 30 E
Ed Deim, *Sudan* **95 E2** 10 10N 28 20 E
Ed Dueim, *Sudan* **95 E3** 14 0N 32 10 E
Edah, *Australia* **113 E2** 28 16 S 117 10 E
Edam, *Canada* **131 C7** 53 11N 108 46W
Edam, *Neths.* **20 C6** 52 31N 5 3 E
Edapally, *India* **83 J4** 11 19N 78 3 E
Eday, *U.K.* **18 B6** 59 11N 2 47W
Edd, *Eritrea* **90 E3** 14 0N 41 38 E
Eddrachillis B., *U.K.* **18 C3** 58 16N 5 10W
Eddystone, *U.K.* **17 G3** 50 11N 4 16W
Eddystone Pt., *Australia* . **114 G4** 40 59 S 148 20 E
Eddyville, *U.S.A.* **140 C4** 41 9N 92 38W
Ede, *Neths.* **20 D7** 52 4N 5 40 E
Ede, *Nigeria* **101 D5** 7 45N 4 29 E
Édea, *Cameroon* **101 E7** 3 51N 10 9 E
Edegem, *Belgium* **21 F4** 51 10N 4 27 E
Edehon L., *Canada* **131 A9** 60 25N 97 15W
Edekel, Adrar, *Algeria* **99 D6** 23 56N 6 47 E
Eden, *Australia* **117 D8** 37 3 S 149 55 E
Eden, *N.C., U.S.A.* **135 G6** 36 29N 79 53W
Eden, *N.Y., U.S.A.* **136 D6** 42 39N 78 55W
Eden, *Tex., U.S.A.* **139 K5** 31 13N 99 51W
Eden, *Wyo., U.S.A.* **142 E9** 42 3N 109 26W
Eden →, *U.K.* **16 C4** 54 57N 3 2W
Eden L., *Canada* **131 B8** 56 38N 100 15W
Edenburg, *S. Africa* **104 D4** 29 43 S 25 58 E
Edendale, *N.Z.* **119 G3** 46 19 S 168 48 E
Edendale, *S. Africa* **105 D5** 29 39 S 30 18 E
Edenderry, *Ireland* **19 C4** 53 21N 7 3W
Edenton, *U.S.A.* **135 G7** 36 4N 76 39W
Edenville, *S. Africa* **105 D4** 27 37 S 27 34 E
Eder →, *Germany* **26 D5** 51 15N 9 25 E
Ederstausee, *Germany* **26 D4** 51 11N 9 0 E
Edgar, *U.S.A.* **138 E5** 40 22N 97 58W
Edgartown, *U.S.A.* **137 E14** 41 23N 70 31W
Edge Hill, *U.K.* **17 E6** 52 7N 1 28W
Edgecumbe, *N.Z.* **118 D5** 37 59 S 176 47 E
Edgefield, *U.S.A.* **135 J5** 33 47N 81 56W
Edgeley, *U.S.A.* **138 B5** 46 22N 98 43W
Edgemont, *U.S.A.* **138 D3** 43 18N 103 50W
Edgeøya, *Svalbard* **6 B9** 77 45N 22 30 E
Edgerton, *Ohio, U.S.A.* . **141 C12** 41 27N 84 45W
Edgerton, *Wis., U.S.A.* . **140 B7** 42 50N 89 4W
Edgewood, *U.S.A.* **141 F8** 38 55N 88 40W
Edhessa, *Greece* **44 D4** 40 48N 22 5 E
Edievale, *N.Z.* **119 F4** 45 49 S 169 22 E
Edina, *Liberia* **100 D2** 6 0N 10 10W
Edina, *U.S.A.* **140 D4** 40 10N 92 11W
Edinburg, *Ill., U.S.A.* **140 E7** 39 39N 89 23W
Edinburg, *Ind., U.S.A.* . **141 E11** 39 21N 85 58W
Edinburg, *Tex., U.S.A.* . **139 M5** 26 18N 98 10W
Edinburgh, *U.K.* **18 F5** 55 57N 3 12W
Edirne, *Turkey* **43 F11** 41 40N 26 34 E
Edirne □, *Turkey* **88 C2** 41 40N 26 30 E
Edison, *U.S.A.* **144 B4** 48 33N 122 27W
Edithburgh, *Australia* **116 C2** 35 5 S 137 43 E
Edjeleh, *Algeria* **99 C6** 28 38N 9 50 E
Edjudina, *Australia* **113 E3** 29 48 S 122 23 E
Edmeston, *U.S.A.* **137 D9** 42 42N 75 15W
Edmond, *U.S.A.* **139 H6** 35 39N 97 29W
Edmonds, *U.S.A.* **144 C4** 47 49N 122 23W
Edmonton, *Australia* **114 B4** 17 2 S 145 46 E
Edmonton, *Canada* **130 C6** 53 30N 113 30W
Edmund L., *Canada* **131 C10** 54 45N 93 17W
Edmundston, *Canada* **129 C6** 47 23N 68 20W
Edna, *U.S.A.* **139 L6** 28 59N 96 39W
Edna Bay, *U.S.A.* **130 B2** 55 55N 133 40W
Edo □, *Nigeria* **101 D6** 6 30N 6 0 E
Edolo, *Italy* **38 B7** 46 10N 10 21 E
Edremit, *Turkey* **88 D2** 39 34N 27 0 E
Edremit Körfezi, *Turkey* . **88 D2** 39 30N 26 45 E
Edsbyn, *Sweden* **14 C9** 61 23N 15 49 E
Edsele, *Sweden* **14 A10** 63 25N 16 32 E
Edson, *Canada* **130 C5** 53 35N 116 28W
Eduardo Castex, *Argentina* **158 D3** 35 50 S 64 18W
Edward →, *Australia* **116 C5** 35 5 S 143 30 E
Edward, L., *Africa* **106 C2** 0 25 S 29 40 E
Edward I., *Canada* **128 C2** 48 22N 88 37W
Edward River, *Australia* . **114 A3** 14 59 S 141 26 E
Edward VII Land,
Antarctica **7 E13** 80 0 S 150 0W
Edwards, *U.S.A.* **145 L9** 34 55N 117 51W
Edwards →, *U.S.A.* **140 C6** 41 9N 90 59W
Edwards Plateau, *U.S.A.* **139 K4** 30 45N 101 20W
Edwardsburg, *U.S.A.* **141 C10** 41 48N 86 6W
Edwardsport, *U.S.A.* **141 F9** 38 49N 87 15W
Edwardsville, *Ill., U.S.A.* **140 F7** 38 49N 89 58W
Edwardsville, *Pa., U.S.A.* **137 E9** 41 15N 75 56W
Edzo, *Canada* **130 A5** 62 49N 116 4W
Eefde, *Neths.* **20 D8** 52 10N 6 13 E
Eekloo, *Belgium* **21 F3** 51 11N 3 33 E
Eel →, *Ind., U.S.A.* **141 E10** 39 7N 86 57W
Eel →, *Ind., U.S.A.* **141 D10** 40 45N 86 22W
Eelde, *Neths.* **20 B9** 53 8N 6 34 E
Eem →, *Neths.* **20 D6** 52 16N 5 20 E
Eems →, *Neths.* **20 B9** 53 26N 6 57 E
Eems Kanaal, *Neths.* **20 B9** 53 18N 6 46 E
Eenrum, *Neths.* **20 B8** 53 22N 6 28 E
Eernegem, *Belgium* **21 F2** 51 8N 3 2 E
Eerste Valthermond,
Neths. **20 C9** 52 53N 6 58 E
Efate, I., *Vanuatu* **121 G6** 17 40 S 168 25 E
Eferding, *Austria* **30 C7** 48 18N 14 1 E
Eferi, *Algeria* **99 D6** 24 30N 9 28 E
Effingham, *U.S.A.* **141 E8** 39 7N 88 33W
Effretikon, *Switz.* **29 B7** 47 25N 8 42 E
Eforie Sud, *Romania* **46 E9** 44 1N 28 37 E
Ega →, *Spain* **34 C3** 42 19N 1 55W
Égadi, Ísole, *Italy* **40 E5** 37 55N 12 16 E
Eganville, *Canada* **128 C4** 45 32N 77 5W
Egeland, *U.S.A.* **138 A5** 48 38N 99 6W
Egenolf L., *Canada* **131 B9** 59 3N 100 0W
Eger = Cheb, *Czech.* **30 A5** 50 9N 12 28 E
Eger, *Hungary* **31 D13** 47 53N 20 27 E
Eger →, *Hungary* **31 D13** 47 38N 20 50 E
Egersund, *Norway* **13 G9** 58 26N 6 1 E
Egg L., *Canada* **131 B7** 55 5N 105 30W
Eggenburg, *Austria* **30 C8** 48 38N 15 50 E
Eggenfelden, *Germany* **27 G8** 48 24N 12 46 E
Eggiwil, *Switz.* **28 C5** 46 52N 7 47 E
Egherta, *Somali Rep.* **108 D2** 2 4N 43 11 E
Éghezée, *Belgium* **21 G5** 50 35N 4 55 E
Eginbah, *Australia* **112 D2** 20 53 S 119 47 E
Egito, *Angola* **103 E2** 12 4 S 13 58 E
Égletons, *France* **24 C6** 45 24N 2 3 E
Eglisau, *Switz.* **29 A7** 47 35N 8 31 E
Egmond-aan-Zee, *Neths.* **20 C5** 52 37N 4 38 E
Egmont, C., *N.Z.* **118 F2** 39 16 S 173 45 E
Egmont, Mt., *N.Z.* **118 F3** 39 17 S 174 5 E
Eğridir, *Turkey* **88 E4** 37 52N 30 51 E
Eğridir Gölü, *Turkey* **88 E4** 37 53N 30 50 E
Egtved, *Denmark* **15 J3** 55 38N 9 18 E
Éguas →, *Brazil* **155 D3** 13 26 S 44 14W
Egume, *Nigeria* **101 D6** 7 30N 7 14 E
Éguzon, *France* **24 B5** 46 27N 1 33 E
Egvekinot, *Russia* **57 C19** 66 19N 179 50W
Egyek, *Hungary* **31 D13** 47 39N 20 52 E
Egypt ■, *Africa* **94 J7** 28 0N 31 0 E
Eha Amufu, *Nigeria* **101 D6** 6 30N 7 46 E
Ehime □, *Japan* **62 D4** 33 30N 132 40 E
Ehingen, *Germany* **27 G5** 48 16N 9 43 E
Ehrenberg, *U.S.A.* **145 M12** 33 36N 114 31W
Ehrwald, *Austria* **30 D3** 47 24N 10 56 E
Eibar, *Spain* **34 B2** 43 11N 2 28W
Eibergen, *Neths.* **20 D9** 52 6N 6 39 E
Eichstatt, *Germany* **27 G7** 48 53N 11 12 E
Eider →, *Germany* **26 A4** 54 19N 8 58 E
Eidsvold, *Australia* **115 D5** 25 25 S 151 12 E
Eidsvoll, *Norway* **13 F11** 60 19N 11 14 E
Eifel, *Germany* **27 E2** 50 10N 6 45 E
Eiffel Flats, *Zimbabwe* **107 F3** 18 20 S 30 0 E
Eigg, *U.K.* **18 E2** 56 54N 6 10W
Eighty Mile Beach,
Australia **112 C3** 19 30 S 120 40 E
Eil, *Somali Rep.* **90 F4** 8 0N 49 50 E
Eil, L., *U.K.* **18 E3** 56 50N 5 15W
Eildon, *Australia* **117 D6** 37 14 S 145 55 E
Eildon, L., *Australia* **115 F4** 37 10 S 146 0 E
Eileen L., *Canada* **131 A7** 62 16N 107 37W
Eilenburg, *Germany* **26 D8** 51 28N 12 38 E
Ein el Luweiqa, *Sudan* **95 E3** 14 5N 33 50 E
Einasleigh, *Australia* **114 B3** 18 32 S 144 5 E
Einasleigh →, *Australia* . **114 B3** 17 30 S 142 17 E
Einbeck, *Germany* **26 D5** 51 48N 9 50 E
Eindhoven, *Neths.* **21 F6** 51 26N 5 28 E
Einsiedeln, *Switz.* **29 B7** 47 7N 8 46 E
Eire ■ = Ireland ■,
Europe **19 D4** 53 0N 8 0W
Eiríksjökull, *Iceland* **12 D3** 64 46N 20 24W
Eirlandsche Gat, *Neths.* **20 B5** 53 12N 4 54 E
Eirunepé, *Brazil* **156 B4** 6 35 S 69 53W
Eisden, *Belgium* **21 G7** 50 59N 5 42 E
Eisenach, *Germany* **26 E6** 50 58N 10 18 E
Eisenberg, *Germany* **26 E7** 50 59N 11 50 E
Eisenerz, *Austria* **30 D7** 47 32N 14 54 E
Eisenhüttenstadt,
Germany **26 C10** 52 9N 14 41 E
Eisenkappel, *Austria* **30 E7** 46 29N 14 36 E
Eisenstadt, *Austria* **31 D9** 47 51N 16 31 E
Eiserfeld, *Germany* **26 E3** 50 50N 7 59 E
Eisfeld, *Germany* **26 E6** 50 25N 10 54 E
Eisleben, *Germany* **26 D7** 51 31N 11 31 E
Eivissa = Ibiza, *Spain* **33 C7** 38 54N 1 26 E
Ejby, *Denmark* **15 J3** 55 25N 9 56 E
Eje, Sierra del, *Spain* **36 C4** 42 24N 6 54W
Ejea de los Caballeros,
Spain **34 C3** 42 7N 1 9W
Ejutla, *Mexico* **147 D5** 16 34N 96 44W
Ekalaka, *U.S.A.* **138 C2** 45 53N 104 33W
Ekalla, *Gabon* **102 C2** 1 27 S 14 0 E
Ekanga, *Zaïre* **102 C4** 2 23 S 23 14 E
Ekawasaki, *Japan* **62 D4** 33 13N 132 46 E
Ekeren, *Belgium* **21 F4** 51 17N 4 25 E
Eket, *Nigeria* **101 E6** 4 38N 7 56 E
Eketahuna, *N.Z.* **118 G4** 40 38 S 175 43 E
Ekhínos, *Greece* **44 C7** 41 16N 25 1 E
Ekibastuz, *Kazakhstan* **56 D8** 51 50N 75 10 E
Ekimchan, *Russia* **57 D14** 53 0N 133 0 E
Ekoli, *Zaïre* **102 C4** 0 23 S 24 13 E
Eksel, *Belgium* **21 F6** 51 9N 5 24 E
Ekwan →, *Canada* **128 B3** 53 12N 82 15W
Ekwan Pt., *Canada* **128 B3** 53 16N 82 7W
El Aaiún, *W. Sahara* **98 C2** 27 9N 13 12W
El Aargub, *Mauritania* **98 D1** 23 37N 15 52W
El Abiodh-Sidi-Cheikh,
Algeria **99 B5** 32 53N 0 31 E
El Adde, *Somali Rep.* **108 D3** 2 35N 46 9 E
El 'Agrûd, *Egypt* **91 E3** 30 14N 34 24 E
El Aïoun, *Morocco* **99 B4** 34 33N 2 30W
El 'Aiyat, *Egypt* **94 J7** 29 36N 31 15 E
El Alamein, *Egypt* **94 H6** 30 48N 28 58 E
El Alto, *Peru* **156 A1** 4 15 S 81 14W
El 'Aqaba, W. →, *Egypt* **91 E2** 30 7N 33 54 E
El 'Arag, *Egypt* **94 B2** 28 40N 26 20 E
El Arahal, *Spain* **37 H5** 37 15N 5 33W
El Arenal, *Spain* **33 B9** 39 30N 2 45 E
El Aricha, *Algeria* **99 B4** 34 13N 1 10W
El Arīhā, *Jordan* **91 D4** 31 52N 35 27 E
El Arish, *Australia* **114 B4** 17 35 S 146 1 E
El 'Arîsh, *Egypt* **91 D2** 31 8N 33 50 E
El 'Arîsh, W. →, *Egypt* . **91 D2** 31 8N 33 47 E
El Arrouch, *Algeria* **99 A6** 36 37N 6 53 E
El Asnam = Ech Cheliff,
Algeria **99 A5** 36 10N 1 20 E
El Astillero, *Spain* **36 B7** 43 24N 3 49W
El Badâri, *Egypt* **94 B3** 27 4N 31 25 E
El Bahreín, *Egypt* **94 B2** 28 30N 26 25 E
El Ballâs, *Egypt* **94 B3** 26 2N 32 43 E
El Balyana, *Egypt* **94 B3** 26 10N 32 3 E
El Banco, *Colombia* **152 B3** 9 0N 73 58W
El Baqeir, *Sudan* **94 D3** 18 40N 33 40 E
El Barco de Ávila, *Spain* **36 E5** 40 21N 5 31W
El Barco de Valdeorras,
Spain **36 C4** 42 23N 6 58W
El Bauga, *Sudan* **94 D3** 18 18N 33 52 E
El Baúl, *Venezuela* **152 B4** 8 57N 68 17W
El Bawiti, *Egypt* **94 J6** 28 25N 28 45 E
El Bayadh, *Algeria* **99 B5** 33 40N 1 1 E
El Bierzo, *Spain* **36 C4** 42 45N 6 30W
El Bluff, *Nic.* **148 D3** 11 59N 83 40W
El Bolsón, *Argentina* **160 B2** 41 55 S 71 30W
El Bonillo, *Spain* **35 G2** 38 57N 2 35W
El Brûk, W. →, *Egypt* . **91 E2** 30 15N 33 50 E
El Buheirat □, *Sudan* **95 F2** 7 0N 30 0 E
El Bur, *Somali Rep.* **108 D3** 4 40N 46 37 E
El Cain, *Argentina* **160 B3** 41 38 S 68 19W
El Cajon, *U.S.A.* **145 N10** 32 48N 116 58W
El Callao, *Venezuela* **153 B5** 7 18N 61 50W
El Camp, *Spain* **34 D6** 41 5N 1 10 E
El Campo, *U.S.A.* **139 L6** 29 12N 96 16W
El Carmen, *Bolivia* **157 C5** 13 40 S 63 55W
El Carmen, *Venezuela* **152 C4** 1 16N 66 52W

Endröd 195

El Castillo, *Spain* **37 H4** 37 41N 6 19W
El Centro, *U.S.A.* **145 N11** 32 48N 115 34W
El Cerro, *Bolivia* **157 D5** 17 30 S 61 40W
El Cerro, *Spain* **37 H4** 37 45N 6 57W
El Cocuy, *Colombia* **152 B3** 6 25N 72 27W
El Compadre, *Mexico* **145 N10** 32 20N 116 14W
El Corcovado, *Argentina* **160 B2** 43 25 S 71 35W
El Coronil, *Spain* **37 H5** 37 5N 5 38W
El Cuy, *Argentina* **160 A3** 39 55 S 68 25W
El Cuyo, *Mexico* **147 C7** 21 30N 87 40W
El Dab'a, *Egypt* **94 H6** 31 0N 28 27 E
El Daheir, *Egypt* **91 D3** 31 13N 34 10 E
El Dambahaddo, *Somali Rep.* **108 D3** 3 17N 46 40 E
El Deir, *Egypt* **94 B3** 25 25N 32 20 E
El Dere, *Ethiopia* **108 C2** 5 6N 43 5 E
El Dere, *Somali Rep.* **108 C3** 5 22N 46 11 E
El Dere, *Somali Rep.* **90 G4** 3 50N 47 8 E
El Descanso, *Mexico* **145 N10** 32 12N 116 58W
El Desemboque, *Mexico* **146 A2** 30 30N 112 57W
El Dilingat, *Egypt* **94 H7** 30 50N 30 31 E
El Diviso, *Colombia* **152 C2** 1 22N 78 14W
El Djem, *Tunisia* **96 A2** 35 18N 10 42 E
El Djouf, *Mauritania* **92 D3** 20 0N 9 0W
El Dorado, *Ark., U.S.A.* **139 J8** 33 12N 92 40W
El Dorado, *Kans., U.S.A.* **139 G6** 37 49N 96 52W
El Dorado, *Venezuela* **153 B5** 6 55N 61 37W
El Eglab, *Algeria* **98 C4** 26 20N 4 30W
El Escorial, *Spain* **36 E6** 40 35N 4 7W
El Eulma, *Algeria* **99 A6** 36 9N 5 42 E
El Faiyûm, *Egypt* **94 J7** 29 19N 30 50 E
El Fâsher, *Sudan* **95 E2** 13 33N 25 26 E
El Fashn, *Egypt* **94 J7** 28 50N 30 54 E
El Ferrol, *Spain* **36 B2** 43 29N 8 15W
El Fifi, *Sudan* **95 E1** 10 4N 25 0 E
El Fud, *Ethiopia* **108 C2** 7 15N 42 52 E
El Fuerte, *Mexico* **146 B3** 26 30N 108 40W
El Gal, *Somali Rep.* **90 E5** 10 58N 50 20 E
El Gebir, *Sudan* **95 E2** 13 40N 29 40 E
El Gedida, *Egypt* **94 B2** 25 40N 28 30 E
El Geteina, *Sudan* **95 E3** 14 50N 32 27 E
El Gezira □, *Sudan* **95 E3** 15 0N 33 0 E
El Gîza, *Egypt* **94 H7** 30 0N 31 10 E
El Goléa, *Algeria* **99 B5** 30 30N 2 50 E
El Guettar, *Algeria* **99 B5** 34 5N 4 38 E
El Hadeb, *W. Sahara* **98 C2** 25 51N 13 0W
El Hadjira, *Algeria* **99 B6** 32 36N 5 30 E
El Hagiz, *Sudan* **95 D4** 15 15N 35 50 E
El Hajeb, *Morocco* **98 B3** 33 43N 5 13W
El Hammam, *Egypt* **94 H6** 30 52N 29 25 E
El Hammâmi, *Mauritania* **98 D2** 23 3N 11 30W
El Hamurre, *Somali Rep.* **108 C3** 7 13N 48 54 E
El Hank, *Mauritania* **98 D3** 24 30N 7 0W
El Harrach, *Algeria* **99 A5** 36 45N 3 5 E
El Hasian, *W. Sahara* **98 C2** 26 20N 14 0W
El Hawata, *Sudan* **95 E3** 13 25N 34 42 E
El Heiz, *Egypt* **94 B2** 27 50N 28 40 E
El 'Idisât, *Egypt* **94 B3** 25 30N 32 35 E
El Iskandarîya, *Egypt* **94 H6** 31 0N 30 0 E
El Jadida, *Morocco* **98 B3** 33 11N 8 17W
El Jebelein, *Sudan* **95 E3** 12 40N 32 55 E
El Kab, *Sudan* **94 D3** 19 27N 32 46 E
El Kabrît, G., *Egypt* **91 F2** 29 42N 33 16 E
El Kala, *Algeria* **99 A6** 36 50N 8 30 E
El Kalâa, *Morocco* **98 B3** 32 4N 7 27W
El Kamlin, *Sudan* **95 D3** 15 3N 33 11 E
El Kantara, *Algeria* **99 A6** 35 14N 5 45 E
El Kantara, *Tunisia* **96 B2** 33 45N 10 58 E
El Karaba, *Sudan* **95 D3** 18 32N 33 41 E
El Kef, *Tunisia* **96 A1** 36 12N 8 47 E
El Khandaq, *Sudan* **94 D3** 18 30N 30 30 E
El Khârga, *Egypt* **94 B3** 25 30N 30 33 E
El Khartûm, *Sudan* **95 D3** 15 31N 32 35 E
El Khartûm □, *Sudan* **95 D3** 16 0N 33 0 E
El Khartûm Bahrî, *Sudan* **95 D3** 15 40N 32 31 E
El Khroub, *Algeria* **99 A6** 36 10N 6 55 E
El Kseur, *Algeria* **99 A5** 36 46N 4 49 E
El Ksiba, *Morocco* **98 B3** 32 45N 6 1W
El Kuntilla, *Egypt* **91 E3** 30 1N 34 45 E
El Laqâwa, *Sudan* **95 E2** 11 25N 29 1 E
El Laqeita, *Egypt* **94 B3** 25 50N 33 15 E
El Leiya, *Sudan* **95 D4** 16 15N 35 28 E
El Mafâza, *Sudan* **95 E3** 13 38N 34 30 E
El Mahalla el Kubra, *Egypt* **94 H7** 31 0N 31 0 E
El Mahârîq, *Egypt* **94 B3** 25 35N 30 35 E
El Mahmûdîya, *Egypt* **94 H7** 31 10N 30 32 E
El Maitén, *Argentina* **160 B2** 42 3 S 71 10W
El Maiz, *Algeria* **99 C4** 28 19N 0 9W
El-Maks el-Bahari, *Egypt* **94 C3** 24 30N 30 40 E
El Manshâh, *Egypt* **94 B3** 26 26N 31 50 E
El Mansour, *Algeria* **99 C4** 27 47N 0 14W
El Mansûra, *Egypt* **94 H7** 31 0N 31 19 E
El Mantico, *Venezuela* **153 B5** 7 38N 62 45W
El Manzala, *Egypt* **94 H7** 31 10N 31 50 E
El Marâgha, *Egypt* **94 B3** 26 35N 31 10 E
El Masid, *Sudan* **95 D3** 15 15N 33 0 E
El Matariya, *Egypt* **94 H8** 31 15N 32 0 E
El Medano, *Canary Is.* **33 F3** 28 3N 16 32W
El Meghaier, *Algeria* **99 B6** 33 55N 5 58 E
El Meraguen, *Algeria* **99 C4** 28 0N 0 7W
El Metemma, *Sudan* **95 D3** 16 50N 33 10 E
El Miamo, *Venezuela* **153 B5** 7 39N 61 46W
El Milagro, *Argentina* **158 C2** 30 59 S 65 59W
El Milia, *Algeria* **99 A6** 36 51N 6 13 E
El Minyâ, *Egypt* **94 J7** 28 7N 30 33 E
El Molar, *Spain* **34 E1** 40 42N 3 45W
El Mreyye, *Mauritania* **100 B3** 18 0N 6 0W
El Nido, *Phil.* **71 F2** 11 10N 119 25 E
El Obeid, *Sudan* **95 E3** 13 8N 30 10 E
El Odaiya, *Sudan* **95 E2** 12 8N 28 12 E
El Oro, *Mexico* **147 D4** 19 48N 100 8W
El Oro □, *Ecuador* **152 D2** 3 30 S 79 50W
El Oued, *Algeria* **99 B6** 33 20N 6 58 E
El Palmar, *Bolivia* **157 D5** 17 50 S 63 9W
El Palmar, *Venezuela* **153 B5** 7 58N 61 53W
El Palmito, Presa, *Mexico* **146 B3** 25 40N 105 30W
El Panadés, *Spain* **34 D6** 41 10N 1 30 E
El Pardo, *Spain* **36 E7** 40 31N 3 47W
El Paso, *Ill., U.S.A.* **140 D7** 40 44N 89 1W
El Paso, *Tex., U.S.A.* **143 L10** 31 45N 106 29W
El Paso Robles, *U.S.A.* **144 K6** 35 38N 120 41W
El Pedernoso, *Spain* **35 F2** 39 29N 2 45W
El Pedroso, *Spain* **37 H5** 37 51N 5 45W
El Pobo de Dueñas, *Spain* **34 E3** 40 46N 1 39W
El Portal, *U.S.A.* **144 H7** 37 41N 119 47W
El Porvenir, *Mexico* **146 A3** 31 15N 105 51W
El Prat de Llobregat, *Spain* **34 D7** 41 18N 2 3 E
El Progreso, *Honduras* **148 C2** 15 26N 87 51W
El Provencío, *Spain* **35 F2** 39 23N 2 35W
El Pueblito, *Mexico* **146 B3** 29 3N 105 4W
El Pueblo, *Canary Is.* **33 F2** 28 36N 17 47W
El Qâhira, *Egypt* **94 H7** 30 1N 31 14 E
El Qantara, *Egypt* **91 E1** 30 51N 32 20 E
El Qasr, *Egypt* **94 B2** 25 44N 28 42 E
El Quseima, *Egypt* **91 E3** 30 40N 34 15 E
El Qusîya, *Egypt* **94 B3** 27 29N 30 44 E
El Râshda, *Egypt* **94 B2** 25 36N 28 57 E
El Reno, *U.S.A.* **139 H6** 35 32N 97 57W
El Ribero, *Spain* **36 C2** 42 30N 8 30W
El Rîdisiya, *Egypt* **94 C3** 24 56N 32 51 E
El Rio, *U.S.A.* **145 L7** 34 14N 119 10W
El Ronquillo, *Spain* **37 H4** 37 44N 6 10W
El Roque, Pta., *Canary Is.* **33 F4** 28 10N 15 25W
El Rosarito, *Mexico* **146 B2** 28 38N 114 4W
El Rubio, *Spain* **37 H5** 37 22N 5 0W
El Saff, *Egypt* **94 J7** 29 34N 31 16 E
El Saheira, W. →, *Egypt* **91 E2** 30 5N 33 25 E
El Salto, *Mexico* **146 C3** 23 47N 105 22W
El Salvador ■, *Cent. Amer.* **148 D2** 13 50N 89 0W
El Sancejo, *Spain* **37 H5** 37 4N 5 6W
El Sauce, *Nic.* **148 D2** 13 0N 86 40W
El Shallal, *Egypt* **94 C3** 24 0N 32 53 E
El Simbillawein, *Egypt* **94 H7** 30 48N 31 13 E
El Sombrero, *Venezuela* **152 B4** 9 23N 67 3W
El Suweis, *Egypt* **94 J8** 29 58N 32 31 E
El Tamarâni, W. →, *Egypt* **91 E3** 30 7N 34 43 E
El Thamad, *Egypt* **91 F3** 29 40N 34 28 E
El Tigre, *Venezuela* **153 B5** 8 44N 64 15W
El Tîh, G., *Egypt* **91 F2** 29 40N 33 50 E
El Tîna, Khalîg, *Egypt* **91 D1** 31 10N 32 40 E
El Tocuyo, *Venezuela* **152 B4** 9 47N 69 48W
El Tofo, *Chile* **158 B1** 29 22 S 71 18W
El Tránsito, *Chile* **158 B1** 28 52 S 70 17W
El Tûr, *Egypt* **94 J8** 28 14N 33 36 E
El Turbio, *Argentina* **160 D2** 51 45 S 72 5W
El Uinle, *Somali Rep.* **108 D2** 3 4N 41 42 E
El Uqsur, *Egypt* **94 B3** 25 41N 32 38 E
El Vado, *Spain* **34 D1** 41 2N 3 18W
El Vallés, *Spain* **34 D7** 41 35N 2 20 E
El Venado, *Mexico* **146 C4** 22 56N 101 10W
El Vigía, *Venezuela* **152 B3** 8 38N 71 39W
El Wabeira, *Egypt* **91 F2** 29 34N 33 6 E
El Wak, *Kenya* **106 B5** 2 49N 40 56 E
El Wak, *Somali Rep.* **108 D2** 2 44N 41 1 E
El Waqf, *Egypt* **94 B3** 25 45N 32 15 E
El Wâsta, *Egypt* **94 J7** 29 19N 31 12 E
El Weguet, *Ethiopia* **95 F5** 5 28N 42 17 E
El Wuz, *Sudan* **95 D3** 15 5N 30 7 E
Elafónisos, *Greece* **45 H4** 36 29N 22 56 E
Elaine, *Australia* **116 D6** 37 44 S 144 2 E
Elamanchili, *India* **82 F6** 17 33N 82 50 E
Elands, *Australia* **117 A10** 31 37 S 152 20 E
Elandsvlei, *S. Africa* **104 E2** 32 19 S 19 31 E
Élassa, *Greece* **45 J8** 35 18N 26 21 E
Elassón, *Greece* **44 E4** 39 53N 22 12 E
Elat, *Israel* **91 F3** 29 30N 34 56 E
Eláthia, *Greece* **45 F4** 38 37N 22 46 E
Elâzığ, *Turkey* **89 D8** 38 37N 39 14 E
Elâzığ □, *Turkey* **89 D8** 38 40N 39 15 E
Elba, *Italy* **38 F7** 42 48N 10 15 E
Elba, *U.S.A.* **135 K2** 31 25N 86 4W
Elbasani, *Albania* **44 C2** 41 9N 20 9 E
Elbasani-Berati □, *Albania* **44 D2** 40 58N 20 0 E
Elbe, *U.S.A.* **144 D4** 46 45N 122 10W
Elbe →, *Europe* **26 B4** 53 50N 9 0 E
Elbe-Seiten Kanal, *Germany* **26 C6** 52 45N 10 32 E
Elberfeld, *U.S.A.* **141 F9** 38 10N 87 27W
Elbert, Mt., *U.S.A.* **143 G10** 39 7N 106 27W
Elberta, *U.S.A.* **134 C2** 44 37N 86 14W
Elberton, *U.S.A.* **135 H4** 34 7N 82 52W
Elbeuf, *France* **22 C8** 49 17N 1 2 E
Elbing = Elbląg, *Poland* **47 A6** 54 10N 19 25 E
Elbistan, *Turkey* **88 D7** 38 12N 36 11 E
Elbląg, *Poland* **47 A6** 54 10N 19 25 E
Elbląg □, *Poland* **47 A6** 54 15N 19 30 E
Elbow, *Canada* **131 C7** 51 7N 106 35W
Elbrus, *Asia* **53 E10** 43 21N 42 30 E
Elburg, *Neths.* **20 D7** 52 26N 5 50 E
Elburn, *U.S.A.* **141 C8** 41 54N 88 28W
Elburz Mts. = Alborz, Reshteh-ye Kūhhā-ye, *Iran* **85 C7** 36 0N 52 0 E
Elche, *Spain* **35 G4** 38 15N 0 42W
Elche de la Sierra, *Spain* **35 G2** 38 27N 2 3W
Elcho I., *Australia* **114 A2** 11 55 S 135 45 E
Elda, *Spain* **35 G4** 38 29N 0 47W
Eldon, *Mo., U.S.A.* **140 F4** 38 21N 92 35W
Eldon, *Wash., U.S.A.* **144 C3** 47 33N 123 3W
Eldora, *U.S.A.* **140 B3** 42 22N 93 5W
Eldorado, *Argentina* **159 B5** 26 28 S 54 43W
Eldorado, *Canada* **131 B7** 59 35N 108 30W
Eldorado, *Mexico* **146 C3** 24 20N 107 22W
Eldorado, *Ill., U.S.A.* **141 G8** 37 49N 88 26W
Eldorado, *Tex., U.S.A.* **139 K4** 30 52N 100 36W
Eldorado Springs, *U.S.A.* **139 G8** 37 52N 94 1W
Eldoret, *Kenya* **106 B4** 0 30N 35 17 E
Eldred, *U.S.A.* **136 E6** 41 58N 78 23W
Eldridge, *U.S.A.* **140 C6** 41 39N 90 35W
Elea, C., *Cyprus* **32 D13** 35 19N 34 4 E
Electra, *U.S.A.* **139 H5** 34 2N 98 55W
Elefantes →, *Mozam.* **105 C5** 24 10 S 32 40 E
Elefantes, G., *Chile* **160 C2** 46 28 S 73 49W
Elektrogorsk, *Russia* **51 D11** 55 56N 38 50 E
Elektrostal, *Russia* **51 D11** 55 41N 38 32 E
Elele, *Nigeria* **101 D6** 5 5N 6 50 E
Elena, *Bulgaria* **43 E10** 42 55N 25 53 E
Elephant Butte Reservoir, *U.S.A.* **143 K10** 33 9N 107 11W
Elephant I., *Antarctica* **7 C18** 61 0 S 55 0W
Elephant Pass, *Sri Lanka* **83 K5** 9 35N 80 25 E
Elesbão Veloso, *Brazil* **154 C3** 6 13 S 42 8W
Eleshnitsa, *Bulgaria* **43 F8** 41 52N 23 36 E
Eleşkirt, *Turkey* **89 D10** 39 50N 42 50 E
Eleuthera, *Bahamas* **148 A4** 25 0N 76 20W
Elevsís, *Greece* **45 F5** 38 4N 23 26 E
Elevtheroúpolis, *Greece* **44 D6** 40 52N 24 20 E
Elgepiggen, *Norway* **14 B5** 62 10N 11 21 E
Elgeyo-Marakwet □, *Kenya* **106 B4** 0 45N 35 30 E
Elgg, *Switz.* **29 B7** 47 29N 8 52 E
Elgin, *N.B., Canada* **129 C6** 45 48N 65 10W
Elgin, *Ont., Canada* **137 B8** 44 36N 76 13W
Elgin, *U.K.* **18 D5** 57 39N 3 20W
Elgin, *Ill., U.S.A.* **141 B8** 42 2N 88 17W
Elgin, *N. Dak., U.S.A.* **138 B4** 46 24N 101 51W
Elgin, *Nebr., U.S.A.* **138 E5** 41 59N 98 5W
Elgin, *Nev., U.S.A.* **143 H6** 37 21N 114 32W
Elgin, *Oreg., U.S.A.* **142 D5** 45 34N 117 55W
Elgin, *Tex., U.S.A.* **139 K6** 30 21N 97 22W
Elgon, Mt., *Africa* **106 B3** 1 10N 34 30 E
Eliase, *Indonesia* **73 C4** 8 21 S 130 48 E
Elida, *U.S.A.* **139 J3** 33 57N 103 39W
Elikón, *Greece* **45 F4** 38 18N 22 45 E
Elim, *S. Africa* **104 E2** 34 35 S 19 45 E
Elin Pelin, *Bulgaria* **43 E8** 42 40N 23 36 E
Elisabethville = Lubumbashi, *Zaïre* **107 E2** 11 40 S 27 28 E
Eliseu Martins, *Brazil* **154 C3** 8 13 S 43 42W
Elista, *Russia* **53 C11** 46 16N 44 14 E
Elizabeth, *Australia* **116 C3** 34 42 S 138 41 E
Elizabeth, *Ill., U.S.A.* **140 B6** 42 19N 90 13W
Elizabeth, *N.J., U.S.A.* **137 F10** 40 40N 74 13W
Elizabeth City, *U.S.A.* **135 G7** 36 18N 76 14W
Elizabethton, *U.S.A.* **135 G4** 36 21N 82 13W
Elizabethtown, *Ky., U.S.A.* **134 G3** 37 42N 85 52W
Elizabethtown, *N.Y., U.S.A.* **137 B11** 44 13N 73 36W
Elizabethtown, *Pa., U.S.A.* **137 F8** 40 9N 76 36W
Elizondo, *Spain* **34 B3** 43 12N 1 30W
Ełk, *Poland* **47 B9** 53 50N 22 21 E
Ełk →, *Poland* **47 B9** 53 41N 22 28 E
Elk City, *U.S.A.* **139 H5** 35 25N 99 25W
Elk Creek, *U.S.A.* **144 F4** 39 36N 122 32W
Elk Grove, *U.S.A.* **144 G5** 38 25N 121 22W
Elk Island Nat. Park, *Canada* **130 C6** 53 35N 112 59W
Elk Lake, *Canada* **128 C3** 47 40N 80 25W
Elk Point, *Canada* **131 C6** 53 54N 110 55W
Elk River, *Idaho, U.S.A.* **142 C5** 46 47N 116 11W
Elk River, *Minn., U.S.A.* **138 C8** 45 18N 93 35W
Elkader, *U.S.A.* **140 B5** 42 51N 91 24W
Elkedra, *Australia* **114 C2** 21 9 S 135 33 E
Elkedra →, *Australia* **114 C2** 21 8 S 136 22 E
Elkhart, *Ind., U.S.A.* **141 C11** 41 41N 85 58W
Elkhart, *Kans., U.S.A.* **139 G4** 37 0N 101 54W
Elkhart →, *U.S.A.* **141 C11** 41 41N 85 58W
Elkhorn, *Canada* **131 D8** 49 59N 101 14W
Elkhorn, *U.S.A.* **141 B8** 42 40N 88 33W
Elkhorn →, *U.S.A.* **138 E6** 41 8N 96 19W
Elkhotovo, *Russia* **53 E11** 43 19N 44 15 E
Elkhovo, *Bulgaria* **43 E11** 42 10N 26 40 E
Elkin, *U.S.A.* **135 G5** 36 15N 80 51W
Elkins, *U.S.A.* **134 F6** 38 55N 79 51W
Elko, *Canada* **130 D5** 49 20N 115 10W
Elko, *U.S.A.* **142 F6** 40 50N 115 46W
Ell, L., *Australia* **113 E4** 29 13 S 127 46 E
Ellecom, *Neths.* **20 D8** 52 2N 6 6 E
Ellef Ringnes I., *Canada* **6 B2** 78 30N 102 2W
Ellendale, *Australia* **112 C3** 17 56 S 124 48 E
Ellendale, *U.S.A.* **138 B5** 46 0N 98 32W
Ellensburg, *U.S.A.* **142 C3** 46 59N 120 34W
Ellenville, *U.S.A.* **137 E10** 41 43N 74 24W
Ellerston, *Australia* **117 A9** 31 49 S 151 20 E
Ellery, Mt., *Australia* **117 D8** 37 28 S 148 47 E
Ellesmere, L., *N.Z.* **119 H7** 47 47 S 172 28 E
Ellesmere I., *Canada* **6 B4** 79 30N 80 0W
Ellesmere Port, *U.K.* **16 D5** 53 17N 2 55W
Ellettsville, *U.S.A.* **141 E10** 39 14N 86 38W
Ellezelles, *Belgium* **21 G3** 50 44N 3 42 E
Ellice Is. = Tuvalu ■, *Pac. Oc.* **122 H9** 8 0 S 178 0 E
Ellinwood, *U.S.A.* **138 F5** 38 21N 98 35W
Elliot, *Australia* **114 B1** 17 33 S 133 32 E
Elliot, *S. Africa* **105 E4** 31 22 S 27 48 E
Elliot Lake, *Canada* **128 C3** 46 25N 82 35W
Elliotdale = Xhora, *S. Africa* **105 E4** 31 55 S 28 38 E
Ellis, *U.S.A.* **138 F5** 38 56N 99 34W
Elliston, *Australia* **115 E1** 33 39 S 134 53 E
Ellisville, *U.S.A.* **139 K10** 31 36N 89 12W
Ellon, *U.K.* **18 D6** 57 21N 2 5W
Ellore = Eluru, *India* **82 F5** 16 48N 81 8 E
Ells →, *Canada* **130 B6** 57 18N 111 40W
Ellsworth, *U.S.A.* **138 F5** 38 44N 98 14W
Ellsworth Land, *Antarctica* **7 D16** 76 0 S 89 0W
Ellsworth Mts., *Antarctica* **7 D16** 78 30 S 85 0W
Ellwangen, *Germany* **27 G6** 48 57N 10 9 E
Ellwood City, *U.S.A.* **136 F4** 40 52N 80 17W
Elm, *Switz.* **29 C8** 46 54N 9 10 E
Elma, *Canada* **131 D9** 49 52N 95 55W
Elma, *U.S.A.* **144 D3** 47 0N 123 25W
Elmadağ, *Turkey* **88 D5** 39 55N 33 14 E
Elmalı, *Turkey* **88 E3** 36 44N 29 56 E
Elmer, *U.S.A.* **140 E4** 39 57N 92 39W
Elmhurst, *U.S.A.* **141 C9** 41 53N 87 56W
Elmina, *Ghana* **101 D4** 5 5N 1 21W
Elmira, *Canada* **136 C4** 43 36N 80 33W
Elmira, *U.S.A.* **136 D8** 42 6N 76 48W
Elmore, *Australia* **116 D6** 36 30 S 144 37 E
Elmore, *Calif., U.S.A.* **145 M11** 33 7N 115 49W
Elmore, *Minn., U.S.A.* **141 C13** 41 29N 83 18W
Elmshorn, *Germany* **26 B5** 53 44N 9 40 E
Elmvale, *Canada* **136 B5** 44 35N 79 52W
Elmwood, *U.S.A.* **140 D6** 40 47N 89 58W
Elne, *France* **24 F6** 42 36N 2 58 E
Elnora, *U.S.A.* **141 F9** 38 53N 87 5W
Elora, *Canada* **136 C4** 43 41N 80 26W
Elorza, *Venezuela* **152 B4** 7 3N 69 31W
Elos, *Greece* **45 H4** 36 46N 22 43 E
Eloúnda, *Greece* **32 D7** 35 16N 25 42 E
Eloy, *U.S.A.* **143 K8** 32 45N 111 33W
Éloyes, *France* **23 D13** 48 6N 6 36 E
Elrose, *Canada* **131 C7** 51 12N 108 0W
Elsas, *Canada* **128 C3** 48 32N 82 55W
Elsie, *U.S.A.* **144 E3** 45 52N 123 36W
Elsinore = Helsingør, *Denmark* **15 H6** 56 2N 12 35 E
Elsinore, *Australia* **117 A6** 31 35 S 145 11 E
Elsinore, *U.S.A.* **143 G7** 38 41N 112 9W
Elspe, *Germany* **26 D4** 51 10N 8 1 E
Elspeet, *Neths.* **20 D7** 52 17N 5 48 E
Elst, *Neths.* **20 E7** 51 55N 5 51 E
Elster →, *Germany* **26 D7** 51 25N 11 57 E
Elsterwerda, *Germany* **26 D9** 51 27N 13 32 E
Elten, *Neths.* **20 E8** 51 52N 6 9 E
Eltham, *Australia* **117 D6** 37 43 S 145 12 E
Eltham, *N.Z.* **118 F3** 39 26 S 174 19 E
Elton, *Russia* **53 B12** 49 5N 46 52 E
Eluanbi, *Taiwan* **69 G13** 21 51N 120 50 E
Eluru, *India* **82 F5** 16 48N 81 8 E
Elvas, *Portugal* **37 G3** 38 50N 7 10W
Elven, *France* **22 E4** 47 44N 2 36W
Elverum, *Norway* **14 D5** 60 53N 11 34 E
Elvire →, *Australia* **112 C4** 17 51 S 128 11 E
Elvo →, *Italy* **38 C5** 45 23N 8 21 E
Elvran, *Norway* **14 A5** 63 24N 11 3 E
Elwood, *Ill., U.S.A.* **141 C8** 41 24N 88 7W
Elwood, *Ind., U.S.A.* **141 D11** 40 17N 85 50W
Elwood, *Nebr., U.S.A.* **138 E5** 40 36N 99 52W
Elx = Elche, *Spain* **35 G4** 38 15N 0 42W
Ely, *U.K.* **17 E8** 52 24N 0 16 E
Ely, *Minn., U.S.A.* **138 B9** 47 55N 91 51W
Ely, *Nev., U.S.A.* **142 G6** 39 15N 114 54W
Elyria, *U.S.A.* **136 E2** 41 22N 82 7W
Elyrus, *Greece* **45 J5** 35 15N 23 45 E
Elz →, *Germany* **27 G3** 48 21N 7 45 E
Emai, *Vanuatu* **121 G6** 17 4 S 168 24 E
Emāmrūd, *Iran* **85 B7** 36 30N 55 0 E
Emba, *Kazakhstan* **56 E6** 48 50N 58 8 E
Emba →, *Kazakhstan* **49 E9** 46 38N 53 14 E
Embarcación, *Argentina* **158 A3** 23 10 S 64 0W
Embarras →, *U.S.A.* **141 F9** 38 39N 87 37W
Embarras Portage, *Canada* **131 B6** 58 27N 111 28W
Embetsu, *Japan* **60 B10** 44 44N 141 47 E
Embira →, *Brazil* **156 B3** 7 19 S 70 15W
Embóna, *Greece* **32 C9** 36 13N 27 51 E
Embrach, *Switz.* **29 A7** 47 30N 8 36 E
Embrun, *France* **25 D10** 44 34N 6 30 E
Embu, *Kenya* **106 C4** 0 32 S 37 38 E
Embu □, *Kenya* **106 C4** 0 30 S 37 35 E
Emden, *Germany* **26 B3** 53 22N 7 12 E
Emerald, *Australia* **114 C4** 23 32 S 148 10 E
Emerson, *Canada* **131 D9** 49 0N 97 10W
Emery, *U.S.A.* **143 G8** 38 55N 111 15W
Emet, *Turkey* **88 D3** 39 20N 29 15 E
Emi Koussi, *Chad* **97 E3** 19 45N 18 55 E
Emilia-Romagna □, *Italy* **38 D7** 44 33N 10 40 E
Emilius, Mte., *Italy* **38 C4** 45 41N 7 23 E
Eminabad, *Pakistan* **80 C6** 32 2N 74 8 E
Emine, Nos, *Bulgaria* **43 E12** 42 40N 27 56 E
Eminence, *U.S.A.* **141 F11** 38 22N 85 11W
Emirdağ, *Turkey* **88 D4** 39 2N 31 8 E
Emlenton, *U.S.A.* **136 E5** 41 11N 79 43W
Emlichheim, *Germany* **26 C2** 52 37N 6 51 E
Emme →, *Switz.* **28 B5** 47 14N 7 32 E
Emmeloord, *Neths.* **20 C7** 52 44N 5 46 E
Emmen, *Neths.* **20 C9** 52 48N 6 57 E
Emmendingen, *Germany* **27 G3** 48 7N 7 51 E
Emmental, *Switz.* **28 C4** 46 55N 7 20 E
Emmer-Compascuum, *Neths.* **20 C10** 52 49N 7 2 E
Emmerich, *Germany* **26 D2** 51 50N 6 12 E
Emmet, *Australia* **114 C3** 24 45 S 144 30 E
Emmetsburg, *U.S.A.* **140 A2** 43 7N 94 41W
Emmett, *U.S.A.* **142 E5** 43 52N 116 30W
Emöd, *Hungary* **31 D13** 47 57N 20 47 E
Emona, *Bulgaria* **43 E12** 42 43N 27 53 E
Empalme, *Mexico* **146 B2** 28 1N 110 49W
Empangeni, *S. Africa* **105 D5** 28 50 S 31 52 E
Empedrado, *Argentina* **158 B4** 28 0 S 58 46W
Emperor Seamount Chain, *Pac. Oc.* **122 D9** 40 0N 170 0 E
Empoli, *Italy* **38 E7** 43 43N 10 57 E
Emporia, *Kans., U.S.A.* **138 F6** 38 25N 96 11W
Emporia, *Va., U.S.A.* **135 G7** 36 42N 77 32W
Emporium, *U.S.A.* **136 E6** 41 31N 78 14W
Empress, *Canada* **131 C6** 50 57N 110 0W
Emptinne, *Belgium* **21 H6** 50 19N 5 8 E
Empty Quarter = Rub' al Khali, *Si. Arabia* **87 C5** 18 0N 48 0 E
Ems →, *Germany* **26 B3** 53 22N 7 15 E
Emsdale, *Canada* **136 A5** 45 32N 79 19W
Emsdetten, *Germany* **26 C3** 52 11N 7 31 E
Emu, *Australia* **116 D5** 36 44 S 143 26 E
Emu, *China* **67 C15** 43 40N 128 6 E
Emu Park, *Australia* **114 C5** 23 13 S 150 50 E
'En 'Avrona, *Israel* **91 F3** 29 43N 35 0 E
En Nahud, *Sudan* **95 E2** 12 45N 28 25 E
Ena, *Japan* **63 B9** 35 25N 137 25 E
Ena-San, *Japan* **63 B9** 35 26N 137 36 E
Enafors, *Sweden* **14 A6** 63 17N 12 20 E
Enambú, *Colombia* **152 C3** 1 1N 70 17W
Enana, *Namibia* **104 B2** 17 30 S 16 23 E
Enånger, *Sweden* **14 C11** 61 30N 17 9 E
Enaratoli, *Indonesia* **73 B5** 3 55 S 136 21 E
Enard B., *U.K.* **18 C3** 58 5N 5 20W
Enare = Inarijärvi, *Finland* **12 B19** 69 0N 28 0 E
Encantadas, Serra, *Brazil* **159 C5** 30 40 S 53 0W
Encarnación, *Paraguay* **159 B4** 27 15 S 55 50W
Encarnación de Diaz, *Mexico* **146 C4** 21 30N 102 13W
Enchi, *Ghana* **100 D4** 5 53N 2 48W
Encinal, *U.S.A.* **139 L5** 28 2N 99 21W
Encinitas, *U.S.A.* **145 M9** 33 3N 117 17W
Encino, *U.S.A.* **143 J11** 34 39N 105 28W
Encontrados, *Venezuela* **152 B3** 9 3N 72 14W
Encounter B., *Australia* **116 C3** 35 45 S 138 45 E
Encruzilhada, *Brazil* **155 E3** 15 31 S 40 54W
Ende, *Indonesia* **72 C2** 8 45 S 121 40 E
Endeavour, *Canada* **131 C8** 52 10N 102 39W
Endeavour Str., *Australia* **114 A3** 10 45 S 142 0 E
Endelave, *Denmark* **15 J4** 55 46N 10 18 E
Enderbury I., *Kiribati* **122 H10** 3 8 S 171 5W
Enderby, *Canada* **130 C5** 50 35N 119 10W
Enderby I., *Australia* **112 D2** 20 35 S 116 30 E
Enderby Land, *Antarctica* **7 C5** 66 0 S 53 0 E
Enderlin, *U.S.A.* **138 B6** 46 38N 97 36W
Endicott, *N.Y., U.S.A.* **137 D8** 42 6N 76 4W
Endicott, *Wash., U.S.A.* **142 C5** 46 56N 117 41W
Endimari →, *Brazil* **156 B4** 8 46 S 66 7W
Endröd, *Hungary* **31 E13** 46 55N 20 47 E

196 Endyalgout I.

Endyalgout I., Australia . 112 B5 11 40 S 132 35 E
Ene →, Peru 156 C3 11 10 S 74 18W
Enewetak Atoll, Pac. Oc. 122 F8 11 30N 162 15 E
Enez, Turkey 44 D8 40 45N 26 5 E
Enfida, Tunisia 96 A2 36 6N 10 28 E
Enfield, U.K. 17 F7 51 39N 0 4W
Enfield, U.S.A. 141 F8 38 6N 88 20W
Engadin, Switz. 27 J6 46 45N 10 10 E
Engaño, C., Dom. Rep. . 149 C6 18 30N 68 20W
Engaño, C., Phil. 70 B4 18 35N 122 23 E
Engcobo, S. Africa 105 E4 31 37 S 28 0 E
Engelberg, Switz. 29 C6 46 48N 8 26 E
Engels = Pokrovsk, Russia 51 F15 51 28N 46 6 E
Engemann L., Canada 131 B7 58 0N 106 55W
Enger, Norway 14 D4 60 35N 10 20 E
Enggano, Indonesia 74 D2 5 20 S 102 40 E
Enghien, Belgium 21 G4 50 37N 4 2 E
Engil, Morocco 98 B4 33 12N 4 32W
Engkilili, Malaysia 75 B4 1 3N 111 42 E
England, U.S.A. 139 H9 34 33N 91 58W
England □, U.K. 11 E5 53 0N 2 0W
Englee, Canada 129 B8 50 45N 56 5W
Englefield, Australia 116 D4 37 21 S 141 48 E
Englehart, Canada 128 C4 47 49N 79 52W
Engler L., Canada 131 B7 59 8N 106 52W
Englewood, Colo., U.S.A. 138 F2 39 39N 104 59W
Englewood, Kans., U.S.A. 139 G5 37 2N 99 59W
Englewood, Ohio, U.S.A. 141 E12 39 53N 84 18W
English, U.S.A. 141 F10 38 20N 86 28W
English →, Canada 131 C10 50 35N 93 30W
English →, U.S.A. 140 C5 41 29N 91 32W
English Bazar = Ingraj Bazar, India 81 G13 24 58N 88 10 E
English Channel, Europe 17 G6 50 0N 2 0W
English River, Canada 128 C1 49 14N 91 0W
Enid, U.S.A. 139 G6 36 24N 97 53W
Enipévs →, Greece 44 E4 39 22N 22 17 E
Enkhuizen, Neths. 20 C6 52 42N 5 17 E
Enköping, Sweden 14 E11 59 37N 17 4 E
Enle, China 68 E3 24 0N 101 9 E
Enna, Italy 41 E7 37 34N 14 15 E
Ennadai, Canada 131 A8 61 8N 100 53W
Ennadai L., Canada 131 A8 61 0N 101 0W
Ennedi, Chad 97 E4 17 15N 22 0 E
Enngonia, Australia 115 D4 29 21 S 145 50 E
Ennis, Ireland 19 D3 52 51N 8 59W
Ennis, Mont., U.S.A. 142 D8 45 21N 111 44W
Ennis, Tex., U.S.A. 139 J6 32 20N 96 38W
Enniscorthy, Ireland 19 D5 52 30N 6 35W
Enniskillen, U.K. 19 B4 54 20N 7 40W
Ennistimon, Ireland 19 D2 52 56N 9 18W
Enns, Austria 30 C7 48 12N 14 28 E
Enns →, Austria 30 C7 48 14N 14 32 E
Enontekiö, Finland 12 B17 68 23N 23 37 E
Enping, China 69 F9 22 16N 112 21 E
Enrekang, Indonesia 72 B1 3 34 S 119 47 E
Enrile, Phil. 70 C3 17 34N 121 42 E
Enriquillo, L., Dom. Rep. 149 C5 18 20N 72 5W
Ens, Neths. 20 C7 52 38N 5 50 E
Enschede, Neths. 20 D9 52 13N 6 53 E
Ensenada, Argentina 158 C4 34 55 S 57 55W
Ensenada, Mexico 146 A1 31 50N 116 50W
Enshi, China 68 B7 30 18N 109 29 E
Enshū-Nada, Japan 63 C9 34 27N 137 38 E
Ensiola, Pta., Spain 33 B9 39 7N 2 55 E
Ensisheim, France 23 E14 47 50N 7 20 E
Entebbe, Uganda 106 B3 0 4N 32 28 E
Enter, Neths. 20 D9 52 17N 6 35 E
Enterprise, Canada 130 A5 60 47N 115 45W
Enterprise, Oreg., U.S.A. 142 D5 45 25N 117 17W
Enterprise, Utah, U.S.A. 143 H7 37 34N 113 43W
Entlebuch, Switz. 28 C6 46 59N 8 4 E
Entre Ríos, Bolivia 158 A3 21 30 S 64 25W
Entre Rios, Bahia, Brazil 155 D4 11 56 S 38 5W
Entre Rios, Pará, Brazil 157 B7 5 24 S 54 21W
Entre Ríos □, Argentina . 158 C4 30 30 S 58 30W
Entrepeñas, Pantano de, Spain 34 E2 40 34N 2 42W
Enugu, Nigeria 101 D6 6 20N 7 30 E
Enugu □, Nigeria 101 D6 6 30N 7 45 E
Enugu Ezike, Nigeria 101 D6 7 0N 7 29 E
Enumclaw, U.S.A. 144 C5 47 12N 121 59W
Envermeu, France 22 C8 49 53N 1 15 E
Envigado, Colombia 152 B2 6 10N 75 35W
Envira, Brazil 156 B3 7 18 S 70 13W
Enz →, Germany 27 F5 49 1N 9 6 E
Enza →, Italy 38 D7 44 54N 10 31 E
Enzan, Japan 63 B10 35 42N 138 44 E
Eólie, Is., Italy 41 D7 38 30N 14 50 E
Epanomí, Greece 44 D4 40 25N 22 59 E
Epe, Neths. 20 D7 52 21N 5 59 E
Epe, Nigeria 101 D5 6 36N 3 59 E
Epéna, Congo 102 B3 1 22N 17 29 E
Épernay, France 23 C10 49 3N 3 56 E
Épernon, France 23 D8 48 35N 1 40 E
Ephesus, Turkey 45 G9 37 50N 27 33 E
Ephraim, U.S.A. 142 G8 39 22N 111 35W
Ephrata, U.S.A. 142 C4 47 19N 119 33W
Epi, Vanuatu 121 F6 16 43 S 168 15 E
Epidaurus Limera, Greece 45 H5 36 46N 23 0 E
Epila, Spain 34 D3 41 36N 1 17W
Épinac-les-Mines, France 23 F11 46 59N 4 31 E
Épinal, France 23 D13 48 10N 6 27 E
Epira, Guyana 153 B6 5 5N 57 20W
Episcopia Bihorulu, Romania 46 B2 47 12N 21 55 E
Episkopi, Cyprus 32 E11 34 40N 32 54 E
Episkopí, Greece 32 D6 35 20N 24 20 E
Episkopi Bay, Cyprus 32 E11 34 35N 32 50 E
Epitálion, Greece 45 G3 37 37N 21 30 E
Epping, U.K. 17 F8 51 42N 0 8 E
Epukiro, Namibia 104 C2 21 40 S 19 9 E
Equality, U.S.A. 141 G8 37 44N 88 20W
Equatorial Guinea ■, Africa 102 B1 2 0N 8 0 E
Equeipa, Venezuela 153 B5 5 22N 62 43W
Er Rahad, Sudan 95 E3 12 45N 30 32 E
Er Rif, Morocco 99 A4 35 1N 4 1W
Er Roseires, Sudan 95 E3 11 55N 34 30 E
Er Yébigué, Chad 97 D3 22 30N 17 30 E
Eran, Phil. 71 G1 9 4N 117 42 E
Erandol, India 82 D2 20 56N 75 20 E
Erap, Papua N. G. 120 D4 6 37 S 146 51 E
Erāwadī Myit = Irrawaddy →, Burma . 78 G5 15 50N 95 6 E
Erba, Italy 38 C6 45 49N 9 12 E
Erba, Sudan 94 D4 19 5N 36 51 E
Erbaa, Turkey 88 C7 40 42N 36 36 E
Erbil = Arbīl, Iraq 84 B5 36 15N 44 5 E
Erçek Gölü, Turkey 89 D10 38 39N 43 35 E
Ercha, Russia 57 C15 69 45N 147 20 E
Erçiş, Turkey 89 D10 39 2N 43 21 E
Erciyaş Dağı, Turkey 88 D6 38 30N 35 30 E
Erdao Jiang →, China 67 C14 43 0N 127 0 E
Erdek, Turkey 88 C2 40 23N 27 47 E
Erdemli, Turkey 88 E6 36 36N 34 19 E
Erdene, Mongolia 66 B6 44 13N 111 10 E
Erding, Germany 27 G7 48 18N 11 55 E
Erdre →, France 22 E5 47 13N 1 32W
Erebato →, Venezuela 153 B5 5 54N 64 16W
Erebus, Mt., Antarctica 7 D11 77 35 S 167 0 E
Erechim, Brazil 159 B5 27 35 S 52 15W
Ereğli, Konya, Turkey 88 E6 37 31N 34 4 E
Ereğli, Zonguldak, Turkey 88 C4 41 15N 31 24 E
Erei, Monti, Italy 41 E7 37 20N 14 20 E
Erembodegem, Belgium 21 G4 50 56N 4 4 E
Erenhot, China 66 C7 43 48N 112 2 E
Eresma →, Spain 36 D6 41 26N 4 45W
Eressós, Greece 45 E7 39 11N 25 57 E
Erfenisdam, S. Africa 104 D4 28 30 S 26 50 E
Erfoud, Morocco 98 B4 31 30N 4 15W
Erft →, Germany 26 D2 51 11N 6 44 E
Erfurt, Germany 26 E7 50 58N 11 2 E
Ergani, Turkey 89 D8 38 17N 39 49 E
Ergene →, Turkey 43 F11 41 1N 26 22 E
Ergeni Vozvyshennost, Russia 53 C11 47 0N 44 0 E
Ērgli, Latvia 50 C4 56 54N 25 38 E
Eria →, Spain 36 C5 42 3N 5 44W
Eriba, Sudan 95 D4 16 40N 36 10 E
Eriboll, L., U.K. 18 C4 58 28N 4 41W
Erica, Neths. 20 C9 52 43N 6 56 E
Érice, Italy 40 D5 38 4N 12 34 E
Erie, Mich., U.S.A. 141 C13 41 47N 83 31W
Erie, Pa., U.S.A. 136 D4 42 8N 80 5W
Erie, L., N. Amer. 136 D3 42 15N 81 0W
Erie Canal, U.S.A. 136 C6 43 5N 78 43W
Erieau, Canada 136 D3 42 16N 81 57W
Erigavo, Somali Rep. 90 E4 10 35N 47 20 E
Erikoúsa, Greece 44 E1 39 55N 19 14 E
Erikoúsa, Kérkira, Greece 32 A3 39 53N 19 34 E
Eriksdale, Canada 131 C9 50 52N 98 7W
Erikslund, Sweden 14 B9 62 31N 15 54 E
Erímanthos, Greece 45 G3 37 57N 21 50 E
Erimo-misaki, Japan 60 D11 41 50N 143 15 E
Eriswil, Switz. 28 B5 47 5N 7 46 E
Erithraí, Greece 45 F5 38 13N 23 20 E
Eritrea □, Africa 95 E4 14 0N 38 30 E
Erjas →, Portugal 37 F3 39 40N 7 1W
Erlangen, Germany 27 F7 49 35N 11 2 E
Erldunda, Australia 114 D1 25 14 S 133 12 E
Erlin, Taiwan 69 F13 23 55N 120 21 E
Ermelo, Neths. 20 D7 52 18N 5 35 E
Ermelo, S. Africa 105 D4 26 31 S 29 59 E
Ermenak, Turkey 88 E5 36 38N 33 0 E
Ermióni, Greece 45 G5 37 23N 23 15 E
Ermones, Greece 32 A3 39 37N 19 46 E
Ermoúpolis = Síros, Greece 45 G6 37 28N 24 57 E
Ernakulam = Cochin, India 83 K3 9 59N 76 22 E
Erne →, Ireland 19 B3 54 30N 8 16W
Erne, Lower L., U.K. 19 B4 54 26N 7 46W
Erne, Upper L., U.K. 19 B4 54 14N 7 22W
Ernée, France 22 D6 48 18N 0 56W
Ernest Giles Ra., Australia 113 E3 27 0 S 123 45 E
Ernstberg, Germany 27 E2 50 14N 6 46 E
Erode, India 83 J3 11 24N 77 45 E
Eromanga, Australia 115 D3 26 40 S 143 11 E
Erongo, Namibia 104 C2 21 39 S 15 58 E
Erp, Neths. 21 E7 51 36N 5 37 E
Erquelinnes, Belgium 21 H4 50 19N 4 8 E
Erquy, France 22 D4 48 38N 2 29W
Erquy, C. d', France 22 D4 48 39N 2 29W
Err, Piz d', Switz. 29 C9 46 34N 9 43 E
Errabiddy, Australia 113 E2 25 25 S 117 5 E
Erramala Hills, India 83 G4 15 30N 78 15 E
Errer →, Ethiopia 95 F5 7 32N 42 35 E
Errigal, Ireland 19 A3 55 2N 8 8W
Erris Hd., Ireland 19 B1 54 19N 10 0W
Erromango, Vanuatu 121 H7 18 45 S 169 5 E
Erseka, Albania 44 D2 40 22N 20 40 E
Erskine, U.S.A. 138 B7 47 40N 96 0W
Erstein, France 23 D14 48 25N 7 38 E
Erstfeld, Switz. 29 C7 46 50N 8 38 E
Ertil, Russia 51 F12 51 55N 40 50 E
Ertis = Irtysh →, Russia 56 C7 61 4N 68 52 E
Ertvelde, Belgium 21 F3 51 11N 3 45 E
Eruh, Turkey 89 E10 37 46N 42 13 E
Eruwa, Nigeria 101 D5 7 33N 3 26 E
Ervy-le-Châtel, France 23 D10 48 2N 3 55 E
Erwin, U.S.A. 135 G4 36 9N 82 25W
Eryuan, China 68 D2 26 7N 99 57 E
Erzgebirge, Germany 26 E9 50 25N 13 0 E
Erzin, Russia 57 D10 50 15N 95 10 E
Erzincan, Turkey 89 D8 39 46N 39 30 E
Erzincan □, Turkey 89 D8 39 45N 39 30 E
Erzurum, Turkey 89 D9 39 57N 41 15 E
Erzurum □, Turkey 89 D9 39 55N 41 15 E
Es Caló, Spain 33 C8 38 40N 1 30 E
Es Caná, Spain 33 B8 39 2N 1 36 E
Es Sahrâ' Esh Sharqîya, Egypt 94 B3 27 30N 32 30 E
Es Sînâ', Egypt 94 J8 29 0N 34 0 E
Es Sûkî, Sudan 95 E3 13 20N 33 58 E
Esa'ala, Papua N. G. 120 E6 9 45 S 150 49 E
Esambo, Zaïre 102 C4 3 48 S 23 30 E
Esan-Misaki, Japan 60 D10 41 40N 141 10 E
Esashi, Hokkaidō, Japan 60 B11 44 56N 142 35 E
Esashi, Hokkaidō, Japan 60 D10 41 52N 140 7 E
Esbjerg, Denmark 15 J2 55 29N 8 29 E
Escada, Brazil 154 C4 8 22 S 35 8W
Escalante, U.S.A. 143 H8 37 47N 111 36W
Escalante →, U.S.A. 143 H8 37 24N 110 57W
Escalente, Phil. 71 F4 10 50N 123 33 E
Escalón, Mexico 146 B4 26 46N 104 20W
Escalona, Spain 36 E6 40 9N 4 29W
Escambia →, U.S.A. 135 K2 30 32N 87 11W
Escanaba, U.S.A. 134 C2 45 45N 87 4W
Escarpada Pt., Phil. 70 B4 18 31N 122 13 E
Escarpé, C., Vanuatu 121 K5 20 41 S 167 13 E
Escaut →, Belgium 21 F3 51 2N 3 45 E
Esch-sur-Alzette, Lux. 21 J7 49 32N 6 0 E
Eschede, Germany 26 C6 52 44N 10 13 E
Escholzmatt, Switz. 28 C5 46 55N 7 56 E
Eschwege, Germany 26 D6 51 10N 10 3 E
Eschweiler, Germany 26 E2 50 49N 6 14 E
Escoma, Bolivia 156 D4 15 40 S 69 8W
Escondido, U.S.A. 145 M9 33 7N 117 5W
Escuinapa, Mexico 146 C3 22 50N 105 50W
Escuintla, Guatemala 148 D1 14 20N 90 48W
Eséka, Cameroon 101 E7 3 41N 10 44 E
Esens, Germany 26 B3 53 40N 7 35 E
Esera →, Spain 34 C5 42 6N 0 15 E
Eşfahān, Iran 85 C6 33 0N 51 30 E
Esfīdeh, Iran 85 C8 33 39N 59 46 E
Esgueva →, Spain 36 D6 41 40N 4 43W
Esh Sham = Dimashq, Syria 91 B5 33 30N 36 18 E
Esh Shamâlîya □, Sudan . 94 D2 19 0N 29 0 E
Eshan, China 68 E4 24 11N 102 24 E
Eshkamesh, Afghan. 79 A3 36 23N 69 19 E
Eshkamish, Tajikistan 55 E5 36 44N 71 37 E
Eshowe, S. Africa 105 D5 28 50 S 31 30 E
Esiama, Ghana 100 E4 4 56N 2 25W
Esil = Ishim →, Russia . 56 D8 57 45N 71 10 E
Esino →, Italy 39 E10 43 39N 13 22 E
Esk →, Dumf. & Gall., U.K. 18 G5 54 58N 3 4W
Esk →, N. Yorks., U.K. 16 C7 54 27N 0 36W
Eskān, Iran 79 D1 26 48N 63 9 E
Eskifjörður, Iceland 12 D7 65 3N 13 55W
Eskilstuna, Sweden 14 E10 59 22N 16 32 E
Eskimalatya, Turkey 89 D8 38 24N 38 22 E
Eskimo Pt., Canada 131 A10 61 10N 94 15W
Eskişehir, Turkey 88 D4 39 50N 30 35 E
Eskişehir □, Turkey 88 D4 39 40N 31 0 E
Esla →, Spain 36 D4 41 29N 6 3W
Esla, Pantano del, Spain . 36 D4 41 29N 6 3W
Eslāmābād-e Gharb, Iran 84 C5 34 10N 46 30 E
Eslöv, Sweden 15 J7 55 50N 13 20 E
Eşme, Turkey 88 D3 38 23N 28 58 E
Esmeralda, I., Chile 160 C1 48 55 S 75 25W
Esmeraldas, Ecuador 152 C2 1 0N 79 40W
Esmeraldas □, Ecuador 152 C2 0 40N 79 30W
Esmeraldas →, Ecuador 152 C2 0 58N 79 38W
Esneux, Belgium 21 G7 50 32N 5 33 E
Espada, Pta., Colombia . 152 A3 12 5N 71 7W
Espalion, France 24 D6 44 32N 2 47 E
Espalmador, I., Spain 33 C7 38 47N 1 26 E
Espanola, Canada 128 C3 46 15N 81 46W
Espardell, I. del, Spain 33 C7 38 48N 1 29 E
Esparraguera, Spain 34 D6 41 33N 1 52 E
Esparta, Costa Rica 148 E3 9 59N 84 40W
Espejo, Spain 37 H6 37 40N 4 34W
Esperança, Brazil 154 C4 7 1 S 35 51W
Esperance, Australia 113 F3 33 45 S 121 55 E
Esperance B., Australia 113 F3 33 48 S 121 55 E
Esperantinópolis, Brazil . 154 B3 4 53 S 44 53W
Esperanza, Santa Cruz, Argentina 160 D2 51 1 S 70 49W
Esperanza, Santa Fe, Argentina 158 C3 31 29 S 61 3W
Esperanza, Masbate, Phil. 71 F5 11 45N 124 3 E
Esperanza, Mindanao, Phil. 71 G5 8 43N 125 36 E
Espéraza, France 24 F6 42 56N 2 14 E
Espichel, C., Portugal 37 G1 38 22N 9 16W
Espiel, Spain 37 G5 38 11N 5 1W
Espigão, Serra do, Brazil 159 B5 26 35 S 50 30W
Espinal, Colombia 152 C3 4 9N 74 53W
Espinar, Peru 156 C3 14 51 S 71 24W
Espinazo, Sierra del = Espinhaço, Serra do, Brazil 155 E3 17 30 S 43 30W
Espinhaço, Serra do, Brazil 155 E3 17 30 S 43 30W
Espinho, Portugal 36 D2 41 1N 8 38W
Espinilho, Serra do, Brazil 159 B5 28 30 S 55 0W
Espino, Venezuela 152 B4 8 34N 66 1W
Espinosa de los Monteros, Spain 36 B7 43 5N 3 34W
Espírito Santo □, Brazil . 155 F3 20 0 S 40 45W
Espíritu Santo, Vanuatu . 121 E4 15 15 S 166 50 E
Espíritu Santo, B. del, Mexico 147 D7 19 15N 87 0W
Espíritu Santo, I., Mexico 146 C2 24 30N 110 23W
Espita, Mexico 147 C7 21 1N 88 19W
Espiye, Turkey 89 C8 40 56N 38 43 E
Esplanada, Brazil 155 D4 11 47 S 37 57W
Espluga de Francolí, Spain 34 D6 41 24N 1 7 E
Espuña, Sierra, Spain 35 H3 37 51N 1 35W
Espungabera, Mozam. 105 C5 20 29 S 32 45 E
Esquel, Argentina 160 B2 42 55 S 71 20W
Esquina, Argentina 158 B4 30 0 S 59 30W
Essaouira, Morocco 98 B3 31 32N 9 42W
Essebie, Zaïre 106 B3 2 58N 30 40 E
Essen, Belgium 21 F4 51 28N 4 28 E
Essen, Germany 26 D2 51 28N 6 59 E
Essendon, Mt., Australia 113 E3 25 0 S 120 29 E
Essequibo →, Guyana 153 B6 6 50N 58 30W
Essex, Canada 136 D2 42 10N 82 49W
Essex, Calif., U.S.A. 145 L11 34 44N 115 15W
Essex, Ill., U.S.A. 141 C8 41 11N 88 11W
Essex, N.Y., U.S.A. 137 B11 44 19N 73 21W
Essex □, U.K. 17 F8 51 48N 0 30 E
Esslingen, Germany 27 G5 48 43N 9 19 E
Essonne □, France 23 D9 48 30N 2 20 E
Essvik, Sweden 14 B11 62 18N 17 24 E
Estaca, Pta. del, Spain 36 B3 43 46N 7 42W
Estadilla, Spain 34 C5 42 4N 0 16 E
Estados, I. de Los, Argentina 160 D4 54 40 S 64 30W
Estagel, France 24 F6 42 47N 2 40 E
Eşţahbānāt, Iran 85 D7 29 8N 54 4 E
Estallenchs, Spain 33 B9 39 39N 2 29 E
Estância, Brazil 154 D4 11 16 S 37 26W
Estancia, U.S.A. 143 J10 34 46N 106 4W
Estārm, Iran 85 D8 28 21N 58 21 E
Estarreja, Portugal 36 E2 40 45N 8 35W
Estats, Pic d', Spain 34 C6 42 40N 1 24 E
Estavayer-le-Lac, Switz. 28 C3 46 51N 6 51 E
Estcourt, S. Africa 105 D4 29 0 S 29 53 E
Este, Italy 39 C8 45 12N 11 40 E
Esteban, Spain 36 B4 43 33N 6 5W
Estelí, Nic. 148 D2 13 9N 86 22W
Estella, Spain 34 C2 42 40N 2 2W
Estelline, S. Dak., U.S.A. 138 C6 44 35N 96 54W
Estelline, Tex., U.S.A. 139 H4 34 33N 100 26W
Estena →, Spain 37 F6 39 23N 4 44W
Estepa, Spain 37 H6 37 17N 4 52W
Estepona, Spain 37 J5 36 24N 5 7W
Esterhazy, Canada 131 C8 50 37N 102 5W
Esternay, France 23 D10 48 44N 3 33 E
Esterri de Aneu, Spain 34 C6 42 38N 1 5 E
Estevan, Canada 131 D8 49 10N 102 59W
Estevan Group, Canada 130 C3 53 3N 129 38W
Estherville, U.S.A. 138 D7 43 24N 94 50W
Estissac, France 23 D10 48 16N 3 48 E
Eston, Canada 131 C7 51 8N 108 40W
Estonia ■, Europe 50 B4 58 30N 25 30 E
Estoril, Portugal 37 G1 38 42N 9 23W
Estouk, Mali 101 B5 18 14N 1 2 E
Estrêla, Serra da, Portugal 36 E3 40 10N 7 45W
Estrella, Spain 35 G1 38 25N 3 35W
Estremoz, Portugal 37 G3 38 51N 7 39W
Estrondo, Serra do, Brazil 154 C2 7 20 S 48 0W
Esztergom, Hungary 31 D11 47 47N 18 44 E
Et Tîdra, Mauritania 100 B1 19 45N 16 20W
Étables-sur-Mer, France . 22 D4 48 38N 2 51W
Etadunna, Australia 115 D2 28 43 S 138 38 E
Etah, India 81 F8 27 35N 78 40 E
Étain, France 23 C12 49 13N 5 38 E
Etalle, Belgium 21 J7 49 40N 5 36 E
Etamamu, Canada 129 B8 50 18N 59 59W
Étampes, France 23 D9 48 26N 2 10 E
Étang-sur-Arroux, France 25 B8 46 51N 4 11 E
Etanga, Namibia 104 B1 17 55 S 13 0 E
Étaples, France 23 B8 50 30N 1 39 E
Etawah, India 81 F8 26 48N 79 6 E
Etawah →, U.S.A. 135 H3 34 20N 84 15W
Etawney L., Canada 131 B9 57 50N 96 50W
Ete, Nigeria 101 D6 7 2N 7 28 E
Éthe, Belgium 21 J7 49 35N 5 35 E
Ethel, U.S.A. 144 D4 46 32N 122 46W
Ethel, Oued el →, Algeria 98 C4 28 31N 3 37W
Ethel Creek, Australia 112 D3 22 55 S 120 11 E
Ethelbert, Canada 131 C8 51 32N 100 25W
Ethiopia ■, Africa 90 F3 8 0N 40 0 E
Ethiopian Highlands, Ethiopia 92 E7 10 0N 37 0 E
Etive, L., U.K. 18 E3 56 30N 5 12W
Etna, Italy 41 E8 37 45N 15 0 E
Etoile, Zaïre 107 E2 11 33 S 27 30 E
Etolin I., U.S.A. 130 B2 56 5N 132 20W
Etosha Pan, Namibia 104 B2 18 40 S 16 30 E
Etoumbi, Congo 102 C2 0 1 S 14 57 E
Etowah, U.S.A. 135 H3 35 20N 84 32W
Étrépagny, France 23 C8 49 18N 1 36 E
Étretat, France 22 C7 49 42N 0 12 E
Etropole, Bulgaria 43 E8 42 50N 24 0 E
Ettelbruck, Lux. 21 J8 49 51N 6 5 E
Etten, Neths. 21 E5 51 34N 4 38 E
Ettlingen, Germany 27 G4 48 58N 8 25 E
Ettrick Water →, U.K. 18 F6 55 31N 2 55W
Etuku, Zaïre 102 C5 3 42 S 25 45 E
Etzatlán, Mexico 146 C4 20 48N 104 5W
Eu, France 22 B8 50 3N 1 26 E
Eua, Tonga 121 Q13 21 22 S 174 56W
Euboea = Évvoia, Greece 45 F5 38 30N 24 0 E
Euchareena, Australia 117 B8 32 57 S 149 6 E
Eucla Motel, Australia 113 F4 31 41 S 128 52 E
Euclid, U.S.A. 136 E3 41 34N 81 32W
Euclides da Cunha, Brazil 154 D4 10 31 S 39 1W
Eucumbene, L., Australia 117 D8 36 2 S 148 40 E
Eudora, U.S.A. 139 J9 33 7N 91 16W
Eudunda, Australia 116 C3 34 12 S 139 7 E
Eufaula, Ala., U.S.A. 135 K3 31 54N 85 9W
Eufaula, Okla., U.S.A. 139 H7 35 17N 95 35W
Eufaula L., U.S.A. 139 H7 35 18N 95 21W
Eugene, U.S.A. 142 E2 44 5N 123 4W
Eugowra, Australia 117 B8 33 22 S 148 24 E
Eulo, Australia 115 D4 28 10 S 145 3 E
Eumungerie, Australia 117 A8 31 56 S 148 36 E
Eunice, La., U.S.A. 139 K8 30 30N 92 25W
Eunice, N. Mex., U.S.A. 139 J3 32 26N 103 10W
Eupen, Belgium 21 G8 50 37N 6 3 E
Euphrates = Furāt, Nahr al →, Asia 84 D5 31 0N 47 25 E
Eure □, France 22 C8 49 10N 1 0 E
Eure →, France 22 C8 49 18N 1 12 E
Eure-et-Loir □, France 22 D8 48 22N 1 30 E
Eureka, Canada 6 B3 80 0N 85 56W
Eureka, Calif., U.S.A. 142 F1 40 47N 124 9W
Eureka, Ill., U.S.A. 140 D7 40 43N 89 16W
Eureka, Kans., U.S.A. 139 G6 37 49N 96 17W
Eureka, Mo., U.S.A. 140 F6 38 30N 90 38W
Eureka, Mont., U.S.A. 142 B6 48 53N 115 3W
Eureka, Nev., U.S.A. 142 G5 39 31N 115 58W
Eureka, S. Dak., U.S.A. 138 C5 45 46N 99 38W
Eureka, Utah, U.S.A. 142 G7 39 58N 112 7W
Eureka, Mt., Australia 113 E3 26 35 S 121 35 E
Eurelia, Australia 116 B3 32 33 S 138 35 E
Euroa, Australia 117 D6 36 44 S 145 35 E
Europa, Picos de, Spain 36 B6 43 10N 4 49W
Europa, Pta. de, Gib. 37 J5 36 3N 5 21W
Europa Pt. = Europa, Pta. de, Gib. 37 J5 36 3N 5 21W
Europe 10 F10 50 0N 20 0 E
Europoort, Neths. 20 E4 51 57N 4 10 E
Euskirchen, Germany 26 E2 50 40N 6 45 E
Eustis, U.S.A. 135 L5 28 51N 81 41W
Eutin, Germany 26 A6 54 7N 10 38 E
Eutsuk L., Canada 130 C3 53 20N 126 45W
Eva, Brazil 153 D6 3 9 S 59 56W
Eva Downs, Australia 114 B1 18 1 S 134 52 E
Evale, Angola 103 F3 16 33 S 15 44 E
Evans, U.S.A. 138 E2 40 23N 104 41W
Evans Head, Australia 115 D5 29 7 S 153 27 E
Evans L., Canada 128 B4 50 50N 77 0W
Evans Mills, U.S.A. 137 B9 44 6N 75 48W
Evansdale, U.S.A. 140 B4 42 30N 92 17W
Evanston, Ill., U.S.A. 141 B9 42 3N 87 41W
Evanston, Wyo., U.S.A. 142 F8 41 16N 110 58W
Evansville, Ill., U.S.A. 140 F7 38 5N 89 56W
Evansville, Ind., U.S.A. 141 G9 37 58N 87 35W
Evansville, Wis., U.S.A. 140 B7 42 47N 89 18W
Évaux-les-Bains, France . 24 B6 46 12N 2 29 E
Evaz, Iran 85 E7 27 46N 53 59 E

Fukue-Shima 199

Fort Klamath, *U.S.A.* ... **142 E3** 42 42N 122 0W
Fort Knox, *U.S.A.* **141 G11** 37 54N 85 57W
Fort Lallemand, *Algeria* . **99 B6** 31 13N 6 17 E
Fort-Lamy = Ndjamena, *Chad* .... **97 F2** 12 10N 14 59 E
Fort Laramie, *U.S.A.* ... **138 D2** 42 13N 104 31W
Fort Lauderdale, *U.S.A.* . **135 M5** 26 7N 80 8W
Fort Leonard Wood, *U.S.A.* **140 G4** 37 46N 92 11W
Fort Liard, *Canada* **130 A4** 60 14N 123 30W
Fort Liberté, *Haiti* **149 C5** 19 42N 71 51W
Fort Lupton, *U.S.A.* **138 E2** 40 5N 104 49W
Fort Mackay, *Canada* ... **130 B6** 57 12N 111 41W
Fort McKenzie, *Canada* . **129 A6** 57 20N 69 0W
Fort Macleod, *Canada* ... **130 D6** 49 45N 113 30W
Fort MacMahon, *Algeria* . **99 C5** 29 43N 1 45 E
Fort McMurray, *Canada* . **130 B6** 56 44N 111 7W
Fort McPherson, *Canada* . **126 B6** 67 30N 134 55W
Fort Madison, *U.S.A.* ... **140 D5** 40 38N 91 27W
Fort Meade, *U.S.A.* **135 M5** 27 45N 81 48W
Fort Miribel, *Algeria* .... **99 C5** 29 25N 2 55 E
Fort Morgan, *U.S.A.* **138 E3** 40 15N 103 48W
Fort Myers, *U.S.A.* **135 M5** 26 39N 81 52W
Fort Nelson, *Canada* **130 B4** 58 50N 122 44W
Fort Nelson →, *Canada* . **130 B4** 59 32N 124 0W
Fort Norman, *Canada* **126 B7** 64 57N 125 30W
Fort Payne, *U.S.A.* **135 H3** 34 26N 85 43W
Fort Peck, *U.S.A.* **142 B10** 48 1N 106 27W
Fort Peck Dam, *U.S.A.* . **142 C10** 48 0N 106 26W
Fort Peck L., *U.S.A.* **142 C10** 48 0N 106 26W
Fort Pierce, *U.S.A.* **135 M5** 27 27N 80 20W
Fort Pierre, *U.S.A.* **138 C4** 44 21N 100 22W
Fort Pierre Bordes = Ti-n-Zaouaténe, *Algeria* .... **99 E5** 19 55N 2 55 E
Fort Plain, *U.S.A.* **137 D10** 42 56N 74 37W
Fort Portal, *Uganda* ..... **106 B3** 0 40N 30 20 E
Fort Providence, *Canada* . **130 A5** 61 3N 117 40W
Fort Qu'Appelle, *Canada* . **131 C8** 50 45N 103 50W
Fort Recovery, *U.S.A.* .. **141 D12** 40 25N 84 47W
Fort Resolution, *Canada* . **130 A6** 61 10N 113 40W
Fort Rixon, *Zimbabwe* .. **107 G2** 20 2 S 29 17 E
Fort Rosebery = Mansa, *Zambia* .... **107 E2** 11 13 S 28 55 E
Fort Ross, *U.S.A.* **144 G3** 38 32N 123 13W
Fort Rousset = Owando, *Congo* .... **102 C3** 0 29 S 15 55 E
Fort Rupert, *Canada* **128 B4** 51 30N 78 40W
Fort Saint, *Tunisia* ...... **96 B1** 30 19N 9 31 E
Fort St. James, *Canada* . **130 C4** 54 30N 124 10W
Fort St. John, *Canada* .. **130 B4** 56 15N 120 50W
Fort Sandeman, *Pakistan* **79 C3** 31 20N 69 31 E
Fort Saskatchewan, *Canada* **130 C6** 53 40N 113 15W
Fort Scott, *U.S.A.* **139 G7** 37 50N 94 42W
Fort Severn, *Canada* **128 A2** 56 0N 87 40W
Fort Shevchenko, *Kazakhstan* .... **53 E14** 43 40N 51 20 E
Fort-Sibut, *C.A.R.* ...... **102 A3** 5 46N 19 10 E
Fort Simpson, *Canada* ... **130 A4** 61 45N 121 15W
Fort Smith, *Canada* **130 B6** 60 0N 111 51W
Fort Smith, *U.S.A.* **139 H7** 35 23N 94 25W
Fort Stanton, *U.S.A.* **143 K11** 33 30N 105 31W
Fort Stockton, *U.S.A.* ... **139 K3** 30 53N 102 53W
Fort Sumner, *U.S.A.* **139 H2** 34 28N 104 15W
Fort Thomas, *U.S.A.* **141 E12** 39 5N 84 27W
Fort Trinquet = Bir Mogrein, *Mauritania* .. **98 C2** 25 10N 11 25W
Fort Valley, *U.S.A.* **135 J4** 32 33N 83 53W
Fort Vermilion, *Canada* . **130 B5** 58 24N 116 0W
Fort Walton Beach, *U.S.A.* **135 K2** 30 25N 86 36W
Fort Wayne, *U.S.A.* **141 C11** 41 4N 85 9W
Fort William, *U.K.* **18 E3** 56 48N 5 8W
Fort Worth, *U.S.A.* **139 J6** 32 45N 97 18W
Fort Yates, *U.S.A.* **138 B4** 46 5N 100 38W
Fort Yukon, *U.S.A.* **126 B5** 66 34N 145 16W
Fortaleza, *Bolivia* ...... **156 C4** 12 6 S 66 49W
Fortaleza, *Brazil* .... **154 B4** 3 45 S 38 35W
Forteau, *Canada* **129 B8** 51 28N 56 58W
Forth →, *U.K.* **18 E5** 56 9N 3 50W
Forth, Firth of, *U.K.* **18 E6** 56 5N 2 55W
Forthassa Rhardia, *Algeria* **99 B4** 32 52N 1 18W
Fortín Coronel Eugenio Garay, *Paraguay* ...... **157 E5** 20 31 S 62 8W
Fortín Garrapatal, *Paraguay* .... **157 E5** 21 27 S 61 30W
Fortín General Pando, *Paraguay* .... **157 D6** 19 45 S 59 47W
Fortín Madrejón, *Paraguay* .... **157 E6** 20 45 S 59 52W
Fortín Uno, *Argentina* ... **160 A3** 38 50 S 65 18W
Fortore →, *Italy* .... **39 G12** 41 55N 15 17 E
Fortrose, *N.Z.* .... **119 G3** 46 38 S 168 45 E
Fortrose, *U.K.* **18 D4** 57 35N 4 10W
Fortuna, *Spain* **35 G3** 38 11N 1 7W
Fortuna, *Calif., U.S.A.* .. **142 F1** 40 36N 124 9W
Fortuna, *N. Dak., U.S.A.* **138 A3** 48 55N 103 47W
Fortune B., *Canada* **129 C8** 47 30N 55 22W
Fos-sur-Mer, *France* ..... **25 E8** 43 26N 4 56 E
Foshan, *China* .... **69 F9** 23 4N 113 5 E
Fossacesia, *Italy* .... **39 F11** 42 15N 14 30 E
Fossano, *Italy* .... **38 D4** 44 33N 7 40 E
Fosses-la-Ville, *Belgium* . **21 H5** 50 24N 4 41 E
Fossil, *U.S.A.* **142 D3** 45 0N 120 9W
Fossilbrook, *Australia* ... **114 B3** 17 47 S 144 29 E
Fossombrone, *Italy* ...... **39 E9** 43 41N 12 49 E
Fosston, *U.S.A.* **138 B7** 47 35N 95 45W
Foster, *Canada* **137 A12** 45 17N 72 30W
Foster, *U.S.A.* **141 F12** 38 48N 84 13W
Foster →, *Canada* **131 B7** 55 47N 105 49W
Fosters Ra., *Australia* ... **114 C1** 21 35 S 133 48 E
Fostoria, *U.S.A.* **141 C13** 41 10N 83 25W
Fotuha'a, *Tonga* .... **121 P13** 19 49 S 174 44W
Fougamou, *Gabon* .... **102 C2** 1 16 S 10 30 E
Fougères, *France* **22 D5** 48 21N 1 14W
Foul Pt., *Sri Lanka* ..... **83 K5** 8 35N 81 18 E
Foula, *U.K.* **18 A6** 60 10N 2 5W
Foulness I., *U.K.* .... **17 F8** 51 36N 0 55 E
Foulpointe, *Madag.* ..... **105 B8** 17 41 S 49 31 E
Foulwind, C., *N.Z.* ..... **119 B6** 41 45 S 171 28 E
Foum Assaka, *Morocco* .. **98 C2** 29 8N 10 24W
Foum Zguid, *Morocco* ... **98 B3** 30 2N 6 59W
Foumban, *Cameroon* .... **101 D7** 5 45N 10 50 E
Foundiougne, *Senegal* ... **100 C1** 14 5N 16 32W
Fountain, *Colo., U.S.A.* . **138 F2** 38 41N 104 42W
Fountain, *Utah, U.S.A.* .. **142 G8** 39 41N 111 37W
Fountain Springs, *U.S.A.* **145 K8** 35 54N 118 51W
Fourchambault, *France* .. **23 E10** 47 2N 3 3 E
Fourchu, *Canada* **129 C7** 45 43N 60 17W
Fouriesburg, *S. Africa* ... **104 D4** 28 38 S 28 14 E
Fourmies, *France* .... **23 B11** 50 1N 4 2 E
Fournás, *Greece* .... **45 E3** 39 3N 21 52 E
Foúrnoi, *Greece* .... **45 G8** 37 36N 26 32 E
Fours, *France* .... **23 F10** 46 50N 3 42 E
Fouta Djalon, *Guinea* ... **100 C2** 11 20N 12 10W
Foux, Cap-à-, *Haiti* **149 C5** 19 43N 73 27W
Foveaux Str., *N.Z.* ...... **119 G3** 46 42 S 168 10 E
Fowey, *U.K.* **17 G3** 50 20N 4 39W
Fowler, *Calif., U.S.A.* ... **144 J7** 36 38N 119 41W
Fowler, *Colo., U.S.A.* ... **138 F3** 38 8N 104 2W
Fowler, *Ind., U.S.A.* **141 D9** 40 37N 87 19W
Fowler, *Kans., U.S.A.* ... **139 G4** 37 23N 100 12W
Fowler, *Mich., U.S.A.* ... **141 B12** 43 0N 84 45W
Fowlers B., *Australia* ... **113 F5** 31 59 S 132 34 E
Fowlerton, *U.S.A.* **139 L5** 28 28N 98 48W
Fowlerville, *U.S.A.* **141 B12** 42 40N 84 4W
Fox →, *Canada* **131 B10** 56 3N 93 18W
Fox Valley, *Canada* **131 C7** 50 30N 109 25W
Foxe Basin, *Canada* **127 B12** 66 0N 77 0W
Foxe Chan., *Canada* **127 B11** 65 0N 80 0W
Foxe Pen., *Canada* **127 B12** 65 0N 76 0W
Foxhol, *Neths.* .... **20 B9** 53 10N 6 43 E
Foxpark, *U.S.A.* **142 F10** 41 5N 106 9W
Foxton, *N.Z.* .... **118 G4** 40 29 S 175 18 E
Foyle, Lough, *U.K.* **19 A4** 55 6N 7 8W
Foynes, *Ireland* **19 D2** 52 37N 9 5W
Foz, *Spain* **36 B3** 43 33N 7 20W
Fóz do Cunene, *Angola* . **103 F2** 17 15 S 11 48 E
Foz do Gregório, *Brazil* . **156 B3** 6 47 S 70 44W
Foz do Iguaçu, *Brazil* ... **159 B5** 25 30 S 54 30W
Foz do Riosinho, *Brazil* . **156 B3** 7 11 S 71 50W
Frackville, *U.S.A.* **137 F8** 40 47N 76 14W
Fraga, *Spain* .... **34 D5** 41 32N 0 21 E
Fraire, *Belgium* .... **21 H5** 50 16N 4 31 E
Frameries, *Belgium* ..... **21 H3** 50 24N 3 54 E
Framingham, *U.S.A.* **137 D13** 42 17N 71 25W
Frampol, *Poland* .... **47 E9** 50 41N 22 40 E
Franca, *Brazil* .... **155 F2** 20 33 S 47 30W
Francavilla al Mare, *Italy* **39 F11** 42 25N 14 16 E
Francavilla Fontana, *Italy* **41 B10** 40 32N 17 35 E
France ■, *Europe* .... **11 F6** 47 0N 3 0 E
Frances, *Australia* ...... **116 D4** 36 41 S 140 55 E
Frances →, *Canada* **130 A3** 60 16N 129 10W
Frances L., *Canada* **130 A3** 61 23N 129 30W
Francés Viejo, C., *Dom. Rep.* **149 C6** 19 40N 69 55W
Francesville, *U.S.A.* **141 D10** 40 59N 86 53W
Franceville, *Gabon* ..... **102 C2** 1 40 S 13 32 E
Franche-Comté, *France* .. **23 F12** 46 50N 5 55 E
Franches Montagnes, *Switz.* .... **28 B4** 47 10N 7 0 E
Francisco de Orellana, *Ecuador* .... **152 D2** 0 28 S 76 58W
Francisco I. Madero, *Coahuila, Mexico* **146 B4** 25 48N 103 18W
Francisco I. Madero, *Durango, Mexico* **146 C4** 24 32N 104 22W
Francisco Sá, *Brazil* .... **155 E3** 16 28 S 43 30W
Francistown, *Botswana* .. **105 C4** 21 7 S 27 33 E
Francofonte, *Italy* ...... **41 E7** 37 13N 14 50 E
François, *Canada* **129 C8** 47 35N 56 45W
François L., *Canada* **130 C3** 54 0N 125 30W
Francorchamps, *Belgium* . **21 H7** 50 27N 5 57 E
Franeker, *Neths.* .... **20 B7** 53 12N 5 33 E
Frankado, *Djibouti* ..... **95 E5** 12 30N 43 12 E
Frankenberg, *Germany* .. **26 D4** 51 3N 8 47 E
Frankenthal, *Germany* .. **27 F4** 49 32N 8 21 E
Frankenwald, *Germany* .. **27 E7** 50 18N 11 36 E
Frankford, *U.S.A.* **140 E5** 39 29N 91 19W
Frankfort, *S. Africa* ..... **105 D4** 27 17 S 28 30 E
Frankfort, *Ind., U.S.A.* .. **141 D10** 40 17N 86 31W
Frankfort, *Kans., U.S.A.* . **138 F6** 39 42N 96 25W
Frankfort, *Ky., U.S.A.* ... **141 F12** 38 12N 84 52W
Frankfort, *Mich., U.S.A.* . **134 C2** 44 38N 86 14W
Frankfort, *Ohio, U.S.A.* . **141 E13** 39 24N 83 11W
Frankfurt am Main, *Germany* .... **27 E4** 50 7N 8 40 E
Frankfurt an der Oder, *Germany* .... **26 C10** 52 20N 14 31 E
Fränkische Alb, *Germany* **27 F7** 49 20N 11 30 E
Fränkische Rezal →, *Germany* .... **27 F7** 49 11N 11 1 E
Fränkische Saale →, *Germany* .... **27 E5** 50 30N 9 42 E
Fränkische Schweiz, *Germany* .... **27 F7** 49 45N 11 10 E
Frankland →, *Australia* . **113 G2** 35 0 S 116 48 E
Franklin, *Ill., U.S.A.* **140 E6** 39 37N 90 3W
Franklin, *Ind., U.S.A.* ... **141 E10** 39 29N 86 3W
Franklin, *Ky., U.S.A.* ... **135 G2** 36 43N 86 35W
Franklin, *La., U.S.A.* ... **139 L9** 29 48N 91 30W
Franklin, *Mass., U.S.A.* . **137 D13** 42 5N 71 24W
Franklin, *N.H., U.S.A.* .. **137 C13** 43 27N 71 39W
Franklin, *Nebr., U.S.A.* . **138 E5** 40 6N 98 57W
Franklin, *Ohio, U.S.A.* .. **141 E12** 39 34N 84 18W
Franklin, *Pa., U.S.A.* ... **136 E5** 41 24N 79 50W
Franklin, *Tenn., U.S.A.* . **135 H2** 35 55N 86 52W
Franklin, *Va., U.S.A.* ... **135 G7** 36 41N 76 56W
Franklin, *W. Va., U.S.A.* **134 F6** 38 39N 79 20W
Franklin B., *Canada* **126 B7** 69 45N 126 0W
Franklin D. Roosevelt L., *U.S.A.* **142 B4** 48 18N 118 9W
Franklin I., *Antarctica* ... **7 D11** 76 10 S 168 30 E
Franklin L., *U.S.A.* **142 F6** 40 25N 115 22W
Franklin Mts., *Canada* .. **126 B7** 65 0N 125 0W
Franklin Mts., *N.Z.* ..... **119 E2** 44 55 S 167 45 E
Franklin Str., *Canada* ... **126 A10** 72 0N 96 0W
Franklinton, *U.S.A.* **139 K9** 30 51N 90 9W
Franklinville, *U.S.A.* ... **136 D6** 42 20N 78 27W
Franklyn Mt., *N.Z.* ..... **119 C7** 42 4 S 172 42 E
Franks Pk., *U.S.A.* **142 E9** 43 58N 109 18W
Frankston, *Australia* .... **117 E6** 38 8 S 145 8 E
Frankton Junc., *N.Z.* ... **118 D4** 37 47 S 175 16 E
Fränsta, *Sweden* .... **14 B10** 62 30N 16 11 E
Frantsa Iosifa, Zemlya, *Russia* .... **56 A6** 82 0N 55 0 E
Franz, *Canada* **128 C3** 48 25N 84 30W
Franz Josef Land = Frantsa Iosifa, Zemlya, *Russia* .... **56 A6** 82 0N 55 0 E
Franzburg, *Germany* .... **26 A8** 54 9N 12 52 E
Frascati, *Italy* .... **40 A5** 41 48N 12 41 E
Fraser →, *B.C., Canada* **130 D4** 49 7N 123 11W
Fraser →, *Nfld., Canada* **129 A7** 56 39N 62 10W
Fraser, Mt., *Australia* ... **113 E2** 25 35 S 118 20 E
Fraser I., *Australia* ..... **115 D5** 25 15 S 153 10 E
Fraser Lake, *Canada* **130 C4** 54 0N 124 50W
Fraserburg, *S. Africa* .... **104 E3** 31 55 S 21 30 E
Fraserburgh, *U.K.* **18 D6** 57 41N 2 3W
Fraserdale, *Canada* **128 C3** 49 55N 81 37W
Frasertown, *N.Z.* .... **118 E6** 38 58 S 177 28 E
Frashëri, *Albania* .... **44 D2** 40 23N 20 26 E
Frasne, *France* .... **23 F13** 46 50N 6 10 E
Frauenfeld, *Switz.* ...... **29 A7** 47 34N 8 54 E
Fray Bentos, *Uruguay* ... **158 C4** 33 10 S 58 15W
Frazier Downs, *Australia* **112 C3** 18 48 S 121 42 E
Frechilla, *Spain* **36 C6** 42 8N 4 50W
Fredericia, *Denmark* .... **15 J3** 55 34N 9 45 E
Frederick, *Md., U.S.A.* .. **134 F7** 39 25N 77 25W
Frederick, *Okla., U.S.A.* **139 H5** 34 23N 99 1W
Frederick, *S. Dak., U.S.A.* **138 C5** 45 50N 98 31W
Frederick Sd., *U.S.A.* ... **130 B2** 57 10N 134 0W
Fredericksburg, *Tex., U.S.A.* **139 K5** 30 16N 98 52W
Fredericksburg, *Va., U.S.A.* **134 F7** 38 18N 77 28W
Fredericktown, *U.S.A.* .. **139 G9** 37 34N 90 18W
Frederico I. Madero, Presa, *Mexico* **146 B3** 28 7N 105 40W
Fredericton, *Canada* **129 C6** 45 57N 66 40W
Fredericton Junc., *Canada* **129 C6** 45 41N 66 40W
Frederikshåb, *Greenland* . **6 C5** 62 0N 49 43W
Frederikshavn, *Denmark* . **15 G4** 57 28N 10 31 E
Frederikssund, *Denmark* . **15 J6** 55 50N 12 3 E
Frederiksted, *Virgin Is.* . **149 C7** 17 43N 64 53W
Fredonia, *Ariz., U.S.A.* .. **143 H7** 36 57N 112 32W
Fredonia, *Kans., U.S.A.* . **139 G7** 37 32N 95 49W
Fredonia, *N.Y., U.S.A.* .. **136 D5** 42 26N 79 20W
Fredrikstad, *Norway* .... **14 E4** 59 13N 10 57 E
Freeburg, *U.S.A.* **140 F5** 38 19N 91 56W
Freehold, *U.S.A.* **137 F10** 40 16N 74 17W
Freel Peak, *U.S.A.* **144 G7** 38 52N 119 54W
Freeland, *U.S.A.* **137 E9** 41 1N 75 54W
Freels, C., *Canada* **129 C9** 49 15N 53 30W
Freeman, *Calif., U.S.A.* . **145 K9** 35 35N 117 53W
Freeman, *Mo., U.S.A.* .. **140 F2** 38 37N 94 30W
Freeman, *S. Dak., U.S.A.* **138 D6** 43 21N 97 26W
Freeport, *Bahamas* **148 A4** 26 30N 78 47W
Freeport, *Canada* **129 D6** 44 15N 66 20W
Freeport, *Ill., U.S.A.* ... **140 B7** 42 17N 89 36W
Freeport, *N.Y., U.S.A.* .. **137 F11** 40 39N 73 35W
Freeport, *Tex., U.S.A.* .. **139 L7** 28 57N 95 21W
Freetown, *S. Leone* **100 D2** 8 30N 13 17W
Frégate, L., *Canada* **128 B5** 53 15N 74 45W
Fregenal de la Sierra, *Spain* **37 G4** 38 10N 6 39W
Fregene, *Italy* .... **40 A5** 41 50N 12 12 E
Fréhel, C., *France* **22 D4** 48 40N 2 20W
Freiberg, *Germany* ..... **26 E9** 50 55N 13 20 E
Freibourg = Fribourg, *Switz.* .... **28 C4** 46 49N 7 9 E
Freiburg, *Baden-W., Germany* .... **27 H3** 48 0N 7 52 E
Freiburg, *Niedersachsen, Germany* .... **26 B5** 53 49N 9 17 E
Freiburger Alpen, *Switz.* . **28 C4** 46 37N 7 10 E
Freire, *Chile* .... **160 A2** 38 54 S 72 38W
Freirina, *Chile* .... **158 B1** 28 30 S 71 10W
Freising, *Germany* ..... **27 G7** 48 24N 11 47 E
Freistadt, *Austria* ...... **30 C7** 48 30N 14 30 E
Freital, *Germany* .... **26 E9** 51 0N 13 40 E
Fréjus, *France* .... **25 E10** 43 25N 6 44 E
Fremantle, *Australia* .... **113 F2** 32 7 S 115 47 E
Fremont, *Calif., U.S.A.* . **144 H4** 37 32N 121 57W
Fremont, *Ind., U.S.A.* .. **141 C12** 41 44N 84 56W
Fremont, *Mich., U.S.A.* . **134 D3** 43 28N 85 57W
Fremont, *Nebr., U.S.A.* . **138 E6** 41 26N 96 30W
Fremont, *Ohio, U.S.A.* .. **141 C13** 41 21N 83 7W
Fremont →, *U.S.A.* **143 G8** 38 24N 110 42W
Fremont L., *U.S.A.* **142 E9** 42 57N 109 48W
French Camp, *U.S.A.* ... **144 H5** 37 53N 121 16W
French Creek →, *U.S.A.* **136 E5** 41 24N 79 50W
French Guiana ■, *S. Amer.* **153 C7** 4 0N 53 0W
French I., *Australia* .... **117 E6** 38 20 S 145 22 E
French Lick, *U.S.A.* **141 F10** 38 33N 86 37W
French Pass, *N.Z.* ...... **119 A8** 40 55 S 173 55 E
French Polynesia ■, *Pac. Oc.* .... **123 J13** 20 0 S 145 0W
French Terr. of Afars & Issas = Djibouti ■, *Africa* .... **90 E3** 12 0N 43 0 E
Frenchburg, *U.S.A.* **141 G13** 37 57N 83 38W
Frenchglen, *U.S.A.* **142 E4** 42 50N 118 55W
Frenchman Butte, *Canada* **131 C7** 53 35N 109 38W
Frenchman Cr. →, *Mont., U.S.A.* **142 B10** 48 31N 107 10W
Frenchman Cr. →, *Nebr., U.S.A.* **138 E4** 40 14N 100 50W
Frenda, *Algeria* .... **99 A5** 35 2N 1 1 E
Fresco →, *Brazil* .... **157 B7** 7 15 S 51 30W
Freshfield, C., *Antarctica* **7 C10** 68 25 S 151 10 E
Fresnay-sur-Sarthe, *France* **22 D7** 48 17N 0 1 E
Fresnillo, *Mexico* **146 C4** 23 10N 103 0W
Fresno, *U.S.A.* **144 J7** 36 44N 119 47W
Fresno Alhandiga, *Spain* . **36 E5** 40 42N 5 37W
Fresno Reservoir, *U.S.A.* **142 B9** 48 36N 109 57W
Freudenstadt, *Germany* .. **27 G4** 48 27N 8 25 E
Freux, *Belgium* .... **21 J6** 49 59N 5 27 E
Frévent, *France* .... **23 B9** 50 15N 2 17 E
Frew →, *Australia* ..... **114 C2** 20 0 S 135 38 E
Frewena, *Australia* ..... **114 B2** 19 25 S 135 25 E
Freycinet Pen., *Australia* **114 G4** 42 10 S 148 25 E
Freyming-Merlebach, *France* .... **23 C13** 49 8N 6 48 E
Freyung, *Germany* ...... **27 G9** 48 48N 13 33 E
Fria, *Guinea* **100 C2** 10 27N 13 38W
Fria, C., *Namibia* ...... **104 B1** 18 0 S 12 0 E
Friant, *U.S.A.* **144 J7** 36 59N 119 43W
Frías, *Argentina* .... **158 B2** 28 40 S 65 5W
Fribourg, *Switz.* .... **28 C4** 46 49N 7 9 E
Fribourg □, *Switz.* ...... **28 C4** 46 40N 7 0 E
Frick, *Switz.* .... **28 A6** 47 31N 8 1 E
Friday Harbor, *U.S.A.* .. **144 B3** 48 32N 123 1W
Friedberg, *Bayern, Germany* .... **27 G6** 48 21N 10 59 E
Friedberg, *Hessen, Germany* .... **27 E4** 50 21N 8 46 E
Friedland, *Germany* ..... **26 B9** 53 40N 13 33 E
Friedrichshafen, *Germany* **27 H5** 47 39N 9 29 E
Friedrichskoog, *Germany* **26 A4** 54 1N 8 52 E
Friedrichstadt, *Germany* . **26 A5** 54 23N 9 6 E
Friendly Is. = Tonga ■, *Pac. Oc.* .... **121 P13** 19 50 S 174 30W
Friesach, *Austria* ...... **30 E7** 46 57N 14 24 E
Friesack, *Germany* ..... **26 C8** 52 43N 12 35 E
Friesche Wad, *Neths.* .... **20 B7** 53 22N 5 44 E
Friesland □, *Neths.* ..... **20 B7** 53 5N 5 50 E
Friesoythe, *Germany* .... **26 B3** 53 1N 7 51 E
Frillesås, *Sweden* ...... **15 G6** 57 20N 12 12 E
Frio →, *U.S.A.* **139 L5** 28 26N 98 11W
Friona, *U.S.A.* **139 H3** 34 38N 102 43W
Frisian Is., *Europe* ..... **26 B2** 53 30N 6 0 E
Fristad, *Sweden* .... **15 G7** 57 50N 13 0 E
Fritch, *U.S.A.* **139 H4** 35 38N 101 36W
Fritsla, *Sweden* .... **15 G6** 57 33N 12 47 E
Fritzlar, *Germany* ...... **26 D5** 51 8N 9 19 E
Friuli-Venezia Giulia □, *Italy* .... **39 B10** 46 0N 13 0 E
Frobisher B., *Canada* ... **127 B13** 62 30N 66 0W
Frobisher Bay = Iqaluit, *Canada* **127 B13** 63 44N 68 31W
Frobisher L., *Canada* **131 B7** 56 20N 108 15W
Frogmore, *Australia* .... **117 C8** 34 15 S 148 52 E
Frohavet, *Norway* ...... **12 E10** 63 50N 9 35 E
Froid, *U.S.A.* **138 A2** 48 20N 104 30W
Froid-Chapelle, *Belgium* . **21 H4** 50 9N 4 19 E
Frolovo, *Russia* .... **53 B10** 49 45N 43 40 E
Fromberg, *U.S.A.* **142 D9** 45 24N 108 54W
Frombork, *Poland* ...... **47 A6** 54 21N 19 41 E
Frome, *U.K.* **17 F5** 51 16N 2 17W
Frome, L., *Australia* .... **116 A3** 30 45 S 139 45 E
Frome Downs, *Australia* . **116 A3** 31 13 S 139 45 E
Frómista, *Spain* **36 C6** 42 16N 4 25W
Front Range, *U.S.A.* **142 G11** 40 25N 105 45W
Front Royal, *U.S.A.* **134 F6** 38 55N 78 12W
Fronteira, *Portugal* **37 F3** 39 3N 7 39W
Fronteiras, *Brazil* ...... **154 C3** 7 5 S 40 37W
Frontera, *Canary Is.* **33 G2** 27 47N 17 59W
Frontera, *Mexico* **147 D6** 18 30N 92 40W
Frontignan, *France* ..... **24 E7** 43 27N 3 45 E
Frosinone, *Italy* .... **40 A6** 41 38N 13 20 E
Frosolone, *Italy* .... **41 A7** 41 34N 14 27 E
Frostburg, *U.S.A.* **134 F6** 39 39N 78 56W
Frostisen, *Norway* ...... **12 B14** 68 14N 17 10 E
Frouard, *France* .... **23 D13** 48 47N 6 8 E
Frøya, *Norway* .... **12 E10** 63 43N 8 40 E
Fruges, *France* .... **23 B9** 50 30N 2 8 E
Frumoasa, *Romania* ..... **46 C6** 46 28N 25 48 E
Frunze = Bishkek, *Kirghizia* .... **55 B7** 42 54N 74 46 E
Fruška Gora, *Serbia* ..... **42 B4** 45 7N 19 30 E
Frutal, *Brazil* .... **155 F2** 20 0 S 49 0W
Frutigen, *Switz.* .... **28 C5** 46 35N 7 38 E
Frýdek-Místek, *Czech.* .. **31 B11** 49 40N 18 20 E
Frýdlant, *Severočeský, Czech.* .... **30 A8** 50 56N 15 9 E
Frýdlant, *Severomoravsky, Czech.* .... **31 B11** 49 35N 18 20 E
Fryvaldov = Jeseník, *Czech.* .... **31 B10** 50 0N 17 8 E
Fthiótis □, *Greece* ..... **45 F4** 38 50N 22 25 E
Fu Jiang →, *China* ..... **68 C6** 30 0N 106 16 E
Fu Xian, *Liaoning, China* **67 E11** 39 38N 121 58 E
Fu Xian, *Shaanxi, China* . **66 F5** 36 0N 109 20 E
Fu'an, *China* .... **69 D12** 27 11N 119 36 E
Fubian, *China* .... **68 B4** 31 17N 102 22 E
Fucécchio, *Italy* .... **38 E7** 43 44N 10 51 E
Fucheng, *China* .... **66 F9** 37 50N 116 10 E
Fuchou = Fuzhou, *China* **69 D12** 26 5N 119 16 E
Fuchū, *Hiroshima, Japan* **62 C5** 34 34N 133 14 E
Fūchū, *Tōkyō, Japan* ... **63 B11** 35 40N 139 29 E
Fuchuan, *China* .... **69 E8** 24 50N 111 5 E
Fuchun Jiang →, *China* . **69 B13** 30 5N 120 5 E
Fúcino, Conca del, *Italy* . **39 F10** 42 1N 13 31 E
Fuding, *China* .... **69 D13** 27 20N 120 12 E
Fuencaliente, *Canary Is.* . **33 F2** 28 28N 17 50W
Fuencaliente, *Spain* **37 G6** 38 25N 4 18W
Fuencaliente, Pta., *Canary Is.* **33 F2** 28 27N 17 51W
Fuengirola, *Spain* **37 J6** 36 32N 4 41W
Fuente Alamo, *Albacete, Spain* **35 G3** 38 44N 1 24W
Fuente Álamo, *Murcia, Spain* **35 H3** 37 42N 1 6W
Fuente de Cantos, *Spain* . **37 G4** 38 15N 6 18W
Fuente del Maestre, *Spain* **37 G4** 38 31N 6 28W
Fuente el Fresno, *Spain* . **37 F7** 39 14N 3 46W
Fuente Ovejuna, *Spain* .. **37 G5** 38 15N 5 25W
Fuentes de Andalucía, *Spain* **37 H5** 37 28N 5 20W
Fuentes de Ebro, *Spain* .. **34 D4** 41 31N 0 38W
Fuentes de León, *Spain* .. **37 G4** 38 5N 6 32W
Fuentes de Oñoro, *Spain* **36 E4** 40 33N 6 52W
Fuentesaúco, *Spain* **36 D5** 41 15N 5 30W
Fuerte →, *Mexico* **146 B3** 25 50N 109 25W
Fuerte Olimpo, *Paraguay* **158 A4** 21 0 S 57 51W
Fuerteventura, *Canary Is.* **33 F6** 28 30N 14 0W
Fufeng, *China* .... **66 G4** 34 22N 108 0 E
Fuga I., *Phil.* .... **70 B3** 18 52N 121 20 E
Fughmah, *Yemen* .... **87 C5** 16 9N 49 26 E
Fugløysund, *Norway* .... **12 A16** 70 15N 20 20 E
Fugong, *China* .... **68 D2** 27 5N 98 47 E
Fugou, *China* .... **66 G8** 34 3N 114 25 E
Fugu, *China* .... **66 E6** 39 2N 111 3 E
Fuhai, *China* .... **64 B3** 47 2N 87 25 E
Fuḥaymī, *Iraq* .... **84 C4** 34 16N 42 10 E
Fuji, *Japan* .... **63 B10** 35 9N 138 39 E
Fuji-San, *Japan* .... **63 B10** 35 22N 138 44 E
Fuji-yoshida, *Japan* ..... **63 B10** 35 30N 138 46 E
Fujian □, *China* .... **69 E12** 26 0N 118 0 E
Fujieda, *Japan* .... **63 C10** 34 52N 138 16 E
Fujinomiya, *Japan* ...... **63 B10** 35 10N 138 40 E
Fujioka, *Japan* .... **63 A11** 36 15N 139 5 E
Fujisawa, *Japan* .... **63 B11** 35 22N 139 29 E
Fukaya, *Japan* .... **63 A11** 36 12N 139 12 E
Fukien = Fujian □, *China* **69 E12** 26 0N 118 0 E
Fukuchiyama, *Japan* .... **63 B7** 35 19N 135 9 E
Fukue-Shima, *Japan* .... **61 H4** 32 40N 128 45 E

Gigen 201

Gashua, *Nigeria* **101 C7** 12 54N 11 0 E
Gaspé, *Canada* **129 C7** 48 52N 64 30W
Gaspé, C. de, *Canada* **129 C7** 48 48N 64 7W
Gaspé, Pén. de, *Canada* **129 C6** 48 45N 65 40W
Gaspésie, Parc Prov. de la, *Canada* **129 C6** 48 55N 65 50W
Gassaway, *U.S.A.* **134 F5** 38 41N 80 47W
Gasselte, *Neths.* **20 C9** 52 58N 6 48 E
Gasselternijveen, *Neths.* **20 C9** 52 59N 6 51 E
Gássino Torinese, *Italy* **38 C4** 45 8N 7 50 E
Gassol, *Nigeria* **101 D7** 8 34N 10 25 E
Gasteiz = Vitoria, *Spain* **34 C2** 42 50N 2 41W
Gastonia, *U.S.A.* **135 H5** 35 16N 81 11W
Gastoúni, *Greece* **45 G3** 37 51N 21 15 E
Gastoúri, *Greece* **44 E1** 39 34N 19 54 E
Gastre, *Argentina* **160 B3** 42 20 S 69 15W
Gata, C., *Cyprus* **32 E12** 34 34N 33 2 E
Gata, C. de, *Spain* **35 J2** 36 41N 2 13W
Gata, Sierra de, *Spain* **36 E4** 40 20N 6 45W
Gataga →, *Canada* **130 B3** 58 35N 126 59W
Gătaia, *Romania* **46 D2** 45 26N 21 30 E
Gatchina, *Russia* **50 B7** 59 35N 30 9 E
Gates, *U.S.A.* **136 C7** 43 9N 77 42W
Gateshead, *U.K.* **16 C6** 54 57N 1 37W
Gatesville, *U.S.A.* **139 K6** 31 26N 97 45W
Gaths, *Zimbabwe* **107 G3** 20 2 S 30 32 E
Gatico, *Chile* **158 A1** 22 29 S 70 20W
Gâtinais, *France* **23 D9** 48 5N 2 40 E
Gâtine, Hauteurs de, *France* **24 B3** 46 35N 0 45W
Gatineau →, *Canada* **128 C4** 45 27N 75 42W
Gatineau, Parc de la, *Canada* **128 C4** 45 40N 76 0W
Gattaran, *Phil.* **70 B3** 18 4N 121 38 E
Gattinara, *Italy* **38 C5** 45 37N 8 22 E
Gatukai, *Solomon Is.* **121 M10** 8 45 S 158 15 E
Gatun, L., *Panama* **148 E4** 9 7N 79 56W
Gatyana, *S. Africa* **105 E4** 32 16 S 28 31 E
Gau, *Fiji* **121 B2** 18 2 S 179 18 E
Gaua, *Vanuatu* **121 D5** 14 15 S 167 30 E
Gaucín, *Spain* **37 J5** 36 31N 5 19W
Gauer L., *Canada* **131 B9** 57 0N 97 50W
Gauhati, *India* **81 F14** 26 10N 91 45 E
Gauja →, *Latvia* **50 C4** 57 10N 24 16 E
Gaula →, *Norway* **12 E11** 63 21N 10 14 E
Gaurain-Ramecroix, *Belgium* **21 G3** 50 36N 3 30 E
Gaurdak, *Turkmenistan* **55 E3** 37 50N 66 4 E
Gausta, *Norway* **14 E2** 59 50N 8 37 E
Gāv Koshī, *Iran* **85 D8** 28 38N 57 12 E
Gavá, *Spain* **34 D6** 41 18N 2 0 E
Gāvakān, *Iran* **85 D7** 29 37N 53 10 E
Gavarnie, *France* **24 F3** 42 44N 0 1W
Gavāter, *Iran* **85 E9** 25 10N 61 31 E
Gāvbandī, *Iran* **85 E7** 27 12N 53 4 E
Gavdhopoúla, *Greece* **32 E6** 34 56N 24 0 E
Gávdhos, *Greece* **32 E6** 34 50N 24 5 E
Gavere, *Belgium* **21 G3** 50 55N 3 40 E
Gavião, *Portugal* **37 F3** 39 28N 7 56W
Gaviota, *U.S.A.* **145 L6** 34 29N 120 13W
Gävleborgs län □, *Sweden* **14 C10** 61 30N 16 15 E
Gavorrano, *Italy* **38 F7** 42 55N 10 49 E
Gavray, *France* **22 D5** 48 55N 1 20W
Gavrilov Yam, *Russia* **51 C11** 57 18N 39 49 E
Gávrion, *Greece* **45 G6** 37 54N 24 44 E
Gawachab, *Namibia* **104 D2** 27 4 S 17 55 E
Gawai, *Burma* **78 B6** 27 56N 97 30 E
Gawilgarh Hills, *India* **82 D3** 21 15N 76 45 E
Gawler, *Australia* **116 C3** 34 30 S 138 42 E
Gaxun Nur, *China* **64 B5** 42 22N 100 30 E
Gay, *Russia* **54 F6** 51 27N 58 27 E
Gaya, *India* **81 G11** 24 47N 85 4 E
Gaya, *Niger* **101 C5** 11 52N 3 28 E
Gaya, *Nigeria* **101 C6** 11 57N 9 0 E
Gaylord, *U.S.A.* **134 C3** 45 2N 84 41W
Gayndah, *Australia* **115 D5** 25 35 S 151 32 E
Gayny, *Russia* **54 A4** 60 18N 54 19 E
Gaysin, *Ukraine* **52 B3** 48 57N 29 25 E
Gayvoron, *Ukraine* **52 B3** 48 22N 29 52 E
Gaza, *Egypt* **91 D3** 31 30N 34 28 E
Gaza □, *Mozam.* **105 C5** 23 10 S 32 45 E
Gaza Strip, *Egypt* **91 D3** 31 29N 34 25 E
Gazaoua, *Niger* **97 F1** 13 32N 7 55 E
Gāzbor, *Iran* **85 D8** 28 5N 58 51 E
Gazelle Pen., *Papua N. G.* **120 C6** 4 40 S 152 0 E
Gazi, *Zaïre* **106 B1** 1 3N 24 30 E
Gaziantep, *Turkey* **88 E7** 37 6N 37 23 E
Gaziantep □, *Turkey* **88 E7** 37 0N 37 0 E
Gazipaşa, *Turkey* **88 E5** 36 16N 32 18 E
Gazli, *Uzbekistan* **56 E7** 40 14N 63 24 E
Gbarnga, *Liberia* **100 D3** 7 19N 9 13W
Gbekebo, *Nigeria* **101 D5** 6 20N 4 56 E
Gboko, *Nigeria* **101 D6** 7 17N 9 4 E
Gbongan, *Nigeria* **101 D5** 7 28N 4 20 E
Gcuwa, *S. Africa* **105 E4** 32 20 S 28 11 E
Gdańsk, *Poland* **47 A5** 54 22N 18 40 E
Gdańsk □, *Poland* **47 A5** 54 10N 18 30 E
Gdańska, Zatoka, *Poland* **47 A6** 54 30N 19 20 E
Gdov, *Russia* **50 B5** 58 48N 27 55 E
Gdynia, *Poland* **47 A5** 54 35N 18 33 E
Gebe, *Indonesia* **73 A3** 0 5N 129 25 E
Gebeit Mine, *Sudan* **94 C4** 21 3N 36 29 E
Gebel Mûsa, *Egypt* **94 J8** 28 32N 33 59 E
Gebze, *Turkey* **88 C3** 40 47N 29 25 E
Gecha, *Ethiopia* **95 F4** 7 30N 35 18 E
Gedaref, *Sudan* **95 E4** 14 2N 35 28 E
Gede, Tanjung, *Indonesia* **74 D3** 6 46 S 105 12 E
Gedinne, *Belgium* **21 J5** 49 59N 4 56 E
Gediz, *Turkey* **88 D3** 39 1N 29 24 E
Gediz →, *Turkey* **88 D2** 38 35N 26 48 E
Gedo, *Ethiopia* **95 F4** 9 2N 37 25 E
Gèdre, *France* **24 F4** 42 47N 0 2 E
Gedser, *Denmark* **15 K5** 54 35N 11 55 E
Gedser Odde, *Denmark* **15 K5** 54 30N 11 58 E
Geegully Cr. →, *Australia* **112 C3** 18 32 S 123 41 E
Geel, *Belgium* **21 F5** 51 10N 4 59 E
Geelong, *Australia* **116 E6** 38 10 S 144 22 E
Geelvink Chan., *Australia* **113 E1** 28 30 S 114 0 E
Geer →, *Belgium* **21 G7** 50 51N 5 42 E
Geesthacht, *Germany* **26 B6** 53 25N 10 20 E
Geffen, *Neths.* **20 E6** 51 44N 5 28 E
Geidam, *Nigeria* **101 C7** 12 57N 11 57 E
Geikie →, *Canada* **131 B8** 57 45N 103 52W
Geili, *Sudan* **95 D3** 16 1N 32 37 E
Geilo, *Norway* **14 D2** 60 32N 8 14 E
Geinica, *Slovak Rep.* **31 C13** 48 51N 20 55 E
Geisingen, *Germany* **27 H4** 47 55N 8 37 E
Geislingen, *Germany* **27 G5** 48 37N 9 51 E
Geita, *Tanzania* **106 C3** 2 48 S 32 12 E
Geita □, *Tanzania* **106 C3** 2 50 S 32 10 E
Gejiu, *China* **68 F4** 23 20N 103 10 E
Gel →, *Sudan* **95 F2** 7 5N 29 10 E
Gel River, *Sudan* **95 F2** 7 5N 29 10 E
Gela, *Italy* **41 E7** 37 6N 14 18 E
Gela, G. di, *Italy* **41 F7** 37 0N 14 8 E
Geladi, *Ethiopia* **90 F4** 6 59N 46 30 E
Gelderland □, *Neths.* **20 D8** 52 5N 6 10 E
Geldermalsen, *Neths.* **20 E6** 51 53N 5 17 E
Geldern, *Germany* **26 D2** 51 32N 6 18 E
Geldrop, *Neths.* **21 F7** 51 25N 5 32 E
Geleen, *Neths.* **21 G7** 50 57N 5 49 E
Gelehun, *S. Leone* **100 D2** 8 20N 11 40W
Gelendost, *Turkey* **88 D4** 38 7N 31 1 E
Gelendzhik, *Russia* **52 D8** 44 33N 38 10 E
Gelib, *Somali Rep.* **108 D2** 0 29N 42 46 E
Gelibolu, *Turkey* **44 D8** 40 28N 26 43 E
Gelidonya Burnu, *Turkey* **88 E4** 36 12N 30 24 E
Gelnhausen, *Germany* **27 E5** 50 12N 9 12 E
Gelsenkirchen, *Germany* **26 D3** 51 30N 7 5 E
Gelting, *Germany* **26 A5** 54 43N 9 53 E
Gemas, *Malaysia* **77 L4** 2 37N 102 36 E
Gembloux, *Belgium* **21 G5** 50 34N 4 43 E
Gemena, *Zaïre* **102 B3** 3 13N 19 48 E
Gemerek, *Turkey* **88 D7** 39 15N 36 10 E
Gemert, *Neths.* **21 E7** 51 33N 5 41 E
Gemlik, *Turkey* **88 C3** 40 26N 29 9 E
Gemona del Friuli, *Italy* **39 B10** 46 16N 13 7 E
Gemsa, *Egypt* **94 B3** 27 39N 33 35 E
Gemünden, *Germany* **27 E5** 50 3N 9 43 E
Genale, *Ethiopia* **95 F4** 6 0N 39 30 E
Genale, *Somali Rep.* **108 D2** 1 48N 44 42 E
Genappe, *Belgium* **21 G4** 50 37N 4 30 E
Genç, *Turkey* **89 D9** 38 44N 40 34 E
Gençay, *France* **24 B4** 46 23N 0 23 E
Gendringen, *Neths.* **20 E8** 51 52N 6 21 E
Gendt, *Neths.* **20 E7** 51 53N 5 59 E
Geneina, Gebel, *Egypt* **94 J8** 29 2N 33 55 E
Genemuiden, *Neths.* **20 C8** 52 38N 6 2 E
General Acha, *Argentina* **158 D3** 37 20 S 64 38W
General Alvear, *Buenos Aires, Argentina* **158 D3** 36 0 S 60 0W
General Alvear, *Mendoza, Argentina* **158 D2** 35 0 S 67 40W
General Artigas, *Paraguay* **158 B4** 26 52 S 56 16W
General Belgrano, *Argentina* **158 D4** 36 35 S 58 47W
General Cabrera, *Argentina* **158 C3** 32 53 S 63 52W
General Carrera, L., *Chile* **160 C2** 46 35 S 72 0W
General Cepeda, *Mexico* **146 B4** 25 23N 101 27W
General Conesa, *Argentina* **160 B4** 40 6 S 64 25W
General Guido, *Argentina* **158 D4** 36 40 S 57 50W
General Juan Madariaga, *Argentina* **158 D4** 37 0 S 57 0W
General La Madrid, *Argentina* **158 D3** 37 17 S 61 20W
General Lorenzo Vintter, *Argentina* **160 B4** 40 45 S 64 26W
General Luna, *Phil.* **70 E4** 13 41N 122 10 E
General MacArthur, *Phil.* **71 F5** 11 18N 125 28 E
General Martin Miguel de Güemes, *Argentina* **158 A3** 24 50 S 65 0W
General Paz, *Argentina* **158 B4** 27 45 S 57 36W
General Pico, *Argentina* **158 D3** 35 45 S 63 50W
General Pinedo, *Argentina* **158 B3** 27 15 S 61 20W
General Pinto, *Argentina* **158 C3** 34 45 S 61 50W
General Sampaio, *Brazil* **154 B4** 4 2 S 39 29W
General Santos, *Phil.* **71 H5** 6 5N 125 14 E
General Tinio, *Phil.* **70 D3** 15 39N 121 10 E
General Toshevo, *Bulgaria* **43 D13** 43 42N 28 6 E
General Trevino, *Mexico* **147 B5** 26 14N 99 29W
General Trías, *Mexico* **146 B3** 28 21N 106 22W
General Viamonte, *Argentina* **158 D3** 35 1 S 61 3W
General Villegas, *Argentina* **158 D3** 35 5 S 63 0W
General Vintter, L., *Argentina* **160 B2** 43 55 S 71 40W
Generoso, Mte., *Switz.* **29 E8** 45 56N 9 2 E
Genesee, *Idaho, U.S.A.* **142 C5** 46 33N 116 56W
Genesee, *Pa., U.S.A.* **136 E7** 41 59N 77 54W
Genesee →, *U.S.A.* **136 C7** 43 16N 77 36W
Geneseo, *Ill., U.S.A.* **140 C6** 41 27N 90 9W
Geneseo, *Kans., U.S.A.* **138 F5** 38 31N 98 10W
Geneseo, *N.Y., U.S.A.* **136 D7** 42 48N 77 49W
Geneva = Genève, *Switz.* **28 D2** 46 12N 6 9 E
Geneva, *Ala., U.S.A.* **135 K3** 31 2N 85 52W
Geneva, *Ill., U.S.A.* **141 C8** 41 53N 88 18W
Geneva, *Ind., U.S.A.* **141 D12** 40 36N 84 58W
Geneva, *N.Y., U.S.A.* **136 D7** 42 52N 76 59W
Geneva, *Nebr., U.S.A.* **138 E6** 40 32N 97 36W
Geneva, *Ohio, U.S.A.* **136 E4** 41 48N 80 57W
Geneva, L. = Léman, Lac, *Switz.* **28 D3** 46 26N 6 30 E
Geneva, L., *U.S.A.* **141 B8** 42 38N 88 30W
Genève, *Switz.* **28 D2** 46 12N 6 9 E
Genève □, *Switz.* **28 D2** 46 10N 6 10 E
Geng, *Afghan.* **79 C1** 31 22N 61 28 E
Gengenbach, *Germany* **27 G4** 48 25N 8 2 E
Gengma, *China* **68 F2** 23 32N 99 20 E
Genichesk, *Ukraine* **52 C6** 46 12N 34 50 E
Genil →, *Spain* **37 H5** 37 42N 5 19W
Génissiat, Barr. de, *France* **25 B9** 46 1N 5 48 E
Genk, *Belgium* **21 G7** 50 58N 5 32 E
Genkai-Nada, *Japan* **62 D2** 34 0N 130 0 E
Genlis, *France* **23 E12** 47 11N 5 12 E
Gennargentu, Mti. del, *Italy* **40 B2** 40 0N 9 10 E
Gennep, *Neths.* **21 E7** 51 41N 5 59 E
Gennes, *France* **22 E6** 47 20N 0 17W
Genoa = Génova, *Italy* **38 D5** 44 24N 8 56 E
Genoa, *Australia* **117 D8** 37 29 S 149 35 E
Genoa, *Ill., U.S.A.* **141 B8** 42 6N 88 42W
Genoa, *N.Y., U.S.A.* **137 D8** 42 40N 76 32W
Genoa, *Nebr., U.S.A.* **138 E6** 41 27N 97 44W
Genoa, *Nev., U.S.A.* **144 F7** 39 2N 119 50W
Genoa →, *Argentina* **160 B2** 44 55 S 70 5W
Genoa City, *U.S.A.* **141 B8** 42 30N 88 20W
Génova, *Italy* **38 D5** 44 24N 8 56 E
Génova, G. di, *Italy* **38 E6** 44 0N 9 0 E
Gent, *Belgium* **21 F3** 51 2N 3 42 E
Gentbrugge, *Belgium* **21 F3** 51 3N 3 47 E
Genthin, *Germany* **26 C8** 52 24N 12 10 E
Gentio do Ouro, *Brazil* **154 D3** 11 25 S 42 30W
Geographe B., *Australia* **113 F2** 33 30 S 115 15 E
Geographe Chan., *Australia* **113 D1** 24 30 S 113 0 E
Geokchay, *Azerbaijan* **53 F12** 40 42N 47 43 E
Georga, Zemlya, *Russia* **56 A5** 80 30N 49 0 E
George, *S. Africa* **104 E3** 33 58 S 22 29 E
George →, *Canada* **129 A6** 58 49N 66 10W
George, L., *N.S.W., Australia* **117 C8** 35 10 S 149 25 E
George, L., *S. Austral., Australia* **116 D4** 37 25 S 140 0 E
George, L., *W. Austral., Australia* **112 D3** 22 45 S 123 40 E
George, L., *Uganda* **106 B3** 0 5N 30 10 E
George, L., *Fla., U.S.A.* **135 L5** 29 17N 81 36W
George, L., *N.Y., U.S.A.* **137 C11** 43 37N 73 33W
George Gill Ra., *Australia* **112 D5** 24 22 S 131 45 E
George River = Port Nouveau-Québec, *Canada* **127 C13** 58 30N 65 59W
George Sound, *N.Z.* **119 E2** 44 52 S 167 25 E
George Town, *Bahamas* **148 B4** 23 33N 75 47W
George Town, *Malaysia* **77 K3** 5 25N 100 15 E
George V Land, *Antarctica* **7 C10** 69 0 S 148 0 E
George VI Sound, *Antarctica* **7 D17** 71 0 S 68 0W
George West, *U.S.A.* **139 L5** 28 20N 98 7W
Georgetown, *Australia* **114 B3** 18 17 S 143 33 E
Georgetown, *Ont., Canada* **128 D4** 43 40N 79 56W
Georgetown, *P.E.I., Canada* **129 C7** 46 13N 62 24W
Georgetown, *Cayman Is.* **148 C3** 19 20N 81 24W
Georgetown, *Gambia* **100 C2** 13 30N 14 47W
Georgetown, *Guyana* **153 B6** 6 50N 58 12W
Georgetown, *Calif., U.S.A.* **144 G6** 38 54N 120 50W
Georgetown, *Colo., U.S.A.* **142 G11** 39 42N 105 42W
Georgetown, *Ill., U.S.A.* **141 E9** 39 59N 87 38W
Georgetown, *Ky., U.S.A.* **134 F3** 38 13N 84 33W
Georgetown, *Ohio, U.S.A.* **141 F13** 38 52N 83 54W
Georgetown, *S.C., U.S.A.* **135 J6** 33 23N 79 17W
Georgetown, *Tex., U.S.A.* **139 K6** 30 38N 97 41W
Georgi Dimitrov, *Bulgaria* **43 E8** 42 15N 23 54 E
Georgi Dimitrov, Yazovir, *Bulgaria* **43 E10** 42 37N 25 18 E
Georgia □, *U.S.A.* **135 J4** 32 50N 83 15W
Georgia ■, *Asia* **53 E10** 42 0N 43 0 E
Georgia, Str. of, *Canada* **130 D4** 49 25N 124 0W
Georgian B., *Canada* **128 C3** 45 15N 81 0W
Georgievsk, *Russia* **53 D10** 44 12N 43 28 E
Georgina →, *Australia* **114 C2** 23 30 S 139 47 E
Georgina Downs, *Australia* **114 C2** 21 10 S 137 40 E
Georgiu-Dezh = Liski, *Russia* **51 F11** 51 3N 39 30 E
Georgiyevka, *Kazakhstan* **55 B7** 43 3N 74 43 E
Gera, *Germany* **26 E8** 50 53N 12 11 E
Geraardsbergen, *Belgium* **21 G3** 50 45N 3 53 E
Geral, Serra, *Bahia, Brazil* **155 D3** 14 0 S 41 0W
Geral, Serra, *Goiás, Brazil* **154 D2** 11 15 S 46 30W
Geral, Serra, *Sta. Catarina, Brazil* **159 B6** 26 25 S 50 0W
Geral de Goiás, Serra, *Brazil* **155 D2** 12 0 S 46 0W
Geral do Paraná Serra, *Brazil* **155 E2** 15 0 S 47 30W
Gerald, *U.S.A.* **140 F5** 38 24N 91 20W
Geraldine, *N.Z.* **119 E6** 44 5 S 171 15 E
Geraldine, *U.S.A.* **142 C8** 47 36N 110 16W
Geraldton, *Australia* **113 E1** 28 48 S 114 32 E
Geraldton, *Canada* **128 C2** 49 44N 86 59W
Geranium, *Australia* **116 C4** 35 23 S 140 11 E
Gérardmer, *France* **23 D13** 48 3N 6 50 E
Gercüş, *Turkey* **89 E9** 37 34N 41 23 E
Gerede, *Turkey* **52 F5** 40 45N 32 10 E
Gereshk, *Afghan.* **79 C2** 31 47N 64 35 E
Gérgal, *Spain* **35 H2** 37 7N 2 31W
Gerik, *Malaysia* **77 K3** 5 50N 101 15 E
Gering, *U.S.A.* **138 E3** 41 50N 103 40W
Gerlach, *U.S.A.* **142 F4** 40 39N 119 21W
Gerlachovka, *Slovak Rep.* **31 B13** 49 11N 20 7 E
Gerlogubi, *Ethiopia* **90 F4** 6 53N 45 3 E
German Planina, *Macedonia* **42 E7** 42 20N 22 0 E
Germansen Landing, *Canada* **130 B4** 55 43N 124 40W
Germantown, *U.S.A.* **141 E12** 39 38N 84 22W
Germany ■, *Europe* **26 E6** 51 0N 10 0 E
Germersheim, *Germany* **27 F4** 49 13N 8 20 E
Germiston, *S. Africa* **105 D4** 26 15 S 28 10 E
Gernsheim, *Germany* **27 F4** 49 44N 8 29 E
Gero, *Japan* **63 B9** 35 48N 137 14 E
Gerolstein, *Germany* **27 E2** 50 12N 6 40 E
Gerolzhofen, *Germany* **27 F6** 49 54N 10 21 E
Gerona, *Spain* **34 D7** 41 58N 2 46 E
Gerona □, *Spain* **34 C7** 42 11N 2 30 E
Gérouville, *Belgium* **21 J6** 49 37N 5 26 E
Gerrard, *Canada* **130 C5** 50 30N 117 17W
Gerringong, *Australia* **117 C9** 34 46 S 150 47 E
Gers □, *France* **24 E4** 43 35N 0 30 E
Gers →, *France* **24 D4** 44 9N 0 39 E
Gersfeld, *Germany* **26 E5** 50 27N 9 57 E
Gersoppa Falls, *India* **83 G2** 14 12N 74 46 E
Gerze, *Turkey* **88 C6** 41 48N 35 12 E
Geseke, *Germany* **26 D4** 51 38N 8 29 E
Geser, *Indonesia* **73 B4** 3 50 S 130 54 E
Gesso →, *Italy* **38 D4** 44 24N 7 33 E
Gestro, Wabi →, *Ethiopia* **95 G5** 4 12N 42 2 E
Gesves, *Belgium* **21 H6** 50 24N 5 4 E
Getafe, *Spain* **36 E7** 40 18N 3 44W
Gethsémani, *Canada* **129 B7** 50 13N 60 40W
Gettysburg, *Pa., U.S.A.* **134 F7** 39 50N 77 14W
Gettysburg, *S. Dak., U.S.A.* **138 C5** 45 1N 99 57W
Getz Ice Shelf, *Antarctica* **7 D14** 75 0 S 130 0W
Geul →, *Neths.* **21 G7** 50 53N 5 43 E
Geureudong, Mt., *Indonesia* **74 B1** 4 13N 96 42 E
Geurie, *Australia* **117 B8** 32 22 S 148 50 E
Gevaş, *Turkey* **89 D10** 38 15N 43 6 E
Gévaudan, *France* **24 D7** 44 40N 3 40 E
Gevgelija, *Macedonia* **42 F7** 41 9N 22 30 E
Gévora →, *Spain* **37 G4** 38 53N 6 57W
Gex, *France* **25 B10** 46 21N 6 3 E
Geyikli, *Turkey* **44 E8** 39 50N 26 12 E
Geyser, *U.S.A.* **142 C8** 47 16N 110 30W
Geyserville, *U.S.A.* **144 G4** 38 42N 122 54W
Geysir, *Iceland* **12 D3** 64 19N 20 18W
Geyve, *Turkey* **88 C4** 40 30N 30 18 E
Ghâbat el Arab = Wang Kai, *Sudan* **95 F2** 9 3N 29 23 E
Ghaghara →, *India* **81 G11** 25 45N 84 40 E
Ghalat, *Oman* **87 B7** 21 6N 58 53 E
Ghalla, Wadi el →, *Sudan* **95 E2** 10 25N 27 32 E
Ghallamane, *Mauritania* **98 D3** 23 15N 10 0W
Ghana ■, *W. Afr.* **101 D4** 8 0N 1 0W
Ghansor, *India* **81 H9** 22 39N 80 1 E
Ghanzi, *Botswana* **104 C3** 21 50 S 21 34 E
Ghanzi □, *Botswana* **104 C3** 21 50 S 21 45 E
Gharb el Istiwa'iya □, *Sudan* **95 F2** 5 0N 30 0 E
Gharbîya, Es Sahrâ el, *Egypt* **94 B2** 27 40N 26 30 E
Ghard Abû Muharik, *Egypt* **94 B2** 26 50N 30 0 E
Ghardaïa, *Algeria* **99 B5** 32 20N 3 37 E
Ghârib, G., *Egypt* **94 J8** 28 6N 32 54 E
Ghârib, Râs, *Egypt* **94 J8** 28 6N 33 18 E
Gharm, W. →, *Oman* **87 C7** 19 57N 57 38 E
Gharyān, *Libya* **96 B2** 32 10N 13 0 E
Gharyān □, *Libya* **96 B2** 30 35N 12 0 E
Ghat, *Libya* **96 D2** 24 59N 10 11 E
Ghatal, *India* **81 H12** 22 40N 87 46 E
Ghatampur, *India* **81 F9** 26 8N 80 13 E
Ghatere, *Solomon Is.* **121 L10** 7 55 S 159 0 E
Ghatprabha →, *India* **83 F2** 16 15N 75 20 E
Ghaṭṭī, *Si. Arabia* **84 D3** 31 16N 37 31 E
Ghawdex = Gozo, *Malta* **32 C1** 36 3N 14 13 E
Ghayl, *Si. Arabia* **86 B4** 21 40N 46 20 E
Ghayl Bā Wazīr, *Yemen* **87 D5** 14 47N 49 22 E
Ghazal, Bahr el →, *Chad* **97 F3** 13 0N 15 47 E
Ghazâl, Bahr el →, *Sudan* **95 F3** 9 31N 30 25 E
Ghazaouet, *Algeria* **99 A4** 35 8N 1 50W
Ghaziabad, *India* **80 E7** 28 42N 77 26 E
Ghazipur, *India* **81 G10** 25 38N 83 35 E
Ghaznī, *Afghan.* **79 B3** 33 30N 68 28 E
Ghaznī □, *Afghan.* **79 B3** 32 10N 68 20 E
Ghedi, *Italy* **38 C7** 45 24N 10 16 E
Ghelari, *Romania* **46 D3** 45 38N 22 45 E
Ghèlinsor, *Somali Rep.* **90 F4** 6 28N 46 39 E
Ghent = Gent, *Belgium* **21 F3** 51 2N 3 42 E
Gheorghe Gheorghiu-Dej, *Romania* **46 C7** 46 17N 26 47 E
Gheorgheni, *Romania* **46 C6** 46 43N 25 41 E
Ghergani, *Romania* **46 E6** 44 37N 25 37 E
Gherla, *Romania* **46 B4** 47 2N 23 57 E
Ghilarza, *Italy* **40 B1** 40 8N 8 50 E
Ghisonaccia, *France* **25 F13** 42 1N 9 26 E
Ghisoni, *France* **25 F13** 42 7N 9 12 E
Ghizao, *Afghan.* **80 C1** 33 20N 65 44 E
Ghizar →, *Pakistan* **81 A5** 36 15N 73 43 E
Ghod →, *India* **82 E2** 18 30N 74 35 E
Ghogha, *India* **80 J5** 21 40N 72 20 E
Ghot Ogrein, *Egypt* **94 A2** 31 10N 25 20 E
Ghotaru, *India* **80 F4** 27 20N 70 1 E
Ghotki, *Pakistan* **80 E3** 28 5N 69 21 E
Ghowr □, *Afghan.* **79 B2** 34 0N 64 20 E
Ghudaf, W. al →, *Iraq* **84 C4** 32 56N 43 30 E
Ghudāmis, *Libya* **96 B1** 30 11N 9 29 E
Ghughri, *India* **81 H9** 22 39N 80 41 E
Ghugus, *India* **82 E4** 19 58N 79 12 E
Ghulam Mohammad Barrage, *Pakistan* **80 G3** 25 30N 68 20 E
Ghurayrah, *Si. Arabia* **86 C3** 18 37N 42 41 E
Ghūrīān, *Afghan.* **79 B1** 34 17N 61 25 E
Gia Dinh, *Vietnam* **77 G6** 10 49N 106 42 E
Gia Lai = Pleiku, *Vietnam* **76 F7** 13 57N 108 0 E
Gia Nghia, *Vietnam* **77 G6** 11 58N 107 42 E
Gia Ngoc, *Vietnam* **76 E7** 14 50N 108 58 E
Gia Vuc, *Vietnam* **76 E7** 14 42N 108 34 E
Giamama, *Somali Rep.* **108 D2** 0 4N 42 44 E
Giannutri, *Italy* **38 F8** 42 16N 11 5 E
Giant Forest, *U.S.A.* **144 J8** 36 36N 118 43W
Giant Mts. = Krkonoše, *Czech.* **30 A8** 50 50N 15 35 E
Giants Causeway, *U.K.* **19 A5** 55 15N 6 30W
Giarabub = Al Jaghbūb, *Libya* **96 C4** 29 42N 24 38 E
Giarre, *Italy* **41 E8** 37 44N 15 10 E
Giaveno, *Italy* **38 C4** 45 3N 7 20 E
Gibara, *Cuba* **148 B4** 21 9N 76 11W
Gibb River, *Australia* **112 C4** 16 26 S 126 26 E
Gibbon, *U.S.A.* **138 E5** 40 45N 98 51W
Gibe →, *Ethiopia* **95 F4** 7 20N 37 36 E
Gibellina, *Italy* **40 E6** 37 48N 13 0 E
Gibraléon, *Spain* **37 H4** 37 23N 6 58W
Gibraltar ■, *Europe* **37 J5** 36 7N 5 22W
Gibraltar, Str. of, *Medit. S.* **37 K5** 35 55N 5 40W
Gibson City, *U.S.A.* **141 D8** 40 28N 88 22W
Gibson Desert, *Australia* **112 D4** 24 0 S 126 0 E
Gibsonburg, *U.S.A.* **141 C13** 41 23N 83 19W
Gibsons, *Canada* **130 D4** 49 24N 123 32W
Gibsonville, *U.S.A.* **144 F6** 39 46N 120 54W
Giddalur, *India* **83 G4** 15 20N 78 57 E
Giddings, *U.S.A.* **139 K6** 30 11N 96 56W
Gidole, *Ethiopia* **95 F4** 5 40N 37 25 E
Gien, *France* **23 E9** 47 40N 2 36 E
Giessen, *Germany* **26 E4** 50 34N 8 40 E
Gieten, *Neths.* **20 B9** 53 1N 6 46 E
Gīfān, *Iran* **85 B8** 37 54N 57 28 E
Gifatin, Geziret, *Egypt* **94 B3** 27 10N 33 50 E
Gifford Creek, *Australia* **112 D2** 24 3 S 116 16 E
Gifhorn, *Germany* **26 C6** 52 29N 10 32 E
Gifu, *Japan* **63 B8** 35 30N 136 45 E
Gifu □, *Japan* **63 B8** 35 40N 137 0 E
Gigant, *Russia* **53 C9** 46 28N 41 20 E
Giganta, Sa. de la, *Mexico* **146 B2** 25 30N 111 30W
Gigen, *Bulgaria* **43 D9** 43 40N 24 28 E

Great Belt 203

Goodenough I., Papua N. G. 120 E6 9 20 S 150 15 E
Gooderham, Canada 128 D4 44 54N 78 21W
Goodeve, Canada 131 C8 51 4N 103 10W
Gooding, U.S.A. 142 E6 42 56N 114 43W
Goodland, U.S.A. 138 F4 39 21N 101 43W
Goodnight, U.S.A. 139 H4 35 2N 101 11W
Goodooga, Australia 115 D4 29 3 S 147 28 E
Goodsoil, Canada 131 C7 54 24N 109 13W
Goodsprings, U.S.A. 143 J6 35 50N 115 26W
Goole, U.K. 16 D7 53 42N 0 52W
Goolgowi, Australia 117 B6 33 58 S 145 41 E
Goolwa, Australia 116 C3 35 30 S 138 47 E
Goomalling, Australia 113 F2 31 15 S 116 49 E
Goombalie, Australia 115 D4 29 59 S 145 26 E
Goonalga, Australia 116 A5 31 45 S 143 37 E
Goonda, Mozam. 107 F3 19 48 S 33 57 E
Goondiwindi, Australia 115 D5 28 30 S 150 21 E
Goongarrie, L., Australia 113 F3 30 3 S 121 9 E
Goonumbla, Australia 117 B8 32 59 S 148 11 E
Goonyella, Australia 114 C4 21 47 S 147 58 E
Goor, Neths. 20 D9 52 13N 6 33 E
Gooray, Australia 115 D5 28 25 S 150 2 E
Goose →, Canada 129 B7 53 20N 60 35W
Goose L., U.S.A. 142 F3 41 56N 120 26W
Gooty, India 83 G3 15 7N 77 41 E
Gopalganj, Bangla. 78 D2 23 1N 89 50 E
Gopalganj, India 81 F11 26 28N 84 30 E
Goppenstein, Switz. 28 D5 46 23N 7 46 E
Göppingen, Germany 27 G5 48 42N 9 40 E
Gor, Spain 35 H2 37 23N 2 58W
Góra, Leszno, Poland 47 D3 51 40N 16 31 E
Góra, Płock, Poland 47 C7 52 39N 20 6 E
Góra Kalwaria, Poland 47 D8 51 59N 21 14 E
Gorakhpur, India 81 F10 26 47N 83 23 E
Goražde, Bos.-H. 42 D3 43 38N 18 58 E
Gorbatov, Russia 51 C13 56 12N 43 2 E
Gorbea, Peña, Spain 34 B2 43 1N 2 50W
Gorda, U.S.A. 144 K5 35 53N 121 26W
Gorda, Pta., Nic. 148 D3 14 20N 83 10W
Gorda, Pta., Canary Is. 33 F2 28 45N 18 0W
Gordan B., Australia 112 B5 11 35 S 130 10 E
Gordon, U.S.A. 138 D3 42 48N 102 12W
Gordon →, Australia 114 G4 42 27 S 145 30 E
Gordon, I., Chile 160 D3 54 55 S 69 30W
Gordon Downs, Australia 112 C4 18 48 S 128 33 E
Gordon L., Alta., Canada 131 B6 56 30N 110 25W
Gordon L., N.W.T., Canada 130 A6 63 5N 113 11W
Gordonia, S. Africa 104 D3 28 13 S 21 10 E
Gordonvale, Australia 114 B4 17 5 S 145 50 E
Gore, Australia 115 D5 28 17 S 151 30 E
Goré, Chad 97 G3 7 59N 16 31 E
Gore, Ethiopia 95 F4 8 12N 35 32 E
Gore, N.Z. 119 G3 46 5 S 168 58 E
Gore Bay, Canada 128 C3 45 57N 82 28W
Görele, Turkey 89 C8 41 2N 39 0 E
Gorey, Ireland 19 D5 52 41N 6 18W
Gorg, Iran 85 D8 29 29N 59 43 E
Gorgān, Iran 85 B7 36 50N 54 29 E
Gorgona, Italy 38 E6 43 27N 9 52 E
Gorgora, Ethiopia 95 E4 12 15N 37 17 E
Gorham, U.S.A. 137 B13 44 23N 71 10W
Gori, Georgia 53 E11 42 0N 44 7 E
Gorin, U.S.A. 140 D4 40 22N 92 1W
Gorinchem, Neths. 20 E5 51 50N 4 59 E
Gorinhatã, Brazil 155 E2 19 15 S 49 45W
Goritsy, Russia 51 C10 57 4N 36 43 E
Gorízia, Italy 39 C10 45 56N 13 37 E
Górka, Poland 47 D3 51 39N 16 58 E
Gorki = Nizhniy Novgorod, Russia 51 C14 56 20N 44 0 E
Gorki, Belorussia 50 D7 54 17N 30 59 E
Gorkiy = Nizhniy Novgorod, Russia 51 C14 56 20N 44 0 E
Gorkovskoye Vdkhr., Russia 51 C13 57 2N 43 4 E
Gørlev, Denmark 15 J5 55 30N 11 15 E
Gorlice, Poland 31 B14 49 35N 21 11 E
Görlitz, Germany 26 D10 51 10N 14 59 E
Gorlovka, Ukraine 52 B8 48 19N 38 5 E
Gorman, Calif., U.S.A. 145 L8 34 47N 118 51W
Gorman, Tex., U.S.A. 139 J5 32 12N 98 41W
Gorna Dzhumayo = Blagoevgrad, Bulgaria 42 E8 42 2N 23 5 E
Gorna Oryakhovitsa, Bulgaria 43 D10 43 7N 25 40 E
Gornja Radgona, Slovenia 39 B13 46 40N 16 2 E
Gornja Tuzla, Bos.-H. 42 C3 44 35N 18 46 E
Gornji Grad, Slovenia 39 B11 46 20N 14 52 E
Gornji Milanovac, Serbia 42 C5 44 0N 20 29 E
Gornji Vakuf, Bos.-H. 42 D2 43 57N 17 34 E
Gorno Ablanovo, Bulgaria 43 D10 43 37N 25 43 E
Gorno-Altaysk, Russia 56 D9 51 50N 86 5 E
Gorno Slinkino, Russia 56 C8 60 5N 70 0 E
Gornyatski, Russia 48 A11 67 32N 64 3 E
Gornyi, Russia 60 B6 44 57N 133 59 E
Gornyy, Russia 51 F16 51 50N 48 30 E
Gorodenka, Ukraine 52 B1 48 41N 25 29 E
Gorodets, Russia 51 C13 56 38N 43 28 E
Gorodishche, Russia 51 E14 53 13N 45 40 E
Gorodishche, Ukraine 52 B4 49 17N 31 27 E
Gorodnitsa, Ukraine 50 F5 50 46N 27 19 E
Gorodnya, Ukraine 50 F7 51 55N 31 33 E
Gorodok, Belorussia 50 D7 55 30N 30 3 E
Gorodok, Ukraine 50 G3 49 46N 23 32 E
Goroka, Papua N. G. 120 D3 6 7 S 145 25 E
Goroke, Australia 116 D4 36 43 S 141 29 E
Gorokhov, Ukraine 50 F4 50 30N 24 45 E
Gorokhovets, Russia 51 C13 56 13N 42 39 E
Gorom Gorom, Burkina Faso 101 C4 14 26N 0 14W
Goromonzi, Zimbabwe 107 F3 17 52 S 31 22 E
Gorongose →, Mozam. 105 C5 20 30 S 34 40 E
Gorongoza, Mozam. 107 F3 18 44 S 34 2 E
Gorongoza, Sa. da, Mozam. 107 F3 18 27 S 34 2 E
Gorontalo, Indonesia 72 A2 0 35N 123 5 E
Goronyo, Nigeria 101 C6 13 29N 5 39 E
Górowo Iławeckie, Poland 47 A7 54 17N 20 30 E
Gorredijk, Neths. 20 C8 53 0N 6 3 E
Gorron, France 22 D6 48 25N 0 50W
Gorssel, Neths. 20 D8 52 12N 6 12 E
Gort, Ireland 19 C3 53 4N 8 50W
Gortis, Greece 32 D6 35 4N 24 58 E
Gorumahisani, India 82 C8 22 20N 86 24 E
Gorzkowice, Poland 47 D6 51 13N 19 36 E
Gorzno, Poland 47 B6 53 12N 19 38 E
Gorzów Śląski, Poland 47 D5 51 3N 18 22 E
Gorzów Wielkopolski, Poland 47 C2 52 43N 15 15 E
Gorzów Wielkopolski □, Poland 47 C2 52 45N 15 30 E
Göschenen, Switz. 29 C7 46 40N 8 36 E
Gose, Japan 63 C7 34 27N 135 44 E
Gosford, Australia 117 B9 33 23 S 151 18 E
Goshen, Calif., U.S.A. 144 J7 36 21N 119 25W
Goshen, Ind., U.S.A. 141 C11 41 35N 85 50W
Goshen, N.Y., U.S.A. 137 E10 41 24N 74 20W
Goshogawara, Japan 60 D10 40 48N 140 27 E
Goslar, Germany 26 D6 51 55N 10 23 E
Gospič, Croatia 39 D12 44 35N 15 23 E
Gosport, U.K. 17 G6 50 48N 1 8W
Gosport, U.S.A. 141 E10 39 21N 86 40W
Gossau, Switz. 29 B8 47 25N 9 15 E
Gosse →, Australia 114 B1 19 32 S 134 37 E
Gostivar, Macedonia 42 F5 41 48N 20 57 E
Gostyń, Poland 47 D4 51 50N 17 3 E
Gostynin, Poland 47 C6 52 26N 19 29 E
Göta älv →, Sweden 15 G5 57 42N 11 54 E
Göta kanal, Sweden 13 G12 58 30N 15 58 E
Göteborg, Sweden 15 G5 57 43N 11 59 E
Göteborgs och Bohus län □, Sweden 13 G11 58 30N 11 30 E
Gotemba, Japan 63 B10 35 18N 138 56 E
Götene, Sweden 15 F7 58 32N 13 30 E
Gotha, Germany 26 E6 50 56N 10 42 E
Gothenburg, U.S.A. 138 E4 40 56N 100 10W
Gotland, Sweden 13 H15 57 30N 18 33 E
Gotse Delchev, Bulgaria 43 F8 41 43N 23 46 E
Gotska Sandön, Sweden 13 G15 58 24N 19 15 E
Gōtsu, Japan 62 B4 35 0N 132 14 E
Göttingen, Germany 26 D5 51 31N 9 55 E
Gottwald = Zmiyev, Ukraine 52 B7 49 39N 36 27 E
Gottwaldov = Zlin, Czech. 31 B10 49 14N 17 40 E
Goubangzi, China 67 D11 41 20N 121 52 E
Gouda, Neths. 20 D5 52 1N 4 42 E
Goúdhoura, Ákra, Greece 32 E8 34 59N 26 6 E
Goudiry, Senegal 100 C2 14 15N 12 45W
Gough I., Atl. Oc. 9 N8 40 10 S 9 45W
Gouin, Rés., Canada 128 C5 48 35N 74 40W
Gouitafla, Ivory C. 100 D3 7 30N 5 53W
Goulburn, Australia 117 C8 34 44 S 149 44 E
Goulburn Is., Australia 114 A1 11 40 S 133 20 E
Goulia, Ivory C. 100 C3 10 1N 7 11W
Goulimine, Morocco 98 C3 28 56N 10 0W
Goulmina, Morocco 98 B4 31 41N 4 57W
Gouménissa, Greece 44 D4 40 56N 22 37 E
Gounou-Gaya, Chad 97 G3 9 38N 15 31 E
Goúra, Greece 45 G4 37 56N 22 20 E
Gouraya, Algeria 99 A5 36 31N 1 56 E
Gourdon, France 24 D5 44 44N 1 23 E
Gouré, Niger 97 F2 14 0N 10 10 E
Gouri, Chad 97 E3 19 36N 19 36 E
Gourits →, S. Africa 104 E3 34 21 S 21 52 E
Gourma Rharous, Mali 101 B4 16 55N 1 50W
Goúrnais, Greece 32 D7 35 19N 25 16 E
Gournay-en-Bray, France 23 C8 49 29N 1 44 E
Gourock Ra., Australia 117 C8 36 0 S 149 25 E
Goursi, Burkina Faso 100 C4 12 42N 2 37W
Gouvêa, Brazil 155 E3 18 27 S 43 44W
Gouverneur, U.S.A. 137 B9 44 20N 75 28W
Gouviá, Greece 32 A3 39 39N 19 50 E
Gouzon, France 24 B6 46 12N 2 14 E
Govan, Canada 131 C8 51 20N 105 0W
Governador Valadares, Brazil 155 E3 18 15 S 41 57W
Governor's Harbour, Bahamas 148 A4 25 10N 76 14W
Gowan Ra., Australia 114 C4 25 0 S 145 0 E
Gowanda, U.S.A. 136 D6 42 28N 78 56W
Gower, U.K. 17 F3 51 35N 4 10W
Gowna, L., Ireland 19 C4 53 52N 7 35W
Gowrie, U.S.A. 140 B2 42 17N 94 17W
Goya, Argentina 158 B4 29 10 S 59 10W
Goyder Lagoon, Australia 115 D2 27 3 S 138 58 E
Goyllarisquisga, Peru 156 C2 10 31 S 76 24W
Göynük, Turkey 88 C4 40 24N 30 48 E
Goz Beïda, Chad 97 F4 12 10N 21 20 E
Goz Regeb, Sudan 95 D4 16 3N 35 33 E
Gozdnica, Poland 47 D2 51 28N 15 4 E
Gozo, Malta 32 C1 36 3N 14 13 E
Graaff-Reinet, S. Africa 104 E3 32 13 S 24 32 E
Grabill, U.S.A. 141 C12 41 13N 84 57W
Grabow, Germany 26 B7 53 17N 11 31 E
Grabów, Poland 47 D5 51 31N 18 7 E
Grabs, Switz. 29 B8 47 11N 9 27 E
Gračac, Croatia 39 D12 44 18N 15 57 E
Gračanica, Bos.-H. 42 C3 44 43N 18 18 E
Graçay, France 23 E8 47 10N 1 50 E
Grace, U.S.A. 142 E8 42 35N 111 44W
Graceville, U.S.A. 138 C6 45 34N 96 26W
Grachevka, Russia 54 E3 52 55N 52 52 E
Gracias a Dios, C., Honduras 148 C3 15 0N 83 10W
Graciosa, I., Canary Is. 33 E6 29 15N 13 32W
Gradačac, Bos.-H. 42 C3 44 52N 18 26 E
Gradaús, Brazil 154 C1 7 43 S 51 11W
Gradaús, Serra dos, Brazil 154 C1 8 0 S 50 45W
Gradeška Planina, Macedonia 42 F7 41 30N 22 15 E
Gradets, Bulgaria 43 E11 42 46N 26 30 E
Grado, Italy 39 C10 45 40N 13 20 E
Grado, Spain 36 B4 43 23N 6 4W
Gradule, Australia 115 D4 28 32 S 149 15 E
Grady, U.S.A. 139 H3 34 49N 103 19W
Graeca, Lacul, Romania 46 E7 44 5N 26 10 E
Graénalon, L., Iceland 12 D5 64 10N 17 20W
Grafenau, Germany 27 G9 48 51N 13 24 E
Gräfenberg, Germany 27 F7 49 39N 11 15 E
Grafton, Australia 115 D5 29 38 S 152 58 E
Grafton, Ill., U.S.A. 140 F6 38 58N 90 26W
Grafton, N. Dak., U.S.A. 138 A6 48 25N 97 25W
Gragnano, Italy 41 B7 40 42N 14 30 E
Graham, Canada 128 C1 49 20N 90 30W
Graham, N.C., U.S.A. 135 G6 36 5N 79 25W
Graham, Tex., U.S.A. 139 J5 33 6N 98 35W
Graham →, Canada 130 B4 56 31N 122 17W
Graham, Mt., U.S.A. 143 K9 32 42N 109 52W
Graham Bell, Os., Russia 56 A7 81 0N 62 0 E
Graham I., Canada 130 C2 53 40N 132 30W
Graham Land, Antarctica 7 C17 65 0 S 64 0W
Grahamdale, Canada 131 C9 51 23N 98 30W
Grahamstown, S. Africa 104 E4 33 19 S 26 31 E
Grahovo, Montenegro 42 E3 42 40N 18 40 E
Graïba, Tunisia 96 B2 34 30N 10 13 E
Graide, Belgium 21 J6 49 58N 5 4 E
Graie, Alpi, Europe 38 C4 45 30N 7 10 E
Grain Coast, W. Afr. 100 E3 4 20N 10 0W
Grajaú, Brazil 154 C2 5 50 S 46 4W
Grajaú →, Brazil 154 B3 3 41 S 44 48W
Grajewo, Poland 47 B9 53 39N 22 30 E
Gramada, Bulgaria 42 D7 43 49N 22 39 E
Gramat, France 24 D5 44 48N 1 43 E
Grammichele, Italy 41 E7 37 12N 14 37 E
Grámmos, Óros, Greece 44 D2 40 18N 20 47 E
Grampian □, U.K. 18 D6 57 20N 3 0W
Grampian Highlands = Grampian Mts., U.K. 18 E5 56 50N 4 0W
Grampian Mts., U.K. 18 E5 56 50N 4 0W
Gran →, Surinam 153 C6 4 1N 55 30W
Gran Altiplanicie Central, Argentina 160 C3 49 0 S 69 30W
Gran Canaria, Canary Is. 33 F4 27 55N 15 35W
Gran Chaco, S. Amer. 158 B3 25 0 S 61 0W
Gran Paradiso, Italy 38 C4 45 33N 7 17 E
Gran Sasso d'Italia, Italy 39 F10 42 25N 13 30 E
Granada, Nic. 148 D2 11 58N 86 0W
Granada, Phil. 71 F4 10 40N 123 2 E
Granada, Spain 35 H1 37 10N 3 35W
Granada, U.S.A. 139 F3 38 4N 102 19W
Granada □, Spain 37 H7 37 18N 3 0W
Granadilla de Abona, Canary Is. 33 F3 28 7N 16 33W
Granard, Ireland 19 C4 53 47N 7 30W
Granbury, U.S.A. 139 J6 32 27N 97 47W
Granby, Canada 128 C5 45 25N 72 45W
Grand →, Mich., U.S.A. 141 A10 43 4N 86 15W
Grand →, Mo., U.S.A. 140 E3 39 23N 93 7W
Grand →, S. Dak., U.S.A. 138 C4 45 40N 100 45W
Grand Bahama, Bahamas 148 A4 26 40N 78 30W
Grand Bank, Canada 129 C8 47 6N 55 48W
Grand Bassam, Ivory C. 100 D4 5 10N 3 49W
Grand Béréby, Ivory C. 100 E3 4 38N 6 55W
Grand Blanc, U.S.A. 141 B13 42 56N 83 38W
Grand-Bourg, Guadeloupe 149 C7 15 53N 61 19W
Grand Canal = Yun Ho →, China 67 E9 39 10N 117 10 E
Grand Canyon, U.S.A. 143 H7 36 3N 112 9W
Grand Canyon National Park, U.S.A. 143 H7 36 15N 112 30W
Grand Cayman, Cayman Is. 148 C3 19 20N 81 20W
Grand Cess, Liberia 100 E3 4 40N 8 12W
Grand Coulee, U.S.A. 142 C4 47 57N 119 0W
Grand Coulee Dam, U.S.A. 142 C4 47 57N 118 59W
Grand Erg de Bilma, Niger 97 E2 18 30N 14 0 E
Grand Erg Occidental, Algeria 99 B5 30 20N 1 0 E
Grand Erg Oriental, Algeria 99 C6 30 0N 6 30 E
Grand Falls, Canada 129 C8 48 56N 55 40W
Grand Forks, Canada 130 D5 49 0N 118 30W
Grand Forks, U.S.A. 138 B6 47 55N 97 3W
Grand-Fougeray, France 22 E5 47 44N 1 43W
Grand Haven, U.S.A. 141 A10 43 4N 86 13W
Grand I., U.S.A. 134 B2 46 31N 86 40W
Grand Island, U.S.A. 138 E5 40 55N 98 21W
Grand Isle, U.S.A. 139 L10 29 14N 90 0W
Grand Junction, Colo., U.S.A. 143 G9 39 4N 108 33W
Grand Junction, Iowa, U.S.A. 140 B2 42 2N 94 14W
Grand L., La., U.S.A. 139 L8 29 55N 92 47W
Grand L., Ohio, U.S.A. 141 D12 40 32N 84 25W
Grand Lac Victoria, Canada 128 C4 47 35N 77 35W
Grand Lahou, Ivory C. 100 D3 5 10N 5 5W
Grand L., N.B., Canada 129 C6 45 57N 66 7W
Grand L., Nfld., Canada 129 C8 49 0N 57 30W
Grand L., Nfld., Canada 129 B7 53 40N 60 30W
Grand Lake, U.S.A. 142 F11 40 15N 105 49W
Grand Ledge, U.S.A. 141 B12 42 45N 84 45W
Grand-Leez, Belgium 21 G5 50 35N 4 45 E
Grand-Lieu, L. de, France 22 E5 47 6N 1 40W
Grand Manan I., Canada 129 D6 44 45N 66 52W
Grand Marais, Canada 138 B9 47 45N 90 25W
Grand Marais, U.S.A. 134 B3 46 40N 85 59W
Grand-Mère, Canada 128 C5 46 36N 72 40W
Grand Popo, Benin 101 D5 6 15N 1 57 E
Grand Portage, U.S.A. 128 C2 47 58N 89 41W
Grand Rapids, Canada 131 C9 53 12N 99 19W
Grand Rapids, Mich., U.S.A. 141 B10 42 58N 85 40W
Grand Rapids, Minn., U.S.A. 138 B8 47 14N 93 31W
Grand River, U.S.A. 140 D3 40 49N 93 58W
Grand St-Bernard, Col du, Switz. 28 E4 45 50N 7 10 E
Grand Santi, Fr. Guiana 153 C7 4 20N 54 24W
Grand Teton, U.S.A. 142 E8 43 54N 111 50W
Grand Valley, U.S.A. 142 G9 39 27N 108 3W
Grand View, Canada 131 C8 51 10N 100 42W
Grandas de Salime, Spain 36 B4 43 13N 6 53W
Grande →, Jujuy, Argentina 158 A2 24 20 S 65 2W
Grande →, Mendoza, Argentina 158 D2 36 52 S 69 45W
Grande →, Bolivia 157 D5 15 51 S 64 39W
Grande →, Bahia, Brazil 154 D3 11 30 S 44 30W
Grande →, Minas Gerais, Brazil 155 F1 20 6 S 51 4W
Grande →, Spain 35 F4 39 6N 0 48W
Grande →, Venezuela 153 B5 8 36N 61 39W
Grande, B., Argentina 160 D3 50 30 S 68 20W
Grande, I., Brazil 155 F3 23 9 S 44 14W
Grande, Rio →, U.S.A. 139 N6 25 58N 97 9W
Grande, Serra, Goiás, Brazil 154 D2 11 15 S 46 30W
Grande, Serra, Piauí, Brazil 154 C2 8 0 S 45 10W
Grande Baie, Canada 129 C5 48 19N 70 52W
Grande Baleine, R. de la →, Canada 128 A4 55 16N 77 47W
Grande Cache, Canada 130 C5 53 53N 119 8W
Grande de Santiago →, Mexico 146 C3 21 20N 105 50W
Grande Dixence, Barr. de la, Switz. 28 D4 46 5N 7 23 E
Grande-Entrée, Canada 129 C7 47 30N 61 40W
Grande Prairie, Canada 130 B5 55 10N 118 50W
Grande-Rivière, Canada 129 C7 48 26N 64 30W
Grande Sauldre →, France 23 E9 47 27N 2 5 E
Grande-Vallée, Canada 129 C6 49 14N 65 8W
Grandes-Bergeronnes, Canada 129 C6 48 16N 69 35W
Grandfalls, U.S.A. 139 K3 31 20N 102 51W
Grandoe Mines, Canada 130 B3 56 29N 129 54W
Grândola, Portugal 37 G2 38 12N 8 35W
Grandpré, France 23 C11 49 20N 4 50 E
Grandson, Switz. 28 C3 46 49N 6 39 E
Grandview, Mo., U.S.A. 140 F2 38 53N 94 32W
Grandview, Wash., U.S.A. 142 C4 46 15N 119 54W
Grandview Heights, U.S.A. 141 E13 39 58N 83 2W
Grandvilliers, France 23 C8 49 40N 1 57 E
Graneros, Chile 158 C1 34 5 S 70 45W
Grangemouth, U.K. 18 E5 56 1N 3 43W
Granger, Wash., U.S.A. 142 C3 46 21N 120 11W
Granger, Wyo., U.S.A. 142 F9 41 35N 109 58W
Grangeville, U.S.A. 142 D5 45 56N 116 7W
Granite City, U.S.A. 140 F6 38 42N 90 9W
Granite Falls, U.S.A. 138 C7 44 49N 95 33W
Granite Mt., U.S.A. 145 M10 33 5N 116 28W
Granite Peak, Australia 113 E3 25 40 S 121 20 E
Granite Peak, U.S.A. 142 D9 45 10N 109 48W
Granitnyy, Pik, Kirghizia 55 D5 39 32N 70 20 E
Granity, N.Z. 119 B6 41 39 S 171 51 E
Granja, Brazil 154 B3 3 7 S 40 50W
Granja de Moreruela, Spain 36 D5 41 48N 5 44W
Granja de Torrehermosa, Spain 37 G5 38 19N 5 35W
Granollers, Spain 34 D7 41 39N 2 18 E
Gransee, Germany 26 B9 53 0N 13 10 E
Grant, U.S.A. 138 E4 40 53N 101 42W
Grant, Mt., U.S.A. 142 G4 38 34N 118 48W
Grant City, U.S.A. 140 D2 40 29N 94 25W
Grant I., Australia 112 B5 11 10 S 132 52 E
Grant Range, U.S.A. 143 G6 38 30N 115 25W
Grantham, U.K. 16 E7 52 55N 0 39W
Grantown-on-Spey, U.K. 18 D5 57 19N 3 36W
Grants, U.S.A. 143 J10 35 9N 107 52W
Grants Pass, U.S.A. 142 E2 42 26N 123 19W
Grantsburg, U.S.A. 138 C8 45 47N 92 41W
Grantsville, U.S.A. 142 F7 40 36N 112 28W
Granville, France 22 D5 48 50N 1 35W
Granville, Ill., U.S.A. 140 C7 41 16N 89 14W
Granville, N. Dak., U.S.A. 138 A4 48 16N 100 47W
Granville, N.Y., U.S.A. 134 D9 43 24N 73 16W
Granville L., Canada 131 B8 56 18N 100 30W
Grao de Gandía, Spain 35 F4 39 0N 0 7W
Grapeland, U.S.A. 139 K7 31 30N 95 29W
Gras, L. de, Canada 126 B8 64 30N 110 30W
Graskop, S. Africa 105 C5 24 56 S 30 49 E
Grass →, Canada 131 B9 56 3N 96 33W
Grass Range, U.S.A. 142 C9 47 0N 109 0W
Grass River Prov. Park, Canada 131 C8 54 40N 100 50W
Grass Valley, Calif., U.S.A. 144 F6 39 13N 121 4W
Grass Valley, Oreg., U.S.A. 142 D3 45 22N 120 47W
Grassano, Italy 41 B9 40 38N 16 17 E
Grasse, France 25 E10 43 38N 6 56 E
Grassmere, Australia 116 A5 31 24 S 142 38 E
Gratis, U.S.A. 141 E12 39 38N 84 32W
Gratz, U.S.A. 141 F12 38 28N 84 57W
Graubünden □, Switz. 29 C9 46 45N 9 30 E
Graulhet, France 24 E5 43 45N 1 59 E
Graus, Spain 34 C5 42 11N 0 20 E
Gravatá, Brazil 154 C4 8 10 S 35 29W
Grave, Neths. 20 E7 51 46N 5 44 E
Grave, Pte. de, France 24 C2 45 34N 1 4W
's-Graveland, Neths. 20 D6 52 15N 5 7 E
Gravelbourg, Canada 131 D7 49 50N 106 35W
Gravelines, France 23 B9 50 59N 2 10 E
's-Gravendeel, Neths. 20 E5 51 47N 4 37 E
's-Gravenhage, Neths. 20 D4 52 7N 4 17 E
Gravenhurst, Canada 136 B5 44 52N 79 20W
's-Gravenpolder, Neths. 21 F3 51 28N 3 54 E
's-Gravensande, Neths. 20 D4 52 0N 4 9 E
Gravesend, Australia 115 D5 29 35 S 150 20 E
Gravesend, U.K. 17 F8 51 25N 0 22 E
Gravina di Púglia, Italy 41 B9 40 48N 16 25 E
Gravois, Pointe-à-, Haiti 149 C5 18 15N 73 56W
Gravone →, France 25 G12 41 58N 8 45 E
Gray, France 23 E12 47 22N 5 35 E
Grayling, U.S.A. 134 C3 44 40N 84 43W
Grayling →, Canada 130 B3 59 21N 125 0W
Grays Harbor, U.S.A. 142 C1 46 59N 124 1W
Grays L., U.S.A. 142 E8 43 4N 111 26W
Grays River, U.S.A. 144 D3 46 21N 123 37W
Grayson, Canada 131 C8 50 45N 102 40W
Grayville, U.S.A. 141 F9 38 16N 88 0W
Graz, Austria 30 D8 47 4N 15 27 E
Grazalema, Spain 37 J5 36 46N 5 23W
Grdelica, Serbia 42 E7 42 55N 22 3 E
Greasy L., Canada 130 A4 62 55N 122 12W
Great Abaco I., Bahamas 148 A4 26 25N 77 10W
Great Artesian Basin, Australia 114 C3 23 0 S 144 0 E
Great Australian Bight, Australia 113 F5 33 30 S 130 0 E
Great Bahama Bank, Bahamas 148 B4 23 15N 78 0W
Great Barrier I., N.Z. 118 C4 36 11 S 175 25 E
Great Barrier Reef, Australia 114 B4 18 0 S 146 50 E
Great Barrington, U.S.A. 137 D11 42 12N 73 22W
Great Basin, U.S.A. 124 F8 40 0N 117 0W
Great Bear →, Canada 126 B7 65 0N 124 0W
Great Bear L., Canada 126 B7 65 30N 120 0W
Great Belt = Store Bælt, Denmark 15 J5 55 20N 11 0 E

Halīl 205

Gudenå, *Denmark* **15 H3** 56 27N 9 40 E
Gudermes, *Russia* **53 E12** 43 24N 46 5 E
Gudivada, *India* **83 F5** 16 30N 81 3 E
Gudiyattam, *India* **83 H4** 12 57N 78 55 E
Gudur, *India* **83 G4** 14 12N 79 55 E
Guebwiller, *France* **23 E14** 47 55N 7 12 E
Guecho, *Spain* **34 B2** 43 21N 2 59W
Guékédou, *Guinea* **100 D2** 8 40N 10 5W
Guelma, *Algeria* **99 A6** 36 25N 7 29 E
Guelph, *Canada* **128 D3** 43 35N 80 20W
Guelt es Stel, *Algeria* **99 A5** 35 12N 3 1 E
Guelttara, *Algeria* **99 C4** 29 23N 2 10W
Guemar, *Algeria* **99 B6** 33 30N 6 49 E
Guéméné-Penfao, *France* **22 E5** 47 38N 1 50W
Guéméné-sur-Scorff, *France* **22 D3** 48 4N 3 13W
Guéné, *Benin* **101 C5** 11 44N 3 16 E
Güepi, *Peru* **152 D2** 0 9 S 75 10W
Guer, *France* **22 E4** 47 54N 2 8W
Güer Aike, *Argentina* **160 D3** 51 39 S 69 35W
Guera Pk., *Chad* **97 F3** 11 55N 18 12 E
Guérande, *France* **22 E4** 47 20N 2 26W
Guercif, *Morocco* **99 B4** 34 14N 3 21W
Guéréda, *Chad* **97 F4** 14 31N 22 5 E
Guéret, *France* **24 B5** 46 11N 1 51 E
Guérigny, *France* **23 E10** 47 6N 3 10 E
Guerneville, *U.S.A.* **144 G4** 38 30N 123 0W
Guernica, *Spain* **34 B2** 43 19N 2 40W
Guernsey, *U.K.* **17 H5** 49 30N 2 35W
Guernsey, *U.S.A.* **138 D2** 42 19N 104 45W
Guerrara, *Oasis, Algeria* **99 B5** 32 51N 4 22 E
Guerrara, *Saoura, Algeria* **99 C4** 28 5N 0 8W
Guerrero □, *Mexico* **147 D5** 17 30N 100 0W
Guerzim, *Algeria* **99 C4** 29 39N 1 40W
Gueugnon, *France* **25 B8** 46 36N 4 4 E
Gueydan, *U.S.A.* **139 K8** 30 2N 92 31W
Gūgher, *Iran* **85 D8** 29 28N 56 27 E
Guglionesi, *Italy* **41 A7** 41 55N 14 54 E
Gui Jiang →, *China* **69 F8** 23 30N 111 15 E
Gui Xian, *China* **68 F7** 23 8N 109 35 E
Guia, *Canary Is.* **33 F4** 28 8N 15 38W
Guia de Isora, *Canary Is.* **33 F3** 28 12N 16 46W
Guia Lopes da Laguna, *Brazil* **159 A4** 21 26 S 56 7W
Guichi, *China* **69 B11** 30 39N 117 27 E
Guider, *Cameroon* **101 D7** 9 56N 13 57 E
Guidimouni, *Niger* **97 F1** 13 42N 9 31 E
Guiding, *China* **68 D6** 26 34N 107 11 E
Guidong, *China* **69 D9** 26 7N 113 57 E
Guiglo, *Ivory C.* **100 D3** 6 45N 7 30W
Guijá, *Mozam.* **105 C5** 24 27 S 33 0 E
Guijo de Coria, *Spain* **36 E4** 40 6N 6 28W
Guildford, *U.K.* **17 F7** 51 14N 0 34W
Guilford, *U.S.A.* **129 C6** 45 10N 69 23W
Guilin, *China* **69 E8** 25 18N 110 15 E
Guillaumes, *France* **25 D10** 44 5N 6 52 E
Guillestre, *France* **25 D10** 44 39N 6 40 E
Guilvinec, *France* **22 E2** 47 48N 4 17W
Güimar, *Canary Is.* **33 F3** 28 18N 16 24W
Guimarães, *Brazil* **154 B3** 2 9 S 44 42W
Guimarães, *Portugal* **36 D2** 41 28N 8 24W
Guimaras, *Phil.* **71 F4** 10 35N 122 37 E
Guimba, *Phil.* **70 D3** 15 40N 120 46 E
Guinda, *U.S.A.* **144 G4** 38 50N 122 12W
Guindulman, *Phil.* **71 G5** 9 46N 124 29 E
Guinea ■, *W. Afr.* **100 C2** 10 20N 11 30W
Guinea, Gulf of, *Atl. Oc.* **101 E5** 3 0N 2 30 E
Guinea-Bissau ■, *Africa* **100 C2** 12 0N 15 0W
Güines, *Cuba* **148 B3** 22 50N 82 0W
Guingamp, *France* **22 D3** 48 34N 3 10W
Guinobatan, *Phil.* **70 E4** 13 11N 123 36 E
Guiom, *Phil.* **71 F4** 11 59N 123 44 E
Guipavas, *France* **22 D2** 48 26N 4 29W
Guiping, *China* **69 F8** 23 21N 110 2 E
Guipúzcoa □, *Spain* **34 B2** 43 12N 2 15W
Guir, O. →, *Algeria* **99 B4** 31 29N 2 17W
Guiratinga, *Brazil* **157 D7** 16 21 S 53 45W
Güiria, *Venezuela* **153 A5** 10 32N 62 18W
Guiscard, *France* **23 C10** 49 40N 3 1 E
Guise, *France* **23 C10** 49 52N 3 35 E
Guitiriz, *Spain* **36 B3** 43 11N 7 50W
Guiuan, *Phil.* **71 F5** 11 5N 125 55 E
Guixi, *China* **69 C11** 28 16N 117 15 E
Guiyang, *Guizhou, China* **68 D6** 26 32N 106 40 E
Guiyang, *Hunan, China* **69 E9** 25 46N 112 42 E
Guizhou □, *China* **68 D6** 27 0N 107 0 E
Gujan-Mestras, *France* **24 D2** 44 38N 1 4W
Gujarat □, *India* **80 H4** 23 20N 71 0 E
Gujiang, *China* **69 D10** 27 11N 114 47 E
Gujranwala, *Pakistan* **79 B4** 32 10N 74 12 E
Gujrat, *Pakistan* **79 B4** 32 40N 74 2 E
Gukovo, *Russia* **53 B8** 48 1N 39 58 E
Gulargambone, *Australia* **117 A8** 31 20 S 148 30 E
Gulbarga, *India* **82 F3** 17 20N 76 50 E
Gulbene, *Latvia* **50 C5** 57 8N 26 52 E
Gulcha, *Kirghizia* **55 C6** 40 19N 73 26 E
Guledagudda, *India* **83 F2** 16 3N 75 48 E
Gulf, The, *Asia* **85 E6** 27 0N 50 0 E
Gulfport, *U.S.A.* **139 K10** 30 22N 89 6W
Gulgong, *Australia* **117 B8** 32 20 S 149 49 E
Gulin, *China* **68 C5** 28 1N 105 50 E
Gulistan, *Pakistan* **80 D2** 30 30N 66 35 E
Gulistan, *Uzbekistan* **55 C4** 40 29N 68 46 E
Gull Lake, *Canada* **131 C7** 50 10N 108 29W
Gullegem, *Belgium* **21 G2** 50 51N 3 13 E
Güllük, *Turkey* **88 E2** 37 14N 27 35 E
Gulma, *Nigeria* **101 C5** 12 40N 4 23 E
Gulmarg, *India* **81 B6** 34 3N 74 25 E
Gülnar, *Turkey* **88 E5** 36 19N 33 24 E
Gulnare, *Australia* **116 B3** 33 27 S 138 27 E
Gulpen, *Neths.* **21 G7** 50 49N 5 53 E
Gülpinar, *Turkey* **44 E8** 39 32N 26 10 E
Gülşehir, *Turkey* **88 D6** 38 44N 34 37 E
Gulshad, *Kazakhstan* **56 E8** 46 45N 74 25 E
Gulsvik, *Norway* **14 D3** 60 24N 9 38 E
Gulu, *Uganda* **106 B3** 2 48N 32 17 E
Gulwe, *Tanzania* **106 D4** 6 30 S 36 25 E
Gulyaypole, *Ukraine* **52 C7** 47 45N 36 21 E
Gum Lake, *Australia* **116 B5** 32 42 S 143 9 E
Gumaca, *Phil.* **70 E4** 13 55N 122 6 E
Gumal →, *Pakistan* **80 D4** 31 40N 71 50 E
Gumbaz, *Pakistan* **80 D3** 30 2N 69 0 E
Gumel, *Nigeria* **101 C6** 12 39N 9 22 E
Gumiel de Hizán, *Spain* **34 D1** 41 46N 3 41W
Gumlu, *Australia* **114 B4** 19 53 S 147 41 E
Gumma □, *Japan* **63 A10** 36 30N 138 20 E
Gummersbach, *Germany* **26 D3** 51 2N 7 32 E
Gummi, *Nigeria* **101 C6** 12 4N 5 9 E
Gümüşhaciköy, *Turkey* **52 F6** 40 50N 35 18 E
Gümüşhane, *Turkey* **89 C8** 40 30N 39 30 E
Gümüşhane □, *Turkey* **89 C8** 40 35N 39 25 E
Gumzai, *Indonesia* **73 C4** 5 28 S 134 42 E
Guna, *Ethiopia* **95 E4** 11 50N 37 40 E
Guna, *India* **80 G7** 24 40N 77 19 E
Gundagai, *Australia* **117 C8** 35 3 S 148 6 E
Gundelfingen, *Germany* **27 G6** 48 33N 10 22 E
Gundih, *Indonesia* **75 D4** 7 10 S 110 56 E
Gundlakamma →, *India* **83 G5** 15 30N 80 15 E
Gunebang, *Australia* **117 B7** 33 1 S 146 38 E
Guneydogu Toroslar, *Turkey* **89 D9** 38 40N 40 30 E
Gungal, *Australia* **117 B9** 32 17 S 150 32 E
Gungu, *Zaïre* **103 D3** 5 43 S 19 20 E
Gunisao →, *Canada* **131 C9** 53 56N 97 53W
Gunisao L., *Canada* **131 C9** 53 33N 96 15W
Gunnbjørn Fjeld, *Greenland* **6 C6** 68 55N 29 47W
Gunnedah, *Australia* **117 A9** 30 59 S 150 15 E
Gunningbar Cr. →, *Australia* **117 A7** 31 14 S 147 6 E
Gunnison, *Colo., U.S.A.* **143 G10** 38 33N 106 56W
Gunnison, *Utah, U.S.A.* **142 G8** 39 9N 111 49W
Gunnison →, *U.S.A.* **143 G9** 39 4N 108 35W
Gunpowder, *Australia* **114 B2** 19 42 S 139 22 E
Guntakal, *India* **83 G3** 15 11N 77 27 E
Guntersville, *U.S.A.* **135 H2** 34 21N 86 18W
Guntong, *Malaysia* **77 K3** 4 36N 101 3 E
Guntur, *India* **83 F5** 16 23N 80 30 E
Gunungapi, *Indonesia* **72 C3** 6 45 S 126 30 E
Gunungsitoli, *Indonesia* **74 B1** 1 15N 97 30 E
Gunupur, *India* **82 E6** 19 5N 83 50 E
Günz →, *Germany* **27 G6** 48 27N 10 16 E
Gunza, *Angola* **103 E2** 10 50 S 13 50 E
Günzburg, *Germany* **27 G6** 48 27N 10 16 E
Gunzenhausen, *Germany* **27 F6** 49 6N 10 45 E
Guo He →, *China* **67 H9** 32 59N 117 10 E
Guoyang, *China* **66 H9** 33 32N 116 12 E
Gupis, *Pakistan* **81 A5** 36 15N 73 20 E
Gura Humorului, *Romania* **46 B6** 47 35N 25 53 E
Gura-Teghii, *Romania* **46 D7** 45 30N 26 25 E
Gurag, *Ethiopia* **95 F4** 8 20N 38 20 E
Gurdaspur, *India* **80 C6** 32 5N 75 31 E
Gurdon, *U.S.A.* **139 J8** 33 55N 93 9W
Gurdzhaani, *Georgia* **53 F11** 41 43N 45 52 E
Gurgaon, *India* **80 E7** 28 27N 77 1 E
Gürgentepe, *Turkey* **88 C7** 40 45N 38 18 E
Gurghiu, Munţii, *Romania* **46 C6** 46 41N 25 15 E
Gurguéia →, *Brazil* **154 C3** 6 50 S 43 24W
Gurha, *India* **80 G4** 25 12N 71 39 E
Guri, Embalse de, *Venezuela* **153 B5** 7 50N 62 52W
Gurk →, *Austria* **30 E7** 46 35N 14 31 E
Gurkha, *Nepal* **81 E11** 28 5N 84 40 E
Gurley, *Australia* **115 D4** 29 45 S 149 48 E
Gurnee, *U.S.A.* **141 B9** 42 22N 87 55W
Gurué, *Mozam.* **107 F4** 15 25 S 36 58 E
Gurun, *Malaysia* **77 K3** 5 49N 100 27 E
Gürün, *Turkey* **88 D7** 38 43N 37 15 E
Gurupá, *Brazil* **153 D7** 1 25 S 51 35W
Gurupá, I. Grande de, *Brazil* **153 D7** 1 25 S 51 45W
Gurupi, *Brazil* **155 D2** 11 43 S 49 4W
Gurupi →, *Brazil* **154 B2** 1 13 S 46 6W
Gurupi, Serra do, *Brazil* **154 C2** 5 0 S 47 50W
Guryev = Atyrau, *Kazakhstan* **53 C14** 47 5N 52 0 E
Gus-Khrustalnyy, *Russia* **51 D12** 55 42N 40 44 E
Gusau, *Nigeria* **101 C6** 12 12N 6 40 E
Gusev, *Russia* **50 D3** 54 35N 22 10 E
Gushan, *China* **67 E12** 39 50N 123 35 E
Gushi, *China* **69 A10** 32 11N 115 41 E
Gushiago, *Ghana* **101 D4** 9 55N 0 15W
Gusinje, *Montenegro* **42 E4** 42 35N 19 50 E
Gusinoozersk, *Russia* **57 D11** 51 16N 106 27 E
Gúspini, *Italy* **40 C1** 39 32N 8 38 E
Güssing, *Austria* **31 D9** 47 3N 16 20 E
Gustanj, *Slovenia* **39 B11** 46 36N 14 59 E
Gustine, *U.S.A.* **144 H6** 37 16N 121 0W
Güstrow, *Germany* **26 B8** 53 47N 12 12 E
Gusum, *Sweden* **15 F10** 58 16N 16 30 E
Guta = Kalárovo, *Slovak Rep.* **31 D11** 47 54N 18 0 E
Gütersloh, *Germany* **26 D4** 51 54N 8 25 E
Gutha, *Australia* **113 E2** 28 58 S 115 55 E
Guthalongra, *Australia* **114 B4** 19 52 S 147 50 E
Guthrie, *U.S.A.* **139 H6** 35 53N 97 25W
Guthrie Center, *U.S.A.* **140 C2** 41 41N 94 30W
Gutian, *China* **69 D12** 26 32N 118 43 E
Gutiérrez, *Bolivia* **157 D5** 19 25 S 63 34W
Guttannen, *Switz.* **29 C6** 46 38N 8 18 E
Guttenberg, *U.S.A.* **140 B5** 42 47N 91 6W
Guyana ■, *S. Amer.* **153 B6** 5 0N 59 0W
Guyane française ■ = French Guiana ■, *S. Amer.* **153 C7** 4 0N 53 0W
Guyang, *China* **66 D6** 41 0N 110 5 E
Guyenne, *France* **24 D4** 44 30N 0 40 E
Guymon, *U.S.A.* **139 G4** 36 41N 101 29W
Guyra, *Australia* **115 E5** 30 15 S 151 40 E
Guyuan, *Hebei, China* **66 D8** 41 37N 115 40 E
Guyuan, *Ningxia Huizu, China* **66 F4** 36 0N 106 20 E
Guzar, *Uzbekistan* **55 D3** 38 36N 66 15 E
Guzhang, *China* **68 C7** 28 42N 109 58 E
Guzhen, *China* **67 H9** 33 22N 117 18 E
Guzmán, L. de, *Mexico* **146 A3** 31 25N 107 25W
Gwa, *Burma* **78 G5** 17 36N 94 34 E
Gwaai, *Zimbabwe* **107 F2** 19 15 S 27 45 E
Gwabegar, *Australia* **117 A8** 30 31 S 149 0 E
Gwadabawa, *Nigeria* **101 C6** 13 28N 5 15 E
Gwādar, *Pakistan* **79 D1** 25 10N 62 18 E
Gwagwada, *Nigeria* **101 C6** 10 15N 7 15 E
Gwalia, *Australia* **113 E3** 28 54 S 121 20 E
Gwalior, *India* **80 F8** 26 12N 78 10 E
Gwanda, *Zimbabwe* **107 G2** 20 55 S 29 0 E
Gwandu, *Nigeria* **101 C5** 12 30N 4 41 E
Gwane, *Zaïre* **106 B2** 4 45N 25 48 E
Gwaram, *Nigeria* **102 C7** 10 15N 10 25 E
Gwarzo, *Nigeria* **101 C6** 12 20N 8 55 E
Gwda →, *Poland* **47 B3** 53 3N 16 44 E
Gweebarra B., *Ireland* **19 B3** 54 52N 8 21W
Gweedore, *Ireland* **19 A3** 55 4N 8 15W
Gwent □, *U.K.* **17 F5** 51 45N 2 55W
Gweru, *Zimbabwe* **107 F2** 19 28 S 29 45 E
Gwi, *Nigeria* **101 D6** 9 0N 7 10 E
Gwinn, *U.S.A.* **134 B2** 46 19N 87 27W
Gwio Kura, *Nigeria* **101 C7** 12 40N 11 2 E
Gwol, *Ghana* **100 C4** 10 58N 1 59W
Gwoza, *Nigeria* **101 C7** 11 5N 13 40 E
Gwydir →, *Australia* **115 D4** 29 27 S 149 48 E
Gwynedd □, *U.K.* **16 E4** 53 0N 4 0W
Gyandzha, *Azerbaijan* **53 F12** 40 45N 46 20 E
Gyaring Hu, *China* **64 C4** 34 50N 97 40 E
Gydanskiy P-ov., *Russia* **56 C8** 70 0N 78 0 E
Gympie, *Australia* **115 D5** 26 11 S 152 38 E
Gyobingauk, *Burma* **78 F5** 18 13N 95 39 E
Gyoda, *Japan* **63 A11** 36 10N 139 30 E
Gyoma, *Hungary* **31 E13** 46 56N 20 50 E
Gyöngyös, *Hungary* **31 D12** 47 48N 19 56 E
Györ, *Hungary* **31 D10** 47 41N 17 40 E
Györ-Sopron □, *Hungary* **31 D10** 47 40N 17 20 E
Gypsum Palace, *Australia* **116 B6** 32 37 S 144 9 E
Gypsum Pt., *Canada* **130 A6** 61 53N 114 35W
Gypsumville, *Canada* **131 C9** 51 45N 98 40W
Gyula, *Hungary* **31 E14** 46 38N 21 17 E
Gyumri = Kumayri, *Armenia* **53 F10** 40 47N 43 50 E
Gzhatsk, *Russia* **50 D9** 55 38N 35 0 E

H

Ha 'Arava →, *Israel* **91 E4** 30 50N 35 20 E
Ha Coi, *Vietnam* **76 B6** 21 26N 107 46 E
Ha Dong, *Vietnam* **76 B5** 20 58N 105 46 E
Ha Giang, *Vietnam* **76 A5** 22 50N 104 59 E
Ha Tien, *Vietnam* **77 G5** 10 23N 104 29 E
Ha Tinh, *Vietnam* **76 C5** 18 20N 105 54 E
Ha Trung, *Vietnam* **76 C5** 19 58N 105 50 E
Haacht, *Belgium* **21 G5** 50 59N 4 37 E
Ha'afeva, *Tonga* **121 P13** 19 57 S 174 43W
Haag, *Germany* **27 G8** 48 11N 12 12 E
Haaksbergen, *Neths.* **20 D9** 52 9N 6 45 E
Haaltert, *Belgium* **21 G4** 50 55N 4 1 E
Haamstede, *Neths.* **21 E3** 51 42N 3 45 E
Ha'ano, *Tonga* **121 P13** 19 41 S 174 18W
Ha'apai Group, *Tonga* **121 P13** 19 47 S 174 27W
Haapamäki, *Finland* **12 E18** 62 18N 24 28 E
Haapsalu, *Estonia* **50 B3** 58 56N 23 30 E
Haarlem, *Neths.* **20 D5** 52 23N 4 39 E
Haast, *N.Z.* **119 D4** 43 51 S 169 1 E
Haast →, *N.Z.* **119 D4** 43 50 S 169 2 E
Haast Bluff, *Australia* **112 D5** 23 22 S 132 0 E
Haast Pass, *N.Z.* **119 E4** 44 6 S 169 21 E
Haastrecht, *Neths.* **20 E5** 52 0N 4 47 E
Hab Nadi Chauki, *Pakistan* **80 G2** 25 0N 66 50 E
Ḩabarūt, *Yemen* **87 C6** 17 18N 52 44 E
Habaswein, *Kenya* **106 B4** 1 2N 39 30 E
Ḩabawnah, W. →, *Si. Arabia* **86 C4** 17 57N 44 58 E
Habay, *Canada* **130 B5** 58 50N 118 44W
Habay-la-Neuve, *Belgium* **21 J7** 49 44N 5 38 E
Ḩabbān, *Yemen* **86 D4** 14 21N 47 5 E
Ḩabbānīyah, *Iraq* **84 C4** 33 17N 43 29 E
Habiganj, *Bangla.* **78 C3** 24 24N 91 30 E
Haboro, *Japan* **60 B10** 44 22N 141 42 E
Haccourt, *Belgium* **21 G7** 50 44N 5 40 E
Hachenburg, *Germany* **26 E3** 50 40N 7 49 E
Hachijō-Jima, *Japan* **63 D11** 33 5N 139 45 E
Hachinohe, *Japan* **60 D10** 40 30N 141 29 E
Hachiōji, *Japan* **63 B11** 35 40N 139 20 E
Hachŏn, *N. Korea* **67 D15** 41 29N 129 2 E
Hachy, *Belgium* **21 J7** 49 42N 5 41 E
Hacıbektaş, *Turkey* **88 D6** 38 56N 34 33 E
Hacılar, *Turkey* **88 D6** 38 38N 35 26 E
Hackensack, *U.S.A.* **137 F10** 40 53N 74 3W
Haçli Gölü, *Turkey* **89 D10** 39 0N 42 17 E
Hadali, *Pakistan* **80 C5** 32 16N 72 11 E
Hadarba, Ras, *Sudan* **94 C4** 22 4N 36 51 E
Hadarom □, *Israel* **91 E3** 31 0N 35 0 E
Ḩadbaram, *Oman* **87 C6** 17 27N 55 15 E
Hadd, Ras al, *Oman* **87 B7** 22 35N 59 50 E
Ḩaddā, *Si. Arabia* **86 B2** 21 27N 39 34 E
Haddington, *U.K.* **18 F6** 55 57N 2 48W
Haddon Rig, *Australia* **117 A7** 31 27 S 147 52 E
Haded Plain, *Somali Rep.* **108 C3** 9 46N 48 2 E
Hadejia, *Nigeria* **101 C7** 12 30N 10 5 E
Hadejia →, *Nigeria* **101 C7** 12 50N 10 51 E
Haden, *Australia* **115 D5** 27 13 S 151 54 E
Ḩadera, *Israel* **91 C3** 32 27N 34 55 E
Ḩadera, N. →, *Israel* **91 C3** 32 28N 34 52 E
Haderslev, *Denmark* **15 J3** 55 15N 9 30 E
Hadháztéglas, *Hungary* **31 D14** 47 40N 21 40 E
Hadhramaut = Hadramawt, *Yemen* **87 D5** 15 30N 49 30 E
Hadım, *Turkey* **88 E5** 36 58N 32 26 E
Hadjeb El Aïoun, *Tunisia* **96 A1** 35 21N 9 32 E
Hadong, *S. Korea* **67 G14** 35 5N 127 44 E
Hadramawt, *Yemen* **87 D5** 15 30N 49 30 E
Hadramawt, W. →, *Yemen* **87 D5** 16 0N 48 53 E
Ḩadrānīyah, *Iraq* **84 C4** 35 38N 43 14 E
Hadrian's Wall, *U.K.* **16 C5** 55 0N 2 30W
Hadsten, *Denmark* **15 H4** 56 19N 10 3 E
Hadsund, *Denmark* **15 H4** 56 44N 10 8 E
Haeju, *N. Korea* **67 E13** 38 3N 125 45 E
Haenam, *S. Korea* **67 G14** 34 34N 126 35 E
Haerhpin = Harbin, *China* **67 B14** 45 48N 126 40 E
Hafar al Bāţin, *Si. Arabia* **84 D5** 28 25N 46 0 E
Hafik, *Turkey* **88 D7** 39 51N 37 23 E
Ḩafīrat al 'Aydā, *Si. Arabia* **84 E3** 26 26N 39 12 E
Ḩafit, *Oman* **87 B6** 23 59N 55 49 E
Hafizabad, *Pakistan* **80 C5** 32 5N 73 40 E
Haflong, *India* **78 C4** 25 10N 93 5 E
Hafnarfjörður, *Iceland* **12 D3** 64 4N 21 57W
Hafun, Ras, *Somali Rep.* **90 E5** 10 29N 51 30 E
Hagalil, *Israel* **91 C4** 32 53N 35 18 E
Hagari →, *India* **83 G3** 15 40N 77 0 E
Hagdan, *Phil.* **71 F4** 11 28N 123 54 E
Hagen, *Germany* **26 D3** 51 21N 7 29 E
Hagenow, *Germany* **26 B7** 53 25N 11 10 E
Hagerman, *U.S.A.* **139 J2** 33 7N 104 20W
Hagerstown, *Ind., U.S.A.* **141 E11** 39 55N 85 10W
Hagerstown, *Md., U.S.A.* **134 F7** 39 39N 77 43W
Hagetmau, *France* **24 E3** 43 39N 0 37W
Hagfors, *Sweden* **13 F12** 60 3N 13 45 E
Häggenås, *Sweden* **14 A8** 63 24N 14 55 E
Hagi, *Iceland* **12 D2** 65 28N 23 25W
Hagi, *Japan* **62 C3** 34 30N 131 22 E
Hagolan, *Syria* **91 B4** 33 0N 35 45 E
Hagondange-Briey, *France* **23 C13** 49 16N 6 11 E
Hagonoy, *Phil.* **70 D3** 14 50N 120 44 E
Hags Hd., *Ireland* **19 D2** 52 57N 9 30W
Hague, C. de la, *France* **22 C5** 49 44N 1 56W
Hague, The = 's-Gravenhage, *Neths.* **20 D4** 52 7N 4 17 E
Haguenau, *France* **23 D14** 48 49N 7 47 E
Hai □, *Tanzania* **106 C4** 3 10 S 37 10 E
Hai Duong, *Vietnam* **76 B6** 20 56N 106 19 E
Hai'an, *Guangdong, China* **69 G8** 20 18N 110 11 E
Hai'an, *Jiangsu, China* **69 A13** 32 37N 120 27 E
Haicheng, *Fujian, China* **69 E11** 24 23N 117 48 E
Haicheng, *Liaoning, China* **67 D12** 40 50N 122 45 E
Haidar Khel, *Afghan.* **80 C3** 33 58N 68 38 E
Haifa = Ḩefa, *Israel* **91 C3** 32 46N 35 0 E
Haifeng, *China* **69 F10** 22 58N 115 10 E
Haig, *Australia* **113 F4** 30 55 S 126 10 E
Haiger, *Germany* **26 E4** 50 44N 8 12 E
Haikang, *China* **69 G8** 20 52N 110 8 E
Haikou, *China* **65 D6** 20 1N 110 16 E
Ḩā'il, *Si. Arabia* **84 E4** 27 28N 41 45 E
Hailakandi, *India* **78 C4** 24 42N 92 34 E
Hailar, *China* **65 B6** 49 10N 119 38 E
Hailey, *U.S.A.* **142 E6** 43 31N 114 19W
Haileybury, *Canada* **128 C4** 47 30N 79 38W
Hailin, *China* **67 B15** 44 37N 129 30 E
Hailing Dao, *China* **69 G8** 21 35N 111 47 E
Hailong, *China* **67 C13** 42 32N 125 40 E
Hailuoto, *Finland* **12 D18** 65 3N 24 45 E
Haimen, *Guangdong, China* **69 F11** 23 15N 116 38 E
Haimen, *Jiangsu, China* **69 B13** 31 52N 121 10 E
Haimen, *Zhejiang, China* **69 C13** 28 40N 121 24 E
Hainan □, *China* **65 E5** 19 0N 109 30 E
Hainaut □, *Belgium* **21 H4** 50 30N 4 0 E
Hainburg, *Austria* **31 C9** 48 9N 16 56 E
Haines, *U.S.A.* **142 D5** 44 55N 117 56W
Haines City, *U.S.A.* **135 L5** 28 7N 81 38W
Haines Junction, *Canada* **130 A1** 60 45N 137 30W
Hainfeld, *Austria* **30 C8** 48 3N 15 48 E
Haining, *China* **69 B13** 30 28N 120 40 E
Haiphong, *Vietnam* **64 D5** 20 47N 106 41 E
Haiti ■, *W. Indies* **149 C5** 19 0N 72 30W
Haiya Junction, *Sudan* **94 D4** 18 20N 36 21 E
Haiyan, *China* **69 B13** 30 28N 120 58 E
Haiyang, *China* **67 F11** 36 47N 121 9 E
Haiyuan, *Guangxi Zhuangzu, China* **68 F6** 22 8N 107 35 E
Haiyuan, *Ningxia Huizu, China* **66 F3** 36 35N 105 52 E
Haizhou, *China* **67 G10** 34 37N 119 7 E
Haizhou Wan, *China* **67 G10** 34 50N 119 20 E
Haja, *Indonesia* **73 B3** 3 19 S 129 37 E
Hajar Bangar, *Sudan* **97 F4** 10 40N 22 45 E
Hajdú-Bihar □, *Hungary* **31 D14** 47 30N 21 30 E
Hajdúböszörmény, *Hungary* **31 D14** 47 40N 21 30 E
Hajdúdurog, *Hungary* **31 D14** 47 48N 21 30 E
Hajdúnánás, *Hungary* **31 D14** 47 50N 21 26 E
Hajdúsámson, *Hungary* **31 D14** 47 37N 21 42 E
Hajdúszoboszló, *Hungary* **31 D14** 47 27N 21 22 E
Hajiganj, *Bangla.* **78 D3** 23 15N 90 50 E
Hajipur, *India* **81 G11** 25 45N 85 13 E
Ḩajjah, *Yemen* **86 D3** 15 42N 43 36 E
Ḩājjī Muḩsin, *Iraq* **84 C5** 32 35N 45 29 E
Ḩājjīābād, *Esfahan, Iran* **85 C7** 33 41N 54 50 E
Ḩājjīābād, *Hormozgān, Iran* **85 D7** 28 19N 55 55 E
Hajnówka, *Poland* **47 C10** 52 47N 23 35 E
Ḩajrah, *Si. Arabia* **86 B3** 20 14N 41 3 E
Haka, *Burma* **78 D4** 22 39N 93 37 E
Hakansson, Mts., *Zaïre* **103 D5** 8 40 S 25 45 E
Håkantorp, *Sweden* **15 F6** 58 18N 12 55 E
Hakataramea, *N.Z.* **119 E5** 44 43 S 170 30 E
Ḩakkan, *Oman* **87 B7** 20 22N 58 47 E
Hakkâri, *Turkey* **89 E10** 37 34N 43 44 E
Hakkâri □, *Turkey* **89 E10** 37 30N 44 0 E
Hakkâri Dağları, *Turkey* **89 E10** 37 45N 42 35 E
Hakken-Zan, *Japan* **63 C7** 34 10N 135 54 E
Hakodate, *Japan* **60 D10** 41 45N 140 44 E
Hakota, *Japan* **63 A12** 36 5N 140 30 E
Haku-San, *Japan* **63 A8** 36 9N 136 46 E
Hakui, *Japan* **61 F8** 36 53N 136 47 E
Hakun, *Burma* **78 B5** 26 46N 95 42 E
Hala, *Pakistan* **79 D3** 25 43N 68 20 E
Ḩalab, *Syria* **84 B3** 36 10N 37 15 E
Ḩalaban, *Si. Arabia* **86 B4** 23 29N 44 23 E
Ḩalabjah, *Iraq* **84 C5** 35 10N 45 58 E
Halaib, *Sudan* **94 C4** 22 12N 36 30 E
Halanzy, *Belgium* **21 J7** 49 33N 5 44 E
Hālāt' Ammār, *Si. Arabia* **84 D3** 29 10N 36 4 E
Halbā, *Lebanon* **91 A5** 34 34N 36 6 E
Halberstadt, *Germany* **26 D7** 51 53N 11 2 E
Halcombe, *N.Z.* **118 G4** 40 8 S 175 30 E
Halcon, Mt., *Phil.* **70 E3** 13 0N 121 30 E
Halden, *Norway* **14 E5** 59 9N 11 23 E
Haldensleben, *Germany* **26 C7** 52 17N 11 30 E
Haldwani, *India* **81 E8** 29 31N 79 30 E
Hale, *U.S.A.* **140 E3** 39 36N 93 20W
Hale →, *Australia* **114 C2** 24 56 S 135 53 E
Haleakala Crater, *U.S.A.* **132 H16** 20 43N 156 16W
Halen, *Belgium* **21 G6** 50 57N 5 6 E
Haleyville, *U.S.A.* **135 H2** 34 14N 87 37W
Half Assini, *Ghana* **100 D4** 5 1N 2 50W
Halfmoon Bay, *N.Z.* **119 G3** 46 50 S 168 5 E
Halfway →, *Canada* **130 B4** 56 12N 121 32W
Haliburton, *Canada* **128 C4** 45 3N 78 30W
Halicarnassus, *Turkey* **45 G9** 37 3N 27 30 E
Halifax, *Australia* **114 B4** 18 32 S 146 22 E
Halifax, *Canada* **129 D7** 44 38N 63 35W
Halifax, *U.K.* **16 D6** 53 43N 1 51W
Halifax B., *Australia* **114 B4** 18 50 S 147 0 E
Halifax I., *Namibia* **104 D2** 26 38 S 15 4 E
Halīl →, *Iran* **85 E8** 27 40N 58 30 E

206 Halin

Halin, *Somali Rep.* 108 C3 9 6N 48 37 E
Hall, *Austria* 30 D4 47 17N 11 30 E
Hall Beach, *Canada* 127 B11 68 46N 81 12W
Hall Pt., *Australia* 112 C3 15 40 S 124 23 E
Hallands län □, *Sweden* 15 H6 56 50N 12 50 E
Hallands Väderö, *Sweden* 15 H6 56 27N 12 34 E
Hallandsås, *Sweden* 15 H7 56 22N 13 0 E
Halle, *Belgium* 21 G4 50 44N 4 13 E
Halle, *Nordrhein-Westfalen, Germany* 26 C4 52 4N 8 20 E
Halle, *Sachsen-Anhalt, Germany* 26 D7 51 29N 12 0 E
Hällefors, *Sweden* 13 G13 59 47N 14 31 E
Hallein, *Austria* 30 D6 47 40N 13 5 E
Hällekis, *Sweden* 15 F7 58 38N 13 27 E
Hallett, *Australia* 116 B3 33 25 S 138 55 E
Hallettsville, *U.S.A.* 139 L6 29 27N 96 57W
Hällevadsholm, *Sweden* 15 F5 58 35N 11 33 E
Hallia →, *India* 82 F4 16 55N 79 20 E
Halliday, *U.S.A.* 138 B3 47 21N 102 20W
Halliday L., *Canada* 131 A7 61 21N 108 56W
Hallim, *S. Korea* 67 H14 33 24N 126 15 E
Hallingdal →, *Norway* 13 F10 60 34N 9 12 E
Hällnäs, *Sweden* 12 D15 64 19N 19 36 E
Hallock, *U.S.A.* 131 D9 48 47N 96 57W
Halls Creek, *Australia* 112 C4 18 16 S 127 38 E
Hallstahammar, *Sweden* 14 E10 59 38N 16 15 E
Hallstatt, *Austria* 30 D6 47 33N 13 38 E
Hallstead, *U.S.A.* 137 E9 41 58N 75 45W
Halmahera, *Indonesia* 72 A3 0 40N 128 0 E
Halmeu, *Romania* 46 B4 47 57N 23 2 E
Halmstad, *Sweden* 15 H6 56 41N 12 52 E
Halq el Oued, *Tunisia* 96 A2 36 53N 10 18 E
Hals, *Denmark* 15 H4 56 59N 10 18 E
Halsafjorden, *Norway* 14 A2 63 5N 8 10 E
Hälsingborg = Helsingborg, *Sweden* 15 H6 56 3N 12 42 E
Halstad, *U.S.A.* 138 B6 47 21N 96 50W
Haltdalen, *Norway* 14 B5 62 56N 11 8 E
Haltern, *Germany* 26 D3 51 44N 7 10 E
Halul, *Qatar* 85 E7 25 40N 52 40 E
Ḥalvān, *Iran* 85 C8 33 57N 56 15 E
Ham, *France* 23 C10 49 45N 3 4 E
Ham Tan, *Vietnam* 77 G6 10 40N 107 45 E
Ham Yen, *Vietnam* 76 A5 22 4N 105 3 E
Hamab, *Namibia* 104 D2 28 7 S 19 16 E
Hamad, *Sudan* 95 D3 15 20N 33 32 E
Hamada, *Japan* 62 C4 34 56N 132 4 E
Hamadān, *Iran* 85 C6 34 52N 48 32 E
Hamadān □, *Iran* 85 C6 35 0N 49 0 E
Hamadia, *Algeria* 99 A5 35 28N 1 57 E
Hamāh, *Syria* 84 C3 35 5N 36 40 E
Hamakita, *Japan* 63 C9 34 45N 137 47 E
Hamamatsu, *Japan* 63 C9 34 45N 137 45 E
Hamar, *Norway* 14 D5 60 48N 11 7 E
Hamarøy, *Norway* 12 B13 68 5N 15 38 E
Hamâta, Gebel, *Egypt* 94 C3 24 17N 35 0 E
Hamber Prov. Park, *Canada* 130 C5 52 20N 118 0W
Hamburg, *Germany* 26 B5 53 32N 9 59 E
Hamburg, *Ark., U.S.A.* 139 J9 33 14N 91 48W
Hamburg, *Iowa, U.S.A.* 138 E7 40 36N 95 39W
Hamburg, *N.Y., U.S.A.* 136 D6 42 43N 78 50W
Hamburg, *Pa., U.S.A.* 137 F9 40 33N 75 59W
Hamburg □, *Germany* 26 B6 53 30N 10 0 E
Ḥamḍ, W. al →, *Si. Arabia* 84 E3 24 55N 36 20 E
Ḥamḍah, *Si. Arabia* 86 C3 19 2N 43 36 E
Ḥamdānah, *Si. Arabia* 86 C3 19 59N 40 34 E
Hamden, *U.S.A.* 137 E12 41 23N 72 54W
Hame □ = Hämeen lääni □, *Finland* 13 F18 61 30N 24 0 E
Hämeen lääni □, *Finland* 13 F18 61 30N 24 0 E
Hämeenlinna, *Finland* 13 F18 61 0N 24 28 E
Hamélé, *Ghana* 100 C4 10 56N 2 45W
Hamelin Pool, *Australia* 113 E1 26 22 S 114 20 E
Hameln, *Germany* 26 C5 52 7N 9 24 E
Hamer Koke, *Ethiopia* 95 F4 5 15N 36 45 E
Hamerkaz □, *Israel* 91 C3 32 15N 34 55 E
Hamersley Ra., *Australia* 112 D2 22 0 S 117 45 E
Hamhung, *N. Korea* 67 E14 39 54N 127 30 E
Hami, *China* 64 B4 42 55N 93 25 E
Hamilton, *Australia* 116 D5 37 45 S 142 2 E
Hamilton, *Canada* 128 D4 43 15N 79 50W
Hamilton, *N.Z.* 118 D4 37 47 S 175 19 E
Hamilton, *U.K.* 18 F4 55 47N 4 2W
Hamilton, *Ill., U.S.A.* 140 D5 40 24N 91 21W
Hamilton, *Ind., U.S.A.* 141 C12 41 33N 84 56W
Hamilton, *Mo., U.S.A.* 138 F8 39 45N 93 59W
Hamilton, *Mo., U.S.A.* 140 E3 39 45N 94 0W
Hamilton, *Mont., U.S.A.* 142 C6 46 15N 114 10W
Hamilton, *N.Y., U.S.A.* 137 D9 42 50N 75 33W
Hamilton, *Ohio, U.S.A.* 141 E12 39 24N 84 34W
Hamilton, *Tex., U.S.A.* 139 K5 31 42N 98 7W
Hamilton →, *Australia* 114 C2 23 30 S 139 47 E
Hamilton City, *U.S.A.* 144 F4 39 45N 122 1W
Hamilton Hotel, *Australia* 114 C3 22 45 S 140 40 E
Hamilton Inlet, *Canada* 129 B8 54 0N 57 30W
Hamiota, *Canada* 131 C8 50 11N 100 38W
Hamlet, *U.S.A.* 135 H6 34 53N 79 42W
Hamley Bridge, *Australia* 116 C3 34 17 S 138 35 E
Hamlin = Hameln, *Germany* 26 C5 52 7N 9 24 E
Hamlin, *N.Y., U.S.A.* 136 C7 43 17N 77 55W
Hamlin, *Tex., U.S.A.* 139 J4 32 53N 100 8W
Hamm, *Germany* 26 D3 51 40N 7 49 E
Hammam Bouhadjar, *Algeria* 99 A4 35 23N 0 58W
Hammamet, *Tunisia* 96 A2 36 24N 10 38 E
Hammamet, G. de, *Tunisia* 96 A2 36 10N 10 48 E
Hammarstrand, *Sweden* 14 A10 63 7N 16 20 E
Hamme, *Belgium* 21 F4 51 6N 4 8 E
Hamme-Mille, *Belgium* 21 G5 50 47N 4 43 E
Hammel, *Denmark* 15 H3 56 16N 9 52 E
Hammelburg, *Germany* 27 E5 50 7N 9 54 E
Hammerfest, *Norway* 12 A17 70 39N 23 41 E
Hammond, *Ill., U.S.A.* 141 E8 39 48N 88 36W
Hammond, *Ind., U.S.A.* 141 C9 41 38N 87 30W
Hammond, *La., U.S.A.* 139 K9 30 30N 90 28W
Hammonton, *U.S.A.* 134 F8 39 39N 74 48W
Hamoir, *Belgium* 21 H7 50 25N 5 32 E
Hamont, *Belgium* 21 F7 51 15N 5 32 E
Hamoyet, Jebel, *Sudan* 94 D4 17 33N 38 2 E
Hampden, *N.Z.* 119 F5 45 18 S 170 50 E
Hampshire □, *U.K.* 17 F6 51 3N 1 20W
Hampshire Downs, *U.K.* 17 F6 51 10N 1 10W
Hampton, *Ark., U.S.A.* 139 J8 33 32N 92 28W
Hampton, *Iowa, U.S.A.* 140 B3 42 45N 93 13W
Hampton, *N.H., U.S.A.* 137 D14 42 57N 70 50W
Hampton, *S.C., U.S.A.* 135 J5 32 52N 81 7W
Hampton, *Va., U.S.A.* 134 G7 37 2N 76 21W
Hampton Tableland, *Australia* 113 F4 32 0 S 127 0 E
Ḥamrā', *Yemen* 86 D3 15 3N 43 0 E
Hamrat esh Sheykh, *Sudan* 95 E2 14 38N 27 55 E
Hamtik, *Phil.* 71 F3 10 42N 121 59 E
Hamur, *Turkey* 89 D10 39 59N 42 36 E
Hamyang, *S. Korea* 67 G14 35 32N 127 42 E
Han Jiang →, *China* 69 F11 23 25N 116 40 E
Han Shui →, *China* 69 B10 30 35N 114 18 E
Hana, *U.S.A.* 132 H17 20 45N 155 59W
Hanak, *Si. Arabia* 84 E3 25 32N 37 0 E
Hanamaki, *Japan* 60 E10 39 23N 141 7 E
Hanang, *Tanzania* 106 C4 4 30 S 35 25 E
Hanau, *Germany* 27 E4 50 8N 8 56 E
Hanbogd, *Mongolia* 66 C4 43 11N 107 10 E
Hancheng, *China* 66 G6 35 31N 110 25 E
Hanchuan, *China* 69 B9 30 40N 113 50 E
Hancock, *Mich., U.S.A.* 138 B10 47 8N 88 35W
Hancock, *Minn., U.S.A.* 138 C7 45 30N 95 48W
Hancock, *N.Y., U.S.A.* 137 E9 41 57N 75 17W
Handa, *Japan* 63 C8 34 53N 136 55 E
Handa, *Somali Rep.* 90 E5 10 37N 51 2 E
Handan, *China* 66 F8 36 35N 114 28 E
Handen, *Sweden* 14 E12 59 12N 18 12 E
Handeni, *Tanzania* 106 D4 5 25 S 38 2 E
Handeni □, *Tanzania* 106 D4 5 30 S 38 0 E
Handlová, *Slovak Rep.* 31 C11 48 45N 18 35 E
Handub, *Sudan* 94 D4 19 15N 37 16 E
Handwara, *India* 81 B6 34 21N 74 20 E
Handzame, *Belgium* 21 F2 51 2N 3 0 E
Hanegev, *Israel* 91 E3 30 50N 35 0 E
Haney, *Canada* 130 D4 49 12N 122 40W
Hanford, *U.S.A.* 144 J7 36 20N 119 39W
Hang Chat, *Thailand* 76 C2 18 20N 99 21 E
Hang Dong, *Thailand* 76 C2 18 41N 98 55 E
Hangang →, *S. Korea* 67 F14 37 50N 126 30 E
Hangayn Nuruu, *Mongolia* 64 B4 47 30N 99 0 E
Hangchou = Hangzhou, *China* 69 B13 30 18N 120 11 E
Hanggin Houqi, *China* 66 D4 40 58N 107 4 E
Hanggin Qi, *China* 66 E5 39 52N 108 50 E
Hangö, *Finland* 13 G17 59 50N 22 57 E
Hangu, *China* 67 E9 39 18N 117 53 E
Hangu, *Pakistan* 79 B3 33 30N 71 10 E
Hangzhou, *China* 69 B13 30 18N 120 11 E
Hangzhou Wan, *China* 69 B13 30 15N 120 45 E
Hanhongor, *Mongolia* 66 C3 43 55N 104 28 E
Ḥanīdh, *Si. Arabia* 85 E6 26 35N 48 38 E
Ḥanīsh, *Yemen* 86 D3 13 45N 42 46 E
Haniska, *Slovak Rep.* 31 C14 48 37N 21 15 E
Hanjiang, *China* 69 E12 25 26N 119 6 E
Hankinson, *U.S.A.* 138 B6 46 4N 96 54W
Hanko = Hangö, *Finland* 13 G17 59 50N 22 57 E
Hanko, *Finland* 13 G17 59 50N 22 57 E
Hankou, *China* 69 B10 30 35N 114 30 E
Hanksville, *U.S.A.* 143 G8 38 22N 110 43W
Hanle, *India* 81 C8 32 42N 79 4 E
Hanmer Springs, *N.Z.* 119 C7 42 32 S 172 50 E
Hann →, *Australia* 112 C4 17 26 S 126 17 E
Hann, Mt., *Australia* 112 C4 15 45 S 126 0 E
Hanna, *Canada* 130 C6 51 40N 111 54W
Hannaford, *U.S.A.* 138 B5 47 19N 98 11W
Hannah, *U.S.A.* 138 A5 48 58N 98 42W
Hannah B., *Canada* 128 B4 51 40N 80 0W
Hannahs Bridge, *Australia* 117 A8 31 55 S 149 41 E
Hannibal, *U.S.A.* 140 E5 39 42N 91 22W
Hannik, *Sudan* 94 D3 18 12N 32 20 E
Hannover, *Germany* 26 C5 52 23N 9 43 E
Hannut, *Belgium* 21 G6 50 40N 5 4 E
Hanoi, *Vietnam* 64 D5 21 5N 105 55 E
Hanover = Hannover, *Germany* 26 C5 52 23N 9 43 E
Hanover, *Canada* 136 B3 44 9N 81 2W
Hanover, *S. Africa* 104 E3 31 4 S 24 29 E
Hanover, *Ind., U.S.A.* 141 F11 38 43N 85 28W
Hanover, *N.H., U.S.A.* 137 C12 43 42N 72 17W
Hanover, *Ohio, U.S.A.* 136 F2 40 4N 82 16W
Hanover, *Pa., U.S.A.* 134 F7 39 48N 76 59W
Hanover, I., *Chile* 160 D2 51 0 S 74 50W
Hanpan, C., *Papua N. G.* 120 C8 5 0 S 154 35 E
Hans Meyer Ra., *Papua N. G.* 120 C7 4 20 S 152 55 E
Hanshou, *China* 69 C8 28 56N 111 50 E
Hansi, *India* 80 E6 29 10N 75 57 E
Hanson, L., *Australia* 116 A2 31 0 S 136 15 E
Hanyang, *China* 69 B10 30 35N 114 2 E
Hanyin, *China* 68 A7 32 54N 108 28 E
Hanyū, *Japan* 63 A11 36 10N 139 32 E
Hanyuan, *China* 68 C4 29 21N 102 40 E
Hanzhong, *China* 66 H4 33 10N 107 1 E
Hanzhuang, *China* 67 G9 34 33N 117 23 E
Haora, *India* 81 H13 22 37N 88 20 E
Haoxue, *China* 69 B9 30 3N 112 24 E
Haparanda, *Sweden* 12 D18 65 52N 24 8 E
Hapert, *Neths.* 21 F6 51 22N 5 15 E
Happy, *U.S.A.* 139 H4 34 45N 101 52W
Happy Camp, *U.S.A.* 142 F2 41 48N 123 23W
Happy Valley-Goose Bay, *Canada* 129 B7 53 15N 60 20W
Hapsu, *N. Korea* 67 D15 41 13N 128 51 E
Hapur, *India* 80 E7 28 45N 77 45 E
Ḥaql, *Si. Arabia* 91 F3 29 10N 34 58 E
Haquira, *Peru* 156 C3 14 14 S 72 12W
Har, *Indonesia* 73 C4 5 16 S 133 14 E
Har-Ayrag, *Mongolia* 66 B5 45 47N 109 16 E
Har Hu, *China* 64 C4 38 20N 97 38 E
Har Us Nuur, *Mongolia* 64 B4 48 0N 92 0 E
Har Yehuda, *Israel* 91 D3 31 35N 34 57 E
Ḥaraḍ, *Si. Arabia* 87 A5 24 22N 49 0 E
Ḥaraḍ, *Yemen* 86 C3 16 26N 43 5 E
Haranomachi, *Japan* 60 F10 37 38N 140 58 E
Harardera, *Somali Rep.* 90 G4 4 33N 47 38 E
Harare, *Zimbabwe* 107 F3 17 43 S 31 2 E
Ḥarāsīs, Jiddat al, *Oman* 87 C7 19 30N 56 0 E
Harat, *Eritrea* 95 D4 16 5N 39 26 E
Harazé, *Chad* 97 G4 9 57N 20 48 E
Harazé, *Chad* 97 F3 14 20N 19 12 E
Harbin, *China* 67 B14 45 48N 126 40 E
Harbiye, *Turkey* 88 E7 36 10N 36 8 E
Harboør, *Denmark* 15 H2 56 38N 8 10 E
Harbor Beach, *U.S.A.* 134 D4 43 51N 82 39W
Harbor Springs, *U.S.A.* 134 C3 45 26N 85 0W
Harbour Breton, *Canada* 129 C8 47 29N 55 50W
Harbour Grace, *Canada* 129 C9 47 40N 53 22W
Harburg, *Germany* 26 B5 53 27N 9 58 E
Hårby, *Denmark* 15 J4 55 13N 10 7 E
Harda, *India* 80 H7 22 27N 77 5 E
Hardangerfjorden, *Norway* 13 F8 60 15N 6 0 E
Hardap Dam, *Namibia* 104 C2 24 32 S 17 50 E
Hardegarijp, *Neths.* 20 B7 53 13N 5 57 E
Harden, *Australia* 117 C8 34 32 S 148 24 E
Hardenberg, *Neths.* 20 C9 52 34N 6 37 E
Harderwijk, *Neths.* 20 D7 52 21N 5 38 E
Hardey →, *Australia* 112 D2 22 45 S 116 8 E
Hardin, *Ill., U.S.A.* 140 E6 39 10N 90 37W
Hardin, *Mont., U.S.A.* 142 D10 45 44N 107 37W
Harding, *S. Africa* 105 E4 30 35 S 29 55 E
Harding Ra., *Australia* 112 C3 16 17 S 124 55 E
Hardinsburg, *U.S.A.* 141 G10 37 47N 86 28W
Hardisty, *Canada* 130 C6 52 40N 111 18W
Hardman, *U.S.A.* 142 D4 45 10N 119 41W
Hardoi, *India* 81 F9 27 26N 80 6 E
Hardwar = Haridwar, *India* 80 E8 29 58N 78 9 E
Hardwick, *U.S.A.* 137 B12 44 30N 72 22W
Hardy, *U.S.A.* 139 G9 36 19N 91 29W
Hardy, Pen., *Chile* 160 E3 55 30 S 68 20W
Hare B., *Canada* 129 B8 51 15N 55 45W
Harelbeke, *Belgium* 21 G2 50 52N 3 20 E
Haren, *Germany* 26 C3 52 47N 7 18 E
Haren, *Neths.* 20 B9 53 11N 6 36 E
Harer, *Ethiopia* 90 F3 9 20N 42 8 E
Harerge □, *Ethiopia* 95 F5 7 12N 42 0 E
Hareto, *Ethiopia* 95 F4 9 23N 37 6 E
Harfleur, *France* 22 C7 49 30N 0 10 E
Hargeisa, *Somali Rep.* 90 F3 9 30N 44 2 E
Harghita □, *Romania* 46 C6 46 30N 25 30 E
Harghita, Mţii., *Romania* 46 C6 46 25N 25 35 E
Hargshamn, *Sweden* 13 F15 60 12N 18 30 E
Hari →, *Indonesia* 74 C2 1 16 S 104 5 E
Haria, *Canary Is.* 33 E6 29 8N 13 32W
Ḥarīb, *Yemen* 86 D4 14 56N 45 30 E
Haricha, Hamada el, *Mali* 98 D4 22 40N 3 15W
Haridwar, *India* 80 E8 29 58N 78 9 E
Harihar, *India* 83 G2 14 32N 75 44 E
Harihari, *N.Z.* 119 D5 43 9 S 170 33 E
Harima-Nada, *Japan* 62 C6 34 30N 134 35 E
Haringhata →, *Bangla.* 78 E2 22 0N 89 58 E
Haringvliet, *Neths.* 20 E4 51 48N 4 10 E
Haripad, *India* 83 K3 9 14N 76 28 E
Harīrūd →, *Asia* 85 B9 37 24N 60 38 E
Harlan, *Iowa, U.S.A.* 138 E7 41 39N 95 19W
Harlan, *Ky., U.S.A.* 135 G4 36 51N 83 19W
Harlech, *U.K.* 16 E3 52 52N 4 7W
Harlem, *U.S.A.* 142 B9 48 32N 108 47W
Harlingen, *Neths.* 20 B6 53 11N 5 25 E
Harlingen, *U.S.A.* 139 M6 26 12N 97 42W
Harlowton, *U.S.A.* 142 C9 46 26N 109 50W
Harmånger, *Sweden* 14 C11 61 55N 17 20 E
Harmil, *Eritrea* 95 D5 16 30N 40 10 E
Harney Basin, *U.S.A.* 142 E4 43 30N 119 0W
Harney L., *U.S.A.* 142 E4 43 14N 119 8W
Harney Peak, *U.S.A.* 138 D3 43 52N 103 32W
Härnön, *Sweden* 14 B12 62 36N 18 0 E
Härnösand, *Sweden* 14 B11 62 38N 17 55 E
Haro, *Spain* 34 C2 42 35N 2 55W
Harp L., *Canada* 129 A7 55 5N 61 50W
Harpanahalli, *India* 83 G3 14 47N 76 2 E
Harper, *Liberia* 100 E3 4 25N 7 43W
Harper Pass, *N.Z.* 119 C6 42 42 S 171 55 E
Harplinge, *Sweden* 15 H6 56 45N 12 45 E
Harrand, *Pakistan* 80 E4 29 28N 70 3 E
Harriman, *U.S.A.* 135 H3 35 56N 84 33W
Harrington Harbour, *Canada* 129 B8 50 31N 59 30W
Harris, *U.K.* 18 D2 57 50N 6 55W
Harris, Sd. of, *U.K.* 18 D1 57 44N 7 6W
Harris L., *Australia* 115 E2 31 10 S 135 10 E
Harris Mts., *N.Z.* 119 E3 44 49 S 168 49 E
Harrisburg, *Ill., U.S.A.* 139 G10 37 44N 88 32W
Harrisburg, *Nebr., U.S.A.* 138 E3 41 33N 103 44W
Harrisburg, *Oreg., U.S.A.* 142 D2 44 16N 123 10W
Harrisburg, *Pa., U.S.A.* 136 F8 40 16N 76 53W
Harrismith, *S. Africa* 105 D4 28 15 S 29 8 E
Harrison, *Ark., U.S.A.* 139 G8 36 14N 93 7W
Harrison, *Idaho, U.S.A.* 142 C5 47 27N 116 47W
Harrison, *Nebr., U.S.A.* 138 D3 42 41N 103 53W
Harrison, C., *Canada* 129 B8 54 55N 57 55W
Harrison Bay, *U.S.A.* 126 A4 70 40N 151 0W
Harrison L., *Canada* 130 D4 49 33N 121 50W
Harrisonburg, *U.S.A.* 134 F6 38 27N 78 52W
Harrisonville, *U.S.A.* 140 F2 38 39N 94 21W
Harriston, *Canada* 128 D3 43 57N 80 53W
Harrisville, *U.S.A.* 136 B1 44 39N 83 17W
Harrodsburg, *Ind., U.S.A.* 141 E10 39 1N 86 33W
Harrodsburg, *Ky., U.S.A.* 141 G12 37 46N 84 51W
Harrogate, *U.K.* 16 D6 53 59N 1 32W
Harrow, *U.K.* 17 F7 51 35N 0 15W
Harry S. Truman Reservoir, *U.S.A.* 140 F3 38 16N 93 24W
Harsefeld, *Germany* 26 B5 53 26N 9 31 E
Harsīn, *Iran* 84 C5 35 12N 46 34 E
Harskamp, *Neths.* 20 D7 52 8N 5 46 E
Harstad, *Norway* 12 B14 68 48N 16 30 E
Hart, *U.S.A.* 134 D2 43 42N 86 22W
Hart, L., *Australia* 116 A2 31 10 S 136 25 E
Hartbees →, *S. Africa* 104 D3 28 45 S 20 32 E
Hartberg, *Austria* 30 D8 47 17N 15 58 E
Hartford, *Conn., U.S.A.* 137 E12 41 46N 72 41W
Hartford, *Ky., U.S.A.* 134 G2 37 27N 86 55W
Hartford, *Mich., U.S.A.* 141 B10 42 13N 86 10W
Hartford, *S. Dak., U.S.A.* 138 D6 43 38N 96 57W
Hartford, *Wis., U.S.A.* 138 D10 43 19N 88 22W
Hartford City, *U.S.A.* 141 D11 40 27N 85 22W
Hartland, *Canada* 129 C6 46 20N 67 32W
Hartland, *U.S.A.* 141 A8 43 6N 88 21W
Hartland Pt., *U.K.* 17 F3 51 2N 4 32W
Hartlepool, *U.K.* 16 C6 54 42N 1 11W
Hartley Bay, *Canada* 130 C3 53 25N 129 15W
Hartmannberge, *Namibia* 104 B1 17 0 S 13 0 E
Hartney, *Canada* 131 D8 49 30N 100 35W
Harts →, *S. Africa* 104 D3 28 24 S 24 17 E
Hartselle, *U.S.A.* 135 H2 34 27N 86 56W
Hartshorne, *U.S.A.* 139 H7 34 51N 95 34W
Hartsville, *U.S.A.* 135 H5 34 23N 80 4W
Hartwell, *U.S.A.* 135 H4 34 21N 82 56W
Harunabad, *Pakistan* 80 E5 29 35N 73 8 E
Harur, *India* 83 H4 12 3N 78 29 E
Harvand, *Iran* 85 D7 28 25N 55 43 E
Harvard, *U.S.A.* 141 B8 42 25N 88 37W
Harvey, *Australia* 113 F2 33 5 S 115 54 E
Harvey, *Ill., U.S.A.* 141 C9 41 36N 87 50W
Harvey, *N. Dak., U.S.A.* 138 B5 47 47N 99 56W
Harwich, *U.K.* 17 F9 51 56N 1 18 E
Haryana □, *India* 80 E7 29 0N 76 10 E
Harz, *Germany* 26 D6 51 40N 10 40 E
Harzé, *Belgium* 21 H7 50 27N 5 40 E
Harzgerode, *Germany* 26 D7 51 38N 11 8 E
Hasaheisa, *Sudan* 95 E3 14 44N 33 20 E
Hasan Kīādeh, *Iran* 85 B6 37 24N 49 58 E
Ḥasanābād, *Iran* 85 C7 32 8N 52 44 E
Hasanpur, *India* 80 E8 28 43N 78 17 E
Haselünne, *Germany* 26 C3 52 40N 7 30 E
Hashima, *Japan* 63 B8 35 20N 136 40 E
Hashimoto, *Japan* 63 C7 34 19N 135 37 E
Hashtjerd, *Iran* 85 C6 35 52N 50 40 E
Ḥāsik, *Oman* 87 C6 17 22N 55 17 E
Håsjö, *Sweden* 14 A10 63 1N 16 5 E
Haskell, *Okla., U.S.A.* 139 H7 35 50N 95 40W
Haskell, *Tex., U.S.A.* 139 J5 33 10N 99 44W
Haslach, *Germany* 27 G4 48 16N 8 7 E
Haslev, *Denmark* 15 J5 55 18N 11 57 E
Hasparren, *France* 24 E2 43 24N 1 18W
Hassa, *Turkey* 88 E7 36 48N 36 29 E
Hasselt, *Belgium* 21 G6 50 56N 5 21 E
Hasselt, *Neths.* 20 C8 52 36N 6 6 E
Hassene, Adrar, *Algeria* 99 D5 21 0N 4 0 E
Hassfurt, *Germany* 27 E6 50 2N 10 30 E
Hassi Berrekrem, *Algeria* 99 B6 33 45N 5 16 E
Hassi bou Khelala, *Algeria* 99 B4 30 17N 0 18W
Hassi Daoula, *Algeria* 99 B6 33 4N 5 38 E
Hassi Djafou, *Algeria* 99 B5 30 55N 3 35 E
Hassi el Abiod, *Algeria* 99 B5 31 47N 3 37 E
Hassi el Biod, *Algeria* 99 C6 28 30N 6 0 E
Hassi el Gassi, *Algeria* 99 B6 30 52N 6 5 E
Hassi el Hadjar, *Algeria* 99 B5 31 28N 4 45 E
Hassi er Rmel, *Algeria* 99 B5 32 56N 3 17 E
Hassi Imoulaye, *Algeria* 99 C6 29 54N 9 10 E
Hassi Inifel, *Algeria* 99 C5 29 50N 3 41 E
Hassi Messaoud, *Algeria* 99 B6 31 43N 6 8 E
Hassi Rhénami, *Algeria* 99 B6 31 50N 5 58 E
Hassi Tartrat, *Algeria* 99 B6 30 5N 6 28 E
Hassi Zerzour, *Morocco* 98 B4 30 51N 3 56W
Hastière-Lavaux, *Belgium* 21 H5 50 13N 4 49 E
Hastings, *Australia* 117 E6 38 18 S 145 12 E
Hastings, *N.Z.* 118 F5 39 39 S 176 52 E
Hastings, *U.K.* 17 G8 50 51N 0 36 E
Hastings, *Mich., U.S.A.* 141 B11 42 39N 85 17W
Hastings, *Minn., U.S.A.* 138 C8 44 44N 92 51W
Hastings, *Nebr., U.S.A.* 138 E5 40 35N 98 23W
Hastings Ra., *Australia* 117 A10 31 15 S 152 14 E
Hat Yai, *Thailand* 77 J3 7 1N 100 27 E
Hatanbulag, *Mongolia* 66 C5 43 8N 109 5 E
Hatano, *Japan* 63 B11 35 22N 139 14 E
Hatay = Antalya, *Turkey* 88 E4 36 52N 30 45 E
Hatay □, *Turkey* 88 E7 36 25N 36 15 E
Hatch, *U.S.A.* 143 K10 32 40N 107 9W
Hatches Creek, *Australia* 114 C2 20 56 S 135 12 E
Hatchet L., *Canada* 131 B8 58 36N 103 40W
Haţeg, *Romania* 46 D3 45 36N 22 55 E
Haţeg, Mţii., *Romania* 46 D4 45 25N 23 0 E
Hatert, *Neths.* 20 E7 51 49N 5 50 E
Hateruma-Shima, *Japan* 61 M1 24 3N 123 47 E
Hatfield P.O., *Australia* 116 B5 33 54 S 143 49 E
Hatgal, *Mongolia* 64 A5 50 26N 100 9 E
Hathras, *India* 80 F8 27 36N 78 6 E
Hato de Corozal, *Colombia* 152 B3 6 11N 71 45W
Hato Mayor, *Dom. Rep.* 149 C6 18 46N 69 15W
Hattah, *Australia* 116 C5 34 48 S 142 17 E
Hattem, *Neths.* 20 D8 52 28N 6 4 E
Hatteras, C., *U.S.A.* 135 H8 35 14N 75 32W
Hattiesburg, *U.S.A.* 139 K10 31 20N 89 17W
Hatvan, *Hungary* 31 D12 47 40N 19 45 E
Hau Bon = Cheo Reo, *Vietnam* 76 F7 13 25N 108 28 E
Hau Duc, *Vietnam* 76 E7 15 20N 108 13 E
Haubstadt, *U.S.A.* 141 F9 38 12N 87 34W
Haug, *Norway* 14 D4 60 23N 10 26 E
Haugastøl, *Norway* 14 D1 60 30N 7 50 E
Haugesund, *Norway* 13 G8 59 23N 5 13 E
Hauhungaroa Ra., *N.Z.* 118 E4 38 42 S 175 40 E
Haulerwijk, *Neths.* 20 B8 53 4N 6 20 E
Haultain →, *Canada* 131 B7 55 51N 106 46W
Haungpa, *Burma* 78 C6 25 29N 96 7 E
Hauraki G., *N.Z.* 118 C4 36 35 S 175 5 E
Hausruck, *Austria* 30 C6 48 6N 13 30 E
Haut Atlas, *Morocco* 98 B3 32 30N 5 0W
Haut-Rhin □, *France* 23 E14 48 0N 7 15 E
Haut Zaïre □, *Zaïre* 106 B2 2 20N 26 0 E
Haute-Corse □, *France* 25 F13 42 30N 9 30 E
Haute-Garonne □, *France* 24 E5 43 30N 1 30 E
Haute-Loire □, *France* 24 C7 45 5N 3 50 E
Haute-Marne □, *France* 23 D12 48 10N 5 20 E
Haute-Saône □, *France* 23 E13 47 45N 6 10 E
Haute-Savoie □, *France* 25 C10 46 0N 6 20 E
Haute-Vienne □, *France* 24 C5 45 50N 1 10 E
Hauterive, *Canada* 129 C6 49 10N 68 16W
Hautes-Alpes □, *France* 25 D10 44 42N 6 20 E
Hautes Fagnes = Hohe Venn, *Belgium* 21 H8 50 30N 6 5 E
Hautes Fagnes, *Belgium* 21 G8 50 34N 6 6 E
Hautes-Pyrénées □, *France* 24 F4 43 0N 0 10 E
Hauteville-Lompnès, *France* 25 C9 45 58N 5 36 E
Hautmont, *France* 23 B10 50 15N 3 55 E
Hautrage, *Belgium* 21 H3 50 29N 3 46 E
Hauts-de-Seine □, *France* 23 D9 48 52N 2 15 E
Hauts Plateaux, *Algeria* 99 B4 35 0N 1 0 E
Hauzenberg, *Germany* 27 G9 48 39N 13 38 E
Havana = La Habana, *Cuba* 148 B3 23 8N 82 22W
Havana, *U.S.A.* 140 D6 40 18N 90 4W
Havant, *U.K.* 17 G7 50 51N 0 59W
Havasu, L., *U.S.A.* 145 L12 34 18N 114 28W

Havel →, *Germany* **26 C8** 52 40N 12 1 E
Havelange, *Belgium* **21 H6** 50 23N 5 15 E
Havelian, *Pakistan* **80 B5** 34 2N 73 10 E
Havelock, *N.B., Canada* **129 C6** 46 2N 65 24W
Havelock, *Ont., Canada* **128 D4** 44 26N 77 53W
Havelock, *N.Z.* **119 B8** 41 17 S 173 48 E
Havelock North, *N.Z.* **118 F5** 39 40 S 176 53 E
Havelte, *Neths.* **20 C8** 52 46N 6 14 E
Haverfordwest, *U.K.* **17 F3** 51 48N 4 59W
Haverhill, *U.S.A.* **137 D13** 42 47N 71 5W
Haveri, *India* **83 G2** 14 53N 75 24 E
Havering, *U.K.* **17 F8** 51 33N 0 20 E
Haverstraw, *U.S.A.* **137 E11** 41 12N 73 58W
Håverud, *Sweden* **15 F6** 58 50N 12 28 E
Havîrna, *Romania* **46 A7** 48 4N 26 43 E
Havlíčkův Brod, *Czech.* **30 B8** 49 36N 15 33 E
Havneby, *Denmark* **15 J2** 55 5N 8 34 E
Havre, *U.S.A.* **142 B9** 48 33N 109 41W
Havre-Aubert, *Canada* **129 C7** 47 12N 61 56W
Havre-St.-Pierre, *Canada* **129 B7** 50 18N 63 33W
Havza, *Turkey* **88 C6** 41 0N 35 35 E
Haw →, *U.S.A.* **135 H6** 35 36N 79 3W
Hawaii □, *U.S.A.* **132 H16** 19 30N 156 30W
Hawaii I., *Pac. Oc.* **132 J17** 20 0N 155 0W
Hawaiian Is., *Pac. Oc.* **132 H17** 20 30N 156 0W
Hawaiian Ridge, *Pac. Oc.* **123 E11** 24 0N 165 0W
Hawarden, *Canada* **131 C7** 51 25N 106 36W
Hawarden, *U.S.A.* **138 D6** 43 0N 96 29W
Hawea, L., *N.Z.* **119 E4** 44 28 S 169 19 E
Hawea Flat, *N.Z.* **119 E4** 44 40 S 169 19 E
Hawera, *N.Z.* **118 F3** 39 35 S 174 19 E
Hawesville, *U.S.A.* **141 G10** 37 54N 86 45W
Hawick, *U.K.* **18 F6** 55 25N 2 48W
Hawk Junction, *Canada* **128 C3** 48 5N 84 38W
Hawk Point, *U.S.A.* **140 F5** 38 58N 91 8W
Hawkdun Ra., *N.Z.* **119 E5** 44 53 S 170 5 E
Hawke B., *N.Z.* **118 F6** 39 25 S 177 20 E
Hawker, *Australia* **116 A3** 31 59 S 138 22 E
Hawke's Bay □, *N.Z.* **118 F5** 39 45 S 176 35 E
Hawkesbury, *Canada* **128 C5** 45 37N 74 37W
Hawkesbury I., *Canada* **130 C3** 53 37N 129 3W
Hawkesbury Pt., *Australia* **114 A1** 11 55 S 134 5 E
Hawkinsville, *U.S.A.* **135 J4** 32 17N 83 28W
Hawkwood, *Australia* **115 D5** 25 45 S 150 50 E
Hawley, *U.S.A.* **138 B6** 46 53N 96 19W
Hawrān, *Syria* **91 C5** 32 45N 36 15 E
Hawsh Mūssá, *Lebanon* **91 B4** 33 45N 35 55 E
Hawthorne, *U.S.A.* **142 G4** 38 32N 118 38W
Hawzen, *Ethiopia* **95 E4** 13 58N 39 28 E
Haxtun, *U.S.A.* **138 E3** 40 39N 102 38W
Hay, *Australia* **117 C6** 34 30 S 144 51 E
Hay →, *Australia* **114 C2** 24 50 S 138 0 E
Hay →, *Canada* **130 A5** 60 50N 116 26W
Hay, C., *Australia* **112 B4** 14 5 S 129 29 E
Hay L., *Canada* **130 B5** 58 50N 118 50W
Hay Lakes, *Canada* **130 C6** 53 12N 113 2W
Hay-on-Wye, *U.K.* **17 E4** 52 4N 3 9W
Hay River, *Canada* **130 A5** 60 51N 115 44W
Hay Springs, *U.S.A.* **138 D3** 42 41N 102 41W
Hayachine-San, *Japan* **60 E10** 39 34N 141 29 E
Hayange, *France* **23 C13** 49 20N 6 2 E
Hayato, *Japan* **62 F2** 31 40N 130 43 E
Hayden, *Ariz., U.S.A.* **143 K8** 33 0N 110 47W
Hayden, *Colo., U.S.A.* **142 F10** 40 30N 107 16W
Haydon, *Australia* **114 B3** 18 0 S 141 30 E
Hayes, *U.S.A.* **138 C4** 44 23N 101 1W
Hayes →, *Canada* **131 B10** 57 3N 92 12W
Hayjān, *Yemen* **86 C4** 16 40N 44 5 E
Haymā', *Oman* **87 C7** 19 56N 56 19 E
Haymana, *Turkey* **88 D5** 39 26N 32 31 E
Haynan, *Yemen* **87 D5** 15 50N 48 18 E
Haynesville, *U.S.A.* **139 J8** 32 58N 93 8W
Hayrabolu, *Turkey* **88 C2** 41 12N 27 5 E
Ḩayrān, *Yemen* **86 C3** 16 8N 43 5 E
Hays, *Canada* **130 C6** 50 6N 111 48W
Hays, *U.S.A.* **138 F5** 38 53N 99 20W
Ḩays, *Yemen* **86 D3** 13 56N 43 29 E
Haysville, *U.S.A.* **141 F10** 38 28N 86 55W
Hayward, *Calif., U.S.A.* **144 H4** 37 40N 122 5W
Hayward, *Wis., U.S.A.* **138 B9** 46 1N 91 29W
Haywards Heath, *U.K.* **17 F7** 51 1N 0 6W
Ḩayy, *Oman* **87 B7** 20 46N 58 18 E
Hazafon □, *Israel* **91 C4** 32 40N 35 20 E
Hazar Gölü, *Turkey* **89 D8** 38 29N 39 25 E
Hazarām, Kūh-e, *Iran* **85 D8** 29 30N 57 18 E
Hazard, *U.S.A.* **134 G4** 37 15N 83 12W
Hazaribag, *India* **81 H11** 23 58N 85 26 E
Hazaribag Road, *India* **81 G11** 24 12N 85 57 E
Hazebrouck, *France* **23 B9** 50 42N 2 31 E
Hazelton, *Canada* **130 B3** 55 20N 127 42W
Hazelton, *U.S.A.* **138 B4** 46 29N 100 17W
Hazen, *N. Dak., U.S.A.* **138 B4** 47 18N 101 38W
Hazen, *Nev., U.S.A.* **142 G4** 39 34N 119 3W
Hazerswoude, *Neths.* **20 D5** 52 5N 4 36 E
Hazlehurst, *Ga., U.S.A.* **135 K4** 31 52N 82 36W
Hazlehurst, *Miss., U.S.A.* **139 K9** 31 52N 90 24W
Hazleton, *Ind., U.S.A.* **141 F9** 38 29N 87 33W
Hazleton, *Pa., U.S.A.* **137 F9** 40 57N 75 59W
Hazlett, L., *Australia* **112 D4** 21 30 S 128 48 E
Hazor, *Israel* **91 B4** 33 2N 35 32 E
He Xian, *Anhui, China* **69 B12** 31 45N 118 20 E
He Xian, *Guangxi Zhuangzu, China* **69 E8** 24 27N 111 30 E
Head of Bight, *Australia* **113 F5** 31 30 S 131 25 E
Headlands, *Zimbabwe* **107 F3** 18 15 S 32 2 E
Healdsburg, *U.S.A.* **144 G4** 38 37N 122 52W
Healdton, *U.S.A.* **139 H6** 34 14N 97 29W
Healesville, *Australia* **117 D6** 37 35 S 145 30 E
Heanor, *U.K.* **16 D6** 53 1N 1 20W
Heard I., *Ind. Oc.* **109 K6** 53 0 S 74 0 E
Hearne, *U.S.A.* **139 K6** 30 53N 96 36W
Hearne B., *Canada* **131 A9** 60 10N 99 10W
Hearne L., *Canada* **130 A6** 62 20N 113 10W
Hearst, *Canada* **128 C3** 49 40N 83 41W
Heart →, *U.S.A.* **138 B4** 46 46N 100 50W
Heart's Content, *Canada* **129 C9** 47 54N 53 27W
Heath →, *Bolivia* **156 C4** 12 31 S 68 38W
Heath Mts., *N.Z.* **119 F2** 45 39 S 167 9 E
Heath Pt., *Canada* **129 C7** 49 8N 61 40W
Heath Steele, *Canada* **129 C6** 47 17N 66 5W
Heathcote, *Australia* **117 D6** 36 56 S 144 45 E
Heavener, *U.S.A.* **139 H7** 34 53N 94 36W
Hebbronville, *U.S.A.* **139 M5** 27 18N 98 41W
Hebei □, *China* **66 E9** 39 0N 116 0 E
Hebel, *Australia* **115 D4** 28 58 S 147 47 E
Heber, *U.S.A.* **145 N11** 32 44N 115 32W
Heber Springs, *U.S.A.* **139 H9** 35 30N 92 2W
Hebert, *Canada* **131 C7** 50 30N 107 10W
Hebgen L., *U.S.A.* **142 D8** 44 52N 111 20W
Hebi, *China* **66 G8** 35 57N 114 7 E
Hebrides, *U.K.* **18 D1** 57 30N 7 0W
Hebron = Al Khalīl, *Jordan* **91 D4** 31 32N 35 6 E
Hebron, *Canada* **127 C13** 58 5N 62 30W
Hebron, *N. Dak., U.S.A.* **138 B3** 46 54N 102 3W
Hebron, *Nebr., U.S.A.* **138 E6** 40 10N 97 35W
Hecate Str., *Canada* **130 C2** 53 10N 130 30W
Hechi, *China* **68 E7** 24 40N 108 2 E
Hechingen, *Germany* **27 G4** 48 20N 8 58 E
Hechtel, *Belgium* **21 F6** 51 8N 5 22 E
Hechuan, *China* **68 B6** 30 2N 106 12 E
Hecla, *U.S.A.* **138 C5** 45 53N 98 9W
Hecla I., *Canada* **131 C9** 51 10N 96 43W
Heddal, *Norway* **14 E3** 59 36N 9 9 E
Hédé, *France* **22 D5** 48 18N 1 49W
Hede, *Sweden* **14 B7** 62 23N 13 30 E
Hedemora, *Sweden* **13 F13** 60 18N 15 58 E
Hedgehope, *N.Z.* **119 G3** 46 12 S 168 34 E
Hedley, *U.S.A.* **139 H4** 34 52N 100 39W
Hedmark fylke □, *Norway* **14 C5** 61 17N 11 40 E
Hedrick, *U.S.A.* **140 C4** 41 11N 92 19W
Hedrum, *Norway* **14 E4** 59 7N 10 5 E
Heeg, *Neths.* **20 C7** 52 58N 5 37 E
Heegermeer, *Neths.* **20 C7** 52 56N 5 32 E
Heemskerk, *Neths.* **20 C5** 52 31N 4 40 E
Heemstede, *Neths.* **20 D5** 52 22N 4 37 E
Heer, *Neths.* **21 G7** 50 50N 5 43 E
Heerde, *Neths.* **20 D8** 52 24N 6 2 E
's Heerenburg, *Neths.* **20 E8** 51 53N 6 16 E
Heerenveen, *Neths.* **20 C7** 52 57N 5 55 E
Heerhugowaard, *Neths.* **20 C5** 52 40N 4 51 E
Heerlen, *Neths.* **21 G7** 50 55N 5 58 E
Heers, *Belgium* **21 G6** 50 45N 5 18 E
Heesch, *Neths.* **20 E7** 51 44N 5 32 E
Heestert, *Belgium* **21 G2** 50 47N 3 25 E
Heeze, *Neths.* **21 F7** 51 23N 5 35 E
Ḩefa, *Israel* **91 C3** 32 46N 35 0 E
Ḩefa □, *Israel* **91 C4** 32 40N 35 0 E
Hefei, *China* **69 B11** 31 52N 117 18 E
Hegang, *China* **65 B8** 47 20N 130 19 E
Hegyalja, *Hungary* **31 C14** 48 25N 21 25 E
Heichengzhen, *China* **66 F4** 36 24N 106 3 E
Heide, *Germany* **26 A5** 54 10N 9 7 E
Heidelberg, *Germany* **27 F4** 49 23N 8 41 E
Heidelberg, *C. Prov., S. Africa* **104 E3** 34 6 S 20 59 E
Heidelberg, *Trans., S. Africa* **105 D4** 26 30 S 28 23 E
Heidenheim, *Germany* **27 G6** 48 40N 10 10 E
Heigun-To, *Japan* **62 D4** 33 47N 132 14 E
Heijing, *China* **68 E3** 25 22N 101 44 E
Heilbron, *S. Africa* **105 D4** 27 16 S 27 59 E
Heilbronn, *Germany* **27 F5** 49 8N 9 13 E
Heiligenblut, *Austria* **30 D5** 47 2N 12 51 E
Heiligenhafen, *Germany* **26 A6** 54 21N 10 58 E
Heiligenstadt, *Germany* **26 D6** 51 22N 10 9 E
Heilongjiang □, *China* **67 B14** 48 0N 126 0 E
Heilunkiang = Heilongjiang □, *China* **67 B14** 48 0N 126 0 E
Heino, *Neths.* **20 D8** 52 26N 6 14 E
Heinola, *Finland* **13 F19** 61 13N 26 2 E
Heinsch, *Belgium* **21 J7** 49 42N 5 44 E
Heinsun, *Burma* **78 C5** 25 52N 95 35 E
Heirnkut, *Burma* **78 C5** 25 14N 94 44 E
Heishan, *China* **67 D12** 41 40N 122 5 E
Heishui, *Liaoning, China* **67 C10** 42 8N 119 30 E
Heishui, *Sichuan, China* **68 A4** 32 4N 103 2 E
Heist, *Belgium* **21 F2** 51 20N 3 15 E
Heist-op-den-Berg, *Belgium* **21 F5** 51 5N 4 44 E
Hejaz = Al Ḩijāz, *Si. Arabia* **86 A2** 26 0N 37 30 E
Hejian, *China* **66 E9** 38 25N 116 5 E
Hejiang, *China* **68 C5** 28 43N 105 46 E
Hejin, *China* **66 G6** 35 35N 110 42 E
Hekelgem, *Belgium* **21 G4** 50 55N 4 7 E
Hekimhan, *Turkey* **89 D7** 38 50N 37 55 E
Hekinan, *Japan* **63 C9** 34 52N 137 0 E
Hekla, *Iceland* **12 E4** 63 56N 19 35W
Hekou, *Gansu, China* **66 F2** 36 10N 103 28 E
Hekou, *Guangdong, China* **69 F9** 23 13N 112 45 E
Hekou, *Yunnan, China* **64 D5** 22 30N 103 59 E
Hel, *Poland* **47 A5** 54 37N 18 47 E
Helagsfjället, *Sweden* **14 B6** 62 54N 12 25 E
Helan Shan, *China* **66 E3** 38 30N 105 55 E
Helchteren, *Belgium* **21 F6** 51 4N 5 22 E
Helden, *Neths.* **21 F7** 51 19N 6 0 E
Helechosa, *Spain* **37 F6** 39 22N 4 53W
Helena, *Ark., U.S.A.* **139 H9** 34 32N 90 36W
Helena, *Mont., U.S.A.* **142 C7** 46 36N 112 2W
Helendale, *U.S.A.* **145 L9** 34 44N 117 19W
Helensburgh, *Australia* **117 C9** 34 11 S 151 1 E
Helensburgh, *U.K.* **18 E4** 56 0N 4 44W
Helensville, *N.Z.* **118 C3** 36 41 S 174 29 E
Helgeroa, *Norway* **14 F3** 59 0N 9 45 E
Helgoland, *Germany* **26 A3** 54 10N 7 51 E
Heligoland = Helgoland, *Germany* **26 A3** 54 10N 7 51 E
Heligoland B. = Deutsche Bucht, *Germany* **26 A4** 54 15N 8 0 E
Heliopolis, *Egypt* **94 H7** 30 6N 31 17 E
Hellebæk, *Denmark* **15 H6** 56 4N 12 32 E
Hellendoorn, *Neths.* **20 D8** 52 24N 6 27 E
Hellevoetsluis, *Neths.* **20 E4** 51 50N 4 8 E
Hellín, *Spain* **35 G3** 38 31N 1 40W
Helmand □, *Afghan.* **79 C2** 31 20N 64 0 E
Helmand →, *Afghan.* **79 C1** 31 12N 61 34 E
Helme →, *Germany* **26 D7** 51 40N 11 20 E
Helmond, *Neths.* **21 F7** 51 29N 5 41 E
Helmsdale, *U.K.* **18 C5** 58 7N 3 40W
Helmstedt, *Germany* **26 C7** 52 16N 11 0 E
Helnæs, *Denmark* **15 J4** 55 9N 10 0 E
Helong, *China* **67 C15** 42 40N 129 0 E
Helper, *U.S.A.* **142 G8** 39 41N 110 51W
Helsingborg, *Sweden* **15 H6** 56 3N 12 42 E
Helsinge, *Denmark* **15 H6** 56 2N 12 12 E
Helsingfors, *Finland* **13 F18** 60 15N 25 3 E
Helsingør, *Denmark* **15 H6** 56 2N 12 35 E
Helsinki, *Finland* **13 F18** 60 15N 25 3 E
Helska, Mierzeja, *Poland* **47 A5** 54 45N 18 40 E
Helston, *U.K.* **17 G2** 50 7N 5 17W
Helvellyn, *U.K.* **16 C4** 54 31N 3 1W
Helvoirt, *Neths.* **21 E6** 51 38N 5 14 E
Helwân, *Egypt* **94 J7** 29 50N 31 20 E
Hemavati →, *India* **83 H3** 12 30N 76 20 E
Hemet, *U.S.A.* **145 M10** 33 45N 116 58W
Hemingford, *U.S.A.* **138 D3** 42 19N 103 4W
Hemphill, *U.S.A.* **139 K8** 31 20N 93 51W
Hempstead, *U.S.A.* **139 K6** 30 6N 96 5W
Hemse, *Sweden* **13 H15** 57 15N 18 22 E
Hemsö, *Sweden* **14 B12** 62 43N 18 5 E
Hen & Chickens Is., *N.Z.* **118 B3** 35 58 S 174 45 E
Henan □, *China* **66 G8** 34 0N 114 0 E
Henares →, *Spain* **34 E1** 40 24N 3 30W
Henashi-Misaki, *Japan* **60 D9** 40 37N 139 51 E
Hendaye, *France* **24 E2** 43 23N 1 47W
Hendek, *Turkey* **88 C4** 40 48N 30 44 E
Henderson, *Argentina* **158 D3** 36 18 S 61 43W
Henderson, *Ky., U.S.A.* **141 G9** 37 50N 87 35W
Henderson, *N.C., U.S.A.* **135 G6** 36 20N 78 25W
Henderson, *Nev., U.S.A.* **145 J12** 36 2N 114 59W
Henderson, *Tenn., U.S.A.* **135 H1** 35 26N 88 38W
Henderson, *Tex., U.S.A.* **139 J7** 32 9N 94 48W
Hendersonville, *U.S.A.* **135 H4** 35 19N 82 28W
Hendījān, *Iran* **85 D6** 30 14N 49 43 E
Hendon, *Australia* **115 D5** 28 5 S 151 50 E
Hendorf, *Romania* **46 C5** 46 4N 24 55 E
Heng Xian, *China* **68 F7** 22 40N 109 17 E
Hengcheng, *China* **66 E4** 38 18N 106 28 E
Hengdaohezi, *China* **67 B15** 44 52N 129 0 E
Hengelo, *Gelderland, Neths.* **20 D8** 52 3N 6 19 E
Hengelo, *Overijssel, Neths.* **20 D9** 52 16N 6 48 E
Hengfeng, *China* **69 C10** 28 12N 115 48 E
Hengshan, *Hunan, China* **69 D9** 27 16N 112 45 E
Hengshan, *Shaanxi, China* **66 F5** 37 58N 109 5 E
Hengshui, *China* **66 F8** 37 41N 115 40 E
Hengyang, *Hunan, China* **69 D9** 26 52N 112 33 E
Hengyang, *Hunan, China* **69 D9** 26 59N 112 22 E
Hénin-Beaumont, *France* **23 B9** 50 25N 2 58 E
Henlopen, C., *U.S.A.* **134 F8** 38 48N 75 6W
Hennan, *Sweden* **14 B9** 62 3N 15 46 E
Hennebont, *France* **22 E3** 47 49N 3 19W
Hennenman, *S. Africa* **104 D4** 27 59 S 27 1 E
Hennepin, *U.S.A.* **140 C7** 41 15N 89 21W
Hennessey, *U.S.A.* **139 G6** 36 6N 97 54W
Hennigsdorf, *Germany* **26 C9** 52 38N 13 13 E
Henrichemont, *France* **23 E9** 47 20N 2 30 E
Henrietta, *U.S.A.* **139 J5** 33 49N 98 12W
Henrietta, Ostrov, *Russia* **57 B16** 77 6N 156 30 E
Henrietta Maria C., *Canada* **128 A3** 55 9N 82 20W
Henry, *U.S.A.* **140 C7** 41 7N 89 22W
Henryetta, *U.S.A.* **139 H6** 35 27N 95 59W
Hensall, *Canada* **136 C3** 43 26N 81 30W
Hentiyn Nuruu, *Mongolia* **65 B5** 48 30N 108 30 E
Henty, *Australia* **115 F4** 35 30 S 147 0 E
Henzada, *Burma* **78 G5** 17 38N 95 26 E
Hephaestia, *Greece* **44 E7** 39 55N 25 14 E
Heping, *China* **69 E10** 24 29N 115 0 E
Heppner, *U.S.A.* **142 D4** 45 21N 119 33W
Hepu, *China* **68 G7** 21 40N 109 12 E
Hepworth, *Canada* **136 B3** 44 37N 81 9W
Heqing, *China* **68 D3** 26 37N 100 11 E
Hequ, *China* **66 E6** 39 20N 111 15 E
Héraðsflói, *Iceland* **12 D6** 65 42N 14 12W
Héraðsvötn →, *Iceland* **12 D4** 65 45N 19 25W
Herald Cays, *Australia* **114 B4** 16 58 S 149 9 E
Herāt, *Afghan.* **79 B1** 34 20N 62 7 E
Herāt □, *Afghan.* **79 B1** 35 0N 62 0 E
Hérault □, *France* **24 E7** 43 34N 3 15 E
Hérault →, *France* **24 E7** 43 17N 3 26 E
Herbault, *France* **22 E8** 47 36N 1 8 E
Herbert →, *Australia* **114 B4** 18 31 S 146 17 E
Herbert Downs, *Australia* **114 C2** 23 7 S 139 9 E
Herberton, *Australia* **114 B4** 17 20 S 145 25 E
Herbertville, *N.Z.* **118 G5** 40 30 S 176 33 E
Herbignac, *France* **22 E4** 47 27N 2 18W
Herborn, *Germany* **26 E4** 50 40N 8 19 E
Herby, *Poland* **47 E5** 50 45N 18 50 E
Hercegnovi, *Montenegro* **42 E3** 42 30N 18 33 E
Herculaneum, *U.S.A.* **140 F6** 38 16N 90 23W
Herðubreið, *Iceland* **12 D5** 65 11N 16 21W
Hereford, *U.K.* **17 E5** 52 4N 2 42W
Hereford, *U.S.A.* **139 H3** 34 49N 102 24W
Hereford and Worcester □, *U.K.* **17 E5** 52 10N 2 30W
Herefoss, *Norway* **15 F2** 58 32N 8 23 E
Herekino, *N.Z.* **118 B2** 35 18 S 173 11 E
Herent, *Belgium* **21 G5** 50 54N 4 40 E
Herentals, *Belgium* **21 F5** 51 12N 4 51 E
Herenthout, *Belgium* **21 F5** 51 8N 4 45 E
Herfølge, *Denmark* **15 J6** 55 26N 12 9 E
Herford, *Germany* **26 C4** 52 7N 8 40 E
Héricourt, *France* **23 E13** 47 32N 6 45 E
Herington, *U.S.A.* **138 F6** 38 40N 96 57W
Herisau, *Switz.* **29 B8** 47 22N 9 17 E
Hérisson, *France* **24 B6** 46 32N 2 42 E
Herjehogna, *Norway* **13 F12** 61 43N 12 7 E
Herk →, *Belgium* **21 G6** 50 56N 5 12 E
Herkenbosch, *Neths.* **21 F8** 51 9N 6 4 E
Herkimer, *U.S.A.* **137 D10** 43 0N 74 59W
Herlong, *U.S.A.* **144 E6** 40 8N 120 8W
Herm, *Chan. Is.* **22 C4** 49 30N 2 28W
Hermagor-Pressegger See, *Austria* **30 E6** 46 38N 13 23 E
Herman, *U.S.A.* **138 C6** 45 49N 96 9W
Hermann, *U.S.A.* **138 F9** 38 42N 91 27W
Hermannsburg, *Germany* **26 C6** 52 49N 10 6 E
Hermannsburg Mission, *Australia* **112 D5** 23 57 S 132 45 E
Hermanus, *S. Africa* **104 E2** 34 27 S 19 12 E
Herment, *France* **24 C6** 45 45N 2 24 E
Hermidale, *Australia* **117 A7** 31 30 S 146 42 E
Hermiston, *U.S.A.* **142 D4** 45 51N 119 17W
Hermitage, *N.Z.* **119 D5** 43 44 S 170 5 E
Hermitage, *U.S.A.* **140 G3** 37 56N 93 19W
Hermite, I., *Chile* **160 E3** 55 50 S 68 0W
Hermon, Mt. = Ash Shaykh, J., *Lebanon* **91 B4** 33 25N 35 50 E
Hermosillo, *Mexico* **146 B2** 29 10N 111 0W
Hernád →, *Hungary* **31 D14** 47 56N 21 8 E
Hernandarias, *Paraguay* **159 B5** 25 20 S 54 40W
Hernandez, *U.S.A.* **144 J6** 36 24N 120 46W
Hernando, *Argentina* **158 C3** 32 28 S 63 40W
Hernando, *U.S.A.* **139 H10** 34 50N 90 0W
Herne, *Belgium* **21 G4** 50 44N 4 2 E
Herne, *Germany* **21 E10** 51 33N 7 12 E
Herne Bay, *U.K.* **17 F9** 51 22N 1 8 E
Herning, *Denmark* **15 H2** 56 8N 8 58 E
Heroica = Caborca, *Mexico* **146 A2** 30 40N 112 10W
Heroica Nogales = Nogales, *Mexico* **146 A2** 31 20N 110 56W
Heron Bay, *Canada* **128 C2** 48 40N 86 25W
Herradura, Pta. de la, *Canary Is.* **33 F5** 28 26N 14 8W
Herreid, *U.S.A.* **138 C4** 45 50N 100 4W
Herrera, *Spain* **37 H6** 37 26N 4 55W
Herrera de Alcántar, *Spain* **37 F3** 39 39N 7 25W
Herrera de Pisuerga, *Spain* **36 C6** 42 35N 4 20W
Herrera del Duque, *Spain* **37 F5** 39 10N 5 3W
Herrick, *Australia* **114 G4** 41 5 S 147 55 E
Herrin, *U.S.A.* **139 G10** 37 48N 89 2W
Herrljunga, *Sweden* **15 F7** 58 5N 13 1 E
Hersbruck, *Germany* **27 F7** 49 30N 11 25 E
Herseaux, *Belgium* **21 G2** 50 43N 3 15 E
Herselt, *Belgium* **21 F5** 51 3N 4 53 E
Hersonissos, *Greece* **32 D7** 35 18N 25 22 E
Herstal, *Belgium* **21 G7** 50 40N 5 38 E
Hertford, *U.K.* **17 F7** 51 47N 0 4W
Hertfordshire □, *U.K.* **17 F7** 51 51N 0 5W
's-Hertogenbosch, *Neths.* **21 E6** 51 42N 5 17 E
Hertzogville, *S. Africa* **104 D4** 28 9 S 25 30 E
Hervás, *Spain* **36 E5** 40 16N 5 52W
Herve, *Belgium* **21 G7** 50 38N 5 48 E
Herwijnen, *Neths.* **20 E6** 51 50N 5 7 E
Herzberg, *Brandenburg, Germany* **26 D9** 51 40N 13 13 E
Herzberg, *Niedersachsen, Germany* **26 D6** 51 38N 10 20 E
Herzele, *Belgium* **21 G3** 50 53N 3 53 E
Herzliyya, *Israel* **91 C3** 32 10N 34 50 E
Herzogenbuchsee, *Switz.* **28 B5** 47 11N 7 42 E
Herzogenburg, *Austria* **30 C8** 48 17N 15 41 E
Ḩeşār, *Fārs, Iran* **85 D6** 29 52N 50 16 E
Ḩeşār, *Markazī, Iran* **85 C6** 35 49N 49 24 E
Hesdin, *France* **23 B9** 50 21N 2 2 E
Hesel, *Germany* **26 B3** 53 18N 7 36 E
Heshui, *China* **66 G5** 36 0N 108 0 E
Heshun, *China* **66 F7** 37 22N 113 32 E
Hesperange, *Lux.* **21 J8** 49 35N 6 10 E
Hesperia, *U.S.A.* **145 L9** 34 25N 117 18W
Hesse = Hessen □, *Germany* **26 E5** 50 40N 9 20 E
Hessen □, *Germany* **26 E5** 50 40N 9 20 E
Hetch Hetchy Aqueduct, *U.S.A.* **144 H5** 37 29N 122 19W
Hettinger, *U.S.A.* **138 C3** 46 0N 102 42W
Hettstedt, *Germany* **26 D7** 51 39N 11 30 E
Heugem, *Neths.* **21 G7** 50 49N 5 42 E
Heule, *Belgium* **21 G2** 50 51N 3 15 E
Heusden, *Belgium* **21 F6** 51 2N 5 17 E
Heusden, *Neths.* **20 E6** 51 44N 5 8 E
Hève, C. de la, *France* **22 C7** 49 30N 0 5 E
Heverlee, *Belgium* **21 G5** 50 52N 4 42 E
Heves □, *Hungary* **31 D13** 47 50N 20 0 E
Hewett, C., *Canada* **127 A13** 70 16N 67 45W
Hexham, *U.K.* **16 C5** 54 58N 2 7W
Hexi, *Yunnan, China* **68 E4** 24 9N 102 38 E
Hexi, *Zhejiang, China* **69 D12** 27 58N 119 38 E
Hexigten Qi, *China* **67 C9** 43 18N 117 30 E
Hexrivier, *S. Africa* **104 E2** 33 30 S 19 35 E
Ḩeydarābād, *Iran* **85 D7** 30 33N 55 38 E
Heyfield, *Australia* **117 D7** 37 59 S 146 47 E
Heysham, *U.K.* **16 C5** 54 5N 2 53W
Heythuysen, *Neths.* **21 F7** 51 15N 5 55 E
Heyuan, *China* **69 F10** 23 39N 114 40 E
Heywood, *Australia* **116 E4** 38 8 S 141 37 E
Heze, *China* **66 G8** 35 14N 115 20 E
Hezhang, *China* **68 D5** 27 8N 104 41 E
Hi-no-Misaki, *Japan* **62 B4** 35 26N 132 38 E
Hi Vista, *U.S.A.* **145 L9** 34 45N 117 46W
Hialeah, *U.S.A.* **135 N5** 25 50N 80 17W
Hiawatha, *Kans., U.S.A.* **138 F7** 39 51N 95 32W
Hiawatha, *Utah, U.S.A.* **142 G8** 39 29N 111 1W
Hibbing, *U.S.A.* **138 B8** 47 25N 92 56W
Hibbs B., *Australia* **114 G4** 42 35 S 145 15 E
Hibernia Reef, *Australia* **112 B3** 12 0 S 123 23 E
Hibiki-Nada, *Japan* **62 C2** 34 0N 130 0 E
Hickory, *U.S.A.* **135 H5** 35 44N 81 21W
Hicks, Pt., *Australia* **117 D8** 37 49 S 149 17 E
Hicks Bay, *N.Z.* **118 D7** 37 34 S 178 21 E
Hicksville, *N.Y., U.S.A.* **137 F11** 40 46N 73 32W
Hicksville, *Ohio, U.S.A.* **141 C12** 41 18N 84 46W
Hida, *Romania* **46 B4** 47 10N 23 19 E
Hida-Gawa →, *Japan* **63 B9** 35 26N 137 3 E
Hida-Sammyaku, *Japan* **63 A9** 36 30N 137 40 E
Hida-Sanchi, *Japan* **63 A9** 36 10N 137 0 E
Hidaka, *Japan* **62 B6** 35 30N 134 44 E
Hidaka-Sammyaku, *Japan* **60 C11** 42 35N 142 45 E
Hidalgo, *Mexico* **147 C5** 24 15N 99 26W
Hidalgo, *U.S.A.* **141 E8** 39 9N 88 9W
Hidalgo □, *Mexico* **147 C5** 20 30N 99 10W
Hidalgo, Presa M., *Mexico* **146 B3** 26 30N 108 35W
Hidalgo, Pta. del, *Canary Is.* **33 F3** 28 33N 16 19W
Hidalgo del Parral, *Mexico* **146 B3** 26 58N 105 40W
Hiddensee, *Germany* **26 A9** 54 30N 13 6 E
Hidrolândia, *Brazil* **155 E2** 17 0 S 49 15W
Hieflau, *Austria* **30 D7** 47 36N 14 46 E
Hiendelaencina, *Spain* **34 D1** 41 5N 3 0W
Hienghène, *N. Cal.* **121 T18** 20 41 S 164 56 E
Hierapolis, *Turkey* **88 E3** 37 57N 28 50 E
Hierro, *Canary Is.* **33 G1** 27 44N 18 0W
Higashi-matsuyama, *Japan* **63 A11** 36 2N 139 25 E
Higashiajima-San, *Japan* **60 F10** 37 40N 140 10 E
Higashiōsaka, *Japan* **63 C7** 34 40N 135 37 E
Higasi-Suidō, *Japan* **62 D1** 34 0N 129 30 E
Higbee, *U.S.A.* **140 E4** 39 19N 92 31W
Higgins, *U.S.A.* **139 G4** 36 7N 100 2W
Higgins Corner, *U.S.A.* **144 F5** 39 2N 121 5W
Higginsville, *Australia* **113 F3** 31 42 S 121 38 E
Higginsville, *U.S.A.* **140 E3** 39 4N 93 43W
High Atlas = Haut Atlas, *Morocco* **98 B3** 32 30N 5 0W
High I., *Canada* **129 A7** 56 40N 61 10W
High Island, *U.S.A.* **139 L7** 29 34N 94 24W

208 High Level

High Level, *Canada* **130 B5** 58 31N 117 8W
High Point, *U.S.A.* **135 H6** 35 57N 80 0W
High Prairie, *Canada* **130 B5** 55 30N 116 30W
High River, *Canada* **130 C6** 50 30N 113 50W
High Springs, *U.S.A.* **135 L4** 29 50N 82 36W
High Tatra = Tatry,
Slovak Rep. .... **31 B12** 49 20N 20 0 E
High Wycombe, *U.K.* ... **17 F7** 51 37N 0 45W
Highbank, *N.Z.* .... **119 D6** 43 37 S 171 45 E
Highbury, *Australia* ..... **114 B3** 16 25 S 143 9 E
Highland, *Ill., U.S.A.* ... **140 F7** 38 44N 89 41W
Highland, *Ind., U.S.A.* .. **141 C9** 41 33N 87 28W
Highland, *Wis., U.S.A.* .. **140 A6** 43 5N 90 22W
Highland □, *U.K.* **18 D4** 57 30N 5 0W
Highland Park, *U.S.A.* .. **141 B9** 42 11N 87 48W
Highmore, *U.S.A.* **138 C5** 44 31N 99 27W
Highrock L., *Canada* **131 B7** 57 5N 105 32W
Higüay, *Dom. Rep.* **149 C6** 18 37N 68 42W
Hihya, *Egypt* .... **94 H7** 30 40N 31 36 E
Hiiumaa, *Estonia* .... **50 B3** 58 50N 22 45 E
Híjar, *Spain* **34 D4** 41 10N 0 27W
Ḥijāz □, *Si. Arabia* ..... **86 A2** 24 0N 40 0 E
Hijāz, Jabal al, *Si. Arabia* **86 C3** 19 45N 41 55 E
Hiji, *Japan* .... **62 D3** 33 22N 131 32 E
Hijken, *Neths.* .... **20 C8** 52 54N 6 30 E
Hijo = Tagum, *Phil.* .... **71 H5** 7 33N 125 53 E
Hikari, *Japan* .... **62 D3** 33 58N 131 58 E
Hiketa, *Japan* .... **62 C6** 34 13N 134 24 E
Hiko, *U.S.A.* **144 H11** 37 32N 115 14W
Hikone, *Japan* .... **63 B8** 35 15N 136 10 E
Hikurangi, *N.Z.* .... **118 B3** 35 36 S 174 17 E
Hikurangi, Mt., *N.Z.* .... **118 E5** 38 21 S 176 52 E
Hilawng, *Burma* .... **78 E4** 21 23N 93 48 E
Hildburghhausen,
Germany .... **27 E6** 50 24N 10 43 E
Hildesheim, *Germany* .... **26 C5** 52 9N 9 55 E
Hill →, *Australia* .... **113 F2** 30 23 S 115 3 E
Hill City, *Idaho, U.S.A.* . **142 E6** 43 18N 115 3W
Hill City, *Kans., U.S.A.* . **138 F5** 39 22N 99 51W
Hill City, *Minn., U.S.A.* . **138 B8** 46 59N 93 36W
Hill City, *S. Dak., U.S.A.* **138 D3** 43 56N 103 35W
Hill End, *Australia* ...... **117 E7** 38 1 S 146 9 E
Hill Island L., *Canada* ... **131 A7** 60 30N 109 50W
Hillared, *Sweden* .... **15 G7** 57 37N 13 10 E
Hillcrest Center, *U.S.A.* .. **145 K8** 35 23N 118 57W
Hillegom, *Neths.* .... **20 D5** 52 18N 4 35 E
Hillerød, *Denmark* ...... **15 J6** 55 56N 12 19 E
Hilli, *Bangla.* .... **78 C2** 25 17N 89 1 E
Hillingdon, *U.K.* **17 F7** 51 33N 0 29W
Hillman, *U.S.A.* **134 C4** 45 4N 83 54W
Hillmond, *Canada* **131 C7** 53 26N 109 41W
Hillsboro, *Ill., U.S.A.* ... **140 E7** 39 9N 89 29W
Hillsboro, *Iowa, U.S.A.* . **140 D5** 40 50N 91 42W
Hillsboro, *Kans., U.S.A.* . **138 F6** 38 21N 97 12W
Hillsboro, *Mo., U.S.A.* .. **140 F6** 38 14N 90 34W
Hillsboro, *N. Dak.,*
U.S.A. **138 B6** 47 26N 97 3W
Hillsboro, *N.H., U.S.A.* . **137 C13** 43 7N 71 54W
Hillsboro, *N. Mex.,*
U.S.A. **143 K10** 32 55N 107 34W
Hillsboro, *Ohio, U.S.A.* . **141 E13** 39 12N 83 37W
Hillsboro, *Oreg., U.S.A.* . **144 E4** 45 31N 122 59W
Hillsboro, *Tex., U.S.A.* .. **139 J6** 32 1N 97 8W
Hillsborough, *Grenada* .. **149 D7** 12 28N 61 28W
Hillsdale, *Mich., U.S.A.* . **141 C12** 41 56N 84 38W
Hillsdale, *N.Y., U.S.A.* .. **137 D11** 42 11N 73 30W
Hillside, *Australia* .... **112 D2** 21 45 S 119 23 E
Hillsport, *Canada* **128 C2** 49 27N 85 34W
Hillston, *Australia* ...... **117 B6** 33 30 S 145 31 E
Hilo, *U.S.A.* **132 J17** 19 44N 155 5W
Hilton, *U.S.A.* **136 C7** 43 17N 77 48W
Hilvan, *Turkey* .... **89 E8** 37 34N 38 58 E
Hilvarenbeek, *Neths.* .... **21 F6** 51 29N 5 8 E
Hilversum, *Neths.* .... **20 D6** 52 14N 5 10 E
Himachal Pradesh □,
India .... **80 D7** 31 30N 77 0 E
Himalaya, *Asia* .... **81 E11** 29 0N 84 0 E
Himamaylan, *Phil.* ...... **71 F4** 10 6N 122 52 E
Himara, *Albania* .... **44 D1** 40 8N 19 43 E
Hime-Jima, *Japan* .... **62 D3** 33 43N 131 40 E
Himeji, *Japan* .... **62 C6** 34 50N 134 40 E
Himi, *Japan* .... **63 A8** 36 50N 136 55 E
Himmerland, *Denmark* .. **15 H3** 56 45N 9 30 E
Ḥimş, *Syria* .... **91 A5** 34 40N 36 45 E
Ḥims □, *Syria* .... **91 A5** 34 30N 37 0 E
Hinatuan, *Phil.* .... **71 G6** 8 23N 126 20 E
Hinatuan Passage, *Phil.* . **71 G5** 9 45N 125 47 E
Hinche, *Haiti* **149 C5** 19 9N 72 1W
Hinchinbrook I., *Australia* **114 B4** 18 20 S 146 15 E
Hinckley, *U.K.* **17 E6** 52 33N 1 21W
Hinckley, *U.S.A.* **142 G7** 39 20N 112 40W
Hindås, *Sweden* .... **15 G6** 57 42N 12 27 E
Hindaun, *India* .... **80 F7** 26 44N 77 5 E
Hindmarsh, L., *Australia* **116 D4** 36 5 S 141 55 E
Hindol, *India* .... **82 D7** 20 40N 85 10 E
Hinds, *N.Z.* .... **119 D6** 43 59 S 171 36 E
Hindsholm, *Denmark* .... **15 J4** 55 30N 10 40 E
Hindu Bagh, *Pakistan* ... **79 C2** 30 56N 67 50 E
Hindu Kush, *Asia* .... **79 B3** 36 0N 71 0 E
Hindupur, *India* .... **83 H3** 13 49N 77 32 E
Hines Creek, *Canada* **130 B5** 56 20N 118 40W
Hinganghat, *India* .... **82 D4** 20 30N 78 52 E
Hingeon, *Belgium* .... **21 G5** 50 32N 4 59 E
Hingham, *U.S.A.* **142 B8** 48 33N 110 25W
Hingoli, *India* .... **82 E3** 19 41N 77 15 E
Hinigaran, *Phil.* .... **71 F4** 10 16N 122 50 E
Hinis, *Turkey* .... **89 D9** 39 22N 41 43 E
Hinna = Imi, *Ethiopia* .. **90 F3** 6 28N 42 10 E
Hinna, *Nigeria* .... **101 C7** 10 25N 11 35 E
Hino, *Japan* .... **63 C8** 35 0N 136 15 E
Hinojosa del Duque, *Spain* **37 G5** 38 30N 5 9W
Hinokage, *Japan* .... **62 E3** 32 39N 131 24 E
Hinsdale, *U.S.A.* **142 B10** 48 24N 107 5W
Hinterrhein →, *Switz.* .. **29 C8** 46 40N 9 25 E
Hinton, *Canada* **130 C5** 53 26N 117 34W
Hinton, *U.S.A.* **134 G5** 37 40N 80 54W
Hinuangan, *Phil.* .... **71 F5** 10 25N 125 12 E
Hinwil, *Switz.* .... **29 B7** 47 18N 8 51 E
Hınzır Burnu, *Turkey* .... **88 E6** 36 19N 35 46 E
Hippolytushoef, *Neths.* .. **20 C5** 52 54N 4 58 E
Hirado, *Japan* .... **62 D1** 33 22N 129 33 E
Hirado-Shima, *Japan* .... **62 D1** 33 20N 129 30 E
Hirakarta, *Japan* .... **63 C7** 34 48N 135 40 E
Hirakud, *India* .... **82 D6** 21 32N 83 51 E
Hirakud Dam, *India* .... **82 D6** 21 32N 83 45 E
Hirata, *Japan* .... **62 B4** 35 24N 132 49 E
Hiratsuka, *Japan* .... **63 B11** 35 19N 139 21 E
Hirfanlı Baraji, *Turkey* .. **88 D5** 39 18N 33 31 E
Hirhafok, *Algeria* .... **99 D6** 23 49N 5 45 E
Hîrlău, *Romania* .... **46 B7** 47 23N 26 55 E
Hiromi, *Japan* .... **62 D4** 33 13N 132 36 E
Hiroo, *Japan* .... **60 C11** 42 17N 143 19 E
Hirosaki, *Japan* .... **60 D10** 40 34N 140 28 E
Hiroshima, *Japan* .... **62 C4** 34 24N 132 30 E
Hiroshima □, *Japan* ..... **62 C4** 34 50N 133 0 E
Hiroshima-Wan, *Japan* .. **62 C4** 34 5N 132 20 E
Hirsholmene, *Denmark* .. **15 G4** 57 30N 10 36 E
Hirson, *France* .... **23 C11** 49 55N 4 4 E
Hîrşova, *Romania* .... **46 E8** 44 40N 27 59 E
Hirtshals, *Denmark* ..... **15 G3** 57 36N 9 57 E
Hisar, *India* .... **80 E6** 29 12N 75 45 E
Hisb →, *Iraq* .... **84 D5** 31 45N 44 17 E
Ḥismá, *Si. Arabia* ...... **84 D3** 28 30N 36 0 E
Ḥisn al 'Abr, *Yemen* .... **86 C4** 16 8N 47 14 E
Ḥiṣn al Qarn, *Yemen* .... **87 D5** 15 8N 49 7 E
Hispaniola, *W. Indies* ... **149 C5** 19 0N 71 0W
Hīt, *Iraq* .... **84 C4** 33 38N 42 49 E
Hita, *Japan* .... **62 D2** 33 20N 130 58 E
Hitachi, *Japan* .... **63 A12** 36 36N 140 39 E
Hitachiota, *Japan* ...... **63 A12** 36 30N 140 30 E
Hitchin, *U.K.* **17 F7** 51 57N 0 16W
Hitoyoshi, *Japan* .... **62 E2** 32 13N 130 45 E
Hitra, *Norway* .... **12 E10** 63 30N 8 45 E
Hitzacker, *Germany* ..... **26 B7** 53 9N 11 1 E
Hiu, *Vanuatu* .... **121 C4** 13 10 S 166 35 E
Hiuchi-Nada, *Japan* .... **62 C5** 34 5N 133 20 E
Ḥiyyon, N. →, *Israel* ... **91 E4** 30 25N 35 10 E
Hjalmar L., *Canada* **131 A7** 61 33N 109 25W
Hjälmare kanal, *Sweden* . **14 E9** 59 20N 15 59 E
Hjälmaren, *Sweden* ..... **14 E9** 59 18N 15 40 E
Hjartdal, *Norway* .... **14 E2** 59 37N 8 41 E
Hjerkinn, *Norway* .... **14 B3** 62 13N 9 33 E
Hjørring, *Denmark* ...... **15 G3** 57 29N 9 59 E
Hjortkvarn, *Sweden* ..... **15 F9** 58 54N 15 26 E
Hko-ut, *Burma* .... **78 E7** 20 58N 98 2 E
Hkyenhpa, *Burma* ...... **78 B6** 27 43N 97 25 E
Hlaingbwe, *Burma* ...... **78 G6** 17 8N 97 50 E
Hlinsko, *Czech.* .... **30 B8** 49 45N 15 54 E
Hlohovec, *Slovak Rep.* .. **31 C10** 48 26N 17 49 E
Hluhluwe, *S. Africa* ..... **105 D5** 28 1 S 32 15 E
Hlwaze, *Burma* .... **78 F6** 18 54N 96 37 E
Ho, *Ghana* .... **101 D5** 6 37N 0 27 E
Ho Chi Minh City =
Phanh Bho Ho Chi
Minh, *Vietnam* .... **77 G6** 10 58N 106 40 E
Ho Thuong, *Vietnam* .... **76 C5** 19 32N 105 48 E
Hoa Binh, *Vietnam* ..... **76 B5** 20 50N 105 20 E
Hoa Da, *Vietnam* .... **77 G7** 11 16N 108 40 E
Hoa Hiep, *Vietnam* ..... **77 G5** 11 34N 105 51 E
Hoai Nhon, *Vietnam* .... **76 E7** 14 28N 109 1 E
Hoare B., *Canada* **127 B13** 65 17N 62 30W
Hobart, *Australia* .... **114 G4** 42 50 S 147 21 E
Hobart, *Ind., U.S.A.* **141 C9** 41 32N 87 15W
Hobart, *Okla., U.S.A.* ... **139 H5** 35 1N 99 6W
Hobbs, *U.S.A.* **139 J3** 32 42N 103 8W
Hobbs Coast, *Antarctica* . **7 D14** 74 50 S 131 0W
Hobo, *Colombia* **152 C2** 2 35N 75 30W
Hoboken, *Belgium* ...... **21 F4** 51 11N 4 21 E
Hoboken, *U.S.A.* **137 F10** 40 45N 74 4W
Hobro, *Denmark* .... **15 H3** 56 39N 9 46 E
Hobscheid, *Lux.* .... **21 J7** 49 42N 5 57 E
Hoburgen, *Sweden* ...... **13 H15** 56 55N 18 7 E
Hochdorf, *Switz.* .... **29 B6** 47 10N 8 17 E
Hochschwab, *Austria* .... **30 D8** 47 35N 15 0 E
Höchstadt, *Germany* .... **27 F6** 49 42N 10 48 E
Hockenheim, *Germany* .. **27 F4** 49 18N 8 33 E
Hodaka-Dake, *Japan* .... **63 A9** 36 17N 137 39 E
Hodgson, *Canada* **131 C9** 51 13N 97 36W
Hódmezövásárhely,
Hungary .... **31 E13** 46 28N 20 22 E
Hodna, Chott el, *Algeria* **99 A5** 35 30N 5 0 E
Hodna, Monts du, *Algeria* **99 A5** 35 52N 4 42 E
Hodonín, *Czech.* .... **31 C10** 48 50N 17 10 E
Hoeamdong, *N. Korea* ... **67 C16** 42 30N 130 16 E
Hœdic, I. de, *France* **22 E4** 47 20N 2 53W
Hoegaarden, *Belgium* .... **21 G5** 50 47N 4 53 E
Hoek van Holland, *Neths.* **20 E4** 52 0N 4 7 E
Hoeksche Waard, *Neths.* . **20 E4** 51 46N 4 25 E
Hoenderloo, *Neths.* ..... **20 D7** 52 7N 5 52 E
Hoengsŏng, *S. Korea* .... **67 F14** 37 29N 127 59 E
Hoensbroek, *Neths.* ..... **21 G7** 50 55N 5 55 E
Hoeryong, *N. Korea* ..... **67 C15** 42 30N 129 45 E
Hoeselt, *Belgium* .... **21 G6** 50 51N 5 29 E
Hoeven, *Neths.* .... **21 E5** 51 35N 4 35 E
Hoeyang, *N. Korea* ..... **67 E14** 38 43N 127 36 E
Hof, *Germany* .... **27 E7** 50 18N 11 55 E
Hof, *Iceland* **12 D6** 64 33N 14 40W
Höfðakaupstaður, *Iceland* **12 D3** 65 50N 20 19W
Hofgeismar, *Germany* ... **26 D5** 51 29N 9 23 E
Hofmeyr, *S. Africa* ..... **104 E4** 31 39 S 25 50 E
Hofsjökull, *Iceland* **12 D4** 64 49N 18 48W
Hofsós, *Iceland* **12 D4** 65 53N 19 26W
Hōfu, *Japan* .... **62 C3** 34 3N 131 34 E
Hogan Group, *Australia* . **114 F4** 39 13 S 147 1 E
Hogansville, *U.S.A.* **135 J3** 33 10N 84 55W
Hogeland, *U.S.A.* **142 B9** 48 51N 108 40W
Hogenakai Falls, *India* .. **83 H3** 12 6N 77 50 E
Hoggar = Ahaggar,
Algeria .... **99 D6** 23 0N 6 30 E
Hōgo-Kaikyō, *Japan* .... **62 D3** 33 20N 131 58 E
Högsäter, *Sweden* .... **15 F6** 58 38N 12 5 E
Hogsty Reef, *Bahamas* .. **149 B5** 21 41N 73 48W
Hoh →, *U.S.A.* **144 C2** 47 45N 124 29W
Hohe Rhön, *Germany* ... **27 E5** 50 24N 9 58 E
Hohe Tauern, *Austria* ... **30 D5** 47 11N 12 40 E
Hohe Venn, *Belgium* .... **21 H8** 50 30N 6 5 E
Hohenau, *Austria* .... **31 C9** 48 36N 16 55 E
Hohenems, *Austria* ...... **30 D2** 47 22N 9 42 E
Hohenstein-Ernstthal,
Germany .... **26 E8** 50 48N 12 43 E
Hohenwald, *U.S.A.* **135 H2** 35 33N 87 33W
Hohenwestedt, *Germany* . **26 A5** 54 6N 9 30 E
Hohhot, *China* .... **66 D6** 40 52N 111 40 E
Hóhlakas, *Greece* .... **32 D9** 35 57N 27 53 E
Hohoe, *Ghana* .... **101 D5** 7 8N 0 32 E
Hoi An, *Vietnam* .... **76 E7** 15 30N 108 19 E
Hoi Xuan, *Vietnam* ..... **76 B5** 20 25N 105 9 E
Hoisington, *U.S.A.* **138 F5** 38 31N 98 47W
Højer, *Denmark* .... **15 K2** 54 58N 8 42 E
Hōjō, *Japan* .... **62 D4** 33 58N 132 46 E
Hökerum, *Sweden* ...... **15 G7** 57 51N 13 16 E
Hokianga Harbour, *N.Z.* . **118 B2** 35 31 S 173 22 E
Hokitika, *N.Z.* .... **119 C5** 42 42 S 171 0 E
Hokkaidō □, *Japan* ..... **60 C11** 43 30N 143 0 E
Hokksund, *Norway* ..... **14 E3** 59 44N 9 59 E
Hol-Hol, *Djibouti* .... **95 E5** 11 20N 42 50 E
Holbæk, *Denmark* ...... **15 J5** 55 43N 11 43 E
Holbrook, *Australia* ..... **117 C7** 35 42 S 147 18 E
Holbrook, *U.S.A.* **143 J8** 34 54N 110 10W
Holden, *Canada* **130 C6** 53 13N 112 11W
Holden, *Mo., U.S.A.* **140 F3** 38 43N 94 1W
Holden, *Utah, U.S.A.* ... **142 G7** 39 6N 112 16W
Holdenville, *U.S.A.* **139 H6** 35 5N 96 24W
Holder, *Australia* .... **116 C3** 34 21 S 140 0 E
Holderness, *U.K.* **16 D7** 53 45N 0 5W
Holdfast, *Canada* **131 C7** 50 58N 105 25W
Holdich, *Argentina* ...... **160 C3** 45 57 S 68 13W
Holdrege, *U.S.A.* **138 E5** 40 26N 99 23W
Hole-Narsipur, *India* .... **83 H3** 12 48N 76 16 E
Holešov, *Czech.* .... **31 B10** 49 20N 17 35 E
Holgate, *U.S.A.* **141 C12** 41 15N 84 8W
Holguín, *Cuba* **148 B4** 20 50N 76 20W
Holíč, *Slovak Rep.* ...... **31 C10** 48 49N 17 10 E
Hollabrunn, *Austria* ..... **30 C9** 48 34N 16 5 E
Hollams Bird I., *Namibia* **104 C1** 24 40 S 14 30 E
Holland, *U.S.A.* **141 B10** 42 47N 86 7W
Hollandia = Jayapura,
Indonesia .... **73 B6** 2 28 S 140 38 E
Hollandsch Diep, *Neths.* . **21 E5** 51 41N 4 30 E
Hollandsch IJssel →,
Neths. .... **20 E5** 51 55N 4 34 E
Hollfeld, *Germany* ...... **27 F7** 49 56N 11 18 E
Hollidaysburg, *U.S.A.* ... **136 F6** 40 26N 78 24W
Hollis, *U.S.A.* **139 H5** 34 41N 99 55W
Hollister, *Calif., U.S.A.* . **144 J5** 36 51N 121 24W
Hollister, *Idaho, U.S.A.* . **142 E6** 42 21N 114 35W
Hollum, *Neths.* .... **20 B7** 53 26N 5 38 E
Holly, *Colo., U.S.A.* **138 F3** 38 3N 102 7W
Holly, *Mich., U.S.A.* **141 B13** 42 48N 83 38W
Holly Hill, *U.S.A.* **135 L5** 29 16N 81 3W
Holly Springs, *U.S.A.* ... **139 H10** 34 46N 89 27W
Hollywood, *Calif., U.S.A.* **143 J4** 34 7N 118 25W
Hollywood, *Fla., U.S.A.* . **135 N5** 26 1N 80 9W
Holm, *Sweden* .... **14 B10** 62 40N 16 40 E
Holman Island, *Canada* .. **126 A8** 70 42N 117 41W
Hólmavík, *Iceland* **12 D3** 65 42N 21 40W
Holmes Reefs, *Australia* . **114 B4** 16 27 S 148 0 E
Holmestrand, *Norway* ... **14 E4** 59 31N 10 14 E
Holmsbu, *Norway* ...... **14 E4** 59 32N 10 27 E
Holmsjön, *Sweden* ...... **14 B9** 62 26N 15 20 E
Holmsland Klit, *Denmark* **15 J2** 56 0N 8 5 E
Holmsund, *Sweden* ...... **12 E16** 63 41N 20 20 E
Holod, *Romania* .... **46 C3** 46 49N 22 8 E
Holroyd →, *Australia* ... **114 A3** 14 10 S 141 36 E
Holstebro, *Denmark* .... **15 H2** 56 22N 8 37 E
Holsworthy, *U.K.* **17 G3** 50 48N 4 21W
Holt, *Iceland* **12 E4** 63 33N 19 48W
Holte, *Denmark* .... **15 J6** 55 50N 12 29 E
Holten, *Neths.* .... **20 D8** 52 17N 6 26 E
Holton, *Canada* **129 B8** 54 31N 57 12W
Holton, *U.S.A.* **138 F7** 39 28N 95 44W
Holtville, *U.S.A.* **145 N11** 32 49N 115 23W
Holwerd, *Neths.* .... **20 B7** 53 22N 5 54 E
Holy Cross, *U.S.A.* **126 B4** 62 12N 159 46W
Holy I., *Gwynedd, U.K.* . **16 D3** 53 17N 4 37W
Holy I., *Northumb., U.K.* **16 B6** 55 42N 1 48W
Holyhead, *U.K.* **16 D3** 53 18N 4 38W
Holyoke, *Colo., U.S.A.* .. **138 E3** 40 35N 102 18W
Holyoke, *Mass., U.S.A.* . **137 D12** 42 12N 72 37W
Holyrood, *Canada* **129 C9** 47 27N 53 8W
Holzkirchen, *Germany* .. **27 H7** 47 53N 11 42 E
Holzminden, *Germany* .. **26 D5** 51 49N 9 31 E
Homa Bay, *Kenya* ...... **106 C3** 0 36 S 34 30 E
Homa Bay □, *Kenya* .... **106 C3** 0 50 S 34 30 E
Homalin, *Burma* .... **78 C5** 24 55N 95 0 E
Homand, *Iran* .... **85 C8** 32 28N 59 37 E
Homberg, *Germany* ..... **26 D5** 51 2N 9 20 E
Hombori, *Mali* **101 B4** 15 20N 1 38W
Homburg, *Germany* ..... **27 F3** 49 19N 7 21 E
Home B., *Canada* **127 B13** 68 40N 67 10W
Home Hill, *Australia* .... **114 B4** 19 43 S 147 25 E
Home Reef, *Tonga* ...... **121 P13** 18 59 S 174 47W
Homedale, *U.S.A.* **142 E5** 43 37N 116 56W
Homer, *Alaska, U.S.A.* .. **126 C4** 59 39N 151 33W
Homer, *Ill., U.S.A.* **141 D9** 40 4N 87 57W
Homer, *La., U.S.A.* **139 J8** 32 48N 93 4W
Homer, *Mich., U.S.A.* .. **141 B12** 42 9N 84 49W
Homestead, *Australia* ... **114 C4** 20 20 S 145 40 E
Homestead, *Fla., U.S.A.* . **135 N5** 25 28N 80 29W
Homestead, *Oreg., U.S.A.* **142 D5** 45 2N 116 51W
Homewood, *Calif., U.S.A.* **144 F6** 39 4N 120 8W
Homewood, *Ill., U.S.A.* .. **141 C9** 41 34N 87 40W
Hominy, *U.S.A.* **139 G6** 36 25N 96 24W
Homnabad, *India* .... **82 F3** 17 45N 77 11 E
Homoine, *Mozam.* ...... **105 C6** 23 55 S 35 8 E
Homoljske Planina, *Serbia* **42 C6** 44 10N 21 45 E
Homonhan I., *Phil.* ..... **71 F5** 10 44N 125 43 E
Homorod, *Romania* ..... **46 C6** 46 5N 25 15 E
Homs = Ḥimş, *Syria* .... **91 A5** 34 40N 36 45 E
Homyel = Gomel,
Belorussia .... **50 E7** 52 28N 31 0 E
Hon Chong, *Vietnam* .... **77 G5** 10 25N 104 30 E
Hon Me, *Vietnam* ...... **76 C5** 19 23N 105 56 E
Hon Quan, *Vietnam* .... **77 G6** 11 40N 106 50 E
Honan = Henan □, *China* **66 G8** 34 0N 114 0 E
Honbetsu, *Japan* .... **60 C11** 43 7N 143 37 E
Honcut, *U.S.A.* **144 F5** 39 20N 121 32W
Honda, *Colombia* **152 B3** 5 12N 74 45W
Honda Bay, *Phil.* .... **71 G2** 9 53N 118 49 E
Hondeklipbaai, *S. Africa* **104 E2** 30 19 S 17 17 E
Hondo, *Japan* .... **62 E2** 32 27N 130 12 E
Hondo, *U.S.A.* **139 L5** 29 21N 99 9W
Hondo →, *Belize* **147 D7** 18 25N 88 21W
Honduras ■, *Cent. Amer.* **148 D2** 14 40N 86 30W
Honduras, G. de,
Caribbean **148 C2** 16 50N 87 0W
Hønefoss, *Norway* ...... **13 F11** 60 10N 10 18 E
Honesdale, *U.S.A.* **137 E9** 41 34N 75 16W
Honey L., *U.S.A.* **144 E6** 40 15N 120 19W
Honfleur, *France* .... **22 C7** 49 25N 0 13 E
Hong Gai, *Vietnam* ..... **76 B6** 20 57N 107 5 E
Hong He →, *China* ..... **66 H8** 32 25N 115 35 E
Hong Kong ■, *Asia* .... **69 F10** 22 11N 114 14 E
Hong'an, *China* .... **69 B10** 31 20N 114 40 E
Hongchŏn, *S. Korea* .... **67 F14** 37 44N 127 53 E
Hongha →, *Vietnam* .... **64 D5** 22 0N 104 0 E
Honghai Wan, *China* .... **69 F10** 22 40N 115 0 E
Honghu, *China* .... **69 C9** 29 50N 113 30 E
Hongjiang, *China* .... **68 D7** 27 7N 109 59 E
Hongliu He →, *China* .. **66 F5** 38 0N 109 50 E
Hongor, *Mongolia* ...... **66 B7** 45 45N 112 50 E
Hongsa, *Laos* .... **76 C3** 19 43N 101 20 E
Hongshui He →, *China* . **68 F7** 23 48N 109 30 E
Hongsŏng, *S. Korea* .... **67 F14** 36 37N 126 38 E
Hongtong, *China* .... **66 F6** 36 16N 111 40 E
Honguedo, Détroit d',
Canada **129 C7** 49 15N 64 0W
Hongwon, *N. Korea* ..... **67 E14** 40 0N 127 56 E
Hongya, *China* .... **68 C4** 29 57N 103 22 E
Hongyuan, *China* .... **68 A4** 32 51N 102 40 E
Hongze Hu, *China* ...... **67 H10** 33 15N 118 35 E
Honiara, *Solomon Is.* ... **121 M10** 9 27 S 159 57 E
Honiton, *U.K.* **17 G4** 50 48N 3 11W
Honjō, *Akita, Japan* .... **60 E10** 39 23N 140 3 E
Honjō, *Gumma, Japan* .. **63 A11** 36 14N 139 11 E
Honkawane, *Japan* ...... **63 B10** 35 5N 138 5 E
Honkorâb, Ras, *Egypt* ... **94 C4** 24 35N 35 10 E
Honolulu, *U.S.A.* **132 H16** 21 19N 157 52W
Honshū, *Japan* .... **61 G9** 36 0N 138 0 E
Hontoria del Pinar, *Spain* **34 D1** 41 50N 3 10W
Hood, Mt., *U.S.A.* **142 D3** 45 23N 121 42W
Hood, Pt., *Australia* ..... **113 F2** 34 23 S 119 34 E
Hood Pt., *Papua N. G.* .. **120 F4** 10 4 S 147 45 E
Hood River, *U.S.A.* **142 D3** 45 43N 121 31W
Hoodsport, *U.S.A.* **144 C3** 47 24N 123 9W
Hooge, *Germany* .... **26 A4** 54 31N 8 36 E
Hoogerheide, *Neths.* .... **21 F4** 51 26N 4 20 E
Hoogeveen, *Neths.* ...... **20 C8** 52 44N 6 28 E
Hoogeveensche Vaart,
Neths. .... **20 C8** 52 42N 6 12 E
Hoogezand, *Neths.* ..... **20 B9** 53 11N 6 45 E
Hooghly → =
Hughli →, *India* ..... **81 J13** 21 56N 88 4 E
Hooghly-Chinsura =
Chunchura, *India* ..... **81 H13** 22 53N 88 27 E
Hoogkerk, *Neths.* .... **20 B9** 53 13N 6 30 E
Hooglede, *Belgium* ...... **21 G2** 50 59N 3 5 E
Hoogstraten, *Belgium* ... **21 F5** 51 24N 4 46 E
Hoogvliet, *Neths.* .... **20 E4** 51 52N 4 21 E
Hook Hd., *Ireland* **19 D5** 52 8N 6 57W
Hook I., *Australia* ...... **114 C4** 20 4 S 149 0 E
Hook of Holland = Hoek
van Holland, *Neths.* ... **20 E4** 52 0N 4 7 E
Hooker, *U.S.A.* **139 G4** 36 52N 101 13W
Hooker Creek, *Australia* . **112 C5** 18 23 S 130 38 E
Hoopeston, *U.S.A.* **141 D9** 40 28N 87 40W
Hoopstad, *S. Africa* ..... **104 D4** 27 50 S 25 55 E
Hoorn, *Neths.* .... **20 C6** 52 38N 5 4 E
Hoover Dam, *U.S.A.* **145 K12** 36 1N 114 44W
Hooversville, *U.S.A.* **136 F6** 40 9N 78 55W
Hop Bottom, *U.S.A.* **137 E9** 41 42N 75 46W
Hopa, *Turkey* .... **53 F9** 41 28N 41 30 E
Hope, *Canada* **130 D4** 49 25N 121 25W
Hope, *Ariz., U.S.A.* **145 M13** 33 43N 113 42W
Hope, *Ark., U.S.A.* **139 J8** 33 40N 93 36W
Hope, *Ind., U.S.A.* **141 E11** 39 18N 85 46W
Hope, *N. Dak., U.S.A.* .. **138 B6** 47 19N 97 43W
Hope, L., *Australia* ..... **115 D2** 28 24 S 139 18 E
Hope, Pt., *U.S.A.* **126 B3** 68 20N 166 50W
Hope Pass, *N.Z.* .... **119 C7** 42 36 S 172 6 E
Hope Town, *Bahamas* ... **148 A4** 26 35N 76 57W
Hopedale, *Canada* **129 A7** 55 28N 60 13W
Hopefield, *S. Africa* ..... **104 E2** 33 3 S 18 22 E
Hopei = Hebei □, *China* **66 E9** 39 0N 116 0 E
Hopelchén, *Mexico* **147 D7** 19 46N 89 50W
Hopetoun, *Vic., Australia* **116 C5** 35 42 S 142 22 E
Hopetoun, *W. Austral.,*
Australia .... **113 F3** 33 57 S 120 7 E
Hopetown, *S. Africa* .... **104 D3** 29 34 S 24 3 E
Hopin, *Burma* .... **78 C6** 24 58N 96 30 E
Hopkins, *Mich., U.S.A.* . **141 B11** 42 37N 85 46W
Hopkins, *Mo., U.S.A.* ... **140 D2** 40 33N 94 49W
Hopkins, L., *Australia* ... **112 D4** 24 15 S 128 35 E
Hopkinsville, *U.S.A.* **135 G2** 36 52N 87 29W
Hopland, *U.S.A.* **144 G3** 38 58N 123 7W
Hoptrup, *Denmark* ..... **15 J3** 55 11N 9 28 E
Hoquiam, *U.S.A.* **144 D3** 46 59N 123 53W
Hōrai, *Japan* .... **63 C9** 34 58N 137 32 E
Horasan, *Turkey* .... **89 C10** 40 3N 42 11 E
Horazdovice, *Czech.* .... **30 B6** 49 19N 13 42 E
Horcajo de Santiago,
Spain **34 F1** 39 50N 3 1W
Hordaland fylke □,
Norway .... **13 F9** 60 25N 6 15 E
Horden Hills, *Australia* .. **112 D5** 20 15 S 130 0 E
Hordio, *Somali Rep.* .... **108 B4** 10 33N 51 6 E
Horezu, *Romania* .... **46 D5** 45 6N 24 0 E
Horgen, *Switz.* .... **29 B7** 47 15N 8 35 E
Horgoš, *Serbia* .... **42 A5** 46 10N 20 0 E
Horice, *Czech.* .... **30 A8** 50 21N 15 39 E
Horinger, *China* .... **66 D6** 40 28N 111 48 E
Horlick Mts., *Antarctica* . **7 E15** 84 0 S 102 0W
Horlivka = Gorlovka,
Ukraine .... **52 B8** 48 19N 38 5 E
Hormoz, *Iran* .... **85 E7** 27 35N 55 0 E
Hormoz, Jaz. ye, *Iran* ... **85 E8** 27 8N 56 28 E
Hormuz Str. of, *The Gulf* **85 E8** 26 30N 56 30 E
Horn, *Austria* .... **30 C8** 48 39N 15 40 E
Horn, *Ísafjarðarsýsla,*
Iceland **12 C2** 66 28N 22 28W
Horn, *Suður-Múlasýsla,*
Iceland **12 D7** 65 10N 13 31W
Horn, *Neths.* .... **21 F7** 51 12N 5 57 E
Horn →, *Canada* **130 A5** 61 30N 118 1W
Horn, Cape = Hornos, C.
de, *Chile* .... **160 E3** 55 50 S 67 30W
Horn, Is., *Wall. & F. Is.* . **111 C15** 14 16 S 178 6W
Horn Head, *Ireland* **19 A3** 55 13N 8 0W
Horn I., *Australia* ...... **114 A3** 10 37 S 142 17 E
Horn I., *U.S.A.* **135 K1** 30 14N 88 39W
Horn Mts., *Canada* **130 A5** 62 15N 119 15W
Hornachuelos, *Spain* **37 H5** 37 50N 5 14W
Hornavan, *Sweden* ..... **12 C14** 66 15N 17 30 E
Hornbæk, *Denmark* ..... **15 H6** 56 5N 12 26 E
Hornbeck, *U.S.A.* **139 K8** 31 20N 93 24W
Hornbrook, *U.S.A.* **142 F2** 41 55N 122 33W
Hornburg, *Germany* .... **26 C6** 52 2N 10 36 E
Hornby, *N.Z.* .... **119 D7** 43 33 S 172 33 E
Horncastle, *U.K.* **16 D7** 53 13N 0 8W
Hornell, *U.S.A.* **136 D7** 42 20N 77 40W

Hyargas Nuur 209

Hornell L., *Canada* **130 A5** 62 20N 119 25W
Hornepayne, *Canada* **128 C3** 49 14N 84 48W
Hornitos, *U.S.A.* **144 H6** 37 30N 120 14W
Hornos, C. de, *Chile* **160 E3** 55 50 S 67 30W
Hornoy, *France* **23 C8** 49 50N 1 54 E
Hornsby, *Australia* **117 B9** 33 42 S 151 2 E
Hornsea, *U.K.* **16 D7** 53 55N 0 10W
Hornslandet, *Sweden* **14 C11** 61 35N 17 37 E
Hornslet, *Denmark* **15 H4** 56 18N 10 19 E
Hornu, *Belgium* **21 H3** 50 26N 3 50 E
Hörnum, *Germany* **26 A4** 54 44N 8 18 E
Horobetsu, *Japan* **60 C10** 42 24N 141 6 E
Horovice, *Czech.* **30 B6** 49 48N 13 53 E
Horqin Youyi Qianqi, *China* **67 A12** 46 5N 122 3 E
Horqueta, *Paraguay* **158 A4** 23 15 S 56 55W
Horred, *Sweden* **15 G6** 57 22N 12 28 E
Horse Creek, *U.S.A.* **138 E3** 41 57N 105 10W
Horse Is., *Canada* **129 B8** 50 15N 55 50W
Horsefly L., *Canada* **130 C4** 52 25N 121 0W
Horsens, *Denmark* **15 J3** 55 52N 9 51 E
Horsens Fjord, *Denmark* **15 J4** 55 50N 10 0 E
Horsham, *Australia* **116 D5** 36 44 S 142 13 E
Horsham, *U.K.* **17 F7** 51 4N 0 20W
Horšovský Týn, *Czech.* **30 B5** 49 31N 12 58 E
Horst, *Neths.* **21 F8** 51 27N 6 3 E
Horten, *Norway* **14 E4** 59 25N 10 32 E
Hortobágy →, *Hungary* **31 D14** 47 30N 21 6 E
Horton, *U.S.A.* **138 F7** 39 40N 95 32W
Horton →, *Canada* **126 B7** 69 56N 126 52W
Horw, *Switz.* **29 B6** 47 1N 8 19 E
Horwood, L., *Canada* **128 C3** 48 5N 82 20W
Hosaina, *Ethiopia* **95 F4** 7 30N 37 47 E
Hosdurga, *India* **83 H3** 13 49N 76 17 E
Ḥoseynābād, *Khuzestān, Iran* **85 C6** 32 45N 48 20 E
Ḥoseynābād, *Kordestān, Iran* **84 C5** 35 33N 47 8 E
Hoshangabad, *India* **80 H7** 22 45N 77 45 E
Hoshiarpur, *India* **80 D6** 31 30N 75 58 E
Hosingen, *Lux.* **21 H8** 50 1N 6 6 E
Hoskins, *Papua N. G.* **120 C6** 5 29 S 150 27 E
Hosmer, *U.S.A.* **138 C5** 45 34N 99 28W
Hososhima, *Japan* **62 E3** 32 26N 131 40 E
Hospental, *Switz.* **29 C7** 46 37N 8 34 E
Hospet, *India* **83 G3** 15 15N 76 20 E
Hospitalet de Llobregat, *Spain* **34 D7** 41 21N 2 6 E
Hoste, I., *Chile* **160 E3** 55 0 S 69 0W
Hostens, *France* **24 D3** 44 30N 0 40W
Hot, *Thailand* **76 C2** 18 8N 98 29 E
Hot Creek Range, *U.S.A.* **142 G5** 38 40N 116 20W
Hot Springs, *Ark., U.S.A.* **139 H8** 34 31N 93 3W
Hot Springs, *S. Dak., U.S.A.* **138 D3** 43 26N 103 29W
Hotagen, *Sweden* **12 E13** 63 50N 14 30 E
Hotan, *China* **64 C2** 37 25N 79 55 E
Hotazel, *S. Africa* **104 D3** 27 17 S 22 58 E
Hotchkiss, *U.S.A.* **143 G10** 38 48N 107 43W
Hotham, C., *Australia* **112 B5** 12 2 S 131 18 E
Hoting, *Sweden* **12 D14** 64 8N 16 15 E
Hotolishti, *Albania* **44 C2** 41 10N 20 25 E
Hotte, Massif de la, *Haiti* **149 C5** 18 30N 73 45W
Hottentotsbaai, *Namibia* **104 D1** 26 8 S 14 59 E
Hotton, *Belgium* **21 H6** 50 16N 5 26 E
Houailou, *N. Cal.* **121 U19** 21 17 S 165 38 E
Houat, I. de, *France* **22 E4** 47 24N 2 58W
Houck, *U.S.A.* **143 J9** 35 20N 109 10W
Houdan, *France* **23 D8** 48 48N 1 35 E
Houdeng-Goegnies, *Belgium* **21 H4** 50 29N 4 10 E
Houei Sai, *Laos* **76 B3** 20 18N 100 26 E
Houffalize, *Belgium* **21 H7** 50 8N 5 48 E
Houghton, *U.S.A.* **138 B10** 47 7N 88 34W
Houghton L., *U.S.A.* **134 C3** 44 21N 84 44W
Houghton-le-Spring, *U.K.* **16 C6** 54 51N 1 28W
Houhora Heads, *N.Z.* **118 A2** 34 49 S 173 9 E
Houille →, *Belgium* **21 H5** 50 8N 4 50 E
Houlton, *U.S.A.* **129 C6** 46 8N 67 51W
Houma, *U.S.A.* **139 L9** 29 36N 90 43W
Houndé, *Burkina Faso* **100 C4** 11 34N 3 31W
Hourtin, *France* **24 C2** 45 11N 1 4W
Hourtin-Carcans, Étang d', *France* **24 C2** 45 10N 1 6W
Houston, *Canada* **130 C3** 54 25N 126 39W
Houston, *Mo., U.S.A.* **139 G9** 37 22N 91 58W
Houston, *Tex., U.S.A.* **139 L7** 29 46N 95 22W
Houten, *Neths.* **20 D6** 52 2N 5 10 E
Houthalen, *Belgium* **21 F6** 51 2N 5 23 E
Houthem, *Belgium* **21 G1** 50 48N 2 57 E
Houthulst, *Belgium* **21 G2** 50 59N 3 20 E
Houtman Abrolhos, *Australia* **113 E1** 28 43 S 113 48 E
Houyet, *Belgium* **21 H6** 50 11N 5 1 E
Hov, *Denmark* **15 J4** 55 55N 10 15 E
Hova, *Sweden* **15 F8** 58 53N 14 14 E
Høvåg, *Norway* **15 F2** 58 10N 8 16 E
Hovd, *Mongolia* **64 B4** 48 2N 91 37 E
Hove, *U.K.* **17 G7** 50 50N 0 10W
Hoveyzeh, *Iran* **85 D6** 31 27N 48 4 E
Hövsgöl, *Mongolia* **66 C5** 43 37N 109 39 E
Hövsgöl Nuur, *Mongolia* **64 A5** 51 0N 100 30 E
Howakil, *Eritrea* **95 D5** 15 10N 40 16 E
Howar, Wadi →, *Sudan* **95 D2** 17 30N 27 8 E
Howard, *Australia* **115 D5** 25 16 S 152 32 E
Howard, *Kans., U.S.A.* **139 G6** 37 28N 96 16W
Howard, *Pa., U.S.A.* **136 E7** 41 1N 77 40W
Howard, *S. Dak., U.S.A.* **138 C6** 44 1N 97 32W
Howard I., *Australia* **114 A2** 12 10 S 135 24 E
Howard L., *Canada* **131 A7** 62 15N 105 57W
Howe, *U.S.A.* **142 E7** 43 48N 113 0W
Howe, C., *Australia* **117 D9** 37 30 S 150 0 E
Howell, *U.S.A.* **141 B13** 42 36N 83 56W
Howick, *Canada* **137 A11** 45 11N 73 51W
Howick, *N.Z.* **118 C3** 36 54 S 174 56 E
Howick, *S. Africa* **105 D5** 29 28 S 30 14 E
Howick Group, *Australia* **114 A4** 14 20 S 145 30 E
Howitt, L., *Australia* **115 D2** 27 40 S 138 40 E
Howley, *Canada* **129 C8** 49 12N 57 2W
Howrah = Haora, *India* **81 H13** 22 37N 88 20 E
Howth Hd., *Ireland* **19 C5** 53 21N 6 3W
Höxter, *Germany* **26 D5** 51 45N 9 26 E
Hoy, *U.K.* **18 C5** 58 50N 3 15W
Hoya, *Germany* **26 C5** 52 47N 9 10 E
Høyanger, *Norway* **13 F9** 61 13N 6 4 E
Hoyerswerda, *Germany* **26 D10** 51 26N 14 14 E
Hoyleton, *Australia* **116 C3** 34 2 S 138 34 E
Hoyos, *Spain* **36 E4** 40 9N 6 45W
Hpawlum, *Burma* **78 B7** 27 12N 98 12 E
Hpettintha, *Burma* **78 C5** 24 14N 95 23 E
Hpizow, *Burma* **78 B7** 26 57N 98 24 E
Hradec Králové, *Czech.* **30 A8** 50 15N 15 50 E
Hrádek, *Czech.* **31 C9** 48 46N 16 16 E
Hranice, *Czech.* **31 B10** 49 34N 17 45 E
Hrodna = Grodno, *Belorussia* **50 E3** 53 42N 23 52 E
Hron →, *Slovak Rep.* **31 D11** 47 49N 18 45 E
Hrubieszów, *Poland* **47 E10** 50 49N 23 51 E
Hrubý Nizký Jeseník, *Czech.* **31 A10** 50 7N 17 10 E
Hrvatska = Croatia ■, *Europe* **39 C13** 45 20N 16 0 E
Hsenwi, *Burma* **78 D6** 23 22N 97 55 E
Hsiamen = Xiamen, *China* **69 E12** 24 25N 118 4 E
Hsian = Xi'an, *China* **66 G5** 34 15N 109 0 E
Hsinhailien = Lianyungang, *China* **67 G10** 34 40N 119 11 E
Hsipaw, *Burma* **78 D6** 22 37N 97 18 E
Hsüchou = Xuzhou, *China* **67 G9** 34 18N 117 10 E
Htawgaw, *Burma* **78 C7** 25 57N 98 23 E
Hu Xian, *China* **66 G5** 34 8N 108 42 E
Hua Hin, *Thailand* **76 F2** 12 34N 99 58 E
Hua Xian, *Henan, China* **66 G8** 35 30N 114 30 E
Hua Xian, *Shaanxi, China* **66 G5** 34 30N 109 48 E
Hua'an, *China* **69 E11** 25 1N 117 32 E
Huacaya, *Bolivia* **157 E5** 20 45 S 63 43W
Huacheng, *China* **69 E10** 24 4N 115 37 E
Huachinera, *Mexico* **146 A3** 30 9N 108 55W
Huacho, *Peru* **156 C2** 11 10 S 77 35W
Huachón, *Peru* **156 C2** 10 35 S 76 0W
Huade, *China* **66 D7** 41 55N 113 59 E
Huadian, *China* **67 C14** 43 0N 126 40 E
Huai He →, *China* **69 A12** 33 0N 118 30 E
Huai Yot, *Thailand* **77 J2** 7 45N 99 37 E
Huai'an, *Hebei, China* **66 D8** 40 30N 114 20 E
Huai'an, *Jiangsu, China* **67 H10** 33 30N 119 10 E
Huaide, *China* **67 C13** 43 30N 124 40 E
Huaidezhen, *China* **67 C13** 43 48N 124 50 E
Huaihua, *China* **68 D7** 27 32N 109 57 E
Huaiji, *China* **69 F9** 23 55N 112 12 E
Huainan, *China* **69 A11** 32 38N 116 58 E
Huaining, *China* **69 B11** 30 24N 116 40 E
Huairen, *China* **66 E7** 39 48N 113 20 E
Huairou, *China* **66 D9** 40 20N 116 35 E
Huaiyang, *China* **66 H8** 33 40N 114 52 E
Huaiyuan, *Anhui, China* **67 H9** 32 55N 117 10 E
Huaiyuan, *Guangxi Zhuangzu, China* **68 E7** 24 31N 108 22 E
Huajianzi, *China* **67 D13** 41 23N 125 20 E
Huajuapan de Leon, *Mexico* **147 D5** 17 50N 97 48W
Hualapai Peak, *U.S.A.* **143 J7** 35 5N 113 54W
Hualian, *Taiwan* **69 F13** 23 59N 121 37 E
Huallaga →, *Peru* **156 B2** 5 15 S 75 30W
Huallanca, *Peru* **156 B2** 8 50 S 77 56W
Huamachuco, *Peru* **156 B2** 7 50 S 78 5W
Huambo, *Angola* **103 E3** 12 42 S 15 54 E
Huambo □, *Angola* **103 E3** 12 50 S 16 0 E
Huan Jiang →, *China* **66 G5** 34 28N 109 0 E
Huan Xian, *China* **66 F4** 36 33N 107 7 E
Huancabamba, *Peru* **156 B2** 5 10 S 79 15W
Huancane, *Peru* **156 D4** 15 10 S 69 44W
Huancapi, *Peru* **156 C3** 13 40 S 74 0W
Huancavelica, *Peru* **156 C2** 12 50 S 75 5W
Huancavelica □, *Peru* **156 C3** 13 0 S 75 0W
Huancayo, *Peru* **156 C2** 12 5 S 75 12W
Huanchaca, *Bolivia* **156 E4** 20 15 S 66 40W
Huanchaca, Serranía de, *Bolivia* **157 C5** 14 30 S 60 39W
Huang Hai = Yellow Sea, *China* **67 G12** 35 0N 123 0 E
Huang He →, *China* **67 F10** 37 55N 118 50 E
Huang Xian, *China* **67 F11** 37 38N 120 30 E
Huangchuan, *China* **69 A10** 32 15N 115 10 E
Huanggang, *China* **69 B10** 30 29N 114 52 E
Huangling, *China* **66 G5** 35 34N 109 15 E
Huanglong, *China* **66 G5** 35 30N 109 59 E
Huanglongtan, *China* **69 A8** 32 40N 110 33 E
Huangmei, *China* **69 B10** 30 5N 115 56 E
Huangpi, *China* **69 B10** 30 50N 114 22 E
Huangping, *China* **68 D6** 26 52N 107 54 E
Huangshi, *China* **69 B10** 30 10N 115 3 E
Huangsongdian, *China* **67 C14** 43 45N 127 25 E
Huangyan, *China* **69 C13** 28 38N 121 19 E
Huangyangsi, *China* **69 D8** 26 33N 111 39 E
Huaning, *China* **68 E4** 24 17N 102 56 E
Huanjiang, *China* **68 E7** 24 50N 108 18 E
Huanta, *Peru* **156 C3** 12 55 S 74 20W
Huantai, *China* **67 F9** 36 58N 117 56 E
Huánuco, *Peru* **156 B2** 9 55 S 76 15W
Huánuco □, *Peru* **156 B2** 9 55 S 76 14W
Huanuni, *Bolivia* **156 D4** 18 16 S 66 51W
Huanzo, Cordillera de, *Peru* **156 C3** 14 35 S 73 20W
Huaping, *China* **68 D3** 26 46N 101 25 E
Huaral, *Peru* **156 C2** 11 32 S 77 13W
Huaraz, *Peru* **156 B2** 9 30 S 77 32W
Huari, *Peru* **156 B2** 9 14 S 77 14W
Huarmey, *Peru* **156 C2** 10 5 S 78 5W
Huarochiri, *Peru* **156 C2** 12 9 S 76 15W
Huarocondo, *Peru* **156 C3** 13 26 S 72 14W
Huarong, *China* **69 C9** 29 29N 112 30 E
Huascarán, *Peru* **156 B2** 9 8 S 77 36W
Huascarán, Nevado, *Peru* **156 B2** 9 7 S 77 37W
Huasco, *Chile* **158 B1** 28 30 S 71 15W
Huasco →, *Chile* **158 B1** 28 27 S 71 13W
Huasna, *U.S.A.* **145 K6** 35 6N 120 24W
Huatabampo, *Mexico* **146 B3** 26 50N 109 50W
Huauchinango, *Mexico* **147 C5** 20 11N 98 3W
Huautla de Jiménez, *Mexico* **147 D5** 18 8N 96 51W
Huaxi, *China* **68 D6** 26 25N 106 40 E
Huay Namota, *Mexico* **146 C4** 21 56N 104 30W
Huayin, *China* **66 G6** 34 35N 110 5 E
Huayllay, *Peru* **156 C2** 11 3 S 76 21W
Huayuan, *China* **68 C7** 28 37N 109 29 E
Huazhou, *China* **69 G8** 21 33N 110 33 E
Hubbard, *Iowa, U.S.A.* **140 B3** 42 18N 93 18W
Hubbard, *Tex., U.S.A.* **139 K6** 31 51N 96 48W
Hubbart Pt., *Canada* **131 B10** 59 21N 94 41W
Hubei □, *China* **69 B9** 31 0N 112 0 E
Hubli-Dharwad = Dharwad, *India* **83 G2** 15 22N 75 15 E
Huchang, *N. Korea* **67 D14** 41 25N 127 2 E
Hückelhoven, *Germany* **26 D2** 51 6N 6 13 E
Huczwa →, *Poland* **47 E10** 50 49N 23 58 E
Huddersfield, *U.K.* **16 D6** 53 38N 1 49W
Hudi, *Sudan* **94 D3** 17 43N 34 18 E
Hudiksvall, *Sweden* **14 C11** 61 43N 17 10 E
Hudson, *Canada* **131 C10** 50 6N 92 9W
Hudson, *Mass., U.S.A.* **137 D13** 42 23N 71 34W
Hudson, *Mich., U.S.A.* **141 C12** 41 51N 84 21W
Hudson, *N.Y., U.S.A.* **137 D11** 42 15N 73 46W
Hudson, *Wis., U.S.A.* **138 C8** 44 58N 92 45W
Hudson, *Wyo., U.S.A.* **142 E9** 42 54N 108 35W
Hudson →, *U.S.A.* **137 F10** 40 42N 74 2W
Hudson Bay, *N.W.T., Canada* **127 C11** 60 0N 86 0W
Hudson Bay, *Sask., Canada* **131 C8** 52 51N 102 23W
Hudson Falls, *U.S.A.* **137 C11** 43 18N 73 35W
Hudson Mts., *Antarctica* **7 D16** 74 32 S 99 20W
Hudson Str., *Canada* **127 B13** 62 0N 70 0W
Hudson's Hope, *Canada* **130 B4** 56 0N 121 54W
Hudsonville, *U.S.A.* **141 B11** 42 52N 85 52W
Hue, *Vietnam* **76 D6** 16 30N 107 35 E
Huebra →, *Spain* **36 D4** 41 2N 6 48W
Huechucuicui, Pta., *Chile* **160 B2** 41 48 S 74 2W
Huedin, *Romania* **46 C4** 46 52N 23 2 E
Huehuetenango, *Guatemala* **148 C1** 15 20N 91 28W
Huejúcar, *Mexico* **146 C4** 22 21N 103 13W
Huelgoat, *France* **22 D3** 48 22N 3 46W
Huelma, *Spain* **35 H1** 37 39N 3 28W
Huelva, *Spain* **37 H4** 37 18N 6 57W
Huelva □, *Spain* **37 H4** 37 40N 7 0W
Huelva →, *Spain* **37 H5** 37 27N 6 0W
Huentelauquén, *Chile* **158 C1** 31 38 S 71 33W
Huércal Overa, *Spain* **35 H3** 37 23N 1 57W
Huerta, Sa. de la, *Argentina* **158 C2** 31 10 S 67 30W
Huertas, C. de las, *Spain* **35 G4** 38 21N 0 24W
Huerva →, *Spain* **34 D4** 41 39N 0 52W
Huesca, *Spain* **34 C4** 42 8N 0 25W
Huesca □, *Spain* **34 C5** 42 20N 0 1 E
Huéscar, *Spain* **35 H2** 37 44N 2 35W
Huetamo, *Mexico* **146 D4** 18 36N 100 54W
Huete, *Spain* **34 E2** 40 10N 2 43W
Hugh →, *Australia* **114 D1** 25 1 S 134 1 E
Hughenden, *Australia* **114 C3** 20 52 S 144 10 E
Hughes, *Australia* **113 F4** 30 42 S 129 31 E
Hughli →, *India* **81 J13** 21 56N 88 4 E
Hugo, *U.S.A.* **138 F3** 39 8N 103 28W
Hugoton, *U.S.A.* **139 G4** 37 11N 101 21W
Hui Xian, *Gansu, China* **66 H4** 33 50N 106 4 E
Hui Xian, *Henan, China* **66 G7** 35 27N 113 12 E
Hui'an, *China* **69 E12** 25 1N 118 43 E
Hui'anbu, *China* **66 F4** 37 28N 106 38 E
Huiarau Ra., *N.Z.* **118 E5** 38 45 S 176 55 E
Huichang, *China* **69 E10** 25 32N 115 45 E
Huichapán, *Mexico* **147 C5** 20 24N 99 40W
Huidong, *China* **68 D4** 26 34N 102 35 E
Huifa He →, *China* **67 C14** 43 0N 127 50 E
Huíla, *Angola* **103 F2** 15 4 S 13 32 E
Huila □, *Colombia* **152 C2** 2 30N 75 45W
Huila, Nevado del, *Colombia* **152 C2** 3 0N 76 0W
Huilai, *China* **69 F11** 23 0N 116 18 E
Huili, *China* **68 D4** 26 35N 102 17 E
Huimin, *China* **67 F9** 37 27N 117 28 E
Huinan, *China* **67 C14** 42 40N 126 2 E
Huinca Renancó, *Argentina* **158 C3** 34 51 S 64 22W
Huining, *China* **66 G3** 35 38N 105 0 E
Huinong, *China* **66 E4** 39 5N 106 35 E
Huiroa, *N.Z.* **118 F3** 39 15 S 174 30 E
Huise, *Belgium* **21 G3** 50 54N 3 36 E
Huishui, *China* **68 D6** 26 7N 106 38 E
Huisne →, *France* **22 E7** 47 59N 0 11 E
Huissen, *Neths.* **20 E7** 51 57N 5 57 E
Huiting, *China* **66 G9** 34 5N 116 5 E
Huitong, *China* **68 D7** 26 51N 109 45 E
Huixtla, *Mexico* **147 D6** 15 9N 92 28W
Huize, *China* **68 D4** 26 24N 103 15 E
Huizen, *Neths.* **20 D6** 52 18N 5 14 E
Huizhou, *China* **69 F10** 23 0N 114 23 E
Hukou, *China* **69 C11** 29 45N 116 21 E
Hukuntsi, *Botswana* **104 C3** 23 58 S 21 45 E
Hula, *Ethiopia* **95 F4** 6 33N 38 30 E
Ḥulayfā', *Si. Arabia* **84 E4** 25 58N 40 45 E
Huld, *Mongolia* **66 B3** 45 5N 105 30 E
Hulin He →, *China* **67 B12** 45 0N 122 10 E
Hull = Kingston upon Hull, *U.K.* **16 D7** 53 45N 0 20W
Hull, *Canada* **128 C4** 45 25N 75 44W
Hull, *U.S.A.* **140 E5** 39 43N 91 13W
Hull →, *U.K.* **16 D7** 53 43N 0 25W
Hulst, *Neths.* **21 F4** 51 17N 4 2 E
Hulun Nur, *China* **65 B6** 49 0N 117 30 E
Humahuaca, *Argentina* **158 A2** 23 10 S 65 25W
Humaitá, *Brazil* **157 B5** 7 35 S 63 1W
Humaitá, *Paraguay* **158 B4** 27 2 S 58 31W
Humansdorp, *S. Africa* **104 E3** 34 2 S 24 46 E
Humansville, *U.S.A.* **140 G3** 37 48N 93 35W
Humbe, *Angola* **103 F2** 16 40 S 14 55 E
Humber →, *U.K.* **16 D7** 53 40N 0 10W
Humberside □, *U.K.* **16 D7** 53 50N 0 30W
Humbert River, *Australia* **112 C5** 16 30 S 130 45 E
Humble, *U.S.A.* **139 L8** 29 59N 93 18W
Humboldt, *Canada* **131 C7** 52 15N 105 9W
Humboldt, *Iowa, U.S.A.* **140 B2** 42 44N 94 13W
Humboldt, *Tenn., U.S.A.* **139 H10** 35 50N 88 55W
Humboldt →, *U.S.A.* **142 F4** 39 59N 118 36W
Humboldt Gletscher, *Greenland* **6 B4** 79 30N 62 0W
Humboldt Mts., *N.Z.* **119 E3** 44 30 S 168 15 E
Humbolt, Massif du, *N. Cal.* **121 U20** 21 53 S 166 25 E
Hume, *Calif., U.S.A.* **144 J8** 36 48N 118 54W
Hume, *Mo., U.S.A.* **140 F2** 38 6N 94 34W
Hume, L., *Australia* **117 D7** 36 0 S 147 5 E
Humenné, *Slovak Rep.* **31 C14** 48 55N 21 50 E
Humeston, *U.S.A.* **140 D3** 40 52N 93 30W
Humpata, *Angola* **103 F2** 15 2 S 13 24 E
Humphreys, Mt., *U.S.A.* **144 H8** 37 17N 118 40W
Humphreys Peak, *U.S.A.* **143 J8** 35 21N 111 41W
Humpolec, *Czech.* **30 B8** 49 31N 15 20 E
Humptulips, *U.S.A.* **144 C3** 47 14N 123 57W
Humula, *Australia* **117 C7** 35 30 S 147 46 E
Hūn, *Libya* **96 C3** 29 2N 16 0 E
Hun Jiang →, *China* **67 D13** 40 50N 125 38 E
Húnaflói, *Iceland* **12 D3** 65 50N 20 50W
Hunan □, *China* **69 D9** 27 30N 112 0 E
Hunchun, *China* **67 C16** 42 52N 130 28 E
Hundested, *Denmark* **15 J5** 55 58N 11 52 E
Hundred Mile House, *Canada* **130 C4** 51 38N 121 18W
Hunedoara, *Romania* **46 D3** 45 40N 22 50 E
Hunedoara □, *Romania* **46 D3** 45 50N 22 54 E
Hünfeld, *Germany* **26 E5** 50 40N 9 47 E
Hung Yen, *Vietnam* **76 B6** 20 39N 106 4 E
Hunga, *Tonga* **121 P13** 18 41 S 174 7W
Hunga Ha'api, *Tonga* **121 Q13** 20 41 S 175 7W
Hungary ■, *Europe* **31 D12** 47 20N 19 20 E
Hungary, Plain of, *Europe* **10 F9** 47 0N 20 0 E
Hungerford, *Australia* **115 D3** 28 58 S 144 24 E
Hŭngnam, *N. Korea* **67 E14** 39 49N 127 45 E
Huni Valley, *Ghana* **100 D4** 5 33N 1 56W
Hunsberge, *Namibia* **104 D2** 27 45 S 17 12 E
Hunsrück, *Germany* **27 F3** 49 30N 7 0 E
Hunstanton, *U.K.* **16 E8** 52 57N 0 30 E
Hunsur, *India* **83 H3** 12 16N 76 16 E
Hunte →, *Germany* **26 C4** 52 30N 8 19 E
Hunter, *N.Z.* **119 E6** 44 36 S 171 2 E
Hunter, *N. Dak., U.S.A.* **138 B6** 47 12N 97 13W
Hunter, *N.Y., U.S.A.* **137 D10** 42 13N 74 13W
Hunter →, *N.Z.* **119 E4** 44 21 S 169 27 E
Hunter, C., *Solomon Is.* **121 M10** 9 48 S 159 50 E
Hunter I., *Australia* **114 G3** 40 30 S 144 45 E
Hunter I., *Canada* **130 C3** 51 55N 128 0W
Hunter Mts., *N.Z.* **119 F2** 45 43 S 167 25 E
Hunter Ra., *Australia* **117 B9** 32 45 S 150 15 E
Hunters Road, *Zimbabwe* **107 F2** 19 9 S 29 49 E
Hunterville, *N.Z.* **118 F4** 39 56 S 175 35 E
Huntingburg, *U.S.A.* **141 F10** 38 18N 86 57W
Huntingdon, *Canada* **128 C5** 45 6N 74 10W
Huntingdon, *U.K.* **17 E7** 52 20N 0 11W
Huntingdon, *U.S.A.* **136 F6** 40 30N 78 1W
Huntington, *Ind., U.S.A.* **141 D11** 40 53N 85 30W
Huntington, *N.Y., U.S.A.* **137 F11** 40 52N 73 26W
Huntington, *Oreg., U.S.A.* **142 D5** 44 21N 117 16W
Huntington, *Utah, U.S.A.* **142 G8** 39 20N 110 58W
Huntington, *W. Va., U.S.A.* **134 F4** 38 25N 82 27W
Huntington Beach, *U.S.A.* **145 M8** 33 40N 118 5W
Huntington Park, *U.S.A.* **143 K4** 33 58N 118 15W
Huntley, *U.S.A.* **141 B8** 42 10N 88 26W
Huntly, *N.Z.* **118 D4** 37 34 S 175 11 E
Huntly, *U.K.* **18 D6** 57 27N 2 48W
Huntsville, *Canada* **128 C4** 45 20N 79 14W
Huntsville, *Ala., U.S.A.* **135 H2** 34 44N 86 35W
Huntsville, *Mo., U.S.A.* **140 E4** 39 26N 92 33W
Huntsville, *Tex., U.S.A.* **139 K7** 30 43N 95 33W
Hunyani →, *Zimbabwe* **107 F3** 15 57 S 30 39 E
Hunyuan, *China* **66 E7** 39 42N 113 42 E
Hunza →, *India* **81 B6** 35 54N 74 20 E
Huo Xian, *China* **66 F6** 36 36N 111 42 E
Huon G., *Papua N. G.* **120 D4** 7 0 S 147 30 E
Huon Pen., *Papua N. G.* **120 D4** 6 20 S 147 30 E
Huong Hoa, *Vietnam* **76 D6** 16 37N 106 45 E
Huong Khe, *Vietnam* **76 C5** 18 13N 105 41 E
Huonville, *Australia* **114 G4** 43 0 S 147 5 E
Huoqiu, *China* **69 A11** 32 20N 116 12 E
Huoshan, *Anhui, China* **69 A12** 32 28N 118 30 E
Huoshan, *Anhui, China* **69 B11** 31 25N 116 20 E
Huoshao Dao, *Taiwan* **69 F13** 22 40N 121 30 E
Hupeh = Hubei □, *China* **69 B9** 31 0N 112 0 E
Ḥūr, *Iran* **85 D8** 30 50N 57 7 E
Hurbanovo, *Slovak Rep.* **31 D11** 47 51N 18 11 E
Hure Qi, *China* **67 C11** 42 45N 121 45 E
Hurezani, *Romania* **46 E4** 44 49N 23 40 E
Hurghada, *Egypt* **94 B3** 27 15N 33 50 E
Hurley, *N. Mex., U.S.A.* **143 K9** 32 42N 108 8W
Hurley, *Wis., U.S.A.* **138 B9** 46 27N 90 11W
Huron, *Calif., U.S.A.* **144 J6** 36 12N 120 6W
Huron, *Ohio, U.S.A.* **136 E2** 41 24N 82 33W
Huron, *S. Dak., U.S.A.* **138 C5** 44 22N 98 13W
Huron, L., *U.S.A.* **136 B2** 44 30N 82 40W
Hurricane, *U.S.A.* **143 H7** 37 11N 113 17W
Hurso, *Ethiopia* **95 F5** 9 35N 41 33 E
Hurum, *Norway* **14 C2** 61 9N 8 46 E
Hurunui →, *N.Z.* **119 C8** 42 54 S 173 18 E
Hurup, *Denmark* **15 H2** 56 46N 8 25 E
Húsavík, *Iceland* **12 C5** 66 3N 17 21W
Huşi, *Romania* **46 C9** 46 41N 28 7 E
Huskvarna, *Sweden* **13 H13** 57 47N 14 15 E
Hussar, *Canada* **130 C6** 51 3N 112 41W
Hustopéce, *Czech.* **31 C9** 48 57N 16 43 E
Husum, *Germany* **26 A5** 54 27N 9 3 E
Husum, *Sweden* **14 A13** 63 21N 19 12 E
Hutchinson, *Kans., U.S.A.* **139 F6** 38 5N 97 56W
Hutchinson, *Minn., U.S.A.* **138 C7** 44 54N 94 22W
Ḥūth, *Yemen* **86 C3** 16 14N 43 58 E
Hutsonville, *U.S.A.* **141 E9** 39 7N 87 40W
Huttenberg, *Austria* **30 E7** 46 56N 14 33 E
Huttig, *U.S.A.* **139 J8** 33 2N 92 11W
Hutton, Mt., *Australia* **115 D4** 25 51 S 148 20 E
Huttwil, *Switz.* **28 B5** 47 7N 7 50 E
Huwun, *Ethiopia* **95 G5** 4 23N 40 6 E
Huy, *Belgium* **21 G6** 50 31N 5 15 E
Hvammur, *Iceland* **12 D3** 65 13N 21 49W
Hvar, *Croatia* **39 E13** 43 11N 16 28 E
Hvarski Kanal, *Croatia* **39 E13** 43 15N 16 35 E
Hvítá, *Iceland* **12 D3** 64 40N 21 5W
Hvítá →, *Iceland* **12 D3** 64 30N 21 58W
Hvítárvatn, *Iceland* **12 D4** 64 37N 19 50W
Hwachon-chosuji, *S. Korea* **67 E14** 38 5N 127 50 E
Hwang Ho = Huang He →, *China* **67 F10** 37 55N 118 50 E
Hwange, *Zimbabwe* **107 F2** 18 18 S 26 30 E
Hwange Nat. Park, *Zimbabwe* **104 B4** 19 0 S 26 30 E
Hwekum, *Burma* **78 B5** 26 7N 95 22 E
Hyannis, *U.S.A.* **138 E4** 42 0N 101 46W
Hyargas Nuur, *Mongolia* **64 B4** 49 0N 93 0 E

Itumbiara 211

Inglewood, Vic., Australia 116 D5 36 29 S 143 53 E
Inglewood, N.Z. 118 F3 39 9 S 174 14 E
Inglewood, U.S.A. 145 M8 33 58N 118 21W
Ingólfshöfði, Iceland 12 E5 63 48N 16 39W
Ingolstadt, Germany 27 G7 48 45N 11 26 E
Ingomar, U.S.A. 142 C10 46 35N 107 23W
Ingonish, Canada 129 C7 46 42N 60 18W
Ingore, Guinea-Biss. 100 C1 12 24N 15 48W
Ingraj Bazar, India 81 G13 24 58N 88 10 E
Ingrid Christensen Coast, Antarctica 7 C6 69 30 S 76 0 E
Ingul →, Ukraine 52 C5 46 50N 32 0 E
Ingulec, Ukraine 52 C5 47 42N 33 14 E
Ingulets →, Ukraine 52 C5 46 35N 32 48 E
Inguri →, Georgia 53 E9 42 38N 41 35 E
Ingwavuma, S. Africa 105 D5 27 9 S 31 59 E
Inhaca, I., Mozam. 105 D5 26 1 S 32 57 E
Inhafenga, Mozam. 105 C5 20 36 S 33 53 E
Inhambane, Mozam. 105 C6 23 54 S 35 30 E
Inhambane □, Mozam. 105 C5 22 30 S 34 20 E
Inhambupe, Brazil 155 D4 11 47 S 38 21W
Inhaminga, Mozam. 107 F4 18 26 S 35 0 E
Inharrime, Mozam. 105 C6 24 30 S 35 0 E
Inharrime →, Mozam. 105 C6 24 30 S 35 0 E
Inhuma, Brazil 154 C3 6 40 S 41 42W
Inhumas, Brazil 155 E2 16 22 S 49 30W
Iniesta, Spain 35 F3 39 27N 1 45W
Ining = Yining, China 56 E9 43 58N 81 10 E
Inini □, Fr. Guiana 153 C7 4 0N 53 0W
Inírida →, Colombia 152 C4 3 55N 67 52W
Inishbofin, Ireland 19 C1 53 35N 10 12W
Inishmore, Ireland 19 C2 53 8N 9 45W
Inishowen, Ireland 19 A4 55 14N 7 15W
Injune, Australia 115 D4 25 53 S 148 32 E
Inklin, Canada 130 B2 58 56N 133 5W
Inklin →, Canada 130 B2 58 50N 133 10W
Inkom, U.S.A. 142 E7 42 48N 112 15W
Inle L., Burma 78 E6 20 30N 96 58 E
Inn →, Austria 27 G9 48 35N 13 28 E
Innamincka, Australia 115 D3 27 44 S 140 46 E
Inner Hebrides, U.K. 18 D2 57 0N 6 30W
Inner Mongolia = Nei Monggol Zizhiqu □, China 66 C6 42 0N 112 0 E
Inner Sound, U.K. 18 D3 57 30N 5 55W
Innerkip, Canada 136 C4 43 13N 80 42W
Innerkirchen, Switz. 28 C6 46 43N 8 14 E
Innerste →, Germany 26 C5 52 45N 9 40 E
Innetalling I., Canada 128 A4 56 0N 79 0W
Innisfail, Australia 114 B4 17 33 S 146 5 E
Innisfail, Canada 130 C6 52 0N 113 57W
In'no-shima, Japan 62 C5 34 19N 133 10 E
Innsbruck, Austria 30 D4 47 16N 11 23 E
Inny →, Ireland 19 C4 53 30N 7 50W
Ino, Japan 62 D5 33 33N 133 26 E
Inocência, Brazil 155 E1 19 47 S 51 48W
Inongo, Zaïre 102 C3 1 55 S 18 30 E
Inoni, Congo 102 C3 3 4 S 15 39 E
Inoucdjouac, Canada 127 C12 58 25N 78 15W
Inowrocław, Poland 47 C5 52 50N 18 12 E
Inpundong, N. Korea 67 D14 41 25N 126 34 E
Inquisivi, Bolivia 156 D4 16 50 S 67 10W
Ins, Switz. 28 B4 47 1N 7 7 E
Inscription, C., Australia 113 E1 25 29 S 112 59 E
Insein, Burma 78 G6 16 50N 96 5 E
Însurăţei, Romania 46 E8 44 50N 27 40 E
Inta, Russia 48 A11 66 5N 60 8 E
Intendente Alvear, Argentina 158 D3 35 12 S 63 32W
Interior, U.S.A. 138 D4 43 44N 101 59W
Interlaken, Switz. 23 F14 46 41N 7 50 E
International Falls, U.S.A. 138 A8 48 36N 93 25W
Intiyaco, Argentina 158 B3 28 43 S 60 5W
Intragna, Switz. 29 D7 46 11N 8 42 E
Intutu, Peru 152 D3 3 32 S 74 48W
Inubō-Zaki, Japan 63 B12 35 42N 140 52 E
Inútil, B., Chile 160 D2 53 30 S 70 15W
Inuvik, Canada 126 B6 68 16N 133 40W
Inuyama, Japan 63 B8 35 23N 136 56 E
Inveraray, U.K. 18 E3 56 13N 5 5W
Inverbervie, U.K. 18 E6 56 50N 2 17W
Invercargill, N.Z. 119 G3 46 24 S 168 24 E
Inverell, Australia 115 D5 29 45 S 151 8 E
Invergordon, U.K. 18 D4 57 41N 4 10W
Inverleigh, Australia 116 E6 38 6 S 144 3 E
Invermere, Canada 130 C5 50 30N 116 2W
Inverness, Canada 129 C7 46 15N 61 19W
Inverness, U.K. 18 D4 57 29N 4 12W
Inverness, U.S.A. 135 L4 28 50N 82 20W
Inverurie, U.K. 18 D6 57 15N 2 21W
Inverway, Australia 112 C4 17 50 S 129 38 E
Investigator Group, Australia 115 E1 34 45 S 134 20 E
Investigator Str., Australia 116 C2 35 30 S 137 0 E
Inya, Russia 56 D9 50 28N 86 37 E
Inyanga, Zimbabwe 107 F3 18 12 S 32 40 E
Inyangani, Zimbabwe 107 F3 18 5 S 32 50 E
Inyantue, Zimbabwe 107 F2 18 30 S 26 40 E
Inyo Mts., U.S.A. 143 H5 36 40N 118 0W
Inyokern, U.S.A. 145 K9 35 39N 117 49W
Inywa, Burma 78 D6 23 56N 96 17 E
Inza, Russia 51 E15 53 55N 46 25 E
Inzer, Russia 54 D5 54 14N 57 34 E
Inzhavino, Russia 51 E13 52 22N 42 30 E
Iō-Jima, Japan 61 J5 30 48N 130 18 E
Ioánnina, Greece 44 E2 39 42N 20 47 E
Ioánnina □, Greece 44 E2 39 39N 20 57 E
Iola, U.S.A. 139 G7 37 55N 95 24W
Ioma, Papua N. G. 120 E4 8 19 S 147 52 E
Ion Corvin, Romania 46 E8 44 7N 27 50 E
Iona, U.K. 18 E2 56 20N 6 25W
Ione, Calif., U.S.A. 144 G6 38 21N 120 56W
Ione, Wash., U.S.A. 142 B5 48 45N 117 25W
Ionia, U.S.A. 141 B11 42 59N 85 4W
Ionian Is. = Iónioi Nísoi, Greece 45 F2 38 40N 20 0 E
Ionian Sea, Europe 10 H9 37 30N 17 30 E
Iónioi Nísoi, Greece 45 F2 38 40N 20 0 E
Iori →, Azerbaijan 53 F12 41 3N 46 17 E
Íos, Greece 45 H7 36 41N 25 20 E
Iowa □, U.S.A. 138 D8 42 18N 93 30W
Iowa →, U.S.A. 140 C5 41 10N 91 1W
Iowa City, U.S.A. 140 C5 41 40N 91 32W
Iowa Falls, U.S.A. 140 B3 42 31N 93 16W
Ipala, Tanzania 106 C3 4 30 S 32 52 E
Ipameri, Brazil 155 E2 17 44 S 48 9W
Iparía, Peru 156 B3 9 17 S 74 29W
Ipáti, Greece 45 F4 38 52N 22 14 E
Ipatinga, Brazil 155 E3 19 32 S 42 30W
Ipatovo, Russia 53 D10 45 45N 42 50 E
Ipel →, Europe 31 C12 48 10N 19 35 E
Ipiales, Colombia 152 C2 0 50N 77 37W
Ipiaú, Brazil 155 D4 14 8 S 39 44W
Ipil, Phil. 71 H4 7 47N 122 35 E
Ipin = Yibin, China 68 C5 28 45N 104 32 E
Ipirá, Brazil 155 D4 12 10 S 39 44W
Ipiranga, Brazil 152 D4 3 13 S 65 57W
Ípiros □, Greece 44 E2 39 30N 20 30 E
Ipixuna, Brazil 156 B3 7 0 S 71 40W
Ipixuna →, Amazonas, Brazil 156 B3 7 11 S 71 51W
Ipixuna →, Amazonas, Brazil 157 B5 5 45 S 63 2W
Ipoh, Malaysia 77 K3 4 35N 101 5 E
Iporá, Brazil 155 D1 11 23 S 50 40W
Ippy, C.A.R. 102 A4 6 5N 21 7 E
Ipsala, Turkey 44 D8 40 55N 26 23 E
Ipsárion Óros, Greece 44 D6 40 40N 24 40 E
Ipswich, Australia 115 D5 27 35 S 152 40 E
Ipswich, U.K. 17 E9 52 4N 1 9 E
Ipswich, Mass., U.S.A. 137 D14 42 41N 70 50W
Ipswich, S. Dak., U.S.A. 138 C5 45 27N 99 2W
Ipu, Brazil 154 B3 4 23 S 40 44W
Ipueiras, Brazil 154 B3 4 33 S 40 43W
Ipupiara, Brazil 155 D3 11 49 S 42 37W
Iput →, Belorussia 50 E7 52 26N 31 2 E
Iqaluit, Canada 127 B13 63 44N 68 31W
Iquique, Chile 156 E3 20 19 S 70 5W
Iquitos, Peru 152 D3 3 45 S 73 10W
Irabu-Jima, Japan 61 M2 24 50N 125 10 E
Iracoubo, Fr. Guiana 153 B7 5 30N 53 10W
Īrafshān, Iran 85 E9 26 42N 61 56 E
Irahuan, Phil. 71 G2 9 48N 118 41 E
Iráklia, Greece 45 H7 36 50N 25 28 E
Iráklion, Greece 32 D7 35 20N 25 12 E
Iráklion □, Greece 32 D7 35 10N 25 10 E
Irako-Zaki, Japan 63 C9 34 35N 137 1 E
Irala, Paraguay 159 B5 25 55 S 54 35W
Iramba □, Tanzania 106 C3 4 30 S 34 30 E
Iran ■, Asia 85 C7 33 0N 53 0 E
Iran, Gunung-Gunung, Malaysia 75 B4 2 20N 114 50 E
Iran Ra. = Iran, Gunung-Gunung, Malaysia 75 B4 2 20N 114 50 E
Iranamadu Tank, Sri Lanka 83 K5 9 23N 80 29 E
Īrānshahr, Iran 85 E9 27 15N 60 40 E
Irapa, Venezuela 153 A5 10 34N 62 35W
Irapuato, Mexico 146 C4 20 40N 101 30W
Iraq ■, Asia 84 C5 33 0N 44 0 E
Irarrar, O. →, Mali 99 D5 20 0N 1 30 E
Irati, Brazil 159 B5 25 25 S 50 38W
Irbid, Jordan 91 C4 32 35N 35 48 E
Irbid □, Jordan 91 C5 32 15N 36 35 E
Irbit, Russia 54 C8 57 41N 63 3 E
Irebu, Zaïre 102 C3 0 40 S 17 46 E
Irecê, Brazil 154 D3 11 18 S 41 52W
Iregua →, Spain 34 C7 42 27N 2 24 E
Ireland ■, Europe 19 D4 53 0N 8 0W
Ireland's Eye, Ireland 19 C5 53 25N 6 4W
Irele, Nigeria 101 D6 7 40N 5 40 E
Iremel, Gora, Russia 54 D6 54 33N 58 50 E
Ireng →, Brazil 153 C6 3 33N 59 51W
Iret, Russia 57 C16 60 3N 154 20 E
Irgiz, Bolshaya →, Russia 51 E16 52 10N 49 10 E
Irhârharene, Algeria 99 C6 27 37N 7 30 E
Irharrhar, O. →, Algeria 99 C6 28 3N 6 15 E
Irherm, Morocco 98 B3 30 7N 8 18W
Irhil Mgoun, Morocco 98 B3 31 30N 6 28W
Irhyangdong, N. Korea 67 D15 41 15N 129 30 E
Iri, S. Korea 67 G14 35 59N 127 0 E
Irian Jaya □, Indonesia 73 B5 4 0 S 137 0 E
Iriba, Chad 97 E4 15 7N 22 15 E
Irid, Mt., Phil. 70 D3 14 47N 121 19 E
Irié, Guinea 100 D3 8 15N 9 10W
Iriga, Phil. 70 E4 13 25N 123 25 E
Iriklinskiy, Russia 54 F6 51 39N 58 38 E
Iriklinskoye Vdkhr., Russia 54 E6 52 0N 59 0 E
Iringa, Tanzania 106 D4 7 48 S 35 43 E
Iringa □, Tanzania 106 D4 7 48 S 35 43 E
Irinjalakuda, India 83 J3 10 21N 76 14 E
Iriomote-Jima, Japan 61 M1 24 19N 123 48 E
Iriona, Honduras 148 C2 15 57N 85 11W
Iriri →, Brazil 153 D7 3 52 S 52 37W
Iriri Novo →, Brazil 157 B7 8 46 S 53 22W
Irish Republic ■, Europe 19 D4 53 0N 8 0W
Irish Sea, Europe 16 D3 54 0N 5 0W
Irkeshtam, Kirghizia 55 D6 39 41N 73 55 E
Irkineyeva, Russia 57 D10 58 30N 96 49 E
Irkutsk, Russia 57 D11 52 18N 104 20 E
Irma, Canada 131 C6 52 55N 111 14W
Irō-Zaki, Japan 63 C10 34 36N 138 51 E
Iroise, Mer d', France 22 D2 48 15N 4 45W
Iron Baron, Australia 116 B2 32 58 S 137 11 E
Iron Gate = Portile de Fier, Europe 46 E3 44 42N 22 30 E
Iron Knob, Australia 116 B2 32 46 S 137 8 E
Iron Mountain, U.S.A. 134 C1 45 49N 88 4W
Iron Ra., Australia 114 A3 12 46 S 143 16 E
Iron River, U.S.A. 138 B10 46 6N 88 39W
Ironbridge, U.K. 17 E5 52 38N 2 29W
Irondequoit, U.S.A. 136 C7 43 13N 77 35W
Ironstone Kopje, Botswana 104 D3 25 17 S 24 5 E
Ironton, Mo., U.S.A. 139 G9 37 36N 90 38W
Ironton, Ohio, U.S.A. 134 F4 38 32N 82 41W
Ironwood, U.S.A. 138 B9 46 27N 90 9W
Iroquois →, U.S.A. 141 C9 41 5N 87 49W
Iroquois Falls, Canada 128 C3 48 46N 80 41W
Irosin, Phil. 70 E5 12 42N 124 2 E
Irpen, Ukraine 50 F7 50 30N 30 15 E
Irrara Cr. →, Australia 115 D4 29 35 S 145 31 E
Irrawaddy □, Burma 78 G5 17 0N 95 0 E
Irrawaddy →, Burma 78 G5 15 50N 95 6 E
Irsina, Italy 41 B9 40 45N 16 15 E
Irtysh →, Russia 56 C7 61 4N 68 52 E
Irumu, Zaïre 106 B2 1 32N 29 53 E
Irún, Spain 34 B3 43 20N 1 52W
Irunea = Pamplona, Spain 34 C3 42 48N 1 38W
Irurzun, Spain 34 C3 42 55N 1 50W
Irvine, Canada 131 D6 49 57N 110 16W
Irvine, U.K. 18 F4 55 37N 4 40W
Irvine, Calif., U.S.A. 145 M9 33 41N 117 46W
Irvine, Ky., U.S.A. 141 G13 37 42N 83 58W
Irvinestown, U.K. 19 B4 54 28N 7 38W
Irving, U.S.A. 139 J6 32 49N 96 56W
Irvington, U.S.A. 141 G10 37 53N 86 17W
Irvona, U.S.A. 136 F6 40 46N 78 33W
Irwin →, Australia 113 E1 29 15 S 114 54 E
Irymple, Australia 116 C5 34 14 S 142 8 E
Is-sur-Tille, France 23 E12 47 30N 5 8 E
Isa, Nigeria 101 C6 13 14N 6 24 E
Isaac →, Australia 114 C4 22 55 S 149 20 E
Isabel, U.S.A. 138 C4 45 24N 101 26W
Isabela, Phil. 71 F4 10 12N 122 59 E
Isabela □, Phil. 70 C4 17 0N 122 0 E
Isabela, I., Mexico 146 C3 21 51N 105 55W
Isabella, Phil. 71 H4 6 40N 122 10 E
Isabella, Cord., Nic. 148 D2 13 30N 85 25W
Isabella Ra., Australia 112 D3 21 0 S 121 4 E
Ísafjarðardjúp, Iceland 12 C2 66 10N 23 0W
Ísafjörður, Iceland 12 C2 66 5N 23 9W
Isagarh, India 80 G7 24 48N 77 51 E
Isahaya, Japan 62 E2 32 52N 130 2 E
Isaka, Tanzania 106 C3 3 56 S 32 59 E
Isakly, Russia 54 D2 54 8N 51 32 E
Isana = Içana →, Brazil 152 C4 0 26N 67 19W
Isangi, Zaïre 102 B4 0 52N 24 10 E
Isar →, Germany 27 G8 48 49N 12 58 E
Isarco →, Italy 39 B8 46 57N 11 18 E
Ísari, Greece 45 G3 37 22N 22 0 E
Isbergues, France 23 B9 50 36N 2 28 E
Isbiceni, Romania 46 F5 43 45N 24 40 E
Iscayachi, Bolivia 157 E4 21 31 S 65 3W
Íschia, Italy 40 B6 40 45N 13 51 E
Iscuandé, Colombia 152 C2 2 28N 77 59W
Isdell →, Australia 112 C3 16 27 S 124 51 E
Ise, Japan 63 C8 34 25N 136 45 E
Ise-Heiya, Japan 63 C8 34 40N 136 30 E
Ise-Wan, Japan 63 C8 34 43N 136 43 E
Isefjord, Denmark 15 J5 55 53N 11 50 E
Iseltwald, Switz. 28 C5 46 43N 7 58 E
Isenthal, Switz. 29 C7 46 55N 8 34 E
Iseo, Italy 38 C7 45 40N 10 3 E
Iseo, L. d', Italy 38 C7 45 45N 10 3 E
Iseramagazi, Tanzania 106 C3 4 37 S 32 10 E
Isère □, France 25 C9 45 15N 5 40 E
Isère →, France 25 D8 44 59N 4 51 E
Iserlohn, Germany 26 D3 51 22N 7 40 E
Isérnia, Italy 41 A7 41 35N 14 12 E
Isesaki, Japan 63 A11 36 19N 139 12 E
Iseyin, Nigeria 101 D5 8 0N 3 36 E
Isfara, Tajikistan 55 C5 40 7N 70 38 E
Isherton, Guyana 153 C6 2 20N 59 25W
Ishigaki-Shima, Japan 61 M2 24 20N 124 10 E
Ishikari-Gawa →, Japan 60 C10 43 15N 141 23 E
Ishikari-Sammyaku, Japan 60 C11 43 30N 143 0 E
Ishikari-Wan, Japan 60 C10 43 25N 141 1 E
Ishikawa □, Japan 63 A8 36 30N 136 30 E
Ishim, Russia 56 D7 56 10N 69 30 E
Ishim →, Russia 56 D8 57 45N 71 10 E
Ishimbay, Russia 54 E5 53 28N 56 2 E
Ishinomaki, Japan 60 E10 38 32N 141 20 E
Ishioka, Japan 63 A12 36 11N 140 16 E
Ishizuchi-Yama, Japan 62 D5 33 45N 133 6 E
Ishkashim = Eshkamish, Tajikistan 55 E5 36 44N 71 37 E
Ishkuman, Pakistan 81 A5 36 30N 73 50 E
Ishmi, Albania 44 C1 41 33N 19 34 E
Ishpeming, U.S.A. 134 B2 46 29N 87 40W
Ishurdi, Bangla. 78 C2 24 9N 89 3 E
Isigny-sur-Mer, France 22 C5 49 19N 1 6W
Isil Kul, Russia 56 D8 54 55N 71 16 E
Isiolo, Kenya 106 B4 0 24N 37 33 E
Isiolo □, Kenya 106 B4 2 30N 37 30 E
Isipingo Beach, S. Africa 105 E5 30 0 S 30 57 E
Isiro, Zaïre 106 B2 2 53N 27 40 E
Isisford, Australia 114 C3 24 15 S 144 21 E
Iskander, Uzbekistan 55 C4 41 36N 69 41 E
İskederun, Turkey 88 E7 36 9N 36 35 E
İskenderun, Turkey 88 E7 36 32N 36 10 E
İskenderun Körfezi, Turkey 88 E6 36 40N 35 50 E
Iski-Naukat, Kirghizia 55 C6 40 16N 72 36 E
İskilip, Turkey 52 F6 40 45N 34 29 E
Iskŭr →, Bulgaria 43 D9 43 45N 24 25 E
Iskŭr, Yazovir, Bulgaria 43 E8 42 23N 23 30 E
Iskut →, Canada 130 B2 56 45N 131 49W
Isla →, U.K. 18 E5 56 32N 3 20W
Isla Cristina, Spain 37 H3 37 13N 7 17W
Isla Vista, U.S.A. 145 L7 34 25N 119 53W
İslâhiye, Turkey 88 E7 37 0N 36 35 E
Islamabad, Pakistan 79 B4 33 40N 73 10 E
Islamkot, Pakistan 80 G4 24 42N 70 13 E
Islampur, India 82 F2 17 2N 74 20 E
Island →, Canada 130 A4 60 25N 121 12W
Island Bay, Phil. 71 G2 9 6N 118 10 E
Island Falls, Canada 128 C3 49 35N 81 20W
Island Falls, U.S.A. 129 C6 46 1N 68 16W
Island L., Canada 131 C10 53 47N 94 25W
Island Lagoon, Australia 116 A2 31 30 S 136 40 E
Island Pond, U.S.A. 137 B13 44 49N 71 53W
Islands, B. of, Canada 129 C8 49 11N 58 15W
Islands, B. of, N.Z. 118 B3 35 15 S 174 6 E
Islay, U.K. 18 F2 55 46N 6 10W
Isle →, France 24 D3 44 55N 0 15W
Isle aux Morts, Canada 129 C8 47 35N 59 0W
Isle of Wight □, U.K. 17 G6 50 40N 1 20W
Isle Royale, U.S.A. 138 A10 48 0N 88 54W
Isleta, U.S.A. 143 J10 34 55N 106 42W
Isleton, U.S.A. 144 G5 38 10N 121 37W
Ismail, Ukraine 52 D3 45 22N 28 46 E
Ismâ'ilîya, Egypt 94 H8 30 37N 32 18 E
Ismaning, Germany 27 G7 48 14N 11 41 E
Ismay, U.S.A. 138 B2 46 30N 104 48W
Isna, Egypt 94 B3 25 17N 32 30 E
Isogstalo, India 81 B8 34 15N 78 46 E
Isola del Gran Sasso d'Italia, Italy 39 F10 42 30N 13 40 E
Ísola del Liri, Italy 40 A6 41 39N 13 32 E
Ísola della Scala, Italy 38 C8 45 16N 11 0 E
Ísola di Capo Rizzuto, Italy 41 D10 38 56N 17 5 E
İsparta, Turkey 88 E4 37 47N 30 30 E
İsparta □, Turkey 88 E4 38 0N 31 0 E
Isperikh, Bulgaria 43 D11 43 43N 26 50 E
Íspica, Italy 41 F7 36 47N 14 53 E
İspir, Turkey 53 F9 40 28N 41 1 E
Israel ■, Asia 91 D3 32 0N 34 50 E
Issano, Guyana 153 B6 5 49N 59 26W
Issia, Ivory C. 100 D3 6 33N 6 33W
Issoire, France 24 C7 45 32N 3 15 E
Issoudun, France 23 F8 46 57N 2 0 E
Issyk-Kul, Kirghizia 55 B8 42 26N 76 12 E
Issyk-Kul, Ozero, Kirghizia 55 B8 42 25N 77 15 E
Ist, Croatia 39 D11 44 17N 14 47 E
Istaihah, U.A.E. 85 F7 23 19N 54 4 E
İstanbul, Turkey 88 C3 41 0N 29 0 E
İstanbul □, Turkey 88 C3 41 0N 29 0 E
Istiaía, Greece 45 F5 38 57N 23 9 E
Istmina, Colombia 152 B2 5 10N 76 39W
Istok, Serbia 42 E5 42 45N 20 24 E
Istokpoga, L., U.S.A. 135 M5 27 23N 81 17W
Istra, Croatia 39 C11 45 10N 14 0 E
Istra, Russia 51 D10 55 55N 36 50 E
İstranca Dağları, Turkey 43 F12 41 48N 27 36 E
Istres, France 25 E8 43 31N 4 59 E
Istria = Istra, Croatia 39 C11 45 10N 14 0 E
Isulan, Phil. 71 H5 6 30N 124 29 E
Itá, Paraguay 158 B4 25 29 S 57 21W
'Itāb, Yemen 87 D5 15 20N 51 29 E
Itabaiana, Paraíba, Brazil 154 C4 7 18 S 35 19W
Itabaiana, Sergipe, Brazil 154 D4 10 41 S 37 37W
Itabaianinha, Brazil 154 D4 11 16 S 37 47W
Itaberaba, Brazil 155 D3 12 32 S 40 18W
Itaberaí, Brazil 155 E2 16 2 S 49 48W
Itabira, Brazil 155 E3 19 37 S 43 13W
Itabirito, Brazil 155 F3 20 15 S 43 48W
Itaboca, Brazil 153 D5 4 50 S 62 40W
Itabuna, Brazil 155 D4 14 48 S 39 16W
Itacajá, Brazil 154 C2 8 19 S 47 46W
Itacaunas →, Brazil 154 C2 5 21 S 49 8W
Itacoatiara, Brazil 153 D6 3 8 S 58 25W
Itacuaí →, Brazil 156 A3 4 20 S 70 12W
Itaguaçu, Brazil 155 E3 19 48 S 40 51W
Itaguari →, Brazil 155 D3 14 11 S 44 40W
Itaguatins, Brazil 154 C2 5 47 S 47 29W
Itaim →, Brazil 154 C3 7 2 S 42 2W
Itainópolis, Brazil 154 C3 7 24 S 41 31W
Itaipu Dam, Brazil 159 B5 25 30 S 54 30W
Itaituba, Brazil 153 D6 4 10 S 55 50W
Itajaí, Brazil 159 B6 27 50 S 48 39W
Itajubá, Brazil 155 F2 22 24 S 45 30W
Itajuípe, Brazil 155 D4 14 41 S 39 22W
Itaka, Tanzania 107 D3 8 50 S 32 49 E
Itako, Japan 63 B12 35 56N 140 33 E
Italy ■, Europe 11 G8 42 0N 13 0 E
Itamataré, Brazil 154 B2 2 16 S 46 24W
Itambacuri, Brazil 155 E3 18 1 S 41 42W
Itambé, Brazil 155 E3 15 15 S 40 37W
Itampolo, Madag. 105 C7 24 41 S 43 57 E
Itanhauã →, Brazil 153 D5 4 45 S 63 48W
Itanhém, Brazil 155 E3 17 9 S 40 20W
Itano, Japan 62 C6 34 7N 134 28 E
Itapaci, Brazil 155 D2 14 57 S 49 34W
Itapagé, Brazil 154 B4 3 41 S 39 34W
Itaparica, I. de, Brazil 155 D4 12 54 S 38 42W
Itapebi, Brazil 155 E4 15 56 S 39 32W
Itapecuru-Mirim, Brazil 154 B3 3 24 S 44 20W
Itaperuna, Brazil 155 F3 21 10 S 41 54W
Itapetinga, Brazil 155 E3 15 15 S 40 15W
Itapetininga, Brazil 159 A6 23 36 S 48 7W
Itapeva, Brazil 159 A6 23 59 S 48 59W
Itapicuru →, Bahia, Brazil 154 D4 11 47 S 37 32W
Itapicuru →, Maranhão, Brazil 154 B3 2 52 S 44 12W
Itapinima, Brazil 157 B5 5 25 S 60 44W
Itapipoca, Brazil 154 B3 3 30 S 39 35W
Itapiranga, Brazil 153 D6 2 45 S 58 1W
Itapiúna, Brazil 154 B4 4 33 S 38 57W
Itaporanga, Brazil 154 C4 7 18 S 38 0W
Itapuá □, Paraguay 159 B4 26 40 S 55 40W
Itapuranga, Brazil 155 E2 15 40 S 49 59W
Itaquari, Brazil 155 F3 20 20 S 40 25W
Itaquatiara, Brazil 153 D6 2 58 S 58 30W
Itaquí, Brazil 158 B4 29 8 S 56 30W
Itararé, Brazil 159 A6 24 6 S 49 23W
Itarsi, India 80 H7 22 36N 77 51 E
Itarumã, Brazil 155 E1 18 42 S 51 25W
Itatí, Argentina 158 B4 27 16 S 58 15W
Itatira, Brazil 154 B4 4 30 S 39 37W
Itatuba, Brazil 157 B5 5 46 S 63 20W
Itatupa, Brazil 153 D7 0 37 S 51 12W
Itaueira, Brazil 154 C3 7 36 S 43 2W
Itaueira →, Brazil 154 C3 6 41 S 42 55W
Itaúna, Brazil 155 F3 20 4 S 44 34W
Itbayat, Phil. 70 A3 20 47N 121 51 E
Itbayat I., Phil. 70 A3 20 46N 121 50 E
Itchen →, U.K. 17 G6 50 57N 1 20W
Ite, Peru 156 D3 17 55 S 70 57W
Itéa, Greece 45 F4 38 25N 22 25 E
Itezhi Tezhi, L., Zambia 107 F2 15 30 S 25 30 E
Ithaca = Itháki, Greece 45 F2 38 25N 20 40 E
Ithaca, U.S.A. 137 D8 42 27N 76 30W
Itháki, Greece 45 F2 38 25N 20 40 E
Itinga, Brazil 155 E3 16 36 S 41 47W
Itiquira, Brazil 157 D7 17 12 S 54 7W
Itiquira →, Brazil 157 D6 17 18 S 56 44W
Itiruçu, Brazil 155 D3 13 31 S 40 9W
Itiúba, Brazil 154 D4 10 43 S 39 51W
Ito, Japan 63 C11 34 58N 139 5 E
Itoigawa, Japan 61 F8 37 2N 137 51 E
Iton →, France 22 C8 49 9N 1 12 E
Itonamas →, Bolivia 157 C5 12 28 S 64 24W
Itsa, Egypt 94 J7 29 15N 30 47 E
Itsukaichi, Japan 62 C4 34 22N 132 22 E
Itsuki, Japan 62 E2 32 24N 130 50 E
Ittiri, Italy 40 B1 40 38N 8 32 E
Ittoqqortoormiit = Scoresbysund, Greenland 6 B6 70 20N 23 0W
Itu, Brazil 159 A6 23 17 S 47 15W
Itu, Nigeria 101 D6 5 10N 7 58 E
Ituaçu, Brazil 155 D3 13 50 S 41 18W
Ituango, Colombia 152 B2 7 4N 75 45W
Ituiutaba, Brazil 155 E2 19 0 S 49 25W
Itumbiara, Brazil 155 E2 18 20 S 49 10W

Junín de los Andes 213

Jelgava, Latvia 13 H17 56 41N 23 49 E
Jelica, Serbia 42 D5 43 50N 20 17 E
Jelli, Sudan 95 F3 5 25N 31 45 E
Jellicoe, Canada 128 C2 49 40N 87 30W
Jelšava, Slovak Rep. 31 C13 48 37N 20 15 E
Jemaja, Indonesia 74 B3 3 5N 105 45 E
Jemaluang, Malaysia 77 L4 2 16N 103 52 E
Jemappes, Belgium 21 H3 50 27N 3 54 E
Jember, Indonesia 75 D4 8 11 S 113 41 E
Jemeppe, Belgium 21 G7 50 37N 5 30 E
Jemnice, Czech. 30 B8 49 1N 15 34 E
Jena, Germany 26 E7 50 56N 11 33 E
Jena, U.S.A. 139 K8 31 41N 92 8W
Jenbach, Austria 30 D4 47 24N 11 47 E
Jendouba, Tunisia 96 A1 36 29N 8 47 E
Jeneponto, Indonesia 72 C1 5 41 S 119 42 E
Jenkins, U.S.A. 134 G4 37 10N 82 38W
Jenner, U.S.A. 144 G3 38 27N 123 7W
Jennings, La., U.S.A. 139 K8 30 13N 92 40W
Jennings, Mo., U.S.A. 140 F6 38 43N 90 16W
Jennings →, Canada 130 B2 59 38N 132 5W
Jepara, Indonesia 75 D3 7 40 S 109 14 E
Jeparit, Australia 116 D5 36 8 S 142 1 E
Jequié, Brazil 155 D3 13 51 S 40 5W
Jequitaí →, Brazil 155 E3 17 4 S 44 50W
Jequitinhonha, Brazil 155 E3 16 30 S 41 0W
Jequitinhonha →, Brazil 155 E4 15 51 S 38 53W
Jerada, Morocco 99 B4 34 17N 2 10W
Jerantut, Malaysia 77 L4 3 56N 102 22 E
Jérémie, Haiti 149 C5 18 40N 74 10W
Jeremoabo, Brazil 154 D4 10 4 S 38 21W
Jerez, Punta, Mexico 147 C5 22 58N 97 40W
Jerez de García Salinas, Mexico 146 C4 22 39N 103 0W
Jerez de la Frontera, Spain 37 J4 36 41N 6 7W
Jerez de los Caballeros, Spain 37 G4 38 20N 6 45W
Jericho = Arīḩā, Syria 84 C3 35 49N 36 35 E
Jericho = El Arīḩā, Jordan 91 D4 31 52N 35 27 E
Jericho, Australia 114 C4 23 38 S 146 6 E
Jerichow, Germany 26 C8 52 30N 12 2 E
Jerico Springs, U.S.A. 140 G2 37 37N 94 1W
Jerilderie, Australia 117 C6 35 20 S 145 41 E
Jermyn, U.S.A. 137 E9 41 31N 75 31W
Jerome, U.S.A. 143 J8 34 45N 112 7W
Jersey, Chan. Is. 17 H5 49 13N 2 7W
Jersey City, U.S.A. 137 F10 40 44N 74 4W
Jersey Shore, U.S.A. 136 E7 41 12N 77 15W
Jerseyville, U.S.A. 140 E6 39 7N 90 20W
Jerusalem, Israel 91 D4 31 47N 35 10 E
Jervis B., Australia 117 C9 35 8 S 150 46 E
Jesenice, Slovenia 39 B11 46 28N 14 3 E
Jeseník, Czech. 31 B10 50 0N 17 8 E
Jesenké, Slovak Rep. 31 C13 48 20N 20 10 E
Jesselton = Kota Kinabalu, Malaysia 75 A5 6 0N 116 4 E
Jessnitz, Germany 26 D8 51 42N 12 19 E
Jessore, Bangla. 78 D2 23 10N 89 10 E
Jesup, Ga., U.S.A. 135 K5 31 36N 81 53W
Jesup, Iowa, U.S.A. 140 B4 42 29N 92 4W
Jesús, Peru 156 B2 7 15 S 78 25W
Jesús Carranza, Mexico 147 D5 17 28N 95 1W
Jesús María, Argentina 158 C3 30 59 S 64 5W
Jetafe, Phil. 71 F5 10 9N 124 9 E
Jetmore, U.S.A. 139 F5 38 4N 99 54W
Jetpur, India 80 J4 21 45N 70 10 E
Jette, Belgium 21 G4 50 53N 4 20 E
Jevnaker, Norway 14 D4 60 15N 10 26 E
Jewell, U.S.A. 140 B3 42 20N 93 39W
Jewett, Ohio, U.S.A. 136 F3 40 22N 81 2W
Jewett, Tex., U.S.A. 139 K6 31 22N 96 9W
Jewett City, U.S.A. 137 E13 41 36N 72 0W
Jeyḩūnābād, Iran 85 C6 34 58N 48 59 E
Jeypore, India 82 E6 18 50N 82 38 E
Jeziorak, Jezioro, Poland 47 B6 53 40N 19 35 E
Jeziorany, Poland 47 B7 53 58N 20 46 E
Jeziorka →, Poland 47 D7 51 59N 20 57 E
Jhajjar, India 80 E7 28 37N 76 42 E
Jhal Jhao, Pakistan 79 D2 26 20N 65 35 E
Jhalakati, Bangla. 78 D3 22 39N 90 12 E
Jhalawar, India 80 G7 24 40N 76 10 E
Jhang Maghiana, Pakistan 79 C4 31 15N 72 22 E
Jhansi, India 81 G8 25 30N 78 36 E
Jharia, India 81 H12 23 45N 86 26 E
Jharsuguda, India 82 D7 21 56N 84 5 E
Jhelum, Pakistan 79 B4 33 0N 73 45 E
Jhelum →, Pakistan 80 D5 31 20N 72 10 E
Jhunjhunu, India 80 E6 28 10N 75 30 E
Ji Xian, Hebei, China 66 F8 37 35N 115 30 E
Ji Xian, Henan, China 66 G8 35 22N 114 5 E
Ji Xian, Shanxi, China 66 F6 36 7N 110 40 E
Jia Xian, Henan, China 66 H7 33 59N 113 12 E
Jia Xian, Shaanxi, China 66 E6 38 12N 110 28 E
Jiading, China 69 B13 31 22N 121 15 E
Jiahe, China 69 E9 25 38N 112 19 E
Jiali, Taiwan 69 F13 23 12N 120 10 E
Jialing Jiang →, China 68 C6 29 30N 106 20 E
Jiamusi, China 65 B8 46 40N 130 26 E
Ji'an, Jiangxi, China 69 D10 27 6N 114 59 E
Ji'an, Jilin, China 67 D14 41 5N 126 10 E
Jianchang, China 67 D11 40 55N 120 35 E
Jianchangying, China 67 D10 40 10N 118 50 E
Jianchuan, China 68 D2 26 38N 99 55 E
Jiande, China 69 C12 29 23N 119 15 E
Jiangbei, China 68 C6 29 40N 106 34 E
Jiangcheng, China 68 F3 22 36N 101 52 E
Jiangdi, China 68 D4 26 57N 103 37 E
Jiange, China 68 A5 32 4N 105 32 E
Jiangjin, China 68 C6 29 14N 106 14 E
Jiangkou, China 68 D7 27 40N 108 49 E
Jiangle, China 69 D11 26 42N 117 23 E
Jiangling, China 69 B9 30 25N 112 12 E
Jiangmen, China 69 F9 22 32N 113 0 E
Jiangshan, China 69 C12 28 40N 118 37 E
Jiangsu □, China 67 H10 33 0N 120 0 E
Jiangxi □, China 69 D10 27 30N 116 0 E
Jiangyin, China 69 B13 31 54N 120 17 E
Jiangyong, China 69 E8 25 20N 111 22 E
Jiangyou, China 68 B5 31 44N 104 43 E
Jianhe, China 68 D7 26 37N 108 31 E
Jianli, China 69 C9 29 46N 112 56 E
Jianning, China 69 D11 26 50N 116 50 E
Jian'ou, China 69 D12 27 3N 118 17 E
Jianshi, China 68 B7 30 37N 109 38 E
Jianshui, China 68 F4 23 36N 102 43 E
Jianyang, Fujian, China 69 D12 27 20N 118 5 E
Jianyang, Sichuan, China 68 B5 30 24N 104 33 E
Jiao Xian, China 67 F11 36 18N 120 1 E
Jiaohe, Hebei, China 66 E9 38 2N 116 20 E
Jiaohe, Jilin, China 67 C14 43 40N 127 22 E
Jiaoling, China 69 E11 24 41N 116 12 E
Jiaozhou Wan, China 67 F11 36 5N 120 10 E
Jiaozuo, China 66 G7 35 16N 113 12 E
Jiashan, China 69 A11 32 46N 117 59 E
Jiawang, China 67 G9 34 28N 117 26 E
Jiaxiang, China 66 G9 35 25N 116 20 E
Jiaxing, China 69 B13 30 49N 120 45 E
Jiayi, Taiwan 69 F13 23 30N 120 24 E
Jiayu, China 69 C9 29 55N 113 55 E
Jibão, Serra do, Brazil 155 D3 14 48 S 45 0W
Jibiya, Nigeria 101 C6 13 5N 7 12 E
Jibou, Romania 46 B4 47 15N 23 17 E
Jibuti = Djibouti ■, Africa 90 E3 12 0N 43 0 E
Jicarón, I., Panama 148 E3 7 10N 81 50W
Jičín, Czech. 30 A8 50 25N 15 28 E
Jiddah, Si. Arabia 86 B2 21 29N 39 10 E
Jieshou, China 66 H8 33 18N 115 22 E
Jiexiu, China 66 F6 37 2N 111 55 E
Jieyang, China 69 F11 23 35N 116 21 E
Jigawa □, Nigeria 101 C6 12 0N 9 45 E
Jiggalong, Australia 112 D3 23 21 S 120 47 E
Jihlava, Czech. 30 B8 49 28N 15 35 E
Jihlava →, Czech. 30 C9 48 55N 16 36 E
Jihočeský □, Czech. 30 B7 49 8N 14 35 E
Jihomoravský □, Czech. 31 B9 49 5N 16 30 E
Jijel, Algeria 99 A6 36 52N 5 50 E
Jijiga, Ethiopia 90 F3 9 20N 42 50 E
Jijona, Spain 35 G4 38 34N 0 30W
Jikamshi, Nigeria 101 C6 12 12N 7 45 E
Jilin, China 67 C14 43 44N 126 30 E
Jilin □, China 67 C13 44 0N 127 0 E
Jiloca →, Spain 34 D3 41 21N 1 39W
Jilong, Taiwan 69 E13 25 8N 121 42 E
Jílové, Czech. 30 B7 49 52N 14 29 E
Jima, Ethiopia 95 F4 7 40N 36 47 E
Jimbolia, Romania 46 D1 45 47N 20 43 E
Jimena de la Frontera, Spain 37 J5 36 27N 5 24W
Jimenbuen, Australia 117 D8 36 42 S 148 53 E
Jiménez, Mexico 146 B4 27 10N 104 54W
Jimenez, Phil. 71 G4 8 20N 123 50 E
Jimo, China 67 F11 36 23N 120 30 E
Jin Jiang →, China 69 C10 28 24N 115 48 E
Jin Xian, Hebei, China 66 E8 38 2N 115 2 E
Jin Xian, Liaoning, China 67 E11 38 55N 121 42 E
Jinan, China 66 F9 36 38N 117 1 E
Jincheng, China 66 G7 35 29N 112 50 E
Jinchuan, China 68 B4 31 30N 102 3 E
Jind, India 80 E7 29 19N 76 22 E
Jindabyne, Australia 117 D8 36 25 S 148 35 E
Jindrichuv Hradeç, Czech. 30 B8 49 10N 15 2 E
Jing He →, China 66 G5 34 27N 109 4 E
Jing Shan, China 69 B8 31 20N 111 35 E
Jing Xian, Anhui, China 69 B12 30 38N 118 25 E
Jing Xian, Hunan, China 68 D7 26 33N 109 40 E
Jing'an, China 69 C10 28 50N 115 17 E
Jingbian, China 66 F5 37 20N 108 30 E
Jingchuan, China 66 G4 35 20N 107 20 E
Jingde, China 69 B12 30 15N 118 27 E
Jingdezhen, China 69 C11 29 20N 117 11 E
Jingdong, China 68 E3 24 23N 100 47 E
Jinggu, China 68 F3 23 35N 100 41 E
Jinghai, China 66 E9 38 55N 116 55 E
Jinghong, China 68 F3 22 0N 100 45 E
Jingjiang, China 69 A13 32 2N 120 16 E
Jingle, China 66 E6 38 20N 111 55 E
Jingmen, China 69 B9 31 0N 112 10 E
Jingning, China 66 G3 35 30N 105 43 E
Jingpo Hu, China 67 C15 43 55N 128 55 E
Jingshan, China 69 B9 31 1N 113 7 E
Jingtai, China 66 F3 37 10N 104 6 E
Jingxi, China 68 F6 23 8N 106 27 E
Jingxing, China 66 E8 38 2N 114 8 E
Jingyang, China 66 G5 34 30N 108 50 E
Jingyu, China 67 C14 42 25N 126 45 E
Jingyuan, China 66 F3 36 30N 104 40 E
Jingziguan, China 66 H6 33 15N 111 0 E
Jinhua, China 69 C12 29 8N 119 38 E
Jining, Nei Mongol Zizhiqu, China 66 D7 41 5N 113 0 E
Jining, Shandong, China 66 G9 35 22N 116 34 E
Jinja, Uganda 106 B3 0 25N 33 12 E
Jinjang, Malaysia 77 L3 3 13N 101 39 E
Jinji, China 66 F4 37 58N 106 8 E
Jinjiang, Fujian, China 69 E12 24 43N 118 33 E
Jinjiang, Yunnan, China 68 D3 26 14N 100 34 E
Jinjie, China 68 F6 23 15N 107 18 E
Jinjini, Ghana 100 D4 7 26N 3 42W
Jinkou, China 69 B10 30 20N 114 8 E
Jinmen Dao, China 69 E12 24 25N 118 25 E
Jinning, China 68 E4 24 38N 102 38 E
Jinotega, Nic. 148 D2 13 6N 85 59W
Jinotepe, Nic. 148 D2 11 50N 86 10W
Jinping, Guizhou, China 68 D7 26 41N 109 10 E
Jinping, Yunnan, China 68 F4 22 45N 103 18 E
Jinsha, China 68 D6 27 29N 106 12 E
Jinsha Jiang →, China 68 C5 28 50N 104 36 E
Jinshan, China 69 B13 30 54N 121 10 E
Jinshi, China 69 C8 29 40N 111 50 E
Jintan, China 69 B12 31 42N 119 36 E
Jintotolo Channel, Phil. 71 F4 11 48N 123 5 E
Jinxi, Jiangxi, China 69 D11 27 56N 116 45 E
Jinxi, Liaoning, China 67 D11 40 52N 120 50 E
Jinxian, China 69 C11 28 26N 116 17 E
Jinxiang, China 66 G9 35 5N 116 22 E
Jinyun, China 69 C13 28 35N 120 5 E
Jinzhai, China 69 B10 31 40N 115 53 E
Jinzhou, China 67 D11 41 5N 121 3 E
Jiparaná →, Brazil 157 B5 8 3 S 62 52W
Jipijapa, Ecuador 152 D1 1 0 S 80 40W
Jiquilpan, Mexico 146 D4 19 57N 102 42W
Jirwān, Si. Arabia 87 B5 23 27N 50 53 E
Jishan, China 66 G6 35 34N 110 58 E
Jishou, China 68 C7 28 21N 109 43 E
Jishui, China 69 D10 27 12N 115 8 E
Jisr ash Shughūr, Syria 84 C3 35 49N 36 18 E
Jitarning, Australia 113 F2 32 48 S 117 57 E
Jitra, Malaysia 77 J3 6 16N 100 25 E
Jiu →, Romania 46 F4 43 47N 23 48 E
Jiudengkou, China 66 E4 39 56N 106 40 E
Jiujiang, Guangdong, China 69 F9 22 50N 113 0 E
Jiujiang, Jiangxi, China 69 C10 29 42N 115 58 E
Jiuling Shan, China 69 C10 28 40N 114 40 E
Jiulong, China 68 C3 28 57N 101 31 E
Jiutai, China 67 B13 44 10N 125 50 E
Jiuxiangcheng, China 66 H8 33 12N 114 50 E
Jiuxincheng, China 66 E8 39 17N 115 59 E
Jiuyuhang, China 69 B12 30 18N 119 56 E
Jixi, Anhui, China 69 B12 30 5N 118 34 E
Jixi, Heilongjiang, China 67 B16 45 20N 130 50 E
Jiyang, China 67 F9 37 0N 117 12 E
Jīz', W. →, Yemen 87 C6 16 12N 52 14 E
Jīzān, Si. Arabia 86 C3 17 0N 42 20 E
Jize, China 66 F8 36 54N 114 56 E
Jizera →, Czech. 30 A7 50 10N 14 43 E
Jizō-Zaki, Japan 62 B5 35 34N 133 20 E
Joaçaba, Brazil 159 B5 27 5 S 51 31W
Joaíma, Brazil 155 E3 16 39 S 41 2W
João, Brazil 154 B1 2 46 S 50 59W
João Amaro, Brazil 155 D3 12 46 S 40 22W
João Câmara, Brazil 154 C4 5 32 S 35 48W
João Pessoa, Brazil 154 C5 7 10 S 34 52W
João Pinheiro, Brazil 155 E2 17 45 S 46 10W
Joaquim Távora, Brazil 155 F2 23 30 S 49 58W
Joaquín V. González, Argentina 158 B3 25 10 S 64 0W
Jobourg, Nez de, France 22 C5 49 41N 1 57W
Jódar, Spain 35 H1 37 50N 3 21W
Jodhpur, India 80 F5 26 23N 73 8 E
Joensuu, Finland 48 B4 62 37N 29 49 E
Jœuf, France 23 C13 49 12N 6 1 E
Jofane, Mozam. 105 C5 21 15 S 34 18 E
Joggins, Canada 129 C7 45 42N 64 27W
Jogjakarta = Yogyakarta, Indonesia 75 D4 7 49 S 110 22 E
Jōhana, Japan 63 A8 36 30N 136 57 E
Johannesburg, S. Africa 105 D4 26 10 S 28 2 E
Johannesburg, U.S.A. 145 K9 35 22N 117 38W
Jōhen, Japan 62 E4 32 58N 132 32 E
John Day, U.S.A. 142 D4 44 25N 118 57W
John Day →, U.S.A. 142 D3 45 44N 120 39W
John H. Kerr Reservoir, U.S.A. 135 G6 36 36N 78 18W
John o' Groats, U.K. 18 C5 58 39N 3 3W
Johnnie, U.S.A. 145 J10 36 25N 116 5W
John's Ra., Australia 114 C1 21 55 S 133 23 E
Johnson, U.S.A. 139 G4 37 34N 101 45W
Johnson City, Ill., U.S.A. 140 G8 37 49N 88 56W
Johnson City, N.Y., U.S.A. 137 D9 42 7N 75 58W
Johnson City, Tenn., U.S.A. 135 G4 36 19N 82 21W
Johnson City, Tex., U.S.A. 139 K5 30 17N 98 25W
Johnsonburg, U.S.A. 136 E6 41 29N 78 41W
Johnsondale, U.S.A. 145 K8 35 58N 118 32W
Johnson's Crossing, Canada 130 A2 60 29N 133 18W
Johnsonville, N.Z. 118 H3 41 13 S 174 48 E
Johnston, L., Australia 113 F3 32 25 S 120 30 E
Johnston Falls = Mambilima Falls, Zambia 107 E2 10 31 S 28 45 E
Johnston I., Pac. Oc. 123 F11 17 10N 169 8W
Johnstone Str., Canada 130 C3 50 28N 126 0W
Johnstown, N.Y., U.S.A. 137 C10 43 0N 74 22W
Johnstown, Pa., U.S.A. 136 F6 40 20N 78 55W
Johor □, Malaysia 74 B2 2 0N 103 30 E
Johor Baharu, Malaysia 77 M4 1 28N 103 46 E
Joigny, France 23 E10 47 58N 3 20 E
Joinvile, Brazil 159 B6 26 15 S 48 55W
Joinville, France 23 D12 48 27N 5 10 E
Joinville I., Antarctica 7 C18 65 0 S 55 30W
Jojutla, Mexico 147 D5 18 37N 99 11W
Jokkmokk, Sweden 12 C15 66 35N 19 50 E
Jökulsá á Bru →, Iceland 12 D6 65 40N 14 16W
Jökulsá á Fjöllum →, Iceland 12 C5 66 10N 16 30W
Jolfā, Āzarbājān-e Sharqī, Iran 84 B5 38 57N 45 38 E
Jolfā, Eşfahan, Iran 85 C6 32 58N 51 37 E
Joliet, U.S.A. 141 C8 41 32N 88 5W
Joliette, Canada 128 C5 46 3N 73 24W
Jolo, Phil. 71 H3 6 0N 121 0 E
Jolo Group, Phil. 71 J3 6 0N 121 9 E
Jolon, U.S.A. 144 K5 35 58N 121 9W
Jomalig, Phil. 70 D4 14 42N 122 22 E
Jombang, Indonesia 75 D4 7 33 S 112 14 E
Jomda, China 68 B2 31 28N 98 12 E
Jome, Indonesia 72 B3 1 16 S 127 30 E
Jomfruland, Norway 15 F3 58 52N 9 36 E
Jönåker, Sweden 15 F10 58 44N 16 40 E
Jonava, Lithuania 50 D4 55 8N 24 12 E
Jones, Phil. 70 C3 16 33N 121 42 E
Jones Sound, Canada 6 B3 76 0N 85 0W
Jonesboro, Ark., U.S.A. 139 H9 35 50N 90 42W
Jonesboro, Ill., U.S.A. 139 G10 37 27N 89 16W
Jonesboro, La., U.S.A. 139 J8 32 15N 92 43W
Jonesburg, U.S.A. 140 F5 38 51N 91 18W
Jonesport, U.S.A. 129 D6 44 32N 67 37W
Jonesville, Ind., U.S.A. 141 E11 39 5N 85 54W
Jonesville, Mich., U.S.A. 141 C12 41 59N 84 40W
Jonglei, Sudan 95 F3 6 25N 30 50 E
Jonglei □, Sudan 95 F3 7 30N 32 30 E
Joniškis, Lithuania 50 C3 56 13N 23 35 E
Jönköping, Sweden 13 H13 57 45N 14 10 E
Jönköpings län □, Sweden 13 H13 57 30N 14 30 E
Jonquière, Canada 129 C5 48 27N 71 14W
Jonsberg, Sweden 15 F10 58 30N 16 48 E
Jonsered, Sweden 15 G6 57 45N 12 10 E
Jonzac, France 24 C3 45 27N 0 28W
Joplin, U.S.A. 139 G7 37 6N 94 31W
Jordan, U.S.A. 142 C10 47 19N 106 55W
Jordan ■, Asia 91 E5 31 0N 36 0 E
Jordan →, Asia 91 D4 31 48N 35 32 E
Jordan Valley, U.S.A. 142 E5 42 59N 117 3W
Jordânia, Brazil 155 E3 15 55 S 40 11W
Jordanów, Poland 31 B12 49 41N 19 49 E
Jorge, C., Chile 160 D1 51 40 S 75 35W
Jorhat, India 78 B5 26 45N 94 12 E
Jorm, Afghan. 79 A3 36 50N 70 52 E
Jörn, Sweden 12 D16 65 4N 20 1 E
Jorong, Indonesia 75 C4 3 58 S 114 56 E
Jorquera →, Chile 158 B2 28 3 S 69 58W
Jos, Nigeria 101 D6 9 53N 8 51 E
Jošanička Banja, Serbia 42 D5 43 24N 20 47 E
Jose Abad Santos, Phil. 71 J5 5 55N 125 39 E
José Batlle y Ordóñez, Uruguay 159 C4 33 20 S 55 10W
José de San Martín, Argentina 160 B2 44 4 S 70 26W
Jose Panganiban, Phil. 70 D4 14 17N 122 41 E
Joseni, Romania 46 C6 46 42N 25 29 E
Joseph, U.S.A. 142 D5 45 21N 117 14W
Joseph, L., Nfld., Canada 129 B6 52 45N 65 18W
Joseph, L., Ont., Canada 136 A5 45 10N 79 44W
Joseph Bonaparte G., Australia 112 B4 14 35 S 128 50 E
Joseph City, U.S.A. 143 J8 34 57N 110 20W
Joshua Tree, U.S.A. 145 L10 34 8N 116 19W
Joshua Tree National Monument, U.S.A. 145 M10 33 55N 116 0W
Josselin, France 22 E4 47 57N 2 33W
Jostedal, Norway 13 F9 61 35N 7 15 E
Jotunheimen, Norway 14 C2 61 35N 8 25 E
Jourdanton, U.S.A. 139 L5 28 55N 98 33W
Joure, Neths. 20 C7 52 58N 5 48 E
Joussard, Canada 130 B5 55 22N 115 50W
Jovellanos, Cuba 148 B3 22 40N 81 10W
Jovellar, Phil. 70 E4 13 4N 123 36 E
Jowai, India 78 C4 25 26N 92 12 E
Jowzjān □, Afghan. 79 A2 36 10N 66 0 E
Joyeuse, France 25 D8 44 29N 4 16 E
Józefów, Poland 47 C8 52 10N 21 11 E
Ju Xian, China 67 F10 36 35N 118 20 E
Juan Aldama, Mexico 146 C4 24 20N 103 23W
Juan Bautista Alberdi, Argentina 158 C3 34 26 S 61 48W
Juan de Fuca Str., Canada 144 B2 48 15N 124 0W
Juan de Nova, Ind. Oc. 105 B7 17 3 S 43 45 E
Juan Fernández, Arch. de, Pac. Oc. 123 L20 33 50 S 80 0W
Juan José Castelli, Argentina 158 B3 25 27 S 60 57W
Juan L. Lacaze, Uruguay 158 C4 34 26 S 57 25W
Juanjuí, Peru 156 B2 7 10 S 76 45W
Juárez, Argentina 158 D4 37 40 S 59 43W
Juárez, Mexico 145 N11 32 20N 115 57W
Juárez, Sierra de, Mexico 146 A1 32 0N 116 0W
Juatinga, Ponta de, Brazil 155 F3 23 17 S 44 30W
Juàzeiro, Brazil 154 C3 9 30 S 40 30W
Juàzeiro do Norte, Brazil 154 C4 7 10 S 39 18W
Jubay, Phil. 71 F5 11 33N 124 18 E
Jubayl, Lebanon 91 A4 34 5N 35 39 E
Jubbah, Si. Arabia 84 D4 28 2N 40 56 E
Jubbulpore = Jabalpur, India 81 H8 23 9N 79 58 E
Jübek, Germany 26 A5 54 31N 9 24 E
Jubga, Russia 53 D8 44 19N 38 48 E
Jubilee L., Australia 113 E4 29 0 S 126 50 E
Júcar →, Spain 35 F4 39 5N 0 10W
Júcaro, Cuba 148 B4 21 37N 78 51W
Juchitán, Mexico 147 D5 16 27N 95 5W
Judaea = Har Yehuda, Israel 91 D3 31 35N 34 57 E
Judenburg, Austria 30 D7 47 12N 14 38 E
Judith →, U.S.A. 142 C9 47 44N 109 39W
Judith, Pt., U.S.A. 137 E13 41 22N 71 29W
Judith Gap, U.S.A. 142 C9 46 41N 109 45W
Jufari →, Brazil 153 D5 1 13 S 62 0W
Jugoslavia = Yugoslavia ■, Europe 42 D5 44 0N 20 0 E
Juigalpa, Nic. 148 D2 12 6N 85 26W
Juillac, France 24 C5 45 20N 1 19 E
Juist, Germany 26 B2 53 40N 7 0 E
Juiz de Fora, Brazil 155 F3 21 43 S 43 19W
Jujuy □, Argentina 158 A2 23 20 S 65 40W
Julesburg, U.S.A. 138 E3 40 59N 102 16W
Juli, Peru 156 D4 16 10 S 69 25W
Julia Cr. →, Australia 114 C3 20 0 S 141 11 E
Julia Creek, Australia 114 C3 20 39 S 141 44 E
Juliaca, Peru 156 D3 15 25 S 70 10W
Julian, U.S.A. 145 M10 33 4N 116 38W
Julian Alps = Julijske Alpe, Slovenia 39 B11 46 15N 14 1 E
Julianakanaal, Neths. 21 F7 51 6N 5 52 E
Julianatop, Surinam 153 C6 3 40N 56 30W
Julianehåb, Greenland 6 C5 60 43N 46 0W
Jülich, Germany 26 E2 50 55N 6 20 E
Julierpass, Switz. 29 D9 46 28N 9 32 E
Julijske Alpe, Slovenia 39 B11 46 15N 14 1 E
Julimes, Mexico 146 B3 28 25N 105 27W
Jullundur, India 80 D6 31 20N 75 40 E
Julu, China 66 F8 37 15N 115 2 E
Jumbo, Zimbabwe 107 F3 17 30 S 30 58 E
Jumbo Pk., U.S.A. 145 J12 36 12N 114 11W
Jumentos Cays, Bahamas 149 B4 23 0N 75 40W
Jumet, Belgium 21 H4 50 27N 4 25 E
Jumilla, Spain 35 G3 38 28N 1 19W
Jumla, Nepal 81 E10 29 15N 82 13 E
Jumna = Yamuna →, India 81 G9 25 30N 81 53 E
Junagadh, India 80 J4 21 30N 70 30 E
Junaynah, Si. Arabia 86 B4 22 33N 46 18 E
Junction, Tex., U.S.A. 139 K5 30 29N 99 46W
Junction, Utah, U.S.A. 143 G7 38 14N 112 13W
Junction B., Australia 114 A1 11 52 S 133 55 E
Junction City, Kans., U.S.A. 138 F6 39 2N 96 50W
Junction City, Oreg., U.S.A. 142 D2 44 13N 123 12W
Junction Pt., Australia 114 A1 11 45 S 133 50 E
Jundah, Australia 114 C3 24 46 S 143 2 E
Jundiaí, Brazil 159 A6 24 30 S 47 0W
Juneau, U.S.A. 126 C6 58 18N 134 25W
Junee, Australia 117 C7 34 53 S 147 35 E
Jungfrau, Switz. 28 C5 46 32N 7 58 E
Junggar Pendi, China 64 B3 44 30N 86 0 E
Junglinster, Lux. 21 J8 49 43N 6 15 E
Jungshahi, Pakistan 80 G2 24 52N 67 44 E
Juniata →, U.S.A. 136 F7 40 30N 77 40W
Junín, Argentina 158 C3 34 33 S 60 57W
Junín, Peru 156 C2 11 12 S 76 0W
Junín □, Peru 156 C3 11 30 S 75 0W
Junín de los Andes, Argentina 160 A2 39 45 S 71 0W

Kaspiyskiy 215

Kampolombo, L., Zambia 107 E2 11 37 S 29 42 E
Kampong To, Thailand .. 77 J3 6 3N 101 13 E
Kampot, Cambodia ..... 77 G5 10 36N 104 10 E
Kampsville, U.S.A. 140 E6 39 18N 90 37W
Kamptee, India .... 82 D4 21 9N 79 19 E
Kampti, Burkina Faso ... 100 C4 10 7N 3 25W
Kampuchea = Cambodia ■, Asia .... 76 F5 12 15N 105 0 E
Kampung →, Indonesia . 73 C5 5 44 S 138 24 E
Kampung Air Putih, Malaysia .... 77 K4 4 15N 103 10 E
Kampung Jerangau, Malaysia .... 77 K4 4 50N 103 10 E
Kampung Raja, Malaysia 77 K4 5 45N 102 35 E
Kampungbaru = Tolitoli, Indonesia .... 72 A2 1 5N 120 50 E
Kamrau, Teluk, Indonesia 73 B4 3 30 S 133 36 E
Kamsack, Canada 131 C8 51 34N 101 54W
Kamskoye Ustye, Russia . 51 D16 55 10N 49 20 E
Kamskoye Vdkhr., Russia 54 B5 58 0N 56 0 E
Kamuchawie L., Canada . 131 B8 56 18N 101 59W
Kamui-Misaki, Japan .... 60 C10 43 20N 140 21 E
Kamyanets-Podilskyy = Kamenets-Podolskiy, Ukraine .... 52 B2 48 45N 26 40 E
Kāmyārān, Iran .... 84 C5 34 47N 46 56 E
Kamyshin, Russia .... 51 F14 50 10N 45 24 E
Kamyshlov, Russia ...... 54 C8 56 50N 62 43 E
Kamyzyak, Russia ...... 53 C13 46 4N 48 10 E
Kan, Burma .... 78 D5 22 25N 94 5 E
Kanaaupscow, Canada ... 128 B4 54 2N 76 30W
Kanab, U.S.A. 143 H7 37 3N 112 32W
Kanab →, U.S.A. 143 H7 36 24N 112 38W
Kanagawa □, Japan ..... 63 B11 35 20N 139 20 E
Kanagi, Japan .... 60 D10 40 54N 140 27 E
Kanairiktok →, Canada . 129 A7 55 2N 60 18W
Kanakapura, India ...... 83 H3 12 33N 77 28 E
Kanália, Greece .... 44 E4 39 30N 22 53 E
Kananga, Zaïre .... 103 D4 5 55 S 22 18 E
Kanarraville, U.S.A. 143 H7 37 32N 113 11W
Kanash, Russia .... 51 D15 55 30N 47 32 E
Kanaskat, U.S.A. 144 C5 47 19N 121 54W
Kanastraíon, Ákra, Greece 44 E5 39 57N 23 45 E
Kanawha →, U.S.A. ... 134 F4 38 50N 82 9W
Kanazawa, Japan .... 63 A8 36 30N 136 38 E
Kanbalu, Burma .... 78 D5 23 12N 95 31 E
Kanchanaburi, Thailand . 76 E2 14 2N 99 31 E
Kanchenjunga, Nepal .... 81 F13 27 50N 88 10 E
Kanchipuram, India ..... 83 H4 12 52N 79 45 E
Kańczuga, Poland .... 31 B15 49 59N 22 25 E
Kanda Kanda, Zaïre .... 103 D4 6 52 S 23 48 E
Kandahar = Qandahār, Afghan. .... 79 C2 31 32N 65 30 E
Kandalaksha, Russia .... 48 A5 67 9N 32 30 E
Kandalakshkiy Zaliv, Russia .... 48 A5 66 0N 35 0 E
Kandangan, Indonesia ... 75 C5 2 50 S 115 20 E
Kandanos, Greece .... 45 J5 35 19N 23 44 E
Kandanos, Kríti, Greece . 32 D5 35 20N 23 45 E
Kandavu, Fiji .... 121 B2 19 0 S 178 15 E
Kandavu Passage, Fiji ... 121 B2 18 45 S 178 0 E
Kandep, Papua N. G. ... 120 C2 5 54 S 143 32 E
Kander →, Switz. ...... 28 C5 46 33N 7 38 E
Kandersteg, Switz. ...... 28 D5 46 28N 7 40 E
Kandhíla, Greece .... 45 G4 37 46N 22 22 E
Kandhkot, Pakistan ..... 80 E3 28 16N 69 8 E
Kandhla, India .... 80 E7 29 18N 77 19 E
Kandi, Benin .... 101 C5 11 7N 2 55 E
Kandi, India .... 81 H13 23 58N 88 5 E
Kandıra, Turkey .... 88 C4 41 4N 30 9 E
Kandla, India .... 80 H4 23 0N 70 10 E
Kandos, Australia .... 117 B8 32 45 S 149 58 E
Kandrian, Papua N. G. .. 120 D5 6 14 S 149 37 E
Kandy, Sri Lanka .... 83 L5 7 18N 80 43 E
Kane, U.S.A. 136 E6 41 40N 78 49W
Kane Basin, Greenland .. 6 B4 79 1N 70 0W
Kanevskaya, Russia ..... 53 C8 46 3N 39 3 E
Kanfanar, Croatia .... 39 C10 45 7N 13 50 E
Kangaba, Mali 100 C3 11 56N 8 25W
Kangal, Turkey .... 88 D7 39 14N 37 23 E
Kangān, Fārs, Iran ...... 85 E7 27 50N 52 3 E
Kangān, Hormozgān, Iran 85 E8 25 48N 57 28 E
Kangar, Malaysia .... 77 J3 6 27N 100 12 E
Kangaroo I., Australia .. 116 C2 35 45 S 137 0 E
Kangavar, Iran .... 85 C6 34 40N 48 0 E
Kangding, China .... 68 B3 30 2N 101 57 E
Kāngdong, N. Korea .... 67 E14 39 9N 126 5 E
Kangean, Kepulauan, Indonesia .... 75 D5 6 55 S 115 23 E
Kangean Is. = Kangean, Kepulauan, Indonesia . 75 D5 6 55 S 115 23 E
Kanggye, N. Korea ..... 67 D14 41 0N 126 35 E
Kanggyŏng, S. Korea .... 67 F14 36 10N 127 0 E
Kanghwa, S. Korea ..... 67 F14 37 45N 126 30 E
Kangnŭng, S. Korea ..... 67 F15 37 45N 128 54 E
Kango, Gabon .... 102 B2 0 11N 10 5 E
Kangoya, Zaïre .... 103 D4 9 55 S 22 48 E
Kangping, China .... 67 C12 42 43N 123 18 E
Kangpokpi, India .... 78 C4 25 8N 93 58 E
Kangyidaung, Burma .... 78 G5 16 56N 94 54 E
Kanhangad, India .... 83 H2 12 21N 74 58 E
Kanheri, India .... 82 E1 19 13N 72 50 E
Kani, Ivory C. 100 D3 8 29N 6 36W
Kaniama, Zaïre .... 103 D4 7 30 S 24 12 E
Kaniapiskau →, Canada 129 A6 56 40N 69 30W
Kaniapiskau L., Canada . 129 B6 54 10N 69 55W
Kanibadam, Tajikistan ... 55 C5 40 17N 70 25 E
Kaniere, L., N.Z. .... 119 C6 42 50 S 171 10 E
Kanin, P-ov., Russia .... 48 A8 68 0N 45 0 E
Kanin Nos, Mys, Russia . 48 A7 68 45N 43 20 E
Kanin Pen. = Kanin, P-ov., Russia .... 48 A8 68 0N 45 0 E
Kanina, Albania .... 44 D1 40 23N 19 30 E
Kaniva, Australia .... 116 D4 36 22 S 141 18 E
Kanjiža, Serbia .... 42 A5 46 3N 20 4 E
Kanjut Sar, Pakistan .... 81 A6 36 7N 75 25 E
Kankakee, U.S.A. 141 C9 41 7N 87 52W
Kankakee →, U.S.A. ... 141 C8 41 23N 88 15W
Kankan, Guinea 100 C3 10 23N 9 15W
Kanker, India .... 82 D5 20 10N 81 40 E
Kankunskiy, Russia ..... 57 D13 57 37N 126 8 E
Kanmuri-Yama, Japan ... 62 C4 34 30N 132 4 E
Kannabe, Japan .... 62 C5 34 32N 133 23 E
Kannapolis, U.S.A. 135 H5 35 30N 80 37W
Kannauj, India .... 81 F8 27 3N 79 56 E
Kano, Nigeria .... 101 C6 12 2N 8 30 E
Kano □, Nigeria .... 101 C6 11 30N 8 30 E
Kan'onji, Japan .... 62 C5 34 7N 133 39 E
Kanoroba, Ivory C. 100 D3 9 7N 6 8W
Kanowha, U.S.A. 140 B3 42 57N 93 47W
Kanowit, Malaysia ...... 75 B4 2 14N 112 20 E
Kanowna, Australia ..... 113 F3 30 32 S 121 31 E
Kanoya, Japan .... 62 F2 31 25N 130 50 E
Kanpetlet, Burma .... 78 E4 21 10N 93 59 E
Kanpur, India .... 81 F9 26 28N 80 20 E
Kansas, U.S.A. 141 E9 39 33N 87 56W
Kansas □, U.S.A. 138 F6 38 30N 99 0W
Kansas →, U.S.A. 138 F7 39 7N 94 37W
Kansas City, Kans., U.S.A. 140 E2 39 7N 94 38W
Kansas City, Mo., U.S.A. 140 E2 39 6N 94 35W
Kansenia, Zaïre .... 107 E2 10 20 S 26 0 E
Kansk, Russia .... 57 D10 56 20N 95 37 E
Kansŏng, S. Korea ...... 67 E15 38 24N 128 30 E
Kansu = Gansu □, China 66 G3 36 0N 104 0 E
Kant, Kirghizia .... 55 B7 42 53N 74 51 E
Kantang, Thailand ...... 77 J2 7 25N 99 31 E
Kantché, Niger .... 97 F1 13 31N 8 30 E
Kanté, Togo .... 101 D5 9 57N 1 3 E
Kantemirovka, Russia ... 53 B8 49 43N 39 55 E
Kantharalak, Thailand ... 76 E5 14 39N 104 39 E
Kantō □, Japan .... 63 A11 36 15N 139 30 E
Kantō-Heiya, Japan .... 63 A11 36 0N 139 30 E
Kantō-Sanchi, Japan .... 63 B10 35 59N 138 50 E
Kantu-long, Burma ..... 78 F6 19 57N 97 36 E
Kanturk, Ireland 19 D3 52 10N 8 55W
Kanuma, Japan .... 63 A11 36 34N 139 42 E
Kanus, Namibia .... 104 D2 27 50 S 18 39 E
Kanye, Botswana .... 104 C4 24 55 S 25 28 E
Kanzenze, Zaïre .... 103 E5 10 30 S 25 12 E
Kanzi, Ras, Tanzania .... 106 D4 7 1 S 39 33 E
Kao, Fiji .... 121 P13 19 40 S 175 1W
Kaohsiung = Gaoxiong, Taiwan .... 69 F13 22 38N 120 18 E
Kaohsiung, Taiwan ...... 65 D7 22 35N 120 16 E
Kaokoveld, Namibia .... 104 B1 19 15 S 14 30 E
Kaolack, Senegal 100 C1 14 5N 16 8W
Kaoshan, China .... 67 B13 44 38N 124 50 E
Kaouar, Niger .... 97 E2 19 5N 12 52 E
Kapadvanj, India .... 80 H5 23 5N 73 0 E
Kapagere, Papua N. G. . 120 E4 9 46 S 147 42 E
Kapanga, Zaïre .... 103 D4 8 30 S 22 40 E
Kapatagan, Phil. .... 71 H4 7 52N 123 44 E
Kapchagai, Kazakhstan .. 55 B8 43 51N 77 14 E
Kapchagaiskoye Vdkhr., Kazakhstan .... 55 B8 43 45N 77 50 E
Kapellen, Belgium ...... 21 F4 51 19N 4 25 E
Kapéllo, Ákra, Greece ... 45 H5 36 9N 23 3 E
Kapema, Zaïre .... 107 E2 10 45 S 28 22 E
Kapfenberg, Austria ..... 30 D8 47 26N 15 18 E
Kapia, Zaïre .... 103 C3 4 17 S 19 46 E
Kapiri Mposhi, Zambia .. 107 E2 13 59 S 28 43 E
Kāpīsā □, Afghan. ...... 79 B3 35 0N 69 20 E
Kapiskau →, Canada ... 128 B3 52 47N 81 55W
Kapit, Malaysia .... 75 B4 2 0N 112 55 E
Kapiti I., N.Z. .... 118 G3 40 50 S 174 56 E
Kapka, Massif du, Chad . 97 E4 15 7N 21 45 E
Kaplice, Czech. .... 30 C7 48 42N 14 30 E
Kapoe, Thailand .... 77 H2 9 34N 98 32 E
Kapoeta, Sudan .... 95 G3 4 50N 33 35 E
Kápolnásnyék, Hungary . 31 D11 47 16N 18 41 E
Kaponga, N.Z. .... 118 F3 39 29 S 174 9 E
Kapos →, Hungary ..... 31 E11 46 44N 18 30 E
Kaposvár, Hungary ..... 31 E10 46 25N 17 47 E
Kapowsin, U.S.A. 144 D4 46 59N 122 13W
Kappeln, Germany ...... 26 A5 54 37N 9 56 E
Kapps, Namibia .... 104 C2 22 32 S 17 18 E
Kaprije, Croatia .... 39 E12 43 42N 15 43 E
Kaprijke, Belgium ...... 21 F3 51 13N 3 38 E
Kapsan, N. Korea ...... 67 D15 41 4N 128 19 E
Kapsukas = Mariyampol, Lithuania .... 50 D3 54 33N 23 19 E
Kapuas, Indonesia ...... 75 C4 3 10 S 114 5 E
Kapuas →, Indonesia ... 75 C3 0 25 S 109 20 E
Kapuas Hulu, Pegunungan, Malaysia . 75 B4 1 30N 113 30 E
Kapuas Hulu Ra. = Kapuas Hulu, Pegunungan, Malaysia . 75 B4 1 30N 113 30 E
Kapulo, Zaïre .... 107 D2 8 18 S 29 15 E
Kapunda, Australia ..... 116 C3 34 20 S 138 56 E
Kapuni, N.Z. .... 118 F3 39 29 S 174 8 E
Kapurthala, India ...... 80 D6 31 23N 75 25 E
Kapuskasing, Canada 128 C3 49 25N 82 30W
Kapuskasing →, Canada 128 C3 49 49N 82 0W
Kapustin Yar, Russia .... 53 B11 48 37N 45 40 E
Kaputar, Australia ...... 115 E5 30 15 S 150 10 E
Kaputir, Kenya .... 106 B4 2 5N 35 28 E
Kapuvár, Hungary ...... 31 D10 47 36N 17 1 E
Kara, Russia .... 56 C7 69 10N 65 0 E
Kara, Turkey .... 45 H9 36 58N 27 30 E
Kara Bogaz Gol, Zaliv, Turkmenistan .... 49 F9 41 0N 53 30 E
Kara Kalpak Republic □, Uzbekistan .... 56 E6 43 0N 58 0 E
Kara Kum = Karakum, Peski, Turkmenistan ... 56 F6 39 30N 60 0 E
Kara-Saki, Japan .... 62 C1 34 41N 129 30 E
Kara Sea, Russia .... 56 B7 75 0N 70 0 E
Kara Su, Kirghizia ...... 55 C6 40 44N 72 53 E
Karabash, Russia .... 54 D7 55 29N 60 14 E
Karabekaul, Turkmenistan 55 D2 38 30N 64 8 E
Karabük, Turkey .... 52 F5 41 12N 32 37 E
Karabulak, Kazakhstan ... 55 A9 44 54N 78 30 E
Karaburun, Turkey ...... 45 F8 38 41N 26 28 E
Karaburuni, Albania ..... 44 D1 40 25N 19 20 E
Karabutak, Kazakhstan .. 56 E7 49 59N 60 14 E
Karacabey, Turkey ...... 88 C3 40 12N 28 21 E
Karacasu, Turkey ...... 88 E3 37 43N 28 35 E
Karachala, Azerbaijan ... 53 G13 39 45N 48 53 E
Karachayevsk, Russia ... 53 E9 43 50N 41 55 E
Karachev, Russia .... 50 E9 53 10N 35 5 E
Karachi, Pakistan ...... 79 D2 24 53N 67 0 E
Karád, Hungary .... 31 E10 46 41N 17 51 E
Karad, India .... 82 F2 17 15N 74 10 E
Karadeniz Boğazı, Turkey 88 C3 41 10N 29 10 E
Karaga, Ghana 101 D4 9 58N 0 28W
Karaganda, Kazakhstan .. 56 E8 49 50N 73 10 E
Karagayly, Kazakhstan .. 56 E8 49 26N 76 0 E
Karaginskiy, Ostrov, Russia .... 57 D17 58 45N 164 0 E
Karagiye Depression, Kazakhstan .... 49 F9 43 27N 51 45 E
Karagüney Dağları, Turkey .... 88 C6 40 30N 34 40 E
Karagwe □, Tanzania ... 106 C3 2 0 S 31 0 E
Karaikal, India .... 83 J4 10 59N 79 50 E
Karaikkudi, India .... 83 J4 10 5N 78 45 E
Karaisali, Turkey .... 88 E6 37 16N 35 2 E
Karaitivu I., Sri Lanka .. 83 K4 9 45N 79 52 E
Karaj, Iran .... 85 C6 35 48N 51 0 E
Karak, Malaysia .... 77 L4 3 25N 102 2 E
Karakas, Kazakhstan .... 56 E9 48 20N 83 30 E
Karakitang, Indonesia ... 72 A3 3 14N 125 28 E
Karaklis, Armenia ...... 53 F11 40 48N 44 30 E
Karakoçan, Turkey ..... 89 D9 38 57N 40 2 E
Karakoram Pass, Pakistan 81 B7 35 33N 77 50 E
Karakoram Ra., Pakistan 81 B7 35 30N 77 0 E
Karakul, Tajikistan ..... 55 D6 39 2N 73 33 E
Karakul, Uzbekistan ..... 55 D1 39 22N 63 50 E
Karakuldzha, Kirghizia .. 55 C6 40 39N 73 26 E
Karakulino, Russia ...... 54 C3 56 1N 53 43 E
Karakum, Peski, Turkmenistan .... 56 F6 39 30N 60 0 E
Karakurt, Turkey ...... 89 C10 40 10N 42 37 E
Karal, Chad .... 97 F2 12 50N 14 46 E
Karalon, Russia .... 57 D12 57 5N 115 50 E
Karaman, Turkey .... 88 E5 37 14N 33 13 E
Karamay, China .... 64 B3 45 30N 84 58 E
Karambu, Indonesia ..... 75 C5 3 53 S 116 6 E
Karamea, N.Z. .... 119 B7 41 14 S 172 6 E
Karamea →, N.Z. ...... 119 B7 41 13 S 172 26 E
Karamea Bight, N.Z. .... 119 B6 41 22 S 171 40 E
Karamet Niyaz, Turkmenistan .... 55 E2 37 45N 64 34 E
Karamoja □, Uganda .... 106 B3 3 0N 34 15 E
Karamsad, India .... 80 H5 22 35N 72 50 E
Karand, Iran .... 84 C5 34 16N 46 15 E
Karanganyar, Indonesia .. 75 D3 7 38 S 109 37 E
Karanja, India .... 82 D3 20 29N 77 31 E
Karapınar, Turkey ...... 88 E5 37 43N 33 32 E
Karapiro, N.Z. .... 118 D4 37 53 S 175 32 E
Karasburg, Namibia .... 104 D2 28 0 S 18 44 E
Karasino, Russia .... 56 C9 66 50N 86 50 E
Karasjok, Norway ...... 12 B18 69 27N 25 30 E
Karasu, Turkey .... 88 C4 41 4N 30 46 E
Karasu →, Turkey ..... 89 D8 39 42N 39 25 E
Karasuk, Russia .... 56 D8 53 44N 78 2 E
Karasuyama, Japan ..... 63 A12 36 39N 140 9 E
Karataş Burnu, Turkey .. 88 E6 36 32N 35 1 E
Karatau, Kazakhstan .... 55 B5 43 10N 70 28 E
Karatau, Khrebet, Kazakhstan .... 55 B4 43 30N 69 30 E
Karatepe, Turkey .... 88 E7 37 22N 36 16 E
Karativu, Sri Lanka .... 83 K4 8 22N 79 47 E
Karatobe, Kazakhstan .... 54 G3 49 44N 53 30 E
Karatoya →, India ..... 78 C2 24 7N 89 36 E
Karaturuk, Kazakhstan .. 55 B8 43 35N 77 50 E
Karaul-Bazar, Uzbekistan 55 D2 39 30N 64 48 E
Karauli, India .... 80 F7 26 30N 77 4 E
Karávi, Greece .... 45 H5 36 49N 23 37 E
Karavostasi, Cyprus ..... 32 D11 35 8N 32 50 E
Karawa, Zaïre .... 102 B4 3 18N 20 17 E
Karawang, Indonesia .... 75 D3 6 30 S 107 15 E
Karawanken, Europe .... 30 E7 46 30N 14 40 E
Karayazı, Turkey .... 89 D10 39 41N 42 9 E
Karazhal, Kazakhstan ... 56 E8 48 2N 70 49 E
Karbalā, Iraq .... 84 C5 32 36N 44 3 E
Kårböle, Sweden .... 14 C9 61 59N 15 22 E
Karcag, Hungary .... 31 D13 47 19N 20 57 E
Karcha →, Pakistan .... 81 B7 34 45N 76 10 E
Karda, Russia .... 57 D11 55 0N 103 16 E
Kardeljovo, Croatia ..... 42 D2 43 4N 17 26 E
Kardhámila, Greece .... 45 F8 38 35N 26 5 E
Kardhítsa, Greece ...... 44 E3 39 23N 21 54 E
Kardhítsa □, Greece .... 44 E3 39 15N 21 50 E
Kärdla, Estonia .... 50 B3 58 50N 22 40 E
Kareeberge, S. Africa ... 104 E3 30 59 S 21 50 E
Kareima, Sudan .... 94 D3 18 30N 31 49 E
Karelian Republic □, Russia .... 48 A5 65 30N 32 30 E
Karema, Papua N. G. ... 120 E4 9 12 S 147 18 E
Kārevāndar, Iran .... 85 E9 27 53N 60 44 E
Kargapolye, Russia ..... 54 D9 55 57N 64 24 E
Kargasok, Russia .... 56 D9 59 3N 80 53 E
Kargat, Russia .... 56 D9 55 10N 80 15 E
Kargı, Turkey .... 52 F6 41 11N 34 30 E
Kargil, India .... 81 B7 34 32N 76 12 E
Kargopol, Russia .... 48 B6 61 30N 38 58 E
Kargowa, Poland .... 47 C2 52 5N 15 51 E
Karguéri, Niger .... 97 F2 13 27N 10 30 E
Karia ba Mohammed, Morocco 98 B3 34 22N 5 12W
Kariaí, Greece .... 44 D6 40 14N 24 19 E
Karīān, Iran .... 85 E8 26 57N 57 14 E
Kariba, Zimbabwe ...... 107 F2 16 28 S 28 50 E
Kariba, L., Zimbabwe ... 107 F2 16 40 S 28 25 E
Kariba Dam, Zimbabwe . 107 F2 16 30 S 28 35 E
Kariba Gorge, Zambia .. 107 F2 16 30 S 28 50 E
Karibib, Namibia ...... 104 C2 22 0 S 15 56 E
Karikari, C., N.Z. ...... 118 A2 34 46 S 173 24 E
Karimata, Kepulauan, Indonesia .... 75 C3 1 25 S 109 0 E
Karimata, Selat, Indonesia 75 C3 2 0 S 108 40 E
Karimata Is. = Karimata, Kepulauan, Indonesia . 75 C3 1 25 S 109 0 E
Karimnagar, India ...... 82 E4 18 26N 79 10 E
Karimunjawa, Kepulauan, Indonesia .... 75 D4 5 50 S 110 30 E
Karin, Somali Rep. ..... 90 E4 10 50N 45 52 E
Káristos, Greece .... 45 F6 38 1N 24 29 E
Karīt, Iran .... 85 C8 33 29N 56 55 E
Kariya, Japan .... 63 C9 34 58N 137 1 E
Karkal, India .... 83 H2 13 15N 74 56 E
Karkar I., Papua N. G. .. 120 C4 4 40 S 146 0 E
Karkaralinsk, Kazakhstan 56 E8 49 26N 75 30 E
Karkinitskiy Zaliv, Ukraine .... 52 D5 45 56N 33 0 E
Karkur Tohl, Egypt ..... 94 C2 22 5N 25 5 E
Karl Libknekht, Russia .. 50 F9 51 40N 35 35 E
Karl-Marx-Stadt = Chemnitz, Germany ... 26 E8 50 50N 12 55 E
Karla, L. = Voiviïs Límni, Greece .... 44 E4 39 30N 22 45 E
Karlino, Poland .... 47 A2 54 3N 15 53 E
Karlobag, Croatia ...... 39 D12 44 32N 15 5 E
Karlovac, Croatia ...... 39 C12 45 31N 15 36 E
Karlovka, Ukraine ...... 52 B6 49 29N 35 8 E
Karlovy Vary, Czech. ... 30 A5 50 13N 12 51 E
Karlsbad = Karlovy Vary, Czech. .... 30 A5 50 13N 12 51 E
Karlsborg, Sweden ...... 15 F8 58 33N 14 33 E
Karlshamn, Sweden ..... 13 H13 56 10N 14 51 E
Karlskoga, Sweden ..... 13 G13 59 22N 14 33 E
Karlskrona, Sweden .... 13 H13 56 10N 15 35 E
Karlsruhe, Germany .... 27 F4 49 3N 8 23 E
Karlstad, Sweden ...... 13 G12 59 23N 13 30 E
Karlstad, U.S.A. 138 A6 48 35N 96 31W
Karlstadt, Germany .... 27 F5 49 57N 9 46 E
Karnal, India .... 80 E7 29 42N 77 2 E
Karnali →, Nepal ...... 81 E9 28 45N 81 16 E
Karnaphuli Res., Bangla. 78 D4 22 40N 92 20 E
Karnataka □, India ..... 83 H3 13 15N 77 0 E
Karnes City, U.S.A. 139 L6 28 53N 97 54W
Karnische Alpen, Europe 30 E6 46 36N 13 0 E
Kärnten □, Austria ..... 30 E6 46 52N 13 30 E
Karo, Mali 100 C4 12 16N 3 18W
Karoi, Zimbabwe .... 107 F2 16 48 S 29 45 E
Karomatan, Phil. .... 71 H4 7 55N 123 44 E
Karonga, Malawi .... 107 D3 9 57 S 33 55 E
Karoonda, Australia .... 116 C3 35 1 S 139 59 E
Karora, Sudan .... 94 D4 17 44N 38 15 E
Káros, Greece .... 45 H7 36 54N 25 40 E
Karousádhes, Greece .... 44 E1 39 47N 19 45 E
Karpasia □, Cyprus ..... 32 D13 35 32N 34 15 E
Kárpathos, Greece ..... 45 J9 35 37N 27 10 E
Kárpathos, Stenón, Greece 45 J9 36 0N 27 30 E
Karpinsk, Russia .... 54 B7 59 45N 60 1 E
Karpogory, Russia ..... 48 B7 63 59N 44 27 E
Karrebæk, Denmark .... 15 J5 55 12N 11 39 E
Kars, Turkey .... 53 F10 40 40N 43 5 E
Kars □, Turkey .... 89 C10 40 40N 43 0 E
Karsakpay, Kazakhstan .. 56 E7 47 55N 66 40 E
Karsha, Kazakhstan ..... 53 B14 49 45N 51 35 E
Karshi, Uzbekistan ..... 55 D2 38 53N 65 48 E
Karsiyang, India .... 81 F13 26 56N 88 18 E
Karst, Croatia .... 39 C11 45 35N 14 0 E
Karsun, Russia .... 51 D15 54 14N 46 57 E
Kartál Óros, Greece .... 44 C7 41 15N 25 13 E
Kartaly, Russia .... 54 E7 53 3N 60 40 E
Kartapur, India .... 80 D6 31 27N 75 32 E
Karthaus, U.S.A. 136 E6 41 8N 78 9W
Kartuzy, Poland .... 47 A5 54 22N 18 10 E
Karuah, Australia ...... 117 B9 32 37 S 151 56 E
Karufa, Indonesia ...... 73 B4 3 50 S 133 20 E
Karumba, Australia ..... 114 B3 17 31 S 140 50 E
Karumo, Tanzania ...... 106 C3 2 25 S 32 50 E
Karumwa, Tanzania ..... 106 C3 3 12 S 32 38 E
Karungu, Kenya .... 106 C3 0 50 S 34 10 E
Karup, Denmark .... 15 H3 56 19N 9 10 E
Karur, India .... 83 J4 10 59N 78 2 E
Karviná, Czech. .... 31 B11 49 53N 18 25 E
Karwi, India .... 81 G9 25 12N 80 57 E
Kaş, Turkey .... 88 E3 36 11N 29 37 E
Kasache, Malawi .... 107 E3 13 25 S 34 20 E
Kasai, Japan .... 62 C6 34 55N 134 52 E
Kasai →, Zaïre .... 103 C3 3 30 S 16 10 E
Kasai Occidental □, Zaïre 103 D4 6 0 S 22 0 E
Kasai Oriental □, Zaïre . 103 D4 5 0 S 24 30 E
Kasaji, Zaïre .... 103 E4 10 25 S 23 27 E
Kasama, Japan .... 63 A12 36 23N 140 16 E
Kasama, Zambia .... 107 E3 10 16 S 31 9 E
Kasan-dong, N. Korea ... 67 D14 41 18N 126 55 E
Kasane, Namibia .... 104 B3 17 34 S 24 50 E
Kasanga, Tanzania ..... 107 D3 8 30 S 31 10 E
Kasangulu, Zaïre .... 103 C3 4 33 S 15 15 E
Kasaoka, Japan .... 62 C5 34 30N 133 30 E
Kasaragod, India ...... 83 H2 12 30N 74 58 E
Kasat, Burma .... 78 G7 15 56N 98 13 E
Kasba, Bangla. .... 78 D3 23 45N 91 2 E
Kasba L., Canada 131 A8 60 20N 102 10W
Kasba Tadla, Morocco ... 98 B3 32 36N 6 17W
Kaseda, Japan .... 62 F2 31 25N 130 19 E
Kāseh Garān, Iran ..... 84 C5 34 5N 46 2 E
Kasempa, Zambia ...... 107 E2 13 30 S 25 44 E
Kasenga, Zaïre .... 107 E2 10 20 S 28 45 E
Kasese, Uganda .... 106 B3 0 13N 30 3 E
Kasewa, Zambia .... 107 E2 14 28 S 28 53 E
Kasganj, India .... 81 F8 27 48N 78 42 E
Kashabowie, Canada 128 C1 48 40N 90 26W
Kāshān, Iran .... 85 C6 34 5N 51 30 E
Kashi, China .... 64 C2 39 30N 76 2 E
Kashihara, Japan ...... 63 C7 34 27N 135 46 E
Kashima, Ibaraki, Japan . 63 B12 35 58N 140 38 E
Kashima, Saga, Japan ... 62 D2 33 7N 130 6 E
Kashima-Nada, Japan ... 63 B12 36 0N 140 45 E
Kashimbo, Zaïre .... 107 E2 11 12 S 26 19 E
Kashin, Russia .... 51 C10 57 20N 37 36 E
Kashipur, Orissa, India .. 82 E6 19 16N 83 3 E
Kashipur, Ut. P., India .. 81 E8 29 15N 79 0 E
Kashira, Russia .... 51 D11 54 45N 38 10 E
Kashiwa, Japan .... 63 B11 35 52N 139 59 E
Kashiwazaki, Japan .... 61 F9 37 22N 138 33 E
Kashk-e Kohneh, Afghan. 79 B1 34 55N 62 30 E
Kashkasu, Kirghizia .... 55 D6 39 54N 72 44 E
Kāshmar, Iran .... 85 C8 35 16N 58 26 E
Kashmir, Asia .... 81 C7 34 0N 76 0 E
Kashmor, Pakistan ..... 79 C3 28 28N 69 32 E
Kashpirovka, Russia .... 51 E16 53 0N 48 30 E
Kashun Noerh = Gaxun Nur, China .... 64 B5 42 22N 100 30 E
Kasimov, Russia .... 51 D12 54 55N 41 20 E
Kasinge, Zaïre .... 106 D2 6 15 S 26 58 E
Kasiruta, Indonesia .... 72 B3 0 25 S 127 12 E
Kaskaskia →, U.S.A. ... 140 G7 37 58N 89 57W
Kaskattama →, Canada . 131 B10 57 3N 90 4W
Kaskelen, Kazakhstan ... 55 B8 43 20N 76 35 E
Kaskinen, Finland ...... 12 E16 62 22N 21 15 E
Kaskö, Finland .... 12 E16 62 22N 21 15 E
Kasli, Russia .... 54 D7 55 53N 60 46 E
Kaslo, Canada 130 D5 49 55N 116 55W
Kasmere L., Canada 131 B8 59 34N 101 10W
Kasongan, Indonesia ... 75 C4 2 0 S 113 23 E
Kasongo, Zaïre .... 106 C2 4 30 S 26 33 E
Kasongo Lunda, Zaïre ... 103 D3 6 35 S 16 49 E
Kásos, Greece .... 45 J8 35 20N 26 55 E
Kásos, Stenón, Greece ... 45 J8 35 30N 26 30 E
Kaspi, Georgia .... 53 F11 41 54N 44 17 E
Kaspichan, Bulgaria .... 43 D12 43 18N 27 11 E
Kaspiysk, Russia .... 53 E12 42 52N 47 40 E
Kaspiyskiy, Russia ..... 53 D12 45 22N 47 23 E

Kinistino 217

Kewanna, U.S.A. 141 C10 41 1N 86 25W
Kewaunee, U.S.A. 134 C2 44 27N 87 31W
Keweenaw B., U.S.A. 134 B1 47 0N 88 15W
Keweenaw Pen., U.S.A. 134 B2 47 30N 88 0W
Keweenaw Pt., U.S.A. 134 B2 47 25N 87 43W
Key Harbour, Canada 128 C3 45 50N 80 45W
Key West, U.S.A. 133 F10 24 33N 81 48W
Keyesport, U.S.A. 140 F7 38 45N 89 17W
Keyser, U.S.A. 134 F6 39 26N 78 59W
Keystone, U.S.A. 138 D3 43 54N 103 25W
Keytesville, U.S.A. 140 E4 39 26N 92 56W
Kez, Russia 54 C3 57 55N 53 46 E
Kezhma, Russia 57 D11 58 59N 101 9 E
Kežmarok, Slovak Rep. 31 B13 49 10N 20 28 E
Khabarovo, Russia 56 C7 69 30N 60 30 E
Khabarovsk, Russia 57 E14 48 30N 135 5 E
Khabr, Iran 85 D8 28 51N 56 22 E
Khābūr →, Syria 84 C4 35 0N 40 30 E
Khachmas, Azerbaijan 53 F13 41 31N 48 42 E
Khachrod, India 80 H6 23 25N 75 20 E
Khadari, W. el →, Sudan 95 E2 10 29N 27 15 E
Khadro, Pakistan 80 F3 26 11N 68 50 E
Khadyzhensk, Russia 53 D8 44 26N 39 32 E
Khadzhilyangar, India 81 B8 35 45N 79 20 E
Khagaria, India 81 G12 25 30N 86 32 E
Khaipur, Bahawalpur, Pakistan 80 E5 29 34N 72 17 E
Khaipur, Hyderabad, Pakistan 80 F3 27 32N 68 49 E
Khair, India 80 F7 27 57N 77 46 E
Khairabad, India 81 F9 27 33N 80 47 E
Khairagarh, India 81 J9 21 27N 81 2 E
Khairpur, Pakistan 79 D3 27 32N 68 49 E
Khāk Dow, Afghan. 79 B2 34 57N 67 16 E
Khakhea, Botswana 104 C3 24 48 S 23 22 E
Khalach, Turkmenistan 55 D2 38 4N 64 52 E
Khalafābād, Iran 85 D6 30 54N 49 24 E
Khalfallah, Algeria 99 B5 34 20N 0 16 E
Khalfūt, Yemen 87 D6 15 52N 52 10 E
Khalilabad, India 81 F10 26 48N 83 5 E
Khalīlī, Iran 85 E7 27 38N 53 17 E
Khalkhāl, Iran 85 B6 37 37N 48 32 E
Khálki, Greece 44 E4 39 36N 22 30 E
Khalkidhikí □, Greece 44 D5 40 25N 23 20 E
Khalkís, Greece 45 F5 38 27N 23 42 E
Khalmer-Sede = Tazovskiy, Russia 56 C8 67 30N 78 44 E
Khalmer Yu, Russia 48 A12 67 58N 65 1 E
Khalturin, Russia 51 B16 58 40N 48 50 E
Khalūf, Oman 90 C6 20 30N 58 13 E
Kham Keut, Laos 76 C5 18 15N 104 43 E
Khamaria, India 82 C5 23 10N 80 52 E
Khamas Country, Botswana 104 C4 21 45 S 26 30 E
Khambat, G. of, India 80 J5 20 45N 72 30 E
Khambhaliya, India 80 H3 22 14N 69 41 E
Khambhat, India 80 H5 22 23N 72 33 E
Khamgaon, India 82 D3 20 42N 76 37 E
Khamilonísion, Greece 45 J8 35 50N 26 15 E
Khamīr, Iran 85 E7 26 57N 55 36 E
Khamir, Yemen 86 C3 16 2N 44 0 E
Khamīs Mushayṭ, Si. Arabia 86 C3 18 18N 42 44 E
Khammam, India 82 F5 17 11N 80 6 E
Khamsa, Egypt 91 E1 30 27N 32 23 E
Khān Abū Shāmat, Syria 91 B5 33 39N 36 53 E
Khān Azād, Iraq 84 C5 33 7N 44 22 E
Khān Mujiddah, Iraq 84 C4 32 21N 43 48 E
Khān Shaykhūn, Syria 84 C3 35 26N 36 38 E
Khān Yūnis, Egypt 91 D3 31 21N 34 18 E
Khānābād, Afghan. 79 A3 36 45N 69 5 E
Khanabad, Uzbekistan 55 C5 40 59N 70 38 E
Khānaqīn, Iraq 84 C5 34 23N 45 25 E
Khānbāghī, Iran 85 B7 36 10N 55 25 E
Khandrá, Greece 45 J8 35 3N 26 8 E
Khandwa, India 82 D3 21 49N 76 22 E
Khandyga, Russia 57 C14 62 42N 135 35 E
Khāneh, Iran 84 B5 36 41N 45 8 E
Khanewal, Pakistan 79 C3 30 20N 71 55 E
Khanh Duong, Vietnam 76 F7 12 44N 108 44 E
Khaniá, Greece 32 D6 35 30N 24 4 E
Khaniá □, Greece 32 D6 35 30N 24 0 E
Khaníon, Kólpos, Greece 32 D5 35 33N 23 55 E
Khanka, Ozero, Asia 57 E14 45 0N 132 24 E
Khankendy, Azerbaijan 89 D12 39 40N 46 25 E
Khanna, India 80 D7 30 42N 76 16 E
Khanpur, Pakistan 79 C3 28 42N 70 35 E
Khantau, Kazakhstan 55 A6 44 13N 73 48 E
Khanty-Mansiysk, Russia 56 C7 61 0N 69 0 E
Khapalu, Pakistan 81 B7 35 10N 76 20 E
Khapcheranga, Russia 57 E12 49 42N 112 24 E
Kharagpur, India 81 H12 22 20N 87 25 E
Khárakas, Greece 32 D7 35 1N 25 7 E
Kharan Kalat, Pakistan 79 C2 28 34N 65 21 E
Kharānaq, Iran 85 C7 32 20N 54 45 E
Kharda, India 82 E2 18 40N 75 34 E
Khardung La, India 81 B7 34 20N 77 43 E
Khârga, El Wâhât el, Egypt 94 B3 25 10N 30 35 E
Khargon, India 82 D2 21 45N 75 40 E
Kharit, Wadi el →, Egypt 94 C3 24 26N 33 3 E
Khārk, Jazireh, Iran 85 D6 29 15N 50 28 E
Kharkiv = Kharkov, Ukraine 52 B7 49 58N 36 20 E
Kharkov, Ukraine 52 B7 49 58N 36 20 E
Kharmanli, Bulgaria 43 F10 41 55N 25 55 E
Kharovsk, Russia 51 B12 59 56N 40 13 E
Khartoum = El Khartûm, Sudan 95 D3 15 31N 32 35 E
Khasan, Russia 60 C5 42 25N 130 40 E
Khasavyurt, Russia 53 E12 43 16N 46 40 E
Khāsh, Iran 85 D9 28 15N 61 15 E
Khashm el Girba, Sudan 95 E4 14 59N 35 58 E
Khashuri, Georgia 53 F10 42 3N 43 35 E
Khasi Hills, India 78 C3 25 30N 91 30 E
Khaskovo, Bulgaria 43 F10 41 56N 25 30 E
Khatanga, Russia 57 B11 72 0N 102 20 E
Khatanga →, Russia 57 B11 72 55N 106 0 E
Khatauli, India 80 E7 29 17N 77 43 E
Khātūnābād, Iran 85 C6 35 30N 51 40 E
Khatyrchi, Uzbekistan 55 C2 40 2N 65 58 E
Khatyrka, Russia 57 C18 62 3N 175 15 E
Khavast, Uzbekistan 55 C4 40 10N 68 49 E
Khawlaf, Ra's, Yemen 87 D6 12 40N 54 7 E
Khay', Si. Arabia 86 C3 18 45N 41 24 E
Khaybar, Harrat, Si. Arabia 84 E4 25 45N 40 0 E
Khaydarken, Kirghizia 55 D5 39 57N 71 20 E
Khāzimiyah, Iraq 84 C4 34 46N 43 37 E
Khazzân Jabal el Awliyâ, Sudan 95 D3 15 24N 32 20 E
Khe Bo, Vietnam 76 C5 19 8N 104 41 E
Khe Long, Vietnam 76 B5 21 29N 104 46 E
Khed, Maharashtra, India 82 F1 17 43N 73 27 E
Khed, Maharashtra, India 82 E1 18 51N 73 56 E
Khekra, India 80 E7 28 52N 77 20 E
Khemarak Phouminville, Cambodia 77 G4 11 37N 102 59 E
Khemelnik, Ukraine 52 B2 49 33N 27 58 E
Khemis Miliana, Algeria 99 A5 36 11N 2 14 E
Khemissèt, Morocco 98 B3 33 50N 6 1W
Khemmarat, Thailand 76 D5 16 10N 105 15 E
Khenāmān, Iran 85 D8 30 27N 56 29 E
Khenchela, Algeria 99 A6 35 28N 7 11 E
Khenifra, Morocco 98 B3 32 58N 5 46W
Kherrata, Algeria 99 A6 36 27N 5 13 E
Khérson, Greece 44 C4 41 5N 22 47 E
Kherson, Ukraine 52 C5 46 35N 32 35 E
Khersónisos Akrotíri, Greece 32 D6 35 30N 24 10 E
Kheta →, Russia 57 B11 71 54N 102 6 E
Khiliomódhion, Greece 45 G4 37 48N 22 51 E
Khilok, Russia 57 D12 51 30N 110 45 E
Khimki, Russia 51 D10 55 50N 37 20 E
Khíos, Greece 45 F8 38 27N 26 9 E
Khirbat Qanāfār, Lebanon 91 B4 33 39N 35 43 E
Khisar-Momina Banya, Bulgaria 43 E9 42 30N 24 44 E
Khiuma = Hiiumaa, Estonia 50 B3 58 50N 22 45 E
Khiva, Uzbekistan 56 E7 41 30N 60 18 E
Khīyāv, Iran 84 B5 38 30N 47 45 E
Khlebarovo, Bulgaria 43 D11 43 37N 26 15 E
Khlong Khlung, Thailand 76 D2 16 12N 99 43 E
Khmelnitskiy, Ukraine 50 G5 49 23N 27 0 E
Khmelnytskyy = Khmelnitskiy, Ukraine 50 G5 49 23N 27 0 E
Khmer Rep. = Cambodia ■, Asia 76 F5 12 15N 105 0 E
Khoai, Hon, Vietnam 77 H5 8 26N 104 50 E
Khodzent, Tajikistan 55 C4 40 17N 69 37 E
Khojak P., Afghan. 79 C2 30 55N 66 30 E
Khok Kloi, Thailand 77 H2 8 17N 98 19 E
Khok Pho, Thailand 77 J3 6 43N 101 6 E
Khokholskiy, Russia 51 F11 51 35N 38 40 E
Kholm, Afghan. 79 A2 36 45N 67 40 E
Kholm, Russia 50 C7 57 10N 31 15 E
Kholmsk, Russia 57 E15 47 40N 142 5 E
Khomas Hochland, Namibia 104 C2 22 40 S 16 0 E
Khomayn, Iran 85 C6 33 40N 50 7 E
Khon Kaen, Thailand 76 D4 16 30N 102 47 E
Khong, Laos 76 E5 14 7N 105 51 E
Khong Sedone, Laos 76 E5 15 34N 105 49 E
Khonu, Russia 57 C15 66 30N 143 12 E
Khoper →, Russia 51 G13 49 30N 42 20 E
Khor el 'Atash, Sudan 95 E3 13 20N 34 15 E
Khóra, Greece 45 G3 37 3N 21 42 E
Khóra Sfakíon, Greece 32 D6 35 15N 24 9 E
Khorāsān □, Iran 85 C8 34 0N 58 0 E
Khorat = Nakhon Ratchasima, Thailand 76 E4 14 59N 102 12 E
Khorat, Cao Nguyen, Thailand 76 E4 15 30N 102 50 E
Khorb el Ethel, Algeria 98 C3 28 30N 6 17W
Khorixas, Namibia 104 C1 20 16 S 14 59 E
Khorog, Tajikistan 55 E5 37 30N 71 36 E
Khorol, Ukraine 52 B5 49 48N 33 15 E
Khorramābād, Khorāsān, Iran 85 C8 35 6N 57 57 E
Khorramābād, Lorestān, Iran 85 C6 33 30N 48 25 E
Khorrāmshahr, Iran 85 D6 30 29N 48 15 E
Khosravī, Iran 85 D6 30 48N 51 28 E
Khosrowābād, Khuzestān, Iran 85 D6 30 10N 48 25 E
Khosrowābād, Kordestān, Iran 84 C5 35 31N 47 38 E
Khosūyeh, Iran 85 D7 28 32N 54 26 E
Khotin, Ukraine 52 B2 48 31N 26 27 E
Khouribga, Morocco 98 B3 32 58N 6 57W
Khowai, Bangla. 78 C3 24 5N 91 40 E
Khoyniki, Belorussia 50 F6 51 54N 29 55 E
Khrami →, Azerbaijan 53 F11 41 25N 45 0 E
Khrenovoye, Russia 51 F12 51 4N 40 16 E
Khristianá, Greece 45 H7 36 14N 25 13 E
Khromtau, Kazakhstan 54 F6 50 17N 58 27 E
Khrysokhou B., Cyprus 32 D11 35 6N 32 25 E
Khtapodhiá, Greece 45 G7 37 24N 25 34 E
Khu Khan, Thailand 76 E5 14 42N 104 12 E
Khudrah, W. →, Yemen 87 C5 18 10N 50 20 E
Khuff, Si. Arabia 84 E5 24 55N 44 53 E
Khūgīānī, Qandahar, Afghan. 79 C2 31 34N 66 32 E
Khūgīānī, Qandahar, Afghan. 79 C2 31 28N 65 14 E
Khulayş, Si. Arabia 86 B2 22 9N 39 19 E
Khulna, Bangla. 78 D2 22 45N 89 34 E
Khulna □, Bangla. 78 D2 22 25N 89 35 E
Khulo, Georgia 53 F10 41 33N 42 19 E
Khumago, Botswana 104 C3 20 26 S 24 32 E
Khumrah, Si. Arabia 86 B2 21 22N 39 13 E
Khūnsorkh, Iran 85 E8 27 9N 56 7 E
Khunzakh, Russia 53 E12 42 35N 46 42 E
Khūr, Iran 85 C8 32 55N 58 18 E
Khurai, India 80 G8 24 3N 78 23 E
Khuraydah, Yemen 87 D5 15 33N 48 18 E
Khurayş, Si. Arabia 85 E6 25 6N 48 2 E
Khūrīyā Mūrīyā, Jazā 'ir, Oman 87 C6 17 30N 55 58 E
Khurja, India 80 E7 28 15N 77 58 E
Khūsf, Iran 85 C8 32 46N 58 53 E
Khushab, Pakistan 79 B4 32 20N 72 20 E
Khuzdar, Pakistan 79 D2 27 52N 66 30 E
Khūzestān □, Iran 85 D6 31 0N 49 0 E
Khvājeh, Iran 84 B5 38 9N 49 35 E
Khvājeh Moḥammad, Kūh-e, Afghan. 79 A3 36 22N 70 17 E
Khvalynsk, Russia 51 E16 52 30N 48 2 E
Khvānsār, Iran 85 D7 29 56N 54 8 E
Khvatovka, Russia 51 E15 52 24N 46 32 E
Khvor, Iran 85 C7 33 45N 55 0 E
Khvorgū, Iran 85 E8 27 34N 56 27 E
Khvormūj, Iran 85 D6 28 40N 51 30 E
Khvoy, Iran 84 B5 38 35N 45 0 E
Khvoynaya, Russia 50 B9 58 58N 34 28 E
Khyber Pass, Afghan. 79 B3 34 10N 71 8 E
Kia, Solomon Is. 121 L10 7 32 S 158 26 E
Kiabukwa, Zaïre 103 D4 8 40 S 24 48 E
Kiadho →, India 82 E3 19 37N 77 40 E
Kiama, Australia 117 C9 34 40 S 150 50 E
Kiamba, Phil. 71 H5 6 2N 124 46 E
Kiambi, Zaïre 106 D2 7 15 S 28 0 E
Kiambu, Kenya 106 C4 1 8 S 36 50 E
Kiangsi = Jiangxi □, China 69 D10 27 30N 116 0 E
Kiangsu = Jiangsu □, China 67 H10 33 0N 120 0 E
Kiáton, Greece 45 F4 38 2N 22 43 E
Kibæk, Denmark 15 H2 56 2N 8 51 E
Kibanga Port, Uganda 106 B3 0 10N 32 58 E
Kibangou, Congo 102 C2 3 26 S 12 22 E
Kibara, Tanzania 106 C3 2 8 S 33 30 E
Kibare, Mts., Zaïre 106 D2 8 25 S 27 10 E
Kibawe, Phil. 71 H5 7 34N 125 0 E
Kibombo, Zaïre 103 C5 3 57 S 25 53 E
Kibondo, Tanzania 106 C3 3 35 S 30 45 E
Kibondo □, Tanzania 106 C3 4 0 S 30 55 E
Kibumbu, Burundi 106 C2 3 32 S 29 45 E
Kibungu, Rwanda 106 C3 2 10 S 30 32 E
Kibuye, Burundi 106 C2 3 39 S 29 59 E
Kibuye, Rwanda 106 C2 2 3 S 29 21 E
Kibwesa, Tanzania 106 D2 6 30 S 29 58 E
Kibwezi, Kenya 106 C4 2 27 S 37 57 E
Kičevo, Macedonia 42 F5 41 31N 20 59 E
Kichiga, Russia 57 D17 59 50N 163 5 E
Kicking Horse Pass, Canada 130 C5 51 28N 116 16W
Kidal, Mali 101 B5 18 26N 1 22 E
Kidapawan, Phil. 71 H5 7 1N 125 3 E
Kidderminster, U.K. 17 E5 52 24N 2 13W
Kidete, Tanzania 106 D4 6 25 S 37 17 E
Kidira, Senegal 100 C2 14 28N 12 13W
Kidnappers, C., N.Z. 118 F6 39 38 S 177 5 E
Kidston, Australia 114 B3 18 52 S 144 8 E
Kidugallo, Tanzania 106 D4 6 49 S 38 15 E
Kidurong, Tanjong, Malaysia 75 B4 3 16N 113 3 E
Kiel, Germany 26 A6 54 16N 10 8 E
Kiel Kanal = Nord-Ostsee Kanal, Germany 26 A5 54 15N 9 40 E
Kielce, Poland 47 E7 50 52N 20 42 E
Kielce □, Poland 47 E7 50 40N 20 40 E
Kieldrecht, Belgium 21 F4 51 17N 4 11 E
Kieler Bucht, Germany 26 A6 54 30N 10 30 E
Kien Binh, Vietnam 77 H5 9 55N 105 19 E
Kien Tan, Vietnam 77 G5 10 7N 105 17 E
Kienge, Zaïre 107 E2 10 30 S 27 30 E
Kiessé, Niger 101 C5 13 29N 4 1 E
Kieta, Papua N. G. 120 D8 6 12 S 155 36 E
Kiev = Kiyev, Ukraine 50 F7 50 30N 30 28 E
Kiffa, Mauritania 100 B2 16 37N 11 24W
Kifisiá, Greece 45 F5 38 4N 23 49 E
Kifissós →, Greece 45 F5 38 35N 23 20 E
Kifrī, Iraq 84 C5 34 45N 45 0 E
Kigali, Rwanda 106 C3 1 59 S 30 4 E
Kigarama, Tanzania 106 C3 1 1 S 31 50 E
Kigoma □, Tanzania 106 D2 5 0 S 30 0 E
Kigoma-Ujiji, Tanzania 106 C2 4 55 S 29 36 E
Kigomasha, Ras, Tanzania 106 C4 4 58 S 38 58 E
Kihee, Australia 115 D3 27 23 S 142 37 E
Kihikihi, N.Z. 118 E4 38 2 S 175 22 E
Kii-Hantō, Japan 63 D7 34 0N 135 45 E
Kii-Sanchi, Japan 63 C8 34 20N 136 0 E
Kii-Suidō, Japan 62 D6 33 40N 134 45 E
Kikaiga-Shima, Japan 61 K4 28 19N 129 59 E
Kikinda, Serbia 42 B5 45 50N 20 30 E
Kikládhes, Greece 45 G6 37 20N 24 30 E
Kikládhes □, Greece 45 G6 37 0N 25 0 E
Kikoira, Australia 117 B7 33 39 S 146 40 E
Kikori, Papua N. G. 120 D3 7 25 S 144 15 E
Kikori →, Papua N. G. 120 D3 7 38 S 144 20 E
Kikuchi, Japan 62 E2 32 59N 130 47 E
Kikwit, Zaïre 103 D3 5 0 S 18 45 E
Kila' Drosh, Pakistan 79 B3 35 33N 71 52 E
Kilakkarai, India 83 K4 9 12N 78 47 E
Kílalki, Greece 45 H9 36 15N 27 35 E
Kilauea Crater, U.S.A. 132 J17 19 25N 155 17W
Kilchberg, Switz. 29 B7 47 18N 8 33 E
Kilcoy, Australia 115 D5 26 59 S 152 30 E
Kildare, Ireland 19 C5 53 10N 6 50W
Kildare □, Ireland 19 C5 53 10N 6 50W
Kilembe, Zaïre 103 D3 5 42 S 19 55 E
Kilgore, U.S.A. 139 J7 32 23N 94 53W
Kilifi, Kenya 106 C4 3 40 S 39 48 E
Kilifi □, Kenya 106 C4 3 30 S 39 40 E
Kilimanjaro, Tanzania 106 C4 3 7 S 37 20 E
Kilimanjaro □, Tanzania 106 C4 4 0 S 38 0 E
Kilinailau Is., Papua N. G. 120 C8 4 45 S 155 20 E
Kilindini, Kenya 106 C4 4 4 S 39 40 E
Kilis, Turkey 88 E7 36 42N 37 6 E
Kiliya, Ukraine 52 D3 45 28N 29 16 E
Kilju, N. Korea 67 D15 40 57N 129 25 E
Kilkee, Ireland 19 D2 52 41N 9 40W
Kilkenny, Ireland 19 D4 52 40N 7 17W
Kilkenny □, Ireland 19 D4 52 35N 7 15W
Kilkieran B., Ireland 19 C2 53 18N 9 45W
Kilkís, Greece 44 D4 40 58N 22 57 E
Kilkís □, Greece 44 C4 41 5N 22 50 E
Killala, Ireland 19 B2 54 13N 9 12W
Killala B., Ireland 19 B2 54 20N 9 12W
Killaloe, Ireland 19 D3 52 48N 8 28W
Killaloe Sta., Canada 136 A7 45 33N 77 25W
Killam, Canada 130 C6 52 47N 111 51W
Killarney, Australia 115 D5 28 20 S 152 18 E
Killarney, Canada 128 C3 45 55N 81 30W
Killarney, Ireland 19 D2 52 2N 9 30W
Killarney, Lakes of, Ireland 19 E2 52 0N 9 30W
Killary Harbour, Ireland 19 C2 53 38N 9 52W
Killdeer, Canada 131 D7 49 6N 106 22W
Killdeer, U.S.A. 138 B3 47 26N 102 48W
Killeen, U.S.A. 139 K6 31 7N 97 44W
Killiecrankie, Pass of, U.K. 18 E5 56 44N 3 46W
Killin, U.K. 18 E4 56 28N 4 20W
Killíni, Ilía, Greece 45 G3 37 55N 21 8 E
Killíni, Korinthía, Greece 45 G4 37 54N 22 25 E
Killybegs, Ireland 19 B3 54 38N 8 26W
Kilmarnock, U.K. 18 F4 55 36N 4 30W
Kilmez, Russia 54 C2 56 58N 50 55 E
Kilmez →, Russia 54 C2 56 58N 50 28 E
Kilmore, Australia 117 D6 37 25 S 144 53 E
Kilondo, Tanzania 107 D3 9 45 S 34 20 E
Kilosa, Tanzania 106 D4 6 48 S 37 0 E
Kilosa □, Tanzania 106 D4 6 48 S 37 0 E
Kilrush, Ireland 19 D2 52 39N 9 30W
Kilwa □, Tanzania 107 D4 9 0 S 39 0 E
Kilwa Kisiwani, Tanzania 107 D4 8 58 S 39 32 E
Kilwa Kivinje, Tanzania 107 D4 8 45 S 39 25 E
Kilwa Masoko, Tanzania 107 D4 8 55 S 39 30 E
Kim, U.S.A. 139 G3 37 15N 103 21W
Kimaam, Indonesia 73 C5 7 58 S 138 53 E
Kimamba, Tanzania 106 D4 6 45 S 37 10 E
Kimba, Australia 116 B2 33 8 S 136 23 E
Kimball, Nebr., U.S.A. 138 E3 41 14N 103 40W
Kimball, S. Dak., U.S.A. 138 D5 43 45N 98 57W
Kimbe, Papua N. G. 120 C6 5 33 S 150 11 E
Kimbe B., Papua N. G. 120 C6 5 15 S 150 30 E
Kimberley, Australia 116 B4 32 50 S 141 4 E
Kimberley, Canada 130 D5 49 40N 115 59W
Kimberley, S. Africa 104 D3 28 43 S 24 46 E
Kimberley Downs, Australia 112 C3 17 24 S 124 22 E
Kimberley Plateau, Australia 110 D4 16 20 S 127 0 E
Kimberly, U.S.A. 142 E6 42 32N 114 22W
Kimchaek, N. Korea 67 D15 40 40N 129 10 E
Kimchŏn, S. Korea 67 F15 36 11N 128 4 E
Kími, Greece 45 F6 38 38N 24 6 E
Kimje, S. Korea 67 G14 35 48N 126 45 E
Kímolos, Greece 45 H6 36 48N 24 37 E
Kimovsk, Russia 51 D11 54 0N 38 29 E
Kimparana, Mali 100 C4 12 48N 5 0W
Kimry, Russia 51 C10 56 55N 37 15 E
Kimsquit, Canada 130 C3 52 45N 126 57W
Kimstad, Sweden 15 F9 58 35N 15 58 E
Kimvula, Zaïre 103 D3 5 44 S 15 58 E
Kinabalu, Gunong, Malaysia 75 A5 6 3N 116 14 E
Kínaros, Greece 45 H8 36 59N 26 15 E
Kinaskan L., Canada 130 B2 57 38N 130 8W
Kinbasket L., Canada 130 C5 52 0N 118 10W
Kincaid, Canada 131 D7 49 40N 107 0W
Kincaid, U.S.A. 140 E7 39 35N 89 25W
Kincardine, Canada 128 D3 44 10N 81 40W
Kinda, Kasai Or., Zaïre 103 D5 9 18 S 25 4 E
Kinda, Shaba, Zaïre 103 C4 4 47 S 21 48 E
Kinder Scout, U.K. 16 D6 53 24N 1 53W
Kindersley, Canada 131 C7 51 30N 109 10W
Kindia, Guinea 100 C2 10 0N 12 52W
Kindu, Zaïre 102 C5 2 55 S 25 50 E
Kinel, Russia 54 E2 53 15N 50 40 E
Kineshma, Russia 51 C13 57 30N 42 5 E
Kinesi, Tanzania 106 C3 1 25 S 33 50 E
King, L., Australia 113 F2 33 10 S 119 35 E
King, Mt., Australia 114 D4 25 10 S 147 30 E
King City, Calif., U.S.A. 144 J5 36 13N 121 8W
King City, Mo., U.S.A. 140 D2 40 3N 94 31W
King Cr. →, Australia 114 C2 24 35 S 139 30 E
King Edward →, Australia 112 B4 14 14 S 126 35 E
King Frederick VI Land = Kong Frederik VI.s Kyst, Greenland 6 C5 63 0N 43 0W
King George B., Falk. Is. 160 D4 51 30 S 60 30W
King George I., Antarctica 7 C18 60 0 S 60 0W
King George Is., Canada 127 C11 57 20N 80 30W
King I., Australia 114 F3 39 50 S 144 0 E
King I., Canada 130 C3 52 10N 127 40W
King Leopold Ras., Australia 112 C4 17 30 S 125 45 E
King Sd., Australia 112 C3 16 50 S 123 20 E
King William I., Canada 126 B10 69 10N 97 25W
King William's Town, S. Africa 104 E4 32 51 S 27 22 E
Kingaroy, Australia 115 D5 26 32 S 151 51 E
Kingfisher, U.S.A. 139 H6 35 52N 97 56W
Kingirbān, Iraq 84 C5 34 40N 44 54 E
Kingisepp = Kuressaare, Estonia 50 B3 58 15N 22 30 E
Kingisepp, Russia 50 B6 59 25N 28 40 E
Kingking, Phil. 71 H5 7 9N 125 54 E
Kingman, Ariz., U.S.A. 145 K12 35 12N 114 4W
Kingman, Ind., U.S.A. 141 E9 39 58N 87 18W
Kingman, Kans., U.S.A. 139 G5 37 39N 98 7W
Kingoonya, Australia 115 E2 30 55 S 135 19 E
Kings →, U.S.A. 144 J7 36 3N 119 50W
Kings Canyon National Park, U.S.A. 144 J8 36 50N 118 40W
King's Lynn, U.K. 16 E8 52 45N 0 25 E
Kings Mountain, U.S.A. 135 H5 35 15N 81 20W
King's Peak, U.S.A. 142 F8 40 46N 110 27W
Kingsbridge, U.K. 17 G4 50 17N 3 46W
Kingsburg, U.S.A. 144 J7 36 31N 119 33W
Kingsbury, U.S.A. 141 C10 41 31N 86 42W
Kingscote, Australia 116 C2 35 40 S 137 38 E
Kingscourt, Ireland 19 C5 53 55N 6 48W
Kingsley, U.S.A. 138 D7 42 35N 95 58W
Kingsport, U.S.A. 135 G4 36 33N 82 33W
Kingston, Canada 128 D4 44 14N 76 30W
Kingston, Jamaica 148 C4 18 0N 76 50W
Kingston, N.Z. 119 F3 45 20 S 168 43 E
Kingston, Mo., U.S.A. 140 E2 39 39N 94 2W
Kingston, N.Y., U.S.A. 137 E10 41 56N 73 59W
Kingston, Pa., U.S.A. 137 E9 41 16N 75 54W
Kingston, R.I., U.S.A. 137 E13 41 29N 71 30W
Kingston Pk., U.S.A. 145 K11 35 45N 115 54W
Kingston South East, Australia 116 D3 36 51 S 139 55 E
Kingston upon Hull, U.K. 16 D7 53 45N 0 20W
Kingston-upon-Thames, U.K. 17 F7 51 23N 0 20W
Kingstown, Australia 117 A9 30 29 S 151 6 E
Kingstown, St. Vincent 149 D7 13 10N 61 10W
Kingstree, U.S.A. 135 J6 33 40N 79 50W
Kingsville, Canada 128 D3 42 2N 82 45W
Kingsville, U.S.A. 139 M6 27 31N 97 52W
Kingussie, U.K. 18 D4 57 5N 4 2W
Kinistino, Canada 131 C7 52 57N 105 2W

218 Kinkala

Kinkala, *Congo* **103 C2** 4 18 S 14 49 E
Kinki □, *Japan* **63 D8** 33 45N 136 0 E
Kinleith, *N.Z.* **118 E4** 38 20 S 175 56 E
Kinmount, *Canada* **136 B6** 44 48N 78 45W
Kinmundy, *U.S.A.* **141 F8** 38 46N 88 51W
Kinna, *Sweden* **15 G6** 57 32N 12 42 E
Kinnaird, *Canada* **130 D5** 49 17N 117 39W
Kinnairds Hd., *U.K.* **18 D7** 57 40N 2 0W
Kinnared, *Sweden* **15 G7** 57 2N 13 7 E
Kinnarodden, *Norway* **10 A11** 71 8N 27 40 E
Kino, *Mexico* **146 B2** 28 45N 111 59W
Kinogitan, *Phil.* **71 G5** 9 0N 124 48 E
Kinoje →, *Canada* **128 B3** 52 8N 81 25W
Kinomoto, *Japan* **63 B8** 35 30N 136 13 E
Kinoni, *Uganda* **106 C3** 0 41 S 30 28 E
Kinrooi, *Belgium* **21 F7** 51 9N 5 45 E
Kinross, *U.K.* **18 E5** 56 13N 3 25W
Kinsale, *Ireland* **19 E3** 51 42N 8 31W
Kinsale, Old Hd. of, *Ireland* **19 E3** 51 37N 8 32W
Kinsha = Chang Jiang →, *China* **69 B13** 31 48N 121 10 E
Kinshasa, *Zaïre* **103 C3** 4 20 S 15 15 E
Kinsley, *U.S.A.* **139 G5** 37 55N 99 25W
Kinston, *U.S.A.* **135 H7** 35 16N 77 35W
Kintampo, *Ghana* **101 D4** 8 5N 1 41W
Kintap, *Indonesia* **75 C5** 3 51 S 115 13 E
Kintore Ra., *Australia* **112 D4** 23 15 S 128 47 E
Kintyre, *U.K.* **18 F3** 55 30N 5 35W
Kintyre, Mull of, *U.K.* **18 F3** 55 17N 5 55W
Kinu, *Burma* **78 D5** 22 46N 95 37 E
Kinu-Gawa →, *Japan* **63 B11** 35 36N 139 57 E
Kinushseo →, *Canada* **128 A3** 55 15N 83 45W
Kinuso, *Canada* **130 B5** 55 20N 115 25W
Kinyangiri, *Tanzania* **106 C3** 4 25 S 34 37 E
Kinzig →, *Germany* **27 G3** 48 37N 7 49 E
Kinzua, *U.S.A.* **136 E6** 41 52N 78 58W
Kinzua Dam, *U.S.A.* **136 E5** 41 53N 79 0W
Kióni, *Greece* **45 F2** 38 27N 20 41 E
Kiosk, *Canada* **128 C4** 46 6N 78 53W
Kiowa, *Kans., U.S.A.* **139 G5** 37 1N 98 29W
Kiowa, *Okla., U.S.A.* **139 H7** 34 43N 95 54W
Kipahigan L., *Canada* **131 B8** 55 20N 101 55W
Kipanga, *Tanzania* **106 D4** 6 15 S 35 20 E
Kiparissía, *Greece* **45 G3** 37 15N 21 40 E
Kiparissiakós Kólpos, *Greece* **45 G3** 37 25N 21 25 E
Kipembawe, *Tanzania* **106 D3** 7 38 S 33 27 E
Kipengere Ra., *Tanzania* **107 D3** 9 12 S 34 15 E
Kipili, *Tanzania* **106 D3** 7 28 S 30 32 E
Kipini, *Kenya* **106 C5** 2 30 S 40 32 E
Kipling, *Canada* **131 C8** 50 6N 102 38W
Kippure, *Ireland* **19 C5** 53 11N 6 23W
Kipungot, *Phil.* **71 H5** 6 24N 124 4 E
Kipushi, *Zaïre* **107 E2** 11 48 S 27 12 E
Kira Kira, *Solomon Is.* **121 N11** 10 27 S 161 56 E
Kirandul, *India* **82 E5** 18 33N 81 10 E
Kiratpur, *India* **80 E8** 29 32N 78 12 E
Kirchberg, *Switz.* **28 B5** 47 5N 7 35 E
Kirchhain, *Germany* **26 E4** 50 49N 8 54 E
Kirchheim, *Germany* **27 G5** 48 38N 9 20 E
Kirchheim-Bolanden, *Germany* **27 F4** 49 40N 8 0 E
Kirchschlag, *Austria* **31 D9** 47 30N 16 19 E
Kirensk, *Russia* **57 D11** 57 50N 107 55 E
Kirgella Rocks, *Australia* **113 F3** 30 5 S 122 50 E
Kirghizia ■, *Asia* **55 C7** 42 0N 75 0 E
Kirghizstan = Kirghizia ■, *Asia* **55 C7** 42 0N 75 0 E
Kirgizia = Kirghizia ■, *Asia* **55 C7** 42 0N 75 0 E
Kirgiziya Steppe, *Kazakhstan* **49 D10** 50 0N 55 0 E
Kiri, *Zaïre* **102 C3** 1 29 S 19 0 E
Kiri Buru, *India* **82 D7** 22 0N 85 0 E
Kiribati ■, *Pac. Oc.* **122 H10** 5 0 S 180 0 E
Kırıkhan, *Turkey* **88 E7** 36 31N 36 21 E
Kırıkkale, *Turkey* **88 D5** 39 51N 33 32 E
Kirikopuni, *N.Z.* **118 B3** 35 50 S 174 1 E
Kirillov, *Russia* **51 B11** 59 51N 38 14 E
Kirin = Jilin, *China* **67 C14** 43 44N 126 30 E
Kirin = Jilin □, *China* **67 C13** 44 0N 127 0 E
Kirindi →, *Sri Lanka* **83 L5** 6 15N 81 20 E
Kirishi, *Russia* **50 B7** 59 28N 31 59 E
Kirishima-Yama, *Japan* **62 F2** 31 58N 130 55 E
Kiritimati, *Kiribati* **123 G12** 1 58N 157 27W
Kırka, *Turkey* **88 D4** 39 16N 30 31 E
Kirkcaldy, *U.K.* **18 E5** 56 7N 3 10W
Kirkcudbright, *U.K.* **18 G4** 54 50N 4 3W
Kirkee, *India* **82 E1** 18 34N 73 56 E
Kirkenær, *Norway* **14 D6** 60 27N 12 3 E
Kirkenes, *Norway* **12 B21** 69 40N 30 5 E
Kirkintilloch, *U.K.* **18 F4** 55 57N 4 10W
Kirkjubæjarklaustur, *Iceland* **12 E4** 63 47N 18 4W
Kirkland, *Ariz., U.S.A.* **143 J7** 34 25N 112 43W
Kirkland, *Ill., U.S.A.* **141 B8** 42 6N 88 51W
Kirkland Lake, *Canada* **128 C3** 48 9N 80 2W
Kırklareli, *Turkey* **43 F12** 41 44N 27 15 E
Kırklareli □, *Turkey* **88 C2** 41 45N 27 15 E
Kirklin, *U.S.A.* **141 D10** 40 12N 86 22W
Kirkliston Ra., *N.Z.* **119 E5** 44 25 S 170 34 E
Kirksville, *U.S.A.* **140 D4** 40 12N 92 35W
Kirkūk, *Iraq* **84 C5** 35 30N 44 21 E
Kirkwall, *U.K.* **18 C6** 58 59N 2 59W
Kirkwood, *S. Africa* **104 E4** 33 22 S 25 15 E
Kirkwood, *U.S.A.* **140 F6** 38 35N 90 24W
Kirlampudi, *India* **82 F6** 17 12N 82 12 E
Kirn, *Germany* **27 F3** 49 46N 7 29 E
Kirov = Vyatka, *Russia* **54 B1** 58 35N 49 40 E
Kirov, *Russia* **50 D9** 54 3N 34 20 E
Kirovabad = Gyandzha, *Azerbaijan* **53 F12** 40 45N 46 20 E
Kirovakan = Karaklis, *Armenia* **53 F11** 40 48N 44 30 E
Kirovo, *Uzbekistan* **55 C5** 40 26N 70 36 E
Kirovo-Chepetsk, *Russia* **51 B17** 58 28N 50 0 E
Kirovograd, *Ukraine* **52 B5** 48 35N 32 20 E
Kirovohrad = Kirovograd, *Ukraine* **52 B5** 48 35N 32 20 E
Kirovsk, *Russia* **48 A5** 67 48N 33 50 E
Kirovsk, *Turkmenistan* **56 F7** 37 42N 60 23 E
Kirovsk, *Ukraine* **53 B8** 48 35N 38 30 E
Kirovski, *Russia* **53 D13** 45 51N 48 11 E
Kirovskiy, *Kazakhstan* **55 A9** 44 52N 78 12 E
Kirovskiy, *Russia* **57 D16** 54 27N 155 42 E
Kirovskiy, *Russia* **60 B6** 45 7N 133 30 E
Kirovskoye, *Kirghizia* **55 B5** 42 39N 71 35 E
Kirriemuir, *U.K.* **18 E6** 56 41N 2 58W
Kirs, *Russia* **54 B3** 59 21N 52 14 E
Kirsanov, *Russia* **51 E13** 52 35N 42 40 E
Kırşehir, *Turkey* **88 D6** 39 14N 34 5 E
Kırşehir □, *Turkey* **88 D6** 39 10N 34 10 E
Kirstonia, *S. Africa* **104 D3** 25 30 S 23 45 E
Kirtachi, *Niger* **101 C5** 12 52N 2 30 E
Kirteh, *Afghan.* **79 B1** 32 15N 63 0 E
Kirthar Range, *Pakistan* **79 D2** 27 0N 67 0 E
Kiruna, *Sweden* **12 C16** 67 52N 20 15 E
Kirundu, *Zaïre* **102 C5** 0 50 S 25 35 E
Kirup, *Australia* **113 F2** 33 40 S 115 50 E
Kirya, *Russia* **51 D15** 55 5N 46 45 E
Kiryū, *Japan* **63 A11** 36 24N 139 20 E
Kisaga, *Tanzania* **106 C3** 4 30 S 34 23 E
Kisalaya, *Nic.* **148 D3** 14 40N 84 3W
Kisambo, *Zaïre* **103 D3** 6 25 S 18 14 E
Kisámou, Kólpos, *Greece* **32 D5** 35 30N 23 38 E
Kisanga, *Zaïre* **106 B2** 2 30N 26 35 E
Kisangani, *Zaïre* **106 B2** 0 35N 25 15 E
Kisantu, *Zaïre* **103 D3** 5 7 S 15 5 E
Kisar, *Indonesia* **72 C3** 8 5 S 127 10 E
Kisaran, *Indonesia* **74 B1** 3 0N 99 37 E
Kisarawe, *Tanzania* **106 D4** 6 53 S 39 0 E
Kisarawe □, *Tanzania* **106 D4** 7 3 S 39 0 E
Kisarazu, *Japan* **63 B11** 35 23N 139 55 E
Kisbér, *Hungary* **31 D11** 47 30N 18 2 E
Kiselevsk, *Russia* **56 D9** 54 5N 86 39 E
Kishanganga →, *Pakistan* **81 B5** 34 18N 73 28 E
Kishanganj, *India* **81 F13** 26 3N 88 14 E
Kishangarh, *India* **80 F4** 27 50N 70 30 E
Kishi, *Nigeria* **101 D5** 9 1N 3 52 E
Kishinev, *Moldavia* **52 C3** 47 0N 28 50 E
Kishiwada, *Japan* **63 C7** 34 28N 135 22 E
Kishorganj, *Bangla.* **78 C3** 24 26N 90 40 E
Kishtwar, *India* **81 C6** 33 20N 75 48 E
Kishwaukee →, *U.S.A.* **140 B7** 42 12N 89 8W
Kisii, *Kenya* **106 C3** 0 40 S 34 45 E
Kisii □, *Kenya* **106 C3** 0 40 S 34 45 E
Kisiju, *Tanzania* **106 D4** 7 23 S 39 19 E
Kısır Dağ, *Turkey* **53 F10** 41 0N 43 5 E
Kisizi, *Uganda* **106 C2** 1 0S 29 58 E
Kiska I., *U.S.A.* **126 C1** 51 59N 177 30 E
Kiskatinaw →, *Canada* **130 B4** 56 8N 120 10W
Kiskittogisu L., *Canada* **131 C9** 54 13N 98 20W
Kiskomárom = Zalakomár, *Hungary* **31 E10** 46 33N 17 10 E
Kiskörös, *Hungary* **31 E12** 46 37N 19 20 E
Kiskundorozsma, *Hungary* **31 E13** 46 16N 20 5 E
Kiskunfélegyháza, *Hungary* **31 E12** 46 42N 19 53 E
Kiskunhalas, *Hungary* **31 E12** 46 28N 19 37 E
Kiskunmajsa, *Hungary* **31 E12** 46 30N 19 48 E
Kislovodsk, *Russia* **53 E10** 43 50N 42 45 E
Kismayu = Chisimaio, *Somali Rep.* **108 E2** 0 22 S 42 32 E
Kiso-Gawa →, *Japan* **63 B8** 35 20N 136 45 E
Kiso-Sammyaku, *Japan* **63 B9** 35 45N 137 45 E
Kisofukushima, *Japan* **63 B9** 35 52N 137 43 E
Kisoro, *Uganda* **106 C2** 1 17 S 29 48 E
Kispest, *Hungary* **31 D12** 47 27N 19 9 E
Kissidougou, *Guinea* **100 D2** 9 5N 10 5W
Kissimmee, *U.S.A.* **135 L5** 28 18N 81 24W
Kissimmee →, *U.S.A.* **135 M5** 27 9N 80 52W
Kississing L., *Canada* **131 B8** 55 10N 101 20W
Kissónerga, *Cyprus* **32 E11** 34 49N 32 24 E
Kistanje, *Croatia* **39 E12** 43 58N 15 55 E
Kisújszállás, *Hungary* **31 D13** 47 12N 20 50 E
Kisuki, *Japan* **62 B4** 35 17N 132 54 E
Kisumu, *Kenya* **106 C3** 0 3 S 34 45 E
Kisvárda, *Hungary* **31 C15** 48 14N 22 4 E
Kiswani, *Tanzania* **106 C4** 4 5 S 37 57 E
Kiswere, *Tanzania* **107 D4** 9 27 S 39 30 E
Kit Carson, *U.S.A.* **138 F3** 38 46N 102 48W
Kita, *Mali* **100 C3** 13 5N 9 25W
Kita-Ura, *Japan* **63 A12** 36 0N 140 34 E
Kitab, *Uzbekistan* **55 D3** 39 7N 66 52 E
Kitaibaraki, *Japan* **61 F10** 36 50N 140 45 E
Kitakami, *Japan* **60 E10** 39 20N 141 10 E
Kitakami-Gawa →, *Japan* **60 E10** 38 25N 141 19 E
Kitakami-Sammyaku, *Japan* **60 E10** 39 30N 141 30 E
Kitakata, *Japan* **60 F9** 37 39N 139 52 E
Kitakyūshū, *Japan* **62 D2** 33 50N 130 50 E
Kitale, *Kenya* **106 B4** 1 0N 35 0 E
Kitami, *Japan* **60 C11** 43 48N 143 54 E
Kitami-Sammyaku, *Japan* **60 B11** 44 22N 142 43 E
Kitangiri, L., *Tanzania* **106 C3** 4 5 S 34 20 E
Kitano-Kaikyō, *Japan* **62 C6** 34 17N 134 58 E
Kitaotao, *Phil.* **71 H5** 7 40N 125 1 E
Kitaya, *Tanzania* **107 E5** 10 38 S 40 8 E
Kitcharao, *Phil.* **71 G5** 9 27N 125 36 E
Kitchener, *Australia* **113 F3** 30 55 S 124 8 E
Kitchener, *Canada* **128 D3** 43 27N 80 29W
Kitega = Gitega, *Burundi* **106 C2** 3 26 S 29 56 E
Kitengo, *Zaïre* **103 D4** 7 26 S 24 8 E
Kiteto □, *Tanzania* **106 C4** 5 0 S 37 0 E
Kitgum, *Uganda* **106 B3** 3 17N 32 52 E
Kíthira, *Greece* **45 H6** 36 9N 23 12 E
Kíthnos, *Greece* **45 G6** 37 26N 24 27 E
Kiti, *Cyprus* **32 E12** 34 50N 33 34 E
Kiti, C., *Cyprus* **32 E12** 34 48N 33 36 E
Kitikmeot □, *Canada* **126 A9** 70 0N 110 0W
Kitimat, *Canada* **130 C3** 54 3N 128 38W
Kitinen →, *Finland* **12 C19** 67 34N 26 40 E
Kitiyab, *Sudan* **95 D3** 17 13N 33 35 E
Kítros, *Greece* **44 D4** 40 22N 22 34 E
Kitsuki, *Japan* **62 D3** 33 25N 131 37 E
Kittakittaooloo, L., *Australia* **115 D2** 28 3 S 138 14 E
Kittanning, *U.S.A.* **136 F5** 40 49N 79 31W
Kittatinny Mts., *U.S.A.* **137 E10** 41 0N 75 0W
Kittery, *U.S.A.* **135 D10** 43 5N 70 45W
Kitui, *Kenya* **106 C4** 1 17 S 38 0 E
Kitui □, *Kenya* **106 C4** 1 30 S 38 25 E
Kitwe, *Zambia* **107 E2** 12 54 S 28 13 E
Kitzbühel, *Austria* **30 D5** 47 27N 12 24 E
Kitzingen, *Germany* **27 F6** 49 44N 10 9 E
Kivalo, *Finland* **12 C19** 66 18N 26 0 E
Kivarli, *India* **80 G5** 24 33N 72 46 E
Kividhes, *Cyprus* **32 E11** 34 46N 32 51 E
Kivotós, *Greece* **44 D3** 40 13N 21 26 E
Kivu □, *Zaïre* **106 C2** 3 10 S 27 0 E
Kivu, L., *Zaïre* **106 C2** 1 48 S 29 0 E
Kiwai I., *Papua N. G.* **120 E2** 8 35 S 143 30 E
Kiyev, *Ukraine* **50 F7** 50 30N 30 28 E
Kiyevskoye Vdkhr., *Ukraine* **50 F7** 51 0N 30 25 E
Kizel, *Russia* **54 B5** 59 3N 57 40 E
Kiziguru, *Rwanda* **106 C3** 1 46 S 30 23 E
Kızıl Irmak →, *Turkey* **52 F6** 41 44N 35 58 E
Kizil Jilga, *India* **81 B8** 35 26N 78 50 E
Kizil Yurt, *Russia* **53 E12** 43 13N 46 54 E
Kızılcahamam, *Turkey* **52 F5** 40 30N 32 30 E
Kızılhisar, *Turkey* **88 E3** 37 32N 29 17 E
Kızılırmak, *Turkey* **88 C5** 40 21N 33 59 E
Kizilskoye, *Russia* **54 E6** 52 44N 58 54 E
Kızıltepe, *Turkey* **89 E9** 37 12N 40 35 E
Kizimkazi, *Tanzania* **106 D4** 6 28 S 39 30 E
Kizlyar, *Russia* **53 E12** 43 51N 46 40 E
Kizyl-Arvat, *Turkmenistan* **56 F6** 38 58N 56 15 E
Kjellerup, *Denmark* **15 H3** 56 17N 9 25 E
Kladanj, *Bos.-H.* **42 C3** 44 14N 18 42 E
Kladnica, *Serbia* **42 D5** 43 23N 20 2 E
Kladno, *Czech.* **30 A7** 50 10N 14 7 E
Kladovo, *Serbia* **42 C7** 44 36N 22 33 E
Klaeng, *Thailand* **76 F3** 12 47N 101 39 E
Klagan, *Malaysia* **75 A5** 5 58N 117 27 E
Klagenfurt, *Austria* **30 E7** 46 38N 14 20 E
Klagshamn, *Sweden* **15 J6** 55 32N 12 53 E
Klagstorp, *Sweden* **15 J7** 55 22N 13 23 E
Klaipėda, *Lithuania* **50 D2** 55 43N 21 10 E
Klamath →, *U.S.A.* **142 F1** 41 33N 124 5W
Klamath Falls, *U.S.A.* **142 E3** 42 13N 121 46W
Klamath Mts., *U.S.A.* **142 F2** 41 20N 123 0W
Klangklang, *Burma* **78 D4** 22 41N 93 26 E
Klanjec, *Croatia* **39 B12** 46 3N 15 45 E
Klappan →, *Canada* **130 B3** 58 0N 129 43W
Klarälven →, *Sweden* **13 G12** 59 23N 13 32 E
Klaten, *Indonesia* **75 D4** 7 43 S 110 36 E
Klatovy, *Czech.* **30 B6** 49 23N 13 18 E
Klawer, *S. Africa* **104 E2** 31 44 S 18 36 E
Klawock, *U.S.A.* **130 B2** 55 33N 133 6W
Klazienaveen, *Neths.* **20 C10** 52 44N 7 0 E
Kłecko, *Poland* **47 C4** 52 38N 17 25 E
Kleczew, *Poland* **47 C5** 52 22N 18 9 E
Kleena Kleene, *Canada* **130 C4** 52 0N 124 59W
Klein, *U.S.A.* **142 C9** 46 24N 108 33W
Klein-Karas, *Namibia* **104 D2** 27 33 S 18 7 E
Kleine Gette →, *Belgium* **21 G6** 50 51N 5 6 E
Kleine Nete →, *Belgium* **21 F5** 51 12N 4 46 E
Klekovača, *Bos.-H.* **39 D13** 44 25N 16 32 E
Klenovec, *Macedonia* **42 F5** 41 32N 20 49 E
Klenovec, *Slovak Rep.* **31 C12** 48 36N 19 54 E
Klerksdorp, *S. Africa* **104 D4** 26 53 S 26 38 E
Kleszczele, *Poland* **47 C10** 52 35N 23 19 E
Kletnya, *Russia* **50 E8** 53 23N 33 12 E
Kletsk, *Belorussia* **50 E5** 53 5N 26 45 E
Kletskiy, *Russia* **53 B10** 49 20N 43 0 E
Kleve, *Germany* **26 D2** 51 46N 6 10 E
Klickitat, *U.S.A.* **142 D3** 45 49N 121 9W
Klickitat →, *U.S.A.* **144 E5** 45 42N 121 17W
Klidhes, *Cyprus* **32 D13** 35 42N 34 36 E
Klimovichi, *Belorussia* **50 E8** 53 36N 32 0 E
Klin, *Russia* **51 C10** 56 20N 36 48 E
Klinaklini →, *Canada* **130 C3** 51 21N 125 40W
Kling, *Phil.* **71 J5** 5 58N 124 42 E
Klintsey, *Russia* **50 E8** 52 50N 32 10 E
Klipdale, *S. Africa* **104 E2** 34 19 S 19 57 E
Klipplaat, *S. Africa* **104 E3** 33 1 S 24 22 E
Klisura, *Bulgaria* **43 E9** 42 40N 24 28 E
Klitmøller, *Denmark* **15 G2** 57 3N 8 30 E
Kljajićevo, *Serbia* **42 B4** 45 45N 19 17 E
Ključ, *Bos.-H.* **39 D13** 44 32N 16 48 E
Kłobuck, *Poland* **47 E5** 50 55N 18 55 E
Kłodawa, *Poland* **47 C5** 52 15N 18 55 E
Kłodzko, *Poland* **47 E3** 50 28N 16 38 E
Kloetinge, *Neths.* **21 F3** 51 30N 3 56 E
Klondike, *Canada* **126 B6** 64 0N 139 26W
Kloosterzande, *Neths.* **21 F4** 51 22N 4 1 E
Klosi, *Albania* **44 C2** 41 28N 20 10 E
Klosterneuburg, *Austria* **31 C9** 48 18N 16 19 E
Klosters, *Switz.* **29 C9** 46 52N 9 52 E
Kloten, *Switz.* **29 B7** 47 27N 8 35 E
Klötze, *Germany* **26 C7** 52 38N 11 9 E
Klouto, *Togo* **101 D5** 6 57N 0 44 E
Kluane L., *Canada* **126 B6** 61 15N 138 40W
Kluczbork, *Poland* **47 E5** 50 58N 18 12 E
Klundert, *Neths.* **21 E5** 51 40N 4 32 E
Klyuchevskaya, Gora, *Russia* **57 D17** 55 50N 160 30 E
Knaresborough, *U.K.* **16 C6** 54 1N 1 29W
Knee L., *Man., Canada* **131 B10** 55 3N 94 45W
Knee L., *Sask., Canada* **131 B7** 55 51N 107 0W
Kneïss, Is., *Tunisia* **96 B2** 34 22N 10 18 E
Knesselare, *Belgium* **21 F2** 51 9N 3 26 E
Knezha, *Bulgaria* **43 D9** 43 30N 24 5 E
Knić, *Serbia* **42 D5** 43 53N 20 45 E
Knight Inlet, *Canada* **130 C3** 50 45N 125 40W
Knighton, *U.K.* **17 E4** 52 21N 3 2W
Knights Ferry, *U.S.A.* **144 H6** 37 50N 120 40W
Knights Landing, *U.S.A.* **144 G5** 38 48N 121 43W
Knightstown, *U.S.A.* **141 E11** 39 48N 85 32W
Knin, *Croatia* **39 D13** 44 1N 16 17 E
Knittelfeld, *Austria* **30 D7** 47 13N 14 51 E
Knjaževac, *Serbia* **42 D7** 43 35N 22 18 E
Knob, C., *Australia* **113 F2** 34 32 S 119 16 E
Knockmealdown Mts., *Ireland* **19 D4** 52 16N 8 0W
Knokke, *Belgium* **21 F2** 51 20N 3 17 E
Knossós, *Greece* **32 D7** 35 16N 25 10 E
Knox, *U.S.A.* **141 C10** 41 18N 86 37W
Knox, C., *Canada* **130 C2** 54 11N 133 5W
Knox City, *U.S.A.* **139 J5** 33 25N 99 49W
Knox Coast, *Antarctica* **7 C8** 66 30 S 108 0 E
Knoxville, *Iowa, U.S.A.* **140 C4** 41 19N 93 6W
Knoxville, *Tenn., U.S.A.* **135 H4** 35 58N 83 55W
Knurów, *Poland* **31 A11** 50 13N 18 38 E
Knutshø, *Norway* **14 B3** 62 18N 9 41 E
Knysna, *S. Africa* **104 E3** 34 2 S 23 2 E
Knyszyn, *Poland* **47 B9** 53 20N 22 56 E
Ko Kha, *Thailand* **76 C2** 18 11N 99 24 E
Kō-Saki, *Japan* **62 C1** 34 5N 129 13 E
Ko Tao, *Thailand* **77 G2** 10 6N 99 48 E
Koartac, *Canada* **127 B13** 60 55N 69 40W
Koba, *Aru, Indonesia* **73 C4** 6 37 S 134 37 E
Koba, *Bangka, Indonesia* **74 C3** 2 26 S 106 14 E
Kobarid, *Slovenia* **39 B10** 46 15N 13 30 E
Kobayashi, *Japan* **62 F2** 31 56N 130 59 E
Kobdo = Hovd, *Mongolia* **64 B4** 48 2N 91 37 E
Kōbe, *Japan* **63 C7** 34 45N 135 10 E
Kobelyaki, *Ukraine* **52 B6** 49 11N 34 9 E
København, *Denmark* **15 J6** 55 41N 12 34 E
Kōbi-Sho, *Japan* **61 M1** 25 56N 123 41 E
Koblenz, *Germany* **27 E3** 50 21N 7 36 E
Koblenz, *Switz.* **28 A6** 47 37N 8 14 E
Kobo, *Ethiopia* **95 E4** 12 2N 39 56 E
Kobo, *Zaïre* **103 C3** 4 54 S 17 9 E
Kobrin, *Belorussia* **50 E4** 52 15N 24 22 E
Kobroor, Kepulauan, *Indonesia* **73 C4** 6 10 S 134 30 E
Kobuchizawa, *Japan* **63 B10** 35 52N 138 19 E
Kobuleti, *Georgia* **53 F9** 41 55N 41 45 E
Kobylin, *Poland* **47 D4** 51 43N 17 12 E
Kobyłka, *Poland* **47 C8** 52 21N 21 10 E
Kobylkino, *Russia* **51 D13** 54 8N 43 56 E
Kobylnik, *Belorussia* **50 D5** 54 58N 26 39 E
Kocaeli = İzmit, *Turkey* **88 C3** 40 45N 29 50 E
Kocaeli □, *Turkey* **88 C3** 40 45N 29 55 E
Kočane, *Serbia* **42 D6** 43 12N 21 52 E
Kočani, *Macedonia* **42 F7** 41 55N 22 25 E
Koçarlı, *Turkey* **45 G9** 37 45N 27 43 E
Koceljevo, *Serbia* **42 C4** 44 28N 19 50 E
Kočevje, *Slovenia* **39 C11** 45 39N 14 50 E
Koch Bihar, *India* **78 B2** 26 22N 89 29 E
Kochang, *S. Korea* **67 G14** 35 41N 127 55 E
Kochas, *India* **81 G10** 25 15N 83 56 E
Kocher →, *Germany* **27 F5** 49 14N 9 12 E
Kocheya, *Russia* **57 D13** 52 32N 120 42 E
Kōchi, *Japan* **62 D5** 33 30N 133 35 E
Kōchi □, *Japan* **62 D5** 33 40N 133 30 E
Kōchi-Heiya, *Japan* **62 D5** 33 28N 133 30 E
Kochiu = Gejiu, *China* **68 F4** 23 20N 103 10 E
Kochkor-Ata, *Kirghizia* **55 C6** 41 1N 72 29 E
Kochkorka, *Kirghizia* **55 B7** 42 13N 75 46 E
Kock, *Poland* **47 D9** 51 38N 22 27 E
Kodaira, *Japan* **63 B11** 35 44N 139 29 E
Koddiyar B., *Sri Lanka* **83 K5** 8 33N 81 15 E
Kodiak, *U.S.A.* **126 C4** 57 47N 152 24W
Kodiak I., *U.S.A.* **126 C4** 57 30N 152 45W
Kodinar, *India* **80 J4** 20 46N 70 46 E
Kodori →, *Georgia* **53 E9** 42 47N 41 10 E
Koekelare, *Belgium* **21 F1** 51 5N 2 59 E
Koersel, *Belgium* **21 F6** 51 3N 5 17 E
Koes, *Namibia* **104 D2** 26 0 S 19 15 E
Koffiefontein, *S. Africa* **104 D4** 29 30 S 25 0 E
Kofiau, *Indonesia* **73 B3** 1 11 S 129 50 E
Köflach, *Austria* **30 D8** 47 4N 15 5 E
Koforidua, *Ghana* **101 D4** 6 3N 0 17W
Kōfu, *Japan* **63 B10** 35 40N 138 30 E
Koga, *Japan* **63 A11** 36 11N 139 43 E
Kogaluk →, *Canada* **129 A7** 56 12N 61 44W
Kogan, *Australia* **115 D5** 27 2 S 150 40 E
Kogi □, *Nigeria* **101 D6** 7 45N 6 45 E
Kogin Baba, *Nigeria* **101 D7** 7 55N 11 35 E
Koh-i-Bābā, *Afghan.* **79 B2** 34 30N 67 0 E
Koh-i-Khurd, *Afghan.* **80 C1** 33 30N 65 59 E
Kohat, *Pakistan* **79 B3** 33 40N 71 29 E
Kohima, *India* **78 C5** 25 35N 94 10 E
Kohkīlūyeh va Būyer Aḥmadi □, *Iran* **85 D6** 31 30N 50 30 E
Kohler Ra., *Antarctica* **7 D15** 77 0 S 110 0W
Kohtla-Järve, *Estonia* **50 B5** 59 20N 27 20 E
Kohukohu, *N.Z.* **118 B2** 35 22 S 173 38 E
Koin-dong, *N. Korea* **67 D14** 40 28N 126 18 E
Kojetín, *Czech.* **31 B10** 49 21N 17 20 E
Kojima, *Japan* **62 C5** 34 30N 133 50 E
Kōjo, *Japan* **62 C5** 34 33N 133 55 E
Kojŏ, *N. Korea* **67 E14** 38 58N 127 58 E
Kojonup, *Australia* **113 F2** 33 48 S 117 10 E
Kojūr, *Iran* **85 B6** 36 23N 51 43 E
Kok Yangak, *Kirghizia* **55 C6** 41 2N 73 12 E
Koka, *Sudan* **94 C3** 20 5N 30 35 E
Kokand, *Uzbekistan* **55 C5** 40 30N 70 57 E
Kokanee Glacier Prov. Park, *Canada* **130 D5** 49 47N 117 10W
Kokas, *Indonesia* **73 B4** 2 42 S 132 26 E
Kokava, *Slovak Rep.* **31 C12** 48 35N 19 50 E
Kokchetav, *Kazakhstan* **56 D7** 53 20N 69 25 E
Kokemäenjoki, *Finland* **13 F16** 61 32N 21 44 E
Kokerite, *Guyana* **153 B6** 7 12N 59 35W
Kokhma, *Russia* **51 C12** 56 55N 41 18 E
Kokiri, *N.Z.* **119 C6** 42 29 S 171 25 E
Kokkola, *Finland* **12 E17** 63 50N 23 8 E
Koko, *Nigeria* **101 C5** 11 28N 4 29 E
Kokoda, *Papua N. G.* **120 E4** 8 54 S 147 47 E
Kokolopozo, *Ivory C.* **100 D3** 5 8N 6 5W
Kokomo, *U.S.A.* **141 D10** 40 29N 86 8W
Kokonau, *Indonesia* **73 B5** 4 43 S 136 26 E
Kokopo, *Papua N. G.* **120 C7** 4 22 S 152 19 E
Kokoro, *Niger* **101 C5** 14 12N 0 55 E
Koksan, *N. Korea* **67 E14** 38 46N 126 40 E
Koksengir, Gora, *Kazakhstan* **55 A2** 44 21N 65 6 E
Koksoak →, *Canada* **127 C13** 58 30N 68 10W
Kokstad, *S. Africa* **105 E4** 30 32 S 29 29 E
Kokubu, *Japan* **62 F2** 31 44N 130 46 E
Kokuora, *Russia* **57 B15** 71 35N 144 50 E
Kola, *Indonesia* **73 C4** 5 35 S 134 30 E
Kola, *Russia* **48 A5** 68 45N 33 8 E
Kola Pen. = Kolskiy Poluostrov, *Russia* **48 A6** 67 30N 38 0 E
Kolachel, *India* **83 K3** 8 10N 77 15 E
Kolahoi, *India* **81 B6** 34 12N 75 22 E
Kolahun, *Liberia* **100 D2** 8 15N 10 4W
Kolaka, *Indonesia* **72 B2** 4 3 S 121 46 E
Kolar, *India* **83 H4** 13 12N 78 15 E
Kolar Gold Fields, *India* **83 H4** 12 58N 78 16 E
Kolari, *Finland* **12 C17** 67 20N 23 48 E
Kolašin, *Montenegro* **42 E4** 42 50N 19 31 E
Kolby Kås, *Denmark* **15 J4** 55 48N 10 32 E
Kolchugino = Leninsk-Kuznetskiy, *Russia* **56 D9** 54 44N 86 10 E
Kolchugino, *Russia* **51 C11** 56 17N 39 22 E
Kolda, *Senegal* **100 C2** 12 55N 14 57W
Kolding, *Denmark* **15 J3** 55 30N 9 29 E
Kole, *Zaïre* **102 C4** 3 16 S 22 42 E
Koléa, *Algeria* **99 A5** 36 38N 2 46 E
Kolepom = Yos Sudarso, Pulau, *Indonesia* **73 C5** 8 0 S 138 30 E
Kolguyev, Ostrov, *Russia* **48 A8** 69 20N 48 30 E
Kolham, *Neths.* **20 B9** 53 11N 6 44 E

Legrad 223

Långsele, *Sweden* **14 A11** 63 12N 17 4 E
Langtao, *Burma* **78 B6** 27 15N 97 34 E
Langting, *India* **78 C4** 25 31N 93 7 E
Langtry, *U.S.A.* **139 L4** 29 49N 101 34W
Langu, *Thailand* **77 J2** 6 53N 99 47 E
Languedoc, *France* **24 E7** 43 58N 3 55 E
Langwies, *Switz.* **29 C9** 46 50N 9 44 E
Langxi, *China* **69 B12** 31 10N 119 12 E
Langxiangzhen, *China* **66 E9** 39 43N 116 8 E
Langzhong, *China* **68 B5** 31 38N 105 58 E
Lanigan, *Canada* **131 C7** 51 51N 105 2W
Lankao, *China* **66 G8** 34 48N 114 50 E
Lannemezan, *France* **24 E4** 43 8N 0 23 E
Lannilis, *France* **22 D2** 48 35N 4 32W
Lannion, *France* **22 D3** 48 46N 3 29W
L'Annonciation, *Canada* **128 C5** 46 25N 74 55W
Lanouaille, *France* **24 C5** 45 24N 1 9 E
Lanping, *China* **68 D2** 26 28N 99 15 E
Lansdale, *U.S.A.* **137 F9** 40 14N 75 17W
Lansdowne, *Australia* **117 A10** 31 48 S 152 30 E
Lansdowne, *Canada* **137 B8** 44 24N 76 1W
Lansdowne House, *Canada* **128 B2** 52 14N 87 53W
L'Anse, *U.S.A.* **128 C2** 46 45N 88 27W
L'Anse au Loup, *Canada* **129 B8** 51 32N 56 50W
Lansford, *U.S.A.* **137 F9** 40 50N 75 53W
Lanshan, *China* **69 E9** 25 24N 112 10 E
Lansing, *U.S.A.* **141 B12** 42 44N 84 33W
Lanslebourg-Mont-Cenis, *France* **25 C10** 45 17N 6 52 E
Lanta Yai, Ko, *Thailand* **77 J2** 7 35N 99 3 E
Lantian, *China* **66 G5** 34 11N 109 20 E
Lanus, *Argentina* **158 C4** 34 45 S 58 27W
Lanusei, *Italy* **40 C2** 39 53N 9 31 E
Lanuza, *Phil.* **71 G6** 9 14N 126 4 E
Lanxi, *China* **69 C12** 29 13N 119 28 E
Lanzarote, *Canary Is.* **33 E6** 29 0N 13 40W
Lanzhou, *China* **66 F2** 36 1N 103 52 E
Lanzo Torinese, *Italy* **38 C4** 45 16N 7 29 E
Lao →, *Italy* **41 C8** 39 45N 15 45 E
Lao Bao, *Laos* **76 D6** 16 35N 106 30 E
Lao Cai, *Vietnam* **76 A4** 22 30N 103 57 E
Laoag, *Phil.* **70 B3** 18 7N 120 34 E
Laoang, *Phil.* **70 E5** 12 32N 125 8 E
Laoha He →, *China* **67 C11** 43 25N 120 35 E
Laois □, *Ireland* **19 D4** 53 0N 7 20W
Laon, *France* **23 C10** 49 33N 3 35 E
Laona, *U.S.A.* **134 C1** 45 34N 88 40W
Laos ■, *Asia* **76 D5** 17 45N 105 0 E
Lapa, *Brazil* **159 B6** 25 46 S 49 44W
Lapalisse, *France* **24 B7** 46 15N 3 38 E
Lapeer, *U.S.A.* **141 A13** 43 3N 83 19W
Lapi □ = Lapin lääni □, *Finland* **12 C19** 67 43N 25 30 E
Lapin lääni □, *Finland* **12 C19** 67 43N 25 30 E
Lapithos, *Cyprus* **32 D12** 35 21N 33 11 E
Lapland = Lappland, *Europe* **12 B18** 68 7N 24 0 E
Lapog, *Phil.* **70 C3** 17 45N 120 27 E
Laporte, *U.S.A.* **137 E8** 41 25N 76 30W
Lapovo, *Serbia* **42 C6** 44 10N 21 2 E
Lappland, *Europe* **12 B18** 68 7N 24 0 E
Laprida, *Argentina* **158 D3** 37 34 S 60 45W
Laptev Sea, *Russia* **57 B13** 76 0N 125 0 E
Lapuş, Munţii, *Romania* **46 B4** 47 20N 23 50 E
Lăpuşul →, *Romania* **46 B4** 47 25N 23 40 E
Łapy, *Poland* **47 C9** 52 59N 22 52 E
L'Aquila, *Italy* **39 F10** 42 21N 13 24 E
Lār, *Āzarbājān-e Sharqī, Iran* **84 B5** 38 30N 47 52 E
Lār, *Fārs, Iran* **85 E7** 27 40N 54 14 E
Lara, *Australia* **116 E6** 38 2 S 144 26 E
Lara, *Phil.* **71 G1** 8 48N 117 52 E
Lara □, *Venezuela* **152 A4** 10 10N 69 50W
Larabanga, *Ghana* **100 D4** 9 16N 1 56W
Laracha, *Spain* **36 B2** 43 15N 8 35W
Larache, *Morocco* **98 A3** 35 10N 6 5W
Laragne-Montéglin, *France* **25 D9** 44 18N 5 49 E
Laramie, *U.S.A.* **138 E2** 41 19N 105 35W
Laramie Mts., *U.S.A.* **138 E2** 42 0N 105 30W
Laranjeiras, *Brazil* **154 D4** 10 48 S 37 10W
Laranjeiras do Sul, *Brazil* **159 B5** 25 23 S 52 23W
Larantuka, *Indonesia* **72 C2** 8 21 S 122 55 E
Larap, *Phil.* **70 D4** 14 18N 122 39 E
Larat, *Indonesia* **73 C4** 7 0 S 132 0 E
L'Arbresle, *France* **25 C8** 45 50N 4 36 E
Larde, *Mozam.* **107 F4** 16 28 S 39 43 E
Larder Lake, *Canada* **128 C4** 48 5N 79 40W
Lardhos, Ákra, *Greece* **32 C10** 36 4N 28 10 E
Lardhos, Órmos, *Greece* **32 C10** 36 4N 28 2 E
Laredo, *Spain* **34 B1** 43 26N 3 28W
Laredo, *U.S.A.* **139 M5** 27 30N 99 30W
Laredo Sd., *Canada* **130 C3** 52 30N 128 53W
Laren, *Neths.* **20 D6** 52 16N 5 14 E
Larena, *Phil.* **71 G4** 9 15N 123 35 E
Largentière, *France* **25 D8** 44 34N 4 18 E
L'Argentière-la-Bessée, *France* **25 D10** 44 47N 6 33 E
Largs, *U.K.* **18 F4** 55 48N 4 51W
Lari, *Italy* **38 E7** 43 34N 10 35 E
Lariang, *Indonesia* **72 B1** 1 26 S 119 17 E
Larimore, *U.S.A.* **138 B6** 47 54N 97 38W
Lārīn, *Iran* **85 C7** 35 55N 52 19 E
Larino, *Italy* **41 A7** 41 48N 14 54 E
Lárisa, *Greece* **44 E4** 39 49N 22 28 E
Lárisa □, *Greece* **44 E4** 39 39N 22 24 E
Larkana, *Pakistan* **79 D3** 27 32N 68 18 E
Larnaca, *Cyprus* **32 E12** 34 55N 33 55 E
Larnaca Bay, *Cyprus* **32 E12** 34 53N 33 45 E
Larne, *U.K.* **19 B6** 54 52N 5 50W
Larned, *U.S.A.* **138 F5** 38 11N 99 6W
Larochette, *Belgium* **21 J8** 49 47N 6 13 E
Laroquebrou, *France* **24 D6** 44 58N 2 12 E
Larrimah, *Australia* **112 C5** 15 35 S 133 12 E
Larsen Ice Shelf, *Antarctica* **7 C17** 67 0 S 62 0W
Larvik, *Norway* **14 E4** 59 4N 10 4 E
Laryak, *Russia* **56 C8** 61 15N 80 0 E
Larzac, Causse du, *France* **24 E7** 43 50N 3 17 E
Las Alpujarras, *Spain* **35 J1** 36 55N 3 20W
Las Animas, *U.S.A.* **138 F3** 38 4N 103 13W
Las Anod, *Somali Rep.* **90 F4** 8 26N 47 19 E
Las Blancos, *Spain* **35 H4** 37 38N 0 49W
Las Brenãs, *Argentina* **158 B3** 27 5 S 61 7W
Las Cabezas de San Juan, *Spain* **37 J5** 37 0N 5 58W
Las Chimeneas, *Mexico* **145 N10** 32 8N 116 5W
Las Coloradas, *Argentina* **160 A2** 39 34 S 70 36W
Las Cruces, *U.S.A.* **143 K10** 32 19N 106 47W
Las Flores, *Argentina* **158 D4** 36 10 S 59 7W
Las Heras, *Argentina* **158 C2** 32 51 S 68 49W
Las Horquetas, *Argentina* **160 C2** 48 14 S 71 11W
Las Khoreh, *Somali Rep.* **90 E4** 11 10N 48 20 E
Las Lajas, *Argentina* **160 A2** 38 30 S 70 25W
Las Lomas, *Peru* **156 A1** 4 40 S 80 10W
Las Lomitas, *Argentina* **158 A3** 24 43 S 60 35W
Las Marismas, *Spain* **37 H4** 37 5N 6 20W
Las Mercedes, *Venezuela* **152 B4** 9 7N 66 24W
Las Navas de la Concepción, *Spain* **37 H5** 37 56N 5 30W
Las Navas de Tolosa, *Spain* **37 G7** 38 18N 3 38W
Las Navas del Marqués, *Spain* **36 E6** 40 36N 4 20W
Las Palmas, *Argentina* **158 B4** 27 8 S 58 45W
Las Palmas, *Canary Is.* **33 F4** 28 7N 15 26W
Las Palmas →, *Mexico* **145 N10** 32 26N 116 54W
Las Piedras, *Uruguay* **159 C4** 34 44 S 56 14W
Las Pipinas, *Argentina* **158 D4** 35 30 S 57 19W
Las Plumas, *Argentina* **160 B3** 43 40 S 67 15W
Las Rosas, *Argentina* **158 C3** 32 30 S 61 35W
Las Tablas, *Panama* **148 E3** 7 49N 80 14W
Las Termas, *Argentina* **158 B3** 27 29 S 64 52W
Las Truchas, *Mexico* **146 D4** 17 57N 102 13W
Las Varillas, *Argentina* **158 C3** 31 50 S 62 50W
Las Vegas, *N. Mex., U.S.A.* **143 J11** 35 36N 105 13W
Las Vegas, *Nev., U.S.A.* **145 J11** 36 10N 115 9W
Lascano, *Uruguay* **159 C5** 33 35 S 54 12W
Lashburn, *Canada* **131 C7** 53 10N 109 40W
Lashio, *Burma* **78 D6** 22 56N 97 45 E
Lashkar, *India* **80 F8** 26 10N 78 10 E
Lashkar Gāh, *Afghan.* **79 C2** 31 35N 64 21 E
Łasin, *Poland* **47 B6** 53 30N 19 2 E
Lasíthi, *Greece* **32 D7** 35 11N 25 31 E
Lasíthi □, *Greece* **32 D7** 35 5N 25 50 E
Lask, *Poland* **47 D6** 51 34N 19 8 E
Łaskarzew, *Poland* **47 D8** 51 48N 21 36 E
Laško, *Slovenia* **39 B12** 46 10N 15 16 E
Lassance, *Brazil* **155 E3** 17 54 S 44 34W
Lassay, *France* **22 D6** 48 27N 0 30W
Lassen Pk., *U.S.A.* **142 F3** 40 29N 121 31W
Last Mountain L., *Canada* **131 C7** 51 5N 105 14W
Lastchance Cr. →, *U.S.A.* **144 E5** 40 2N 121 15W
Lastoursville, *Gabon* **102 C2** 0 55 S 12 38 E
Lastovo, *Croatia* **39 F13** 42 46N 16 55 E
Lastovski Kanal, *Croatia* **39 F13** 42 50N 17 0 E
Lat Yao, *Thailand* **76 E2** 15 45N 99 48 E
Latacunga, *Ecuador* **152 D2** 0 50 S 78 35W
Latakia = Al Lādhiqīyah, *Syria* **84 C2** 35 30N 35 45 E
Latchford, *Canada* **128 C4** 47 20N 79 50W
Late, *Tonga* **121 P13** 18 48 S 174 39W
Laterza, *Italy* **41 B9** 40 38N 16 47 E
Latham, *Australia* **113 E2** 29 44 S 116 20 E
Lathen, *Germany* **26 C3** 52 51N 7 21 E
Lathrop, *U.S.A.* **140 E2** 39 33N 94 20W
Lathrop Wells, *U.S.A.* **145 J10** 36 39N 116 24W
Latiano, *Italy* **41 B10** 40 33N 17 43 E
Latina, *Italy* **40 A5** 41 26N 12 53 E
Latisana, *Italy* **39 C10** 45 47N 13 1 E
Latium = Lazio □, *Italy* **39 F9** 42 10N 12 30 E
Laton, *U.S.A.* **144 J7** 36 26N 119 41W
Latorica →, *Slovak Rep.* **31 C14** 48 28N 21 50 E
Latouche Treville, C., *Australia* **112 C3** 18 27 S 121 49 E
Latrobe, *Australia* **114 G4** 41 14 S 146 30 E
Latrobe, *U.S.A.* **136 F5** 40 19N 79 23W
Latrónico, *Italy* **41 B9** 40 5N 16 0 E
Latur, *India* **82 E3** 18 25N 76 40 E
Latvia ■, *Europe* **50 C3** 56 50N 24 0 E
Lau Group, *Fiji* **121 A3** 17 0 S 178 30W
Lauca →, *Bolivia* **156 D4** 19 9 S 68 10W
Lauchhammer, *Germany* **26 D9** 51 35N 13 48 E
Lauenburg, *Germany* **26 B6** 53 23N 10 33 E
Läufelfingen, *Switz.* **28 B5** 47 24N 7 52 E
Laufen, *Switz.* **28 B5** 47 25N 7 30 E
Lauffen, *Germany* **27 F5** 49 4N 9 9 E
Laugarbakki, *Iceland* **12 D3** 65 20N 20 55W
Laujar, *Spain* **35 J2** 37 0N 2 54W
Launceston, *Australia* **114 G4** 41 24 S 147 8 E
Launceston, *U.K.* **17 G3** 50 38N 4 21W
Laune →, *Ireland* **19 D2** 52 5N 9 40W
Laupheim, *Germany* **27 G5** 48 13N 9 53 E
Laur, *Phil.* **70 D3** 15 35N 121 11 E
Laura, *Queens., Australia* **114 B3** 15 32 S 144 32 E
Laura, *S. Austral., Australia* **116 B3** 33 10 S 138 18 E
Laureana di Borrello, *Italy* **41 D9** 38 28N 16 5 E
Laurel, *Ind., U.S.A.* **141 E11** 39 31N 85 11W
Laurel, *Miss., U.S.A.* **139 K10** 31 41N 89 8W
Laurel, *Mont., U.S.A.* **142 D9** 45 40N 108 46W
Laurencekirk, *U.K.* **18 E6** 56 50N 2 30W
Laurens, *U.S.A.* **135 H4** 34 30N 82 1W
Laurentian Plateau, *Canada* **129 B6** 52 0N 70 0W
Laurentides, Parc Prov. des, *Canada* **129 C5** 47 45N 71 15W
Lauria, *Italy* **41 B8** 40 3N 15 50 E
Laurie L., *Canada* **131 B8** 56 35N 101 57W
Laurinburg, *U.S.A.* **135 H6** 34 47N 79 28W
Laurium, *U.S.A.* **134 B1** 47 14N 88 27W
Lausanne, *Switz.* **28 C3** 46 32N 6 38 E
Laut, *Indonesia* **75 B3** 4 45N 108 0 E
Laut, Pulau, *Indonesia* **75 C5** 3 40 S 116 10 E
Laut Ketil, Kepulauan, *Indonesia* **75 C5** 4 45 S 115 40 E
Lautaro, *Chile* **160 A2** 38 31 S 72 27W
Lauterbach, *Germany* **26 E5** 50 39N 9 23 E
Lauterbrunnen, *Switz.* **28 C5** 46 36N 7 55 E
Lauterecken, *Germany* **27 F3** 49 38N 7 35 E
Lautoka, *Fiji* **121 A1** 17 37 S 177 27 E
Lauwe, *Belgium* **21 G2** 50 47N 3 12 E
Lauwers, *Neths.* **20 A8** 53 32N 6 23 E
Lauwers Zee, *Neths.* **20 B8** 53 21N 6 13 E
Lauzon, *Canada* **129 C5** 46 48N 71 10W
Lava Hot Springs, *U.S.A.* **142 E7** 42 37N 112 1W
Lavadores, *Spain* **36 C2** 42 14N 8 41W
Lavagna, *Italy* **38 D6** 44 18N 9 22 E
Laval, *France* **22 D6** 48 4N 0 48W
Lavalle, *Argentina* **158 B2** 28 15 S 65 15W
Lávara, *Greece* **44 C8** 41 19N 26 22 E
Lavardac, *France* **24 D4** 44 12N 0 20 E
Lavaur, *France* **24 E5** 43 40N 1 49 E
Lavaux, *Switz.* **28 D3** 46 30N 6 45 E
Lavelanet, *France* **24 F5** 42 57N 1 51 E
Lavello, *Italy* **41 A8** 41 4N 15 47 E
Laverne, *U.S.A.* **139 G5** 36 43N 99 54W
Lavers Hill, *Australia* **116 E5** 38 40 S 143 25 E
Laverton, *Australia* **113 E3** 28 44 S 122 29 E
Lávkos, *Greece* **45 E5** 39 9N 23 14 E
Lavos, *Portugal* **36 E2** 40 6N 8 49W
Lavras, *Brazil* **155 F3** 21 20 S 45 0W
Lavre, *Portugal* **37 G2** 38 46N 8 22W
Lavrentiya, *Russia* **57 C19** 65 35N 171 0W
Lávrion, *Greece* **45 G6** 37 40N 24 4 E
Lávris, *Greece* **32 D6** 35 25N 24 40 E
Lavumisa, *Swaziland* **105 D5** 27 20 S 31 55 E
Lawa, *Phil.* **71 H5** 6 12N 125 41 E
Lawa-an, *Phil.* **71 F5** 11 51N 125 5 E
Lawas, *Malaysia* **75 B5** 4 55N 115 25 E
Lawdar, *Yemen* **86 D4** 13 53N 45 52 E
Lawele, *Indonesia* **72 C2** 5 16 S 123 3 E
Lawksawk, *Burma* **78 E6** 21 15N 96 52 E
Lawn Hill, *Australia* **114 B2** 18 36 S 138 33 E
Lawqar, *Si. Arabia* **84 D4** 29 49N 42 45 E
Lawra, *Ghana* **100 C4** 10 39N 2 51W
Lawrence, *N.Z.* **119 F4** 45 55 S 169 41 E
Lawrence, *Ind., U.S.A.* **141 E10** 39 50N 86 2W
Lawrence, *Kans., U.S.A.* **138 F7** 38 58N 95 14W
Lawrence, *Mass., U.S.A.* **137 D13** 42 43N 71 10W
Lawrenceburg, *Ind., U.S.A.* **141 E12** 39 6N 84 52W
Lawrenceburg, *Ky., U.S.A.* **141 F12** 38 2N 84 54W
Lawrenceburg, *Tenn., U.S.A.* **135 H2** 35 14N 87 20W
Lawrenceville, *Ga., U.S.A.* **135 J4** 33 57N 83 59W
Lawrenceville, *Ill., U.S.A.* **141 F9** 38 44N 87 41W
Laws, *U.S.A.* **144 H8** 37 24N 118 20W
Lawson, *U.S.A.* **140 E2** 39 26N 94 12W
Lawton, *Mich., U.S.A.* **141 B11** 42 10N 85 50W
Lawton, *Okla., U.S.A.* **139 H5** 34 37N 98 25W
Lawu, *Indonesia* **75 D4** 7 40 S 111 13 E
Laxford, L., *U.K.* **18 C3** 58 25N 5 10W
Layht, Ra's, *Yemen* **87 D6** 12 38N 53 25 E
Laylá, *Si. Arabia* **86 B4** 22 10N 46 40 E
Laylān, *Iraq* **84 C5** 35 18N 44 31 E
Layon →, *France* **22 E6** 47 20N 0 45W
Laysan I., *Pac. Oc.* **123 E11** 25 30N 167 0W
Laytonville, *U.S.A.* **142 G2** 39 41N 123 29W
Laza, *Burma* **78 B6** 26 30N 97 38 E
Lazarevac, *Serbia* **42 C5** 44 23N 20 17 E
Lazi, *Phil.* **71 G4** 9 8N 123 38 E
Lazio □, *Italy* **39 F9** 42 10N 12 30 E
Lazo, *Russia* **60 C6** 43 25N 133 55 E
Łazy, *Poland* **47 E6** 50 27N 19 24 E
Le Barcarès, *France* **24 F7** 42 47N 3 2 E
Le Beausset, *France* **25 E9** 43 12N 5 48 E
Le Blanc, *France* **24 B5** 46 37N 1 3 E
Le Bleymard, *France* **24 D7** 44 30N 3 42 E
Le Bourgneuf-la-Fôret, *France* **22 D6** 48 10N 0 59W
Le Bouscat, *France* **24 D3** 44 53N 0 37W
Le Brassus, *Switz.* **28 C2** 46 35N 6 13 E
Le Bugue, *France* **24 D4** 44 55N 0 56 E
Le Canourgue, *France* **24 D7** 44 26N 3 13 E
Le Cateau, *France* **23 B10** 50 7N 3 32 E
Le Chambon-Feugerolles, *France* **25 C8** 45 24N 4 19 E
Le Château-d'Oléron, *France* **24 C2** 45 54N 1 12W
Le Châtelard, *Switz.* **28 D3** 46 4N 6 57 E
Le Châtelet, *France* **24 B6** 46 38N 2 16 E
Le Châtelet-en-Brie, *France* **23 D9** 48 31N 2 48 E
Le Chesne, *France* **23 C11** 49 30N 4 45 E
Le Cheylard, *France* **25 D8** 44 55N 4 25 E
Le Claire, *U.S.A.* **140 C6** 41 36N 90 21W
Le Conquet, *France* **22 D2** 48 21N 4 46W
Le Creusot, *France* **23 F11** 46 48N 4 24 E
Le Croisic, *France* **22 E4** 47 18N 2 30W
Le Donjon, *France* **24 B7** 46 22N 3 48 E
Le Dorat, *France* **24 B5** 46 14N 1 5 E
Le François, *Martinique* **149 D7** 14 38N 60 57W
Le Grand-Lucé, *France* **22 E7** 47 52N 0 28 E
Le Grand-Pressigny, *France* **22 F7** 46 55N 0 48 E
Le Havre, *France* **22 C7** 49 30N 0 5 E
Le Lavandou, *France* **25 E10** 43 8N 6 22 E
Le Lion-d'Angers, *France* **22 E6** 47 37N 0 43W
Le Locle, *Switz.* **28 B3** 47 3N 6 44 E
Le Louroux-Béconnais, *France* **22 E6** 47 30N 0 55W
Le Luc, *France* **25 E10** 43 23N 6 21 E
Le Madonie, *Italy* **40 E6** 37 50N 13 50 E
Le Maire, Est. de, *Argentina* **160 D4** 54 50 S 65 0W
Le Mans, *France* **22 E7** 48 0N 0 10 E
Le Marinel, *Zaïre* **103 E5** 10 25 S 25 17 E
Le Mars, *U.S.A.* **138 D6** 42 47N 96 10W
Le Mêle-sur-Sarthe, *France* **22 D7** 48 31N 0 22 E
Le Merlerault, *France* **22 D7** 48 41N 0 16 E
Le Monastier-sur-Gazeille, *France* **24 D7** 44 57N 3 59 E
Le Monêtier-les-Bains, *France* **25 D10** 44 58N 6 30 E
Le Mont d'Or, *France* **23 F13** 46 45N 6 18 E
Le Mont-Dore, *France* **24 C6** 45 35N 2 49 E
Le Mont-St.-Michel, *France* **22 D5** 48 40N 1 30W
Le Moule, *Guadeloupe* **149 C7** 16 20N 61 22W
Le Muy, *France* **25 E10** 43 28N 6 34 E
Le Palais, *France* **22 E3** 47 20N 3 10W
Le Perthus, *France* **24 F6** 42 30N 2 53 E
Le Pont, *Switz.* **28 C2** 46 41N 6 20 E
Le Pouldu, *France* **22 E3** 47 41N 3 36W
Le Puy, *France* **24 C7** 45 3N 3 52 E
Le Quesnoy, *France* **23 B10** 50 15N 3 38 E
Le Roy, *Ill., U.S.A.* **141 D8** 40 21N 88 46W
Le Roy, *Kans., U.S.A.* **139 F7** 38 5N 95 38W
Le Sentier, *Switz.* **28 C2** 46 37N 6 15 E
Le Sueur, *U.S.A.* **138 C8** 44 28N 93 55W
Le Teil, *France* **25 D8** 44 33N 4 40 E
Le Teilleul, *France* **22 D6** 48 32N 0 53W
Le Theil, *France* **22 D7** 48 16N 0 42 E
Le Thillot, *France* **23 E13** 47 53N 6 46 E
Le Thuy, *Vietnam* **76 D6** 17 14N 106 49 E
Le Touquet-Paris-Plage, *France* **23 B8** 50 30N 1 36 E
Le Tréport, *France* **22 B8** 50 3N 1 20 E
Le Val-d'Ajol, *France* **23 E13** 47 55N 6 30 E
Le Verdon-sur-Mer, *France* **24 C2** 45 33N 1 4W
Le Vigan, *France* **24 E7** 43 59N 3 36 E
Lea →, *U.K.* **17 F7** 51 30N 0 10W
Leach, *Cambodia* **77 F4** 12 21N 103 46 E
Lead, *U.S.A.* **138 C3** 44 21N 103 46W
Leader, *Canada* **131 C7** 50 50N 109 30W
Leadhills, *U.K.* **18 F5** 55 25N 3 47W
Leadville, *U.S.A.* **143 G10** 39 15N 106 18W
Leaf →, *U.S.A.* **139 K10** 30 59N 88 44W
Leakey, *U.S.A.* **139 L5** 29 44N 99 46W
Lealui, *Zambia* **103 F4** 15 10 S 23 2 E
Leamington, *Canada* **128 D3** 42 3N 82 36W
Leamington, *N.Z.* **118 D4** 37 55 S 175 30 E
Leamington, *U.S.A.* **142 G7** 39 32N 112 17W
Leamington Spa = Royal Leamington Spa, *U.K.* **17 E6** 52 18N 1 32W
Le'an, *China* **69 D10** 27 22N 115 48 E
Leandro Norte Alem, *Argentina* **159 B4** 27 34 S 55 15W
Learmonth, *Australia* **112 D1** 22 13 S 114 10 E
Leask, *Canada* **131 C7** 53 5N 106 45W
Leavenworth, *Ind., U.S.A.* **141 F10** 38 12N 86 21W
Leavenworth, *Kans., U.S.A.* **138 F7** 39 19N 94 55W
Leavenworth, *Wash., U.S.A.* **142 C3** 47 36N 120 40W
Leawood, *U.S.A.* **140 F2** 38 57N 94 37W
Łeba, *Poland* **47 A4** 54 45N 17 32 E
Łeba →, *Poland* **47 A4** 54 46N 17 33 E
Lebak, *Phil.* **71 H5** 6 32N 124 5 E
Lebam, *U.S.A.* **144 D3** 46 34N 123 33W
Lebane, *Serbia* **42 E6** 42 56N 21 44 E
Lebango, *Congo* **102 B2** 0 39N 14 21 E
Lebanon, *Ill., U.S.A.* **140 F7** 38 38N 89 49W
Lebanon, *Ind., U.S.A.* **141 D10** 40 3N 86 28W
Lebanon, *Kans., U.S.A.* **138 F5** 39 49N 98 33W
Lebanon, *Ky., U.S.A.* **134 G3** 37 34N 85 15W
Lebanon, *Mo., U.S.A.* **139 G8** 37 41N 92 40W
Lebanon, *Ohio, U.S.A.* **141 E12** 39 26N 84 13W
Lebanon, *Oreg., U.S.A.* **142 D2** 44 32N 122 55W
Lebanon, *Pa., U.S.A.* **137 F8** 40 20N 76 26W
Lebanon, *Tenn., U.S.A.* **135 G2** 36 12N 86 18W
Lebanon ■, *Asia* **91 B4** 34 0N 36 0 E
Lebanon Junction, *U.S.A.* **141 G11** 37 50N 85 44W
Lebbeke, *Belgium* **21 G4** 50 58N 4 8 E
Lebec, *U.S.A.* **145 L8** 34 50N 118 52W
Lebedin, *Ukraine* **50 F9** 50 35N 34 30 E
Lebedyan, *Russia* **51 E11** 53 0N 39 10 E
Lebomboberge, *S. Africa* **105 C5** 24 30 S 32 0 E
Lębork, *Poland* **47 A4** 54 33N 17 46 E
Lebrija, *Spain* **37 J4** 36 53N 6 5W
Łebsko, Jezioro, *Poland* **47 A4** 54 40N 17 25 E
Lebu, *Chile* **158 D1** 37 40 S 73 47W
Lecce, *Italy* **41 B11** 40 20N 18 10 E
Lecco, *Italy* **38 C6** 45 50N 9 27 E
Lecco, L. di, *Italy* **38 C6** 45 51N 9 22 E
Lécera, *Spain* **34 D4** 41 13N 0 43W
Lech, *Austria* **30 D3** 47 13N 10 9 E
Lech →, *Germany* **27 G6** 48 44N 10 56 E
Lechang, *China* **69 E9** 25 10N 113 20 E
Lechtaler Alpen, *Austria* **30 D3** 47 15N 10 30 E
Lectoure, *France* **24 E4** 43 56N 0 38 E
Łeczna, *Poland* **47 D9** 51 18N 22 53 E
Łęczyca, *Poland* **47 C6** 52 5N 19 15 E
Ledang, Gunong, *Malaysia* **74 B2** 2 22N 102 37 E
Ledbury, *U.K.* **17 E5** 52 3N 2 25W
Lede, *Belgium* **21 G3** 50 58N 3 59 E
Ledeberg, *Belgium* **21 F3** 51 2N 3 45 E
Ledeč, *Czech.* **30 B8** 49 41N 15 18 E
Ledesma, *Spain* **36 D5** 41 6N 5 59W
Ledong, *China* **76 C7** 18 41N 109 5 E
Leduc, *Canada* **130 C6** 53 15N 113 30W
Ledyczek, *Poland* **47 B3** 53 33N 16 59 E
Lee, *U.S.A.* **137 D11** 42 19N 73 15W
Lee →, *Ireland* **19 E3** 51 50N 8 30W
Lee Vining, *U.S.A.* **144 H7** 37 58N 119 7W
Leech L., *U.S.A.* **138 B7** 47 10N 94 24W
Leedey, *U.S.A.* **139 H5** 35 52N 99 21W
Leeds, *U.K.* **16 D6** 53 48N 1 34W
Leeds, *U.S.A.* **135 J2** 33 33N 86 33W
Leek, *Neths.* **20 B8** 53 10N 6 24 E
Leek, *U.K.* **16 D5** 53 7N 2 2W
Leende, *Neths.* **21 F7** 51 21N 5 33 E
Leer, *Germany* **26 B3** 53 13N 7 29 E
Leerdam, *Neths.* **20 E6** 51 54N 5 6 E
Leersum, *Neths.* **20 E6** 52 0N 5 26 E
Lee's Summit, *U.S.A.* **140 F2** 38 55N 94 23W
Leesburg, *Fla., U.S.A.* **135 L5** 28 49N 81 53W
Leesburg, *Ohio, U.S.A.* **141 E13** 39 21N 83 33W
Leeston, *N.Z.* **119 D7** 43 45 S 172 19 E
Leesville, *U.S.A.* **139 K8** 31 9N 93 16W
Leeton, *Australia* **117 C7** 34 33 S 146 23 E
Leetonia, *U.S.A.* **136 F4** 40 53N 80 45W
Leeu Gamka, *S. Africa* **104 E3** 32 47 S 21 59 E
Leeuwarden, *Neths.* **20 B7** 53 15N 5 48 E
Leeuwin, C., *Australia* **113 F2** 34 20 S 115 9 E
Leeward Is., *Atl. Oc.* **149 C7** 16 30N 63 30W
Léfini, *Congo* **102 C3** 2 55 S 15 39 E
Lefka, *Cyprus* **32 D11** 35 6N 32 51 E
Lefkoniko, *Cyprus* **32 D12** 35 18N 33 44 E
Lefors, *U.S.A.* **139 H4** 35 26N 100 48W
Lefroy, L., *Australia* **113 F3** 31 21 S 121 40 E
Łeg →, *Poland* **47 E8** 50 42N 21 50 E
Legal, *Canada* **130 C6** 53 55N 113 35W
Leganés, *Spain* **36 E7** 40 19N 3 45W
Legazpi, *Phil.* **70 E4** 13 10N 123 45 E
Legendre I., *Australia* **112 D2** 20 22 S 116 55 E
Leghorn = Livorno, *Italy* **38 E7** 43 32N 10 18 E
Legionowo, *Poland* **47 C7** 52 25N 20 50 E
Léglise, *Belgium* **21 J7** 49 48N 5 32 E
Legnago, *Italy* **39 C8** 45 10N 11 19 E
Legnano, *Italy* **38 C5** 45 35N 8 55 E
Legnica, *Poland* **47 D3** 51 12N 16 10 E
Legnica □, *Poland* **47 D3** 51 30N 16 0 E
Legrad, *Croatia* **39 B13** 46 17N 16 51 E

McCusker 227

Luanda, *Angola* **103 D2** 8 50 S 13 15 E
Luanda □, *Angola* **103 D2** 9 0 S 13 10 E
Luang Prabang, *Laos* **76 C4** 19 52N 102 10 E
Luang Thale, *Thailand* **77 J3** 7 30N 100 15 E
Luangwa, *Zambia* **107 F3** 15 35 S 30 16 E
Luangwa →, *Zambia* **107 E3** 14 25 S 30 25 E
Luangwa Valley, *Zambia* **107 E3** 13 30 S 31 30 E
Luanne, *China* **67 D9** 40 55N 117 40 E
Luanping, *China* **67 D9** 40 53N 117 23 E
Luanshya, *Zambia* **107 E2** 13 3 S 28 28 E
Luapula □, *Zambia* **107 E2** 11 0 S 29 0 E
Luapula →, *Africa* **107 D2** 9 26 S 28 33 E
Luarca, *Spain* **36 B4** 43 32N 6 32W
Luashi, *Zaïre* **103 E4** 10 50 S 23 36 E
Luau, *Angola* **103 E4** 10 40 S 22 10 E
Luba, *Phil.* **70 C3** 17 19N 120 42 E
Lubaczów, *Poland* **47 E10** 50 10N 23 8 E
Lubalo, *Angola* **103 D3** 9 10 S 19 15 E
Luban, *Phil.* **71 H6** 6 26N 126 13 E
Lubań, *Poland* **47 D2** 51 5N 15 15 E
Lubana, Ozero, *Latvia* **50 C5** 56 45N 27 0 E
Lubang, *Phil.* **70 E3** 13 52N 120 7 E
Lubang Is., *Phil.* **70 E3** 13 50N 120 12 E
Lubango, *Angola* **103 E2** 14 55 S 13 30 E
Lubao, *Phil.* **70 D3** 14 56N 120 36 E
Lubartów, *Poland* **47 D9** 51 28N 22 42 E
Lubawa, *Poland* **47 B6** 53 30N 19 48 E
Lubbeek, *Belgium* **21 G5** 50 54N 4 50 E
Lübben, *Germany* **26 D9** 51 56N 13 54 E
Lübbenau, *Germany* **26 D9** 51 49N 13 59 E
Lubbock, *U.S.A.* **139 J4** 33 35N 101 51W
Lübeck, *Germany* **26 B6** 53 52N 10 41 E
Lübecker Bucht, *Germany* **26 A7** 54 3N 11 0 E
Lubefu, *Zaïre* **103 C4** 4 47 S 24 27 E
Lubefu →, *Zaïre* **103 C4** 4 10 S 23 0 E
Lubero = Luofu, *Zaïre* **106 C2** 0 10 S 29 15 E
Lubicon L., *Canada* **130 B5** 56 23N 115 56W
Lubień Kujawski, *Poland* **47 C6** 52 23N 19 9 E
Lubin, *Poland* **47 D3** 51 24N 16 11 E
Lublin, *Poland* **47 D9** 51 12N 22 38 E
Lublin □, *Poland* **47 D9** 51 5N 22 30 E
Lubliniec, *Poland* **47 E5** 50 43N 18 45 E
Lubnān, J., *Lebanon* **91 B4** 33 50N 35 45 E
Lubny, *Ukraine* **50 F8** 50 3N 32 58 E
Lubon, *Poland* **47 C3** 52 21N 16 51 E
Lubongola, *Zaïre* **106 C2** 2 35 S 27 50 E
Lubotin, *Slovak Rep.* **31 B13** 49 17N 20 53 E
Lubraniec, *Poland* **47 C5** 52 33N 18 50 E
Lubsko, *Poland* **47 D1** 51 45N 14 57 E
Lübtheen, *Germany* **26 B7** 53 18N 11 4 E
Lubuagan, *Phil.* **70 C3** 17 21N 121 10 E
Lubudi →, *Zaïre* **103 D5** 9 0 S 25 35 E
Lubuklinggau, *Indonesia* **74 C2** 3 15 S 102 55 E
Lubuksikaping, *Indonesia* **74 B2** 0 10N 100 15 E
Lubumbashi, *Zaïre* **107 E2** 11 40 S 27 28 E
Lubunda, *Zaïre* **103 D5** 5 12 S 26 41 E
Lubungu, *Zambia* **107 E2** 14 35 S 26 24 E
Lubutu, *Zaïre* **106 C2** 0 45 S 26 30 E
Luc An Chau, *Vietnam* **76 A5** 22 6N 104 43 E
Luc-en-Diois, *France* **25 D9** 44 36N 5 28 E
Lucala, *Angola* **103 D3** 9 7 S 15 58 E
Lucan, *Canada* **136 C3** 43 11N 81 24W
Lucban, *Phil.* **70 D3** 14 6N 121 33 E
Lucca, *Italy* **38 E7** 43 50N 10 30 E
Luce Bay, *U.K.* **18 G4** 54 45N 4 48W
Lucea, *Jamaica* **148 C4** 18 25N 78 10W
Lucedale, *U.S.A.* **135 K1** 30 56N 88 35W
Lucena, *Phil.* **70 E3** 13 56N 121 37 E
Lucena, *Spain* **37 H6** 37 27N 4 31W
Lucena del Cid, *Spain* **34 E4** 40 9N 0 17W
Lučenec, *Slovak Rep.* **31 C12** 48 18N 19 42 E
Lucens, *Switz.* **28 C3** 46 43N 6 51 E
Lucera, *Italy* **41 A8** 41 30N 15 20 E
Lucerne = Luzern, *Switz.* **29 B6** 47 3N 8 18 E
Lucerne, *U.S.A.* **144 F4** 39 6N 122 48W
Lucerne Valley, *U.S.A.* **145 L10** 34 27N 116 57W
Lucero, *Mexico* **146 A3** 30 49N 106 30W
Luchena →, *Spain* **35 H3** 37 44N 1 50W
Lucheng, *China* **66 F7** 36 20N 113 11 E
Lucheringo →, *Mozam.* **107 E4** 11 43 S 36 17 E
Lüchow, *Germany* **26 C7** 52 58N 11 8 E
Luchuan, *China* **69 F8** 22 21N 110 12 E
Lucie →, *Surinam* **153 C6** 3 35N 57 38W
Lucira, *Angola* **103 E2** 14 0 S 12 35 E
Luckau, *Germany* **26 D9** 51 50N 13 43 E
Luckenwalde, *Germany* **26 C9** 52 5N 13 11 E
Luckey, *U.S.A.* **141 C13** 41 27N 83 29W
Lucknow, *India* **81 F9** 26 50N 81 0 E
Luçon, *France* **24 B2** 46 28N 1 10W
Lucusse, *Angola* **103 E4** 12 32 S 20 48 E
Lüda = Dalian, *China* **67 E11** 38 50N 121 40 E
Luda Kamchiya →, *Bulgaria* **43 D12** 43 3N 27 29 E
Ludbreg, *Croatia* **39 B13** 46 15N 16 38 E
Lüdenscheid, *Germany* **26 D3** 51 13N 7 37 E
Lüderitz, *Namibia* **104 D2** 26 41 S 15 8 E
Ludewe □, *Tanzania* **107 D3** 10 0 S 34 50 E
Ludhiana, *India* **80 D6** 30 57N 75 56 E
Ludian, *China* **68 D4** 27 10N 103 33 E
Luding Qiao, *China* **68 C4** 29 53N 102 12 E
Lüdinghausen, *Germany* **26 D3** 51 46N 7 28 E
Ludington, *U.S.A.* **134 D2** 43 57N 86 27W
Ludlow, *U.K.* **17 E5** 52 23N 2 42W
Ludlow, *Calif., U.S.A.* **145 L10** 34 43N 116 10W
Ludlow, *Vt., U.S.A.* **137 C12** 43 24N 72 42W
Ludus, *Romania* **46 C5** 46 29N 24 5 E
Ludvika, *Sweden* **13 F13** 60 8N 15 14 E
Ludwigsburg, *Germany* **27 G5** 48 53N 9 11 E
Ludwigshafen, *Germany* **27 F4** 49 27N 8 27 E
Ludwigslust, *Germany* **26 B7** 53 19N 11 28 E
Ludza, *Latvia* **50 C5** 56 32N 27 43 E
Lue, *Australia* **117 B8** 32 38 S 149 50 E
Luebo, *Zaïre* **103 D4** 5 21 S 21 23 E
Lueki, *Zaïre* **102 C5** 3 20 S 25 48 E
Luena, *Angola* **103 E3** 12 13 S 19 51 E
Luena, *Zaïre* **107 D2** 9 28 S 25 43 E
Luena, *Zambia* **107 E3** 10 40 S 30 25 E
Luepa, *Venezuela* **153 B5** 5 43N 61 31W
Lüeyang, *China* **66 H4** 33 22N 106 10 E
Lufeng, *Guangdong, China* **69 F10** 22 57N 115 38 E
Lufeng, *Yunnan, China* **68 E4** 25 0N 102 5 E
Lufico, *Angola* **103 D2** 6 24 S 13 23 E
Lufira →, *Zaïre* **107 D2** 9 30 S 27 0 E
Lufkin, *U.S.A.* **139 K7** 31 21N 94 44W
Lufupa, *Zaïre* **103 E4** 10 37 S 24 56 E
Luga, *Russia* **50 B6** 58 40N 29 55 E
Luga →, *Russia* **50 B6** 59 40N 28 18 E
Lugang, *Taiwan* **69 E13** 24 4N 120 23 E
Lugano, *Switz.* **29 D7** 46 0N 8 57 E
Lugano, L. di, *Switz.* **29 E8** 46 0N 9 0 E
Lugansk, *Ukraine* **53 B8** 48 38N 39 15 E
Lugard's Falls, *Kenya* **106 C4** 3 6 S 38 41 E
Lugela, *Mozam.* **107 F4** 16 25 S 36 43 E
Lugenda →, *Mozam.* **107 E4** 11 25 S 38 33 E
Lugh Ganana, *Somali Rep.* **90 G3** 3 48N 42 34 E
Lugnaquilla, *Ireland* **19 D5** 52 58N 6 28W
Lugnvik, *Sweden* **14 B11** 62 56N 17 55 E
Lugo, *Italy* **39 D8** 44 25N 11 53 E
Lugo, *Spain* **36 B3** 43 2N 7 35W
Lugo □, *Spain* **36 C3** 43 0N 7 30W
Lugoj, *Romania* **42 B6** 45 42N 21 57 E
Lugones, *Spain* **36 B5** 43 26N 5 50W
Lugovoye, *Kazakhstan* **55 B6** 42 55N 72 43 E
Luhansk = Lugansk, *Ukraine* **53 B8** 48 38N 39 15 E
Luhe, *China* **69 A12** 32 19N 118 50 E
Luhe →, *Germany* **26 B6** 53 18N 10 11 E
Luhuo, *China* **68 B3** 31 21N 100 48 E
Luiana, *Angola* **103 F4** 17 25 S 22 59 E
Luino, *Italy* **38 C5** 45 58N 8 42 E
Luís Correia, *Brazil* **154 B3** 3 0 S 41 35W
Luís Gonçalves, *Brazil* **154 C1** 5 37 S 50 25W
Luitpold Coast, *Antarctica* **7 D1** 78 30 S 32 0W
Luiza, *Zaïre* **103 D4** 7 40 S 22 30 E
Luizi, *Zaïre* **106 D2** 6 0 S 27 25 E
Luján, *Argentina* **158 C4** 34 45 S 59 5W
Lujiang, *China* **69 B11** 31 20N 117 15 E
Lukala, *Zaïre* **103 D2** 5 31 S 14 32 E
Lukanga Swamp, *Zambia* **107 E2** 14 30 S 27 40 E
Lukenie →, *Zaïre* **102 C3** 3 0 S 18 50 E
Lukhisaral, *India* **81 G12** 25 11N 86 5 E
Lŭki, *Bulgaria* **43 F9** 41 50N 24 43 E
Lukk, *Libya* **96 B4** 32 1N 24 46 E
Lukolela, *Equateur, Zaïre* **102 C3** 1 10 S 17 12 E
Lukolela, *Kasai Or., Zaïre* **103 D4** 5 23 S 24 32 E
Lukosi, *Zimbabwe* **107 F2** 18 30 S 26 30 E
Lukovit, *Bulgaria* **43 D9** 43 13N 24 11 E
Łuków, *Poland* **47 D9** 51 55N 22 23 E
Lukoyanov, *Russia* **51 D14** 55 2N 44 29 E
Lule älv →, *Sweden* **12 D17** 65 35N 22 10 E
Luleå, *Sweden* **12 D17** 65 35N 22 10 E
Lüleburgaz, *Turkey* **43 F12** 41 23N 27 22 E
Luliang, *China* **68 E4** 25 0N 103 40 E
Luling, *U.S.A.* **139 L6** 29 41N 97 39W
Lulong, *China* **67 E10** 39 53N 118 51 E
Lulonga →, *Zaïre* **102 B3** 1 0N 18 10 E
Lulua →, *Zaïre* **103 C4** 4 30 S 20 30 E
Luluabourg = Kananga, *Zaïre* **103 D4** 5 55 S 22 18 E
Lumai, *Angola* **103 E4** 13 13 S 21 25 E
Lumajang, *Indonesia* **75 D4** 8 8 S 113 13 E
Lumaku, Gunong, *Malaysia* **75 B5** 4 52N 115 38 E
Lumbala Kaquengue, *Angola* **103 E4** 12 39 S 22 34 E
Lumbala N'guimbo, *Angola* **103 E4** 14 18 S 21 18 E
Lumberton, *Miss., U.S.A.* **139 K10** 31 0N 89 27W
Lumberton, *N.C., U.S.A.* **135 H6** 34 37N 79 0W
Lumberton, *N. Mex., U.S.A.* **143 H10** 36 56N 106 56W
Lumbres, *France* **23 B9** 50 40N 2 5 E
Lumbwa, *Kenya* **106 C4** 0 12 S 35 28 E
Lumding, *India* **78 C4** 25 46N 93 10 E
Lumi, *Papua N. G.* **120 B2** 3 30 S 142 2 E
Lummen, *Belgium* **21 G6** 50 59N 5 12 E
Lumsden, *N.Z.* **119 F3** 45 44 S 168 27 E
Lumut, *Malaysia* **77 K3** 4 13N 100 37 E
Lumut, Tg., *Indonesia* **74 C3** 3 50 S 105 58 E
Luna, *Luzon, Phil.* **70 B3** 18 18N 121 21 E
Luna, *Luzon, Phil.* **70 C3** 16 51N 120 23 E
Lunan, *China* **68 E4** 24 40N 103 18 E
Lunavada, *India* **80 H5** 23 8N 73 37 E
Lunca, *Romania* **46 B6** 47 22N 25 1 E
Lund, *Sweden* **15 J7** 55 44N 13 12 E
Lund, *U.S.A.* **142 G6** 38 52N 115 0W
Lunda Norte □, *Angola* **103 D3** 8 0 S 20 0 E
Lunda Sul □, *Angola* **103 D4** 10 0 S 20 0 E
Lundazi, *Zambia* **107 E3** 12 20 S 33 7 E
Lunde, *Norway* **14 E3** 59 17N 9 5 E
Lunderskov, *Denmark* **15 J3** 55 29N 9 19 E
Lundi →, *Zimbabwe* **107 G3** 21 43 S 32 34 E
Lundu, *Malaysia* **75 B3** 1 40N 109 50 E
Lundy, *U.K.* **17 F3** 51 10N 4 41W
Lune →, *U.K.* **16 C5** 54 0N 2 51W
Lüneburg, *Germany* **26 B6** 53 15N 10 23 E
Lüneburg Heath = Lüneburger Heide, *Germany* **26 C6** 53 0N 10 0 E
Lüneburger Heide, *Germany* **26 C6** 53 0N 10 0 E
Lunel, *France* **25 E8** 43 39N 4 9 E
Lünen, *Germany* **26 D3** 51 36N 7 31 E
Lunenburg, *Canada* **129 D7** 44 22N 64 18W
Lunéville, *France* **23 D13** 48 36N 6 30 E
Lunga →, *Zambia* **107 E2** 14 34 S 26 25 E
Lungern, *Switz.* **28 C6** 46 48N 8 10 E
Lungi Airport, *S. Leone* **100 D2** 8 40N 13 17W
Lunglei, *India* **78 D4** 22 55N 92 45 E
Lungngo, *Burma* **78 E4** 21 57N 93 36 E
Luni, *India* **80 F5** 26 0N 73 6 E
Luni →, *India* **80 G4** 24 41N 71 14 E
Luninets, *Belorussia* **50 E5** 52 15N 26 50 E
Luning, *U.S.A.* **142 G4** 38 30N 118 11W
Lunino, *Russia* **51 E14** 53 35N 45 6 E
Luninyets = Luninets, *Belorussia* **50 E5** 52 15N 26 50 E
Lunner, *Norway* **14 D4** 60 19N 10 35 E
Lunsemfwa →, *Zambia* **107 E3** 14 54 S 30 12 E
Lunsemfwa Falls, *Zambia* **107 E2** 14 30 S 29 6 E
Lunteren, *Neths.* **20 D7** 52 5N 5 38 E
Luo He →, *China* **66 G6** 34 35N 110 20 E
Luocheng, *China* **68 E7** 24 48N 108 53 E
Luochuan, *China* **66 G5** 35 45N 109 26 E
Luoci, *China* **68 E4** 25 19N 102 18 E
Luodian, *China* **68 E6** 25 24N 106 43 E
Luoding, *China* **69 F8** 22 45N 111 40 E
Luodong, *Taiwan* **69 E13** 24 41N 121 46 E
Luofu, *Zaïre* **106 C2** 0 10 S 29 15 E
Luohe, *China* **66 H8** 33 32N 114 2 E
Luojiang, *China* **68 B5** 31 18N 104 33 E
Luonan, *China* **66 G6** 34 5N 110 10 E
Luoning, *China* **66 G6** 34 35N 111 40 E
Luoshan, *China* **69 A10** 32 13N 114 30 E
Luotian, *China* **69 B10** 30 46N 115 22 E
Luoyang, *China* **66 G7** 34 40N 112 26 E
Luoyuan, *China* **69 D12** 26 28N 119 30 E
Luozi, *Zaïre* **103 C2** 4 54 S 14 0 E
Luozigou, *China* **67 C16** 43 42N 130 18 E
Lupeni, *Romania* **46 D4** 45 21N 23 13 E
Lupilichi, *Mozam.* **107 E4** 11 47 S 35 13 E
Lupire, *Angola* **103 E3** 14 36 S 19 29 E
Łupków, *Poland* **31 B15** 49 15N 22 4 E
Lupoing, *China* **68 E5** 24 53N 104 21 E
Lupon, *Phil.* **71 H5** 6 54N 126 0 E
Luquan, *China* **68 E4** 25 35N 102 25 E
Luque, *Paraguay* **158 B4** 25 19 S 57 25W
Luque, *Spain* **37 H6** 37 35N 4 16W
Luray, *U.S.A.* **134 F6** 38 40N 78 28W
Lure, *France* **23 E13** 47 40N 6 30 E
Luremo, *Angola* **103 D3** 8 30 S 17 50 E
Lurgan, *U.K.* **19 B5** 54 28N 6 20W
Luribay, *Bolivia* **156 D4** 17 6 S 67 39W
Lurin, *Peru* **156 C2** 12 17 S 76 52W
Lusaka, *Zambia* **107 F2** 15 28 S 28 16 E
Lusambo, *Zaïre* **103 C4** 4 58 S 23 28 E
Lusangaye, *Zaïre* **103 C5** 4 54 S 26 0 E
Luseland, *Canada* **131 C7** 52 5N 109 24W
Lushan, *Henan, China* **66 H7** 33 45N 112 55 E
Lushan, *Sichuan, China* **68 B4** 30 12N 102 52 E
Lushi, *China* **66 G6** 34 3N 111 3 E
Lushnja, *Albania* **44 D1** 40 55N 19 41 E
Lushoto, *Tanzania* **106 C4** 4 47 S 38 20 E
Lushoto □, *Tanzania* **106 C4** 4 45 S 38 20 E
Lushui, *China* **68 E2** 25 58N 98 44 E
Lüshun, *China* **67 E11** 38 45N 121 15 E
Lusignan, *France* **24 B4** 46 26N 0 8 E
Lusigny-sur-Barse, *France* **23 D11** 48 16N 4 15 E
Lusk, *U.S.A.* **138 D2** 42 46N 104 27W
Lussac-les-Châteaux, *France* **24 B4** 46 24N 0 43 E
Lussanvira, *Brazil* **155 F1** 20 42 S 51 7W
Luta = Dalian, *China* **67 E11** 38 50N 121 40 E
Lutembo, *Angola* **103 E4** 13 26 S 21 16 E
Luti, *Solomon Is.* **121 L9** 7 14 S 157 0 E
Luton, *U.K.* **17 F7** 51 53N 0 24W
Lutong, *Malaysia* **75 B4** 4 28N 114 0 E
Lutry, *Switz.* **28 C3** 46 31N 6 42 E
Lutsk, *Ukraine* **50 F4** 50 50N 25 15 E
Lutuai, *Angola* **103 E4** 12 41 S 20 7 E
Lützow Holmbukta, *Antarctica* **7 C4** 69 10 S 37 30 E
Lutzputs, *S. Africa* **104 D3** 28 3 S 20 40 E
Luverne, *U.S.A.* **138 D6** 43 39N 96 13W
Luvo, *Angola* **103 D2** 5 51 S 14 5 E
Luvua, *Zaïre* **103 D5** 8 48 S 25 17 E
Luvua →, *Zaïre* **106 D2** 6 50 S 27 30 E
Luwegu →, *Tanzania* **107 D4** 8 31 S 37 23 E
Luwuk, *Indonesia* **72 B2** 0 56 S 122 47 E
Luxembourg, *Lux.* **21 J8** 49 37N 6 9 E
Luxembourg □, *Belgium* **21 J7** 49 58N 5 30 E
Luxembourg ■, *Europe* **21 J8** 49 45N 6 0 E
Luxeuil-les-Bains, *France* **23 E13** 47 49N 6 24 E
Luxi, *Hunan, China* **69 C8** 28 20N 110 7 E
Luxi, *Yunnan, China* **68 E4** 24 40N 103 55 E
Luxi, *Yunnan, China* **68 E2** 24 27N 98 36 E
Luxor = El Uqsur, *Egypt* **94 B3** 25 41N 32 38 E
Luy →, *France* **24 E2** 43 39N 1 9W
Luy-de-Béarn →, *France* **24 E3** 43 39N 0 48W
Luy-de-France →, *France* **24 E3** 43 39N 0 48W
Luyi, *China* **66 H8** 33 50N 115 35 E
Luyksgestel, *Neths.* **21 F6** 51 17N 5 20 E
Luz-St.-Sauveur, *France* **24 F4** 42 53N 0 0 E
Luza, *Russia* **48 B8** 60 39N 47 10 E
Luzern, *Switz.* **29 B6** 47 3N 8 18 E
Luzern □, *Switz.* **28 B5** 47 2N 7 55 E
Luzhai, *China* **68 E7** 24 29N 109 42 E
Luzhou, *China* **68 C5** 28 52N 105 20 E
Luziânia, *Brazil* **155 E2** 16 20 S 48 0W
Luzilândia, *Brazil* **154 B3** 3 28 S 42 22W
Luzon, *Phil.* **70 C3** 16 0N 121 0 E
Luzy, *France* **23 F10** 46 47N 3 58 E
Luzzi, *Italy* **41 C9** 39 28N 16 17 E
Lviv = Lvov, *Ukraine* **50 G4** 49 50N 24 0 E
Lvov, *Ukraine* **50 G4** 49 50N 24 0 E
Lwówek, *Poland* **47 C3** 52 28N 16 10 E
Lwówek Śląski, *Poland* **47 D2** 51 7N 15 38 E
Lyakhovichi, *Belorussia* **50 E5** 53 2N 26 32 E
Lyakhovskiye, Ostrova, *Russia* **57 B15** 73 40N 141 0 E
Lyaki, *Azerbaijan* **53 F12** 40 34N 47 22 E
Lyall Mt., *N.Z.* **119 F2** 45 16 S 167 32 E
Lyallpur = Faisalabad, *Pakistan* **79 C4** 31 30N 73 5 E
Lyalya →, *Russia* **54 B7** 59 9N 61 29 E
Lyaskovets, *Bulgaria* **43 D10** 43 6N 25 44 E
Lycaonia, *Turkey* **88 D5** 38 0N 33 0 E
Lychen, *Germany* **26 B9** 53 13N 13 20 E
Lycia, *Turkey* **88 E3** 36 30N 29 30 E
Lycksele, *Sweden* **12 D15** 64 38N 18 40 E
Lycosura, *Greece* **45 G4** 37 20N 22 3 E
Lydda = Lod, *Israel* **91 D3** 31 57N 34 54 E
Lydenburg, *S. Africa* **105 D5** 25 10 S 30 29 E
Lydia, *Turkey* **88 D3** 39 0N 28 0 E
Lyell, *N.Z.* **119 B7** 41 48 S 172 4 E
Lyell I., *Canada* **130 C2** 52 40N 131 35W
Lygnern, *Sweden* **15 G6** 57 30N 12 15 E
Lyman, *U.S.A.* **142 F8** 41 20N 110 18W
Lyme Regis, *U.K.* **17 G5** 50 44N 2 57W
Lymington, *U.K.* **17 G6** 50 46N 1 32W
Łyna →, *Poland* **47 A8** 54 37N 21 14 E
Lynchburg, *Ohio, U.S.A.* **141 E13** 39 15N 83 48W
Lynchburg, *Va., U.S.A.* **134 G6** 37 25N 79 9W
Lynd →, *Australia* **114 B3** 16 28 S 143 18 E
Lynd Ra., *Australia* **115 D4** 25 30 S 149 20 E
Lynden, *Canada* **136 C4** 43 14N 80 9W
Lynden, *U.S.A.* **144 B4** 48 57N 122 27W
Lyndhurst, *Queens., Australia* **114 B3** 19 12 S 144 20 E
Lyndhurst, *S. Austral., Australia* **115 E2** 30 15 S 138 18 E
Lyndon →, *Australia* **113 D1** 23 29 S 114 6 E
Lyndonville, *N.Y., U.S.A.* **136 C6** 43 20N 78 23W
Lyndonville, *Vt., U.S.A.* **137 B12** 44 31N 72 1W
Lyngdal, *Norway* **14 E3** 59 54N 9 32 E
Lynher Reef, *Australia* **112 C3** 15 27 S 121 55 E
Lynn, *Ind., U.S.A.* **141 D12** 40 3N 84 56W
Lynn, *Mass., U.S.A.* **137 D14** 42 28N 70 57W
Lynn Canal, *U.S.A.* **130 B1** 58 50N 135 15W
Lynn Lake, *Canada* **131 B8** 56 51N 101 3W
Lynnwood, *U.S.A.* **144 C4** 47 49N 122 19W
Lynton, *U.K.* **17 F4** 51 14N 3 50W
Lyntupy, *Belorussia* **50 D5** 55 4N 26 23 E
Lynx L., *Canada* **131 A7** 62 25N 106 15W
Lyø, *Denmark* **15 J4** 55 3N 10 9 E
Lyon, *France* **25 C8** 45 46N 4 50 E
Lyonnais, *France* **25 C8** 45 45N 4 15 E
Lyons = Lyon, *France* **25 C8** 45 46N 4 50 E
Lyons, *Colo., U.S.A.* **138 E2** 40 14N 105 16W
Lyons, *Ga., U.S.A.* **135 J4** 32 12N 82 19W
Lyons, *Kans., U.S.A.* **138 F5** 38 21N 98 12W
Lyons, *N.Y., U.S.A.* **136 C8** 43 5N 77 0W
Lyrestad, *Sweden* **15 F8** 58 48N 14 4 E
Lys = Leie →, *Belgium* **23 A10** 51 2N 3 45 E
Lysá, *Czech.* **30 A7** 50 11N 14 51 E
Lysekil, *Sweden* **15 F5** 58 17N 11 26 E
Lyskovo, *Russia* **51 D14** 56 0N 45 3 E
Lyss, *Switz.* **28 B4** 47 4N 7 19 E
Lysva, *Russia* **54 B5** 58 7N 57 49 E
Lytle, *U.S.A.* **139 L5** 29 14N 98 48W
Lyttelton, *N.Z.* **119 D7** 43 35 S 172 44 E
Lytton, *Canada* **130 C4** 50 13N 121 31W
Lyuban, *Russia* **50 B7** 59 16N 31 18 E
Lyubcha, *Belorussia* **50 E5** 53 46N 26 1 E
Lyubertsy, *Russia* **51 D10** 55 39N 37 50 E
Lyubim, *Russia* **51 B12** 58 20N 40 39 E
Lyubimets, *Bulgaria* **43 F11** 41 50N 26 5 E
Lyuboml, *Ukraine* **50 F4** 51 11N 24 4 E
Lyubotin, *Ukraine* **52 B6** 50 0N 36 0 E
Lyubytino, *Russia* **50 B8** 58 50N 33 16 E
Lyudinovo, *Russia* **50 E9** 53 52N 34 28 E

M

Ma →, *Vietnam* **76 C5** 19 47N 105 56 E
Ma'adaba, *Jordan* **91 E4** 30 43N 35 47 E
Maamba, *Zambia* **104 B4** 17 17 S 26 28 E
Ma'ān, *Jordan* **91 E4** 30 12N 35 44 E
Ma'ān □, *Jordan* **91 F5** 30 0N 36 0 E
Ma'anshan, *China* **69 B12** 31 44N 118 29 E
Maarheeze, *Neths.* **21 F7** 51 19N 5 36 E
Maarianhamina, *Finland* **13 F15** 60 5N 19 55 E
Maarn, *Neths.* **20 D6** 52 3N 5 22 E
Ma'arrat an Nu'mān, *Syria* **84 C3** 35 43N 36 43 E
Maarssen, *Neths.* **20 D6** 52 9N 5 2 E
Maartensdijk, *Neths.* **20 D6** 52 9N 5 10 E
Maas →, *Neths.* **20 E5** 51 45N 4 32 E
Maasbracht, *Belgium* **21 F7** 51 9N 5 54 E
Maasbree, *Neths.* **21 F8** 51 22N 6 3 E
Maasdam, *Neths.* **20 E5** 51 48N 4 34 E
Maasdijk, *Neths.* **20 E4** 51 58N 4 13 E
Maaseik, *Belgium* **21 F7** 51 6N 5 45 E
Maasland, *Neths.* **20 E4** 51 57N 4 16 E
Maasniel, *Neths.* **21 F8** 51 12N 6 1 E
Maassluis, *Neths.* **20 E4** 51 56N 4 16 E
Maastricht, *Neths.* **21 G7** 50 50N 5 40 E
Maave, *Mozam.* **105 C5** 21 4 S 34 47 E
Ma'bar, *Yemen* **86 D4** 14 48N 44 17 E
Mabaruma, *Guyana* **153 B6** 8 10N 59 50W
Mabein, *Burma* **78 D6** 23 29N 96 37 E
Mabel L., *Canada* **130 C5** 50 35N 118 43W
Mabenge, *Zaïre* **106 B1** 4 15N 24 12 E
Mabian, *China* **68 C4** 28 47N 103 37 E
Mablethorpe, *U.K.* **16 D8** 53 21N 0 14 E
Maboma, *Zaïre* **106 B2** 2 30N 28 10 E
Maboukou, *Congo* **102 C2** 3 39 S 12 31 E
Mabrouk, *Mali* **101 B4** 19 29N 1 15W
Mabton, *U.S.A.* **142 C3** 46 13N 120 0W
Mabungo, *Somali Rep.* **108 D2** 0 49N 42 35 E
Mac Bac, *Vietnam* **77 H6** 9 46N 106 7 E
Macachín, *Argentina* **158 D3** 37 10 S 63 43W
Macaé, *Brazil* **155 F3** 22 20 S 41 43W
Macaíba, *Brazil* **154 C4** 5 51 S 35 21W
Macajuba, *Brazil* **155 D3** 12 9 S 40 22W
Macalelon, *Phil.* **70 E4** 13 45N 122 8 E
McAlester, *U.S.A.* **139 H7** 34 56N 95 46W
McAllen, *U.S.A.* **139 M5** 26 12N 98 14W
Macamic, *Canada* **128 C4** 48 45N 79 0W
Macao = Macau ■, *China* **69 F9** 22 16N 113 35 E
Macão, *Portugal* **37 F3** 39 35N 7 59W
Macapá, *Brazil* **153 C7** 0 5N 51 4W
Macará, *Ecuador* **152 D2** 4 23 S 79 57W
Macarani, *Brazil* **155 E3** 15 33 S 40 24W
Macarena, Serranía de la, *Colombia* **152 C3** 2 45N 73 55W
Macarthur, *Australia* **116 E5** 38 5 S 142 0 E
McArthur →, *Australia* **114 B2** 15 54 S 136 40 E
McArthur, Port, *Australia* **114 B2** 16 4 S 136 23 E
McArthur River, *Australia* **114 B2** 16 27 S 136 7 E
Macas, *Ecuador* **152 D2** 2 19 S 78 7W
Macate, *Peru* **156 B2** 8 48 S 78 7W
Macau, *Brazil* **154 C4** 5 15 S 36 40W
Macau ■, *China* **69 F9** 22 16N 113 35 E
Macaúbas, *Brazil* **155 D3** 13 2 S 42 42W
Macaya →, *Colombia* **152 C3** 0 59N 72 20W
McBride, *Canada* **130 C4** 53 20N 120 19W
McCall, *U.S.A.* **142 D5** 44 55N 116 6W
McCamey, *U.S.A.* **139 K3** 31 8N 102 14W
McCammon, *U.S.A.* **142 E7** 42 39N 112 12W
McCauley I., *Canada* **130 C2** 53 40N 130 15W
McCleary, *U.S.A.* **144 C3** 47 3N 123 16W
Macclesfield, *U.K.* **16 D5** 53 16N 2 9W
McClintock, *Canada* **131 B10** 57 50N 94 10W
McClintock Ra., *Australia* **112 C4** 18 44 S 127 38 E
McCloud, *U.S.A.* **142 F2** 41 15N 122 8W
McCluer I., *Australia* **112 B5** 11 5 S 133 0 E
McClure, *U.S.A.* **136 F7** 40 42N 77 19W
McClure, L., *U.S.A.* **144 H6** 37 35N 120 16W
M'Clure Str., *Canada* **124 B8** 75 0N 119 0W
McClusky, *U.S.A.* **138 B4** 47 29N 100 27W
McComb, *U.S.A.* **139 K9** 31 15N 90 27W
McConaughy, L., *U.S.A.* **138 E4** 41 14N 101 40W
McCook, *U.S.A.* **138 E4** 40 12N 100 38W
McCullough Mt., *U.S.A.* **145 K11** 35 35N 115 13W
McCusker →, *Canada* **131 B7** 55 32N 108 39W

228 McDame

McDame, *Canada* **130 B3** 59 44N 128 59W
McDermitt, *U.S.A.* **142 F5** 41 59N 117 43W
Macdonald, L., *Australia* **112 D4** 23 30 S 129 0 E
Macdonald, Mt., *Vanuatu* **121 G6** 17 36 S 168 23 E
McDonald Is., *Ind. Oc.* **109 K6** 53 0 S 73 0 E
Macdonnell Ras., *Australia* **112 D5** 23 40 S 133 0 E
McDouall Peak, *Australia* **115 D1** 29 51 S 134 55 E
Macdougall L., *Canada* **126 B10** 66 0N 98 27W
McDougalls Well, *Australia* **116 A4** 31 8 S 141 15 E
MacDowell L., *Canada* **128 B1** 52 15N 92 45W
Macduff, *U.K.* **18 D6** 57 40N 2 30W
Maceda, *Spain* **36 C3** 42 16N 7 39W
Macedonia = Makedhonía □, *Greece* **44 D3** 40 39N 22 0 E
Macedonia ■, *Europe* **42 F6** 41 53N 21 40 E
Maceió, *Brazil* **154 C4** 9 40 S 35 41W
Maceira, *Portugal* **37 F2** 39 41N 8 55W
Macenta, *Guinea* **100 D3** 8 35N 9 32W
Macerata, *Italy* **39 E10** 43 19N 13 28 E
McFarland, *U.S.A.* **145 K7** 35 41N 119 14W
McFarlane →, *Canada* **131 B7** 59 12N 107 58W
Macfarlane, L., *Australia* **116 B2** 32 0 S 136 40 E
McGehee, *U.S.A.* **139 J9** 33 38N 91 24W
McGill, *U.S.A.* **142 G6** 39 23N 114 47W
Macgillycuddy's Reeks, *Ireland* **19 D2** 52 2N 9 45W
MacGregor, *Canada* **131 D9** 49 57N 98 48W
McGregor, *U.S.A.* **140 A5** 43 1N 91 11W
McGregor →, *Canada* **130 B4** 55 10N 122 0W
McGregor Ra., *Australia* **115 D3** 27 0 S 142 45 E
Māch Kowr, *Iran* **85 E9** 25 48N 61 28 E
Machacalis, *Brazil* **155 E3** 17 5 S 40 45W
Machado = Jiparaná →, *Brazil* **157 B5** 8 3 S 62 52W
Machagai, *Argentina* **158 B3** 26 56 S 60 2W
Machakos, *Kenya* **106 C4** 1 30 S 37 15 E
Machakos □, *Kenya* **106 C4** 1 30 S 37 15 E
Machala, *Ecuador* **152 D2** 3 20 S 79 57W
Machanga, *Mozam.* **105 C6** 20 59 S 35 0 E
Machattie, L., *Australia* **114 C2** 24 50 S 139 48 E
Machava, *Mozam.* **105 D5** 25 54 S 32 28 E
Machece, *Mozam.* **107 F4** 19 15 S 35 32 E
Machecoul, *France* **22 F5** 47 0N 1 49W
Machelen, *Belgium* **21 G4** 50 55N 4 26 E
Macheng, *China* **69 B10** 31 12N 115 2 E
McHenry, *U.S.A.* **141 B8** 42 21N 88 16W
Machevna, *Russia* **57 C18** 61 20N 172 20 E
Machezo, *Spain* **37 F6** 39 21N 4 20W
Machias, *U.S.A.* **129 D6** 44 43N 67 28W
Machichaco, C., *Spain* **34 B2** 43 28N 2 47W
Machichi →, *Canada* **131 B10** 57 3N 92 6W
Machico, *Madeira* **33 D3** 32 43N 16 44W
Machida, *Japan* **63 B11** 35 28N 139 23 E
Machilipatnam, *India* **83 F5** 16 12N 81 8 E
Machiques, *Venezuela* **152 A3** 10 4N 72 34W
Machupicchu, *Peru* **156 C3** 13 8 S 72 30W
Machynlleth, *U.K.* **17 E4** 52 36N 3 51W
Maciejowice, *Poland* **47 D8** 51 36N 21 26 E
McIlwraith Ra., *Australia* **114 A3** 13 50 S 143 20 E
Măcin, *Romania* **46 D9** 45 16N 28 8 E
Macina, *Mali* **100 C4** 14 50N 5 0W
McIntosh, *U.S.A.* **138 C4** 45 55N 101 21W
McIntosh L., *Canada* **131 B8** 55 45N 105 0W
Macintosh Ra., *Australia* **113 E4** 27 39 S 125 32 E
Macintyre →, *Australia* **115 D5** 28 37 S 150 47 E
Macizo Galaico, *Spain* **36 C3** 42 30N 7 30W
Mackay, *Australia* **114 C4** 21 8 S 149 11 E
Mackay, *U.S.A.* **142 E7** 43 55N 113 37W
MacKay →, *Canada* **130 B6** 57 10N 111 38W
Mackay, L., *Australia* **112 D4** 22 30 S 129 0 E
McKay Ra., *Australia* **112 D3** 23 0 S 122 30 E
McKeesport, *U.S.A.* **136 F5** 40 21N 79 52W
McKenna, *U.S.A.* **144 D4** 46 56N 122 33W
Mackenzie, *Canada* **130 B4** 55 20N 123 5W
Mackenzie, *Guyana* **153 B6** 6 0N 58 17W
McKenzie, *U.S.A.* **135 G1** 36 8N 88 31W
Mackenzie →, *Australia* **114 C4** 23 38 S 149 46 E
Mackenzie →, *Canada* **126 B6** 69 10N 134 20W
McKenzie →, *U.S.A.* **142 D2** 44 7N 123 6W
Mackenzie Bay, *Canada* **6 B1** 69 0N 137 30W
Mackenzie City = Linden, *Guyana* **153 B6** 6 0N 58 10W
Mackenzie Highway, *Canada* **130 B5** 58 0N 117 15W
Mackenzie Mts., *Canada* **126 B6** 64 0N 130 0W
Mackenzie Plains, *N.Z.* **119 E5** 44 10 S 170 25 E
McKerrow L., *N.Z.* **119 E3** 44 25 S 168 5 E
Mackinaw, *U.S.A.* **140 D7** 40 32N 89 21W
Mackinaw →, *U.S.A.* **140 D7** 40 33N 89 44W
Mackinaw City, *U.S.A.* **134 C3** 45 47N 84 44W
McKinlay, *Australia* **114 C3** 21 16 S 141 18 E
McKinlay →, *Australia* **114 C3** 20 50 S 141 28 E
McKinley, Mt., *U.S.A.* **126 B4** 63 4N 151 0W
McKinley Sea, *Arctic* **6 A7** 84 0N 10 0W
McKinney, *U.S.A.* **139 J6** 33 12N 96 37W
McKinnon Pass, *N.Z.* **119 E3** 44 52 S 168 12 E
Mackinnon Road, *Kenya* **106 C4** 3 40 S 39 1 E
Macksville, *Australia* **117 A10** 30 40 S 152 56 E
McLaren Vale, *Australia* **116 C3** 35 13 S 138 31 E
McLaughlin, *U.S.A.* **138 C4** 45 49N 100 49W
Maclean, *Australia* **115 D5** 29 26 S 153 16 E
McLean, *Ill., U.S.A.* **140 D7** 40 19N 89 10W
McLean, *Tex., U.S.A.* **139 H4** 35 14N 100 36W
McLeansboro, *U.S.A.* **138 F10** 38 6N 88 32W
Maclear, *S. Africa* **105 E4** 31 2 S 28 23 E
Macleay →, *Australia* **117 A10** 30 56 S 153 0 E
McLennan, *Canada* **130 B5** 55 42N 116 50W
MacLeod, B., *Canada* **131 A7** 62 53N 110 0W
McLeod, L., *Australia* **113 D1** 24 9 S 113 47 E
MacLeod Lake, *Canada* **130 C4** 54 58N 123 0W
M'Clintock Chan., *Canada* **126 A9** 72 0N 102 0W
McLoughlin, Mt., *U.S.A.* **142 E2** 42 27N 122 19W
McLure, *Canada* **130 C4** 51 2N 120 13W
McMechen, *U.S.A.* **136 G4** 39 57N 80 44W
McMillan, L., *U.S.A.* **139 J2** 32 36N 104 21W
McMinnville, *Oreg., U.S.A.* **142 D2** 45 13N 123 12W
McMinnville, *Tenn., U.S.A.* **135 H3** 35 41N 85 46W
McMorran, *Canada* **131 C7** 51 19N 108 42W
McMurdo Sd., *Antarctica* **7 D11** 77 0 S 170 0 E
McMurray = Fort McMurray, *Canada* **130 B6** 56 44N 111 7W
McMurray, *U.S.A.* **144 B4** 48 19N 122 14W
McNary, *U.S.A.* **143 J9** 34 4N 109 51W
MacNutt, *Canada* **131 C8** 51 5N 101 36W
Maco, *Phil.* **71 H5** 7 20N 125 50 E
Macocolo, *Angola* **103 D3** 6 47 S 16 8 E
Macodoene, *Mozam.* **105 C6** 23 32 S 35 5 E
Macomb, *U.S.A.* **140 D6** 40 27N 90 40W
Macomer, *Italy* **40 B1** 40 16N 8 48 E
Mâcon, *France* **25 B8** 46 19N 4 50 E
Macon, *Ga., U.S.A.* **135 J4** 32 51N 83 38W
Macon, *Ill., U.S.A.* **140 E7** 39 43N 89 0W
Macon, *Miss., U.S.A.* **135 J1** 33 7N 88 34W
Macon, *Mo., U.S.A.* **140 E4** 39 44N 92 28W
Macondo, *Angola* **103 E4** 12 37 S 23 46 E
Macossa, *Mozam.* **107 F3** 17 55 S 33 56 E
Macoun L., *Canada* **131 B8** 56 32N 103 40W
Macoupin Cr. →, *U.S.A.* **140 E6** 39 11N 90 38W
Macovane, *Mozam.* **105 C6** 21 30 S 35 2 E
McPherson, *U.S.A.* **138 F6** 38 22N 97 40W
McPherson Pk., *U.S.A.* **145 L7** 34 53N 119 53W
McPherson Ra., *Australia* **115 D5** 28 15 S 153 15 E
Macquarie Harbour, *Australia* **114 G4** 42 15 S 145 23 E
Macquarie Is., *Pac. Oc.* **122 N7** 54 36 S 158 55 E
MacRobertson Land, *Antarctica* **7 D6** 71 0 S 64 0 E
Macroom, *Ireland* **19 E3** 51 54N 8 57W
Macroy, *Australia* **112 D2** 20 53 S 118 2 E
MacTier, *Canada* **136 A5** 45 9N 79 46W
Macubela, *Mozam.* **107 F4** 16 53 S 37 49 E
Macugnaga, *Italy* **38 C4** 45 57N 7 58 E
Macuiza, *Mozam.* **107 F3** 18 7 S 34 29 E
Macujer, *Colombia* **152 C3** 0 24N 73 10W
Macusani, *Peru* **156 C3** 14 4 S 70 29W
Macuse, *Mozam.* **107 F4** 17 45 S 37 10 E
Macuspana, *Mexico* **147 D6** 17 46N 92 36W
Macusse, *Angola* **103 F4** 17 48 S 20 23 E
McVille, *U.S.A.* **138 B5** 47 46N 98 11W
Madadeni, *S. Africa* **105 D5** 27 43 S 30 3 E
Madadi, *Chad* **97 E4** 18 28N 20 45 E
Madagali, *Nigeria* **101 C7** 10 56N 13 33 E
Madagascar ■, *Africa* **105 C8** 20 0 S 47 0 E
Madā'in Sālih, *Si. Arabia* **84 E3** 26 46N 37 57 E
Madalag, *Phil.* **71 F4** 11 32N 122 18 E
Madama, *Niger* **97 D2** 22 0N 13 40 E
Madame I., *Canada* **129 C7** 45 30N 60 58W
Madan, *Bulgaria* **43 F9** 41 30N 24 57 E
Madanapalle, *India* **83 H4** 13 33N 78 28 E
Madang, *Papua N. G.* **120 C3** 5 12 S 145 49 E
Madaoua, *Niger* **101 C6** 14 5N 6 27 E
Madara, *Nigeria* **101 C7** 11 45N 10 35 E
Madaripur, *Bangla.* **78 D3** 23 19N 90 15 E
Madauk, *Burma* **78 G6** 17 56N 96 52 E
Madawaska, *Canada* **136 A7** 45 30N 78 0W
Madawaska →, *Canada* **128 C4** 45 27N 76 21W
Madaya, *Burma* **78 D6** 22 12N 96 10 E
Madbar, *Sudan* **95 F3** 6 17N 30 45 E
Maddaloni, *Italy* **41 A7** 41 4N 14 23 E
Made, *Neths.* **21 E5** 51 41N 4 49 E
Madeira, *Atl. Oc.* **33 D3** 32 50N 17 0W
Madeira, *U.S.A.* **141 E12** 39 11N 84 22W
Madeira →, *Brazil* **153 D6** 3 22 S 58 45W
Madeleine, Is. de la, *Canada* **129 C7** 47 30N 61 40W
Maden, *Turkey* **89 D8** 38 23N 39 40 E
Madera, *U.S.A.* **144 J6** 36 57N 120 3W
Madgaon, *India* **83 G1** 15 12N 73 58 E
Madha, *India* **82 F2** 18 0N 75 30 E
Madhubani, *India* **81 F12** 26 21N 86 7 E
Madhumati →, *Bangla.* **78 D2** 22 53N 89 52 E
Madhya Pradesh □, *India* **80 J7** 21 50N 78 0 E
Madian, *China* **69 A11** 33 0N 116 6 E
Madidi →, *Bolivia* **156 C4** 12 32 S 66 52W
Madikeri, *India* **83 H2** 12 30N 75 45 E
Madill, *U.S.A.* **139 H6** 34 6N 96 46W
Madimba, *Angola* **103 D2** 6 36 S 14 23 E
Madimba, *Zaïre* **103 C3** 4 58 S 15 5 E
Ma'din, *Syria* **84 C3** 35 45N 39 36 E
Madīnat ash Sha'b, *Yemen* **86 D4** 12 50N 45 0 E
Madingou, *Congo* **102 C2** 4 10 S 13 33 E
Madirovalo, *Madag.* **105 B8** 16 26 S 46 32 E
Madison, *Calif., U.S.A.* **144 G5** 38 41N 121 59W
Madison, *Fla., U.S.A.* **135 K4** 30 28N 83 25W
Madison, *Ind., U.S.A.* **141 F11** 38 44N 85 23W
Madison, *Mo., U.S.A.* **140 E4** 39 28N 92 13W
Madison, *Nebr., U.S.A.* **138 E6** 41 50N 97 27W
Madison, *Ohio, U.S.A.* **136 E3** 41 46N 81 3W
Madison, *S. Dak., U.S.A.* **138 D6** 44 0N 97 7W
Madison, *Wis., U.S.A.* **140 A7** 43 4N 89 24W
Madison →, *U.S.A.* **142 D8** 45 56N 111 31W
Madisonville, *Ky., U.S.A.* **134 G2** 37 20N 87 30W
Madisonville, *Tex., U.S.A.* **139 K7** 30 57N 95 55W
Madista, *Botswana* **104 C4** 21 15 S 25 6 E
Madiun, *Indonesia* **75 D4** 7 38 S 111 32 E
Madley, *U.K.* **17 E5** 52 3N 2 51W
Madol, *Sudan* **95 F2** 9 3N 27 45 E
Madon →, *France* **23 D13** 48 36N 6 6 E
Madona, *Latvia* **50 C5** 56 53N 26 5 E
Madrakah, Ra's al, *Oman* **87 C7** 19 0N 57 50 E
Madras = Tamil Nadu □, *India* **83 J3** 11 0N 77 0 E
Madras, *India* **83 H5** 13 8N 80 19 E
Madras, *U.S.A.* **142 D3** 44 38N 121 8W
Madre, L., *Mexico* **147 B5** 25 0N 97 30W
Madre, Laguna, *U.S.A.* **139 M6** 27 0N 97 30W
Madre, Sierra, *Phil.* **70 C4** 17 0N 122 0 E
Madre de Dios □, *Peru* **156 C3** 12 0 S 70 15W
Madre de Dios →, *Bolivia* **156 C4** 10 59 S 66 8W
Madre de Dios, I., *Chile* **160 D1** 50 20 S 75 10W
Madre del Sur, Sierra, *Mexico* **147 D5** 17 30N 100 0W
Madre Occidental, Sierra, *Mexico* **146 B3** 27 0N 107 0W
Madre Oriental, Sierra, *Mexico* **146 C4** 25 0N 100 0W
Madri, *India* **80 G5** 24 16N 73 32 E
Madrid, *Spain* **36 E7** 40 25N 3 45W
Madrid, *U.S.A.* **140 C3** 41 53N 93 49W
Madrid □, *Spain* **36 E7** 40 30N 3 45W
Madridejos, *Spain* **37 F7** 39 28N 3 33W
Madrigal de las Altas Torres, *Spain* **36 D6** 41 5N 5 0W
Madrona, Sierra, *Spain* **37 G6** 38 27N 4 16W
Madroñera, *Spain* **37 F5** 39 26N 5 42W
Madu, *Sudan* **95 E2** 14 37N 26 4 E
Madura, Selat, *Indonesia* **75 D4** 7 30 S 113 20 E
Madura Motel, *Australia* **113 F4** 31 55 S 127 0 E
Madurai, *India* **83 K4** 9 55N 78 10 E
Madurantakam, *India* **83 H4** 12 30N 79 50 E
Madzhalis, *Russia* **53 E12** 42 9N 47 47 E
Mae Chan, *Thailand* **76 B2** 20 9N 99 52 E
Mae Hong Son, *Thailand* **76 C2** 19 16N 98 1 E
Mae Khlong →, *Thailand* **76 F3** 13 24N 100 0 E
Mae Phrik, *Thailand* **76 D2** 17 27N 99 7 E
Mae Ramat, *Thailand* **76 D2** 16 58N 98 31 E
Mae Rim, *Thailand* **76 C2** 18 54N 98 57 E
Mae Sot, *Thailand* **76 D2** 16 43N 98 34 E
Mae Suai, *Thailand* **76 C2** 19 39N 99 33 E
Mae Tha, *Thailand* **76 C2** 18 28N 99 8 E
Maebaru, *Japan* **62 D2** 33 33N 130 12 E
Maebashi, *Japan* **63 A11** 36 24N 139 4 E
Maella, *Spain* **34 D5** 41 8N 0 7 E
Măeruş, *Romania* **46 D6** 45 53N 25 31 E
Maesteg, *U.K.* **17 F4** 51 36N 3 40W
Maestra, Sierra, *Cuba* **148 B4** 20 15N 77 0W
Maestrazgo, Mts. del, *Spain* **34 E4** 40 30N 0 25W
Maestre de Campo I., *Phil.* **70 E3** 12 56N 121 42 E
Maevatanana, *Madag.* **105 B8** 16 56 S 46 49 E
Maewo, *Vanuatu* **121 E6** 15 10 S 168 10 E
Ma'fan, *Libya* **96 C2** 25 56N 14 29 E
Mafeking = Mafikeng, *S. Africa* **104 D4** 25 50 S 25 38 E
Mafeking, *Canada* **131 C8** 52 40N 101 10W
Maféré, *Ivory C.* **100 D4** 5 30N 3 2W
Mafeteng, *Lesotho* **104 D4** 29 51 S 27 15 E
Maffe, *Belgium* **21 H6** 50 21N 5 19 E
Maffra, *Australia* **117 D7** 37 53 S 146 58 E
Mafia I., *Tanzania* **106 D4** 7 45 S 39 50 E
Mafikeng, *S. Africa* **104 D4** 25 50 S 25 38 E
Mafra, *Brazil* **159 B6** 26 10 S 49 55W
Mafra, *Portugal* **37 G1** 38 55N 9 20W
Mafungabusi Plateau, *Zimbabwe* **107 F2** 18 30 S 29 8 E
Magadan, *Russia* **57 D16** 59 38N 150 50 E
Magadi, *Kenya* **106 C4** 1 54 S 36 19 E
Magadi, L., *Kenya* **106 C4** 1 54 S 36 19 E
Magaliesburg, *S. Africa* **105 D4** 26 0 S 27 32 E
Magallanes, *Phil.* **70 E4** 12 50N 123 50 E
Magallanes □, *Chile* **160 D2** 52 0 S 72 0W
Magallanes, Estrecho de, *Chile* **160 D2** 52 30 S 75 0W
Magangué, *Colombia* **152 B3** 9 14N 74 45W
Maganoy, *Phil.* **71 H5** 6 51N 124 31 E
Magaria, *Niger* **97 F1** 13 4N 9 5 E
Magburaka, *S. Leone* **100 D2** 8 47N 12 0W
Magdalen Is. = Madeleine, Is. de la, *Canada* **129 C7** 47 30N 61 40W
Magdalena, *Argentina* **158 D4** 35 5 S 57 30W
Magdalena, *Bolivia* **157 C5** 13 13 S 63 57W
Magdalena, *Mexico* **146 A2** 30 50N 112 0W
Magdalena, *U.S.A.* **143 J10** 34 7N 107 15W
Magdalena □, *Colombia* **152 A3** 10 0N 74 0W
Magdalena →, *Colombia* **152 A3** 11 6N 74 51W
Magdalena →, *Mexico* **146 A2** 30 40N 112 25W
Magdalena, B., *Mexico* **146 C2** 24 30N 112 10W
Magdalena, I., *Chile* **160 B2** 44 40 S 73 0W
Magdalena, Llano de la, *Mexico* **146 C2** 25 0N 111 30W
Magdeburg, *Germany* **26 C7** 52 8N 11 36 E
Magdelaine Cays, *Australia* **114 B5** 16 33 S 150 18 E
Magdub, *Sudan* **95 E2** 13 42N 25 5 E
Magee, *U.S.A.* **139 K10** 31 52N 89 44W
Magee, I., *U.K.* **19 B6** 54 48N 5 44W
Magelang, *Indonesia* **75 D4** 7 29 S 110 13 E
Magellan's Str. = Magallanes, Estrecho de, *Chile* **160 D2** 52 30 S 75 0W
Magenta, *Australia* **116 B5** 33 51 S 143 34 E
Magenta, *Italy* **38 C5** 45 28N 8 53 E
Magenta, L., *Australia* **113 F2** 33 30 S 119 2 E
Maggea, *Australia* **116 C4** 34 28 S 140 2 E
Maggia, *Switz.* **29 D7** 46 15N 8 42 E
Maggia →, *Switz.* **29 D7** 46 18N 8 36 E
Maggiorasca, Mte., *Italy* **38 D6** 44 33N 9 29 E
Maggiore, L., *Italy* **38 C5** 46 0N 8 35 E
Maghama, *Mauritania* **100 B2** 15 32N 12 57W
Magherafelt, *U.K.* **19 B5** 54 44N 6 37W
Maghnia, *Algeria* **99 B4** 34 50N 1 43W
Magione, *Italy* **39 E9** 43 10N 12 12 E
Maglaj, *Bos.-H.* **42 C3** 44 33N 18 7 E
Magliano in Toscana, *Italy* **39 F8** 42 36N 11 18 E
Máglie, *Italy* **41 B11** 40 8N 18 17 E
Magnac-Laval, *France* **24 B5** 46 13N 1 11 E
Magnetic Pole (North) = North Magnetic Pole, *Canada* **6 B2** 77 58N 102 8W
Magnetic Pole (South) = South Magnetic Pole, *Antarctica* **7 C9** 64 8 S 138 8 E
Magnisía □, *Greece* **44 E4** 39 15N 22 45 E
Magnitogorsk, *Russia* **54 E6** 53 27N 59 4 E
Magnolia, *Ark., U.S.A.* **139 J8** 33 16N 93 14W
Magnolia, *Miss., U.S.A.* **139 K9** 31 9N 90 28W
Magnor, *Norway* **14 E6** 59 56N 12 15 E
Magny-en-Vexin, *France* **23 C8** 49 9N 1 47 E
Magog, *Canada* **129 C5** 45 18N 72 9W
Magoro, *Uganda* **106 B3** 1 45N 34 12 E
Magosa = Famagusta, *Cyprus* **32 D12** 35 8N 33 55 E
Magouládhes, *Greece* **32 A3** 39 45N 19 42 E
Magoye, *Zambia* **107 F2** 16 1 S 27 30 E
Magpie L., *Canada* **129 B7** 51 0N 64 41W
Magrath, *Canada* **130 D6** 49 25N 112 50W
Magro →, *Spain* **35 F4** 39 11N 0 25W
Magrur, Wadi →, *Sudan* **95 D2** 16 5N 26 30 E
Magsingal, *Phil.* **70 C3** 17 41N 120 25 E
Magu □, *Tanzania* **106 C3** 2 31 S 33 28 E
Maguan, *China* **68 F5** 23 0N 104 21 E
Maguarinho, C., *Brazil* **154 B2** 0 15 S 48 30W
Maguindanao □, *Phil.* **71 H5** 7 5N 124 0 E
Maguse L., *Canada* **131 A9** 61 40N 95 10W
Maguse Pt., *Canada* **131 A10** 61 20N 93 50W
Magwe, *Burma* **78 E5** 20 10N 95 0 E
Maha Sarakham, *Thailand* **76 D4** 16 12N 103 16 E
Mahābād, *Iran* **84 B5** 36 50N 45 45 E
Mahabaleshwar, *India* **82 F1** 17 58N 73 43 E
Mahabharat Lekh, *Nepal* **81 E9** 28 30N 82 0 E
Mahabo, *Madag.* **105 C7** 20 23 S 44 40 E
Mahad, *India* **82 E1** 18 6N 73 29 E
Mahaddei Uen, *Somali Rep.* **108 D3** 2 58N 45 32 E
Mahadeo Hills, *India* **80 H8** 22 20N 78 30 E
Mahadeopur, *India* **82 E5** 18 48N 80 0 E
Mahagi, *Zaïre* **106 B3** 2 20N 31 0 E
Mahaicony, *Guyana* **153 B6** 6 36N 57 48W
Mahajamba →, *Madag.* **105 B8** 15 33 S 47 8 E
Mahajamba, Helodranon' i, *Madag.* **105 B8** 15 24 S 47 5 E
Mahajan, *India* **80 E5** 28 48N 73 56 E
Mahajanga, *Madag.* **105 B8** 15 40 S 46 25 E
Mahajanga □, *Madag.* **105 B8** 17 0 S 47 0 E
Mahajilo →, *Madag.* **105 B8** 19 42 S 45 22 E
Mahakam →, *Indonesia* **75 C5** 0 35 S 117 17 E
Mahalapye, *Botswana* **104 C4** 23 1 S 26 51 E
Maḩallāt, *Iran* **85 C6** 33 55N 50 30 E
Māhān, *Iran* **85 D8** 30 5N 57 18 E
Mahanadi →, *India* **82 D8** 20 20N 86 25 E
Mahanoro, *Madag.* **105 B8** 19 54 S 48 48 E
Mahanoy City, *U.S.A.* **137 F8** 40 49N 76 9W
Mahaplag, *Phil.* **71 F5** 10 35N 124 57 E
Maharashtra □, *India* **82 D2** 20 30N 75 30 E
Maharès, *Tunisia* **96 B2** 34 32N 10 29 E
Mahari Mts., *Tanzania* **106 D2** 6 20 S 30 0 E
Mahasham, W. →, *Egypt* **91 E3** 30 15N 34 10 E
Mahasolo, *Madag.* **105 B8** 19 7 S 46 22 E
Mahattat ash Shīdīyah, *Jordan* **91 F4** 29 55N 35 55 E
Mahattat 'Unayzah, *Jordan* **91 E4** 30 30N 35 47 E
Mahaweli →, *Sri Lanka* **83 K5** 8 30N 81 15 E
Mahaxay, *Laos* **76 D5** 17 22N 105 12 E
Mahbes, *W. Sahara* **98 C3** 27 10N 9 50W
Mahbubabad, *India* **82 F5** 17 42N 80 2 E
Mahbubnagar, *India* **82 F3** 16 45N 77 59 E
Maḩḑah, *Oman* **85 E7** 24 24N 55 59 E
Mahdia, *Guyana* **153 B6** 5 13N 59 8W
Mahdia, *Tunisia* **96 A2** 35 28N 11 0 E
Mahe, *Jammu & Kashmir, India* **81 C8** 33 10N 78 32 E
Mahé, *Pondicherry, India* **83 J2** 11 42N 75 34 E
Mahé, *Seychelles* **109 E4** 5 0 S 55 30 E
Mahendra Giri, *India* **83 K3** 8 20N 77 30 E
Mahendraganj, *India* **78 C2** 25 20N 89 45 E
Mahenge, *Tanzania* **107 D4** 8 45 S 36 41 E
Maheno, *N.Z.* **119 F5** 45 10 S 170 50 E
Mahesana, *India* **80 H5** 23 39N 72 26 E
Mahia Pen., *N.Z.* **118 F6** 39 9 S 177 55 E
Mahilyow = Mogilev, *Belorussia* **50 E7** 53 55N 30 18 E
Mahirija, *Morocco* **99 B4** 34 0N 3 16W
Mahlaing, *Burma* **78 E5** 21 6N 95 39 E
Mahmiya, *Sudan* **95 D3** 17 12N 33 43 E
Mahmud Kot, *Pakistan* **80 D4** 30 16N 71 0 E
Mahmudia, *Romania* **46 D10** 45 5N 29 5 E
Mahnomen, *U.S.A.* **138 B7** 47 19N 95 58W
Mahoba, *India* **81 G8** 25 15N 79 55 E
Mahomet, *U.S.A.* **141 D8** 40 12N 88 24W
Mahón, *Spain* **33 B11** 39 53N 4 16 E
Mahone Bay, *Canada* **129 D7** 44 30N 64 20W
Mahuta, *Nigeria* **101 C5** 11 32N 4 58 E
Mai-Ndombe, L., *Zaïre* **102 C3** 2 0 S 18 20 E
Mai-Sai, *Thailand* **76 B2** 20 20N 99 55 E
Maibara, *Japan* **63 B8** 35 19N 136 17 E
Maicao, *Colombia* **152 A3** 11 23N 72 13W
Maîche, *France* **23 E13** 47 16N 6 48 E
Maici →, *Brazil* **157 B5** 6 30 S 61 43W
Maicurú →, *Brazil* **153 D7** 2 14 S 54 17W
Máida, *Italy* **41 D9** 38 51N 16 21 E
Maidan Khula, *Afghan.* **80 C3** 33 36N 69 50 E
Maidenhead, *U.K.* **17 F7** 51 31N 0 42W
Maidi, *Yemen* **95 D5** 16 20N 42 45 E
Maidstone, *Canada* **131 C7** 53 5N 109 20W
Maidstone, *U.K.* **17 F8** 51 16N 0 31 E
Maiduguri, *Nigeria* **101 C7** 12 0N 13 20 E
Maignelay, *France* **23 C9** 49 32N 2 30 E
Maigo, *Phil.* **71 G4** 8 10N 123 57 E
Maigualida, Sierra, *Venezuela* **153 B4** 5 30N 65 10W
Maigudo, *Ethiopia* **95 F4** 7 30N 37 8 E
Maijdi, *Bangla.* **78 D3** 22 48N 91 10 E
Maikala Ra., *India* **82 D5** 22 0N 81 0 E
Maikoor, *Indonesia* **73 C4** 6 8 S 134 6 E
Mailly-le-Camp, *France* **23 D11** 48 41N 4 12 E
Mailsi, *Pakistan* **80 E5** 29 48N 72 15 E
Maimbung, *Phil.* **71 J3** 5 56N 121 2 E
Main →, *Germany* **27 F4** 50 0N 8 18 E
Main →, *U.K.* **19 B5** 54 49N 6 20W
Main Centre, *Canada* **131 C7** 50 35N 107 21W
Mainburg, *Germany* **27 G7** 48 37N 11 49 E
Maine, *France* **22 E6** 47 55N 0 25W
Maine □, *U.S.A.* **129 C6** 45 20N 69 0W
Maine →, *Ireland* **19 D2** 52 10N 9 40W
Maine-et-Loire □, *France* **22 E6** 47 31N 0 30W
Maïne-Soroa, *Niger* **101 C7** 13 13N 12 2 E
Maingkwan, *Burma* **78 B6** 26 15N 96 37 E
Mainit, *Phil.* **71 G5** 9 32N 125 32 E
Mainit, L., *Phil.* **71 G5** 9 31N 125 30 E
Mainkaing, *Burma* **78 C5** 24 48N 95 16 E
Mainland, *Orkney, U.K.* **18 C5** 59 0N 3 10W
Mainland, *Shet., U.K.* **18 A7** 60 15N 1 22W
Mainpuri, *India* **81 F8** 27 18N 79 4 E
Maintenon, *France* **23 D8** 48 35N 1 35 E
Maintirano, *Madag.* **105 B7** 18 3 S 44 1 E
Mainvault, *Belgium* **21 G3** 50 39N 3 43 E
Mainz, *Germany* **27 F4** 50 0N 8 17 E
Maipú, *Argentina* **158 D4** 36 52 S 57 50W
Maiquetía, *Venezuela* **152 A4** 10 36N 66 57W
Maira →, *Italy* **38 D4** 44 49N 7 38 E
Mairabari, *India* **78 B4** 26 30N 92 22 E
Mairipotaba, *Brazil* **155 E2** 17 18 S 49 28W
Maisí, *Cuba* **149 B5** 20 17N 74 9W
Maisi, Pta. de, *Cuba* **149 B5** 20 10N 74 10W
Maisse, *France* **23 D9** 48 24N 2 21 E
Maissin, *Belgium* **21 J6** 49 58N 5 10 E
Maitland, *N.S.W., Australia* **117 B9** 32 33 S 151 36 E
Maitland, *S. Austral., Australia* **116 C2** 34 23 S 137 40 E
Maitland →, *Canada* **136 C3** 43 45N 81 43W
Maitland, Banjaran, *Malaysia* **75 B5** 4 55N 116 37 E

Mangyshlakskiy Zaliv 229

Maiyema, *Nigeria* **101 C5** 12 5N 4 25 E
Maiyuan, *China* **69 E11** 25 34N 117 28 E
Maiz, Is. del, *Nic.* **148 D3** 12 15N 83 4W
Maizuru, *Japan* **63 B7** 35 25N 135 22 E
Majagual, *Colombia* **152 B3** 8 33N 74 38W
Majalengka, *Indonesia* **75 D3** 6 50 S 108 13 E
Majari →, *Brazil* **153 C5** 3 29N 60 58W
Majene, *Indonesia* **72 B1** 3 38 S 118 57 E
Majes →, *Peru* **156 D3** 16 40 S 72 44W
Majevica, *Bos.-H.* **42 C3** 44 45N 18 50 E
Maji, *Ethiopia* **95 F4** 6 12N 35 30 E
Majiang, *China* **68 D6** 26 28N 107 32 E
Major, *Canada* **131 C7** 51 52N 109 37W
Majorca = Mallorca,
Spain **33 B10** 39 30N 3 0 E
Majors Creek, *Australia* **117 C8** 35 33 S 149 45 E
Majuriã, *Brazil* **157 B5** 7 30 S 64 55W
Maka, *Senegal* **100 C2** 13 40N 14 10W
Makak, *Cameroon* **101 E7** 3 36N 11 0 E
Makakou, *Gabon* **102 C2** 0 11 S 12 12 E
Makale, *Indonesia* **72 B1** 3 6 S 119 51 E
Makamba, *Burundi* **106 C2** 4 8 S 29 49 E
Makarewa, *N.Z.* **119 G3** 46 20 S 168 21 E
Makarikari =
Makgadikgadi Salt Pans,
Botswana **104 C4** 20 40 S 25 45 E
Makarovo, *Russia* **57 D11** 57 40N 107 45 E
Makarska, *Croatia* **42 D2** 43 20N 17 2 E
Makaryev, *Russia* **51 C13** 57 52N 43 50 E
Makasar = Ujung
Pandang, *Indonesia* **72 C1** 5 10 S 119 20 E
Makasar, Selat, *Indonesia* **72 B1** 1 0 S 118 20 E
Makasar, Str. of =
Makasar, Selat,
Indonesia **72 B1** 1 0 S 118 20 E
Makat, *Kazakhstan* **49 E9** 47 39N 53 19 E
Makedhonía □, *Greece* **44 D3** 40 39N 22 0 E
Makedonija =
Macedonia ■, *Europe* **42 F6** 41 53N 21 40 E
Makena, *U.S.A.* **132 H16** 20 39N 156 27W
Makeni, *S. Leone* **100 D2** 8 55N 12 5W
Makeyevka, *Ukraine* **52 B7** 48 0N 38 0 E
Makgadikgadi Salt Pans,
Botswana **104 C4** 20 40 S 25 45 E
Makhachkala, *Russia* **53 E12** 43 0N 47 30 E
Makhambet, *Kazakhstan* **53 C14** 47 43N 51 40 E
Makharadze = Ozurgety,
Georgia **53 F10** 41 55N 42 2 E
Makhmūr, *Iraq* **84 C4** 35 46N 43 35 E
Makhyah, W. →, *Yemen* **87 C5** 17 40N 49 1 E
Makian, *Indonesia* **72 A3** 0 20N 127 20 E
Makindu, *Kenya* **106 C4** 2 18 S 37 50 E
Makinsk, *Kazakhstan* **56 D8** 52 37N 70 26 E
Makiyivka = Makeyevka,
Ukraine **52 B7** 48 0N 38 0 E
Makkah, *Si. Arabia* **86 B2** 21 30N 39 54 E
Makkovik, *Canada* **129 A8** 55 10N 59 10W
Makkum, *Neths.* **20 B6** 53 3N 5 25 E
Makó, *Hungary* **31 E13** 46 14N 20 33 E
Makok, *Gabon* **102 C1** 0 1 S 9 35 E
Makokou, *Gabon* **102 B2** 0 40N 12 50 E
Makongo, *Zaïre* **106 B2** 3 25N 26 17 E
Makoro, *Zaïre* **106 B2** 3 10N 29 59 E
Makoua, *Congo* **102 C3** 0 5 S 15 50 E
Maków Mazowiecki,
Poland **47 C8** 52 52N 21 6 E
Maków Podhal, *Poland* **31 B12** 49 43N 19 45 E
Makrá, *Greece* **45 H7** 36 15N 25 54 E
Makran, *Asia* **79 D1** 26 13N 61 30 E
Makran Coast Range,
Pakistan **79 D2** 25 40N 64 0 E
Makrana, *India* **80 F6** 27 2N 74 46 E
Mákri, *Greece* **44 D7** 40 52N 25 40 E
Makriyialos, *Greece* **32 D7** 35 2N 25 59 E
Maksimkin Yar, *Russia* **56 D9** 58 42N 86 50 E
Maktar, *Tunisia* **96 A1** 35 48N 9 12 E
Mākū, *Iran* **84 B5** 39 15N 44 31 E
Makum, *India* **78 B5** 27 30N 95 23 E
Makumbi, *Zaïre* **103 D4** 5 50 S 20 43 E
Makunda, *Botswana* **104 C3** 22 30 S 20 7 E
Makurazaki, *Japan* **62 F2** 31 15N 130 20 E
Makurdi, *Nigeria* **101 D6** 7 43N 8 35 E
Makūyeh, *Iran* **85 D7** 28 7N 53 9 E
Makwassie, *S. Africa* **104 D4** 27 17 S 26 0 E
Mal, *India* **78 B2** 26 51N 88 45 E
Mal B., *Ireland* **19 D2** 52 50N 9 30W
Mal i Gjalicës së Lumës,
Albania **44 B2** 42 2N 20 25 E
Mal i Gribës, *Albania* **44 D1** 40 17N 19 45 E
Mal i Nemërçkës, *Albania* **44 D2** 40 15N 20 15 E
Mal i Tomorit, *Albania* **44 D2** 40 42N 20 11 E
Mala, *Peru* **156 C2** 12 40 S 76 38W
Mala, Pta., *Panama* **148 E3** 7 28N 80 2W
Mala Kapela, *Croatia* **39 D12** 44 45N 15 30 E
Malabang, *Phil.* **71 H5** 7 36N 124 3 E
Malabar Coast, *India* **83 J2** 11 0N 75 0 E
Malabo = Rey Malabo,
Eq. Guin. **101 E6** 3 45N 8 50 E
Malabon, *Phil.* **70 D3** 14 21N 121 0 E
Malabrigo Pt., *Phil.* **70 E3** 13 36N 121 15 E
Malabungan, *Phil.* **71 G1** 9 3N 117 38 E
Malacca, Str. of, *Indonesia* **77 L3** 3 0N 101 0 E
Malacky, *Slovak Rep.* **31 C10** 48 27N 17 0 E
Malad City, *U.S.A.* **142 E7** 42 12N 112 15W
Maladzyechna =
Molodechno, *Belorussia* **50 D5** 54 20N 26 50 E
Málaga, *Colombia* **152 B3** 6 42N 72 44W
Málaga, *Spain* **37 J6** 36 43N 4 23W
Malaga, *U.S.A.* **139 J2** 32 14N 104 4W
Málaga □, *Spain* **37 J6** 36 38N 4 58W
Malagarasi, *Tanzania* **106 D3** 5 5 S 30 50 E
Malagarasi →, *Tanzania* **106 D2** 5 12 S 29 47 E
Malagón, *Spain* **37 F7** 39 11N 3 52W
Malagón →, *Spain* **37 H3** 37 35N 7 29W
Malaimbandy, *Madag.* **105 C8** 20 20 S 45 36 E
Malaita, *Pac. Oc.* **121 M11** 9 0 S 161 0 E
Malakâl, *Sudan* **95 F3** 9 33N 31 40 E
Malakand, *Pakistan* **79 B3** 34 40N 71 55 E
Malakoff, *U.S.A.* **139 J7** 32 10N 96 1W
Malalag, *Phil.* **71 H5** 6 36N 125 24 E
Malam, *Chad* **97 F4** 11 27N 20 59 E
Malamyzh, *Russia* **57 E14** 49 50N 136 50 E
Malang, *Indonesia* **75 D4** 7 59 S 112 45 E
Malangas, *Phil.* **71 H4** 7 37N 123 1 E
Malange □, *Angola* **103 D3** 9 30 S 16 0 E
Malanje, *Angola* **103 D3** 9 36 S 16 17 E
Mälaren, *Sweden* **14 E11** 59 30N 17 10 E
Malargüe, *Argentina* **158 D2** 35 32 S 69 30W
Malartic, *Canada* **128 C4** 48 9N 78 9W
Malatya, *Turkey* **89 D8** 38 25N 38 20 E
Malatya □, *Turkey* **89 D8** 38 15N 38 0 E
Malawali, *Malaysia* **75 A5** 7 3N 117 18 E
Malawi ■, *Africa* **107 E3** 11 55 S 34 0 E
Malawi, L., *Africa* **107 E3** 12 30 S 34 30 E
Malay, *Phil.* **71 F3** 11 54N 121 55 E
Malay Pen., *Asia* **77 J3** 7 25N 100 0 E
Malaya Belozërka,
Ukraine **52 C6** 47 12N 34 56 E
Malaya Vishera, *Russia* **50 B8** 58 55N 32 25 E
Malaya Viska, *Ukraine* **52 B4** 48 39N 31 36 E
Malaybalay, *Phil.* **71 G5** 8 5N 125 7 E
Malāyer, *Iran* **85 C6** 34 19N 48 51 E
Malaysia ■, *Asia* **74 B4** 5 0N 110 0 E
Malazgirt, *Turkey* **89 D10** 39 10N 42 33 E
Malbon, *Australia* **114 C3** 21 5 S 140 17 E
Malbooma, *Australia* **115 E1** 30 41 S 134 11 E
Malbork, *Poland* **47 A6** 54 3N 19 1 E
Malca Dube, *Ethiopia* **108 C2** 6 47N 42 4 E
Malcésine, *Italy* **38 C7** 45 46N 10 48 E
Malchin, *Germany* **26 B8** 53 43N 12 44 E
Malchow, *Germany* **26 B8** 53 29N 12 25 E
Malcolm, *Australia* **113 E3** 28 51 S 121 25 E
Malcolm, Pt., *Australia* **113 F3** 33 48 S 123 45 E
Malczyce, *Poland* **47 D3** 51 14N 16 29 E
Maldegem, *Belgium* **21 F2** 51 14N 3 26 E
Malden, *Mass., U.S.A.* **137 D13** 42 26N 71 4W
Malden, *Mo., U.S.A.* **139 G10** 36 34N 89 57W
Malden I., *Kiribati* **123 H12** 4 3 S 155 1W
Maldives ■, *Ind. Oc.* **59 J11** 5 0N 73 0 E
Maldon, *Australia* **116 D6** 37 0 S 144 6 E
Maldonado, *Uruguay* **159 C5** 34 59 S 55 0W
Maldonado, Punta, *Mexico* **147 D5** 16 19N 98 35W
Malé, *Italy* **38 B7** 46 20N 10 55 E
Malé Karpaty,
Slovak Rep. **31 C10** 48 30N 17 20 E
Maléa, Ákra, *Greece* **45 H5** 36 28N 23 7 E
Malebo, Pool, *Africa* **103 C3** 4 17 S 15 20 E
Malegaon, *India* **82 D2** 20 30N 74 38 E
Malei, *Mozam.* **107 F4** 17 12 S 36 58 E
Malek Kandī, *Iran* **84 B5** 37 9N 46 6 E
Malekula, *Vanuatu* **121 F5** 16 15 S 167 30 E
Malela, *Bas Zaïre, Zaïre* **103 D2** 5 59 S 12 37 E
Malela, *Kivu, Zaïre* **103 C5** 4 22 S 26 8 E
Malema, *Mozam.* **107 E4** 14 57 S 37 20 E
Máleme, *Greece* **32 D5** 35 31N 23 49 E
Malerkotla, *India* **80 D6** 30 32N 75 58 E
Máles, *Greece* **32 D7** 35 6N 25 35 E
Malesherbes, *France* **23 D9** 48 15N 2 24 E
Maleshevska Planina,
Europe **42 F8** 41 38N 23 7 E
Malestroit, *France* **22 E4** 47 49N 2 25W
Malfa, *Italy* **41 D7** 38 35N 14 50 E
Malgobek, *Russia* **53 E11** 43 30N 44 34 E
Malgomaj, *Sweden* **12 D14** 64 40N 16 30 E
Malgrat, *Spain* **34 D7** 41 39N 2 46 E
Malha, *Sudan* **95 D2** 15 8N 25 10 E
Malheur →, *U.S.A.* **142 D5** 44 4N 116 59W
Malheur L., *U.S.A.* **142 E4** 43 20N 118 48W
Mali, *Guinea* **100 C2** 12 10N 12 20W
Mali ■, *Africa* **100 B4** 17 0N 3 0W
Mali Hka →, *Burma* **78 C6** 25 42N 97 30 E
Mali Kanal, *Serbia* **42 B4** 45 36N 19 24 E
Malibu, *U.S.A.* **145 L8** 34 2N 118 41W
Maligaya, *Phil.* **70 E3** 12 59N 121 30 E
Malik, *Indonesia* **72 B2** 0 39 S 123 16 E
Malili, *Indonesia* **72 B2** 2 42 S 121 6 E
Malimba, Mts., *Zaïre* **106 D2** 7 30 S 29 30 E
Malin, *Ukraine* **50 F6** 50 46N 29 3 E
Malin Hd., *Ireland* **19 A4** 55 18N 7 24W
Malindang, Mt., *Phil.* **71 G4** 8 13N 123 38 E
Malindi, *Kenya* **106 C5** 3 12 S 40 5 E
Malines = Mechelen,
Belgium **21 F4** 51 2N 4 29 E
Maling, *Indonesia* **72 A2** 1 0N 121 0 E
Malinyi, *Tanzania* **107 D4** 8 56 S 36 0 E
Malipo, *China* **68 F5** 23 7N 104 42 E
Maliqi, *Albania* **44 D2** 40 45N 20 48 E
Malita, *Phil.* **71 H5** 6 19N 125 39 E
Maljenik, *Serbia* **42 D6** 43 59N 21 55 E
Malkapur, *Maharashtra*,
India **82 F3** 16 57N 76 17 E
Malkapur, *Maharashtra*,
India **82 D1** 20 53N 73 58 E
Malkara, *Turkey* **88 C2** 40 53N 26 53 E
Małkinia Górna, *Poland* **47 C9** 52 42N 22 5 E
Malko Tŭrnovo, *Bulgaria* **43 F12** 41 59N 27 31 E
Mallacoota, *Australia* **117 D8** 37 40 S 149 40 E
Mallacoota Inlet, *Australia* **117 D8** 37 34 S 149 40 E
Mallaig, *U.K.* **18 E3** 57 0N 5 50W
Mallala, *Australia* **116 C3** 34 26 S 138 30 E
Mallard, *U.S.A.* **140 B2** 42 56N 94 41W
Mallawan, *India* **81 F9** 27 4N 80 12 E
Mallawi, *Egypt* **94 B3** 27 44N 30 44 E
Malleco □, *Chile* **160 A2** 38 10 S 72 20W
Mallemort, *France* **25 E9** 43 43N 5 11 E
Málles Venosta, *Italy* **38 B7** 46 42N 10 32 E
Mállia, *Greece* **32 D7** 35 17N 25 27 E
Mallicolo = Malekula,
Vanuatu **121 F5** 16 15 S 167 30 E
Mallig, *Phil.* **70 C3** 17 8N 121 42 E
Mallión, Kólpos, *Greece* **32 D7** 35 19N 25 27 E
Mallorca, *Spain* **33 B10** 39 30N 3 0 E
Mallorytown, *Canada* **137 B9** 44 29N 75 53W
Mallow, *Ireland* **19 D3** 52 8N 8 40W
Malmberget, *Sweden* **12 C16** 67 11N 20 40 E
Malmédy, *Belgium* **21 H8** 50 25N 6 2 E
Malmesbury, *S. Africa* **104 E2** 33 28 S 18 41 E
Malmö, *Sweden* **15 J6** 55 36N 12 59 E
Malmöhus län □, *Sweden* **15 J7** 55 45N 13 30 E
Malmslätt, *Sweden* **15 F9** 58 27N 15 33 E
Malmyzh, *Russia* **54 C2** 56 31N 50 41 E
Malnaş, *Romania* **46 C6** 46 2N 25 49 E
Malo, *Vanuatu* **121 E5** 15 40 S 167 11 E
Malo Konare, *Bulgaria* **43 E9** 42 12N 24 24 E
Maloarkhangelsk, *Russia* **51 E10** 52 28N 36 30 E
Maloca, *Brazil* **153 C6** 0 43N 55 57W
Maloja, *Switz.* **29 D9** 46 25N 9 35 E
Maloja, P., *Switz.* **29 D9** 46 23N 9 42 E
Malolos, *Phil.* **70 D3** 14 50N 120 49 E
Malomalsk, *Russia* **54 B6** 58 45N 59 53 E
Malombe L., *Malawi* **107 E4** 14 40 S 35 15 E
Malomir, *Bulgaria* **43 E11** 42 16N 26 30 E
Malone, *U.S.A.* **137 B10** 44 51N 74 18W
Malong, *China* **68 E4** 25 24N 103 34 E
Malonga, *Zaïre* **103 E4** 10 24 S 23 10 E
Malorad, *Bulgaria* **43 D8** 43 28N 23 41 E
Malorita, *Belorussia* **50 F4** 51 50N 24 3 E
Maloyaroslovets, *Russia* **51 D10** 55 2N 36 20 E
Malozemelskaya Tundra,
Russia **48 A9** 67 0N 50 0 E
Malpartida, *Spain* **37 F4** 39 26N 6 30W
Malpaso, *Canary Is.* **33 G1** 27 43N 18 3W
Malpica, *Spain* **36 B2** 43 19N 8 50W
Malprabha →, *India* **83 F3** 16 20N 76 5 E
Malta, *Brazil* **154 C4** 6 54 S 37 31W
Malta, *Idaho, U.S.A.* **142 E7** 42 18N 113 22W
Malta, *Mont., U.S.A.* **142 B10** 48 21N 107 52W
Malta ■, *Europe* **32 D1** 35 50N 14 30 E
Malta Channel, *Medit. S.* **40 F6** 36 40N 14 0 E
Maltahöhe, *Namibia* **104 C2** 24 55 S 17 0 E
Malters, *Switz.* **28 B6** 47 3N 8 11 E
Malton, *Canada* **136 C5** 43 42N 79 38W
Malton, *U.K.* **16 C7** 54 9N 0 48W
Malu'a, *Solomon Is.* **121 M11** 8 0 S 160 0 E
Maluku, *Indonesia* **72 B3** 1 0 S 127 0 E
Maluku □, *Indonesia* **72 B3** 3 0 S 128 0 E
Maluku Sea, *Indonesia* **72 A3** 2 0 S 124 0 E
Malumfashi, *Nigeria* **101 C6** 11 48N 7 39 E
Malungun, *Phil.* **71 H5** 6 16N 125 14 E
Maluso, *Phil.* **71 H3** 6 33N 121 53 E
Malvalli, *India* **83 H3** 12 28N 77 8 E
Malvan, *India* **83 F1** 16 2N 73 30 E
Malvern, *U.S.A.* **139 H8** 34 22N 92 49W
Malvern Hills, *U.K.* **17 E5** 52 0N 2 19W
Malvik, *Norway* **14 A4** 63 25N 10 40 E
Malvinas, Is. = Falkland
Is. ■, *Atl. Oc.* **160 D5** 51 30 S 59 0W
Malya, *Tanzania* **106 C3** 3 5 S 33 38 E
Malybay, *Kazakhstan* **55 B9** 43 30N 78 25 E
Malyy Lyakhovskiy,
Ostrov, *Russia* **57 B15** 74 7N 140 36 E
Mama, *Russia* **57 D12** 58 18N 112 54 E
Mamadysh, *Russia* **54 D2** 55 44N 51 23 E
Mamaia, *Romania* **46 E9** 44 18N 28 37 E
Mamaku, *N.Z.* **118 E5** 38 5 S 176 8 E
Mamanguape, *Brazil* **154 C4** 6 50 S 35 4W
Mamasa, *Indonesia* **72 B1** 2 55 S 119 20 E
Mambajao, *Phil.* **71 G5** 9 15N 124 43 E
Mambasa, *Zaïre* **106 B2** 1 22N 29 3 E
Mamberamo →,
Indonesia **73 B5** 2 0 S 137 50 E
Mambilima Falls, *Zambia* **107 E2** 10 31 S 28 45 E
Mambirima, *Zaïre* **107 E2** 11 25 S 27 33 E
Mambo, *Tanzania* **106 C4** 4 52 S 38 22 E
Mambrui, *Kenya* **106 C5** 3 5 S 40 5 E
Mamburao, *Phil.* **70 E3** 13 13N 120 39 E
Mameigwess L., *Canada* **128 B2** 52 35N 87 50W
Mamer, *Lux.* **21 J8** 49 38N 6 2 E
Mamers, *France* **22 D7** 48 21N 0 22 E
Mamfe, *Cameroon* **101 D6** 5 50N 9 15 E
Māmī, Ra's, *Yemen* **87 D6** 12 32N 54 30 E
Mamiña, *Chile* **156 E4** 20 5 S 69 14W
Mámmola, *Italy* **41 D9** 38 23N 16 13 E
Mammoth, *U.S.A.* **143 K8** 32 43N 110 39W
Mamoré →, *Bolivia* **157 C4** 10 23 S 65 53W
Mamou, *Guinea* **100 C2** 10 15N 12 0W
Mamparang Mts., *Phil.* **70 C3** 16 21N 121 28 E
Mampatá, *Guinea-Biss.* **100 C2** 11 54N 14 53W
Mampong, *Ghana* **101 D4** 7 6N 1 26W
Mamry, Jezioro, *Poland* **47 A8** 54 5N 21 50 E
Mamuil Malal, Paso,
S. Amer. **160 A2** 39 35 S 71 28W
Mamuju, *Indonesia* **72 B1** 2 41 S 118 50 E
Ma'mūl, *Oman* **87 C6** 18 8N 55 16 E
Man, *Ivory C.* **100 D3** 7 30N 7 40W
Man →, *India* **82 F2** 17 31N 75 32 E
Man, I. of, *U.K.* **16 C3** 54 15N 4 30W
Man Na, *Burma* **78 D6** 23 27N 97 19 E
Man Tun, *Burma* **78 D7** 23 52N 98 38 E
Mana, *Fr. Guiana* **153 B7** 5 45N 53 55W
Mana →, *Fr. Guiana* **153 B7** 5 45N 53 55W
Måna →, *Norway* **14 E2** 59 55N 8 50 E
Manaar, G. of = Mannar,
G. of, *Asia* **83 K4** 8 30N 79 0 E
Manabí □, *Ecuador* **152 D1** 0 40 S 80 5W
Manacacías →, *Colombia* **152 C3** 4 23N 72 4W
Manacapuru, *Brazil* **153 D5** 3 16 S 60 37W
Manacapuru →, *Brazil* **153 D5** 3 18 S 60 37W
Manacor, *Spain* **33 B10** 39 34N 3 13 E
Manado, *Indonesia* **72 A2** 1 29N 124 51 E
Manage, *Belgium* **21 G4** 50 31N 4 15 E
Managua, *Nic.* **148 D2** 12 6N 86 20W
Managua, L., *Nic.* **148 D2** 12 20N 86 30W
Manaia, *N.Z.* **118 F3** 39 33 S 174 8 E
Manakara, *Madag.* **105 C8** 22 8 S 48 1 E
Manakau Mt., *N.Z.* **119 C8** 42 15 S 173 42 E
Manākhah, *Yemen* **86 D3** 15 5N 43 44 E
Manakino, *N.Z.* **118 E4** 38 22 S 175 47 E
Manam I., *Papua N. G.* **120 C3** 4 5 S 145 0 E
Manama = Al Manāmah,
Bahrain **85 E6** 26 10N 50 30 E
Manambao →, *Madag.* **105 B7** 17 35 S 44 0 E
Manambato, *Madag.* **105 A8** 13 43 S 49 7 E
Manambolo →, *Madag.* **105 B7** 19 18 S 44 22 E
Manambolosy, *Madag.* **105 B8** 16 2 S 49 40 E
Mananara, *Madag.* **105 B8** 16 10 S 49 46 E
Mananara →, *Madag.* **105 C8** 23 21 S 47 42 E
Mananjary, *Madag.* **105 C8** 21 13 S 48 20 E
Manantenina, *Madag.* **105 C8** 24 17 S 47 19 E
Manaos = Manaus, *Brazil* **153 D6** 3 0 S 60 0W
Manapala, *Phil.* **71 F4** 10 58N 123 5 E
Manapire →, *Venezuela* **152 B4** 7 42N 66 7W
Manapouri, *N.Z.* **119 F2** 45 34 S 167 39 E
Manapouri, L., *N.Z.* **119 F2** 45 32 S 167 32 E
Manar →, *India* **82 E3** 18 50N 77 20 E
Manār, Jabal, *Yemen* **86 D4** 14 2N 44 17 E
Manas, *China* **64 B3** 44 17N 85 56 E
Manas, *Somali Rep.* **108 D2** 2 57N 43 28 E
Manas, Gora, *Kirghizia* **55 B5** 42 22N 71 2 E
Manaslu, *Nepal* **81 E11** 28 33N 84 33 E
Manasquan, *U.S.A.* **137 F10** 40 8N 74 3W
Manassa, *U.S.A.* **143 H11** 37 11N 105 56W
Manaung, *Burma* **78 F4** 18 45N 93 40 E
Manaus, *Brazil* **153 D6** 3 0 S 60 0W
Manavgat, *Turkey* **88 E4** 36 47N 31 26 E
Manawan L., *Canada* **131 B8** 55 24N 103 14W
Manawatu →, *N.Z.* **118 G4** 40 28 S 175 12 E
Manay, *Phil.* **71 H6** 7 17N 126 33 E
Manbij, *Syria* **84 B3** 36 31N 37 57 E
Mancelona, *U.S.A.* **134 C3** 44 54N 85 4W
Mancha Real, *Spain* **37 H7** 37 48N 3 39W
Manche □, *France* **22 C5** 49 10N 1 20W
Manchegorsk, *Russia* **48 A5** 67 40N 32 40 E
Manchester, *U.K.* **16 D5** 53 30N 2 15W
Manchester, *Calif., U.S.A.* **144 G3** 38 58N 123 41W
Manchester, *Conn.*,
U.S.A. **137 E12** 41 47N 72 31W
Manchester, *Ga., U.S.A.* **135 J3** 32 51N 84 37W
Manchester, *Iowa, U.S.A.* **140 B5** 42 29N 91 27W
Manchester, *Ky., U.S.A.* **134 G4** 37 9N 83 46W
Manchester, *Mich.*,
U.S.A. **141 B12** 42 9N 84 2W
Manchester, *N.H., U.S.A.* **137 D13** 42 59N 71 28W
Manchester, *N.Y., U.S.A.* **136 D7** 42 56N 77 16W
Manchester, *Vt., U.S.A.* **137 C11** 43 10N 73 5W
Manchester L., *Canada* **131 A7** 61 28N 107 29W
Manchuria = Dongbei,
China **67 D13** 42 0N 125 0 E
Manciano, *Italy* **39 F8** 42 35N 11 30 E
Mancifa, *Ethiopia* **95 F5** 6 53N 41 50 E
Mancora, Pta., *Peru* **156 A1** 4 9 S 81 1W
Mand →, *Iran* **85 D7** 28 20N 52 30 E
Manda, *Chunya, Tanzania* **106 D3** 6 51 S 32 29 E
Manda, *Ludewe, Tanzania* **107 E3** 10 30 S 34 40 E
Mandabé, *Madag.* **105 C7** 21 0 S 44 55 E
Mandaguari, *Brazil* **159 A5** 23 32 S 51 42W
Mandah, *Mongolia* **66 B5** 44 27N 108 2 E
Mandal, *Norway* **13 G9** 58 2N 7 25 E
Mandalay, *Burma* **78 D6** 22 0N 96 4 E
Mandale = Mandalay,
Burma **78 D6** 22 0N 96 4 E
Mandalgovi, *Mongolia* **66 B4** 45 45N 106 10 E
Mandalī, *Iraq* **84 C5** 33 43N 45 28 E
Mandalya Körfezı, *Turkey* **45 G9** 37 15N 27 20 E
Mandan, *U.S.A.* **138 B4** 46 50N 100 54W
Mandaon, *Phil.* **70 E4** 12 13N 123 17 E
Mandapeta, *India* **82 F5** 16 47N 81 56 E
Mandar, Teluk, *Indonesia* **72 B1** 3 35 S 119 15 E
Mandas, *Italy* **40 C2** 39 40N 9 8 E
Mandasor = Mandsaur,
India **80 G6** 24 3N 75 8 E
Mandaue, *Phil.* **71 F4** 10 20N 123 56 E
Mandayar, *Phil.* **71 H6** 7 34N 126 14 E
Mandelieu-la-Napoule,
France **25 E10** 43 34N 6 57 E
Mandera, *Kenya* **106 B5** 3 55N 41 53 E
Mandera □, *Kenya* **106 B5** 3 30N 41 0 E
Manderfeld, *Belgium* **21 H8** 50 20N 6 20 E
Mandi, *India* **80 D7** 31 39N 76 58 E
Mandimba, *Mozam.* **107 E4** 14 20 S 35 40 E
Mandioli, *Indonesia* **72 B3** 0 40 S 127 20 E
Mandioré, L., *S. Amer.* **157 D6** 18 8 S 57 33W
Mandji I. = Lopez I.,
Gabon **102 C1** 0 50 S 8 47 E
Mandla, *India* **81 H9** 22 39N 80 30 E
Mandø, *Denmark* **15 J2** 55 18N 8 33 E
Mandoto, *Madag.* **105 B8** 19 34 S 46 17 E
Mandoúdhion, *Greece* **45 F5** 38 48N 23 29 E
Mandra, *Pakistan* **80 C5** 33 23N 73 12 E
Mandráki, *Greece* **45 H9** 36 36N 27 11 E
Mandrare →, *Madag.* **105 D8** 25 10 S 46 30 E
Mandritsara, *Madag.* **105 B8** 15 50 S 48 49 E
Mandsaur, *India* **80 G6** 24 3N 75 8 E
Mandurah, *Australia* **113 F2** 32 36 S 115 48 E
Mandúria, *Italy* **41 B10** 40 25N 17 38 E
Mandvi, *India* **80 H3** 22 51N 69 22 E
Mandya, *India* **83 H3** 12 30N 77 0 E
Mandzai, *Pakistan* **80 D2** 30 55N 67 6 E
Mané, *Burkina Faso* **101 C4** 12 59N 1 21W
Maneh, *Iran* **85 B8** 37 39N 57 7 E
Manengouba, Mts.,
Cameroon **101 D6** 5 0N 9 50 E
Maner →, *India* **82 E4** 18 30N 79 40 E
Maneroo, *Australia* **114 C3** 23 22 S 143 53 E
Maneroo Cr. →,
Australia **114 C3** 23 21 S 143 53 E
Manfalût, *Egypt* **94 B3** 27 20N 30 52 E
Manfred, *Australia* **116 B5** 33 19 S 143 45 E
Manfredónia, *Italy* **41 A8** 41 40N 15 55 E
Manfredónia, G. di, *Italy* **41 A9** 41 30N 16 10 E
Manga, *Brazil* **155 D3** 14 46 S 43 56W
Manga, *Burkina Faso* **101 C4** 11 40N 1 4W
Manga, *Niger* **97 F2** 15 0N 14 0 E
Mangabeiras, Chapada
das, *Brazil* **154 D2** 10 0 S 46 30W
Mangal, *Phil.* **71 H3** 6 25N 121 58 E
Mangalagiri, *India* **83 F5** 16 26N 80 36 E
Mangaldai, *India* **78 B4** 26 26N 92 2 E
Mangalia, *Romania* **46 F9** 43 50N 28 35 E
Mangalore, *Australia* **117 D6** 36 56 S 145 10 E
Mangalore, *India* **83 H2** 12 55N 74 47 E
Manganeses, *Spain* **36 D5** 41 45N 5 43W
Mangaon, *India* **82 E1** 18 15N 73 20 E
Mangaweka, *N.Z.* **118 F4** 39 48 S 175 47 E
Mangaweka, Mt., *N.Z.* **118 F5** 39 49 S 176 5 E
Mange, *Zaïre* **102 B4** 0 54N 20 30 E
Manggar, *Indonesia* **75 C3** 2 50 S 108 10 E
Manggawitu, *Indonesia* **73 B4** 4 8 S 133 32 E
Mangin Range, *Burma* **78 C5** 24 15N 95 45 E
Mangkalihat, Tanjung,
Indonesia **75 B5** 1 2N 118 59 E
Mangla Dam, *Pakistan* **81 C5** 33 9N 73 44 E
Manglares, C., *Colombia* **152 C2** 1 36N 79 2W
Manglaur, *India* **80 E7** 29 44N 77 49 E
Mangnai, *China* **64 C4** 37 52N 91 43 E
Mango, *Togo* **101 C5** 10 20N 0 30 E
Mangoche, *Malawi* **107 E4** 14 25 S 35 16 E
Mangoky →, *Madag.* **105 C7** 21 29 S 43 41 E
Mangole, *Indonesia* **72 B3** 1 50 S 125 55 E
Mangombe, *Zaïre* **106 C2** 1 20 S 26 48 E
Mangonui, *N.Z.* **118 B2** 35 1 S 173 32 E
Mangualde, *Portugal* **36 E3** 40 38N 7 48W
Mangueigne, *Chad* **97 F4** 10 30N 21 15 E
Mangueira, L. da, *Brazil* **159 C5** 33 0 S 52 50W
Manguéni, Hamada, *Niger* **96 D2** 22 35N 12 40 E
Mangum, *U.S.A.* **139 H5** 34 53N 99 30W
Mangyshlak Poluostrov,
Kazakhstan **53 D15** 44 30N 52 30 E
Mangyshlakskiy Zaliv,
Kazakhstan **53 D14** 44 40N 50 50 E

Mawlaik 231

Marla, Australia 115 D1 27 19 S 133 33 E
Marlboro, U.S.A. 137 D13 42 19N 71 33W
Marlborough, Australia 114 C4 22 46 S 149 52 E
Marlborough Downs, U.K. 17 F6 51 25N 1 55W
Marle, France 23 C10 49 43N 3 47 E
Marlin, U.S.A. 139 K6 31 18N 96 54W
Marlow, Germany 26 A8 54 8N 12 34 E
Marlow, U.S.A. 139 H6 34 39N 97 58W
Marly-le-Grand, Switz. 28 C4 46 47N 7 10 E
Marmagao, India 83 G1 15 25N 73 56 E
Marmande, France 24 D4 44 30N 0 10 E
Marmara, Turkey 52 F2 40 35N 27 38 E
Marmara, Sea of =
Marmara Denizi, Turkey 88 C3 40 45N 28 15 E
Marmara Denizi, Turkey 88 C3 40 45N 28 15 E
Marmara Gölü, Turkey 88 D3 38 37N 28 0 E
Marmaris, Turkey 88 E3 36 50N 28 14 E
Marmarth, U.S.A. 138 B3 46 18N 103 54W
Marmelos →, Brazil 157 B5 6 6 S 61 46W
Marmion, Mt., Australia 113 E2 29 16 S 119 50 E
Marmion L., Canada 128 C1 48 55N 91 20W
Marmolada, Mte., Italy 39 B8 46 25N 11 55 E
Marmolejo, Spain 37 G6 38 3N 4 13W
Marmora, Canada 128 D4 44 28N 77 41W
Marnay, France 23 E12 47 16N 5 48 E
Marne, Germany 26 B5 53 57N 9 1 E
Marne □, France 23 D11 48 50N 4 10 E
Marne →, France 23 D9 48 48N 2 24 E
Marneuli, Georgia 53 F11 41 30N 44 48 E
Maro, Chad 97 G3 8 30N 19 0 E
Maroa, Venezuela 152 C4 2 43N 67 33W
Maroala, Madag. 105 B8 15 23 S 47 59 E
Maroantsetra, Madag. 105 B8 15 26 S 49 44 E
Maromandia, Madag. 105 A8 14 13 S 48 5 E
Marondera, Zimbabwe 107 F3 18 5 S 31 42 E
Maroni →, Fr. Guiana 153 B7 5 30N 54 0W
Marónia, Greece 44 D7 40 53N 25 24 E
Maronne →, France 24 C5 45 5N 1 56 E
Maroochydore, Australia 115 D5 26 29 S 153 5 E
Maroona, Australia 116 D5 37 27 S 142 54 E
Maros, Indonesia 72 C1 5 0 S 119 34 E
Maros →, Hungary 31 E13 46 15N 20 13 E
Marosakoa, Madag. 105 B8 15 26 S 46 38 E
Marostica, Italy 39 C8 45 44N 11 40 E
Maroua, Cameroon 101 C7 10 40N 14 20 E
Marovoay, Madag. 105 B8 16 6 S 46 39 E
Marowijne □, Surinam 153 C7 4 0N 55 0W
Marowijne →, Surinam 153 B7 5 45N 53 58W
Marquard, S. Africa 104 D4 28 40 S 27 28 E
Marqueira, Portugal 37 G1 38 41N 9 9W
Marquesas Is. =
Marquises, Is., Pac. Oc. 123 H14 9 30 S 140 0W
Marquette, U.S.A. 134 B2 46 33N 87 24W
Marquise, France 23 B8 50 50N 1 40 E
Marquises, Is., Pac. Oc. 123 H14 9 30 S 140 0W
Marra, Gebel, Sudan 95 F2 7 20N 27 35 E
Marracuene, Mozam. 105 D5 25 45 S 32 35 E
Marradi, Italy 39 D8 44 5N 11 37 E
Marrakech, Morocco 98 B3 31 9N 8 0W
Marrawah, Australia 114 G3 40 55 S 144 42 E
Marrecas, Serra das,
Brazil 154 C3 9 0 S 41 0W
Marree, Australia 115 D2 29 39 S 138 1 E
Marrilla, Australia 112 D1 22 31 S 114 25 E
Marrimane, Mozam. 105 C5 22 58 S 33 34 E
Marromeu, Mozam. 105 B6 18 15 S 36 25 E
Marroquí, Punta, Spain 37 K5 36 0N 5 37W
Marrowie Cr. →,
Australia 117 B6 33 23 S 145 40 E
Marrubane, Mozam. 107 F4 18 0 S 37 0 E
Marrum, Neths. 20 B7 53 19N 5 48 E
Marrupa, Mozam. 107 E4 13 8 S 37 30 E
Marsa Brega, Libya 96 B3 30 24N 19 37 E
Marsá Matrûh, Egypt 94 A2 31 19N 27 9 E
Marsá Susah, Libya 96 B4 32 52N 21 59 E
Marsabit, Kenya 106 B4 2 18N 38 0 E
Marsabit □, Kenya 106 B4 2 45N 37 45 E
Marsala, Italy 40 E5 37 48N 12 25 E
Marsalforn, Malta 32 C1 36 4N 14 15 E
Marsberg, Germany 26 D4 51 28N 8 52 E
Marsciano, Italy 39 F9 42 54N 12 20 E
Marsden, Australia 117 B7 33 47 S 147 32 E
Marsdiep, Neths. 20 C5 52 58N 4 46 E
Marseillan, France 24 E7 43 23N 3 31 E
Marseille, France 25 E9 43 18N 5 23 E
Marseilles = Marseille,
France 25 E9 43 18N 5 23 E
Marseilles, U.S.A. 141 C8 41 20N 88 43W
Marsh I., U.S.A. 139 L9 29 34N 91 53W
Marsh L., U.S.A. 138 C6 45 5N 96 0W
Marshall, Liberia 100 D2 6 8N 10 22W
Marshall, Ark., U.S.A. 139 H8 35 55N 92 38W
Marshall, Ill., U.S.A. 141 E9 39 23N 87 42W
Marshall, Mich., U.S.A. 141 B12 42 16N 84 58W
Marshall, Minn., U.S.A. 138 C7 44 25N 95 45W
Marshall, Mo., U.S.A. 140 E3 39 7N 93 12W
Marshall, Tex., U.S.A. 139 J7 32 33N 94 23W
Marshall →, Australia 114 C2 22 59 S 136 59 E
Marshall Is. ■, Pac. Oc. 122 G9 9 0N 171 0 E
Marshalltown, U.S.A. 140 B4 42 3N 92 55W
Marshfield, Mo., U.S.A. 139 G8 37 15N 92 54W
Marshfield, Wis., U.S.A. 138 C9 44 40N 90 10W
Marshūn, Iran 85 B6 36 19N 49 23 E
Mársico Nuovo, Italy 41 B8 40 26N 15 43 E
Märsta, Sweden 14 E11 59 37N 17 52 E
Marstal, Denmark 15 K4 54 51N 10 30 E
Marstrand, Sweden 15 G5 57 53N 11 35 E
Mart, U.S.A. 139 K6 31 33N 96 50W
Marta →, Italy 39 F8 42 14N 11 42 E
Martaban, Burma 78 G6 16 30N 97 35 E
Martaban, G. of, Burma 78 G6 16 5N 96 30 E
Martano, Italy 41 B11 40 14N 18 18 E
Martapura, Kalimantan,
Indonesia 75 C4 3 22 S 114 47 E
Martapura, Sumatera,
Indonesia 74 C2 4 19 S 104 22 E
Marte, Nigeria 101 C7 12 23N 13 46 E
Martel, France 24 D5 44 57N 1 37 E
Martelange, Belgium 21 J7 49 49N 5 43 E
Martensdale, U.S.A. 140 C3 41 23N 93 45W
Martés, Sierra, Spain 35 F4 39 20N 1 0W
Martha's Vineyard, U.S.A. 137 E14 41 25N 70 38W
Martigné-Ferchaud, France 22 E5 47 50N 1 20W
Martigny, Switz. 28 D4 46 6N 7 3 E
Martigues, France 25 E9 43 24N 5 4 E
Martil, Morocco 98 A3 35 36N 5 15W
Martin, Slovak Rep. 31 B11 49 6N 18 48 E
Martin, S. Dak., U.S.A. 138 D4 43 11N 101 44W
Martin, Tenn., U.S.A. 139 G10 36 21N 88 51W
Martín →, Spain 34 D4 41 18N 0 19W
Martin L., U.S.A. 135 J3 32 41N 85 55W
Martina, Switz. 29 C10 46 53N 10 28 E
Martina Franca, Italy 41 B10 40 42N 17 20 E
Martinborough, N.Z. 118 H4 41 14 S 175 29 E
Martinez, U.S.A. 144 G4 38 1N 122 8W
Martinho Campos, Brazil 155 E2 19 20 S 45 13W
Martinique ■, W. Indies 149 D7 14 40N 61 0W
Martinique Passage,
W. Indies 149 C7 15 15N 61 0W
Martínon, Greece 45 F5 38 35N 23 15 E
Martinópolis, Brazil 159 A5 22 11 S 51 12W
Martins Ferry, U.S.A. 136 F4 40 6N 80 44W
Martinsberg, Austria 30 C8 48 22N 15 9 E
Martinsburg, Pa., U.S.A. 136 F6 40 19N 78 20W
Martinsburg, W. Va.,
U.S.A. 134 F7 39 27N 77 58W
Martinsville, Ill., U.S.A. 141 E9 39 20N 87 53W
Martinsville, Ind., U.S.A. 141 E10 39 26N 86 25W
Martinsville, Va., U.S.A. 135 G6 36 41N 79 52W
Marton, N.Z. 118 G4 40 4 S 175 23 E
Martorell, Spain 34 D6 41 28N 1 56 E
Martos, Spain 37 H7 37 44N 3 58W
Martūbah, Libya 96 B4 32 35N 22 46 E
Martuk, Kazakhstan 54 F5 50 46N 56 31 E
Martuni, Armenia 53 F11 40 9N 45 10 E
Maru, Nigeria 101 C6 12 22N 6 22 E
Marudi, Malaysia 75 B4 4 11N 114 19 E
Ma'ruf, Afghan. 79 C2 31 30N 67 6 E
Marugame, Japan 62 C5 34 15N 133 40 E
Marúggio, Italy 41 B10 40 20N 17 33 E
Marui, Papua N. G. 120 C2 4 4 S 143 2 E
Maruia →, N.Z. 119 B7 41 47 S 172 13 E
Maruim, Brazil 154 D4 10 45 S 37 5W
Marulan, Australia 117 C9 34 43 S 150 3 E
Marum, Neths. 20 B8 53 9N 6 16 E
Marum, Mt., Vanuatu 121 F6 16 15 S 168 7 E
Marunga, Angola 103 F4 17 28 S 20 2 E
Marungu, Mts., Zaïre 106 D2 7 30 S 30 0 E
Maruoka, Japan 63 A8 36 9N 136 16 E
Marvast, Iran 85 D7 30 30N 54 15 E
Marvejols, France 24 D7 44 33N 3 19 E
Marwar, India 80 G5 25 43N 73 45 E
Mary, Turkmenistan 56 F7 37 40N 61 50 E
Mary Frances L., Canada 131 A7 63 19N 106 13W
Mary Kathleen, Australia 114 C2 20 44 S 139 48 E
Maryborough = Port
Laoise, Ireland 19 C4 53 2N 7 20W
Maryborough, Queens.,
Australia 115 D5 25 31 S 152 37 E
Maryborough, Vic.,
Australia 116 D5 37 0 S 143 44 E
Maryfield, Canada 131 D8 49 50N 101 35W
Maryland □, U.S.A. 134 F7 39 0N 76 30W
Maryland Junction,
Zimbabwe 107 F3 17 45 S 30 31 E
Maryport, U.K. 16 C4 54 43N 3 30W
Mary's Harbour, Canada 129 B8 52 18N 55 51W
Marystown, Canada 129 C8 47 10N 55 10W
Marysvale, U.S.A. 143 G7 38 27N 112 14W
Marysville, Canada 130 D5 49 35N 116 0W
Marysville, Calif., U.S.A. 144 F5 39 9N 121 35W
Marysville, Kans., U.S.A. 138 F6 39 51N 96 39W
Marysville, Mich., U.S.A. 136 D2 42 54N 82 29W
Marysville, Ohio, U.S.A. 141 D13 40 14N 83 22W
Marysville, Wash., U.S.A. 144 B4 48 3N 122 11W
Maryvale, Australia 115 D5 28 4 S 152 12 E
Maryville, Mo., U.S.A. 140 D2 40 21N 94 52W
Maryville, Tenn., U.S.A. 135 H4 35 46N 83 58W
Marzo, Punta, Colombia 152 B2 6 50N 77 42W
Marzūq, Libya 96 C2 25 53N 13 57 E
Masahunga, Tanzania 106 C3 2 6 S 33 18 E
Masai, Malaysia 77 M4 1 29N 103 55 E
Masai Steppe, Tanzania 106 C4 4 30 S 36 30 E
Masaka, Uganda 106 C3 0 21 S 31 45 E
Masalembo, Kepulauan,
Indonesia 75 D4 5 35 S 114 30 E
Masalima, Kepulauan,
Indonesia 75 D5 5 4 S 117 5 E
Masamba, Indonesia 72 B2 2 30 S 120 15 E
Masan, S. Korea 67 G15 35 11N 128 32 E
Masanasa, Spain 35 F4 39 25N 0 25W
Masasi, Tanzania 107 E4 10 45 S 38 52 E
Masasi □, Tanzania 107 E4 10 45 S 38 50 E
Masaya, Nic. 148 D2 12 0N 86 7W
Masba, Nigeria 101 C7 10 35N 13 1 E
Masbate, Phil. 70 E4 12 21N 123 36 E
Masbate Pass, Phil. 70 E4 12 30N 123 35 E
Mascara, Algeria 99 A5 35 26N 0 6 E
Mascarene Is., Ind. Oc. 109 G4 22 0 S 55 0 E
Mascota, Mexico 146 C4 20 30N 104 50W
Mascoutah, U.S.A. 140 F7 38 29N 89 48W
Masela, Indonesia 73 C3 8 9 S 129 51 E
Maseru, Lesotho 104 D4 29 18 S 27 30 E
Mashaba, Zimbabwe 107 G3 20 2 S 30 29 E
Mashābih, Si. Arabia 84 E3 25 35N 36 30 E
Mashan, China 68 F7 23 40N 108 11 E
Masherbrum, Pakistan 81 B7 35 38N 76 18 E
Mashhad, Iran 85 B8 36 20N 59 35 E
Mashi, Nigeria 101 C6 13 0N 7 54 E
Mashiki, Japan 62 E2 32 51N 130 53 E
Mashīz, Iran 85 D8 29 56N 56 37 E
Mashkel, Hamun-i-,
Pakistan 79 C1 28 30N 63 0 E
Mashki Chāh, Pakistan 79 C1 29 5N 62 30 E
Mashonaland Central □,
Zimbabwe 105 B5 17 30 S 31 0 E
Mashonaland East □,
Zimbabwe 105 B5 18 0 S 32 0 E
Mashonaland West □,
Zimbabwe 105 B4 17 30 S 29 30 E
Mashtaga, Azerbaijan 53 F13 40 35N 49 57 E
Masi, Norway 12 B17 69 26N 23 40 E
Masi Manimba, Zaïre 103 C3 4 40 S 17 54 E
Masindi, Uganda 106 B3 1 40N 31 43 E
Masindi Port, Uganda 106 B3 1 43N 32 2 E
Masinloc, Phil. 70 D2 15 32N 119 57 E
Maşīrah, Khalīj, Oman 87 B7 20 10N 58 10 E
Maşīrah, Tur'at, Oman 87 B7 20 15N 58 40 E
Masisea, Peru 156 B3 8 35 S 74 22W
Masisi, Zaïre 106 C2 1 23 S 28 49 E
Masjed Soleyman, Iran 85 D6 31 55N 49 18 E
Mask, L., Ireland 19 C2 53 36N 9 24W
Maskelyne Is., Vanuatu 121 F5 16 32 S 167 49 E
Maski, India 83 G3 15 56N 76 46 E
Maslen Nos, Bulgaria 43 E12 42 18N 27 48 E
Maslinica, Croatia 39 E13 43 24N 16 13 E
Maşna'ah, Yemen 87 D5 14 27N 48 17 E
Masnou, Spain 34 D7 41 28N 2 20 E
Masoala, Tanjon' i,
Madag. 105 B9 15 59 S 50 13 E
Masoarivo, Madag. 105 B7 19 3 S 44 19 E
Masohi, Indonesia 73 B3 3 20 S 128 55 E
Masomeloka, Madag. 105 C8 20 17 S 48 37 E
Mason, Mich., U.S.A. 141 B12 42 35N 84 27W
Mason, Nev., U.S.A. 144 G7 38 56N 119 8W
Mason, Ohio, U.S.A. 141 E12 39 22N 84 19W
Mason, Tex., U.S.A. 139 K5 30 45N 99 14W
Mason B., N.Z. 119 G2 46 55 S 167 45 E
Mason City, Ill., U.S.A. 140 D7 40 12N 89 42W
Mason City, Iowa, U.S.A. 140 A3 43 9N 93 12W
Maspalomas, Canary Is. 33 G4 27 46N 15 35W
Maspalomas, Pta.,
Canary Is. 33 G4 27 43N 15 36W
Masqat, Oman 87 B7 23 37N 58 36 E
Massa, Congo 102 C3 3 45 S 15 29 E
Massa, Italy 38 D7 44 2N 10 7 E
Massa, O. →, Morocco 98 B3 30 2N 9 40W
Massa Maríttima, Italy 38 E7 43 3N 10 52 E
Massachusetts □, U.S.A. 137 D12 42 30N 72 0W
Massachusetts B., U.S.A. 137 D14 42 20N 70 50W
Massafra, Italy 41 B10 40 35N 17 8 E
Massaguet, Chad 97 F3 12 28N 15 26 E
Massakory, Chad 97 F3 13 0N 15 49 E
Massanella, Spain 33 B9 39 48N 2 51 E
Massangena, Mozam. 105 C5 21 34 S 33 0 E
Massapê, Brazil 154 B3 3 31 S 40 19W
Massarosa, Italy 38 E7 43 53N 10 17 E
Massat, France 24 F5 42 53N 1 21 E
Massava, Russia 54 A8 60 40N 62 6 E
Massawa = Mitsiwa,
Eritrea 95 D4 15 35N 39 25 E
Massena, U.S.A. 137 B10 44 56N 74 54W
Massénya, Chad 97 F3 11 21N 16 9 E
Masset, Canada 130 C2 54 2N 132 10W
Massiac, France 24 C7 45 15N 3 11 E
Massif Central, France 24 D7 44 55N 3 0 E
Massillon, U.S.A. 136 F3 40 48N 81 32W
Massinga, Mozam. 105 C6 23 15 S 35 22 E
Masson, Canada 137 A9 45 32N 75 25W
Masson I., Antarctica 7 C7 66 10 S 93 20 E
Mastābah, Si. Arabia 86 B2 20 49N 39 26 E
Mastanli = Momchilgrad,
Bulgaria 43 F10 41 33N 25 23 E
Masterton, N.Z. 118 G4 40 56 S 175 39 E
Mástikho, Ákra, Greece 45 F8 38 10N 26 2 E
Mastuj, Pakistan 81 A5 36 20N 72 36 E
Mastung, Pakistan 79 C2 29 50N 66 56 E
Mastūrah, Si. Arabia 86 B2 23 7N 38 52 E
Masuda, Japan 62 C3 34 40N 131 51 E
Masuika, Zaïre 103 D4 7 37 S 22 32 E
Masvingo, Zimbabwe 107 G3 20 8 S 30 49 E
Masvingo □, Zimbabwe 107 G3 21 0 S 31 30 E
Maswa □, Tanzania 106 C3 3 30 S 34 0 E
Maşyāf, Syria 84 C3 35 4N 36 20 E
Mata de São João, Brazil 155 D4 12 31 S 38 17W
Mata Utu, Wall. & F. Is. 111 C15 13 17 S 176 8W
Matabeleland North □,
Zimbabwe 107 F2 19 0 S 28 0 E
Matabeleland South □,
Zimbabwe 107 G2 21 0 S 29 0 E
Mataboor, Indonesia 73 B5 1 41 S 138 3 E
Matachel →, Spain 37 G4 38 50N 6 17W
Matachewan, Canada 128 C3 47 56N 80 39W
Matacuni →, Venezuela 153 C4 3 2N 65 16W
Matadi, Zaïre 103 D2 5 52 S 13 31 E
Matagalpa, Nic. 148 D2 13 0N 85 58W
Matagami, Canada 128 C4 49 45N 77 34W
Matagami, L., Canada 128 C4 49 50N 77 40W
Matagorda, U.S.A. 139 L7 28 42N 95 58W
Matagorda B., U.S.A. 139 L6 28 40N 96 0W
Matagorda I., U.S.A. 139 L6 28 15N 96 30W
Mataguinao, Phil. 70 E5 12 5N 124 55 E
Matak, P., Indonesia 77 L6 3 18N 106 16 E
Matakana, Australia 117 B6 32 59 S 145 54 E
Matakana, N.Z. 118 C3 36 21 S 174 43 E
Matakana I., N.Z. 118 C3 36 21 S 174 43 E
Matala, Angola 103 E3 14 46 S 15 4 E
Mátala, Greece 32 E6 34 59N 24 45 E
Matalaque, Peru 156 D3 16 26 S 70 49W
Matale, Sri Lanka 83 L5 7 30N 80 37 E
Matam, Phil. 71 G4 8 25N 123 19 E
Matam, Senegal 100 B2 15 34N 13 17W
Matamata, N.Z. 118 D4 37 48 S 175 47 E
Matameye, Niger 97 F1 13 26N 8 28 E
Matamoros, Campeche,
Mexico 147 D6 18 50N 90 50W
Matamoros, Coahuila,
Mexico 146 B4 25 33N 103 15W
Matamoros, Puebla,
Mexico 147 D5 18 2N 98 17W
Matamoros, Tamaulipas,
Mexico 147 B5 25 50N 97 30W
Ma'ţan as Sarra, Libya 97 D4 21 45N 22 0 E
Matandu →, Tanzania 107 D3 8 45 S 34 19 E
Matane, Canada 129 C6 48 50N 67 33W
Matang, China 68 F5 23 30N 104 7 E
Matankari, Niger 101 C5 13 46N 4 1 E
Matanzas, Cuba 148 B3 23 0N 81 40W
Matapan, C. = Taínaron,
Ákra, Greece 45 H4 36 22N 22 27 E
Matapédia, Canada 129 C6 48 0N 66 59W
Matara, Sri Lanka 83 M5 5 58N 80 30 E
Mataram, Indonesia 75 D5 8 41 S 116 10 E
Matarani, Peru 156 D3 17 0 S 72 10W
Mataranka, Australia 112 B5 14 55 S 133 4 E
Matarma, Râs, Egypt 91 E1 30 27N 32 44 E
Mataró, Spain 34 D7 41 32N 2 29 E
Matarraña →, Spain 34 D5 41 14N 0 22 E
Mataruška Banja, Serbia 42 D5 43 40N 20 45 E
Matase, Vanuatu 121 G6 17 14 S 168 26 E
Matata, N.Z. 118 D5 37 54 S 176 48 E
Matatiele, S. Africa 105 E4 30 20 S 28 49 E
Mataura, N.Z. 119 G3 46 11 S 168 51 E
Mataura →, N.Z. 119 G3 46 34 S 168 44 E
Mategua, Bolivia 157 C5 13 1 S 62 48W
Matehuala, Mexico 146 C4 23 40N 100 40W
Mateira, Brazil 155 E1 18 54 S 50 30W
Mateke Hills, Zimbabwe 107 G3 21 48 S 31 0 E
Matélica, Italy 39 E10 43 15N 13 0 E
Matera, Italy 41 B9 40 40N 16 37 E
Mátészalka, Hungary 31 D15 47 58N 22 20 E
Matetsi, Zimbabwe 107 F2 18 12 S 26 0 E
Mateur, Tunisia 96 A1 37 0N 9 40 E
Matfors, Sweden 14 B11 62 21N 17 2 E
Matha, France 24 C3 45 52N 0 20W
Matheson Island, Canada 131 C9 51 45N 96 56W
Mathis, U.S.A. 139 L6 28 6N 97 50W
Mathoura, Australia 117 C6 35 50 S 144 55 E
Mathura, India 80 F7 27 30N 77 40 E
Mati, Phil. 71 H6 6 55N 126 15 E
Mati →, Albania 44 C1 41 40N 19 35 E
Matías Romero, Mexico 147 D5 16 53N 95 2W
Matibane, Mozam. 107 E5 14 49 S 40 45 E
Matican, Phil. 71 H3 6 39N 121 53 E
Matima, Botswana 104 C3 20 15 S 24 26 E
Matiri Ra., N.Z. 119 B7 41 38 S 172 20 E
Matlock, U.K. 16 D6 53 8N 1 32W
Matmata, Tunisia 96 B1 33 37N 9 59 E
Matna, Sudan 95 E4 13 49N 35 10 E
Matnog, Phil. 70 E5 12 35N 124 5 E
Mato →, Venezuela 153 B4 7 9N 65 7W
Mato, Serrania de,
Venezuela 152 B4 6 25N 65 25W
Mato Grosso □, Brazil 157 C6 14 0 S 55 0W
Mato Grosso, Planalto do,
Brazil 157 C7 15 0 S 55 0W
Mato Grosso do Sul □,
Brazil 157 D7 18 0 S 55 0W
Matochkin Shar, Russia 56 B6 73 10N 56 40 E
Matong, Papua N. G. 120 C6 5 36 S 151 50 E
Matopo Hills, Zimbabwe 107 G2 20 36 S 28 20 E
Matopos, Zimbabwe 107 G2 20 20 S 28 29 E
Matosinhos, Portugal 36 D2 41 11N 8 42W
Matour, France 25 B8 46 19N 4 29 E
Matrah, Oman 87 B7 23 37N 58 30 E
Matsena, Nigeria 101 C7 13 5N 10 5 E
Matsesta, Russia 53 E8 43 34N 39 51 E
Matsubara, Japan 63 C7 34 33N 135 34 E
Matsudo, Japan 63 B11 35 47N 139 54 E
Matsue, Japan 62 B5 35 25N 133 10 E
Matsumae, Japan 60 D10 41 26N 140 7 E
Matsumoto, Japan 63 A9 36 15N 138 0 E
Matsusaka, Japan 63 C8 34 34N 136 32 E
Matsutō, Japan 63 A8 36 31N 136 34 E
Matsuura, Japan 62 D1 33 20N 129 49 E
Matsuyama, Japan 62 D4 33 45N 132 45 E
Matsuzaki, Japan 63 C10 34 43N 138 50 E
Mattagami →, Canada 128 B3 50 43N 81 29W
Mattancheri, India 83 K3 9 50N 76 15 E
Mattawa, Canada 128 C4 46 20N 78 45W
Mattawamkeag, U.S.A. 129 C6 45 32N 68 21W
Matterhorn, Switz. 28 E5 45 58N 7 39 E
Mattersburg, Austria 31 D9 47 44N 16 24 E
Matteson, U.S.A. 141 C9 41 30N 87 42W
Matthew Town, Bahamas 149 B5 20 57N 73 40W
Matthews, U.S.A. 141 D11 40 23N 85 30W
Matthew's Ridge, Guyana 153 B5 7 37N 60 10W
Mattice, Canada 128 C3 49 40N 83 20W
Mattituck, U.S.A. 137 F12 40 59N 72 32W
Mattmar, Sweden 14 A7 63 18N 13 45 E
Matuba, Mozam. 105 C5 24 28 S 32 49 E
Matucana, Peru 156 C2 11 55 S 76 25W
Matuku, Fiji 121 B2 19 10 S 179 44 E
Matun, Afghan. 80 C3 33 22N 69 58 E
Maturín, Venezuela 153 B5 9 45N 63 11W
Matutum, Mt., Phil. 71 H5 6 22N 125 5 E
Matveyev Kurgan, Russia 53 C8 47 35N 38 47 E
Mau, India 81 G10 25 56N 83 33 E
Mau Escarpment, Kenya 106 C4 0 40 S 36 0 E
Mau Ranipur, India 81 G8 25 16N 79 8 E
Mauban, Phil. 70 D3 14 12N 121 44 E
Maubeuge, France 23 B10 50 17N 3 57 E
Maubourguet, France 24 E4 43 29N 0 1 E
Maud, Pt., Australia 112 D1 23 6 S 113 45 E
Maude, Australia 116 C6 34 29 S 144 18 E
Maués, Brazil 153 D6 3 20 S 57 45W
Maui, U.S.A. 132 H16 20 48N 156 20W
Maulamyaing =
Moulmein, Burma 78 G6 16 30N 97 40 E
Maule □, Chile 158 D1 36 5 S 72 30W
Mauléon-Licharre, France 24 E3 43 14N 0 54W
Maullín, Chile 160 B2 41 38 S 73 37W
Maulvibazar, Bangla. 78 C3 24 29N 91 42 E
Maumee, U.S.A. 141 C13 41 34N 83 39W
Maumee →, U.S.A. 141 C13 41 42N 83 28W
Maumere, Indonesia 72 C2 8 38 S 122 13 E
Maun, Botswana 104 B3 20 0 S 23 26 E
Mauna Kea, U.S.A. 132 J17 19 50N 155 28W
Mauna Loa, U.S.A. 132 J17 19 30N 155 35W
Maungaturoto, N.Z. 118 C3 36 6 S 174 23 E
Maungdow, Burma 78 E4 20 50N 92 21 E
Maupin, U.S.A. 142 D3 45 11N 121 5W
Maure-de-Bretagne,
France 22 E5 47 53N 1 58W
Maurepas, L., U.S.A. 139 K9 30 15N 90 30W
Maures, France 25 E10 43 15N 6 15 E
Mauriac, France 24 C6 45 13N 2 19 E
Maurice, L., Australia 113 E5 29 30 S 131 0 E
Mauriceville, N.Z. 118 G4 40 45 S 175 42 E
Mauritania ■, Africa 98 D3 20 50N 10 0W
Mauritius ■, Ind. Oc. 93 J9 20 0 S 57 0 E
Mauron, France 22 D4 48 9N 2 18W
Maurs, France 24 D6 44 43N 2 12 E
Mauston, U.S.A. 138 D9 43 48N 90 5W
Mauterndorf, Austria 30 D6 47 9N 13 40 E
Mauvezin, France 24 E4 43 44N 0 53 E
Mauzé-sur-le-Mignon,
France 24 B3 46 12N 0 41W
Mavaca →, Venezuela 153 C4 2 31N 65 11W
Mavelikara, India 83 K3 9 14N 76 32 E
Mavinga, Angola 103 F4 15 50 S 20 21 E
Mavli, India 80 G5 24 45N 73 55 E
Mavrova, Albania 44 D1 40 26N 19 32 E
Mavuradonha Mts.,
Zimbabwe 107 F3 16 30 S 31 30 E
Mawa, Zaïre 106 B2 2 45N 26 40 E
Mawana, India 80 E7 29 6N 77 58 E
Mawand, Pakistan 80 E3 29 33N 68 38 E
Mawk Mai, Burma 78 E6 20 14N 97 37 E
Mawlaik, Burma 78 D5 23 40N 94 26 E

232 Mawlawkho

Mawlawkho, *Burma* **78 G6** 17 50N 97 38 E
Mawquq, *Si. Arabia* **84 E4** 27 25N 41 8 E
Mawshij, *Yemen* **86 D3** 13 43N 43 17 E
Mawson Coast, *Antarctica* **7 C6** 68 30 S 63 0 E
Max, *U.S.A.* **138 B4** 47 49N 101 18W
Maxcanú, *Mexico* **147 C6** 20 40N 92 0W
Maxesibeni, *S. Africa* **105 E4** 30 49 S 29 23 E
Maxhamish L., *Canada* **130 B4** 59 50N 123 17W
Maxixe, *Mozam.* **105 C6** 23 54 S 35 17 E
Maxville, *Canada* **137 A10** 45 17N 74 51W
Maxwell, *N.Z.* **118 F3** 39 51 S 174 49 E
Maxwell, *U.S.A.* **144 F4** 39 17N 122 11W
Maxwelton, *Australia* **114 C3** 20 43 S 142 41 E
May Downs, *Australia* **114 C4** 22 38 S 148 55 E
May Pen, *Jamaica* **148 C4** 17 58N 77 15W
May River, *Papua N. G.* **120 C1** 4 19 S 141 58 E
Maya, *Indonesia* **75 C3** 1 10 S 109 35 E
Maya, *Spain* **34 B3** 43 12N 1 29W
Maya →, *Russia* **57 D14** 60 28N 134 28 E
Maya Mts., *Belize* **147 D7** 16 30N 89 0W
Mayaguana, *Bahamas* **149 B5** 22 30N 72 44W
Mayagüez, *Puerto Rico* **149 C6** 18 12N 67 9W
Mayahi, *Niger* **101 C6** 13 58N 7 40 E
Mayals, *Spain* **34 D5** 41 22N 0 30 E
Mayama, *Congo* **102 C2** 3 51 S 14 54 E
Mayāmey, *Iran* **85 B7** 36 24N 55 42 E
Mayang, *China* **68 D7** 27 53N 109 49 E
Mayarí, *Cuba* **149 B4** 20 40N 75 41W
Mayavaram = Mayuram, *India* **83 J4** 11 3N 79 42 E
Maybell, *U.S.A.* **142 F9** 40 31N 108 5W
Maychew, *Ethiopia* **95 E4** 12 50N 39 31 E
Maydān, *Iraq* **84 C5** 34 55N 45 37 E
Maydena, *Australia* **114 G4** 42 45 S 146 30 E
Maydī, *Yemen* **86 C3** 16 19N 42 48 E
Maydos, *Turkey* **44 D8** 40 13N 26 20 E
Mayen, *Germany* **27 E3** 50 18N 7 10 E
Mayenne, *France* **22 D6** 48 20N 0 38W
Mayenne □, *France* **22 D6** 48 10N 0 40W
Mayenne →, *France* **22 E6** 47 30N 0 32W
Mayer, *U.S.A.* **143 J7** 34 24N 112 14W
Mayerthorpe, *Canada* **130 C5** 53 57N 115 8W
Mayfield, *U.S.A.* **135 G1** 36 44N 88 38W
Mayhill, *U.S.A.* **143 K11** 32 53N 105 29W
Maykop, *Russia* **53 D9** 44 35N 40 10 E
Mayli-Say, *Kirghizia* **55 C6** 41 17N 72 24 E
Maymyo, *Burma* **76 A1** 22 2N 96 28 E
Maynard, *U.S.A.* **144 C4** 47 59N 122 55W
Maynard Hills, *Australia* **113 E2** 28 28 S 119 49 E
Mayne →, *Australia* **114 C3** 23 40 S 141 55 E
Maynooth, *Ireland* **19 C5** 53 22N 6 38W
Mayo, *Canada* **126 B6** 63 38N 135 57W
Mayo □, *Ireland* **19 C2** 53 47N 9 7W
Mayo →, *Argentina* **160 C3** 45 45 S 69 45W
Mayo →, *Peru* **156 B2** 6 38 S 76 15W
Mayo Bay, *Phil.* **71 H6** 6 56N 126 22 E
Mayo L., *Canada* **126 B6** 63 45N 135 0W
Mayoko, *Zaïre* **102 C2** 2 18 S 12 49 E
Mayon Volcano, *Phil.* **70 E4** 13 15N 123 41 E
Mayor I., *N.Z.* **118 D5** 37 16 S 176 17 E
Mayorga, *Spain* **36 C5** 42 10N 5 16W
Mayoyao, *Phil.* **70 C3** 16 59N 121 14 E
Mayraira Pt., *Phil.* **70 B3** 18 39N 120 51 E
Mayskiy, *Russia* **53 E11** 43 47N 44 2 E
Mayson L., *Canada* **131 B7** 57 55N 107 10W
Maysville, *Ky., U.S.A.* **141 F13** 38 39N 83 46W
Maysville, *Mo., U.S.A.* **140 E2** 39 53N 94 22W
Mayu, *Indonesia* **72 A3** 1 30N 126 30 E
Mayumba, *Gabon* **102 C2** 3 25 S 10 39 E
Mayuram, *India* **83 J4** 11 3N 79 42 E
Mayville, *N. Dak., U.S.A.* **138 B6** 47 30N 97 20W
Mayville, *N.Y., U.S.A.* **136 D5** 42 15N 79 30W
Mayya, *Russia* **57 C14** 61 44N 130 18 E
Mazabuka, *Zambia* **107 F2** 15 52 S 27 44 E
Mazagán = El Jadida, *Morocco* **98 B3** 33 11N 8 17W
Mazagão, *Brazil* **153 D7** 0 7 S 51 16W
Mazamet, *France* **24 E6** 43 30N 2 20 E
Mazán, *Peru* **152 D3** 3 30 S 73 0W
Māzandarān □, *Iran* **85 B7** 36 30N 52 0 E
Mazapil, *Mexico* **146 C4** 24 38N 101 34W
Mazar, O. →, *Algeria* **99 B5** 31 50N 1 36 E
Mazar-e Sharīf, *Afghan.* **79 A2** 36 41N 67 0 E
Mazara del Vallo, *Italy* **40 E5** 37 40N 12 34 E
Mazarredo, *Argentina* **160 C3** 47 10 S 66 50W
Mazarrón, *Spain* **35 H3** 37 38N 1 19W
Mazarrón, G. de, *Spain* **35 H3** 37 27N 1 19W
Mazaruni →, *Guyana* **153 B6** 6 25N 58 35W
Mazatán, *Mexico* **146 B2** 29 0N 110 8W
Mazatenango, *Guatemala* **148 D1** 14 35N 91 30W
Mazatlán, *Mexico* **146 C3** 23 10N 106 30W
Mažeikiai, *Lithuania* **50 C3** 56 20N 22 20 E
Māzhān, *Iran* **85 C8** 32 30N 59 0 E
Mazīnān, *Iran* **85 B8** 36 19N 56 56 E
Mazoe, *Mozam.* **107 F3** 16 42 S 33 7 E
Mazoe →, *Mozam.* **107 F3** 16 20 S 33 30 E
Mazomanie, *U.S.A.* **140 A7** 43 11N 89 48W
Mazon, *U.S.A.* **141 C8** 41 14N 88 25W
Mazowe, *Zimbabwe* **107 F3** 17 28 S 30 58 E
Mazrûb, *Sudan* **95 E2** 14 0N 29 20 E
Mazu Dao, *China* **69 D12** 26 10N 119 55 E
Mazurian Lakes = Mazurski, Pojezierze, *Poland* **47 B7** 53 50N 21 0 E
Mazurski, Pojezierze, *Poland* **47 B7** 53 50N 21 0 E
Mazzarino, *Italy* **41 E7** 37 19N 14 12 E
Mba, *Fiji* **121 A1** 17 33 S 177 41 E
Mbaba, *Senegal* **100 C1** 14 59N 16 44W
Mbabane, *Swaziland* **105 D5** 26 18 S 31 6 E
Mbagne, *Mauritania* **100 B2** 16 6N 14 47W
M'bahiakro, *Ivory C.* **100 D4** 7 33N 4 19W
Mbaïki, *C.A.R.* **102 B3** 3 53N 18 1 E
Mbakana, Mt. de, *Cameroon* **102 A3** 7 57N 15 6 E
Mbala, *Zambia* **107 D3** 8 46 S 31 24 E
Mbale, *Uganda* **106 B3** 1 8N 34 12 E
Mbalmayo, *Cameroon* **101 E7** 3 33N 11 33 E
Mbamba Bay, *Tanzania* **107 E3** 11 13 S 34 49 E
Mbandaka, *Zaïre* **102 B3** 0 1N 18 18 E
Mbanga, *Cameroon* **101 E6** 4 30N 9 33 E
Mbanza Congo, *Angola* **103 D2** 6 18 S 14 16 E
Mbanza Ngungu, *Zaïre* **103 D2** 5 12 S 14 53 E
Mbarara, *Uganda* **106 C3** 0 35 S 30 40 E
Mbashe →, *S. Africa* **105 E4** 32 15 S 28 54 E
Mbatto, *Ivory C.* **100 D4** 6 28N 4 22W
Mbengga, *Fiji* **121 B2** 18 23 S 178 8 E
Mbenkuru →, *Tanzania* **107 D4** 9 25 S 39 50 E
Mberengwa, *Zimbabwe* **107 G2** 20 29 S 29 57 E
Mberengwa, Mt., *Zimbabwe* **107 G2** 20 37 S 29 55 E
Mberubu, *Nigeria* **101 D6** 6 10N 7 38 E
Mbesuma, *Zambia* **107 D3** 10 0 S 32 2 E
Mbeya, *Tanzania* **107 D3** 8 54 S 33 29 E
Mbeya □, *Tanzania* **106 D3** 8 15 S 33 30 E
Mbigou, *Gabon* **102 C2** 1 53 S 11 56 E
Mbinga, *Tanzania* **107 E4** 10 50 S 35 0 E
Mbinga □, *Tanzania* **107 E3** 10 50 S 35 0 E
Mbini □, *Eq. Guin.* **102 B2** 1 30N 10 0 E
Mboki, *C.A.R.* **95 F2** 5 19N 25 58 E
Mboli, *Zaïre* **102 B4** 4 8N 23 9 E
Mboro, *Senegal* **100 B1** 15 9N 16 54W
Mboune, *Senegal* **100 C2** 14 42N 13 34W
Mbouoma, *Congo* **102 C3** 0 52 S 15 4 E
Mbour, *Senegal* **100 C1** 14 22N 16 54W
Mbout, *Mauritania* **100 B2** 16 1N 12 38W
Mbozi □, *Tanzania* **107 D3** 9 0 S 32 50 E
Mbrés, *C.A.R.* **102 A3** 6 40N 19 48 E
Mbuji-Mayi, *Zaïre* **103 D4** 6 9 S 23 40 E
Mbulu, *Tanzania* **106 C4** 3 45 S 35 30 E
Mbulu □, *Tanzania* **106 C4** 3 52 S 35 33 E
Mburucuyá, *Argentina* **158 B4** 28 1 S 58 14W
Mcherrah, *Algeria* **98 C4** 27 0N 4 30W
Mchinja, *Tanzania* **107 D4** 9 44 S 39 45 E
Mchinji, *Malawi* **107 E3** 13 47 S 32 58 E
Mdennah, *Mauritania* **98 D3** 24 37N 6 0W
Mead, L., *U.S.A.* **145 J12** 36 1N 114 44W
Meade, *U.S.A.* **139 G4** 37 17N 100 20W
Meadow, *Australia* **113 E1** 26 35 S 114 40 E
Meadow Lake, *Canada* **131 C7** 54 10N 108 26W
Meadow Lake Prov. Park, *Canada* **131 C7** 54 27N 109 0W
Meadow Valley Wash →, *U.S.A.* **145 J12** 36 40N 114 34W
Meadville, *Mo., U.S.A.* **140 E3** 39 47N 93 18W
Meadville, *Pa., U.S.A.* **136 E4** 41 39N 80 9W
Meaford, *Canada* **128 D3** 44 36N 80 35W
Mealhada, *Portugal* **36 E2** 40 22N 8 27W
Mealy Mts., *Canada* **129 B8** 53 10N 58 0W
Meander River, *Canada* **130 B5** 59 2N 117 42W
Meares, C., *U.S.A.* **142 D2** 45 37N 124 0W
Mearim →, *Brazil* **154 B3** 3 4 S 44 35W
Meath □, *Ireland* **19 C5** 53 32N 6 40W
Meath Park, *Canada* **131 C7** 53 27N 105 22W
Meatian, *Australia* **116 C5** 35 34 S 143 21 E
Meaulne, *France* **24 B6** 46 36N 2 36 E
Meaux, *France* **23 D9** 48 58N 2 50 E
Mebechi-Gawa →, *Japan* **60 D10** 40 31N 141 31 E
Mecanhelas, *Mozam.* **107 F4** 15 12 S 35 54 E
Mecaya →, *Colombia* **152 C2** 0 29N 75 11W
Mecca = Makkah, *Si. Arabia* **86 B2** 21 30N 39 54 E
Mecca, *U.S.A.* **145 M10** 33 34N 116 5W
Mechanicsburg, *U.S.A.* **136 F8** 40 13N 77 1W
Mechanicsville, *U.S.A.* **140 C5** 41 54N 91 16W
Mechanicville, *U.S.A.* **137 D11** 42 54N 73 41W
Mechara, *Ethiopia* **95 F5** 8 36N 40 20 E
Mechelen, *Antwerpen, Belgium* **21 F4** 51 2N 4 29 E
Mechelen, *Limburg, Belgium* **21 G7** 50 58N 5 41 E
Mecheria, *Algeria* **99 B4** 33 35N 0 18W
Mechernich, *Germany* **26 E2** 50 35N 6 39 E
Mechetinskaya, *Russia* **53 C9** 46 45N 40 32 E
Mechra Benâbbou, *Morocco* **98 B3** 32 39N 7 48W
Mecidiye, *Turkey* **44 D8** 40 38N 26 32 E
Mecitözü, *Turkey* **52 F6** 40 32N 35 17 E
Mecklenburg-Vorpommern □, *Germany* **26 B8** 53 50N 12 0 E
Mecklenburger Bucht, *Germany* **26 A7** 54 20N 11 40 E
Meconta, *Mozam.* **107 E4** 14 59 S 39 50 E
Meda, *Australia* **112 C3** 17 22 S 123 59 E
Meda, *Portugal* **36 E3** 40 57N 7 18W
Medak, *India* **82 E4** 18 1N 78 15 E
Medan, *Indonesia* **74 B1** 3 40N 98 38 E
Médanos, *Argentina* **160 A4** 38 50 S 62 42W
Medanosa, Pta., *Argentina* **160 C3** 48 8 S 66 0W
Medaryville, *U.S.A.* **141 C10** 41 5N 86 55W
Medawachchiya, *Sri Lanka* **83 K5** 8 30N 80 30 E
Medéa, *Algeria* **99 A5** 36 12N 2 50 E
Mededa, *Bos.-H.* **42 D4** 43 44N 19 15 E
Médégué, *Gabon* **102 B2** 0 37N 10 8 E
Medeiros Neto, *Brazil* **155 E3** 17 20 S 40 14W
Medel, Pic, *Switz.* **29 C7** 46 34N 8 55 E
Medellín, *Colombia* **152 B2** 6 15N 75 35W
Medemblik, *Neths.* **20 C6** 52 46N 5 8 E
Médenine, *Tunisia* **96 B2** 33 21N 10 30 E
Mederdra, *Mauritania* **100 B1** 17 0N 15 38W
Medford, *Mass., U.S.A.* **137 D13** 42 25N 71 7W
Medford, *Oreg., U.S.A.* **142 E2** 42 19N 122 52W
Medford, *Wis., U.S.A.* **138 C9** 45 9N 90 20W
Medgidia, *Romania* **46 E9** 44 15N 28 19 E
Medi, *Sudan* **95 F3** 5 4N 30 42 E
Media Agua, *Argentina* **158 C2** 31 58 S 68 25W
Media Luna, *Argentina* **158 C2** 34 45 S 66 44W
Mediapolis, *U.S.A.* **140 C5** 41 0N 91 10W
Mediaş, *Romania* **46 C5** 46 9N 24 22 E
Medical Lake, *U.S.A.* **142 C5** 47 34N 117 41W
Medicina, *Italy* **39 D8** 44 29N 11 38 E
Medicine Bow, *U.S.A.* **142 F10** 41 54N 106 12W
Medicine Bow Pk., *U.S.A.* **142 F10** 41 21N 106 19W
Medicine Bow Ra., *U.S.A.* **142 F10** 41 10N 106 25W
Medicine Hat, *Canada* **131 D6** 50 0N 110 45W
Medicine Lake, *U.S.A.* **138 A2** 48 30N 104 30W
Medicine Lodge, *U.S.A.* **139 G5** 37 17N 98 35W
Medina = Al Madīnah, *Si. Arabia* **84 E3** 24 35N 39 52 E
Medina, *Brazil* **155 E3** 16 15 S 41 29W
Medina, *Colombia* **152 C3** 4 30N 73 21W
Medina, *N. Dak., U.S.A.* **138 B5** 46 54N 99 18W
Medina, *N.Y., U.S.A.* **136 C6** 43 13N 78 23W
Medina, *Ohio, U.S.A.* **136 E3** 41 8N 81 52W
Medina →, *U.S.A.* **139 L5** 29 16N 98 29W
Medina de Ríoseco, *Spain* **36 D5** 41 53N 5 3W
Medina del Campo, *Spain* **36 D6** 41 18N 4 55W
Medina L., *U.S.A.* **139 L5** 29 32N 98 56W
Medina-Sidonia, *Spain* **37 J5** 36 28N 5 57W
Medinaceli, *Spain* **34 D2** 41 12N 2 30W
Medinipur, *India* **81 H12** 22 25N 87 21 E
Mediterranean Sea, *Europe* **92 C5** 35 0N 15 0 E
Medjerda, O. →, *Tunisia* **96 A2** 37 7N 10 13 E
Medley, *Canada* **131 C6** 54 25N 110 16W
Mednogorsk, *Russia* **54 F5** 51 24N 57 37 E
Médoc, *France* **24 C3** 45 10N 0 50W
Medora, *U.S.A.* **141 F10** 38 49N 86 10W
Médouneu, *Gabon* **102 B2** 0 57N 10 47 E
Medstead, *Canada* **131 C7** 53 19N 108 5W
Medulin, *Croatia* **39 D10** 44 49N 13 55 E
Medveda, *Serbia* **42 E6** 42 50N 21 32 E
Medveditsa →, *Russia* **51 G13** 49 35N 42 41 E
Medveditsa →, *Russia* **51 C10** 57 5N 37 30 E
Medvedok, *Russia* **54 C2** 57 20N 50 1 E
Medvezhi, Ostrava, *Russia* **57 B17** 71 0N 161 0 E
Medvezhyegorsk, *Russia* **48 B5** 63 0N 34 25 E
Medway →, *U.K.* **17 F8** 51 28N 0 45 E
Medyn, *Russia* **51 D9** 54 58N 35 52 E
Medzev, *Slovak Rep.* **31 C13** 48 43N 20 55 E
Medzilaborce, *Slovak Rep.* **31 B14** 49 17N 21 52 E
Meeberrie, *Australia* **113 E2** 26 57 S 115 51 E
Meekatharra, *Australia* **113 E2** 26 32 S 118 29 E
Meeker, *U.S.A.* **142 F10** 40 2N 107 55W
Meeniyan, *Australia* **117 E7** 38 35 S 146 0 E
Meer, *Belgium* **21 F5** 51 27N 4 45 E
Meerane, *Germany* **26 E8** 50 51N 12 30 E
Meerbeke, *Belgium* **21 G4** 50 50N 4 3 E
Meerhout, *Belgium* **21 F6** 51 7N 5 4 E
Meerle, *Belgium* **21 F5** 51 29N 4 48 E
Meersburg, *Germany* **27 H5** 47 42N 9 16 E
Meerssen, *Neths.* **21 G7** 50 53N 5 50 E
Meerut, *India* **80 E7** 29 1N 77 42 E
Meeteetse, *U.S.A.* **142 D9** 44 9N 108 52W
Meeuwen, *Belgium* **21 F7** 51 6N 5 31 E
Mega, *Ethiopia* **95 G4** 3 57N 38 19 E
Megálo Khorío, *Greece* **45 H9** 36 27N 27 24 E
Megálo Petalí, *Greece* **45 G6** 38 0N 24 15 E
Megalópolis, *Greece* **45 G4** 37 25N 22 7 E
Meganísi, *Greece* **45 F2** 38 39N 20 48 E
Mégara, *Greece* **45 G5** 37 58N 23 22 E
Megarine, *Algeria* **99 B6** 33 14N 6 2 E
Megdhova →, *Greece* **45 E3** 39 10N 21 45 E
Megève, *France* **25 C10** 45 51N 6 37 E
Meghalaya □, *India* **78 C3** 25 50N 91 0 E
Meghezez, *Ethiopia* **95 F4** 9 18N 39 26 E
Meghna →, *Bangla.* **78 D3** 22 50N 90 50 E
Mégiscane, L., *Canada* **128 C4** 48 35N 75 55W
Mehadia, *Romania* **46 E3** 44 56N 22 23 E
Mehaigne →, *Belgium* **21 G6** 50 32N 5 13 E
Mehaïguene, O. →, *Algeria* **99 B5** 32 15N 2 59 E
Mehedinţi □, *Romania* **46 E3** 44 40N 22 45 E
Meheisa, *Sudan* **94 D3** 19 38N 32 57 E
Mehndawal, *India* **81 F10** 26 58N 83 5 E
Mehr Jān, *Iran* **85 C7** 33 50N 55 6 E
Mehrābād, *Iran* **84 B5** 36 53N 47 55 E
Mehrān, *Iran* **84 C5** 33 7N 46 10 E
Mehrīz, *Iran* **85 D7** 31 35N 54 28 E
Mehun-sur-Yèvre, *France* **23 E9** 47 10N 2 13 E
Mei Jiang →, *China* **69 E11** 24 25N 116 35 E
Mei Xian, *Guangdong, China* **69 E11** 24 16N 116 6 E
Mei Xian, *Shaanxi, China* **66 G4** 34 18N 107 55 E
Meia Ponte →, *Brazil* **155 E2** 18 32 S 49 36W
Meicheng, *China* **69 C12** 29 29N 119 16 E
Meichengzhen, *China* **69 C8** 28 9N 111 40 E
Meichuan, *China* **69 B10** 30 8N 115 31 E
Meiganga, *Cameroon* **102 A2** 6 30N 14 25 E
Meijel, *Neths.* **21 F7** 51 21N 5 53 E
Meiktila, *Burma* **78 E5** 20 53N 95 54 E
Meilen, *Switz.* **29 B7** 47 16N 8 39 E
Meiningen, *Germany* **26 E6** 50 32N 10 25 E
Meio →, *Brazil* **155 D3** 13 36 S 44 7W
Meira, Sierra de, *Spain* **36 B3** 43 15N 7 15W
Meiringen, *Switz.* **28 C6** 46 43N 8 12 E
Meishan, *China* **68 B4** 30 3N 103 23 E
Meissen, *Germany* **26 D9** 51 10N 13 29 E
Meissner, *Germany* **26 D5** 51 13N 9 51 E
Meitan, *China* **68 D6** 27 45N 107 29 E
Mejillones, *Chile* **158 A1** 23 10 S 70 30W
Meka, *Australia* **113 E2** 27 25 S 116 48 E
Mékambo, *Gabon* **102 B2** 1 2N 13 50 E
Mekdela, *Ethiopia* **95 E4** 11 24N 39 10 E
Mekele, *Ethiopia* **95 E4** 13 33N 39 30 E
Mekhtar, *Pakistan* **79 C3** 30 30N 69 15 E
Meknès, *Morocco* **98 B3** 33 57N 5 33W
Meko, *Nigeria* **101 D5** 7 27N 2 52 E
Mekong →, *Asia* **77 H6** 9 30N 106 15 E
Mekongga, *Indonesia* **72 B2** 3 39 S 121 15 E
Melagiri Hills, *India* **83 H3** 12 20N 77 30 E
Melah, Sebkhet el, *Algeria* **99 C4** 29 20N 1 30W
Melaka, *Malaysia* **77 L4** 2 15N 102 15 E
Melaka □, *Malaysia* **74 B2** 2 15N 102 15 E
Mélambes, *Greece* **32 D6** 35 8N 24 40 E
Melanesia, *Pac. Oc.* **122 H7** 4 0 S 155 0 E
Melapalaiyam, *India* **83 K3** 8 39N 77 44 E
Melawi →, *Indonesia* **75 B4** 0 5N 111 29 E
Melbourne, *Australia* **117 D6** 37 50 S 145 0 E
Melbourne, *Fla., U.S.A.* **135 L5** 28 5N 80 37W
Melbourne, *Iowa, U.S.A.* **140 C3** 41 57N 93 6W
Melcher, *U.S.A.* **140 C3** 41 14N 93 15W
Melchor Múzquiz, *Mexico* **146 B4** 27 50N 101 30W
Melchor Ocampo, *Mexico* **146 C4** 24 52N 101 40W
Méldola, *Italy* **39 D9** 44 7N 12 3 E
Meldorf, *Germany* **26 A5** 54 5N 9 5 E
Meleden, *Somali Rep.* **108 B3** 10 25N 49 51 E
Melegnano, *Italy* **38 C6** 45 21N 9 20 E
Melenci, *Serbia* **42 B5** 45 32N 20 20 E
Melenki, *Russia* **51 D12** 55 20N 41 37 E
Meleuz, *Russia* **54 E4** 52 58N 55 55 E
Mélèzes →, *Canada* **127 C12** 57 30N 71 0W
Melfi, *Chad* **97 F3** 11 0N 17 59 E
Melfi, *Italy* **41 B8** 41 0N 15 33 E
Melfort, *Canada* **131 C8** 52 50N 104 37W
Melfort, *Zimbabwe* **107 F3** 18 0 S 31 25 E
Melgaço, *Madeira* **36 C2** 42 7N 8 15W
Melgar de Fernamental, *Spain* **36 C6** 42 27N 4 17W
Melhus, *Norway* **14 A4** 63 17N 10 18 E
Melick, *Neths.* **21 F8** 51 10N 6 1 E
Melide, *Switz.* **29 E7** 45 57N 8 57 E
Meligalá, *Greece* **45 G3** 37 15N 21 59 E
Melilla, *Morocco* **99 A4** 35 21N 2 57W
Melipilla, *Chile* **158 C1** 33 42 S 71 15W
Mélissa, Ákra, *Greece* **32 D6** 35 6N 24 33 E
Mélissa Óros, *Greece* **45 G8** 37 32N 26 4 E
Melita, *Canada* **131 D8** 49 15N 101 0W
Mélito di Porto Salvo, *Italy* **41 E8** 37 55N 15 47 E
Melitopol, *Ukraine* **52 C6** 46 50N 35 22 E
Melk, *Austria* **30 C8** 48 13N 15 20 E
Mellansel, *Sweden* **12 E15** 63 25N 18 17 E
Melle, *Belgium* **21 G3** 51 0N 3 49 E
Melle, *France* **24 B3** 46 14N 0 10W
Melle, *Germany* **26 C4** 52 12N 8 20 E
Mellégue, O. →, *Tunisia* **96 A1** 36 32N 8 51 E
Mellen, *U.S.A.* **138 B9** 46 20N 90 40W
Mellerud, *Sweden* **15 F6** 58 41N 12 28 E
Mellette, *U.S.A.* **138 C5** 45 9N 98 30W
Mellid, *Spain* **36 C2** 42 55N 8 1W
Mellieha, *Malta* **32 D1** 35 57N 14 21 E
Mellit, *Sudan* **95 E2** 14 7N 25 34 E
Mellizo Sur, Cerro, *Chile* **160 C2** 48 33 S 73 10W
Mellrichstadt, *Germany* **27 E6** 50 26N 10 19 E
Melnik, *Bulgaria* **43 F8** 41 30N 23 25 E
Mělník, *Czech.* **30 A7** 50 22N 14 23 E
Melo, *Uruguay* **159 C5** 32 20 S 54 10W
Melolo, *Indonesia* **72 C2** 9 53 S 120 40 E
Melouprey, *Cambodia* **76 F5** 13 48N 105 16 E
Melovoye, *Ukraine* **53 B9** 49 25N 40 5 E
Melrhir, Chott, *Algeria* **99 B6** 34 25N 6 24 E
Melrose, *N.S.W., Australia* **117 B7** 32 42 S 146 57 E
Melrose, *W. Austral., Australia* **113 E3** 27 50 S 121 15 E
Melrose, *U.K.* **18 F6** 55 35N 2 44W
Melrose, *Iowa, U.S.A.* **140 D3** 40 59N 93 3W
Melrose, *N. Mex., U.S.A.* **139 H3** 34 26N 103 38W
Mels, *Switz.* **29 B8** 47 3N 9 25 E
Melsele, *Belgium* **21 F4** 51 13N 4 17 E
Melstone, *U.S.A.* **142 C10** 46 36N 107 52W
Melsungen, *Germany* **26 D5** 51 8N 9 34 E
Melton Mowbray, *U.K.* **16 E7** 52 46N 0 52W
Melun, *France* **23 D9** 48 32N 2 39 E
Melur, *India* **83 J4** 10 2N 78 23 E
Melut, *Sudan* **95 E3** 10 30N 32 13 E
Melville, *Canada* **131 C8** 50 55N 102 50W
Melville, C., *Australia* **114 A3** 14 11 S 144 30 E
Melville, L., *Canada* **129 B8** 53 30N 60 0W
Melville B., *Australia* **114 A2** 12 0 S 136 45 E
Melville I., *Australia* **112 B5** 11 30 S 131 0 E
Melville I., *Canada* **124 B8** 75 30N 112 0W
Melville Pen., *Canada* **127 B11** 68 0N 84 0W
Melvin →, *Canada* **130 B5** 59 11N 117 31W
Mélykút, *Hungary* **31 E12** 46 11N 19 25 E
Memaliaj, *Albania* **44 D1** 40 25N 19 58 E
Memba, *Mozam.* **107 E5** 14 11 S 40 30 E
Memboro, *Indonesia* **72 C1** 9 30 S 119 30 E
Membrilla, *Spain* **35 G1** 38 59N 3 21W
Memel = Klaìpéda, *Lithuania* **50 D2** 55 43N 21 10 E
Memel, *S. Africa* **105 D4** 27 38 S 29 36 E
Memmingen, *Germany* **27 H6** 47 59N 10 12 E
Mempawah, *Indonesia* **75 B3** 0 30N 109 5 E
Memphis, *Mo., U.S.A.* **140 D4** 40 28N 92 10W
Memphis, *Tenn., U.S.A.* **139 H10** 35 8N 90 3W
Memphis, *Tex., U.S.A.* **139 H4** 34 44N 100 33W
Mena, *U.S.A.* **139 H7** 34 35N 94 15W
Mena →, *Ethiopia* **95 F5** 5 40N 40 50 E
Menai Strait, *U.K.* **16 D3** 53 14N 4 10W
Ménaka, *Mali* **101 B5** 15 59N 2 18 E
Menaldum, *Neths.* **20 B7** 53 13N 5 40 E
Menamurtee, *Australia* **116 A5** 31 25 S 143 11 E
Menan = Chao Phraya →, *Thailand* **76 F3** 13 32N 100 36 E
Menarandra →, *Madag.* **105 D7** 25 17 S 44 30 E
Menard, *U.S.A.* **139 K5** 30 55N 99 47W
Menasha, *U.S.A.* **134 C1** 44 13N 88 26W
Menate, *Indonesia* **75 C4** 0 12 S 113 3 E
Mendawai →, *Indonesia* **75 C4** 3 30 S 113 0 E
Mende, *France* **24 D7** 44 31N 3 30 E
Mendebo, *Ethiopia* **95 F4** 7 0N 39 22 E
Mendez, *Mexico* **147 B5** 25 7N 98 34W
Mendez Nunez, *Phil.* **70 D3** 14 8N 120 54 E
Mendhar, *India* **81 C6** 33 35N 74 10 E
Mendi, *Ethiopia* **95 F4** 9 47N 35 4 E
Mendi, *Papua N. G.* **120 D2** 6 11 S 143 39 E
Mendip Hills, *U.K.* **17 F5** 51 17N 2 40W
Mendocino, *U.S.A.* **142 G2** 39 19N 123 48W
Mendocino, C., *U.S.A.* **142 F1** 40 26N 124 25W
Mendon, *U.S.A.* **141 B11** 42 0N 85 27W
Mendota, *Calif., U.S.A.* **144 J6** 36 45N 120 23W
Mendota, *Ill., U.S.A.* **140 C7** 41 33N 89 7W
Mendoza, *Argentina* **158 C2** 32 50 S 68 52W
Mendoza □, *Argentina* **158 C2** 33 0 S 69 0W
Mendrisio, *Switz.* **29 E7** 45 52N 8 59 E
Mene Grande, *Venezuela* **152 B3** 9 49N 70 56W
Menemen, *Turkey* **88 D2** 38 34N 27 3 E
Menen, *Belgium* **21 G2** 50 47N 3 7 E
Menéndez, L., *Argentina* **160 B2** 42 40 S 71 51W
Menfi, *Italy* **40 E5** 37 36N 12 57 E
Mengcheng, *China* **69 A11** 33 18N 116 31 E
Mengdingjie, *China* **68 F2** 23 31N 98 58 E
Mengeš, *Slovenia* **39 B11** 46 10N 14 35 E
Menggala, *Indonesia* **74 C3** 4 30 S 105 15 E
Menghai, *China* **68 G3** 21 49N 100 55 E
Mengíbar, *Spain* **37 H7** 37 58N 3 48W
Mengjin, *China* **66 G7** 34 55N 112 45 E
Mengla, *China* **68 G3** 21 20N 101 25 E
Menglian, *China* **68 F2** 22 21N 99 27 E
Mengoub, *Algeria* **98 C3** 29 49N 5 26W
Mengshan, *China* **69 E8** 24 14N 110 55 E
Mengyin, *China* **67 G9** 35 40N 117 58 E
Mengzhe, *China* **68 F3** 22 2N 100 15 E
Mengzi, *China* **68 F4** 23 20N 103 22 E
Menihek L., *Canada* **129 B6** 54 0N 67 0W
Menin = Menen, *Belgium* **21 G2** 50 47N 3 7 E
Menindee, *Australia* **116 B5** 32 20 S 142 25 E
Menindee L., *Australia* **116 B5** 32 20 S 142 25 E
Meningie, *Australia* **116 C3** 35 50 S 139 18 E
Menlo Park, *U.S.A.* **144 H4** 37 27N 122 12W
Menominee, *U.S.A.* **134 C2** 45 6N 87 37W
Menominee →, *U.S.A.* **134 C2** 45 6N 87 36W
Menomonee Falls, *U.S.A.* **141 A8** 43 11N 88 7W
Menomonie, *U.S.A.* **138 C9** 44 53N 91 55W
Menongue, *Angola* **103 E3** 14 48 S 17 52 E
Menorca, *Spain* **33 B11** 40 0N 4 0 E

Mentakab, *Malaysia* **77 L4** 3 29N 102 21 E
Mentawai, Kepulauan, *Indonesia* **74 C1** 2 0 S 99 0 E
Menton, *France* **25 E11** 43 50N 7 29 E
Mentone, *U.S.A.* **141 C10** 41 10N 86 2W
Mentor, *U.S.A.* **136 E3** 41 40N 81 21W
Mentz Dam, *S. Africa* **104 E4** 33 10 S 25 9 E
Menyamya, *Papua N. G.* **120 D3** 7 10 S 145 59 E
Menzel-Bourguiba, *Tunisia* **96 A1** 37 9N 9 49 E
Menzel Chaker, *Tunisia* **96 B2** 35 0N 10 26 E
Menzel-Temime, *Tunisia* **96 A2** 36 46N 11 0 E
Menzelinsk, *Russia* **54 D3** 55 53N 53 1 E
Menzies, *Australia* **113 E3** 29 40 S 121 2 E
Me'ona, *Israel* **91 B4** 33 1N 35 15 E
Meoqui, *Mexico* **146 B3** 28 17N 105 29W
Mepaco, *Mozam.* **107 F3** 15 57 S 30 48 E
Meppel, *Neths.* **20 C8** 52 42N 6 12 E
Meppen, *Germany* **26 C3** 52 41N 7 20 E
Mequinenza, *Spain* **34 D5** 41 22N 0 17 E
Mequon, *U.S.A.* **141 A9** 43 14N 87 59W
Mer Rouge, *U.S.A.* **139 J9** 32 47N 91 48W
Mera Lava, *Vanuatu* **121 D6** 14 25 S 168 3 E
Merabéllou, Kólpos, *Greece* **32 D7** 35 10N 25 50 E
Merai, *Papua N. G.* **120 C7** 4 52 S 152 19 E
Meramangye, L., *Australia* **113 E5** 28 25 S 132 13 E
Meramec →, *U.S.A.* **140 F6** 38 24N 90 21W
Meran = Merano, *Italy* **39 B8** 46 40N 11 10 E
Merano, *Italy* **39 B8** 46 40N 11 10 E
Merate, *Italy* **38 C6** 45 42N 9 23 E
Merauke, *Indonesia* **73 C6** 8 29 S 140 24 E
Merbabu, *Indonesia* **75 D4** 7 30 S 110 40 E
Merbein, *Australia* **116 C5** 34 10 S 142 2 E
Merca, *Somali Rep.* **90 G3** 1 48N 44 50 E
Mercadal, *Spain* **33 B11** 39 59N 4 5 E
Mercato Saraceno, *Italy* **39 E9** 43 57N 12 11 E
Merced, *U.S.A.* **144 H6** 37 18N 120 29W
Merced Pk., *U.S.A.* **144 H7** 37 36N 119 24W
Mercedes, *Buenos Aires, Argentina* **158 C4** 34 40 S 59 30W
Mercedes, *Corrientes, Argentina* **158 B4** 29 10 S 58 5W
Mercedes, *San Luis, Argentina* **158 C2** 33 40 S 65 21W
Mercedes, *Camarines N., Phil.* **70 D4** 14 7N 123 1 E
Mercedes, *Leyte, Phil.* **71 F5** 10 41N 124 24 E
Mercedes, *Zamboanga del S., Phil.* **71 H4** 6 57N 122 9 E
Mercedes, *Uruguay* **158 C4** 33 12 S 58 0W
Merceditas, *Chile* **158 B1** 28 20 S 70 35W
Mercer, *N.Z.* **118 D4** 37 16 S 175 5 E
Mercer, *Mo., U.S.A.* **140 D3** 40 31N 93 32W
Mercer, *Pa., U.S.A.* **136 E4** 41 14N 80 15W
Merchtem, *Belgium* **21 G4** 50 58N 4 14 E
Mercier, *Bolivia* **156 C4** 10 42 S 68 5W
Mercury, *U.S.A.* **145 J11** 36 40N 115 58W
Mercury B., *N.Z.* **118 C4** 36 48 S 175 45 E
Mercury Is., *N.Z.* **118 C4** 36 37 S 175 52 E
Mercy C., *Canada* **127 B13** 65 0N 63 30W
Merdrignac, *France* **22 D4** 48 11N 2 27W
Mere, *Belgium* **21 G3** 50 55N 3 58 E
Meredith, C., *Falk. Is.* **160 D4** 52 15 S 60 40W
Meredith, L., *U.S.A.* **139 H4** 35 43N 101 33W
Meredosia, *U.S.A.* **140 E6** 39 50N 90 34W
Meregh, *Somali Rep.* **108 D3** 3 46N 47 18 E
Merei, *Romania* **46 D7** 45 7N 26 43 E
Merelbeke, *Belgium* **21 G3** 51 0N 3 45 E
Méréville, *France* **23 D9** 48 20N 2 5 E
Merga = Nukheila, *Sudan* **94 D2** 19 1N 26 21 E
Mergenevsky, *Kazakhstan* **53 B14** 49 59N 51 15 E
Mergui Arch. = Myeik Kyunzu, *Burma* **77 G1** 11 30N 97 30 E
Meribah, *Australia* **116 C4** 34 43 S 140 51 E
Mérida, *Mexico* **147 C7** 20 9N 89 40W
Merida, *Phil.* **71 F5** 10 55N 124 32 E
Mérida, *Spain* **37 G4** 38 55N 6 25W
Mérida, *Venezuela* **152 B3** 8 24N 71 8W
Mérida □, *Venezuela* **152 B3** 8 30N 71 10W
Mérida, Cord. de, *Venezuela* **152 B3** 9 0N 71 0W
Meriden, *U.S.A.* **137 E12** 41 32N 72 48W
Meridian, *Calif., U.S.A.* **144 F5** 39 9N 121 55W
Meridian, *Idaho, U.S.A.* **142 E5** 43 37N 116 24W
Meridian, *Miss., U.S.A.* **135 J1** 32 22N 88 42W
Meridian, *Tex., U.S.A.* **139 K6** 31 56N 97 39W
Mering, *Germany* **27 G7** 48 15N 11 0 E
Meriruma, *Brazil* **153 C7** 1 15N 54 50W
Merke, *Kazakhstan* **55 B6** 42 52N 73 11 E
Merkel, *U.S.A.* **139 J4** 32 28N 100 1W
Merksem, *Belgium* **21 F4** 51 16N 4 25 E
Merksplas, *Belgium* **21 F5** 51 22N 4 52 E
Mermaid Reef, *Australia* **112 C2** 17 6 S 119 36 E
Mern, *Denmark* **15 J6** 55 3N 12 3 E
Merowe, *Sudan* **94 D3** 18 29N 31 46 E
Merredin, *Australia* **113 F2** 31 28 S 118 18 E
Merrick, *U.K.* **18 F4** 55 8N 4 30W
Merrickville, *Canada* **137 B9** 44 55N 75 50W
Merrill, *Oreg., U.S.A.* **142 E3** 42 1N 121 36W
Merrill, *Wis., U.S.A.* **138 C10** 45 11N 89 41W
Merrillville, *U.S.A.* **141 C9** 41 29N 87 20W
Merriman, *U.S.A.* **138 D4** 42 55N 101 42W
Merritt, *Canada* **130 C4** 50 10N 120 45W
Merriwa, *Australia* **117 B9** 32 6 S 150 22 E
Merriwagga, *Australia* **117 B6** 33 47 S 145 43 E
Merry I., *Canada* **128 A4** 55 29N 77 31W
Merrygoen, *Australia* **117 A8** 31 51 S 149 12 E
Merryville, *U.S.A.* **139 K8** 30 45N 93 33W
Mersa Fatma, *Eritrea* **90 E3** 14 57N 40 17 E
Mersch, *Lux.* **21 J8** 49 44N 6 7 E
Merseburg, *Germany* **26 D7** 51 20N 12 0 E
Mersey →, *U.K.* **16 D5** 53 20N 2 56W
Merseyside □, *U.K.* **16 D5** 53 25N 2 55W
Mersin, *Turkey* **88 E6** 36 51N 34 36 E
Mersing, *Malaysia* **77 L4** 2 25N 103 50 E
Merta, *India* **80 F6** 26 39N 74 4 E
Mertert, *Lux.* **21 J8** 49 43N 6 29 E
Merthyr Tydfil, *U.K.* **17 F4** 51 45N 3 23W
Mértola, *Portugal* **37 H3** 37 40N 7 40W
Mertzig, *Lux.* **21 J8** 49 51N 6 1 E
Mertzon, *U.S.A.* **139 K4** 31 16N 100 49W
Méru, *France* **23 C9** 49 13N 2 8 E
Meru, *Kenya* **106 B4** 0 3N 37 40 E
Meru, *Tanzania* **106 C4** 3 15 S 36 46 E
Meru □, *Kenya* **106 B4** 0 3N 37 46 E
Merville, *France* **23 B9** 50 38N 2 38 E
Méry-sur-Seine, *France* **23 D10** 48 31N 3 54 E
Merzifon, *Turkey* **52 F6** 40 53N 35 32 E
Merzig, *Germany* **27 F2** 49 26N 6 37 E
Merzouga, Erg Tin, *Algeria* **99 D7** 24 0N 11 4 E
Mesa, *U.S.A.* **143 K8** 33 25N 111 50W
Mesach Mellet, *Libya* **96 D2** 24 30N 11 30 E
Mesagne, *Italy* **41 B10** 40 34N 17 48 E
Mesanagrós, *Greece* **32 C9** 36 1N 27 49 E
Mesaoría □, *Cyprus* **32 D12** 35 12N 33 14 E
Mesarás, Kólpos, *Greece* **32 D6** 35 6N 24 47 E
Meschede, *Germany* **26 D4** 51 20N 8 17 E
Mesfinto, *Ethiopia* **95 E4** 13 20N 37 22 E
Mesgouez, L., *Canada* **128 B4** 51 20N 75 0W
Meshchovsk, *Russia* **50 D9** 54 22N 35 17 E
Meshed = Mashhad, *Iran* **85 B8** 36 20N 59 35 E
Meshoppen, *U.S.A.* **137 E8** 41 36N 76 3W
Meshra er Req, *Sudan* **95 F2** 8 25N 29 18 E
Mesick, *U.S.A.* **134 C3** 44 24N 85 43W
Mesilinka →, *Canada* **130 B4** 56 6N 124 30W
Mesilla, *U.S.A.* **143 K10** 32 16N 106 48W
Meslay-du-Maine, *France* **22 E6** 47 58N 0 33W
Mesocco, *Switz.* **29 D8** 46 23N 9 12 E
Mesolóngion, *Greece* **45 F3** 38 21N 21 28 E
Mesopotamia = Al Jazirah, *Iraq* **84 C5** 33 30N 44 0 E
Mesoraca, *Italy* **41 C9** 39 5N 16 47 E
Mésou Volímais, *Greece* **45 G2** 37 53N 20 35 E
Mesquite, *U.S.A.* **143 H6** 36 47N 114 6W
Mess Cr. →, *Canada* **130 B2** 57 55N 131 14W
Messac, *France* **22 E5** 47 49N 1 50W
Messad, *Algeria* **99 B5** 34 8N 3 30 E
Messalo →, *Mozam.* **107 E4** 12 25 S 39 15 E
Méssaména, *Cameroon* **101 E7** 3 48N 12 49 E
Messancy, *Belgium* **21 J7** 49 36N 5 49 E
Messeue, *Greece* **45 G3** 37 12N 21 58 E
Messier, Canal, *Chile* **160 C2** 48 20 S 74 33W
Messina, *Italy* **41 D8** 38 10N 15 32 E
Messina, *S. Africa* **105 C5** 22 20 S 30 5 E
Messina, Str. di, *Italy* **41 D8** 38 5N 15 35 E
Messíni, *Greece* **45 G4** 37 4N 22 1 E
Messínia □, *Greece* **45 G3** 37 10N 22 0 E
Messiniakós Kólpos, *Greece* **45 H4** 36 45N 22 5 E
Messkirch, *Germany* **27 H5** 47 59N 9 7 E
Messonghi, *Greece* **32 B3** 39 29N 19 56 E
Mesta →, *Bulgaria* **43 F9** 41 30N 24 12 E
Mestà, Ákra, *Greece* **45 F7** 38 16N 25 53 E
Mestanza, *Spain* **37 G6** 38 35N 4 4W
Město Teplá, *Czech.* **30 B5** 49 59N 12 52 E
Mestre, *Italy* **39 C9** 45 30N 12 13 E
Mestre, Espigão, *Brazil* **155 D2** 12 30 S 46 10W
Městys Zelezná Ruda, *Czech.* **30 B6** 49 8N 13 15 E
Meta, *U.S.A.* **140 F4** 38 19N 92 10W
Meta □, *Colombia* **152 C3** 3 30N 73 0W
Meta →, *S. Amer.* **152 B4** 6 12N 67 28W
Metairie, *U.S.A.* **139 L9** 29 58N 90 10W
Metalici, Munţii, *Romania* **46 C3** 46 15N 22 50 E
Metaline Falls, *U.S.A.* **142 B5** 48 52N 117 22W
Metamora, *U.S.A.* **140 D7** 40 47N 89 22W
Metán, *Argentina* **158 B3** 25 30 S 65 0W
Metangula, *Mozam.* **107 E3** 12 40 S 34 50 E
Metauro →, *Italy* **39 E10** 43 50N 13 3 E
Metema, *Ethiopia* **95 E4** 12 56N 36 13 E
Metengobalame, *Mozam.* **107 E3** 14 49 S 34 30 E
Méthana, *Greece* **45 G5** 37 35N 23 23 E
Methóni, *Greece* **45 H3** 36 49N 21 42 E
Methven, *N.Z.* **119 D6** 43 38 S 171 40 E
Methy L., *Canada* **131 B7** 56 28N 109 30W
Metil, *Mozam.* **107 F4** 16 24 S 39 0 E
Metkovets, *Bulgaria* **43 D8** 43 37N 23 10 E
Metković, *Croatia* **42 D2** 43 6N 17 39 E
Metlakatla, *U.S.A.* **130 B2** 55 8N 131 35W
Metlaoui, *Tunisia* **96 B1** 34 24N 8 24 E
Metlika, *Slovenia* **39 C12** 45 40N 15 20 E
Metro, *Indonesia* **74 D3** 5 5 S 105 20 E
Metropolis, *U.S.A.* **139 G10** 37 9N 88 44W
Métsovon, *Greece* **44 E3** 39 48N 21 12 E
Mettet, *Belgium* **21 H5** 50 19N 4 41 E
Mettuppalaiyam, *India* **83 J3** 11 18N 76 59 E
Mettur, *India* **83 J3** 11 48N 77 47 E
Metz, *France* **23 C13** 49 8N 6 10 E
Meulaboh, *Indonesia* **74 B1** 4 11N 96 3 E
Meulan, *France* **23 C8** 49 3N 1 55 E
Meung-sur-Loire, *France* **23 E8** 47 50N 1 40 E
Meureudu, *Indonesia* **74 A1** 5 19N 96 10 E
Meurthe →, *France* **23 D13** 48 47N 6 9 E
Meurthe-et-Moselle □, *France* **23 D13** 48 52N 6 0 E
Meuse □, *France* **23 C12** 49 8N 5 25 E
Meuse →, *Europe* **21 G7** 50 45N 5 41 E
Meuselwitz, *Germany* **26 D8** 51 3N 12 18 E
Meutapok, Mt., *Malaysia* **75 A5** 5 40N 117 0 E
Mexborough, *U.K.* **16 D6** 53 29N 1 18W
Mexia, *U.S.A.* **139 K6** 31 41N 96 29W
Mexiana, I., *Brazil* **154 A2** 0 0 49 30W
Mexicali, *Mexico* **146 A1** 32 40N 115 30W
México, *Mexico* **147 D5** 19 20N 99 10W
Mexico, *Maine, U.S.A.* **137 B14** 44 34N 70 33W
Mexico, *Mo., U.S.A.* **140 E5** 39 10N 91 53W
México □, *Mexico* **146 D5** 19 20N 99 10W
Mexico ■, *Cent. Amer.* **146 C4** 25 0N 105 0W
Mexico, G. of, *Cent. Amer.* **147 C7** 25 0N 90 0W
Meyenburg, *Germany* **26 B8** 53 19N 12 15 E
Meymac, *France* **24 C6** 45 32N 2 10 E
Meymaneh, *Afghan.* **79 B2** 35 53N 64 38 E
Meyrargues, *France* **25 E9** 43 38N 5 32 E
Meyrueis, *France* **24 D7** 44 12N 3 27 E
Meyssac, *France* **24 C5** 45 3N 1 40 E
Mezdra, *Bulgaria* **43 D8** 43 12N 23 42 E
Mèze, *France* **24 E7** 43 27N 3 36 E
Mezen, *Russia* **48 A7** 65 50N 44 20 E
Mezen →, *Russia* **48 A7** 66 11N 43 59 E
Mézenc, Mt., *France* **25 D8** 44 54N 4 11 E
Mezeş, Munţii, *Romania* **46 B4** 47 5N 23 5 E
Mezha →, *Russia* **50 D7** 55 50N 31 45 E
Mezhdurechenskiy, *Russia* **54 B9** 59 36N 65 56 E
Mézidon, *France* **22 C6** 49 5N 0 1W
Mézilhac, *France* **25 D8** 44 49N 4 21 E
Mézin, *France* **24 D4** 44 4N 0 16 E
Mezöberény, *Hungary* **31 E14** 46 49N 21 3 E
Mezöfalva, *Hungary* **31 E11** 46 55N 18 49 E
Mezöhegyes, *Hungary* **31 E13** 46 19N 20 49 E
Mezökövácsháza, *Hungary* **31 E13** 46 25N 20 57 E
Mezökövesd, *Hungary* **31 D13** 47 49N 20 35 E
Mézos, *France* **24 D2** 44 5N 1 10W
Mezötúr, *Hungary* **31 E13** 46 58N 20 41 E
Mezquital, *Mexico* **146 C4** 23 29N 104 23W
Mezzolombardo, *Italy* **38 B8** 46 13N 11 5 E
Mgeta, *Tanzania* **107 D4** 8 22 S 36 6 E
Mglin, *Russia* **50 E8** 53 2N 32 50 E
Mhlaba Hills, *Zimbabwe* **107 F3** 18 30 S 30 30 E
Mhow, *India* **80 H6** 22 33N 75 50 E
Mi-Shima, *Japan* **62 C3** 34 46N 131 9 E
Miahuatlán, *Mexico* **147 D5** 16 21N 96 36W
Miajadas, *Spain* **37 F5** 39 9N 5 54W
Miallo, *Australia* **114 B4** 16 28 S 145 22 E
Miami, *Ariz., U.S.A.* **143 K8** 33 24N 110 52W
Miami, *Fla., U.S.A.* **135 N5** 25 47N 80 11W
Miami, *Tex., U.S.A.* **139 H4** 35 42N 100 38W
Miami →, *U.S.A.* **134 F3** 39 20N 84 40W
Miami Beach, *U.S.A.* **135 N5** 25 47N 80 8W
Miamisburg, *U.S.A.* **141 E12** 39 38N 84 17W
Mian Xian, *China* **66 H4** 33 10N 106 32 E
Mianchi, *China* **66 G6** 34 48N 111 48 E
Mīāndowāb, *Iran* **84 B5** 37 0N 46 5 E
Miandrivazo, *Madag.* **105 B8** 19 31 S 45 29 E
Mīāneh, *Iran* **84 B5** 37 30N 47 40 E
Mianning, *China* **68 C4** 28 32N 102 9 E
Mianwali, *Pakistan* **79 B3** 32 38N 71 28 E
Mianyang, *Hubei, China* **69 B9** 30 25N 113 25 E
Mianyang, *Sichuan, China* **68 B5** 31 22N 104 47 E
Mianzhu, *China* **68 B5** 31 22N 104 7 E
Miaoli, *Taiwan* **69 E13** 24 37N 120 49 E
Miarinarivo, *Madag.* **105 B8** 18 57 S 46 55 E
Miass, *Russia* **54 D7** 54 59N 60 6 E
Miass →, *Russia* **54 C9** 56 6N 64 30 E
Miasteczko Kraj, *Poland* **47 B4** 53 7N 17 1 E
Miastko, *Poland* **47 B3** 54 0N 16 58 E
Micăsasa, *Romania* **46 C5** 46 7N 24 7 E
Michael, Mt., *Papua N. G.* **120 D3** 6 27 S 145 22 E
Michalovce, *Slovak Rep.* **31 C14** 48 47N 21 58 E
Michelstadt, *Germany* **27 F5** 49 40N 9 0 E
Michigan □, *U.S.A.* **134 C3** 44 0N 85 0W
Michigan, L., *U.S.A.* **134 C2** 44 0N 87 0W
Michigan Center, *U.S.A.* **141 B12** 42 14N 84 20W
Michigan City, *U.S.A.* **141 C10** 41 43N 86 54W
Michikamau L., *Canada* **129 B7** 54 20N 63 10W
Michipicoten, *Canada* **128 C3** 47 55N 84 55W
Michipicoten I., *Canada* **128 C2** 47 40N 85 40W
Michoacan □, *Mexico* **146 D4** 19 0N 102 0W
Michurin, *Bulgaria* **43 E12** 42 9N 27 51 E
Michurinsk, *Russia* **51 E12** 52 58N 40 27 E
Miclere, *Australia* **114 C4** 22 34 S 147 32 E
Mico, Pta. , *Nic.* **148 D3** 12 0N 83 30W
Micronesia, Federated States of ■, *Pac. Oc.* **122 G7** 9 0N 150 0 E
Mid Glamorgan □, *U.K.* **17 F4** 51 40N 3 25W
Mid-Indian Ridge, *Ind. Oc.* **109 H6** 30 0 S 75 0 E
Midai, P., *Indonesia* **75 B3** 3 0N 107 47 E
Midale, *Canada* **131 D8** 49 25N 103 20W
Middagsfjället, *Sweden* **14 A6** 63 27N 12 19 E
Middelbeers, *Neths.* **21 F6** 51 28N 5 15 E
Middelburg, *Neths.* **21 F3** 51 30N 3 36 E
Middelburg, *C. Prov., S. Africa* **104 E3** 31 30 S 25 0 E
Middelburg, *Trans., S. Africa* **105 D4** 25 49 S 29 28 E
Middelfart, *Denmark* **15 J3** 55 30N 9 43 E
Middelharnis, *Neths.* **20 E4** 51 46N 4 10 E
Middelkerke, *Belgium* **21 F1** 51 11N 2 49 E
Middelrode, *Neths.* **21 E6** 51 41N 5 26 E
Middelwit, *S. Africa* **104 C4** 24 51 S 27 3 E
Middle →, *U.S.A.* **140 C3** 41 26N 93 30W
Middle Alkali L., *U.S.A.* **142 F3** 41 27N 120 5W
Middle Fork Feather →, *U.S.A.* **144 F5** 38 33N 121 30W
Middle I., *Australia* **113 F3** 34 6 S 123 11 E
Middle Loup →, *U.S.A.* **138 E5** 41 17N 98 24W
Middle Raccoon →, *U.S.A.* **140 C3** 41 35N 93 35W
Middleboro, *U.S.A.* **137 E14** 41 54N 70 55W
Middleburg, *N.Y., U.S.A.* **137 D10** 42 36N 74 20W
Middleburg, *Pa., U.S.A.* **136 F7** 40 47N 77 3W
Middlebury, *Ind., U.S.A.* **141 C11** 41 41N 85 42W
Middlebury, *Vt., U.S.A.* **137 B11** 44 1N 73 10W
Middlemarch, *N.Z.* **119 F5** 45 30 S 170 9 E
Middleport, *U.S.A.* **134 F4** 39 0N 82 3W
Middlesboro, *Ky., U.S.A.* **133 C10** 36 36N 83 43W
Middlesboro, *Ky., U.S.A.* **135 G4** 36 36N 83 43W
Middlesbrough, *U.K.* **16 C6** 54 35N 1 14W
Middlesex, *Belize* **148 C2** 17 2N 88 31W
Middlesex, *U.S.A.* **137 F10** 40 36N 74 30W
Middleton, *Australia* **114 C3** 22 22 S 141 32 E
Middleton, *Canada* **129 D6** 44 57N 65 4W
Middleton, *U.S.A.* **140 A7** 43 6N 89 30W
Middletown, *Calif., U.S.A.* **144 G4** 38 45N 122 37W
Middletown, *Conn., U.S.A.* **137 E12** 41 34N 72 39W
Middletown, *N.Y., U.S.A.* **137 E10** 41 27N 74 25W
Middletown, *Ohio, U.S.A.* **141 E12** 39 31N 84 24W
Middletown, *Pa., U.S.A.* **137 F8** 40 12N 76 44W
Middleville, *U.S.A.* **141 B11** 42 43N 85 28W
Midelt, *Morocco* **98 B4** 32 46N 4 44W
Midhirst, *N.Z.* **118 F3** 39 17 S 174 18 E
Midi, Canal du →, *France* **24 E5** 43 45N 1 21 E
Midi d'Ossau, Pic du, *France* **24 F3** 42 50N 0 26W
Midland, *Canada* **128 D4** 44 45N 79 50W
Midland, *Calif., U.S.A.* **145 M12** 33 52N 114 48W
Midland, *Mich., U.S.A.* **134 D3** 43 37N 84 14W
Midland, *Pa., U.S.A.* **136 F4** 40 39N 80 27W
Midland, *Tex., U.S.A.* **139 K3** 32 0N 102 3W
Midlands □, *Zimbabwe* **107 F2** 19 40 S 29 0 E
Midleton, *Ireland* **19 E3** 51 52N 8 12W
Midlothian, *U.S.A.* **139 J6** 32 30N 97 0W
Midongy, Tangorombohitr' i, *Madag.* **105 C8** 23 30 S 47 0 E
Midongy Atsimo, *Madag.* **105 C8** 23 35 S 47 1 E
Midou →, *France* **24 E3** 43 54N 0 30W
Midouze →, *France* **24 E3** 43 48N 0 51W
Midsayap, *Phil.* **71 H5** 7 12N 124 32 E
Midu, *China* **68 E3** 25 18N 100 30 E
Midway Is., *Pac. Oc.* **122 E10** 28 13N 177 22W
Midway Wells, *U.S.A.* **145 N11** 32 41N 115 7W
Midwest, *U.S.A.* **133 B9** 42 0N 90 0W
Midwest, *Wyo., U.S.A.* **142 E10** 43 25N 106 16W
Midwolda, *Neths.* **20 B9** 53 12N 6 52 E
Midyat, *Turkey* **89 E9** 37 25N 41 23 E
Midzur, *Bulgaria* **42 D7** 43 24N 22 40 E
Mie □, *Japan* **63 C8** 34 30N 136 10 E
Miechów, *Poland* **47 E7** 50 21N 20 5 E
Miedwie, Jezioro, *Poland* **47 B1** 53 17N 14 54 E
Międzybód, *Poland* **47 D4** 51 25N 17 34 E
Międzychód, *Poland* **47 C2** 52 35N 15 53 E
Międzylesie, *Poland* **47 E3** 50 8N 16 40 E
Międzyrzec Podlaski, *Poland* **47 D9** 51 58N 22 45 E
Międzyrzecz, *Poland* **47 C2** 52 26N 15 35 E
Międzyzdroje, *Poland* **47 B1** 53 56N 14 26 E
Miejska, *Poland* **47 D3** 51 39N 16 58 E
Miélan, *France* **24 E4** 43 27N 0 19 E
Mielec, *Poland* **47 E8** 50 15N 21 25 E
Mienga, *Angola* **103 F3** 17 12 S 19 48 E
Miercurea Ciuc, *Romania* **46 C6** 46 21N 25 48 E
Mieres, *Spain* **36 B5** 43 18N 5 48W
Mierlo, *Neths.* **21 F7** 51 27N 5 37 E
Mieroszów, *Poland* **47 E3** 50 40N 16 11 E
Mieso, *Ethiopia* **95 F5** 9 15N 40 43 E
Mieszkowice, *Poland* **47 C1** 52 47N 14 30 E
Mifflintown, *U.S.A.* **136 F7** 40 34N 77 24W
Mifraz Hefa, *Israel* **91 C4** 32 52N 35 0 E
Migdāl, *Israel* **91 C4** 32 51N 35 30 E
Migennes, *France* **23 E10** 47 58N 3 31 E
Migliarino, *Italy* **39 D8** 44 45N 11 56 E
Miguel Alemán, Presa, *Mexico* **147 D5** 18 15N 96 40W
Miguel Alves, *Brazil* **154 B3** 4 11 S 42 55W
Miguel Calmon, *Brazil* **154 D3** 11 26 S 40 36W
Mihaliççık, *Turkey* **88 D4** 39 53N 31 30 E
Mihara, *Japan* **62 C5** 34 24N 133 5 E
Mihara-Yama, *Japan* **63 C11** 34 43N 139 23 E
Mijares →, *Spain* **34 F4** 39 55N 0 1W
Mijas, *Spain* **37 J6** 36 36N 4 40W
Mikese, *Tanzania* **106 D4** 6 48 S 37 55 E
Mikha-Tskhakaya = Senaki, *Georgia* **53 E10** 42 15N 42 7 E
Mikhailovka, *Ukraine* **52 C6** 47 36N 35 16 E
Mikhaylovgrad, *Bulgaria* **43 D8** 43 27N 23 16 E
Mikhaylovka, *Azerbaijan* **53 F13** 41 31N 48 52 E
Mikhaylovka, *Russia* **51 D11** 54 14N 39 0 E
Mikhaylovka, *Russia* **51 F13** 50 3N 43 5 E
Mikhaylovskiy, *Russia* **54 C6** 56 27N 59 7 E
Mikhnevo, *Russia* **51 D10** 55 4N 37 59 E
Miki, *Hyōgo, Japan* **62 C6** 34 48N 134 59 E
Miki, *Kagawa, Japan* **62 C6** 34 12N 134 7 E
Mikínai, *Greece* **45 G4** 37 43N 22 46 E
Mikkeli, *Finland* **13 F19** 61 43N 27 15 E
Mikkeli □ = Mikkelin lääni □, *Finland* **12 F20** 61 56N 28 0 E
Mikkelin lääni □, *Finland* **12 F20** 61 56N 28 0 E
Mikkwa →, *Canada* **130 B6** 58 25N 114 46W
Mikniya, *Sudan* **95 D3** 17 0N 33 45 E
Mikołajki, *Poland* **47 B8** 53 49N 21 37 E
Mikołów, *Poland* **31 A11** 50 10N 18 50 E
Míkonos, *Greece* **45 G7** 37 30N 25 25 E
Mikrí Préspa, Límni, *Greece* **44 D3** 40 47N 21 3 E
Mikrón Dhérion, *Greece* **44 C8** 41 19N 26 6 E
Mikstat, *Poland* **47 D4** 51 32N 17 59 E
Mikulov, *Czech.* **31 C9** 48 48N 16 39 E
Mikumi, *Tanzania* **106 D4** 7 26 S 37 0 E
Mikun, *Russia* **48 B9** 62 20N 50 0 E
Mikuni, *Japan* **63 A8** 36 13N 136 9 E
Mikuni-Tōge, *Japan* **63 A10** 36 50N 138 50 E
Mikura-Jima, *Japan* **63 D11** 33 52N 139 36 E
Milaca, *U.S.A.* **138 C8** 45 45N 93 39W
Milagro, *Ecuador* **152 D2** 2 11 S 79 36W
Milagros, *Phil.* **70 E4** 12 13N 123 30 E
Milan = Milano, *Italy* **38 C6** 45 28N 9 10 E
Milan, *Ill., U.S.A.* **140 C6** 41 27N 90 34W
Milan, *Mich., U.S.A.* **141 B13** 42 5N 83 41W
Milan, *Mo., U.S.A.* **140 D3** 40 12N 93 7W
Milan, *Tenn., U.S.A.* **135 H1** 35 55N 88 46W
Milang, *S. Austral., Australia* **115 E2** 32 2 S 139 10 E
Milang, *S. Austral., Australia* **116 C3** 35 24 S 138 58 E
Milange, *Mozam.* **107 F4** 16 3 S 35 45 E
Milano, *Italy* **38 C6** 45 28N 9 10 E
Milâs, *Turkey* **88 E2** 37 20N 27 50 E
Mílatos, *Greece* **32 D7** 35 18N 25 34 E
Milazzo, *Italy* **41 D8** 38 13N 15 13 E
Milbank, *U.S.A.* **138 C6** 45 13N 96 38W
Milden, *Canada* **131 C7** 51 29N 107 32W
Mildmay, *Canada* **136 B3** 44 3N 81 7W
Mildura, *Australia* **116 C5** 34 13 S 142 9 E
Mile, *China* **68 E4** 24 28N 103 20 E
Miléai, *Greece* **44 E5** 39 20N 23 9 E
Milh Tharthār, *Iraq* **84 C4** 34 0N 43 15 E
Miles, *Australia* **115 D5** 26 40 S 150 9 E
Miles, *U.S.A.* **139 K4** 31 36N 100 11W
Miles City, *U.S.A.* **138 B2** 46 25N 105 51W
Milestone, *Canada* **131 D8** 49 59N 104 31W
Mileto, *Italy* **41 D9** 38 37N 16 3 E
Miletto, Mte., *Italy* **41 A7** 41 26N 14 23 E
Miletus, *Turkey* **45 G9** 37 30N 27 18 E
Mileura, *Australia* **113 E2** 26 22 S 117 20 E
Milevsko, *Czech.* **30 B7** 49 27N 14 21 E
Milford, *Calif., U.S.A.* **144 E6** 40 10N 120 22W
Milford, *Conn., U.S.A.* **137 E11** 41 14N 73 3W
Milford, *Del., U.S.A.* **134 F8** 38 55N 75 26W
Milford, *Ill., U.S.A.* **141 D9** 40 38N 87 42W
Milford, *Mass., U.S.A.* **137 D13** 42 8N 71 31W
Milford, *Mich., U.S.A.* **141 B13** 42 35N 83 36W
Milford, *Pa., U.S.A.* **137 E10** 41 19N 74 48W
Milford, *Utah, U.S.A.* **143 G7** 38 24N 113 1W
Milford Haven, *U.K.* **17 F2** 51 43N 5 2W
Milford Sd., *N.Z.* **119 E2** 44 41 S 167 47 E
Milgun, *Australia* **113 D2** 24 56 S 118 18 E
Milḥ, Baḥr al, *Iraq* **84 C4** 32 40N 43 35 E
Miliana, *Aïn Salah, Algeria* **99 C5** 27 20N 2 32 E
Miliana, *Médéa, Algeria* **99 A5** 36 20N 2 15 E
Milicz, *Poland* **47 D4** 51 31N 17 19 E
Miling, *Australia* **113 F2** 30 30 S 116 17 E
Militello in Val di Catánia, *Italy* **41 E7** 37 16N 14 46 E
Milk →, *U.S.A.* **142 B10** 48 4N 106 19W

234 Milk, Wadi el

Milk, Wadi el →, *Sudan* **94 D3** 17 55N 30 20 E
Milk River, *Canada* **130 D6** 49 10N 112 5W
Mill, *Neths.* **21 E7** 51 41N 5 48 E
Mill City, *U.S.A.* **142 D2** 44 45N 122 29W
Mill I., *Antarctica* **7 C8** 66 0 S 101 30 E
Mill Shoals, *U.S.A.* **141 F8** 38 15N 88 21W
Mill Valley, *U.S.A.* **144 H4** 37 54N 122 32W
Millau, *France* **24 D7** 44 8N 3 4 E
Millbridge, *Canada* **136 B7** 44 41N 77 36W
Millbrook, *Canada* **136 B6** 44 10N 78 29W
Mille Lacs, L. des, *Canada* **128 C1** 48 45N 90 35W
Mille Lacs L., *U.S.A.* **138 B8** 46 15N 93 39W
Milledgeville, *Ga., U.S.A.* **135 J4** 33 5N 83 14W
Milledgeville, *Ill., U.S.A.* **140 C7** 41 58N 89 46W
Millen, *U.S.A.* **135 J5** 32 48N 81 57W
Miller, *U.S.A.* **138 C5** 44 31N 98 59W
Millerovo, *Russia* **53 B9** 48 57N 40 28 E
Miller's Flat, *N.Z.* **119 F4** 45 39 S 169 23 E
Millersburg, *Ind., U.S.A.* **141 C11** 41 32N 85 42W
Millersburg, *Ohio, U.S.A.* **136 F3** 40 33N 81 55W
Millersburg, *Pa., U.S.A.* **136 F8** 40 32N 76 58W
Millerton, *N.Z.* **119 B6** 41 39 S 171 54 E
Millerton, *U.S.A.* **137 E11** 41 57N 73 31W
Millerton L., *U.S.A.* **144 J7** 37 1N 119 41W
Millevaches, Plateau de, *France* **24 C6** 45 45N 2 0 E
Millicent, *Australia* **116 D4** 37 34 S 140 21 E
Millingen, *Neths.* **20 E8** 51 52N 6 2 E
Millinocket, *U.S.A.* **129 C6** 45 39N 68 43W
Millmerran, *Australia* **115 D5** 27 53 S 151 16 E
Mills L., *Canada* **130 A5** 61 30N 118 20W
Millsboro, *U.S.A.* **136 G4** 40 0N 80 0W
Milltown Malbay, *Ireland* **19 D2** 52 51N 9 25W
Millville, *U.S.A.* **134 F8** 39 24N 75 2W
Millwood L., *U.S.A.* **139 J8** 33 42N 93 58W
Milly-la-Forêt, *France* **23 D9** 48 24N 2 28 E
Milna, *Croatia* **39 E13** 43 20N 16 28 E
Milne →, *Australia* **114 C2** 21 10 S 137 33 E
Milne Inlet, *Canada* **127 A11** 72 30N 80 0W
Milnor, *U.S.A.* **138 B6** 46 16N 97 27W
Milo, *Canada* **130 C6** 50 34N 112 53W
Mílos, *Greece* **45 H6** 36 44N 24 25 E
Miloševo, *Serbia* **42 B5** 45 42N 20 20 E
Miłosław, *Poland* **47 C4** 52 12N 17 32 E
Milparinka P.O., *Australia* **115 D3** 29 46 S 141 57 E
Milroy, *U.S.A.* **141 E11** 39 30N 85 28W
Miltenberg, *Germany* **27 F5** 49 41N 9 13 E
Milton, *Canada* **136 C5** 43 31N 79 53W
Milton, *N.Z.* **119 G4** 46 7 S 169 59 E
Milton, *U.K.* **18 D4** 57 18N 4 32W
Milton, *Calif., U.S.A.* **144 G6** 38 3N 120 51W
Milton, *Fla., U.S.A.* **135 K2** 30 38N 87 3W
Milton, *Iowa, U.S.A.* **140 D4** 40 41N 92 10W
Milton, *Pa., U.S.A.* **136 F8** 41 1N 76 51W
Milton, *Wis., U.S.A.* **141 B8** 42 47N 88 56W
Milton-Freewater, *U.S.A.* **142 D4** 45 56N 118 23W
Milton Keynes, *U.K.* **17 E7** 52 3N 0 42W
Miltou, *Chad* **97 F3** 10 14N 17 26 E
Milverton, *Canada* **136 C4** 43 34N 80 55W
Milwaukee, *U.S.A.* **141 A9** 43 2N 87 55W
Milwaukee Deep, *Atl. Oc.* **8 G2** 19 50N 68 0W
Milwaukie, *U.S.A.* **144 E4** 45 27N 122 38W
Mim, *Ghana* **100 D4** 6 57N 2 33W
Mimizan, *France* **24 D2** 44 12N 1 13W
Mimon, *Czech.* **30 A7** 50 38N 14 43 E
Mimongo, *Gabon* **102 C2** 1 11 S 11 36 E
Mimoso, *Brazil* **155 E2** 15 10 S 48 5W
Min Chiang →, *China* **69 E12** 26 0N 119 35 E
Min Jiang →, *China* **68 C5** 28 45N 104 40 E
Min-Kush, *Kirghizia* **55 C7** 41 40N 74 28 E
Min Xian, *China* **66 G3** 34 25N 104 5 E
Mina, *U.S.A.* **143 G4** 38 24N 118 7W
Mina Pirquitas, *Argentina* **158 A2** 22 40 S 66 30W
Mīnā Su'ud, *Si. Arabia* **85 D6** 28 45N 48 28 E
Mīnā'al Aḥmadī, *Kuwait* **85 D6** 29 5N 48 10 E
Mīnāb, *Iran* **85 E8** 27 10N 57 1 E
Minago →, *Canada* **131 C9** 54 33N 98 59W
Minakami, *Japan* **63 A10** 36 49N 138 59 E
Minaki, *Canada* **131 D10** 49 59N 94 40W
Minakuchi, *Japan* **63 C8** 34 58N 136 10 E
Minamata, *Japan* **62 E2** 32 10N 130 30 E
Minami-Tori-Shima, *Pac. Oc.* **122 E7** 24 0N 153 45 E
Minas, *Uruguay* **159 C4** 34 20 S 55 10W
Minas, Sierra de las, *Guatemala* **148 C2** 15 9N 89 31W
Minas Basin, *Canada* **129 C7** 45 20N 64 12W
Minas de Rio Tinto, *Spain* **37 H4** 37 42N 6 35W
Minas de San Quintín, *Spain* **37 G6** 38 49N 4 23W
Minas Gerais □, *Brazil* **155 E2** 18 50 S 46 0W
Minas Novas, *Brazil* **155 E3** 17 15 S 42 36W
Minatitlán, *Mexico* **147 D6** 17 58N 94 35W
Minbu, *Burma* **78 E5** 20 10N 94 52 E
Minbya, *Burma* **78 E4** 20 22N 93 16 E
Mincio →, *Italy* **38 C7** 45 4N 10 59 E
Mindanao, *Phil.* **71 H5** 8 0N 125 0 E
Mindanao Sea = Bohol Sea, *Phil.* **71 G5** 9 0N 124 0 E
Mindanao Trench, *Pac. Oc.* **70 E5** 12 0N 126 6 E
Mindel →, *Germany* **27 G6** 48 31N 10 23 E
Mindelheim, *Germany* **27 G6** 48 4N 10 30 E
Minden, *Canada* **136 B6** 44 55N 78 43W
Minden, *Germany* **26 C4** 52 18N 8 45 E
Minden, *La., U.S.A.* **139 J8** 32 37N 93 17W
Minden, *Nev., U.S.A.* **144 G7** 38 57N 119 46W
Mindiptana, *Indonesia* **73 C6** 5 55 S 140 22 E
Mindon, *Burma* **78 F5** 19 21N 94 44 E
Mindoro, *Phil.* **70 E3** 13 0N 121 0 E
Mindoro Occidental □, *Phil.* **70 E3** 13 0N 120 55 E
Mindoro Oriental □, *Phil.* **70 E3** 13 0N 121 5 E
Mindoro Str., *Phil.* **70 E3** 12 30N 120 30 E
Mindouli, *Congo* **103 C2** 4 12 S 14 28 E
Mine, *Japan* **62 C3** 34 12N 131 7 E
Minehead, *U.K.* **17 F4** 51 12N 3 29W
Mineiros, *Brazil* **157 D7** 17 34 S 52 34W
Mineola, *U.S.A.* **139 J7** 32 40N 95 29W
Mineral King, *U.S.A.* **144 J8** 36 27N 118 36W
Mineral Point, *U.S.A.* **140 B6** 42 52N 90 11W
Mineral Wells, *U.S.A.* **139 J5** 32 48N 98 7W
Mineralnyye Vody, *Russia* **53 D10** 44 15N 43 8 E
Minersville, *Pa., U.S.A.* **137 F8** 40 41N 76 16W
Minersville, *Utah, U.S.A.* **143 G7** 38 13N 112 56W
Minerva, *U.S.A.* **136 F3** 40 44N 81 6W
Minervino Murge, *Italy* **41 A9** 41 6N 16 4 E
Minetto, *U.S.A.* **137 C8** 43 24N 76 28W
Mingan, *Canada* **129 B7** 50 20N 64 0W
Mingary, *Australia* **116 B4** 32 8 S 140 45 E
Mingechaur, *Azerbaijan* **53 F12** 40 45N 47 0 E
Mingechaurskoye Vdkhr., *Azerbaijan* **53 F12** 40 56N 47 20 E
Mingela, *Australia* **114 B4** 19 52 S 146 38 E
Mingenew, *Australia* **113 E2** 29 12 S 115 21 E
Mingera Cr. →, *Australia* **114 C2** 20 38 S 137 45 E
Minggang, *China* **69 A10** 32 24N 114 3 E
Mingin, *Burma* **78 D5** 22 50N 94 30 E
Minglanilla, *Spain* **34 F3** 39 34N 1 38W
Minglun, *China* **68 E7** 25 10N 108 21 E
Mingorria, *Spain* **36 E6** 40 45N 4 40W
Mingt'iehkaitafan = Mintaka Pass, *Pakistan* **81 A6** 37 0N 74 58 E
Mingxi, *China* **69 D11** 26 18N 117 12 E
Mingyuegue, *China* **67 C15** 43 2N 128 50 E
Minhou, *China* **69 E12** 26 0N 119 15 E
Minićevo, *Serbia* **42 D7** 43 42N 22 18 E
Minidoka, *U.S.A.* **142 E7** 42 45N 113 29W
Minier, *U.S.A.* **140 D7** 40 26N 89 19W
Minigwal, L., *Australia* **113 E3** 29 31 S 123 14 E
Minilya, *Australia* **113 D1** 23 55 S 114 0 E
Minilya →, *Australia* **113 D1** 23 45 S 114 0 E
Mininera, *Australia* **116 D5** 37 37 S 142 58 E
Minipi, L., *Canada* **129 B7** 52 25N 60 45W
Minj, *Papua N. G.* **120 C3** 5 54 S 144 37 E
Mink L., *Canada* **130 A5** 61 54N 117 40W
Minlaton, *Australia* **116 C2** 34 45 S 137 35 E
Minna, *Nigeria* **101 D6** 9 37N 6 30 E
Minneapolis, *Kans., U.S.A.* **138 F6** 39 8N 97 42W
Minneapolis, *Minn., U.S.A.* **138 C8** 44 59N 93 16W
Minnedosa, *Canada* **131 C9** 50 14N 99 50W
Minnesota □, *U.S.A.* **138 B7** 46 0N 94 15W
Minnesund, *Norway* **14 D5** 60 23N 11 14 E
Minnie Creek, *Australia* **113 D2** 24 3 S 115 42 E
Minnipa, *Australia* **115 E2** 32 51 S 135 9 E
Minnitaki L., *Canada* **128 C1** 49 57N 92 10W
Mino, *Japan* **63 B8** 35 32N 136 55 E
Miño →, *Spain* **36 D2** 41 52N 8 40W
Mino-Kamo, *Japan* **63 B9** 35 23N 137 2 E
Mino-Mikawa-Kōgen, *Japan* **63 B9** 35 10N 137 23 E
Minoa, *Greece* **45 J7** 35 6N 25 45 E
Minobu, *Japan* **63 B10** 35 22N 138 26 E
Minobu-Sanchi, *Japan* **63 B10** 35 14N 138 20 E
Minonk, *U.S.A.* **140 D7** 40 54N 89 2W
Minooka, *U.S.A.* **141 C8** 41 27N 88 16W
Minorca = Menorca, *Spain* **33 B11** 40 0N 4 0 E
Minore, *Australia* **117 B8** 32 14 S 148 27 E
Minot, *U.S.A.* **138 A4** 48 14N 101 18W
Minqin, *China* **66 E2** 38 38N 103 20 E
Minqing, *China* **69 D12** 26 15N 118 50 E
Minsen, *Germany* **26 B3** 53 43N 7 58 E
Minsk, *Belorussia* **50 E5** 53 52N 27 30 E
Mińsk Mazowiecki, *Poland* **47 C8** 52 10N 21 33 E
Minster, *U.S.A.* **141 D12** 40 24N 84 23W
Mintaka Pass, *Pakistan* **81 A6** 37 0N 74 58 E
Minthami, *Burma* **78 D5** 23 55N 94 16 E
Minto, *U.S.A.* **126 B5** 64 53N 149 11W
Minton, *Canada* **131 D8** 49 10N 104 35W
Mintoum, *Gabon* **102 B2** 0 27N 12 16 E
Minturn, *U.S.A.* **142 G10** 39 35N 106 26W
Minturno, *Italy* **40 A6** 41 15N 13 43 E
Minûf, *Egypt* **94 H7** 30 26N 30 52 E
Minusinsk, *Russia* **57 D10** 53 50N 91 20 E
Minutang, *India* **78 A6** 28 15N 96 30 E
Minvoul, *Gabon* **102 B2** 2 9N 12 8 E
Minwakh, *Yemen* **87 C5** 16 48N 48 6 E
Minya el Qamh, *Egypt* **94 H7** 30 31N 31 21 E
Minyar, *Russia* **54 D5** 55 4N 57 33 E
Minyip, *Australia* **116 D5** 36 29 S 142 36 E
Mionica, *Serbia* **42 C5** 44 14N 20 6 E
Mir, *Niger* **97 F2** 14 5N 11 59 E
Mir-Bashir, *Azerbaijan* **53 F12** 40 20N 46 58 E
Mīr Kūh, *Iran* **85 E8** 26 22N 58 55 E
Mīr Shahdād, *Iran* **85 E8** 26 15N 58 29 E
Mira, *Italy* **39 C9** 45 26N 12 9 E
Mira, *Portugal* **36 E2** 40 26N 8 44W
Mira →, *Colombia* **152 C2** 1 36N 79 1W
Mira →, *Portugal* **37 H2** 37 43N 8 47W
Mira por vos Cay, *Bahamas* **149 B5** 22 9N 74 30W
Mīrābād, *Afghan.* **79 C1** 30 25N 61 50 E
Mirabella Eclano, *Italy* **41 A7** 41 3N 14 59 E
Miracema do Norte, *Brazil* **154 C2** 9 33 S 48 24W
Mirador, *Brazil* **154 C3** 6 22 S 44 22W
Miraflores, *Colombia* **152 C3** 1 25N 72 13W
Miraj, *India* **82 F2** 16 50N 74 45 E
Miram Shah, *Pakistan* **79 B3** 33 0N 70 2 E
Miramar, *Argentina* **158 D4** 38 15 S 57 50W
Miramar, *Mozam.* **105 C6** 23 50 S 35 35 E
Miramas, *France* **25 E8** 43 33N 4 59 E
Mirambeau, *France* **24 C3** 45 23N 0 35W
Miramichi B., *Canada* **129 C7** 47 15N 65 0W
Miramont-de-Guyenne, *France* **24 D4** 44 37N 0 21 E
Miranda, *Brazil* **157 E6** 20 10 S 56 15W
Miranda □, *Venezuela* **152 A4** 10 15N 66 25W
Miranda →, *Brazil* **157 D6** 19 25 S 57 20W
Miranda de Ebro, *Spain* **34 C2** 42 41N 2 57W
Miranda do Corvo, *Spain* **36 E2** 40 6N 8 20W
Miranda do Douro, *Portugal* **36 D4** 41 30N 6 16W
Mirande, *France* **24 E4** 43 31N 0 25 E
Mirandela, *Portugal* **36 D3** 41 32N 7 10W
Mirando City, *U.S.A.* **139 M5** 27 26N 99 0W
Mirandola, *Italy* **38 D8** 44 53N 11 2 E
Mirandópolis, *Brazil* **159 A5** 21 9 S 51 6W
Mirango, *Malawi* **107 E3** 13 32 S 34 58 E
Mirani, *Australia* **114 C4** 21 9 S 148 53 E
Mirano, *Italy* **39 C9** 45 29N 12 6 E
Mirassol, *Brazil* **159 A6** 20 46 S 49 28W
Mirbāṭ, *Oman* **87 C6** 17 0N 54 45 E
Mirboo North, *Australia* **117 E7** 38 24 S 146 10 E
Mirear, *Egypt* **94 C4** 23 15N 35 41 E
Mirebeau, *Côte-d'Or, France* **23 E12** 47 25N 5 20 E
Mirebeau, *Vienne, France* **22 F7** 46 49N 0 10 E
Mirecourt, *France* **23 D13** 48 20N 6 10 E
Mirgorod, *Ukraine* **50 G8** 49 58N 33 37 E
Miri, *Malaysia* **75 B4** 4 23N 113 59 E
Miriam Vale, *Australia* **114 C5** 24 20 S 151 33 E
Mirim, L., *S. Amer.* **159 C5** 32 45 S 52 50W
Mirimire, *Venezuela* **152 A4** 11 10N 68 43W
Miriti, *Brazil* **157 B6** 6 15 S 59 0W
Mirnyy, *Russia* **57 C12** 62 33N 113 53 E
Miroč, *Serbia* **42 C7** 44 32N 22 16 E
Mirond L., *Canada* **131 B8** 55 6N 102 47W
Mirosławiec, *Poland* **47 B3** 53 20N 16 5 E
Mirpur, *Pakistan* **79 B4** 33 32N 73 56 E
Mirpur Bibiwari, *Pakistan* **80 E2** 28 33N 67 44 E
Mirpur Khas, *Pakistan* **79 D3** 25 30N 69 0 E
Mirpur Sakro, *Pakistan* **80 G2** 24 33N 67 41 E
Mirria, *Niger* **97 F1** 13 43N 9 7 E
Mirror, *Canada* **130 C6** 52 30N 113 7W
Mîrşani, *Romania* **46 E4** 44 1N 23 59 E
Mirsk, *Poland* **47 E2** 50 58N 15 23 E
Miryang, *S. Korea* **67 G15** 35 31N 128 44 E
Mirzaani, *Georgia* **53 F12** 41 24N 46 5 E
Mirzapur, *India* **81 G10** 25 10N 82 34 E
Mirzapur-cum-Vindhyachal = Mirzapur, *India* **81 G10** 25 10N 82 34 E
Misamis Occidental □, *Phil.* **71 G4** 8 20N 123 42 E
Misamis Oriental □, *Phil.* **71 G5** 8 45N 125 0 E
Misantla, *Mexico* **147 D5** 19 56N 96 50W
Misawa, *Japan* **60 D10** 40 41N 141 24 E
Miscou I., *Canada* **129 C7** 47 57N 64 31W
Mish'āb, Ra'as al, *Si. Arabia* **85 D6** 28 15N 48 43 E
Mishagua →, *Peru* **156 C3** 11 12 S 72 58W
Mishan, *China* **65 B8** 45 37N 131 48 E
Mishawaka, *U.S.A.* **141 C10** 41 40N 86 11W
Mishbih, Gebel, *Egypt* **94 C3** 22 38N 34 44 E
Mishima, *Japan* **63 B10** 35 10N 138 52 E
Mishkino, *Russia* **54 D8** 55 20N 63 55 E
Mishmi Hills, *India* **78 A5** 29 0N 96 0 E
Misilmeri, *Italy* **40 D6** 38 2N 13 25 E
Misima I., *Papua N. G.* **120 F7** 10 40 S 152 45 E
Misión, *Mexico* **145 N10** 32 6N 116 53W
Misión Fagnano, *Argentina* **160 D3** 54 32 S 67 17W
Misiones □, *Argentina* **159 B5** 27 0 S 55 0W
Misiones □, *Paraguay* **158 B4** 27 0 S 56 0W
Miskah, *Si. Arabia* **84 E4** 24 49N 42 56 E
Miskitos, Cayos, *Nic.* **148 D3** 14 26N 82 50W
Miskolc, *Hungary* **31 C13** 48 7N 20 50 E
Misoke, *Zaïre* **106 C2** 0 42 S 28 2 E
Misool, *Indonesia* **73 B4** 1 52 S 130 10 E
Misrātah, *Libya* **96 B3** 32 24N 15 3 E
Misrātah □, *Libya* **96 C3** 29 0N 16 0 E
Missanabie, *Canada* **128 C3** 48 20N 84 6W
Missão Velha, *Brazil* **154 C4** 7 15 S 39 10W
Missinaibi →, *Canada* **128 B3** 50 43N 81 29W
Missinaibi L., *Canada* **128 C3** 48 23N 83 40W
Mission, *S. Dak., U.S.A.* **138 D4** 43 18N 100 39W
Mission, *Tex., U.S.A.* **139 M5** 26 13N 98 20W
Mission City, *Canada* **130 D4** 49 10N 122 15W
Mission Viejo, *U.S.A.* **145 M9** 33 36N 117 40W
Missisa L., *Canada* **128 B2** 52 20N 85 7W
Missisagi →, *Canada* **128 C3** 46 15N 83 9W
Mississinewa Res., *U.S.A.* **141 D10** 40 46N 86 3W
Mississippi □, *U.S.A.* **139 J10** 33 0N 90 0W
Mississippi →, *U.S.A.* **139 L10** 29 9N 89 15W
Mississippi L., *Canada* **137 A8** 45 5N 76 10W
Mississippi River Delta, *U.S.A.* **139 L9** 29 10N 89 15W
Mississippi Sd., *U.S.A.* **139 K10** 30 20N 89 0W
Missoula, *U.S.A.* **142 C6** 46 52N 114 1W
Missour, *Morocco* **98 B4** 33 3N 4 0W
Missouri □, *U.S.A.* **138 F8** 38 25N 92 30W
Missouri →, *U.S.A.* **138 F9** 38 49N 90 7W
Missouri Valley, *U.S.A.* **138 E7** 41 34N 95 53W
Mist, *U.S.A.* **144 E3** 45 59N 123 15W
Mistake B., *Canada* **131 A10** 62 8N 93 0W
Mistassini →, *Canada* **129 C5** 48 42N 72 20W
Mistassini L., *Canada* **128 B5** 51 0N 73 30W
Mistastin L., *Canada* **129 A7** 55 57N 63 20W
Mistatim, *Canada* **131 C8** 52 52N 103 22W
Mistelbach, *Austria* **31 C9** 48 34N 16 34 E
Misterbianco, *Italy* **41 E8** 37 32N 15 2 E
Mistretta, *Italy* **41 E7** 37 56N 14 20 E
Misty L., *Canada* **131 B8** 58 53N 101 40W
Misugi, *Japan* **63 C8** 34 31N 136 16 E
Misumi, *Japan* **62 E2** 32 37N 130 27 E
Misurata = Misrātah, *Libya* **96 B3** 32 24N 15 3 E
Mît Ghamr, *Egypt* **94 H7** 30 42N 31 12 E
Mitaka, *Japan* **63 B11** 35 40N 139 33 E
Mitan, *Uzbekistan* **55 C3** 40 5N 66 35 E
Mitatib, *Sudan* **95 D4** 15 59N 36 12 E
Mitchell, *Australia* **115 D4** 26 29 S 147 58 E
Mitchell, *Canada* **136 C3** 43 28N 81 12W
Mitchell, *Ind., U.S.A.* **141 F10** 38 44N 86 28W
Mitchell, *Nebr., U.S.A.* **138 E3** 41 57N 103 49W
Mitchell, *Oreg., U.S.A.* **142 D3** 44 34N 120 9W
Mitchell, *S. Dak., U.S.A.* **138 D5** 43 43N 98 2W
Mitchell →, *Australia* **114 B3** 15 12 S 141 35 E
Mitchell, Mt., *U.S.A.* **135 H4** 35 46N 82 16W
Mitchell Ras., *Australia* **114 A2** 12 49 S 135 36 E
Mitchelstown, *Ireland* **19 D3** 52 16N 8 18W
Mitha Tiwana, *Pakistan* **80 C5** 32 13N 72 6 E
Míthimna, *Greece* **44 E8** 39 20N 26 12 E
Mitiamo, *Australia* **116 D6** 36 12 S 144 15 E
Mitilíni, *Greece* **45 E8** 39 6N 26 35 E
Mitilinoí, *Greece* **45 G8** 37 42N 26 56 E
Mito, *Japan* **63 A12** 36 20N 140 30 E
Mitre, Mt., *N.Z.* **118 G4** 40 50 S 175 30 E
Mitsinjo, *Madag.* **105 B8** 16 1 S 45 52 E
Mitsiwa, *Eritrea* **95 D4** 15 35N 39 25 E
Mitsiwa Channel, *Eritrea* **95 D5** 15 30N 40 0 E
Mitsukaidō, *Japan* **63 A11** 36 1N 139 59 E
Mittagong, *Australia* **117 C9** 34 28 S 150 29 E
Mittelland, *Switz.* **28 C4** 46 50N 7 23 E
Mittelland Kanal, *Germany* **26 C3** 52 23N 7 45 E
Mittenwalde, *Germany* **26 C9** 52 16N 13 33 E
Mitterteich, *Germany* **27 F8** 49 57N 12 15 E
Mittweida, *Germany* **26 E8** 50 59N 12 59 E
Mitú, *Colombia* **152 C3** 1 8N 70 3W
Mituas, *Colombia* **152 C4** 3 52N 68 49W
Mitumba, *Tanzania* **106 D3** 7 8 S 31 2 E
Mitumba, Chaîne des, *Zaïre* **106 D2** 7 0 S 27 30 E
Mitumba Mts. = Mitumba, Chaîne des, *Zaïre* **106 D2** 7 0 S 27 30 E
Mitwaba, *Zaïre* **107 D2** 8 2 S 27 17 E
Mityana, *Uganda* **106 B3** 0 23N 32 2 E
Mitzic, *Gabon* **102 B2** 0 45N 11 40 E
Miura, *Japan* **63 B11** 35 12N 139 40 E
Mixteco →, *Mexico* **147 D5** 18 11N 98 30W
Miyagi □, *Japan* **60 E10** 38 15N 140 45 E
Miyâh, W. el →, *Egypt* **94 B3** 25 0N 33 23 E
Miyah, W. el →, *Syria* **84 C3** 34 44N 39 57 E
Miyake-Jima, *Japan* **63 C11** 34 5N 139 30 E
Miyako, *Japan* **60 E10** 39 40N 141 59 E
Miyako-Jima, *Japan* **61 M2** 24 45N 125 20 E
Miyako-Rettō, *Japan* **61 M2** 24 24N 125 0 E
Miyakonojō, *Japan* **62 F3** 31 40N 131 5 E
Miyanojō, *Japan* **62 F2** 31 54N 130 27 E
Miyanoura-Dake, *Japan* **61 J5** 30 20N 130 31 E
Miyata, *Japan* **62 D2** 33 49N 130 42 E
Miyazaki, *Japan* **62 F3** 31 56N 131 30 E
Miyazaki □, *Japan* **62 E3** 32 30N 131 30 E
Miyazu, *Japan* **63 B7** 35 35N 135 10 E
Miyet, Bahr el = Dead Sea, *Asia* **91 D4** 31 30N 35 30 E
Miyi, *China* **68 D4** 26 47N 102 9 E
Miyoshi, *Japan* **62 C4** 34 48N 132 51 E
Miyun, *China* **66 D9** 40 28N 116 50 E
Miyun Shuiku, *China* **67 D9** 40 30N 117 0 E
Mizamis = Ozamiz, *Phil.* **71 G4** 8 15N 123 50 E
Mizdah, *Libya* **96 B2** 31 30N 13 0 E
Mizen Hd., *Cork, Ireland* **19 E2** 51 27N 9 50W
Mizen Hd., *Wick., Ireland* **19 D5** 52 52N 6 4W
Mizhi, *China* **66 F6** 37 47N 110 12 E
Mizil, *Romania* **46 E7** 44 59N 26 29 E
Mizoram □, *India* **78 D4** 23 30N 92 40 E
Mizpe Ramon, *Israel* **91 E3** 30 34N 34 49 E
Mizuho, *Japan* **63 B7** 35 6N 135 17 E
Mizunami, *Japan* **63 B9** 35 22N 137 15 E
Mizusawa, *Japan* **60 E10** 39 8N 141 8 E
Mjöbäck, *Sweden* **15 G6** 57 28N 12 53 E
Mjölby, *Sweden* **15 F9** 58 20N 15 10 E
Mjörn, *Sweden* **15 G6** 57 55N 12 25 E
Mjøsa, *Norway* **14 D5** 60 48N 11 0 E
Mkata, *Tanzania* **106 D4** 5 45 S 38 20 E
Mkokotoni, *Tanzania* **106 D4** 5 55 S 39 15 E
Mkomazi, *Tanzania* **106 C4** 4 40 S 38 7 E
Mkomazi →, *S. Africa* **105 E5** 30 12 S 30 50 E
Mkulwe, *Tanzania* **107 D3** 8 37 S 32 20 E
Mkumbi, Ras, *Tanzania* **106 D4** 7 38 S 39 55 E
Mkushi, *Zambia* **107 E2** 14 25 S 29 15 E
Mkushi River, *Zambia* **107 E2** 13 32 S 29 45 E
Mkuze, *S. Africa* **105 D5** 27 10 S 32 0 E
Mkuze →, *S. Africa* **105 D5** 27 45 S 32 30 E
Mladá Boleslav, *Czech.* **30 A7** 50 27N 14 53 E
Mladenovac, *Serbia* **42 C5** 44 28N 20 44 E
Mlala Hills, *Tanzania* **106 D3** 6 50 S 31 40 E
Mlange, *Malawi* **107 F4** 16 2 S 35 33 E
Mlava →, *Serbia* **42 C6** 44 45N 21 13 E
Mława, *Poland* **47 B7** 53 9N 20 25 E
Mlinište, *Bos.-H.* **39 D13** 44 15N 16 50 E
Mljet, *Croatia* **42 E2** 42 43N 17 30 E
Mljetski Kanal, *Croatia* **42 E2** 42 48N 17 35 E
Młynary, *Poland* **47 A6** 54 12N 19 46 E
Mmabatho, *S. Africa* **104 D4** 25 49 S 25 30 E
Mme, *Cameroon* **101 D7** 6 18N 10 14 E
Mo i Rana, *Norway* **12 C13** 66 15N 14 7 E
Moa, *Indonesia* **72 C3** 8 0 S 128 0 E
Moa →, *S. Leone* **100 D2** 6 59N 11 36W
Moab, *U.S.A.* **143 G9** 38 35N 109 33W
Moabi, *Gabon* **102 C2** 2 24 S 10 59 E
Moaco →, *Brazil* **156 B4** 7 41 S 68 18W
Moala, *Fiji* **121 B2** 18 36 S 179 53 E
Moalie Park, *Australia* **115 D3** 29 42 S 143 3 E
Moaña, *Spain* **36 C2** 42 18N 8 43W
Moba, *Zaïre* **106 D2** 7 0 S 29 48 E
Mobara, *Japan* **63 B12** 35 25N 140 18 E
Mobārakābād, *Iran* **85 D7** 28 24N 53 20 E
Mobārakīyeh, *Iran* **85 C6** 35 5N 51 47 E
Mobaye, *C.A.R.* **102 B4** 4 25N 21 5 E
Mobayi, *Zaïre* **102 B4** 4 15N 21 8 E
Moberly, *U.S.A.* **140 E4** 39 25N 92 26W
Moberly →, *Canada* **130 B4** 56 12N 120 55W
Mobile, *U.S.A.* **135 K1** 30 41N 88 3W
Mobile B., *U.S.A.* **135 K2** 30 30N 88 0W
Mobridge, *U.S.A.* **138 C4** 45 32N 100 26W
Mobutu Sese Seko, L., *Africa* **106 B3** 1 30N 31 0 E
Moc Chau, *Vietnam* **76 B5** 20 50N 104 38 E
Moc Hoa, *Vietnam* **77 G5** 10 46N 105 56 E
Mocabe, Sa. de, *Angola* **103 D3** 7 12 S 15 0 E
Mocabe Kasari, *Zaïre* **107 D2** 9 58 S 26 12 E
Mocajuba, *Brazil* **154 B2** 2 35 S 49 30W
Moçambique, *Mozam.* **107 F5** 15 3 S 40 42 E
Moçâmedes = Namibe, *Angola* **103 F2** 15 7 S 12 11 E
Mocapra →, *Venezuela* **152 B4** 7 56N 66 46W
Mocha, I., *Chile* **160 A2** 38 22 S 73 56W
Mochudi, *Botswana* **104 C4** 24 27 S 26 7 E
Mocimboa da Praia, *Mozam.* **107 E5** 11 25 S 40 20 E
Mociu, *Romania* **46 C5** 46 46N 24 3 E
Moclips, *U.S.A.* **144 C2** 47 14N 124 13W
Mocoa, *Colombia* **152 C2** 1 7N 76 35W
Mococa, *Brazil* **159 A6** 21 28 S 47 0W
Mocorito, *Mexico* **146 B3** 25 30N 107 53W
Moctezuma, *Mexico* **146 B3** 29 50N 109 0W
Moctezuma →, *Mexico* **147 C5** 21 59N 98 34W
Mocuba, *Mozam.* **107 F4** 16 54 S 36 57 E
Mocúzari, Presa, *Mexico* **146 B3** 27 10N 109 10W
Moda, *Burma* **78 C6** 24 22N 96 29 E
Modane, *France* **25 C10** 45 12N 6 40 E
Modasa, *India* **80 H5** 23 30N 73 21 E
Modave, *Belgium* **21 H6** 50 27N 5 18 E
Modder →, *S. Africa* **104 D3** 29 2 S 24 37 E
Modderrivier, *S. Africa* **104 D3** 29 2 S 24 38 E
Módena, *Italy* **38 D7** 44 39N 10 55 E
Modena, *U.S.A.* **143 H7** 37 48N 113 56W
Modesto, *U.S.A.* **144 H6** 37 39N 121 0W
Módica, *Italy* **41 F7** 36 52N 14 45 E
Modigliana, *Italy* **39 D8** 44 9N 11 48 E
Modjamboli, *Zaïre* **102 B4** 2 28N 22 6 E
Modlin, *Poland* **47 C7** 52 24N 20 41 E
Mödling, *Austria* **31 C9** 48 5N 16 17 E
Modo, *Sudan* **95 F3** 5 31N 30 33 E
Modra, *Slovak Rep.* **31 C10** 48 19N 17 20 E

236 Montmoreau-St.-Cybard

Montmoreau-St.-Cybard, France 24 C4 45 23N 0 8 E
Montmorency, Canada 129 C5 46 53N 71 11W
Montmorillon, France 24 B4 46 26N 0 50 E
Montmort, France 23 D10 48 55N 3 49 E
Monto, Australia 114 C5 24 52 S 151 6 E
Montoir-sur-le-Loir, France 22 E7 47 45N 0 52 E
Montório al Vomano, Italy 39 F10 42 35N 13 38 E
Montoro, Spain 37 G6 38 1N 4 27W
Montour Falls, U.S.A. 136 D8 42 21N 76 51W
Montpelier, Idaho, U.S.A. 142 E8 42 19N 111 18W
Montpelier, Ind., U.S.A. 141 D11 40 33N 85 17W
Montpelier, Ohio, U.S.A. 141 C12 41 35N 84 37W
Montpelier, Vt., U.S.A. 137 B12 44 16N 72 35W
Montpellier, France 24 E7 43 37N 3 52 E
Montpezat-de-Quercy, France 24 D5 44 15N 1 30 E
Montpon-Ménestérol, France 24 D4 45 0N 0 11 E
Montréal, Canada 128 C5 45 31N 73 34W
Montréal, France 24 E6 43 13N 2 8 E
Montreal L., Canada 131 C7 54 20N 105 45W
Montreal Lake, Canada 131 C7 54 3N 105 46W
Montredon-Labessonnié, France 24 E6 43 45N 2 18 E
Montréjeau, France 24 E4 43 6N 0 35 E
Montrésor, France 22 E8 47 10N 1 10 E
Montreuil, France 23 B8 50 27N 1 45 E
Montreuil-Bellay, France 22 E6 47 8N 0 9W
Montreux, Switz. 28 D3 46 26N 6 55 E
Montrevault, France 22 E5 47 17N 1 2W
Montrevel-en-Bresse, France 25 B9 46 21N 5 8 E
Montrichard, France 22 E8 47 20N 1 10 E
Montrose, U.K. 18 E6 56 43N 2 28W
Montrose, Colo., U.S.A. 143 G10 38 29N 107 53W
Montrose, Pa., U.S.A. 137 E9 41 50N 75 53W
Montrose, L., U.S.A. 140 F3 38 18N 93 50W
Monts, Pte. des, Canada 129 C6 49 20N 67 12W
Monts-sur-Guesnes, France 22 F7 46 55N 0 13 E
Montsalvy, France 24 D6 44 41N 2 30 E
Montsant, Sierra de, Spain 34 D5 41 17N 1 0 E
Montsauche, France 23 E11 47 13N 4 2 E
Montsech, Sierra del, Spain 34 C5 42 0N 0 45 E
Montseny, Spain 34 D2 41 55N 2 25W
Montserrat, Spain 34 D6 41 36N 1 49 E
Montserrat ■, W. Indies 149 C7 16 40N 62 10W
Montuenga, Spain 36 D6 41 3N 4 38W
Montuiri, Spain 33 B9 39 34N 2 59 E
Monveda, Zaïre 102 B4 2 52N 21 30 E
Monyo, Burma 78 G5 17 59N 95 30 E
Monywa, Burma 78 D5 22 7N 95 11 E
Monza, Italy 38 C6 45 35N 9 15 E
Monze, Zambia 107 F2 16 17 S 27 29 E
Monze, C., Pakistan 79 D2 24 47N 66 37 E
Monzón, Spain 34 D5 41 52N 0 10 E
Mooi River, S. Africa 105 D4 29 13 S 29 50 E
Mook, Neths. 20 E7 51 46N 5 54 E
Mo'oka, Japan 63 A12 36 26N 140 1 E
Moolawatana, Australia 115 D2 29 55 S 139 45 E
Mooleulooloo, Australia 116 A4 31 36 S 140 32 E
Mooliabeenee, Australia 113 F2 31 20 S 116 2 E
Mooloogool, Australia 113 E2 26 2 S 119 5 E
Moomin Cr. →, Australia 115 D4 29 44 S 149 20 E
Moonah →, Australia 114 C2 22 3 S 138 33 E
Moonbeam, Canada 128 C3 49 20N 82 10W
Moonda, L., Australia 114 D3 25 52 S 140 25 E
Moonie, Australia 115 D5 27 46 S 150 20 E
Moonie →, Australia 115 D4 29 19 S 148 43 E
Moonta, Australia 116 C2 34 6 S 137 32 E
Moora, Australia 113 F2 30 37 S 115 58 E
Mooraberree, Australia 114 D3 25 13 S 140 54 E
Moorarie, Australia 113 E2 25 56 S 117 35 E
Moorcroft, U.S.A. 138 C2 44 16N 104 57W
Moore →, Australia 113 F2 31 22 S 115 30 E
Moore, L., Australia 113 E2 29 50 S 117 35 E
Moore Reefs, Australia 114 B4 16 0 S 149 5 E
Moorefield, U.S.A. 134 F6 39 5N 78 59W
Moores Res., U.S.A. 137 B13 44 45N 71 50W
Mooresville, Ind., U.S.A. 141 E10 39 37N 86 22W
Mooresville, N.C., U.S.A. 135 H5 35 35N 80 48W
Moorfoot Hills, U.K. 18 F5 55 44N 3 8W
Moorhead, U.S.A. 138 B6 46 53N 96 45W
Moorland, Australia 117 A10 31 46 S 152 38 E
Mooroopna, Australia 117 D6 36 25 S 145 22 E
Moorpark, U.S.A. 145 L8 34 17N 118 53W
Moorreesburg, S. Africa 104 E2 33 6 S 18 38 E
Moorslede, Belgium 21 G2 50 54N 3 4 E
Moosburg, Germany 27 G7 48 28N 11 57 E
Moose →, Canada 128 B3 51 20N 80 25W
Moose Factory, Canada 128 B3 51 16N 80 32W
Moose I., Canada 131 C9 51 42N 97 10W
Moose Jaw, Canada 131 C7 50 24N 105 30W
Moose Jaw →, Canada 131 C7 50 34N 105 18W
Moose Lake, Canada 131 C8 53 43N 100 20W
Moose Lake, U.S.A. 138 B8 46 27N 92 46W
Moose Mountain Cr. →, Canada 131 D8 49 13N 102 12W
Moose Mountain Prov. Park, Canada 131 D8 49 48N 102 25W
Moose River, Canada 128 B3 50 48N 81 17W
Moosehead L., U.S.A. 129 C6 45 38N 69 40W
Moosomin, Canada 131 C8 50 9N 101 40W
Moosonee, Canada 128 B3 51 17N 80 39W
Moosup, U.S.A. 137 E13 41 43N 71 53W
Mopeia Velha, Mozam. 107 F4 17 30 S 35 40 E
Mopipi, Botswana 104 C3 21 6 S 24 55 E
Mopoi, C.A.R. 102 A5 5 6N 26 54 E
Mopti, Mali 100 C4 14 30N 4 0W
Moqatta, Sudan 95 E4 14 38N 35 50 E
Moquegua, Peru 156 D3 17 15 S 70 46W
Moquegua □, Peru 156 D3 16 50 S 70 55W
Mór, Hungary 31 D11 47 25N 18 12 E
Móra, Portugal 37 G2 38 55N 8 10W
Mora, Sweden 13 F13 61 2N 14 38 E
Mora, Minn., U.S.A. 138 C8 45 53N 93 18W
Mora, N. Mex., U.S.A. 143 J11 35 58N 105 20W
Mora de Ebro, Spain 34 D5 41 6N 0 38 E
Mora de Rubielos, Spain 34 E4 40 15N 0 45W
Mora la Nueva, Spain 34 D5 41 7N 0 39 E
Morača →, Montenegro 42 E4 42 20N 19 9 E
Morada Nova, Brazil 154 C4 5 7 S 38 23W
Morada Nova de Minas, Brazil 155 E2 18 37 S 45 22W
Moradabad, India 81 E8 28 50N 78 50 E
Morafenobe, Madag. 105 B7 17 50 S 44 53 E
Morąg, Poland 47 B6 53 55N 19 56 E
Moral de Calatrava, Spain 35 G1 38 51N 3 33W
Moraleja, Spain 36 E4 40 6N 6 43W
Morales, Colombia 152 C2 2 45N 76 38W
Moramanga, Madag. 105 B8 18 56 S 48 12 E
Moran, Kans., U.S.A. 139 G7 37 55N 95 10W
Moran, Wyo., U.S.A. 142 E8 43 53N 110 37W
Moranbah, Australia 114 C4 22 1 S 148 6 E
Morano Cálabro, Italy 41 C9 39 51N 16 8 E
Morant Cays, Jamaica 148 C4 17 22N 76 0W
Morant Pt., Jamaica 148 C4 17 55N 76 12W
Morar, L., U.K. 18 E3 56 57N 5 40W
Moratalla, Spain 35 G3 38 14N 1 49W
Moratuwa, Sri Lanka 83 L4 6 45N 79 55 E
Morava →, Europe 31 C9 48 10N 16 59 E
Moravia, U.S.A. 140 D4 40 53N 92 49W
Moravian Hts. = Ceskomoravská Vrchovina, Czech. 30 B8 49 30N 15 40 E
Moravica →, Serbia 42 D5 43 52N 20 8 E
Moravice →, Czech. 31 B10 49 50N 17 43 E
Moraviţa, Romania 46 E2 45 17N 21 14 E
Moravská Třebová, Czech. 31 B9 49 45N 16 40 E
Moravské Budějovice, Czech. 30 B8 49 4N 15 49 E
Morawa, Australia 113 E2 29 13 S 116 0 E
Morawhanna, Guyana 153 B6 8 30N 59 40W
Moray Firth, U.K. 18 D5 57 50N 3 30W
Morbach, Germany 27 F3 49 48N 7 7 E
Morbegno, Italy 38 B6 46 8N 9 34 E
Morbi, India 80 H4 22 50N 70 42 E
Morbihan □, France 22 E4 47 55N 2 50W
Morcenx, France 24 D3 44 3N 0 55W
Mordelles, France 22 D5 48 5N 1 52W
Morden, Canada 131 D9 49 15N 98 10W
Mordovian Republic □, Russia 51 D14 54 20N 44 30 E
Mordovo, Russia 51 E12 52 6N 40 50 E
Mordvinia = Mordovian Republic □, Russia 51 D14 54 20N 44 30 E
Mordy, Poland 47 C9 52 13N 22 31 E
Møre og Romsdal fylke □, Norway 14 B2 62 30N 8 0 E
Morea, Australia 116 D4 36 45 S 141 18 E
Morea, Greece 10 H10 37 45N 22 10 E
Moreau →, U.S.A. 138 C4 45 18N 100 43W
Morecambe, U.K. 16 C5 54 5N 2 52W
Morecambe B., U.K. 16 C5 54 7N 3 0W
Moree, Australia 115 D4 29 28 S 149 54 E
Morehead, Papua N. G. 120 E1 8 41 S 141 41 E
Morehead, U.S.A. 141 F13 38 11N 83 26W
Morehead City, U.S.A. 135 H7 34 43N 76 43W
Morelia, Mexico 146 D4 19 40N 101 11W
Morella, Australia 114 C3 23 0 S 143 52 E
Morella, Spain 34 E4 40 35N 0 5W
Morelos, Mexico 146 B3 26 42N 107 40W
Morelos □, Mexico 147 D5 18 40N 99 10W
Morena, Sierra, Spain 37 G7 38 20N 4 0W
Morenci, Ariz., U.S.A. 143 K9 33 5N 109 22W
Morenci, Mich., U.S.A. 141 C12 41 43N 84 13W
Moreni, Romania 46 E6 44 59N 25 36 E
Morero, Bolivia 157 C4 11 9 S 66 15W
Moreru →, Brazil 157 C6 10 10 S 59 15W
Moresby I., Canada 130 C2 52 30N 131 40W
Morestel, France 25 C9 45 40N 5 28 E
Moret-sur-Loing, France 23 D9 48 22N 2 58 E
Moreton, Australia 114 A3 12 22 S 142 40 E
Moreton I., Australia 115 D5 27 10 S 153 25 E
Moreuil, France 23 C9 49 46N 2 30 E
Morey, Spain 33 B10 39 44N 3 20 E
Morez, France 25 B10 46 31N 6 2 E
Morgan, Australia 116 C3 34 2 S 139 35 E
Morgan, U.S.A. 142 F8 41 2N 111 41W
Morgan City, U.S.A. 139 L9 29 42N 91 12W
Morgan Hill, U.S.A. 144 H5 37 8N 121 39W
Morgan Vale, Australia 116 B4 33 10 S 140 32 E
Morganfield, U.S.A. 134 G2 37 41N 87 55W
Morganton, U.S.A. 135 H5 35 45N 81 41W
Morgantown, Ind., U.S.A. 141 E10 39 22N 86 16W
Morgantown, W. Va., U.S.A. 134 F6 39 38N 79 57W
Morgat, France 22 D2 48 15N 4 32W
Morgenzon, S. Africa 105 D4 26 45 S 29 36 E
Morges, Switz. 28 C2 46 31N 6 29 E
Morghak, Iran 85 D8 29 7N 57 54 E
Morhange, France 23 D13 48 55N 6 38 E
Mori, Italy 38 C7 45 51N 10 59 E
Morialmée, Belgium 21 H5 50 17N 4 35 E
Morice L., Canada 130 C3 53 50N 127 40W
Morichal, Colombia 152 C3 2 10N 70 34W
Morichal Largo →, Venezuela 153 B5 9 27N 62 25W
Moriguchi, Japan 63 C7 34 44N 135 34 E
Moriki, Nigeria 101 C6 12 52N 6 30 E
Morinville, Canada 130 C6 53 49N 113 41W
Morioka, Japan 60 E10 39 45N 141 8 E
Moris, Mexico 146 B3 28 8N 108 32W
Morisset, Australia 117 B9 33 6 S 151 30 E
Morlaàs, France 24 E3 43 21N 0 18W
Morlaix, France 22 D3 48 36N 3 52W
Morlanwelz, Belgium 21 H4 50 28N 4 15 E
Mormanno, Italy 41 C8 39 53N 15 59 E
Mormant, France 23 D9 48 37N 2 52 E
Mornington, Vic., Australia 117 E6 38 15 S 145 5 E
Mornington, W. Austral., Australia 112 C4 17 31 S 126 6 E
Mornington, I., Chile 160 C1 49 50 S 75 30W
Mornington I., Australia 114 B2 16 30 S 139 30 E
Mórnos →, Greece 45 F3 38 25N 21 50 E
Moro, Sudan 95 E3 10 50N 30 9 E
Moro G., Phil. 71 H4 6 30N 123 0 E
Morobe, Papua N. G. 120 D4 7 49 S 147 38 E
Morocco, U.S.A. 141 D9 40 57N 87 27W
Morocco ■, N. Afr. 98 B3 32 0N 5 50W
Morococha, Peru 156 C2 11 40 S 76 5W
Morogoro, Tanzania 106 D4 6 50 S 37 40 E
Morogoro □, Tanzania 106 D4 8 0 S 37 0 E
Moroleón, Mexico 146 C4 20 8N 101 32W
Morombe, Madag. 105 C7 21 45 S 43 22 E
Moron, Argentina 158 C4 34 39 S 58 37W
Morón, Cuba 148 B4 22 8N 78 39W
Morón de Almazán, Spain 34 D2 41 29N 2 27W
Morón de la Frontera, Spain 37 H5 37 6N 5 28W
Morona →, Peru 152 D2 4 40 S 77 10W
Morona-Santiago □, Ecuador 152 D2 2 30 S 78 0W
Morondava, Madag. 105 C7 20 17 S 44 17 E
Morondo, Ivory C. 100 D3 8 57N 6 47W
Morong, Phil. 70 D3 14 41N 120 16 E
Morongo Valley, U.S.A. 145 L10 34 3N 116 37W
Moronou, Ivory C. 100 D4 6 16N 4 59W
Morotai, Indonesia 72 A3 2 10N 128 30 E
Moroto, Uganda 106 B3 2 28N 34 42 E
Moroto Summit, Kenya 106 B3 2 30N 34 43 E
Morozov, Bulgaria 43 E10 42 30N 25 10 E
Morozovsk, Russia 53 B9 48 25N 41 50 E
Morpeth, U.K. 16 B6 55 11N 1 41W
Morphou, Cyprus 32 D11 35 12N 32 59 E
Morphou Bay, Cyprus 32 D11 35 15N 32 50 E
Morrelganj, Bangla. 78 D2 22 28N 89 51 E
Morrilton, U.S.A. 139 H8 35 9N 92 44W
Morrinhos, Ceara, Brazil 154 B3 3 14 S 40 7W
Morrinhos, Minas Gerais, Brazil 155 E2 17 45 S 49 10W
Morrinsville, N.Z. 118 D4 37 40 S 175 32 E
Morris, Canada 131 D9 49 25N 97 22W
Morris, Ill., U.S.A. 141 C8 41 22N 88 26W
Morris, Minn., U.S.A. 138 C7 45 35N 95 55W
Morris, Mt., Australia 113 E5 26 9 S 131 4 E
Morrisburg, Canada 128 D4 44 55N 75 7W
Morrison, U.S.A. 140 C7 41 49N 89 58W
Morrisonville, U.S.A. 140 E7 39 25N 89 27W
Morristown, Ariz., U.S.A. 143 K7 33 51N 112 37W
Morristown, Ind., U.S.A. 141 E11 39 40N 85 42W
Morristown, N.J., U.S.A. 137 F10 40 48N 74 29W
Morristown, S. Dak., U.S.A. 138 C4 45 56N 101 43W
Morristown, Tenn., U.S.A. 135 G4 36 13N 83 18W
Morro, Pta., Chile 158 B1 27 6 S 71 0W
Morro Bay, U.S.A. 144 K6 35 22N 120 51W
Morro del Jable, Canary Is. 33 F5 28 3N 14 23W
Morro do Chapéu, Brazil 155 D3 11 33 S 41 9W
Morro Jable, Pta. de, Canary Is. 33 F5 28 2N 14 20W
Morros, Brazil 154 B3 2 52 S 44 3W
Morrosquillo, G. de, Colombia 148 E4 9 35N 75 40W
Morrumbene, Mozam. 105 C6 23 31 S 35 16 E
Mors, Denmark 15 H2 56 50N 8 45 E
Morshansk, Russia 51 E12 53 28N 41 50 E
Mörsil, Sweden 14 A7 63 19N 13 40 E
Mortagne →, France 23 D13 48 33N 6 27 E
Mortagne-au-Perche, France 22 D7 48 31N 0 33 E
Mortagne-sur-Gironde, France 24 C3 45 28N 0 47W
Mortagne-sur-Sèvre, France 22 F6 46 59N 0 57W
Mortain, France 22 D6 48 40N 0 57W
Mortara, Italy 38 C5 45 15N 8 43 E
Mortcha, Chad 97 E4 16 0N 21 10 E
Morteau, France 23 E13 47 3N 6 35 E
Morteros, Argentina 158 C3 30 50 S 62 0W
Mortes, R. das →, Brazil 155 D1 11 45 S 50 44W
Mortlake, Australia 116 E5 38 5 S 142 50 E
Morton, Ill., U.S.A. 140 D7 40 37N 89 28W
Morton, Tex., U.S.A. 139 J3 33 44N 102 46W
Morton, Wash., U.S.A. 144 D4 46 34N 122 17W
Mortsel, Belgium 21 F4 51 11N 4 27 E
Morundah, Australia 117 C7 34 57 S 146 19 E
Moruya, Australia 117 C9 35 58 S 150 3 E
Morvan, France 23 E11 47 5N 4 3 E
Morven, Australia 115 D4 26 22 S 147 5 E
Morven, N.Z. 119 E6 44 50 S 171 6 E
Morvern, U.K. 18 E3 56 38N 5 44W
Morwell, Australia 117 E7 38 10 S 146 22 E
Moryn, Poland 47 C1 52 51N 14 22 E
Morzhovets, Ostrov, Russia 48 A7 66 44N 42 35 E
Mosalsk, Russia 50 D9 54 30N 34 55 E
Mosbach, Germany 27 F5 49 21N 9 9 E
Mošćenice, Croatia 39 C11 45 17N 14 16 E
Mosciano Sant' Ángelo, Italy 39 F10 42 42N 13 52 E
Moscos Is., Burma 76 E1 14 0N 97 30 E
Moscow = Moskva, Russia 51 D10 55 45N 37 35 E
Moscow, U.S.A. 142 C5 46 44N 117 0W
Mosel →, Europe 27 E3 50 22N 7 36 E
Moselle = Mosel →, Europe 27 E3 50 22N 7 36 E
Moselle □, France 23 D13 48 59N 6 33 E
Moses Lake, U.S.A. 142 C4 47 8N 119 17W
Mosgiel, N.Z. 119 F5 45 53 S 170 21 E
Moshi, Tanzania 106 C4 3 22 S 37 18 E
Moshi □, Tanzania 106 C4 3 22 S 37 18 E
Moshupa, Botswana 104 C4 24 46 S 25 29 E
Mośina, Poland 47 C3 52 15N 16 50 E
Mosjøen, Norway 12 D12 65 51N 13 12 E
Moskenesøya, Norway 12 C12 67 58N 13 0 E
Moskenstraumen, Norway 12 C12 67 47N 12 45 E
Moskva, Russia 51 D10 55 45N 37 35 E
Moskva →, Russia 51 D11 55 5N 38 51 E
Moslavačka Gora, Croatia 39 C13 45 40N 16 37 E
Moso, Vanuatu 121 G6 17 30 S 168 15 E
Mosomane, Botswana 104 C4 24 2 S 26 19 E
Mosonmagyaróvár, Hungary 31 D10 47 52N 17 18 E
Mošorin, Serbia 42 B5 45 19N 20 4 E
Mospino, Ukraine 52 C7 47 52N 38 0 E
Mosquera, Colombia 152 C2 2 35N 78 24W
Mosquero, U.S.A. 139 H3 35 47N 103 58W
Mosqueruela, Spain 34 E4 40 21N 0 27W
Mosquitia, Honduras 148 C3 15 20N 84 10W
Mosquitos, G. de los, Panama 148 E3 9 15N 81 10W
Moss, Norway 14 E4 59 27N 10 40 E
Moss Vale, Australia 117 C9 34 32 S 150 25 E
Mossaka, Congo 102 C3 1 15 S 16 45 E
Mossâmedes, Brazil 155 E1 16 7 S 50 11W
Mossbank, Canada 131 D7 49 56N 105 56W
Mossburn, N.Z. 119 F3 45 41 S 168 15 E
Mosselbaai, S. Africa 104 E3 34 11 S 22 8 E
Mossendjo, Congo 102 C2 2 55 S 12 42 E
Mosses, Col des, Switz. 28 D4 46 25N 7 7 E
Mossgiel, Australia 116 B6 33 15 S 144 5 E
Mossman, Australia 114 B4 16 21 S 145 15 E
Mossoró, Brazil 154 C4 5 10 S 37 15W
Mossuril, Mozam. 107 E5 14 58 S 40 42 E
Mossy →, Canada 131 C8 54 5N 102 58W
Most, Czech. 30 A6 50 31N 13 38 E
Mosta, Malta 32 D1 35 54N 14 24 E
Moşţafáābād, Iran 85 C7 33 39N 54 53 E
Mostaganem, Algeria 99 A5 35 54N 0 5 E
Mostar, Bos.-H. 42 D2 43 22N 17 50 E
Mostardas, Brazil 159 C5 31 2 S 50 51W
Mostefa, Rass, Tunisia 96 A2 36 55N 11 3 E
Mostiska, Ukraine 50 G3 49 48N 23 4 E
Móstoles, Spain 36 E7 40 19N 3 53W
Mosty, Belorussia 50 E4 53 27N 24 38 E
Mosul = Al Mawşil, Iraq 84 B4 36 15N 43 5 E
Mosulpo, S. Korea 67 H14 33 20N 126 17 E
Mota, Vanuatu 121 C5 13 49 S 167 42 E
Mota del Cuervo, Spain 34 F2 39 30N 2 52W
Mota del Marqués, Spain 36 D5 41 38N 5 11W
Mota Lava, Vanuatu 121 C5 13 40 S 167 40 E
Motagua →, Guatemala 148 C2 15 44N 88 14W
Motala, Sweden 15 F9 58 32N 15 1 E
Motegi, Japan 63 A12 36 32N 140 11 E
Motherwell, U.K. 18 F5 55 48N 4 0W
Motihari, India 81 F11 26 30N 84 55 E
Motilla del Palancar, Spain 34 F3 39 34N 1 55W
Motiti I., N.Z. 118 D5 37 38 S 176 25 E
Motnik, Slovenia 39 B11 46 14N 14 54 E
Motocurunya, Venezuela 153 C5 4 24N 64 5W
Motovun, Croatia 39 C10 45 20N 13 50 E
Motozintla de Mendoza, Mexico 147 D6 15 21N 92 14W
Motril, Spain 35 J1 36 31N 3 37W
Motru →, Romania 46 E4 44 32N 23 31 E
Mott, U.S.A. 138 B3 46 23N 102 20W
Móttola, Italy 41 B10 40 38N 17 2 E
Motu, N.Z. 118 E6 38 18 S 177 40 E
Motu →, N.Z. 118 D6 37 51 S 177 35 E
Motueka, N.Z. 119 B8 41 7 S 173 1 E
Motueka →, N.Z. 119 B8 41 5 S 173 1 E
Motul, Mexico 147 C7 21 0N 89 20W
Motupena Pt., Papua N. G. 120 D8 6 30 S 155 10 E
Mouanda, Gabon 102 C2 1 28 S 13 7 E
Mouchalagane →, Canada 129 B6 50 56N 68 41W
Moúdhros, Greece 44 E7 39 50N 25 18 E
Mouding, China 68 E3 25 20N 101 28 E
Moudjeria, Mauritania 100 B2 17 50N 12 28W
Moudon, Switz. 28 C3 46 40N 6 49 E
Mougoundou, Congo 102 C2 2 40 S 12 41 E
Mouila, Gabon 102 C2 1 50 S 11 0 E
Mouka, C.A.R. 102 A4 7 16N 21 52 E
Moulamein, Australia 116 C6 35 3 S 144 1 E
Moulianá, Greece 32 D7 35 10N 25 59 E
Moulins, France 24 B7 46 35N 3 19 E
Moulmein, Burma 78 G6 16 30N 97 40 E
Moulmeingyun, Burma 78 G5 16 23N 95 16 E
Moulouya, O. →, Morocco 99 A4 35 5N 2 25W
Moulton, Iowa, U.S.A. 140 D4 40 41N 92 41W
Moulton, Tex., U.S.A. 139 L6 29 35N 97 9W
Moultrie, U.S.A. 135 K4 31 11N 83 47W
Moultrie, L., U.S.A. 135 J5 33 20N 80 5W
Mound City, Mo., U.S.A. 138 E7 40 7N 95 14W
Mound City, S. Dak., U.S.A. 138 C4 45 44N 100 4W
Moúnda, Ákra, Greece 45 F2 38 5N 20 45 E
Moundou, Chad 97 G3 8 40N 16 10 E
Moundsville, U.S.A. 136 G4 39 55N 80 44W
Mounembé, Congo 102 C2 3 20 S 12 32 E
Moung, Cambodia 76 F4 12 46N 103 27 E
Moungoudi, Congo 102 C2 2 45 S 11 46 E
Mount Airy, U.S.A. 135 G5 36 31N 80 37W
Mount Albert, Canada 136 B5 44 8N 79 19W
Mount Amherst, Australia 112 C4 18 24 S 126 58 E
Mount Angel, U.S.A. 142 D2 45 4N 122 48W
Mount Augustus, Australia 112 D2 24 20 S 116 56 E
Mount Ayr, U.S.A. 140 D2 40 43N 94 14W
Mount Barker, S. Austral., Australia 116 C3 35 5 S 138 52 E
Mount Barker, W. Austral., Australia 113 F2 34 38 S 117 40 E
Mount Beauty, Australia 117 D7 36 47 S 147 10 E
Mount Carmel, U.S.A. 141 F9 38 25N 87 46W
Mount Carroll, U.S.A. 140 B7 42 6N 89 59W
Mount Clemens, U.S.A. 128 D3 42 35N 82 53W
Mount Coolon, Australia 114 C4 21 25 S 147 25 E
Mount Darwin, Zimbabwe 107 F3 16 47 S 31 38 E
Mount Desert I., U.S.A. 129 D6 44 21N 68 20W
Mount Dora, U.S.A. 135 L5 28 48N 81 38W
Mount Douglas, Australia 114 C4 21 35 S 146 50 E
Mount Eba, Australia 115 E2 30 11 S 135 40 E
Mount Eden, U.S.A. 141 F11 38 3N 85 9W
Mount Edgecumbe, U.S.A. 130 B1 57 3N 135 21W
Mount Elizabeth, Australia 112 C4 16 0 S 125 50 E
Mount Fletcher, S. Africa 105 E4 30 40 S 28 30 E
Mount Forest, Canada 128 D3 43 59N 80 43W
Mount Gambier, Australia 116 D4 37 50 S 140 46 E
Mount Garnet, Australia 114 B4 17 37 S 145 6 E
Mount Hagen, Papua N. G. 120 C3 5 52 S 144 16 E
Mount Hope, N.S.W., Australia 117 B6 32 51 S 145 51 E
Mount Hope, S. Austral., Australia 115 E2 34 7 S 135 23 E
Mount Hope, U.S.A. 134 G5 37 54N 81 10W
Mount Horeb, U.S.A. 140 A7 43 1N 89 44W
Mount Howitt, Australia 115 D3 26 31 S 142 16 E
Mount Isa, Australia 114 C2 20 42 S 139 26 E
Mount Keith, Australia 113 E3 27 15 S 120 30 E
Mount Laguna, U.S.A. 145 N10 32 52N 116 25W
Mount Larcom, Australia 114 C5 23 48 S 150 59 E
Mount Lofty Ra., Australia 116 C3 34 35 S 139 5 E
Mount McKinley National Park, U.S.A. 126 B5 63 30N 150 0W
Mount Magnet, Australia 113 E2 28 2 S 117 47 E
Mount Manara, Australia 116 B5 32 29 S 143 58 E
Mount Margaret, Australia 115 D3 26 54 S 143 21 E
Mount Maunganui, N.Z. 118 D5 37 40 S 176 14 E

Müritz See 237

Mount Molloy, Australia . 114 B4 16 42 S 145 20 E
Mount Monger, Australia 113 F3 31 0 S 122 0 E
Mount Morgan, Australia 114 C5 23 40 S 150 25 E
Mount Morris, U.S.A. ... 136 D7 42 44N 77 52W
Mount Mulligan, Australia 114 B3 16 45 S 144 47 E
Mount Narryer, Australia 113 E2 26 30 S 115 55 E
Mount Olive, U.S.A. 140 E7 39 4N 89 44W
Mount Olivet, U.S.A. ... 141 F12 38 32N 84 2W
Mount Olympus = Uludağ, Turkey .... 88 C3 40 4N 29 13 E
Mount Orab, U.S.A. 141 E13 39 2N 83 55W
Mount Oxide Mine, Australia .... 114 B2 19 30 S 139 29 E
Mount Pearl, Canada 129 C9 47 31N 52 47W
Mount Perry, Australia .. 115 D5 25 13 S 151 42 E
Mount Phillips, Australia 112 D2 24 25 S 116 15 E
Mount Pleasant, Iowa, U.S.A. 140 D5 40 58N 91 33W
Mount Pleasant, Mich., U.S.A. 134 D3 43 36N 84 46W
Mount Pleasant, Pa., U.S.A. 136 F5 40 9N 79 33W
Mount Pleasant, S.C., U.S.A. 135 J6 32 47N 79 52W
Mount Pleasant, Tenn., U.S.A. 135 H2 35 32N 87 12W
Mount Pleasant, Tex., U.S.A. 139 J7 33 9N 94 58W
Mount Pleasant, Utah, U.S.A. 142 G8 39 33N 111 27W
Mount Pocono, U.S.A. .. 137 E9 41 7N 75 22W
Mount Pulaski, U.S.A. .. 140 D7 40 1N 89 17W
Mount Rainier National Park, U.S.A. 144 D5 46 55N 121 50W
Mount Revelstoke Nat. Park, Canada 130 C5 51 5N 118 30W
Mount Robson Prov. Park, Canada 130 C5 53 0N 119 0W
Mount Roskill, N.Z. .... 118 C3 36 55 S 174 45 E
Mount Sandiman, Australia .... 113 D2 24 25 S 115 30 E
Mount Shasta, U.S.A. ... 142 F2 41 19N 122 19W
Mount Signal, U.S.A. ... 145 N11 32 39N 115 37W
Mount Somers, N.Z. .... 119 D6 43 45 S 171 27 E
Mount Sterling, Ill., U.S.A. 140 E6 39 59N 90 45W
Mount Sterling, Ky., U.S.A. 141 F13 38 4N 83 56W
Mount Sterling, Ohio, U.S.A. 141 E13 39 43N 83 16W
Mount Surprise, Australia 114 B3 18 10 S 144 17 E
Mount Union, U.S.A. ... 136 F7 40 23N 77 53W
Mount Vernon, Australia 112 D2 24 9 S 118 2 E
Mount Vernon, Ind., U.S.A. 138 F10 38 17N 88 57W
Mount Vernon, Ind., U.S.A. 141 F8 37 56N 87 54W
Mount Vernon, Iowa, U.S.A. 140 C5 41 55N 91 23W
Mount Vernon, N.Y., U.S.A. 137 F11 40 55N 73 50W
Mount Vernon, Ohio, U.S.A. 136 F2 40 23N 82 29W
Mount Vernon, Wash., U.S.A. 144 B4 48 25N 122 20W
Mount Victor, Australia . 116 B3 32 11 S 139 44 E
Mount Washington, U.S.A. 141 F11 38 3N 85 33W
Mount Wellington, N.Z. . 118 C3 36 55 S 174 52 E
Mount Zion, U.S.A. 141 E8 39 46N 88 53W
Mountain □, Phil. ...... 70 C3 17 20N 121 10 E
Mountain Center, U.S.A. 145 M10 33 42N 116 44W
Mountain City, Nev., U.S.A. 142 F6 41 50N 115 58W
Mountain City, Tenn., U.S.A. 135 G5 36 29N 81 48W
Mountain Grove, U.S.A. 139 G8 37 8N 92 16W
Mountain Home, Ark., U.S.A. 139 G8 36 20N 92 23W
Mountain Home, Idaho, U.S.A. 142 E6 43 8N 115 41W
Mountain Iron, U.S.A. .. 138 B8 47 32N 92 37W
Mountain Park, Canada . 130 C5 52 50N 117 15W
Mountain Pass, U.S.A. .. 145 K11 35 29N 115 35W
Mountain View, Ark., U.S.A. 139 H8 35 52N 92 7W
Mountain View, Calif., U.S.A. 144 H4 37 23N 122 5W
Mountainair, U.S.A. 143 J10 34 31N 106 15W
Mountmellick, Ireland ... 19 C4 53 7N 7 20W
Moura, Australia .... 114 C4 24 35 S 149 58 E
Moura, Brazil .... 153 D5 1 32 S 61 38W
Moura, Portugal 37 G3 38 7N 7 30W
Mourão, Portugal 37 G3 38 22N 7 22W
Mourdi, Dépression du, Chad .... 97 E4 18 10N 23 0 E
Mourdiah, Mali 100 C3 14 35N 7 25W
Mourenx-Ville-Nouvelle, France 24 E3 43 22N 0 38W
Mouri, Ghana 101 D4 5 6N 1 14W
Mourilyan, Australia .... 114 B4 17 35 S 146 3 E
Mourmelon-le-Grand, France .... 23 C11 49 8N 4 22 E
Mourne →, U.K. 19 B4 54 45N 7 39W
Mourne Mts., U.K. 19 B5 54 10N 6 0W
Mournies, Greece .... 32 D6 35 29N 24 1 E
Mouscron, Belgium ...... 21 G2 50 45N 3 12 E
Moussoro, Chad .... 97 F3 13 41N 16 35 E
Mouthe, France .... 23 F13 46 44N 6 12 E
Moutier, Switz. .... 28 B4 47 16N 7 21 E
Moûtiers, France .... 25 C10 45 29N 6 32 E
Moutohara, N.Z. .... 118 E6 38 27 S 177 32 E
Moutong, Indonesia ..... 72 A2 0 28N 121 13 E
Mouy, France .... 23 C9 49 18N 2 20 E
Mouzáki, Greece .... 44 E3 39 25N 21 37 E
Movas, Mexico 146 B3 28 10N 109 25W
Moville, Ireland 19 A4 55 11N 7 3W
Moweaqua, U.S.A. 140 E7 39 38N 89 1W
Moxhe, Belgium .... 21 G6 50 38N 5 5 E
Moxico □, Angola ...... 103 E4 12 0 S 20 30 E
Moxotó →, Brazil ...... 154 C4 9 19 S 38 14W
Moy →, Ireland 19 B3 54 5N 8 50W
Moyale, Kenya .... 90 G2 3 30N 39 0 E
Moyamba, S. Leone 100 D2 8 4N 12 30W
Moyen Atlas, Morocco .. 98 B3 33 0N 5 0W
Moyle □, U.K. 19 A5 55 10N 6 15W
Moyo, Indonesia .... 72 C1 8 10 S 117 40 E
Moyobamba, Peru .... 156 B2 6 0 S 77 0W
Moyyero →, Russia .... 57 C11 68 44N 103 42 E
Mozambique = Moçambique, Mozam. . 107 F5 15 3 S 40 42 E
Mozambique ■, Africa .. 107 F4 19 0 S 35 0 E
Mozambique Chan., Africa .... 105 B7 17 30 S 42 30 E
Mozdok, Russia .... 53 E11 43 45N 44 48 E
Mozdūrān, Iran .... 85 B9 36 9N 60 35 E
Mozhaysk, Russia .... 51 D10 55 30N 36 2 E
Mozhga, Russia .... 54 C3 56 26N 52 15 E
Mozhnābād, Iran .... 85 C9 34 7N 60 6 E
Mozirje, Slovenia .... 39 B11 46 22N 14 58 E
Mozyr, Belorussia .... 50 E6 51 59N 29 15 E
Mpanda, Tanzania ...... 106 D3 6 23 S 31 1 E
Mpanda □, Tanzania .... 106 D3 6 23 S 31 40 E
Mpésoba, Mali 100 C3 12 31N 5 39W
Mpika, Zambia .... 107 E3 11 51 S 31 25 E
Mpulungu, Zambia ...... 107 D3 8 51 S 31 5 E
Mpumalanga, S. Africa .. 105 D5 29 50 S 30 33 E
Mpwapwa, Tanzania .... 106 D4 6 23 S 36 30 E
Mpwapwa □, Tanzania .. 106 D4 6 30 S 36 20 E
Mrągowo, Poland .... 47 B8 53 52N 21 18 E
Mrakovo, Russia .... 54 E5 52 43N 56 38 E
Mramor, Serbia .... 42 D6 43 20N 21 45 E
Mrimina, Morocco 98 C3 29 50N 7 9W
Mrkonjić Grad, Bos.-H. . 42 C2 44 26N 17 4 E
Mrkopalj, Croatia .... 39 C11 45 21N 14 52 E
Mrocza, Poland .... 47 B4 53 16N 17 35 E
Msab, Oued en →, Algeria .... 99 B6 32 25N 5 20 E
Msaken, Tunisia .... 96 A2 35 49N 10 33 E
Msambansovu, Zimbabwe 107 F3 15 50 S 30 3 E
M'sila, Algeria .... 99 A5 35 46N 4 30 E
Msoro, Zambia .... 107 E3 13 35 S 31 50 E
Msta →, Russia .... 50 B7 58 25N 31 20 E
Mstislavl, Belorussia ..... 50 D7 54 0N 31 50 E
Mszana Dolna, Poland ... 31 B13 49 41N 20 5 E
Mszczonów, Poland ..... 47 D7 51 58N 20 33 E
Mtama, Tanzania .... 107 E4 10 17 S 39 21 E
Mtilikwe →, Zimbabwe . 107 G3 21 9 S 31 30 E
Mtsensk, Russia .... 51 E10 53 25N 36 30 E
Mtskheta, Georgia ...... 53 F11 41 52N 44 45 E
Mtubatuba, S. Africa ... 105 D5 28 30 S 32 8 E
Mtwara-Mikindani, Tanzania .... 107 E5 10 20 S 40 20 E
Mu →, Burma .... 78 E5 21 56N 95 38 E
Mu Gia, Deo, Vietnam .. 76 D5 17 40N 105 47 E
Mu Us Shamo, China .... 66 E5 39 0N 109 0 E
Muacandalo, Angola .... 103 E3 10 2 S 19 40 E
Muaná, Brazil .... 154 B2 1 25 S 49 15W
Muanda, Zaïre .... 103 D2 6 0 S 12 20 E
Muang Chiang Rai, Thailand .... 76 C2 19 52N 99 50 E
Muang Lamphun, Thailand .... 76 C2 18 40N 99 2 E
Muang Pak Beng, Laos .. 76 C3 19 54N 101 8 E
Muar, Malaysia .... 77 L4 2 3N 102 34 E
Muarabungo, Indonesia .. 74 C2 1 28 S 102 52 E
Muaraenim, Indonesia ... 74 C2 3 40 S 103 50 E
Muarajuloi, Indonesia ... 75 C4 0 12 S 114 3 E
Muarakaman, Indonesia . 75 C5 0 2 S 116 45 E
Muaratebo, Indonesia ... 74 C2 1 30 S 102 26 E
Muaratembesi, Indonesia 74 C2 1 42 S 103 8 E
Muaratewe, Indonesia ... 75 C4 0 58 S 114 52 E
Mubarakpur, India ...... 81 F10 26 6N 83 18 E
Mubarraz = Al Mubarraz, Si. Arabia .... 85 E6 25 30N 49 40 E
Mubende, Uganda .... 106 B3 0 33N 31 22 E
Mubi, Nigeria .... 101 C7 10 18N 13 16 E
Mubur, P., Indonesia .... 77 L6 3 20N 106 12 E
Mucajaí →, Brazil 153 C5 2 25N 60 52W
Mucajaí, Serra do, Brazil 153 C5 2 23N 61 10W
Mucari, Angola .... 103 D3 9 30 S 16 54 E
Muchachos, Roque de los, Canary Is. 33 F2 28 44N 17 52W
Mücheln, Germany ...... 26 D7 51 18N 11 49 E
Muchinga Mts., Zambia . 107 E3 11 30 S 31 30 E
Muchkapskiy, Russia .... 51 F13 51 52N 42 28 E
Muck, U.K. 18 E2 56 50N 6 15W
Muckadilla, Australia .... 115 D4 26 35 S 148 23 E
Muco →, Colombia 152 C3 4 15N 70 21W
Mucoma, Angola .... 103 F2 15 18 S 13 39 E
Muconda, Angola .... 103 E4 10 31 S 21 15 E
Mucuim →, Brazil ...... 157 B5 6 33 S 64 18W
Mucur, Turkey .... 88 D6 39 3N 34 22 E
Mucura, Brazil .... 153 D5 2 31 S 62 43W
Mucuri, Brazil .... 155 E4 18 0 S 39 36W
Mucurici, Brazil .... 155 E3 18 6 S 40 31W
Mucusso, Angola .... 103 F4 18 1 S 21 25 E
Muda, Canary Is. 33 F6 28 34N 13 57W
Mudan Jiang →, China .. 67 A15 46 20N 129 30 E
Mudanjiang, China ...... 67 B15 44 38N 129 30 E
Mudanya, Turkey .... 52 F3 40 25N 28 50 E
Muddy Cr. →, U.S.A. 143 H8 38 24N 110 42W
Mudgee, Australia ...... 117 B8 32 32 S 149 31 E
Mudjatik →, Canada 131 B7 56 1N 107 36W
Mudon, Burma .... 78 G6 16 15N 97 44 E
Mudugh, Somali Rep. .... 108 C3 7 0N 47 30 E
Mudurnu, Turkey .... 88 C4 40 27N 31 12 E
Muecate, Mozam. .... 107 E4 14 55 S 39 40 E
Muêda, Mozam. .... 107 E4 11 36 S 39 28 E
Mueller Ra., Australia ... 112 C4 18 18 S 126 46 E
Muende, Mozam. .... 107 E3 14 28 S 33 0 E
Muerto, Mar, Mexico 147 D6 16 10N 94 10W
Muertos, Punta de los, Spain 35 J3 36 57N 1 54W
Mufindi □, Tanzania .... 107 D4 8 30 S 35 20 E
Mufu Shan, China ...... 69 C10 29 20N 114 30 E
Mufulira, Zambia ...... 107 E2 12 32 S 28 15 E
Mufumbiro Range, Africa 106 C2 1 25 S 29 30 E
Mugardos, Spain 36 B2 43 27N 8 15W
Muge, Portugal 37 F2 39 3N 8 40W
Muge →, Portugal 37 F2 39 8N 8 44W
Múggia, Italy .... 39 C10 45 36N 13 47 E
Mughayrā', Si. Arabia ... 84 D3 29 17N 37 41 E
Mugi, Japan .... 62 D6 33 40N 134 25 E
Mugia, Spain 36 B1 43 3N 9 10W
Mugila, Mts., Zaïre ..... 106 D2 7 0 S 28 50 E
Muğla, Turkey .... 88 E3 37 15N 28 22 E
Muğla □, Turkey .... 88 E3 37 0N 28 0 E
Müglizh, Bulgaria ...... 43 E10 42 37N 25 32 E
Mugu, Nepal .... 81 E10 29 45N 82 30 E
Muhammad, Râs, Egypt . 94 B3 27 44N 34 16 E
Muhammad Qol, Sudan . 94 C4 20 53N 37 9 E
Muhammadabad, India .. 81 F10 26 4N 83 25 E
Muḩayriqah, Si. Arabia .. 86 B4 23 59N 45 4 E
Muhesi →, Tanzania ... 106 D4 7 0 S 35 20 E
Muheza □, Tanzania .... 106 C4 5 0 S 39 0 E
Mühldorf, Germany ..... 27 G8 48 14N 12 33 E
Mühlhausen, Germany .. 26 D6 51 12N 10 29 E
Mühlig Hofmann fjella, Antarctica .... 7 D3 72 30 S 5 0 E
Muhutwe, Tanzania ..... 106 C3 1 35 S 31 45 E
Muiden, Neths. .... 20 D6 52 20N 5 4 E
Muikamachi, Japan ..... 61 F9 37 15N 138 50 E
Muine Bheag, Ireland ... 19 D5 52 42N 6 57W
Muiños, Spain 36 D3 41 58N 7 59W
Muir, L., Australia ...... 113 F2 34 30 S 116 40 E
Mukachevo, Ukraine .... 50 G3 48 27N 22 45 E
Mukah, Malaysia .... 75 B4 2 55N 112 5 E
Mukawwa, Geziret, Egypt 94 C4 23 55N 35 53 E
Mukdahan, Thailand .... 76 D5 16 32N 104 43 E
Mukden = Shenyang, China .... 67 D12 41 48N 123 27 E
Mukhtolovo, Russia ..... 51 D13 55 29N 43 15 E
Mukhtuya = Lensk, Russia .... 57 C12 60 48N 114 55 E
Mukinbudin, Australia ... 113 F2 30 55 S 118 5 E
Mukishi, Zaïre .... 103 D4 8 30 S 24 44 E
Mukomuko, Indonesia ... 74 C2 2 30 S 101 10 E
Mukomwenze, Zaïre .... 106 D2 6 49 S 27 15 E
Mukry, Turkmenistan ... 55 E2 37 54N 65 12 E
Muktsar, India .... 80 D6 30 30N 74 30 E
Mukur, Afghan. .... 80 C2 32 50N 67 42 E
Mukutawa →, Canada .. 131 C9 53 10N 97 24W
Mukwela, Zambia ...... 107 F2 17 0 S 26 40 E
Mukwonago, U.S.A. 141 B8 42 52N 88 20W
Mula, Spain 35 G3 38 3N 1 33W
Mula →, India .... 82 E2 18 34N 74 21 E
Mulanay, Phil. .... 70 E4 13 31N 122 24 E
Mulange, Zaïre .... 106 C2 3 40 S 27 10 E
Mulberry Grove, U.S.A. . 140 F7 38 56N 89 16W
Mulchén, Chile .... 158 D1 37 45 S 72 20W
Mulde →, Germany ..... 26 D8 51 50N 12 15 E
Muldraugh, U.S.A. 141 G11 37 56N 85 59W
Mule Creek, U.S.A. 138 D2 43 19N 104 8W
Muleba, Tanzania .... 106 C3 1 50 S 31 37 E
Muleba □, Tanzania .... 106 C3 2 0 S 31 30 E
Mulegns, Switz. .... 29 C9 46 32N 9 38 E
Muleshoe, U.S.A. 139 H3 34 13N 102 43W
Mulga Valley, Australia .. 116 A4 31 8 S 141 3 E
Mulgathing, Australia ... 115 E1 30 15 S 134 8 E
Mulgrave, Canada 129 C7 45 38N 61 31W
Mulgrave I., Papua N. G. 120 F2 10 5 S 142 10 E
Mulhacén, Spain 35 H1 37 4N 3 20W
Mülheim, Germany ..... 26 D2 51 26N 6 53 E
Mulhouse, France ...... 23 E14 47 40N 7 20 E
Muli, China .... 68 D3 27 52N 101 8 E
Mulifanua, W. Samoa ... 121 W24 13 50 S 171 59W
Muling, China .... 67 B16 44 35N 130 10 E
Mull, U.K. 18 E3 56 27N 6 0W
Mullaittvu, Sri Lanka ... 83 K5 9 15N 80 49 E
Mullen, U.S.A. 138 D4 42 3N 101 1W
Mullengudgery, Australia 117 A7 31 43 S 147 23 E
Mullens, U.S.A. 134 G5 37 35N 81 23W
Muller, Pegunungan, Indonesia .... 75 B4 0 30N 113 30 E
Mullet Pen., Ireland 19 B1 54 10N 10 2W
Mullewa, Australia ...... 113 E2 28 29 S 115 30 E
Müllheim, Germany ..... 27 H3 47 48N 7 37 E
Mulligan →, Australia ... 114 C2 25 0 S 139 0 E
Mullin, U.S.A. 139 K5 31 33N 98 40W
Mullingar, Ireland 19 C4 53 31N 7 20W
Mullins, U.S.A. 135 H6 34 12N 79 15W
Mullumbimby, Australia . 115 D5 28 30 S 153 30 E
Mulobezi, Zambia ...... 107 F2 16 45 S 25 7 E
Mulshi L., India .... 82 E1 18 30N 73 48 E
Multai, India .... 82 D4 21 50N 78 21 E
Multan, Pakistan .... 79 C3 30 15N 71 36 E
Multrå, Sweden .... 14 A11 63 10N 17 24 E
Mulu, Gunong, Malaysia 75 B4 4 3N 114 56 E
Mulumbe, Mts., Zaïre ... 107 D2 8 40 S 27 30 E
Mulungushi Dam, Zambia 107 E2 14 48 S 28 48 E
Mulvane, U.S.A. 139 G6 37 29N 97 15W
Mulwad, Sudan .... 94 D3 18 45N 30 39 E
Mulwala, Australia ..... 117 C7 35 59 S 146 0 E
Mumbondo, Angola ..... 103 E2 10 9 S 14 15 E
Mumbwa, Zambia ...... 107 E2 15 0 S 27 0 E
Mumeng, Papua N. G. ... 120 D4 7 1 S 146 37 E
Mumra, Russia .... 53 D12 45 45N 47 41 E
Mun →, Thailand .... 76 E5 15 19N 105 30 E
Muna, Indonesia .... 72 B2 5 0 S 122 30 E
Munamagi, Estonia ..... 50 C5 57 43N 27 4 E
Münchberg, Germany .... 27 E7 50 11N 11 48 E
Müncheberg, Germany .. 26 C10 52 30N 14 9 E
München, Germany ..... 27 G7 48 8N 11 33 E
Munchen-Gladbach = Mönchengladbach, Germany .... 26 D2 51 12N 6 23 E
Muncho Lake, Canada ... 130 B3 59 0N 125 50W
Munchŏn, N. Korea ..... 67 E14 39 14N 127 19 E
Münchwilen, Switz. ..... 29 B7 47 28N 8 59 E
Muncie, U.S.A. 141 D11 40 12N 85 23W
Muncoonie, L., Australia 114 D2 25 12 S 138 40 E
Munda, Solomon Is. .... 121 M9 8 20 S 157 16 E
Mundakayam, India .... 83 K3 9 30N 76 50 E
Mundala, Indonesia .... 73 B6 4 30 S 141 0 E
Mundare, Canada 130 C6 53 35N 112 20W
Munday, U.S.A. 139 J5 33 27N 99 38W
Münden, Germany ...... 26 D5 51 25N 9 42 E
Mundiwindi, Australia ... 112 D3 23 47 S 120 9 E
Mundo →, Spain 35 G2 38 30N 2 15W
Mundo Novo, Brazil .... 155 D3 11 50 S 40 29W
Mundra, India .... 80 H3 22 54N 69 48 E
Mundrabilla, Australia .. 113 F4 31 52 S 127 51 E
Munducurus, Brazil ..... 153 D6 4 47 S 58 16W
Munenga, Angola ...... 103 E2 10 2 S 14 41 E
Munera, Spain 35 F2 39 2N 2 29W
Muneru →, India ...... 83 F5 16 45N 80 3 E
Mungallala, Australia ... 115 D4 26 28 S 147 34 E
Mungallala Cr. →, Australia .... 115 D4 28 53 S 147 5 E
Mungana, Australia ..... 114 B3 17 8 S 144 27 E
Mungaoli, India .... 80 G8 24 24N 78 7 E
Mungari, Mozam. ...... 107 F3 17 12 S 33 30 E
Mungbere, Zaïre ...... 106 B2 2 36N 28 28 E
Munger, India .... 81 G12 25 23N 86 30 E
Mungindi, Australia ..... 115 D4 28 58 S 149 1 E
Munhango, Angola ...... 103 E3 12 10 S 18 38 E
Munich = München, Germany .... 27 G7 48 8N 11 33 E
Munising, U.S.A. 134 B2 46 25N 86 40W
Munka-Ljungby, Sweden . 15 H6 56 16N 12 58 E
Munkedal, Sweden ...... 15 F5 58 28N 11 40 E
Munku-Sardyk, Russia ... 57 D11 51 45N 100 20 E
Münnerstadt, Germany .. 27 E6 50 15N 10 11 E
Munoz, Phil. .... 70 D3 15 43N 120 54 E
Muñoz Gamero, Pen., Chile .... 160 D2 52 30 S 73 5W
Munro, Australia .... 117 D7 37 56 S 147 11 E
Munroe L., Canada 131 B9 59 13N 98 35W
Munsan, S. Korea ...... 67 F14 37 51N 126 48 E
Munshiganj, Bangla. .... 78 D3 23 33N 90 32 E
Münsingen, Switz. ...... 28 C5 46 52N 7 32 E
Munster, France .... 23 D14 48 2N 7 8 E
Munster, Niedersachsen, Germany .... 26 C6 52 59N 10 5 E
Münster, Nordrhein-Westfalen, Germany .... 26 D3 51 58N 7 37 E
Münster, Switz. .... 29 D6 46 29N 8 17 E
Munster □, Ireland 19 D3 52 20N 8 40W
Muntadgin, Australia .... 113 F2 31 45 S 118 33 E
Muntele Mare, Romania . 46 C4 46 30N 23 12 E
Muntok, Indonesia ...... 74 C3 2 5 S 105 10 E
Munyak, Uzbekistan .... 56 E6 43 30N 59 15 E
Munyama, Zambia ...... 107 F2 16 5 S 28 31 E
Muong Beng, Laos ..... 76 B3 20 23N 101 46 E
Muong Boum, Vietnam .. 76 A4 22 24N 102 49 E
Muong Et, Laos .... 76 B5 20 49N 104 1 E
Muong Hai, Laos ...... 76 B3 21 3N 101 49 E
Muong Hiem, Laos ..... 76 B4 20 5N 103 22 E
Muong Houn, Laos ..... 76 B3 20 8N 101 23 E
Muong Hung, Vietnam .. 76 B4 20 56N 103 53 E
Muong Kau, Laos ...... 76 E5 15 6N 105 47 E
Muong Khao, Laos ..... 76 C4 19 38N 103 32 E
Muong Khoua, Laos .... 76 B4 21 5N 102 31 E
Muong Liep, Laos ..... 76 C3 18 29N 101 40 E
Muong May, Laos ...... 76 E6 14 49N 106 56 E
Muong Ngeun, Laos .... 76 B3 20 36N 101 3 E
Muong Ngoi, Laos ..... 76 B4 20 43N 102 41 E
Muong Nhie, Vietnam .. 76 A4 22 12N 102 28 E
Muong Nong, Laos ..... 76 D6 16 22N 106 30 E
Muong Ou Tay, Laos ... 76 A3 22 7N 101 48 E
Muong Oua, Laos ...... 76 C3 18 18N 101 20 E
Muong Peun, Laos ..... 76 B4 20 13N 103 52 E
Muong Phalane, Laos ... 76 D5 16 39N 105 34 E
Muong Phieng, Laos .... 76 C3 19 6N 101 32 E
Muong Phine, Laos ..... 76 D6 16 32N 106 2 E
Muong Sai, Laos ...... 76 B3 20 42N 101 59 E
Muong Saiapoun, Laos .. 76 C3 18 24N 101 31 E
Muong Sen, Vietnam ... 76 C5 19 24N 104 8 E
Muong Sing, Laos ..... 76 B3 21 11N 101 9 E
Muong Son, Laos ...... 76 B4 20 27N 103 19 E
Muong Soui, Laos ..... 76 C4 19 33N 102 52 E
Muong Va, Laos .... 76 B4 21 53N 102 19 E
Muong Xia, Vietnam .... 76 B5 20 19N 104 50 E
Muonio, Finland .... 12 C17 67 57N 23 40 E
Muotathal, Switz. ...... 29 C7 46 58N 8 46 E
Mupa, Angola .... 103 F3 16 5 S 15 50 E
Muping, China .... 67 F11 37 22N 121 36 E
Muqaddam, Wadi →, Sudan .... 94 D3 18 4N 31 30 E
Muqdisho, Somali Rep. .. 90 G4 2 2N 45 25 E
Muqshin, W. →, Oman . 87 C6 19 44N 55 14 E
Muquequete, Angola .... 103 E2 14 50 S 14 16 E
Mur →, Austria .... 30 E9 46 35N 16 3 E
Mur-de-Bretagne, France 22 D4 48 12N 3 0W
Mura →, Slovenia ..... 39 B13 46 30N 16 33 E
Muradiye, Turkey ...... 89 D10 39 0N 43 44 E
Murakami, Japan .... 60 E9 38 14N 139 29 E
Murallón, Cuerro, Chile . 160 C2 49 48 S 73 30W
Muralto, Switz. .... 29 D7 46 11N 8 49 E
Muranda, Rwanda ...... 106 C2 1 52 S 29 20 E
Murang'a, Kenya ...... 106 C4 0 45 S 37 9 E
Murashi, Russia .... 51 B16 59 30N 49 0 E
Murat, France .... 24 C6 45 7N 2 53 E
Murat →, Turkey ...... 89 D8 38 39N 39 50 E
Muratlı, Turkey .... 88 C2 41 10N 27 29 E
Murau, Austria .... 30 D7 47 6N 14 10 E
Muravera, Italy .... 40 C2 39 25N 9 35 E
Murayama, Japan ...... 60 E10 38 30N 140 25 E
Murban, U.A.E. .... 85 F7 23 50N 53 45 E
Murça, Portugal 36 D3 41 24N 7 28W
Murchison, N.Z. .... 119 B7 41 49 S 172 21 E
Murchison →, Australia . 113 E1 27 45 S 114 0 E
Murchison, Mt., Antarctica 7 D11 73 0 S 168 0 E
Murchison Falls = Kabarega Falls, Uganda 106 B3 2 15N 31 30 E
Murchison House, Australia .... 113 E1 27 39 S 114 14 E
Murchison Mt., N.Z. .... 119 D6 43 0 S 171 22 E
Murchison Mts., N.Z. ... 119 F2 45 13 S 167 23 E
Murchison Ra., Australia 114 C1 20 0 S 134 10 E
Murchison Rapids, Malawi 107 F3 15 55 S 34 35 E
Murcia, Spain 35 G3 38 5N 1 10W
Murcia □, Spain 35 H3 37 50N 1 30W
Murdo, U.S.A. 138 D4 43 53N 100 43W
Murdoch Pt., Australia .. 114 A3 14 37 S 144 55 E
Mureş □, Romania ..... 46 C5 46 45N 24 40 E
Mureş →, Romania .... 46 C1 46 15N 20 13 E
Mureşul = Mureş →, Romania .... 46 C1 46 15N 20 13 E
Muret, France .... 24 E5 43 30N 1 20 E
Murfatlar, Romania ..... 46 E9 44 10N 28 26 E
Murfreesboro, U.S.A. ... 135 H2 35 51N 86 24W
Murg, Switz. .... 29 B8 47 6N 9 13 E
Murg →, Germany ..... 27 G4 48 55N 8 10 E
Murgab, Tajikistan ..... 55 D7 38 10N 74 2 E
Murgeni, Romania ..... 46 C9 46 12N 28 1 E
Murgenthal, Switz. ..... 28 B5 47 16N 7 50 E
Murgon, Australia ...... 115 D5 26 15 S 151 54 E
Murgoo, Australia ...... 113 E2 27 24 S 116 28 E
Muri, Switz. .... 29 B6 47 17N 8 21 E
Muria, Indonesia ...... 75 D4 6 36 S 110 53 E
Muriaé, Brazil .... 155 F3 21 8 S 42 23W
Murias de Paredes, Spain 36 C4 42 52N 6 11W
Murici, Brazil .... 154 C4 9 19 S 35 56W
Muriége, Angola .... 103 D4 9 58 S 21 11 E
Muriel Mine, Zimbabwe . 107 F3 17 14 S 30 40 E
Murila, Angola .... 103 E4 10 44 S 20 20 E
Müritz See, Germany .... 26 B8 53 25N 12 40 E

Nelson 239

Namur □, Belgium 21 H6 50 17N 5 0 E
Namutoni, Namibia 104 B2 18 49 S 16 55 E
Namwala, Zambia 107 F2 15 44 S 26 30 E
Namwŏn, S. Korea 67 G14 35 23N 127 23 E
Namysłów, Poland 47 D4 51 6N 17 42 E
Nan, Thailand 76 C3 18 48N 100 46 E
Nan →, Thailand 76 E3 15 42N 100 9 E
Nan Xian, China 69 C9 29 20N 112 22 E
Nana, Romania 46 E7 44 17N 26 34 E
Nanaimo, Canada 130 D4 49 10N 124 0W
Nanam, N. Korea 67 D15 41 44N 129 40 E
Nanan, China 69 E12 24 59N 118 21 E
Nanango, Australia 115 D5 26 40 S 152 0 E
Nan'ao, China 69 F11 23 28N 117 5 E
Nanao, Japan 61 F8 37 0N 137 0 E
Nanbu, China 68 B6 31 18N 106 3 E
Nanchang, China 69 C10 28 42N 115 55 E
Nancheng, China 69 D11 27 33N 116 35 E
Nanching = Nanjing, China 69 A12 32 2N 118 47 E
Nanchong, China 68 B6 30 43N 106 2 E
Nanchuan, China 68 C6 29 9N 107 6 E
Nancy, France 23 D13 48 42N 6 12 E
Nanda Devi, India 81 D8 30 23N 79 59 E
Nandan, China 68 E6 24 58N 107 29 E
Nandan, Japan 62 C6 34 10N 134 42 E
Nanded, India 82 E3 19 10N 77 20 E
Nandewar Ra., Australia 115 E5 30 15 S 150 35 E
Nandi □, Kenya 106 B4 0 15N 35 0 E
Nandikotkur, India 83 G4 15 52N 78 18 E
Nandura, India 82 D3 20 52N 76 25 E
Nandurbar, India 82 D2 21 20N 74 15 E
Nandyal, India 83 G4 15 30N 78 30 E
Nanfeng, Guangdong, China 69 F8 23 45N 111 47 E
Nanfeng, Jiangxi, China 69 D11 27 12N 116 28 E
Nanga, Australia 113 E1 26 7 S 113 45 E
Nanga-Eboko, Cameroon 101 E7 4 41N 12 22 E
Nanga Parbat, Pakistan 81 B6 35 10N 74 35 E
Nangade, Mozam. 107 E4 11 5 S 39 36 E
Nangapinoh, Indonesia 75 C4 0 20 S 111 44 E
Nangarhár □, Afghan. 79 B3 34 20N 70 0 E
Nangatayap, Indonesia 75 C4 1 32 S 110 34 E
Nangeya Mts., Uganda 106 B3 3 30N 33 30 E
Nangis, France 23 D10 48 33N 3 1 E
Nangong, China 66 F8 37 23N 115 22 E
Nangwarry, Australia 116 D4 37 33 S 140 48 E
Nanhua, China 68 E3 25 13N 101 21 E
Nanhuang, China 67 F11 36 58N 121 48 E
Nanhui, China 69 B13 31 5N 121 44 E
Nanjangud, India 83 H3 12 6N 76 43 E
Nanjeko, Zambia 107 F1 15 31 S 23 30 E
Nanji Shan, China 69 D13 27 27N 121 4 E
Nanjian, China 68 E3 25 2N 100 25 E
Nanjiang, China 68 A6 32 28N 106 51 E
Nanjing, Fujian, China 69 E11 24 25N 117 20 E
Nanjing, Jiangsu, China 69 A12 32 2N 118 47 E
Nanjirinji, Tanzania 107 D4 9 41 S 39 5 E
Nankana Sahib, Pakistan 80 D5 31 27N 73 38 E
Nankang, China 69 E10 25 40N 114 45 E
Nanking = Nanjing, China 69 A12 32 2N 118 47 E
Nankoku, Japan 62 D5 33 39N 133 44 E
Nanling, China 69 B12 30 55N 118 20 E
Nanning, China 68 F7 22 48N 108 20 E
Nannup, Australia 113 F2 33 59 S 115 48 E
Nanpan Jiang →, China 68 E6 25 10N 106 5 E
Nanpara, India 81 F9 27 52N 81 33 E
Nanpi, China 66 E9 38 2N 116 45 E
Nanping, Fujian, China 69 D12 26 38N 118 10 E
Nanping, Henan, China 69 C9 29 55N 112 3 E
Nanri Dao, China 69 E12 25 15N 119 25 E
Nanripe, Mozam. 107 E4 13 52 S 38 52 E
Nansei-Shotō = Ryūkyū-rettō, Japan 61 M2 26 0N 126 0 E
Nansen Sd., Canada 6 A3 81 0N 91 0W
Nansio, Tanzania 106 C3 2 3 S 33 4 E
Nant, France 24 D7 44 1N 3 18 E
Nantes, France 22 E5 47 12N 1 33W
Nanteuil-le-Haudouin, France 23 C9 49 9N 2 48 E
Nantiat, France 24 B5 46 1N 1 11 E
Nanticoke, U.S.A. 137 E8 41 12N 76 0W
Nanton, Canada 130 C6 50 21N 113 46W
Nantong, China 69 A13 32 1N 120 52 E
Nantua, France 25 B9 46 10N 5 35 E
Nantucket I., U.S.A. 124 E12 41 16N 70 5W
Nanuku Passage, Fiji 121 A3 16 45 S 179 15W
Nanuque, Brazil 155 E3 17 50 S 40 21W
Nanutarra, Australia 112 D2 22 32 S 115 30 E
Nanxiong, China 69 E10 25 6N 114 15 E
Nanyang, China 66 H7 33 11N 112 30 E
Nanyi Hu, China 69 B12 31 5N 119 0 E
Nan'yō, Japan 62 C3 34 3N 131 49 E
Nanyuan, China 66 E9 39 44N 116 22 E
Nanyuki, Kenya 106 B4 0 2N 37 4 E
Nanzhang, China 69 B8 31 45N 111 50 E
Náo, C. de la, Spain 35 G5 38 44N 0 14 E
Naococane L., Canada 129 B5 52 50N 70 45W
Naoetsu, Japan 61 F9 37 12N 138 10 E
Naogaon, Bangla. 78 C2 24 52N 88 52 E
Náousa, Greece 44 D4 40 42N 22 9 E
Naozhou Dao, China 69 G8 20 55N 110 20 E
Napa, U.S.A. 144 G4 38 18N 122 17W
Napa →, U.S.A. 144 G4 38 10N 122 19W
Napanee, Canada 128 D4 44 15N 77 0W
Napanoch, U.S.A. 137 E10 41 44N 74 22W
Nape, Laos 76 C5 18 18N 105 6 E
Nape Pass = Keo Neua, Deo, Vietnam 76 C5 18 23N 105 10 E
Naperville, U.S.A. 141 C8 41 46N 88 9W
Napf, Switz. 28 B5 47 1N 7 56 E
Napier, N.Z. 118 F5 39 30 S 176 56 E
Napier Broome B., Australia 112 B4 14 2 S 126 37 E
Napier Downs, Australia 112 C3 17 11 S 124 36 E
Napier Pen., Australia 114 A2 12 4 S 135 43 E
Naples = Nápoli, Italy 41 B7 40 50N 14 17 E
Naples, U.S.A. 135 M5 26 8N 81 48W
Napo, China 68 F5 23 22N 105 50 E
Napo □, Ecuador 152 D2 0 30 S 77 0W
Napo →, Peru 152 D3 3 20 S 72 40W
Napoleon, N. Dak., U.S.A. 138 B5 46 30N 99 46W
Napoleon, Ohio, U.S.A. 141 C12 41 23N 84 8W
Nápoli, Italy 41 B7 40 50N 14 17 E
Nápoli, G. di, Italy 41 B7 40 40N 14 10 E
Napopo, Zaïre 106 B2 4 15N 28 0 E
Nappa Merrie, Australia 115 D3 27 36 S 141 7 E
Nappanee, U.S.A. 141 C11 41 27N 86 0W
Naqâda, Egypt 94 B3 25 53N 32 42 E
Naqqāsh, Iran 85 C6 35 40N 49 6 E
Nara, Japan 63 C7 34 40N 135 49 E
Nara, Mali 100 B3 15 10N 7 20W
Nara □, Japan 63 C7 34 30N 136 0 E
Nara Canal, Pakistan 80 G3 24 30N 69 20 E
Nara Visa, U.S.A. 139 H3 35 37N 103 6W
Naracoorte, Australia 116 D4 36 58 S 140 45 E
Naradhan, Australia 117 B7 33 34 S 146 17 E
Narasapur, India 83 F5 16 26N 81 40 E
Narasaropet, India 83 F5 16 14N 80 4 E
Narathiwat, Thailand 77 J3 6 30N 101 48 E
Narayanganj, Bangla. 78 D3 23 40N 90 33 E
Narayanpet, India 82 F3 16 45N 77 30 E
Narbonne, France 24 E7 43 11N 3 0 E
Narcea →, Spain 36 B4 43 33N 6 44W
Nardīn, Iran 85 B7 37 3N 55 59 E
Nardò, Italy 41 B11 40 10N 18 0 E
Narembeen, Australia 113 F2 32 7 S 118 24 E
Nares Str., Arctic 124 B13 80 0N 70 0W
Naretha, Australia 113 F3 31 0 S 124 45 E
Narew, Poland 47 C10 52 55N 23 31 E
Narew →, Poland 47 C7 52 26N 20 41 E
Nari →, Pakistan 80 E2 28 0N 67 40 E
Narindra, Helodranon' i, Madag. 105 A8 14 55 S 47 30 E
Narino □, Colombia 152 C2 1 30N 78 0W
Narita, Japan 63 B12 35 47N 140 19 E
Narmada →, India 80 J5 21 38N 72 36 E
Narman, Turkey 89 C9 40 26N 41 57 E
Narnaul, India 80 E7 28 5N 76 11 E
Narni, Italy 39 F9 42 30N 12 30 E
Naro, Ghana 100 C4 10 22N 2 27W
Naro, Italy 40 E6 37 18N 13 48 E
Naro Fominsk, Russia 51 D10 55 23N 36 43 E
Narodnaya, Russia 48 A10 65 5N 59 58 E
Narok, Kenya 106 C4 1 55 S 35 52 E
Narok □, Kenya 106 C4 1 20 S 36 30 E
Narón, Spain 36 B2 43 32N 8 9W
Narooma, Australia 117 D9 36 14 S 150 4 E
Narowal, Pakistan 79 B4 32 6N 74 52 E
Narrabri, Australia 115 E4 30 19 S 149 46 E
Narran →, Australia 115 D4 28 37 S 148 12 E
Narrandera, Australia 117 C7 34 42 S 146 31 E
Narraway →, Canada 130 B5 55 44N 119 55W
Narrogin, Australia 113 F2 32 58 S 117 14 E
Narromine, Australia 117 B8 32 12 S 148 12 E
Narsampet, India 82 F4 17 57N 79 58 E
Narsimhapur, India 81 H8 22 54N 79 14 E
Nartkala, Russia 53 E10 43 33N 43 51 E
Naruto, Kantō, Japan 62 C6 34 11N 134 37 E
Narutō, Shikoku, Japan 63 B12 35 36N 140 25 E
Naruto-Kaikyō, Japan 62 C6 34 14N 134 39 E
Narva, Estonia 50 B6 59 23N 28 12 E
Narva →, Russia 50 B6 59 27N 28 2 E
Narvacan, Phil. 70 C3 17 25N 120 28 E
Narvik, Norway 12 B14 68 28N 17 26 E
Narvskoye Vdkhr., Russia 50 B6 59 18N 28 14 E
Narwana, India 80 E7 29 39N 76 6 E
Naryan-Mar, Russia 48 A9 68 0N 53 0 E
Naryilco, Australia 115 D3 28 37 S 141 53 E
Narym, Russia 56 D9 59 0N 81 30 E
Narymskoye, Kazakhstan 56 E9 49 10N 84 15 E
Naryn, Kirghizia 55 C7 41 26N 75 58 E
Naryn →, Uzbekistan 55 C5 40 52N 71 36 E
Nasa, Norway 12 C13 66 29N 15 23 E
Nasarawa, Nigeria 101 D6 8 32N 7 41 E
Năsăud, Romania 46 B5 47 19N 24 29 E
Nasawa, Vanuatu 121 E6 15 0 S 168 0 E
Naseby, N.Z. 119 F5 45 1 S 170 10 E
Naselle, U.S.A. 144 D3 46 22N 123 49W
Naser, Buheirat en, Egypt 94 C3 23 0N 32 30 E
Nashua, Iowa, U.S.A. 140 B4 42 57N 92 32W
Nashua, Mont., U.S.A. 142 B10 48 8N 106 22W
Nashua, N.H., U.S.A. 137 D13 42 45N 71 28W
Nashville, Ark., U.S.A. 139 J8 33 57N 93 51W
Nashville, Ga., U.S.A. 135 K4 31 12N 83 15W
Nashville, Ill., U.S.A. 140 F7 38 21N 89 23W
Nashville, Ind., U.S.A. 141 E10 39 12N 86 15W
Nashville, Mich., U.S.A. 141 B11 42 36N 85 5W
Nashville, Tenn., U.S.A. 135 G2 36 10N 86 47W
Našice, Croatia 42 B3 45 32N 18 4 E
Nasielsk, Poland 47 C7 52 35N 20 50 E
Nasik, India 82 E1 19 58N 73 50 E
Nasipit, Phil. 71 G5 8 57N 125 19 E
Nasirabad, India 80 F6 26 15N 74 45 E
Naskaupi →, Canada 129 B7 53 47N 60 51W
Naso, Italy 41 D7 38 8N 14 46 E
Naso Pt., Phil. 71 F3 10 25N 121 57 E
Naṣrīān-e Pā'īn, Iran 84 C5 32 52N 46 52 E
Nass →, Canada 130 B3 55 0N 129 40W
Nassau, Bahamas 148 A4 25 5N 77 20W
Nassau, U.S.A. 137 D11 42 31N 73 37W
Nassau, B., Chile 160 E3 55 20 S 68 0W
Nasser, L. = Naser, Buheirat en, Egypt 94 C3 23 0N 32 30 E
Nasser City = Kôm Ombo, Egypt 94 C3 24 25N 32 52 E
Nassian, Ivory C. 100 D4 8 28N 3 28W
Nässjö, Sweden 13 H13 57 39N 14 42 E
Nasugbu, Phil. 70 D3 14 5N 120 38 E
Näsviken, Sweden 14 C10 61 46N 16 52 E
Nata, Botswana 104 C4 20 12 S 26 12 E
Natagaima, Colombia 152 C2 3 37N 75 6W
Natal, Brazil 154 C4 5 47 S 35 13W
Natal, Canada 130 D6 49 43N 114 51W
Natal, Indonesia 74 B1 0 35N 99 7 E
Natal □, S. Africa 105 D5 28 30 S 30 30 E
Natalinci, Serbia 42 C5 44 15N 20 49 E
Naṭanz, Iran 85 C6 33 30N 51 55 E
Natashquan, Canada 129 B7 50 14N 61 46W
Natashquan →, Canada 129 B7 50 7N 61 50W
Natchez, U.S.A. 139 K9 31 34N 91 24W
Natchitoches, U.S.A. 139 K8 31 46N 93 5W
Naters, Switz. 28 D5 46 19N 7 58 E
Natewa B., Fiji 121 A2 16 35 S 179 40 E
Nathalia, Australia 117 D6 36 1 S 145 13 E
Nathdwara, India 80 G5 24 55N 73 50 E
Nati, Pta., Spain 33 A10 40 3N 3 50 E
Natimuk, Australia 116 D4 36 42 S 142 0 E
Nation →, Canada 130 B4 55 30N 123 32W
National City, U.S.A. 145 N9 32 41N 117 6W
Natitingou, Benin 101 C5 10 20N 1 26 E
Natividad, I., Mexico 146 B1 27 50N 115 10W
Natogyi, Burma 78 E5 21 25N 95 39 E
Natoma, U.S.A. 138 F5 39 11N 99 2W
Natonin, Phil. 70 C3 17 6N 121 18 E
Natron, L., Tanzania 106 C4 2 20 S 36 0 E
Natrona Heights, U.S.A. 136 F5 40 37N 79 44W
Natrûn, W. el →, Egypt 94 H7 30 25N 30 13 E
Natuna Besar, Kepulauan, Indonesia 77 L7 4 0N 108 15 E
Natuna Is. = Natuna Besar, Kepulauan, Indonesia 77 L7 4 0N 108 15 E
Natuna Selatan, Kepulauan, Indonesia 75 B3 2 45N 109 0 E
Natural Bridge, U.S.A. 137 B9 44 5N 75 30W
Naturaliste, C., Australia 114 G4 40 50 S 148 15 E
Natya, Australia 116 C5 34 57 S 143 13 E
Nau, Tajikistan 55 C4 40 9N 69 22 E
Nau Qala, Afghan. 80 B3 34 5N 68 5 E
Naubinway, U.S.A. 128 C2 46 6N 85 27W
Naucelle, France 24 D6 44 13N 2 20 E
Nauders, Austria 30 E3 46 54N 10 30 E
Nauen, Germany 26 C8 52 36N 12 52 E
Naugatuck, U.S.A. 137 E11 41 30N 73 3W
Naujan, Phil. 70 E3 13 20N 121 18 E
Naujoji Vilnia, Lithuania 50 D4 54 48N 25 27 E
Naumburg, Germany 26 D7 51 10N 11 48 E
Nā'ūr at Tunayb, Jordan 91 D4 31 48N 35 57 E
Nauru ■, Pac. Oc. 122 H8 1 0 S 166 0 E
Naurzum, Kazakhstan 54 F9 51 32N 64 34 E
Naushahra = Nowshera, Pakistan 79 B3 34 0N 72 0 E
Nausori, Fiji 121 B2 18 2 S 178 32 E
Nauta, Peru 152 D3 4 31 S 73 35W
Nautla, Mexico 147 C5 20 20N 96 50W
Nauvoo, U.S.A. 140 D5 40 33N 91 23W
Nava, Mexico 146 B4 28 25N 100 46W
Nava del Rey, Spain 36 D5 41 22N 5 6W
Navacerrada, Puerto de, Spain 36 E7 40 47N 4 0W
Navadwip, India 81 H13 23 34N 88 20 E
Navahermosa, Spain 37 F6 39 41N 4 28W
Navajo Reservoir, U.S.A. 143 H10 36 48N 107 36W
Naval, Phil. 71 F5 11 34N 124 23 E
Navalcarnero, Spain 36 E6 40 17N 4 5W
Navalmoral de la Mata, Spain 36 F5 39 52N 5 33W
Navalvillar de Pela, Spain 37 F5 39 9N 5 24W
Navan = An Uaimh, Ireland 19 C5 53 39N 6 40W
Navarino, I., Chile 160 E3 55 0 S 67 40W
Navarra □, Spain 34 C3 42 40N 1 40W
Navarre, U.S.A. 136 F3 40 43N 81 31W
Navarrenx, France 24 E3 43 20N 0 45W
Navarro →, U.S.A. 144 F3 39 11N 123 45W
Navasota, U.S.A. 139 K6 30 23N 96 5W
Navassa, W. Indies 149 C4 18 30N 75 0W
Nave, Italy 38 C7 45 35N 10 17 E
Naver →, U.K. 18 C4 58 34N 4 15W
Navia, Spain 36 B4 43 35N 6 42W
Navia →, Spain 36 B4 43 15N 6 50W
Navia de Suarna, Spain 36 C4 42 58N 6 59W
Navidad, Chile 158 C1 33 57 S 71 50W
Navlya, Russia 50 E9 52 53N 34 30 E
Navoi, Uzbekistan 55 C2 40 9N 65 22 E
Navojoa, Mexico 146 B3 27 0N 109 30W
Navolato, Mexico 146 C3 24 47N 107 42W
Navolok, Russia 48 B6 62 33N 39 57 E
Návpaktos, Greece 45 F3 38 23N 21 50 E
Návplion, Greece 45 G4 37 33N 22 50 E
Navrongo, Ghana 101 C4 10 51N 1 3W
Navsari, India 82 D1 20 57N 72 59 E
Nawa Kot, Pakistan 80 E4 28 21N 71 24 E
Nawabganj, Bangla. 78 C2 24 35N 88 14 E
Nawabganj, Ut. P., India 81 F9 26 56N 81 14 E
Nawabganj, Ut. P., India 81 E8 28 32N 79 40 E
Nawabshah, Pakistan 79 D3 26 15N 68 25 E
Nawada, India 81 G11 24 50N 85 33 E
Nāwah, Afghan. 79 B2 32 19N 67 53 E
Nawakot, Nepal 81 F11 27 55N 85 10 E
Nawalgarh, India 80 F6 27 50N 75 15 E
Nawanshahr, India 81 C6 32 33N 74 48 E
Nawapara, India 82 D6 20 46N 82 33 E
Nawāsīf, Harrat, Si. Arabia 86 B3 21 20N 42 10 E
Nawi, Sudan 94 D3 18 32N 30 50 E
Nawng Hpa, Burma 78 D7 22 30N 98 30 E
Nawş, Ra's, Oman 87 C6 17 15N 55 16 E
Náxos, Greece 45 G7 37 8N 25 25 E
Nay, France 24 E3 43 10N 0 18W
Nāy Band, Iran 85 E7 27 20N 52 40 E
Naya →, Colombia 152 C2 3 13N 77 22W
Nayakhan, Russia 57 C16 61 56N 159 0 E
Nayarit □, Mexico 146 C4 22 0N 105 0W
Nayé, Senegal 100 C2 14 28N 12 12W
Nayong, China 68 D5 26 50N 105 20 E
Nayoro, Japan 60 B11 44 21N 142 28 E
Nayyāl, W. →, Si. Arabia 84 D3 28 35N 39 4 E
Nazaré, Bahia, Brazil 155 D4 13 2 S 39 0W
Nazaré, Goiás, Brazil 154 C2 6 23 S 47 40W
Nazaré, Pará, Brazil 157 B7 6 25 S 52 29W
Nazaré, Portugal 37 F1 39 36N 9 4W
Nazareth = Nazerat, Israel 91 C4 32 42N 35 17 E
Nazas, Mexico 146 B4 25 10N 104 6W
Nazas →, Mexico 146 B4 25 35N 103 25W
Naze, The, U.K. 17 F9 51 53N 1 19 E
Nazerat, Israel 91 C4 32 42N 35 17 E
Nāzīk, Iran 84 B5 39 1N 45 4 E
Nazik Gölü, Turkey 89 D10 38 50N 42 16 E
Nazilli, Turkey 88 E3 37 55N 28 15 E
Nazir Hat, Bangla. 78 D3 22 35N 91 49 E
Nazko, Canada 130 C4 53 1N 123 37W
Nazko →, Canada 130 C4 53 7N 123 34W
Nazret, Ethiopia 95 F4 8 32N 39 22 E
Nazwá, Oman 87 B7 22 56N 57 32 E
Nchanga, Zambia 107 E2 12 30 S 27 49 E
Ncheu, Malawi 107 E3 14 50 S 34 47 E
Ndala, Tanzania 106 C3 4 45 S 33 15 E
Ndalatando, Angola 103 D2 9 12 S 14 48 E
Ndali, Benin 101 D5 9 50N 2 46 E
Ndareda, Tanzania 106 C4 4 12 S 35 30 E
Ndélé, C.A.R. 102 A4 8 25N 20 36 E
Ndendé, Gabon 102 C2 2 22 S 11 23 E
Ndjamena, Chad 97 F2 12 10N 14 59 E
Ndjolé, Gabon 102 C2 0 10 S 10 45 E
Ndola, Zambia 107 E2 13 0 S 28 34 E
Ndoto Mts., Kenya 106 B4 2 0N 37 0 E
Ndoua, C., N. Cal. 121 V20 22 24 S 166 56 E
Nduguti, Tanzania 106 C3 4 18 S 34 41 E
Nduindui, Vanuatu 121 E5 15 24 S 167 46 E
Nea →, Norway 14 A5 63 15N 11 0 E
Néa Epídhavros, Greece 45 G5 37 40N 23 7 E
Néa Flippiás, Greece 44 E2 39 12N 20 53 E
Néa Kallikrátia, Greece 44 D5 40 21N 23 1 E
Néa Víssi, Greece 44 C8 41 34N 26 33 E
Neagari, Japan 63 A8 36 26N 136 25 E
Neagh, Lough, U.K. 19 B5 54 35N 6 25W
Neah Bay, U.S.A. 144 B2 48 22N 124 37W
Neale, L., Australia 112 D5 24 15 S 130 0 E
Neamţ □, Romania 46 C7 47 0N 26 20 E
Neápolis, Kozan, Greece 44 D3 40 20N 21 24 E
Neápolis, Kríti, Greece 32 D7 35 15N 25 37 E
Neápolis, Lakonia, Greece 45 H5 36 27N 23 8 E
Near Is., U.S.A. 126 C1 53 0N 172 0 E
Neath, U.K. 17 F4 51 39N 3 49W
Nebbou, Burkina Faso 101 C4 11 9N 1 51W
Nebine Cr. →, Australia 115 D4 29 27 S 146 56 E
Nebit Dag, Turkmenistan 49 G9 39 30N 54 22 E
Nebolchy, Russia 50 B8 59 8N 33 18 E
Nebraska □, U.S.A. 138 E5 41 30N 99 30W
Nebraska City, U.S.A. 138 E7 40 41N 95 52W
Nébrodi, Monti, Italy 41 E7 37 55N 14 50 E
Necedah, U.S.A. 138 C9 44 2N 90 4W
Nechako →, Canada 130 C4 53 30N 122 44W
Neches →, U.S.A. 139 L8 29 58N 93 51W
Neckar →, Germany 27 F4 49 31N 8 26 E
Necochea, Argentina 158 D4 38 30 S 58 50W
Nectar Brook, Australia 116 B2 32 43 S 137 57 E
Nedelišće, Croatia 39 B13 46 23N 16 22 E
Neder Rijn →, Neths. 20 E8 51 57N 6 2 E
Nederbrakel, Belgium 21 G3 50 48N 3 46 E
Nederweert, Neths. 21 F7 51 17N 5 45 E
Nédha →, Greece 45 G3 37 25N 21 45 E
Nedroma, Algeria 99 A4 35 1N 1 45W
Nee Soon, Singapore 74 B2 1 24N 103 49 E
Neede, Neths. 20 D9 52 8N 6 37 E
Needles, U.S.A. 145 L12 34 51N 114 37W
Needles, The, U.K. 17 G6 50 39N 1 35W
Needles Pt., N.Z. 118 C4 36 3 S 175 25 E
Ñeembucú □, Paraguay 158 B4 27 0 S 58 0W
Neemuch = Nimach, India 80 G6 24 30N 74 56 E
Neenah, U.S.A. 134 C1 44 11N 88 28W
Neepawa, Canada 131 C9 50 15N 99 30W
Neer, Neths. 21 F7 51 16N 5 59 E
Neerpelt, Belgium 21 F6 51 13N 5 26 E
Neft-chala = imeni 26 Bakinskikh Komissarov, Azerbaijan 89 D13 39 19N 49 12 E
Nefta, Tunisia 96 B1 33 53N 7 50 E
Neftah Sidi Boubekeur, Algeria 99 A5 35 1N 0 4 E
Neftegorsk, Russia 53 D8 44 25N 39 45 E
Neftekumsk, Russia 53 D11 44 46N 44 50 E
Neftenbach, Switz. 29 A7 47 32N 8 41 E
Neftyannyye Kamni, Azerbaijan 49 F9 40 20N 50 55 E
Negapatam = Nagappattinam, India 83 J4 10 46N 79 51 E
Negaunee, U.S.A. 134 B2 46 30N 87 36W
Negele, Ethiopia 90 F2 5 20N 39 36 E
Negeri Sembilan □, Malaysia 74 B2 2 45N 102 10 E
Negev Desert = Hanegev, Israel 91 E3 30 50N 35 0 E
Negoiul, Vf., Romania 46 D5 45 38N 24 35 E
Negombo, Sri Lanka 83 L4 7 12N 79 50 E
Negotin, Serbia 42 C7 44 16N 22 37 E
Negotino, Macedonia 42 F7 41 29N 22 9 E
Negra, Peña, Spain 36 C4 42 11N 6 30W
Negra, Pta., Mauritania 98 D1 22 54N 16 18W
Negra, Pta., Peru 156 B1 6 6 S 81 10W
Negra Pt., Phil. 70 B3 18 40N 120 50 E
Negrais C., Burma 78 G5 16 0N 94 12 E
Negreira, Spain 36 C2 42 54N 8 45W
Negreşti, Romania 46 C8 46 50N 27 30 E
Négrine, Algeria 99 B6 34 30N 7 30 E
Negro →, Argentina 160 B4 41 2 S 62 47W
Negro →, Bolivia 157 C5 14 11 S 63 7W
Negro →, Brazil 153 D6 3 0 S 60 0W
Negro →, Uruguay 159 C4 33 24 S 58 22W
Negros, Phil. 71 G4 9 30N 122 40 E
Negru Vodă, Romania 46 F9 43 47N 28 21 E
Nehalem →, U.S.A. 144 E3 45 40N 123 56W
Nehāvand, Iran 85 C6 35 56N 49 31 E
Nehbandān, Iran 85 D9 31 35N 60 5 E
Neheim, Germany 26 D3 51 27N 7 58 E
Nehoiaşu, Romania 46 D7 45 24N 26 20 E
Nei Monggol Zizhiqu □, China 66 C6 42 0N 112 0 E
Neiafu, Tonga 121 P14 18 39 S 173 59W
Neidpath, Canada 131 C7 50 12N 107 20W
Neihart, U.S.A. 142 C8 47 0N 110 44W
Neijiang, China 68 C5 29 35N 104 55 E
Neilrex, Australia 117 A8 31 44 S 149 20 E
Neilton, U.S.A. 142 C2 47 25N 123 53W
Neiqiu, China 66 F8 37 15N 114 30 E
Neira de Jusá, Spain 36 C3 42 53N 7 14W
Neiva, Colombia 152 C2 2 56N 75 18W
Neixiang, China 66 H6 33 10N 111 52 E
Nejanilini L., Canada 131 B9 59 33N 97 48W
Nejo, Ethiopia 95 F4 9 30N 35 28 E
Nekā, Iran 85 B7 36 39N 53 19 E
Nekemte, Ethiopia 95 F4 9 4N 36 30 E
Nêkheb, Egypt 94 B3 25 10N 32 48 E
Neksø, Denmark 13 J13 55 4N 15 8 E
Nelas, Portugal 36 E3 40 32N 7 52W
Nelia, Australia 114 C3 20 39 S 142 12 E
Nelidovo, Russia 50 C8 56 13N 32 49 E
Neligh, U.S.A. 138 D5 42 8N 98 2W
Nelkan, Russia 57 D14 57 40N 136 4 E
Nellikuppam, India 83 J4 11 46N 79 43 E
Nellore, India 83 G4 14 27N 79 59 E
Nelma, Russia 57 E14 47 39N 139 0 E
Nelson, Canada 130 D5 49 30N 117 20W
Nelson, N.Z. 119 B8 41 18 S 173 16 E
Nelson, U.K. 16 D5 53 50N 2 14W
Nelson, U.S.A. 143 J7 35 31N 113 19W
Nelson →, Canada 131 C9 54 33N 98 2W

Olascoaga 243

Nurzec →, *Poland* **47 C9** 52 37N 22 25 E
Nusa Barung, *Indonesia* **75 D4** 8 10 S 113 30 E
Nusa Kambangan, *Indonesia* **75 D3** 7 40 S 108 10 E
Nusa Tenggara Barat □, *Indonesia* **75 D5** 8 50 S 117 30 E
Nusa Tenggara Timur □, *Indonesia* **72 C2** 9 30 S 122 0 E
Nusaybin, *Turkey* **49 G7** 37 3N 41 10 E
Nushki, *Pakistan* **79 C2** 29 35N 66 0 E
Nutak, *Canada* **127 C13** 57 28N 61 59W
Nuth, *Neths.* **21 G7** 50 55N 5 53 E
Nutwood Downs, *Australia* **114 B1** 15 49 S 134 10 E
Nuuk = Godthåb, *Greenland* **127 B14** 64 10N 51 35W
Nuwakot, *Nepal* **81 E10** 28 10N 83 55 E
Nuwara Eliya, *Sri Lanka* **83 L5** 6 58N 80 48 E
Nuweiba', *Egypt* **94 B3** 28 59N 34 39 E
Nuweveldberge, *S. Africa* **104 E3** 32 10 S 21 45 E
Nuyts, C., *Australia* **113 F5** 32 2 S 132 21 E
Nuyts Arch., *Australia* **115 E1** 32 35 S 133 20 E
Nuzvid, *India* **82 F5** 16 47N 80 53 E
Nxau-Nxau, *Botswana* **104 B3** 18 57 S 21 4 E
Nyaake, *Liberia* **100 E3** 4 52N 7 37W
Nyack, *U.S.A.* **137 E11** 41 5N 73 55W
Nyadal, *Sweden* **14 B11** 62 48N 17 59 E
Nyah West, *Australia* **116 C5** 35 16 S 143 21 E
Nyahanga, *Tanzania* **106 C3** 2 20 S 33 37 E
Nyahua, *Tanzania* **106 D3** 5 25 S 33 23 E
Nyahururu, *Kenya* **106 B4** 0 2N 36 27 E
Nyainqentanglha Shan, *China* **64 D3** 30 0N 90 0 E
Nyakanazi, *Tanzania* **106 C3** 3 2 S 31 10 E
Nyakrom, *Ghana* **101 D4** 5 40N 0 50W
Nyâlâ, *Sudan* **95 E1** 12 2N 24 58 E
Nyamandhlovu, *Zimbabwe* **107 F2** 19 55 S 28 16 E
Nyambiti, *Tanzania* **106 C3** 2 48 S 33 27 E
Nyamwaga, *Tanzania* **106 C3** 1 27 S 34 33 E
Nyandekwa, *Tanzania* **106 C3** 3 57 S 32 32 E
Nyanding →, *Sudan* **95 F3** 8 40N 32 41 E
Nyandoma, *Russia* **48 B7** 61 40N 40 12 E
Nyanga →, *Gabon* **102 C2** 2 58 S 10 15 E
Nyangana, *Namibia* **104 B3** 18 0 S 20 40 E
Nyanguge, *Tanzania* **106 C3** 2 30 S 33 12 E
Nyankpala, *Ghana* **101 D4** 9 21N 0 58W
Nyanza, *Burundi* **106 C2** 4 21 S 29 36 E
Nyanza, *Rwanda* **106 C2** 2 20 S 29 42 E
Nyanza □, *Kenya* **106 C3** 0 10 S 34 15 E
Nyarling →, *Canada* **130 A6** 60 41N 113 23W
Nyasa, L. = Malawi, L., *Africa* **107 E3** 12 30 S 34 30 E
Nyaunglebin, *Burma* **78 G6** 17 52N 96 42 E
Nyazepetrovsk, *Russia* **54 C6** 56 3N 59 36 E
Nyazura, *Zimbabwe* **107 F3** 18 40 S 32 16 E
Nyazwidzi →, *Zimbabwe* **107 F3** 20 0 S 31 17 E
Nyborg, *Denmark* **15 J4** 55 18N 10 47 E
Nybro, *Sweden* **13 H13** 56 44N 15 55 E
Nyda, *Russia* **56 C8** 66 40N 72 58 E
Nyeri, *Kenya* **106 C4** 0 23 S 36 56 E
Nyerol, *Sudan* **95 F3** 8 41N 32 1 E
Nyhem, *Sweden* **14 B9** 62 54N 15 37 E
Nyiel, *Sudan* **95 F3** 6 9N 31 13 E
Nyinahin, *Ghana* **100 D4** 6 43N 2 3W
Nyirbátor, *Hungary* **31 D15** 47 49N 22 9 E
Nyíregyháza, *Hungary* **31 D14** 47 58N 21 47 E
Nykarleby, *Finland* **12 E17** 63 22N 22 31 E
Nykøbing, *Sjælland, Denmark* **15 J5** 55 55N 11 40 E
Nykøbing, *Storstrøm, Denmark* **15 K5** 54 56N 11 52 E
Nykøbing, *Viborg, Denmark* **15 H2** 56 48N 8 51 E
Nyköping, *Sweden* **15 F11** 58 45N 17 0 E
Nykvarn, *Sweden* **14 E11** 59 11N 17 25 E
Nyland, *Sweden* **14 A11** 63 1N 17 45 E
Nylstroom, *S. Africa* **105 C4** 24 42 S 28 22 E
Nymagee, *Australia* **117 B7** 32 7 S 146 20 E
Nymburk, *Czech.* **30 A8** 50 10N 15 1 E
Nynäshamn, *Sweden* **14 F11** 58 54N 17 57 E
Nyngan, *Australia* **115 E4** 31 30 S 147 8 E
Nyon, *Switz.* **28 D2** 46 23N 6 14 E
Nyong →, *Cameroon* **101 E6** 3 17N 9 54 E
Nyons, *France* **25 D9** 44 22N 5 10 E
Nyora, *Australia* **117 E6** 38 20 S 145 41 E
Nyord, *Denmark* **15 J6** 55 4N 12 13 E
Nyou, *Burkina Faso* **101 C4** 12 42N 2 1W
Nysa, *Poland* **47 E4** 50 30N 17 22 E
Nysa →, *Europe* **26 C10** 52 4N 14 46 E
Nyssa, *U.S.A.* **142 E5** 43 53N 117 0W
Nysted, *Denmark* **15 K5** 54 40N 11 44 E
Nytva, *Russia* **54 C4** 57 56N 55 20 E
Nyūgawa, *Japan* **62 D5** 33 56N 133 5 E
Nyunzu, *Zaïre* **106 D2** 5 57 S 27 58 E
Nyurba, *Russia* **57 C12** 63 17N 118 28 E
Nzega, *Tanzania* **106 C3** 4 10 S 33 12 E
Nzega □, *Tanzania* **106 C3** 4 10 S 33 10 E
N'Zérékoré, *Guinea* **100 D3** 7 49N 8 48W
Nzeto, *Angola* **103 D2** 7 10 S 12 52 E
Nzilo, Chutes de, *Zaïre* **103 E5** 10 18 S 25 27 E
Nzubuka, *Tanzania* **106 C3** 4 45 S 32 50 E

O

Ō-Shima, *Fukuoka, Japan* **62 D2** 33 54N 130 25 E
Ō-Shima, *Nagasaki, Japan* **62 C1** 34 29N 129 33 E
Ō-Shima, *Shizuoka, Japan* **63 C11** 34 44N 139 24 E
Oacoma, *U.S.A.* **138 D5** 43 48N 99 24W
Oahe, L., *U.S.A.* **138 C4** 44 27N 100 24W
Oahe Dam, *U.S.A.* **138 C4** 44 27N 100 24W
Oahu, *U.S.A.* **132 H16** 21 28N 157 58W
Oak Creek, *Colo., U.S.A.* **142 F10** 40 16N 106 57W
Oak Creek, *Wis., U.S.A.* **141 B9** 42 52N 87 55W
Oak Harbor, *U.S.A.* **144 B4** 48 18N 122 39W
Oak Hill, *U.S.A.* **134 G5** 37 59N 81 9W
Oak Lawn, *U.S.A.* **141 C9** 41 43N 87 44W
Oak Park, *U.S.A.* **141 C9** 41 53N 87 47W
Oak Ridge, *U.S.A.* **135 G3** 36 1N 84 16W
Oak View, *U.S.A.* **145 L7** 34 24N 119 18W
Oakan-Dake, *Japan* **60 C12** 43 27N 144 10 E
Oakbank, *Australia* **116 B4** 33 4 S 140 33 E
Oakdale, *Calif., U.S.A.* **144 H6** 37 46N 120 51W
Oakdale, *La., U.S.A.* **139 K8** 30 49N 92 40W
Oakengates, *U.K.* **16 E5** 52 42N 2 29W
Oakes, *U.S.A.* **138 B5** 46 8N 98 6W
Oakesdale, *U.S.A.* **142 C5** 47 8N 117 15W
Oakey, *Australia* **115 D5** 27 25 S 151 43 E
Oakford, *U.S.A.* **140 D7** 40 6N 89 58W
Oakham, *U.K.* **16 E7** 52 40N 0 43W
Oakhurst, *U.S.A.* **144 H7** 37 19N 119 40W
Oakland, *Calif., U.S.A.* **144 H4** 37 49N 122 16W
Oakland, *Ill., U.S.A.* **141 E8** 39 39N 88 2W
Oakland, *Oreg., U.S.A.* **142 E2** 43 25N 123 18W
Oakland City, *U.S.A.* **141 F9** 38 20N 87 21W
Oaklands, *Australia* **117 C7** 35 34 S 146 10 E
Oakley, *Idaho, U.S.A.* **142 E7** 42 15N 113 53W
Oakley, *Kans., U.S.A.* **138 F4** 39 8N 100 51W
Oakley Creek, *Australia* **117 A8** 31 37 S 149 46 E
Oakover →, *Australia* **112 D3** 21 0 S 120 40 E
Oakridge, *U.S.A.* **142 E2** 43 45N 122 28W
Oaktown, *U.S.A.* **141 F9** 38 52N 87 26W
Oakville, *U.S.A.* **144 D3** 46 51N 123 14W
Oakwood, *U.S.A.* **141 C12** 41 6N 84 23W
Oamaru, *N.Z.* **119 F5** 45 5 S 170 59 E
Ōamishirasato, *Japan* **63 B12** 35 31N 140 18 E
Oarai, *Japan* **63 A12** 36 21N 140 34 E
Oasis, *Calif., U.S.A.* **145 M10** 33 28N 116 6W
Oasis, *Nev., U.S.A.* **144 H9** 37 29N 117 55W
Oates Land, *Antarctica* **7 C11** 69 0 S 160 0 E
Oatman, *U.S.A.* **145 K12** 35 1N 114 19W
Oaxaca, *Mexico* **147 D5** 17 2N 96 40W
Oaxaca □, *Mexico* **147 D5** 17 0N 97 0W
Ob →, *Russia* **56 C7** 66 45N 69 30 E
Oba, *Canada* **128 C3** 49 4N 84 7W
Obala, *Cameroon* **101 E7** 4 9N 11 32 E
Obama, *Fukui, Japan* **63 B7** 35 30N 135 45 E
Obama, *Nagasaki, Japan* **62 E2** 32 43N 130 13 E
Oban, *U.K.* **18 E3** 56 25N 5 30W
Obbia, *Somali Rep.* **90 F4** 5 25N 48 30 E
Obdam, *Neths.* **20 C5** 52 41N 4 55 E
Obed, *Canada* **130 C5** 53 30N 117 10W
Ober-Aagau, *Switz.* **28 B5** 47 10N 7 45 E
Obera, *Argentina* **159 B4** 27 21 S 55 2W
Oberalppass, *Switz.* **29 C7** 46 39N 8 35 E
Oberalpstock, *Switz.* **29 C7** 46 45N 8 47 E
Oberammergau, *Germany* **27 H7** 47 35N 11 3 E
Oberdrauburg, *Austria* **30 E5** 46 44N 12 58 E
Oberengadin, *Switz.* **29 C9** 46 35N 9 55 E
Oberentfelden, *Switz.* **28 B6** 47 21N 8 2 E
Oberhausen, *Germany* **26 D2** 51 28N 6 50 E
Oberkirch, *Germany* **27 G4** 48 31N 8 5 E
Oberland, *Switz.* **28 C5** 46 35N 7 38 E
Oberlin, *Kans., U.S.A.* **138 F4** 39 49N 100 32W
Oberlin, *La., U.S.A.* **139 K8** 30 37N 92 46W
Oberlin, *Ohio, U.S.A.* **136 E2** 41 18N 82 13W
Obernai, *France* **23 D14** 48 28N 7 30 E
Oberndorf, *Germany* **27 G4** 48 17N 8 35 E
Oberon, *Australia* **117 B8** 33 45 S 149 52 E
Oberösterreich □, *Austria* **30 C6** 48 10N 14 0 E
Oberpfälzer Wald, *Germany* **27 F8** 49 30N 12 25 E
Obersiggenthal, *Switz.* **29 B6** 47 29N 8 18 E
Oberstdorf, *Germany* **27 H6** 47 25N 10 16 E
Oberting, *Gabon* **102 C1** 0 22 S 9 46 E
Oberwil, *Switz.* **28 A5** 47 32N 7 33 E
Obi, Kepulauan, *Indonesia* **72 B3** 1 23 S 127 45 E
Obi Is. = Obi, Kepulauan, *Indonesia* **72 B3** 1 23 S 127 45 E
Obiaruku, *Nigeria* **101 D6** 5 51N 6 9 E
Óbidos, *Brazil* **153 D6** 1 50 S 55 30W
Óbidos, *Portugal* **37 F1** 39 19N 9 10W
Obihiro, *Japan* **60 C11** 42 56N 143 12 E
Obilatu, *Indonesia* **72 B3** 1 25 S 127 20 E
Obilnoye, *Russia* **53 C11** 47 32N 44 30 E
Obing, *Germany* **27 H8** 48 0N 12 25 E
Öbisfelde, *Germany* **26 C6** 52 27N 10 57 E
Objat, *France* **24 C5** 45 16N 1 24 E
Oblong, *U.S.A.* **141 E9** 39 0N 87 55W
Obluchye, *Russia* **57 E14** 49 1N 131 4 E
Obninsk, *Russia* **51 D10** 55 8N 36 37 E
Obo, *C.A.R.* **102 A5** 5 20N 26 32 E
Obo, *Ethiopia* **95 G4** 3 46N 38 52 E
Oboa, Mt., *Uganda* **106 B3** 1 45N 34 45 E
Obock, *Djibouti* **95 E5** 12 0N 43 20 E
Oborniki, *Poland* **47 C3** 52 39N 16 50 E
Oborniki Śląskie, *Poland* **47 D3** 51 17N 16 53 E
Obouya, *Congo* **102 C3** 0 56 S 15 43 E
Oboyan, *Russia* **51 F10** 51 13N 36 37 E
Obozerskaya, *Russia* **56 C5** 63 20N 40 15 E
Obrenovac, *Serbia* **42 C5** 44 40N 20 11 E
Obrovac, *Croatia* **39 D12** 44 11N 15 41 E
Obruk, *Turkey* **88 D5** 38 18N 33 12 E
Observatory Inlet, *Canada* **130 B3** 55 10N 129 54W
Obshchi Syrt, *Kazakhstan* **10 E16** 52 0N 53 0 E
Obskaya Guba, *Russia* **56 C8** 69 0N 73 0 E
Obuasi, *Ghana* **101 D4** 6 17N 1 40W
Obubra, *Nigeria* **101 D6** 6 8N 8 20 E
Obwalden □, *Switz.* **28 C6** 46 55N 8 15 E
Obyachevo, *Russia* **54 A1** 60 20N 49 37 E
Obzor, *Bulgaria* **43 E12** 42 50N 27 52 E
Ocala, *U.S.A.* **135 L4** 29 11N 82 8W
Ocamo →, *Venezuela* **153 C4** 2 48N 65 14W
Ocampo, *Mexico* **146 B3** 28 9N 108 24W
Ocaña, *Colombia* **152 B3** 8 15N 73 20W
Ocaña, *Spain* **34 F1** 39 55N 3 30W
Ocanomowoc, *U.S.A.* **138 D10** 43 7N 88 30W
Ocate, *U.S.A.* **139 G2** 36 11N 105 3W
Occidental, Cordillera, *Colombia* **152 C3** 5 0N 76 0W
Occidental, Cordillera, *Peru* **156 C3** 14 0 S 74 0W
Ocean City, *N.J., U.S.A.* **134 F8** 39 17N 74 35W
Ocean City, *Wash., U.S.A.* **144 C2** 47 4N 124 10W
Ocean I. = Banaba, *Kiribati* **122 H8** 0 45 S 169 50 E
Ocean Park, *U.S.A.* **144 D2** 46 30N 124 3W
Oceano, *U.S.A.* **145 K6** 35 6N 120 37W
Oceanport, *U.S.A.* **137 F10** 40 19N 74 3W
Oceanside, *U.S.A.* **145 M9** 33 12N 117 23W
Ochagavia, *Spain* **34 C3** 42 55N 1 5W
Ochamchire, *Georgia* **53 E9** 42 46N 41 32 E
Ochamps, *Belgium* **21 J6** 49 56N 5 16 E
Ocher, *Russia* **54 C4** 57 53N 54 42 E
Ochiai, *Japan* **62 B5** 35 1N 133 45 E
Ochil Hills, *U.K.* **18 E5** 56 14N 3 40W
Ochre River, *Canada* **131 C9** 51 4N 99 47W
Ochsenfurt, *Germany* **27 F6** 49 38N 10 3 E
Ochsenhausen, *Germany* **27 G5** 48 4N 9 57 E
Ocilla, *U.S.A.* **135 K4** 31 36N 83 15W
Ocmulgee →, *U.S.A.* **135 K4** 31 58N 82 33W
Ocna Mureş, *Romania* **46 C4** 46 23N 23 55 E
Ocna Sibiului, *Romania* **46 D5** 45 52N 24 2 E
Ocnele Mari, *Romania* **46 D5** 45 8N 24 18 E
Ocoña, *Peru* **156 D3** 16 26 S 73 8W
Ocoña →, *Peru* **156 D3** 16 28 S 73 8W
Oconee →, *U.S.A.* **135 K4** 31 58N 82 33W
Oconomowoc, *U.S.A.* **141 A8** 43 7N 88 30W
Oconto, *U.S.A.* **134 C2** 44 53N 87 52W
Oconto Falls, *U.S.A.* **134 C1** 44 52N 88 9W
Ocosingo, *Mexico* **147 D6** 17 10N 92 15W
Ocotal, *Nic.* **148 D2** 13 41N 86 31W
Ocotlán, *Mexico* **146 C4** 20 21N 102 42W
Ocquier, *Belgium* **21 H6** 50 24N 5 24 E
Ocreza →, *Portugal* **37 F3** 39 32N 7 50W
Ócsa, *Hungary* **31 D12** 47 17N 19 15 E
Octave, *U.S.A.* **143 J7** 34 10N 112 43W
Octeville, *France* **22 C5** 49 38N 1 40W
Ocumare del Tuy, *Venezuela* **152 A4** 10 7N 66 46W
Ocuri, *Bolivia* **157 D4** 18 45 S 65 50W
Oda, *Ghana* **101 D4** 5 50N 0 51W
Ōda, *Ehime, Japan* **62 D4** 33 36N 132 53 E
Ōda, *Shimane, Japan* **62 B4** 35 11N 132 30 E
Oda, J., *Sudan* **94 C4** 20 21N 36 39 E
Ódáðahraun, *Iceland* **12 D5** 65 5N 17 0W
Ödåkra, *Sweden* **15 H6** 56 7N 12 45 E
Odate, *Japan* **60 D10** 40 16N 140 34 E
Odawara, *Japan* **63 B11** 35 20N 139 6 E
Odda, *Norway* **13 F9** 60 3N 6 35 E
Odder, *Denmark* **15 J4** 55 58N 10 10 E
Oddur, *Somali Rep.* **90 G3** 4 11N 43 52 E
Ödeborg, *Sweden* **15 F5** 58 32N 11 58 E
Odei →, *Canada* **131 B9** 56 6N 96 54W
Odell, *U.S.A.* **141 D8** 41 0N 88 31W
Odemira, *Portugal* **37 H2** 37 35N 8 40W
Ödemiş, *Turkey* **88 D3** 38 15N 28 0 E
Odendaalsrus, *S. Africa* **104 D4** 27 48 S 26 45 E
Odense, *Denmark* **15 J4** 55 22N 10 23 E
Odenwald, *Germany* **27 F5** 49 30N 9 0 E
Oder →, *Germany* **26 B10** 53 33N 14 38 E
Oderzo, *Italy* **39 C9** 45 47N 12 29 E
Odesa = Odessa, *Ukraine* **52 C4** 46 30N 30 45 E
Odessa, *Canada* **137 B8** 44 17N 76 43W
Odessa, *Ukraine* **52 C4** 46 30N 30 45 E
Odessa, *Mo., U.S.A.* **140 F3** 39 0N 93 57W
Odessa, *Tex., U.S.A.* **139 K3** 31 52N 102 23W
Odessa, *Wash., U.S.A.* **142 C4** 47 20N 118 41W
Odiakwe, *Botswana* **104 C4** 20 12 S 25 17 E
Odiel →, *Spain* **37 H4** 37 10N 6 55W
Odienné, *Ivory C.* **100 D3** 9 30N 7 34W
Odintsovo, *Russia* **51 D10** 55 39N 37 15 E
Odiongan, *Phil.* **70 E3** 12 24N 121 59 E
Odobeşti, *Romania* **46 D8** 45 43N 27 4 E
Odolanów, *Poland* **47 D4** 51 34N 17 40 E
O'Donnell, *Phil.* **70 D3** 15 21N 120 27 E
O'Donnell, *U.S.A.* **139 J4** 32 58N 101 50W
Odoorn, *Neths.* **20 C9** 52 51N 6 51 E
Odorheiu Secuiesc, *Romania* **46 C6** 46 21N 25 21 E
Odoyevo, *Russia* **51 E10** 53 56N 36 42 E
Odra →, *Poland* **47 B1** 53 33N 14 38 E
Odra →, *Spain* **36 C6** 42 14N 4 17W
Odweina, *Somali Rep.* **108 C3** 9 25N 45 4 E
Odžaci, *Serbia* **42 B4** 45 30N 19 17 E
Odžak, *Bos.-H.* **42 B3** 45 3N 18 18 E
Odzi, *Zimbabwe* **105 B5** 19 0 S 32 20 E
Oedelem, *Belgium* **21 F2** 51 10N 3 21 E
Oegstgeest, *Neths.* **20 D4** 52 11N 4 29 E
Oeiras, *Brazil* **154 C3** 7 0 S 42 8W
Oeiras, *Portugal* **37 G1** 38 41N 9 18W
Oelrichs, *U.S.A.* **138 D3** 43 11N 103 14W
Oelsnitz, *Germany* **26 E8** 50 24N 12 11 E
Oelwein, *U.S.A.* **138 D9** 42 41N 91 55W
Oenpelli, *Australia* **112 B5** 12 20 S 133 4 E
Of, *Turkey* **89 C9** 40 59N 40 23 E
O'Fallon, *U.S.A.* **140 F6** 38 49N 90 42W
Ofanto →, *Italy* **41 A9** 41 22N 16 13 E
Offa, *Nigeria* **101 D5** 8 13N 4 42 E
Offaly □, *Ireland* **19 C4** 53 15N 7 30W
Offenbach, *Germany* **27 E4** 50 6N 8 46 E
Offenburg, *Germany* **27 G3** 48 29N 7 56 E
Offerdal, *Sweden* **14 A8** 63 28N 14 0 E
Offida, *Italy* **39 F10** 42 56N 13 40 E
Offranville, *France* **22 C8** 49 52N 1 1 E
Ofidhousa, *Greece* **45 H8** 36 33N 26 8 E
Ofotfjorden, *Norway* **12 B14** 68 27N 16 40 E
Ofu, *Amer. Samoa* **121 X25** 14 11 S 169 41W
Ōfunato, *Japan* **60 E10** 39 4N 141 43 E
Oga, *Japan* **60 E9** 39 55N 139 50 E
Oga-Hantō, *Japan* **60 E9** 39 58N 139 47 E
Ogaden, *Ethiopia* **108 C3** 7 30N 45 30 E
Ogahalla, *Canada* **128 B2** 50 6N 85 51W
Ōgaki, *Japan* **63 B8** 35 21N 136 37 E
Ogallala, *U.S.A.* **138 E4** 41 8N 101 43W
Ogan →, *Indonesia* **74 C2** 3 1 S 104 44 E
Ogasawara Gunto, *Pac. Oc.* **122 E6** 27 0N 142 0 E
Ogbomosho, *Nigeria* **101 D5** 8 1N 4 11 E
Ogden, *Iowa, U.S.A.* **140 B2** 42 2N 94 2W
Ogden, *Utah, U.S.A.* **142 F7** 41 13N 111 58W
Ogdensburg, *U.S.A.* **137 B9** 44 42N 75 30W
Ogeechee →, *U.S.A.* **135 K5** 31 50N 81 3W
Ogilby, *U.S.A.* **145 N12** 32 49N 114 50W
Oglesby, *U.S.A.* **140 C7** 41 18N 89 4W
Oglio →, *Italy* **38 C7** 45 2N 10 39 E
Ogmore, *Australia* **114 C4** 22 37 S 149 35 E
Ognon →, *France* **23 E12** 47 16N 5 28 E
Ogo Mas, *Indonesia* **72 A2** 0 50N 120 5 E
Ogoja, *Nigeria* **101 D6** 6 38N 8 39 E
Ogoki →, *Canada* **128 B2** 51 38N 85 57W
Ogoki L., *Canada* **128 B2** 50 50N 87 10W
Ogoki Res., *Canada* **128 B2** 50 45N 88 15W
Ogooué →, *Gabon* **102 C1** 1 0 S 9 0 E
Ōgori, *Japan* **62 C3** 34 6N 131 24 E
Ogosta →, *Bulgaria* **43 D8** 43 48N 23 55 E
Ogowe = Ogooué →, *Gabon* **102 C1** 1 0 S 9 0 E
Ogr = Sharafa, *Sudan* **95 E2** 11 59N 27 7 E
Ograźden, *Macedonia* **42 F7** 41 30N 22 50 E
Ogrein, *Sudan* **94 D3** 17 55N 34 50 E
Ogulin, *Croatia* **39 C12** 45 16N 15 16 E
Ogun □, *Nigeria* **101 D5** 7 0N 3 0 E
Oguni, *Japan* **62 D3** 33 11N 131 8 E
Oguta, *Nigeria* **101 D6** 5 44N 6 44 E
Ogwashi-Uku, *Nigeria* **101 D6** 6 15N 6 30 E
Ogwe, *Nigeria* **101 E6** 5 0N 7 14 E
Ohai, *N.Z.* **119 F3** 45 55 S 168 0 E
Ohakune, *N.Z.* **118 F4** 39 24 S 175 24 E
Ohanet, *Algeria* **99 C6** 28 44N 8 46 E
Ōhara, *Japan* **63 B12** 35 15N 140 23 E
Ohata, *Japan* **60 D10** 41 24N 141 10 E
Ohau, L., *N.Z.* **119 E4** 44 15 S 169 53 E
Ohaupo, *N.Z.* **118 D4** 37 56 S 175 20 E
Ohey, *Belgium* **21 H6** 50 26N 5 8 E
Ohio □, *U.S.A.* **134 E3** 40 15N 82 45W
Ohio →, *U.S.A.* **134 G1** 36 59N 89 8W
Ohio City, *U.S.A.* **141 D12** 40 46N 84 37W
Ohiwa Harbour, *N.Z.* **118 D6** 37 59 S 177 10 E
Ohre →, *Czech.* **30 A7** 50 30N 14 10 E
Ohre →, *Germany* **26 C7** 52 18N 11 47 E
Ohrid, *Macedonia* **42 F5** 41 8N 20 52 E
Ohridsko, Jezero, *Macedonia* **42 F5** 41 8N 20 52 E
Ohrigstad, *S. Africa* **105 C5** 24 39 S 30 36 E
Öhringen, *Germany* **27 F5** 49 11N 9 31 E
Ohura, *N.Z.* **118 E3** 38 51 S 174 59 E
Oiapoque →, *Brazil* **153 C7** 4 8N 51 40W
Oikou, *China* **67 E9** 38 35N 117 42 E
Oil City, *U.S.A.* **136 E5** 41 26N 79 42W
Oildale, *U.S.A.* **145 K7** 35 25N 119 1W
Oinousa, *Greece* **45 F8** 38 33N 26 14 E
Oirschot, *Neths.* **21 E6** 51 30N 5 18 E
Oise □, *France* **23 C9** 49 28N 2 30 E
Oise →, *France* **23 D9** 49 0N 2 4 E
Oisterwijk, *Neths.* **21 E6** 51 35N 5 12 E
Ōita, *Japan* **62 D3** 33 14N 131 36 E
Ōita □, *Japan* **62 D3** 33 15N 131 30 E
Oiticica, *Brazil* **154 C3** 5 3 S 41 5W
Ojai, *U.S.A.* **145 L7** 34 27N 119 15W
Ojinaga, *Mexico* **146 B4** 29 34N 104 25W
Ojiya, *Japan* **61 F9** 37 18N 138 48 E
Ojos del Salado, Cerro, *Argentina* **158 B2** 27 0 S 68 40W
Oka →, *Russia* **51 C13** 56 20N 43 59 E
Okaba, *Indonesia* **73 C5** 8 6 S 139 42 E
Okahandja, *Namibia* **104 C2** 22 0 S 16 59 E
Okahukura, *N.Z.* **118 E4** 38 48 S 175 14 E
Okaihau, *N.Z.* **118 B2** 35 19 S 173 47 E
Okanagan L., *Canada* **130 C5** 50 0N 119 30W
Okandja, *Gabon* **102 C2** 0 35 S 13 45 E
Okanogan, *U.S.A.* **142 B4** 48 22N 119 35W
Okanogan →, *U.S.A.* **142 B4** 48 6N 119 44W
Okány, *Hungary* **31 E14** 46 52N 21 21 E
Okapa, *Papua N. G.* **120 D3** 6 38 S 145 39 E
Okaputa, *Namibia* **104 C2** 20 5 S 17 0 E
Okara, *Pakistan* **79 C4** 30 50N 73 31 E
Okarito, *N.Z.* **119 D5** 43 15 S 170 9 E
Okato, *N.Z.* **118 F2** 39 12 S 173 53 E
Okaukuejo, *Namibia* **104 B2** 19 10 S 16 0 E
Okavango Swamps, *Botswana* **104 B3** 18 45 S 22 45 E
Okawa, *Japan* **62 D2** 33 9N 130 21 E
Okawville, *U.S.A.* **140 F7** 38 26N 89 33W
Okaya, *Japan* **63 A10** 36 5N 138 10 E
Okayama, *Japan* **62 C5** 34 40N 133 54 E
Okayama □, *Japan* **62 C5** 35 0N 133 50 E
Okazaki, *Japan* **63 C9** 34 57N 137 10 E
Oke-Iho, *Nigeria* **101 D5** 8 1N 3 18 E
Okeechobee, *U.S.A.* **135 M5** 27 15N 80 50W
Okeechobee, L., *U.S.A.* **135 M5** 27 0N 80 50W
Okefenokee Swamp, *U.S.A.* **135 K4** 30 40N 82 20W
Okehampton, *U.K.* **17 G3** 50 44N 4 1W
Okene, *Nigeria* **101 D6** 7 32N 6 11 E
Oker →, *Germany* **26 C6** 52 30N 10 22 E
Okha, *Russia* **57 D15** 53 40N 143 0 E
Ókhi Óros, *Greece* **45 F6** 38 5N 24 25 E
Okhotsk, *Russia* **57 D15** 59 20N 143 10 E
Okhotsk, Sea of, *Asia* **57 D15** 55 0N 145 0 E
Okhotskiy Perevoz, *Russia* **57 C14** 61 52N 135 35 E
Okhotsko Kolymskoye, *Russia* **57 C16** 63 0N 157 0 E
Oki-no-Shima, *Japan* **62 E4** 32 44N 132 33 E
Oki-Shotō, *Japan* **62 A5** 36 5N 133 15 E
Okiep, *S. Africa* **104 D2** 29 39 S 17 53 E
Okigwi, *Nigeria* **101 D6** 5 52N 7 20 E
Okija, *Nigeria* **101 D6** 5 54N 6 55 E
Okinawa □, *Japan* **61 L3** 26 40N 128 0 E
Okinawa-Guntō, *Japan* **61 L3** 26 40N 128 0 E
Okinawa-Jima, *Japan* **61 L4** 26 32N 128 0 E
Okino-erabu-Shima, *Japan* **61 L4** 27 21N 128 33 E
Okitipupa, *Nigeria* **101 D5** 6 31N 4 50 E
Oklahoma □, *U.S.A.* **139 H6** 35 20N 97 30W
Oklahoma City, *U.S.A.* **139 H6** 35 30N 97 30W
Okmulgee, *U.S.A.* **139 H7** 35 37N 95 58W
Oknitsa, *Ukraine* **52 B2** 48 25N 27 30 E
Okolo, *Uganda* **106 B3** 2 37N 31 8 E
Okolona, *Ky., U.S.A.* **141 F11** 38 8N 85 41W
Okolona, *Miss., U.S.A.* **139 H10** 34 0N 88 45W
Okonek, *Poland* **47 B3** 53 32N 16 51 E
Okrika, *Nigeria* **101 E6** 4 40N 7 10 E
Oktabrsk, *Kazakhstan* **49 E10** 49 28N 57 25 E
Oktyabr, *Kazakhstan* **55 B8** 43 41N 77 12 E
Oktyabrsk, *Russia* **51 E16** 53 11N 48 40 E
Oktyabrskiy, *Belorussia* **50 E6** 52 38N 28 53 E
Oktyabrskiy, *Russia* **54 D3** 54 28N 53 28 E
Oktyabrskoy Revolyutsii, Os., *Russia* **57 B10** 79 30N 97 0 E
Oktyabrskoye = Zhovtnevoye, *Ukraine* **52 C5** 46 54N 32 3 E
Oktyabrskoye, *Russia* **56 C7** 62 28N 66 3 E
Ōkuchi, *Japan* **62 E2** 32 4N 130 37 E
Okulovka, *Russia* **50 B8** 58 25N 33 19 E
Okuru, *N.Z.* **119 D3** 43 55 S 168 55 E
Okushiri-Tō, *Japan* **60 C9** 42 15N 139 30 E
Okuta, *Nigeria* **101 D5** 9 14N 3 12 E
Okwa →, *Botswana* **104 C3** 22 30 S 23 0 E
Ola, *U.S.A.* **139 H8** 35 2N 93 13W
Ólafsfjörður, *Iceland* **12 C4** 66 4N 18 39W
Ólafsvík, *Iceland* **12 D2** 64 53N 23 43W
Olancha, *U.S.A.* **145 J8** 36 17N 118 1W
Olancha Pk., *U.S.A.* **145 J8** 36 15N 118 7W
Olanchito, *Honduras* **148 C2** 15 30N 86 30W
Öland, *Sweden* **13 H14** 56 45N 16 38 E
Olargues, *France* **24 E6** 43 34N 2 53 E
Olary, *Australia* **116 B4** 32 18 S 140 19 E
Olascoaga, *Argentina* **158 D3** 35 15 S 60 39W

244 Olathe

Olathe, *U.S.A.* **138 F7** 38 53N 94 49W
Olavarría, *Argentina* **158 D3** 36 55 S 60 20W
Oława, *Poland* **47 E4** 50 57N 17 20 E
Ólbia, *Italy* **40 B2** 40 55N 9 30 E
Ólbia, G. di, *Italy* **40 B2** 40 55N 9 35 E
Old Bahama Chan. = Bahama, Canal Viejo de, *W. Indies* **148 B4** 22 10N 77 30W
Old Baldy Pk. = San Antonio, Mt., *U.S.A.* **145 L9** 34 17N 117 38W
Old Castile = Castilla y Leon □, *Spain* **36 D6** 42 0N 5 0W
Old Castle, *Ireland* **19 C4** 53 46N 7 10W
Old Cork, *Australia* **114 C3** 22 57 S 141 52 E
Old Crow, *Canada* **126 B6** 67 30N 139 55W
Old Dale, *U.S.A.* **145 L11** 34 8N 115 47W
Old Dongola, *Sudan* **94 D3** 18 11N 30 44 E
Old Fletton, *U.K.* **17 E7** 52 34N 0 13W
Old Forge, *N.Y., U.S.A.* **137 C10** 43 43N 74 58W
Old Forge, *Pa., U.S.A.* **137 E9** 41 22N 75 45W
Old Fort →, *Canada* **131 B6** 58 36N 110 24W
Old Shinyanga, *Tanzania* **106 C3** 3 33 S 33 27 E
Old Speck Mt., *U.S.A.* **137 B14** 44 34N 70 57W
Old Town, *U.S.A.* **129 D6** 44 56N 68 39W
Old Wives L., *Canada* **131 C7** 50 5N 106 0W
Oldbury, *U.K.* **17 F5** 51 38N 2 30W
Oldeani, *Tanzania* **106 C4** 3 22 S 35 35 E
Oldenburg, *Niedersachsen, Germany* **26 B4** 53 10N 8 10 E
Oldenburg, *Schleswig-Holstein, Germany* **26 A6** 54 16N 10 53 E
Oldenzaal, *Neths.* **20 D9** 52 19N 6 53 E
Oldham, *U.K.* **16 D5** 53 33N 2 8W
Oldman →, *Canada* **130 D6** 49 57N 111 42W
Olds, *Canada* **130 C6** 51 50N 114 10W
Olean, *U.S.A.* **136 D6** 42 5N 78 26W
Olecko, *Poland* **47 A9** 54 2N 22 31 E
Oléggio, *Italy* **38 C5** 45 36N 8 38 E
Oleiros, *Portugal* **36 F3** 39 56N 7 56W
Olekma →, *Russia* **57 C13** 60 22N 120 42 E
Olekminsk, *Russia* **57 C13** 60 25N 120 30 E
Olema, *U.S.A.* **144 G4** 38 3N 122 47W
Olen, *Belgium* **21 F5** 51 9N 4 52 E
Olenegorsk, *Russia* **48 A5** 68 9N 33 18 E
Olenek, *Russia* **57 C12** 68 28N 112 18 E
Olenek →, *Russia* **57 B13** 73 0N 120 10 E
Olenino, *Russia* **50 C8** 56 15N 33 30 E
Oléron, I. d', *France* **24 C2** 45 55N 1 15W
Oleśnica, *Poland* **47 D4** 51 13N 17 22 E
Olesno, *Poland* **47 E5** 50 51N 18 26 E
Olevsk, *Ukraine* **50 F5** 51 12N 27 39 E
Olga, *Russia* **57 E14** 43 50N 135 14 E
Olga, L., *Canada* **128 C4** 49 47N 77 15W
Olga, Mt., *Australia* **113 E5** 25 20 S 130 50 E
Ølgod, *Denmark* **15 J2** 55 49N 8 36 E
Olhão, *Portugal* **37 H3** 37 3N 7 48W
Olib, *Croatia* **39 D11** 44 23N 14 44 E
Oliena, *Italy* **40 B2** 40 18N 9 22 E
Oliete, *Spain* **34 D4** 41 1N 0 41W
Olifants →, *Africa* **105 C5** 23 57 S 31 58 E
Olifantshoek, *S. Africa* **104 D3** 27 57 S 22 42 E
Ólimbos, *Greece* **45 J9** 35 44N 27 11 E
Ólimbos, Óros, *Greece* **44 D4** 40 6N 22 23 E
Olímpia, *Brazil* **159 A6** 20 44 S 48 54W
Olin, *U.S.A.* **140 B5** 42 0N 91 9W
Olinda, *Brazil* **154 C5** 8 1 S 34 51W
Olindiná, *Brazil* **154 D4** 11 22 S 38 21W
Olite, *Spain* **34 C3** 42 29N 1 40W
Oliva, *Argentina* **158 C3** 32 0 S 63 38W
Oliva, *Spain* **35 G4** 38 58N 0 9W
Oliva, Punta del, *Spain* **36 B5** 43 37N 5 28W
Oliva de la Frontera, *Spain* **37 G4** 38 17N 6 54W
Olivares, *Spain* **34 F2** 39 46N 2 20W
Olive Hill, *U.S.A.* **141 F13** 38 18N 83 13W
Olivehurst, *U.S.A.* **144 F5** 39 6N 121 34W
Oliveira, *Brazil* **155 F3** 20 39 S 44 50W
Oliveira de Azemeis, *Portugal* **36 E2** 40 49N 8 29W
Oliveira dos Brejinhos, *Brazil* **155 D3** 12 19 S 42 54W
Olivenza, *Spain* **37 G3** 38 41N 7 9W
Oliver, *Canada* **130 D5** 49 13N 119 37W
Oliver L., *Canada* **131 B8** 56 56N 103 22W
Olivine Ra., *N.Z.* **119 E3** 44 15 S 168 30 E
Olivone, *Switz.* **29 C7** 46 32N 8 57 E
Olkhovka, *Russia* **53 B11** 49 48N 44 32 E
Olkusz, *Poland* **47 E6** 50 18N 19 33 E
Ollagüe, *Chile* **158 A2** 21 15 S 68 10W
Olloy, *Belgium* **21 H5** 50 5N 4 36 E
Olmedo, *Spain* **36 D6** 41 20N 4 43W
Olmos, *Peru* **156 B2** 5 59 S 79 46W
Olney, *Ill., U.S.A.* **141 F8** 38 44N 88 5W
Olney, *Tex., U.S.A.* **139 J5** 33 22N 98 45W
Oloma, *Cameroon* **101 E7** 3 29N 11 19 E
Olomane →, *Canada* **129 B7** 50 14N 60 37W
Olombo, *Congo* **102 C3** 1 18 S 15 53 E
Olomouc, *Czech.* **31 B10** 49 38N 17 12 E
Olonets, *Russia* **48 B5** 61 10N 33 0 E
Olongapo, *Phil.* **70 D3** 14 50N 120 18 E
Oloron, Gave d' →, *France* **24 E2** 43 33N 1 5W
Oloron-Ste.-Marie, *France* **24 E3** 43 11N 0 38W
Olot, *Spain* **34 C7** 42 11N 2 30 E
Olovo, *Bos.-H.* **42 C3** 44 8N 18 35 E
Olovo, *Yugoslavia* **42 C3** 44 3N 19 0 E
Olovyannaya, *Russia* **57 D12** 50 58N 115 35 E
Oloy →, *Russia* **57 C16** 66 29N 159 29 E
Olpe, *Germany* **26 D3** 51 2N 7 50 E
Olshanka, *Ukraine* **52 B4** 48 16N 30 58 E
Olshany, *Ukraine* **50 F9** 50 3N 35 53 E
Olst, *Neths.* **20 D8** 52 20N 6 7 E
Olsztyn, *Poland* **47 B7** 53 48N 20 29 E
Olsztyn □, *Poland* **47 B7** 54 0N 21 0 E
Olsztynek, *Poland* **47 B7** 53 34N 20 19 E
Olt □, *Romania* **46 E5** 44 20N 24 30 E
Olt →, *Romania* **46 F5** 43 43N 24 51 E
Olten, *Switz.* **28 B5** 47 21N 7 53 E
Oltenița, *Romania* **46 E7** 44 7N 26 42 E
Olton, *U.S.A.* **139 H3** 34 11N 102 8W
Oltu, *Turkey* **89 C9** 40 35N 41 58 E
Olur, *Turkey* **89 C10** 40 49N 42 8 E
Olutanga, *Phil.* **71 H4** 7 26N 122 54 E
Olutanga I., *Phil.* **71 H4** 7 22N 122 52 E
Olvega, *Spain* **34 D3** 41 47N 2 0W
Olvera, *Spain* **37 J5** 36 55N 5 18W
Olymbos, *Cyprus* **32 D12** 35 21N 33 45 E
Olympia, *Greece* **45 G3** 37 39N 21 39 E
Olympia, *U.S.A.* **144 D4** 47 3N 122 53W
Olympic Mts., *U.S.A.* **144 C3** 47 55N 123 45W
Olympic Nat. Park, *U.S.A.* **144 C3** 47 48N 123 30W
Olympus, *Cyprus* **32 E11** 34 56N 32 52 E
Olympus, Mt. = Ólimbos, Óros, *Greece* **44 D4** 40 6N 22 23 E
Olympus, Mt., *U.S.A.* **144 C3** 47 48N 123 43W
Olyphant, *U.S.A.* **137 E9** 41 27N 75 36W
Om →, *Russia* **56 D8** 54 59N 73 22 E
Om Hajer, *Eritrea* **95 E4** 14 20N 36 41 E
Om Koi, *Thailand* **76 D2** 17 48N 98 22 E
Ōma, *Japan* **60 D10** 41 45N 141 5 E
Ōmachi, *Japan* **63 A9** 36 30N 137 50 E
Omae-Zaki, *Japan* **63 C10** 34 36N 138 14 E
Ōmagari, *Japan* **60 E10** 39 27N 140 29 E
Omagh, *U.K.* **19 B4** 54 36N 7 20W
Omagh □, *U.K.* **19 B4** 54 35N 7 15W
Omaha, *U.S.A.* **138 E7** 41 17N 95 58W
Omak, *U.S.A.* **142 B4** 48 25N 119 31W
Omalos, *Greece* **32 D5** 35 19N 23 55 E
Oman ■, *Asia* **87 B7** 23 0N 58 0 E
Oman, G. of, *Asia* **85 E8** 24 30N 58 30 E
Omapere, *N.Z.* **118 B2** 35 37 S 173 25 E
Omar Combon, *Somali Rep.* **108 D3** 3 10N 45 47 E
Omaruru, *Namibia* **104 C2** 21 26 S 16 0 E
Omaruru →, *Namibia* **104 C1** 22 7 S 14 15 E
Omate, *Peru* **156 D3** 16 45 S 71 0W
Ombai, Selat, *Indonesia* **72 C2** 8 30 S 124 50 E
Omboué, *Gabon* **102 C1** 1 35 S 9 15 E
Ombrone →, *Italy* **38 F8** 42 39N 11 0 E
Omchi, *Chad* **97 D3** 21 22N 17 53 E
Omdurmân, *Sudan* **95 D3** 15 40N 32 28 E
Ōme, *Japan* **63 B11** 35 47N 139 15 E
Omegna, *Italy* **38 C5** 45 52N 8 23 E
Omeonga, *Zaïre* **102 C4** 3 40 S 24 22 E
Ometepe, I. de, *Nic.* **148 D2** 11 32N 85 35W
Ometepec, *Mexico* **147 D5** 16 39N 98 23W
Ōmi-Shima, *Ehime, Japan* **62 C5** 34 15N 133 0 E
Ōmi-Shima, *Yamaguchi, Japan* **62 C3** 34 25N 131 9 E
Omihachiman, *Japan* **63 B8** 35 7N 136 3 E
Ominato, *Japan* **60 D10** 41 17N 141 10 E
Omineca →, *Canada* **130 B4** 56 3N 124 16W
Omiš, *Croatia* **39 E13** 43 28N 16 40 E
Omišalj, *Croatia* **39 C11** 45 13N 14 32 E
Omitara, *Namibia* **104 C2** 22 16 S 18 2 E
Ōmiya, *Japan* **63 B11** 35 54N 139 38 E
Omme Å →, *Denmark* **15 J2** 55 56N 8 32 E
Ommen, *Neths.* **20 C8** 52 31N 6 26 E
Ömnögovĭ □, *Mongolia* **66 C3** 43 15N 104 0 E
Omo →, *Ethiopia* **95 F4** 6 25N 36 10 E
Omodhos, *Cyprus* **32 E11** 34 51N 32 48 E
Omolon →, *Russia* **57 C16** 68 42N 158 36 E
Omono-Gawa →, *Japan* **60 E10** 39 46N 140 3 E
Omsk, *Russia* **56 D8** 55 0N 73 12 E
Omsukchan, *Russia* **57 C16** 62 32N 155 48 E
Ōmu, *Japan* **60 B11** 44 34N 142 58 E
Omul, Vf., *Romania* **46 D6** 45 27N 25 29 E
Omulew →, *Poland* **47 B8** 53 5N 21 33 E
Ōmura, *Japan* **62 E1** 32 56N 129 57 E
Omura-Wan, *Japan* **62 E1** 32 57N 129 52 E
Omurtag, *Bulgaria* **43 D11** 43 8N 26 26 E
Ōmuta, *Japan* **62 D2** 33 5N 130 26 E
Omutninsk, *Russia* **54 B3** 58 45N 52 4 E
On, *Belgium* **21 H6** 50 11N 5 18 E
On-Take, *Japan* **62 F2** 31 35N 130 39 E
Oña, *Spain* **34 C1** 42 43N 3 25W
Onaga, *U.S.A.* **138 F6** 39 29N 96 10W
Onalaska, *U.S.A.* **138 D9** 43 53N 91 14W
Onamia, *U.S.A.* **138 B8** 46 4N 93 40W
Onancock, *U.S.A.* **134 G8** 37 43N 75 45W
Onang, *Indonesia* **72 B1** 3 2 S 118 49 E
Onaping L., *Canada* **128 C3** 47 3N 81 30W
Onarga, *U.S.A.* **141 D8** 40 43N 88 1W
Onarhā, *Afghan.* **79 B3** 35 30N 71 0 E
Oñate, *Spain* **34 B2** 43 3N 2 25W
Onavas, *Mexico* **146 B3** 28 28N 109 30W
Onawa, *U.S.A.* **138 D6** 42 2N 96 6W
Onaway, *U.S.A.* **134 C3** 45 21N 84 14W
Oncesti, *Romania* **46 F6** 43 56N 25 52 E
Oncócua, *Angola* **103 F2** 16 30 S 13 25 E
Onda, *Spain* **34 F4** 39 55N 0 17W
Ondaejin, *N. Korea* **67 D15** 41 34N 129 40 E
Ondangua, *Namibia* **104 B2** 17 57 S 16 4 E
Ondárroa, *Spain* **34 B2** 43 19N 2 25W
Ondas →, *Brazil* **155 D3** 12 8 S 44 55W
Ondava →, *Slovak Rep.* **31 C14** 48 27N 21 48 E
Onderdijk, *Neths.* **20 C6** 52 45N 5 8 E
Ondjiva, *Angola* **103 F3** 16 48 S 15 50 E
Ondo, *Japan* **62 C4** 34 11N 132 32 E
Ondo, *Nigeria* **101 D5** 7 4N 4 47 E
Ondo □, *Nigeria* **101 D6** 7 0N 5 0 E
Öndörshil, *Mongolia* **66 B5** 45 13N 108 5 E
Öndverðarnes, *Iceland* **12 D1** 64 52N 24 0W
Onega, *Russia* **48 B6** 64 0N 38 10 E
Onega →, *Russia* **48 B6** 63 58N 37 55 E
Onega, G. of = Onezhskaya Guba, *Russia* **48 B6** 64 30N 37 0 E
Onega, L. = Onezhskoye Ozero, *Russia* **48 B6** 62 0N 35 30 E
Onehunga, *N.Z.* **118 C3** 36 55 S 174 48 E
Oneida, *Ill., U.S.A.* **140 C6** 41 4N 90 13W
Oneida, *N.Y., U.S.A.* **137 C9** 43 6N 75 39W
Oneida L., *U.S.A.* **137 C9** 43 12N 75 54W
O'Neill, *U.S.A.* **138 D5** 42 27N 98 39W
Onekotan, Ostrov, *Russia* **57 E16** 49 25N 154 45 E
Onema, *Zaïre* **103 C4** 4 35 S 24 30 E
Oneonta, *Ala., U.S.A.* **135 J2** 33 57N 86 28W
Oneonta, *N.Y., U.S.A.* **137 D9** 42 27N 75 4W
Onerahi, *N.Z.* **118 B3** 35 45 S 174 22 E
Onezhskaya Guba, *Russia* **48 B6** 64 30N 37 0 E
Onezhskoye Ozero, *Russia* **48 B6** 62 0N 35 30 E
Ongarue, *N.Z.* **118 E4** 38 42 S 175 19 E
Ongea Levu, *Fiji* **121 B3** 19 8 S 178 24W
Ongerup, *Australia* **113 F2** 33 58 S 118 28 E
Ongjin, *N. Korea* **67 F13** 37 56N 125 21 E
Ongkharak, *Thailand* **76 E3** 14 8N 101 1 E
Ongniud Qi, *China* **67 C10** 43 0N 118 38 E
Ongoka, *Zaïre* **106 C2** 1 20 S 26 0 E
Ongole, *India* **83 G5** 15 33N 80 2 E
Ongon, *Mongolia* **66 B7** 45 41N 113 5 E
Onguren, *Russia* **57 D11** 53 38N 107 36 E
Onhaye, *Belgium* **21 H5** 50 15N 4 50 E
Oni, *Georgia* **53 E10** 42 33N 43 26 E
Onida, *U.S.A.* **138 C4** 44 42N 100 4W
Onilahy →, *Madag.* **105 C7** 23 34 S 43 45 E
Onitsha, *Nigeria* **101 D6** 6 6N 6 42 E
Onmaka, *Burma* **78 D6** 22 17N 96 41 E
Ono, *Fiji* **121 B2** 18 55 S 178 29 E
Ono, *Fukui, Japan* **63 B8** 35 59N 136 29 E
Ono, *Hyōgo, Japan* **62 C6** 34 51N 134 56 E
Onoda, *Japan* **62 C3** 34 2N 131 25 E
Onoke, L., *N.Z.* **118 H4** 41 22 S 175 8 E
Onomichi, *Japan* **62 C5** 34 25N 133 12 E
Onpyŏng-ni, *S. Korea* **67 H14** 33 25N 126 55 E
Ons, Is. d', *Spain* **36 C2** 42 23N 8 55W
Onsala, *Sweden* **15 G6** 57 26N 12 0 E
Onslow, *Australia* **112 D2** 21 40 S 115 12 E
Onslow B., *U.S.A.* **135 H7** 34 20N 77 15W
Onstwedde, *Neths.* **20 B10** 53 2N 7 4 E
Ontake-San, *Japan* **63 B9** 35 53N 137 29 E
Ontaneda, *Spain* **36 B7** 43 12N 3 57W
Ontario, *Calif., U.S.A.* **145 L9** 34 4N 117 39W
Ontario, *Oreg., U.S.A.* **142 D5** 44 2N 116 58W
Ontario □, *Canada* **128 B2** 48 0N 83 0W
Ontario, L., *U.S.A.* **128 D4** 43 20N 78 0W
Onteniente, *Spain* **35 G4** 38 50N 0 35W
Ontonagon, *U.S.A.* **138 B10** 46 52N 89 19W
Ontur, *Spain* **35 G3** 38 38N 1 29W
Onyx, *U.S.A.* **145 K8** 35 41N 118 14W
Oodnadatta, *Australia* **115 D2** 27 33 S 135 30 E
Ooldea, *Australia* **113 F5** 30 27 S 131 50 E
Ooltgensplaat, *Neths.* **21 E4** 51 41N 4 21 E
Oombulgurri, *Australia* **112 C4** 15 15 S 127 45 E
Oona River, *Canada* **130 C2** 53 57N 130 16W
Oordegem, *Belgium* **21 G3** 50 58N 3 54 E
Oorindi, *Australia* **114 C3** 20 40 S 141 1 E
Oost-Vlaanderen □, *Belgium* **21 F3** 51 5N 3 50 E
Oost-Vlieland, *Neths.* **20 B6** 53 18N 5 4 E
Oostakker, *Belgium* **21 F3** 51 6N 3 46 E
Oostburg, *Neths.* **21 F3** 51 19N 3 30 E
Oostduinkerke, *Belgium* **21 F1** 51 7N 2 41 E
Oostelijk-Flevoland, *Neths.* **20 C7** 52 31N 5 38 E
Oostende, *Belgium* **21 F1** 51 15N 2 54 E
Oosterbeek, *Neths.* **20 E7** 51 59N 5 51 E
Oosterdijk, *Neths.* **20 C6** 52 44N 5 14 E
Oosterend, *Friesland, Neths.* **20 B6** 53 24N 5 23 E
Oosterend, *Noord-Holland, Neths.* **20 B5** 53 5N 4 52 E
Oosterhout, *Noord-Brabant, Neths.* **21 E7** 51 53N 5 50 E
Oosterhout, *Noord-Brabant, Neths.* **21 E5** 51 39N 4 47 E
Oosterschelde, *Neths.* **21 E4** 51 33N 4 0 E
Oosterwolde, *Neths.* **20 B8** 53 0N 6 17 E
Oosterzele, *Belgium* **21 G3** 50 57N 3 48 E
Oostkamp, *Belgium* **21 F2** 51 9N 3 14 E
Oostmalle, *Belgium* **21 F5** 51 18N 4 44 E
Oostrozebekke, *Belgium* **21 G2** 50 55N 3 21 E
Oostvleteven, *Belgium* **21 G1** 50 56N 2 45 E
Oostvoorne, *Neths.* **20 E4** 51 55N 4 5 E
Oostzaan, *Neths.* **20 D5** 52 26N 4 52 E
Ootacamund, *India* **83 J3** 11 30N 76 44 E
Ootha, *Australia* **117 B7** 33 6 S 147 29 E
Ootmarsum, *Neths.* **20 D9** 52 24N 6 54 E
Ootsa L., *Canada* **130 C3** 53 50N 126 2W
Opaka, *Bulgaria* **43 D11** 43 28N 26 10 E
Opala, *Russia* **57 D16** 51 58N 156 30 E
Opala, *Zaïre* **102 C4** 0 40 S 24 20 E
Opalenica, *Poland* **47 C3** 52 18N 16 24 E
Opan, *Bulgaria* **43 E10** 42 13N 25 41 E
Opanake, *Sri Lanka* **83 L5** 6 35N 80 40 E
Opapa, *N.Z.* **118 F5** 39 47 S 176 42 E
Opasatika, *Canada* **128 C3** 49 30N 82 50W
Opasquia, *Canada* **131 C10** 53 16N 93 34W
Opatija, *Croatia* **39 C11** 45 21N 14 17 E
Opatów, *Poland* **47 E8** 50 50N 21 27 E
Opava, *Czech.* **31 B10** 49 57N 17 58 E
Opeinde, *Neths.* **20 B8** 53 8N 6 4 E
Opelousas, *U.S.A.* **139 K8** 30 32N 92 5W
Opémisca, L., *Canada* **128 C5** 49 56N 74 52W
Open Bay Is., *N.Z.* **119 D3** 43 51 S 168 51 E
Opglabbeek, *Belgium* **21 F7** 51 3N 5 35 E
Opheim, *U.S.A.* **142 B10** 48 51N 106 24W
Ophthalmia Ra., *Australia* **112 D2** 23 15 S 119 30 E
Opi, *Nigeria* **101 D6** 6 36N 7 28 E
Opinaca →, *Canada* **128 B4** 52 15N 78 2W
Opinaca L., *Canada* **128 B4** 52 39N 76 20W
Opiskotish, L., *Canada* **129 B6** 53 10N 67 50W
Oploo, *Neths.* **21 E7** 51 37N 5 52 E
Opmeer, *Neths.* **20 C5** 52 42N 4 57 E
Opobo, *Nigeria* **101 E6** 4 35N 7 34 E
Opochka, *Russia* **50 C6** 56 42N 28 45 E
Opoczno, *Poland* **47 D7** 51 22N 20 18 E
Opol, *Phil.* **71 G5** 8 31N 124 34 E
Opole, *Poland* **47 E4** 50 42N 17 58 E
Opole □, *Poland* **47 E4** 50 40N 17 56 E
Opon = Capu-Lapu, *Phil.* **71 F4** 10 20N 123 55 E
Oporto = Porto, *Portugal* **36 D2** 41 8N 8 40W
Opotiki, *N.Z.* **118 E6** 38 1 S 177 19 E
Opp, *U.S.A.* **135 K2** 31 17N 86 16W
Oppenheim, *Germany* **27 F4** 49 50N 8 22 E
Opperdoes, *Neths.* **20 C6** 52 45N 5 4 E
Óppido Mamertina, *Italy* **41 D8** 38 16N 15 59 E
Oppland fylke □, *Norway* **14 C3** 61 15N 9 40 E
Oppstad, *Norway* **14 D5** 60 17N 11 40 E
Oprtalj, *Croatia* **39 C10** 45 23N 13 50 E
Opua, *N.Z.* **118 B3** 35 19 S 174 9 E
Opunake, *N.Z.* **118 F2** 39 26 S 173 52 E
Opuzen, *Croatia* **42 D2** 43 1N 17 34 E
Oquawka, *U.S.A.* **140 D6** 40 56N 90 57W
Ora, *Cyprus* **32 E12** 34 51N 33 12 E
Ora, *Italy* **39 B8** 46 20N 11 19 E
Ora Banda, *Australia* **113 F3** 30 20 S 121 0 E
Oracle, *U.S.A.* **143 K8** 32 37N 110 46W
Oradea, *Romania* **46 B2** 47 2N 21 58 E
Öræfajökull, *Iceland* **12 D5** 64 2N 16 39W
Orahovac, *Serbia* **42 E5** 42 24N 20 40 E
Orahovica, *Croatia* **42 B2** 45 35N 17 52 E
Orai, *India* **81 G8** 25 58N 79 30 E
Oraison, *France* **25 E9** 43 55N 5 55 E
Oral = Ural →, *Kazakhstan* **53 C14** 47 0N 51 48 E
Oral = Uralsk, *Kazakhstan* **54 F2** 51 20N 51 20 E
Oran, *Algeria* **99 A4** 35 45N 0 39W
Oran, *Argentina* **158 A3** 23 10 S 64 20W
Orange = Oranje →, *S. Africa* **104 D2** 28 41 S 16 28 E
Orange, *Australia* **117 B8** 33 15 S 149 7 E
Orange, *France* **25 D8** 44 8N 4 47 E
Orange, *Calif., U.S.A.* **145 M9** 33 47N 117 51W
Orange, *Mass., U.S.A.* **137 D12** 42 35N 72 19W
Orange, *Tex., U.S.A.* **139 K8** 30 6N 93 44W
Orange, *Va., U.S.A.* **134 F6** 38 15N 78 7W
Orange, C., *Brazil* **153 C7** 4 20N 51 30W
Orange Cove, *U.S.A.* **144 J7** 36 38N 119 19W
Orange Free State □, *S. Africa* **104 D4** 28 30 S 27 0 E
Orange Grove, *U.S.A.* **139 M6** 27 58N 97 56W
Orange Walk, *Belize* **147 D7** 18 6N 88 33W
Orangeburg, *U.S.A.* **135 J5** 33 30N 80 52W
Orangeville, *Canada* **128 D3** 43 55N 80 5W
Orangeville, *U.S.A.* **140 B7** 42 28N 89 39W
Orani, *Phil.* **70 D3** 14 49N 120 32 E
Oranienburg, *Germany* **26 C9** 52 45N 13 15 E
Oranje →, *S. Africa* **104 D2** 28 41 S 16 28 E
Oranje Vrystaat = Orange Free State □, *S. Africa* **104 D4** 28 30 S 27 0 E
Oranjemund, *Namibia* **104 D2** 28 38 S 16 29 E
Oranjerivier, *S. Africa* **104 D3** 29 40 S 24 12 E
Oras, *Phil.* **70 E5** 12 9N 125 28 E
Orašje, *Bos.-H.* **42 B3** 45 1N 18 42 E
Orăştie, *Romania* **46 D4** 45 50N 23 10 E
Orașul Stalin = Brașov, *Romania* **46 D6** 45 38N 25 35 E
Orava →, *Slovak Rep.* **31 B12** 49 24N 19 20 E
Oravita, *Romania* **42 B6** 45 2N 21 43 E
Orawia, *N.Z.* **119 G2** 46 1 S 167 50 E
Orb →, *France* **24 E7** 43 15N 3 18 E
Orba →, *Italy* **38 D5** 44 53N 8 37 E
Ørbæk, *Denmark* **15 J4** 55 17N 10 39 E
Orbe, *Switz.* **28 C3** 46 43N 6 32 E
Orbec, *France* **22 C7** 49 1N 0 23 E
Orbetello, *Italy* **39 F8** 42 26N 11 11 E
Órbigo →, *Spain* **36 C5** 42 5N 5 42W
Orbost, *Australia* **117 D8** 37 40 S 148 29 E
Orce, *Spain* **35 H2** 37 44N 2 28W
Orce →, *Spain* **35 H2** 37 44N 2 28W
Orchies, *France* **23 B10** 50 28N 3 14 E
Orchila, I., *Venezuela* **152 A4** 11 48N 66 10W
Orco →, *Italy* **38 C4** 45 10N 7 52 E
Orcopampa, *Peru* **156 D3** 15 20 S 72 23W
Orcutt, *U.S.A.* **145 L6** 34 52N 120 27W
Ord →, *Australia* **112 C4** 15 33 S 128 15 E
Ord, Mt., *Australia* **112 C4** 17 20 S 125 34 E
Ordenes, *Spain* **36 B2** 43 5N 8 29W
Orderville, *U.S.A.* **143 H7** 37 17N 112 38W
Ording, *Germany* **26 A4** 54 23N 8 32 E
Ordos = Mu Us Shamo, *China* **66 E5** 39 0N 109 0 E
Ordu, *Turkey* **89 C7** 40 55N 37 53 E
Ordu □, *Turkey* **89 C7** 41 0N 37 50 E
Orduña, *Álava, Spain* **34 C7** 42 58N 2 58 E
Orduña, *Granada, Spain* **35 H1** 37 20N 3 30W
Ordway, *U.S.A.* **138 F3** 38 13N 103 46W
Ordzhonikidze = Vladikavkaz, *Russia* **53 E11** 43 0N 44 35 E
Ordzhonikidze, *Ukraine* **52 C6** 47 39N 34 3 E
Ordzhonikidze, *Uzbekistan* **55 C4** 41 21N 69 22 E
Ordzhonikidzeabad, *Tajikistan* **55 D4** 38 34N 69 1 E
Ore, *Zaïre* **106 B2** 3 17N 29 30 E
Ore Mts. = Erzgebirge, *Germany* **26 E9** 50 25N 13 0 E
Orealla, *Guyana* **153 B6** 5 15N 57 23W
Orebić, *Croatia* **42 D2** 43 0N 17 11 E
Örebro, *Sweden* **13 G13** 59 20N 15 18 E
Örebro län □, *Sweden* **13 G13** 59 27N 15 0 E
Oregon, *Ill., U.S.A.* **140 B7** 42 1N 89 20W
Oregon, *Ohio, U.S.A.* **141 C13** 41 38N 83 25W
Oregon, *Wis., U.S.A.* **140 B7** 42 56N 89 23W
Oregon □, *U.S.A.* **142 E3** 44 0N 121 0W
Oregon City, *U.S.A.* **144 E4** 45 21N 122 36W
Orekhov, *Ukraine* **52 C6** 47 30N 35 48 E
Orekhovo-Zuyevo, *Russia* **51 D11** 55 50N 38 55 E
Orel, *Russia* **51 E10** 52 57N 36 3 E
Orel →, *Ukraine* **52 B6** 48 45N 34 20 E
Orellana, Canal de, *Spain* **37 F5** 39 2N 6 0W
Orellana, Pantano de, *Spain* **37 F5** 39 5N 5 10W
Orellana la Vieja, *Spain* **37 F5** 39 1N 5 32W
Orem, *U.S.A.* **142 F8** 40 19N 111 42W
Ören, *Turkey* **45 G9** 37 3N 27 57 E
Orenburg, *Russia* **54 F4** 51 45N 55 6 E
Orense, *Spain* **36 C3** 42 19N 7 55W
Orense □, *Spain* **36 C3** 42 15N 7 51W
Orepuki, *N.Z.* **119 G2** 46 19 S 167 46 E
Orestiás, *Greece* **44 C8** 41 30N 26 33 E
Øresund, *Europe* **15 J6** 55 45N 12 45 E
Oreti →, *N.Z.* **119 G3** 46 28 S 168 14 E
Orford Ness, *U.K.* **17 E9** 52 6N 1 31 E
Orgañà, *Spain* **34 C6** 42 13N 1 20 E
Organos, Pta. de los, *Canary Is.* **33 F2** 28 12N 17 17W
Orgaz, *Spain* **37 F7** 39 39N 3 53W
Orgeyev, *Moldavia* **52 C3** 47 24N 28 50 E
Orgon, *France* **25 E9** 43 47N 5 3 E
Orgūn, *Afghan.* **79 B3** 32 55N 69 12 E
Orhaneli, *Turkey* **88 D3** 39 54N 28 59 E
Orhangazi, *Turkey* **88 C3** 40 29N 29 18 E
Orhon Gol →, *Mongolia* **64 A5** 50 21N 106 0 E
Ória, *Italy* **41 B10** 40 30N 17 38 E
Orient, *Australia* **115 D3** 28 7 S 142 50 E
Orient, *U.S.A.* **140 C2** 41 12N 94 25W
Oriental, Cordillera, *Bolivia* **157 D4** 17 0 S 66 0W
Oriental, Cordillera, *Colombia* **152 B3** 6 0N 73 0W
Oriente, *Argentina* **158 D3** 38 44 S 60 37W
Origny-Ste.-Benoîte, *France* **23 C10** 49 50N 3 30 E
Orihuela, *Spain* **35 G4** 38 7N 0 55W
Orihuela del Tremedal, *Spain* **34 E3** 40 33N 1 39W

Owensboro 245

Oriku, Albania 44 D1 40 20N 19 30 E
Orinduik, Guyana 153 C5 4 40N 60 3W
Orinoco →, Venezuela 153 B5 9 15N 61 30W
Orion, U.S.A. 140 C6 41 21N 90 23W
Orissa □, India 82 D6 20 0N 84 0 E
Oristano, Italy 40 C1 39 54N 8 35 E
Oristano, G. di, Italy 40 C1 39 50N 8 22 E
Orituco →, Venezuela 152 B4 8 45N 67 27W
Orizaba, Mexico 147 D5 18 50N 97 10W
Orizare, Bulgaria 43 E12 42 44N 27 39 E
Orizona, Brazil 155 E2 17 3 S 48 18W
Orjen, Bos.-H. 42 E3 42 35N 18 34 E
Orjiva, Spain 35 J1 36 53N 3 24W
Orkanger, Norway 14 A3 63 18N 9 52 E
Örkelljunga, Sweden 15 H7 56 17N 13 17 E
Örkény, Hungary 31 D12 47 9N 19 26 E
Orkla →, Norway 14 A3 63 18N 9 51 E
Orkney, S. Africa 104 D4 26 58 S 26 40 E
Orkney □, U.K. 18 C6 59 0N 3 0W
Orkney Is., U.K. 18 C6 59 0N 3 0W
Orla, Poland 47 C10 52 42N 23 20 E
Orland, Calif., U.S.A. 144 F4 39 45N 122 12W
Orland, Ind., U.S.A. 141 C11 41 47N 85 12W
Orlando, U.S.A. 135 L5 28 33N 81 23W
Orlando, C. d', Italy 41 D7 38 10N 14 43 E
Orléanais, France 23 E9 48 0N 2 0 E
Orléans, France 23 E8 47 54N 1 52 E
Orleans, U.S.A. 137 B12 44 49N 72 12W
Orléans, I. d', Canada 129 C5 46 54N 70 58W
Orlice →, Czech. 30 A9 50 5N 16 10 E
Orlické Hory, Czech. 31 A9 50 15N 16 30 E
Orlov, Slovak Rep. 31 B13 49 17N 20 51 E
Orlov Gay, Russia 51 F16 50 56N 48 19 E
Orlovat, Serbia 42 B5 45 14N 20 33 E
Ormara, Pakistan 79 D2 25 16N 64 33 E
Ormea, Italy 38 D4 44 9N 7 54 E
Ormília, Greece 44 D5 40 16N 23 39 E
Ormoc, Phil. 71 F5 11 0N 124 37 E
Ormond, N.Z. 118 E6 38 33 S 177 56 E
Ormond Beach, U.S.A. 135 L5 29 17N 81 3W
Ormondville, N.Z. 118 G5 40 5 S 176 19 E
Ormož, Slovenia 39 B13 46 25N 16 10 E
Ormstown, Canada 137 A11 45 8N 74 0W
Ornans, France 23 E13 47 7N 6 10 E
Orne □, France 22 D7 48 40N 0 5 E
Orne →, France 22 C6 49 18N 0 15W
Orneta, Poland 47 A7 54 8N 20 9 E
Ørnhøj, Denmark 15 H2 56 13N 8 34 E
Ornö, Sweden 14 E12 59 4N 18 24 E
Örnsköldsvik, Sweden 14 A12 63 17N 18 40 E
Oro, N. Korea 67 D14 40 1N 127 27 E
Oro →, Mexico 146 B3 25 35N 105 2W
Oro Grande, U.S.A. 145 L9 34 36N 117 20W
Orobie, Alpi, Italy 38 B6 46 7N 10 0 E
Orocué, Colombia 152 C3 4 48N 71 20W
Orodo, Nigeria 101 D6 5 34N 7 4 E
Orogrande, U.S.A. 143 K10 32 24N 106 5W
Orol, Spain 36 B3 43 34N 7 39W
Oromocto, Canada 129 C6 45 54N 66 29W
Oron, Nigeria 101 E6 4 48N 8 14 E
Oron, Switz. 28 C3 46 34N 6 50 E
Orono, Canada 136 C6 43 59N 78 37W
Oropesa, Spain 36 F5 39 57N 5 10W
Oroqen Zizhiqi, China 65 A7 50 34N 123 43 E
Oroquieta, Phil. 71 G4 8 32N 123 44 E
Orós, Brazil 154 C4 6 15 S 38 55W
Orosei, G. di, Italy 40 B2 40 15N 9 40 E
Orosháza, Hungary 31 E13 46 32N 20 42 E
Orote Pen., Guam 121 R15 13 26N 144 38 E
Orotukan, Russia 57 C16 62 16N 151 42 E
Oroville, Calif., U.S.A. 144 F5 39 31N 121 33W
Oroville, Wash., U.S.A. 142 B4 48 56N 119 26W
Oroville, L., U.S.A. 144 F5 39 33N 121 29W
Orrick, U.S.A. 140 E2 39 13N 94 7W
Orroroo, Australia 116 B3 32 43 S 138 38 E
Orrville, U.S.A. 136 F3 40 50N 81 46W
Orsara di Púglia, Italy 41 A8 41 17N 15 16 E
Orsha, Belorussia 50 D7 54 30N 30 25 E
Orsières, Switz. 28 D4 46 2N 7 9 E
Orsk, Russia 54 F6 51 12N 58 34 E
Ørslev, Denmark 15 J5 55 3N 11 56 E
Orsogna, Italy 39 F11 42 13N 14 17 E
Orşova, Romania 46 E3 44 41N 22 25 E
Ørsted, Denmark 15 H4 56 30N 10 20 E
Orta, L. d', Italy 38 C5 45 48N 8 21 E
Orta Nova, Italy 41 A8 41 20N 15 40 E
Ortaca, Turkey 88 E3 36 49N 28 45 E
Ortaköy, Çorum, Turkey 88 C6 40 16N 35 15 E
Ortaköy, Niğde, Turkey 88 D6 38 44N 34 3 E
Orte, Italy 39 F9 42 28N 12 23 E
Ortegal, C., Spain 36 B3 43 43N 7 52W
Orteguaza →, Colombia 152 C2 0 43N 75 16W
Orthez, France 24 E3 43 29N 0 48W
Ortho, Belgium 21 H7 50 8N 5 37 E
Ortigueira, Spain 36 B3 43 40N 7 50W
Orting, U.S.A. 144 C4 47 6N 122 12W
Ortles, Italy 38 B7 46 31N 10 33 E
Orto, Tokay, Kirghizia 55 B8 42 20N 76 1 E
Ortón →, Bolivia 156 C4 10 50 S 67 0W
Ortona, Italy 39 F11 42 21N 14 24 E
Orūmīyeh, Iran 84 B5 37 40N 45 0 E
Orūmīyeh, Daryācheh-ye, Iran 84 B5 37 50N 45 30 E
Orune, Italy 40 B2 40 25N 9 20 E
Oruro, Bolivia 156 D4 18 0 S 67 9W
Oruro□, Bolivia 156 D4 18 40 S 67 30W
Orust, Sweden 15 F5 58 10N 11 40 E
Oruzgān □, Afghan. 79 B2 33 30N 66 0 E
Orvault, France 22 E5 47 17N 1 38W
Orvieto, Italy 39 F9 42 43N 12 8 E
Orwell, U.S.A. 136 E4 41 32N 80 52W
Orwell →, U.K. 17 E9 52 2N 1 12 E
Oryakhovo, Bulgaria 43 D8 43 40N 23 57 E
Orzinuovi, Italy 38 C6 45 24N 9 55 E
Orzyc →, Poland 47 C8 52 46N 21 14 E
Orzysz, Poland 47 B8 53 50N 21 58 E
Osa, Russia 54 C4 57 17N 55 26 E
Osa →, Poland 47 B5 53 33N 18 46 E
Osa, Pen. de, Costa Rica 148 E3 8 0N 84 0W
Osage, Iowa, U.S.A. 138 D8 43 17N 92 49W
Osage, Wyo., U.S.A. 138 D2 43 59N 104 25W
Osage →, U.S.A. 140 F5 38 35N 91 57W
Osage City, U.S.A. 138 F7 38 38N 95 50W
Ōsaka, Japan 63 C7 34 40N 135 30 E
Ōsaka □, Japan 63 C7 34 30N 135 30 E
Ōsaka-Wan, Japan 63 C7 34 30N 135 18 E
Osan, S. Korea 67 F14 37 11N 127 4 E
Osawatomie, U.S.A. 138 F7 38 31N 94 57W
Osborne, U.S.A. 138 F5 39 26N 98 42W
Osceola, Ark., U.S.A. 139 H10 35 42N 89 58W
Osceola, Iowa, U.S.A. 140 C3 41 2N 93 46W
Osceola, Mo., U.S.A. 140 F3 38 3N 93 42W
Oschatz, Germany 26 D9 51 17N 13 8 E
Oschersleben, Germany 26 C7 52 2N 11 13 E
Óschiri, Italy 40 B2 40 43N 9 7 E
Oscoda, U.S.A. 136 B1 44 26N 83 20W
Osečina, Serbia 42 C4 44 23N 19 34 E
Ösel = Saaremaa, Estonia 50 B3 58 30N 22 30 E
Osëry, Russia 51 D11 54 52N 38 28 E
Osgood, U.S.A. 141 E11 39 8N 85 18W
Osh, Kirghizia 55 C6 40 37N 72 49 E
Oshawa, Canada 128 D4 43 50N 78 50W
Oshima, Japan 62 D4 33 55N 132 14 E
Oshkosh, Nebr., U.S.A. 138 E3 41 24N 102 21W
Oshkosh, Wis., U.S.A. 138 C10 44 1N 88 33W
Oshmyany, Belorussia 50 D4 54 26N 25 52 E
Oshnovīyeh, Iran 84 B5 37 2N 45 6 E
Oshogbo, Nigeria 101 D5 7 48N 4 37 E
Oshtorīnān, Iran 85 C6 34 1N 48 38 E
Oshwe, Zaïre 102 C3 3 25 S 19 28 E
Osica de Jos, Romania 46 E5 44 14N 24 20 E
Osieczna, Poland 47 D3 51 55N 16 40 E
Osijek, Croatia 42 B3 45 34N 18 41 E
Ósilo, Italy 40 B1 40 45N 8 41 E
Ósimo, Italy 39 E10 43 28N 13 30 E
Osintorf, Belorussia 50 D7 54 40N 30 39 E
Osipenko = Berdyansk, Ukraine 52 C7 46 45N 36 50 E
Osipovichi, Belorussia 50 E6 53 19N 28 33 E
Osizweni, S. Africa 105 D5 27 49 S 30 7 E
Oskaloosa, U.S.A. 140 C4 41 18N 92 39W
Oskarshamn, Sweden 13 H14 57 15N 16 27 E
Oskélanéo, Canada 128 C4 48 5N 75 15W
Öskemen = Ust-Kamenogorsk, Kazakhstan 56 E9 50 0N 82 36 E
Oskol →, Ukraine 51 G10 49 6N 37 25 E
Oslo, Norway 14 E4 59 55N 10 45 E
Oslob, Phil. 71 G4 9 31N 123 26 E
Oslofjorden, Norway 14 E4 59 20N 10 35 E
Osmanabad, India 82 E3 18 5N 76 10 E
Osmancık, Turkey 52 F6 40 58N 34 47 E
Osmaniye, Turkey 88 E7 37 5N 36 10 E
Ösmo, Sweden 14 F11 58 58N 17 55 E
Osnabrück, Germany 26 C4 52 16N 8 2 E
Ośno Lubuskie, Poland 47 C1 52 28N 14 51 E
Osobláha, Czech. 31 A10 50 17N 17 44 E
Osogovska Planina, Macedonia 42 E7 42 10N 22 30 E
Osor, Italy 39 D11 44 42N 14 24 E
Osorio, Brazil 159 B5 29 53 S 50 17W
Osorno, Chile 160 B2 40 25 S 73 0W
Osorno, Spain 36 C6 42 24N 4 22W
Osorno □, Chile 160 B2 40 34 S 73 9W
Osorno, Vol., Chile 160 B2 41 0 S 72 30W
Osoyoos, Canada 130 D5 49 0N 119 30W
Ospika →, Canada 130 B4 56 20N 124 0W
Osprey Reef, Australia 114 A4 13 52 S 146 36 E
Oss, Neths. 20 E7 51 46N 5 32 E
Ossa, Mt., Australia 114 G4 41 52 S 146 3 E
Óssa, Oros, Greece 44 E4 39 47N 22 42 E
Ossa de Montiel, Spain 35 G2 38 58N 2 45W
Ossabaw I., U.S.A. 135 K5 31 50N 81 5W
Osse →, France 24 D4 44 7N 0 17 E
Ossendrecht, Neths. 21 F4 51 24N 4 20 E
Ossining, U.S.A. 137 E11 41 10N 73 55W
Ossipee, U.S.A. 137 C13 43 41N 71 7W
Ossokmanuan L., Canada 129 B7 53 25N 65 0W
Ossora, Russia 57 D17 59 20N 163 13 E
Ostashkov, Russia 50 C8 57 4N 33 2 E
Oste →, Germany 26 B5 53 30N 9 12 E
Ostend = Oostende, Belgium 21 F1 51 15N 2 54 E
Oster, Ukraine 50 F7 50 57N 30 53 E
Osterburg, Germany 26 C7 52 47N 11 44 E
Osterburken, Germany 27 F5 49 26N 9 25 E
Österdalälven →, Sweden 13 F12 61 30N 13 45 E
Östergötlands län □, Sweden 15 F9 58 35N 15 45 E
Osterholz-Scharmbeck, Germany 26 B4 53 14N 8 48 E
Østerild, Denmark 15 G2 57 2N 8 51 E
Ostermundigen, Switz. 28 C4 46 58N 7 27 E
Östersund, Sweden 14 A8 63 10N 14 38 E
Østfold fylke □, Norway 14 E5 59 25N 11 25 E
Ostfriesische Inseln, Germany 26 B3 53 45N 7 15 E
Ostfriesland, Germany 26 B3 53 20N 7 30 E
Óstia, Lido di, Italy 40 A5 41 43N 12 17 E
Ostiglía, Italy 39 C8 45 4N 11 9 E
Ostra, Italy 39 E10 43 40N 13 5 E
Ostrava, Czech. 31 B11 49 51N 18 18 E
Ostróda, Poland 47 B6 53 42N 19 58 E
Ostrog, Ukraine 50 F5 50 20N 26 30 E
Ostrogozhsk, Russia 51 F11 50 55N 39 7 E
Ostrogróg Sźamotuły, Poland 47 C3 52 37N 16 33 E
Ostrołęka, Poland 47 B8 53 4N 21 32 E
Ostrołeka □, Poland 47 C8 53 0N 21 30 E
Ostrov, Bulgaria 43 D9 43 40N 24 9 E
Ostrov, Romania 46 E8 44 6N 27 24 E
Ostrov, Russia 50 C5 57 25N 28 20 E
Ostrów Lubelski, Poland 47 D9 51 29N 22 51 E
Ostrów Mazowiecka, Poland 47 C8 52 50N 21 51 E
Ostrów Wielkopolski, Poland 47 D4 51 36N 17 44 E
Ostrowiec-Świętokrzyski, Poland 47 E8 50 55N 21 22 E
Ostrozac, Bos.-H. 42 D2 43 43N 17 49 E
Ostrzeszów, Poland 47 D4 51 25N 17 52 E
Ostseebad-Kühlungsborn, Germany 26 A7 54 10N 11 40 E
Osttirol □, Austria 27 J8 46 50N 12 30 E
Ostuni, Italy 41 B10 40 44N 17 34 E
Osum →, Bulgaria 43 D9 43 40N 24 50 E
Osumi →, Albania 44 D2 40 40N 20 10 E
Ōsumi-Hantō, Japan 62 F2 31 20N 130 55 E
Ōsumi-Kaikyō, Japan 61 J5 30 55N 131 0 E
Ōsumi-Shotō, Japan 61 J5 30 30N 130 0 E
Osun □, Nigeria 101 D5 7 30N 4 30 E
Osuna, Spain 37 H5 37 14N 5 8W
Oswego, U.S.A. 137 C8 43 27N 76 31W
Oswestry, U.K. 16 E4 52 52N 3 3W
Oświecim, Poland 31 A12 50 2N 19 11 E
Ōta, Japan 63 A11 36 18N 139 22 E
Ota-Gawa →, Japan 62 C4 34 21N 132 18 E
Otago □, N.Z. 119 E4 45 15 S 170 0 E
Otago Harbour, N.Z. 119 F5 45 47 S 170 42 E
Otago Pen., N.Z. 119 F5 45 48 S 170 39 E
Otahuhu, N.Z. 118 C3 36 56 S 174 51 E
Ōtake, Japan 62 C4 34 12N 132 13 E
Ōtaki, Japan 63 B12 35 17N 140 15 E
Otaki, N.Z. 118 G4 40 45 S 175 10 E
Otane, N.Z. 118 F5 39 54 S 176 39 E
Otar, Kazakhstan 55 B7 43 32N 75 12 E
Otaru, Japan 60 C10 43 10N 141 0 E
Otaru-Wan = Ishikari-Wan, Japan 60 C10 43 25N 141 1 E
Otautau, N.Z. 119 G3 46 9 S 168 1 E
Otava →, Czech. 30 B7 49 26N 14 12 E
Otavalo, Ecuador 152 C2 0 13N 78 20W
Otavi, Namibia 104 B2 19 40 S 17 24 E
Otchinjau, Angola 103 F2 16 30 S 13 56 E
Otelec, Romania 46 D1 45 36N 20 50 E
Otero de Rey, Spain 36 B3 43 6N 7 36W
Othello, U.S.A. 142 C4 46 50N 119 10W
Othonoí, Greece 44 E1 39 52N 19 22 E
Óthris, Óros, Greece 45 E4 39 4N 22 42 E
Otira, N.Z. 119 C6 42 49 S 171 35 E
Otira Gorge, N.Z. 119 C6 42 53 S 171 33 E
Otis, U.S.A. 138 E3 40 9N 102 58W
Otjiwarongo, Namibia 104 C2 20 30 S 16 33 E
Otmuchów, Poland 47 E4 50 28N 17 10 E
Oto Tolu Group, Tonga 121 Q13 20 21 S 174 32W
Otočac, Croatia 39 D12 44 53N 15 12 E
Otoineppu, Japan 60 B11 44 44N 142 16 E
Oton, Phil. 71 F4 10 42N 122 29 E
Otorohanga, N.Z. 118 E4 38 12 S 175 14 E
Otoskwin →, Canada 128 B2 52 13N 88 6W
Otosquen, Canada 131 C8 53 17N 102 1W
Ōtoyo, Japan 62 D5 33 43N 133 45 E
Otranto, Italy 41 B11 40 9N 18 28 E
Otranto, C. d', Italy 41 B11 40 7N 18 30 E
Otranto, Str. of, Italy 41 B11 40 15N 18 40 E
Otse, S. Africa 104 D4 25 2 S 25 45 E
Otsego, U.S.A. 141 B11 42 27N 85 42W
Ōtsu, Japan 63 B7 35 0N 135 50 E
Ōtsuki, Japan 63 B10 35 36N 138 57 E
Otta, Norway 14 C3 61 46N 9 32 E
Ottapalam, India 83 J3 10 46N 76 23 E
Ottawa = Outaouais →, Canada 128 C5 45 27N 74 8W
Ottawa, Canada 128 C4 45 27N 75 42W
Ottawa, Ill., U.S.A. 138 E10 41 21N 88 51W
Ottawa, Kans., U.S.A. 138 F7 38 37N 95 16W
Ottawa, Ohio, U.S.A. 141 C12 41 1N 84 3W
Ottawa Is., Canada 127 C11 59 35N 80 10W
Ottélé, Cameroon 101 E7 3 38N 11 19 E
Ottensheim, Austria 30 C7 48 21N 14 12 E
Otter L., Canada 131 B8 55 35N 104 39W
Otter Rapids, Ont., Canada 128 B3 50 11N 81 39W
Otter Rapids, Sask., Canada 131 B8 55 38N 104 44W
Otterbein, U.S.A. 141 D9 40 29N 87 6W
Otterndorf, Germany 26 B4 53 47N 8 52 E
Otterup, Denmark 15 J4 55 30N 10 22 E
Otterville, Canada 136 D4 42 55N 80 36W
Otterville, U.S.A. 140 F4 38 42N 93 0W
Ottignies, Belgium 21 G5 50 40N 4 33 E
Otto Beit Bridge, Zimbabwe 107 F2 15 59 S 28 56 E
Ottosdal, S. Africa 104 D4 26 46 S 25 59 E
Ottoshoop, S. Africa 104 D4 25 45 S 25 58 E
Ottoville, U.S.A. 141 D12 40 57N 84 22W
Ottsjön, Sweden 14 A7 63 13N 13 2 E
Ottumwa, U.S.A. 140 C4 41 1N 92 25W
Otu, Nigeria 101 D5 8 14N 3 22 E
Otukpa, Nigeria 101 D6 7 9N 7 41 E
Oturkpo, Nigeria 101 D6 7 16N 8 8 E
Otway, B., Chile 160 D2 53 30 S 74 0W
Otway, C., Australia 116 E5 38 52 S 143 30 E
Otwock, Poland 47 C8 52 5N 21 20 E
Ötz, Austria 30 D3 47 13N 10 53 E
Ötz →, Austria 30 D3 47 14N 10 50 E
Ötztaler Alpen, Austria 30 E4 46 56N 11 0 E
Ou →, Laos 76 B4 20 4N 102 13 E
Ou Neua, Laos 76 A3 22 18N 101 48 E
Ou-Sammyaku, Japan 60 E10 39 20N 140 35 E
Ouachita →, U.S.A. 139 K9 31 38N 91 49W
Ouachita, L., U.S.A. 139 H8 34 34N 93 12W
Ouachita Mts., U.S.A. 139 H7 34 40N 94 25W
Ouaco, N. Cal. 121 T18 20 50 S 164 29 E
Ouadâne, Mauritania 98 D2 20 50N 11 40W
Ouadda, C.A.R. 102 A4 8 15N 22 20 E
Ouagadougou, Burkina Faso 101 C4 12 25N 1 30W
Ouagam, Chad 97 F2 14 22N 14 42 E
Ouahigouya, Burkina Faso 100 C4 13 31N 2 25W
Ouahila, Algeria 98 C3 27 50N 5 0W
Ouahran = Oran, Algeria 99 A4 35 45N 0 39W
Oualâta, Mauritania 100 B3 17 20N 6 55W
Ouallene, Algeria 99 D5 24 41N 1 11 E
Ouanda Djallé, C.A.R. 102 A4 8 55N 22 53 E
Ouandago, C.A.R. 102 A3 7 13N 18 50 E
Ouango, C.A.R. 102 B4 4 19N 22 30 E
Ouarâne, Mauritania 98 D2 21 0N 10 30W
Ouargla, Algeria 99 B6 31 59N 5 16 E
Ouarkziz, Djebel, Algeria 98 C3 28 50N 8 0W
Ouarzazate, Morocco 98 B3 30 55N 6 50W
Ouatagouna, Mali 101 B5 15 11N 0 43 E
Ouatere, C.A.R. 102 A3 5 30N 19 8 E
Oubangi →, Zaïre 102 C3 0 30 S 17 50 E
Oubarakai, O. →, Algeria 99 C6 27 20N 9 0 E
Oubatche, N. Cal. 121 T18 20 26 S 164 39 E
Ouche →, France 23 E12 47 6N 5 16 E
Oud-Beijerland, Neths. 20 E4 51 50N 4 25 E
Oud-Gastel, Neths. 21 E4 51 35N 4 28 E
Oud Turnhout, Belgium 21 F6 51 19N 5 0 E
Ouddorp, Neths. 20 E3 51 50N 3 57 E
Oude-Pekela, Neths. 20 B10 53 6N 7 0 E
Oude Rijn →, Neths. 20 D4 52 12N 4 24 E
Oudega, Neths. 20 B8 53 8N 6 0 E
Oudenaarde, Belgium 21 G3 50 50N 3 37 E
Oudenbosch, Neths. 21 E5 51 35N 4 32 E
Oudenburg, Belgium 21 F2 51 11N 3 1 E
Ouderkerk, Utrecht, Neths. 20 D5 52 18N 4 55 E
Ouderkerk, Zuid-Holland, Neths. 20 E5 51 56N 4 38 E
Oudeschild, Neths. 20 B5 53 2N 4 50 E
Oudewater, Neths. 20 D5 52 2N 4 52 E
Oudkarspel, Neths. 20 C5 52 43N 4 49 E
Oudon, France 22 E5 47 22N 1 19W
Oudtshoorn, S. Africa 104 E3 33 35 S 22 14 E
Oued Zem, Morocco 98 B3 32 52N 6 34W
Ouégoa, N. Cal. 121 T18 20 20 S 164 26 E
Ouellé, Ivory C. 100 D4 7 26N 4 1W
Ouen, I., N. Cal. 121 V20 22 26 S 166 49 E
Ouenza, Algeria 99 A6 35 57N 8 4 E
Ouessa, Burkina Faso 100 C4 11 4N 2 47W
Ouessant, I. d', France 22 D1 48 28N 5 6W
Ouesso, Congo 102 B3 1 37N 16 5 E
Ouest, Pte., Canada 129 C7 49 52N 64 40W
Ouezzane, Morocco 98 B3 34 51N 5 35W
Ouffet, Belgium 21 H6 50 26N 5 28 E
Ouidah, Benin 101 D5 6 25N 2 0 E
Ouistreham, France 22 C6 49 17N 0 18W
Oujda, Morocco 99 B4 34 41N 1 55W
Oujeft, Mauritania 98 D2 20 2N 13 0W
Ould Yenjé, Mauritania 100 B2 15 38N 12 16W
Ouled Djellal, Algeria 99 B6 34 28N 5 2 E
Ouled Naïl, Mts. des, Algeria 99 B5 34 30N 3 30 E
Oulmès, Morocco 98 B3 33 17N 6 0W
Oulu, Finland 12 D18 65 1N 25 29 E
Oulu □ = Oulun lääni □, Finland 12 D19 64 36N 27 20 E
Oulujärvi, Finland 12 D19 64 25N 27 15 E
Oulujoki →, Finland 12 D18 65 1N 25 30 E
Oulun lääni □, Finland 12 D19 64 36N 27 20 E
Oulx, Italy 38 C3 45 2N 6 49 E
Oum Chalouba, Chad 97 E4 15 48N 20 46 E
Oum-el-Bouaghi, Algeria 99 A6 35 55N 7 6 E
Oum el Ksi, Algeria 98 C3 29 4N 6 59W
Oum-er-Rbia, O. →, Morocco 98 B3 33 19N 8 21W
Oumè, Ivory C. 100 D3 6 21N 5 27W
Ounane, Dj., Algeria 99 C6 25 4N 7 19 E
Ounguati, Namibia 104 C2 22 0 S 15 46 E
Ounianga-Kébir, Chad 97 E4 19 4N 20 29 E
Ounianga Sérir, Chad 97 E4 18 54N 20 51 E
Our →, Lux. 21 J8 49 55N 6 5 E
Ouray, U.S.A. 143 G10 38 1N 107 40W
Ourcq →, France 23 C10 49 1N 3 1 E
Oureg, Oued el →, Algeria 99 B5 32 34N 2 10 E
Ourém, Brazil 154 B2 1 33 S 47 6W
Ourense = Orense, Spain 36 C3 42 19N 7 55W
Ouricuri, Brazil 154 C3 7 53 S 40 5W
Ourinhos, Brazil 159 A6 23 0 S 49 54W
Ourique, Portugal 37 H2 37 38N 8 16W
Ouro Fino, Brazil 159 A6 22 16 S 46 25W
Ouro Prêto, Brazil 155 F3 20 20 S 43 30W
Ouro Sogui, Senegal 100 B2 15 36N 13 19W
Oursi, Burkina Faso 101 C4 14 41N 0 27W
Ourthe →, Belgium 21 H7 50 29N 5 35 E
Ouse, Australia 114 G4 42 38 S 146 42 E
Ouse →, E. Susx., U.K. 17 G8 50 43N 0 3 E
Ouse →, N. Yorks., U.K. 16 C8 54 3N 0 7 E
Oust, France 24 F5 42 52N 1 13 E
Oust →, France 22 E4 47 35N 2 6W
Outaouais →, Canada 128 C5 45 27N 74 8W
Outardes →, Canada 129 C6 49 24N 69 30W
Outat Oulad el Haj, Morocco 99 B4 33 22N 3 42W
Outer Hebrides, U.K. 18 D1 57 30N 7 40W
Outer I., Canada 129 B8 51 10N 58 35W
Outes, Spain 36 C2 42 52N 8 55W
Outjo, Namibia 104 C2 20 5 S 16 7 E
Outlook, Canada 131 C7 51 30N 107 0W
Outlook, U.S.A. 138 A2 48 53N 104 47W
Outreau, France 23 B8 50 40N 1 36 E
Ouvèze →, France 25 E8 43 59N 4 51 E
Ouyen, Australia 116 C5 35 1 S 142 22 E
Ouzouer-le-Marché, France 23 E8 47 54N 1 32 E
Ovada, Italy 38 D5 44 39N 8 40 E
Ovalau, Fiji 121 A2 17 40 S 178 48 E
Ovalle, Chile 158 C1 30 33 S 71 18W
Ovar, Portugal 36 E2 40 51N 8 40W
Ovejas, Colombia 152 B2 9 32N 75 14W
Ovens, Australia 117 D7 36 35 S 146 46 E
Overdinkel, Neths. 20 D10 52 14N 7 2 E
Overflakkee, Neths. 20 E4 51 44N 4 10 E
Overijse, Belgium 21 G5 50 47N 4 32 E
Overijssel □, Neths. 20 D9 52 25N 6 35 E
Overijsselsch Kanaal →, Neths. 20 C8 52 31N 6 6 E
Overland, U.S.A. 140 F6 38 41N 90 22W
Overpelt, Belgium 21 F6 51 12N 5 20 E
Overton, U.S.A. 145 J12 36 33N 114 27W
Övertorneå, Sweden 12 C17 66 23N 23 38 E
Ovid, Colo., U.S.A. 138 E3 40 58N 102 23W
Ovid, Mich., U.S.A. 141 A12 43 1N 84 22W
Ovidiopol, Ukraine 52 C4 46 15N 30 30 E
Oviedo, Spain 36 B5 43 25N 5 50W
Oviedo □, Spain 36 B5 43 20N 6 0W
Oviken, Sweden 14 A8 63 0N 14 23 E
Oviksfjällen, Sweden 14 B7 63 0N 13 49 E
Övör Hangay □, Mongolia 66 B2 45 0N 102 30 E
Ovoro, Nigeria 101 D6 5 26N 7 16 E
Ovruch, Ukraine 50 F6 51 25N 28 45 E
Owaka, N.Z. 119 G4 46 27 S 169 40 E
Owando, Congo 102 C3 0 29 S 15 55 E
Owase, Japan 63 C8 34 7N 136 12 E
Owatonna, U.S.A. 138 C8 44 5N 93 14W
Owbeh, Afghan. 79 B1 34 28N 63 10 E
Owego, U.S.A. 137 D8 42 6N 76 16W
Owen, Australia 116 C3 34 15 S 138 32 E
Owen Falls, Uganda 106 B3 0 30N 33 5 E
Owen Mt., N.Z. 119 B7 41 35 S 172 33 E
Owen Sound, Canada 128 D3 44 35N 80 55W
Owen Stanley Ra., Papua N. G. 120 E4 8 30 S 147 0 E
Owendo, Gabon 102 B1 0 17N 9 30 E
Owens →, U.S.A. 144 J9 36 32N 117 59W
Owens L., U.S.A. 145 J9 36 26N 117 57W
Owensboro, U.S.A. 141 G9 37 46N 87 7W

Pazin 247

Panguipulli, Chile 160 A2 39 38 S 72 20W
Panguitch, U.S.A. 143 H7 37 50N 112 26W
Pangutaran, Phil. 71 H3 6 18N 120 35 E
Pangutaran Group, Phil. 71 H3 6 18N 120 34 E
Panhandle, U.S.A. 139 H4 35 21N 101 23W
Pani Mines, India 80 H5 22 29N 73 50 E
Pania-Mutombo, Zaïre 103 D4 5 11 S 23 51 E
Panié, Mt., N. Cal. 121 T18 20 36 S 164 46 E
Panipat, India 80 E7 29 25N 77 2 E
Panitan, Phil. 71 F4 11 28N 122 46 E
Panjal Range, India 80 C7 32 30N 76 50 E
Panjgur, Pakistan 79 D2 27 0N 64 5 E
Panjim = Panaji, India 83 G1 15 25N 73 50 E
Panjwai, Afghan. 80 D1 31 26N 65 27 E
Pankshin, Nigeria 101 D6 9 16N 9 25 E
Panmunjŏm, N. Korea 67 F14 37 59N 126 38 E
Panna, India 81 G9 24 40N 80 15 E
Panna Hills, India 81 G9 24 40N 81 15 E
Pano Lefkara, Cyprus 32 E12 34 53N 33 20 E
Pano Panayia, Cyprus 32 E11 34 55N 32 38 E
Panora, U.S.A. 140 C2 41 42N 94 22W
Panorama, Brazil 159 A5 21 21 S 51 51W
Pánormon, Greece 32 D6 35 25N 24 41 E
Panruti, India 83 J4 11 46N 79 35 E
Panshan, China 67 D12 41 3N 122 2 E
Panshi, China 67 C14 42 58N 126 5 E
Pantao, Phil. 70 E4 13 12N 123 20 E
Pantar, Indonesia 72 C2 8 28 S 124 10 E
Pante Macassar, Indonesia 72 C2 9 30 S 123 58 E
Pantelleria, Italy 40 F5 36 52N 12 0 E
Pantha, Burma 78 D5 23 55N 94 35 E
Pantin Sakan, Burma 78 F6 18 38N 97 33 E
Pantón, Spain 36 C3 42 31N 7 37W
Pánuco, Mexico 147 C5 22 0N 98 15W
Panukulan, Phil. 70 D3 14 56N 121 49 E
Panyam, Nigeria 101 D6 9 27N 9 8 E
Panyu, China 69 F9 22 51N 113 20 E
Pao →, Anzoátegui, Venezuela 153 B5 8 6N 64 17W
Pao →, Apure, Venezuela 152 B4 8 33N 68 1W
Páola, Italy 41 C9 39 21N 16 2 E
Paola, Malta 32 D2 35 52N 14 30 E
Paola, U.S.A. 138 F7 38 35N 94 53W
Paoli, U.S.A. 141 F10 38 33N 86 28W
Paonia, U.S.A. 143 G10 38 52N 107 36W
Paoting = Baoding, China 66 E8 38 50N 115 28 E
Paot'ou = Baotou, China 66 D6 40 32N 110 2 E
Paoua, C.A.R. 102 A3 7 9N 16 20 E
Pápa, Hungary 31 D10 47 22N 17 30 E
Papagayo →, Mexico 147 D5 16 36N 99 43W
Papagayo, G. de, Costa Rica 148 D2 10 30N 85 50W
Papagni →, India 83 G3 15 35N 77 45 E
Papakura, N.Z. 118 D3 37 4 S 174 59 E
Papantla, Mexico 147 C5 20 30N 97 30W
Paparoa, N.Z. 118 C3 36 6 S 174 16 E
Paparoa Nat. Park, N.Z. 119 C6 42 7 S 171 26 E
Paparoa Ra., N.Z. 119 C6 42 5 S 171 35 E
Pápas, Ákra, Greece 45 F3 38 13N 21 20 E
Papatoetoe, N.Z. 118 C3 36 59 S 174 51 E
Papenburg, Germany 26 B3 53 7N 7 25 E
Paphlagonia, Turkey 88 C5 41 30N 33 0 E
Paphos, Cyprus 32 E11 34 46N 32 25 E
Papien Chiang = Da →, Vietnam 76 B5 21 15N 105 20 E
Papigochic →, Mexico 146 B3 29 9N 109 40W
Paposo, Chile 158 B1 25 0 S 70 30W
Papoutsa, Cyprus 32 E12 34 54N 33 4 E
Papua, G. of, Papua N. G. 120 E3 9 0 S 144 50 E
Papua New Guinea ■, Oceania 120 D3 8 0 S 145 0 E
Papuča, Croatia 39 D12 44 22N 15 30 E
Papudo, Chile 158 C1 32 29 S 71 27W
Papuk, Croatia 42 B2 45 30N 17 30 E
Papun, Burma 78 F6 18 2N 97 30 E
Papunya, Australia 112 D5 23 15 S 131 54 E
Pará = Belém, Brazil 154 B2 1 20 S 48 30W
Pará □, Brazil 157 A7 3 20 S 52 0W
Pará □, Surinam 153 B6 5 20N 55 5W
Parábita, Italy 41 B11 40 3N 18 8 E
Paraburdoo, Australia 112 D2 23 14 S 117 32 E
Paracale, Phil. 70 D4 14 17N 122 48 E
Paracas, Pen., Peru 156 C2 13 53 S 76 20W
Paracatu, Brazil 155 E2 17 10 S 46 50W
Paracatu →, Brazil 155 E2 16 30 S 45 4W
Parachilna, Australia 116 A3 31 10 S 138 21 E
Parachinar, Pakistan 79 B3 33 55N 70 5 E
Paraćin, Serbia 42 D6 43 54N 21 27 E
Paracuru, Brazil 154 B4 3 24 S 39 4W
Parada, Punta, Peru 156 D2 15 22 S 75 11W
Paradas, Spain 37 H5 37 18N 5 29W
Paradela, Spain 36 C3 42 44N 7 37W
Paradhísi, Greece 32 C10 36 18N 28 7 E
Paradip, India 82 D8 20 15N 86 35 E
Paradise, Calif., U.S.A. 144 F5 39 46N 121 37W
Paradise, Mont., U.S.A. 142 C6 47 23N 114 48W
Paradise, Nev., U.S.A. 145 J11 36 9N 115 10W
Paradise →, Canada 129 B8 53 27N 57 19W
Paradise Valley, U.S.A. 142 F5 41 30N 117 32W
Parado, Indonesia 75 D5 8 42 S 118 30 E
Paradyz, Poland 47 D7 51 19N 20 2 E
Paragould, U.S.A. 139 G9 36 3N 90 29W
Paraguá →, Bolivia 157 C5 13 34 S 61 53W
Paragua →, Venezuela 153 B5 6 55N 62 55W
Paraguaçu →, Brazil 155 D4 12 45 S 38 54W
Paraguaçu Paulista, Brazil 159 A5 22 22 S 50 35W
Paraguaipoa, Venezuela 152 A3 11 21N 71 57W
Paraguaná, Pen. de, Venezuela 152 A3 12 0N 70 0W
Paraguarí, Paraguay 158 B4 25 36 S 57 0W
Paraguarí □, Paraguay 158 B4 26 0 S 57 10W
Paraguay ■, S. Amer. 158 A4 23 0 S 57 0W
Paraguay →, Paraguay 158 B4 27 18 S 58 38W
Paraíba = João Pessoa, Brazil 154 C5 7 10 S 34 52W
Paraíba □, Brazil 154 C4 7 0 S 36 0W
Paraíba do Sul →, Brazil 155 F3 21 37 S 41 3W
Parainen, Finland 13 F17 60 18N 22 18 E
Paraiso, Mexico 147 D6 18 24N 93 14W
Parak, Iran 85 E7 27 38N 52 25 E
Parakhino Paddubye, Russia 50 B8 58 26N 33 10 E
Parakou, Benin 101 D5 9 25N 2 40 E
Parakylia, Australia 116 A2 30 24 S 136 25 E
Paralimni, Cyprus 32 D12 35 2N 33 58 E
Parálion-Astrous, Greece 45 G4 37 25N 22 45 E
Paramakkudi, India 83 K4 9 31N 78 39 E
Paramaribo, Surinam 153 B6 5 50N 55 10W
Parambu, Brazil 154 C3 6 13 S 40 43W
Paramillo, Nudo del, Colombia 152 B2 7 4N 75 55W
Paramirim, Brazil 155 D3 13 26 S 42 15W
Paramirim →, Brazil 155 D3 11 34 S 43 18W
Paramithiá, Greece 44 E2 39 30N 20 35 E
Paramushir, Ostrov, Russia 57 D16 50 24N 156 0 E
Paran →, Israel 91 E4 30 20N 35 10 E
Paraná, Argentina 158 C3 31 45 S 60 30W
Paranã, Brazil 155 D2 12 30 S 47 48W
Paraná □, Brazil 159 A5 24 30 S 51 0W
Paraná →, Argentina 158 C4 33 43 S 59 15W
Paranaguá, Brazil 159 B6 25 30 S 48 30W
Paranaíba →, Brazil 155 F1 20 6 S 51 4W
Paranapanema →, Brazil 159 A5 22 40 S 53 9W
Paranapiacaba, Serra do, Brazil 159 A6 24 31 S 48 35W
Paranavaí, Brazil 159 A5 23 4 S 52 56W
Parang, Jolo, Phil. 71 J3 5 55N 120 54 E
Parang, Mindanao, Phil. 71 H5 7 23N 124 16 E
Parangaba, Brazil 154 B4 3 45 S 38 33W
Parangippettai, India 83 J4 11 30N 79 38 E
Paraparauma, N.Z. 118 G4 40 57 S 175 3 E
Parapóla, Greece 45 H5 36 55N 23 27 E
Paraspóri, Ákra, Greece 45 J9 35 55N 27 15 E
Paratinga, Brazil 155 D3 12 40 S 43 10W
Paratoo, Australia 116 B3 32 42 S 139 20 E
Parattah, Australia 114 G4 42 22 S 147 23 E
Paraúna, Brazil 155 E1 16 55 S 50 26W
Paray-le-Monial, France 25 B8 46 27N 4 7 E
Parbati →, India 80 G7 25 50N 76 30 E
Parbatipur, Bangla. 78 C2 25 39N 88 55 E
Parbhani, India 82 E3 19 8N 76 52 E
Parchim, Germany 26 B7 53 25N 11 50 E
Parczew, Poland 47 D9 51 40N 22 52 E
Pardes Hanna, Israel 91 C3 32 28N 34 57 E
Pardilla, Spain 36 D7 41 33N 3 43W
Pardo →, Bahia, Brazil 155 E4 15 40 S 39 0W
Pardo →, Mato Grosso, Brazil 159 A5 21 46 S 52 9W
Pardo →, Minas Gerais, Brazil 155 E3 15 48 S 44 48W
Pardo →, São Paulo, Brazil 155 F2 20 10 S 48 38W
Pardubice, Czech. 30 A8 50 3N 15 45 E
Pare, Indonesia 75 D4 7 43 S 112 12 E
Pare □, Tanzania 106 C4 4 10 S 38 0 E
Pare Mts., Tanzania 106 C4 4 0 S 37 45 E
Parecis, Serra dos, Brazil 157 C6 13 0 S 60 0W
Paredes de Nava, Spain 36 C6 42 9N 4 42W
Pareh, Iran 84 B5 38 52N 45 42 E
Parelhas, Brazil 154 C4 6 41 S 36 39W
Paren, Russia 57 C17 62 30N 163 15 E
Parengarenga Harbour, N.Z. 118 A1 34 31 S 173 0 E
Parent, Canada 128 C5 47 55N 74 35W
Parent, L., Canada 128 C4 48 31N 77 1W
Parentis-en-Born, France 24 D2 44 21N 1 4W
Parepare, Indonesia 72 B1 4 0 S 119 40 E
Parfino, Russia 50 C7 57 59N 31 34 E
Pargo, Pta. do, Madeira 33 D2 32 49N 17 17W
Parguba, Russia 48 B5 62 20N 34 27 E
Paria, G. de, Venezuela 153 A5 10 20N 62 0W
Paria, Pen. de, Venezuela 153 A5 10 50N 62 30W
Pariaguán, Venezuela 153 B5 8 51N 64 34W
Pariaman, Indonesia 74 C2 0 47 S 100 11 E
Paricatuba, Brazil 153 D5 4 26 S 61 53W
Paricutín, Cerro, Mexico 146 D4 19 28N 102 15W
Parigi, Java, Indonesia 75 D3 7 42 S 108 29 E
Parigi, Sulawesi, Indonesia 72 B2 0 50 S 120 5 E
Parika, Guyana 153 B6 6 50N 58 20W
Parima, Serra, Brazil 153 C5 2 30N 64 0W
Parinari, Peru 156 A3 4 35 S 74 25W
Parincea, Romania 46 C8 46 27N 27 9 E
Parîng, Romania 46 D4 45 20N 23 37 E
Parintins, Brazil 153 D6 2 40 S 56 50W
Paris, Canada 128 D3 43 12N 80 25W
Paris, France 23 D9 48 50N 2 20 E
Paris, Idaho, U.S.A. 142 E8 42 14N 111 24W
Paris, Ill., U.S.A. 141 E9 39 36N 87 42W
Paris, Ky., U.S.A. 141 F12 38 13N 84 15W
Paris, Mo., U.S.A. 140 E5 39 29N 92 0W
Paris, Tenn., U.S.A. 135 G1 36 18N 88 19W
Paris, Tex., U.S.A. 139 J7 33 40N 95 33W
Paris, Ville de □, France 23 D9 48 50N 2 20 E
Parish, U.S.A. 137 C8 43 25N 76 8W
Pariti, Indonesia 72 D2 10 15 S 123 45 E
Park, U.S.A. 144 B4 48 45N 122 18W
Park City, U.S.A. 142 F8 40 39N 111 30W
Park Falls, U.S.A. 138 C9 45 56N 90 27W
Park Forest, U.S.A. 141 C9 41 29N 87 40W
Park Range, U.S.A. 142 G10 40 0N 106 30W
Park Rapids, U.S.A. 138 B7 46 55N 95 4W
Park Ridge, U.S.A. 141 B9 42 2N 87 51W
Park River, U.S.A. 138 A6 48 24N 97 45W
Park Rynie, S. Africa 105 E5 30 25 S 30 45 E
Parkā Bandar, Iran 85 E8 25 55N 59 35 E
Parkent, Uzbekistan 55 C4 41 18N 69 40 E
Parker, Ariz., U.S.A. 145 L12 34 9N 114 17W
Parker, S. Dak., U.S.A. 138 D6 43 24N 97 8W
Parker Dam, U.S.A. 145 L12 34 18N 114 8W
Parkersburg, Iowa, U.S.A. 140 B4 42 35N 92 47W
Parkersburg, W. Va., U.S.A. 134 F5 39 16N 81 34W
Parkerview, Canada 131 C8 51 21N 103 18W
Parkes, Australia 117 B8 33 9 S 148 11 E
Parkfield, U.S.A. 144 K6 35 54N 120 26W
Parkhar, Tajikistan 55 E4 37 30N 69 34 E
Parkland, U.S.A. 144 C4 47 9N 122 26W
Parkside, Canada 131 C7 53 10N 106 33W
Parkston, U.S.A. 138 D5 43 24N 97 59W
Parksville, Canada 130 D4 49 20N 124 21W
Parlakimidi, India 82 E7 18 45N 84 5 E
Parli, India 82 E3 18 50N 76 35 E
Parma, Italy 38 D7 44 50N 10 20 E
Parma, Idaho, U.S.A. 142 E5 43 47N 116 57W
Parma, Ohio, U.S.A. 136 E3 41 23N 81 43W
Parma →, Italy 38 D7 44 56N 10 26 E
Parnaguá, Brazil 154 D3 10 10 S 44 38W
Parnaíba, Piauí, Brazil 154 B3 2 54 S 41 47W
Parnaíba, São Paulo, Brazil 157 D7 19 34 S 51 14W
Parnaíba →, Brazil 154 B3 3 0 S 41 50W
Parnamirim, Brazil 154 C4 8 5 S 39 34W
Parnarama, Brazil 154 C3 5 31 S 43 6W
Parnassós, Greece 45 F4 38 35N 22 30 E
Parnassus, N.Z. 119 C8 42 42 S 173 23 E
Párnis, Greece 45 F5 38 14N 23 45 E
Párnon Óros, Greece 45 G4 37 15N 22 45 E
Pärnu, Estonia 50 B4 58 28N 24 33 E
Parola, India 82 D2 20 47N 75 7 E
Paroo →, Australia 115 E3 31 28 S 143 32 E
Páros, Greece 45 G7 37 5N 25 12 E
Parowan, U.S.A. 143 H7 37 51N 112 50W
Parpaillon, France 25 D10 44 30N 6 40 E
Parral, Chile 158 D1 36 10 S 71 52W
Parramatta, Australia 117 B9 33 48 S 151 1 E
Parras, Mexico 146 B4 25 30N 102 20W
Parrett →, U.K. 17 F5 51 7N 2 58W
Parris I., U.S.A. 135 J5 32 20N 80 41W
Parrsboro, Canada 129 C7 45 30N 64 25W
Parry Is., Canada 6 B2 77 0N 110 0W
Parry Sound, Canada 128 C3 45 20N 80 0W
Parsberg, Germany 27 F7 49 10N 11 43 E
Parseta →, Poland 47 A2 54 11N 15 34 E
Parshall, U.S.A. 138 B3 47 57N 102 8W
Parsnip →, Canada 130 B4 55 10N 123 2W
Parsons, U.S.A. 139 G7 37 20N 95 16W
Parsons Ra., Australia 114 A2 13 30 S 135 15 E
Partabpur, India 82 E5 20 0N 80 42 E
Partanna, Italy 40 E5 37 43N 12 51 E
Parthenay, France 22 F6 46 38N 0 16W
Partinico, Italy 40 D6 38 3N 13 6 E
Partur, India 82 E3 19 40N 76 14 E
Paru →, Brazil 153 D7 1 33 S 52 38W
Parú →, Venezuela 152 C4 4 20N 66 27W
Paru de Oeste →, Brazil 153 C6 1 30N 56 0W
Parubcan, Phil. 70 E4 13 43N 123 45 E
Parucito →, Venezuela 152 B4 5 18N 65 59W
Parur, India 83 J3 10 13N 76 14 E
Paruro, Peru 156 C3 13 45 S 71 50W
Parvān □, Afghan. 79 B3 35 0N 69 0 E
Parvatipuram, India 82 E6 18 50N 83 25 E
Parys, S. Africa 104 D4 26 52 S 27 29 E
Pas-de-Calais □, France 23 B9 50 30N 2 10 E
Pasadena, Calif., U.S.A. 145 L8 34 9N 118 9W
Pasadena, Tex., U.S.A. 139 L7 29 43N 95 13W
Pasaje, Ecuador 152 D2 3 23 S 79 50W
Pasaje →, Argentina 158 B3 25 39 S 63 56W
Pasay, Phil. 70 D3 14 33N 121 0 E
Pascagoula, U.S.A. 139 K10 30 21N 88 33W
Pascagoula →, U.S.A. 139 K10 30 23N 88 37W
Paşcani, Romania 46 B7 47 14N 26 45 E
Pasco, U.S.A. 142 C4 46 14N 119 6W
Pasco □, Peru 156 C2 10 40 S 75 0W
Pasco, Cerro de, Peru 156 C2 10 45 S 76 10W
Pascua, I. de, Pac. Oc. 123 K17 27 0 S 109 0W
Pasewalk, Germany 26 B10 53 30N 14 0 E
Pasfield L., Canada 131 B7 58 24N 105 20W
Pasha →, Russia 50 B8 60 29N 32 55 E
Pashiwari, Pakistan 81 B6 34 40N 75 10 E
Pashiya, Russia 54 B6 58 33N 58 26 E
Pashmakli = Smolyan, Bulgaria 43 F9 41 36N 24 38 E
Pasighat, India 78 A5 28 4N 95 21 E
Pasinler, Turkey 89 D9 39 59N 41 41 E
Pasir Mas, Malaysia 74 A2 6 2N 102 8 E
Pasirian, Indonesia 75 D4 8 13 S 113 8 E
Paskūh, Iran 85 E9 27 34N 61 39 E
Pasłęka →, Poland 47 A6 54 26N 19 46 E
Pasley, C., Australia 113 F3 33 52 S 123 35 E
Pašman, Croatia 39 E12 43 58N 15 20 E
Pasmore →, Australia 116 A3 31 5 S 139 49 E
Pasni, Pakistan 79 D1 25 15N 63 27 E
Paso Cantinela, Mexico 145 N11 32 33N 115 47W
Paso de Indios, Argentina 160 B3 43 55 S 69 0W
Paso de los Libres, Argentina 158 B4 29 44 S 57 10W
Paso de los Toros, Uruguay 158 C4 32 45 S 56 30W
Paso Flores, Argentina 160 B2 40 35 S 70 38W
Paso Robles, U.S.A. 143 J3 35 38N 120 41W
Pasorapa, Bolivia 157 D5 18 16 S 64 37W
Paspébiac, Canada 129 C6 48 3N 65 17W
Pasrur, Pakistan 80 C6 32 16N 74 43 E
Passage West, Ireland 19 E3 51 52N 8 20W
Passaic, U.S.A. 137 F10 40 51N 74 7W
Passau, Germany 27 G9 48 34N 13 27 E
Passendale, Belgium 21 G2 50 54N 3 2 E
Passero, C., Italy 41 F8 36 42N 15 8 E
Passi, Phil. 71 F4 11 6N 122 38 E
Passo Fundo, Brazil 159 B5 28 10 S 52 20W
Passos, Brazil 155 F2 20 45 S 46 37W
Passow, Germany 26 B10 53 13N 14 10 E
Passwang, Switz. 28 B5 47 22N 7 41 E
Passy, France 25 C10 45 55N 6 41 E
Pastaza □, Ecuador 152 D2 2 0 S 77 0W
Pastaza →, Peru 152 D2 4 50 S 76 52W
Pastęk, Poland 47 A6 54 3N 19 41 E
Pasto, Colombia 152 C2 1 13N 77 17W
Pastos Bons, Brazil 154 C3 6 36 S 44 5W
Pastrana, Spain 34 E2 40 27N 2 53W
Pasuquin, Phil. 70 B3 18 20N 120 37 E
Pasuruan, Indonesia 75 D4 7 40 S 112 44 E
Pasym, Poland 47 B7 53 48N 20 49 E
Pásztó, Hungary 31 D12 47 52N 19 43 E
Patagonia, Argentina 160 C2 45 0 S 69 0W
Patagonia, U.S.A. 143 L8 31 33N 110 45W
Patambar, Iran 85 D9 29 45N 60 17 E
Patan, Gujarat, India 82 F1 17 22N 73 57 E
Patan, Maharashtra, India 80 H5 23 54N 72 14 E
Patani, Indonesia 72 A3 0 20N 128 50 E
Pataudi, India 80 E7 28 18N 76 48 E
Patay, France 23 D8 48 2N 1 40 E
Patchewollock, Australia 116 C5 35 22 S 142 12 E
Patchogue, U.S.A. 137 F11 40 46N 73 1W
Patea, N.Z. 118 F3 39 45 S 174 30 E
Pategi, Nigeria 101 D6 8 50N 5 45 E
Patensie, S. Africa 104 E3 33 46 S 24 49 E
Paternò, Italy 41 E7 37 34N 14 53 E
Pateros, U.S.A. 142 B4 48 3N 119 54W
Paterson, Australia 117 B9 32 35 S 151 36 E
Paterson, U.S.A. 137 F10 40 55N 74 11W
Paterson Inlet, N.Z. 119 G3 46 56 S 168 12 E
Paterson Ra., Australia 112 D3 21 45 S 122 10 E
Paterswolde, Neths. 20 B9 53 9N 6 34 E
Pathankot, India 80 C6 32 18N 75 45 E
Patharghata, Bangla. 78 D2 22 2N 89 58 E
Pathfinder Reservoir, U.S.A. 142 E10 42 28N 106 51W
Pathiu, Thailand 77 G2 10 42N 99 19 E
Pathum Thani, Thailand 76 E3 14 1N 100 32 E
Pati, Indonesia 75 D4 6 45 S 111 1 E
Pati Pt., Guam 121 R15 13 40N 144 50 E
Patía, Colombia 152 C2 2 4N 77 4W
Patía →, Colombia 152 C2 2 13N 78 40W
Patiala, India 80 D7 30 23N 76 26 E
Patine Kouka, Senegal 100 C2 12 45N 13 45W
Pativilca, Peru 156 C2 10 42 S 77 48W
Patkai Bum, India 78 B5 27 0N 95 30 E
Pátmos, Greece 45 G8 37 21N 26 36 E
Patna, India 81 G11 25 35N 85 12 E
Patnongon, Phil. 71 F3 10 55N 122 0 E
Patnos, Turkey 89 D10 39 13N 42 51 E
Patonga, Uganda 106 B3 2 45N 33 15 E
Patos, Brazil 154 C4 6 55 S 37 16W
Patos, L. dos, Brazil 159 C5 31 20 S 51 0W
Patos de Minas, Brazil 155 E2 18 35 S 46 32W
Patosi, Albania 44 D1 40 42N 19 38 E
Patquía, Argentina 158 C2 30 2 S 66 55W
Pátrai, Greece 45 F3 38 14N 21 47 E
Pátraikós Kólpos, Greece 45 F3 38 17N 21 30 E
Patricio Lynch, I., Chile 160 C1 48 35 S 75 30W
Patrocínio, Brazil 155 E2 18 57 S 47 0W
Patta, Kenya 106 C5 2 10 S 41 0 E
Pattada, Italy 40 B2 40 35N 9 7 E
Pattanapuram, India 83 K3 9 6N 76 50 E
Pattani, Thailand 77 J3 6 48N 101 15 E
Patten, U.S.A. 129 C6 46 0N 68 38W
Patterson, Calif., U.S.A. 144 H5 37 28N 121 8W
Patterson, La., U.S.A. 139 L9 29 42N 91 18W
Patterson, Mt., U.S.A. 144 G7 38 29N 119 20W
Patteson, Passage, Vanuatu 121 E6 15 26 S 168 12 E
Patti, India 80 D6 31 17N 74 54 E
Patti, Italy 41 D7 38 8N 14 57 E
Pattoki, Pakistan 80 D5 31 5N 73 52 E
Patton, U.S.A. 136 F6 40 38N 78 39W
Pattonsburg, U.S.A. 140 D2 40 3N 94 8W
Pattukkattai, India 83 J4 10 25N 79 20 E
Patu, Brazil 154 C4 6 6 S 37 38W
Patuakhali, Bangla. 78 D3 22 20N 90 25 E
Patuca →, Honduras 148 C3 15 50N 84 18W
Patuca, Punta, Honduras 148 C3 15 49N 84 14W
Pâturages, Belgium 21 H3 50 25N 3 52 E
Pátzcuaro, Mexico 146 D4 19 30N 101 40W
Pau, France 24 E3 43 19N 0 25W
Pau, Gave de →, France 24 E2 43 33N 1 12W
Pau d' Arco, Brazil 154 C2 7 30 S 49 22W
Pau dos Ferros, Brazil 154 C4 6 7 S 38 10W
Paucartambo, Peru 156 C3 13 19 S 71 35W
Pauillac, France 24 C3 45 11N 0 46W
Pauini, Brazil 156 B4 7 40 S 66 58W
Pauini →, Brazil 153 D5 1 42 S 62 50W
Pauk, Burma 78 E5 21 27N 94 30 E
Paul I., Canada 129 A7 56 30N 61 20W
Paul Isnard, Fr. Guiana 153 C7 4 47N 54 1W
Paulding, U.S.A. 141 C12 41 8N 84 35W
Paulhan, France 24 E7 43 33N 3 28 E
Paulis = Isiro, Zaïre 106 B2 2 53N 27 40 E
Paulista, Brazil 154 C5 7 57 S 34 53W
Paulistana, Brazil 154 C3 8 9 S 41 9W
Paullina, U.S.A. 138 D7 42 59N 95 41W
Paulo Afonso, Brazil 154 C4 9 21 S 38 15W
Paulo de Faria, Brazil 155 F2 20 2 S 49 24W
Paulpietersburg, S. Africa 105 D5 27 23 S 30 50 E
Pauls Valley, U.S.A. 139 H6 34 44N 97 13W
Pauma Valley, U.S.A. 145 M10 33 16N 116 58W
Paungde, Burma 78 F5 18 29N 95 30 E
Pauni, India 82 D4 20 48N 79 40 E
Pausa, Peru 156 D3 15 16 S 73 22W
Pauto →, Colombia 152 B3 5 9N 70 55W
Pāveh, Iran 84 C5 35 3N 46 22 E
Pavelets, Russia 51 E11 53 49N 39 14 E
Pavia, Italy 38 C6 45 10N 9 10 E
Pavlikeni, Bulgaria 43 D10 43 14N 25 20 E
Pavlodar, Kazakhstan 56 D8 52 33N 77 0 E
Pavlograd, Ukraine 52 B6 48 30N 35 52 E
Pavlovo, Russia 51 D13 55 58N 43 5 E
Pavlovo, Russia 57 C12 63 5N 115 25 E
Pavlovsk, Russia 51 F12 50 26N 40 5 E
Pavlovskaya, Russia 53 C8 46 17N 39 47 E
Pavlovskiy-Posad, Russia 51 D11 55 47N 38 42 E
Pavullo nel Frignano, Italy 38 D7 44 20N 10 50 E
Pavuvu, Solomon Is. 121 M10 9 4 S 159 8 E
Paw Paw, U.S.A. 141 B11 42 13N 85 53W
Pawahku, Burma 78 B7 26 11N 98 40 E
Pawan →, Indonesia 75 C4 1 55 S 110 0 E
Pawhuska, U.S.A. 139 G6 36 40N 96 20W
Pawling, U.S.A. 137 E11 41 34N 73 36W
Pawnee, Ill., U.S.A. 140 E7 39 36N 89 35W
Pawnee, Okla., U.S.A. 139 G6 36 20N 96 48W
Pawnee City, U.S.A. 138 E6 40 7N 96 9W
Pawpaw, U.S.A. 140 C8 41 41N 88 59W
Pawtucket, U.S.A. 137 E13 41 53N 71 23W
Paximádhia, Greece 32 D6 35 0N 24 35 E
Paxoí, Greece 44 E2 39 14N 20 12 E
Paxton, Ill., U.S.A. 141 D8 40 27N 88 6W
Paxton, Nebr., U.S.A. 138 E4 41 7N 101 21W
Payakumbuh, Indonesia 74 C2 0 20 S 100 35 E
Payerne, Switz. 28 C3 46 49N 6 56 E
Payette, U.S.A. 142 D5 44 5N 116 56W
Paymogo, Spain 37 H3 37 44N 7 21W
Payne, U.S.A. 141 C12 41 5N 84 44W
Payne Bay = Bellin, Canada 127 B13 60 0N 70 0W
Payne L., Canada 127 C12 59 30N 74 30W
Paynes Find, Australia 113 E2 29 15 S 117 42 E
Paynesville, Liberia 100 D2 6 20N 10 45W
Paynesville, U.S.A. 138 C7 45 23N 94 43W
Paysandú, Uruguay 158 C4 32 19 S 58 8W
Payson, Ariz., U.S.A. 143 J8 34 14N 111 20W
Payson, Utah, U.S.A. 142 F8 40 3N 111 44W
Paz →, Guatemala 148 D1 13 44N 90 10W
Paz, B. la, Mexico 146 C2 24 15N 110 25W
Pāzanān, Iran 85 D6 30 35N 49 59 E
Pazar, Turkey 89 C9 41 10N 40 50 E
Pazarcık, Turkey 88 E7 37 30N 37 17 E
Pazardzhik, Bulgaria 43 E9 42 12N 24 20 E
Pazin, Croatia 39 C10 45 14N 13 56 E

248 Pazña

Pazña, *Bolivia* **156 D4** 18 36 S 66 55W
Pčinja →, *Macedonia* **42 F6** 41 50N 21 45 E
Pe Ell, *U.S.A.* **144 D3** 46 34N 123 18W
Peabody, *U.S.A.* **137 D14** 42 31N 70 56W
Peace →, *Canada* **130 B6** 59 0N 111 25W
Peace Point, *Canada* **130 B6** 59 7N 112 27W
Peace River, *Canada* **130 B5** 56 15N 117 18W
Peach Springs, *U.S.A.* **143 J7** 35 32N 113 25W
Peak, The = Kinder Scout, *U.K.* **16 D6** 53 24N 1 53W
Peak Downs, *Australia* **114 C4** 22 55 S 148 5 E
Peak Downs Mine, *Australia* **114 C4** 22 17 S 148 11 E
Peak Hill, *N.S.W., Australia* **117 B8** 32 47 S 148 11 E
Peak Hill, *W. Austral., Australia* **113 E2** 25 35 S 118 43 E
Peak Ra., *Australia* **114 C4** 22 50 S 148 20 E
Peake, *Australia* **116 C3** 35 25 S 139 55 E
Peake Cr. →, *Australia* **115 D2** 28 2 S 136 7 E
Peale, Mt., *U.S.A.* **143 G9** 38 26N 109 14W
Pearblossom, *U.S.A.* **145 L9** 34 30N 117 55W
Pearl, *U.S.A.* **140 E6** 39 28N 90 38W
Pearl →, *U.S.A.* **139 K10** 30 11N 89 32W
Pearl Banks, *Sri Lanka* **83 K4** 8 45N 79 45 E
Pearl City, *Hawaii, U.S.A.* **132 H16** 21 24N 157 59W
Pearl City, *Ill., U.S.A.* **140 B7** 42 16N 89 50W
Pearsall, *U.S.A.* **139 L5** 28 54N 99 6W
Pearse I., *Canada* **130 C2** 54 52N 130 14W
Peary Land, *Greenland* **6 A6** 82 40N 33 0W
Pease →, *U.S.A.* **139 H5** 34 12N 99 2W
Pebane, *Mozam.* **107 F4** 17 10 S 38 8 E
Pebas, *Peru* **152 D3** 3 10 S 71 46W
Pebble, I., *Falk. Is.* **160 D5** 51 20 S 59 40W
Pebble Beach, *U.S.A.* **144 J5** 36 34N 121 57W
Peč, *Serbia* **42 E5** 42 40N 20 17 E
Peçanha, *Brazil* **155 E3** 18 33 S 42 34W
Pecatonica, *U.S.A.* **140 B7** 42 19N 89 22W
Pecatonica →, *U.S.A.* **140 B7** 42 26N 89 12W
Péccioli, *Italy* **38 E7** 43 32N 10 43 E
Pechea, *Romania* **46 D8** 45 36N 27 49 E
Pechenezhin, *Ukraine* **52 B1** 48 30N 24 48 E
Pechenga, *Russia* **48 A5** 69 30N 31 25 E
Pechiguera, Pta., *Canary Is.* **33 F6** 28 51N 13 53W
Pechnezhskoye Vdkhr., *Ukraine* **52 A7** 50 0N 37 10 E
Pechora →, *Russia* **48 A9** 68 13N 54 15 E
Pechorskaya Guba, *Russia* **48 A9** 68 40N 54 0 E
Pecica, *Romania* **46 C2** 46 10N 21 3 E
Pečka, *Serbia* **42 C4** 44 18N 19 33 E
Pécora, C., *Italy* **40 C1** 39 28N 8 23 E
Pečory, *Russia* **50 C5** 57 48N 27 40 E
Pecos, *U.S.A.* **139 K3** 31 26N 103 30W
Pecos →, *U.S.A.* **139 L3** 29 42N 101 22W
Pécs, *Hungary* **31 E11** 46 5N 18 15 E
Peddapalli, *India* **82 E4** 18 40N 79 24 E
Peddapuram, *India* **82 F6** 17 6N 82 8 E
Pedder, L., *Australia* **114 G4** 42 55 S 146 10 E
Peddie, *S. Africa* **105 E4** 33 14 S 27 7 E
Pédernales, *Dom. Rep.* **149 C5** 18 2N 71 44W
Pedieos →, *Cyprus* **32 D12** 35 10N 33 54 E
Pedirka, *Australia* **115 D2** 26 40 S 135 14 E
Pedra Azul, *Brazil* **155 E3** 16 2 S 41 17W
Pedra Grande, Recifes de, *Brazil* **155 E4** 17 45 S 38 58W
Pedras Negras, *Brazil* **157 C5** 12 51 S 62 54W
Pedreiras, *Brazil* **154 B3** 4 32 S 44 40W
Pedro Afonso, *Brazil* **154 C2** 9 0 S 48 10W
Pedro Cays, *Jamaica* **148 C4** 17 5N 77 48W
Pedro Chico, *Colombia* **152 C3** 1 4N 70 25W
Pedro de Valdivia, *Chile* **158 A2** 22 55 S 69 38W
Pedro Juan Caballero, *Paraguay* **159 A4** 22 30 S 55 40W
Pedro Muñoz, *Spain* **35 F2** 39 25N 2 56W
Pedrógão Grande, *Portugal* **36 F2** 39 55N 8 9W
Peebinga, *Australia* **116 C4** 34 52 S 140 57 E
Peebles, *U.K.* **18 F5** 55 40N 3 12W
Peebles, *U.S.A.* **141 F13** 38 57N 83 24W
Peekskill, *U.S.A.* **137 E11** 41 17N 73 55W
Peel, *U.K.* **16 C3** 54 13N 4 41W
Peel →, *Australia* **117 A9** 30 50 S 150 29 E
Peel →, *Canada* **126 B6** 67 0N 135 0W
Peelwood, *Australia* **117 C8** 34 7 S 149 27 E
Peene →, *Germany* **26 A9** 54 9N 13 46 E
Peera Peera Poolanna L., *Australia* **115 D2** 26 30 S 138 0 E
Peers, *Canada* **130 C5** 53 40N 116 0W
Pegasus Bay, *N.Z.* **119 D8** 43 20 S 173 10 E
Peggau, *Austria* **30 D8** 47 12N 15 21 E
Pegnitz, *Germany* **27 F7** 49 45N 11 33 E
Pegnitz →, *Germany* **27 F6** 49 29N 10 59 E
Pego, *Spain* **35 G4** 38 51N 0 8W
Pegu, *Burma* **78 G6** 17 20N 96 29 E
Pegu Yoma, *Burma* **78 F5** 19 0N 96 0 E
Pehčevo, *Macedonia* **42 F7** 41 41N 22 55 E
Pehuajó, *Argentina* **158 D3** 35 45 S 62 0W
Pei Xian, *China* **66 G9** 34 44N 116 55 E
Peine, *Chile* **158 A2** 23 45 S 68 8W
Peine, *Germany* **26 C6** 52 19N 10 12 E
Peip'ing = Beijing, *China* **66 E9** 39 55N 116 20 E
Peissenberg, *Germany* **27 H7** 47 48N 11 4 E
Peitz, *Germany* **26 D10** 51 50N 14 23 E
Peixe, *Brazil* **155 D2** 12 0 S 48 40W
Peixe →, *Brazil* **155 F1** 21 31 S 51 58W
Peixoto de Azeredo →, *Brazil* **157 C6** 10 6 S 55 31W
Peize, *Neths.* **20 B8** 53 9N 6 30 E
Pek →, *Serbia* **42 C6** 44 45N 21 29 E
Pekalongan, *Indonesia* **75 D3** 6 53 S 109 40 E
Pekan, *Malaysia* **77 L4** 3 30N 103 25 E
Pekanbaru, *Indonesia* **74 B2** 0 30N 101 15 E
Pekin, *U.S.A.* **140 D7** 40 35N 89 40W
Peking = Beijing, *China* **66 E9** 39 55N 116 20 E
Pelabuhan Kelang, *Malaysia* **77 L3** 3 0N 101 23 E
Pelabuhan Ratu, Teluk, *Indonesia* **74 D3** 7 5 S 106 30 E
Pelabuhanratu, *Indonesia* **74 D3** 7 0 S 106 32 E
Pélagos, *Greece* **44 E6** 39 17N 24 4 E
Pelaihari, *Indonesia* **75 C4** 3 55 S 114 45 E
Pelat, Mt., *France* **25 D10** 44 16N 6 42 E
Pełczyce, *Poland* **47 B2** 53 3N 15 16 E
Peleaga, *Romania* **46 D3** 45 22N 22 55 E
Pelechuco, *Bolivia* **156 C4** 14 48 S 69 4W
Pelée, Mt., *Martinique* **149 D7** 14 48N 61 10W
Pelee, Pt., *Canada* **128 D3** 41 54N 82 31W
Pelee I., *Canada* **128 D3** 41 47N 82 40W
Pelejo, *Peru* **156 B2** 6 10 S 75 49W
Pelekech, *Kenya* **106 B4** 3 52N 35 8 E
Peleng, *Indonesia* **72 B2** 1 20 S 123 30 E
Pelham, *U.S.A.* **135 K3** 31 8N 84 9W
Pelhřimov, *Czech.* **30 B8** 49 24N 15 12 E
Pelican L., *Canada* **131 C8** 52 28N 100 20W
Pelican Narrows, *Canada* **131 B8** 55 10N 102 56W
Pelican Rapids, *Canada* **131 C8** 52 45N 100 42W
Peljesac, *Croatia* **42 E2** 42 55N 17 25 E
Pelkosenniemi, *Finland* **12 C19** 67 6N 27 28 E
Pella, *Greece* **44 D4** 40 46N 22 23 E
Pella, *S. Africa* **104 D2** 29 1 S 19 6 E
Pella, *U.S.A.* **140 C4** 41 25N 92 55W
Pélla □, *Greece* **44 D4** 40 52N 22 0 E
Péllaro, *Italy* **41 D8** 38 1N 15 40 E
Pellworm, *Germany* **26 A4** 54 30N 8 40 E
Pelly →, *Canada* **126 B6** 62 47N 137 19W
Pelly Bay, *Canada* **127 B11** 68 38N 89 50W
Pelly L., *Canada* **126 B9** 66 0N 102 0W
Peloponnese = Pelopónnisos □, *Greece* **45 G4** 37 10N 22 0 E
Pelopónnisos □, *Greece* **45 G4** 37 10N 22 0 E
Peloritani, Monti, *Italy* **41 D8** 38 2N 15 25 E
Peloro, C., *Italy* **41 D8** 38 15N 15 40 E
Pelorus →, *N.Z.* **119 B8** 41 16 S 173 45 E
Pelorus Sd., *N.Z.* **119 A8** 40 59 S 173 59 E
Pelotas, *Brazil* **159 C5** 31 42 S 52 23W
Pelòvo, *Bulgaria* **43 D9** 43 26N 24 17 E
Pelvoux, Massif de, *France* **25 D10** 44 52N 6 20 E
Pelym →, *Russia* **54 B8** 59 39N 63 26 E
Pemalang, *Indonesia* **75 D3** 6 53 S 109 23 E
Pematangsiantar, *Indonesia* **74 B1** 2 57N 99 5 E
Pemba, *Mozam.* **107 E5** 12 58 S 40 30 E
Pemba, *Zambia* **107 F2** 16 30 S 27 28 E
Pemba Channel, *Tanzania* **106 D4** 5 0 S 39 37 E
Pemba I., *Tanzania* **106 D4** 5 0 S 39 45 E
Pemberton, *Australia* **113 F2** 34 30 S 116 0 E
Pemberton, *Canada* **130 C4** 50 25N 122 50W
Pembina, *N. Dak., U.S.A.* **131 D9** 48 58N 97 15W
Pembina, *N. Dak., U.S.A.* **138 A6** 48 58N 97 15W
Pembina →, *U.S.A.* **131 D9** 48 58N 97 14W
Pembine, *U.S.A.* **134 C2** 45 38N 87 59W
Pembroke, *Canada* **128 C4** 45 50N 77 7W
Pembroke, *U.K.* **17 F3** 51 41N 4 57W
Pembroke, *U.S.A.* **135 J5** 32 8N 81 37W
Pembuang →, *Indonesia* **75 C4** 3 24 S 112 33 E
Pen-y-Ghent, *U.K.* **16 C5** 54 10N 2 15W
Peña, Sierra de la, *Spain* **34 C4** 42 32N 0 45W
Peña de Francia, Sierra de, *Spain* **36 E4** 40 32N 6 10W
Penafiel, *Portugal* **36 D2** 41 12N 8 17W
Peñafiel, *Spain* **36 D6** 41 35N 4 7W
Peñaflor, *Spain* **37 H5** 37 43N 5 21W
Peñalara, Pico, *Spain* **36 E7** 40 51N 3 57W
Penalva, *Brazil* **154 B2** 3 18 S 45 10W
Penamacôr, *Portugal* **36 E3** 40 10N 7 10W
Penang = Pinang, *Malaysia* **77 K3** 5 25N 100 15 E
Penápolis, *Brazil* **159 A6** 21 30 S 50 0W
Peñaranda de Bracamonte, *Spain* **36 E5** 40 53N 5 13W
Peñarroya-Pueblonuevo, *Spain* **37 G5** 38 19N 5 16W
Peñas, C. de, *Spain* **36 B5** 43 42N 5 52W
Penas, G. de, *Chile* **160 C2** 47 0 S 75 0W
Peñas, Pta., *Venezuela* **153 A5** 11 17N 62 0W
Peñas de San Pedro, *Spain* **35 G2** 38 44N 2 0W
Peñas del Chache, *Canary Is.* **33 E6** 29 6N 13 33W
Peñausende, *Spain* **36 D5** 41 17N 5 52W
Pench'i = Benxi, *China* **67 D12** 41 20N 123 48 E
Pend Oreille →, *U.S.A.* **142 B5** 49 4N 117 37W
Pend Oreille L., *U.S.A.* **142 C5** 48 10N 116 21W
Pendálofon, *Greece* **44 D3** 40 14N 21 12 E
Pendelikón, *Greece* **45 F5** 38 10N 23 53 E
Pendembu, *S. Leone* **100 D2** 9 7N 12 14W
Pendências, *Brazil* **154 C4** 5 15 S 36 43W
Pender B., *Australia* **112 C3** 16 45 S 122 42 E
Pendleton, *Calif., U.S.A.* **145 M9** 33 16N 117 23W
Pendleton, *Ind., U.S.A.* **141 E11** 40 0N 85 45W
Pendleton, *Oreg., U.S.A.* **142 D4** 45 40N 118 47W
Pendzhikent, *Tajikistan* **55 D3** 39 29N 67 37 E
Penedo, *Brazil* **154 D4** 10 15 S 36 36W
Penetanguishene, *Canada* **128 D4** 44 50N 79 55W
Peng Xian, *China* **68 B4** 31 4N 103 32 E
Pengalengan, *Indonesia* **75 D3** 7 9 S 107 30 E
Penge, *Kasai Or., Zaïre* **103 D4** 5 30 S 24 33 E
Penge, *Kivu, Zaïre* **106 C2** 4 27 S 28 25 E
Penglai, *China* **67 F11** 37 48N 120 42 E
Pengshui, *China* **68 C7** 29 17N 108 12 E
Penguin, *Australia* **114 G4** 41 8 S 146 6 E
Pengxi, *China* **68 B5** 30 44N 105 45 E
Pengze, *China* **69 C11** 29 52N 116 32 E
Penhalonga, *Zimbabwe* **107 F3** 18 52 S 32 40 E
Peniche, *Portugal* **37 F1** 39 19N 9 22W
Penicuik, *U.K.* **18 F5** 55 50N 3 14W
Penida, *Indonesia* **75 D5** 8 45 S 115 30 E
Peninsular Malaysia □, *Malaysia* **77 L4** 4 0N 102 0 E
Peñíscola, *Spain* **34 E5** 40 22N 0 24 E
Penitente, Serra dos, *Brazil* **154 C2** 8 45 S 46 20W
Penmarch, *France* **22 E2** 47 49N 4 21W
Penmarch, Pte. de, *France* **22 E2** 47 48N 4 22W
Penn Hills, *U.S.A.* **136 F5** 40 28N 79 52W
Penn Yan, *U.S.A.* **136 D7** 42 40N 77 3W
Pennabilli, *Italy* **39 E9** 43 50N 12 17 E
Pennant, *Canada* **131 C7** 50 32N 108 14W
Penne, *Italy* **39 F10** 42 28N 13 56 E
Penner →, *India* **83 G5** 14 35N 80 10 E
Penneshaw, *Australia* **116 C2** 35 44 S 137 56 E
Pennine, Alpi, *Alps* **38 B4** 46 4N 7 30 E
Pennines, *U.K.* **16 C5** 54 50N 2 20W
Pennington, *U.S.A.* **144 F5** 39 15N 121 47W
Pennino, Mte., *Italy* **39 E9** 43 6N 12 54 E
Pennsylvania □, *U.S.A.* **134 E6** 40 45N 77 30W
Pennville, *U.S.A.* **141 D11** 40 30N 85 9W
Penny, *Canada* **130 C4** 53 51N 121 20W
Peno, *Russia* **50 C8** 57 2N 32 49 E
Penola, *Australia* **116 D4** 37 25 S 140 48 E
Penong, *Australia* **110 G5** 31 59 S 133 5 E
Penong, *S. Austral., Australia* **113 F5** 31 56 S 133 1 E
Penonomé, *Panama* **148 E3** 8 31N 80 21W
Penot, Mt., *Vanuatu* **121 F5** 16 20 S 167 31 E
Penrith, *Australia* **117 B9** 33 43 S 150 38 E
Penrith, *U.K.* **16 C5** 54 40N 2 45W
Pensacola, *U.S.A.* **135 K2** 30 25N 87 13W
Pensacola Mts., *Antarctica* **7 E1** 84 0 S 40 0W
Pense, *Canada* **131 C8** 50 25N 104 59W
Penshurst, *Australia* **116 D5** 37 49 S 142 20 E
Pensiangan, *Malaysia* **75 B5** 4 33N 116 19 E
Pentecost = Pentecôte, *Vanuatu* **121 E6** 15 42 S 168 10 E
Pentecoste, *Brazil* **154 B4** 3 48 S 39 17W
Pentecôte, *Vanuatu* **121 E6** 15 42 S 168 10 E
Penticton, *Canada* **130 D5** 49 30N 119 38W
Pentland, *Australia* **114 C4** 20 32 S 145 25 E
Pentland Firth, *U.K.* **18 C5** 58 43N 3 10W
Pentland Hills, *U.K.* **18 F5** 55 48N 3 25W
Penukonda, *India* **83 G3** 14 5N 77 38 E
Penylan L., *Canada* **131 A7** 61 50N 106 20W
Penza, *Russia* **51 E14** 53 15N 45 5 E
Penzance, *U.K.* **17 G2** 50 7N 5 32W
Penzberg, *Germany* **27 H7** 47 46N 11 23 E
Penzhino, *Russia* **57 C17** 63 30N 167 55 E
Penzhinskaya Guba, *Russia* **57 C17** 61 30N 163 0 E
Penzlin, *Germany* **26 B9** 53 32N 13 6 E
Peoria, *Ariz., U.S.A.* **143 K7** 33 35N 112 14W
Peoria, *Ill., U.S.A.* **140 D7** 40 42N 89 36W
Peoria Heights, *U.S.A.* **140 D7** 40 45N 89 35W
Peotone, *U.S.A.* **141 C9** 41 20N 87 48W
Pepingen, *Belgium* **21 G4** 50 46N 4 10 E
Pepinster, *Belgium* **21 G7** 50 34N 5 47 E
Peqini, *Albania* **44 C1** 41 4N 19 44 E
Pera Hd., *Australia* **114 A3** 12 55 S 141 37 E
Perabumilih, *Indonesia* **74 C2** 3 27 S 104 15 E
Perak □, *Malaysia* **74 A2** 5 0N 101 0 E
Perakhóra, *Greece* **45 F4** 38 2N 22 56 E
Perales de Alfambra, *Spain* **34 E3** 40 38N 1 0W
Perales del Puerto, *Spain* **36 E4** 40 10N 6 40W
Peralta, *Spain* **34 C3** 42 21N 1 49W
Pérama, *Kérkira, Greece* **32 A3** 39 34N 19 54 E
Pérama, *Kríti, Greece* **32 D6** 35 20N 24 40 E
Perast, *Montenegro* **42 E3** 42 31N 18 47 E
Percé, *Canada* **129 C7** 48 31N 64 13W
Perche, *France* **22 D8** 48 31N 1 1 E
Perche, Collines du, *France* **22 D7** 48 30N 0 40 E
Percival Lakes, *Australia* **112 D4** 21 25 S 125 0 E
Percy, *France* **22 D5** 48 55N 1 11W
Percy, *U.S.A.* **140 F7** 38 5N 89 41W
Percy Is., *Australia* **114 C5** 21 39 S 150 16 E
Perdido →, *Argentina* **160 B3** 42 55 S 67 0W
Perdido, Mte., *Spain* **24 F4** 42 40N 0 5 E
Perdu, Mt. = Perdido, Mte., *Spain* **24 F4** 42 40N 0 5 E
Pereira, *Colombia* **152 C2** 4 49N 75 43W
Pereira Barreto, *Brazil* **155 F1** 20 38 S 51 7W
Perekerten, *Australia* **116 C5** 34 55 S 143 40 E
Perené →, *Peru* **156 C3** 11 9 S 74 14W
Perenjori, *Australia* **113 E2** 29 26 S 116 16 E
Pereslavi-Zalesskiy, *Russia* **51 C11** 56 45N 38 50 E
Pereyaslav Khmelnitskiy, *Ukraine* **50 F7** 50 3N 31 28 E
Pérez, I., *Mexico* **147 C7** 22 24N 89 42W
Perg, *Austria* **30 C7** 48 15N 14 38 E
Pergamino, *Argentina* **158 C3** 33 52 S 60 30W
Pérgine Valsugano, *Italy* **39 B8** 46 4N 11 15 E
Pérgola, *Italy* **39 E9** 43 35N 12 50 E
Perham, *U.S.A.* **138 B7** 46 36N 95 34W
Perhentian, Kepulauan, *Malaysia* **77 K4** 5 54N 102 42 E
Peri L., *Australia* **116 A5** 30 45 S 143 35 E
Periam, *Romania* **46 C1** 46 2N 20 59 E
Péribonca →, *Canada* **129 C5** 48 45N 72 5W
Péribonca, L., *Canada* **129 B5** 50 1N 71 10W
Perico, *Argentina* **158 A2** 24 20 S 65 5W
Pericos, *Mexico* **146 B3** 25 3N 107 42W
Périers, *France* **22 C5** 49 11N 1 25W
Périgord, *France* **24 D4** 45 0N 0 40 E
Périgueux, *France* **24 C4** 45 10N 0 42 E
Perijá, Sierra de, *Colombia* **152 B3** 9 30N 73 3W
Peristéra, *Greece* **45 E5** 39 15N 23 58 E
Peristerona →, *Cyprus* **32 D12** 35 8N 33 5 E
Perito Moreno, *Argentina* **160 C2** 46 36 S 70 56W
Peritoró, *Brazil* **154 B3** 4 20 S 44 18W
Perivol = Dragovishtitsa, *Bulgaria* **42 E7** 42 22N 22 39 E
Periyakulam, *India* **83 J3** 10 5N 77 30 E
Periyar →, *India* **83 J3** 10 15N 76 10 E
Periyar, L., *India* **83 K3** 9 25N 77 10 E
Perković, *Croatia* **39 E13** 43 41N 16 10 E
Perlas, Arch. de las, *Panama* **148 E4** 8 41N 79 7W
Perlas, Punta de, *Nic.* **148 D3** 12 30N 83 30W
Perleberg, *Germany* **26 B7** 53 5N 11 50 E
Perlevka, *Russia* **51 F11** 51 58N 38 57 E
Perlez, *Serbia* **42 B5** 45 11N 20 22 E
Perlis □, *Malaysia* **74 A2** 6 30N 100 15 E
Perm, *Russia* **54 C5** 58 0N 56 10 E
Përmeti, *Albania* **44 D2** 40 15N 20 21 E
Pernambuco = Recife, *Brazil* **154 C5** 8 0 S 35 0W
Pernambuco □, *Brazil* **154 C4** 8 0 S 37 0W
Pernatty Lagoon, *Australia* **116 A2** 31 30 S 137 12 E
Pernik, *Bulgaria* **42 E8** 42 35N 23 2 E
Peron, C., *Australia* **113 E1** 25 30 S 113 30 E
Peron Is., *Australia* **112 B5** 13 9 S 130 4 E
Peron Pen., *Australia* **113 E1** 26 0 S 113 10 E
Péronne, *France* **23 C9** 49 55N 2 57 E
Péronnes, *Belgium* **21 H4** 50 27N 4 9 E
Perosa Argentina, *Italy* **38 D4** 44 57N 7 11 E
Perow, *Canada* **130 C3** 54 35N 126 10W
Perpendicular Pt., *Australia* **115 E5** 31 37 S 152 52 E
Perpignan, *France* **24 F6** 42 42N 2 53 E
Perris, *U.S.A.* **145 M9** 33 47N 117 14W
Perros-Guirec, *France* **22 D3** 48 49N 3 28W
Perry, *Fla., U.S.A.* **135 K4** 30 7N 83 35W
Perry, *Ga., U.S.A.* **135 J4** 32 28N 83 44W
Perry, *Iowa, U.S.A.* **140 C2** 41 51N 94 6W
Perry, *Maine, U.S.A.* **135 C12** 44 58N 67 5W
Perry, *Mich., U.S.A.* **141 B12** 42 50N 84 13W
Perry, *Mo., U.S.A.* **140 E5** 39 26N 91 40W
Perry, *Okla., U.S.A.* **139 G6** 36 17N 97 14W
Perrysburg, *U.S.A.* **141 C13** 41 34N 83 38W
Perryton, *U.S.A.* **139 G4** 36 24N 100 48W
Perryville, *U.S.A.* **139 G10** 37 43N 89 52W
Perşembe, *Turkey* **89 C7** 41 5N 37 46 E
Perseverancia, *Bolivia* **157 C5** 14 44 S 62 48W
Persia = Iran ■, *Asia* **85 C7** 33 0N 53 0 E
Persian Gulf = Gulf, The, *Asia* **85 E6** 27 0N 50 0 E
Perstorp, *Sweden* **15 H7** 56 10N 13 25 E
Pertek, *Turkey* **89 D8** 38 51N 39 19 E
Perth, *Australia* **113 F2** 31 57 S 115 52 E
Perth, *Canada* **128 D4** 44 55N 76 15W
Perth, *U.K.* **18 E5** 56 24N 3 27W
Perth Amboy, *U.S.A.* **137 F10** 40 31N 74 16W
Pertuis, *France* **25 E9** 43 42N 5 30 E
Peru, *Ill., U.S.A.* **140 C7** 41 20N 89 8W
Peru, *Ind., U.S.A.* **141 D10** 40 45N 86 4W
Peru ■, *S. Amer.* **152 D2** 4 0 S 75 0W
Peru-Chile Trench, *Pac. Oc.* **123 K20** 20 0 S 72 0W
Perúgia, *Italy* **39 E9** 43 6N 12 24 E
Perušić, *Croatia* **39 D12** 44 40N 15 22 E
Péruwelz, *Belgium* **21 G3** 50 31N 3 36 E
Pervomaysk, *Russia* **51 D13** 54 56N 43 58 E
Pervomaysk, *Ukraine* **52 B4** 48 10N 30 46 E
Pervouralsk, *Russia* **54 C6** 56 55N 59 45 E
Perwez, *Belgium* **21 G5** 50 38N 4 48 E
Pes, Pta. del, *Spain* **33 C7** 38 46N 1 26 E
Pésaro, *Italy* **39 E9** 43 55N 12 53 E
Pescara, *Italy* **39 F11** 42 28N 14 13 E
Pescara →, *Italy* **39 F11** 42 28N 14 13 E
Peschanokopskoye, *Russia* **53 C9** 46 14N 41 4 E
Péscia, *Italy* **38 E7** 43 54N 10 40 E
Pescina, *Italy* **39 G10** 42 0N 13 39 E
Peseux, *Switz.* **28 C3** 46 59N 6 53 E
Peshawar, *Pakistan* **79 B3** 34 2N 71 37 E
Peshkopia, *Albania* **44 C2** 41 41N 20 25 E
Peshtera, *Bulgaria* **43 E9** 42 2N 24 18 E
Peshtigo, *U.S.A.* **134 C2** 45 4N 87 46W
Peski, *Russia* **51 F13** 51 14N 42 29 E
Peskovka, *Russia* **51 B18** 59 23N 52 20 E
Peskovka, *Russia* **54 B3** 59 4N 52 22 E
Pêso da Régua, *Portugal* **36 D3** 41 10N 7 47W
Pesqueira, *Brazil* **154 C4** 8 20 S 36 42W
Pessac, *France* **24 D3** 44 48N 0 37W
Pessoux, *Belgium* **21 H6** 50 17N 5 11 E
Pest □, *Hungary* **31 D12** 47 29N 19 5 E
Pestovo, *Russia* **50 B9** 58 33N 35 42 E
Pestravka, *Russia* **51 E16** 52 28N 49 57 E
Péta, *Greece* **45 E3** 39 10N 21 2 E
Petah Tiqwa, *Israel* **91 C3** 32 6N 34 53 E
Petalídhion, *Greece* **45 H3** 36 57N 21 55 E
Petaling Jaya, *Malaysia* **77 L3** 3 4N 101 42 E
Petaloudhes, *Greece* **32 C10** 36 18N 28 5 E
Petaluma, *U.S.A.* **144 G4** 38 14N 122 39W
Petange, *Lux.* **21 J7** 49 33N 5 55 E
Petatlán, *Mexico* **146 D4** 17 31N 101 16W
Petauke, *Zambia* **107 E3** 14 14 S 31 20 E
Petawawa, *Canada* **128 C4** 45 54N 77 17W
Petegem, *Belgium* **21 G3** 50 59N 3 32 E
Petén Itzá, L., *Guatemala* **148 C2** 16 58N 89 50W
Peter I.s Øy, *Antarctica* **7 C16** 69 0 S 91 0W
Peter Pond L., *Canada* **131 B7** 55 55N 108 44W
Peterbell, *Canada* **128 C3** 48 36N 83 21W
Peterborough, *Australia* **116 B3** 32 58 S 138 51 E
Peterborough, *Canada* **127 D12** 44 20N 78 20W
Peterborough, *U.K.* **17 E7** 52 35N 0 14W
Peterborough, *U.S.A.* **137 D13** 42 53N 71 57W
Peterhead, *U.K.* **18 D7** 57 30N 1 49W
Petermann Bjerg, *Greenland* **124 B17** 73 7N 28 25W
Peter's Mine, *Guyana* **153 B6** 6 14N 59 20W
Petersburg, *Alaska, U.S.A.* **130 B2** 56 48N 132 58W
Petersburg, *Ill., U.S.A.* **140 D7** 40 1N 89 51W
Petersburg, *Ind., U.S.A.* **141 F9** 38 30N 87 17W
Petersburg, *Va., U.S.A.* **134 G7** 37 14N 77 24W
Petersburg, *W. Va., U.S.A.* **134 F6** 39 1N 79 5W
Petford, *Australia* **114 B3** 17 20 S 144 58 E
Petília Policastro, *Italy* **41 C9** 39 7N 16 48 E
Petit Bois I., *U.S.A.* **135 K1** 30 12N 88 26W
Petit-Cap, *Canada* **129 C7** 49 3N 64 30W
Petit Goâve, *Haiti* **149 C5** 18 27N 72 51W
Petit Lac Manicouagan, *Canada* **129 B6** 51 25N 67 40W
Petit Saint Bernard, Col du, *Italy* **38 C3** 45 40N 6 52 E
Petitcodiac, *Canada* **129 C6** 45 57N 65 11W
Petite Baleine →, *Canada* **128 A4** 56 0N 76 45W
Petite Saguenay, *Canada* **129 C5** 48 15N 70 4W
Petitsikapau, L., *Canada* **129 B6** 54 37N 66 25W
Petlad, *India* **80 H5** 22 30N 72 45 E
Peto, *Mexico* **147 C7** 20 10N 88 53W
Petone, *N.Z.* **118 H3** 41 13 S 174 53 E
Petoskey, *U.S.A.* **134 C3** 45 22N 84 57W
Petra, *Jordan* **91 E4** 30 20N 35 22 E
Petra, *Spain* **33 B10** 39 37N 3 6 E
Petra, Ostrova, *Russia* **6 B13** 76 15N 118 30 E
Petra Velikogo, Zaliv, *Russia* **60 C5** 42 40N 132 0 E
Petralia, *Italy* **41 E7** 37 49N 14 4 E
Petrel, *Spain* **35 G4** 38 30N 0 46W
Petreto-Bicchisano, *France* **25 G12** 41 47N 8 58 E
Petrich, *Bulgaria* **43 F8** 41 24N 23 13 E
Petrijanec, *Croatia* **39 B13** 46 23N 16 17 E
Petrikov, *Belorussia* **50 E6** 52 11N 28 29 E
Petrila, *Romania* **46 D4** 45 29N 23 29 E
Petrinja, *Croatia* **39 C13** 45 28N 16 18 E
Petrograd = Sankt-Peterburg, *Russia* **50 B7** 59 55N 30 20 E
Petrolândia, *Brazil* **154 C4** 9 5 S 38 20W
Petrolia, *Canada* **128 D3** 42 54N 82 9W
Petrolina, *Brazil* **154 C3** 9 24 S 40 30W
Petromagoúla, *Greece* **45 F5** 38 31N 23 0 E
Petropavlovsk, *Kazakhstan* **56 D7** 54 53N 69 13 E
Petropavlovsk-Kamchatskiy, *Russia* **57 D16** 53 3N 158 43 E
Petropavlovskiy = Akhtubinsk, *Russia* **53 B12** 48 13N 46 7 E
Petrópolis, *Brazil* **155 F3** 22 33 S 43 9W

Piteşti 249

Petroşeni, *Romania* **46 D4** 45 28N 23 20 E
Petrova Gora, *Croatia* **39 C12** 45 15N 15 45 E
Petrovac, *Montenegro* **42 E3** 42 13N 18 57 E
Petrovac, *Serbia* **42 C6** 44 22N 21 26 E
Petrovaradin, *Serbia* **42 B4** 45 16N 19 55 E
Petrovsk, *Russia* **51 E14** 52 22N 45 19 E
Petrovsk-Zabaykalskiy, *Russia* **57 D11** 51 20N 108 55 E
Petrovskoye = Svetlograd, *Russia* **53 D10** 45 25N 42 58 E
Petrovskoye, *Russia* **54 E5** 53 37N 56 23 E
Petrozavodsk, *Russia* **48 B5** 61 41N 34 20 E
Petrus Steyn, *S. Africa* **105 D4** 27 38 S 28 8 E
Petrusburg, *S. Africa* **104 D4** 29 4 S 25 26 E
Pettitts, *Australia* **117 C8** 34 56 S 148 10 E
Petukhovka, *Belorussia* **50 E7** 53 42N 30 54 E
Peumo, *Chile* **158 C1** 34 21 S 71 12W
Peureulak, *Indonesia* **74 B1** 4 48N 97 45 E
Peusangan →, *Indonesia* **74 A1** 5 16N 96 51 E
Pevek, *Russia* **57 C18** 69 41N 171 19 E
Peveragno, *Italy* **38 D4** 44 20N 7 37 E
Peyrehorade, *France* **24 E2** 43 34N 1 7W
Peyruis, *France* **25 D9** 44 1N 5 56 E
Pézenas, *France* **24 E7** 43 28N 3 24 E
Pezinok, *Slovak Rep.* **31 C10** 48 17N 17 17 E
Pfaffenhofen, *Germany* **27 G7** 48 31N 11 31 E
Pfäffikon, *Switz.* **29 B7** 47 13N 8 46 E
Pfarrkirchen, *Germany* **27 G8** 48 25N 12 57 E
Pfeffenhausen, *Germany* **27 G7** 48 40N 11 58 E
Pforzheim, *Germany* **27 G4** 48 53N 8 43 E
Pfullendorf, *Germany* **27 H5** 47 55N 9 15 E
Pfungstadt, *Germany* **27 F4** 49 47N 8 36 E
Phaistós, *Greece* **32 D6** 35 2N 24 50 E
Phala, *Botswana* **104 C4** 23 45 S 26 50 E
Phalera = Phulera, *India* **80 F6** 26 52N 75 16 E
Phalodi, *India* **80 F5** 27 12N 72 24 E
Phalsbourg, *France* **23 D14** 48 46N 7 15 E
Phan, *Thailand* **76 C2** 19 28N 99 43 E
Phan Rang, *Vietnam* **77 G7** 11 34N 109 0 E
Phan Ri = Hoa Da, *Vietnam* **77 G7** 11 16N 108 40 E
Phan Thiet, *Vietnam* **77 G7** 11 1N 108 9 E
Phanae, *Greece* **45 F7** 38 8N 25 57 E
Phanat Nikhom, *Thailand* **76 F3** 13 27N 101 11 E
Phangan, Ko, *Thailand* **77 H3** 9 45N 100 0 E
Phangnga, *Thailand* **77 H2** 8 28N 98 30 E
Phanh Bho Ho Chi Minh, *Vietnam* **77 G6** 10 58N 106 40 E
Phanom Sarakham, *Thailand* **76 F3** 13 45N 101 21 E
Pharenda, *India* **81 F10** 27 5N 83 17 E
Phatthalung, *Thailand* **77 J3** 7 39N 100 6 E
Phayao, *Thailand* **76 C2** 19 11N 99 55 E
Phelps, *N.Y., U.S.A.* **136 D7** 42 58N 77 3W
Phelps, *Wis., U.S.A.* **138 B10** 46 4N 89 5W
Phelps L., *Canada* **131 B8** 59 15N 103 15W
Phenix City, *U.S.A.* **135 J3** 32 28N 85 0W
Phet Buri, *Thailand* **76 F2** 13 1N 99 55 E
Phetchabun, *Thailand* **76 D3** 16 25N 101 8 E
Phetchabun, Thiu Khao, *Thailand* **76 E3** 16 0N 101 20 E
Phetchaburi = Phet Buri, *Thailand* **76 F2** 13 1N 99 55 E
Phi Phi, Ko, *Thailand* **77 J2** 7 45N 98 46 E
Phiafay, *Laos* **76 E6** 14 48N 106 0 E
Phibun Mangsahan, *Thailand* **76 E5** 15 14N 105 14 E
Phichai, *Thailand* **76 D3** 17 22N 100 10 E
Phichit, *Thailand* **76 D3** 16 26N 100 22 E
Philadelphia, *Miss., U.S.A.* **139 J10** 32 46N 89 7W
Philadelphia, *N.Y., U.S.A.* **137 B9** 44 9N 75 43W
Philadelphia, *Pa., U.S.A.* **137 F9** 39 57N 75 10W
Philip, *U.S.A.* **138 C4** 44 2N 101 40W
Philippeville, *Belgium* **21 H5** 50 12N 4 33 E
Philippi, *Greece* **44 C6** 41 1N 24 16 E
Philippi L., *Australia* **114 C2** 24 20 S 138 55 E
Philippines ■, *Asia* **70 E4** 12 0N 123 0 E
Philippolis, *S. Africa* **104 E4** 30 15 S 25 16 E
Philippopolis = Plovdiv, *Bulgaria* **43 E9** 42 8N 24 44 E
Philipsburg, *Mont., U.S.A.* **142 C7** 46 20N 113 18W
Philipsburg, *Pa., U.S.A.* **136 F6** 40 54N 78 13W
Philipstown, *S. Africa* **104 E3** 30 28 S 24 30 E
Phillip I., *Australia* **117 E6** 38 30 S 145 12 E
Phillips, *Tex., U.S.A.* **139 H4** 35 42N 101 22W
Phillips, *Wis., U.S.A.* **138 C9** 45 42N 90 24W
Phillipsburg, *Kans., U.S.A.* **138 F5** 39 45N 99 19W
Phillipsburg, *N.J., U.S.A.* **137 F9** 40 42N 75 12W
Phillott, *Australia* **115 D4** 27 53 S 145 50 E
Philmont, *U.S.A.* **137 D11** 42 15N 73 39W
Philomath, *U.S.A.* **142 D2** 44 32N 123 22W
Phimai, *Thailand* **76 E4** 15 13N 102 30 E
Phitsanulok, *Thailand* **76 D3** 16 50N 100 12 E
Phnom Dangrek, *Thailand* **76 E5** 14 20N 104 0 E
Phnom Penh, *Cambodia* **77 G5** 11 33N 104 55 E
Phoenix, *Ariz., U.S.A.* **143 K7** 33 27N 112 4W
Phoenix, *N.Y., U.S.A.* **137 C8** 43 14N 76 18W
Phoenix Is., *Kiribati* **122 H10** 3 30 S 172 0W
Phoenixville, *U.S.A.* **137 F9** 40 8N 75 31W
Phon, *Thailand* **76 E4** 15 49N 102 36 E
Phon Tiou, *Laos* **76 D5** 17 53N 104 37 E
Phong →, *Thailand* **76 D4** 16 23N 102 56 E
Phong Saly, *Laos* **76 B4** 21 42N 102 9 E
Phong Tho, *Vietnam* **76 A4** 22 32N 103 21 E
Phonhong, *Laos* **76 C4** 18 30N 102 25 E
Phonum, *Thailand* **77 H2** 8 49N 98 48 E
Phosphate Hill, *Australia* **114 C2** 21 53 S 139 58 E
Photharam, *Thailand* **76 F2** 13 41N 99 51 E
Phra Chedi Sam Ong, *Thailand* **76 E2** 15 16N 98 23 E
Phra Nakhon Si Ayutthaya, *Thailand* **76 E3** 14 25N 100 30 E
Phra Thong, Ko, *Thailand* **77 H2** 9 5N 98 17 E
Phrae, *Thailand* **76 C3** 18 7N 100 9 E
Phrom Phiram, *Thailand* **76 D3** 17 2N 100 12 E
Phrygia, *Turkey* **88 D3** 38 40N 30 0 E
Phu Dien, *Vietnam* **76 C5** 18 58N 105 31 E
Phu Loi, *Laos* **76 B4** 20 14N 103 14 E
Phu Ly, *Vietnam* **76 B5** 20 35N 105 50 E
Phu Tho, *Vietnam* **76 B5** 21 24N 105 13 E
Phuc Yen, *Vietnam* **76 B5** 21 16N 105 45 E
Phuket, *Thailand* **77 J2** 7 52N 98 22 E
Phuket, Ko, *Thailand* **77 J2** 8 0N 98 22 E
Phulbari, *India* **78 C3** 25 55N 90 2 E
Phulera, *India* **80 F6** 26 52N 75 16 E
Phumiphon, Khuan, *Thailand* **76 D2** 17 15N 98 58 E
Phun Phin, *Thailand* **77 H2** 9 7N 99 12 E
Piacá, *Brazil* **154 C2** 7 42 S 47 18W
Piacenza, *Italy* **38 C6** 45 2N 9 42 E
Piaçubaçu, *Brazil* **154 D4** 10 24 S 36 25W
Piádena, *Italy* **38 C7** 45 8N 10 22 E
Piako →, *N.Z.* **118 D4** 37 12 S 175 30 E
Pialba, *Australia* **115 D5** 25 20 S 152 45 E
Pian Cr. →, *Australia* **115 E4** 30 2 S 148 12 E
Piana, *France* **25 F12** 42 15N 8 34 E
Pianella, *Italy* **39 F11** 42 24N 14 5 E
Piangil, *Australia* **116 C5** 35 5 S 143 20 E
Pianoro, *Italy* **39 D8** 44 20N 11 20 E
Pianosa, *Puglia, Italy* **39 F12** 42 12N 15 44 E
Pianosa, *Toscana, Italy* **38 F7** 42 36N 10 4 E
Piapot, *Canada* **131 D7** 49 59N 109 8W
Piare →, *Italy* **39 C9** 45 32N 12 44 E
Pias, *Portugal* **37 G3** 38 1N 7 29W
Piaseczno, *Poland* **47 C8** 52 5N 21 2 E
Piaski, *Poland* **47 D9** 51 8N 22 52 E
Piastów, *Poland* **47 C7** 52 12N 20 48 E
Piatã, *Brazil* **155 D3** 13 9 S 41 48W
Piatra, *Romania* **46 F6** 43 51N 25 9 E
Piatra Neamţ, *Romania* **46 C7** 46 56N 26 21 E
Piatra Olt, *Romania* **46 E5** 44 22N 24 16 E
Piauí □, *Brazil* **154 C3** 7 0 S 43 0W
Piaui →, *Brazil* **154 C3** 6 38 S 42 42W
Piave →, *Italy* **39 C9** 45 32N 12 44 E
Piazza Ármerina, *Italy* **41 E7** 37 21N 14 20 E
Pibor →, *Sudan* **95 F3** 7 35N 33 0 E
Pibor Post, *Sudan* **95 F3** 6 47N 33 3 E
Pica, *Chile* **156 E4** 20 35 S 69 25W
Picardie, *France* **23 C9** 49 50N 3 0 E
Picardie, Plaine de, *France* **23 C9** 50 0N 2 0 E
Picardy = Picardie, *France* **23 C9** 49 50N 3 0 E
Picayune, *U.S.A.* **139 K10** 30 32N 89 41W
Picerno, *Italy* **41 B8** 40 40N 15 37 E
Pichilemu, *Chile* **158 C1** 34 22 S 72 0W
Pichincha, □, *Ecuador* **152 D2** 0 10 S 78 40W
Pickerel L., *Canada* **128 C1** 48 40N 91 25W
Pickle Lake, *Canada* **128 B1** 51 30N 90 12W
Pico Truncado, *Argentina* **160 C3** 46 40 S 68 0W
Picos, *Brazil* **154 C3** 7 5 S 41 28W
Picos Ancares, Sierra de, *Spain* **36 C4** 42 51N 6 52W
Picota, *Peru* **156 B2** 6 54 S 76 24W
Picquigny, *France* **23 C9** 49 56N 2 10 E
Picton, *Australia* **117 C9** 34 12 S 150 34 E
Picton, *Canada* **128 D4** 44 1N 77 9W
Picton, *N.Z.* **119 B9** 41 18 S 174 3 E
Picton, I., *Chile* **160 E3** 55 2 S 66 57W
Pictou, *Canada* **129 C7** 45 41N 62 42W
Picture Butte, *Canada* **130 D6** 49 55N 112 45W
Picuí, *Brazil* **154 C4** 6 31 S 36 21W
Picún Leufú, *Argentina* **160 A3** 39 30 S 69 5W
Pidurutalagala, *Sri Lanka* **83 L5** 7 10N 80 50 E
Piedecuesta, *Colombia* **152 B3** 6 59N 73 3W
Piedicavallo, *Italy* **38 C4** 45 41N 7 57 E
Piedmont = Piemonte □, *Italy* **38 D4** 45 0N 7 30 E
Piedmont, *U.S.A.* **135 J3** 33 55N 85 37W
Piedmont Plateau, *U.S.A.* **135 J5** 34 0N 81 30W
Piedmonte d'Alife, *Italy* **41 A7** 41 22N 14 22 E
Piedra →, *Spain* **34 D3** 41 18N 1 47W
Piedra del Anguila, *Argentina* **160 B2** 40 2 S 70 4W
Piedra Lais, *Venezuela* **152 C4** 3 10N 65 50W
Piedrabuena, *Spain* **37 F6** 39 0N 4 10W
Piedrahita, *Spain* **36 E5** 40 28N 5 23W
Piedras, R. de las →, *Peru* **156 C4** 12 30 S 69 15W
Piedras Negras, *Mexico* **146 B4** 28 35N 100 35W
Piedras Pt., *Phil.* **71 F2** 10 11N 118 48 E
Piemonte □, *Italy* **38 D4** 45 0N 7 30 E
Piensk, *Poland* **47 D2** 51 16N 15 2 E
Pier Millan, *Australia* **116 C5** 35 14 S 142 40 E
Pierce, *U.S.A.* **142 C6** 46 30N 115 48W
Piercefield, *U.S.A.* **137 B10** 44 13N 74 35W
Piería □, *Greece* **44 D4** 40 13N 22 25 E
Pierre, *U.S.A.* **138 C4** 44 22N 100 21W
Pierre Bénite, Barrage de la, *France* **25 C8** 45 42N 4 49 E
Pierre-de-Bresse, *France* **25 B9** 46 54N 5 13 E
Pierrefeu-du-Var, *France* **25 E10** 43 13N 6 9 E
Pierrefonds, *France* **23 C9** 49 20N 2 58 E
Pierrefontaine-les-Varans, *France* **23 E13** 47 14N 6 32 E
Pierrefort, *France* **24 D6** 44 55N 2 50 E
Pierrelatte, *France* **25 D8** 44 23N 4 43 E
Piešťany, *Slovak Rep.* **31 C10** 48 38N 17 55 E
Piesting →, *Austria* **31 C9** 48 6N 16 40 E
Pieszyce, *Poland* **47 E3** 50 43N 16 33 E
Piet Retief, *S. Africa* **105 D5** 27 1 S 30 50 E
Pietarsaari = Jakobstad, *Finland* **12 E17** 63 40N 22 43 E
Pietermaritzburg, *S. Africa* **105 D5** 29 35 S 30 25 E
Pietersburg, *S. Africa* **105 C4** 23 54 S 29 25 E
Pietraperzia, *Italy* **41 E7** 37 26N 14 8 E
Pietrasanta, *Italy* **38 E7** 43 57N 10 12 E
Pietrosu, *Romania* **46 B6** 47 12N 25 8 E
Pietrosul, *Romania* **46 B5** 47 35N 24 43 E
Pieve di Cadore, *Italy* **39 B9** 46 25N 12 22 E
Pieve di Teco, *Italy* **38 D4** 44 3N 7 54 E
Pievepélago, *Italy* **38 D7** 44 12N 10 35 E
Pigádhia, *Greece* **45 J9** 35 30N 27 12 E
Pigadhítsa, *Greece* **44 E3** 39 59N 21 23 E
Pigeon, *U.S.A.* **134 D4** 43 50N 83 16W
Pigeon I., *India* **83 G2** 14 2N 74 20 E
Piggott, *U.S.A.* **139 G9** 36 23N 90 11W
Pigna, *Italy* **38 E4** 43 57N 7 40 E
Pigüe, *Argentina* **158 D3** 37 36 S 62 25W
Pihani, *India* **81 F9** 27 36N 80 15 E
Pijnacker, *Neths.* **20 D4** 52 1N 4 26 E
Pikalevo, *Russia* **50 B9** 59 37N 34 0 E
Pikes Peak, *U.S.A.* **138 F2** 38 50N 105 3W
Piketberg, *S. Africa* **104 E2** 32 55 S 18 40 E
Pikeville, *U.S.A.* **134 G4** 37 29N 82 31W
Pikou, *China* **67 E12** 39 18N 122 22 E
Pikwitonei, *Canada* **131 B9** 55 35N 97 9W
Piła, *Poland* **47 B3** 53 10N 16 48 E
Pila, *Spain* **35 G3** 38 16N 1 11W
Piła □, *Poland* **47 B3** 53 0N 17 0 E
Pilaía, *Greece* **44 D4** 40 32N 22 59 E
Pilani, *India* **80 E6** 28 22N 75 33 E
Pilar, *Brazil* **154 C4** 9 36 S 35 56W
Pilar, *Paraguay* **158 B4** 26 50 S 58 20W
Pilas Group, *Phil.* **71 H3** 6 45N 121 35 E
Pilawa, *Poland* **47 D8** 51 57N 21 32 E
Pilaya →, *Bolivia* **157 E5** 20 55 S 64 4W
Pilcomayo →, *Paraguay* **158 B4** 25 21 S 57 42W
Píli, *Greece* **45 H9** 36 50N 27 15 E
Pili, *Phil.* **70 E4** 13 33N 123 19 E
Pilibhit, *India* **81 E8** 28 40N 79 50 E
Pilica →, *Poland* **47 D8** 51 52N 21 17 E
Pilion, *Greece* **44 E5** 39 27N 23 7 E
Pilis, *Hungary* **31 D12** 47 17N 19 35 E
Pilisvörösvár, *Hungary* **31 D11** 47 38N 18 56 E
Pilkhawa, *India* **80 E7** 28 43N 77 42 E
Pillaro, *Ecuador* **152 D2** 1 10 S 78 32W
Pílos, *Greece* **45 H3** 36 55N 21 42 E
Pilot Grove, *U.S.A.* **140 F4** 38 53N 92 55W
Pilot Mound, *Canada* **131 D9** 49 15N 98 54W
Pilot Point, *U.S.A.* **139 J6** 33 24N 96 58W
Pilot Rock, *U.S.A.* **142 D4** 45 29N 118 50W
Pilsen = Plzeň, *Czech.* **30 B6** 49 45N 13 22 E
Pilštanj, *Slovenia* **39 B12** 46 8N 15 39 E
Pilzno, *Poland* **31 B14** 49 58N 21 16 E
Pima, *U.S.A.* **143 K9** 32 54N 109 50W
Pimba, *Australia* **116 A2** 31 18 S 136 46 E
Pimenta Bueno, *Brazil* **157 C5** 11 35 S 61 10W
Pimentel, *Peru* **156 B2** 6 45 S 79 55W
Pina, *Spain* **34 D4** 41 29N 0 33W
Pinamalayan, *Phil.* **70 E3** 13 2N 121 29 E
Pinang, *Malaysia* **77 K3** 5 25N 100 15 E
Pinang □, *Malaysia* **74 A2** 5 20N 100 20 E
Pinar, C. del, *Spain* **33 B10** 39 53N 3 12 E
Pinar del Río, *Cuba* **148 B3** 22 26N 83 40W
Pinarbaşi, *Turkey* **88 D7** 38 43N 36 23 E
Pincehely, *Hungary* **31 E11** 46 41N 18 27 E
Pinchang, *China* **68 B6** 31 36N 107 3 E
Pincher Creek, *Canada* **130 D6** 49 30N 113 57W
Pinchi L., *Canada* **130 C4** 54 38N 124 30W
Pinckneyville, *U.S.A.* **140 F7** 38 5N 89 23W
Pîncota, *Romania* **42 A6** 46 20N 21 45 E
Pińczów, *Poland* **47 E7** 50 32N 20 32 E
Pind Dadan Khan, *Pakistan* **80 C5** 32 36N 73 7 E
Pindar, *Australia* **113 E2** 28 30 S 115 47 E
Pindaré →, *Brazil* **154 B3** 3 17 S 44 47W
Pindaré Mirim, *Brazil* **154 B2** 3 37 S 45 21W
Pindi Gheb, *Pakistan* **80 C5** 33 14N 72 21 E
Pindiga, *Nigeria* **101 D7** 9 58N 10 53 E
Pindobal, *Brazil* **154 B2** 3 16 S 48 25W
Pindos Óros, *Greece* **44 E3** 40 0N 21 0 E
Pindus Mts. = Pindos Óros, *Greece* **44 E3** 40 0N 21 0 E
Pine, *U.S.A.* **143 J8** 34 23N 111 27W
Pine →, *Canada* **131 B7** 58 50N 105 38W
Pine, C., *Canada* **129 C9** 46 37N 53 32W
Pine Bluff, *U.S.A.* **139 H8** 34 13N 92 1W
Pine City, *U.S.A.* **138 C8** 45 50N 92 59W
Pine Falls, *Canada* **131 C9** 50 34N 96 11W
Pine Flat L., *U.S.A.* **144 J7** 36 50N 119 20W
Pine Pass, *Canada* **130 B4** 55 25N 122 42W
Pine Point, *Canada* **130 A6** 60 50N 114 28W
Pine Ridge, *Australia* **117 A9** 31 30 S 150 28 E
Pine Ridge, *U.S.A.* **138 D3** 43 2N 102 33W
Pine River, *Canada* **131 C8** 51 45N 100 30W
Pine River, *U.S.A.* **138 B7** 46 43N 94 24W
Pine Valley, *U.S.A.* **145 N10** 32 50N 116 32W
Pinecrest, *U.S.A.* **144 G6** 38 12N 120 1W
Pinedale, *U.S.A.* **144 J7** 36 50N 119 48W
Pinega →, *Russia* **48 B8** 64 8N 46 54 E
Pinehill, *Australia* **114 C4** 23 38 S 146 57 E
Pinerolo, *Italy* **38 D4** 44 47N 7 21 E
Pineto, *Italy* **39 F11** 42 36N 14 4 E
Pinetop, *U.S.A.* **143 J9** 34 8N 109 56W
Pinetown, *S. Africa* **105 D5** 29 48 S 30 54 E
Pinetree, *U.S.A.* **142 E11** 43 42N 105 52W
Pineville, *Ky., U.S.A.* **135 G4** 36 46N 83 42W
Pineville, *La., U.S.A.* **139 K8** 31 19N 92 26W
Piney, *France* **23 D11** 48 22N 4 21 E
Ping →, *Thailand* **76 E3** 15 42N 100 9 E
Pingaring, *Australia* **113 F2** 32 40 S 118 32 E
Pingba, *China* **68 D6** 26 23N 106 12 E
Pingchuan, *China* **68 D3** 27 35N 101 55 E
Pingding, *China* **66 F7** 37 47N 113 38 E
Pingdingshan, *China* **66 H7** 33 43N 113 27 E
Pingdong, *Taiwan* **69 F13** 22 39N 120 30 E
Pingdu, *China* **67 F10** 36 42N 119 59 E
Pingelly, *Australia* **113 F2** 32 32 S 117 5 E
Pingguo, *China* **68 F6** 23 19N 107 36 E
Pinghe, *China* **69 E11** 24 17N 117 21 E
Pinghu, *China* **69 B13** 30 40N 121 2 E
Pingjiang, *China* **69 C9** 28 45N 113 36 E
Pingle, *China* **69 E8** 24 40N 110 40 E
Pingli, *China* **68 A7** 32 27N 109 22 E
Pingliang, *China* **66 G4** 35 35N 106 31 E
Pinglu, *China* **66 E7** 39 31N 112 30 E
Pingluo, *China* **66 E4** 38 52N 106 30 E
Pingnan, *Fujian, China* **69 D12** 26 55N 119 0 E
Pingnan, *Guangxi Zhuangzu, China* **69 F8** 23 33N 110 22 E
Pingquan, *China* **67 D10** 41 1N 118 37 E
Pingrup, *Australia* **113 F2** 33 32 S 118 29 E
Pingtan, *China* **69 E12** 25 31N 119 47 E
Pingtang, *China* **68 E6** 25 49N 107 17 E
Pingwu, *China* **66 H3** 32 25N 104 30 E
Pingxiang, *Guangxi Zhuangzu, China* **68 F6** 22 6N 106 46 E
Pingxiang, *Jiangxi, China* **69 D9** 27 43N 113 48 E
Pingyao, *China* **66 F7** 37 12N 112 10 E
Pingyi, *China* **67 G9** 35 30N 117 35 E
Pingyin, *China* **66 F9** 36 20N 116 25 E
Pingyuan, *Guangdong, China* **69 E10** 24 37N 115 57 E
Pingyuan, *Shandong, China* **66 F9** 37 10N 116 22 E
Pingyuanjie, *China* **68 F4** 23 45N 103 48 E
Pinhal, *Brazil* **159 A6** 22 10 S 46 46W
Pinheiro, *Brazil* **154 B2** 2 31 S 45 5W
Pinhel, *Portugal* **36 E3** 40 50N 7 1W
Pinhuá →, *Brazil* **157 B4** 6 21 S 65 0W
Pini, *Indonesia* **74 B1** 0 10N 98 40 E
Piniós →, *Ilía, Greece* **45 G3** 37 48N 21 20 E
Piniós →, *Trikkala, Greece* **44 E4** 39 55N 22 10 E
Pinjarra, *Australia* **113 F2** 32 37 S 115 52 E
Pink →, *Canada* **131 B8** 56 50N 103 50W
Pinkafeld, *Austria* **31 D9** 47 22N 16 9 E
Pinlebu, *Burma* **78 C5** 24 5N 95 22 E
Pinnacles, *Australia* **113 E3** 28 12 S 120 26 E
Pinnacles, *U.S.A.* **144 J5** 36 33N 121 19W
Pinnaroo, *Australia* **116 C4** 35 17 S 140 53 E
Pinneberg, *Germany* **26 B5** 53 39N 9 48 E
Pino Hachado, Paso, *S. Amer.* **160 A2** 38 39 S 70 54W
Pinon Hills, *U.S.A.* **145 L9** 34 26N 117 39W
Pinos, *Mexico* **146 C4** 22 20N 101 40W
Pinos, Mt., *U.S.A.* **145 L7** 34 49N 119 8W
Pinos Pt., *U.S.A.* **143 H3** 36 38N 121 57W
Pinos Puente, *Spain* **37 H7** 37 15N 3 45W
Pinotepa Nacional, *Mexico* **147 D5** 16 19N 98 3W
Pinrang, *Indonesia* **72 B1** 3 46 S 119 41 E
Pins, I. des, *N. Cal.* **121 V21** 22 37 S 167 30 E
Pinsk, *Belorussia* **50 E5** 52 10N 26 1 E
Pintados, *Chile* **156 E4** 20 35 S 69 40W
Pintumba, *Australia* **113 F5** 31 30 S 132 12 E
Pintuyan, *Phil.* **71 G5** 9 57N 125 15 E
Pinukpuk, *Phil.* **70 C3** 17 35N 121 22 E
Pinyang, *China* **69 D13** 27 42N 120 31 E
Pinyug, *Russia* **48 B8** 60 5N 48 0 E
Pinzolo, *Italy* **38 B7** 46 9N 10 45 E
Pio V. Corpuz, *Phil.* **71 F5** 11 55N 124 2 E
Pio XII, *Brazil* **154 B2** 3 53 S 45 17W
Pioche, *U.S.A.* **143 H6** 37 56N 114 27W
Pioduran, *Phil.* **70 E4** 13 2N 123 25 E
Piombino, *Italy* **38 F7** 42 54N 10 30 E
Piombino, Canale di, *Italy* **38 F7** 42 50N 10 25 E
Pioner, Os., *Russia* **57 B10** 79 50N 92 0 E
Pionki, *Poland* **47 D8** 51 29N 21 28 E
Piorini →, *Brazil* **153 D5** 3 23 S 63 30W
Piorini, L., *Brazil* **153 D5** 3 15 S 62 35W
Piotrków Trybunalski, *Poland* **47 D6** 51 23N 19 43 E
Piotrków Trybunalski □, *Poland* **47 D6** 51 30N 19 45 E
Piove di Sacco, *Italy* **39 C9** 45 18N 12 1 E
Pip, *Iran* **85 E9** 26 45N 60 10 E
Pipar, *India* **80 F5** 26 25N 73 31 E
Piparia, *India* **80 H8** 22 45N 78 23 E
Pipéri, *Greece* **44 E6** 39 20N 24 19 E
Pipestone, *U.S.A.* **138 D6** 44 0N 96 19W
Pipestone →, *Canada* **128 B2** 52 53N 89 23W
Pipestone Cr. →, *Canada* **131 D8** 49 38N 100 15W
Pipiriki, *N.Z.* **118 F4** 39 28 S 175 5 E
Pipmuacan, Rés., *Canada* **129 C5** 49 45N 70 30W
Pippingarra, *Australia* **112 D2** 20 27 S 118 42 E
Pipriac, *France* **22 E5** 47 49N 1 58W
Piqua, *U.S.A.* **141 D12** 40 9N 84 15W
Piquet Carneiro, *Brazil* **154 C4** 5 48 S 39 25W
Piquiri →, *Brazil* **159 A5** 24 3 S 54 14W
Pīr Sohrāb, *Iran* **85 E9** 25 44N 60 54 E
Piracanjuba, *Brazil* **155 E2** 17 18 S 49 1W
Piracicaba, *Brazil* **159 A6** 22 45 S 47 40W
Piracuruca, *Brazil* **154 B3** 3 50 S 41 50W
Piræus = Piraiévs, *Greece* **45 G5** 37 57N 23 42 E
Piraiévs, *Greece* **45 G5** 37 57N 23 42 E
Piraiévs □, *Greece* **45 G5** 37 0N 23 30 E
Piráino, *Italy* **41 D7** 38 10N 14 52 E
Pirajuí, *Brazil* **159 A6** 21 59 S 49 29W
Piran, *Slovenia* **39 C10** 45 31N 13 33 E
Pirané, *Argentina* **158 B4** 25 42 S 59 6W
Piranhas, *Brazil* **154 C4** 9 27 S 37 46W
Pirano = Piran, *Slovenia* **39 C10** 45 31N 13 33 E
Pirapemas, *Brazil* **154 B3** 3 43 S 44 14W
Pirapora, *Brazil* **155 E3** 17 20 S 44 56W
Piray →, *Bolivia* **157 D5** 16 32 S 63 45W
Pirdop, *Bulgaria* **43 E9** 42 40N 24 10 E
Pires do Rio, *Brazil* **155 E2** 17 18 S 48 17W
Pirganj, *Bangla.* **78 C2** 25 51N 88 24 E
Pírgos, *Ilía, Greece* **45 G3** 37 40N 21 27 E
Pírgos, *Messinía, Greece* **45 H4** 36 50N 22 16 E
Pirgovo, *Bulgaria* **43 D10** 43 44N 25 43 E
Piriac-sur-Mer, *France* **22 E4** 47 22N 2 33W
Piribebuy, *Paraguay* **158 B4** 25 26 S 57 2W
Pirin Planina, *Bulgaria* **43 F8** 41 40N 23 30 E
Pirineos, *Spain* **34 C6** 42 40N 1 0 E
Piripiri, *Brazil* **154 B3** 4 15 S 41 46W
Piritu, *Venezuela* **152 B4** 9 23N 69 12W
Pirmasens, *Germany* **27 F3** 49 12N 7 30 E
Pirna, *Germany* **26 E9** 50 57N 13 57 E
Pirojpur, *Bangla.* **78 D3** 22 35N 90 1 E
Pirot, *Serbia* **42 D7** 43 9N 22 39 E
Piru, *Indonesia* **72 B3** 3 4 S 128 12 E
Piru, *U.S.A.* **145 L8** 34 25N 118 48W
Piryatin, *Ukraine* **50 F8** 50 15N 32 25 E
Piryí, *Greece* **45 F7** 38 13N 25 59 E
Pisa, *Italy* **38 E7** 43 43N 10 23 E
Pisa →, *Poland* **47 B8** 53 14N 21 52 E
Pisa Ra., *N.Z.* **119 E4** 44 52 S 169 12 E
Pisac, *Peru* **156 C3** 13 25 S 71 50W
Pisagua, *Chile* **156 D3** 19 40 S 70 15W
Pisarovina, *Croatia* **39 C12** 45 35N 15 50 E
Pisau, Tanjong, *Malaysia* **75 A5** 6 4N 117 59 E
Pisciotta, *Italy* **41 B8** 40 7N 15 12 E
Pisco, *Peru* **156 C2** 13 50 S 76 12W
Piscu, *Romania* **46 D8** 45 30N 27 43 E
Písek, *Czech.* **30 B7** 49 19N 14 10 E
Pishan, *China* **64 C2** 37 30N 78 33 E
Pishin Lora →, *Pakistan* **80 E1** 29 9N 64 5 E
Pisidia, *Turkey* **88 E4** 37 30N 31 40 E
Pising, *Indonesia* **72 C2** 5 8 S 121 53 E
Pismo Beach, *U.S.A.* **145 K6** 35 9N 120 38W
Pissos, *France* **24 D3** 44 19N 0 49W
Pissouri, *Cyprus* **32 E11** 34 40N 32 42 E
Pisticci, *Italy* **41 B9** 40 24N 16 33 E
Pistóia, *Italy* **38 E7** 43 57N 10 53 E
Pistol B., *Canada* **131 A10** 62 25N 92 37W
Pisuerga →, *Spain* **36 D6** 41 33N 4 52W
Pisz, *Poland* **47 B8** 53 38N 21 49 E
Pitalito, *Colombia* **152 C2** 1 51N 76 2W
Pitanga, *Brazil* **155 F1** 24 46 S 51 44W
Pitangui, *Brazil* **155 E3** 19 40 S 44 54W
Pitarpunga, L., *Australia* **116 C5** 34 24 S 143 30 E
Pitcairn I., *Pac. Oc.* **123 K14** 25 5 S 130 5W
Pite älv →, *Sweden* **12 D16** 65 20N 21 25 E
Piteå, *Sweden* **12 D16** 65 20N 21 25 E
Piterka, *Russia* **51 F15** 50 41N 47 29 E
Piteşti, *Romania* **46 E5** 44 52N 24 54 E

250 Pithapuram

Pithapuram, India 82 F6 17 10N 82 15 E
Pithara, Australia 113 F2 30 20 S 116 35 E
Píthion, Greece 44 C8 41 24N 26 40 E
Pithiviers, France 23 D9 48 10N 2 13 E
Pitigliano, Italy 39 F8 42 38N 11 40 E
Pitlochry, U.K. 18 E5 56 43N 3 43W
Pitoco, Phil. 71 F5 10 8N 124 33 E
Pitrufquén, Chile 160 A2 38 59 S 72 39W
Pitsilia □, Cyprus 32 E12 34 55N 33 0 E
Pitt I., Canada 130 C3 53 30N 129 50W
Pittem, Belgium 21 F2 51 1N 3 13 E
Pittsburg, Kans., U.S.A. 139 G7 37 25N 94 42W
Pittsburg, Tex., U.S.A. 139 J7 33 0N 94 59W
Pittsburgh, U.S.A. 136 F5 40 26N 80 1W
Pittsfield, Ill., U.S.A. 140 E6 39 36N 90 49W
Pittsfield, Mass., U.S.A. 137 D11 42 27N 73 15W
Pittsfield, N.H., U.S.A. 137 C13 43 18N 71 20W
Pittston, U.S.A. 137 E9 41 19N 75 47W
Pittsworth, Australia 115 D5 27 41 S 151 37 E
Pituri →, Australia 114 C2 22 35 S 138 30 E
Piuí, Brazil 155 F2 20 28 S 45 58W
Pium, Brazil 154 D2 10 27 S 49 11W
Piura, Peru 156 B1 5 15 S 80 38W
Piura □, Peru 156 A2 5 10 S 80 0W
Piva →, Montenegro 42 D3 43 20N 18 50 E
Pivijay, Colombia 152 A3 10 28N 74 37W
Piwniczna, Poland 31 B13 49 27N 20 42 E
Pixley, U.S.A. 144 K7 35 58N 119 18W
Piyai, Greece 44 E3 39 17N 21 25 E
Pizarro, Colombia 152 C2 4 58N 77 22W
Pizol, Switz. 29 C8 46 57N 9 23 E
Pizzo, Italy 41 D9 38 44N 16 10 E
Placentia, Canada 129 C9 47 20N 54 0W
Placentia B., Canada 129 C9 47 0N 54 40W
Placer, Phil. 71 F4 11 52N 123 55 E
Placerville, U.S.A. 144 G6 38 44N 120 48W
Placetas, Cuba 148 B4 22 15N 79 44W
Plačkovica, Macedonia 42 F7 41 45N 22 30 E
Plaffeien, Switz. 28 C4 46 45N 7 17 E
Plain Dealing, U.S.A. 139 J8 32 54N 93 42W
Plainfield, Ill., U.S.A. 141 C8 41 37N 88 12W
Plainfield, N.J., U.S.A. 137 F10 40 37N 74 25W
Plains, Kans., U.S.A. 139 G4 37 16N 100 35W
Plains, Mont., U.S.A. 142 C6 47 28N 114 53W
Plains, Tex., U.S.A. 139 J3 33 11N 102 50W
Plainview, Nebr., U.S.A. 138 D6 42 21N 97 47W
Plainview, Tex., U.S.A. 139 H4 34 11N 101 43W
Plainville, U.S.A. 138 F5 39 14N 99 18W
Plainwell, U.S.A. 134 D3 42 27N 85 38W
Plaisance, France 24 E4 43 36N 0 3 E
Pláka, Greece 44 E7 40 0N 25 24 E
Pláka, Ákra, Greece 32 D8 35 11N 26 19 E
Plakenska Planina, Macedonia 42 F6 41 14N 21 2 E
Plakhino, Russia 56 C9 67 45N 86 5 E
Planá, Czech. 30 B5 49 50N 12 44 E
Plana Cays, Bahamas 149 B5 22 38N 73 30W
Planada, U.S.A. 144 H6 37 16N 120 19W
Plancoët, France 22 D4 48 32N 2 13W
Plandište, Serbia 42 B6 45 16N 21 10 E
Planeta Rica, Colombia 152 B2 8 25N 75 36W
Planina, Slovenia 39 B12 46 10N 15 20 E
Planina, Slovenia 39 C11 45 47N 14 19 E
Plankinton, U.S.A. 138 D5 43 43N 98 29W
Plano, U.S.A. 139 J6 33 1N 96 42W
Plant City, U.S.A. 135 L4 28 1N 82 7W
Plaquemine, U.S.A. 139 K9 30 17N 91 14W
Plaridel, Phil. 71 G4 8 37N 123 43 E
Plasencia, Spain 36 E4 40 3N 6 8W
Plaški, Croatia 39 C12 45 4N 15 22 E
Plast, Russia 54 D7 54 22N 60 50 E
Plaster City, U.S.A. 145 N11 32 47N 115 51W
Plaster Rock, Canada 129 C6 46 53N 67 22W
Plastun, Russia 60 B8 44 45N 136 19 E
Plata, Río de la, S. Amer. 158 C4 34 45 S 57 30W
Platani →, Italy 40 E6 37 23N 13 16 E
Plátanos, Greece 32 D5 35 28N 23 33 E
Plateau □, Nigeria 101 D6 8 0N 8 30 E
Plateau du Coteau du Missouri, U.S.A. 138 B4 47 9N 101 5W
Platí, Ákra, Greece 44 D5 40 27N 24 0 E
Plato, Colombia 152 B3 9 47N 74 47W
Platta, Piz, Switz. 29 D9 46 28N 9 35 E
Platte, U.S.A. 138 D5 43 23N 98 51W
Platte →, U.S.A. 140 E2 39 16N 94 50W
Platte City, U.S.A. 140 E2 39 22N 94 47W
Platteville, Colo., U.S.A. 138 E2 40 13N 104 49W
Platteville, Wis., U.S.A. 140 B6 42 44N 90 29W
Plattling, Germany 27 G8 48 46N 12 53 E
Plattsburg, U.S.A. 140 E2 39 34N 94 27W
Plattsburgh, U.S.A. 137 B11 44 42N 73 28W
Plattsmouth, U.S.A. 138 E7 41 1N 95 53W
Plau, Germany 26 B8 53 27N 12 16 E
Plauen, Germany 26 E8 50 29N 12 9 E
Plav, Montenegro 42 E4 42 38N 19 57 E
Plavinas, Latvia 50 C4 56 35N 25 46 E
Plavnica, Montenegro 42 E4 42 20N 19 13 E
Plavsk, Russia 51 E10 53 40N 37 18 E
Playa Blanca, Canary Is. 33 F6 28 55N 13 37W
Playa Blanca Sur, Canary Is. 33 F6 28 51N 13 50W
Playa de las Americas, Canary Is. 33 F3 28 5N 16 43W
Playa de Mogán, Canary Is. 33 G4 27 48N 15 47W
Playa del Inglés, Canary Is. 33 G4 27 45N 15 33W
Playa Esmerelda, Canary Is. 33 F5 28 8N 14 16W
Playgreen L., Canada 131 C9 54 0N 98 15W
Pleasant Bay, Canada 129 C7 46 51N 60 48W
Pleasant Hill, Calif., U.S.A. 144 H4 37 57N 122 4W
Pleasant Hill, Ill., U.S.A. 140 E6 39 27N 90 52W
Pleasant Hill, Mo., U.S.A. 140 F2 38 47N 94 16W
Pleasant Hills, Australia 117 C7 35 28 S 146 50 E
Pleasant Pt., N.Z. 119 E6 44 16 S 171 9 E
Pleasanton, U.S.A. 139 L5 28 58N 98 29W
Pleasantville, Iowa, U.S.A. 140 C3 41 23N 93 18W
Pleasantville, N.J., U.S.A. 134 F8 39 24N 74 32W
Pleasure Ridge Park, U.S.A. 141 F11 38 9N 85 50W
Pléaux, France 24 C6 45 8N 2 13 E
Pleiku, Vietnam 76 F7 13 57N 108 0 E
Plélan-le-Grand, France 22 D4 48 0N 2 7W
Plémet-la-Pierre, France 22 D4 48 11N 2 36W
Pléneuf-Val-André, France 22 D4 48 35N 2 32W
Pleniţa, Romania 46 E4 44 14N 23 10 E
Plenty →, Australia 114 C2 23 25 S 136 31 E
Plenty, B. of, N.Z. 118 D6 37 45 S 177 0 E
Plentywood, U.S.A. 138 A2 48 47N 104 34W
Plesetsk, Russia 48 B7 62 40N 40 10 E
Plessisville, Canada 129 C5 46 14N 71 47W
Plestin-les-Grèves, France 22 D3 48 40N 3 39W
Pleszew, Poland 47 D4 51 53N 17 47 E
Pleternica, Croatia 42 B2 45 17N 17 48 E
Pletipi L., Canada 129 B5 51 44N 70 6W
Pleven, Bulgaria 43 D9 43 26N 24 37 E
Plevlja, Montenegro 42 D4 43 21N 19 21 E
Ploče = Kardeljovo, Croatia 42 D2 43 4N 17 26 E
Płock, Poland 47 C6 52 32N 19 40 E
Płock □, Poland 47 C6 52 30N 19 45 E
Plöcken Passo, Italy 39 B9 46 37N 12 57 E
Ploegsteert, Belgium 21 G1 50 44N 2 53 E
Ploemeur, France 22 E3 47 44N 3 26W
Ploërmel, France 22 E4 47 55N 2 26W
Ploieşti, Romania 46 E7 44 57N 26 5 E
Plomárion, Greece 45 F8 38 58N 26 24 E
Plombières-les-Bains, France 23 E13 47 58N 6 27 E
Plomin, Croatia 39 C11 45 8N 14 10 E
Plön, Germany 26 A6 54 8N 10 22 E
Plöner See, Germany 26 A6 54 10N 10 22 E
Plonge, Lac la, Canada 131 B7 55 8N 107 20W
Płońsk, Poland 47 C7 52 37N 20 21 E
Płoty, Poland 47 B2 53 48N 15 18 E
Plouaret, France 22 D3 48 37N 3 28W
Plouay, France 22 E3 47 55N 3 21W
Ploučnice →, Czech. 30 A7 50 46N 14 13 E
Ploudalmézeau, France 22 D2 48 34N 4 41W
Plougasnou, France 22 D3 48 42N 3 49W
Plouha, France 22 D4 48 41N 2 57W
Plouhinec, France 22 E2 48 0N 4 29W
Plovdiv, Bulgaria 43 E9 42 8N 24 44 E
Plum, U.S.A. 136 F5 40 29N 79 47W
Plum I., U.S.A. 137 E12 41 11N 72 12W
Plumas, U.S.A. 144 F7 39 45N 119 4W
Plummer, U.S.A. 142 C5 47 20N 116 53W
Plumtree, Zimbabwe 107 G2 20 27 S 27 55 E
Plunge, Lithuania 50 D2 55 53N 21 59 E
Pluvigner, France 22 E3 47 46N 3 1W
Plymouth, U.K. 17 G3 50 23N 4 9W
Plymouth, Calif., U.S.A. 144 G6 38 29N 120 51W
Plymouth, Ill., U.S.A. 140 D6 40 18N 90 58W
Plymouth, Ind., U.S.A. 141 C10 41 21N 86 19W
Plymouth, Mass., U.S.A. 137 E14 41 57N 70 40W
Plymouth, N.C., U.S.A. 135 H7 35 52N 76 43W
Plymouth, N.H., U.S.A. 137 C13 43 46N 71 41W
Plymouth, Pa., U.S.A. 137 E9 41 14N 75 57W
Plymouth, Wis., U.S.A. 134 D2 43 45N 87 59W
Plynlimon = Pumlumon Fawr, U.K. 17 E4 52 29N 3 47W
Plyussa, Russia 50 B6 58 40N 29 20 E
Plyussa →, Russia 50 B6 59 10N 29 10 E
Plzeň, Czech. 30 B6 49 45N 13 22 E
Pniewy, Poland 47 C3 52 31N 16 16 E
Pô, Burkina Faso 101 C4 11 14N 1 5W
Po →, Italy 39 D9 44 57N 12 4 E
Po, Foci del, Italy 39 D9 44 55N 12 30 E
Po Hai = Bo Hai, China 67 E10 39 0N 119 0 E
Pobé, Benin 101 D5 7 0N 2 56 E
Pobeda, Russia 57 C15 65 12N 146 12 E
Pobedino, Russia 57 E15 49 51N 142 49 E
Pobedy Pik, Kirghizia 56 E8 40 45N 79 58 E
Pobiedziska, Poland 47 C4 52 29N 17 11 E
Pobla de Segur, Spain 34 C5 42 15N 0 58 E
Pobladura de Valle, Spain 36 C5 42 6N 5 44W
Pocahontas, Ark., U.S.A. 139 G9 36 16N 90 58W
Pocahontas, Ill., U.S.A. 140 F7 38 50N 89 33W
Pocahontas, Iowa, U.S.A. 140 B2 42 44N 94 40W
Pocatello, U.S.A. 142 E7 42 52N 112 27W
Počátky, Czech. 30 B8 49 15N 15 14 E
Pochep, Russia 50 E8 52 58N 33 29 E
Pochinki, Russia 51 D14 54 41N 44 59 E
Pochinok, Russia 50 D8 54 28N 32 29 E
Pöchlarn, Austria 30 C8 48 12N 15 12 E
Pochutla, Mexico 147 D5 15 50N 96 31W
Poci, Venezuela 153 B5 5 57N 61 29W
Pocinhos, Brazil 154 C4 7 4 S 36 3W
Pocito Casas, Mexico 146 B2 28 32N 111 6W
Poções, Brazil 155 D3 14 31 S 40 21W
Pocomoke City, U.S.A. 134 F8 38 5N 75 34W
Poconé, Brazil 157 D6 16 15 S 56 37W
Poços de Caldas, Brazil 159 A6 21 50 S 46 33W
Poddebice, Poland 47 D5 51 54N 18 58 E
Poděbrady, Czech. 30 A8 50 9N 15 8 E
Podensac, France 24 D3 44 40N 0 22W
Podgorač, Croatia 42 B3 45 27N 18 13 E
Podgorica, Montenegro 42 E4 42 30N 19 19 E
Podkamennaya Tunguska →, Russia 57 C10 61 50N 90 13 E
Podlapac, Croatia 39 D12 44 37N 15 47 E
Podmokly, Czech. 30 A7 50 48N 14 10 E
Podoleni, Romania 46 C7 46 46N 26 39 E
Podolínec, Slovak Rep. 31 B13 49 16N 20 31 E
Podolsk, Russia 51 D10 55 25N 37 30 E
Podor, Senegal 100 B1 16 40N 15 2W
Podporozhy, Russia 48 B5 60 55N 34 2 E
Podravska Slatina, Croatia 42 B2 45 42N 17 45 E
Podu Turcului, Romania 46 C8 46 11N 27 25 E
Podujevo, Serbia 42 E6 42 54N 21 10 E
Poel, Germany 26 B7 54 0N 11 25 E
Pofadder, S. Africa 104 D2 29 10 S 19 22 E
Pogamasing, Canada 128 C3 46 55N 81 50W
Poggiardo, Italy 41 B11 40 3N 18 21 E
Poggibonsi, Italy 39 E8 43 27N 11 8 E
Pogoanele, Romania 46 E8 44 55N 27 0 E
Pogorzela, Poland 47 D4 51 50N 17 12 E
Pogoso, Zaïre 103 D3 6 46 S 17 12 E
Pogradeci, Albania 44 D2 40 57N 20 37 E
Pogranitšnyi, Russia 60 B5 44 25N 131 24 E
Poh, Indonesia 72 B2 0 46 S 122 51 E
Pohang, S. Korea 67 F15 36 1N 129 23 E
Pohnpei, Pac. Oc. 122 G7 6 55N 158 10 E
Pohorelá, Slovak Rep. 31 C13 48 50N 20 2 E
Pohořelice, Czech. 31 C9 48 59N 16 31 E
Pohorje, Slovenia 39 B12 46 30N 15 20 E
Poiana Mare, Romania 46 F4 43 57N 23 5 E
Poiana Ruscăi, Munţii, Romania 46 D3 45 45N 22 25 E
Poindimié, N. Cal. 121 T19 20 56 S 165 20 E
Poinsett, C., Antarctica 7 C8 65 42 S 113 18 E
Point Edward, Canada 128 D3 43 0N 82 30W
Point Pass, Australia 116 C3 34 5 S 139 5 E
Point Pedro, Sri Lanka 83 K5 9 50N 80 15 E
Point Pleasant, N.J., U.S.A. 137 F10 40 5N 74 4W
Point Pleasant, W. Va., U.S.A. 134 F4 38 51N 82 8W
Pointe-à-la Hache, U.S.A. 139 L10 29 35N 89 55W
Pointe-à-Pitre, Guadeloupe 149 C7 16 10N 61 30W
Pointe Noire, Congo 103 C2 4 48 S 11 53 E
Poirino, Italy 38 D4 44 55N 7 50 E
Poisonbush Ra., Australia 112 D3 22 30 S 121 30 E
Poissy, France 23 D9 48 55N 2 2 E
Poitiers, France 22 F7 46 35N 0 20 E
Poitou, France 24 B3 46 40N 0 10W
Poitou, Seuil du, France 24 B4 46 20N 0 10 E
Poix de Picardie, France 23 C8 49 47N 1 58 E
Poix-Terron, France 23 C11 49 38N 4 38 E
Pojoaque Valley, U.S.A. 143 J11 35 54N 106 1W
Pokataroo, Australia 115 D4 29 30 S 148 36 E
Poko, Sudan 95 F3 5 41N 31 55 E
Poko, Zaïre 106 B2 3 7N 26 52 E
Pokrov, Russia 51 D11 55 55N 39 7 E
Pokrovka, Kirghizia 55 B9 42 20N 78 0 E
Pokrovsk, Russia 51 F15 51 28N 46 6 E
Pokrovsk, Russia 57 C13 61 29N 129 0 E
Pokrovsk-Uralskiy, Russia 54 A6 60 10N 59 49 E
Pol, Spain 36 B3 43 9N 7 20W
Pola = Pula, Croatia 39 D10 44 54N 13 57 E
Pola de Allande, Spain 36 B4 43 16N 6 37W
Pola de Lena, Spain 36 B5 43 10N 5 49W
Pola de Siero, Spain 36 B5 43 24N 5 39W
Pola de Somiedo, Spain 36 B4 43 5N 6 15W
Polacca, U.S.A. 143 J8 35 50N 110 23W
Polan, Iran 85 E9 25 30N 61 10 E
Poland ■, Europe 47 D7 52 0N 20 0 E
Polanów, Poland 47 A3 54 7N 16 41 E
Polatsk = Polotsk, Belorussia 50 D6 55 30N 28 50 E
Polcura, Chile 158 D1 37 17 S 71 43W
Połczyn Zdrój, Poland 47 B3 53 47N 16 5 E
Polden Hills, U.K. 17 F5 51 7N 2 50W
Polessk, Russia 50 D2 54 50N 21 8 E
Polesye, Belorussia 50 E6 52 10N 28 10 E
Polevskoy, Russia 54 C7 56 26N 60 11 E
Polewali, Indonesia 72 B1 3 21 S 119 23 E
Polgar, Hungary 31 D14 47 54N 21 6 E
Pŏlgyo-ri, S. Korea 67 G14 34 51N 127 21 E
Poli, Cameroon 102 A2 8 34N 13 15 E
Políaigos, Greece 45 H6 36 45N 24 38 E
Policastro, G. di, Italy 41 C8 39 55N 15 35 E
Police, Poland 47 B1 53 33N 14 33 E
Polička, Czech. 31 B9 49 43N 16 15 E
Polignano a Mare, Italy 41 B10 41 0N 17 12 E
Poligny, France 23 F12 46 50N 5 42 E
Polîkhnitas, Greece 45 E8 39 4N 26 10 E
Polillo, Phil. 70 D3 14 43N 121 56 E
Polillo Is., Phil. 70 D4 14 56N 122 0 E
Polillo Strait, Phil. 70 D3 14 44N 121 51 E
Polis, Cyprus 32 D11 35 2N 32 26 E
Polístena, Italy 41 D9 38 25N 16 4 E
Políyiros, Greece 44 D5 40 23N 23 25 E
Polk, U.S.A. 136 E5 41 22N 79 56W
Polkowice, Poland 47 D3 51 29N 16 3 E
Polla, Italy 41 B8 40 31N 15 27 E
Pollachi, India 83 J3 10 35N 77 0 E
Pollensa, Spain 33 B10 39 54N 3 1 E
Pollensa, B. de, Spain 33 B10 39 53N 3 8 E
Póllica, Italy 41 B8 40 13N 15 3 E
Pollino, Mte., Italy 41 C9 39 54N 16 13 E
Pollock, U.S.A. 138 C4 45 55N 100 17W
Polna, Russia 50 B6 58 31N 28 5 E
Polnovat, Russia 56 C7 63 50N 65 54 E
Polo, Ill., U.S.A. 140 C7 41 59N 89 35W
Polo, Mo., U.S.A. 140 E2 39 33N 94 3W
Pologi, Ukraine 52 C7 47 29N 36 15 E
Polonnoye, Ukraine 50 F5 50 6N 27 30 E
Polotsk, Belorussia 50 D6 55 30N 28 50 E
Polski Trŭmbesh, Bulgaria 43 D10 43 20N 25 38 E
Polsko Kosovo, Bulgaria 43 D10 43 23N 25 38 E
Polson, U.S.A. 142 C6 47 41N 114 9W
Poltava, Ukraine 52 B6 49 35N 34 35 E
Polunochnoye, Russia 48 B11 60 52N 60 25 E
Polur, India 83 H4 12 32N 79 11 E
Polyanovgrad, Bulgaria 43 E11 42 39N 26 59 E
Polyarny, Russia 48 A5 69 8N 33 20 E
Polynesia, Pac. Oc. 123 H11 10 0 S 162 0W
Polynésie française □ = French Polynesia ■, Pac. Oc. 123 J13 20 0 S 145 0W
Pomarance, Italy 38 E7 43 18N 10 51 E
Pomarico, Italy 41 B9 40 31N 16 33 E
Pomaro, Mexico 146 D4 18 20N 103 18W
Pombal, Brazil 154 C4 6 45 S 37 50W
Pombal, Portugal 36 F2 39 55N 8 40W
Pómbia, Greece 32 D6 35 0N 24 51 E
Pomeroy, Ohio, U.S.A. 134 F4 39 2N 82 2W
Pomeroy, Wash., U.S.A. 142 C5 46 28N 117 36W
Pomio, Papua N. G. 120 C6 5 32 S 151 33 E
Pomme de Terre L., U.S.A. 140 G3 37 54N 93 19W
Pomona, U.S.A. 145 L9 34 4N 117 45W
Pomorie, Bulgaria 43 E12 42 32N 27 41 E
Pomos, Cyprus 32 D11 35 9N 32 33 E
Pomos, C., Cyprus 32 D11 35 10N 32 33 E
Pomoshnaya, Ukraine 52 B4 48 13N 31 36 E
Pompano Beach, U.S.A. 135 M5 26 14N 80 8W
Pompei, Italy 41 B7 40 45N 14 30 E
Pompey, France 23 D13 48 46N 6 6 E
Pompeys Pillar, U.S.A. 142 D10 45 59N 107 57W
Ponape = Pohnpei, Pac. Oc. 122 G7 6 55N 158 10 E
Ponask, L., Canada 128 B1 54 0N 92 41W
Ponass L., Canada 131 C8 52 16N 103 58W
Ponca, U.S.A. 138 D6 42 34N 96 43W
Ponca City, U.S.A. 139 G6 36 42N 97 5W
Ponce, Puerto Rico 149 C6 18 1N 66 37W
Ponchatoula, U.S.A. 139 K9 30 26N 90 26W
Poncheville, L., Canada 128 B4 50 10N 76 55W
Poncin, France 25 B9 46 6N 5 25 E
Pond, U.S.A. 145 K7 35 43N 119 20W
Pond Inlet, Canada 127 A12 72 40N 77 0W
Pondicherry, India 83 J4 11 59N 79 50 E
Pondooma, Australia 116 B2 33 29 S 136 59 E
Pondrôme, Belgium 21 H6 50 6N 5 0 E
Ponds, I. of, Canada 129 B8 53 27N 55 52W
Ponérihouen, N. Cal. 121 U19 21 5 S 165 24 E
Ponferrada, Spain 36 C4 42 32N 6 35W
Pongo, Wadi →, Sudan 95 F2 8 42N 27 40 E
Poniatowa, Poland 47 D9 51 11N 22 3 E
Poniec, Poland 47 D3 51 48N 16 50 E
Ponikva, Slovenia 39 B12 46 16N 15 26 E
Ponnaiyar →, India 83 J4 11 50N 79 45 E
Ponnani, India 83 J2 10 45N 75 59 E
Ponneri, India 83 H5 13 20N 80 15 E
Ponnuru, India 83 F5 16 5N 80 34 E
Ponoi, Russia 48 A7 67 0N 41 0 E
Ponoi →, Russia 48 A7 66 59N 41 17 E
Ponoka, Canada 130 C6 52 42N 113 40W
Ponomarevka, Russia 54 E4 53 19N 54 8 E
Ponorogo, Indonesia 75 D4 7 52 S 111 27 E
Ponot, Phil. 71 G4 8 25N 123 0 E
Pons, France 24 C3 45 35N 0 34W
Pons, Spain 34 D6 41 55N 1 12 E
Ponsul →, Portugal 37 F3 39 40N 7 31W
Pont-à-Celles, Belgium 21 G4 50 30N 4 22 E
Pont-à-Mousson, France 23 D13 48 54N 6 1 E
Pont-Audemer, France 22 C7 49 21N 0 30 E
Pont-Aven, France 22 E3 47 51N 3 47W
Pont Canavese, Italy 38 C4 45 24N 7 33 E
Pont-de-Roide, France 23 E13 47 23N 6 45 E
Pont-de-Salars, France 24 D6 44 18N 2 44 E
Pont-de-Vaux, France 23 F11 46 26N 4 56 E
Pont-de-Veyle, France 25 B8 46 17N 4 53 E
Pont-l'Abbé, France 22 E2 47 52N 4 15W
Pont-l'Évêque, France 22 C7 49 18N 0 11 E
Pont-St.-Esprit, France 25 D8 44 16N 4 40 E
Pont-sur-Yonne, France 23 D10 48 18N 3 10 E
Ponta de Pedras, Brazil 154 B2 1 23 S 48 52W
Ponta do Sol, Madeira 33 D2 32 42N 17 7W
Ponta Grossa, Brazil 159 B5 25 7 S 50 10W
Ponta Pora, Brazil 159 A4 22 20 S 55 35W
Pontacq, France 24 E3 43 11N 0 8W
Pontailler-sur-Saône, France 23 E12 47 13N 5 25 E
Pontal →, Brazil 154 C3 9 8 S 40 12W
Pontalina, Brazil 155 E2 17 31 S 49 27W
Pontarlier, France 23 F13 46 54N 6 20 E
Pontassieve, Italy 39 E8 43 47N 11 25 E
Pontaubault, France 22 D5 48 40N 1 20W
Pontaumur, France 24 C6 45 52N 2 40 E
Pontcharra, France 25 C10 45 26N 6 1 E
Pontchartrain L., U.S.A. 139 K9 30 5N 90 5W
Pontchâteau, France 22 E4 47 25N 2 5W
Ponte Alta, Serra do, Brazil 155 E2 19 42 S 47 40W
Ponte Alta do Norte, Brazil 154 D2 10 45 S 47 34W
Ponte Branca, Brazil 157 D7 16 27 S 52 40W
Ponte da Barca, Portugal 36 D2 41 48N 8 25W
Ponte de Sor, Portugal 37 F3 39 17N 7 57W
Ponte dell 'Olio, Italy 38 D6 44 52N 9 39 E
Ponte di Legno, Italy 38 B7 46 15N 10 30 E
Ponte do Lima, Portugal 36 D2 41 46N 8 35W
Ponte do Pungué, Mozam. 107 F3 19 30 S 34 33 E
Ponte-Leccia, France 25 F13 42 28N 9 13 E
Ponte nell' Alpi, Italy 39 B9 46 10N 12 18 E
Ponte Nova, Brazil 155 F3 20 25 S 42 54W
Ponte San Martino, Italy 38 C4 45 36N 7 47 E
Ponte San Pietro, Italy 38 C6 45 42N 9 35 E
Pontebba, Italy 39 B10 46 30N 13 17 E
Pontecorvo, Italy 40 A6 41 28N 13 40 E
Pontedera, Italy 38 E7 43 40N 10 37 E
Pontefract, U.K. 16 D6 53 42N 1 19W
Ponteix, Canada 131 D7 49 46N 107 29W
Pontelandolfo, Italy 41 A7 41 17N 14 41 E
Pontevedra, Negros, Phil. 71 F4 10 22N 122 52 E
Pontevedra, Panay, Phil. 71 F4 11 29N 122 50 E
Pontevedra, Spain 36 C2 42 26N 8 40W
Pontevedra □, Spain 36 C2 42 25N 8 39W
Pontevedra, R. de →, Spain 36 C2 42 22N 8 45W
Pontevico, Italy 38 C7 45 16N 10 6 E
Pontiac, Ill., U.S.A. 138 E10 40 53N 88 38W
Pontiac, Mich., U.S.A. 141 B13 42 38N 83 18W
Pontian Kecil, Malaysia 77 M4 1 29N 103 23 E
Pontianak, Indonesia 75 C3 0 3 S 109 15 E
Pontic Mts. = Kuzey Anadolu Dağlari, Turkey 88 C6 41 30N 35 0 E
Pontine Is. = Ponziane, Isole, Italy 40 B5 40 55N 13 0 E
Pontine Mts. = Kuzey Anadolu Dağlari, Turkey 88 C6 41 30N 35 0 E
Pontínia, Italy 40 A6 41 25N 13 2 E
Pontivy, France 22 D4 48 5N 2 58W
Pontoise, France 23 C9 49 3N 2 5 E
Ponton →, Canada 130 B5 58 27N 116 11W
Pontorson, France 22 D5 48 34N 1 30W
Pontrémoli, Italy 38 D6 44 22N 9 52 E
Pontresina, Switz. 29 D9 46 29N 9 48 E
Pontrieux, France 22 D3 48 42N 3 10W
Pontypool, Canada 136 B6 44 6N 78 38W
Pontypool, U.K. 17 F4 51 42N 3 1W
Pontypridd, U.K. 17 F4 51 36N 3 21W
Ponza, Italy 40 B5 40 55N 12 57 E
Ponziane, Isole, Italy 40 B5 40 55N 13 0 E
Poochera, Australia 115 E1 32 43 S 134 51 E
Poole, U.K. 17 G6 50 42N 1 58W
Pooley I., Canada 130 C3 52 45N 128 15W
Poona = Pune, India 82 E1 18 29N 73 57 E
Poona Bayabao, Phil. 71 H5 7 56N 124 17 E
Poonamallee, India 83 H5 13 3N 80 10 E
Pooncarie, Australia 116 B5 33 22 S 142 31 E
Poonindie, Australia 116 C1 34 34 S 135 54 E
Poopelloe L., Australia 116 A6 31 40 S 144 0 E
Poopó, Bolivia 156 D4 18 23 S 66 59W
Poopó, L. de, Bolivia 156 D4 18 30 S 67 35W
Poor Knights Is., N.Z. 118 B3 35 29 S 174 43 E
Popanyinning, Australia 113 F2 32 40 S 117 2 E
Popayán, Colombia 152 C2 2 27N 76 36W
Poperinge, Belgium 21 G1 50 51N 2 42 E
Popigay, Russia 57 B12 72 1N 110 39 E
Popilta, L., Australia 116 B4 33 10 S 141 42 E
Popina, Bulgaria 43 C11 44 7N 26 57 E

Pravara 251

Popio L., Australia 116 B4 33 10 S 141 52 E
Poplar, U.S.A. 138 A2 48 7N 105 12W
Poplar →, Man., Canada 131 C9 53 0N 97 19W
Poplar →, N.W.T., Canada 130 A4 61 22N 121 52W
Poplar Bluff, U.S.A. 139 G9 36 46N 90 24W
Poplarville, U.S.A. 139 K10 30 51N 89 32W
Popocatepetl, Mexico 147 D5 19 10N 98 40W
Popokabaka, Zaïre 103 D3 5 41 S 16 40 E
Pópoli, Italy 39 F10 42 12N 13 50 E
Popondetta, Papua N. G. 120 E5 8 48 S 148 17 E
Popovača, Croatia 39 C13 45 30N 16 41 E
Popovo, Bulgaria 43 D11 43 21N 26 18 E
Poppel, Belgium 21 F6 51 27N 5 2 E
Poprád, Slovak Rep. 31 B13 49 3N 20 18 E
Poprád →, Slovak Rep. 31 B13 49 38N 20 42 E
Poradaha, Bangla. 78 D2 23 51N 89 1 E
Porali →, Pakistan 79 D2 25 35N 66 26 E
Porangaba, Brazil 156 B3 8 48 S 57 36W
Porangahau, N.Z. 118 G5 40 17 S 176 37 E
Porangatu, Brazil 155 D2 13 26 S 49 10W
Porbandar, India 80 J3 21 44N 69 43 E
Porce →, Colombia 152 B3 7 28N 74 53W
Porcher I., Canada 130 C2 53 50N 130 30W
Porco, Bolivia 157 D4 19 50 S 65 59W
Porcos →, Brazil 155 D2 12 42 S 45 7W
Porcuna, Spain 37 H6 37 52N 4 11W
Porcupine →, Canada 131 B8 59 11N 104 46W
Porcupine →, U.S.A. 126 B5 66 34N 145 19W
Pordenone, Italy 39 C9 45 58N 12 40 E
Pordim, Bulgaria 43 D9 43 23N 24 51 E
Poreč, Croatia 39 C10 45 14N 13 36 E
Porecatu, Brazil 155 F1 22 43 S 51 24W
Poretskoye, Russia 51 D15 55 9N 46 21 E
Pori, Finland 13 F16 61 29N 21 48 E
Porí, Greece 45 J5 35 58N 23 13 E
Porjus, Sweden 12 C15 66 57N 19 50 E
Porkhov, Russia 50 C6 57 45N 29 38 E
Porkkala, Finland 13 G18 59 59N 24 26 E
Porlamar, Venezuela 153 A5 10 57N 63 51W
Porlezza, Italy 38 B6 46 2N 9 8 E
Porma →, Spain 36 C5 42 49N 5 28W
Pornic, France 22 E4 47 7N 2 5W
Poronaysk, Russia 57 E15 49 13N 143 0 E
Póros, Greece 45 G5 37 30N 23 30 E
Poroshiri-Dake, Japan 60 C11 42 41N 142 52 E
Poroszló, Hungary 31 D13 47 39N 20 40 E
Poroto Mts., Tanzania 107 D3 9 0 S 33 30 E
Porpoise B., Antarctica 7 C9 66 0 S 127 0 E
Porquerolles, I. de, France 25 F10 43 0N 6 13 E
Porrentruy, Switz. 28 B4 47 25N 7 6 E
Porreras, Spain 33 B10 39 31N 3 2 E
Porretta, Passo di, Italy 38 D7 44 2N 10 56 E
Porsangen, Norway 12 A18 70 40N 25 40 E
Porsgrunn, Norway 14 E3 59 10N 9 40 E
Port Adelaide, Australia 116 C3 34 46 S 138 30 E
Port Alberni, Canada 130 D4 49 14N 124 50W
Port Albert, Australia 117 E7 38 42 S 146 42 E
Port Alfred, Canada 129 C5 48 18N 70 53W
Port Alfred, S. Africa 104 E4 33 36 S 26 55 E
Port Alice, Canada 130 C3 50 20N 127 25W
Port Allegany, U.S.A. 136 E6 41 48N 78 17W
Port Allen, U.S.A. 139 K9 30 27N 91 12W
Port Alma, Australia 114 C5 23 38 S 150 53 E
Port Angeles, U.S.A. 144 B3 48 7N 123 27W
Port Antonio, Jamaica 148 C4 18 10N 76 30W
Port Aransas, U.S.A. 139 M6 27 50N 97 4W
Port Arthur = Lüshun, China 67 E11 38 45N 121 15 E
Port Arthur, Australia 114 G4 43 7 S 147 50 E
Port Arthur, U.S.A. 139 L8 29 54N 93 56W
Port au Port B., Canada 129 C8 48 40N 58 50W
Port-au-Prince, Haiti 149 C5 18 40N 72 20W
Port Augusta, Australia 116 B2 32 30 S 137 50 E
Port Augusta West, Australia 116 B2 32 29 S 137 29 E
Port Austin, U.S.A. 128 D3 44 3N 83 1W
Port Bell, Uganda 106 B3 0 18N 32 35 E
Port Bergé Vaovao, Madag. 105 B8 15 33 S 47 40 E
Port Blandford, Canada 129 C9 48 20N 54 10W
Port Bou, Spain 34 C8 42 25N 3 9 E
Port Bouët, Ivory C. 100 D4 5 16N 3 57W
Port Bradshaw, Australia 114 A2 12 30 S 137 20 E
Port Broughton, Australia 116 B2 33 37 S 137 56 E
Port Burwell, Canada 128 D3 42 40N 80 48W
Port Campbell, Australia 116 E5 38 37 S 143 1 E
Port Canning, India 81 H13 22 23N 88 40 E
Port-Cartier, Canada 129 B6 50 2N 66 50W
Port Chalmers, N.Z. 119 F5 45 49 S 170 30 E
Port Charles, N.Z. 118 C4 36 33 S 175 30 E
Port Chester, U.S.A. 137 F11 41 0N 73 40W
Port Clements, Canada 130 C2 53 40N 132 10W
Port Clinton, U.S.A. 141 C14 41 31N 82 56W
Port Colborne, Canada 128 D4 42 50N 79 10W
Port Coquitlam, Canada 130 D4 49 15N 122 45W
Port Credit, Canada 136 C5 43 33N 79 35W
Port Curtis, Australia 114 C5 23 57 S 151 20 E
Port Dalhousie, Canada 136 C5 43 13N 79 16W
Port Darwin, Australia 112 B5 12 24 S 130 45 E
Port Darwin, Falk. Is. 160 D5 51 50 S 59 0W
Port Davey, Australia 114 G4 43 16 S 145 55 E
Port-de-Bouc, France 25 E8 43 24N 4 59 E
Port-de-Paix, Haiti 149 C5 19 50N 72 50W
Port Dickson, Malaysia 77 L3 2 30N 101 49 E
Port Douglas, Australia 114 B4 16 30 S 145 30 E
Port Dover, Canada 136 D4 42 47N 80 12W
Port Edward, Canada 130 C2 54 12N 130 10W
Port Elgin, Canada 128 D3 44 25N 81 25W
Port Elizabeth, S. Africa 104 E4 33 58 S 25 40 E
Port Ellen, U.K. 18 F2 55 38N 6 10W
Port-en-Bessin, France 22 C6 49 21N 0 45W
Port Erin, I. of Man 16 C3 54 5N 4 45W
Port Essington, Australia 112 B5 11 15 S 132 10 E
Port Etienne = Nouâdhibou, Mauritania 98 D1 20 54N 17 0W
Port Fairy, Australia 116 E5 38 22 S 142 12 E
Port Fitzroy, N.Z. 118 C4 36 8 S 175 20 E
Port Fouâd = Bûr Fuad, Egypt 94 H8 31 15N 32 20 E
Port Gamble, U.S.A. 144 C4 47 51N 122 35W
Port-Gentil, Gabon 102 C1 0 40 S 8 50 E
Port Gibson, U.S.A. 139 K9 31 58N 90 59W
Port Glasgow, U.K. 18 F4 55 57N 4 40W
Port Harcourt, Nigeria 101 E6 4 40N 7 10 E
Port Hardy, Canada 130 C3 50 41N 127 30W
Port Harrison = Inoucdjouac, Canada 127 C12 58 25N 78 15W
Port Hawkesbury, Canada 129 C7 45 36N 61 22W
Port Hedland, Australia 112 D2 20 25 S 118 35 E
Port Henry, U.S.A. 137 B11 44 3N 73 28W
Port Hood, Canada 129 C7 46 0N 61 32W
Port Hope, Canada 128 D4 43 56N 78 20W
Port Hueneme, U.S.A. 145 L7 34 7N 119 12W
Port Huron, U.S.A. 134 D4 42 58N 82 26W
Port Isabel, U.S.A. 139 M6 26 5N 97 12W
Port Jefferson, U.S.A. 137 F11 40 57N 73 3W
Port Jervis, U.S.A. 137 E10 41 22N 74 41W
Port-Joinville, France 22 F4 46 45N 2 23W
Port Katon, Russia 53 C8 46 52N 38 46 E
Port Kelang = Pelabuhan Kelang, Malaysia 77 L3 3 0N 101 23 E
Port Kembla, Australia 117 C9 34 52 S 150 49 E
Port Kenny, Australia 115 E1 33 10 S 134 41 E
Port-la-Nouvelle, France 24 E7 43 1N 3 3 E
Port Laoise, Ireland 19 C4 53 2N 7 20W
Port Lavaca, U.S.A. 139 L6 28 37N 96 38W
Port-Leucate, France 24 F7 42 53N 3 3 E
Port Lincoln, Australia 116 C1 34 42 S 135 52 E
Port Loko, S. Leone 100 D2 8 48N 12 46W
Port Louis, France 22 E3 47 42N 3 22W
Port Louis, Mauritius 109 G4 20 10 S 57 30 E
Port Lyautey = Kenitra, Morocco 98 B3 34 15N 6 40W
Port MacDonnell, Australia 116 E4 38 5 S 140 48 E
Port Macquarie, Australia 117 A10 31 25 S 152 25 E
Port Maria, Jamaica 148 C4 18 25N 76 55W
Port Mellon, Canada 130 D4 49 32N 123 31W
Port-Menier, Canada 129 C7 49 51N 64 15W
Port Morant, Jamaica 148 C4 17 54N 76 19W
Port Moresby, Papua N. G. 120 E4 9 24 S 147 8 E
Port Mourant, Guyana 153 B6 6 15N 57 20W
Port Mouton, Canada 129 D7 43 58N 64 50W
Port Musgrave, Australia 114 A3 11 55 S 141 50 E
Port-Navalo, France 22 E4 47 34N 2 54W
Port Nelson, Canada 131 B10 57 3N 92 36W
Port Nicholson, N.Z. 118 H3 41 20 S 174 52 E
Port Nolloth, S. Africa 104 D2 29 17 S 16 52 E
Port Nouveau-Québec, Canada 127 C13 58 30N 65 59W
Port O'Connor, U.S.A. 139 L6 28 26N 96 24W
Port of Spain, Trin. & Tob. 149 D7 10 40N 61 31W
Port Orchard, U.S.A. 144 C4 47 32N 122 38W
Port Orford, U.S.A. 142 E1 42 45N 124 30W
Port Pegasus, N.Z. 119 H2 47 12 S 167 41 E
Port Perry, Canada 128 D4 44 6N 78 56W
Port Phillip B., Australia 115 F3 38 10 S 144 50 E
Port Pirie, Australia 116 B3 33 10 S 138 1 E
Port Pólnocny, Poland 47 A5 54 25N 18 42 E
Port Radium = Echo Bay, Canada 126 B8 66 5N 117 55W
Port Renfrew, Canada 130 D4 48 30N 124 20W
Port Roper, Australia 114 A2 14 45 S 135 25 E
Port Rowan, Canada 128 D3 42 40N 80 30W
Port Safaga = Bûr Safâga, Egypt 94 B3 26 43N 33 57 E
Port Said = Bûr Sa'îd, Egypt 94 H8 31 16N 32 18 E
Port St. Joe, U.S.A. 135 L3 29 49N 85 18W
Port St. Johns, S. Africa 105 E4 31 38 S 29 33 E
Port-St.-Louis-du-Rhône, France 25 E8 43 23N 4 49 E
Port San Vicente, Phil. 70 B4 18 30N 122 8 E
Port Sanilac, U.S.A. 128 D3 43 26N 82 33W
Port Saunders, Canada 129 B8 50 40N 57 18W
Port Severn, Canada 136 B5 44 48N 79 43W
Port Shepstone, S. Africa 105 E5 30 44 S 30 28 E
Port Simpson, Canada 130 C2 54 30N 130 20W
Port Stanley = Stanley, Falk. Is. 160 D5 51 40 S 59 51W
Port Stanley, Canada 128 D3 42 40N 81 10W
Port Sudan = Bûr Sûdân, Sudan 94 D4 19 32N 37 9 E
Port-sur-Saône, France 23 E13 47 42N 6 2 E
Port Talbot, U.K. 17 F4 51 35N 3 48W
Port Taufîq = Bûr Taufiq, Egypt 94 J8 29 54N 32 32 E
Port Townsend, U.S.A. 144 B4 48 7N 122 45W
Port-Vendres, France 24 F7 42 32N 3 8 E
Port Victoria, Australia 116 C2 34 30 S 137 29 E
Port Vila, Pac. Oc. 111 D12 17 45 S 168 18 E
Port Vladimir, Russia 48 A5 69 25N 33 6 E
Port Wakefield, Australia 116 C3 34 12 S 138 10 E
Port Washington, U.S.A. 134 D2 43 23N 87 53W
Port Weld, Malaysia 77 K3 4 50N 100 38 E
Portachuelo, Bolivia 157 D5 17 10 S 63 20W
Portadown, U.K. 19 B5 54 27N 6 26W
Portage, Mich., U.S.A. 141 B11 42 12N 85 35W
Portage, Wis., U.S.A. 138 D10 43 33N 89 28W
Portage →, U.S.A. 141 C14 41 31N 83 5W
Portage La Prairie, Canada 131 D9 49 58N 98 18W
Portageville, U.S.A. 139 G10 36 26N 89 42W
Portalegre, Portugal 37 F3 39 19N 7 25W
Portalegre □, Portugal 37 F3 39 20N 7 40W
Portales, U.S.A. 139 H3 34 11N 103 20W
Portarlington, Ireland 19 C4 53 10N 7 10W
Porteirinha, Brazil 155 E3 15 44 S 43 2W
Portel, Brazil 154 B1 1 57 S 50 49W
Portel, Portugal 37 G3 38 19N 7 41W
Porter, U.S.A. 141 C9 41 36N 87 4W
Porter L., N.W.T., Canada 131 A7 61 41N 108 5W
Porter L., Sask., Canada 131 B7 56 20N 107 20W
Porterville, S. Africa 104 E2 33 0 S 19 0 E
Porterville, U.S.A. 144 J8 36 4N 119 1W
Porthcawl, U.K. 17 F4 51 28N 3 42W
Porthill, U.S.A. 142 B5 48 59N 116 30W
Portile de Fier, Europe 46 E3 44 42N 22 30 E
Portimão, Portugal 37 H2 37 8N 8 32W
Portland, N.S.W., Australia 117 B8 33 20 S 150 0 E
Portland, Vic., Australia 116 E4 38 20 S 141 35 E
Portland, Canada 137 B8 44 42N 76 12W
Portland, Conn., U.S.A. 137 E12 41 34N 72 38W
Portland, Ind., U.S.A. 141 D12 40 26N 84 59W
Portland, Maine, U.S.A. 129 D5 43 39N 70 16W
Portland, Mich., U.S.A. 141 B12 42 52N 84 54W
Portland, Oreg., U.S.A. 144 E4 45 32N 122 37W
Portland, I. of, U.K. 17 G5 50 32N 2 25W
Portland B., Australia 116 E4 38 15 S 141 45 E
Portland Bill, U.K. 17 G5 50 31N 2 27W
Portland I., N.Z. 118 F6 39 20 S 177 51 E
Portland Prom., Canada 127 C12 58 40N 78 33W
Portlands Roads, Australia 114 A3 12 36 S 143 25 E
Portneuf, Canada 129 C5 46 43N 71 55W
Pôrto, Brazil 154 B3 3 54 S 42 42W
Porto, France 25 F12 42 16N 8 42 E
Porto, Portugal 36 D2 41 8N 8 40W
Porto □, Portugal 36 D2 41 8N 8 20W
Porto, G. de, France 25 F12 42 17N 8 34 E
Pôrto Acre, Brazil 156 B4 9 34 S 67 31W
Pôrto Alegre, Pará, Brazil 153 D7 4 22 S 52 44W
Pôrto Alegre, Rio Grande do S., Brazil 159 C5 30 5 S 51 10W
Porto Amboim = Gunza, Angola 103 E2 10 50 S 13 50 E
Porto Argentera, Italy 38 D4 44 15N 7 27 E
Porto Azzurro, Italy 38 F7 42 46N 10 24 E
Porto Botte, Italy 40 C1 39 3N 8 33 E
Pôrto Cajueiro, Brazil 157 C6 11 3 S 55 53W
Porto Civitanova, Italy 39 E10 43 19N 13 44 E
Porto Cristo, Spain 33 B10 39 33N 3 20 E
Pôrto da Fôlha, Brazil 154 C4 9 55 S 37 17W
Pôrto de Móz, Brazil 153 D7 1 41 S 52 13W
Pôrto de Pedras, Brazil 154 C4 9 10 S 35 17W
Pôrto des Meinacos, Brazil 157 C7 12 33 S 53 7W
Porto Empédocle, Italy 40 E6 37 18N 13 30 E
Pôrto Esperança, Brazil 157 D6 19 37 S 57 29W
Pôrto Esperidão, Brazil 157 D6 15 51 S 58 28W
Pôrto Franco, Brazil 154 C2 6 20 S 47 24W
Porto Garibaldi, Italy 39 D9 44 41N 12 14 E
Pôrto Grande, Brazil 153 C7 0 42N 51 24W
Pôrto Jofre, Brazil 157 D6 17 20 S 56 48W
Pórto Lágo, Greece 44 D7 40 58N 25 6 E
Porto Mendes, Brazil 159 A5 24 30 S 54 15W
Porto Moniz, Madeira 33 D2 32 52N 17 11W
Pôrto Murtinho, Brazil 157 E6 21 45 S 57 55W
Pôrto Nacional, Brazil 154 D2 10 40 S 48 30W
Porto Novo, Benin 101 D5 6 23N 2 42 E
Porto Petro, Spain 33 B10 39 22N 3 13 E
Porto Recanati, Italy 39 E10 43 26N 13 40 E
Porto San Giórgio, Italy 39 E10 43 11N 13 49 E
Pôrto Santana, Brazil 153 D7 0 3 S 51 11W
Porto Santo Stefano, Italy 38 F8 42 26N 11 7 E
Pôrto São José, Brazil 159 A5 22 43 S 53 10W
Pôrto Seguro, Brazil 155 E4 16 26 S 39 5W
Porto Tolle, Italy 39 D9 44 57N 12 20 E
Porto Tórres, Italy 40 B1 40 50N 8 23 E
Pôrto União, Brazil 159 B5 26 10 S 51 10W
Pôrto Válter, Brazil 156 B3 8 15 S 72 40W
Porto-Vecchio, France 25 G13 41 35N 9 16 E
Pôrto Velho, Brazil 157 B5 8 46 S 63 54W
Portobelo, Panama 148 E4 9 35N 79 42W
Portoferráio, Italy 38 F7 42 50N 10 20 E
Portogruaro, Italy 39 C9 45 47N 12 50 E
Portola, U.S.A. 144 F6 39 49N 120 28W
Portomaggiore, Italy 39 D8 44 41N 11 47 E
Portoscuso, Italy 40 C1 39 12N 8 22 E
Portovénere, Italy 38 D6 44 2N 9 50 E
Portovíejo, Ecuador 152 D1 1 7 S 80 28W
Portpatrick, U.K. 18 G3 54 50N 5 7W
Portree, U.K. 18 D2 57 25N 6 11W
Portrush, U.K. 19 A5 55 13N 6 40W
Portsall, France 22 D2 48 37N 4 45W
Portsmouth, Domin. 149 C7 15 34N 61 27W
Portsmouth, U.K. 17 G6 50 48N 1 6W
Portsmouth, N.H., U.S.A. 137 C14 43 5N 70 45W
Portsmouth, Ohio, U.S.A. 134 F4 38 44N 82 57W
Portsmouth, R.I., U.S.A. 137 E13 41 36N 71 15W
Portsmouth, Va., U.S.A. 134 G7 36 50N 76 18W
Portsoy, U.K. 18 D6 57 41N 2 41W
Porttipahta, Finland 12 B19 68 5N 26 40 E
Portugal ■, Europe 36 F3 40 0N 8 0W
Portugalete, Spain 34 B1 43 19N 3 4W
Portuguesa □, Venezuela 152 B4 9 10N 69 15W
Portuguese-Guinea = Guinea-Bissau ■, Africa 100 C2 12 0N 15 0W
Portumna, Ireland 19 C3 53 5N 8 12W
Portville, U.S.A. 136 D6 42 3N 78 20W
Porvenir, Bolivia 156 C4 11 10 S 68 50W
Porvenir, Chile 160 D2 53 10 S 70 16W
Porvoo = Borgå, Finland 13 F18 60 24N 25 40 E
Porzuna, Spain 37 F6 39 9N 4 9W
Posada →, Italy 40 B2 40 40N 9 45 E
Posadas, Argentina 159 B4 27 30 S 55 50W
Posadas, Spain 37 H5 37 47N 5 11W
Poschiavo, Switz. 29 D10 46 19N 10 4 E
Posets, Spain 34 C5 42 39N 0 25 E
Poseyville, U.S.A. 141 F9 38 10N 87 47W
Poshan = Boshan, China 67 F9 36 28N 117 49 E
Posht-e-Badam, Iran 85 C7 33 2N 55 23 E
Posídhion, Ákra, Greece 44 E5 39 57N 23 30 E
Posidium, Greece 45 J9 35 30N 27 10 E
Poso, Indonesia 72 B2 1 20 S 120 55 E
Posoegroenoe, Surinam 153 C6 4 23N 55 43W
Posong, S. Korea 67 G14 34 46N 127 5 E
Posse, Brazil 155 D2 14 4 S 46 18W
Possel, C.A.R. 102 A3 5 5N 19 10 E
Possession I., Antarctica 7 D11 72 4 S 172 0 E
Pössneck, Germany 26 E7 50 42N 11 34 E
Post, U.S.A. 139 J4 33 12N 101 23W
Post Falls, U.S.A. 142 C5 47 43N 116 57W
Postavy, Belorussia 50 D5 55 4N 26 50 E
Poste Maurice Cortier, Algeria 99 D5 22 14N 1 2 E
Postmasburg, S. Africa 104 D3 28 18 S 23 5 E
Postojna, Slovenia 39 C11 45 46N 14 12 E
Poston, U.S.A. 145 M12 34 0N 114 24W
Postville, U.S.A. 140 A5 43 5N 91 34W
Potamós, Andikíthira, Greece 45 H4 35 52N 23 15 E
Potamós, Kíthira, Greece 45 H4 36 15N 22 58 E
Potchefstroom, S. Africa 104 D4 26 41 S 27 7 E
Potcoava, Romania 46 E5 44 30N 24 39 E
Poté, Brazil 155 E3 17 49 S 41 49W
Poteau, U.S.A. 139 H7 35 3N 94 37W
Poteet, U.S.A. 139 L5 29 2N 98 35W
Potelu, Lacul, Romania 46 F5 43 44N 24 20 E
Potenza, Italy 41 B8 40 40N 15 50 E
Potenza →, Italy 39 E10 43 27N 13 38 E
Potenza Picena, Italy 39 E10 43 22N 13 37 E
Poteriteri, L., N.Z. 119 G2 46 5 S 167 10 E
Potes, Spain 36 B6 43 15N 4 42W
Potgietersrus, S. Africa 105 C4 24 10 S 28 55 E
Poti, Georgia 53 E9 42 10N 41 38 E
Potiraguá, Brazil 155 E4 15 36 S 39 53W
Potiskum, Nigeria 101 C7 11 39N 11 2 E
Potlogi, Romania 46 E6 44 34N 25 34 E
Potomac →, U.S.A. 134 F7 38 0N 76 23W
Potosí, Bolivia 157 D4 19 38 S 65 50W
Potosi, U.S.A. 140 G6 37 56N 90 47W
Potosí □, Bolivia 156 E4 20 31 S 67 0W
Potosi Mt., U.S.A. 145 K11 35 57N 115 29W
Pototan, Phil. 71 F4 10 54N 122 38 E
Potrerillos, Chile 158 B2 26 30 S 69 30W
Potsdam, Germany 26 C9 52 23N 13 4 E
Potsdam, U.S.A. 137 B10 44 40N 74 59W
Pottenstein, Germany 27 F7 49 46N 11 25 E
Potter, U.S.A. 138 E3 41 13N 103 19W
Pottery Hill = Abû Ballas, Egypt 94 C2 24 26N 27 36 E
Pottstown, U.S.A. 137 F9 40 15N 75 39W
Pottsville, U.S.A. 137 F8 40 41N 76 12W
Pouancé, France 22 E5 47 44N 1 10W
Pouce Coupé, Canada 130 B4 55 40N 120 10W
Pouembout, N. Cal. 121 U18 21 8 S 164 53 E
Poughkeepsie, U.S.A. 137 E11 41 42N 73 56W
Pouilly-sur-Loire, France 23 E9 47 17N 2 57 E
Poulaphouca Res., Ireland 19 C5 53 8N 6 30W
Poulsbo, U.S.A. 144 C4 47 44N 122 39W
Poum, N. Cal. 121 T18 20 14 S 164 2 E
Poumadji, C.A.R. 102 A4 5 56N 22 10 E
Pounga-Nganda, Gabon 102 C2 2 58 S 10 51 E
Pourri, Mt., France 25 C10 45 32N 6 52 E
Pouso Alegre, Mato Grosso, Brazil 157 C6 11 46 S 57 16W
Pouso Alegre, Minas Gerais, Brazil 159 A6 22 14 S 45 57W
Pouzauges, France 22 F6 46 47N 0 50W
Povenets, Russia 48 B5 62 50N 34 50 E
Poverty B., N.Z. 118 E7 38 43 S 178 2 E
Povlen, Serbia 42 C4 44 9N 19 44 E
Póvoa de Lanhosa, Portugal 36 D2 41 33N 8 15W
Póvoa de Varzim, Portugal 36 D2 41 25N 8 46W
Povorino, Russia 51 F13 51 12N 42 5 E
Powassan, Canada 128 C4 46 5N 79 25W
Poway, U.S.A. 145 N9 32 58N 117 2W
Powder →, U.S.A. 138 B2 46 45N 105 26W
Powder River, U.S.A. 142 E10 43 2N 106 59W
Powell, U.S.A. 142 D9 44 45N 108 46W
Powell L., U.S.A. 143 H8 36 57N 111 29W
Powell River, Canada 130 D4 49 50N 124 35W
Powers, Mich., U.S.A. 134 C2 45 41N 87 32W
Powers, Oreg., U.S.A. 142 E1 42 53N 124 4W
Powers Lake, U.S.A. 138 A3 48 34N 102 39W
Powys □, U.K. 17 E4 52 20N 3 20W
Poxoreu, Brazil 157 D7 15 50 S 54 23W
Poya, N. Cal. 121 U19 21 19 S 165 7 E
Poyang Hu, China 69 C11 29 5N 116 20 E
Poyarkovo, Russia 57 E13 49 36N 128 41 E
Poysdorf, Austria 31 C9 48 40N 16 37 E
Poza de la Sal, Spain 34 C1 42 35N 3 31W
Poza Rica, Mexico 147 C5 20 33N 97 27W
Pozanti, Turkey 88 E6 37 25N 34 50 E
Požarevac, Serbia 42 C6 44 35N 21 18 E
Požega, Serbia 42 D5 43 53N 20 2 E
Pozhva, Russia 54 B5 59 5N 56 5 E
Pozi, Taiwan 69 F13 23 30N 120 13 E
Poznań, Poland 47 C3 52 25N 16 55 E
Poznań □, Poland 47 C4 52 30N 17 0 E
Pozo, U.S.A. 145 K6 35 20N 120 24W
Pozo Alcón, Spain 35 H2 37 42N 2 56W
Pozo Almonte, Chile 156 E4 20 10 S 69 50W
Pozo Colorado, Paraguay 158 A4 23 30 S 58 45W
Pozo del Dátil, Mexico 146 B2 30 0N 112 15W
Pozoblanco, Spain 37 G6 38 23N 4 51W
Pozorrubio, Phil. 70 C3 16 7N 120 33 E
Pozuzo, Peru 156 C2 10 5 S 75 35W
Pozzallo, Italy 41 F7 36 44N 14 52 E
Pozzuoli, Italy 41 B7 40 46N 14 6 E
Pra →, Ghana 101 D4 5 1N 1 37W
Prabuty, Poland 47 B6 53 47N 19 15 E
Prača, Bos.-H. 42 D3 43 47N 18 43 E
Prachatice, Czech. 30 B7 49 1N 14 0 E
Prachin Buri, Thailand 76 E3 14 0N 101 25 E
Prachuap Khiri Khan, Thailand 77 G2 11 49N 99 48 E
Pradelles, France 24 D7 44 46N 3 52 E
Pradera, Colombia 152 C2 3 25N 76 15W
Prades, France 24 F6 42 38N 2 23 E
Prado, Brazil 155 E4 17 20 S 39 13W
Prado del Rey, Spain 37 J5 36 48N 5 33W
Præstø, Denmark 15 J6 55 8N 12 2 E
Pragersko, Slovenia 39 B12 46 27N 15 42 E
Prague = Praha, Czech. 30 A7 50 5N 14 22 E
Praha, Czech. 30 A7 50 5N 14 22 E
Prahecq, France 24 B3 46 19N 0 26W
Prahita →, India 82 E4 19 0N 79 55 E
Prahova □, Romania 46 D6 45 10N 26 0 E
Prahova →, Romania 46 E6 44 50N 25 50 E
Prahovo, Serbia 42 C7 44 18N 22 39 E
Praid, Romania 46 C6 46 32N 25 10 E
Prainha, Amazonas, Brazil 157 B5 7 10 S 60 30W
Prainha, Pará, Brazil 153 D7 1 45 S 53 30W
Prairie, Australia 114 C3 20 50 S 144 35 E
Prairie →, U.S.A. 139 H5 34 30N 99 23W
Prairie City, U.S.A. 142 D4 44 28N 118 43W
Prairie du Chien, U.S.A. 140 A5 43 3N 91 9W
Prairie du Rocher, U.S.A. 140 F6 38 5N 90 6W
Prairies, Canada 126 C9 52 0N 108 0W
Pramánda, Greece 44 E3 39 32N 21 8 E
Pran Buri, Thailand 76 F2 12 23N 99 55 E
Prang, Ghana 101 D4 8 1N 0 56W
Prasonísi, Ákra, Greece 32 D9 35 42N 27 46 E
Praszka, Poland 47 D5 51 5N 18 31 E
Prata, Brazil 155 E2 19 25 S 48 54W
Pratapgarh, India 80 G6 24 2N 74 40 E
Prática di Mare, Italy 40 A5 41 40N 12 26 E
Prätigau, Switz. 29 C9 46 56N 9 44 E
Prato, Italy 38 E8 43 53N 11 5 E
Prátola Peligna, Italy 39 F10 42 7N 13 51 E
Pratovécchio, Italy 39 E8 43 44N 11 43 E
Prats-de-Mollo-la-Preste, France 24 F6 42 25N 2 27 E
Pratt, U.S.A. 139 G5 37 39N 98 44W
Pratteln, Switz. 28 A5 47 31N 7 41 E
Prattville, U.S.A. 135 J2 32 28N 86 29W
Pravara →, India 82 E2 19 35N 74 45 E

Quqon 253

Punta de Díaz, Chile 158 B1 28 0 S 70 45W
Punta Delgado, Argentina 160 B4 42 43 S 63 38W
Punta Gorda, Belize 147 D7 16 10N 88 45W
Punta Gorda, U.S.A. 135 M5 26 56N 82 3W
Punta Prieta, Mexico 146 B2 28 58N 114 17W
Punta Prima, Spain 33 B11 39 48N 4 16 E
Puntabie, Australia 115 E1 32 12 S 134 13 E
Puntarenas, Costa Rica 148 E3 10 0N 84 50W
Punto Fijo, Venezuela 152 A3 11 50N 70 13W
Punxsatawney, U.S.A. 136 F5 40 57N 78 59W
Puqi, China 69 C9 29 40N 113 50 E
Puquio, Peru 156 C3 14 45 S 74 10W
Pur →, Russia 56 C8 67 31N 77 55 E
Purace, Vol., Colombia 152 C2 2 21N 76 23W
Puračić, Bos.-H. 42 C3 44 33N 18 28 E
Puralia = Puruliya, India 81 H12 23 17N 86 24 E
Purari →, Papua N. G. 120 D3 7 49 S 145 0 E
Purbeck, Isle of, U.K. 17 G5 50 40N 2 5W
Purcell, U.S.A. 139 H6 35 1N 97 22W
Purchena Tetica, Spain 35 H2 37 21N 2 21W
Puri, India 82 E7 19 50N 85 58 E
Purificación, Colombia 152 C3 3 51N 74 55W
Purmerend, Neths. 20 C5 52 32N 4 58 E
Purna →, India 82 E3 19 6N 77 2 E
Purnia, India 81 G12 25 45N 87 31 E
Purukcahu, Indonesia 75 C4 0 35 S 114 35 E
Puruliya, India 81 H12 23 17N 86 24 E
Purus →, Brazil 153 D5 3 42 S 61 28W
Pŭrvomay, Bulgaria 43 E10 42 8N 25 17 E
Purwakarta, Indonesia 75 D3 6 35 S 107 29 E
Purwodadi, Jawa, Indonesia 75 D4 7 7 S 110 55 E
Purwodadi, Jawa, Indonesia 75 D3 7 51 S 110 0 E
Purwokerto, Indonesia 75 D3 7 25 S 109 14 E
Purworejo, Indonesia 75 D4 7 43 S 110 2 E
Puryŏng, N. Korea 67 C15 42 5N 129 43 E
Pus →, India 82 E3 19 55N 77 55 E
Pusad, India 82 E3 19 56N 77 36 E
Pusan, S. Korea 67 G15 35 5N 129 0 E
Pushchino, Russia 57 D16 54 10N 158 0 E
Pushkin, Russia 50 B7 59 45N 30 25 E
Pushkino, Russia 51 F15 51 16N 47 0 E
Pushkino, Russia 51 C10 56 2N 37 49 E
Püspökladány, Hungary 31 D14 47 19N 21 6 E
Pustoshka, Russia 50 C6 56 20N 29 30 E
Puszczykowo, Poland 47 C3 52 18N 16 49 E
Putahow L., Canada 131 B8 59 54N 100 40W
Putao, Burma 78 B6 27 28N 97 30 E
Putaruru, N.Z. 118 E4 38 2 S 175 50 E
Putbus, Germany 26 A9 54 19N 13 29 E
Puţeni, Romania 46 D8 45 49N 27 42 E
Putian, China 69 E12 25 23N 119 0 E
Putignano, Italy 41 B10 40 50N 17 5 E
Putina, Peru 156 C4 14 55 S 69 55W
Puting, Tanjung, Indonesia 75 C4 3 31 S 111 46 E
Putlitz, Germany 26 B8 53 15N 12 3 E
Putna, Romania 46 B6 47 50N 25 33 E
Putna →, Romania 46 D8 45 42N 27 26 E
Putnam, U.S.A. 137 E13 41 55N 71 55W
Putnok, Hungary 31 C13 48 18N 20 26 E
Putorana, Gory, Russia 57 C10 69 0N 95 0 E
Putorino, N.Z. 118 F5 39 4 S 176 58 E
Putre, Chile 156 D4 18 12 S 69 35W
Puttalam Lagoon, Sri Lanka 83 K4 8 15N 79 45 E
Putte, Neths. 21 F4 51 22N 4 24 E
Putten, Neths. 20 D7 52 16N 5 36 E
Puttgarden, Germany 26 A7 54 28N 11 15 E
Puttur, India 83 H2 12 46N 75 12 E
Putty, Australia 117 B9 32 57 S 150 42 E
Putumayo →, S. Amer. 152 D4 3 7 S 67 58W
Putuo, China 69 C14 29 56N 122 20 E
Putussibau, Indonesia 75 B4 0 50N 112 56 E
Pututahi, N.Z. 118 E6 38 39 S 177 53 E
Puurs, Belgium 21 F4 51 5N 4 17 E
Puy-de-Dôme, France 24 C6 45 46N 2 57 E
Puy-de-Dôme □, France 24 C7 45 40N 3 5 E
Puy-Guillaume, France 24 C7 45 57N 3 29 E
Puy-l'Êvêque, France 24 D5 44 31N 1 9 E
Puyallup, U.S.A. 144 C4 47 12N 122 18W
Puyang, China 66 G8 35 40N 115 1 E
Puyehue, Chile 160 B2 40 40 S 72 37W
Puylaurens, France 24 E6 43 35N 2 0 E
Puyo, Ecuador 152 D2 1 28 S 77 59W
Puysegur Pt., N.Z. 119 G1 46 9 S 166 37 E
Pūzeh Rīg, Iran 85 E8 27 20N 58 40 E
Pwani □, Tanzania 106 D4 7 0 S 39 0 E
Pweto, Zaïre 107 D2 8 25 S 28 51 E
Pwinbyu, Burma 78 E5 20 23N 94 40 E
Pwllheli, U.K. 16 E3 52 54N 4 26W
Pya-ozero, Russia 48 A5 66 5N 30 58 E
Pyana →, Russia 51 D15 55 30N 46 0 E
Pyandzh, Tajikistan 55 E4 37 14N 69 6 E
Pyandzh →, Afghan. 79 A2 37 15N 67 15 E
Pyandzh →, Tajikistan 55 E4 37 6N 68 20 E
Pyapon, Burma 78 G5 16 20N 95 40 E
Pyasina →, Russia 57 B9 73 30N 87 0 E
Pyatigorsk, Russia 53 D10 44 2N 43 6 E
Pyatikhatki, Ukraine 52 B5 48 28N 33 38 E
Pyaye, Burma 78 F5 19 12N 95 10 E
Pydna, Greece 44 D4 40 20N 22 34 E
Pyè, Burma 78 F5 18 49N 95 13 E
Pyinbauk, Burma 78 F5 19 10N 95 12 E
Pyinmana, Burma 78 F6 19 45N 96 12 E
Pyla, C., Cyprus 32 E12 34 56N 33 51 E
Pyŏktong, N. Korea 67 D13 40 50N 125 50 E
Pyŏnggang, N. Korea 67 E14 38 24N 127 17 E
Pyŏngtaek, S. Korea 67 F14 37 1N 127 4 E
P'yŏngyang, N. Korea 67 E13 39 0N 125 30 E
Pyote, U.S.A. 139 K3 31 32N 103 8W
Pyramid L., U.S.A. 142 G4 40 1N 119 35W
Pyramid Pk., U.S.A. 145 J10 36 25N 116 37W
Pyramids, Egypt 94 J7 29 58N 31 9 E
Pyrénées, Europe 24 F4 42 45N 0 18 E
Pyrénées-Atlantiques □, France 24 E3 43 10N 0 50W
Pyrénées-Orientales □, France 24 F6 42 35N 2 26 E
Pyrzyce, Poland 47 B1 53 10N 14 55 E
Pyshchug, Russia 51 B14 58 57N 45 47 E
Pytalovo, Russia 50 C5 57 5N 27 55 E
Pyttegga, Norway 14 B1 62 13N 7 42 E
Pyu, Burma 78 F6 18 30N 96 28 E
Pyzdry, Poland 47 C4 52 11N 17 42 E

Q

Qaanaaq = Thule, Greenland 6 B4 77 40N 69 0W
Qabr Hūd, Yemen 87 C5 16 9N 49 34 E
Qachasnek, S. Africa 105 E4 30 6 S 28 42 E
Qādib, Yemen 87 D6 12 37N 53 57 E
Qa'el Jafr, Jordan 91 E5 30 20N 36 25 E
Qa'emābād, Iran 85 D9 31 44N 60 2 E
Qā'emshahr, Iran 85 B7 36 30N 52 53 E
Qagan Nur, China 66 C8 43 30N 114 55 E
Qahar Youyi Zhongqi, China 66 D7 41 12N 112 40 E
Qahremānshahr = Bākhtarān, Iran 84 C5 34 23N 47 0 E
Qaidam Pendi, China 64 C4 37 0N 95 0 E
Qajarīyeh, Iran 85 D6 31 1N 48 22 E
Qala, Ras il, Malta 32 C1 36 1N 14 20 E
Qala-i-Jadid, Afghan. 80 D2 31 1N 66 25 E
Qala Yangi, Afghan. 80 B2 34 20N 66 30 E
Qalācheh, Afghan. 79 B2 35 3N 66 25 E
Qalansīyah, Yemen 87 D6 12 41N 53 29 E
Qalāt, Afghan. 79 B2 32 15N 66 58 E
Qal'at al Akhḑar, Si. Arabia 86 B3 28 0N 37 10 E
Qal'at Bīshah, Si. Arabia 86 C3 20 0N 42 36 E
Qal'at Sukkar, Iraq 84 D5 31 51N 46 5 E
Qal'eh Darreh, Iran 84 B5 38 47N 47 2 E
Qal'eh-ye Best, Afghan. 79 C2 31 30N 64 21 E
Qal'eh-ye Now, Afghan. 79 B1 35 0N 63 5 E
Qal'eh-ye Panjeh, Afghan. 79 A4 37 0N 72 35 E
Qal'eh-ye Sarkari, Afghan. 79 B2 35 54N 67 17 E
Qal'eh-ye Valī, Afghan. 79 B1 35 46N 63 45 E
Qalyûb, Egypt 94 H7 30 12N 31 11 E
Qamar, Ghubbat al, Yemen 87 C6 16 20N 52 30 E
Qamar, Jabal al, Oman 87 C6 16 48N 53 15 E
Qamdo, China 68 B1 31 15N 97 6 E
Qamruddin Karez, Pakistan 79 C3 31 45N 68 20 E
Qandahār, Afghan. 79 C2 31 32N 65 30 E
Qandahār □, Afghan. 79 C2 31 0N 65 0 E
Qapān, Iran 85 B7 37 40N 55 47 E
Qaqortoq = Julianehåb, Greenland 6 C5 60 43N 46 0W
Qâra, Egypt 94 B2 29 38N 26 30 E
Qarā', Jabal al, Oman 87 C6 17 15N 54 15 E
Qara Qash →, India 81 B8 35 0N 78 30 E
Qaraghandy = Karaganda, Kazakhstan 56 E8 49 50N 73 10 E
Qārah, Si. Arabia 84 D4 29 55N 40 3 E
Qarāvol, Afghan. 79 A3 37 14N 68 46 E
Qardud, Sudan 95 E2 10 20N 29 56 E
Qareh →, Iran 84 B5 39 25N 47 22 E
Qareh Tekān, Iran 85 B6 36 38N 49 29 E
Qarqan He →, China 64 C3 39 30N 88 30 E
Qarrasa, Sudan 95 E3 14 38N 32 5 E
Qarshi = Karshi, Uzbekistan 55 D2 38 53N 65 48 E
Qartabā, Lebanon 91 A4 34 4N 35 50 E
Qaryat al Gharab, Iraq 84 D5 31 27N 44 48 E
Qaryat al 'Ulyā, Si. Arabia 84 E5 27 33N 47 42 E
Qasr 'Amra, Jordan 84 D3 31 48N 36 35 E
Qaşr Bū Hadi, Libya 96 B3 31 1N 16 45 E
Qaşr-e Qand, Iran 85 E9 26 15N 60 45 E
Qasr Farâfra, Egypt 94 B2 27 0N 28 1 E
Qat Lesh, Afghan. 79 B2 34 40N 66 18 E
Qa'ṭabah, Yemen 86 D4 13 51N 44 42 E
Qatanā, Syria 91 B5 33 26N 36 4 E
Qaţānan, Ra's, Yemen 87 D6 12 21N 53 33 E
Qatar ■, Asia 85 E6 25 30N 51 15 E
Qatlīsh, Iran 85 B8 37 50N 57 19 E
Qattâra, Egypt 94 A2 30 12N 27 3 E
Qattâra, Munkhafed el, Egypt 94 B2 29 30N 27 30 E
Qattâra Depression = Qattâra, Munkhafed el, Egypt 94 B2 29 30N 27 30 E
Qawām al Ḩamzah, Iraq 84 D5 31 43N 44 58 E
Qāyen, Iran 85 C8 33 40N 59 10 E
Qazaqstan = Kazakhstan ■, Asia 56 E7 50 0N 70 0 E
Qazvin, Iran 85 B6 36 15N 50 0 E
Qena, Egypt 94 B3 26 10N 32 43 E
Qena, Wadi →, Egypt 94 B3 26 12N 32 44 E
Qeqertarsuag = Disko, Greenland 6 C5 69 45N 53 30W
Qeqertarsuaq = Godhavn, Greenland 6 C5 69 15N 53 38W
Qeshlāq, Iran 84 C5 34 55N 46 28 E
Qeshm, Iran 85 E8 26 55N 56 10 E
Qezi'ot, Israel 91 E3 30 52N 34 26 E
Qi Xian, China 66 G8 34 40N 114 48 E
Qian Gorlos, China 67 B13 45 5N 124 42 E
Qian Xian, China 66 G5 34 31N 108 15 E
Qiancheng, China 68 D7 27 12N 109 50 E
Qianjiang, Guangxi Zhuangzu, China 68 F7 23 38N 108 58 E
Qianjiang, Hubei, China 69 B9 30 24N 112 55 E
Qianjiang, Sichuan, China 68 C7 29 33N 108 47 E
Qianshan, China 69 B11 30 37N 116 35 E
Qianwei, China 68 C4 29 13N 103 56 E
Qianxi, China 68 D6 27 3N 106 3 E
Qianyang, Hunan, China 69 D8 27 18N 110 10 E
Qianyang, Shaanxi, China 66 G4 34 40N 107 8 E
Qianyang, Zhejiang, China 69 B12 30 11N 119 25 E
Qiaojia, China 68 D4 26 56N 102 58 E
Qibā', Si. Arabia 84 E5 27 24N 44 20 E
Qichun, China 69 B10 30 18N 115 25 E
Qidong, Hunan, China 69 D9 26 49N 112 7 E
Qidong, Jiangsu, China 69 B13 31 48N 121 38 E
Qijiang, China 68 C6 28 57N 106 35 E
Qila Saifullāh, Pakistan 80 D3 30 45N 68 17 E
Qilian Shan, China 64 C4 38 30N 96 0 E
Qimen, China 69 C11 29 50N 117 42 E
Qin He →, China 66 G7 35 1N 113 22 E
Qin Jiang →, China 69 D10 26 15N 115 55 E
Qin Ling = Qinling Shandi, China 66 H5 33 50N 108 10 E
Qināb, W. →, Yemen 87 C5 17 55N 49 59 E
Qin'an, China 66 G3 34 48N 105 40 E
Qing Xian, China 66 E9 38 35N 116 45 E
Qingcheng, China 67 F9 37 15N 117 40 E
Qingdao, China 67 F11 36 5N 120 20 E
Qingfeng, China 66 G8 35 52N 115 8 E
Qinghai □, China 64 C4 36 0N 98 0 E
Qinghai Hu, China 64 C5 36 40N 100 10 E
Qinghecheng, China 67 D13 41 15N 124 30 E
Qinghemen, China 67 D11 41 48N 121 25 E
Qingjian, China 66 F6 37 8N 110 8 E
Qingjiang, Jiangsu, China 67 H10 33 30N 119 2 E
Qingjiang, Jiangxi, China 69 C10 28 4N 115 29 E
Qingliu, China 69 D11 26 11N 116 48 E
Qinglong, China 68 E5 25 49N 105 12 E
Qingping, China 68 D6 26 39N 107 47 E
Qingpu, China 69 B13 31 10N 121 6 E
Qingshui, China 66 G4 34 48N 106 8 E
Qingshuihe, China 66 E6 39 55N 111 35 E
Qingtian, China 69 C13 28 12N 120 15 E
Qingtongxia Shuiku, China 66 F3 37 50N 105 58 E
Qingxi, China 68 D7 27 8N 108 43 E
Qingxu, China 66 F7 37 34N 112 22 E
Qingyang, Anhui, China 69 B11 30 38N 117 50 E
Qingyang, Gansu, China 66 F4 36 2N 107 55 E
Qingyi Jiang →, China 68 C4 29 32N 103 44 E
Qingyuan, Guangdong, China 69 F9 23 40N 112 59 E
Qingyuan, Liaoning, China 67 C13 42 10N 124 55 E
Qingyuan, Zhejiang, China 69 D12 27 36N 119 3 E
Qingyun, China 67 F9 37 45N 117 20 E
Qingzhen, China 68 D6 26 31N 106 25 E
Qinhuangdao, China 67 E10 39 56N 119 30 E
Qinling Shandi, China 66 H5 33 50N 108 10 E
Qinshui, China 66 G7 35 40N 112 8 E
Qinyang, China 66 G7 35 7N 112 57 E
Qinyuan, China 66 F7 36 29N 112 20 E
Qinzhou, China 68 G7 21 58N 108 38 E
Qionghai, China 76 C8 19 15N 110 26 E
Qionglai, China 68 B4 30 25N 103 31 E
Qionglai Shan, China 68 B4 31 0N 102 30 E
Qiongshan, China 76 C8 19 51N 110 26 E
Qiongzhou Haixia, China 76 B8 20 10N 110 15 E
Qiqihar, China 57 E13 47 26N 124 0 E
Qiraîya, W. →, Egypt 91 E3 30 27N 34 0 E
Qiryat Ata, Israel 91 C4 32 47N 35 6 E
Qiryat Gat, Israel 91 D3 31 32N 34 46 E
Qiryat Mal'akhi, Israel 91 D3 31 44N 34 44 E
Qiryat Shemona, Israel 91 B4 33 13N 35 35 E
Qiryat Yam, Israel 91 C4 32 51N 35 4 E
Qishan, China 66 G4 34 25N 107 38 E
Qishan, Taiwan 69 F13 22 52N 120 25 E
Qishn, Yemen 87 D5 15 26N 51 40 E
Qitai, China 64 B3 44 2N 89 35 E
Qitbīt, W. →, Oman 87 C6 19 15N 54 23 E
Qiubei, China 68 E5 24 2N 104 12 E
Qixia, China 67 F11 37 17N 120 52 E
Qiyang, China 69 D8 26 35N 111 50 E
Qojūr, Iran 84 B5 36 12N 47 55 E
Qom, Iran 85 C6 34 40N 51 0 E
Qomsheh, Iran 85 D6 32 0N 51 55 E
Qondūz, Afghan. 79 A3 36 50N 68 50 E
Qondūz □, Afghan. 79 A3 36 50N 68 50 E
Qostanay = Kustanay, Kazakhstan 54 E8 53 10N 63 35 E
Qu Jiang →, China 68 B6 30 1N 106 24 E
Qu Xian, Sichuan, China 68 B6 30 48N 106 58 E
Qu Xian, Zhejiang, China 69 C12 28 57N 118 54 E
Quackenbrück, Germany 26 C3 52 40N 7 59 E
Quairading, Australia 113 F2 32 0 S 117 21 E
Quakertown, U.S.A. 137 F9 40 26N 75 21W
Qualeup, Australia 113 F2 33 48 S 116 48 E
Quambatook, Australia 116 C5 35 49 S 143 34 E
Quambone, Australia 117 A7 30 57 S 147 53 E
Quamby, Australia 114 C3 20 22 S 140 17 E
Quan Long, Vietnam 77 H5 9 7N 105 8 E
Quanah, U.S.A. 139 H5 34 18N 99 44W
Quandialla, Australia 117 C7 34 1 S 147 47 E
Quang Ngai, Vietnam 76 E7 15 13N 108 58 E
Quang Yen, Vietnam 76 B6 20 56N 106 52 E
Quannan, China 69 E10 24 45N 114 33 E
Quantock Hills, U.K. 17 F4 51 8N 3 10W
Quanzhou, Fujian, China 69 E12 24 55N 118 34 E
Quanzhou, Guangxi Zhuangzu, China 69 E8 25 57N 111 5 E
Quaraí, Brazil 158 C4 30 15 S 56 20W
Quarré-les-Tombes, France 23 E10 47 21N 4 0 E
Quartu Sant' Elena, Italy 40 C2 39 15N 9 10 E
Quartzsite, U.S.A. 145 M12 33 40N 114 13W
Quatsino, Canada 130 C3 50 30N 127 40W
Quatsino Sd., Canada 130 C3 50 25N 127 58W
Qūchān, Iran 85 B8 37 10N 58 27 E
Queanbeyan, Australia 117 C8 35 17 S 149 14 E
Québec, Canada 129 C5 46 52N 71 13W
Québec □, Canada 129 B6 48 0N 74 0W
Quedlinburg, Germany 26 D7 51 47N 11 9 E
Queen Alexandra Ra., Antarctica 7 E11 85 0 S 170 0 E
Queen Charlotte, Canada 130 C2 53 15N 132 2W
Queen Charlotte Bay, Falk. Is. 160 D4 51 50 S 60 40W
Queen Charlotte Is., Canada 130 C2 53 20N 132 10W
Queen Charlotte Sd., N.Z. 119 B9 41 10 S 174 15 E
Queen Charlotte Str., Canada 130 C3 51 0N 128 0W
Queen City, U.S.A. 140 D4 40 25N 92 34W
Queen Elizabeth Is., Canada 124 B10 76 0N 95 0W
Queen Elizabeth Nat. Park, Uganda 106 C3 0 0 30 0 E
Queen Mary Land, Antarctica 7 D7 70 0 S 95 0 E
Queen Maud G., Canada 126 B9 68 15N 102 30W
Queen Maud Land, Antarctica 7 D3 72 30 S 12 0 E
Queen Maud Mts., Antarctica 7 E13 86 0 S 160 0W
Queens Chan., Australia 112 C4 15 0 S 129 30 E
Queenscliff, Australia 115 F3 38 16 S 144 39 E
Queensland □, Australia 114 C3 22 0 S 142 0 E
Queenstown, Australia 114 G4 42 4 S 145 35 E
Queenstown, N.Z. 119 F3 45 1 S 168 40 E
Queenstown, S. Africa 104 E4 31 52 S 26 52 E
Queets, U.S.A. 144 C2 47 32N 124 20W
Queguay Grande →, Uruguay 158 C4 32 9 S 58 9W
Queimadas, Brazil 154 D4 11 0 S 39 38W
Queiros, C., Vanuatu 121 D5 14 55 S 167 1 E
Quela, Angola 103 D3 9 10 S 16 56 E
Quelimane, Mozam. 107 F4 17 53 S 36 58 E
Quelpart = Cheju Do, S. Korea 67 H14 33 29N 126 34 E
Quemado, N. Mex., U.S.A. 143 J9 34 20N 108 30W
Quemado, Tex., U.S.A. 139 L4 28 58N 100 35W
Quemú-Quemú, Argentina 158 D3 36 3 S 63 36W
Quequén, Argentina 158 D4 38 30 S 58 30W
Querco, Peru 156 C3 13 50 S 74 52W
Querétaro, Mexico 146 C4 20 40N 100 23W
Querétaro □, Mexico 146 C5 20 30N 100 0W
Querfurt, Germany 26 D7 51 22N 11 33 E
Quesada, Spain 35 H1 37 51N 3 4W
Queshan, China 66 H8 32 55N 114 2 E
Quesnel, Canada 130 C4 53 0N 122 30W
Quesnel →, Canada 130 C4 52 58N 122 29W
Quesnel L., Canada 130 C4 52 30N 121 20W
Questa, U.S.A. 143 H11 36 42N 105 36W
Questembert, France 22 E4 47 40N 2 28W
Quetena, Bolivia 156 E4 22 10 S 67 25W
Quetico Prov. Park, Canada 128 C1 48 30N 91 45W
Quetrequile, Argentina 160 B3 41 33 S 69 22W
Quetta, Pakistan 79 C2 30 15N 66 55 E
Quevedo, Ecuador 152 D2 1 2 S 79 29W
Quezaltenango, Guatemala 148 D1 14 50N 91 30W
Quezon □, Phil. 70 D3 14 40N 121 30 E
Quezon City, Phil. 70 D3 14 38N 121 0 E
Qufār, Si. Arabia 84 E4 27 26N 41 37 E
Qui Nhon, Vietnam 76 F7 13 40N 109 13 E
Quibala, Angola 103 E2 10 46 S 14 59 E
Quibaxe, Angola 103 D2 8 24 S 14 27 E
Quibdo, Colombia 152 B2 5 42N 76 40W
Quiberon, France 22 E3 47 29N 3 9W
Quíbor, Venezuela 152 B4 9 56N 69 37W
Quick, Canada 130 C3 54 36N 126 54W
Quickborn, Germany 26 B5 53 42N 9 52 E
Quiet L., Canada 130 A2 61 5N 133 5W
Quiévrain, Belgium 21 H3 50 24N 3 41 E
Quiindy, Paraguay 158 B4 25 58 S 57 14W
Quila, Mexico 146 C3 24 23N 107 13W
Quilán, C., Chile 160 B2 43 15 S 74 30W
Quilcene, U.S.A. 144 C4 47 49N 122 53W
Quilengues, Angola 103 E2 14 12 S 14 12 E
Quilimarí, Chile 158 C1 32 5 S 71 30W
Quilino, Argentina 158 C3 30 14 S 64 29W
Quillabamba, Peru 156 C3 12 50 S 72 50W
Quillacollo, Bolivia 156 D4 17 26 S 66 17W
Quillagua, Chile 158 A2 21 40 S 69 40W
Quillaicillo, Chile 158 C1 31 17 S 71 40W
Quillan, France 24 F6 42 53N 2 10 E
Quillebeuf-sur-Seine, France 22 C7 49 28N 0 30 E
Quillota, Chile 158 C1 32 54 S 71 16W
Quilmes, Argentina 158 C4 34 43 S 58 15W
Quilon, India 83 K3 8 50N 76 38 E
Quilpie, Australia 115 D3 26 35 S 144 11 E
Quilpué, Chile 158 C1 33 5 S 71 33W
Quilua, Mozam. 107 F4 16 17 S 39 54 E
Quimbele, Angola 103 D3 6 17 S 16 41 E
Quimbonge, Angola 103 D3 8 36 S 18 30 E
Quime, Bolivia 156 D4 17 2 S 67 15W
Quimilí, Argentina 158 B3 27 40 S 62 30W
Quimper, France 22 D2 48 0N 4 9W
Quimperlé, France 22 E3 47 53N 3 33W
Quinault →, U.S.A. 144 C2 47 21N 124 18W
Quincemil, Peru 156 C3 13 15 S 70 40W
Quincy, Calif., U.S.A. 144 F6 39 56N 120 57W
Quincy, Fla., U.S.A. 135 K3 30 35N 84 34W
Quincy, Ill., U.S.A. 138 F9 39 56N 91 23W
Quincy, Mass., U.S.A. 137 D14 42 15N 71 0W
Quincy, Wash., U.S.A. 142 C4 47 22N 119 56W
Quines, Argentina 158 C2 32 13 S 65 48W
Quinga, Mozam. 107 F5 15 49 S 40 15 E
Quingey, France 23 E12 47 7N 5 52 E
Quiniluban Group, Phil. 71 F3 11 27N 120 48 E
Quintana de la Serena, Spain 37 G5 38 45N 5 40W
Quintana Roo □, Mexico 147 D7 19 0N 88 0W
Quintanar de la Orden, Spain 34 F1 39 36N 3 5W
Quintanar de la Sierra, Spain 34 D2 41 57N 2 55W
Quintanar del Rey, Spain 35 F3 39 21N 1 56W
Quintero, Chile 158 C1 32 45 S 71 30W
Quintin, France 22 D4 48 26N 2 56W
Quinto, Spain 34 D4 41 25N 0 32W
Quinyambie, Australia 115 E3 30 15 S 141 0 E
Quípar →, Spain 35 G3 38 15N 1 40W
Quipungo, Angola 103 E2 14 37 S 14 40 E
Quirihue, Chile 158 D1 36 15 S 72 35W
Quirimbo, Angola 103 E2 10 36 S 14 12 E
Quirindi, Australia 117 A9 31 28 S 150 40 E
Quirino □, Phil. 70 C3 16 15N 121 40 E
Quiroga, Spain 36 C3 42 28N 7 18W
Quiruvilca, Peru 156 B2 8 1 S 78 19W
Quissac, France 25 E8 43 55N 4 0 E
Quissanga, Mozam. 107 E5 12 24 S 40 28 E
Quitapa, Angola 103 E3 10 20 S 18 19 E
Quitilipi, Argentina 158 B3 26 50 S 60 13W
Quitman, Ga., U.S.A. 135 K4 30 47N 83 34W
Quitman, Miss., U.S.A. 135 J1 32 2N 88 44W
Quitman, Tex., U.S.A. 139 J7 32 48N 95 27W
Quito, Ecuador 152 D2 0 15 S 78 35W
Quixadá, Brazil 154 B4 4 55 S 39 0W
Quixaxe, Mozam. 107 F5 15 17 S 40 4 E
Quixeramobim, Brazil 154 C4 5 12 S 39 17W
Quixinge, Angola 103 D2 9 52 S 14 23 E
Quizenga, Angola 103 D3 9 21 S 15 28 E
Qujing, China 68 E4 25 32N 103 41 E
Qul'ân, Jazâ'ir, Egypt 94 C4 24 22N 35 31 E
Qumbu, S. Africa 105 E4 31 10 S 28 48 E
Quneitra, Syria 91 B4 33 7N 35 48 E
Qunfudh, Yemen 87 C5 16 39N 49 33 E
Quoin I., Australia 112 B4 14 54 S 129 32 E
Quoin Pt., S. Africa 104 E2 34 46 S 19 37 E
Quondong, Australia 116 B4 33 6 S 140 18 E
Quorn, Australia 116 B3 32 25 S 138 5 E
Quqon = Kokand, Uzbekistan 55 C5 40 30N 70 57 E

254 Qurein

Qurein, *Sudan* **95 E3** 13 30N 34 50 E
Qurnat as Sawdā', *Lebanon* **91 A5** 34 18N 36 6 E
Qûs, *Egypt* **94 B3** 25 55N 32 50 E
Qusaybah, *Iraq* **84 C4** 34 24N 40 59 E
Quşay'ir, *Yemen* **87 D5** 14 55N 50 20 E
Quseir, *Egypt* **94 B3** 26 7N 34 16 E
Qūshchī, *Iran* **84 B5** 37 59N 45 3 E
Quthing, *Lesotho* **105 E4** 30 25 S 27 36 E
Qūţīābād, *Iran* **85 C6** 35 47N 48 30 E
Quwo, *China* **66 G6** 35 38N 111 25 E
Quyang, *China* **66 E8** 38 35N 114 40 E
Quynh Nhai, *Vietnam* **76 B4** 21 49N 103 33 E
Quzi, *China* **66 F4** 36 20N 107 20 E
Qytet Stalin, *Albania* **44 D1** 40 47N 19 57 E
Qyzylorda = Kzyl-Orda, *Kazakhstan* **55 A2** 44 48N 65 28 E

R

Ra, Ko, *Thailand* **77 H2** 9 13N 98 16 E
Råå, *Sweden* **15 J6** 56 0N 12 45 E
Raab, *Austria* **30 C6** 48 21N 13 39 E
Raahe, *Finland* **12 D18** 64 40N 24 28 E
Raalte, *Neths.* **20 D8** 52 23N 6 16 E
Raamsdonksveer, *Neths.* **21 E5** 51 43N 4 52 E
Raasay, *U.K.* **18 D2** 57 25N 6 4W
Raasay, Sd. of, *U.K.* **18 D2** 57 30N 6 8W
Rab, *Croatia* **39 D11** 44 45N 14 45 E
Raba, *Indonesia* **72 C1** 8 36 S 118 55 E
Rába →, *Hungary* **31 D10** 47 38N 17 38 E
Raba →, *Poland* **31 A13** 50 8N 20 30 E
Rabaçal →, *Portugal* **36 D3** 41 30N 7 12W
Rabah, *Nigeria* **101 C6** 13 5N 5 30 E
Rabai, *Kenya* **106 C4** 3 50 S 39 31 E
Rabaraba, *Papua N. G.* **120 E5** 9 58 S 149 49 E
Rabastens, *France* **24 E5** 43 50N 1 43 E
Rabastens-de-Bigorre, *France* **24 E4** 43 23N 0 9 E
Rabat, *Malta* **32 D1** 35 53N 14 25 E
Rabat, *Morocco* **98 B3** 34 2N 6 48W
Rabaul, *Papua N. G.* **120 C7** 4 24 S 152 18 E
Rabbit →, *Canada* **130 B3** 59 41N 127 12W
Rabbit Lake, *Canada* **131 C7** 53 8N 107 46W
Rabbitskin →, *Canada* **130 A4** 61 47N 120 42W
Rābigh, *Si. Arabia* **86 B2** 22 50N 39 5 E
Rabka, *Poland* **31 B12** 49 37N 19 59 E
Rābor, *Iran* **85 D8** 29 17N 56 55 E
Rača, *Serbia* **42 C5** 44 14N 21 0 E
Răcale, *Italy* **41 C11** 39 57N 18 6 E
Racalmuto, *Italy* **40 E6** 37 25N 13 41 E
Răcăşdia, *Romania* **42 C6** 44 59N 21 36 E
Racconigi, *Italy* **38 D4** 44 47N 7 41 E
Raccoon →, *U.S.A.* **140 C3** 41 35N 93 37W
Raccoon Cr. →, *U.S.A.* **141 E9** 39 47N 87 23W
Race, C., *Canada* **129 C9** 46 40N 53 5W
Rach Gia, *Vietnam* **77 G5** 10 5N 105 5 E
Raciąż, *Poland* **47 C7** 52 46N 20 10 E
Racibórz, *Poland* **31 A11** 50 7N 18 18 E
Racine, *U.S.A.* **141 B9** 42 41N 87 51W
Rackerby, *U.S.A.* **144 F5** 39 26N 121 22W
Radama, Nosy, *Madag.* **105 A8** 14 0 S 47 47 E
Radama, Saikanosy, *Madag.* **105 A8** 14 16 S 47 53 E
Radan, *Serbia* **42 E6** 42 59N 21 29 E
Rădăuţi, *Romania* **46 B6** 47 50N 25 59 E
Radbuza →, *Czech.* **30 B6** 49 35N 13 5 E
Radcliff, *U.S.A.* **141 G11** 37 51N 85 57W
Radeburg, *Germany* **26 D9** 51 6N 13 55 E
Radeče, *Slovenia* **39 B12** 46 5N 15 14 E
Radekhov, *Ukraine* **50 F4** 50 25N 24 32 E
Radew →, *Poland* **47 A2** 54 2N 15 52 E
Radford, *U.S.A.* **134 G5** 37 8N 80 34W
Radhanpur, *India* **80 H4** 23 50N 71 38 E
Radiska →, *Macedonia* **42 F5** 41 38N 20 37 E
Radisson, *Canada* **131 C7** 52 30N 107 20W
Radium Hot Springs, *Canada* **130 C5** 50 35N 116 2W
Radków, *Poland* **47 E3** 50 30N 16 24 E
Radlin, *Poland* **31 A11** 50 3N 18 29 E
Radna, *Romania* **42 A6** 46 7N 21 41 E
Radnevo, *Bulgaria* **43 E10** 42 17N 25 58 E
Radnice, *Czech.* **30 B6** 49 51N 13 35 E
Radnor Forest, *U.K.* **17 E4** 52 17N 3 10W
Radolfzell, *Germany* **27 H4** 47 44N 8 58 E
Radom, *Poland* **47 D8** 51 23N 21 12 E
Radom □, *Poland* **47 D8** 51 30N 21 0 E
Radomir, *Bulgaria* **42 E8** 42 37N 23 4 E
Radomka →, *Poland* **47 D8** 51 31N 21 11 E
Radomsko, *Poland* **47 D6** 51 5N 19 28 E
Radomyshl, *Ukraine* **50 F6** 50 30N 29 12 E
Radomysl Wielki, *Poland* **31 A14** 50 14N 21 15 E
Radoszyce, *Poland* **47 D7** 51 4N 20 15 E
Radoviš, *Macedonia* **42 F7** 41 38N 22 28 E
Radovljica, *Slovenia* **39 B11** 46 22N 14 12 E
Radstadt, *Austria* **30 D6** 47 24N 13 28 E
Radstock, *U.K.* **17 F5** 51 17N 2 25W
Radstock, C., *Australia* **115 E1** 33 12 S 134 20 E
Răducăneni, *Romania* **46 C8** 46 58N 27 54 E
Raduša, *Serbia* **42 E6** 42 7N 21 15 E
Radviliškis, *Lithuania* **50 D3** 55 49N 23 33 E
Radville, *Canada* **131 D8** 49 30N 104 15W
Radymno, *Poland* **31 B15** 49 59N 22 52 E
Radzanów, *Poland* **47 C7** 52 56N 20 8 E
Radziejów, *Poland* **47 C5** 52 40N 18 30 E
Radzymin, *Poland* **47 C8** 52 25N 21 11 E
Radzyń Chełmiński, *Poland* **47 B5** 53 23N 18 55 E
Radzyń Podlaski, *Poland* **47 D9** 51 47N 22 37 E
Rae, *Canada* **130 A5** 62 50N 116 3W
Rae Bareli, *India* **81 F9** 26 18N 81 20 E
Rae Isthmus, *Canada* **127 B11** 66 40N 87 30W
Raeren, *Belgium* **21 G8** 50 41N 6 7 E
Raeside, L., *Australia* **113 E3** 29 20 S 122 0 E
Raetihi, *N.Z.* **118 F4** 39 25 S 175 17 E
Rafaela, *Argentina* **158 C3** 31 10 S 61 30W
Rafah, *Egypt* **91 D3** 31 18N 34 14 E
Rafai, *C.A.R.* **102 B4** 4 59N 23 58 E
Raffadali, *Italy* **40 E6** 37 23N 13 29 E
Rafḩā, *Si. Arabia* **84 D4** 29 35N 43 35 E
Rafsanjān, *Iran* **85 D8** 30 30N 56 5 E
Raft Pt., *Australia* **112 C3** 16 4 S 124 26 E
Ragag, *Sudan* **95 E1** 10 59N 24 40 E
Ragang, Mt., *Phil.* **71 H5** 7 43N 124 32 E
Ragay, *Phil.* **70 E4** 13 49N 122 47 E
Ragay G., *Phil.* **70 E4** 13 30N 122 45 E
Ragged, Mt., *Australia* **113 F3** 33 27 S 123 25 E
Raglan, *Australia* **114 C5** 23 42 S 150 49 E
Raglan, *N.Z.* **118 D3** 37 55 S 174 55 E
Raglan Harbour, *N.Z.* **118 D3** 37 47 S 174 50 E
Ragunda, *Sweden* **14 A10** 63 6N 16 23 E
Ragusa, *Italy* **41 F7** 36 56N 14 42 E
Raha, *Indonesia* **72 B2** 4 55 S 123 0 E
Rahad, Nahr ed →, *Sudan* **95 E3** 14 28N 33 31 E
Rahad al Bardī, *Sudan* **97 F4** 11 20N 23 40 E
Rahaeng = Tak, *Thailand* **76 D2** 16 52N 99 8 E
Rahden, *Germany* **26 C4** 52 26N 8 36 E
Raheita, *Eritrea* **95 E5** 12 46N 43 4 E
Raḩīmah, *Si. Arabia* **85 E6** 26 42N 50 4 E
Rahimyar Khan, *Pakistan* **79 C3** 28 30N 70 25 E
Rāhjerd, *Iran* **85 C6** 34 22N 50 22 E
Rahotu, *N.Z.* **118 F2** 39 20 S 173 49 E
Raichur, *India* **83 F3** 16 10N 77 20 E
Raiganj, *India* **81 G13** 25 37N 88 10 E
Raigarh, *India* **82 D6** 21 56N 83 25 E
Raighar, *India* **82 E6** 19 51N 82 6 E
Raijua, *Indonesia* **72 D2** 10 37 S 121 36 E
Railton, *Australia* **114 G4** 41 25 S 146 28 E
Rainbow, *Australia* **116 C5** 35 55 S 142 0 E
Rainbow Lake, *Canada* **130 B5** 58 30N 119 23W
Rainier, *U.S.A.* **144 D4** 46 53N 122 41W
Rainier, Mt., *U.S.A.* **144 D5** 46 52N 121 46W
Rainy L., *Canada* **131 D10** 48 42N 93 10W
Rainy River, *Canada* **131 D10** 48 43N 94 29W
Raipur, *India* **82 D5** 21 17N 81 45 E
Raj Nandgaon, *India* **82 D5** 21 5N 81 5 E
Raja, Ujung, *Indonesia* **74 B1** 3 40N 96 25 E
Raja Ampat, Kepulauan, *Indonesia* **73 B4** 0 30 S 130 0 E
Rajahmundry, *India* **82 F5** 17 1N 81 48 E
Rajajooseppi, *Finland* **12 B20** 68 28N 28 29 E
Rajang →, *Malaysia* **75 B4** 2 30N 112 0 E
Rajapalaiyam, *India* **83 K3** 9 25N 77 35 E
Rajasthan □, *India* **80 F5** 26 45N 73 30 E
Rajasthan Canal, *India* **80 E5** 28 0N 72 0 E
Rajauri, *India* **81 C6** 33 25N 74 21 E
Rajbari, *Bangla.* **78 D2** 23 47N 89 41 E
Rajgarh, *Mad. P., India* **80 G7** 24 2N 76 45 E
Rajgarh, *Raj., India* **80 E6** 28 40N 75 25 E
Rajgród, *Poland* **47 B9** 53 42N 22 42 E
Rajhenburg, *Slovenia* **39 B12** 46 1N 15 29 E
Rajkot, *India* **80 H4** 22 15N 70 56 E
Rajmahal Hills, *India* **81 G12** 24 30N 87 30 E
Rajpipla, *India* **82 D1** 21 50N 73 30 E
Rajpura, *India* **80 D7** 30 25N 76 32 E
Rajshahi, *Bangla.* **78 C2** 24 22N 88 39 E
Rajshahi □, *Bangla.* **81 G13** 25 0N 89 0 E
Rakaia, *N.Z.* **119 D7** 43 45 S 172 1 E
Rakaia →, *N.Z.* **119 D7** 43 36 S 172 15 E
Rakan, Ra's, *Qatar* **85 E6** 26 10N 51 20 E
Rakaposhi, *Pakistan* **81 A6** 36 10N 74 25 E
Rakata, Pulau, *Indonesia* **74 D3** 6 10 S 105 20 E
Rakhawt, W. →, *Yemen* **87 C5** 18 16N 51 50 E
Rakhneh-ye Jamshīdī, *Afghan.* **79 B1** 34 22N 62 19 E
Rakhni, *Pakistan* **80 D3** 30 4N 69 56 E
Rakhyūt, *Oman* **87 C6** 16 44N 53 20 E
Rakitnoye, *Russia* **60 B7** 45 36N 134 17 E
Rakitovo, *Bulgaria* **43 F9** 41 59N 24 5 E
Rakkestad, *Norway* **14 E5** 59 25N 11 21 E
Rakoniewice, *Poland* **47 C3** 52 10N 16 16 E
Rakops, *Botswana* **104 C3** 21 1 S 24 28 E
Rákospalota, *Hungary* **31 D12** 47 30N 19 5 E
Rakov, *Belorussia* **50 E5** 53 58N 26 59 E
Rakovica, *Croatia* **39 D12** 44 59N 15 38 E
Rakovník, *Czech.* **30 A6** 50 6N 13 42 E
Rakovski, *Bulgaria* **43 E9** 42 21N 24 57 E
Rakvere, *Estonia* **50 B5** 59 20N 26 25 E
Raleigh, *U.S.A.* **135 H6** 35 47N 78 39W
Raleigh B., *U.S.A.* **135 H7** 34 50N 76 15W
Ralja, *Serbia* **42 C5** 44 33N 20 34 E
Ralls, *U.S.A.* **139 J4** 33 41N 101 24W
Ram →, *Canada* **130 A4** 62 1N 123 41W
Rām Allāh, *Jordan* **91 D4** 31 55N 35 10 E
Ram Hd., *Australia* **117 D8** 37 47 S 149 30 E
Rama, *Nic.* **148 D3** 12 9N 84 15W
Ramacca, *Italy* **41 E7** 37 24N 14 40 E
Ramachandrapuram, *India* **82 F6** 16 50N 82 4 E
Ramales de la Victoria, *Spain* **34 B1** 43 15N 3 28W
Ramalho, Serra do, *Brazil* **155 D3** 13 45 S 44 0W
Raman, *Thailand* **77 J3** 6 29N 101 18 E
Ramanathapuram, *India* **83 K4** 9 25N 78 55 E
Ramanetaka, B. de, *Madag.* **105 A8** 14 13 S 47 52 E
Ramas C., *India* **83 G1** 15 5N 73 55 E
Ramat Gan, *Israel* **91 C3** 32 4N 34 48 E
Ramatlhabama, *S. Africa* **104 D4** 25 37 S 25 33 E
Ramban, *India* **81 C6** 33 14N 75 12 E
Rambervillers, *France* **23 D13** 48 20N 6 38 E
Rambi, *Fiji* **121 A3** 16 30 S 179 59W
Rambipuji, *Indonesia* **75 D4** 8 12 S 113 37 E
Rambouillet, *France* **23 D8** 48 39N 1 50 E
Ramdurg, *India* **83 G2** 15 58N 75 22 E
Ramea, *Canada* **129 C8** 47 31N 57 23W
Ramechhap, *Nepal* **81 F12** 27 25N 86 10 E
Ramelau, *Indonesia* **72 C3** 8 55 S 126 22 E
Ramenskoye, *Russia* **51 D11** 55 32N 38 15 E
Ramgarh, *Bihar, India* **81 H11** 23 40N 85 35 E
Ramgarh, *Raj., India* **80 F6** 27 16N 75 14 E
Ramgarh, *Raj., India* **80 F4** 27 30N 70 36 E
Rāmhormoz, *Iran* **85 D6** 31 15N 49 35 E
Ramīān, *Iran* **85 B7** 37 3N 55 16 E
Ramingining, *Australia* **114 A2** 12 19 S 135 3 E
Ramla, *Israel* **91 D3** 31 55N 34 52 E
Ramlat Zalṭan, *Libya* **96 C3** 28 30N 19 30 E
Ramlu, *Eritrea* **95 E5** 13 32N 41 40 E
Ramme, *Denmark* **15 H2** 56 30N 8 11 E
Ramnad = Ramanathapuram, *India* **83 K4** 9 25N 78 55 E
Ramnagar, *India* **81 C6** 32 47N 75 18 E
Ramnäs, *Sweden* **14 E10** 59 46N 16 12 E
Ramon, *Russia* **51 F11** 51 55N 39 21 E
Ramona, *U.S.A.* **145 M10** 33 2N 116 52W
Ramore, *Canada* **128 C3** 48 30N 80 25W
Ramotswa, *Botswana* **104 C4** 24 50 S 25 52 E
Rampur, *H.P., India* **80 D7** 31 26N 77 43 E
Rampur, *Mad. P., India* **80 H5** 23 25N 73 53 E
Rampur, *Orissa, India* **82 D6** 21 48N 83 58 E
Rampur, *Ut. P., India* **81 E8** 28 50N 79 5 E
Rampur Hat, *India* **81 G12** 24 10N 87 50 E
Rampura, *India* **80 G6** 24 30N 75 27 E
Rāmsar, *Iran* **85 B6** 36 53N 50 41 E
Ramsel, *Belgium* **21 F5** 51 2N 4 50 E
Ramsey, *Canada* **128 C3** 47 25N 82 20W
Ramsey, *U.K.* **16 C3** 54 20N 4 21W
Ramsey, *U.S.A.* **140 E7** 39 8N 89 7W
Ramsgate, *U.K.* **17 F9** 51 20N 1 25 E
Ramshai, *India* **78 B2** 26 44N 88 51 E
Ramsjö, *Sweden* **14 B9** 62 11N 15 37 E
Ramtek, *India* **82 D4** 21 20N 79 15 E
Ramu →, *Papua N. G.* **120 C3** 4 0 S 144 41 E
Ramvik, *Sweden* **14 B11** 62 49N 17 51 E
Ranaghat, *India* **81 H13** 23 15N 88 35 E
Ranahu, *Pakistan* **80 G3** 25 55N 69 45 E
Rancagua, *Chile* **158 C1** 34 10 S 70 50W
Rance, *Belgium* **21 H4** 50 9N 4 16 E
Rance →, *France* **22 D5** 48 34N 1 59W
Rance, Barrage de la, *France* **22 D4** 48 30N 2 3W
Rancharia, *Brazil* **155 F1** 22 15 S 50 55W
Rancheria →, *Canada* **130 A3** 60 13N 129 7W
Ranchester, *U.S.A.* **142 D10** 44 54N 107 10W
Ranchi, *India* **81 H11** 23 19N 85 27 E
Ranco, L., *Chile* **160 B2** 40 15 S 72 25W
Rancu, *Romania* **46 E5** 44 32N 24 15 E
Rand, *Australia* **117 C7** 35 33 S 146 32 E
Randan, *France* **24 B7** 46 2N 3 21 E
Randazzo, *Italy* **41 E7** 37 53N 14 56 E
Randers, *Denmark* **15 H4** 56 29N 10 1 E
Randers Fjord, *Denmark* **15 H4** 56 37N 10 20 E
Randfontein, *S. Africa* **105 D4** 26 8 S 27 45 E
Randle, *U.S.A.* **144 D5** 46 32N 121 57W
Randolph, *Mass., U.S.A.* **137 D13** 42 10N 71 2W
Randolph, *N.Y., U.S.A.* **136 D6** 42 10N 78 59W
Randolph, *Utah, U.S.A.* **142 F8** 41 40N 111 11W
Randolph, *Vt., U.S.A.* **137 C12** 43 55N 72 40W
Randsfjord, *Norway* **14 D4** 60 15N 10 25 E
Råne älv →, *Sweden* **12 D17** 65 50N 22 20 E
Ranfurly, *N.Z.* **119 F5** 45 7 S 170 6 E
Rangae, *Thailand* **77 J3** 6 19N 101 44 E
Rangamati, *Bangla.* **78 D4** 22 38N 92 12 E
Rangataua, *N.Z.* **118 F4** 39 26 S 175 28 E
Rangaunu B., *N.Z.* **118 A2** 34 51 S 173 15 E
Rångedala, *Sweden* **15 G7** 57 47N 13 9 E
Rangeley, *U.S.A.* **137 B14** 44 58N 70 39W
Rangely, *U.S.A.* **142 F9** 40 5N 108 48W
Ranger, *U.S.A.* **139 J5** 32 28N 98 41W
Rangia, *India* **78 B3** 26 28N 91 38 E
Rangiora, *N.Z.* **119 D7** 43 19 S 172 36 E
Rangitaiki, *N.Z.* **118 E5** 38 52 S 176 24 E
Rangitaiki →, *N.Z.* **118 D5** 37 54 S 176 49 E
Rangitata →, *N.Z.* **119 D6** 43 45 S 171 15 E
Rangitikei →, *N.Z.* **118 G4** 40 17 S 175 15 E
Rangitoto Ra., *N.Z.* **118 E4** 38 25 S 175 35 E
Rangkasbitung, *Indonesia* **74 D3** 6 21 S 106 15 E
Rangoon, *Burma* **78 G6** 16 45N 96 20 E
Rangpur, *Bangla.* **78 C2** 25 42N 89 22 E
Rangsang, *Indonesia* **74 B2** 1 20N 103 30 E
Rangsit, *Thailand* **76 F3** 13 59N 100 37 E
Ranibennur, *India* **83 G2** 14 35N 75 30 E
Raniganj, *India* **81 H12** 23 40N 87 5 E
Ranippettai, *India* **83 H4** 12 56N 79 23 E
Rāniyah, *Iraq* **84 B5** 36 15N 44 53 E
Ranken →, *Australia* **114 C2** 20 31 S 137 36 E
Rankin, *Ill., U.S.A.* **141 D9** 40 28N 87 54W
Rankin, *Tex., U.S.A.* **139 K4** 31 13N 101 56W
Rankin Inlet, *Canada* **126 B10** 62 30N 93 0W
Rankins Springs, *Australia* **117 B7** 33 49 S 146 14 E
Rannoch, L., *U.K.* **18 E4** 56 41N 4 20W
Rannoch Moor, *U.K.* **18 E4** 56 38N 4 48W
Ranobe, Helodranon' i, *Madag.* **105 C7** 23 3 S 43 33 E
Ranohira, *Madag.* **105 C8** 22 29 S 45 24 E
Ranomafana, *Toamasina, Madag.* **105 B8** 18 57 S 48 50 E
Ranomafana, *Toliara, Madag.* **105 C8** 24 34 S 47 0 E
Ranong, *Thailand* **77 H2** 9 56N 98 40 E
Rānsa, *Iran* **85 C6** 33 39N 48 18 E
Ransiki, *Indonesia* **73 B4** 1 30 S 134 10 E
Ransom, *U.S.A.* **141 C8** 41 9N 88 39W
Rantau, *Indonesia* **75 C5** 2 56 S 115 9 E
Rantauprapat, *Indonesia* **74 B1** 2 15N 99 50 E
Rantekombola, *Indonesia* **72 B1** 3 15 S 119 57 E
Rantoul, *U.S.A.* **141 D8** 40 19N 88 9W
Ranum, *Denmark* **15 H3** 56 54N 9 14 E
Ranyah, W. →, *Si. Arabia* **86 B3** 21 18N 43 20 E
Raon l'Étape, *France* **23 D13** 48 24N 6 50 E
Raoui, Erg er, *Algeria* **99 C4** 29 0N 2 0W
Raoyang, *China* **66 E8** 38 15N 115 45 E
Rapa, *Pac. Oc.* **123 K13** 27 35 S 144 20W
Rapallo, *Italy* **38 D6** 44 21N 9 12 E
Rāpch, *Iran* **85 E8** 25 40N 59 15 E
Rapid →, *Canada* **130 B3** 59 15N 129 5W
Rapid City, *U.S.A.* **138 D3** 44 5N 103 14W
Rapid River, *U.S.A.* **134 C2** 45 55N 86 58W
Rapides des Joachims, *Canada* **128 C4** 46 13N 77 43W
Rapla, *Estonia* **50 B4** 59 1N 24 52 E
Rapperswil, *Switz.* **29 B7** 47 14N 8 45 E
Rapu Rapu I., *Phil.* **70 E5** 13 12N 124 9 E
Rarotonga, *Cook Is.* **123 K12** 21 30 S 160 0W
Ra's al' Ayn, *Syria* **84 B4** 36 51N 40 4 E
Ra's al Khaymah, *U.A.E.* **85 E8** 25 50N 56 5 E
Ra's al-Unuf, *Libya* **96 B3** 30 25N 18 15 E
Ra's an Naqb, *Jordan* **91 F4** 30 0N 35 29 E
Ras Bânâs, *Egypt* **94 C4** 23 57N 35 59 E
Ras Dashen, *Ethiopia* **95 E4** 13 8N 38 26 E
Ras el Ma, *Algeria* **99 B4** 34 26N 0 50W
Ras Mallap, *Egypt* **94 J8** 29 18N 32 50 E
Râs Timirist, *Mauritania* **100 B1** 19 21N 16 30W
Rasa, Punta, *Argentina* **160 B4** 40 50 S 62 15W
Rasca, Pta. de la, *Canary Is.* **33 G3** 27 59N 16 41W
Raseiniai, *Lithuania* **50 D3** 55 25N 23 5 E
Rashad, *Sudan* **95 E3** 11 55N 31 0 E
Rashîd, *Egypt* **94 H7** 31 21N 30 22 E
Rashîd, Masabb, *Egypt* **94 H7** 31 22N 30 17 E
Rasht, *Iran* **85 B6** 37 20N 49 40 E
Rasi Salai, *Thailand* **76 E5** 15 20N 104 9 E
Rasipuram, *India* **83 J4** 11 30N 78 15 E
Raška, *Serbia* **42 D5** 43 19N 20 39 E
Rason L., *Australia* **113 E3** 28 45 S 124 25 E
Raşova, *Romania* **46 E8** 44 15N 27 55 E
Rasovo, *Bulgaria* **43 D8** 43 42N 23 17 E
Rasra, *India* **81 G10** 25 50N 83 50 E
Rass el Oued, *Algeria* **99 A6** 35 57N 5 2 E
Rasskazovo, *Russia* **51 E12** 52 35N 41 50 E
Rastatt, *Germany* **27 G4** 48 50N 8 12 E
Rastu, *Romania* **46 F4** 43 53N 23 16 E
Raszków, *Poland* **47 D4** 51 43N 17 40 E
Rat Buri, *Thailand* **76 F2** 13 30N 99 54 E
Rat Islands, *U.S.A.* **126 C1** 52 0N 178 0 E
Rat River, *Canada* **130 A6** 61 7N 112 36W
Ratangarh, *India* **80 E6** 28 5N 74 35 E
Raţāwī, *Iraq* **84 D5** 30 38N 47 13 E
Rath, *India* **81 G8** 25 36N 79 37 E
Rath Luirc, *Ireland* **19 D3** 52 21N 8 40W
Rathbun Res., *U.S.A.* **140 D4** 40 49N 92 53W
Rathdrum, *Ireland* **19 D5** 52 57N 6 13W
Rathedaung, *Burma* **78 E4** 20 29N 92 45 E
Rathenow, *Germany* **26 C8** 52 38N 12 23 E
Rathkeale, *Ireland* **19 D3** 52 32N 8 57W
Rathlin, *U.K.* **19 A5** 55 18N 6 14W
Rathlin O'Birne I., *Ireland* **19 B3** 54 40N 8 50W
Ratibor = Racibórz, *Poland* **31 A11** 50 7N 18 18 E
Rätikon, *Austria* **30 D2** 47 0N 9 55 E
Ratlam, *India* **80 H6** 23 20N 75 0 E
Ratnagiri, *India* **82 F1** 16 57N 73 18 E
Ratnapura, *Sri Lanka* **83 L5** 6 40N 80 20 E
Raton, *U.S.A.* **139 G2** 36 54N 104 24W
Rattaphum, *Thailand* **77 J3** 7 8N 100 16 E
Ratten, *Austria* **30 D8** 47 28N 15 44 E
Rattray Hd., *U.K.* **18 D7** 57 38N 1 50W
Ratz, Mt., *Canada* **130 B2** 57 23N 132 12W
Ratzeburg, *Germany* **26 B6** 53 41N 10 46 E
Raub, *Malaysia* **77 L3** 3 47N 101 52 E
Rauch, *Argentina* **158 D4** 36 45 S 59 5W
Raufarhöfn, *Iceland* **12 C6** 66 27N 15 57W
Raufoss, *Norway* **14 D4** 60 44N 10 37 E
Raukumara Ra., *N.Z.* **118 E6** 38 5 S 177 55 E
Raul Soares, *Brazil* **155 F3** 20 5 S 42 22W
Rauland, *Norway* **14 E2** 59 43N 8 0 E
Rauma, *Finland* **13 F16** 61 10N 21 30 E
Rauma →, *Norway* **14 B1** 62 34N 7 43 E
Raurkela, *India* **81 H11** 22 14N 84 50 E
Rausu-Dake, *Japan* **60 B12** 44 4N 145 7 E
Rava Russkaya, *Ukraine* **50 F3** 50 15N 23 42 E
Ravānsar, *Iran* **84 C5** 34 43N 46 40 E
Ravanusa, *Italy* **40 E6** 37 16N 13 58 E
Rāvar, *Iran* **85 D8** 31 20N 56 51 E
Ravels, *Belgium* **21 F6** 51 22N 5 0 E
Ravena, *U.S.A.* **137 D11** 42 28N 73 49W
Ravenna, *Italy* **39 D9** 44 28N 12 15 E
Ravenna, *Ky., U.S.A.* **141 G13** 37 42N 83 55W
Ravenna, *Nebr., U.S.A.* **138 E5** 41 1N 98 55W
Ravenna, *Ohio, U.S.A.* **136 E3** 41 9N 81 15W
Ravensburg, *Germany* **27 H5** 47 48N 9 38 E
Ravenshoe, *Australia* **114 B4** 17 37 S 145 29 E
Ravenstein, *Neths.* **20 E7** 51 47N 5 39 E
Ravensthorpe, *Australia* **113 F3** 33 35 S 120 2 E
Ravenswood, *Australia* **114 C4** 20 6 S 146 54 E
Ravenswood, *U.S.A.* **134 F5** 38 57N 81 46W
Ravensworth, *Australia* **117 B9** 32 26 S 151 4 E
Ravenwood, *U.S.A.* **140 D2** 40 22N 94 41W
Ravi →, *Pakistan* **80 D4** 30 35N 71 49 E
Ravna Gora, *Croatia* **39 C11** 45 24N 14 50 E
Ravna Reka, *Serbia* **42 D6** 43 59N 21 35 E
Rawa Mazowiecka, *Poland* **47 D7** 51 46N 20 12 E
Rawalpindi, *Pakistan* **79 B4** 33 38N 73 8 E
Rawāndūz, *Iraq* **84 B5** 36 40N 44 30 E
Rawang, *Malaysia* **77 L3** 3 20N 101 35 E
Rawdon, *Canada* **128 C5** 46 3N 73 40W
Rawene, *N.Z.* **118 B2** 35 25 S 173 32 E
Rawicz, *Poland* **47 D3** 51 36N 16 52 E
Rawka →, *Poland* **47 C7** 52 9N 20 8 E
Rawlinna, *Australia* **113 F4** 30 58 S 125 28 E
Rawlins, *U.S.A.* **142 F10** 41 47N 107 14W
Rawlinson Ra., *Australia* **113 D4** 24 40 S 128 30 E
Rawson, *Argentina* **160 B3** 43 15 S 65 5W
Ray, *U.S.A.* **138 A3** 48 21N 103 10W
Ray, C., *Canada* **129 C8** 47 33N 59 15W
Rayachoti, *India* **83 G4** 14 4N 78 50 E
Rayadurg, *India* **83 G3** 14 40N 76 50 E
Rayagada, *India* **82 E6** 19 15N 83 20 E
Raychikhinsk, *Russia* **57 E13** 49 46N 129 25 E
Rāyen, *Iran* **85 D8** 29 34N 57 26 E
Rayevskiy, *Russia* **54 D4** 54 4N 54 56 E
Raymond, *Canada* **130 D6** 49 30N 112 35W
Raymond, *Calif., U.S.A.* **144 H7** 37 13N 119 54W
Raymond, *Ill., U.S.A.* **140 E7** 39 19N 89 34W
Raymond, *Wash., U.S.A.* **144 D3** 46 41N 123 44W
Raymond Terrace, *Australia* **117 B9** 32 45 S 151 44 E
Raymondville, *U.S.A.* **139 M6** 26 29N 97 47W
Raymore, *Canada* **131 C8** 51 25N 104 31W
Rayne, *U.S.A.* **139 K8** 30 14N 92 16W
Rayón, *Mexico* **146 B2** 29 43N 110 35W
Rayong, *Thailand* **76 F3** 12 40N 101 20 E
Raytown, *U.S.A.* **140 E2** 39 1N 94 28W
Rayville, *U.S.A.* **139 J9** 32 29N 91 46W
Raz, Pte. du, *France* **22 D2** 48 2N 4 47W
Razan, *Iran* **85 C6** 35 23N 49 2 E
Ražana, *Serbia* **42 C4** 44 6N 19 55 E
Ražanj, *Serbia* **42 D6** 43 40N 21 31 E
Razdelna, *Bulgaria* **43 D12** 43 13N 27 41 E
Razdel'naya, *Ukraine* **52 C4** 46 50N 30 2 E
Razdolnoye, *Russia* **60 C5** 43 30N 131 52 E
Razdolnoye, *Ukraine* **52 D5** 45 46N 33 29 E
Razeh, *Iran* **85 C6** 32 47N 48 9 E
Razelm, Lacul, *Romania* **46 E10** 44 50N 29 0 E
Razgrad, *Bulgaria* **43 D11** 43 33N 26 34 E
Razlog, *Bulgaria* **43 F8** 41 53N 23 28 E
Razmak, *Pakistan* **79 B3** 32 45N 69 50 E
Razole, *India* **83 F5** 16 36N 81 48 E
Ré, I. de, *France* **24 B2** 46 12N 1 30W
Reading, *U.K.* **17 F7** 51 27N 0 57W
Reading, *Mich., U.S.A.* **141 C12** 41 50N 84 45W
Reading, *Ohio, U.S.A.* **141 E12** 39 13N 84 26W
Reading, *Pa., U.S.A.* **137 F9** 40 20N 75 56W
Real, Cordillera, *Bolivia* **156 D4** 17 0 S 67 10W
Realicó, *Argentina* **158 D3** 35 0 S 64 15W
Réalmont, *France* **24 E6** 43 48N 2 10 E

256 Rimrock

Rimrock, *U.S.A.* **144 D5** 46 38N 121 10W
Rinca, *Indonesia* **72 C1** 8 45 S 119 35 E
Rincón de Romos, *Mexico* **146 C4** 22 14N 102 18W
Rinconada, *Argentina* **158 A2** 22 26 S 66 10W
Ringarum, *Sweden* **15 F10** 58 21N 16 26 E
Ringe, *Denmark* **15 J4** 55 13N 10 28 E
Ringgold Is., *Fiji* **121 A3** 16 15 S 179 25W
Ringim, *Nigeria* **101 C6** 12 13N 9 10 E
Ringkøbing, *Denmark* **15 H2** 56 5N 8 15 E
Ringling, *U.S.A.* **142 C8** 46 16N 110 49W
Ringsaker, *Norway* **14 D4** 60 54N 10 45 E
Ringsted, *Denmark* **15 J5** 55 25N 11 46 E
Ringvassøy, *Norway* **12 B15** 69 56N 19 15 E
Rinía, *Greece* **45 G7** 37 23N 25 13 E
Rinjani, *Indonesia* **75 D5** 8 24 S 116 28 E
Rinteln, *Germany* **26 C5** 52 11N 9 3 E
Río, Punta del, *Spain* **35 J2** 36 49N 2 24W
Rio Branco, *Brazil* **156 B4** 9 58 S 67 49W
Río Branco, *Uruguay* **159 C5** 32 40 S 53 40W
Rio Brilhante, *Brazil* **159 A5** 21 48 S 54 33W
Río Bueno, *Chile* **160 B2** 40 19 S 72 58W
Río Chico, *Venezuela* **152 A4** 10 19N 65 59W
Rio Claro, *Brazil* **159 A6** 22 19 S 47 35W
Rio Claro, *Trin. & Tob.* **149 D7** 10 20N 61 25W
Río Colorado, *Argentina* **160 A4** 39 0 S 64 0W
Río Cuarto, *Argentina* **158 C3** 33 10 S 64 25W
Rio das Pedras, *Mozam.* **105 C6** 23 8 S 35 28 E
Rio de Contas, *Brazil* **155 D3** 13 36 S 41 48W
Rio de Janeiro, *Brazil* **155 F3** 23 0 S 43 12W
Rio de Janeiro □, *Brazil* **155 F3** 22 50 S 43 0W
Rio do Prado, *Brazil* **155 E3** 16 35 S 40 34W
Rio do Sul, *Brazil* **159 B6** 27 13 S 49 37W
Río Gallegos, *Argentina* **160 D3** 51 35 S 69 15W
Río Grande, *Argentina* **160 D3** 53 50 S 67 45W
Río Grande, *Bolivia* **156 E4** 20 51 S 67 17W
Rio Grande, *Brazil* **159 C5** 32 0 S 52 20W
Río Grande, *Mexico* **146 C4** 23 50N 103 2W
Río Grande, *Nic.* **148 D3** 12 54N 83 33W
Rio Grande →, *U.S.A.* **139 N6** 25 57N 97 9W
Rio Grande City, *U.S.A.* **139 M5** 26 23N 98 49W
Río Grande del Norte →, *N. Amer.* **133 E7** 26 0N 97 0W
Rio Grande do Norte □, *Brazil* **154 C4** 5 40 S 36 0W
Rio Grande do Sul □, *Brazil* **159 C5** 30 0 S 53 0W
Río Hato, *Panama* **148 E3** 8 22N 80 10W
Rio Lagartos, *Mexico* **147 C7** 21 36N 88 10W
Rio Largo, *Brazil* **154 C4** 9 28 S 35 50W
Rio Maior, *Portugal* **37 F2** 39 19N 8 57W
Rio Marina, *Italy* **38 F7** 42 48N 10 25 E
Río Mayo, *Argentina* **160 C2** 45 40 S 70 15W
Río Mulatos, *Bolivia* **156 D4** 19 40 S 66 50W
Río Muni = Mbini □, *Eq. Guin.* **102 B2** 1 30N 10 0 E
Rio Negro, *Brazil* **159 B6** 26 0 S 49 55W
Río Negro, *Chile* **160 B2** 40 47 S 73 14W
Rio Negro, Pantanal do, *Brazil* **157 D6** 19 0 S 56 0W
Rio Pardo, *Brazil* **159 C5** 30 0 S 52 30W
Río Pico, *Argentina* **160 B2** 44 0 S 70 22W
Rio Real, *Brazil* **155 D4** 11 28 S 37 56W
Río Segundo, *Argentina* **158 C3** 31 40 S 63 59W
Río Tercero, *Argentina* **158 C3** 32 15 S 64 8W
Rio Tinto, *Brazil* **154 C4** 6 48 S 35 5W
Rio Tinto, *Portugal* **36 D2** 41 11N 8 34W
Rio Verde, *Brazil* **155 E1** 17 50 S 51 0W
Río Verde, *Mexico* **147 C5** 21 56N 99 59W
Rio Verde de Mato Grosso, *Brazil* **157 D7** 18 56 S 54 52W
Rio Vista, *U.S.A.* **144 G5** 38 10N 121 42W
Ríobamba, *Ecuador* **152 D2** 1 50 S 78 45W
Ríohacha, *Colombia* **152 A3** 11 33N 72 55W
Rioja, *Peru* **156 B2** 6 11 S 77 5W
Riom, *France* **24 C7** 45 54N 3 7 E
Riom-ès-Montagnes, *France* **24 C6** 45 17N 2 39 E
Rion-des-Landes, *France* **24 E3** 43 55N 0 56W
Rionegro, *Colombia* **152 B2** 6 9N 75 22W
Rionero in Vúlture, *Italy* **41 B8** 40 55N 15 40 E
Rioni →, *Georgia* **53 E9** 42 5N 41 50 E
Rios, *Spain* **36 D3** 41 58N 7 16W
Riosucio, *Caldas, Colombia* **152 B2** 5 30N 75 40W
Ríosucio, *Choco, Colombia* **152 B2** 7 27N 77 7W
Riou L., *Canada* **131 B7** 59 7N 106 25W
Rioz, *France* **23 E13** 47 26N 6 5 E
Riozinho →, *Brazil* **152 D4** 2 55 S 67 7W
Riparia, Dora →, *Italy* **38 C4** 45 7N 7 24 E
Ripatransone, *Italy* **39 F10** 43 0N 13 45 E
Ripley, *Canada* **136 B3** 44 4N 81 35W
Ripley, *Calif., U.S.A.* **145 M12** 33 32N 114 39W
Ripley, *N.Y., U.S.A.* **136 D5** 42 16N 79 43W
Ripley, *Ohio, U.S.A.* **141 F13** 38 45N 83 51W
Ripley, *Tenn., U.S.A.* **139 H10** 35 45N 89 32W
Ripoll, *Spain* **34 C7** 42 15N 2 13 E
Ripon, *U.K.* **16 C6** 54 8N 1 31W
Ripon, *Calif., U.S.A.* **144 H5** 37 44N 121 7W
Ripon, *Wis., U.S.A.* **134 D1** 43 51N 88 50W
Riposto, *Italy* **41 E8** 37 44N 15 12 E
Risalpur, *Pakistan* **80 B4** 34 3N 71 59 E
Risan, *Montenegro* **42 E3** 42 32N 18 42 E
Risaralda □, *Colombia* **152 B2** 5 0N 76 10W
Riscle, *France* **24 E3** 43 39N 0 5W
Rishā', W. ar →, *Si. Arabia* **84 E5** 25 33N 44 5 E
Rishiri-Tō, *Japan* **60 B10** 45 11N 141 15 E
Rishon le Ziyyon, *Israel* **91 D3** 31 58N 34 48 E
Rising Sun, *U.S.A.* **141 F12** 38 57N 84 51W
Risle →, *France* **22 C7** 49 26N 0 23 E
Rîsnov, *Romania* **46 D6** 45 35N 25 27 E
Rison, *U.S.A.* **139 J8** 33 58N 92 11W
Risør, *Norway* **15 F3** 58 43N 9 13 E
Rissani, *Morocco* **98 B4** 31 18N 4 12W
Riti, *Nigeria* **101 D6** 7 57N 9 41 E
Ritidian Pt., *Guam* **121 R15** 13 39N 144 51 E
Rittman, *U.S.A.* **136 F3** 40 58N 81 47W
Ritzville, *U.S.A.* **142 C4** 47 8N 118 23W
Riu, *India* **78 A5** 28 19N 95 3 E
Riva Bella, *France* **22 C6** 49 17N 0 18W
Riva del Garda, *Italy* **38 C7** 45 53N 10 50 E
Rivadavia, *Buenos Aires, Argentina* **158 D3** 35 29 S 62 59W
Rivadavia, *Mendoza, Argentina* **158 C2** 33 13 S 68 30W
Rivadavia, *Salta, Argentina* **158 A3** 24 5 S 62 54W
Rivadavia, *Chile* **158 B1** 29 57 S 70 35W
Rivarolo Canavese, *Italy* **38 C4** 45 20N 7 42 E
Rivas, *Nic.* **148 D2** 11 30N 85 50W
Rive-de-Gier, *France* **25 C8** 45 32N 4 37 E
River Cess, *Liberia* **100 D3** 5 30N 9 32W
Rivera, *Uruguay* **159 C4** 31 0 S 55 50W
Riverdale, *U.S.A.* **144 J7** 36 26N 119 52W
Riverhead, *U.S.A.* **137 F12** 40 55N 72 40W
Riverhurst, *Canada* **131 C7** 50 55N 106 50W
Riverina, *Australia* **113 E3** 29 45 S 120 40 E
Rivers, *Canada* **131 C8** 50 2N 100 14W
Rivers □, *Nigeria* **101 E6** 5 0N 6 30 E
Rivers, L. of the, *Canada* **131 D7** 49 49N 105 44W
Rivers Inlet, *Canada* **130 C3** 51 42N 127 15W
Riversdale, *N.Z.* **119 F3** 45 54 S 168 44 E
Riversdale, *S. Africa* **104 E3** 34 7 S 21 15 E
Riverside, *Calif., U.S.A.* **145 M9** 33 59N 117 22W
Riverside, *Wyo., U.S.A.* **142 F10** 41 13N 106 47W
Riversleigh, *Australia* **114 B2** 19 5 S 138 40 E
Riverton, *Australia* **116 C3** 34 10 S 138 46 E
Riverton, *Canada* **131 C9** 51 1N 97 0W
Riverton, *N.Z.* **119 G2** 46 21 S 168 0 E
Riverton, *Ill., U.S.A.* **140 E7** 39 51N 89 33W
Riverton, *Wyo., U.S.A.* **142 E9** 43 2N 108 23W
Riverton Heights, *U.S.A.* **144 C4** 47 28N 122 17W
Rives, *France* **25 C9** 45 21N 5 31 E
Rivesaltes, *France* **24 F6** 42 47N 2 50 E
Riviera, *Europe* **38 E5** 44 0N 8 30 E
Rivière-à-Pierre, *Canada* **129 C5** 46 59N 72 11W
Rivière-au-Renard, *Canada* **129 C7** 48 59N 64 23W
Rivière-du-Loup, *Canada* **129 C6** 47 50N 69 30W
Rivière-Pentecôte, *Canada* **129 C6** 49 57N 67 1W
Rivière-Pilote, *Martinique* **149 D7** 14 26N 60 53W
Rivne = Rovno, *Ukraine* **50 F5** 50 40N 26 10 E
Rívoli, *Italy* **38 C4** 45 3N 7 31 E
Rivoli B., *Australia* **116 D4** 37 32 S 140 3 E
Riwaka, *N.Z.* **119 B7** 41 5 S 172 59 E
Rixensart, *Belgium* **21 G5** 50 43N 4 32 E
Riyadh = Ar Riyāḍ, *Si. Arabia* **84 E5** 24 41N 46 42 E
Rizal, *Cagayan, Phil.* **70 C3** 17 51N 121 21 E
Rizal, *Nueva Ecija, Phil.* **70 D3** 15 43N 121 6 E
Rizal, *Zamboanga del N., Phil.* **71 G4** 8 35N 123 26 E
Rize, *Turkey* **89 C9** 41 0N 40 30 E
Rize □, *Turkey* **89 C9** 41 0N 40 30 E
Rizhao, *China* **67 G10** 35 25N 119 30 E
Rizokarpaso, *Cyprus* **32 D13** 35 36N 34 23 E
Rizzuto, C., *Italy* **41 D10** 38 54N 17 5 E
Rjukan, *Norway* **14 E2** 59 54N 8 33 E
Rô, *N. Cal.* **121 U21** 21 22 S 167 50 E
Roa, *Norway* **14 D4** 60 17N 10 37 E
Roa, *Spain* **36 D7** 41 41N 3 56W
Roachdale, *U.S.A.* **141 E10** 39 51N 86 48W
Road Town, *Virgin Is.* **149 C7** 18 27N 64 37W
Roag, L., *U.K.* **18 C2** 58 10N 6 55W
Roanne, *France* **25 B8** 46 3N 4 4 E
Roanoke, *Ala., U.S.A.* **135 J3** 33 9N 85 22W
Roanoke, *Ind., U.S.A.* **141 D11** 40 58N 85 22W
Roanoke, *Va., U.S.A.* **134 G6** 37 16N 79 56W
Roanoke →, *U.S.A.* **135 H7** 35 57N 76 42W
Roanoke I., *U.S.A.* **135 H8** 35 55N 75 40W
Roanoke Rapids, *U.S.A.* **135 G7** 36 28N 77 40W
Roatán, *Honduras* **148 C2** 16 18N 86 35W
Rob Roy, *Solomon Is.* **121 L9** 7 23 S 157 36 E
Robbins I., *Australia* **114 G4** 40 42 S 145 0 E
Robe →, *Australia* **112 D2** 21 42 S 116 15 E
Robe →, *Ireland* **19 C2** 53 38N 9 10W
Röbel, *Germany* **26 B8** 53 24N 12 37 E
Robert Lee, *U.S.A.* **139 K4** 31 54N 100 29W
Roberts, *Idaho, U.S.A.* **142 E7** 43 43N 112 8W
Roberts, *Ill., U.S.A.* **141 D8** 40 37N 88 11W
Robertsganj, *India* **81 G10** 24 44N 83 4 E
Robertson, *Australia* **117 C9** 34 37 S 150 36 E
Robertson, *S. Africa* **104 E2** 33 46 S 19 50 E
Robertson I., *Antarctica* **7 C18** 65 15 S 59 30W
Robertson Ra., *Australia* **112 D3** 23 15 S 121 0 E
Robertsport, *Liberia* **100 D2** 6 45N 11 26W
Robertstown, *Australia* **116 B3** 33 58 S 139 5 E
Roberval, *Canada* **129 C5** 48 32N 72 15W
Robeson Chan., *Greenland* **6 A4** 82 0N 61 30W
Robinson, *U.S.A.* **141 E9** 39 0N 87 44W
Robinson →, *Australia* **114 B2** 16 3 S 137 16 E
Robinson Ra., *Australia* **113 E2** 25 40 S 119 0 E
Robinson River, *Australia* **114 B2** 16 45 S 136 58 E
Robinvale, *Australia* **116 C5** 34 40 S 142 45 E
Roblin, *Canada* **131 C8** 51 14N 101 21W
Roboré, *Bolivia* **157 D6** 18 10 S 59 45W
Robson, Mt., *Canada* **130 C5** 53 10N 119 10W
Robstown, *U.S.A.* **139 M6** 27 47N 97 40W
Roca, C. da, *Portugal* **10 H4** 38 40N 9 31W
Roca Partida, I., *Mexico* **146 D2** 19 1N 112 2W
Rocas, I., *Brazil* **154 B5** 4 0 S 34 1W
Rocca d'Aspidé, *Italy* **41 B8** 40 27N 15 10 E
Rocca San Casciano, *Italy* **39 D8** 44 3N 11 45 E
Roccalbegna, *Italy* **39 F8** 42 47N 11 30 E
Roccastrada, *Italy* **39 F8** 43 0N 11 10 E
Roccella Iónica, *Italy* **41 D9** 38 20N 16 24 E
Rocha, *Uruguay* **159 C5** 34 30 S 54 25W
Rochdale, *U.K.* **16 D5** 53 36N 2 10W
Rochechouart, *France* **24 C4** 45 50N 0 49 E
Rochedo, *Brazil* **157 D7** 19 57 S 54 52W
Rochefort, *Belgium* **21 H6** 50 9N 5 12 E
Rochefort, *France* **24 C3** 45 56N 0 57W
Rochefort-en-Terre, *France* **22 E4** 47 42N 2 22W
Rochelle, *U.S.A.* **140 C7** 41 56N 89 4W
Rocher River, *Canada* **130 A6** 61 23N 112 44W
Rocherath, *Belgium* **21 H8** 50 26N 6 18 E
Rocheservière, *France* **22 F5** 46 57N 1 30W
Rochester, *Australia* **116 D6** 36 22 S 144 41 E
Rochester, *Canada* **130 C6** 54 22N 113 27W
Rochester, *U.K.* **17 F8** 51 22N 0 30 E
Rochester, *Ind., U.S.A.* **141 C10** 41 4N 86 13W
Rochester, *Mich., U.S.A.* **141 B13** 42 41N 83 8W
Rochester, *Minn., U.S.A.* **138 C8** 44 1N 92 28W
Rochester, *N.H., U.S.A.* **137 C14** 43 18N 70 59W
Rochester, *N.Y., U.S.A.* **136 C7** 43 10N 77 37W
Rociana, *Spain* **37 H4** 37 19N 6 35W
Rociu, *Romania* **46 E6** 44 43N 25 2 E
Rock →, *Canada* **130 A3** 60 7N 127 7W
Rock Falls, *U.S.A.* **140 C7** 41 47N 89 41W
Rock Flat, *Australia* **117 D8** 36 21 S 149 13 E
Rock Hill, *U.S.A.* **135 H5** 34 56N 81 1W
Rock Island, *U.S.A.* **140 C6** 41 30N 90 34W
Rock Rapids, *U.S.A.* **138 D6** 43 26N 96 10W
Rock River, *U.S.A.* **142 F11** 41 44N 105 58W
Rock Sound, *Bahamas* **148 B4** 24 54N 76 12W
Rock Springs, *Mont., U.S.A.* **142 C10** 46 49N 106 15W
Rock Springs, *Wyo., U.S.A.* **142 F9** 41 35N 109 14W
Rock Valley, *U.S.A.* **138 D6** 43 12N 96 18W
Rockall, *Atl. Oc.* **10 D3** 57 37N 13 42W
Rockanje, *Neths.* **20 E4** 51 52N 4 4 E
Rockdale, *Tex., U.S.A.* **139 K6** 30 39N 97 0W
Rockdale, *Wash., U.S.A.* **144 C5** 47 22N 121 28W
Rockefeller Plateau, *Antarctica* **7 E14** 80 0 S 140 0W
Rockford, *Ill., U.S.A.* **140 B7** 42 16N 89 6W
Rockford, *Iowa, U.S.A.* **140 A4** 43 3N 92 57W
Rockford, *Mich., U.S.A.* **141 A11** 43 7N 85 34W
Rockford, *Ohio, U.S.A.* **141 D12** 40 41N 84 39W
Rockglen, *Canada* **131 D7** 49 11N 105 57W
Rockhampton, *Australia* **114 C5** 23 22 S 150 32 E
Rockhampton Downs, *Australia* **114 B2** 18 57 S 135 10 E
Rockingham, *Australia* **113 F2** 32 15 S 115 38 E
Rockingham B., *Australia* **114 B4** 18 5 S 146 10 E
Rockingham Forest, *U.K.* **17 E7** 52 28N 0 42W
Rocklake, *U.S.A.* **138 A5** 48 47N 99 15W
Rockland, *Canada* **137 A9** 45 33N 75 17W
Rockland, *Idaho, U.S.A.* **142 E7** 42 34N 112 53W
Rockland, *Maine, U.S.A.* **129 D6** 44 6N 69 7W
Rockland, *Mich., U.S.A.* **138 B10** 46 44N 89 11W
Rocklin, *U.S.A.* **144 G5** 38 48N 121 14W
Rockmart, *U.S.A.* **135 H3** 34 0N 85 3W
Rockport, *Ind., U.S.A.* **141 G9** 37 53N 87 3W
Rockport, *Mo., U.S.A.* **138 E7** 40 25N 95 31W
Rockport, *Tex., U.S.A.* **139 L6** 28 2N 97 3W
Rocksprings, *U.S.A.* **139 K4** 30 1N 100 13W
Rockville, *Conn., U.S.A.* **137 E12** 41 52N 72 28W
Rockville, *Ind., U.S.A.* **141 E9** 39 46N 87 14W
Rockville, *Md., U.S.A.* **134 F7** 39 5N 77 9W
Rockwall, *U.S.A.* **139 J6** 32 56N 96 28W
Rockwell City, *U.S.A.* **140 B2** 42 24N 94 38W
Rockwood, *U.S.A.* **135 H3** 35 52N 84 41W
Rocky Ford, *U.S.A.* **138 F3** 38 3N 103 43W
Rocky Fork Lake, *U.S.A.* **141 E13** 39 12N 83 23W
Rocky Gully, *Australia* **113 F2** 34 30 S 116 57 E
Rocky Lane, *Canada* **130 B5** 58 31N 116 22W
Rocky Mount, *U.S.A.* **135 H7** 35 57N 77 48W
Rocky Mountain House, *Canada* **130 C6** 52 22N 114 55W
Rocky Mts., *N. Amer.* **130 C4** 55 0N 121 0W
Rockyford, *Canada* **130 C6** 51 14N 113 10W
Rocroi, *France* **23 C11** 49 55N 4 30 E
Rod, *Pakistan* **79 C1** 28 10N 63 5 E
Rødberg, *Norway* **14 D2** 60 17N 8 56 E
Rødby, *Denmark* **15 K5** 54 41N 11 23 E
Rødbyhavn, *Denmark* **15 K5** 54 39N 11 22 E
Roddickton, *Canada* **129 B8** 50 51N 56 8W
Rødding, *Denmark* **15 J3** 55 23N 9 3 E
Rødekro, *Denmark* **15 J3** 55 4N 9 20 E
Roden, *Neths.* **20 B8** 53 8N 6 26 E
Rødenes, *Norway* **14 E5** 59 35N 11 34 E
Rodenkirchen, *Germany* **26 B4** 53 24N 8 26 E
Roderick I., *Canada* **130 C3** 52 38N 128 22W
Rodez, *France* **24 D6** 44 21N 2 33 E
Rodholívas, *Greece* **44 D5** 40 55N 24 0 E
Rodhópi □, *Greece* **44 C7** 41 5N 25 30 E
Rodhopoú, *Greece* **32 D5** 35 34N 23 45 E
Ródhos, *Greece* **32 C10** 36 15N 28 10 E
Rodi Garganico, *Italy* **41 A8** 41 55N 15 53 E
Rodna, *Romania* **46 B5** 47 25N 24 50 E
Rodnei, Munţii, *Romania* **46 B5** 47 35N 24 35 E
Rodney, *Canada* **136 D3** 42 34N 81 41W
Rodney, C., *N.Z.* **118 C3** 36 17 S 174 50 E
Rodniki, *Russia* **51 C12** 57 7N 41 47 E
Rodriguez, *Ind. Oc.* **109 F5** 19 45 S 63 20 E
Roe →, *U.K.* **19 A5** 55 10N 6 59W
Roebling, *U.S.A.* **137 F10** 40 7N 74 47W
Roebourne, *Australia* **112 D2** 20 44 S 117 9 E
Roebuck B., *Australia* **112 C3** 18 5 S 122 20 E
Roebuck Plains, *Australia* **112 C3** 17 56 S 122 28 E
Roer →, *Neths.* **21 F7** 51 12N 5 59 E
Roermond, *Neths.* **21 F7** 51 12N 6 0 E
Roes Welcome Sd., *Canada* **127 B11** 65 0N 87 0W
Roeselare, *Belgium* **21 G2** 50 57N 3 7 E
Rœulx, *Belgium* **21 G4** 50 31N 4 7 E
Rogachev, *Belorussia* **50 E7** 53 8N 30 5 E
Rogaçica, *Serbia* **42 C4** 44 4N 19 40 E
Rogagua, L., *Bolivia* **156 C4** 13 43 S 66 50W
Rogaland fylke □, *Norway* **13 G9** 59 12N 6 20 E
Rogaška Slatina, *Slovenia* **39 B12** 46 15N 15 42 E
Rogatec, *Slovenia* **39 B12** 46 15N 15 46 E
Rogatica, *Bos.-H.* **42 D4** 43 47N 19 0 E
Rogatin, *Ukraine* **50 G4** 49 24N 24 36 E
Rogdhia, *Greece* **32 D7** 35 22N 25 1 E
Rogers, *U.S.A.* **139 G7** 36 20N 94 7W
Rogers City, *U.S.A.* **134 C4** 45 25N 83 49W
Rogerson, *U.S.A.* **142 E6** 42 13N 114 36W
Rogersville, *U.S.A.* **135 G4** 36 24N 83 1W
Roggan River, *Canada* **128 B4** 54 25N 79 32W
Roggel, *Neths.* **21 F7** 51 16N 5 56 E
Roggeveldberge, *S. Africa* **104 E3** 32 10 S 20 10 E
Roggiano Gravina, *Italy* **41 C9** 39 37N 16 9 E
Rogliano, *France* **25 F13** 42 57N 9 30 E
Rogliano, *Italy* **41 C9** 39 11N 16 20 E
Rogoaguado, L., *Bolivia* **157 C4** 13 0 S 65 30W
Rogowo, *Poland* **47 C4** 52 43N 17 38 E
Rogozno, *Poland* **47 C3** 52 45N 16 59 E
Rogue →, *U.S.A.* **142 E1** 42 26N 124 26W
Rohan, *France* **22 D4** 48 4N 2 45W
Róhda, *Greece* **32 A3** 39 48N 19 46 E
Rohnert Park, *U.S.A.* **144 G4** 38 16N 122 40W
Rohrbach-lès-Bitche, *France* **23 C14** 49 3N 7 15 E
Rohri, *Pakistan* **79 D3** 27 45N 68 51 E
Rohri Canal, *Pakistan* **80 F3** 26 15N 68 27 E
Rohtak, *India* **80 E7** 28 55N 76 43 E
Roi Et, *Thailand* **76 D4** 16 4N 103 40 E
Roisel, *France* **23 C10** 49 58N 3 6 E
Rojas, *Argentina* **158 C3** 34 10 S 60 45W
Rojo, C., *Mexico* **147 C5** 21 33N 97 20W
Rokan →, *Indonesia* **74 B2** 2 0N 100 50 E
Rokeby, *Australia* **114 A3** 13 39 S 142 40 E
Rokiškis, *Lithuania* **50 D4** 55 55N 25 35 E
Rokitno, *Russia* **50 F9** 50 57N 35 56 E
Rokycany, *Czech.* **30 B6** 49 43N 13 35 E
Rolândia, *Brazil* **159 A5** 23 18 S 51 23W
Rolde, *Neths.* **20 C9** 52 59N 6 39 E
Rolette, *U.S.A.* **138 A5** 48 40N 99 51W
Rolfe, *U.S.A.* **140 B2** 42 49N 94 31W
Rolla, *Kans., U.S.A.* **139 G4** 37 7N 101 38W
Rolla, *Mo., U.S.A.* **139 G9** 37 57N 91 46W
Rolla, *N. Dak., U.S.A.* **138 A5** 48 52N 99 37W
Rollag, *Norway* **14 D3** 60 2N 9 18 E
Rollands Plains, *Australia* **117 A10** 31 17 S 152 42 E
Rolle, *Switz.* **28 D2** 46 28N 6 20 E
Rolleston, *Australia* **114 C4** 24 28 S 148 35 E
Rolleston, *N.Z.* **119 D7** 43 35 S 172 24 E
Rolling Fork →, *U.S.A.* **141 G11** 37 55N 85 50W
Rollingstone, *Australia* **114 B4** 19 2 S 146 24 E
Rom, *Sudan* **95 F3** 9 54N 32 16 E
Roma, *Australia* **115 D4** 26 32 S 148 49 E
Roma, *Italy* **40 A5** 41 54N 12 30 E
Roma, *Sweden* **13 H15** 57 32N 18 26 E
Roman, *Bulgaria* **43 D8** 43 8N 23 54 E
Roman, *Romania* **46 C7** 46 57N 26 55 E
Roman, *Russia* **57 C12** 60 4N 112 14 E
Roman-Kosh, Gora, *Ukraine* **52 D6** 44 37N 34 15 E
Romanche →, *France* **25 C9** 45 5N 5 43 E
Romang, *Indonesia* **72 C3** 7 30 S 127 20 E
Români, *Egypt* **91 E1** 30 59N 32 38 E
Romania ■, *Europe* **46 C5** 46 0N 25 0 E
Romanija, *Bos.-H.* **42 D3** 43 50N 18 45 E
Romano, Cayo, *Cuba* **148 B4** 22 0N 77 30W
Romano di Lombardía, *Italy* **38 C6** 45 32N 9 45 E
Romanovka = Bessarabka, *Moldavia* **52 C3** 46 21N 28 58 E
Romans-sur-Isère, *France* **25 C9** 45 3N 5 3 E
Romanshorn, *Switz.* **29 A8** 47 33N 9 22 E
Romblon, *Phil.* **70 E4** 12 33N 122 17 E
Romblon □, *Phil.* **70 E4** 12 30N 122 15 E
Romblon Pass, *Phil.* **70 E4** 12 27N 122 12 E
Rombo □, *Tanzania* **106 C4** 3 10 S 37 30 E
Rome = Roma, *Italy* **40 A5** 41 54N 12 30 E
Rome, *Ga., U.S.A.* **135 H3** 34 15N 85 10W
Rome, *N.Y., U.S.A.* **137 C9** 43 13N 75 27W
Romeleåsen, *Sweden* **15 J7** 55 34N 13 33 E
Romenay, *France* **25 B9** 46 30N 5 1 E
Romerike, *Norway* **14 D5** 60 7N 11 10 E
Romilly-sur-Seine, *France* **23 D10** 48 31N 3 44 E
Romîni, *Romania* **46 E5** 44 59N 24 11 E
Rommani, *Morocco* **98 B3** 33 31N 6 40W
Romney, *U.S.A.* **134 F6** 39 21N 78 45W
Romney Marsh, *U.K.* **17 F8** 51 4N 0 58 E
Romny, *Ukraine* **50 F8** 50 48N 33 28 E
Rømø, *Denmark* **15 J2** 55 10N 8 30 E
Romodan, *Ukraine* **50 G8** 49 55N 33 15 E
Romodanovo, *Russia* **51 D14** 54 26N 45 23 E
Romont, *Switz.* **28 C3** 46 42N 6 54 E
Romorantin-Lanthenay, *France* **23 E8** 47 21N 1 45 E
Rompin →, *Malaysia* **74 B2** 2 49N 103 29 E
Romsdalen, *Norway* **14 B2** 62 25N 8 0 E
Ron, *Vietnam* **76 D6** 17 53N 106 27 E
Rona, *U.K.* **18 D3** 57 33N 5 57W
Ronan, *U.S.A.* **142 C6** 47 32N 114 6W
Roncador, Cayos, *Caribbean* **148 D3** 13 32N 80 4W
Roncador, Serra do, *Brazil* **155 D1** 12 30 S 52 30W
Roncesvalles, Paso, *Spain* **34 B3** 43 1N 1 19W
Ronceverte, *U.S.A.* **134 G5** 37 45N 80 28W
Ronciglione, *Italy* **39 F9** 42 18N 12 12 E
Ronco →, *Italy* **39 D9** 44 24N 12 12 E
Ronda, *Spain* **37 J5** 36 46N 5 12W
Ronda, Serranía de, *Spain* **37 J5** 36 44N 5 3W
Rondane, *Norway* **14 C3** 61 57N 9 50 E
Rondón, *Colombia* **152 B3** 6 17N 71 6W
Rondônia, *Brazil* **157 C5** 10 52 S 61 57W
Rondônia □, *Brazil* **157 C5** 11 0 S 63 0W
Rondonópolis, *Brazil* **157 D7** 16 28 S 54 38W
Rong Jiang →, *China* **68 E7** 24 35N 109 20 E
Rong Xian, *Guangxi Zhuangzu, China* **69 F8** 22 50N 110 31 E
Rong Xian, *Sichuan, China* **68 C5** 29 23N 104 22 E
Rong'an, *China* **68 E7** 25 14N 109 22 E
Rongchang, *China* **68 C5** 29 20N 105 32 E
Ronge, L. la, *Canada* **131 B7** 55 6N 105 17W
Rongjiang, *China* **68 E7** 25 57N 108 28 E
Rongotea, *N.Z.* **118 G4** 40 19 S 175 25 E
Rongshui, *China* **68 E7** 25 5N 109 12 E
Ronne Ice Shelf, *Antarctica* **7 D18** 78 0 S 60 0W
Ronsard, C., *Australia* **113 D1** 24 46 S 113 10 E
Ronse, *Belgium* **21 G3** 50 45N 3 35 E
Ronuro →, *Brazil* **157 C7** 11 56 S 53 33W
Roodepoort, *S. Africa* **105 D4** 26 11 S 27 54 E
Roodeschool, *Neths.* **20 B9** 53 25N 6 46 E
Roodhouse, *U.S.A.* **140 E6** 39 29N 90 24W
Roof Butte, *U.S.A.* **143 H9** 36 28N 109 5W
Roompot, *Neths.* **21 E3** 51 37N 3 44 E
Roorkee, *India* **80 E7** 29 52N 77 59 E
Roosendaal, *Neths.* **21 E4** 51 32N 4 29 E
Roosevelt, *Minn., U.S.A.* **138 A7** 48 48N 95 6W
Roosevelt, *Utah, U.S.A.* **142 F8** 40 18N 109 59W
Roosevelt →, *Brazil* **157 B5** 7 35 S 60 20W
Roosevelt, Mt., *Canada* **130 B3** 58 26N 125 20W
Roosevelt I., *Antarctica* **7 D12** 79 30 S 162 0W
Roosevelt Res., *U.S.A.* **143 K8** 33 46N 111 0W
Ropczyce, *Poland* **31 A14** 50 4N 21 38 E
Roper →, *Australia* **114 A2** 14 43 S 135 27 E
Ropesville, *U.S.A.* **139 J3** 33 26N 102 9W
Roque Pérez, *Argentina* **158 D4** 35 25 S 59 24W
Roquefort, *France* **24 D3** 44 2N 0 20W
Roquemaure, *France* **25 D8** 44 3N 4 48 E
Roquetas, *Spain* **34 E5** 40 50N 0 30 E
Roquevaire, *France* **25 E9** 43 20N 5 36 E
Roraima □, *Brazil* **153 C5** 2 0N 61 30W
Roraima, Mt., *Venezuela* **153 B5** 5 10N 60 40W
Rorketon, *Canada* **131 C9** 51 24N 99 35W
Røros, *Norway* **14 B5** 62 35N 11 23 E
Rorschach, *Switz.* **29 B8** 47 28N 9 28 E

258 Sabadell

Sabadell, *Spain* **34 D7** 41 28N 2 7 E
Sabae, *Japan* **63 B8** 35 57N 136 11 E
Sabah □, *Malaysia* **75 A5** 6 0N 117 0 E
Sabak Bernam, *Malaysia* **77 L3** 3 46N 100 58 E
Sábana de la Mar, *Dom. Rep.* **149 C6** 19 7N 69 24W
Sábanalarga, *Colombia* **152 A3** 10 38N 74 55W
Sabang, *Indonesia* **74 A1** 5 50N 95 15 E
Sabangan, *Phil.* **70 C3** 17 0N 120 55 E
Sabará, *Brazil* **155 E3** 19 55 S 43 46W
Sabarania, *Indonesia* **73 B5** 2 5 S 138 18 E
Sabari →, *India* **82 F5** 17 35N 81 16 E
Sab'atayn, Ramlat as, *Yemen* **86 D4** 15 30N 46 10 E
Sabattis, *U.S.A.* **137 B10** 44 6N 74 40W
Sabáudia, *Italy* **40 A6** 41 17N 13 2 E
Sabaya, *Bolivia* **156 D4** 19 1 S 68 23W
Sabāyā, Jaz., *Si. Arabia* **86 C3** 18 35N 41 3 E
Sabhah, *Libya* **96 C2** 27 9N 14 29 E
Sabhah □, *Libya* **96 C2** 26 0N 14 0 E
Sabie, *S. Africa* **105 D5** 25 10 S 30 48 E
Sabina, *U.S.A.* **141 E13** 39 29N 83 38W
Sabinal, *Mexico* **146 A3** 30 58N 107 25W
Sabinal, *U.S.A.* **139 L5** 29 19N 99 28W
Sabinal, Punta del, *Spain* **35 J2** 36 43N 2 44W
Sabinas, *Mexico* **146 B4** 27 50N 101 10W
Sabinas →, *Mexico* **146 B4** 27 37N 100 42W
Sabinas Hidalgo, *Mexico* **146 B4** 26 33N 100 10W
Sabine →, *U.S.A.* **139 L8** 29 59N 93 47W
Sabine L., *U.S.A.* **139 L8** 29 53N 93 51W
Sabine Pass, *U.S.A.* **139 L8** 29 44N 93 54W
Sabinópolis, *Brazil* **155 E3** 18 40 S 43 6W
Sabinov, *Slovak Rep.* **31 B14** 49 6N 21 5 E
Sabirabad, *Azerbaijan* **53 F13** 40 5N 48 30 E
Sabkhat Tāwurghā', *Libya* **96 B3** 31 48N 15 30 E
Sabkhet el Bardawîl, *Egypt* **91 D2** 31 10N 33 15 E
Sablayan, *Phil.* **70 E3** 12 50N 120 50 E
Sable, C., *U.S.A.* **133 E10** 25 9N 81 8W
Sable, C., *Canada* **129 D6** 43 29N 65 38W
Sable I., *Canada* **129 D8** 44 0N 60 0W
Sablé-sur-Sarthe, *France* **22 E6** 47 50N 0 20W
Saboeiro, *Brazil* **154 C4** 6 32 S 39 54W
Sabolev, *Russia* **57 D16** 54 20N 155 30 E
Sabor →, *Portugal* **36 D3** 41 10N 7 7W
Sabou, *Burkina Faso* **100 C4** 12 1N 2 15W
Sabrātah, *Libya* **96 B2** 32 47N 12 29 E
Sabria, *Tunisia* **96 B1** 33 22N 8 45 E
Sabrina Coast, *Antarctica* **7 C9** 68 0 S 120 0 E
Sabtang I., *Phil.* **70 A3** 20 19N 121 52 E
Sabugal, *Portugal* **36 E3** 40 20N 7 5W
Sabula, *U.S.A.* **140 B6** 42 4N 90 10W
Sabulubek, *Indonesia* **74 C1** 1 36 S 98 40 E
Şabyā, *Si. Arabia* **86 C3** 17 9N 42 37 E
Sabzevār, *Iran* **85 B8** 36 15N 57 40 E
Sabzvārān, *Iran* **85 D8** 28 45N 57 50 E
Sac City, *U.S.A.* **140 B2** 42 25N 95 0W
Sacedón, *Spain* **34 E2** 40 29N 2 41W
Sachigo →, *Canada* **128 A2** 55 6N 88 58W
Sachigo, L., *Canada* **128 B1** 53 50N 92 12W
Sachkhere, *Georgia* **53 E10** 42 25N 43 28 E
Sachseln, *Switz.* **29 C6** 46 52N 8 15 E
Sachsen □, *Germany* **26 E9** 51 0N 13 0 E
Sachsen-Anhalt □, *Germany* **26 D8** 52 0N 12 0 E
Sacile, *Italy* **39 C9** 45 58N 12 30 E
Sackets Harbor, *U.S.A.* **137 C8** 43 57N 76 7W
Saco, *Maine, U.S.A.* **135 D10** 43 30N 70 27W
Saco, *Mont., U.S.A.* **142 B10** 48 28N 107 21W
Sacramento, *Brazil* **155 E2** 19 53 S 47 27W
Sacramento, *U.S.A.* **144 G5** 38 35N 121 29W
Sacramento →, *U.S.A.* **144 G5** 38 3N 121 56W
Sacramento Mts., *U.S.A.* **143 K11** 32 30N 105 30W
Sacramento Valley, *U.S.A.* **144 G5** 39 30N 122 0W
Sacratif, C., *Spain* **35 J1** 36 42N 3 28W
Săcueni, *Romania* **46 B3** 47 20N 22 5 E
Sada, *Spain* **36 B2** 43 22N 8 15W
Sada-Misaki-Hantō, *Japan* **62 D4** 33 22N 132 1 E
Sádaba, *Spain* **34 C3** 42 19N 1 12W
Sadani, *Tanzania* **106 D4** 5 58 S 38 35 E
Sadao, *Thailand* **77 J3** 6 38N 100 26 E
Sadaseopet, *India* **82 F3** 17 38N 77 59 E
Sadd el Aali, *Egypt* **94 C3** 23 54N 32 54 E
Saddle Mt., *U.S.A.* **144 E3** 45 58N 123 41W
Sade, *Nigeria* **101 C7** 11 22N 10 45 E
Şadh, *Oman* **87 C6** 17 3N 55 4 E
Sadieville, *U.S.A.* **141 F12** 38 23N 84 32W
Sadimi, *Zaïre* **103 D4** 9 25 S 23 32 E
Sadiya, *India* **78 B5** 27 50N 95 40 E
Sado, *Japan* **60 E9** 38 0N 138 25 E
Sado →, *Portugal* **37 G2** 38 29N 8 55W
Sadon, *Russia* **53 E10** 42 52N 43 58 E
Sæby, *Denmark* **15 G4** 57 21N 10 30 E
Saegerstown, *U.S.A.* **136 E4** 41 43N 80 9W
Saelices, *Spain* **34 F2** 39 55N 2 49W
Safaga, *Egypt* **94 B3** 26 42N 34 0 E
Şafājah, *Si. Arabia* **84 E3** 26 25N 39 0 E
Šafárikovo = Tornala, *Slovak Rep.* **31 C13** 48 25N 20 20 E
Safata B., *W. Samoa* **121 X24** 14 0 S 171 50W
Safed Koh, *Afghan.* **79 B3** 34 0N 70 0 E
Säffle, *Sweden* **13 G12** 59 8N 12 55 E
Safford, *U.S.A.* **143 K9** 32 50N 109 43W
Saffron Walden, *U.K.* **17 E8** 52 2N 0 15 E
Safi, *Morocco* **98 B3** 32 18N 9 20W
Şafīābād, *Iran* **85 B8** 36 45N 57 58 E
Safīd Dasht, *Iran* **85 C6** 33 27N 48 11 E
Safīd Kūh, *Afghan.* **79 B1** 34 45N 63 0 E
Safonovo, *Russia* **50 D8** 55 4N 33 16 E
Safranbolu, *Turkey* **52 F5** 41 15N 32 41 E
Safwān, *Iraq* **84 D5** 30 7N 47 43 E
Sag Harbor, *U.S.A.* **137 F12** 41 0N 72 18W
Sag Sag, *Papua N. G.* **120 C5** 5 32 S 148 23 E
Saga, *Indonesia* **73 B4** 2 40 S 132 55 E
Saga, *Kōchi, Japan* **62 D5** 33 5N 133 6 E
Saga, *Saga, Japan* **62 D2** 33 15N 130 16 E
Saga □, *Japan* **62 D2** 33 15N 130 20 E
Sagae, *Japan* **60 E10** 38 22N 140 17 E
Sagaing □, *Burma* **78 D5** 23 55N 95 56 E
Sagala, *Mali* **100 C3** 14 9N 6 38W
Sagami-Nada, *Japan* **63 C11** 34 58N 139 30 E
Sagami-Wan, *Japan* **63 B11** 35 15N 139 25 E
Sagamihara, *Japan* **63 B11** 35 33N 139 25 E
Saganoseki, *Japan* **62 D3** 33 15N 131 53 E
Sagar, *India* **83 G2** 14 14N 75 6 E
Sagara, *Japan* **63 C10** 34 41N 138 12 E
Sagara, L., *Tanzania* **106 D3** 5 20 S 31 0 E
Sagawa, *Japan* **62 D5** 33 28N 133 11 E
Sagay, *Phil.* **71 F4** 10 57N 123 25 E
Saginaw, *U.S.A.* **134 D4** 43 26N 83 56W
Saginaw B., *U.S.A.* **134 D4** 43 50N 83 40W
Sagīr, Zab as →, *Iraq* **84 C4** 35 10N 43 20 E
Sagleipie, *Liberia* **100 D3** 7 0N 8 52W
Saglouc, *Canada* **127 B12** 62 14N 75 38W
Sagŏ-ri, *S. Korea* **67 G14** 35 25N 126 49 E
Sagone, *France* **25 F12** 42 7N 8 42 E
Sagone, G. de, *France* **25 F12** 42 4N 8 40 E
Sagres, *Portugal* **37 J2** 37 0N 8 58W
Sagu, *Burma* **78 E5** 20 13N 94 46 E
Sagua la Grande, *Cuba* **148 B3** 22 50N 80 10W
Saguache, *U.S.A.* **143 G10** 38 5N 106 8W
Saguenay →, *Canada* **129 C5** 48 22N 71 0W
Sagunto, *Spain* **34 F4** 39 42N 0 18W
Sahaba, *Sudan* **94 D3** 18 57N 30 25 E
Sahagún, *Colombia* **152 B2** 8 57N 75 27W
Sahagún, *Spain* **36 C5** 42 18N 5 2W
Saḩam al Jawlān, *Syria* **91 C4** 32 45N 35 55 E
Sahand, Kūh-e, *Iran* **84 B5** 37 44N 46 27 E
Sahara, *Africa* **92 D4** 23 0N 5 0 E
Saharan Atlas = Saharien, Atlas, *Algeria* **99 B5** 33 30N 1 0 E
Saharanpur, *India* **80 E7** 29 58N 77 33 E
Saharien, Atlas, *Algeria* **99 B5** 33 30N 1 0 E
Sahasinaka, *Madag.* **105 C8** 21 49 S 47 49 E
Sahaswan, *India* **81 E8** 28 5N 78 45 E
Sahel, Canal du, *Mali* **100 C3** 14 20N 6 0W
Sahibganj, *India* **81 G12** 25 12N 87 40 E
Sahiwal, *Pakistan* **79 C4** 30 45N 73 8 E
Şaḩneh, *Iran* **84 C5** 34 29N 47 41 E
Sahtaneh →, *Canada* **130 B4** 59 2N 122 28W
Sahuaripa, *Mexico* **146 B3** 29 0N 109 13W
Sahuarita, *U.S.A.* **143 L8** 31 57N 110 58W
Sahuayo, *Mexico* **146 C4** 20 4N 102 43W
Sahy, *Slovak Rep.* **31 C11** 48 4N 18 55 E
Sai Buri, *Thailand* **77 J3** 6 43N 101 45 E
Sai-Cinza, *Brazil* **157 B6** 6 17 S 57 42W
Saibai I., *Australia* **120 E2** 9 25 S 142 40 E
Sa'id Bundas, *Sudan* **97 G4** 8 24N 24 48 E
Saïda, *Algeria* **99 B5** 34 50N 0 11 E
Saʻīdābād, *Kermān, Iran* **85 D7** 29 30N 55 45 E
Saʻīdābād, *Semnān, Iran* **85 B7** 36 8N 54 11 E
Saïdia, *Morocco* **99 A4** 35 5N 2 14W
Sa'idiyeh, *Iran* **85 B6** 36 20N 48 55 E
Saidor, *Papua N. G.* **120 C4** 5 40 S 146 29 E
Saidpur, *Bangla.* **78 C2** 25 48N 89 0 E
Saidu, *Pakistan* **79 B4** 34 43N 72 24 E
Saignelégier, *Switz.* **28 B3** 47 15N 7 0 E
Saignes, *France* **24 C6** 45 20N 2 31 E
Saigō, *Japan* **62 A5** 36 12N 133 20 E
Saigon = Phanh Bho Ho Chi Minh, *Vietnam* **77 G6** 10 58N 106 40 E
Saijō, *Ehime, Japan* **62 D5** 33 55N 133 11 E
Saijō, *Hiroshima, Japan* **62 C4** 34 25N 132 45 E
Saiki, *Japan* **62 E3** 32 58N 131 51 E
Saillans, *France* **25 D9** 44 42N 5 12 E
Sailolof, *Indonesia* **73 B4** 1 7 S 130 46 E
Saimbeyli, *Turkey* **88 E7** 37 59N 36 6 E
Şa'in Dezh, *Iran* **84 B5** 36 40N 46 25 E
St. Abb's Head, *U.K.* **18 F6** 55 55N 2 10W
St. Aegyd, *Austria* **30 D8** 47 52N 15 33 E
St.-Affrique, *France* **24 E6** 43 57N 2 53 E
St.-Agrève, *France* **25 C8** 45 0N 4 23 E
St.-Aignan, *France* **22 E8** 47 16N 1 22 E
St. Alban's, *Canada* **129 C8** 47 51N 55 50W
St. Albans, *U.K.* **17 F7** 51 44N 0 19W
St. Albans, *Vt., U.S.A.* **137 B11** 44 49N 73 5W
St. Albans, *W. Va., U.S.A.* **134 F5** 38 23N 81 50W
St. Alban's Head, *U.K.* **17 G5** 50 34N 2 3W
St. Albert, *Canada* **130 C6** 53 37N 113 32W
St.-Amand-en-Puisaye, *France* **23 E10** 47 32N 3 5 E
St.-Amand-les-Eaux, *France* **23 B10** 50 27N 3 25 E
St.-Amand-Mont-Rond, *France* **24 B6** 46 43N 2 30 E
St.-Amarin, *France* **23 E14** 47 54N 7 2 E
St.-Amour, *France* **25 B9** 46 26N 5 21 E
St.-André-de-Cubzac, *France* **24 D3** 44 59N 0 26W
St.-André-de-l'Eure, *France* **22 D8** 48 54N 1 16 E
St.-André-les-Alpes, *France* **25 E10** 43 58N 6 30 E
St. Andrew's, *Canada* **129 C8** 47 45N 59 15W
St. Andrews, *N.Z.* **119 E6** 44 33 S 171 10 E
St. Andrews, *U.K.* **18 E6** 56 20N 2 48W
St-Anicet, *Canada* **137 A10** 45 8N 74 22W
St. Ann B., *Canada* **129 C7** 46 22N 60 25W
St. Anne, *U.K.* **22 C4** 49 43N 2 11W
St. Anne, *U.S.A.* **141 C9** 41 1N 87 43W
St. Ann's Bay, *Jamaica* **148 C4** 18 26N 77 15W
St. Anthony, *Canada* **129 B8** 51 22N 55 35W
St. Anthony, *U.S.A.* **142 E8** 43 58N 111 41W
St.-Antonin-Noble-Val, *France* **24 D5** 44 10N 1 45 E
St. Arnaud, *Australia* **116 D5** 36 40 S 143 16 E
St. Arnaud Ra., *N.Z.* **119 C7** 42 1 S 172 53 E
St. Arthur, *Canada* **129 C6** 47 33N 67 46W
St. Asaph, *U.K.* **16 D4** 53 15N 3 27W
St.-Astier, *France* **24 C4** 45 8N 0 31 E
St.-Aubin, *Switz.* **28 C3** 46 54N 6 47 E
St.-Aubin-du-Cormier, *France* **22 D5** 48 15N 1 26W
St-Augustin-Saguenay, *Canada* **129 B8** 51 13N 58 38W
St. Augustine, *U.S.A.* **135 L5** 29 54N 81 19W
St. Austell, *U.K.* **17 G3** 50 20N 4 48W
St.-Avold, *France* **23 C13** 49 6N 6 43 E
St.-Barthélemy, I., *W. Indies* **149 C7** 17 50N 62 50W
St. Bathans, *N.Z.* **119 E4** 44 53 S 169 50 E
St. Bathan's Mt., *N.Z.* **119 E4** 44 45 S 169 45 E
St. Bee's Hd., *U.K.* **16 C4** 54 30N 3 38W
St.-Benoît-du-Sault, *France* **24 B5** 46 26N 1 24 E
St.-Bernard, Col du Grand, *Europe* **28 E4** 45 53N 7 11 E
St.-Bernard, Col du Petit, *France* **25 C10** 45 41N 6 51 E
St.-Blaise, *Switz.* **28 B3** 47 1N 6 59 E
St. Boniface, *Canada* **131 D9** 49 53N 97 5W
St.-Bonnet, *France* **25 D10** 44 40N 6 5 E
St.-Brévin-les-Pins, *France* **22 E4** 47 14N 2 10W
St.-Brice-en-Coglès, *France* **22 D5** 48 25N 1 22W
St. Bride's, *Canada* **129 C9** 46 56N 54 10W
St. Brides B., *U.K.* **17 F2** 51 48N 5 15W
St.-Brieuc, *France* **22 D4** 48 30N 2 46W
St.-Calais, *France* **22 E7** 47 55N 0 45 E
St.-Cast-le-Guildo, *France* **22 D4** 48 37N 2 18W
St. Catharines, *Canada* **128 D4** 43 10N 79 15W
St. Catherines I., *U.S.A.* **135 K5** 31 40N 81 10W
St. Catherine's Pt., *U.K.* **17 G6** 50 34N 1 18W
St.-Céré, *France* **24 D5** 44 51N 1 54 E
St.-Cergue, *Switz.* **28 D2** 46 27N 6 10 E
St.-Cernin, *France* **24 C6** 45 5N 2 25 E
St.-Chamond, *France* **25 C8** 45 28N 4 31 E
St. Charles, *Ill., U.S.A.* **141 C8** 41 54N 88 19W
St. Charles, *Mo., U.S.A.* **140 F6** 38 47N 90 29W
St.-Chély-d'Apcher, *France* **24 D7** 44 48N 3 17 E
St.-Chinian, *France* **24 E6** 43 25N 2 56 E
St. Christopher = St. Kitts, *W. Indies* **149 C7** 17 20N 62 40W
St. Christopher-Nevis ■, *W. Indies* **149 C7** 17 20N 62 40W
St.-Ciers-sur-Gironde, *France* **24 C3** 45 17N 0 37W
St. Clair, *Mich., U.S.A.* **136 D2** 42 50N 82 30W
St. Clair, *Mo., U.S.A.* **140 F6** 38 21N 90 59W
St. Clair, *Pa., U.S.A.* **137 F8** 40 43N 76 12W
St. Clair, L., *Canada* **128 D3** 42 30N 82 45W
St. Clair Shores, *U.S.A.* **141 B14** 42 30N 82 53W
St. Clairsville, *U.S.A.* **136 F4** 40 5N 80 54W
St.-Claud, *France* **24 C4** 45 54N 0 28 E
St. Claude, *Canada* **131 D9** 49 40N 98 20W
St.-Claude, *France* **25 B9** 46 22N 5 52 E
St. Cloud, *Fla., U.S.A.* **135 L5** 28 15N 81 17W
St. Cloud, *Minn., U.S.A.* **138 C7** 45 34N 94 10W
St-Coeur de Marie, *Canada* **129 C5** 48 39N 71 43W
St. Cricq, C., *Australia* **113 E1** 25 17 S 113 6 E
St. Croix, *Virgin Is.* **149 C7** 17 45N 64 45W
St. Croix →, *U.S.A.* **138 C8** 44 45N 92 48W
St. Croix Falls, *U.S.A.* **138 C8** 45 24N 92 38W
St.-Cyr-sur-Mer, *France* **25 E9** 43 11N 5 43 E
St. David, *U.S.A.* **140 D6** 40 30N 90 3W
St. David's, *Canada* **129 C8** 48 12N 58 52W
St. David's, *U.K.* **17 F2** 51 54N 5 16W
St. David's Head, *U.K.* **17 F2** 51 55N 5 16W
St.-Denis, *France* **23 D9** 48 56N 2 22 E
St.-Denis, *Réunion* **109 G4** 20 52 S 55 27 E
St.-Denis-d'Orques, *France* **22 D6** 48 2N 0 17W
St.-Dié, *France* **23 D13** 48 17N 6 56 E
St.-Dizier, *France* **23 D11** 48 38N 4 56 E
St.-Égrève, *France* **25 C9** 45 14N 5 41 E
St. Elias, Mt., *U.S.A.* **126 B5** 60 18N 140 56W
St. Elias Mts., *Canada* **130 A1** 60 33N 139 28W
St.-Élie, *Fr. Guiana* **153 C7** 4 49N 53 17W
St. Elmo, *U.S.A.* **141 E8** 39 2N 88 51W
St.-Eloy-les-Mines, *France* **24 B6** 46 10N 2 51 E
St.-Émilion, *France* **24 D3** 44 53N 0 9W
St.-Étienne, *France* **25 C8** 45 27N 4 22 E
St.-Étienne-de-Tinée, *France* **25 D10** 44 16N 6 56 E
St. Eugène, *Canada* **137 A10** 45 30N 74 28W
St. Eustatius, *W. Indies* **149 C7** 17 20N 63 0W
St-Félicien, *Canada* **128 C5** 48 40N 72 25W
St.-Florent, *France* **25 F13** 42 41N 9 18 E
St.-Florent-sur-Cher, *France* **23 F9** 46 59N 2 15 E
St.-Florentin, *France* **23 D10** 48 0N 3 45 E
St.-Flour, *France* **24 C7** 45 2N 3 6 E
St.-Fons, *France* **25 C8** 45 42N 4 52 E
St. Francis, *U.S.A.* **138 F4** 39 47N 101 48W
St. Francis →, *U.S.A.* **139 H9** 34 38N 90 36W
St. Francis, C., *S. Africa* **104 E3** 34 14 S 24 49 E
St. Francisville, *Ill., U.S.A.* **141 F9** 38 36N 87 39W
St. Francisville, *La., U.S.A.* **139 K9** 30 47N 91 23W
St-François, L., *Canada* **137 A10** 45 10N 74 22W
St.-Fulgent, *France* **22 F5** 46 50N 1 10W
St-Gabriel-de-Brandon, *Canada* **128 C5** 46 17N 73 24W
St. Gallen = Sankt Gallen, *Switz.* **29 B8** 47 26N 9 22 E
St.-Gaudens, *France* **24 E4** 43 6N 0 44 E
St.-Gengoux-le-National, *France* **25 B8** 46 37N 4 40 E
St.-Geniez-d'Olt, *France* **24 D6** 44 27N 2 58 E
St. George, *Australia* **115 D4** 28 1 S 148 30 E
St. George, *Canada* **129 C6** 45 11N 66 50W
St. George, *S.C., U.S.A.* **135 J5** 33 11N 80 35W
St. George, *Utah, U.S.A.* **143 H7** 37 6N 113 35W
St. George, C., *Canada* **129 C8** 48 30N 59 16W
St. George, C., *Papua N. G.* **120 C7** 4 49 S 152 53 E
St. George, C., *U.S.A.* **135 L3** 29 40N 85 5W
St. George Ra., *Australia* **112 C4** 18 40 S 125 0 E
St-Georges, *Belgium* **21 G6** 50 37N 5 20 E
St. George's, *Canada* **129 C8** 48 26N 58 31W
St-Georges, *Canada* **129 C5** 46 8N 70 40W
St.-Georges, *Fr. Guiana* **153 C7** 4 0N 52 0W
St. George's, *Grenada* **149 D7** 12 5N 61 43W
St. George's B., *Canada* **129 C8** 48 24N 58 53W
St. Georges Basin, *Australia* **112 C4** 15 23 S 125 2 E
St. George's Channel, *Papua N. G.* **120 C7** 4 10 S 152 20 E
St. George's Channel, *U.K.* **19 E6** 52 0N 6 0W
St.-Georges-de-Didonne, *France* **24 C3** 45 36N 1 0W
St. Georges Hd., *Australia* **117 C9** 35 12 S 150 42 E
St.-Gérard, *Belgium* **21 H5** 50 21N 4 44 E
St.-Germain-de-Calberte, *France* **24 D7** 44 13N 3 48 E
St.-Germain-des-Fossés, *France* **24 B7** 46 12N 3 26 E
St.-Germain-du-Plain, *France* **23 F11** 46 42N 4 58 E
St.-Germain-en-Laye, *France* **23 D9** 48 54N 2 6 E
St.-Germain-Laval, *France* **25 C8** 45 50N 4 1 E
St.-Germain-Lembron, *France* **24 C7** 45 27N 3 14 E
St.-Gervais-d'Auvergne, *France* **24 B6** 46 4N 2 50 E
St.-Gervais-les-Bains, *France* **25 C10** 45 53N 6 42 E
St.-Gildas, Pte. de, *France* **22 E4** 47 8N 2 14W
St.-Gilles, *France* **25 E8** 43 40N 4 26 E
St.-Gilles-Croix-de-Vie, *France* **24 B2** 46 41N 1 55W
St.-Gingolph, *Switz.* **28 D3** 46 24N 6 48 E
St.-Girons, *France* **24 F5** 42 59N 1 8 E
St. Gotthard P. = San Gottardo, Paso del, *Switz.* **29 C7** 46 33N 8 33 E
St.-Gualtier, *France* **22 F8** 46 39N 1 26 E
St.-Guénolé, *France* **22 E2** 47 49N 4 23W
St. Helena, *U.S.A.* **142 G2** 38 30N 122 28W
St. Helena ■, *Atl. Oc.* **9 K8** 15 55 S 5 44W
St. Helena, Mt., *U.S.A.* **144 G4** 38 40N 122 36W
St. Helena B., *S. Africa* **104 E2** 32 40 S 18 10 E
St. Helens, *Australia* **114 G4** 41 20 S 148 15 E
St. Helens, *U.K.* **16 D5** 53 28N 2 44W
St. Helens, *U.S.A.* **144 E4** 45 52N 122 48W
St. Helens, Mt., *U.S.A.* **144 D4** 46 12N 122 12W
St. Helier, *U.K.* **17 H5** 49 11N 2 6W
St.-Hilaire-du-Harcouët, *France* **22 D5** 48 35N 1 5W
St.-Hippolyte, *France* **23 E13** 47 19N 6 50 E
St.-Hippolyte-du-Fort, *France* **24 E7** 43 58N 3 52 E
St.-Honoré-les-Bains, *France* **23 F10** 46 54N 3 50 E
St-Hubert, *Belgium* **21 H6** 50 2N 5 23 E
St-Hyacinthe, *Canada* **128 C5** 45 40N 72 58W
St. Ignace, *U.S.A.* **134 C3** 45 52N 84 44W
St. Ignace I., *Canada* **128 C2** 48 45N 88 0W
St. Ignatius, *U.S.A.* **142 C6** 47 19N 114 6W
St-Imier, *Switz.* **28 B3** 47 9N 6 58 E
St. Ives, *Cambs., U.K.* **17 E7** 52 20N 0 5W
St. Ives, *Corn., U.K.* **17 G2** 50 13N 5 29W
St.-James, *France* **22 D5** 48 31N 1 20W
St. James, *Minn., U.S.A.* **138 D7** 43 59N 94 38W
St. James, *Mo., U.S.A.* **140 G5** 38 0N 91 37W
St-Jean, *Canada* **128 C5** 45 20N 73 20W
St-Jean →, *Canada* **129 B7** 50 17N 64 20W
St-Jean, L., *Canada* **129 C5** 48 40N 72 0W
St. Jean Baptiste, *Canada* **131 D9** 49 15N 97 20W
St.-Jean-d'Angély, *France* **24 C3** 45 57N 0 31W
St.-Jean-de-Bournay, *France* **25 C9** 45 30N 5 9 E
St.-Jean-de-Luz, *France* **24 E2** 43 23N 1 39W
St.-Jean-de-Maurienne, *France* **25 C10** 45 16N 6 21 E
St.-Jean-de-Monts, *France* **22 F4** 46 47N 2 4W
St.-Jean-du-Gard, *France* **24 D7** 44 7N 3 52 E
St.-Jean-en-Royans, *France* **25 C9** 45 1N 5 18 E
St-Jean-Port-Joli, *Canada* **129 C5** 47 15N 70 13W
St-Jérôme, *Qué., Canada* **128 C5** 45 47N 74 0W
St-Jérôme, *Qué., Canada* **129 C5** 48 26N 71 53W
St. Joe, *U.S.A.* **141 C12** 41 19N 84 54W
St. John, *Canada* **129 C6** 45 20N 66 8W
St. John, *Kans., U.S.A.* **139 G5** 38 0N 98 46W
St. John, *N. Dak., U.S.A.* **138 A5** 48 57N 99 43W
St. John →, *U.S.A.* **129 C6** 45 12N 66 5W
St. John, C., *Canada* **129 B8** 50 0N 55 32W
St. John's, *Antigua* **149 C7** 17 6N 61 51W
St. John's, *Canada* **129 C9** 47 35N 52 40W
St. Johns, *Ariz., U.S.A.* **143 J9** 34 30N 109 22W
St. Johns, *Mich., U.S.A.* **141 A12** 43 0N 84 33W
St. Johns →, *U.S.A.* **135 K5** 30 24N 81 24W
St. Johnsbury, *U.S.A.* **137 B12** 44 25N 72 1W
St. Johnsville, *U.S.A.* **137 C10** 43 0N 74 43W
St.-Joseph, *N. Cal.* **121 K4** 20 27 S 166 36 E
St. Joseph, *Ill., U.S.A.* **141 D8** 40 7N 88 2W
St. Joseph, *La., U.S.A.* **139 K9** 31 55N 91 14W
St. Joseph, *Mich., U.S.A.* **141 B10** 42 6N 86 29W
St. Joseph, *Mo., U.S.A.* **140 E2** 39 46N 94 50W
St. Joseph →, *U.S.A.* **141 B10** 42 7N 86 29W
St. Joseph, I., *Canada* **128 C3** 46 12N 83 58W
St. Joseph, L., *Canada* **128 B1** 51 10N 90 35W
St-Jovite, *Canada* **128 C5** 46 8N 74 38W
St.-Juéry, *France* **24 E6** 43 57N 2 12 E
St.-Julien-Chapteuil, *France* **25 C8** 45 2N 4 4 E
St.-Julien-du-Sault, *France* **23 D10** 48 1N 3 17 E
St.-Julien-en-Genevois, *France* **25 B10** 46 9N 6 5 E
St.-Junien, *France* **24 C4** 45 53N 0 55 E
St.-Just-en-Chaussée, *France* **23 C9** 49 30N 2 25 E
St.-Just-en-Chevalet, *France* **24 C7** 45 55N 3 50 E
St.-Justin, *France* **24 E3** 43 59N 0 14W
St. Kilda, *N.Z.* **119 F5** 45 53 S 170 31 E
St. Kitts, *W. Indies* **149 C7** 17 20N 62 40W
St. Kitts-Nevis = St. Christopher-Nevis ■, *W. Indies* **149 C7** 17 20N 62 40W
St. Laurent, *Canada* **131 C9** 50 25N 97 58W
St.-Laurent, *Fr. Guiana* **153 B7** 5 29N 54 3W
St.-Laurent-du-Pont, *France* **25 C9** 45 23N 5 45 E
St.-Laurent-en-Grandvaux, *France* **25 B9** 46 35N 5 58 E
St. Lawrence, *Australia* **114 C4** 22 16 S 149 31 E
St. Lawrence, *Canada* **129 C8** 46 54N 55 23W
St. Lawrence →, *Canada* **129 C6** 49 30N 66 0W
St. Lawrence, Gulf of, *Canada* **129 C7** 48 25N 62 0W
St. Lawrence I., *U.S.A.* **126 B3** 63 30N 170 30W
St.-Léger, *Belgium* **21 J7** 49 37N 5 39 E
St. Leonard, *Canada* **129 C6** 47 12N 67 58W
St.-Léonard-de-Noblat, *France* **24 C5** 45 49N 1 29 E
St. Lewis →, *Canada* **129 B8** 52 26N 56 11W
St.-Lô, *France* **22 C5** 49 7N 1 5W
St-Louis, *Senegal* **100 B1** 16 8N 16 27W
St. Louis, *Mich., U.S.A.* **134 D3** 43 25N 84 36W
St. Louis, *Mo., U.S.A.* **140 F6** 38 37N 90 12W
St. Louis →, *U.S.A.* **138 B8** 47 15N 92 45W
St.-Loup-sur-Semouse, *France* **23 E13** 47 53N 6 16 E

Sambawizi 259

St. Lucia ■, *W. Indies* . . . **149 D7** 14 0N 60 50W
St. Lucia, L., *S. Africa* . . **105 D5** 28 5 S 32 30 E
St. Lucia Channel, *W. Indies* **149 D7** 14 15N 61 0W
St. Lunaire-Griquet, *Canada* **129 B8** 51 31N 55 28W
St. Maarten, *W. Indies* . . **149 C7** 18 0N 63 5W
St.-Maixent-l'École, *France* **24 B3** 46 24N 0 12W
St.-Malo, *France* **22 D4** 48 39N 2 1W
St.-Malo, G. de, *France* . **22 D4** 48 50N 2 30W
St.-Mandrier-sur-Mer, *France* . . . . **25 E9** 43 4N 5 57 E
St-Marc, *Haiti* **149 C5** 19 10N 72 41W
St.-Marcellin, *France* . . . . **25 C9** 45 9N 5 20 E
St.-Marcouf, Is., *France* . **22 C5** 49 30N 1 10W
St. Maries, *U.S.A.* **142 C5** 47 19N 116 35W
St-Martin, *W. Indies* **149 C7** 18 0N 63 0W
St. Martin, L., *Canada* . . **131 C9** 51 40N 98 30W
St.-Martin-de-Ré, *France* **24 B2** 46 12N 1 21W
St.-Martin-Vésubie, *France* **25 D11** 44 4N 7 15 E
St. Martins, *Canada* **129 C6** 45 22N 65 34W
St. Martinville, *U.S.A.* . . **139 K9** 30 7N 91 50W
St.-Martory, *France* . . . . . **24 E4** 43 9N 0 56 E
St. Mary, Mt., *Papua N. G.* . . . . **120 E4** 8 8 S 147 2 E
St. Mary Is., *India* . . . . . . **83 H2** 13 20N 74 35 E
St. Mary Pk., *Australia* . . **116 A3** 31 32 S 138 34 E
St. Marys, *Australia* . . . . . **114 G4** 41 35 S 148 11 E
St. Marys, *Canada* **136 C3** 43 20N 81 10W
St. Mary's, *U.K.* **17 H1** 49 55N 6 18W
St. Marys, *Mo., U.S.A.* . . **140 G7** 37 53N 89 57W
St. Marys, *Pa., U.S.A.* . . **136 E6** 41 26N 78 34W
St. Mary's, C., *Canada* . . **129 C9** 46 50N 54 12W
St. Mary's B., *Canada* . . . **129 C9** 46 50N 53 50W
St. Marys Bay, *Canada* . . **129 D6** 44 25N 66 10W
St.-Mathieu, Pte., *France* **22 D2** 48 20N 4 45W
St. Matthews, *U.S.A.* . . . **141 F11** 38 15N 85 39W
St. Matthews, I. = Zadetkyi Kyun, *Burma* **77 H2** 10 0N 98 25 E
St. Matthias Group, *Papua N. G.* . . . . **120 A5** 1 30 S 150 0 E
St.-Maur-des-Fossés, *France* . . . . **23 D9** 48 48N 2 30 E
St. Maurice, *Switz.* . . . . . . **28 D4** 46 13N 7 0 E
St-Maurice →, *Canada* . . **128 C5** 46 21N 72 31W
St.-Médard-de-Guizières, *France* **24 C3** 45 1N 0 4W
St.-Méen-le-Grand, *France* **22 D4** 48 11N 2 12W
St. Meinrad, *U.S.A.* **141 F10** 38 10N 86 49W
St. Michael's Mount, *U.K.* **17 G2** 50 7N 5 30W
St.-Michel-de-Maurienne, *France* . . . . **25 C10** 45 12N 6 28 E
St.-Mihiel, *France* . . . . **23 D12** 48 54N 5 32 E
St.-Nazaire, *France* **22 E4** 47 17N 2 12W
St. Neots, *U.K.* **17 E7** 52 14N 0 16W
St.-Nicolas-de-Port, *France* **23 D13** 48 38N 6 18 E
St. Niklass = Sint Niklaas, *Belgium* . . . . **21 F4** 51 10N 4 9 E
St. Niklaus, *Switz.* . . . . . . **28 D5** 46 10N 7 49 E
St.-Omer, *France* . . . . **23 B9** 50 45N 2 15 E
St-Pacome, *Canada* **129 C6** 47 24N 69 58W
St.-Palais-sur-Mer, *France* **24 C2** 45 38N 1 5W
St-Pamphile, *Canada* **129 C6** 46 58N 69 48W
St.-Pardoux-la-Rivière, *France* . . . . **24 C4** 45 29N 0 45 E
St. Paris, *U.S.A.* **141 D13** 40 8N 83 58W
St. Pascal, *Canada* **129 C6** 47 32N 69 48W
St. Paul, *Canada* **130 C6** 54 0N 111 17W
St. Paul, *Ind., U.S.A.* . . . **141 E11** 39 26N 85 38W
St. Paul, *Minn., U.S.A.* . . **138 C8** 44 57N 93 6W
St. Paul, *Nebr., U.S.A.* . . **138 E5** 41 13N 98 27W
St. Paul, I., *Ind. Oc.* . . . . **109 H6** 38 55 S 77 34 E
St.-Paul-de-Fenouillet, *France* . . . . **24 F6** 42 48N 2 30 E
St. Paul I., *Canada* **129 C7** 47 12N 60 9W
St.-Paul-lès-Dax, *France* . **24 E2** 43 44N 1 3W
St.-Péray, *France* . . . . **25 D8** 44 57N 4 50 E
St.-Père-en-Retz, *France* . **22 E4** 47 11N 2 2W
St. Peter, *U.S.A.* **138 C8** 44 20N 93 57W
St. Peter Port, *Chan. Is.* . **17 H5** 49 27N 2 31W
St. Peters, *N.S., Canada* . **129 C7** 45 40N 60 53W
St. Peters, *P.E.I., Canada* **129 C7** 46 25N 62 35W
St. Petersburg = Sankt-Peterburg, *Russia* . . . . . **50 B7** 59 55N 30 20 E
St. Petersburg, *U.S.A.* . . . **135 M4** 27 46N 82 39W
St.-Philbert-de-Grand-Lieu, *France* **22 E5** 47 2N 1 39W
St.-Pierre, *St- P. & M.* . . **129 C8** 46 46N 56 12W
St. Pierre, *Seychelles* . . . . **109 E3** 9 20 S 46 0 E
St-Pierre, L., *Canada* **128 C5** 46 12N 72 52W
St.-Pierre-d'Oléron, *France* **24 C2** 45 57N 1 19W
St.-Pierre-Église, *France* . **22 C5** 49 40N 1 24W
St.-Pierre-en-Port, *France* **22 C7** 49 48N 0 30 E
St.-Pierre et Miquelon □, *St- P. & M.* **129 C8** 46 55N 56 10W
St.-Pierre-le-Moûtier, *France* . . . . **23 F10** 46 47N 3 7 E
St.-Pierre-sur-Dives, *France* **22 C6** 49 2N 0 1W
St.-Pieters Leew, *Belgium* **21 G4** 50 47N 4 16 E
St.-Pol-de-Léon, *France* . **22 D2** 48 41N 4 0W
St.-Pol-sur-Mer, *France* . **23 A9** 51 1N 2 20 E
St.-Pol-sur-Ternoise, *France* . . . . **23 B9** 50 23N 2 20 E
St.-Pons, *France* . . . . **24 E6** 43 30N 2 45 E
St.-Pourçain-sur-Sioule, *France* . . . . **24 B7** 46 18N 3 18 E
St.-Quay-Portrieux, *France* **22 D4** 48 39N 2 51W
St.-Quentin, *France* . . . . . **23 C10** 49 50N 3 16 E
St.-Rambert-d'Albon, *France* . . . . **25 C8** 45 17N 4 49 E
St.-Raphaël, *France* . . . . . **25 E10** 43 25N 6 46 E
St. Regis, *U.S.A.* **142 C6** 47 18N 115 6W
St.-Rémy-de-Provence, *France* . . . . **25 E8** 43 48N 4 50 E
St.-Renan, *France* **22 D2** 48 26N 4 37W
St.-Saëns, *France* . . . . **22 C8** 49 41N 1 16 E
St.-Sauveur-en-Puisaye, *France* . . . . **23 E10** 47 37N 3 12 E
St.-Sauveur-le-Vicomte, *France* **22 C5** 49 23N 1 32W
St.-Savin, *France* . . . . **24 B4** 46 34N 0 53 E
St.-Savinien, *France* **24 C3** 45 53N 0 42W
St. Sebastien, Tanjon' i, *Madag.* . . . . **105 A8** 12 26 S 48 44 E
St.-Seine-l'Abbaye, *France* **23 E11** 47 26N 4 47 E
St.-Sernin-sur-Rance, *France* . . . . **24 E6** 43 54N 2 35 E
St.-Servan-sur-Mer, *France* **22 D4** 48 38N 2 2W
St.-Sever, *France* **24 E3** 43 45N 0 35W
St.-Sever-Calvados, *France* **22 D5** 48 50N 1 3W
St-Siméon, *Canada* **129 C6** 47 51N 69 54W
St. Stephen, *Canada* **129 C6** 45 16N 67 17W
St.-Sulpice, *France* . . . . . . **24 E5** 43 46N 1 41 E
St.-Sulpice-Laurière, *France* . . . . **24 B5** 46 3N 1 29 E
St.-Syprien, *France* . . . . . . **24 F7** 42 37N 3 2 E
St.-Thégonnec, *France* . . . **22 D3** 48 31N 3 57W
St. Thomas, *Canada* **128 D3** 42 45N 81 10W
St. Thomas I., *Virgin Is.* . **149 C7** 18 20N 64 55W
St-Tite, *Canada* **128 C5** 46 45N 72 34W
St.-Tropez, *France* . . . . . . **25 E10** 43 17N 6 38 E
St. Troud = Sint Truiden, *Belgium* . . . . **21 G6** 50 48N 5 10 E
St.-Vaast-la-Hougue, *France* **22 C5** 49 35N 1 17W
St.-Valéry-en-Caux, *France* . . . . **22 C7** 49 52N 0 43 E
St.-Valéry-sur-Somme, *France* . . . . **23 B8** 50 11N 1 38 E
St.-Vallier, *France* . . . . . . **25 C8** 45 11N 4 50 E
St.-Vallier-de-Thiey, *France* . . . . **25 E10** 43 42N 6 51 E
St.-Varent, *France* **22 F6** 46 53N 0 13W
St. Vincent, *C. Verde Is.* . **8 G6** 18 0N 26 1W
St. Vincent, *W. Indies* . . . **149 D7** 13 10N 61 10W
St. Vincent, G., *Australia* **116 C3** 35 0 S 138 0 E
St. Vincent & the Grenadines ■, *W. Indies* **149 D7** 13 0N 61 10W
St.-Vincent-de-Tyrosse, *France* **24 E2** 43 39N 1 19W
St. Vincent Passage, *W. Indies* **149 D7** 13 30N 61 0W
St-Vith, *Belgium* . . . . **21 H8** 50 17N 6 9 E
St.-Yrieix-la-Perche, *France* . . . . **24 C5** 45 31N 1 12 E
Ste.-Adresse, *France* . . . . **22 C7** 49 31N 0 5 E
Ste-Agathe-des-Monts, *Canada* **128 C5** 46 3N 74 17W
Ste-Anne de Beaupré, *Canada* **129 C5** 47 2N 70 58W
Ste-Anne-des-Monts, *Canada* **129 C6** 49 8N 66 30W
Ste-Croix, *Switz.* . . . . **28 C3** 46 49N 6 34 E
Ste.-Enimie, *France* . . . . . **24 D7** 44 22N 3 26 E
Ste.-Foy-la-Grande, *France* . . . . **24 D4** 44 50N 0 13 E
Ste. Genevieve, *U.S.A.* . . **140 G6** 37 59N 90 2W
Ste.-Hermine, *France* **24 B2** 46 32N 1 4W
Ste.-Livrade-sur-Lot, *France* . . . . **24 D4** 44 24N 0 36 E
Ste-Marguerite →, *Canada* **129 B6** 50 9N 66 36W
Ste-Marie, *Martinique* . . **149 D7** 14 48N 61 1W
Ste.-Marie-aux-Mines, *France* . . . . **23 D14** 48 15N 7 12 E
Ste-Marie de la Madeleine, *Canada* . . . **129 C5** 46 26N 71 0W
Ste.-Maure-de-Touraine, *France* . . . . **22 E7** 47 7N 0 37 E
Ste.-Maxime, *France* . . . . . **25 E10** 43 19N 6 39 E
Ste.-Menehould, *France* . . **23 C11** 49 5N 4 54 E
Ste.-Mère-Église, *France* . **22 C5** 49 24N 1 19W
Ste.-Rose, *Guadeloupe* . . **149 C7** 16 20N 61 45W
Ste. Rose du Lac, *Canada* **131 C9** 51 4N 99 30W
Saintes, *France* **24 C3** 45 45N 0 37W
Saintes, I. des, *Guadeloupe* **149 C7** 15 50N 61 35W
Stes.-Maries-de-la-Mer, *France* . . . . **25 E8** 43 26N 4 26 E
Saintonge, *France* **24 C3** 45 40N 0 50W
Saipan, *Pac. Oc.* . . . . **122 F6** 15 12N 145 45 E
Sairecábur, Cerro, *Bolivia* **158 A2** 22 43 S 67 54W
Saitama □, *Japan* . . . . . . **63 A11** 36 25N 139 30 E
Saito, *Japan* . . . . **62 E3** 32 3N 131 24 E
Sajama, *Bolivia* . . . . **156 D4** 18 7 S 69 0W
Sajan, *Serbia* . . . . **42 B5** 45 50N 20 20 E
Sajószentpéter, *Hungary* . **31 C13** 48 12N 20 44 E
Sajum, *India* . . . . **81 C8** 33 20N 79 0 E
Sak →, *S. Africa* . . . . **104 E3** 30 52 S 20 25 E
Sakai, *Japan* . . . . **63 C7** 34 30N 135 30 E
Sakaide, *Japan* . . . . **62 C5** 34 15N 133 50 E
Sakaiminato, *Japan* . . . . . **62 B5** 35 38N 133 11 E
Sakākah, *Si. Arabia* . . . . . **84 D4** 30 0N 40 8 E
Sakakawea, L., *U.S.A.* . . . **138 B3** 47 30N 101 25W
Sakami, L., *Canada* **128 B4** 53 15N 77 0W
Sâkâne, 'Erg i-n, *Mali* . . . **98 D4** 20 30N 1 30W
Sakania, *Zaïre* . . . . **107 E2** 12 43 S 28 30 E
Sakarya = Adapazarı, *Turkey* . . . . **88 C4** 40 48N 30 25 E
Sakarya □, *Turkey* . . . . . . **88 C4** 40 45N 30 25 E
Sakarya →, *Turkey* . . . . . **52 F4** 41 7N 30 39 E
Sakashima-Guntō, *Japan* . **61 M2** 24 46N 124 0 E
Sakata, *Japan* . . . . **60 E9** 38 55N 139 50 E
Sakchu, *N. Korea* . . . . **67 D13** 40 23N 125 2 E
Sakeny →, *Madag.* . . . . . . **105 C8** 20 0 S 45 25 E
Sakété, *Benin* . . . . **101 D5** 6 40N 2 45 E
Sakha = Yakut Republic □, *Russia* . . . **57 C13** 62 0N 130 0 E
Sakhalin, *Russia* . . . . **57 D15** 51 0N 143 0 E
Sakhalinskiy Zaliv, *Russia* **57 D15** 54 0N 141 0 E
Sakhi Gopal, *India* . . . . . . **82 E7** 19 58N 85 50 E
Saki, *Ukraine* . . . . **52 D5** 45 9N 33 34 E
Šakiai, *Lithuania* . . . . **50 D3** 54 59N 23 0 E
Sakmara, *Russia* . . . . **54 E4** 52 0N 55 20 E
Sakmara →, *Russia* . . . . . **54 F4** 51 46N 55 1 E
Sakon Nakhon, *Thailand* . **76 D5** 17 10N 104 9 E
Sakrand, *Pakistan* . . . . . . **80 F3** 26 10N 68 15 E
Sakri, *India* . . . . **82 D2** 21 2N 74 20 E
Sakrivier, *S. Africa* . . . . . **104 E3** 30 54 S 20 28 E
Sakskøbing, *Denmark* . . . . **15 K5** 54 49N 11 39 E
Saku, *Japan* . . . . **63 A10** 36 17N 138 31 E
Sakuma, *Japan* . . . . **63 B9** 35 3N 137 49 E
Sakura, *Japan* . . . . **63 B12** 35 43N 140 14 E
Sakurai, *Japan* . . . . **63 C7** 34 30N 135 51 E
Sal →, *Russia* . . . . **53 C9** 47 31N 40 45 E
Šal'a, *Slovak Rep.* . . . . . . **31 C10** 48 10N 17 50 E
Sala, *Sweden* . . . . **13 G14** 59 58N 16 35 E
Sala Consilina, *Italy* . . . . . **41 B8** 40 23N 15 35 E
Sala-y-Gómez, *Pac. Oc.* . **123 K17** 26 28 S 105 28W
Salaberry-de-Valleyfield, *Canada* **128 C5** 45 15N 74 8W
Saladas, *Argentina* . . . . . . **158 B4** 28 15 S 58 40W
Saladillo, *Argentina* . . . . . **158 D4** 35 40 S 59 55W
Salado →, *Buenos Aires, Argentina* . . . . **158 D4** 35 44 S 57 22W
Salado →, *La Pampa, Argentina* . . . . **160 A3** 37 30 S 67 0W
Salado →, *Río Negro, Argentina* . . . . **160 B3** 41 34 S 65 3W
Salado →, *Santa Fe, Argentina* . . . . **158 C3** 31 40 S 60 41W
Salado →, *Mexico* **146 B5** 26 52N 99 19W
Salaga, *Ghana* **101 D4** 8 31N 0 31W
Sālah, *Syria* . . . . **91 C5** 32 40N 36 45 E
Sălaj □, *Romania* . . . . **46 B4** 47 15N 23 0 E
Sálakhos, *Greece* . . . . **32 C9** 36 17N 27 57 E
Salala, *Liberia* **100 D2** 6 42N 10 7W
Salala, *Sudan* . . . . **94 C4** 21 17N 36 16 E
Salālah, *Oman* . . . . **87 C6** 16 56N 53 59 E
Salamanca, *Chile* . . . . **158 C1** 31 46 S 70 59W
Salamanca, *Spain* **36 E5** 40 58N 5 39W
Salamanca, *U.S.A.* **136 D6** 42 10N 78 43W
Salamanca □, *Spain* **36 E5** 40 57N 5 40W
Salāmatābād, *Iran* . . . . . . **84 C5** 35 39N 47 50 E
Salamina, *Colombia* **152 B2** 5 25N 75 29W
Salamis, *Cyprus* . . . . **32 D12** 35 11N 33 54 E
Salamis, *Greece* . . . . **45 G5** 37 56N 23 30 E
Salamonie L., *U.S.A.* **141 D11** 40 46N 85 37W
Salar de Atacama, *Chile* . **158 A2** 23 30 S 68 25W
Salar de Uyuni, *Bolivia* . . **156 E4** 20 30 S 67 45W
Sălard, *Romania* . . . . **46 B3** 47 12N 22 3 E
Salas, *Spain* **36 B4** 43 25N 6 15W
Salas de los Infantes, *Spain* **34 C1** 42 2N 3 17W
Salatiga, *Indonesia* . . . . . . **75 D4** 7 19 S 110 30 E
Salavat, *Russia* . . . . **54 E4** 53 21N 55 55 E
Salaverry, *Peru* . . . . **156 B2** 8 15 S 79 0W
Salawati, *Indonesia* . . . . . . **73 B4** 1 7 S 130 52 E
Salay, *Phil.* . . . . **71 G5** 8 52N 124 47 E
Salayar, *Indonesia* . . . . . . **72 C2** 6 7 S 120 30 E
Salazar →, *Spain* **34 C3** 42 40N 1 20W
Salbris, *France* . . . . **23 E9** 47 25N 2 3 E
Salcia, *Romania* . . . . **46 F5** 43 56N 24 55 E
Salcombe, *U.K.* **17 G4** 50 14N 3 47W
Salda Gölü, *Turkey* . . . . . . **88 E3** 37 22N 29 41 E
Saldaña, *Spain* **36 C6** 42 32N 4 48W
Saldanha, *S. Africa* . . . . . **104 E2** 33 0 S 17 58 E
Saldanha B., *S. Africa* . . . **104 E2** 33 6 S 18 0 E
Saldus, *Latvia* . . . . **50 C3** 56 38N 22 30 E
Sale, *Australia* . . . . **117 E7** 38 6 S 147 6 E
Salé, *Morocco* **98 B3** 34 3N 6 48W
Sale, *U.K.* **16 D5** 53 26N 2 19W
Salekhard, *Russia* . . . . **48 A12** 66 30N 66 35 E
Salem, *India* . . . . **83 J4** 11 40N 78 11 E
Salem, *Ill., U.S.A.* **140 F8** 38 38N 88 57W
Salem, *Ind., U.S.A.* **141 F10** 38 36N 86 6W
Salem, *Mass., U.S.A.* **137 D14** 42 31N 70 53W
Salem, *Mo., U.S.A.* **139 G9** 37 39N 91 32W
Salem, *N.J., U.S.A.* **134 F8** 39 34N 75 28W
Salem, *Ohio, U.S.A.* **136 F4** 40 54N 80 52W
Salem, *Oreg., U.S.A.* **142 D2** 44 56N 123 2W
Salem, *S. Dak., U.S.A.* . . . **138 D6** 43 44N 97 23W
Salem, *Va., U.S.A.* **134 G5** 37 18N 80 3W
Salemi, *Italy* . . . . **40 E5** 37 49N 12 47 E
Salernes, *France* . . . . **25 E10** 43 34N 6 15 E
Salerno, *Italy* . . . . **41 B7** 40 40N 14 44 E
Salerno, G. di, *Italy* . . . . . **41 B7** 40 35N 14 45 E
Salford, *U.K.* **16 D5** 53 30N 2 17W
Salgir →, *Ukraine* . . . . . . **52 D6** 45 38N 35 1 E
Salgótarján, *Hungary* . . . . **31 C12** 48 5N 19 47 E
Salgueiro, *Brazil* . . . . **154 C4** 8 4 S 39 6W
Salida, *U.S.A.* **132 C5** 38 32N 106 0W
Salies-de-Béarn, *France* . . **24 E3** 43 28N 0 56W
Şalif, *Yemen* . . . . **86 D3** 15 18N 42 41 E
Salihli, *Turkey* . . . . **88 D3** 38 28N 28 8 E
Salin, *Burma* . . . . **78 E5** 20 35N 94 40 E
Salina, *Italy* . . . . **41 D7** 38 35N 14 50 E
Salina, *U.S.A.* **138 F6** 38 50N 97 37W
Salina Cruz, *Mexico* **147 D5** 16 10N 95 10W
Salinas, *Brazil* . . . . **155 E3** 16 10 S 42 10W
Salinas, *Chile* . . . . **158 A2** 23 31 S 69 29W
Salinas, *Ecuador* . . . . **152 D1** 2 10 S 80 58W
Salinas, *U.S.A.* **144 J5** 36 40N 121 39W
Salinas →, *Guatemala* . . . **147 D6** 16 28N 90 31W
Salinas →, *U.S.A.* **144 J5** 36 45N 121 48W
Salinas, B. de, *Nic.* **148 D2** 11 4N 85 45W
Salinas, C. de, *Spain* . . . . **33 B10** 39 16N 3 4 E
Salinas, Pampa de las, *Argentina* . . . . **158 C2** 31 58 S 66 42W
Salinas Ambargasta, *Argentina* . . . . **158 B3** 29 0 S 65 0W
Salinas de Hidalgo, *Mexico* **146 C4** 22 30N 101 40W
Salinas Grandes, *Argentina* **158 B2** 30 0 S 65 0W
Saline →, *Ark., U.S.A.* . . . **139 J8** 33 10N 92 8W
Saline →, *Kans., U.S.A.* . . **138 F6** 38 52N 97 30W
Salines, *Spain* . . . . **33 B10** 39 21N 3 3 E
Salinópolis, *Brazil* . . . . . . **154 B2** 0 40 S 47 20W
Salins-les-Bains, *France* . . **23 F12** 46 58N 5 52 E
Salir, *Portugal* **37 H2** 37 14N 8 2W
Salisbury = Harare, *Zimbabwe* . . . . **107 F3** 17 43 S 31 2 E
Salisbury, *Australia* . . . . . **116 C3** 34 46 S 138 40 E
Salisbury, *U.K.* **17 F6** 51 4N 1 48W
Salisbury, *Md., U.S.A.* . . . **134 F8** 38 22N 75 36W
Salisbury, *Mo., U.S.A.* . . . **140 E4** 39 25N 92 48W
Salisbury, *N.C., U.S.A.* . . **135 H5** 35 40N 80 29W
Salisbury Plain, *U.K.* **17 F6** 51 13N 1 50W
Săliştea, *Romania* . . . . **46 D4** 45 45N 23 56 E
Salitre →, *Brazil* . . . . **154 C3** 9 29 S 40 39W
Salka, *Nigeria* . . . . **101 C5** 10 20N 4 58 E
Salkhad, *Jordan* . . . . **91 C5** 32 30N 36 43 E
Sallent, *Spain* . . . . **34 D6** 41 49N 1 54 E
Salles-Curan, *France* . . . . **24 D6** 44 11N 2 48 E
Salling, *Denmark* . . . . **15 H2** 56 40N 8 55 E
Sallisaw, *U.S.A.* **139 H7** 35 28N 94 47W
Sallom Junction, *Sudan* . . **94 D4** 19 17N 37 6 E
Salmās, *Iran* . . . . **84 B5** 38 11N 44 47 E
Salmerón, *Spain* **34 E2** 40 33N 2 29W
Salmo, *Canada* **130 D5** 49 10N 117 20W
Salmon, *U.S.A.* **142 D7** 45 11N 113 54W
Salmon →, *Canada* **130 C4** 54 3N 122 40W
Salmon →, *U.S.A.* **142 D5** 45 51N 116 47W
Salmon Arm, *Canada* **130 C5** 50 40N 119 15W
Salmon Falls, *U.S.A.* **142 E6** 42 48N 114 59W
Salmon Gums, *Australia* . **113 F3** 32 59 S 121 38 E
Salmon Res., *Canada* . . . **129 C8** 48 5N 56 0W
Salmon River Mts., *U.S.A.* **142 D6** 45 0N 114 30W
Salo, *Finland* . . . . **13 F17** 60 22N 23 10 E
Salò, *Italy* . . . . **38 C7** 45 37N 10 32 E
Salobreña, *Spain* **37 J7** 36 44N 3 35W
Salome, *U.S.A.* **145 M13** 33 47N 113 37W
Salon-de-Provence, *France* **25 E9** 43 39N 5 6 E
Salonica = Thessaloníki, *Greece* . . . . **44 D4** 40 38N 22 58 E
Salonta, *Romania* . . . . **46 C2** 46 49N 21 42 E
Salor →, *Spain* **37 F3** 39 39N 7 3W
Salou, C., *Spain* . . . . **34 D6** 41 3N 1 10 E
Salsacate, *Argentina* . . . . . **158 C2** 31 20 S 65 5W
Salses, *France* . . . . **24 F6** 42 50N 2 55 E
Salsette I., *India* . . . . **82 E1** 19 5N 72 50 E
Salsk, *Russia* . . . . **53 C9** 46 28N 41 30 E
Salso →, *Italy* . . . . **40 E6** 37 6N 13 55 E
Salsomaggiore, *Italy* . . . . . **38 D6** 44 48N 9 59 E
Salt →, *Canada* **130 B6** 60 0N 112 25W
Salt →, *Ariz., U.S.A.* . . . **143 K7** 33 23N 112 19W
Salt →, *Mo., U.S.A.* **140 E5** 39 28N 91 4W
Salt Creek, *Australia* . . . . **116 D3** 36 8 S 139 38 E
Salt Fork Arkansas →, *U.S.A.* **139 G6** 36 36N 97 3W
Salt Lake City, *U.S.A.* . . **142 F8** 40 45N 111 53W
Salt Range, *Pakistan* . . . . **80 C5** 32 30N 72 25 E
Salta, *Argentina* . . . . **158 A2** 24 57 S 65 25W
Salta □, *Argentina* . . . . . . **158 A2** 24 48 S 65 30W
Saltcoats, *U.K.* **18 F4** 55 38N 4 47W
Saltee Is., *Ireland* **19 D5** 52 7N 6 37W
Saltfjorden, *Norway* . . . . . **12 C13** 67 15N 14 10 E
Saltholm, *Denmark* . . . . . . **15 J6** 55 38N 12 43 E
Salthólmavík, *Iceland* **12 D3** 65 24N 21 57W
Saltillo, *Mexico* **146 B4** 25 30N 100 57W
Salto, *Argentina* . . . . **158 C3** 34 20 S 60 15W
Salto, *Uruguay* . . . . **158 C4** 31 27 S 57 50W
Salto da Divisa, *Brazil* . . . **155 E4** 16 0 S 39 57W
Salton City, *U.S.A.* **145 M11** 33 29N 115 51W
Salton Sea, *U.S.A.* **145 M11** 33 15N 115 45W
Saltpond, *Ghana* **101 D4** 5 15N 1 3W
Saltsjöbaden, *Sweden* . . . . **14 E12** 59 15N 18 20 E
Saltville, *U.S.A.* **134 G5** 36 53N 81 46W
Saluda →, *U.S.A.* **135 H5** 34 1N 81 4W
Salûm, *Egypt* . . . . **94 A2** 31 31N 25 7 E
Salûm, Khâlig el, *Egypt* . **94 A2** 31 30N 25 9 E
Salur, *India* . . . . **82 E6** 18 27N 83 18 E
Salut, Is. du, *Fr. Guiana* . **153 B7** 5 15N 52 35W
Saluzzo, *Italy* . . . . **38 D4** 44 39N 7 29 E
Salvacion, *Phil.* . . . . **71 G2** 9 56N 118 47 E
Salvación, B., *Chile* . . . . . **160 D1** 50 50 S 75 10W
Salvador, *Brazil* . . . . **155 D4** 13 0 S 38 30W
Salvador, *Canada* **131 C7** 52 10N 109 32W
Salvador, L., *U.S.A.* **139 L9** 29 43N 90 15W
Salvaterra, *Brazil* . . . . **154 B2** 0 46 S 48 31W
Salvaterra de Magos, *Portugal* **37 F2** 39 1N 8 47W
Salvisa, *U.S.A.* **141 G12** 37 54N 84 51W
Sálvora, I., *Spain* **36 C2** 42 30N 8 58W
Salween →, *Burma* . . . . . **78 G6** 16 31N 97 37 E
Salyany, *Azerbaijan* . . . . . **89 D13** 39 10N 48 50 E
Salyersville, *U.S.A.* **134 G4** 37 45N 83 4W
Salza →, *Austria* . . . . **30 D7** 47 40N 14 43 E
Salzach →, *Austria* . . . . . **30 C5** 48 12N 12 56 E
Salzburg, *Austria* . . . . **30 D6** 47 48N 13 2 E
Salzburg □, *Austria* . . . . . **30 D6** 47 15N 13 0 E
Salzgitter, *Germany* . . . . . **26 C6** 52 13N 10 22 E
Salzwedel, *Germany* . . . . . **26 C7** 52 50N 11 11 E
Sam, *Gabon* . . . . **102 B2** 0 58N 11 16 E
Sam Neua, *Laos* . . . . **76 B5** 20 29N 104 5 E
Sam Ngao, *Thailand* . . . . . **76 D2** 17 18N 99 0 E
Sam Rayburn Reservoir, *U.S.A.* **139 K7** 31 4N 94 5W
Sam Son, *Vietnam* . . . . **76 C5** 19 44N 105 54 E
Sam Teu, *Laos* . . . . **76 C5** 19 59N 104 38 E
Sama, *Russia* . . . . **54 A7** 60 12N 60 22 E
Sama de Langreo, *Spain* . . **36 B5** 43 18N 5 40W
Samacimbo, *Angola* . . . . . . **103 E3** 13 33 S 16 59 E
Samagaltai, *Russia* . . . . . . **57 D10** 50 36N 95 3 E
Samā'il, *Oman* . . . . **87 B7** 23 40N 57 50 E
Samaipata, *Bolivia* . . . . . . **157 D5** 18 9 S 63 52W
Samal, *Phil.* . . . . **71 H5** 7 5N 125 42 E
Samal I., *Phil.* . . . . **71 H5** 7 3N 125 44 E
Samales Group, *Phil.* . . . . . **71 J3** 6 0N 122 0 E
Samalkot, *India* . . . . **82 F6** 17 3N 82 13 E
Samâlût, *Egypt* . . . . **94 J7** 28 20N 30 42 E
Samana, *India* . . . . **80 D7** 30 10N 76 13 E
Samana Cay, *Bahamas* . . **149 B5** 23 3N 73 45W
Samandağı, *Turkey* . . . . . . **88 E6** 36 5N 35 59 E
Samanga, *Tanzania* . . . . . . **107 D4** 8 20 S 39 13 E
Samangán □, *Afghan.* . . . . **79 A3** 36 15N 68 3 E
Samangwa, *Zaïre* . . . . **103 C4** 4 23 S 24 10 E
Samani, *Japan* . . . . **60 C11** 42 7N 142 56 E
Samar, *Phil.* . . . . **71 E5** 12 0N 125 0 E
Samar □, *Phil.* . . . . **71 F5** 11 50N 125 0 E
Samar Sea, *Phil.* . . . . **70 E5** 12 0N 124 15 E
Samara, *Russia* . . . . **51 E17** 53 8N 50 6 E
Samara →, *Russia* . . . . . . **54 E2** 53 10N 50 4 E
Samarai, *Papua N. G.* . . . **120 F6** 10 39 S 150 41 E
Samaria = Shōmrōn, *Jordan* . . . . **91 C4** 32 15N 35 13 E
Samariá, *Greece* . . . . **32 D5** 35 17N 23 58 E
Samarinda, *Indonesia* . . . **75 C5** 0 30 S 117 9 E
Samarkand, *Uzbekistan* . . **55 D3** 39 40N 66 55 E
Samarqand = Samarkand, *Uzbekistan* . . . . **55 D3** 39 40N 66 55 E
Sāmarrā, *Iraq* . . . . **84 C4** 34 12N 43 52 E
Samastipur, *India* . . . . **81 G11** 25 50N 85 50 E
Samatan, *France* . . . . **24 E4** 43 29N 0 55 E
Samaúma, *Brazil* . . . . **157 B5** 7 50 S 60 2W
Samba, *India* . . . . **81 C6** 32 32N 75 10 E
Samba, *Zaïre* . . . . **103 C5** 4 38 S 26 22 E
Samba Caju, *Angola* . . . . . **103 D3** 8 46 S 15 24 E
Sambaíba, *Brazil* . . . . **154 C2** 7 8 S 45 21W
Sambalpur, *India* . . . . **82 D7** 21 28N 84 4 E
Sambar, Tanjung, *Indonesia* . . . . **75 C4** 2 59 S 110 19 E
Sambas, *Indonesia* . . . . . . **75 B3** 1 20N 109 20 E
Sambava, *Madag.* . . . . **105 A9** 14 16 S 50 10 E
Sambawizi, *Zimbabwe* . . . **107 F2** 18 24 S 26 13 E

260 Sambhal

Sambhal, *India* **81 E8** 28 35N 78 37 E
Sambhar, *India* **80 F6** 26 52N 75 6 E
Sambiase, *Italy* **41 D9** 38 58N 16 16 E
Sambonifacio, *Italy* **38 C8** 45 24N 11 16 E
Sambor, *Cambodia* **76 F6** 12 46N 106 0 E
Sambor, *Ukraine* **50 G3** 49 30N 23 10 E
Sambre →, *Europe* **21 H5** 50 27N 4 52 E
Sambuca di Sicilia, *Italy* **40 E6** 37 39N 13 6 E
Samburu □, *Kenya* **106 B4** 1 10N 37 0 E
Samchŏk, *S. Korea* **67 F15** 37 30N 129 10 E
Samchonpo, *S. Korea* **67 G15** 35 0N 128 6 E
Same, *Tanzania* **106 C4** 4 2 S 37 38 E
Samedan, *Switz.* **29 C9** 46 32N 9 52 E
Samer, *France* **23 B8** 50 38N 1 44 E
Samfya, *Zambia* **107 E2** 11 22 S 29 31 E
Samḥān, Jabal, *Oman* **87 C6** 17 12N 54 55 E
Sámi, *Greece* **45 F2** 38 15N 20 39 E
Samnah, *Si. Arabia* **84 E3** 25 10N 37 15 E
Samnaun, *Switz.* **29 C10** 46 57N 10 22 E
Samnū, *Libya* **96 C2** 27 15N 14 55 E
Samo Alto, *Chile* **158 C1** 30 22 S 71 0W
Samoan Is., *Pac. Oc.* **121 X24** 14 0 S 171 0W
Samobor, *Croatia* **39 C12** 45 47N 15 44 E
Samoëns, *France* **25 B10** 46 5N 6 45 E
Samokov, *Bulgaria* **43 E8** 42 18N 23 35 E
Samoorombón, B., *Argentina* **158 D4** 36 5 S 57 20W
Samorogouan, *Burkina Faso* **100 C4** 11 21N 4 57W
Sámos, *Greece* **45 G8** 37 45N 26 50 E
Samoš, *Serbia* **42 B5** 45 13N 20 49 E
Samos, *Spain* **36 C3** 42 44N 7 20W
Samosir, *Indonesia* **74 B1** 2 55N 98 50 E
Samothráki, *Évros, Greece* **44 D7** 40 28N 25 28 E
Samothráki, *Ionioi Nísoi, Greece* **44 E1** 39 48N 19 31 E
Samothráki, *Kérkira, Greece* **32 A3** 39 48N 19 31 E
Samoylovka, *Russia* **51 F13** 51 12N 43 43 E
Sampa, *Ghana* **100 D4** 8 0N 2 36W
Sampacho, *Argentina* **158 C3** 33 20 S 64 50W
Sampang, *Indonesia* **75 D4** 7 11 S 113 13 E
Samper de Calanda, *Spain* **34 D4** 41 11N 0 28W
Sampit, *Indonesia* **75 C4** 2 34 S 113 0 E
Sampit →, *Indonesia* **75 C4** 2 44 S 112 54 E
Sampit, Teluk, *Indonesia* **75 C4** 3 5 S 113 3 E
Samrée, *Belgium* **21 H7** 50 13N 5 39 E
Samrong, *Cambodia* **76 E4** 14 15N 103 30 E
Samrong, *Thailand* **76 E3** 15 10N 100 40 E
Samsø, *Denmark* **15 J4** 55 50N 10 35 E
Samsø Bælt, *Denmark* **15 J4** 55 45N 10 45 E
Samsonovo, *Turkmenistan* **55 E2** 37 53N 65 15 E
Samsun, *Turkey* **88 C7** 41 15N 36 22 E
Samsun Dağı, *Turkey* **45 G9** 37 45N 27 10 E
Samtredia, *Georgia* **53 E10** 42 7N 42 24 E
Samui, Ko, *Thailand* **77 H3** 9 30N 100 0 E
Samun □, *Turkey* **88 C7** 41 10N 36 10 E
Samur →, *Azerbaijan* **53 F13** 41 53N 48 32 E
Samusole, *Zaïre* **103 E4** 10 2 S 24 0 E
Samut Prakan, *Thailand* **76 F3** 13 32N 100 40 E
Samut Sakhon, *Thailand* **76 F3** 13 31N 100 13 E
Samut Songkhram →, *Thailand* **76 F3** 13 24N 100 1 E
Samwari, *Pakistan* **80 E2** 28 30N 66 46 E
San, *Mali* **100 C4** 13 15N 4 57W
San →, *Cambodia* **76 F5** 13 32N 105 57 E
San →, *Poland* **31 A14** 50 45N 21 51 E
San Adrián, C. de, *Spain* **36 B2** 43 21N 8 50W
San Agustín, *Colombia* **152 C2** 1 53N 76 16W
San Agustin, C., *Phil.* **71 H6** 6 20N 126 13 E
San Agustín de Valle Fértil, *Argentina* **158 C2** 30 35 S 67 30W
San Ambrosio, *Pac. Oc.* **123 K20** 26 28 S 79 53W
San Andreas, *U.S.A.* **144 G6** 38 12N 120 41W
San Andres, *Phil.* **70 E4** 13 19N 122 41 E
San Andrés, I. de, *Caribbean* **148 D3** 12 42N 81 46W
San Andres Mts., *U.S.A.* **143 K10** 33 0N 106 30W
San Andrés Tuxtla, *Mexico* **147 D5** 18 30N 95 20W
San Angelo, *U.S.A.* **139 K4** 31 28N 100 26W
San Anselmo, *U.S.A.* **144 H4** 37 59N 122 34W
San Antonio, *Belize* **147 D7** 16 15N 89 2W
San Antonio, *Chile* **158 C1** 33 40 S 71 40W
San Antonio, *Phil.* **70 D3** 14 57N 120 5 E
San Antonio, *N. Mex., U.S.A.* **143 K10** 33 55N 106 52W
San Antonio, *Tex., U.S.A.* **139 L5** 29 25N 98 30W
San Antonio, *Venezuela* **152 C4** 3 30N 66 44W
San Antonio →, *U.S.A.* **139 L6** 28 30N 96 54W
San Antonio, C., *Argentina* **158 D4** 36 15 S 56 40W
San Antonio, C., *Cuba* **148 B3** 21 50N 84 57W
San Antonio, C. de, *Spain* **35 G5** 38 48N 0 12 E
San Antonio, Mt., *U.S.A.* **145 L9** 34 17N 117 38W
San Antonio Abad, *Spain* **33 C7** 38 59N 1 19 E
San Antonio Bay, *Phil.* **71 G1** 8 38N 117 35 E
San Antonio de los Baños, *Cuba* **148 B3** 22 54N 82 31W
San Antonio de los Cobres, *Argentina* **158 A2** 24 10 S 66 17W
San Antonio Oeste, *Argentina* **160 B4** 40 40 S 65 0W
San Arcángelo, *Italy* **41 B9** 40 14N 16 14 E
San Ardo, *U.S.A.* **144 J6** 36 1N 120 54W
San Augustín, *Canary Is.* **33 G4** 27 47N 15 32W
San Augustine, *U.S.A.* **139 K7** 31 30N 94 7W
San Bartolomé, *Canary Is.* **33 F6** 28 59N 13 37W
San Bartolomé de Tirajana, *Canary Is.* **33 G4** 27 54N 15 34W
San Bartolomeo in Galdo, *Italy* **41 A8** 41 23N 15 2 E
San Benedetto, *Italy* **38 C7** 45 2N 10 57 E
San Benedetto del Tronto, *Italy* **39 F10** 42 57N 13 52 E
San Benedicto, I., *Mexico* **146 D2** 19 18N 110 49W
San Benito, *U.S.A.* **139 M6** 26 8N 97 38W
San Benito →, *U.S.A.* **144 J5** 36 53N 121 34W
San Benito Mt., *U.S.A.* **144 J6** 36 22N 120 37W
San Bernardino, *U.S.A.* **145 L9** 34 7N 117 19W
San Bernardino, Paso del, *Switz.* **29 D8** 46 28N 9 11 E
San Bernardino Mts., *U.S.A.* **145 L10** 34 10N 116 45W
San Bernardino Str., *Phil.* **70 E5** 13 0N 125 0 E
San Bernardo, *Chile* **158 C1** 33 40 S 70 50W
San Bernardo, I. de, *Colombia* **152 B2** 9 45N 75 50W
San Blas, *Mexico* **146 B3** 26 4N 108 46W
San Blas, Arch. de, *Panama* **148 E4** 9 50N 78 31W
San Blas, C., *U.S.A.* **135 L3** 29 40N 85 21W
San Borja, *Bolivia* **156 C4** 14 50 S 66 52W
San Buenaventura, *Bolivia* **156 C4** 14 28 S 67 35W
San Buenaventura, *Mexico* **146 B4** 27 5N 101 32W
San Carlos = Butuku-Luba, *Eq. Guin.* **101 E6** 3 29N 8 33 E
San Carlos, *Argentina* **158 C2** 33 50 S 69 0W
San Carlos, *Bolivia* **157 D5** 17 24 S 63 45W
San Carlos, *Chile* **158 D1** 36 10 S 72 0W
San Carlos, *Mexico* **146 B4** 29 0N 100 54W
San Carlos, *Nic.* **148 D3** 11 12N 84 50W
San Carlos, *Negros, Phil.* **71 F4** 10 29N 123 25 E
San Carlos, *Pangasinan, Phil.* **70 D3** 15 55N 120 20 E
San Carlos, *Spain* **33 B8** 39 3N 1 34 E
San Carlos, *Uruguay* **159 C5** 34 46 S 54 58W
San Carlos, *U.S.A.* **143 K8** 33 21N 110 27W
San Carlos, *Amazonas, Venezuela* **152 C4** 1 55N 67 4W
San Carlos, *Cojedes, Venezuela* **152 B4** 9 40N 68 36W
San Carlos de Bariloche, *Argentina* **160 B2** 41 10 S 71 25W
San Carlos de la Rápita, *Spain* **34 E5** 40 37N 0 35 E
San Carlos del Zulia, *Venezuela* **152 B3** 9 1N 71 55W
San Carlos L., *U.S.A.* **143 K8** 33 11N 110 32W
San Cataldo, *Italy* **40 E6** 37 30N 13 58 E
San Celoni, *Spain* **34 D7** 41 42N 2 30 E
San Clemente, *Chile* **158 D1** 35 30 S 71 29W
San Clemente, *Spain* **35 F2** 39 24N 2 25W
San Clemente, *U.S.A.* **145 M9** 33 26N 117 37W
San Clemente I., *U.S.A.* **145 N8** 32 53N 118 29W
San Constanzo, *Italy* **39 E10** 43 46N 13 5 E
San Cristóbal, *Argentina* **158 C3** 30 20 S 61 10W
San Cristóbal, *Colombia* **152 D3** 2 18 S 73 2W
San Cristóbal, *Dom. Rep.* **149 C5** 18 25N 70 6W
San Cristóbal, *Mexico* **147 D6** 16 50N 92 33W
San Cristóbal, *Solomon Is.* **121 N11** 10 30 S 161 0 E
San Cristóbal, *Spain* **33 B11** 39 57N 4 3 E
San Cristóbal, *Venezuela* **152 B3** 7 46N 72 14W
San Damiano d'Asti, *Italy* **38 D5** 44 51N 8 4 E
San Daniele del Friuli, *Italy* **39 B10** 46 10N 13 0 E
San Demétrio Corone, *Italy* **41 C9** 39 34N 16 22 E
San Diego, *Calif., U.S.A.* **145 N9** 32 43N 117 9W
San Diego, *Tex., U.S.A.* **139 M5** 27 46N 98 14W
San Diego, C., *Argentina* **160 D3** 54 40 S 65 10W
San Diego de la Unión, *Mexico* **146 C4** 21 28N 100 52W
San Dimitri, Ras, *Malta* **32 C1** 36 4N 14 11 E
San Dionosio, *Phil.* **71 F4** 11 16N 123 6 E
San Donà di Piave, *Italy* **39 C9** 45 38N 12 34 E
San Elpídio a Mare, *Italy* **39 E10** 43 16N 13 41 E
San Emilio, *Phil.* **70 C3** 17 14N 120 37 E
San Estanislao, *Paraguay* **158 A4** 24 39 S 56 26W
San Esteban de Gormaz, *Spain* **34 D1** 41 34N 3 13W
San Fabian, *Phil.* **70 C3** 16 5N 120 25 E
San Felice sul Panaro, *Italy* **38 D8** 44 51N 11 9 E
San Felipe, *Chile* **158 C1** 32 43 S 70 42W
San Felipe, *Colombia* **152 C4** 1 55N 67 6W
San Felipe, *Mexico* **146 A2** 31 0N 114 52W
San Felipe, *Phil.* **70 D3** 15 4N 120 4 E
San Felipe, *Venezuela* **152 A4** 10 20N 68 44W
San Felipe →, *U.S.A.* **145 M11** 33 12N 115 49W
San Felíu de Guíxols, *Spain* **34 D8** 41 45N 3 1 E
San Felíu de Llobregat, *Spain* **34 D7** 41 23N 2 2 E
San Félix, *Pac. Oc.* **123 K20** 26 23 S 80 0W
San Fernando, *Chile* **158 C1** 34 30 S 71 0W
San Fernando, *Mexico* **146 B1** 29 55N 115 10W
San Fernando, *Cebu, Phil.* **71 F4** 10 10N 123 42 E
San Fernando, *La Union, Phil.* **70 C3** 16 40N 120 23 E
San Fernando, *Pampanga, Phil.* **70 D3** 15 5N 120 37 E
San Fernando, *Tablas, Phil.* **70 E4** 12 18N 122 36 E
San Fernando, *Baleares, Spain* **33 C7** 38 42N 1 28 E
San Fernando, *Cádiz, Spain* **37 J4** 36 28N 6 17W
San Fernando, *Trin. & Tob.* **149 D7** 10 20N 61 30W
San Fernando, *U.S.A.* **145 L8** 34 17N 118 26W
San Fernando →, *Mexico* **146 C5** 24 55N 98 10W
San Fernando de Apure, *Venezuela* **152 B4** 7 54N 67 15W
San Fernando de Atabapo, *Venezuela* **152 C4** 4 3N 67 42W
San Fernando di Púglia, *Italy* **41 A9** 41 18N 16 5 E
San Francisco, *Argentina* **158 C3** 31 30 S 62 5W
San Francisco, *Bolivia* **157 D4** 15 16 S 65 31W
San Francisco, *Cebu, Phil.* **71 F5** 10 39N 124 23 E
San Francisco, *Leyte, Phil.* **71 F5** 10 4N 125 9 E
San Francisco, *Mindanao, Phil.* **71 G5** 8 30N 125 56 E
San Francisco, *U.S.A.* **144 H4** 37 47N 122 25W
San Francisco →, *U.S.A.* **143 K9** 32 59N 109 22W
San Francisco, Paso de, *S. Amer.* **158 B2** 27 0 S 68 0W
San Francisco de Macorîs, *Dom. Rep.* **149 C5** 19 19N 70 15W
San Francisco del Monte de Oro, *Argentina* **158 C2** 32 36 S 66 8W
San Francisco del Oro, *Mexico* **146 B3** 26 52N 105 50W
San Francisco Javier, *Spain* **33 C7** 38 42N 1 26 E
San Francisco Solano, Pta., *Colombia* **152 B2** 6 18N 77 29W
San Fratello, *Italy* **41 D7** 38 1N 14 33 E
San Gabriel, *Ecuador* **152 C2** 0 36N 77 49W
San Gavino Monreale, *Italy* **40 C1** 39 33N 8 47 E
San Gil, *Colombia* **152 B3** 6 33N 73 8W
San Gimignano, *Italy* **38 E8** 43 28N 11 3 E
San Giórgio di Nogaro, *Italy* **39 C10** 45 50N 13 13 E
San Giórgio Iónico, *Italy* **41 B10** 40 27N 17 23 E
San Giovanni Bianco, *Italy* **38 C6** 45 52N 9 40 E
San Giovanni in Fiore, *Italy* **41 C9** 39 16N 16 42 E
San Giovanni in Persiceto, *Italy* **39 D8** 44 39N 11 12 E
San Giovanni Rotondo, *Italy* **41 A8** 41 41N 15 42 E
San Giovanni Valdarno, *Italy* **39 E8** 43 32N 11 30 E
San Giuliano Terme, *Italy* **38 E7** 43 45N 10 26 E
San Gorgonio Mt., *U.S.A.* **145 L10** 34 7N 116 51W
San Gottardo, Paso del, *Switz.* **29 C7** 46 33N 8 33 E
San Gregorio, *Uruguay* **159 C4** 32 37 S 55 40W
San Gregorio, *U.S.A.* **144 H4** 37 20N 122 23W
San Guiseppe Iato, *Italy* **40 E6** 37 57N 13 11 E
San Ignacio, *Belize* **147 D7** 17 10N 89 0W
San Ignacio, *Bolivia* **157 D5** 16 20 S 60 55W
San Ignacio, *Mexico* **146 B2** 27 27N 113 0W
San Ignacio, *Paraguay* **158 B4** 26 52 S 57 3W
San Ignacio, L., *Mexico* **146 B2** 26 50N 113 11W
San Ildefonso, *Phil.* **70 D3** 15 5N 120 56 E
San Ildefonso, C., *Phil.* **70 C4** 16 0N 122 1 E
San Isidro, *Argentina* **158 C4** 34 29 S 58 31W
San Jacinto, *Colombia* **152 B2** 9 50N 75 8W
San Jacinto, *Phil.* **70 E4** 12 34N 123 44 E
San Jacinto, *U.S.A.* **145 M10** 33 47N 116 57W
San Jaime, *Spain* **33 B11** 39 54N 4 4 E
San Javier, *Misiones, Argentina* **159 B4** 27 55 S 55 5W
San Javier, *Santa Fe, Argentina* **158 C4** 30 40 S 59 55W
San Javier, *Beni, Bolivia* **157 C5** 14 34 S 64 42W
San Javier, *Santa Cruz, Bolivia* **157 D5** 16 18 S 62 30W
San Javier, *Chile* **158 D1** 35 40 S 71 45W
San Javier, *Spain* **35 H4** 37 49N 0 50W
San Jerónimo, Sa. de, *Colombia* **152 B2** 8 0N 75 50W
San Jeronimo Taviche, *Mexico* **147 D5** 16 38N 96 32W
San Joaquín, *Bolivia* **157 C5** 13 4 S 64 49W
San Joaquin, *Phil.* **71 F4** 10 35N 122 8 E
San Joaquin, *U.S.A.* **144 J6** 36 36N 120 11W
San Joaquín, *Venezuela* **152 A4** 10 16N 67 47W
San Joaquín →, *Bolivia* **157 C5** 13 8 S 63 41W
San Joaquin →, *U.S.A.* **144 G5** 38 4N 121 51W
San Joaquin Valley, *U.S.A.* **144 J6** 37 20N 121 0W
San Jordi, *Spain* **33 B9** 39 33N 2 46 E
San Jorge, *Argentina* **158 C3** 31 54 S 61 50W
San Jorge, *Spain* **33 C7** 38 54N 1 24 E
San Jorge, B. de, *Mexico* **146 A2** 31 20N 113 20W
San Jorge, G., *Argentina* **160 C3** 46 0 S 66 0W
San Jorge, G. de, *Spain* **34 E4** 40 50N 0 55W
San José, *Bolivia* **157 D5** 17 53 S 60 50W
San José, *Costa Rica* **148 E3** 9 55N 84 2W
San José, *Guatemala* **148 D1** 14 0N 90 50W
San José, *Mexico* **146 C2** 25 0N 110 50W
San Jose, *Phil.* **70 D3** 15 45N 120 55 E
San José, *Spain* **33 C7** 38 55N 1 18 E
San Jose, *Calif., U.S.A.* **144 H5** 37 20N 121 53W
San Jose, *Ill., U.S.A.* **140 D7** 40 18N 89 36W
San Jose →, *U.S.A.* **143 J10** 34 25N 106 45W
San Jose de Buenovista, *Phil.* **70 E3** 12 27N 121 4 E
San José de Feliciano, *Argentina* **158 C4** 30 26 S 58 46W
San José de Jáchal, *Argentina* **158 C2** 30 15 S 68 46W
San José de Mayo, *Uruguay* **158 C4** 34 27 S 56 40W
San José de Ocune, *Colombia* **152 C3** 4 15N 70 20W
San José de Uchapiamonas, *Bolivia* **156 C4** 14 13 S 68 5W
San José del Cabo, *Mexico* **146 C3** 23 0N 109 40W
San José del Guaviare, *Colombia* **152 C3** 2 35N 72 38W
San José do Anauá, *Brazil* **153 C5** 0 58N 61 22W
San Juan, *Argentina* **158 C2** 31 30 S 68 30W
San Juan, *Colombia* **152 B2** 8 46N 76 32W
San Juan, *Mexico* **146 C4** 21 20N 102 50W
San Juan, *Ica, Peru* **156 D2** 15 22 S 75 7W
San Juan, *Puno, Peru* **156 C4** 14 2 S 69 30W
San Juan, *Luzon, Phil.* **70 C3** 16 40N 120 20 E
San Juan, *Mindanao, Phil.* **71 G6** 8 25N 126 20 E
San Juan, *Puerto Rico* **149 C6** 18 28N 66 7W
San Juan □, *Argentina* **158 C2** 31 9 S 69 0W
San Juan →, *Argentina* **158 C2** 32 20 S 67 25W
San Juan →, *Bolivia* **157 E4** 21 2 S 65 19W
San Juan →, *Colombia* **152 C2** 4 3N 77 27W
San Juan →, *Nic.* **148 D3** 10 56N 83 42W
San Juan →, *U.S.A.* **143 H8** 37 16N 110 26W
San Juan →, *Venezuela* **153 A5** 10 14N 62 38W
San Juan, C., *Eq. Guin.* **102 B1** 1 5N 9 20 E
San Juan Bautista, *Paraguay* **158 B4** 26 37 S 57 6W
San Juan Bautista, *Spain* **33 B8** 39 5N 1 31 E
San Juan Bautista, *U.S.A.* **144 J5** 36 51N 121 32W
San Juan Bautista Valle Nacional, *Mexico* **147 D5** 17 47N 96 19W
San Juan Capistrano, *U.S.A.* **145 M9** 33 30N 117 40W
San Juan Cr. →, *U.S.A.* **144 J5** 35 40N 120 22W
San Juan de Guadalupe, *Mexico* **146 C4** 24 38N 102 44W
San Juan de los Morros, *Venezuela* **152 B4** 9 55N 67 21W
San Juan del César, *Colombia* **152 A3** 10 46N 73 1W
San Juan del Norte, *Nic.* **148 D3** 10 58N 83 40W
San Juan del Norte, B. de, *Nic.* **148 D3** 11 0N 83 40W
San Juan del Puerto, *Spain* **37 H4** 37 20N 6 50W
San Juan del Río, *Mexico* **147 C5** 20 25N 100 0W
San Juan del Sur, *Nic.* **148 D2** 11 20N 85 51W
San Juan I., *U.S.A.* **144 B3** 48 32N 123 5W
San Juan Mts., *U.S.A.* **143 H10** 37 30N 107 0W
San Julián, *Argentina* **160 C3** 49 15 S 67 45W
San Julian, *Phil.* **71 F5** 11 45N 125 27 E
San Just, Sierra de, *Spain* **34 E4** 40 45N 0 49W
San Justo, *Argentina* **158 C3** 30 47 S 60 30W
San Kamphaeng, *Thailand* **76 C2** 18 45N 99 8 E
San Lázaro, C., *Mexico* **146 C2** 24 50N 112 18W
San Lázaro, Sa., *Mexico* **146 C3** 23 25N 110 0W
San Leandro, *U.S.A.* **144 H4** 37 44N 122 9W
San Leonardo, *Spain* **34 D1** 41 51N 3 5W
San Lorenzo, *Argentina* **158 C3** 32 45 S 60 45W
San Lorenzo, *Beni, Bolivia* **157 D4** 15 22 S 65 48W
San Lorenzo, *Tarija, Bolivia* **157 E5** 21 26 S 64 47W
San Lorenzo, *Ecuador* **152 C2** 1 15N 78 50W
San Lorenzo, *Paraguay* **158 B4** 25 20 S 57 32W
San Lorenzo, *Spain* **33 B10** 39 37N 3 17 E
San Lorenzo, *Venezuela* **152 B3** 9 47N 71 4W
San Lorenzo →, *Mexico* **146 C3** 24 15N 107 24W
San Lorenzo, I., *Mexico* **146 B2** 28 35N 112 50W
San Lorenzo, I., *Peru* **156 C2** 12 7 S 77 15W
San Lorenzo, Mt., *Argentina* **160 C2** 47 40 S 72 20W
San Lorenzo de la Parrilla, *Spain* **34 F2** 39 51N 2 22W
San Lorenzo de Morunys, *Spain* **34 C6** 42 8N 1 35 E
San Lucas, *Bolivia* **157 E4** 20 5 S 65 7W
San Lucas, *Baja Calif. S., Mexico* **146 C3** 22 53N 109 54W
San Lucas, *Baja Calif. S., Mexico* **146 B2** 27 10N 112 14W
San Lucas, *U.S.A.* **144 J5** 36 8N 121 1W
San Lucas, C., *Mexico* **146 C3** 22 50N 110 0W
San Lúcido, *Italy* **41 C9** 39 18N 16 3 E
San Luis, *Argentina* **158 C2** 33 20 S 66 20W
San Luis, *Cuba* **148 B3** 22 17N 83 46W
San Luis, *Guatemala* **148 C2** 16 14N 89 27W
San Luis, *U.S.A.* **143 H11** 37 12N 105 25W
San Luis □, *Argentina* **158 C2** 34 0 S 66 0W
San Luis, I., *Mexico* **146 B2** 29 58N 114 26W
San Luis, L. de, *Bolivia* **157 C5** 13 45 S 64 0W
San Luis, Sierra de, *Argentina* **158 C2** 32 30 S 66 10W
San Luis de la Paz, *Mexico* **146 C4** 21 19N 100 32W
San Luis Obispo, *U.S.A.* **145 K6** 35 17N 120 40W
San Luis Potosí, *Mexico* **146 C4** 22 9N 100 59W
San Luis Potosí □, *Mexico* **146 C4** 22 10N 101 0W
San Luis Reservoir, *U.S.A.* **144 H5** 37 4N 121 5W
San Luis Río Colorado, *Mexico* **146 A2** 32 29N 114 58W
San Manuel, *Phil.* **70 C3** 16 4N 120 40 E
San Marco Argentano, *Italy* **41 C9** 39 34N 16 8 E
San Marco dei Cavoti, *Italy* **41 A7** 41 20N 14 50 E
San Marco in Lámis, *Italy* **41 A8** 41 43N 15 38 E
San Marcos, *Colombia* **152 B2** 8 39N 75 8W
San Marcos, *Guatemala* **148 D1** 14 59N 91 52W
San Marcos, *Mexico* **146 B2** 27 13N 112 6W
San Marcos, *U.S.A.* **139 L6** 29 53N 97 56W
San Marino ■, *Europe* **39 E9** 43 56N 12 25 E
San Martín, *Argentina* **158 C2** 33 5 S 68 28W
San Martín, *Colombia* **152 C3** 3 42N 73 42W
San Martin →, *Bolivia* **157 C5** 13 8 S 63 43W
San Martín, L., *Argentina* **160 C2** 48 50 S 72 50W
San Martin de los Andes, *Argentina* **160 B2** 40 10 S 71 20W
San Martín de Valdeiglesias, *Spain* **36 E6** 40 21N 4 24W
San Martino de Calvi, *Italy* **38 C6** 45 57N 9 41 E
San Mateo, *Agusan del N., Phil.* **71 G5** 8 48N 125 33 E
San Mateo, *Isabela, Phil.* **70 C3** 16 54N 121 33 E
San Mateo, *Baleares, Spain* **33 B7** 39 3N 1 23 E
San Mateo, *Valencia, Spain* **34 E5** 40 28N 0 10 E
San Mateo, *U.S.A.* **144 H4** 37 34N 122 19W
San Matías, *Bolivia* **157 D6** 16 25 S 58 20W
San Matías, G., *Argentina* **160 B4** 41 30 S 64 0W
San Miguel = Linapacan, *Phil.* **71 F2** 11 30N 119 52 E
San Miguel, *El Salv.* **148 D2** 13 30N 88 12W
San Miguel, *Panama* **148 E4** 8 27N 78 55W
San Miguel, *Lanao del N., Phil.* **71 G5** 9 3N 125 59 E
San Miguel, *Lanao del S., Phil.* **71 G5** 8 13N 124 14 E
San Miguel, *Spain* **33 B7** 39 3N 1 26 E
San Miguel, *U.S.A.* **144 K6** 35 45N 120 42W
San Miguel, *Venezuela* **152 B4** 9 40N 65 11W
San Miguel →, *Bolivia* **157 C5** 13 52 S 63 56W
San Miguel →, *S. Amer.* **152 C2** 0 25N 76 30W
San Miguel de Huachi, *Bolivia* **156 D4** 15 40 S 67 15W
San Miguel de Salinas, *Spain* **35 H4** 37 59N 0 47W
San Miguel de Tucumán, *Argentina* **158 B2** 26 50 S 65 20W
San Miguel del Monte, *Argentina* **158 D4** 35 23 S 58 50W
San Miguel I., *U.S.A.* **145 L6** 34 2N 120 23W
San Miguel Is., *Phil.* **71 H2** 7 45N 118 28 E
San Miniato, *Italy* **38 E7** 43 40N 10 50 E
San Narciso, *Quezon, Phil.* **70 E4** 13 34N 122 34 E
San Narciso, *Zambales, Phil.* **70 D3** 15 2N 120 3 E
San Nicolás, *Canary Is.* **33 G4** 27 58N 15 47W
San Nicolas, *Phil.* **70 B3** 18 10N 120 36 E
San Nicolás de los Arroyos, *Argentina* **158 C3** 33 25 S 60 10W
San Nicolas I., *U.S.A.* **145 M7** 33 15N 119 30W
San Onofre, *Colombia* **152 B2** 9 44N 75 32W
San Onofre, *U.S.A.* **145 M9** 33 22N 117 34W
San Pablo, *Bolivia* **158 A2** 21 43 S 66 38W
San Pablo, *Isabela, Phil.* **70 C3** 17 27N 121 48 E
San Pablo, *Laguna, Phil.* **70 D3** 14 11N 121 31 E
San Paolo di Civitate, *Italy* **41 A8** 41 44N 15 16 E
San Pascual, *Phil.* **70 E4** 13 8N 122 59 E
San Pedro, *Buenos Aires, Argentina* **159 B5** 26 30 S 54 10W

Santa Rosa de Osos 261

San Pedro, *Jujuy, Argentina* **158 A3** 24 12 S 64 55W
San Pedro, *Colombia* **152 C3** 4 56N 71 53W
San-Pédro, *Ivory C.* **100 E3** 4 50N 6 33W
San Pedro, *Mexico* **146 C2** 23 55N 110 17W
San Pedro, *Peru* **156 C3** 14 49 S 74 5W
San Pedro □, *Paraguay* **158 A4** 24 0 S 57 0W
San Pedro →, *Chihuahua, Mexico* **146 B3** 28 20N 106 10W
San Pedro →, *Michoacan, Mexico* **146 D4** 19 23N 103 51W
San Pedro →, *Nayarit, Mexico* **146 C3** 21 45N 105 30W
San Pedro →, *U.S.A.* **143 K8** 32 59N 110 47W
San Pedro, Pta., *Chile* **158 B1** 25 30 S 70 38W
San Pedro, Sierra de, *Spain* **37 F4** 39 18N 6 40W
San Pedro Channel, *U.S.A.* **145 M8** 33 30N 118 25W
San Pedro de Arimena, *Colombia* **152 C3** 4 37N 71 42W
San Pedro de Atacama, *Chile* **158 A2** 22 55 S 68 15W
San Pedro de Jujuy, *Argentina* **158 A3** 24 12 S 64 55W
San Pedro de las Colonias, *Mexico* **146 B4** 25 50N 102 59W
San Pedro de Lloc, *Peru* **156 B2** 7 15 S 79 28W
San Pedro de Macorís, *Dom. Rep.* **149 C6** 18 30N 69 18W
San Pedro del Norte, *Nic.* **148 D3** 13 4N 84 33W
San Pedro del Paraná, *Paraguay* **158 B4** 26 43 S 56 13W
San Pedro del Pinatar, *Spain* **35 H4** 37 50N 0 50W
San Pedro Mártir, Sierra, *Mexico* **146 A1** 31 0N 115 30W
San Pedro Mixtepec, *Mexico* **147 D5** 16 2N 97 7W
San Pedro Ocampo = Melchor Ocampo, *Mexico* **146 C4** 24 52N 101 40W
San Pedro Sula, *Honduras* **148 C2** 15 30N 88 0W
San Pietro, I., *Italy* **40 C1** 39 9N 8 17 E
San Pietro Vernótico, *Italy* **41 B11** 40 28N 18 0 E
San Quintín, *Mexico* **146 A1** 30 29N 115 57W
San Rafael, *Argentina* **158 C2** 34 40 S 68 21W
San Rafael, *Calif., U.S.A.* **144 H4** 37 58N 122 32W
San Rafael, *N. Mex., U.S.A.* **143 J10** 35 7N 107 53W
San Rafael, *Venezuela* **152 A3** 10 58N 71 46W
San Rafael Mt., *U.S.A.* **145 L7** 34 41N 119 52W
San Rafael Mts., *U.S.A.* **145 L7** 34 40N 119 50W
San Ramón, *Bolivia* **157 C5** 13 17 S 64 43W
San Ramón, *Peru* **156 C2** 11 8 S 75 20W
San Ramón de la Nueva Orán, *Argentina* **158 A3** 23 10 S 64 20W
San Remo, *Italy* **38 E4** 43 48N 7 47 E
San Román, C., *Venezuela* **152 A3** 12 12N 70 0W
San Roque, *Argentina* **158 B4** 28 25 S 58 45W
San Roque, *Phil.* **70 E5** 12 37N 124 52 E
San Roque, *Spain* **37 J5** 36 17N 5 21W
San Rosendo, *Chile* **158 D1** 37 16 S 72 43W
San Saba, *U.S.A.* **139 K5** 31 12N 98 43W
San Salvador, *Bahamas* **149 B5** 24 0N 74 40W
San Salvador, *El Salv.* **148 D2** 13 40N 89 10W
San Salvador, *Spain* **33 B10** 39 27N 3 11 E
San Salvador de Jujuy, *Argentina* **158 A3** 24 10 S 64 48W
San Salvador I., *Bahamas* **149 B5** 24 0N 74 32W
San Sebastián, *Argentina* **160 D3** 53 10 S 68 30W
San Sebastián, *Spain* **34 B3** 43 17N 1 58W
San Sebastián, *Venezuela* **152 B4** 9 57N 67 11W
San Sebastian de la Gomera, *Canary Is.* **33 F2** 28 5N 17 7W
San Serra, *Spain* **33 B10** 39 43N 3 13 E
San Serverino Marche, *Italy* **39 E10** 43 13N 13 10 E
San Simeon, *U.S.A.* **144 K5** 35 39N 121 11W
San Simon, *U.S.A.* **143 K9** 32 16N 109 14W
San Stéfano di Cadore, *Italy* **39 B9** 46 34N 12 33 E
San Telmo, *Mexico* **146 A1** 30 58N 116 6W
San Telmo, *Spain* **33 B9** 39 35N 2 21 E
San Teodoro, *Phil.* **70 E3** 13 26N 121 1 E
San Tiburcio, *Mexico* **146 C4** 24 8N 101 32W
San Valentin, Mte., *Chile* **160 C2** 46 30 S 73 30W
San Vicente de Alcántara, *Spain* **37 F3** 39 22N 7 8W
San Vicente de la Barquera, *Spain* **36 B6** 43 23N 4 29W
San Vicente del Caguán, *Colombia* **152 C3** 2 7N 74 46W
San Vincenzo, *Italy* **38 E7** 43 6N 10 29 E
San Vito, *Italy* **40 C2** 39 26N 9 32 E
San Vito, C., *Italy* **40 D5** 38 11N 12 41 E
San Vito al Tagliamento, *Italy* **39 C9** 45 55N 12 50 E
San Vito Chietino, *Italy* **39 F11** 42 19N 14 27 E
San Vito dei Normanni, *Italy* **41 B10** 40 40N 17 40 E
San Yanaro, *Colombia* **152 C4** 2 47N 69 42W
San Ygnacio, *U.S.A.* **139 M5** 27 3N 99 26W
Saña, *Peru* **156 B2** 6 54 S 79 36W
Sana', *Yemen* **86 D4** 15 27N 44 12 E
Sana →, *Bos.-H.* **39 C13** 45 3N 16 23 E
Sanaba, *Burkina Faso* **100 C4** 12 25N 3 47W
Şanāfīr, *Si. Arabia* **94 B3** 27 56N 34 42 E
Sanaga →, *Cameroon* **101 E6** 3 35N 9 38 E
Sanaloa, Presa, *Mexico* **146 C3** 24 50N 107 20W
Sanām, *Si. Arabia* **86 B4** 23 40N 44 45 E
Sanana, *Indonesia* **72 B3** 2 5 S 125 59 E
Sanana, *Indonesia* **72 B3** 2 4 S 125 58 E
Sanand, *India* **80 H5** 22 59N 72 25 E
Sanandaj, *Iran* **84 C5** 35 18N 47 1 E
Sanandita, *Bolivia* **158 A3** 21 40 S 63 45W
Sanary-sur-Mer, *France* **25 E9** 43 7N 5 49 E
Sanāw, *Yemen* **87 C5** 17 50N 51 5 E
Sanawad, *India* **80 H7** 22 11N 76 5 E
Sanbe-San, *Japan* **62 B4** 35 6N 132 38 E
Sancellas, *Spain* **33 B9** 39 39N 2 54 E
Sancergues, *France* **23 E9** 47 10N 2 54 E
Sancerre, *France* **23 E9** 47 20N 2 50 E
Sancerrois, Collines du, *France* **23 E9** 47 20N 2 40 E
Sancha He →, *China* **68 D6** 26 48N 106 7 E
Sanchahe, *China* **67 B14** 44 50N 126 2 E
Sánchez, *Dom. Rep.* **149 C6** 19 15N 69 36W
Sanchor, *India* **80 G4** 24 45N 71 55 E
Sanco Pt., *Phil.* **71 G6** 8 15N 126 27 E
Sancoins, *France* **23 F9** 46 47N 2 55 E
Sancti-Spíritus, *Cuba* **148 B4** 21 52N 79 33W
Sancy, Puy de, *France* **24 C6** 45 32N 2 50 E
Sand →, *S. Africa* **105 C5** 22 25 S 30 5 E
Sand Cr. →, *U.S.A.* **141 E11** 39 3N 85 51W
Sand Springs, *U.S.A.* **139 G6** 36 9N 96 7W
Sanda, *Japan* **63 C7** 34 53N 135 14 E
Sandakan, *Malaysia* **75 A5** 5 53N 118 4 E
Sandalwood, *Australia* **116 C4** 34 55 S 140 9 E
Sandan = Sambor, *Cambodia* **76 F6** 12 46N 106 0 E
Sandanski, *Bulgaria* **43 F8** 41 35N 23 16 E
Sandaré, *Mali* **100 C2** 14 40N 10 15W
Sanday, *U.K.* **18 B6** 59 15N 2 30W
Sandefjord, *Norway* **14 G4** 59 10N 10 15 E
Sanders, *Ariz., U.S.A.* **143 J9** 35 13N 109 20W
Sanders, *Ky., U.S.A.* **141 F12** 38 40N 84 56W
Sanderson, *U.S.A.* **139 K3** 30 9N 102 24W
Sanderston, *Australia* **116 C3** 34 46 S 139 15 E
Sandfly L., *Canada* **131 B7** 55 43N 106 6W
Sandgate, *Australia* **115 D5** 27 18 S 153 3 E
Sandía, *Peru* **156 C4** 14 10 S 69 30W
Sandıklı, *Turkey* **88 D4** 38 30N 30 20 E
Sandnes, *Norway* **13 G8** 58 50N 5 45 E
Sandness, *U.K.* **18 A7** 60 18N 1 38W
Sandoa, *Zaïre* **103 D4** 9 41 S 23 0 E
Sandomierz, *Poland* **47 E8** 50 40N 21 43 E
Sandona, *Colombia* **152 C2** 1 17N 77 28W
Sandongo, *Angola* **103 F4** 15 30 S 21 28 E
Sandoval, *U.S.A.* **140 F7** 38 37N 89 7W
Sandover →, *Australia* **114 C2** 21 43 S 136 32 E
Sandpoint, *U.S.A.* **142 B5** 48 17N 116 33W
Sandringham, *U.K.* **16 E8** 52 50N 0 30 E
Sandslån, *Sweden* **14 A11** 63 2N 17 49 E
Sandspit, *Canada* **130 C2** 53 14N 131 49W
Sandstone, *Australia* **113 E2** 27 59 S 119 16 E
Sandu, *China* **68 E6** 26 0N 107 52 E
Sandusky, *Mich., U.S.A.* **128 D3** 43 25N 82 50W
Sandusky, *Ohio, U.S.A.* **136 E2** 41 27N 82 42W
Sandusky →, *U.S.A.* **141 C14** 41 27N 83 0W
Sandvig, *Sweden* **15 J8** 55 18N 14 47 E
Sandviken, *Sweden* **13 F14** 60 38N 16 46 E
Sandwich, *U.S.A.* **141 C8** 41 39N 88 37W
Sandwich, C., *Australia* **114 B4** 18 14 S 146 18 E
Sandwich B., *Canada* **129 B8** 53 40N 57 15W
Sandwich B., *Namibia* **104 C1** 23 25 S 14 20 E
Sandy, *Nev., U.S.A.* **145 K11** 35 49N 115 36W
Sandy, *Oreg., U.S.A.* **144 E4** 45 24N 122 16W
Sandy Bight, *Australia* **113 F3** 33 50 S 123 20 E
Sandy C., *Queens., Australia* **114 C5** 24 42 S 153 15 E
Sandy C., *Tas., Australia* **114 G3** 41 25 S 144 45 E
Sandy Cay, *Bahamas* **149 B4** 23 13N 75 18W
Sandy Cr. →, *U.S.A.* **142 F9** 41 51N 109 47W
Sandy L., *Canada* **128 B1** 53 2N 93 0W
Sandy Lake, *Canada* **128 B1** 53 0N 93 15W
Sandy Narrows, *Canada* **131 B8** 55 5N 103 4W
Sanford, *Fla., U.S.A.* **135 L5** 28 48N 81 16W
Sanford, *Maine, U.S.A.* **137 C14** 43 27N 70 47W
Sanford, *N.C., U.S.A.* **135 H6** 35 29N 79 10W
Sanford →, *Australia* **113 E2** 27 22 S 115 53 E
Sanford, Mt., *U.S.A.* **126 B5** 62 13N 144 8W
Sang-i-Masha, *Afghan.* **80 C2** 33 8N 67 27 E
Sanga, *Mozam.* **107 E4** 12 22 S 35 21 E
Sanga →, *Congo* **102 C3** 1 5 S 17 0 E
Sanga-Tolon, *Russia* **57 C15** 61 50N 149 40 E
Sangamner, *India* **82 E2** 19 37N 74 15 E
Sangamon →, *U.S.A.* **140 D6** 40 7N 90 20W
Sangar, *Afghan.* **80 C1** 32 56N 65 30 E
Sangar, *Russia* **57 C13** 64 2N 127 31 E
Sangar Sarai, *Afghan.* **80 B4** 34 27N 70 35 E
Sangasangadalam, *Indonesia* **75 C5** 0 36 S 117 13 E
Sangay, *Ecuador* **152 D2** 2 0 S 78 20W
Sange, *Zaïre* **106 D2** 6 58 S 28 21 E
Sangeang, *Indonesia* **72 C1** 8 12 S 119 6 E
Sanger, *U.S.A.* **144 J7** 36 42N 119 33W
Sangerhausen, *Germany* **26 D7** 51 28N 11 18 E
Sanggan He →, *China* **66 E9** 38 12N 117 15 E
Sanggau, *Indonesia* **75 B4** 0 5N 110 30 E
Sangihe, Kepulauan, *Indonesia* **72 A3** 3 0N 126 0 E
Sangihe, P., *Indonesia* **72 A3** 3 45N 125 30 E
Sangju, *S. Korea* **67 F15** 36 25N 128 10 E
Sangkapura, *Indonesia* **75 D4** 5 52 S 112 40 E
Sangkhla, *Thailand* **76 E2** 14 57N 98 28 E
Sangli, *India* **82 F2** 16 55N 74 33 E
Sangmélina, *Cameroon* **101 E7** 2 57N 12 1 E
Sangonera →, *Spain* **35 H3** 37 59N 1 4W
Sangpang Bum, *Burma* **78 B5** 26 30N 95 50 E
Sangre de Cristo Mts., *U.S.A.* **139 G2** 37 0N 105 0W
Sangro →, *Italy* **39 F11** 42 14N 14 32 E
Sangudo, *Canada* **130 C6** 53 50N 114 54W
Sangue →, *Brazil* **157 C6** 11 1 S 58 39W
Sangüesa, *Spain* **34 C3** 42 37N 1 17W
Sanguinaires, Is., *France* **25 G12** 41 51N 8 36 E
Sangzhi, *China* **69 C8** 29 25N 110 12 E
Sanhala, *Ivory C.* **100 C3** 10 3N 6 51W
Sāniyah, *Iraq* **84 C4** 33 49N 42 43 E
Sanje, *Uganda* **106 C3** 0 49 S 31 30 E
Sanjiang, *China* **68 E7** 25 48N 109 37 E
Sanjo, *Japan* **60 F9** 37 37N 138 57 E
Sankarankovil, *India* **83 K3** 9 10N 77 35 E
Sankeshwar, *India* **83 F2** 16 23N 74 32 E
Sankosh →, *India* **78 B2** 26 24N 89 47 E
Sankt Andrä, *Austria* **30 E7** 46 46N 14 50 E
Sankt Antönien, *Switz.* **29 C9** 46 58N 9 48 E
Sankt Blasien, *Germany* **27 H4** 47 47N 8 7 E
Sankt Gallen, *Switz.* **29 B8** 47 26N 9 22 E
Sankt Gallen □, *Switz.* **29 B8** 47 25N 9 22 E
Sankt Goar, *Germany* **27 E3** 50 12N 7 43 E
Sankt Ingbert, *Germany* **27 F3** 49 16N 7 6 E
Sankt Johann, *Salzburg, Austria* **30 D6** 47 22N 13 12 E
Sankt Johann, *Tirol, Austria* **30 D5** 47 30N 12 25 E
Sankt Margrethen, *Switz.* **29 B9** 47 28N 9 37 E
Sankt Moritz, *Switz.* **29 D9** 46 30N 9 50 E
Sankt-Peterburg, *Russia* **50 B7** 59 55N 30 20 E
Sankt Pölten, *Austria* **30 C8** 48 12N 15 38 E
Sankt Valentin, *Austria* **30 C7** 48 11N 14 33 E
Sankt Veit, *Austria* **30 E7** 46 54N 14 22 E
Sankt Wendel, *Germany* **27 F3** 49 27N 7 9 E
Sankt Wolfgang, *Austria* **30 D6** 47 43N 13 27 E
Sankuru →, *Zaïre* **103 C4** 4 17 S 20 25 E
Sanlúcar de Barrameda, *Spain* **37 J4** 36 46N 6 21W
Sanlúcar la Mayor, *Spain* **37 H4** 37 26N 6 18W
Sanluri, *Italy* **40 C1** 39 35N 8 55 E
Sanmenxia, *China* **66 G6** 34 47N 111 12 E
Sanming, *China* **65 D6** 26 13N 117 35 E
Sanming, *Fujian, China* **69 D11** 26 15N 117 40 E
Sannan, *Japan* **63 B7** 35 2N 135 1 E
Sannaspos, *S. Africa* **104 D4** 29 6 S 26 34 E
Sannicandro Gargánico, *Italy* **41 A8** 41 50N 15 34 E
Sannidal, *Norway* **14 F3** 58 55N 9 15 E
Sannieshof, *S. Africa* **104 D4** 26 30 S 25 47 E
Sannīn, J., *Lebanon* **91 B4** 33 57N 35 52 E
Sano, *Japan* **63 A11** 36 19N 139 35 E
Sanok, *Poland* **31 B15** 49 35N 22 10 E
Sanquhar, *U.K.* **18 F5** 55 21N 3 56W
Sansanding Dam, *Mali* **100 C3** 13 48N 6 0W
Sansepolcro, *Italy* **39 E9** 43 34N 12 8 E
Sansha, *China* **69 D13** 26 58N 120 12 E
Sanshui, *China* **69 F9** 23 10N 112 56 E
Sanski Most, *Bos.-H.* **39 D13** 44 46N 16 40 E
Sansui, *China* **68 D7** 26 58N 108 39 E
Santa, *Peru* **156 B2** 8 59 S 78 40W
Sant' Ágata de Goti, *Italy* **41 A7** 41 6N 14 30 E
Sant' Ágata di Militello, *Italy* **41 D7** 38 2N 14 8 E
Santa Ana, *Beni, Bolivia* **157 C4** 13 50 S 65 40W
Santa Ana, *Santa Cruz, Bolivia* **157 D6** 18 43 S 58 44W
Santa Ana, *Santa Cruz, Bolivia* **157 D5** 16 37 S 60 43W
Santa Ana, *Ecuador* **152 D1** 1 16 S 80 20W
Santa Ana, *El Salv.* **148 D2** 14 0N 89 31W
Santa Ana, *Mexico* **146 A2** 30 31N 111 8W
Santa Ana, *Phil.* **70 B4** 18 28N 122 20 E
Santa Ana, *U.S.A.* **145 M9** 33 46N 117 52W
Santa Ana →, *Venezuela* **152 B3** 9 30N 71 57W
Sant' Ángelo Lodigiano, *Italy* **38 C6** 45 14N 9 25 E
Sant' Antíoco, *Italy* **40 C1** 39 2N 8 30 E
Sant' Arcángelo di Romagna, *Italy* **39 D9** 44 4N 12 26 E
Santa Bárbara, *Colombia* **152 B2** 5 53N 75 35W
Santa Bárbara, *Honduras* **148 D2** 14 53N 88 14W
Santa Bárbara, *Mexico* **146 B3** 26 48N 105 50W
Santa Barbara, *Phil.* **71 F4** 10 50N 122 32 E
Santa Bárbara, *Spain* **34 E5** 40 42N 0 29 E
Santa Barbara, *U.S.A.* **145 L7** 34 25N 119 42W
Santa Bárbara, *Venezuela* **152 B3** 7 47N 71 10W
Santa Bárbara, Mt., *Spain* **35 H2** 37 23N 2 50W
Santa Barbara Channel, *U.S.A.* **145 L7** 34 15N 120 0W
Santa Barbara I., *U.S.A.* **145 M7** 33 29N 119 2W
Santa Catalina, *Colombia* **152 A2** 10 36N 75 17W
Santa Catalina, *Mexico* **146 B2** 25 40N 110 50W
Santa Catalina, Gulf of, *U.S.A.* **145 N9** 33 10N 117 50W
Santa Catalina I., *U.S.A.* **145 M8** 33 23N 118 25W
Santa Catarina □, *Brazil* **159 B6** 27 25 S 48 30W
Santa Catarina, I. de, *Brazil* **159 B6** 27 30 S 48 40W
Santa Caterina Villarmosa, *Italy* **41 E7** 37 37N 14 1 E
Santa Cecília, *Brazil* **159 B5** 26 56 S 50 18W
Santa Clara, *Cuba* **148 B4** 22 20N 80 0W
Santa Clara, *Calif., U.S.A.* **144 H5** 37 21N 121 57W
Santa Clara, *Utah, U.S.A.* **143 H7** 37 8N 113 39W
Santa Clara de Olimar, *Uruguay* **159 C5** 32 50 S 54 54W
Santa Clotilde, *Peru* **152 D3** 2 33 S 73 45W
Santa Coloma de Farners, *Spain* **34 D7** 41 50N 2 39 E
Santa Coloma de Gramanet, *Spain* **34 D7** 41 27N 2 13 E
Santa Comba, *Spain* **36 B2** 43 2N 8 49W
Santa Croce Camerina, *Italy* **41 F7** 36 50N 14 30 E
Santa Croce di Magliano, *Italy* **41 A7** 41 43N 14 59 E
Santa Cruz, *Argentina* **160 D3** 50 0 S 68 32W
Santa Cruz, *Bolivia* **157 D5** 17 43 S 63 10W
Santa Cruz, *Brazil* **154 C4** 6 13 S 36 1W
Santa Cruz, *Chile* **158 C1** 34 38 S 71 27W
Santa Cruz, *Costa Rica* **148 D2** 10 15N 85 35W
Santa Cruz, *Madeira* **33 D3** 32 42N 16 46W
Santa Cruz, *Peru* **156 B2** 5 40 S 75 56W
Santa Cruz, *Davao del S., Phil.* **71 H5** 6 50N 125 25 E
Santa Cruz, *Laguna, Phil.* **70 D3** 14 20N 121 24 E
Santa Cruz, *Marinduque, Phil.* **70 E4** 13 28N 122 2 E
Santa Cruz, *U.S.A.* **144 J4** 36 58N 122 1W
Santa Cruz, *Venezuela* **153 B5** 8 3N 64 27W
Santa Cruz □, *Argentina* **160 C3** 49 0 S 70 0W
Santa Cruz □, *Bolivia* **157 D5** 17 43 S 63 10W
Santa Cruz →, *Argentina* **160 D3** 50 10 S 68 20W
Santa Cruz Cabrália, *Brazil* **155 E4** 16 17 S 39 2W
Santa Cruz de la Palma, *Canary Is.* **33 F2** 28 41N 17 46W
Santa Cruz de Mudela, *Spain* **35 G1** 38 39N 3 28W
Santa Cruz de Tenerife, *Canary Is.* **33 F3** 28 28N 16 15W
Santa Cruz del Norte, *Cuba* **148 B3** 23 9N 81 55W
Santa Cruz del Retamar, *Spain* **36 E6** 40 8N 4 14W
Santa Cruz del Sur, *Cuba* **148 B4** 20 44N 78 0W
Santa Cruz do Rio Pardo, *Brazil* **159 A6** 22 54 S 49 37W
Santa Cruz do Sul, *Brazil* **159 B5** 29 42 S 52 25W
Santa Cruz I., *Solomon Is.* **122 J8** 10 30 S 166 0 E
Santa Cruz I., *U.S.A.* **145 M7** 34 1N 119 43W
Santa Domingo, Cay, *Bahamas* **148 B4** 21 25N 75 15W
Santa Elena, *Argentina* **158 C4** 30 58 S 59 47W
Santa Elena, *Ecuador* **152 D1** 2 16 S 80 52W
Santa Elena, C., *Costa Rica* **148 D2** 10 54N 85 56W
Sant' Eufémia, G. di, *Italy* **41 D9** 38 50N 16 10 E
Santa Eugenia, Pta., *Mexico* **146 B1** 27 50N 115 5W
Santa Eulalia, *Spain* **33 C8** 38 59N 1 32 E
Santa Fe, *Argentina* **158 C3** 31 35 S 60 41W
Santa Fe, *Nueva Viscaya, Phil.* **70 C3** 16 10N 120 57 E
Santa Fe, *Tablas, Phil.* **70 E4** 12 10N 122 0 E
Santa Fe, *Spain* **37 H7** 37 11N 3 43W
Santa Fe, *U.S.A.* **143 J11** 35 41N 105 57W
Santa Fé □, *Argentina* **158 C3** 31 50 S 60 55W
Santa Filomena, *Brazil* **154 C2** 9 6 S 45 50W
Santa Galdana, *Spain* **33 B10** 39 56N 3 58 E
Santa Gertrudis, *Spain* **33 B7** 39 0N 1 26 E
Santa Helena, *Brazil* **154 B2** 2 14 S 45 18W
Santa Helena de Goiás, *Brazil* **155 E1** 17 53 S 50 35W
Santa Inês, *Brazil* **155 D4** 13 17 S 39 48W
Santa Inés, *Baleares, Spain* **33 B7** 39 3N 1 21 E
Santa Inés, *Extremadura, Spain* **37 G5** 38 32N 5 37W
Santa Inés, I., *Chile* **160 D2** 54 0 S 73 0W
Santa Isabel = Rey Malabo, *Eq. Guin.* **101 E6** 3 45N 8 50 E
Santa Isabel, *Argentina* **158 D2** 36 10 S 66 54W
Santa Isabel, *Brazil* **155 D1** 11 45 S 51 30W
Santa Isabel, *Solomon Is.* **121 M10** 8 0 S 159 0 E
Santa Isabel, Pico, *Eq. Guin.* **101 E6** 3 36N 8 49 E
Santa Isabel do Araguaia, *Brazil* **154 C2** 6 7 S 48 19W
Santa Isabel do Morro, *Brazil* **155 D1** 11 34 S 50 40W
Santa Lucía, *Corrientes, Argentina* **158 B4** 28 58 S 59 5W
Santa Lucía, *San Juan, Argentina* **158 C2** 31 30 S 68 30W
Santa Lucia, *Phil.* **70 C3** 17 7N 120 27 E
Santa Lucía, *Spain* **35 H4** 37 35N 0 58W
Santa Lucía, *Uruguay* **158 C4** 34 27 S 56 24W
Santa Lucia Range, *U.S.A.* **144 K5** 36 0N 121 20W
Santa Magdalena, I., *Mexico* **146 C2** 24 40N 112 15W
Santa Margarita, *Argentina* **158 D3** 38 28 S 61 35W
Santa Margarita, *Mexico* **146 C2** 24 30N 111 50W
Santa Margarita, *Spain* **33 B10** 39 42N 3 6 E
Santa Margarita, *U.S.A.* **144 K6** 35 23N 120 37W
Santa Margarita →, *U.S.A.* **145 M9** 33 13N 117 23W
Santa Margherita, *Italy* **38 D6** 44 20N 9 11 E
Santa María, *Argentina* **158 B2** 26 40 S 66 0W
Santa Maria, *Brazil* **159 B5** 29 40 S 53 48W
Santa Maria, *Ilocos S., Phil.* **70 C3** 17 22N 120 29 E
Santa Maria, *Isabela, Phil.* **70 C3** 17 28N 121 45 E
Santa Maria, *Spain* **33 B9** 39 38N 2 47 E
Santa Maria, *Switz.* **29 C10** 46 36N 10 25 E
Santa Maria, *U.S.A.* **145 L6** 34 57N 120 26W
Santa María →, *Mexico* **146 A3** 31 0N 107 14W
Santa María, B. de, *Mexico* **146 B3** 25 10N 108 40W
Santa Maria, C. de, *Portugal* **37 J3** 36 58N 7 53W
Santa Maria Capua Vetere, *Italy* **41 A7** 41 3N 14 15 E
Santa Maria da Vitória, *Brazil* **155 D3** 13 24 S 44 12W
Santa María de Ipire, *Venezuela* **153 B4** 8 49N 65 19W
Santa Maria di Leuca, C., *Italy* **41 C11** 39 48N 18 20 E
Santa Maria do Suaçuí, *Brazil* **155 E3** 18 12 S 42 25W
Santa Maria dos Marmelos, *Brazil* **157 B5** 6 7 S 61 51W
Santa María la Real de Nieva, *Spain* **36 D6** 41 4N 4 24W
Santa Marta, *Colombia* **152 A3** 11 15N 74 13W
Santa Marta, *Spain* **37 G4** 38 37N 6 39W
Santa Marta, Ría de, *Spain* **36 B3** 43 44N 7 45W
Santa Marta, Sierra Nevada de, *Colombia* **152 A3** 10 55N 73 50W
Santa Marta Grande, C., *Brazil* **159 B6** 28 43 S 48 50W
Santa Maura = Levkás, *Greece* **45 F2** 38 40N 20 43 E
Santa Monica, *U.S.A.* **145 M8** 34 1N 118 29W
Santa Olalla, *Huelva, Spain* **37 H4** 37 54N 6 14W
Santa Olalla, *Toledo, Spain* **36 E6** 40 2N 4 25W
Sant' Onofrio, *Italy* **41 D9** 38 42N 16 10 E
Santa Pola, *Spain* **35 G4** 38 13N 0 35W
Santa Ponsa, *Spain* **33 B9** 39 30N 2 28 E
Santa Quitéria, *Brazil* **154 B3** 4 20 S 40 10W
Santa Rita, *U.S.A.* **143 K10** 32 48N 108 4W
Santa Rita, *Guarico, Venezuela* **152 B4** 8 8N 66 16W
Santa Rita, *Zulia, Venezuela* **152 A3** 10 32N 71 32W
Santa Rita do Araquaia, *Brazil* **157 D7** 17 20 S 53 12W
Santa Rosa, *La Pampa, Argentina* **158 D3** 36 40 S 64 17W
Santa Rosa, *San Luis, Argentina* **158 C2** 32 21 S 65 10W
Santa Rosa, *Bolivia* **156 C4** 10 36 S 67 20W
Santa Rosa, *Brazil* **159 B5** 27 52 S 54 29W
Santa Rosa, *Colombia* **152 C4** 3 32N 69 48W
Santa Rosa, *Ecuador* **152 D2** 3 27 S 79 58W
Santa Rosa, *Peru* **156 C3** 14 30 S 70 50W
Santa Rosa, *Phil.* **70 D3** 15 25N 120 57 E
Santa Rosa, *Calif., U.S.A.* **144 G4** 38 26N 122 43W
Santa Rosa, *N. Mex., U.S.A.* **139 H2** 34 57N 104 41W
Santa Rosa, *Venezuela* **152 C4** 1 29N 66 55W
Santa Rosa de Cabal, *Colombia* **152 C2** 4 52N 75 38W
Santa Rosa de Copán, *Honduras* **148 D2** 14 47N 88 46W
Santa Rosa de Osos, *Colombia* **152 B2** 6 39N 75 28W

Sierra Blanca Peak 265

Shawano, U.S.A. 134 C1 44 47N 88 36W
Shawinigan, Canada 128 C5 46 35N 72 50W
Shawnee, Kans., U.S.A. 140 E2 39 1N 94 43W
Shawnee, Okla., U.S.A. 139 H6 35 20N 96 55W
Shaybārā, Si. Arabia 84 E3 25 26N 36 47 E
Shayib el Banat, Gebel, Egypt 94 B3 26 59N 33 29 E
Shaykh Sa'īd, Iraq 84 C5 32 34N 46 17 E
Shaykh 'Uthmān, Yemen 86 D4 12 52N 44 59 E
Shaymak, Tajikistan 55 E7 37 33N 74 50 E
Shchekino, Russia 51 D10 54 1N 37 34 E
Shcherbakov = Rybinsk, Russia 51 B11 58 5N 38 50 E
Shchigri, Russia 51 F10 51 55N 36 58 E
Shchors, Ukraine 50 F7 51 48N 31 56 E
Shchuchiosk, Kazakhstan 56 D8 52 56N 70 12 E
Shchuchye, Russia 54 D8 55 12N 62 46 E
She Xian, Anhui, China 69 C12 29 50N 118 25 E
She Xian, Hebei, China 66 F7 36 30N 113 40 E
Shea, Guyana 153 C6 2 48N 59 4W
Shebekino, Russia 51 F10 50 28N 36 54 E
Shebele = Scebeli, Wabi →, Somali Rep. 90 G3 2 0N 44 0 E
Sheboygan, U.S.A. 134 D2 43 46N 87 45W
Shediac, Canada 129 C7 46 14N 64 32W
Sheelin, L., Ireland 19 C4 53 48N 7 20W
Sheep Haven, Ireland 19 A4 55 12N 7 55W
Sheerness, U.K. 17 F8 51 26N 0 47 E
Sheet Harbour, Canada 129 D7 44 56N 62 31W
Sheffield, N.Z. 119 D7 43 23 S 172 1 E
Sheffield, U.K. 16 D6 53 23N 1 28W
Sheffield, Ala., U.S.A. 135 H2 34 46N 87 41W
Sheffield, Ill., U.S.A. 140 C7 41 21N 89 44W
Sheffield, Iowa, U.S.A. 140 B3 42 54N 93 13W
Sheffield, Mass., U.S.A. 137 D11 42 5N 73 21W
Sheffield, Pa., U.S.A. 136 E5 41 42N 79 3W
Sheffield, Tex., U.S.A. 139 K4 30 41N 101 49W
Shegaon, India 82 D3 20 48N 76 47 E
Sheho, Canada 131 C8 51 35N 103 13W
Shehojele, Ethiopia 95 E4 10 40N 35 9 E
Shehong, China 68 B5 30 54N 105 18 E
Shehuen →, Argentina 160 C3 49 35 S 69 34W
Sheikhpura, India 81 G11 25 9N 85 53 E
Shek Hasan, Ethiopia 95 E4 12 5N 35 58 E
Shekhupura, Pakistan 79 C4 31 42N 73 58 E
Sheki, Azerbaijan 53 F12 41 10N 47 5 E
Sheksna →, Russia 51 B11 59 0N 38 30 E
Shelbina, U.S.A. 140 E4 39 47N 92 2W
Shelburn, U.S.A. 141 E9 39 11N 87 24W
Shelburne, N.S., Canada 129 D6 43 47N 65 20W
Shelburne, Ont., Canada 128 D3 44 4N 80 15W
Shelburne, U.S.A. 137 B11 44 23N 73 14W
Shelburne B., Australia 114 A3 11 50 S 142 50 E
Shelburne Falls, U.S.A. 137 D12 42 36N 72 45W
Shelby, Mich., U.S.A. 134 D2 43 37N 86 22W
Shelby, Mont., U.S.A. 142 B8 48 30N 111 51W
Shelby, N.C., U.S.A. 135 H5 35 17N 81 32W
Shelby, Ohio, U.S.A. 136 F2 40 53N 82 40W
Shelbyville, Ill., U.S.A. 138 F10 39 24N 88 48W
Shelbyville, Ind., U.S.A. 141 E11 39 31N 85 47W
Shelbyville, Ky., U.S.A. 141 F11 38 13N 85 14W
Shelbyville, Mo., U.S.A. 140 E4 39 48N 92 2W
Shelbyville, Tenn., U.S.A. 135 H2 35 29N 86 28W
Shelbyville, L., U.S.A. 141 E8 39 26N 88 46W
Sheldon, Iowa, U.S.A. 138 D7 43 11N 95 51W
Sheldon, Mo., U.S.A. 140 G2 37 40N 94 18W
Sheldrake, Canada 129 B7 50 20N 64 51W
Shelikhova, Zaliv, Russia 57 D16 59 30N 157 0 E
Shell Lake, Canada 131 C7 53 19N 107 2W
Shell Lakes, Australia 113 E4 29 20 S 127 30 E
Shellbrook, Canada 131 C7 53 13N 106 24W
Shellharbour, Australia 117 C9 34 31 S 150 51 E
Shelling Rocks, Ireland 19 E1 51 45N 10 35W
Shellsburg, U.S.A. 140 B5 42 6N 91 52W
Shelon →, Russia 50 B7 58 10N 30 30 E
Shelton, Conn., U.S.A. 137 E11 41 19N 73 5W
Shelton, Wash., U.S.A. 144 C3 47 13N 123 6W
Shemakha, Azerbaijan 53 F13 40 38N 48 37 E
Shen Xian, China 66 F8 36 15N 115 40 E
Shenandoah, Iowa, U.S.A. 138 E7 40 46N 95 22W
Shenandoah, Pa., U.S.A. 137 F8 40 49N 76 12W
Shenandoah, Va., U.S.A. 134 F6 38 29N 78 37W
Shenandoah →, U.S.A. 134 F7 39 19N 77 44W
Shenchi, China 66 E7 39 8N 112 10 E
Shencottah, India 83 K3 8 59N 77 18 E
Shendam, Nigeria 101 D6 8 49N 9 30 E
Shendî, Sudan 95 D3 16 46N 33 22 E
Shendurni, India 82 D2 20 39N 75 36 E
Sheng Xian, China 69 C13 29 35N 120 50 E
Shengfang, China 66 E9 39 3N 116 42 E
Shëngjergji, Albania 44 C2 41 17N 20 10 E
Shëngjini, Albania 44 C1 41 50N 19 35 E
Shenjingzi, China 67 B13 44 40N 124 30 E
Shenmëria, Albania 44 B2 42 7N 20 13 E
Shenmu, China 66 E6 38 50N 110 29 E
Shennongjia, China 69 B8 31 43N 110 44 E
Shenqiu, China 66 H8 33 25N 115 5 E
Shenqiucheng, China 66 H8 33 24N 115 2 E
Shensi = Shaanxi □, China 66 G5 35 0N 109 0 E
Shenyang, China 67 D12 41 48N 123 27 E
Shepetovka, Ukraine 50 F5 50 10N 27 10 E
Shepherd Is., Vanuatu 121 F6 16 55 S 168 36 E
Shepherdsville, U.S.A. 141 G11 37 59N 85 43W
Shepparton, Australia 117 D6 36 23 S 145 26 E
Sheqi, China 66 H7 33 12N 112 57 E
Sher Qila, Pakistan 81 A6 36 7N 74 2 E
Sherborne, U.K. 17 G5 50 56N 2 31W
Sherbro I., S. Leone 100 D2 7 30N 12 40W
Sherbrooke, Canada 129 C5 45 28N 71 57W
Sherda, Chad 97 D3 20 7N 16 46 E
Shereik, Sudan 94 D3 18 44N 33 47 E
Sheridan, Ark., U.S.A. 139 H8 34 19N 92 24W
Sheridan, Ill., U.S.A. 141 C8 41 32N 88 41W
Sheridan, Ind., U.S.A. 141 D10 40 8N 86 13W
Sheridan, Mo., U.S.A. 140 D2 40 31N 94 37W
Sheridan, Wyo., U.S.A. 142 D10 44 48N 106 58W
Sherkot, India 81 E8 29 22N 78 35 E
Sherman, U.S.A. 139 J6 33 40N 96 35W
Sherpur, Afghan. 79 B3 34 32N 69 10 E
Sherpur, Bangla. 78 C3 25 0N 90 0 E
Sherridon, Canada 131 B8 55 8N 101 5W
Sherwood, N. Dak., U.S.A. 138 A4 48 57N 101 38W
Sherwood, Ohio, U.S.A. 141 C12 41 17N 84 33W
Sherwood, Tex., U.S.A. 139 K4 31 18N 100 45W
Sherwood Forest, U.K. 16 D6 53 5N 1 5W
Sheslay, Canada 130 B2 58 17N 131 52W
Sheslay →, Canada 130 B2 58 48N 132 5W
Shethanei L., Canada 131 B9 58 48N 97 50W
Shetland □, U.K. 18 A7 60 30N 1 30W
Shetland Is., U.K. 18 A7 60 30N 1 30W
Shevaroy Hills, India 83 J4 11 58N 78 12 E
Shewa □, Ethiopia 95 F4 9 33N 38 10 E
Shewa Gimira, Ethiopia 95 F4 7 4N 35 51 E
Sheyenne, U.S.A. 138 B5 47 50N 99 7W
Sheyenne →, U.S.A. 138 B6 47 2N 96 50W
Shibām, Yemen 87 D5 16 0N 48 36 E
Shibata, Japan 60 F9 37 57N 139 20 E
Shibecha, Japan 60 C12 43 17N 144 36 E
Shibetsu, Japan 60 B11 44 10N 142 23 E
Shibîn el Kôm, Egypt 94 H7 30 31N 30 55 E
Shibîn el Qanâtir, Egypt 94 H7 30 19N 31 19 E
Shibing, China 68 D7 27 2N 108 7 E
Shibogama L., Canada 128 B2 53 35N 88 15W
Shibukawa, Japan 63 A10 36 29N 139 0 E
Shibushi, Japan 62 F3 31 25N 131 8 E
Shibushi-Wan, Japan 62 F3 31 24N 131 8 E
Shicheng, China 69 D11 26 22N 116 20 E
Shickshock Mts. = Chic-Chocs, Mts., Canada 129 C6 48 55N 66 0W
Shidād, Si. Arabia 86 B3 21 19N 40 3 E
Shidao, China 67 F12 36 50N 122 25 E
Shidian, China 68 E2 24 40N 99 5 E
Shido, Japan 62 C6 34 19N 134 10 E
Shiel, L., U.K. 18 E3 56 48N 5 32W
Shield, C., Australia 114 A2 13 20 S 136 20 E
Shiga □, Japan 63 B8 35 20N 136 0 E
Shigaib, Sudan 97 E4 15 5N 23 35 E
Shigaraki, Japan 63 C8 34 57N 136 2 E
Shigu, China 68 D2 26 51N 99 56 E
Shiguaigou, China 66 D6 40 52N 110 15 E
Shihan, W. →, Yemen 87 C5 17 24N 51 26 E
Shihchiachuangi = Shijiazhuang, China 66 E8 38 2N 114 28 E
Shiiba, Japan 62 E3 32 29N 131 4 E
Shijaku, Albania 44 C1 41 21N 19 33 E
Shijiazhuang, China 66 E8 38 2N 114 28 E
Shijiu Hu, China 69 B12 31 25N 118 50 E
Shikarpur, India 80 E8 28 17N 78 7 E
Shikarpur, Pakistan 79 D3 27 57N 68 39 E
Shikine-Jima, Japan 63 C11 34 19N 139 13 E
Shikoku, Japan 62 D5 33 30N 133 30 E
Shikoku □, Japan 62 D5 33 30N 133 30 E
Shikoku-Sanchi, Japan 62 D5 33 30N 133 30 E
Shilabo, Ethiopia 90 F3 6 22N 44 32 E
Shilda, Russia 54 F6 51 49N 59 47 E
Shiliguri, India 78 B2 26 45N 88 25 E
Shilka, Russia 57 D12 52 0N 115 55 E
Shilka →, Russia 57 D13 53 20N 121 26 E
Shillelagh, Ireland 19 D5 52 46N 6 32W
Shillong, India 78 C3 25 35N 91 53 E
Shilo, Jordan 91 C4 32 4N 35 18 E
Shilong, China 69 F9 23 5N 113 52 E
Shilou, China 66 F6 37 0N 110 48 E
Shilovo, Russia 51 D12 54 25N 40 57 E
Shima-Hantō, Japan 63 C8 34 22N 136 45 E
Shimabara, Japan 62 E2 32 48N 130 20 E
Shimada, Japan 63 C10 34 49N 138 10 E
Shimane □, Japan 62 C4 35 0N 132 30 E
Shimane-Hantō, Japan 62 B4 35 30N 133 0 E
Shimanovsk, Russia 57 D13 52 15N 127 30 E
Shimen, China 69 C8 29 35N 111 20 E
Shimenjie, China 69 C11 29 29N 116 48 E
Shimian, China 68 C4 29 17N 102 23 E
Shimizu, Japan 63 C10 35 0N 138 30 E
Shimo-Jima, Japan 62 E2 32 15N 130 7 E
Shimo-Koshiki-Jima, Japan 62 F1 31 40N 129 43 E
Shimoda, Japan 63 C10 34 40N 138 57 E
Shimodate, Japan 63 A11 36 20N 139 55 E
Shimoga, India 83 H2 13 57N 75 32 E
Shimoni, Kenya 106 C4 4 38 S 39 20 E
Shimonita, Japan 63 A10 36 13N 138 47 E
Shimonoseki, Japan 62 D2 33 58N 130 55 E
Shimotsuma, Japan 63 A11 36 11N 139 58 E
Shimpuru Rapids, Angola 103 F3 17 45 S 19 55 E
Shimsha →, India 83 H3 13 15N 77 10 E
Shimsk, Russia 50 B7 58 15N 30 50 E
Shin, L., U.K. 18 C4 58 7N 4 30W
Shin-Tone →, Japan 63 B12 35 44N 140 51 E
Shinan, China 68 F7 22 44N 109 53 E
Shinano →, Japan 61 F9 36 50N 138 30 E
Shīndand, Afghan. 79 B1 33 12N 62 8 E
Shingbwiyang, Burma 78 B6 26 41N 96 13 E
Shingleton, U.S.A. 128 C2 46 21N 86 28W
Shingū, Japan 63 D7 33 40N 135 55 E
Shinji, Japan 62 B4 35 24N 132 54 E
Shinji Ko, Japan 62 B4 35 26N 132 57 E
Shinjō, Japan 60 E10 38 46N 140 18 E
Shinkafe, Nigeria 101 C6 13 8N 6 29 E
Shīnkay, Afghan. 79 C2 31 57N 67 26 E
Shinminato, Japan 63 A9 36 47N 137 4 E
Shinonoi, Japan 63 A10 36 35N 138 9 E
Shinshār, Syria 91 A5 34 36N 36 43 E
Shinshiro, Japan 63 C9 34 54N 137 30 E
Shinyanga, Tanzania 106 C3 3 45 S 33 27 E
Shinyanga □, Tanzania 106 C3 3 50 S 34 0 E
Shio-no-Misaki, Japan 63 D7 33 25N 135 45 E
Shiogama, Japan 60 E10 38 19N 141 1 E
Shiojiri, Japan 63 A9 36 6N 137 58 E
Ship I., U.S.A. 139 K10 30 13N 88 55W
Shipehenski Prokhod, Bulgaria 43 E10 42 45N 25 15 E
Shiping, China 68 F4 23 45N 102 23 E
Shippegan, Canada 129 C7 47 45N 64 45W
Shippensburg, U.S.A. 136 F7 40 3N 77 31W
Shiprock, U.S.A. 143 H9 36 47N 108 41W
Shiqian, China 68 D7 27 32N 108 13 E
Shiqma, N. →, Israel 91 D3 31 37N 34 30 E
Shiquan, China 66 H5 33 5N 108 15 E
Shīr Kūh, Iran 85 D7 31 39N 54 3 E
Shirabad, Uzbekistan 55 E3 37 40N 67 1 E
Shiragami-Misaki, Japan 60 D10 41 24N 140 12 E
Shirahama, Japan 63 D7 33 41N 135 20 E
Shirakawa, Fukushima, Japan 61 F10 37 7N 140 13 E
Shirakawa, Gifu, Japan 63 A8 36 17N 136 56 E
Shirane-San, Gumma, Japan 63 A11 36 48N 139 22 E
Shirane-San, Yamanashi, Japan 63 B10 35 42N 138 9 E
Shiraoi, Japan 60 C10 42 33N 141 21 E
Shīrāz, Iran 85 D7 29 42N 52 30 E
Shirbîn, Egypt 94 H7 31 11N 31 32 E
Shire →, Africa 107 F4 17 42 S 35 19 E
Shiretoko-Misaki, Japan 60 B12 44 21N 145 20 E
Shirinab →, Pakistan 80 D2 30 15N 66 28 E
Shiringushi, Russia 51 E13 53 51N 42 46 E
Shiriya-Zaki, Japan 60 D10 41 25N 141 30 E
Shirley, U.S.A. 141 E11 39 53N 85 35W
Shiroishi, Japan 60 E10 38 0N 140 37 E
Shirol, India 82 F2 16 47N 74 41 E
Shirpur, India 82 D2 21 21N 74 57 E
Shīrvān, Iran 85 B8 37 30N 57 50 E
Shirwa, L. = Chilwa, L., Malawi 107 F4 15 15 S 35 40 E
Shishmanova, Bulgaria 43 E8 42 58N 23 12 E
Shishou, China 69 C9 29 38N 112 22 E
Shitai, China 69 B11 30 12N 117 25 E
Shively, U.S.A. 141 F11 38 12N 85 49W
Shivpuri, India 80 G7 25 26N 77 42 E
Shixian, China 67 C15 43 5N 129 50 E
Shixing, China 69 E10 24 46N 114 5 E
Shiyan, China 69 A8 32 35N 110 45 E
Shiyata, Egypt 94 B2 29 25N 25 7 E
Shizhu, China 68 C7 29 58N 108 7 E
Shizong, China 68 E5 24 50N 104 0 E
Shizuishan, China 66 E4 39 15N 106 50 E
Shizuoka, Japan 63 C10 34 57N 138 24 E
Shizuoka □, Japan 63 B10 35 15N 138 40 E
Shklov, Belorussia 50 D7 54 16N 30 15 E
Shkoder = Shkodra, Albania 44 B1 42 6N 19 20 E
Shkodra, Albania 44 B1 42 6N 19 20 E
Shkodra □, Albania 44 B1 42 25N 19 20 E
Shkumbini →, Albania 44 C1 41 5N 19 50 E
Shmidta, O., Russia 57 A10 81 0N 91 0 E
Shō-Gawa →, Japan 63 A9 36 47N 137 4 E
Shoal Cr. →, U.S.A. 140 E3 39 44N 93 32W
Shoal Lake, Canada 131 C8 50 30N 100 35W
Shoals, U.S.A. 141 F10 38 40N 86 47W
Shōbara, Japan 62 C5 34 51N 133 1 E
Shōdo-Shima, Japan 62 C6 34 30N 134 15 E
Shoeburyness, U.K. 17 F8 51 31N 0 49 E
Shokpar, Kazakhstan 55 B7 43 49N 74 21 E
Sholapur = Solapur, India 82 F2 17 43N 75 56 E
Shologontsy, Russia 57 C12 66 13N 114 0 E
Shōmrōn, Jordan 91 C4 32 15N 35 13 E
Shoranur, India 83 J3 10 46N 76 19 E
Shorapur, India 83 F3 16 31N 76 48 E
Shortland I., Solomon Is. 121 L8 7 0 S 155 45 E
Shoshone, Calif., U.S.A. 145 K10 35 58N 116 16W
Shoshone, Idaho, U.S.A. 142 E6 42 56N 114 25W
Shoshone L., U.S.A. 142 D8 44 22N 110 43W
Shoshone Mts., U.S.A. 142 G5 39 20N 117 25W
Shoshong, Botswana 104 C4 22 56 S 26 31 E
Shoshoni, U.S.A. 142 E9 43 14N 108 7W
Shostka, Ukraine 50 F8 51 57N 33 32 E
Shou Xian, China 69 A11 32 37N 116 42 E
Shouchang, China 69 C12 29 18N 119 12 E
Shouguang, China 67 F10 37 52N 118 45 E
Shouning, China 69 D12 27 27N 119 31 E
Shouyang, China 66 F7 37 54N 113 8 E
Show Low, U.S.A. 143 J9 34 15N 110 2W
Shpola, Ukraine 52 B4 49 1N 31 30 E
Shreveport, U.S.A. 139 J8 32 31N 93 45W
Shrewsbury, U.K. 16 E5 52 42N 2 45W
Shrirampur, India 81 H13 22 44N 88 21 E
Shrirangapattana, India 83 H3 12 26N 76 43 E
Shropshire □, U.K. 17 E5 52 36N 2 45W
Shuangbai, China 68 E3 24 42N 101 38 E
Shuangcheng, China 67 B14 45 20N 126 15 E
Shuangfeng, China 69 D9 27 29N 112 11 E
Shuanggou, China 67 G9 34 2N 117 30 E
Shuangjiang, China 68 F2 23 26N 99 58 E
Shuangliao, China 67 C12 43 29N 123 30 E
Shuangshanzi, China 67 D10 40 20N 119 8 E
Shuangyang, China 67 C13 43 28N 125 40 E
Shuangyashan, China 65 B8 46 28N 131 5 E
Shu'b, Ra's, Yemen 87 D6 12 30N 53 25 E
Shucheng, China 69 B11 31 28N 116 57 E
Shuguri Falls, Tanzania 107 D4 8 33 S 37 22 E
Shuḩayr, Yemen 87 D5 14 41N 49 23 E
Shuicheng, China 68 D5 26 38N 104 48 E
Shuiji, China 69 D12 27 13N 118 20 E
Shuiye, China 66 F8 36 7N 114 8 E
Shujalpur, India 80 H7 23 18N 76 46 E
Shukpa Kunzang, India 81 B8 34 22N 78 22 E
Shulan, China 67 B14 44 28N 127 0 E
Shule, China 64 C2 39 25N 76 3 E
Shullsburg, U.S.A. 140 B6 42 35N 90 13W
Shumagin Is., U.S.A. 126 C4 55 7N 159 45W
Shumerlya, Russia 51 D15 55 30N 46 25 E
Shumikha, Russia 54 D8 55 10N 63 15 E
Shunchang, China 69 D11 26 54N 117 48 E
Shunde, China 69 F9 22 42N 113 14 E
Shungay, Kazakhstan 53 B12 48 30N 46 45 E
Shungnak, U.S.A. 126 B4 66 52N 157 9W
Shuo Xian, China 66 E7 39 20N 112 33 E
Shūr →, Iran 85 D7 28 30N 55 0 E
Shūr Āb, Iran 85 C6 34 23N 51 11 E
Shūr Gaz, Iran 85 D8 29 10N 59 20 E
Shūrāb, Iran 85 C8 33 43N 56 29 E
Shurab, Tajikistan 55 C5 40 3N 70 33 E
Shurchi, Uzbekistan 55 E3 37 59N 67 47 E
Shūrjestān, Iran 85 D7 31 24N 52 25 E
Shurkhua, Burma 78 D4 22 15N 93 38 E
Shurma, Russia 54 C2 56 58N 50 21 E
Shurugwi, Zimbabwe 107 F3 19 40 S 30 0 E
Shūsf, Iran 85 D9 31 50N 60 5 E
Shūshtar, Iran 85 D6 32 0N 48 50 E
Shuswap L., Canada 130 C5 50 55N 119 3W
Shuya, Russia 51 C12 56 50N 41 28 E
Shuyang, China 67 G10 34 10N 118 42 E
Shuzenji, Japan 63 C10 34 58N 138 56 E
Shūzū, Iran 85 D7 29 52N 54 30 E
Shwebo, Burma 78 D5 22 30N 95 45 E
Shwegu, Burma 78 C6 24 15N 96 26 E
Shwegun, Burma 78 G6 17 9N 97 39 E
Shwenyaung, Burma 78 E6 20 46N 96 57 E
Shymkent = Chimkent, Kazakhstan 55 B4 42 18N 69 36 E
Shyok, India 81 B8 34 13N 78 12 E
Shyok →, Pakistan 81 B6 35 13N 75 53 E
Si Chon, Thailand 77 H2 9 0N 99 54 E
Si Kiang = Xi Jiang →, China 69 F9 22 5N 113 20 E
Si-ngan = Xi'an, China 66 G5 34 15N 109 0 E
Si Prachan, Thailand 76 E3 14 37N 100 9 E
Si Racha, Thailand 76 F3 13 10N 100 48 E
Si Xian, China 67 H9 33 30N 117 50 E
Siahan Range, Pakistan 79 D2 27 30N 64 40 E
Siak →, Indonesia 74 B2 1 13N 102 9 E
Siaksrindrapura, Indonesia 74 B2 0 51N 102 0 E
Sialkot, Pakistan 79 B4 32 32N 74 30 E
Sialsuk, India 78 D4 23 24N 92 45 E
Siam = Thailand ■, Asia 76 E4 16 0N 102 0 E
Siam, Australia 116 B2 32 35 S 136 41 E
Siantan, P., Indonesia 77 L6 3 10N 106 15 E
Siàpo →, Venezuela 152 C4 2 7N 66 28W
Sīāreh, Iran 85 D9 28 5N 60 14 E
Siargao, Phil. 71 G6 9 52N 126 3 E
Siari, Pakistan 81 B7 34 55N 76 40 E
Siari, Phil. 71 G4 8 19N 122 58 E
Siasi I., Phil. 71 J3 5 33N 120 51 E
Siassi, Papua N. G. 120 C4 5 40 S 147 51 E
Siátista, Greece 44 D3 40 15N 21 33 E
Siaton, Phil. 71 G4 9 4N 123 2 E
Siau, Indonesia 72 A3 2 50N 125 25 E
Šiauliai, Lithuania 50 D3 55 56N 23 15 E
Siaya □, Kenya 106 B3 0 0 34 20 E
Siazan, Azerbaijan 53 F13 41 3N 49 10 E
Sibâi, Gebel el, Egypt 94 B3 25 45N 34 10 E
Sibang, Gabon 102 B1 0 25N 9 31 E
Sibari, Italy 41 C9 39 47N 16 27 E
Sibasa, S. Africa 105 C5 22 53 S 30 33 E
Sibay, Russia 54 E6 52 42N 58 39 E
Sibay I., Phil. 71 F3 11 51N 121 29 E
Sibayi, L., S. Africa 105 D5 27 20 S 32 45 E
Šibenik, Croatia 39 E12 43 48N 15 54 E
Siberia, Russia 58 D14 60 0N 100 0 E
Siberut, Indonesia 74 C1 1 30 S 99 0 E
Sibi, Pakistan 79 C2 29 30N 67 54 E
Sibil, Indonesia 73 B6 4 59 S 140 35 E
Sibiti, Congo 102 C2 3 38 S 13 19 E
Sibiu, Romania 46 D5 45 45N 24 9 E
Sibiu □, Romania 46 D5 45 50N 24 15 E
Sibley, Ill., U.S.A. 141 D8 40 35N 88 23W
Sibley, Iowa, U.S.A. 138 D7 43 24N 95 45W
Sibley, La., U.S.A. 139 J8 32 33N 93 18W
Sibolga, Indonesia 74 B1 1 42N 98 45 E
Sibret, Belgium 21 J7 49 58N 5 38 E
Sibsagar, India 78 B5 27 0N 94 36 E
Sibu, Malaysia 75 B4 2 18N 111 49 E
Sibuco, Phil. 71 H4 7 20N 122 10 E
Sibuguey B., Phil. 71 H4 7 50N 122 45 E
Sibutu, Phil. 71 J2 4 45N 119 30 E
Sibutu Group, Phil. 71 J2 4 45N 119 20 E
Sibutu Passage, E. Indies 71 J2 4 50N 120 0 E
Sibuyan, Phil. 70 E4 12 25N 122 40 E
Sibuyan Sea, Phil. 70 E4 12 30N 122 20 E
Sicamous, Canada 130 C5 50 49N 119 0W
Sicapoo, Mt., Phil. 70 B3 18 1N 120 56 E
Sichuan □, China 68 B5 31 0N 104 0 E
Sicilia, Italy 41 E7 37 30N 14 30 E
Sicilia □, Italy 41 E7 37 30N 14 30 E
Sicilia, Canale di, Italy 40 E5 37 25N 12 30 E
Sicilian Channel = Sicilia, Canale di, Italy 40 E5 37 25N 12 30 E
Sicily = Sicilia, Italy 41 E7 37 30N 14 30 E
Sicuani, Peru 156 C3 14 21 S 71 10W
Siculiana, Italy 40 E6 37 20N 13 23 E
Šid, Serbia 42 B4 45 8N 19 14 E
Sidamo □, Ethiopia 95 G4 5 0N 37 50 E
Sidaouet, Niger 97 E1 18 34N 8 3 E
Sidári, Greece 32 A3 39 47N 19 41 E
Siddeburen, Neths. 20 B9 53 15N 6 52 E
Siddhapur, India 80 H5 23 56N 72 25 E
Siddipet, India 82 E4 18 5N 78 51 E
Side, Turkey 88 E4 36 45N 31 23 E
Sidell, U.S.A. 141 E9 39 55N 87 49W
Sidéradougou, Burkina Faso 100 C4 10 42N 4 12W
Siderno Marina, Italy 41 D9 38 16N 16 17 E
Sídheros, Ákra, Greece 32 D8 35 19N 26 19 E
Sidhirókastron, Greece 44 C5 41 13N 23 24 E
Sîdi Abd el Rahmân, Egypt 94 H6 30 55N 29 44 E
Sîdi Barrâni, Egypt 94 A2 31 38N 25 58 E
Sidi-bel-Abbès, Algeria 99 A4 35 13N 0 39W
Sidi Bennour, Morocco 98 B3 32 40N 8 25W
Sidi Haneish, Egypt 94 A2 31 10N 27 35 E
Sidi Kacem, Morocco 98 B3 34 11N 5 49W
Sidi Omar, Egypt 94 A1 31 24N 24 57 E
Sidi Slimane, Morocco 98 B3 34 16N 5 56W
Sidi Smaïl, Morocco 98 B3 32 50N 8 31W
Sidi 'Uzayz, Libya 96 B4 31 41N 24 55 E
Sidlaw Hills, U.K. 18 E5 56 32N 3 10W
Sidley, Mt., Antarctica 7 D14 77 2 S 126 2W
Sidmouth, U.K. 17 G4 50 40N 3 13W
Sidmouth, C., Australia 114 A3 13 25 S 143 36 E
Sidney, Canada 130 D4 48 39N 123 24W
Sidney, Mont., U.S.A. 138 B2 47 43N 104 9W
Sidney, N.Y., U.S.A. 137 D9 42 19N 75 24W
Sidney, Nebr., U.S.A. 138 E3 41 8N 102 59W
Sidney, Ohio, U.S.A. 141 D12 40 17N 84 9W
Sidoarjo, Indonesia 75 D4 7 27 S 112 43 E
Sidoktaya, Burma 78 E5 20 27N 94 15 E
Sidon = Saydā, Lebanon 91 B4 33 35N 35 25 E
Sidra, G. of = Surt, Khalīj, Libya 96 B3 31 40N 18 30 E
Siedlce, Poland 47 C9 52 10N 22 20 E
Siedlce □, Poland 47 C9 52 0N 22 0 E
Sieg →, Germany 26 E3 50 46N 7 7 E
Siegburg, Germany 26 E3 50 48N 7 12 E
Siegen, Germany 26 E4 50 52N 8 2 E
Siem Pang, Cambodia 76 E6 14 7N 106 23 E
Siem Reap, Cambodia 76 F4 13 20N 103 52 E
Siena, Italy 39 E8 43 20N 11 20 E
Sieniawa, Poland 31 A15 50 11N 22 38 E
Sieradź, Poland 47 D5 51 37N 18 41 E
Sieraków, Poland 47 C3 52 39N 16 2 E
Sierck-les-Bains, France 23 C13 49 26N 6 20 E
Sierpc, Poland 47 C6 52 55N 19 43 E
Sierpe, Bocas de la, Venezuela 153 B5 10 0N 61 30W
Sierra Blanca, U.S.A. 143 L11 31 11N 105 22W
Sierra Blanca Peak, U.S.A. 143 K11 33 23N 105 49W

Sudeten Mts. 269

Stanislaus →, U.S.A. 144 H5 37 40N 121 14W
Stanislav = Ivano-Frankovsk, Ukraine 50 G4 48 40N 24 40 E
Stanisławów, Poland 47 C8 52 18N 21 33 E
Stanke Dimitrov, Bulgaria 42 E8 42 17N 23 9 E
Stanley, Australia 114 G4 40 46 S 145 19 E
Stanley, N.B., Canada 129 C6 46 20N 66 44W
Stanley, Sask., Canada 131 B8 55 24N 104 22W
Stanley, Falk. Is. 160 D5 51 40 S 59 51W
Stanley, Idaho, U.S.A. 142 D6 44 13N 114 56W
Stanley, N. Dak., U.S.A. 138 A3 48 19N 102 23W
Stanley, N.Y., U.S.A. 136 D7 42 48N 77 6W
Stanley, Wis., U.S.A. 138 C9 44 58N 90 56W
Stanley Res., India 83 J3 11 50N 77 40 E
Stanovoy Khrebet, Russia 57 D13 55 0N 130 0 E
Stanovoy Ra. = Stanovoy Khrebet, Russia 57 D13 55 0N 130 0 E
Stans, Switz. 29 C6 46 58N 8 21 E
Stansmore Ra., Australia 112 D4 21 23 S 128 33 E
Stanthorpe, Australia 115 D5 28 36 S 151 59 E
Stanton, U.S.A. 139 J4 32 8N 101 48W
Stantsiya Karshi, Uzbekistan 55 D2 38 49N 65 47 E
Stanwood, U.S.A. 144 B4 48 15N 122 23W
Staphorst, Neths. 20 C8 52 39N 6 12 E
Staples, U.S.A. 138 B7 46 21N 94 48W
Stapleton, U.S.A. 138 E4 41 29N 100 31W
Staporków, Poland 47 D7 51 9N 20 31 E
Star City, Canada 131 C8 52 50N 104 20W
Stara-minskaya, Russia 53 C8 46 33N 39 0 E
Stara Moravica, Serbia 42 B4 45 50N 19 30 E
Stara Pazova, Serbia 42 C5 44 58N 20 10 E
Stara Planina, Bulgaria 43 D8 43 15N 23 0 E
Stara Zagora, Bulgaria 43 E10 42 26N 25 39 E
Starachowice, Poland 47 D8 51 3N 21 2 E
Starashcherbinovskaya, Russia 53 C8 46 40N 38 53 E
Staraya Russa, Russia 50 C7 57 58N 31 23 E
Starbuck I., Kiribati 123 H12 5 37 S 155 55W
Stargard Szczeciński, Poland 47 B2 53 20N 15 0 E
Stari Bar, Montenegro 42 E4 42 7N 19 13 E
Stari Trg, Slovenia 39 C12 45 29N 15 7 E
Staritsa, Russia 50 C9 56 33N 34 55 E
Starke, U.S.A. 135 K4 29 57N 82 7W
Starkville, Colo., U.S.A. 139 G2 37 8N 104 30W
Starkville, Miss., U.S.A. 135 J1 33 28N 88 49W
Starnberg, Germany 27 G7 48 0N 11 20 E
Starnberger See, Germany 27 H7 47 55N 11 20 E
Starobelsk, Ukraine 53 B8 49 16N 39 0 E
Starodub, Russia 50 E8 52 30N 32 50 E
Starogard, Poland 47 B5 53 59N 18 30 E
Starokonstantinov, Ukraine 52 B2 49 48N 27 10 E
Starosielce, Poland 47 B10 53 8N 23 5 E
Start Pt., U.K. 17 G4 50 13N 3 38W
Stary Sącz, Poland 31 B13 49 33N 20 35 E
Staryy Biryuzyak, Russia 53 D12 44 46N 46 50 E
Staryy Chartoriysk, Ukraine 50 F4 51 15N 25 54 E
Staryy Kheydzhan, Russia 57 C15 60 0N 144 50 E
Staryy Krym, Ukraine 52 D6 45 3N 35 8 E
Staryy Oskol, Russia 51 F10 51 19N 37 55 E
Stassfurt, Germany 26 D7 51 51N 11 34 E
Staszów, Poland 47 E8 50 33N 21 10 E
State Center, U.S.A. 140 B3 42 1N 93 10W
State College, U.S.A. 136 F7 40 48N 77 52W
Stateline, U.S.A. 144 G7 38 57N 119 56W
Staten, I. = Estados, I. de Los, Argentina 160 D4 54 40 S 64 30W
Staten I., U.S.A. 137 F10 40 35N 74 9W
Statesboro, U.S.A. 135 J5 32 27N 81 47W
Statesville, U.S.A. 135 H5 35 47N 80 53W
Stauffer, U.S.A. 145 L7 34 45N 119 3W
Staunton, Ill., U.S.A. 140 E7 39 1N 89 47W
Staunton, Va., U.S.A. 134 F6 38 9N 79 4W
Stavanger, Norway 13 G8 58 57N 5 40 E
Staveley, N.Z. 119 D6 43 40 S 171 32 E
Stavelot, Belgium 21 H7 50 23N 5 55 E
Stavenhagen, Germany 26 B8 53 41N 12 54 E
Stavenisse, Neths. 21 E4 51 35N 4 1 E
Staveren, Neths. 20 C6 52 53N 5 22 E
Stavern, Norway 14 F4 59 0N 10 1 E
Stavre, Sweden 14 B9 62 51N 15 19 E
Stavropol, Russia 53 D10 45 5N 42 0 E
Stavros, Cyprus 32 D11 35 1N 32 38 E
Stavrós, Greece 32 D6 35 12N 24 45 E
Stavros, Ákra, Greece 32 D6 35 26N 24 58 E
Stavroúpolis, Greece 44 C6 41 12N 24 45 E
Stawell, Australia 116 D5 37 5 S 142 47 E
Stawell →, Australia 114 C3 20 20 S 142 55 E
Stawiski, Poland 47 B9 53 22N 22 9 E
Stawiszyn, Poland 47 D5 51 56N 18 4 E
Stayner, Canada 136 B4 44 25N 80 5W
Steamboat Springs, U.S.A. 142 F10 40 29N 106 50W
Stębark, Poland 47 B7 53 30N 20 10 E
Stebleva, Albania 44 C2 41 18N 20 33 E
Steckborn, Switz. 29 A7 47 44N 8 59 E
Steele, U.S.A. 138 B5 46 51N 99 55W
Steelton, U.S.A. 136 F8 40 14N 76 50W
Steelville, U.S.A. 139 G9 37 58N 91 22W
Steen River, Canada 130 B5 59 40N 117 12W
Steenbergen, Neths. 21 E4 51 35N 4 19 E
Steenkool = Bintuni, Indonesia 73 B4 2 7 S 133 32 E
Steenvoorde, France 23 B9 50 48N 2 33 E
Steenwijk, Neths. 20 C8 52 47N 6 7 E
Steep Pt., Australia 113 E1 26 8 S 113 8 E
Steep Rock, Canada 131 C9 51 30N 98 48W
Ştefăneşti, Romania 46 B8 47 44N 27 15 E
Stefanie L. = Chew Bahir, Ethiopia 95 G4 4 40N 36 50 E
Stefansson Bay, Antarctica 7 C5 67 20 S 59 8 E
Steffisburg, Switz. 28 C5 46 47N 7 38 E
Stege, Denmark 15 K6 55 0N 12 18 E
Steiermark □, Austria 30 D8 47 26N 15 0 E
Steigerwald, Germany 27 F6 49 45N 10 30 E
Steilacoom, U.S.A. 144 C4 47 10N 122 36W
Stein, Neths. 21 G7 50 58N 5 45 E
Steinbach, Canada 131 D9 49 32N 96 40W
Steinfort, Lux. 21 J7 49 39N 5 55 E
Steinfurt, Germany 26 C3 52 9N 7 23 E
Steinheim, Germany 26 D5 51 50N 9 6 E
Steinhuder Meer, Germany 26 C5 52 48N 9 20 E
Steinkjer, Norway 12 E11 63 59N 11 31 E
Steinkopf, S. Africa 104 D2 29 18 S 17 43 E
Stekene, Belgium 21 F4 51 12N 4 2 E
Stellarton, Canada 129 C7 45 32N 62 30W
Stellenbosch, S. Africa 104 E2 33 58 S 18 50 E
Stellendam, Neths. 20 E4 51 49N 4 1 E
Stelvio, Paso dello, Italy 29 C10 46 32N 10 27 E
Stemshaug, Norway 14 A2 63 19N 8 44 E
Stendal, Germany 26 C7 52 36N 11 50 E
Stene, Belgium 21 F1 51 12N 2 56 E
Stensele, Sweden 12 D14 65 3N 17 8 E
Stenstorp, Sweden 15 F7 58 17N 13 45 E
Stepanakert = Khankendy, Azerbaijan 89 D12 39 40N 46 25 E
Stephen, U.S.A. 138 A6 48 27N 96 53W
Stephens, C., N.Z. 119 A8 40 42 S 173 58 E
Stephens Creek, Australia 116 A4 31 50 S 141 30 E
Stephens I., Canada 130 C2 54 10N 130 45W
Stephens I., N.Z. 119 A9 40 40 S 174 1 E
Stephenville, Canada 129 C8 48 31N 58 35W
Stephenville, U.S.A. 139 J5 32 13N 98 12W
Stepnica, Poland 47 B1 53 38N 14 36 E
Stepnoi = Elista, Russia 53 C11 46 16N 44 14 E
Stepnoye, Russia 54 D7 54 4N 60 26 E
Stepnyak, Kazakhstan 56 D8 52 50N 70 50 E
Steppe, Asia 58 E9 50 0N 50 0 E
Stereá Ellas □, Greece 45 F4 38 50N 22 0 E
Sterkstroom, S. Africa 104 E4 31 32 S 26 32 E
Sterling, Colo., U.S.A. 138 E3 40 37N 103 13W
Sterling, Ill., U.S.A. 140 C7 41 48N 89 42W
Sterling, Kans., U.S.A. 138 F5 38 13N 98 12W
Sterling City, U.S.A. 139 K4 31 51N 101 0W
Sterling Heights, U.S.A. 141 B13 42 35N 83 0W
Sterling Run, U.S.A. 136 E6 41 25N 78 12W
Sterlitamak, Russia 54 E4 53 40N 56 0 E
Sternberg, Germany 26 B7 53 42N 11 48 E
Šternberk, Czech. 31 B10 49 45N 17 15 E
Stérnes, Greece 32 D6 35 30N 24 9 E
Stettin = Szczecin, Poland 47 B1 53 27N 14 27 E
Stettiner Haff, Germany 26 B10 53 50N 14 25 E
Stettler, Canada 130 C6 52 19N 112 40W
Steubenville, U.S.A. 136 F4 40 22N 80 37W
Stevens Point, U.S.A. 138 C10 44 31N 89 34W
Stevenson, U.S.A. 144 E5 45 42N 121 53W
Stevenson L., Canada 131 C9 53 55N 96 0W
Stevns Klint, Denmark 15 J6 55 17N 12 28 E
Steward, U.S.A. 140 C7 41 51N 89 1W
Stewardson, U.S.A. 141 E8 39 16N 88 38W
Stewart, B.C., Canada 130 B3 55 56N 129 57W
Stewart, N.W.T., Canada 126 B6 63 19N 139 26W
Stewart, U.S.A. 144 F7 39 5N 119 46W
Stewart, C., Australia 114 A1 11 57 S 134 56 E
Stewart, I., Chile 160 D2 54 50 S 71 15W
Stewart I., N.Z. 119 G2 46 58 S 167 54 E
Stewarts Point, U.S.A. 144 G3 38 39N 123 24W
Stewartsville, U.S.A. 140 E2 39 45N 94 30W
Stewiacke, Canada 129 C7 45 9N 63 22W
Steynsburg, S. Africa 104 E4 31 15 S 25 49 E
Steyr, Austria 30 C7 48 3N 14 25 E
Steyr →, Austria 30 C7 48 17N 14 15 E
Steytlerville, S. Africa 104 E3 33 17 S 24 19 E
Stia, Italy 39 E8 43 48N 11 41 E
Stiens, Neths. 20 B7 53 16N 5 46 E
Stigler, U.S.A. 139 H7 35 15N 95 8W
Stigliano, Italy 41 B9 40 24N 16 13 E
Stigsnæs, Denmark 15 J5 55 13N 11 18 E
Stigtomta, Sweden 15 F10 58 47N 16 48 E
Stikine →, Canada 130 B2 56 40N 132 30W
Stilfontein, S. Africa 104 D4 26 51 S 26 50 E
Stilís, Greece 45 F4 38 55N 22 47 E
Stillwater, N.Z. 119 C6 42 27 S 171 20 E
Stillwater, Minn., U.S.A. 138 C8 45 3N 92 49W
Stillwater, N.Y., U.S.A. 137 D11 42 55N 73 41W
Stillwater, Okla., U.S.A. 139 G6 36 7N 97 4W
Stillwater Range, U.S.A. 142 G4 39 50N 118 5W
Stilwell, U.S.A. 139 H7 35 49N 94 38W
Stimfalías, L., Greece 45 G4 37 51N 22 27 E
Štip, Macedonia 42 F7 41 42N 22 10 E
Stíra, Greece 45 F6 38 9N 24 14 E
Stirling, Australia 114 B3 17 12 S 141 35 E
Stirling, Canada 130 D6 49 30N 112 30W
Stirling, N.Z. 119 G4 46 14 S 169 49 E
Stirling, U.K. 18 E5 56 7N 3 57W
Stirling Ra., Australia 113 F2 34 23 S 118 0 E
Stittsville, Canada 137 A9 45 15N 75 55W
Stockach, Germany 27 H5 47 51N 9 1 E
Stockbridge, U.S.A. 141 B12 42 27N 84 11W
Stockerau, Austria 31 C9 48 24N 16 12 E
Stockett, U.S.A. 142 C8 47 21N 111 10W
Stockholm, Sweden 14 E12 59 20N 18 3 E
Stockholms län □, Sweden 14 E12 59 30N 18 20 E
Stockhorn, Switz. 28 C5 46 42N 7 33 E
Stockport, U.K. 16 D5 53 25N 2 11W
Stockton, Australia 117 B9 32 50 S 151 47 E
Stockton, Calif., U.S.A. 144 H5 37 58N 121 17W
Stockton, Ill., U.S.A. 140 B6 42 21N 90 1W
Stockton, Kans., U.S.A. 138 F5 39 26N 99 16W
Stockton, Mo., U.S.A. 139 G8 37 42N 93 48W
Stockton-on-Tees, U.K. 16 C6 54 34N 1 20W
Stockvik, Sweden 14 B11 62 17N 17 23 E
Stoczek Łukowski, Poland 47 D8 51 58N 21 58 E
Stöde, Sweden 14 B10 62 28N 16 35 E
Stogovo, Macedonia 42 F5 41 31N 20 38 E
Stoke, N.Z. 119 B8 41 19 S 173 14 E
Stoke on Trent, U.K. 16 D5 53 1N 2 11W
Stokes Bay, Canada 128 C3 45 0N 81 28W
Stokes Pt., Australia 114 G3 40 10 S 143 56 E
Stokes Ra., Australia 112 C5 15 50 S 130 50 E
Stokkseyri, Iceland 12 E3 63 50N 21 2W
Stokksnes, Iceland 12 D6 64 14N 14 58W
Stolac, Bos.-H. 42 D2 43 8N 17 59 E
Stolberg, Germany 26 E2 50 48N 6 13 E
Stolbovaya, Russia 51 D10 55 10N 37 32 E
Stolbovaya, Russia 57 C16 64 50N 153 50 E
Stolbovoy, Ostrov, Russia 57 D17 74 44N 135 14 E
Stolbtsy, Belorussia 50 E5 53 30N 26 43 E
Stolin, Belorussia 50 F5 51 53N 26 50 E
Stolnici, Romania 46 E5 44 31N 24 48 E
Stolwijk, Neths. 20 E5 51 59N 4 47 E
Stomíon, Greece 32 D5 35 21N 23 32 E
Ston, Croatia 42 E2 42 51N 17 43 E
Stonehaven, U.K. 18 E6 56 58N 2 11W
Stonehenge, Australia 114 C3 24 22 S 143 17 E
Stonewall, Canada 131 C9 50 10N 97 19W
Stonington, U.S.A. 140 E7 39 44N 89 12W
Stony L., Man., Canada 131 B9 58 51N 98 40W
Stony L., Ont., Canada 136 B6 44 30N 78 5W
Stony Rapids, Canada 131 B7 59 16N 105 50W
Stony Tunguska = Podkamennaya Tunguska →, Russia 57 C10 61 50N 90 13 E
Stonyford, U.S.A. 144 F4 39 23N 122 33W
Stopnica, Poland 47 E7 50 27N 20 57 E
Stora Lulevatten, Sweden 12 C15 67 10N 19 30 E
Stora Sjöfallet, Sweden 12 C15 67 29N 18 40 E
Storavan, Sweden 12 D15 65 45N 18 10 E
Store Bælt, Denmark 15 J5 55 20N 11 0 E
Store Creek, Australia 117 B8 32 54 S 149 6 E
Store Heddinge, Denmark 15 J6 55 18N 12 23 E
Støren, Norway 14 A4 63 3N 10 18 E
Storlulea = Stora Lulevatten, Sweden 12 C15 67 10N 19 30 E
Storm B., Australia 114 G4 43 10 S 147 30 E
Storm Lake, U.S.A. 138 D7 42 39N 95 13W
Stormberge, S. Africa 104 E4 31 16 S 26 17 E
Stormsrivier, S. Africa 104 E3 33 59 S 23 52 E
Stornoway, U.K. 18 C2 58 12N 6 23W
Storozhinets, Ukraine 52 B1 48 14N 25 45 E
Storsjö, Sweden 14 B7 62 49N 13 5 E
Storsjøen, Hedmark, Norway 14 D5 60 20N 11 40 E
Storsjøen, Hedmark, Norway 14 C5 61 30N 11 14 E
Storsjön, Sweden 14 B7 62 50N 13 8 E
Storstrøms Amt. □, Denmark 15 K5 54 50N 11 45 E
Storuman, Sweden 12 D14 65 5N 17 10 E
Story City, U.S.A. 140 B3 42 11N 93 36W
Stoughton, Canada 131 D8 49 40N 103 0W
Stoughton, U.S.A. 140 B8 42 55N 89 13W
Stour →, Dorset, U.K. 17 G5 50 48N 2 7W
Stour →, Here. & Worcs., U.K. 17 E5 52 25N 2 13W
Stour →, Kent, U.K. 17 F9 51 15N 1 20 E
Stour →, Suffolk, U.K. 17 F9 51 55N 1 5 E
Stourbridge, U.K. 17 E5 52 28N 2 8W
Stout, L., Canada 131 C10 52 0N 94 40W
Stove Pipe Wells Village, U.S.A. 145 J9 36 35N 117 11W
Stowmarket, U.K. 17 E9 52 11N 1 0 E
Strabane, U.K. 19 B4 54 50N 7 28W
Strabane □, U.K. 19 B4 54 45N 7 25W
Stracin, Macedonia 42 E7 42 13N 22 2 E
Stradella, Italy 38 C6 45 4N 9 20 E
Strahan, Australia 114 G4 42 9 S 145 20 E
Strakonice, Czech. 30 B6 49 15N 13 53 E
Straldzha, Bulgaria 43 E11 42 35N 26 40 E
Stralsund, Germany 26 A9 54 17N 13 5 E
Strand, S. Africa 104 E2 34 9 S 18 48 E
Strangford L., U.K. 19 B6 54 30N 5 37W
Strängnäs, Sweden 14 E11 59 23N 17 2 E
Strangsville, U.S.A. 136 E3 41 19N 81 50W
Stranraer, U.K. 18 G3 54 54N 5 0W
Strasbourg, Canada 131 C8 51 4N 104 55W
Strasbourg, France 23 D14 48 35N 7 42 E
Strasburg, Germany 26 B9 53 30N 13 44 E
Strasburg, U.S.A. 138 B4 46 8N 100 10W
Strassen, Lux. 21 J8 49 37N 6 4 E
Stratford, N.S.W., Australia 117 B9 32 7 S 151 55 E
Stratford, Vic., Australia 117 D7 37 59 S 147 7 E
Stratford, Canada 128 D3 43 23N 81 0W
Stratford, N.Z. 118 F3 39 20 S 174 19 E
Stratford, Calif., U.S.A. 144 J7 36 11N 119 49W
Stratford, Conn., U.S.A. 137 E11 41 12N 73 8W
Stratford, Tex., U.S.A. 139 G3 36 20N 102 4W
Stratford-upon-Avon, U.K. 17 E6 52 12N 1 42W
Strath Spey, U.K. 18 D5 57 15N 3 40W
Strathalbyn, Australia 116 C3 35 13 S 138 53 E
Strathclyde □, U.K. 18 F4 56 0N 4 50W
Strathcona Prov. Park, Canada 130 D3 49 38N 125 40W
Strathmore, Australia 114 B3 17 50 S 142 35 E
Strathmore, Canada 130 C6 51 5N 113 18W
Strathmore, U.K. 18 E5 56 40N 3 4W
Strathmore, U.S.A. 144 J7 36 9N 119 4W
Strathnaver, Canada 130 C4 53 20N 122 33W
Strathpeffer, U.K. 18 D4 57 35N 4 32W
Strathroy, Canada 128 D3 42 58N 81 38W
Strathy Pt., U.K. 18 C4 58 35N 4 3W
Stratton, U.S.A. 138 F3 39 19N 102 36W
Straubing, Germany 27 G8 48 53N 12 35 E
Straumnes, Iceland 12 C2 66 26N 23 8W
Strausberg, Germany 26 C9 52 40N 13 52 E
Strawberry Point, U.S.A. 140 B5 42 41N 91 32W
Strawberry Reservoir, U.S.A. 142 F8 40 8N 111 9W
Strawn, U.S.A. 139 J5 32 33N 98 30W
Strážnice, Czech. 31 C10 48 54N 17 19 E
Streaky B., Australia 115 E1 32 48 S 134 13 E
Streaky Bay, Australia 115 E1 32 51 S 134 18 E
Streator, U.S.A. 138 E10 41 8N 88 50W
Středočeský □, Czech. 30 B7 49 55N 14 30 E
Středoslovenský □, Slovak Rep. 31 C12 48 30N 19 15 E
Streé, Belgium 21 H4 50 17N 4 18 E
Streeter, U.S.A. 138 B5 46 39N 99 21W
Streetsville, Canada 136 C5 43 35N 79 42W
Strehaia, Romania 46 E4 44 37N 23 10 E
Strelcha, Bulgaria 43 E9 42 25N 24 19 E
Strelka, Russia 57 D10 58 5N 93 3 E
Streng →, Cambodia 76 F4 13 12N 103 37 E
Strésa, Italy 38 C5 45 52N 8 28 E
Strezhevoy, Russia 56 C8 60 42N 77 34 E
Stříbro, Czech. 30 B6 49 44N 13 2 E
Strickland →, Papua N. G. 120 D1 7 35 S 141 36 E
Strijen, Neths. 20 E5 51 45N 4 33 E
Strimón →, Greece 44 D5 40 46N 23 51 E
Strimonikós Kólpos, Greece 44 D5 40 33N 24 0 E
Stroeder, Argentina 160 B4 40 12 S 62 37W
Strofádhes, Greece 45 G3 37 15N 21 0 E
Strömbacka, Sweden 14 C10 61 58N 16 44 E
Strómboli, Italy 41 D8 38 48N 15 12 E
Stromeferry, U.K. 18 D3 57 20N 5 33W
Stromness, U.K. 18 C5 58 58N 3 18W
Ströms vattudal, Sweden 12 D13 64 15N 14 55 E
Stromsburg, U.S.A. 138 E6 41 7N 97 36W
Strömstad, Sweden 13 G11 58 55N 11 15 E
Strömsund, Sweden 12 E13 63 51N 15 33 E
Stronghurst, U.S.A. 140 D6 40 45N 90 55W
Stróngoli, Italy 41 C10 39 16N 17 2 E
Stronsay, U.K. 18 B6 59 8N 2 38W
Stropkov, Slovak Rep. 31 B14 49 13N 21 39 E
Stroud, U.K. 17 F5 51 44N 2 12W
Stroud Road, Australia 117 B9 32 18 S 151 57 E
Stroudsburg, U.S.A. 137 F9 40 59N 75 12W
Stroumbi, Cyprus 32 E11 34 53N 32 29 E
Struer, Denmark 15 H2 56 30N 8 35 E
Struga, Macedonia 42 F5 41 13N 20 44 E
Strugi Krasnyye, Russia 50 B6 58 21N 29 1 E
Strumica, Macedonia 42 F7 41 28N 22 41 E
Strumica →, Europe 42 F8 41 20N 23 22 E
Struthers, Canada 128 C2 48 41N 85 51W
Struthers, U.S.A. 136 E4 41 4N 80 39W
Stryama, Bulgaria 43 E9 42 16N 24 54 E
Stryi, Ukraine 50 G3 49 16N 23 48 E
Stryker, U.S.A. 142 B6 48 41N 114 46W
Stryków, Poland 47 D6 51 55N 19 33 E
Strzegom, Poland 47 E3 50 58N 16 20 E
Strzelce Krajeńskie, Poland 47 C2 52 52N 15 33 E
Strzelce Opolskie, Poland 47 E5 50 31N 18 18 E
Strzelecki Cr. →, Australia 115 D2 29 37 S 139 59 E
Strzelin, Poland 47 E4 50 46N 17 2 E
Strzelno, Poland 47 C5 52 35N 18 9 E
Strzybnica, Poland 47 E5 50 28N 18 48 E
Strzyzów, Poland 31 B14 49 52N 21 47 E
Stuart, Fla., U.S.A. 135 M5 27 12N 80 15W
Stuart, Iowa, U.S.A. 140 C2 41 30N 94 19W
Stuart, Nebr., U.S.A. 138 D5 42 36N 99 8W
Stuart →, Canada 130 C4 54 0N 123 35W
Stuart Bluff Ra., Australia 112 D5 22 50 S 131 52 E
Stuart L., Canada 130 C4 54 30N 124 30W
Stuart Mts., N.Z. 119 F2 45 2 S 167 39 E
Stuart Ra., Australia 115 D1 29 10 S 134 56 E
Stubbekøbing, Denmark 15 K6 54 53N 12 9 E
Stuben, Austria 30 D3 47 10N 10 8 E
Studen Kladenets, Yazovir, Bulgaria 43 F10 41 37N 25 30 E
Studholme, N.Z. 119 E6 44 42 S 171 9 E
Stugun, Sweden 14 A9 63 10N 15 40 E
Stull, L., Canada 128 B1 54 24N 92 34W
Stung Treng, Cambodia 76 F5 13 31N 105 58 E
Stupart →, Canada 131 B10 56 0N 93 25W
Stupino, Russia 51 D11 54 57N 38 2 E
Sturgeon B., Canada 131 C9 52 0N 97 50W
Sturgeon Bay, U.S.A. 134 C2 44 50N 87 23W
Sturgeon Falls, Canada 128 C4 46 25N 79 57W
Sturgeon L., Alta., Canada 130 B5 55 6N 117 32W
Sturgeon L., Ont., Canada 128 B1 50 0N 90 45W
Sturgeon L., Ont., Canada 136 B6 44 28N 78 43W
Sturgis, Mich., U.S.A. 141 C11 41 48N 85 25W
Sturgis, S. Dak., U.S.A. 138 C3 44 25N 103 31W
Štúrovo, Slovak Rep. 31 D11 47 48N 18 41 E
Sturt Cr. →, Australia 112 C4 19 8 S 127 50 E
Sturt Creek, Australia 112 C4 19 12 S 128 8 E
Sturts Meadows, Australia 116 A4 31 18 S 141 42 E
Stutterheim, S. Africa 104 E4 32 33 S 27 28 E
Stuttgart, Germany 27 G5 48 46N 9 10 E
Stuttgart, U.S.A. 139 H9 34 30N 91 33W
Stuyvesant, U.S.A. 137 D11 42 23N 73 45W
Stykkishólmur, Iceland 12 D2 65 2N 22 40W
Styr →, Belorussia 50 E5 52 7N 26 35 E
Styria = Steiermark □, Austria 30 D8 47 26N 15 0 E
Su-no-Saki, Japan 63 C11 34 58N 139 45 E
Su Xian, China 66 H9 33 41N 116 59 E
Suakin, Sudan 94 D4 19 8N 37 20 E
Sual, Phil. 70 C3 16 4N 120 5 E
Suan, N. Korea 67 E14 38 42N 126 22 E
Suapure →, Venezuela 152 B4 6 48N 67 1W
Suaqui, Mexico 146 B3 29 12N 109 41W
Suatá →, Venezuela 153 B4 7 52N 65 22W
Subang, Indonesia 75 D3 6 34 S 107 45 E
Subansiri →, India 78 B4 26 48N 93 50 E
Subayhah, Si. Arabia 84 D3 30 2N 38 50 E
Subi, Indonesia 75 B3 2 58N 108 50 E
Subiaco, Italy 39 G10 41 56N 13 5 E
Subotica, Serbia 42 A4 46 6N 19 39 E
Success, Canada 131 C7 50 28N 108 6W
Suceava, Romania 46 B7 47 38N 26 16 E
Suceava □, Romania 46 B6 47 37N 25 40 E
Suceava →, Romania 46 B7 47 38N 26 16 E
Sucha-Beskidzka, Poland 31 B12 49 44N 19 35 E
Suchan, Poland 47 B2 53 18N 15 18 E
Suchan, Russia 60 C6 43 8N 133 9 E
Suchedniów, Poland 47 D7 51 3N 20 49 E
Suchitoto, El Salv. 148 D2 13 56N 89 0W
Suchou = Suzhou, China 69 B13 31 19N 120 38 E
Süchow = Xuzhou, China 67 G9 34 18N 117 10 E
Suchowola, Poland 47 B10 53 33N 23 3 E
Sucio →, Colombia 152 B2 7 27N 77 7W
Suck →, Ireland 19 C3 53 17N 8 18W
Suckling, Mt., Papua N. G. 120 E5 9 49 S 148 53 E
Sucre, Bolivia 157 D4 19 0 S 65 15W
Sucre, Colombia 152 B3 8 49N 74 44W
Sucre □, Colombia 152 B2 8 50N 75 40W
Sucre □, Venezuela 153 A5 10 25N 63 30W
Sucuaro, Colombia 152 C4 4 34N 68 50W
Sućuraj, Croatia 39 E14 43 10N 17 8 E
Sucuriju, Brazil 154 A2 1 39N 49 57W
Sucuriú →, Brazil 157 E7 20 47 S 51 38W
Sud, Pte., Canada 129 C7 49 3N 62 14W
Sud-Ouest, Pte. du, Canada 129 C7 49 23N 63 36W
Suda →, Russia 51 B10 59 0N 37 40 E
Sudak, Ukraine 52 D6 44 51N 34 57 E
Sudan, U.S.A. 139 H3 34 4N 102 32W
Sudan ■, Africa 95 E3 15 0N 30 0 E
Suday, Russia 51 B13 59 0N 43 0 E
Sudbury, Canada 128 C3 46 30N 81 0W
Sudbury, U.K. 17 E8 52 2N 0 44 E
Sûdd, Sudan 95 F2 8 20N 30 0 E
Suddie, Guyana 153 B6 7 8N 58 29W
Süderbrarup, Germany 26 A5 54 38N 9 47 E
Süderlügum, Germany 26 A4 54 50N 8 55 E
Süderoog-Sand, Germany 26 A4 54 27N 8 30 E
Sudeten Mts. = Sudety, Europe 31 A9 50 20N 16 45 E

270 Sudety

Sudety, *Europe* 31 **A9** 50 20N 16 45 E
Sudi, *Tanzania* 107 **E4** 10 11 S 39 57 E
Sudirman, Pegunungan, *Indonesia* 73 **B5** 4 30 S 137 0 E
Suditi, *Romania* 46 **E8** 44 35N 27 38 E
Sudogda, *Russia* 51 **D12** 55 55N 40 50 E
Sudr, *Egypt* 94 **J8** 29 40N 32 42 E
Sudzha, *Russia* 50 **F9** 51 14N 35 17 E
Sueca, *Spain* 35 **F4** 39 12N 0 21W
Suedala, *Sweden* 15 **J7** 55 30N 13 15 E
Suez = El Suweis, *Egypt* 94 **J8** 29 58N 32 31 E
Suez, G. of = Suweis, Khalîg el, *Egypt* 94 **J8** 28 40N 33 0 E
Suez Canal = Suweis, Qanâl es, *Egypt* 94 **H8** 31 0N 32 20 E
Suffield, *Canada* 131 **C6** 50 12N 111 10W
Suffolk, *U.S.A.* 134 **G7** 36 44N 76 35W
Suffolk □, *U.K.* 17 **E9** 52 16N 1 0 E
Sufi-Kurgan, *Kirghizia* 55 **C6** 40 2N 73 30 E
Suga no-Sen, *Japan* 62 **B6** 35 25N 134 25 E
Sugag, *Romania* 46 **D4** 45 47N 23 37 E
Sugar →, *Ill., U.S.A.* 140 **B7** 42 26N 89 12W
Sugar →, *Ind., U.S.A.* 141 **E9** 39 50N 87 23W
Sugar City, *U.S.A.* 138 **F3** 38 14N 103 40W
Sugar Cr. →, *U.S.A.* 140 **D7** 40 9N 89 38W
Sugbai Passage, *Phil.* 71 **J3** 5 22N 120 33 E
Suğla Gölü, *Turkey* 88 **E5** 37 20N 32 0 E
Sugluk = Saglouc, *Canada* 127 **B12** 62 14N 75 38W
Sugny, *Belgium* 21 **J5** 49 49N 4 54 E
Suhaia, L., *Romania* 46 **F6** 43 45N 25 15 E
Suhār, *Oman* 85 **E8** 24 20N 56 40 E
Sühbaatar □, *Mongolia* 66 **B8** 45 30N 114 0 E
Suhl, *Germany* 26 **E6** 50 35N 10 40 E
Suhr, *Switz.* 28 **B6** 47 22N 8 5 E
Şuhut, *Turkey* 88 **D4** 38 31N 30 32 E
Sui Xian, *Henan, China* 66 **G8** 34 25N 115 2 E
Sui Xian, *Henan, China* 69 **B9** 31 42N 113 24 E
Suiá Missu →, *Brazil* 157 **C7** 11 13 S 53 15W
Suichang, *China* 69 **C12** 28 29N 119 15 E
Suichuan, *China* 69 **D10** 26 20N 114 32 E
Suide, *China* 66 **F6** 37 30N 110 12 E
Suifenhe, *China* 67 **B16** 44 25N 131 10 E
Suihua, *China* 65 **B7** 46 32N 126 55 E
Suijiang, *China* 68 **C4** 28 40N 103 59 E
Suining, *Hunan, China* 68 **D8** 26 35N 110 10 E
Suining, *Jiangsu, China* 67 **H9** 33 56N 117 58 E
Suining, *Sichuan, China* 68 **B5** 30 26N 105 35 E
Suiping, *China* 66 **H7** 33 10N 113 59 E
Suippes, *France* 23 **C11** 49 8N 4 30 E
Suir →, *Ireland* 19 **D4** 52 15N 7 10W
Suita, *Japan* 63 **C7** 34 45N 135 32 E
Suixi, *China* 69 **G8** 21 19N 110 18 E
Suiyang, *Guizhou, China* 68 **D6** 27 58N 107 18 E
Suiyang, *Heilongjiang, China* 67 **B16** 44 30N 130 56 E
Suizhong, *China* 67 **D11** 40 21N 120 20 E
Sujangarh, *India* 80 **F6** 27 42N 74 31 E
Sujica, *Bos.-H.* 42 **D2** 43 52N 17 11 E
Sukabumi, *Indonesia* 74 **D3** 6 56 S 106 50 E
Sukadana, *Kalimantan, Indonesia* 75 **C4** 1 10 S 110 0 E
Sukadana, *Sumatera, Indonesia* 74 **D3** 5 5 S 105 33 E
Sukagawa, *Japan* 61 **F10** 37 17N 140 23 E
Sukaraja, *Indonesia* 75 **C4** 2 28 S 110 25 E
Sukarnapura = Jayapura, *Indonesia* 73 **B6** 2 28 S 140 38 E
Sukchŏn, *N. Korea* 67 **E13** 39 22N 125 35 E
Sukhindol, *Bulgaria* 43 **D10** 43 11N 25 10 E
Sukhinichi, *Russia* 50 **D9** 54 8N 35 10 E
Sukhona →, *Russia* 48 **C6** 59 40N 39 45 E
Sukhothai, *Thailand* 76 **D2** 17 1N 99 49 E
Sukhoy Log, *Russia* 54 **C8** 56 55N 62 1 E
Sukhumi, *Georgia* 53 **E9** 43 0N 41 0 E
Sukkur, *Pakistan* 79 **D3** 27 42N 68 54 E
Sukkur Barrage, *Pakistan* 80 **F3** 27 40N 68 50 E
Sukma, *India* 82 **E5** 18 24N 81 45 E
Sukovo, *Serbia* 42 **D7** 43 4N 22 37 E
Sukumo, *Japan* 62 **E4** 32 56N 132 44 E
Sukunka →, *Canada* 130 **B4** 55 45N 121 15W
Sul, Canal do, *Brazil* 154 **B2** 0 10 S 48 30W
Sula →, *Ukraine* 50 **G8** 49 40N 32 41 E
Sula, Kepulauan, *Indonesia* 72 **B3** 1 45 S 125 0 E
Sulaco →, *Honduras* 148 **C2** 15 2N 87 44W
Sulaiman Range, *Pakistan* 80 **D3** 30 30N 69 50 E
Sulak →, *Russia* 53 **E12** 43 20N 47 34 E
Sūlār, *Iran* 85 **D6** 31 53N 51 54 E
Sulawesi □, *Indonesia* 72 **B2** 2 0 S 120 0 E
Sulawesi Sea, *Indonesia* 72 **A2** 3 0N 123 0 E
Sulechów, *Poland* 47 **C2** 52 5N 15 40 E
Sulęcin, *Poland* 47 **C2** 52 26N 15 10 E
Sulejów, *Poland* 47 **D6** 51 26N 19 53 E
Sulejówek, *Poland* 47 **C8** 52 13N 21 17 E
Sulgen, *Switz.* 29 **A8** 47 33N 9 7 E
Sulima, *S. Leone* 100 **D2** 6 58N 11 32W
Sulina, *Romania* 46 **D10** 45 10N 29 40 E
Sulina, Braţul →, *Romania* 46 **D10** 45 10N 29 20 E
Sulingen, *Germany* 26 **C4** 52 41N 8 47 E
Sulita, *Romania* 46 **B7** 47 39N 26 59 E
Sulitälma, *Sweden* 12 **C14** 67 17N 17 28 E
Sulitjelma, *Norway* 12 **C14** 67 9N 16 3 E
Sułkowice, *Poland* 31 **B12** 49 50N 19 49 E
Sullana, *Peru* 156 **A1** 4 52 S 80 39W
Sullivan, *Ill., U.S.A.* 138 **F10** 39 36N 88 37W
Sullivan, *Ind., U.S.A.* 141 **E9** 39 6N 87 24W
Sullivan, *Mo., U.S.A.* 140 **F6** 38 13N 91 10W
Sullivan Bay, *Canada* 130 **C3** 50 55N 126 50W
Sully, *U.S.A.* 140 **C4** 41 34N 92 50W
Sully-sur-Loire, *France* 23 **E9** 47 45N 2 20 E
Sulmierzyce, *Poland* 47 **D4** 51 37N 17 32 E
Sulmona, *Italy* 39 **F10** 42 3N 13 55 E
Sulphur, *La., U.S.A.* 139 **K8** 30 14N 93 23W
Sulphur, *Okla., U.S.A.* 139 **H6** 34 31N 96 58W
Sulphur Pt., *Canada* 130 **A6** 60 56N 114 48W
Sulphur Springs, *U.S.A.* 139 **J7** 33 8N 95 36W
Sulphur Springs Draw →, *U.S.A.* 139 **J4** 32 12N 101 36W
Sulsul, *Ethiopia* 108 **C2** 5 5N 44 50 E
Sultan, *Canada* 128 **C3** 47 36N 82 47W
Sultan, *U.S.A.* 144 **C5** 47 52N 121 49W
Sultan Kudarat □, *Phil.* 71 **H5** 6 30N 124 10 E
Sultan sa Barongis, *Phil.* 71 **H5** 6 45N 124 35 E
Sultanpur, *India* 81 **F10** 26 18N 82 4 E
Sultsa, *Russia* 48 **B8** 63 27N 46 2 E
Sulu □, *Phil.* 71 **J3** 5 30N 120 30 E
Sulu Arch., *Phil.* 71 **J3** 6 0N 121 0 E
Sulu Sea, *E. Indies* 71 **G3** 8 0N 120 0 E
Sülüklü, *Turkey* 88 **D5** 38 53N 32 20 E
Sululta, *Ethiopia* 95 **F4** 9 10N 38 43 E
Suluova, *Turkey* 88 **C6** 40 46N 35 32 E
Suluq, *Libya* 96 **B4** 31 44N 20 14 E
Sulyukta, *Kirghizia* 55 **D4** 39 56N 69 34 E
Sulzbach, *Germany* 27 **F3** 49 18N 7 4 E
Sulzbach-Rosenberg, *Germany* 27 **F7** 49 30N 11 46 E
Sulzberger Ice Shelf, *Antarctica* 7 **D10** 78 0 S 150 0 E
Sumalata, *Indonesia* 72 **A2** 1 0N 122 31 E
Sumampa, *Argentina* 158 **B3** 29 25 S 63 29W
Sumatera □, *Indonesia* 74 **B2** 0 40N 100 20 E
Sumatra = Sumatera □, *Indonesia* 74 **B2** 0 40N 100 20 E
Sumatra, *U.S.A.* 142 **C10** 46 37N 107 33W
Sumba, *Indonesia* 72 **C1** 9 45 S 119 35 E
Sumba, Selat, *Indonesia* 72 **C1** 9 0 S 118 40 E
Sumbawa, *Indonesia* 72 **C1** 8 26 S 117 30 E
Sumbawa Besar, *Indonesia* 72 **C1** 8 30 S 117 26 E
Sumbawanga □, *Tanzania* 106 **D3** 8 0 S 31 30 E
Sumbe, *Angola* 103 **E2** 11 10 S 13 48 E
Sumburgh Hd., *U.K.* 18 **B7** 59 52N 1 17W
Sumdo, *India* 81 **B8** 35 6N 78 41 E
Sumé, *Brazil* 154 **C4** 7 39 S 36 55W
Sumedang, *Indonesia* 75 **D3** 6 52 S 107 55 E
Sümeg, *Hungary* 31 **E10** 46 59N 17 20 E
Šumen, *Bulgaria* 43 **D11** 43 18N 26 55 E
Sumenep, *Indonesia* 75 **D4** 7 1 S 113 52 E
Sumgait, *Azerbaijan* 53 **F13** 40 34N 49 38 E
Sumisu-Jima, *Japan* 63 **F12** 31 27N 140 3 E
Sumiswald, *Switz.* 28 **B5** 47 2N 7 44 E
Summer L., *U.S.A.* 142 **E3** 42 50N 120 45W
Summerland, *Canada* 130 **D5** 49 32N 119 41W
Summerside, *Canada* 129 **C7** 46 24N 63 47W
Summerville, *Ga., U.S.A.* 135 **H3** 34 29N 85 21W
Summerville, *S.C., U.S.A.* 135 **J5** 33 1N 80 11W
Summit Lake, *Canada* 130 **C4** 54 20N 122 40W
Summit Peak, *U.S.A.* 143 **H10** 37 21N 106 42W
Sumner, *N.Z.* 119 **D7** 43 35 S 172 48 E
Sumner, *Ill., U.S.A.* 141 **F9** 38 42N 87 53W
Sumner, *Iowa, U.S.A.* 140 **B4** 42 51N 92 6W
Sumner, *Wash., U.S.A.* 144 **C4** 47 12N 122 14W
Sumner L., *N.Z.* 119 **C7** 42 42 S 172 15 E
Sumoto, *Japan* 62 **C6** 34 21N 134 54 E
Sumpangbinangae, *Indonesia* 72 **B1** 4 24 S 119 36 E
Sumperk, *Czech.* 31 **B9** 49 59N 17 0 E
Sumprabum, *Burma* 78 **B6** 26 33N 97 36 E
Sumqayit = Sumgait, *Azerbaijan* 53 **F13** 40 34N 49 38 E
Sumter, *U.S.A.* 135 **J5** 33 55N 80 21W
Sumy, *Ukraine* 50 **F9** 50 57N 34 50 E
Sun City, *Ariz., U.S.A.* 143 **K7** 33 36N 112 17W
Sun City, *Calif., U.S.A.* 145 **M9** 33 42N 117 11W
Sun Prairie, *U.S.A.* 140 **A7** 43 11N 89 13W
Sunagawa, *Japan* 60 **C10** 43 29N 141 55 E
Sunan, *N. Korea* 67 **E13** 39 15N 125 40 E
Sunart, L., *U.K.* 18 **E3** 56 42N 5 43W
Sunburst, *U.S.A.* 142 **B8** 48 53N 111 55W
Sunbury, *Australia* 117 **D6** 37 35 S 144 44 E
Sunbury, *U.S.A.* 137 **F8** 40 52N 76 48W
Sunchales, *Argentina* 158 **C3** 30 58 S 61 35W
Suncho Corral, *Argentina* 158 **B3** 27 55 S 63 27W
Sunchon, *S. Korea* 67 **G14** 34 52N 127 31 E
Suncook, *U.S.A.* 137 **C13** 43 8N 71 27W
Sunda, Selat, *Indonesia* 74 **D3** 6 20 S 105 30 E
Sunda Is., *Indonesia* 58 **K14** 5 0 S 105 0 E
Sunda Str. = Sunda, Selat, *Indonesia* 74 **D3** 6 20 S 105 30 E
Sundance, *U.S.A.* 138 **C2** 44 24N 104 23W
Sundarbans, The, *Asia* 78 **E2** 22 0N 89 0 E
Sundargarh, *India* 82 **C7** 22 4N 84 5 E
Sundays = Sondags →, *S. Africa* 104 **E4** 33 44 S 25 51 E
Sundbyberg, *Sweden* 14 **E11** 59 22N 17 58 E
Sunderland, *Canada* 136 **B5** 44 16N 79 4W
Sunderland, *U.K.* 16 **C6** 54 54N 1 22W
Sundre, *Canada* 130 **C6** 51 49N 114 38W
Sundridge, *Canada* 128 **C4** 45 45N 79 25W
Sunds, *Denmark* 15 **H3** 56 13N 9 1 E
Sundsjö, *Sweden* 14 **B9** 62 59N 15 9 E
Sundsvall, *Sweden* 14 **B11** 62 23N 17 17 E
Sung Hei, *Vietnam* 77 **G6** 10 20N 106 2 E
Sungai Kolok, *Thailand* 77 **J3** 6 2N 101 58 E
Sungai Lembing, *Malaysia* 77 **L4** 3 55N 103 3 E
Sungai Patani, *Malaysia* 77 **K3** 5 37N 100 30 E
Sungaigerong, *Indonesia* 74 **C2** 2 59 S 104 52 E
Sungailiat, *Indonesia* 74 **C3** 1 51 S 106 8 E
Sungaipenuh, *Indonesia* 74 **C2** 2 1 S 101 20 E
Sungaitiram, *Indonesia* 75 **C5** 0 45 S 117 8 E
Sungari = Songhua Jiang →, *China* 65 **B8** 47 45N 132 30 E
Sungguminasa, *Indonesia* 72 **C1** 5 17 S 119 30 E
Sunghua Chiang = Songhua Jiang →, *China* 65 **B8** 47 45N 132 30 E
Sungikai, *Sudan* 95 **E2** 12 20N 29 51 E
Sungurlu, *Turkey* 52 **F6** 40 12N 34 21 E
Sunja, *Croatia* 39 **C13** 45 21N 16 35 E
Sunkar, Gora, *Kazakhstan* 55 **A6** 44 15N 73 50 E
Sunnyside, *Utah, U.S.A.* 142 **G8** 39 34N 110 23W
Sunnyside, *Wash., U.S.A.* 142 **C3** 46 20N 120 0W
Sunnyvale, *U.S.A.* 144 **H4** 37 23N 122 2W
Sunray, *U.S.A.* 139 **G4** 36 1N 101 49W
Sunshine, *Australia* 117 **D6** 37 48 S 144 52 E
Suntar, *Russia* 57 **C12** 62 15N 117 30 E
Sunyani, *Ghana* 100 **D4** 7 21N 2 22W
Suō-Nada, *Japan* 62 **D3** 33 50N 131 30 E
Suoyarvi, *Russia* 48 **B5** 62 12N 32 23 E
Supai, *U.S.A.* 143 **H7** 36 15N 112 41W
Supamo →, *Venezuela* 153 **B5** 6 48N 61 50W
Supaul, *India* 81 **F12** 26 10N 86 40 E
Supe, *Peru* 156 **C2** 11 0 S 77 30W
Superior, *Ariz., U.S.A.* 143 **K8** 33 18N 111 6W
Superior, *Mont., U.S.A.* 142 **C6** 47 12N 114 53W
Superior, *Nebr., U.S.A.* 138 **E5** 40 1N 98 4W
Superior, *Wis., U.S.A.* 138 **B8** 46 44N 92 6W
Superior, L., *U.S.A.* 128 **C2** 47 0N 87 0W
Supetar, *Croatia* 39 **E13** 43 25N 16 32 E
Suphan Buri, *Thailand* 76 **E3** 14 14N 100 10 E
Suphan Daği, *Turkey* 89 **D10** 38 54N 42 48 E
Supraśl, *Poland* 47 **B10** 53 13N 23 19 E
Supriori, Kepulauan, *Indonesia* 73 **B5** 1 0 S 136 0 E
Supung Sk., *China* 67 **D13** 40 35N 124 50 E
Sūq' Abs, *Yemen* 86 **D3** 16 0N 43 12 E
Suq al Jum'ah, *Libya* 96 **B2** 32 58N 13 12 E
Sūq Suwayq, *Si. Arabia* 84 **E3** 24 23N 38 27 E
Suqian, *China* 67 **H10** 33 54N 118 8 E
Sūr, *Lebanon* 91 **B4** 33 19N 35 16 E
Sur, Pt., *U.S.A.* 144 **J5** 36 18N 121 54W
Sura →, *Russia* 51 **C15** 56 6N 46 0 E
Surab, *Pakistan* 79 **C2** 28 25N 66 15 E
Surabaja = Surabaya, *Indonesia* 75 **D4** 7 17 S 112 45 E
Surabaya, *Indonesia* 75 **D4** 7 17 S 112 45 E
Suraia, *Romania* 46 **D8** 45 40N 27 25 E
Surakarta, *Indonesia* 75 **D4** 7 35 S 110 48 E
Surakhany, *Azerbaijan* 53 **F14** 40 25N 50 1 E
Surandai, *India* 83 **K3** 8 58N 77 26 E
Šurany, *Slovak Rep.* 31 **C11** 48 6N 18 10 E
Surat, *Australia* 115 **D4** 27 10 S 149 6 E
Surat, *India* 82 **D1** 21 12N 72 55 E
Surat Thani, *Thailand* 77 **H2** 9 6N 99 20 E
Suratgarh, *India* 80 **E5** 29 18N 73 55 E
Suraz, *Poland* 47 **C9** 52 57N 22 57 E
Surazh, *Belorussia* 50 **D7** 55 25N 30 44 E
Surazh, *Russia* 50 **E8** 53 5N 32 27 E
Surduc, *Romania* 46 **B4** 47 15N 23 25 E
Surduc Pasul, *Romania* 46 **D4** 45 21N 23 23 E
Surdulica, *Serbia* 42 **E7** 42 41N 22 11 E
Sûre = Sauer →, *Germany* 21 **J9** 49 44N 6 31 E
Surendranagar, *India* 80 **H4** 22 45N 71 40 E
Surf, *U.S.A.* 145 **L6** 34 41N 120 36W
Surgères, *France* 24 **B3** 46 7N 0 47W
Surgut, *Russia* 56 **C8** 61 14N 73 20 E
Surhuisterveen, *Neths.* 20 **B8** 53 11N 6 10 E
Surianu, *Romania* 46 **D4** 45 33N 23 31 E
Suriapet, *India* 82 **F4** 17 10N 79 40 E
Surigao, *Phil.* 71 **G5** 9 47N 125 29 E
Surigao del Norte □, *Phil.* 71 **G5** 10 0N 125 40 E
Surigao del Sur □, *Phil.* 71 **G6** 8 45N 126 0 E
Surigao Strait, *Phil.* 71 **F5** 10 15N 125 23 E
Surin, *Thailand* 76 **E4** 14 50N 103 34 E
Surin Nua, Ko, *Thailand* 77 **H1** 9 30N 97 55 E
Surinam ■, *S. Amer.* 153 **C6** 4 0N 56 0W
Suriname □, *Surinam* 153 **B6** 5 30N 55 0W
Suriname ■ = Surinam ■, *S. Amer.* 153 **C6** 4 0N 56 0W
Suriname →, *Surinam* 153 **B6** 5 50N 55 15W
Surkhandarya →, *Uzbekistan* 55 **E3** 37 12N 67 20 E
Sūrmaq, *Iran* 85 **D7** 31 3N 52 48 E
Sürmene, *Turkey* 53 **F9** 41 0N 40 1 E
Surovikino, *Russia* 53 **B10** 48 32N 42 55 E
Surprise L., *Canada* 130 **B2** 59 40N 133 15W
Surrey □, *U.K.* 17 **F7** 51 16N 0 30W
Sursee, *Switz.* 28 **B6** 47 11N 8 6 E
Sursk, *Russia* 51 **E14** 53 3N 45 40 E
Surt, *Libya* 96 **B3** 31 11N 16 39 E
Surt, Al Hammadah al, *Libya* 96 **B3** 30 0N 17 50 E
Surt, Khalīj, *Libya* 96 **B3** 31 40N 18 30 E
Surtsey, *Iceland* 12 **E3** 63 20N 20 30W
Surubim, *Brazil* 154 **C4** 7 50 S 35 45W
Sürüç, *Turkey* 89 **E8** 36 58N 38 25 E
Surud Ad, *Somali Rep.* 108 **B3** 10 42N 47 9 E
Suruga-Wan, *Japan* 63 **C10** 34 45N 138 30 E
Surumu →, *Brazil* 153 **C5** 3 22N 60 19W
Susa, *Italy* 38 **C4** 45 8N 7 3 E
Suså →, *Denmark* 15 **J5** 55 20N 11 42 E
Sušac, *Croatia* 39 **F13** 42 46N 16 30 E
Susak, *Croatia* 39 **D11** 44 30N 14 18 E
Susaki, *Japan* 62 **D5** 33 22N 133 17 E
Susamyr, *Kirghizia* 55 **B6** 42 12N 73 58 E
Susamyrtau, Khrebet, *Kirghizia* 55 **B6** 42 8N 73 15 E
Sūsangerd, *Iran* 85 **D6** 31 35N 48 6 E
Susanino, *Russia* 57 **D15** 52 50N 140 14 E
Susanville, *U.S.A.* 142 **F3** 40 25N 120 39W
Susch, *Switz.* 29 **C10** 46 46N 10 5 E
Suşehri, *Turkey* 89 **C8** 40 10N 38 6 E
Sušice, *Czech.* 30 **B6** 49 17N 13 30 E
Susong, *China* 69 **B11** 30 10N 116 5 E
Susquehanna →, *U.S.A.* 137 **G8** 39 33N 76 5W
Susquehanna Depot, *U.S.A.* 137 **E9** 41 57N 75 36W
Susques, *Argentina* 158 **A2** 23 35 S 66 25W
Sussex, *Canada* 129 **C6** 45 45N 65 37W
Sussex, *U.S.A.* 137 **E10** 41 13N 74 37W
Sussex, E. □, *U.K.* 17 **G8** 51 0N 0 20 E
Sussex, W. □, *U.K.* 17 **G7** 51 0N 0 30W
Susteren, *Neths.* 21 **F7** 51 4N 5 51 E
Sustut →, *Canada* 130 **B3** 56 20N 127 30W
Susubona, *Solomon Is.* 121 **M10** 8 19 S 159 27 E
Susuman, *Russia* 57 **C15** 62 47N 148 10 E
Susunu, *Indonesia* 73 **B4** 3 20 S 133 25 E
Susurluk, *Turkey* 88 **D3** 39 54N 28 8 E
Susuz, *Turkey* 89 **C10** 40 46N 43 8 E
Susz, *Poland* 47 **B6** 53 44N 19 20 E
Sütçüler, *Turkey* 88 **E4** 37 29N 30 57 E
Şuţeşti, *Romania* 46 **D8** 45 13N 27 27 E
Sutherland, *Australia* 117 **C9** 34 2 S 151 4 E
Sutherland, *S. Africa* 104 **E3** 32 24 S 20 40 E
Sutherland, *U.S.A.* 138 **E4** 41 10N 101 8W
Sutherland Falls, *N.Z.* 119 **E2** 44 48 S 167 46 E
Sutherlin, *U.S.A.* 142 **E2** 43 23N 123 19W
Sutivan, *Croatia* 39 **E13** 43 23N 16 30 E
Sutlej →, *Pakistan* 79 **C3** 29 23N 71 3 E
Sutter, *U.S.A.* 144 **F5** 39 10N 121 45W
Sutter Creek, *U.S.A.* 144 **G6** 38 24N 120 48W
Sutton, *Canada* 137 **A12** 45 6N 72 37W
Sutton, *N.Z.* 119 **F5** 45 34 S 170 8 E
Sutton, *U.S.A.* 138 **E6** 40 36N 97 52W
Sutton →, *Canada* 128 **A3** 55 15N 83 45W
Sutton in Ashfield, *U.K.* 16 **D6** 53 7N 1 20W
Suttor →, *Australia* 114 **C4** 21 36 S 147 2 E
Suttsu, *Japan* 60 **C10** 42 48N 140 14 E
Su'u, *Solomon Is.* 121 **M11** 9 11 S 160 56 E
Suva, *Fiji* 121 **B2** 18 6 S 178 30 E
Suva Gora, *Macedonia* 42 **F6** 41 45N 21 3 E
Suva Planina, *Serbia* 42 **D7** 43 10N 22 5 E
Suva Reka, *Serbia* 42 **E5** 42 21N 20 50 E
Suvo Rudište, *Serbia* 42 **D5** 43 17N 20 49 E
Suvorov, *Russia* 51 **D10** 54 7N 36 30 E
Suvorov Is. = Suwarrow Is., *Cook Is.* 123 **J11** 15 0 S 163 0W
Suvorovo, *Bulgaria* 43 **D12** 43 20N 27 35 E
Suwa, *Japan* 63 **A10** 36 2N 138 8 E
Suwa-Ko, *Japan* 63 **A10** 36 3N 138 5 E
Suwałki, *Poland* 47 **A9** 54 8N 22 59 E
Suwałki □, *Poland* 47 **B9** 54 0N 22 30 E
Suwannaphum, *Thailand* 76 **E4** 15 33N 103 47 E
Suwannee →, *U.S.A.* 135 **L4** 29 17N 83 10W
Suwanose-Jima, *Japan* 61 **K4** 29 38N 129 43 E
Suwarrow Is., *Cook Is.* 123 **J11** 15 0 S 163 0W
Suwayq aş Şuqban, *Iraq* 84 **D5** 31 32N 46 7 E
Suweis, Khalîg el, *Egypt* 94 **J8** 28 40N 33 0 E
Suweis, Qanâl es, *Egypt* 94 **H8** 31 0N 32 20 E
Suwŏn, *S. Korea* 67 **F14** 37 17N 127 1 E
Suykbulak, *Kazakhstan* 54 **F8** 50 25N 62 33 E
Suyo, *Phil.* 70 **C3** 16 59N 120 31 E
Suzak, *Kazakhstan* 55 **A4** 44 9N 68 27 E
Suzaka, *Japan* 63 **A10** 36 39N 138 19 E
Suzdal, *Russia* 51 **C12** 56 29N 40 26 E
Suzhou, *China* 69 **B13** 31 19N 120 38 E
Suzu, *Japan* 61 **F8** 37 25N 137 17 E
Suzu-Misaki, *Japan* 61 **F8** 37 31N 137 21 E
Suzuka, *Japan* 63 **C8** 34 55N 136 36 E
Suzuka-Sam, *Japan* 63 **B8** 35 5N 136 30 E
Suzzara, *Italy* 38 **C7** 45 0N 10 45 E
Svalbard, *Arctic* 6 **B8** 78 0N 17 0 E
Svalbarð, *Iceland* 12 **C6** 66 12N 15 43W
Svalöv, *Sweden* 15 **J7** 55 57N 13 8 E
Svanvik, *Norway* 12 **B21** 69 25N 30 3 E
Svappavaara, *Sweden* 12 **C16** 67 40N 21 3 E
Svarstad, *Norway* 14 **E3** 59 27N 9 56 E
Svartisen, *Norway* 12 **C12** 66 40N 13 50 E
Svartvik, *Sweden* 14 **B11** 62 19N 17 24 E
Svatovo, *Ukraine* 52 **B8** 49 35N 38 11 E
Svay Chek, *Cambodia* 76 **F4** 13 48N 102 58 E
Svay Rieng, *Cambodia* 77 **G5** 11 5N 105 48 E
Svealand □, *Sweden* 13 **G13** 59 55N 15 0 E
Sveg, *Sweden* 13 **E13** 62 2N 14 21 E
Svendborg, *Denmark* 15 **J4** 55 4N 10 35 E
Svene, *Norway* 14 **E3** 59 45N 9 31 E
Svenljunga, *Sweden* 15 **G7** 57 29N 13 5 E
Svenstrup, *Denmark* 15 **H3** 56 58N 9 50 E
Sverdlovsk = Yekaterinburg, *Russia* 54 **C7** 56 50N 60 30 E
Sverdlovsk, *Ukraine* 53 **B8** 48 5N 39 47 E
Sverdrup Is., *Canada* 124 **B10** 79 0N 97 0W
Svetac, *Croatia* 39 **E12** 43 3N 15 43 E
Sveti Ivan Zelina, *Croatia* 39 **C13** 45 57N 16 16 E
Sveti Jurij, *Slovenia* 39 **B12** 46 14N 15 24 E
Sveti Lenart, *Slovenia* 39 **B12** 46 36N 15 48 E
Sveti Nikola, Prokhad, *Europe* 42 **D7** 43 27N 22 6 E
Sveti Nikole, *Macedonia* 42 **F6** 41 51N 21 56 E
Sveti Trojica, *Slovenia* 39 **B12** 46 37N 15 50 E
Svetlaya, *Russia* 60 **A9** 46 33N 138 18 E
Svetlogorsk, *Belorussia* 50 **E6** 52 38N 29 46 E
Svetlograd, *Russia* 53 **D10** 45 25N 42 58 E
Svetlovodsk, *Ukraine* 50 **G8** 49 2N 33 13 E
Svetlyy, *Russia* 54 **F7** 50 48N 60 51 E
Svetozarevo, *Serbia* 42 **C6** 44 5N 21 15 E
Svidník, *Slovak Rep.* 31 **B14** 49 20N 21 37 E
Svilaja Planina, *Croatia* 39 **E13** 43 49N 16 31 E
Svilajnac, *Serbia* 42 **C6** 44 15N 21 11 E
Svilengrad, *Bulgaria* 43 **F11** 41 49N 26 12 E
Svir →, *Russia* 48 **B5** 60 30N 32 48 E
Svishtov, *Bulgaria* 43 **D10** 43 36N 25 23 E
Svisloch, *Belorussia* 50 **E4** 53 3N 24 2 E
Svitava →, *Czech.* 31 **B9** 49 30N 16 37 E
Svitavy, *Czech.* 31 **B9** 49 47N 16 28 E
Svobodnyy, *Russia* 57 **D13** 51 20N 128 0 E
Svoge, *Bulgaria* 43 **E8** 42 59N 23 23 E
Svolvær, *Norway* 12 **B13** 68 15N 14 34 E
Svratka →, *Czech.* 31 **B9** 49 11N 16 38 E
Svrljig, *Serbia* 42 **D7** 43 25N 22 6 E
Swa, *Burma* 78 **F6** 19 15N 96 17 E
Swa Tende, *Zaïre* 103 **D3** 7 9 S 17 7 E
Swabian Alps = Schwäbische Alb, *Germany* 27 **G5** 48 30N 9 30 E
Swainsboro, *U.S.A.* 135 **J4** 32 36N 82 20W
Swakopmund, *Namibia* 104 **C1** 22 37 S 14 30 E
Swale →, *U.K.* 16 **C6** 54 5N 1 20W
Swalmen, *Neths.* 21 **F8** 51 13N 6 2 E
Swan Hill, *Australia* 116 **C5** 35 20 S 143 33 E
Swan Hills, *Canada* 130 **C5** 54 42N 115 24W
Swan Is., *W. Indies* 148 **C3** 17 22N 83 57W
Swan L., *Canada* 131 **C8** 52 30N 100 40W
Swan Reach, *Australia* 116 **C3** 34 35 S 139 37 E
Swan River, *Canada* 131 **C8** 52 10N 101 16W
Swanage, *U.K.* 17 **G6** 50 36N 1 59W
Swansea, *Australia* 117 **B9** 33 3 S 151 35 E
Swansea, *U.K.* 17 **F4** 51 37N 3 57W
Swar →, *Pakistan* 81 **B5** 34 40N 72 5 E
Swartberge, *S. Africa* 104 **E3** 33 20 S 22 0 E
Swartmodder, *S. Africa* 104 **D3** 28 1 S 20 32 E
Swartruggens, *S. Africa* 104 **D4** 25 39 S 26 42 E
Swarzędz, *Poland* 47 **C4** 52 25N 17 4 E
Swastika, *Canada* 128 **C3** 48 7N 80 6W
Swatow = Shantou, *China* 69 **F11** 23 18N 116 40 E
Swaziland ■, *Africa* 105 **D5** 26 30 S 31 30 E
Sweden ■, *Europe* 13 **H13** 57 0N 15 0 E
Swedru, *Ghana* 101 **D4** 5 32N 0 41W
Sweet Home, *U.S.A.* 142 **D2** 44 24N 122 44W
Sweet Springs, *U.S.A.* 140 **F3** 38 58N 93 25W
Sweetwater, *Nev., U.S.A.* 144 **G7** 38 27N 119 9W
Sweetwater, *Tex., U.S.A.* 139 **J4** 32 28N 100 25W
Sweetwater →, *U.S.A.* 142 **E10** 42 31N 107 2W
Swellendam, *S. Africa* 104 **E3** 34 1 S 20 26 E
Świder →, *Poland* 47 **C8** 52 6N 21 14 E
Świdnica, *Poland* 47 **E3** 50 50N 16 30 E
Świdnik, *Poland* 47 **D9** 51 13N 22 39 E
Świdwin, *Poland* 47 **B2** 53 47N 15 49 E
Świebodzice, *Poland* 47 **E3** 50 51N 16 20 E
Świebodzin, *Poland* 47 **C2** 52 15N 15 31 E
Świecie, *Poland* 47 **B5** 53 25N 18 30 E
Świętokrzyskie, Góry, *Poland* 47 **E7** 51 0N 20 30 E
Swift Current, *Canada* 131 **C7** 50 20N 107 45W
Swiftcurrent →, *Canada* 131 **C7** 50 38N 107 44W
Swilly, L., *Ireland* 19 **A4** 55 12N 7 35W
Swindle, I., *Canada* 130 **C3** 52 30N 128 35W
Swindon, *U.K.* 17 **F6** 51 33N 1 47W
Swinemünde = Świnoujście, *Poland* 47 **B1** 53 54N 14 16 E

Tamerza 271

Świnoujście, *Poland* **47 B1** 53 54N 14 16 E
Switzerland ■, *Europe* **28 D6** 46 30N 8 0 E
Swords, *Ireland* **19 C5** 53 27N 6 15W
Syasstroy, *Russia* **50 A8** 60 5N 32 15 E
Sychevka, *Russia* **50 D9** 55 59N 34 16 E
Syców, *Poland* **47 D4** 51 19N 17 40 E
Sydney, *Australia* **117 B9** 33 53 S 151 10 E
Sydney, *Canada* **129 C7** 46 7N 60 7W
Sydney Mines, *Canada* **129 C7** 46 18N 60 15W
Sydprøven, *Greenland* **6 C5** 60 30N 45 35W
Sydra G. of = Surt, Khalīj, *Libya* **96 B3** 31 40N 18 30 E
Syke, *Germany* **26 C4** 52 55N 8 50 E
Syktyvkar, *Russia* **48 B9** 61 45N 50 40 E
Sylacauga, *U.S.A.* **135 J2** 33 10N 86 15W
Sylarna, *Sweden* **12 E12** 63 2N 12 13 E
Sylhet, *Bangla.* **78 C3** 24 54N 91 52 E
Sylt, *Germany* **26 A4** 54 50N 8 20 E
Sylva →, *Russia* **54 B5** 58 0N 56 54 E
Sylvan Lake, *Canada* **130 C6** 52 20N 114 3W
Sylvania, *Ga., U.S.A.* **135 J5** 32 45N 81 38W
Sylvania, *Ohio, U.S.A.* **141 C13** 41 43N 83 42W
Sylvester, *U.S.A.* **135 K4** 31 32N 83 50W
Sym, *Russia* **56 C9** 60 20N 88 18 E
Symón, *Mexico* **146 C4** 24 42N 102 35W
Synnott Ra., *Australia* **112 C4** 16 30 S 125 20 E
Syracuse, *Ind., U.S.A.* **141 C11** 41 26N 85 45W
Syracuse, *Kans., U.S.A.* **139 F4** 37 59N 101 45W
Syracuse, *N.Y., U.S.A.* **137 C8** 43 3N 76 9W
Syrdarya, *Uzbekistan* **55 C4** 40 50N 68 40 E
Syrdarya →, *Kazakhstan* **56 E7** 46 3N 61 0 E
Syria ■, *Asia* **84 C3** 35 0N 38 0 E
Syriam, *Burma* **78 G6** 16 44N 96 19 E
Sysert, *Russia* **54 C7** 56 29N 60 49 E
Syul'dzhyukyor, *Russia* **57 C12** 63 14N 113 32 E
Syutkya, *Bulgaria* **43 F9** 41 50N 24 16 E
Syzran, *Russia* **51 E16** 53 12N 48 30 E
Szabolcs-Szatmár □, *Hungary* **31 C14** 48 2N 21 45 E
Szamocin, *Poland* **47 B4** 53 2N 17 7 E
Szamos →, *Hungary* **31 C15** 48 7N 22 20 E
Szaraz →, *Hungary* **31 E13** 46 28N 20 44 E
Szarvas, *Hungary* **31 E13** 46 50N 20 38 E
Szazhalombatta, *Hungary* **31 D11** 47 20N 18 58 E
Szczawnica, *Poland* **31 B13** 49 26N 20 30 E
Szczebrzeszyn, *Poland* **47 E9** 50 42N 22 59 E
Szczecin, *Poland* **47 B1** 53 27N 14 27 E
Szczecin □, *Poland* **47 B1** 53 25N 14 32 E
Szczecinek, *Poland* **47 B3** 53 43N 16 41 E
Szczekocimy, *Poland* **47 E6** 50 38N 19 48 E
Szczucin, *Poland* **47 E8** 50 18N 21 4 E
Szczuczyn, *Poland* **47 B9** 53 36N 22 19 E
Szczytno, *Poland* **47 B8** 53 33N 21 0 E
Szechwan = Sichuan □, *China* **68 B5** 31 0N 104 0 E
Szécsény, *Hungary* **31 C12** 48 7N 19 30 E
Szeged, *Hungary* **31 E13** 46 16N 20 10 E
Szeghalom, *Hungary* **31 D14** 47 1N 21 10 E
Székesfehérvár, *Hungary* **31 D11** 47 15N 18 25 E
Szekszárd, *Hungary* **31 E11** 46 22N 18 42 E
Szendrö, *Hungary* **31 C13** 48 24N 20 41 E
Szentendre, *Hungary* **31 D12** 47 39N 19 4 E
Szentes, *Hungary* **31 E13** 46 39N 20 21 E
Szentgotthárd, *Hungary* **31 E9** 46 58N 16 19 E
Szentlörinc, *Hungary* **31 E11** 46 3N 18 1 E
Szerencs, *Hungary* **31 C14** 48 10N 21 12 E
Szigetvár, *Hungary* **31 E10** 46 3N 17 46 E
Szikszó, *Hungary* **31 C13** 48 12N 20 56 E
Szkwa →, *Poland* **47 B8** 53 11N 21 43 E
Szlichtyngowa, *Poland* **47 D3** 51 42N 16 15 E
Szob, *Hungary* **31 D11** 47 48N 18 53 E
Szolnok, *Hungary* **31 D13** 47 10N 20 15 E
Szolnok □, *Hungary* **31 D13** 47 15N 20 30 E
Szombathely, *Hungary* **31 D9** 47 14N 16 38 E
Szprotawa, *Poland* **47 D2** 51 33N 15 35 E
Sztum, *Poland* **47 B6** 53 55N 19 1 E
Sztutowo, *Poland* **47 A6** 54 20N 19 15 E
Szubin, *Poland* **47 B4** 53 1N 17 45 E
Szydłowiec, *Poland* **47 D7** 51 15N 20 51 E
Szypliszki, *Poland* **47 A10** 54 17N 23 2 E

T

't Harde, *Neths.* **20 D7** 52 24N 5 54 E
't Zandt, *Neths.* **20 B9** 53 22N 6 46 E
Ta Khli Khok, *Thailand* **76 E3** 15 18N 100 20 E
Ta Lai, *Vietnam* **77 G6** 11 24N 107 23 E
Tabacal, *Argentina* **158 A3** 23 15 S 64 15W
Tabaco, *Phil.* **70 E4** 13 22N 123 44 E
Tabagné, *Ivory C.* **100 D4** 7 59N 3 4W
Ţabah, *Si. Arabia* **84 E4** 26 55N 42 38 E
Tabajara, *Brazil* **157 B5** 8 56 S 62 8W
Tabalos, *Peru* **156 B2** 6 26 S 76 37W
Tabango, *Phil.* **71 F5** 11 19N 124 22 E
Tabar Is., *Papua N. G.* **120 B7** 2 50 S 152 0 E
Tabarca, I. de, *Spain* **35 G4** 38 17N 0 30W
Tabarka, *Tunisia* **96 A1** 36 56N 8 46 E
Ţabas, *Khorāsān, Iran* **85 C9** 32 48N 60 12 E
Ţabas, *Khorāsān, Iran* **85 C8** 33 35N 56 55 E
Tabasará, Serranía de, *Panama* **148 E3** 8 35N 81 40W
Tabasco □, *Mexico* **147 D6** 17 45N 93 30W
Tabatinga, Serra da, *Brazil* **154 D3** 10 30 S 44 0W
Tabayin, *Burma* **78 D5** 22 42N 95 20 E
Tabāzīn, *Iran* **85 D8** 31 12N 57 54 E
Tabelbala, Kahal de, *Algeria* **99 C4** 28 47N 2 0W
Taber, *Canada* **130 D6** 49 47N 112 8W
Tabernas, *Spain* **35 H2** 37 4N 2 26W
Tabernes de Valldigna, *Spain* **35 F4** 39 5N 0 13W
Tabi, *Angola* **103 D2** 8 10 S 13 18 E
Tabira, *Brazil* **154 C4** 7 35 S 37 33W
Tablas, *Phil.* **70 E4** 12 25N 122 2 E
Tablas Strait, *Phil.* **70 E3** 12 40N 121 48 E
Table B. = Tafelbaai, *S. Africa* **104 E2** 33 35 S 18 25 E
Table B., *Canada* **129 B8** 53 40N 56 25W
Table Grove, *U.S.A.* **140 D6** 40 20N 90 27W
Table Mt., *S. Africa* **104 E2** 34 0 S 18 22 E
Tableland, *Australia* **112 C4** 17 16 S 126 51 E
Tabletop, Mt., *Australia* **114 C4** 23 24 S 147 11 E
Tabogon, *Phil.* **71 F5** 10 57N 124 2 E
Tábor, *Czech.* **30 B7** 49 25N 14 39 E
Tabora, *Tanzania* **106 D3** 5 2 S 32 50 E
Tabora □, *Tanzania* **106 D3** 5 0 S 33 0 E
Tabory, *Russia* **54 B9** 58 31N 64 33 E
Tabou, *Ivory C.* **100 E3** 4 30N 7 20W
Tabrīz, *Iran* **84 B5** 38 7N 46 20 E
Tabuaeran, *Pac. Oc.* **123 G12** 3 51N 159 22W
Tabuelan, *Phil.* **71 F4** 10 49N 123 52 E
Tabuenca, *Spain* **34 D3** 41 42N 1 33W
Tabuk, *Phil.* **70 C3** 17 24N 121 25 E
Tabūk, *Si. Arabia* **84 D3** 28 23N 36 36 E
Tabwemasana, Mt., *Vanuatu* **121 E4** 15 20 S 166 44 E
Tacámbaro de Codallos, *Mexico* **146 D4** 19 14N 101 28W
Tacheng, *China* **64 B3** 46 40N 82 58 E
Tachibana-Wan, *Japan* **62 E2** 32 45N 130 7 E
Tachikawa, *Japan* **63 B11** 35 42N 139 25 E
Tach'ing Shan = Daqing Shan, *China* **66 D6** 40 40N 111 0 E
Táchira □, *Venezuela* **152 B3** 8 7N 72 15W
Tachov, *Czech.* **30 B5** 49 47N 12 39 E
Tácina →, *Italy* **41 D9** 38 57N 16 55 E
Tacloban, *Phil.* **71 F5** 11 15N 124 58 E
Tacna, *Peru* **156 D3** 18 0 S 70 20W
Tacna □, *Peru* **156 D3** 17 40 S 70 20W
Tacoma, *U.S.A.* **144 C4** 47 14N 122 26W
Tacuarembó, *Uruguay* **159 C4** 31 45 S 56 0W
Tacutu →, *Brazil* **153 C5** 3 1N 60 29W
Tademaït, Plateau du, *Algeria* **99 C5** 28 30N 2 30 E
Tadent, O. →, *Algeria* **99 D6** 22 25N 6 40 E
Tadjerdjeri, O. →, *Algeria* **99 C6** 26 0N 8 0 E
Tadjerouna, *Algeria* **99 B5** 33 31N 2 3 E
Tadjettaret, O. →, *Algeria* **99 D6** 21 20N 7 22 E
Tadjmout, *Oasis, Algeria* **99 B5** 33 52N 2 30 E
Tadjmout, *Saoura, Algeria* **99 C5** 25 37N 3 48 E
Tadjoura, *Djibouti* **90 E3** 11 50N 42 55 E
Tadjoura, Golfe de, *Djibouti* **95 E5** 11 50N 43 0 E
Tadmor, *N.Z.* **119 B7** 41 27 S 172 45 E
Tadotsu, *Japan* **62 C5** 34 16N 133 45 E
Tadoule, L., *Canada* **131 B9** 58 36N 98 20W
Tadoussac, *Canada* **129 C6** 48 11N 69 42W
Tadzhikistan = Tajikistan ■, *Asia* **55 D5** 38 30N 70 0 E
Taechŏn-ni, *S. Korea* **67 F14** 36 21N 126 36 E
Taegu, *S. Korea* **67 G15** 35 50N 128 37 E
Taegwan, *N. Korea* **67 D13** 40 13N 125 12 E
Taejŏn, *S. Korea* **67 F14** 36 20N 127 28 E
Tafalla, *Spain* **34 C3** 42 30N 1 41W
Tafar, *Sudan* **95 F2** 6 52N 28 15 E
Tafassasset, O. →, *Algeria* **99 D6** 22 0N 9 57 E
Tafelbaai, *S. Africa* **104 E2** 33 35 S 18 25 E
Tafelney, C., *Morocco* **98 B3** 31 3N 9 51W
Tafermaar, *Indonesia* **73 C4** 6 47 S 134 10 E
Taffermit, *Morocco* **98 C3** 29 37N 9 15W
Tafí Viejo, *Argentina* **158 B2** 26 43 S 65 17W
Tafīhān, *Iran* **85 D7** 29 25N 52 39 E
Tafiré, *Ivory C.* **100 D3** 9 4N 5 4W
Tafnidilt, *Morocco* **98 C2** 28 47N 10 58W
Tafraoute, *Morocco* **98 C3** 29 50N 8 58W
Taft, *Iran* **85 D7** 31 45N 54 14 E
Taft, *Phil.* **71 F5** 11 57N 125 30 E
Taft, *Calif., U.S.A.* **145 K7** 35 8N 119 28W
Taft, *Tex., U.S.A.* **139 M6** 27 59N 97 24W
Taga, *W. Samoa* **121 W23** 13 46 S 172 28W
Taga Dzong, *Bhutan* **78 B2** 27 5N 89 55 E
Tagana-an, *Phil.* **71 G5** 9 42N 125 35 E
Taganrog, *Russia* **53 C8** 47 12N 38 50 E
Taganrogskiy Zaliv, *Russia* **52 C8** 47 0N 38 30 E
Tagânt, *Mauritania* **100 B2** 18 20N 11 0W
Tagap Ga, *Burma* **78 B6** 26 56N 96 13 E
Tagapula I., *Phil.* **70 E5** 12 4N 124 12 E
Tagatay, *Phil.* **70 D3** 14 6N 120 56 E
Tagauayan I., *Phil.* **71 F3** 10 58N 121 13 E
Tagbilaran, *Phil.* **71 G4** 9 39N 123 51 E
Tage, *Papua N. G.* **120 D2** 6 19 S 143 20 E
Tàggia, *Italy* **38 E4** 43 52N 7 50 E
Taghrīfat, *Libya* **96 C3** 29 5N 17 26 E
Taghzout, *Morocco* **98 B4** 33 30N 4 49W
Tagish, *Canada* **130 A2** 60 19N 134 16W
Tagish L., *Canada* **130 A2** 60 10N 134 20W
Tagkawayan, *Phil.* **70 E4** 13 58N 122 32 E
Tagliacozzo, *Italy* **39 F10** 42 4N 13 13 E
Tagliamento →, *Italy* **39 C10** 45 38N 13 5 E
Táglio di Po, *Italy* **39 D9** 45 0N 12 12 E
Tagna, *Colombia* **152 D3** 2 24 S 70 37W
Tago, *Phil.* **71 G6** 9 2N 126 13 E
Tago, Mt., *Phil.* **71 G5** 8 23N 125 5 E
Tagomago, I. de, *Spain* **33 B8** 39 2N 1 39 E
Taguatinga, *Brazil* **155 D3** 12 16 S 42 26W
Tagudin, *Phil.* **70 C3** 16 56N 120 27 E
Tagula, *Papua N. G.* **120 F7** 11 22 S 153 15 E
Tagula I., *Papua N. G.* **120 F7** 11 30 S 153 30 E
Tagum, *Phil.* **71 H5** 7 33N 125 53 E
Tagus = Tejo →, *Europe* **37 G1** 38 40N 9 24W
Tahakopa, *N.Z.* **119 G4** 46 30 S 169 23 E
Tahala, *Morocco* **98 B4** 34 0N 4 28W
Tahan, Gunong, *Malaysia* **77 K4** 4 34N 102 17 E
Tahānah-ye sūr Gol, *Afghan.* **79 C2** 31 43N 67 53 E
Tahara, *Japan* **63 C9** 34 40N 137 16 E
Tahat, *Algeria* **99 D6** 23 18N 5 33 E
Tāherī, *Iran* **85 E7** 27 43N 52 20 E
Tahiti, *Pac. Oc.* **123 J13** 17 37 S 149 27W
Tahoe, L., *U.S.A.* **144 G6** 39 6N 120 2W
Tahoe City, *U.S.A.* **144 F6** 39 10N 120 9W
Taholah, *U.S.A.* **144 C2** 47 21N 124 17W
Tahora, *N.Z.* **118 F3** 39 2 S 174 49 E
Tahoua, *Niger* **101 C6** 14 57N 5 16 E
Tahta, *Egypt* **94 B3** 26 44N 31 32 E
Tahtali Dağları, *Turkey* **88 D6** 38 20N 36 0 E
Tahuamanu →, *Bolivia* **156 C4** 11 6 S 67 36W
Tahulandang, *Indonesia* **72 A3** 2 27N 125 23 E
Tahuna, *Indonesia* **72 A3** 3 38N 125 30 E
Taï, *Ivory C.* **100 D3** 5 55N 7 30W
Tai Shan, *China* **67 F9** 36 25N 117 20 E
Tai Xian, *China* **69 A13** 32 30N 120 7 E
Tai'an, *China* **67 F9** 36 12N 117 8 E
Taibei, *Taiwan* **69 E13** 25 4N 121 29 E
Taibique, *Canary Is.* **33 G2** 27 42N 17 58W
Taibus Qi, *China* **66 D8** 41 54N 115 22 E
T'aichung = Taizhong, *Taiwan* **69 E13** 24 12N 120 35 E
Taidong, *Taiwan* **69 F13** 22 43N 121 9 E
Taieri →, *N.Z.* **119 G5** 46 3 S 170 12 E
Taiga Madema, *Libya* **96 D3** 23 46N 15 25 E
Taigu, *China* **66 F7** 37 28N 112 30 E
Taihang Shan, *China* **66 G7** 36 0N 113 30 E
Taihape, *N.Z.* **118 F4** 39 41 S 175 48 E
Taihe, *Anhui, China* **66 H8** 33 20N 115 42 E
Taihe, *Jiangxi, China* **69 D10** 26 47N 114 52 E
Taihu, *China* **69 B11** 30 22N 116 20 E
Taijiang, *China* **68 D7** 26 39N 108 21 E
Taikang, *China* **66 G8** 34 5N 114 50 E
Taikkyi, *Burma* **78 G6** 17 20N 96 0 E
Tailem Bend, *Australia* **116 C3** 35 12 S 139 29 E
Tailfingen, *Germany* **27 G5** 48 15N 9 1 E
Taimyr Peninsula = Taymyr, Poluostrov, *Russia* **57 B11** 75 0N 100 0 E
Tain, *U.K.* **18 D4** 57 49N 4 4W
Tainan, *Taiwan* **69 F13** 23 17N 120 18 E
Taínaron, Ákra, *Greece* **45 H4** 36 22N 22 27 E
Tainggyo, *Burma* **78 G5** 17 49N 94 29 E
Taining, *China* **69 D11** 26 54N 117 9 E
Taintignies, *Belgium* **21 G2** 50 33N 3 22 E
Taiobeiras, *Brazil* **155 E3** 15 49 S 42 14W
T'aipei = Taibei, *Taiwan* **69 E13** 25 4N 121 29 E
T'aipei, *Taiwan* **65 D7** 25 2N 121 30 E
Taiping, *China* **69 B12** 30 15N 118 6 E
Taiping, *Malaysia* **77 K3** 4 51N 100 44 E
Taipingzhen, *China* **66 H6** 33 35N 111 42 E
Taipu, *Brazil* **154 C4** 5 37 S 35 36W
Taisha, *Japan* **62 B4** 35 24N 132 40 E
Taishan, *China* **69 F9** 22 14N 112 41 E
Taishun, *China* **69 D12** 27 30N 119 42 E
Taita □, *Kenya* **106 C4** 4 0 S 38 30 E
Taita Hills, *Kenya* **106 C4** 3 25 S 38 15 E
Taitao, C., *Chile* **160 C1** 45 53 S 75 5W
Taitao, Pen. de, *Chile* **160 C2** 46 30 S 75 0W
Taivalkoski, *Finland* **12 D20** 65 33N 28 12 E
Taiwan ■, *Asia* **69 F13** 23 30N 121 0 E
Taiwan Shan, *Taiwan* **69 F13** 23 40N 121 20 E
Taixing, *China* **69 A13** 32 11N 120 0 E
Taïyetos Óros, *Greece* **45 H4** 37 0N 22 23 E
Taiyiba, *Israel* **91 C4** 32 36N 35 27 E
Taiyuan, *China* **66 F7** 37 52N 112 33 E
Taizhong, *Taiwan* **69 E13** 24 12N 120 35 E
Taizhou, *China* **69 A12** 32 28N 119 55 E
Taizhou Liedao, *China* **69 C13** 28 30N 121 55 E
Ta'izz, *Yemen* **86 D4** 13 35N 44 2 E
Tājābād, *Iran* **85 D7** 30 2N 54 24 E
Tajapuru, Furo do, *Brazil* **154 B1** 1 50 S 50 25W
Tajarḩī, *Libya* **96 D2** 24 21N 14 28 E
Tajikistan ■, *Asia* **55 D5** 38 30N 70 0 E
Tajima, *Japan* **61 F9** 37 12N 139 46 E
Tajimi, *Japan* **63 B9** 35 19N 137 8 E
Tajo = Tejo →, *Europe* **37 G1** 38 40N 9 24W
Tajrīsh, *Iran* **85 C6** 35 48N 51 25 E
Tājūrā, *Libya* **96 B2** 32 51N 13 21 E
Tak, *Thailand* **76 D2** 16 52N 99 8 E
Takāb, *Iran* **84 B5** 36 24N 47 7 E
Takachiho, *Japan* **62 E3** 32 42N 131 18 E
Takada, *Japan* **61 F9** 37 7N 138 15 E
Takahagi, *Japan* **61 F10** 36 43N 140 45 E
Takahashi, *Japan* **62 C5** 34 51N 133 39 E
Takaka, *N.Z.* **119 A7** 40 51 S 172 50 E
Takamatsu, *Japan* **62 C6** 34 20N 134 5 E
Takanabe, *Japan* **62 E3** 32 8N 131 30 E
Takaoka, *Japan* **63 A8** 36 47N 137 0 E
Takapau, *N.Z.* **118 G5** 40 2 S 176 21 E
Takapuna, *N.Z.* **118 C3** 36 47 S 174 47 E
Takasago, *Japan* **62 C6** 34 45N 134 48 E
Takasaki, *Japan* **63 A10** 36 20N 139 0 E
Takase, *Japan* **62 C5** 34 7N 133 48 E
Takatsuki, *Japan* **63 C7** 34 51N 135 37 E
Takaungu, *Kenya* **106 C4** 3 38 S 39 52 E
Takawa, *Japan* **62 D2** 33 38N 130 51 E
Takayama, *Japan* **63 A9** 36 18N 137 11 E
Takayama-Bonchi, *Japan* **63 B9** 36 0N 137 18 E
Take-Shima, *Japan* **61 J5** 30 49N 130 26 E
Takefu, *Japan* **63 B8** 35 50N 136 10 E
Takehara, *Japan* **62 C4** 34 21N 132 55 E
Takengon, *Indonesia* **74 B1** 4 45N 96 50 E
Takeo, *Cambodia* **77 G5** 10 59N 104 47 E
Takeo, *Japan* **62 D2** 33 12N 130 1 E
Tåkern, *Sweden* **15 F8** 58 22N 14 45 E
Tākestān, *Iran* **85 C6** 36 0N 49 40 E
Taketa, *Japan* **62 E3** 32 58N 131 24 E
Takh, *India* **81 C7** 33 6N 77 32 E
Takhār □, *Afghan.* **79 A3** 36 40N 70 0 E
Takhman, *Cambodia* **77 G5** 11 29N 104 57 E
Taki, *Papua N. G.* **120 D8** 6 29 S 155 52 E
Takikawa, *Japan* **60 C10** 43 33N 141 54 E
Takla L., *Canada* **130 B3** 55 15N 125 45W
Takla Landing, *Canada* **130 B3** 55 30N 125 50W
Takla Makan = Taklamakan Shamo, *China* **58 F12** 38 0N 83 0 E
Taklamakan Shamo, *China* **58 F12** 38 0N 83 0 E
Taku, *Japan* **62 D2** 33 18N 130 3 E
Taku →, *Canada* **130 B2** 58 30N 133 50W
Takum, *Nigeria* **101 D6** 7 18N 9 36 E
Takuma, *Japan* **62 C5** 34 13N 133 40 E
Takundi, *Zaïre* **103 C3** 4 45 S 16 34 E
Takuran, *Phil.* **71 H4** 7 51N 123 34 E
Takutu →, *Guyana* **153 C5** 3 1N 60 29W
Tal Halāl, *Iran* **85 D7** 28 54N 55 1 E
Tala, *Uruguay* **159 C4** 34 21 S 55 46W
Talacogan, *Phil.* **71 G5** 8 32N 125 39 E
Talagante, *Chile* **158 C1** 33 40 S 70 50W
Talaïnt, *Morocco* **98 C3** 29 41N 9 40W
Talak, *Niger* **101 B6** 18 0N 5 0 E
Talakag, *Phil.* **71 G5** 8 16N 124 37 E
Talamanca, Cordillera de, *Cent. Amer.* **148 E3** 9 20N 83 20W
Talara, *Peru* **156 A1** 4 38 S 81 18W
Talas, *Kirghizia* **55 B6** 42 30N 72 13 E
Talas, *Turkey* **88 D6** 38 41N 35 33 E
Talas →, *Kazakhstan* **55 B5** 44 0N 70 20 E
Talasea, *Papua N. G.* **120 C6** 5 20 S 150 2 E
Talasskiy Alatau, Khrebet, *Kirghizia* **55 B6** 42 15N 72 0 E
Talâta, *Egypt* **91 E1** 30 36N 32 20 E
Talata Mafara, *Nigeria* **101 C6** 12 38N 6 4 E
Talaud, Kepulauan, *Indonesia* **72 A3** 4 30N 127 10 E
Talaud Is. = Talaud, Kepulauan, *Indonesia* **72 A3** 4 30N 127 10 E
Talavera de la Reina, *Spain* **36 F6** 39 55N 4 46W
Talawana, *Australia* **112 D3** 22 51 S 121 9 E
Talawgyi, *Burma* **78 C6** 25 4N 97 19 E
Talayan, *Phil.* **71 H5** 6 52N 124 24 E
Talbert, Sillon de, *France* **22 D3** 48 53N 3 5W
Talbot, C., *Australia* **112 B4** 13 48 S 126 43 E
Talbragar →, *Australia* **117 B8** 32 12 S 148 37 E
Talca, *Chile* **158 D1** 35 28 S 71 40W
Talca □, *Chile* **158 D1** 35 20 S 71 46W
Talcahuano, *Chile* **158 D1** 36 40 S 73 10W
Talcher, *India* **82 D7** 21 0N 85 18 E
Talcho, *Niger* **101 C5** 14 44N 3 28 E
Taldy Kurgan, *Kazakhstan* **56 E8** 45 10N 78 45 E
Taldyqorghan = Taldy Kurgan, *Kazakhstan* **56 E8** 45 10N 78 45 E
Talesh, *Iran* **85 B6** 37 58N 48 58 E
Ţalesh, Kūhhā-ye, *Iran* **85 B6** 39 0N 48 30 E
Talgar, *Kazakhstan* **55 B8** 43 19N 77 15 E
Talgar, Pik, *Kazakhstan* **55 B8** 43 5N 77 20 E
Talguharai, *Sudan* **94 D4** 18 19N 35 56 E
Tali Post, *Sudan* **95 F3** 5 55N 30 44 E
Taliabu, *Indonesia* **72 B2** 1 45 S 125 0 E
Talibon, *Phil.* **71 F5** 10 9N 124 20 E
Talibong, Ko, *Thailand* **77 J2** 7 15N 99 23 E
Talihina, *U.S.A.* **139 H7** 34 45N 95 3W
Talikota, *India* **83 F3** 16 29N 76 17 E
Talimardzhan, *Turkmenistan* **55 D2** 38 23N 65 37 E
Talisay, *Phil.* **71 F4** 10 44N 122 58 E
Talisayan, *Phil.* **71 G5** 9 0N 124 55 E
Talitsa, *Russia* **54 C8** 57 0N 63 43 E
Taliwang, *Indonesia* **72 C1** 8 50 S 116 55 E
Tall 'Asūr, *Jordan* **91 D4** 31 59N 35 17 E
Tall Kalakh, *Syria* **91 A5** 34 41N 36 15 E
Talla, *Egypt* **94 J7** 28 5N 30 43 E
Talladega, *U.S.A.* **135 J2** 33 26N 86 6W
Tallahassee, *U.S.A.* **135 K3** 30 27N 84 17W
Tallangatta, *Australia* **117 D7** 36 15 S 147 19 E
Tallarook, *Australia* **117 D6** 37 5 S 145 6 E
Tallawang, *Australia* **117 B8** 32 12 S 149 28 E
Tallering Pk., *Australia* **113 E2** 28 6 S 115 37 E
Tallinn, *Estonia* **50 B4** 59 22N 24 48 E
Tallulah, *U.S.A.* **139 J9** 32 25N 91 11W
Tălmaciu, *Romania* **46 D5** 45 38N 24 19 E
Talmest, *Morocco* **98 B3** 31 48N 9 21W
Talmont, *France* **24 B2** 46 27N 1 37W
Talnoye, *Ukraine* **52 B4** 48 50N 30 44 E
Taloda, *India* **82 D2** 21 34N 74 11 E
Talodi, *Sudan* **95 E3** 10 35N 30 22 E
Talomo, *Phil.* **71 H5** 7 3N 125 32 E
Talovaya, *Russia* **51 F12** 51 6N 40 45 E
Talpa de Allende, *Mexico* **146 C4** 20 23N 104 51W
Tālqān, *Afghan.* **79 A3** 36 44N 69 33 E
Talsi, *Latvia* **50 C3** 57 10N 22 30 E
Talsinnt, *Morocco* **99 B4** 32 33N 3 27W
Taltal, *Chile* **158 B1** 25 23 S 70 33W
Taltson →, *Canada* **130 A6** 61 24N 112 46W
Talwood, *Australia* **115 D4** 28 29 S 149 29 E
Talyawalka Cr. →, *Australia* **116 B5** 32 28 S 142 22 E
Tam Chau, *Vietnam* **77 G5** 10 48N 105 12 E
Tam Ky, *Vietnam* **76 E7** 15 34N 108 29 E
Tam Quan, *Vietnam* **76 E7** 14 35N 109 3 E
Tama, *U.S.A.* **140 C4** 41 58N 92 35W
Tamala, *Australia* **113 E1** 26 42 S 113 47 E
Tamalameque, *Colombia* **152 B3** 8 52N 73 49W
Tamale, *Ghana* **101 D4** 9 22N 0 50W
Taman, *Russia* **52 D7** 45 14N 36 41 E
Tamana, *Japan* **62 E2** 32 58N 130 32 E
Tamanar, *Morocco* **98 B3** 31 1N 9 46W
Tamano, *Japan* **62 C5** 34 29N 133 59 E
Tamanrasset, *Algeria* **99 D6** 22 50N 5 30 E
Tamanrasset, O. →, *Algeria* **99 D5** 22 0N 2 0 E
Tamanthi, *Burma* **78 C5** 25 19N 95 17 E
Tamaqua, *U.S.A.* **137 F9** 40 48N 75 58W
Tamar →, *U.K.* **17 G3** 50 33N 4 15W
Támara, *Colombia* **152 B3** 5 50N 72 10W
Tamarang, *Australia* **117 A9** 31 27 S 150 5 E
Tamarinda, *Spain* **33 B10** 39 55N 3 49 E
Tamarite de Litera, *Spain* **34 D5** 41 52N 0 25 E
Tamaroa, *U.S.A.* **140 F7** 38 8N 89 14W
Tamashima, *Japan* **62 C5** 34 32N 133 40 E
Tamási, *Hungary* **31 E11** 46 40N 18 18 E
Tamaské, *Niger* **101 C6** 14 49N 5 43 E
Tamaulipas □, *Mexico* **147 C5** 24 0N 99 0W
Tamaulipas, Sierra de, *Mexico* **147 C5** 23 30N 98 20W
Tamazula, *Mexico* **146 C3** 24 55N 106 58W
Tamazunchale, *Mexico* **147 C5** 21 16N 98 47W
Tamba-Dabatou, *Guinea* **100 C2** 11 50N 10 40W
Tambacounda, *Senegal* **100 C2** 13 45N 13 40W
Tambelan, Kepulauan, *Indonesia* **74 B3** 1 0N 107 30 E
Tambellup, *Australia* **113 F2** 34 4 S 117 37 E
Tambo, *Australia* **114 C4** 24 54 S 146 14 E
Tambo, *Peru* **156 C3** 12 57 S 74 1W
Tambo →, *Peru* **156 C3** 10 42 S 73 47W
Tambo de Mora, *Peru* **156 C2** 13 30 S 76 8W
Tambobamba, *Peru* **156 C3** 13 54 S 72 8W
Tambohorano, *Madag.* **105 B7** 17 30 S 43 58 E
Tambopata →, *Peru* **156 C4** 13 21 S 69 36W
Tambora, *Indonesia* **72 C1** 8 12 S 118 5 E
Tamboritha, Mt., *Australia* **117 D7** 37 31 S 146 40 E
Tambov, *Russia* **51 E12** 52 45N 41 28 E
Tambre →, *Spain* **36 C2** 42 49N 8 53W
Tambuku, *Indonesia* **75 D4** 7 8 S 113 40 E
Tambun Sigumbal, *Phil.* **71 H3** 6 5N 121 47 E
Tamburâ, *Sudan* **95 F2** 5 40N 27 25 E
Tambuyukan, Gunong, *Malaysia* **75 A5** 6 13N 116 39 E
Tâmchekket, *Mauritania* **100 B2** 17 25N 10 40W
Tamdybulak, *Uzbekistan* **55 C2** 41 46N 64 36 E
Tame, *Colombia* **152 B3** 6 28N 71 44W
Tamega →, *Portugal* **36 D2** 41 5N 8 21W
Tamelelt, *Morocco* **98 B3** 31 50N 7 32W
Tamenglong, *India* **78 C4** 25 0N 93 35 E
Tamerlanovka, *Kazakhstan* **55 B4** 42 36N 69 17 E
Tamerza, *Tunisia* **96 B1** 34 23N 7 58 E

The Hamilton 273

Tchibanga, *Gabon* **102 C2** 2 45 S 11 0 E
Tchien, *Liberia* **100 D3** 5 59N 8 15W
Tchikala-Tcholohanga, *Angola* **103 E3** 12 38 S 16 3 E
Tchin Tabaraden, *Niger* **101 B6** 15 58N 5 56 E
Tchingou, Massif de, *N. Cal.* **121 T19** 20 54 S 165 0 E
Tcholliré, *Cameroon* **102 A2** 8 24N 14 10 E
Tch'ong-k'ing = Chongqing, *China* **68 C6** 29 35N 106 25 E
Tczew, *Poland* **47 A5** 54 8N 18 50 E
Te Anau, *N.Z.* **119 F2** 45 25 S 167 43 E
Te Anau, L., *N.Z.* **119 F2** 45 15 S 167 45 E
Te Araroa, *N.Z.* **118 D7** 37 39 S 178 25 E
Te Aroha, *N.Z.* **118 D4** 37 32 S 175 44 E
Te Awamutu, *N.Z.* **118 E4** 38 1 S 175 20 E
Te Kaha, *N.Z.* **118 D6** 37 44 S 177 52 E
Te Karaka, *N.Z.* **118 E6** 38 26 S 177 53 E
Te Kauwhata, *N.Z.* **118 D4** 37 25 S 175 9 E
Te Kopuru, *N.Z.* **118 C2** 36 2 S 173 56 E
Te Kuiti, *N.Z.* **118 E4** 38 20 S 175 11 E
Te Puke, *N.Z.* **118 D5** 37 46 S 176 22 E
Te Teko, *N.Z.* **118 E5** 38 2 S 176 48 E
Te Waewae B., *N.Z.* **119 G2** 46 13 S 167 33 E
Tea →, *Brazil* **152 D4** 0 30 S 65 9W
Tea Tree, *Australia* **114 C1** 22 5 S 133 22 E
Teaca, *Romania* **46 C5** 46 55N 24 30 E
Teague, *U.S.A.* **139 K6** 31 38N 96 17W
Teano, *Italy* **41 A7** 41 15N 14 1 E
Teapa, *Mexico* **147 D6** 18 35N 92 56W
Teba, *Spain* **37 J6** 36 59N 4 55W
Teberau, *Malaysia* **74 B2** 1 32N 103 45 E
Teberda, *Russia* **53 E9** 43 30N 41 46 E
Tébessa, *Algeria* **99 A6** 35 22N 8 8 E
Tebicuary →, *Paraguay* **158 B4** 26 36 S 58 16W
Tebingtinggi, *Indonesia* **74 B1** 3 20N 99 9 E
Tebintingii, *Indonesia* **74 B2** 1 0N 102 45 E
Tébourba, *Tunisia* **96 A1** 36 49N 9 51 E
Téboursouk, *Tunisia* **96 A1** 36 29N 9 10 E
Tebulos, *Russia* **53 E11** 42 36N 45 17 E
Tecate, *Mexico* **145 N10** 32 34N 116 38W
Tecer Dağı, *Turkey* **88 D7** 39 39N 37 15 E
Tech →, *France* **24 F7** 42 36N 3 3 E
Techa →, *Russia* **54 C8** 56 13N 62 58 E
Techiman, *Ghana* **100 D4** 7 35N 1 58W
Techirghiol, *Romania* **46 E9** 44 4N 28 32 E
Tecka, *Argentina* **160 B2** 43 29 S 70 48W
Tecomán, *Mexico* **146 D4** 18 55N 103 53W
Tecopa, *U.S.A.* **145 K10** 35 51N 116 13W
Tecoripa, *Mexico* **146 B3** 28 37N 109 57W
Tecuala, *Mexico* **146 C3** 22 23N 105 27W
Tecuci, *Romania* **46 D8** 45 51N 27 27 E
Tecumseh, *U.S.A.* **141 B13** 42 0N 83 57W
Ted, *Somali Rep.* **108 D2** 4 24N 43 55 E
Tedzhen, *Turkmenistan* **56 F7** 37 23N 60 31 E
Tees →, *U.K.* **16 C6** 54 36N 1 25W
Teesside, *U.K.* **16 C6** 54 37N 1 13W
Teeswater, *Canada* **136 C3** 43 59N 81 17W
Tefé, *Brazil* **153 D5** 3 25 S 64 50W
Tefé →, *Brazil* **153 D5** 3 35 S 64 47W
Tefenni, *Turkey* **88 E3** 37 18N 29 45 E
Tegal, *Indonesia* **75 D3** 6 52 S 109 8 E
Tegelen, *Neths.* **21 F8** 51 20N 6 9 E
Tegernsee, *Germany* **27 H7** 47 43N 11 46 E
Teggiano, *Italy* **41 B8** 40 24N 15 32 E
Teghra, *India* **81 G11** 25 30N 85 34 E
Tegid, L. = Bala, L., *U.K.* **16 E4** 52 53N 3 38W
Tegina, *Nigeria* **101 C6** 10 5N 6 11 E
Tegua, *Vanuatu* **121 C4** 13 15 S 166 37 E
Tegucigalpa, *Honduras* **148 D2** 14 5N 87 14W
Tehachapi, *U.S.A.* **145 K8** 35 8N 118 27W
Tehachapi Mts., *U.S.A.* **145 L8** 35 0N 118 30W
Tehamiyam, *Sudan* **94 D4** 18 20N 36 32 E
Tehilla, *Sudan* **94 D4** 17 42N 36 6 E
Téhini, *Ivory C.* **100 D4** 9 39N 3 40W
Tehrān, *Iran* **85 C6** 35 44N 51 30 E
Tehuacán, *Mexico* **147 D5** 18 30N 97 30W
Tehuantepec, *Mexico* **147 D5** 16 21N 95 13W
Tehuantepec, G. de, *Mexico* **147 D5** 15 50N 95 12W
Tehuantepec, Istmo de, *Mexico* **147 D6** 17 0N 94 30W
Teide, *Canary Is.* **33 F3** 28 15N 16 38W
Teifi →, *U.K.* **17 E3** 52 4N 4 14W
Teign →, *U.K.* **17 G4** 50 41N 3 42W
Teignmouth, *U.K.* **17 G4** 50 33N 3 30W
Teiuş, *Romania* **46 C4** 46 12N 23 40 E
Teixeira, *Brazil* **154 C4** 7 13 S 37 15W
Teixeira Pinto, *Guinea-Biss.* **100 C1** 12 3N 16 0W
Tejo →, *Europe* **37 G1** 38 40N 9 24W
Tejon Pass, *U.S.A.* **145 L8** 34 49N 118 53W
Tekamah, *U.S.A.* **138 E6** 41 47N 96 13W
Tekapo →, *N.Z.* **119 E5** 44 13 S 170 21 E
Tekapo, L., *N.Z.* **119 D5** 43 53 S 170 33 E
Tekax, *Mexico* **147 C7** 20 11N 89 18W
Tekeli, *Kazakhstan* **55 A9** 44 50N 79 0 E
Tekeze →, *Ethiopia* **95 E4** 14 20N 35 50 E
Tekija, *Serbia* **42 C7** 44 42N 22 26 E
Tekirdağ, *Turkey* **88 C2** 40 58N 27 30 E
Tekirdağ □, *Turkey* **88 C2** 41 0N 27 0 E
Tekkali, *India* **82 E7** 18 37N 84 15 E
Tekke, *Turkey* **88 C7** 40 42N 36 12 E
Tekman, *Turkey* **89 D9** 39 38N 41 29 E
Tekoa, *U.S.A.* **142 C5** 47 14N 117 4W
Tekouiât, O. →, *Algeria* **99 D5** 22 25N 2 35 E
Tel Aviv-Yafo, *Israel* **91 C3** 32 4N 34 48 E
Tel Lakhish, *Israel* **91 D3** 31 34N 34 51 E
Tel Megiddo, *Israel* **91 C4** 32 35N 35 11 E
Tela, *Honduras* **148 C2** 15 40N 87 28W
Télagh, *Algeria* **99 B4** 34 51N 0 32W
Telanaipura = Jambi, *Indonesia* **74 C2** 1 38 S 103 30 E
Telavi, *Georgia* **53 F11** 42 0N 45 30 E
Telciu, *Romania* **46 B5** 47 25N 24 24 E
Telde, *Canary Is.* **33 G4** 27 59N 15 25W
Telefomin, *Papua N. G.* **120 C1** 5 10 S 141 31 E
Telegraph Creek, *Canada* **130 B2** 58 0N 131 10W
Telekhany, *Belorussia* **50 E4** 52 30N 25 46 E
Telemark fylke □, *Norway* **14 E2** 59 25N 8 30 E
Telén, *Argentina* **158 D2** 36 15 S 65 31W
Telen →, *Indonesia* **75 C5** 0 10 S 117 20 E
Teleng, *Iran* **85 E9** 25 47N 61 3 E
Teleño, *Spain* **36 C4** 42 23N 6 22W
Teleorman □, *Romania* **46 E6** 44 0N 25 0 E
Teleorman →, *Romania* **46 E6** 44 15N 25 20 E
Teles Pires →, *Brazil* **157 B6** 7 21 S 58 3W
Telescope Pk., *U.S.A.* **145 J9** 36 10N 117 5W
Teletaye, *Mali* **101 B5** 16 31N 1 30 E
Telford, *U.K.* **16 E5** 52 42N 2 31W
Telfs, *Austria* **30 D4** 47 19N 11 4 E
Télimélé, *Guinea* **100 C2** 10 54N 13 2W
Telkwa, *Canada* **130 C3** 54 41N 127 5W
Tell City, *U.S.A.* **141 G10** 37 57N 86 46W
Tellicherry, *India* **83 J2** 11 45N 75 30 E
Tellin, *Belgium* **21 H6** 50 5N 5 13 E
Telluride, *U.S.A.* **143 H10** 37 56N 107 49W
Telok Datok, *Malaysia* **74 B2** 2 49N 101 31 E
Teloloapán, *Mexico* **147 D5** 18 21N 99 51W
Telpos Iz, *Russia* **48 B10** 63 35N 57 30 E
Telsen, *Argentina* **160 B3** 42 30 S 66 50W
Telšiai, *Lithuania* **50 D3** 55 59N 22 14 E
Teltow, *Germany* **26 C9** 52 24N 13 15 E
Teluk Anson, *Malaysia* **77 K3** 4 3N 101 0 E
Teluk Betung = Tanjungkarang Telukbetung, *Indonesia* **74 D3** 5 20 S 105 10 E
Teluk Intan = Teluk Anson, *Malaysia* **77 K3** 4 3N 101 0 E
Telukbutun, *Indonesia* **75 B3** 4 13N 108 12 E
Telukdalem, *Indonesia* **74 B1** 0 33N 97 50 E
Tema, *Ghana* **101 D5** 5 41N 0 0 E
Temanggung, *Indonesia* **75 D4** 7 18 S 110 10 E
Temapache, *Mexico* **147 C5** 21 4N 97 38W
Temax, *Mexico* **147 C7** 21 10N 88 50W
Temba, *S. Africa* **105 D4** 25 20 S 28 17 E
Tembe, *Zaïre* **106 C2** 0 16 S 28 14 E
Tembesi, *Indonesia* **74 C2** 1 43 S 103 6 E
Tembilahan, *Indonesia* **74 C2** 0 19 S 103 9 E
Temblador, *Venezuela* **153 B5** 8 59N 62 44W
Tembleque, *Spain* **34 F1** 39 41N 3 30W
Temblor Range, *U.S.A.* **145 K7** 35 20N 119 50W
Teme →, *U.K.* **17 E5** 52 23N 2 15W
Temecula, *U.S.A.* **145 M9** 33 30N 117 9W
Temerloh, *Malaysia* **77 L4** 3 27N 102 25 E
Temir, *Kazakhstan* **56 E6** 49 21N 57 3 E
Temirtau, *Kazakhstan* **56 D8** 50 5N 72 56 E
Temirtau, *Russia* **56 D9** 53 10N 87 30 E
Témiscaming, *Canada* **128 C4** 46 44N 79 5W
Temma, *Australia* **114 G3** 41 12 S 144 48 E
Temnikov, *Russia* **51 D13** 54 40N 43 11 E
Temo →, *Italy* **40 B1** 40 20N 8 30 E
Temora, *Australia* **117 C7** 34 30 S 147 30 E
Temosachic, *Mexico* **146 B3** 28 58N 107 50W
Tempe, *U.S.A.* **143 K8** 33 25N 111 56W
Tempe Downs, *Australia* **112 D5** 24 22 S 132 24 E
Témpio Pausania, *Italy* **40 B2** 40 53N 9 6 E
Tempiute, *U.S.A.* **144 H11** 37 39N 115 38W
Temple, *U.S.A.* **139 K6** 31 6N 97 21W
Temple B., *Australia* **114 A3** 12 15 S 143 3 E
Templemore, *Ireland* **19 D4** 52 48N 7 50W
Templeton, *U.S.A.* **144 K6** 35 33N 120 42W
Templeton →, *Australia* **114 C2** 21 0 S 138 40 E
Templeuve, *Belgium* **21 G2** 50 39N 3 17 E
Templin, *Germany* **26 B9** 53 8N 13 31 E
Tempoal, *Mexico* **147 C5** 21 31N 98 23W
Temryuk, *Russia* **52 D7** 45 15N 37 24 E
Temse, *Belgium* **21 F4** 51 7N 4 13 E
Temska →, *Serbia* **42 D7** 43 17N 22 33 E
Temuco, *Chile* **160 A2** 38 45 S 72 40W
Temuka, *N.Z.* **119 E6** 44 14 S 171 17 E
Ten Boer, *Neths.* **20 B9** 53 16N 6 42 E
Tena, *Ecuador* **152 D2** 0 59 S 77 49W
Tenabo, *Mexico* **147 C6** 20 2N 90 12W
Tenaha, *U.S.A.* **139 K7** 31 57N 94 15W
Tenali, *India* **83 F5** 16 15N 80 35 E
Tenancingo, *Mexico* **147 D5** 19 0N 99 33W
Tenango, *Mexico* **147 D5** 19 7N 99 33W
Tenasserim, *Burma* **77 F2** 12 6N 99 3 E
Tenasserim □, *Burma* **76 F2** 14 0N 98 30 E
Tenay, *France* **25 C9** 45 55N 5 31 E
Tenby, *U.K.* **17 F3** 51 40N 4 42W
Tenda, Col di, *France* **25 D11** 44 7N 7 36 E
Tendaho, *Ethiopia* **90 E3** 11 48N 40 54 E
Tende, *France* **25 D11** 44 5N 7 35 E
Tendelti, *Sudan* **95 E3** 13 1N 31 55 E
Tendjedi, Adrar, *Algeria* **99 D6** 23 41N 7 32 E
Tendrara, *Morocco* **99 B4** 33 3N 1 58W
Tendre, Mt., *Switz.* **28 C2** 46 35N 6 18 E
Teneida, *Egypt* **94 B2** 25 30N 29 19 E
Tenente Marques →, *Brazil* **157 C6** 11 10 S 59 56W
Ténéré, *Niger* **97 E2** 19 0N 10 30 E
Ténéré, Erg du, *Niger* **97 E2** 17 35N 10 55 E
Tenerife, *Canary Is.* **33 F3** 28 15N 16 35W
Tenerife, Pico, *Canary Is.* **33 G1** 27 43N 18 1W
Ténès, *Algeria* **99 A5** 36 31N 1 14 E
Teng Xian, *Guangxi Zhuangzu, China* **69 F8** 23 21N 110 56 E
Teng Xian, *Shandong, China* **67 G9** 35 5N 117 10 E
Tengah □, *Indonesia* **72 B2** 2 0 S 122 0 E
Tengah Kepulauan, *Indonesia* **75 D5** 7 5 S 118 15 E
Tengchong, *China* **68 E2** 25 0N 98 28 E
Tengchowfu = Penglai, *China* **67 F11** 37 48N 120 42 E
Tenggara □, *Indonesia* **72 B2** 3 0 S 122 0 E
Tenggarong, *Indonesia* **75 C5** 0 24 S 116 58 E
Tenggol, P., *Malaysia* **77 K4** 4 48N 103 41 E
Tengiz, Ozero, *Kazakhstan* **56 D7** 50 30N 69 0 E
Tenigerbad, *Switz.* **29 C7** 46 42N 8 57 E
Tenino, *U.S.A.* **144 D4** 46 51N 122 51W
Tenkasi, *India* **83 K3** 8 55N 77 20 E
Tenke, *Shaba, Zaïre* **107 E2** 11 22 S 26 40 E
Tenke, *Shaba, Zaïre* **107 E2** 10 32 S 26 7 E
Tenkodogo, *Burkina Faso* **101 C4** 11 54N 0 19W
Tenna →, *Italy* **39 E10** 43 12N 13 47 E
Tennant Creek, *Australia* **114 B1** 19 30 S 134 15 E
Tennessee □, *U.S.A.* **135 H2** 36 0N 86 30W
Tennessee →, *U.S.A.* **134 G1** 37 4N 88 34W
Tenneville, *Belgium* **21 H7** 50 6N 5 32 E
Tennille, *U.S.A.* **135 J4** 32 56N 82 48W
Tennsift, Oued →, *Morocco* **98 B3** 32 3N 9 28W
Tennyson, *U.S.A.* **141 F9** 38 5N 87 7W
Teno, Pta. de, *Canary Is.* **33 F3** 28 21N 16 55W
Tenom, *Malaysia* **75 A5** 5 4N 115 57 E
Tenosique, *Mexico* **147 D6** 17 30N 91 24W
Tenri, *Japan* **63 C7** 34 39N 135 49 E
Tenryū, *Japan* **63 C9** 34 52N 137 49 E
Tenryū-Gawa →, *Japan* **63 B9** 35 39N 137 48 E
Tent L., *Canada* **131 A7** 62 25N 107 54W
Tentelomatinan, *Indonesia* **72 A2** 0 56N 121 48 E
Tenterfield, *Australia* **115 D5** 29 0 S 152 0 E
Teófilo Otoni, *Brazil* **155 E3** 17 50 S 41 30W
Teotihuacán, *Mexico* **147 D5** 19 44N 98 50W
Tepa, *Indonesia* **73 C3** 7 52 S 129 31 E
Tepalcatepec →, *Mexico* **146 D4** 18 35N 101 59W
Tepehuanes, *Mexico* **146 B3** 25 21N 105 44W
Tepelena, *Albania* **44 D2** 40 17N 20 2 E
Tepequem, Serra, *Brazil* **153 C5** 3 45N 61 45W
Tepetongo, *Mexico* **146 C4** 22 28N 103 9W
Tepic, *Mexico* **146 C4** 21 30N 104 54W
Teplice, *Czech.* **30 A6** 50 40N 13 48 E
Teploklyuchenka, *Kirghizia* **55 B9** 42 30N 78 30 E
Tepoca, C., *Mexico* **146 A2** 30 20N 112 25W
Tequila, *Mexico* **146 C4** 20 54N 103 47W
Ter →, *Spain* **34 C8** 42 2N 3 12 E
Ter Apel, *Neths.* **20 C10** 52 53N 7 5 E
Téra, *Niger* **101 C5** 14 0N 0 45 E
Tera →, *Spain* **36 D5** 41 54N 5 44W
Teraina, *Kiribati* **123 G11** 4 43N 160 25W
Téramo, *Italy* **39 F10** 42 40N 13 40 E
Terang, *Australia* **116 E5** 38 15 S 142 55 E
Terawhiti, C., *N.Z.* **118 H3** 41 16 S 174 38 E
Terazit, Massif de, *Niger* **97 D1** 20 2N 8 30 E
Terborg, *Neths.* **20 E8** 51 56N 6 22 E
Tercan, *Turkey* **89 D9** 39 47N 40 23 E
Tercero →, *Argentina* **158 C3** 32 58 S 61 47W
Terdal, *India* **82 F2** 16 33N 75 3 E
Terebovlya, *Ukraine* **50 G4** 49 18N 25 44 E
Teregova, *Romania* **46 D3** 45 10N 22 16 E
Terek →, *Russia* **53 E12** 44 0N 47 30 E
Terek-Say, *Kirghizia* **55 C5** 41 30N 71 11 E
Terengganu □, *Malaysia* **74 B2** 4 55N 103 0 E
Terenos, *Brazil* **157 E7** 20 26 S 54 50W
Tereshka →, *Russia* **51 F15** 51 48N 46 26 E
Teresina, *Brazil* **154 C3** 5 9 S 42 45W
Teresinha, *Brazil* **153 C7** 0 58N 52 2W
Terespol, *Poland* **47 C10** 52 5N 23 37 E
Terewah, L., *Australia* **115 D4** 29 52 S 147 35 E
Terges →, *Portugal* **37 H3** 37 49N 7 41W
Tergnier, *France* **23 C10** 49 40N 3 17 E
Terhazza, *Mali* **98 D3** 23 38N 5 22W
Terheijden, *Neths.* **21 E5** 51 38N 4 45 E
Teridgerie Cr. →, *Australia* **115 E4** 30 25 S 148 50 E
Terifa, *Yemen* **86 D3** 14 24N 43 48 E
Terlizzi, *Italy* **41 A9** 41 8N 16 32 E
Terme, *Turkey* **52 F7** 41 11N 37 0 E
Termez, *Uzbekistan* **55 E3** 37 15N 67 15 E
Términi Imerese, *Italy* **40 E6** 37 58N 13 42 E
Términos, L. de, *Mexico* **147 D6** 18 35N 91 30W
Térmoli, *Italy* **39 F12** 42 0N 15 0 E
Ternate, *Indonesia* **72 A3** 0 45N 127 25 E
Terneuzen, *Neths.* **21 F3** 51 20N 3 50 E
Terney, *Russia* **57 E14** 45 3N 136 37 E
Terni, *Italy* **39 F9** 42 34N 12 38 E
Ternitz, *Austria* **30 D9** 47 43N 16 2 E
Ternopol, *Ukraine* **52 B1** 49 30N 25 40 E
Terowie, *N.S.W., Australia* **115 E4** 32 27 S 147 52 E
Terowie, *S. Austral., Australia* **115 E2** 33 8 S 138 55 E
Terra Bella, *U.S.A.* **145 K7** 35 58N 119 3W
Terrace, *Canada* **130 C3** 54 30N 128 35W
Terrace Bay, *Canada* **128 C2** 48 47N 87 5W
Terracina, *Italy* **40 A6** 41 17N 13 12 E
Terralba, *Italy* **40 C1** 39 42N 8 38 E
Terranova = Ólbia, *Italy* **40 B2** 40 55N 9 30 E
Terranuova Bracciolini, *Italy* **39 E8** 43 31N 11 35 E
Terrasini Favarotta, *Italy* **40 D6** 38 10N 13 4 E
Terrassa = Tarrasa, *Spain* **34 D7** 41 34N 2 1 E
Terrasson-la-Villedieu, *France* **24 C5** 45 8N 1 18 E
Terre Haute, *U.S.A.* **141 E9** 39 28N 87 25W
Terrebonne B., *U.S.A.* **139 L9** 29 5N 90 35W
Terrecht, *Mali* **99 D4** 20 10N 0 10W
Terrell, *U.S.A.* **139 J6** 32 44N 96 17W
Terrenceville, *Canada* **129 C9** 47 40N 54 44W
Terrick Terrick, *Australia* **114 C4** 24 44 S 145 5 E
Terry, *U.S.A.* **138 B2** 46 47N 105 19W
Terschelling, *Neths.* **20 B6** 53 25N 5 20 E
Terskey Alatau, Khrebet, *Kirghizia* **55 C8** 41 50N 77 0 E
Terter →, *Azerbaijan* **53 F12** 40 25N 47 10 E
Teruel, *Spain* **34 E3** 40 22N 1 8W
Teruel □, *Spain* **34 E4** 40 48N 1 0W
Tervel, *Bulgaria* **43 D12** 43 45N 27 28 E
Tervola, *Finland* **12 C18** 66 6N 24 49 E
Teryaweyna L., *Australia* **116 B5** 32 18 S 143 22 E
Tešanj, *Bos.-H.* **42 C2** 44 38N 18 1 E
Teseney, *Eritrea* **95 D4** 15 5N 36 42 E
Tesha →, *Russia* **51 D13** 55 38N 42 9 E
Teshio, *Japan* **60 B10** 44 53N 141 44 E
Teshio-Gawa →, *Japan* **60 B10** 44 53N 141 45 E
Tešica, *Serbia* **42 D6** 43 27N 21 45 E
Tesiyn Gol →, *Mongolia* **64 A4** 50 40N 93 20 E
Teslić, *Bos.-H.* **42 C2** 44 37N 17 54 E
Teslin, *Canada* **130 A2** 60 10N 132 43W
Teslin →, *Canada* **130 A2** 61 34N 134 35W
Teslin L., *Canada* **130 A2** 60 15N 132 57W
Tesouro, *Brazil* **157 D7** 16 4 S 53 34W
Tessalit, *Mali* **101 A5** 20 12N 1 0 E
Tessaoua, *Niger* **97 F1** 13 47N 7 56 E
Tessenderlo, *Belgium* **21 F6** 51 4N 5 5 E
Tessin, *Germany* **26 A8** 54 2N 12 28 E
Tessit, *Mali* **101 B5** 15 13N 0 18 E
Test →, *U.K.* **17 F6** 51 7N 1 30W
Testa del Gargano, *Italy* **41 A9** 41 50N 16 10 E
Tét, *Hungary* **31 D10** 47 30N 17 33 E
Têt →, *France* **24 F7** 42 44N 3 2 E
Tetachuck L., *Canada* **130 C3** 53 18N 125 55W
Tetas, Pta., *Chile* **158 A1** 23 31 S 70 38W
Tete, *Mozam.* **107 F3** 16 13 S 33 33 E
Tete □, *Mozam.* **107 F3** 15 15 S 32 40 E
Teterev →, *Ukraine* **50 F7** 51 1N 30 5 E
Teteringen, *Neths.* **21 E5** 51 37N 4 49 E
Teterow, *Germany* **26 B8** 53 45N 12 34 E
Teteven, *Bulgaria* **43 E9** 42 58N 24 17 E
Tethul →, *Canada* **130 A6** 60 35N 112 12W
Tetiyev, *Ukraine* **52 B3** 49 22N 29 38 E
Teton →, *U.S.A.* **142 C8** 47 56N 110 31W
Tétouan, *Morocco* **98 A3** 35 35N 5 21W
Tetovo, *Macedonia* **42 E6** 42 1N 21 2 E
Tetuán = Tétouan, *Morocco* **98 A3** 35 35N 5 21W
Tetyukhe Pristan, *Russia* **60 B7** 44 22N 135 48 E
Tetyushi, *Russia* **51 D16** 54 55N 48 49 E
Teuco →, *Argentina* **158 B3** 25 35 S 60 11W
Teufen, *Switz.* **29 B8** 47 24N 9 23 E
Teulada, *Italy* **40 D1** 38 59N 8 47 E
Teulon, *Canada* **131 C9** 50 23N 97 16W
Teun, *Indonesia* **73 C3** 6 59 S 129 8 E
Teutoburger Wald, *Germany* **26 C4** 52 5N 8 20 E
Tevere →, *Italy* **39 G9** 41 44N 12 14 E
Teverya, *Israel* **91 C4** 32 47N 35 32 E
Teviot →, *U.K.* **18 F6** 55 21N 2 51W
Tewantin, *Australia* **115 D5** 26 27 S 153 3 E
Tewkesbury, *U.K.* **17 F5** 51 59N 2 8W
Texada I., *Canada* **130 D4** 49 40N 124 25W
Texarkana, *Ark., U.S.A.* **139 J8** 33 26N 94 2W
Texarkana, *Tex., U.S.A.* **139 J7** 33 26N 94 3W
Texas, *Australia* **115 D5** 28 49 S 151 9 E
Texas □, *U.S.A.* **139 K5** 31 40N 98 30W
Texas City, *U.S.A.* **139 L7** 29 24N 94 54W
Texel, *Neths.* **20 B5** 53 5N 4 50 E
Texhoma, *U.S.A.* **139 G4** 36 30N 101 47W
Texline, *U.S.A.* **139 G3** 36 23N 103 2W
Texoma, L., *U.S.A.* **139 J6** 33 50N 96 34W
Teykovo, *Russia* **51 C12** 56 55N 40 30 E
Teyvareh, *Afghan.* **79 B2** 33 30N 64 24 E
Teza →, *Russia* **51 C12** 56 32N 41 53 E
Tezin, *Afghan.* **80 B3** 34 24N 69 30 E
Teziutlán, *Mexico* **147 D5** 19 50N 97 22W
Tezpur, *India* **78 B4** 26 40N 92 45 E
Tezzeron L., *Canada* **130 C4** 54 43N 124 30W
Tha-anne →, *Canada* **131 A10** 60 31N 94 37W
Tha Deua, *Laos* **76 D4** 17 57N 102 53 E
Tha Deua, *Laos* **76 C3** 19 26N 101 50 E
Tha Pla, *Thailand* **76 D3** 17 48N 100 32 E
Tha Rua, *Thailand* **76 E3** 14 34N 100 44 E
Tha Sala, *Thailand* **77 H2** 8 40N 99 56 E
Tha Song Yang, *Thailand* **76 D1** 17 34N 97 55 E
Thaba Nchu, *S. Africa* **104 D4** 29 17 S 26 52 E
Thaba Putsoa, *Lesotho* **105 D4** 29 45 S 28 0 E
Thabana Ntlenyana, *Lesotho* **105 D4** 29 30 S 29 16 E
Thabazimbi, *S. Africa* **105 C4** 24 40 S 27 21 E
Thabeikkyin, *Burma* **78 D5** 22 53N 95 59 E
Thai Binh, *Vietnam* **76 B6** 20 35N 106 1 E
Thai Hoa, *Vietnam* **76 C5** 19 20N 105 20 E
Thai Muang, *Thailand* **77 H2** 8 24N 98 16 E
Thai Nguyen, *Vietnam* **76 B5** 21 35N 105 55 E
Thailand ■, *Asia* **76 E4** 16 0N 102 0 E
Thailand, G. of, *Asia* **77 G3** 11 30N 101 0 E
Thakhek, *Laos* **76 D5** 17 25N 104 45 E
Thakurgaon, *Bangla.* **78 B2** 26 2N 88 34 E
Thal, *Pakistan* **79 B3** 33 28N 70 33 E
Thal Desert, *Pakistan* **80 D4** 31 10N 71 30 E
Thala, *Tunisia* **96 A1** 35 35N 8 40 E
Thalabarivat, *Cambodia* **76 F5** 13 33N 105 57 E
Thalkirch, *Switz.* **29 C8** 46 39N 9 17 E
Thallon, *Australia* **115 D4** 28 39 S 148 49 E
Thalwil, *Switz.* **29 B7** 47 17N 8 35 E
Thamarīt, *Oman* **87 C6** 17 39N 54 2 E
Thame →, *U.K.* **17 F6** 51 35N 1 8W
Thames, *N.Z.* **118 D4** 37 7 S 175 34 E
Thames →, *Canada* **128 D3** 42 20N 82 25W
Thames →, *U.K.* **17 F8** 51 30N 0 35 E
Thames →, *U.S.A.* **137 E12** 41 18N 72 5W
Thames, Firth of, *N.Z.* **118 D4** 37 0 S 175 25 E
Thamesford, *Canada* **136 C3** 43 4N 81 0W
Thamesville, *Canada* **136 D3** 42 33N 81 59W
Thāmit, W. →, *Libya* **96 B3** 30 51N 16 14 E
Thamūd, *Yemen* **87 C5** 17 18N 49 55 E
Than Uyen, *Vietnam* **76 B4** 22 0N 103 54 E
Thanbyuzayat, *Burma* **78 G6** 15 58N 97 44 E
Thane, *India* **82 E1** 19 12N 72 59 E
Thanesar, *India* **80 D7** 30 1N 76 52 E
Thanet, I. of, *U.K.* **17 F9** 51 21N 1 20 E
Thangoo, *Australia* **112 C3** 18 10 S 122 22 E
Thangool, *Australia* **114 C5** 24 38 S 150 42 E
Thanh Hoa, *Vietnam* **76 C5** 19 48N 105 46 E
Thanh Hung, *Vietnam* **77 H5** 9 55N 105 43 E
Thanh Pho Ho Chi Minh = Phanh Bho Ho Chi Minh, *Vietnam* **77 G6** 10 58N 106 40 E
Thanh Thuy, *Vietnam* **76 A5** 22 55N 104 51 E
Thanjavur, *India* **83 J4** 10 48N 79 12 E
Thann, *France* **23 E14** 47 48N 7 5 E
Thaon-les-Vosges, *France* **23 D13** 48 15N 6 24 E
Thap Sakae, *Thailand* **77 G2** 11 30N 99 37 E
Thap Than, *Thailand* **76 E2** 15 27N 99 54 E
Thar Desert, *India* **80 F4** 28 0N 72 0 E
Tharad, *India* **80 G4** 24 30N 71 44 E
Thargomindah, *Australia* **115 D3** 27 58 S 143 46 E
Tharrawaddy, *Burma* **78 G5** 17 38N 95 48 E
Tharrawaw, *Burma* **78 G5** 17 41N 95 28 E
Tharthar, W. →, *Iraq* **84 C4** 33 59N 43 12 E
Thasopoúla, *Greece* **44 D6** 40 49N 24 45 E
Thásos, *Greece* **44 D6** 40 40N 24 40 E
That Khe, *Vietnam* **76 A6** 22 16N 106 28 E
Thatcher, *Ariz., U.S.A.* **143 K9** 32 51N 109 46W
Thatcher, *Colo., U.S.A.* **139 G2** 37 33N 104 7W
Thaton, *Burma* **78 G6** 16 55N 97 22 E
Thau, Bassin de, *France* **24 E7** 43 23N 3 36 E
Thaungdut, *Burma* **78 C5** 24 30N 94 40 E
Thayer, *U.S.A.* **139 G9** 36 31N 91 33W
Thayetmyo, *Burma* **78 F5** 19 20N 95 10 E
Thayngen, *Switz.* **29 A7** 47 49N 8 43 E
The Alberga →, *Australia* **115 D2** 27 6 S 135 33 E
The Bight, *Bahamas* **149 B4** 24 19N 75 24W
The Brothers, *Yemen* **87 D6** 12 8N 53 10 E
The Coorong, *Australia* **116 C3** 35 50 S 139 20 E
The Dalles, *U.S.A.* **142 D3** 45 36N 121 10W
The English Company's Is., *Australia* **114 A2** 11 50 S 136 32 E
The Entrance, *Australia* **117 B9** 33 21 S 151 30 E
The Frome →, *Australia* **115 D2** 29 8 S 137 54 E
The Grampians, *Australia* **116 D5** 37 0 S 142 20 E
The Great Divide = Great Dividing Ra., *Australia* **114 C4** 23 0 S 146 0 E
The Hague = 's-Gravenhage, *Neths.* **20 D4** 52 7N 4 17 E
The Hamilton →, *Australia* **115 D2** 26 40 S 135 19 E

Uffenheim 277

Tsurumi-Saki, Japan 62 E4 32 56N 132 5 E
Tsuruoka, Japan 60 E9 38 44N 139 50 E
Tsurusaki, Japan 62 D3 33 14N 131 41 E
Tsushima, Gifu, Japan 63 B8 35 10N 136 43 E
Tsushima, Nagasaki, Japan 62 C1 34 20N 129 20 E
Tsvetkovo, Ukraine 52 B4 49 8N 31 33 E
Tu →, Burma 78 E6 21 50N 96 15 E
Tua →, Portugal 36 D3 41 13N 7 26W
Tuai, N.Z. 118 E6 38 47 S 177 10 E
Tuakau, N.Z. 118 D3 37 16 S 174 59 E
Tual, Indonesia 73 C4 5 38 S 132 44 E
Tuam, Ireland 19 C3 53 30N 8 50W
Tuamarina, N.Z. 119 B8 41 25 S 173 59 E
Tuamotu Arch. = Tuamotu Is., Pac. Oc. 123 J13 17 0 S 144 0W
Tuamotu Is., Pac. Oc. 123 J13 17 0 S 144 0W
Tuamotu Ridge, Pac. Oc. 123 K14 20 0 S 138 0W
Tuanfeng, China 69 B10 30 38N 114 52 E
Tuanxi, China 68 D6 27 28N 107 8 E
Tuao, Phil. 70 C3 17 55N 121 22 E
Tuapse, Russia 53 D8 44 5N 39 10 E
Tuas, Singapore 74 B2 1 19N 103 39 E
Tuatapere, N.Z. 119 G2 46 8 S 167 41 E
Tuba City, U.S.A. 143 H8 36 8N 111 14W
Tuban, Indonesia 75 D4 6 54 S 112 3 E
Tubarão, Brazil 159 B6 28 30 S 49 0W
Tūbās, Jordan 91 C4 32 20N 35 22 E
Tubau, Malaysia 75 B4 3 10N 113 40 E
Tubbergen, Neths. 20 D9 52 24N 6 48 E
Tübingen, Germany 27 G5 48 31N 9 4 E
Tubize, Belgium 21 G4 50 42N 4 13 E
Tubruq, Libya 96 B4 32 7N 23 55 E
Tubuai Is., Pac. Oc. 123 K12 25 0 S 150 0W
Tuburan, Phil. 71 H4 6 39N 122 16 E
Tuc Trung, Vietnam 77 G6 11 1N 107 12 E
Tucacas, Venezuela 152 A4 10 48N 68 19W
Tucano, Brazil 154 D4 10 58 S 38 48W
Tuchang, Taiwan 69 E13 24 59N 121 30 E
Tuchodi →, Canada 130 B4 58 17N 123 42W
Tuchola, Poland 47 B4 53 33N 17 52 E
Tuchów, Poland 31 B14 49 54N 21 1 E
Tucson, U.S.A. 143 K8 32 13N 110 58W
Tucumán □, Argentina 158 B2 26 48 S 66 2W
Tucumcari, U.S.A. 139 H3 35 10N 103 44W
Tucunaré, Brazil 157 B6 5 18 S 55 51W
Tucupido, Venezuela 152 B4 9 17N 65 47W
Tucupita, Venezuela 153 B5 9 2N 62 3W
Tucuruí, Brazil 154 B2 3 42 S 49 44W
Tuczno, Poland 47 B3 53 13N 16 10 E
Tudela, Spain 34 C3 42 4N 1 39W
Tudela de Duero, Spain 36 D6 41 37N 4 39W
Tudmur, Syria 84 C3 34 36N 38 15 E
Tudor, L., Canada 129 A6 55 50N 65 25W
Tudora, Romania 46 B7 47 31N 26 45 E
Tuella →, Portugal 36 D3 41 30N 7 12W
Tuen, Australia 115 D4 28 33 S 145 37 E
Tueré →, Brazil 154 B1 2 48 S 50 59W
Tufi, Papua N. G. 120 E5 9 8 S 149 19 E
Tugela →, S. Africa 105 D5 29 14 S 31 30 E
Tuguegarao, Phil. 70 C3 17 35N 121 42 E
Tugur, Russia 57 D14 53 44N 136 45 E
Tuineje, Canary Is. 33 F5 28 19N 14 3W
Tukangbesi, Kepulauan, Indonesia 72 C2 6 0 S 124 0 E
Tukarak I., Canada 128 A4 56 15N 78 45W
Tukayyid, Iraq 84 D5 29 47N 45 36 E
Tûkh, Egypt 94 H7 30 21N 31 12 E
Tukituki →, N.Z. 118 F5 39 36 S 176 56 E
Tukobo, Ghana 100 D4 5 1N 2 47W
Tūkrah, Libya 96 B4 32 30N 20 37 E
Tuktoyaktuk, Canada 126 B6 69 27N 133 2W
Tukums, Latvia 50 C3 57 2N 23 10 E
Tukuyu, Tanzania 107 D3 9 17 S 33 35 E
Tula, Hidalgo, Mexico 147 C5 20 5N 99 20W
Tula, Tamaulipas, Mexico 147 C5 23 0N 99 40W
Tula, Nigeria 101 D7 9 51N 11 27 E
Tula, Russia 51 D10 54 13N 37 38 E
Tulak, Afghan. 79 B1 33 55N 63 40 E
Tulancingo, Mexico 147 C5 20 5N 99 22W
Tulangbawang →, Indonesia 74 C3 4 24 S 105 52 E
Tulare, U.S.A. 144 J7 36 13N 119 21W
Tulare Lake Bed, U.S.A. 144 K7 36 0N 119 48W
Tularosa, U.S.A. 143 K10 33 5N 106 1W
Tulbagh, S. Africa 104 E2 33 16 S 19 6 E
Tulcán, Ecuador 152 C2 0 48N 77 43W
Tulcea, Romania 46 D9 45 13N 28 46 E
Tulcea □, Romania 46 D9 45 0N 28 30 E
Tulchin, Ukraine 52 B3 48 41N 28 49 E
Tūleh, Iran 85 C7 34 35N 52 33 E
Tulemalu L., Canada 131 A9 62 58N 99 25W
Tulgheş, Romania 46 C6 46 58N 25 45 E
Tuli, Indonesia 72 B2 1 24 S 122 26 E
Tuli, Zimbabwe 107 G2 21 58 S 29 13 E
Tulia, U.S.A. 139 H4 34 32N 101 46W
Ṭūlkarm, Jordan 91 C4 32 19N 35 2 E
Tullahoma, U.S.A. 135 H2 35 22N 86 13W
Tullamore, Australia 117 B7 32 39 S 147 36 E
Tullamore, Ireland 19 C4 53 17N 7 30W
Tulle, France 24 C5 45 16N 1 46 E
Tullibigeal, Australia 117 B7 33 25 S 146 44 E
Tullins, France 25 C9 45 18N 5 29 E
Tulln, Austria 30 C9 48 20N 16 4 E
Tullow, Ireland 19 D4 52 48N 6 45W
Tullus, Sudan 95 E1 11 7N 24 31 E
Tully, Australia 114 B4 17 56 S 145 55 E
Ṭulmaythah, Libya 96 B4 32 40N 20 55 E
Tulmur, Australia 114 C3 22 40 S 142 20 E
Tulnici, Romania 46 D7 45 51N 26 38 E
Tulovo, Bulgaria 43 E10 42 33N 25 32 E
Tulsa, U.S.A. 139 G7 36 10N 95 55W
Tulsequah, Canada 130 B2 58 39N 133 35W
Tulu Milki, Ethiopia 95 F4 9 55N 38 20 E
Tulu Welel, Ethiopia 95 F3 8 56N 34 47 E
Tulua, Colombia 152 C2 4 6N 76 11W
Tulun, Russia 57 D11 54 32N 100 35 E
Tulungagung, Indonesia 75 D4 8 5 S 111 54 E
Tum, Indonesia 73 B4 3 36 S 130 21 E
Tuma, Russia 51 D12 55 10N 40 30 E
Tuma →, Nic. 148 D3 13 6N 84 35W
Tumaco, Colombia 152 C2 1 50N 78 45W
Tumaco, Ensenada, Colombia 152 C2 1 55N 78 45W
Tumatumari, Guyana 153 B6 5 20N 58 55W
Tumauini, Phil. 70 C3 17 17N 121 49 E
Tumba, Sweden 14 E11 59 12N 17 48 E
Tumba, L., Zaïre 102 C3 0 50 S 18 0 E
Tumbarumba, Australia 117 C8 35 44 S 148 0 E
Tumbaya, Argentina 158 A2 23 50 S 65 26W
Túmbes, Peru 156 A1 3 37 S 80 27W
Tumbes □, Peru 156 A1 3 50 S 80 30W
Tumbwe, Zaïre 107 E2 11 25 S 27 15 E
Tumby Bay, Australia 116 C2 34 21 S 136 8 E
Tumd Youqi, China 66 D6 40 30N 110 30 E
Tumen, China 67 C15 43 0N 129 50 E
Tumen Jiang →, China 67 C16 42 20N 130 35 E
Tumeremo, Venezuela 153 B5 7 18N 61 30W
Tumiritinga, Brazil 155 E3 18 58 S 41 38W
Tumkur, India 83 H3 13 18N 77 6 E
Tummel, L., U.K. 18 E5 56 43N 3 55W
Tump, Pakistan 79 D1 26 7N 62 16 E
Tumpat, Malaysia 77 J4 6 11N 102 10 E
Tumsar, India 82 D4 21 26N 79 45 E
Tumu, Ghana 100 C4 10 56N 1 56W
Tumucumaque, Serra, Brazil 153 C7 2 0N 55 0W
Tumupasa, Bolivia 156 C4 14 9 S 67 55W
Tumut, Australia 117 C8 35 16 S 148 13 E
Tumutuk, Russia 54 D3 55 1N 53 19 E
Tumwater, U.S.A. 142 C2 47 1N 122 54W
Tunas de Zaza, Cuba 148 B4 21 39N 79 34W
Tunbridge Wells, U.K. 17 F8 51 7N 0 16 E
Tunceli, Turkey 89 D8 39 6N 39 31 E
Tunceli □, Turkey 89 D8 39 5N 39 35 E
Tuncurry, Australia 117 B10 32 17 S 152 29 E
Tunduru, Tanzania 107 E4 11 8 S 37 25 E
Tunduru □, Tanzania 107 E4 11 5 S 37 22 E
Tundzha →, Bulgaria 43 F11 41 40N 26 35 E
Tunga →, India 83 G2 15 0N 75 50 E
Tunga Pass, India 78 A5 29 0N 94 14 E
Tungabhadra →, India 83 G4 15 57N 78 15 E
Tungabhadra Dam, India 83 G2 15 0N 75 50 E
Tungaru, Sudan 95 E3 10 9N 30 52 E
Tungi, Bangla. 78 D3 23 53N 90 24 E
Tungla, Nic. 148 D3 13 24N 84 21W
Tungnafellsjökull, Iceland 12 D5 64 45N 17 55W
Tungsten, Canada 130 A3 61 57N 128 16W
Tungurahua □, Ecuador 152 D2 1 15 S 78 35W
Tunguska, Nizhnyaya →, Russia 57 C9 65 48N 88 4 E
Tuni, India 82 F6 17 22N 82 36 E
Tunia, Colombia 152 C2 2 41N 76 31W
Tunica, U.S.A. 139 H9 34 41N 90 23W
Tunis, Tunisia 96 A2 36 50N 10 11 E
Tunis, Golfe de, Tunisia 96 A2 37 0N 10 30 E
Tunisia ■, Africa 96 B1 33 30N 9 10 E
Tunja, Colombia 152 B3 5 33N 73 25W
Tunkhannock, U.S.A. 137 E9 41 32N 75 57W
Tunliu, China 66 F7 36 13N 112 52 E
Tunnsjøen, Norway 12 D12 64 45N 13 25 E
Tunungayualok I., Canada 129 A7 56 0N 61 0W
Tunuyán, Argentina 158 C2 33 35 S 69 0W
Tunuyán →, Argentina 158 C2 33 33 S 67 30W
Tunxi, China 69 C12 29 42N 118 25 E
Tuo Jiang →, China 68 C5 28 50N 105 35 E
Tuolumne, U.S.A. 144 H6 37 58N 120 15W
Tuolumne →, U.S.A. 144 H5 37 36N 121 13W
Tuoy-Khaya, Russia 57 C12 62 32N 111 25 E
Tūp Āghāj, Iran 84 B5 36 3N 47 50 E
Tupã, Brazil 159 A5 21 57 S 50 28W
Tupaciguara, Brazil 155 E2 18 35 S 48 42W
Tupelo, U.S.A. 135 H1 34 16N 88 43W
Tupik, Russia 50 D8 55 42N 33 22 E
Tupik, Russia 57 D12 54 26N 119 57 E
Tupinambaranas, Brazil 153 D6 3 0 S 58 0W
Tupirama, Brazil 154 C2 8 58 S 48 12W
Tupiratins, Brazil 154 C2 8 23 S 48 8W
Tupiza, Bolivia 158 A2 21 30 S 65 40W
Tupižnica, Serbia 42 D7 43 43N 22 10 E
Tupman, U.S.A. 145 K7 35 18N 119 21W
Tupper, Canada 130 B4 55 32N 120 1W
Tupper Lake, U.S.A. 137 B10 44 14N 74 28W
Tupungato, Cerro, S. Amer. 158 C2 33 15 S 69 50W
Tuquan, China 67 B11 45 18N 121 38 E
Túquerres, Colombia 152 C2 1 5N 77 37W
Tura, India 78 C3 25 30N 90 16 E
Tura, Russia 57 C11 64 20N 100 17 E
Turabah, Si. Arabia 84 D4 28 20N 43 15 E
Turagua, Serranía, Venezuela 153 B5 7 20N 64 35W
Turaiyur, India 83 J4 11 9N 78 38 E
Turakina, N.Z. 118 G4 40 3 S 175 16 E
Turakina →, N.Z. 118 G4 40 5 S 175 8 E
Turakirae Hd., N.Z. 118 H3 41 26 S 174 56 E
Tūrān, Iran 85 C8 35 39N 56 42 E
Turan, Russia 57 D10 51 55N 95 0 E
Turayf, Si. Arabia 84 D3 31 41N 38 39 E
Turbacz, Poland 31 B13 49 30N 20 8 E
Turbe, Bos.-H. 42 C2 44 15N 17 35 E
Turbenthal, Switz. 29 B7 47 27N 8 51 E
Turda, Romania 46 C4 46 34N 23 47 E
Turégano, Spain 36 D6 41 9N 4 1W
Turek, Poland 47 C5 52 3N 18 30 E
Turen, Venezuela 152 B4 9 17N 69 6W
Turfan = Turpan, China 64 B3 43 58N 89 10 E
Turgay, Kazakhstan 54 G8 49 38N 63 30 E
Tŭrgovishte, Bulgaria 43 D11 43 17N 26 38 E
Turgutlu, Turkey 88 D2 38 30N 27 48 E
Turhal, Turkey 52 F7 40 24N 36 5 E
Turia →, Spain 35 F4 39 27N 0 19W
Turiaçu, Brazil 154 B2 1 40 S 45 19W
Turiaçu →, Brazil 154 B2 1 36 S 45 19W
Turiec →, Slovak Rep. 31 B11 49 7N 18 55 E
Turin = Torino, Italy 38 C4 45 4N 7 40 E
Turin, Canada 130 D6 49 58N 112 31W
Turinsk, Russia 54 B8 58 3N 63 42 E
Turka, Ukraine 50 G3 49 10N 23 2 E
Turkana □, Kenya 106 B4 3 0N 35 30 E
Turkana, L., Africa 106 B4 3 30N 36 5 E
Turkestan, Kazakhstan 55 B4 43 17N 68 16 E
Turkestanskiy, Khrebet, Tajikistan 55 D4 39 35N 69 0 E
Túrkeve, Hungary 31 D13 47 6N 20 44 E
Turkey ■, Eurasia 88 D7 39 0N 36 0 E
Turkey →, U.S.A. 140 B5 42 43N 91 2W
Turkey Creek, Australia 112 C4 17 2 S 128 12 E
Turki, Russia 51 F13 52 0N 43 15 E
Turkmenistan ■, Asia 56 F6 39 0N 59 0 E
Türkoğlu, Turkey 88 E7 37 23N 36 50 E
Turks & Caicos Is. ■, W. Indies 149 B5 21 20N 71 20W
Turks Island Passage, W. Indies 149 B5 21 30N 71 30W
Turku, Finland 13 F17 60 30N 22 19 E
Turkwe →, Kenya 106 B4 3 6N 36 6 E
Turlock, U.S.A. 144 H6 37 30N 120 51W
Turnagain →, Canada 130 B3 59 12N 127 35W
Turnagain, C., N.Z. 118 G5 40 28 S 176 38 E
Turneffe Is., Belize 147 D7 17 20N 87 50W
Turner, Australia 112 C4 17 52 S 128 16 E
Turner, U.S.A. 142 B9 48 51N 108 24W
Turner Pt., Australia 114 A1 11 47 S 133 32 E
Turner Valley, Canada 130 C6 50 40N 114 17W
Turners Falls, U.S.A. 137 D12 42 36N 72 33W
Turnhout, Belgium 21 F5 51 19N 4 57 E
Türnitz, Austria 30 D8 47 55N 15 29 E
Turnor L., Canada 131 B7 56 35N 108 35W
Turnov, Czech. 30 A8 50 34N 15 10 E
Tŭrnovo, Bulgaria 43 D10 43 5N 25 41 E
Turnu Măgurele, Romania 46 F5 43 46N 24 56 E
Turnu Rosu Pasul, Romania 46 D5 45 33N 24 17 E
Turobin, Poland 47 E9 50 50N 22 44 E
Turon, U.S.A. 139 G5 37 48N 98 26W
Tuross Head, Australia 117 D9 36 3 S 150 8 E
Turpan, China 64 B3 43 58N 89 10 E
Turrës, Kalaja e, Albania 44 C1 41 10N 19 28 E
Turriff, U.K. 18 D6 57 32N 2 28W
Tursāq, Iraq 84 C5 33 27N 45 47 E
Tursha, Russia 51 C15 56 55N 47 36 E
Tursi, Italy 41 B9 40 15N 16 27 E
Turtle Head I., Australia 114 A3 10 56 S 142 37 E
Turtle Is., Phil. 71 H2 6 7N 118 14 E
Turtle L., Canada 131 C7 53 36N 108 38W
Turtle Lake, N. Dak., U.S.A. 138 B4 47 31N 100 53W
Turtle Lake, Wis., U.S.A. 138 C8 45 24N 92 8W
Turtleford, Canada 131 C7 53 23N 108 57W
Turua, N.Z. 118 D4 37 14 S 175 35 E
Turukhansk, Russia 57 C9 65 21N 88 5 E
Turun ja Porin lääni □, Finland 13 F17 60 27N 22 15 E
Turzovka, Slovak Rep. 31 B11 49 25N 18 35 E
Tuscaloosa, U.S.A. 135 J2 33 12N 87 34W
Tuscánia, Italy 39 F8 42 25N 11 53 E
Tuscany = Toscana, Italy 38 E8 43 30N 11 5 E
Tuscola, Ill., U.S.A. 141 E8 39 48N 88 17W
Tuscola, Tex., U.S.A. 139 J5 32 12N 99 48W
Tuscumbia, Ala., U.S.A. 135 H2 34 44N 87 42W
Tuscumbia, Mo., U.S.A. 140 F4 38 14N 92 28W
Tuskar Rock, Ireland 19 D5 52 12N 6 10W
Tuskegee, U.S.A. 135 J3 32 25N 85 42W
Tustna, Norway 14 A2 63 10N 8 5 E
Tuszyn, Poland 47 D6 51 36N 19 33 E
Tutak, Turkey 89 D10 39 31N 42 46 E
Tutayev, Russia 51 C11 57 53N 39 32 E
Tuticorin, India 83 K4 8 50N 78 12 E
Tutin, Serbia 42 E5 42 58N 20 20 E
Tutóia, Brazil 154 B3 2 45 S 42 20W
Tutong, Brunei 75 B4 4 47N 114 40 E
Tutova →, Romania 46 C8 46 20N 27 30 E
Tutrakan, Bulgaria 43 C11 44 2N 26 40 E
Tutshi L., Canada 130 B2 59 56N 134 30W
Tuttle, U.S.A. 138 B5 47 9N 100 0W
Tuttlingen, Germany 27 H4 47 59N 8 50 E
Tutuala, Indonesia 72 C3 8 25 S 127 15 E
Tutuila, Amer. Samoa 121 X24 14 19 S 170 50W
Tutuko Mt., N.Z. 119 E3 44 35 S 168 1 E
Tututepec, Mexico 147 D5 16 9N 97 38W
Tutye, Australia 116 C4 35 12 S 141 29 E
Tuva Republic □, Russia 57 D10 51 30N 95 0 E
Tuvalu ■, Pac. Oc. 122 H9 8 0 S 178 0 E
Tuwal, Si. Arabia 86 B2 22 17N 39 6 E
Tuxpan, Mexico 147 C5 20 58N 97 23W
Tuxtla Gutiérrez, Mexico 147 D6 16 50N 93 10W
Tuy, Spain 36 C2 42 3N 8 39W
Tuy An, Vietnam 76 F7 13 17N 109 16 E
Tuy Duc, Vietnam 77 F6 12 15N 107 27 E
Tuy Hoa, Vietnam 76 F7 13 5N 109 10 E
Tuy Phong, Vietnam 77 G7 11 14N 108 43 E
Tuya L., Canada 130 B2 59 7N 130 35W
Tuyen Hoa, Vietnam 76 D6 17 50N 106 10 E
Tuyen Quang, Vietnam 76 B5 21 50N 105 10 E
Tuymazy, Russia 54 D3 54 36N 53 42 E
Tūysarkān, Iran 85 C6 34 33N 48 27 E
Tuz Gölü, Turkey 88 D5 38 45N 33 30 E
Ṭūz Khurmātū, Iraq 84 C5 34 56N 44 38 E
Tuzkan, Ozero, Uzbekistan 55 C3 40 35N 67 28 E
Tuzla, Bos.-H. 42 C3 44 34N 18 41 E
Tuzla Gölü, Turkey 88 D6 39 1N 35 49 E
Tuzlov →, Russia 53 C8 47 10N 39 10 E
Tvååker, Sweden 15 G6 57 4N 12 25 E
Tvedestrand, Norway 15 F2 58 38N 8 58 E
Tver, Russia 51 C9 56 55N 35 55 E
Tvŭrditsa, Bulgaria 43 E10 42 42N 25 53 E
Twain, U.S.A. 144 E5 40 1N 121 3W
Twain Harte, U.S.A. 144 G6 38 2N 120 14W
Twardogóra, Poland 47 D4 51 23N 17 28 E
Tweed, Canada 136 B7 44 29N 77 19W
Tweed →, U.K. 18 F7 55 42N 1 59W
Tweed Heads, Australia 115 D5 28 10 S 153 31 E
Tweedsmuir Prov. Park, Canada 130 C3 53 0N 126 20W
Twello, Neths. 20 D8 52 14N 6 6 E
Twentynine Palms, U.S.A. 145 L10 34 8N 116 3W
Twillingate, Canada 129 C9 49 42N 54 45W
Twin Bridges, U.S.A. 142 D7 45 33N 112 20W
Twin Falls, U.S.A. 142 E6 42 34N 114 28W
Twin Valley, U.S.A. 138 B6 47 16N 96 16W
Twinnge, Burma 78 D6 23 0N 96 0 E
Twisp, U.S.A. 142 B3 48 22N 120 7W
Twistringen, Germany 26 C4 52 48N 8 38 E
Two Harbors, U.S.A. 138 B9 47 2N 91 40W
Two Hills, Canada 130 C6 53 43N 111 52W
Two Rivers, U.S.A. 134 C2 44 9N 87 34W
Two Thumbs Ra., N.Z. 119 D5 43 45 S 170 44 E
Twofold B., Australia 117 D8 37 8 S 149 59 E
Tychy, Poland 31 A11 50 9N 18 59 E
Tyczyn, Poland 31 B15 49 58N 22 2 E
Tykocin, Poland 47 B9 53 13N 22 46 E
Tyldal, Norway 14 B4 62 8N 10 48 E
Tyler, U.S.A. 133 D7 32 18N 95 17W
Tyler, Minn., U.S.A. 138 C6 44 18N 96 8W
Tyler, Tex., U.S.A. 139 J7 32 21N 95 18W
Týn nad Vltavou, Czech. 30 B7 49 13N 14 26 E
Tynda, Russia 57 D13 55 10N 124 43 E
Tyne →, U.K. 16 C6 54 58N 1 28W
Tyne & Wear □, U.K. 16 C6 54 55N 1 35W
Tynemouth, U.K. 16 B6 55 1N 1 27W
Tynset, Norway 14 B4 62 17N 10 47 E
Tyre = Sūr, Lebanon 91 B4 33 19N 35 16 E
Tyrifjorden, Norway 14 D4 60 2N 10 8 E
Tyringe, Sweden 15 H7 56 9N 13 35 E
Tyristrand, Norway 14 D4 60 5N 10 5 E
Tyrnyauz, Russia 53 E10 43 21N 42 45 E
Tyrol = Tirol □, Austria 30 D3 47 3N 10 43 E
Tyrone, U.S.A. 136 F6 40 40N 78 14W
Tyrrell →, Australia 116 C5 35 26 S 142 51 E
Tyrrell, L., Australia 116 C5 35 20 S 142 50 E
Tyrrell Arm, Canada 131 A9 62 27N 97 30W
Tyrrell L., Canada 131 A7 63 7N 105 27W
Tyrrhenian Sea, Europe 40 B5 40 0N 12 30 E
Tysfjorden, Norway 12 B14 68 7N 16 25 E
Tystberga, Sweden 15 F11 58 51N 17 15 E
Tyub Karagan, Mys, Kazakhstan 53 D14 44 40N 50 19 E
Tyuleniy, Russia 53 D12 44 28N 47 30 E
Tyulgan, Russia 54 E5 52 22N 56 12 E
Tyumen, Russia 54 C9 57 11N 65 29 E
Tyumen-Aryk, Kazakhstan 55 A3 44 2N 67 1 E
Tyup, Kirghizia 55 B9 42 45N 78 20 E
Tywi →, U.K. 17 F3 51 48N 4 20W
Tywyn, U.K. 17 E3 52 36N 4 5W
Tzaneen, S. Africa 105 C5 23 47 S 30 9 E
Tzermiádhes, Greece 32 D7 35 12N 25 29 E
Tzermiádhes Neápolis, Greece 45 J7 35 11N 25 29 E
Tzoumérka, Óros, Greece 44 E3 39 30N 21 26 E
Tzukong = Zigong, China 68 C5 29 15N 104 48 E
Tzummarum, Neths. 20 B7 53 14N 5 32 E

U

U Taphao, Thailand 76 F3 12 35N 101 0 E
U.S.A. = United States of America ■, N. Amer. 132 C7 37 0N 96 0W
Uacalla Iero, Somali Rep. 108 D2 1 48N 42 38 E
Uachadi, Sierra, Venezuela 153 C4 4 54N 65 18W
Uainambi, Colombia 152 C4 1 43N 69 51W
Uanda, Australia 114 C3 21 37 S 144 55 E
Uanle Uen, Somali Rep. 108 D2 2 37N 44 54 E
Uarsciek, Somali Rep. 90 G4 2 28N 45 55 E
Uascen, Somali Rep. 108 D2 4 11N 43 13 E
Uasin □, Kenya 106 B4 0 30N 35 20 E
Uato-Udo, Indonesia 72 C3 4 3 S 126 6 E
Uatumã →, Brazil 153 D6 2 26 S 57 37W
Uauá, Brazil 154 C4 9 50 S 39 28W
Uaupés, Brazil 152 D4 0 8 S 67 5W
Uaupés →, Brazil 152 C4 0 2N 67 16W
Uaxactún, Guatemala 148 C2 17 25N 89 29W
Ub, Serbia 42 C5 44 28N 20 6 E
Ubá, Brazil 155 F3 21 8 S 43 0W
Ubaitaba, Brazil 155 D4 14 18 S 39 20W
Ubangi = Oubangi →, Zaïre 102 C3 0 30 S 17 50 E
Ubaté, Colombia 152 B3 5 19N 73 49W
Ubauro, Pakistan 80 E3 28 15N 69 45 E
Ubay, Phil. 71 F5 10 3N 124 28 E
'Ubaydīyah, Yemen 86 D3 13 7N 43 20 E
Ubaye →, France 25 D10 44 28N 6 18 E
Ube, Japan 62 D3 33 56N 131 15 E
Ubeda, Spain 35 G1 38 3N 3 23W
Uberaba, Brazil 155 E2 19 50 S 47 55W
Uberaba, L., Brazil 157 D6 17 30 S 57 50W
Uberlândia, Brazil 155 E2 19 0 S 48 20W
Überlingen, Germany 27 H5 47 46N 9 10 E
Ubiaja, Nigeria 101 D6 6 41N 6 22 E
Ubolratna Res., Thailand 76 D4 16 45N 102 30 E
Ubombo, S. Africa 105 D5 27 31 S 32 4 E
Ubon Ratchathani, Thailand 76 E5 15 15N 104 50 E
Ubondo, Zaïre 106 C2 0 55 S 25 42 E
Ubort →, Belorussia 50 E6 52 6N 28 30 E
Ubrique, Spain 37 J5 36 41N 5 27W
Ubundu, Zaïre 102 C5 0 22 S 25 30 E
Ucayali →, Peru 156 A3 4 30 S 73 30W
Uccle, Belgium 21 G4 50 48N 4 22 E
Uchaly, Russia 54 D6 54 19N 59 27 E
Uchi Lake, Canada 131 C10 51 5N 92 35W
Uchiko, Japan 62 D4 33 33N 132 39 E
Uchiura-Wan, Japan 60 C10 42 25N 140 40 E
Uchiza, Peru 156 B2 8 25 S 76 20W
Uchte, Germany 26 C4 52 29N 8 52 E
Uchur →, Russia 57 D14 58 48N 130 35 E
Ucluelet, Canada 130 D3 48 57N 125 32W
Ucuriş, Romania 46 C2 46 41N 21 58 E
Uda →, Russia 57 D14 54 42N 135 14 E
Udaipur, India 80 G5 24 36N 73 44 E
Udaipur Garhi, Nepal 81 F12 27 0N 86 35 E
Udbina, Croatia 39 D12 44 31N 15 47 E
Uddel, Neths. 20 D7 52 15N 5 48 E
Uddevalla, Sweden 15 F5 58 21N 11 55 E
Uddjaur, Sweden 12 D16 65 25N 21 15 E
Uden, Neths. 21 E7 51 40N 5 37 E
Udgir, India 82 E3 18 25N 77 5 E
Udhampur, India 81 C6 33 0N 75 5 E
Udi, Nigeria 101 D6 6 17N 7 21 E
Údine, Italy 39 B10 46 5N 13 10 E
Udmurt Republic □, Russia 54 C3 57 30N 52 30 E
Udon Thani, Thailand 76 D4 17 29N 102 46 E
Udumalaippettai, India 83 J3 10 35N 77 15 E
Udupi, India 83 H2 13 25N 74 42 E
Udvoy Balkan, Bulgaria 43 E11 42 50N 26 50 E
Udzungwa Range, Tanzania 107 D4 9 30 S 35 10 E
Ueckermünde, Germany 26 B10 53 45N 14 1 E
Ueda, Japan 63 A10 36 24N 138 16 E
Uedineniya, Os., Russia 6 B12 78 0N 85 0 E
Uel Scimbirro, Somali Rep. 108 D2 2 23N 44 14 E
Uele →, Zaïre 102 B4 3 45N 24 45 E
Uelen, Russia 57 C19 66 10N 170 0W
Uelzen, Germany 26 C6 53 0N 10 33 E
Ueno, Japan 63 C8 34 45N 136 8 E
Uetendorf, Switz. 28 C5 46 47N 7 34 E
Ufa, Russia 54 D4 54 45N 55 55 E
Ufa →, Russia 54 D5 54 40N 56 0 E
Uffenheim, Germany 27 F6 49 32N 10 15 E

Veliki Popović 279

Uudenmaan lääni □, Finland 13 F18 60 25N 25 0 E
Uusikaarlepyy, Finland 12 E17 63 32N 22 31 E
Uusikaupunki, Finland 13 F16 60 47N 21 25 E
Uva, Russia 54 C3 56 59N 52 13 E
Uvá →, Colombia 152 C3 3 41N 70 3W
Uvac →, Serbia 42 D4 43 35N 19 30 E
Uvalde, U.S.A. 139 L5 29 13N 99 47W
Uvarovo, Russia 51 F13 51 59N 42 14 E
Uvat, Russia 56 D7 59 5N 68 50 E
Uvéa, I., Vanuatu 111 E12 20 30 S 166 35 E
Uvelskiy, Russia 54 D7 54 26N 61 22 E
Uvinza, Tanzania 106 D3 5 5 S 30 24 E
Uvira, Zaïre 106 C2 3 22 S 29 3 E
Uvs Nuur, Mongolia 64 A4 50 20N 92 30 E
Uwa, Japan 62 D4 33 22N 132 31 E
Uwajima, Japan 62 D4 33 10N 132 35 E
'Uwayfī, Oman 87 B7 22 15N 56 59 E
Uweinat, Jebel, Sudan 94 C1 21 54N 24 58 E
Uxbridge, Canada 136 B5 44 6N 79 7W
Uxin Qi, China 66 E5 38 50N 109 5 E
Uxmal, Mexico 147 C7 20 22N 89 46W
Uyandi, Russia 57 C15 69 19N 141 0 E
Uyo, Nigeria 101 D6 5 1N 7 53 E
Uyu →, Burma 78 C5 24 51N 94 57 E
Uyuk, Kazakhstan 55 B5 43 36N 71 16 E
Uyuni, Bolivia 156 E4 20 28 S 66 47W
Uzbekistan ■, Asia 55 C2 41 30N 65 0 E
Uzen, Kazakhstan 49 F9 43 27N 53 10 E
Uzen, Bol. →, Kazakhstan 51 G16 49 0N 49 30 E
Uzen, Mal. →, Kazakhstan 51 G16 50 0N 48 30 E
Uzerche, France 24 C5 45 25N 1 34 E
Uzès, France 25 D8 44 1N 4 26 E
Uzgen, Kirghizia 55 C6 40 46N 73 18 E
Uzh →, Ukraine 50 F7 51 15N 30 12 E
Uzhgorod, Ukraine 50 G3 48 36N 22 18 E
Uzlovaya, Russia 51 E11 54 0N 38 5 E
Uzun-Agach, Kazakhstan 55 B8 43 35N 76 20 E
Uzunköprü, Turkey 43 F11 41 16N 26 43 E
Uzwil, Switz. 29 B8 47 26N 9 9 E

V

Vaal →, S. Africa 104 D3 29 4 S 23 38 E
Vaal Dam, S. Africa 105 D4 27 0 S 28 14 E
Vaals, Neths. 21 G8 50 46N 6 1 E
Vaalwater, S. Africa 105 C4 24 15 S 28 8 E
Vaasa, Finland 12 E16 63 6N 21 38 E
Vaasan lääni □, Finland 12 E17 63 2N 22 50 E
Vaassen, Neths. 20 D7 52 17N 5 58 E
Vabre, France 24 E6 43 42N 2 24 E
Vác, Hungary 31 D12 47 49N 19 10 E
Vacaria, Brazil 159 B5 28 31 S 50 52W
Vacaville, U.S.A. 144 G5 38 21N 121 59W
Vaccarès, Étang de, France 25 E8 43 32N 4 34 E
Vach →, Russia 56 C8 60 45N 76 45 E
Vache, I.-à-, Haiti 149 C5 18 2N 73 35W
Vadnagar, India 80 H5 23 47N 72 40 E
Vado Lígure, Italy 38 D5 44 16N 8 26 E
Vadodara, India 80 H5 22 20N 73 10 E
Vadsø, Norway 12 A20 70 3N 29 50 E
Vadstena, Sweden 15 F8 58 28N 14 54 E
Vaduz, Liech. 29 B9 47 8N 9 31 E
Værøy, Norway 12 C12 67 40N 12 40 E
Vagnhärad, Sweden 14 F11 58 57N 17 33 E
Vagos, Portugal 36 E2 40 33N 8 42W
Váh →, Slovak Rep. 31 D11 47 43N 18 7 E
Vahsel B., Antarctica 7 D1 75 0 S 35 0W
Vaï, Greece 32 D8 35 15N 26 18 E
Vaigach, Russia 56 B6 70 10N 59 0 E
Vaigai →, India 83 K4 9 15N 79 10 E
Vaiges, France 22 D6 48 2N 0 30W
Vaihingen, Germany 27 G4 48 55N 8 58 E
Vaijapur, India 82 E2 19 58N 74 45 E
Vaikam, India 83 K3 9 45N 76 25 E
Vailly-sur-Aisne, France 23 C10 49 24N 3 31 E
Vaippar →, India 83 K4 9 0N 78 25 E
Vaison-la-Romaine, France 25 D9 44 14N 5 4 E
Vajpur, India 82 D1 21 24N 73 17 E
Vakarel, Bulgaria 43 E8 42 35N 23 40 E
Vakfikebir, Turkey 89 C8 41 2N 39 17 E
Vakhsh →, Tajikistan 55 E4 37 6N 68 18 E
Vál, Hungary 31 D11 47 22N 18 40 E
Val-de-Marne □, France 23 D9 48 45N 2 28 E
Val-d'Oise □, France 23 C9 49 5N 2 10 E
Val d'Or, Canada 128 C4 48 7N 77 47W
Val Marie, Canada 131 D7 49 15N 107 45W
Valadares, Portugal 36 D2 41 5N 8 38W
Valahia, Romania 46 E5 44 35N 25 0 E
Valais □, Switz. 28 D5 46 12N 7 45 E
Valais, Alpes du, Switz. 28 D5 46 5N 7 35 E
Valandovo, Macedonia 42 F7 41 19N 22 34 E
Valašské Meziříčí, Czech. 31 B10 49 29N 17 59 E
Valáxa, Greece 45 F6 38 50N 24 29 E
Vălcani, Romania 42 A5 46 0N 20 26 E
Valcheta, Argentina 160 B3 40 40 S 66 8W
Valdagno, Italy 39 C8 45 38N 11 18 E
Valday, Russia 50 C8 57 58N 33 9 E
Valdayskaya Vozvyshennost, Russia 50 C8 57 0N 33 30 E
Valdeazogues →, Spain 37 G6 38 45N 4 55W
Valdemarsvik, Sweden 15 F10 58 14N 16 40 E
Valdepeñas, Ciudad Real, Spain 37 G7 38 43N 3 25W
Valdepeñas, Jaén, Spain 37 H7 37 33N 3 47W
Valderaduey →, Spain 36 D5 41 31N 5 42W
Valderrobres, Spain 34 E5 40 53N 0 9 E
Valdés, Pen., Argentina 160 B4 42 30 S 63 45W
Valdez, Ecuador 152 C2 1 15N 79 0W
Valdez, U.S.A. 126 B5 61 7N 146 16W
Valdivia, Chile 160 A2 39 50 S 73 14W
Valdivia, Colombia 152 B2 7 11N 75 27W
Valdivia □, Chile 160 B2 40 0 S 73 0W
Valdobbiádene, Italy 39 C9 45 53N 12 0 E
Valdosta, U.S.A. 135 K4 30 50N 83 17W
Valdoviño, Spain 36 B2 43 36N 8 8W
Valdres, Norway 14 D3 60 55N 9 28 E
Vale, Georgia 53 F10 41 30N 42 58 E
Vale, U.S.A. 142 E5 43 59N 117 15W
Valea lui Mihai, Romania 46 B3 47 32N 22 11 E
Valença, Brazil 155 D4 13 20 S 39 5W
Valença, Portugal 36 C2 42 1N 8 34W
Valença do Piauí, Brazil 154 C3 6 20 S 41 45W
Valençay, France 23 E8 47 9N 1 34 E
Valence, Drôme, France 25 D8 44 57N 4 54 E
Valence, Tarn-et-Garonne, France 24 D4 44 6N 0 53 E
Valencia, Phil. 71 H5 7 57N 125 3 E
Valencia, Spain 35 F4 39 27N 0 23W
Valencia, Venezuela 152 A4 10 11N 68 0W
Valencia □, Spain 35 F4 39 20N 0 40W
Valencia, Albufera de, Spain 35 F4 39 20N 0 27W
Valencia, G. de, Spain 35 F5 39 30N 0 20 E
Valencia de Alcántara, Spain 37 F3 39 25N 7 14W
Valencia de Don Juan, Spain 36 C5 42 17N 5 31W
Valencia del Ventoso, Spain 37 G4 38 15N 6 29W
Valenciennes, France 23 B10 50 20N 3 34 E
Văleni, Romania 46 E5 44 15N 24 45 E
Valensole, France 25 E9 43 50N 5 59 E
Valentia Harbour, Ireland 19 E1 51 56N 10 17W
Valentia I., Ireland 19 E1 51 54N 10 22W
Valentim, Sa. do, Brazil 154 C3 6 0 S 43 30W
Valentin, Russia 60 C7 43 8N 134 17 E
Valentine, Nebr., U.S.A. 138 D4 42 52N 100 33W
Valentine, Tex., U.S.A. 139 K2 30 35N 104 30W
Valenza, Italy 38 C5 45 2N 8 39 E
Valera, Venezuela 152 B3 9 19N 70 37W
Valguarnera Caropepe, Italy 41 E7 37 30N 14 22 E
Valier, U.S.A. 142 B7 48 18N 112 16W
Valinco, G. de, France 25 G12 41 40N 8 52 E
Valjevo, Serbia 42 C4 44 18N 19 53 E
Valka, Estonia 50 C5 57 44N 26 5 E
Valkeakoski, Finland 13 F18 61 16N 24 2 E
Valkenburg, Neths. 21 G7 50 52N 5 50 E
Valkenswaard, Neths. 21 F6 51 21N 5 29 E
Vall de Uxó, Spain 34 F4 39 49N 0 15W
Valla, Sweden 14 E10 59 2N 16 20 E
Valladolid, Mexico 147 C7 20 40N 88 11W
Valladolid, Spain 36 D6 41 38N 4 43W
Valladolid □, Spain 36 D6 41 38N 4 43W
Vallata, Italy 41 A8 41 3N 15 16 E
Valldemosa, Spain 33 B9 39 43N 2 37 E
Valle d'Aosta □, Italy 38 C4 45 45N 7 22 E
Valle de Arán, Spain 34 C5 42 50N 0 55 E
Valle de Cabuérniga, Spain 36 B6 43 14N 4 18W
Valle de la Pascua, Venezuela 152 B4 9 13N 66 0W
Valle de las Palmas, Mexico 145 N10 32 20N 116 43W
Valle de Santiago, Mexico 146 C4 20 25N 101 15W
Valle de Suchil, Mexico 146 C4 23 38N 103 55W
Valle de Zaragoza, Mexico 146 B3 27 28N 105 49W
Valle del Cauca □, Colombia 152 C2 3 45N 76 30W
Valle Fértil, Sierra del, Argentina 158 C2 30 20 S 68 0W
Valle Hermoso, Mexico 147 B5 25 35N 97 40W
Vallecas, Spain 36 E7 40 23N 3 41W
Valledupar, Colombia 152 A3 10 29N 73 15W
Vallehermoso, Canary Is. 33 F2 28 10N 17 15W
Vallejo, U.S.A. 144 G4 38 7N 122 14W
Vallenar, Chile 158 B1 28 30 S 70 50W
Valleraugue, France 24 D7 44 6N 3 39 E
Vallet, France 22 E5 47 10N 1 15W
Valletta, Malta 32 D2 35 54N 14 31 E
Valley Center, U.S.A. 145 M9 33 13N 117 2W
Valley City, U.S.A. 138 B6 46 55N 98 0W
Valley Falls, U.S.A. 142 E3 42 29N 120 17W
Valley Park, U.S.A. 140 F6 38 33N 90 29W
Valley Springs, U.S.A. 144 G6 38 12N 120 50W
Valley Station, U.S.A. 141 F11 38 6N 85 52W
Valley Wells, U.S.A. 145 K11 35 27N 115 46W
Valleyview, Canada 130 B5 55 5N 117 17W
Valli di Comácchio, Italy 39 D9 44 40N 12 15 E
Vallimanca, Arroyo, Argentina 158 D4 35 40 S 59 10W
Vallo della Lucánia, Italy 41 B8 40 14N 15 16 E
Vallon-Pont-d'Arc, France 25 D8 44 24N 4 24 E
Vallorbe, Switz. 28 C2 46 42N 6 20 E
Valls, Spain 34 D6 41 18N 1 15 E
Vallsta, Sweden 14 C10 61 31N 16 22 E
Valmaseda, Spain 34 B1 43 11N 3 12W
Valmeyer, U.S.A. 140 F6 38 18N 90 19W
Valmiera, Latvia 50 C4 57 37N 25 29 E
Valmont, France 22 C7 49 45N 0 30 E
Valmontone, Italy 40 A5 41 48N 12 55 E
Valmy, France 23 C11 49 5N 4 45 E
Valnera, Mte., Spain 34 B1 43 9N 3 40W
Valognes, France 22 C5 49 30N 1 28W
Valona = Vlóra, Albania 44 D1 40 32N 19 28 E
Valongo, Portugal 36 D2 41 8N 8 30W
Valpaços, Portugal 36 D3 41 36N 7 17W
Valparaíso, Chile 158 C1 33 2 S 71 40W
Valparaíso, Mexico 146 C4 22 50N 103 32W
Valparaiso, U.S.A. 141 C9 41 28N 87 4W
Valparaíso □, Chile 158 C1 33 2 S 71 40W
Valpovo, Croatia 42 B3 45 39N 18 25 E
Valréas, France 25 D8 44 24N 5 0 E
Vals, Switz. 29 C8 46 39N 9 11 E
Vals →, S. Africa 104 D4 27 23 S 26 30 E
Vals, Tanjung, Indonesia 73 C5 8 26 S 137 25 E
Vals-les-Bains, France 25 D8 44 42N 4 24 E
Valsad, India 82 D1 20 40N 72 58 E
Valskog, Sweden 14 E9 59 27N 15 57 E
Válta, Greece 44 D5 40 3N 23 25 E
Valtellina, Italy 38 B6 46 9N 9 55 E
Valuyki, Russia 51 F11 50 10N 38 5 E
Valverde, Canary Is. 33 G2 27 48N 17 55W
Valverde del Camino, Spain 37 H4 37 35N 6 47W
Valverde del Fresno, Spain 36 E4 40 15N 6 51W
Vama, Romania 46 B6 47 34N 25 42 E
Vámos, Greece 32 D6 35 24N 24 13 E
Vamsadhara →, India 82 E7 18 21N 84 8 E
Van, Turkey 89 D10 38 30N 43 20 E
Van □, Turkey 89 D10 38 30N 43 20 E
Van, L. = Van Gölü, Turkey 89 D10 38 30N 43 0 E
Van Alstyne, U.S.A. 139 J6 33 25N 96 35W
Van Bruyssel, Canada 129 C5 47 56N 72 9W
Van Buren, Canada 129 C6 47 10N 67 55W
Van Buren, Ark., U.S.A. 139 H7 35 26N 94 21W
Van Buren, Maine, U.S.A. 135 B11 47 10N 67 58W
Van Buren, Mo., U.S.A. 139 G9 37 0N 91 1W
Van Canh, Vietnam 76 F7 13 37N 109 0 E
Van Diemen, C., N. Terr., Australia 112 B5 11 9 S 130 24 E
Van Diemen, C., Queens., Australia 114 B2 16 30 S 139 46 E
Van Diemen G., Australia 112 B5 11 45 S 132 0 E
Van Gölü, Turkey 89 D10 38 30N 43 0 E
Van Horn, U.S.A. 139 K2 31 3N 104 50W
Van Horne, U.S.A. 140 B4 42 1N 92 4W
Van Ninh, Vietnam 76 F7 12 42N 109 14 E
Van Reenen P., S. Africa 105 D4 28 22 S 29 27 E
Van Rees, Pegunungan, Indonesia 73 B5 2 35 S 138 15 E
Van Tassell, U.S.A. 138 D2 42 40N 104 5W
Van Tivu, India 83 K4 8 51N 78 15 E
Van Wert, U.S.A. 141 D12 40 52N 84 35W
Van Yen, Vietnam 76 B5 21 4N 104 42 E
Vanavara, Russia 57 C11 60 22N 102 16 E
Vanceburg, U.S.A. 141 F13 38 36N 83 19W
Vancouver, Canada 130 D4 49 15N 123 10W
Vancouver, U.S.A. 144 E4 45 38N 122 40W
Vancouver, C., Australia 113 G2 35 2 S 118 11 E
Vancouver I., Canada 130 D3 49 50N 126 0W
Vandalia, Ill., U.S.A. 140 F7 38 58N 89 6W
Vandalia, Mo., U.S.A. 140 E5 39 19N 91 29W
Vandalia, Ohio, U.S.A. 141 E12 39 54N 84 12W
Vandavasi, India 83 H4 12 30N 79 30 E
Vandeloos B., Sri Lanka 83 K5 8 0N 81 45 E
Vandenburg, U.S.A. 145 L6 34 35N 120 33W
Vanderbijlpark, S. Africa 105 D4 26 42 S 27 54 E
Vandergrift, U.S.A. 136 F5 40 36N 79 34W
Vanderhoof, Canada 130 C4 54 0N 124 0W
Vanderlin I., Australia 114 B2 15 44 S 137 2 E
Vandyke, Australia 114 C4 24 10 S 147 51 E
Vänern, Sweden 15 F7 58 47N 13 30 E
Vänersborg, Sweden 15 F6 58 26N 12 19 E
Vang Vieng, Laos 76 C4 18 58N 102 32 E
Vanga, Kenya 106 C4 4 35 S 39 12 E
Vangaindrano, Madag. 105 C8 23 21 S 47 36 E
Vanguard, Canada 131 D7 49 55N 107 20W
Vangunu, Solomon Is. 121 M10 8 40 S 158 5 E
Vanier, Canada 128 C4 45 27N 75 40W
Vanimo, Papua N. G. 120 B1 2 42 S 141 21 E
Vanivilasa Sagara, India 83 H3 13 45N 76 30 E
Vaniyambadi, India 83 H4 12 46N 78 44 E
Vankarem, Russia 57 C18 67 51N 175 50W
Vankleek Hill, Canada 128 C5 45 32N 74 40W
Vanna, Norway 12 A15 70 6N 19 50 E
Vännäs, Sweden 12 E15 63 58N 19 48 E
Vannes, France 22 E4 47 40N 2 47W
Vanoise, Massif de la, France 25 C10 45 25N 6 40 E
Vanrhynsdorp, S. Africa 104 E2 31 36 S 18 44 E
Vanrook, Australia 114 B3 16 57 S 141 57 E
Vansbro, Sweden 13 F13 60 32N 14 15 E
Vansittart B., Australia 112 B4 14 3 S 126 17 E
Vanthli, India 80 J4 21 28N 70 25 E
Vanua Levu, Fiji 121 A2 16 33 S 179 15 E
Vanuatu ■, Pac. Oc. 121 E6 15 0 S 168 0 E
Vanwyksvlei, S. Africa 104 E3 30 18 S 21 49 E
Vanzylsrus, S. Africa 104 D3 26 52 S 22 4 E
Vapnyarka, Ukraine 52 B3 48 32N 28 45 E
Var □, France 25 E10 43 27N 6 18 E
Var →, France 25 E11 43 39N 7 12 E
Vara, Sweden 15 F6 58 16N 12 55 E
Varada →, India 83 G2 15 0N 75 40 E
Varades, France 22 E5 47 25N 1 1W
Varaita →, Italy 38 D4 44 49N 7 36 E
Varallo, Italy 38 C5 45 50N 8 13 E
Varanasi, India 81 G10 25 22N 83 0 E
Varangerfjorden, Norway 12 A20 70 3N 29 25 E
Varaždin, Croatia 39 B13 46 20N 16 20 E
Varazze, Italy 38 D5 44 21N 8 36 E
Varberg, Sweden 15 G6 57 6N 12 20 E
Vardar = Axiós →, Greece 44 D4 40 57N 22 35 E
Vardar →, Macedonia 42 F7 41 15N 22 33 E
Varde, Denmark 15 J2 55 38N 8 29 E
Varde Å →, Denmark 15 J2 55 35N 8 19 E
Varel, Germany 26 B4 53 23N 8 9 E
Varella, Mui, Vietnam 76 F7 12 54N 109 26 E
Varena, Lithuania 50 D4 54 12N 24 30 E
Varennes-sur-Allier, France 24 B7 46 19N 3 24 E
Vareš, Bos.-H. 42 C3 44 12N 18 23 E
Varese, Italy 38 C5 45 49N 8 50 E
Varese Lígure, Italy 38 D6 44 22N 9 33 E
Vårgårda, Sweden 15 F6 58 2N 12 49 E
Vargem Bonita, Brazil 155 F2 20 20 S 46 22W
Vargem Grande, Brazil 154 B3 3 33 S 43 56W
Varginha, Brazil 159 A6 21 33 S 45 25W
Vargön, Sweden 15 F6 58 22N 12 20 E
Variadero, U.S.A. 139 H2 35 43N 104 17W
Varillas, Chile 158 A1 24 0 S 70 10W
Väring, Sweden 15 F8 58 30N 14 0 E
Värmlands län □, Sweden 13 G12 60 0N 13 20 E
Varna, Bulgaria 43 D12 43 13N 27 56 E
Varna, Russia 54 E7 53 24N 60 58 E
Varna, U.S.A. 140 C7 41 2N 89 14W
Varna →, India 82 F2 16 48N 74 32 E
Värnamo, Sweden 13 H13 57 10N 14 3 E
Varnsdorf, Czech. 30 A7 50 55N 14 35 E
Värö, Sweden 15 G6 57 16N 12 11 E
Vars, Canada 137 A9 45 21N 75 21W
Varsseveld, Neths. 20 E8 51 56N 6 29 E
Varto, Turkey 89 D9 39 10N 41 27 E
Varvarin, Serbia 42 D6 43 43N 21 20 E
Varzaneh, Iran 85 C7 32 25N 52 40 E
Várzea Alegre, Brazil 154 C4 6 47 S 39 17W
Várzea da Palma, Brazil 155 E3 17 36 S 44 44W
Várzea Grande, Brazil 157 D6 15 39 S 56 8W
Varzi, Italy 38 D6 44 50N 9 12 E
Varzo, Italy 38 B5 46 12N 8 15 E
Varzy, France 23 E10 47 22N 3 20 E
Vas □, Hungary 31 D9 47 10N 16 55 E
Vasa, Finland 12 E16 63 6N 21 38 E
Vasa Barris →, Brazil 154 D4 11 10 S 37 10W
Vásárosnamény, Hungary 31 C15 48 9N 22 19 E
Vascão →, Portugal 37 H3 37 31N 7 31W
Vaşcău, Romania 46 C3 46 28N 22 30 E
Vascongadas = País Vasco □, Spain 34 C2 42 50N 2 45W
Vāshīr, Afghan. 79 B1 32 16N 63 51 E
Vasht = Khāsh, Iran 85 D9 28 15N 61 15 E
Vasilevichi, Belorussia 50 E6 52 15N 29 50 E
Vasilikón, Greece 45 F5 38 25N 23 40 E
Vasilkov, Ukraine 50 F7 50 7N 30 15 E
Vaslui, Romania 46 C8 46 38N 27 42 E
Vaslui □, Romania 46 C8 46 30N 27 45 E
Vassar, Canada 131 D9 49 10N 95 55W
Vassar, U.S.A. 134 D4 43 22N 83 35W
Västerås, Sweden 14 E10 59 37N 16 38 E
Västerbottens län □, Sweden 12 D14 64 58N 18 0 E
Västernorrlands län □, Sweden 14 A11 63 30N 17 30 E
Västervik, Sweden 13 H14 57 43N 16 43 E
Västmanlands län □, Sweden 13 G14 59 45N 16 20 E
Vasto, Italy 39 F11 42 8N 14 40 E
Vasvár, Hungary 31 D9 47 3N 16 47 E
Vatan, France 23 E8 47 4N 1 50 E
Vaté = Efate, I., Vanuatu 121 G6 17 40 S 168 25 E
Vathí, Itháki, Greece 45 F2 38 18N 20 40 E
Vathí, Sámos, Greece 45 G9 37 46N 27 1 E
Váthia, Greece 45 H4 36 29N 22 29 E
Vatican City ■, Europe 39 G9 41 54N 12 27 E
Vaticano, C., Italy 41 D8 38 40N 15 48 E
Vatili, Cyprus 32 D12 35 6N 33 40 E
Vatin, Serbia 42 B6 45 12N 21 20 E
Vatnajökull, Iceland 12 D5 64 30N 16 48W
Vatnås, Norway 14 E3 59 58N 9 37 E
Vatneyri, Iceland 12 D2 65 35N 24 0W
Vatólakkos, Greece 32 D5 35 27N 23 53 E
Vatoloha, Madag. 105 B8 17 52 S 47 48 E
Vatomandry, Madag. 105 B8 19 20 S 48 59 E
Vatra-Dornei, Romania 46 B6 47 22N 25 22 E
Vättern, Sweden 15 F8 58 25N 14 30 E
Vättis, Switz. 29 C8 46 55N 9 27 E
Vatulele, Fiji 121 B1 18 33 S 177 37 E
Vaucluse □, France 25 E9 43 50N 5 20 E
Vaucouleurs, France 23 D12 48 37N 5 40 E
Vaud □, Switz. 28 C2 46 35N 6 30 E
Vaughn, Mont., U.S.A. 142 C8 47 33N 111 33W
Vaughn, N. Mex., U.S.A. 143 J11 34 36N 105 13W
Vaulruz, Switz. 28 C3 46 38N 6 58 E
Vaupés = Uaupés →, Brazil 152 C4 0 2N 67 16W
Vaupes □, Colombia 152 C3 1 0N 71 0W
Vauvert, France 25 E8 43 42N 4 17 E
Vauxhall, Canada 130 C6 50 5N 112 9W
Vava'u, Tonga 121 P14 18 36 S 174 0W
Vavoua, Ivory C. 100 D3 7 23N 6 29W
Vaxholm, Sweden 14 E12 59 25N 18 20 E
Växjö, Sweden 13 H13 56 52N 14 50 E
Vaygach, Ostrov, Russia 56 C6 70 0N 60 0 E
Váyia, Ákra, Greece 32 C10 36 15N 28 11 E
Vazovgrad, Bulgaria 43 E9 42 39N 24 45 E
Veadeiros, Brazil 155 D2 14 7 S 47 31W
Vechta, Germany 26 C4 52 47N 8 18 E
Vechte →, Neths. 20 C8 52 34N 6 6 E
Vecsés, Hungary 31 D12 47 26N 19 19 E
Vedaranniyam, India 83 J4 10 25N 79 50 E
Veddige, Sweden 15 G6 57 17N 12 20 E
Vedea →, Romania 46 F6 43 53N 25 59 E
Vedia, Argentina 158 C3 34 30 S 61 31W
Vedra, I. del, Spain 33 C7 38 52N 1 12 E
Vedrin, Belgium 21 G5 50 30N 4 52 E
Veendam, Neths. 20 B9 53 5N 6 52 E
Veenendaal, Neths. 20 D7 52 2N 5 34 E
Veerle, Belgium 21 F5 51 4N 4 59 E
Vefsna →, Norway 12 D12 65 48N 13 10 E
Vega, Norway 12 D11 65 40N 11 55 E
Vega, U.S.A. 139 H3 35 15N 102 26W
Vegadeo, Spain 36 B3 43 27N 7 4W
Vegafjorden, Norway 12 D12 65 37N 12 0 E
Veghel, Neths. 21 E7 51 37N 5 32 E
Vegorritis, Límni, Greece 44 D3 40 45N 21 45 E
Vegreville, Canada 130 C6 53 30N 112 5W
Vegusdal, Norway 15 F2 58 32N 8 10 E
Veii, Italy 39 F9 42 0N 12 24 E
Veitch, Australia 116 C4 34 39 S 140 31 E
Vejen, Denmark 15 J3 55 30N 9 9 E
Vejer de la Frontera, Spain 37 J5 36 15N 5 59W
Vejle, Denmark 15 J3 55 43N 9 30 E
Vejle Fjord, Denmark 15 J3 55 40N 9 50 E
Vela Luka, Croatia 39 F13 42 59N 16 44 E
Velanai I., Sri Lanka 83 K4 9 45N 79 45 E
Velas, C., Costa Rica 148 D2 10 21N 85 52W
Velasco, Sierra de, Argentina 158 B2 29 20 S 67 10W
Velay, Mts. du, France 24 D7 45 0N 3 40 E
Velddrif, S. Africa 104 E2 32 42 S 18 11 E
Veldegem, Belgium 21 F2 51 7N 3 10 E
Velden, Neths. 21 F8 51 25N 6 10 E
Veldhoven, Neths. 21 F6 51 24N 5 25 E
Velebit Planina, Croatia 39 D12 44 50N 15 20 E
Velebitski Kanal, Croatia 39 D11 44 45N 14 55 E
Veleka →, Bulgaria 43 E12 42 4N 27 58 E
Velenje, Slovenia 39 B12 46 23N 15 8 E
Velestínon, Greece 44 E4 39 23N 22 43 E
Velež, Bos.-H. 42 D3 43 19N 18 2 E
Vélez, Colombia 152 B3 6 1N 73 41W
Vélez Blanco, Spain 35 H2 37 41N 2 5W
Vélez Málaga, Spain 37 J6 36 48N 4 5W
Vélez Rubio, Spain 35 H2 37 41N 2 5W
Velhas →, Brazil 155 E3 17 13 S 44 49W
Velik Jastrebac, Serbia 42 D6 43 25N 21 30 E
Velika, Croatia 42 B2 45 27N 17 40 E
Velika Gorica, Croatia 39 C13 45 44N 16 5 E
Velika Gradište, Serbia 42 C6 44 46N 21 29 E
Velika Kapela, Croatia 39 C12 45 10N 15 5 E
Velika Kladuša, Bos.-H. 39 C12 45 11N 15 48 E
Velika Morava →, Serbia 42 C6 44 43N 21 3 E
Velika Plana, Serbia 42 C6 44 20N 21 1 E
Velikaya →, Russia 50 C6 57 48N 28 10 E
Velikaya Kema, Russia 60 B8 45 30N 137 12 E
Velikaya Lepetikha, Ukraine 52 C5 47 2N 33 58 E
Veliké Kapušany, Slovak Rep. 31 C15 48 34N 22 5 E
Velike Lašče, Slovenia 39 C11 45 49N 14 45 E
Veliki Backu Kanal, Serbia 42 B4 45 45N 19 15 E
Veliki Popović, Serbia 42 C6 44 8N 21 18 E

Vrakhnéïka 281

Villafranca, Spain 34 C3 42 17N 1 46W
Villafranca de los Barros, Spain 37 G4 38 35N 6 18W
Villafranca de los Caballeros, Spain 33 B10 39 34N 3 25 E
Villafranca de los Caballeros, Spain 35 F1 39 26N 3 21W
Villafranca del Bierzo, Spain 36 C4 42 38N 6 50W
Villafranca del Cid, Spain 34 E4 40 26N 0 16W
Villafranca del Panadés, Spain 34 D6 41 21N 1 40 E
Villafranca di Verona, Italy 38 C7 45 20N 10 51 E
Villagarcía de Arosa, Spain 36 C2 42 34N 8 46W
Villagrán, Mexico 147 C5 24 29N 99 29W
Villaguay, Argentina 158 C4 32 0 S 59 0W
Villaharta, Spain 37 G6 38 9N 4 54W
Villahermosa, Mexico 147 D6 18 0N 92 50W
Villahermosa, Spain 35 G2 38 46N 2 52W
Villaines-la-Juhel, France 22 D6 48 21N 0 20W
Villajoyosa, Spain 35 G4 38 30N 0 12W
Villalba, Spain 36 B3 43 26N 7 40W
Villalba de Guardo, Spain 36 C6 42 42N 4 49W
Villalcampo, Pantano de, Spain 36 D4 41 31N 6 0W
Villalón de Campos, Spain 36 C5 42 5N 5 4W
Villalpando, Spain 36 D5 41 51N 5 25W
Villaluenga, Spain 36 E7 40 2N 3 54W
Villamanán, Spain 36 C5 42 19N 5 35W
Villamartín, Spain 37 J5 36 52N 5 38W
Villamayor, Spain 34 F2 39 50N 2 59W
Villamblard, France 24 C4 45 2N 0 32 E
Villanova Monteleone, Italy 40 B1 40 30N 8 28 E
Villanueva, Colombia 152 A3 10 37N 72 59W
Villanueva, U.S.A. 143 J11 35 16N 105 22W
Villanueva de Castellón, Spain 35 F4 39 5N 0 31W
Villanueva de Córdoba, Spain 37 G6 38 20N 4 38W
Villanueva de la Fuente, Spain 35 G2 38 42N 2 42W
Villanueva de la Serena, Spain 37 G5 38 59N 5 50W
Villanueva de la Sierra, Spain 36 E4 40 12N 6 24W
Villanueva de los Castillejos, Spain 37 H3 37 30N 7 15W
Villanueva del Arzobispo, Spain 35 G1 38 10N 3 0W
Villanueva del Duque, Spain 37 G5 38 20N 5 0W
Villanueva del Fresno, Spain 37 G3 38 23N 7 10W
Villanueva y Geltrú, Spain 34 D6 41 13N 1 40 E
Villaodrid, Spain 36 B3 43 20N 7 11W
Villaputzu, Italy 40 C2 39 28N 9 33 E
Villar del Arzobispo, Spain 34 F4 39 44N 0 50W
Villar del Rey, Spain 37 F4 39 7N 6 50W
Villarcayo, Spain 34 C1 42 56N 3 34W
Villard-Bonnot, France 25 C9 45 14N 5 53 E
Villard-de-Lans, France 25 C9 45 3N 5 33 E
Villarino de los Aires, Spain 36 D4 41 18N 6 23W
Villarosa, Italy 41 E7 37 36N 14 9 E
Villarramiel, Spain 36 C6 42 2N 4 55W
Villarreal, Spain 34 F4 39 55N 0 3W
Villarrica, Chile 160 A2 39 15 S 72 15W
Villarrica, Paraguay 158 B4 25 40 S 56 30W
Villarrobledo, Spain 35 F2 39 18N 2 36W
Villarroya de la Sierra, Spain 34 D3 41 27N 1 46W
Villarrubia de los Ojos, Spain 35 F1 39 14N 3 36W
Villars-les-Dombes, France 25 B9 46 0N 5 3 E
Villarta de San Juan, Spain 35 F1 39 15N 3 25W
Villasayas, Spain 34 D2 41 24N 2 39W
Villaseca de los Gamitos, Spain 36 D4 41 2N 6 7W
Villastar, Spain 34 E3 40 17N 1 9W
Villatobas, Spain 34 F1 39 54N 3 20W
Villavicencio, Argentina 158 C2 32 28 S 69 0W
Villavicencio, Colombia 152 C3 4 9N 73 37W
Villaviciosa, Spain 36 B5 43 32N 5 27W
Villazón, Bolivia 158 A2 22 0 S 65 35W
Ville-Marie, Canada 128 C4 47 20N 79 30W
Ville Platte, U.S.A. 139 K8 30 41N 92 17W
Villedieu-les-Poêlles, France 22 D5 48 50N 1 13W
Villefort, France 24 D7 44 28N 3 56 E
Villefranche-de-Lauragais, France 24 E5 43 25N 1 44 E
Villefranche-de-Rouergue, France 24 D6 44 21N 2 2 E
Villefranche-du-Périgord, France 24 D5 44 38N 1 5 E
Villefranche-sur-Cher, France 23 E8 47 18N 1 46 E
Villefranche-sur-Saône, France 25 C8 45 59N 4 43 E
Villegrande, Bolivia 157 D5 18 30 S 64 10W
Villel, Spain 34 E3 40 14N 1 12W
Villemaur-sur-Vanne, France 23 D10 48 15N 3 44 E
Villemur-sur-Tarn, France 24 E5 43 51N 1 31 E
Villena, Spain 35 G4 38 39N 0 52W
Villenauxe-la-Grande, France 23 D10 48 35N 3 33 E
Villenave-d'Ornon, France 24 D3 44 46N 0 33W
Villeneuve, Italy 38 C4 45 40N 7 10 E
Villeneuve, Switz. 28 D3 46 24N 6 56 E
Villeneuve-l'Archevêque, France 23 D10 48 14N 3 32 E
Villeneuve-lès-Avignon, France 25 E8 43 58N 4 49 E
Villeneuve-St.-Georges, France 23 D9 48 44N 2 28 E
Villeneuve-sur-Allier, France 24 B7 46 40N 3 13 E
Villeneuve-sur-Lot, France 24 D4 44 24N 0 42 E
Villeréal, France 24 D4 44 38N 0 45 E
Villers-Bocage, France 22 C6 49 3N 0 40W
Villers-Bretonneux, France 23 C9 49 50N 2 30 E
Villers-Cotterêts, France 23 C10 49 15N 3 4 E
Villers-le-Bouillet, Belgium 21 G6 50 34N 5 15 E
Villers-le-Gambon, Belgium 21 H5 50 11N 4 37 E
Villers-sur-Mer, France 22 C6 49 21N 0 2W
Villersexel, France 23 E13 47 33N 6 26 E
Villerupt, France 23 C12 49 28N 5 55 E
Villerville, France 22 C7 49 26N 0 5 E
Villiers, S. Africa 105 D4 27 2 S 28 36 E
Villingen, Germany 27 G4 48 4N 8 28 E
Villisca, U.S.A. 140 D2 40 56N 94 59W
Villupuram, India 83 J4 11 59N 79 31 E
Vilna, Canada 130 C6 54 7N 111 55W
Vilnius, Lithuania 50 D4 54 38N 25 19 E
Vils →, Germany 27 G8 48 38N 13 11 E
Vilsbiburg, Germany 27 G8 48 27N 12 23 E
Vilshofen, Germany 27 G9 48 38N 13 11 E
Vilskutskogo, Proliv, Russia 57 B11 78 0N 103 0 E
Vilusi, Montenegro 42 E3 42 44N 18 34 E
Vilvoorde, Belgium 21 G4 50 56N 4 26 E
Vilyuy →, Russia 57 C13 64 24N 126 26 E
Vilyuysk, Russia 57 C13 63 40N 121 35 E
Vimercate, Italy 38 C6 45 38N 9 25 E
Vimiosa, Portugal 36 D4 41 35N 6 31W
Vimoutiers, France 22 D7 48 57N 0 10 E
Vimperk, Czech. 30 B6 49 3N 13 46 E
Viña del Mar, Chile 158 C1 33 0 S 71 30W
Vinaroz, Spain 34 E5 40 30N 0 27 E
Vincennes, U.S.A. 141 F9 38 41N 87 32W
Vincent, U.S.A. 145 L8 34 33N 118 11W
Vinces, Ecuador 152 D2 1 32 S 79 45W
Vinchina, Argentina 158 B2 28 45 S 68 15W
Vindel älven →, Sweden 12 E15 63 55N 19 50 E
Vindeln, Sweden 12 D15 64 12N 19 43 E
Vinderup, Denmark 15 H2 56 29N 8 45 E
Vindhya Ra., India 80 H7 22 50N 77 0 E
Vine Grove, U.S.A. 141 G11 37 49N 85 59W
Vineland, U.S.A. 134 F8 39 29N 75 2W
Vinga, Romania 46 C2 46 0N 21 14 E
Vingnes, Norway 14 C4 61 7N 10 26 E
Vinh, Vietnam 76 C5 18 45N 105 38 E
Vinh Linh, Vietnam 76 D6 17 4N 107 2 E
Vinh Long, Vietnam 77 G5 10 16N 105 57 E
Vinh Yen, Vietnam 76 B5 21 21N 105 35 E
Vinhais, Portugal 36 D3 41 50N 7 5W
Vinica, Croatia 39 B13 46 20N 16 9 E
Vinica, Slovenia 39 C12 45 28N 15 16 E
Vinita, U.S.A. 139 G7 36 39N 95 9W
Vinkeveen, Neths. 20 D5 52 13N 4 56 E
Vinkovci, Croatia 42 B3 45 19N 18 48 E
Vinnitsa, Ukraine 52 B3 49 15N 28 30 E
Vinnytsya = Vinnitsa, Ukraine 52 B3 49 15N 28 30 E
Vinstra, Norway 14 C3 61 37N 9 44 E
Vintar, Phil. 70 B3 18 14N 120 39 E
Vinton, Calif., U.S.A. 144 F6 39 48N 120 10W
Vinton, Iowa, U.S.A. 140 B4 42 10N 92 1W
Vinton, La., U.S.A. 139 K8 30 11N 93 35W
Vințu de Jos, Romania 46 D4 46 0N 23 30 E
Viöl, Germany 26 A5 54 32N 9 12 E
Viola, U.S.A. 140 C6 41 12N 90 35W
Violet Town, Australia 117 D6 36 38 S 145 42 E
Vipava, Slovenia 39 C10 45 51N 13 58 E
Vipiteno, Italy 39 B8 46 55N 11 25 E
Viqueque, Indonesia 72 C3 8 52 S 126 23 E
Vir, Croatia 39 D12 44 17N 15 3 E
Vir, Tajikistan 55 E6 37 45N 72 5 E
Virac, Phil. 70 E5 13 30N 124 20 E
Virachei, Cambodia 76 F6 13 59N 106 49 E
Virago Sd., Canada 130 C2 54 0N 132 30W
Virajpet = Virarajendrapet, India 83 H2 12 10N 75 50 E
Viramgam, India 80 H5 23 5N 72 0 E
Viranşehir, Turkey 89 E8 37 13N 39 45 E
Virarajendrapet, India 83 H2 12 10N 75 50 E
Viravanallur, India 83 K3 8 40N 77 30 E
Virden, Canada 131 D8 49 50N 100 56W
Virden, U.S.A. 140 E7 39 30N 89 46W
Vire, France 22 D6 48 50N 0 53W
Vire →, France 22 C5 49 20N 1 7W
Virgem da Lapa, Brazil 155 E3 16 49 S 42 21W
Virgenes, C., Argentina 160 D3 52 19 S 68 21W
Virgin →, Canada 131 B7 57 2N 108 17W
Virgin →, U.S.A. 143 H6 36 28N 114 21W
Virgin Gorda, Virgin Is. 149 C7 18 30N 64 26W
Virgin Is. (British) ■, W. Indies 149 C7 18 30N 64 30W
Virgin Is. (U.S.) ■, W. Indies 149 C7 18 20N 65 0W
Virginia, S. Africa 104 D4 28 8 S 26 55 E
Virginia, Ill., U.S.A. 140 E6 39 57N 90 13W
Virginia, Minn., U.S.A. 138 B8 47 31N 92 32W
Virginia □, U.S.A. 134 G7 37 30N 78 45W
Virginia Beach, U.S.A. 134 G8 36 51N 75 59W
Virginia City, Mont., U.S.A. 142 D8 45 18N 111 56W
Virginia City, Nev., U.S.A. 144 F7 39 19N 119 39W
Virginia Falls, Canada 130 A3 61 38N 125 42W
Virginiatown, Canada 128 C4 48 9N 79 36W
Virieu-le-Grand, France 25 C9 45 51N 5 39 E
Virje, Croatia 42 A1 46 4N 16 59 E
Viroqua, U.S.A. 138 D9 43 34N 90 53W
Virovitica, Croatia 42 B2 45 51N 17 21 E
Virpazar, Montenegro 42 E4 42 14N 19 6 E
Virton, Belgium 21 J7 49 35N 5 32 E
Virtsu, Estonia 50 B3 58 32N 23 33 E
Virú, Peru 156 B2 8 25 S 78 45W
Virudunagar, India 83 K3 9 30N 77 58 E
Vis, Croatia 39 E13 43 0N 16 10 E
Vis Kanal, Croatia 39 E13 43 4N 16 5 E
Visalia, U.S.A. 144 J7 36 20N 119 18W
Visayan Sea, Phil. 71 F4 11 30N 123 30 E
Visby, Sweden 13 H15 57 37N 18 18 E
Viscount Melville Sd., Canada 6 B2 74 10N 108 0W
Visé, Belgium 21 G7 50 44N 5 41 E
Višegrad, Bos.-H. 42 D4 43 47N 19 17 E
Viseu, Brazil 154 B2 1 10 S 46 5W
Viseu, Portugal 36 E3 40 40N 7 55W
Viseu □, Portugal 36 E3 40 40N 7 55W
Vişeu de Sus, Romania 46 B5 47 45N 24 25 E
Vishakhapatnam, India 82 F6 17 45N 83 20 E
Vishera →, Russia 54 B5 59 55N 56 25 E
Viskafors, Sweden 15 G6 57 37N 12 50 E
Visnagar, India 80 H5 23 45N 72 32 E
Višnja Gora, Slovenia 39 C11 45 58N 14 45 E
Viso, Mte., Italy 38 D4 44 38N 7 5 E
Viso del Marqués, Spain 35 G1 38 32N 3 34W
Visoko, Bos.-H. 42 D3 43 58N 18 10 E
Visokoi I., Antarctica 7 B1 56 43 S 27 15W
Visp, Switz. 28 D5 46 17N 7 52 E
Vispa →, Switz. 28 D5 46 9N 7 48 E
Visselhövede, Germany 26 C5 52 59N 9 36 E
Vissoie, Switz. 28 D5 46 13N 7 36 E
Vista, U.S.A. 145 M9 33 12N 117 14W
Vistonikos, Ormos, Greece 44 D7 41 0N 25 7 E
Vistula = Wisła →, Poland 47 A5 54 22N 18 55 E
Vit →, Bulgaria 43 D9 43 30N 24 30 E
Vitanje, Slovenia 39 B12 46 25N 15 18 E
Vitebsk, Belorussia 50 D7 55 10N 30 15 E
Viterbo, Italy 39 F9 42 25N 12 8 E
Viti Levu, Fiji 121 A1 17 30 S 177 30 E
Vitiaz Str., Papua N. G. 120 C4 5 40 S 147 10 E
Vitigudino, Spain 36 D4 41 1N 6 26W
Vitim, Russia 57 D12 59 28N 112 35 E
Vitim →, Russia 57 D12 59 26N 112 34 E
Vitina, Bos.-H. 42 D2 43 17N 17 29 E
Vitína, Greece 45 G4 37 40N 22 10 E
Vitória, Brazil 155 F3 20 20 S 40 22W
Vitoria, Spain 34 C2 42 50N 2 41W
Vitória da Conquista, Brazil 155 D3 14 51 S 40 51W
Vitória de São Antão, Brazil 154 C4 8 10 S 35 20W
Vitorino Friere, Brazil 154 B2 4 4 S 45 10W
Vitré, France 22 D5 48 8N 1 12W
Vitry-le-François, France 23 D11 48 43N 4 33 E
Vitsi, Óros, Greece 44 D3 40 40N 21 25 E
Vitsyebsk = Vitebsk, Belorussia 50 D7 55 10N 30 15 E
Vitteaux, France 23 E11 47 24N 4 30 E
Vittel, France 23 D12 48 12N 5 57 E
Vittória, Italy 41 F7 36 58N 14 30 E
Vittório Véneto, Italy 39 C9 45 59N 12 18 E
Vitu Is., Papua N. G. 120 C5 4 50 S 149 25 E
Vivario, France 25 F13 42 10N 9 11 E
Vivegnis, Belgium 21 G7 50 42N 5 39 E
Viver, Spain 34 F4 39 55N 0 36W
Vivero, Spain 36 B3 43 39N 7 38W
Viviers, France 25 D8 44 30N 4 40 E
Vivonne, Australia 116 C2 35 59 S 137 9 E
Vivonne, France 24 B4 46 25N 0 15 E
Vivonne B., Australia 116 C2 35 59 S 137 9 E
Vizcaíno, Desierto de, Mexico 146 B2 27 40N 113 50W
Vizcaíno, Sierra, Mexico 146 B2 27 30N 114 0W
Vizcaya □, Spain 34 B2 43 15N 2 45W
Vize, Turkey 88 C2 41 34N 27 45 E
Vizianagaram, India 82 E6 18 6N 83 30 E
Vizille, France 25 C9 45 5N 5 46 E
Viziñada, Croatia 39 C10 45 20N 13 46 E
Viziru, Romania 46 D8 45 0N 27 43 E
Vizovice, Czech. 31 B10 49 12N 17 56 E
Vizzini, Italy 41 E7 37 9N 14 43 E
Vjosa →, Albania 44 D1 40 37N 19 42 E
Vlaardingen, Neths. 20 E4 51 55N 4 21 E
Vlădeasa, Romania 46 C3 46 47N 22 50 E
Vladicin Han, Serbia 42 E7 42 42N 22 1 E
Vladikavkaz, Russia 53 E11 43 0N 44 35 E
Vladimir, Russia 51 C12 56 15N 40 30 E
Vladimir Volynskiy, Ukraine 50 F4 50 50N 24 18 E
Vladimirci, Serbia 42 C4 44 36N 19 45 E
Vladimirovac, Serbia 42 B5 45 1N 20 53 E
Vladimirovka, Russia 53 B12 48 27N 46 10 E
Vladimirovka, Russia 53 D11 44 45N 44 41 E
Vladimirovo, Bulgaria 43 D8 43 32N 23 22 E
Vladislavovka, Ukraine 52 D6 45 15N 35 15 E
Vladivostok, Russia 57 E14 43 10N 131 53 E
Vlamertinge, Belgium 21 G1 50 51N 2 49 E
Vlasenica, Bos.-H. 42 C3 44 11N 18 59 E
Vlašić, Bos.-H. 42 C2 44 19N 17 37 E
Vlašim, Czech. 30 B7 49 40N 14 53 E
Vlasinsko Jezero, Serbia 42 E7 42 44N 22 22 E
Vlasotinci, Serbia 42 E7 42 59N 22 7 E
Vleuten, Neths. 20 D6 52 6N 5 1 E
Vlieland, Neths. 20 B5 53 16N 4 55 E
Vliestroom, Neths. 20 B6 53 19N 5 8 E
Vlijmen, Neths. 21 E6 51 42N 5 14 E
Vlissingen, Neths. 21 F3 51 26N 3 34 E
Vlóra, Albania 44 D1 40 32N 19 28 E
Vlóra □, Albania 44 D2 40 12N 20 0 E
Vlorës, Gjiri i, Albania 44 D1 40 29N 19 27 E
Vltava →, Czech. 30 A7 50 21N 14 30 E
Vo Dat, Vietnam 77 G6 11 9N 107 31 E
Vobarno, Italy 38 C7 45 38N 10 30 E
Voćin, Croatia 42 B2 45 37N 17 33 E
Vöcklabruck, Austria 30 C6 48 1N 13 39 E
Vodice, Croatia 39 E12 43 47N 15 47 E
Vodňany, Czech. 30 B7 49 9N 14 11 E
Vodnjan, Croatia 39 D10 44 59N 13 52 E
Vogelkop = Doberai, Jazirah, Indonesia 73 B4 1 25 S 133 0 E
Vogelsberg, Germany 26 E5 50 37N 9 15 E
Voghera, Italy 38 D6 44 59N 9 1 E
Voh, N. Cal. 121 T18 20 58 S 164 42 E
Vohibinany, Madag. 105 B8 18 49 S 49 4 E
Vohimarina, Madag. 105 A9 13 25 S 50 0 E
Vohimena, Tanjon' i, Madag. 105 D8 25 36 S 45 8 E
Vohipeno, Madag. 105 C8 22 22 S 47 51 E
Voi, Kenya 106 C4 3 25 S 38 32 E
Void, France 23 D12 48 40N 5 36 E
Voineşti, Iaşi, Romania 46 B8 47 5N 27 27 E
Voineşti, Prahova, Romania 46 D6 45 5N 25 14 E
Voiótía □, Greece 45 F5 38 20N 23 0 E
Voiron, France 25 C9 45 22N 5 35 E
Voisey B., Canada 129 A7 56 15N 61 50W
Voitsberg, Austria 30 D8 47 3N 15 9 E
Voiviïs Límni, Greece 44 E4 39 30N 22 45 E
Vojens, Denmark 15 J3 55 16N 9 18 E
Vojmsjön, Sweden 12 D14 64 55N 16 40 E
Vojnić, Croatia 39 C12 45 19N 15 43 E
Vojnik, Italy 39 B12 46 18N 15 19 E
Vojvodina □, Serbia 42 B4 45 20N 20 0 E
Vokhma, Russia 51 B15 59 0N 46 45 E
Vokhma →, Russia 51 C15 56 20N 46 20 E
Vokhtoga, Russia 51 B12 58 46N 41 8 E
Volary, Czech. 30 C6 48 54N 13 52 E
Volborg, U.S.A. 138 C2 45 51N 105 41W
Volcano Is. = Kazan-Rettō, Pac. Oc. 122 E6 25 0N 141 0 E
Volchansk, Ukraine 52 A7 50 17N 36 58 E
Volchayevka, Russia 57 E14 48 40N 134 30 E
Volchya →, Ukraine 52 C7 48 32N 36 0 E
Volda, Norway 12 E9 62 9N 6 5 E
Volendam, Neths. 20 D6 52 30N 5 4 E
Volga, Russia 51 C11 57 58N 38 16 E
Volga →, Russia 53 C13 46 0N 48 30 E
Volga Hts. = Privolzhskaya Vozvyshennost, Russia 51 F15 51 0N 46 0 E
Volgodonsk, Russia 53 C10 47 33N 42 5 E
Volgograd, Russia 53 B11 48 40N 44 25 E
Volgogradskoye Vdkhr., Russia 51 F14 50 0N 45 20 E
Volgorechensk, Russia 51 C12 57 28N 41 14 E
Volissós, Greece 45 F7 38 29N 25 54 E
Volkach, Germany 27 F6 49 52N 10 14 E
Volkerak, Neths. 21 E4 51 39N 4 18 E
Völkermarkt, Austria 30 E7 46 39N 14 39 E
Volkhov, Russia 50 B8 59 55N 32 15 E
Volkhov →, Russia 50 A8 60 8N 32 20 E
Völklingen, Germany 27 F2 49 15N 6 50 E
Volkovysk, Belorussia 50 E4 53 9N 24 30 E
Volksrust, S. Africa 105 D4 27 24 S 29 53 E
Vollenhove, Neths. 20 C7 52 40N 5 58 E
Vol'n'ansk, Ukraine 52 C6 48 2N 35 29 E
Volnovakha, Ukraine 52 C7 47 35N 37 30 E
Volochanka, Russia 57 B10 71 0N 94 28 E
Volodarsk, Russia 51 C13 56 12N 43 15 E
Vologda, Russia 51 B11 59 10N 39 45 E
Volokolamsk, Russia 51 C9 56 5N 35 57 E
Volokonovka, Russia 51 F10 50 33N 37 52 E
Vólos, Greece 44 E4 39 24N 22 59 E
Volosovo, Russia 50 B6 59 27N 29 32 E
Volozhin, Belorussia 50 D5 54 3N 26 30 E
Volsk, Russia 51 E15 52 5N 47 22 E
Volta →, Ghana 101 D5 5 46N 0 41 E
Volta, L., Ghana 101 D5 7 30N 0 15 E
Volta Blanche = White Volta →, Ghana 101 D4 9 10N 1 15W
Volta Redonda, Brazil 155 F3 22 31 S 44 5W
Voltaire, C., Australia 112 B4 14 16 S 125 35 E
Volterra, Italy 38 E7 43 24N 10 50 E
Voltri, Italy 38 D5 44 25N 8 43 E
Volturara Áppula, Italy 41 A8 41 30N 15 2 E
Volturno →, Italy 40 A6 41 1N 13 55 E
Volubilis, Morocco 98 B3 34 2N 5 33W
Volujak, Bos.-H. 42 D2 43 53N 17 47 E
Vólvi, L., Greece 44 D5 40 40N 23 34 E
Volvo, Australia 116 A5 31 41 S 143 57 E
Volzhsk, Russia 51 D16 55 57N 48 23 E
Volzhskiy, Russia 53 B11 48 56N 44 46 E
Vondrozo, Madag. 105 C8 22 49 S 47 20 E
Vónitsa, Greece 45 F2 38 53N 20 58 E
Voorburg, Neths. 20 D4 52 5N 4 24 E
Voorne Putten, Neths. 20 E4 51 52N 4 10 E
Voorst, Neths. 20 D8 52 10N 6 8 E
Voorthuizen, Neths. 20 D7 52 11N 5 36 E
Vopnafjörður, Iceland 12 D6 65 45N 14 40W
Vorarlberg □, Austria 30 D2 47 20N 10 0 E
Vóras Óros, Greece 44 D3 40 57N 21 45 E
Vorbasse, Denmark 15 J3 55 39N 9 6 E
Vorden, Neths. 20 D8 52 6N 6 19 E
Vorderrhein →, Switz. 29 C8 46 49N 9 25 E
Vordingborg, Denmark 15 K5 55 0N 11 54 E
Voreppe, France 25 C9 45 18N 5 39 E
Voríai Sporádhes, Greece 45 E5 39 15N 23 30 E
Vórios Evvoïkos Kólpos, Greece 45 F5 38 45N 23 15 E
Vorkuta, Russia 48 A11 67 48N 64 20 E
Vorma →, Norway 14 D5 60 9N 11 27 E
Vorona →, Russia 51 F13 51 22N 42 3 E
Voronezh, Russia 51 F11 51 40N 39 10 E
Voronezh, Ukraine 50 F8 51 47N 33 28 E
Voronezh →, Russia 51 F10 51 32N 39 0 E
Vorontsovo-Aleksandrovskoye = Zelenokumsk, Russia 53 D10 44 24N 44 0 E
Voroshilovgrad = Lugansk, Ukraine 53 B8 48 38N 39 15 E
Voroshilovsk = Kommunarsk, Ukraine 53 B8 48 30N 38 45 E
Vorovskoye, Russia 57 D16 54 30N 155 50 E
Vorselaar, Belgium 21 F5 51 12N 4 46 E
Vorskla →, Ukraine 52 B6 48 50N 34 10 E
Võru, Estonia 50 C5 57 48N 26 54 E
Vorukh, Kirghizia 55 D5 39 52N 70 35 E
Vorupør, Denmark 15 H2 56 58N 8 22 E
Vosges, France 23 D14 48 20N 7 10 E
Vosges □, France 23 D13 48 12N 6 20 E
Voskopoja, Albania 44 D2 40 40N 20 33 E
Voskresensk, Russia 51 D11 55 19N 38 43 E
Voskresenskoye, Russia 51 C14 56 51N 45 30 E
Voss, Norway 13 F9 60 38N 6 26 E
Vosselaar, Belgium 21 F5 51 19N 4 52 E
Vostok I., Kiribati 123 J12 10 5 S 152 23W
Votice, Czech. 30 B7 49 38N 14 39 E
Votkinsk, Russia 54 C3 57 0N 53 55 E
Votkinskoye Vdkhr., Russia 54 C4 57 30N 55 0 E
Vouga →, Portugal 36 E2 40 41N 8 40W
Vouillé, France 22 F7 46 38N 0 10 E
Voulou, C.A.R. 102 A4 8 33N 22 36 E
Vouvray, France 22 E7 47 25N 0 48 E
Vouvry, Switz. 28 D3 46 21N 6 51 E
Voúxa, Ákra, Greece 32 D5 35 37N 23 32 E
Vouzela, Portugal 36 E2 40 43N 8 7W
Vouziers, France 23 C11 49 22N 4 40 E
Voves, France 23 D8 48 15N 1 38 E
Voxna, Sweden 14 C9 61 20N 15 40 E
Vozhe Oz., Russia 48 B6 60 45N 39 0 E
Vozhgaly, Russia 51 B17 58 9N 50 11 E
Voznesenka, Russia 57 D10 56 40N 95 3 E
Voznesensk, Ukraine 52 C4 47 35N 31 21 E
Voznesenye, Russia 48 B6 61 0N 35 45 E
Vráble, Slovak Rep. 31 C11 48 15N 18 16 E
Vraćevšnica, Serbia 42 C5 44 2N 20 34 E
Vrådal, Norway 14 E2 59 20N 8 25 E
Vraka, Albania 44 B1 42 8N 19 28 E
Vrakhnéïka, Greece 45 F3 38 10N 21 40 E

W

West Point 283

Warora, *India* 82 D4 20 14N 79 1 E
Warracknabeal, *Australia* 116 D5 36 9 S 142 26 E
Warragul, *Australia* 117 E6 38 10 S 145 58 E
Warrawagine, *Australia* 112 D3 20 51 S 120 42 E
Warrego →, *Australia* 115 E4 30 24 S 145 21 E
Warrego Ra., *Australia* 114 C4 24 58 S 146 0 E
Warren, *Australia* 117 A7 31 42 S 147 51 E
Warren, *Ark., U.S.A.* 139 J8 33 37N 92 4W
Warren, *Ill., U.S.A.* 140 B7 42 29N 90 0W
Warren, *Mich., U.S.A.* 141 B13 42 30N 83 0W
Warren, *Minn., U.S.A.* 138 A6 48 12N 96 46W
Warren, *Ohio, U.S.A.* 136 E4 41 14N 80 49W
Warren, *Pa., U.S.A.* 136 E5 41 51N 79 9W
Warrenpoint, *U.K.* 19 B5 54 7N 6 15W
Warrensburg, *Ill., U.S.A.* 140 E7 39 56N 89 4W
Warrensburg, *Mo., U.S.A.* 138 F8 38 46N 93 44W
Warrenton, *S. Africa* 104 D3 28 9 S 24 47 E
Warrenton, *Mo., U.S.A.* 140 F5 38 49N 91 9W
Warrenton, *Oreg., U.S.A.* 144 D3 46 10N 123 56W
Warrenville, *Australia* 115 D4 25 48 S 147 22 E
Warri, *Nigeria* 101 D6 5 30N 5 41 E
Warrina, *Australia* 115 D2 28 12 S 135 50 E
Warrington, *N.Z.* 119 F5 45 43 S 170 35 E
Warrington, *U.K.* 16 D5 53 25N 2 38W
Warrington, *U.S.A.* 135 K2 30 23N 87 17W
Warrnambool, *Australia* 116 E5 38 25 S 142 30 E
Warroad, *U.S.A.* 138 A7 48 54N 95 19W
Warsa, *Indonesia* 73 B5 0 47 S 135 55 E
Warsaw = Warszawa, *Poland* 47 C8 52 13N 21 0 E
Warsaw, *Ill., U.S.A.* 140 D5 40 22N 91 26W
Warsaw, *Ind., U.S.A.* 141 C11 41 14N 85 51W
Warsaw, *Ky., U.S.A.* 141 F12 38 47N 84 54W
Warsaw, *Mo., U.S.A.* 140 F3 38 15N 93 23W
Warsaw, *N.Y., U.S.A.* 136 D6 42 45N 78 8W
Warsaw, *Ohio, U.S.A.* 136 F2 40 20N 82 0W
Warstein, *Germany* 26 D4 51 26N 8 20 E
Warszawa, *Poland* 47 C8 52 13N 21 0 E
Warszawa □, *Poland* 47 C8 52 30N 21 0 E
Warta, *Poland* 47 D5 51 43N 18 38 E
Warta →, *Poland* 47 C1 52 35N 14 39 E
Warthe = Warta →, *Poland* 47 C1 52 35N 14 39 E
Waru, *Indonesia* 73 B4 3 30 S 130 36 E
Warud, *India* 82 D4 21 30N 78 16 E
Warwick, *Australia* 115 D5 28 10 S 152 1 E
Warwick, *U.K.* 17 E6 52 17N 1 36W
Warwick, *U.S.A.* 137 E13 41 42N 71 28W
Warwickshire □, *U.K.* 17 E6 52 20N 1 30W
Wasaga Beach, *Canada* 136 B4 44 31N 80 1W
Wasatch Ra., *U.S.A.* 142 F8 40 30N 111 15W
Wasbank, *S. Africa* 105 D5 28 15 S 30 9 E
Wasco, *Calif., U.S.A.* 145 K7 35 36N 119 20W
Wasco, *Oreg., U.S.A.* 142 D3 45 36N 120 42W
Waseca, *U.S.A.* 138 C8 44 5N 93 30W
Wasekamio L., *Canada* 131 B7 56 45N 108 45W
Wash, The, *U.K.* 16 E8 52 58N 0 20 E
Washago, *Canada* 136 B5 44 45N 79 20W
Washburn, *Ill., U.S.A.* 140 D7 40 55N 89 17W
Washburn, *N. Dak., U.S.A.* 138 B4 47 17N 101 2W
Washburn, *Wis., U.S.A.* 138 B9 46 40N 90 54W
Washim, *India* 82 D3 20 3N 77 0 E
Washington, *D.C., U.S.A.* 134 F7 38 54N 77 2W
Washington, *Ga., U.S.A.* 135 J4 33 44N 82 44W
Washington, *Ind., U.S.A.* 141 F9 38 40N 87 10W
Washington, *Iowa, U.S.A.* 140 C5 41 18N 91 42W
Washington, *Mo., U.S.A.* 140 F5 38 33N 91 1W
Washington, *N.C., U.S.A.* 135 H7 35 33N 77 3W
Washington, *N.J., U.S.A.* 137 F10 40 46N 74 59W
Washington, *Pa., U.S.A.* 136 F4 40 10N 80 15W
Washington, *Utah, U.S.A.* 143 H7 37 8N 113 31W
Washington □, *U.S.A.* 142 C3 47 30N 120 30W
Washington, Mt., *U.S.A.* 137 B13 44 16N 71 18W
Washington Court House, *U.S.A.* 141 E13 39 32N 83 26W
Washington I., *U.S.A.* 134 C2 45 23N 86 54W
Washougal, *U.S.A.* 144 E4 45 35N 122 21W
Washuk, *Pakistan* 79 D2 27 42N 64 45 E
Wasian, *Indonesia* 73 B4 1 47 S 133 19 E
Wasilków, *Poland* 47 B10 53 12N 23 13 E
Wasior, *Indonesia* 73 B4 2 43 S 134 30 E
Waskaiowaka, L., *Canada* 131 B9 56 33N 96 23W
Waskesiu Lake, *Canada* 131 C7 53 55N 106 5W
Wasmes, *Belgium* 21 H3 50 25N 3 50 E
Waspik, *Neths.* 21 E5 51 41N 4 57 E
Wassen, *Switz.* 29 C7 46 42N 8 36 E
Wassenaar, *Neths.* 20 D4 52 8N 4 24 E
Wasserburg, *Germany* 27 G8 48 4N 12 15 E
Wasserkuppe, *Germany* 26 E5 50 30N 9 56 E
Wassy, *France* 23 D11 48 30N 4 58 E
Waswanipi, *Canada* 128 C4 49 40N 76 29W
Waswanipi, L., *Canada* 128 C4 49 35N 76 40W
Watangpone, *Indonesia* 72 B2 4 29 S 120 25 E
Watansoppeng, *Indonesia* 72 B1 4 10 S 119 56 E
Water Park Pt., *Australia* 114 C5 22 56 S 150 47 E
Water Valley, *U.S.A.* 139 H10 34 10N 89 38W
Waterberge, *S. Africa* 105 C4 24 10 S 28 0 E
Waterbury, *Conn., U.S.A.* 137 E11 41 33N 73 3W
Waterbury, *Vt., U.S.A.* 137 B12 44 20N 72 46W
Waterbury L., *Canada* 131 B8 58 10N 104 22W
Waterdown, *Canada* 136 C5 43 20N 79 53W
Waterford, *Canada* 136 D4 42 56N 80 17W
Waterford, *Ireland* 19 D4 52 16N 7 8W
Waterford, *Calif., U.S.A.* 144 H6 37 38N 120 46W
Waterford, *Wis., U.S.A.* 141 B8 42 46N 88 13W
Waterford □, *Ireland* 19 D4 52 10N 7 40W
Waterford Harbour, *Ireland* 19 D5 52 10N 6 58W
Waterhen L., *Man., Canada* 131 C9 52 10N 99 40W
Waterhen L., *Sask., Canada* 131 C7 54 28N 108 25W
Wateringen, *Neths.* 20 D4 52 2N 4 16 E
Waterloo, *Belgium* 21 G4 50 43N 4 25 E
Waterloo, *Ont., Canada* 128 D3 43 30N 80 32W
Waterloo, *Qué., Canada* 137 A12 45 22N 72 32W
Waterloo, *S. Leone* 100 D2 8 26N 13 8W
Waterloo, *Ill., U.S.A.* 140 F6 38 20N 90 9W
Waterloo, *Ind., U.S.A.* 141 C11 41 26N 85 1W
Waterloo, *Iowa, U.S.A.* 140 B4 42 30N 92 21W
Waterloo, *N.Y., U.S.A.* 136 D8 42 54N 76 52W
Waterloo, *Wis., U.S.A.* 140 A8 43 11N 88 59W
Waterman, *U.S.A.* 141 C8 41 46N 88 47W
Watermeal-Boitsford, *Belgium* 21 G4 50 48N 4 25 E
Watersmeet, *U.S.A.* 138 B10 46 16N 89 11W
Waterton-Glacier International Peace Park, *U.S.A.* 142 B7 48 45N 115 0W
Watertown, *Conn., U.S.A.* 137 E11 41 36N 73 7W
Watertown, *N.Y., U.S.A.* 137 C9 43 59N 75 55W
Watertown, *S. Dak., U.S.A.* 138 C6 44 54N 97 7W
Watertown, *Wis., U.S.A.* 138 D10 43 12N 88 43W
Waterval-Boven, *S. Africa* 105 D5 25 40 S 30 18 E
Waterville, *Canada* 137 A13 45 16N 71 54W
Waterville, *Maine, U.S.A.* 129 D6 44 33N 69 38W
Waterville, *N.Y., U.S.A.* 137 D9 42 56N 75 23W
Waterville, *Pa., U.S.A.* 136 E7 41 19N 77 21W
Waterville, *Wash., U.S.A.* 142 C3 47 39N 120 4W
Watervliet, *Belgium* 21 F3 51 17N 3 38 E
Watervliet, *Mich., U.S.A.* 141 B10 42 11N 86 18W
Watervliet, *N.Y., U.S.A.* 137 D11 42 44N 73 42W
Wates, *Indonesia* 75 D4 7 51 S 110 10 E
Watford, *Canada* 136 D3 42 57N 81 53W
Watford, *U.K.* 17 F7 51 38N 0 23W
Watford City, *U.S.A.* 138 B3 47 48N 103 17W
Wathaman →, *Canada* 131 B8 57 16N 102 59W
Watheroo, *Australia* 113 F2 30 15 S 116 0 E
Wating, *China* 66 G4 35 40N 106 38 E
Watkins Glen, *U.S.A.* 136 D8 42 23N 76 52W
Watling I. = San Salvador, *Bahamas* 149 B5 24 0N 74 40W
Watonga, *U.S.A.* 139 H5 35 51N 98 25W
Watou, *Belgium* 21 G1 50 51N 2 38 E
Watrous, *Canada* 131 C7 51 40N 105 25W
Watrous, *U.S.A.* 139 H2 35 48N 104 59W
Watsa, *Zaïre* 106 B2 3 4N 29 30 E
Watseka, *U.S.A.* 141 D9 40 47N 87 44W
Watson, *Australia* 113 F5 30 29 S 131 31 E
Watson, *Canada* 131 C8 52 10N 104 30W
Watson Lake, *Canada* 130 A3 60 6N 128 49W
Watsonville, *U.S.A.* 144 J5 36 55N 121 45W
Wattenwil, *Switz.* 28 C5 46 46N 7 30 E
Wattiwarriganna Cr. →, *Australia* 115 D2 28 57 S 136 10 E
Wattwil, *Switz.* 29 B8 47 18N 9 6 E
Watuata = Batuata, *Indonesia* 72 C2 6 12 S 122 42 E
Watubela, Kepulauan, *Indonesia* 73 B4 4 28 S 131 35 E
Watubela Is. = Watubela, Kepulauan, *Indonesia* 73 B4 4 28 S 131 35 E
Wau, *Papua N. G.* 120 D4 7 21 S 146 47 E
Waubach, *Neths.* 21 G8 50 55N 6 3 E
Waubamik, *Canada* 136 A4 45 27N 80 1W
Waubay, *U.S.A.* 138 C6 45 20N 97 18W
Waubra, *Australia* 116 D5 37 21 S 143 39 E
Wauchope, *Australia* 117 A10 31 28 S 152 45 E
Wauchula, *U.S.A.* 135 M5 27 33N 81 49W
Waugh, *Canada* 131 D9 49 40N 95 11W
Waukarlycarly, L., *Australia* 112 D3 21 18 S 121 56 E
Waukegan, *U.S.A.* 141 B9 42 22N 87 50W
Waukesha, *U.S.A.* 141 B8 43 1N 88 14W
Waukon, *U.S.A.* 138 D9 43 16N 91 29W
Wauneta, *U.S.A.* 138 E4 40 25N 101 23W
Waupaca, *U.S.A.* 138 C10 44 21N 89 5W
Waupun, *U.S.A.* 138 D10 43 38N 88 44W
Waurika, *U.S.A.* 139 H6 34 10N 98 0W
Wausau, *U.S.A.* 138 C10 44 58N 89 38W
Wauseon, *U.S.A.* 141 C12 41 33N 84 8W
Wautoma, *U.S.A.* 138 C10 44 4N 89 18W
Wauwatosa, *U.S.A.* 141 A9 43 3N 88 0W
Wave Hill, *Australia* 112 C5 17 32 S 131 0 E
Waveland, *U.S.A.* 141 E9 39 53N 87 3W
Waveney →, *U.K.* 17 E9 52 24N 1 20 E
Waverley, *N.Z.* 118 F3 39 46 S 174 37 E
Waverly, *Ill., U.S.A.* 140 E7 39 36N 89 57W
Waverly, *Iowa, U.S.A.* 140 B4 42 44N 92 29W
Waverly, *Mo., U.S.A.* 140 E3 39 13N 93 31W
Waverly, *N.Y., U.S.A.* 137 D8 42 1N 76 32W
Wavre, *Belgium* 21 G5 50 43N 4 38 E
Wavreille, *Belgium* 21 H6 50 7N 5 15 E
Wâw, *Sudan* 95 F2 7 45N 28 1 E
Wāw al Kabīr, *Libya* 96 C3 25 20N 16 43 E
Wāw an Nāmūs, *Libya* 96 D3 24 55N 17 46 E
Wawa, *Canada* 128 C3 47 59N 84 47W
Wawa, *Nigeria* 101 D5 9 54N 4 27 E
Wawa, *Sudan* 94 C3 20 30N 30 22 E
Wawanesa, *Canada* 131 D9 49 36N 99 40W
Wawasee, L., *U.S.A.* 141 C11 41 24N 85 42W
Wawoi →, *Papua N. G.* 120 D2 7 48 S 143 16 E
Wawona, *U.S.A.* 144 H7 37 32N 119 39W
Waxahachie, *U.S.A.* 139 J6 32 24N 96 51W
Way, L., *Australia* 113 E3 26 45 S 120 16 E
Wayabula Rau, *Indonesia* 72 A3 2 29N 128 17 E
Wayatinah, *Australia* 114 G4 42 19 S 146 27 E
Waycross, *U.S.A.* 135 K4 31 13N 82 21W
Wayi, *Sudan* 95 F3 5 8N 30 10 E
Wayland, *U.S.A.* 141 B11 42 40N 85 39W
Wayne, *Nebr., U.S.A.* 138 D6 42 14N 97 1W
Wayne, *W. Va., U.S.A.* 134 F4 38 13N 82 27W
Wayne City, *U.S.A.* 141 F8 38 21N 88 35W
Waynesboro, *Ga., U.S.A.* 135 J4 33 6N 82 1W
Waynesboro, *Miss., U.S.A.* 135 K1 31 40N 88 39W
Waynesboro, *Pa., U.S.A.* 134 F7 39 45N 77 35W
Waynesboro, *Va., U.S.A.* 134 F6 38 4N 78 53W
Waynesburg, *U.S.A.* 134 F5 39 54N 80 11W
Waynesville, *Mo., U.S.A.* 140 G4 37 50N 92 12W
Waynesville, *N.C., U.S.A.* 135 H4 35 28N 82 58W
Waynesville, *Ohio, U.S.A.* 141 E12 39 32N 84 5W
Waynoka, *U.S.A.* 139 G5 36 35N 98 53W
Wazay, *Afghan.* 79 B3 33 22N 69 26 E
Wāzin, *Libya* 96 B2 31 58N 10 40 E
Wazirabad, *Pakistan* 80 C6 32 30N 74 8 E
Wda →, *Poland* 47 B5 53 25N 18 29 E
We, *Indonesia* 74 A1 5 51N 95 18 E
Weald, The, *U.K.* 17 F8 51 7N 0 29 E
Wear →, *U.K.* 16 C6 54 55N 1 22W
Weatherford, *Okla., U.S.A.* 139 H5 35 32N 98 43W
Weatherford, *Tex., U.S.A.* 139 J6 32 46N 97 48W
Weaubleau, *U.S.A.* 140 G3 37 54N 93 32W
Weaverville, *U.S.A.* 142 F2 40 44N 122 56W
Webb City, *U.S.A.* 139 G7 37 9N 94 28W
Weber, *N.Z.* 118 G5 40 24 S 176 20 E
Webo = Nyaake, *Liberia* 100 E3 4 52N 7 37W
Webster, *Mass., U.S.A.* 137 D13 42 3N 71 53W
Webster, *N.Y., U.S.A.* 136 C7 43 13N 77 26W
Webster, *S. Dak., U.S.A.* 138 C6 45 20N 97 31W
Webster, *Wis., U.S.A.* 138 C8 45 53N 92 22W
Webster City, *U.S.A.* 140 B3 42 28N 93 49W
Webster Green, *U.S.A.* 138 F9 38 38N 90 20W
Webster Springs, *U.S.A.* 134 F5 38 29N 80 25W
Weda, *Indonesia* 72 A3 0 21N 127 50 E
Weda, Teluk, *Indonesia* 72 A3 0 30N 127 50 E
Weddell I., *Falk. Is.* 160 D4 51 50 S 61 0W
Weddell Sea, *Antarctica* 7 D1 72 30 S 40 0W
Wedderburn, *Australia* 116 D5 36 26 S 143 33 E
Wedgeport, *Canada* 129 D6 43 44N 65 59W
Wedza, *Zimbabwe* 107 F3 18 40 S 31 33 E
Wee Elwah, *Australia* 117 B6 33 2 S 145 14 E
Wee Waa, *Australia* 115 E4 30 11 S 149 26 E
Weed, *U.S.A.* 142 F2 41 25N 122 23W
Weed Heights, *U.S.A.* 144 G7 38 59N 119 13W
Weedsport, *U.S.A.* 137 C8 43 3N 76 35W
Weedville, *U.S.A.* 136 E6 41 17N 78 30W
Weemelah, *Australia* 115 D4 29 2 S 149 15 E
Weenen, *S. Africa* 105 D5 28 48 S 30 7 E
Weener, *Germany* 26 B3 53 10N 7 23 E
Weert, *Neths.* 21 F7 51 15N 5 43 E
Weesp, *Neths.* 20 D6 52 18N 5 2 E
Weggis, *Switz.* 29 B6 47 2N 8 26 E
Wegierska-Gorka, *Poland* 31 B12 49 36N 19 7 E
Węgliniec, *Poland* 47 D2 51 18N 15 10 E
Węgorzewo, *Poland* 47 A8 54 13N 21 43 E
Węgrów, *Poland* 47 C9 52 24N 22 0 E
Wehl, *Neths.* 20 E8 51 58N 6 13 E
Wei He →, *Hebei, China* 66 F8 36 10N 115 45 E
Wei He →, *Shaanxi, China* 66 G6 34 38N 110 15 E
Weichang, *China* 67 D9 41 58N 117 49 E
Weichuan, *China* 66 G7 34 20N 113 59 E
Weida, *Germany* 26 E8 50 47N 12 3 E
Weiden, *Germany* 27 F8 49 40N 12 10 E
Weifang, *China* 65 C6 36 47N 119 10 E
Weifang, *Shandong, China* 67 F10 36 44N 119 7 E
Weihai, *China* 67 F12 37 30N 122 6 E
Weilburg, *Germany* 26 E4 50 28N 8 17 E
Weilheim, *Germany* 27 H7 47 50N 11 9 E
Weimar, *Germany* 26 E7 51 0N 11 20 E
Weinan, *China* 66 G5 34 31N 109 29 E
Weinfelden, *Switz.* 29 A8 47 34N 9 6 E
Weingarten, *Germany* 27 H5 47 49N 9 39 E
Weinheim, *Germany* 27 F4 49 33N 8 40 E
Weining, *China* 68 D5 26 50N 104 17 E
Weipa, *Australia* 114 A3 12 40 S 141 50 E
Weir →, *Australia* 115 D4 28 20 S 149 50 E
Weir →, *Canada* 131 B10 56 54N 93 21W
Weir River, *Canada* 131 B10 56 49N 94 6W
Weirton, *U.S.A.* 136 F4 40 24N 80 35W
Weisen, *Switz.* 29 C9 46 42N 9 43 E
Weiser, *U.S.A.* 142 D5 44 10N 117 0W
Weishan, *Shandong, China* 67 G9 34 47N 117 5 E
Weishan, *Yunnan, China* 68 E3 25 12N 100 20 E
Weissenburg, *Germany* 27 F6 49 2N 10 58 E
Weissenfels, *Germany* 26 D8 51 11N 12 0 E
Weisshorn, *Switz.* 28 D5 46 7N 7 43 E
Weissmies, *Switz.* 28 D6 46 8N 8 1 E
Weisstannen, *Switz.* 29 C8 46 59N 9 22 E
Weisswasser, *Germany* 26 D10 51 30N 14 36 E
Weiswampach, *Belgium* 21 H8 50 8N 6 5 E
Wéitra, *Austria* 30 C7 48 41N 14 54 E
Weixi, *China* 68 D2 27 10N 99 10 E
Weixin, *China* 68 D5 27 48N 105 3 E
Weiyuan, *China* 66 G3 35 7N 104 10 E
Weiz, *Austria* 30 D8 47 13N 15 39 E
Weizhou Dao, *China* 68 G7 21 0N 109 5 E
Wejherowo, *Poland* 47 A5 54 35N 18 12 E
Wekusko L., *Canada* 131 C9 54 40N 99 50W
Welbourn Hill, *Australia* 115 D1 27 21 S 134 6 E
Welch, *U.S.A.* 134 G5 37 26N 81 35W
Weldya, *Ethiopia* 95 E4 11 50N 39 34 E
Welega □, *Ethiopia* 95 F3 9 25N 34 20 E
Welkenraedt, *Belgium* 21 G7 50 39N 5 58 E
Welkite, *Ethiopia* 95 F4 8 15N 37 42 E
Welkom, *S. Africa* 104 D4 28 0 S 26 46 E
Welland, *Canada* 128 D4 43 0N 79 15W
Welland →, *U.K.* 16 E7 52 43N 0 10W
Wellen, *Belgium* 21 G6 50 50N 5 21 E
Wellesley Is., *Australia* 114 B2 16 42 S 139 30 E
Wellin, *Belgium* 21 H6 50 5N 5 6 E
Wellingborough, *U.K.* 17 E7 52 18N 0 41W
Wellington, *Australia* 117 B8 32 35 S 148 59 E
Wellington, *Canada* 128 D4 43 57N 77 20W
Wellington, *N.Z.* 118 H3 41 19 S 174 46 E
Wellington, *S. Africa* 104 E2 33 38 S 19 1 E
Wellington, *Shrops., U.K.* 16 E5 52 42N 2 31W
Wellington, *Somst., U.K.* 17 G4 50 58N 3 13W
Wellington, *Colo., U.S.A.* 138 E2 40 42N 105 0W
Wellington, *Kans., U.S.A.* 139 G6 37 16N 97 24W
Wellington, *Mo., U.S.A.* 140 E3 39 8N 93 59W
Wellington, *Nev., U.S.A.* 144 G7 38 45N 119 23W
Wellington, *Ohio, U.S.A.* 136 E2 41 10N 82 13W
Wellington, *Tex., U.S.A.* 139 H4 34 51N 100 13W
Wellington □, *N.Z.* 118 G4 41 0 S 175 30 E
Wellington, I., *Chile* 160 C2 49 30 S 75 0W
Wellington, L., *Australia* 117 E7 38 6 S 147 20 E
Wells, *Norfolk, U.K.* 16 E8 52 57N 0 51 E
Wells, *Somst., U.K.* 17 F5 51 12N 2 39W
Wells, *Maine, U.S.A.* 137 C14 43 20N 70 35W
Wells, *Minn., U.S.A.* 138 D8 43 45N 93 44W
Wells, *Nev., U.S.A.* 142 F6 41 7N 114 58W
Wells, L., *Australia* 113 E3 26 44 S 123 15 E
Wells Gray Prov. Park, *Canada* 130 C4 52 30N 120 15W
Wells River, *U.S.A.* 137 B12 44 9N 72 4W
Wellsboro, *U.S.A.* 136 E7 41 45N 77 18W
Wellsburg, *U.S.A.* 136 F4 40 16N 80 37W
Wellsford, *N.Z.* 118 C3 36 16 S 174 32 E
Wellsville, *Mo., U.S.A.* 140 E5 39 4N 91 34W
Wellsville, *N.Y., U.S.A.* 136 D7 42 7N 77 57W
Wellsville, *Ohio, U.S.A.* 136 F4 40 36N 80 39W
Wellsville, *Utah, U.S.A.* 142 F8 41 38N 111 56W
Wellton, *U.S.A.* 143 K6 32 40N 114 8W
Welmel, Wabi →, *Ethiopia* 95 F5 5 38N 40 47 E
Welna →, *Poland* 47 C4 52 46N 17 32 E
Welo, *Somali Rep.* 108 C3 9 25N 48 55 E
Welo □, *Ethiopia* 95 E4 11 50N 39 48 E
Wels, *Austria* 30 C7 48 9N 14 1 E
Welshpool, *U.K.* 17 E4 52 40N 3 9W
Wem, *U.K.* 16 E5 52 52N 2 45W
Wembere →, *Tanzania* 106 C3 4 10 S 34 15 E
Wemmel, *Belgium* 21 G4 50 55N 4 18 E
Wen Xian, *Gansu, China* 66 H3 32 43N 104 36 E
Wen Xian, *Henan, China* 66 G7 34 55N 113 5 E
Wenatchee, *U.S.A.* 142 C3 47 25N 120 19W
Wenchang, *China* 76 C8 19 38N 110 42 E
Wencheng, *China* 69 D13 27 46N 120 4 E
Wenchi, *Ghana* 100 D4 7 46N 2 8W
Wenchow = Wenzhou, *China* 69 C13 28 0N 120 38 E
Wenchuan, *China* 68 B4 31 22N 103 35 E
Wendell, *U.S.A.* 142 E6 42 47N 114 42W
Wenden, *U.S.A.* 145 M13 33 49N 113 33W
Wendeng, *China* 67 F12 37 15N 122 5 E
Wendesi, *Indonesia* 73 B4 2 30 S 134 17 E
Wendo, *Ethiopia* 95 F4 6 40N 38 27 E
Wendover, *U.S.A.* 142 F6 40 44N 114 2W
Wenduine, *Belgium* 21 F2 51 18N 3 5 E
Weng'an, *China* 68 D6 27 5N 107 25 E
Wengcheng, *China* 69 E9 24 22N 113 50 E
Wengen, *Switz.* 28 C5 46 37N 7 55 E
Wengyuan, *China* 69 E10 24 20N 114 9 E
Wenjiang, *China* 68 B4 30 44N 103 55 E
Wenling, *China* 69 C13 28 21N 121 20 E
Wenlock →, *Australia* 114 A3 12 2 S 141 55 E
Wenona, *U.S.A.* 140 C7 41 3N 89 3W
Wenshan, *China* 68 F5 23 20N 104 18 E
Wenshang, *China* 66 G9 35 45N 116 30 E
Wenshui, *Guizhou, China* 68 C6 28 27N 106 28 E
Wenshui, *Shanxi, China* 66 F7 37 26N 112 1 E
Wensu, *China* 64 B3 41 15N 80 10 E
Wentworth, *Australia* 116 C4 34 2 S 141 54 E
Wentzville, *U.S.A.* 140 F6 38 49N 90 51W
Wenut, *Indonesia* 73 B4 3 11 S 133 19 E
Wenxi, *China* 66 G6 35 20N 111 10 E
Wenzhou, *China* 69 C13 28 0N 120 38 E
Weott, *U.S.A.* 142 F2 40 20N 123 55W
Wepener, *S. Africa* 104 D4 29 42 S 27 3 E
Werbomont, *Belgium* 21 H7 50 23N 5 41 E
Werda, *Botswana* 104 D3 25 24 S 23 15 E
Werdau, *Germany* 26 E8 50 45N 12 20 E
Werder, *Ethiopia* 90 F4 6 58N 45 1 E
Werder, *Germany* 26 C8 52 23N 12 56 E
Werdohl, *Germany* 26 D3 51 15N 7 47 E
Wereilu, *Ethiopia* 95 E4 10 40N 39 28 E
Weri, *Indonesia* 73 B4 3 10 S 132 38 E
Werkendam, *Neths.* 20 E5 51 50N 4 53 E
Werne, *Germany* 26 D3 51 38N 7 38 E
Werneck, *Germany* 27 F6 49 59N 10 6 E
Wernigerode, *Germany* 26 D6 51 49N 10 45 E
Werra →, *Germany* 26 D5 51 26N 9 39 E
Werribee, *Australia* 116 D6 37 54 S 144 40 E
Werrimull, *Australia* 116 C4 34 25 S 141 38 E
Werris Creek, *Australia* 117 A9 31 18 S 150 38 E
Wersar, *Indonesia* 73 B4 1 30 S 131 55 E
Wertach →, *Germany* 27 G6 48 24N 10 53 E
Wertheim, *Germany* 27 F5 49 44N 9 32 E
Wertingen, *Germany* 27 G6 48 33N 10 41 E
Wervershoof, *Neths.* 20 C6 52 44N 5 10 E
Wervik, *Belgium* 21 G2 50 47N 3 3 E
Wesel, *Germany* 26 D2 51 39N 6 34 E
Weser →, *Germany* 26 B4 53 33N 8 30 E
Wesiri, *Indonesia* 72 C3 7 30 S 126 30 E
Wesley Vale, *U.S.A.* 143 J10 35 3N 106 2W
Wesleyville, *Canada* 129 C9 49 8N 53 36W
Wesleyville, *U.S.A.* 136 D4 42 9N 80 0W
Wessel, C., *Australia* 114 A2 10 59 S 136 46 E
Wessel Is., *Australia* 114 A2 11 10 S 136 45 E
Wesselburen, *Germany* 26 A4 54 11N 8 53 E
Wessem, *Neths.* 21 F7 51 11N 5 49 E
Wessington, *U.S.A.* 138 C5 44 27N 98 42W
Wessington Springs, *U.S.A.* 138 C5 44 5N 98 34W
West, *U.S.A.* 139 K6 31 48N 97 6W
West Allis, *U.S.A.* 141 A10 43 1N 88 0W
West B., *U.S.A.* 139 L10 29 3N 89 22W
West Baines →, *Australia* 112 C4 15 38 S 129 59 E
West Bend, *U.S.A.* 134 D1 43 25N 88 11W
West Bengal □, *India* 81 H12 23 0N 88 0 E
West Beskids = Západné Beskydy, *Europe* 31 B12 49 30N 19 0 E
West Branch, *U.S.A.* 134 C3 44 17N 84 14W
West Bromwich, *U.K.* 17 E5 52 32N 2 1W
West Cape Howe, *Australia* 113 G2 35 8 S 117 36 E
West Carrollton, *U.S.A.* 141 E12 39 40N 84 17W
West Chazy, *U.S.A.* 137 B11 44 49N 73 28W
West Chester, *U.S.A.* 134 F8 39 58N 75 36W
West Chicago, *U.S.A.* 141 C8 41 53N 88 12W
West Columbia, *U.S.A.* 139 L7 29 9N 95 39W
West Covina, *U.S.A.* 145 L9 34 4N 117 54W
West Des Moines, *U.S.A.* 140 C3 41 35N 93 43W
West End, *Bahamas* 148 A4 26 41N 78 58W
West Falkland, *Falk. Is.* 160 D4 51 40 S 60 0W
West Fjord = Vestfjorden, *Norway* 12 C13 67 55N 14 0 E
West Frankfort, *U.S.A.* 140 G8 37 54N 88 55W
West Glamorgan □, *U.K.* 17 F4 51 40N 3 55W
West Hartford, *U.S.A.* 137 E12 41 45N 72 44W
West Haven, *U.S.A.* 137 E12 41 17N 72 57W
West Helena, *U.S.A.* 139 H9 34 33N 90 38W
West Ice Shelf, *Antarctica* 7 C7 67 0 S 85 0 E
West Indies, *Cent. Amer.* 149 C7 15 0N 65 0W
West Lafayette, *U.S.A.* 141 D10 40 27N 86 55W
West Liberty, *Iowa, U.S.A.* 140 C5 41 34N 91 16W
West Liberty, *Ky., U.S.A.* 141 G13 37 55N 83 16W
West Liberty, *Ohio, U.S.A.* 141 D13 40 15N 83 45W
West Lorne, *Canada* 136 D3 42 36N 81 36W
West Lunga →, *Zambia* 107 E1 13 6 S 24 39 E
West Manchester, *U.S.A.* 141 E12 39 55N 84 38W
West Memphis, *U.S.A.* 139 H9 35 9N 90 11W
West Midlands □, *U.K.* 17 E6 52 30N 1 55W
West Mifflin, *U.S.A.* 136 F5 40 22N 79 52W
West Milton, *U.S.A.* 141 E12 39 58N 84 20W
West Monroe, *U.S.A.* 139 J8 32 31N 92 9W
West Newton, *U.S.A.* 136 F5 40 14N 79 46W
West Nicholson, *Zimbabwe* 107 G2 21 2 S 29 20 E
West Palm Beach, *U.S.A.* 135 M5 26 43N 80 3W
West Plains, *U.S.A.* 139 G9 36 44N 91 51W
West Pt. = Ouest, Pte., *Canada* 129 C7 49 52N 64 40W
West Pt., *Australia* 116 C1 35 1 S 135 56 E
West Point, *Ga., U.S.A.* 135 J3 32 53N 85 11W
West Point, *Ill., U.S.A.* 140 D5 40 15N 91 11W
West Point, *Iowa, U.S.A.* 140 D5 40 43N 91 27W

284 West Point

West Point, *Ky., U.S.A.* **141 G11** 37 59N 85 57W
West Point, *Miss., U.S.A.* **135 J1** 33 36N 88 39W
West Point, *Nebr., U.S.A.* **138 E6** 41 51N 96 43W
West Point, *Va., U.S.A.* **134 G7** 37 32N 76 48W
West Pokot □, *Kenya* **106 B4** 1 30N 35 15 E
West Road —►, *Canada* **130 C4** 53 18N 122 53W
West Rutland, *U.S.A.* **137 C11** 43 38N 73 5W
West Salem, *U.S.A.* **141 F8** 38 31N 88 1W
West Schelde = Westerschelde —►, *Neths.* **21 F2** 51 25N 3 25 E
West Seneca, *U.S.A.* **136 D6** 42 51N 78 48W
West Siberian Plain, *Russia* **58 C11** 62 0N 75 0 E
West Sussex □, *U.K.* **17 G7** 50 55N 0 30W
West Terre Haute, *U.S.A.* **141 E9** 39 28N 87 27W
West-Terschelling, *Neths.* **20 B6** 53 22N 5 13 E
West Union, *Iowa, U.S.A.* **140 B5** 42 57N 91 49W
West Union, *Ohio, U.S.A.* **141 F13** 38 48N 83 33W
West Unity, *U.S.A.* **141 C12** 41 35N 84 26W
West Virginia □, *U.S.A.* **134 F5** 38 45N 80 30W
West-Vlaanderen □, *Belgium* **21 G2** 51 0N 3 0 E
West Walker —►, *U.S.A.* **144 G7** 38 54N 119 9W
West Wyalong, *Australia* **117 B7** 33 56 S 147 10 E
West Yellowstone, *U.S.A.* **142 D8** 44 40N 111 6W
West Yorkshire □, *U.K.* **16 D6** 53 45N 1 40W
Westall Pt., *Australia* **115 E1** 32 55 S 134 4 E
Westbrook, *Maine, U.S.A.* **135 D10** 43 41N 70 22W
Westbrook, *Tex., U.S.A.* **139 J4** 32 21N 101 1W
Westbury, *Australia* **114 G4** 41 30 S 146 51 E
Westby, *U.S.A.* **138 A2** 48 52N 104 3W
Westend, *U.S.A.* **145 K9** 35 42N 117 24W
Westerbork, *Neths.* **20 C9** 52 51N 6 37 E
Westerland, *Germany* **26 A4** 54 51N 8 20 E
Western □, *Kenya* **106 B3** 0 30N 34 30 E
Western □, *Uganda* **106 B3** 1 45N 31 30 E
Western □, *Zambia* **107 F1** 15 15 S 24 30 E
Western Australia □, *Australia* **113 E2** 25 0 S 118 0 E
Western Ghats, *India* **83 H2** 14 0N 75 0 E
Western Isles □, *U.K.* **18 D1** 57 30N 7 10W
Western River, *Australia* **116 C2** 35 42 S 136 56 E
Western Sahara ■, *Africa* **98 D2** 25 0N 13 0W
Western Samoa ■, *Pac. Oc.* **121 X24** 14 0 S 172 0W
Westernport, *U.S.A.* **134 F6** 39 29N 79 3W
Westerschelde —►, *Neths.* **21 F2** 51 25N 3 25 E
Westerstede, *Germany* **26 B3** 53 15N 7 55 E
Westervoort, *Neths.* **20 E7** 51 58N 5 59 E
Westerwald, *Germany* **26 E4** 50 39N 8 0 E
Westfield, *Ill., U.S.A.* **141 E8** 39 27N 88 0W
Westfield, *Ind., U.S.A.* **141 D10** 40 2N 86 8W
Westfield, *Mass., U.S.A.* **137 D12** 42 7N 72 45W
Westfield, *N.Y., U.S.A.* **136 D5** 42 20N 79 35W
Westfield, *Pa., U.S.A.* **136 E7** 41 55N 77 32W
Westgat, *Neths.* **21 E3** 51 39N 3 44 E
Westhope, *U.S.A.* **138 A4** 48 55N 101 1W
Westkapelle, *Belgium* **21 F2** 51 19N 3 19 E
Westkapelle, *Neths.* **21 E2** 51 31N 3 28 E
Westland, *U.S.A.* **141 B13** 42 15N 83 20W
Westland Bight, *N.Z.* **119 C5** 42 55 S 170 5 E
Westlock, *Canada* **130 C6** 54 9N 113 55W
Westmalle, *Belgium* **21 F5** 51 18N 4 42 E
Westmeath □, *Ireland* **19 C4** 53 30N 7 30W
Westminster, *U.S.A.* **134 F7** 39 34N 76 59W
Westmorland, *U.S.A.* **143 K6** 33 2N 115 37W
Weston, *Malaysia* **75 A5** 5 10N 115 35 E
Weston, *Ohio, U.S.A.* **141 C13** 41 21N 83 47W
Weston, *Oreg., U.S.A.* **142 D4** 45 49N 118 26W
Weston, *W. Va., U.S.A.* **134 F5** 39 2N 80 28W
Weston I., *Canada* **128 B4** 52 33N 79 36W
Weston-super-Mare, *U.K.* **17 F5** 51 20N 2 59W
Westphalia, *U.S.A.* **140 F5** 38 26N 92 0W
Westport, *Canada* **137 B8** 44 40N 76 25W
Westport, *Ireland* **19 C2** 53 44N 9 31W
Westport, *N.Z.* **119 B6** 41 46 S 171 37 E
Westport, *Ind., U.S.A.* **141 E11** 39 11N 85 34W
Westport, *Oreg., U.S.A.* **144 D3** 46 8N 123 23W
Westport, *Wash., U.S.A.* **142 C1** 46 53N 124 6W
Westray, *Canada* **131 C8** 53 36N 101 24W
Westray, *U.K.* **18 B6** 59 18N 3 0W
Westree, *Canada* **128 C3** 47 26N 81 34W
Westville, *Calif., U.S.A.* **144 F6** 39 8N 120 42W
Westville, *Ill., U.S.A.* **141 D9** 40 2N 87 38W
Westville, *Ind., U.S.A.* **141 C10** 41 35N 86 55W
Westville, *Okla., U.S.A.* **139 G7** 35 58N 94 40W
Westwood, *U.S.A.* **142 F3** 40 18N 121 0W
Wetar, *Indonesia* **72 C3** 7 30 S 126 30 E
Wetaskiwin, *Canada* **130 C6** 52 55N 113 24W
Wethersfield, *U.S.A.* **137 E12** 41 42N 72 40W
Wetlet, *Burma* **78 D5** 22 20N 95 53 E
Wetteren, *Belgium* **21 G3** 51 0N 3 52 E
Wettingen, *Switz.* **29 B6** 47 28N 8 20 E
Wetzikon, *Switz.* **29 B7** 47 19N 8 48 E
Wetzlar, *Germany* **26 E4** 50 33N 8 30 E
Wevelgem, *Belgium* **21 G2** 50 49N 3 12 E
Wewak, *Papua N. G.* **120 B2** 3 38 S 143 41 E
Wewoka, *U.S.A.* **139 H6** 35 9N 96 30W
Wexford, *Ireland* **19 D5** 52 20N 6 28W
Wexford □, *Ireland* **19 D5** 52 20N 6 25W
Wexford Harbour, *Ireland* **19 D5** 52 20N 6 25W
Weyburn, *Canada* **131 D8** 49 40N 103 50W
Weyburn L., *Canada* **130 A5** 63 0N 117 59W
Weyer, *Austria* **30 D7** 47 51N 14 40 E
Weyib —►, *Ethiopia* **95 F5** 7 15N 40 15 E
Weymouth, *Canada* **129 D6** 44 30N 66 1W
Weymouth, *U.K.* **17 G5** 50 36N 2 28W
Weymouth, *U.S.A.* **137 D14** 42 13N 70 58W
Weymouth, C., *Australia* **114 A3** 12 37 S 143 27 E
Wezemaal, *Belgium* **21 G5** 50 57N 4 45 E
Wezep, *Neths.* **20 D7** 52 28N 6 0 E
Whakamaru, *N.Z.* **118 E4** 38 23 S 175 50 E
Whakatane, *N.Z.* **118 D6** 37 57 S 177 1 E
Whakatane —►, *N.Z.* **118 D6** 37 57 S 177 1 E
Whale —►, *Canada* **129 A6** 58 15N 67 40W
Whale Cove, *Canada* **131 A10** 62 11N 92 36W
Whales, B. of, *Antarctica* **7 D12** 78 0 S 165 0W
Whalsay, *U.K.* **18 A7** 60 22N 1 0W
Whangaehu —►, *N.Z.* **118 G4** 40 3 S 175 6 E
Whangamata, *N.Z.* **118 D4** 37 12 S 175 53 E
Whangamomona, *N.Z.* **118 F3** 39 8 S 174 44 E
Whangarei, *N.Z.* **118 B3** 35 43 S 174 21 E
Whangarei Harb., *N.Z.* **118 B3** 35 45 S 174 28 E
Whangaroa Harb., *N.Z.* **118 B2** 35 4 S 173 46 E
Whangaruru Harb., *N.Z.* **118 B3** 35 24 S 174 23 E
Wharanui, *N.Z.* **119 B9** 41 55 S 174 6 E
Wharfe —►, *U.K.* **16 D6** 53 55N 1 30W
Wharfedale, *U.K.* **16 C5** 54 7N 2 4W
Wharton, *N.J., U.S.A.* **137 F10** 40 54N 74 35W
Wharton, *Pa., U.S.A.* **136 E6** 41 31N 78 1W
Wharton, *Tex., U.S.A.* **139 L6** 29 19N 96 6W
Whataroa, *N.Z.* **119 D5** 43 18 S 170 24 E
Whataroa —►, *N.Z.* **119 D5** 43 7 S 170 16 E
Wheatfield, *U.S.A.* **141 C9** 41 13N 87 4W
Wheatland, *Calif., U.S.A.* **144 F5** 39 1N 121 25W
Wheatland, *Ind., U.S.A.* **141 F9** 38 40N 87 19W
Wheatland, *Wyo., U.S.A.* **138 D2** 42 3N 104 58W
Wheatley, *Canada* **136 D2** 42 6N 82 27W
Wheaton, *Ill., U.S.A.* **141 C8** 41 52N 88 6W
Wheaton, *Minn., U.S.A.* **138 C6** 45 48N 96 30W
Wheelbarrow Pk., *U.S.A.* **144 H10** 37 26N 116 5W
Wheeler, *Oreg., U.S.A.* **142 D2** 45 41N 123 53W
Wheeler, *Tex., U.S.A.* **139 H4** 35 27N 100 16W
Wheeler —►, *Canada* **131 B7** 57 25N 105 30W
Wheeler Pk., *N. Mex., U.S.A.* **143 H11** 36 34N 105 25W
Wheeler Pk., *Nev., U.S.A.* **143 G6** 38 57N 114 15W
Wheeler Ridge, *U.S.A.* **145 L8** 35 0N 118 57W
Wheeling, *U.S.A.* **136 F4** 40 4N 80 43W
Whernside, *U.K.* **16 C5** 54 14N 2 24W
Whidbey I., *U.S.A.* **130 D4** 48 12N 122 17W
Whiskey Gap, *Canada* **130 D6** 49 0N 113 3W
Whiskey Jack L., *Canada* **131 B8** 58 23N 101 55W
Whistleduck Cr. —►, *Australia* **114 C2** 20 15 S 135 18 E
Whitby, *Canada* **136 C6** 43 52N 78 56W
Whitby, *U.K.* **16 C7** 54 29N 0 37W
Whitcombe Pass, *N.Z.* **119 D5** 43 13 S 170 55 E
White —►, *Ark., U.S.A.* **139 J9** 33 57N 91 5W
White —►, *Ind., U.S.A.* **141 F9** 38 25N 87 45W
White —►, *S. Dak., U.S.A.* **138 D5** 43 42N 99 27W
White —►, *Utah, U.S.A.* **142 F9** 40 4N 109 41W
White —►, *Wash., U.S.A.* **144 C4** 47 12N 122 15W
White, East Fork —►, *U.S.A.* **141 F9** 38 33N 87 14W
White, L., *Australia* **112 D4** 21 9 S 128 56 E
White B., *Canada* **129 B8** 50 0N 56 35W
White Bear Res., *Canada* **129 C8** 48 10N 57 5W
White Bird, *U.S.A.* **142 D5** 45 46N 116 18W
White Butte, *U.S.A.* **138 B3** 46 23N 103 18W
White City, *U.S.A.* **138 F6** 38 48N 96 44W
White Cliffs, *Australia* **116 A5** 30 50 S 143 10 E
White Deer, *U.S.A.* **139 H4** 35 26N 101 10W
White Hall, *U.S.A.* **140 E6** 39 26N 90 24W
White Haven, *U.S.A.* **137 E9** 41 4N 75 47W
White I., *N.Z.* **118 D6** 37 30 S 177 13 E
White L., *Canada* **137 A8** 45 18N 76 31W
White L., *U.S.A.* **139 L8** 29 44N 92 30W
White Mts., *Calif., U.S.A.* **144 H8** 37 30N 118 15W
White Mts., *N.H., U.S.A.* **137 B13** 44 15N 71 15W
White Nile = Nîl el Abyad —►, *Sudan* **95 D3** 15 38N 32 31 E
White Nile Dam = Khazzân Jabal el Awliyâ, *Sudan* **95 D3** 15 24N 32 20 E
White Otter L., *Canada* **128 C1** 49 5N 91 55W
White Pass, *Canada* **130 B1** 59 40N 135 3W
White Pass, *U.S.A.* **144 D5** 46 38N 121 24W
White Pigeon, *U.S.A.* **141 C11** 41 48N 85 39W
White Plains, *U.S.A.* **137 E11** 41 2N 73 46W
White River, *Canada* **128 C2** 48 35N 85 20W
White River, *S. Africa* **105 D5** 25 20 S 31 0 E
White River, *U.S.A.* **138 D4** 43 34N 100 45W
White Russia = Belorussia ■, *Europe* **50 E5** 53 30N 27 0 E
White Sea = Beloye More, *Russia* **48 A6** 66 30N 38 0 E
White Sulphur Springs, *Mont., U.S.A.* **142 C8** 46 33N 110 54W
White Sulphur Springs, *W. Va., U.S.A.* **134 G5** 37 48N 80 18W
White Swan, *U.S.A.* **144 D6** 46 23N 120 44W
White Volta —►, *Ghana* **101 D4** 9 10N 1 15W
Whitecliffs, *N.Z.* **119 D6** 43 26 S 171 55 E
Whitecourt, *Canada* **130 C5** 54 10N 115 45W
Whiteface, *U.S.A.* **139 J3** 33 36N 102 37W
Whitefield, *U.S.A.* **137 B13** 44 23N 71 37W
Whitefish, *U.S.A.* **142 B6** 48 25N 114 20W
Whitefish Bay, *U.S.A.* **141 A9** 43 23N 87 54W
Whitefish L., *Canada* **131 A7** 62 41N 106 48W
Whitefish Point, *U.S.A.* **134 B3** 46 45N 84 59W
Whitegull, L., *Canada* **129 A7** 55 27N 64 17W
Whitehall, *Mich., U.S.A.* **134 D2** 43 24N 86 21W
Whitehall, *Mont., U.S.A.* **142 D7** 45 52N 112 6W
Whitehall, *N.Y., U.S.A.* **137 C11** 43 33N 73 24W
Whitehall, *Wis., U.S.A.* **138 C9** 44 22N 91 19W
Whitehaven, *U.K.* **16 C4** 54 33N 3 35W
Whitehorse, *Canada* **130 A1** 60 43N 135 3W
Whitehorse, Vale of, *U.K.* **17 F6** 51 37N 1 30W
Whiteman, *U.S.A.* **140 F3** 38 45N 93 40W
Whiteman Ra., *Papua N. G.* **120 C5** 5 55 S 150 0 E
Whitemark, *Australia* **114 G4** 40 7 S 148 3 E
Whitemouth, *Canada* **131 D9** 49 57N 95 58W
Whiteplains, *Liberia* **100 D2** 6 28N 10 40W
Whitesboro, *N.Y., U.S.A.* **137 C9** 43 7N 75 18W
Whitesboro, *Tex., U.S.A.* **139 J6** 33 39N 96 54W
Whiteshell Prov. Park, *Canada* **131 C9** 50 0N 95 40W
Whiteside, *U.S.A.* **140 E5** 39 12N 91 2W
Whiteside, Canal, *Chile* **160 D2** 53 55 S 70 15W
Whitetail, *U.S.A.* **138 A2** 48 54N 105 10W
Whiteville, *U.S.A.* **135 H6** 34 20N 78 42W
Whitewater, *U.S.A.* **141 B8** 42 50N 88 44W
Whitewater Baldy, *U.S.A.* **143 K9** 33 20N 108 39W
Whitewater L., *Canada* **128 B2** 50 50N 89 10W
Whitewood, *Australia* **114 C3** 21 28 S 143 30 E
Whitewood, *Canada* **131 C8** 50 20N 102 20W
Whitfield, *Australia* **117 D7** 36 42 S 146 24 E
Whithorn, *U.K.* **18 G4** 54 44N 4 25W
Whitianga, *N.Z.* **118 C4** 36 47 S 175 41 E
Whiting, *U.S.A.* **141 C9** 41 41N 87 29W
Whitman, *U.S.A.* **137 D14** 42 5N 70 56W
Whitmire, *U.S.A.* **135 H5** 34 30N 81 37W
Whitney, *Canada* **128 C4** 45 31N 78 14W
Whitney, Mt., *U.S.A.* **144 J8** 36 35N 118 18W
Whitney Point, *U.S.A.* **137 D9** 42 20N 75 58W
Whitstable, *U.K.* **17 F9** 51 21N 1 2 E
Whitsunday I., *Australia* **114 C4** 20 15 S 149 4 E
Whittemore, *U.S.A.* **140 A2** 43 4N 94 26W
Whittier, *U.S.A.* **145 M8** 33 58N 118 3W
Whittlesea, *Australia* **117 D6** 37 27 S 145 9 E
Whitwell, *U.S.A.* **135 H3** 35 12N 85 31W
Wholdaia L., *Canada* **131 A8** 60 43N 104 20W
Whyalla, *Australia* **116 B2** 33 2 S 137 30 E
Whyjonta, *Australia* **115 D3** 29 41 S 142 28 E
Wiarton, *Canada* **128 D3** 44 40N 81 10W
Wiawso, *Ghana* **100 D4** 6 10N 2 25W
Wiazów, *Poland* **47 E4** 50 50N 17 10 E
Wibaux, *U.S.A.* **138 B2** 46 59N 104 11W
Wichabai, *Guyana* **153 C6** 2 57N 59 35W
Wichian Buri, *Thailand* **76 E3** 15 39N 101 7 E
Wichita, *U.S.A.* **139 G6** 37 42N 97 20W
Wichita Falls, *U.S.A.* **139 J5** 33 54N 98 30W
Wick, *U.K.* **18 C5** 58 26N 3 5W
Wickenburg, *U.S.A.* **143 K7** 33 58N 112 44W
Wickepin, *Australia* **113 F2** 32 50 S 117 30 E
Wickham, C., *Australia* **114 F3** 39 35 S 143 57 E
Wickliffe, *U.S.A.* **136 E3** 41 36N 81 28W
Wicklow, *Ireland* **19 D5** 53 0N 6 2W
Wicklow □, *Ireland* **19 D5** 52 59N 6 25W
Wicklow Hd., *Ireland* **19 D5** 52 59N 6 3W
Widawa, *Poland* **47 D5** 51 27N 18 51 E
Widawka, *Poland* **47 D6** 51 7N 19 36 E
Widgiemooltha, *Australia* **113 F3** 31 30 S 121 34 E
Widnes, *U.K.* **16 D5** 53 22N 2 44W
Więcbork, *Poland* **47 B4** 53 21N 17 30 E
Wiedenbrück, *Germany* **26 D4** 51 52N 8 15 E
Wiek, *Germany* **26 A9** 54 37N 13 17 E
Wielbark, *Poland* **47 B7** 53 24N 20 55 E
Wieleń, *Poland* **47 C3** 52 53N 16 9 E
Wieliczka, *Poland* **31 B13** 50 0N 20 5 E
Wieluń, *Poland* **47 D5** 51 15N 18 34 E
Wien, *Austria* **31 C9** 48 12N 16 22 E
Wiener Neustadt, *Austria* **31 D9** 47 49N 16 16 E
Wieprz —►, Koszalin, *Poland* **47 A3** 54 26N 16 35 E
Wieprz —►, Lublin, *Poland* **47 D8** 51 34N 21 49 E
Wierden, *Neths.* **20 D9** 52 22N 6 35 E
Wiers, *Belgium* **21 H3** 50 30N 3 32 E
Wieruszów, *Poland* **47 D5** 51 19N 18 9 E
Wiesbaden, *Germany* **27 E4** 50 7N 8 17 E
Wiesental, *Germany* **27 F4** 49 15N 8 30 E
Wigan, *U.K.* **16 D5** 53 33N 2 38W
Wiggins, *Colo., U.S.A.* **138 E2** 40 14N 104 4W
Wiggins, *Miss., U.S.A.* **139 K10** 30 51N 89 8W
Wight, I. of □, *U.K.* **17 G6** 50 40N 1 20W
Wigry, Jezioro, *Poland* **47 A10** 54 2N 23 8 E
Wigtown, *U.K.* **18 G4** 54 52N 4 27W
Wigtown B., *U.K.* **18 G4** 54 46N 4 15W
Wijchen, *Neths.* **20 E7** 51 48N 5 44 E
Wijhe, *Neths.* **20 D8** 52 23N 6 8 E
Wijk bij Duurstede, *Neths.* **20 E6** 51 59N 5 21 E
Wil, *Switz.* **29 B8** 47 28N 9 3 E
Wilamowice, *Poland* **31 B12** 49 55N 19 9 E
Wilangee, *Australia* **116 A4** 31 28 S 141 20 E
Wilber, *U.S.A.* **138 E6** 40 29N 96 58W
Wilberforce, *Canada* **136 A6** 45 2N 78 13W
Wilberforce, C., *Australia* **114 A2** 11 54 S 136 35 E
Wilburton, *U.S.A.* **139 H7** 34 55N 95 19W
Wilcannia, *Australia* **116 A5** 31 30 S 143 26 E
Wilcox, *U.S.A.* **136 E6** 41 35N 78 41W
Wildbad, *Germany* **27 G4** 48 44N 8 32 E
Wildcat —►, *U.S.A.* **141 D10** 40 28N 86 52W
Wildervank, *Neths.* **20 B9** 53 5N 6 52 E
Wildeshausen, *Germany* **26 C4** 52 54N 8 25 E
Wildhorn, *Switz.* **28 D4** 46 22N 7 21 E
Wildon, *Austria* **30 E8** 46 52N 15 31 E
Wildrose, *Calif., U.S.A.* **145 J9** 36 14N 117 11W
Wildrose, *N. Dak., U.S.A.* **138 A3** 48 38N 103 11W
Wildspitze, *Austria* **30 E3** 46 53N 10 53 E
Wildstrubel, *Switz.* **28 D5** 46 24N 7 32 E
Wildwood, *U.S.A.* **134 F8** 38 59N 74 50W
Wilga —►, *Poland* **47 D8** 51 52N 21 18 E
Wilgaroon, *Australia* **117 A6** 30 52 S 145 42 E
Wilge —►, *S. Africa* **105 D4** 27 3 S 28 20 E
Wilhelm, Mt., *Papua N. G.* **120 C3** 5 50 S 145 1 E
Wilhelm II Coast, *Antarctica* **7 C7** 68 0 S 90 0 E
Wilhelm-Pieck-Stadt Guben, *Germany* **26 D10** 51 59N 14 48 E
Wilhelmina, Geb., *Surinam* **153 C6** 3 50N 56 30W
Wilhelmina Kanaal, *Neths.* **21 E6** 51 36N 5 6 E
Wilhelmsburg, *Austria* **30 C8** 48 6N 15 36 E
Wilhelmshaven, *Germany* **26 B4** 53 30N 8 9 E
Wilhelmstal, *Namibia* **104 C2** 21 58 S 16 21 E
Wilkes-Barre, *U.S.A.* **137 E9** 41 15N 75 53W
Wilkesboro, *U.S.A.* **135 G5** 36 9N 81 10W
Wilkie, *Canada* **131 C7** 52 27N 108 42W
Wilkinsburg, *U.S.A.* **136 F5** 40 26N 79 53W
Wilkinson Lakes, *Australia* **113 E5** 29 40 S 132 39 E
Willamina, *U.S.A.* **142 D2** 45 5N 123 29W
Willamulka, *Australia* **116 B2** 33 55 S 137 52 E
Willandra Billabong Creek —►, *Australia* **116 B6** 33 22 S 145 52 E
Willapa B., *U.S.A.* **142 C2** 46 40N 124 0W
Willapa Hills, *U.S.A.* **144 D3** 46 35N 123 25W
Willard, *N. Mex., U.S.A.* **143 J10** 34 36N 106 2W
Willard, *Utah, U.S.A.* **142 F7** 41 25N 112 2W
Willaura, *Australia* **116 D5** 37 31 S 142 45 E
Willbriggie, *Australia* **117 C7** 34 28 S 146 2 E
Willcox, *U.S.A.* **143 K9** 32 15N 109 50W
Willebroek, *Belgium* **21 F4** 51 4N 4 22 E
Willemstad, *Neth. Ant.* **149 D6** 12 5N 69 0W
Willeroo, *Australia* **112 C5** 15 14 S 131 37 E
William —►, *Canada* **131 B7** 59 8N 109 19W
William, Mt., *Australia* **116 D5** 37 17 S 142 35 E
William Creek, *Australia* **115 D2** 28 58 S 136 22 E
Williambury, *Australia* **113 D2** 23 45 S 115 12 E
Williams, *Australia* **113 F2** 33 2 S 116 52 E
Williams, *Ariz., U.S.A.* **143 J7** 35 15N 112 11W
Williams, *Calif., U.S.A.* **144 F4** 39 9N 122 9W
Williams Lake, *Canada* **130 C4** 52 10N 122 10W
Williamsburg, *Ky., U.S.A.* **135 G3** 36 44N 84 10W
Williamsburg, *Pa., U.S.A.* **136 F6** 40 28N 78 12W
Williamsburg, *Va., U.S.A.* **134 G7** 37 17N 76 44W
Williamsfield, *U.S.A.* **140 D6** 40 55N 90 1W
Williamson, *N.Y., U.S.A.* **136 C7** 43 14N 77 15W
Williamson, *W. Va., U.S.A.* **134 G4** 37 41N 82 17W
Williamsport, *Ind., U.S.A.* **141 D9** 40 17N 87 17W
Williamsport, *Pa., U.S.A.* **136 E7** 41 15N 77 0W
Williamston, *Mich., U.S.A.* **141 B12** 42 41N 84 17W
Williamston, *N.C., U.S.A.* **135 H7** 35 51N 77 4W
Williamstown, *Australia* **117 D6** 37 51 S 144 52 E
Williamstown, *Ky., U.S.A.* **141 F12** 38 38N 84 34W
Williamstown, *Mass., U.S.A.* **137 D11** 42 41N 73 12W
Williamstown, *N.Y., U.S.A.* **137 C9** 43 26N 75 53W
Williamsville, *Ill., U.S.A.* **140 E7** 39 57N 89 33W
Williamsville, *Mo., U.S.A.* **139 G9** 36 58N 90 33W
Willimantic, *U.S.A.* **137 E12** 41 43N 72 13W
Willis Group, *Australia* **114 B5** 16 18 S 150 0 E
Willisau, *Switz.* **28 B6** 47 7N 8 0 E
Willisburg, *U.S.A.* **141 G11** 37 49N 85 8W
Williston, *S. Africa* **104 E3** 31 20 S 20 53 E
Williston, *Fla., U.S.A.* **135 L4** 29 23N 82 27W
Williston, *N. Dak., U.S.A.* **138 A3** 48 9N 103 37W
Williston L., *Canada* **130 B4** 56 0N 124 0W
Willits, *U.S.A.* **142 G2** 39 25N 123 21W
Willmar, *U.S.A.* **138 C7** 45 7N 95 3W
Willoughby, *U.S.A.* **136 E3** 41 39N 81 24W
Willow Bunch, *Canada* **131 D7** 49 20N 105 35W
Willow L., *Canada* **130 A5** 62 10N 119 8W
Willow Lake, *U.S.A.* **138 C6** 44 38N 97 38W
Willow Springs, *U.S.A.* **139 G8** 37 0N 91 58W
Willow Tree, *Australia* **117 A9** 31 40 S 150 45 E
Willow Wall, The, *China* **67 C12** 42 10N 122 0 E
Willowlake —►, *Canada* **130 A4** 62 42N 123 8W
Willowmore, *S. Africa* **104 E3** 33 15 S 23 30 E
Willows, *Australia* **114 C4** 23 39 S 147 25 E
Willows, *U.S.A.* **144 F4** 39 31N 122 12W
Willowvale = Gatyana, *S. Africa* **105 E4** 32 16 S 28 31 E
Wills, L., *Australia* **112 D4** 21 25 S 128 51 E
Wills Cr. —►, *Australia* **114 C3** 22 43 S 140 2 E
Wills Point, *U.S.A.* **139 J7** 32 43N 96 1W
Willunga, *Australia* **116 C3** 35 15 S 138 30 E
Wilmette, *U.S.A.* **134 D2** 42 5N 87 42W
Wilmington, *Australia* **116 B3** 32 39 S 138 7 E
Wilmington, *Del., U.S.A.* **134 F8** 39 45N 75 33W
Wilmington, *Ill., U.S.A.* **141 C8** 41 18N 88 9W
Wilmington, *N.C., U.S.A.* **135 H7** 34 14N 77 55W
Wilmington, *Ohio, U.S.A.* **141 E13** 39 27N 83 50W
Wilpena Cr. —►, *Australia* **116 A3** 31 25 S 139 29 E
Wilrijk, *Belgium* **21 F4** 51 9N 4 22 E
Wilsall, *U.S.A.* **142 D8** 45 59N 110 38W
Wilson, *U.S.A.* **135 H7** 35 44N 77 55W
Wilson —►, *Queens., Australia* **115 D3** 27 38 S 141 24 E
Wilson —►, *W. Austral., Australia* **112 C4** 16 48 S 128 16 E
Wilson Bluff, *Australia* **113 F4** 31 41 S 129 0 E
Wilson Str., *Solomon Is.* **121 M9** 8 0 S 156 39 E
Wilsons Promontory, *Australia* **117 E7** 38 55 S 146 25 E
Wilster, *Germany* **26 B5** 53 55N 9 23 E
Wilton, *U.K.* **17 F6** 51 5N 1 52W
Wilton, *U.S.A.* **138 B4** 47 10N 100 47W
Wilton —►, *Australia* **114 A1** 14 45 S 134 33 E
Wiltshire □, *U.K.* **17 F6** 51 20N 2 0W
Wiltz, *Lux.* **21 J7** 49 57N 5 55 E
Wiluna, *Australia* **113 E3** 26 36 S 120 14 E
Wimereux, *France* **23 B8** 50 45N 1 37 E
Wimmera —►, *Australia* **116 D4** 36 8 S 141 56 E
Winam G., *Kenya* **106 C3** 0 20 S 34 15 E
Winamac, *U.S.A.* **141 C10** 41 3N 86 36W
Winburg, *S. Africa* **104 D4** 28 30 S 27 2 E
Winchelsea, *Australia* **116 E6** 38 10 S 144 1 E
Winchendon, *U.S.A.* **137 D12** 42 41N 72 3W
Winchester, *N.Z.* **119 E6** 44 11 S 171 17 E
Winchester, *U.K.* **17 F6** 51 4N 1 19W
Winchester, *Conn., U.S.A.* **137 E11** 41 53N 73 9W
Winchester, *Idaho, U.S.A.* **142 C5** 46 14N 116 38W
Winchester, *Ill., U.S.A.* **140 E6** 39 38N 90 27W
Winchester, *Ind., U.S.A.* **141 D12** 40 10N 84 59W
Winchester, *Ky., U.S.A.* **141 G12** 38 0N 84 11W
Winchester, *N.H., U.S.A.* **137 D12** 42 46N 72 23W
Winchester, *Nev., U.S.A.* **145 J11** 36 6N 115 10W
Winchester, *Ohio, U.S.A.* **141 F13** 38 57N 83 40W
Winchester, *Tenn., U.S.A.* **135 H2** 35 11N 86 7W
Winchester, *Va., U.S.A.* **134 F6** 39 11N 78 10W
Wind —►, *U.S.A.* **142 E9** 43 12N 108 12W
Wind Point, *U.S.A.* **141 B9** 42 47N 87 46W
Wind River Range, *U.S.A.* **142 E9** 43 0N 109 30W
Windau = Ventspils, *Latvia* **13 H16** 57 25N 21 32 E
Windber, *U.S.A.* **136 F6** 40 14N 78 50W
Windermere, L., *U.K.* **16 C5** 54 20N 2 57W
Windfall, *Canada* **130 C5** 54 12N 116 13W
Windfall, *U.S.A.* **141 D11** 40 22N 85 57W
Windflower L., *Canada* **130 A5** 62 52N 118 30W
Windhoek, *Namibia* **104 C2** 22 35 S 17 4 E
Windischgarsten, *Austria* **30 D7** 47 42N 14 21 E
Windom, *U.S.A.* **138 D7** 43 52N 95 7W
Windorah, *Australia* **114 D3** 25 24 S 142 36 E
Window Rock, *U.S.A.* **143 J9** 35 41N 109 3W
Windrush —►, *U.K.* **17 F6** 51 48N 1 35W
Windsor, *Australia* **117 B9** 33 37 S 150 50 E
Windsor, *N.S., Canada* **129 D7** 44 59N 64 5W
Windsor, *Nfld., Canada* **129 C8** 48 57N 55 40W
Windsor, *Ont., Canada* **128 D3** 42 18N 83 0W
Windsor, *N.Z.* **119 E5** 44 59 S 170 49 E
Windsor, *U.K.* **17 F7** 51 28N 0 36W
Windsor, *Colo., U.S.A.* **138 E2** 40 29N 104 54W
Windsor, *Conn., U.S.A.* **137 E12** 41 50N 72 39W
Windsor, *Ill., U.S.A.* **141 E8** 39 26N 88 36W
Windsor, *Mo., U.S.A.* **140 F3** 38 32N 93 31W
Windsor, *N.Y., U.S.A.* **137 D9** 42 5N 75 37W
Windsor, *Vt., U.S.A.* **137 C12** 43 29N 72 24W
Windsorton, *S. Africa* **104 D3** 28 16 S 24 44 E
Windward Is., *W. Indies* **149 D7** 13 0N 61 0W
Windward Passage = Vientos, Paso de los, *Caribbean* **149 C5** 20 0N 74 0W
Windy L., *Canada* **131 A8** 60 20N 100 2W
Winefred L., *Canada* **131 B6** 55 30N 110 30W
Winejok, *Sudan* **95 F2** 9 1N 27 30 E
Winfield, *Iowa, U.S.A.* **140 C5** 41 7N 91 26W
Winfield, *Kans., U.S.A.* **139 G6** 37 15N 96 59W
Winfield, *Mo., U.S.A.* **140 E6** 39 0N 90 44W
Wingate Mts., *Australia* **112 B5** 14 25 S 130 40 E
Wingen, *Australia* **117 A9** 31 54 S 150 54 E
Wingene, *Belgium* **21 F2** 51 3N 3 17 E

Z

KEY TO WORLD MAP PAGES

NORTH AMERICA

ARCTIC OCEAN 6

Arctic Circle

126-127

12

12-1

18

19   16-17   26

22-23   20-21

24-25   28-2

130-131

128-129

142-143   138-139   134-135

136-137

140-141

144-145

ATLANTIC

OCEAN

ATLANTIC OCEAN 8-9

36-37   34-35   38-3

33
33

98-99

33

33

Tropic of Cancer

132

PACIFIC OCEAN 122-123

146-147

148-149

152-153

100-101   96-

SOUTH AMERICA

154-155

Equator

AFRICA

156-157

Tropic of Capricorn

PACIFIC   OCEAN

158-159

160